S0-BZC-427

AMERICAN CRIMINAL PROCEDURE

CASES AND COMMENTARY

Fourth Edition

By

Stephen A. Saltzburg
Howrey Professor of Trial Advocacy
George Washington University National Law Center

Daniel J. Capra
Professor of Law
Fordham University School of Law

AMERICAN CASEBOOK SERIES®

WEST PUBLISHING CO.
ST. PAUL, MINN., 1992

610 Opperman Drive
P.O. Box 64526
St. Paul, MN 55164–0526

Printed in the United States of America

Library of Congress Cataloging-in-Publication Data

Saltzburg, Stephen A.
American criminal procedure : cases and commentary / by Stephen A. Saltzburg and Daniel J. Capra. — 4th ed.
p. cm. — (American casebook series)
Includes bibliographical references and index.
ISBN 0–314–00351–7
1. Criminal procedure—United States—Cases. I. Capra, Daniel J., 1953– . II. Title. III. Series.
KF9618.S24 1992
345.73'05—dc20
[347.3055] 92–5160
CIP

ISBN 0–314–00351–7

(S. & C.) Amer.Crim.Proc. 4th Ed. ACB
2nd Reprint—1995

To Our Wives,
Susan Lee and Anne Capra

*

Preface

This Fourth Edition plays to what we feel were the strengths of the first three editions. While the predominant focus is on Supreme Court jurisprudence, we have tried wherever possible to give the reader a sense of what the lower courts are doing with the interesting and exciting issues that abound in criminal procedure. The lower courts are where the day-to-day law is made, and many of the most interesting fact situations arise. Since our topic is "American" Criminal Procedure, we have made an effort to include cases from all the circuits and state courts throughout the book. As with prior editions, extensive commentary and interesting fact situations are included to assist in doctrinal development. Finally, the book covers all problems of criminal investigation and adjudication. It is not limited to constitutional issues. Yet despite the breadth of the book, we have made a special effort to keep it to a manageable and readable length.

The format of the book is the same as the prior editions, although much of the material has been reorganized and updated. Citations to Supreme Court opinions are limited to United States Reports, unless the case is so recent that the U.S. cite is not available. Certiorari denied citations are omitted on the ground that they unnecessarily clutter a book that is primarily for classroom use. Citations included in cases are often omitted without so specifying. Lettered footnotes are from the original materials. Numbered footnotes are ours. Omissions from the text of original material are indicated by asterisks and brackets.

This Edition gives special treatment to some of the more active areas of criminal procedure in the past four years. The case law on peremptory challenges has burgeoned, and is thoroughly discussed in the material on *Batson* and its progeny in Chapter Ten. Important questions concerning the right to retained counsel and to counsel's role are also explored in Chapter Ten. The fundamental changes wrought by the Sentencing Guidelines, which take up much of the lower courts' time and effort and which have resulted in a shift of power from courts to prosecutors, are explored in Chapter Eleven. Chapter Eleven also considers recent death penalty jurisprudence, by which the Supreme Court has largely left the States to their own discretion. Finally, Chapter Thirteen gives extensive treatment to the Court's recent efforts to limit habeas corpus review.

We would like to thank those authors, editors, printers and publishers who gave us permission to reprint from their works. They are as follows:

ALI Model Code of Pre-Arraignment Procedure; Copyright © 1975 by the American Law Institute. Reprinted with the permission of the American Law Institute.

Allen, The Restoration of In re Winship: A comment on Burdens of Persuasion in Criminal Cases after Patterson v. New York, 76 Mich.L.Rev. 30 (1977); reprinted with the permission of the Michigan Law Review.

Barkai, Accuracy Inquiries for all Felony and Misdemeanor Pleas; Voluntary Pleas But Innocent Defendants, 126 U.Pa.L.Rev. 88 (1977); reprinted with the permission of the University of Pennsylvania Law Review and Fred B. Rothman & Co.

Friendly, The Fifth Amendment Tomorrow: The Case for Constitutional Change, 37 U.Cin.L.Rev. 671 (1968); reprinted with the permission of the University of Cincinnati Law Review.

L. Levy, The Origins of the Fifth Amendment (1968). Reprinted with the permission of Oxford University Press. Copyright © 1968 by CLIO Enterprises, Inc.

H. Miller, W. McDonald, J. Cramer, Plea Bargaining in the United States (1979); reprinted with the permission of the Georgetown University Law Center.

Moylan, Hearsay and Probable Cause: An Aguilar and Spinelli Primer, 25 Mercer L.Rev. 741 (1974); reprinted with permission of the author.

Perlman, Sentencing System Ineffective and Disparate, 30 Virginia Law Weekly, No. 15 (1978); reprinted with the permission of the Virginia Law Weekly and the author.

Scheininger, United States v. Nobles: A Prosecutor's Perspective, 14 Am.Crim.L.Rev. 1 (1976); reprinted with the permission of the author and the ABA Criminal Justice Section.

Serrill, Determinate Sentencing: History, Theory, Debate, 2 Corrections Magazine, No. 3 (Sept. 1977); reprinted with the permission of Corrections Magazine.

Traynor, Mapp v. Ohio at Large in the Fifty States, 1962 Duke L.J. 319; reprinted with the permission of the Duke Law Journal. Copyright © 1962.

P. Wice, Bail and Its Reform: A National Survey (1973); reprinted with permission of LEAA.

Wilkey, Why Suppress Valid Evidence?, Wall Street Journal, Oct. 7, 1977; reprinted with the permission of the author and the Wall Street Journal.

The Fourth Edition covers all Supreme Court cases decided in the 1990 term, and those of the 1991 term that were decided before the book went to press. We will provide yearly supplements to cover new Supreme Court cases and major lower court cases.

Because every criminal procedure teacher likes to cover different material, we have tried to divide the book into numerous subdivisions to enable teachers to pick and choose the subjects they most want to cover. We think that an advanced criminal procedure course is a useful and popular addition to the curriculum. If an advanced course is contemplated, Chapters Nine through Thirteen could be reserved for that course. An alternative approach is to include Chapter Nine in the basic course and move Chapters Eight and Five into the advanced course. A third approach is to cover parts of all, or almost all, chapters in the basic course, and to finish them in the advanced course. We believe and hope that the material lends itself to several different divisions that all work well in class and make either a single course or a tandem interesting for all students.

We would like to thank Bruce Green and Will Hellerstein for their helpful comments. We gratefully acknowledge the excellent work of our research assistant, Jill Moskowitz.

STEPHEN A. SALTZBURG,
Washington, D.C.

DANIEL J. CAPRA
New York, N.Y.

March 1992

*

Introduction

Criminal procedure is one of the courses in law school that generates classroom excitement that continues from the first to the last day of class without significant abatement. Whether it is the opportunity to compare the Warren and the Burger Courts and to predict the likely course of the Rehnquist Court, the fact that criminal procedure as a subject of study has developed only recently so that one is almost always on the cutting edge of the law, a fascination with the battle between government and individual and the true adversary clash that often results, the fact that the Bill of Rights holds an important place in the hearts and minds of future lawyers, or all of these things to some extent, people like to talk and argue about criminal procedure, and they mind studying it less than they mind studying many other things.

As excited as students of criminal procedure are, too often they leave their courses feeling somewhat frustrated. They have learned a lot of recent law and they know what the latest decisions of the Supreme Court are, but they do not feel comfortable in their understanding of the criminal justice system (to the extent that it is accurate to call the way criminal cases are handled a system) as a whole, or in their knowledge of the doctrinal roots of the numerous concepts that they have examined. This book is an effort to remove some of that frustration, to clarify the way in which the parts of the criminal justice system relate to one another, and to explain how we arrived where we now find ourselves.

To accomplish this task, the book utilizes far more original text than is typically found in casebooks on the subject. The text attempts to develop the history of the rules discussed, to point out how judicial treatment of various concepts has changed over time, and to indicate the vices and the virtues of various approaches, past and present. An effort is made to provide students with citations to law journals, books and cases not presented in this book so that those who are interested can examine topics more fully on their own with easy access to the relevant literature.

When a subject is examined, an effort is made to point out inadequacies in judicial opinions or legislative reactions to judicial opinions. Sometimes our own views are stated, either explicitly or implicitly, in an effort to stimulate thinking about new approaches to familiar problems. Where appropriate, students are asked to think about the concepts they have learned in connection with problems that encourage them to develop their own ideas about how best to handle hard cases and close questions.

An effort has been made to reproduce only those Supreme Court cases that are most important. Less important cases are discussed in the textual material. Some of the cases that are offered are not yesterday's Supreme Court decisions, but those of a more distant Court, because the important opinions may be those that were seminal.

The emphasis on the development of concepts over time indicates a bias that should be confessed here: We believe that the judiciary, especially the Supreme Court, and legislatures, to the extent that they become involved in establishing procedures for criminal cases, attempt to articulate and apply doctrines that will hold their own over time. In other words, we believe that they struggle "to get it right" eventually, if not always at the first crack.

This is not to suggest that right answers are clear or easy to ascertain. In many instances, reasonable minds will differ on the proper solution to questions, and often reasonable minds will find proper solutions to be elusive. We suggest only that approaches that are plainly defective are almost always abandoned or changed, and that it seems that courts and legislatures do attempt to refine the procedures that govern criminal investigations and prosecutions as a result of experience.

Like most criminal procedure books, this one places much emphasis on constitutional rules. This hardly can be avoided, since the Constitution as now interpreted does set minimum standards for many parts of the criminal justice system. But, an attempt is made to indicate when nonconstitutional rules may be more important or more useful than constitutional ones.

To sum up, this book combines elements of traditional casebooks with textual material that might more typically be found in a treatise or hornbook, and it intersperses problems in many chapters. Overall, the idea is to identify clearly the problems of criminal procedure, to offer various ideas about how to handle the problems, and to describe the work that still needs to be done if criminal cases are to be processed fairly.

Some comments on the particular chapters of the book may help to explain how we have approached various topics.

Chapter One begins with a development of the criminal justice system. The importance of constitutional rules is discussed, and the incorporation and retroactivity doctrines are examined, since they arise again and again in the cases that are discussed in the following chapters.

Chapter Two examines all aspects of Fourth Amendment law. It begins with a careful examination of the Amendment's language and an exploration of the relationship between the warrant clause and the reasonableness clause. The concepts of probable cause, valid warrants, arrest, stop and frisk, and scrutiny by a detached magistrate are all covered at length. Eavesdropping and wiretapping are looked at afterwards. The chapter reserves an examination of the exclusionary rule until the end and attempts thereby to promote an understanding of what the rule is and what its true costs are. This is the longest chapter of the book, covering the many facets of search and seizure law.

Chapter Three covers self-incrimination and confessions. More than usual attention is paid to traditional Fifth Amendment law and how it relates to the law of confessions. Much space is devoted to laying the historical foundation for present law. Only then are *Miranda, Massiah, Brewer, Henry* and other major cases discussed.

Identification evidence is scrutinized in Chapter Four. The major Supreme Court cases take up most of the chapter, but an attempt is made to point out the shortcomings in the Court's work and to suggest how identification procedures might be improved and how fairer trials might result.

Chapter Five is about the right to counsel. Since the right to counsel may be important in connection with confessions and identifications, as well as later in the process, it might seem strange for this chapter to follow the two previous ones. But we believe that the order works and that it is helpful to treat the counsel cases in one place—at the point at which counsel is likely to be involved for the remainder of the process. The doctrines of ineffective assistance and self-representation are not treated here, but are reserved for Chapter Ten.

Chapter Six looks at the decision whether or not to charge a suspect. The roles of the police, the prosecutor and the grand jury are examined, and an effort is made to show how interdependent they are. The current controversy over the utility of the grand jury as a screening device and the dangers of the grand jury serving as an arm of the executive are described and discussed. Preliminary hearings and their relationship to grand juries and charging decisions generally are considered in some detail.

Chapter Seven covers bail and pretrial release. Both constitutional and nonconstitutional rules, especially the 1984 and 1966 Federal Bail Reform Acts, are analyzed. The purposes of bail and the controversy over preventive detention are discussed. Some emphasis is placed on the traditional role of the bondsman and the need for bail reform.

Chapter Eight presents criminal discovery. After a general overview, attention is paid to what the defendant can get from the prosecutor and what the prosecutor can get from the defendant without violating the Constitution. Proposals for liberalizing dscovery are considered.

Chapter Nine is devoted to guilty pleas and plea bargaining. An extensive exerpt from a comprehensive study of plea bargaining in the United States begins the chapter. It is followed by a discussion of the requirements of a valid plea and an analysis of the finality of a plea.

Trial and trial-related rights are treated in Chapter Ten. Among the topics covered are speedy trial, joinder of defendants and charges, burdens of persuasion, jury trial, fair-trial—free press conflicts, confrontation and compulsory process, and effective representation and self-representation. This is the second longest chapter in the book. It addresses in the context of criminal trials many issues that are considered in the context of civil trials in the typical course in Civil Procedure.

Sentencing is the exclusive concern of Chapter Eleven. Basic options in sentencing are described, as are the roles of judge and jury. The determinate versus indeterminate sentencing controversy is explored, and the Federal Sentencing Guidelines are carefully examined. Also, the procedures that are generally employed in sentencing, and the applicable constitutional rules are set forth. Special attention is paid to capital punishment procedures.

Chapter Twelve covers all aspects of double jeopardy. Most attention is paid to recent decisions of the Supreme Court that clarify (or further confuse, depending on how the decisions are read) a subject that has been puzzling criminal procedure students for years. Collateral estoppel and vindictive prosecutorial conduct also are discussed.

Finally, Chapter Thirteen focuses on post-trial motions, appeals, and collateral attacks on convictions. An effort is made to examine all important post-sentencing challenges that can be made to a conviction. The section on collateral attack endeavors to explain the development of habeas corpus by the Supreme Court and the high points of the debate over how much post-conviction attack is desirable in a criminal justice system.

It should be obvious that we have tried to cover all of the significant parts of the criminal justice system and to do so in a reasonable number of pages. To accomplish this, we have worked hard to make the textual portions of the book as informative as possible. This Edition cannot yet be called a short book, but criminal procedure is not a subject that is easily confined to a few pages. To make the length somewhat more tolerable, we have endeavored to use several different typesizes, not only for purposes of emphasis, but also to break the monotony of the printed page. To make the book easier to read, we also delete most internal citations in material that we quote from other sources. Thus, most internal cites in the Supreme Court opinions found throughout the book are missing. Footnotes in quoted material generally are deleted also. When we leave internal citations and original footnotes in the quoted material, we do so in the belief that they make a contribution to the overall coverage of the materials. Footnotes that are taken from the original source all have small letters to identify them—i.e., a, b, c, etc. Our own footnotes are identified by number—i.e., 1, 2, 3, etc. We hope that these choices enhance the "readability" of the book, and that by choosing to delete unnecessary baggage in quoted material, we have been able to pay more attention to the important and interesting questions that make criminal procedure a joy to study.

STEPHEN A. SALTZBURG
Washington, D.C.

DANIEL J. CAPRA
New York, N.Y.

March, 1992

*

Summary of Contents

*

Table of Contents

*

Table of Cases

The principal cases are in bold type. Cases cited or discussed in the text are roman type. References are to pages. Cases cited in principal cases and within other quoted materials are not included.

Table of Authorities

Hale, M., Pleas of the Crown (1st Am. ed. 1847), 149

Hale, M., The Law of Arrest in both Civil and Criminal Cases, by an Attorney at Law (2d ed. 1753), 57

Hall, Objectives of Federal Criminal Procedural Revision, 51 Yale L.J. 723 (1942), 5

Hall, Police and Law in a Democratic Society, 28 Ind.L.J. 133 (1953), 656

Hall, The Prosecutor's Subpoena Power, 33 Ark.L.Rev. 122 (1979), 697

Hall & Fennell, Due Process at Sentencing: An Empirical and Legal Analysis of the Disclosure of Presentence Reports in Federal Courts, 93 Harv.L.Rev. 1615 (1980), 1142

Halpern, Federal Habeas Corpus and the Mapp Exclusionary Rule After *Stone v. Powell*, 82 Colum.L.Rev. 1 (1982), 1313

Hancock, State Court Activism and Searches Incident to Arrest, 68 Va.L.Rev. 1085 (1982), 15

Harland, Monetary Remedies for the Victims of Crime: Assessing the Role of the Criminal Courts, 30 U.C.L.A.L.Rev. 52 (1982), 1119

Harris, *Ake* Revisited: Expert Psychiatric Witnesses Remain Beyond Reach for the Indigent, 68 No.Car.L.Rev. 763 (1990), 651

Harrison, Federalism & Double Jeopardy: A Study in the Frustration of Human Rights, 17 U.Miami L.Rev. 306 (1963), 1241

Hayman, Beyond Penry: The Remedial Use of the Mentally Retarded Label in Death Penalty Sentencing, 59 U.M.K.C.L.Rev. 17 (1990), 1165

Heaney, The Reality of Guidelines Sentencing: No End to Disparity, 28 Am.Crim.L.Rev. 161 (1991), 1101

Heffernan, On Justifying Fourth Amendment Exclusion, 1989 Wis.L.Rev. 1193, p. 367

Heidt, The Conjurer's Circle, The Fifth Amendment Privilege in Civil Cases, 91 Yale L.J. 1062 (1982), 452

Heller, F., The Sixth Amendment (1951), 628

Herman, The New Liberty: The Procedural Due Process Rights of Prisoners and Others under the Burger Court, 59 N.Y.U.L.Rev. 482 (1984), 1148

Herman & Thompson, *Scott v. Illinois* and the Right to Counsel: A Decision in Search of a Doctrine? 17 Am.Crim. L.Rev. 71 (1979), 639

Hixson, Bringing Down the Curtain on the Absurd Drama of Entrances and Exits—Witness Representation in the Grand Jury Room, 15 Am.Cr.L.Rev. 307 (1978), 692

Hoffmand, The Privilege Against Self-Incrimination and Immunity Statutes: Permissible Uses of Immunized Testimony, 16 Crim.L.Bull. 421 (1980), 487

Hogan & Snee, The *McNabb-Mallory* Rule: Its Rise, Rationale and Rescue, 47 Geo.L.J. 1 (1958), 503

Holmes, The Path of the Law in Harv.L.Rev. 457 (1897), 65

Holt, Mech, Davis Kerr & Atkin, The Decision Processes of 6– and 12–Person Mock Juries Assigned Unanimous and Two-Thirds Majority Rules, 32 J. of Personality & Soc.Psych. 1 (1975), 894

Holtzoff, The Right of Counsel Under the Sixth Amendment, 20 N.Y.U.L.Rev. 1–22 (1944), 628

Hood & Radzinowicz, Judicial Discretion and Sentencing Standards: Victorian Attempts to Solve a Perennial Problem, 127 U.Pa.L.Rev. 1288 (1979), 1124

Hudson, J., Police Review Boards and Police Accountability, 36 L. & Contemp.Prob. 515 (1971), 438

Hudson & Galaway, Restitution in Criminal Justice (1977), 1118

Hughes, English Criminal Justice: Is it Better Than Ours?, 26 Ariz.L.Rev. 507 (1984), 799

Humble, Nonevidentiary Use of Compelled Testimony: Beyond the Fifth Amendment, 66 Tex.L.Rev. 351 (1987), 486

Identification Parades, Part I, (1963) Crim.L.Rev. 479, p. 599

Inbau & Manak, *Miranda v. Arizona*: Is It Worth the Cost? (A Sample Survey, with Commentary, of the Expenditure of Court Time and Effort), 24 Cal. Western L.Rev, 185 (1988), 524

Israel, Criminal Procedure, The Burger Court and the Legacy of the Warren Court, 75 Mich.L.Rev. 1320 (1977), 819

Israel, *Gideon v. Wainwright*: The "Art" of Overruling, 1963 Sup.Ct.Rev. 211, p. 633

Israel, Selective Incorporation: Revisited, 71 Geo.L.J. 253 (1982), 14

Jacobson, The Unanimous Verdict: Politics and the Jury Trial, 1977 Wash.U.L.Q. 39, p. 901

James, G., Constitutional Limitations on Evidence in Criminal Cases (1973), 490

Jeffries & Stephan, Defenses, Presumptions and Burden of Proof in the Criminal Law, 88 Yale L.J. 1325 (1979), 868

Joseph & Saltzburg, Evidence in America (1989), 1006

Joseph & Saltzburg, Evidence in America (1991 Supp.), 1012

Kadane, Lehoczky & Kairys, Jury Representativeness: A Mandate for Multiple Source Lists, 65 Calif.L.Rev. 776 (1977), 909

*

AMERICAN CRIMINAL PROCEDURE

CASES AND COMMENTARY

Fourth Edition

*

Chapter One

FORESHADOWING THE COURSE

I. A CRIMINAL CASE

A course in criminal procedure obviously is intended to cover the procedures that are employed as a criminal case is processed. It could be said that the course covers the processing of those cases that are studied in criminal law. Although such a statement would be fairly accurate, it would fail to address the question of when a case is sufficiently "criminal" to require the procedures which are the focus of this book.

To answer this question, it is not necessary to ponder the limits of the criminal sanction; nor is it vital to consider whether, as a matter of policy, a criminal sanction, some other sanction, or none at all should be addressed to designated conduct. Whether or not to invoke a criminal sanction in given circumstances is a subject left for a course in substantive criminal law. This course analyzes what happens once the decision is made to utilize a particular sanction. This is not to suggest that the basic question of whether to use the criminal law to control, or to attempt to control, human behavior should be made irrespective of the procedures that attend the criminal process. It should be plain that an accurate assessment of the costs and benefits of any sanction must focus in part on the procedural mechanism by which law is enforced. The point to be made here, however, is that a cost-benefit analysis of criminal sanctions is not part of this course.

What is part of the course is deciding whether a sanction that has been chosen is properly classified as "criminal" for purposes of assigning procedural rights to parties. The threshold question is what distinguishes criminal cases from other cases.

An answer that is frequently given is that criminal cases require proof beyond a reasonable doubt, whereas civil and administrative cases generally do not. But this answer is too circular to be helpful. Proof beyond a reasonable doubt is required once a case is identified as criminal. Similarly, rights to counsel, to invoke the privilege against self-incrimination, to suppress illegally seized evidence, and others as well, may be triggered when a case is identified as criminal. But these rights arise after the identification is made. Similarly it puts the cart before the horse to identify a criminal case as one that stigmatizes. Cases usually stigmatize in a special way because they are criminal. And one reason they stigmatize is that the world is told that someone who is found guilty is guilty beyond any reasonable doubt.

Another answer is that the label "criminal" implies jail and prison. But jail and prison are not the usual penalties for many lesser criminal offenses. It is probably true that if jail and prison are prescribed penalties for a violation of the law, the law is criminal.[1] But, fines, restitution and other sanctions might be employed as criminal sanctions. If the existence or absence of jail and prison penalties does not determine whether or not a case is criminal, could the determinative factor be whether a penalty is a punishment or not? This would appear to be somewhat closer to the mark. Yet, deciding whether a sanction is a penalty itself may present difficulties. Moreover, punitive damages and civil fines are hardly unknown to American law. Thus, the penalty aspect alone cannot identify a criminal case.

Another answer might be that the party seeking to impose the penalty is the state. One characteristic of criminal cases is that they are brought in the name of the government on behalf of the community. The decision whether to bring a criminal case and what kind of a case to bring generally is left to government officials. The penalty scheme prescribed for crimes and the actual penalty imposed in any case may bear no direct relation to the harm suffered by any individual victim. The decision on whether to settle the case generally is left to the government, and there is no counterclaim that can be made against the plaintiff (always the government).

Although the presence of the state as a party is a feature of criminal cases, it is also a feature of many civil cases and of administrative proceedings brought by government agencies, which are generally thought to be civil. Thus, something more is needed to identify criminal cases. That something is so obvious that it may appear unsatisfactory at first; it is the label that the legislature chooses to give a sanction. If the legislature calls something criminal, presumably it wants the public to treat an offense as criminal. When this happens, the special procedures of criminal cases will be invoked. See generally Cheh, Constitutional Limits on Using Civil Remedies To Achieve Criminal Law Objectives: Understanding and Transcending the Criminal–Civil Law Distinction, 42 Hastings L.J. 1325 (1991) (proceeding is criminal where labelled as such by the legislature).

Thus, if the legislature prescribes jail and prison as sanctions for violations of law and the characteristics of a criminal case, described above, are present, the case will be treated as a criminal case. When jail or prison are not prescribed, the labeling of conduct as "criminal," added to the previously described characteristics, results in similar treatment.[2]

Usually, the issue whether a violation is civil or criminal is raised by a defendant seeking to take advantage of certain constitutional rights that are only available in criminal prosecutions. A decision that the defendant faces a civil sanction means that the claim of right will be denied. In United States v. L. O. Ward, 448 U.S. 242 (1980), for example, the Supreme Court held that a

1. There are exceptions to the general rule. For example, imposition of civil contempt can result in incarceration. See Hicks on Behalf of Feiock v. Feiock, discussed in this section. Also, there may be certain other punishments—e.g., physical hardship or loss of citizenship—which, if not violative of the Eighth Amendment, would be treated as "infamous" or as reserved for criminal cases.

2. There are provisions of the United States Constitution that protect against punishment, whether or not it is criminal. See generally Clark, Civil and Criminal Penalties and Forfeitures: A Framework for Constitutional Analysis, 60 Minn.L.Rev. 379 (1976). These are not considered in this book.

penalty imposed upon persons discharging hazardous substances into navigable waters was a civil penalty and, therefore, that a reporting requirement for violators did not violate the Fifth Amendment's privilege against self-incrimination. The Court said that the question whether a penalty is criminal or civil is a matter of statutory construction.

> Our inquiry in this regard has traditionally proceeded on two levels. First, we have set out to determine whether Congress, in establishing the penalizing mechanism, indicated either expressly or impliedly a preference for one label or the other. Second, where Congress has indicated an intention to establish a civil penalty, we have inquired further whether the statutory scheme was so punitive either in purpose or effect as to negate that intention. In regard to this latter inquiry, we have noted that "only the clearest proof could suffice to establish the unconstitutionality of a statute on such a ground."

The Court accepted the congressional label of "civil," although Justice Stevens dissented. In United States v. One Assortment of 89 Firearms, 465 U.S. 354 (1984), the Court unanimously held that a proceeding to forfeit firearms used in violation of federal law was civil in nature, even though Congress labeled forfeiture a "penalty." Chief Justice Burger's opinion reasoned that there are civil and criminal penalties and the statutory scheme evinced a congressional intent to make forfeiture a civil proceeding. See also Allen v. Illinois, 478 U.S. 364 (1986) (commitment proceedings under the Illinois Sexually Dangerous Persons Act held not criminal for self-incrimination purposes). In *Allen,* the Court found that the legislature's characterization of the statute as civil and treatment-oriented was crucial, even though persons committed under the Act were kept in a maximum security institution that also housed prisoners in need of psychiatric care.

The Supreme Court explained its approach to distinguishing criminal and civil contempt proceedings in Hicks on Behalf of Feiock v. Feiock, 485 U.S. 624 (1988), a case involving a father's failure to make support payments as ordered by a state court. The father was ordered to make payments for his three children, complied only sporadically, and was ordered a second time to provide support. The state court adjudged him in contempt on five of nine counts of failing to comply with the order and sentenced him to 25 days in jail. The court suspended the jail sentence, however, placed the father on probation and ordered him to provide support as a condition of probation. In finding the father in contempt, the court relied upon a state presumption that he was able to comply with the order. The father challenged the validity of the presumption at the hearing and on appeal.

Justice White's opinion for the Court observed that the state appellate court treated the contempt citation as quasi-criminal contempt. The majority stated that "state law provides strong guidance about whether or not the State is exercising its authority 'in a nonpunitive, noncriminal manner,' and one who challenges the State's classification of the relief imposed as 'civil' or 'criminal' may be required to show 'the clearest proof' that it is not correct as a matter of federal law." (Citing *Allen*). The Court reasoned that in contempt cases "the critical features are the substance of the proceeding and the character of the relief that the proceeding will afford." It suggested that remedial relief for the benefit of the complainant is civil, while punitive relief to vindicate the authority of the court is criminal. The Court added that "[i]f the relief provided is a sentence of imprisonment, it is remedial 'if the defendant stands committed unless and until he performs the affirmative act required by the court order,' and is criminal if 'the sentence is limited to imprisonment for a definite period.' "

The Court rejected the argument that the classification of the relief should turn on an assessment of the underlying purpose of a contempt citation, since "both civil and criminal relief have aspects that can be seen as either remedial or punitive or both; when a court imposes fines and punishments on a contemnor, it is not only vindicating its legal authority to enter the initial order, but it also is seeking to give effect to the law's purpose of modifying the contemnor's behavior to conform to the terms required in the order."

The Court remanded the case for application of its approach to the facts presented.

Justice O'Connor, joined by Chief Justice Rehnquist and Justice Scalia, dissented and argued that "[c]ontempt proceedings often will be useless if the parent seeking enforcement of valid support orders must prove that the obligor can comply with the court order." Although she agreed with Justice White that the question whether a proceeding was criminal or civil was a federal question, she contended that "[t]he most important indication is whether the judgment inures to the benefit of another party to the proceeding" and concluded that the thrust of the sanction imposed upon the father was to inure to the benefit of the children. Justice Kennedy did not participate in the case.

Occasionally, constitutional guarantees covered in the criminal procedure course will arise in a civil context. The most prevalent situation is an action for damages brought against a police officer under 42 U.S.C. § 1983 for violation of the plaintiff's constitutional rights. If the plaintiff claims that he was wrongly arrested or illegally searched, the court applies Fourth Amendment principles in the same way as if a criminal defendant moves to suppress evidence allegedly obtained in violation of the Fourth Amendment.

II. THE NATURE OF THE PROCEDURAL SYSTEM AND THE SOURCES OF PROCEDURAL RULES

Many of the procedural rules that will be discussed in this book have their roots in the United States Constitution. The Bill of Rights contains several provisions that have exclusive applicability to criminal cases, and others that have had their principal impact on the criminal justice system. Many of these same rights are found in the constitutions of the fifty states, and as the next section of this Chapter will explain, most of the Bill of Rights is now binding on the states.

The constitutional rights discussed in this book—to counsel; to indictment by grand jury; to a speedy trial; to trial by an impartial jury; to freedom from cruel and unusual punishment, excessive bail, excessive fines and double jeopardy; to freedom also from unreasonable searches and seizures; and to confront one's accusers and to have compulsory process for one's witnesses, but not to incriminate oneself—suggest a great deal about the nature of American criminal justice. Concepts such as the presumption of innocence, proof beyond a reasonable doubt, and general notions of fair procedures are not specifically mentioned in the Constitution, but they have assumed the same importance as if they were found in the document itself.

These concepts combine to produce a process that is protective of persons suspected and accused of crime. There are limits placed on the ability of government to gather and to use evidence, and to prosecute suspects. In many ways, the constitutional rules reflect a fundamental distrust of government power generally and of certain particular powers.

It must be recognized that constitutional rules represent only the minimum protections that must be afforded criminal defendants. Statutes and court rules can and do build upon or add to constitutional minima and fill out the interstices of the criminal justice process.

As you examine American criminal justice, you will not be surprised to see that law enforcement officials, whose job it is to investigate criminal activity, to solve crimes, to prosecute offenders, to convict the guilty and to punish those convicted, find that constitutional, statutory and judge-made rules may make it difficult for them to carry out the duties assigned to them. Throughout criminal procedure, there is a tension between goals having to do with protecting individual defendants and promoting individual freedom, and goals having to do with ferreting out, prosecuting, and, ultimately, stopping crime. See generally Hall, Objectives of Federal Criminal Procedural Revision, 51 Yale L.J. 723 (1942). Professor Packer described the conflict by positing two possible, competing models of the criminal justice system: the crime control model and the due process model. See generally, The Limits of the Criminal Sanction (1968). As you go through the course, another model will present itself. For lack of a better term, it might be called the "individual human rights" model. Some support for it can be found in R. Dworkin, Taking Rights Seriously (1977).

Pay attention to the kind of system that develops in the pages that follow. Like so many systems, it hardly is perfect. And, like so many systems, its attempts to reconcile competing values result in compromises. As you wonder about the worth of the end product, remember that many of the rules that have been developed, constitutional and non-constitutional alike, attempt to separate power in the processing of criminal cases. Others are designed to assure that the defendant can participate in and take control of her own case. Rules that decentralize power and that place party control in the hands of a defendant have political and sociological significance, aside from more instrumental importance. In each section, and with each new rule, it will be helpful to ask what kind of system would be created if the rules were changed.

III. TWO SPECIAL ASPECTS OF CONSTITUTIONAL LAW: THE INCORPORATION DOCTRINE AND PROSPECTIVE DECISIONMAKING

A. INCORPORATION

Few individual rights were guaranteed by the original Constitution prior to the adoption of the Bill of Rights. But the ratification of the first ten Amendments in 1791 provided procedural protections that comprise much of what will be examined in this book.

In Barron v. Baltimore, 32 U.S. (7 Pet.) 243 (1833), Chief Justice Marshall, writing for the Court, had little difficulty in concluding that the Bill of Rights applied against the federal government, but not against the states. Because of restrictions on appellate review in criminal cases, the Court had few opportunities to reaffirm the decision in its early days. Although the clarity of the Marshall view leaves little doubt as to his reluctance to apply any of the original Amendments against the states, there have been suggestions that some Amendments might have been intended to be generally applicable to states and the federal government. See 2 Crosskey, Politics and the Constitution in the History of the United States 1050 (1953). Prior to the Civil War, the Court never had occasion to approve any of these suggestions.

After the Civil War and the adoption of the Thirteenth, Fourteenth and Fifteenth Amendments, a new question arose: whether these Amendments, particularly the Fourteenth, incorporated the Bill of Rights, making it applicable against the states. Early cases, like the *Slaughter-House Cases*, 83 U.S. (16 Wall.) 36 (1873), took a narrow view of the Amendments. But four dissenters would have read the Fourteenth Amendment more broadly, as altering the fundamental relationship of the federal government and the states, and of the states and all persons within their reach.[3]

For approximately three quarters of a century the Court struggled to interpret the open-ended language of the Fourteenth Amendment. In 1884, in Hurtado v. California, 110 U.S. 516, the Court held that California could permit criminal proceedings to be instituted by information, rather than by grand jury indictment. And in 1908, the Court, in Twining v. New Jersey, 211 U.S. 78, held that the privilege against self-incrimination was not binding on the states. But in 1932, in Powell v. Alabama, 287 U.S. 45, the Court held that denial of counsel in a capital case effectively denied defendants the right to be heard and thus denied them a fundamental right.

Five years later, in Palko v. Connecticut, 302 U.S. 319 (1937), Justice Cardozo wrote for the Court to uphold a state procedure that permitted the state to appeal in a criminal case and obtain a new trial. He assumed that the double jeopardy clause of the Fifth Amendment would have invalidated such an appeal and retrial by the federal government, but found that the states could take a different approach. Discussing the question whether the Bill of Rights was "absorbed" into the Fourteenth Amendment, Justice Cardozo wrote that the "specific pledges of particular amendments have been found to be implicit in the concept of ordered liberty, and thus, through the Fourteenth Amendment, become valid as against the states." But the double jeopardy clause was not one.

A decade after *Palko*, a majority of the Court reaffirmed *Twining* in Adamson v. California, 332 U.S. 46 (1947). Justice Black, joined by Justice Douglas, dissented. Justice Black argued that the language of the first section of the Fourteenth Amendment was intended to assure that no state could deprive its citizens of the privileges and protections of the Bill of Rights. Also, Justice Black rejected what he called the "natural law" formula of *Palko,* which invited the Court to recognize rights not found in the Bill of Rights.[4]

3. Professor Ely has observed that the opinions in the case can be read to support a claim that all nine justices would have incorporated the Bill of Rights into the Fourteenth Amendment. J. Ely, Democracy and Distrust 196 n. 59 (1980).

4. Justice Murphy, joined by Justice Rutledge, also dissented. Justice Murphy would have reserved the right to recognize procedural protections not explicitly recognized in the Bill of Rights. Later, Justice Douglas also would move to this position.

Responding to the opinion by Justice Black and its appendix of constitutional history, Justice Frankfurter took vigorous exception to Black's argument.[5]

Justices Black and Frankfurter continued to disagree for years over the relationship of the Bill of Rights and the Fourteenth Amendment, with Justice Frankfurter generally prevailing on the theory, although not necessarily on its application. See, e.g., Wolf v. Colorado, 338 U.S. 25 (1949); Rochin v. California, 342 U.S. 165 (1952); Irvine v. California, 347 U.S. 128 (1954); Breithaupt v. Abram, 352 U.S. 432 (1957).

In the 1960's a shift took place, subtle at first, but less so over time. The Warren Court—without ever formally abandoning the fundamental fairness standard—began to incorporate more and more Bill of Rights guarantees into the Fourteenth Amendment, pursuant to an approach referred to by Justice Black as "selective incorporation." The Court paid little attention to the facts of the case presenting the incorporation issue, and proceeded instead to determine whether the right asserted was fundamental to the American system of justice. Moreover, the Court insisted that, once incorporated, the scope of the guarantee would be the same in state as in federal cases: every detail of the incorporated provision was applicable "jot-for-jot" to the states. See G. Gunther, Cases and Materials on Constitutional Law 420–21 (12th ed. 1991).

The current approach of the Court, and the competing theories also, are well illustrated by Duncan v. Louisiana. *Duncan* held that the right to jury trial, guaranteed by the Sixth Amendment, is binding on the states. That particular holding is not the subject of attention here; rather, the focus is on how the Court reached its result.

DUNCAN v. LOUISIANA

Supreme Court of the United States, 1968.
391 U.S. 145.

MR. JUSTICE WHITE delivered the opinion of the Court.

* * *

I

The Fourteenth Amendment denies the States the power to "deprive any person of life, liberty, or property, without due process of law." In resolving conflicting claims concerning the meaning of this spacious language, the Court has looked increasingly to the Bill of Rights for guidance; many of the rights guaranteed by the first eight Amendments to the Constitution have been held to be protected against state action by the Due Process Clause of the Fourteenth Amendment. That clause now protects the right to compensation for property taken by the State;[a] the rights of speech, press, and religion covered by the First Amendment;[b] the Fourth Amendment rights to be free from unreasonable searches and seizures and to have excluded from criminal trials any evidence illegally seized;[c] the right guaranteed by the Fifth Amendment to be free of compelled self-incrimina-

5. For additional criticism, see Fairman, Does the Fourteenth Amendment Incorporate the Bill of Rights? The Original Understanding, 2 Stan.L.Rev. 5 (1949). Both Justice Black and Professor Fairman are criticized in Kelly, Clio and the Court: An Illicit Love Affair, 1965 Sup.Ct.Rev. 119.

a. Chicago, B. & Q. R. Co. v. Chicago, 166 U.S. 226 (1897).

b. See, e.g., Fiske v. Kansas, 274 U.S. 380 (1927).

c. See Mapp v. Ohio, 367 U.S. 643 (1961).

tion;[d] and the Sixth Amendment rights to counsel,[e] to a speedy[f] and public[g] trial, to confrontation of opposing witnesses,[h] and to compulsory process for obtaining witnesses.[i]

The test for determining whether a right extended by the Fifth and Sixth Amendments with respect to federal criminal proceedings is also protected against state action by the Fourteenth Amendment has been phrased in a variety of ways in the opinions of this Court. The question has been asked whether a right is among those " 'fundamental principles of liberty and justice which lie at the base of all our civil and political institutions,' " Powell v. Alabama, 287 U.S. 45, 67 (1932);[j] whether it is "basic in our system of jurisprudence," In re Oliver, 333 U.S. 257, 273 (1948); and whether it is "a fundamental right, essential to a fair trial," Gideon v. Wainwright, 372 U.S. 335, 343–344 (1963); Malloy v. Hogan, 378 U.S. 1 (1964); Pointer v. Texas, 380 U.S. 400, 403 (1965). The claim before us is that the right to trial by jury guaranteed by the Sixth Amendment meets these tests. The position of Louisiana, on the other hand, is that the Constitution imposes upon the States no duty to give a jury trial in any criminal case, regardless of the seriousness of the crime or the size of the punishment which may be imposed. Because we believe that trial by jury in criminal cases is fundamental to the American scheme of justice, we hold that the Fourteenth Amendment guarantees a right of jury trial in all criminal cases which—were they to be tried in a federal court—would come within the Sixth Amendment's guarantee.[k] Since we

d. Malloy v. Hogan, 378 U.S. 1 (1964).

e. Gideon v. Wainwright, 372 U.S. 335 (1963).

f. Klopfer v. North Carolina, 386 U.S. 213 (1967).

g. In re Oliver, 333 U.S. 257 (1948).

h. Pointer v. Texas, 380 U.S. 400 (1965).

i. Washington v. Texas, 388 U.S. 14 (1967).

j. Quoting from Hebert v. Louisiana, 272 U.S. 312, 316 (1926).

k. In one sense recent cases applying provisions of the first eight Amendments to the States represent a new approach to the "incorporation" debate. Earlier the Court can be seen as having asked, when inquiring into whether some particular procedural safeguard was required of a State, if a civilized system could be imagined that would not accord the particular protection. For example, Palko v. Connecticut, 302 U.S. 319, 325 (1937) stated: "The right to trial by jury and the immunity from prosecution except as the result of an indictment may have value and importance. Even so, they are not of the very essence of a scheme of ordered liberty * * *. Few would be so narrow or provincial as to maintain that a fair and enlightened system of justice would be impossible without them." The recent cases, on the other hand, have proceeded upon the valid assumption that state criminal processes are not imaginary and theoretical schemes but actual systems bearing virtually every characteristic of the common-law system that has been developing contemporaneously in England and in this country. The question thus is whether given this kind of system a particular procedure is fundamental—whether, that is, a procedure is necessary to an Anglo-American regime of ordered liberty. It is this sort of inquiry that can justify the conclusions that state courts must exclude evidence seized in violation of the Fourth Amendment, Mapp v. Ohio, 367 U.S. 643 (1961); that state prosecutors may not comment on a defendant's failure to testify, Griffin v. California, 380 U.S. 609 (1965); and that criminal punishment may not be imposed for the status of narcotics addiction, Robinson v. California, 370 U.S. 660 (1962). Of immediate relevance for this case are the Court's holdings that the States must comply with certain provisions of the Sixth Amendment, specifically that the States may not refuse a speedy trial, confrontation of witnesses, and the assistance, at state expense if necessary, of counsel. See cases cited in nn. e–i, supra. Of each of these determinations that a constitutional provision originally written to bind the Federal Government should bind the States as well it might be said that the limitation in question is not necessarily fundamental to fairness in every criminal system that might be imagined but is fundamental in the context of the criminal processes maintained by the American States.

When the inquiry is approached in this way the question whether the States can impose criminal punishment without granting a jury trial appears quite different from the way it appeared in the older cases opining that

consider the appeal before us to be such a case, we hold that the Constitution was violated when appellant's demand for jury trial was refused.

* * *

MR. JUSTICE BLACK, with whom MR. JUSTICE DOUGLAS joins, concurring.

The Court today holds that the right to trial by jury guaranteed defendants in criminal cases in federal courts by Art. III of the United States Constitution and by the Sixth Amendment is also guaranteed by the Fourteenth Amendment to defendants tried in state courts. With this holding I agree for reasons given by the Court.

* * *

All of these holdings making Bill of Rights' provisions applicable as such to the States mark, of course, a departure from the *Twining* doctrine holding that none of those provisions were enforceable as such against the States. The dissent in this case, however, makes a spirited and forceful defense of that now discredited doctrine. I do not believe that it is necessary for me to repeat the historical and logical reasons for my challenge to the *Twining* holding contained in my *Adamson* dissent and Appendix to it. What I wrote there in 1947 was the product of years of study and research. My appraisal of the legislative history followed 10 years of legislative experience as a Senator of the United States, not a bad way, I suspect, to learn the value of what is said in legislative debates, committee discussions, committee reports, and various other steps taken in the course of passage of bills, resolutions, and proposed constitutional amendments. My Brother Harlan's objections to my *Adamson* dissent history, like that of most of the objectors, relies most heavily on a criticism written by Professor Charles Fairman and published in the Stanford Law Review. 2 Stan.L.Rev. 5 (1949). I have read and studied this article extensively, including the historical references, but am compelled to add that in my view it has completely failed to refute the inferences and arguments that I suggested in my *Adamson* dissent. Professor Fairman's "history" relies very heavily on what was *not* said in the state legislatures that passed on the Fourteenth Amendment. Instead of relying on this kind of negative pregnant, my legislative experience has convinced me that it is far wiser to rely on what *was* said, and most importantly, said by the men who actually sponsored the Amendment in the Congress. * * *

In addition to the adoption of Professor Fairman's "history," the dissent states that "the great words of the four clauses of the first section of the Fourteenth Amendment would have been an exceedingly peculiar way to say that 'The rights heretofore guaranteed against federal intrusion by the first eight Amendments are henceforth guaranteed against state intrusion as well.'" In response to this I can say only that the words "No State shall make or enforce any law which shall abridge the privileges or immunities of citizens of the United States" seem to me an eminently reasonable way of expressing the idea that henceforth the Bill of Rights

States might abolish jury trial. See, e.g., Maxwell v. Dow, 176 U.S. 581 (1900). A criminal process, which was fair and equitable but used no juries is easy to imagine. It would make use of alternative guarantees and protections which would serve the purposes that the jury serves in the English and American systems. Yet no American State has undertaken to construct such a system. Instead, every American State, including Louisiana, uses the jury extensively, and imposes very serious punishments only after a trial at which the defendant has a right to a jury's verdict. In every State, including Louisiana, the structure and style of the criminal process—the supporting framework and the subsidiary procedures—are of the sort that naturally complement jury trial, and have developed in connection with and in reliance upon jury trial.

shall apply to the States.[1] What more precious "privilege" of American citizenship could there be than that privilege to claim the protections of our great Bill of Rights? I suggest that any reading of "privileges or immunities of citizens of the United States" which excludes the Bill of Rights' safeguards renders the words of this section of the Fourteenth Amendment meaningless. * * *

While I do not wish at this time to discuss at length my disagreement with Brother Harlan's forthright and frank restatement of the now discredited *Twining* doctrine, I do want to point out what appears to me to be the basic difference between us. His view, as was indeed the view of *Twining,* is that "due process is an evolving concept" and therefore that it entails a "gradual process of judicial inclusion and exclusion" to ascertain those "immutable principles * * * of free government which no member of the Union may disregard." Thus the Due Process Clause is treated as prescribing no specific and clearly ascertainable constitutional command that judges must obey in interpreting the Constitution, but rather as leaving judges free to decide at any particular time whether a particular rule or judicial formulation embodies an "immutable principl[e] of free government" or is "implicit in the concept of ordered liberty," or whether certain conduct "shocks the judge's conscience" or runs counter to some other similar, undefined and undefinable standard. Thus due process, according to my Brother Harlan, is to be a phrase with no permanent meaning, but one which is found to shift from time to time in accordance with judges' predilections and understandings of what is best for the country. If due process means this, the Fourteenth Amendment, in my opinion, might as well have been written that "no person shall be deprived of life, liberty or property except by laws that the judges of the United States Supreme Court shall find to be consistent with the immutable principles of free government." It is impossible for me to believe that such unconfined power is given to judges in our Constitution that is a written one in order to limit governmental power.

Another tenet of the *Twining* doctrine as restated by my Brother Harlan is that "due process of law requires only fundamental fairness." But the "fundamental fairness" test is one on a par with that of shocking the conscience of the Court. Each of such tests depends entirely on the particular judge's idea of ethics and morals instead of requiring him to depend on the boundaries fixed by the written words of the Constitution. Nothing in the history of the phrase "due process of law" suggests that constitutional controls are to depend on any particular judge's sense of values. * * * There is not one word of legal history that justifies making the term "due process of law" mean a guarantee of a trial free from laws and conduct which the courts deem at the time to be "arbitrary," "unreasonable," "unfair," or "contrary to civilized standards." The due process of law standard for a trial is one in accordance with the Bill of Rights and laws passed pursuant to constitutional power, guaranteeing to all alike a trial under the general law of the land.

Finally I want to add that I am not bothered by the argument that applying the Bill of Rights to the States, "according to the same standards that protect those personal rights against federal encroachment," interferes with our concept of federalism in that it may prevent States from trying novel social and eco-

1. My view has been and is that the Fourteenth Amendment, *as a whole,* makes the Bill of Rights applicable to the States. This would certainly include the language of the Privileges and Immunities Clause, as well as the Due Process Clause.

nomic experiments. I have never believed that under the guise of federalism the States should be able to experiment with the protections afforded our citizens through the Bill of Rights. It seems to me totally inconsistent to advocate, on the one hand, the power of this Court to strike down any state law or practice which it finds "unreasonable" or "unfair" and, on the other hand, urge that the States be given maximum power to develop their own laws and procedures. Yet the due process approach of my Brothers Harlan and Fortas does just that since in effect it restricts the States to practices which a majority of this Court is willing to approve on a case-by-case basis. No one is more concerned than I that the States be allowed to use the full scope of their powers as their citizens see fit. And that is why I have continually fought against the expansion of this Court's authority over the States through the use of a broad, general interpretation of due process that permits judges to strike down state laws they do not like.

In closing I want to emphasize that I believe as strongly as ever that the Fourteenth Amendment was intended to make the Bill of Rights applicable to the States. I have been willing to support the selective incorporation doctrine, however, as an alternative, although perhaps less historically supportable than complete incorporation. The selective incorporation process, if used properly, does limit the Supreme Court in the Fourteenth Amendment field to specific Bill of Rights' protections only and keeps judges from roaming at will in their own notions of what policies outside the Bill of Rights are desirable and what are not. And, most importantly for me, the selective incorporation process has the virtue of having already worked to make most of the Bill of Rights' protections applicable to the States.

MR. JUSTICE HARLAN, whom MR. JUSTICE STEWART joins, dissenting.

* * *

The Court's approach to this case is an uneasy and illogical compromise among the views of various Justices on how the Due Process Clause should be interpreted. The Court does not say that those who framed the Fourteenth Amendment intended to make the Sixth Amendment applicable to the States. And the Court concedes that it finds nothing unfair about the procedure by which the present appellant was tried. Nevertheless, the Court reverses his conviction: it holds, for some reason not apparent to me that the Due Process Clause incorporates the particular clause of the Sixth Amendment that requires trial by jury in federal criminal cases—including, as I read its opinion, the sometimes trivial accompanying baggage of judicial interpretation in federal contexts. I have raised my voice many times before against the Court's continuing undiscriminating insistence upon fastening on the States federal notions of criminal justice and I must do so again in this instance. With all respect, the Court's approach and its reading of history are altogether topsy-turvy.

I

I believe I am correct in saying that every member of the Court for at least the last 135 years has agreed that our Founders did not consider the requirements of the Bill of Rights so fundamental that they should operate directly against the States. They were wont to believe rather that the security of liberty in America rested primarily upon the dispersion of governmental power across a federal system. The Bill of Rights was considered unnecessary by some but insisted upon by others in order to curb the possibility of abuse of power by the strong central government they were creating.

The Civil War Amendments dramatically altered the relation of the Federal Government to the States. The first section of the Fourteenth Amendment imposes highly significant restrictions on state action. But the restrictions are couched in very broad and general terms: citizenship; privileges and immunities; due process of law; equal protection of the laws. Consequently, for 100 years this Court has been engaged in the difficult process Professor Jaffe has well called "the search for intermediate premises." The question has been, Where does the Court properly look to find the specific rules that define and give content to such terms as "life, liberty, or property" and "due process of law"?

A few members of the Court have taken the position that the intention of those who drafted the first section of the Fourteenth Amendment was simply, and exclusively, to make the provisions of the first eight Amendments applicable to state action. This view has never been accepted by this Court. In my view, often expressed elsewhere, the first section of the Fourteenth Amendment was meant neither to incorporate, nor to be limited to, the specific guarantees of the first eight Amendments. The overwhelming historical evidence marshalled by Professor Fairman demonstrates, to me conclusively, that the Congressmen and state legislators who wrote, debated, and ratified the Fourteenth Amendment did not think they were "incorporating" the Bill of Rights [m] and the very breadth and generality of the Amendment's provisions suggest that its authors did not suppose that the Nation would always be limited to mid-19th century conceptions of "liberty" and "due process of law" but that the increasing experience and evolving conscience of the American people would add new "intermediate premises." In short, neither history, nor sense, supports using the Fourteenth Amendment to put the States in a constitutional straitjacket with respect to their own development in the administration of criminal or civil law.

Although I therefore fundamentally disagree with the total incorporation view of the Fourteenth Amendment, it seems to me that such a position does at least have the virtue, lacking in the

m. Fairman, Does the Fourteenth Amendment Incorporate the Bill of Rights? The Original Understanding, 2 Stan.L.Rev. 5 (1949). Professor Fairman was not content to rest upon the overwhelming fact that the great words of the four clauses of the first section of the Fourteenth Amendment would have been an exceedingly peculiar way to say that "The rights heretofore guaranteed against federal intrusion by the first eight Amendments are henceforth guaranteed against state intrusion as well." He therefore sifted the mountain of material comprising the debates and committee reports relating to the Amendment in both Houses of Congress and in the state legislatures that passed upon it. He found that in the immense corpus of comments on the purpose and effects of the proposed amendment, and on its virtues and defects, there is almost no evidence whatever for "incorporation." The first eight Amendments are so much as mentioned by only two members of Congress, one of whom effectively demonstrated (a) that he did not understand Barron v. Baltimore, 7 Pet. 243, and therefore did not understand the question of incorporation, and (b) that he was not himself understood by his colleagues. One state legislative committee report, rejected by the legislature as a whole, found § 1 of the Fourteenth Amendment superfluous because it duplicated the Bill of Rights: the committee obviously did not understand Barron v. Baltimore either. That is all Professor Fairman could find, in hundreds of pages of legislative discussion prior to passage of the Amendment, that even suggests incorporation.

To this negative evidence the judicial history of the Amendment could be added. For example, it proved possible for a Court whose members had lived through Reconstruction to reiterate the doctrine of Barron v. Baltimore, that the Bill of Rights did not apply to the States, without so much as questioning whether the Fourteenth Amendment had any effect on the continued validity of that principle. E.g., Walker v. Sauvinet, 92 U.S. 90; see generally Morrison, Does the Fourteenth Amendment Incorporate the Bill of Rights? The Judicial Interpretation, 2 Stan.L.Rev. 140 (1949).

Court's selective incorporation approach, of internal consistency: we look to the Bill of Rights, word for word, clause for clause, precedent for precedent because, it is said, the men who wrote the Amendment wanted it that way. For those who do not accept this "history," a different source of "intermediate premises" must be found. The Bill of Rights is not necessarily irrelevant to the search for guidance in interpreting the Fourteenth Amendment, but the reason for and the nature of its relevance must be articulated.

Apart from the approach taken by the absolute incorporationists, I can see only one method of analysis that has any internal logic. That is to start with the words "liberty" and "due process of law" and attempt to define them in a way that accords with American traditions and our system of government. This approach, involving a much more discriminating process of adjudication than does "incorporation," is, albeit difficult, the one that was followed throughout the 19th and most of the present century. It entails a "gradual process of judicial inclusion and exclusion," seeking, with due recognition of constitutional tolerance for state experimentation and disparity, to ascertain those "immutable principles * * * of free government which no member of the Union may disregard." Due process was not restricted to rules fixed in the past, for that "would be to deny every quality of the law but its age, and to render it incapable of progress or improvement." Nor did it impose nationwide uniformity in details * * *.

Through this gradual process, this Court sought to define "liberty" by isolating freedoms that Americans of the past and of the present considered more important than any suggested countervailing public objective. The Court also, by interpretation of the phrase "due process of law," enforced the Constitution's guarantee that no State may imprison an individual except by fair and impartial procedures.

The relationship of the Bill of Rights to this "gradual process" seems to me to be twofold. In the first place it has long been clear that the Due Process Clause imposes some restrictions on state action that parallel Bill of Rights restrictions on federal action. Second, and more important than this accidental overlap, is the fact that the Bill of Rights is evidence, at various points, of the content Americans find in the term "liberty" and of American standards of fundamental fairness.

Today's Court still remains unwilling to accept the total incorporationists' view of the history of the Fourteenth Amendment. This, if accepted, would afford a cogent reason for applying the Sixth Amendment to the States. The Court is also, apparently, unwilling to face the task of determining whether denial of trial by jury in the situation before us, or in other situations, is fundamentally unfair. Consequently, the Court has compromised on the ease of the incorporationist position, without its internal logic. It has simply assumed that the question before us is whether the Jury Trial Clause of the Sixth Amendment should be incorporated into the Fourteenth, jot-for-jot and case-for-case, or ignored. Then the Court merely declares that the clause in question is "in" rather than "out."

The Court has justified neither its starting place nor its conclusion. * * *

Justice Fortas' concurring opinion is deleted here. His approach is close to that of Justice Harlan—i.e., the Bill of Rights provides guidance as to the meaning of due process, but not all the "bag and baggage" of a right necessarily must be incorporated. One difference between Justice Fortas and Justice Harlan was that Justice Fortas did not quarrel with the results of earlier incorporation cases, whereas Justice Harlan did.

The Court has not accepted Justice Black's view that the Fourteenth Amendment incorporates the Bill of Rights. Thus, the right to indictment by grand jury is not binding on the states. The Seventh Amendment jury trial right is not binding upon the states in civil cases. And the bail clause of the Eighth Amendment has not yet been incorporated into the Fourteenth Amendment by the Supreme Court. But, the "fundamental fairness" approach of *Palko* and *Adamson* has given way to a selective incorporation view that, as Justice Black properly notes in *Duncan,* has moved the Court a long way toward the total incorporation result that he advocated. The selective incorporation used by the Court is "selective incorporation *plus,*" the *plus* being the recognition of constitutional, procedural rights not explicitly mentioned in the Constitution, a process which Justice Black disapproved.[6]

If Justice Black was wrong about the intent of the drafters of the Fourteenth Amendment and they did not intend incorporation, is there any rhyme or reason to the selective incorporation idea? If there is, it has to be that the Court has been willing to assume that the drafters of the Fourteenth Amendment wanted to enforce against the states only those portions of the Bill of Rights whose fundamentality remained evident many years after the first ten Amendments were adopted. Justice Black argued that incorporation of the Bill of Rights is preferable to a case-by-case, fundamental fairness approach, because the latter gives rise to judicial subjectivity in applying the vague term "due process." Are the Bill of Rights protections less susceptible to judicial subjectivity? For instance, does the term "unreasonable searches and seizures" in the Fourth Amendment provide more limitation on judicial subjectivity than the term "due process"?

As you go through the book, you will see that other Justices, particularly Justice Powell, have urged adoption of the Harlan-Fortas analysis—i.e., when a portion of the Bill of Rights is incorporated, it need not be incorporated "jot-for-jot," and states might have more flexibility than the federal government. For example, in Apodaca v. Oregon, 406 U.S. 404 (1972), Justice Powell was of the view that while the Sixth Amendment requires a jury verdict to be unanimous, the unanimity requirement was not so fundamental that it should be forced upon the states under the due process clause. This position has never commanded a majority of the Court, however. Justice Harlan warned that if the 05 Court compelled all states to conform to the same procedural standards binding on federal courts, ultimately the standards would be interpreted to be less demanding across the board. There is evidence that he may have been right. In the case of jury trials, for example, the Supreme Court has permitted both the federal government and the states to reduce jury size from 12 to 6, Williams v. Florida, 399 U.S. 78 (1969). There is also reason to believe, however, that the Court's decisions have established basic procedural protections that might not have been recognized in all jurisdictions.

One of the interesting developments in recent years is that law enforcement officers, who once fought incorporation, now resist efforts by state courts

6. The development of the selective incorporation approach to the Bill of Rights is explored in Israel, Selective Incorporation: Revisited, 71 Geo.L.J. 253 (1982).

to provide enhanced protection of constitutional rights through reliance on state constitutions. Advocates of expansive readings of constitutional protections, who once asserted that state courts could not be trusted to protect fundamental liberties, are now turning to those courts and asking them to use their state constitutions to go beyond the decisions of the United States Supreme Court. The incorporation of federal constitutional law through the Fourteenth Amendment has been accomplished, and the number of decisions and the votes over time of the Justices suggest that incorporation will remain a part of American constitutional law. The result is that states may not experiment in ways that provide less protection than is guaranteed by the Bill of Rights, but they may provide more. Whether or not they should is a question that you might ask as you examine the Supreme Court's decisions in the chapters that follow. For extensive discussions about what has come to be called "state court activism," see Brennan, J., State Constitutions and the Protection of Individual Rights, 90 Harv.L.Rev. 489 (1977); Hancock, State Court Activism and Searches Incident to Arrest, 68 Va.L.Rev. 1085, 1110 (1982).

B. RETROACTIVITY

1. *The Impact of New Decisions*

When the Supreme Court decides criminal cases it renders legal decisions and to some extent political decisions as well. The Court is concerned not only about protecting rights of defendants and assuring uniform application of the law, but it also is concerned about the disruptive effects its decisions may have on law enforcement officials and lower courts.

For example, when the Supreme Court overrules a prior decision establishing guidelines for police behavior, the Court might reasonably be concerned that law enforcement officers who relied on the overruled case acted as competent officers should. The Court might, therefore, be reluctant to see the officers disadvantaged as a result of their reliance. The Court also might be concerned that trial courts that relied on the old rule may be burdened with numerous retrials once the new decision is announced.

Of course, if a decision is important enough to be called a "constitutional decision," it is arguable that it ought to be enforced on behalf of as many persons who claim the relevant constitutional right as possible. For many years, this argument did not persuade the Supreme Court. It differentiated constitutional decisions that are directed to assuring that guilt is accurately determined from decisions meant to control law enforcement behavior. It differentiated rulings that surprised law enforcement officials and lower courts from those where the handwriting was on the wall well before the new decisions were announced. And it distinguished decisions that were highly burdensome from those that were not.

One rule that the Court always has followed is to give the benefit of the new rule to the litigant who establishes it, even if the rule is meant to control police behavior rather than to enhance the reliability of the determination of guilt or innocence and even though it comes as a great surprise to most people. The Court has done so for two reasons: to provide litigants with incentives to improve past decisions of the Court, for few litigants would ask the Court to establish a new rule that they could not use; and to assure that there is a concrete case or controversy before the Court, even though it might be constitutional for the Court to announce a new rule for future cases only.

When the Court has limited the effect of a decision to the litigant who won the case and others whose claims relate to things that happened after the announcement of the decision, the limitation often is referred to as prospective (applying to future conduct) decisionmaking. When the Court applies its decisions to past conduct, often this is referred to as retroactive or retrospective decisionmaking. If a decision is to be retrospective, the Court must decide whether it will be recognized in habeas corpus cases or only while a case is proceeding through the appellate courts for the first time. What justification could exist for distinguishing, for retroactivity purposes, between habeas corpus cases and those still on direct review?

As you examine the constitutional issues that pervade the book, you will see how the Court once softened the impact of some of its new decisions by prospective decisionmaking or limited retrospective decisionmaking, an approach that it significantly modified in 1987, as explained below. In deciding who, other than the litigant who establishes a precedent, should benefit from it, the Court once opted for a variety of different approaches. The list that follows describes some of the situations that the Court confronted. The defendant in each situation seeks the benefit of a decision previously rendered on behalf of another defendant.

2. *Possible Beneficiaries of a New Supreme Court Decision*

1. A defendant claims before trial that after the decision was announced police officers violated the principle established by the Court. Once the Court announces a decision, it expects government officers to comply, and the defendant almost surely will win.

2. A defendant claims before trial that before the decision was announced police officers violated the principle established by the Court. In this situation the Court might be concerned with law enforcement reliance, not with burdens on lower courts.

3. A defendant claims that before the decision was announced police officers violated the principle established by the Court and raises his claim during or after trial. In this situation, the Court will be concerned with the burden of retrials as well as with law enforcement reliance.

4. A defendant claims that the trial court is violating a principle established by the Court. Once the decision is announced, the Court will expect judges to obey, and this defendant will get the benefit of the decision.

5. A defendant, having already lost an appeal and failed in a petition for certiorari, files a habeas corpus petition and claims that before the decision was announced the police, the trial court or an appellate court violated a principle established by the Court. Depending on the claim, the Court will be concerned with law enforcement expectancies, retrial burdens, or both, and also will have to consider the scope of habeas corpus. If this defendant could have raised the claim at trial or on direct review, but failed to do so, his failure to raise the claim earlier might be deemed a procedural default that would bar habeas corpus relief. The Court will also be concerned about the impact on federalism

when a state judgment is overturned even though the state court applied federal law properly at the time of the decision.

A few cases can illustrate how the Court handled some of these situations.

After the Court made the Fourth Amendment exclusionary rule binding on the states, the Court held that the rule would not be applied to state convictions that had become final prior to the date that the exclusionary rule was extended to the states. Linkletter v. Walker, 381 U.S. 618 (1965). It should be noted that *Linkletter* was a habeas corpus case; the Court did apply its decision extending the exclusionary rule to cases still pending on direct review (i.e., where the process of petitioning higher courts for relief had not ended) at the time of the decision. In other words, Linkletter, as a habeas corpus petitioner whose direct review efforts ended before the decision was announced applying the exclusionary rule to the states, could not claim the benefit of the rule. But defendants whose cases remained alive on direct review could. See also Tehan v. United States ex. rel. Shott, 382 U.S. 406 (1966) (declining to apply a holding that adverse comment on a defendant's election not to testify by the prosecutor or judge violated the Fifth Amendment to state cases "finalized" before the Court's holding).

Over time, the retroactivity decisions began to change. Miranda v. Arizona, 384 U.S. 436 (1966), which required the now famous *Miranda* warnings and its predecessor case, Escobedo v. Illinois, 378 U.S. 478 (1964), were held to apply only in cases in which the trial began after the date of decision in those cases. Johnson v. New Jersey, 384 U.S. 719 (1966).[7] Thus, *Johnson* held that some persons would not benefit from the new decisions even though direct review of their cases was ongoing.

Next, in Stovall v. Denno, 388 U.S. 293 (1967) and Desist v. United States, 394 U.S. 244, 248 (1969), the Court refused to apply its decisions requiring counsel at certain lineups and its holding in an earlier Fourth Amendment case, Katz v. United States, 389 U.S. 347 (1967), to other cases still pending on direct review.[8] Rather, the Court applied its earlier decision to reach only the police activity that followed the announcement of the new rules. Essentially, the rulings had only prospective effect, other than for the litigants in the cases in which the new rule was established.

Justice Harlan dissented in *Desist* and concluded that new constitutional rules must be applied, at a minimum, to all cases pending on direct review when the rules are handed down. He would not have allowed all constitutional claims to be raised on collateral attack, however. The Harlan view finds support in Mishkin, The High Court, the Great Writ, and the Due Process of Time and Law, 79 Harv.L.Rev. 56 (1965). Justice Harlan reiterated his views with some modifications in Mackey v. United States, 401 U.S. 667 (1971). Essentially, he concluded that the Supreme Court was "an appellate court charged with the responsibility of adjudicating cases or controversies according to the law of the land and * * * the law applicable to any * * * dispute necessarily includes the Federal Constitution." He concluded that "[i]f we do not resolve all cases before us on direct review in light of our best under-

7. In Jenkins v. Delaware, 395 U.S. 213 (1969), the Court held that *Miranda* did not apply to retrials after *Miranda* of cases initially tried before *Miranda*.

8. *Stovall* itself was a habeas corpus case, so the Court's language was dictum. But it was holding in *Desist*.

standing of governing constitutional principles, it is difficult to see why we should so adjudicate any case at all." He charged that a decision to apply a ruling on direct review of one case, but not another, is an assertion of legislative, not adjudicatory, power. Also, he questioned whether litigants and counsel would continue to litigate cases all the way to the Supreme Court, if they were denied the benefits of a new rule on direct review.

Justice Harlan argued that, as a general matter, a new rule should not be applied in collateral attack proceedings. He contended that a distinction for retroactivity purposes between direct and collateral review could be justified, because of the purpose behind the writ of habeas corpus. He argued that the purpose of the writ is to assure that state courts apply constitutional law properly, as the law exists at the time the state system applies it. The writ deters the states from incorrect application of then-prevailing constitutional standards. In Justice Harlan's view, the writ was not designed to assure a trial free from all constitutional error; at some point, there must be finality to litigation. Justice Harlan asserted that it was necessary to assure that states applied constitutional law properly, but it was wrong to demoralize states by overturning expensive convictions where they properly applied the law at the time, only to see the law change retroactively—especially where convictions may have been obtained long ago and retrials may be a practical impossibility.

Justice Harlan was disturbed that the Court might grant relief to litigant A, whose petition for certiorari, fortuitously granted, established a new constitutional rule, but deny relief to litigants B, C, D, and E, whose identical petitions followed A's. But does it make sense to say that if the Court denied their petitions for review before the Court decided A's case—perhaps while A's case was docketed, but before certiorari was granted—litigants B, C, D, and E could properly be denied the benefit of a new rule; but if the Court granted review, or decided to hold the cases while A's was decided, it would have to give them the benefit of the new rule? If the process of granting review itself is arbitrary, and if the Court admittedly does not sit to correct all errors in all cases, does it follow that the Court must choose between taking the cases of B, C, D, and E and applying the rule of A's case, or denying them review, which would mean that none of their claims would be heard?

Under the Harlan view, defendants are subject to different treatment depending on the efficiency of the appellate courts in the state in which they are convicted. In fact, the slower the appellate system, the more likely that the defendant will benefit from new rules. Another criticism of the Harlan approach is that if new rules are generally applicable to cases not finalized, the cost of a new rule will often be significant. That may deter the Court from promulgating new rules in the first place. See Jenkins v. Delaware, 395 U.S. 213 (1969) (non-retroactivity provides an impetus for the "implementation of long overdue reforms which otherwise could not be practicably effected.").

Justice Harlan identified two situations in which the presumption of nonretroactivity of new rules for habeas corpus cases could be overcome; these were exceptions to the general principle of nonretroactivity. The first exception encompassed habeas corpus petitioners who sought the benefit of a new rule that is so fundamental that it is "implicit in the concept of ordered liberty" (quoting Justice Cardozo's opinion in *Palko*). The second exception covered a petitioner who relied upon a new rule to demonstrate that the conduct for which the petitioner was tried is constitutionally protected, so that a trial should never have occurred in the first place. As Justice Harlan put it in *Mackey:* "There is little societal interest in permitting the criminal process to rest at a point where it ought properly never to repose."

In a series of cases, the Court finally adopted the Harlan approach to retroactivity, with one slight modification as to the "fundamental fairness" exception to non-retroactivity on habeas. In Griffith v. Kentucky, 479 U.S. 314 (1987), the Court held that its decision the previous term in Batson v. Kentucky, 476 U.S. 79 (1986) (defendant could establish a prima facie case of racial discrimination based on the prosecution's use of peremptory challenges in a single case), would be applied retroactively to all cases still pending on direct review when the decision was announced. Although *Batson* overruled a decision that had withstood attack for more than twenty years, Swain v. Alabama, 380 U.S. 202 (1965), the Court declined to follow *Stovall* and other cases which had barred some or all defendants from benefiting from recently announced decisions even while pursuing direct appeal or review in the Supreme Court. Instead the Court adopted Justice Harlan's analysis of direct review.

Justice Blackmun wrote in *Griffith* for six Justices, declaring that "failure to apply a newly declared constitutional rule to criminal cases pending on direct review violates basic norms of constitutional adjudication," and that "selective application of new rules violates the principle of treating similarly situated defendants the same." Justice Powell added a short concurring opinion, observing that the Court did not address the question whether constitutional decisions should be retroactively applied in habeas corpus cases, and suggesting that "habeas [corpus] petitions generally should be judged according to the constitutional standards existing at the time of conviction."

Justice White joined by Chief Justice Rehnquist and Justice O'Connor, dissented. Justice White argued that *Stovall* was sound and that the Court should "recognize no distinction for retroactivity purposes between cases on direct and collateral review, and alternatively, if there were to be a distinction, that retroactivity should be denied when there are "clear breaks" with past decisions on which lower courts and government agents have relied.

In Teague v. Lane, 489 U.S. 288 (1989), the Court adopted the Harlan view that new rules are generally inapplicable to habeas cases. The Court narrowed the Harlan "fundamental fairness" exception to non-retroactivity, stating that the exception would apply only for a rule which goes to the integrity of the criminal justice system and raises a substantial question whether without application of the rule, the risk exists that an innocent person may have been convicted. With respect to this exception, Justice O'Connor noted that "[b]ecause we operate from the premise that such procedures would be so central to an accurate determination of innocence or guilt, we believe it unlikely that many such components of basic due process have yet to emerge." Teague's claim, that the Sixth Amendment guaranteed a fair cross section of the community on the petit jury, did not seek to establish a watershed rule of criminal procedure which fit the exception; even if the jury was not a fair cross-section, the jury may have been eminently fair.

The Court in *Teague* further reasoned that since a new rule of law cannot be applied on habeas corpus as a general rule, a habeas petitioner generally cannot argue for the *adoption* of a new rule in his own case. The Court therefore held that habeas petitioners cannot seek to establish new rules of law, unless such a rule could be applied retroactively to all habeas petitioners. This will only be the case if the new rule fits within one of the two very limited exceptions discussed above. Applying the Harlan principles of equitable treatment, the Court concluded that since a new rule could not generally be applied to anyone else on habeas if promulgated in a petitioner's case, it would be inequitable to apply it to the petitioner himself. Consequently, not only do habeas claimants not get the benefit of a new rule, in most cases they cannot compel a federal court to consider an argument that a new rule should be adopted. *Teague* was a plurality opinion, written by Justice O'Connor and joined by Chief Justice Rehnquist and Justices Scalia and Kennedy. Justice White concurred in the judgment, preferring the *Stovall* approach, but concluding that the Court's decision was consistent with the theory developed in *Griffith.* Justice Stevens, joined by Justice Blackmun, concurred in the judgment, but objected to the plurality's narrowing of the Harlan "fundamental fairness" exception to non-retroactivity. Justice Brennan, joined by Justice Marshall, dissented, arguing that the Court was making "massive changes, unsupported by precedent" and had impermissibly curtailed the writ of habeas corpus. Subsequently, the Court adopted the plurality opinion in *Teague* as controlling the question of retroactivity of new rules on habeas. See Penry v. Lynaugh, 492 U.S. 302 (1989) (applying *Teague* to collateral attack of a death sentence). For a vigorous critique of *Teague,* see Liebman, More Than "Slightly Retro": The Rehnquist Court's Rout of Habeas Corpus Jurisdiction in Teague v. Lane, 18 N.Y.U. Rev. of Law & Social Change 537 (1991).

After *Teague,* new rules are generally inapplicable to those whose convictions have been finalized. However, Justice Harlan, whose views were generally adopted in *Teague,* emphasized that some "new" holdings are not "new" at all, but are merely applications of well-settled principles to different fact situations.

The Court, following Justice Harlan's approach, has mandated that when a decision merely applies settled precedent it is not a "new" rule at all, and is thus completely retroactive. See Yates v. Aiken, 484 U.S. 211 (1988). The difficulty is in determining if a rule is "new" or merely an old rule applied to a different fact situation. In *Teague,* the Court stated that a case announces a new rule when it breaks new ground or imposes a new obligation on the government. This will occur if the result was "not dictated by existing precedent."

In Butler v. McKellar, 494 U.S. 407 (1990), the Court expounded further on the *Teague* definition of a "new" rule. The issue was whether Arizona v. Roberson was a new rule or merely an application of Edwards v. Arizona[9] (holding that once a person has requested counsel, the police may not conduct further interrogation unless counsel is provided or the suspect initiates communications) to a somewhat different fact situation. The petitioner in *Butler* argued that the rule in *Roberson* should be completely retroactive, on the ground that the Court itself in that case stated that the rule was not new but merely an application of *Edwards.*

9. Both of these cases are discussed in the material on confessions in Chapter Three.

Chief Justice Rehnquist, writing for the majority, stated that a rule is "new" if reasonable minds could have differed about the result of the decision before it was rendered. The majority accordingly held that *Roberson* was a new rule, since reasonable-minded lower courts before *Roberson* had differed about whether *Edwards* would apply to questioning about unrelated investigations (which was the fact situation in *Roberson*). The fact that the majority in *Roberson* characterized its decision as indistinguishable from *Edwards* and as a refusal to create an "exception" was not dispositive. According to the Chief Justice, "courts frequently view their decisions as being 'controlled' or 'governed' by prior opinions even when aware of reasonable contrary conclusions reached by lower courts." Justice Rehnquist stated that "[t]he 'new rule' principle * * * validates reasonable, good-faith interpretations of existing precedents made by state courts even though they are shown to be contrary to later decisions."

Justice Brennan, joined by Justices Marshall, Blackmun and Stevens, dissented. Justice Brennan complained that *Butler,* when combined with *Teague,* drastically limits the scope of habeas corpus relief by a "virtually all-encompassing definition of 'new rule'." The Federal court reviewing a state court decision cannot grant the petition if reasonable minds could differ about the state court result: that would be tantamount to applying a new rule on habeas, which is prohibited by *Teague.* Consequently, the petition will only be granted if the state court was so incorrect as to be completely unreasonable. According to Justice Brennan, such a permissive standard is contrary to the "deterrence function" of habeas review.

The test in *Butler* for whether a rule is new might mean that all Supreme Court decisions will be "new" and hence non-retroactive to habeas cases. Almost by definition, the Supreme Court does not take a case unless reasonable minds could differ about its resolution. The major ground for granting certiorari is a split in the lower courts. Does the *Butler* test also mean that if a Supreme Court decision is non-unanimous, it will be non-retroactive on habeas? Is disagreement among the Justices always reasonable? Can a plurality opinion of the Supreme Court be applied retroactively in habeas cases? What is the effect on subsequent cases when the Supreme Court declines to decide an issue on habeas because it would be a "new" rule?

In Chapter Two, see whether there is a similarity between the standards adopted by the Court in *Butler* and the Court's earlier adoption of the "good faith exception" to the exclusionary rule in United States v. Leon (discussed in Chapter Two). What do *Butler* and *Leon* say about the Court's interest in deterring incorrect applications of constitutional law? Professor Kinports offers three contexts in which the courts require accurate predictions concerning developments in constitutional law: (1) the qualified immunity defense in cases brought under 42 U.S.C. § 1983 (which is the same standard applied to the good faith exception to the exclusionary rule); (2) the rules governing procedural default by petitioners in habeas corpus cases (see Chapter Thirteen, supra); and (3) the retroactive application of new Supreme Court rulings on habeas. She argues that the federal courts have readily excused state court judges and public officials from erroneous interpretation of constitutional norms, while prisoners and their attorneys are held to a much higher standard. See Kinports, Habeas Corpus, Qualified Immunity, and Crystal Balls: Predicting the Course of Constitutional Law, 53 Ariz.L.Rev. 115 (1991).

Is it possible to separate the question of whether a proposed rule is "new" from the question whether a proposed rule is meritorious? See Arkin, The Prisoner's Dilemma: Life in the Lower Federal Courts After Teague v. Lane, 69 No.Car.L.Rev. 371 (1991) (whether a rule is new requires a view into the merits of the rule).

In Collins v. Youngblood, 110 S.Ct. 2715 (1990), the Court held that the rule in *Teague,* prohibiting retroactive application or promulgation of new rules to habeas corpus cases, was not jurisdictional and therefore would not be raised by the Court sua sponte.

With the Court committed to applying all new rules to all cases pending on direct review, the question that naturally arises is what effect, if any, will expanded retroactivity have on the Court's willingness to broaden its interpretation of constitutional rights. *Stovall* gave the Court a means to correct its past errors or to depart from past decisions in light of changing circumstances or additional information and to move the law forward while simultaneously limiting the dislocative effects of change. *Griffith* requires that the dislocative effects be fully borne for all cases on direct review when a decision is announced. Is it possible that in close cases the Court will rule against constitutional claims because of the dislocative effects? The Court could deny certiorari in all cases pending before it except one and uphold a constitutional claim in that one case in an effort to minimize the effects of a new decision. Would this be consistent with treating "like cases alike?" If not, will the Court simply disregard the effects of change?

It is difficult to appreciate the lines the Court has drawn between prospective and retrospective decisions without focusing on specific holdings. The subject is raised at the outset of the book to put you on notice that it is an important part of the Court's work. See whether you would have cushioned the force of some decisions even more than the Court did by prospective decisions, or whether you would adopt a rule giving all defendants the benefit of constitutional decisions no matter when a precedent is established. In the final chapter you will have a chance to examine habeas corpus and the subject of collateral remedies generally.

Chapter Two

SEARCHES AND SEIZURES OF PERSONS AND THINGS

I. AN INTRODUCTION TO THE FOURTH AMENDMENT

A. THE PROBLEM OF GATHERING EVIDENCE

The principal job of the police force, whether it is local, state or federal, is to deal with actual and potential violations of the law. Crimes that are committed must be investigated, and evidence must be sought so that law breakers can be sanctioned in an appropriate way for their activities. Prospective crimes must be anticipated and measures must be taken to prevent the physical, emotional and economic harm associated with criminal behavior.

When government focuses its attention on crime detection and crime prevention, frequently it encounters uncooperative individuals. Those suspected of past criminal activity are not likely to want the government to find them out and punish them, and those who see the future as holding out the promise of satisfaction from crime too are unlikely to welcome governmental efforts intended to eliminate or minimize their returns.

The police cannot expect the guilty, prospective criminals and even many citizens with knowledge of either past or planned crimes to volunteer to share with the police their knowledge and any evidence they might possess. But the police are not compelled to forego investigative and preventive measures for lack of voluntary cooperation. They can exert themselves in order to gather information, evidence and suspects. When they do, they must comply with the requirements of law, especially with the Fourth Amendment, which reads as follows:

> The right of the people to be secure in their persons, houses, papers and effects, against unreasonable searches and seizures shall not be violated, and no Warrants shall issue, but upon probable cause, supported by Oath or affirmation, and particularly describing the place to be searched, and the persons or things to be seized.

B. THE BASICS OF THE FOURTH AMENDMENT

A number of points will seem obvious from a reading of the language of the Amendment, even without knowledge of its history and interpretation. They are briefly summarized here with foreshadowing as to whether the courts, especially the Supreme Court, have found that what seems obvious also is what the Amendment's proponents intended.

First, the language ascribes the right to the people, not to one person as under the Fifth Amendment, or to an accused as under the Sixth Amendment. Hence, the wording resembles that found in the Ninth and Tenth Amendments. Professor Amsterdam has suggested that the framer's choice of language might well be important in properly interpreting the Amendment; in his view the courts might be well advised to focus on problems of how to regulate or control the conduct of the government so that Fourth Amendment violations do not occur rather than on fashioning remedies for only those individuals who have suffered a personal Fourth Amendment wrong. See Perspectives on the Fourth Amendment, 58 Minn.L.Rev. 335, 367 (1974). But the decided cases have placed little reliance on this particular language in the Amendment, even though the Supreme Court's opinions implicitly do seem to recognize the regulatory nature of the Fourth Amendment. Where it has been invoked, the term "the people" has been used instead to narrow the class of people protected by the Fourth Amendment.

Thus, in United States v. Verdugo—Urquidez, 494 U.S. 259 (1990), a Mexican citizen and resident was apprehended by Mexican police and transported to the United States for trial on drug charges. After his arrest, United States law enforcement officials, working with Mexican officials, conducted warrantless searches of the defendant's residences in Mexico. The lower courts held that the searches violated the Fourth Amendment.

The Supreme Court held that the Fourth Amendment does not apply to a search of property owned by a non-resident alien and located in a foreign country. Chief Justice Rehnquist for the Court reasoned that the Fourth Amendment's reference to "the people," as opposed to a particular person, was a "term of art." He asserted that this term of art was intended to refer only to a class of persons "who are part of a national community or who have otherwise developed sufficient connection with this country to be considered a part of that community."

The Court held that the defendant, who had been involuntarily transported to the United States three days before the foreign search was conducted, lacked sufficient connection with the United States to be one of "the people" protected by the Fourth Amendment. The Chief Justice looked to the history of the Amendment and concluded that its purpose was to protect the people of the United States from abuses by their own government; he contended that this history could not be fairly read to limit government actions against aliens, outside the United States.

Justice Brennan, joined by Justice Marshall, dissented. Justice Brennan argued that it was unfair of the Federal Government to require aliens outside the country to obey federal laws (through extraterritorial application), and then to refuse to obey its own laws in the course of investigating the very extraterritorial activity that the government has criminalized. According to Justice Brennan, the Fourth Amendment is an "unavoidable correlative" of the Government's power to enforce the criminal law. Justice Brennan further argued that the term "the people" refers to everyone to whom American governmental power extends: to the governed. Justice Brennan found it clear that an alien defendant subjected to criminal prosecution in the United States is one of the governed. The government treats him as a member of the community by prosecuting him. Justice Blackmun wrote a separate dissenting opinion.

In *Verdugo–Urquidez,* the Court specifically refused to decide whether an illegal alien who lived in the United States would be one of "the people" protected by the Fourth Amendment. Presumably, however, the Fourth Amendment would apply, since an illegal alien living in the United States would have the "connection" with this country required to be one of "the people". Five Justices (Justices Stevens, Kennedy, Brennan, Marshall and Blackmun), in various opinions in *Verdugo–Urquidez,* indicated that they would hold the Fourth Amendment applicable to searches of illegal aliens conducted within the United States.

As a second introductory point, the Amendment covers searches and seizures of "persons, houses, papers and effects," and draws no apparent line between persons and objects. That no distinction was intended is a proposition that finds some support also in the final six words of the amendment. Yet, the cases reveal important differences between the treatment of arrests of people and concomitant searches on the one hand, and searches and seizures of places and things on the other hand. Surprisingly, the person often gets less protection than his property. The words used in the Amendment focus on people and objects. Frequently, law enforcement officers wish to "search" for conversations and to intercept them. Eavesdropping techniques, many of which were probably unforeseen by the framers, raise special problems. Do they involve searches and seizures within the meaning of the Amendment? Courts have used the Amendment to limit some new forms of surveillance, but they have struggled to make the Amendment meaningful in a technological society.

Third, the Amendment has two parts, the first dealing with unreasonable searches and the second dealing with warrants. Because the term "unreasonable" is used first, it might be thought to predominate so that all searches and seizures must satisfy its command, whereas the warrant clause would come into play only when a warrant is sought to justify government action. But the Supreme Court has purported not to read the language in this way. One observer has suggested that the Court has "stood the amendment on its head" by reading the warrant clause as the controlling clause of the Amendment. T. Taylor, Two Studies in Constitutional Interpretation 23–24 (1969). The Court has stated that searches and seizures are presumed to be *per se* constitutionally unreasonable unless carried out pursuant to a warrant. The warrant is deemed to be a necessary part of a showing of reasonableness. But important exceptions to the *per se* warrant requirement have been created. When they apply, only the reasonableness requirement must be satisfied. It must also be noted that in recent years, the Court has in some cases explicitly invoked the reasonableness clause as the predominant clause of the Fourth Amendment, most notably when the Government's search or seizure serves "special needs" beyond mere law enforcement.

Fourth, the term "probable cause" is used to define the minimum showing necessary to support a warrant application; it is not used to demarcate reasonableness generally in search and seizure situations. Despite the placement of the words, the decisions make probable cause a limitation on many searches and seizures even though no warrant is deemed necessary under the circumstances. Also, the Amendment does not identify to what the probable cause showing is to relate. Does probable cause to believe X committed murder by shotgun justify a search of X's house for the gun, or must there also be probable cause to believe the gun is there? The answer is by no means clear in the cases, although both probable cause showings probably are required. Even the definition of probable cause is not altogether clear; the Amendment itself contains not a hint as to its meaning. The judicially created definition probably is adequate, although you may conclude otherwise as you work with it.

Fifth, the Amendment plainly recognizes a right, but does not indicate against whom it applies. Arguably, the people have a right to be free from all searches and seizures that are not reasonable, even if conducted by private persons. But, unlike the Thirteenth Amendment, the Fourth is interpreted as providing protection only against the government and those acting in conjunction with it. On the other hand, nothing in the language of the Amendment limits the applicability to criminal investigations or to the police. The protection is against all unreasonable searches and seizures conducted by government officials regardless of the purpose of the investigation or the identity of the investigator. Courts have accepted this reading, but do take the nature of the investigation into account in assessing the reasonableness of particular searches and in defining the requirements of a proper warrant.

Sixth, the Amendment establishes a right, but does not mention the consequences of a violation of that right; as with other provisions of the Bill of Rights, remedies are not specified. Whether the Constitution mandates certain remedies for a violation of the Fourth Amendment is a question considered in connection with the exclusionary rule.

C. THE PURPOSE OF THE AMENDMENT

These points will become clearer as the cases that interpret the Amendment are examined. It is sufficient now to observe that the Fourth Amendment, like most provisions of the Constitution, is hardly a black letter expression of an easily grasped rule of law. It is more an expression of a philosophy that grew out of offensive British procedures prior to the Revolution and was written into the fundamental law of the land by framers who hoped to assure that government must always respect the sanctity of the people and the effects they hold dear.

The cases, especially those decided after 1960, will suggest that the Amendment protects privacy. To some extent this must be true. Insofar as the Amendment restricts the availability of warrants and bars all unreasonable searches, the capacity of people to keep things secret (or private) from the government is enhanced. But on the face of the Amendment it is apparent that privacy is not absolutely protected. In fact, the Amendment implicitly recognizes the legitimacy of reasonable searches, the propriety of warrants directing the seizure of persons and things, and perhaps most importantly, that the probable cause standard for a warrant (and for warrantless searches and seizures) requires less of the government than the proof beyond a reasonable doubt required in a criminal case, or even the preponderant proof necessary in a civil case. Privacy is thus protected by language implying the government's authority to search and seize. The tension between the protection afforded the people and the power of their government is what this Chapter is about.

D. THE AMENDMENT AND THE EXCLUSIONARY RULE

Before turning to specifics, one suggestion is in order: It is useful to distinguish two questions in thinking about Fourth Amendment problems. First, there is the question whether the Amendment prohibits the kind of conduct described in the cases. If so, the second question is whether evidence obtained by means of a Fourth Amendment violation should be available as proof in criminal trials and other proceedings. The debate over the wisdom of an exclusionary rule is a debate over the second question. Yet, too often analysis of the first question is confused in the process of debating the second. Consider, for example, the following personal editorial by Judge Wilkey of the United States Court of Appeals for the District of Columbia Circuit:

> Among nations of the civilized world we are unique in two respects: (1) We suffer the most extraordinary crime rate with firearms. (2) In criminal prosecutions, by a rule of evidence which exists in no other country, we exclude the most trustworthy and convincing evidence.
>
> These two aberrations are not unconnected. In fact, the "exclusionary rule" has made unenforceable the gun control laws we have and will make ineffective any stricter controls which may be devised. Its fetters particularly paralyze police efforts to prevent, detect and punish street crimes involving not only weapons but narcotics.
>
> * * *
>
> The exclusionary rule has been devastating to gun control laws. Unless a police officer has "probable cause" to make a reasonable search, nothing found during the search—no sawed-off shotgun, automatic pistol or submachine gun—can be introduced as evidence. Therefore, since it is virtually impossible to be convicted in the U.S. of carrying a weapon illegally, American criminals do carry guns and use them. Since police know they carry and use them, they engage in far more searches and seizures than in the countries mentioned above, and some of those searches and seizures are blatantly illegal.
>
> * * *

Why Suppress Valid Evidence, Wall Street Journal, Oct. 7, 1977, at 1, col. 1. See also Wilkey, The Exclusionary Rule: Why Suppress Valid Evidence, 62 Judicature 214 (1978).

This is an argument by a distinguished jurist who has pondered search and seizure problems for years. Yet, it is fundamentally flawed. Can you see the logical error on the basis of your brief exposure to the language of the Fourth Amendment? The error may become more readily apparent if one additional paragraph by Judge Wilkey is set forth.

> What is this "exclusionary rule" that permits a professional criminal to swagger down the street with a handgun bulging in his hip pocket, immune to police search and seizure? It is not required by the Constitution. The Fourth Amendment only forbids "unreasonable searches and seizures." The exclusionary rule is a judge-made rule of evidence which bars "the use of evidence secured through an illegal search and seizure."

The exclusionary rule is a judge-made rule in the sense that it is not explicitly required by the Amendment's language. (It can also be viewed as judicial interpretation of the Constitution, which is implicitly *required* by the Amendment, but detailed discussion of the propriety of such a judge-fashioned rule is reserved for the end of the chapter.) But "probable cause" is a term found in the language chosen by the framers. If the Court correctly interprets the Fourth Amendment as requiring probable cause for particular police action, then it is the Amendment itself, not the remedy for a violation, that truly concerns Judge Wilkey. Immediate abolition of the exclusionary rule does not signify that police officers may engage in searches and seizures without probable cause. They remain bound by the Constitution.[1] Hence, even with the demise of the exclusionary rule, gun control laws still will be hard to enforce. If more vigorous enforcement is desired, the Constitution can be amended or the prevailing interpretation challenged. But changing the reach, as it is now understood, of the Amendment raises issues different from those raised by the exclusionary rule debate.

This is not to suggest that the two questions—has the Amendment been violated and, if so, what remedy, if any, is to be provided—are totally unconnected. Knowledge of the demands placed upon the police by the Fourth Amendment might inform the debate over what police conduct should trigger various kinds of remedies, and knowledge of remedies, both those currently in effect and those that are possible, might even assist in understanding what is a reasonable search and seizure.

The cases that comprise the bulk of this Chapter assume that the remedy for an unconstitutional search and seizure is exclusion. The costs and benefits of the exclusionary rule are not discussed until late in the Chapter. Delay should provide an adequate opportunity for an understanding of the different circumstances in which a Fourth Amendment violation occurs. But delay in no way is intended to imply that the exclusionary rule is plainly desirable and that the debate over it is not important. The debate is important for practical and symbolic reasons, and delay in reaching it is tantamount to deference to its significance. But, it is true that even without the exclusionary rule, the basic problems of deciding what the Amendment means, which form the heart of most of the cases considered herein, would remain. With or without an exclusionary rule, the government is bound by the Fourth Amendment. As you read the cases, keep in mind that despite the fact that the issues usually are cast in terms of whether evidence should have been excluded at trial, the same issues could arise in some form or other—perhaps in civil suits rather than criminal cases—even without an exclusionary rule. Hence, you cannot avoid grappling with the meaning and proper interpretation of the Fourth Amendment simply by doing away with the exclusionary rule. If you ultimately decide that the guilty should not go free (because of suppressed evidence) because the constable has blundered, you must be prepared to guide the constable's future actions, at least if you believe in the rule of law and the oath to support the Constitution demanded of public officers.

1. This point is made by another experienced jurist, Justice Stewart, in The Road to *Mapp v. Ohio* and Beyond: The Origins, Development, and Future of the Exclusionary Rule in Search-and-Seizure Cases, 83 Colum.L.Rev. 1365 (1989).

II. THRESHOLD REQUIREMENTS FOR FOURTH AMENDMENT PROTECTIONS: WHAT IS A "SEARCH?" WHAT IS A "SEIZURE?"

The Fourth Amendment prohibits unreasonable searches and seizures. Unless the government activity is either a "search" or a "seizure" it is not regulated by the Fourth Amendment, and therefore it does not have to be reasonable.

It has been argued that in deciding the threshold question whether a Government intrusion is a search or seizure, one should err on the side of the individual. The consequence of finding a search or seizure is merely that the Government is required to act reasonably, whereas the consequence of not finding a search or seizure is that Government officials can act unreasonably and arbitrarily. See Amsterdam, Perspectives on the Fourth Amendment, 58 Minn.L.Rev. 349 (1974). In fact the Court in recent years has often held police activity to be not a search, and thus free from the strictures of the Fourth Amendment.

A. THE REASONABLE EXPECTATION TEST

In the following landmark case, the Court established a general test for determining whether Government activity rises to the level of a search or a seizure.

KATZ v. UNITED STATES

Supreme Court of the United States, 1967.
389 U.S. 347.

MR. JUSTICE STEWART delivered the opinion of the Court.

The petitioner was convicted in the District Court for the Southern District of California under an eight-count indictment charging him with transmitting wagering information by telephone from Los Angeles to Miami and Boston, in violation of a federal statute. At trial the Government was permitted, over the petitioner's objection, to introduce evidence of the petitioner's end of telephone conversations, overheard by FBI agents who had attached an electronic listening and recording device to the outside of the public telephone booth from which he had placed his calls. In affirming his conviction, the Court of Appeals rejected the contention that the recordings had been obtained in violation of the Fourth Amendment, because "[t]here was no physical entrance into the area occupied by [the petitioner]." We granted certiorari in order to consider the constitutional questions thus presented.

The petitioner has phrased those questions as follows:

"A. Whether a public telephone booth is a constitutionally protected area so that evidence obtained by attaching an electronic listening recording device to the top of such a booth is obtained in violation of the right to privacy of the user of the booth.

"B. Whether physical penetration of a constitutionally protected area is necessary before a search and seizure can be said to be violative of the Fourth Amendment to the United States Constitution."

We decline to adopt this formulation of the issues. In the first place, the correct solution of Fourth Amendment problems is not necessarily promoted by incantation of the phrase "constitutionally protected area." Secondly, the Fourth Amendment cannot be translated into a general constitutional "right to privacy." That Amendment protects individual privacy against certain kinds of governmental intrusion, but its protections go further, and often have nothing to do with privacy at all. Other provisions of the Constitution protect personal privacy from other forms of governmental invasion. But the protection of a person's *general* right to privacy—his right to be let alone by other people—is like the protection of his property and of his very life, left largely to the law of the individual States.

Because of the misleading way the issues have been formulated, the parties have attached great significance to the characterization of the telephone booth from which the petitioner placed his calls. The petitioner has strenuously argued that the booth was a "constitutionally protected area." The Government has maintained with equal vigor that it was not. But this effort to decide whether or not a given "area," viewed in the abstract, is "constitutionally protected" deflects attention from the problem presented by this case. For the Fourth Amendment protects people, not places. What a person knowingly exposes to the public, even in his own home or office, is not a subject of Fourth Amendment protection. But what he seeks to preserve as private, even in an area accessible to the public, may be constitutionally protected.

The Government stresses the fact that the telephone booth from which the petitioner made his calls was constructed partly of glass, so that he was as visible after he entered it as he would have been if he had remained outside. But what he sought to exclude when he entered the booth was not the intruding eye—it was the uninvited ear. He did not shed his right to do so simply because he made his calls from a place where he might be seen. No less than an individual in a business office, in a friend's apartment, or in a taxicab, a person in a telephone booth may rely upon the protection of the Fourth Amendment. One who occupies it, shuts the door behind him, and pays the toll that permits him to place a call is surely entitled to assume that the words he utters into the mouthpiece will not be broadcast to the world. To read the Constitution more narrowly is to ignore the vital role that the public telephone has come to play in private communication.

The Government contends, however, that the activities of its agents in this case should not be tested by Fourth Amendment requirements, for the surveillance technique they employed involved no physical penetration of the telephone booth from which the petitioner placed his calls. It is true that the absence of such penetration was at one time thought to foreclose further Fourth Amendment inquiry, Olmstead v. United States, 277 U.S. 438, 457, 464, 466; Goldman v. United States, 316 U.S. 129, 134–136, for that Amendment was thought to limit only searches and seizures of tangible property. But "[t]he premise that property interests control the right of the Government to search and seize has been discredited." Warden v. Hayden, 387 U.S. 294, 304. Thus, although a closely divided Court supposed in *Olmstead* that surveillance without any trespass and without the seizure of any material object fell outside the ambit of the Constitution, we have since departed from the narrow view on which that decision rested. Indeed, we have expressly held that the Fourth Amendment governs not only the seizure of tangible items, but extends as well to the recording of oral statements, overheard without any "technical trespass under * * * local property law." Silverman v. United States, 365 U.S. 505, 511. Once this much is acknowledged, and once it is recognized that the Fourth Amendment protects people—and not simply "areas"—against unreasonable searches and seizures, it becomes clear that the reach of that Amendment cannot turn upon the presence or absence of a physical intrusion into any given enclosure.

We conclude that the underpinnings of *Olmstead* and *Goldman* have been so eroded by our subsequent decisions that the "trespass" doctrine there enunciated can no longer be regarded as controlling. The Government's activities in electronically listening to and recording the petitioner's words violated the privacy upon which he justifiably relied while using the telephone booth and thus constituted a "search and seizure" within the meaning of the Fourth Amendment. The fact that the electronic device employed to achieve that end did not happen to penetrate the wall of the booth can have no constitutional significance.

The question remaining for decision, then, is whether the search and seizure conducted in this case complied with constitutional standards. In that regard, the Government's position is that its agents acted in an entirely defensible manner: They did not begin their electronic surveillance until investigation of the petitioner's activities had established a strong probability that he was using the telephone in question to transmit gambling information to persons in other States, in violation of federal law. Moreover, the surveillance was limited, both in scope and in duration, to the specific purpose of establishing the contents of the petitioner's unlawful telephonic communications. The agents confined their surveillance to the brief periods during which he used the telephone booth,[a] and they took great care to overhear only the conversations of the petitioner himself.[b]

Accepting this account of the Government's actions as accurate, it is clear that this surveillance was so narrowly circumscribed that a duly authorized magistrate, properly notified of the need for such investigation, specifically informed of the basis on which it was to proceed, and clearly apprised of the precise intrusion it would entail, could constitutionally have authorized, with appropriate safeguards, the very limited search and seizure that the Government asserts in fact took place. * * *

The Government urges that, because its agents relied upon the decisions in *Olmstead* and *Goldman,* and because they did no more here than they might properly have done with prior judicial sanction, we should retroactively validate their conduct. That we cannot do. It is apparent that the agents in this case acted with restraint. Yet the inescapable fact is that this restraint was imposed by the agents themselves, not by a judicial officer. They were not required, before commencing the search, to present their estimate of probable cause for detached scrutiny by a neutral magistrate. They were not compelled, during the conduct of the search itself, to observe precise limits established in advance by a specific court order. Nor were they directed, after the search had been completed, to notify the authoriz-

a. Based upon their previous visual observations of the petitioner, the agents correctly predicted that he would use the telephone booth for several minutes at approximately the same time each morning. The petitioner was subjected to electronic surveillance only during this predetermined period. Six recordings, averaging some three minutes each, were obtained and admitted in evidence. They preserved the petitioner's end of conversations concerning the placing of bets and the receipt of wagering information.

b. On the single occasion when the statements of another person were inadvertently intercepted, the agents refrained from listening to them.

ing magistrate in detail of all that had been seized. In the absence of such safeguards, this Court has never sustained a search upon the sole ground that officers reasonably expected to find evidence of a particular crime and voluntarily confined their activities to the least intrusive means to that end * * *.

* * *

The Government does not question these basic principles. Rather, it urges the creation of a new exception to cover this case. It argues that surveillance of a telephone booth should be exempted from the usual requirement of advance authorization by a magistrate upon a showing of probable cause. We cannot agree. Omission of such authorization

> "bypasses the safeguards provided by an objective predetermination of probable cause, and substitutes instead the far less reliable procedure of an after-the-event justification for the * * * search, too likely to be subtly influenced by the familiar shortcomings of hindsight judgment." Beck v. Ohio, 379 U.S. 89, 96.

And bypassing a neutral predetermination of the *scope* of a search leaves individuals secure from Fourth Amendment violations "only in the discretion of the police."

These considerations do not vanish when the search in question is transferred from the setting of a home, an office, or a hotel room to that of a telephone booth. Wherever a man may be, he is entitled to know that he will remain free from unreasonable searches and seizures. The government agents here ignored "the procedure of antecedent justification * * * that is central to the Fourth Amendment," a procedure that we hold to be a constitutional precondition of the kind of electronic surveillance involved in this case. Because the surveillance here failed to meet that condition, and because it led to the petitioner's conviction, the judgment must be reversed.

MR. JUSTICE MARSHALL took no part in the consideration or decision of this case.[c]

* * *

MR. JUSTICE HARLAN, concurring.

I join the opinion of the Court, which I read to hold only (a) that an enclosed telephone booth is an area where, like a home, Weeks v. United States, 232 U.S. 383, and unlike a field, Hester v. United States, 265 U.S. 57, a person has a constitutionally protected reasonable expectation of privacy; (b) that electronic as well as physical intrusion into a place that is in this sense private may constitute a violation of the Fourth Amendment; and (c) that the invasion of a constitutionally protected area by federal authorities is, as the Court has long held, presumptively unreasonable in the absence of a search warrant.

As the Court's opinion states, "the Fourth Amendment protects people, not places." The question, however, is what protection it affords to those people. Generally, as here, the answer to that question requires reference to a "place." My understanding of the rule that has emerged from prior decisions is that there is a twofold requirement, first that a person have exhibited an actual (subjective) expectation of privacy[d] and, second, that the expectation be one that society is prepared to recognize as "reasonable." Thus a man's home is, for most purposes, a place where he expects privacy, but objects, activities,

c. Concurring opinions by Douglas, J., joined by Brennan, J., and by White, J. are omitted.

d. In United States v. White, considered supra, at p. 39, Justice Harlan said that "[t]he analysis must * * * transcend the search for subjective expectations or legal attributions of assumptions of risk."

or statements that he exposes to the "plain view" of outsiders are not "protected" because no intention to keep them to himself has been exhibited. On the other hand, conversations in the open would not be protected against being overheard, for the expectation of privacy under the circumstances would be unreasonable. Cf. Hester v. United States, supra.

The critical fact in this case is that "[o]ne who occupies it, [a telephone booth] shuts the door behind him, and pays the toll that permits him to place a call is surely entitled to assume" that his conversation is not being intercepted. The point is not that the booth is "accessible to the public" at other times, but that it is a temporarily private place whose momentary occupants' expectations of freedom from intrusion are recognized as reasonable.

* * * This case requires us to reconsider *Goldman,* and I agree that it should now be overruled. Its limitation on Fourth Amendment protection is, in the present day, bad physics as well as bad law, for reasonable expectations of privacy may be defeated by electronic as well as physical invasion.

Finally, I do not read the Court's opinion to declare that no interception of a conversation one-half of which occurs in a public telephone booth can be reasonable in the absence of a warrant. As elsewhere under the Fourth Amendment, warrants are the general rule, to which the legitimate needs of law enforcement may demand specific exceptions. It will be time enough to consider any such exceptions when an appropriate occasion presents itself, and I agree with the Court that this is not one.

* * *

MR. JUSTICE BLACK, dissenting.

* * *

My basic objection is twofold: (1) I do not believe that the words of the Amendment will bear the meaning given them by today's decision, and (2) I do not believe that it is the proper role of this Court to rewrite the Amendment in order "to bring it into harmony with the times" and thus reach a result that many people believe to be desirable.

While I realize that an argument based on the meaning of words lacks the scope, and no doubt the appeal, of broad policy discussions and philosophical discourses on such nebulous subjects as privacy, for me the language of the Amendment is the crucial place to look in construing a written document such as our Constitution. * * *

The first clause protects "persons, houses, papers, and effects, against unreasonable searches and seizures * * *." These words connote the idea of tangible things with size, form, and weight, things capable of being searched, seized, or both. The second clause of the Amendment still further establishes its Framers' purpose to limit its protection to tangible things by providing that no warrants shall issue but those "particularly describing the place to be searched, and the persons or things to be seized." A conversation overheard by eavesdropping, whether by plain snooping or wiretapping, is not tangible and, under the normally accepted meanings of the words, can neither be searched nor seized. In addition the language of the second clause indicates that the Amendment refers not only to something tangible so it can be seized but to something already in existence so it can be described. Yet the Court's interpretation would have the Amendment apply to overhearing future conversations which by their very nature are nonexistent until they take place. How can one "describe" a future conversation, and, if one cannot, how can a magistrate issue a warrant to eavesdrop one in the future? * * *

Tapping telephone wires, of course, was an unknown possibility at the time the Fourth Amendment was adopted. But eavesdropping (and wiretapping is nothing more than eavesdropping by telephone) was * * * "an ancient practice which at common law was condemned as a nuisance. 4 Blackstone, Commentaries 168. In those days the eavesdropper listened by naked ear under the eaves of houses or their windows, or beyond their walls seeking out private discourse." 388 U.S., at 45. There can be no doubt that the Framers were aware of this practice, and if they had desired to outlaw or restrict the use of evidence obtained by eavesdropping, I believe that they would have used the appropriate language to do so in the Fourth Amendment. They certainly would not have left such a task to the ingenuity of language-stretching judges. No one, it seems to me, can read the debates on the Bill of Rights without reaching the conclusion that its Framers and critics well knew the meaning of the words they used, what they would be understood to mean by others, their scope and their limitations. Under these circumstances it strikes me as a charge against their scholarship, their common sense and their candor to give to the Fourth Amendment's language the eavesdropping meaning the Court imputes to it today.

* * *

B. INTERESTS PROTECTED BY THE FOURTH AMENDMENT AFTER *KATZ*

The Court has held on several occasions after *Katz* that there is no legitimate privacy interest in illegal activity. See United States v. Place, page 45 (no privacy interest in possession of contraband). If that is the case, it may be wondered why Katz was entitled to protection in the phone booth. Katz was not expressing private, personal thoughts; he was engaging in illegal betting transactions.

One possible answer is that Katz received the protection of the Fourth Amendment because the Government was not certain that his activity was illegal until officials listened to the conversations. Permitting a Government intrusion on the ground that the citizen is engaged in illegal activity is question-begging, since the police have to make the intrusion to determine whether the citizen's activity is illegal. In the process, the police may be invading the legitimate privacy and possessory interests of those who are innocent. See Loewy, The Fourth Amendment as a Device for Protecting the Innocent, 81 Mich.L.Rev. 907 (1983) (Fourth Amendment can be invoked by the guilty "when necessary to protect the innocent").

Couldn't the Government in *Katz* have argued that if Katz were placing a legitimate call, he should have no complaint about Government surveillance? If the private activity is legitimate, what does the citizen have to hide? Courts after *Katz* have found three legitimate interests which can be affected by a Government intrusion. First, there is an interest in being free from physical disruption and inconvenience. Thus, an innocent person who is subject to a body search or an arrest suffers a Fourth Amendment intrusion; the fact that he or she had nothing to hide is irrelevant. Second, certain information, even though not indicative of criminal activity, may be personal or embarrassing; innocent citizens have a legitimate interest in keeping such information private. Third, the Fourth Amendment prohibits unreasonable seizures as well as searches. The citizen has a legitimate interest in control over and use of his or her property, and that interest is obviously implicated when the Government exercises dominion and control over such property.

Note that a seizure may occur without a search, and a search may occur without a seizure. As Justice Stevens explained in his concurring opinion in Texas v. Brown, 460 U.S. 730, 747–48 (1983):

> Although our Fourth Amendment cases sometimes refer indiscriminately to searches and seizures, there are important differences between the two * * *. The Amendment protects two different interests of the citizen—the interest in retaining possession of property and the interest in maintaining personal privacy. A seizure threatens the former, a search the latter. As a matter of timing, a seizure is usually preceded by a search, but when a container is involved the converse is often true. Significantly, the two protected interests are not always present to the same extent; for example, the seizure of a locked suitcase does not necessarily compromise the secrecy of its contents, and the search of a stopped vehicle does not necessarily deprive its owner of possession.

Whether a seizure of property has or has not occurred is usually obvious and is rarely contested. More difficult questions have arisen concerning whether police efforts to detain an individual constitute a seizure of the person triggering Fourth Amendment protection. These questions are considered in the discussion of stop and frisk, later in this Chapter.

C. APPLICATIONS OF THE *KATZ* PRINCIPLE:

The Court has on many occasions applied the *Katz* principle, usually by referring to the concurring opinion of Justice Harlan, which set forth a two-pronged test for whether a government intrusion triggers the Fourth Amendment. First, has the individual manifested a subjective expectation of privacy? Second, is the expectation one that society is prepared to accept as reasonable?

1. *Manifestation of a Subjective Interest in Privacy*

In United States v. Dunn, 480 U.S. 294 (1987), officers entered defendant's property by crossing several fences, two with barbed wire, and then came upon a barn. The barn had no windows. The door of the barn was six feet high; above the door was a heavy mesh fabric, which was opaque from a distance of a few feet. However, if one were to jump up on the door and press one's face to the mesh, one could see inside the barn. The officers did this, and saw evidence of a drug laboratory. The Supreme Court held that the officers' activity did not constitute a search, since the defendant had not sufficiently manifested an expectation of privacy in the interior of the barn, even presuming that society was prepared to accept such an expectation as legitimate. What steps should Dunn have taken to sufficiently manifest an interest in privacy?

Abandonment of property is inconsistent with the retention of any subjective privacy or possessory interests. Suppose that officers at an airport suspect that a deplaning passenger is a drug courier. They follow the suspect to the baggage claim area. The suspect appears aware of surveillance, and appears very nervous. The officers approach the suspect and ask if he is picking up any luggage. The suspect denies that he checked any luggage. Can the suspect complain of a search when the officers later open a suitcase remaining unclaimed on the baggage carousel? See United States v. McBean, 861 F.2d 1570 (11th Cir.1988) (no).

2. *Open Fields*

Katz appeared to make certain doctrines more understandable. For example, the open fields exception to the warrant requirement was relatively easy to square with *Katz*. It was developed in Hester v. United States, 265 U.S. 57 (1924). The Court distinguished open fields from constitutionally protected areas like houses. The doctrine was reaffirmed in Air Pollution Variance Bd. v. Western Alfalfa Corp., 416 U.S. 861 (1974).

Everyone is familiar with privately owned land which neighbors traverse and the community knows is not quite as "private" as the small yard in front of a home. Arguably, the open fields doctrine is well applied to these situations. See United States v. Edmonds, 611 F.2d 1386 (5th Cir. 1980) (no trespassing sign may be disregarded where it is clear that an area is open to the public). A similar doctrine is also applicable to a police officer's intrusion onto the walk leading up to the door of a home when the officer wishes to ask for the cooperation of persons in a house.

The Court broadened the "open fields" doctrine in Oliver v. United States, 466 U.S. 170 (1984). Two defendants complained of police searches. Oliver complained that two state police officers went to his farm to investigate reports that he was growing marijuana. They drove past his house to a locked gate with a "No Trespassing" sign on it. A footpath led around one side of the gate. The officers took it, walked around the gate and along the road for several hundred yards, and passed a barn and a parked camper. An investigation of the farm revealed a field of marijuana about a mile from Oliver's house.

Thornton complained that two police officers, having received an anonymous tip that marijuana was being grown in woods behind his house, entered the woods by a path between his and a neighbor's house, followed a footpath through the woods, and found two marijuana patches which were determined to be on Thornton's property.

Justice Powell wrote the Court's opinion and was fully supported by four other Justices. Justice White joined the majority on the proposition that the Fourth Amendment "indicates with some precision the places and things encompassed by its protections" and that open fields are not "effects" within the coverage of the Amendment. Justice White did not join the longer parts of the majority opinion. The lengthy opinion reached the following conclusions: "an individual may not legitimately demand privacy for activities conducted out of doors in fields, except in the area immediately surrounding the home"; "open fields do not provide the setting for those intimate activities that the Amendment is intended to shelter from government interference or surveillance"; "[i]t is not generally true that fences or no trespassing signs effectively bar the public from viewing open fields in rural areas"; "courts * * * have extended Fourth Amendment protection to the curtilage; and they have defined the curtilage, as did the common law, by reference to the factors that determine whether an individual may expect that an area immediately adjacent to the home will remain private".

The majority rejected "the suggestion that steps taken to protect privacy establish that expectations of privacy in an open field are legitimate." Although it recognized that Oliver and Thornton "planted the marijuana upon secluded land and erected fences and no trespassing signs around the property," the Court found that these efforts did not establish that any expectation of privacy was legitimate.

The majority concluded that even if the officers committed a trespass, the Fourth Amendment was not violated: "in the case of open fields, the general rights of property protected by the common law of trespass have little or no relevancy to the applicability of the Fourth Amendment." Finally, the Court rejected the suggestion that a case-by-case approach be used to determine whether a person had sufficiently closed off the property beyond the curtilage to public access. Justice Powell stated that such an approach would not provide "a workable accommodation between the needs of law enforcement and the interests protected by the Fourth Amendment."

Justice Marshall, joined by Justices Brennan and Stevens, dissented. He challenged the majority's reasoning that real property is not protected by the Fourth Amendment, observing that telephone booths and commercial establishments do not fit the language of the Amendment any more than open fields do, yet Supreme Court decisions have found them to be protected by the Fourth Amendment. Moreover, he urged that "[w]e do not construe constitutional provisions of this sort the way we do statutes, whose drafters can be expected to indicate with some comprehensiveness and exactitude the conduct they wish to forbid or control and to change those prescriptions when they become obsolete."

Justice Marshall disagreed also with the majority's assertion that a person has no reasonable expectation of privacy in open fields irrespective of the circumstances of any particular case. He argued that the fact that ownership of property is protected provides considerable support for a privacy claim; that many private activities take place in privately owned woods and fields; that a privacy claim is strengthened where a person takes precautions to exclude others; and that a clearly administrable rule can be devised to protect "[p]rivate land marked in a fashion sufficient to render entry thereon a criminal trespass under the law of the state in which the land lies."

Which analysis do you find preferable? Is it now the case that no one—scientist, naturalist, lover, or simply a private person who prefers outdoors to indoors—can rely on the Fourth Amendment to protect against police surveillance of land areas not immediately adjacent to a house? May the police engage in as much surveillance as they care to as often as they want on the theory that there is no violation of any reasonable expectation of privacy? Does the Supreme Court's decision mean that police may plant hidden microphones and cameras in fields that are fenced off, since the majority seems to have held there are no expectations of privacy in these fields?

The Court in *Oliver* takes a literal approach to the words of the Fourth Amendment, and finds that a field is neither a person, house, paper, or effect. Recall Justice Black's dissent in *Katz.* Does Katz's telephone conversation fit within the literal terms of the Fourth Amendment?

What may officers do if they come upon a container in a fenced, privately owned open field? If, for instance, they come upon a barrel with a lid, may they pry open the lid? Does it make any difference what condition the barrel is in? May officers lift up a tarpaulin to see what is beneath it? Does it make a difference if the tarpaulin is tied to the ground with stakes? If you would not be willing to let officers open barrels or lift up covers on objects, are you more willing to permit them to roam about and look at uncovered objects? Might the reason that objects are uncovered be that landowners rely on their fence to keep out intruders?

Finally, if there is no reasonable expectation of privacy in fenced land, may officers refuse a landowner's demand that they leave his land and not return? May the officers use physical force to overcome a landowner's attempts to remove the officers from his property? If not, does this suggest that the landowner does have a reasonable expectation of privacy, at least in some circumstances?

In Husband v. Bryan, 946 F.2d 27 (5th Cir.1991), officers looking for a body used bulldozers to dig up three acres of a pasture owned by Husband. They had no warrant or probable cause, and a body was never found. Husband sued the officers, alleging a violation of her Fourth Amendment rights. The officers contended that under the open fields doctrine, Husband had no right to be free from unreasonable searches of her pasture. The court held that the open fields doctrine could not be extended to anything beyond "observation searches" and accordingly that Husband's Fourth Amendment rights had been violated. Do you agree? Would the Supreme Court agree?

How far the curtilage extends is now an issue that every police officer must confront. In United States v. Dunn, 480 U.S. 294 (1987), the Supreme Court held that a barn located approximately fifty yards from the fence surrounding a residence on almost two hundred acres of property was outside the curtilage. Although Dunn's entire ranch was encircled by a fence and interior fences constructed of posts and barbed wires also were present, federal and state officers ignored the fences and trespassed without a warrant upon Dunn's land. They crossed over the outer fence and one interior fence before smelling the odor of an acid used in the manufacture of certain drugs. The officers then crossed an interior barbed wire fence surrounding one smaller barn, and another barbed wire interior fence surrounding a larger barn. The larger barn had an open overhang, a wooden fence around it, locked, waist-high gates barring entry into the barn, and netting above the gates. From a distance the officers could not see through the netting. They approached the gates, shined a light through the netting and saw what appeared to a drug laboratory. They left the property without entering the barn, but twice reentered the property without a warrant before obtaining a warrant to search the barn from a federal magistrate.

Justice White's opinion for the Court reasoned "that curtilage questions should be resolved with particular reference to four factors: the proximity of the area claimed to be curtilage to the home; whether the area is included within an enclosure surrounding the home; the nature of the uses to which the area is put; and the steps taken by the resident to protect the area from observation by people passing by." He rejected the government's "invitation to adopt a 'bright-line' rule that 'the curtilage should extend no farther than the nearest fence surrounding a fenced house.'" Justice White applied the factors and found that the barn was 60 yards from the house itself, not within the area enclosed by the house fence, there was no objective indication that the barn was used for intimate activities associated with the home, and there was no protection from observation by those standing in open fields. The Court accepted arguendo, but did not decide, Dunn's contention that an entry into the barn would have been impermissible under the open fields doctrine.

Justice Scalia concurred in the opinion, except for the portion that focused on whether law enforcement officials possessed objective data indicating that the barn was not being used for intimate activities of the home. He indicated that the significant point was that the barn was not being so used, not whether the law enforcement officers knew that.

Justice Brennan, joined by Justice Marshall, dissented. He argued that the barn was within the curtilage and that the agents infringed upon Dunn's reasonable expectation of privacy. He also suggested that the decision might have an unforeseen consequence: preventing law enforcement officers who have a warrant to search a house (traditionally considered to include curtilage) from searching exterior buildings.

How would you resolve the open question of whether the officers could have entered the barn? Does a farmer have a reasonable expectation of privacy in his barn? Do *Oliver* and *Dunn* provide sensible guidance for police? Do they reflect common understandings as to the importance of private property?

3. *Access by Members of the Public*

Even if a citizen tries to keep information private, it is sometimes the case in society that the citizen will not get his or her wish. One cannot walk along a public street and have a reasonable expectation that the walk will be free from public viewing. A homeowner cannot demand that planes not fly overhead. Society is not prepared to accept such demands as legitimate. After *Katz,* the Supreme Court has held in a series of cases that if an aspect of a person's life is subject to scrutiny by society, then that person has no legitimate expectation in denying equivalent access to police. There is thus no search if the police obtain information that members of the public could obtain.

a. *Consensual Electronic Surveillance*

In United States v. White, 401 U.S. 745 (1971), a government informer carrying a radio transmitter engaged the defendant in conversations in the informer's home and car, in the defendant's home, and in a restaurant, which were overheard by an agent using a radio receiver. Justice White's opinion for himself, Chief Justice Burger, Justice Stewart and Justice Blackmun concluded that the defendant had no reasonable expectation of privacy in the conversations. The plurality stated that "the law permits the frustration of actual expectations of privacy by permitting authorities to use the testimony of those associates who for one reason or another have determined to turn to the police" and that "one contemplating illegal activities must realize and risk that his companions may be reporting to the police." Justice Black concurred in the judgment for the reasons he stated in *Katz.* Justice Douglas dissented, questioning whether a citizen must "live in fear that every word he speaks may be transmitted or recorded and later repeated to the entire world." Justice

Harlan in dissent argued that the assumption of risk approach was not an adequate guide to controlling new threats to privacy. As he put the question, it was not whether the defendant knew there was a risk of third party bugging but whether "we should impose on our citizens the risks of the electronic listener or observer without at least the protection of a warrant requirement." He concluded that "[t]he impact of third-party bugging must * * * be considered to undermine that confidence and sense of security in dealing with another that is characteristic of individual relationships between citizens in a free society." Justice Marshall also dissented.[2] Justice Brennan concurred in the result on a different ground. Where do you come out on the question?[3]

b. Financial Records

California Bankers Ass'n v. Shultz, 416 U.S. 21 (1974), analyzed whether the record keeping and reporting requirements imposed upon banks and individuals by the Bank Secrecy Act of 1970 violated the Fourth Amendment. Banks were required by Title I of the Act to maintain records of their client's identities and to microfilm certain checks and to keep records of other items. Part of Title II authorized the Secretary of the Treasury to require financial institutions to file reports of certain payments, receipts, or transfers of currency or other monetary instruments. Implementing regulations required banks to report each deposit, withdrawal, exchange of currency, or other payment or transfer involving more than $10,000. The information could be made available to other agencies of the government. The ACLU and other persons challenging the record keeping provisions argued that the Act made banks agents of the government and, thus, the record keeping provisions amounted to a seizure of customers' records. The Court rejected the argument on the ground that banks were parties to any transactions and their records were covered by the Act and regulations. A similar analysis was used to uphold the currency reporting requirement. The Court also upheld provisions of Title II that required individuals to report transportation into or out of the United States of monetary instruments valued in excess of $5,000. It held that reporting requirements do not violate the Fourth Amendment. Justice Powell's concurring opinion, joined by Justice Blackmun, warned that "[a] significant extension of the regulations' reporting requirements * * * would pose substantial and difficult constitutional questions * * *." Justice Douglas dissented, arguing that "[o]ne's bank accounts are within the 'expectations of privacy' category. For they mirror not only one's finances but his interests, his debts, his way of life, his family, and his civil commitments." Justice Marshall

2. Some state courts have sided with the dissenters. See, e.g., People v. Beavers, 393 Mich. 554, 227 N.W.2d 511 (1975); State v. Glass, 583 P.2d 872 (Alaska 1978).

3. Justice O'Connor wrote for seven Justices in Maryland v. Macon, 472 U.S. 463 (1985), as the Court held that undercover officers did not engage in a "search" or "seizure" within the ambit of the Fourth Amendment when they purchased magazines from a bookstore salesclerk with a marked bill prior to making a warrantless arrest of the clerk for distributing obscene materials. The Court reasoned that "[a]n undercover officer does not violate the Fourth Amendment by accepting an offer to do business that is freely made to the public." The fact that the officers retrieved the marked bill used to make the purchase did not transform the purchase into a search. Justice Brennan, joined by Justice Marshall, dissented and argued that seizure of a person for distributing obscene materials should be preceded by a prior judicial determination of probable obscenity.

Macon did not involve electronic surveillance. If First Amendment interests are put aside, the case is no different from any other use of undercover agents.

agreed in his dissent, as he relied heavily on *Katz.* "The fact that one has disclosed private papers to the bank, for a limited purpose, within the context of a confidential customer-bank relationship, does not mean that one has waived all right to the privacy of the papers." Justice Brennan also dissented, but did not reach the privacy question.

In United States v. Miller, 425 U.S. 435 (1976), Justice Powell's opinion for the Court rejected the claim that the Act's allowance of a subpoena to a bank to obtain the records compiled by the bank without notice to the depositor violated the Fourth Amendment. Over dissents by Justices Brennan and Marshall, the Court found that there was no reasonable expectation of privacy to be protected; the depositor took the risk that the bank would disclose records.

Justice Marshall's opinion for a unanimous Court relied upon *Miller* in SEC v. Jerry T. O'Brien, Inc., 467 U.S. 735 (1984), to hold that the SEC need not give notice to a target of a "nonpublic investigation" that it has subpoenaed documents from third parties. The Court reasoned that "[i]t is established that, when a person communicates information to a third party even on the understanding that the communication is confidential, he cannot object if the third party conveys that information or records thereof to law enforcement authorities."

c. *Pen Registers*

In Smith v. Maryland, 442 U.S. 735 (1979), police installed a pen register device in the phone company offices. This device recorded the numbers called by the defendant on his home telephone. Justice Blackmun, writing for six members of the Court, found that the use of the pen register did not constitute a search, and hence no warrant was required. The majority stated that "a person has no legitimate expectation of privacy in information he voluntarily turns over to third parties" and that "when he used his phone, petitioner voluntarily conveyed numerical information to the telephone company." The Court held that Smith "assumed the risk that the company would reveal to the police the numbers he dialed." Justice Stewart, joined by Justice Brennan, dissented, arguing that since private telephone conversations were protected by *Katz,* the numbers dialed from a private telephone were equally protected. Justice Marshall's dissent asserted that "privacy is not a discrete commodity, possessed absolutely or not at all" and that those who disclose information for "a limited business purpose need not assume that this information will be released to other persons for other purposes." Justice Powell did not participate in the decision. Is the majority correct in its assessment of societal expectations? Is the dissent?

d. *Trash*

In California v. Greenwood, 486 U.S. 35 (1988), police officers asked a neighborhood trash collector to pick up plastic garbage bags that Greenwood left on the curb in front of his house and to turn the bags over to the police. The police rummaged through the bags and found items indicative of narcotics use. This information was used to obtain warrants to search Greenwood's house. Greenwood challenged the warrants as having been obtained as the result of an illegal search of his trash. Justice White, writing for seven members of the Court, concluded that the officer's inspection of the trash was not a search and therefore did not require a warrant or probable cause. Justice White relied on *Smith* (the pen register case) and asserted that "respondents exposed their garbage to the public sufficiently to defeat their claim to Fourth Amendment protection. It is common knowledge that plastic garbage bags left on or at the side of a public street are readily accessible to animals, children, scavengers, snoops, and other members of the public." Since the public had access to the trash, Justice White reasoned that "the police cannot be reasonably expected to avert their eyes from evidence of criminal activity that could have been observed by any member of the public." Justice White therefore found it irrelevant that Greenwood was prohibited by city ordinance from disposing of his trash in any way other than leaving it for the trash service.

Justice Brennan, joined by Justice Marshall, dissented. He argued that "scrutiny of another's trash is contrary to commonly accepted notions of civilized behavior" and that "society will be shocked to learn that the Court, the ultimate guarantor of liberty, deems unreasonable our expectation that the aspects of our private lives that are concealed safely in a trash bag will not become public." Justice Brennan concluded as follows:

> The mere *possibility* that unwelcome meddlers *might* open and rummage through the containers does not negate the expectation of privacy in its contents any more than the possibility of a burglary negates an expectation of privacy in the home; or the possibility of a private intrusion negates an expectation of privacy in an unopened package; or the possibility that an operator will listen in on a telephone conversation negates an expectation of privacy in the words spoken on the telephone.

Who more accurately captures the objective beliefs of the American people, Justice White or Justice Brennan? What if Greenwood had placed his garbage bags in a trash can inside his fenced-in backyard? See United States v. Hedrick, 922 F.2d 396 (7th Cir.1991) (not a search even though trash was located near garage, well inside defendant's property).

Can police officers look through the effects of a homeless person (such as a closed cardboard box) without a warrant? Is *Greenwood* good authority for holding that such an inspection is not a search? In Connecticut v. Mooney, 218 Conn. 85, 588 A.2d 145 (1991) the court held that a homeless person had a reasonable expectation of privacy in the contents of a duffel bag and cardboard box kept on public property. The court distinguished *Greenwood* as a case in which defendants placed trash at the curb for the purpose of conveying it to a third party. Is this distinction persuasive?

e. *Aerial Surveillance*

The Court has applied the public access rationale of *Smith* and *Greenwood* to aerial surveillance of private areas. In California v. Ciraolo, 476 U.S. 207 (1986), Chief Justice Burger wrote for the Court as it held, 5–4, that the Fourth Amendment is not violated by aerial observation without a warrant from an altitude of 1,000 feet of a fenced-in backyard within the curtilage of a home. Ciraolo had erected two fences, a six foot outer and a ten foot inner fence, to protect his backyard from observation on the ground. The majority reasoned that "the mere fact that an individual has taken measures to restrict some views of his activities [does not] preclude an officer's observations from a public vantage point where he has a right to be and which renders the activities clearly visible." Since any member of the public flying in the public airspace could have made the observations of marijuana in the yard that the police made, the majority concluded that there was no reasonable expectation of privacy against aerial surveillance. The majority rejected a distinction between flights for law enforcement investigatory purposes and ordinary commercial or private flights and had "difficulty understanding exactly how respondent's expectations of privacy from aerial observation might differ when two airplanes pass overhead at identical altitudes, simply for different purposes."

Justice Powell, joined by Justices Brennan, Marshall and Blackmun, dissented. He relied upon *Katz* and argued that the Court erred in relying solely on the manner of surveillance rather than "focusing on the interests of the individual and of a free society" and suggested that "[a]erial surveillance is nearly as intrusive on family privacy as physical trespass into the curtilage."

Dow Chemical Co. v. United States, 476 U.S. 227 (1986), was decided the same day by the same vote as *Ciraolo.* The Environmental Protection Agency engaged in aerial photographing of Dow Chemical Co.'s manufacturing plant in Michigan. Dow had maintained elaborate ground security that barred public views of its plant from the ground and had investigated low flights over the plant. It sued for injunctive relief against the EPA. Dow prevailed in the district court before losing in the court of appeals. Chief Justice Burger's majority opinion affirmed the appeals court, concluding that "the open areas of an industrial plant complex with numerous plant structures spread over an area of 2,000 acres are not analogous to the 'curtilage' of a dwelling for purposes of aerial surveillance; such an industrial complex is more comparable to an open field and as such it is open to the public view and observation of persons in aircraft lawfully in the public airspace immediately above or sufficiently near the area for the reach of cameras." Thus, "the taking of aerial photographs of an industrial plant complex from navigable airspace is not a search prohibited by the Fourth Amendment."

Again Justice Powell wrote for the four dissenters. He relied upon *Katz* to argue that trade secrets laws demonstrate societal recognition of legitimate interests in business privacy and distinguished *Ciraolo* on the ground that the EPA needed to use a sophisticated camera to discover the details revealed in its photographs. Since Dow had controlled its property to exclude outsiders, Justice Powell reasoned that the 2,000 acres did not fall within the open fields rule and represented "a private commercial enclave, an area in which society has recognized that privacy interests legitimately may be claimed."

Are these decisions persuasive? In answering the question, suppose that police attach one end of a rope near the top of a tree just outside a homeowner's fenced property and the other end near the top of another tall tree just outside the other side of the property, stretch the rope tight, and have an officer climb in the air over a suspect's house and yard. Would this be a search? What if an officer is given a propulsion package that enables him to fly from one border of the property over the property to the other side? Would this be a search? See e.g. West v. State, 588 So.2d 248 (Fla.App.1991) (peering over a fence into a yard from atop a ladder is a search; while the yard may have been visible from an airplane, it was not visible from the ground). The Supreme Court's open field cases are criticized in Saltzburg, Another Victim of Illegal Narcotics: The Fourth Amendment (As Illustrated By the Open Fields Doctrine) 48 U.Pitt.L.Rev. 1 (1986). See also Wilkins, Defining the "Reasonable Expectation of Privacy": An Emerging Tripartite Analysis, 40 Vand.L.Rev. 1077 (1987).

The Court applied *Ciraolo* in Florida v. Riley, 488 U.S. 445 (1989), and held that surveillance of a backyard from a helicopter hovering at 400 feet was not a search. Justice White, writing for a plurality, relied on prior cases for the proposition that if information is available to the public, the police can act as any member of the public could, and obtain the information free from Fourth Amendment restrictions. The crucial question in *Riley* was whether the public could have access to the information in Riley's backyard by way of aerial surveillance; the information was partially obscured by a greenhouse, rendering observation by airplane as in *Ciraolo* insufficient. Justice White contended that since the public could legally hover over Riley's property in a helicopter at a low level, the police could do so as well. Justice White relied on FAA regulations which allow helicopters to be operated at virtually any altitude so long as they do not pose a safety hazard. He added that there was no injury to the property or any dust or threat from the visual inspection, and that no intimate activities in the house or curtilage had been observed.

Justice O'Connor concurred in the judgment. She disagreed with the plurality's analysis and contended that the proper test for determining the reasonableness of an expectation of privacy was whether the public *ordinarily* had access to the information sought by the police, not whether it was legal for a member of the public to obtain it. Thus, for Justice O'Connor, the question was whether members of the public ordinarily hovered over Riley's property at 400 feet in helicopters—if so, it would be unreasonable to expect that the police could not do so. Justice O'Connor nonetheless concurred in the result, asserting that the burden was on the defendant to show that members of the public did not regularly hover over his property in helicopters. Since Riley had offered no proof on this point in the lower court, she agreed that a search was not shown on the facts in *Riley.*

Justice Brennan wrote a dissenting opinion joined by Justices Marshall and Stevens. He agreed with Justice O'Connor that the reasonableness of a privacy expectation should be determined by whether the public ordinarily has access to the information, not by whether it is legally possible to obtain access. Justice Brennan urged that judicial notice could be taken of the infrequent nature of similar intrusions, and that the burden should be placed upon the government to show that such aerial surveillance is so frequent as to render unreasonable a privacy expectation. Justice Blackmun also dissented. He agreed with Justices Brennan and O'Connor that the appropriate test is one of frequent public access to the property, and agreed with Justice Brennan that the burden should be placed upon the government to show frequency of public access. He argued that a remand would give the government the opportunity to satisfy the burden.

In *Riley* five members of the Court agree that the mere *possibility* of public access is not enough to render a privacy expectation unreasonable. Isn't that the same point that Justice Brennan made in dissent in *Greenwood*? How can *Riley* and *Greenwood* be reconciled?

4. *Investigation Which Can Only Uncover Illegal Activity*

Investigation which threatens to uncover innocent, private activity can constitute a search, because it invades a legitimate Fourth Amendment secrecy interest. In several cases, however, the Supreme Court has held that if an investigative activity cannot reveal innocent information, but only uncovers illegal activity if it exists, then it is not a search.

a. Canine Sniffs

In United States v. Place, 462 U.S. 696 (1983), the Supreme Court held that a canine sniff of closed luggage was not a search.

The majority said this about "canine sniffs":

> A "canine sniff" by a well-trained narcotics detection dog * * * does not require opening the luggage. It does not expose noncontraband items that otherwise would remain hidden from public view, as does, for example, an officer's rummaging through the contents of the luggage. Thus, the manner in which information is obtained through this investigative technique is much less intrusive than a typical search. Moreover, the sniff discloses only the presence or absence of narcotics, a contraband item. Thus, despite the fact that the sniff tells the authorities something about the contents of the luggage, the information obtained is limited. This limited disclosure also ensures that the owner of the property is not subjected to the embarrassment and inconvenience entailed in less discriminate and more intrusive investigative methods.
>
> In these respects, the canine sniff is sui generis. We are aware of no other investigative procedure that is so limited both in the manner in which the information is obtained and in the content of the information revealed by the procedure. Therefore, we conclude that the particular course of investigation that the agents intended to pursue here—exposure of respondent's luggage, which was located in a public place, to a trained canine—did not constitute a "search" within the meaning of the Fourth Amendment.

While the dog sniff in *Place* was not a search, the Court nonetheless held that the cocaine found in Place's luggage was illegally obtained. This was because, in order to conduct the dog sniff, the police detained the luggage for 90 minutes. This detention was an exercise of dominion and control over the luggage, which implicated the Fourth Amendment's prohibition against unreasonable seizures; and the Court found the 90 minute seizure unreasonable under the circumstances, because the officers were not diligent in their investigation and had no probable cause to detain the luggage.

If a trained dog alerts to the luggage, can the officers open the luggage immediately? Is there anything more that they ought to do?

Do the police implicate the Fourth Amendment if they conduct a dog sniff of a person? What if they send the dog down the block in a neighborhood, and the dog alerts to a certain house? What if they send the dog down the aisle of a passenger train, and the dog alerts to a sleeper compartment? In United States v. Thomas, 757 F.2d 1359 (2d Cir.1985) the court held that the use of a marijuana-sniffing dog outside an apartment was a search. The court reasoned that because of the greater expectation of privacy in the home, the dog sniff outside Thomas' apartment was a greater intrusion that the dog sniff outside Place's luggage. Was it? In contrast, in United States v. Colyer, 878 F.2d 469 (D.C.Cir.1989), the court held that a dog sniff outside an Amtrak sleeping compartment was not a search. The court stated that *Place* stood for the proposition that "governmental conduct that can reveal nothing about noncontraband items * * * interferes with no legitimate privacy expectation." The court was also concerned about the spectre of police officer liability if canine sniffs were searches:

> [I]f we were to hold that the corridor sniff were a search, those whose sleeper cars were sniffed in order to ensure that Max 25 was not falsely alerting—and of whom the agents had no reason to suspect possession of illicit drugs—could maintain a civil action, although no information pertaining to their private affairs was obtained, and neither they nor their belongings were seized.

Would you hold a canine sniff to be a search under some circumstances? Would you distinguish the sniffing of a person from the sniffing of property?

b. Chemical Testing for Drugs

The Court extended the reasoning in *Place* when it upheld the warrantless chemical field-testing of a powder that a federal agent obtained from Federal Express employees in United States v. Jacobsen, 466 U.S. 109 (1984). The portion of the Court's opinion upholding the visual examination and seizure of the plastic bags containing the powder is discussed in the section on mixed public and private searches, infra.

Justice Stevens' opinion for the Court stated that "[t]he concept of an interest in privacy that society is prepared to recognize as reasonable is, by its very nature, critically different from the mere expectation, however well justified, that certain facts will not come to the attention of the authorities." He concluded that "[a] chemical test that merely discloses whether or not a particular substance is cocaine does not compromise any legitimate interest in privacy." Even if the results of the test are negative, the results reveal "nothing of special interest." Thus, "[h]ere, as in *Place,* the likelihood that official conduct * * * will actually compromise any legitimate interest in privacy seems much too remote to characterize the testing as a search subject to the Fourth Amendment," even though "the field test did affect respondents' possessory interests protected by the Amendment, since by destroying a quantity of the powder it converted what had been only a temporary deprivation of possessory interests into a permanent one."

Justice Brennan, joined by Justice Marshall, wrote a dissenting opinion. He argued that "[t]he prohibitions of the Fourth Amendment are not * * * limited to any preconceived conceptions of what constitutes a search or a seizure; instead we must apply the constitutional language to modern developments according to the fundamental principles that the Fourth Amendment embodies. * * * Before excluding a class of surveillance techniques from the reach of the Fourth Amendment, therefore, we must be certain that none of the techniques so excluded threatens the areas of personal security and privacy that the Amendment is intended to protect."

The dissent found it "most startling" that in this case and in *Place* the Court placed "its exclusive focus on the nature of the information or item sought and revealed through the use of a surveillance technique, rather than on the context in which the information or item is concealed." Justice Brennan expressed concern about the implications of *Place* and this case:

> It is certainly true that a surveillance technique that identifies only the presence or absence of contraband is less intrusive than a technique that reveals the precise nature of an item regardless of whether it is contraband. But, by seizing upon this distinction alone to conclude that the first type of technique, as a general matter, is not a search, the Court has foreclosed any consideration of the circumstances under which the technique is used, and may very well have paved the way for technology to override the limits of law in the area of criminal investigation.

As an example, Justice Brennan posited the use of cocaine-sensitive dogs to roam the streets at random or the use of street-corner scanners for drugs. He suggested that in past cases the Court had analyzed reasonable expectations of privacy in terms of the location of an item and the manner in which an individual sought to preserve the private nature of a particular fact. Rather than hold that a technique either always or never violates reasonable expectations of privacy, Justice Brennan urged the Court to examine the private nature of the area or item subjected to intrusion. He indicated that a warrantless dog-sniff of a container, as in *Place,* would be improper if the container is the kind that ordinarily gives rise to a reasonable expectation of privacy. In the case of the Federal Express package, he concluded that "the context in which the powder was found could not support a reasonable expectation of privacy," since once it was observed it was so clearly contraband that agents could identify it with "virtual certainty."

Note that despite the labeling of Justice Brennan's opinion as a dissent, he agrees with the conclusion reached by the majority on the facts of the case. His opinion attacks the notion that a field test of a narcotic could never be an invasion of a legitimate expectation of privacy. Consider a situation in which a chemist, suspected of manufacturing drugs, consents to talk with an agent in his home, where he works, and shows the agent his laboratory. If the agent sees something that gives him cause to believe that some of the chemist's work product might be illicit drugs, does the agent have authority to field test the drugs in the home without a warrant and without additional consent? Would the majority and the dissenters resolve this case differently? Whose analysis would you prefer?

In one of the most highly publicized cases in recent memory, State v. von Bulow, 475 A.2d 995 (R.I.1984), the state supreme court reversed a husband's convictions on two counts of attempted murder. It relied on both federal and state constitutional principles to conclude that chemical testing of pills received by the state from the victim's children, who had searched the defendant's closet, bathroom, desk and study without permission, was improper without a warrant. The court cited *Jacobsen,* but reasoned that the field test conducted in this case was dissimilar. In this case, government agents could not know in advance what they would find, it was not clear that the pills were contraband, and this was not a case, therefore, in which the sole purpose of the test was to quickly determine whether what appeared to be contraband really was. Is the distinction persuasive?

Does *Jacobsen* mean that drug tests on urine samples are not searches? In Skinner v. Railway Labor Executives' Ass'n, 489 U.S. 602 (1989), the Court unanimously held that such testing was a search. The Court noted that unlike the field testing in *Jacobsen,* drug testing of blood and urine samples could uncover such innocent secret information as epilepsy, pregnancy, or the use of prescription drugs. Moreover, the process of collecting urine samples (including aural observation) was intrusive and embarrassing. The Court concluded that "the collection and testing of urine intrudes upon expectations of privacy that society has long recognized as reasonable."

5. *Sensory Enhancement Devices*

If a police officer uses binoculars, or microphones, to see or hear something that could not otherwise be seen or heard, does the use of the device constitute a search? What if the information could be detected through the naked eye or ear, but the officer uses the enhancement device to make his or her job easier?

a. Electronic Beepers

Beepers are becoming ever more common. "The beeper is a miniature, battery-powered radio transmitter that emits recurrent signals at a set frequency. By covertly attaching the beeper to a subject's property and monitoring its signals with a separate receiver, the police can electronically track the property, and often the subject, for distances of several miles and for as long as several weeks." Note, Tracking *Katz:* Beepers, Privacy and the Fourth Amendment, 86 Yale L.J. 1461 (1977).

The Supreme Court left most of the interesting questions concerning beepers undecided in United States v. Knotts, 460 U.S. 276 (1983). State officers, suspicious that a purchaser of chemicals, Armstrong, might be using them to manufacture drugs, obtained the consent of the company selling the drugs to install a beeper inside a 5 gallon container of chloroform before Armstrong picked it up. Armstrong placed the container in his car. The officers monitored the beeper signal from the container and followed Armstrong to Petschen's house where the container was transferred to his car. After losing contact at one point, the officers found the signal once more via a helicopter monitoring device. Ultimately the signal became stationary at a location identified as a cabin belonging to Knotts. Because Knotts did not (and could not, for lack of standing) challenge the warrantless installation of the beeper in the container, the Court had no occasion to address the permissibility of this intrusion. Justice Rehnquist's majority opinion quoted from *Katz* and *Smith* (pen register case) and framed the question presented as whether the officers had invaded a legitimate expectation of privacy. The opinion reasoned as follows:

> Visual surveillance from public places along Petschen's route or adjoining Knott's premises would have sufficed to reveal all of these facts to the police. The fact that the officers in this case relied not only on visual surveillance, but on the use of the beeper to signal the presence of Petschen's automobile to the police receiver, does not alter the situation. Nothing in the Fourth Amendment prohibited the police from augmenting the sensory faculties bestowed

upon them at birth with such enhancement as science and technology afforded them in this case.

The Court responded to the argument that under its ruling, unlimited surveillance of any citizen would be possible without judicial supervision, by saying that "if such dragnet type law enforcement practices * * * should eventually occur, there will be time enough then to determine whether different constitutional principles may be applicable." It noted too that nothing in the record indicated that the beeper signal was used to monitor any activity in the cabin.

Justice Stevens, joined by Justices Brennan and Marshall, concurred in the judgment, noting that the language used by the majority concerning enhancement of sensory faculties was inconsistent with *Katz*.

United States v. Karo, 468 U.S. 705 (1984), answered some of the questions left open in *Knotts*. A Drug Enforcement Agency agent learned that Karo, Horton and Harley had ordered 50 gallons of ether from a government informant, who told the agent that the ether was to be used to extract cocaine from clothing that had been imported into the United States. The government obtained a court order, which was later held to be invalid, that authorized the installation and monitoring of a beeper in one of the cans of ether. Agents saw Karo pick up the ether from the informant and followed him to his house. They used the beeper to determine that the ether was still in the house, and they subsequently used it to detect that the ether had been moved to Horton's house. From this house, agents could smell the ether while standing on the sidewalk. A third use of the beeper helped agents discover that the ether had been moved to Horton's father's house, and a fourth use revealed it had been taken to a commercial storage facility. Agents could smell the ether in a row of lockers and used the beeper a fifth time to discover the exact location of the ether. The sixth use led agents to another storage facility where they detected the smell of ether from a locker. They obtained consent to install a closed-circuit camera in the facility and observed a man and woman load the ether into Horton's pick-up truck. While undertaking to follow the truck to another house, the agents used the beeper a seventh time. The eighth use assured the agents that the ether remained in the house when the truck left. Finally, agents obtained a search warrant for the house. They found cocaine and laboratory equipment and made arrests.

Justice White wrote for the Court. He concluded that no authorization was necessary to place a beeper in the can of ether:

> It is clear that the actual placement of the beeper into the can violated no one's Fourth Amendment rights. The can into which the beeper was placed belonged at the time to the DEA, and by no stretch of the imagination could it be said that respondents then had any legitimate expectation of privacy in it. The ether and the original 10 cans, on the other hand, belonged to, and were in the possession of, Muehlenweg, who had given his consent to any invasion of those items that occurred. Thus, even if there had been no substitution of cans and the agents had placed the beeper into one of the original 10 cans, Muehlenweg's consent was sufficient to validate the placement of the beeper in the can.
>
> * * *
>
> The mere transfer to Karo of a can containing an unmonitored beeper infringed no privacy interest. It conveyed no information that Karo wished to

keep private, for it conveyed no information at all. To be sure, it created a *potential* for an invasion of privacy, but we have never held that potential, as opposed to actual, invasions of privacy constitute searches for purposes of the Fourth Amendment. A holding to that effect would mean that a policeman walking down the street carrying a parabolic microphone capable of picking up conversations in nearby homes would be engaging in a search even if the microphone were not turned on. It is the exploitation of technological advances that implicates the Fourth Amendment, not their mere existence.

We likewise do not believe that the transfer of the container constituted a seizure. A "seizure" of property occurs when "there is some meaningful interference with an individual's possessory interests in that property." Although the can may have contained an unknown and unwanted foreign object, it cannot be said that anyone's possessory interest was interfered with in a meaningful way. At most, there was a technical trespass on the space occupied by the beeper. The existence of a physical trespass is only marginally relevant to the question of whether the Fourth Amendment has been violated, however, for an actual trespass is neither necessary nor sufficient to establish a constitutional violation. * * * Of course, if the presence of a beeper in the can constituted a seizure merely because of its occupation of space, it would follow that the presence of any object, regardless of its nature, would violate the Fourth Amendment.

We conclude that no Fourth Amendment interest of Karo or of any other respondent was infringed by the installation of the beeper. Rather, any impairment of their privacy interests that may have occurred was occasioned by the monitoring of the beeper.

Justice White reached a different conclusion as to the monitoring of the beeper "in a private residence, a location not open to visual surveillance".

The monitoring of an electronic device such as a beeper is, of course, less intrusive than a full-scale search, but it does reveal a critical fact about the interior of the premises that the Government is extremely interested in knowing and that it could not have otherwise obtained without a warrant. The case is thus not like *Knotts*, for there the beeper told the authorities nothing about the interior of *Knotts'* cabin. The information obtained in *Knotts* was "voluntarily conveyed to anyone who wanted to look. * * *"; here, as we have said, the monitoring indicated that the beeper was inside the house, a fact that could not have been visually verified.

We cannot accept the Government's contention that it should be completely free from the constraints of the Fourth Amendment to determine by means of an electronic device, without a warrant and without probable cause or reasonable suspicion, whether a particular article—or a person, for that matter—is in an individual's home at a particular time. Indiscriminate monitoring of property that has been withdrawn from public view would present far too serious a threat to privacy interests in the home to escape entirely some sort of Fourth Amendment oversight.

Although the Court condemned warrantless monitoring of a beeper inside a private house, it sustained the search warrant that agents obtained at the end of their surveillance. The knowledge that the agents obtained without using the beeper and their proper use of the beeper in monitoring travel provided sufficient information to justify the issuance of a search warrant.

Justice Stevens, joined by Justices Brennan and Marshall, dissented in part. Justice Stevens observed that "the character of the property is profoundly different when infected with an electronic bug than when it is entirely germ free." He found that agents asserted dominion and control over the property when they inserted the beeper and that this amounted to a seizure covered by the Fourth Amendment. Central to his analysis was the proposition that "the private citizen is entitled to assume, and in fact does assume, that his possessions are not infected with concealed electronic devices." He found "little comfort in the Court's notion that no invasion of privacy occurs until a listener obtains some significant information by use of the device." Justice Stevens concluded that "absent exigent circumstances government agents have a constitutional duty to obtain a warrant before they install an electronic device on a citizen's property."

Justice O'Connor, joined by Justice Rehnquist, added an opinion concurring in most of the Court's opinion and in its judgment. She wrote separately to state her view that a home owner might not be able to claim that his privacy rights are violated if he permits a third person to enter the home with property that contains a beeper. If, for example, a government undercover agent entered a suspect's home and carried a beeper, the home owner might not have a valid complaint. Justice White responded in a footnote by saying that he did not necessarily disagree with this analysis. Justice White found it inapplicable to the instant case. The point that Justice O'Connor raised might well be crucial in future cases if an informant agrees to have a beeper placed in property that he acquires and brings to the homes of other suspects. It might also have bearing on who will have standing to complain about the use of beepers.

Is the Court's treatment of beepers consistent with *Katz*? Who owned the telephone booth in *Katz*? Should the user of a telephone booth be able to complain if the owner permits electronic eavesdropping? Would *Katz* have been decided differently had the phone company consented to the FBI's actions?

b. *Visual and Aural Surveillance*

United States v. Taborda, 635 F.2d 131 (2d Cir.1980), holds that agents invaded a person's reasonable expectation of privacy when they used a telescope to see activities not visible with the naked eye from across the street from a suspect's apartment. The same court opined that observations made with binoculars or other visual aids were not proscribed in places where a suspect otherwise had exposed himself to public view, United States v. Lace, 669 F.2d 46 (2d Cir.1982). A concurring judge expressed disagreement with any approval of "open-ended, long-term surveillance conducted on private residential property in the hope of seeing evidence of crime." See also United States v. Gibson, 636 F.2d 761 (D.C.Cir.1980). Would you agree that use of a telescope may violate *Katz?*

The court found no constitutional violation in United States v. Mankani, 738 F.2d 538 (2d Cir.1984), where a federal agent managed to overhear conversations in an adjoining hotel room through a pre-existing hole in the wall. The court reasoned that the agent had a legal right to be in the adjoining room and that the transitory nature of a hotel diminished the expectation of privacy that a person may rely upon while there. Would this reasoning have authorized the agent to drill a hole?

If the police officer shines a flashlight into a darkened car, is that a search? Can it be argued that the flashlight does not prejudice the citizen, since it does not provide the officer with information beyond what could be obtained from sensory perception? See Texas v. Brown, 460 U.S. 730 (1983) ("the use of artificial means to illuminate a darkened area simply does not constitute a search, and thus triggers no Fourth Amendment protection").

In Dow Chemical Co. v. United States, 476 U.S. 227 (1986), Government officials flew over Dow's commercial property, and used a $22,000 camera to take pictures of the areas between Dow's buildings. The photographs could be magnified so that objects one-half inch in diameter could be seen. Chief Justice Burger, writing for the Court, relied on *Knotts* and *Oliver* and held that Dow had no privacy interest in the area between its buildings, at least not from aerial surveillance, and hence the use of the camera was not a search. The majority noted that "surveillance of private property by using highly sophisticated surveillance equipment not generally available to the public, such as satellite technology, might be constitutionally proscribed absent a warrant." However, the Court found that the photographs at issue did not rise to that level. The Chief Justice stated that "the mere fact that human vision is enhanced somewhat, at least to the degree here, does not give rise to constitutional problems," and that "Fourth Amendment cases must be decided on the facts of each case, not by extravagant generalizations."

Justice Powell, joined by Justices Brennan, Marshall, and Blackmun, dissented. Justice Powell argued that the Government activity constituted a search, because the magnification gave information that could not have been obtained through the senses. Is *Dow* based on the fact that the photographic magnification would never be problematic, or on the fact that Dow had no expectation of privacy in the first place?

6. *Jails, Prison Cells, and Convicts*

Chief Justice Burger wrote for the Court in Hudson v. Palmer, 468 U.S. 517 (1984), as it held that a prisoner has no constitutionally protected expectation of privacy in his prison cell or in papers or property in his cell. The Court rejected a court of appeals' holding that "shakedown" searches of a cell should be performed only "pursuant to an established program of conducting random searches * * * reasonably designed to deter or discover the possession of contraband." The Court concluded that "[t]he uncertainty that attends random searches of cells renders these searches perhaps the most effective weapon of the prison administrator in the constant fight against the proliferation of knives and guns, illicit drugs, and other contraband." It added that prison officials must be free to seize any articles from cells when necessary to serve legitimate institutional interests. They may not destroy a prisoner's property with impunity, however, since due process requires that a state provide a prisoner with a meaningful remedy against negligent or intentional destruction of property.

Justice Stevens, joined by Justices Brennan, Marshall and Blackmun, dissented. He did not disagree that prison officials should be able to conduct random searches to protect prison security, but he took exception to the holding that "no matter how malicious, destructive or arbitrary a cell search and seizure may be, it cannot constitute an unreasonable invasion of any privacy or possessory interest that society is prepared to recognize as reasonable." In his opinion, "[t]o hold that a prisoner's possession of a letter from his wife, or a picture of his baby, has no protection against arbitrary or malicious perusal, seizure or destruction would not * * * comport with any civilized standard of decency." Justice Stevens expressed concern that "[d]epriving inmates of any residuum of privacy or possessory rights is in fact plainly *contrary* to institutional goals" and is inconsistent with any rehabilitative functions that an institution might serve. He argued that the Fourth Amendment requires an evaluation of the reasonableness of all seizures and that the Court's blanket endorsement of any and all seizures of a prisoner's property could not be squared with either the Constitution or with common sense.

Justice Stevens noted that the majority's holding was limited to a prisoner's papers and effects located in his cell, and that the the Court apparently "believes that at least a prisoner's person is secure from unreasonable search and seizure." In Bell v. Wolfish, 441 U.S. 520 (1979), the Court stated that at best prisoners have a reasonable expectation of privacy "of diminished scope" and that strip searches and body cavity searches of pretrial detainees after contact visits were reasonable.

Is it possible for a prison or jail to create reasonable expectations of privacy that the Fourth Amendment would protect? [4]

7. *Public Schools and Public Employees*

In New Jersey v. T.L.O., 469 U.S. 325 (1985), the Court rejected a state's arguments that students have no reasonable expectation of privacy in public schools. Although the Court recognized the need for schools to maintain discipline, it declined to apply its decision in *Hudson* to the school context. Justice White wrote for the Court and stated that "[w]e are not yet ready to hold that the schools and the prisons need be equated for purposes of the Fourth Amendment." His opinion also rejected the state's suggestion that school children have no need to bring personal property to school and thus could not claim a legitimate expectation of privacy in personal property. The opinion concluded that "schoolchildren may find it necessary to carry with them a variety of legitimate, noncontraband items, and there is no reason to conclude that they have necessarily waived all rights to privacy in such items merely by bringing them onto school grounds." The Court adopted the "reasonable suspicion" standard for searches of students by teachers.

The Supreme Court, in O'Connor v. Ortega, 480 U.S. 709 (1987), unanimously rejected an argument made by California officials and supported by the Solicitor General that governmental employees "can never have a reasonable expectation of privacy in their place of work," although the Justices could not

4. In the pretrial investigation of the man accused of attempting to assassinate President Reagan, the government seized handwritten notes and a diary made by the suspect while incarcerated. The district court found that the suspect had a reasonable expectation of privacy in the materials and suppressed them. United States v. Hinckley, 525 F.Supp. 1342 (D.D.C.1981). The Court of Appeals affirmed, 672 F.2d 115 (D.C.Cir.1982). This was before *Hudson*, however.

agree on an opinion for the Court. State hospital officials, investigating various charges made against a psychiatrist, entered the psychiatrist's office and seized various items from his desk and file cabinets. The psychiatrist brought a civil rights action against the officials, claiming that they had violated his Fourth Amendment rights.

Justice O'Connor's plurality opinion, joined by Chief Justice Rehnquist and Justices White and Powell, declined to decide whether the psychiatrist had a reasonable expectation of privacy in his office, but found that he definitely had one in his desk and file cabinets. The plurality concluded "that public employers' intrusions upon the constitutionally protected privacy interests of government employees for noninvestigatory, work-related purposes, as well as for investigations of work-related misconduct should be judged by the standard of reasonableness under all the circumstances."

Justice Scalia concurred in the judgment. He objected to the vagueness of the plurality opinion and "would hold ... that the offices of government employees, and a fortiori the drawers and files within those offices, are covered by the Fourth Amendment protections as a general matter. (The qualification is necessary to cover such unusual situations as that in which the office is subject to unrestricted public access * * *.)" But, Justice Scalia also "would hold that government searches to retrieve work-related materials or to investigate violations of workplace rules—searches of the sort that are regarded as reasonable and normal in the private-employer context—do not violate the Fourth Amendment."

Justice Blackmun, joined by Justices Brennan, Marshall, and Stevens, dissented. He stated that the plurality failed to demonstrate that the traditional probable cause standard would not adequately protect public employers.

Which of the three approaches is most persuasive? May the government effectively assure that Justice Scalia's approach will prevail by announcing to employees that their offices, desks and cabinets are subject to inspection for work-related matters? In the end, which approach protects privacy more, Justice O'Connor's or Justice Scalia's?

8. Traditional "Searches" Not Covered by the Fourth Amendment After Katz

At the time of *Katz,* it could have been argued that there was general agreement that traditional entries and inspections by law enforcement officers were regulated by the Fourth Amendment, and that the *Katz* test was designed to limit government activity at the margins, such as electronic surveillance. Since *Katz,* however, the courts have used the expectation of privacy test not only to expand but also to limit Fourth Amendment protection, so that much law enforcement activity which looks like a search (as that word would be commonly understood) is not a search for Fourth Amendment purposes. Recall *Greenwood* and *Hudson,* where the police rummaged through property, and yet the activity was found not a search.

An officer's entry into and visual inspection of the interior of the home has traditionally been considered a search. Yet this may not always be the case after *Katz.* Consider United States v. York, 895 F.2d 1026 (5th Cir.1990). Officers responding to a distress call found a man named Bill and his two minor sons waiting on the street outside York's home. Bill told the officers that he and his family had been living as guests in York's home. Bill complained that York had threatened Bill and his children; Bill had then departed with his two sons, leaving behind his daughter who was taking a bath at the time in York's home. Bill asked an officer to accompany him so that he and his family could retrieve their belongings from York's home. Bill and his family then led the officers into the house, and the family began loading their belongings into Bill's truck. The officers entered and stood inside the entrance foyer. From there, they saw a gun cabinet, which contained two machine guns. York then came from the back of the house, ordered the officers to leave, and stated that he was going to the back of the house to call his attorney. An officer followed York into his bedroom, and observed a sawed-off shotgun near the bed. The officers reported what they had seen to federal authorities, who obtained a search warrant for York's home and seized the guns. York was convicted of illegally receiving and possessing firearms. The court found that the guns were properly admitted at trial, since the officers' conduct did not constitute a search. It reasoned as follows:

> [A]lthough the right to privacy in the home is certainly a reasonable expectation, it has also been noted that this expectation can be reduced as a result of the activities of the home's occupants. * * * [A]ctivities or circumstances within a dwelling may lessen the owner's reasonable expectation of privacy by creating a risk of intrusion which is reasonably foreseeable. * * *
>
> In the present case the actions of the Harris County deputies were made reasonably foreseeable when York became intoxicated and belligerent and threatened Bill and his children, whom he had allowed to occupy his home. * * * York's threats of violence to Bill and his children made it foreseeable that Bill would seek help in removing his possessions. * * * No fourth amendment "search" took place.

Was there any way for the court in *York* to uphold the officers' actions, other than to declare that no search took place? Has *Katz* been turned on its head so as to limit rather than expand Fourth Amendment protection, or were such limitations anticipated by the Court which decided *Katz?*

III. THE TENSION BETWEEN THE REASONABLENESS AND THE WARRANT CLAUSES

A. THE IMPORTANCE OF THE WARRANT CLAUSE GENERALLY

Today it is well established in the opinions of the Supreme Court that searches and seizures conducted without a warrant are suspect. In fact, they are presumed to be unreasonable. The language of the Court, which is by now quite familiar is that "searches conducted outside the judicial process, without prior approval by judge or magistrate are *per se* unreasonable under the Fourth Amendment—subject only to a few specifically established and well-delineated exceptions." Katz v. United States, 389 U.S. 347, 357 (1967). The Court has deemed this "a cardinal principle" of Fourth Amendment law. Mincey v. Arizona, 437 U.S. 385 (1978).

Actually, the thought of a tough, sweeping per se rule yielding only to the most demanding claims for exceptions is at odds with reality. Despite the

Court's ringing language, the so-called per se rule can be restated as follows: A search and seizure in some circumstances is presumed to be unconstitutional if no prior warrant is obtained, but in other circumstances the prior warrant is unnecessary to justify a search and seizure. The line of demarcation is most difficult to draw. Undoubtedly, there is a per se rule that applies in *some* situations, but it would be gross exaggeration, as the cases, infra, will demonstrate, for anyone to suggest even that most searches and seizures require a warrant. Most probably they do not. As Justice Scalia stated in his concurring opinion in California v. Acevedo, 111 S.Ct. 1982 (1991), the Court's jurisprudence with respect to the warrant requirement has "lurched back and forth between imposing a categorical warrant requirement and looking to reasonableness alone." According to Justice Scalia, the result is that the warrant requirement has become "so riddled with exceptions that it [is] basically unrecognizable."

The theory of the Fourth Amendment, which in large part is the theory of the warrant clause, is removed from the everyday practice under the Amendment. Whether this is as it should be is a subject that can be better addressed once the "per se" rule and its numerous exceptions are fully explored.

B. SOME HISTORY OF THE FOURTH AMENDMENT

1. *Early Search Authorizations*

Search warrants "crept into the law by imperceptible practice." Entick v. Carrington, 18 How.St.Trials 1030 (1765). As late as 1641, Lord Coke insisted that it was illegal for a justice of the peace to break into a man's house to search for a felon or stolen goods. Coke, 4 Institutes, Cap. 31, at 176. The use of warrants can be traced to three distinct sources. See T. Taylor, Two Studies in Constitutional Interpretation 24–27 (1969). First, the common law warrant to search for stolen goods, which arose sometime in the late 16th century, was issued by a justice of the peace and executed by a constable in the company of the victim of the theft. To be valid, the victim had to swear under oath that a theft had occurred and that he had probable cause to believe that the goods were lodged in a specific place. If the search failed to reveal the stolen goods, the victim was liable for trespass. Most of the present-day safeguards in search and seizure procedures arose in this area.

Second, searches in particular cases were authorized by statute in England as early as the 14th century, and with the expiration of the statutes, they continued on a common-law footing. For example, an act in 1335 authorized innkeepers in ports to search guests for counterfeit money. N. Lasson, The History and Development of the Fourth Amendment 23 (1937). General warrants, which were used extensively in the 1600's and 1700's under the auspices of the seditious libel laws to suppress the press, were also of this type. Briefly, general warrants were issued by executive officers, and did not specify the goods or person sought or the premises to be searched. The officer in possession of such a warrant could legally search any house or shop without a showing of probable cause, regardless of whether or not the goods or person were actually found. Early commentators agreed that a general warrant to search for stolen goods was illegal, although there was some precedent for granting them. 2 M. Hale, Historia Placitorum Coronae, Ch. XVIII, § 1, at

149–150 (1847); The Law of Arrest in both Civil and Criminal Cases, by an Attorney at Law (2d ed. 1753) 173. There was much controversy in 18th century England over the legality of such warrants where the statutory justification had ceased to exist. This controversy, discussed in detail, infra (*Wilkes* and *Entick*), had a substantial effect on the development of Fourth Amendment liberties.

Third, searches were authorized by statute in the 17th and 18th centuries, and these were often similar in scope to the general warrants discussed above. In this category were the writs of assistance issued by the Court of Exchequer which authorized a constable (or in America, any person) to break into and search any place for the seizure of uncustomed or prohibited goods. The use of these writs by customs officials was a major source of colonial discontent, and led directly to the search and seizure guarantees in the Fourth Amendment and the various states' Bills of Rights.

The origins and use of warrantless searches are difficult to document since there is virtually no case or statutory law in point. Taylor, supra, at 27–29, suggests several reasons for believing that they were common practice throughout this period, reasons drawn from the relationship of search and seizure to arrest law. First, as a practical matter, few people could read during the middle ages, rendering useless warrants for either search or arrest. Second, he suggests that search incident to arrest was necessary since most arrests were in hot pursuit of a felon or upon hue and cry, where delay would be detrimental. It was such commonplace and ancient practice that it was taken for granted (which explains the lack of early records) and was of little concern since it involved only suspected felons. A brief look at the law of arrest sheds light on the scope of warrantless searches.

2. *Arrests*

Under the common law, arrest could be made by any officer of the law or by a private person. Arrests without a warrant were justified when treason, felony, dangerous wounding, or breach of the peace occurred in the presence of an officer, or where there was good reason to suspect another of treason, felony or dangerous wounding. Officers of the law were required to arrest in these circumstances and were also afforded greater protection against suits for false arrest than were private persons who were only required to arrest when treason, felony or dangerous wounding occurred in their presence. Private persons could, however, be compelled to aid an officer in pursuing a felon or executing a warrant.

Another instance of warrantless arrest was "upon hue and cry" wherein the victim or an officer gave information that a felony had occurred, and as near a description of the felon as was possible, and the constable was then authorized to search for him in all suspected places. Unlike the first category of cases above, "hue and cry" required not probable cause, but mere information, and authorized search upon suspicion. However, a constable broke into a house at his peril: if the suspected felon was there, it was justified; if not, he was liable as a trespasser. M. Hale, supra, at 103. And a person raising a hue and cry against an innocent person could also be punished.

A final type of warrantless arrest was that pursuant to a statute such as an English law which authorized watchmen to arrest nightwalkers upon mere suspicion or information. Id. at 97. An example in colonial law is a Massachusetts statute which authorized a constable to arrest without a warrant those who "are overtaken with drink, swearing, Sabbath breaking, lying," etc., if such occurs in his presence or if he learns of it by present information.

A warrant for arrest could be issued by a court or justice of the peace upon oath or affirmation showing probable cause that a specific person was involved in a crime.

Search incident to arrest was thus not always based on the existence of an arrest warrant, or even on probable cause. However, civil and criminal liabilities often attached where persons wrongly raised a hue and cry, or otherwise gave information against an innocent person, and thus Taylor suggests that few arrests occurred except where actual felons were involved. At any rate, no warrantless search incident to arrest was ever challenged in England till the end of the 19th century, and that challenge was rejected. Dillon v. O'Brien, 16 Cox C.C. 245 (Exch.Ireland 1887).

3. *Wilkes and Entick*

The *Wilkes* and *Entick* cases were the culmination of over 200 years of executive and legislative control over the press in England through the use of broad search and seizure provisions. Beginning in 1538, the King, and later Parliament, initiated licensing schemes enforceable by general warrants as a means of prior state censorship of the press. Originally, the enforcement of these provisions was in the hands of the Stationers' Company, a private guild organization, whose incentive to strictly enforce the laws was the protection of its monopoly printing rights. The authority to enforce seditious libel laws was vested in the Court of Star Chamber, who in turn granted increasingly broader powers of search and seizure to the Company. When the Star Chamber was abolished in 1640, Parliament passed its own censorship and search laws, enforceable by general warrants from the secretary of state. When this Printing Act expired in 1679, Chief Justice Scrogg, in response to the King's inquiry, ruled that general warrants to control the press had a basis in common law, needing no statutory justification. He was later impeached for the decision, marking the first recognition by Parliament that general warrants were an arbitrary exercise of government power against which the public needed protection. However, in that same year, Parliament renewed the Printing Act, and it continued in force until 1694.

The first protections against search and seizure came in the early 1700's when several taxes failed in Parliament because their broad, abusive search powers imposed "a badge of slavery on the whole people." J. Landynski, Search and Seizure and the Supreme Court 25 (1966). At the same time, safeguards had been gradually developing in the courts to limit search and seizure powers under the common law: A warrant had to be issued by a judicial officer, and it required specificity as to the person or thing sought, and probable cause to search. However, even after the expiration of the Printing Act, secretaries of state continued to issue broad oppressive general warrants to enforce the seditious libel laws. As a result of these warrants, a search and seizure controversy arose in England in the mid-1700's.

In 1763, Lord Halifax, as Secretary of State, issued a general warrant for the arrest and seizure of the papers of the author of the anonymous *North Briton* # 5 which severely criticized George III's cider excise tax. Many unrelated persons were arrested and dozens of houses and shops searched. The author, John Wilkes, sued the messengers who executed the warrants and Halifax for trespass. Justice Pratt (later to become Lord Camden) upheld high jury verdicts against the messengers in the lower court, although recognizing that Wilkes had suffered little damage. Pratt held that the Secretary had no authority to issue the warrants, and that, alternatively, they were invalid because they were too general and vested such broad discretion in the messengers as to be subversive of liberty. Wilkes v. Weed, Lofft 1, 98 Eng.Rep. 489 (1763). Also Wilkes v. Halifax, XIX Howell St.Tr. 1401 (1769). On appeal, Lord Mansfield affirmed the lower court ruling, but on narrower grounds. He recognized Halifax's power to issue the warrant, but found it invalid since it failed to name the person sought.

During this same period, Halifax issued a warrant for the arrest of John Entick for suspicion of seditious libel, and for the seizure of all his papers. In 1765, Entick sued the messengers in trespass and the case was heard by Lord Camden. The case was decided on two grounds: First, Camden held that neither Halifax nor the messengers had statutory authority to issue or execute the warrants, and that, even if they did, they had exceeded this authority by not adhering strictly to the terms of the warrant. Second, Camden held that the executive's power to issue general warrants did not, in the absence of statute, derive from the common law. He rejected the analogy to the common law warrant to search for stolen goods on the grounds that the Entick warrant contained none of the procedural safeguards afforded by the common law rules of search and seizure. Specifically, the warrant was defective because it failed to name the specific libelous papers to be sought, because no oath of probable cause had been required, and because no record of goods seized had been kept. Entick v. Carrington, 18 How.St.Trials 1030 (1765).

In response to *Entick,* the House of Commons in 1766 adopted a resolution to the effect that general warrants for arrests, or for search in seditious libel cases, were illegal.

4. The Colonies

The fight for protection of personal liberty, taking place in England, had a parallel in the colonies which, as has been noted, had statutes purporting to authorize broad searches and seizures. Two acts of Parliament were used to justify the use of writs of assistance by customs officials in the colonies. T. Taylor, supra, at 35. The first, in 1662, authorized officials to enter and search any house suspected of containing prohibited or uncustomed goods, pursuant to a writ issued by the Court of Exchequer. The second, in 1696, authorized colonial customs officials to exercise the same powers. In 1755, the Massachusetts Superior Court issued a writ to the Surveyor of the Port of Boston, which expired automatically six months after the death of the sovereign under whom it was issued. When George II died in 1760, several merchants in Massachusetts requested the court to hear arguments on the validity of general warrants before issuing a new writ to the Surveyor.

The case was argued twice before Thomas Hutchinson, with James Otis, Jr., and Oxenbridge Thatcher representing the merchants. Thatcher's argument was based on statutory construction: he contended that Parliament had not authorized the Massachusetts court to issue writs of assistance, and that they were therefore invalid unless issued directly by the Court of Exchequer. Otis argued, on broad libertarian principles, that the writs were repugnant to the Magna Charta and fundamental principles of law which recognized the privilege of the home. He maintained that even if the writs had a statutory basis, the statute must be void and unenforceable as against the constitution and natural equity. The writs were defective in several ways: first, they were universal, authorizing any person to enforce them; second, they were perpetual, i.e., they need not be returned to the issuing court, and thus there were no judicial restraints on their enforcement; and third, they gave overly broad authority to enter any house on bare suspicion, i.e., no oath of probable cause was required.

There is some evidence that the right to be free from disturbances in one's home was recognized in the common law. In Anglo-Saxon England, forcible entry into another's dwelling justified killing of the perpetrator, and Alfred the Great is said to have hanged men in several cases because they had executed others pursuant to false or invalid warrants. N. Lasson, supra, at 19. Chapter 39 of the Magna Charta is often cited as the foundation for the principle of reasonable search and seizure, although Lasson suggests that the chapter was included to safeguard against specific abuses of power by King John, and read in context, had nothing to do with search and seizure law. Id. at 20–21. However, its authority was cited by Lords Camden and Mansfield, and James Otis in the cases discussed above, as the source of that right, and therefore, it had symbolic value, if nothing else.

Hutchinson naturally sought guidance from the law of England, and discovering that writs were granted there, held that the Massachusetts Court could issue new writs of assistance. The importance of the case lies in its effect on the revolutionary spirit in the colonies. According to John Adams, Otis' oratory inspired every man to take up arms against writs of assistance. "Then and there the Child Independence was born." 2 Legal Papers of John Adams 106–47 (Wroth & Zobel ed. 1965). In fact, the enforcement of the new writs provoked violent riots in Massachusetts in 1765 and 1768.

In the other colonies, courts simply refused to grant the writs, claiming no authority initially, and later, when the Townshend Acts effectively obviated that objection, claiming that they were unconstitutional. In 1774, the Continental Congress listed the abuse of search power by customs officials in its petition to the King for a redress of grievances.

It is clear, therefore, that at the time of the Revolution, the primary concern of the colonists *viz.* search and seizure was general writs and warrants which gave unbridled discretion to the enforcing officers. It does not appear that warrantless searches were in issue, and this contention receives support from the earliest Bills of Rights drawn up by individual states.

C. PREDECESSORS OF THE AMENDMENT

Neither colonial charters nor early codifications of colonial law refer to any right which parallels the Fourth Amendment, although many of them contain liberal and far-reaching declarations of rights. Furthermore, several of the earliest codes specifically rejected the common law and laws of England, and thus might not have recognized a "sanctity of the home" even if it were an established part of the common law. P. Reinsch, English Common Law in American Colonies (1889) at 25, 40, 53, 56. These codes were based instead on natural law and the Word of God, and while Otis also found freedom in one's home to be a natural law right, it appears that the early colonists either did not recognize, or were not sufficiently concerned with, that freedom to insure its protection. It is more likely that the development of that right—or at least the concern which gave rise to its articulation—was relatively contemporaneous with the growth of the revolutionary spirit in the colonies. The Fourth Amendment was a direct response to a current problem more than the codification of a fundamental right. It is interesting to note here that the author of the first draft of the Virginia Declaration of Rights (the first state declaration of rights in 1776) did not include the right to be free from unreasonable searches in that document. That provision was drafted by a committee and included in the final document, over the original author's objections that it was not fundamental.

Article X of the Virginia Declaration of Rights stated that "General warrants * * * are grievous and oppressive and ought not to be granted." In the next few years, six states adopted declarations of rights which included search and seizure provisions. Also in 1776, Pennsylvania adopted a provision which specified a right to be free from searches and seizures as a general principle underlying its prohibition of general warrants. The Massachusetts Bill of 1780, was the first to use the phrase "unreasonable searches and seizures," and thus, by that year, all the elements of the Fourth Amendment had been introduced in some form in the Bill of Rights of a state constitution.

However, the Declaration of Independence, the Articles of Confederation and the Constitution all failed to mention any such right, and the latter two documents contained no declarations of rights whatsoever, on the premise that a limited government required no articulation of the reserved rights of its citizens. Thus, the adoption of the Fourth Amendment is tied strongly to the debates over the Bill of Rights as a whole, and in fact, there is little specific mention of the search and seizure provision in either the state conventions for ratification of the Constitution, or in the Federal Congress which had approved the Bill of Rights that was sent to the states. The Virginia debates on ratification contain some discussion of the right to be free from unreasonable searches, but the issue is never whether the right exists, or its scope, but only whether citizens are protected against abuses of that right without a federal guarantee in the Constitution. Most of the arguments are specifically directed to general warrants, but the amendment proposed by that convention contained a general principle of freedom from unreasonable searches in addition to the prohibition against general warrants, and also warrants without probable cause. Debates and Other Proceedings of the Convention of Virginia, 1788, (1805), "Proposed Bill of Rights" Section 14, pp. 318, 420. This marked a change from the provision in that state's bill of rights.

The circumstances surrounding the adoption of the Fourth Amendment indicate that nuances in the language used cannot readily be construed as clear evidence of the framers' intent. It appears that the House never consciously agreed to the present form of the Amendment. As proposed by the Committee of Eleven, the provision read:

> "the right * * * to be secured in their persons, papers, houses, and effects shall not be violated by warrants issuing * * *"
>
> That was corrected to read:
>
> "The right * * * to be secure * * * against unreasonable searches and seizures shall not be violated by warrants issuing * * *"

At that point, Mr. Benson objected to the words "by warrants issuing," as not being sufficient. His proposal that they be altered to read: "and no warrant shall issue" lost by a considerable majority. Annals of Congress, 1st Congress, 1st Sess. at 783. However, Benson, as chairman of the Committee appointed to arrange the amendments, reported his version—the rejected version—of the Amendment. The alteration was never noticed, and was subsequently agreed to by the Senate and ratified by the states in that form. Thus, arguments based on the intent of the framers, as evidenced by the existence of a two-clause amendment, have little foundation in fact.

D. THE SIGNIFICANCE OF THE HISTORY

To this additional history one more fact should be added. Taylor, supra, at 47–48, concludes that, traditionally, most searches and seizures were incident to arrest and that, because no warrant was required to justify them, the better reading of the Fourth Amendment is not that the warrant is presumptively required, but that reasonableness is the key.

There is reason to doubt his conclusion, however. The history is rather clear that even searches explicitly authorized by statute were not accepted by those who fought England for freedom. The claim they made apparently was that the warrant is the protection against government to which free people are entitled. That an arrest might justify a warrantless search incident thereto may have been a common and accepted idea. But there is no reason to think that the framers viewed this limited search as anything but a necessary and wise exception to their fundamental preference for warrants. Indeed, as Justice Jackson argues in his dissent in Harris v. United States, 331 U.S. 145 (1947), it would be an odd reading of the history of the Amendment to conclude that the framers, who "believed that by thus controlling search warrants they had controlled searches" would have been indifferent to the suggestion that searches without a warrant could be conducted without restriction, or in any manner that might be deemed reasonable.

History rarely provides conclusive answers to constitutional problems; this is certainly true with respect to interpreting the Fourth Amendment. But, even where the framers of the Constitution have not provided a clear answer to a problem, history does foster insights into their purpose in choosing to rely on certain language to promote freedom throughout the years that would follow.

E. THE IMPORTANCE OF THE WARRANT

The case which follows is probably the Supreme Court's most thorough explication and justification of the warrant requirement. It lays the foundation of the current "per se" rule that warrants are required for searches and seizures, subject to "a few carefully delineated" exceptions.

JOHNSON v. UNITED STATES

Supreme Court of the United States, 1948.
333 U.S. 10.

MR. JUSTICE JACKSON delivered the opinion of the Court.

Petitioner was convicted of four counts charging violation of federal narcotic laws. The only question which brings the case here is whether it was lawful, without a warrant of any kind, to arrest petitioner and to search her living quarters.

Taking the Government's version of disputed events, decision would rest on these facts:

At about 7:30 p.m. Detective Lieutenant Belland, an officer of the Seattle police force narcotic detail, received information from a confidential informer, who was also a known narcotic user, that unknown persons were smoking opium in the Europe Hotel. The informer was taken back to the hotel to interview the manager, but he returned at once saying he could smell burning opium in the hallway. Belland communicated with federal narcotic agents and between 8:30 and 9 o'clock went back to the hotel with four such agents. All were experienced in narcotic work and recognized at once a strong odor of burning opium which to them was distinctive and unmistakable. The odor led to Room 1. The officers did not know who was occupying that room. They knocked and a voice inside asked who was there. "Lieutenant Belland," was the reply. There was a slight delay, some "shuffling or noise" in the room and then the defendant opened the door. The officer said, "I want to talk to you a little bit." She then, as he describes it, "stepped back acquiescently and admitted us." He said, "I want to talk to you about this opium smell in the room here." She denied that there was such a smell. Then he said, "I want you to consider yourself under arrest because we are going to search the room." The search turned up incriminating opium and smoking apparatus, the latter being warm, apparently from recent use. This evidence the District Court refused to suppress before trial and admitted over defendant's objection at the trial. Conviction resulted and the Circuit Court of Appeals affirmed.

The defendant challenged the search of her home as a violation of the rights secured to her, in common with others, by the Fourth Amendment to the Constitution.

I

* * *

* * * The Government defends the search as legally justifiable, more particularly as incident to what it urges was a lawful arrest of the person.

Entry to defendant's living quarters, which was the beginning of the search, was demanded under color of office. It was granted in submission to authority rather than as an understanding and intentional waiver of a constitutional right.

At the time entry was demanded the officers were possessed of evidence which a magistrate might have found to be probable cause for issuing a search warrant. We cannot sustain defendant's contention, erroneously made, on the strength of Taylor v. United States, 286 U.S. 1, that odors cannot be evidence sufficient to constitute probable grounds for any search. That decision held only that odors alone do not authorize a search without warrant. If the presence of odors is testified to before a magistrate and he finds the affiant qualified to know the odor, and it is one sufficiently distinctive to identify a forbidden substance, this Court has never held such a basis insufficient to justify issuance of a search warrant. Indeed it might very well be found to be evidence of most persuasive character.

The point of the Fourth Amendment, which often is not grasped by zealous officers, is not that it denies law enforcement the support of the usual inferences which reasonable men draw from evidence. Its protection consists in requiring that those inferences be drawn by a neutral and detached magistrate instead of being judged by the officer engaged in the often competitive enterprise of ferreting out crime.[a] Any assumption that evidence sufficient to support a magistrate's disinterested determination to issue a search warrant will justify the officers in making a search without a warrant would reduce the Amendment to a nullity and leave the people's homes secure only in the discretion of police officers.[b] Crime, even in the privacy of one's own quarters, is, of course, of grave concern to society, and the law allows such crime to be reached on proper showing. The right of officers to thrust themselves into a home is also a grave concern, not only to the individual but to a society which chooses to dwell in reasonable security and freedom from surveillance. When the right of privacy must reasonably yield to the right of search is, as a rule, to be decided by a judicial officer, not by a policeman or government enforcement agent.

There are exceptional circumstances in which, on balancing the need for effective law enforcement against the right of privacy, it may be contended that a magistrate's warrant for search may be dispensed with. But this is not such a case. No reason is offered for not obtaining a search warrant except the inconvenience to the officers and some slight delay necessary to prepare papers and present the evidence to a magistrate. These are never very convincing reasons and, in these circumstances, certainly are not enough to bypass the constitutional requirement. No suspect was fleeing or likely to take flight. The search was of permanent premises, not of a movable vehicle. No evidence or contraband was threatened with removal or destruction, except perhaps the fumes which we suppose in time would disappear. But they were not capable at any time of being reduced to possession for presentation to court. The evidence of their existence before the search was adequate and the testimony of the officers to that effect would not perish from the delay of getting a warrant.

If the officers in this case were excused from the constitutional duty of presenting their evidence to a magistrate, it is difficult to think of a case in which it should be required.

II

[The Court held that the officers had no probable cause to arrest the defendant until they entered the defendant's quarters, and reasoned that the search (entry and visual inspection) preceded the arrest. It was not possible, therefore, to justify the officers' conduct on a search incident to a valid arrest theory.

a. In United States v. Lefkowitz, 285 U.S. 452, 464, this Court said: "* * * the informed and deliberate determinations of magistrates empowered to issue warrants as to what searches and seizures are permissible under the Constitution are to be preferred over the hurried action of officers and others who may happen to make arrests. Security against unlawful searches is more likely to be attained by resort to search warrants than by reliance upon the caution and sagacity of petty officers while acting under the excitement that attends the capture of persons accused of crime. * * *"

b. "Belief, however well founded, that an article sought is concealed in a dwelling house furnishes no justification for a search of that place without a warrant. And such searches are held unlawful notwithstanding facts unquestionably showing probable cause." Agnello v. United States, 269 U.S. 20, 33.

Justices Black, Reed, and Burton, together with Chief Justice Vinson, dissented without opinion.]

Note

Johnson represents a victory for those who would have the police secure warrants. As the majority intimates, there almost certainly was enough evidence known to the police to justify a magistrate's issuance of a warrant. Yet, because no warrant was sought, the search is deemed constitutionally "unreasonable" or invalid. Why is this the correct result? If you would answer that the framers assumed that warrants generally would be required, you must recognize that those same framers were familiar with warrantless searches incident to arrest and therefore presumably had in mind that some searches would not require warrants. Could *Johnson* have been viewed as a case in which no warrant was necessary? To answer this to your own satisfaction it may be important to think about why the framers assumed that warrants were generally necessary to justify searches and seizures. You might agree with Justice Holmes that "[i]t is revolting to have no better reason for a rule of law than that it was laid down in the time of Henry IV." The Path of the Law in Harv.L.Rev. 457, 469 (1897).

F. THE THEORY OF THE WARRANT CLAUSE

Professor Amsterdam has made the following suggestion:

> Indiscriminate searches or seizures might be thought to be bad for either or both of two reasons. The first is that they expose people and their possessions to interferences by government when there is no good reason to do so. The concern here is against *unjustified* searches and seizures: it rests upon the principle that every citizen is entitled to security of his person and property unless and until an adequate justification for disturbing that security is shown. The second is that indiscriminate searches and seizures are conducted at the discretion of executive officials, who may act despotically and capriciously in the exercise of the power to search and seize. This latter concern runs against arbitrary searches and seizures: it condemns the petty tyranny of unregulated rummagers.

Perspectives on the Fourth Amendment, 58 Minn.L.Rev. 349, 411 (1974). The history of searches and seizures in England and America, plus the language of the Fourth Amendment itself, which both have received some attention, supra, should help to elucidate the concerns so well identified by Professor Amsterdam.

With searches and seizures that are subject to the warrant requirement, probable cause represents the threshold of proof that must be satisfied before the power to search and seize is legitimated. The existence of such a proof requirement strongly suggests that the government must be able to demonstrate an interest in people, places or things *before* using its power to disturb them. The proof requirement protects against *unjustified* searches and seizures.

Related to the proof requirement are the "Oath or affirmation" and particularity provisions of the Amendment. Probable cause is to be shown by persons willing to swear to or affirm the truth of their statements and thus to be held accountable for their representations. In addition, the applicant for the warrant is committing to a public record the information that is known *before* the search so that, after the search takes place, there is no confusion between the ex-post and ex-ante positions of the applicant. Without an antecedent warrant requirement, an officer questioned about probable cause can work backwards from the search, and fill in the facts as if they were known beforehand. The specificity requirement implies that the government can only interfere with those persons, places or things that it has shown a valid interest in. Here, too, the written record made in advance of the search may decrease the danger that after a search is completed, the police will claim that whatever is found is exactly what was sought. Also, the specification of objects sought to be seized may inform the magistrate's decision on whether the search is reasonable, as the next paragraph explains. A showing of probable cause, then, does not mean any search and seizure authorized by a warrant is valid; it means that any search and seizure directed by warrant at the people, places, or things to which the probable cause specifically relates satisfies the warrant clause of the Fourth Amendment. These limitations guard against what Amsterdam called *arbitrary* searches and seizures.

By placing a magistrate between the citizen and the police, the Amendment, in the words of the *Johnson* majority, establishes that a neutral observer is to decide whether the probable cause and specificity requirements have been satisfied. This is one way in which the Amendment operates to prevent unjustified searches and seizures; the presumption is that a magistrate will make fewer errors than "the officer engaged in the often competitive enterprise of ferreting out crime." *Johnson,* 333 U.S., at 14. By interposing the magistrate between the "competitors"—the police and the suspect—the Amendment may also serve another function. It may afford the neutral magistrate an opportunity to refuse a warrant, even if the application is supported by oath, probable cause and specifics, on the ground that a search and seizure is unreasonable under the circumstances. For example, if the police have probable cause to believe that A has marijuana cigarettes in his home, and if possession of small quantities of marijuana is punishable by fine only, a magistrate might be inclined to disapprove a warrant to search A's entire house on the ground that the scope of the search would be beyond what reasonable persons would call reasonable in light of the government's professed interest in small quantities of cannabis. The same magistrate might be persuaded to permit a search of A's briefcase. Similarly, if the police obtain a warrant to search A's house on Monday and execute the warrant that same day, but find nothing, a magistrate might hesitate to issue another warrant to search on Tuesday, and perhaps another to look again on Wednesday, even if the police still have probable cause. Or, in an income tax evasion case, if the police asked for authority to search for and seize everything found in a home as evidence of an income greater than that recorded on a tax return, a magistrate might balk at issuing such a warrant. However, the same magistrate might authorize an entry into the house to take photographs. By imposing limitations on searches, a magistrate may prevent *excessive* governmental intrusions.

As you go through the remainder of the chapter, see if you can identify other goals of the warrant requirement. Might one be to assure citizens that the persons invading their homes have actual authority to do so? If so, a related goal might be to regularly remind police of their obligation to comply with the legal constraints placed upon them. Could it also be argued that without the specific limitation of the warrant requirement, the Fourth Amendment's general command that a search be "reasonable" would be inherently ambiguous and subject to the case-by-case balancing of shifting majorities of the courts? Is it possible for the Supreme Court to give specific and principled guidance under the reasonableness clause?

It is surprising that the Supreme Court has not more clearly articulated the rationale for the warrant requirement in a century of litigation. Looking back on the Court's efforts, Justice Stewart wrote for the Court (three other Justices joined the entire opinion and Justice Harlan joined in this part of the opinion) in Coolidge v. New Hampshire, 403 U.S. 443, 474–75 (1971) (footnotes omitted), as follows:

> Much the most important part of the conflict that has been so notable in this Court's attempts over a hundred years to develop a coherent body of Fourth Amendment law has been caused by disagreement over the importance of requiring law enforcement officers to secure warrants. Some have argued that a determination by a magistrate of probable cause as a precondition of any search or seizure is so essential that the Fourth Amendment is violated whenever the police might reasonably have obtained a warrant but failed to do so. Others have argued with equal force that a test of reasonableness, applied after the fact of search or seizure when the police attempt to introduce the fruits in evidence, affords ample safeguard for the rights in question, so that "[t]he relevant test is not whether it is reasonable to procure a search warrant, but whether the search was reasonable."

As noted earlier, the conflict has been resolved in favor of magisterial screening prior to searches and seizures. See, e.g., Mincey v. Arizona, 437 U.S. 385 (1978) (holding invalid warrantless search of murder scene); Michigan v. Tyler, 436 U.S. 499 (1978) (holding invalid re-entry by fire officials after extinguishing blaze to search for evidence of arson). But, because the explication of the rationale for the warrant requirement has left something to be desired, the decisions of the Court that recognize exceptions often are unpersuasive and chaotic. It is difficult to make a persuasive case for an exception, unless one can explicate the purpose of the rule from which the exception is to depart. The exceptions will be considered shortly. Before reaching them, it is useful to understand what practical protections the warrant application procedure affords, so that you know what it really means to say that the warrant clause, with its dependence on the neutral magistrate, is a fundamental part of American freedom. In the decisions that prescribe the various aspects of the warrant process, there is further evidence that the Court's inadequate articulation of the protections that the warrant clause is intended to afford leads to decisions that ill serve its purposes.

IV. OBTAINING A SEARCH WARRANT: CONSTITUTIONAL PREREQUISITES

A. DEMONSTRATING PROBABLE CAUSE

1. *The Creation of a Two-Pronged Test*

The Fourth Amendment mandates a showing of probable cause as justification for a search warrant. As noted above, this is the threshold proof requirement. The higher it is set, the greater are the theoretical role of the magistrate in the warrant process and the protection against police searches and seizures. Scant attention was paid to the term probable cause until the 1960's, when two major cases were decided, Aguilar v. Texas, 378 U.S. 108 (1964) and Spinelli v. United States, 393 U.S. 410 (1969). *Spinelli* is set forth below; the earlier *Aguilar* decision is discussed in the majority opinion.

SPINELLI v. UNITED STATES

Supreme Court of the United States, 1969.
393 U.S. 410.

Appendix to Opinion of the Court

Affidavit in Support of Search Warrant

I, Robert L. Bender, being duly sworn, depose and say that I am a Special Agent of the Federal Bureau of Investigation, and as such am authorized to make searches and seizures.

That on August 6, 1965, at approximately 11:44 a.m., William Spinelli was observed by an Agent of the Federal Bureau of Investigation driving a 1964 Ford convertible, Missouri license HC3–649, onto the Eastern approach of the Veterans Bridge leading from East St. Louis, Illinois, to St. Louis, Missouri.

That on August 11, 1965, at approximately 11:16 a.m., William Spinelli was observed by an Agent of the Federal Bureau of Investigation driving a 1964 Ford convertible, Missouri license HC3–649, onto the Eastern approach of the Eads Bridge leading from East St. Louis, Illinois, to St. Louis, Missouri.

Further, at approximately 11:18 a.m. on August 11, 1965, I observed William Spinelli driving the aforesaid Ford convertible from the Western approach of the Eads Bridge into St. Louis, Missouri.

Further, at approximately 4:40 p.m. on August 11, 1965, I observed the aforesaid Ford convertible, bearing Missouri license HC3–649, parked in a parking lot used by residents of The Chieftain Manor Apartments, approximately one block east of 1108 Indian Circle Drive.

On August 12, 1965, at approximately 12:07 p.m., William Spinelli was observed by an Agent of the Federal Bureau of Investigation driving the aforesaid 1964 Ford convertible onto the Eastern approach of the Veterans Bridge from East St. Louis, Illinois, in the direction of St. Louis, Missouri.

Further, on August 12, 1965, at approximately 3:46 p.m., I observed William Spinelli driving the aforesaid 1964 Ford convertible onto the parking lot used by the residents of The Chieftain Manor Apartments approximately one block east of 1108 Indian Circle Drive.

Further, on August 12, 1965, at approximately 3:49 p.m., William Spinelli was observed by an Agent of the Federal Bureau of Investigation entering the front entrance of the two-story apartment building located at 1108 Indian Circle Drive, this building being one of The Chieftain Manor Apartments.

On August 13, 1965, at approximately 11:08 a.m., William Spinelli was observed by an Agent of the Federal Bureau of Investigation driving the aforesaid Ford convertible onto the Eastern approach of the Eads Bridge from East St. Louis, Illinois, heading towards St. Louis, Missouri.

Further, on August 13, 1965, at approximately 11:11 a.m., I observed William Spinelli driving the aforesaid Ford convertible from the Western approach of the Eads Bridge into St. Louis, Missouri.

Further, on August 13, 1965, at approximately 3:45 p.m., I observed William Spinelli driving the aforesaid 1964 Ford convertible onto the parking area used by residents of The Chieftain Manor Apartments, said parking area being approximately one block from 1108 Indian Circle Drive.

Further, on August 13, 1965, at approximately 3:55 p.m., William Spinelli was observed by an Agent of the Federal Bureau of Investigation entering the corner apartment located on the second floor in the southwest corner, known as Apartment F, of the two-story apartment building known and numbered as 1108 Indian Circle Drive.

On August 16, 1965, at approximately 3:22 p.m., I observed William Spinelli driving the aforesaid Ford convertible onto the parking lot used by the residents of The Chieftain Manor Apartments approximately one block east of 1108 Indian Circle Drive.

Further, an Agent of the F.B.I. observed William Spinelli alight from the aforesaid Ford convertible and walk toward the apartment building located at 1108 Indian Circle Drive.

The records of the Southwestern Bell Telephone Company reflect that there are two telephones located in the southwest corner apartment on the second floor of the apartment building located at 1108 Indian Circle Drive under the name of Grace P. Hagen. The numbers listed in the Southwestern Bell Telephone Company records for the aforesaid telephones are WYdown 4–0029 and WYdown 4–0136.

William Spinelli is known to this affiant and to federal law enforcement agents and local law enforcement agents as a bookmaker, an associate of bookmakers, a gambler, and an associate of gamblers.

The Federal Bureau of Investigation has been informed by a confidential reliable informant that William Spinelli is operating a handbook and accepting wagers and disseminating wagering information by means of the telephones which have been assigned the numbers WYdown 4–0029 and WYdown 4–0136.

/s/Robert L. Bender,
Robert L. Bender,
Special Agent, Federal Bureau of Investigation.

Subscribed and sworn to before me this 18th day of August, 1965, at St. Louis, Missouri.

/s/William R. O'Toole.

MR. JUSTICE HARLAN delivered the opinion of the Court.

William Spinelli was convicted under 18 U.S.C.A. § 1952 of traveling to St. Louis, Missouri, from a nearby Illinois suburb with the intention of conducting gambling activities proscribed by Missouri law. See Mo.Rev.Stat. § 563.360 (1959). At every appropriate stage in the proceedings in the lower courts, the petitioner challenged the constitutionality of the warrant which authorized the FBI search that uncovered the evidence necessary for his conviction. * * *

In *Aguilar,* a search warrant had issued upon an affidavit of police officers who swore only that they had "received reliable information from a credible person and do believe" that narcotics were being illegally stored on the described premises. While recognizing that the constitutional requirement of probable cause can be satisfied by hearsay information, this Court held the affidavit inadequate for two reasons. First, the application failed to set forth any of the "underlying circumstances" necessary to enable the magistrate independently to judge of the validity of the informant's conclusion that the narcotics were where he said they were. Second, the affiant-officers did not attempt to support their claim that their informant was " 'credible' or his information 'reliable.' "[5] The Government is, however, quite right in saying that the FBI affidavit in the present case is more ample than that in *Aguilar.* Not only does it contain a report from an anonymous informant, but it also contains a report of an independent FBI investigation which is said to corroborate the informant's tip. We are, then, required to delineate the manner in which *Aguilar's* two-pronged test should be applied in these circumstances.

In essence, the affidavit, reproduced in full in the Appendix to this opinion, contained the following allegations: [a]

1. The FBI had kept track of Spinelli's movements on five days during the month of August 1965. On four of these occasions, Spinelli was seen crossing one of two bridges leading from Illinois into St. Louis, Missouri, between 11 a.m. and 12:15 p.m. On four of the five days, Spinelli was also seen parking his car in a lot used by residents of an apartment house at 1108 Indian Circle Drive in St. Louis, between 3:30 p.m. and 4:45 p.m. On one day, Spinelli was followed further and seen to enter a particular apartment in the building.

2. An FBI check with the telephone company revealed that this apartment contained two telephones listed under the name of Grace P. Hagen, and carrying the numbers WYdown 4–0029 and WYdown 4–0136.

3. The application stated that "William Spinelli is known to this affiant and to federal law enforcement agents and local law enforcement agents as a bookmaker, an associate of bookmakers, a gambler, and an associate of gamblers."

4. Finally, it was stated that the FBI "has been informed by a confidential reliable informant that William Spinelli is operating a handbook and accepting wagers and disseminating wagering information by means of the telephones which have been assigned the numbers WYdown 4–0029 and WYdown 4–0136."

There can be no question that the last item mentioned, detailing the informant's tip, has a fundamental place in this warrant application. Without it, probable cause could not be established. The first two items reflect only innocent-seeming activity and data. Spinelli's travels to and from the apartment building and his entry into a particular apartment on one occasion could hardly be taken as bespeaking gambling activi-

5. The majority in *Aguilar* relied upon Nathanson v. United States, 290 U.S. 41 (1933), which held invalid a warrant issued upon the sworn allegation that the affiant "has cause to suspect and does believe" that certain merchandise was at the premises described, and Giordenello v. United States, 357 U.S. 480 (1958), which held that an *arrest* warrant was invalid because the underlying affidavit alleged in a conclusory fashion that the suspect had received and concealed narcotic drugs. Justice Clark dissented in *Aguilar* and was joined by Justices Black and Stewart. They argued that in *Aguilar* the fact that the affidavit relied on "reliable information from a credible person" plus the additional fact that the officers who sought the warrant had engaged in a week's surveillance of the suspect (something not stated in the affidavit) distinguished the prior cases. The dissent charged "that the Court has substituted a rigid, academic formula for the unified standards of reasonableness and 'probable cause' laid down by the Fourth Amendment itself—a substitution of technicality for practicality—and * * * that the Court's holding will tend to obstruct the administration of criminal justice throughout the country." 378 U.S. at 122.

a. It is, of course, of no consequence that the agents might have had additional information which could have been given to the Commissioner. "It is elementary that in passing on the validity of a warrant, the reviewing court may consider *only* information brought to the magistrate's attention." Aguilar v. Texas, 378 U.S. 108, 109, n. 1 (emphasis in original). Since the Government does not argue that whatever additional information the agents may have possessed was sufficient to provide probable cause for the arrest, thereby justifying the resultant search as well, we need not consider that question.

ty; and there is surely nothing unusual about an apartment containing two separate telephones. Many a householder indulges himself in this petty luxury. Finally, the allegation that Spinelli was "known" to the affiant and to other federal and local law enforcement officers as a gambler and an associate of gamblers is but a bald and unilluminating assertion of suspicion that is entitled to no weight in appraising the magistrate's decision.

So much indeed the Government does not deny. Rather, following the reasoning of the Court of Appeals, the Government claims that the informant's tip gives a suspicious color to the FBI's reports detailing Spinelli's innocent-seeming conduct and that, conversely, the FBI's surveillance corroborates the informant's tip, thereby entitling it to more weight. It is true, of course that the magistrate is obligated to render a judgment based upon a common-sense reading of the entire affidavit. We believe, however, that the "totality of circumstances" approach taken by the Court of Appeals paints with too broad a brush. Where, as here, the informer's tip is a necessary element in a finding of probable cause, its proper weight must be determined by a more precise analysis.

The informer's report must first be measured against *Aguilar's* standards so that its probative value can be assessed. If the tip is found inadequate under *Aguilar,* the other allegations which corroborate the information contained in the hearsay report should then be considered. At this stage as well, however, the standards enunciated in *Aguilar* must inform the magistrate's decision. He must ask: Can it fairly be said that the tip, even when certain parts of it have been corroborated by independent sources, is as trustworthy as a tip which would pass *Aguilar's* tests without independent corroboration? *Aguilar* is relevant at this stage of the inquiry as well because the tests it establishes were designed to implement the long-standing principle that probable cause must be determined by a "neutral and detached magistrate," and not by "the officer engaged in the often competitive enterprise of ferreting out crime." Johnson v. United States, 333 U.S. 10 (1948). A magistrate cannot be said to have properly discharged his constitutional duty if he relies on an informer's tip which—even when partially corroborated—is not as reliable as one which passes *Aguilar's* requirements when standing alone.

Applying these principles to the present case, we first consider the weight to be given the informer's tip when it is considered apart from the rest of the affidavit. It is clear that a Commissioner could not credit it without abdicating his constitutional function. Though the affiant swore that his confidant was "reliable," he offered the magistrate no reason in support of this conclusion. Perhaps even more important is the fact that *Aguilar's* other test has not been satisfied. The tip does not contain a sufficient statement of the underlying circumstances from which the informer concluded that Spinelli was running a bookmaking operation. We are not told how the FBI's source received his information—it is not alleged that the informant personally observed Spinelli at work or that he had ever placed a bet with him. Moreover, if the informant came by the information indirectly, he did not explain why his sources were reliable. In the absence of a statement detailing the manner in which the information was gathered, it is especially important that the tip describe the accused's criminal activity in sufficient detail that the magistrate may know that he is relying on something more substantial than a casual rumor circulating in the underworld or an accusation based merely on an individual's general reputation.

The detail provided by the informant in Draper v. United States, 358 U.S. 307 (1959), provides a suitable benchmark. While Hereford, the Government's informer in that case, did not state the way in which he had obtained his information, he reported that Draper had gone to Chicago the day before by train and that he would return to Denver by train with three ounces of heroin on one of two specified mornings. Moreover, Hereford, went on to describe, with minute particularity, the clothes that Draper would be wearing upon his arrival at the Denver station. A magistrate, when confronted with such detail, could reasonably infer that the informant had gained his information in a reliable way.[b] Such an inference cannot be made in the present case. Here, the only facts supplied were that Spinelli was using two specified telephones and that these phones were being used in gambling operations. This meager report could easily have been obtained from an offhand remark heard at a neighborhood bar.

Nor do we believe that the patent doubts *Aguilar* raises as to the report's reliability are adequately resolved by a consideration of the allegations detailing the FBI's independent investigative efforts. At most, these allegations indicated that Spinelli could have used the telephones specified by the informant for some purpose. This cannot by itself be said to support both the inference that the informer was generally trustworthy and that he had made his charge against Spinelli on the basis of information obtained in a reliable way. Once again, *Draper* provides a relevant comparison. Independent police work in that case corroborated much more than one small detail that had been provided by the informant. There, the police, upon meeting the inbound Denver train on the second morning specified by informer Hereford, saw a man whose dress corresponded precisely to Hereford's detailed description. It was then apparent that the informant had not been fabricating his report out of whole cloth; since the report was of the sort which in common experience may be recognized as having been obtained in a reliable way, it was perfectly clear that probable cause had been established.

We conclude, then, that in the present case the informant's tip—even when corroborated to the extent indicated—was not sufficient to provide the basis for a finding of probable cause. This is not to say that the tip was so insubstantial that it could not properly have counted in the magistrate's determination. Rather, it needed some further support. When we look to the other parts of the application, however, we find nothing alleged which would permit the suspicions engendered by the informant's report to ripen into a judgment that a crime was probably being committed. As we have already seen, the allegations detailing the FBI's surveillance of Spinelli and its investigation of the telephone company records contain no suggestion of criminal conduct when taken by themselves—and they are not endowed with an aura of suspicion by virtue of the informer's tip. Nor do we find that the FBI's reports take on a sinister color when read in light of common knowledge that bookmaking is often carried on over the telephone and from premises ostensibly used by others for perfectly normal purposes. Such an argument would carry weight in a situation in which the premises contain an unusual number of telephones or abnormal activity is observed, cf. McCray v. Illinois, 386 U.S. 300,

b. While *Draper* involved the question whether the police had probable cause for an arrest without a warrant, the analysis required for an answer to this question is basically similar to that demanded of a magistrate when he considers whether a search warrant should issue.

302 (1967), but it does not fit this case where neither of these factors is present.[c] All that remains to be considered is the flat statement that Spinelli was "known" to the FBI and others as a gambler. But just as a simple assertion of police suspicion is not itself a sufficient basis for a magistrate's finding of probable cause, we do not believe it may be used to give additional weight to allegations that would otherwise be insufficient.

The affidavit, then, falls short of the standards set forth in *Aguilar, Draper,* and our other decisions that give content to the notion of probable cause. In holding as we have done, we do not retreat from the established propositions that only the probability, and not a prima facie showing, of criminal activity is the standard of probable cause; that affidavits of probable cause are tested by much less rigorous standards than those governing the admissibility of evidence at trial; that in judging probable cause issuing magistrates are not to be confined by niggardly limitations or by restrictions on the use of their common sense; and that their determination of probable cause should be paid great deference by reviewing courts. But we cannot sustain this warrant without diluting important safeguards that assure that the judgment of a disinterested judicial officer will interpose itself between the police and the citizenry.

* * *

MR. JUSTICE MARSHALL took no part in the consideration or decision of this case.

MR. JUSTICE WHITE, concurring.

An investigator's affidavit that he has seen gambling equipment being moved into a house at a specified address will support the issuance of a search warrant. The oath affirms the honesty of the statement and negatives the lie or imagination. Personal observation attests to the facts asserted—that there is gambling equipment on the premises at the named address.

But if the officer simply avers, without more, that there is gambling paraphernalia on certain premises, the warrant should not issue, even though the belief of the officer is an honest one, as evidenced by his oath, and even though the magistrate knows him to be an experienced, intelligent officer who has been reliable in the past. This much was settled in Nathanson v. United States, 290 U.S. 41 (1933), where the Court held insufficient an officer's affidavit swearing he had cause to believe that there was illegal liquor on the premises for which the warrant was sought. The unsupported assertion or belief of the officer does not satisfy the requirement of probable cause.

What is missing in *Nathanson* and like cases is a statement of the basis for the affiant's believing the facts contained in the affidavit—the good "cause" which the officer in *Nathanson* said he had. If an officer swears that there is gambling equipment at a certain address, the possibilities are (1) that he has seen the equipment; (2) that he has observed or perceived facts from which the presence of the equipment may reasonably be inferred; and (3) that he has obtained the information from someone else. If (1) is true, the affidavit is good. But in (2), the affidavit is insufficient unless the perceived facts are given, for it is the magistrate, not the officer, who is to judge the existence of probable cause. With respect to (3), where the officer's information is hearsay, no warrant should issue absent good cause for crediting that hearsay. Because an affidavit asserting, without more, the location of

c. A box containing three uninstalled telephones was found in the apartment, but only after execution of the search warrant.

gambling equipment at a particular address does not claim personal observation of any of the facts by the officer, and because of the likelihood that the information came from an unidentified third party, affidavits of this type are unacceptable.

Neither should the warrant issue if the officer states that there is gambling equipment in a particular apartment and that his information comes from an informant, named or unnamed, since the honesty of the informant and the basis for his report are unknown. Nor would the missing elements be completely supplied by the officer's oath that the informant has often furnished reliable information in the past. This attests to the honesty of the informant, but Aguilar v. Texas, supra, requires something more—did the information come from observation, or did the informant in turn receive it from another? Absent additional facts for believing the informant's report, his assertion stands no better than the oath of the officer to the same effect. * * *

If the affidavit rests on hearsay—an informant's report—what is necessary under *Aguilar* is one of two things: the informant must declare either (1) that he has himself seen or perceived the fact or facts asserted; or (2) that his information is hearsay, but there is good reason for believing it—perhaps one of the usual grounds for crediting hearsay information. The first presents few problems: since the report, although hearsay, purports to be first-hand observation, remaining doubt centers on the honesty of the informant, and that worry is dissipated by the officer's previous experience with the informant. The other basis for accepting the informant's report is more complicated. But if, for example, the informer's hearsay comes from one of the actors in the crime in the nature of admission against interest, the affidavit giving this information should be held sufficient.

I am inclined to agree with the majority that there are limited special circumstances in which an "honest" informant's report, if sufficiently detailed, will in effect verify itself—that is, the magistrate when confronted with such detail could reasonably infer that the informant had gained his information in a reliable way. * * *

So too in the special circumstances of Draper v. United States, 358 U.S. 307 (1959), the kind of information related by the informant is not generally sent ahead of a person's arrival in a city except to those who are intimately connected with making careful arrangements for meeting him. The informant, posited as honest, somehow had the reported facts, very likely from one of the actors in the plan, or as one of them himself. The majority's suggestion is that a warrant could have been obtained based only on the informer's report. I am inclined to agree, although it seems quite plain that if it may be so easily inferred from the affidavit that the informant has himself observed the facts or has them from an actor in the event, no possible harm could come from requiring a statement to that effect, thereby removing the difficult and recurring questions which arise in such situations.

Of course, *Draper* itself did not proceed on this basis. Instead, the Court pointed out that when the officer saw a person getting off the train at the specified time, dressed and conducting himself precisely as the informant had predicted, all but the critical fact with respect to possessing narcotics had then been verified and for that reason the officer had "reasonable grounds" to believe also that Draper was carrying narcotics. Unquestionably, verification of arrival time, dress, and gait reinforced the honesty of the informant—he had not reported a made-up story. But if what *Draper* stands for is that the existence of the tenth and critical fact is made sufficiently probable to justify the issuance of a warrant by verifying nine other facts coming from the same source, I have my doubts about that case.

In the first place, the proposition is not that the tenth fact may be logically inferred from the other nine or that the tenth fact is usually found in conjunction with the other nine. No one would suggest that just anyone getting off the 10:30 train dressed as Draper was, with a brisk walk and carrying a zipper bag, should be arrested for carrying narcotics. The thrust of *Draper* is not that the verified facts have independent significance with respect to proof of the tenth. The argument instead relates to the reliability of the source: because an informant is right about some things, he is more probably right about other facts, usually the critical, unverified facts.

But the Court's cases have already rejected for Fourth Amendment purposes the notion that the past reliability of an officer is sufficient reason for believing his current assertions. Nor would it suffice, I suppose, if a reliable informant states there is gambling equipment in Apartment 607 and then proceeds to describe in detail Apartment 201, a description which is verified before applying for the warrant. He was right about 201, but that hardly makes him more believable about the equipment in 607. But what if he states that there are narcotics locked in a safe in Apartment 300, which is described in detail, and the apartment manager verifies everything but the contents of the safe? I doubt that the report about the narcotics is made appreciably more believable by the verification. The informant could still have gotten his information concerning the safe from others about whom nothing is known or could have inferred the presence of narcotics from circumstances which a magistrate would find unacceptable.

The tension between *Draper* and the *Nathanson-Aguilar* line of cases is evident from the course followed by the majority opinion. First, it is held that the report from a reliable informant that Spinelli is using two telephones with specified numbers to conduct a gambling business plus Spinelli's reputation in police circles as a gambler does not add up to probable cause. This is wholly consistent with *Aguilar* and *Nathanson:* the informant did not reveal whether he had personally observed the facts or heard them from another and, if the latter, no basis for crediting the hearsay was presented. Nor were the facts, as Mr. Justice Harlan says, of such a nature that they normally would be obtainable only by the personal observation of the informant himself. The police, however, did not stop with the informant's report. Independently, they established the existence of two phones having the given numbers and located them in an apartment house which Spinelli was regularly frequenting away from his home. * * * The *Draper* approach would reasonably justify the issuance of a warrant in this case, particularly since the police had some awareness of Spinelli's past activities. The majority, however, while seemingly embracing *Draper,* confines that case to its own facts. Pending full-scale reconsideration of that case, on the one hand, or of the *Nathanson-Aguilar* cases on the other, I join the opinion of the Court and the judgment of reversal, especially since a vote to affirm would produce an equally divided Court.

MR. JUSTICE BLACK, dissenting.

In my view, this Court's decision in Aguilar v. Texas, 378 U.S. 108 (1964), was bad enough. That decision went very far toward elevating the magistrate's hearing for issuance of a search warrant to a full-fledged trial, where witnesses must be brought forward to attest personally to all the facts alleged. But not content with this, the Court today expands *Aguilar* to almost unbelievable proportions. Of course, it would strengthen the probable-cause presentation if eyewitnesses could testify that they saw the defendant commit the crime. It would be stronger still if these witnesses could explain in detail the nature of the sensual perceptions on which they based their "conclusion" that the person they had seen was the defendant and that he was responsible for the events they observed. Nothing in our Constitution, however, requires that the facts be established with that degree of certainty and with such elaborate specificity before a policeman can be authorized by a disinterested magistrate to conduct a carefully limited search.

* * *

MR. JUSTICE FORTAS, dissenting.

* * *

Today's decision deals, not with the necessity of obtaining a warrant prior to search, but with the difficult problem of the nature of the showing that must be made before the magistrate to justify his issuance of a search warrant. While I do not subscribe to the criticism of the majority expressed by my Brother Black in dissent, I believe—with all respect—that the majority is in error in holding that the affidavit supporting the warrant in this case is constitutionally inadequate.

* * *

A policeman's affidavit should not be judged as an entry in an essay contest. It is not "abracadabra." As the majority recognizes, a policeman's affidavit is entitled to common-sense evaluation. * * *

MR. JUSTICE STEWART, dissenting.

For substantially the reasons stated by my Brothers Black and Fortas, I believe the warrant in this case was supported by a sufficient showing of probable cause. * * *

Note

For most people *Spinelli* is a difficult case to understand, at least at first meeting. In Hearsay and Probable Cause: An Aguilar and Spinelli Primer, 25 Mercer L.Rev. 741 (1974), Associate Judge Charles Moylan, Jr. of the Maryland Court of Special Appeals has explained as well as anyone what the case means:

* * *

"The clear and unremitting command of the Supreme Court throughout this century has been that search and seizure by authority of a warrant is always to be preferred over a warrantless intrusion, and indeed, wherever feasible is to be required. Implicit in that command is the concept that any decision as to whether probable cause exists so that a warrant should issue should always be made where possible, by a 'neutral and detached magistrate' rather than by a policeman. The constitutional protection consists of interposing an impartial judicial figure between the investigator and his quarry. * * *

* * *

"The simple thrust of these decisions is that whatever rules govern the evaluation of information from the primary source—the affiant—govern also the evaluation of information from the secondary source—the non-swearing, nonappearing, off-warrant declarant, i.e., the informant. Whether the magistrate is dealing with a primary, a secondary or even, theoretically, a tertiary source, he must still (1) assess the credibility of that source and (2) then weigh the information furnished if he believes it to be true.

* * *

"Once the magistrate has decided that the informant is believable, he has still only half completed his ultimate determination. He must still decide what the information is worth. He has decided that the source is not lying, but he has not yet decided whether the source is mistaken. The magistrate's second function is now to evaluate the information which he is accepting as true and to see what probabilities emerge from that available data. Again, he may not accept the conclusion of either the affiant-observer or the non-swearing informant. He must take from either of those sources his facts and then arrive at his own conclusion as to the significance of those facts."

Judge Moylan's explication is a great first step in understanding the aim of the Court in *Spinelli*. By adding some specifics, we can take a further step. Those who have never had a course in evidence may not fully comprehend the use of the term "hearsay" by the Court in these probable cause cases. Those who know evidence law may comprehend its use, but question the precision of the Court's terminology. A brief detour into the law of evidence should suffice to clarify for all what the Court means by its use of the word hearsay.

In trials, both civil and criminal, the preferred mode of offering evidence, other than physical evidence from which the judge or jury can draw its own conclusions without the help of other knowledgable persons, is to present live testimony by putting witnesses on the stand, who are under oath and subject to examination and cross-examination, and whose demeanor is subject to evaluation by judge or jury. Out of court statements offered for their truth—which means statements made by a person offered to the judge or jury with the hope that they will be accepted as true in the same way they might be accepted if the person who made the statement said the same thing on the witness stand—generally are classified as hearsay and disfavored by rules of evidence. Hearsay statements are presumed to be inadmissible unless covered by an exception. Exceptions are created for classes of statements or for particular statements that are made under circumstances guaranteeing some of the same kind of reliability produced by cross-examination, oath and observation of demeanor.

When a police officer fills out an affidavit in support of a warrant or swears out a warrant, the officer is taking an oath. But there is no opportunity for cross-examination by opposing parties. The proceeding is ex parte. Demeanor is generally not observed because the sworn statements are made in writing, not orally.

Because of the nature of the warrant procedure, the magistrate almost always is asked to issue warrants on the basis of hearsay, because the affidavit is not live testimony and it is offered for the truth of its contents. But this is not the hearsay problem to which the Supreme Court refers. An assumption is made by the Court that the affidavit is not hearsay if it represents the personal knowledge of the affiant. Hearsay problems, for the Court, arise when the affiant bases his statements on communications from others.

Spinelli can be discussed without using the word "hearsay." The majority appears to accept the following propositions:

a. A police officer is presumed to be honest when making an affidavit. Thus, credibility of the officer is never to be questioned.[6]

6. Courts have not hesitated to assume that all police officers who supply information to one officer-affiant who seeks a warrant are as credible as the affiant herself is presumed to be. See, e.g., United States v. Romano, 482 F.2d 1183 (5th Cir. 1973). Even an undercov-

b. What may be questioned, however, is the source of the officer's information.

c. If the officer has first-hand knowledge of the facts used to demonstrate probable cause, the only question is whether the sworn facts are sufficient to meet the threshold. The magistrate is informed of what the officer knows and makes an independent determination of sufficiency.

d. If the officer is relying on someone else for part or all of the information, then it is necessary to make three additional determinations:

(i.) Who is the source of the information, and is the source reliable? Reliability is the first prong of the *Spinelli* test.

(ii.) What are the bases and details of the source's knowledge? Credible information is the second prong of the test.

(iii.) Assuming reliability of the source, are the facts, either standing alone or taken together with other facts provided by the affiant, sufficient to satisfy the proof threshold, probable cause?

e. If the source is not known to the police to be reliable under d, i, above, the police may be able to demonstrate reliability by corroborating the details provided by the informant (although the amount of corroboration required is unclear).

f. If it is unclear what the basis of the information provided by the informant is, the fact that the information is such that it seemingly could have only come from the informant's personal observation may satisfy d, ii, above.

g. If the information provided by the informant falls short of demonstrating probable cause, the police can gather other information to be included in the application for a warrant.

h. When the magistrate looks at all the information provided to assess whether probable cause is shown, she is to take a common sense approach to the application and ask whether the government has shown "the probability" of criminal activity. (The portion of the Court's opinion setting forth this standard is murky. The Court cited a case, Beck v. Ohio, 379 U.S. 89, 96 (1964), as support for its view. *Beck* was an arrest case, and the officer had no warrant. But *Beck* did analyze the question of what probable cause means. The standard set forth is a useful, albeit indefinite, one: "whether at that moment [in *Beck* the time of arrest; in search warrant cases the time when the application is made] the facts and circumstances within their [the police] knowledge and of which they had reasonably trustworthy information were sufficient to warrant a prudent man in believing [in *Beck*] that the petitioner had committed or was committing an offense" [or in search cases that the evidence sought is in the place to be searched]).

Spinelli does not purport to deal with circumstances in which a crime victim or eyewitness reports an alleged crime immediately after he or she says it took place. It addresses warrant applications in which the police rely on tipsters who generally are not themselves personally involved as participants or witnesses in the very criminal activity they report, but who have an ongoing relationship with police.

When *Spinelli* is fully understood, is it properly viewed as an anti-police opinion? Or is it an opinion that substantially defers to the integrity of the police at the same time that it attempts to explain the magistrate's function in the warrant process?

er agent for a private detective agency may benefit from the presumption of credibility. See, e.g., Schmidt v. State, 17 Md.App. 492, 302 A.2d 714 (1973).

Whatever your own opinion is, you should know that *Spinelli* was not well received by law enforcement officials. This reaction was predictable, especially in view of the dissenters' warning that law enforcement efforts would suffer greatly from the majority's position. Also, the decision may have appeared to be more complicated and even more hostile to police than it was intended to be.

2. *Rejection of the Two-Pronged Test*

In one of the Court's most important changes in direction in the past two decades, it abandoned the two-pronged test of *Aguilar* and *Spinelli.*

ILLINOIS v. GATES

Supreme Court of the United States, 1983.
462 U.S. 213.

JUSTICE REHNQUIST delivered the opinion of the Court.

Respondents Lance and Susan Gates were indicted for violation of state drug laws after police officers, executing a search warrant, discovered marijuana and other contraband in their automobile and home. Prior to trial the Gates' moved to suppress evidence seized during this search. The Illinois Supreme Court affirmed the decisions of lower state courts granting the motion. * * *

We granted certiorari to consider the application of the Fourth Amendment to a magistrate's issuance of a search warrant on the basis of a partially corroborated anonymous informant's tip. * * *

* * *

II

* * * Bloomingdale, Ill., is a suburb of Chicago located in DuPage County. On May 3, 1978, the Bloomingdale Police Department received by mail an anonymous handwritten letter which read as follows:

> "This letter is to inform you that you have a couple in your town who strictly make their living on selling drugs. They are Sue and Lance Gates, they live on Greenway, off Bloomingdale Rd. in the condominiums. Most of their buys are done in Florida. Sue his wife drives their car to Florida, where she leaves it to be loaded up with drugs, then Lance flys down and drives it back. Sue flys back after she drops the car off in Florida. May 3 she is driving down there again and Lance will be flying down in a few days to drive it back. At the time Lance drives the car back he has the trunk loaded with over $100,000.00 in drugs. Presently they have over $100,000.00 worth of drugs in their basement.
>
> They brag about the fact they never have to work, and make their entire living on pushers.
>
> I guarantee if you watch them carefully you will make a big catch. They are friends with some big drugs dealers, who visit their house often.
>
> Lance & Susan Gates
>
> Greenway
>
> in Condominiums"

The letter was referred by the Chief of Police of the Bloomingdale Police Department to Detective Mader, who decided to pursue the tip. Mader learned, from the office of the Illinois Secretary of State, that an Illinois driver's license had been issued to one Lance Gates, residing at a stated address in Bloomingdale. He contacted a confidential informant, whose examination of certain financial records revealed a more recent address for the Gates, and he also learned from a police officer assigned to O'Hare Airport that "L. Gates" had made a reservation on Eastern Airlines flight 245 to West Palm Beach, Fla., scheduled to depart from Chicago on May 5 at 4:15 p.m.

Mader then made arrangements with an agent of the Drug Enforcement Administration for surveillance of the May 5 Eastern Airlines flight. The agent later reported to Mader that Gates had boarded the flight, and that federal agents in Florida had observed him arrive in West Palm Beach and take a taxi to the nearby Holiday Inn. They also reported that Gates went to a room registered to one Susan Gates and that, at 7:00 a.m. the next morning, Gates and an unidentified woman left the motel in a Mercury bearing Illinois license plates and drove northbound on an interstate frequently used by travelers to the Chicago area. In addition, the DEA agent informed Mader that the license plate number on the Mercury registered to a Hornet station wagon owned by Gates. The agent also advised Mader that the driving time between West Palm Beach and Bloomingdale was approximately 22 to 24 hours.

Mader signed an affidavit setting forth the foregoing facts, and submitted it to a judge of the Circuit Court of DuPage County, together with a copy of the anonymous letter. The judge of that court thereupon issued a search warrant for the Gates' residence and for their automobile. The judge, in deciding to issue the warrant, could have determined that the *modus operandi* of the Gates had been substantially corroborated. As the anonymous letter predicted, Lance Gates had flown from Chicago to West Palm Beach late in the afternoon of May 5th, had checked into a hotel room registered in the name of his wife, and, at 7:00 a.m. the following morning, had headed north, accompanied by an unidentified woman, out of West Palm Beach on an interstate highway used by travelers from South Florida to Chicago in an automobile bearing a license plate issued to him.

At 5:15 a.m. on March 7th, only 36 hours after he had flown out of Chicago, Lance Gates, and his wife, returned to their home in Bloomingdale, driving the car in which they had left West Palm Beach some 22 hours earlier. The Bloomingdale police were awaiting them, searched the trunk of the Mercury, and uncovered approximately 350 pounds of marijuana. A search of the Gates' home revealed marijuana, weapons, and other contraband. The Illinois Circuit Court ordered suppression of all these items, on the ground that the affidavit submitted to the Circuit Judge failed to support the necessary determination of probable cause to believe that the Gates' automobile and home contained the contraband in question. This decision was affirmed in turn by the Illinois Appellate Court and by a divided vote of the Supreme Court of Illinois.

The Illinois Supreme Court concluded—and we are inclined to agree—that, standing alone, the anonymous letter sent to the Bloomingdale Police Department would not provide the basis for a magistrate's determination that there was probable cause to believe contraband would be found in the Gates' car and home. The letter provides virtually nothing from which one might conclude that its author is either honest or his information reliable; likewise, the letter gives absolutely no indication of the basis for the writer's predictions regarding the Gates' criminal activities. Something more was required, then, before a magistrate could conclude that there was probable cause to believe that contraband would be found in the Gates' home and car.

The Illinois Supreme Court also properly recognized that Detective Mader's affidavit might be capable of supplementing the anonymous letter with information sufficient to permit a determination of probable cause. In holding that the affidavit in fact did not contain sufficient additional information to sustain a determination of probable cause, the Illinois court applied a "two-pronged test," derived from our decision in Spinelli v. United States. The Illinois Supreme Court, like some others, apparently understood *Spinelli* as requiring that the anonymous letter satisfy each of two independent requirements before it could be relied on. According to this view, the letter, as supplemented by Mader's affidavit, first had to adequately reveal the "basis of knowledge" of the letter writer—the particular means by which he came by the information given in his report. Second, it had to provide facts sufficiently establishing either the "veracity" of the affiant's informant, or, alternatively, the "reliability" of the informant's report in this particular case.

The Illinois court, alluding to an elaborate set of legal rules that have developed among various lower courts to enforce the "two-pronged test," found that the test had not been satisfied. First, the "veracity" prong was not satisfied because, "there was simply no basis [for] * * * conclud[ing] that the anonymous person [who wrote the letter to the Bloomingdale Police Department] was credible." The court indicated that corroboration by police of details contained in the letter might never satisfy the "veracity" prong, and in any event, could not do so if, as in the present case, only "innocent" details are corroborated. In addition, the letter gave no indication of the basis of its writer's knowledge of the Gates' activities. The Illinois court understood *Spinelli* as permitting the detail contained in a tip to be used to infer that the informant had a reliable basis for his statements, but it thought that the anonymous letter failed to provide sufficient detail to permit such an inference. Thus, it concluded that no showing of probable cause had been made.

We agree with the Illinois Supreme Court that an informant's "veracity," "reliability" and "basis of knowledge" are all highly relevant in determining the value of his report. We do not agree, however, that these elements should be understood as entirely separate and independent requirements to be rigidly exacted in every case,[a] which the opinion of the Supreme Court of Illinois would imply. Rather, as detailed below, they should be understood simply as closely intertwined issues that may usefully illuminate the commonsense, practical question whether there is "probable cause" to believe that contraband or evidence is located in a particular place.

III

This totality of the circumstances approach is far more consistent with our prior treatment of probable cause [b] than

a. The entirely independent character that the *Spinelli* prongs have assumed is indicated both by the opinion of the Illinois Supreme Court in this case, and by decisions of other courts. One frequently cited decision, Stanley v. State, 313 A.2d 847, 861 (Md.App. 1974), remarks that "the dual requirements represented by the 'two-pronged test' are 'analytically severable' and an 'overkill' on one prong will not carry over to make up for a deficit on the other prong."

b. Our original phrasing of the so-called "two-pronged test" in Aguilar v. Texas, suggests that the two prongs were intended simply as guides to a magistrate's determination of probable cause, not as inflexible, independent requirements applicable in every case. In *Aguilar,* we required only that:

"the magistrate must be informed of *some of the underlying circumstances* from which the informant concluded that * * * narcotics were where he claimed they were, and *some of the underlying circumstances* from

is any rigid demand that specific "tests" be satisfied by every informant's tip. Perhaps the central teaching of our decisions bearing on the probable cause standard is that it is a "practical, nontechnical conception." * * *

[P]robable cause is a fluid concept—turning on the assessment of probabilities in particular factual contexts—not readily, or even usefully, reduced to a neat set of legal rules. Informants' tips doubtless come in many shapes and sizes from many different types of persons. * * *

[T]he "two-pronged test" directs analysis into two largely independent channels—the informant's "veracity" or "reliability" and his "basis of knowledge." There are persuasive arguments against according these two elements such independent status. Instead, they are better understood as relevant considerations in the totality of circumstances analysis that traditionally has guided probable cause determinations: a deficiency in one may be compensated for, in determining the overall reliability of a tip, by a strong showing as to the other, or by some other indicia of reliability.

* * * Unlike a totality of circumstances analysis, which permits a balanced assessment of the relative weights of all the various indicia of reliability (and unreliability) attending an informant's tip, the "two-pronged test" has encouraged an excessively technical dissection of informants' tips,[c] with undue attention being focused on isolated issues that cannot sensibly be divorced from the other facts presented to the magistrate.

* * * Finely-tuned standards such as proof beyond a reasonable doubt or by a preponderance of the evidence, useful in formal trials, have no place in the magistrate's decision. While an effort to fix some general, numerically precise degree of certainty corresponding to "probable cause" may not be helpful, it is clear that "only the probability, and not a prima facie showing, of criminal activity is the standard of probable cause." *Spinelli,* supra.

which the officer concluded that the informant * * * was 'credible' or his information 'reliable.'"

As our language indicates, we intended neither a rigid compartmentalization of the inquiries into an informant's "veracity," "reliability" and "basis of knowledge," nor that these inquiries be elaborate exegeses of an informant's tip. Rather, we required only that *some* facts bearing on two particular issues be provided to the magistrate. * * *

c. Some lower court decisions, brought to our attention by the State, reflect a rigid application of such rules. In Bridger v. State, 503 S.W.2d 801 (Tex.Cr.App. 1974), the affiant had received a confession of armed robbery from one of two suspects in the robbery; in addition, the suspect had given the officer $800 in cash stolen during the robbery. The suspect also told the officer that the gun used in the robbery was hidden in the other suspect's apartment. A warrant issued on the basis of this was invalidated on the ground that the affidavit did not satisfactorily describe how the accomplice had obtained his information regarding the gun.

Likewise, in People v. Palanza, 371 N.E.2d 687 (Ill.App. 1978), the affidavit submitted in support of an application for a search warrant stated that an informant of proven and uncontested reliability had seen, in specifically described premises, "a quantity of a white crystalline substance which was represented to the informant by a white male occupant of the premises to be cocaine. Informant has observed cocaine on numerous occasions in the past and is thoroughly familiar with its appearance. The informant states that the white crystalline powder he observed in the above described premises appeared to him to be cocaine." The warrant issued on the basis of the affidavit was invalidated because "There is no indication as to how the informant or for that matter any other person could tell whether a white substance was cocaine and not some other substance such as sugar or salt."

Finally, in People v. Brethauer, 482 P.2d 369 (Colo. 1971), an informant, stated to have supplied reliable information in the past, claimed that L.S.D. and marijuana were located on certain premises. The affiant supplied police with drugs, which were tested by police and confirmed to be illegal substances. The affidavit setting forth these, and other, facts was found defective under both prongs of *Spinelli.*

We have also recognized that affidavits are normally drafted by nonlawyers in the midst and haste of a criminal investigation. * * * The rigorous inquiry into the *Spinelli* prongs and the complex superstructure of evidentiary and analytical rules that some have seen implicit in our *Spinelli* decision, cannot be reconciled with the fact that many warrants are—quite properly—issued on the basis of nontechnical, common-sense judgments of laymen applying a standard less demanding than those used in formal legal proceedings.

* * *

If the affidavits submitted by police officers are subjected to the type of scrutiny some courts have deemed appropriate, police might well resort to warrantless searches, with the hope of relying on consent or some other exception to the warrant clause that might develop at the time of the search. In addition, the possession of a warrant by officers conducting an arrest or search greatly reduces the perception of unlawful or intrusive police conduct, by assuring "the individual whose property is searched or seized of the lawful authority of the executing officer, his need to search, and the limits of his power to search." Reflecting this preference for the warrant process, the traditional standard for review of an issuing magistrate's probable cause determination has been that so long as the magistrate had a "substantial basis for * * * conclud[ing]" that a search would uncover evidence of wrongdoing, the Fourth Amendment requires no more.[d] * * *

Finally, the direction taken by decisions following *Spinelli* poorly serves "the most basic function of any government": "to provide for the security of the individual and of his property." The strictures that inevitably accompany the "two-pronged test" cannot avoid seriously impeding the task of law enforcement. If, as the Illinois Supreme Court apparently thought, that test must be rigorously applied in every case, anonymous tips would be of greatly diminished value in police work. Ordinary citizens * * * generally do not provide extensive recitations of the basis of their everyday observations. Likewise, as the Illinois Supreme Court recognized in this case, the veracity of persons supplying anonymous tips is by hypothesis largely unknown, and unknowable. As a result, anonymous tips seldom could survive a rigorous application of either of the *Spinelli* prongs. Yet, such tips, particularly when supplemented by independent police investigation, frequently contribute to the solution of otherwise "perfect crimes." While a conscientious assessment of the basis for crediting such tips is required by the Fourth Amendment, a standard that leaves virtually no place for anonymous citizen informants is not.

For all these reasons, we conclude that it is wiser to abandon the "two-pronged test" established by our decisions in *Aguilar* and *Spinelli*.[e] In its

d. We also have said that "Although in a particular case it may not be easy to determine when an affidavit demonstrates the existence of probable cause, the resolution of doubtful or marginal cases in this area should be largely determined by the preference to be accorded to warrants." This reflects both a desire to encourage use of the warrant process by police officers and a recognition that once a warrant has been obtained, intrusion upon interests protected by the Fourth Amendment is less severe than otherwise may be the case. Even if we were to accept the premise that the accurate assessment of probable cause would be furthered by the "two-pronged test," which we do not,these Fourth Amendment policies would require a less rigorous standard than that which appears to have been read into *Aguilar* and *Spinelli*.

e. The Court's decision in *Spinelli* has been the subject of considerable criticism, both by members of this Court and others. * * *

Whether the allegations submitted to the magistrate in *Spinelli* would, under the view we now take, have supported a finding of probable cause, we think it would not be profitable to decide. There are so many variables in the probable cause equation that one deter-

place we reaffirm the totality of the circumstances analysis that traditionally has informed probable cause determinations. The task of the issuing magistrate is simply to make a practical, common-sense decision whether, given all the circumstances set forth in the affidavit before him, including the "veracity" and "basis of knowledge" of persons supplying hearsay information, there is a fair probability that contraband or evidence of a crime will be found in a particular place. And the duty of a reviewing court is simply to ensure that the magistrate had a "substantial basis for * * * conclud[ing]" that probable cause existed. * * *

Our earlier cases illustrate the limits beyond which a magistrate may not venture in issuing a warrant. A sworn statement of an affiant that "he has cause to suspect and does believe that" liquor illegally brought into the United States is located on certain premises will not do. Nathanson v. United States. An affidavit must provide the magistrate with a substantial basis for determining the existence of probable cause, and the wholly conclusory statement at issue in *Nathanson* failed to meet this requirement. An officer's statement that "affiants have received reliable information from a credible person and believe" that heroin is stored in a home, is likewise inadequate. Aguilar v. Texas. As in *Nathanson,* this is a mere conclusory statement that gives the magistrate virtually no basis at all for making a judgment regarding probable cause. Sufficient information must be presented to the magistrate to allow that official to determine probable cause; his action cannot be a mere ratification of the bare conclusions of others. In order to ensure that such an abdication of the magistrate's duty does not occur, courts, must continue to conscientiously review the sufficiency of affidavits on which warrants are issued. But when we move beyond the "bare bones" affidavits present in cases such as *Nathanson* and *Aguilar,* this area simply does not lend itself to a prescribed set of rules, like that which had developed from *Spinelli.* Instead, the flexible, common-sense standard * * * better serves the purposes of the Fourth Amendment's probable cause requirement.

Justice Brennan's dissent suggests in several places that the approach we take today somehow downgrades the role of the neutral magistrate, because *Aguilar* and *Spinelli* "preserve the role of magistrates as independent arbiters of probable cause. * * *" Quite the contrary, we believe, is the case. * * * Nothing in our opinion in any way lessens the authority of the magistrate to draw such reasonable inferences as he will from the material supplied to him by applicants for a warrant; indeed, he is freer than under the regime of *Aguilar* and *Spinelli* to draw such inferences, or to refuse to draw them if he is so minded.

* * *

IV

[The Court describes Draper v. United States.]

The showing of probable cause in the present case was fully as compelling as that in *Draper.* Even standing alone, the facts obtained through the independent investigation of Mader and the DEA at least suggested that the Gateses were involved in drug trafficking. In addition to being a popular vacation site, Florida is well-known as a source of narcotics and other illegal drugs. Lance Gates' flight to Palm Beach, his brief,

mination will seldom be a useful "precedent" for another. Suffice it to say that while we in no way abandon *Spinelli*'s concern for the trustworthiness of informers and for the principle that it is the magistrate who must ultimately make a finding of probable cause, we reject the rigid categorization suggested by some of its language.

overnight stay in a motel, and apparent immediate return north to Chicago in the family car, conveniently awaiting him in West Palm Beach, is as suggestive of a pre-arranged drug run, as it is of an ordinary vacation trip.

In addition, the magistrate could rely on the anonymous letter which had been corroborated in major part by Mader's efforts—just as had occurred in *Draper.*[f] The Supreme Court of Illinois reasoned that *Draper* involved an informant who had given reliable information on previous occasions, while the honesty and reliability of the anonymous informant in this case were unknown to the Bloomingdale police. While this distinction might be an apt one at the time the police department received the anonymous letter, it became far less significant after Mader's independent investigative work occurred. The corroboration of the letter's predictions that the Gateses' car would be in Florida, that Lance Gates would fly to Florida in the next day or so, and that he would drive the car north toward Bloomingdale all indicated, albeit not with certainty, that the informant's other assertions also were true. "Because an informant is right about some things, he is more probably right about other facts"—including the claim regarding the Gateses' illegal activity. This may well not be the type of "reliability" or "veracity" necessary to satisfy some views of the "veracity prong" of *Spinelli,* but we think it suffices for the practical, common-sense judgment called for in making a probable cause determination. It is enough, for purposes of assessing probable cause, that "corroboration through other sources of information reduced the chances of a reckless or prevaricating tale," thus providing "a substantial basis for crediting the hearsay."

Finally, the anonymous letter contained a range of details relating not just to easily obtained facts and conditions existing at the time of the tip, but to future actions of third parties ordinarily not easily predicted. The letter writer's accurate information as to the travel plans of each of the Gateses' was of a character likely obtained only from the Gateses' themselves, or from someone familiar with their not entirely ordinary travel plans. If the informant had access to accurate information of this type a magistrate could properly conclude that it was not unlikely that he also had access to reliable information of the Gateses' alleged illegal activities.[g]

f. The Illinois Supreme Court thought that the verification of details contained in the anonymous letter in this case amounted only to "the corroboration of innocent activity," and that this was insufficient to support a finding of probable cause. We are inclined to agree, however with the observation of Justice Moran in his dissenting opinion that "In this case, just as in *Draper,* seemingly innocent activity became suspicious in the light of the initial tip." And it bears noting that *all* of the corroborating detail established in *Draper, supra,* was of entirely innocent activity * * *.

This is perfectly reasonable. As discussed previously, probable cause requires only a probability or substantial chance of criminal activity, not an actual showing of such activity. By hypothesis, therefore, innocent behavior frequently will provide the basis for a showing of probable cause; to require otherwise would be to *sub silentio* impose a drastically more rigorous definition of probable cause than the security of our citizens demands. We think the Illinois court attempted a too rigid classification of the types of conduct that may be relied upon in seeking to demonstrate probable cause. In making a determination of probable cause the relevant inquiry is not whether particular conduct is "innocent" or "guilty," but the degree of suspicion that attaches to particular types of non-criminal acts.

g. Justice Stevens' dissent seizes on one inaccuracy in the anonymous informant's letter—its statement the Sue Gates would fly from Florida to Illinois, when in fact she drove—and argues that the probative value of the entire tip was undermined by this allegedly "material mistake." We have never required that informants used by the police be infallible, and can see no reason to impose such a requirement in this case. Probable cause, particularly when police have obtained a warrant, simply does not require the perfection the dissent finds necessary.

Of course, the Gateses' travel plans might have been learned from a talkative neighbor or travel agent; under the "two-pronged test" developed from *Spinelli*, the character of the details in the anonymous letter might well not permit a sufficiently clear inference regarding the letter writer's "basis of knowledge." But, as discussed previously, probable cause does not demand the certainty we associate with formal trials. It is enough that there was a fair probability that the writer of the anonymous letter had obtained his entire story either from the Gateses or someone they trusted. And corroboration of major portions of the letter's predictions provides just this probability. It is apparent, therefore, that the judge issuing the warrant had a "substantial basis for * * * conclud[ing]" that probable cause to search the Gateses' home and car existed. The judgment of the Supreme Court of Illinois therefore must be

Reversed.

JUSTICE WHITE, concurring in the judgment.

[Justice White first argued against suppression because the police reasonably believed they were acting lawfully.]

III

* * *

B

The Court agrees that the warrant was valid, but, in the process of reaching this conclusion, it overrules the *Aguilar-Spinelli* tests and replaces them with a "totality of the circumstances" standard. As shown above, it is not at all necessary to overrule *Aguilar-Spinelli* in order to reverse the judgment below. Therefore, because I am inclined to believe that, when applied properly, the *Aguilar-Spinelli* rules play an appropriate role in probable cause determinations, and because the Court's holding may foretell an evisceration of the probable cause standard, I do not join the Court's holding.

The Court reasons that the "veracity" and "basis of knowledge" tests are not independent, and that a deficiency as to one can be compensated for by a strong showing as to the other. Thus, a finding of probable cause may be based on a tip from an informant "known for the unusual reliability of his predictions" or from "an unquestionably honest citizen," even if the report fails thoroughly to set forth the basis upon which the information was obtained. If this is so, then it must follow *a fortiori* that "the affidavit of an officer, known by the magistrate to be honest and experienced, stating that [contraband] is located in a certain building" must be ac-

Likewise, there is no force to the dissent's argument that the Gateses' action in leaving their home unguarded undercut the informant's claim that drugs were hidden there. Indeed, the line-by-line scrutiny that the dissent applies to the anonymous letter is akin to that we find inappropriate in reviewing magistrate's decisions. The dissent apparently attributes to the magistrate who issued the warrant in this case the rather implausible notion that persons dealing in drugs always stay at home, apparently out of fear that to leave might risk intrusion by criminals. If accurate, one could not help sympathizing with the self-imposed isolation of people so situated. In reality, however, it is scarcely likely that the magistrate ever thought that the anonymous tip "kept one spouse" at home, much less that he relied on the theory advanced by the dissent. The letter simply says that Sue would fly from Florida to Illinois, without indicating whether the Gateses' made the bitter choice of leaving the drugs in their house, or those in their car, unguarded. The magistrate's determination that there might be drugs or evidence of criminal activity in the Gateses' home was well-supported by the less speculative theory, noted in text, that if the informant could predict with considerable accuracy the somewhat unusual travel plans of the Gateses, he probably also had a reliable basis for his statements that the Gateses kept a large quantity of drugs in their home and frequently were visited by other drug traffickers there.

ceptable. It would be "quixotic" if a similar statement from an honest informant, but not one from an honest officer, could furnish probable cause. But we have repeatedly held that the unsupported assertion or belief of an officer does not satisfy the probable cause requirement. Thus, this portion of today's holding can be read as implicitly rejecting the teachings of these prior holdings.

The Court may not intend so drastic a result. Indeed, the Court expressly reaffirms the validity of cases such as *Nathanson* that have held that, no matter how reliable the affiant-officer may be, a warrant should not be issued unless the affidavit discloses supporting facts and circumstances. The Court limits these cases to situations involving affidavits containing only "bare conclusions" and holds that, if an affidavit contains anything more, it should be left to the issuing magistrate to decide, based solely on "practical[ity]" and "common-sense," whether there is a fair probability that contraband will be found in a particular place.

Thus, as I read the majority opinion, it appears that the question whether the probable cause standard is to be diluted is left to the common-sense judgments of issuing magistrates. I am reluctant to approve any standard that does not expressly require, as a prerequisite to issuance of a warrant, some showing of facts from which an inference may be drawn that the informant is credible and that his information was obtained in a reliable way. * * *

JUSTICE BRENNAN, with whom JUSTICE MARSHALL joins, dissenting.

Although I join Justice Stevens' dissenting opinion and agree with him that the warrant is invalid even under the Court's newly announced "totality of the circumstances" test, I write separately to dissent from the Court's unjustified and ill-advised rejection of the two-prong test for evaluating the validity of a warrant based on hearsay announced in Aguilar v. Texas and refined in Spinelli v. United States.

I

* * * Properly understood * * * *Spinelli* stands for the proposition that corroboration of certain details in a tip may be sufficient to satisfy the veracity, but not the basis of knowledge, prong of *Aguilar.* As noted, *Spinelli* also suggests that in some limited circumstances considerable detail in an informant's tip may be adequate to satisfy the basis of knowledge prong of *Aguilar.*

Although the rules drawn from the cases discussed above are cast in procedural terms, they advance an important underlying substantive value: Findings of probable cause, and attendant intrusions, should not be authorized unless there is some assurance that the information on which they are based has been obtained in a reliable way by an honest or credible person. As applied to police officers, the rules focus on the way in which the information was acquired. As applied to informants, the rules focus both on the honesty or credibility of the informant and on the reliability of the way in which the information was acquired. Insofar as it is more complicated, an evaluation of affidavits based on hearsay involves a more difficult inquiry. This suggests a need to structure the inquiry in an effort to insure greater accuracy. The standards announced in *Aguilar,* as refined by *Spinelli,* fulfill that need. The standards inform the police of what information they have to provide and magistrates of what information they should demand. The standards also inform magistrates of the subsidiary findings they must make in order to arrive at an ultimate finding of probable cause. *Spinelli,* properly understood, directs the magistrate's attention to the possibility that the presence of self-verifying detail might satisfy

Aguilar's basis of knowledge prong and that corroboration of the details of a tip might satisfy *Aguilar*'s veracity prong. By requiring police to provide certain crucial information to magistrates and by structuring magistrates' probable cause inquiries, *Aguilar* and *Spinelli* assure the magistrate's role as an independent arbiter of probable cause, insure greater accuracy in probable cause determinations, and advance the substantive value identified above.

Until today the Court has never squarely addressed the application of the *Aguilar* and *Spinelli* standards to tips from anonymous informants. Both *Aguilar* and *Spinelli* dealt with tips from informants known at least to the police. And surely there is even more reason to subject anonymous informants' tips to the tests established by *Aguilar* and *Spinelli.* By definition nothing is known about an anonymous informant's identity, honesty, or reliability. * * * [T]here certainly is no basis for treating anonymous informants as presumptively reliable. Nor is there any basis for assuming that the information provided by an anonymous informant has been obtained in a reliable way. If we are unwilling to accept conclusory allegations from the police, who are presumptively reliable, or from informants who are known, at least to the police, there cannot possibly be any rational basis for accepting conclusory allegations from anonymous informants.

To suggest that anonymous informants' tips are subject to the tests established by *Aguilar* and *Spinelli* is not to suggest that they can never provide a basis for a finding of probable cause. It is conceivable that police corroboration of the details of the tip might establish the reliability of the informant under *Aguilar*'s veracity prong, as refined in *Spinelli*, and that the details in the tip might be sufficient to qualify under the "self-verifying detail" test established by *Spinelli* as a means of satisfying *Aguilar*'s basis of knowledge prong. The *Aguilar* and *Spinelli* tests must be applied to anonymous informants' tips, however, if we are to continue to insure that findings of probable cause, and attendant intrusions, are based on information provided by an honest or credible person who has acquired the information in a reliable way.[h]

In light of the important purposes served by *Aguilar* and *Spinelli*, I would

h. * * * *Aguilar* and *Spinelli* inform the police of what information they have to provide and magistrates of what information they should demand. This advances the important process value, which is intimately related to substantive Fourth Amendment concerns, of having magistrates, rather than police, or informants, determine whether there is probable cause to support the issuance of a warrant. We want the police to provide magistrates with the information on which they base their conclusions so that magistrates can perform their important function. When the police rely on facts about which they have personal knowledge, requiring them to disclose those facts to magistrates imposes no significant burden on the police. When the police rely on information obtained from confidential informants, requiring the police to disclose the facts on which the informants based their conclusions imposes a more substantial burden on the police, but it is one that they can meet because they presumably have access to their confidential informants.

In cases in which the police rely on information obtained from an anonymous informant, the police, by hypothesis, cannot obtain further information from the informant regarding the facts and circumstances on which the informant based his conclusion. When the police seek a warrant based solely on an anonymous informants' tip, therefore, they are providing the magistrate with all the information on which they have based their conclusion. In this respect, the command of *Aguilar* and *Spinelli* has been met and the process value identified above has been served. But *Aguilar* and *Spinelli* advance other values which argue for their application even to anonymous informants' tips. They structure the magistrate's probable cause inquiry and, more importantly, they guard against findings of probable cause, and attendant intrusions, based on anything other than information which magistrates reasonably can conclude has been obtained in a reliable way by an honest or credible person.

not reject the standards they establish. * * *

II

In rejecting the *Aguilar-Spinelli* standards, the Court suggests that a "totality of the circumstances approach is far more consistent with our prior treatment of probable cause than is any rigid demand that specific 'tests' be satisfied by every informant's tip." * * *

[O]ne can concede that probable cause is a "practical, nontechnical" concept without betraying the values that *Aguilar* and *Spinelli* reflect. *Aguilar* and *Spinelli* require the police to provide magistrates with certain crucial information. They also provide structure for magistrates' probable cause inquiries. In so doing, *Aguilar* and *Spinelli* preserve the role of magistrates as independent arbiters of probable cause, insure greater accuracy in probable cause determinations, and advance the substantive value of precluding findings of probable cause, and attendant intrusions, based on anything less than information from an honest or credible person who has acquired his information in a reliable way. Neither the standards nor their effects are inconsistent with a "practical, nontechnical" conception of probable cause. Once a magistrate has determined that he has information before him that he can reasonably say has been obtained in a reliable way by a credible person, he has ample room to use his common sense and to apply a practical, nontechnical conception of probable cause.

* * *

The Court also insists that the *Aguilar-Spinelli* standards must be abandoned because they are inconsistent with the fact that non-lawyers frequently serve as magistrates. To the contrary, the standards help to structure probable cause inquiries and, properly interpreted, may actually help a non-lawyer magistrate in making a probable cause determination. Moreover, the *Aguilar* and *Spinelli* tests are not inconsistent with deference to magistrates' determinations of probable cause. * * *

* * *

JUSTICE STEVENS, with whom JUSTICE BRENNAN joins, dissenting.

The fact that Lance and Sue Gates made a 22-hour nonstop drive from West Palm Beach, Florida, to Bloomingdale, Illinois, only a few hours after Lance had flown to Florida provided persuasive evidence that they were engaged in illicit activity. That fact, however, was not known to the magistrate when he issued the warrant to search their home.

What the magistrate did know at that time was that the anonymous informant had not been completely accurate in his or her predictions. The informant had indicated that "Sue drives their car to Florida *where she leaves it to be loaded up with drugs * * *. Sue flies back after she drops the car off in Florida.*" Yet Detective Mader's affidavit reported that she "left the West Palm Beach area driving the Mercury northbound."

The discrepancy between the informant's predictions and the facts known to Detective Mader is significant for three reasons. First, it cast doubt on the informant's hypothesis that the Gateses already had "over $100,000 worth of drugs in their basement." The informant had predicted an itinerary that always kept one spouse in Bloomingdale, suggesting that the Gateses did not want to leave their home unguarded because something valuable was hidden within. That inference obviously could not be drawn when it was known that the pair was actually together over a thousand miles from home.

Second, the discrepancy made the Gateses' conduct seem substantially less unusual than the informant had predicted it would be. It would have been odd if, as predicted, Sue had driven down to Florida on Wednesday, left the car, and flown right back to Illinois. But the mere facts that Sue was in West Palm Beach with the car, that she was joined by her husband at the Holiday Inn on Friday, and that the couple drove north together the next morning are neither unusual nor probative of criminal activity.

Third, the fact that the anonymous letter contained a material mistake undermines the reasonableness of relying on it as a basis for making a forcible entry into a private home.

Of course, the activities in this case did not stop when the magistrate issued the warrant. The Gateses drove all night to Bloomingdale, the officers searched the car and found 400 pounds of marijuana, and then they searched the house. However, none of these subsequent events may be considered in evaluating the warrant, and the search of the house was legal only if the warrant was valid. I cannot accept the Court's casual conclusion that, *before the Gateses arrived in Bloomingdale,* there was probable cause to justify a valid entry and search of a private home. No one knows who the informant in this case was, or what motivated him or her to write the note. Given that the note's predictions were faulty in one significant respect, and were corroborated by nothing except ordinary innocent activity, I must surmise that the Court's evaluation of the warrant's validity has been colored by subsequent events.

* * *

Note

The Court moves to a totality of the circumstances test and abandons the two-pronged test that it had previously established. Can a magistrate avoid examining the two prongs of the Court's previous test in attempting to assess the totality of the circumstances? Is there any way for a magistrate to independently screen applications for warrants without looking at who provides the underlying information that appears in the applications and how these people obtained their information? Does the substitution of a totality of the circumstances test for the two-pronged test mean that the two-pronged test is no longer relevant? Or does Illinois v. Gates in large measure reaffirm the logical importance of both prongs of the *Aguilar* and *Spinelli* test while establishing that one prong may be strong enough to overcome weaknesses in the other?

If you were teaching magistrates, which test, the two-pronged *Spinelli* test or the *Gates* totality of the circumstances test, would be more helpful to you in explaining how magistrates are to evaluate warrant applications?

Gates finds scholarly support in Grano, Probable Cause and Common Sense: A Reply to the Critics of Illinois v. Gates, 17 Mich.J.L.Reform 465 (1984). But, the two-pronged test remains the choice of some lower courts and some judges.

Gates arose, of course, in Illinois, but it was not until People v. Tisler, 103 Ill.2d 226, 82 Ill.Dec. 613, 469 N.E.2d 147 (1984), that the state supreme court had occasion to decide whether to adhere to the two-pronged test under its state constitution. It decided to follow the United States Supreme Court, although three justices dissented from this decision.

The New York Court of Appeals rejected *Gates* in the context of warrantless police activity in People v. Johnson, 66 N.Y.2d 398, 497 N.Y.S.2d 618, 488 N.E.2d 439 (1985). In so holding, the court followed the lead of the Washington Supreme Court in State v. Jackson, 102 Wn.2d 432, 688 P.2d 136 (1984). See also State v.

Jacumin, 778 S.W.2d 430 (Tenn.1989) and State v. Jones, 706 P.2d 317 (Alaska 1985) both rejecting *Gates* in favor of the *Spinelli* two-pronged test.

Does it make sense that a strong showing on one of the *Spinelli* prongs can make up for a weak showing on the other? For cases in which courts used this reasoning in *Gates* to uphold a finding of probable cause, see Carter v. United States, 729 F.2d 935 (8th Cir.1984) (no specific statement as to informant's basis of knowledge for stating that marijuana was growing on certain property; however, some detail concerning the location of the property was given, and any deficiency in basis of knowledge is compensated for by informant's prior track record of reliable tips); United States v. Phillips, 727 F.2d 392 (5th Cir.1984) (questionable veracity of citizen-informant who hated defendant was overcome by wealth of detail in the tip).

The biggest effect of *Gates* is its more permissive view of the nature and extent of corroboration necessary to shore up a defective tip. For a post-*Gates* example of the use of corroboration, consider United States v. Warner, 894 F.2d 957 (8th Cir.1990). A "confidential and reliable source" informed the Sheriff's office that he had seen Warner fire a machinegun at Warner's residence. The next day, an anonymous caller reported that Warner had shot a machinegun the previous day at Warner's residence. The officer checked firearms registrations and found that Warner had no registered firearms. On the basis of this information, a warrant was issued to search Warner's house. The court of appeals upheld the magistrate's determination of probable cause, reasoning that the tips were "mutually corroborative," and that the officer's check of firearms records provided further crucial corroboration. Would this corroboration have been sufficient under *Spinelli*?

The effect of *Gates* is apparent in cases like United States v. Peyko, 717 F.2d 741 (2d Cir.1983) (upholding warrantless seizure of package by agent who received an anonymous tip that Peyko was receiving weekly deliveries of drugs by Federal Express and who corroborated fact that Peyko had been using Federal Express).

The Court reiterated its "totality of the circumstances" test in Massachusetts v. Upton, 466 U.S. 727 (1984), a per curiam disposition reversing the state supreme court which had found a warrant invalid in reliance on *Aguilar* and *Spinelli*. The Supreme Court described the facts as follows:

> At noon on September 11, 1980, Lt. Beland of the Yarmouth Police Department assisted in the execution of a search warrant for a motel room reserved by one Richard Kelleher at the Snug Harbor Motel in West Yarmouth. The search produced several items of identification, including credit cards, belonging to two persons whose homes had recently been burglarized. Other items taken in the burglaries, such as jewelry, silver and gold, were not found at the motel.
>
> At 3:20 p.m. on the same day, Lt. Beland received a call from an unidentified female who told him that there was "a motor home full of stolen stuff" parked behind # 5 Jefferson Ave., the home of respondent George Upton and his mother. She stated that the stolen items included jewelry, silver and gold. As set out in Lt. Beland's affidavit in support of a search warrant:
>
>> She further stated that George Upton was going to move the motor home any time now because of the fact that Ricky Kelleher's motel room was raided and that George Upton had purchased these stolen items from Ricky Kelleher. This unidentified female stated that she had seen the

> stolen items but refused to identify herself because "he'll kill me," referring to George Upton. I then told this unidentified female that I knew who she was, giving her the name of Lynn Alberico, who I had met on May 16, 1980, at George Upton's repair shop off Summer St., in Yarmouthport. She was identified to me by George Upton as being his girlfriend, Lynn Alberico. The unidentified female admitted that she was the girl that I had named, stating that she was surprised that I knew who she was. She then told me that she'd broken up with George Upton and wanted to burn him. She also told me that she wouldn't give me her address or phone number but that she would contact me in the future, if need be.

> Following the phone call, Lt. Beland went to Upton's house to verify that a motor home was parked on the property. Then, while other officers watched the premises, Lt. Beland prepared the application for a search warrant, setting out all the information noted above in an accompanying affidavit. He also attached the police reports on the two prior burglaries, along with lists of the stolen property. A magistrate issued the warrant, and a subsequent search of the motor home produced the items described by the caller and other incriminating evidence. The discovered evidence led to Upton's conviction on multiple counts of burglary, receiving stolen property, and related crimes.

The Court explained why the state supreme court's approach was inconsistent with *Gates*:

> Prior to *Gates*, the Fourth Amendment was understood by many courts to require strict satisfaction of a "two-pronged test" whenever an affidavit supporting the issuance of a search relies on an informant's tip. It was thought that the affidavit, first, must establish the "basis of knowledge" of the informant—the particular means by which he came by the information given in his report; and, second, that it must provide facts establishing either the general "veracity" of the informant or the specific "reliability" of his report in the particular case. The Massachusetts court apparently viewed *Gates* as merely adding a new wrinkle to this two-pronged test: where an informant's veracity and/or basis of knowledge are not sufficiently clear, substantial corroboration of the tip may save an otherwise invalid warrant.
>
> > "We do not view the Gates opinion as decreeing a standardless 'totality of the circumstances' test. The informant's veracity and the basis of his knowledge are still important but, where the tip is adequately corroborated, they are not elements indispensible [sic] to a finding of probable cause. It seems that, in a given case, the corroboration may be so strong as to satisfy probable cause in the absence of any other showing of the informant's 'veracity' and any direct statement of the 'basis of [his] knowledge.'"
>
> Turning to the facts of this case, the Massachusetts court reasoned, first, that the basis of the informant's knowledge was not "forcefully apparent" in the affidavit. Although the caller stated that she had seen the stolen items and that they were in the motor home, she did not specifically state that she saw them in the motor home. Second, the court concluded that "[n]one of the common bases for determining the credibility of an informant or the reliability of her information is present here." The caller was not a "tried and true" informant, her statement was not against penal interest, and she was not an "ordinary citizen" providing information as a witness to a crime. "She was an anonymous informant, and her unverified assent to the suggestion that she was Lynn Alberico does not take her out of that category."

Finally, the court felt that there was insufficient corroboration of the informant's tip to make up for its failure to satisfy the two-pronged test. The facts that tended to corroborate the informant's story were that the motor home was where it was supposed to be, that the caller knew of the motel raid which took place only three hours earlier, and that the caller knew the name of Upton and his girlfriend. But, much as the Supreme Court of Illinois did in the opinion we reviewed in *Gates*, the Massachusetts court reasoned that each item of corroborative evidence either related to innocent, nonsuspicious conduct or related to an event that took place in public. To sustain the warrant, the court concluded, more substantial corroboration was needed. The court therefore held that the warrant violated the Fourth Amendment to the United States Constitution and reversed respondent's convictions.

We think that the Supreme Judicial Court of Massachusetts misunderstood our decision in *Gates*. We did not merely refine or qualify the "two-pronged test." We rejected it as hypertechnical and divorced from "the factual and practical considerations of everyday life on which reasonable and prudent men, not legal technicians, act." Our statement on that score was explicit. "[W]e conclude that it is wiser to abandon the 'two-pronged test' established by our decisions in *Aguilar* and *Spinelli*. In its place we reaffirm the totality of the circumstances analysis that traditionally has informed probable cause determinations." This "totality of the circumstances" analysis is more in keeping with the "practical, common-sense decision" demanded of the magistrate.

We noted in *Gates* that "the 'two-pronged test' has encouraged an excessively technical dissection of informants' tips, with undue attention being focused on isolated issues that cannot sensibly be divorced from the other facts presented to the magistrate." This, we think, is the error of the Massachusetts court in this case. The court did not consider Lt. Beland's affidavit in its entirety, giving significance to each relevant piece of information and balancing the relative weights of all the various indicia of reliability (and unreliability) attending the tip. Instead, the court insisted on judging bits and pieces of information in isolation against the artificial standards provided by the two-pronged test.

The Supreme Judicial Court also erred in failing to grant any deference to the decision of the magistrate to issue a warrant. Instead of merely deciding whether the evidence viewed as a whole provided a "substantial basis" for the magistrate's finding of probable cause, the court conducted a de novo probable cause determination. We rejected just such after-the-fact, de novo scrutiny in *Gates*. * * *

Examined in light of *Gates*, Lt. Beland's affidavit provides a substantial basis for the issuance of the warrant. No single piece of evidence in it is conclusive. But the pieces fit neatly together and, so viewed, support the magistrate's determination that there was "a fair probability that contraband or evidence of crime" would be found in Upton's motor home. The informant claimed to have seen the stolen goods and gave a description of them which tallied with the items taken in recent burglaries. She knew of the raid on the motel room—which produced evidence connected to those burglaries—and that the room had been reserved by Kelleher. She explained the connection between Kelleher's motel room and the stolen goods in Upton's motor home. And she provided a motive both for her attempt at anonymity—fear of Upton's retaliation—and for furnishing the information—her recent breakup with Upton and her desire "to burn him."

The Massachusetts court dismissed Lt. Beland's identification of the caller as a mere "unconfirmed guess." But "probable cause does not demand the certainty we associate with formal trials." Lt. Beland noted that the caller "admitted that she was the girl I had named, stating that she was surprised that I knew who she was." It is of course possible that the caller merely adopted Lt. Beland's suggestion as "a convenient cover for her true identity." But given the caller's admission, her obvious knowledge of who Alberico was and how she was connected with Upton, and her explanation of her motive in calling, Lt. Beland's inference appears stronger than a mere uninformed and unconfirmed guess. It is enough that the inference was a reasonable one and conformed with the other pieces of evidence making up the total showing of probable cause.

Justice Stevens concurred in the judgment, expressing the opinion that the state supreme court should have indicated whether the warrant was valid under state law. Justices Brennan and Marshall dissented from the summary reversal of the state court.

Note

On remand in *Upton,* the Massachusetts Supreme Judicial Court declined to follow *Gates* and reaffirmed its commitment to the two-pronged test under the state constitution. Commonwealth v. Upton, 394 Mass. 363, 476 N.E.2d 548 (1985). It reasoned that the two-pronged test "aids lay people, such as the police and certain lay magistrates, in a way that the 'totality of the circumstances' test never could." Do you believe that the state supreme court correctly applied the *Spinelli* test to the *Upton* facts?

Application of the probable cause standard requires careful attention to the specific facts presented in a warrant application. Consider, for example, Woodard v. State, 567 P.2d 512 (Okl.Cr.1977). A police officer sought a search warrant that the appellate court described as follows:

> The section of the affidavit going to reliability of the informant follows:
>
> "That affiants [sic] informant is known to affiant and has provided reliable information on two occasions [sic] in the past and that convictions have resulted from the use of said informants [sic] prior information. This information involved controlled dangerous substances and was provided within the past 18 months."
>
> The affidavit also states that "the informant has seen the LSD and marijuana at said location." Further, the affidavit states that the affiant "has received information from other sources, who have not provided information in the past * * *"; that LSD and marijuana is located at the location or in the possession of the defendant.

Does the affidavit satisfy *Gates*? Would it have satisfied the *Aguilar-Spinelli* test? Would the affidavit be more troublesome if it did not state the number of prior occasions on which the informant provided information? Should the affidavit be required to disclose whether the informant ever provided information that resulted in a fruitless search or arrest?

3. *The Citizen Informant*

It is important to have the police believe that reasonable care in investigation of cases and preparation of warrants will not be met with judicially created pleading requirements that make every warrant application a painful experience. *Aguilar* and *Spinelli* attempted, probably without much success, to provide guidance to officers. *Gates* abandons the two-pronged test, but its totality of the circumstances approach is unlikely to assist police and magistrates in assessing the importance of particular facts. Prior to *Gates,* a number of courts had suggested that only one prong of the two-pronged test need be satisfied when a citizen-informer, rather than a more typical police informer, provides information used to support a warrant application. The trend is to distinguish sharply the "traditional police informer" from "an ordinary citizen who reports a crime" on the ground that the nature of the former and the information he supplies "convey a certain impression of unreliability" whereas the latter is presumed reliable because the motivations, which are "concern for society or for his own safety," suggest that there is little chance of fabrication. State v. Paszek, 50 Wis.2d 619, 184 N.W.2d 836 (1971). See also United States v. Decoteau, 932 F.2d 1205 (7th Cir.1991) (where citizen-informant known to the officer told him that she had seen the defendant with a sawed-off shotgun, the informant's statement provides probable cause and corroboration is unnecessary). Some courts have bucked the trend and suggested that corroboration by police officers of statements of an eyewitness victim may be necessary to sustain a finding of reliability of the informant. See United States v. Hunley, 567 F.2d 822, 826 (8th Cir. 1977) and cases therein cited.

Are you persuaded that citizen informants should be presumed reliable? If you are, would you require that an officer applying for a warrant demonstrate that the informant is an ordinary citizen and not a routine informant? For such a requirement, see People v. Smith, 17 Cal.3d 845, 132 Cal.Rptr. 397, 553 P.2d 557 (1976). Would you be willing to presume reliability as readily in some cases as others? Or would you carefully scrutinize the circumstances that result in an informant's emerging to cooperate with the police?

Who qualifies as a citizen informant? In Rutledge v. United States, 392 A.2d 1062 (D.C.App.1978), the Court concluded that a first-time volunteer, paid informant was closer to a typical or ordinary informant than to the usual unrewarded citizen who comes forward. Do you agree?

4. *Delay and Corroboration*

These hypothetical situations raise a question not often considered in decided cases: i.e., can the possible harmful effects of delaying the issuance of a warrant be considered in judging whether probable cause has been demonstrated? It will be clear in the upcoming sections on arrest and the various exceptions to the warrant requirement that the costs of delay can be considered in deciding whether to dispense with a warrant altogether. But can one set of facts establish probable cause in a case in which delay might be very costly, when it would not suffice in a case in which delay would be unlikely to disadvantage the government's law enforcement efforts? If the costs of delay can be considered, should a warrant that is issued on a less than optimal probable cause showing be more limited in scope than an ordinary warrant? If delay is a factor, then cases in which police use information supplied by persons at the scene of a crime to make arrests of fleeing suspects—e.g., King v. State, 16 Md.App. 546, 298 A.2d 446 (1973)—may not be apposite in other cases when there is time to get a warrant and a more deliberate search is planned.

Rules of thumb may be more elusive than police officers and courts would like. No cases illustrate this better than those that discuss the amount of corroboration necessary to transform information supplied by an informant that, standing alone, is inadequate to establish probable cause into that which is necessary to satisfy the Fourth Amendment. See generally LaFave, Probable Cause from Informants: The Effects of Murphy's Law on Fourth Amendment Adjudication, 1977 U.Ill.L.For. 1 (1977). What is rarely noticed is that corroboration can remedy either or both of two problems: inadequate information about the informant's credibility and an inadequate showing of the basis of an informant's tip. If an informant known to be reliable hurriedly passes information to a police contact, there may be a question about the source of the information. If the officer can independently determine that the informant was situated so as to have first-hand knowledge from personal observation of the information supplied, a magistrate might decide that a warrant should issue.[7] If the credibility of an informant is not easily established, verification of some facts may tend to show truthfulness. *Gates* makes this point. Almost certainly the amount of verification evidence required will appear to be a sliding scale, since the weaker the initial showing of credibility of the basis of information the greater the need for additional facts. See, e.g., Dawson v. State, 14 Md.App. 18, 284 A.2d 861 (1971).

The term verification sometimes is used in other ways to justify the issuance of a warrant. First, Justice Harlan's *Spinelli* opinion discusses "self-verifying detail" in connection with the *Draper* precedent. Some information from a person known to be reliable may be so complete that a magistrate could find that it must have been obtained in a reliable way. The Supreme Court uses similar reasoning in *Gates*. This is not really as much verification as it is inference drawing. Second, an informant who is demonstrably reliable and possesses information obtained in the most reliable way may supply insufficient facts to amount to probable cause. By adding facts through their own investigation, the police may be able to obtain a warrant. This "verification" concerns itself with adding to demonstrably reliable information, rather than demonstrating reliability.

Whatever terms are used, the Fourth Amendment requires police seeking warrants to present reliable information to the magistrate. The thing that the police must keep in mind is that the magistrate is constitutionally required to ask of them "why should I conclude that what you have told me represents the true state of affairs," and an appropriate answer requires that the police tell the magistrate "who knows what and why I should believe both who and what."

5. *Quantity of Information Required for Probable Cause*

Gates dealt with the quality of information which could be considered in the probable cause determination, i.e. whether the informant's tip is reliable enough to be considered as proof of probable cause. Assuming that all the information is reliable, another question arises: has the information submitted established a "fair probability" of criminal activity? This question arises not

7. People v. Elwell, 50 N.Y.2d 231, 428 N.Y.S.2d 655, 406 N.E.2d 471 (1980), discusses the way in which the specificity of information may lead to a conclusion that it was based on an informant's personal observation.

only with respect to affidavits submitted to magistrates, but also with warrantless searches and seizures; even if the search or seizure is done pursuant to an exception to the warrant requirement, the officer is ordinarily required to have probable cause.

One context in which the question of fair probability arises is where police know that a crime has been committed, but they are not certain that a suspect is the perpetrator. Consider United States v. Valez, 796 F.2d 24 (2d Cir.1986) where the court set forth the following facts and analysis:

> At 4:30 p.m. on October 16, 1984, New York City Police Sergeant Albert Zarr and Officer James Allen were parked in a surveillance vehicle on West 48th Street between Eighth and Ninth Avenues in Manhattan. Zarr sat near the rear window watching the street with binoculars; Allen remained in the front seat. After observing what appeared to be a narcotics sale on the southeast corner of 48th and Ninth, Zarr sent one of his undercover police officers to make a drug buy.
>
> Zarr saw the undercover officer hand money to two men at the corner and in return receive two packets that later proved to contain cocaine. Zarr observed that one of the sellers was an Hispanic male in his twenties, wearing a black leather jacket, grey pants with a comb in the back pocket, and a white or off-white V-neck shirt with dark trim on the collar.
>
> Zarr described the sellers to Allen and radioed the description to the field team. At that point, the seller with the black jacket walked around the corner and disappeared from view. Zarr instructed Allen to follow the subject and make an arrest.
>
> Allen left the van immediately and proceeded west on 48th Street and then south on Ninth Avenue in search of the seller. Allen walked to the next corner, but did not see his subject. He decided to turn back on the hunch that the seller had ducked into one of the stores. When Allen returned to the corner of 48th and Ninth, he saw a man coming out of a Blimpie's fast food restaurant who matched the description that Zarr had given him. At 4:40 p.m., five to ten minutes after Allen left the surveillance van, he arrested the man. The person whom Allen had arrested was Valez. [Valez was brought to the station, and a search of his person uncovered packets of cocaine.]
>
> When Sergeant Zarr and the undercover officer who made the "buy" returned to the stationhouse, they realized that Allen had arrested the wrong man. [Valez moved to suppress the cocaine on the ground that the arrest was illegal for lack of probable cause.] Valez relied primarily on the fact that Zarr's description did not include any mention of facial hair, whereas Valez had a small goatee and a thick moustache. Valez also argued that Zarr's description of the seller was overly general and that the mistaken arrest resulted from the negligent and unorganized conduct of the surveillance team.
>
> * * *
>
> Given Zarr's detailed description of the seller's clothing, his failure to mention that the seller was cleanshaven does not constitute an unreasonable oversight. * * * [T]he police may justifiably place little reliance on the presence or absence of facial hair on a suspect who otherwise matches a description because facial hair may be worn or taken off as a disguise. * * *
>
> We also believe that Zarr's description was sufficiently detailed to provide Allen with probable cause to believe that Valez was the seller, particularly

> because Allen encountered Valez, who matched every detail of the description, within the immediate vicinity of the drug sale and not more than 10 minutes after Zarr gave Allen the description. * * *
>
> We find that there was probable cause to arrest Valez. Thus, although Valez may be the victim of a mistake, no purpose would be served by suppressing clear evidence of Valez's guilt, which evidence came to the attention of the police as a result of their well-intentioned but misguided actions.

Dissenting Judge Oakes argued that Officer Zarr's description was too general to support probable cause to arrest:

> By sending an officer into the area with a description only of race, approximate age, and clothing and, oh yes, of a comb in the hip pocket—but not mentioning facial hair or its absence, or the length of the suspect's haircut—Zarr was insufficiently distinguishing the person who made the sale from other Latin males of not uncommon appearance in the immediate area. It was the equivalent of "identifying" a suspect in the Wall Street area by describing him as a white, thirty-ish man with a button-down shirt and dark pinstripe suit, carrying a leather attache case.

Who has the better of the argument on probable cause, the majority or the dissent? Would it have mattered if Zarr had arrested the real seller before Allen had arrested Valez?

As is indicated by *Valez,* probable cause can exist even though the police are mistaken. See Hill v. California, 401 U.S. 797 (1971) (if police have probable cause to arrest Hill and have probable cause to believe that Miller is Hill, they act properly if they arrest Miller).

State v. Howe, 136 Vt. 53, 386 A.2d 1125 (1978), illustrates the difficulty of deciding whether probable cause as to identity exists early in an investigation when few facts have been assembled. An elderly woman was sexually assaulted and murdered in her hotel room. Human bitemarks were found on her neck and one of her breasts, and hairs not matching hers were found in her bed. The discovery of the body was reported to the hotel clerk by Howe who occupied the room next to the woman's. Howe subsequently told the police that he had been in bed, heard a scream, put on a pair of pants, gone into the hallway where he found a man scurrying away toward a fire exit, entered the open door of the victim's room, saw the body, checked both wrists for a pulse, and reported the crime to the desk clerk. The police prepared an affidavit, which the Supreme Court of Vermont described as follows:

> The affidavit states that it appeared to the affiant and his fellow officers that the victim had been strangled and sexually assaulted. It described the position of the victim's body and her state of undress and noted that a pair of glasses, "which is believed to belong to" appellant, had been found on the floor near the bed. The affidavit goes on to describe appellant as an acquaintance of the victim and states that appellant "supposedly discovered the victim's body." The affidavit recounts appellant's story of the scream and the man seen running down the hall.
>
> The affidavit goes on to recite the statement of the hotel desk clerk, named in the affidavit, that only the victim and her son had a key to the room and that she always kept her door locked. The affidavit then states that appellant lived next door to the victim and that when he reported the discovery of the body to the desk clerk he was wearing only a pair of pants. Finally, the

affidavit recounts the desk clerk's statements concerning the reporting of the crime; appellant came down the stairs yelling that the victim had been murdered; the clerk noticed that appellant was not wearing his glasses and asked appellant where they were, appellant replying that he didn't know, he had lost them; the two men went upstairs and entered the victim's room; appellant lifted the bed covers. The affidavit next recited the desk clerk's statement that he told appellant not to touch anything, pushed him out of the room and then left the room. * * * [N]othing appears in the affidavit to sustain the credibility of the desk clerk * * *.

On the basis of this information, could a magistrate issue a warrant to search the person of Howe to obtain a sample of his pubic hair and a search of his room for the clothes he was wearing on the night of the murder?

Assume that the warrant did issue and that a pubic hair sample was taken, and further that the police seek another warrant to search Howe and to take fingerprints, a blood sample and dental impressions. Would it be constitutional for a magistrate to issue the warrant on the same affidavit if, the second time, the affidavit also states the following things:

> that bitemarks were found on the victim's left breast, that cigarettes found in the victim's room had been shown by laboratory tests to have been smoked by a person with blood type "O" and that fingerprints were found in the victim's room. Finally, the affidavit states that pubic hair found in the victim's bed shared with pubic hair samples taken from appellant (pursuant to search warrant) the characteristic that they had been trimmed.

In answering, remember that appellant told the police that twice he was at the bed of the victim—once to check her pulse and once with the desk clerk.

Another circumstance in which the probable cause issue arises is where there is a question whether a crime has been or is being committed at all, i.e. the officer has a specific person in mind as a perpetrator, but is not certain whether there is any criminal activity afoot. For example, what if the officer sees a person at 2:00 a.m. carrying a television and a stereo down the street in a shopping cart? There are many innocent explanations for this activity. Does that mean that there is no fair probability of criminal activity? Consider United States v. Raborn, 872 F.2d 589 (5th Cir.1989). Acting on a tip, officers investigated a secluded farmhouse. They detected the odor of phenylacetic acid and of ether, two chemicals commonly used in the manufacture of amphetamines. The next day, they found that the farmhouse had been boarded up and the only opening other than the doors was a large vent equipped with a fan. A pickup truck entered the driveway of the farmhouse, its driver honked the horn, and the vehicle remained there for five minutes before someone came from the farmhouse and entered the passenger side. The officers followed the pickup truck for several miles, to a point where it appeared to be leaving the area. They stopped the truck and placed the driver and passenger under arrest. The driver challenged the arrest as lacking probable cause. The Court of Appeals rejected the driver's argument. The court recognized that there is no probable cause to arrest someone merely because he associates with a criminal, but the court found more than mere association in this case: the farmhouse was in an isolated location; the driver drove directly up to the farmhouse in a manner that indicated he knew his destination and was not lost; he did not appear to be seeking directions, or to be engaged in an innocent errand like delivering milk; he blew the truck's horn as if he were expected, and someone came from the house in response. Do you think that these facts indicate a fair probability of criminal activity?

6. *First Amendment Concerns*

In New York v. P.J. Video, 475 U.S. 868 (1986), Justice Rehnquist wrote for the Court as it held that warrants authorizing the seizure of "adult" tapes from a video store were supported by probable cause to believe that the tapes were pornographic. Justice Rehnquist first noted that "an application for a warrant authorizing the seizure of materials presumptively protected by the First Amendment should be evaluated under the same standard of probable cause used to review warrants generally." [8] The Court found that the affidavits in the instant case contained more than enough information to conclude that there was a "fair probability" that the movies satisfied the statutory definition of obscenity (i.e., predominant appeal to prurient interest in sex, specific sexual conduct presented in patently offensive manner, and no serious scientific, artistic value). Justice Marshall, joined by Justices Brennan and Stevens, dissented. He argued that the affidavits described no more than excerpted scenes, and the magistrate could not have determined that the sex acts pervaded the films or that the films as a whole lacked artistic value. The Supreme Court appended five affidavits of an investigator to its opinion. One is set forth below. Assuming it is fairly typical, who has the better of the argument, the majority or the dissent?

AFFIDAVIT

STATE OF NEW YORK)
COUNTY OF ERIE) SS:
CITY OF BUFFALO)

DAVID J. GROBLEWSKI, being duly sworn, deposes and says:

I am presently a Confidential Criminal Investigator assigned to the Erie County District Attorney's Office and prior to this, a member of the New York State Police for approximately 25 years.

On September 26th, 1983 I viewed the video tape movie "CALIFORNIA VALLEY GIRLS," which was rented on September 20th, 1983, from Network Video, 5868 Transit Road, Depew, New York. This movie was rented by Detective Sergeant Vincent Costanza, a member of the Erie County Sheriff's Department. This movie was viewed in my office starting at 12:00 Noon and lasted until 1:33 P.M.

8. The Court observed that First Amendment decisions in Roaden v. Kentucky, 413 U.S. 496 (1973), A Quantity of Copies of Books v. Kansas, 378 U.S. 205 (1964), Marcus v. Search Warrants, 367 U.S. 717 (1961), Heller v. New York, 413 U.S. 483 (1973), and Lee Art Theatre, Inc. v. Virginia, 392 U.S. 636 (1968), provided various protections against seizure of films and books on the basis of their content. *Roaden* barred reliance on "exigent circumstances" to seize allegedly obscene materials if the seizure would amount to a prior restraint. *A Quantity of Books* and *Marcus* prohibited large-scale seizures constituting a prior restraint without an adversary hearing first. *Heller* restricted seizure of allegedly obscene materials, even where there is no prior restraint, to searches pursuant to a warrant with a prompt post-seizure hearing provided. *Lee Art Theatres* barred the issuance of a warrant based upon the conclusory statements of a police officer that materials are obscene. After *P.J. Video,* the Court held in Fort Wayne Books, Inc. v. Indiana, 489 U.S. 46 (1989) that the First Amendment prohibits the seizure of more than one copy of a book or film until there has been a determination of obscenity following an adversary hearing.

The content and character of the above mentioned video movie is as follows: Six white females, approximately 18 to 25 years of age, are unemployed and attempt to make a living by becoming prostitutes. The first scene is a bedroom scene where two females are involved in lovemaking, fondling and cunnilingus. The second scene depicts a white male and a white female having intercourse in the back of a van. The third scene is a house scene where six girls, all white females are introduced to the art of lovemaking. One male, approximately 35 years of age, is teaching the girls the art of fellatio with each one of them performing this act on him. The next scene is a bedroom scene in a home where a husband and wife, a white male and a white female, alone with a girl, a white female, perform various sexual acts which include intercourse, fellatio, anal intercourse and cunnilingus. The movie ends with some lesbianism where the wife performs cunnilingus on the girl while she performs fellatio on the husband and they engage in intercourse and anal intercourse.

[Signature]

David J. Groblewski
Confidential Criminal
Investigator

Subscribed and sworn to
before me this [21] day
of November, 1983.

[Signature]

Notary Public

When *P.J. Video* returned to the state courts, the New York Court of Appeals held in New York v. P.J. Video, Inc., 68 N.Y.2d 296, 508 N.Y.S.2d 907, 501 N.E.2d 556 (1986), that the state constitution barred reliance on the totality of circumstances approach for warrants directed at allegedly obscene materials. It reasoned that all aspects of the statutory definition of obscenity are significant and that the Supreme Court's approach effectively ignores some of the statutory elements.

B. PROBABLE CAUSE, SPECIFICITY AND REASONABLENESS

1. The Place to be Searched

It is sometimes the case that police have probable cause to believe that a suspect has committed a crime and is in control of certain evidence, but they are less sure where the evidence is located. Can they obtain a search warrant of the premises where the suspect lives on the theory that it is the most likely place to search for evidence? The premises where the suspect works? The premises that the suspect frequents? Some courts hold that a showing of probable cause to believe a suspect guilty does not automatically justify a search of her residence. See, e.g., United States v. Bailey, 458 F.2d 408 (9th Cir. 1972). Other courts are much quicker to issue warrants for places with which a suspect has continuous contact. See, e.g., Commonwealth v. De Masi, 362 Mass. 53, 283 N.E.2d 845 (1972). In Zurcher v. Stanford Daily, 436 U.S. 547, 556 (1978), the majority stated that "[t]he critical element * * * is reasonable cause to believe that the specific 'things' to be searched for and seized are located on the property to which entry is sought."

In United States v. Chesher, 678 F.2d 1353 (9th Cir. 1982), the Court of Appeals, in the course of explaining why a remand for a hearing on the validity of a search warrant was needed, stated that a racketeering indictment does not establish probable cause to search a defendant's house for evidence of racketeering, since the charge might relate to an earlier time period. The same court also stressed in United States v. Flores, 679 F.2d 173 (9th Cir. 1982), that "[s]tanding alone, a suspect's presence or arrest at a residence is too insignificant a connection with that residence" to justify a search for evidence. Similarly, United States v. Freeman, 685 F.2d 942 (5th Cir. 1982), states that "the fact that there is probable cause to believe that a person has committed a crime does not automatically give the police probable cause to search his residence for evidence of that crime. * * * [F]acts must exist which establish a nexus between the house to be searched and the evidence sought. * * * However, that nexus may be established either through direct observation or through normal inferences as to where the article sought would be located." Compare these cases with People v. Easley, 33 Cal.3d 65, 187 Cal.Rptr. 745, 654 P.2d 1272, (1982), which states that a search warrant affidavit must enable a magistrate to conclude that evidence of crime could be found at either of a defendant's residences or in either of his cars, and that the fact that a warrant enabled the police to search four separate locations for the same item did not invalidate the warrant.

See also United States v. Green, 634 F.2d 222 (5th Cir. 1981):

> The justification for allowing a search of a person's residence when that person is suspected of criminal activity is the commonsense realization that one tends to conceal fruits and instrumentalities of a crime in a place to which easy access may be had and in which privacy is nevertheless maintained. In normal situations, few places are more convenient than one's residence for use in planning criminal activities and hiding fruits of a crime. But we are confronted with a different situation: in this case defendant Green allegedly engaged in criminal activity several thousand miles from his residence. The convenience of the residence for use as a place to plan and hide fruits of the crime is thus diminished, if not eliminated. Assuming, as the affidavits indicate, that all criminal activity took place in California, we find no justification for a reasonable person to conclude that there was probable cause to believe that fruits or instrumentalities of crimes could be found at the Florida residence.

Considering the purposes of the warrant requirement, what do you think the correct standard is? Try and apply it to the following illustrative cases.

In United States v. Scott, 555 F.2d 522 (5th Cir. 1977), the FBI investigated several persons suspected of operating a numbers lottery. Part of a 49 page affidavit filed by FBI agent Burgess was as follows:

> Affiant [Burgess] has learned from his prior experience in investigating illegal numbers lotteries that the persons engaged therein customarily keep wagering paraphernalia, such as lottery slips, rundown sheets, ribbons, tapes, collection sheets, books of accounts, miscellaneous records of bets, code books, lists of telephone numbers, checks, money orders, and records of bank accounts in conducting such lotteries * * *. They also maintain safety deposit boxes with local banking concerns for the purpose of hiding lottery records, account

ledgers and money. Normally, pass keys to such safety deposit boxes are kept by lottery participants on their person as well as in their headquarters, residences and vehicles. Based on all the information, facts, and circumstances set forth heretofore, Affiant has probable cause to believe that the foregoing described wagering paraphernalia and money is now being concealed on the premises, persons and in the automobiles previously described, and more particularly described in each of Affiant's individual Affidavits for Search Warrants, which are attached hereto.

Was this a sufficient showing to justify the search of the areas mentioned? See also United States v. Lamon, 930 F.2d 1183 (7th Cir.1991) (probable cause existed to search the car of a known drug dealer, because a magistrate can credit an officer's observance that drug dealers often store drugs in their cars). Does *Lamon* stand for the proposition that there is per se probable cause to search the car of a drug dealer?

In State v. Ernest, 200 Neb. 615, 264 N.W.2d 677 (1978), the opinion discusses an affidavit used to obtain a search warrant relating to a person suspected of setting fire to a tavern. The affidavit was issued seven months after the crime and listed three locations, "all of which were residences where the defendant was known to stay from time to time." The evidence consisted of photographs of the defendant and a companion who testified for the state and claimed to be an eyewitness and two newspapers containing stories about the tavern fire. Could a valid warrant be issued to search the three residences?

2. *Searches of Non-Suspects' Premises*

State v. Ernest introduces the concept of searches of one person's premises for evidence against another. That and several other problems arose in *Zurcher*, infra, one of the Supreme Court's Fourth Amendment cases that have been heavily criticized, not for tying the hands of the police, but for providing them with too much authority to seek evidence through a search warrant.

ZURCHER v. STANFORD DAILY

Supreme Court of the United States, 1978.
436 U.S. 547.

MR. JUSTICE WHITE delivered the opinion of the Court.

* * *

I

Late in the day on Friday, April 9, 1971, officers of the Palo Alto Police Department and of the Santa Clara County Sheriff's Department responded to a call from the director of the Stanford University Hospital requesting the removal of a large group of demonstrators who had seized the hospital's administrative offices and occupied them since the previous afternoon. After several futile efforts to persuade the demonstrators to leave peacefully, more drastic measures were employed. The demonstrators had barricaded the doors at both ends of a hall adjacent to the administrative offices. The police chose to force their way in at the west end of the corridor. As they did so, a group of demonstrators emerged through the doors at the east end and, armed with sticks and clubs, attacked the group of nine police officers stationed there. One officer was knocked to the floor and struck repeatedly on the head; another suffered a broken shoulder. All nine were injured. There were no police photographers at the east doors, and most bystanders and reporters were on the west side. The officers themselves were able to identify only two of their assailants, but one of them did see at least one person photographing the assault at the east doors.

On Sunday, April 11, a special edition of the Stanford Daily (Daily), a student newspaper published at Stanford University, carried articles and photographs devoted to the hospital protest and the violent clash between demonstrators and police. The photographs carried the byline of a Daily staff member and indicated that he had been at the east end of the hospital hallway where he could have photographed the assault on the nine officers. The next day, the Santa Clara County District Attorney's Office secured a warrant from the Municipal Court for an immediate search of the Daily's offices for negatives, film, and pictures showing the events and occurrences at the hospital on the evening of April 9. The warrant issued on a finding of "just, probable and reasonable cause for believing that: Negatives and photographs and films, evidence material and relevant to the identity of the perpetrators of felonies, to wit, Battery on a Peace Officer, and Assault with Deadly Weapon, will be located [on the premises of the Daily]." The warrant affidavit contained no allegation or indication that members of the Daily staff were in any way involved in unlawful acts at the hospital.

The search pursuant to the warrant was conducted later that day by four police officers and took place in the presence of some members of the Daily staff. The Daily's photographic laboratories, filing cabinets, desks, and wastepaper baskets were searched. Locked drawers and rooms were not opened. The officers apparently had opportunity to read notes and correspondence during the search; but, contrary to claims of the staff, the officers denied that they had exceeded the limits of the warrant. They had not been advised by the staff that the areas they were searching contained confidential materials. The search revealed only the photographs that had already been published on April 11, and no materials were removed from the Daily's office.

A month later the Daily and various members of its staff, respondents here, brought a civil action in the United States District Court for the Northern District of California seeking declaratory and injunctive relief * * *.

The District Court denied the request for an injunction but on respondents' motion for summary judgment, granted declaratory relief. 353 F.Supp. 124 (ND Cal.1972). The court did not question the existence of probable cause to believe that a crime had been committed and to believe that relevant evidence would be found on the Daily's premises. It held, however, that the Fourth and Fourteenth Amendments forbade the issuance of a warrant to search for materials in possession of one not suspected of crime unless there is probable cause to believe, based on facts presented in a sworn affidavit, that a subpoena *duces tecum* would be impracticable. Moreover, the failure to honor a subpoena would not alone justify a warrant; it must also appear that the possessor of the objects sought would disregard a court order not to remove or destroy them. The District Court further held that where the innocent object of the search is a newspaper, First Amendment interests are also involved and that such a search is constitutionally permissible "only in the rare circumstance where there is a *clear showing* that (1) important materials will be destroyed or removed from the jurisdiction; *and* (2) a restraining order would be futile." Since these preconditions to a valid warrant had not been satisfied here, the search of the Daily's offices was declared to have been illegal. The Court of Appeals affirmed *per curiam,* adopting the opinion of the District Court. 550 F.2d 464 (CA9 1977). We issued the writs of certiorari requested by petitioners. We reverse.

II

The issue here is how the Fourth Amendment is to be construed and applied to the "third party" search, the recurring situation where state authorities have probable cause to believe that fruits, instrumentalities, or other evidence of crime is located on identified property but do not then have probable cause to believe that the owner or possessor of the property is himself implicated in the crime that has occurred or is occurring. Because under the District Court's rule impracticability can be shown only by furnishing facts demonstrating that the third party will not only disobey the subpoena but also ignore a restraining order not to move or destroy the property, it is apparent that only in unusual situations could the State satisfy such a severe burden and that for all practical purposes the effect of the rule is that fruits, instrumentalities, and evidence of crime may be recovered from third parties only by subpoena, not by search warrant. * * *

It is an understatement to say that there is no direct authority in this or any other federal court for the District Court's sweeping revision of the Fourth Amendment. Under existing law, valid warrants may be issued to search *any* property, whether or not occupied by a third party, at which there is probable cause to believe that fruits, instrumentalities, or evidence of a crime will be found. Nothing on the face of the Amendment suggests that a third-party search warrant should not normally issue. The Warrant Clause speaks of search warrants issued on "probable cause" and "particularly describing the place to be searched, and the persons or things to be seized." In situations where the State does not seek to seize "persons" but only those "things" which there is probable cause to believe are located on the place to be searched, there is no apparent basis in the language of the Amendment for also imposing the requirements for a valid arrest—probable cause to believe that the third party is implicated in the crime.

* * *

The critical element in a reasonable search is not that the owner of the property is suspected of crime but that there is reasonable cause to believe that the specific "things" to be searched for and seized are located on the property to which entry is sought. * * *

Against this background, it is untenable to conclude that property may not be searched unless its occupant is reasonably suspected of crime and is subject to arrest. * * * As we understand the structure and language of the Fourth Amendment and our cases expounding it, valid warrants to search property may be issued when it is satisfactorily demonstrated to the magistrate that fruits, instrumentalities, or evidence of crime is located on the premises. The Fourth Amendment has itself struck the balance between privacy and public need, and there is no occasion or justification for a court to revise the Amendment and strike a new balance by denying the search warrant in the circumstances present here and by insisting that the investigation proceed by subpoena *duces tecum,* whether on the theory that the latter is a less intrusive alternative or otherwise.

This is not to question that "reasonableness" is the overriding test of compliance with the Fourth Amendment or to assert that searches, however or whenever executed, may never be unreasonable if supported by a warrant issued on probable cause and properly identifying the place to be searched and the property to be seized. We do hold, however, that the courts may not, in the name of Fourth Amendment reasonableness, forbid the States from issuing warrants to search for evidence simply because the owner or possessor of the place to be searched is not then reasonably suspected of criminal involvement.

III

In any event, the reasons presented by the District Court and adopted by the Court of Appeals for arriving at its remarkable conclusion do not withstand analysis. First, as we have said, it is apparent that whether the third-party occupant is suspect or not, the State's interest in enforcing the criminal law and recovering the evidence remains the same; and it is the seeming innocence of the property owner that the District Court relied on to foreclose the warrant to search. But, as respondents themselves now concede, if the third party knows that contraband or other illegal materials are on his property, he is sufficiently culpable to justify the issuance of a search warrant. Similarly, if his ethical stance is the determining factor, it seems to us that whether or not he knows that the sought-after articles are secreted on his property and whether or not he knows that the articles are in fact the fruits, instrumentalities, or evidence of crime, he will be so informed when the search warrant is served, and it is doubtful that he should then be permitted to object to the search, to withhold, if it is there, the evidence of crime reasonably believed to be possessed by him or secreted on his property, and to forbid the search and insist that the officers serve him with a subpoena *duces tecum.*

Second, we are unpersuaded that the District Court's new rule denying search warrants against third parties and insisting on subpoenas would substantially further privacy interests without seriously undermining law enforcement efforts. Because of the fundamental public interest in implementing the criminal law, the search warrant, a heretofore effective and constitutionally acceptable enforcement tool, should not be suppressed on the basis of surmise and without solid evidence supporting the change. As the District Court understands it, denying third-party search warrants would not have substantial adverse effects on criminal investigations because the nonsuspect third party, once served with a subpoena, will preserve the evidence and ultimately lawfully respond. The difficulty with this assumption is that search warrants are often employed early in an investigation, perhaps before the identity of any likely criminal and certainly before all the perpetrators are or could be known. The seemingly blameless third party in possession of the fruits or evidence may not be innocent at all; and if he is, he may nevertheless be so related to or so sympathetic with the culpable that he cannot be relied upon to retain and preserve the articles that may implicate his friends, or at least not to notify those who would be damaged by the evidence that the authorities are aware of its location. In any event, it is likely that the real culprits will have access to the property, and the delay involved in employing the subpoena *duces tecum,* offering as it does the opportunity to litigate its validity, could easily result in the disappearance of the evidence, whatever the good faith of the third party.

* * *

We are also not convinced that the net gain to privacy interests by the District Court's new rule would be worth the candle. In the normal course of events, search warrants are more difficult to obtain than subpoenas, since the latter do not involve the judiciary and do not require proof of probable cause. Where, in the real world, subpoenas would suffice, it can be expected that they will be employed by the rational prosecutor. On the other hand, when choice is available under local law and the prosecutor chooses to use the search warrant, it is unlikely that he has needlessly selected the more difficult course. His choice is more likely to be based on the solid belief, arrived at through experience but difficult, if not impossible, to sustain in a specific case, that the warranted search is necessary to secure and to avoid the destruction of evidence.[a]

IV

The District Court held, and respondents assert here, that whatever may be true of third-party searches generally, where the third party is a newspaper, there are additional factors derived from the First Amendment that justify a nearly *per se* rule forbidding the search warrant and permitting only the subpoena *duces tecum.* * * *

* * *

There is no reason to believe * * * that magistrates cannot guard against searches of the type, scope, and intrusiveness that would actually interfere with the timely publication of a newspaper. Nor, if the requirements of specificity and reasonableness are properly applied, policed, and observed, will there be any occasion or opportunity for officers to rummage at large in newspaper files or to intrude into or to deter normal editorial and publication decisions. The warrant issued in this case authorized nothing of this sort. Nor are we convinced * * * that confidential sources will disappear and that the press will suppress news because of fears of warranted searches. Whatever incremental effect there may be in this regard if search warrants, as well as subpoenas, are permissible in proper circumstances, it does not make a constitutional difference in our judgment.

* * *

MR. JUSTICE BRENNAN took no part in the consideration or decision of this case.

MR. JUSTICE POWELL, concurring.

I join the opinion of the Court, and I write simply to emphasize what I take to be the fundamental error of Mr. Justice Stewart's dissenting opinion. As I understand that opinion, it would read into the Fourth Amendment, as a new and *per se* exception, the rule that any search of an entity protected by the Press Clause of the First Amendment is unreasonable so long as a subpoena could be used as a substitute procedure. Even aside from the difficulties involved in deciding on a case-by-case basis whether a subpoena can serve as an adequate substitute,[b] I agree with the Court that there is no constitutional basis for such a reading.

a. Petitioners assert that the District Court ignored the realities of California law and practice that are said to preclude or make very difficult the use of subpoenas as investigatory techniques. If true, the choice of procedures may not always be open to the diligent prosecutor in the State of California.

b. For example, respondents had announced a policy of destroying any photographs that might aid prosecution of protesters. While this policy probably reflected the deep feelings of the Vietnam era, and one may assume that under normal circumstances few, if any, press entities would adopt a policy so hostile to law enforcement, respondents' policy at least illustrates the possibility of such hostility. Use of a subpoena, as proposed by the dissent would be of no utility in face of a policy of destroying evidence. And unless the policy were publicly announced, it probably would be difficult to show the impracticality of a subpoena as opposed to a search warrant.

* * *

If the Framers had believed that the press was entitled to a special procedure, not available to others, when government authorities required evidence in its possession, one would have expected the terms of the Fourth Amendment to reflect that belief. * * *

* * * While there is no justification for the establishment of a separate Fourth Amendment procedure for the press, a magistrate asked to issue a warrant for the search of press offices can and should take cognizance of the independent values protected by the First Amendment—such as those highlighted by Mr. Justice Stewart—when he weighs such factors. If the reasonableness and particularity requirements are thus applied, the dangers are likely to be minimal.[c]

In any event, considerations such as these are the province of the Fourth Amendment. There is no authority either in history or in the Constitution itself for exempting certain classes of persons or entities from its reach.

MR. JUSTICE STEWART, with whom MR. JUSTICE MARSHALL joins, dissenting.

Believing that the search by the police of the offices of the Stanford Daily infringed the First and Fourteenth Amendments' guarantee of a free press, I respectfully dissent.[d]

I

It seems to me self-evident that police searches of newspaper offices burden the freedom of the press. The most immediate and obvious First Amendment injury caused by such a visitation by the police is physical disruption of the operation of the newspaper. Policemen occupying a newsroom and searching it thoroughly for what may be an extended period of time will inevitably interrupt its normal operations, and thus impair or even temporarily prevent the processes of news-gathering, writing, editing, and publishing. By contrast, a subpoena would afford the newspaper itself an opportunity to locate whatever material might be requested and produce it.

But there is another and more serious burden on a free press imposed by an unannounced police search of a newspaper office: the possibility of disclosure of information received from confidential sources, or of the identity of the sources themselves. Protection of those sources is necessary to ensure that the press can fulfill its constitutionally designated function of informing the public, because important information can often be obtained only by an assurance that the source will not be revealed. * * *

* * *

A search warrant allows police officers to ransack the files of a newspaper, reading each and every document until they have found the one named in the warrant,[e] while a subpoena would per-

c. Similarly, the magnitude of a proposed search directed at *any* third party, together with the nature and significance of the material sought, are factors properly considered as bearing on the reasonableness and particularity requirements. Moreover, there is no reason why police officers executing a warrant should not seek the cooperation of the subject party, in order to prevent needless disruption.

d. I agree with the Court that the *Fourth* Amendment does not forbid the issuance of search warrants "simply because the owner or possessor of the place to be searched is not then reasonably suspected of criminal involvement." Thus, contrary to the understanding expressed in the concurring opinion, I do not "read" anything "into the Fourth Amendment." Instead, I would simply enforce the provisions of the *First* Amendment.

e. The Court says that "if the requirements of specificity and reasonableness are properly applied, policed, and observed" there will be no opportunity for the police to "rummage at large in newspaper files." But in order to find a particular document, no matter how specifically it is identified in the warrant, the police will have to search every place where it might be—including, presumably, every file in the office—and to examine each document they find to see if it is the correct

mit the newspaper itself to produce only the specific documents requested. A search, unlike a subpoena, will therefore lead to the needless exposure of confidential information completely unrelated to the purpose of the investigation. The knowledge that police officers can make an unannounced raid on a newsroom is thus bound to have a deterrent effect on the availability of confidential news sources. The end result, wholly inimical to the First Amendment, will be a diminishing flow of potentially important information to the public.

One need not rely on mere intuition to reach this conclusion. The record in this case includes affidavits not only from members of the staff of the Stanford Daily but from many professional journalists and editors, attesting to precisely such personal experience.[f] Despite the Court's rejection of this uncontroverted evidence, I believe it clearly establishes that unannounced police searches of newspaper offices will significantly burden the constitutionally protected function of the press to gather news and report it to the public.

* * *

MR. JUSTICE STEVENS, dissenting.

The novel problem presented by this case is an outgrowth of the profound change in Fourth Amendment law that occurred in 1967, when Warden v. Hayden, 387 U.S. 294, was decided. The question is what kind of "probable cause" must be established in order to obtain a warrant to conduct an unannounced search for documentary evidence in the private files of a person not suspected of involvement in any criminal activity. The Court holds that a reasonable belief that the files contain relevant evidence is a sufficient justification. This holding rests on a misconstruction of history and of the Fourth Amendment's purposely broad language.

The Amendment contains two Clauses, one protecting "persons, houses, papers, and effects, against unreasonable searches and seizures," the other regulating the issuance of warrants: "no Warrants shall issue, but upon probable cause, supported by Oath or affirmation, and particularly describing the place to be searched, and the persons or things to be seized." When these words were written, the procedures of the Warrant Clause were not the primary protection against oppressive searches. It is unlikely that the authors expected private papers ever to be among the "things" that could be seized with a warrant, for only a few years earlier, in 1765, Lord Camden had delivered his famous opinion denying that any magistrate had power to authorize the seizure of private papers.[g] Because

one. I thus fail to see how the Fourth Amendment would provide an effective limit to these searches.

f. According to these uncontradicted affidavits, when it becomes known that a newsman cannot guarantee confidentiality, potential sources of information often become unavailable. Moreover, efforts are sometimes made, occasionally by force, to prevent reporters and photographers from covering newsworthy events, because of fear that the police will seize the newsman's notes or photographs as evidence. The affidavits of the members of the staff of the Stanford Daily give examples of how this very search produced such an impact on the Daily's own journalistic functions.

g. "Papers are the owner's goods and chattels: they are his dearest property; and are so far from enduring a seizure, that they will hardly bear an inspection; and though the eye cannot by the laws of England be guilty of a trespass, yet where private papers are removed and carried away, the secret nature of those goods will be an aggravation of the trespass, and demand more considerable damages in that respect. Where is the written law that gives any magistrate such a power? I can safely answer, there is none; and therefore it is too much for us without such authority to pronounce a practice legal, which would be subversive of all the comforts of society." Entick v. Carrington, 19 How.St.Tr. 1029, 1066 (1765).

all such seizures were considered unreasonable, the Warrant Clause was not framed to protect against them.

* * *

In the pre-*Hayden* era warrants were used to search for contraband, weapons, and plunder, but not for "mere evidence."[h] The practical effect of the rule prohibiting the issuance of warrants to search for mere evidence was to narrowly limit not only the category of objects, but also the category of persons and the character of the privacy interests that might be affected by an unannounced police search.

Just as the witnesses who participate in an investigation or a trial far outnumber the defendants, the persons who possess evidence that may help to identify an offender, or explain an aspect of a criminal transaction, far outnumber those who have custody of weapons or plunder. Countless law-abiding citizens—doctors, lawyers, merchants, customers, bystanders—may have documents in their possession that relate to an ongoing criminal investigation. The consequences of subjecting this large category of persons to unannounced police searches are extremely serious. The *ex parte* warrant procedure enables the prosecutor to obtain access to privileged documents that could not be examined if advance notice gave the custodian an opportunity to object. The search for the documents described in a warrant may involve the inspection of files containing other private matter. The dramatic character of a sudden search may cause an entirely unjustified injury to the reputation of the persons searched.

* * *

A showing of probable cause that was adequate to justify the issuance of a warrant to search for stolen goods in the 18th century does not automatically satisfy the new dimensions of the Fourth Amendment in the post-*Hayden* era. In *Hayden* itself, the Court recognized that the meaning of probable cause should be reconsidered in the light of the new authority it conferred on the police. The only conceivable justification for an unannounced search of an innocent citizen is the fear that, if notice were given, he would conceal or destroy the object of the search. Probable cause to believe that the custodian is a criminal, or that he holds a criminal's weapons, spoils, or the like, justifies that fear, and therefore such a showing complies with the Clause. But if nothing said under oath in the warrant application demonstrates the need for an unannounced search by force, the probable-cause requirement is not satisfied. In the absence of some other showing of reasonableness, the ensuing search violates the Fourth Amendment.

In this case, the warrant application set forth no facts suggesting that respondents were involved in any wrongdoing or would destroy the desired evidence if given notice of what the police desired. I would therefore hold that the warrant did not comply with the Warrant Clause and that the search was unreasonable within the meaning of the first Clause of the Fourth Amendment.

I respectfully dissent.

h. Until 1967, when Warden v. Hayden was decided, our cases interpreting the Fourth Amendment had drawn a "'distinction between merely evidentiary materials, on the one hand, which may not be seized either under the authority of a search warrant or during the course of a search incident to arrest, and on the other hand, those objects which may validly be seized including the instrumentalities and means by which a crime is committed, the fruits of crime such as stolen property, weapons by which escape of the person arrested might be effected, and property the possession of which is a crime.'" See Warden v. Hayden, 387 U.S., at 295–296, quoting from Harris v. United States, 331 U.S. 145, 154.

Note

The officer who swore out the affidavit in *Zurcher* was present at the scene of the demonstration and was a victim of the student violence. Although he did not swear that he or any other officer saw a photographer from the Daily at the demonstration, he did swear that he "personally saw cameras being pointed in the direction of the officers and demonstrators during the course of the evening." He also said that he examined the pictures in the paper and that "they depict the location, occurrences and activity during the period of time the felonies of assault were occurring." Finally, he swore that the photos bore the by-line of Bill Cooke, who was listed on the Daily's masthead as a "photo labman." Is this enough to justify the issuance of a warrant? When the Stanford Daily brought its suit, it was the typical victim of a third party search—it had no other effective remedy, given the immunities of the officers and the magistrate and the absence of evidence to suppress. Is the absence of another remedy for a bad search and seizure something that offers support for Justice Stevens' approach?

The search warrant was issued because a photographer from the paper "could have photographed the assault on nine officers." It authorized a search for negatives and films that no one suggested ever existed. Was there probable cause to believe that evidence of criminal activity was located at the newspaper office? Would you have required some greater probability that specific evidence existed? Did anyone on the Court ever consider the question?

If the government cannot identify with specificity the evidence that it hopes to find in a search, isn't the intrusion caused by the search likely to be greater than when specific objects are sought? Absent identification of that which is sought in advance of the search, the searchers will be deciding as they go exactly what they are looking for and they will examine everything that possibly could be evidence rather than only those things that match a pre-existing description. If no specific description is available prior to the search, should a greater showing of cause be required than if evidence can be identified with more precision?

Warden v. Hayden is discussed in the text and footnotes of Justice Stevens' opinion. Prior to that case, the kinds of things that could be seized pursuant to a warrant were limited. Justice Brennan's opinion in *Warden* rejected "[t]he distinction made by some of our cases between seizure of items of evidential value only and seizure of instrumentalities, fruits or contraband." 387 U.S. at 300. He concluded that

> [a] magistrate can intervene in both situations, and the requirements of probable cause and specificity can be preserved intact. Moreover, nothing in the nature of property seized as evidence renders it more private than property seized, for example, as an instrumentality; quite the opposite may be true.

Id. at 302. Only Justice Douglas dissented. However, Justice Fortas joined by Chief Justice Warren, concurred in the treatment of evidence relating to an identification, but warned that to move too quickly to allow all evidence to be seized is to invoke spectres of the writs of assistance so abhorred by the framers of the Fourth Amendment.

In considering whether the Court might have decided *Zurcher* differently if a more traditional Fourth Amendment argument had been made, consider Lo-Ji Sales, Inc. v. New York, 442 U.S. 319 (1979). An investigator for the New York State Police purchased two reels of film from an "adult" bookstore and took them to a magistrate for a determination whether there was reasonable cause to believe that the films violated state obscenity laws. The magistrate apparently concluded that there was reasonable cause, and he issued an arrest warrant for the store clerk and a search warrant that was designed to allow him to determine whether the store had other obscene material. The magistrate signed a warrant that described copies of the two films that the investigator had obtained, but that listed no other items. With the help of state and local police and a local prosecutor, the magistrate went to the store and viewed various films and magazines and made determinations whether there was probable cause to believe they were obscene and subject to seizure. A unanimous Supreme Court, in an opinion by Chief Justice Burger, described the warrant as "reminiscent of the general warrant or writ of assistance of the 18th century." It held that the search procedure was invalid, because when the search began there was insufficient cause to believe that there was seizable material beyond the copies of the film purchased by the investigator. The Court was critical of the magistrate's allowing himself to become a member of the search party and held that he acted improperly when he found an item to be obscene in instructing the police to seize all "similar" items, since this left the officers with discretion to determine what was similar. Although the magistrate did not accompany the police on the *Zurcher* search, did he do enough to control police discretion?

After *Zurcher,* the Minnesota Supreme Court held that under the state constitution and the Fourth Amendment it was unreasonable for police to secure a warrant to search an attorney's office for records belonging to a client, unless the attorney also is suspected of wrongdoing or there is a threat of destruction of the records. O'Connor v. Johnson, 287 N.W.2d 400 (Minn.1979). Wisconsin has accomplished the same thing as Minnesota, but through legislation. Wis.Stat.Ann. § 968.13 (1979).

The problems of law office searches are fully discussed in Bloom, The Law Office Search: An Emerging Problem and Some Suggested Solutions, 69 Geo.L.J. 1 (1980). National City Trading Corp. v. United States, 635 F.2d 1020 (2d Cir.1980), illustrates how broad the search of an office can be: the court approved the search of a suite of rooms which were used for business purposes and as a lawyer's office.

In Klitzman, Klitzman & Gallagher v. Krut, 744 F.2d 955 (3d Cir.1984), the court affirmed an injunction requiring the return of documents and records seized at a law office pursuant to three search warrants. The warrants were directed at an attorney who was the target of an investigation into an alleged conspiracy to use the mails to defraud insurance companies in personal injury cases by submitting fraudulent medical reports and inflated medical bills. The court found that the search was overbroad and expressed concern for privileged material. It noted that no effort was made to protect privileged communications and that lawyers other than the one who was under investigation and their clients were affected by the search. In condemning the United States Attorney's office for affixing its imprimatur to "a rampant trampling of the attorney-client privilege," the court cited the guidelines that the Department of Justice has promulgated pursuant to the Privacy Protection Act. 28 C.F.R. §§ 59.1–59.6. Those guidelines forbid a search for documents against third parties unless the use of a less intrusive alternative appears to jeopardize substantially the availability or usefulness of the material sought.

Sections 220.2 and 220.5 of the ALI Model Code of Pre–Arraignment Procedure provide that a magistrate may direct that documents be impounded, not examined, by the police. Before the documents are examined, interested persons may seek to have them returned or to limit the scope of the search. This approach finds support in United States v. Tamura, 694 F.2d 591 (9th Cir.1982).

In the Privacy Protection Act of 1980, 42 U.S.C. § 200aa, Congress confined the application of *Zurcher.* Congress used its commerce power and regulated searches by government officers and employees (state or federal) of "a person reasonably believed to have a purpose to disseminate to the public a newspaper, book, broadcast, or other similar form of public communication, in or affecting interstate or foreign commerce." Government agents may not search for work product—i.e., materials, other than fruits or instrumentalities of crime that are prepared or created in anticipation of communicating information to the public in the possession of someone (whether or not she herself prepared it) who holds them for the purpose of public communications—unless (1) there is probable cause to believe that the person possessing the materials is involved in the crime to which the materials relate (except that probable cause is not enough to warrant a search if the offense consists only of possession, communication or withholding of the materials themselves, unless national security is involved); or (2) there is reason to believe that the immediate seizure of work product is necessary to prevent the death or serious bodily injury of a human being. Documents (including films, negatives and tapes) not qualifying as work product are subject to search under similar circumstances and also when there is reason to believe that giving notice by subpoena would result in the loss of the evidence or the documents have not been produced as ordered by a court and all appellate remedies have been exhausted, or there is reason to believe that further delay would threaten the interests of justice (although the possessor of the documents should be given an opportunity to respond here by affidavit).

Violation of the statute permits a suit for damages against the United States. States that have waived sovereign immunity may be sued, and state officers may be sued personally in states that retain their immunity. The damage action against the United States or state governments is an exclusive remedy (to encourage states to waive immunity to protect individual officers). Minimum damages of $1,000 must be awarded for violations. Attorneys' fees and other litigation costs also may be awarded to successful plaintiffs. An officer sued personally has a defense of good faith belief in the lawfulness of his conduct, but no governmental unit may assert the good faith of its officers (except for judicial officers) as a defense.

3. Reasonable Warrants

In *Zurcher,* Justice White leaves open the possibility that reasonableness is a limitation on searches even when probable cause exists. But he states that the Constitution should not be read to absolutely prohibit searches of third parties absent a showing that a subpoena would be inadequate to gather evidence. He also states that no one told the officers who executed the warrant that they might be reading confidential material. Why is this relevant? The magistrate who authorized the police search must have known that files of the newspaper were going to be examined and, therefore, that unpublished material might be viewed. Isn't the magistrate in an *ex parte* proceeding obliged to consider the likely impact of the police search on the person or organization at whom the warrant is directed?

Unless magistrates exercise some care in screening warrant affidavits and requests to search, the impact of Warden v. Hayden may be enormous.

Certain rules, like Fed.R.Crim.P. 41(c) provide that "[i]f the * * * magistrate * * * is satisfied that grounds for the application exist or that there is probable cause to believe that they exist, he shall issue a warrant identifying the property and naming or describing the person or place to be searched." Although the language appears to be mandatory, no matter how strong the showing of cause, a magistrate cannot issue a warrant that violates the reasonableness portion of the Fourth Amendment.

Most of the cases in which courts have hesitated to issue warrants despite the existence of probable cause involve medical procedures. A federal court granted an injunction in Lee v. Winston, 551 F.Supp. 247 (E.D.Va.1982), aff'd, 717 F.2d 888 (4th Cir.1983), to prevent a state from forcing a defendant to undergo surgery under a general anesthetic to remove a bullet lodged at least 2.5 to 3 centimeters beneath the surface of his skin. Justice Brennan wrote for the Court in Winston v. Lee, 470 U.S. 753 (1985), affirming the court of appeals. He noted that the medical risks of the operation were disputed and reasoned that the uncertainty militated against a finding that the operation was a reasonable search. Moreover, the Commonwealth failed to show a compelling need for the bullet, since it had substantial other evidence tying the defendant to the robbery and could offer evidence of the location of the bullet in the defendant's body. Chief Justice Burger added a one sentence concurrence which stated that he "read the Court's opinion as not preventing detention of an individual if there are reasonable grounds to believe that natural bodily functions will disclose the presence of contraband materials secreted internally." Justices Blackmun and Rehnquist concurred in the judgment without opinion. The Chief Justice's reading was proved correct in United States v. Montoya de Hernandez, 473 U.S. 531 (1985).

It is possible, in light of Supreme Court cases like *Lee,* Griswold v. Connecticut, 381 U.S. 479 (1965) (asking "[w]ould we allow the police to search the sacred precincts of marital bedrooms for telltale signs of the use of contraceptives?"), and Stanley v. Georgia, 394 U.S. 557 (1969) (private possession of obscene material in home constitutionally protected), and statutes like the Privacy Protection Act of 1980, that some magistrates might decline to issue warrants that would invade areas that traditionally have been regarded as off limits to the government.

4. *Breadth of an Authorized Seizure*

Little, if any, effort was expended by the Court in *Warden* and *Zurcher* to explain what it means to be able to seize evidence. Can anything be seized that would be relevant at trial? If so, rules like Federal Rule of Evidence 401, which defines relevant evidence as that "having any tendency to make the existence of any fact that is of consequence to the determination of the action more probable or less probable than it would be without the evidence," suggest that any evidence that sheds even the smallest light on a case could be seized, even if it were cumulative. As broad as this seizure power would be, it probably is not nearly as broad as what actually is permitted. Your knowledge of civil procedure is likely to include the fact that discovery in most jurisdictions is not limited to admissible evidence, but extends to any matter relevant to the subject matter of a dispute. See, e.g., Fed.R.Civ.P. 26(b)(1). Criminal discovery rules are much more limited. See, e.g., Fed.R.Crim.P. 16. Moreover, the privilege against self-incrimination is more likely to stand as a barrier to discovery attempts in criminal cases. Precisely because discovery is limited, the government relies on searches and seizures to gather as much evidence as possible. Hence, search warrants take on special importance in criminal cases as means of obtaining evidence prior to trial. They, like grand jury subpoenas, are substitutes for discovery, and like subpoenas, probably reach all evidence relevant to the subject matter of potential litigation, whether or not admissible at trial. Since searches take place before exact charges are filed—i.e., before the prosecution or grand jury specifies the charge or charges to be disposed of—the potential reach of a search warrant for evidence is enormous.

The breadth of possible searches makes the probable cause and specificity requirements of the warrant clause critical, if the magistrate is to limit "unreasonable" searches and seizures. Should the *Zurcher* Court be criticized for a lack of concern about probable cause as it related to the evidence sought and the place it might be found? In the following case, should the Court be criticized for a lack of concern about the specificity requirement?

ANDRESEN v. MARYLAND

Supreme Court of the United States, 1976.
427 U.S. 463.

MR. JUSTICE BLACKMUN delivered the opinion of the Court.

* * *

I

In early 1972, a Bi-County Fraud Unit, acting under the joint auspices of the State's Attorneys' Offices of Montgomery and Prince George's Counties, Md., began an investigation of real estate settlement activities in the Washington, D.C., area. At the time, petitioner Andresen was an attorney who, as a sole practitioner, specialized in real estate settlements in Montgomery County. During the Fraud Unit's investigation, his activities came under scrutiny, particularly in connection with a transaction involving Lot 13T in the Potomac Woods subdivision of Montgomery County. The investigation, which included interviews with the purchaser, the mortgage holder, and other lienholders of Lot 13T, as well as an examination of county land records, disclosed that petitioner, acting as settlement attorney, had defrauded Standard-Young Associates, the purchaser of Lot 13T. Petitioner had represented that the property was free of liens and that, accordingly, no title insurance was necessary, when in fact, he knew that there were two outstanding liens on the property. In addition, investigators learned that the lienholders, by threatening to foreclose their liens, had forced a halt to the purchaser's construction on the property. When Standard-Young had confronted petitioner with this information, he responded by issuing, as an agent of a title insurance company, a title policy guaranteeing clear title to the property. By this action, petitioner also defrauded that insurance company by requiring it to pay the outstanding liens.

The investigators * * * applied for warrants to search petitioner's law office and the separate office of Mount Vernon Development Corporation, of which petitioner was incorporator, sole shareholder, resident agent, and director. The application sought permission to search for specified documents pertaining to the sale and conveyance of Lot 13T. A judge of the Sixth Judicial Circuit of Montgomery County concluded that there was probable cause and issued the warrants.

The searches of the two offices were conducted simultaneously during daylight hours on October 31, 1972.[a] Petitioner was present during the search of his law office and was free to move about. Counsel for him was present during the latter half of the search. Between 2% and 3% of the files in the office were seized. A single investigator, in the presence of a police officer, conducted the search of Mount Vernon Development Corporation. This search, taking about four hours, resulted in the seizure of less than 5% of the corporation's files.

* * *

III

[Petitioner contends] that rights guaranteed him by the Fourth Amendment were violated because the descriptive terms of the search warrants were so broad as to make them impermissible "general" warrants, and because certain items were seized in violation of the principles of Warden v. Hayden, 387 U.S. 294 (1967).

The specificity of the search warrants. Although petitioner concedes that the warrants for the most part were models of particularity, he contends that they were rendered fatally "general" by the addition, in each warrant, to the exhaustive list of particularly described documents, of the phrase "together with other fruits, instrumentalities and evidence of crime at this [time] unknown." The quoted language, it is argued, must be read in isolation and without reference to the rest of the long sentence at the end of which it appears. When read "properly," petitioner contends, it permits the search for and seizure of any evidence of any crime.

* * *

In this case we agree with the determination of the Court of Special Appeals of Maryland that the challenged phrase must be read as authorizing only the search for and seizure of evidence relating to "the crime of false pretenses with respect to Lot 13T." 24 Md.App., at 167, 331 A.2d, at 103. The challenged phrase is not a separate sentence. Instead, it appears in each warrant at the end of a sentence containing a lengthy list of specified and particular items to be seized, all pertaining to Lot 13T.[b] We think it clear from the con-

a. Before these search warrants were executed, the Bi-County Fraud Unit had also received complaints concerning other Potomac Woods real estate transactions conducted by petitioner. The gist of the complaints was that petitioner, as settlement attorney, took money from three sets of home purchasers upon assurances that he would use it to procure titles to their properties free and clear of all encumbrances. It was charged that he had misappropriated the money so that they had not received clear title to the properties as promised.

b. "[T]he following items pertaining to sale, purchase, settlement and conveyance of lot 13, block T, Potomac Woods subdivision, Montgomery County, Maryland:

"title notes, title abstracts, title rundowns; contracts of sale and/or assignments from Raffaele Antonelli and Rocco Caniglia to Mount Vernon Development Corporation and/or others; lien payoff correspondence and lien payoff memoranda to and from lienholders and noteholders; correspondence and memoranda to and from trustees of deeds of trust; lenders instructions for a construction loan or construction and permanent loan; disbursement sheets and disbursement memoranda; checks, check stubs and ledger sheets indicating disbursement upon settlement; correspondence and memoranda concerning disbursements upon settlement; settlement statements and settlement memoranda; fully or partially prepared deed of trust releases, whether or not executed and whether or not recorded; books, records, documents, papers, memoranda and correspondence, showing or tending to show a fraudulent intent, and/or knowledge as elements of the crime of false pretenses, in violation of Article 27, Section 140, of the Annotated Code of Maryland, 1957 Edition, as amended and revised, together with other fruits, instrumentalities and evidence of crime at this [time] unknown."

Petitioner also suggests that the specific list of the documents to be seized constitutes a

text that the term "crime" in the warrants refers only to the crime of false pretenses with respect to the sale of Lot 13T. The "other fruits" clause is one of a series that follows the colon after the word "Maryland." All clauses in the series are limited by what precedes that colon, namely, "items pertaining to * * * lot 13, block T." The warrants, accordingly, did not authorize the executing officers to conduct a search for evidence of other crimes but only to search for and seize evidence relevant to the crime of false pretenses and Lot 13T.[c]

The admissibility of certain items of evidence in light of Warden v. Hayden. Petitioner charges that the seizure of documents pertaining to a lot other than Lot 13T violated the principles of Warden v. Hayden and therefore should have been suppressed. His objection appears to be that these papers were not relevant to the Lot 13T charge and were admissible only to prove another crime with which he was charged after the search. The fact that these documents were used to help form the evidentiary basis for another charge, it is argued, shows that the documents were seized solely for that purpose.

The State replies that Warden v. Hayden was not violated and that this is so because the challenged evidence is relevant to the question whether petitioner committed the crime of false pretenses with respect to Lot 13T. In Maryland, the crime is committed when a person makes a false representation of a past or existing fact, with intent to defraud and knowledge of its falsity, and obtains any chattel, money, or valuable security from another, who relies on the false representation to his detriment. Thus, the State is required to prove intent to defraud beyond a reasonable doubt. The State consequently argues that the documents pertaining to another lot in the Potomac Woods subdivision demonstrate that the misrepresentation with respect to Lot 13T was not the result of mistake on the part of petitioner.

In Warden v. Hayden, the Court stated that when the police seize " 'mere evidence,' probable cause must be examined in terms of cause to believe that the evidence sought will aid in a particular apprehension or conviction. In so doing, consideration of police purposes will be required." In this case, we conclude that the trained special investigators reasonably could have believed that the evidence specifically dealing with another lot in the Potomac Woods

"general" warrant. We disagree. Under investigation was a complex real estate scheme whose existence could be proved only by piecing together many bits of evidence. Like a jigsaw puzzle, the whole "picture" of petitioner's false-pretense scheme with respect to Lot 13T could be shown only by placing in the proper place the many pieces of evidence that, taken singly, would show comparatively little. The complexity of an illegal scheme may not be used as a shield to avoid detection when the State has demonstrated probable cause to believe that a crime has been committed and probable cause to believe that evidence of this crime is in the suspect's possession.

c. The record discloses that the officials executing the warrants seized numerous papers that were not introduced into evidence. Although we are not informed of their content, we observe that to the extent such papers were not within the scope of the warrants or were otherwise improperly seized, the State was correct in returning them voluntarily and the trial judge was correct in suppressing others.

We recognize that there are grave dangers inherent in executing a warrant authorizing a search and seizure of a person's papers that are not necessarily present in executing a warrant to search for physical objects whose relevance is more easily ascertainable. In searches for papers, it is certain that some innocuous documents will be examined, at least cursorily, in order to determine whether they are, in fact among those papers authorized to be seized. Similar dangers, of course, are present in executing a warrant for the "seizure" of telephone conversations. In both kinds of searches, responsible officials, including judicial officials, must take care to assure that they are conducted in a manner that minimizes unwarranted intrusions upon privacy.

subdivision could be used to show petitioner's intent with respect to the Lot 13T transaction.

* * * In the present case, when the special investigators secured the search warrants, they had been informed of a number of similar charges against petitioner arising out of Potomac Woods transactions. And, by reading numerous documents and records supplied by the Lot 13T and other complainants, and by interviewing witnesses, they had become familiar with petitioner's method of operation. Accordingly, the relevance of documents pertaining specifically to a lot other than Lot 13T, and their admissibility to show the Lot 13T offense, would have been apparent. Lot 13T and the other lot had numerous features in common. Both were in the same section of the Potomac Woods subdivision; both had been owned by the same person; and transactions concerning both had been handled extensively by petitioner. Most important was the fact that there were two deeds of trust in which both lots were listed as collateral. Unreleased liens respecting both lots were evidenced by these deeds of trusts. Petitioner's transactions relating to the other lot, subject to the same liens as Lot 13T, therefore, were highly relevant to the question whether his failure to deliver title to Lot 13T free of all encumbrances was mere inadvertence. Although these records subsequently were used to secure additional charges against petitioner, suppression of this evidence in this case was not required. The fact that the records could be used to show intent to defraud with respect to Lot 13T permitted the seizure and satisfied the requirements of Warden v. Hayden.

* * *

MR. JUSTICE BRENNAN, dissenting.

* * *

II

[T]he warrants under which those papers were seized were impermissibly general. General warrants are specially prohibited by the Fourth Amendment. * * *

The Court recites these requirements, [of the Fourth Amendment's warrant Clause] but their application in this case renders their limitation on unlawful governmental conduct an empty promise. After a lengthy and admittedly detailed listing of items to be seized, the warrants in this case further authorized the seizure of "other fruits, instrumentalities and evidence of crime at this [time] unknown." The Court construes this sweeping authorization to be limited to evidence pertaining to the crime of false pretenses with respect to the sale of Lot 13T. However, neither this Court's construction of the warrants nor the similar construction by the Court of Special Appeals of Maryland was available to the investigators at the time they executed the warrants. The question is not how those warrants are to be viewed in hindsight, but how they were in fact viewed by those executing them. The overwhelming quantity of seized material that was either suppressed or returned to petitioner is irrefutable testimony to the unlawful generality of the warrants. The Court's attempt to cure this defect by *post hoc* judicial construction evades principles settled in this Court's Fourth Amendment decisions. * * *

[Justice Marshall also dissented, agreeing with Justice Brennan's Fourth Amendment analysis.]

Note

Justice Blackmun reads the last portion of the *Andresen* warrant as authorizing the police "only to search for and seize evidence relevant to the crime of false pretenses and Lot 13T." Justice Brennan complains that the police reasonably believed the warrant was broader and authorized a search for evidence of other crimes. If a warrant is drafted in such a way that it is subject to two readings, one which would render it valid and another which would invalidate it, should a reviewing court adopt the reading that the police give the warrant, or the reading that the reviewing court believes that the magistrate, presumed to be acting constitutionally, intended? Which approach is more in line with the goals of the Fourth Amendment? Arguably, Justice Brennan failed to address adequately the important problems with the majority opinion. Assuming that the majority's reading of the warrant is correct, the majority is holding that it is acceptable for a magistrate to authorize the search for and seizure of any and all evidence that relates to a particular crime. There would appear to be problems of the absence of a showing of probable cause to believe such additional evidence exists and might be found in the place to be searched, of the total absence of particularity, and of the impossibility once such a warrant is issued that the magistrate can review, before it occurs, a wholesale seizure of anything that might in any way touch upon a case. What kind of screening is this? Could a magistrate in the next *Andresen*—type case issue a warrant devoid of any particulars and simply order the seizure of "all fruits, instrumentalities and evidence" of a crime? If not, why should the magistrate be able to add such an order to a particularized warrant? Notice that if all of the particular papers described in the warrant were found in Andresen's office in a single file folder, the last clause of the warrant still would justify a search of the remainder of the office.

The majority opinion engages in some nice sleight of hand to mask another problem with the warrant. The majority first holds that the last portion of the warrant was limited to evidence concerning Lot 13T. Then it proceeds to argue later that evidence of other crimes was relevant to showing intent regarding Lot 13T. Although this might be a permissible use of other crime evidence at trial, what justified a police officer in looking for such evidence during a search? Was there probable cause to believe that specific other crime evidence existed? The majority put its imprimatur on a warrant that let the police decide what discovery to engage in. Isn't this the magistrate's task under the warrant clause of the Fourth Amendment?

Some courts have been more demanding than *Andresen.* See, e.g., United States v. Abrams, 615 F.2d 541 (1st Cir. 1980) (warrant for "certain business and medical records of patients * * * showing actual medical services performed and fraudulent services claimed to have been performed" is not particular enough); Application of Lafayette Academy, 610 F.2d 1 (1st Cir. 1979) (invalidating warrant for all books and papers relating to designated statutes); United States v. Cardwell, 680 F.2d 75 (9th Cir. 1982) (similar to *Lafayette Academy*); Kinsey v. State, 602 P.2d 240 (Okl.Cr.App.) (holding search warrant language "and other stolen property" invalid as "general warrant"); Walthall v. State, 594 S.W.2d 74 (Tex.Cr.App.1980) (phrases "all items of personal property commonly used in commission of a criminal offense" and "all implements used in the commission of a crime" were too vague).

In re Search Warrant Dated July 4, 1977, 667 F.2d 117 (D.C.Cir. 1981), rejected a district court's finding that a search warrant was impermissibly broad. It also rejected the lower court's ruling that when officers exceed the bounds of a warrant all evidence seized must be suppressed. It cited *Andresen* for the proposition that only extraneous items must be suppressed; designated items need not be. Similarly, in LeBron v. Vitek, 751 F.2d 311 (8th Cir. 1985) the court "affirmed the concept of severability" and held that an item seized pursuant to a particularized clause in a warrant was properly admitted at trial, even though other items were improperly seized pursuant to a clause allowing seizure of "records and other stolen property."

In United States v. Strand, 761 F.2d 449 (8th Cir.1985) postal inspectors suspected that Strand, a mail carrier, was stealing items from the mail. They obtained a warrant authorizing the seizure of "stolen mail" from Strand's house. The court held that some items seized from Strand's home were legally obtained, others illegally obtained. The court explained as follows:

> We believe that the term "stolen mail" is sufficiently definite to enable a postal inspector to identify and seize items which clearly fit within such a generic class, such as letters and parcels, neither addressed to nor sent by the person whose property is being searched, bearing postage stamps or marks. A search for "stolen mail" does not, however, permit the seizure of items which do not fit into the generic category. Many of the items seized in the present case under the rubric of stolen mail were not found in parcels of mail, and included items such as socks, a sweatshirt, cosmetics, a sweater, a thermometer, a china plate, and gloves; * * *

Has the court in *Strand* given the searching officers too much or too little discretion to determine whether an item constitutes "stolen mail"?

In connection with Warden v. Hayden's expansion of the type of things which can be seized, and the crucial role of the particularity requirement after *Warden,* consider the dissenting opinion of Judge Weinstein, sitting on a panel of the Second Circuit, in United States v. Riley, 906 F.2d 841 (2d Cir.1990). The majority in *Riley* held that a locker rental agreement was properly seized under the portion of the warrant listing "other items that constitute evidence of the offenses of conspiracy to distribute controlled substances." Judge Weinstein objected that such "boilerplate language * * * gives police officers carte blanche to search every nook and cranny of a home from basement to attic; to examine every item, including clothing, linens and the like, to open and rifle every closet, cabinet, drawer, briefcase and piece of luggage; to remove bedding, carpets, floors and walls; to seize garbage and the residue in plumbing drains, and to read every book and piece of paper." Judge Weinstein argued that the particularity requirement should be vigorously enforced in light of Warden v. Hayden, and especially in light of technological advancement in forensic techniques. He explained as follows:

> The increasing sensitivity and sophistication of forensic science means that almost any object in a person's house could provide evidence of drug activity and be the subject of seizure under the warrant and search procedures allowed by the majority. Because of these scientific advances, it has become even more necessary than heretofore to forcefully uphold the Fourth Amendment's protections against general searches and seizures.
>
> Under the warrant in this case as interpreted by the majority, all cash would be subject to seizure since bills would have to be examined for markings or contact with drugs. Kitchen utensils might have residues if used in the mixing of drugs. Baggies, saran wrap and garbage bags might be used in the packaging and transportation of drugs. Any table or desk and the floor under it might contain a trace of drugs spilled if the surface was used for cutting, weighing or packaging. If cocaine was free-based or marijuana or other drugs smoked, there might be residue on the walls. All of these items could be seized and brought to the laboratory for analysis since present techniques allow the detection of minute traces of drugs invisible to the naked eye and undetectable by the most sensitive olfactory organs of man or dog. See, e.g., Neilson & Katz, A Processing Protocol for Drug Residue and Latent Print Evidence, 33 J.

Forensic Sci. 1463 (1988) (describing method of detecting cocaine residue and latent fingerprints on a variety of surfaces). * * *

Furniture, carpeting and parts of the walls could also be removed, both to detect drug residues, and in an effort to prove that drugs seized elsewhere were once stored in the house, by linking the residues to the drugs seized, see, e.g. United States v. Kelly, 420 F.2d 26 (2d Cir.1969) (technique of neutron activation analysis, used to link drugs found in two different locations, is sufficiently reliable), or by linking minute particles of foreign objects such as fibers or paint chips found on drugs to objects in the house. See, e.g., Williams v. State, 251 Ga. 749, 312 S.E.2d 40 (1983) (allowing expert evidence linking fibers in defendant's home to fibers found on homicide victims); People v. Mackins, 17 Ill.App.3d 24, 308 N.E.2d 92 (1st Dist., 1st Div.1974) (allowing expert evidence of laser emission spectroscopy to identify paint fragments, linking defendant's car to crime scene).

The sheets on the bed could be taken to the laboratory because hair, blood, semen or saliva stains found there could be analyzed to show use of narcotics. * * * Razors in the bathroom, tops of vanities, portions of the floor and the residue of drains might also lead to hair or other organic material that could evidence drug use.

Residues of blood and semen (and possibly hair and saliva) could be subjected to DNA analysis that might show the presence and identities of people other than the defendant. In this way, other people might be implicated in a conspiracy by their connection with the defendant, or, if these other people were known to law enforcement officials as drug dealers, the defendant might be further compromised. Growing data banks will ultimately permit DNA evidence to be used like a giant data bank to determine involvement in similar crimes. * * *

The house could be swept for fingernail clippings, since their uniqueness could be used as evidence of the presence of a particular individual. See State v. Shaw, 124 Wis.2d 363, 369 N.W.2d 772 (Ct.App.1985) (allowing such evidence); * * *.

Any object in the house could be seized as possibly containing fingerprints identifying the presence of specific people. See, e.g. United States v. Giese, 597 F.2d 1170, 1184–85 (9th Cir.) (fingerprints of several individuals on a book owned by defendant used as evidence of conspiracy). Modern fluorescence techniques, using new reagents and illumination by laser light, permit the examination of latent fingerprints on almost any surface, from paper or plastic to human skin. See e.g., People v. Eyler, 133 Ill.2d 173, 549 N.E.2d 268 (1989) (admitting fingerprint evidence produced by cyanoacrylate esters ("super-glue") method).

Cosmetics or any object with traces of cosmetics could be seized and analyzed in order to link the cosmetics to that possessed or worn by a particular person, thus demonstrating that person's presence in the house. See Keagy, Examinations of Cosmetic Smudges Including Transesterification and Gas Chromatographic/Mass Spectrometric Analysis, 28 J. Forensic Sci. 623 (1983) (describing method for determining common source of traces of cosmetics).

Such developments may sound like science fiction, but they are becoming standard forensic techniques. The appeal of scientific theory and technology is so great that once these methods are developed they are almost certain to be used. * * *

The way to protect against potentially limitless searches and seizures is to follow the words of the Fourth Amendment. A warrant must be narrowly drawn. The items specified must be keyed to detailed and specific information contained in an affidavit presented to the magistrate that is the product of good investigative work. Vague general language, or exhaustive lists of everything in a house that might conceivably be of assistance to investigators must not be tolerated.

5. *Details of the Warrant*

Section 220.2(2) of the ALI Model Code of Pre-Arraignment Procedure sets forth all of the things supposedly particularized in the warrant itself.

Section 220.2. Contents of Search Warrant

(1) **Date and Address.** A search warrant issued pursuant to [this Code] shall be dated, and shall be addressed to and authorize its execution by an officer authorized by law to execute search warrants issued by the issuing authority.

(2) **Scope of Contents.** The warrant shall state, or describe with particularity:

(a) the identity of the issuing authority, and the date when and place where application for the warrant was made;

(b) the identity of the applicant and all persons whose affidavits were submitted in support of the application;

(c) the issuing authority's finding of sufficiency of the application and of reasonable cause for issuance of the warrant;

(d) the identity of the individual to be searched, and the location and designation of the places to be searched;

(e) the individuals or things constituting the object of the search and authorized to be seized;

(f) the times of day or night and the period of time during which execution of the warrant is authorized; and

(g) the period of time, not to exceed five days, after execution of the warrant, within which the warrant is to be returned to the issuing authority.

The date on which a warrant is sought is important, since stale information may result in a finding of no probable cause. See United States v. Harris, 403 U.S. 573 (1971); Henry v. State, 373 A.2d 575 (Del.1977). Deciding when information is stale may require careful attention to the nature of the evidence sought. In United States v. Beltempo, 675 F.2d 472 (2d Cir. 1982), a search warrant was issued on April 1, 1981 to search an apartment for heroin traces and heroin related equipment that an informant said were present on February 7, 1981. Since the affidavit supporting the warrant did not indicate that there was a continuing offense occurring, the court was faced with the question whether the warrant was based on stale information. Unwilling to adopt any arbitrary "cut-off" for warrants, the court concluded that the heroin traces that the affidavit indicated had fallen into a rug were small enough that they were not likely to have been removed and that the equipment was not the kind that ordinarily would have been washed or cleaned. Thus, it upheld the warrant.

See also United States v. Lamon, 930 F.2d 1183 (7th Cir.1991) (where informant stated that defendant sold cocaine out of his residence, had an ounce remaining 72 hours earlier, and that defendant also sold drugs out of his car, the information was not stale, since it suggested a pattern of ongoing drug activity).

The requirement that affiants be disclosed does not require that the names of informants be revealed. It is included so that the person served can decide whether to challenge the warrant and is, therefore, not really a limitation on searches and seizures. The Commentary to § 220.2, at 512, states that "[u]pon occasion, a warrant is applied for on the basis of an affidavit signed with a fictitious name. Recent decisions holding warrants so issued to be constitutionally defective are clearly correct under the 'oath or affirmation' requirement of the Fourth Amendment." The warrant must indicate that the magistrate has found the supporting application to be sufficient. Can you see why this is required? Individuals and things to be searched and seized, the times when service is authorized and the time for the return are all to be specified. Time limits on execution are often found in statutes or court rules.

Fed.R.Crim.P. 41(c) places the following restriction on a search warrant.

> It shall command the officer to search, within a specified period of time not to exceed 10 days, the person or place named for the property specified. The warrant shall be served in the daytime, unless the issuing authority, by appropriate provision in the warrant, and for reasonable cause shown, authorizes its execution at times other than daytime. It shall designate a federal magistrate to whom it shall be returned.

Daytime means the hours from 6:00 a.m. to 10:00 p.m. according to local time. Fed.R.Crim.P. 41(h).

Slightly less than half of the states restrict the execution of searches to daylight hours absent special circumstances. There is, however, some trend toward relaxing the requirement. See Commentary to § 220.2(3) of the ALI Model Code of Pre-Arraignment Procedure, at 512–13. In Gooding v. United States, 416 U.S. 430 (1974), the Court held that a federal statute governing searches for "controlled substances" and authorizing execution of a warrant at any time of the day or night "if the * * * magistrate * * * is satisfied that there is probable cause to believe that grounds exist for the warrant and for its service at such time" controlled the search in question, rather than a District of Columbia Code provision requiring a special showing of need to justify a search at night. The Court concluded that the federal statute "requires no special showing for a nighttime search, other than a showing that the contraband is likely to be on the property or person to be searched at that time." Justice Marshall's dissenting opinion, joined by Justices Douglas and Brennan, argued that "there is no expectation of privacy more reasonable and more demanding of constitutional protection than our right to expect that we will be let alone in the privacy of our homes during the night." He suggested that the majority's interpretation of the statute raised a substantial constitutional question (one not argued to the Court). Is there support, either in the history or the policies of the Fourth Amendment, for a constitutional rule forbidding nighttime searches, except in special circumstances?

In describing the place or person to be searched, the warrant should be as specific as possible. For example, "[f]or purposes of the Fourth Amendment, two or more apartments in the same building stand on the same footing as two or more houses. A single warrant cannot describe an entire building when cause is shown for searching only one apartment." Moore v. United States, 461 F.2d 1236, 1238 (D.C.Cir. 1972). Accord, State v. Gordon, 221 Kan. 253, 559 P.2d 312 (1977).[9] In rural areas, less particularized descriptions may be reasonable due to the absence of street addresses. In some cases, warrants have misdescribed an address, especially where the residence is on a corner. For example, in Lyons v. Robinson, 783 F.2d 737 (8th Cir. 1985), the warrant listed the place to be searched as 325 Adkinson Street; Lyons' residence was actually 325 Short Street, on the corner of Short and Adkinson. The court stated that the test for determining the sufficiency of the description of the place to be searched is whether the warrant enables "the executing officer to locate and identify the premises with reasonable effort, and whether there is any reasonable probability that another premises might be mistakenly searched." Can you see why, under that test, the court in *Lyons* found the warrant sufficiently particular?

An arrest warrant must describe the person to be seized with sufficient particularity. Does the fact that the officers have probable cause to arrest a person mean that the person can be specifically described? Is a warrant authorizing the arrest of "John Doe a/k/a Ed" sufficiently particular? The court in United States v. Doe, 703 F.2d 745 (3d Cir. 1983) held that such a warrant was overbroad, and held further that the insufficient description was not cured by the fact that the officer who executed the warrant had independent personal knowledge that the arrestee was the person for whom the warrant was intended. Why doesn't the officer's personal knowledge solve the problem? Would the warrant have been sufficiently particular if it described "John Doe, a/k/a Ed, a white male six feet tall and 200 pounds"?

Regarding the things to be seized, one commentator has suggested that "[t]he nature of the property will often give some indication as to how detailed a description is necessary." LaFave, Search and Seizure, The Course of True Law * * * Has Not * * * Run Smooth, 1966 U.Ill.L.For. 255, 268. Some property may by its very nature be described generally. "But, if the items sought are of a kind generally found in various places, then there is a need to be more specific." Id. See United States v. Fuccillo, 808 F.2d 173 (1st Cir.1987) (warrant to seize "stolen clothing" held insufficiently particular where officers were given a detailed list of the articles stolen before applying for the warrant). If police discover seizable items not listed in the warrant during the course of executing it, they may seize those items pursuant to the plain view rule, discussed infra.

Can government agents obtain an "anticipatory" search warrant conditioned upon future events which, if fulfilled, would create probable cause? The court in United States v. Garcia, 882 F.2d 699 (2d Cir.1989) found such a warrant valid. The warrant in *Garcia* was issued before cocaine was delivered to the house to be searched. Execution of the warrant was contingent upon the

9. If the police reasonably believe that a building is one living unit, but it actually is more than one, a warrant to search the entire building still may be valid. The Supreme Court held in Maryland v. Garrison, 480 U.S. 79 (1987), that a search warrant satisfied that particularity requirement when it was issued to police officers who reasonably believed, at the time they applied for and executed the warrant, that one apartment occupied the entire third floor of a building. Later the officers learned that they had actually searched two apartments.

delivery of cocaine by two designated messengers. The court found itself presented with the following choice:

> whether the objective of the Fourth Amendment is better served by allowing an agent to obtain a warrant in advance of the delivery, or whether it is better served by forcing him to go to the scene without a warrant, and, if necessary, proceed under the constraints of the exigent circumstances exception, subject always to the risk of being second-guessed by judicial authorities at a later date as to whether the known facts legally justified the search.

In essence the court found that the anticipatory warrant was better than no warrant at all. The court noted, however, that to be valid, the warrant must set forth explicit conditions to limit the discretion of the officers in determining whether the triggering event has occurred. Many other lower courts have upheld anticipatory warrants. See the thorough discussion in Adams, Anticipatory Search Warrants: Constitutionality, Requirements, and Scope, 79 Ky. L.J. 681 (1991). Is an anticipatory warrant consistent with the theory of the warrant clause?

One of the most difficult problems for the courts has been the scope of the search of the property of persons who happen to be on the premises to be searched under a warrant. One of the most useful analytical approaches is found in United States v. Micheli, 487 F.2d 429, 430–32 (1st Cir. 1973). The opinion analyses the search issue in terms of a person's relationship to a place. If a person has a special relationship to a place so that "it could reasonably be expected that some of his belongings would be there," then a warrant includes the property of such a person. A warrant would not reach the property of someone who visits the premises infrequently, but who happens to be present at the time of a search.[10] Some courts focus on whether property is in the physical possession of a person, in which case it cannot be searched. See e.g., United States v. Robertson, 833 F.2d 777 (9th Cir. 1987) (shoulder bag carried by visitor not covered by warrant authorizing the search of premises and curtilage).

C. EXECUTING THE WARRANT

1. *Notice of Purpose and Authority*

As noted above, it is common for statutes or court rules to regulate the execution of a warrant. Typical of these statutes is 18 U.S.C.A. § 3109.

> The officer may break open any outer or inner door or window of a house, or any part of a house, or anything therein, to execute a search warrant, if, after

10. Although this is one of the rare judicial efforts to harmonize law enforcement and privacy interests, is it successful? Are police officers who execute warrants capable of making the determination required by the court? Would it be better to adopt a different rule: to wit, police officers may search any property that is found on the premises described in a warrant except property that they have reason to believe has been deposited on the premises after the warrant was issued; but property deposited after a warrant issued may be searched if, at the time the warrant is sought, the police demonstrate probable cause to believe that specifically identified property not presently on the premises will be found there at the time they expect to execute the warrant and this property is included in the warrant. Such a test would turn on what the magistrate authorized, not on whether the person whose property was searched had a permanent tie to the searched premises. Which approach is better? The Supreme Court held 6–3 in Ybarra v. Illinois, 444 U.S. 85 (1979), that police executing a search warrant cannot automatically frisk persons found at the premises to be searched.

> notice of his authority and purpose, he is refused admittance or when necessary to liberate himself or a person aiding him in the execution of the warrant.

The statute provides that an officer can break open premises if he has announced his authority and purpose and is refused admission. "The rule seems to require notice in the form of an express announcement by the officers of their purpose for demanding admission." Miller v. United States, 357 U.S. 301 (1958). But refusal of admittance may be implied under various circumstances. See, e.g., United States v. Allende, 486 F.2d 1351 (9th Cir. 1973).

In Miller v. United States, supra, the government conceded that 18 U.S.C.A. § 3109 applied to entries into premises to effect an arrest as well as to execute a search warrant. But the question whether the announcement (or notice) rule was constitutionally required was not decided in that case. The issue arose in Ker v. California, 374 U.S. 23 (1963). The context, as in *Miller,* was a warrantless arrest, not execution of a search warrant, but there is no reason to believe the opinion would have been different if a warrant had been involved. California had a statute like the federal statute, but it permitted an exception from the notice requirement in exigent circumstances. Justice Clark, writing for himself and Justices Black, Stewart and White addressed the question "whether, notwithstanding its legality under state law, the method of entering the home may offend federal constitutional standards of reasonableness and therefore vitiate the legality of an accompanying search." After stating the question he wrote that

> [W]e find no such offensiveness on the facts here. * * * [I]t has been recognized from the early common law that such breaking is permissible in executing an arrest under certain circumstances. See Wilgus, Arrest Without a Warrant, 22 Mich.L.Rev. 541, 798, 800–806 (1924). Indeed, 18 U.S.C.A. § 3109, dealing with the execution of search warrants by federal officers, authorizes breaking of doors in words very similar to those of the California statute, both statutes including a requirement of notice of authority and purpose.

He went on to write as follows:

> Here justification for the officers' failure to give notice is uniquely present. In addition to the officers' belief that Ker was in possession of narcotics, which could be quickly and easily destroyed, Ker's furtive conduct in eluding them shortly before the arrest was ground for the belief that he might well have been expecting the police. We therefore hold that in the particular circumstances of this case the officers' method of entry, sanctioned by the law of California, was not unreasonable under the standards of the Fourth Amendment as applied to the States through the Fourteenth Amendment.

Justice Harlan provided the fifth vote to affirm the California courts' judgment with respect to the search. He concurred in the result, however, because he, alone on the Court, did not believe that the Fourth Amendment bound the states. Justice Brennan, joined by Chief Justice Warren, and Justices Douglas and Goldberg, dissented. Part of that opinion follows:

> Even if probable cause exists for the arrest of a person within, the Fourth Amendment is violated by an unannounced police intrusion into a private home, with or without an arrest warrant, except (1) where the persons within already know of the officers' authority and purpose, or (2) where the officers are justified in the belief that persons within are in imminent peril of bodily harm, or (3) where those within, made aware of the presence of someone

outside (because, for example, there has been a knock at the door), are then engaged in activity which justifies the officers in the belief that an escape or the destruction of evidence is being attempted.

Justice Brennan went on to disagree with Justice Clark's conclusion that the facts of the case supported invocation of the exception to prevent destruction of evidence.

Were there five votes in *Ker* for the proposition that the Fourth Amendment requires notice before premises are forcibly entered to effect an arrest or search? Arguably, there were eight. The problem is that Justice Clark's opinion did not explicitly state his support for the proposition. Absence of an explicit statement has caused some courts to conclude that "[a] careful reading of the opinions in *Ker* reveals that the majority of the court did not address whether the Constitution itself required police to announce their authority and purpose." People v. Wolgemuth, 69 Ill.2d 154, 13 Ill.Dec. 40, 370 N.E.2d 1067 (1977). Some courts even cite Justice Clark's opinion as holding that "[e]ntry without prior announcement does not render a search unreasonable under the fourth amendment, * * * nor is compliance with the rule mandated by any other provision of the federal constitution." State v. Anonymous, 34 Conn.Sup. 531, 375 A.2d 417 (1977). Other courts have had no difficulty in reading *Ker* as establishing a Fourth Amendment rule at the same time that it recognized exceptions. See, e.g., United States v. Price, 441 F.Supp. 814 (E.D.Ark.1977). Whether or not *Ker* decided the point, a number of state courts have adopted the view that the approach of the federal statute is a good definition of a reasonable execution of a warrant. See, e.g., Commonwealth v. Newman, 429 Pa. 441, 240 A.2d 795 (1968). And a number of states, as noted above, have statutes or rules that mirror the federal law.

Generally, the burden of establishing a prima facie claim that the notice rule has been violated is on a defendant. United States v. Murrie, 534 F.2d 695 (6th Cir. 1976). In United States v. Mueller, 902 F.2d 336 (5th Cir. 1990) the court stated that the defendant must establish a prima facie case that entry was unannounced. In *Mueller,* defendant averred that at the time of entry, he was sleeping on the other side of the house, and that he would have heard the officers knock if they had done so. The court found that this assertion was not enough to establish a prima facie case; even though the state offered no affirmative evidence of knocking, defendant had not met his burden of going forward. For a description of opinions analyzing the notice rule in various circumstances, see Annot., What Constitutes Compliance with Knock-and-Announce Rules in Search of Private Premises—State Cases, 70 ALR 3d 217 (1976).

2. *Exceptions to the Notice Rule*

If the door to a residence is already open, are police required to announce their presence before entering? In United States v. Remigio, 767 F.2d 730 (10th Cir.1985) the court held that such conduct was not a "breaking" so that the knock and announce statute was inapplicable. The court noted that this was the majority view. See also United States v. Salter, 815 F.2d 1150 (7th Cir.1987) (police officers' action in inducing defendant to unlock and partially open her door by means of a ruse, and forcefully preventing the door from being closed, did not constitute a "breaking").

Section 220.3(3) of the ALI Model Code of Pre-Arraignment Procedure provides that "[i]f the executing officer has reasonable cause to believe that the notice * * * would endanger the successful execution of the warrant with all practicable safety, the officer may execute the warrant without such prior notice." The Commentary to the section, at 514, states that "[g]oods not, in an objective sense, easily destroyed or disposed of, may in fact be in danger of such handling as will frustrate successful execution of the warrant." This explains the choice of the standard.

Notice that the Code makes a judgment that the executing officers, not the magistrate, should decide whether to dispense with notice. Compare this approach with that prescribed in State v. Lien, 265 N.W.2d 833 (Minn.1978) (magistrate should decide).

After *Ker* the courts have held that the emergency circumstances which excuse the knock and announce requirement are determined by the same standards that govern whether exigent circumstances exist to excuse the warrant requirement. See e.g. United States v. Ramirez, 770 F.2d 1458 (9th Cir.1985) (officer had reasonable fear that if he announced his presence he would put himself and others in physical peril); United States v. Tracy, 835 F.2d 1267 (8th Cir.1988) (reasonable fear that announcement would cause evidence to be destroyed). The knock and announce requirement is also excused if facts known to the officers justify them in assuming that the persons in the home already know the officers' purpose. Id.

3. *No-Knock Laws*

One of the most controversial notice statutes ever enacted involved approval of entry without notice by a magistrate. D.C.Code § 23–591(c), which was popularly (or unpopularly) known as the "no-knock" law prior to repeal in 1974, authorized magistrates to issue warrants authorizing "breaking and entry without * * * prior announcement" even though exigent circumstances were not shown. Its federal counterpart, 21 U.S.C.A. § 879, was more limited.

During the debate on the repealer, constitutional and practical problems were discussed. Ultimately, the view that prevailed was that expressed by Senator Bayh, 120 Cong.Rec. 35904 (Oct. 16, 1974):

> [T]he marginal utility of the no-knock provisions is outweighed by the grave dangers which they pose to the fundamental and constitutionally guaranteed right to privacy. Recent reports have documented how Government agents have broken into the homes of, and terrorized, unsuspecting and even innocent individuals. These reports have also documented how the mere existence of the no-knock authority can breed an attitude which leads to Government agents placing themselves above the law.
>
> By repealing the no-knock provisions, our report would leave intact the constitutional and common law principles concerning Government searches. Under those principles, as noted above, the no-knock searches would be permitted but only when exigent circumstances become known to Government agents immediately prior to their contemplated search.

4. *Timing and Scope of Execution*

It is frequently the case that statutes or rules of court define a time period in which a warrant must be served. Some courts hold that the exact time of execution within that period should be left to the officer's discretion. See, e.g., State v. Morgan, 222 Kan. 149, 563 P.2d 1056 (1977). However, delay may leave officers unable to execute their warrant if intervening circumstances negate the previous showing of probable cause. See United States v. Nepstead, 424 F.2d 269 (9th Cir. 1970).

In view of the number of search and seizure cases that have been decided, it is surprising that few have discussed the permissible latitude that officers have in executing a warrant. Clearly they can only look in places where the objects specified might be found. But can they break open walls, tear up floors and ceilings and inflict other permanent damage? The case law, most of it old, offers little guidance. One case which contains a helpful discussion is Buckley v. Beaulieu, 104 Me. 56, 71 A. 70 (1908), where the court held that officers acted excessively and unreasonably when they searched unsuccessfully for liquor by tearing out the interior walls of a house. The court noted that the officers could have searched for any liquor concealed within the walls by using "some slender probe with comparatively little injury."

In a civil rights action against police officers and others, the court reasoned in Tarpley v. Greene, 684 F.2d 1 (D.C. Cir. 1982), that officers could be held liable if they damaged property as a result of unreasonable conduct in executing a warrant. Reasonableness must be determined by looking at the facts of each case, including the scope of the warrant. The court noted that officers may not remain on premises once a search is concluded and they must avoid unnecessary damage to premises.

If a search is likely to result in damage to property, should officers executing the warrant have the authority to decide how far they should go in conducting a search? Or should they have to seek special permission from a magistrate before damaging property? See State v. Thisius, 281 N.W.2d 645 (Minn.1978) ("[t]he ultimate test is one of reasonableness"). One state supreme court recognized in Langford v. Superior Court, 43 Cal.3d 21, 233 Cal.Rptr. 387, 729 P.2d 822 (1987), the possible role of a magistrate in deciding whether police should be permitted to engage in searches that threaten to damage property. The court held that a motorized battering ram used to enter dwellings was so destructive that it infringed on occupants' and owners' rights to be secure against unreasonable searches and seizures. No use of the battering ram was permitted unless approved by a magistrate who would determine whether the ram could be used with relative safety against a particular building if the need arose. If the magistrate approved the use of the ram, officers on the scene would have to determine whether an exigency required its use.

Should officers be required to conduct searches in the presence of the owner or possessor of property, unless it would be unduly burdensome for them to do so? Most courts recognize the advisability of such a procedure. See, e.g., State v. Jacques, 2 Kan.App.2d 277, 579 P.2d 146 (1978). But most also hold that it is not a necessary one. See, e.g. United States v. Gervato, 474 F.2d 40 (3d Cir. 1973).

Must the officer who executes a search warrant actually have the warrant in hand at the time of the search? Courts have held that while Fed.R.Crim.P. 41(d) requires the officer to serve upon the person searched a copy of the warrant, it does not require that this be done before the search takes place. See e.g. United States v. Bonner, 808 F.2d 864 (1st Cir.1986); United States v. Hepperle, 810 F.2d 836, 839 (8th Cir.1987) ("[w]hile it may be foolhardy to proceed in the absence of the physical presence of the warrant, it is not unconstitutional"). Considering that one reason for the warrant is to provide the executing officer with a lawful show of authority, do these decisions make sense?

5. *Enlisting Private Citizens to Help Search*

In United States v. New York Tel. Co., 434 U.S. 159 (1977), the Court, per Justice White, held that, upon a showing of probable cause, a district judge had power to order an unwilling telephone company to assist the government in installing pen registers (mechanical devices that record the numbers dialed on a telephone by monitoring the electrical impulses caused when the dial on the telephone is released). The All Writs Act, 28 U.S.C.A. § 1651(a) ("The Supreme Court and all courts established by Act of Congress may issue all writs necessary or appropriate in aid of their respective jurisdictions and agreeable to the usages and principles of law") was thought to be sufficient authority for a court to compel a private person to act. Justice Stevens wrote for himself and Justices Brennan and Marshall in dissent. Their position was that Congress did not empower federal courts to compel private parties to carry out this kind of surveillance. Justice Stewart, also in dissent, agreed with this point. Justice Stevens argued that the majority's decision

> provides a sweeping grant of authority without precedent in our Nation's history. Of course, there is precedent for such authority in the common law—the writ of assistance.

If a warrant is otherwise valid, why shouldn't a person be subject to an order to help the police enforce it? [11] Sometimes such an order might minimize the intrusion the police otherwise would have to make. Is such minimization undesirable? In *Zurcher,* the newspaper really wanted to "search itself"—i.e., it argued that if the government wanted evidence from it, the government should subpoena the evidence and the newspaper would then search for and produce what it had. Would a search warrant that required the newspaper to do the same thing, but to turn over evidence to the police, be unconstitutional? Would people like Andresen be worse off if secretaries and employees could be compelled to participate in searches in order to minimize intrusions? [12] In the *New York Telephone* case, the majority said that without assistance from the company the government could not have conducted the surveillance. Should this make a difference in Fourth Amendment analysis?

11. Plum Creek Lumber Co. v. Hutton, 608 F.2d 1283 (9th Cir. 1979), limits the reliance on the All Writs Act to compel employers to assist OSHA investigators.

12. People v. Superior Court, 25 Cal.3d 67, 157 Cal.Rptr. 716, 598 P.2d 877 (1979), holds that in the light of the number and nature of the objects named in a search warrant, the presence of burglary victims, acting as police agents, represented no improper intrusion into the privacy of persons whose premises were searched. There were three dissents.

D. THE SCREENING MAGISTRATE

1. *Neutral and Detached*

Because of the important position the magistrate holds under the Supreme Court's view of the warrant requirement, it would be natural to expect that the magistrate should be a person of some learning, good legal sense and sensitivity to constitutional doctrines. In many jurisdictions, the sad truth is that there are few, if any, magistrates who possess these qualifications. See generally Nock, The Point of the Fourth Amendment and the Myth of Magisterial Discretion, 23 Conn. L.Rev. 1 (1990) (arguing that the fact that most state magistrates are elected impairs their neutral and detached function).

In Coolidge v. New Hampshire, 403 U.S. 443, 449–453 (1971), the Court invalidated a warrant issued by the state's Attorney General, who was authorized by state law to act as a justice of the peace because the executive officer was not the neutral and detached magistrate required by the Constitution. See also Mancusi v. DeForte, 392 U.S. 364 (1968). From the *Coolidge* holding, Justice Black, joined by Chief Justice Burger and Justice Blackmun, dissented. That three justices were willing to hold that a law enforcement officer could be the screener in the warrant process suggests something about the teeth they wanted to see that process have. However, in Connally v. Georgia, 429 U.S. 245 (1977), the Court was unanimous in holding that a magistrate who was paid a fee if he issued a warrant and nothing if he denied an application was not neutral and detached.[13]

In United States v. McKeever, 906 F.2d 129 (5th Cir.1990) the defendant complained of the magistrate's neutrality on the following grounds: she was formerly involved in law enforcement and retained reserve officer status; her husband was a deputy; and she visited the site of the search while it was being conducted. The court found these factors "troubling" but not enough to show a lack of neutrality. The court stated that a magistrate may retain certain law enforcement duties without losing neutrality; that no showing was made that the magistrate's husband participated in the issuance of the warrant or the search; and that the magistrate went to the site solely out of "curiosity" and did not assist in the search.

2. *Legal Training*

Are there any other qualities constitutionally required in a magistrate other than impartiality? The next case suggests that the answer may be "no."

13. For a discussion of the importance of the screening function, see United States v. Kalscheuer, 11 M.J. 373 (C.M.A.1981) (holding that a search performed by permission of a commander's delagatee did not satisfy the Fourth Amendment unless the delagatee was a military judge or magistrate). State v. Slaughter, 252 Ga. 435, 315 S.E.2d 865 (1984), examines the issuance of a search warrant by a lawyer-magistrate against a defendant who was also the defendant in a civil case in which the magistrate was counsel for the plaintiff. Although the court declined to hold that no magistrate who represents someone in unrelated litigation against a warrant target can be neutral and detached, it recognized that in some instances the magistrate cannot be and remanded for a hearing on the specific circumstances of the case.

SHADWICK v. CITY OF TAMPA

Supreme Court of the United States, 1972.
407 U.S. 345.

MR. JUSTICE POWELL delivered the opinion of the Court.

The charter of Tampa, Florida, authorizes the issuance of certain arrest warrants by clerks of the Tampa Municipal Court. The sole question in this case is whether these clerks qualify as neutral and detached magistrates for purposes of the Fourth Amendment. We hold that they do.

Appellant was arrested for impaired driving on a warrant issued by a clerk of the municipal court. He moved the court to quash the warrant on the ground that it was issued by a nonjudicial officer in violation of the Fourth and Fourteenth Amendments. * * *

I

A clerk of the municipal court is appointed by the city clerk from a classified list of civil servants and assigned to work in the municipal court. The statute does not specify the qualifications necessary for this job, but no law degree or special legal training is required. The clerk's duties are to receive traffic fines, prepare the court's dockets and records, fill out commitment papers and perform other routine clerical tasks. Apparently he may issue subpoenas. He may not, however, sit as a judge, and he may not issue a search warrant or even a felony or misdemeanor arrest warrant for violations of state laws. The only warrants he may issue are for the arrest of those charged with having breached municipal ordinances of the city of Tampa.

Appellant, contending that the Fourth Amendment requires that warrants be issued by "judicial officers," argues that even this limited warrant authority is constitutionally invalid. He reasons that warrant applications of whatever nature cannot be assured the discerning, independent review compelled by the Fourth Amendment when the review is performed by less than a judicial officer. It is less than clear, however, as to who would qualify as a "judicial officer" under appellant's theory. There is some suggestion in appellant's brief that a judicial officer must be a lawyer or the municipal court judge himself. A more complete portrayal of appellant's position would be that the Tampa clerks are disqualified as judicial officers not merely because they are not lawyers or judges, but because they lack the institutional independence associated with the judiciary in that they are members of the civil service, appointed by the city clerk, "an executive official," and enjoy no statutorily specified tenure in office.

II

Past decisions of the Court have mentioned review by a "judicial officer" prior to issuance of a warrant, Whiteley v. Warden, 401 U.S. 560, 564 (1971); Katz v. United States, 389 U.S. 347, 356 (1967); Wong Sun v. United States, 371 U.S. 471, 481–482 (1963); Jones v. United States, 362 U.S. 257, 270 (1960); Johnson v. United States, 333 U.S. 10, 14 (1948). In some cases the term "judicial officer" appears to have been used interchangeably with that of "magistrate." In others, it was intended simply to underscore the now accepted fact that someone independent of the police and prosecution must determine probable cause. The very term "judicial officer" implies, of course, some connection with the judicial branch. But it has never been held that only a lawyer or judge could grant a warrant, regardless of the court system or the type of warrant involved. * * *

* * *

An examination of the Court's decisions reveals that the terms "magistrate" and "judicial officer" have been used interchangeably. Little attempt was made to define either term, to distinguish the one from the other, or to advance one as the definitive Fourth Amendment requirement. We find no commandment in either term, however, that all warrant authority must reside exclusively in a lawyer or judge. Such a requirement would have been incongruous when even within the federal system warrants were until recently widely issued by nonlawyers.

* * * The substance of the Constitution's warrant requirements does not turn on the labeling of the issuing party. The warrant traditionally has represented an independent assurance that a search and arrest will not proceed without probable cause to believe that a crime has been committed and that the person or place named in the warrant is involved in the crime. Thus, an issuing magistrate must meet two tests. He must be neutral and detached, and he must be capable of determining whether probable cause exists for the requested arrest or search. * * *

III

The requisite detachment is present in the case at hand. Whatever else neutrality and detachment might entail, it is clear that they require severance and disengagement from activities of law enforcement. There has been no showing whatever here of partiality, or affiliation of these clerks with prosecutors or police. The record shows no connection with any law enforcement activity or authority which would distort the independent judgment the Fourth Amendment requires.[14] Appellant himself expressly refused to allege anything to that effect. The municipal court clerk is assigned not to the police or prosecutor but to the municipal court judge for whom he does much of his work. In this sense, he may well be termed a "judicial officer." While a statutorily specified term of office and appointment by someone other than "an executive authority" might be desirable, the absence of such features is hardly disqualifying. Judges themselves take office under differing circumstances. Some are appointed, but many are elected by legislative bodies or by the people. Many enjoy but limited terms and are subject to re-appointment or re-election. Most depend for their salary level upon the legislative branch. We will not elevate requirements for the independence of a municipal clerk to a level higher than that prevailing with respect to many judges. The clerk's neutrality has not been impeached: he is removed from prosecutor or police and works within the judicial branch subject to the supervision of the municipal court judge.

Appellant likewise has failed to demonstrate that these clerks lack capacity to determine probable cause. The clerk's authority extends only to the issuance of arrest warrants for breach of municipal ordinances. We presume from the nature of the clerk's position that he would be able to deduce from the facts on an affidavit before him whether there was probable cause to believe a citizen guilty of impaired driving, breach of peace, drunkenness, trespass, or the multiple other common offenses covered by a municipal code. There has been no showing that this is too difficult a task for a clerk to accomplish. Our legal system has long entrusted nonlawyers to evaluate more complex and significant factual data

14. United States v. Device, Labeled Theramatic, 641 F.2d 1289 (9th Cir. 1981), invalidates an "in rem arrest warrant" for a diathermy machine where the government's complaint was conclusory and the clerk who issued the warrant was without discretion to examine its substantive adequacy.

than that in the case at hand. Grand juries daily determine probable cause prior to rendering indictments, and trial juries assess whether guilt is proved beyond a reasonable doubt. The significance and responsibility of these lay judgments betray any belief that the Tampa clerks could not determine probable cause for arrest.

* * *

Nor need we determine whether a State may lodge warrant authority in someone entirely outside the sphere of the judicial branch. Many persons may not qualify as the kind of "public civil officers" we have come to associate with the term "magistrate." Had the Tampa clerk been entirely divorced from a judicial position, this case would have presented different considerations. Here, however, the clerk is an employee of the judicial branch of the city of Tampa, disassociated from the role of law enforcement. On the record in this case, the independent status of the clerk cannot be questioned.

What we do reject today is any *per se* invalidation of a state or local warrant system on the ground that the issuing magistrate is not a lawyer or judge. Communities may have sound reasons for delegating the responsibility of issuing warrants to competent personnel other than judges or lawyers.[a] Many municipal courts face stiff and unrelenting caseloads. A judge pressured with the docket before him may give warrant applications more brisk and summary treatment than would a clerk. All this is not to imply that a judge or lawyer would not normally provide the most desirable review of warrant requests. But our federal system warns of converting desirable practice into constitutional commandment. It recognizes in plural and diverse state activities one key to national innovation and vitality. States are entitled to some flexibility and leeway in their designation of magistrates, so long as all are neutral and detached and capable of the probable-cause determination required of them.

* * *

Note

Of course, *Shadwick* dealt with arrest warrants, not search warrants. But, the Court's disclaimers notwithstanding, it is clear that the Court was defining the term magistrate for Fourth Amendment purposes. Notice that it cites arrest and search cases simultaneously. In Illinois v. Gates, 462 U.S. 213 (1983), considered supra, the Court assumed that non-lawyers may issue search warrants. Those jurisdictions that provide that search warrants can be approved by non-lawyers must get comfort from *Shadwick* and *Gates*. See, e.g., 4A Code of Virginia § 19.2–52 (1986); State v. Porter, 88 Wn.2d 512, 563 P.2d 829 (1977).

Do you believe that the warrant clause is meaningful when the magistrate is not a lawyer? What message, if any, does *Shadwick* send to magistrates about the importance of their screening function? After all the Court has had to say about the role of the magistrate under the Fourth Amendment, does *Shadwick* signify that the great protections of the warrant requirement rest on a foundation of sand? For suggestions that magistrates really screen very little, see LaFave, Warrantless Searches and the Supreme Court: Further Ventures Into the "Quagmire," 8 Crim.L.Bull. 9 (1972); Miller & Tiffany, Prosecutor Dominance of the Warrant Decision: A Study of Current Practices, 1964 Wash.U.L.Q. 1.

a. Some communities, such as those in rural or sparsely settled areas, may have a shortage of available lawyers and judges and must entrust responsibility for issuing warrants to other qualified persons. The Federal Magistrates Act, for example, explicitly makes provision for nonlawyers to be appointed in those communities where members of the bar are not available. 28 U.S.C.A. § 631(b)(1).

In thinking about whether a jurisdiction would be burdened by having to provide legally trained magistrates, you might be interested in various programs around the country that use volunteer "lawyer-judges," particularly to reduce case backlogs. See generally, Aikman, Volunteer lawyer-judges bolster court resources, NIJ Reports 2 (January 1986).

Notice that in Fed.R.Crim.P. 41, Congress limited the class of persons who could issue warrants.

> (a) **Authority to Issue Warrant.** A search warrant authorized by this rule may be issued by a federal magistrate or a judge of a state court of record within the district wherein the property or person sought is located, upon request of a federal law enforcement officer or an attorney for the government.

Why do you suppose Congress drafted the rule this way? Since the holding of *Shadwick* is far more limited than its reasoning, a future case might limit it to minor offenses like traffic infractions. If so, the door would be open in other situations to adopt a more restrictive view of the term "magistrate." What approach would you take? The same as *Shadwick*?

3. *Magistrate Decisions*

There is no requirement that a magistrate give reasons for finding probable cause or for rejecting a warrant application. Is there an argument that magistrates should have to signify in writing their reasons for finding probable cause before issuing a warrant? Would you be persuaded by a counter-argument that it does not matter whether the magistrate reasoned properly as long as the Fourth Amendment probable cause standard actually is satisfied by the warrant application? Can the Fourth Amendment be satisfied if the magistrate is not reasoning properly? Could it be satisfied, for example, if the issuing magistrate never reads the warrant, but approves it in reliance on the professionalism of the police? Rooker v. Commonwealth, 508 S.W.2d 570 (Ky.App.1974), rejects the notion that it is acceptable for the magistrate to be a "rubber stamp for the police."[15] Do you also reject the idea? Even if it is agreed that a "rubber stamp" magistrate is unacceptable, how is that issue determined? Consider United States v. Brown, 832 F.2d 991 (7th Cir. 1987), where Brown submitted into evidence hundreds of search warrants issued by the municipal judge who issued the warrant against Brown. Most of the affidavits submitted and approved by the judge were form affidavits. The court stated that the volume of warrants issued, especially in comparison to lesser amounts issued by other judges, proved only that the judge had "extraordinary experience in reviewing warrant applications." The court noted that "it might be difficult for a litigant to establish" that a judge has abandoned her neutral and detached role.

What assurance can you ever have that the magistrate is all that you want her to be? If your answer depends upon your hope for appellate review and remedies for improprieties, you will find a discussion of these subjects at the end of this chapter. Think back at the goals of the Fourth Amendment. Even if you could assume perfect appellate review, would this mean that the evils of

15. See also People v. Potwora, 48 N.Y.2d 91, 421 N.Y.S.2d 850, 397 N.E.2d 361 (1979) (holding that warrant is suspect where magistrate is a "rubber stamp", and that a neutral and detached magistrate cannot delegate his screening function, even by relying on other magistrates' conclusions that magazines were obscene).

a magistrate who shirked the screening function envisioned by the Supreme Court's opinions would be harmless?

V. TO APPLY OR NOT APPLY THE WARRANT CLAUSE

A. ARRESTS AND OTHER SEARCHES AND SEIZURES OF THE PERSON

1. *Standards for Warrantless Arrests*

Once the point is made that warrants are necessary to search for property and seize it, it might seem that to search and seize a person would *a fortiori* require a warrant. But this is not the law.

Section 120.1 of the ALI Model Code of Pre-Arraignment Procedure illustrates the powers that police may be given to proceed without a warrant.

Section 120.1. Arrest Without a Warrant

(1) **Authority to Arrest Without a Warrant.** A law enforcement officer may arrest a person without a warrant if the officer has reasonable cause to believe that such person has committed

(a) a felony;

(b) a misdemeanor, and the officer has reasonable cause to believe that such person

(i) will not be apprehended unless immediately arrested; or

(ii) may cause injury to himself or others or damage to property unless immediately arrested; or

(c) a misdemeanor or petty misdemeanor in the officer's presence.

* * *

2. *The Constitutional Rule: Arrests Generally*

No law, state or federal, could validly authorize action outside the Fourth Amendment. Thus it is important to know how the Amendment has been applied to arrests.

UNITED STATES v. WATSON

Supreme Court of the United States, 1975.
423 U.S. 411.

MR. JUSTICE WHITE delivered the opinion of the Court.

This case presents questions under the Fourth Amendment as to the legality of a warrantless arrest * * *.

I

The relevant events began on August 17, 1972, when an informant, one Khoury, telephoned a postal inspector informing him that respondent Watson was in possession of a stolen credit card and had asked Khoury to cooperate in using the card to their mutual advantage. On five to 10 previous occasions Khoury had provided the inspector with reliable information on postal inspection matters, some involving Watson. Later that day Khoury delivered the card to the inspector. On learning that Watson had agreed to furnish additional cards, the inspector asked Khoury to arrange to meet with Watson. * * * Khoury met with Watson at a restaurant designated by the latter. Khoury had been instructed that if Watson had additional stolen credit cards, Khoury was to give a designated signal. The signal was given, the officers closed in, and Watson was forthwith arrested. * * * A search having revealed that Watson had no credit cards on his person, the inspector asked if he could look inside Watson's car, which was standing within view. Watson said, "Go ahead," and repeated these words when the inspector cautioned that "[i]f I find anything, it is going to go against you." Using keys furnished by Watson, the inspector entered the car and found under the floor mat an envelope containing two credit cards in the names of other persons. * * *

Prior to trial, Watson moved to suppress the cards, claiming that his arrest was illegal for want of probable cause and an arrest warrant * * . The motion was denied, and Watson was convicted of illegally possessing the two cards seized from his car.

A divided panel of the Court of Appeals for the Ninth Circuit reversed, 504 F.2d 849 (1974), ruling that the admission in evidence of the two credit cards found in the car was prohibited by the Fourth Amendment. * * *

II

* * *

Contrary to the Court of Appeals' view, Watson's arrest was not invalid because executed without a warrant. Title 18 U.S.C.A. § 3061(a)(3) expressly empowers the Board of Governors of the Postal Service to authorize Postal Service officers and employees "performing duties related to the inspection of postal matters" to

> "make arrests without warrant for felonies cognizable under the laws of the United States if they have reasonable grounds to believe that the person to be arrested has committed or is committing such a felony."

By regulation, 39 CFR § 232.5(a)(3) (1975), and in identical language, the Board of Governors has exercised that power and authorized warrantless arrests. * * * The effect of the judgment of the Court of Appeals was to invalidate the statute as applied in this case and as applied to all the situations where a court fails to find exigent circumstances justifying a warrantless arrest. We reverse that judgment.

* * * Section 3061 represents a judgment by Congress that it is not unreasonable under the Fourth Amendment for postal inspectors to arrest without a warrant provided they have probable cause to do so. This was not an isolated or quixotic judgment of the legislative branch. Other federal law enforcement officers have been expressly authorized by statute for many years to make felony arrests on probable cause but without a warrant. This is true of United States marshals, 18 U.S.C.A. § 3053, and of agents of the Federal Bureau of Investigation, 18 U.S.C.A. § 3052; the Drug Enforcement Administration, 84 Stat. 1273, 21 U.S.C.A. § 878; the Secret Service, 18 U.S.C.A. § 3056(a); and the Customs Service, 26 U.S.C.A. § 7607.

* * *

Moreover, there is nothing in the Court's prior cases indicating that under the Fourth Amendment a warrant is required to make a valid arrest for a felony. Indeed, the relevant prior decisions are uniformly to the contrary.

"The usual rule is that a police officer may arrest without warrant one believed by the officer upon reasonable cause to have been guilty of a felony

* * *." Carroll v. United States, 267 U.S. 132, 156 (1925). * * *

The cases construing the Fourth Amendment thus reflect the ancient common-law rule that a peace officer was permitted to arrest without a warrant for a misdemeanor or felony committed in his presence as well as for a felony not committed in his presence if there was reasonable ground for making the arrest. This has also been the prevailing rule under state constitutions and statutes. * * *.

* * *

The balance struck by the common law in generally authorizing felony arrests on probable cause, but without a warrant, has survived substantially intact. It appears in almost all of the States in the form of express statutory authorization. * * *

This is the rule Congress has long directed its principal law enforcement officers to follow. Congress has plainly decided against conditioning warrantless arrest power on proof of exigent circumstances. Law enforcement officers may find it wise to seek arrest warrants where practicable to do so, and their judgments about probable cause may be more readily accepted where backed by a warrant issued by a magistrate. But we decline to transform this judicial preference into a constitutional rule when the judgment of the Nation and Congress has for so long been to authorize warrantless public arrests on probable cause rather than to encumber criminal prosecutions with endless litigation with respect to the existence of exigent circumstances, whether it was practicable to get a warrant, whether the suspect was about to flee, and the like.

Watson's arrest did not violate the Fourth Amendment, and the Court of Appeals erred in holding to the contrary.

* * *

MR. JUSTICE STEVENS took no part in the consideration or decision of this case.

[Justice Stewart's one paragraph opinion concurring in the judgment is omitted.]

MR. JUSTICE POWELL, concurring.

* * *

I

* * *

In reversing the Court of Appeals, the Court concludes that nothing in our previous cases involving warrantless arrests supports the position of respondent and the Court of Appeals. But it is fair to say, I think, that the prior decisions of the Court have assumed the validity of such arrests without addressing in a reasoned way the analysis advanced by respondent.[a] Today's deci-

a. None of the decisions cited by the Court today squarely faced the issue. In Henry v. United States, 361 U.S. 98 (1959), for example, the Court declared that 18 U.S.C.A. § 3052, which authorizes an FBI agent to make a warrantless arrest when he has reasonable grounds to believe that a person has committed a felony, "states the constitutional standard." But that declaration was made without discussion, and the issue actually presented to and addressed by the Court was whether there was in fact probable cause for the arrest in that case. Similarly, Draper v. United States, 358 U.S. 307 (1959), stands only for the validity of a warrantless arrest made with probable cause to believe that the arrestee had committed an offense in the arresting officer's presence. As this Court had noted in an earlier case, such an arrest presents no danger that an innocent person might be ensnared, since the officer observes both the crime and the culprit with his own eyes; there thus would be no reason to require a warrant in that particular situation even if there might be in others. Trupiano v. United States, 334 U.S. 699, 705 (1948). Another case cited by the Court, Carroll v. United States, 267 U.S. 132 (1925), involved no challenge to an arrest. Nor did Abel v. United States, 362 U.S. 217 (1960), in which the Court refused to consider petitioner's challenge to his arrest under less than a judicial warrant because of his failure to raise the issue in the lower

sion is the first square holding that the Fourth Amendment permits a duly authorized law enforcement officer to make a warrantless arrest in a public place even though he had adequate opportunity to procure a warrant after developing probable cause for arrest.

On its face, our decision today creates a certain anomaly. There is no more basic constitutional rule in the Fourth Amendment area than that which makes a warrantless search unreasonable except in a few "jealously and carefully drawn" exceptional circumstances. * * *

* * *

Since the Fourth Amendment speaks equally to both searches and seizures, and since an arrest, the taking hold of one's person, is quintessentially a seizure, it would seem that the constitutional provision should impose the same limitations upon arrests that it does upon searches. Indeed, as an abstract matter an argument can be made that the restrictions upon arrest perhaps should be greater. A search may cause only annoyance and temporary inconvenience to the law-abiding citizen, assuming more serious dimension only when it turns up evidence of criminality. An arrest, however, is a serious personal intrusion regardless of whether the person seized is guilty or innocent. * * *.

But logic sometimes must defer to history and experience. The Court's opinion emphasizes the historical sanction accorded warrantless felony arrests. * * *

The historical momentum for acceptance of warrantless arrests, already strong at the adoption of the Fourth Amendment, has gained strength during the ensuing two centuries. Both the judiciary and the legislative bodies of this Nation repeatedly have placed their imprimaturs upon the practice and, as the Government emphasizes, law enforcement agencies have developed their investigative and arrest procedures upon an assumption that warrantless arrests were valid so long as based upon probable cause. The decision of the Court of Appeals in this case was virtually unprecedented. Of course, no practice that is inconsistent with constitutional protections can be saved merely by appeal to previous uncritical acceptance. But the warrantless felony arrest, long preferred at common law and unimpeached at the passage of the Fourth Amendment, is not such a practice. Given the revolutionary implications of such a holding, a declaration at this late date that warrantless felony arrests are constitutionally infirm would have to rest upon reasons more substantial than a desire to harmonize the rules for arrest with those governing searches.

Moreover, a constitutional rule permitting felony arrests only with a warrant or in exigent circumstances could severely hamper effective law enforcement. Good police practice often requires postponing an arrest, even after probable cause has been established, in order to place the suspect under surveillance or otherwise develop further evidence necessary to prove guilt to a jury. Under the holding of the Court of Appeals such additional investigative work could imperil the entire prosecution. Should the officers fail to obtain a warrant initially, and later be required by unforeseen circumstances to arrest immediately with no chance to procure a last-minute warrant, they would risk a court decision that the subsequent exigency did not excuse their failure to get

courts. Finally, in Ker v. California, 374 U.S. 23 (1963), the Court addressed only the questions of whether there was probable cause for arrest and whether the method of entry for the purpose of arrest was reasonable; no issue arose as to whether a warrant was necessary for either the arrest or the entry.

a warrant in the interim since they first developed probable cause. If the officers attempted to meet such a contingency by procuring a warrant as soon as they had probable cause and then merely held it during their subsequent investigation, they would risk a court decision that the warrant had grown stale by the time it was used.[b] Law enforcement personnel caught in this squeeze could ensure validity of their arrests only by obtaining a warrant and arresting as soon as probable cause existed, thereby foreclosing the possibility of gathering vital additional evidence from the suspect's continued actions.

In sum, the historical and policy reasons sketched above fully justify the Court's sustaining of a warrantless arrest upon probable cause, despite the resulting divergence between the constitutional rule governing searches and that now held applicable to seizures of the person.

* * *

MR. JUSTICE MARSHALL, with whom MR. JUSTICE BRENNAN joins, dissenting.

By granting police broad powers to make warrantless arrests, the Court today sharply reverses the course of our modern decisions construing the Warrant Clause of the Fourth Amendment. * * *

I

Before addressing what the Court does today, I note what it does not do. It does not decide this case on the narrow question that is presented. That is unfortunate for this is, fundamentally, a simple case.

* * *

The signal of the reliable informant that Watson was in possession of stolen credit cards gave the postal inspectors probable cause to make the arrest. This probable cause was separate and distinct from the probable cause relating to the offense six days earlier, and provided an adequate independent basis for the arrest. Whether or not a warrant ordinarily is required prior to making an arrest, no warrant is required when exigent circumstances are present. When law enforcement officers have probable cause to believe that an offense is taking place in their presence and that the suspect is at that moment in possession of the evidence, exigent circumstances exist. Delay could cause the escape of the suspect or the destruction of the evidence. Accordingly, Watson's warrantless arrest was valid under the recognized exigent circumstances exception to the warrant requirement, and the Court has no occasion to consider whether a warrant would otherwise be necessary.

* * *

II

Since, for reasons it leaves unexpressed, the Court does not take this traditional course, I am constrained to express my views on the issues it unnecessarily decides. * * *

* * * There is no doubt that by the reference to the seizure of persons, the Fourth Amendment was intended to apply to arrests. Indeed, we have often considered whether arrests were made in conformity with the Fourth Amendment. Admittedly, as the Court ob-

b. The probable cause to support issuance of an arrest warrant normally would not grow stale as easily as that which supports a warrant to search a particular place for particular objects. This is true because once there is probable cause to believe that someone is a felon the passage of time often will bring new supporting evidence. But in some cases the original grounds supporting the warrant could be disproved by subsequent investigation that at the same time turns up wholly new evidence supporting probable cause on a different theory. In those cases the warrant could be stale because based upon discredited information.

serves, some of our decisions make passing reference to the common-law rule on arrests. However, none of the cases cited by the Court, nor any other warrantless arrest case in this Court mandates the decision announced today. * * * [A]s the case-by-case analysis undertaken by my Brother Powell demonstrates, the dicta relied upon by the Court in support of its decision today are just that—dicta. They are no substitute for reasoned analysis of the relationship between the warrant requirement and the law of arrest.

The Court next turns to history. It relies on the English common-law rule of arrest and the many state and federal statutes following it. There are two serious flaws in this approach. First, as a matter of factual analysis, the substance of the ancient common-law rule provides no support for the far-reaching modern rule that the Court fashions on its model. Second, as a matter of doctrine, the long-standing existence of a Government practice does not immunize the practice from scrutiny under the mandate of our Constitution.

* * *

Both at common law and today, felonies find definition in the penal consequences of crime rather than the nature of the crime itself. At common law, as this Court has several times recognized,

> "No crime was considered a felony which did not occasion a total forfeiture of the offender's lands, or goods, or both." Kurtz v. Moffitt, 115 U.S. at 499.

See also 4 W. Blackstone, Commentaries *95. At present, on the other hand,

> "Any offense punishable by death or imprisonment for a term exceeding one year is a felony." 18 U.S.C.A. § 1(1).[c]

This difference reflects more than changing notions of penology. It reflects a substantive change in the kinds of crimes called felonies.[d] Only the most serious crimes were felonies at common law, and many crimes now classified as felonies under federal or state law were treated as misdemeanors. * * * See also 9 Halsbury's Laws of England 450–793 (1909).[e] To make an arrest for any of these crimes at common law, the police officer was required to obtain a warrant, unless the crime was committed in his presence. Since many of these same crimes are commonly classified as felonies today,[f] however, under the Court's holding a warrant is no longer needed to make such arrests, a result in contravention of the common law.

Thus the lesson of the common law, and those courts in this country that have accepted its rule, is an ambiguous

c. In the States the most common rule is that any crime punishable by death or imprisonment in the state prison is a felony.

d. "In England at the common law the difference in punishment between felonies and misdemeanors was very great. Under our present federal statutes, it is much less important and Congress may exercise a relatively wide discretion in classing particular offenses as felonies or misdemeanors." Carroll v. United States, 267 U.S., at 158.

e. Indeed, by statute, it was no more than a high misdemeanor wilfully to discharge or attempt to discharge a pistol at or near the King of England. 9 Halsbury's Laws of England 459 (1909). Cf. 18 U.S.C.A. § 871 (felony to make threats against President of United States); § 1751 (felony to assault President of United States).

f. For example, under federal law these are some of the common-law misdemeanors, or their modern equivalents, now considered felonies: assault, 18 U.S.C.A. §§ 111–112; assault with intent to commit murder, rape or any other felony, § 113; forging securities of the United States, § 471; bribing voters, § 597; escape, § 751; kidnaping, § 1201; obstruction of congressional or executive investigations, § 1505; obstruction of criminal investigations, § 1510; perjury, § 1621; riots, § 2101; interception of wire or oral communications, § 2511.

* * *

one. Applied in its original context, the common-law rule would allow the warrantless arrest of some, but not all, of those we call felons today. Accordingly, the Court is simply historically wrong when it tells us that "[t]he balance struck by the common law in generally authorizing felony arrests on probable cause, but without a warrant, has survived substantially intact." As a matter of substance, the balance struck by the common law in accommodating the public need for the most certain and immediate arrest of criminal suspects with the requirement of magisterial oversight to protect against mistaken insults to privacy decreed that only in the most serious of cases could the warrant be dispensed with. This balance is not recognized when the common-law rule is unthinkingly transposed to our present classifications of criminal offenses. Indeed, the only clear lesson of history is contrary to the one the Court draws: the common law considered the arrest warrant far more important than today's decision leaves it.

* * *

Lastly, the Court relies on the numerous state and federal statutes codifying the common-law rule. But this, too, is no substitute for reasoned analysis. True enough, the national and state legislatures have steadily ratified the drift of the balance struck by the common-law rule past the bounds of its original intent. And it is true as well, as the Court observes, that a presumption of constitutionality attaches to every Act of Congress. But neither observation is determinative of the constitutional issue, and the doctrine of deference that the Court invokes is contrary to the principles of constitutional analysis practiced since Marbury v. Madison, 1 Cranch 137 (1803). * * *

* * *

III

My Brother Powell concludes: "Logic * * * would seem to dictate that arrests be subject to the warrant requirement at least to the same extent as searches." I agree.

* * *

A warrant requirement for arrests would, of course, minimize the possibility that * * * an intrusion into the individual's sacred sphere of personal privacy would occur on less than probable cause. Primarily for this reason, a warrant is required for searches. Surely there is no reason to place greater trust in the partisan assessment of a police officer that there is probable cause for an arrest than in his determination that probable cause exists for a search. * * *

We come then to the second part of the warrant test: whether a warrant requirement would unduly burden legitimate law enforcement interests. * * * I believe that the suggested concerns are wholly illusory. Indeed, the argument that a warrant requirement for arrests would be an onerous chore for the police seems somewhat anomalous in light of the Government's concession that "it is the standard practice of the Federal Bureau of Investigation [FBI] to present its evidence to the United States Attorney, and to obtain a warrant, before making an arrest." Brief for United States 26 n.15. In the past, the practice and experience of the FBI have been taken as a substantial indication that no intolerable burden would be presented by a proposed rule of procedure. There is no reason to accord less deference to the FBI practice here.

The Government's assertion that a warrant requirement would impose an intolerable burden stems, in large part, from the specious supposition that procurement of an arrest warrant would be necessary as soon as probable cause ripens. There is no requirement that a search warrant be obtained the moment police have probable cause to search. The rule is only that present probable cause be shown and a warrant obtained before a search is undertaken.[g] The same rule should obtain for arrest warrants, where it may even make more sense. Certainly, there is less need for prompt procurement of a warrant in the arrest situation. Unlike probable cause to search, probable cause to arrest, once formed, will continue to exist for the indefinite future, at least if no intervening exculpatory facts come to light.

* * *

It is suggested, however, that even if application of this rule does not require police to secure a warrant as soon as they obtain probable cause, the confused officer would nonetheless be prone to do so. If so, police "would risk a court decision that the warrant had grown stale by the time it was used." This fear is groundless. First, as suggested above, the requirement that police procure a warrant before an arrest is made is rather simple of application. Thus, there is no need for the police to find themselves in this "squeeze." Second, the "squeeze" is nonexistent. Just as it is virtually impossible for probable cause for an arrest to grow stale between the time of formation and the time a warrant is procured, it is virtually impossible for probable cause to become stale between procurement and arrest. Delay by law enforcement officers in executing an arrest warrant does not ordinarily affect the legality of the arrest. In short, staleness should be the least of an arresting officer's worries.[h]

Thus, the practical reasons marshaled against an arrest warrant requirement are unimpressive.[i] * * *

* * *

IV

* * *

[B]y paying no attention whatever to the substance of the offense, and considering only whether it is labeled "felony," the Court, in the guise of "constitutionalizing" the common-law rule, actually does away with it altogether, replacing it with the rule that the police may, consistent with the Constitution, arrest on probable cause anyone who they believe has committed any sort of crime at all. Certainly this rule would follow if the legislatures redenominated all crimes as "felonies." As a matter of substance, it would seem to follow in any event from the holding of this case, for the Court surely does not intend to accord constitutional status to a distinc-

g. The police will, however, encounter problems of "staleness" of their information if they delay too long in seeking a search warrant. E.g., Sgro v. United States, 287 U.S. 206 (1932); United States v. Sawyer, 213 F.Supp. 38, 40 (ED Pa. 1963). This problem relates, however, to the existence at the time the warrant is applied for of probable cause to believe the object to be seized remains where it was, not to whether the earlier probable cause mandated immediate application for a warrant. Mascolo, The Staleness of Probable Cause in Affidavits for Search Warrants: Resolving the Issue of Timeliness, 43 Conn.B.J. 189 (1969). This problem has no bearing, of course, in connection with a warrant to arrest.

h. It is suggested that staleness would be most serious in situations where the original probable cause justifying a warrant is undercut by exculpatory evidence, only to be reaffirmed by further inculpatory evidence. Why this should be a problem baffles me. It should be obvious that when the probable cause supporting a warrant no longer exists, the warrant is void and the suspect cannot be arrested. That probable cause is thereafter again found only tells us that, absent exigency, a subsequent warrant should be obtained, not that the void warrant should somehow be resurrected.

i. The fear that "endless litigation" will result from a warrant rule cannot be credited as an additional practical reason against such a rule. Recognition of a constitutional right inevitably results in litigation to enforce that right. We would quickly lose all protection from our Constitution if it could successfully be argued that its guarantees should be ignored because if they were recognized our citizens would begin to assert them.

tion that can be readily changed by legislative fiat.[j]

[T]he Court surrenders the opportunity to put teeth in our oft-expressed preference for the use of arrest warrants. While some incentives for police to obtain arrest warrants remain,[k] they are only indirect and have proved ineffective in the past in assuring routine application for arrest warrants when the circumstances permit it. By our holding today, the preference for an arrest warrant, which the Court has conceded is the optimal method to protect our citizens from the affront of an unlawful arrest, will remain only an ideal, one that the Court will espouse but not enforce.

* * *

Note

Based on your knowledge of the background and purposes of the Fourth Amendment, are you satisfied with the balance struck by the *Watson* court? In evaluating the need for pre-arrest screening, you might want to consider that police can use force to effect an arrest.

The Supreme Court limited the use of deadly force by police in Tennessee v. Garner, 471 U.S. 1 (1985), as it ruled pursuant to the Fourth Amendment that deadly force may not be used to prevent the escape of a felon unless it is necessary to prevent the escape and the officer has probable cause to believe that the suspect poses a significant threat of death or serious physical injury to the officer or others. Justice White wrote for six Justices that "[i]t is not better that all felony suspects die than that they escape." The majority declined to interpret the Fourth Amendment in light of the common-law rule which permitted the use of deadly force to prevent the escape of fleeing felons. It observed that "[b]ecause of sweeping change in the legal and technological context, reliance on the common-law rule in this case would be a mistaken literalism that ignores the purposes of a historical inquiry." The Court noted that the common law made most felonies punishable by death and recognized most felons as especially dangerous while few felonies are punishable by death today and numerous modern misdemeanors involve conduct more dangerous than felonies. Moreover, the common law rule developed when weapons were rudimentary and deadly force was inflicted by hand-to-hand combat in many instances, whereas today the ever-present gun makes the use of deadly force very

j. Thus the Court calls into question the line of state cases holding unconstitutional statutes authorizing warrantless arrests for misdemeanors not committed in the presence of the arresting officer. In re Kellam, 55 Kan. 700, 41 P. 960 (1895); Robison v. Miner, 68 Mich. 549, 37 N.W. 21 (1888); Pinkerton v. Verberg, 78 Mich. 573, 44 N.W. 579 (1889); Gunderson v. Struebing, 125 Wis. 173, 104 N.W. 149 (1905); Ex parte Rhodes, 79 So. 462 (Ala.1918). Of course, such a result (or, indeed, the result I espouse herein) may still be sustained under the pertinent provisions of the state constitution. Cf. Oregon v. Hass, 420 U.S. 714, 726 (1975) (Marshall, J., dissenting).

k. After today there are two primary incentives for the police to obtain an arrest warrant. First, the Court has suggested, but never held, that a stronger showing of probable cause may be needed to justify a warrantless arrest than would be required if a warrant had been obtained. Wong Sun v. United States, 371 U.S. 471, 479–480 (1963). Cf. United States v. Ventresca, 380 U.S. 102, 106 (1965) (searches). This two-tier standard of probable cause may prove too slippery for ready application, however, especially given the already imprecise definition of probable cause itself, Carroll v. United States, 267 U.S., at 161. What the Court intends, I suspect, is simply that the evidence of probable cause supporting a warrantless arrest will be subjected to closer scrutiny than that underlying a warrant-supported arrest.

The second incentive for police to obtain a warrant is that they may desire to present their evidence to a magistrate so as to be sure that they have probable cause. If probable cause is lacking, the police will then have an opportunity to gather more evidence rather than make an illegal arrest that would result in suppression of any evidence seized.

different. Although most states had not abandoned the common law rule, the majority of police departments in the United States had forbidden the use of deadly force against nonviolent suspects.

Justice O'Connor, joined by Chief Justice Burger and Justice Rehnquist, dissented. She argued "the Court effectively creates a Fourth Amendment right allowing a burglary suspect to flee unimpeded from a police officer who has probable cause to arrest, who has ordered the suspect to halt, and who has no means short of firing his weapon to prevent escape."

3. *Protections Against Erroneous Arrest*

Watson holds that no warrant generally is required before an arrest is made in a felony case. The Supreme Court has held, however, that after a warrantless arrest is effected, the arrestee is entitled to screening by a magistrate. Gerstein v. Pugh, 420 U.S. 103 (1975). The Court in *Gerstein* held that the screening must be conducted promptly after the arrest, but that the state need not provide the adversary safeguards associated with a trial. The Court reasoned that the probable cause standard traditionally has been decided by a magistrate in a nonadversary hearing on the basis of hearsay and written testimony. In the following case the Court considered how prompt the probable cause hearing must be.

COUNTY OF RIVERSIDE v. McLAUGHLIN

Supreme Court of the United States, 1991.
111 S.Ct. 1661.

JUSTICE O'CONNOR delivered the opinion of the Court.

In Gerstein v. Pugh, this Court held that the Fourth Amendment requires a prompt judicial determination of probable cause as a prerequisite to an extended pretrial detention following a warrantless arrest. This case requires us to define what is "prompt" under *Gerstein.*

I

This is a class action brought under 42 U.S.C. § 1983 challenging the manner in which the County of Riverside, California (County), provides probable cause determinations to persons arrested without a warrant. At issue is the County's policy of combining probable cause determinations with its arraignment procedures. Under County policy, * * * arraignments must be conducted without unnecessary delay and, in any event, within two days of arrest. This two-day requirement excludes from computation weekends and holidays. Thus, an individual arrested without a warrant late in the week may in some cases be held for as long as five days before receiving a probable cause determination. Over the Thanksgiving holiday, a 7–day delay is possible.

* * *

Plaintiffs asked the District Court to issue a preliminary injunction requiring the County to provide all persons arrested without a warrant a judicial determination of probable cause within 36 hours of arrest. The District Court issued the injunction, holding that the County's existing practice violated this Court's decision in *Gerstein.* Without discussion, the District Court adopted a rule that the County provide probable cause determinations within 36 hours of arrest, except in exigent circumstances.
* * *

The Court of Appeals * * * determined that the County's policy of providing probable cause determinations at arraignment within 48 hours was "not in accord with *Gerstein*'s requirement of a determination 'promptly after arrest' " because no more than 36 hours were needed "to complete the administrative steps incident to arrest."

* * *

III

A

In *Gerstein,* this Court held unconstitutional Florida procedures under which persons arrested without a warrant could remain in police custody for 30 days or more without a judicial determination of probable cause. In reaching this conclusion we attempted to reconcile important competing interests. On the one hand, States have a strong interest in protecting public safety by taking into custody those persons who are reasonably suspected of having engaged in criminal activity, even where there has been no opportunity for a prior judicial determination of probable cause. On the other hand, prolonged detention based on incorrect or unfounded suspicion may unjustly "imperil [a] suspect's job, interrupt his source of income, and impair his family relationships." We sought to balance these competing concerns by holding that States "must provide a fair and reliable determination of probable cause as a condition for any significant pretrial restraint of liberty, and this determination must be made by a judicial officer either before *or promptly after* arrest."

The Court thus established a "practical compromise" between the rights of individuals and the realities of law enforcement. * * * Significantly, the Court stopped short of holding that jurisdictions were constitutionally compelled to provide a probable cause hearing immediately upon taking a suspect into custody and completing booking procedures. We acknowledged the burden that proliferation of pretrial proceedings places on the criminal justice system and recognized that the interests of everyone involved, including those persons who are arrested, might be disserved by introducing further procedural complexity into an already intricate system. Accordingly, we left it to the individual States to integrate prompt probable cause determinations into their differing systems of pretrial procedures.

In so doing, we gave proper deference to the demands of federalism. * * * Our purpose in *Gerstein* was to make clear that the Fourth Amendment requires every State to provide prompt determinations of probable cause, but that the Constitution does not impose on the States a rigid procedural framework. Rather, individual States may choose to comply in different ways.

Inherent in *Gerstein*'s invitation to the States to experiment and adapt was the recognition that the Fourth Amendment does not compel an immediate determination of probable cause upon completing the administrative steps incident to arrest. Plainly, if a probable cause hearing is constitutionally compelled the moment a suspect is finished being "booked," there is no room whatsoever for "flexibility and experimentation by the States." * * * Waiting even a few hours so that a bail hearing or arraignment could take place at the same time as the probable cause determination would amount to a constitutional violation. Clearly, *Gerstein* is not that inflexible.

Notwithstanding *Gerstein*'s discussion of flexibility, the Ninth Circuit Court of Appeals held that no flexibility was permitted. It construed *Gerstein* as "requir[ing] a probable cause determination to be made *as soon as the administrative steps incident to arrest were completed,* and that such steps should require only a brief period." This same reading is advanced by the dissent. The foregoing discussion readily demonstrates the error of this approach. *Gerstein* held that probable cause determinations must be prompt—not immediate. * * * As we have explained, *Gerstein* struck a balance between competing interests; a proper understanding of the decision is possible only if one takes into account both sides of the equation.

The dissent claims to find support for its approach in the common law. It points to several statements from the early 1800's to the effect that an arresting officer must bring a person arrested without a warrant before a judicial officer " 'as soon as he *reasonably* can.' " This vague admonition offers no more support for the dissent's inflexible standard than does *Gerstein*'s statement that a hearing follow "promptly after arrest." * * * The question before us today is what is "prompt" under *Gerstein.* We answer that question by recognizing that *Gerstein* struck a balance between competing interests.

B

Given that *Gerstein* permits jurisdictions to incorporate probable cause determinations into other pretrial procedures, some delays are inevitable. For example, where, as in Riverside County, the probable cause determination is combined with arraignment, there will be delays caused by paperwork and logistical problems. * * * On weekends, when the number of arrests is often higher and available resources tend to be limited, arraignments may get pushed back even further. In our view, the Fourth Amendment permits a reasonable postponement of a probable cause determination while the police cope with the everyday problems of processing suspects through an overly burdened criminal justice system.

But flexibility has its limits; *Gerstein* is not a blank check. A State has no legitimate interest in detaining for extended periods individuals who have been arrested without probable cause. The Court recognized in *Gerstein* that a person arrested without a warrant is entitled to a fair and reliable determination of probable cause and that this determination must be made promptly.

Unfortunately, as lower court decisions applying *Gerstein* have demonstrated, it is not enough to say that probable cause determinations must be "prompt." This vague standard simply has not provided sufficient guidance. * * *

Our task in this case is to articulate more clearly the boundaries of what is permissible under the Fourth Amendment. Although we hesitate to announce that the Constitution compels a specific time limit, it is important to provide some degree of certainty so that States and counties may establish procedures with confidence that they fall within constitutional bounds. Taking into account the competing interests articulated in *Gerstein,* we believe that a jurisdiction that provides judicial determinations of probable cause within 48 hours of arrest will, as a general matter, comply with the promptness requirement of *Gerstein.* For this reason, such jurisdictions will be immune from systemic challenges.

This is not to say that the probable cause determination in a particular case passes constitutional muster simply because it is provided within 48 hours. Such a hearing may nonetheless violate *Gerstein* if the arrested individual can prove that his or her probable cause determination was delayed unreasonably. Examples of unreasonable delay are delays for the purpose of gathering additional evidence to justify the arrest, a delay motivated by ill will against the arrested individual, or delay for delay's sake. In evaluating whether the delay in a particular case is unreasonable, however, courts must allow a substantial degree of flexibility. Courts cannot ignore the often unavoidable delays in transporting arrested persons from one facility to another, handling late-night bookings where no magistrate is readily available, obtaining the presence of an arresting officer who may be busy processing other suspects or securing the premises of an arrest, and other practical realities.

Where an arrested individual does not receive a probable cause determination within 48 hours, the calculus changes. In such a case, the arrested individual does not bear the burden of proving an unreasonable delay. Rather, the burden shifts to the government to demonstrate the existence of a bona fide emergency or other extraordinary circumstance. The fact that in a particular case it may take longer than 48 hours to consolidate pretrial proceedings does not qualify as an extraordinary circumstance. Nor, for that matter, do intervening weekends. A jurisdiction that chooses to offer combined proceedings must do so as soon as is reasonably feasible, but in no event later than 48 hours after arrest.

* * * In advocating a 24-hour rule, the dissent would compel Riverside County—and countless others across the Nation—to speed up its criminal justice mechanisms substantially, presumably by allotting local tax dollars to hire additional police officers and magistrates. There may be times when the Constitution compels such direct interference with local control, but this is not one. As we have explained, *Gerstein* clearly contemplated a reasonable accommodation between legitimate competing concerns. We do no more than recognize that such accommodation can take place without running afoul of the Fourth Amendment.

Everyone agrees that the police should make every attempt to minimize the time a presumptively innocent individual spends in jail. One way to do so is to provide a judicial determination of probable cause immediately upon completing the administrative steps incident to arrest—*i.e.,* as soon as the suspect has been booked, photographed, and fingerprinted. As the dissent explains, several States, laudably, have adopted this approach. The Constitution does not compel so rigid a schedule, however. Under *Gerstein,* jurisdictions may choose to combine probable cause determinations with other pretrial proceedings, so long as they do so promptly. This necessarily means that only certain proceedings are candidates for combination. Only those proceedings that arise very early in the pretrial process—such as bail hearings and arraignments—may be chosen. Even then, every effort must be made to expedite the combined proceedings.

* * *

JUSTICE MARSHALL, with whom JUSTICE BLACKMUN and JUSTICE STEVENS join, dissenting.

In Gerstein v. Pugh, this Court held that an individual detained following a warrantless arrest is entitled to a "prompt" judicial determination of probable cause as a prerequisite to any further restraint on his liberty. I agree with Justice Scalia that a probable-cause hearing is sufficiently "prompt" under *Gerstein* only when provided immediately upon completion of the "administrative steps incident to arrest."

JUSTICE SCALIA, dissenting.

* * *

I

The Court views the task before it as one of "balanc[ing] [the] competing concerns" of "protecting public safety," on the one hand, and avoiding "prolonged detention based on incorrect or unfounded suspicion," on the other hand. It purports to reaffirm the "practical compromise" between these concerns struck in Gerstein v. Pugh.

There is assuredly room for such an approach in resolving novel questions of search and seizure under the "reasonableness" standard that the Fourth Amendment sets forth. But not, I think, in resolving those questions on which a clear answer already existed in 1791 and has been generally adhered to by the traditions of our society ever since. As to those matters, the "balance" has already been struck, the "practical compromise" reached—and it is the function of the Bill of Rights to *preserve* that judgment, not only against the changing views of Presidents and Members of Congress, but also against the changing views of Justices whom Presidents appoint and Members of Congress confirm to this Court.

The issue before us today is of precisely that sort. As we have recently had occasion to explain, the Fourth Amendment's prohibition of "unreasonable seizures," insofar as it applies to seizure of the person, preserves for our citizens the traditional protections against unlawful arrest afforded by the common law. See California v. Hodari D. [page 188, infra]. One of those—one of the most important of those—was that a person arresting a suspect without a warrant must deliver the arrestee to a magistrate "as soon as he reasonably can." 2 M. Hale, Pleas of the Crown 95, n. 13 (1st Am. ed. 1847). See also 4 W. Blackstone, Commentaries * 289, * 293 * * *. The practice in the United States was the same. See e.g., Perkins, The Law of Arrest, 25 Iowa L.Rev. 201, 254 (1940). It was clear, moreover, that the only element bearing upon the reasonableness of delay was, not such circumstances as the pressing need to conduct further investigation, but the arresting officer's ability, once the prisoner had been secured, to reach a magistrate who could issue the needed warrant for further detention. Any detention beyond the period within which a warrant could have been obtained rendered the officer liable for false imprisonment. See, e.g., Annot., 98 A.L.R.2d 966 (1964).

We discussed and relied upon this common-law understanding in *Gerstein,* holding that the period of warrantless detention must be limited to the time necessary to complete the arrest and obtain the magistrate's review. * * * We said that "the Fourth Amendment requires a judicial determination of probable cause as a prerequisite to extended restraint of liberty," "either before or promptly after arrest." Though *how* "promptly" we did not say, it was plain enough that the requirement left no room for intentional delay unrelated to the completion of "the administrative steps incident to arrest." * * *

* * *

Since the Court's opinion hangs so much upon *Gerstein,* it is worth quoting the allegedly relevant passage in its entirety.

> "Although we conclude that the Constitution does not require an adversary determination of probable cause, we recognize that state systems of criminal procedure vary widely. There is no single preferred pretrial procedure, and the nature of the probable cause determination usually will be shaped to accord with a State's pretrial procedure viewed as a whole. While we limit our holding to the precise requirement of the Fourth Amendment, we recognize the desirability of flexibility and experimentation by the States. It may be found desirable, for example, to make the probable cause determination at the suspect's first appearance before a judicial officer, ... or the determination may be incorporated into the procedure for setting bail or fixing other conditions of pretrial release. In some States, existing procedures may satisfy the requirement of the

Fourth Amendment. Others may require only minor adjustment, *such as acceleration of existing preliminary hearings.* Current proposals for criminal procedure reform suggest other ways of testing probable cause for detention. Whatever procedure a State may adopt, it must provide a fair and reliable determination of probable cause as a condition for any significant pretrial restraint of liberty, and this determination must be made by a judicial officer *either before or promptly after arrest.*"

The Court's holding today rests upon the statement that "we recognize the desirability of flexibility and experimentation." But in its context that statement plainly refers to the *nature* of the hearing and not to its *timing.* That the timing is a given and a constant is plain from the italicized phrases, especially that which concludes the relevant passage. * * *

Of course even if the implication of the dictum in *Gerstein* were what the Court says, that would be poor reason for keeping a wrongfully arrested citizen in jail contrary to the clear dictates of the Fourth Amendment. What is most revealing of the frailty of today's opinion is that it relies upon *nothing* but that implication from a dictum, plus its own (quite irrefutable because entirely value laden) "balancing" of the competing demands of the individual and the State. With respect to the point at issue here, different times and different places—even highly liberal times and places—have struck that balance in different ways. * * * It was the purpose of the Fourth Amendment to put this matter beyond time, place and judicial predilection, incorporating the traditional common-law guarantees against unlawful arrest. The Court says not a word about these guarantees, and they are determinative. * * * Mr. McLaughlin was entitled to have a *prompt* impartial determination that there was reason to deprive him of his liberty—not according to a schedule that suits the State's convenience in piggybacking various proceedings, but as soon as his arrest was completed and the magistrate could be procured.

II

* * *

I do not know how the Court calculated its outer limit of 48 hours. I must confess, however, that I do not know how I would do so either, if I thought that one justification for delay could be the State's "desire to combine." There are no standards for "combination," and as we acknowledged in *Gerstein* the various procedures that might be combined "vary widely" from State to State. So as far as I can discern (though I cannot pretend to be able to do better), the Court simply decided that, given the administrative convenience of "combining," it is not so bad for an utterly innocent person to wait 48 hours in jail before being released.

If one eliminates (as one should) that novel justification for delay, determining the outer boundary of reasonableness is a more objective and more manageable task. * * *

With one exception, no federal court considering the question has regarded 24 hours as an inadequate amount of time to complete arrest procedures, and with the same exception every court actually setting a limit for probable-cause determination based on those procedures has selected 24 hours. (The exception would not count Sunday within the 24–hour limit.) See Brandes, Post–Arrest Detention and the Fourth Amendment: Refining the Standard of *Gerstein v. Pugh,* 22 Colum.J.L. & Soc. Prob. 445, 474–475 (1989). Federal courts have reached a similar conclusion in applying Federal Rules of Criminal Procedure 5(a), which requires presentment before a federal magistrate "without unnecessary delay." See, e.g., Thomas, The Poisoned Fruit of Pretrial Detention, 61 N.Y.U.L.Rev. 413, 450, n. 238 (1986) (citing cases). And state courts have similarly applied a 24-hour limit under state statutes requiring presentment without "unreasonable delay." New York, for example, has concluded that no more than 24 hours is necessary from arrest to *arraignment.* Twenty-nine States have statutes similar to New York's, which require either presentment or arraignment "without unnecessary delay" or "forthwith"; eight States explicitly require presentment or arraignment within 24 hours; and only seven States have statutes explicitly permitting a period longer than 24 hours. Since the States requiring a probable-cause hearing within 24 hours include both New York and Alaska, it is unlikely that circumstances of population or geography demand a longer period. Twenty-four hours is consistent with the American Law Institute's Model Code. ALI, Model Code of Pre-Arraignment Procedure § 310.1 (1975). * * *

In my view, absent extraordinary circumstances, it is an "unreasonable seizure" within the meaning of the Fourth Amendment for the police, having arrested a suspect without a warrant, to delay a determination of probable cause for the arrest either (1) for reasons unrelated to arrangement of the probable-cause determination or completion of the steps incident to arrest, or (2) beyond 24 hours after the arrest. Like the Court, I would treat the time limit as a presumption; when the 24 hours are exceeded the burden shifts to the police to adduce unforeseeable circumstances justifying the additional delay.

* * *

* * * One hears the complaint, nowadays, that the Fourth Amendment has become constitutional law for the guilty; that it benefits the career criminal (through the exclusionary rule) often and directly, but the ordinary citizen remotely if at all. By failing to protect the innocent arrestee, today's opinion reinforces that view. The common law rule of *prompt* hearing had as its primary beneficiaries the innocent—not those whose fully justified convictions must be overturned to scold the police; nor those who avoid conviction because the evidence, while convincing, does not establish guilt beyond a reasonable doubt; but those so blameless that there was not even good reason to arrest them. While in recent years we have invented novel applications of the Fourth Amendment to release the unquestionably guilty, we today repudiate one of its core applications so that the presumptively innocent may be left in jail. Hereafter a law-abiding citizen wrongfully arrested may be compelled to await the grace of a Dickensian bureaucratic machine, as it churns its cycle for up to two days—never once given the opportunity to show a judge that there is absolutely no reason to hold him, that a mistake has been made. In my view, this is the image of a system of justice that has lost its ancient sense of priority, a system that few Americans would recognize as our own.

I respectfully dissent.

4. *Arrests in the Home*

Watson and *Gerstein* left open the question whether a warrant is necessary to enter a home to make an arrest. The Court answered the question concerning arrests in the home in Payton v. New York, 445 U.S. 573 (1980). The Court described the facts as follows:

> On January 14, 1970, after two days of intensive investigation, New York detectives had assembled evidence sufficient to establish probable cause to

believe that Theodore Payton had murdered the manager of a gas station two days earlier. At about 7:30 a.m. on January 15, six officers went to Payton's apartment in the Bronx, intending to arrest him. They had not obtained a warrant. Although light and music emanated from the apartment, there was no response to their knock on the metal door. They summoned emergency assistance and, about 30 minutes later, used crowbars to break open the door and enter the apartment. No one was there. In plain view, however, was a .30-caliber shell casing that was seized and later admitted into evidence at Payton's murder trial.

In due course Payton surrendered to the police, was indicted for murder, and moved to suppress the evidence taken from his apartment.

The New York Court of Appeals held, 4–3, that no warrant was required to enter a home to make an arrest. The Supreme Court disagreed.

Justice Stevens' majority opinion emphasized that the house has always been viewed as an especially private place; set forth a history that indicated there were doubts at common law concerning authority to invade a home to make an arrest; conceded that a majority of state courts addressing the question had permitted warrantless arrests in the home, but observed a trend in the opposite direction in the last decade; and finally decided that the home deserved special protection. Justice Stevens concluded that "the Fourth Amendment has drawn a firm line at the entrance to the house" and that "absent exigent circumstances, that threshold may not reasonably be crossed without a warrant."

In its penultimate paragraph, the opinion addressed the kind of warrant it required:

> Finally, we note the State's suggestion that only a search warrant based upon probable cause to believe the suspect is at home at a given time can adequately protect the privacy interests at stake, and since such a warrant requirement is manifestly impractical, there need be no warrant of any kind. We find this ingenious argument unpersuasive. It is true that an arrest warrant requirement may afford less protection than a search warrant requirement, but it will suffice to interpose the magistrate's determination of probable cause between the zealous officer and the citizen. If there is sufficient evidence of a citizen's participation in a felony to persuade a judicial officer that his arrest is justified, it is constitutionally reasonable to require him to open his doors to the officers of the law. Thus, for Fourth Amendment purposes, an arrest warrant founded on probable cause implicitly carries with it the limited authority to enter a dwelling in which the suspect lives when there is reason to believe the suspect is within.

Justice Blackmun wrote a one paragraph concurring opinion. Justice White dissented and was joined by the Chief Justice and Justice Rehnquist. Justice Rehnquist also added a short dissent.

Payton leaves it to the officer executing the arrest warrant to determine whether there is "reason to believe the suspect is within" the home. Is this consistent with the theory of the warrant clause? Is the officer who executes a search warrant free to determine whether probable cause exists to believe that evidence described in the warrant is located in a certain place?

In light of *Payton* and *Watson,* it becomes important to determine whether the arrest occurs at the home or in public. In United States v. Holland, 755

F.2d 253 (2d Cir.1985), defendant was in his second-floor apartment in a two-family house when he heard someone ring the doorbell to his apartment. To answer the bell, he had to walk down a flight of stairs through a common hallway and open the door in the front of the building. There he was arrested without a warrant. The court found no intent in *Payton* to broaden the definition of "home" so as to include the entranceway to a common hallway. Judge Newman in dissent noted that if Holland had been living in a modern building with a buzzer mechanism, the officer would have had to arrest him at the door to his apartment. He concluded that *Payton* should apply as well to the "humble surroundings" in which defendant lived. See also United States v. Berkowitz, 927 F.2d 1376 (7th Cir.1991) (whether *Payton* or *Watson* applies depends on whether officers inform defendant that he is under arrest before or after entering his home).

If the defendant is in his home, can the officer wait for ten hours for the defendant to come outside and then arrest him without a warrant? See United States v. Bustamante–Saenz, 894 F.2d 114 (5th Cir.1990) (yes). The holding in *Bustamante–Saenz* receives support from the recent Supreme Court decision of New York v. Harris, 495 U.S. 14 (1990), in which the Court held that a violation of *Payton* constitutes an illegal *search* of the home, but that the warrantless in-home arrest itself is not illegal. *Harris* concerned the fruits of an alleged *Payton* violation, and is discussed in the material on the exclusionary rule later in this Chapter.

After *Payton*, the Court addressed the standard to be used when an arrest of one suspect is made in the home of a third person in Steagald v. United States, 451 U.S. 204 (1981). The Court related the following facts:

> In early January 1978, an agent of the Drug Enforcement Administration (DEA) was contacted in Detroit, Mich., by a confidential informant who suggested that he might be able to locate Ricky Lyons, a federal fugitive wanted on drug charges. On January 14, 1978, the informant called the agent again, and gave him a telephone number in the Atlanta, Ga., area where, according to the informant, Ricky Lyons could be reached during the next 24 hours. On January 16, 1978, the agent called fellow DEA Agent Kelly Goodowens in Atlanta and relayed the information he had obtained from the informant. Goodowens contacted Southern Bell Telephone Company, and secured the address corresponding to the telephone number obtained by the informant. Goodowens also discovered that Lyons was the subject of a six-month-old arrest warrant.
>
> Two days later, Goodowens and 11 other officers drove to the address supplied by the telephone company to search for Lyons. The officers observed two men standing outside the house to be searched. These men were Hoyt Gaultney and petitioner Gary Steagald. The officers approached with guns drawn, frisked both men, and, after demanding identification, determined that neither man was Lyons. Several agents proceeded to the house. Gaultney's wife answered the door, and informed the agents that she was alone in the house. She was told to place her hands against the wall and was guarded in that position while one agent searched the house. Ricky Lyons was not found, but during the search of the house the agent observed what he believed to be cocaine. Upon being informed of this discovery, Agent Goodowens sent an officer to obtain a search warrant and in the meantime conducted a second search of the house, which uncovered additional incriminating evidence. Dur-

ing a third search conducted pursuant to a search warrant, the agents uncovered 43 pounds of cocaine. Petitioner was arrested and indicted on federal drug charges.

Prior to trial, petitioner moved to suppress all evidence uncovered during the various searches on the ground that it was illegally obtained because the agents had failed to secure a search warrant before entering the house.

Justice Marshall's majority opinion concluded that a search warrant must be obtained to look for a suspect in the home of a third party absent exigent circumstances or consent. The majority held that an arrest warrant did not sufficiently protect the privacy interests of the third party homeowner. Justice Marshall noted that Steagald's only protection from an illegal search "was the agent's personal determination of probable cause." The majority was concerned with the possibility of abuse that could arise if a search warrant were not required in the absence of exigent circumstances: "Armed solely with an arrest warrant for a single person, the police could search all the homes of that individual's friends and acquaintances." The Chief Justice concurred in the judgment without opinion. Justice Rehnquist's dissent was joined by Justice White. They focused on the mobility of fugitives and the likelihood of escape. They also observed that when a suspect lives in another's place for a significant period, this may convert the place into the suspect's home and thus justify a search under an arrest warrant.

The majority in *Steagald* showed concern that a third party may be the victim of a search where there is no probable cause to believe that the arrestee is on the premises. But what about those third parties who live with the arrestee? Since an arrest warrant is sufficient to arrest a person in his home, aren't those who live with him subject to the same risk that concerned the Court in *Steagald?* Is the real difference between *Payton* and *Steagald* that the officer's error as to probable cause can be more pervasive in the latter case than in the former?

After *Steagald,* it is important for the officer to determine whether the suspect lives in the premises (in which case an arrest warrant is sufficient) or is just a visitor (in which case a search warrant is required). What considerations should an officer take into account? See United States v. Pallais, 921 F.2d 684 (7th Cir.1990) (suspect who was staying in garage overseeing the renovation of his children's home was a resident, so that arrest warrant was sufficient).

The Court concluded in Minnesota v. Olson, 495 U.S. 91 (1990), that an arrest warrant was required under *Payton* to arrest an overnight guest in the home of a third person. Justice White wrote the majority opinion. Chief Justice Rehnquist and Justice Blackmun dissented without opinion. Justice White stressed that a person's "status as an overnight guest is alone enough to show that he had an expectation of privacy in the home that society is prepared to accept as reasonable." The Court specifically rejected the State's argument that a place must be one's home in order to have a legitimate expectation of privacy there.

It is of course true that one can have a legitimate expectation of privacy outside one's own home. But is that the issue in a case like *Olson?* Should the Court in *Olson* have focussed on the home or the suspect? Should a search warrant have been required? Should both a search and an arrest warrant have been required? Is *Payton* concerned with protection of the home or the homeowner?

In Welsh v. Wisconsin, 466 U.S. 740 (1984), Justice Brennan's opinion for six members of the Court observed that *Payton* did not decide what sort of emergency or dangerous situation might permit a warrantless arrest in the home. *Welsh* provided the Court with an opportunity to begin to address that question.

Police officers arrested Welsh in his home shortly after receiving a report from an observer that Welsh had been driving his car while being intoxicated or very sick. After seeing Welsh driving erratically and ultimately swerving off the road into a ditch, the observer blocked Welsh's car with his own car and saw Welsh walk away from the ditch after being refused a ride. Another observer called the police who came to the scene and discovered a motor vehicle registration in Welsh's abandoned car. The police went to the address listed on the registration and arrested Welsh for driving while under the influence of an intoxicant. Welsh subsequently refused to submit to a breathalyzer test.

The state supreme court held that Welsh lost his license as a result of his refusal because his arrest was valid and the refusal was therefore unreasonable. It found the warrantless arrest to be valid because the police were in "hot pursuit" of a suspect and they needed to prevent harm to both Welsh and the public and also to protect against destruction of evidence. The United States Supreme Court reversed.

Justice Brennan's opinion reiterated the importance of protecting the home from warrantless intrusions and stated that the concept of exigent circumstances must be narrowly construed when the home is the target of police conduct, "especially when the underlying offense for which there is probable cause to arrest is relatively minor."

Justice Brennan explained the proper approach to exigent circumstances as follows:

> [C]ourts have permitted warrantless home arrests for major felonies if identifiable exigencies, independent of the gravity of the offense, existed at the time of the arrest. But of those courts addressing the issue, most have refused to permit warrantless home arrests for nonfelonious crimes. The approach taken in these cases should not be surprising. Indeed, without necessarily approving any of these particular holdings or considering every possible factual situation, we note that it is difficult to conceive of a warrantless home arrest that would not be unreasonable under the Fourth Amendment when the underlying offense is extremely minor.
>
> We therefore conclude that the commonsense approach utilized by most lower courts is required by the Fourth Amendment prohibition on "unreasonable searches and seizures," and hold that an important factor to be considered when determining whether any exigency exists is the gravity of the underlying offense for which the arrest is being made. Moreover, although no exigency is created simply because there is probable cause to believe that a serious crime has been committed, application of the exigent-circumstances exception in the context of a home entry should rarely be sanctioned when there is probable cause to believe that only a minor offense, such as the kind at issue in this case, has been committed.

Applying this principle to the facts, the opinion emphasized that there was no continuous immediate pursuit of Welsh; that Welsh had already arrived home and therefore was not dangerous when arrested; and that the only potential loss of evidence related to blood-alcohol level. Assuming that destruction of such evidence might in some circumstances amount to a sufficient exigent circumstance to permit a warrantless arrest in the home, the opinion reasoned that "[t]he State of Wisconsin has chosen to classify the first offense for driving while intoxicated as a noncriminal, civil forfeiture offense for which no imprisonment is possible," and that "[g]iven this expression of the state's interest, a warrantless home arrest cannot be upheld simply because evidence of the petitioner's blood-alcohol level might have dissipated while the police obtained a warrant."

Justice White, joined by Justice Rehnquist, dissented. He accepted the notion that the gravity of the underlying offense might be relevant to a determination of the likelihood that a suspect will flee, but he argued that exigent circumstances exist when an officer has probable cause to believe that any suspect will escape or that evidence will be destroyed while a warrant is sought. He reasoned that a warrantless home entry is no more intrusive for a minor offense than a major one and that the majority's approach will force officers who must make quick decisions to assess whether a violation is major or minor for purposes of making an exigency determination. Justice White noted that a misdemeanor-felony distinction could have been adopted, but opined that the majority wisely did not adopt it, since "the category of misdemeanors today includes enough serious offenses to call into question the desirability of such line drawing."

Chief Justice Burger would have dismissed the writ of certiorari as improvidently granted. Justice Blackmun added a two-paragraph concurring opinion expressing his amazement that a state would still classify drunk driving as a civil violation.

Note

What justifies the rule that no warrant is required for an arrest? Is it anything more than the assumed need for immediate action, either to protect the community by beginning the enforcement process or to prevent the escape of the suspect? If not, is the need less when a suspect is at home than when he is in the office? If the idea of *Payton* is that the home is a private place, why shouldn't a search warrant be required to invade the place? The Court's answer, that an arrest warrant is enough because a magistrate has found probable cause, does not establish a special need to enter a house. At most it suggests that once the magistrate makes an independent determination, the person may be seized. But if there is time for a magistrate to make a determination as to a suspect who is home, and if the Court will insist on this determination as a prerequisite for a valid arrest in the home, isn't there time to make the same determination as to any suspect whose location is known and who is not thought to present a risk of flight? If there is time, why is the warrant not required?

After *Welsh,* should the Court have reconsidered *Watson* and the subsequent home-warrant cases? If it was unreasonable to arrest Welsh at home, even shortly after he left his car, would it have been reasonable to arrest him at work the next day without a warrant? The next day in the park while he was playing with his children? What if Wisconsin responds to the Supreme Court's decision by making the crime of driving under the influence an offense punishable by six months in jail? Does this change the result?

Which do you find to be the more reasonable police action—a warrantless arrest of a person suspected of a felony as to whom there is no reason to suspect flight or destruction of evidence, or an effort, as in *Welsh,* to gather blood-alcohol evidence before it dissipates and a drunk driver escapes detention and sanction?

The Court declined to decide in Maryland v. Macon, 472 U.S. 463 (1985), whether a warrantless arrest for distribution of obscene materials violated the Fourth Amendment, since nothing of evidentiary value was seized as a result of the arrest. Justice Brennan, joined by Justice Marshall, dissented. He argued that no seizure of a person for distribution of allegedly obscene materials should be permitted until a judicial determination of probable obscenity has been made and that the remedy for invalid arrest in this circumstance should be invalidation of a conviction. Would you impose a warrant requirement when First Amendment interests might be jeopardized by an arrest? Do *Zurcher* and *P.J. Video* imply that First Amendment and Fourth Amendment issues are separate and distinct? Was it important in those cases that the police secured warrants before conducting searches?

5. *Arrest Versus Summons*

Neither *Watson* nor *Gerstein* explains why it is reasonable under the Fourth Amendment to begin the criminal process by means of an arrest. In 1791, when the Fourth Amendment was adopted, the availability of the death penalty and the incentive it provided offenders to escape might have provided a reason for seizing a person at the time he was charged with any felony. Then, and now, arresting someone who is committing an offense in the officer's presence, especially one who is disturbing the public peace, could be defended on the ground that officers should stop criminal activities before they are completed, if reasonably possible. But, why should other cases begin with forcible detention? They need not in most places. Consider, e.g., Fed. R.Crim.P. 4(a).

A complaint is defined in Fed.R.Crim.P. 3 as a written statement of the essential facts of the offense charged, which "shall be made upon oath before a magistrate." See also Uniform Rule of Criminal Procedure 221 (officer may issue citation instead of arresting); ALI Model Code of Pre-Arraignment Procedure § 120.2 (requirement that regulations providing for maximum use of citations be adopted, but not requiring use of citations in any particular cases). If the prosecutor asks that a summons issue, it shall be used in lieu of a warrant. But there is no requirement that the government demonstrate a need for an arrest in lieu of ordinary judicial process. Is it clear that persons charged with criminal offenses are much more likely to flee than persons named as defendants in civil actions? Once they were arrested too. See Levy, Mesne Process in Personal Actions, 78 Yale L.J. 52 (1968). Could civil defendants be arrested today without a special showing of need? It is hardly likely in light of cases like Sniadach v. Family Finance Corp., 395 U.S. 337 (1969) and North Georgia Finishing, Inc. v. Di-Chem, Inc., 419 U.S. 601 (1975), which strictly limit the ability to seize property as a way of beginning a suit, even though the many seizures now barred under the Fourteenth Amendment's due process clause have firm historical roots. What justifies different treatment for criminal defendants? In Gustafson v. Florida, 414 U.S. 260, 267 (1973), Justice Stewart suggested that "a persuasive claim might have been made * * * that the custodial arrest of the petitioner for a minor traffic offense violated his rights under the Fourth and Fourteenth Amendments." But his suggestion has received little attention.

Cases like Dobbs v. Huff, 446 F.Supp. 35 (N.D.Ga.1977) (civil rights suit following arrest), continue to arise. The facts stated in the opinion are as follows:

> The plaintiffs were individuals engaged in the business of preparing income tax returns for individuals. The plaintiffs, on April 10, 1973, were arrested by special agents of the I.R.S. pursuant to arrest warrants. Plaintiffs were arrested at their place of business, in the presence of some of their clientele, searched and Bryan T. Dobbs was placed in handcuffs. Defendants Marshall and Benson, with other agents, then took plaintiffs to the United States District Courthouse in Atlanta, Georgia. * * *
>
> At that time, due to information divulged by agents of the I.R.S., numerous reporters, cameramen, photographers and other members of the news media were present to film, photograph and report the arrest of the plaintiffs.
>
> * * *
>
> The defendants were present at a meeting on March 28, 1973 (nearly two weeks before the arrest of plaintiffs) when plaintiffs' counsel requested that plaintiffs be allowed to surrender voluntarily, should they be charged with any criminal offense or any warrant issue for their arrest.

Apparently, plaintiffs were so upset about the procedure that they sued on the same day they were arrested. The District Court held that nothing in the Constitution required that the plaintiffs be afforded a chance to turn themselves in without being arrested. Do you agree?

Notice that nothing in *Watson* or *Gerstein* bars the police from seeking a warrant before they arrest someone or from avoiding arrest and utilizing citations or summons whenever possible. Those cases signify only that, absent a nonconstitutional rule requiring a warrant, an arrest can be made on the basis of probable cause without prior scrutiny by a magistrate. And there is nothing to prevent courts and legislatures from adopting rules that require warrants for some or most arrests. Some states have such rules. See Commentary to Section 120.1 of the ALI Model Code of Pre-Arraignment Procedure, at 389 n. 1. See also People v. Casias, 193 Colo. 66, 563 P.2d 926 (1977) (adopting the *Watson* dissent). Similarly, rules requiring use of citations in lieu of warrants in some instances can be adopted. See, e.g., Uniform Rule of Criminal Procedure 226. If more warrants were required, would magistrates tend to be less careful in issuing them? This is one possible danger in increasing the scope of the warrant requirement. Can it be eliminated?

Absent special rules, the authority of police to arrest and to do so without warrant is broad. Rule 4 of the Federal Rules of Criminal Procedure illustrates the procedures that are likely to be employed if an officer seeks a warrant or summons.

Why would an officer seek a warrant if none is required by the Fourth Amendment or applicable statutes and rules? A number of reasons are suggested in W. LaFave, Arrest 36–52 (1965).

a. The person named in the warrant cannot presently be arrested, because his whereabouts are unknown, and the police hope to get help from officers elsewhere in finding and arresting the subject. "While arrests merely upon the request of another officer or department are sometimes subject to question [e.g., whether the offense is a felony or misdemeanor], statutes often make arrest upon notice that a warrant exists clearly legal." Id. at 38. Also, the warrant may be needed to obtain the cooperation of the FBI; it helps demonstrate that flight across state lines by a suspect is for purposes of avoiding prosecution. Moreover, in cases in which one state wants to have a fugitive extradited from another state, pursuant to Article IV, Section 2 of the Constitution, 18 U.S.C.A. § 3182, and the Uniform Extradition Act (in force almost everywhere), it may be necessary that a magistrate have found probable cause.[16]

b. Immediate arrest for a misdemeanor committed in the officer's presence would reveal identity of informants or undercover agents. A warrant may be a useful way of protecting the identity of the undercover agent or informant, and after a delay in arresting, necessary to comply with misdemeanor arrest statutes.

c. "[B]y applying for a warrant before arrest, the police can better determine whether the arrest will later stand up in court." This may be important if a search incident to arrest is made.

d. Existence of the warrant may encourage the suspect to believe that the case against him is great and to confess.

e. Police may seek to minimize chances of individual or police objections regarding arrest or manner of arrest.

f. Police may want advice of the prosecutor before deciding whether to arrest.

g. Police may want to involve the victim or witness in the complaint-warrant process.

To this list may be added two further considerations. First, an arrest warrant permits entry into the arrestee's home, with the opportunity for at

16. In Michigan v. Doran, 439 U.S. 282 (1978), the Court held under Art. IV, § 2 of the Constitution ("A person charged in any State with Treason, Felony, or other Crime, who shall flee from Justice, and be found in another State, shall on Demand of the executive Authority of the state from which he fled, be delivered up, to be removed to the State having Jurisdiction of the Crime"), implemented by 18 U.S.C.A. § 3182, that when a neutral judicial officer of the demanding state has determined that probable cause exists, the courts of the asylum state are without power to review the determination. The Court was not concerned with the power of the executive of the asylum state to refuse extradition, since the governor of the asylum state indicated that he wanted to cooperate with the requesting state. Also, a majority of the Court did not reach the question whether the demanding state must recite in its papers that an arrest warrant was issued after a finding of probable cause by a magistrate, since the demand papers in *Doran* satisfied any such requirement. Justice Blackmun, joined by Justices Brennan and Marshall, concurred in the result, arguing that Fourth Amendment values are implicated in extradition and that "there must be a determination of probable cause by a neutral and detached magistrate, and * * * the asylum state need not grant extradition unless that determination has been made. The demanding State * * * has the burden of so demonstrating."

least a limited visual inspection of the premises while effectuating the arrest. Second, the officer relying on the magistrate's determination of probable cause is protected by the good faith exception to the exclusionary rule, discussed later in this Chapter. This means that even if the arrest is illegal for lack of probable cause, the evidence obtained pursuant to the arrest will ordinarily be admissible since it was the magistrate, and not the officer, who was in error.

In Whiteley v. Warden, 401 U.S. 560 (1971), the Supreme Court said that "[c]ertainly police officers called upon to aid other officers in executing arrest warrants are entitled to assume that the officers requesting aid offered the magistrate the information requisite to support an independent judicial assessment of probable cause." This sensible approach means that once Officer A demonstrates to a magistrate probable cause to arrest a suspect, any other officer can make the arrest on the assumption that the warrant is valid. The arresting officer need have no independent knowledge of the arrestee's criminal activity. The same rule applies in warrantless arrest cases. If Officer B makes an arrest pursuant to orders from Officer A, and the latter had probable cause for the order, the arrest is valid. Sometimes courts sustain arrests by reasoning as follows:

> Defendant argues that because the arresting officer did not have sufficient knowledge or information to establish probable cause, the arrest was illegal. This is not the correct test. The test is whether the law enforcement agency as corporate body possessed sufficient information to establish probable cause.

State v. Stark, 288 Minn. 286, 179 N.W.2d 597 (1970). This reasoning is questionable. The person who decides that an arrest should take place must herself have probable cause in order to satisfy the Fourth Amendment. Can you see why?

6. *Material Witness*

The power to arrest is usually applied to persons suspected of criminal activity. However, the police also have the power to arrest and detain a material witness to a crime "if it is shown that it may become impracticable to secure his presence by subpoena." 18 U.S.C.A. § 3144. In addition to the federal statutes, every state has provisions for detention of material witnesses. The Supreme Court has cited the practice with approval in Stein v. New York, 346 U.S. 156, 184 (1953) and Barry v. United States ex rel. Cunningham, 279 U.S. 597, 617 (1929).

What are the constitutional limitations on this power? In Bacon v. United States, 449 F.2d 933 (9th Cir. 1971), it was held that a warrant to arrest a material witness must be based on probable cause to believe first, that the testimony of the witness will be material, and second, that it may become impracticable to secure his presence by a subpoena. Should arrests without warrant ever be permitted? Only in exigent circumstances?

18 U.S.C.A. § 3144 provides for release if the witness' testimony can be adequately secured by deposition. But in most states, there is no statutory limit on the permissible length of detention of a witness who cannot pay the required bond. See e.g., Quince v. State, 94 R.I. 200, 179 A.2d 485 (1962) (witness confined with convicted offenders for 158 days). States differ widely in the procedural protections they afford to detained witness, e.g., preliminary

hearing, assistance of counsel, appeal, and compensation. See Application of Cochran, 434 F.Supp. 1207 (D.C.Neb.1977) (outlining minimum due process requirements).

There is no constitutional right to monetary compensation for time spent in confinement as a material witness. In Hurtado v. United States, 410 U.S. 578 (1973), the Court held that payment of one dollar per day as compensation did not constitute a "taking" without just compensation or a denial of equal protection. For a comprehensive study of the constitutional problems involved with this practice, see Carlson, Jailing the Innocent: The Plight of the Material Witness, 55 Iowa L.Rev. 1 (1969) and Comment, Pretrial Detention of Witnesses, 117 U.Pa.L.Rev. 700 (1969). Carlson & Voelpel, Material Witness and Material Injustice, 58 Wash.U.L.Q. 1 (1980), describes the historical antecedents of current law and some common plights of innocent witnesses and urges reform.

One of the rare opinions devoted to the plight of persons incarcerated as material witnesses is In re Class Action Application, 612 F.Supp. 940 (W.D.Tex. 1985). The court held that Congress intended to require appointment of counsel for indigent persons whom the government seeks to incarcerate as material witnesses. It also indicated that the due process clause of the Fifth Amendment requires counsel in order for an indigent to receive a fair hearing on whether detention is necessary.

7. *Defining "Arrest"*

Arrest has been described in LaFave, Arrest 3.4 (1965) as the decision to take custody to the extent of removal to the police station of a person suspected of criminal behavior. Is this the definition you have been using? If not, have you a better one?

There are numerous situations in which the police recognize that they do not have probable cause to act, but want "to stop suspicious persons for questioning and, occasionally, to search these persons for dangerous weapons." LaFave, "Street Encounters" and the Constitution: Terry, Sibron, Peters and Beyond, 67 Mich.L.Rev. 40, 42 (1968). Following the adoption in 1964 of a New York statute that became known as the "stop and frisk" law and the conclusion of several important studies of what police do in the real world, the United States Supreme Court placed its first imprimatur on searches and seizures of persons and things without probable cause.

8. *Stop and Frisk Established*

TERRY v. OHIO

Supreme Court of the United States, 1968.
392 U.S. 1.

MR. CHIEF JUSTICE WARREN delivered the opinion of the Court.

This case presents serious questions concerning the role of the Fourth Amendment in the confrontation on the street between the citizen and the policeman investigating suspicious circumstances.

Petitioner Terry was convicted of carrying a concealed weapon and sentenced to the statutorily prescribed term of one to three years in the penitentiary. Following the denial of a pretrial motion to suppress, the prosecution introduced in evidence two revolvers and a number of bullets seized from Terry and a codefendant, Richard Chilton, by Cleveland Police Detective Martin McFadden. At the hearing on the motion to suppress this evidence, Officer McFadden testified that while he was patrolling in plain clothes in downtown Cleveland at approximately 2:30 in the afternoon of October 31, 1963, his attention was attracted by two men, Chilton and Terry, standing on the corner of Huron Road and Euclid Avenue. He had never seen the two men before, and he was unable to say precisely what first drew his eye to them. However, he testified that he had been a policeman for 39 years and a detective for 35 and that he had been assigned to patrol this vicinity of downtown Cleveland for shoplifters and pickpockets for 30 years. He explained that he had developed routine habits of observation over the years and that he would "stand and watch people or walk and watch people at many intervals of the day." He added: "Now, in this case when I looked over they didn't look right to me at the time."

His interest aroused, Officer McFadden took up a post of observation in the entrance to a store 300 to 400 feet away from the two men. * * * He saw one of the men leave the other one and walk southwest on Huron Road, past some stores. The man paused for a moment and looked in a store window, then walked on a short distance, turned around and walked back toward the corner, pausing once again to look in the same store window. He rejoined his companion at the corner, and the two conferred briefly. Then the second man went through the same series of motions, strolling down Huron Road, looking in the same window, walking on a short distance, turning back, peering in the store window again, and returning to confer with the first man at the corner. The two men repeated this ritual alternately between five and six times apiece—in all, roughly a dozen trips. At one point, while the two were standing together on the corner, a third man approached them and engaged them briefly in conversation. This man then left the two others and walked west on Euclid Avenue. Chilton and Terry resumed their measured pacing, peering, and conferring. After this had gone on for 10 to 12 minutes, the two men walked off together, heading west on Euclid Avenue, following the path taken earlier by the third man.

By this time Officer McFadden had become thoroughly suspicious. He testified that after observing their elaborately casual and oft-repeated reconnaissance of the store window on Huron Road, he suspected the two men of "casing a job, a stick-up," and that he considered it his duty as a police officer to investigate further. He added that he feared "they may have a gun." Thus, Officer McFadden followed Chilton and Terry and saw them stop in front of Zucker's store to talk to the same man who had conferred with them earlier on the street corner. Deciding that the situation was ripe for direct action, Officer McFadden approached the three men, identified himself as a police officer and asked for their names. * * * When the men "mumbled something" in response to his inquiries, Officer McFadden grabbed petitioner Terry, spun him around so that they were facing the other two, with Terry between McFadden and the others, and patted down the outside of his clothing. In the left breast pocket of Terry's overcoat Officer McFadden felt a pistol. He reached inside the overcoat pocket, but was unable to remove the gun. At this point, keeping Terry between himself and the others, the officer ordered all three men to enter Zucker's store. As they went in, he removed Terry's overcoat completely, removed a .38-caliber revolver from the pocket and ordered all three men to face the wall with their hands raised. Officer McFadden proceeded to pat down the outer clothing of Chilton and the third man, Katz. He discovered another revolver in the outer pocket of Chilton's overcoat, but no weapons were found on Katz. The officer testified that he only patted the men down to see whether they had weapons, and that he did not put his hands beneath the outer garments of either Terry or Chilton until he felt their guns. So far as appears from the record, he never placed his hands beneath Katz' outer garments. Officer McFadden seized Chilton's gun, asked the proprietor of the store to call a police wagon, and took all three men to the station, where Chilton and Terry were formally charged with carrying concealed weapons.

On the motion to suppress the guns the prosecution took the position that they had been seized following a search incident to a lawful arrest. The trial court rejected this theory, stating that it "would be stretching the facts beyond reasonable comprehension" to find that Officer McFadden had had probable cause to arrest the men before he patted them down for weapons. However, the court denied the defendants' motion on the ground that Officer McFadden, on the basis of his experience, "had reasonable cause to believe * * * that the defendants were conducting themselves suspiciously, and some interrogation should be made of their action." Purely for his own protection, the court held, the officer had the right to pat down the outer clothing of these men, who he had reasonable cause to believe might be armed. The court distinguished between an investigatory "stop" and an arrest, and between a "frisk" of the outer clothing for weapons and a full-blown search for evidence of crime. The frisk, it held, was essential to the proper performance of the officer's investigatory duties, for without it "the answer to the police officer may be a bullet, and a loaded pistol discovered during the frisk is admissible."

* * *

I

The Fourth Amendment provides that "the right of the people to be secure in their persons, houses, papers, and effects, against unreasonable searches and seizures shall not be violated * * *." This inestimable right of personal security belongs as much to the citizen on the streets of our cities as to the homeowner closeted in his study to dispose of his secret affairs. * * *

We would be less than candid if we did not acknowledge that this question thrusts to the fore difficult and troublesome issues regarding a sensitive area of police activity—issues which have never before been squarely presented to this Court. Reflective of the tensions involved are the practical and constitutional arguments pressed with great vigor on both sides of the public debate over the power of the police to "stop and frisk"—as it is sometimes euphemistically termed—suspicious persons.

* * *

In this context we approach the issues in this case mindful of the limitations of the judicial function in controlling the myriad daily situations in which policemen and citizens confront each other on the street. The State has characterized the issue here as "the right of a police officer * * * to make an on-the-street stop, interrogate and pat down for weapons (known in street vernacular as 'stop and frisk')." But this is only partly accurate. For the issue is not the abstract propriety of the police conduct, but the admissibility against petitioner of the evidence uncovered by the search and seizure. [The Court suggests that the exclusionary rule may not deter all Fourth Amendment violations.]

* * *

Proper adjudication of cases in which the exclusionary rule is invoked demands a constant awareness of these limitations. The wholesale harassment by certain elements of the police community, of which minority groups, particularly Negroes, frequently complain,[a] will not be stopped by the exclusion of any evidence from any criminal trial. Yet a rigid and unthinking application of the exclusionary rule, in futile protest against practices which it can never be used effectively to control, may exact a high toll in human injury and frustration of efforts to prevent crime. * * *

* * *

II

Our first task is to establish at what point in this encounter the Fourth Amendment becomes relevant. That is, we must decide whether and when Officer McFadden "seized" Terry and whether and when he conducted a "search." There is some suggestion in the use of such terms as "stop" and "frisk" that such police conduct is outside the purview of the Fourth Amendment because neither action rises to the level of a "search" or "seizure" within the meaning of the Constitution. We emphatically reject this notion. It is quite plain that the Fourth Amendment governs "seizures" of the person which do not eventuate in a trip to the station house and prosecution for crime—"arrests" in traditional terminology. It must be recognized that whenever a police officer accosts an individual and restrains his freedom to walk away, he has "seized" that person. And it is nothing less than sheer torture of the English language to suggest that a careful exploration of the outer surfaces of a person's clothing all over his or her body in an attempt to find weapons is not a "search." Moreover, it is simply fantastic to urge that such a procedure performed in public by a policeman while the citizen stands helpless, perhaps facing a wall with his hands raised, is a "petty indignity." It is a serious intrusion upon the sanctity of the person, which may inflict great indignity and arouse strong resentment, and it is not to be undertaken lightly.

The danger in the logic which proceeds upon distinctions between a "stop" and an "arrest," or "seizure" of the person, and between a "frisk" and a "search" is twofold. It seeks to isolate from constitutional scrutiny the initial stages of the contact between the policeman and the citizen. And by suggesting a rigid all-or-nothing model of justification and regulation under the

a. The President's Commission on Law Enforcement and Administration of Justice found that "[i]n many communities, field interrogations are a major source of friction between the police and minority groups." President's Commission on Law Enforcement and Administration of Justice, Task Force Report: The Police 183 (1967). It was reported that the friction caused by "[m]isuse of field interrogations" increases "as more police departments adopt 'aggressive patrol' in which officers are encouraged routinely to stop and question persons on the street who are unknown to them, who are suspicious, or whose purpose for being abroad is not readily evident." Id., at 184. While the frequency with which "frisking" forms a part of field interrogation practice varies tremendously with the locale, the objective of the interrogation, and the particular officer, it cannot help but be a severely exacerbating factor in police-community tensions. This is particularly true in situations where the "stop and frisk" of youths or minority group members is "motivated by the officers' perceived need to maintain the power image of the beat officer, an aim sometimes accomplished by humiliating anyone who attempts to undermine police control of the streets."

[For a general discussion of problems of police stopping suspects for reasons other than arrest, see Dix, Nonarrest Investigatory Detentions in Search and Seizure Law, 1985 Duke L.J. 849.]

Amendment, it obscures the utility of limitations upon the scope, as well as the initiation, of police action as a means of constitutional regulation. This Court has held in the past that a search which is reasonable at its inception may violate the Fourth Amendment by virtue of its intolerable intensity and scope. * * *

The distinctions of classical "stop-and-frisk" theory thus serve to divert attention from the central inquiry under the Fourth Amendment—the reasonableness in all the circumstances of the particular governmental invasion of a citizen's personal security. "Search" and "seizure" are not talismans. We therefore reject the notions that the Fourth Amendment does not come into play at all as a limitation upon police conduct if the officers stop short of something called a "technical arrest" or a "full-blown search."

In this case there can be no question, then, that Officer McFadden "seized" petitioner and subjected him to a "search" when he took hold of him and patted down the outer surfaces of his clothing. We must decide whether at that point it was reasonable for Officer McFadden to have interfered with petitioner's personal security as he did.[b] And in determining whether the seizure and search were "unreasonable" our inquiry is a dual one—whether the officer's action was justified at its inception, and whether it was reasonably related in scope to the circumstances which justified the interference in the first place.

III

If this case involved police conduct subject to the Warrant Clause of the Fourth Amendment, we would have to ascertain whether "probable cause" existed to justify the search and seizure which took place. However, that is not the case. We do not retreat from our holdings that the police must, whenever practicable, obtain advance judicial approval of searches and seizures through the warrant procedure or that in most instances failure to comply with the warrant requirement can only be excused by exigent circumstances. But we deal here with an entire rubric of police conduct—necessarily swift action predicated upon the on-the-spot observations of the officer on the beat—which historically has not been, and as a practical matter could not be, subjected to the warrant procedure. Instead the conduct involved in this case must be tested by the Fourth Amendment's general proscription against unreasonable searches and seizures.

Nonetheless, the notions which underlie both the warrant procedure and the requirement of probable cause remain fully relevant in this context. In order to assess the reasonableness of Officer McFadden's conduct as a general proposition, it is necessary "first to focus upon the governmental interest which allegedly justifies official intrusion upon the constitutionally protected interests of the private citizen," for there is "no ready test for determining reasonableness other than by balancing the need to search [or seize] against the invasion which the search [or seizure] entails." Camara v. Municipal Court, 387 U.S. 523, 534–535, 536–537 (1967). And in justifying the particular

b. We thus decide nothing today concerning the constitutional propriety of an investigative "seizure" upon less than probable cause for purposes of "detention" and/or interrogation. Obviously, not all personal intercourse between policemen and citizens involves "seizures" of persons. Only when the officer, by means of physical force or show of authority, has in some way restrained the liberty of a citizen may we conclude that a "seizure" has occurred. We cannot tell with any certainty upon this record whether any such "seizure" took place here prior to Officer McFadden's initiation of physical contact for purposes of searching Terry for weapons, and we thus may assume that up to that point no intrusion upon constitutionally protected rights had occurred.

intrusion the police officer must be able to point to specific and articulable facts which, taken together with rational inferences from those facts, reasonably warrant that intrusion. The scheme of the Fourth Amendment becomes meaningful only when it is assured that at some point the conduct of those charged with enforcing the laws can be subjected to the more detached, neutral scrutiny of a judge who must evaluate the reasonableness of a particular search or seizure in light of the particular circumstances. And in making that assessment it is imperative that the facts be judged against an objective standard: would the facts available to the officer at the moment of the seizure or the search "warrant a man of reasonable caution in the belief" that the action taken was appropriate? Anything less would invite intrusions upon constitutionally guaranteed rights based on nothing more substantial than inarticulate hunches, a result this Court has consistently refused to sanction. And simple " 'good faith on the part of the arresting officer is not enough.' * * * If subjective good faith alone were the test, the protections of the Fourth Amendment would evaporate, and the people would be 'secure in their persons, houses, papers, and effects,' only in the discretion of the police."

Applying these principles to this case, we consider first the nature and extent of the governmental interests involved. One general interest is of course that of effective crime prevention and detection; it is this interest which underlies the recognition that a police officer may in appropriate circumstances and in an appropriate manner approach a person for purposes of investigating possibly criminal behavior even though there is no probable cause to make an arrest. It was this legitimate investigative function Officer McFadden was discharging when he decided to approach petitioner and his companions. He had observed Terry, Chilton, and Katz go through a series of acts, each of them perhaps innocent in itself, but which taken together warranted further investigation. There is nothing unusual in two men standing together on a street corner, perhaps waiting for someone. Nor is there anything suspicious about people in such circumstances strolling up and down the street, singly or in pairs. Store windows, moreover, are made to be looked in. But the story is quite different where, as here, two men hover about a street corner for an extended period of time, at the end of which it becomes apparent that they are not waiting for anyone or anything; where these men pace alternately along an identical route, pausing to stare in the same store window roughly 24 times; where each completion of this route is followed immediately by a conference between the two men on the corner; where they are joined in one of these conferences by a third man who leaves swiftly; and where the two men finally follow the third and rejoin him a couple of blocks away. It would have been poor police work indeed for an officer of 30 years' experience in the detection of thievery from stores in this same neighborhood to have failed to investigate this behavior further.

The crux of this case, however, is not the propriety of Officer McFadden's taking steps to investigate petitioner's suspicious behavior, but rather, whether there was justification for McFadden's invasion of Terry's personal security by searching him for weapons in the course of that investigation. We are now concerned with more than the governmental interest in investigating crime; in addition, there is the more immediate interest of the police officer in taking steps to assure himself that the person with whom he is dealing is not armed with a weapon that could unexpectedly and fatally be used against him. Certainly it would be unreasonable to require that police officers take unnecessary risks in the performance of their duties. American criminals have a long tradition of armed violence, and every year in this country many law enforcement officers are killed in the line of duty, and thousands more are wounded. Virtually all of these deaths and a substantial portion of the injuries are inflicted with guns and knives.

In view of these facts, we cannot blind ourselves to the need for law enforcement officers to protect themselves and other prospective victims of violence in situations where they may lack probable cause for an arrest. When an officer is justified in believing that the individual whose suspicious behavior he is investigating at close range is armed and presently dangerous to the officer or to others, it would appear to be clearly unreasonable to deny the officer the power to take necessary measures to determine whether the person is in fact carrying a weapon and to neutralize the threat of physical harm.

* * *

Petitioner does not argue that a police officer should refrain from making any investigation of suspicious circumstances until such time as he has probable cause to make an arrest; nor does he deny that police officers in properly discharging their investigative function may find themselves confronting persons who might well be armed and dangerous. Moreover, he does not say that an officer is always unjustified in searching a suspect to discover weapons. Rather, he says it is unreasonable for the policeman to take that step until such time as the situation evolves to a point where there is probable cause to make an arrest. When that point has been reached, petitioner would concede the officer's right to conduct a search of the suspect for weapons, fruits or instrumentalities of the crime, or "mere" evidence, incident to the arrest.

There are two weaknesses in this line of reasoning, however. First, it fails to take account of traditional limitations upon the scope of searches, and thus recognizes no distinction in purpose, character, and extent between a search incident to an arrest and a limited search for weapons. The former, although justified in part by the acknowledged necessity to protect the arresting officer from assault with a concealed weapon, is also justified on other grounds, and can therefore involve a relatively extensive exploration of the person. A search for weapons in the absence of probable cause to arrest, however, must, like any other search, be strictly circumscribed by the exigencies which justify its initiation. Thus it must be limited to that which is necessary for the discovery of weapons which might be used to harm the officer or others nearby, and may realistically be characterized as something less than a "full" search, even though it remains a serious intrusion.

A second, and related, objection to petitioner's argument is that it assumes that the law of arrest has already worked out the balance between the particular interests involved here—the neutralization of danger to the policeman in the investigative circumstance and the sanctity of the individual. But this is not so. * * *

Our evaluation of the proper balance that has to be struck in this type of case leads us to conclude that there must be a narrowly drawn authority to permit a reasonable search for weapons for the protection of the police officer, where he has reason to believe that he is dealing with an armed and dangerous individual, regardless of whether he has probable cause to arrest the individual for a crime. The officer need not be absolutely certain that the individual is armed; the issue is whether a reasonably prudent man in the circumstances would be warranted in the belief that his safety or that of others was in danger. And in determining whether the officer acted reasonably in such circumstances, due weight must be given, not to his inchoate and unparticularized suspicion or "hunch," but to the specific reasonable inferences which he is entitled to draw from the facts in light of his experience.

IV

* * *

We need not develop at length in this case * * * the limitations which the Fourth Amendment places upon a protective seizure and search for weapons. These limitations will have to be developed in the concrete factual circumstances of individual cases. Suffice it to note that such a search, unlike a search without a warrant incident to arrest, is not justified by any need to prevent the disappearance or destruction of evidence of crime. The sole justification of the search in the present situation is the protection of the police officer and others nearby, and it must therefore be confined in scope to an intrusion reasonably designed to discover guns, knives, clubs, or other hidden instruments for the assault of the police officer.

The scope of the search in this case presents no serious problem in light of these standards. * * *

V

We conclude that the revolver seized from Terry was properly admitted in evidence against him. At the time he seized petitioner and searched him for weapons, Officer McFadden had reasonable grounds to believe that petitioner was armed and dangerous, and it was necessary for the protection of himself and others to take swift measures to discover the true facts and neutralize the threat of harm if it materialized. The policeman carefully restricted his search to what was appropriate to the discovery of the particular items which he sought. Each case of this sort will, of course, have to be decided on its own facts. We merely hold today that where a police officer observes unusual conduct which leads him reasonably to conclude in light of his experience that criminal activity may be afoot and that the persons with whom he is dealing may be armed and presently dangerous, where in the course of investigating this behavior he identifies himself as a policeman and makes reasonable inquiries, and where nothing in the initial stages of the encounter serves to dispel his reasonable fear for his own or others' safety, he is entitled for the protection of himself and others in the area to conduct a carefully limited search of the outer clothing of such persons in an attempt to discover weapons which might be used to assault him. Such a search is a reasonable search under the Fourth Amendment, and any weapons seized may properly be introduced in evidence against the person from whom they were taken.

MR. JUSTICE BLACK concurs in the judgment and the opinion except where the opinion quotes from and relies upon this Court's opinion in Katz v. United States and the concurring opinion in Warden v. Hayden.

MR. JUSTICE HARLAN, concurring.

While I unreservedly agree with the Court's ultimate holding in this case, I am constrained to fill in a few gaps, as I see them, in its opinion. I do this because what is said by this Court today will serve as initial guidelines for law enforcement authorities and courts throughout the land as this important new field of law develops.

A police officer's right to make an on-the-street "stop" and an accompanying "frisk" for weapons is of course bounded by the protections afforded by the Fourth and Fourteenth Amendments. The Court holds, and I agree, that while the right does not depend upon possession by the officer of a valid warrant, nor upon the existence of probable cause, such activities must be reasonable under the circumstances as the officer credibly relates them in court. * * *

* * * The holding has, however, two logical corollaries that I do not think the Court has fully expressed.

In the first place, if the frisk is justified in order to protect the officer during an encounter with a citizen, the officer must first have constitutional grounds to insist on an encounter, to make a *forcible* stop. Any person, including a policeman, is at liberty to avoid a person he considers dangerous. If and when a policeman has a right instead to disarm such a person for his own protection, he must first have a right not to avoid him but to be in his presence. That right must be more than the liberty (again, possessed by every citizen) to address questions to other persons, for ordinarily the person addressed has an equal right to ignore his interrogator and walk away; he certainly need not submit to a frisk for the questioner's protection. I would make it perfectly clear that the right to frisk in this case depends upon the reasonableness of a forcible stop to investigate a suspected crime.

Where such a stop is reasonable, however, the right to frisk must be immediate and automatic if the reason for the stop is, as here, an articulable suspicion of a crime of violence. Just as a full search incident to a lawful arrest requires no additional justification, a limited frisk incident to a lawful stop must often be rapid and routine. There is no reason why an officer, rightfully but forcibly confronting a person suspected of a serious crime, should have to ask one question and take the risk that the answer might be a bullet.

* * *

MR. JUSTICE WHITE, concurring.

* * * I think an additional word is in order concerning the matter of interrogation during an investigative stop. There is nothing in the Constitution which prevents a policeman from addressing questions to anyone on the street. Absent special circumstances, the person approached may not be detained or frisked but may refuse to cooperate and go on his way. However, given the proper circumstances, such as those in this case, it seems to me the person may be briefly detained against his will while pertinent questions are directed to him. Of course, the person stopped is not obliged to answer, answers may not be compelled, and refusal to answer furnishes no basis for an arrest, although it may alert the officer to the need for continued observation. In my view, it is temporary detention, warranted by the circumstances, which chiefly justifies the protective frisk for weapons. Perhaps the frisk itself, where proper, will have beneficial results whether questions are asked or not. If weapons are found, an arrest will follow. If none are found, the frisk may nevertheless serve preventive ends because of its unmistakable message that suspicion has been aroused. But if the investigative stop is sustainable at all, constitutional rights are not necessarily violated if pertinent questions are asked and the person is restrained briefly in the process.

MR. JUSTICE DOUGLAS, dissenting.

I agree that petitioner was "seized" within the meaning of the Fourth Amendment. I also agree that frisking petitioner and his companions for guns was a "search." But it is a mystery how that "search" and that "seizure" can be constitutional by Fourth Amendment standards, unless there was "probable cause" to believe that (1) a crime had been committed or (2) a crime was in the process of being committed or (3) a crime was about to be committed.

* * *

The infringement on personal liberty of any "seizure" of a person can only be "reasonable" under the Fourth Amendment if we require the police to possess "probable cause" before they seize him. Only that line draws a meaningful distinction between an officer's mere inkling and the presence of facts within the officer's personal knowledge which would convince a reasonable man that the person seized has committed, is committing, or is about to commit a particular crime. "In dealing with probable cause, * * * as the very name implies, we deal with probabilities. These are not technical; they are the factual and practical considerations of everyday life on which reasonable and prudent men, not legal technicians, act." Brinegar v. United States, 338 U.S. 160, 175.

To give the police greater power than a magistrate is to take a long step down the totalitarian path. Perhaps such a step is desirable to cope with modern forms of lawlessness. But if it is taken, it should be the deliberate choice of the people through a constitutional amendment. Until the Fourth Amendment, which is closely allied with the Fifth, is rewritten, the person and the effects of the individual are beyond the reach of all government agencies until there are reasonable grounds to believe (probable cause) that a criminal venture has been launched or is about to be launched.

There have been powerful hydraulic pressures throughout our history that bear heavily on the Court to water down constitutional guarantees and give the police the upper hand. That hydraulic pressure has probably never been greater than it is today.

Yet if the individual is no longer to be sovereign, if the police can pick him up whenever they do not like the cut of his jib, if they can "seize" and "search" him in their discretion, we enter a new regime. The decision to enter it should be made only after a full debate by the people of this country.

Note

Chief Justice Warren's opinion is reprinted with few major deletions. It is not only long; it is repetitious. Most of the repetition appears to be an intentional effort to make as clear as possible what the Court was approving. Justice Harlan's opinion implies that the Court missed a step in its reasoning. It suggests that the right to frisk depends upon the right to stop. Can you see any reasons for the Chief Justice choosing to write his opinion as he did?

Is it surprising that the Court does not dwell on Fourth Amendment history in its opinion? Are you impressed by the way in which the Court articulates the policies of the Fourth Amendment and squares *Terry* with them?

A poll of citizens on stop and frisk probably would produce a vote much like that of the Justices—i.e., an overwhelming majority would approve. But what is the case for stop and frisk on less than probable cause?

It would be hard to overestimate the effect of *Terry* on Fourth Amendment jurisprudence. The Court not only permitted stops and frisks on less than probable cause; it also explicitly invoked the reasonableness clause over the warrant clause as the governing standard. Perhaps the Court intended to limit use of the reasonableness clause and its balancing approach to the area of stop and frisk; but once that balancing process was undertaken in one area, it became difficult to prevent its application to other searches and seizures. See Sundby, A Return to

Fourth Amendment Basics: Undoing the Mischief of *Camara* and *Terry*, 72 Minn. L.Rev. 383 (1988).

9. *Stop and Frisk Applied*

The *Terry* decision with its companion cases—Sibron v. New York, and Peters v. New York, 392 U.S. 40 (1968)—was only the first step in the articulation of what the Fourth Amendment permits the police to do without probable cause. The Supreme Court's first post-*Terry* effort is illustrative of the difficulty that courts have had in applying general standards to specific facts.

ADAMS v. WILLIAMS

Supreme Court of the United States, 1972.
407 U.S. 143.

MR. JUSTICE REHNQUIST delivered the opinion of the Court.

Respondent Robert Williams was convicted in a Connecticut state court of illegal possession of a handgun found during a "stop and frisk," as well as of possession of heroin that was found during a full search incident to his weapons arrest. After respondent's conviction was affirmed by the Supreme Court of Connecticut, this Court denied certiorari. Williams' petition for federal habeas corpus relief was denied by the District Court and by a divided panel of the Second Circuit, but on rehearing *en banc* the Court of Appeals granted relief. That court held that evidence introduced at Williams' trial had been obtained by an unlawful search of his person and car, and thus the state court judgments of conviction should be set aside. Since we conclude that the policeman's actions here conformed to the standards this Court laid down in Terry v. Ohio, we reverse.

Police Sgt. John Connolly was alone early in the morning on car patrol duty in a high-crime area of Bridgeport, Connecticut. At approximately 2:15 a.m. a person known to Sgt. Connolly approached his cruiser and informed him that an individual seated in a nearby vehicle was carrying narcotics and had a gun at his waist.

After calling for assistance on his car radio, Sgt. Connolly approached the vehicle to investigate the informant's report. Connolly tapped on the car window and asked the occupant, Robert Williams, to open the door. When Williams rolled down the window instead, the sergeant reached into the car and removed a fully loaded revolver from Williams' waistband. The gun had not been visible to Connolly from outside the car, but it was in precisely the place indicated by the informant. Williams was then arrested by Connolly for unlawful possession of the pistol. A search incident to that arrest was conducted after other officers arrived. They found substantial quantities of heroin on Williams' person and in the car, and they found a machete and a second revolver hidden in the automobile.

Respondent contends that the initial seizure of his pistol, upon which rested the later search and seizure of other weapons and narcotics, was not justified by the informant's tip to Sgt. Connolly. He claims that absent a more reliable informant, or some corroboration of the tip, the policeman's actions were unreasonable under the standards set forth in Terry v. Ohio, supra.

In *Terry* this Court recognized that "a police officer may in appropriate circumstances and in an appropriate manner approach a person for purposes of investigating possibly criminal behavior even though there is no probable cause to make an arrest." The Fourth Amendment does not require a policeman who lacks the precise level of information necessary for probable cause to arrest to simply shrug his shoulders and allow a crime to occur or a criminal to escape. On the contrary, *Terry* recognizes that it may be the essence of good police work to adopt an intermediate response. A brief stop of a suspicious individual, in order to determine his identity or to maintain the status quo momentarily while obtaining more information, may be most reasonable in light of the facts known to the officer at the time.

The Court recognized in *Terry* that the policeman making a reasonable investigatory stop should not be denied the opportunity to protect himself from attack by a hostile suspect. "When an officer is justified in believing that the individual whose suspicious behavior he is investigating at close range is armed and presently dangerous to the officer or to others," he may conduct a limited protective search for concealed weapons. The purpose of this limited search is not to discover evidence of crime, but to allow the officer to pursue his investigation without fear of violence, and thus the frisk for weapons might be equally necessary and reasonable, whether or not carrying a concealed weapon violated any applicable state law. So long as the officer is entitled to make a forcible stop, and has reason to believe that the suspect is armed and dangerous, he may conduct a weapons search limited in scope to this protective purpose.

Applying these principles to the present case, we believe that Sgt. Connolly acted justifiably in responding to his informant's tip. The informant was known to him personally and had provided him with information in the past. This is a stronger case than obtains in the case of an anonymous telephone tip. The informant here came forward personally to give information that was immediately verifiable at the scene. Indeed, under Connecticut law, the informant might have been subject to immediate arrest for making a false complaint had Sgt. Connolly's investigation proved the tip incorrect. Thus, while the Court's decisions indicate that this informant's unverified tip may have been insufficient for a narcotics arrest or search warrant, the information carried enough indicia of reliability to justify the officer's forcible stop of Williams.

In reaching this conclusion, we reject respondent's argument that reasonable cause for a stop and frisk can only be based on the officer's personal observation rather than on information supplied by another person. Informants' tips, like all other clues and evidence coming to a policeman on the scene, may vary greatly in their value and reliability. * * *

While properly investigating the activity of a person who was reported to be carrying narcotics and a concealed weapon and who was sitting alone in a car in a high-crime area at 2:15 in the morning, Sgt. Connolly had ample reason to fear of his safety.[a] When Williams rolled down his window, rather than complying with the policeman's request to step out of the car so that his

a. Figures reported by the Federal Bureau of Investigation indicate that 125 policemen were murdered in 1971, with all but five of them having been killed by gunshot wounds. Federal Bureau of Investigation Law Enforcement Bulletin, Feb. 1972, p. 33. According to one study, approximately 30% of police shootings occurred when a police officer approached a suspect seated in an automobile. Bristow, Police Officer Shootings—A Tactical Evaluation, 54 J. Crim.L.C. & P.S. 93 (1963). [For a skeptical view of these figures, see the opinion of Justice Stevens in Pennsylvania v. Mimms, infra.]

movements could more easily be seen, the revolver allegedly at Williams' waist became an even greater threat. Under these circumstances the policeman's action in reaching to the spot where the gun was thought to be hidden constituted a limited intrusion designed to insure his safety, and we conclude that it was reasonable. * * *

Once Sgt. Connolly had found the gun precisely where the informant had predicted, probable cause existed to arrest Williams for unlawful possession of the weapon. * * * In the present case the policeman found Williams in possession of a gun in precisely the place predicted by the informant. This tended to corroborate the reliability of the informant's further report of narcotics and, together with the surrounding circumstances, certainly suggested no lawful explanation for possession of the gun. * * * Under the circumstances surrounding Williams' possession of the gun seized by Sgt. Connolly, the arrest on the weapons charge was supported by probable cause, and the search of his person and of the car incident to that arrest was lawful. The fruits of the search were therefore properly admitted at Williams' trial, and the Court of Appeals erred in reaching a contrary conclusion.

Reversed.

MR. JUSTICE DOUGLAS, with whom MR. JUSTICE MARSHALL concurs, dissenting.

My views have been stated in substance by Judge Friendly, dissenting, in the Court of Appeals. 436 F.2d 30, 35. Connecticut allows its citizens to carry weapons, concealed or otherwise, at will, provided they have a permit. Conn.Gen.Stat.Rev. §§ 29–35, 29–38. Connecticut law gives its police no authority to frisk a person for a permit. Yet the arrest was for illegal possession of a gun. The only basis for that arrest was the informer's tip on the narcotics. Can it be said that a man in possession of narcotics will not have a permit for his gun? Is that why the arrest for possession of a gun in the free-and-easy State of Connecticut becomes constitutional?

* * *

MR. JUSTICE BRENNAN, dissenting.

The crucial question on which this case turns, as the Court concedes, is whether, there being no contention that Williams acted voluntarily in rolling down the window of his car, the State had shown sufficient cause to justify Sgt. Connolly's "forcible" stop. I would affirm, believing, for the following reasons stated by Judge, now Chief Judge, Friendly, dissenting, 436 F.2d 30, 38–39, that the State did not make that showing:

> "To begin, I have the gravest hesitancy in extending [*Terry*] to crimes like the possession of narcotics. * * * There is too much danger that, instead of the stop being the object and the protective frisk an incident thereto, the reverse will be true. Against that we have here the added fact of the report that Williams had a gun on his person. * * * [But] Connecticut allows its citizens to carry weapons, concealed or otherwise, at will, provided only they have a permit, Conn.Gen.Stat. §§ 29–35 and 29–38, and gives its police officers no special authority to stop for the purpose of determining whether the citizen has one. * * *
>
> "If I am wrong in thinking that *Terry* should not be applied at all to mere possessory offenses, * * * I would not find the combination of Officer Connolly's almost meaningless observation and the tip in this case to be sufficient justification for the intrusion. * * *

* * *

MR. JUSTICE MARSHALL, with whom MR. JUSTICE DOUGLAS joins, dissenting.

* * *

In today's decision the Court ignores the fact that *Terry* begrudgingly accepted the necessity for creating an exception from the warrant requirement of the Fourth Amendment and treats this case as if warrantless searches were the rule rather than the "narrowly drawn" exception. This decision betrays the careful balance that *Terry* sought to strike between a citizen's right to privacy and his government's responsibility for effective law enforcement and expends the concept of warrantless searches far beyond anything heretofore recognized as legitimate. I dissent.

I

* * *

The only information that the informant had previously given the officer involved homosexual conduct in the local railroad station. The following colloquy took place between respondent's counsel and the officer at the hearing on respondent's motion to suppress the evidence that had been seized from him.

> "Q. Now, with respect to the information that was given you about homosexuals in the Bridgeport Police Station [*sic*], did that lead to an arrest? A. No.
>
> "Q. An arrest was not made. A. No. There was no substantiating evidence.
>
> * * *
>
> "Q. And what do you mean by that? A. I didn't have occasion to witness these individuals committing any crime of any nature.
>
> "Q. In other words, after this person gave you the information, you checked for corroboration before you made an arrest. Is that right? A. Well, I checked to determine the possibility of homosexual activity.
>
> * * *
>
> "Q. Since an arrest was not made, I presume you didn't find any substantiating information. A. No.
>
> "Q. So that, you don't recall any other specific information given you about the commission of crimes by this informant. A. No.
>
> "Q. And you still thought this person was reliable. A. Yes."

Were we asked to determine whether the information supplied by the informant was sufficient to provide probable cause for an arrest and search rather than a stop and frisk, there can be no doubt that we would hold that it was insufficient. * * *

Assuming, *arguendo*, that this case truly involves, not an arrest and a search incident thereto, but a stop and frisk,[b] we must decide whether or not the information possessed by the officer justified this interference with respondent's liberty. *Terry*, our only case to actually uphold a stop and frisk, is not directly in point, because the police officer in that case acted on the basis of his own personal observations. No informant was involved. But the rationale of *Terry* is still controlling, and it requires that we condemn the conduct of the police officer in encountering the respondent.

Terry did not hold that whenever a policeman has a hunch that a citizen is engaging in criminal activity, he may engage in a stop and frisk. It held that if police officers want to stop and frisk,

b. Terry v. Ohio, 392 U.S. 1 (1968), makes it clear that a stop and frisk is a search and seizure within the meaning of the Fourth Amendment. When I use the term stop and frisk herein, I merely intend to emphasize that it is, as *Terry* held, a lesser intrusion than a full-scale search and seizure.

they must have specific facts from which they can reasonably infer that an individual is engaged in criminal activity and is armed and dangerous. * * * When we legitimated the conduct of the officer in *Terry* we did so because of the substantial *reliability* of the information on which the officer based his decision to act.

If the Court does not ignore the care with which we examined the knowledge possessed by the officer in *Terry* when he acted, then I cannot see how the actions of the officer in this case can be upheld. The Court explains what the officer knew about respondent before accosting him. But what is more significant is what he did not know. With respect to the scene generally, the officer had no idea how long respondent had been in the car, how long the car had been parked, or to whom the car belonged. With respect to the gun,[c] the officer did not know if or when the informant had ever seen the gun, or whether the gun was carried legally, as Connecticut law permitted, or illegally. And with respect to the narcotics, the officer did not know what kind of narcotics respondent allegedly had, whether they were legally or illegally possessed, what the basis of the informant's knowledge was, or even whether the informant was capable of distinguishing narcotics from other substances.

Unable to answer any of these questions, the officer nevertheless determined that it was necessary to intrude on respondent's liberty. I believe that his determination was totally unreasonable. As I read *Terry*, an officer may act on the basis of *reliable* information short of probable cause to make a stop, and ultimately a frisk, if necessary; but the officer may not use unreliable, unsubstantiated, conclusory hearsay to justify an invasion of liberty. *Terry* never meant to approve the kind of knee-jerk police reaction that we have before us in this case.

* * *

II

Even if I could agree with the Court that the stop and frisk in this case was proper, I could not go further and sustain the arrest and the subsequent searches. * * *

Once the officer seized the gun from respondent, it is uncontradicted that he did not ask whether respondent had a license to carry it, or whether respondent carried it for any legal reason under Connecticut law. Rather, the officer placed him under arrest immediately and hastened to search his person. Since Connecticut has not made it illegal for private citizens to carry guns, there is nothing in the facts of this case to warrant a man "of prudence and caution" to believe that any offense had been committed merely because respondent had a gun on his person.[d]

* * *

c. The fact that the respondent carried his gun in a high-crime area is irrelevant. In such areas it is more probable than not that citizens would be more likely to carry weapons authorized by the State to protect themselves.

d. The Court appears to rely on the fact that the existence of the gun corroborated the information supplied to the officer by the informant. It cannot be disputed that there is minimal corroboration here, but the fact remains that the officer still lacked any knowledge that respondent had done anything illegal. Since carrying a gun is not *per se* illegal in Connecticut, the fact that respondent carried a gun is no more relevant to probable cause than the fact that his shirt may have been blue, or that he was wearing a jacket. Moreover, the fact that the informant can identify a gun on sight does not indicate an ability to do the same with narcotics. The corroboration of this one fact is a far cry from the corroboration that the Court found sufficient to sustain an arrest in Draper v. United States, 358 U.S. 307 (1959).

Note

What guidance do the police have from the Supreme Court after Adams v. Williams? Do they know what kinds of information can be used to satisfy *Terry*? Does *Adams* answer the question left open in *Terry*, whether the police can make a forcible investigative stop? Does *Adams* mean that stop and frisk techniques can be used in dealing with all criminal activity? (In connection with this last question, examine closely how Justice Rehnquist attempts to avoid Judge Friendly's problems with extending *Terry* to drug possession cases. Justice Brennan may not have fully realized the shift Justice Rehnquist made. This might explain why Justice Marshall wrote about the application of *Terry* to the facts rather than the nature of the crime under investigation.) Does the Court identify the points when a stop under *Terry* occurs and when a touching of a person amounts to a frisk? Did the *Adams* court improperly ignore language used by Chief Justice Warren in *Terry* that implied that a suspect should have an opportunity to dispel an officer's fear before being searched?

10. Stop and Frisk Extended

PENNSYLVANIA v. MIMMS

Supreme Court of the United States, 1977.
434 U.S. 106.

Per Curiam.

* * *

The facts are not in dispute. While on routine patrol, two Philadelphia police officers observed respondent Harry Mimms driving an automobile with an expired license plate. The officers stopped the vehicle for the purpose of issuing a traffic summons. One of the officers approached and asked respondent to step out of the car and produce his owner's card and operator's license. Respondent alighted, whereupon the officer noticed a large bulge under respondent's sports jacket. Fearing that the bulge might be a weapon, the officer frisked respondent and discovered in his waistband a .38-caliber revolver loaded with five rounds of ammunition. The other occupant of the car was carrying a .32-caliber revolver. Respondent was immediately arrested and subsequently indicted for carrying a concealed deadly weapon and for unlawfully carrying a firearm without a license. His motion to suppress the revolver was denied; and, after a trial at which the revolver was introduced into evidence, respondent was convicted on both counts.

The Supreme Court of Pennsylvania reversed respondent's conviction, however, holding that the revolver should have been suppressed because it was seized contrary to the guarantees contained in the Fourth and Fourteenth Amendments to the United States Constitution. The Pennsylvania court did not doubt that the officers acted reasonably in stopping the car. It was also willing to assume, *arguendo*, that the limited search for weapons was proper once the officer observed the bulge under respondent's coat. But the court nonetheless thought the search constitutionally infirm because the officer's order to respondent to get out of the car was an impermissible "seizure." This was so because the officer could not point to "objective observable facts to support a suspicion that criminal activity was afoot or that the occupants of the vehicle posed a threat to police safety." Since this unconstitutional intrusion led directly to observance of the bulge and to the subsequent "pat down," the revolver was the fruit of an unconstitutional search, and, in the view of the Supreme court of Pennsylvania, should have been suppressed.

We do not agree with this conclusion.
* * *

In this case, unlike Terry v. Ohio, there is no question about the propriety of the initial restrictions on respondent's freedom of movement. Respondent was driving an automobile with expired license tags in violation of the Pennsylvania Motor Vehicle Code. Deferring for a moment the legality of the "frisk" once the bulge had been observed, we need presently deal only with the narrow question of whether the order to get out of the car, issued after the driver was lawfully detained, was reasonable and thus permissible under the Fourth Amendment. This inquiry must therefore focus not on the intrusion resulting from the request to stop the vehicle or from the later "pat-down," but on the incremental intrusion resulting from the request to get out of the car once the vehicle was lawfully stopped.

Placing the question in this narrowed frame, we look first to that side of the balance which bears the officer's interest in taking the action that he did. The State freely concedes the officer had no reason to suspect foul play from the particular driver at the time of the stop, there having been nothing unusual or suspicious about his behavior. It was apparently his practice to order all drivers out of their vehicles as a matter of course whenever they had been stopped for a traffic violation. The State argues that this practice was adopted as a precautionary measure to afford a degree of protection to the officer and that it may be justified on that ground. Establishing a face-to-face confrontation diminishes the possibility, otherwise substantial, that the driver can make unobserved movements; this, in turn, reduces the likelihood that the officer will be the victim of an assault.

We think it too plain for argument that the State's proffered justification—the safety of the officer—is both legitimate and weighty. * * * "According to one study, approximately 30% of police shootings occurred when a police officer approached a suspect seated in an automobile. Bristow, Police Officer Shootings—A Tactical Evaluation, 54 J.Crim.L.C. & P.S. 93 (1963)." Adams v. Williams. We are aware that not all these assaults occur when issuing traffic summons, but we have before expressly declined to accept the argument that traffic violations necessarily involve less danger to officers than other types of confrontations. * * *

The hazard of accidental injury from passing traffic to an officer standing on the driver's side of the vehicle may also be appreciable in some situations. Rather than conversing while standing exposed to moving traffic, the officer prudently may prefer to ask the driver of the vehicle to step out of the car and off onto the shoulder of the road where the inquiry may be pursued with greater safety to both.

Against this important interest we are asked to weigh the intrusion into the driver's personal liberty occasioned not by the initial stop of the vehicle, which was admittedly justified, but by the order to get out of the car. We think this additional intrusion can only be described as *de minimis.* The driver is being asked to expose to view very little more of his person than is already exposed. * * * What is at most a mere inconvenience cannot prevail when balanced against legitimate concerns for the officer's safety.[a]

a. Contrary to the suggestion in the dissent of our Brother Stevens, we do not hold today that "whenever an officer has an occasion to speak with the driver of a vehicle, he may also order the driver out of the car." We hold only that once a motor vehicle has been lawfully detained for a traffic violation, the police officers may order the driver to get out of the vehicle without violating the Fourth Amendment's proscription of unreasonable searches and seizures.

There remains the second question of the propriety of the search once the bulge in the jacket was observed. We have as little doubt on this point as on the first; the answer is controlled by Terry v. Ohio, supra. * * *

* * *

MR. JUSTICE MARSHALL, dissenting.

* * *

In the instant case, the officer did not have even the slightest hint, prior to ordering respondent out of the car, that respondent might have a gun. As the Court notes, "the officer had no reason to suspect foul play." The car was stopped for the most routine of police procedures, the issuance of a summons for an expired license plate. Yet the Court holds that, once the officer had made this routine stop, he was justified in imposing the additional intrusion of ordering respondent out of the car, regardless of whether there was any individualized reason to fear respondent.

Such a result cannot be explained by *Terry,* which limited the nature of the intrusion by reference to the reason for the stop. * * * In the instant case "the circumstance * * * which justified the interference in the first place" was an expired license plate. There is simply no relation at all between that circumstance and the order to step out of the car.

* * *

MR. JUSTICE STEVENS, with whom MR. JUSTICE BRENNAN and MR. JUSTICE MARSHALL join, dissenting.

* * *

Today, without argument, the Court adopts still another—and even lesser—standard of justification for a major category of police seizures.[b] More important, it appears to abandon "the central teaching of this Court's Fourth Amendment jurisprudence"—which has ordinarily required individualized inquiry into the particular facts justifying every police intrusion—in favor of a general rule covering countless situations. But what is most disturbing is the fact that this important innovation is announced almost casually, in the course of explaining the summary reversal of a decision the Court should not even bother to review.

* * *

This case illustrates two ways in which haste can introduce a new element of confusion into an already complex set of rules. First, the Court has based its legal ruling on a factual assumption about police safety that is dubious at best; second, the Court has created an entirely new legal standard of justification for intrusions on the liberty of the citizen.

Without any attempt to differentiate among the multitude of varying situations in which an officer may approach a person seated in an automobile, the Court characterizes the officer's risk as "inordinate" on the basis of this statement:

> " 'According to one study, approximately 30% of police shootings occurred when a police officer approached a suspect seated in an automobile."

That statement does not fairly characterize the study to which it refers. Moreover, the study does not indicate that police officers can minimize the risk of being shot by ordering drivers stopped for routine traffic violations out of their cars. * * *

* * *

[The] figures tell us very little about the risk associated with the routine traf-

b. The Court does not dispute, nor do I, that ordering Mimms out of his car was a seizure. A seizure occurs whenever an "officer, by means of physical force or show of authority, * * * in some way restrain[s] the liberty of a citizen * * *".

fic stop;[c] and they lend no support to the Court's assumption that ordering the routine traffic offender out of his car significantly enhances the officer's safety. Arguably, such an order could actually aggravate the officer's danger because the fear of a search might cause a serious offender to take desperate action that would be unnecessary if he remained in the vehicle while being ticketed. Whatever the reason, it is significant that some experts in this area of human behavior strongly recommend that the police officer "never allow the violator to get out of the car * * *."[d]

Obviously it is not my purpose to express an opinion on the safest procedure to be followed in making traffic arrests or to imply that the arresting officer faces no significant hazard, even in the apparently routine situation. I do submit, however, that no matter how hard we try we cannot totally eliminate the danger associated with law enforcement, and that, before adopting a nationwide rule, we should give further consideration to the infinite variety of situations in which today's holding may be applied.

* * *

Until today the law applicable to seizures of a person has required individualized inquiry into the reason for each intrusion, or some comparable guarantee against arbitrary harassment.[e] A factual demonstration of probable cause is required to justify an arrest; an articulable reason to suspect criminal activity and possible violence is needed to justify a stop and frisk. But to eliminate any requirement that an officer be able to explain the reasons for his actions signals an abandonment of effective judicial supervision of this kind of seizure and leaves police discretion utterly without limits. Some citizens will be subjected to this minor indignity while others—perhaps those with more expensive cars, or different bumper stickers, or different-colored skin—may escape it entirely.

* * *

Note

Two arguments are accepted by the majority—one is that officers should be able to order drivers stopped for violations out of their cars to avoid assaults, and the other is that such an order is a valid attempt to avoid traffic injuries. It is not clear whether the state pressed the second argument. Are you persuaded by it? Is

c. Over the past 10 years, more than 1,000 police officers have been murdered. FBI, Uniform Crime Reports 289 (1976). Approximately 10% of those killings, or about 11 each year, occurred during "traffic pursuits and stops," but it is not clear how many of those pursuits and stops involved offenses such as reckless or highspeed driving, rather than offenses such as driving on an expired license, or how often the shootings could have been avoided by ordering the driver to dismount.

d. "2. *Never allow the violator to get out of the car* and stand to its left. If he does get out, which should be avoided, walk him to the rear and right side of the car. Quite obviously this is a much safer area to conduct a conversation." V. Folley, Police Patrol Techniques and Tactics 95 (1973) (emphasis in original).

Another authority is even more explicit:

"The officer should stand slightly to the rear of the front door and doorpost. This will prevent the violator from suddenly opening the door and striking the officer. In order to thoroughly protect himself as much as possible, the officer should reach with his weak hand and push the lock button down if the window is open. This will give an indication to the driver that he is to remain inside the vehicle. * * * A. Yount, Vehicle Stops Manual, Misdemeanor and Felony 2–3 (1976).

e. Government intrusions must be justified with particularity in all but a few narrowly cabined contexts. Inspections pursuant to a general regulatory scheme and stops at border checkpoints are the best known exceptions to the particularity requirement. And even these limited exceptions fit within a broader rule—that the general populace should never be subjected to seizures without some assurance that the intruding officials are acting under a carefully limited grant of discretion.

it an argument that depends on the facts of a particular case or one that justifies a rule uniformly applicable in all cases? The first argument is not new. It was made in Adams v. Williams and in a case decided one year after *Adams,* United States v. Robinson, which is presented infra.

Do the statistics help either the majority or the dissent? [17] Assume that you know that no officer ever was killed or seriously wounded making a traffic stop. Would you know whether the reason for the zero figure was an absence of danger in such stops or the taking of precautions like ordering people out of cars? Of course not.

The dissent argues that a major category of police seizures now can be justified without any standard of proof. But in *Mimms* there was probable cause to stop the car initially. Are you persuaded that ordering someone out of a car—at least as long as no frisk or other touching of the person can occur without independent justification—amounts to an additional seizure that should be controlled by a reasonable suspicion standard? What if the driver of the car wants to get out, and the officer (perhaps relying on Justice Stevens' police authorities) wants the driver to stay in the car? Is this an additional seizure for Fourth Amendment purposes? Is the dissent's position that the driver can do whatever she wants? What if the officer permits the driver to remain in the car, but says "keep your hands where I can see them"? Is this an invalid seizure if unaccompanied by articulable suspicion? If the intrusion here is less than in *Terry,* why does the dissent opt for the *Terry* standard?

Do real possibilities of harassment exist under the majority's view? Identify them. Does the *Terry* standard provide protection against harassment in contexts like *Mimms? Mimms* is far removed from the general warrants and writs of assistance that generated the desire for a Fourth Amendment. Is it fruitless to look to history and to the ideals of the framers in deciding how to treat police decisions like that in *Mimms?*

Mimms is extended to passengers in State v. Webster, ___ Ariz. ___, 824 P.2d 768 (App.1991), and State v. Ferrise, 269 N.W.2d 888 (Minn.1978). A contrary view is found in Cousart v. United States, 1991 WL 188785 (D.C.App.1991), where the court reasoned that "the intrusion on the passenger's privacy interest is clearly greater than on the driver" since the passenger is "an innocent bystander." The court also noted that "the risk of accidental injury from passing traffic, of concern to the Court in *Mimms,* is less likely when the officer is on the passenger side of the car."

In New York v. Class, 475 U.S. 106 (1986), the Court held that "in order to observe a Vehicle Identification Number (VIN) generally visible from outside an automobile, a police officer may reach into the passenger compartment of a vehicle to move papers obscuring the VIN after its driver has been stopped for a traffic violation and has exited the car." Justice O'Connor wrote for the Court. She reasoned that "[t]he VIN is a significant thread in the web of regulation of the automobile" and that "[a] motorist must surely expect that such regulation will on occasion require the State to determine the VIN of his or her vehicle, and the individual's reasonable expectation of privacy in the VIN is thereby diminished," especially for a driver who has committed a traffic violation. Thus, she concluded that police officers acted properly, after stopping a car for speeding and having a cracked windshield, in detaining the driver briefly outside the car while entering the car to move papers blocking the VIN after the driver voluntarily exited the car.

17. For a criticism of the statistics, see Sherman, Enforcement Workshop: Traffic Stops and Police Officers' Authority: A Comment on Pennsylvania v. Mimms, 14 Crim. L.Bull. 343 (1978).

When an officer found a gun, he was authorized to seize it in plain view. She relied upon *Mimms* to reason that officers may detain an individual outside a car to protect themselves from danger. Justice O'Connor noted that the Court's holding "does not authorize a police officer to enter a vehicle to obtain a dashboard-mounted VIN when the VIN is visible from outside the automobile," since "[i]f the VIN is in the plain view of someone outside the vehicle, there is no justification for governmental intrusion into the passenger compartment to see it."

Justice Powell, joined by Chief Justice Burger, concurred, emphasized the important governmental interest in the VIN, and stated that "the Fourth Amendment question may be stated simply as whether the officer's efforts to inspect the VIN were reasonable." Justice Brennan, joined by Justices Marshall and Stevens, dissented. He argued that "[t]he police had no justification whatever, let alone probable cause, to *search* for the VIN, and therefore no amount of 'balancing' can make the *search* of respondent's car constitutional." He added that "[r]egardless of whether he had a reasonable expectation of privacy in the VIN, respondent clearly retained a reasonable expectation of privacy with respect to the area searched by the police—the car's interior." Justice Brennan concluded that "the mere fact that the state utilizes the VIN in conjunction with regulations designed to promote highway safety does not give the police a reason to *search* for such information every time a motorist violates a traffic law. Justice White, joined by Justice Stevens, also dissented, stating that he was unprepared to accept the Court's reasoning that "the governmental interest in obtaining the VIN by entering a protected area is sufficient to outweigh the owner's privacy interest in the interior of the car."

Class is assailed in Maclin, New York v. Class: A Little–Noticed Case with Disturbing Implications, 78 J. Crim.L. & Crim. 1 (1987). The author asks whether the police could search a glove compartment for a registration certificate? Whether they could enter a vehicle to search for a driver's license inadvertently left behind in a purse, suitcase, or other container? Whether they could enter a car to inspect the VIN after stopping a motorist at a roadblock to check for license and registrations? Are these situations distinguishable from the facts of *Class*? The author argues that "the assertion that a motorist cannot reasonably expect any privacy in an object required by law to be in plain view is irrelevant to a logical resolution of the constitutional question under review." Is the argument correct? If Class had remained in his car, could he have been validly ordered to move the papers?

In Michigan v. Summers, 452 U.S. 692 (1981), the Court held, 6–3, that police officers with a search warrant for a home can require persons on the premises, even if leaving when the police arrive, to remain while the search warrant is executed. The Court held that such a seizure would always be reasonable, given the state's interest in preventing flight, and the risk that persons leaving the premises would attempt to destroy evidence. The Court noted that the intrusion was less serious than the public stops sanctioned in *Terry,* and that the search warrant provided protection against overreaching by the police officers. Does *Mimms* lend support to the result in *Summers*?

11. When Does a Seizure Occur? The Line Between "Stop" and "Encounter"

In *Terry,* it was not difficult to determine the precise point at which the stop occurred: the officer physically grabbed Terry and spun him around.

However, the Court has had more difficulty determining whether a stop has occurred when the police conduct is not as affirmatively coercive as in *Terry.* In United States v. Mendenhall, 446 U.S. 544 (1980), Mendenhall was observed by Drug Enforcement Administration agents at the Detroit Airport as she arrived on a flight from Los Angeles. They suspected her of being a drug courier. The agents approached her as she was walking through the concourse, identified themselves as federal agents, and one agent asked to see her identification and airline ticket. The driver's license she produced was in her name, but her ticket was not. She became extremely nervous. The agent gave her back her license and ticket and asked Mendenhall to accompany him to the airport DEA office for further questions. Without saying anything, she did so. In the office Mendenhall said she would allow a search of her person and handbag when asked by the agent to do so. In a strip search of her person drugs were found. Mendenhall was arrested, prosecuted and convicted.

Justice Stewart, joined only by Justice Rehnquist, addressed an argument that the government had not made in the lower courts and concluded that

> no "seizure" of the respondent occurred [when she was first approached]. The events took place in the public concourse. The agents wore no uniforms and displayed no weapons. They did not summon the respondent to their presence, but instead approached her and identified themselves as federal agents. They requested, but did not demand to see the respondent's identification and ticket. Such conduct, without more, did not amount to an intrusion upon any constitutionally protected interest. * * *

This conclusion resulted from application of the following rule:

> [a] person has been "seized" within the meaning of the Fourth Amendment only if, in view of all the circumstances surrounding the incident, a reasonable person would have believed that he was not free to leave. Examples of circumstances that might indicate a seizure, even where the person did not attempt to leave, would be the threatening presence of several officers, the display of a weapon by an officer, some physical touching of the person of the citizen, or the use of language or tone of voice indicating that compliance with the officer's request might be compelled.

Justice Stewart's "free to walk away test" did not command a majority of the Court in *Mendenhall;* seven Justices found that the question of whether a seizure had occurred had not been properly raised in the lower court. A plurality of the Court applied the Stewart test in Florida v. Royer, 460 U.S. 491 (1983). Justice White, writing for himself and Justices Marshall, Powell and Stevens, stated the facts:

> On January 3, 1978, Royer was observed at Miami International Airport by two plain-clothes detectives of the Dade County, Florida, Public Safety Department assigned to the County's Organized Crime Bureau, Narcotics Investigation Section. Detectives Johnson and Magdalena believed that Royer's appearance, mannerisms, luggage, and actions fit the so-called "drug courier profile." Royer, apparently unaware of the attention he had attracted, purchased a one-way ticket to New York City and checked his two suitcases, placing on each suitcase an identification tag bearing the name "Holt" and the destination, "LaGuardia". As Royer made his way to the concourse which led to the airline boarding area, the two detectives approached him, identified themselves as policemen working out of the sheriff's office, and asked if Royer had a "moment" to speak with them; Royer said "Yes."

Upon request, but without oral consent, Royer produced for the detectives his airline ticket and his driver's license. The airline ticket, like the baggage identification tags, bore the name "Holt," while the driver's license carried respondent's correct name, "Royer." When the detectives asked about the discrepancy, Royer explained that a friend had made the reservation in the name of "Holt." Royer became noticeably more nervous during this conversation, whereupon the detectives informed Royer that they were in fact narcotics investigators and that they had reason to suspect him of transporting narcotics.

The detectives did not return his airline ticket and identification but asked Royer to accompany them to a room, approximately forty feet away, adjacent to the concourse. Royer said nothing in response but went with the officers as he had been asked to do. The room was later described by Detective Johnson as a "large storage closet," located in the stewardesses' lounge and containing a small desk and two chairs. Without Royer's consent or agreement, Detective Johnson, using Royer's baggage check stubs, retrieved the "Holt" luggage from the airline and brought it to the room where respondent and Detective Magdalena were waiting. Royer was asked if he would consent to a search of the suitcases. Without orally responding to this request, Royer produced a key and unlocked one of the suitcases, which the detective then opened without seeking further assent from Royer. Drugs were found in that suitcase. According to Detective Johnson, Royer stated that he did not know the combination to the lock on the second suitcase. When asked if he objected to the detective opening the second suitcase, Royer said "no, go ahead," and did not object when the detective explained that the suitcase might have to be broken open. The suitcase was pried open by the officers and more marihuana was found. Royer was then told that he was under arrest. Approximately fifteen minutes had elapsed from the time the detectives initially approached respondent until his arrest upon the discovery of the contraband.

Justice White observed that Royer had testified that he believed he was not free to leave the officers' presence and that Detective Johnson stated that he did not believe he had probable cause to arrest until after he opened the suitcases. He summarized some of the law regarding "stops."

Some preliminary observations are in order. First, it is unquestioned that without a warrant to search Royer's luggage and in the absence of probable cause and exigent circumstances, the validity of the search depended on Royer's purported consent. Neither is it disputed that where the validity of a search rests on consent, the State has the burden of proving that the necessary consent was obtained and that it was freely and voluntarily given, a burden that is not satisfied by showing a mere submission to a claim of lawful authority.

Second, law enforcement officers do not violate the Fourth Amendment by merely approaching an individual on the street or in another public place, by asking him if he is willing to answer some questions, by putting questions to him if the person is willing to listen, or by offering in evidence in a criminal prosecution his voluntary answers to such questions. Nor would the fact that the officer identifies himself as a police officer, without more, convert the encounter into a seizure requiring some level of objective justification. The person approached, however, need not answer any question put to him; indeed, he may decline to listen to the questions at all and may go on his way. He may not be detained even momentarily without reasonable, objective grounds for doing so; and his refusal to listen or answer does not, without more, furnish

> those grounds. If there is no detention—no seizure within the meaning of the Fourth Amendment—then no constitutional rights have been infringed.

The plurality rejected the State's argument that the police activity could be justified as a consensual encounter, and thus that no "seizure" ever occurred.

> We find this submission untenable. Asking for and examining Royer's ticket and his driver's license were no doubt permissible in themselves, but when the officers identified themselves as narcotics agents, told Royer that he was suspected of transporting narcotics, and asked him to accompany them to the police room, while retaining his ticket and driver's license and without indicating in any way that he was free to depart, Royer was effectively seized for the purposes of the Fourth Amendment. These circumstances surely amount to a show of official authority such that "a reasonable person would have believed he was not free to leave." United States v. Mendenhall, 446 U.S. 544, 554 (Opinion of Stewart, J.). * * *
>
> Here, Royer's ticket and identification remained in the possession of the officers throughout the encounter; the officers also seized and had possession of his luggage. As a practical matter, Royer could not leave the airport without them. In *Mendenhall,* no luggage was involved, the ticket and identification were immediately returned, and the officers were careful to advise that the suspect could decline to be searched. Here, the officers had seized Royer's luggage and made no effort to advise him that he need not consent to the search.

Justice Brennan concurred in the result. Four Justices dissented in *Royer* on the ground that, while Royer may have been seized, the seizure was supported by reasonable suspicion and the police lawfully obtained Royer's consent. Does the Court give sufficient guidance to the police to determine what type of conduct triggers a Fourth Amendment seizure? Lower courts have tried to impart some guidance. See United States v. Jefferson, 906 F.2d 346 (8th Cir.1990) (implying that failing to return necessary documentation such as driver's license always constitutes a stop); United States v. High, 921 F.2d 112 (7th Cir.1990) (suggesting that officers "preface their questions with a statement that the encounter is consensual and that the citizen is free to go").

Can you determine when a seizure occurs under *Mendenhall* and *Royer*? It remains apparent that lower courts find *Royer* to be no more helpful in determining when a seizure occurred during an airport confrontation than *Mendenhall* was. See, e.g., United States v. Berryman, 717 F.2d 650 (1st Cir.1983), a case in which the court sitting en banc voted, 3–1, to overturn a 2–1 panel decision that a seizure occurred when two officers stood on opposite sides of a suspect and identified themselves as DEA agents. The en banc court found that there was no seizure. See also United States v. $84,000 United States Currency, 717 F.2d 1090 (7th Cir.1983) (holding, 2–1, that no seizure occurred when two officers approached two suspects, identified themselves and asked to see the suspects' tickets). In Wilson v. Superior Court, 34 Cal.3d 777, 195 Cal.Rptr. 671, 670 P.2d 325 (1983), the court found that a seizure had taken place when a police officer approached a passenger who had picked up his luggage and put it into a car, told him that the police had received information that the passenger would be carrying a lot of drugs, and asked the passenger for permission to search the luggage. Compare United States v. Berke, 930 F.2d 1219 (7th Cir.1991) (police contact was an encounter where officers sat on either side of the defendant in a bus terminal, notified him that they were officers looking for narcotics, asked for consent to search, and informed the defendant that he had the right to leave and to refuse consent).

A majority of the Court finally adopted and applied the *Mendenhall* test in Immigration and Naturalization Service v. Delgado, 466 U.S. 210 (1984), which held that INS officers did not seize workers when they conducted factory surveys in search of illegal aliens. Justice Rehnquist described the surveys as follows:

> At the beginning of the surveys several agents positioned themselves near the buildings' exits, while other agents dispersed throughout the factory to question most, but not all, employees at their work stations. The agents displayed badges, carried walkie-talkies, and were armed, although at no point during any of the surveys was a weapon ever drawn. Moving systematically through the factory, the agents approached employees and, after identifying themselves, asked them from one to three questions relating to their citizenship. If the employee gave a credible reply that he was a United States citizen, the questioning ended, and the agent moved on to another employee. If the employee gave an unsatisfactory response or admitted that he was an alien, the employee was asked to produce his immigration papers. During the survey, employees continued with their work and were free to walk around within the factory.

Four employees questioned in one of the surveys filed suit seeking declaratory and injunctive relief. They lost in the district court, prevailed in the court of appeals, and lost again in the Supreme Court.

The majority noted that "police questioning, by itself, is unlikely to result in a Fourth Amendment violation. While most citizens will respond to a police request, the fact that people do so, and do so without being told they are free not to respond, hardly eliminates the consensual nature of the response." The Justices rejected the argument that the employees were seized during the entire survey, finding that even though there were agents at the exits, they obviously were placed there to insure that questions were put to all employees. The majority reasoned that "[t]his conduct should have given [the employees] no reason to believe that they would be detained if they gave truthful answers to the questions put to them or if they simply refused to answer." And the majority also rejected an argument that individual employees were seized when they were questioned.

Justice Powell concurred in the result with an opinion stating that the majority opinion was "persuasive," but that the question of whether a seizure took place was a close one. He found it unnecessary to resolve the question, since he concluded that any seizure was reasonable given the importance of the government's interest in finding illegal aliens.

Justice Brennan, joined by Justice Marshall, dissented from the holding that the individual interrogations were not seizures and argued that the testimony in the case "paints a frightening picture of people subjected to wholesale interrogation under conditions designed not to respect personal security and privacy, but rather to elicit prompt answers from completely intimidated workers."

Put yourself in the workers' place. Would you feel free to leave? Would you assume the armed guards at the exits were not placed there to keep you inside the factory? Suppose the building was a law school rather than a factory and you were present as a student who had read *Delgado.* Would you attempt to leave a building secured in the way the *Delgado* factory was? How sure would you be that the INS agents had read *Delgado*? In LaDuke v. Nelson, 762 F.2d 1318 (9th Cir.1985), the Court distinguished *Delgado* and found that the INS had seized aliens when armed agents "cordoned off migrant housing during early morning or late evening hours, surrounded the residences in emergency vehicles with flashing lights, approached the homes with flashlights, and stationed officers at all doors and windows." At that point, the officers would knock on the doors and ask questions similar to those asked by the officers in *Delgado.* How can *Delgado* be distinguished?

In Florida v. Bostick, 111 S.Ct. 2382 (1991), the Court considered the question whether the recent law enforcement practice of boarding buses at scheduled stops to obtain consent to search the luggage of passengers constitutes a seizure within the Fourth Amendment. The officers' conduct was described by the Court as follows:

> Two officers, complete with badges, insignia and one of them holding a recognizable zipper pouch, containing a pistol, boarded a bus bound from Miami to Atlanta during a stopover in Fort Lauderdale. Eyeing the passengers, the officers admittedly without articulable suspicion picked out the defendant passenger and asked to inspect his ticket and identification. The ticket, from Miami to Atlanta, matched the defendant's identification and both were immediately returned to him as unremarkable. However, the two police officers persisted and explained their presence as narcotics agents on the lookout for illegal drugs. In pursuit of that aim, they then requested the defendant's consent to search his luggage. [The trial court found that Bostick gave voluntary consent to search.]

Justice O'Connor, writing for the Court, considered the Florida Supreme Court to have established a *per se* rule that "working the buses" without articulable suspicion is unconstitutional. She found that such a *per se* rule was inconsistent with *Royer* and *Delgado.* She stated that "there is no doubt that if this same encounter had taken place before Bostick boarded the bus or in the lobby of the bus terminal, it would not rise to the level of a seizure." She noted that the fact that the encounter takes place in the cramped confines of a bus is one factor; but that fact alone is not so significant as to warrant a *per se* rule that an encounter therein is always a seizure.

Bostick argued that because of the limited confines of the bus, the fact that the officers were blocking the aisle, and the fact that the bus was soon scheduled to depart, a seizure occurred because he did not feel "free to leave." Justice O'Connor responded that the term "free to leave" should be construed in accordance with "the principle that those words were intended to capture." She explained as follows:

> When police attempt to question a person who is walking down the street or through an airport lobby, it makes sense to inquire whether a reasonable person would feel free to continue walking. But when the person is seated on a bus and has no desire to leave, the degree to which a reasonable person would feel that he or she could leave is not an accurate measure of the coercive effect of the encounter.
>
> Here, for example, the mere fact that Bostick did not feel free to leave the bus does not mean the police seized him. Bostick was a passenger on a bus

that was scheduled to depart. He would not have felt free to leave the bus even if the police had not been present. Bostick's movements were "confined" in a sense, but this was the natural result of his decision to take the bus; it says nothing about whether or not the police conduct at issue was coercive.

The Court remanded to determine whether, under the totality of circumstances, "the police conduct would have communicated to a reasonable person that the person was not free to decline the officers' requests or otherwise terminate the encounter."

Justice Marshall, joined by Justices Blackmun and Stevens, dissented. The dissenters argued that the suspicionless police sweep of buses "bears all the indicia of coercion and unjustified intrusion associated with the general warrant." Justice Marshall complained that instead of requiring the police to justify their conduct, "the majority blames respondent for his own sensation of constraint." He argued:

> Obviously, a person's voluntary decision to place himself in a room with only one exit does not authorize the police to force an encounter upon him by placing themselves in front of the exit. It is no more acceptable for the police to force an encounter upon a person by exploiting his voluntary decision to expose himself to perfectly legitimate personal or social constraints. By consciously deciding to single out persons who have undertaken interstate or intrastate travel, officers who conduct suspicionless, dragnet-style sweeps put passengers to the choice of cooperating or of exiting their buses and possibly being stranded in unfamiliar locations. It is exactly because this "choice" is no "choice" at all that police engage in this technique.

Is Justice O'Connor correct that *per se* rules are never permissible in the stop and frisk area? Didn't the Court in *Mimms* adopt a *per se* rule? Does *Bostick* mean that police activity on a bus will *never* constitute a seizure? See In re J.M., 596 A.2d 961 (D.C.App.1991), where the court distinguished *Bostick* and found that the officers seized the defendant, a juvenile who had no prior experience with police officers. The officers boarded the bus at 2:30 a.m. and announced over the intercom that they were looking for drugs; they approached the defendant and asked for consent to search his belongings; defendant was never informed that he had the right to refuse consent.

If the bus is detained for longer than a scheduled stop while the officers are "working" the bus, have the passengers' Fourth Amendment rights been violated?

For a criticism of *Bostick,* see Slobogin, The World Without a Fourth Amendment, 39 U.C.L.A. L.Rev. 1 (1991).

Must an officer have a certain state of mind in order to seize a person? Justice Scalia wrote for the Court in Brower v. County of Inyo, 489 U.S. 593 (1989), as it held that a plaintiff stated a claim that a seizure occurred when police established a roadblock which was designed to produce a stop by physical impact if the driver of a car did not stop voluntarily. Justice Scalia reasoned that "a Fourth Amendment seizure does not occur whenever there is a governmentally caused termination of an individual's freedom of movement * * *, nor even whenever there is a governmentally *desired* termination of an individual's freedom of movement * * *, but only when there is a governmental termination of freedom of movement *through means intentionally applied.*" He did not address the question whether the seizure was unreasonable.

Justice Stevens, joined by Justices Brennan, Marshall, and Blackmun, concurred in the judgment. He objected to Justice Scalia's emphasis on an intentional acquisition of physical control as marking the onset of a seizure, and suggested that, since it was clear in the instant case that the roadblock was intended to stop the deceased, "[d]ecision in the case before us is thus not advanced by pursuing a hypothetical inquiry concerning whether an unintentional act might also violate the Fourth Amendment."

Michigan v. Chesternut, 486 U.S. 567 (1988), emphasized that the objective approach to deciding whether a person has been seized under *Terry* examines whether a reasonable person under all the circumstances surrounding the incident would have believed that he was not free to leave. Justice Blackmun wrote for a unanimous Court that "[t]he test is necessarily imprecise, because it is designed to assess the coercive effect of police conduct, taken as a whole, rather than to focus on particular details of that conduct in isolation." The Court held that there was no seizure when police officers in a patrol car neared a corner where Chesternut was standing, he began to run, the officers followed around a corner and came alongside him to see what he was doing, and he began to discard a number of packets from his pocket. Justice Blackmun wrote as follows:

> The record does not reflect that the police activated a siren or flashers; or that they commanded respondent to halt, or displayed any weapons; or that they operated the car in an aggressive manner to block respondent's course or otherwise control the direction or speed of his movement. While the very presence of a police car driving parallel to a running pedestrian could be somewhat intimidating, this kind of police presence does not, standing alone, constitute a seizure.

Justice Kennedy, joined by Justice Scalia, filed a brief concurring opinion. He observed that "[i]t is at least plausible to say that whether or not the officers' conduct communicates to a person a reasonable belief that they intend to apprehend him, such conduct does not implicate the Fourth Amendment until it achieves a restraining effect," and suggested that the Court had not foreclosed such a holding.

The holding which Justice Kennedy found not foreclosed by *Chesternut* was made law in Justice Scalia's majority opinion in California v. Hodari D., 111 S.Ct. 1547 (1991). The Court noted the limits of the *Mendenhall* test and held that a seizure does not necessarily take place when a person reasonably believes that he is not free to leave a scene; a non-physical show of force becomes a seizure only when the citizen submits or is subdued. The case arose when officers encountered a group of youths who were huddled around a car and who fled when they saw the officers. Hodari, one of the group who ran, threw away a small rock as a pursuing officer was about to catch him. The officer tackled Hodari, handcuffed him and radioed for assistance. Subsequently, the officer discovered that the discarded rock was crack cocaine. Hodari claimed that the pursuit was a seizure, and since there was no legal cause for the pursuit, it violated the Fourth Amendment, requiring suppression of the fruits including the cocaine.

Justice Scalia "consulted the common law" and cited law dictionaries to support the notion that the word "seizure" has meant a "taking possession." Justice Scalia separated seizures into two types: those in which the officer has physically touched the citizen, and those in which the officer has used a non-physical show of authority. As to the former category, Justice Scalia noted that "[t]o constitute an arrest, * * *—the quintessential 'seizure of the person' under our Fourth Amendment jurisprudence—the mere grasping or application of physical force with lawful authority, whether or not it succeeded in subduing the arrestee, was sufficient." Although "an arrest is effected by the slightest application of physical force," Justice Scalia rejected the idea that "there is a *continuing* arrest during the period of fugitivity."

As to the latter category of a non-physical show of force, at issue under the facts of *Hodari,* Justice Scalia framed the question before the Court as "whether, with respect to a show of authority as with respect to application of physical force, a seizure occurs even though the subject does not yield." The answer was "that it does not."

Justice Scalia recognized that *Mendenhall* and *Chesternut* dealt with non-physical shows of authority, and focused only on whether a reasonable person would feel that he or she was not free to leave, not on actual submission. Justice Scalia concluded, however, that the objective test of reasonableness was necessary, but not sufficient, to constitute a seizure. He stated that the *Mendenhall* test when "read carefully" says that a person has been seized "only if", not "whenever" the officer uses a show of authority. Thus, where the officer engages in a non-physical show of authority, it must be such that a reasonable person would not feel free to leave, *and* the citizen must actually submit. This is in contrast to physical touching or grasping, which is a seizure whether or not the citizen submits.

As a matter of policy, Justice Scalia reasoned that the public should be encouraged to comply with police orders, and also that unlawful orders will not be deterred by excluding evidence obtained when suspects disobey them, since police do not issue orders expecting them to be ignored.

Justice Stevens, joined by Justice Marshall, dissented. He criticized the majority's "narrow construction" of the word seizure as meaning "that a police officer may now fire his weapon at an innocent citizen and not implicate the Fourth Amendment—as long as he misses his target." The dissenters argued that the common law distinction between touching and a show of force was not determinative for Fourth Amendment purposes. Justice Stevens suggested that the common law ought not to govern analyses of current law enforcement practices, and that, even if it did govern, an attempted arrest was unlawful at common law and could amount to a seizure.

Justice Stevens wrote that "[e]ven though momentary, a seizure occurs whenever an objective evaluation of a police officer's show of force conveys the message that the citizen is not entirely free to leave—in other words, that his or her liberty is being restrained in a significant way." Hodari, he concluded, was not free to leave, since the officer's show of force in giving chase adequately communicated that Hodari was objectively under restraint. Justice Stevens observed that the question of when a seizure takes place may arise when an officer commands a suspect to "freeze," fires a warning shot or sounds a siren in a patrol car. He concluded that the majority erred in focusing on the citizen's reaction to an officer's conduct rather than on the officer's conduct itself. He asked whether an officer, who has flashed his lights to stop a car without adequate cause, can claim that observations made before the car comes to a complete stop are not fruits of a seizure, and whether a drug enforcement agent may approach a group of passengers in an airport with a drawn gun, announce a baggage search, and rely on the passengers' reaction to justify a subsequent investigative stop.

Justice Stevens concluded that it was "anomalous, at best" to establish different rules for seizures effected by touching and those effected by a show of force. He argued that it was important for an officer to know in advance whether certain conduct would constitute a seizure, and that the majority's test made this impossible when the officer is using a non-physical show of force.

Which approach to "seizure" makes more sense, the majority's or the dissenters'? Suppose an officer pulls a gun, tells a suspect to stop, the suspect turns toward the officer, and has a heart attack and dies. Has the suspect been seized? What if an officer fires a warning shot in the air and a fleeing suspect stops suddenly and a package falls from his pocket as a result of this sudden stop? Is the package the fruit of a seizure? Is there a danger that law enforcement agents will seek to engage in displays of unlawful force short of actual touchings in order to frighten suspects into making statements, disgorging evidence, or engaging in acts that would justify arrest or detention?

Is there any merit to the following argument? A person who discards evidence before being searched should not be able to later complain that the evidence was obtained unlawfully merely because he or she was illegally stopped; since the police might have decided to refrain from searching, the act of discarding evidence is not a necessary result (thus not a fruit) of an improper seizure of the person.

Had such an argument been accepted, the result would be to condemn arbitrary and unjustified attempts by police to seize individuals, but to treat flight or actions undertaken by the individuals prior to actually being forced by police to submit to a search as independent of the seizure. Would this have recognized the interests which both the majority and the dissenters in *Hodari* believed were important?

What if Hodari had not thrown the cocaine, and the officer tackled him? That would be a seizure; would the seizure be reasonable? This would depend on whether a suspect's flight upon spotting police officers could give rise to reasonable suspicion for a seizure. The Court left this question unanswered in *Hodari,* though Justice Scalia implied in a footnote that such flight would lead to reasonable suspicion: he cited the proverb that the "wicked flee when no man pursueth." Justice Scalia did not consider whether a young African–American male might flee upon the approach of white police officers for reasons other than "wickedness". See United States v. Jackson, 741 F.2d 223 (8th Cir.1984) (flight upon seeing police officers constitutes reasonable suspicion for a stop).

12. Grounds for a Stop: Reasonable Suspicion

The degree of suspicion required to make a stop is referred to as "reasonable suspicion" by the courts. See United States v. Brignoni–Ponce, 422 U.S. 873 (1975). As with the higher standard of probable cause, two separate questions arise in determining whether reasonable suspicion exists. The court must investigate the *source* of information upon which reasonable suspicion is based; and the court must evaluate whether that information creates *sufficient* cause to justify a stop.

a. Source of Information

In Adams v. Williams, *supra,* the Court considered whether an informant's tip could be credited toward reasonable suspicion. *Adams* did not consider, however, whether reasonable suspicion could be based on a tip from an anonymous informant.

The Court relied heavily on *Adams* and Illinois v. Gates (discussed in the material on probable cause) in Alabama v. White, 496 U.S. 325 (1990), and held that an anonymous informant's tip which was "significantly corroborated" provided reasonable suspicion for a stop. The police received an anonymous tip that White would be leaving a particular apartment in a brown Plymouth station wagon with the right taillight lens broken, and would be driving to Dobey's Motel with a brown attache case containing cocaine. The officers went to the apartment, and saw White enter a brown Plymouth station wagon with a broken right taillight. She was not carrying an attache case. They followed the station wagon as it took the most direct route to Dobey's Motel. White was stopped just short of Dobey's Motel, and consented to the search of a brown attache case that was in the car. The officers found marijuana in the attache case, and three milligrams of cocaine in White's purse, which was searched during processing at the station.

Justice White, writing for a six-person majority, held that the stop was supported by reasonable suspicion. He noted that under the *Gates* "totality of the circumstances" approach to probable cause, an informant's veracity and basis of knowledge remain "highly relevant" in determining the value of the report of an informant. Justice White stated: "These factors are also relevant in the reasonable suspicion context, although allowance must be made in applying them for the lesser showing required to meet that standard."

Even given the lesser showing required, Justice White acknowledged that the anonymous tip did not itself provide reasonable suspicion, since it did not show that the informant was reliable, or give any indication of the informant's basis for predicting White's activities. But the majority stated: "As there was in *Gates,* however, in this case there is more than the tip itself."

Justice White determined that the corroboration in *White* was not as substantial as that in *Gates.* Yet this was not fatal, since reasonable suspicion is a less stringent standard than probable cause. Justice White explained as follows:

> Reasonable suspicion is a less demanding standard than probable cause not only in the sense that reasonable suspicion can be established with information that is different in quantity or content than that required to establish probable cause, but also in the sense that reasonable suspicion can arise from information that is less reliable than that required to show probable cause. Adams v. Williams * * * demonstrates as much. We there assumed that the unverified tip from the known informant might not have been reliable enough to establish probable cause, but nevertheless found it sufficiently reliable to justify a *Terry* stop. * * * Both factors—quantity and quality—are considered in the totality

of the circumstances * * * that must be taken into account when evaluating whether there is reasonable suspicion.

The Court found that the stop of White was based on reasonable suspicion, even though the corroboration of the tip was not complete, and in fact the tip was not correct in some details. Justice White acknowledged that corroboration of the existence of the car was insignificant, since "anyone could have predicted that fact because it was a condition presumably existing at the time of the call." However, the caller's ability to predict White's future behavior was "important," because

> [I]t demonstrated inside information—a special familiarity with respondent's affairs. The general public would have had no way of knowing that respondent would shortly leave the building, get in the described car, and drive the most direct route to Dobey's Motel. Because only a small number of people are generally privy to an individual's itinerary, it is reasonable for police to believe that a person with access to such information is likely to also have access to reliable information about that individual's illegal activities. * * * When significant aspects of the caller's predictions were verified, there was reason to believe not only that the caller was honest but also that he was well informed, at least well enough to justify the stop.

Justice Stevens wrote a short dissenting opinion, joined by Justices Brennan and Marshall. The dissenters argued that the activity predicted by the informant and corroborated by the police (i.e. leaving an apartment and driving toward a motel) was completely innocent. Justice Stevens concluded as follows:

> Millions of people leave their apartments at about the same time every day carrying an attache case and heading for a destination known to their neighbors. Usually, however, the neighbors do not know what the briefcase contains. An anonymous neighbor's prediction about somebody's time of departure and probable destination is anything but a reliable basis for assuming that the commuter is in possession of an illegal substance—particularly when the person is not even carrying the attache case described by the tipster.

Does it make sense that the reasonable suspicion standard is less demanding as to both quantity and *quality* of information? Does the Court mean that certain information may be too unreliable to credit toward probable cause, but reliable enough to credit toward reasonable suspicion? Has the Court in *Adams* and *White* given clear guidelines about the degree of corroboration necessary to support reasonable suspicion? Does it follow that an informant's prediction of future innocent activity makes it more likely that the informant is correct in his conclusion about the suspect's criminal activity? Reconsider Justice White's concurring opinion in *Spinelli* (discussed in the material on probable cause). Is it consistent with his majority opinion in *White?*

In evaluating the reasonableness of reliance on an anonymous tip, is it relevant that such tips to the police may be rare occurrences? Does the infrequency of volunteering information suggest that those who do volunteer are accurate? Or, perhaps, that they are unusually suspicious or vindictive? Is it important for future courts to know whether anonymous tips increase after *White?* See Generally Rudstein, White on *White:* Anonymous Tips, Reasonable Suspicion, and the Constitution, 79 Ky.L.J. 661 (1991).

b. *Quantum of Suspicion*

The Supreme Court in United States v. Cortez, 449 U.S. 411 (1981) set forth the following oft-cited test for determining whether reasonable suspicion exists:

> [T]he totality of the circumstances—the whole picture—must be taken into account. Based upon that whole picture the detaining officers must have a particularized and objective basis for suspecting the particular person stopped of criminal activity. * * * [P]articularized suspicion contains two elements, each of which must be present before a stop is permissible. First, the assessment must be based upon all the circumstances. The analysis proceeds with various objective observations, information from police reports, if such are available, and considerations of the modes or patterns of operation of certain kinds of lawbreakers. From these data, a trained officer draws inferences and makes deductions—inferences and deductions that might well elude an untrained person.
>
> The process does not deal with hard certainties, but with probabilities. Long before the law of probabilities was articulated as such, practical people formulated certain common sense conclusions about human behavior; * * *.
>
> The second element contained in the idea that an assessment of the whole picture must yield a particularized suspicion is the concept that the process just described must raise a suspicion that the particular individual being stopped is engaged in wrongdoing.

How would you apply the above test from *Cortez* to the following facts?

> At 1:00 p.m. two Boston police detectives in an unmarked car were patrolling that portion of Boston known as the "Combat Zone." The Combat Zone is a high crime area known for prostitution and drug-dealing. As the officers were stopped at a light, they noticed a grey Thunderbird automobile stopped on the curb of Washington Street with a man at the wheel. As the officers watched, a second man approached the Thunderbird from the sidewalk and engaged the driver in a twenty second conversation through the open passenger-side window. The second man got into the car and had an additional five or ten second conversation with the driver. The car then pulled out and proceeded for two blocks until it made a right turn onto Hayward Place, a short street which connects Washington Street and Harrison Avenue. The officers followed in their unmarked car. Hayward Place was deserted. The Thunderbird parked on Hayward Place, and the officers parked well behind it with an unobstructed view. The officers observed the driver and passenger engaged in a thirty second discussion with their heads inclined toward each other. The passenger then got out of the car and walked back toward Washington Street. One officer approached the car, ordered the driver out, noticed a bulge, and pursuant to a pat-down frisk uncovered a spring-activated knife. The officer arrested the driver for carrying an illegal weapon, and in a search incident to arrest eleven grams of cocaine were uncovered.

The court confronted with these facts in United States v. Trullo, 809 F.2d 108 (1st Cir.1987) stated that the officer's seizure of the driver went to the "outermost reaches of a permissible *Terry* stop," and that "today's satisfactory explanation may very well be tomorrow's lame excuse." But the court did uphold the conduct, relying on the high crime area, the officers' expertise in determining whether drug activity was afoot, the short nature of the conversation between the driver and passenger, and the fact that the passenger walked back toward the place where he had met the car. This latter factor meant that it was "unlikely that the man was seeking transportation." The court concluded that while it would be possible to "hypothesize some innocent explanation" for the conduct, the test for a stop is whether there is reasonable suspicion of criminal activity, and not whether the facts can be construed as innocent. Judge Bownes, in dissent, asked the following question: "If a citizen lets another person into his car on Washington Street, where must he let him off to avoid an armed stop by the police?" Judge Bownes claimed that the majority "seems to allow armed stops of individuals who meet in the Combat Zone on the basis of unlimited deference to police discretion." Who has the better of the argument, the majority or the dissent? Who has more accurately applied the *Cortez* test, the majority or the dissent?

Can the suspect's race be taken into account in determining reasonable suspicion? How would the test articulated in *Cortez* apply to the following facts?

> A St. Paul police officer observed Uber's vehicle at about 2:15 a.m. The officer saw the vehicle again about 30 minutes later in the same area. At that time the officer ran a check on the license number and determined that the vehicle was registered to a person in Moundsview, Minnesota, a suburb about 20 miles from St. Paul. Upon learning this information, the officer decided to stop the vehicle, because he thought the driver was seeking to solicit a prostitute. The Summit–University area, in which Uber's car was spotted, is well known as one where prostitution flourishes. The officer did not at that time see prostitutes in the area, nor had Uber slowed down or talked to anyone.

The court in City of St. Paul v. Uber, 450 N.W.2d 623 (Minn.App.1990) held that this information did not create reasonable suspicion to support a stop. The court stated as follows:

> We know of no authority that requires a resident of the State of Minnesota to have any reason to be on the public streets of another town * * *. No one from any suburb needs to justify his or her lawful presence on a public street in Minneapolis or St. Paul. * * * The officer's assumption that [Uber] was seeking prostitution was an inadvertent, but nevertheless invidious, form of discrimination. We would not tolerate the blatant discriminatory proposition that any member of a minority group found on a public street in Edina [an affluent suburb] had better live there, or be required to stop and justify his or her presence to the authorities. * * * Once we clear away the smoke from this case, it is clear that the stop of [Uber] is premised on the belief that after midnight, Caucasian males from the suburbs are only in the Summit–University area for no good, and that after midnight, no good is all the Summit–University area has to offer. Neither the residents of Summit–University nor the residents of Moundsview deserve the implications of this case. * * * Simply being on a public street in an area where one "might" find a prostitute or a drug dealer does not, without more, meet any constitutional standard for a stop by the authorities. See e.g. Brown v. Texas, 443 U.S. 47 (1979) (defendant's mere presence in a neighborhood frequented by drug users held insufficient to justify a stop).

While a person's race, or the existence of a high crime area may not "without more" constitute reasonable suspicion, how much more is required? What if Uber had been driving ten miles below the speed limit?

In Sibron v. New York, 392 U.S. 40 (1968) a companion case to *Terry,* the following facts arose:

> * * * Sibron * * * was convicted of the unlawful possession of heroin. He moved before trial to suppress the heroin seized from his person by the arresting officer, Brooklyn Patrolman Anthony Martin. After the trial court denied his motion, Sibron pleaded guilty to the charge, preserving his right to appeal the evidentiary ruling. At the hearing on the motion to suppress, Officer Martin testified that while he was patrolling his beat in uniform on March 9, 1965, he observed Sibron "continually from the hours of 4:00 P.M. to 12:00, midnight * * * in the vicinity of 742 Broadway." He stated that during this period of time he saw Sibron in conversation with six or eight persons whom he (Patrolman Martin) knew from past experience to be narcotics addicts. The officer testified that he did not overhear any of these conversations, and that he did not see anything pass between Sibron and any of the others. Late in the evening Sibron entered a restaurant. Patrolman Martin saw Sibron speak with three more known addicts inside the restaurant. Once again, nothing was overheard and nothing was seen to pass between Sibron and the addicts. Sibron sat down and ordered pie and coffee, and, as he was eating, Patrolman Martin approached him and told him to come outside. Once outside, the officer said to Sibron, "You know what I am after." According to the officer, Sibron "mumbled something and reached into his pocket." Simultaneously, Patrolman Martin thrust his hand into the same pocket, discovering several glassine envelopes, which, it turned out, contained heroin.

The Court found that *Terry* could not justify the officer's actions. Do you see why?

Officers often use profiles to determine whether citizens should be stopped for suspicion of criminal activity. A profile is a list of characteristics compiled by a law enforcement agency, which characteristics have been found through experience to be common to those engaged in a certain type of criminal activity. An example is the drug courier profile; another example is the gang member profile. See United States v. Malone, 886 F.2d 1162 (9th Cir.1989). The use of drug courier profiles was discussed extensively in United States v. Berry, 670 F.2d 583 (5th Cir.1982) (en banc).

> The precise characteristics in the profile appear to vary, but those most commonly mentioned in cases in this Circuit as constituting the profile are described in Elmore v. United States, 595 F.2d 1036, 1039 n. 3 (5th Cir.1979), cert. denied, 447 U.S. 910 (1980):
>
> > The seven primary characteristics are: (1) arrival from or departure to an identified source city; (2) carrying little or no luggage, or large quantities of empty suitcases; (3) unusual itinerary, such as rapid turnaround time for a very lengthy airplane trip; (4) use of an alias; (5) carrying unusually large amounts of currency in the many thousands of dollars, usually on their person, in briefcases or bags; (6) purchasing airline tickets with a large amount of small denomination currency; and (7) unusual nervousness beyond that ordinarily exhibited by passengers.
> >
> > The secondary characteristics are (1) the almost exclusive use of public transportation, particularly taxicabs, in departing from the airport; (2) immediately making a telephone call after deplaning; (3) leaving a false or fictitious call-back telephone number with the airline being utilized; and (4) excessively frequent travel to source or distribution cities.

> We use the opportunity presented by the occasion of this en banc sitting to consider the proper role of the profile characteristics in a court's determination of the existence of reasonable suspicion. We conclude that the profile is nothing more than an administrative tool of the police. The presence or absence of a particular characteristic on any particular profile is of *no* legal significance in the determination of reasonable suspicion.
>
> Two consequences stem from this holding. First, a match between certain characteristics listed on the profile and characteristics exhibited by a defendant does not automatically establish reasonable suspicion. Rather, critical to any finding that reasonable suspicion existed is an evaluation of "the reasonableness of a particular search or seizure *in light of the particular circumstances.*" Terry v. Ohio, 392 U.S. 1, 21 (1968) (emphasis supplied). Subsequent cases have elaborated on this holding and have required that the suspicion must be focused on the particular individual seized. Any checklist of suspicious characteristics cannot be mechanically applied by a court to determine whether a particular search or seizure meets the Supreme Court's standards. A profile does not focus on the particular circumstances at issue. Nor does such a profile indicate in every case that a specific individual who happens to match some of the profile's vague characteristics is involved in actions sufficiently suspicious as to justify a stop.
>
> The second consequence of our holding flows from the first. Although a match between a defendant's characteristics and some of the characteristics on a drug courier profile does not automatically support a finding of reasonable suspicion, the fact that a characteristic of a defendant also happens to appear on the profile does not preclude its use as a justification providing reasonable suspicion for a stop. If an officer can demonstrate why some factor, interpreted with due regard for the officer's experience and not merely in light of its presence on the profile, was, in the particular circumstances of the facts at issue, of such import as to support a reasonable suspicion that an individual was involved in drug smuggling, we do not believe that a court should downgrade the importance of that factor merely because it happens to be part of the profile. Our holding is only that we will assign no characteristic greater or lesser weight merely because the characteristic happens to be present on, or absent from, the profile.

In United States v. Sokolow, 490 U.S. 1 (1989), DEA agents stopped Sokolow after they learned that he paid $2100 for two airplane tickets from a roll of $20 bills, he traveled under a name that did not match the name under which his telephone was listed, he traveled to Honolulu from Miami and stayed only 48 hours even though a round-trip flight takes 20 hours, he appeared nervous during the trip, and he checked no luggage. Chief Justice Rehnquist wrote for the majority, which found that the above facts, taken together, amounted to reasonable suspicion. He rejected the lower court's two-tiered approach which distinguished between evidence of ongoing criminal behavior (such as the use of an alias) and evidence of personal characteristics of couriers shared by the public at large (such as cash payment for tickets). The Chief Justice stated that the lower court had impermissibly drawn a "sharp line between types of evidence, the probative value of which varies only in degree." He asserted that "the concept of reasonable suspicion, like probable cause, is not readily or even usefully reduced to a neat set of legal rules." The Chief Justice reviewed the facts known to the officers concerning Sokolow, and recognized that "any one of these factors is not by itself proof of any illegal conduct and is quite consistent with innocent travel." But he stated that the relevant inquiry "is not whether particular conduct is innocent or guilty, but the degree of suspicion that attaches to particular types of noncriminal acts."

The Chief Justice rejected Sokolow's argument that the officer's use of a drug courier profile tainted the stop:

> A court sitting to determine the existence of reasonable suspicion must require the agent to articulate the factors leading to that conclusion, but the fact that these factors may be set forth in a "profile" does not somehow detract from their evidentiary significance as seen by a trained agent.

The Chief Justice also rejected Sokolow's argument that agents were obligated to use the least intrusive means available to verify or dispel their suspicions—in this case by engaging in an encounter rather than a stop. The majority reasoned that any rule requiring a least intrusive approach would hamper the police in making on-the-spot decisions.

Justice Marshall, joined by Justice Brennan, dissented and complained about the officers' use of the drug courier profile.

> It is highly significant that the DEA agents stopped Sokolow because he matched one of the DEA's "profiles" of a paradigmatic drug courier. In my view, a law enforcement officer's mechanistic application of a formula of personal and behavioral traits in deciding whom to detain can only dull the officer's ability and determination to make sensitive and fact-specific inferences "in light of his experience," *Terry*, particularly in ambiguous or borderline cases. Reflexive reliance on a profile of drug courier characteristics runs a far greater risk than does ordinary, case-by-case police work, of subjecting innocent individuals to unwarranted police harassment and detention. This risk is enhanced by the profile's "chameleon-like way of adapting to any particular set of observations." 831 F.2d 1413, 1418 (CA9 1987). Compare, e.g., United States v. Moore, 675 F.2d 802, 803 (CA6 1982), cert. denied, 460 U.S. 1068 (1983) (suspect was first to deplane), with United States v. Mendenhall, 446 U.S. 544, 564 (1980) (last to deplane), with United States v. Buenaventura–Ariza, 615 F.2d 29, 31 (CA2 1980) (deplaned from middle); United States v. Sullivan, 625 F.2d 9, 12 (CA4 1980) (one-way tickets), with United States v. Craemer, 555 F.2d 594, 595 (CA6 1977) (round-trip tickets), with United States v. McCaleb, 552 F.2d 717, 720 (CA6 1977) (non-stop flight), with United States v. Sokolow, 808 F.2d 1366, 1370 (CA9 1987), vacated, 831 F.2d 1413 (CA9 1987) (changed planes); *Craemer,* supra, at 595 (no luggage), with United States v. Sanford, 658 F.2d 342, 343 (CA5 1981) (gym bag), with *Sullivan,* supra, at 12 (new suitcases); United States v. Smith, 574 F.2d 882, 883 (CA6 1978) (traveling alone), with United States v. Fry, 622 F.2d 1218, 1219 (CA5 1980) (traveling with companion); United States v. Andrews, 600 F.2d 563, 566 (CA6 1979) (acted nervously), with United States v. Himmelwright, 551 F.2d 991, 992 (CA5), cert. denied, 434 U.S. 902 (1977) (acted too calmly). In asserting that it is not "somehow" relevant that the agents who stopped Sokolow did so in reliance on a prefabricated profile of criminal characteristics, the majority thus ducks serious issues relating to a questionable law enforcement practice * * *.

Can a *Terry* stop be made on the basis of reasonable suspicion to believe that a crime has already been committed? A unanimous Court held in United States v. Hensley, 469 U.S. 221 (1985), that "police officers may stop and briefly detain a person who is the subject of a 'wanted flyer' while they attempt to find out whether an arrest warrant has been issued." The facts are set forth in the next two paragraphs.

> Several days after a tavern robbery in St. Bernard, Ohio (a Cincinnati suburb), a St. Bernard police officer interviewed an informant who stated that Hensley drove the getaway car. The officer obtained a written statement from the informant and immediately issued a "wanted flyer" to other police departments in the metropolitan area. The flyer stated that Hensley was wanted for investigation of an aggravated robbery, described Hensley and the date and location of the robbery, warned that Hensley should be considered armed and dangerous, and asked other departments to pick up and hold Hensley for the St. Bernard police.
>
> In a Kentucky suburb of Cincinnati, an officer who had heard the flyer read aloud several times stopped a car driven by Hensley. Although the officer let Hensley drive away, he inquired whether there was an outstanding warrant for his arrest. Two other officers in separate patrol cars interrupted to say that there might be an Ohio warrant on Hensley. The three officers then looked for Hensley while the dispatcher looked for the flyer and mistakenly telephoned Cincinnati to inquire about the flyer. One of the officers spotted Hensley's car and, after being advised by the dispatcher that Cincinnati was hunting for a warrant, he pulled the car over and approached with a drawn service revolver. A second officer arrived at the scene, saw a gun under the seat of a passenger known to be a convicted felon, arrested the passenger, and searched the car. When another gun was found, Hensley was arrested for illegal handgun possession.

Justice O'Connor reasoned for the Court that *Terry* was not confined to prospective crimes; it also may apply to completed crimes. She recognized, however, that a stop relating to a completed offense might not promote crime prevention as directly as a stop relating to a prospective crime and that public safety might be less threatened by a suspect who had finished his criminal act and who thereafter appeared to be "going about his lawful business" than by a suspect planning to commit an offense. Her opinion approved stops where "police have a reasonable suspicion, grounded in specific and articulable facts, that a person they encounter was involved in or is wanted in connection with a completed felony." It did not decide whether *Terry* would permit a stop relating to all past crimes.

Relying on Whiteley v. Warden, [page 160, supra] Justice O'Connor concluded that one department or officer could act to make a stop if another officer or department had sufficient cause to make the stop and asked for assistance. She applied her analysis to the facts and concluded that the St. Bernard police had a reasonable suspicion concerning Hensley, that the Kentucky officers properly relied on the flyer, and that the stop was carried out in compliance with *Terry*.

13. Limited Searches for Police Protection Under the Terry Doctrine

Terry and *Adams* indicate that an officer can frisk a suspect, and pull out objects from the suspect, if there is reasonable suspicion to believe that he or she presents a threat of bodily harm to the officer. Are you concerned that an officer may testify in support of the frisk that she felt a fear of bodily harm, when in fact she was looking for evidence without probable cause? Is there an easy way to distinguish *Terry* frisks from impermissible searches for evidence?

Evaluate the following facts in light of *Terry* and *Adams*.

> The officer received a radio report of an anonymous 911 call in which the informant stated that he had seen a woman in a blue car with a white top parked in front of 123 West 112th Street, a high crime area in New York City. The woman had passed a handgun to a man seated in the car with her. Finding defendant in a car meeting the description at the specific location indicated by the informant, the officer ordered the defendant out of the car, frisked her, and took a pistol from the area of her waistband.

The New York Court of Appeals held that while the stop was permissible, the frisk was not. The court reasoned as follows:

> A frisk requires reliable knowledge of facts providing reasonable basis for suspecting that the individual to be subjected to that intrusion is armed and may be dangerous. Here, there was no such predicate either in the information received, which indicated that defendant had given a gun to the man but provided no basis for inferring that she had another or that it had been returned to her, or in what occurred during the officer's encounter with defendant. No inquiry was made of defendant so she neither refused to answer nor answered evasively; no suspicious bulge was perceived in her clothing; no furtive movements were made by her; her appearance and movements were not concealed by darkness.

People v. Russ, 61 N.Y.2d 693, 472 N.Y.S.2d 601, 460 N.E.2d 1086 (1984). If you were a police officer, would you have found it necessary to frisk Russ for a gun, after she had already passed a gun in a high crime area?

The Court held in Michigan v. Long, 463 U.S. 1032 (1983), that *Terry* is not restricted to protective frisks of a person and that it also extends to protective examinations of areas. Long was stopped by officers who saw him driving erratically before he swerved into a ditch. When the officers stopped, Long was out of his car and he appeared to be under the influence of something. Long failed to respond to initial requests that he produce a license and registration and then began to walk toward the passenger compartment of his car. An officer flashed a light into the car and saw a hunting knife. A protective search for weapons was conducted in the passenger compartment and marijuana was found and seized. Justice O'Connor's opinion for the Court reasoned that *Terry* permits a limited examination of an area from which a person, who police reasonably believe is dangerous, might gain immediate control of a weapon. The Court upheld the examination of the passenger compartment. Justice Blackmun concurred in part and in the judgment. Justice Brennan, joined by Justice Marshall, and Justice Stevens filed dissenting opinions.

Considering that Long was outside the car at the time that it was searched, how could the officers have had a reasonable fear that harm could come from something inside the car? The New York Court of Appeals, in People v. Torres, 74 N.Y.2d 224, 544 N.Y.S.2d 796, 543 N.E.2d 61 (1989) rejected *Long* as a matter of state constitutional law. The court reasoned as follows:

> [I]t is unrealistic to assume, as the Supreme Court did in Michigan v. Long, that having been stopped and questioned without incident, a suspect who is about to be released and permitted to proceed on his way would, upon reentry

into his vehicle, reach for a concealed weapon and threaten the departing police officer's safety. Certainly, such a far-fetched scenario is an insufficient basis upon which to predicate the substantial intrusion that occurred here.

Is it "far-fetched" to believe that a suspect could present a risk of harm to the officer in a post-stop situation? Would you think it far-fetched if you were a police officer?

Is it reasonable to assume that those suspected of drug dealing always present a risk of harm to the officer when stopped? In United States v. Brown, 913 F.2d 570 (8th Cir.1990), the court relied upon *Long* to uphold a search of a locked glove compartment, when the officers had reasonable suspicion of drug activity. The court concluded that "since weapons and violence are frequently associated with drug transactions, the officers reasonably believed that the individuals with whom they were dealing were armed and dangerous." Is there now a per se rule that a full-fledged search of a passenger compartment can be conducted upon reasonable suspicion to believe the driver is a drug dealer?

The *Long* rationale is not, of course, limited to protective searches of cars. Thus, in United States v. Johnson, 932 F.2d 1068 (5th Cir.1991), the court upheld a cursory inspection of a pair of overalls located a few feet away from a suspect who appeared to be attempting to burglarize a house. The court found that merely separating the suspect from his effects during the stop would not be a sufficient protection, since if the stop was terminated, the officers would have to return the property to the suspect.

In the course of making arrests, officers are often confronted with whether persons other than the arrestee can be frisked for self-protection. In United States v. Berryhill, 445 F.2d 1189 (9th Cir.1971), the court adopted an "automatic companion" rule, whereby the companion of an arrestee could automatically be subject to a frisk. Other courts have rejected this rule on the ground that it is inconsistent with the case-by-case approach to reasonable suspicion mandated by *Terry*. See United States v. Bell, 762 F.2d 495 (6th Cir.1985). See also United States v. Flett, 806 F.2d 823 (8th Cir.1986) (rejecting the automatic companion rule but finding that the officer had reasonable suspicion on the facts to conduct a frisk of the companion of an arrestee).

In Ybarra v. Illinois, 444 U.S. 85 (1979), the Court refused to uphold the frisk of a patron of a bar who happened to be present when the police arrived to conduct a search of the bar pursuant to a valid search warrant. The Court noted that the patron's mere presence in the bar was not enough to indicate reasonable suspicion of bodily harm, and that no specific facts were shown to indicate that Ybarra was armed and dangerous. Does *Ybarra* support the courts which have adopted the automatic companion rule, or the courts which have rejected it?

In Maryland v. Buie, 494 U.S. 325 (1990) the Court considered the legality of a "protective sweep" which it defined as a "quick and limited search of a premises, incident to an arrest and conducted to protect the safety of police officers or others." Buie argued that such a sweep could not be conducted in the absence of probable cause to believe that there were individuals on the premises who would harm the officers or others. The Court, by a 7–2 vote, rejected Buie's argument. Justice White, writing for the majority, relied heavily on *Terry* and *Long* to find that a protective sweep could be justified by reasonable suspicion of bodily harm. According to Justice White, the reasonable suspicion standard was an appropriate balance between the arrestee's remaining privacy interest in the home and the officer's interest in safety. Justice Stevens concurred to emphasize that a protective sweep could only be conducted for safety purposes, not to prevent destruction of evidence. Justice Brennan, joined by Justice Marshall dissented and noted his continuing criticism "of the emerging tendency on the part of the Court to convert the *Terry* decision from a narrow exception into one that swallows the general rule that searches are 'reasonable' only if based upon probable cause."

14. Brief and Limited Detentions: The Line Between "Stop" and "Arrest"

Terry allows a stop upon a standard of proof less than probable cause, in part because a stop is a more limited intrusion than an arrest. But it is often difficult to determine when an intrusion crosses over from a stop to an arrest requiring probable cause. What is there about an arrest that makes it different from a stop? Is it that the officers force the suspect to move to a detention area? Is it that the officers draw their guns or use handcuffs? Is it the length of the detention? What guidelines would you set to determine whether the officer has crossed the line and effectuated an arrest?

a. Forced Movement of the Suspect to a Custodial Area

In Florida v. Royer, supra, Royer was taken from the public area of an airport into a small room, where the officers sought and obtained Royer's consent to a search of his luggage. The plurality in *Royer* held that the consent was invalid because it was obtained pursuant to an arrest without probable cause. Justice White, writing for the plurality, first set forth general principles governing stops and arrests:

> [N]ot all seizures of the person must be justified by probable cause to arrest for a crime. Prior to Terry v. Ohio, any restraint on the person amounting to a seizure for the purposes of the Fourth Amendment was invalid unless justified by probable cause. *Terry* created a limited exception to this general rule: certain seizures are justifiable under the Fourth Amendment if there is articulable suspicion that a person has committed or is about to commit a crime.
>
> * * *
>
> *Terry* and its progeny nevertheless created only limited exceptions to the general rule that seizures of the person require probable cause to arrest. Detentions may be "investigative" yet violative of the Fourth Amendment absent probable cause. In the name of investigating a person who is no more than suspected of criminal activity, the police may not carry out a full search of the person or of his automobile or other effects. Nor may the police seek to verify their suspicions by means that approach the conditions of arrest. * * *
>
> The predicate permitting seizures on suspicion short of probable cause is that law enforcement interests warrant a limited intrusion on the personal security of the suspect. The scope of the intrusion permitted will vary to some extent with the particular facts and circumstances of each case. This much, however, is clear: an investigative detention must be temporary and last no

longer than is necessary to effectuate the purpose of the stop. Similarly, the investigative methods employed should be the least intrusive means reasonably available to verify or dispel the officer's suspicion in a short period of time. It is the State's burden to demonstrate that the seizure it seeks to justify on the basis of a reasonable suspicion was sufficiently limited in scope and duration to satisfy the conditions of an investigative seizure.

The plurality found that Royer had been illegally detained.

[A]t the time Royer produced the key to his suitcase, the detention to which he was then subjected was a more serious intrusion on his personal liberty than is allowable on mere suspicion of criminal activity.

By the time Royer was informed that the officers wished to examine his luggage, he had identified himself when approached by the officers and had attempted to explain the discrepancy between the name shown on his identification and the name under which he had purchased his ticket and identified his luggage. The officers were not satisfied, for they informed him they were narcotics agents and had reason to believe that he was carrying illegal drugs. They requested him to accompany them to the police room. Royer went with them. He found himself in a small room—a large closet—equipped with a desk and two chairs. He was alone with two police officers who again told him that they thought he was carrying narcotics. He also found that the officers, without his consent, had retrieved his checked luggage from the airlines. What had begun as a consensual inquiry in a public place had escalated into an investigatory procedure in a police interrogation room, where the police, unsatisfied with previous explanations, sought to confirm their suspicions. The officers had Royer's ticket, they had his identification, and they had seized his luggage. Royer was never informed that he was free to board his plane if he so chose, and he reasonably believed that he was being detained. At least as of that moment, any consensual aspects of the encounter had evaporated, and we cannot fault the Florida Court of Appeal for concluding that Terry v. Ohio and the cases following it did not justify the restraint to which Royer was then subjected. As a practical matter, Royer was under arrest. * * *

We also think that the officers' conduct was more intrusive than necessary to effectuate an investigative detention otherwise authorized by the *Terry* line of cases. First, by returning his ticket and driver's license, and informing him that he was free to go if he so desired, the officers may have obviated any claim that the encounter was anything but a consensual matter from start to finish. Second, there are undoubtedly reasons of safety and security that would justify moving a suspect from one location to another during an investigatory detention, such as from an airport concourse to a more private area. There is no indication in this case that such reasons prompted the officers to transfer the site of the encounter from the concourse to the interrogation room. It appears, rather, that the primary interest of the officers was not in having an extended conversation with Royer but in the contents of his luggage, a matter which the officers did not pursue orally with Royer until after the encounter was relocated to the police room. The record does not reflect any facts which would support a finding that the legitimate law enforcement purposes which justified the detention in the first instance were furthered by removing Royer to the police room prior to the officer's attempt to gain his consent to a search of his luggage. As we have noted, had Royer consented to a search on the spot, the search could have been conducted with Royer present in the area where the bags were retrieved by Officer Johnson and any evidence recovered would have been admissible against him. If the search proved negative, Royer would have been free to go much earlier and with less likelihood of missing his flight, which in itself can be a very serious matter in a variety of circumstances.

Third, the State has not touched on the question whether it would have been feasible to investigate the contents of Royer's bags in a more expeditious way. The courts are not strangers to the use of trained dogs to detect the presence of controlled substances in luggage. There is no indication here that this means was not feasible and available. If it had been used, Royer and his luggage could have been momentarily detained while this investigative procedure was carried out. Indeed, it may be that no detention at all would have been necessary. A negative result would have freed Royer in short order; a positive result would have resulted in his justifiable arrest on probable cause.

Justice Blackmun dissented and argued as follows:

* * *

The officers in this case began their encounter with Royer with reasonable suspicion. They continued their questioning and requested further cooperation only as more facts, heightening their suspicion, came to their attention. Certainly, as any such detention continues or escalates, a greater degree of reasonable suspicion is necessary to sustain it, and at some point probable cause will be required. But here, the intrusion was short-lived and minimal. Only 15 minutes transpired from the initial approach to the opening of the suitcases. The officers were polite, and sought and immediately obtained Royer's consent at each significant step of the process. Royer knew that if the search of the suitcases did not turn up contraband, he would be free to go on his way. Thus, it seems clear to me that " 'the police [were] diligently pursuing a means of investigation which [was] likely to resolve the matter one way or another very soon * * *.' "

The special need for flexibility in uncovering illicit drug couriers is hardly debatable. * * * In light of the extraordinary and well-documented difficulty of identifying drug couriers, the minimal intrusion in this case, based on particularized suspicion, was eminently reasonable.

Justice Rehnquist, joined by the Chief Justice and Justice O'Connor, also dissented, arguing as follows:

* * *

The plurality inferentially concedes, as of course it must, that at the time the suitcases were opened and 65 pounds of marijuana were disclosed, the officers had probable cause to arrest and detain Royer. But working backward through this very brief encounter, the plurality manages to sufficiently fault the officers' conduct so as to require that Royer's conviction for smuggling drugs be set aside. Analyzed in terms of the "reasonableness" which must attend any search and seizure under the requirements of the Fourth Amendment, I find it impossible to conclude that any step in the officers' efforts to apprehend Royer fails to meet that test.

The plurality concedes that after their initial conversation with Royer, the officers had "grounds for suspecting Royer of carrying drugs and for temporarily detaining him and his luggage while they attempted to verify or dispel their suspicions * * *." I agree that their information reached at least this level.

* * *

The point at which I part company with the plurality's opinion is in the assessment of the reasonableness of the officers' conduct following their initial conversation with Royer. The plurality focuses on the transfer of the place of the interview from the main concourse of the airport to the room off the concourse and observes that Royer "found himself in a small room—a large closet—equipped with a desk and two chairs. He was alone with two police officers who again told him that they thought he was carrying narcotics. He also found that the officers, without his consent, had retrieved his checked luggage from the airlines."

Obviously, this quoted language is intended to convey stern disapproval of the described conduct of the officers. To my mind, it merits no such disapproval and was eminently reasonable. Would it have been preferable for the officers to have detained Royer for further questioning, as they concededly had a right to do, without paying any attention to the fact that his luggage had already been checked on the flight to New York, and might be put aboard the flight even though Royer himself was not on the plane? Would it have been more "reasonable" to interrogate Royer about the contents of his suitcases, and to seek his permission to open the suitcases when they were retrieved, in the busy main concourse of the Miami Airport, rather than to find a room off the concourse where the confrontation would surely be less embarrassing to Royer? If the room had been large and spacious, rather than small, if it had possessed three chairs rather than two, would the officers' conduct have been made reasonable by these facts?

The plurality's answers to these questions, to the extent that it attempts any, are scarcely satisfying. * * *

The plurality in *Royer* faulted the officers in part because they used means more intrusive than necessary to conduct their investigation. How does this square with the Court's holding in the later case of *Sokolow,* that an officer is permitted to conduct a stop even though an encounter would effectuate the officer's purpose? Does the availability of less intrusive means indicate that the course chosen by the officer was unreasonable?

b. *Forced Movement for Identification Purposes*

In *Royer,* the Court held that an arrest occurred when Royer was forcibly moved to a custodial atmosphere, for purposes of extracting consent to search. The Court noted, however, that an officer can, within the confines of a *Terry* stop, force the suspect to move for purposes of safety and security. Are there any other legitimate reasons to force a suspect to move without probable cause to arrest? Many courts have found that if reasonable suspicion exists, it is permissible to transport the suspect a short distance for purposes of identification. In People v. Hicks, 68 N.Y.2d 234, 508 N.Y.S.2d 163, 500 N.E.2d 861 (1986), the New York Court of Appeals was presented with the following facts:

Shortly after 4:00 a.m. on November 12, 1981, Police Officer Murray Wright and his partner heard a radio report that a holdup had occurred at a nearby factory. As they headed toward the factory in their patrol car, another broadcast seconds later identified the robbers as two black men, both about five-feet five-inches tall, in a green Pontiac with black trim. At approximately that moment, at an intersection about a quarter mile from the factory, the officers saw two black men in a grey and black Buick sedan, turning out of the street near the factory, with no other traffic at the intersection. Both men appeared to Wright to be "sitting low in their seats", indicating their height. Suspecting that they might be the robbers, the officers pulled them over.

Upon approaching the car, Wright (a police officer for 15 years) observed that both men seemed about five-feet five-inches tall. Asked where they had been, they responded that they were coming from work at American Brass, which Wright knew was not in the area, and in fact was miles away in the opposite direction. The officer then ordered the men out of the car and patted them down for weapons. He told them about the robbery, that he was going to take them to the factory for possible identification; he intended to release them if they were not identified. The passenger got into the back seat of the patrol car while defendant, the driver, first went to park the car nearby and then also got into the patrol car. Neither was handcuffed, and both accompanied the police without objection. There is no evidence that guns were drawn at any point. No additional questions were asked. Less than a minute later the patrol car arrived at the factory—these were the first police officers on the scene—where three of the victims identified both suspects. They were then placed under arrest, and they and the car were searched, revealing weapons, as well as other implements and fruits of the crime. In Wright's estimation, approximately 10 minutes had elapsed between completion of the holdup and the identification.

The Court in *Hicks* found that the officer had reasonable suspicion to detain the two suspects. Do you agree? The Court further found that the coercive movement to the crime scene for purposes of identification was within the confines of a permissible *Terry* stop. It explained as follows:

An arrest and search of a suspect are unquestionably unlawful without probable cause. But not every seizure is an arrest. By the same token, the police testimony that defendant was arrested only after identification by the victims is not conclusive of the issue. Even without a technical formal arrest, a suspect's detention may in fact be the equivalent of an arrest, requiring probable cause. As with many other questions in this troubling, sensitive area of police encounters with private citizens, the desire for a fixed list of factors that will guide persons in the field and courts sitting in review is frustrated by the speed and individuality with which such situations develop. No checklist has yet been assembled that would facilitate mechanical determination of when a given set of circumstances equals an arrest (*see,* Dix, *Nonarrest Investigatory Detentions in Search and Seizure Law,* 1985 Duke L.J. 849, 921). * * *

Defendant was not handcuffed, there was no show of force, he was permitted to park the car nearby before accompanying the police, he was not taken to the police station, the total time and distance involved were very brief, he was told the specific, limited purpose of the detention, and no information was asked of him after the initial inquiry. * * * There were witnesses within a quarter mile of the place of inquiry—approximately one minute away by car—who had just seen the perpetrators and would either identify defendant (in which event he would be arrested) or not identify him (in which event he would be released). A speedy on-the-scene viewing thus was of value both to law enforcement authorities and to defendant, and was appropriate here. The transportation did not unduly prolong the detention. Defendant might, alternatively, have been momentarily detained where he had been stopped and the witnesses brought there, but such a procedure would have entailed first securing defendant and his companion and then arranging transportation for the witnesses, possibly even a more time-consuming process than that chosen. At all events, given the time and distance involved this is a difference without constitutional significance.

* * * A fixed yardstick by which to measure the reasonableness of such detentions may be impossible, but by the same token a test of what was unreasonable in the circumstances, applying common sense, seems to us to be unduly elastic, furnish little guidance, and provide inadequate protection of individual rights. Moreover, such analysis, in its emphasis on law enforcement objectives, does not accord sufficient weight to the fact that the *Terry* exception is limited and should not swallow up the probable cause requirement of the State and Federal Constitutions. * * * It should therefore be made clear that, in the case before us, we uphold the scope of the police action not only because its purpose was to confirm or dispel reasonable suspicion quickly, but also because of the presence of the following particular factors: the authorities knew that a crime had actually been committed; the total period of detention was less than 10 minutes, the crime scene to which defendant was taken was very close, and eyewitnesses were there; and there is no proof of significantly less intrusive means available to accomplish the same purpose.

c. *Interrogations and Fingerprinting Pursuant to a Terry Stop*

In Dunaway v. New York, 442 U.S. 200 (1979), the Court distinguished cases where police have reasonable suspicion to believe that criminal activity is occurring, has just occurred, or is about to occur from cases in which the police detain a suspect for sustained interrogation. The Court emphasized that *Terry* was a narrow decision and concluded that police cannot detain a suspect and transport him to the stationhouse for questioning without probable cause, even if the detention is not deemed to be an arrest under state law (and there would be no arrest record or formal booking procedure). Justice Brennan, writing for the Court, concluded that "detention for custodial interrogation—regardless of its label—intrudes so severely on interests protected by the Fourth Amendment as necessarily to trigger the traditional safeguards against illegal arrest." He noted that "any 'exception' that could cover a seizure as intrusive as that in this case would threaten to swallow the general rule that Fourth Amendment seizures are reasonable only if based upon probable cause." Justice White wrote a short opinion concurring in the judgment. Justice Stevens also wrote a brief concurring opinion. Justice Rehnquist, joined by Chief Justice Burger, dissented.

In Kolender v. Lawson, 461 U.S. 352 (1983), the Court found unconstitutionally vague a statute requiring persons who loiter or wander on the streets to provide a "credible and reliable" identification and to account for their presence when an officer has *Terry* cause to stop them. Only Justice Brennan addressed the question whether a state could compel a person to identify or explain himself to officers under a properly drawn statute. He concluded that the Fourth Amendment prohibited states from authorizing "the arrest and criminal prosecution of an individual for failing to produce identification or further information on demand by a police officer."

In Davis v. Mississippi, 394 U.S. 721 (1969), cited in *Dunaway,* the Court held that a round-up of twenty-five Negro youths for questioning and fingerprinting in an effort to match prints found around a window entered by a rape suspect violated the Fourth Amendment. Justice Brennan wrote for the Court that "[i]t is arguable * * * that because of the unique nature of the fingerprinting process, such detentions might, under narrowly defined circumstances, be found to comply with the Fourth Amendment even though there is no probable cause in the traditional sense." He explained that fingerprinting is less serious an intrusion on liberty than other searches, that repeated fingerprinting is not a real danger, that fingerprinting is extremely reliable, and that it can be done at a convenient time and does not offer opportunities for harassment. But he added that "the general requirement that the authorization of a judicial officer be obtained in advance of detention would seem not to admit of any exception in the fingerprinting context." If a police officer has reasonable suspicion to justify a stop and frisk but not probable cause, should the officer be able to fingerprint the suspect if the suspect refuses to cooperate by supplying a name and address? If there is reasonable suspicion but not probable cause, and the officer who makes a stop knows that there were fingerprints found at the scene of a crime, is it permissible for the officer to take fingerprints and delay the suspect long enough to obtain a match?

Justice White wrote for the Court in Hayes v. Florida, 470 U.S. 811 (1985), as it held that police officers who were investigating a series of rapes violated *Davis* when they took a suspect to the stationhouse to be fingerprinted without probable cause or consent. He indicated that the Court adhered to the view that when police forcibly remove a person from his home or other place where he is entitled to be and take him to the stationhouse, they are making a seizure that must be treated like an arrest—i.e., as requiring probable cause. Justice White added, however, that the Court's reasoning did not imply "that a brief detention in the field for the purpose of fingerprinting, where there is only reasonable suspicion not amounting to probable cause, is necessarily impermissible under the Fourth Amendment."

Justice Brennan, joined by Justice Marshall, concurred in the judgment. He objected to "the Court's strained effort to reach the question" of "[t]he validity of on-site fingerprinting." Justice Blackmun concurred in the judgment without opinion. Justice Powell did not participate in the case.

Would you permit fingerprinting as part of a *Terry* stop? Would you permit the police to photograph persons who are stopped?

d. Time Limits on Terry Stops

The Supreme Court rejected an absolute time limit for *Terry* stops in United States v. Sharpe, 470 U.S. 675 (1985). The facts are described in the next two paragraphs.

A Drug Enforcement agent was on patrol in an unmarked car on a coastal road in North Carolina at approximately 6:30 a.m. when he saw a blue pickup truck with an attached camper "traveling in tandem with a blue Pontiac Bonneville." The agent saw that the truck was riding low, the camper did not bounce or sway appreciably around turns, and that a quilted material covered the rear and side windows of the camper. The agent followed the vehicles for 20 miles into South Carolina where he decided to make an "investigative stop." He radioed the highway patrol for help and a trooper in a marked patrol car responded to the call. Almost immediately after the trooper caught up with the vehicles, the Pontiac and the pickup turned off the highway onto a campground road. The agent and trooper followed the two vehicles as they sped along the road at double the legal speed until they returned to the main road. The trooper pulled alongside the Pontiac, which was in the lead, turned on his flashing light and motioned for the driver to pull over. As the Pontiac moved to the side, the pickup truck cut between it and the trooper's car, nearly hitting the latter. The trooper pursued the truck while the agent approached the Pontiac and requested identification.

The agent examined the driver's license. After unsuccessfully attempting to radio the trooper, he radioed the local police for assistance. Two local officers arrived and the agent asked them to "maintain the situation" while he went to find the trooper. The trooper had stopped the pickup, removed the driver from the truck, examined his license and a bill of sale for the truck, and patted him down. When the trooper told the driver that he would be held until a DEA agent arrived, the driver became nervous, stated that he wanted to leave, and asked for the return of the driver's license. Approximately 15 minutes after the truck was stopped, the agent arrived and learned that the name on the registration was the same as the name on the driver's license of the Pontiac's driver. The driver of the pickup denied two requests for permission to search the truck before the agent examined the truck and stated that he could smell marijuana. Without asking again for permission, he removed the keys from the ignition, opened the rear of the camper, and observed a large number of burlap-wrapped bales resembling marijuana. The agent arrested the driver and returned to the Pontiac to arrest its occupants. The total time between his initial stop of the Pontiac and the arrests of its occupants was between 30 and 40 minutes.

Chief Justice Burger wrote for the Court as it approved the conduct of the law enforcement officials and overturned a divided court of appeals' decision holding that the marijuana had to be suppressed. He found it unnecessary to consider the length of the detention of the Pontiac because it bore no relation to the discovery of the marijuana. Focusing instead on the detention of the pickup, the Chief Justice noted the "difficult linedrawing problems in distinguishing an investigative stop from a de facto arrest". He recognized that "if an investigative stop continues indefinitely, at some point it can no longer be justified as an investigative stop." But he rejected a "hard-and-fast time limit" and concluded that it was "appropriate to examine whether the police diligently pursued a means of investigation that was likely to confirm or dispel their suspicions quickly, during which time it was necessary to detain the defendant." The DEA agent satisfied the test, since the case did "not involve any delay unnecessary to the legitimate investigation of the law enforcement officers" and the suspects contributed to the delay by their actions.

Justice Marshall concurred in the judgment because the evasive actions of the suspects turned a brief encounter with the officers into an extended one. He emphasized that *Terry* stops must be brief "no matter what the needs of law enforcement in the particular case." Thus, the suspect was responsible for whatever delay occurred.

Justice Brennan dissented. Justice Brennan objected to treating the brevity limitation upon a stop as an "accordian-like concept that may be expanded outward depending on 'the law enforcement purposes to be served by the stop.'" He criticized the officers' handling of the investigation and found that the stop was unduly and unnecessarily lengthy. Justice Stevens dissented without reaching the merits.

After *Sharpe* what kind of conduct, if any, will be considered impermissible delay, as opposed to diligent investigation? See United States v. Davies, 768 F.2d 893 (7th Cir.1985) (reasonable to detain suspects for an additional thirty minutes to await advice from superiors, where detaining officers were inexperienced). Is it consistent for the Court to say that at some point a stop can continue for so long as to constitute an arrest, and yet that there is no hard and fast rule on the effect of time upon a *Terry* stop?

e. *Show of Force During a Terry Stop*

A traditional arrest is sometimes accompanied by the officer's use of handcuffs and drawn gun. Can the officer use such coercive tactics within the confines of a *Terry* stop? Courts have routinely relied on *Terry* and *Adams* to uphold the use of handcuffs and guns where there is reasonable suspicion to believe that they are necessary to protect the officer from harm. See People v. Allen, 73 N.Y.2d 378, 540 N.Y.S.2d 971, 538 N.E.2d 323 (1989) (officers handcuffed suspect who matched the description of an armed bank robber, after chasing him down a dark alley in a high crime area). In United States v. Alexander, 907 F.2d 269 (2d Cir.1990) the court held that officers acted properly when they unholstered their guns to detain two men suspected of purchasing drugs. The two men were in a Jaguar at 6:00 p.m., parked in an area known for drug activity. The court emphasized the "dangerous nature of the drug trade and the genuine need of law enforcement agents to protect themselves from the deadly threat it may pose." Has the court established a per se rule for those who are reasonably suspected of drug activity? Compare United States v. Novak, 870 F.2d 1345 (7th Cir.1989) where nine law enforcement officers working in an airport stopped two suspected drug couriers. One officer drew her gun and pointed it directly at one suspect's head at close range. The court found that an arrest had occurred. Do you agree?

15. Detention of Property Under Terry

Terry concerned seizures of the person, but its principles have been applied to seizures of property as well. The Court in United States v. Van Leeuwen, 397 U.S. 249 (1970) held that some detentions of property could occur upon reasonable suspicion. Officers detained a mailed package for more than a day, while an investigation was made for purposes of obtaining a warrant. A unanimous Court recognized that detention of mail could at some point become an unreasonable seizure, but found that in the instant case the investigation was conducted promptly. Compare United States v. Dass, 849 F.2d 414 (9th Cir.1988) (reasonable suspicion does not justify detention of mail for 7–23 days, where the delay could have been reduced to 32 hours if officers had acted diligently); United States v. Aldaz, 921 F.2d 227 (9th Cir.1990) (three day detention of mail permissible upon reasonable suspicion, where drug-sniffing dogs were 700 air miles away, and other delays were caused by remoteness of post office).

The Court in *Van Leeuwen* upheld a one-day detention without probable cause, while an investigation was conducted. Recall the facts of *Sharpe*. Do you think the Court would have allowed the suspects to be detained without probable cause for more than a day, while a diligent investigation was being conducted? If not, what is the difference between the seizure in *Sharpe* and that in *Van Leeuwen?* Could it be argued that the detention in *Van Leeuwen* was no seizure at all, since the person who receives mail has no legitimate expectation of receiving it on a particular day?

In United States v. LaFrance, 879 F.2d 1 (1st Cir.1989), police had reasonable suspicion to believe that a Federal Express package contained drugs. The package was guaranteed for delivery that day by noon. The officers arranged for a dog sniff, but the dog was several miles away. The sniff began at 1:15 p.m., and was completed by 2:15; the test was positive. Then a warrant was obtained to search the package. LaFrance challenged the reasonableness of the detention pending a warrant. He testified at the suppression hearing that on the basis of prior experience, he expected to receive the package by 11:00 a.m. The court held that "LaFrance's anticipation that he would receive the goods soon after 11 a.m., though based on earlier experiences, is irrelevant. It is hornbook contract law that where a delivery time is agreed upon, a court should not intrude to imply a different reasonable time for delivery." The court recognized that "once noon arrived, the constitutional chemistry was altered" but that the detention from that point was for a limited time, and that the police were diligent in their investigation during that time.

The Court held in United States v. Place, 462 U.S. 696 (1983), that if officers have reasonable suspicion, they may under some circumstances temporarily detain personal luggage, pending further investigation or the obtaining of a warrant. Applying the *Terry* balance of interests approach, the Court noted that it is often necessary to seize property while an investigation of criminal activity continues or while a warrant is being obtained. The Court recognized, however, that a seizure of property "intrudes on both the suspect's possessory interest in his luggage as well as his liberty interest in proceeding with his itinerary." It concluded that "the limitations applicable to investigative detentions of the person should define the permissible scope of the person's luggage on less than probable cause."

On the facts, the Court held that reasonable suspicion was not sufficient to support the lengthy detention that occurred in *Place.* Police officers seized Place's luggage as he arrived at LaGuardia Airport on a flight from Miami. 90 minutes later, they subjected the luggage to a canine sniff. Justice O'Connor, writing for the Court, stated that the 90 minute detention was unreasonable because the delay was caused by the failure to transport the drug detecting dog from one New York metropolitan airport to another. She reasoned that the dog could have been transported while Place was in the air en route to New York, since the officers had reasonable suspicion during that time. She concluded that the officers had not diligently pursued the investigation, and that "we have never approved a seizure of the person for the prolonged 90–minute period involved here." Finally, the Court noted that the Fourth Amendment violation was "exacerbated by the failure of the agents to inform the respondent of the place to which they were transporting his luggage, of the length of time he might be dispossessed, and of what arrangements would be made for return of the luggage if the investigation dispelled the suspicion." Therefore, the detention of the luggage could not be supported in the absence of probable cause. Justice Brennan, joined by Justice Marshall, concurred in the result. He argued that the *Terry* balancing approach "should not be conducted except in the most limited circumstances." Justice Blackmun also concurred in the result, similarly expressing concern "with what appears to me to be an emerging tendency on the part of the Court to convert the *Terry* decision into a general statement that the Fourth Amendment requires only that any seizure be reasonable." Does *Place* mean that a 90–minute detention of luggage is always unreasonable in the absence of probable cause? Does *Place* mean that officers must have the drug sniffing dog on the premises at the time the luggage is seized? See United States v. Alpert, 816 F.2d 958 (4th Cir.1987) (50–minute detention of luggage reasonable, and *Place* does not contemplate a per se rule requiring that narcotics dogs be kept at each airport).

16. Limited Searches for Evidence by Law Enforcement Officers Under Terry

Terry allows limited investigative seizures of the person or property on the basis of reasonable suspicion. *Terry* also allows limited searches for self-protection on the basis of reasonable suspicion. Does *Terry* permit limited, cursory inspections by law enforcement officers searching for evidence on the basis of reasonable suspicion? This was one question encountered by the Court in Arizona v. Hicks, 480 U.S. 321 (1987). Police lawfully entered premises from which a weapon had been fired and noticed two sets of expensive stereo components in an otherwise squalid apartment. Suspecting that the components were stolen, one officer moved a turntable in order to read its serial number. This led to information that the turntable had been taken in an armed robbery. The State did not argue that probable cause existed to move the turntable, but rather that the movement and inspection was a "cursory" search that was supported by reasonable suspicion. Justice Scalia, writing for the Court, rejected this argument and held that probable cause was required for the search. He declared that "a search is a search, even if it happens to disclose nothing but the bottom of a turntable." He concluded that "we are unwilling to send police and judges into a new thicket of Fourth Amendment law, to seek a creature of uncertain description that is neither a plain-view inspection nor yet a full-blown search. Nothing in the prior opinions of this Court supports such a distinction." Why doesn't the prior opinion of *Terry* support the distinction that Justice Scalia rejected?

Justice O'Connor, joined by Chief Justice Rehnquist and Justice Powell, dissented. She argued that police officers who have reasonable, articulable suspicion that an object they come across in a lawful search is evidence of crime may make a cursory inspection of the object to verify their suspicion. Justice Powell added a dissenting opinion, joined by the Chief Justice and Justice O'Connor, that suggested that the majority's distinction between observing a serial number while searching (permissible) and moving an object to read a serial number (impermissible) trivialized the Fourth Amendment and would cause uncertainty.

There is a potential problem with Justice O'Connor's approach. Suppose that the officer first had the thought that the stereo equipment might be stolen after he left the apartment, and the officer then went before a magistrate to set forth a reasonable suspicion that the property was stolen. Could a magistrate issue a warrant that would entitle the officer to do a cursory investigation? If the answer is "no," is there any justification for permitting an officer to do the same investigation without a warrant? In thinking about these questions, it is useful to reconsider the basic *Terry* doctrine. That doctrine permits police to act on less than probable cause. Why is reasonable suspicion not enough in *Hicks*? Are the exigencies the same in both *Terry* and *Hicks*? Suppose the officer thought he had probable cause to search in *Hicks* and wanted to prevent removal of the stereo equipment while seeking a warrant. Could he invoke *Terry* to keep anyone from taking the equipment from the premises for a brief period in which a warrant was sought? *Place* suggests an affirmative answer. Why can the officer "freeze" the equipment but not move it?

The State in *Hicks* did not argue that the existence of two new stereos in a squalid apartment constituted probable cause to believe they were stolen. Should this argument have been made?

The holding in *Hicks* has not deterred the Government from arguing that cursory inspections can be conducted on reasonable suspicion. In United States v. Winsor, 846 F.2d 1569 (9th Cir.1988) officers chased suspected bank robbers fleeing from the crime into a hotel. Given the large number of rooms in the hotel, the court found that there was reasonable suspicion, but not probable cause, to believe that the robbers were in any particular room. At each room, the officers knocked on the door and announced "Police, open the door." After checking a few rooms, they knocked on a door answered by Dennis Winsor. They recognized him as the robber. At this point, the police had probable cause to enter, whereupon they found Peter Winsor, the other robber, as well as incriminating evidence. The Winsors argued that under *Hicks,* the police conducted a search when they knocked on the door and commanded that it be opened. The Government argued that the officers' conduct was not a full-blown search for evidence, but at most a limited intrusion requiring reasonable suspicion. The court of appeals, in an en banc decision, held that the evidence discovered when the door opened and thereafter was illegally obtained, and concluded as follows:

> We refuse the government's invitation to decide this case by balancing the competing interests at stake. Instead, we adhere to the bright-line rule that *Hicks* appears to have announced: The Fourth Amendment prohibits searches of dwellings without probable cause.

Would *Winsor* have come out differently if the officers had searched all but 30 rooms before finding the Winsors? All but 20? All but 10?

In United States v. Colyer, 878 F.2d 469 (D.C.Cir.1989), the court found it difficult to reconcile the *Terry* doctrine with the Court's rejection of Justice O'Connor's approach in *Hicks.*

> To be sure, the Supreme Court has upheld on reasonable suspicion a variety of minimally intrusive *seizures* * * *. Although there may be no compelling reason to differentiate between seizures on the basis of their intrusiveness and failing to likewise differentiate between types of searches, the fact remains that we are unable to point to a single Supreme Court case that has upheld a search on reasonable suspicion merely because it was minimally intrusive.

Other courts have taken the contrary view and held that a minimally intrusive search for evidence is permissible if supported by reasonable suspicion. For example, in United States v. Concepcion, 942 F.2d 1170 (7th Cir.

1991), officers took a key found on the defendant, and inserted it into a lock on a door to an apartment in which drugs had been found. The court held that this was a search, since the use of the key in the lock gave the officers information they did not otherwise have, i.e. that the defendant had a key to the apartment. But the search was upheld even though, at the time they used the key, the officers had only reasonable suspicion and not probable cause to connect the defendant with the apartment. The court reasoned that the search was minimally intrusive. It distinguished *Hicks* on the ground that the information uncovered in *Hicks* was more private: the officers in *Concepcion* could have connected the defendant with the apartment in a variety of ways. Is this a meaningful distinction?

Is there any persuasive distinction between searches and seizures which supports the difference in result between *Terry* and *Hicks*?

17. Search Incident to Arrest

As discussed in the introduction to the Fourth Amendment, a warrantless search incident to a valid arrest was an accepted practice at the time the Bill of Rights was adopted. While the principle was and is well-accepted, its application to various fact situations, and even the rationale underlying the exception, have been subject to dispute and inconsistent application in the Supreme Court. In the following case, the Court sought to explain the rationale of the search incident to arrest exception, and to limit the scope of an incident search to the rationale supporting the exception.

a. Spatial Limitations

CHIMEL v. CALIFORNIA

Supreme Court of the United States, 1969.
395 U.S. 752.

MR. JUSTICE STEWART delivered the opinion of the Court.

This case raises basic questions concerning the permissible scope under the Fourth Amendment of a search incident to a lawful arrest.

The relevant facts are essentially undisputed. Late in the afternoon of September 13, 1965, three police officers arrived at the Santa Ana, California, home of the petitioner with a warrant authorizing his arrest for the burglary of a coin shop. The officers knocked on the door, identified themselves to the petitioner's wife, and asked if they might come inside. She ushered them into the house, where they waited 10 or 15 minutes until the petitioner returned home from work. When the petitioner entered the house, one of the officers handed him the arrest warrant and asked for permission to "look around." The petitioner objected, but was advised that "on the basis of the lawful arrest," the officers would nonetheless conduct a search. No search warrant had been issued.

Accompanied by the petitioner's wife, the officers then looked through the entire three-bedroom house, including the attic, the garage, and a small workshop. In some rooms the search was relatively cursory. In the master bedroom and sewing room, however, the officers directed the petitioner's wife to open drawers and "to physically move contents of the drawers from side to side so that [they] might view any items that would have come from [the] burglary." After completing the search, they seized numerous items—primarily coins, but also several medals, tokens, and a few other objects. The entire search took between 45 minutes and an hour.

At the petitioner's subsequent state trial on two charges of burglary, the items taken from his house were admitted into evidence against him, over his objection that they had been unconstitutionally seized. * * *

Without deciding the question, we proceed on the hypothesis that the California courts were correct in holding that the arrest of the petitioner was valid under the Constitution. This brings us directly to the question whether the warrantless search of the petitioner's entire house can be constitutionally justified as incident to that arrest. The decisions of this Court bearing upon that question have been far from consistent, as even the most cursory review makes evident.

* * *

[The Court describes its erratic decisions beginning with dictum in Weeks v. United States, 232 U.S. 383 (1914), and continuing through Harris v. United States, 331 U.S. 145 (1947), Trupiano v. United States, 334 U.S. 699 (1948), and United States v. Rabinowitz, 339 U.S. 56 (1950).]

Rabinowitz has come to stand for the proposition, *inter alia,* that a warrantless search "incident to a lawful arrest" may generally extend to the area that is considered to be in the "possession" or under the "control" of the person arrested. And it was on the basis of that proposition that the California courts upheld the search of the petitioner's entire house in this case. That doctrine, however, at least in the broad sense in which it was applied by the California courts in this case, can withstand neither historical nor rational analysis.

Even limited to its own facts, the *Rabinowitz* decision was, as we have seen, hardly founded on an unimpeachable line of authority. * * *

* * *

* * * When an arrest is made, it is reasonable for the arresting officer to search the person arrested in order to remove any weapons that the latter might seek to use in order to resist arrest or effect his escape. Otherwise, the officer's safety might well be endangered, and the arrest itself frustrated. In addition, it is entirely reasonable for the arresting officer to search for and seize any evidence on the arrestee's person in order to prevent its concealment or destruction. And the area into which an arrestee might reach in order to grab a weapon or evidentiary items must, of course, be governed by a like rule. A gun on a table or in a drawer in front of one who is arrested can be as dangerous to the arresting officer as one concealed in the clothing of the person arrested. There is ample justification, therefore, for a search of the arrestee's person and the area "within his immediate control"—construing that phrase to mean the area from within which he might gain possession of a weapon or destructible evidence.

There is no comparable justification, however, for routinely searching any room other than that in which an arrest occurs—or, for that matter, for searching through all the desk drawers or other closed or concealed areas in that room itself. Such searches, in the absence of well-recognized exceptions, may be made only under the authority of a search warrant. The "adherence to judicial processes" mandated by the Fourth Amendment requires no less.

* * *

It is argued in the present case that it is "reasonable" to search a man's house when he is arrested in it. But that argument is founded on little more than a subjective view regarding the acceptability of certain sorts of police conduct, and not on considerations relevant to Fourth Amendment interests. Under such an unconfined analysis, Fourth Amendment protection in this area would approach the evaporation point. It is not easy to explain why, for instance, it is less subjectively "reasonable" to search a man's house when he is arrested on his front lawn—or just down the street—than it is when he happens to be in the house at the time of arrest. * * * Thus, although "[t]he recurring questions of the reasonableness of searches" depend upon "the facts and circumstances—the total atmosphere of the case," those facts and circumstances must be viewed in the light of established Fourth Amendment principles.

It would be possible, of course, to draw a line between *Rabinowitz* and *Harris* on the one hand, and this case on the other. For *Rabinowitz* involved a single room, and *Harris* a four-room apartment, while in the case before us an entire house was searched. But such a distinction would be highly artificial. The rationale that allowed the searches and seizures in *Rabinowitz* and *Harris* would allow the searches and seizures in this case. No consideration relevant to the Fourth Amendment suggests any point of rational limitation, once the search is allowed to go beyond the area from which the person arrested might obtain weapons or evidentiary items. The only reasoned distinction is one between a search of the person arrested and the area within his reach on the one hand, and more extensive searches on the other.[a]

The petitioner correctly points out that one result of decisions such as *Rabinowitz* and *Harris* is to give law enforcement officials the opportunity to engage in searches not justified by probable cause, by the simple expedient of arranging to arrest suspects at home rather than elsewhere. We do not suggest that the petitioner is necessarily correct in his assertion that such a strategy was utilized here,[b] but the fact remains that had he been arrested earlier in the day, at his place of employment rather than at home, no search of his house could have been made without a search warrant. * * *

* * *

MR. JUSTICE HARLAN, concurring.

a. It is argued in dissent that so long as there is probable cause to search the place where an arrest occurs, a search of that place should be permitted even though no search warrant has been obtained. This position seems to be based principally on two premises: first, that once an arrest has been made, the additional invasion of privacy stemming from the accompanying search is "relatively minor"; and second, that the victim of the search may "shortly thereafter" obtain a judicial determination of whether the search was justified by probable cause. With respect to the second premise, one may initially question whether all of the States in fact provide the speedy suppression procedures the dissent assumes. More fundamentally, however, we cannot accept the view that Fourth Amendment interests are vindicated so long as "the rights of the criminal" are "protect[ed] * * * against introduction of evidence seized without probable cause." The Amendment is designed to prevent, not simply to redress, unlawful police action. In any event, we cannot join in characterizing the invasion of privacy that results from a top-to-bottom search of a man's house as "minor." And we can see no reason why, simply because some interference with an individual's privacy and freedom of movement has lawfully taken place, further intrusions should automatically be allowed despite the absence of a warrant that the Fourth Amendment would otherwise require.

b. Although the warrant was issued at 10:39 a.m. and the arrest was not made until late in the afternoon, the State suggests that the delay is accounted for by normal police procedures and by the heavy workload of the officer in charge. In addition, that officer testified that he and his colleagues went to the petitioner's house "to keep from approaching him at his place of business to cause him any problem there."

I join the Court's opinion with these remarks concerning a factor to which the Court has not alluded. The only thing that has given me pause in voting to overrule *Harris* and *Rabinowitz* is that as a result of Mapp v. Ohio, 367 U.S. 643, (1961), and Ker v. California, 374 U.S. 23 (1963), every change in Fourth Amendment law must now be obeyed by state officials facing widely different problems of local law enforcement. We simply do not know the extent to which cities and towns across the Nation are prepared to administer the greatly expanded warrant system which will be required by today's decision; nor can we say with assurance that in each and every local situation, the warrant requirement plays an essential role in the protection of those fundamental liberties protected against state infringement by the Fourteenth Amendment.

* * *

This federal-state factor has not been an easy one for me to resolve, but in the last analysis I cannot in good conscience vote to perpetuate bad Fourth Amendment law.

* * *

MR. JUSTICE WHITE, with whom MR. JUSTICE BLACK joins, dissenting.

* * *

II

* * *

* * * Search of an arrested man and of the items within his immediate reach must in almost every case be reasonable. There is always a danger that the suspect will try to escape, seizing concealed weapons with which to overpower and injure the arresting officers, and there is a danger that he may destroy evidence vital to the prosecution. Circumstances in which these justifications would not apply are sufficiently rare that inquiry is not made into searches of this scope, which have been considered reasonable throughout.

The justifications which make such a search reasonable obviously do not apply to the search of areas to which the accused does not have ready physical access. This is not enough, however, to prove such searches unconstitutional. The Court has always held, and does not today deny, that when there is probable cause to search and it is "impracticable" for one reason or another to get a search warrant, then a warrantless search may be reasonable. This is the case whether an arrest was made at the time of the search or not.

This is not to say that a search can be reasonable without regard to the probable cause to believe that seizable items are on the premises. But when there are exigent circumstances, and probable cause, then the search may be made without a warrant, reasonably. An arrest itself may often create an emergency situation making it impracticable to obtain a warrant before embarking on a related search. Again assuming that there is probable cause to search premises at the spot where a suspect is arrested, it seems to me unreasonable to require the police to leave the scene in order to obtain a search warrant when they are already legally there to make a valid arrest, and when there must almost always be a strong possibility that confederates of the arrested man will in the meanwhile remove the items for which the police have probable cause to search. This must so often be the case that it seems to me as unreasonable to require a warrant for a search of the premises as to require a warrant for search of the person and his very immediate surroundings.

* * *

Note

What are the precise spatial limitations on search incident to arrest after *Chimel*? Is the permissible scope of the search determined by where the suspect was arrested, or by where the search occurred? Does it make a difference that the suspect is handcuffed? Infirm? Consider United States v. Lucas, 898 F.2d 606 (8th Cir.1990), where the defendant was convicted of bank robbery based in part upon evidence found in the following search incident to arrest:

> The magistrate found that Lucas was seated at a kitchen table with two other men as the officers stood in the front doorway of the apartment in which he was arrested. As Lucas began to get up from the table, the officers entered the apartment and ran into the kitchen. Two officers attempted to apprehend Lucas, and one officer monitored the other two men seated at the table. By the time the officers reached Lucas, his hand was within inches of the handle on a cabinet door. During the ensuing struggle, which lasted for approximately forty seconds, Lucas and the two officers slid around on the slick floor. At one point, Lucas fell to the floor, and the skirmish continued until Lucas was handcuffed. As an officer pulled Lucas from the floor and moved him toward the living room, another officer immediately stood up, opened the cabinet door that Lucas had been attempting to reach, and found a chrome automatic pistol inside the cabinet. The two men seated at the kitchen table were not handcuffed until after the gun was discovered.

The Court upheld the search under *Chimel:*

> Lucas argues that *Chimel* does not justify the search here because he was being escorted, handcuffed, from the kitchen when the search occurred. While relevant under *Chimel,* this is not a determinative factor. Rather, the question is whether, in light of all of the circumstances, the police conducted a valid search incident to Lucas' arrest. Considering the totality of the circumstances, we hold that they did.
>
> [A] warrantless search incident to an arrest may be valid even though a court, operating with the benefit of hindsight in an environment well removed from the scene of the arrest, doubts that the defendant could have reached the items seized during the search. The officers in this case searched a cabinet in a small kitchen immediately after handcuffing Lucas and while removing him from the kitchen. Moreover, two of Lucas' friends who had not been handcuffed were still at the kitchen table when the search took place. On these facts, we conclude that this was a valid warrantless search incident to Lucas' arrest. This conclusion is consistent not only with [this Circuit's opinions] but also with opinions from other circuits. See United States v. Queen, 847 F.2d at 352–54 (holding search valid even though it occurred when arrestee was handcuffed and guarded by two police officers several feet from the searched area); United States v. Silva, 745 F.2d 840, 847 (4th Cir.1984) (upholding search begun after arrestees were handcuffed, placed on beds, and monitored by federal agents); United States v. Fleming, 677 F.2d 602, 606–08 (7th Cir.1982) (approving the search, after arrestees were handcuffed, of a paper bag that was in police custody).
>
> In upholding the search here, we are persuaded by the Seventh Circuit's reasoning in *Fleming.* While acknowledging that "[i]t is surely possible for a *Chimel* search to be undertaken too long after the arrest and too far from the arrestee's person," the court recognized in *Fleming* that "it does not make

sense to prescribe a constitutional test that is entirely at odds with safe and sensible police procedures."

Does the court in *Lucas* show too much or just enough concern for the safety of the officers? See also Davis v. Robbs, 794 F.2d 1129 (6th Cir.1986) where the court upheld the seizure of a rifle which had been in close proximity to the arrestee at the time of the arrest. Judge Wellford dissented on this point, noting that the seizure occurred after the arrestee was put in the squad car:

> The rationale justifying the search incident to arrest exception is that some exigency exists at the time of the search or seizure, not arrest. Otherwise, no actual exigency, such as danger to the safety of the police or others, would exist. The actual exigency at the time of arrest would become fictional through transplantation to the time of the search and seizure. At the time the police seized the rifle in the present case, [the arrestee] was handcuffed and in the squad car. He no longer had access to the gun nor posed any danger to the police. Neither does the record suggest that the rifle would have been later unavailable for seizure had the police obtained a warrant. Thus, the rationale justifying the exception does not support the seizure of the rifle. The danger had passed.

Does the rationale of *Chimel,* allowing search incident to arrest to protect the officer and preserve the evidence, apply to every arrest? Does it apply even if the arrestee is allowed to move about? In Washington v. Chrisman, 455 U.S. 1 (1982), Chief Justice Burger, writing for the Court, declared that "the absence of an affirmative indication that an arrested person might have a weapon available or might attempt to escape does not diminish the arresting officer's authority to maintain custody over the arrested person." The Court stated that "every arrest must be presumed to present a risk of danger to the arresting officer," because "there is no way for an officer to predict reliably how a particular subject will react to arrest of the degree of potential danger." The Court upheld a search and seizure incident to arrest under the following circumstances: A police officer saw a person who appeared to be underage carrying liquor. He asked for identification and the suspect said it was in his dormitory room. The suspect agreed that the officer could accompany him while he retrieved it. As the suspect entered the room the officer remained in the open doorway from where he saw the suspect's roommate become nervous. The officer entered the room and noticed seeds and a small pipe that he concluded were used in marijuana smoking. After warning both roommates of their rights, the officer asked about other drugs and was given additional marijuana. The officer subsequently obtained consent to search the room and found LSD.

Chief Justice Burger's opinion reasoned that once the officer placed his suspect under arrest before returning to the suspect's room "[t]he officer had a right to remain literally at the suspect's elbow at all times." The opinion referred to the initial actions of the officer in waiting in the doorway as exhibiting restraint and concluded that since he had a valid right to enter the room at any time to monitor the movements of the arrested person, he had a right to be where he was when he first saw the seeds and the pipe.

Justice White, joined by Justices Brennan and Marshall, dissented. He agreed that if it had been reasonably necessary for the officer to enter the room to protect himself or to maintain control over the arrestee, his entry would have been proper. But he concluded that the officer did not enter for either purpose, but rather to get a better look at things he had seen from the doorway. The thrust of the dissent was that an officer "should not be permitted to invade living quarters any more than is necessary to maintain control and protect himself," which were not the reasons for the invasion in this case.[18]

Justice White, dissenting in *Chimel,* argues that the fact of arrest will in almost all cases give rise to exigent circumstances to search beyond the control area of the arrestee, because the family or the associates of the arrestee will try to destroy evidence when they learn about the arrest. Justice White does not contend that exigent circumstances will *always* arise, nor could he: if Chimel had been arrested while his wife was at work, there could be no threat that the wife would immediately destroy evidence. Rather, Justice White argues that exigent circumstances will arise so often upon an arrest that it makes sense to establish a bright line rule to that effect, so as to avoid the negative effects of ad hoc judgments and a case-by-case approach. Why did this argument not persuade the majority? If, as *Chrisman* states, we presume that the arrestee will destroy evidence or harm the officer even if that is not so in a particular case, why do we not presume that the arrestee's associates will learn about the arrest and destroy evidence or harm the officer?

The exigent circumstances exception will be discussed later in this Chapter, but for now it is important to note that the Court requires a showing of exigency on the facts of each case, and that the fact of arrest, while pertinent, is not dispositive of whether there is a risk of destruction of evidence or harm to the officers or public that would excuse the requirement that a warrant be obtained. Illustrative is Vale v. Louisiana, 399 U.S. 30 (1970). Officers observing Vale had probable cause to believe that he had engaged in a drug transaction outside his house. When they approached, Vale walked quickly toward the house. He was arrested on his front steps. The officers searched the house, and found narcotics in the back bedroom. Three minutes after the officers entered the house, Vale's mother and brother came home carrying groceries. Justice Stewart wrote for the Court as it held that the officers' warrantless search of the bedroom violated the Fourth Amendment. The Court found that the State had not met its burden of showing that exigent circumstances existed. Justice Stewart stated that "the goods ultimately seized were not in the process of destruction," and rejected the argument that "an arrest on the street can provide its own exigent circumstance so as to justify a warrantless search of the arrestee's house." Justice Blackmun did not take part. Justice Black, joined by Chief Justice Burger, dissented. He concluded that the State's burden of showing exigent circumstances was met:

> I do not suggest that all arrests necessarily provide the basis for a search of the arrestee's house. In this case there is far more than a mere street arrest. The police also observed Vale's use of the house as a base of operations for his commercial business, his attempt to return hurriedly to the house on seeing the officers, and the apparent destruction of evidence by the man with whom Vale

18. Although the Supreme Court reversed the Washington Supreme Court in *Chrisman,* it was the state supreme court that was to have the last word. On remand, it held that the officer violated the state constitution, which it interpreted to prohibit warrantless entry into a private dwelling by an officer unless he has specific articulable facts justifying the entry. The court found that the officer had no reason to perceive a threat to his safety or to fear destruction of evidence or escape, and that his entry was therefore invalid. State v. Chrisman, 100 Wn.2d 814, 676 P.2d 419 (1984).

was dealing. Furthermore the police arrival and Vale's arrest were plainly visible to anyone within the house, and the police had every reason to believe that someone in the house was likely to destroy the contraband if the search were postponed.

Notwithstanding *Vale,* in many cases the fact of arrest will create exigent circumstances due to the risk of destruction of evidence by the arrestee's associates. See United States v. Chavez, 812 F.2d 1295 (10th Cir.1987) (exigent circumstances allowed warrantless entry into garage, where lights therein were turned off shortly after drug seller was arrested in front of the garage). In United States v. Socey, 846 F.2d 1439 (D.C.Cir.1988), the Court set forth the following standard for determining the existence of exigent circumstances after an arrest:

> Consistent with *Vale,* we believe that a police officer can show an objectively reasonable belief that contraband is being, or will be, destroyed within a home if he can show 1) a reasonable belief that third persons were inside a private dwelling and 2) a reasonable belief that these third persons are aware of an * * * arrest of a confederate outside the premises so that they might see a need to destroy evidence.

The Court in *Socey* found that exigent circumstances existed where an arrest was made outside a house in which a large-scale drug operation was being conducted. The court stated that it was not unreasonable for the officers to believe "that such an operation would have some type of look-out system." The court also emphasized the fact that drugs are easily destroyed. Has the court in *Socey* applied a per se rule of exigent circumstances for arrests outside suspected drug operations? Is that consistent with *Chimel* and *Vale?*

Even in the absence of exigent circumstances, police may, pursuant to the *Terry* doctrine, search beyond the *Chimel* spatial limitations if it is necessary to conduct a "protective sweep" of the place where the arrest is made. In Maryland v. Buie, 494 U.S. 325 (1990), the Court defined a "protective sweep" as a "quick and limited search of a premises, incident to an arrest and conducted to protect the safety of police officers or others." The Court held that a protective sweep could be justified by reasonable suspicion "that the area swept harbored an individual posing a danger to the officer or others." Justice White, writing for the Court, stated that the reasonable suspicion standard was an appropriate balance between the arrestee's remaining privacy interest in the home and the officer's interest in safety. Justice White rejected the contention that a probable cause standard was mandated by Arizona v. Hicks. *Hicks* was distinguished as a search for evidence, rather than a search for safety purposes as in *Terry.* The majority also concluded that the spatial limitations of *Chimel* were not undermined by allowing a protective sweep on reasonable suspicion. Unlike a search incident to arrest, the protective sweep is limited to areas where persons may be hidden. Nor does the officer have an automatic right to conduct a protective sweep (unlike the automatic right to conduct a search incident to arrest). Justice Stevens concurred to emphasize that a protective sweep could not be conducted to root out those who might destroy evidence but who would not present a safety risk. Justice Brennan, joined by Justice Marshall dissented.

In *Buie,* defendant was arrested in the home. Could a protective sweep be conducted if, as in *Vale,* the arrest was made just outside the home?

b. Temporal Limitations

Generally, a search incident to arrest takes place immediately after the arrest itself. But courts will not concern themselves with the technicality of which came first—the arrest or the search—when both are nearly simultaneous and probable cause to arrest existed before the search was conducted. As the Court stated in Rawlings v. Kentucky, 448 U.S. 98 (1980): "Where the formal arrest followed quickly on the heels of the challenged search of petitioner's person, we do not believe it particularly important that the search preceded the arrest rather than vice versa." In Cupp v. Murphy, 412 U.S. 291 (1973), the Court upheld as legitimate under *Chimel* the scraping of a murder suspect's fingernails at a time when there was probable cause to arrest, the suspect was informed of the police suspicion, and he moved in a manner that suggested he was trying to wipe his fingernails clean. But the Court noted that a person not under formal arrest "might well be less hostile to the police and less likely to take conspicuous, immediate steps to destroy incriminating evidence on his person." The Court emphasized that it was not holding that "a full *Chimel* search would have been justified in this case without a formal arrest and without a warrant."

While a search can precede the arrest it cannot be used to provide probable cause to make the arrest. As the Court stated in the per curiam opinion in Smith v. Ohio, 494 U.S. 541 (1990): "That reasoning, . . . justifying the arrest by the search and at the same time . . . the search by the arrest, just will not do."

The term "incident to" implies that if the search is conducted too long after the arrest is completed, it will not qualify for the exception. But how long is too long? In Chambers v. Maroney, 399 U.S. 42 (1970), officers searched an automobile which had been impounded and brought to the police station after the arrest of its occupants. The Court held that the search could not be justified as incident to arrest, stating that "once an accused is under arrest and in custody, then a search made at another place, without a warrant, is simply not incident to the arrest," and that the reasons for a search incident to arrest "no longer obtain when the accused is safely in custody at the station house." The Court applied the same principle in United States v. Chadwick, 433 U.S. 1 (1977), where a footlocker was searched at the police station, 90 minutes after the arrest of its owner. The Court stated that the search "cannot be viewed as incidental to the arrest or as justified by any other exigency."

In United States v. Edwards, 415 U.S. 800 (1974), the Court held that a suspect, who was arrested for attempting to break into a post office and was jailed close to midnight, could be searched incident to arrest the next morning. After the arrest, the police discovered that entry into the post office apparently involved prying open a window with an iron bar that caused paint to chip. They seized Edwards' shirt and trousers in the morning and subjected them to analysis that revealed paint chips. Justice White's majority opinion said "that searches and seizures that could be made on the spot at the time of arrest may legally be conducted later when the accused arrives at the place of detention." He went on to conclude "that the normal processes incident to arrest and custody had not yet been completed when Edwards was placed in his cell." In addition he left open the possibility that the warrant clause might govern some post-seizure searches of arrestees, but strongly implied that most searches and seizures of the arrestee's person and things in his possession at the time of the arrest could be automatically examined. Justice Stewart, joined by Justices Douglas, Brennan and Marshall dissented, taking the view that "the considerations that typically justify a warrantless search incident to a lawful arrest were wholly absent here." [19]

Edwards was cited by Justice Blackmun in dissent in *Chadwick.* Is there any way to reconcile the two cases? Do they take a different view of what is incident to arrest, or do they merely deal with different types of searches? The next case may have some bearing on this question.

c. *Searches of the Person Incident to Arrest*

UNITED STATES v. ROBINSON

Supreme Court of the United States, 1973.
414 U.S. 218.

MR. JUSTICE REHNQUIST delivered the opinion of the Court.

Respondent Robinson was convicted in United States District Court for the District of Columbia of the possession and facilitation of concealment of heroin * * *. [T]he Court of Appeals en banc reversed the judgment of conviction, holding that the heroin introduced in evidence against respondent had been obtained as a result of a search which violated the Fourth Amendment to the United States Constitution. * * *

On April 23, 1968, at approximately 11 p.m., Officer Richard Jenks, a 15-year veteran of the District of Columbia Metropolitan Police Department, observed the respondent driving a 1965 Cadillac near the intersection of 8th and C Streets, N.E., in the District of Columbia. Jenks, as a result of previous investigation following a check of respondent's operator's permit four days earlier, determined there was reason to believe that respondent was operating a motor vehicle after the revocation of his operator's permit. This is an offense defined by statute in the District of Columbia which carries a mandatory minimum jail term, a mandatory minimum fine, or both.

Jenks signaled respondent to stop the automobile, which respondent did, and all three of the occupants emerged from the car. At that point Jenks informed respondent that he was under arrest for "operating after revocation and obtaining a permit by misrepresentation." It was assumed by the Court of Appeals, and is conceded by the respondent here, that Jenks had probable cause to arrest respondent, and that he effected a full-custody arrest.[a]

19. The reasonableness clause of the Fourth Amendment may limit some searches incident to arrest. Thus, a vaginal cavity search without a warrant was condemned in State v. Clark, 65 Hawaii 488, 654 P.2d 355 (1982). The court limited searches incident to arrest that go beyond the outer surface of the body to situations where there is a "clear indication that evidence will be found, and there is an emergency which makes the delay in getting a warrant" a threat that the evidence will be destroyed.

a. The Court of Appeals noted that there was a difference in the presentation of the facts in the various proceedings that were conducted in the District Court. Counsel for respondent on appeal stressed that respondent had a record of two prior narcotics convictions, and suggested that Officer Jenks may have been aware of that record through his investigation of criminal records, while Jenks was checking out the discrepancies in the birthdates on the operator's permit and on the Selective Service card that had been given to him for examination when he had confronted

In accordance with procedures prescribed in police department instructions, Jenks then began to search respondent. He explained at a subsequent hearing that he was "face-to-face" with the respondent, and "placed [his] hands on [the respondent], my right-hand to his left breast like this (demonstrating) and proceeded to pat him down thus [with the right hand]." During this patdown, Jenks felt an object in the left breast pocket of the heavy coat respondent was wearing, but testified that he "couldn't tell what it was" and also that he "couldn't actually tell the size of it." Jenks then reached into the pocket and pulled out the object, which turned out to be a "crumpled up cigarette package." Jenks testified that at this point he still did not know what was in the package:

> "As I felt the package I could feel objects in the package but I couldn't tell what they were. * * * I knew they weren't cigarettes."

The officer then opened the cigarette pack and found 14 gelatin capsules of white powder which he thought to be, and which later analysis proved to be, heroin. Jenks then continued his search of respondent to completion, feeling around his waist and trouser legs, and examining the remaining pockets. The heroin seized from the respondent was admitted into evidence at the trial which resulted in his conviction in the District Court.

* * * We conclude that the search conducted by Jenks in this case did not offend the limits imposed by the Fourth Amendment, and we therefore reverse the judgment of the Court of Appeals.

I

It is well settled that a search incident to a lawful arrest is a traditional exception to the warrant requirement of the Fourth Amendment. This general exception has historically been formulated into two distinct propositions. The first is that a search may be made of the *person* of the arrestee by virtue of the lawful arrest. The second is that a search may be made of the area within the control of the arrestee.

Examination of this Court's decisions shows that these two propositions have been treated quite differently. The validity of the search of a person incident to a lawful arrest has been regarded as settled from its first enunciation, and has remained virtually unchallenged until the present case. The validity of the second proposition, while likewise conceded in principle, has been subject to differing interpretations as to the extent of the area which may be searched. * * *

* * *

Throughout the series of cases in which the Court has addressed the second proposition relating to a search incident to a lawful arrest—the permissible area beyond the person of the arrestee which such a search may cover—no doubt has been expressed as to the unqualified authority of the arresting authority to search the person of the arrestee.

* * * Since the statements in the cases speak not simply in terms of an

the respondent on the previous occasion. Respondent argued below that Jenks may have used the subsequent traffic violation arrest as a mere pretext for a narcotics search which would not have been allowed by a neutral magistrate had Jenks sought a warrant. The Court of Appeals found that Jenks had denied he had any such motive, and for the purposes of its opinion accepted the Government's version of that factual question, since even accepting that version it still found the search involved to be unconstitutional. We think it is sufficient for purposes of our decision that respondent was lawfully arrested for an offense, and that Jenks' placing him in custody following that arrest was not a departure from established police department practice. We leave for another day questions which would arise on facts different from these.

exception to the warrant requirement, but in terms of an affirmative authority to search, they clearly imply that such searches also meet the Fourth Amendment's requirement of reasonableness.

II

In its decision of this case, the Court of Appeals decided that even after a police officer lawfully places a suspect under arrest for the purpose of taking him into custody, he may not ordinarily proceed to fully search the prisoner. He must, instead, conduct a limited frisk of the outer clothing and remove such weapons that he may, as a result of that limited frisk, reasonably believe and ascertain that the suspect has in his possession. While recognizing that Terry v. Ohio dealt with a permissible "frisk" incident to an investigative stop based on less than probable cause to arrest, the Court of Appeals felt that the principles of that case should be carried over to this probable-cause arrest for driving while one's license is revoked. Since there would be no further evidence of such a crime to be obtained in a search of the arrestee, the court held that only a search for weapons could be justified.

* * *

III

* * *

The Court of Appeals in effect determined that the *only* reason supporting the authority for a *full* search incident to lawful arrest was the possibility of discovery of evidence or fruits. Concluding that there could be no evidence or fruits in the case of an offense such as that with which respondent was charged, it held that any protective search would have to be limited by the conditions laid down in *Terry* for a search upon less than probable cause to arrest. Quite apart from the fact that *Terry* clearly recognized the distinction between the two types of searches, and that a different rule governed one than governed the other, we find additional reason to disagree with the Court of Appeals.

The justification or reason for the authority to search incident to a lawful arrest rests quite as much on the need to disarm the suspect in order to take him into custody as it does on the need to preserve evidence on his person for later use at trial. The standards traditionally governing a search incident to lawful arrest are not, therefore, commuted to the stricter *Terry* standards by the absence of probable fruits or further evidence of the particular crime for which the arrest is made.

Nor are we inclined, on the basis of what seems to us to be a rather speculative judgment, to qualify the breadth of the general authority to search incident to a lawful custodial arrest on an assumption that persons arrested for the offense of driving while their licenses have been revoked are less likely to possess dangerous weapons than are those arrested for other crimes. It is scarcely open to doubt that the danger to an officer is far greater in the case of the extended exposure which follows the taking of a suspect into custody and transporting him to the police station than in the case of the relatively fleeting contact resulting from the typical *Terry*-type stop. This is an adequate basis for treating all custodial arrests alike for purposes of search justification.

But quite apart from these distinctions, our more fundamental disagreement with the Court of Appeals arises from its suggestion that there must be litigated in each case the issue of whether or not there was present one of the reasons supporting the authority for a search of the person incident to a lawful arrest. We do not think the long line of authorities of this Court * * *, or what we can glean from the history of practice in this country and in England, requires such a case-by-case adjudication. A police officer's determination as to how and where to search the person of a suspect whom he has arrested is necessarily a quick *ad hoc* judgment which the Fourth Amendment does not require to be broken down in each instance into an analysis of each step in the search. The authority to search the person incident to a lawful custodial arrest, while based upon the need to disarm and to discover evidence, does not depend on what a court may later decide was the probability in a particular arrest situation that weapons or evidence would in fact be found upon the person of the suspect. A custodial arrest of a suspect based on probable cause is a reasonable intrusion under the Fourth Amendment; that intrusion being lawful, a search incident to the arrest requires no additional justification. It is the fact of the lawful arrest which establishes the authority to search, and we hold that in the case of a lawful custodial arrest a full search of the person is not only an exception to the warrant requirement of the Fourth Amendment, but is also a "reasonable" search under that Amendment.

* * *

MR. JUSTICE POWELL, concurring.

* * *

* * * I believe that an individual lawfully subjected to a custodial arrest retains no significant Fourth Amendment interest in the privacy of his person. Under this view the custodial arrest is the significant intrusion of state power into the privacy of one's person. If the arrest is lawful, the privacy interest guarded by the Fourth Amendment is subordinated to a legitimate and overriding governmental concern. No reason then exists to frustrate law enforcement by requiring some independent justification for a search incident to a lawful custodial arrest. This seems to me the reason that a valid arrest justifies a full search of the person, even if that search is not narrowly limited by the twin rationales of seizing evidence and disarming the arrestee. The search incident to arrest is reasonable under the Fourth Amendment because the privacy interest protected by that constitutional guarantee is legitimately abated by the fact of arrest.

MR. JUSTICE MARSHALL, with whom MR. JUSTICE DOUGLAS and MR. JUSTICE BRENNAN join, dissenting.

* * *

II

* * * The majority's fear of overruling the "quick *ad hoc* judgment" of the police officer is * * * inconsistent with the very function of the Amendment—to ensure that the quick *ad hoc* judgments of police officers are subject to review and control by the judiciary.

* * *

The majority's attempt to avoid case-by-case adjudication of Fourth Amendment issues is not only misguided as a matter of principle, but is also doomed to fail as a matter of practical application. As the majority itself is well aware, the powers granted the police in this case are strong ones, subject to potential abuse. Although, in this particular case, Officer Jenks was required by police department regulations to make an in-custody arrest rather than to issue a citation, in most jurisdictions and for most traffic offenses the determination of whether to issue a citation or effect a full arrest is discretionary with the officer. There is always the possibility that a police officer, lacking probable cause to obtain a search warrant, will use a traffic arrest as a pretext to conduct a search. * * *

III

* * *

As I view the matter, the search in this case divides into three distinct phases: the patdown of respondent's coat pocket; the removal of the unknown object from the pocket; and the opening of the crumpled-up cigarette package.

A

No question is raised here concerning the lawfulness of the patdown of respondent's coat pocket. The Court of Appeals unanimously affirmed the right of a police officer to conduct a limited frisk for weapons when making an in-custody arrest, regardless of the nature of the crime for which the arrest was made. * * *

B

With respect to the removal of the unknown object from the coat pocket, the first issue presented is whether that aspect of the search can be sustained as part of the limited frisk for weapons. The weapons search approved by the Court of Appeals was modeled upon the narrowly drawn protective search for weapons authorized in *Terry,* which consists "of a limited patting of the outer clothing of the suspect for concealed objects which might be used as instruments of assault."

It appears to have been conceded by the Government below that the removal of the object from respondent's coat pocket exceeded the scope of a *Terry* frisk for weapons, since, under *Terry,* an officer may not remove an object from the suspect's pockets unless he has reason to believe it to be a dangerous weapon.

In the present case, however, Officer Jenks had no reason to believe and did not in fact believe that the object in respondent's coat pocket was a weapon. He admitted later that the object did not feel like a gun. In fact, he did not really have any thoughts one way or another about what was in the pocket. As Jenks himself testified, "I just searched him. I didn't think about what I was looking for. I just searched him." Since the removal of the object from the pocket cannot be justified as part of a limited *Terry* weapons frisk, the question arises whether it is reasonable for a police officer, when effecting an in-custody arrest of a traffic offender, to make a fuller search of the person than is permitted pursuant to *Terry.*

* * *

The Government does not now contend that the search of respondent's pocket can be justified by any need to find and seize evidence in order to prevent its concealment or destruction, for, as the Court of Appeals found, there is no evidence or fruits of the offense with which respondent was charged. The only rationale for a search in this case, then, is the removal of weapons which the arrestee might use to harm the officer and attempt an escape. This rationale, of course, is identical to the rationale of the search permitted in *Terry.* * * * Since the underlying rationale of a *Terry* search and the search of a traffic violator are identical, the Court of Appeals held that the scope of the searches must be the same. * * *

The problem with this approach, however, is that it ignores several significant differences between the context in which a search incident to arrest for a traffic violation is made, and the situation presented in *Terry.* Some of these differences would appear to suggest permitting a more thorough search in this case than was permitted in *Terry;* other differences suggest a narrower, more limited right to search than was there recognized.

The most obvious difference between the two contexts relates to whether the officer has cause to believe that the individual he is dealing with possesses weapons which might be used against him. *Terry* did not permit an officer to conduct a weapons frisk of anyone he lawfully stopped on the street, but rather, only where "he has reason to believe that he is dealing with an armed and dangerous individual * * *." 392 U.S., at 27. While the policeman who arrests a suspected rapist or robber may well have reason to believe he is dealing with an armed and dangerous person, certainly this does not hold true with equal force with respect to a person arrested for a motor vehicle violation of the sort involved in this case.

Nor was there any particular reason in this case to believe that respondent was dangerous. He had not attempted to evade arrest, but had quickly complied with the police both in bringing his car to a stop after being signaled to do so and in producing the documents Officer Jenks requested. In fact, Jenks admitted that he searched respondent face to face rather than in spread-eagle fashion because he had no reason to believe respondent would be violent.

While this difference between the situation presented in *Terry* and the context presented in this case would tend to suggest a lesser authority to search here than was permitted in *Terry,* other distinctions between the two cases suggest just the opposite. As the Court of Appeals noted, a crucial feature distinguishing the in-custody arrest from the *Terry* context " 'is not the greater likelihood that a person taken into custody is armed, but rather the increased likelihood of danger to the officer *if* in fact the person is armed.' " A *Terry* stop involves a momentary encounter between officer and suspect, while an in-custody arrest places the two in close proximity for a much longer period of time. If the individual happens to have a weapon on his person, he will certainly have much more opportunity to use it against the officer in the in-custody situation. The prolonged proximity also makes it more likely that the individual will be able to extricate any small hidden weapon which might go undetected in a weapons frisk, such as a safety pin or razor blade. In addition, a suspect taken into custody may feel more threatened by the serious restraint on his liberty than a person who is simply stopped by an officer for questioning, and may therefore be more likely to resort to force.

* * * Balancing these competing considerations in order to determine what is a reasonable warrantless search in the traffic arrest context is a difficult process, one for which there may be no easy analytical guideposts. We are dealing with factors not easily quantified and, therefore, not easily weighed one against the other. And the competing interests we are protecting—the individual's interest in remaining free from unnecessarily intrusive invasions of privacy and society's interest that police officers not take unnecessary risks in the performance of their duties—are each deserving of our most serious attention and do not themselves tip the balance in any particular direction.

* * *

C

The majority opinion fails to recognize that the search conducted by Officer Jenks did not merely involve a search of respondent's person. It also included a separate search of effects found on his person. And even were we to assume, *arguendo,* that it was reasonable for Jenks to remove the object he felt in respondent's pocket, clearly there was no justification consistent with the Fourth Amendment which would authorize his opening the package and looking inside.

To begin with, after Jenks had the cigarette package in his hands, there is no indication that he had reason to believe or did in fact believe that the package contained a weapon. More importantly, even if the crumpled-up cigarette package had in fact contained some sort of small weapon, it would have been impossible for respondent to have used it once the package was in the officer's hands. Opening the package, therefore, did not further the protective purpose of the search. * * *

It is suggested, however, that since the custodial arrest itself represents a significant intrusion into the privacy of the person, any additional intrusion by way of opening or examining effects found on the person is not worthy of constitutional protection. But such an approach was expressly rejected by the Court in *Chimel.* * * *

* * *

The Government argues that it is difficult to see what constitutionally protected "expectation of privacy" a prisoner has in the interior of a cigarette pack. One wonders if the result in this case would have been the same were respondent a businessman who was lawfully taken into custody for driving without a license and whose wallet was taken from him by the police. Would it be reasonable for the police officer, because of the possibility that a razor blade was hidden somewhere in the wallet, to open it, remove all the contents, and examine each item carefully? Or suppose a lawyer lawfully arrested for a traffic offense is found to have a sealed envelope on his person. Would it be permissible for the arresting officer to tear open the envelope in order to make sure that it did not contain a clandestine weapon—perhaps a pin or a razor blade? Would it not be more consonant with the purpose of the Fourth Amendment and the legitimate needs of the police to require the officer, if he has any question whatsoever about what the wallet or letter contains, to hold on to it until the arrestee is brought to the precinct station? [b]

* * *

Note

What is the principle that gives rise to two decisions like *Chimel* and *Robinson?* The first marks an attempt to make the warrant clause a meaningful protection

b. Nor would it necessarily have been reasonable for the police to have opened the cigarette package at the police station. The Government argued below, as an alternative theory to justify the search in this case, that when a suspect is booked and is about to be placed in station house detention, it is reasonable to search his person to prevent the introduction of weapons or contraband into the jail facility and to inventory the personal effects found on the suspect. Since respondent's cigarette package would have been removed and opened at the station house anyway, the argument goes, the search might just as well take place in the field at the time of the arrest. This argument fails * * *. [A]s the Court of Appeals had indicated in its opinion in United States v. Mills, 153 U.S.App.D.C. 156, 472 F.2d 1231 (1972) (en banc), the justification for station-house searches is not the booking process itself, but rather the fact that the suspect will be placed in jail. In the District of Columbia, petty offenses of the sort involved in the present case are bailable, and, as the Government stipulated in *Mills,* the normal procedure is for offenders to be advised of the opportunity to post collateral at the station house and to avoid an inventory search unless they are unable or refuse to do so. One cannot justify a full search in the field on a subsequent event that quite possibly may never take place.

The Government also suggested in oral argument before this Court that it would be administratively inconvenient to require a police officer, after removing an object from an arrestee, to hold on to the object rather than to look inside and determine what it contained. Mere administrative inconvenience, however, cannot justify invasion of Fourth Amendment rights. See Chimel v. California, 395 U.S., at 768. One can no doubt imagine cases where the inconvenience might be so substantial as to interfere with the task of transporting the suspect into custody. While these situations might necessitate a different rule, certainly in this case there would have been no inconvenience whatsoever. Officer Jenks could easily have placed the cigarette package in his own pocket or handed it to his partner to hold onto until they reached the precinct station.

against searches not approved in advance by a magistrate. The intent of the second is less clear. What argument does the majority finally accept as a justification for a search beyond what the dissenters would accept? Do you find the approach of the majority to be consistent with the Court's approach in *Terry?* With the theory of the predominating warrant clause? Several state courts have rejected the majority's approach by relying on their state constitutions. See e.g., People v. Brisendine, 13 Cal.3d 528, 119 Cal.Rptr. 315, 531 P.2d 1099 (1975); Dunn v. Alaska, 653 P.2d 1071 (Alaska, 1982).

The history of search incident to arrest is hardly likely to be of much assistance in deciding what the Fourth Amendment requires since so few early cases discussed the goals of the Amendment. It is especially unhelpful in deciding what is reasonable in the modern world with relatively large and professionalized police forces. Do you believe that the position of the *Robinson* dissenters would have unduly burdened the police?

Decided together with *Robinson* was Gustafson v. Florida, 414 U.S. 260 (1973). In that case, both the decision whether to arrest for a traffic offense (or issue a citation) and whether to conduct a full scale search were left to the officer on the scene. The majority said that "we do not find these differences determinative of the constitutional issue." The lineup of the Justices was the same as in *Robinson,* except that Mr. Justice Stewart noted in a one paragraph concurrence "that a persuasive claim might have been made in this case that the custodial arrest * * * for a minor traffic offense violated * * * rights under the Fourth and Fourteenth Amendments." 414 U.S. at 266–67. Professor Amsterdam argued that had the Court condemned the amount of discretion left the officer in *Gustafson* and distinguished *Robinson's* rule-oriented system, "it would * * * have made by far the greatest contribution to the jurisprudence of the fourth amendment since James Otis argued against the writs of assistance in 1761." Perspectives on the Fourth Amendment, 58 Minn.L.Rev. 349, 416 (1974). Would police regulations be helpful? What Fourth Amendment problems would they solve? Can it be argued that Professor Amsterdam overestimates the effect of a contrary result in *Gustafson*? That case allowed the officer discretion to determine whether to make a custodial or non-custodial arrest. But didn't the officer in *Robinson* have discretion as to whether to place the suspect under arrest? Can an officer be required to arrest a person when the officer determines that probable cause exists? Would that be a beneficial rule?

Justice Powell's concurring view in *Robinson* and *Gustafson* poses the Fourth Amendment issue sharply. He argues that once an arrest is made there is "a legitimate and overriding governmental concern" to which "the privacy interest guarded by the Fourth Amendment is subordinated." But what is the governmental concern that would not be satisfied by the dissenters' approach? One view of the Fourth Amendment is that once there is a justifiable intrusion, other smaller intrusions should not be of concern. The other view is that all intrusions are of concern and that although the government's real needs may be recognized and served, a need of the government should be served in the manner that is least intrusive. If the warrant clause is the dominant clause, which view is correct?

Lower courts have consistently rejected Justice Powell's argument that an arrest renders reasonable any incremental intrusion pursuant to that arrest. See Mary Beth G. v. City of Chicago, 723 F.2d 1263 (7th Cir.1983), where the court held that the City violated the Fourth Amendment by promoting a policy of strip searching all those placed in custody for misdemeanors, even though many of the arrestees would be in custody for only a short time pending posting of bail.

In United States v. Chadwick, supra, the Court held that a search of a footlocker at the police station could not be justified as a search incident to arrest because it occurred long after Chadwick was in custody. In a footnote, the Court referred to *Robinson* and stated as follows:

> Unlike searches of the person, searches of possessions within an arrestee's immediate control cannot be justified by any reduced expectations of privacy caused by the arrest. Respondents' privacy interest in the contents of the footlocker was not eliminated simply because they were under arrest.

Does this passage mean that the officer does not have an automatic right to search containers incident to arrest when they are within the control area but not on the person? This would mean that briefcases, pocketbooks and bookbags could be seized but not searched without a warrant or exigent circumstances (such as a ticking briefcase); whereas wallets and cigarette packs could be thoroughly and automatically searched under *Robinson.* Does this distinction make sense? Most lower courts have applied the automatic arrest power rule of *Robinson* to searches of briefcases and the like. See e.g. United States v. Morales, 923 F.2d 621 (8th Cir.1991) (distinguishing *Chadwick* as a case involving a search which occurred too long after the arrest was completed); United States v. Herrera, 810 F.2d 989 (10th Cir.1987) (same). But see United States v. Gorski, 852 F.2d 692 (2d Cir.1988) (search of bag during arrest must be justified by exigent circumstances, otherwise seizure is all that is permitted). The following case, though ostensibly dealing with automobiles, may have some bearing on whether any container in the control area may be searched incident to a lawful arrest.

d. Search Incident to Arrest Applied to Automobiles

NEW YORK v. BELTON

Supreme Court of the United States, 1981.
453 U.S. 454.

JUSTICE STEWART delivered the opinion of the Court.

When the occupant of an automobile is subjected to a lawful custodial arrest, does the constitutionally permissible scope of a search incident to his arrest include the passenger compartment of the automobile in which he was riding? That is the question at issue in the present case.

I

On April 9, 1978, Trooper Douglas Nicot, a New York State policeman driving an unmarked car on the New York Thruway, was passed by another automobile travelling at an excessive rate of speed. Nicot gave chase, overtook the speeding vehicle, and ordered its driver to pull it over to the side of the road and stop. There were four men in the car, one of whom was Roger Belton, the respondent in this case. The policeman asked to see the driver's license and automobile registration, and discovered that none of the men owned the vehicle or was related to its owner. Meanwhile, the policeman had smelled burnt marihuana and had seen on the floor of the car an envelope marked "Supergold" that he associated with marihuana. He therefore directed the men to get out of the car, and placed them under arrest for the unlawful possession of marihuana. He patted down each of the men and "split them up into four separate areas of the Thruway at this time so they would not be in physical touching area of each other." He then picked up the envelope marked "Supergold" and found that it contained marihuana. After giving the arrestees the warnings required by Miranda v. Arizona, the state policeman searched each one of them. He then searched the passenger compartment of the car. On the back seat he found a black leather jacket belonging to Belton. He unzipped one of the pockets of the jacket and discovered cocaine. Placing the jacket in his automobile, he drove the four arrestees to a nearby police station.

Belton was subsequently indicted for criminal possession of a controlled substance. In the trial court he moved that the cocaine the trooper had seized from the jacket pocket be suppressed. The court denied the motion. * * *

The New York Court of Appeals reversed, holding that "[a] warrantless search of the zippered pockets of an unaccessible jacket may not be upheld as a search incident to a lawful arrest where there is no longer any danger that the arrestee or a confederate might gain access to the article." Two judges dissented. * * *

II

* * *

Although the principle that limits a search incident to a lawful custodial arrest may be stated clearly enough, courts have discovered the principle difficult to apply in specific cases. Yet, as one commentator has pointed out, the protection of the Fourth and Fourteenth Amendments "can only be realized if the police are acting under a set of rules which, in most instances, makes it possible to reach a correct determination beforehand as to whether an invasion of privacy is justified in the interest of law enforcement." LaFave, "Case-by-Case Adjudication" versus "Standardized Procedures": The Robinson Dilemma, 1974 Sup.Ct.Rev. 127, 142. * * * In short, "A single, familiar standard is essential to guide police officers, who have only limited time and expertise to reflect on and balance the social and individual interests involved in the specific circumstances they confront."

So it was that, in United States v. Robinson, the Court hewed to a straightforward rule, easily applied, and predictably enforced. * * *

But no straightforward rule has emerged from the litigated cases respecting the question involved here—the question of the proper scope of a search of the interior of an automobile incident to a lawful custodial arrest of its occupants. * * *

When a person cannot know how a court will apply a settled principle to a recurring factual situation, that person cannot know the scope of his constitutional protection, nor can a policeman know the scope of his authority. While the *Chimel* case established that a search incident to an arrest may not stray beyond the area within the immediate control of the arrestee, courts have found no workable definition of "the area within the immediate control of the arrestee" when that area arguably includes the interior of an automobile and the arrestee is its recent occupant. Our reading of the cases suggests the generalization that articles inside the relatively narrow compass of the passenger compartment of an automobile are in fact generally, even if not inevitably, within "the area into which an arrestee might reach in order to grab a weapon or evidentiary item." In order to establish the workable rule this category of cases requires, we read *Chimel's* definition of the limits of the area that may be searched in light of that generalization. Accordingly, we hold that when a policeman has made a lawful custodial arrest of the occupant of an automobile, he may, as a contemporaneous incident of that arrest, search the passenger compartment of that automobile.[a]

It follows from this conclusion that the police may also examine the contents of any containers found within the passenger compartment, for if the passenger compartment is within reach of the arrestee, so also will containers in it be within his reach.[b] Such a container may, of course, be searched whether it is open or closed, since the justification for the search is not that the arrestee has no privacy interest in the container, but that the lawful custodial arrest justifies the infringement of any privacy interest the arrestee may have. * * *

It is true, of course, that these containers will sometimes be such that they could hold neither a weapon nor evidence of the criminal conduct for which the suspect was arrested. However, in United States v. Robinson, supra, the Court rejected the argument that such a container—there a "crumpled up cigarette package"—located during a search of Robinson incident to his arrest could not be searched * * *.[c]

[The Court distinguishes automobile search cases and upholds the search and seizure.]

JUSTICE BRENNAN, with whom JUSTICE MARSHALL, joins, dissenting.

* * *

In its attempt to formulate a " 'single, familiar standard * * * to guide police officers, who have only limited time and expertise to reflect on and balance the social and individual interests involved in the specific circumstances they confront,' " the Court today disregards these principles, and instead adopts a fiction—that the interior of a car is *always* within the immediate control of an arrestee who has recently been in the car. * * * In so holding, the Court ignores both precedent and principle and fails to achieve its objective of providing police officers with a more workable standard for determining the permissible scope of searches incident to arrest.

* * *

The Court seeks to justify its departure from the principles underlying *Chimel* by proclaiming the need for a new bright line rule to guide the officer in the field. As we pointed out in Mincey v. Arizona, however, "the mere fact that law enforcement may be made more efficient can never by itself justify disregard of the Fourth Amendment." Moreover, the Court's attempt to forge a "bright line" rule fails on its own terms. While the "interior/trunk" distinction may provide a workable guide in certain routine cases—for example, where the officer arrests the driver of a car and then immediately searches the seats and floor—in the long run, I suspect it will create far more problems than it solves. The Court's new approach leaves open too many questions and, more important, it provides the

a. Our holding today does no more than determine the meaning of *Chimel's* principles in this particular and problematic context. It in no way alters the fundamental principles established in the *Chimel* case regarding the basic scope of searches incident to lawful custodial arrests.

b. "Container" here denotes any object capable of holding another object. It thus includes closed or open glove compartments, consoles, or other receptacles located anywhere within the passenger compartment, as well as luggage, boxes, bags, clothing, and the like. Our holding encompasses only the interior of the passenger compartment of an automobile and does not encompass the trunk.

c. It seems to have been the theory of the Court of Appeals that the search and seizure in the present case could not have been incident to the respondent's arrest, because Trooper Nicot, by the very act of searching the respondent's jacket and seizing the contents of its pocket, had gained "exclusive control" of them. But under this fallacious theory no search or seizure incident to a lawful arrest could ever be valid; by seizing an article even on the arrestee's person, an officer may be said to have reduced that article to his "exclusive control."

police and the courts with too few tools with which to find the answers.

Thus, although the Court concludes that a warrantless search of a car may take place even though the suspect was arrested outside the car, it does not indicate how long after the suspect's arrest that search may validly be conducted. Would a warrantless search incident to arrest be valid if conducted five minutes after the suspect left his car? Thirty minutes? Three hours? Does it matter whether the suspect is standing in close proximity to the car when the search is conducted? Does it matter whether the police formed probable cause to arrest before or after the suspect left his car? And *why* is the rule announced today necessarily limited to searches of cars? What if a suspect is seen walking out of a house where the police, peering in from outside, had formed probable cause to believe a crime was being committed? Could the police then arrest that suspect and enter the house to conduct a search incident to arrest? Even assuming today's rule is limited to searches of the "interior" of cars—an assumption not demanded by logic—what is meant by "interior"? Does it include locked glove compartments, the interior of door panels, or the area under the floorboards? Are special rules necessary for station wagons and hatchbacks, where the luggage compartment may be reached through the interior, or taxicabs, where a glass panel might separate the driver's compartment from the rest of the car? Are the only containers that may be searched those that are large enough to be "capable of holding another object"? Or does the new rule apply to any container, even if it "could hold neither a weapon nor evidence of the criminal conduct for which the suspect was arrested"?

The Court does not give the police any "bright line" answers to these questions. More important, because the Court's new rule abandons the justifications underlying *Chimel, it offers no guidance to the police officer seeking to work out these answers for himself.* As we warned in *Chimel,* "no consideration relevant to the Fourth Amendment suggests any point of rational limitation, once the search is allowed to go beyond the area from which the person arrested might obtain weapons or evidentiary items." By failing to heed this warning, the Court has undermined rather than furthered the goal of consistent law enforcement: it has failed to offer any principles to guide the police and the courts in their application of the new rule to nonroutine situations.

The standard announced in *Chimel* is not nearly as difficult to apply as the Court suggests. To the contrary, I continue to believe that *Chimel* provides a sound, workable rule for determining the constitutionality of a warrantless search incident to arrest. Under *Chimel,* searches incident to arrest may be conducted without a warrant only if limited to the person of the arrestee, or to the area within the arrestee's "immediate control." While it may be difficult in some cases to measure the exact scope of the arrestee's immediate control, relevant factors would surely include the relative number of police officers and arrestees, the manner of restraint placed on the arrestee, and the ability of the arrestee to gain access to a particular area or container. Certainly there will be some close cases, but when in doubt the police can always turn to the rationale underlying *Chimel*—the need to prevent the arrestee from reaching weapons or contraband—before exercising their judgment. A rule based on that rationale should provide more guidance than the rule announced by the Court today. Moreover, unlike the Court's rule, it would be faithful to the Fourth Amendment.

[The one paragraph concurring opinion of Justice Rehnquist, the one paragraph opinion concurring in the judgment by Justice Stevens, and the one paragraph dissent by Justice White (joined by Justice Marshall) are omitted.]

Note

The result in *Belton* is hardly shocking after *Robinson.* Both are "bright line" rule cases. In fact, the entire search incident to arrest doctrine assumes a necessity for a single rule by positing danger of physical harm and destruction of evidence in all arrest situations. Can you think of a more narrow statement of the basic search incident to arrest exception that would (1) protect police against dangers to their safety and against destruction of evidence that they have reasonable cause to believe is within the control or reach of an arrestee, (2) that would be understandable to the police, and (3) that would recognize that a person's body and intimate effects ought to receive some respect even though there may be probable cause to believe that a person has committed a crime?

United States v. Cotton, 751 F.2d 1146 (10th Cir.1985), expounds upon *Belton* and holds that "where an officer has made a lawful arrest of a suspect in an automobile, he may seize articles found within the interior of the automobile as part of a search incident to a lawful arrest, even where the arrestee is outside of the vehicle and handcuffed." What justifies this result?

Is the Court in *Belton* justified in establishing a bright line rule that the passenger compartment is always in the control area of the arrestee? Is that true as an empirical matter? Why not establish a bright line rule that the passenger compartment is *never* within the control area of the arrestee? For a criticism of the Court's bright-line adjudication in *Belton,* see Alschuler, Bright Line Fever and the Fourth Amendment, 45 U.Pitt.L.Rev. 227 (1981).

Despite the footnote in *Belton* limiting its application to automobiles, lower Courts have looked at *Belton* more expansively. For example, in United States v. Palumbo, 735 F.2d 1095 (8th Cir.1984), the court held that a search incident to arrest of a dresser drawer in a motel room was within the arrestee's control area, even though the defendant was handcuffed and surrounded by several officers. The court relied on *Belton* for the proposition that the arrest power rule "is not constrained because the arrestee is unlikely at the time of the arrest to actually reach into an area." Is this a fair reading of *Belton*? In United States v. Johnson, 846 F.2d 279 (5th Cir.1988), the court relied on *Belton* to hold that containers within the "grab" area could be immediately searched, even though the arrest did not occur in or near a car. The court reasoned as follows:

> Although the Court in *Chadwick* seemed to have drawn a distinction between searches of persons and searches of possessions in the arrestee's immediate control, the Court discarded that distinction in *Belton.* * * * We conclude that *Belton* eradicates any differences between searches of the person and searches within the arrestee's immediate control. Law enforcement officers may, pursuant to a valid arrest, search any container on the person or within his reach. Of course, the search must be contemporaneous with the arrest. Cf. *Chadwick.*

Judge Williams, concurring, went even further and stated that

> *Belton* constituted a virtual overruling of the rationale of *Chimel. Belton* overruled this rationale in spite of the fact that the opinion * * * stated its limitation upon *Chimel* solely in terms of the search of the passenger compart-

ment of an automobile * * *. The only limitation upon this conclusion was contained in a footnote * * *. I am now convinced that the Supreme Court * * * would push *Belton* beyond its facts and treat the *Chimel* rationale as no longer accurately reflecting the law.

Do you agree with Judge Williams' prediction? What could be the rationale, and corresponding limitation, of the search incident to arrest exception if *Chimel* is overruled?

18. The Problem of Pretext

Belton, Robinson, and the *Terry* doctrine give police officers the right to conduct certain searches on the basis of a stop or arrest for a minor offense, such as a traffic offense. Is it possible that these investigatory powers as to minor crimes can be used to search for evidence of a more serious crime for which probable cause or reasonable suspicion does not exist? Are you concerned with that possibility? One view is that a detention on a minor offense should not be used as a pretext to search for evidence of a greater offense. Another view is that if the officer has probable cause or reasonable suspicion to detain a person for a minor offense, and if the investigation does not proceed beyond the scope allowed for that offense, then the officer is complying with the objective reasonableness standards of the Fourth Amendment. Which view do you take?

In the en banc decision of United States v. Causey, 834 F.2d 1179 (1987) the Fifth Circuit reversed a panel opinion and adopted the objective reasonableness approach applied by the majority of federal courts. The facts are stated by the court as follows:

> An anonymous tipster identified appellant Causey as the robber of a Baton Rouge bank, but the city police believed that they lacked probable cause to arrest and interrogate him about that crime. Casting about for means to apprehend and question him, they discovered an outstanding warrant for Causey's arrest, issued some years earlier when he had failed to appear in court to answer a petty theft charge. After verifying the warrant's continued validity with the issuing judge, the city officers arrested Causey, gave him *Miranda* warnings, interrogated him about the bank robbery, and called in the FBI. Some time and several *Miranda* warnings later, Causey made a voluntary confession of robbing the bank.
>
> At a hearing on Causey's motion to suppress the confession, one of the city officers testified that their *only* reason for arresting Causey on the warrant was "to take him downtown and continue [the] investigation of the bank robbery . . . ."

The majority found that Causey's confession on the major offense was admissible, because his arrest on the minor offense was permissible. The court reasoned as follows:

> [T]he police who arrested Causey were empowered to do so by a valid warrant and * * * they took no action that they were not legally authorized to take. Nor is it suggested that anything improper occurs when police officers question a suspect who is under arrest for one crime about others of which he may be guilty or have knowledge. * * * [H]ad the arresting police done exactly the same things with Causey from start to finish as they did in fact, but had they in addition entertained a subjective intention at the time of his arrest to

question him about the lesser offense for which the arrest warrant issued as well as about the bank robbery, his confession to the robbery would have been properly admitted at his trial. But since one of the arresting officers testified that their *only* purpose in arresting Causey was to investigate the robbery, the panel declares that his confession is just as tainted as if it had been coerced by torture. For several reasons, we decline to countenance such a rule.

* * * [I]t is hard to see what police misconduct it is that is sought to be deterred by such a ruling: Is it acting to execute a valid warrant? to investigate a bank robbery by all means at hand not unlawful? or perhaps to question a suspect without coercion or force after giving proper *Miranda* warnings? In fact, the only conduct likely to be deterred by such a rule as that confected by the panel would be a prosecutor's act of leniency in omitting to prosecute the less serious offense on which the warrant had issued, a matter of small consequence to the police or prosecutor and of further *detriment* to the arrestee.

* * * To inject a new constitutional issue of subjective police intent into every case in which a suspect is arrested for one offense and later confesses to another (or others) seems to us unwarranted and to rest on no apparent constitutional basis or foundation.

Judge Rubin, who had written the original panel decision holding that the arrest was pretextual and thus illegal, dissented from the en banc decision:

In the kind of society in which we live, few persons have a life so blameless that some reason to arrest them cannot be found, whether it be for entering an intersection when the light is on caution, or for violating a zoning regulation, or for having an expired brake tag. The fourth amendment protection against arrests without probable cause is designed to protect citizens against being arrested for such a matter when there is no objective justification for the arrest save the police's desire to question the person in custody about a matter for which they lack the authority to make an arrest.

Untold thousands of Americans are subject to arrest for failing to pay parking tickets, failure to respond to summonses for traffic violations, and similar minor offenses. Even though the charges themselves and the warrants based on them are not stored or "warehoused" for a use other than to support an arrest for the offense charged, the result reached in the majority opinion makes the earlier charges readily available for later use. Police who desire to arrest an individual without probable cause may merely leaf through the files or turn to the computer to determine whether they can find some reasons to arrest a suspect for whose arrest they otherwise lack probable cause, just as the police did when they set out to find some pretext to arrest Causey. While I do not condone the possible law violations that led to the imposition of the earlier charges, I do not think such prior derelictions strip the alleged lawbreakers of fourth amendment protection if they should later be suspected of other offenses.

* * *

Current technology has made it possible for every police system in the nation to record in a computer the name of every traffic offender and every other person wanted for any offense, however trivial, and for a national system to collate all of these records. The majority opinion permits any police officer who suspects anyone of any crime to turn to the computer, determine whether the suspect is listed as subject to an outstanding charge of running a red light or some other misdemeanor, obtain a warrant if none has previously been issued, and arrest the suspect without probable cause to detain him for the offense being investigated, then interrogate him at the jail.

To uphold the Constitution is not "to punish the public for naughty intent on the part of the police," as the majority chooses to characterize it. The public is not punished but served when the constitutional rights of the nation's citizens are safeguarded. When other branches of the government fail in their duty, it is our responsibility in the cases that come before us to call the foul. The police conduct in arresting Causey was just such a foul, and I condemn it not because it was motivated by naughty intent but because it violated the fourth amendment.

For cases similar to *Causey,* see United States v. Cummins, 920 F.2d 498 (8th Cir.1990) (officer trailed a suspect for a mile until he committed a traffic infraction; search of the car pursuant to that offense uncovered drugs and guns: "Officer Bernal had a legitimate reason—the traffic violation—for stopping the green Volkswagen and that is the end of our inquiry."); United States v. Kordosky, 878 F.2d 991 (7th Cir.1989) (officer who suspected defendant of drug activity, and who trailed defendant for a month and then arrested him on an outstanding traffic ticket, conducted a legal search of the passenger compartment; drugs found in the search were admissible because the officer had probable cause to arrest for the traffic violation).

A contrary view is expressed by the Eleventh Circuit in United States v. Miller, 821 F.2d 546 (11th Cir.1987). There, a state trooper suspected that a driver on I–95 in Florida was a drug courier, but he did not have reasonable suspicion to stop him for that offense. (Miller was suspected because he drove below the speed limit, he was driving a car with out-of-state plates, and he did not turn his head to look at the trooper when the trooper shined his headlights at Miller's car. The trooper found this conduct to be "overly cautious"). The trooper stopped Miller when Miller drove with his wheels across the lane marker for six seconds; this was a violation of Florida traffic laws. In the course of the stop, the officer discovered narcotics. The court of appeals held that the narcotics had to be excluded as the product of a pretextual stop. The court stated that "the proper inquiry is whether a reasonable officer *would* have made the seizure in the absence of illegitimate motivation." It reasoned that a reasonable officer would not have stopped Miller for going over the lane marker for six seconds, absent motivation to search for drugs.

Does Fourth Amendment protection depend on the subjective judgment of police officers? Assume that in *Miller,* the officer had, objectively, reasonable suspicion to stop Miller for the narcotics offense, but subjectively, he thought he didn't and was using the traffic offense as an excuse. Would the court in *Miller* have suppressed the evidence? If not, does *Miller* make sense?

Presuming that there is sufficient proof to arrest or stop an individual for a minor offense, and that the officer has certain legitimate investigatory powers pursuant to that offense, has a citizen been prejudiced if the officer's subjective motivation is to search for evidence of a major offense? Isn't the real complaint not one of pretext, but that the Supreme Court has allowed extensive investigatory powers to be exercised as to minor offenses? So long as *Robinson, Belton* and *Terry* remain the law, why should the courts accept a complaint that a stop or arrest, legal on its face, must be invalidated as pretextual?

19. *Plain View Seizures*

The concept of plain view underlies much of the law and practice under the *Terry* doctrine and search incident to arrest, and it applies as well during searches conducted pursuant to a warrant or another exception to the warrant requirement. For example, the officers in *Robinson* and *Belton* seized narcotics in plain view during the course of a search incident to arrest; the officers in *Long* seized weapons in Long's car during the course of a search for self-protection under *Terry;* and an officer searching pursuant to a warrant can seize contraband which comes into view during the lawful course of that search. In Coolidge v. New Hampshire, 403 U.S. 443 (1971) Justice Stewart's plurality opinion stated that if officers have a right to be in a particular place and come upon evidence that they have probable cause to believe is subject to seizure, they may seize it. In the following case, the Court explains the plain view doctrine in detail, and revisits some of the problems of applying that doctrine which divided the Court in *Coolidge.*

HORTON v. CALIFORNIA

Supreme Court of the United States, 1990.
496 U.S. 128.

JUSTICE STEVENS delivered the opinion of the Court.

In this case we revisit an issue that was considered, but not conclusively resolved, in Coolidge v. New Hampshire: Whether the warrantless seizure of evidence of crime in plain view is prohibited by the Fourth Amendment if the discovery of the evidence was not inadvertent. We conclude that even though inadvertence is a characteristic of most legitimate "plain view" seizures, it is not a necessary condition.

I

Petitioner was convicted of the armed robbery of Erwin Wallaker, the treasurer of the San Jose Coin Club. * * *

Sergeant LaRault, an experienced police officer, investigated the crime and determined that there was probable cause to search petitioner's home for the proceeds of the robbery and for the weapons used by the robbers. His affidavit for a search warrant referred to police reports that described the weapons as well as the proceeds, but the warrant issued by the Magistrate only authorized a search for the proceeds, including three specifically described rings.

Pursuant to the warrant, LaRault searched petitioner's residence, but he did not find the stolen property. During the course of the search, however, he discovered the weapons in plain view and seized them. * * * LaRault testified that while he was searching for the rings, he also was interested in finding other evidence connecting petitioner to the robbery. Thus, the seized evidence was not discovered "inadvertently."

* * *

II

* * *

The right to security in person and property protected by the Fourth Amendment may be invaded in quite different ways by searches and seizures. A search compromises the individual interest in privacy; a seizure deprives the individual of dominion over his or her person or property. The "plain view" doctrine is often considered an exception to the general rule that warrantless searches are presumptively unreasonable, but this characterization overlooks the important difference between searches and seizures. If an article is already in plain view, neither its observation nor its seizure would involve any invasion of privacy. A seizure of the article, however, would obviously invade the owner's possessory interest. If "plain view" justifies an exception from an otherwise applicable warrant requirement, therefore, it must be an exception that is addressed to the concerns that are implicated by seizures rather than by searches.

The criteria that generally guide "plain view" seizures were set forth in Coolidge v. New Hampshire. The Court held that the seizure of two automobiles parked in plain view on the defendant's driveway in the course of arresting the defendant violated the Fourth Amendment. Accordingly, particles of gun powder that had been subsequently found in vacuum sweepings from one of the cars could not be introduced in evidence against the defendant. The State endeavored to justify the seizure of the automobiles, and their subsequent search at the police station, on four different grounds, including the "plain view" doctrine. The scope of that doctrine as it had developed in earlier cases was fairly summarized in * * * Justice Stewart's opinion:

> "It is well established that under certain circumstances the police may seize evidence in plain view without a warrant. But it is important to keep in mind that, in the vast majority of cases, *any* evidence seized by the police will be in plain view, at least at the moment of seizure. The problem with the 'plain view' doctrine has been to identify the circumstances in which plain view has legal significance rather than being simply the normal concomitant of any search, legal or illegal.

> "An example of the applicability of the 'plain view' doctrine is the situation in which the police have a warrant to search a given area for specified objects, and in the course of the search come across some other article of incriminating character. Where the initial intrusion that brings the police within plain view of such an article is supported, not by a warrant, but by one of the recognized exceptions to the warrant requirement, the seizure is also legitimate. Thus * * * an object that comes into view during a search incident to arrest that is appropriately limited in scope under existing law may be seized without a warrant. Chimel v. California. * * *
>
> "What the 'plain view' cases have in common is that the police officer in each of them had a prior justification for an intrusion in the course of which he came inadvertently across a piece of evidence incriminating the accused. The doctrine serves to supplement the prior justification—whether it be a warrant for another object, hot pursuit, search incident to lawful arrest, or some other legitimate reason for being present unconnected with a search directed against the accused—and permits the warrantless seizure. Of course, the extension of the original justification is legitimate only where it is immediately apparent to the police that they have evidence before them; the 'plain view' doctrine may not be used to extend a general exploratory search from one object to another until something incriminating at last emerges."

Justice Stewart then described the two limitations on the doctrine that he found implicit in its rationale: First, "that plain view *alone* is never enough to justify the warrantless seizure of evidence; and second, "that the discovery of evidence in plain view must be inadvertent."

Justice Stewart's analysis of the "plain view" doctrine did not command a majority and a plurality of the Court has since made clear that the discussion is "not a binding precedent." Texas v. Brown, 460 U.S., at 737 (opinion of REHNQUIST, J.). Justice Harlan, who concurred in the Court's judgment and in its response to the dissenting opinions, did not join the plurality's discussion of the "plain view" doctrine. The decision nonetheless is a binding precedent. Before discussing the second limitation, which is implicated in this case, it is therefore necessary to explain why the first adequately supports the Court's judgment.

It is, of course, an essential predicate to any valid warrantless seizure of incriminating evidence that the officer did not violate the Fourth Amendment in arriving at the place from which the evidence could be plainly viewed. There are, moreover, two additional conditions that must be satisfied to justify the warrantless seizure. First, not only must the item be in plain view, its incriminating character must also be "immediately apparent." Thus, in *Coolidge,* the cars were obviously in plain view, but their probative value remained uncertain until after the interiors were swept and examined microscopically. Second, not only must the officer be lawfully located in a place from which the object can be plainly seen, but he or she must also have a lawful right of access to the object itself. * * * Justice Harlan's vote in *Coolidge* may have rested on the fact that the seizure of the cars was accomplished by means of a warrantless trespass on the defendant's property. In all events, we are satisfied that the absence of inadvertence was not essential to the Court's rejection of the State's "plain view" argument in *Coolidge.*

III

Justice Stewart concluded that the inadvertence requirement was necessary to avoid a violation of the express constitutional requirement that a valid warrant must particularly describe the things to be seized. He explained:

> "The rationale of the exception to the warrant requirement, as just stated, is that a plain-view seizure will not turn an initially valid (and therefore limited) search into a 'general' one, while the inconvenience of procuring a warrant to cover an inadvertent discovery is great. But where the discovery is anticipated, where the police know in advance the location of the evidence and intend to seize it, the situation is altogether different. The requirement of a warrant to seize imposes no inconvenience whatever, or at least none which is constitutionally cognizable in a legal system that regards warrantless searches as '*per se* unreasonable' in the absence of 'exigent circumstances.' "

* * *

We find two flaws in this reasoning. First, evenhanded law enforcement is best achieved by the application of objective standards of conduct, rather than standards that depend upon the subjective state of mind of the officer. The fact that an officer is interested in an item of evidence and fully expects to find it in the course of a search should not invalidate its seizure if the search is confined in area and duration by the terms of a warrant or a valid exception to the warrant requirement. If the officer has knowledge approaching certainty that the item will be found, we see no reason why he or she would deliberately omit a particular description of the item to be seized from the application for a search warrant. Specification of the additional item could only permit the officer to expand the scope of the search. On the other hand, if he or she has a valid warrant to search for one item and merely a suspicion concerning the second, whether or not it amounts to probable cause, we fail to see why that suspicion should immunize the second item from seizure if it is found during a lawful search for the first.

* * *

Second, the suggestion that the inadvertence requirement is necessary to prevent the police from conducting general searches, or from converting specific warrants into general warrants, is not persuasive because that interest is already served by the requirements that no warrant issue unless it "particularly describ[es] the place to be searched and the persons or things to be seized," and that a warrantless search be circumscribed by the exigencies which justify its initiation. Scrupulous adherence to these requirements serves the interests in limiting the area and duration of the search that the inadvertence requirement inadequately protects. Once those commands have been satisfied and the officer has a lawful right of access, however, no additional Fourth Amendment interest is furthered by requiring that the discovery of evidence be inadvertent. If the scope of the search exceeds that permitted by the terms of a validly issued warrant or the character of the relevant exception from the warrant requirement, the subsequent seizure is unconstitutional without more.

* * *

In this case, the scope of the search was not enlarged in the slightest by the omission of any reference to the weapons in the warrant. Indeed, if the three rings and other items named in the warrant had been found at the outset—or if petitioner had them in his possession and had responded to the warrant by producing them immediately—no search for weapons could have taken place. * * * JUSTICE WHITE's dissenting opinion in *Coolidge* is instructive:

"Police with a warrant for a rifle may search only places where rifles might be and must terminate the search once the rifle is found; the inadvertence rule will in no way reduce the number of places into which they may lawfully look."

* * * The prohibition against general searches and general warrants serves primarily as a protection against unjustified intrusions on privacy. But reliance on privacy concerns that support that prohibition is misplaced when the inquiry concerns the scope of an exception that merely authorizes an officer with a lawful right of access to an item to seize it without a warrant.

* * *

JUSTICE BRENNAN, with whom JUSTICE MARSHALL joins, dissenting.

* * * In eschewing the inadvertent discovery requirement, the majority ignores the Fourth Amendment's express command that warrants particularly describe not only the *places* to be searched, but also the *things* to be seized. I respectfully dissent from this rewriting of the Fourth Amendment.

I

The Fourth Amendment * * * protects two distinct interests. The prohibition against unreasonable searches and the requirement that a warrant "particularly describ[e] the place to be searched" protect an interest in privacy. The prohibition against unreasonable seizures and the requirement that a warrant "particularly describ[e] . . . the . . . things to be seized" protect a possessory interest in property. * * *

The Amendment protects these equally important interests in precisely the same manner: by requiring a neutral and detached magistrate to evaluate, before the search or seizure, the government's showing of probable cause and its particular description of the place to be searched and the items to be seized. * * * A decision to invade a possessory interest in property is too important to be left to the discretion of zealous officers "engaged in the often competitive enterprise of ferreting out crime." Johnson v. United States.

* * * The rationale behind the inadvertent discovery requirement is simply that we will not excuse officers from the general requirement of a warrant to seize if the officers know the location of evidence, have probable cause to seize it, intend to seize it, and yet do not bother to obtain a warrant particularly describing that evidence. * * *

[T]here are a number of instances in which a law enforcement officer might deliberately choose to omit certain items from a warrant application even though he has probable cause to seize them, knows they are on the premises, and intends to seize them when they are discovered in plain view. For example, the warrant application process can often be time-consuming, especially when the police attempt to seize a large number of items. An officer interested in conducting a search as soon as possible might decide to save time by listing only one or two hard-to-find items, such as the stolen rings in this case, confident that he will find in plain view all of the other evidence he is looking for before he discovers the listed items. Because rings could be located almost anywhere inside or outside a house, it is unlikely that a warrant to search for and seize the rings would restrict the scope of the search. An officer might rationally find the risk of immediately discovering the items listed in the warrant—thereby forcing him to conclude the search immediately—outweighed by the time saved in the application process.

The majority also contends that, once an officer is lawfully in a house and the scope of his search is adequately circumscribed by a warrant, * * * " 'the inadvertence rule will in no way reduce the number of places into which [law enforcement officers] may lawfully look.' " The majority is correct, but it has asked the wrong question. It is true that the inadvertent discovery requirement furthers no privacy interests. * * * But it does protect possessory interests. The inadvertent discovery requirement is essential if we are to take seriously the Fourth Amendment's protection of possessory interests as well as privacy interests. The Court today eliminates a rule designed to further possessory interests on the ground that it fails to further privacy interests. I cannot countenance such constitutional legerdemain.

II

Fortunately, this decision should have only a limited impact, for the Court is not confronted today with what lower courts have described as a "pretextual" search. For example, if an officer enters a house pursuant to a warrant to search for evidence of one crime when he is really interested only in seizing evidence relating to another crime, for which he does not have a warrant, his search is "pretextual" and the fruits of that search should be suppressed. See, e.g., State v. Kelsey, 592 S.W.2d 509 (Mo.App.1979) (evidence suppressed because officers, who had ample opportunity to obtain warrant relating to murder investigation, entered the premises instead pursuant to a warrant relating to a drug investigation, and searched only the hiding place of the murder weapon, rather than conducting a "top to bottom" search for drugs).

* * * The Court's opinion today does not address pretextual searches, but I have no doubt that such searches violate the Fourth Amendment.

III

* * * The Court today ignores the explicit language of the Fourth Amend-

ment, which protects possessory interests in the same manner as it protects privacy interests, in order to eliminate a generally accepted element of the plain view doctrine that has caused no apparent difficulties for law enforcement officers. I am confident, however, that when confronted with more egregious police conduct than that found in this case, such as pretextual searches, the Court's interpretation of the Constitution will be less parsimonious than it is today. I respectfully dissent.

Note

What dangers, if any, exist when an officer omits items from a warrant request? Does omission impair the magistrate's ability to make the probable cause determination before a search is conducted? Does omission threaten the viability of the magistrate's role in determining the reasonableness of what may be seized?

Recall the previous discussion of pretext stops and arrests, and the Court's statement in *Horton* that "evenhanded law enforcement is best achieved by the application of objective standards of conduct." Are you as confident as Justice Brennan that the Court will invalidate a pretextual search for a serious offense, where the officer could lawfully do the same search for a lesser offense?

One of the difficult plain view issues is how closely the police may examine an object to decide whether it is subject to seizure. As one court wrote, the "core issue" in plain view determinations is "how much movement, probing or testing of an apparently innocuous object, aimed at uncovering an incriminating characteristic is permitted." Anderson v. State, 555 P.2d 251, 256–57 (Alaska, 1976).

In the 6–3 decision in Arizona v. Hicks, 480 U.S. 321 (1987), Justice Scalia wrote for the Court as it squarely held for the first time that probable cause is necessary to justify a search that precedes a plain view seizure. Arizona police entered Hicks' apartment after a bullet was fired through its floor into the apartment below, injuring a man. The officers looked for the shooter, other victims and weapons. One officer noticed two sets of expensive stereo components that seemed out of place in an "ill-appointed four-room apartment." The officer moved some of the components in order to find serial numbers, telephoned in the numbers, and learned that one turntable he had moved was stolen. He seized the turntable immediately. Later it was learned that other equipment was stolen, and a warrant was obtained for it.

Justice Scalia rejected the state's argument that the officer's actions did not amount to a search: "A search is a search, even if it happens to disclose nothing but the bottom of a turntable." He also rejected the argument that the officer had sufficient cause to justify his actions. The state conceded that the officer lacked probable cause for a search, but sought to justify his actions on the basis of reasonable suspicion. Justice Scalia described the plain view doctrine as resting on the "desirability of sparing police, whose viewing of the object in the course of a lawful search is as legitimate as it would have been in a public place, the inconvenience and the risk—to themselves or to preservation of the evidence—of going to get a warrant." He further observed that "[n]o reason is apparent why an object should routinely be seizable on lesser grounds, during an unrelated search and seizure, than would have been needed to obtain a warrant for that same object if it had been known to be on the premises," but he also noted that exigent circumstances may justify a seizure on less than probable cause. Justice O'Connor, joined by Chief Justice Rehnquist and Justice Powell, dissented.

B. AUTOMOBILES AND OTHER MOVABLE OBJECTS

One of the well-recognized exceptions to the warrant requirement is that which is commonly referred to as the "automobile exception." Broadly stated, the doctrine holds that the police may search an automobile without a warrant if they have probable cause to believe it contains evidence of criminal activity. The circumstances which justify such a warrantless intrusion have been repeatedly delineated by the Supreme Court since it first created the exception in Carroll v. United States, 267 U.S. 132 (1925). As you study the following material, consider three questions: whether the rationale for the exception can withstand analysis, how consistently the Court has applied the articulated rationale to new sets of facts, and whether acceptance of the rationale might logically require its extension to objects other than cars.

1. *The Carroll Doctrine*

Carroll v. United States involved a violation of the National Prohibition Act, as did many early search and seizure cases. In December 1921, the two defendants were driving westward on a highway between Detroit and Grand Rapids when they were stopped by federal prohibition agents who were patrolling the road. Bootlegging traffic was known to be heavy in the area, due to its proximity to Ontario, which apparently had not seen the same virtues in abstinence as did her neighbor to the south. The defendant's car was searched without a warrant, and 68 quarts of whiskey and gin were found behind the upholstering of the seats. The officers had not anticipated that the defendants would be traveling the highway at that particular time, but their past experiences with these men led them to believe that the defendants were presently engaged in transporting liquor. Three months earlier, two of the agents had met the defendants in an apartment in Grand Rapids to arrange for delivery of three cases of bootleg whiskey. That deal never came off, possibly because the defendants' suspicions had been aroused, but the agents were able to note the make and license number of the defendants' car. A few weeks later, the officers spotted the car traveling eastward from Grand Rapids to Detroit, but an attempt to follow it was unsuccessful. When they again sighted the car some two months later coming from Detroit, they stopped it and made the warrantless search which was at issue in the case. The defendants were convicted of illegal transportation of intoxicating liquor, a misdemeanor.

The Court, in a 7–2 decision written by Chief Justice Taft, found the search to be reasonable because the agents had probable cause to search but had no time in which to obtain a warrant. Probable cause was found in the fact that known bootleggers were traveling on a road, which was judicially noticed as an important route for transporting liquor into the country, in a direction away from the source of that liquor—i.e., Detroit.

Taft began his analysis by considering revenue statutes passed by the earliest Congresses, in addition to the legislative history of the National Prohibition Act. He concluded that:

> [T]he guaranty of freedom from unreasonable searches and seizures by the Fourth Amendment has been construed, practically since the beginning of the Government, as recognizing a necessary difference between a search of a store,

dwelling house or other structure in respect of which a proper official warrant readily may be obtained, and a search of a ship, motor boat, wagon or automobile, for contraband goods, where it is not practicable to secure a warrant because the vehicle can be quickly moved out of the locality or jurisdiction in which the warrant must be sought.

Taft further noted that the right to search and the validity of the seizure were not dependent on the right to arrest, thus clearly distinguishing this search from that of an automobile incident to the arrest of the driver.

It is not apparent from the opinion why it was necessary for the Court to create an automobile exception in order to uphold the search in *Carroll*. If one accepts the majority's view that probable cause existed to believe that liquor was in the car, then one must also conclude that the officers had probable cause to believe that a misdemeanor was being committed before their eyes. If so, they could have arrested and the search could have been upheld as incident to arrest. But recall the history of the search incident doctrine set forth in Justice Stewart's *Chimel* opinion; the first case in which the Court developed the doctrine was *Marron*, decided two years after *Carroll*. Considering the 40 years of circuitous decisions which predated *Chimel*, it is conceivable that the Court was merely avoiding the necessity of deciding whether a search of the upholstery of a car was within the scope of a legal search incident to arrest.

2. *Distinguishing Carroll From Search Incident to Arrest*

Judge Moylan decries the tendency of judges and lawyers to confuse search incident to an arrest in an automobile with the automobile exception. The Automobile Exception: What It Is and What It Is Not—A Rationale in Search of a Clearer Label, 27 Mercer L.Rev. 987 (1976). Although both may apply in a given situation, he emphasizes that the analysis must be kept distinct.

No matter how tangled a set of facts, when we analyze those facts under the *Carroll* Doctrine we are interested in but two things: (1) Was there probable cause to believe that the automobile contained evidence? and (2) Was there an exigency requiring an immediate warrantless search? * * * We do not care one whit whether the driver or any of his passengers were arrested at all, let alone whether they were arrested lawfully. We do not care where the driver or passengers are located at the time of the search. They may still be in the car; they may be shackled in a police car a hundred yards away; they may be shot dead in the middle of the street; they may be in jail. Such questions are irrelevant under the *Carroll* Doctrine.

When we have finished that analysis and move on to a distinct analysis under the "search incident" exception, however, such questions suddenly become important. We are looking to the legality of an underlying arrest. * * * [T]he question of exigency loses all relevance. It is not a necessary condition to a warrantless arrest or to its attendant search incident. All the opportunity in the world to obtain a warrant will not defeat a warrantless arrest or a warrantless search incident to that arrest. We are concerned only with the status, as a lawful arrestee, of the person searched and with the restricted compass of the search incident—the two things which suddenly take on a significance under "search incident" law which they lacked under *Carroll* Doctrine analysis.

Judge Moylan accurately describes what the Court did in *Carroll.* But is it sensible to create an automobile exception that disregards the likely mobility of the car under a given set of facts? This is the basic problem of *Carroll.*

On the other hand, at least it can be said for the automobile exception that the officer must still have probable cause to search. As Judge Moylan points out, all that is needed for a search incident to arrest is probable cause to arrest—and as shown in *Belton,* that probable cause could be for a minor crime such as a traffic offense. Recall the discussion on pretextual stops and arrests. Which exception will more likely be invoked to justify a pretextual search? Justice Stevens concurred in the judgment in *Belton* on the ground that it could and should have been decided under the automobile exception. He argued that under the majority opinion in *Belton,* the officer may find reason to make a custodial arrest on a minor offense "whenever he sees an interesting looking briefcase or package in a vehicle that has been stopped for a traffic violation." He contended that by taking "the giant step of permitting searches in the absence of probable cause, the Court misses the shorter step of relying on the automobile exception." Is the automobile exception a shorter step than the search incident to arrest exception? When would the government seek to justify a search under one exception but not the other?

3. *The Progeny of Carroll*

Most cases decided under *Carroll* were concerned with the existence of probable cause rather than exigencies of any sort, and later decisions did little to expand or restrict the exception: United States v. Lee, 274 U.S. 559 (1927) (search of motorboat upheld); Scher v. United States, 305 U.S. 251 (1938) (search of car after it had pulled into a garage upheld).

In 1970, in Chambers v. Maroney, the issue of exigency came to the fore, when the Court considered the question whether a warrantless automobile search conducted after the car had been removed to the police station could be valid under *Carroll.*

CHAMBERS v. MARONEY

Supreme Court of the United States, 1970.
399 U.S. 42.

MR. JUSTICE WHITE delivered the opinion of the Court.

The principal question in this case concerns the admissibility of evidence seized from an automobile, in which petitioner was riding at the time of his arrest, after the automobile was taken to a police station and was there thoroughly searched without a warrant. The Court of Appeals for the Third Circuit found no violation of petitioner's Fourth Amendment rights. We affirm.

I

During the night of May 20, 1963, a Gulf service station in North Braddock, Pennsylvania, was robbed by two men, each of whom carried and displayed a gun. The robbers took the currency from the cash register; the service station attendant, one Stephen Kovacich, was directed to place the coins in his right-hand glove, which was then taken by the robbers. Two teen-agers, who had earlier noticed a blue compact station wagon circling the block in the vicinity of the Gulf station, then saw the station wagon speed away from a parking lot close to the Gulf station. About the same time, they learned that the Gulf station had been robbed. They reported to police, who arrived immediately, that four men were in the station wagon and one was wearing a green sweater. Kovacich told the police that one of the men who robbed him was wearing a green sweater and the other was wearing a trench coat. A description of the car and the two robbers was broadcast over the police radio. Within an hour, a light blue compact station wagon answering the description and carrying four men was stopped by the police about two miles from the Gulf station. Petitioner was one of the men in the station wagon. He was wearing a green sweater and there was a trench coat in the car. The occupants were arrested and the car was driven to the police station. In the course of a thorough search of the car at the station, the police found concealed in a compartment under the dashboard two .38-caliber revolvers (one loaded with dumdum bullets), a right-hand glove containing small change, and certain cards bearing the name of Raymond Havicon, the attendant at a Boron service station in McKeesport, Pennsylvania, who had been robbed at gunpoint on May 13, 1963. * * *

Petitioner was indicted for both robberies. His first trial ended in a mistrial but he was convicted of both robberies at the second trial. Both Kovacich and Havicon identified petitioner as one of the robbers. The materials taken from the station wagon were introduced into evidence, Kovacich identifying his glove and Havicon the cards taken in the May 13 robbery. * * *

II

We pass quickly the claim that the search of the automobile was the fruit of an unlawful arrest. Both the courts below thought the arresting officers had probable cause to make the arrest. We agree. Having talked to the teen-age observers and to the victim Kovacich, the police had ample cause to stop a light blue compact station wagon carrying four men and to arrest the occupants, one of whom was wearing a green sweater and one of whom had a trench coat with him in the car.[a]

[The Court holds that the search of the car at the police station could not be justified as a search incident to arrest.]

In terms of the circumstances justifying a warrantless search, the Court has long distinguished between an automobile and a home or office. * * * [The Court quotes from *Carroll* and cites its other early cases.]

* * *

Neither *Carroll,* supra, nor other cases in this Court require or suggest that in every conceivable circumstance the search of an auto even with probable cause may be made without the extra protection for privacy that a warrant affords. But the circumstances that furnish probable cause to search a particular auto for particular articles are most often unforeseeable; moreover, the opportunity to search is fleeting since a car is readily movable. Where this is true, as in *Carroll* and the case before us now, if an effective search is to be made at any time, either the search must be made immediately without a warrant or the car itself must be seized and held without a warrant for whatever period is necessary to obtain a

a. In any event, as we point out below, the validity of an arrest is not necessarily determinative of the right to search a car if there is probable cause to make the search. Here, as will be true in many cases, the circumstances justifying the arrest are also those furnishing probable cause for the search.

warrant for the search.[b]

* * * Only in exigent circumstances will the judgment of the police as to probable cause serve as a sufficient authorization for a search. *Carroll,* supra, holds a search warrant unnecessary where there is probable cause to search an automobile stopped on the highway; the car is movable, the occupants are alerted, and the car's contents may never be found again if a warrant must be obtained. Hence an immediate search is constitutionally permissible.

Arguably, because of the preference for a magistrate's judgment only the immobilization of the car should be permitted until a search warrant is obtained; arguably, only the "lesser" intrusion is permissible until the magistrate authorizes the "greater." But which is the "greater" and which the "lesser" intrusion is itself a debatable question and the answer may depend on a variety of circumstances. For constitutional purposes, we see no difference between on the one hand seizing and holding a car before presenting the probable cause issue to a magistrate and on the other hand carrying out an immediate search without a warrant. Given probable cause to search, either course is reasonable under the Fourth Amendment.

On the facts before us, the blue station wagon could have been searched on the spot when it was stopped since there was probable cause to search and it was a fleeting target for a search. The probable-cause factor still obtained at the station house and so did the mobility of the car unless the Fourth Amendment permits a warrantless seizure of the car and the denial of its use to anyone until a warrant is secured. In that event there is little to choose in terms of practical consequences between an immediate search without a warrant and the car's immobilization until a warrant is obtained.[c] The same consequences may not follow where there is unforeseeable cause to search a house. Compare Vale v. Louisiana. But as *Carroll,* supra, held, for the purposes of the Fourth Amendment there is a constitutional difference between houses and cars.

* * *

MR. JUSTICE BLACKMUN took no part in the consideration or decision of this case.

MR. JUSTICE HARLAN, concurring in part and dissenting in part.

* * *

II

* * *

Where officers have probable cause to search a vehicle on a public way, a * * * limited exception to the warrant requirement is reasonable because "the vehicle can be quickly moved out of the locality or jurisdiction in which the warrant must be sought." Carroll v. United States. Because the officers might be deprived of valuable evidence if required to obtain a warrant before effecting any search or seizure, I agree with the Court that they should be permitted to take the steps necessary to preserve evidence and to make a search possible. The Court holds that those steps include making a warrantless search of the en-

b. Following the car until a warrant can be obtained seems an impractical alternative since, among other things, the car may be taken out of the jurisdiction. Tracing the car and searching it hours or days later would of course permit instruments or fruits of crime to be removed from the car before the search.

c. It was not unreasonable in this case to take the car to the station house. All occupants in the car were arrested in a dark parking lot in the middle of the night. A careful search at that point was impractical and perhaps not safe for the officers, and it would serve the owner's convenience and the safety of his car to have the vehicle and the keys together at the station house.

tire vehicle on the highway—a conclusion reached by the Court in *Carroll* without discussion—and indeed appears to go further and to condone the removal of the car to the police station for a warrantless search there at the convenience of the police. I cannot agree that this result is consistent with our insistence in other areas that departures from the warrant requirement strictly conform to the exigency presented.

The Court concedes that the police could prevent removal of the evidence by temporarily seizing the car for the time necessary to obtain a warrant. It does not dispute that such a course would fully protect the interests of effective law enforcement; rather it states that whether temporary seizure is a "lesser" intrusion than warrantless search "is itself a debatable question and the answer may depend on a variety of circumstances." [d] I believe it clear that a warrantless search involves the greater sacrifice of Fourth Amendment values.

* * * [I]n the circumstances in which this problem is likely to occur, the lesser intrusion will almost always be the simple seizure of the car for the period—perhaps a day—necessary to enable the officers to obtain a search warrant. In the first place, as this case shows, the very facts establishing probable cause to search will often also justify arrest of the occupants of the vehicle. Since the occupants themselves are to be taken into custody, they will suffer minimal further inconvenience from the temporary immobilization of their vehicle. Even where no arrests are made, persons who wish to avoid a search—either to protect their privacy or to conceal incriminating evidence—will almost certainly prefer a brief loss of the use of the vehicle in exchange for the opportunity to have a magistrate pass upon the justification for the search. To be sure, one can conceive of instances in which the occupant, having nothing to hide and lacking concern for the privacy of the automobile, would be more deeply offended by a temporary immobilization of his vehicle than by a prompt search of it. However, such a person always remains free to consent to an immediate search, thus avoiding any delay. Where consent is not forthcoming, the occupants of the car have an interest in privacy that is protected by the Fourth Amendment even where the circumstances justify a temporary seizure. The Court's endorsement of a warrantless invasion of that privacy where another course would suffice is simply inconsistent with our repeated stress on the Fourth Amendment's mandate of " 'adherence to judicial processes.' " [e]

* * *

d. The Court, unable to decide whether search or temporary seizure is the "lesser" intrusion, in this case authorizes both. The Court concludes that it was reasonable for the police to take the car to the station, where they searched it once to no avail. The searching officers then entered the station, interrogated petitioner and the car's owner, and returned later for another search of the car—this one successful. At all times the car and its contents were secure against removal or destruction. Nevertheless, the Court approves the searches without even an inquiry into the officers' ability promptly to take their case before a magistrate.

e. Circumstances might arise in which it would be impracticable to immobilize the car for the time required to obtain a warrant—for example, where a single police officer must take arrested suspects to the station, and has no way of protecting the suspects' car during his absence. In such situations it might be wholly reasonable to perform an on-the-spot search based on probable cause. However, where nothing in the situation makes impracticable the obtaining of a warrant, I cannot join the Court in shunting aside that vital Fourth Amendment safeguard.

Note

Do you agree with Justice White's major premise, i.e., that there is no constitutional difference between an immediate warrantless search and the seizure of a car until a warrant can be obtained? If that premise is valid, then the legality of a search under the *Carroll* doctrine should be determined by the existence of probable cause and exigency at the time of the initial stop, not at the time the search is actually conducted. If it is not valid—if, as the dissent suggests, there is a significant difference in the intrusiveness of a search as opposed to a seizure—then should the police be required to choose the least intrusive alternative? Is that proposition consistent with *Carroll?*

What implications does the majority holding have for searches of parked cars, where the police do not make an initial stop? Does it matter where the car is parked, or whether the initial police-vehicle encounter is deliberate or by chance? Not surprisingly, a discussion of these issues had to arise. It did in Coolidge v. New Hampshire, 403 U.S. 443 (1971). In *Coolidge,* the police obtained warrants to arrest the defendant and to search his car. The automobile was seized from his driveway shortly after the defendant's arrest, and was searched two days later at the police station, and twice more in the following months. The warrants were held to be defective, because they had not been issued by a neutral magistrate. Thus, the Court considered whether the search could be justified under any other theories, including the *Carroll* doctrine. A plurality held *Carroll* to be inapplicable here, because of the absence of exigency. This is the first and last Supreme Court case where a warrantless automobile search was held to be unconstitutional for that reason. Obviously, it could not be seriously argued that it was impracticable to obtain a warrant when a warrant had in fact been obtained, albeit a defective one. The Court nevertheless considered whether an exigency existed justifying the warrantless seizure of the car because of its potential mobility.

Justice Stewart wrote for the plurality as follows:

> Coolidge was arrested inside the house, without resistance of any kind on his part, after he had voluntarily admitted the officers at both front and back doors. There was no way in which he could conceivably have gained access to the automobile after the police arrived on his property. When Coolidge had been taken away, the police informed Mrs. Coolidge, the only other adult occupant of the house, that she and her baby had to spend the night elsewhere and that she could not use either of the Coolidge cars. Two police officers then drove her in a police car to the house of a relative in another town, and they stayed with her there until around midnight, long after the police had had the Pontiac towed to the station house. The Coolidge premises were guarded throughout the night by two policemen.
>
> The word "automobile" is not a talisman in whose presence the Fourth Amendment fades away and disappears. And surely there is nothing in this case to invoke the meaning and purpose of the rule of Carroll v. United States—no alerted criminal bent on flight, no fleeting opportunity on an open highway after a hazardous chase, no contraband or stolen goods or weapons, no confederates waiting to move the evidence, not even the inconvenience of a special police detail to guard the immobilized automobile. In short, by no possible stretch of the legal imagination can this be made into a case where "it is not practicable to secure a warrant," *Carroll,* supra, at 153, and the "automobile exception," despite its label, is simply irrelevant.

Justice Stewart distinguished *Chambers* on the ground that, in the present case, the initial intrusion by the police was unjustified. Was it unjustified because there was no urgency, or because the police entered "private property to seize and search an unoccupied, parked vehicle not then being used for any illegal purpose"? Or does this combination of facts add up to "no exigency"? Is it possible to isolate the factors that were most important? Was it the fact that the police-vehicle encounter was planned rather than spontaneous? Was it that the car was parked rather than moving? Would such a distinction make sense? Once the driver and passenger in the *Carroll* car were arrested and removed from the car, wasn't it "parked"?

Several state courts have imposed an "exigency" requirement on warrantless automobile searches.[20] But the Supreme Court has narrowed *Coolidge* to its facts and has abjured fact-specific analysis.

In one post-*Coolidge* case, Cardwell v. Lewis, 417 U.S. 583 (1974), a plurality of the Court explicitly rejected the contention that motion makes a difference: "The fact that the car in *Chambers* was seized after being stopped on a highway, whereas Lewis' car was seized from a public parking lot, has little, if any, legal significance."

After *Chambers, Coolidge,* and *Cardwell,* what constitutes exigent circumstances? In Texas v. White, 423 U.S. 67 (1975), Justice White's opinion for the Court reaffirmed *Chambers* over the dissent of Justice Marshall, joined by Justice Brennan. The dissent would have required a justification for removing a car to the stationhouse, rather than searching it on the spot of the arrest. See also Michigan v. Thomas, 458 U.S. 259 (1982) (holding "that the justification to conduct such a warrantless search does not vanish once the car has been immobilized"). An impatient Supreme Court summarily reversed a Florida intermediate appellate court in Florida v. Meyers, 466 U.S. 380 (1984) (per curiam), and, as in Michigan v. Thomas, reiterated the *Chambers* holding that a warrantless search of an auto may be conducted after the auto has been immobilized, as long as there is probable cause to believe that the auto contains contraband, evidence or fruits of criminal activity.

In light of *White* and *Thomas,* lower courts have interpreted *Coolidge* to mean that a warrant is required only if the officers had a reasonable opportunity to obtain a warrant before *seizing* the car. Under this view, *Chambers* is based on the rationale that due to its mobility, a car can be seized pending the obtaining of a warrant; and a search without a warrant is permitted because the search of a car is no more intrusive than would be the seizure of the car pending a warrant. But if the original seizure itself could have been preceded by a warrant, then the premise of *Chambers* is missing and the car exception ought not to apply. This explanation is consistent with the facts of *Chambers,* where the officers clearly could not have obtained a warrant before seizing the car, and with the facts of *Coolidge,* where the officers could have obtained a warrant (in fact they did so, but it was invalid because issued by a law enforcement officer) before seizing the car. See e.g. United States v. Moscatiello, 771 F.2d 589 (1st Cir.1985) (*Coolidge* distinguished where officers seized car after pursuing it in a rapidly developing situation).

20. See State v. Clark, 574 P.2d 1261 (Alaska, 1978) (factual circumstances must be considered rather than abstract potentiality for mobility or destruction; search of car parked in public place was reasonable when known accomplice was at large); State v. Parker, 355 So.2d 900 (La.1978) (no exigent circumstances existed when van was parked and unattended and guard could have been posted till warrant was obtained).

State v. Luna, 93 N.M. 773, 606 P.2d 183 (1980), holds that a warrantless stationhouse search of an automobile was improper, even if there was probable cause, since there were no exigent circumstances and therefore no reason not to get a warrant. Fields v. State, 382 So.2d 1098 (Miss.1980), reaches a similar conclusion, as do State v. Agnasan, 62 Hawaii 252, 614 P.2d 393 (1980); State v. Benoit, 417 A.2d 895 (R.I.1980). State courts that rely on state constitutional provisions had better do so explicitly, however. See Colorado v. Bannister, 449 U.S. 1 (1980) (vacating and remanding state court judgment suppressing evidence).

It is apparent that exigency is not a sufficient basis for the automobile exception after cases like *Chambers, White* and *Thomas*. In California v. Carney, 471 U.S. 386 (1985), the Court considered its prior cases and concluded that "the reasons for the vehicle exception are twofold." Chief Justice Burger, writing for the Court, explained as follows:

> The capacity to be quickly moved was clearly the basis of the holding in *Carroll*, and our cases have consistently recognized ready mobility as one of the principle bases of the automobile exception. * * *
>
> However, although ready mobility alone was perhaps the original justification for the vehicle exception, our later cases have made clear that ready mobility is not the only basis for the exception. * * * Besides the element of mobility, less rigorous warrant requirements govern because the expectation of privacy with respect to one's automobile is significantly less than that relating to one's home or office.
>
> Even in cases where an automobile was not immediately mobile, the lesser expectation of privacy resulting from its use as a readily mobile vehicle justified application of the vehicular exception.

Why do citizens have a diminished expectation of privacy with respect to their automobiles? The Chief Justice stated that these reduced expectations "derive not from the fact that the area to be searched is in plain view, but from the pervasive regulation of vehicles capable of traveling on the public highways." He stressed that automobiles are "subjected to pervasive and continuing governmental regulation and controls." Has the Court correctly assessed societal expectations with regard to automobiles?

The Court in *Carney* considered whether the dual justification for the automobile exception applied to the warrantless search of a mobile home. A six-person majority held that police officers validly searched a "Dodge Mini Motor Home" with probable cause but no warrant when the home was parked in a lot in a downtown area. Officers had received uncorroborated information that the home was used by a person who exchanged marijuana for sex. They watched a youth enter the home and remain there for more than an hour. When he left, the officers stopped him and learned that he had received marijuana in exchange for sexual contacts. The officers knocked on the door and the suspect stepped out. They identified themselves as officers and entered the home where they saw marijuana and related equipment.

Chief Justice Burger rejected the argument that the motor home was different from other vehicles because it was capable of functioning as a home as well as a vehicle, reasoning that "[t]o distinguish between respondent's motor home and an ordinary sedan for purposes of the vehicle exception would require that we apply the exception depending upon the size of the vehicle and the quality of its appointments" and "to fail to apply the exception to vehicles such as a motor home ignores the fact that a motor home lends itself easily to use as an instrument of illicit drug traffic and other illegal activity." Thus, the Court declined "to distinguish between 'worthy' and 'unworthy' vehicles which are either on the public roads and highways, or situated such that it is reasonable to conclude that the vehicle is not being used as a residence." In a footnote, the Court noted that it did not "pass on the application of the vehicle to a motor home that is situated in a way or place that objectively indicates that it is being used as a residence." It suggested, however, some factors that might be relevant in determining whether a warrant should be required: "its location, whether the vehicle is licensed, whether it is connected to utilities, and whether it has convenient access to a public road."

Justice Stevens, joined by Justices Brennan and Marshall, dissented. He argued that the Court "entered new territory prematurely" (since lower courts had little occasion to address the warrant requirement as applied to various hybrid vehicles and the California decision to require a warrant at worst provided more protection than the Constitution required); that the decision "accorded priority to an exception rather than to the general rule" (since motor homes were a combination of homes and autos, and the general preference for a warrant should govern a close case); and that the Court "abandoned the limits on the exception imposed by prior cases" (since a motor home that is removed from a public highway is different from other vehicles and is the functional equivalent of a hotel room, vacation or retirement home, or a hunting and fishing cabin).

In deciding who has the better of the argument, think about the lines that might have to be drawn between motor homes, vans, converted vans, minivans, station wagons and other different vehicles. If it is true, as many people believe, that many vehicles house personal possessions, especially when they are used to transport occupants from one house to another or to a cabin or vacation home, and that many occupants use their vehicles for a variety of purposes—to shelter them from storms, to rest, to travel privately rather than by public transportation, to converse privately—is the automobile exception justifiable as an independent exception to the warrant requirement?

Suppose that a motor home is parked in the garage of a private home, and that officers learn that marijuana has been traded for sexual contact inside the home while it was in the garage. Does the warrant clause apply since officers have to enter the garage to search the van? Would it make a difference if the van were parked in the driveway outside the garage rather than inside it? What if the van is parked in front of the house on the street? Is the van more or less mobile in one situation than in another? If the officers seize the van, is it mobile at all? What if officers learn that a suspect has marijuana in his house and a motor home parked in front of the house. May they enter the house without a warrant on the theory that the suspect has a vehicle that could be used to move the marijuana?

The automobile exception extends to airplanes, according to United States v. Nigro, 727 F.2d 100 (6th Cir.1984) (en banc). Three dissenters argued that once officers had immobilized a plane, they should have obtained a warrant before searching it. But, the majority cited the Supreme Court's auto search cases and concluded that "[t]he automobile exception has always depended on the inherent mobility of the vehicle to be searched, not on whether it could in fact be used immediately to effect a removal of evidence once investigating officers have determined that they have probable cause to search it and have taken steps to prevent its departure." Do you believe the automobile cases should apply to commercial carriers? May police search a 747 without a warrant? May they search a cruise liner without a warrant?

4. *Movable Property—In and Out of Cars*

If the automobile exception were based totally on exigency due to mobility, then it should also permit warrantless searches of other mobile containers such as briefcases, suitcases, and footlockers. However, as seen in *Carney,* the exception is also based on the reduced expectation of privacy accorded an automobile. Is there any way to distinguish mobile containers from automobiles on privacy grounds? The Supreme Court did just that in United States v. Chadwick, 433 U.S. 1 (1977), where it held that the mobility of a footlocker justified its seizure, but that a warrant was required to search the footlocker, unless emergency circumstances rendered a seizure insufficient to protect the state interest (e.g. if the footlocker was ticking). Chief Justice Burger, writing for the Court, distinguished mobile containers from cars on the following grounds:

> The factors which diminish the privacy aspects of an automobile do not apply to respondents' footlocker. Luggage contents are not open to public view, except as a condition to a border entry or common carrier travel; nor is luggage subject to regular inspections and official scrutiny on a continuing basis. Unlike an automobile, whose primary function is transportation, luggage is intended as a repository of personal effects. In sum, a person's expectations of privacy in personal luggage are substantially greater than in an automobile.

Because of the higher expectation of privacy in the footlocker, it could not be said, as it could in *Chambers,* that an immediate search would be no more intrusive than a seizure pending a warrant. As the Chief Justice explained in a footnote:

> A search of the interior [of the footlocker] was therefore a far greater intrusion into Fourth Amendment values than the impoundment of the footlocker. Though surely a substantial infringement of respondents' use and possession, the seizure did not diminish respondents' legitimate expectation that the footlocker's contents would remain private.
>
> It was the greatly reduced expectation of privacy in the automobile, coupled with the transportation function of the vehicle, which made the Court in *Chambers* unwilling to decide whether an immediate search of an automobile, or its seizure and indefinite mobilization, constituted a greater interference with the rights of the owner. This is clearly not the case with locked luggage.

The crux of the majority's argument lies in the contention that one has a lesser expectation of privacy in one's car than in movable chattel such as luggage. Is this argument convincing? Is the only reason that a lesser expectation of privacy surrounds autos, if it does, that the Supreme Court has said so? If the Court overruled *Carroll, Chambers, White, Thomas* and *Meyers,* the expectation of privacy would increase, would it not?

Does the fact that vehicles are used essentially for transportation demand, or even allow, the conclusion that they are seldom used as repositories for personal effects? Would that assertion hold true in the case of a traveling salesman who lives out of his car for several days each week?

The Fourth Amendment extends beyond homes to all effects, including cars and suitcases. Searches of particular kinds of effects may pose special problems, but shouldn't these be addressed on a particularized, rather than a wholesale, basis? If the least intrusive alternative to searches must be taken when a suitcase is involved, why not when a car is involved? Is the difference between the intrusiveness of a search, and that of a seizure, negligible if the object searched is a car, but of constitutional dimensions where a footlocker is concerned?

With a warrant required for a mobile container, but not for an automobile, it was of course only a matter of time before the Court was presented with cases in which the two rules collided: the search of a container in an automobile. In Arkansas v. Sanders, 442 U.S. 753 (1979), the Court held that a warrant was required to search a suitcase which had been placed in the trunk of a taxi. However, in United States v. Ross, 456 U.S. 798 (1982), the Court upheld the warrantless search of a paper bag and pouch found during the search of a car. Justice Stevens, writing for a six-person majority, noted that "in neither *Chadwick* nor *Sanders* did the police have probable cause to search the vehicle or anything within it except the footlocker in the former case and the green suitcase in the latter." In contrast, in *Ross* the officers had probable cause to search the entire car for drugs. Justice Stevens noted that the *Carroll* doctrine would largely be nullified if it did not extend to containers such as the brown paper bag in *Ross,* since "contraband goods rarely are strewn across the trunk or floor of a car." Justice Stevens concluded that, in light of *Carroll,* "the scope of a warrantless search of a car based on probable cause is no narrower—and no broader—than the scope of a search authorized by a warrant supported by probable cause."

Justice Marshall, joined by Justice Brennan in dissent in *Ross,* emphasized the anomalous results that could occur due to the fine lines drawn between *Ross* and *Sanders.* For example, if officers are informed that a person has drugs in a bag in the trunk, it would appear that probable cause is localized in the bag, and hence *Sanders* would apply. But if they are more generally informed that there are drugs in the trunk, *Ross* would apply. Yet it is notable that the *Ross* dissenters did not challenge the primacy of the *Carroll* doctrine, and accepted the majority's premise that there is a diminished expectation of privacy attendant to the automobile. *Sanders, Ross,* and *Chadwick* are extensively discussed in the next case, in which the Court again tries to resolve the question of whether a warrant is required to search a container placed in a car.

CALIFORNIA v. ACEVEDO

Supreme Court of the United States, 1991.
111 S.Ct. 1982.

JUSTICE BLACKMUN delivered the opinion of the Court.

This case requires us once again to consider the so-called "automobile exception" to the warrant requirement of the Fourth Amendment and its application to the search of a closed container in the trunk of a car.

I

On October 28, 1987, Officer Coleman of the Santa Ana, Cal., Police Department received a telephone call from a federal drug enforcement agent in Hawaii. The agent informed Coleman that he had seized a package containing marijuana which was to have been delivered to the Federal Express office in Santa Ana and which was addressed to J.R. Daza at 805 West Stevens Avenue in that city. The agent arranged to send the package to Coleman instead. Coleman then was to take the package to the Federal Express office and arrest the person who arrived to claim it.

* * * At about 10:30 a.m. on October 30, a man, who identified himself as Jamie Daza, arrived to claim the package. He accepted it and drove to his apartment on West Stevens. He carried the package into the apartment.

* * *

At 12:30 p.m., respondent Charles Steven Acevedo arrived. He entered Daza's apartment, stayed for about 10 minutes, and reappeared carrying a brown paper bag that looked full. The officers noticed that the bag was the size of one of the wrapped marijuana packages sent from Hawaii. Acevedo walked to a silver Honda in the parking lot. He placed the bag in the trunk of the car and started to drive away. Fearing the loss of evidence, officers in a marked police car stopped him. They opened the trunk and the bag, and found marijuana.

* * *

The California Court of Appeal, Fourth District, concluded that the marijuana found in the paper bag in the car's trunk should have been suppressed. The court concluded that the officers had probable cause to believe that the paper bag contained drugs but lacked probable cause to suspect that Acevedo's car, itself, otherwise contained contraband. Because the officers' probable cause was directed specifically at the bag, the court held that the case was controlled by United States v. Chadwick rather than by United States v. Ross. Although the court agreed that the officers could seize the paper bag, it held that, under *Chadwick,* they could not open the bag without first obtaining a warrant for that purpose. The court then recognized "the anomalous nature" of the dichotomy between the rule in *Chadwick* and the rule in *Ross.* That dichotomy dictates that if there is probable cause to search a car, then the entire car—including any closed container found therein—may be searched without a warrant, but if there is probable cause only as to a container in the car, the container may be held but not searched until a warrant is obtained.

* * *

II

* * * Contemporaneously with the adoption of the Fourth Amendment, the First Congress, and, later, the Second and Fourth Congresses, distinguished between the need for a warrant to search for contraband concealed in "a dwelling house or similar place" and the need for a warrant to search for contraband concealed in a movable vessel. See Carroll v. United States. * * *

[*Carroll*] held that a warrantless search of an automobile based upon probable cause to believe that the vehicle contained evidence of crime in the light of an exigency arising out of the likely disappearance of the vehicle did not contravene the Warrant Clause of the Fourth Amendment.

The Court refined the exigency requirement in Chambers v. Maroney, when it held that the existence of exigent circumstances was to be determined at the time the automobile is seized. * * * The Court reasoned in *Chambers* that the police could search later whenever they could have searched earlier, had they so chosen. Following *Chambers* if the police have probable cause to justify a warrantless seizure of an automobile on a public roadway, they may conduct either an immediate or a delayed search of the vehicle.

In United States v. Ross, we held that a warrantless search of an automobile under the *Carroll* doctrine could include a search of a container or package found inside the car when such a search was supported by probable cause. The warrantless search of Ross' car occurred after an informant told the police that he had seen Ross complete a drug transaction using drugs stored in the trunk of his car. The police stopped the car, searched it, and discovered in the trunk a brown paper bag containing drugs. We decided that the search of Ross' car was not unreasonable under the Fourth Amendment: "The scope of a warrantless search based on probable cause is no narrower—and no broader—than the scope of a search authorized by a warrant supported by probable cause." Thus, "[i]f probable cause justifies the search of a lawfully stopped vehicle, it justifies the search of every part of the vehicle and its contents that may conceal the object of the search." In *Ross,* therefore, we clarified the scope of the *Carroll* doctrine as properly including a "probing search" of compartments and containers within the automobile so long as the search is supported by probable cause.

In addition to this clarification, *Ross* distinguished the *Carroll* doctrine from the separate rule that governed the search of closed containers. The Court had announced this separate rule, unique to luggage and other closed packages, bags, and containers, in United States v. Chadwick. In *Chadwick,* federal narcotics agents had probable cause to believe that a 200–pound double-locked footlocker contained marijuana. The agents tracked the locker as the defendants removed it from a train and carried it through the station to a waiting car. As soon as the defendants lifted the locker into the trunk of the car, the agents arrested them, seized the locker, and searched it. In this Court, the United States did not contend that the locker's brief contact with the automobile's trunk sufficed to make the *Carroll* doctrine applicable. Rather, the United States urged that the search of movable luggage could be considered analogous to the search of an automobile.

The Court rejected this argument because, it reasoned, a person expects more privacy in his luggage and personal effects than he does in his automobile. * * *

In Arkansas v. Sanders, the Court extended *Chadwick's* rule to apply to a suitcase actually being transported in the trunk of a car. In *Sanders,* the police had probable cause to believe a suitcase contained marijuana. They watched as the defendant placed the suitcase in the trunk of a taxi and was driven away. The police pursued the taxi for several blocks, stopped it, found the suitcase in the trunk, and searched it. Although the Court had applied the *Carroll* doctrine to searches of integral parts of the automobile itself, (indeed, in *Carroll,* contraband whiskey was in the upholstery of the seats) it did not extend the doctrine to the warrantless search of personal luggage "merely because it was located in an automobile lawfully stopped by the police." Again, the *Sanders* majority stressed the heightened privacy expectation in personal luggage and concluded that the presence of luggage in an automobile did not diminish the owner's expectation of privacy in his personal items.

In *Ross,* the Court endeavored to distinguish between *Carroll,* which governed the *Ross* automobile search, and *Chadwick,* which governed the *Sanders* automobile search. It held that the *Carroll* doctrine covered searches of automobiles when the police had probable cause to search an entire vehicle but that the *Chadwick* doctrine governed searches of luggage when the officers had probable cause to search only a container within the vehicle. Thus, in a *Ross* situation, the police could conduct a reasonable search under the Fourth Amendment without obtaining a warrant, whereas in a *Sanders* situation, the police had to obtain a warrant before they searched.

* * * Ross held that closed containers encountered by the police during a warrantless search of a car pursuant to the automobile exception could also be searched. Thus, this Court in *Ross* took the critical step of saying that closed containers in cars could be searched without a warrant because of their presence within the automobile. Despite the protection that *Sanders* purported to extend to closed containers, the privacy

interest in those closed containers yielded to the broad scope of an automobile search.

III

* * *

This Court in *Ross* rejected *Chadwick's* distinction between containers and cars. It concluded that the expectation of privacy in one's vehicle is equal to one's expectation of privacy in the container, and noted that "the privacy interests in a car's trunk or glove compartment may be no less than those in a movable container." It also recognized that it was arguable that the same exigent circumstances that permit a warrantless search of an automobile would justify the warrantless search of a movable container. In deference to the rule of *Chadwick* and *Sanders,* however, the Court put that question to one side. It concluded that the time and expense of the warrant process would be misdirected if the police could search every cubic inch of an automobile until they discovered a paper sack, at which point the Fourth Amendment required them to take the sack to a magistrate for permission to look inside. We now must decide the question deferred in *Ross:* whether the Fourth Amendment requires the police to obtain a warrant to open the sack in a movable vehicle simply because they lack probable cause to search the entire car. We conclude that it does not.

IV

Dissenters in *Ross* asked why the suitcase in *Sanders* was "more private, less difficult for police to seize and store, or in any other relevant respect more properly subject to the warrant requirement, than a container that police discover in a probable-cause search of an entire automobile?" We now agree that a container found after a general search of the automobile and a container found in a car after a limited search for the container are equally easy for the police to store and for the suspect to hide or destroy. In fact, we see no principled distinction in terms of either the privacy expectation or the exigent circumstances between the paper bag found by the police in *Ross* and the paper bag found by the police here. Furthermore, by attempting to distinguish between a container for which the police are specifically searching and a container which they come across in a car, we have provided only minimal protection for privacy and have impeded effective law enforcement.

The line between probable cause to search a vehicle and probable cause to search a package in that vehicle is not always clear, and separate rules that govern the two objects to be searched may enable the police to broaden their power to make warrantless searches and disserve privacy interests. * * * At the moment when officers stop an automobile, it may be less than clear whether they suspect with a high degree of certainty that the vehicle contains drugs in a bag or simply contains drugs. If the police know that they may open a bag only if they are actually searching the entire car, they may search more extensively than they otherwise would in order to establish the general probable cause required by *Ross.*

* * * We cannot see the benefit of a rule that requires law enforcement officers to conduct a more intrusive search in order to justify a less intrusive one.

To the extent that the *Chadwick–Sanders* rule protects privacy, its protection is minimal. Law enforcement officers may seize a container and hold it until they obtain a search warrant. *Chadwick.* "Since the police, by hypothesis, have probable cause to seize the property, we can assume that a warrant will be routinely forthcoming in the overwhelming majority of cases." *Sanders* (dissenting opinion). And the police often will be able to search containers without a warrant, despite the *Chadwick–Sanders* rule, as a search incident to a lawful arrest. New York v. Belton.

* * *

Finally, the search of a paper bag intrudes far less on individual privacy than does the incursion sanctioned long ago in *Carroll.* In that case, prohibition agents slashed the upholstery of the automobile. This Court nonetheless found their search to be reasonable under the Fourth Amendment. If destroying the interior of an automobile is not unreasonable, we cannot conclude that looking inside a closed container is. In light of the minimal protection to privacy afforded by the *Chadwick–Sanders* rule, and our serious doubt whether that rule substantially serves privacy interests, we now hold that the Fourth Amendment does not compel separate treatment for an automobile search that extends only to a container within the vehicle.

V

The *Chadwick–Sanders* rule not only has failed to protect privacy but it has also confused courts and police officers and impeded effective law enforcement. * * *

The discrepancy between the two rules has led to confusion for law enforcement officers. For example, when an officer, who has developed probable cause to believe that a vehicle contains drugs, begins to search the vehicle and immediately discovers a closed container, which rule applies? The defendant will argue that the fact that the officer first chose to search the container indicates that his probable cause extended only to the container and that *Chadwick* and *Sanders* therefore require a warrant. On the other hand, the fact that the officer first chose to search in the most obvious location should not restrict the propriety of the search. The *Chadwick* rule, as applied in *Sanders,* has devolved into an anomaly such that the more likely the police are to discover drugs in a container, the less authority they have to search it. We have noted the virtue of providing "clear and unequivocal guidelines to the law enforcement profession." The *Chadwick–Sanders* rule is the antithesis of a "clear and unequivocal guideline."

* * *

The *Chadwick* dissenters predicted that the container rule would have "the perverse result of allowing fortuitous circumstances to control the outcome" of various searches. The rule also was so confusing that within two years after *Chadwick,* this Court found it necessary to expound on the meaning of that decision and explain its application to luggage in general. *Sanders.* Again, dissenters bemoaned the "inherent opaqueness" of the difference between the *Carroll* and *Chadwick* principles and noted "the confusion to be created for all concerned." Three years after *Sanders,* we returned in *Ross* to "this troubled area," in order to assert that *Sanders* had not cut back on *Carroll.*

Although we have recognized firmly that the doctrine of stare decisis serves profoundly important purposes in our legal system, this Court has overruled a prior case on the comparatively rare occasion when it has bred confusion or been a derelict or led to anomalous results. * * * [T]he existence of the dual regimes for automobile searches that uncover containers has proved as confusing as the *Chadwick* and *Sanders* dissenters predicted. We conclude that it is better to adopt one clear-cut rule to govern automobile searches and eliminate the warrant requirement for closed containers set forth in *Sanders.*

VI

* * *

Until today, this Court has drawn a curious line between the search of an automobile that coincidentally turns up a container and the search of a container that coincidentally turns up in an automobile. The protections of the Fourth Amendment must not turn on such coincidences. We therefore interpret *Carroll* as providing one rule to govern all automobile searches. The police may search an automobile and the containers within it where they have probable cause to believe contraband or evidence is contained.

* * *

JUSTICE SCALIA, concurring in the judgment.

I agree with the dissent that it is anomalous for a briefcase to be protected by the "general requirement" of a prior warrant when it is being carried along the street, but for that same briefcase to become unprotected as soon as it is carried into an automobile. On the other hand, I agree with the Court that it would be anomalous for a locked compartment in an automobile to be unprotected by the "general requirement" of a prior warrant, but for an unlocked briefcase within the automobile to be protected. I join in the judgment of the Court because I think its holding is more faithful to the text and tradition of the Fourth Amendment, and if these anomalies in our jurisprudence are ever to be eliminated that is the direction in which we should travel.

The Fourth Amendment does not by its terms require a prior warrant for searches and seizures; it merely prohibits searches and seizures that are "unreasonable." What it explicitly states regarding warrants is by way of limitation upon their issuance rather than requirement of their use. For the warrant was a means of insulating officials from personal liability assessed by colonial juries. An officer who searched or seized without a warrant did so at his own risk; he would be liable for trespass, including exemplary damages, unless the jury found that his action was "reasonable." Amar, The Bill of Rights as a Constitution, 100 Yale L.J. 1131, 1178–1180 (1991). If, however, the officer acted pursuant to a proper warrant, he would be absolutely immune. See Bell v. Clapp, 10 Johns 263 (N.Y.1813); 4 W. Blackstone, Commentaries 288 (1769). By restricting the issuance of warrants, the Framers endeavored to preserve the jury's role in regulating searches and seizures. Amar, supra; Posner, Rethinking the Fourth Amendment, 1981 S.Ct.Rev. 49, 72–73; see also T. Taylor, Two Studies in Constitutional Interpretation 41 (1969).

Although the Fourth Amendment does not explicitly impose the requirement of a warrant, it is of course textually possible to consider that implicit within the requirement of reasonableness. For some years after the (still continuing) explosion in Fourth Amendment litigation that followed our announcement of the exclusionary rule in Weeks v United States, our jurisprudence lurched back and forth between imposing a categorical warrant requirement and looking to reasonableness alone. (The opinions preferring a warrant involved searches of structures.) See generally Chimel v. California. By the late 1960's, the preference for a warrant had won out, at least rhetorically. See *Chimel;* Coolidge v. New Hampshire.

The victory was illusory. Even before today's decision, the "warrant requirement" had become so riddled with exceptions that it was basically unrecognizable. In 1985, one commentator cataloged nearly 20 such exceptions, including "searches incident to arrest . . . automobile searches . . . border searches ... administrative searches of regulated businesses ... exigent circumstances ... search[es] incident to nonarrest when there is probable cause to arrest ... boat boarding for document checks ... welfare searches ... inventory searches ... airport searches ... school search[es]. ..." Bradley, Two Models of the Fourth Amendment, 83 Mich.L.Rev. 1468, 1473–1474 (1985) (footnotes omitted). * * * Our intricate body of law regarding "reasonable expectation of privacy" has been developed largely as a means of creating these exceptions, enabling a search to be denominated not a Fourth Amendment "search" and therefore not subject to the general warrant requirement.

Unlike the dissent, therefore, I do not regard today's holding as some momentous departure, but rather as merely the continuation of an inconsistent jurisprudence that has been with us for years. Cases like United States v. Chadwick, and Arkansas v. Sanders have taken the "preference for a warrant" seriously, while cases like United States v. Ross and Carroll v. United States have not. There can be no clarity in this area unless we make up our minds, and unless the principles we express comport with the actions we take.

In my view, the path out of this confusion should be sought by returning to the first principle that the "reasonableness" requirement of the Fourth Amendment affords the protection that the common law afforded. I have no difficulty with the proposition that that includes the requirement of a warrant, where the common law required a warrant; and it may even be that changes in the surrounding legal rules * * * may make a warrant indispensable to reasonableness where it once was not. But the supposed "general rule" that a warrant is always required does not appear to have any basis in the common law and confuses rather than facilitates any attempt to develop rules of reasonableness in light of changed legal circumstances, as the anomaly eliminated and the anomaly created by today's holding both demonstrate.

And there are more anomalies still. Under our precedents (as at common law), a person may be arrested outside the home on the basis of probable cause, without an arrest warrant. United States v. Watson. Upon arrest, the person, as well as the area within his grasp, may be searched for evidence related to the crime. Chimel v. California. Under these principles, if a known drug dealer is carrying a briefcase reasonably believed to contain marijuana (the unauthorized possession of which is a crime), the police may arrest him and search his person on the basis of probable cause alone. And, under our precedents, upon arrival at the station house, the police may inventory his possessions, including the briefcase, even if there is no reason to suspect that they contain contraband. Illinois v. Lafayette [discussed in the section on inventory searches in this Chapter]. According to our current law, however, the police may not, on the basis of the same probable cause, take the less intrusive step of stopping the individual on the street and demanding to see the contents of his briefcase. That makes no sense a priori, and in the absence of any common law tradition supporting such a distinction, I see no reason to continue it.

* * *

JUSTICE WHITE, dissenting.

Agreeing as I do with most of Justice Stevens' opinion and with the result he reaches, I dissent and would affirm the judgment below.

JUSTICE STEVENS, with whom JUSTICE MARSHALL joins, dissenting.

* * *

I

* * *

We held in *Ross* that "the scope of the warrantless search authorized by [the automobile] exception is no broader and no narrower than a magistrate could legitimately authorize by warrant." The inherent mobility of the vehicle justified the immediate search without a warrant, but did not affect the scope of the search. Thus, the search could encompass containers, which might or might not conceal the object of the search, as well as the remainder of the vehicle.

Our conclusion was supported not only by prior cases defining the proper scope of searches authorized by warrant, as well as cases involving the automobile exception, but also by practical considerations that apply to searches in which the police have only generalized probable cause to believe that contraband is somewhere in a vehicle. We explained that, in such instances, "prohibiting police from opening immediately a container in which the object of the search is most likely to be found and instead forcing them first to comb the entire vehicle would actually exacerbate the intrusion on privacy interests." Indeed, because "the police could never be certain that the contraband was not secreted in a yet undiscovered portion of the vehicle," the most likely result would be that "the vehicle would need to be secured while a warrant was obtained."

These concerns that justified our holding in *Ross* are not implicated in cases like *Chadwick* and *Sanders* in which the police have probable cause to search a *particular* container rather than the *entire* vehicle. Because the police can seize the container which is the object of their search, they have no need either to search or to seize the entire vehicle. Indeed, as even the Court today recognizes, they have no authority to do so.

In reaching our conclusion in *Ross,* we therefore did not retreat at all from the holding in either *Chadwick* or *Sanders.* * * * We explained repeatedly that *Ross* involved the *scope* of the warrantless search authorized by the automobile exception, and, unlike *Chadwick* and *Sanders,* did not involve the *applicability* of the exception to closed containers.

Thus, we recognized in *Ross* that *Chadwick* and *Sanders* had not created a special rule for container searches, but rather had merely applied the cardinal principle that warrantless searches are per se unreasonable unless justified by an exception to the general rule. * * *

II

* * *

To the extent there was any "anomaly" in our prior jurisprudence, the Court has "cured" it at the expense of creating a more serious paradox. For, surely it is anomalous to prohibit a search of a briefcase while the owner is carrying it exposed on a public street yet to permit a search once the owner has placed the briefcase in the locked trunk of his car. One's privacy interest in one's luggage can certainly not be diminished by one's removing it from a public thoroughfare and placing it—out of sight—in a privately owned vehicle. Nor is the danger that evidence will escape increased if the luggage is in a car rather than on the street. In either location, if the police have probable cause, they are authorized to seize the luggage and to detain it until they obtain judicial approval for a search. Any line demarking an exception to the warrant requirement will appear blurred at the edges, but the Court has certainly erred if it believes that, by erasing one line and drawing another, it has drawn a clearer boundary.

* * *

To support its argument that today's holding works only a minimal intrusion on privacy, the Court suggests that "[i]f the police know that they may open a bag only if they are actually searching the entire car, they may search more extensively than they otherwise would in order to establish the general probable cause required by *Ross.*" * * * [T]his fear is unexplained and inexplicable. Neither evidence uncovered in the course of a search nor the scope of the search conducted can be used to provide post hoc justification for a search unsupported by probable cause at its inception.

The Court also justifies its claim that its holding inflicts only minor damage by suggesting that, under New York v. Belton, the police could have arrested respondent and searched his bag if respondent had placed the bag in the passenger compartment of the automobile instead of the trunk. * * * Even accepting *Belton's* application to a case like this one, however, the Court's logic extends its holding to a container placed in the *trunk* of a vehicle, rather than in the passenger compartment. And the Court makes this extension without any justification whatsoever other than convenience to law enforcement.

The Court's suggestion that *Chadwick* and *Sanders* have created a significant burden on effective law enforcement is unsupported, inaccurate, and, in any event, an insufficient reason for creating a new exception to the warrant requirement.

* * * No impartial observer could criticize this Court for hindering the progress of the war on drugs. On the contrary, decisions like the one the Court makes today will support the conclusion that this Court has become a loyal foot soldier in the Executive's fight against crime.

* * *

Note

The Court in *Acevedo* had three choices available: overrule *Carroll* and its progeny, overrule *Sanders,* or reaffirm *Ross.* Which choice is most consistent with the exigent circumstance rationale that supports the creation of an exception from the warrant requirement? Which choice is most consistent with the diminished expectation of privacy rationale used by the Court to justify warrantless searches of cars? Are you persuaded by Justice Blackmun's argument that a warrant should not be required where a warrant would be routinely forthcoming in the overwhelming majority of cases?

After *Acevedo,* is there anything left of *Chadwick?*

Are you surprised by the argument of the dissenters in *Ross* and *Acevedo,* which appears to accept the "lesser expectation of privacy" argument for autos generally? Once this argument is accepted, are the holdings really very surprising? Could the dissenters really have thought that a person who stores items in a locked trunk of a car or in a locked glove compartment has a lesser expectation of privacy than one who puts items in a zipped luggage bag in the back seat of the car?

Professor Green points out that the rule in *Acevedo* does not eliminate all the uncertainty of the previous law. Prior to *Acevedo,* a defendant might argue that a search of a container was excessive under the car exception because the police had probable cause to believe that evidence was in the container and nowhere else. After *Acevedo,* a defendant may challenge a search of areas of the car other than the container on precisely the same ground. Therefore, the difficult issues of probable cause as to location still exist. See Green, "Power, Not Reason": Justice Marshall's Valedictory and the Fourth Amendment in the Supreme Court's 1990–91 Term, 70 No.Car. L.Rev. 373 (1992).

If probable cause to search an automobile exists but there is no probable cause to arrest any of the occupants, may an occupant be searched if the goods sought are small enough to be concealed on his person? In United States v. Di Re, 332 U.S. 581 (1948), the Court dismissed the contention that the question should be answered affirmatively, noting that a warrant to search a car or house would not permit search of its occupants. "How then could we say that the right to search a car without a warrant confers greater latitude than a search by warrant would permit?" 332 U.S. at 589. Compare A.L.I. Model Code of Pre-Arraignment Procedure § 260.3, which would permit the search of occupants if the items sought are not found in the automobile, and if there is reason to suspect that an occupant is concealing the items. What does the rationale of *Carroll* suggest the proper answer is? Is this the correct answer?

Some courts have extended the automobile cases to permit warrantless seizures of vehicles thought to be subject to forfeiture. See generally Note, The Forfeiture Exception to the Warrant Requirement: A Distinction Without a Difference, 67 Va.L.Rev. 1035 (1981). United States v. Bagley, 765 F.2d 836 (9th Cir.1985), reasoned that after *Carney* "if the existence of probable cause alone justifies the warrantless search of a vehicle parked in a public place, certainly a warrantless seizure of such a vehicle, based only on probable cause, also falls within the automobile exception." Thus, the court rejected its prior interpretation of the exception—see, e.g., United States v. Spetz, 721 F.2d 1457 (9th Cir.1983)—which required exigent circumstances as well as probable cause. Is the court correct in its reading of *Carney* and the Supreme Court's other auto cases? Is there a difference between a seizure and a search that might justify limits on the former that are not placed on the latter? The problem the courts struggle with derives from the Supreme Court's simplistic assertion that vehicles are always mobile and thus almost always subject to warrantless seizures and searches for evidence. If they are so mobile, then presumably they could disappear before forfeiture is accomplished. If there really are no exigent circumstances, arguably warrants should be required for cars just like other places in all situations.

One lower court's effort to limit the scope of the automobile exception was repudiated by the Supreme Court, in United States v. Johns, 469 U.S. 478 (1985). The Court held that after customs agents removed packages from a trunk and placed them in a Drug Enforcement Agency warehouse, it was permissible for DEA agents to open the packages and search them without a warrant, even if their actions took place three days after the packages were first removed from the trunk. Writing for the Court, Justice O'Connor reasoned that *Ross* would have authorized a warrantless search of the packages when they were removed from the trunk, that previous cases—e.g., Chambers v. Maroney, Texas v. White—authorized a delayed search of the trunk, and that "searches of containers discovered in the course of a vehicle search are [not] subject to temporal restrictions not applicable to the vehicle search itself." The Court indicated that it did not intend to authorize indefinite retention of vehicles or "to foreclose the possibility that the owner of a vehicle or its contents might attempt to prove that delay in the completion of a vehicle search was unreasonable because it adversely affected a privacy or possessory interest." Justice Brennan, joined by Justice Marshall, dissented and argued that no exigency precluded reasonable efforts to obtain a warrant.

C. EXIGENT CIRCUMSTANCES

1. *Exigent Circumstances Generally*

The rationale of the Supreme Court's decisions in the arrest, auto and related cases—that the warrant clause, if applied, would produce unfortunate consequences—has been applied to situations in which the delay involved in obtaining a warrant would create untoward results. The exigent circumstance cases concern fact-specific situations in which the state must show that immediate action was reasonably necessary to safeguard the police or public or to protect against the loss of evidence.

The very concept of exigent circumstances has a tendency to distort analysis, and the term should be used with care. As you examine cases in which courts identify exigencies, note that the future of the nation does not depend on the success of the searches that are challenged. Nor would the lives of the officers or of third persons always be directly threatened by a failure to make the searches. In many cases it cannot even be shown that people, places or things that are searched in an "emergency" could not be searched pursuant to a warrant at a later time; all that can be shown is that a certain possibility exists that the government's agents will have greater difficulty in making a subsequent search with a warrant than an immediate warrantless search.

In fact-specific exigent circumstance cases, courts address circumstances in which an officer had probable cause to search, but had no time or insufficient time to seek a warrant. The exigent circumstances exception merely excuses the officer from having to obtain a magistrate's determination that probable cause exists; it does not permit a search in the absence of probable cause. Besides having probable cause to search, the officer must have probable cause to believe that the persons or items to be searched might be gone, or that some other danger would arise, before a warrant could be obtained and the search conducted.

The argument for warrantless, exigent circumstance searches is attractive. Because probable cause exists, a magistrate could issue a warrant to make the search; where there is no time to consult the magistrate, the warrant clause should not stand in the way of gathering the same evidence that could be gathered pursuant to a warrant when there is time to obtain one. But, the problems with the argument are almost self-evident by now. It assumes that probable cause exists, whereas the warrant clause cases assume that the zealous officer may overreact to observed facts. Moreover, the argument is inattentive to the reasonable concern that the very exigencies that justify immediate action may affect an officer's perceptions and distort his usual judgment on the cause question. It assumes that a magistrate who could issue a warrant would issue one, when, in theory at least, the magistrate might refuse in an effort to prevent an unreasonable search. Also, the argument blinks the fact that the officer who makes an exigent circumstance search is personally deciding the scope and particulars of the intrusion.

Thus, the fact-specific exigent circumstance cases pit a reasonable claim that the warrant clause should not be read to apply when there is no time to get a warrant against both the argument that the usual dangers of warrantless action are compounded by the pressure for immediate action and the reality that not all evidence must be seized if the government is to effectively enforce the law. Which side should prevail?

The answer may be that neither should, and that the Fourth Amendment should be read as requiring a compromise approach. The Fourth Amendment, as explicated at the outset of the chapter, implicitly approves of searches as a way of gathering evidence. Its limitations are most appropriate in the context of planned police action with time to consult a magistrate. If police are permitted to execute exigent circumstance searches and seizures with a limitation—that, if possible, the places, objects or things will be secured and not fully searched, while a warrant is sought to justify a further intrusion—would enforcement and privacy interests be appropriately accommodated? This compromise would mean that police would have to justify the level of intrusion by the emergency they confronted, and they would know that they had permission only for the slightest intrusion necessary to preserve an opportunity for consulting a magistrate. As you examine the material on exigent circumstances, see whether this compromise would work and whether it differs from the views the courts seem to have expressed.

2. *Danger to the Police*

People v. Crawl, 401 Mich. 1, 257 N.W.2d 86 (1977), according to a majority of the Michigan Supreme Court, involved a need for a warrantless search and seizure. Officers investigated an armed robbery and shooting at a bar. One of the robbers had been shot and taken to the hospital. The robber told the officers that Crawl had shot the bartender, gave Crawl's address and apartment number, and stated that an unidentified third man had participated. Crawl's apartment building had been the scene of several recent shootings. Three officers knocked on the door of the apartment and were admitted, while Sergeant Ewald waited outside the building. The occupants were scurrying throughout the apartment and there was general confusion. At that point, Sergeant Ewald saw a man climb out the apartment window; this was Crawl, whom Ewald placed under arrest. Ewald then brought Crawl back into the apartment in handcuffs. Officers in the apartment were still trying to gain control of the situation. Ewald then did a search of the bedroom. Nobody was there. He looked under the bed and saw a black bag, which he opened. The bag contained a gun, shells and identification cards, all offered against Crawl at trial.

The majority held that the evidence obtained by Ewald was admissible under the exigent circumstances exception to the warrant requirement. The court reasoned as follows:

> When Sergeant Ewald captured Crawl outside the apartment, he was not thereby prohibited from returning to the apartment to assist his fellow officers. When he entered the apartment, about two minutes after the raid began, the situation was not under police control. An unidentified man and two women were milling or running around the living room of this small apartment. There was a great deal of confusion. The man could have been the third robber. The other handgun used in the crime was not accounted for. The officers had every reason to believe they were in a life endangering situation. There had been trouble, including shootings, at this apartment building in the

past. It was dark and late at night. They were looking for a murderer and an accomplice who might well be prepared to kill again.

Under these circumstances, we cannot say that Sergeant Ewald's cursory search was unreasonable or illegal. The lack of police control and the dangerousness of the situation justified his proceeding without first obtaining a search warrant. To have delayed would have needlessly endangered the lives of his fellow officers.

The dissenters responded:

We acknowledge that if the police officers had reason to believe that the other robber was in the apartment and might escape, endanger the officers or destroy evidence, they would have been justified in entering the bedroom to avoid those dangers. Assuming then that Officer Ewald was justified in entering the bedroom, once he determined that no one was in the bedroom there was no justification for opening the bag. All four occupants (Crawl and the other three persons) were in the living room; there was no danger that anyone in the apartment could grab the bag and destroy it or any evidence in it or make use of any weapon contained in the bag. When the officers left the apartment, all four occupants were taken to police headquarters.

Who had the better of the argument? Note that *Crawl* was decided before Maryland v. Buie (discussed after both *Terry* and *Chimel*) which relied on *Terry* to hold that officers could conduct a protective sweep of premises incident to an arrest where there is reasonable suspicion to believe that such a sweep is necessary to protect the safety of the officers. Could the search that occurred in *Crawl* be upheld under the standards set forth in *Buie*? If so, is there ever a need for the officers to invoke the exigent circumstances exception, given that the exception requires a showing of probable cause as opposed to the lesser standard of reasonable suspicion?

3. *Danger to Individuals*

A different kind of emergency was examined in State v. Boggess, 115 Wis.2d 443, 340 N.W.2d 516 (1983), where the court upheld the entry into a home by a police officer and social worker in response to an anonymous telephone call that reported that children in the home may have been battered and were in need of medical attention. The caller identified the children by their last names and indicated that they lived with Boggess. The Court found corroboration in the fact that Boggess answered the door, identified himself, did not deny that two children lived there, and asked whether the social worker and the officer had a warrant. Are these facts sufficient to justify a warrantless entry into a home? See also United States v. Gillenwaters, 890 F.2d 679 (4th Cir.1989) where an officer responded to a radio report that a stabbing had occurred at a certain address, and entered the home while paramedics were still attending to the victim. The officer saw narcotics on the table in the room where the victim was being treated. The court found that exigent circumstances justified the entry, and that the officer's observations during the entry were thus justified by the plain view doctrine.

In United States v. Riccio, 726 F.2d 638 (10th Cir.1984), officers had probable cause to believe that Riccio had committed armed robbery. They surrounded his trailer, and then announced that fact over a loudspeaker and asked Riccio to come out of the trailer with his hands in the air. A shoot-out ensued, Riccio was hit by gunfire, and then the officers entered the trailer to attend to Riccio, who was laying on the floor with a bullet wound in his chest. In the course of the entry, incriminating evidence was found. The court held that the entry was justified by exigent circumstances, since the officers "had reason to believe that appellant was shot and might be in need of immediate aid." Is there any reason to think that the police should be prevented from invoking exigent circumstances in a case like *Riccio*? What would the consequences be if the police could not invoke the exception?

4. *The Risk of Destruction of Evidence*

In the en banc decision of United States v. MacDonald, 916 F.2d 766 (2d Cir.1990), the court of appeals reversed a panel decision which had held that exigent circumstances did not exist under the following facts:

> In May 1988, an informant alerted the New York Drug Enforcement Task Force ("Task Force") of a possible narcotics operation utilizing two apartments in a Manhattan apartment building located at 321 Edgecombe Avenue. On the evening of September 8, 1988, agents of the Task Force established surveillance outside the apartment building. The agents observed numerous indications that a retail narcotics exchange was being operated out of Apartment 1–O, a one-room efficiency on the first floor.
>
> Shortly before ten o'clock that evening, one of the agents of the Task Force, James Agee, went to Apartment 1–O in an attempt to transact an undercover purchase of narcotics. After knocking and being admitted by an unidentified man, Agent Agee encountered Paul Thomas, who was sitting in a chair next to the door and pointing a cocked 9 mm. semi-automatic weapon at the floor, but in Agee's direction. Defendant Errol MacDonald, who was sitting on a couch counting a stack of money, was within easy reach of a .357 magnum revolver. There were four other men, including the man who admitted Agee, in the apartment which contained large quantities of what appeared to Agee to be marijuana and cocaine. Agee detected the distinct odor of marijuana smoke. He handed the unidentified doorman a prerecorded five dollar bill in return for a package of marijuana. Agee then immediately left the building and reported his observations to the other Task Force members waiting outside.
>
> Approximately ten minutes after the controlled purchase, Agee returned to the apartment with reinforcements. After knocking on the door and identifying themselves, the agents heard the sounds of shuffling feet. They also simultaneously received a radio communication from agents remaining outside the building informing them that the occupants of the first floor apartment were attempting to escape through a bathroom window. The agents at the apartment door then used a battering ram to force entry.
>
> The agents arrested five men in the apartment, four in the bathroom and one hiding in a closet. As they performed a security sweep of the apartment, they discovered in plain view the two loaded weapons, large quantities of cocaine and marijuana, narcotics paraphernalia, packaging materials and several thousand dollars in cash. Additional cash was recovered from the persons of the suspects.

The majority of the en banc court found that exigent circumstances existed even before the officers knocked on the door and heard people scurrying around. The court stated as follows:

The essential question in determining whether exigent circumstances justified a warrantless entry is whether law enforcement agents were confronted by an "urgent need" to render aid or take action. Dorman v. United States, 435 F.2d 385, 391 (D.C.Cir.1970) (in banc). We have adopted the factors set out in *Dorman* as guideposts intended to facilitate the district court's determination. The *Dorman* factors have been summarized as follows:

> (1) the gravity or violent nature of the offense with which the suspect is to be charged; (2) whether the suspect "is reasonably believed to be armed"; (3) "a clear showing of probable cause ... to believe that the suspect committed the crime"; (4) "strong reason to believe that the suspect is in the premises being entered"; (5) "a likelihood that the suspect will escape if not swiftly apprehended"; and (6) the peaceful circumstances of the entry.

We have consistently emphasized that the *Dorman* factors are intended not as an exhaustive canon, but as an illustrative sampling of the kinds of facts to be taken into account. Sometimes the presence of a solitary factor suffices, see, e.g., United States v. Gallo–Roman, 816 F.2d 76, 79–80 (2d Cir.1987) (destruction of evidence), alternatively, a combination of several, see, e.g., United States v. Callabrass, 607 F.2d 559, 563–64 (2d Cir.1979), cert. denied, 446 U.S. 940, 100 S.Ct. 2163, 64 L.Ed.2d 794 (1980) (destruction of evidence and danger to public).

Applying the *Dorman* factors to the case at hand, the district court's determination [that exigent circumstances existed] was far from clearly erroneous. First, the ongoing sale and distribution of narcotics constituted a grave offense. Second, the defendant and at least one of his associates were armed with loaded, semi-automatic weapons. Third, the law enforcement agents had not only probable cause to suspect that a crime had been perpetrated but firsthand knowledge that ongoing crimes were transpiring. Fourth, the agents further knew that the defendant and his associates were in the apartment. Fifth, the likelihood that a suspect might escape if not swiftly apprehended was confirmed by the fact that the man who actually made the sale to Agent Agee had apparently escaped during the ten-minute interval that elapsed after the controlled purchase and before the agents entered the apartment. Sixth, the agents acted in accordance with the law, and first attempted to effect a peaceful entry by knocking and announcing themselves.

* * * In addition, the district court's finding that the agents were confronted by an urgent need to prevent the possible loss of evidence cannot be said to be clearly erroneous in light of the information that the suspects were using an unidentified apartment in the building to store narcotics, the ease with which the suspects could have disposed of the cocaine by flushing it down the toilet, and the possibility that the prerecorded five dollar bill used by Agent Agee in the undercover buy would be lost if the ongoing drug transactions were permitted to continue while the agents sought a warrant. Finally, the dangers of harm to law enforcement agents and the public, of the loss of evidence and of the escape of the suspects were aggravated by the additional time required for, and the impracticability of, obtaining a warrant at the late hour of day, while the apartment continued to be used as a retail drug outlet.

The *MacDonald* majority was unsympathetic to the defendant's claim that it had created a per se exigent circumstances exception in narcotics cases.

The defendant also argues that narcotics-related crimes so frequently involve exigent circumstances that the exception threatens to eviscerate the rule. * * * If it is true that ongoing retail narcotics operations often confront law enforcement agents with exigent circumstances, we fail to see how such a sad reality constitutes a ground for declaring that the exigencies do not, in fact, exist. To disallow the exigent circumstances exception in these cases would be to tie the hands of law enforcement agents who are entrusted with the responsibility of combatting grave, ongoing crimes * * *.

Judge Kearse, who had written the panel opinion in *MacDonald,* dissented from the majority's en banc decision. In her view, the government had not made a factual showing that a risk of destruction of evidence existed at the time that the officers decided to knock on the door.

> The principal factor relied on by the majority in the present case to reach the conclusion that there was an urgent need to enter without a warrant is that narcotics trafficking is a grave offense. Indeed it is; but though certain types of crimes, such as attempted murder or arson, create an inherent exigency while in progress, narcotics trafficking is not of that genre. There has never been an exigent circumstances exception permitting a warrantless entry simply because the offense involves narcotics. Nor was an exigency created in the present case by the fact that there were firearms in the apartment. We often have taken judicial notice that, to substantial dealers in narcotics, firearms are as much tools of the trade as are the commonly recognized articles of narcotics paraphernalia. Thus, emphasis on the presence of firearms for the view that the circumstances were exigent suggests that whenever there is probable cause to believe that narcotics offenses are being committed, the agents should be allowed to ignore the warrant requirement.
>
> * * *
>
> The total lack of awareness by the suspects in the present case, prior to the agents' return to the apartment, is virtually ignored by the majority. Thus, in concluding that there was a likelihood that the suspects would escape and evidence would be destroyed, the majority apparently sees no significance in the fact that this operation had been ongoing in Apartment 1–O since May, i.e., some four months before the agents' surveillance, and that there was no reason to believe it would be moved. * * * There was no basis for believing that the occupants of the apartment had been alerted to the September 8 surveillance prior to the agents' announcement of their official presence. The agents had received no information and had seen no indication that the suspects had any kind of security devices in the apartment or had posted any lookouts in the area. The surveillance was conducted by a team of agents whose ethnic makeup matched that of the civilians coming and going in the neighborhood. The surveillance was inconspicuous; the building was large, and there was a good deal of traffic in and out with respect to apartments other than 1–O; the agents' vehicles were placed so circumspectly that even Agee did not know where those other than his own were parked. * * * Nor did anything that occurred during Agee's subsequent purchase appear to alert the suspects. Agee testified that none of the occupants of the apartment knew who he was. He had never seen any of them before. There was simply nothing in the record to suggest that the suspects would suddenly, after at least four months of operation, start to destroy their business assets * * *.
>
> Finally, though the majority also relies on the difficulty that the agents would have had in obtaining a search warrant speedily because of the lateness of the hour at which they entered, I do not believe the government met its burden of showing that the timing was a permissible justification. Agee

testified that there was never any discussion whatever of the possibility of obtaining a warrant. Further, the government concedes that the agents had probable cause to obtain a warrant at least a half-hour before their forced entry, i.e., as of the time they obtained statements from persons who had just come from the apartment, confirming the agents' existing information from the informant and from their own observations of the stream of 15–20 quick visits to the apartment. I do not believe we should allow law enforcement officers who have probable cause early to tarry and then justify a warrantless entry on the basis of the lateness of the hour.

* * *

The majority's ruling today gives law enforcement officers broad license to enter premises without a warrant. Apparently, they need no more than to have probable cause for belief that there is ongoing narcotics trafficking within and to request entry; if they hear any sounds in response other than the purest of verbal refusals, they can justify a warrantless entry by their fear that evidence will be destroyed or that suspects will escape. Indeed, it appears that the majority would allow the agents to enter simply on the basis that one agent had recently been on the premises by consent and witnessed the trafficking. After this decision there appears to be little left of the warrant requirement in narcotics cases.

Judge Kearse's dissent was joined by Judge Oakes who had also dissented in United States v. Cattouse, 846 F.2d 144 (2d Cir.1988), a similar narcotics case in which the court found exigent circumstances due to the risk of destruction of evidence. In *Cattouse,* Judge Oakes stated that "we should be more forthright and say that the Fourth Amendment's warrant requirement is simply inapplicable in drug buy cases."

Is the en banc decision in *MacDonald* consistent with the Supreme Court's decision in Vale v. Louisiana, page 219, supra? In *Vale,* the Court emphasized the fact-based nature of the exigent circumstances inquiry, and held that exigent circumstances did not exist to search Vale's home, when Vale was arrested outside his home for engaging in a drug transaction. The Court noted that at the time of the officers' entry into the home, the narcotics were not "in the process of destruction." Does the Court in *Vale* mean that the destruction must have already begun before a warrant is excused? Is the issue whether destruction is "imminent?" Was there an imminent risk of destruction of narcotics in *MacDonald?* Would the court in *MacDonald* have come out the same way if the officers were staking out a counterfeiting operation as opposed to a drug operation?

5. *Impermissibly Created Exigency*

In some cases, suspects are alerted to the presence of police activity, and there is little dispute that there is a risk of destruction of evidence or other danger at the time the officers make an entry. Rather, defendants argue that the police acted impermissibly in revealing their presence, and thus manufactured the exigent circumstances. It is well-recognized that officers should not be allowed to evade the warrant requirement by impermissibly creating exigent circumstances; but it is often difficult to determine whether the officers in revealing themselves were acting impermissibly.

The issue of manufactured exigency arose in *MacDonald,* discussed above. Recall that the officers went to the door of the drug operation and knocked on it, announcing their presence. At that point, they heard people scurrying around, and used a battering ram, which they happened to have with them, to knock down the door. An officer who testified at the suppression hearing stated that they knocked on the door to obtain consent. The court held first that exigent circumstances existed even before the officers knocked on the door. But even assuming that was not the case, the court found that exigent circumstances existed after the knocking and that the officers did not impermissibly create the exigency. The majority analyzed this issue as follows:

> [T]he agents' conduct was perfectly proper. By knocking and announcing themselves, they acted in accordance with the law, attempting the "peaceful entry" contemplated in *Dorman,* 435 F.2d at 393. See Miller v. United States, 357 U.S. 301 (1958) (the requirement of notice before forcing entry is a tradition deeply rooted in Anglo–American common law). See also 18 U.S.C. § 3109 (establishing a notice requirement in executing a warrant). Exigent circumstances are not to be disregarded simply because the suspects chose to respond to the agents' lawful conduct by attempting to escape, destroy evidence, or engage in any other unlawful activity. The fact that the suspects may reasonably be expected to behave illegally does not prevent law enforcement agents from acting lawfully to afford the suspects the opportunity to do so. Thus, assuming *arguendo* that there were no exigent circumstances before the knock, the agents' conduct did not impermissibly create the circumstances occurring thereafter.
>
> The argument that law enforcement agents created exigent circumstances in bad faith has been rejected in numerous other contexts. We have previously reasoned that agents did not intentionally design exigent circumstances by using: (1) an all white surveillance team in a predominantly black neighborhood, and thus exposing the agents to a great risk of detection, [United States v.] Cattouse, 846 F.2d at 147, 148; (2) marked buy money in a controlled drug deal, and thus compelling the agents to act immediately lest the money be dissipated, id.; and (3) counterfeit tickets marked void, and thus endangering the lives of agents and occasioning the possibility of destruction of evidence when the suspect unwrapped the package and discovered the markings, [United States] v. Zabare, 871 F.2d at 290. The United States Court of Appeals for the First Circuit has held that a deceptive telephone call by agents advising the occupants of a motel room to vacate since their associates in a narcotics deal had been arrested was "a creative investigative effort and simply an example of good police work" rather than an impermissible effort to circumvent the arrest warrant requirement. United States v. Rengifo, 858 F.2d 800, 803 (1st Cir. 1988).
>
> The defendant asserts that United States v. Segura, 663 F.2d 411, 415 (2d Cir.1981), aff'd on other grounds, 468 U.S. 796 (1984), betokens a contrary result here. First, the facts of *Segura* are distinguishable from those of the case at hand. In that case, agents brought a suspect under arrest to the front door, displayed him to the occupants, and then sought to rely on the scurrying that occurred as an exigency to enter. That kind of contrived behavior on the part of law enforcement agents is far different than the agents' compliance with the law involved here.
>
> In addition, *Segura* ought not to be understood to suggest that a district court in reaching a determination about exigent circumstances should attribute any significance to the subjective state of mind of law enforcement agents. * * * [W]e have repeatedly held that the determination of exigent circum-

stances is an objective one based on the totality of the circumstances confronting law enforcement agents. The Supreme Court's recent decision in Horton v. California [page 238, supra] confirms our approach.

* * * We simply shall not engage in futile speculation as to whether the agents actually expected the suspects to respond lawfully to their knock at the door. The fact that the agents brought along a battering ram changes nothing. The exigent circumstances known to the agents before they knocked sufficiently alerted them to the possibility that a forced entry would be necessary.

* * * Therefore, we hold that when law enforcement agents act in an entirely lawful manner, they do not impermissibly create exigent circumstances. Law enforcement agents are required to be innocent but not naive.

Judge Kearse in dissent argued that the officers had impermissibly created exigent circumstances.

I find it difficult to conceive of the officers' return to the apartment as anything other than pretext, in an effort to precipitate a crisis that did not then exist. Though Agee stated that he returned in the hope that the occupants would give him consent to search the apartment, that explanation should, in the circumstances, be found not credible as a matter of law. Agee testified that when he made his undercover purchase, he saw two firearms in the apartment, and one of them was held cocked and pointed in his direction while he was in the apartment. It was not objectively reasonable for the officers to hold any belief that suspects who took such precautions during an apparently innocuous buy would voluntarily consent to a search by law enforcement officers. Since the agents' suggestion that they returned because they thought they could gain entrance to search by consent defies credulity, and since the agents plainly anticipated that the announcement of their identity would precipitate an exigency, for they came armed with a battering ram, I think the agents must be regarded as having deliberately created the exigency precisely to justify their warrantless entry. We should not endorse such contrivances by law enforcement officials in their efforts to circumvent the Fourth Amendment's warrant requirement.

Recall the discussion of pretext stops and arrests, and the Supreme Court's rejection of an inadvertence requirement for plain view seizures in Horton v. California. Are the results in those cases determinative of the result in a case like *MacDonald?* For a case with facts similar to *MacDonald,* see United States v. Timberlake, 896 F.2d 592 (D.C.Cir.1990). In that case, the court stated that "once the officers knocked on the door and shouted 'police, open up', those inside the apartment had some reason to know who the officers were." It noted that "police officers cannot deliberately create exigent circumstances," and held the entry invalid because there was "no evidence that the police, when they knocked on the door, intended anything other than a warrantless search of the apartment." Compare that same court's opinion in United States v. Socey, 846 F.2d 1439 (D.C.Cir.1988), where a risk of destruction of evidence arose when officers staked out an apartment housing a retail drug operation, and arrested one of the drug dealers when he came outside. The court found that the arrest was "not deliberately designed to invent exigent circumstances." How does the court know what was in the mind of the arresting officer? Why is that relevant?

6. *Prior Opportunity to Obtain a Warrant*

If the police can foresee that an exigency would arise at a certain time, and have probable cause and sufficient time to obtain a warrant before that exigency occurs, then the opportunity to obtain the warrant precludes the later invocation of the exigent circumstances exception. For example, assume that an officer knows that a murder suspect vacuums his carpet every Wednesday morning, and that such activity may destroy relevant hair and fiber samples. On Wednesday morning, there are exigent circumstances due to the risk of destruction of evidence. But if the officer learned this information on Monday, and had probable cause to search at that time, then he should not be able to invoke the exigent circumstances exception two days later. The decided cases are not usually that clear, however. In the typical case, the state argues that the officer did not have probable cause until the exigency arose, and therefore had no prior opportunity to obtain a warrant. The defendant then makes the anomalous argument that the officer had probable cause well before that. The state also argues that the officer should not be required to go to the magistrate at the very first moment that probable cause exists, and that a contrary rule would jeopardize undercover activity and ongoing investigations. See United States v. Hultgren, 713 F.2d 79 (5th Cir.1983) (noting that "the fluidity of an ongoing investigation of the distribution of narcotics makes the obtaining of an adequate search warrant more difficult to time in the flow of events," and distinguishing such an investigation from a routine felony arrest where a given individual and a distinct crime is involved).

How the court resolves these contentions will depend on the facts. In United States v. Miles, 889 F.2d 382 (2d Cir.1989), the court was confronted with the following facts: Joy, a reliable informant for the DEA, had arranged a cocaine buy in Miles' apartment. He gave DEA agents Miles' name and address, and the agents monitored a phone call between Joy and Miles indicating Miles' willingness to make the narcotics deal. Several hours later, the transaction took place in the apartment. The seller was one Rodriguez, with Miles acting as a broker. Joy was present when Rodriguez delivered a kilogram of cocaine to Miles' apartment. Joy so notified DEA agents outside the building by beeper. Then Joy left the apartment telling Rodriguez and Miles that he was going to get the money for the buy. At that point, the DEA agents entered the apartment. The court found that the warrantless search was supported by exigent circumstances, stating that "Joy's absence for an extended period of time while the agents sought a warrant would create a substantial risk of alerting Miles and Rodriguez to the imminence of an arrest" and that, if alerted, they might destroy the cocaine. The court rejected Miles' argument that the officer had a prior opportunity to obtain a warrant, which existed at least from the time they monitored Joy's phone conversation with Miles. The court stated that "law enforcement officers may delay obtaining a warrant until events have proceeded to a point where the agents could be reasonably certain that the evidence would ultimately support a conviction;" and it was not until the transaction actually took place that this reasonable certainty existed. The court further concluded that "even if the agents might have been able to obtain a warrant earlier in the day, their failure to do so at the first opportunity does not bar them from acting on an exigency that arises later." Does the court in *Miles* mean that officers must have even more proof than probable cause before they are required to go to a magistrate? In what type of factual situation will a court hold that the officer had a prior opportunity to obtain a warrant so as to preclude resort to exigent circumstances?

7. *Telephone Warrants*

Fed.R.Crim.P. 41(c)(2) authorizes telephone warrants, and such warrants are available in many states as well. Basically, however, the telephone warrant merely saves travel time, since a duplicate original warrant must be prepared by the officer, and must be read verbatim to the magistrate, who must transcribe it and prepare an original warrant for the record. Still, the time involved in obtaining a telephone warrant can be significantly less than it would take to obtain a warrant in person. In United States v. Cuaron, 700 F.2d 582 (10th Cir.1983), the court held that exigent circumstances must be determined by whether the officer could have obtained a telephone warrant before the entry:

> The time necessary to obtain a warrant is relevant to a determination whether circumstances are exigent. Therefore, courts should consider the amount of time required to obtain a telephone warrant in assessing the urgency of the situation. Although warrants obtained by telephone generally take less time to procure than traditional warrants, the time required for a telephone warrant varies from case to case. * * * [T]rial courts must consider the availability of a telephone warrant in determining whether exigent circumstances existed, unless the critical nature of the circumstances clearly prevented the effective use of *any* warrant procedure.

See also United States v. Berick, 710 F.2d 1035 (5th Cir.1983) (risk of destruction of evidence resulting from arrest of drug seller was so imminent that recourse to even a telephone warrant was unavailable); United States v. Patino, 830 F.2d 1413 (7th Cir.1987) (agent who observed fugitive in defendant's yard had adequate opportunity to obtain a telephone warrant during 30–minute wait for back-up assistance).

8. *Seizing Premises in the Absence of Exigent Circumstances*

If exigent circumstances do not exist to search a house or other premises, the officers must obtain a search warrant. But can the officers take any protective action to preserve the status quo while a warrant is being obtained? In Segura v. United States, 468 U.S. 796 (1984), officers had probable cause to believe that two individuals, Segura and Luz Colon, were trafficking in cocaine from their New York apartment. They established surveillance, and arrested Segura as he entered the lobby of his apartment building. The agents took Segura to his apartment, and knocked on the door. Luz Colon answered the door. The agents entered without receiving permission, placed Luz Colon under arrest, and conducted a limited security sweep. In the process of the sweep, they saw evidence of drug activity. Luz Colon and Segura were incarcerated, and two officers waited in Segura's apartment while a search warrant was being obtained. Due to "administrative delay" it was 19 hours before the search of the apartment was eventually conducted.

A majority of the Court found it unnecessary to reach the question of whether the officers acted illegally, since, even if they had, the later search conducted pursuant to a warrant was based on an independent legal source, i.e., the information the officers already had before they seized the premises. This aspect of the opinion will be discussed later in this Chapter. Chief Justice Burger, joined by Justice O'Connor, went further and stated that the seizure of the premises pending a warrant was reasonable, even in the absence of exigent circumstances.

> The Court has not had occasion to consider whether, when officers have probable cause to believe that evidence of criminal activity is on the premises, the temporary securing of a dwelling to prevent the removal or destruction of evidence violates the Fourth Amendment. However, in two cases we have suggested that securing of premises under these circumstances does not violate the Fourth Amendment, at least when undertaken to preserve the status quo while a search warrant is being sought. In Mincey v. Arizona, 437 U.S. 385 (1978), we noted with approval that, to preserve evidence, a police guard had been stationed at the entrance to an apartment in which a homicide had been committed, even though "[t]here was no indication that evidence would be lost, destroyed, or removed during the time required to obtain a search warrant." Similarly, in Rawlings v. Kentucky, 448 U.S. 98 (1980), although officers secured, from within, the home of a person for whom they had an arrest warrant, and detained all occupants while other officers were obtaining a search warrant, the Court did not question the admissibility of evidence discovered pursuant to the warrant later issued.
>
> * * * The sanctity of the home is not to be disputed. But the home is sacred in Fourth Amendment terms not primarily because of the occupants' *possessory* interests in the premises, but because of their *privacy* interests in the activities that take place within. * * *
>
> As we have noted, however, a seizure affects only possessory interests, not privacy interests. Therefore, the heightened protection we accord privacy interests is simply not implicated where a *seizure* of premises, not a search, is at issue. We hold, therefore, that securing a dwelling, on the basis of probable cause, to prevent the destruction or removal of evidence while a search warrant is being sought is not itself an unreasonable seizure of either the dwelling or its contents. We reaffirm at the same time, however, that, absent exigent circumstances, a warrantless search—such as that invalidated in Vale v. Louisiana, 399 U.S. 30, 33–34 (1970)—is illegal.

The Chief Justice recognized that the officers not only seized the premises—they also entered the premises without exigent circumstances. But he found this fact irrelevant to the reasonableness of the seizure.

> In this case, the agents entered and secured the apartment from within. Arguably, the wiser course would have been to depart immediately and secure the premises from the outside by a "stakeout" once the security check revealed that no one other than those taken into custody were in the apartment. But the method actually employed does not require a different result under the Fourth Amendment, insofar as the *seizure* is concerned. As the Court of Appeals held, absent exigent circumstances, the entry may have constituted an illegal *search,* or interference with petitioners' privacy interests, requiring suppression of all evidence observed during the entry. Securing of the premises from within, however, was no more an interference with the petitioners' possessory interests in the contents of the apartment than a perimeter "stakeout." In other words, the initial entry—legal or not—does not affect the reasonableness of the seizure. Under either method—entry and securing from

within or a perimeter stakeout—agents control the apartment pending arrival of the warrant; both an internal securing and a perimeter stakeout interfere to the same extent with the possessory interests of the owners.

Finally, the Chief Justice rejected the argument that the lengthy nature of the seizure rendered it unreasonable.

Of course, a seizure reasonable at its inception because based upon probable cause may become unreasonable as a result of its duration or for other reasons. Cf. United States v. Place. Here, because of the delay in securing the warrant, the occupation of the apartment continued throughout the night and into the next day. Such delay in securing a warrant in a large metropolitan center unfortunately is not uncommon; this is not, in itself, evidence of bad faith. And there is no suggestion that the officers, in bad faith, purposely delayed obtaining the warrant. The asserted explanation is that the officers focused first on the task of processing those whom they had arrested before turning to the task of securing the warrant. It is not unreasonable for officers to believe that the former should take priority, given, as was the case here, that the proprietors of the apartment were in the custody of the officers throughout the period in question.

* * *

Here, of course, Segura and Colon, whose possessory interests were interfered with by the occupation, were under arrest and in the custody of the police throughout the entire period the agents occupied the apartment. The actual interference with their possessory interests in the apartment and its contents was, thus, virtually nonexistent. We are not prepared to say under these limited circumstances that the seizure was unreasonable under the Fourth Amendment.

Justice Stevens, joined by Justices Brennan, Marshall, and Blackmun, dissented. He argued that the duration of the seizure was unreasonably long. While the portion of *Segura* concerning seizure of the premises was joined by only two Justices, the principle established by Chief Justice Burger has become well-accepted. See Murray v. United States, 487 U.S. 533 (1988); United States v. Veillette, 778 F.2d 899 (1st Cir.1985) (48 hour seizure of premises held reasonable under *Segura*); United States v. Rodriguez, 869 F.2d 479 (9th Cir.1989) (seizure of premises found reasonable under *Segura*). Does the *Segura* rule adequately balance the individual's possessory interests and the state interests at stake while a warrant is being obtained? If those who live in the premises are in custody, will the seizure of the premises ever be so long as to be unreasonable? Is the Chief Justice correct when he states that the officers' entry to secure the premises was an illegal search but not an illegal seizure? What difference does that make?

9. *Fire Safety*

Michigan v. Tyler, 436 U.S. 499 (1978), is another exigent circumstance case.

Shortly before midnight on January 21, 1970, a fire broke out at Tyler's Auction, a furniture store in Oakland County, Mich. The building was leased to respondent Loren Tyler, who conducted the business in association with respondent Robert Tompkins. According to the trial testimony of various witnesses, the fire department responded to the fire and was "just watering down smoldering embers" when Fire Chief See arrived on the scene around 2 a.m. It was Chief See's responsibility "to determine the cause and make out all reports." Chief See was met by Lt. Lawson, who informed him that two plastic containers of flammable liquid had been found in the building. Using portable lights, they entered the gutted store, which was filled with smoke and steam, to examine the containers. Concluding that the fire "could possibly have been an arson," Chief See called Police Detective Webb, who arrived around 3:30 a.m. Detective Webb took several pictures of the containers and of the interior of the store, but finally abandoned his efforts because of the smoke and steam. Chief See briefly "[l]ooked throughout the rest of the building to see if there was any further evidence, to determine what the cause of the fire was." By 4 a.m. the fire had been extinguished and the firefighters departed. See and Webb took the two containers to the fire station, where they were turned over to Webb for safekeeping. There was neither consent nor a warrant for any of these entries into the building, nor for the removal of the containers. * * *

Four hours after he had left Tyler's Auction, Chief See returned with Assistant Chief Somerville, whose job was to determine the "origin of all fires that occur within the Township." The fire had been extinguished and the building was empty. After a cursory examination they left, and Somerville returned with Detective Webb around 9 a.m. In Webb's words, they discovered suspicious "burn marks in the carpet, which [Webb] could not see earlier that morning, because of the heat, steam, and the darkness." They also found "pieces of tape, with burn marks, on the stairway." After leaving the building to obtain tools, they returned and removed pieces of the carpet and sections of the stairs to preserve these bits of evidence suggestive of a fuse trail. Somerville also searched through the rubble "looking for any other signs or evidence that showed how this fire was caused." Again, there was neither consent nor a warrant for these entries and seizures. * * *

On February 16 Sergeant Hoffman of the Michigan State Police Arson Section returned to Tyler's Auction to take photographs. During this visit or during another at about the same time, he checked the circuit breakers, had someone inspect the furnace, and had a television repairman examine the remains of several television sets found in the ashes. He also found a piece of fuse. Over the course of his several visits, Hoffman secured physical evidence and formed opinions that played a substantial role at trial in establishing arson as the cause of the fire and in refuting the respondents' testimony about what furniture had been lost.

Justice Stewart's opinion for the Court held that firefighters without a warrant may enter a burning building to extinguish a blaze and that, for a reasonable time thereafter, they may investigate the causes of the fire.

Fire officials are charged not only with extinguishing fires, but with finding their causes. Prompt determination of the fire's origin may be necessary to prevent its recurrence, as through the detection of continuing dangers such as faulty wiring or a defective furnace. Immediate investigation may also be necessary to preserve evidence from intentional or accidental destruction. And, of course, the sooner the officials complete their duties, the less will be their subsequent interference with the privacy and the recovery efforts of the victims. For these reasons, officials need no warrant to remain in a building for a reasonable time to investigate the cause of a blaze after it has been extinguished. And if the warrantless entry to put out the fire and determine its cause is constitutional, the warrantless seizure of evidence while inspecting the premises for these purposes also is constitutional.

The January 22nd entries thus were approved by the Court, but the post-January 22nd entries were condemned.

Justice White, joined by Justice Marshall would have found that all of the subsequent re-entries were invalid.

> Those investigating fires and their causes deserve a clear demarcation of the constitutional limits of their authority. Today's opinion recognizes the need for speed and focuses attention on fighting an ongoing blaze. The fire truck need not stop at the courthouse in rushing to the flames. But once the fire has been extinguished and the firemen have left the premises, the emergency is over. Further intrusion on private property can and should be accompanied by a warrant indicating the authority under which the firemen presume to enter and search.

In dissent, Justice Rehnquist wrote that the warrant clause was inapplicable to routine, regulatory inspections of business premises and would have found the search reasonable under the Fourth Amendment.

In Michigan v. Clifford, 464 U.S. 287 (1984), the Court attempted to clarify the scope of *Tyler*. However, the absence of a majority opinion makes it unlikely that much clarity was achieved. The facts were as follows: In the early morning hours, a fire erupted at the Clifford home while the Cliffords were away camping. Fire units arrived at the house, extinguished the fire and left the premises at 7:00 a.m. An hour later, an arson investigator learned that arson was suspected, but he did not reach the house until 1:00 p.m. because of other duties. He learned from a neighbor that the Cliffords were away and saw a work crew boarding up the house and pumping water from the basement. The officer entered the house, began a search in the basement and determined that the fire had started there. Finding evidence that suggested arson, the officer searched the remainder of the house.

Justice Powell, joined by Justices Brennan, White and Marshall, recognized that "[t]he aftermath of a fire often presents exigencies that will not tolerate the delay necessary to obtain a warrant or to secure the owner's consent to inspect fire-damaged premises. Because determining the cause and origin of a fire serves a compelling public interest, the warrant requirement does not apply in such cases." The warrant requirement does apply, however, when the exigencies disappear.

Justice Powell found that there was no exigency to excuse a warrant when the arson investigation took place because at that time an effort was being made to secure the fire-damaged home and fire and police units had left the scene.

Justice Stevens concurred in the judgment only. He agreed, however, that firefighters may make a warrantless nonconsensual entry into a home to put out a fire and to investigate the blaze, and that once the firefighters have determined the cause of the fire and its origins a warrant is needed to search other portions of the premises.

Justice Rehnquist's dissent was joined by Chief Justice Burger and Justices Blackmun and O'Connor. He would have held that concerns about discretionary searches and unwarranted invasions of privacy did not require a warrant to justify the post-fire inspection of premises, a practice of "long-standing and widespread acceptance."

Which view would you adopt? Would you consider too extreme an argument that without a warrant no investigation into the cause of the fire should be conducted and that the fire-fighters' function, absent a warrant, should be to put the fire out and nothing more?

10. Murder Scene

Is the argument made above more extreme than the one accepted by the Court in Mincey v. Arizona, 437 U.S. 385 (1978)? The relevant facts as set out by the Court were these:

> On the afternoon of October 28, 1974, undercover police officer Barry Headricks of the Metropolitan Area Narcotics Squad knocked on the door of an apartment in Tucson, Ariz., occupied by the petitioner, Rufus Mincey. Earlier in the day, Officer Headricks had allegedly arranged to purchase a quantity of heroin from Mincey and had left, ostensibly to obtain money. On his return he was accompanied by nine other plainclothes policemen and a deputy county attorney. The door was opened by John Hodgman, one of three acquaintances of Mincey who were in the living room of the apartment. Officer Headricks slipped inside and moved quickly into the bedroom. Hodgman attempted to slam the door in order to keep the other officers from entering, but was pushed back against the wall. As the police entered the apartment, a rapid volley of shots was heard from the bedroom. Officer Headricks emerged and collapsed on the floor. When other officers entered the bedroom they found Mincey lying on the floor, wounded and semiconscious. Officer Headricks died a few hours later in the hospital.
>
> * * *
>
> * * * After the shooting, the narcotics agents, thinking that other persons in the apartment might have been injured, looked about quickly for other victims. They found a young woman wounded in the bedroom closet and Mincey apparently unconscious in the bedroom, as well as Mincey's three acquaintances (one of whom had been wounded in the head) in the living room. Emergency assistance was requested and some medical aid administered to Officer Headricks. But the agents refrained from further investigation, pursuant to a Tucson Police Department directive that police officers should not investigate incidents in which they are involved. They neither searched further nor seized any evidence; they merely guarded the suspects and the premises.
>
> Within 10 minutes, however, homicide detectives who had heard a radio report of the shooting arrived and took charge of the investigation. They supervised the removal of Officer Headricks and the suspects, trying to make sure that the scene was disturbed as little as possible, and then proceeded to gather evidence. Their search lasted four days, during which period the entire apartment was searched, photographed, and diagrammed. The officers opened drawers, closets, and cupboards, and inspected their contents; they emptied clothing pockets; they dug bullet fragments out of the walls and floors; they pulled up sections of the carpet and removed them for examination. Every item in the apartment was closely examined and inventoried, and two to three hundred objects were seized. In short, Mincey's apartment was subjected to an exhaustive and intrusive search. No warrant was ever obtained.

Justice Stewart wrote for a unanimous Court. He rejected a "scene of the homicide" exception to the warrant requirement and stated that the state must make a factual showing of exigent circumstances.

Justice Stewart wrote as follows:

> * * * We do not question the right of the police to respond to emergency situations. Numerous state and federal cases have recognized that the Fourth Amendment does not bar police officers from making warrantless entries and searches when they reasonably believe that a person within is in need of immediate aid. Similarly, when the police come upon the scene of a homicide they may make a prompt warrantless search of the area to see if there are other victims or if a killer is still on the premises. * * *
>
> But a warrantless search must be "strictly circumscribed by the exigencies which justify its initiation," and it simply cannot be contended that this search was justified by any emergency threatening life or limb. All the persons in Mincey's apartment had been located before the investigating homicide officers arrived there and began their search. And a four-day search that included opening dresser drawers and ripping up carpets can hardly be rationalized in terms of the legitimate concerns that justify an emergency search.
>
> [T]he State points to the vital public interest in the prompt investigation of the extremely serious crime of murder. No one can doubt the importance of this goal. But the public interest in the investigation of other serious crimes is comparable. If the warrantless search of a homicide scene is reasonable, why not the warrantless search of the scene of a rape, a robbery, or a burglary? "No consideration relevant to the Fourth Amendment suggests any point of rational limitation" of such a doctrine.
>
> Moreover, the mere fact that law enforcement may be made more efficient can never by itself justify disregard of the Fourth Amendment. The investigation of crime would always be simplified if warrants were unnecessary. But the Fourth Amendment reflects the view of those who wrote the Bill of Rights that the privacy of a person's home and property may not be totally sacrificed in the name of maximum simplicity in enforcement of the criminal law. * * *

Does *Mincey* leave open the possibility of any search of the scene of a homicide other than one to look for the killer? If not, is the decision acceptable? Plain view would allow a seizure of obvious evidence, but is it sensible to require a warrant to search the area in the immediate vicinity of the body? What would be wrong with a rule that allowed automatic searches at the scene of a homicide, rape, or robbery? Won't there be an automatic search warrant issued? If the warrant application is perfunctory, what is gained by having the police, who are already at the scene of the crime, seek a warrant? Does the fact that particular homicides, rapes and robberies will not be anticipated by the police, who must react to these crimes without prior notice and planning, suggest that no warrant is needed to protect against harassment and erroneous searches? Would a warrant requirement have prevented the abuse that most bothered the Court in *Mincey?*

In a unanimous per curiam opinion in Thompson v. Louisiana, 469 U.S. 17 (1984), the Court found that *Mincey* required reversal of a state court decision upholding the warrantless "murder scene" search of the defendant's home. Sheriff's deputies came to the defendant's home in response to a call from her daughter reporting a homicide. The deputies entered the home, made a cursory search and found the defendant's husband dead of a gunshot wound in a bedroom and the defendant unconscious in another bedroom due to an apparent drug overdose. The daughter apparently told the deputies that the defendant had shot her husband, took a large quantity of pills in a suicide attempt, changed her mind, and called the daughter and asked for help. The daughter had arrived at the defendant's home before the deputies, admitted them into the home, and directed them to the rooms with the bodies. The deputies transported the defendant to the hospital and secured the scene after searching for other victims or suspects. Thirty-five minutes later, officers from the homicide unit arrived and conducted a two hour follow-up investigation in which they examined each room of the house. The defendant moved to suppress a pistol taken from a chest of drawers in the room where the deceased's body was found, a torn up note found in a wastepaper basket in an adjoining bathroom, and a letter (alleged to be a suicide note) found inside an envelope containing a Christmas card on the top of a chest of drawers. The Court found that *Mincey* was squarely in point. Do you agree? If so, are you more or less convinced that *Mincey* was correctly decided?

D. ADMINISTRATIVE SEARCHES AND OTHER SEARCHES AND SEIZURES BASED ON "SPECIAL NEEDS"

While the warrant clause is still, at least rhetorically, the predominant clause of the Fourth Amendment, the Supreme Court has applied the reasonableness clause to searches and seizures conducted for purposes other than traditional criminal law enforcement. The Court has reasoned that the traditional requirement of a warrant based on probable cause is not well-suited to searches for purposes as varied as enforcing school discipline, public safety, and administrative efficiency. If the search is supported by special needs beyond criminal law enforcement, then the Court engages in a balancing of interests under the reasonableness clause to determine what safeguards must apply. Reasonableness analysis balances the need for a particular search against the degree of invasion upon personal rights which the search entails. And if the probable cause standard and/or the warrant requirement takes insufficient account of the state interest in light of the degree of the intrusion, then the Court finds it reasonable to dispense with such requirements in favor of lesser standards such as reasonable suspicion, area warrants, or other controls on official discretion. If there is no special need beyond law enforcement, then a search to obtain evidence for law enforcement purposes presumptively requires probable cause. See Arizona v. Hicks (page 211, supra).

As you go through the following cases, it may be helpful to keep the following questions in mind. Has the state established a special need beyond criminal law enforcement for conducting the search? Does the establishment of such a special need by definition mean that the state interest is so high as to outweigh the individual's privacy interest? Why is a need to search for purposes other than criminal law enforcement more important than the need to search to enforce the criminal law? And most importantly, does it make any difference to the citizen that the state intrusion is for a purpose other than traditional criminal law enforcement?

1. *Safety Inspections of Homes*

In Camara v. Municipal Court, 387 U.S. 523 (1967), a homeowner claimed the right to refuse a warrantless entry by a health inspector who desired to inspect the house as provided for in the San Francisco housing code. The Court overruled Frank v. Maryland, 359 U.S. 360 (1959) (upholding conviction of person who refused to permit warrantless entry to locate and abate a nuisance) and held that the Fourth Amendment covered these administrative searches. But Justice White's majority opinion said that no showing was required that there was probable cause to believe that a particular dwelling was in violation of the code being enforced. Rather, area investigations are permissible and "it is obvious that 'probable cause' to issue a warrant to inspect must exist if reasonable legislative or administrative standards for conducting an area inspection are satisfied with respect to a particular dwelling." Finally, the opinion noted that "nothing we say today is intended to foreclose prompt inspections, even without a warrant, that the law had traditionally upheld in emergency situations."

In a companion case, See v. City of Seattle, 387 U.S. 541 (1967), the Court, per Justice White, extended *Camara* to inspections of non-residential commercial structures. But, the Court did "not in any way imply that business premises may not reasonably be inspected in many more situations than private homes."

Justice Clark, joined by Justices Harlan and Stewart, dissented from *Camara* and *See*. They argued that the area warrant concept and the "boxcar" warrant would degrade the Fourth Amendment, and asked: "Why the ceremony, the delay, the expense, the abuse of the search warrant?"

What danger does an area-wide warrant, which is not based upon probable cause as to any specific home, guard against? What would be wrong with a rule that safety inspectors could not enter a house without probable cause to believe that there was a safety violation? How would a safety inspector obtain enough information to constitute probable cause? Is a safety inspection of a home less intrusive than a search of a home by law enforcement officers investigating a crime?

2. *Administrative Searches of Businesses*

The Court applied the *Camara* protections to businesses in *See,* but it is apparent that administrative searches of businesses involve different issues from searches of residences. For one thing, some entries into business premises may not be searches at all, since the area searched is open to the general public. Thus, if the inspector walks through a hotel lobby and looks for fire exits, no reasonable expectation of privacy is implicated. See Donovan v. Lone Steer, Inc., 464 U.S. 408 (1984). Also, an administrative search of a business implicates more complex regulatory concerns; the state has an administrative interest not only in whether the business structure is safe, but also in whether the business is being safely and properly conducted. Moreover, the businessperson may have a diminished expectation of privacy given the nature of the business conducted. But on the other hand, the risk of an arbitrary use of power to conduct a regulatory search of a business must be a cause for special concern. It is no secret that businesspersons have occasionally been subject to harassment and extortion by unscrupulous investigators. All of these considerations are discussed in the following case.

NEW YORK v. BURGER

Supreme Court of the United States, 1987.
482 U.S. 691.

JUSTICE BLACKMUN delivered the opinion of the Court.

This case presents the question whether the warrantless search of an automobile junkyard, conducted pursuant to a statute authorizing such a search, falls within the exception to the warrant requirement for administrative inspections of pervasively regulated industries. The case also presents the question whether an otherwise proper administrative inspection is unconstitutional because the ultimate purpose of the regulatory statute pursuant to which the search is done—the deterrence of criminal behavior—is the same as that of penal laws, with the result that the inspection may disclose violations not only of the regulatory statute but also of the penal statutes.

I

Respondent Joseph Burger is the owner of a junkyard in Brooklyn, N.Y. His business consists, in part, of the dismantling of automobiles and the selling of their parts. * * * At approximately noon on November 17, 1982, Officer Joseph Vega and four other plainclothes officers, all members of the Auto Crimes Division of the New York City Police Department, entered respondent's junkyard to conduct an inspection pursuant to N.Y.Veh. & Traf. Law § 415–a5 (McKinney 1986).[a] On any given day, the Division conducts from 5 to 10 inspections of vehicle dismantlers, automobile junkyards, and related businesses.[b]

Upon entering the junkyard, the officers asked to see Burger's license and his "police book"—the record of the automobiles and vehicle parts in his possession. Burger replied that he had neither a license nor a police book. The officers then announced their intention to conduct a § 415–a5 inspection. Burger did not object. In accordance with their practice, the officers copied down the Vehicle Identification Numbers (VINs) of several vehicles and parts of vehicles that were in the junkyard. After checking these numbers against a police computer, the officers determined that respondent was in possession of stolen vehicles and parts. Accordingly, Burger was arrested and charged with five counts of possession of stolen property and one count of

a. This statute reads in pertinent part:

"Records and identification. (a) * * * Every person required to be registered pursuant to this section shall maintain a record of all motor vehicles, trailers, and major component parts thereof, coming into his possession together with a record of the disposition of any such motor vehicle, trailer or part thereof and shall maintain proof of ownership for any motor vehicle, trailer or major component part thereof while in his possession. * * * Upon request of an agent of the commissioner or of any police officer and during his regular and usual business hours, a vehicle dismantler shall produce such records and permit said agent or police officer to examine them and any vehicles or parts of vehicles which are subject to the record keeping requirements of this section and which are on the premises. . . . The failure to produce such records or to permit such inspection on the part of any person required to be registered pursuant to this section as required by this paragraph shall be a class A misdemeanor."

b. It was unclear from the record why, on that particular day, Burger's junkyard was selected for inspection. The junkyards designated for inspection apparently were selected from a list of such businesses compiled by New York City police detectives.

unregistered operation as a vehicle dismantler, in violation of § 415–a1.

[The trial court denied a motion to suppress, but the New York Court of Appeals reversed, finding that the statute was unconstitutional.]

II

A

The Court long has recognized that the Fourth Amendment's prohibition on unreasonable searches and seizures is applicable to commercial premises, as well as to private homes. See v. City of Seattle. An owner or operator of a business thus has an expectation of privacy in commercial property, which society is prepared to consider to be reasonable, see Katz v. United States (Harlan, J., concurring). This expectation exists not only with respect to traditional police searches conducted for the gathering of criminal evidence but also with respect to administrative inspections designed to enforce regulatory statutes. See Marshall v. Barlow's, Inc., 436 U.S. 307, 312–313 (1978). An expectation of privacy in commercial premises, however, is different from, and indeed less than, a similar expectation in an individual's home. See Donovan v. Dewey, 452 U.S. 594, 598–599 (1981). This expectation is particularly attenuated in commercial property employed in "closely regulated" industries. * * *

The Court first examined the "unique" problem of inspections of "closely regulated" businesses in two enterprises that had "a long tradition of close government supervision." In Colonnade Corp. v. United States, 397 U.S. 72 (1970), it considered a warrantless search of a catering business pursuant to several federal revenue statutes authorizing the inspection of the premises of liquor dealers. Although the Court disapproved the search because the statute provided that a sanction be imposed when entry was refused, and because it did not authorize entry without a warrant as an alternative in this situation, it recognized that "the liquor industry [was] long subject to close supervision and inspection." We returned to this issue in United States v. Biswell, 406 U.S. 311 (1972), which involved a warrantless inspection of the premises of a pawnshop operator, who was federally licensed to sell sporting weapons pursuant to the Gun Control Act of 1968. While noting that "[f]ederal regulation of the interstate traffic in firearms is not as deeply rooted in history as is governmental control of the liquor industry," we nonetheless concluded that the warrantless inspections authorized by the Gun Control Act would "pose only limited threats to the dealer's justifiable expectations of privacy." We observed: "When a dealer chooses to engage in this pervasively regulated business and to accept a federal license, he does so with the knowledge that his business records, firearms, and ammunition will be subject to effective inspection."

The *"Colonnade–Biswell"* doctrine, stating the reduced expectation of privacy by an owner of commercial premises in a "closely regulated" industry, has received renewed emphasis in more recent decisions. In Marshall v. Barlow's, Inc., we noted its continued vitality but declined to find that warrantless inspections, made pursuant to the Occupational Safety and Health Act of 1970, of *all* businesses engaged in interstate commerce fell within the narrow focus of this doctrine. However, we found warrantless inspections made pursuant to the Federal Mine Safety and Health Act of 1977, proper because they were of a "closely regulated" industry. Donovan v. Dewey, supra.

Indeed, in Donovan v. Dewey, we declined to limit our consideration to the length of time during which the business in question—stone quarries—had been subject to federal regulation.

We pointed out that the doctrine is essentially defined by "the pervasiveness and regularity of the federal regulation" and the effect of such regulation upon an owner's expectation of privacy. We observed, however, that "the duration of a particular regulatory scheme" would remain an "important factor" in deciding whether a warrantless inspection pursuant to the scheme is permissible.[c]

B

Because the owner or operator of commercial premises in a "closely regulated" industry has a reduced expectation of privacy, the warrant and probable-cause requirements, which fulfill the traditional Fourth Amendment standard of reasonableness for a government search have lessened application in this context. Rather, we conclude that, as in other situations of "special need" where the privacy interests of the owner are weakened and the government interests in regulating particular businesses are concomitantly heightened, a warrantless inspection of commercial premises may well be reasonable within the meaning of the Fourth Amendment.

This warrantless inspection, however, even in the context of a pervasively regulated business, will be deemed to be reasonable only so long as three criteria are met. First, there must be a "substantial" government interest that informs the regulatory scheme pursuant to which the inspection is made. See Donovan v. Dewey ("substantial federal interest in improving the health and safety conditions in the Nation's underground and surface mines"); United States v. Biswell (regulation of firearms is "of central importance to federal efforts to prevent violent crime and to assist the States in regulating the firearms traffic within their borders"); Colonnade Corp. v. United States (federal interest "in protecting the revenue against various types of fraud").

Second, the warrantless inspections must be "necessary to further [the] regulatory scheme." For example, in *Dewey* we recognized that forcing mine inspectors to obtain a warrant before every inspection might alert mine owners or operators to the impending inspection, thereby frustrating the purposes of the Mine Safety and Health Act—to detect and thus to deter safety and health violations.

Finally, "the statute's inspection program, in terms of the certainty and regularity of its application, [must] provid[e] a constitutionally adequate substitute for a warrant." Ibid. In other words, the regulatory statute must perform the two basic functions of a warrant: it must advise the owner of the commercial premises that the search is being made pursuant to the law and has a properly defined scope, and it must limit the discretion of the inspecting officers. To perform this first function, the statute must be "sufficiently comprehensive and defined that the owner of commercial property cannot help but be aware that his property will be subject to periodic inspections undertaken for specific purposes." Donovan v. Dewey. In addition, in defining how a statute limits the discretion of the inspectors, we have observed that it must be "carefully limited in time, place, and scope." United States v. Biswell.

III

A

Searches made pursuant to § 415–a5, in our view, clearly fall within this es-

c. We explained in Donovan v. Dewey: "If the length of regulation were the only criterion, absurd results would occur. Under appellees' view, new or emerging industries, including ones such as the nuclear power industry that pose enormous potential safety and health problems, could never be subject to warrantless searches even under the most carefully structured inspection program simply because of the recent vintage of regulation."

tablished exception to the warrant requirement for administrative inspections in "closely regulated" businesses. First, the nature of the regulatory statute reveals that the operation of a junkyard, part of which is devoted to vehicle dismantling, is a "closely regulated" business in the State of New York. The provisions regulating the activity of vehicle dismantling are extensive. An operator cannot engage in this industry without first obtaining a license, which means that he must meet the registration requirements and must pay a fee. Under § 415–a5(a), the operator must maintain a police book recording the acquisition and disposition of motor vehicles and vehicle parts, and make such records and inventory available for inspection by the police or any agent of the Department of Motor Vehicles. The operator also must display his registration number prominently at his place of business, on business documentation, and on vehicles and parts that pass through his business. Moreover, the person engaged in this activity is subject to criminal penalties, as well as to loss of license or civil fines, for failure to comply with these provisions. That other States besides New York have imposed similarly extensive regulations on automobile junkyards further supports the "closely regulated" status of this industry.

In determining whether vehicle dismantlers constitute a "closely regulated" industry, the "duration of [this] particular regulatory scheme" has some relevancy. Section 415–a could be said to be of fairly recent vintage, and the inspection provision of § 415–a5 was added only in 1979. But because the automobile is a relatively new phenomenon in our society and because its widespread use is even newer, automobile junkyards and vehicle dismantlers have not been in existence very long and thus do not have an ancient history of government oversight. * * *

The automobile-junkyard business, however, is simply a new branch of an industry that has existed, and has been closely regulated, for many years. The automobile junkyard is closely akin to the secondhand shop or the general junkyard. * * * As such, vehicle dismantlers represent a modern, specialized version of a traditional activity. In New York, general junkyards and secondhand shops long have been subject to regulation. * * * The history of government regulation of junk-related activities argues strongly in favor of the "closely regulated" status of the automobile junkyard.

Accordingly, in light of the regulatory framework governing his business and the history of regulation of related industries, an operator of a junkyard engaging in vehicle dismantling has a reduced expectation of privacy in this "closely regulated" business.

B

The New York regulatory scheme satisfies the three criteria necessary to make reasonable warrantless inspections pursuant to § 415–a5. First, the State has a substantial interest in regulating the vehicle-dismantling and automobile-junkyard industry because motor vehicle theft has increased in the State and because the problem of theft is associated with this industry. In this day, automobile theft has become a significant social problem, placing enormous economic and personal burdens upon the citizens of different States. * * *

Second, regulation of the vehicle-dismantling industry reasonably serves the State's substantial interest in eradicating automobile theft. It is well established that the theft problem can be addressed effectively by controlling the receiver of, or market in, stolen property. Automobile junkyards and vehicle dismantlers provide the major market for stolen vehicles and vehicle parts. Thus, the State rationally may believe that it will reduce car theft by regulations that prevent automobile junkyards from becoming markets for stolen vehicles and that help trace the origin and destination of vehicle parts.

Moreover, the warrantless administrative inspections pursuant to § 415–a5 "are necessary to further [the] regulatory scheme." Donovan v. Dewey. In this respect, we see no difference between these inspections and those approved by the Court in United States v. Biswell and Donovan v. Dewey. We explained in *Biswell:*

> "[I]f inspection is to be effective and serve as a credible deterrent, unannounced, even frequent, inspections are essential. In this context, the prerequisite of a warrant could easily frustrate inspection; and if the necessary flexibility as to time, scope, and frequency is to be preserved, the protections afforded by a warrant would be negligible."

* * * Because stolen cars and parts often pass quickly through an automobile junkyard, "frequent" and "unannounced" inspections are necessary in order to detect them. In sum, surprise is crucial if the regulatory scheme aimed at remedying this major social problem is to function at all.

Third, § 415–a5 provides a "constitutionally adequate substitute for a warrant." The statute informs the operator of a vehicle dismantling business that inspections will be made on a regular basis. Thus, the vehicle dismantler knows that the inspections to which he is subject do not constitute discretionary acts by a government official but are conducted pursuant to statute. Section 415–a5 also sets forth the scope of the inspection and, accordingly, places the operator on notice as to how to comply with the statute. In addition, it notifies the operator as to who is authorized to conduct an inspection.

Finally, the "time, place, and scope" of the inspection is limited to place appropriate restraints upon the discretion of the inspecting officers. The officers are allowed to conduct an inspection only "during [the] regular and usual business hours."[d] The inspections can be made only of vehicle-dismantling and related industries. And the permissible scope of these searches is narrowly defined: the inspectors may examine the records, as well as "any vehicles or parts of vehicles which are subject to the record keeping requirements of this section and which are on the premises."

IV

* * * The Court of Appeals, nevertheless, struck down the statute as violative of the Fourth Amendment because, in its view, the statute had no truly administrative purpose but was "designed simply to give the police an expedient means of enforcing penal sanctions for possession of stolen property." The court rested its conclusion that the administrative goal of the statute was pretextual and that § 415–a5 really "authorize[d] searches undertaken solely to uncover evidence of criminality" particularly on the fact that, even if an operator failed to produce his police book, the inspecting officers could continue their inspection for stolen vehicles and parts. The court also suggested that the identity of the inspectors—police officers—was significant in revealing the true nature of the statutory scheme.

d. Respondent contends that § 415–a5 is unconstitutional because it fails to limit the number of searches that may be conducted of a particular business during any given period. While such limitations, or the absence thereof, are a factor in an analysis of the adequacy of a particular statute, they are not determinative of the result so long as the statute, as a whole, places adequate limits upon the discretion of the inspecting officers. * * *

In arriving at this conclusion, the Court of Appeals failed to recognize that a State can address a major social problem *both* by way of an administrative scheme *and* through penal sanctions. Administrative statutes and penal laws may have the same *ultimate* purpose of remedying the social problem, but they have different subsidiary purposes and prescribe different methods of addressing the problem. An administrative statute establishes how a particular business in a "closely regulated" industry should be operated, setting forth rules to guide an operator's conduct of the business and allowing government officials to ensure that those rules are followed. Such a regulatory approach contrasts with that of the penal laws, a major emphasis of which is the punishment of individuals for specific acts of behavior.

* * * The New York penal laws address automobile theft by punishing it or the possession of stolen property, including possession by individuals in the business of buying and selling property. In accordance with its interest in regulating the automobile-junkyard industry, the State also has devised a regulatory manner of dealing with this problem. Section 415–a, as a whole, serves the regulatory goals of seeking to ensure that vehicle dismantlers are legitimate businesspersons and that stolen vehicles and vehicle parts passing through automobile junkyards can be identified. * * *

If the administrative goals of § 415–a5 are recognized, the difficulty the Court of Appeals perceives in allowing inspecting officers to examine vehicles and vehicle parts even in the absence of records evaporates. The regulatory purposes of § 415–a5 certainly are served by having the inspecting officers compare the records of a particular vehicle dismantler with vehicles and vehicle parts in the junkyard. The purposes of maintaining junkyards in the hands of legitimate businesspersons and of tracing vehicles that pass through these businesses, however, *also* are served by having the officers examine the operator's inventory even when the operator, for whatever reason, fails to produce the police book. Forbidding inspecting officers to examine the inventory in this situation would permit an illegitimate vehicle dismantler to thwart the purposes of the administrative scheme and would have the absurd result of subjecting his counterpart who maintained records to a more extensive search.

Nor do we think that this administrative scheme is unconstitutional simply because, in the course of enforcing it, an inspecting officer may discover evidence of crimes, besides violations of the scheme itself. * * * The discovery of evidence of crimes in the course of an otherwise proper administrative inspection does not render that search illegal or the administrative scheme suspect.

Finally, we fail to see any constitutional significance in the fact that police officers, rather than "administrative" agents, are permitted to conduct the § 415–a5 inspection. The significance respondent alleges lies in the role of police officers as enforcers of the penal laws and in the officers' power to arrest for offenses other than violations of the administrative scheme. It is, however, important to note that state police officers, like those in New York, have numerous duties in addition to those associated with traditional police work. As a practical matter, many States do not have the resources to assign the enforcement of a particular administrative scheme to a specialized agency. So long as a regulatory scheme is properly administrative, it is not rendered illegal by the fact that the inspecting officer has the power to arrest individuals for violations other than those created by the scheme itself. In sum, we decline to impose upon the States the burden of requiring the enforcement of their regulatory statutes to be carried out by specialized agents.

* * *

JUSTICE BRENNAN, with whom JUSTICE MARSHALL joins, and with whom JUSTICE O'CONNOR joins as to all but Part III, dissenting.

Warrantless inspections of pervasively regulated businesses are valid if necessary to further an urgent state interest, and if authorized by a statute that carefully limits their time, place, and scope. I have no objection to this general rule. Today, however, the Court finds pervasive regulation in the barest of administrative schemes. Burger's vehicle-dismantling business is not closely regulated (unless most New York City businesses are), and an administrative warrant therefore was required to search it. The Court also perceives careful guidance and control of police discretion in a statute that is patently insufficient to eliminate the need for a warrant. Finally, the Court characterizes as administrative a search for evidence of only criminal wrongdoing. As a result, the Court renders virtually meaningless the general rule that a warrant is required for administrative searches of commercial property.

I

In See v. City of Seattle, we held that an administrative search of commercial property generally must be supported by a warrant. We make an exception to this rule, and dispense with the warrant requirement, in cases involving "closely regulated" industries, where we believe that the commercial operator's privacy interest is adequately protected by detailed regulatory schemes authorizing warrantless inspections. The Court has previously made clear that "the closely regulated industry . . . is the exception." Marshall v. Barlow's, Inc. Unfortunately, today's holding makes it the rule.

* * *

The provisions governing vehicle dismantling in New York simply are not extensive. A vehicle dismantler must register and pay a fee, display the registration in various circumstances, maintain a police book, and allow inspections. Of course, the inspections themselves cannot be cited as proof of pervasive regulation justifying elimination of the warrant requirement; that would be obvious bootstrapping. Nor can registration and recordkeeping requirements be characterized as close regulation. New York City, like many States and municipalities, imposes similar, and often more stringent licensing, recordkeeping, and other regulatory requirements on a myriad of trades and businesses. Few substantive qualifications are required of an aspiring vehicle dismantler; no regulation governs the condition of the premises, the method of operation, the hours of operation, the equipment utilized, etc. This scheme stands in marked contrast to, e.g., the mine safety regulations relevant in Donovan v. Dewey.

In sum, if New York City's administrative scheme renders the vehicle-dismantling business closely regulated, few businesses will escape such a finding. Under these circumstances, the warrant requirement is the exception not the rule, and *See* has been constructively overruled.

II

Even if vehicle dismantling were a closely regulated industry, I would nonetheless conclude that this search violated the Fourth Amendment. * * * In order to serve as the equivalent of a warrant, an administrative statute must create "a predictable and guided [governmental] presence," *Dewey,*

452 U.S., at 604. Section 415–a5 does not approach the level of "certainty and regularity of . . . application" necessary to provide "a constitutionally adequate substitute for a warrant."

* * * There is neither an upper nor a lower limit on the number of searches that may be conducted at any given operator's establishment in any given time period. Neither the statute, nor any regulations, nor any regulatory body, provides limits or guidance on the selection of vehicle dismantlers for inspection. * * *

The Court also maintains that this statute effectively limits the scope of the search. * * * Plainly, a statute authorizing a search which can uncover *no* administrative violations is not sufficiently limited in scope to avoid the warrant requirement. This statute fails to tailor the scope of administrative inspection to the particular concerns posed by the regulated business. I conclude that "the frequency and purpose of the inspections [are left] to the unchecked discretion of Government officers." The conduct of the police in this case underscores this point. The police removed identification numbers from a walker and a wheelchair, neither of which fell within the statutory scope of a permissible administrative search.

The Court also finds significant that an operator is on notice as to who is authorized to search the premises; I do not find the statutory limitation—to "any police officer" or "agent of the commissioner"—significant. The *sole* limitation I see on a police search of the premises of a vehicle dismantler is that it must occur during business hours; otherwise it is open season. The unguided discretion afforded police in this scheme precludes its substitution for a warrant.

III

The fundamental defect in § 415–a5 is that it authorizes searches intended solely to uncover evidence of criminal acts. * * *

Here the State has used an administrative scheme as a pretext to search without probable cause for evidence of criminal violations. It thus circumvented the requirements of the Fourth Amendment by altering the label placed on the search. This crucial point is most clearly illustrated by the fact that the police copied the serial numbers from a wheelchair and a handicapped person's walker that were found on the premises, and determined that these items had been stolen. * * * The scope of the search alone reveals that it was undertaken solely to uncover evidence of criminal wrongdoing.

Moreover, it is factually impossible that the search was intended to discover wrongdoing subject to administrative sanction. Burger stated that he was not registered to dismantle vehicles as required by § 415–a1, and that he did not have a police book, as required by § 415–a5(a). At that point he had violated every requirement of the administrative scheme. There is no administrative provision forbidding possession of stolen automobiles or automobile parts. The inspection became a search for evidence of criminal acts when all possible administrative violations had been uncovered.

The State contends that acceptance of this argument would allow a vehicle dismantler to thwart its administrative scheme simply by failing to register and keep records. This is false. A failure to register or keep required records violates the scheme and results in both administrative sanctions and criminal penalties. Neither is the State's further criminal investigation thwarted; the police need only obtain a warrant and then proceed to search the premises. If respondent's failure to register and maintain records amounted to probable cause, then the inspecting police officers, who worked in the Auto Crimes Division of the New York City Police Department, possessed probable cause to obtain a criminal warrant authorizing a search of Burger's premises.[e] Several of the officers might have stayed on the premises to ensure that this unlicensed dismantler did no further business, while the others obtained a warrant. * * *

The Court thus implicitly holds that if an administrative scheme has certain goals and if the search serves those goals, it may be upheld even if no concrete administrative consequences could follow from a particular search. This is a dangerous suggestion, for the goals of administrative schemes often overlap with the goals of the criminal law. Thus, on the Court's reasoning, administrative inspections would evade the requirements of the Fourth Amendment so long as they served an abstract administrative goal, such as the prevention of automobile theft. * * * If the Fourth Amendment is to retain meaning in the commercial context, it must be applied to searches for evidence of criminal acts even if those searches would also serve an administrative purpose, unless that administrative purpose takes the concrete form of seeking an administrative violation.[f]

IV

The implications of the Court's opinion, if realized, will virtually eliminate Fourth Amendment protection of commercial entities in the context of administrative searches. No State may require, as a condition of doing business, a blanket submission to warrantless searches for any purpose. I respectfully dissent.

Note

What precisely are the limitations on administrative inspections of businesses after *Burger?* Has the Court imposed sufficient controls on discretion? Did Justice Brennan overreact? Analysis in some lower court cases after *Burger* would suggest that he did not. In United States v. Hernandez, 901 F.2d 1217 (5th Cir.1990), an FBI agent who suspected that a commercial truck was carrying drugs followed the truck for twenty-four hours and 600 miles. He then notified the Texas Department of Public Safety that a truck believed to be carrying drugs was traveling on the interstate with no license plates. The DPS officer stopped the truck and demanded a driver's license and a bill of lading describing the cargo. The driver failed to produce evidence of Texas Interstate Commerce Commission Motor Carrier authorization. The officer then walked to the back of the truck and opened an inspection port, a small door used to check the temperature of the cargo. He smelled marijuana, obtained the keys to the cargo door, and a search of the truck uncovered 98 bales of marijuana. The court of appeals found that, while there was probable cause to arrest for the license plate violation, this did not provide probable cause to

e. Although the fact that the police conducted the search is not dispositive as to its administrative or criminal nature, it should caution the Court to proceed with care, because "[s]earches by the police are inherently more intrusive than purely administrative inspections. Moreover, unlike administrative agents, the police have general criminal investigative duties which exceed the legitimate scope and purposes of purely administrative inspections." Commonwealth v. Lipomi, 385 Mass. 370, 378, 432 N.E.2d 86, 91 (1982). * * *

f. This case thus does not present the more difficult question whether a State could take any criminal conduct, make it an administrative violation, and then search without probable cause for violations of the newly created administrative rule. The increasing overlap of administrative and criminal violations creates an obvious temptation for the State to do so, and plainly toleration of this type of pretextual search would allow an end run around the protections of the Fourth Amendment.

search the truck; nor was the search permissible as a search incident to arrest, because it went beyond the passenger compartment; nor was it permissible as a protective search under *Terry*, because the officer had no reasonable suspicion of bodily harm. But the search was permissible as an administrative search under *Burger*. The court concluded that a Texas civil statute regulating motor carriers authorized any Department of Public Safety Officer to inspect any load of commodities being transported for hire over the highways of the state. To similar effect is United States v. Dominguez–Prieto, 923 F.2d 464 (6th Cir.1991), upholding the search of the trailer portion of a truck pursuant to a statute authorizing inspection by Public Service Commissioners, and relying on *Burger* to conclude that the commercial trucking industry is a heavily regulated business.

Cases such as *Burger* and *Hernandez* again demonstrate the possibility of pretextual searches, discussed earlier in the Chapter. In light of that previous discussion, are you convinced that the Supreme Court will invalidate a search due to an officer's pretextual motivation, if it is conducted in accordance with a proper regulatory scheme?

Departures from the probable cause-based, particularized warrant requirement in the administrative search cases are based upon the importance of overall enforcement schemes and procedural substitutes for the warrant. If legislation or administrative regulations specify places to be searched, things to be examined, items that may be seized, and the particulars of when and how searches may be conducted, arguably the limitations are as effective a control on executive action as the limitations found in a warrant. But *Burger* suggests that the statutory limitations need not be as vigorous as those that would be imposed if a warrant were required.

Besides establishing a broad exception to the administrative warrant requirement in *Burger*, the Court has recently addressed the more fundamental question of whether a warrant which is not based upon particularized probable cause can ever be mandated. In Griffin v. Wisconsin, 483 U.S. 868 (1987), the Court invoked its "special needs" analysis to uphold the warrantless search of a probationer's home. The Court held that the search could be conducted upon reasonable suspicion of a probation violation. In dissent, Justice Blackmun agreed that the reasonable suspicion standard represented an appropriate balance between state and individual interests. But he argued that in the absence of exigent circumstances, the probation officer should have obtained a warrant based upon reasonable suspicion. He cited *Camara* for this proposition. Justice Scalia, writing for the Court, contended that the Fourth Amendment did not permit the issuance of a judicial warrant on the basis of reasonable suspicion.

> This * * * is a combination that neither the text of the Constitution nor any of our prior decisions permits. While it is possible to say that Fourth Amendment reasonableness demands probable cause without a judicial warrant, the reverse runs up against the constitutional provision that "no warrants shall issue, but upon probable cause." Although we have arguably come to permit an exception to that prescription for administrative search warrants, which may but do not necessarily have to be issued by courts, we have never done so for constitutionally mandated judicial warrants. There it remains true that if a search warrant be constitutionally required, the requirement cannot be flexibly interpreted to dispense with the rigorous constitutional restrictions for its issue.

Has Justice Scalia persuasively distinguished *Camara* and *Marshall?*

3. *Searches of Individuals Pursuant to "Special Needs"*

The Court has used its special needs balancing analysis in a series of cases to uphold civil-based searches of individuals in the absence of a warrant and probable cause. In New Jersey v. T.L.O., 469 U.S. 325 (1985), the Court held that a warrantless search of a student's purse was reasonable when the school administrator had reasonable suspicion to believe that cigarettes were in the student's purse. The special need invoked was the state's interest in maintaining discipline in its schools. The Court did not decide whether its special needs analysis would be applicable if the search of the student was conducted by a law enforcement official. On this question, recall *Burger,* where the Court stated that it would not impose upon the states the burden of requiring their regulatory interests to be carried out by administrative agents. After *Burger,* should the search of a student by a police officer, ostensibly to enforce school regulations, be treated any differently from a search by the principal? Does it matter that marijuana was discovered in T.L.O.'s purse by the school administrator and it was used against T.L.O. in a juvenile proceeding?

The *T.L.O.* analysis was used by the Court to uphold warrantless searches of the office of a government official, and of the house of a probationer. O'Connor v. Ortega, 480 U.S. 709 (1987); Griffin v. Wisconsin, supra. In both *O'Connor* and *Griffin,* as in *T.L.O.,* the Court found that conditioning searches on probable cause would be deleterious to the state interest, and that the reasonable suspicion standard was an appropriate balance between state and individual interests. These cases are discussed in the next case, although the case presents a somewhat different question—whether the special needs balancing of interests can be used to allow a search without any suspicion at all.

SKINNER v. RAILWAY LABOR EXECUTIVES' ASS'N

Supreme Court of the United States, 1989.
489 U.S. 602.

JUSTICE KENNEDY delivered the opinion of the Court.

* * * Finding that alcohol and drug abuse by railroad employees poses a serious threat to safety, the Federal Railroad Administration (FRA) has promulgated regulations that mandate blood and urine tests of employees who are involved in certain train accidents. The FRA also has adopted regulations that do not require, but do authorize, railroads to administer breath and urine tests to employees who violate certain safety rules. The question presented is whether these regulations violate the Fourth Amendment.

I

A

[The Court discusses the history of alcohol and drug use on American railroads, and the attempts before 1985 to regulate the problem.]

B

After reviewing further comments from representatives of the railroad industry, labor groups, and the general public, the FRA, in 1985, promulgated regulations addressing the problem of alcohol and drugs on the railroads. * * *

To the extent pertinent here, two subparts of the regulations relate to testing. Subpart C, which is entitled "Post–Accident Toxicological Testing," is mandatory. It provides that railroads "shall take all practicable steps to assure that all covered employees of the railroad directly involved ... provide blood and urine samples for toxicological testing by FRA," upon the occurrence of certain specified events. Toxicological testing is required following a "major train accident," which is defined as any train accident that involves (i) a fatality, (ii) the release of hazardous material accompanied by an evacuation or a reportable injury, or (iii) damage to railroad property of $500,000 or more. The railroad has the further duty of collecting blood and urine samples for testing after an "impact accident," which is defined as a collision that results in a reportable injury, or in damage to railroad property of $50,000 or more. Finally, the railroad is also obligated to test after "[a]ny train incident that involves a fatality to any onduty railroad employee."

After occurrence of an event which activates its duty to test, the railroad must transport all crew members and other covered employees directly involved in the accident or incident to an independent medical facility, where both blood and urine samples must be obtained from each employee. * * *

The regulations require that the FRA notify employees of the results of the tests and afford them an opportunity to respond in writing before preparation of any final investigative report. Employees who refuse to provide required blood or urine samples may not perform covered service for nine months, but they are entitled to a hearing concerning their refusal to take the test.

Subpart D of the regulations, which is entitled "Authorization to Test for Cause," is permissive. It authorizes railroads to require covered employees to submit to breath or urine tests in certain circumstances not addressed by Subpart C. Breath or urine tests, or both, may be ordered (1) after a reportable accident or incident, where a supervisor has a "reasonable suspicion" that an employee's acts or omissions contributed to the occurrence or severity of the accident or incident, or (2) in the event of certain specific rule violations, including noncompliance with a signal and excessive speeding. A railroad also may require breath tests where a supervisor has a "reasonable suspicion" that an employee is under the influence of alcohol, based upon specific, personal observations concerning the appearance, behavior, speech, or body odors of the employee. Where impairment is suspected, a railroad, in addition, may require urine tests, but only if two supervisors make the appropriate determination, and, where the supervisors suspect impairment due to a substance other than alcohol, at least one of those supervisors must have received specialized training in detecting the signs of drug intoxication.

* * *

II

The Fourth Amendment provides that "[t]he right of the people to be secure in their persons, houses, papers, and effects, against unreasonable searches and seizures, shall not be violated ...." The Amendment guarantees the privacy, dignity, and security of persons against certain arbitrary and invasive acts by officers of the Government or those acting at their direction. Before we consider whether the tests in question are reasonable under the Fourth Amendment, we must inquire whether the tests are attributable to the Government or its agents, and whether they amount to searches or seizures. We turn to those matters.

A

Although the Fourth Amendment does not apply to a search or seizure, even an arbitrary one, effected by a private party on his own initiative, the Amendment protects against such intrusions if the private party acted as an instrument or agent of the Government. * * *

* * * Whether a private party should be deemed an agent or instrument of the Government for Fourth Amendment purposes necessarily turns on the degree of the Government's participation in the private party's activities. The fact that the Government has not compelled a private party to perform a search does not, by itself, establish that the search is a private one. Here, specific features of the regulations combine to convince us that the Government did more than adopt a passive position toward the underlying private conduct.

* * * The Government has removed all legal barriers to the testing authorized by Subpart D, and indeed has made plain not only its strong preference for testing, but also its desire to share the fruits of such intrusions. In addition, it has mandated that the railroads not bargain away the authority to perform tests granted by Subpart D. These are clear indices of the Government's encouragement, endorsement, and participation, and suffice to implicate the Fourth Amendment.

B

* * *

It is not disputed * * * that chemical analysis of urine, like that of blood, can reveal a host of private medical facts about an employee, including whether he or she is epileptic, pregnant, or diabetic. Nor can it be disputed that the process of collecting the sample to be tested, which may in some cases involve visual or aural monitoring of the act of urination, itself implicates privacy interests. * * * Because it is clear that the collection and testing of urine intrudes upon expectations of privacy that society has long recognized as reasonable, the Federal Courts of Appeals have concluded unanimously, and we agree, that these intrusions must be deemed searches under the Fourth Amendment.

* * *

III

A

To hold that the Fourth Amendment is applicable to the drug and alcohol testing prescribed by the FRA regulations is only to begin the inquiry into the standards governing such intrusions. For the Fourth Amendment does not proscribe all searches and seizures, but only those that are unreasonable. What is reasonable, of course, "depends on all of the circumstances surrounding the search or seizure and the nature of the search or seizure itself." Thus, the permissibility of a particular practice "is judged by balancing its intrusion on the individual's Fourth Amendment interests against its promotion of legitimate governmental interests."

In most criminal cases, we strike this balance in favor of the procedures described by the Warrant Clause of the Fourth Amendment. Except in certain well-defined circumstances, a search or seizure in such a case is not reasonable unless it is accomplished pursuant to a judicial warrant issued upon probable cause. We have recognized exceptions to this rule, however, "when 'special needs, beyond the normal need for law enforcement, make the warrant and probable-cause requirement impracticable.'" Griffin v. Wisconsin, 483 U.S. 868, 873 (1987), quoting New Jersey v. T.L.O., 469 U.S., at 351 (Blackmun, J., concurring in judgment). When faced with such special needs, we have not hesitated to balance the governmental and privacy interests to assess the practicality of the warrant and probable cause requirements in the particular context. See, e.g., Griffin v. Wisconsin (search of probationer's home); New York v. Burger (search of premises of certain highly regulated businesses); O'Connor v. Ortega (work-related searches of employees' desks and offices); New Jersey v. T.L.O. (search of student's property by school officials); Bell v. Wolfish, 441 U.S. 520, 558–560 (1979) (body cavity searches of prison inmates).

The Government's interest in regulating the conduct of railroad employees to ensure safety, like its supervision of probationers or regulated industries, or its operation of a government office, school, or prison, "likewise presents 'special needs' beyond normal law enforcement that may justify departures from the usual warrant and probable-cause requirements." * * *

The FRA has prescribed toxicological tests, not to assist in the prosecution of employees, but rather "to prevent accidents and casualties in railroad operations that result from impairment of employees by alcohol or drugs." [a] This governmental interest in ensuring the safety of the traveling public and of the employees themselves plainly justifies prohibiting covered employees from using alcohol or drugs on duty, or while subject to being called for duty. * * * The question that remains, then, is whether the Government's need to monitor compliance with these restrictions justifies the privacy intrusions at issue absent a warrant or individualized suspicion.

B

An essential purpose of a warrant requirement is to protect privacy interests by assuring citizens subject to a search or seizure that such intrusions are not the random or arbitrary acts of government agents. * * * A warrant also provides the detached scrutiny of a neutral magistrate, and thus ensures an objective determination whether an intrusion is justified in any given case. In the present context, however, a warrant would do little to further these aims. Both the circumstances justifying toxicological testing and the permissible limits of such intrusions are defined narrowly and specifically in the regulations that authorize them, and doubtless are well known to covered employees. Indeed, in light of the standardized nature of the tests and the minimal discretion vested in those charged with administering the program, there are virtually no facts for a neutral magistrate to evaluate.[b]

a. The regulations provide that "[e]ach sample provided under [Subpart C] is retained for not less than six months following the date of the accident or incident and may be made available to . . . a party in litigation upon service of appropriate compulsory process on the custodian . . . ." * * * While this provision might be read broadly to authorize the release of biological samples to law enforcement authorities, the record does not disclose that it was intended to be, or actually has been, so used. * * * Absent a persuasive showing that the FRA's testing program is pretextual, we assess the FRA's scheme in light of its obvious administrative purpose. We leave for another day the question whether routine use in criminal prosecutions of evidence obtained pursuant to the administrative scheme would give rise to an inference of pretext, or otherwise impugn the administrative nature of the FRA's program.

b. Subpart C of the regulations, for example, does not permit the exercise of any discretion in choosing the employees who must submit to testing, except in limited circumstances and then only if warranted by objective criteria. Subpart D, while conferring some discretion to choose those who may be required to submit to testing, also imposes specific constraints on the exercise of that discretion. * * * To be sure, some discretion necessarily must be used in determining whether an employee's acts or omissions contributed to the occurrence or severity of an event, but this limited assessment of the objective circumstances surrounding the event does not devolve unbridled discretion upon the supervisor in the field.

* * *

We have recognized, moreover, that the Government's interest in dispensing with the warrant requirement is at its strongest when, as here, "the burden of obtaining a warrant is likely to frustrate the governmental purpose behind the search." * * * Although the metabolites of some drugs remain in the urine for longer periods of time and may enable the FRA to estimate whether the employee was impaired by those drugs at the time of a covered accident, incident, or rule violation, the delay necessary to procure a warrant nevertheless may result in the destruction of valuable evidence.

The Government's need to rely on private railroads to set the testing process in motion also indicates that insistence on a warrant requirement would impede the achievement of the Government's objective. Railroad supervisors, like school officials, see New Jersey v. T.L.O., supra, and hospital administrators, see O'Connor v. Ortega, are not in the business of investigating violations of the criminal laws or enforcing administrative codes, and otherwise have little occasion to become familiar with the intricacies of this Court's Fourth Amendment jurisprudence. "Imposing unwieldy warrant procedures ... upon supervisors, who would otherwise have no reason to be familiar with such procedures, is simply unreasonable."

In sum, imposing a warrant requirement in the present context would add little to the assurances of certainty and regularity already afforded by the regulations, while significantly hindering, and in many cases frustrating, the objectives of the Government's testing program. We do not believe that a warrant is essential to render the intrusions here at issue reasonable under the Fourth Amendment.

C

Our cases indicate that even a search that may be performed without a warrant must be based, as a general matter, on probable cause to believe that the person to be searched has violated the law. When the balance of interests precludes insistence on a showing of probable cause, we have usually required "some quantum of individualized suspicion" before concluding that a search is reasonable. We made it clear, however, that a showing of individualized suspicion is not a constitutional floor, below which a search must be presumed unreasonable. In limited circumstances, where the privacy interests implicated by the search are minimal, and where an important governmental interest furthered by the intrusion would be placed in jeopardy by a requirement of individualized suspicion, a search may be reasonable despite the absence of such suspicion. We believe this is true of the intrusions in question here.

By and large, intrusions on privacy under the FRA regulations are limited. To the extent transportation and like restrictions are necessary to procure the requisite blood, breath, and urine samples for testing, this interference alone is minimal given the employment context in which it takes place. Ordinarily, an employee consents to significant restrictions in his freedom of movement where necessary for his employment, and few are free to come and go as they please during working hours. Any additional interference with a railroad employee's freedom of movement that occurs in the time it takes to procure a blood, breath, or urine sample for testing cannot, by itself, be said to infringe significant privacy interests.

[The Court finds that the blood and breath tests are minimally intrusive.]

A more difficult question is presented by urine tests. Like breath tests, urine tests are not invasive of the body and, under the regulations, may not be used as an occasion for inquiring into private facts unrelated to alcohol or drug use. We recognize, however, that the procedures for collecting the necessary samples, which require employees to perform an excretory function traditionally shielded by great privacy, raise concerns not implicated by blood or breath tests. While we would not characterize these additional privacy concerns as minimal in most contexts, we note that the regulations endeavor to reduce the intrusiveness of the collection process. The regulations do not require that samples be furnished under the direct observation of a monitor, despite the desirability of such a procedure to ensure the integrity of the sample. The sample is also collected in a medical environment, by personnel unrelated to the railroad employer, and is thus not unlike similar procedures encountered often in the context of a regular physical examination.

More importantly, the expectations of privacy of covered employees are diminished by reason of their participation in an industry that is regulated pervasively to ensure safety, a goal dependent, in substantial part, on the health and fitness of covered employees. * * *

We do not suggest, of course, that the interest in bodily security enjoyed by those employed in a regulated industry must always be considered minimal. Here, however, the covered employees have long been a principal focus of regulatory concern. * * * We conclude, therefore, that the testing procedures contemplated by Subparts C and D pose only limited threats to the justifiable expectations of privacy of covered employees.

By contrast, the Government interest in testing without a showing of individualized suspicion is compelling. Employees subject to the tests discharge duties fraught with such risks of injury to others that even a momentary lapse of attention can have disastrous consequences. Much like persons who have routine access to dangerous nuclear power facilities, see, e.g., Rushton v. Nebraska Public Power Dist. 844 F.2d 562, 566 (C.A.8 1988), employees who are subject to testing under the FRA regulations can cause great human loss before any signs of impairment become noticeable to supervisors or others. An impaired employee, the FRA found, will seldom display any outward "signs detectable by the lay person or, in many cases, even the physician." * * * Indeed, while respondents posit that impaired employees might be detected without alcohol or drug testing,[c] the premise of respondents' lawsuit is that even the occurrence of a major calamity will not give rise to a suspicion of impairment with respect to any particular employee.

While no procedure can identify all impaired employees with ease and perfect accuracy, the FRA regulations supply an effective means of deterring employees engaged in safety-sensitive tasks from using controlled substances or alcohol in the first place. * * * By en-

c. Respondents offer a list of "less drastic and equally effective means" of addressing the Government's concerns, including reliance on the private proscriptions already in force, and training supervisory personnel "to effectively detect employees who are impaired by drug or alcohol use without resort to such intrusive procedures as blood and urine tests." We have repeatedly stated, however, that "[t]he reasonableness of any particular government activity does not necessarily or invariably turn on the existence of alternative 'less intrusive' means." It is obvious that "[t]he logic of such elaborate less-restrictive-alternative arguments could raise insuperable barriers to the exercise of virtually all search-and-seizure powers," because judges engaged in post hoc evaluations of government conduct " 'can almost always imagine some alternative means by which the objectives of the [Government] might have been accomplished.' " At bottom, respondents' insistence on less drastic alternatives would require us to second-guess the reasonable conclusions drawn by the FRA after years of investigation and study. This we decline to do.

suring that employees in safety-sensitive positions know they will be tested upon the occurrence of a triggering event, the timing of which no employee can predict with certainty, the regulations significantly increase the deterrent effect of the administrative penalties associated with the prohibited conduct, concomitantly increasing the likelihood that employees will forgo using drugs or alcohol while subject to being called for duty.

The testing procedures contemplated by Subpart C also help railroads obtain invaluable information about the causes of major accidents, and to take appropriate measures to safeguard the general public. Positive test results would point toward drug or alcohol impairment on the part of members of the crew as a possible cause of an accident, and may help to establish whether a particular accident, otherwise not drug related, was made worse by the inability of impaired employees to respond appropriately. Negative test results would likewise furnish invaluable clues, for eliminating drug impairment as a potential cause or contributing factor would help establish the significance of equipment failure, inadequate training, or other potential causes, and suggest a more thorough examination of these alternatives. Tests performed following the rule violations specified in Subpart D likewise can provide valuable information respecting the causes of those transgressions, which the FRA found to involve "the potential for a serious train accident or grave personal injury, or both."

A requirement of particularized suspicion of drug or alcohol use would seriously impede an employer's ability to obtain this information, despite its obvious importance. Experience confirms the FRA's judgment that the scene of a serious rail accident is chaotic. * * * Obtaining evidence that might give rise to the suspicion that a particular employee is impaired, a difficult endeavor in the best of circumstances, is most impracticable in the aftermath of a serious accident. While events following the rule violations that activate the testing authority of Subpart D may be less chaotic, objective indicia of impairment are absent in these instances as well. Indeed, any attempt to gather evidence relating to the possible impairment of particular employees likely would result in the loss or deterioration of the evidence furnished by the tests. * * *

* * *

We conclude that the compelling Government interests served by the FRA's regulations would be significantly hindered if railroads were required to point to specific facts giving rise to a reasonable suspicion of impairment before testing a given employee. In view of our conclusion that, on the present record, the toxicological testing contemplated by the regulations is not an undue infringement on the justifiable expectations of privacy of covered employees, the Government's compelling interests outweigh privacy concerns.

* * *

* * * We hold that the alcohol and drug tests contemplated by Subparts C and D of the FRA's regulations are reasonable within the meaning of the Fourth Amendment. The judgment of the Court of Appeals is accordingly reversed.

Justice Stevens, concurring in part and concurring in the judgment.

In my opinion the public interest in determining the causes of serious railroad accidents adequately supports the validity of the challenged regulations. I am not persuaded, however, that the interest in deterring the use of alcohol or drugs is either necessary or sufficient to justify the searches authorized by these regulations.

I think it a dubious proposition that the regulations significantly deter the use of alcohol and drugs by hours of service employees. Most people—and I would think most railroad employees as well—do not go to work with the expectation that they may be involved in a major accident, particularly one causing such catastrophic results as loss of life or the release of hazardous material requiring an evacuation. Moreover, even if they are conscious of the possibilities that such an accident might occur and that alcohol or drug use might be a contributing factor, if the risk of serious personal injury does not deter their use of these substances, it seems highly unlikely that the additional threat of loss of employment would have any effect on their behavior.

For this reason, I do not join the portions of Part III of the Court's opinion that rely on a deterrence rationale; I do, however, join the balance of the opinion and the Court's judgment.

JUSTICE MARSHALL, with whom JUSTICE BRENNAN joins, dissenting.

* * *

I

The Court today takes its longest step yet toward reading the probable-cause requirement out of the Fourth Amendment. For the fourth time in as many years, a majority holds that a " 'special nee[d], beyond the normal need for law enforcement,' " makes the " 'requirement' " of probable cause " 'impracticable.' " With the recognition of "[t]he Government's interest in regulating the conduct of railroad employees to ensure safety" as such a need, the Court has now permitted "special needs" to displace constitutional text in each of the four categories of searches enumerated in the Fourth Amendment: searches of "persons," "houses," Griffin v. Wisconsin (1987); "papers," O'Connor v. Ortega; and "effects," New Jersey v. T.L.O.

The process by which a constitutional "requirement" can be dispensed with as "impracticable" is an elusive one to me. The Fourth Amendment provides that "[t]he right of the people to be secure in their persons, houses, papers, and effects, against unreasonable searches and seizures, shall not be violated; and no Warrants shall issue, but upon probable cause, supported by Oath or affirmation, and particularly describing the place to be searched, and the persons or things to be seized." The majority's recitation of the Amendment, remarkably, leaves off after the word "violated," but the remainder of the Amendment—the Warrant Clause—is not so easily excised. As this Court has long recognized, the Framers intended the provisions of that Clause—a warrant and probable cause—to "provide the yardstick against which official searches and seizures are to be measured." Without the content which those provisions give to the Fourth Amendment's overarching command that searches and seizures be "reasonable," the Amendment lies virtually devoid of meaning, subject to whatever content shifting judicial majorities, concerned about the problems of the day, choose to give to that supple term. Constitutional requirements like probable cause are not fair-weather friends, present when advantageous, conveniently absent when "special needs" make them seem not.

Until recently, an unbroken line of cases had recognized probable cause as an indispensable prerequisite for a full-scale search, regardless of whether such a search was conducted pursuant to a warrant or under one of the recognized exceptions to the warrant requirement. Only where the Government action in question had a "substantially less intrusive" impact on privacy, and thus clearly fell short of a full-scale search, did we relax the probable-cause standard. Even in this class of cases, we almost always required the Government to show some individualized suspicion to justify the search.[d] The few searches which we upheld in the absence of individualized justification were routinized, fleeting, and nonintrusive encounters conducted pursuant to regulatory programs which entailed no contact with the person.[e]

In the four years since this Court, in *T.L.O.,* first began recognizing "special needs" exceptions to the Fourth Amendment, the clarity of Fourth Amendment doctrine has been badly distorted, as the Court has eclipsed the probable-cause requirement in a patchwork quilt of settings: public school principals' searches of students' belongings, *T.L.O.;* public employers' searches of employees' desks, *O'Connor;* and probation officers' searches of probationers' homes, *Griffin.*[f] Tellingly, each time the Court has found that "special needs" counseled ignoring the literal requirements of the Fourth Amendment for such full-scale searches in favor of a formless and unguided "reasonableness" balancing inquiry, it has concluded that the search in question satisfied that test. I have joined dissenting opinions in each of these cases, protesting the "jettison[ing of] ... the only standard that finds support in the text of the Fourth Amendment" and predicting that the majority's "Rohrschach-like 'balancing test' " portended "a dangerous weakening of the purpose of the Fourth Amendment to protect the privacy and security of our citizens." *T.L.O.* (opinion of Brennan, J.).

The majority's decision today bears out that prophecy. After determining that the Fourth Amendment applies to the FRA's testing regime, the majority embarks on an extended inquiry into whether that regime is "reasonable," an inquiry in which it balances " 'all of the circumstances surrounding the search or seizure and the nature of the search or seizure itself.' " The result is "special needs" balancing analysis' deepest incursion yet into the core protections of the Fourth Amendment. Until today, it was conceivable that, when a Government search was aimed at a person and not simply the person's possessions, balancing analysis had no place. No longer: with nary a word of explanation or acknowledgment of the novelty of its approach, the majority extends the "special needs" framework to a regulation involving compulsory blood withdrawal and urinary excretion, and chemical testing of the bodily fluids collected through these procedures. And until today, it was conceivable that a prerequisite for surviving "special needs" analysis was the existence of individualized suspicion. No longer: in contrast to the searches in *T.L.O., O'Connor,* and *Griffin,* which were supported by individualized evidence suggesting the culpability of the persons whose property was searched,[g] the regu-

d. The first, and leading, case of a minimally intrusive search held valid when based on suspicion short of probable cause is Terry v. Ohio, where we held that a police officer who observes unusual conduct suggesting criminal activity by persons he reasonably suspects are armed and presently dangerous may "conduct a carefully limited search of the outer clothing of such persons."

e. See, e.g., United States v. Martinez–Fuerte, 428 U.S. 543 (brief interrogative stop at permanent border checkpoint to ascertain motorist's residence status); Camara v. Municipal Court of San Francisco (routine annual inspection by city housing department).

f. The "special needs" the Court invoked to justify abrogating the probable-cause requirement were, in New Jersey v. T.L.O., "the substantial need of teachers and administrators for freedom to maintain order in the schools"; in O'Connor v. Ortega, "the efficient and proper operation of the workplace"; and in Griffin v. Wisconsin, the need to preserve "the deterrent effect of the supervisory arrangement" of probation.

g. See *T.L.O.* (teacher's report that student had been smoking provided reasonable suspicion that purse contained cigarettes); *O'Connor* (charges of specific financial improprieties gave employer individualized suspicion of mis-

latory regime upheld today requires the postaccident collection and testing of the blood and urine of *all* covered employees—even if every member of this group gives every indication of sobriety and attentiveness.

In widening the "special needs" exception to probable cause to authorize searches of the human body unsupported by *any* evidence of wrongdoing, the majority today completes the process begun in T.L.O. of eliminating altogether the probable-cause requirement for civil searches—those undertaken for reasons "beyond the normal need for law enforcement." In its place, the majority substitutes a manipulable balancing inquiry under which, upon the mere assertion of a "special need," even the deepest dignitary and privacy interests become vulnerable to governmental incursion. By its terms, however, the Fourth Amendment—unlike the Fifth and Sixth—does not confine its protections to either criminal or civil actions. Instead, it protects generally "[t]he right of the people to be secure." [h]

The fact is that the malleable "special needs" balancing approach can be justified only on the basis of the policy results it allows the majority to reach. * * * There is no drug exception to the Constitution, any more than there is a communism exception or an exception for other real or imagined sources of domestic unrest. Because abandoning the explicit protections of the Fourth Amendment seriously imperils "the right to be let alone—the most comprehensive of rights and the right most valued by civilized men," Olmstead v. United States, 277 US 438, 478 (Brandeis, J., dissenting), I reject the majority's "special needs" rationale as unprincipled and dangerous.

II

* * *

Our decisions in the regulatory search area refute the suggestion that the heavy regulation of the railroad industry eclipses workers' rights under the Fourth Amendment to insist upon a showing of probable cause when their bodily fluids are being extracted. This line of cases has exclusively involved searches of employer *property,* * * *. Never have we intimated that regulatory searches reduce employees' rights of privacy in their *persons.* * * * These rights mean little indeed if, having passed through these portals, an individual may remain subject to a suspicionless search of his person justified solely on the grounds that the Government already is permitted to conduct a search of the inanimate contents of the surrounding area.

* * *

III

Even accepting the majority's view that the FRA's collection and testing program is appropriately analyzed under a multifactor balancing test, and not under the literal terms of the Fourth Amendment, I would still find the program invalid. The benefits of suspicionless blood and urine testing are far outstripped by the costs imposed on personal liberty by such sweeping searches. Only by erroneously deriding as "minimal" the privacy and dignity interests at stake, and by uncritically

conduct by employee); *Griffin* (tip to police officer that probationer was storing guns in his apartment provided reasonable suspicion).

h. That the Fourth Amendment applies equally to criminal and civil searches was emphasized, ironically enough, in the portion of T.L.O. holding the Fourth Amendment applicable to schoolhouse searches. The malleability of "special needs" balancing thus could not be clearer: the majority endorses the applicability of the Fourth Amendment to civil searches in determining whether a search has taken place, but then wholly ignores it in the subsequent inquiry into the validity of that search.

inflating the likely efficacy of the FRA's testing program, does the majority strike a different balance.

* * * I find nothing minimal about the intrusion on individual liberty that occurs whenever the Government forcibly draws and analyzes a person's blood and urine. Several aspects of the FRA's testing program exacerbate the intrusiveness of these procedures. Most strikingly, the agency's regulations not only do not forbid, but, in fact, appear to invite criminal prosecutors to obtain the blood and urine samples drawn by the FRA and use them as the basis of criminal investigations and trials. This is an unprecedented invitation, leaving open the possibility of criminal prosecutions based on suspicionless searches of the human body.

* * * [T]he majority's refusal to restrict the release of test results casts considerable doubt on the conceptual basis of its decision—that the "special need" of railway safety is one "beyond the normal need for law enforcement."

* * *

The majority's trivialization of the intrusions on worker privacy posed by the FRA's testing program is matched at the other extreme by its blind acceptance of the Government's assertion that testing will "dete[r] employees engaged in safety-sensitive tasks from using controlled substances or alcohol," and "help railroads obtain invaluable information about the causes of major accidents." With respect, first, to deterrence, it is simply implausible that testing employees *after* major accidents occur will appreciably discourage them from using drugs or alcohol. * * * Under the majority's deterrence rationale, people who skip school or work to spend a sunny day at the zoo will not taunt the lions because their truancy or absenteeism might be discovered in the event they are mauled. It is, of course, the fear of the accident, not the fear of a postaccident revelation, that deters. * * *

The poverty of the majority's deterrence rationale leaves the Government's interest in diagnosing the causes of major accidents as the sole remaining justification for the FRA's testing program. I do not denigrate this interest, but it seems a slender thread from which to hang such an intrusive program, particularly given that the knowledge that one or more workers were impaired at the time of an accident falls far short of proving that substance abuse caused or exacerbated that accident. Some corroborative evidence is needed: witness or co-worker accounts of a worker's misfeasance, or at least indications that the cause of the accident was within a worker's area of responsibility. Such particularized facts are, of course, the very essence of the individualized suspicion requirement which the respondent railroad workers urge, and which the Court of Appeals found to "pos[e] no insuperable burden on the government." * * *

Note

In National Treasury Employees Union v. Von Raab, 489 U.S. 656 (1989), a case decided the same day as *Skinner,* the Court upheld compelled urinalysis of certain Customs Service employees. Drug tests were made a condition of obtaining employment for three types of positions in the Customs Service: those involving drug interdiction, those requiring the employee to carry a firearm, and those in which the employee would handle "classified documents." The plan calls for urinalysis to be monitored by an independent contractor, at a time agreed to by the employee who sought a covered position. The employee is allowed to produce the sample privately, but to protect against adulteration, "a monitor of the same sex as the employee remains close at hand to listen for the normal sounds of urination." Customs employees who test positive for drugs and who can offer no satisfactory explanation are subject to dismissal from the Service. However, unlike the regulations in *Skinner,* the Customs Service regulations specifically provide that the testing results cannot be turned over to a criminal prosecutor without the employee's consent.

Justice Kennedy again wrote the opinion for the Court. He found that the drug-testing served special needs beyond criminal law enforcement. This question was easier than the same question presented in *Skinner,* since the plan in *Von Raab* prohibited use of the test results in a criminal prosecution.

Balancing the state and individual interests, Justice Kennedy concluded that a warrant was not required for the testing. Again, this issue was easier to resolve than in *Skinner,* since the event which triggered the testing in *Von Raab* could admit of no discretion. Justice Kennedy stated as follows:

> The process becomes automatic when the employee elects to apply for, and thereafter pursue, a covered position. Because the Service does not make a discretionary determination to search based on a judgment that certain conditions are present, there are simply no special facts for a neutral magistrate to evaluate.

The Court found suspicionless testing was reasonable as applied to two of the three covered types of employees—those involved in drug interdiction and those carrying handguns. Justice Kennedy noted that "the Government has a compelling interest in ensuring that front-line personnel are physically fit, and have unimpeachable integrity and judgment," and that the public interest "likewise demands effective measures to prevent the promotion of drug users to positions that require the incumbent to carry a firearm." The majority asserted that these two classes of employees had a diminished expectation of privacy, because the positions depended uniquely on the employees' "judgment and dexterity." Justice Kennedy also emphasized that the testing procedures were designed to minimize the intrusion involved, to the extent possible without sacrificing the reliability of the test.

The most difficult issue for the majority was that the Customs Service had implemented the drug-testing program even though the Commissioner admitted that there was no drug problem among Customs employees. This was unlike the situation in *Skinner,* where the drug problem among railroad employees, and the risk therefrom, was well-documented. Those who challenged the plan in *Von Raab* argued that suspicionless drug-testing was unreasonable unless it could be justified as responsive to and effective against a documented drug problem. Justice Kennedy rejected this argument in the following analysis:

> Petitioners' * * * contention evinces an unduly narrow view of the context in which the Service's testing program was implemented. Petitioners do not dispute, nor can there be doubt, that drug abuse is one of the most serious problems confronting our society today. There is little reason to believe that American workplaces are immune from this pervasive social problem, as is amply illustrated by our decision in *Railway Labor Executives.* Detecting drug impairment on the part of employees can be a difficult task, especially where, as here, it is not feasible to subject employees and their work product to the kind of day-to-day scrutiny that is the norm in more traditional office environments. Indeed, the almost unique mission of the Service gives the Government a compelling interest in ensuring that many of these covered employees do not use drugs even off duty, for such use creates risks of bribery and blackmail

against which the Government is entitled to guard. In light of the extraordinary safety and national security hazards that would attend the promotion of drug users to positions that require the carrying of firearms or the interdiction of controlled substances, the Service's policy of deterring drug users from seeking such promotions cannot be deemed unreasonable.

The mere circumstance that all but a few of the employees tested are entirely innocent of wrongdoing does not impugn the program's validity. The same is likely to be true of householders who are required to submit to suspicionless housing code inspections, see Camara v. Municipal Court of San Francisco, and of motorists who are stopped at the checkpoints we approved in United States v. Martinez–Fuerte, 428 U.S. 543 (1976). The Service's program is designed to prevent the promotion of drug users to sensitive positions as much as it is designed to detect those employees who use drugs. Where, as here, the possible harm against which the Government seeks to guard is substantial, the need to prevent its occurrence furnishes an ample justification for reasonable searches calculated to advance the Government's goal.

In a footnote, Justice Kennedy compared suspicionless drug-testing to suspicionless magnetometer searches at airports.

The point is well illustrated also by the Federal Government's practice of requiring the search of all passengers seeking to board commercial airliners, as well as the search of their carry-on luggage, without any basis for suspecting any particular passenger of an untoward motive. Applying our precedents dealing with administrative searches, the lower courts that have considered the question have consistently concluded that such searches are reasonable under the Fourth Amendment. As Judge Friendly explained in a leading case upholding such searches:

> "When the risk is the jeopardy to hundreds of human lives and millions of dollars of property inherent in the pirating or blowing up of a large airplane, that danger *alone* meets the test of reasonableness, so long as the search is conducted in good faith for the purpose of preventing hijacking or like damage and with reasonable scope and the passenger has been given advance notice of his liability to such a search so that he can avoid it by choosing not to travel by air." United States v. Edwards, 498 F.2d 496, 500 (C.A.2 1974) (emphasis in original).

See also United States v. Skipwith, 482 F.2d 1272, 1275–1276 (C.A.5 1973); United States v. Davis, 482 F.2d 893, 907–912 (C.A.9 1973). It is true * * * that these air piracy precautions were adopted in response to an observable national and international hijacking crisis. Yet we would not suppose that, if the validity of these searches be conceded, the Government would be precluded from conducting them absent a demonstration of danger as to any particular airport or airline. It is sufficient that the Government have a compelling interest in preventing an otherwise pervasive societal problem from spreading to the particular context.

Nor would we think, in view of the obvious deterrent purpose of these searches, that the validity of the Government's airport screening program necessarily turns on whether significant numbers of putative air pirates are actually discovered by the searches conducted under the program. In the 15 years the program has been in effect, more than 9.5 *billion* persons have been screened, and over 10 *billion* pieces of luggage have been inspected. By far the overwhelming majority of those persons who have been searched, like Customs employees who have been tested under the Service's drug-screening scheme, have proved entirely innocent—only 42,000 firearms have been detected during the same period. When the Government's interest lies in deterring highly hazardous conduct, a low incidence of such conduct, far from impugning the validity of the scheme for implementing this interest, is more logically viewed as a hallmark of success.

The Court found itself unable to assess the reasonableness of suspicionless testing as applied to the third category of employees, those handling classified documents. The Court explained as follows:

> It is not clear * * * whether the category defined by the Service's testing directive encompasses only those Customs employees likely to gain access to sensitive information. Employees who are tested under the Service's scheme include those holding such diverse positions as "Accountant," "Accounting Technician," "Animal Caretaker," "Attorney (All)," "Baggage Clerk," "Co-op Student (All)," "Electric Equipment Repairer," "Mail Clerk/Assistant," and "Messenger." * * * [I]t is not evident that those occupying these positions are likely to gain access to sensitive information, and this apparent discrepancy raises in our minds the question whether the Service has defined this category of employees more broadly than is necessary to meet the purposes of the Commissioner's directive.
>
> * * * Upon remand the Court of Appeals should examine the criteria used by the Service in determining what materials are classified and in deciding whom to test under this rubric. In assessing the reasonableness of requiring tests of these employees, the court should also consider pertinent information bearing upon the employees' privacy expectations, as well as the supervision to which these employees are already subject.

Justice Marshall, joined by Justice Brennan, dissented for the reasons stated in *Skinner*. Justice Scalia, joined by Justice Stevens, both of whom found suspicionless drug-testing to be reasonable in *Skinner*, dissented in *Von Raab*. Justice Scalia explained his differing votes in the two cases as follows:

> I joined the Court's opinion [in *Skinner*] because the demonstrated frequency of drug and alcohol use by the targeted class of employees, and the demonstrated connection between such use and grave harm, rendered the search a reasonable means of protecting society. I decline to join the Court's opinion in the present case because neither frequency of use nor connection to harm is demonstrated or even likely. In my view the Customs Service rules are a kind of immolation of privacy and human dignity in symbolic opposition to drug use.

Justice Scalia rejected the majority's generalization that no American workplace is free from the drug problem. He responded that such a generalization could perhaps suffice "if the workplace at issue could produce such catastrophic social harm that no risk whatever is tolerable—the secured areas of a nuclear power plant for example." Justice Scalia noted that suspicionless testing for nuclear power plant employees in sensitive jobs had been upheld even without a showing of a drug problem. See Rushton v. Nebraska Public Power District, 844 F.2d 562 (8th Cir.1988). See also Thomson v. Marsh, 884 F.2d 113 (4th Cir.1989) (suspicionless testing of personnel in chemical weapons plant upheld). He responded, however, that if the majority considered that the threat posed by drug-addicted Customs officials was comparable to that found in *Rushton*, "then the Fourth Amendment has become frail protection indeed." He noted that this reasoning would extend approval of suspicionless drug testing to vast numbers of public employees:

> Logically, of course, if those who carry guns can be treated in this fashion, so can all others whose work, if performed under the influence of drugs, may endanger others—automobile drivers, operators of other potentially dangerous equipment, construction workers, school crossing guards. A similarly broad scope attaches to the Court's approval of drug testing for those with access to "sensitive information." * * * Since drug use is not a particular problem in the Customs Service, employees throughout the government are no less likely to violate the public trust by taking bribes to feed their drug habit, or by yielding to blackmail. * * *
>
> I do not believe for a minute that the driving force behind these drug-testing rules was any of the feeble justifications * * * accepted by the Court. The only plausible explanation, in my view, is what the Commissioner himself offered in the concluding sentence of his memorandum to Customs Service employees announcing the program: "Implementation of the drug screening program would set an important example in our country's struggle with this most serious threat to our national health and security." * * * What better way to show that the Government is serious about its "war on drugs" than to subject its employees on the front line of that war to this invasion of their privacy and affront to their dignity? * * * I think it obvious that this justification is unacceptable; that the impairment of individual liberties cannot be the means of making a point; that symbolism, even symbolism for so worthy a cause as the abolition of unlawful drugs, cannot validate an otherwise unreasonable search.

* * *

Does *Von Raab* mean, as Justice Scalia implies, that all public employees can be subject to suspicionless drug testing? In light of the remand in *Von Raab* to determine the state interest in testing employees with access to classified information, lower courts have not read *Von Raab* so broadly. See Harmon v. Thornburgh, 878 F.2d 484 (D.C.Cir.1989), where the court upheld suspicionless drug-testing of Justice Department employees with top secret security clearances, but required reasonable suspicion as to others such as attorneys responsible for conducting grand jury hearings. With respect to the latter category, the court found that the risk to the public from drug use by such attorneys was too remote to justify suspicionless testing. See also National Federation of Federal Employees v. Cheney, 884 F.2d 603 (D.C.Cir.1989), where the same court again distinguished between employees who could be subject to suspicionless testing and those who could not. Civilian drug counselors working for the Defense Department were held properly subject to suspicionless testing, since drug use by them was found completely antithetical to their job, and contrary to the strong governmental interest in rehabilitating army personnel with drug problems. But the court held that civilian lab technicians who conducted the drug tests could not themselves be tested in the absence of reasonable suspicion. The court reasoned that their drug usage could be detected, since they worked in an office context, and that the consequences of drug use by such personnel were not as serious as those invoked by the Supreme Court in *Skinner* and *Von Raab.* Do you agree? Would the court have allowed suspicionless testing of the lab technicians if they had been military, instead of civilian, personnel?

Assume that the Secretary of the Interior promulgates a random drug testing program, which imposes suspicionless testing on, among others, switchboard operators and mail handlers. Presumably the plan is unreasonable. But what if the plan imposed such testing of these employees upon reasonable suspicion—not probable cause—of drug use? Would the plan then be reasonable?

In evaluating the above cases, consider how the courts have justified a search on reasonable suspicion rather than probable cause, or on no suspicion at all rather than reasonable suspicion. The lesser standard of proof is ordinarily justified on one or both of the following grounds: (1) a higher standard of proof would be too difficult to satisfy because suspicious facts would be too difficult to detect (as in *Von Raab,* where the Customs officials were out in the field rather than in the office); (2) waiting for the higher standard of proof to develop would itself be deleterious to the state interest (because by then, for instance, the Customs agent with a gun could already have harmed someone), thus a lower standard of proof is required to "nip the problem in the bud." Are either of these justifications persuasive? If so, have they been properly applied to the facts of the above cases?

Can suspicionless, mandatory testing for AIDS ever be considered reasonable? Does AIDS testing raise different privacy concerns than drug-testing? In Glover v. Eastern Nebraska Community Office of Retardation, 867 F.2d 461 (8th Cir.1989), the court invalidated suspicionless AIDS testing of employees who cared for institutionalized mental patients. The state justified the plan on the ground that these patients often exhibited aggressive behavior such as biting, and therefore risked contracting AIDS from the bitten employee. The court found that the risk of the patients contracting AIDS from the employees was "extraordinarily low, theoretical, and approaches zero." But after *Von Raab,* and its discussion of the airport magnetometer cases, is the relevant question the likelihood of harm, or the gravity of harm if it occurs? In Dunn v. White, 880 F.2d 1188 (10th Cir.1989), the court upheld suspicionless AIDS testing of prisoners, even though no showing was made that there was an AIDS problem in the prison. Can *Glover* and *Dunn* be reconciled? See also Love v. Superior Court, 226 Cal.App.3d 736, 276 Cal.Rptr. 660 (1990), upholding suspicionless AIDS testing of persons convicted of soliciting an act of prostitution.

4. *Roadblocks and Suspicionless Seizures*

In Delaware v. Prouse, 440 U.S. 648 (1979), the Court held that an officer could not, in the absence of reasonable suspicion, stop an automobile and detain the driver in order to check his license and registration. The officer in *Prouse* made an ad hoc, suspicionless stop, and the Court expressed its concern with "the unconstrained exercise of discretion." The Court noted that such an ad hoc stop was not "a sufficiently productive mechanism to justify the intrusion" and that there were other, better ways to effectuate the state interest in vehicle registration and safety, such as yearly inspections. The majority emphasized that it was not foreclosing as one possible alternative the "questioning of all oncoming traffic at roadblock-type stops." In response to the majority's roadblock alternative, Justice Rehnquist argued in dissent that the majority had "elevated the adage 'misery loves company' to a novel role in Fourth Amendment jurisprudence." Why is it better to stop everybody rather than anybody?

The dictum in *Prouse* was supported by the Court's earlier decision in United States v. Martinez—Fuerte, 428 U.S. 543 (1976). In that case, the Court, invoking *Terry* principles, approved suspicionless stops at permanent checkpoints removed from the border. The Court emphasized that suspicionless stops were necessary to implement the state interest in regulating the flow of illegal aliens, and noted that the fixed checkpoint was minimally intrusive. Justice Powell, writing for the Court, argued that motorists are not surprised by a fixed checkpoint; that such checkpoints limit the discretion of the officer; and that "the location of a fixed checkpoint is not chosen by officers in the field, but by officials responsible for making overall decisions as to the most effective allocation of limited enforcement resources." Justice Powell stressed that it was permissible to dispense with particularized suspicion because "we deal neither with searches nor with the sanctuary of private dwellings."

The Court upheld suspicionless stops at sobriety checkpoints in Michigan Department of State Police v. Sitz, 110 S.Ct. 2481 (1990). The Michigan program allowed checkpoints to be set up by officers in the field according to a list of considerations including "safety of the location," "minimum inconvenience for the driver," and available space "to pull the vehicle off the traveled portion of the roadway for further inquiry if necessary." Under the program, all motorists passing through the checkpoint would be stopped and briefly examined for signs of intoxication. If such signs were detected, the motorist would be directed to another area where license and registration would be checked, and further sobriety tests would be conducted if warranted. The only checkpoint operated under the program resulted in a stop of 126 vehicles, and one arrest for drunk driving. The challenge in the Supreme Court focussed solely on the original detention and associated preliminary investigation of motorists.

Chief Justice Rehnquist's opinion for five members of the Court relied heavily on *Martinez—Fuerte,* and applied the "misery loves company" rationale that then-Justice Rehnquist had criticized in *Prouse.*

Respondents in *Sitz* argued that a reasonableness balancing approach could not be employed to evaluate sobriety checkpoints, since there was no special interest beyond criminal law enforcement at stake. They argued that sobriety checkpoints are solely used to enforce criminal laws prohibiting drunk driving.

The majority responded that a special need beyond criminal law enforcement was not required to support reasonableness balancing for stops at fixed checkpoints. The Chief Justice stated that the special needs analysis of *Skinner* et al. "was in no way designed to repudiate our prior cases dealing with police stops." The Court relied on the *Terry* line of cases. Of course, *Terry* also employs reasonableness balancing, but on grounds different from those employed in the "special needs" cases: *Terry* allows a stop upon less than probable cause, because the nature of the intrusion is limited. *Martinez—Fuerte* took *Terry* one step further and allowed a stop without suspicion, given the limited intrusiveness of and controlled discretion attendant to fixed checkpoints. In contrast, the line of "special needs" cases allows a seizure and search for evidence, but the motive of the search is to effectuate a special need beyond criminal law enforcement.

Balancing the interests of the state and the individual, the Chief Justice quoted from *Martinez—Fuerte,* and concluded that the intrusiveness of a sobriety checkpoint was extremely limited:

> At traffic checkpoints the motorist can see that other vehicles are being stopped, he can see visible signs of the officers' authority, and he is much less likely to be frightened or annoyed by the intrusion. * * * Here, checkpoints

are selected pursuant to the guidelines, and uniformed police officers stop every approaching vehicle. The intrusion resulting from the brief stop at the sobriety checkpoint is for constitutional purposes indistinguishable from the checkpoint stops we upheld in *Martinez—Fuerte.*

Against this limited intrusion, the Court balanced the State's heavy interest in eradicating drunken driving. Chief Justice Rehnquist rejected the argument that sobriety checkpoints did not effectively advance this undeniable state interest. He stated that references to effectiveness of searches and seizures in previous cases, such as *Prouse,* were not intended "to transfer from politically accountable officials to the courts the decision as to which among reasonable alternative law enforcement techniques should be employed to deal with a serious public danger." The Court concluded that "the choice among such reasonable alternatives remains with the government officials who have a unique understanding of, and a responsibility for, limited public resources." The majority faulted the lower court for its "searching examination" of the effectiveness of sobriety checkpoints. Justice Blackmun wrote a short opinion concurring in the judgment.

Justice Brennan wrote a dissenting opinion joined by Justice Marshall. Justice Brennan argued that "some level of individualized suspicion is a core component of the protection the Fourth Amendment provides against arbitrary government action," and that the majority's allowance of suspicionless detentions "potentially subjects the general public to arbitrary or harassing conduct by the police."

Justice Stevens wrote a dissenting opinion joined in large part by Justices Brennan and Marshall. Justice Stevens complained that the Court had misapplied the reasonableness balancing test:

> The Court overvalues the law enforcement interest in using sobriety checkpoints, undervalues the citizen's interest in freedom from random, unannounced investigatory seizures, and mistakenly assumes that there is virtually no difference between a routine stop at a permanent, fixed checkpoint and a surprise stop at a sobriety checkpoint.

Justice Stevens found the majority's reliance on *Martinez—Fuerte* to be unpersuasive. He argued that unlike the permanent, fixed checkpoint, the police operating a sobriety checkpoint "have extremely broad discretion in determining the exact timing and placement of the roadblock." Moreover, a temporary checkpoint is more intrusive because of the element of surprise that it presents:

> A driver who discovers an unexpected checkpoint on a familiar local road will be startled and distressed. She may infer, correctly, that the checkpoint is not simply 'business as usual,' and may likewise infer, again correctly, that the police have made a discretionary decision to focus their law enforcement efforts upon her and others who pass the chosen point.

Finally, Justice Stevens criticized the majority's determination that the sobriety checkpoint was sufficiently effective to outweigh its intrusiveness:

> The Court's analysis of this issue resembles a business decision that measures profits by counting gross receipts and ignoring expenses * * * [S]obriety checkpoints result in the arrest of a fraction of one percent of the drivers who are stopped but there is absolutely no evidence that this figure represents

any increase over the number of arrests that would have been made by using the same law enforcement resources in conventional patrols.

Should it make a difference under the Fourth Amendment whether sobriety checkpoints result in few arrests or many? Suppose only one person is arrested among two thousand who are stopped. Are the two thousand stops reasonable? Does *Sitz* mean that so long as the state can articulate an interest furthered by a seizure, the court is not allowed to investigate whether the intrusions actually further the expressed interest?

If *Martinez—Fuerte* is the correct analogy, can *Sitz* stand for the proposition that daily stops are permissible at various locations? Can *Martinez—Fuerte* justify roving or moveable checkpoints? If so, who decides where these checkpoints should be placed? Does it make a difference that the location of the checkpoint in *Martinez—Fuerte* was chosen by high level officials rather than by officers in the field? Do the considerations set forth in the Michigan program restrict police discretion or promote it?

After *Sitz,* is there anything wrong with the following scenario? Officers established a license and registration checkpoint on a road known for drug-trafficking. They stopped all oncoming traffic. When they stopped Morales–Zamora's car to check his license and registration, they sent a narcotics-detecting dog, which happened to be present at the registration checkpoint, around the car. The dog gave a positive alert, so the officers conducted a warrantless search of the car, and seized narcotics. The court in United States v. Morales—Zamora, 914 F.2d 200 (10th Cir.1990), held that the evidence was legally obtained. The checkpoint was valid after *Sitz,* without regard to its placement or its degree of success in uncovering registration violations. The dog sniff was not a search under United States v. Place (page 45; the positive alert created probable cause to search, and the warrantless search of the car upon probable cause was permissible under the automobile exception. The court recognized that the officers may have used the registration checkpoint as a pretext, but under the predominant view (see United States v. Causey, page 235) a search or seizure cannot be invalidated as pretextual where the officer has the objective justification to conduct it.

At least one court after *Sitz* has sought to limit the discretion of field officers in choosing checkpoint sites. In Hall v. Commonwealth, 406 S.E.2d 674 (Va.App.1991), the court held invalid a plan which gave the field officer discretion to place a checkpoint in any one of 54 pre-approved sites in a county, at any time. The court noted that an officer who had already decided to stop a particular person "could do so within these guidelines by ascertaining at what time that person would travel through a particular intersection and set up a roadblock accordingly." Accepting that the conduct described is arbitrary and pretextual, does that make any difference after *Sitz* and the pretext cases?

It is important to note that *Sitz* is a *seizure* case. It does not allow a search for law enforcement purposes on less than probable cause. The Court has allowed searches on less than probable cause in only two circumstances: (1) a search for weapons and dangerous people, not evidence, made for purposes of self-protection (*Terry*); and (2) a search for evidence, where there are special needs beyond criminal law enforcement at stake (*Von Raab*). In contrast, a search by law enforcement officers for evidence of criminal activity has been held not subject to reasonableness balancing, and must be supported by probable cause. In Arizona v. Hicks (page 211) the Court specifically rejected a reasonableness balancing approach to a search for evidence by law enforcement officials.

5. *Inventory Searches*

By now it should be apparent that the line between regulatory searches and law enforcement searches is often blurred. Another example of this overlap occurs with inventory searches. In most jurisdictions it is standard procedure for the police to inventory the contents of automobiles being held in their custody. An inventory search has nothing to do with probable cause, and *ostensibly,* is unrelated to criminal investigation of any kind. Rather it is justified by interests in protecting the owner's property while it is in police custody, protecting the police against claims for lost or stolen property, and protecting both the police and the public from danger.

The Supreme Court has discussed these warrantless searches in several instances. In Cady v. Dombrowski, 413 U.S. 433 (1973), the Court approved the search of a car towed to a private garage after an accident which resulted in the hospitalization of the driver. The driver was a Chicago policeman, and the officer who conducted the search testified that he was looking for the driver's service revolver, which he believed Chicago policemen were required to carry at all times. In the course of the search, blood-stained garments were discovered in the trunk, which were later used to convict the defendant of murder. In a 5–4 decision, Justice Rehnquist found that the initial intrusion to search for the gun was reasonable as a "community caretaking function," to protect the public from the possibility that it would fall into the hands of vandals. Therefore, the seizure of evidence found in plain view was also justified. (Note that this search could not have been justified under *Carroll* even though there was reasonable cause to believe that the car contained a revolver. The defendant was under arrest for drunk driving, and since he was permitted to carry a gun, the search could not be explained as a search for evidence of crime or contraband.)

Two years later, the Court addressed the issue of whether the warrantless inventory search of a car impounded for a parking violation was valid under the Fourth Amendment. In South Dakota v. Opperman, 428 U.S. 364 (1976), the Court per Chief Justice Burger, upheld such a search when conducted pursuant to standard police procedures, a factor which would tend to ensure that the intrusion was neither arbitrary nor beyond the scope necessary to carry out the caretaking function of the police. The majority found the search reasonable when motivated by a desire to protect valuables, which could be seen in plain view on the dashboard. The facts that the car had to be forcibly unlocked in order to conduct the protective inventory, and that the search included the contents of a closed glove compartment, which revealed a bag of marijuana, did not make the search unreasonable, since standard police procedures were being followed. As with other special needs cases, the Court balanced the state interest against the nature of the intrusion to determine whether inventory searches were reasonable. The Court found that inventory searches furthered three important state interests—protection of the police department from false property claims, protection of the property interests of the owner of the car, and protection of the public from dangerous items which may be concealed in cars. The majority found that these interests outweighed the owner's privacy interests, especially given the diminished expectation of privacy in automobiles.

Justice Powell, in a concurring opinion, explained why the warrant requirement is inapposite where inventory searches conducted pursuant to departmental regulations are involved. First, there are no special facts for a neutral magistrate to evaluate so as to determine whether probable cause exists, since inventory searches are non-criminal in nature. Second, there is no danger of discretionary searches or hindsight justifications when searches are conducted in accordance with standard procedure. Third, the danger of arbitrariness, inherent in other administrative searches where warrants are now required, is not present where routine searches of all impounded cars are conducted.

Justice Marshall—in a dissent joined by Justices Brennan and Stewart, and in part by Justice White—critically analyzed the Court's asserted justifications for allowing inventory searches, and found them inadequate.

Justice Marshall examined the "protective needs" supposedly advanced by inventories. He found the safety rationale, i.e., that such searches protected the police from dangerous items concealed in cars kept in custody, and the public from vandals who might find firearms or contraband, to be unconvincing. Such an "undifferentiated possibility of harm" cannot serve as a basis for an inventory, except where specific circumstances indicate the possibility of a particular danger. Furthermore, this asserted rationale would justify the search of all automobiles, whether impounded or not, located in a similar area.

Next, Justice Marshall considered the assertion that inventories are necessary to protect the police against lost property claims. In this case, the concern was irrelevant since South Dakota law absolved police of responsibility as "gratuitous depositors" beyond inventorying objects in plain view and locking the car. Furthermore, an inventory does not discourage false claims that an item was stolen prior to it, or was intentionally omitted from police records. Nor does it ensure that such police misconduct did not in fact occur. Thus, the contention that an inventory protects the owner's valuables was found debatable.

Justice Marshall concluded that the Fourth Amendment does not permit routine searches of impounded cars absent specific consent. He discredited the assumption that, since inventories are, hypothetically, for the benefit of the owner, the law may presume consent. Even if most persons would want a protective inventory of their cars to be conducted upon impoundment, that fact would not be sufficient to justify routine searches, since even a majority lacks authority to consent to the search of all cars in order to assure the search of theirs. In the absence of explicit consent, Justice Marshall argued that two requirements must be met:

> * * * First, there must be specific cause to believe that a search of the scope to be undertaken is necessary in order to preserve the integrity of particular valuable property threatened by the impoundment. * * * Second, even where a search might be appropriate, such an intrusion may only follow the exhaustion and failure of reasonable efforts under the circumstances to identify and reach the owner of the property in order to facilitate alternative

means of security or to obtain his consent to the search, for in this context the right to refuse the search remains with the owner.

The Supreme Court relied on South Dakota v. Opperman in Illinois v. Lafayette, 462 U.S. 640 (1983), as it upheld the inventory search at the police station of a shoulder bag belonging to a man arrested for disturbing the peace. The search uncovered drugs. Chief Justice Burger reasoned that the government's interests in an inventory search at the stationhouse "may in some circumstances be even greater that those supporting a search incident to arrest" and that police conduct that might be embarrassingly intrusive on the street could be handled privately at the stationhouse. He observed that police need to protect the property of arrested persons, to protect themselves from claims of theft or damage to property, and to remove dangerous instrumentalities from arrestees.

The lower court in *Lafayette* had found the inventory search unreasonable on the ground that preservation of the property could have been achieved by a less intrusive manner, such as by storing the bag rather than investigating its contents. Chief Justice Burger rejected this reasoning, stating as follows:

> [T]he real question is not what 'could have been achieved,' but whether the Fourth Amendment *requires* such steps; it is not our function to write a manual on administering routine, neutral procedures of the stationhouse. * * * The reasonableness of any particular governmental activity does not necessarily or invariably turn on the existence of alternative 'less intrusive' means. * * * Even if less intrusive means existed of protecting some particular types of property, it would be unreasonable to expect police officers in the everyday course of business to make fine and subtle distinctions in deciding which containers or items may be searched and which must be sealed as a unit. [citing New York v. Belton]

In a footnote, the Court stated that the inventory search of Lafayette's bag may have been impermissible if he was not going to be incarcerated after being booked for disturbing the peace.[21] Justice Marshall, joined by Justice Brennan, concurred in the judgment.

Opperman and *Lafayette* supported the Supreme Court's decision in Colorado v. Bertine, 479 U.S. 367 (1987), holding that police officers could inventory the contents of a van, including a closed backpack and a nylon bag and other containers within it. Chief Justice Rehnquist's opinion for the Court rejected an argument that there was no safety reason for the inventory, since, after the driver was arrested for driving under the influence of alcohol, the van was towed to a secure, lighted facility and the driver could have been offered the opportunity to make arrangements for the safekeeping of his property. The Court concluded that "reasonable police regulations relating to inventory procedures administered in good faith satisfy the Fourth Amendment, even though courts might as a matter of hindsight be able to devise equally reasonable rules requiring a different procedure." It also rejected the defen-

21. A number of courts have held that a preincarceration inventory search is improper if the arrestee, upon posting collateral, has a right to release without any incarceration. United States v. Mills, 472 F.2d 1231 (D.C.Cir. 1972); People v. Dixon, 392 Mich. 691, 222 N.W.2d 749 (1974). In Zehrung v. State, 569 P.2d 189 (Alaska 1977), the court held that such inventories are unreasonable even absent a clear statutory right to release on bail. The existence of routine procedures permitting preincarceration inventories did not validate the search.

dant's claim that the inventory was impermissible because departmental regulations gave police officers discretion whether to impound the van or to park and lock it in a public parking lot. The Chief Justice noted that the regulations established several factors by which the officer was to determine whether to impound the vehicle or instead exercise a park and lock alternative. The regulations did not permit the use of the park and lock alternative if there was a reasonable risk of damage or vandalism to the vehicle or if the approval of the arrestee could not be obtained. The majority held that these conditions sufficiently circumscribed the discretion of the officer. The Court concluded that "nothing in *Opperman* or *Lafayette* prohibits the exercise of police discretion so long as that discretion is exercised according to standard criteria and on the basis of something other than suspicion of criminal activity."

Bertine challenged the opening of the containers in his car, on the ground that the inventorying officer did not properly weigh the privacy interest in the container against the risk that it might serve as a repository for dangerous or valuable items. The majority, relying on the above-quoted language in *Lafayette,* rejected a less intrusive means analysis for opening containers in an inventory search. In a footnote, the Court emphasized that "the police department procedures mandated the opening of closed containers and the listing of their contents."

Justice Blackmun, joined by Justices Powell and O'Connor, concurred and wrote "separately to underscore the importance of having such inventories conducted only pursuant to standardized police procedures." Justice Marshall, joined by Justice Brennan, dissented. He urged that the officers did not act according to standards that sufficiently controlled their discretion and he repeated the arguments he made in *Opperman* that the government's interests in conducting an inventory did not outweigh the property owner's privacy interests.[22]

The Court revisited the subject of police discretion in conducting inventory searches in Florida v. Wells, 495 U.S. 1 (1990). The Court unanimously found that the opening of a locked suitcase could not be justified as an inventory search where the Florida Highway Patrol had no policy whatever concerning the opening of closed containers. Chief Justice Rehnquist, writing for the Court, found the search to be insufficiently regulated. However, the Chief Justice took issue with a statement by the Florida Supreme Court that "the police under *Bertine* must mandate either that all containers will be opened during an inventory search, or that no containers will be opened. There can be no room for discretion." According to the majority, the Fourth Amendment does allow the officer some latitude to decide whether a container may be opened in an inventory search. This discretion can be exercised "in light of the nature of the search and the characteristics of the container itself." The Chief Justice concluded:

22. Even before *Opperman*, the Oregon Supreme Court had used the state Constitution to limit inventories of closed containers seized from an arrestee, finding that the container could have been listed on the inventory without opening it. State v. Keller, 265 Or. 622, 510 P.2d 568 (1973). In State v. Perry, 298 Or. 21, 688 P.2d 827 (1984), the court found that an inventory of a closed container seized from an intoxicated person who is held "in civil custody" also was improper. A person is entitled to even more privacy in a civil "hold" situation than in a criminal case, the court reasoned.

While policies of opening all containers or of opening no containers are unquestionably permissible, it would be equally permissible, for example, to allow the opening of closed containers whose contents officers determine they are unable to ascertain from examining the contents' exteriors. The allowance of the exercise of judgment based on concerns related to the purpose of an inventory search does not violate the Fourth Amendment.

This dictum prompted sharp responses in opinions by Justice Brennan (joined by Justice Marshall), Justice Blackmun, and Justice Stevens, all of whom concurred in the judgment. These Justices generally argued that to allow the individual officer any discretion to determine whether a container should be opened would create an unacceptable risk of abuse. Justice Brennan noted that the *Bertine* Court had allowed the officer some discretion as to whether to impound a car, but no discretion as to whether to open a container therein. He concluded that "attempting to cast doubt on the vitality of the holding in *Bertine* in this otherwise easy case is not justified." After *Wells,* would a policy allowing police officers to open containers "if they reasonably appear to contain valuables" be upheld? Why does Justice Brennan prefer that all containers be opened rather than some? Is it better that everybody suffer an invasion of privacy rather than a few?

A consideration of the foregoing Supreme Court cases raises several issues concerning the scope and justification for inventory searches. First, when is the initial impoundment of a vehicle permissible? Authority to impound is statutory in most states. Most states provide for the towing and impoundment of automobiles left unattended or abandoned for prescribed lengths of time on public highways. Impoundment for repeated parking violations is also permitted. Circumstances may justify the temporary seizure of a car, as where a suspect is arrested while driving on a public road, and it is not safe to leave the car at the side of the road until other arrangements can be made.

A second issue which arises from a consideration of the justifications for an inventory is whether the procedure is a pretext for conducting a warrantless search of a vehicle. The emphasis in *Opperman* and *Bertine* on standardized inventory procedures reflects concern that, absent such guidelines, investigatory searches may be conducted under the guise of inventories. As we have seen in other areas, however (most notably with roadblocks and searches incident to arrest), the fact that the officer is guided by bright line, all-or-nothing rules does not eliminate the possibility of pretextual searches. And as in other areas, the fact that the officer may have a pretextual motive is usually held irrelevant if the search itself is objectively reasonable. Recall the material on pretextual stops and arrests earlier in the Chapter. Applying those principles to inventory searches means that if the officer follows guidelines and makes the search look like an inventory search, the existence of an investigatory motive will be irrelevant. See United States v. Porter, 859 F.2d 83 (8th Cir. 1988) ("an officer's suspicion that evidence may be present does not invalidate an otherwise lawful inventory search"; United States v. Walker, 931 F.2d 1066 (5th Cir.1991) (inventory search was not pretextual where conducted pursuant to standardized procedures; inventory procedures need not be in writing). On the other hand, if the officer is acting without guidelines, as in *Wells,* or if the officer disregards guidelines to obtain evidence, then the search cannot be justified as an inventory search. An example of the latter is where the officer opens only a few containers in an impounded automobile, or fails to file an inventory list. See United States v. Parr, 716 F.2d 796 (11th Cir. 1983) (search cannot be justified as an inventory search where items were selectively investigated).

The problem of pretext impoundments is greatest where non-statutory seizures are involved, as where the police take an arrestee's car to the station rather than leave it unattended at the roadside. In these situations, the decision as to what to do with the automobile may be highly discretionary, and the danger of an impoundment for the purpose of conducting an investigatory search is great. When no passengers are present at the time of an arrest, what alternatives are available for disposition of the arrestee's car? Would the car be better protected from theft or vandalism if left at roadside till the arrestee or family members can retrieve it? Should the car be driven to a nearby parking area, or to the arrestee's home if it is on the way to the station? Are Fourth Amendment rights better protected by allowing officers flexibility to respond to the circumstances surrounding a particular arrest, or by mandating impoundment—and subsequent inventory—of all cars in which a person is arrested?

Several courts and commentators suggest that the owner's desires should be accommodated when the police have no justification for seizing the car. South Dakota v. Opperman, supra (Marshall, J., dissenting); Dixon v. State, 23 Md.App. 19, 327 A.2d 516 (1974); State v. Slockbower, 79 N.J. 1, 397 A.2d 1050 (1979). Judge Moylan maintains that impoundment in an arrest situation, under the guise of doing the owner a favor by protecting his property, is "an epic hypocrisy" and "flagrantly unconstitutional." The Inventory Search of an Automobile: A Willing Suspension of Disbelief, 5 U. of Baltimore L.Rev. 203, 220 (1976). The fact that routine police policy is being followed does little to guarantee that a particular inventory is not "a case more of investigative opportunism than of genuine solicitude for personal property." However, these arguments are based on a less intrusive means analysis which the Supreme Court has rejected in *Lafayette* and *Bertine*. An impoundment or search which effectuates the state interests supporting an inventory search, even though those interests could be met less intrusively, must be distinguished from an impoundment or search which effectuates none of those state interests. It is reasonable under *Bertine* and *Lafayette* to impound a vehicle where alternative arrangements could be made to protect the car, or to open a container which could otherwise be secured. It is not reasonable to impound a vehicle which is parked in a locked garage attached to the arrestee's home, or to vacuum a car's interior to "inventory" carpet fibers. See United States v. Showalter, 858 F.2d 149 (3d Cir. 1988), where the government sought to justify the search of a residence under the inventory exception. The court stated that "none of the factors which have been used to justify the warrantless inventory search of an automobile are present * * * when generally applied to the home."

In the end, there may be no way to completely limit the exercise of discretion in an inventory search. Certainly an all-or-nothing rule of impoundment would not be practicable, given the various fact situations in which officers come upon cars subject to impoundment. While an all-or-nothing rule could be applied to opening containers, discretion would still have to be exercised to determine whether a certain item is a container. See generally United States v. Judge, 864 F.2d 1144 (5th Cir.1989). Assuming that discretion cannot be completely eliminated, are you satisfied with the approach of the Court in *Bertine* and *Wells?*

6. *Border Searches*

Courts are not always persuasive in their inventory search opinions, but they try to state a rationale for not requiring a warrant. This is in sharp contrast with the cases establishing the border search exception to the warrant and probable cause requirements. They make little effort to justify the exception on policy grounds. The most persuasive rationale is similar to that used in *Skinner* and *Von Raab*—border searches serve a special need beyond traditional criminal law enforcement. The special need is the interest in protecting American borders, and regulating the goods which flow into the country. As the Court stated in United States v. Montoya de Hernandez, 473 U.S. 531 (1985):

> At the border, customs officials have more than merely an investigative law enforcement role. They are also charged, along with immigration officials, with protecting this Nation from entrants who may bring anything harmful into this country, whether that be communicable diseases, narcotics, or explosives.

Because the search serves special needs, it is evaluated under the reasonableness clause of the Fourth Amendment. And given the heavy state interest just stated, as well as the diminished expectation of privacy attendant to a border crossing, border searches are ordinarily reasonable even without a warrant or probable cause, and often without any suspicion at all.

Routine border searches have been authorized by statute to prevent entrance into the country of illegal aliens or goods, and to enforce customs regulations. The constitutionality of routine border searches, conducted without warrant or probable cause, has been assumed since the beginning of the nation. In 1976, the Supreme Court repeated the assumption in a case in which the Court was asked by the government to uphold the warrantless search of first class international mail by customs officials, who had reasonable cause to suspect that it contained illegally imported merchandise.[23]

23. On the subject of searches of vessels, see Note, High on the Seas: Drug Smuggling, The Fourth Amendment, and Warrantless Searches at Sea, 93 Harv.L.Rev. 725 (1980) (arguing for more restrictions on searches of ships); United States v. Williams, 617 F.2d 1063 (5th Cir. 1980) (en banc).

The Court distinguished stops of ships from automobile stops in United States v. Villamonte-Marquez, 462 U.S. 579 (1983). It traced 19 U.S.C. § 1581(a), which authorizes a customs officer to board any vessel to examine the manifest and other documents and papers, to a similar 1790 statute and concluded that the framers of the Fourth Amendment considered it reasonable for officials to board vessels in waters providing ready access to the open sea without any suspicion of wrongdoing. The Court found that permanent checkpoints would not be practical on the water, that smugglers could operate without entering ports, and that documentation of autos made tracing them considerably easier than tracing ships.

An analysis of possible Fourth Amendment restrictions on sea searches is found in Saltzburg, The Reach of the Bill of Rights Beyond the Terra Firma of the United States, 20 Va. J.Int'l L. 741 (1980).

If a vessel on the high seas is owned by a non-resident alien, the search need not be justified under the border exception, because the Fourth Amendment is not applicable to searches of a non-resident alien's property which is located outside the United States. Such an alien is not one of "the people" entitled to Fourth Amendment protection. See United States v. Verdugo-Urquidez (page 24); United States v. Davis, 905 F.2d 245 (9th Cir.1990) (applying *Verdugo-Urquidez* to a search on the high seas).

UNITED STATES v. RAMSEY

Supreme Court of the United States, 1976.
431 U.S. 606.

MR. JUSTICE REHNQUIST delivered the opinion of the Court.

[The case involved an investigation of a heroin-by-mail enterprise in the Washington, D.C. area. Customs officials developed a reasonable suspicion that eight envelopes from Thailand might contain heroin. The envelopes were opened without a warrant and each did, in fact, contain heroin.]

* * *

III

A

That searches made at the border, pursuant to the longstanding right of the sovereign to protect itself by stopping and examining persons and property crossing into this country, are reasonable simply by virtue of the fact that they occur at the border should, by now, require no extended demonstration. The Congress which proposed the Bill of Rights, including the Fourth Amendment, to the state legislatures on September 25, 1789, 1 Stat. 97, had, some two months prior to that proposal, enacted the first customs statute, Act of July 31, 1789, c. 5, 1 Stat. 29. Section 24 of this statute granted customs officials "full power and authority" to enter and search "any ship or vessel, in which they shall have reason to suspect any goods, wares or merchandise subject to duty shall be concealed * * *." This acknowledgment of plenary customs power was differentiated from the more limited power to enter and search "any particular dwelling-house, store, building, or other place * * *" where a warrant upon "cause to suspect" was required. The historical importance of the enactment of this customs statute by the same Congress which proposed the Fourth Amendment is, we think, manifest. * * *

* * *

Border searches, then, from before the adoption of the Fourth Amendment, have been considered to be "reasonable" by the single fact that the person or item in question had entered into our country from outside. There has never been any additional requirement that the reasonableness of a border search depended on the existence of probable cause. This longstanding recognition that searches at our borders without probable cause and without a warrant are nonetheless "reasonable" has a history as old as the Fourth Amendment itself. We reaffirm it now.

B

Respondents urge upon us, however, the position that mailed letters are somehow different, and, whatever may be the normal rule with respect to border searches, different considerations, requiring the full panoply of Fourth Amendment protections, apply to international mail. * * *

The border-search exception is grounded in the recognized right of the sovereign to control, subject to substantive limitations imposed by the Constitution, who and what may enter the country. It is clear that there is nothing in the rationale behind the border-search exception which suggests that the mode of entry will be critical. It was conceded at oral argument that customs officials could search, without probable cause and without a warrant, envelopes carried by an entering traveler, whether in his luggage or on his person. Surely no different constitutional standard should apply simply because the envelopes were mailed, not carried. The critical fact is that the envelopes cross the border and enter this country, not that they are brought in by one mode of transportation rather than another. It is their entry into this country from without it that makes a resulting search "reasonable."

* * *

* * * The historically recognized scope of the border-search doctrine, suggest no distinction in constitutional doctrine stemming from the mode of transportation across our borders. The contrary view of the Court of Appeals and respondents stems, we think, from an erroneous reading of Carroll v. United States, 267 U.S. at 153, under which the Court of Appeals reasoned that "the rationale of the border search exception * * * is based upon * * * the difficulty of obtaining a warrant when the subject of the search is mobile, as a car or person * * *." 176 U.S.App. D.C., at 70, 538 F.2d at 418.

The fundamental difficulty with this position is that the "border search" exception is not based on the doctrine of "exigent circumstances" at all. It is a longstanding, historically recognized exception to the Fourth Amendment's general principle that a warrant be obtained, and in this respect is like the similar "search incident to lawful arrest" exception treated in United States v. Robinson, 414 U.S. 218, 224 (1973). We think that the language in Carroll v. United States, supra, makes this point abundantly clear. * * * *Carroll* thus recognized that there was no "probable cause" requirement at the border. This determination simply has nothing to do with "exigent circumstances."

* * *

In view of the wealth of authority establishing the border search as "reasonable" within the Fourth Amendment even though there be neither probable cause nor a warrant, we reject the distinctions made by the Court of Appeals in its opinion.

Note

Justice Stevens, joined by Justices Brennan and Marshall, dissented, arguing that Congress did not confer authority to open letters without probable cause. Justice Powell's concurring opinion indicated that he did not join any suggestion in the Court's opinion that a lesser standard of suspicion could be employed.

The court in United States v. Charleus, 871 F.2d 265 (2d Cir.1989) states the well-accepted proposition that "routine border searches of the personal belongings and effects of entrants may be conducted without regard to probable cause or reasonable suspicion." Such searches are deemed reasonable because of the important state interest, the diminished expectation of privacy attendant to crossing the border, and the limited intrusiveness of a routine border search. The justification for routine border searches is discussed in Note, Border Searches and the Fourth Amendment, 77 Yale L.J. 1007, 1012 (1968):

> First, since an individual crossing a border belongs to a class whose members frequently violate certain laws in the process of entering, the fact of his crossing is by itself some evidence that he may be violating some law. Second, since the individual crossing a border is on notice that certain types of searches are likely to be made, his privacy is arguably less invaded by those searches. Third, since non-intrusive personal searches at the border are administered to a class (international travelers) which is not deemed unworthy, such searches lack the quality of insult felt by an individual singled out for a search.

Additional factors which are relevant to the distinction between border and other criminal investigations are the government's interest in preventing the entrance of illegal aliens and merchandise, the scope and intensity of the illicit international narcotics trade, the probability that smuggling attempts will occur at the border, and the difficulties of detecting narcotics smuggling. Id. at 1014. Accepting the need to prevent the flow of narcotics and aliens into the country as an important government interest, do the exigencies of law enforcement justify the invasion of privacy entailed in conducting warrantless border searches of any person entering the country? In judging the reasonableness of such searches, should the fact that they are the most effective and efficient means of enforcing a legitimate government interest be considered? The possibility that they are the only effective means? See Almeida–Sanchez v. United States, 413 U.S. 266, 273 (1973). Does the lesser expectation of privacy in luggage carried into the country justify warrantless border searches, or does the existence of such searches reduce one's expectation of privacy?

While suspicionless routine border searches have been well-accepted, controversy has arisen with respect to two questions. First, what standard of proof is required for a search which is beyond the scope of a routine border search? Second, what factors distinguish routine from non-routine border searches? In United States v. Montoya de Hernandez, 473 U.S. 531 (1985), the Court answered the first question. It did not have to deal with the second, since the intrusion in *Montoya* was by any account beyond the routine. Justice Rehnquist, writing for a six-person majority, stated that "the detention of a traveler at the border, beyond the scope of a routine customs search and inspection, is justified at its inception if customs agents, considering all the facts surrounding the traveler and her trip, reasonably suspect that the traveler is smuggling contraband in her alimentary canal."

Montoya de Hernandez went though customs in Los Angeles after arriving on a plane from Colombia. Her eight recent trips to either Miami or Los Angeles caused agents to question her about the purpose for her trip. She carried $5,000 cash, mostly $50 bills, with no billfold and stated that she came to purchase goods for her husband's store in Colombia. Although she had no appointments with sellers or hotel reservation, she stated that she planned to ride around the city visiting retail stores and that she planned to stay at a Holiday Inn. She could not recall how her airline reservation was purchased. In her valise inspectors found four changes of "cold weather" clothing.

These facts, the Court held, were sufficient to warrant seasoned inspectors in arriving at reasonable suspicion that Montoya de Hernandez was a "balloon swallower" attempting to smuggle drugs into the country. A strip search by a female inspector revealed a fullness in the suspect's abdomen, as if she were wearing a girdle. The inspector noticed that the suspect was wearing two pair of elastic underpants with a paper towel lining the crotch area. Upon receiving this information, the inspector in charge informed the suspect of his suspicion. The inspector gave her the option of returning to Colombia on the next available flight, agreeing to an x-ray or remaining in detention until she produced a monitored bowel movement. She chose the first option, but inspectors were unable to arrange a flight. Sixteen hours later, the suspect had not defecated or urinated and had refused food or drink. It appeared that she was struggling to avoid use of the toilet. Inspectors sought and obtained a warrant authorizing a rectal examination and x-ray, provided that the physician consider the suspect's claim of pregnancy. A pregnancy test was negative, and a rectal examination produced a balloon containing a foreign substance. Investigators arrested the suspect. She later passed 88 balloons through her system containing 80% pure cocaine hydrochloride.

The Supreme Court upheld both the initial inspection and the detention, finding that the delay was attributable to the suspect's "heroic" efforts "to resist the call of nature" and that the detention was not unreasonably long even though it "undoubtedly exceed[ed] any other detention we have approved under reasonable suspicion." Justice Rehnquist emphasized not only the suspect-created delay, but also the heavy state interest and diminished expectation of privacy attendant to a border crossing. He noted that "alimentary canal smuggling cannot be detected in the amount of time in which other illegal activity may be investigated through brief *Terry*-type stops." Justice Stevens concurred in the judgment on the ground that the prolonged detention was attributable to the suspect's choice not to consent to an x-ray. Justice Brennan, joined by Justice Marshall, described the facts as a "disgusting and saddening episode" involving a detention based upon a profile that justified at most reasonable suspicion, and he dissented. He argued that "[i]ndefinite involuntary *incommunicado* detentions 'for investigation' are the hallmark of a police state, not a free society."

Were the inspectors' actions reasonable or disgusting (assuming they could not be both)?

The lower court in *Montoya* had found that the intrusion was so severe that it had to be justified by a "clear indication" of criminal activity. This was a standard of proof somewhere between reasonable suspicion and probable cause. In *Montoya,* the majority emphatically rejected this approach, and stated that as in *Terry,* there is no relevant standard of proof between reasonable suspicion and probable cause. Justice Rehnquist concluded as follows:

> We do not think that the Fourth Amendment's emphasis upon reasonableness is consistent with the creation of a third verbal standard in addition to reasonable suspicion and probable cause; * * * subtle verbal gradations may obscure rather than elucidate the meaning of the provision in question.
>
> The reasonable suspicion standard has been applied in a number of contexts and effects a needed balance between private and public interests when law enforcement officials must make a limited intrusion on less than probable cause.

After *Montoya,* there are apparently two types of intrusions at the border—a routine border search which can be done without suspicion, and a non-routine border search which requires reasonable suspicion. It could be argued that some intrusions at the border could be so severe as to require probable cause, but given the facts of *Montoya* and the state interest supporting border searches, can you envision such an intrusion?

There are many lower court decisions concerning whether a border search is so intrusive as to be beyond the routine. In United States v. Sandoval Vargas, 854 F.2d 1132 (9th Cir.1988), Customs Inspectors referred defendant's car to a secondary inspection area, and conducted a thorough search of the passenger compartment and the trunk. The court found this a routine search, noting that it was "typical of those conducted at the border." In United States v. Puig, 810 F.2d 1085 (11th Cir.1987), the court held that reasonable suspicion allowed the Customs Official to drill a hole into the hull of a boat. In United States v. Sanders, 663 F.2d 1 (2d Cir.1981), customs officials forced the defendant to take off his artificial leg and inspected it, finding drugs. The court likened the police activity to a body cavity search, well-recognized as more intrusive than the routine border search.

In contrast, in United States v. Charleus, 871 F.2d 265 (2d Cir.1989), a customs inspector patted down the defendant, felt a hard lump under his clothing, and lifted the back of his shirt, whereupon he found packages of narcotics taped to the defendant's body. The court analyzed the intrusion as follows:

> The [intrusion] arguably straddles the line between the two categories of border searches—searching more than personal belongings or effects such as a purse, wallet, or even outer jacket was involved; but the search was not nearly as intrusive as a body cavity or full strip search. [The Court discusses cases finding such activity as removal of shoes, pulling down a girdle in a private room, and lifting up a skirt to be routine border searches]. Since the potential indignity resulting from a pat on the back followed by a lifting of one's shirt simply fails to compare with the much greater level of intrusion associated with a body cavity or full strip search, we decline to hold that reasonable suspicion was here required.

In a footnote, the court rejected the suggestion that an intrusion which falls somewhere between a routine search and a strip search should be governed by a standard of proof somewhere between no suspicion and reasonable suspicion. The court reasoned that the Supreme Court's rejection in *Montoya* of a standard of proof between reasonable suspicion and probable cause "applies equally to the creation of new standards based on levels of suspicion between no suspicion and reasonable suspicion." For a case which takes the opposite view, over a dissent stating that the holding is inconsistent with *Montoya,* see People v. Luna, 73 N.Y.2d 173, 538 N.Y.S.2d 765, 535 N.E.2d 1305 (1989) ("some" suspicion required before a patdown border search can be conducted).

While the constitutionality of border searches has never been questioned, considerable controversy has arisen over the question, "what is a border?" The right to search at the border has generally been recognized as extending to its functional equivalent as well. In *Almeida-Sanchez* the Court cited as examples "searches at an established station near the border, at a point marking the confluence of two or more roads that extend from the border," or "a search of the passengers and cargo of an airplane arriving at a St. Louis airport after a non-stop flight from Mexico City." Id. at 273. Before aircraft may be searched at an internal checkpoint, however, there must be a high degree of probability that a border crossing took place, or that the object of search has just entered the country. United States v. Ivey, 546 F.2d 139 (5th Cir. 1977). The same standard applies to searches of ships. United States v. Tilton, 534 F.2d 1363 (9th Cir. 1976). In Torres v. Puerto Rico, 442 U.S. 465 (1979), the Court unanimously agreed that a trip from the mainland to Puerto Rico did not result in the crossing of an *international* border and that the border search exception to the warrant requirement did not apply.

A more troubling problem has arisen in connection with searches of vehicles inside the border, pursuant to § 287(a) of the Immigration and Nationality Act [8 U.S.C.A. § 1357(a)] which allows searches for aliens "within a reasonable distance from any external boundary of the United States." A reasonable distance has been defined as 100 air miles from any external border, 8 CFR § 287.1. The reasons for this legislative extension of border search powers, and the regulatory response is explained in the following excerpt from United States v. Martinez-Fuerte, 428 U.S. 543, 552–53 (1976):

> Interdicting the flow of illegal entrants from Mexico poses formidable law enforcement problems. The principal problem arises from surreptitious entries. The United States shares a border with Mexico that is almost 2,000 miles long, and much of the border area is uninhabited desert or thinly populated arid land. Although the Border Patrol maintains personnel, elec-

tronic equipment, and fences along portions of the border, it remains relatively easy for individuals to enter the United States without detection. It also is possible for an alien to enter unlawfully at a port of entry by the use of falsified papers or to enter lawfully but violate restrictions of entry in an effort to remain in the country unlawfully. Once within the country, the aliens seek to travel inland to areas where employment is believed to be available, frequently meeting by prearrangement with friends or professional smugglers who transport them in private vehicles.

The Border Patrol conducts three kinds of inland traffic-checking operations in an effort to minimize illegal immigration. Permanent checkpoints, such as those at San Clemente and Sarita, are maintained at or near intersections of important roads leading away from the border. They operate on a coordinated basis designed to avoid circumvention by smugglers and others who transport the illegal aliens. Temporary checkpoints, which operate like permanent ones, occasionally are established in other strategic locations. Finally, roving patrols are maintained to supplement the checkpoint system. In fiscal 1973, 175,511 deportable aliens were apprehended throughout the Nation by "line watch" agents stationed at the border itself. Traffic-checking operations in the interior apprehended approximately 55,300 more deportable aliens.

* * *

[P]ermanent checkpoints are chosen on the basis of a number of factors. The Border Patrol believes that to assure effectiveness, a checkpoint must be (i) distant enough from the border to avoid interference with traffic in populated areas near the border, (ii) close to the confluence of two or more significant roads leading away from the border, (iii) situated in terrain that restricts vehicle passage around the checkpoint, (iv) on a stretch of highway compatible with safe operation, and (v) beyond the 25-mile zone in which "border passes" are valid.

The operation of the checkpoints is outlined in United States v. Ortiz, 422 U.S. 891, 910–911, 914 (1975) (Appendix to Burger, C.J., concurring).

When the checkpoints, whether permanent or temporary, are in operation, an officer standing at the "point" in full dress uniform on the highway will view the decelerating oncoming vehicles and their passengers, and will visually determine whether he has reason to believe the occupants of the vehicle are aliens (i.e., "breaks the pattern" of usual traffic). If so, the vehicle will be stopped (if the traffic at the checkpoint is heavy, as at the San Clemente checkpoint, the vehicle will be actually directed off the highway) for inquiries to be made by the agent. If the agent does not have reason to believe that the vehicle approaching the checkpoint is carrying aliens, he may exchange salutations, or merely wave the vehicle through the checkpoint.

If, after questioning the occupants, the agent then believes that illegal aliens may be secreted in the vehicle (because of a break in the "pattern" indicating the possibility of smuggling) he will inspect the vehicle by giving a cursory visual inspection of those areas of the vehicle not visible from the outside (i.e. trunk, interior portion of camper, etc.).

At the point of location of the sites now in regular use few aliens have reached the locale on foot, with 99 percent having entered a vehicle of one type or another. Approximately 12 percent of all apprehensions of deportable aliens throughout the nation are made at checkpoints.

* * *

The deterrent impact of these checkpoints has been noted on several occasions when they resumed operation unexpectedly and a great number of aliens were apprehended.

The evidence presented before this court clearly established that there is no reasonable or effective alternative method of detection and apprehension available to the Border Patrol in the absence of the checkpoints, for even a geometric increase in its personnel or line watch would not leave any control over those admitted as temporary visitors from Mexico.

In addition to the permanent and temporary checkpoints described in *Ortiz,* a third regulatory solution to the illegal alien problem was roving patrols in border areas. These patrols were used only on roads with light traffic, or when weather conditions precluded regular traffic checking. As originally designed, these roving patrols had complete discretion to stop all cars, or any random vehicle.

Beginning with *Almeida-Sanchez* in 1973, the Supreme Court decided a series of cases dealing with the constitutionality of these law enforcement efforts in border areas. In *Almeida-Sanchez* the defendant was stopped by a roving Border Patrol on an east-west road in California about 25 air miles north of the Mexican border. The patrol had no warrant and no probable cause to stop or search. They nevertheless searched the defendant's vehicle for illegal aliens, discovering instead a large quantity of marijuana. The Court held the search unconstitutional since it was neither a border search nor a functional equivalent thereof. In a 5–4 decision, Justice Stewart wrote for the majority that a roving border patrol could not conduct a vehicle search without probable cause.

Justice White's dissent found the search to be a reasonable response to the unique problems of enforcing immigration laws in border areas. Furthermore, it argued the Court should defer to the judgment of Congress and the Circuit Courts in that region, who had authorized and approved these searches as reasonable in light of the practicalities of border-area law enforcement.

Two years later, the Court held that stops by roving border patrols, absent reasonable cause to suspect that aliens were being illegally transported, were unconstitutional. However, in light of significant enforcement needs and the limited intrusion entailed in a stop for questioning, reasonable suspicion rather than probable cause would justify the stop. Any additional detention, however, would require probable cause. United States v. Brignoni-Ponce, 422 U.S. 873 (1975).

The use of traffic checkpoints removed from the border also came under scrutiny. In United States v. Ortiz, supra, warrantless searches at internal checkpoints were held unconstitutional unless based on probable cause. The Court found that no less discretion was operated at checkpoints than by roving patrols, at least insofar as searches were concerned, since officers at the former were free to decide which cars to search, and only 3% of the vehicles which were stopped were also searched.

The following year, the Court approved warrantless stops of vehicles at permanent checkpoints for limited questioning of the occupants. United States v. Martinez-Fuerte, 428 U.S. 543 (1976). No probable cause or reasonable suspicion was required to justify the stops. The rationale for allowing them was that they were necessary tools of law enforcement, and that the public interest in making them outweighed the constitutionally protected interests of private citizens. In addition, Justice Powell, writing for the Court, stated that motorists could be selectively referred to secondary inspection areas for further questioning, again without any articulable suspicion. He argued that the additional intrusion—although admittedly a seizure—was limited and inoffensive and that use of the questioning techniques tended to minimize the intrusion on the general motoring public, thus protecting other Fourth Amendment interests.

A final issue dealt with in *Martinez-Fuerte* was whether a judicial warrant is required to authorize a particular checkpoint location and the practice of routine stops. Justice Powell contrasted the border checkpoint situation with those circumstances which justified the administrative warrant requirement in *Camara*. He argued that *Martinez-Fuerte* involved a lesser intrusion, that the motorist at a checkpoint knows that the officers present have authority to act, and that high ranking executive officials make decisions on the location of checkpoints, thereby minimizing the field officer's discretion.

Justice Brennan, in a dissent joined by Justice Marshall, ignored the warrant issue. Instead, he attacked the majority's distinction between roving patrol and checkpoint stops, finding both to be unreasonable under the Fourth Amendment.

> [T]he governmental interests relied on as warranting intrusion here are the same as those in *Almeida-Sanchez* and *Ortiz,* which required a showing of probable cause for roving-patrol and fixed checkpoint searches, and *Brignoni-Ponce,* which required at least a showing of reasonable suspicion based on specific articulable facts to justify roving-patrol stops. Absent some difference in the nature of the intrusion, the same minimal requirement should be imposed for checkpoint stops.

Justice Brennan dismissed the contentions that checkpoint stops were subjectively less intrusive, and that selective referral to secondary detention areas was any less discretionary or stigmatizing than roving patrol stops. He suggested that reasonable suspicion should be required for checkpoint stops, or, at the very least, for the additional detention. He concluded that the Court was allowing constitutional limitations to be dispensed with merely because they could not be conveniently satisfied.

As the dissent points out, there is not an appreciable difference between the amount of discretion exercised by roving patrols or checkpoint agents, at least insofar as the decision to detain a motorist for additional questioning is concerned. Why has the majority been willing to dispense with the *Terry* standard of reasonable suspicion, even as a prerequisite to secondary detention? Has the Court created a new category which combines border, *Carroll* and administrative justifications into a super-exception to the warrant and probable cause requirement?

In asserting that there are no other viable solutions to the illegal alien problem, is the majority essentially adopting a reasonableness test in lieu of the warrant requirement? Has it lowered its standard of reasonableness to accommodate law enforcement necessities?

The problem of determining the temporal and geographical scope of a border search, i.e., what is the functional equivalent thereof, arises in cases outside the context of routine enforcement policies. Broadly speaking, the issue becomes: under what circumstances is a search that does not take place in a border area or at a port of entry justified as a border search? When a person entering the country flees through a checkpoint, and is caught and searched at a point several miles away, courts have generally upheld the search as a border search. United States v. Moya, 549 F.2d 340 (5th Cir. 1977). Does it matter whether the fugitive is immediately pursued and seized, or whether agents lose sight of him for some time or distance? One court has held that an inland search is valid if there were circumstances known to customs officers at the time of entry which justify the subsequent search. Marsh v. United States, 344 F.2d 317 (5th Cir. 1965). In cases such as these, is the border search exception necessary? Couldn't these searches often fall under the *Carroll* or exigent circumstances doctrines?

A related problem involves goods which enter the country through the mail or other type of shipment, and are searched before they reach their destination, but at a point other than the port of entry. In United States v. Gallagher, 557 F.2d 1041 (4th Cir. 1977), the search of a camper imported from Portugal was upheld as a border search although it had entered the country in Baltimore, but was not searched until it reached Norfolk, Virginia. In United States v. King, 517 F.2d 350 (1975) the search of international mail which had entered the United States at San Francisco and had been routed, uninspected to Birmingham, was similarly upheld. The inspection, which occurred in Alabama before delivery to the defendant's post office box, was distinguished from *Almeida-Sanchez.* The delayed customs inspection did not infringe any greater expectation of privacy, did not cause any more of an intrusion, and did not increase the danger that goods not subject to search (e.g., domestic mail) would be inspected. Since the envelopes could have been searched without a warrant in San Francisco, the court held that the later search was a reasonable border inspection. Would you distinguish *Gallagher* from *King* on the grounds that the delayed search in the former case raised greater problems of controlling discretion?

Should border officials have the same broad powers to search outgoing persons and vehicles as they do to search those entering the country? Do any of the considerations which justify regular border searches apply to searches of things leaving the country? See United States v. Duncan, 693 F.2d 971 (9th Cir. 1982) (holding, 2–1, that search of departing passenger was a border search, requiring no cause or suspicion). In United States v. Berisha, 925 F.2d 791 (5th Cir. 1991), the court stated that "both incoming and outgoing border searches have several features in common; for example, the government is interested in protecting some interest of United States citizens, there is a likelihood of smuggling attempts at the border, and the individual is on notice that his privacy may be invaded when he crosses the border." The court therefore upheld a warrantless, suspicionless patdown search of a departing traveler, which uncovered $17,000 of domestic currency. Do you agree that the principles supporting the border exception apply equally to the "reverse" border exception? Consider the arguments of Judge Kozinski, dissenting in United States v. Nates, 831 F.2d 860 (9th Cir. 1987), a case in which the court upheld the suspicionless search of outgoing luggage under the reverse border exception, after the defendant had checked it with the airline:

> Nates' suitcase contained an unusually large amount of currency, which led the officers to confront Nates and, eventually, arrest him. We therefore know a good deal about this particular search. What we don't know much about are the searches conducted of other people's luggage * * *. We also don't know precisely how many suitcases are opened and searched every day without the knowledge or consent of their owners, but the number appears to be very substantial. In a case recently decided by the Eleventh Circuit, the record disclosed that in a seven-month period during 1985, *a single customs agent* surreptitiously "opened about 50,000 suitcases." United States v. Hernandez–Salazar, 813 F.2d 1126, 1130 n. 16 (11th Cir.1987). If this rate is typical, it would amount to about 100,000 bags opened per agent per year. Assuming that the customs service assigns even a modest number of agents to this task, the number of surreptitious intrusions into the property and privacy

of travelers is potentially staggering. It is a matter that should give us serious pause lest we overlook, and implicitly approve, what may amount to wholesale violations of the fourth amendment rights of the traveling public.

Here, there is no indication that signs were posted or that passengers were otherwise advised that agents would be rummaging through their personal possessions. Moreover, because exit searches are quite uncommon in the United States, passengers have no expectation or common understanding that they may suffer a fairly serious intrusion into their privacy as a condition for leaving the country. Indeed, given the above-board procedure employed in entry searches, where passengers are required to line up with their luggage for spot-checks by customs agents, travelers can reasonably infer from the absence of such procedure that no exit checks are conducted. My guess is that most passengers would be shocked to learn that, as they are waiting to board the plane, faceless bureaucrats are breaking into their luggage and pawing through it at will.

On a more mundane level, when the search is conducted outside the passengers' presence, they are unable to protect the physical security or integrity of their possessions. Thus, bags might be damaged when they are forced open, or their contents might be broken, lost or stolen. When passengers are present during the search, they can minimize the risk by opening suitcases themselves and alerting the agents about any items that may be subject to damage. Also, they can witness any mishap and hold the agent responsible. Agents, for their part, may be more careful if passengers are watching. * * * The fact of the matter is, when agents secretly break into people's suitcases and search through them by the hundreds of thousands, occasionally something will go wrong—someone will be tempted, or careless, or even do something that seems perfectly reasonable yet causes damage, such as opening a canister of undeveloped film.

Finally, there is a separate intrusion because passengers whose luggage is searched are generally never told about it. This means that when something is lost, stolen, mislaid or broken, the passenger will be completely mystified as to what happened. He will have no idea where to inquire as to its whereabouts or demand compensation. He may spend countless hours looking for the item in places he might have left it, harassing people who might have taken it, never suspecting that a government agent used a passkey to go through his luggage. Being subject to a secret search and then never being told about it is something I think most people would find especially offensive, and this then bears on the reasonableness of the procedure employed by the government.

All of this might be beside the point if there were no reasonably available alternatives. But there clearly are. * * *

One simple way of handling the matter would be for passengers to exit the country through customs—with occasional spot checks—much as they do when entering.

Is there an aspect of border searches that has not yet been articulated, but which helps to distinguish permanent borders from internal, temporary checkpoints? Arguably, the fact that people and goods are moving into the country from foreign lands means that there is no way that law enforcement persons in the United States could be expected to have probable cause to justify searches. Were no searches permitted without probable cause, criminal activity with roots outside the country would be difficult to investigate and prevent. Does this help explain the routine search of incoming passengers and goods? As for departing passengers and things, there is the argument that once outside the United States evidence that would be discovered here might be forever lost.

E. CONSENT SEARCHES

1. *Voluntary Consent*

A search based upon valid consent is reasonable even in the absence of a warrant or any articulable suspicion. The Supreme Court addressed the requirements for valid consent in Schneckloth v. Bustamonte, 412 U.S. 218 (1973). A California police officer at 2:40 a.m. stopped an automobile with a headlight and a license plate light burned out. Six men were in the car. The driver had no license, only one passenger produced his license, and he explained that the car was his brother's. The officer asked the men to step out of the car, they complied, and after two additional officers arrived, the officer asked the person who produced the license if he could search the car. The man replied, "Sure, go ahead," and opened the trunk for the officer. The search produced three stolen checks. The California courts held that the consent was valid and justified the search. But in a habeas corpus action, the court of appeals held that consent was not valid unless the government demonstrated that the consenting party understood that it could be freely and effectively withheld. The Supreme Court disagreed.

Justice Stewart's majority opinion cited voluntariness concepts developed in confession cases and concluded that "the question whether a consent to a search was in fact voluntary or was the product of duress or coercion, express or implied, is a question of fact to be determined from the totality of the circumstances. While knowledge of the right to refuse consent is one factor to be taken into account, the government need not establish such knowledge as the sine qua non of an effective consent." Justice Stewart explained that there were reasonable law enforcement interests served by consent searches, but that "the Fourth and Fourteenth Amendments require that a consent not be coerced, by explicit or implicit means, by implied threat or covert force."

An argument was made that warnings, like the *Miranda* warnings, which we shall examine in connection with police interrogation, should be required before consent is actually requested. The majority said that it would be impractical to give such warnings under the "informal and unstructured conditions" in which consent requests are usually made.

Justice Stewart distinguished the traditional concept of waiver of "the safeguards of a fair criminal trial" from consent to search. He concluded that a defendant was to be given "the greatest possible opportunity to utilize every facet of the constitutional model of a fair criminal trial," and that "[a]ny trial conducted in derogation of that model leaves open the possibility that the trial reached an unfair result." But, he found, that "[t]he protections of the Fourth Amendment are of a wholly different order." Justice Stewart concluded that the proper test in consent search cases is not whether there was a waiver of the defendant's Fourth Amendment rights, but whether the consent to search was voluntary under the totality of circumstances. A search upon voluntary consent is thus a reasonable search in compliance with the Fourth Amendment. Justice Stewart argued that there was nothing unfair or suspect about consent to a search, and that the Fourth and Fourteenth Amendments did not require that citizens be discouraged from cooperating with the police.

Justice Douglas' dissent implied that he agreed with the court of appeals. Justice Brennan dissented also, writing that "[i]t wholly escapes me how our citizens can meaningfully be said to have waived something as precious as a constitutional guarantee without ever being aware of its existence." The longest dissent was that of Justice Marshall. He said that the issue was not "coercion" but "consent" and urged that the substantive right at stake was the right to be free from warrantless searches. He said that consent searches are permissible because we permit our citizens to choose not to exercise their constitutional rights, not because of law enforcement needs. At the heart of his opinion, he wrote that "[i]f consent to search means that a person has chosen to forego his right to exclude the police from the place they seek to search, it follows that his consent cannot be considered a meaningful choice unless he knew that he could in fact exclude the police." His solution was to have the government bear the burden of showing knowledge, which burden could be satisfied by a warning before asking for consent.

In *Schneckloth,* consent was obtained from a person not in the custody of the police, a fact emphasized by the Court in its conclusion that its decision was "a narrow one." But in United States v. Watson, 423 U.S. 411 (1976), the Court found that the absence of warnings or of proof that Watson knew he could withhold consent was not controlling where the defendant "had been arrested and was in custody, but his consent was given while on a public street, not in the confines of the police station." The majority added that "to hold that illegal coercion is made out from the fact of arrest and the failure to inform the arrestee that he could withhold consent would not be consistent with *Schneckloth.*" *Watson* made clear that *Schneckloth* was not quite as narrow as Justice Stewart had proclaimed. Justice Marshall, joined by Justice Brennan, adhered to his opinion in *Schneckloth,* but added that "even short of this position there are valid reasons for application of such a rule to consents procured from suspects held in custody." Not surprisingly, *Watson* has been extended to consent extracted at the police station. See e.g., United States v. Smith, 543 F.2d 1141 (5th Cir. 1976); State v. Flores, 280 Or.App. 273, 570 P.2d 965 (1977). Contrast *Watson* with Sims v. State, 274 Ind. 495, 413 N.E.2d 556 (1980), which recognizes the right of persons in custody to have the advice of counsel and requires that the state bear the burden of showing an explicit waiver of counsel as a condition of establishing consent to a search.

The opinions in *Schneckloth* pass like ships in the night. Neither the majority nor the dissents exhibited any apparent understanding of each other, and neither did a very good job of explaining the rationale for the approach chosen.

Putting aside all of Justice Stewart's comments about different kinds of waiver and the impracticality of giving warnings before asking for consent, there remains a very straight-forward, powerful argument in support of the majority's result. That argument can be summarized as follows: The Fourth Amendment protects against unreasonable searches; prior decisions indicate that where the government wants to use power to force a search and seizure, the warrant clause is the basic definition of reasonableness; but where the government, rather than using coercive power to force and seize, asks people for their permission to conduct a search, the warrant clause is inapplicable; and, when the warrant clause is inapplicable, the basic test is reasonableness under the circumstances.

Putting aside much of the rhetoric of the dissents, a strong and easily stated argument remains to support their position: When the government seeks to invade the privacy (i.e., the area protected by the Fourth Amendment) of a person, even if the government asks permission the person asked may take the most polite request by a government official, especially a police officer, to be equivalent to an order, or at a minimum, a prelude to the coercive search that surely would take place if permission is refused. Essentially, this view holds that police officers exert force, whether they intend to or not, unless the person from whom permission is requested understands the rules of the consent game. The right to be free from warrantless searches extends to all coercive searches, and thus extends to situations in which a polite request is actually coercive. The interrelationship of the doctrines of "search" and "consent" is explored in Goldberger, Consent, Expectations of Privacy, and the Meaning of "Searches" in the Fourth Amendment, 75 J.Crim.L. & Crim. 319 (1984).

Which view is preferable? What warnings should a person be given under the dissenting view? For example, would a warning explaining that a right exists to refuse consent be adequate? Is it necessary to explain the right to provide a limited consent? See United States v. Dichiarinte, 445 F.2d 126 (7th Cir. 1971); State v. Koucoules, 343 A.2d 860 (Me.1974). Does the person warned have to understand what happens if consent is refused? If so, what should the police say about the consequences of refusing consent? Should the person be told of the right to revoke consent? See United States v. Bily, 406 F.Supp. 726 (E.D.Pa.1975).

Sections 240.2(2) and (3) of the Model Code of Pre-Arraignment Procedure would require a warning that the requested person "is under no obligation to give such consent and that anything found may be taken and used in evidence." If the person is in custody or under arrest, the additional warning that the person has the right to consult with counsel and to communicate with relatives and friends before deciding whether to consent must be given. Section 240.3 would limit the scope of the search to the consent, would confine the things subject to seizure to items seizable pursuant to other valid searches, and would allow consent to be withdrawn or limited prior to the completion of the search (although objects seized prior to the change of mind remain seized).

The ALI adopted its rule despite *Schneckloth* and opted for a provision that would be workable. The Comment to Section 240.2, at 533, states that "[i]f there is one thing that comes through clearly from almost all of the cases * * *, whichever way they come out on the warning requirement, it is the extreme difficulty of determining from the record the extent to which the person whose consent was sought acted on the assumption that the police had a right to make the search." Thus, the Code is written to avoid confusion and to assure that consent determinations after the fact can be made with greater ease. The ALI Comment, at pages 536–37, goes on to say that "if there is the slightest doubt that the person in question is not aware of his right, and no such information is given him, the police are eliciting consent on the basis of withheld information. It is hard to describe such conduct as other than deceptive, or the Court's decision as other than retrograde." This is strong criticism. Is it so clear that the *Schneckloth* Court was misguided? Would the Court have been better advised to have required a warrant if there was an opportunity, before requesting consent, to obtain one? See Weinreb, Generalities of the Fourth Amendment, 42 U.Chi.L.Rev. 47, 57–58 (1974).[24]

After *Schneckloth* the totality of the circumstances must be examined. In Bumper v. North Carolina, 391 U.S. 543 (1968), the Court placed the burden of proving that consent "was, in fact, freely and voluntarily given" on the prosecutor, and "[t]his burden cannot be discharged by showing no more than acquiescence to a claim of lawful authority." See also United States v. Lindsay, 506 F.2d 166 (D.C.Cir.1974) (silence not consent). In *Bumper*, the defendant's grandmother was told by police that they had a warrant to search her home and she allowed them to search. The Supreme Court wrote as follows:

> A search conducted in reliance upon a warrant cannot later be justified on the basis of consent if it turns out that the warrant was invalid. The result can be no different when it turns out that the State does not even attempt to rely upon the validity of the warrant, or fails to show that there was, in fact, any warrant at all. When a law enforcement officer claims authority to search a home under a warrant, he announces in effect that the occupant has no right to resist the search. The situation is instinct with coercion—albeit colorably lawful coercion. Where there is coercion there cannot be consent.

See also Evans v. State, 530 S.W.2d 932 (Tex.Cr.App.1975) (consent involuntary when invalid arrest warrant used).

The Supreme Court applied *Schneckloth* and found a valid consent in United States v. Mendenhall, 446 U.S. 544 (1980). The facts are set forth in the stop and frisk material, supra. Although a majority of the Court did not agree on whether to treat a woman who arrived in Detroit on a plane from Los Angeles as "seized" when federal agents first approached her, a majority did agree that she consented to accompany the agents to their airport office and to have her purse and person searched. In deciding that Mendenhall voluntarily accompanied the agents to their office, the Court observed that she was simply asked to go and was not threatened or physically forced. In deciding that the searches in the office were consensual, the Court emphasized that Mendenhall was twice told that she was free to decline consent. Justice White's dissent for four members of the Court argued that the government failed to meet its burden of proving that Mendenhall consented to accompany the officers to their office. "[T]he Court's conclusion can only be based on the notion that consent can be assumed from the absence of proof that a suspect resisted police authority. This is a notion that we have squarely rejected." [Citing Bumper v. North Carolina.] He added the following observation:

> Since the defendant was not present to testify at the suppression hearing, we can only speculate about her state of mind as her encounter with the DEA

24. In United States v. Prescott, 581 F.2d 1343 (9th Cir. 1978), the Court held that a person had a right to refuse an officer's request for permission to make a warrantless search. The majority went on to say that one cannot be penalized for exercising the right and that "passive refusal to consent to a warrantless search is privileged conduct which cannot be considered as evidence of criminal wrongdoing." The majority said that its reasoning was not to promote any deterrent function of the exclusionary rule, but "to protect the exercise of a constitutional right." Surprisingly, there was a dissenting opinion that argued that no harm would come if a citizen's decision to invoke Fourth Amendment rights were admissible in evidence against the citizen.

agents progressed from surveillance, to detention, to questioning, to seclusion in a private office, to the female officer's command to remove her clothing. Nevertheless, it is unbelievable that this sequence of events involved no invasion of a citizen's constitutionally protected interest in privacy. The rule of law requires a different conclusion.

In United States v. Gonzalez–Basulto, 898 F.2d 1011 (5th Cir.1990), the court set forth a non-exclusive list of six factors relevant to whether consent is voluntarily obtained.

(1) the voluntariness of the defendant's custodial status; (2) the presence of coercive police procedures; (3) the extent and level of the defendant's cooperation with the police; (4) the defendant's awareness of his right to refuse consent; (5) the defendant's education and intelligence; and (6) the defendant's belief that no evidence will be found.

Obviously, none of these factors are dispositive. For example, *Watson* found a consent voluntary even though the defendant was under arrest, and *Schneckloth* found voluntary consent even though the defendant was unaware of his right to refuse. However, a weak showing by the government on several of the factors substantially increases the likelihood that consent will be found involuntary. Illustrative is United States v. Shaibu, 920 F.2d 1423 (9th Cir.1990). Four officers looking for Bazuaye, a suspect in a bank fraud, went to an apartment complex, which had a front gate and buzzer system. They pressed the button for apartment 115, Shaibu's apartment. The door release sounded, and they entered the complex. As they approached apartment 115, they saw that Shaibu had stepped out of his apartment, leaving the door open, and was walking towards them. One of the officers asked Shaibu if Bazuaye was in the apartment; without answering, Shaibu walked back into the apartment, leaving the door open, and the officers followed him inside. The officers found evidence incriminating Shaibu inside the apartment. The court of appeals found that Shaibu had not voluntarily consented to the entry.

[T]his court has never sanctioned entry to the home based on inferred consent. * * * In Shaibu's case, no affirmative acts took place. He opened the door not to let the police enter, but only for himself to step out of the apartment to meet visitors outside rather than inside. * * * It is one thing to infer consent from actions responding to a police request. It is quite another to sanction the police walking in to a person's home without stopping at the door to ask permission. * * *

We do not expect others to walk in to our homes, even if the door is open, without first requesting permission to enter. That the police would so enter, without request, creates an impression of authority to do so. * * * [W]e interpret failure to object to the police officer's thrusting himself into Shaibu's apartment as more likely suggesting submission to authority than implied or voluntary consent.

The court in *Shaibu* considered whether Shaibu's lack of objection to entry was a voluntary consent. But isn't there more to it than that? Shaibu not only failed to object to entry; he left the door open. If he wasn't consenting to entry, what was he doing? For a case arguably at odds with *Shaibu*, see United States v. Griffin, 530 F.2d 739 (7th Cir.1976), where officers suspecting a burglary was taking place knocked on the door of an apartment where Griffin and his co-defendant Russell lived. Russell answered, the officers requested admission, but Russell said he was busy and slammed the door in their faces.

The police knocked again, and stated that they had reason to believe that a burglary was taking place in the apartment, and again asked to be admitted. Russell stepped back into the apartment, leaving the door partially open. The officers entered and found incriminating evidence. The court held that Russell had voluntarily consented to the entry. The *Shaibu* court distinguished *Griffin*. On what grounds?

The facts and resolution of *Gonzalez–Basulto,* supra are typical of consent cases after *Schneckloth.* Border patrol agents at a permanent checkpoint suspected that Gonzalez–Basulto was carrying drugs in a refrigerated tractor-trailer rig. He was referred to a secondary inspection area to verify his claim that he was an American citizen. Gonzalez produced immigration documentation, and looked nervously about at the drug sniffing dogs present at the checkpoint. The agent asked whether Gonzalez would mind opening the trailer for an inspection. Gonzalez replied "no problem" and unlocked and opened the trailer, which contained boxes of oranges and lemons. A drug-sniffing dog was hoisted into the trailer, and gave a positive alert. The agents opened many boxes, and finally found cocaine in boxes near the front of the trailer. The court found that Gonzalez voluntarily consented to the search.

> The agents did not brandish weapons or threaten Gonzalez in any way. Gonzalez was not placed under arrest until the search uncovered the cocaine. Gonzalez cooperated with the agent who requested permission to search by responding "no problem" to the request and by unlocking and opening the trailer doors. While the agent admitted that he did not inform Gonzalez of his right to refuse to consent, the agent emphasized that he did not put any kind of pressure on Gonzalez to get his consent. He merely asked for permission. Gonzalez was not well-educated but he exhibited a sufficient degree of understanding to indicate his "no problem" response was intelligent. Gonzalez may well have believed that no drugs would be found because the cocaine was hidden in boxes toward the front of the trailer and there was little crawl space in the trailer.

Compare United States v. Jones, 846 F.2d 358 (6th Cir.1988), where the court held that a convicted felon did not voluntarily consent to a search of his home which uncovered guns. Jones' car was stopped by three police cars, he was not told of his right to refuse consent, and he had no formal education. He testified that he felt he was under arrest at the time he gave consent. But at the time Jones was asked for permission to search his home, he had served a prison sentence for murder and two felony drug offenses, and he was on parole. Judge Ryan, dissenting in *Jones,* argued that a court "should not be quick to ignore the distinction between a defendant's general intelligence and formal schooling and his familiarity, rooted in experience, with police practices." What type of "education" do you think should be most relevant to whether a person gave voluntary consent?

Consider the sixth factor discussed in *Gonzalez–Basulto,* i.e. the defendant's belief that no evidence would be found. In United States v. Mendenhall, (discussed in the stop and frisk section at page 182) the Court categorically rejected the argument that Mendenhall could not have voluntarily consented to a strip search because it would disclose the drugs that she carried. The Court stated that, while the suspect may later regret having given consent, "the question is not whether she acted in her ultimate self-interest, but whether she acted voluntarily." Wouldn't the contrary view—that a person could not give voluntary consent if the search would be likely to uncover incriminating evidence—all but do away with consent searches? Is there any plausible reason for a suspect to voluntarily consent to a search which will uncover evidence? Can the sixth factor of *Gonzalez–Basulto* be reconciled with the Court's statements in *Mendenhall?*

Voluntary consent cannot be obtained by trickery. United States v. Tweel, 550 F.2d 297 (5th Cir.1977). But determining whether police conduct is trickery can be difficult. In United States v. Andrews, 746 F.2d 247 (5th Cir.1984), the defendant was in the custody of a federal agent, and told the agent that he had two guns at home. The agent asked if he could inspect the guns, stating that he was investigating an armed robbery. The agent did not state another reason for the inspection—to establish that Andrews, a convicted felon, was illegally possessing firearms. Andrews, who was apparently not involved in the armed robbery, consented to the inspection, and was later charged with illegal possession of firearms. The court held that "the mere failure of the officer to give an encyclopedic catalogue of everything he might be interested in does not render the consent to search involuntary." The court stated that the officer's subjective intent to trick Andrews into producing the guns was irrelevant. Recall the discussion on pretext, earlier in the Chapter. Is the result in *Andrews* consistent with the courts' treatment of pretextual stops and arrests?

In Graves v. Beto, 424 F.2d 524 (5th Cir.1970), the defendant, who had initially refused to give a blood sample, gave his consent after being told that the sample would be used only to determine the alcohol content of his blood. The court refused to allow the blood sample to be used later to establish identity in a rape case. Is this result consistent with *Andrews?* Is *Graves* better understood as a trickery case, or as a case dealing with the scope of consent?

2. *Third Party Consent*

Can a third party consent to the search of an area in which a suspect has an expectation of privacy? Frazier v. Cupp, 394 U.S. 731 (1969), upheld the search of a defendant's duffle bag when his cousin, a joint user of the bag, consented. The Court rejected the argument that because the cousin had authority to use only one compartment of the bag, he could not consent to a search of the remainder, stating that it would not "engage in such metaphysical subtleties," and that the defendant, who allowed his cousin to use the bag, must "have assumed the risk" he would consent to let others see inside.

The leading third-party consent case is United States v. Matlock, 415 U.S. 164 (1974). Matlock was arrested in the front yard of a house. Mrs. Graff admitted the police to the house and told them she shared the house with Matlock. She consented to a search. The lower courts held that the third party consent doctrine depended upon not only the reasonable appearance of authority to consent but also upon actual authority to consent, and they found insufficient evidence to show actual authority. The Supreme Court reversed, finding actual authority. It did not reach the question whether apparent authority is sufficient. In a footnote the Court wrote that "[c]ommon authority is * * * not to be implied from the mere property interest a third party has in the property. The authority which justifies the third-party consent does not rest upon the law of property, with its attendant historical and legal refinements, but rests rather on mutual use of the property by persons generally having joint access or control for most purposes, so that it is reasonable to recognize that any of the co-inhabitants has the right to permit the inspection in his own right and that the others have assumed the risk that one of their number might permit the common area to be searched."

The Court in Illinois v. Rodriguez, 110 S.Ct. 2793 (1990), considered the issue it left open in *Matlock:* whether a search is valid when based on the consent of a third party who has apparent but not actual authority. The third party in *Rodriguez* was Rodriguez's woman friend, who had, unknown to the officers, moved out of his apartment a month before the search and retained a key without permission. When speaking to the officers, she referred to the premises as "our apartment."

Justice Scalia, writing for a six-person majority, agreed with the lower courts that the friend did not have actual authority to consent to a search of the apartment, in that she had no joint access or control of the premises after moving out. According to the majority, however, the officers' reasonable belief that the friend had authority to consent would validate the entry. The Court rejected the defendant's argument that permitting a reasonable belief of common authority to validate a search would be tantamount to a vicarious waiver of Fourth Amendment rights. Relying on *Schneckloth,* Justice Scalia distinguished between a waiver of constitutional rights and the voluntary consent to search. He explained that while a waiver of a constitutional right must be personal, the validity of a consent search is determined by whether the search is reasonable:

> We would assuredly not permit * * * evidence seized in violation of the Fourth Amendment to be introduced on the basis of a trial court's mere 'reasonable belief'—derived from statements by unauthorized persons—that the defendant has waived his objection. But one must make a distinction between, on the one hand, trial rights that derive from the violation of constitutional guarantees and, on the other hand, the nature of those constitutional guarantees themselves. * * *
>
> What Rodriguez is assured by the trial right of the exclusionary rule, where it applies, is that no evidence seized in violation of the Fourth Amendment will be introduced at his trial unless he consents. What he is assured by the Fourth Amendment itself, however, is not that no government search of his house will occur unless he consents; but that no search will occur that is 'unreasonable.' * * * There are various elements, of course, that can make a search of a person's house 'reasonable'—one of which is the consent of the person or his cotenant. The essence of respondent's argument is that we should impose upon this element a requirement that we have not imposed upon other elements that regularly compel government officers to exercise judgment regarding the facts: namely, the requirement that their judgment be not only responsible but correct.

Justice Scalia concluded that the question of authority to consent should be governed by the same standard of reasonableness—and allowance for reasonable mistakes—as had been applied in other areas of Fourth Amendment jurisprudence, such as probable cause, the execution of a warrant, and the existence of exigent circumstances. According to the Court, it would be anomalous that a reasonable mistake of fact could support probable cause or exigent circumstances, but that a similar mistake could not support the validity of a consent. The Court remanded for a determination of whether the officers could have reasonably believed that Rodriguez's friend had actual authority to consent to a search of his apartment.

Justice Marshall, joined by Justices Brennan and Stevens, dissented. Justice Marshall contended that third party consent searches are permissible not because they are reasonable, but because a person "may voluntarily limit his expectation of privacy by allowing others to exercise authority over his possessions" and thus they are not searches at all. Justice Marshall concluded that if an individual did not actually voluntarily assume the risk of third party consent, there would then be a "search" and the consent of a third party does not make a search reasonable.

In Stoner v. California, 376 U.S. 483 (1964), the government argued that the officers relied on the apparent authority of the hotel desk clerk to consent to a search of Stoner's room. The Court rejected that argument, stating that "the rights protected by the Fourth Amendment are not to be eroded by unrealistic doctrines of apparent authority." Is the result and language in *Stoner* inconsistent with *Rodriguez?* Or can it be explained by the reasonableness standards that are applicable to third party consent searches? Is *Stoner* really an apparent authority case?

Does *Rodriguez* mean that the police can presume third party consent upon the assertion of the third party that he has common authority? If a babysitter answers the door, and asserts that she has common authority over the entire premises, can police search the entire house upon the babysitter's consent? Professor Weinreb argues that such a search would be unreasonable in Generalities of the Fourth Amendment, 42 U.Chi.L.Rev. 47 (1974). What if the babysitter really had actual authority, but could not reasonably be believed to have apparent authority? What if the officer did not believe that the babysitter had either apparent or actual authority, but in fact she had actual authority? In light of the pretext cases discussed throughout this Chapter, would the courts find that a search pursuant to such consent was reasonable? See e.g. United States v. Chaidez, 919 F.2d 1193, 1201–02 (7th Cir.1990) (it was unreasonable to infer authority when person consenting to search said that she did not live in the house and was there only to do laundry, and that she rented the property for her father; however, the fact that she had actual authority justified the search).

Most lower courts before *Rodriguez* had held that police officers must make reasonable inquiries concerning apparent authority when they find themselves in ambiguous circumstances, and more facts can be easily obtained. See United States v. Poole, 307 F.Supp. 1185 (E.D.La.1969) (officers who obtained consent searched around a person in the bedroom; the court found a duty to inquire whether some of the property searched was owned by that person). Compare People v. Adams, 53 N.Y.2d 1, 439 N.Y.S.2d 877, 422 N.E.2d 537 (1981) (duty of further inquiry excused given exigencies of situation in which consent was given and search was made). Does *Rodriguez* change these results?

Courts seem puzzled by cases involving consents by parents and children. But there appears to be some sense in allowing parents with control over entire premises to consent, see, e.g., United States v. Peterson, 524 F.2d 167 (4th Cir.

1975), but not to allow such consent when a part of premises is exclusively reserved for a child, see, e.g., In re Scott K, 24 Cal.3d 395, 595 P.2d 104, 155 Cal.Rptr. 671 (1979); People v. Nunn, 55 Ill.2d 344, 304 N.E.2d 81 (1973). Courts have been reluctant to let minor children consent to searches of homes. See, e.g., Padron v. State, 328 So.2d 216 (Fla.App.1976); May v. State, 199 So.2d 635 (Miss.1967). Siblings frequently have been permitted to consent to searches of jointly occupied premises. See, e.g., United States v. Boston, 508 F.2d 1171 (2d Cir. 1974).

Problems involving the relationship between principal and agent, employer and employee, bailor and bailee, school officials and students abound. If the relationship is such that, without the permission of the other party to the relationship, one party could freely invite third persons, who are not law enforcement officers, to inspect the shared premises or property, then the Fourth Amendment permits the same party to invite all persons, including law enforcement officers. See generally United States v. Klotz, 943 F.2d 707 (7th Cir.1991) (wife has authority to consent to the search of a storage locker leased in her name, even if she was unaware that the locker was currently being rented).

3. *Scope of Consent*

Even where a person voluntarily gives consent, there may be a question about whether the consent extended to the areas actually searched by the officer. A search beyond the scope of consent cannot be justified as a consent search. The question is whether a given search is beyond the scope of a given consent. In United States v. Blake, 888 F.2d 795 (11th Cir.1989), officers approached Blake while he was walking to his plane at an airport. After receiving identification and examining his tickets, the officers asked Blake if he would consent to a search of his "person." They informed him of his right to refuse. Within seconds of receiving consent, one officer reached into Blake's groin region where he did a "frontal touching" of Blake's genitals. The officer felt an object and heard a crinkling sound, and a subsequent search incident to arrest revealed crack cocaine. The court held that the frontal touching was a search beyond the scope of Blake's consent. It stated that, given the public location of the police-citizen encounter, "it cannot be said that a reasonable individual would understand that a search of one's person would entail an officer touching his or her genitals." Do you agree? Recall the facts of *Gonzalez–Basulto,* supra, where the defendant consented to an inspection of his truck, and officers at the border checkpoint brought a drug-sniffing dog onto the truck. Gonzalez argued that the entry of the dog into the truck was beyond the scope of the consent given, but the court stated that Gonzalez had seen the dogs before giving consent, and so could reasonably expect that a dog would be used. Is this consistent with *Blake?* What if, before asking Blake for permission to search his person, the officers had conducted frontal touchings of five other people in the airport in full view of Blake? See also United States v. Towns, 913 F.2d 434 (7th Cir.1990) (consent for entry into an apartment to look at defendant's identification did not permit thorough seven hour search of the apartment).

In Florida v. Jimeno, 111 S.Ct. 1801 (1991), Chief Justice Rehnquist, writing for a majority of seven justices, relied on *Rodriguez* and *Schneckloth* to conclude that the scope of a consent is determined by a standard of objective reasonableness. The Court held that an officer could reasonably conclude that when a suspect gave general consent to a search of his car, he also consented to a search of a paper bag lying on the floor of the car. The officer had informed Jimeno that he was looking for narcotics in the car and obtained consent to search. Jimeno did not place any explicit limitation on the scope of the search. The Chief Justice reasoned that the general consent to search the car included consent to search containers in the car that might contain drugs. He stated that "the scope of a search is generally defined by its expressed object" and that "a reasonable person might be expected to know that narcotics are carried in some form of container." The Chief Justice distinguished the instant case from one in which an officer, given consent to search the trunk of a car, pried open a locked briefcase found inside the trunk. He explained that "it is very likely unreasonable to think that a suspect, by consenting to the search of his trunk, has agreed to the breaking open of a locked briefcase within the trunk, but it is otherwise with a paper bag."

The majority rejected the defendant's argument that police officers should be required to separately request permission to search each container found in a car. The Chief Justice saw "no basis for adding this sort of superstructure to the Fourth Amendment's basic tenet of reasonableness" and noted the community's interest in encouraging consent searches.

Justice Marshall, joined by Justice Stevens, dissented. He argued that a person has distinct privacy expectations in a car and in containers which might be found therein. Thus, consent to relinquish some privacy is not consent to relinquish all privacy. Justice Marshall noted that, at best, general consent is ambiguous, and police can avoid ambiguity by asking at the outset for permission to search a car and its contents or by asking for additional permission to search a container when it is found within a car. Justice Marshall concluded by attacking the majority's expressed interest in encouraging consent searches:

> The majority's real concern is that if the police were required to ask for additional consent to search a closed container * * *, an individual who did not mean to authorize such additional searching would have an opportunity to say no. In essence, then, the majority is claiming that 'the community has a real interest' not in encouraging citizens to *consent* to investigatory efforts of their law enforcement agents, but rather in encouraging individuals to be *duped* by them. That is not the community that the Fourth Amendment contemplates.

In terms of providing guidance to the police, is the dissent's approach less helpful than the majority's? Which approach provides a suspect with the clearest choice? Which approach is more likely to communicate to a suspect that consent may be limited or general? Which approach is most likely to generate consent? Are the arguments of the majority and dissent in *Jimeno* different from those of the majority and dissent in *Schneckloth?*

After *Jimeno,* it is up to the citizen rather than the officer to clarify any ambiguity concerning the scope of consent. See United States v. Berke, 930 F.2d 1219 (7th Cir.1991) (consent to officer's "looking" into bag allows a thorough search of the bag; defendant did not ask for clarification of what the officers meant when they said they wanted to "look"); United States v. Ibarra, 948 F.2d 903 (5th Cir.1991) (consent to search "the house" implicitly includes consent for officers to enter the attic by breaking down a wooden barricade with a sledgehammer).

VI. THE REACH OF THE FOURTH AMENDMENT

A. SEARCHES BY INDIVIDUALS NOT COVERED BY THE FOURTH AMENDMENT

1. *Private Citizens*

Although the language of the Fourth Amendment is broad enough to encompass searches by all persons, whether or not they are agents of the government, the Amendment was part of the Bill of Rights that the Supreme Court said was directed at the federal government in 1791, and parts of which have been incorporated through the Fourteenth Amendment to operate against the states.

In Burdeau v. McDowell, 256 U.S. 465 (1921), the Supreme Court held that private papers stolen from office safes that were blown open, and a desk that was forced open, could be presented to a grand jury by a government prosecutor, because there was no unconstitutional government search and hence no violation of the Fourth Amendment. The Court noted that the victim of the thefts had a private right of action against the thieves, but refused to bar the government from using the evidence. Justice Brandeis, joined by Justice Holmes, dissented.

Some years later the Court decided Elkins v. United States, 364 U.S. 206 (1960), holding that evidence improperly obtained by state officials (who were bound by the Fourth Amendment after Wolf v. Colorado, 338 U.S. 25 (1949), but not by an exclusionary rule) could not be used in a federal prosecution, and rejecting the theory that when federal agents have not violated the Constitution they may use in federal prosecutions evidence illegally seized by state officers. Some argued that after *Elkins'* abolished the "silver platter" doctrine—i.e., receipt and use of the tainted evidence by federal officials—the same approach should be taken to receipt and use of evidence illegally seized by private persons. But *Elkins* dealt with officials, all of whom were covered by the Fourth Amendment, whereas private persons are not within the Amendment's reach. "The thrust of the Fourth Amendment is to assure protection from official, not private intrusion." United States v. McGuire, 381 F.2d 306, 313 n. 5 (2d Cir. 1967). Thus, *Burdeau* was not overruled by *Elkins.*

Judge Moylan has argued that if *Burdeau* were decided otherwise, then "it would cease to be a Bill of Rights and would become a code of substantive law." The Fourth Amendment Inapplicable Vs. the Fourth Amendment Satisfied: The Neglected Threshold of "So What?" 1977 So.Ill.L.J. 75, 103 (1977). On the other hand, it could be argued that the costs of excluding evidence would be low in light of the few private invasions that take place and that use of stolen evidence violates a basic sense of fairness. You might want to consider how you would respond when you consider the exclusionary rule in the last section of the chapter.

State v. Helfrich, 183 Mont. 484, 600 P.2d 816 (1979), holds that an illegal search by a private person tainted a warrant. The Montana Supreme Court also held, 4–3 in State v. Hyem, 630 P.2d 202 (Mont.1981), that all searches without a warrant, whether by government officials or private persons, are per se unreasonable unless they fall within one of the recognized exceptions and that illegally seized evidence by private persons must be suppressed. For a scholarly argument supporting this result, see Burkhoff, Not So Private Searches and the Constitution, 66 Corn.L.Rev. 627 (1981).

For more typical analyses, see United States v. McGreevy, 652 F.2d 849 (9th Cir. 1981) (police officer working at second job as security officer is not governed by Amendment); United States v. Walther, 652 F.2d 788 (9th Cir. 1981) (airline employee acted as government agent when he expected a DEA reward for his actions and the agency had encouraged him).

2. *Mixed Public and Private Action*

Sticky questions arise as to when public officials are so involved in private action that the Fourth Amendment governs the conduct of all participants. In Coolidge v. New Hampshire, 403 U.S. 443 (1971), which seems to be a case for all Fourth Amendment issues, all the Justices apparently agreed that when police officers went to the Coolidge's house in order to talk with his wife and "to check his story against what she might say," there was no government action within the reach of the Fourth Amendment arising from the officers questioning the wife about her husband's guns and her response, "Yes, I will get them in the bedroom." The test for whether the Amendment applied, said the Court, was "whether Mrs. Coolidge, in light of all the circumstances of the case, must be regarded as having acted as an 'instrument' or agent of the state when she produced her husband's belongings." The Court noted that "the simple but often powerful convention of openness and honesty, the fear that secretive behavior will intensify suspicion, and uncertainty as to what course is most likely to be helpful to the absent spouse" are forces pushing the spouse to cooperate with the police. The Court concluded with the comment that "[t]o hold that the conduct of the police here was a search and seizure would be to hold, in effect, that a criminal suspect has constitutional protection against the adverse consequences of a spontaneous, good-faith effort by his wife to clear him of suspicion."

Unfortunately, the Court's comment about spontaneous action hardly was appropriate when the police arrived at the Coolidge home while Mr. Coolidge was in custody, asked about guns and found that Mrs. Coolidge was willing to cooperate because she felt she had nothing to hide. It is interesting to note that in its important consent search case, Schneckloth v. Bustamonte, 412 U.S. 218, 245 (1973), the majority opinion of Justice Stewart referred to his *Coolidge* opinion for the Court as a consent case.

When the police are requesting specific cooperation to secure particular evidence from someone who would have authority to let the police search for themselves, differentiating a consent search from a non-search is difficult, if not impossible. It also is irrelevant, since consent validates the action. But, if a person has no authority to consent, it is crucial to a Fourth Amendment claim to know whether a search by the person is attributed to the police. See, e.g., People v. Hamilton, 74 Ill.2d 457, 386 N.E.2d 53 (1979). Whenever a claim is made that a private person is acting as a police agent, the claim probably will turn on the question whether the private person believed at the time of a search or seizure that her action had been explicitly or implicitly requested or required by police or other government agents, who had reason to know that their actions well might give rise to such belief or that such a belief existed. If the belief existed and the government had reason to know that it might or actually did exist, the private person will be treated as agreeing to participate in government action, and the search by the private person will come within the reach of the Fourth Amendment. See generally United States v. Mekjian, 505 F.2d 1320 (5th Cir. 1975). Thus, in Skinner v. Railway Labor Executives' Ass'n, (page 294), the Court held that drug-testing procedures promulgated by private railroad companies, pursuant to Federal regulations granting authority to the railroads, implicated the Fourth Amendment. The government had mandated that the railroads not bargain away the drug-testing authority granted by the Federal regulations. Also, the Federal regulations made plain a strong preference for testing as well as the Government's desire to have access to the results. The Court held that the Fourth Amendment could be applicable even if the Government does not actually compel a search by a private party. The Court found "clear indices of the Government's encouragement, endorsement, and participation" sufficient to make the drug testing a Government search. See also United States v. Pierce, 893 F.2d 669 (5th Cir. 1990) (for a search by a private person to trigger Fourth Amendment protection, the Government must have known about the search in advance, and the private party must be acting for law enforcement purposes).

3. *Government Investigative Activity Subsequent to Private and Other Legal Searches*

Difficult questions can arise when Government agents follow up on a private search. Walter v. United States, 447 U.S. 649 (1980), divided the Court on the question whether FBI agents, who received a package of films from a recipient to whom it was misdelivered by a private carrier, could view the films without a warrant. The recipient had opened the package but had not viewed the films. Justice Stevens' opinion, joined by Justice Stewart, concluded that "the unauthorized exhibition of the films constituted an unreasonable invasion of their owner's constitutionally protected interest in privacy," and that "an officer's authority to possess a package is distinct from his authority to examine its contents." Hence, although the agents could receive the films, they could not view them without a warrant, even though the recipient not covered by the Fourth Amendment had opened the package; "[a] partial invasion of privacy cannot automatically justify a total invasion." Justice White, joined by Justice Brennan, concurred in part and disagreed with a footnote of Justice Stevens that left open the question "whether the Government projection of the films would have infringed any Fourth Amendment interest if private parties had projected the films before turning them over to the Government." Justice White agreed that a search by private persons could provide probable cause for a warrant, but said it could not excuse the government from the warrant requirement for its own search. Apparently, both opinions agreed that what the FBI observed in plain view was properly observed. Justice Marshall concurred in the judgment without opinion. Justice Blackmun's dissent, joined by the Chief Justice and Justices Powell and Rehnquist, argued "that, by the time the FBI received the films, these petitioners had no remaining expectation of privacy in their contents."

The extent to which government agents may search or seize evidence following searches by private individuals again divided the Court in United States v. Jacobsen, 466 U.S. 109 (1984). A Federal Express supervisor asked an office manager to examine a package that had been torn by a fork lift. Inside a cardboard outer container, the supervisor and manager found, cushioned by five or six pieces of crumpled newspaper, a ten-inch long tube wrapped with the kind of silver tape used on basement ducts. They cut open the tube and found a series of zip-lock bags that contained white powder. They notified the Drug Enforcement Administration of their finding, and an agent arrived at the office after the plastic bags had been placed back into the tube and the cardboard box. The agent opened the bags, removed a trace of the powder from each, did a "field test," and discovered that the powder was cocaine.

Although a magistrate found that the powder was in plain view when the agent arrived, the Court noted that the District Judge who ruled on the suppression motion did not rely on the magistrate's finding. The Court, also choosing not to rely on the finding, sustained the agent's actions. Justice Stevens' opinion commanded six votes. He reasoned that the Federal Express employees' actions were not covered by the Fourth Amendment and that *Walter* required an analysis of the extent to which the government exceeded the bounds of the private search.

Justice Stevens observed that there was no Fourth Amendment violation in the employees' describing what they saw and reasoned as follows: when the agent first saw the package he knew that it contained "nothing of significance except a tube containing plastic bags and, ultimately, white powder"; "a manual inspection of the tube and its contents would not tell [the agent] anything more than he already had been told"; the only reason for the inspection was to avoid "the risk of a flaw in the employees' recollection," which did not involve an infringing of privacy rights; the removal of the plastic bags from the tube and the agent's visual inspection "enabled the agent to learn nothing that had not previously been learned during the private search"; the agent's seizure was reasonable since the package already had been opened, it remained unsealed, and the employees invited the agent to inspect its contents; and the warrantless seizure of the bags was reasonable on the ground that they probably contained contraband.

Finally, Justice Stevens reasoned that the field test—to determine only one thing, whether the powder was cocaine—compromised "no legitimate privacy interest." This portion of his opinion is examined in connection with "reasonable expectations of privacy," supra.

Justice White concurred in part and in the judgment. He would have relied upon the magistrate's finding of plain view and expressed strong disagreement with the majority's approach to "government inspections following on the heels of private searches." He agreed that a private party may permissibly reveal to government agents the results of a private search, but disagreed that this automatically justifies additional government searches following private searches. He also agreed that agents may use information supplied by private parties to obtain search warrants, but disagreed that they could use this information as a justification for a warrantless search.

Justice White argued that the effect of the Court's decision was to permit police to break into a locked car, suitcase, or even a house, if a private person previously did so and reported what he found to the police. He stated he "would be hard-pressed" to distinguish this case from three others: "(1) one in which the private party's knowledge, later communicated to the government, that a particular container concealed contraband and nothing else arose from his presence at the time the container was sealed; (2) one in which the private party learned that a container concealed contraband and nothing else when it was previously opened in his presence; or (3) one in which the private party knew to a certainty that a container concealed contraband and nothing else as a result of conversations with its owner." Justice White concluded that a warrant should be required in these cases and that one would have been required in the instant case had there been no plain view. Justice Brennan, joined by Justice Marshall, dissented and agreed with Justice White's criticism of the majority opinion. He would have remanded for further consideration of the plain view question.

Who has the better of the argument, Justice Stevens or Justice White? In thinking about the majority's approach, consider whether it really is important that the employees told the agent that the package contained only the bags with the powder. Assume that the package also had some kind of document in it and that the employees had not examined the document and could not describe it in any detail. Would the agent's uncertainty about the document bar a search of the bags with the powder? What if the employees had opened only part of the package and had called the agent as soon as they found the bags? Would the agent be barred from reopening and examining the package—at least to the extent that the employees did—because he would not know exactly what else might be in the package? Justice Stevens states that there was nothing of significance in the package other than the bags. On these facts, he probably is correct. What, however, if the newspapers had not been crumpled, or if something else was in the package besides the bags? Does the agent decide what is significant? Or should a magistrate decide?

If you prefer Justice White's approach, would you have found the agent's conduct to be valid if the bags had been visible from outside the package when he got there? If so, do you conclude that it should be outcome determinative for Fourth Amendment purposes whether the Federal Express employees actually resealed the package? If they had left it open and invited the agent to examine it and you conclude that he legitimately could have done so, should their act of closing the package—after they called the government and, in essence, invited a governmental examination—be viewed as restoring expectations of privacy on the part of the persons who mailed and awaited receipt of the package?

Jacobsen establishes that if an initial intrusion is not covered by the Fourth Amendment, a later intrusion to the same effect is also free from Fourth Amendment constraints. While *Jacobsen* dealt with an initial search to which the Fourth Amendment did not apply, its principle has been held equally applicable to initial searches which are valid under the Fourth Amendment. In Illinois v. Andreas, 463 U.S. 765 (1983), Government agents conducted a legal customs search of a wooden crate that was being shipped to an address in the United States, and found drugs hidden in a table therein. They then resealed the crate, and followed it to its destination using a surveillance process called a "controlled delivery." Surveilling police ultimately saw Andreas drag the container into his apartment; when he re-emerged with it 30 to 45 minutes later, the agents searched the container without a warrant. Chief Justice Burger, writing for the Court, concluded that "the simple act of resealing the container to enable the police to make a controlled delivery does not operate to revive or restore the lawfully invaded privacy rights."

What if Andreas came out with the crate two days later? If a Customs official searches a suitcase, can Government agents search the same suitcase without a warrant a year later? In *Andreas,* Chief Justice Burger noted that there may be a gap in surveillance, during which "it is possible that the container will be put to other uses—for example, the contraband may be removed or other items may be placed inside." He concluded, however, that the Fourth Amendment would only be applicable to a subsequent reopening if there is "a substantial likelihood that the contents of the container have been changed during the gap in surveillance." Otherwise, "there is no legitimate expectation of privacy in the contents of a container previously opened under lawful authority." On the facts, the Court found that the re-opening did not implicate a revived privacy interest, due to the unusual size of the container, its specialized purpose, and the relatively short time that Andreas had the container in his apartment. If *Andreas* and *Jacobsen* are correctly decided, can an officer who receives information about the interior of a home from an informant then enter the home without a warrant?

4. *Foreign Officials*

Several decisions hold that the Fourth Amendment is not violated if American officials receive and use evidence seized outside the United States by foreign officials whose procedures would violate the Fourth Amendment if conducted here. See, e.g., Stonehill v. United States, 405 F.2d 738 (9th Cir.1968); Brulay v. United States, 383 F.2d 345 (9th Cir.1967). See also Note, Searches South of the Border: Admission of Evidence Seized by Foreign Officials, 53 Cornell L.Rev. 886 (1968).[25] Of course, the Fourth Amendment is not intended to control the activities of foreign officials. But, if an American agent participates in a foreign search, should the Fourth Amendment apply? United States v. Marzano, 537 F.2d 257 (7th Cir.1976), suggests that it should. Do you agree? If a search is conducted pursuant to a treaty, is the treaty invalid if it explicitly provides for foreign searches that would violate the Fourth Amendment? Does the United States have an obligation, if it requests foreign officials to search on its behalf, to also request that they comply with our concept of reasonableness and even our warrant requirement if it is similar to local procedure?

United States v. Phillips, 479 F.Supp. 423 (M.D.Fla.1979), concludes that evidence illegally seized in Canada could not be used in United States courts if the seizure also would have been unlawful under federal law, and suggests that the usual exclusionary rule might apply if foreign officers are "in privity" with American officials.

25. If the conscience of the Court is shocked, however, evidence may be suppressed. See United States v. Rose, 570 F.2d 1358, 1362 (9th Cir.1978). The usual statement that the exclusionary rule does not apply when foreign searches are conducted by foreign officials is repeated in United States v. Mount, 757 F.2d 1315 (D.C.Cir.1985). Judge Bork offers a concurring opinion in which he rejects the argument that exclusion might be required if the foreign conduct were to "shock the judicial conscience."

A suggested approach for identifying foreign searches subject to American constitutional restraints is offered in Saltzburg, The Reach of the Bill of Rights Beyond the Terra Firma of the United States, 20 Va.J.Int'l L. 741 (1980).

Even if the foreign search is conducted by or at the behest of American officials, it will not implicate the Fourth Amendment if the victim of the search is a non-resident alien. In United States v. Verdugo–Urquidez, discussed at page 24, the Court held that non-resident aliens lack sufficient connection with this Country to be considered as part of "the people" covered by the Fourth Amendment.

B. EAVESDROPPING, WIRETAPPING, UNDERCOVER ACTIVITY, AND THE OUTER REACHES OF THE FOURTH AMENDMENT

The Court has struggled in its attempts to consider the Fourth Amendment's applicability to various types of undercover investigative activity.

1. *The Early Cases*

In 1928, Chief Justice Taft's majority opinion in Olmstead v. United States, 277 U.S. 438, declared that the interception of voice communications over telephone lines without entry into Olmstead's premises was not within the coverage of the Amendment. "The evidence was secured by the use of the sense of hearing and that only. There was no entry of the house or offices of the defendants." Justices Brandeis and Holmes wrote separate dissenting opinions. Brandeis observed that "[t]he makers of our Constitution * * * conferred, as against the government, the right to be let alone—the most comprehensive of rights and the right most valued by civilized men." He argued that "every unjustifiable intrusion upon the privacy of the individual, by whatever means employed, must be deemed a violation of the Fourth Amendment." And he warned, in now familiar words, that "[o]ur government is the potent, the omnipresent teacher. For good or ill, it teaches the whole people by its example. Crime is contagious. If the government becomes a lawbreaker, it breeds contempt for law; it invites every man to become a law unto himself; it invites anarchy."

In Goldman v. United States, 316 U.S. 129 (1942), the Court found that the use of a detectaphone placed against an office wall to hear conversations next door did not violate the Fourth Amendment because there was no trespass. A decade later the Court held by a 5–4 majority in On Lee v. United States, 343 U.S. 747 (1952), that the Fourth Amendment was not implicated when the government wired an undercover agent for sound by means of a microphone that transmitted sounds to another officer outside the laundry in which the undercover agent was conversing with On Lee. There was no trespass, and the majority found the use of the electronic equipment to be no different from the use of bifocals, field glasses or telescopes. Justice Burton, joined by Justice Frankfurter in dissent, relied on the invasion of the "house." In a separate opinion, Justice Frankfurter said that the dissenting view in *Goldman* was correct: *Olmstead* should be overruled. Justice Douglas' dissent expressed dissatisfaction that he had voted with the majority in *Goldman*. And Justice Black's dissent relied on the Court's supervisory powers over federal criminal trials.

Nine years later came the first Supreme Court condemnation of eavesdropping under the Fourth Amendment. Justice Stewart's unanimous opinion in Silverman v. United States, 365 U.S. 505 (1961), found a constitutional violation in the placement of a spike, a foot long with a microphone attached, under a baseboard into a party wall, so that it made contact with the heating duct that ran through the entire house and served as a sounding board. The Court said that its decision did "not turn upon the technicality of a trespass upon a party wall as a matter of local law. It is based upon the reality of an intrusion into a constitutionally protected area." Three years later a per curiam opinion applied *Silverman* to an electronic listening device stuck into an adjoining wall by a thumb tack. Clinton v. Virginia, 377 U.S. 158 (1964).

2. *The 1960's*

The decade of the 1960's saw several more cases challenging the practices of undercover agents reach the Court. Lopez v. United States, 373 U.S. 427 (1963), involved an IRS agent who, having received an unsolicited bribe and having reported it to his superiors, concealed a wire recorder on his person, as directed by his superiors, when he met Lopez. Justice Harlan's majority opinion relied on *On Lee.* "[T]he device was used only to obtain the most reliable evidence possible of a conversation in which the Government's own agent was a participant and which that agent was fully entitled to disclose." The opinion concluded that "the risk that petitioner took in offering a bribe * * * fairly included the risk that the offer would be accurately reproduced in court, whether by faultless memory or mechanical recording." Chief Justice Warren's concurring opinion argued that *On Lee* was wrongly decided but distinguishable because the recording there was a substitute for the undercover agent's testimony, whereas in *Lopez* the agent testified, was subject to cross-examination, and the tape was used to support credibility. Justice Brennan's dissenting opinion, joined by Justices Douglas and Goldberg, viewed *On Lee* as wrongly decided and indistinguishable from *Lopez.* It argued that On Lee and Lopez both assumed the risk that persons to whom they spoke would divulge their conversation, but that "the risk which both *On Lee* and today's decision impose is of a different order. It is the risk that third parties, whether mechanical auditors * * * or human transcribers of mechanical transmissions as in *On Lee*—third parties who cannot be shut out of a conversation, as conventional eavesdroppers can be, merely by a lowering of voices, or withdrawing to a private place—may give independent evidence of any conversation."

Three years later three cases decided the same day shed additional light on the Fourth Amendment's application to undercover government investigative activities. Chief Justice Warren wrote for the Court in Lewis v. United States, 385 U.S. 206 (1966). An undercover narcotics agent had telephoned Lewis' home asking about the possibility of purchasing marijuana. Arrangements were made and a sale was consummated. Subsequently, another sale took place in Lewis' home. Only Justice Douglas dissented from the Warren view that, because Lewis invited the agent into his home "for the specific purpose of executing a felonious sale of narcotics," the fact that Lewis believed he was dealing with a fellow lawbreaker did not require constitutional protection for the belief. Justice Brennan, with whom Justice Fortas concurred, emphasized that "the agent, in the same manner as any private person, entered the premises for the very purpose contemplated by the occupant and took nothing away except what would be taken away by any willing purchaser." But Justice Douglas argued that "[w]hen the agent in *Lewis* had reason for believing that petitioner possessed narcotics, a search warrant should have been obtained."

The petitioner in *Lewis* had relied on Gouled v. United States, 255 U.S. 298 (1921). In *Gouled,* a business associate of the defendant, acting under orders from federal officers, obtained entry into defendant's office by pretending that he was paying a social visit, when in fact he searched the office in the defendant's absence. The Court in *Gouled* invalidated the search. But the Court in *Lewis* distinguished *Gouled:*

> During neither of his visits to [Lewis'] home did the agent see, hear, or take anything that was not contemplated and in fact intended by petitioner as a necessary part of his illegal business. * * * When, as here, the home is converted into a commercial center to which outsiders are invited for purposes of transacting unlawful business, that business is entitled to no greater sanctity than if it were carried on in a store, a garage, a car or on the street.

Does the foregoing passage adequately explain why a person assumes the risk that a business associate in an illegal enterprise is an undercover agent, but does not assume the same risk with respect to a business associate in a legal enterprise? If an officer masquerades as a television repairman, is his undercover investigative activity in a home covered by the Fourth Amendment?

A similar result to that in *Lewis* was reached in Hoffa v. United States, 385 U.S. 293 (1966). Union leader James Hoffa was convicted for attempting to bribe jurors in a previous trial. Much of the government's case depended on the testimony of a local union official who, after being released from jail with federal and state charges pending against him, spent a great deal of time in the Hoffa camp at the time of the bribe attempts. Justice Stewart's majority opinion assumed that the witness had been an undercover agent from the first visit to Hoffa, but found that "no interest legitimately protected by the Fourth Amendment" was involved in the case. Justice Stewart wrote that "[w]hat the Fourth Amendment protects is the security a man relies upon when he places himself or his property within a constitutionally protected area * * *." He concluded that the undercover agent invaded no protected area because he was invited into Hoffa's hotel room. Under these circumstances, Hoffa was not relying on the security of the hotel room, but upon his "misplaced confidence" that the union official would not reveal his statements. Such a risk, according to Justice Stewart, is "the kind of risk we necessarily assume whenever we speak." Citing *Lopez,* he concluded that although some members of the Court had believed that recording the conversation was improper, no one on the *Lopez* Court expressed doubt that concealment of the true identity of an undercover agent is permissible. Chief Justice Warren dissented and would have exercised the Court's supervisory powers to prevent the use of an informer with a poor background and strong incentives to assure that Hoffa was convicted. Justice Clark was joined by Justice Douglas in an opinion stating that the district court's finding that the government did not place the witness in Hoffa's midst was not clearly erroneous and that the case should have been dismissed without reaching the constitutional argument.

The third case, Osborn v. United States, 385 U.S. 323 (1966), arose out of the attempt to bribe the Hoffa jurors. A man (Vick) hired by Hoffa's lawyer to investigate prospective jurors was cooperating with the government. He related a conversation during which a juror bribe was discussed. Responding to a government request for court authorization, two district judges approved the utilization of a tape recorder on Vick's person during his next scheduled meeting with the lawyer. The recording was used as evidence leading to the lawyer's conviction. Justice Stewart's majority opinion found *Lopez* good authority for sustaining the use of the evidence but added that the judicial approval for a "narrow and particularized purpose" also validated the procedure. Justice Douglas dissented, because the government planted Vick in Hoffa's entourage and thereby participated in a breach of Hoffa's privacy.

The Court struggled in the early wiretapping and eavesdropping cases just to identify the right issues. Faced with new techniques of evidence gathering, the Court first found no Fourth Amendment violation unless a trespass occurred. Then, it suggested that any trespass was enough to require a finding that the Fourth Amendment was violated. Why should trespass be the measure of the constitutional right? Recall that *Katz,* supra, ultimately rejected a trespass test and substituted a reasonable expectation of privacy test. But the *Katz* test does not change the results in *Lewis, Hoffa,* or *Osborn,* since the Court in those cases held that the defendants had no reasonable expectation of privacy from undercover activity, having assumed the risk that their friends or associates would disclose their guilty secrets. Similar analysis has been used to hold that there is no expectation of privacy in trash, or against consensual electronic surveillance. See California v. Greenwood, page 41, supra. United States v. White, page 39, supra. Is the assumption of risk analysis a better way to handle these problems than the old trespass analysis? How do we know what risks we assume until the Court tells us? Why does a person assume the risk that a friend will record an incriminating conversation, but not the risk that the Government will use a wiretap and record an incriminating conversation?

In *Lewis,* the Court emphasized that the narcotics agent was invited into the seller's house. In *Hoffa* it also relied on the fact that the local official was invited to be with Hoffa. But were the cases the same? The agent-buyer in *Lewis* was a stranger. In *Hoffa* the undercover official was a supposed friend, a turncoat in Hoffa's camp. Should the cases have been treated the same way? What about *Osborn,* where the undercover agent Vick was an employee, presumably working with the attorney and client on an important part of the defense; was this an "invitation" case also? In *Osborn,* the Court did not simply cite its earlier *Lopez* opinion. Do you think this was because the defendant in *Lopez,* a stranger, initiated the meeting with the IRS agent? Are the risks in these cases the same?

Is there any place in undercover police work for a warrant requirement? If you find the warrant to be especially satisfying in *Osborn,* ask yourself how the government got the information to provide the two judges. It was by the use of the same agent whom the judges later authorized the government to wire. Should a warrant be required only when a conversation is to be recorded?

Chief Justice Warren's concurrence in *Lopez* suggested that the cases could be explained in part on the basis of how seized conversations were used—i.e., were they independent or corroborative evidence. But can the use of the evidence at trial really be the test of a valid search and seizure?

3. *Wiretapping and Eavesdropping Statutes*

Berger v. New York, 388 U.S. 41 (1967), seemed to evince a different judicial attitude toward electronic eavesdropping. The case arose out of a state investigation of alleged bribery of officials responsible for liquor licenses. An eavesdropping order was obtained pursuant to a New York statute, which read as follows:

> An ex parte order for eavesdropping * * * may be issued by any justice of the supreme court or judge of a county court or of the court of general sessions of the county of New York upon oath or affirmation of a district attorney, or of the attorney-general or of an officer above the rank of sergeant of any police department of the state or of any political subdivision thereof, that there is reasonable ground to believe that evidence of crime may be thus obtained, and particularly describing the person or persons whose communications, conversations or discussions are to be overheard or recorded and the purpose thereof, and, in the case of a telegraphic or telephonic communication, identifying the particular telephone number or telegraph line involved. In connection with the issuance of such an order the justice or judge may examine on oath the applicant and any other witness he may produce and shall satisfy himself of the existence of reasonable grounds for the granting of such application. Any such order shall be effective for the time specified therein but not for a period of more than two months unless extended or renewed by the justice or judge who signed and issued the original order upon satisfying himself that such extension or renewal is in the public interest. Any such order together with the papers upon which the application was based, shall be delivered to and retained by the applicant as authority for the eavesdropping authorized therein.

The order permitted the installation of a recording device in an attorney's office for 60 days. A second order to put another recording device in a second person's office was approved also. After two weeks, a conspiracy was uncovered and Berger was indicted as part of it. Relevant portions of the recordings were admitted into evidence. Justice Clark's majority opinion found serious fault with the New York statute. Justice Clark viewed the statute as a "blanket grant" of permission to eavesdrop, "without adequate supervision or protective procedures." Among the procedural flaws, Justice Clark noted that there was a conspicuous absence of any requirement that a particular crime be named, there was no requirement of a particular description of the conversations sought, the length of time eavesdropping was permitted was too extensive, extensions of the time period were granted on an insufficient showing that such extensions were "in the public interest," there was no provision for terminating the conversation once the evidence sought was found, and the statute lacked notice and return procedures. The opinion recognized that no statute might satisfy its demands, but indicated its willingness to bar much eavesdropping absent a better statute. It concluded as follows: "Our concern with the statute here is whether its language permits a trespassory invasion of the home, by general warrant, contrary to the command of the Fourth Amendment. As it is written, we believe that it does." Justice Douglas' concurring opinion observed that the Court "at long last * * * overrules sub silentio *Olmstead* and its offspring and brings wiretapping and other electronic eavesdropping fully within the purview of the Fourth Amendment."

Justices Black, Harlan, and White dissented. All agreed that the statute passed constitutional muster. Justice Stewart agreed with them, although he found the affidavits in *Berger* to be constitutionally defective. Justice Black said "I am by no means satisfied that the Amendment controls the constitutionality of such [electronic] eavesdropping." Together, Justices Harlan and White argued that the New York procedure as used in *Berger* provided sufficient particularity and sufficient restrictions on the area to be searched, and that the particular judicial order in *Berger* was based upon probable cause and was executed properly.

One year later Congress enacted a new scheme of regulating wiretapping and electronic eavesdropping as part of the 1968 Omnibus Crime Control and Safe Streets Act. Title III was modified by Title I of the 1986 Electronic Communications Privacy Act, to account for technological advances and to correct perceived gaps in the statute. Portions of Title III, as modified by Title I, are set forth below. Compare these provisions with the New York statute invalidated in *Berger*.

TITLE III OF THE OMNIBUS CRIME CONTROL AND SAFE STREETS ACT OF 1968, AS MODIFIED BY TITLE I OF THE 1986 ELECTRONIC COMMUNICATIONS PRIVACY ACT, 18 U.S.C.A. §§ 2510–2520.

CHAPTER 119—WIRE INTERCEPTION AND INTERCEPTION OF ORAL COMMUNICATIONS

§ 2510. Definitions

As used in this chapter—

(1) "wire communication" means any aural transfer made in whole or in part through the use of facilities for the transmission of communications by the aid of wire, cable, or other like connection between the point of origin and the point of reception (including the use of such connection in a switching station) furnished or operated by any person engaged in providing or operating such facilities for the transmission of interstate or foreign communications or communications affecting interstate or foreign commerce and such term includes any electronic storage of such communication, but such term does not include the radio portion of a cordless telephone communication that is transmitted between the cordless telephone handset and the base unit;

(2) "oral communication" means any oral communication uttered by a person exhibiting an expectation that such communication is not subject to interception under circumstances justifying such expectation, but such term does not include any electronic communication;

* * *

(4) "intercept" means the aural acquisition or other acquisition of the contents of any wire, electronic, or oral communication through the use of any electronic, mechanical, or other device; [26]

26. In United States v. New York Tel. Co., 434 U.S. 159 (1977), the Court held that pen registers were not interceptions within the meaning of the statute.

* * *

(9) ["Judges" mean federal district and appeals judges and state court of general jurisdiction judges authorized by state statute to authorize interceptions.]

* * *

(11) "aggrieved person" means a person who was a party to any intercepted wire, oral, or electronic communication or a person against whom the interception was directed.

§ 2511. Interception and disclosure of wire or oral communications prohibited

[This section bars interception, use, and disclosure of wire, oral, or electronic communications obtained in violation of the Act.]

* * *

(2)(f) Nothing contained [herein], shall be deemed to affect the acquisition by the United States Government of foreign intelligence information from international or foreign communications, or foreign intelligence activities conducted in accordance with otherwise applicable Federal law involving a foreign electronic communications system, utilizing a means other than electronic surveillance as defined in section 101 of the Foreign Intelligence Surveillance Act of 1978, and procedures in this chapter and the Foreign Intelligence Surveillance Act of 1978 shall be the exclusive means by which electronic surveillance, as defined in section 101 of such Act, and the interception of domestic wire and oral communications may be conducted.[27]

The result in *New York Tel. Co.* is now codified in 18 U.S.C. § 2511(2)(h). In the 1986 Electronic Communications Privacy Act, 18 U.S.C. § 3121, Congress provided that pen register surveillance must be court-approved; however, it is not subject to all the procedural safeguards governing court-ordered electronic surveillance.

The language "or other acquisition" was added in 1986 to cover such techniques as video surveillance. See generally United States v. Koyomejian, 946 F.2d 1450 (9th Cir. 1991) (provisions of Title I are applicable to the conduct of video surveillance). Some courts have held that Title I leaves domestic video surveillance unregulated, but that such surveillance is subject to the Fourth Amendment's particularity and probable cause requirements as codified by Title I. See United States v. Mesa–Rincon, 911 F.2d 1433 (10th Cir.1990).

27. In United States v. United States District Court, 407 U.S. 297 (1972), the Court, without a dissent, held that the President had no power to conduct warrantless searches in domestic security investigations. But the Court left open the question whether there could be warrantless taps in foreign security investigations.

United States v. Truong Dinh Hung, 629 F.2d 908 (4th Cir. 1980), discusses the Congressional response to the Supreme Court's national security wiretap case, the Foreign Intelligence Surveillance Act of 1978, 50 U.S.C.A. § 1801 et seq., (referred to in the statute quoted above) which requires judicial approval for some foreign intelligence surveillance and authorizes approval upon a less demanding showing than is required for ordinary warrants. The court upheld warrantless electronic surveillance in the instant case, concluding that the government did not need a warrant "when the object of the search or the surveillance is a foreign power, its agent or collaborators," and the surveillance is conducted "primarily" for foreign intelligence reasons. Even when a warrant is not required, the court said that the search must satisfy the reasonableness requirement of the Fourth Amendment. The FISA also is discussed in Note, The Foreign Intelligence Surveillance Act: Legislating a Judicial Role in National Security Surveillance, 78 Mich.L.Rev. 1116 (1980).

Ex parte scrutiny of exhibits in determining compliance with the FISA was upheld in United States v. Belfield, 692 F.2d 141 (D.C.Cir. 1982). Two defendants convicted of first degree murder and perjury had been overheard during the course of surveillance authorized under the Act. After examining logs of the surveillance in camera, the trial judge ruled that the overhearing was irrelevant and not discoverable. As it is permitted to do by stat-

§ 2515. Prohibition of use as evidence of intercepted wire or oral communications

Whenever any wire or oral communication has been intercepted, no part of the contents of such communication and no evidence derived therefrom may be received in evidence in any trial, hearing, or other proceeding in or before any court, grand jury, department, officer, agency, regulatory body, legislative committee, or other authority of the United States, a State, or a political subdivision thereof if the disclosure of that information would be in violation of this chapter.

§ 2516. Authorization for interception of wire or oral communications

(1) The Attorney General, Deputy Attorney General, Associate Attorney General, or any Assistant Attorney General, any acting Assistant Attorney General, or any Deputy Assistant Attorney General in the Criminal Division specially designated by the Attorney General, may authorize an application to a Federal judge of competent jurisdiction for * * * an order authorizing or approving the interception of wire or oral communications * * *

(2) The principal prosecuting attorney of any State, or the principal prosecuting attorney of any political subdivision thereof,[28] if such attorney is authorized by a statute of that State to make application to a State court judge of competent jurisdiction for an order authorizing or approving the interception of wire or oral communications, may apply to such judge for * * * an order * * *.

* * *

§ 2518. Procedure for interception of wire or oral communications

* * *

(3) Upon such application the judge may enter an ex parte order, as requested or as modified, authorizing or approving interception of wire or oral communications within the territorial jurisdiction of the court in which the judge is sitting (and outside that jurisdiction but within the United States in the case of a mobile interception device authorized by a Federal court within such jurisdiction), if the judge determines on the basis of the facts submitted by the applicant that—

(a) there is probable cause for belief that an individual is committing, has committed, or is about to commit a particular offense enumerated in section 2516 of this chapter;

(b) there is probable cause for belief that particular communications concerning that offense will be obtained through such interception;

(c) normal investigative procedures have been tried and have failed or

ute, the government subsequently filed a petition in the District Court in the District of Columbia for a judicial determination as to the validity of the surveillance. This determination was made by the district judge without the convicted defendants having an opportunity to see the government's submission. The court found that Congress intended an ex parte, in camera review under the Act. It upheld the constitutionality of the statute, noting the need "for the Executive to engage in and employ the fruits of clandestine surveillance without being constantly hamstrung by disclosure requirements." United States v. Duggan, 743 F.2d 59 (2d Cir.1984), also sustains the constitutionality of the procedures under the Foreign Intelligence Surveillance Act.

28. State v. Daniels, 389 So.2d 631 (Fla. 1980), indicates the importance of compliance with the federal requirements when states accept the Congressional invitation to adopt statutes based on the federal model. The court found that an assistant state's attorney was not a person who could authorize an application for a wiretap order.

reasonably appear to be unlikely to succeed if tried or to be too dangerous;[29]

(d) there is probable cause for belief that the facilities from which, or the place where, the wire or oral communications are to be intercepted are being used, or are about to be used, in connection with the commission of such offense, or are leased to, listed in the name of, or commonly used by such person.

(4) Each order authorizing or approving the interception of any wire or oral communication shall specify—

(a) the identity of the person, if known, whose communications are to be intercepted;[30]

(b) the nature and location of the communications facilities as to which, or the place where, authority to intercept is granted;

(c) a particular description of the type of communication sought to be intercepted, and a statement of the particular offense to which it relates;

(d) the identity of the agency authorized to intercept the communications, and of the person authorizing the application; and

(e) the period of time during which such interception is authorized, including a statement as to whether or not the interception shall automatically terminate when the described communication has been first obtained.[31]

* * *

(5) No order entered under this section may authorize or approve the interception of any wire, oral, or electronic communication for any period longer than is necessary to achieve the objective of the authorization, nor in any event longer than thirty days. * * * Every order and extension thereof shall contain a provision that the authorization to intercept shall be executed as soon as practicable, shall be conducted in such a way as to minimize the interception of communications not otherwise subject to interception under this chapter, and must terminate upon attainment of the authorized objective, or in any event in thirty days.[32]

29. This is known as the exhaustion requirement. But, as the Court stated in United States v. Giordano, 416 U.S. 505 (1974), the term "exhaustion" is a misnomer. The statute was intended to ensure not that wiretaps are used only as a last resort, "but that they were not to be routinely employed as the initial step in a criminal investigation." Thus, the statute does not require that alternative investigative procedures have been tried and failed, "but only that the success of other methods of investigation appear unlikely." United States v. Thompson, 944 F.2d 1331 (7th Cir.1991) (wiretap properly authorized where it was unlikely that infiltration with confidential informants would be successful).

30. In United States v. Kahn, 415 U.S. 143 (1974), the Court held that where the government knew of the existence of a person but did not know she was using the phone for illegal purposes, she was not a person within this section.

31. In Dalia v. United States, 441 U.S. 238 (1979), the Supreme Court held that the electronic surveillance statute permits courts to authorize electronic surveillance that requires entry into private premises for installation of the necessary equipment. The Court also held that such authorization need not include a specific statement by the court indicating approval of the covert entry. Although the Court recognized that one of the purposes of a warrant is to reduce or eliminate executive discretion when it comes to intrusions into protected areas, the Court concluded that executive officers must have some leeway in deciding how best to execute a warrant.

32. In Scott v. United States, 436 U.S. 128 (1978), the Court held that whether or not agents subjectively intended to comply with the minimization section of the statute was not controlling. What is controlling, said the court, is what the agents actually did. As long as the conduct is reasonable, the statute is not violated. Justice Brennan, joined by Justice Marshall, dissented and charged that the decision eviscerated the protection that Congress attempted to codify.

* * *

(8)(d) Within a reasonable time but not later than ninety days after the filing of an application for an order of approval under section 2518(7)(b) which is denied or the termination of the period of an order or extensions thereof, the issuing or denying judge shall cause to be served, on the persons named in the order or the application, and such other parties to intercepted communications as the judge may determine in his discretion that is in the interest of justice, an inventory which shall include notice of—

(1) the fact of the entry of the order or the application;

(2) the date of the entry and the period of authorized, approved or disapproved interception, or the denial of the application; and

(3) the fact that during the period wire or oral communications were or were not intercepted.

The judge, upon the filing of a motion, may in his discretion make available to such person or his counsel for inspection such portions of the intercepted communications, applications and orders as the judge determines to be in the interest of justice. On an ex parte showing of good cause to a judge of competent jurisdiction the serving of the inventory required by this subsection may be postponed.[33]

* * *

Do you believe the statute satisfies the concerns expressed by the *Berger* Court? For an attack on the statute, see Schwartz, The Legitimation of Electronic Eavesdropping: The Politics of "Law and Order," 67 Mich.L.Rev. 455 (1969). Are wiretaps and eavesdropping devices inherently unreasonable? See Spritzer, Electronic Surveillance by Leave of the Magistrate: The Case in Opposition, 118 U.Pa.L.Rev. 169 (1969). Does electronic surveillance remove some of the danger law enforcement officials face when using undercover techniques? The Supreme Court's handling of important questions under the statute is criticized in Goldsmith, The Supreme Court and Title III; Rewriting the Law of Electronic Surveillance, 74 J.Crim.L. & Crim. 1 (1983).

VII. REMEDIES FOR FOURTH AMENDMENT VIOLATIONS

A. THE BACKGROUND OF THE EXCLUSIONARY RULE

At the outset of the chapter, the point was made that the debate over what the Fourth Amendment requires often is confused with another debate: what to do about Fourth Amendment violations. Thus far we have suspended any discussion of the exclusionary rule, which is at the heart of most search and seizure disputes. Whether there is an exclusionary rule or not, virtually every problem presented up to this point in the chapter still exists, because there is a

33. In United States v. Donovan, 429 U.S. 413 (1977), the Court held that when the government inadvertently excluded persons from its list of those intercepted and thus deprived them of the inventory notice, suppression of evidence was not warranted since the requirements did not play a "substantive role" in the statutory scheme. The Court in United States v. Ojeda Rios, 495 U.S. 257 (1990), held that a failure to comply with the Title III requirement that tapes be immediately sealed would not result in suppression if the Government's error was the result of a good faith, objectively reasonable misinterpretation of the statute. Justice White wrote the majority opinion. Justices Stevens, Brennan and Marshall dissented.

Fourth Amendment. This is no small point, since those who view abolition of the exclusionary rule as a way of simplifying Fourth Amendment law should be able to see how complicated the law would remain even after its abolition. It is true that were there no rule of exclusion, some issues considered infra would not arise. But these are relatively few in number. Moreover, there is no guarantee that the remedy used in place of exclusion would not create as many extra issues for judicial resolution. This is not an argument for the exclusionary rule. It is only recognition that one evil associated with it—i.e., it unduly complicates constitutional decisionmaking—may be overstated. Of course, it would be possible to treat the Amendment as hortatory and to deny that there should be any remedy for its violation. The right that remained, however, hardly would be worth inclusion in a Bill of Rights. Some remedy is necessary, then. But what it should be remains to be determined.

Once it has been determined that a violation of the Fourth Amendment has occurred, the usual remedy today is exclusion of any evidence gathered as a result of that violation—i.e., evidence seized in an illegal search and evidence directly associated with the illegal search (the "fruits" thereof). But the exclusionary rule was not born contemporaneously with the Fourth Amendment. The Bill of Rights is not explicit as to remedies. For over a century after the adoption of the Fourth Amendment, virtually the only remedies available to victims of illegal searches were suits in trespass for damages, or in replevin for return of the goods seized. The trespass alternative was usually impractical, and replevin had no chance of success if the goods seized were contraband, or the fruits or instrumentalities of crime, since these items were considered forfeited to the state regardless of the legality of the seizure. Warden, Md. Penitentiary v. Hayden, 387 U.S. 294, 303–304 (1967).

Why did it take the Supreme Court so long to formulate the exclusionary rule? Did the first 100 years plus indicate that the Court believed that the Amendment did not require exclusion of evidence seized unconstitutionally? In a discussion of Fifth Amendment protections in United States v. Scott, 437 U.S. 82 (1978), the Supreme Court explained that one reason the earlier years provide little guidance to the remedial requirements of the Bill of Rights is that at the time the Bill of Rights was adopted, there was little opportunity for the Supreme Court to address criminal cases:

> [M]ost criminal prosecutions proceeded to final judgment, and neither the United States nor the defendant had any right to appeal an adverse verdict. The verdict in such a case was unquestionably final, and could be raised in bar against any further prosecution for the same offense.
>
> Soon thereafter, Congress made provision for review of certain criminal cases by this Court, but only upon a certificate of division from the Circuit Court, and not at the instigation of the defendant. It was not until 1889 that Congress permitted criminal defendants to seek a writ of error in this Court, and then only in capital cases. Only then did it become necessary for this Court to deal with the issues presented by the challenge of verdicts on appeal.

The exclusionary rule was created in Weeks v. United States, 232 U.S. 383 (1914). Justice Day wrote for a unanimous court:

> The case in the aspect in which we are dealing with it involves the right of the court in a criminal prosecution to retain for the purposes of evidence the letters and correspondence of the accused, seized in his house in his absence

and without his authority, by a United States Marshal holding no warrant for his arrest and none for the search of his premises. The accused, without awaiting his trial, made timely application to the court for an order for the return of these letters, as well as other property. This application was denied, the letters retained and put in evidence, after a further application at the beginning of the trial, both applications asserting the rights of the accused under the Fourth and Fifth Amendments to the Constitution. If letters and private documents can thus be seized and held and used in evidence against a citizen accused of an offense, the protection of the Fourth Amendment declaring his right to be secure against such searches and seizures is of no value, and, so far as those thus placed are concerned, might as well be stricken from the Constitution. The efforts of the courts and their officials to bring the guilty to punishment, praiseworthy as they are, are not to be aided by the sacrifice of those great principles established by years of endeavor and suffering which have resulted in their embodiment in the fundamental law of the land. The United States Marshal could only have invaded the house of the accused when armed with a warrant issued as required by the Constitution, upon sworn information and describing with reasonable particularity the thing for which the search was to be made. Instead, he acted without sanction of law, doubtless prompted by the desire to bring further proof to the aid of the Government, and under color of his office undertook to make a seizure of private papers in direct violation of the constitutional prohibition against such action. * * * To sanction such proceedings would be to affirm by judicial decision a manifest neglect if not an open defiance of the prohibitions of the Constitution intended for the protection of the people against such unauthorized action.

Weeks was limited to cases where the illegal search was conducted by federal officers and the evidence was sought to be admitted in a federal criminal proceeding.

Two themes articulated in *Weeks,* and finding recurrent expression in later cases dealing with the rationale for excluding evidence, were that the exclusionary rule is the only effective means of protecting Fourth Amendment rights, and that the interest in judicial integrity requires that the courts not sanction illegal searches by admitting the fruits of illegality into evidence. In Silverthorne Lumber Co. v. United States, 251 U.S. 385 (1920), these considerations were held to prohibit the copying of illegally seized documents, and their use as the basis for a subpoena of the originals, which had been returned pursuant to a motion by the defendant. The Court stressed that "[t]he essence of a provision forbidding the acquisition of evidence in a certain way is [not merely that] evidence so acquired shall not be used before the Court but that it shall not be used at all."

B. THE EXCLUSIONARY RULE AND THE STATES

In the next thirty years, the Supreme Court had several opportunities to discuss the Fourth Amendment in the context of the incorporation doctrine, and federal-state relations. *Weeks* had explicitly rejected the notion that the exclusionary rule should apply to violations by state or local police. Dicta in Byars v. United States, 273 U.S. 28 (1927) and Gambino v. United States, 275 U.S. 310 (1927), established what came to be known as the "silver platter doctrine". This doctrine made evidence obtained in an illegal state search admissible in federal court as long as there was no federal participation in the search. While the definition of "federal participation" broadened considerably in the ensuing years so as to more readily trigger the exclusion of evidence, Lustig v. United States, 338 U.S. 74 (1949), the silver platter doctrine remained in force till 1960 when Elkins v. United States, 364 U.S. 206, abolished it. Shortly thereafter, the issue became largely academic with the application of the exclusionary rule to the states. Mapp v. Ohio, 367 U.S. 643 (1961).

The rationale underlying these developments in Fourth Amendment remedies can best be understood by contrasting two major opinions of that period: Wolf v. Colorado, 338 U.S. 25 (1949), where unreasonable state searches and seizures were held to violate the Due Process Clause of the Fourteenth Amendment, and Mapp v. Ohio, where that violation was held to require the exclusion of evidence. As you study the two opinions, consider not only the debate over the efficacy of the exclusionary rule, but also the sensitive issues of federal-state relations.

WOLF v. COLORADO

Supreme Court of the United States, 1949.
338 U.S. 25.

MR. JUSTICE FRANKFURTER delivered the opinion of the Court.

* * *

The security of one's privacy against arbitrary intrusion by the police—which is at the core of the Fourth Amendment—is basic to a free society. It is therefore implicit in "the concept of ordered liberty" and as such enforceable against the States through the Due Process Clause. The knock at the door, whether by day or by night, as a prelude to a search, without authority of law but solely on the authority of the police, did not need the commentary of recent history to be condemned as inconsistent with the conception of human rights enshrined in the history and the basic constitutional documents of English-speaking peoples.

Accordingly, we have no hesitation in saying that were a State affirmatively to sanction such police incursion into privacy it would run counter to the guaranty of the Fourteenth Amendment. But the ways of enforcing such a basic right raise questions of a different order. How such arbitrary conduct should be checked, what remedies against it should be afforded, the means by which the right should be made effective, are all questions that are not to be so dogmatically answered as to preclude the varying solutions which spring from an allowable range of judgment on issues not susceptible of quantitative solution.

In Weeks v. United States, this Court held that in a federal prosecution the Fourth Amendment barred the use of evidence secured through an illegal search and seizure. This ruling was made for the first time in 1914. It was not derived from the explicit requirements of the Fourth Amendment; it was not based on legislation expressing Congressional policy in the enforcement of the Constitution. The decision was a matter of judicial implication. Since then it has been frequently applied and we stoutly adhere to it. But the immediate question is whether the basic right to protection against arbitrary intrusion by the police demands the exclusion of logically relevant evidence obtained by an unreasonable search and seizure because, in a federal prosecution for a federal crime, it would be excluded. As a matter of inherent reason, one would suppose this to be an issue as to which men with complete devotion to the protection of the right of privacy might give different answers. When we find that in fact most of the English-speaking world does not regard as vital to such protection the exclusion of evidence thus obtained, we must hesitate to treat this remedy as an essential ingredient of the right. The contrariety of views of the States is particularly impressive in view of the careful reconsideration which they have given the problem in the light of the *Weeks* decision.

[Justice Frankfurter summarized state case law on the issue of admissibility of evidence, contrasting pre- and post-*Weeks* decisions. In 1949, 31 states had rejected the *Weeks* doctrine and 16 states were in agreement with it.]

The jurisdictions which have rejected the *Weeks* doctrine have not left the right to privacy without other means of protection. Indeed, the exclusion of evidence is a remedy which directly serves only to protect those upon whose person or premises something incriminating has been found. We cannot, therefore, regard it as a departure from basic standards to remand such persons, together with those who emerge scatheless from a search, to the remedies of private action and such protection as the internal discipline of the police, under the eyes of an alert public opinion, may afford. Granting that in practice the exclusion of evidence may be an effective way of deterring unreasonable searches, it is not for this Court to condemn as falling below the minimal standards assured by the Due Process Clause a State's reliance upon other methods which, if consistently enforced, would be equally effective. Weighty testimony against such an insistence on our own view is furnished by the opinion of Mr. Justice (then Judge) Cardozo in People v. Defore, 242 N.Y. 13, 150 N.E. 585.[a] We cannot brush aside the experience of States which deem the incidence of such conduct by the police too slight to call for a deterrent remedy not by way of disciplinary measures but by overriding the relevant rules of evidence. There are, moreover, reasons for excluding evidence unreasonably obtained by the federal police which are less compelling in the case of police under State or local authority. The public opinion of a community can far more effectively be exerted against oppressive conduct on the part of police

a. "We hold, then, with the defendant that the evidence against him was the outcome of a trespass. The officer might have been resisted, or sued for damages, or even prosecuted for oppression. He was subject to removal or other discipline at the hands of his superiors. These consequences are undisputed. The defendant would add another. We must determine whether evidence of criminality, procured by an act of trespass, is to be rejected as incompetent for the misconduct of the trespasser. * * *

"In so holding [i.e., that evidence procured by unlawful search is not incompetent], we are not unmindful of the argument that unless the evidence is excluded, the statute becomes a form and its protection an illusion. This has a strange sound when the immunity is viewed in the light of its origin and history. The rule now embodied in the statute was received into English law as the outcome of the prosecution of Wilkes and Entick * * *. Wilkes sued the messengers who had ransacked his papers, and recovered a verdict of £ 4,000 against one and £ 1,000 against the other. Entick, too, had a substantial verdict * * *. We do not know whether the public, represented by its juries, is today more indifferent to its liberties than it was when the immunity was born. If so, the change of sentiment without more does not work a change of remedy. Other sanctions, penal and disciplinary, supplementing the right to damages, have already been enumerated. No doubt the protection of the statute would be greater from the point of view of the individual whose privacy had been invaded if the government were required to ignore what it had learned through the invasion. The question is whether protection for the individual would not be gained at a disproportionate loss of protection for society. On the one side is the social need that crime shall be repressed. On the other, the social need that law shall not be flouted by the insolence of office. There are dangers in any choice. * * *"

directly responsible to the community itself than can local opinion, sporadically aroused, be brought to bear upon remote authority pervasively exerted throughout the country.

We hold, therefore, that in a prosecution in a State court for a State crime the Fourteenth Amendment does not forbid the admission of evidence obtained by an unreasonable search and seizure. * * *

MR. JUSTICE MURPHY, with whom MR. JUSTICE RUTLEDGE joins, dissenting.

It is disheartening to find so much that is right in an opinion which seems to me so fundamentally wrong. Of course I agree with the Court that the Fourteenth Amendment prohibits activities which are proscribed by the search and seizure clause of the Fourth Amendment. * * *

* * * It is difficult for me to understand how the Court can go this far and yet be unwilling to make the step which can give some meaning to the pronouncements it utters.

Imagination and zeal may invent a dozen methods to give content to the commands of the Fourth Amendment. But this Court is limited to the remedies currently available. It cannot legislate the ideal system. If we would attempt the enforcement of the search and seizure clause in the ordinary case today, we are limited to three devices: judicial exclusion of the illegally obtained evidence; criminal prosecution of violators; and civil action against violators in the action of trespass.

Alternatives are deceptive. Their very statement conveys the impression that one possibility is as effective as the next. In this case their statement is blinding. For there is but one alternative to the rule of exclusion. That is no sanction at all.

[Justice Murphy then analyzed the merits of the two proposed alternatives to the exclusionary rule: criminal prosecution of police, and civil actions in trespass against violators. He found both remedies to be "illusory," if deterrence of violations was the goal to be achieved.]

The conclusion is inescapable that but one remedy exists to deter violations of the search and seizure clause. That is the rule which excludes illegally obtained evidence. Only by exclusion can we impress upon the zealous prosecutor that violation of the Constitution will do him no good. And only when that point is driven home can the prosecutor be expected to emphasize the importance of observing constitutional demands in his instructions to the police.

* * *

[Justice Rutledge's separate dissent is omitted, as is Justice Douglas' dissent. Justice Black's concurring opinion, stating that the exclusionary rule "is not a command of the Fourth Amendment" also is omitted.]

Although the Court was divided 6–3 in *Wolf,* the division was over the applicability of the exclusionary rule to the States. The Justices unanimously agreed that the prohibition against unreasonable searches and seizures applied to the States. They disagreed as to whether the exclusionary rule was a constitutionally required remedy.

In the next decade, the issue received the Court's attention twice more. In Rochin v. California, 342 U.S. 165 (1952), the shocking methods used by the State to obtain incriminating evidence were held to so offend "a sense of justice" as to require exclusion at a state trial. The evidence had been obtained by pumping the defendant's stomach. Two years later, in Irvine v. California, 347 U.S. 128 (1954), *Wolf* was reaffirmed, 5–4, and evidence was admitted where the search of a home, although shocking, did not involve a physical assault on the suspect's person.

In 1961, the Supreme Court once again considered the question in Mapp v. Ohio. *Mapp* appeared to be exclusively a First Amendment case; the exclusionary rule issue was neither briefed nor argued. Yet, *Wolf* was overruled 5–3. The change is partly explained by the fact that six members of the *Wolf* court were no longer on the Bench. Consider, however, whether other factors might account for the complete rejection of *Wolf* in that short period of time.

MAPP v. OHIO

Supreme Court of the United States, 1961.
367 U.S. 643.

MR. JUSTICE CLARK delivered the opinion of the Court.

* * *

[I]n the year 1914, in the *Weeks* case, this Court "for the first time" held that "in a federal prosecution the Fourth Amendment barred the use of evidence secured through an illegal search and seizure." This Court has ever since required of federal law officers a strict adherence to that command which this Court has held to be a clear, specific, and constitutionally required—even if judicially implied—deterrent safeguard without insistence upon which the Fourth Amendment would have been reduced to "a form of words." It meant, quite simply, that "conviction by means of unlawful seizures and enforced confessions * * * should find no sanction in the judgments of the courts * * *," Weeks v. United States, and that such evidence "shall not be used at all." Silverthorne Lumber Co. v. United States.

There are in the cases of this Court some passing references to the *Weeks* rule as being one of evidence. But the plain and unequivocal language of *Weeks*—and its later paraphrase in *Wolf*—to the effect that the *Weeks* rule is of constitutional origin, remains entirely undisturbed. * * * The Court, in Olmstead v. United States, 277 U.S. 438 at 462 (1928), in unmistakable language restated the *Weeks* rule:

"The striking outcome of the *Weeks* case and those which followed it was the sweeping declaration that the Fourth Amendment, although not referring to or limiting the use of evidence in courts, really forbade its introduction if obtained by government officers through a violation of the Amendment." At p. 462.

[Justice Clark considered the current validity of the factual grounds on which *Wolf* was based and found them to be no longer controlling. In particular, he noted that the trend among the States since *Wolf* had been toward acceptance of the exclusionary rule, and that experience had proved other remedies to be worthless. However, these considerations "are not basically relevant to a decision that the exclusionary rule is an essential ingredient of the Fourth Amendment as the right it embodies is vouchsafed against the States by the Due Process Clause."]

III

Some five years after *Wolf,* in answer to a plea made here Term after Term that we overturn its doctrine on applicability of the *Weeks* exclusionary rule, this Court indicated that such should not be done until the States had "adequate opportunity to adopt or reject the [*Weeks*] rule." Irvine v. California. * * *

And only last Term, after again carefully re-examining the *Wolf* doctrine in Elkins v. United States, the Court pointed out that "the controlling principles" as to search and seizure and the problem of admissibility "seemed clear" until the announcement in *Wolf* "that the Due Process Clause of the Fourteenth Amendment does not itself require state courts to adopt the exclusionary rule" of the *Weeks* case. At the same time, the Court pointed out, "the underlying constitutional doctrine which *Wolf* established * * * that the Federal Constitution * * * prohibits unreasonable searches and seizures by state officers" had undermined the "foundation upon which the admissibility of state-seized evidence in a federal trial originally rested * * *." The Court concluded that it was therefore obliged to hold, although it chose the narrower ground on which to do so, that all evidence obtained by an unconstitutional search and seizure was inadmissible in a federal court regardless of its source. Today we once again examine *Wolf's* constitutional documentation of the right to privacy free from unreasonable state intrusion, and, after its dozen years on our books, are led by it to close the only courtroom door remaining open to evidence secured by official lawlessness in flagrant abuse of that basic right, reserved to all persons as a specific guarantee against that very same unlawful conduct. We hold that all evidence obtained by searches and seizures in violation of the Constitution is, by that same authority, inadmissible in a state court.

IV

Since the Fourth Amendment's right of privacy has been declared enforceable against the States through the Due Process Clause of the Fourteenth, it is enforceable against them by the same sanction of exclusion as is used against the Federal Government. Were it otherwise, then just as without the *Weeks* rule the assurance against unreasonable federal searches and seizures would be "a form of words," valueless and undeserving of mention in a perpetual charter of inestimable human liberties, so too, without that rule the freedom from state invasions of privacy would be so ephemeral and so neatly severed from its conceptual nexus with the freedom from all brutish means of coercing evidence as not to merit this Court's high regard as a freedom "implicit in the concept of ordered liberty." At the time that the Court held in *Wolf* that the Amendment was applicable to the States through the Due Process Clause, the cases of this Court, as we have seen, had steadfastly held that as to federal officers the Fourth Amendment included the exclusion of the evidence seized in violation of its provisions. Even *Wolf* "stoutly adhered" to that proposition. The right to privacy, when conceded operatively enforceable against the States, was not susceptible of destruction by avulsion of the sanction upon which its protection and enjoyment had always been deemed dependent under the *Boyd, Weeks* and *Silverthorne* cases. Therefore, in extending the substantive protections of due process to all constitutionally unreasonable searches—state or federal—it was logically and constitutionally necessary that the exclusion doctrine—an essential part of the right to privacy—be also insisted upon as an essential ingredient of the right newly recognized by the *Wolf* case. In short, the admission of the new constitutional right by *Wolf* could not consistently tolerate denial of its most important constitutional privilege, namely, the exclusion of the evidence which an accused had been forced to give by reason of the unlawful seizure. To hold otherwise is to grant the right but in reality to withhold its privilege and enjoyment. Only last year the Court itself recognized that the purpose of the exclusionary rule "is to deter—to compel respect for the constitutional guaranty in the only effectively available way—by removing the incentive to disregard it." Elkins v. United States.

Indeed, we are aware of no restraint, similar to that rejected today, conditioning the enforcement of any other basic constitutional right. The right to privacy, no less important than any other right carefully and particularly reserved to the people, would stand in marked contrast to all other rights declared as basic to a free society. This Court has not hesitated to enforce as strictly against the States as it does against the Federal Government the rights of free speech and of a free press, the rights to notice and to a fair, public trial, including, as it does, the right not to be convicted by use of a coerced confession, however logically relevant it be, and without regard to its reliability. * * * Why should not the same rule apply to what is tantamount to coerced testimony by way of unconstitutional seizure of goods, papers, effects, documents, etc.? * * *

V

[The Court focuses on the incentives *Wolf* provided for federal officials to provide state courts unconstitutionally obtained evidence.]

There are those who say, as did Justice (then Judge) Cardozo, that under our constitutional exclusionary doctrine "[t]he criminal is to go free because the constable has blundered." People v. Defore, 242 N.Y. at 21, 150 N.E. at 587. In some cases this will undoubtedly be the result. But, as was said in *Elkins,* "there is another consideration—the imperative of judicial integrity." 364 U.S. at 222. The criminal goes free, if he must, but it is the law that sets him free. Nothing can destroy a government more quickly than its failure to observe its own laws, or worse, its disregard of the charter of its own existence. * * *

The ignoble shortcut to conviction left open to the States tends to destroy the entire system of constitutional restraints on which the liberties of the people rest. Having once recognized that the right to privacy embodied in the Fourth Amendment is enforceable against the States, and that the right to be secure against rude invasions of privacy by state officers is, therefore, constitutional in origin, we can no longer permit that right to remain an empty promise. Because it is enforceable in the same manner and to like effect as other basic rights secured by the Due Process Clause, we can no longer permit it to be revocable at the whim of any police officer who, in the name of law enforcement itself, chooses to suspend its enjoyment. Our decision, founded on reason and truth, gives to the individual no more than that which the Constitution guarantees him, to the police officer no less than that to which honest law enforcement is entitled, and, to the courts, that judicial integrity so necessary in the true administration of justice. * * *

* * *

[Justice Black concurred in a separate opinion, arguing that the Constitutional basis for the majority rule was the Fourth Amendment in conjunction with the Fifth Amendment's ban against compelled self-incrimination. The concurrences of Justices Douglas and Stewart have been omitted. Justice Stewart did not reach the Fourth Amendment question, preferring to decide the case on First Amendment grounds.]

MR. JUSTICE HARLAN, whom MR. JUSTICE FRANKFURTER and JUSTICE WHITTAKER join, dissenting.

* * *

I would not impose upon the States this federal exclusionary remedy. The reasons given by the majority for now suddenly turning its back on *Wolf* seem to me notably unconvincing.

First, it is said that "the factual grounds upon which *Wolf* was based" have since changed, in that more States now follow the *Weeks* exclusionary rule than was so at the time *Wolf* was decided. While that is true, a recent survey indicates that at present one-half of the States still adhere to the common-law non-exclusionary rule, and one, Maryland, retains the rule as to felonies. But in any case surely all this is beside the point, as the majority itself indeed seems to recognize. Our concern here, as it was in *Wolf,* is not with the desirability of that rule but only with the question whether the States are Constitutionally free to follow it or not as they may themselves determine, and the relevance of the disparity of views among the States on this point lies simply in the fact that the judgment involved is a debatable one. Moreover, the very fact on which the majority relies, instead of lending support to what is now being done, points away from the need of replacing voluntary state action with federal compulsion.

* * *

Further, we are told that imposition of the *Weeks* rule on the States makes "very good sense," in that it will promote recognition by state and federal officials of their "mutual obligation to respect the same fundamental criteria" in their approach to law enforcement, and will avoid "needless conflict between state and federal courts." Indeed the majority now finds an incongruity in *Wolf's* discriminating perception between the demands of "ordered liberty" as respects the basic right of "privacy" and the means of securing it among the States. That perception, resting both on a sensitive regard for our federal system and a sound recognition of this Court's remoteness from particular state problems, is for me the strength of that decision.

An approach which regards the issue as one of achieving procedural symmetry or of serving administrative convenience surely disfigures the boundaries of this Court's functions in relation to the state and federal courts. * * *

Finally, it is said that the overruling of *Wolf* is supported by the established doctrine that the admission in evidence of an involuntary confession renders a state conviction Constitutionally invalid. Since such a confession may often be entirely reliable, and therefore of the greatest relevance to the issue of the trial, the argument continues, this doctrine is ample warrant in precedent that the way evidence was obtained, and not just its relevance, is Constitutionally significant to the fairness of a trial. I believe this analogy is not a true one. The "coerced confession" rule is certainly not a rule that any illegally obtained statements may not be used in evidence. I would suppose that a statement which is procured during a period of illegal detention, McNabb v. United States, 318 U.S. 332, is, as much as unlawfully seized evidence, illegally obtained, but this Court has consistently refused to reverse state convictions resting on the use of such statements. * * *

The point, then, must be that in requiring exclusion of an involuntary statement of an accused, we are concerned not with an appropriate remedy for what the police have done, but with something which is regarded as going to the heart of our concepts of fairness in judicial procedure. * * * The pressures brought to bear against an accused leading to a confession, unlike an unconstitutional violation of privacy, do not, apart from the use of the confession at trial, necessarily involve independent Constitutional violations. What is crucial is that the trial defense to which an accused is entitled should not be rendered an empty formality by reason of statements wrung from him, for then "a prisoner * * * [has been] made the deluded instrument of his own conviction." 2 Hawkins, Pleas of the Crown (8th ed., 1824), c. 46, § 34. That this is a *procedural right,* and that its violation occurs at the time his improperly obtained statement is admitted at trial, is manifest. For without this right all the careful safeguards erected around the giving of testimony, whether by an accused or any other witness, would become empty formalities in a procedure where the most compelling possible evidence of guilt, a confession, would have already been obtained at the unsupervised pleasure of the police.

This, and not the disciplining of the police, as with illegally seized evidence, is surely the true basis for excluding a statement of the accused which was unconstitutionally obtained. In sum, I think the coerced confession analogy works strongly *against* what the Court does today.

* * *

Note

Both the majority and dissent in *Mapp* stressed that the issue was not the effectiveness of the exclusionary rule or the ineffectiveness of alternative remedies, but whether the exclusion of evidence illegally obtained was constitutionally mandated. Are the two issues really distinct? What is the basis for the majority's conclusion that the exclusionary rule is required? Obviously, the texts of the Fourth and Fourteenth Amendments lend no support to the proposition. The recent origins of the rule likewise throw no historical weight behind its acceptance. In the final analysis, isn't the majority implicitly deciding that the exclusion of evidence is the only effective sanction, and that the right to be free from unreasonable searches is "a dead letter" without a sanction? If other alternatives had proved effective in deterring violations, would the Court have found exclusion to be a constitutional requirement? Would a showing that exclusion of evidence has no deterrent effects whatsoever have required a different result? Professor Dripps, in Living with *Leon,* 95 Yale L.J. 906 (1986), argues that if no sanction attaches to a Fourth Amendment violation, the Amendment does not qualify as a law, and such disqualification "betrays the fundamental principle of constitutionalism, which is after all that the Constitution states the law." He argues that "even if the sanction does not deter, the refusal to apply it or anything else expresses the judgment that the underlying norm is of little importance." Do you agree? Dripps gives the following example: "Even if we were absolutely certain that a convicted murderer would never murder again, we would still feel obliged to impose a relatively severe sentence in order to vindicate the principle that life is dear and may not be unlawfully taken without paying a price." Is this example persuasive?

Both the majority and the dissent in *Mapp* discuss the constitutional rule of exclusion of coerced confessions. Who has the better of the argument on this point? As we will see in *Leon,* the Court has held that the exclusionary rule is not constitutionally required, in part because the violation of a Fourth Amendment right occurs at the time of the original police intrusion. The argument is that later exclusion from the trial has nothing to do with the completed violation, and conversely that introduction of the evidence at trial is not a separate violation of privacy. When does the constitutional violation occur if the police coerce a confession? See Schulhofer, Confessions and the Court, 79 Mich.L.Rev. 569 (1981) (violation of right to be free from coerced confession occurs when the confession is admitted at trial). Does this mean that the dissent in *Mapp* was right? For an argument that the Fourth Amendment violation is not complete at the time of the intrusion, and that the exclusionary rule is constitutionally required, see Heffernan, On Justifying Fourth Amendment Exclusion, 1989 Wis.L.Rev. 1193.

The majority cites People v. Cahan, 44 Cal.2d 434, 282 P.2d 905 (1955), in which Justice Traynor, writing for the California Supreme Court, accepted the exclusionary rule for that state, thus overruling his previous decision in People v. Gonzalez, 20 Cal.2d 165, 124 P.2d 44 (1942). In *Cahan,* Justice Traynor explained his shift in thinking as a recognition that illegal searches were a routine procedure which could only be deterred through application of the exclusionary rule. He further explains both his "conversion" and his analysis of the Supreme Court's decision in *Mapp,* in Mapp v. Ohio at Large in the 50 States, 1962 Duke L.J. 319:

> By 1961, roughly half of the states had adopted the exclusionary rule, with local variations. There was no uniformity of interpretation, however, and less than consistency in either the federal or state gloss of the rule. There emanated from the federal cases a sensitivity to federal-state relations that goes far to explain the willingness of the United States Supreme Court to afford the states ample time and latitude to determine how to enforce the right it had announced in Wolf v. Colorado in 1949. However guarded the Court was about state remedies, it left no doubt that the right was of constitutional dimension, for
>
> "Security of one's privacy against arbitrary intrusion by the police—which is at the core of the Fourth Amendment—is basic to a free society. It is therefore implicit in "the concept of ordered liberty" and as such enforceable against the States through the Due Process Clause."
>
> It was quickly apparent that this otherwise eloquent declaration went limp on the key word *enforceable.* In many states there had not yet loomed any effective remedies to attend the right that loomed so large. Wearing its rich constitutional cloak, it went begging for recognition. Alone of the princely rights it often went begging in vain. It became a classic right without a remedy. In California six years elapsed between Wolf v. Colorado and People v. Cahan, and all during that time we were painfully aware of the right begging in our midst. We remained mindful of the cogent reasons for the admission of illegally obtained evidence and clung to the fragile hope that the very brazenness of lawless police methods would bring on effective deterrents other than the exclusionary rule. Accordingly we were proceeding with caution before responding to the message in Wolf v. Colorado, to the long and short of the handwriting on the distant wall. We needed no more than Irvine v. California to read the handwriting on our own wall. In the interim between Irvine v. California and People v. Cahan it became all too clear in our state that there was no recourse but to the exclusionary rule. In the interim between Irvine v. California and Mapp v. Ohio a like reflection of nation-wide import must also have been developing in the Supreme Court of the United States. Its decision in *Irvine* had intimated a hope that in time the many states still uncommitted to the exclusionary rule would reconsider their evidentiary rules in the light of the *Wolf* doctrine that the fourth amendment is enforceable against the states through the fourteenth. The indifferent response must have been disheartening to a Court that had expressed its reluctance to invoke federal power to upset state convictions based on unconstitutionally obtained evidence.

The many states that failed even to re-examine their evidentiary rules merely postponed the day of reckoning. They had clear warning in *Irvine* that if they defaulted and there were no demonstrably effective deterrents to unreasonable searches and seizures in lieu of the exclusionary rule, the Supreme Court might yet decide that they had not complied with "minimal standards" of due process. When in 1961 it so decided in Mapp v. Ohio and made the exclusionary rule mandatory in all states, it could hardly have taken anyone by surprise. For all their distracting, discordantly nay-saying chimes, the hours had been successively striking that the zero hour was coming.

Individual judges can change their mind about the exclusionary rule. Justice Black, for example, was part of the majority in *Wolf,* but cast one of the five votes for Justice Clark's position in *Mapp.* Arguably, this was more important than many of the changes in personnel on the court. Note also Justice Traynor's description of how judicial attitudes changed over time. Justice Stewart, who voted for Mrs. Mapp on other grounds, originally was reluctant to bind the states to follow federal rules, but he became more willing to do so as time passed. Chief Justice Burger had some extremely harsh words for exclusionary rules generally in Brewer v. Williams, considered in Chapter Three. Yet, he actually extended the doctrine utilized in *Brewer* in United States v. Henry, also considered infra, in Chapter Three. It may be that the more a judge sees cases in which the Constitution is violated, the more the judge is inclined to look for a powerful remedy. Also, the absence of serious efforts to develop alternative remedies with teeth may leave experienced judges reconciled to the exclusionary rule as the only judicially created remedy that is likely to work. Thus, seers who predict the demise of the rule generally do so with caution, since vote-counting on the Supreme Court must be done year-to-year. Supporters of the rule always watch the Court with concern, however, knowing that the rule was made binding on the states by a divided vote, and there are justices who delight in attacking it. For example, Judge Bowman, who has been mentioned as being on the "short list" for recent Supreme Court appointments, had this to say about the exclusionary rule in United States v. Jefferson, 906 F.2d 346 (8th Cir.1990), a case in which the entire court agreed that evidence obtained pursuant to a stop made without reasonable suspicion was properly excluded at trial:

> This case vividly illustrates the perversity of the exclusionary rule. Here, an officer's educated hunch led to the discovery of evidence (nine kilograms of cocaine) of substantial criminal activity. This discovery occurred as a result of information the officer developed by asking questions and examining documents in the course of his routine check of a parked car and its occupants at a highway rest stop. The ordinary law-abiding citizen, I believe, would think the officer should be commended for his fine work, and the cocaine dealers punished. Instead, because we hold (as I agree, under the existing case law, we must) that a "seizure" within the meaning of the Fourth Amendment occurred before the officer had formed an objectively reasonable basis for suspecting the defendants of criminal activity, the exclusionary rule requires that the evidence be suppressed. The defendants thus exit unpunished, free to continue dealing illegal drugs to the pathetic addicts and contemptible scofflaws who comprise the national market for these substances. As for the officer, far from his being commended, it is judicially recorded that he blundered, and the point once again is driven home that legalistic observance of even the most technical of the judge-created rules of search and seizure—rules which, like the Fourth Amendment itself, seek to protect law-abiding citizens from intrusive conduct by officers of the state—is more important than intelligent, courageous, and vigorous initiative to expose criminal activity and bring those responsible for it to the bar of justice.

> It has been reported that since 1961, when [*Mapp* was decided], "the murder rate has doubled, rape has quadrupled and robbery has quintupled." *Wall St.J.*, May 7, 1990, at A14, Col. 1. While it would be foolish to blame the exclusionary rule for all of this alarming increase in violent crime, I believe it is equally foolish to pretend that the exclusionary rule, and the *zeitgeist* it has created, is to blame for none of it.

Judge Bowman's comments prompted Chief Judge Lay, who has not been mentioned as being on the "short list", to respond as follows:

> If police are not deterred from illegal intrusions of privacy by excluding whatever evidence is seized, the fourth amendment will have no meaning or force. Surely an appreciation for the history and purpose of our basic freedoms will never allow emotional fear to justify an environment where there is no check on the abuse of police power.
>
> The fourth amendment protects the good guy as well as the bad. It would mean very little to anyone if it did not. The argument that since 1961 murders have doubled, rapes quadrupled, and robbery quintupled in part because of the exclusionary rule is a statement more fitting for headlines of the National Enquirer. It is irrational hyperbole totally unsupported in fact or in law.

A fascinating description of how Justice Clark fashioned a majority in *Mapp* and especially how he won the vote of Justice Black is found in Dorin, "Seize the Time: Justice Tom Clark's Role in Mapp v. Ohio (1961)," in Law and the Legal Process (Swigert ed. 1982).

In Robbins v. California, 453 U.S. 420 (1981), Justice Rehnquist expresses concern about the exclusionary rule and the warrant requirement. He suggests that these rules make it almost impossible for police officers to have clear guidance as to what is expected of them:

> I think that probably any search for "bright lines" short of overruling Mapp v. Ohio is apt to be illusory. Our entire profession is trained to attack "bright lines" the way hounds attack foxes. Acceptance by the courts of arguments that one thing is the "functional equivalent" of the other, for example, soon breaks down what might have been a bright line into a blurry impressionistic pattern.

But would overruling *Mapp* really make the limits of the Constitution more understandable to police? Would requiring fewer warrants make police work that much easier? As long as some warrants are required, won't police officers be called upon to make judgments about which circumstances demand immediate action and which do not? Could bright lines be established as well by cutting back on exceptions to the warrant requirement?

One of the most interesting developments is the increasing focus on whether exclusion of illegally seized evidence is a necessary remedy generally, rather than on the question whether the rule first announced in *Weeks* should still bind the states. If the exclusionary rule is ultimately rejected, it might fall as to both state and federal courts.

C. EVIDENCE SEIZED ILLEGALLY, BUT CONSTITUTIONALLY

1. *Violations of State Law*

Generally speaking, a violation of state law which is not itself a violation of the Fourth Amendment will not result in exclusion of evidence in federal court.

Whether exclusion will occur in state court is a matter of state law. Some states require exclusion of evidence obtained in violation of nonconstitutional law; other states do not. In Elkins v. United States, 364 U.S. 206 (1960), the Court held that evidence obtained by state officers in violation of the federal Constitution could not be handed over to federal officers and used in federal court, but it implied that violations of state law governing searches would not require the same result. Justice Frankfurter's dissent noted that a line was drawn between unconstitutional searches and those that merely violated state law. Today, federal courts, whenever possible, try to duck the question of whether state law applies. See, e.g., United States v. Boyer, 574 F.2d 951 (8th Cir. 1978). Some cases, however, purport to hold that state law need not be followed by either Federal or State officers, when the evidence is offered at a Federal trial. See, e.g., United States v. Hodge, 539 F.2d 898 (6th Cir.1976); United States v. Chavez–Vernaza, 844 F.2d 1368 (9th Cir.1987) (evidence seized by state officials in compliance with Federal law is admissible in Federal court even though state law was violated). Doesn't this result create a reverse "silver platter" doctrine?

In some cases, however, state standards are effectively incorporated into Federal law, and a violation of these standards will result in exclusion in a Federal trial. In United States v. Wanless, 882 F.2d 1459 (9th Cir.1989), the court held that evidence obtained in an inventory search of a car by a Washington State Trooper was improperly admitted, because the Trooper did not follow state guidelines requiring him to ask for the owner's consent before impounding the car. The court distinguished other cases in which it found state law to be irrelevant, reasoning that "the federal law on inventory searches by state or local police officers is that they must be conducted in accordance with the official procedures of the relevant state or local police department." (Citing South Dakota v. Opperman and Colorado v. Bertine, supra).

Because federal officers may move from state to state, and because federal interests in certain procedures not permitted by some states may be great, a federal standard makes some sense. But the argument for following state law still has force—i.e., federal officers can find out from state officers peculiarities of state law, federal law enforcement interests rarely are much stronger than state interests, and state law creates expectations of privacy that federal agents should respect. Whether or not state law should control federal officers, there is an argument that federal courts should suppress evidence seized by state officers if the state courts would suppress. The argument rests on notions of comity. Failure to suppress may undercut state efforts at deterrence.[34] Pre-

34. Should a forum state exclude evidence illegally but not unconstitutionally seized in another state? Generally, courts have said no. For an argument supporting this view, see Theis, Choice of Law and the Administration of the Exclusionary Rule in Criminal Cases, 44 Tenn.L.Rev. 1043 (1977). Are the arguments for exclusion by a federal court of evidence seized in violation of state law stronger because of the likelihood that state officers probably will know of the possibility of a federal prosecution if their evidence is not excluded by a federal court?

In People v. Blair, 25 Cal.3d 640, 159 Cal. Rptr. 818, 602 P.2d 738 (1979), the court held that evidence seized in a manner that would have been unconstitutional in California could be admitted in that state's courts when it was seized in Pennsylvania in compliance with state and federal law.

Even a violation of state constitutional law by state officers does not require suppression of evidence by a federal court as long as federal constitutional rules were not violated, according to United States v. Rickus, 737 F.2d 360 (3d Cir. 1984). The court stated that it

sumably, the same comity issue arises when federal agents violate a federal statute so that their evidence is illegally, but not unconstitutionally, seized and the evidence is offered in a state court. The only difference here is that, under the Supremacy Clause, Congress probably can force the state courts to exclude the evidence, whereas a state legislature could not force exclusion upon federal courts.

Should a violation of a state ethical standard by a federal prosecutor result in the exclusion of evidence from a federal trial? In United States v. Hammad, 858 F.2d 834 (2d Cir.1988), the court held that if a prosecutor violated DR 7–104 of the New York Code of Professional Responsibility, which prohibits direct communication with an opposing party in the absence of counsel, then any statements derived from that direct communication would be excluded from a federal trial. In response to *Hammad,* former Attorney General Thornburgh took the position that state ethical standards found in the Code of Professional Responsibility and the Model Rules of Professional Conduct were not binding on federal prosecutors. See 45 The Record of the Association of the Bar of the City of New York 834 (1990), discussing and criticizing the Justice Department's response to *Hammad.* One federal judge dismissed an indictment after she found a violation of DR 7–104. She called the Justice Department's position, that federal prosecutors were not governed by state ethical standards, "alarming." United States v. Lopez, 765 F.Supp. 1433 (N.D.Cal.1991). Should federal prosecutors be subject to state ethical standards? If they are, should exclusion result from a violation of these standards?

2. *Violations of Federal Statutes, Regulations and Federal Rules of Criminal Procedure*

The courts have been reluctant to impose exclusion as a judicial remedy for a violation of a federal statute or regulation, or a Federal Rule of Criminal Procedure. For example, violations of the procedural limitations on warrants contained in Fed.R.Crim.P. 41 do not usually result in exclusion. As stated by the court in United States v. Schoenheit, 856 F.2d 74 (8th Cir.1988), exclusion is not required "unless the search would not have otherwise occurred or would not have been so abrasive if the Rule had been followed, or there was evidence of an intentional and deliberate disregard of Fed.R.Crim.P. 41." In *Schoenheit,* a search was made at 10:30 p.m.; the warrant provided for execution at night, but the application and affidavits did not establish reasonable cause authorizing execution at times other than between 6:00 a.m. and 10:00 p.m., as required by Rule 41. The court refused to suppress the evidence, finding that the search would have occurred anyway, and that no showing was made that the search would have been less abrasive if conducted before 10:00 p.m. See also United States v. Charles, 883 F.2d 355 (5th Cir.1989) (violation of Rule 41 provision requiring officer to conduct a search with the warrant in hand does not require exclusion where the search would have occurred anyway).

With respect to statutes, Congress has in some cases provided expressly for exclusion, such as in the wiretapping statute, Title III, discussed supra. Where Congress has not so provided, the courts have ordinarily not imposed exclusion

was not "insensitive to the claim that we should not encourage state officials to violate principles central to the state's social and governmental order," but it concluded that the loss of evidence in state proceedings was a sufficient deterrent to control state officers.

as a remedy. See United States v. Blue Diamond Coal Co., 667 F.2d 510 (6th Cir.1981) (no suppression required for violation of statute requiring consent or administrative warrant for seizure of lawfully inspected records). Similar results occur with violations of agency regulations or other non-constitutional law. See United States v. Caceres, 440 U.S. 741 (1979) (violation of IRS regulations concerning recording of conversations does not require suppression); United States v. Hensel, 699 F.2d 18 (1st Cir.1983) (no suppression even if international law and coast guard regulations were violated).

D. THE EXCLUSIONARY RULE IN DETAIL: PROCEDURES, SCOPE AND PROBLEMS

1. *Procedures for Return of Property and Motions to Suppress*

Before addressing the coverage of the exclusionary rule, it is helpful to understand the procedures that trigger its application. Previously, we have seen that a copy of the search warrant is either provided to the person whose premises are searched or left at unoccupied premises. Accompanying the copy of the warrant is a list of things seized. In Berger v. New York, you will recall, the Supreme Court complained about New York's failure to provide some form of notice to search victims. The federal statute, 18 U.S.C.A. § 2518(8)(d), attempts to remedy the defect.

When the person whose property is taken wants to challenge the validity of the search, a motion to return the evidence can be made. See, e.g., Fed.R.Crim.P. 41(e). Also, a motion to suppress evidence can be made, even if the evidence seized is contraband, someone else's property, or otherwise not returnable. The motion to suppress is directed to the use of the evidence rather than its return. See, e.g., Fed.R.Crim.P. 41(g). See also Uniform R.Crim.P. 461 (1974). Since it is usually more efficient for courts to hear suppression motions prior to trial, rather than in the midst of trying the merits (especially when a jury is used), court rules may encourage or require pretrial motions. Failure to make a pre-trial motion could in some jurisdictions result in the loss of the claim absent a good reason for the failure. If a motion at trial is permitted, generally it will have to be made when the evidence is offered.

Some states allow the same magistrates who issue warrants to rule on motions to return and suppress evidence, but the Model Code provides for disposition only by a judge of the court having jurisdiction of the offense to be tried. Pre-trial hearings obviously are outside the presence of the jury. Generally, mid-trial hearings also will be outside the hearing of the jury. Whether a search and seizure is lawful is a question for the judge, but in some jurisdictions the judge who finds the search to be lawful will resubmit the issue to the jury with an instruction on search and seizure law. Naturally, the judge's determination will not be revealed to the jury.

Model Code § 280.3(3) provides that "[i]n granting a motion for return or restoration of seized things, the court may postpone execution of the order for return or restoration until such time as such things no longer remain available for evidentiary use." Once the evidence is no longer needed, it should be returned if the defendant has a proper claim to it. See United States v. Wilson, 540 F.2d 1100 (D.C.Cir.1976); United States v. Palmer, 565 F.2d 1063

(9th Cir. 1977). But if there has been no unconstitutional search and seizure, the government may be able to keep copies of seized material.

2. *Attacking the Warrant*

If the search was pursuant to a warrant, the judge ruling on the motion to suppress will consider the sworn evidence presented to the magistrate who issued the warrant. The Fourth Amendment determination will be made on the basis of only this evidence. See generally Kaiser v. Lief, 874 F.2d 732 (10th Cir.1989) (magistrate may rely on affidavit, complaint, and other affidavits contemporaneously presented for other warrants).

Prior to the Supreme Court's decision in Franks v. Delaware, 438 U.S. 154 (1978), there was a split of authority on the question whether the sworn statements in warrant applications could be attacked as having been made in bad faith, and if so, what form of attack would be proper. In *Franks,* the Supreme Court held that the moving party had a limited right to challenge the good faith of the sworn statements.

> * * * There is, of course, a presumption of validity with respect to the affidavit supporting the search warrant. To mandate an evidentiary hearing, the challenger's attack must be more than conclusory and must be supported by more than a mere desire to cross-examine. There must be allegations of deliberate falsehood or of reckless disregard for the truth, and those allegations must be accompanied by an offer of proof. They should point out specifically the portion of the warrant affidavit that is claimed to be false; and they should be accompanied by a statement of supporting reasons. Affidavits or sworn or otherwise reliable statements of witnesses should be furnished, or their absence satisfactorily explained. Allegations of negligence or innocent mistake are insufficient. The deliberate falsity or reckless disregard whose impeachment is permitted today is only that of the affiant, not of any nongovernmental informant. Finally, if these requirements are met, and if, when material that is the subject of the alleged falsity or reckless disregard is set to one side, there remains sufficient content in the warrant affidavit to support a finding of probable cause, no hearing is required. On the other hand, if the remaining content is insufficient, the defendant is entitled, under the Fourth Amendment, to his hearing. Whether he will prevail at that hearing is, of course, another issue.

The Court found that the need to assure that the police act in good faith outweighed the drain on resources that its hearing requirement would necessitate. Justice Rehnquist, joined by Chief Justice Burger, dissented, arguing that, even if "some inaccurate or falsified information may have gone into the making of the determination" to issue a warrant, "I simply do not think the game is worth the candle in this situation." When you recall that the warrant application is made ex parte and the magistrate makes nothing like a credibility determination, what would become of the warrant clause of the Amendment if Justice Rehnquist's view had prevailed?

Why is the *Franks* deliberate falsity or reckless disregard standard applicable to statements of the affiant, but not to statements of a non-governmental informant? See United States v. Henry, 933 F.2d 553 (7th Cir. 1991) (even if an informant lied, this does not establish a knowing falsehood which would invalidate the warrant; the relevant question is whether the officer acted in reckless disregard of the truth). Can probable cause be based on a deliberate, material misstatement from an informant? To answer this question it may be helpful to recall the Court's discussion in Illinois v. Gates, supra.

An example of a showing sufficient to warrant a *Franks* hearing is United States v. Johns, 851 F.2d 1131 (9th Cir.1988), where probable cause was based in material part on the officer's averment that he had detected the odor of metamphetamine emanating from defendant's premises. Defendant submitted affidavits from two experts stating that in light of the way the metamphetamine was stored, it would have been impossible for the officer outside the premises to smell it. *Johns* was distinguished in United States v. Mueller, 902 F.2d 336 (5th Cir.1990), where the officer averred that he could smell metamphetamine emanating from a house while standing across the street. Defendant submitted an expert affidavit to the effect that it would have been unlikely to pick up such a smell given the distance and the prevailing winds. The court denied a *Franks* hearing, noting that Mueller's expert merely concluded that the officer's story was "unlikely," while the experts in *Johns* concluded that the officer's story was "impossible."

Several courts before *Franks* had ruled that negligent misstatements that are material to a showing of probable cause invalidate a search warrant. In United States v. Astroff, 556 F.2d 1369 (5th Cir. 1977), for example, the court said "that negligent misstatements by the police should and theoretically could be deterred":

> Our refusal to countenance affidavits which fail to establish probable cause absent negligent misrepresentations will effectuate those assumptions underlying the integrity of the warrant procedure. The materiality inquiry is a sufficient counterbalance to any judicial tendency to demand semantic precision from those engaged in the harried and often hurried pursuit of crime.

Other courts had held that only perjury would invalidate an affidavit. See, e.g., Kahn v. Flood, 550 F.2d 784 (2d Cir. 1974). Are either of these views preferable to the *Franks* approach? Some decisions stated that, in the case of deliberate perjury, the warrant is invalid even if probable cause exists aside from the perjurious statements. See, e.g., United States v. Collins, 549 F.2d 557 (8th Cir. 1977). Some courts will follow the pre-*Franks* approach and protect against all intentional misstatements under their state constitutions. See State v. Paster, 373 So.2d 170 (La.1979). Is there merit in this approach?

The Supreme Court's *Franks* approach is rejected in part in State v. Malkin, 722 P.2d 943 (Alaska 1986), as the court held that once the defendant proves that an affidavit contains material false statements, the burden shifts to the prosecution to justify the misstatements by proving that they were not made intentionally or recklessly. Unless the prosecution satisfies the burden, the warrant will be invalid, since "[a] deliberate attempt to mislead a judicial officer in a sworn affidavit deserves the most severe deterrent sanction that the exclusionary rule can provide." Is this burden-shifting approach preferable to *Franks*?

An officer's misstatement is not material under *Franks* if probable cause would exist even without the misstatement. See United States v. Campbell, 878 F.2d 170 (6th Cir.1989), citing cases in every circuit applying this test. In *Campbell,* the court found the search warrant valid even though the affidavit included a statement attributed to an informant known by the affiant to be fictitious. The court found that untainted information in the affidavit from three reliable informants was sufficient to establish probable cause under Illinois v. Gates, supra.

3. *Challenging A Warrantless Search*

The burden of producing evidence placed on the moving party in *Franks* is different from the burden placed on the moving party when a warrantless search is challenged. Once it is established that no warrant was obtained, and that the motion to suppress claims that the search violated the Constitution, the government must justify the search. Generally, the state must prove by a preponderance of the evidence that an exception to the warrant requirement was satisfied. See United States v. Matlock, 415 U.S. 164 (1974); United States v. Hurtado, 905 F.2d 74 (5th Cir.1990) (government must prove voluntariness of consent by a preponderance of the evidence). See generally Saltzburg, Standards of Proof and Preliminary Questions of Fact, 27 Stan.L.Rev. 271 (1975). A few states purport to place the burdens of producing evidence and of persuasion on the prosecution even when a warrant has been obtained. But they require the defendant to identify the defect complained of; this, plus the fact that they judge the warrant on the face of the sworn statements, make these burdens less consequential than in warrantless arrest cases. On certain non-constitutional claims the defendant may have the burden of putting on evidence that persuades the judge. See, e.g., United States v. Phillips, 540 F.2d 319 (8th Cir. 1976) (defendant had burden under 18 U.S.C.A. § 2511(2)(d) to show that private person "unlawfully" recorded conversations).

4. *The Hearing and Judicial Review*

At the hearing on the motion to suppress evidence, the government will have a privilege to protect the identity of informants. See McCray v. Illinois, 386 U.S. 300 (1967) (holding that it is constitutional to withhold informant's identity on issue of probable cause). Of course, the judge can require the government to reveal the informant's identity if that is necessary "to decide whether the officer is a believable witness." State v. Burnett, 42 N.J. 377, 201 A.2d 39 (1964). "[T]he judge may in his discretion require the prosecution, *in camera,* to disclose to him the identity of the informant, or produce the informant for questioning. If the judge does so require, the information or testimony so obtained shall be kept securely under seal and, in the event of an appeal from the judge's disposition of the motion, transmitted to the appellate court." § 290.4, ALI Model Code of Pre-Arraignment Procedure. At the hearing, the usual rules of evidence do not apply. Thus, hearsay evidence may be received. See Fed.R.Evid. 1101.

At the hearing, the defendant may testify in support of his claim of a Fourth Amendment violation. Simmons v. United States, 390 U.S. 377 (1968), holds that when a defendant testifies on the question of "standing" (a subject discussed infra) at a suppression hearing, the government may not use his testimony against him on the question of guilt or innocence. Justice Harlan's opinion for the 6–2 majority said that"[s]ince search-and-seizure claims depend heavily upon their individual facts, and since the law of search and seizure is in a state of flux," defendants would be unduly inhibited from making Fourth

Amendment claims absent protection against automatic use of suppression hearing testimony at trial. In light of the way the opinion is written, it is likely that it extends to all Fourth Amendment questions considered at the hearing, not just to "standing" questions. It may be, however that the testimony at the suppression hearing could be used at trial to impeach a defendant who changes his testimony. Cf. United States v. Havens, 446 U.S. 620 (1980). Also, if the defendant calls a witness to testify at the suppression hearing, the government may use that witness (or the suppression hearing testimony if the witness is unavailable) against the defendant at trial. This is because *Simmons* was designed to protect defendants from sacrificing one constitutional right (the Fifth Amendment right against self-incrimination) for another (the Fourth Amendment right). When the defendant calls a witness at the suppression hearing, the defendant's Fifth Amendment rights are not implicated. As the court stated in United States. v. Boruff, 870 F.2d 316 (5th Cir.1989):

> While a defendant's decision to call third-parties to corroborate his testimony at a suppression hearing might be affected by his knowledge that the government may subsequently utilize that testimony at trial, this dilemma does not rise to the level of a constitutional problem.

If a motion to suppress is granted, more and more jurisdictions permit immediate appellate review of the ruling. Title VIII of the 1968 Crime Control Act added a new paragraph to 18 U.S.C.A. § 3731, authorizing direct appeals from district court orders granting pre-trial motions for the return of seized property or the suppression of evidence. In 1971, the section was amended to provide appeal to circuit courts, not the Supreme Court. The ALI Model Code of Pre-Arraignment Procedure, § 290.1(4), and the ABA Standards Relating to Criminal Appeals § 21–1.4 (2d ed. 1980), approve the procedure. A few states allow a defendant to appeal a denial of a motion to suppress if the trial judge or appellate tribunal certifies that the issue is substantial and an immediate appeal would expedite litigation; but most jurisdictions deny the defendant the right to an immediate appeal. It must be kept in mind that prosecutors cannot appeal the merits of an acquittal; only defendants can. Thus, the prosecutors will get an immediate appeal or none at all. If the defendant is convicted, an issue on appeal may be the denial of a suppression motion.

Great deference is paid by reviewing courts to issuing magistrates and to judges making suppression rulings. The Court in Illinois v. Gates, supra, stated that "after the fact scrutiny by courts of the sufficiency of an affidavit should not take the form of *de novo* review." The Court declared that the magistrate's determination was entitled to "great deference," and that the reviewing court should uphold the warrant so long as the magistrate had a "substantial basis" for issuing it. The Court found that this deferential review was necessary to further the Fourth Amendment's "strong preference" for warrants.

Should magistrates defer to each other? If one magistrate refuses to issue a warrant because of perceived inadequacies in the application, can another magistrate issue a warrant on the same showing? Some courts have been bothered by the unseemliness of prosecutors and police, who are turned down in attempts to obtain judicial approval of searches and seizures, seeking to find somebody, anybody, willing to issue a warrant. See People v. Cocilova, 132

Misc.2d 106, 503 N.Y.S.2d 258 (1986) (suppressing evidence on grounds that "judge shopping" cannot be permitted). Other courts permit the practice, so long as the magistrate who issues the warrant is neutral and detached, and the warrant is sufficiently particular and supported by probable cause. See United States v. Pace, 898 F.2d 1218 (7th Cir.1990). If probable cause exists and the second magistrate is neutral and detached, why should it matter that prior magistrates refused to issue a warrant? What if the officer had been to 15 magistrates, all of whom denied the application, before a friendly magistrate was found?

Gates might suggest that an appellate court should defer to the magistrate who issued the warrant, but not necessarily to the magistrate who rules on a motion to suppress. When testimony about a warrantless search is taken, the factual determinations of the hearing magistrate (or the trial judge, depending on whether she ruled on a suppression motion) may not appear on the record, since only a few states require the magistrate to state findings of fact. The decision of the hearing magistrate or trial judge is accepted on appeal unless it is clearly erroneous. See Jackson v. United States, 353 F.2d 862 (D.C.Cir.1965); United States v. Flickinger, 573 F.2d 1349 (9th Cir. 1978). "[A]n appellate court will usually not limit itself to the testimony received on the pre-trial motion to suppress, but will also consider pertinent testimony given at the trial." 3 C. Wright, Federal Practice and Procedure § 678, at 805 (2d ed. 1982).

If an appellate court finds that a motion to suppress was erroneously granted, the case will continue toward trial with the error corrected. If, after trial, the appellate court finds that evidence admitted by the trial court should have been excluded, it will reverse any affected conviction unless the error can be deemed "harmless beyond a reasonable doubt." Chapman v. California, 386 U.S. 18 (1967). See Franks v. Delaware, 438 U.S. 154 (1978). See generally Saltzburg, The Harm of Harmless Error, 59 Va.L.Rev. 988 (1973).

5. *The Fruits of the Search: Causation and Attenuation*

Turning now to the scope of the exclusionary rule, the first point to be made is that it is a remedy that is useful only when evidence is seized as a result of a search. If no evidence is obtained, there obviously is nothing to exclude. In Ker v. Illinois, 119 U.S. 436 (1886), and Frisbie v. Collins, 342 U.S. 519 (1952), the Supreme Court held that an illegal or unconstitutional arrest of a person did not deprive a court of jurisdiction to try the person—i.e., the body of the person, which is not being used as evidence, need not be released from the jurisdiction. United States ex rel. Lujan v. Gengler, 510 F.2d 62 (2d Cir. 1975) and United States v. Toscanino, 500 F.2d 267 (2d Cir. 1974), together suggest that a set of facts that shocks the conscience of the court could result in dismissal of a case. *Ker* and *Frisbie* remain good law. See Kester, Some Myths of United States Extradition Law, 76 Geo.L.J. 1441 (1988). However, it has been held that if an arrest is in violation of a treaty, the *Ker-Frisbie* doctrine does not apply and a United States court lacks jurisdiction to try the defendant. See United States v. Verdugo-Urquidez, 939 F.2d 1341 (9th Cir. 1991) (on remand from the Supreme Court), where the court held that if the United States authorizes or sponsors the abduction of a Mexican national from that country, without the consent of the Mexican government, it breaches its obligations under the the extradition treaty between the two countries. The court further held that if the Mexican government formally objects to the treaty breach, United States courts have no jurisdiction to try the Mexican national. The court remanded the case to determine whether the United States sponsored the defendant's abduction without the consent of the Mexican government.

If an illegal arrest produces evidence—pursuant to a search incident thereto, as a result of a plain view search, or through an interrogation tainted by the arrest—the evidence falls within the scope of the exclusionary rule. This evidence is the "fruit" of the illegal search.

The language quoted above from Silverthorne Lumber Co. v. United States in the section on the history of the exclusionary rule represents the beginning of the "fruit of the poisonous tree" doctrine. But the phrase itself was coined in Nardone v. United States, 308 U.S. 338 (1939), as Justice Frankfurter's opinion for the Court addressed the question "whether the [trial] judge improperly refused to allow the accused to examine the prosecution as to the uses to which it had put the information" obtained by wiretaps which an earlier case with the same name, 302 U.S. 379 (1937), had held were accomplished in violation of the 1934 Communications Act. Although he recognized that "[a]ny claim for the exclusion of evidence logically relevant in criminal prosecutions is heavily handicapped" and "must be justified by an over-riding public policy expressed in the Constitution or the law of the land," Justice Frankfurter cited and quoted from *Silverthorne* and concluded that "[t]o forbid the direct use of methods thus characterized but to put no curb on their full indirect use would only invite the very methods deemed 'inconsistent with ethical standards and personal liberty.'" Thus, he found that the trial judge erred. His opinion suggests a limit on the exclusionary principle: "A causal connection between information obtained through illicit wiretapping and the Government's proof * * * may have become so attenuated as to dissipate the taint."

Wong Sun v. United States, 371 U.S. 471 (1963) and the following case, Brown v. Illinois, are the Court's leading cases on causation and attenuation. *Wong Sun* is discussed in detail in *Brown.*

BROWN v. ILLINOIS

Supreme Court of the United States, 1975.
422 U.S. 590.

MR. JUSTICE BLACKMUN delivered the opinion of the Court.

* * *

I

As petitioner Richard Brown was climbing the last of the stairs leading to the rear entrance of his Chicago apartment in the early evening of May 13, 1968, he happened to glance at the window near the door. He saw, pointed at him through the window, a revolver held by a stranger who was inside the apartment. The man said: "Don't move, you are under arrest." Another man, also with a gun, came up behind Brown and repeated the statement that he was under arrest. It was about 7:45 p.m. The two men turned out to be Detectives William Nolan and William Lenz of the Chicago police force. * * * As both officers held him at gunpoint, the three entered the apartment. Brown was ordered to stand against the wall and was searched. No weapon was found. * * * Detective Lenz informed him that he was under arrest for the murder of Roger Corpus, handcuffed him, and escorted him to the squad car.

The two detectives took petitioner to the Maxwell Street police station. [While at the station, Brown was twice given *Miranda* warnings and twice confessed. The first confession occurred 90 minutes after the arrest, the second occurred seven hours after the arrest. Brown moved to suppress the confessions as the fruit of an arrest without probable cause. The trial court denied the motion, and Brown was convicted. The Illinois Supreme Court found that Brown had been arrested without probable cause, but nonetheless held that the motion to suppress was properly denied because the confessions were not tainted fruit].

* * * The court appears to have held that the *Miranda* warnings in and of themselves broke the causal chain so that any subsequent statement, even one induced by the continuing effects of unconstitutional custody, was admissible so long as, in the traditional sense, it was voluntary and not coerced in violation of the Fifth and Fourteenth Amendments.

* * *

II

In *Wong Sun,* the Court pronounced the principles to be applied where the issue is whether statements and other evidence obtained after an illegal arrest or search should be excluded. In that case, federal agents elicited an oral statement from defendant Toy after forcing entry at 6 a.m. into his laundry, at the back of which he had his living quarters. The agents had followed Toy down the hall to the bedroom and there had placed him under arrest. The Court of Appeals found that there was no probable cause for the arrest. This Court concluded that that finding was "amply justified by the facts clearly shown on this record." Toy's statement, which bore upon his participation in the sale of narcotics, led the agents to question another person, Johnny Yee, who actually possessed narcotics. Yee stated that heroin had been brought to him earlier by Toy and another Chinese known to him only as "Sea Dog." Under questioning, Toy said that "Sea Dog" was Wong Sun. Toy led agents to a multifamily dwelling where, he said, Wong Sun lived. Gaining admittance to the building through a bell and buzzer, the agents climbed the stairs and entered the apartment. One went into the back room and brought Wong Sun out in handcuffs. After arraignment, Wong Sun was released on his own recognizance. Several days later, he returned voluntarily to give an unsigned confession.

This Court ruled that Toy's declarations and the contraband taken from Yee were the fruits of the agents' illegal action and should not have been admitted as evidence against Toy. It held that the statement did not result from " 'an intervening independent act of a free will,' " and that it was not "sufficiently an act of free will to purge the primary taint of the unlawful invasion." With respect to Wong Sun's confession, however, the Court held that in the light of his lawful arraignment and release on his own recognizance, and of his return voluntarily several days later to make the statement, the connection between his unlawful arrest and the statement "had 'become so attenuated as to dissipate the taint.' " The Court said:

"We need not hold that all evidence is 'fruit of the poisonous tree' simply because it would not have come to light but for the illegal actions of the police. Rather, the more apt question in such a case is 'whether, granting establishment of the primary illegality, the evidence to which instant objection is made has been come at by exploitation of that illegality or instead by means sufficiently distinguishable to be purged of the primary taint.' "

* * *

III

The Illinois courts refrained from resolving the question, as apt here as it was in *Wong Sun,* whether Brown's statements were obtained by exploitation of the illegality of his arrest. They assumed that the *Miranda* warnings, by themselves, assured that the statements (verbal acts, as contrasted with physical evidence) were of sufficient free will as to purge the primary taint of the unlawful arrest. *Wong Sun,* of course, preceded *Miranda.*

* * *

* * * The exclusionary rule, however, when utilized to effectuate the Fourth Amendment, serves interests and policies that are distinct from those it serves under the Fifth. It is directed at all unlawful searches and seizures, and not merely those that happen to produce incriminating material or testimony as fruits. In short, exclusion of a confession made without *Miranda* warnings might be regarded as necessary to effectuate the Fifth Amendment, but it would not be sufficient fully to protect the Fourth. * * *

Thus, even if the statements in this case were found to be voluntary under the Fifth Amendment, the Fourth Amendment issue remains. In order for the causal chain, between the illegal arrest and the statements made subsequent thereto, to be broken, *Wong Sun* requires not merely that the statement meet the Fifth Amendment standard of voluntariness but that it be "sufficiently an act of free will to purge the primary taint." * * *

If *Miranda* warnings, by themselves, were held to attenuate the taint of an unconstitutional arrest, regardless of how wanton and purposeful the Fourth Amendment violation, the effect of the exclusionary rule would be substantially diluted. * * * Any incentive to avoid Fourth Amendment violations would be eviscerated by making the warnings, in effect, a "cure-all," and the constitutional guarantee against unlawful searches and seizures could be said to be reduced to "a form of words."

* * *

While we therefore reject the *per se* rule which the Illinois courts appear to have accepted, we also decline to adopt any alternative *per se* or "but for" rule. * * * The question whether a confession is the product of a free will under *Wong Sun* must be answered on the facts of each case. No single fact is dispositive. The workings of the human mind are too complex, and the possibilities of misconduct too diverse, to permit protection of the Fourth Amendment to turn on such a talismanic test. The *Miranda* warnings are an important factor, to be sure, in determining whether the confession is obtained by exploitation of an illegal arrest. But they are not the only factor to be considered. The temporal proximity of the arrest and the confession, the presence of intervening circumstances, and, particularly, the purpose and flagrancy of the official misconduct are all relevant. * * * And the burden of showing admissibility rests, of course, on the prosecution.

IV

* * * We conclude that the State failed to sustain the burden of showing that the evidence in question was admissible under *Wong Sun.*

Brown's first statement was separated from his illegal arrest by less than two hours, and there was no intervening event of significance whatsoever. In its essentials, his situation is remarkably like that of James Wah Toy in *Wong*

Sun.[a] We could hold Brown's first statement admissible only if we overrule *Wong Sun.* We decline to do so. And the second statement was clearly the result and the fruit of the first.

The illegality here, moreover, had a quality of purposefulness. The impropriety of the arrest was obvious; awareness of that fact was virtually conceded by the two detectives when they repeatedly acknowledged, in their testimony, that the purpose of their action was "for investigation" or for "questioning." The arrest, both in design and in execution, was investigatory. The detectives embarked upon this expedition for evidence in the hope that something might turn up. The manner in which Brown's arrest was effected gives the appearance of having been calculated to cause surprise, fright, and confusion.

[The concurring opinion of Justice White is omitted.]

MR. JUSTICE POWELL, with whom MR. JUSTICE REHNQUIST joins, concurring in part.

I join the Court insofar as it holds that the *per se* rule adopted by the Illinois Supreme Court for determining the admissibility of petitioner's two statements inadequately accommodates the diverse interests underlying the Fourth Amendment exclusionary rule. I would, however, remand the case for reconsideration under the general standards articulated in the Court's opinion and elaborated herein.

A

* * * The statements at issue in *Wong Sun* were on the temporal extremes in relation to the illegal arrest. Toy's statement was obtained immediately after his pursuit and arrest by six agents. It appears to have been a spontaneous response to a question put to him in the frenzy of that event, and there is no indication that the agents made any attempt to inform him of his right to remain silent. Wong Sun's statement, by contrast, was not given until after he was arraigned and released on his own recognizance. Wong Sun voluntarily returned to the station a few days after the arrest for questioning. His statement was preceded by an official warning of his right to remain silent and to have counsel if he desired. The Court rejected the Government's assertion that Toy's statement resulted from an independent act of free will sufficient to purge the consequences of the illegal arrest. Wong Sun's statement, however, was deemed admissible. Given the circumstances in which Wong Sun's statement was obtained, the Court concluded that "the connection between the arrest and the statement had 'become so attenuated as to dissipate the taint.' "

Like most cases in which the admissibility of statements obtained subsequent to an illegal arrest is contested, this case concerns statements more removed than that of Toy from the time and circumstances of the illegal arrest. Petitioner made his first statement some two hours following his arrest, after he had been given *Miranda* warnings. The Court is correct in noting that no other significant intervening event altered the relationship established between petitioner and the officers by the illegal arrest. But the Court's conclusion that admission of this statement could be allowed only by overruling *Wong Sun* rests either on an overly restrictive interpretation of the attenuation doctrine, to which I cannot subscribe, or on its view that the arrest was made for investigato-

a. The situation here is thus in dramatic contrast to that of Wong Sun himself. Wong Sun's confession, which the Court held admissible, came several days after the illegality, and was preceded by a lawful arraignment and a release from custody on his own recognizance.

ry purposes, a factual determination that I think more appropriately should have been left for decision in the first instance by the state courts.

B

* * * If an illegal arrest merely provides the occasion of initial contact between the police and the accused, and because of time or other intervening factors the accused's eventual statement is the product of his own reflection and free will, application of the exclusionary rule can serve little purpose: the police normally will not make an illegal arrest in the hope of eventually obtaining such a truly volunteered statement. * * * Bearing these considerations in mind, and recognizing that the deterrent value of the Fourth Amendment exclusionary rule is limited to certain kinds of police conduct, the following general categories can be identified.

Those most readily identifiable are on the extremes: the flagrantly abusive violation of Fourth Amendment rights, on the one hand, and "technical" Fourth Amendment violations, on the other. In my view, these extremes call for significantly different judicial responses.

I would require the clearest indication of attenuation in cases in which official conduct was flagrantly abusive of Fourth Amendment rights. * * * In such cases the deterrent value of the exclusionary rule is most likely to be effective, and the corresponding mandate to preserve judicial integrity most clearly demands that the fruits of official misconduct be denied. I thus would require some demonstrably effective break in the chain of events leading from the illegal arrest to the statement, such as actual consultation with counsel or the accused's presentation before a magistrate for a determination of probable cause, before the taint can be deemed removed.

At the opposite end of the spectrum lie "technical" violations of Fourth Amendment rights * * *.

* * * [In such cases] with the exception of statements given in the immediate circumstances of the illegal arrest—a constraint I think is imposed by existing exclusionary-rule law—I would not require more than proof that effective *Miranda* warnings were given and that the ensuing statement was voluntary in the Fifth Amendment sense. * * *

Between these extremes lies a wide range of situations that defy ready categorization, and I will not attempt to embellish on the factors set forth in the Court's opinion other than to emphasize that the *Wong Sun* inquiry always should be conducted with the deterrent purpose of the Fourth Amendment exclusionary rule sharply in focus. * * *

Note

Brown is followed in Dunaway v. New York, 439 U.S. 979 (1978), where the defendant was arrested without probable cause, taken down to the station, and confessed after *Miranda* warnings. The Court found that Dunaway's situation was "virtually a replica of the situation in *Brown.*" As in *Brown,* the Court was concerned that officers would "violate the Fourth Amendment with impunity, safe in the knowledge that they could wash their hands in the procedural safeguards of the Fifth."

Brown and *Dunaway* were deemed to be dispositive in Taylor v. Alabama, 455 U.S. 1014 (1982). On the basis of a tip that was insufficient to provide probable cause, police arrested Taylor without a warrant for a grocery store robbery, searched him, took him to the station for questioning and gave him Miranda warnings. At the station, he was fingerprinted, re-advised of his rights, questioned and placed in a lineup. Police told Taylor that his fingerprints matched those on some grocery items that had been handled by a participant in the robbery, and after a short visit with his girlfriend and a male companion, Taylor signed a Miranda waiver and confessed. Although the length of time between the illegal arrests and the confessions in *Brown* and *Dunaway* was two hours and in this case it was six hours, the Court said that "a difference of a few hours is not significant where, as here, petitioner was in police custody, unrepresented by counsel, and he was questioned on several occasions, fingerprinted and subjected to a line-up." Although Taylor was given Miranda warnings three times, the Court found that this was insufficient to break the connection with the illegal arrest and detention. It also found irrelevant the fact that the police obtained an arrest warrant after fingerprinting Taylor and matching his prints to those found at the robbery scene. And it declined to limit the prior cases to "flagrant or purposeful" illegal police conduct. Four dissenters agreed on the applicable law but disagreed on its application to the facts of the case. Citing *Taylor*, the Supreme Court summarily vacated and remanded in Lanier v. South Carolina, 474 U.S. 25 (1985). The Court observed that the fact that a confession was voluntary did not mean that it would not be suppressed as the fruit of an illegal arrest.

Brown, Dunaway and *Taylor* each excluded confessions as the fruit of an arrest unsupported by probable cause. In New York v. Harris, 495 U.S. 14 (1990), the defendant confessed at the station after a warrantless in-home arrest in violation of Payton v. New York, supra (holding that an arrest warrant was necessary for an in-home arrest). The challenged confession was made at the station an hour after the illegal arrest. Justice White concluded for the Court that the confession was not tainted, because unlike the prior cases, the defendant was not unlawfully in custody when he made the confession. Justice White reasoned that "the rule in *Payton* was designed to protect the physical integrity of the home; it was not intended to grant criminal suspects * * * protection for statements made outside their premises where the police have probable cause to arrest the suspect." Thus, the violation of *Payton* constitutes an illegal *search* of the home, but not an illegal arrest; and while evidence obtained in the search of the home is subject to exclusion, there is no connection between that search and a subsequent confession outside the home.

The majority further noted that exclusion of the confession was not necessary to serve the deterrent function of the exclusionary rule. Justice White argued that sufficient deterrence flows from the exclusion of any evidence found in the home during the arrest. The incremental deterrence of excluding the confession would be minimal, since police have probable cause to arrest outside the home and "it is doubtful therefore that the desire to secure a statement from a criminal suspect would motivate the police to violate *Payton*."

Justice Marshall dissented in an opinion joined by Justices Brennan, Blackmun and Stevens. The dissenters objected to the categorical rule that the mere physical exit from the home necessarily breaks the chain of causation between the illegal entry and a subsequent statement. Justice Marshall also contended that the rule adopted by the majority would give the police an incentive to violate *Payton*. He reasoned that the officer would enter illegally to save time, and perhaps exploit the in-home nature of the arrest to rattle the suspect and increase the likelihood of a confession. Excluding evidence found in the house would be no deterrent, since such suppression would make the officer no worse off than if he had waited outside to make the arrest.

In *Harris* the *Payton* violation turned up no evidence. Where the *Payton* violation does produce evidence and is followed by a stationhouse confession that is influenced by the seizure of the tainted evidence, the fruit of the poisonous tree doctrine is applicable. There is thus a distinction between a confession which is the product of the *Payton* arrest (which is legal) and one which is the product of the *Payton* search (which is illegal). For example, in United States v. Beltran, 917 F.2d 641, 645 (1st Cir.1990), police arrested Beltran in her home without a warrant. During the arrest the police saw cocaine in plain view. They took the defendant to the stationhouse where she made incriminating statements. The court stated that "whether or the extent to which *Harris* applies may turn on questions of fact such as when the police seized the items in question or what motivated Ms. Beltran's statements" and remanded the case to the district court for a factual determination. Thus if Beltran was rattled into a confession not by the arrest but by the fact that the police saw the cocaine, *Harris* would not apply.

Brown was distinguished in Rawlings v. Kentucky, 448 U.S. 98 (1980). The Court assumed that Rawlings and others were improperly detained in a house while police went to get a search warrant, but found that the improper detention did not require suppression of statements made by Rawlings after evidence was discovered. Justice Rehnquist's majority opinion observed that *Miranda* warnings were given (also true in *Brown*); that the 45 minute detention was in a congenial atmosphere; that the statements were apparently spontaneous reactions to the discovery of evidence rather than the product of the illegal detention; that the police action did not involve flagrant misconduct; and that no argument was made that the statements were involuntary. Justices White and Stewart would have remanded for consideration of the "fruit" question. Justices Marshall and Brennan thought that the statements "were obviously the fruit of the illegal detention."

6. *Independent Source*

In addition to the concept of attenuation, two additional doctrines soften the impact of the fruit of the poisonous tree rule. The first doctrine is that of the independent source.[35] "It applies * * * when the independent source of information provides a distinct evidentiary trail that leads to the same destination [as the fruits], evidence of guilt," United States v. Villarreal, 565 F.2d 932, 941 (5th Cir. 1978) (Wisdom, J., dissenting). Following an illegal arrest, police may establish probable cause through independent means. If so, they will not have to release the suspect and rearrest him. If statements are made after legal cause to arrest exists they will not be suppressed. See, e.g., United States v. Morris, 451 F.Supp. 361 (E.D.N.Y.1978).

In Segura v. United States, 468 U.S. 796 (1984), and in the following case, Murray v. United States, the Court considered whether an illegal search of premises could be cured when the officers later obtained a warrant, and where the probable cause supporting the warrant was not derived from information obtained in the illegal search. *Segura* is discussed in detail in *Murray.*

35. Another limitation on the exclusionary rule is the doctrine of curative admissibility. It is explained in Thomas v. State, 572 S.W.2d 507, 512–13 (Tex.Cr.App.1976):

> It has long been the rule of this state that the admission of improper evidence cannot be urged as grounds for reversal where the defendant gives testimony on direct examination which establishes the same facts as those objected to. Cameron v. State, 530 S.W.2d 841 (Tex.Cr.App.1975); Palmer v. State, 475 S.W.2d 797 (Tex.Cr.App.1972). This principle is sometimes referred to as the doctrine of curative admissibility. 5A C.J.S. Appeal and Error § 1724(3)(b) at 954 (1958). A corollary to this rule is that the harmful effect of improperly admitted evidence is not cured by the fact that the accused sought to meet, destroy, or explain it by the introduction of rebutting evidence. * * * Thus if a defendant takes the witness stand to refute, deny, contradict, or impeach evidence or testimony properly objected to, no waiver of the objection occurs.

MURRAY v. UNITED STATES

Supreme Court of the United States, 1988.
487 U.S. 533.

JUSTICE SCALIA delivered the opinion of the Court.

In Segura v. United States, 468 U.S. 796 (1984), we held that police officers' illegal entry upon private premises did not require suppression of evidence subsequently discovered at those premises when executing a search warrant obtained on the basis of information wholly unconnected with the initial entry. In these consolidated cases we are faced with the question whether, again assuming evidence obtained pursuant to an independently obtained search warrant, the portion of such evidence that had been observed in plain view at the time of a prior illegal entry must be suppressed.

I

* * * Based on information received from informants, federal law enforcement agents had been surveilling petitioner Murray and several of his co-conspirators. At about 1:45 p.m. on April 6, 1983, they observed Murray drive a truck and Carter drive a green camper, into a warehouse in South Boston. When the petitioners drove the vehicles out about 20 minutes later, the surveilling agents saw within the warehouse two individuals and a tractor-trailer rig bearing a long, dark container. Murray and Carter later turned over the truck and camper to other drivers, who were in turn followed and ultimately arrested, and the vehicles lawfully seized. Both vehicles were found to contain marijuana.

After receiving this information, several of the agents converged on the South Boston warehouse and forced entry. They found the warehouse unoccupied, but observed in plain view numerous burlap-wrapped bales that were later found to contain marijuana. They left without disturbing the bales, kept the warehouse under surveillance, and did not reenter it until they had a search warrant. In applying for the warrant, the agents did not mention the prior entry, and did not rely on any observations made during that entry. When the warrant was issued—at 10:40 p.m., approximately eight hours after the initial entry—the agents immediately reentered the warehouse and seized 270 bales of marijuana and notebooks listing customers for whom the bales were destined.

[The motion to suppress was denied and the Court of Appeals affirmed.]

II

* * *

Almost simultaneously with our development of the exclusionary rule, * * * we also announced what has come to be known as the "independent source" doctrine. That doctrine, which has been applied to evidence acquired not only through Fourth Amendment violations but also through Fifth and Sixth Amendment violations, has recently been described as follows:

> "[T]he interest of society in deterring unlawful police conduct and the public interest in having juries receive all probative evidence of a crime are properly balanced by putting the police in the same, not a *worse,* position that they would have been in if no police error or misconduct had occurred.... When the challenged evidence has an independent source, exclusion of such evidence would put the police in a worse position than they would have been in absent any error or violation." Nix v. Williams, 467 U.S. 431, 443 (1984).

The dispute here is over the scope of this doctrine. Petitioners contend that it applies only to evidence obtained for the first time during an independent lawful search. The Government argues that it applies also to evidence initially discovered during, or as a consequence of, an unlawful search, but later obtained independently from activities untainted by the initial illegality. We think the Government's view has better support in both precedent and policy.

Our cases have used the concept of "independent source" in a more general and a more specific sense. The more general sense identifies *all* evidence acquired in a fashion untainted by the illegal evidence-gathering activity. Thus, where an unlawful entry has given investigators knowledge of facts *x* and *y*, but fact *z* has been learned by other means, fact *z* can be said to be admissible because derived from an "independent source." This is how we used the term in Segura v. United States. In that case, agents unlawfully entered the defendant's apartment and remained there until a search warrant was obtained. The admissibility of what they discovered while waiting in the apartment was not before us, but we held that the evidence found for the first time during the execution of the valid and untainted search warrant was admissible because it was discovered pursuant to an "independent source."

The original use of the term, however, and its more important use for purposes of this case, was more specific. It was originally applied in the exclusionary rule context * * *, with reference to that particular category of evidence acquired by an untainted search *which is identical to the evidence unlawfully acquired*—that is, in the example just given, to knowledge of facts *x* and *y* derived from an independent source.

* * *

We recently assumed this application of the independent source doctrine (in the Sixth Amendment context) in Nix v. Williams. There incriminating statements obtained in violation of the defendant's right to counsel had led the police to the victim's body. The body had not in fact been found through an independent source as well, and so the independent source doctrine was not itself applicable. We held, however, that evidence concerning the body was nonetheless admissible because a search had been under way which would have discovered the body, had it not been called off because of the discovery produced by the unlawfully obtained statements. This "inevitable discovery" doctrine obviously assumes the validity of the independent source doctrine as applied to evidence initially acquired unlawfully. It would make no sense to admit the evidence because the independent search, had it not been aborted, would have found the body, but to exclude the evidence if the search had continued and had in fact found the body. The inevitable discovery doctrine, with its distinct requirements, is in reality an extrapolation from the independent source doctrine: *Since* the tainted evidence would be admissible if in fact discovered through an independent source, it should be admissible if it inevitably would have been discovered.

Petitioners' asserted policy basis for excluding evidence which is initially discovered during an illegal search, but is subsequently acquired through an independent and lawful source, is that a contrary rule will remove all deterrence to, and indeed positively encourage, unlawful police searches. As petitioners see the incentives, law enforcement officers will routinely enter without a warrant to make sure that what they expect to be on the premises is in fact there. If it is not, they will have spared themselves the time and trouble of getting a warrant; if it is, they can get the warrant and use the evidence despite the unlawful entry. We see the incentives differently. An officer with probable cause sufficient to obtain a search warrant would be foolish to enter the premises first in an unlawful manner. By doing so, he would risk suppression of all evidence on the premises, both seen and unseen, since his action would add to the normal burden of convincing a magistrate that there is probable cause the much more onerous burden of convincing a trial court that no information gained from the illegal entry affected either the law enforcement officers' decision to seek a warrant or the magistrate's decision to grant it. Nor would the officer *without* sufficient probable cause to obtain a search warrant have any added incentive to conduct an unlawful entry, since whatever he finds cannot be used to establish probable cause before a magistrate.[a]

It is possible to read petitioners' briefs as asserting the more narrow position that the "independent source" doctrine does apply to independent acquisition of evidence previously derived *indirectly* from the unlawful search, but does not apply to what they call "primary evidence," that is, evidence acquired during the course of the search itself. In addition to finding no support in our precedent, this strange distinction would produce results bearing no relation to the policies of the exclusionary rule. It would mean, for example, that the government's knowledge of the existence and condition of a dead body, knowledge lawfully acquired through independent sources, would have to be excluded if government agents had previously observed the body during an unlawful search of the defendant's apartment; but not if they had observed a notation that the body was buried in a certain location, producing consequential discovery of the corpse.

III

To apply what we have said to the present cases: Knowledge that the marijuana was in the warehouse was assuredly acquired at the time of the unlawful entry. But it was also acquired at the time of entry pursuant to the warrant, and if that later acquisition was not the result of the earlier entry there is no reason why the independent source doctrine should not apply. Invoking the exclusionary rule would put the police (and society) not in the *same* position they would have occupied if no violation occurred, but in a *worse* one.

We think this is also true with respect to the tangible evidence, the bales of marijuana. It would make no more sense to exclude that than it would to exclude tangible evidence found upon the corpse in *Nix,* if the search in that case had not been abandoned and had in fact come upon the body. * * * The independent source doctrine does not rest upon such metaphysical analysis, but upon the policy that, while the government should not profit from its illegal activity, neither should it be placed in a worse position than it would otherwise have occupied.

The ultimate question, therefore, is whether the search pursuant to warrant was in fact a genuinely independent

a. * * * To say that a district court must be satisfied that a warrant would have been sought without the illegal entry is not to give dispositive effect to police officers' assurances on the point. Where the facts render those assurances implausible, the independent source doctrine will not apply.

We might note that there is no basis for pointing to the present cases as an example of a "search first, warrant later" mentality. The District Court found that the agents entered the warehouse "in an effort to apprehend any participants who might have remained inside and to guard against the destruction of possibly critical evidence." While they may have misjudged the existence of sufficient exigent circumstances to justify the warrantless entry * * * there is nothing to suggest that they went in merely to see if there was anything worth getting a warrant for.

source of the information and tangible evidence at issue here. This would not have been the case if the agents' decision to seek the warrant was prompted by what they had seen during the initial entry, or if information obtained during that entry was presented to the Magistrate and affected his decision to issue the warrant. * * * The District Court found that the agents did not reveal their warrantless entry to the Magistrate and that they did not include in their application for a warrant any recitation of their observations in the warehouse. It did not, however, explicitly find that the agents would have sought a warrant if they had not earlier entered the warehouse. * * * To be sure, the District Court did determine that the purpose of the warrantless entry was in part "to guard against the destruction of possibly critical evidence," and one could perhaps infer from this that the agents who made the entry already planned to obtain that "critical evidence" through a warrant-authorized search. That inference is not, however, clear enough to justify the conclusion that the District Court's findings amounted to a determination of independent source.

Accordingly, we vacate the judgment and remand these cases to the Court of Appeals with instructions that it remand to the District Court for determination whether the warrant-authorized search of the warehouse was an independent source of the challenged evidence in the sense we have described.

JUSTICE BRENNAN and JUSTICE KENNEDY took no part in the consideration or decision of this litigation.

JUSTICE MARSHALL, with whom JUSTICE STEVENS and JUSTICE O'CONNOR join, dissenting.

The Court today holds that the "independent source" exception to the exclusionary rule may justify admitting evidence discovered during an illegal warrantless search that is later "rediscovered" by the same team of investigators during a search pursuant to a warrant obtained immediately after the illegal search. I believe the Court's decision, by failing to provide sufficient guarantees that the subsequent search was, in fact, independent of the illegal search, emasculates the Warrant Clause and undermines the deterrence function of the exclusionary rule. * * *

This Court has stated frequently that the exclusionary rule is principally designed to deter violations of the Fourth Amendment. The independent source exception, like the inevitable discovery exception, is primarily based on a practical view that under certain circumstances the beneficial deterrent effect that exclusion will have on future constitutional violations is too slight to justify the social cost of excluding probative evidence from a criminal trial. When the seizure of the evidence at issue is "wholly independent of" the constitutional violation, then exclusion arguably will have no effect on a law enforcement officer's incentive to commit an unlawful search.

* * * In holding that the independent source exception may apply to the facts of these cases, I believe the Court loses sight of the practical moorings of the independent source exception and creates an affirmative incentive for unconstitutional searches. * * *

* * * Obtaining a warrant is inconvenient and time consuming. Even when officers have probable cause to support a warrant application, therefore, they have an incentive first to determine whether it is worthwhile to obtain a warrant. Probable cause is much less than certainty, and many "confirmatory" searches will result in the discovery that no evidence is present, thus saving the police the time and trouble of getting a warrant. If contraband is discovered, however, the officers may later seek a warrant to shield the evidence

from the taint of the illegal search. The police thus know in advance that they have little to lose and much to gain by forgoing the bother of obtaining a warrant and undertaking an illegal search.

Under the Court's view, today's decision does not provide an incentive for unlawful searches, because the officer undertaking the search would know that "his action would add to the normal burden of convincing a magistrate that there is probable cause the much more onerous burden of convincing a trial court that no information gained from the illegal entry affected either the law enforcement officers' decision to seek a warrant or the magistrate's decision to grant it." The Court, however, provides no hint of why this risk would actually seem significant to the officers. Under the circumstances of these cases, the officers committing the illegal search have both knowledge and control of the factors central to the trial court's determination. First, it is a simple matter, as was done in these cases, to exclude from the warrant application any information gained from the initial entry so that the magistrate's determination of probable cause is not influenced by the prior illegal search. Second, today's decision makes the application of the independent source exception turn entirely on an evaluation of the officers' intent. It normally will be difficult for the trial court to verify, or the defendant to rebut, an assertion by officers that they always intended to obtain a warrant, regardless of the results of the illegal search.[b] The testimony of the officers conducting the illegal search is the only direct evidence of intent, and the defendant will be relegated simply to arguing that the officers should not be believed. Under these circumstances, the litigation risk described by the Court seems hardly a risk at all; it does not significantly dampen the incentive to conduct the initial illegal search.

* * *

[The dissenting opinion of Justice Stevens is omitted.]

Note

Isn't there a distinction between the body in *Nix* and the bales that the officers saw upon their illegal entry in *Murray?* In *Nix,* the body itself was not illegally seized or searched; the illegality dealt with the statement which led to the body. Does that make a difference?

The majority in *Murray* expresses concern about a "confirmatory" search, and states that the subsequent search will be invalidated if the officer's testimony denying a confirmatory motivation is "implausible." The officer denying a confirmatory motivation will explain why he or she did the original search without a warrant, and after *Murray* this explanation must rise only to the level of plausibility. In *Murray,* the explanation found plausible was that the officers thought they had exigent circumstances, even though in fact they did not (if they did, *Murray* would not be a fruits case, since the original search would have been legal). Recall the discussion of exigent circumstances earlier in the Chapter. Under what facts could the officers be so wrong about exigent circumstances that their explanation on that point would be implausible? Could that ever happen in a narcotics case? Has the Court in *Murray* established a good faith exception for warrantless searches that are later sanitized by a warrant? As in *Leon,* discussed infra, the

b. * * * The Court fails to describe how a trial court will properly evaluate whether the law enforcement officers fully intended to obtain a warrant regardless of what they discovered during the illegal search. The obvious question is whose intent is relevant? Intentions clearly may differ both among supervisory officers and among officers who initiate the illegal search.

search, though illegal, does not result in exclusion so long as the officers are not totally unreasonable in believing that they were acting legally. For criticism of *Murray* on these points, see Bradley, Murray v. United States: The Bell Tolls for the Search Warrant Requirement, 64 Ind.L.J. 907 (1989).

Is the primary purpose of the exclusionary rule to deter police misconduct, or to restore the situation as it existed before the illegal search? If the primary purpose is deterrence, can it be argued that it is sometimes necessary to place the State in a worse position than if the illegal search had not occurred? Is *Murray* one of those times?

The court in United States v. Curtis, 931 F.2d 1011 (4th Cir.1991) applied *Murray* where an undercover agent bought drugs in Curtis' house, and then the officers went to get a warrant, but while they were gone the officers remaining for surveillance purposes entered Curtis' house for an ostensible protective sweep. The court found that, presuming the protective sweep was illegal, it did not affect the officers' decision to get a warrant. Is *Curtis* an easier or harder case than *Murray?*

7. *Inevitable Discovery*

The inevitable discovery exception, discussed in *Murray,* has been termed the "hypothetical independent source" exception. See Note, the Inevitable Discovery Exception, Primary Evidence, and the Emasculation of the Fourth Amendment, 55 Fordham L.Rev. 1221 (1987). For the exception to apply, the government must show that the illegally obtained evidence would have been discovered through legitimate means independent of the official misconduct. Note that if the evidence had been actually discovered through legitimate independent means, the independent source exception would apply. So the inevitable discovery exception is one step removed from the independent source exception.

A variation on the inevitable discovery doctrine is the rule in most courts that, if an arrest warrant is invalid but the arrest could have been made without a warrant, evidence will not be suppressed. See, e.g., United States v. Hall, 348 F.2d 837 (2d Cir. 1965). A few courts hold the arrest to be invalid and suppress. See, e.g., Isaacks v. State, 350 So.2d 1340 (Miss.1977). What are the opposing arguments?

The Supreme Court approved the inevitable discovery limitation upon the exclusionary rule for the first time in Nix v. Williams, 467 U.S. 431 (1984), which is discussed in *Murray.* Seven years earlier, the Court had held by a 5–4 vote that Williams' conviction for murdering a 10-year-old girl was tainted when a police officer managed to obtain statements from Williams in derogation of Williams' Sixth Amendment right to counsel. In the course of making statements, Williams led police to the girl's body. Although the Court held that the statements must be suppressed, it left open the question whether evidence as to the location and condition of the body might be admissible.

At the second trial, a state court judge found that the government proved by a preponderance of the evidence that a search party, which had suspended its activities once Williams agreed to lead the police to the body, would have found the body shortly afterwards anyway and that the body would have been found in essentially the same condition as when Williams led the police to it. Thus, he admitted evidence concerning its location and condition. The state supreme court affirmed, but a federal appellate court found that the inevitable discovery rule could not be invoked where a police officer acted in bad faith, as it found the officer had in dealing with Williams.

Chief Justice Burger wrote for a majority as it reversed the court of appeals. He treated the independent source and inevitable discovery doctrines as related, since both limit the exclusionary rule so that the government is not denied evidence it would have had even without its officers' overstepping constitutional boundaries. The Court indicated that the exclusionary rule works to assure that police do not believe they will benefit from constitutional violations, and that the inevitable discovery rule limitation simply recognizes that the government actually obtains no advantage over a defendant when it is permitted to use evidence obtained following a constitutional violation, *if* the government can prove that absent the violation it still would have had the evidence. The Court declined to restrict the inevitable discovery limitation to situations in which an officer acts in good faith. It found that the limitation is not needed to deter officers from violating constitutional rules, since officers seeking to gather evidence must be careful since they cannot know whether the government will be able to prove that their evidence would have been discovered inevitably. The Chief Justice found that a bad faith limitation "would put the police in a *worse* position than they would have been if no unlawful conduct had transpired" and that the exclusionary rule could not be used to punish the state in that way. The Court held that to invoke the exception the government must prove by a preponderance that the evidence would have been discovered through independent legal means. Chief Justice Burger rejected the clear and convincing evidence standard, stating that "we are unwilling to impose added burdens on the already difficult task of proving guilt in criminal cases by enlarging the barrier to placing evidence of unquestioned truth before juries."

Justice Stevens concurred in the judgment. He agreed that as long as the government must prove that evidence would have been inevitably found, officers are unlikely to violate the Constitution in the hope that the inevitable discovery doctrine will save them, since they have no way of knowing at the time they act whether the government will have sufficient proof to invoke the doctrine. He expressed concern, however, that the majority emphasized the "societal costs" of the exclusionary rule without also emphasizing the "societal costs" of unconstitutional police conduct.

Although Justice Brennan, joined by Justice Marshall, dissented, he accepted the inevitable discovery doctrine. He emphasized that inevitable discovery was a more hypothetical exception than independent source, and consequently would have required the government to prove inevitability by clear and convincing evidence.

Although *Williams* is a Sixth Amendment case, the Court discussed the exclusionary rules it has adopted to enforce Fourth, Fifth and Sixth Amendment standards. The Court's opinion strongly suggests that the inevitable discovery doctrine will limit the exclusionary rule under all three amendments. Both before and after *Nix,* lower courts have applied the inevitable discovery exception to Fourth Amendment violations. See, e.g., United States v. Jackson, 901 F.2d 83 (7th Cir.1990) (even if defendant did not give voluntary consent to a search of his person, officers would have inevitably conducted a *Terry* frisk and uncovered crack cocaine in defendant's pockets).

In *Nix,* the inevitable discovery exception was applied to admit the fruit of the poisonous tree; the condition of the body was admitted, but not the illegally obtained confession that led to the body. Questions have arisen whether the exception can be applied to the illegally obtained evidence itself, which some have called "primary" as opposed to "derivative" evidence. See Capra, Independent Source and Inevitable Discovery, N.Y.L.J. Dec. 8, 1989, p. 4, col. 3. In United States v. Andrade, 784 F.2d 1431 (9th Cir.1986) officers searched Andrade's bag and found cocaine after he was arrested for a drug violation. The search did not occur until an hour after the arrest. The court held that even if the search could not be justified as incident to arrest and was thus unlawful (see United States v. Chadwick, supra), "the cocaine was admissible because it would have been inevitably discovered through a routine inventory search." The court noted that it was normal DEA procedure to inventory the contents of bags held by arrestees, and that such a procedure was valid under Illinois v. Lafayette, supra. Judge Reinhardt, concurring, agreed that the "confluence" of *Nix* and *Lafayette* required this result, but concluded that "the result we are required to reach will serve only to encourage illegal and unconstitutional searches."

If *Andrade* is correct that the existence of routine inventory procedures allows admission of evidence obtained directly from the illegal search of a car or container, then why would an officer ever have to comply with the rules which still limit searches of cars or containers? For example, the trunk of a car cannot be searched without probable cause. But does that probable cause requirement mean anything if the inevitable discovery exception applies by way of the inventory exception to anything found in the trunk? The New York Court of Appeals rejected the argument that primary evidence could be admitted if it would have been inevitably discovered in an inventory. The court in People v. Stith, 69 N.Y.2d 313, 514 N.Y.S.2d 201, 506 N.E.2d 911 (1987) reasoned as follows:

> [A]pplying the inevitable discovery rule in these circumstances, and effecting what would amount to a *post hoc* rationalization of the initial wrong would be an unacceptable dilution of the exclusionary rule. It would defeat a primary purpose of that rule, deterrence of police misconduct.

The court in *Stith* distinguished primary evidence, which it thought not subject to the inevitable discovery exception, from secondary evidence derived from the illegal activity—such as leads from an address book found in the trunk, as opposed to the address book itself. The court stated that "as distinguished from secondary evidence, failing to exclude wrongfully obtained primary evidence would encourage unlawful searches in the hope that probable cause would be developed after the fact." Is this distinction persuasive? If the primary evidence found in the illegal search of a trunk would have been discovered in a lawful inventory search, doesn't exclusion put the officers in a worse position than they would have been if the illegal conduct had never occurred? Isn't that contrary to *Nix* and *Murray?* Is it necessary to punish in order to deter illegality in cases like *Stith* and *Andrade?*

If the inevitable discovery exception applies to the very evidence obtained in an illegal search, what is to stop the government from making the following argument: "We realize that we did an illegal warrantless search. However, we had probable cause, and we would have obtained a warrant on that basis.

Since the warrant would have inevitably issued, and we would have searched pursuant to it (if we had bothered to obtain it) then all the evidence we obtained is admissible under the inevitable discovery exception." Do *Nix* and *Murray* require that such an argument must be accepted? If so, is there anything left of the warrant requirement? See United States v. Satterfield, 743 F.2d 827 (11th Cir.1984) (acceptance of such an argument would "destroy the requirement that a warrant for the search of a home be obtained before the search takes place"). But see Bradley, 64 Ind.L.J. 907, supra (noting that the "we would have obtained a warrant" argument is creditable and persuasive in light of *Murray,* which applied the independent source exception to primary evidence, i.e. evidence discovered during the illegal search itself). At least two courts have relied on *Nix* to hold that evidence found in an illegal warrantless search was admissible because a warrant could and would have been obtained. See United States v. Levasseur, 620 F.Supp. 624 (E.D.N.Y.1985); State v. Butler, 676 S.W.2d 809 (Mo.1984).

It is possible to argue that even with probable cause, there is no assurance that a warrant would have inevitably been obtained, since the magistrate may not actually have found probable cause; moreover, a magistrate is not required to issue a warrant even if he or she finds that probable cause exists. But this argument is tempered by several considerations. First, the government need only establish inevitability by a preponderance of the evidence. Second, most courts do not prevent the officer from going to another magistrate if the first magistrate denies the application. Third, the officer need only establish a fair probability of criminal activity to support a warrant application.

A few courts have imposed the requirement that in order to invoke the inevitable discovery exception, the police must be actively pursuing the lawful means at the time the illegal search is conducted. See United States v. Khoury, 901 F.2d 948 (11th Cir.1990), rejecting the argument that evidence obtained in an illegal search of a car would have been inevitably discovered in an inventory, since at the time of the search an inventory had not yet begun. Other courts, such as the court in *Andrade,* reject the "active pursuit" limitation on the inevitable discovery exception. Would an active pursuit limitation solve some of the concerns posed in applying the inevitable discovery exception to primary evidence?

In United States v. Feldhacker, 849 F.2d 293 (8th Cir.1988), the court cautioned that in deciding whether the inevitable discovery exception applies, courts must focus on what the officers would have done, not on what they could possibly have done.

> There are reasonable limits to the scope that courts will impute to the hypothetical untainted investigation. An investigation conducted over an infinite time with infinite thoroughness will, of course, ultimately or inevitably turn up any and all pieces of evidence in the world. Prosecutors may not justify unlawful extractions of information post hoc where lawful methods present only a theoretical possibility of discovery. While the hypothetical discovery by lawful means need not be reached as rapidly as that actually reached by unlawful means, the lawful discovery must be inevitable through means that would actually have been employed.

8. *Identifications After Illegal Arrests and Searches*

Courts are reluctant to suppress the testimony from a live witness which is alleged to be the result of an illegal search or arrest. In United States v. Ceccolini, 435 U.S. 268 (1978), an officer stopped to talk with a friend who was in Ceccolini's flower shop. While there, the officer illegally picked up and opened an envelope, and found money and gambling slips. He then learned from his friend, who did not know about his discovery, that the envelope belonged to Ceccolini. The officer relayed his information to detectives who in turn transmitted it to the FBI. Four months later, an FBI agent questioned the officer's friend who had been in the flower shop, without mentioning the illegally discovered gambling slips. The friend expressed a willingness to testify against Ceccolini, and did so before the grand jury and at Ceccolini's trial. Justice Rehnquist, writing for the Court, declined to adopt a rule that the testimony of a live witness should never be excluded. But he stated that "the exclusionary rule should be invoked with much greater reluctance where the claim is based on a causal relationship between a constitutional violation and the discovery of a live witness than when a similar claim is advanced to support suppression of an inanimate object." The Court noted that the willingness of the witness to testify is very likely, if not certain, to break the chain of causation under *Wong Sun.* Justice Rehnquist also noted that exclusion of a live witness would have a serious cost, since it would "perpetually disable a witness from testifying about relevant and material facts, regardless of how unrelated such testimony might be to the purpose of the originally illegal search or the evidence discovered thereby." Because of this cost, the Court concluded that the exclusionary rule should only apply if there was a very close and direct link between the illegality and the witness' testimony. The Court found no such close link under the facts in *Ceccolini,* where the witness was willing to testify, four months passed between the illegality and the agent's contact with the witness, and the witness was unaware of the illegality. Chief Justice Burger concurred and would have gone further and held that the testimony of a live witness should never be suppressed. Justice Marshall, in a dissent joined by Justice Brennan, found no meaningful distinction between live witnesses and inanimate evidence. He argued that "the same tree" cannot bear "two different kinds of fruit, with one kind less susceptible than the other to exclusion." After *Ceccolini,* can you think of facts which will result in the exclusion of a live witness? For a case distinguishing *Ceccolini,* see United States v. Ramirez–Sandoval, 872 F.2d 1392 (9th Cir.1989) (witnesses were tainted fruit where illegally obtained information was used in questioning them, no time elapsed between the illegal search and the questioning, officer did not know the identity of the witnesses beforehand, and witnesses expressed no willingness to come forward).

In Crews v. United States, 445 U.S. 463 (1980), the question was whether an armed robber's in-court identification should have been suppressed as the fruit of an illegal arrest. In between the arrest and testimony came the photographing of defendant by the police, who conducted a photo identification session with the victim and a court-ordered lineup. Justice Brennan, writing for the Court, identified three distinct elements of a victim's in-court identification: the presence of the victim to testify at trial; the ability of the victim to reconstruct the crime; and the physical presence of the defendant. He concluded "that none of these three elements 'has been come at by exploitation' of the violation of the defendant's Fourth Amendment rights." The majority concluded that a person who can be brought to trial following an illegal arrest can be identified, as long as the in-court identification is free from any improper taint attributable to unconstitutional extra-judicial identification procedures.

The argument has been made that evidence is tainted if it would not have been found "but for" the unconstitutional police practice. See Comment, The Inevitable Discovery Exception to the Constitutional Exclusionary Rules, 74 Colum.L.Rev. 88 (1974). But this ignores the theory of attenuation, which really focuses on the deterrent efficacy of exclusion. See Pitlen, "The Fruit of the Poisonous Tree" Revisited and Shepardized, 56 Calif.L.Rev. 579 (1968).

9. *Standing*

In all courts one must have standing to successfully move to suppress evidence. Standing, as applied to the exclusionary rule, does not refer to community reputation; it refers to the moving party's relationship to the search and seizure that is challenged. Standing in the federal system and some states is, in part, a tool to identify under rules of procedure like Fed.R.Crim.P. 41(e) who is a person "aggrieved" by an unlawful search and seizure. But, since the exclusionary rule has been deemed part of Fourth and Fourteenth Amendment rights, any limitation like standing also must satisfy the demands of the Fourth Amendment. Assuming, then, that the Supreme Court's decisions are more than interpretations of local rules, they probably signify that no state could provide for less standing than is required by the decisions. A state could, however, provide for more, if it wished.

Jones v. United States, 362 U.S. 257 (1960), held that a defendant had automatic standing to challenge the legality of the search that produced the very drugs that he was charged with possessing at the time of the search. The Court in *Jones* also stated that anyone "legitimately on the premises where a search occurs" had standing to challenge its legality. In the following case the Court substantially cut back on *Jones* and, more importantly, recharacterized standing questions so that they are now resolved by substantive principles of Fourth Amendment law.

RAKAS v. ILLINOIS

Supreme Court of the United States, 1978.
439 U.S. 128.

MR. JUSTICE REHNQUIST delivered the opinion of the Court.

[Officers received a radio call concerning a robbery and describing the getaway car. They stopped a vehicle which matched the description. Petitioners and two female companions were in the car. They were ordered out of the car, the officers searched the passenger compartment, and found a box of rifle shells in the glove compartment and a sawed-off rifle under the front passenger seat. Petitioners were passengers in the car; the owner of the car had been the driver when the car was stopped. The lower court denied the motion to suppress, reasoning that petitioners lacked standing, and the Illinois appellate courts affirmed. The Supreme Court found that petitioners had the burden of proof as to standing, and that they failed to meet their burden of showing ownership of the rifle or shells. The Court proceeded to consider whether standing could be established in the absence of ownership of the property seized].

* * *

II

Petitioners first urge us to relax or broaden the rule of standing enunciated in Jones v. United States, so that any criminal defendant at whom a search was "directed" would have standing to contest the legality of that search and object to the admission at trial of evidence obtained as a result of the search. Alternatively, petitioners argue that they have standing to object to the search under *Jones* because they were "legitimately on [the] premises" at the time of the search.

The concept of standing discussed in *Jones* focuses on whether the person seeking to challenge the legality of a search as a basis for suppressing evidence was himself the "victim" of the search or seizure. Adoption of the so-called "target" theory advanced by petitioners would in effect permit a defendant to assert that a violation of the Fourth Amendment rights of a third party entitled him to have evidence suppressed at his trial. If we reject petitioners' request for a broadened rule of standing such as this, and reaffirm the holding of *Jones* and other cases that Fourth Amendment rights are personal rights that may not be asserted vicariously, we will have occasion to re-examine the "standing" terminology emphasized in *Jones.* For we are not at all sure that the determination of a motion to suppress is materially aided by labeling the inquiry identified in *Jones* as one of standing, rather than simply recognizing it as one involving the substantive question of whether or not the proponent of the motion to suppress has had his own Fourth Amendment rights infringed by the search and seizure which he seeks to challenge. * * *

A

We decline to extend the rule of standing in Fourth Amendment cases in the manner suggested by petitioners. As we stated in Alderman v. United States, 394 U.S. 165, 174 (1969), "Fourth Amendment rights are personal rights which, like some other constitutional rights, may not be vicariously asserted." A person who is aggrieved by an illegal search and seizure only through the introduction of damaging evidence secured by a search of a third person's premises or property has not had any of his Fourth Amendment rights infringed. And since the exclusionary rule is an attempt to effectuate the guarantees of the Fourth Amendment, it is proper to permit only defendants whose Fourth Amendment rights have been violated to benefit from the rule's protections.[a] There is no reason to think that a party whose rights have been infringed will not, if evidence is used against him, have ample motivation to move to suppress it. Even if such a person is not a defendant in the action, he may be able to recover damages for the violation of his Fourth Amendment rights, see Monroe v. Pape, 365 U.S. 167 (1961), or seek redress under state law for invasion of privacy or trespass.

a. The necessity for a showing of a violation of personal rights is not obviated by recognizing the deterrent purpose of the exclusionary rule. Despite the deterrent aim of the exclusionary rule, we never have held that unlawfully seized evidence is inadmissible in all proceedings or against all persons. * * *

* * * In *Jones,* the Court set forth two alternative holdings: It established a rule of "automatic" standing to contest an allegedly illegal search where the same possession needed to establish standing is an essential element of the offense charged; and second, it stated that "anyone legitimately on premises where a search occurs may challenge its legality by way of a motion to suppress." Had the Court intended to adopt the target theory now put forth by petitioners, neither of the above two holdings would have been necessary since Jones was the "target" of the police search in that case. * * *

In Alderman v. United States, Mr. Justice Fortas, in a concurring and dissenting opinion, argued that the Court should "include within the category of those who may object to the introduction of illegal evidence 'one against whom the search was directed.'" The Court did not directly comment on Mr. Justice Fortas' suggestion, but it left no doubt that it rejected this theory by holding that persons who were not parties to unlawfully overheard conversations or who did not own the premises on which such conversations took place did not have standing to contest the legality of the surveillance, regardless of whether or not they were the "targets" of the surveillance. Mr. Justice Harlan, concurring and dissenting, did squarely address Mr. Justice Fortas' arguments and declined to accept them. He identified administrative problems posed by the target theory:

> "[T]he [target] rule would entail very substantial administrative difficulties. In the majority of cases, I would imagine that the police plant a bug with the expectation that it may well produce leads to a large number of crimes. A lengthy hearing would, then, appear to be necessary in order to determine whether the police knew of an accused's criminal activity at the time the bug was planted and whether the police decision to plant a bug was motivated by an effort to obtain information against the accused or some other individual. I do not believe that this administrative burden is justified in any substantial degree by the hypothesized marginal increase in Fourth Amendment protection."

When we are urged to grant standing to a criminal defendant to assert a violation, not of his own constitutional rights but of someone else's, we cannot but give weight to practical difficulties such as those foreseen by Mr. Justice Harlan in the quoted language.

Conferring standing to raise vicarious Fourth Amendment claims would necessarily mean a more widespread invocation of the exclusionary rule during criminal trials. * * * Each time the exclusionary rule is applied it exacts a substantial social cost for the vindication of Fourth Amendment rights. Relevant and reliable evidence is kept from the trier of fact and the search for truth at trial is deflected. * * *

B

* * * [H]aving rejected petitioners' target theory and reaffirmed the principle that the "rights assured by the Fourth Amendment are personal rights, [which] . . . may be enforced by exclusion of evidence only at the instance of one whose own protection was infringed by the search and seizure," the question necessarily arises whether it serves any useful analytical purpose to consider this principle a matter of standing, distinct from the merits of a defendant's Fourth Amendment claim. We can think of no decided cases of this Court that would have come out differently had we concluded, as we do now, that the type of standing requirement discussed in *Jones* and reaffirmed today is more properly subsumed under substantive Fourth Amendment doctrine. Rig-

orous application of the principle that the rights secured by this Amendment are personal, in place of a notion of "standing," will produce no additional situations in which evidence must be excluded. The inquiry under either approach is the same.[b] But we think the better analysis forthrightly focuses on the extent of a particular defendant's rights under the Fourth Amendment, rather than on any theoretically separate, but invariably intertwined concept of standing.

* * *

Analyzed in these terms, the question is whether the challenged search and seizure violated the Fourth Amendment rights of a criminal defendant who seeks to exclude the evidence obtained during it. That inquiry in turn requires a determination of whether the disputed search and seizure has infringed an interest of the defendant which the Fourth Amendment was designed to protect. We are under no illusion that by dispensing with the rubric of standing used in *Jones* we have rendered any simpler the determination of whether the proponent of a motion to suppress is entitled to contest the legality of a search and seizure. But by frankly recognizing that this aspect of the analysis belongs more properly under the heading of substantive Fourth Amendment doctrine than under the heading of standing, we think the decision of this issue will rest on sounder logical footing.

C

Here petitioners, who were passengers occupying a car which they neither owned nor leased, seek to analogize their position to that of the defendant in Jones v. United States. In *Jones,* petitioner was present at the time of the search of an apartment which was owned by a friend. The friend had given Jones permission to use the apartment and a key to it, with which Jones had admitted himself on the day of the search. He had a suit and shirt at the apartment and had slept there "maybe a night," but his home was elsewhere. At the time of the search, Jones was the only occupant of the apartment because the lessee was away for a period of several days. Under these circumstances, this Court stated that while one wrongfully on the premises could not move to suppress evidence obtained as a result of searching them, "anyone legitimately on premises where a search occurs may challenge its legality." Petitioners argue that their occupancy of the automobile in question was comparable to that of Jones in the apartment and that they therefore have standing to contest the legality of the search—or as we have rephrased the inquiry, that they, like Jones, had their Fourth Amendment rights violated by the search.

We do not question the conclusion in *Jones* that the defendant in that case suffered a violation of his personal Fourth Amendment rights if the search in question was unlawful. Nonetheless, we believe that the phrase "legitimately on premises" coined in *Jones* creates too broad a gauge for measurement of Fourth Amendment rights. For example, applied literally, this statement would permit a casual visitor who has never seen, or been permitted to visit, the basement of another's house to ob-

b. So, for example, in Katz v. United States (1967), the Court focused on substantive Fourth Amendment law, concluded that a person in a telephone booth "may rely upon the protection of the Fourth Amendment," and then proceeded to determine whether the search was "unreasonable." In Mancusi v. DeForte, 392 U.S. 364 (1968), on the other hand, the Court concentrated on the issue of standing, decided that the defendant possessed it, and with barely any mention of the threshold substantive question of whether the search violated DeForte's own Fourth Amendment rights, went on to decide whether the search was "unreasonable." In both cases, however, the first inquiry was much the same.

ject to a search of the basement if the visitor happened to be in the kitchen of the house at the time of the search. Likewise, a casual visitor who walks into a house one minute before a search of the house commences and leaves one minute after the search ends would be able to contest the legality of the search. * * *

We think that *Jones* on its facts merely stands for the unremarkable proposition that a person can have a legally sufficient interest in a place other than his own home so that the Fourth Amendment protects him from unreasonable governmental intrusion into that place. * * *

Katz v. United States, provides guidance in defining the scope of the interest protected by the Fourth Amendment. * * * [T]he Court in *Katz* held that capacity to claim the protection of the Fourth Amendment depends not upon a property right in the invaded place but upon whether the person who claims the protection of the Amendment has a legitimate expectation of privacy in the invaded place. Viewed in this manner, the holding in *Jones* can best be explained by the fact that Jones had a legitimate expectation of privacy in the premises he was using and therefore could claim the protection of the Fourth Amendment with respect to a governmental invasion of those premises, even though his "interest" in those premises might not have been a recognized property interest at common law.[c]

Our Brother WHITE in dissent expresses the view that by rejecting the phrase "legitimately on [the] premises" as the appropriate measure of Fourth Amendment rights, we are abandoning a thoroughly workable, "bright line" test in favor of a less certain analysis of whether the facts of a particular case give rise to a legitimate expectation of privacy. If "legitimately on premises" were the successful litmus test of Fourth Amendment rights that he assumes it is, his approach would have at least the merit of easy application, whatever it lacked in fidelity to the history and purposes of the Fourth Amendment. But a reading of lower court cases that have applied the phrase "legitimately on premises," and of the dissent itself, reveals that this expression is not a shorthand summary for a bright-line rule which somehow encapsulates the "core" of the Fourth Amendment's protections.

* * * The dissenters concede that "there comes a point when use of an area is shared with so many that one simply cannot reasonably expect seclusion." But surely the "point" referred to is not one demarcating a line which is black on one side and white on another; it is inevitably a point which separates one shade of gray from another. We are likewise told by the dissent that a person "legitimately on *private* premises . . ., though his privacy is *not absolute,* is entitled to expect that he is sharing it only with those persons [allowed there] and that governmental officials will intrude only with *consent* or by complying with the Fourth Amendment." This single sentence describing

c. Obviously, however, a "legitimate" expectation of privacy by definition means more than a subjective expectation of not being discovered. A burglar plying his trade in a summer cabin during the off season may have a thoroughly justified subjective expectation of privacy, but it is not one which the law recognizes as "legitimate." His presence, in the words of *Jones,* 362 U.S., at 267, is "wrongful"; his expectation is not "one that society is prepared to recognize as 'reasonable.'" Katz v. United States, 389 U.S., at 361 (Harlan, J., concurring). And it would, of course, be merely tautological to fall back on the notion that those expectations of privacy which are legitimate depend primarily on cases deciding exclusionary-rule issues in criminal cases. Legitimation of expectations of privacy by law must have a source outside of the Fourth Amendment, either by reference to concepts of real or personal property law or to understandings that are recognized and permitted by society. * * *

the contours of the supposedly easily applied rule virtually abounds with unanswered questions: What are "private" premises? Indeed, what are the "premises?" It may be easy to describe the "premises" when one is confronted with a 1–room apartment, but what of the case of a 10–room house, or of a house with an attached garage that is searched?

* * * In abandoning "legitimately on premises" for the doctrine that we announce today, we are not forsaking a time-tested and workable rule, which has produced consistent results when applied, solely for the sake of fidelity to the values underlying the Fourth Amendment. Rather, we are rejecting blind adherence to a phrase which at most has superficial clarity and which conceals underneath that thin veneer all of the problems of line drawing which must be faced in any conscientious effort to apply the Fourth Amendment. Where the factual premises for a rule are so generally prevalent that little would be lost and much would be gained by abandoning case-by-case analysis, we have not hesitated to do so. See United States v. Robinson [page 222]. But the phrase "legitimately on premises" has not been shown to be an easily applicable measure of Fourth Amendment rights so much as it has proved to be simply a label placed by the courts on results which have not been subjected to careful analysis. We would not wish to be understood as saying that legitimate presence on the premises is irrelevant to one's expectation of privacy, but it cannot be deemed controlling.

D

Judged by the foregoing analysis, petitioners' claims must fail. They asserted neither a property nor a possessory interest in the automobile, nor an interest in the property seized. And as we have previously indicated, the fact that they were "legitimately on [the] premises" in the sense that they were in the car with the permission of its owner is not determinative of whether they had a legitimate expectation of privacy in the particular areas of the automobile searched. * * *

Jones v. United States and Katz v. United States, involved significantly different factual circumstances. Jones not only had permission to use the apartment of his friend, but had a key to the apartment with which he admitted himself on the day of the search and kept possessions in the apartment. Except with respect to his friend, Jones had complete dominion and control over the apartment and could exclude others from it. Likewise in *Katz,* the defendant occupied the telephone booth, shut the door behind him to exclude all others and paid the toll, which "entitled [him] to assume that the words he utter[ed] into the mouthpiece [would] not be broadcast to the world." Katz and Jones could legitimately expect privacy in the areas which were the subject of the search and seizure each sought to contest. No such showing was made by these petitioners with respect to those portions of the automobile which were searched and from which incriminating evidence was seized.[d]

* * *

MR. JUSTICE POWELL, with whom THE CHIEF JUSTICE joins, concurring.

* * *

* * * Here there were three passengers and a driver in the automobile

d. * * * The case before us involves the search of and seizure of property from the glove compartment and area under the seat of a car in which petitioners were riding as passengers. Petitioners claimed only that they were "legitimately on [the] premises" and did not claim that they had any legitimate expectation of privacy in the areas of the car which were searched. We cannot, therefore, agree with the dissenters' insistence that our decision will encourage the police to violate the Fourth Amendment.

searched. None of the passengers is said to have had control of the vehicle or the keys. It is unrealistic—as the shared experience of us all bears witness—to suggest that these passengers had any reasonable expectation that the car in which they had been riding would not be searched after they were lawfully stopped and made to get out. The minimal privacy that existed simply is not comparable to that, for example, of an individual in his place of abode, see Jones v. United States, supra; of one who secludes himself in a telephone booth, Katz v. United States, supra; or of the traveler who secures his belongings in a locked suitcase or footlocker. See United States v. Chadwick.[e]

This is not an area of the law in which any "bright line" rule would safeguard both Fourth Amendment rights and the public interest in a fair and effective criminal justice system. The range of variables in the fact situations of search and seizure is almost infinite. Rather than seek facile solutions, it is best to apply principles broadly faithful to Fourth Amendment purposes.

MR. JUSTICE WHITE, with whom MR. JUSTICE BRENNAN, MR. JUSTICE MARSHALL, and MR. JUSTICE STEVENS join, dissenting.

The Court today holds that the Fourth Amendment protects property, not people, and specifically that a legitimate occupant of an automobile may not invoke the exclusionary rule and challenge a search of that vehicle unless he happens to own or have a possessory interest in it. Though professing to acknowledge that the primary purpose of the Fourth Amendment's prohibition of unreasonable searches is the protection of privacy—not property—the Court nonetheless effectively ties the application of the Fourth Amendment and the exclusionary rule in this situation to property law concepts. Insofar as passengers are concerned, the Court's opinion today declares an "open season" on automobiles. However unlawful stopping and searching a car may be, absent a possessory or ownership interest, no "mere" passenger may object, regardless of his relationship to the owner. * * * If the Court is troubled by the practical impact of the exclusionary rule, it should face the issue of that rule's continued validity squarely instead of distorting other doctrines in an attempt to reach what are perceived as the correct results in specific cases.

* * * The *Jones* rule is relatively easily applied by police and courts; the rule announced today will not provide law enforcement officials with a bright line between the protected and the unprotected. Only rarely will police know whether one private party has or has not been granted a sufficient possessory or other interest by another private party. Surely in this case the officers had no such knowledge. The Court's rule will ensnare defendants and police in needless litigation over factors that should not be determinative of Fourth Amendment rights.

More importantly, the ruling today undercuts the force of the exclusionary rule in the one area in which its use is most certainly justified—the deterrence

e. I do not share the dissenters' concern that the Court's ruling will "invit[e] police to engage in patently unreasonable searches every time an automobile contains more than one occupant." A police officer observing an automobile carrying several passengers will not know the circumstances surrounding each occupant's presence in the automobile, and certainly will not know whether an occupant will be able to establish that he had a reasonable expectation of privacy. Thus, there will continue to be a significant incentive for the police to comply with the requirements of the Fourth Amendment, lest otherwise valid prosecutions be voided. Moreover, any marginal diminution in this incentive that might result from the Court's decision today is more than justified by society's interest in restricting the scope of the exclusionary rule to those cases where in fact there is a reasonable expectation of privacy.

of bad-faith violations of the Fourth Amendment. This decision invites police to engage in patently unreasonable searches every time an automobile contains more than one occupant. Should something be found, only the owner of the vehicle, or of the item, will have standing to seek suppression, and the evidence will presumably be usable against the other occupants. The danger of such bad faith is especially high in cases such as this one where the officers are only after the passengers and can usually infer accurately that the driver is the owner. The suppression remedy for those owners in whose vehicles something is found and who are charged with crime is small consolation for all those owners *and* occupants whose privacy will be needlessly invaded by officers following mistaken hunches not rising to the level of probable cause but operated on in the knowledge that someone in a crowded car will probably be unprotected if contraband or incriminating evidence happens to be found. After this decision, police will have little to lose by unreasonably searching vehicles occupied by more than one person.

* * *

Note

The Court rejects the bright-line rule of *Jones.* In other cases in this Chapter, such as *Mimms, Robinson,* and *Belton,* the Court has adopted bright line rules for ease of administration and to provide necessary guidance to police officers. Has the Court been consistent in deciding when to draw a bright line and when not to draw one?

Rakas was relied upon by the Supreme Court in United States v. Salvucci, 448 U.S. 83 (1980), which finally overruled *Jones* and abolished the automatic standing doctrine. Justice Rehnquist's majority opinion concluded that *Jones* no longer was necessary and that possession of a seized good should not be used as a substitute for a factual finding that the owner of the good had a legitimate expectation of privacy in the area searched. *Rakas* and other cases, said the majority, "clearly establish that a prosecutor may simultaneously maintain that a defendant criminally possessed the seized good, but was not subject to a Fourth Amendment deprivation, without legal contradiction." This was because, after *Rakas,* a "person in legal possession of a good seized during an illegal search has not necessarily been subject to a Fourth Amendment deprivation." [36]

A companion case, Rawlings v. Kentucky, 448 U.S. 98 (1980), demonstrated the significance of *Salvucci.* Rawlings was convicted of trafficking in and possession of various controlled substances. These substances were seized from the purse of a woman who, along with Rawlings, was visiting the premises when police arrived. The Supreme Court found that Rawlings had no standing to object to the search of the purse, since he had no legitimate expectation of privacy in the purse. The Court added that even assuming that the woman consented to have the drugs stored in the purse, "the precipitous nature of the transaction hardly supports a reasonable inference that petitioner took normal precautions to maintain his privacy." Ownership of the drugs was not enough to confer standing. Justice Marshall, joined by Justice Brennan, dissented.

36. The *Salvucci* approach is rejected and automatic standing is preserved under the state constitution in State v. Simpson, 95 Wn.2d 170, 622 P.2d 1199 (1980). State v. Alston, 88 N.J. 211, 440 A.2d 1311 (1981), also clings to the *Jones* automatic standing rule under the state constitution. Accord, State v. Sidebotham, 124 N.H. 682, 474 A.2d 1377 (1984) (defendant has standing to challenge search of a stolen car).

United States v. Payner, 447 U.S. 727 (1980), shows the consequences of the Court's rejection of the "target" theory of standing in *Rakas.* An IRS investigation of American citizens doing business in the Bahamas focussed on a certain Bahamian bank. When an official of that bank visited the United States, IRS agents stole his briefcase, and removed and photographed hundreds of documents. They did this to obtain evidence against Payner. Under *Rakas,* Payner had no standing to object to the search of the briefcase, but he argued that the Federal District Court should exercise its supervisory power to exclude the evidence and thus to sanction the purposefully illegal tactics. The District Court agreed with Payner and excluded the evidence, but the Supreme Court held "that the supervisory power does not authorize a federal court to suppress otherwise admissible evidence on the ground that it was seized unlawfully from a third party not before the court." *Rakas* and other standing cases were relied upon. Justice Marshall, joined by Justices Brennan and Blackmun, dissented and argued that since the district court found that the government agents manipulated the standing rules in order to conduct intentionally and in bad faith an unconstitutional search, suppression of the illegally seized evidence was essential to protect the integrity of the judiciary whose rules were being manipulated. The dissent also charged that the decision made the supervisory power superfluous, since the majority would require a showing of a Fourth or Fifth Amendment violation before suppressing. But, the majority in two separate footnotes indicated that its focus was on whether the evidence was "taken from the *defendant,*" not simply on whether there was a constitutional violation.

United States v. Lopez, 474 F.Supp. 943 (C.D.Cal.1979), holds that defendants who had been given keys to a truck, who had permission to use it and who did use it, had standing to challenge a search of the truck. Standing was also found in Minnesota v. Olson, (page 154), when a defendant was staying overnight at an apartment with the permission of the tenant. But see United States v. Dall, 608 F.2d 910 (1st Cir. 1979) (holds that ownership of truck is not sufficient to establish reasonable expectation of privacy); United States v. Vicknair, 610 F.2d 372 (5th Cir. 1980) (holds that people with keys to a boat, who sometimes slept on it, did not have a privacy interest therein). In United States v. Greer, 939 F.2d 1076 (5th Cir.1991), the court held that passengers in a car had standing to object to the *stop* of the car, but not to a search, since they claimed no ownership interest in the car or in the property seized. Does it make sense that a person could have standing to object to the stop but not to the search? In United States v. Powell, 929 F.2d 1190 (7th Cir.1991), the court reached the opposite conclusion with respect to the owner of a car, where he was absent at the time the car was stopped and searched: the owner had standing to object to the search but not to the stop. Does this make sense?

In United States v. Boruff, 909 F.2d 111 (5th Cir.1990), a pick-up truck driven by Taylor and a rented car driven by Boruff were involved in a drug-smuggling scheme. The truck had been purchased by Boruff, but title, registration and insurance were put in Taylor's name. Boruff added improvements to the truck, and it was understood that if the truck were sold, the money would go to Boruff. The car was rented by Boruff's girlfriend in her own name. The standard rental agreement signed by the girlfriend stated that only she would drive the car and that the car would not be used for any illegal purpose. Boruff and Taylor drove to Mexico, loaded marijuana into the pick-up truck, and started back. They travelled 100 yards apart on the highway. When a suspicious Border Patrol agent began to pursue the pick-up truck, Boruff did two u-turns in an effort to divert the agent's attention. A second agent pursued Boruff, while the first agent stopped the truck, searched it, and placed Taylor under arrest. The second agent stopped Boruff, searched the rented car and found incriminating evidence. Boruff argued that both searches were illegal and moved to suppress all the evidence. As to the truck, the court held that Boruff had failed to establish an expectation of privacy, even though he paid for it.

> Despite his asserted ownership interest, Boruff did everything he could to disassociate himself from the truck in the event it was stopped by law enforcement officials. [Besides placing all documentation in Taylor's name], during the smuggling operation, Taylor, not Boruff, drove the truck. Boruff travelled in a separate vehicle, * * * and left his position in front of the truck after spotting the Border Patrol vehicle. * * * In addition, Boruff was not present when the truck was stopped or searched. See Rakas v. Illinois (legitimate presence at time of search an important factor). * * * Boruff also disavowed any knowledge of the truck and its contents after his own vehicle was stopped.

As to the rental car, the court found that Boruff had no standing to contest the search because his girlfriend was the only legal operator of the vehicle under the terms of the agreement and thus "had no authority to give control of the car to Boruff. The rental agreement also expressly forbade any use of the vehicle for illegal purposes." Do you agree with the court? Shouldn't Boruff have had some expectation of privacy somewhere? Why is the rental agreement controlling? Does the court mean that even Boruff's girlfriend would have had no standing if she had been driving the car and engaged in illegal activity?

The doctrine of standing is difficult to understand because it is inconsistent with almost everything else in the search and seizure area. Attenuation, inevitable discovery and independent source limit the application of the exclusionary rule in recognition of its deterrent purpose. The basic idea is that exclusion is a proper remedy when it could reasonably be thought to affect police behavior and to remove an incentive—i.e., the ability to use illegally seized evidence—for unconstitutional action. Standing actually undercuts the disincentive. If A and B are suspected of being coconspirators, the police can illegally search the house of each for evidence to be used against the other. The larger the suspected membership in the conspiracy, the greater the incentive to make a search, even if it is unconstitutional.

The Alaska Supreme Court had occasion to reexamine the state's law of standing in Waring v. State, 670 P.2d 357 (Alaska, 1983). It agreed with the United States Supreme Court that "allowing standing to assert the violation of a co-defendant's rights would not deter unlawful conduct in most situations," but it also reasoned that deterrence could be achieved and judicial integrity promoted if evidence were excluded whenever the police "knowingly and intentionally violate a co-defendant's rights," and also whenever the police direct their search at a particular co-defendant. If the focus is on the nature of an investigation, more than on the knowledge the police had at the time of a search about specific individuals, can some of the difficulties of judging motivation be avoided? Is this a more difficult analysis to undertake than that required by the fruit of the poisonous tree cases?

10. Using Illegally Seized Evidence

Assuming that standing exists and that evidence clearly is the fruit of a search that plainly violated the Fourth Amendment, a motion to suppress the evidence at trial will be granted—at least, the government will not be able to use the evidence as part of its case in chief (i.e., its opening presentation of evidence, before the defense offers its evidence). But it can use the evidence in numerous other proceedings.

In United States v. Calandra, 414 U.S. 338 (1974), the Court held that a grand jury witness, who claimed illegally seized evidence was used by the grand jury as a basis for interrogation, had no right to refuse to answer questions. The Court emphasized the deterrent thrust of the exclusionary rule in concluding that the marginal deterrent effect of allowing a witness to raise a Fourth Amendment claim before the grand jury did not warrant utilization of the exclusionary rule in grand jury proceedings in light of the disruption of investigations which the rule might produce. The Court concluded that sufficient deterrence flowed from exclusion of the illegally obtained evidence at trial. Justice Brennan, whose dissent was joined by Justices Douglas and Marshall, de-emphasized the deterrent rationale of the rule and focused instead on the benefits of keeping courts from lending their assistance to unconstitutional practices.

Justice Powell's majority opinion fails to address the obvious question that arises from the Court's holding: i.e., if, as a direct result of using illegally seized evidence, the grand jury gathers all the evidence that the government can find, is all the evidence to be suppressed at trial? If so, the administrative inconvenience of allowing witnesses to challenge questions put by the grand jury may pale before the inconvenience of "untainting" evidence at trial. If not, then it would seem that *Calandra* substantially undermines *Weeks* and *Mapp* by allowing the government to profit in a readily foreseeable way from violating the Constitution in its investigations.

Even if *Calandra* meant to require suppression of evidence at trial, the fact that indictments can be based on illegally seized evidence is another arrow in the government's quiver. One of the most obvious trends in the decisions of the Supreme Court and lower courts is to restrict the use of exclusion to the government's case-in-chief at trial. Viewed in isolation, each decision might not be troublesome. But the end result is that police know that illegally seized evidence often can be used in a variety of proceedings.

For example, although the Court once held that the exclusionary rule applies in quasi-criminal forfeiture proceedings, One 1958 Plymouth Sedan v. Pennsylvania, 380 U.S. 693 (1965), more recently it held that evidence illegally seized by state police could be used by federal tax officials and that the evidence would not be suppressed in civil tax litigation despite the fact, pointed out by one of the three dissenters, that federal and local law enforcement personnel regularly provide federal tax officials with information. United States v. Janis, 428 U.S. 433 (1976). The Court in *Janis* found the deterrent effect of the exclusionary rule "attenuated when the punishment imposed upon the offending criminal enforcement officer is the removal of that evidence from a civil suit by or against a different sovereign." This attenuation, coupled with the "existing deterrence" effected by exclusion of the evidence from both state and federal criminal trials, tilted the cost-benefit analysis in favor of admitting the evidence.

In Immigration and Naturalization Service v. Lopez-Mendoza, 468 U.S. 1032 (1984), Justice O'Connor's opinion for the Court reasoned that "the deterrence value of applying the exclusionary rule in deportation proceedings would be higher than it was in *Janis,*" because, unlike in *Janis,* INS law enforcement efforts are geared specifically toward deportation proceedings rather than toward criminal prosecutions. But the Court found that the social costs of exclusion would be much greater as well, since exclusion could mean that a person who is committing a criminal offense at the time of the proceeding would be allowed to go free. Applying the *Janis* balancing test, the Court held that illegally seized evidence may be used in a deportation proceeding.

Justice O'Connor reasoned as follows: no matter how an arrest is made, deportation will still be possible when evidence derived independently of the arrest is available, and evidence of alienage alone might be sufficient to warrant deportation; as a practical matter, it is highly unlikely that deportees will raise exclusionary rule claims and therefore unlikely that the rule would deter INS agents; the INS has its own scheme for deterring Fourth Amendment violations by its agents; declaratory relief is available to restrain institutional practices by the INS that violate the Fourth Amendment; deportation currently requires only a simple hearing; INS agents handle so many cases that they might have difficulty accounting for exactly how they handled each suspected alien; and "[a]pplying the exclusionary rule in proceedings that are intended not to punish past transgressions but to prevent their continuance or renewal would require the courts to close their eyes to ongoing violations of the law."

Justice White dissented. He reasoned that INS agents seek to gather evidence to use in deportation proceedings and that their activities are closely analogous to those of police officers who seek evidence for criminal trials. And he disagreed with each of the majority's reasons for not applying the rule. He argued that: the fact that independent evidence might justify deportation is not a reason to reject the exclusionary rule, since independent evidence might also support a criminal conviction; even if many illegal aliens will not challenge INS conduct, those who do should have the benefit of the rule just as defendants who go to trial rather than plead guilty do; there is no instance in which INS has actually punished agents for violating the Constitution, making the claim for an administrative substitute for the rule suspect; alternative remedies are unavailable for aliens who are removed from the country; presence in the country is not a continuous offense, since it is illegal entry that is prohibited; hearing officers should be able to consider Fourth Amendment claims, especially if INS agents are expected to comply with the Constitution; and the failure to require INS agents to account for their treatment of arrested persons is tantamount to excusing them from Fourth Amendment coverage.

Justices Brennan, Marshall and Stevens each filed a short dissenting opinion. Each agreed with most of Justice White's analysis, but declined to adopt his suggestion that INS agents acting in good faith would not have to fear exclusion of evidence.

Even in proceedings that have a lot to do with ordinary criminal litigation, there is a tendency to cut back on the rule. For example in Stone v. Powell, 428 U.S. 465 (1976), the Court, using its familiar cost-benefit analysis, held that the exclusionary rule could not be invoked in habeas corpus proceedings to challenge Fourth Amendment violations. The Court stated that in the context of habeas proceedings, "the contribution of the exclusionary rule, if any, to the effectuation of the Fourth Amendment is minimal and the substantial societal costs of application of the rule persist with special force." Why is the deterrent effect especially low and the cost especially high in the habeas context?

While the Supreme Court has not considered the applicability of the exclusionary rule to sentencing proceedings or to parole and probation revocation hearings, most lower courts have found the exclusionary rule inapplicable in these circumstances. See United States v. Torres, 926 F.2d 321 (3d Cir.1991) (relying on *Calandra* and holding that illegally seized evidence can be used in sentencing); United States v. Finney, 897 F.2d 1047 (10th Cir.1990) ("application of the exclusionary rule to revocation proceedings will not achieve the deterrent effect behind the rule;" citing cases). See also People v. Drain, 73 N.Y.2d 107, 538 N.Y.S.2d 500, 535 N.E.2d 630 (1989) (exclusionary rule inapplicable in perjury prosecution, since sufficient deterrence flows from exclusion in a direct prosecution for the underlying offense); Garrett v. Lehman, 751 F.2d 997 (9th Cir.1985) (exclusionary rule inapplicable to military discharge proceedings).

Can it realistically be said that the police are indifferent as to whether illegally seized evidence is admissible in civil litigation, sentencing, parole and probation revocation proceedings, etc.? If they are not indifferent, then the failure to adopt an exclusionary rule can affect police behavior.

Certainly, there are arguments for holding the exclusionary rule inapplicable in some proceedings, sometimes even at trials. For example, in In re Diane P., 110 A.D.2d 354, 494 N.Y.S.2d 881 (1985), a 13–year–old girl went to the police and complained that her mother hit her with a broom. The officers went to the mother's apartment at 3 a.m. and did a warrantless search. They seized a broom and a shoe. These were offered not at a criminal trial but at a child protective proceeding. The court held that the exclusionary rule did not apply to child protective proceedings. It found that sufficient deterrence flowed from exclusion in a criminal prosecution, and that exclusion in a child protection proceeding would impose an extraordinary cost. Do you agree?

11. Use of Illegally Obtained Evidence for Impeachment Purposes

In Walder v. United States, 347 U.S. 62 (1954), Walder testified on direct examination in a trial on narcotics charges that he had never possessed or sold narcotics in his life. The Supreme Court held that he was properly impeached with evidence of heroin which had been illegally seized from his home in an earlier, unrelated case. The Court reasoned that Walder had "opened the door" to this evidence and that the exclusionary rule could not be used as a license for perjury.

In United States v. Havens, 446 U.S. 620 (1980), officers stopped McLeroth and Havens coming off a flight. They illegally searched Havens' suitcase and found a shirt from which the pocket had been torn out. McLeroth was also searched, and officers found a pocket, matching the shirt found in Havens' bag, sewn into McLeroth's clothing. The officers found cocaine in the pocket. At his trial, Havens took the stand and denied being involved with McLeroth in the transportation of cocaine. On cross-examination, Havens was asked whether he had been involved in sewing a pocket into McLeroth's clothing, and whether he had a shirt in his own suitcase from which that pocket had been torn out. Havens answered in the negative, and this testimony was impeached by introduction of the illegally seized shirt. The court of appeals held that the evidence was improperly admitted. It reasoned that *Walder* permitted impeachment only if the illegally obtained evidence contradicted the defendant's direct testimony, and that there was no such contradiction between the evidence and the direct testimony in this case. In a 5–4 decision by Justice White, the Supreme Court held that illegally obtained evidence can be used to impeach the defendant's testimony no matter when it is elicited. Justice White argued that there was no difference of constitutional magnitude between impeachment of direct testimony and impeachment of testimony elicited on cross-examination, so long as the questions put to the defendant on cross-examination "are plainly within the scope" of the direct. He noted that a contrary rule would severely impede the normal function of cross-examination. Justice White concluded as follows:

> [T]he policies of the exclusionary rule no more bar impeachment here than they did in *Walder* * * *. [The incremental deterrence which occurs] by forbidding impeachment of the defendant who testifies was deemed [in *Walder*] insufficient to permit or require that false testimony go unchallenged, with the resulting impairment of the integrity of the fact-finding goals of the criminal trial. We reaffirm this assessment of the competing interests * * *.

Justice Brennan, joined by Justices Stewart, Marshall and Stevens, dissented. He complained that the majority had passed control of the impeachment exception to the government, "since the prosecutor can lay the predicate for admitting otherwise suppressible evidence with his own questioning." He argued that the practical effect of *Havens* was that a defendant who has been the victim of an illegal search will be compelled to forego testifying on his own behalf.

The cost-benefit analysis as applied to the impeachment exception is argued as follows. Since the officer is not motivated by a desire to obtain impeachment evidence, but rather by a desire to obtain substantive evidence of guilt, exclusion of illegally obtained evidence when offered for impeachment purposes has minimal deterrent effect. Against the minimal deterrence is the significant cost of excluding illegally obtained evidence for impeachment purposes. Not only would the jury be deprived of reliable information, but the defendant would be able to commit perjury on the stand, secure in the knowledge that he is free from impeachment. Thus the costs of the rule outweigh the benefits in the impeachment context. But is that true when it is the defendant's testimony on cross-examination, rather than direct, that is being impeached?

In James v. Illinois, 493 U.S. 307 (1990), the Court refused to extend the impeachment exception to allow impeachment of defendant's witnesses with illegally obtained evidence. James made a statement to police officers that he had changed his hair color and style the day after taking part in a shooting. The trial court suppressed this statement because it was the fruit of an arrest without probable cause. Prosecution witnesses at trial identified James, even though they admitted that his hair color at trial was different from that of the perpetrator at the time of the shooting. James called a family friend, who testified that just before the shooting, James' hair color and style was the same as it was at trial. The trial court, relying on the impeachment exception to the exclusionary rule, allowed the prosecution to introduce James' suppressed statement to impeach the credibility of the defense witness.

The Supreme Court reversed in an opinion by Justice Brennan. Justice Brennan found a compelling distinction between impeachment of a defendant's own testimony and that of defense witnesses. Despite his prior dissents on the impeachment exception, Justice Brennan argued that as applied to the defendant, the impeachment exception serves salutary purposes: it "penalizes defendants for committing perjury," and yet "leaves defendants free to testify truthfully on their own behalf." According to the Court, the impeachment exception keeps perjury out and allows truthful testimony in, thus furthering in both ways the search for truth.

In contrast, the Court found that expanding the impeachment exception to encompass the testimony of all defense witnesses would result in the loss of truthful testimony. Justice Brennan argued that the fear of impeachment of one's witnesses likely would discourage defendants from presenting the testimony of others. Unlike the defendant who could carefully tailor truthful testimony to avoid reference to illegally obtained evidence, the defendant's witnesses could not be so easily controlled.

> Defendants might reasonably fear that one or more of their witnesses, in a position to offer truthful and favorable testimony, would also make some statement in sufficient tension with the tainted evidence to allow the prosecutor to introduce that evidence for impeachment * * *. As a result, an expanded impeachment exception likely would chill some defendants from calling witnesses who would otherwise offer probative evidence * * *.
>
> Given the potential chill created * * *, the conceded gains to the truthseeking process from discouraging or disclosing perjured testimony would be offset to some extent by the concomitant loss of probative witness testimony.

Justice Brennan also argued that it was unnecessary to apply the impeachment exception to deter defense witnesses from offering perjurious testimony. Unlike the defendant, defense witnesses are sufficiently deterred by the threat of a perjury prosecution.

Justice Brennan concluded that the exclusionary rule would be robbed of significant deterrent effect if illegally obtained evidence could be used to impeach not only the defendant but the defendant's witnesses. He argued that illegally obtained evidence would have greater value to the government because it could be used to deter defendants from calling witnesses to give truthful testimony. Consequently, officers would have a strong incentive to violate the law in order to obtain evidence even though it could only be used for impeachment purposes. Justice Brennan asserted that a rule allowing impeachment of defense witnesses "would leave officers with little to lose and much to gain by overstepping constitutional limits on evidence gathering."

Justice Kennedy, joined by Chief Justice Rehnquist and Justices O'Connor and Scalia, dissented. The dissenters complained that the majority had granted the defendant "broad immunity to introduce whatever false testimony it can produce from the mouth of a friendly witness." Justice Kennedy was particularly concerned with the costs to the truthseeking process if defense witnesses could testify without fear of impeachment with probative evidence. He argued that impeachment is even more vital for attacking untruthful testimony of a defense witness than it is for attacking the defendant's testimony:

> The potential for harm to the truth-seeking process resulting from the majority's new rule in fact will be greater than if the defendant himself had testified. It is natural for jurors to be skeptical of self-serving testimony by the defendant. Testimony by a witness said to be independent has the greater potential to deceive. And if a defense witness can present false testimony with impunity, the jurors may find the rest of the prosecution's case suspect, for ineffective and artificial cross-examination will be viewed as a real weakness in the State's case. Jurors will assume that if the prosecution had any proof the statement was false, it would make the proof known * * *. The State must * * * suffer the introduction of false testimony and appear to bolster the falsehood by its own silence.

Justice Kennedy advocated a rule that illegally obtained evidence could be used to impeach defense witnesses, but only where there was a direct conflict between the evidence and the witness' testimony. According to Justice Kennedy, the requirement of a direct conflict would alleviate the majority's concern that the defendant would not present truthful witnesses for fear they would be impeached in virtually all cases.

Has the majority drawn a well-reasoned distinction between impeachment of the defendant and impeachment of defense witnesses? Does it matter that the defendant who is impeached has already decided to take the stand before any impeachment occurs? If defense witnesses could be impeached with a defendant's statement, what impact would the impeachment have on a defendant's decision not to testify?

The majority in *James* bases its decision on the assumption that the defendant can tailor his testimony to avoid impeachment while the defendant's witnesses cannot. After *Havens,* which allowed impeachment on cross-examination even though the direct testimony was carefully tailored to avoid any reference to the shirt, is it ever possible for the defendant to avoid impeachment with illegally obtained evidence? *James* is criticized in Note, The Pinocchio Defense Witness Impeachment Exception to the Exclusionary Rule: Combatting a Defendant's Right to Use with Impunity the Perjurious Testimony of Defense Witnesses, 1990 U.Ill.L.Rev. 375.

12. Good Faith

Do you see a need for a good faith exception to the exclusionary rule? In United States v. Williams, 622 F.2d 830 (5th Cir. 1980) (en banc), thirteen of 24 judges expressed the view that evidence seized pursuant to a search incident to an unauthorized arrest should not be suppressed as long as police act in "good faith" in making the arrest.

For an attack on attempts to place a good faith limitation on the exclusionary rule, see Mertens & Wasserstrom, Foreword: The Good Faith Exception to the Exclusionary Rule: Deregulating the Police and Derailing the Law, 70 Geo.L.J. 365 (1981).

In the 1982 term, the Supreme Court asked for arguments in Illinois v. Gates on the desirability of a "good faith" exception to the exclusionary rule when officers rely on a warrant subsequently found invalid. Ultimately it decided to postpone consideration of such an exception. Only Justice White indicated his view on the merits of the exception in these circumstances.

Justice White's view of the good faith exception became law in United States v. Leon and Massachusetts v. Sheppard. The Court's analysis is contained in *Leon*. The facts of *Sheppard* are offered in the Note following the case.

UNITED STATES v. LEON

Supreme Court of the United States, 1984.
468 U.S. 897.

JUSTICE WHITE delivered the opinion of the Court.

This case presents the question whether the Fourth Amendment exclusionary rule should be modified so as not to bar the use in the prosecution's case-in-chief of evidence obtained by officers acting in reasonable reliance on a search warrant issued by a detached and neutral magistrate but ultimately found to be unsupported by probable cause. * * *

I

In August 1981, a confidential informant of unproven reliability informed an officer of the Burbank Police Department that two persons known to him as "Armando" and "Patsy" were selling large quantities of cocaine and methaqualone from their residence at 620 Price Drive in Burbank, Cal. The informant also indicated that he had witnessed a sale of methaqualone by "Patsy" at the residence approximately five months earlier and had observed at that time a shoebox containing a large amount of cash that belonged to "Patsy." He further declared that "Armando" and "Patsy" generally kept only small quantities of drugs at their residence and stored the remainder at another location in Burbank.

On the basis of this information, the Burbank police initiated an extensive investigation focusing first on the Price Drive residence and later on two other residences as well. Cars parked at the Price Drive residence were determined to belong to respondents Armando Sanchez, who had previously been arrested for possession of marihuana, and Patsy Stewart, who had no criminal record. During the course of the investigation, officers observed an automobile belonging to respondent Ricardo Del Castillo, who had previously been arrested for possession of 50 pounds of marihuana, arrive at the Price Drive residence. The driver of that car entered the house, exited shortly thereafter carrying a small paper sack, and drove away. A check of Del Castillo's probation records led the officers to respondent Alberto Leon, whose telephone number Del Castillo had listed as his employer's. Leon had been arrested in 1980 on drug charges, and a companion had informed the police at that time that Leon was heavily involved in the importation of drugs into this country. Before the current investigation began, the Burbank officers had learned that an informant had told a Glendale police officer that Leon stored a large quantity of methaqualone at his residence in Glendale. During the course of this investigation, the Burbank officers learned that Leon was living at 716 South Sunset Canyon in Burbank.

Subsequently, the officers observed several persons, at least one of whom had prior drug involvement, arriving at the Price Drive residence and leaving with small packages; observed a variety of other material activity at the two residences as well as at a condominium at 7902 Via Magdalena; and witnessed a variety of relevant activity involving respondents' automobiles. The officers also observed respondents Sanchez and Stewart board separate flights for Miami. The pair later returned to Los

Angeles together, consented to a search of their luggage that revealed only a small amount of marihuana, and left the airport. Based on these and other observations summarized in the affidavit, Officer Cyril Rombach of the Burbank Police Department, an experienced and well-trained narcotics investigator, prepared an application for a warrant to search 620 Price Drive, 716 South Sunset Canyon, 7902 Via Magdalena, and automobiles registered to each of the respondents for an extensive list of items believed to be related to respondents' drug-trafficking activities. Officer Rombach's extensive application was reviewed by several Deputy District Attorneys.

A facially valid search warrant was issued in September 1981 by a state superior court judge. The ensuing searches produced large quantities of drugs at the Via Magdalena and Sunset Canyon addresses and a small quantity at the Price Drive residence. Other evidence was discovered at each of the residences and in Stewart's and Del Castillo's automobiles. Respondents were indicted by a grand jury in the District Court for the Central District of California and charged with conspiracy to possess and distribute cocaine and a variety of substantive counts.

The respondents then filed motions to suppress the evidence seized pursuant to the warrant. The District Court held an evidentiary hearing and, while recognizing that the case was a close one, granted the motions to suppress in part. It concluded that the affidavit was insufficient to establish probable cause, but did not suppress all of the evidence as to all of the respondents because none of the respondents had standing to challenge all of the searches. In response to a request from the Government, the court made clear that Officer Rombach had acted in good faith, but it rejected the Government's suggestion that the Fourth Amendment exclusionary rule should not apply where evidence is seized in reasonable, good-faith reliance on a search warrant.

The District Court denied the Government's motion for reconsideration, and a divided panel of the Court of Appeals for the Ninth Circuit affirmed. The Court of Appeals first concluded that Officer Rombach's affidavit could not establish probable cause to search the Price Drive residence. To the extent that the affidavit set forth facts demonstrating the basis of the informant's knowledge of criminal activity, the information included was fatally stale. The affidavit, moreover, failed to establish the informant's credibility. Accordingly, the Court of Appeals concluded that the information provided by the informant was inadequate under both prongs of the two-part test established in Aguilar v. Texas, and Spinelli v. United States. The officers' independent investigation neither cured the staleness nor corroborated the details of the informant's declarations. The Court of Appeals then considered whether the affidavit formed a proper basis for the search of the Sunset Canyon residence. In its view, the affidavit included no facts indicating the basis for the informant's statements concerning respondent Leon's criminal activities and was devoid of information establishing the informants' reliability. Because these deficiencies had not been cured by the police investigation, the District Court properly suppressed the fruits of the search. The Court of Appeals refused the Government's invitation to recognize a good-faith exception to the Fourth Amendment exclusionary rule.

The Government's petition for certiorari expressly declined to seek review of the lower courts' determinations that the search warrant was unsupported by probable cause and presented only the question "[w]hether the Fourth Amendment exclusionary rule should be modified so as not to bar the admission of evidence seized in reasonable, good-faith reliance on a search warrant that is subsequently held to be defective." We granted certiorari to consider the propriety of such a modification. Although it undoubtedly is within our power to consider the question whether probable cause existed under the "totality of the circumstances" test announced last Term in Illinois v. Gates, that question has not been briefed or argued; and it is also within our authority, which we choose to exercise, to take the case as it comes to us, accepting the Court of Appeals' conclusion that probable cause was lacking under the prevailing legal standards.

We have concluded that, in the Fourth Amendment context, the exclusionary rule can be modified somewhat without jeopardizing its ability to perform its intended functions. Accordingly, we reverse the judgment of the Court of Appeals.

II

Language in opinions of this Court and of individual Justices has sometimes implied that the exclusionary rule is a necessary corollary of the Fourth Amendment, or that the rule is required by the conjunction of the Fourth and Fifth Amendments. These implications need not detain us long. The Fifth Amendment theory has not withstood critical analysis or the test of time, and the Fourth Amendment "has never been interpreted to proscribe the introduction of illegally seized evidence in all proceedings or against all persons."

A

The Fourth Amendment contains no provision expressly precluding the use of evidence obtained in violation of its commands, and an examination of its origin and purposes makes clear that the use of fruits of a past unlawful search or seizure "works no new Fourth Amendment wrong." The wrong condemned by the Amendment is "fully accomplished" by the unlawful search or seizure itself, and the exclusionary rule is neither intended nor able to "cure the invasion of the defendant's rights which he has already suffered." The rule thus operates as "a judicially created remedy designed to safeguard Fourth Amendment rights generally through its deterrent effect, rather than a personal constitutional right of the party aggrieved."

Whether the exclusionary sanction is appropriately imposed in a particular case, our decisions make clear, is "an issue separate from the question whether the Fourth Amendment rights of the party seeking to invoke the rule were violated by police conduct." Only the former question is currently before us, and it must be resolved by weighing the costs and benefits of preventing the use in the prosecution's case-in-chief of inherently trustworthy tangible evidence obtained in reliance on a search warrant issued by a detached and neutral magistrate that ultimately is found to be defective.

The substantial social costs exacted by the exclusionary rule for the vindication of Fourth Amendment rights have long been a source of concern. * * * An objectionable collateral consequence of this interference with the criminal justice system's truth-finding function is that some guilty defendants may go free or receive reduced sentences as a result of favorable plea bargains.[a] Particular-

a. Researchers have only recently begun to study extensively the effects of the exclusionary rule on the disposition of felony arrests. One study suggests that the rule results in the nonprosecution or nonconviction of between 0.6% and 2.35% of individuals arrested for felonies. Davies, A Hard Look at What We Know (and Still Need to Learn) About the "Costs" of the Exclusionary Rule: the NIJ Study and Other Studies of "Lost" Arrests, 1983 A.B.F. Res. J. 611, 621. The estimates are higher for particular crimes the prosecu-

ly when law enforcement officers have acted in objective good faith or their transgressions have been minor, the magnitude of the benefit conferred on such guilty defendants offends basic concepts of the criminal justice system. * * *

B

Close attention to those remedial objectives has characterized our recent decisions concerning the scope of the Fourth Amendment exclusionary rule.

[Justice White discusses some of the limitations that the Court has placed upon the exclusionary rule and notes that the Court has: confined the rule to criminal trials; required standing on the part of defendants who seek suppression; permitted impeachment use of illegally seized evidence; and allowed evidence to be admitted where its link to a violation is attenuated.]

As yet, we have not recognized any form of good-faith exception to the Fourth Amendment exclusionary rule. But the balancing approach that has evolved during the years of experience with the rule provides strong support for the modification currently urged upon us. * * *

III

A

Because a search warrant "provides the detached scrutiny of a neutral magistrate, which is a more reliable safeguard against improper searches than the hurried judgment of a law enforcement officer 'engaged in the often competitive enterprise of ferreting out crime,'" we have expressed a strong preference for warrants and declared that "in a doubtful or marginal case a search under a warrant may be sustainable where without one it would fail." Reasonable minds frequently may differ on the question whether a particular affidavit establishes probable cause, and we have thus concluded that the preference for warrants is most appropriately effectuated by according "great deference" to a magistrate's determination.

Deference to the magistrate, however, is not boundless. It is clear, first, that the deference accorded to a magistrate's finding of probable cause does not preclude inquiry into the knowing or reckless falsity of the affidavit on which that determination was based. Second, the courts must also insist that the magistrate purport to "perform his 'neutral and detached' function and not

tion of which depends heavily on physical evidence. Thus, the cumulative loss due to nonprosecution or nonconviction of individuals arrested on felony drug charges is probably in the range of 2.8% to 7.1%. Id., at 680. Davies' analysis of California data suggests that screening by police and prosecutors results in the release because of illegal searches or seizures of as many as 1.4% of all felony arrestees, id., at 650, that 0.9% of felony arrestees are released because of illegal searches or seizures at the preliminary hearing or after trial, id., at 653, and that roughly 0.5% of all felony arrestees benefit from reversals on appeal because of illegal searches. Id., at 654. See also K. Brosi, A Cross-City Comparison of Felony Case Processing 16, 18–19 (1979); Report of the Comptroller General of the United States, Impact of the Exclusionary Rule on Federal Criminal Prosecutions 10–11, 14 (1979); F. Feeney, F. Dill & A. Weir, Arrests Without Convictions: How Often They Occur and Why 203–206 (1983); National Institute of Justice, The Effects of the Exclusionary Rule: A Study in California 1–2 (1982); Nardulli, The Societal Cost of the Exclusionary Rule: An Empirical Assessment, 1983 A.B.F. Res. J. 585, 600. The exclusionary rule also has been found to affect the plea-bargaining process. S. Schlesinger, Exclusionary Injustice: The Problem of Illegally Obtained Evidence 63 (1977). But see Davies, supra, at 668–669; Nardulli, supra, at 604–606.

Many of these researchers have concluded that the impact of the exclusionary rule is insubstantial, but the small percentages with which they deal mask a large absolute number of felons who are released because the cases against them were based in part on illegal searches or seizures. * * * Because we find that the rule can have no substantial deterrent effect in the sorts of situations under consideration in this case, we conclude that it cannot pay its way in those situations.

serve merely as a rubber stamp for the police." A magistrate failing to "manifest that neutrality and detachment demanded of a judicial officer when presented with a warrant application" and who acts instead as "an adjunct law enforcement officer" cannot provide valid authorization for an otherwise unconstitutional search.

Third, reviewing courts will not defer to a warrant based on an affidavit that does not "provide the magistrate with a substantial basis for determining the existence of probable cause." "Sufficient information must be presented to the magistrate to allow that official to determine probable cause; his action cannot be a mere ratification of the bare conclusions of others." Even if the warrant application was supported by more than a "bare bones" affidavit, a reviewing court may properly conclude that notwithstanding the deference that magistrates deserve, the warrant was invalid because the magistrate's probable-cause determination reflected an improper analysis of the totality of the circumstances, or because the form of the warrant was improper in some respect.

Only in the first of these three situations, however, has the Court set forth a rationale for suppressing evidence obtained pursuant to a search warrant; in the other areas, it has simply excluded such evidence without considering whether Fourth Amendment interests will be advanced. To the extent that proponents of exclusion rely on its behavioral effects on judges and magistrates in these areas, their reliance is misplaced. First, the exclusionary rule is designed to deter police misconduct rather than to punish the errors of judges and magistrates. Second, there exists no evidence suggesting that judges and magistrates are inclined to ignore or subvert the Fourth Amendment or that lawlessness among these actors requires application of the extreme sanction of exclusion.

Third, and most important, we discern no basis, and are offered none, for believing that exclusion of evidence seized pursuant to a warrant will have a significant deterrent effect on the issuing judge or magistrate. * * * Judges and magistrates are not adjuncts to the law enforcement team; as neutral judicial officers, they have no stake in the outcome of particular criminal prosecutions. The threat of exclusion thus cannot be expected significantly to deter them. Imposition of the exclusionary sanction is not necessary to inform judicial officers of their errors, and we cannot conclude that admitting evidence obtained pursuant to a warrant while at the same time declaring that the warrant was somehow defective will in any way reduce judicial officers' professional incentives to comply with the Fourth Amendment, encourage them to repeat their mistakes, or lead to the granting of all colorable warrant requests.[b]

B

If exclusion of evidence obtained pursuant to a subsequently invalidated warrant is to have any deterrent effect, therefore, it must alter the behavior of individual law enforcement officers or the policies of their departments. One could argue that applying the exclusion-

b. Limiting the application of the exclusionary sanction may well increase the care with which magistrates scrutinize warrant applications. We doubt that magistrates are more desirous of avoiding the exclusion of evidence obtained pursuant to warrants they have issued than of avoiding invasions of privacy.

Federal magistrates, moreover, are subject to the direct supervision of district courts. They may be removed for "incompetency, misconduct, neglect of duty, or physical or mental disability." 28 U.S.C.A. § 631(i). If a magistrate serves merely as a "rubber stamp" for the police or is unable to exercise mature judgment, closer supervision or removal provides a more effective remedy than the exclusionary rule.

ary rule in cases where the police failed to demonstrate probable cause in the warrant application deters future inadequate presentations or "magistrate shopping" and thus promotes the ends of the Fourth Amendment. Suppressing evidence obtained pursuant to a technically defective warrant supported by probable cause also might encourage officers to scrutinize more closely the form of the warrant and to point out suspected judicial errors. We find such arguments speculative and conclude that suppression of evidence obtained pursuant to a warrant should be ordered only on a case-by-case basis and only in those unusual cases in which exclusion will further the purposes of the exclusionary rule.[c]

We have frequently questioned whether the exclusionary rule can have any deterrent effect when the offending officers acted in the objectively reasonable belief that their conduct did not violate the Fourth Amendment. * * * But even assuming that the rule effectively deters some police misconduct and provides incentives for the law enforcement profession as a whole to conduct itself in accord with the Fourth Amendment, it cannot be expected, and should not be applied, to deter objectively reasonable law enforcement activity. * * * [d]

This is particularly true, we believe, when an officer acting with objective good faith has obtained a search warrant from a judge or magistrate and acted within its scope. In most such cases, there is no police illegality and thus nothing to deter. It is the magistrate's responsibility to determine whether the officer's allegations establish probable cause and, if so, to issue a warrant comporting in form with the requirements of the Fourth Amendment. In the ordinary case, an officer cannot be expected to question the magistrate's probable cause determination or his judgment that the form of the warrant is technically sufficient. * * * Penalizing the officer for the magistrate's error, rather than his own, cannot logically contribute to the deterrence of Fourth Amendment violations.[e]

C

We conclude that the marginal or nonexistent benefits produced by suppressing evidence obtained in objective-

c. Our discussion of the deterrent effect of excluding evidence obtained in reasonable reliance on a subsequently invalidated warrant assumes, of course, that the officers properly executed the warrant and searched only those places and for those objects that it was reasonable to believe were covered by the warrant. * * *

d. We emphasize that the standard of reasonableness we adopt is an objective one. Many objections to a good-faith exception assume that the exception will turn on the subjective good faith of individual officers. "Grounding the modification in objective reasonableness, however, retains the value of the exclusionary rule as an incentive for the law enforcement profession as a whole to conduct themselves in accord with the Fourth Amendment." Illinois v. Gates, 462 U.S., at 261, n. 15 (White, J., concurring in the judgment); see Dunaway v. New York, 442 U.S., at 221 (Stevens, J., concurring). The objective standard we adopt, moreover, requires officers to have a reasonable knowledge of what the law prohibits.

e. To the extent that Justice Stevens' conclusions concerning the integrity of the courts, rest on a foundation other than his judgment, which we reject, concerning the effects of our decision on the deterrence of police illegality, we find his argument unpersuasive. "Judicial integrity clearly does not mean that the courts must never admit evidence obtained in violation of the Fourth Amendment." * * * Our cases establish that the question whether the use of illegally obtained evidence in judicial proceedings represents judicial participation in a Fourth Amendment violation and offends the integrity of the courts "is essentially the same as the inquiry into whether exclusion would serve a deterrent purpose. * * * The analysis showing that exclusion in this case has no demonstrated deterrent effect and is unlikely to have any significant such effect shows, by the same reasoning that the admission of the evidence is unlikely to encourage violations of the Fourth Amendment." * * *

ly reasonable reliance on a subsequently invalidated search warrant cannot justify the substantial costs of exclusion. We do not suggest, however, that exclusion is always inappropriate in cases where an officer has obtained a warrant and abided by its terms. * * * [T]he officer's reliance on the magistrate's probable-cause determination and on the technical sufficiency of the warrant he issues must be objectively reasonable, and it is clear that in some circumstances the officer[f] will have no reasonable grounds for believing that the warrant was properly issued.

Suppression therefore remains an appropriate remedy if the magistrate or judge in issuing a warrant was misled by information in an affidavit that the affiant knew was false or would have known was false except for his reckless disregard of the truth. The exception we recognize today will also not apply in cases where the issuing magistrate wholly abandoned his judicial role in the manner condemned in Lo–Ji Sales, Inc. v. New York; in such circumstances, no reasonably well-trained officer should rely on the warrant. Nor would an officer manifest objective good faith in relying on a warrant based on an affidavit "so lacking in indicia of probable cause as to render official belief in its existence entirely unreasonable." Finally, depending on the circumstances of the particular case, a warrant may be so facially deficient—i.e., in failing to particularize the place to be searched or the things to be seized—that the executing officers cannot reasonably presume it to be valid.

In so limiting the suppression remedy, we leave untouched the probable-cause standard and the various requirements for a valid warrant. * * *

Nor are we persuaded that application of a good-faith exception to searches conducted pursuant to warrants will preclude review of the constitutionality of the search or seizure, deny needed guidance from the courts, or freeze Fourth Amendment law in its present state. * * *

If the resolution of a particular Fourth Amendment question is necessary to guide future action by law enforcement officers and magistrates, nothing will prevent reviewing courts from deciding that question before turning to the good-faith issue. Indeed, it frequently will be difficult to determine whether the officers acted reasonably without resolving the Fourth Amendment issue. Even if the Fourth Amendment question is not one of broad import, reviewing courts could decide in particular cases that magistrates under their supervision need to be informed of their errors and so evaluate the officers' good faith only after finding a violation. * * *

IV

When the principles we have enunciated today are applied to the facts of this case, it is apparent that the judgment of the Court of Appeals cannot stand. The Court of Appeals applied the prevailing legal standards to Officer Rombach's warrant application and concluded that the application could not support the magistrate's probable-cause determination. In so doing, the court clearly informed the magistrate that he had erred in issuing the challenged war-

f. References to "officer" throughout this opinion should not be read too narrowly. It is necessary to consider the objective reasonableness, not only of the officers who eventually executed a warrant, but also of the officers who originally obtained it or who provided information material to the probable-cause determination. Nothing in our opinion suggests, for example, that an officer could obtain a warrant on the basis of a "bare bones" affidavit and then rely on colleagues who are ignorant of the circumstances under which the warrant was obtained to conduct the search. See Whitely v. Warden, 401 U.S. 560, 568 (1971).

rant. This aspect of the court's judgment is not under attack in this proceeding.

* * *

In the absence of an allegation that the magistrate abandoned his detached and neutral role, suppression is appropriate only if the officers were dishonest or reckless in preparing their affidavit or could not have harbored an objectively reasonable belief in the existence of probable cause. * * * Officer Rombach's application for a warrant clearly was supported by much more than a "bare bones" affidavit. The affidavit related the results of an extensive investigation and, as the opinions of the divided panel of the Court of Appeals make clear, provided evidence sufficient to create disagreement among thoughtful and competent judges as to the existence of probable cause. Under these circumstances, the officers' reliance on the magistrate's determination of probable cause was objectively reasonable, and application of the extreme sanction of exclusion is inappropriate.

Accordingly, the judgment of the Court of Appeals is

Reversed.

JUSTICE BLACKMUN, concurring.

* * * I join the Court's opinion in this case and the one in Massachusetts v. Sheppard, post, because I believe that the rule announced today advances the legitimate interests of the criminal justice system without sacrificing the individual rights protected by the Fourth Amendment. I write separately, however, to underscore what I regard as the unavoidably provisional nature of today's decisions.

* * *

* * * By their very nature, the assumptions on which we proceed today cannot be cast in stone. To the contrary, they now will be tested in the real world of state and federal law enforcement, and this Court will attend to the results. If it should emerge from experience that, contrary to our expectations, the good faith exception to the exclusionary rule results in a material change in police compliance with the Fourth Amendment, we shall have to reconsider what we have undertaken here. The logic of a decision that rests on untested predictions about police conduct demands no less.

* * *

JUSTICE BRENNAN, with whom JUSTICE MARSHALL joins, dissenting.[g]

* * *

I

The Court holds that physical evidence seized by police officers reasonably relying upon a warrant issued by a detached and neutral magistrate is admissible in the prosecution's case-in-chief, even though a reviewing court has subsequently determined either that the warrant was defective, or that those officers failed to demonstrate when applying for the warrant that there was probable cause to conduct the search. I have no doubt that these decisions will prove in time to have been a grave mistake. But, as troubling and important as today's new doctrine may be for the administration of criminal justice in this country, the mode of analysis used to generate that doctrine also requires critical examination, for it may prove in the long run to pose the greater threat to our civil liberties.

A

At bottom, the Court's decision turns on the proposition that the exclusionary rule is merely a " 'judicially created remedy designed to safeguard Fourth Amendment rights generally through its

g. The dissent addresses both *Leon* and the companion case, *Sheppard*.

deterrent effect, rather than a personal constitutional right.' " * * * The essence of this view * * * is that the sole "purpose of the Fourth Amendment is to prevent unreasonable governmental intrusions into the privacy of one's person, house, papers, or effects. The wrong condemned is the unjustified governmental invasion of these areas of an individual's life. That wrong * * * is *fully accomplished* by the original search without probable cause." * * * This view of the scope of the Amendment relegates the judiciary to the periphery. * * * [T]he most the judge can do is wring his hands and hope that perhaps by excluding such evidence he can deter future transgressions by the police.

Such a reading appears plausible, because, as critics of the exclusionary rule never tire of repeating, the Fourth Amendment makes no express provision for the exclusion of evidence secured in violation of its commands. A short answer to this claim, of course, is that many of the Constitution's most vital imperatives are stated in general terms and the task of giving meaning to these precepts is therefore left to subsequent judicial decisionmaking. * * *

A more direct answer may be supplied by recognizing that the Amendment, like other provisions of the Bill of Rights, restrains the power of the government as a whole; * * *. The judiciary is responsible, no less than the executive, for ensuring that constitutional rights are respected.

* * * Because seizures are executed principally to secure evidence, and because such evidence generally has utility in our legal system only in the context of a trial supervised by a judge, it is apparent that the admission of illegally obtained evidence implicates the same constitutional concerns as the initial seizure of that evidence. Indeed, by admitting unlawfully seized evidence, the judiciary becomes a part of what is in fact a single governmental action prohibited by the terms of the Amendment. * * *

[I]f the Amendment is to have any meaning, police and the courts cannot be regarded as constitutional strangers to each other; because the evidence-gathering role of the police is directly linked to the evidence-admitting function of the courts, an individual's Fourth Amendment rights may be undermined as completely by one as by the other.

B

* * *

[T]he Court has frequently bewailed the "cost" of excluding reliable evidence. In large part, this criticism rests upon a refusal to acknowledge the function of the Fourth Amendment itself. If nothing else, the Amendment plainly operates to disable the government from gathering information and securing evidence in certain ways. * * * Thus, some criminals will go free *not,* in Justice (then Judge) Cardozo's misleading epigram, "because the constable has blundered," but rather because official compliance with Fourth Amendment requirements makes it more difficult to catch criminals. Understood in this way, the Amendment directly contemplates that some reliable and incriminating evidence will be lost to the government; therefore, it is not the exclusionary rule, but the Amendment itself that has imposed this cost.

[T]he Court's decisions over the past decade have made plain that the entire enterprise of attempting to assess the benefits and costs of the exclusionary rule in various contexts is a virtually impossible task for the judiciary to perform honestly or accurately. Although the Court's language in those cases suggests that some specific empirical basis may support its analyses, the reality is that the Court's opinions represent inherently unstable compounds of intuition, hunches, and occasional pieces of partial and often inconclusive data. * * *

By remaining within its redoubt of empiricism and by basing the rule solely on the deterrence rationale, the Court has robbed the rule of legitimacy. * * *

II

[Justice Brennan reasoned that the warrant should not have issued in this case.]

III

Even if I were to accept the Court's general approach to the exclusionary rule, I could not agree with today's result. There is no question that in the hands of the present Court the deterrence rationale has proved to be a powerful tool for confining the scope of the rule. * * *

* * *

At the outset, the Court suggests that society has been asked to pay a high price—in terms either of setting guilty persons free or of impeding the proper functioning of trials—as a result of excluding relevant physical evidence in cases where the police, in conducting searches and seizing evidence, have made only an "objectively reasonable" mistake concerning the constitutionality of their actions. But what evidence is there to support such a claim?

Significantly, the Court points to none, and, indeed, as the Court acknowledges, recent studies have demonstrated that the "costs" of the exclusionary rule—calculated in terms of dropped prosecutions and lost convictions—are quite low. Contrary to the claims of the rule's critics that exclusion leads to "the release of countless guilty criminals," these studies have demonstrated that federal and state prosecutors very rarely drop cases because of potential search and seizure problems. For example, a 1979 study prepared at the request of Congress by the General Accounting Office reported that only 0.4% of all cases actually declined for prosecution by federal prosecutors were declined primarily because of illegal search problems. Report of the Comptroller General of the United States, Impact of the Exclusionary Rule on Federal Criminal Prosecutions 14 (1979). If the GAO data are restated as a percentage of *all* arrests, the study shows that only 0.2% of all felony arrests are declined for prosecution because of potential exclusionary rule problems. See Davies, A Hard Look at What We Know (and Still Need to Learn) About the "Costs" of the Exclusionary Rule: The NIJ Study and Other Studies of "Lost" Arrests, 1983 Am.Bar Found. Res.J. 611, 635.[h] Of course, these data

h. In a series of recent studies, researchers have attempted to quantify the actual costs of the rule. A recent National Institute of Justice study based on data for the four year period 1976–1979 gathered by the California Bureau of Criminal Statistics showed that 4.8% of all cases that were declined for prosecution by California prosecutors were rejected because of illegally seized evidence. National Institute of Justice, Criminal Justice Research Report—The Effects of the Exclusionary Rule: A Study in California 1 (1982). However, if these data are calculated as a percentage of all arrests that were declined for prosecution, they show that only 0.8% of all arrests were rejected for prosecution because of illegally seized evidence. See Davies, supra, at 619.

In another measure of the rule's impact—the number of prosecutions that are dismissed or result in acquittals in cases where evidence has been excluded—the available data again show that the Court's past assessment of the rule's costs has generally been exaggerated. For example, a study based on data from 9 mid-sized counties in Illinois, Michigan and Pennsylvania reveals that motions to suppress physical evidence were filed in approximately 5% of the 7,500 cases studied, but that such motions were successful in only 0.7% of all these cases. Nardulli, The Societal Cost of the Exclusionary Rule: An Empirical Assessment, 1983 Am.Bar Found.Res.J. 585, 596. The study also shows that only 0.6% of all cases resulted in acquittals because evidence had

described only the costs attributable to the exclusion of evidence in all cases; the costs due to the exclusion of evidence in the narrower category of cases where police have made objectively reasonable mistakes must necessarily be even smaller. The Court, however, ignores this distinction and mistakenly weighs the aggregated costs of exclusion in *all* cases, irrespective of the circumstances that led to exclusion, against the potential benefits associated with only those cases in which evidence is excluded because police reasonably but mistakenly believe that their conduct does not violate the Fourth Amendment. When such faulty scales are used, it is little wonder that the balance tips in favor of restricting the application of the rule.

What then supports the Court's insistence that this evidence be admitted? Apparently, the Court's only answer is that even though the costs of exclusion are not very substantial, the potential deterrent effect in these circumstances is so marginal that exclusion cannot be justified. The key to the Court's conclusion in this respect is its belief that the prospective deterrent effect of the exclusionary rule operates only in those situations in which police officers, when deciding whether to go forward with some particular search, have reason to know that their planned conduct will violate the requirements of the Fourth Amendment. If these officers in fact understand (or reasonably should understand because the law is well-settled) that their proposed conduct will offend the Fourth Amendment and that, consequently, any evidence they seize will be suppressed in court, they will refrain from conducting the planned search. In those circumstances, the incentive system created by the exclusionary rule will have the hoped-for deterrent effect. But in situations where police officers reasonably (but mistakenly) believe that their planned conduct satisfies Fourth Amendment requirements—presumably either (a) because they are acting on the basis of an apparently valid warrant, or (b) because their conduct is only later determined to be invalid as a result of a subsequent change in the law or the resolution of an unsettled question of law—then such officers will have no reason to refrain from conducting the search and the exclusionary rule will have no effect.

At first blush, there is some logic to this position. Undoubtedly, in the situation hypothesized by the Court, the existence of the exclusionary rule cannot be expected to have any deterrent effect on the particular officers at the moment they are deciding whether to go forward with the search. * * *

The flaw in the Court's argument, however, is that its logic captures only one comparatively minor element of the generally acknowledged deterrent purposes of the exclusionary rule. To be sure, the rule operates to some extent to deter future misconduct by individual officers who have had evidence suppressed in their own cases. But what the Court overlooks is that the deterrence rationale for the rule is not designed to be, nor should it be thought of as, a form of "punishment" of individual police officers for their failures to obey the restraints imposed by the

been excluded. Id., at 600. In the GAO study, suppression motions were filed in 10.5% of all federal criminal cases surveyed, but of the motions filed, approximately 80–90% were denied. GAO Report, supra, at 8, 10. Evidence was actually excluded in only 1.3% of the cases studied, and only 0.7% of all cases resulted in acquittals or dismissals after evidence was excluded. Id., at 9–11. See Davies, supra, at 660. And in another study based on data from cases during 1978 and 1979 in San Diego and Jacksonville, it was shown that only 1% of all cases resulting in nonconviction were caused by illegal searches. Feeney, Dill & Weir, Arrests Without Conviction: How Often They Occur and Why (1983). See generally Davies, supra, at 663.

Fourth Amendment. Instead, the chief deterrent function of the rule is its tendency to promote institutional compliance with Fourth Amendment requirements on the part of law enforcement agencies generally. * * *

If the overall educational effect of the exclusionary rule is considered, application of the rule to even those situations in which individual police officers have acted on the basis of a reasonable but mistaken belief that their conduct was authorized can still be expected to have a considerable long-term deterrent effect. If evidence is consistently excluded in these circumstances, police departments will surely be prompted to instruct their officers to devote greater care and attention to providing sufficient information to establish probable cause when applying for a warrant, and to review with some attention the form of the warrant that they have been issued, rather than automatically assuming that whatever document the magistrate has signed will necessarily comport with Fourth Amendment requirements.

* * *

Although the Court brushes these concerns aside, a host of grave consequences can be expected to result from its decision to carve this new exception out of the exclusionary rule. A chief consequence of today's decision will be to convey a clear and unambiguous message to magistrates that their decisions to issue warrants are now insulated from subsequent judicial review. * * *

Moreover, the good faith exception will encourage police to provide only the bare minimum of information in future warrant applications. The police will now know that if they can secure a warrant, so long as the circumstances of its issuance are not "entirely unreasonable," all police conduct pursuant to that warrant will be protected from further judicial review. * * *

[E]ven if one were to believe, as the Court apparently does, that police are hobbled by inflexible and hypertechnical warrant procedures, today's decision cannot be justified. This is because, given the relaxed standard for assessing probable cause established just last Term in Illinois v. Gates, the Court's newly fashioned good faith exception, when applied in the warrant context, will rarely, if ever, offer any greater flexibility for police than the *Gates* standard already supplies. In *Gates,* the Court held that "the task of an issuing magistrate is simply to make a practical, common-sense decision whether, given all the circumstances set forth in the affidavit before him, * * * there is a fair probability that contraband or evidence of a crime will be found in a particular place." The task of a reviewing court is confined to determining whether "the magistrate had a 'substantial basis' for concluding that probable cause existed." Given such a relaxed standard, it is virtually inconceivable that a reviewing court, when faced with a defendant's motion to suppress, could first find that a warrant was invalid under the new *Gates* standard, but then, at the same time, find that a police officer's reliance on such an invalid warrant was nevertheless "objectively reasonable" under the test announced today. Because the two standards overlap so completely, it is unlikely that a warrant could be found invalid under *Gates* and yet the police reliance upon it could be seen as objectively reasonable; otherwise, we would have to entertain the mindboggling concept of objectively reasonable reliance upon an objectively unreasonable warrant.

This paradox * * * perhaps explains the Court's unwillingness to remand for reconsideration in light of *Gates,* for it is quite likely that on remand the Court of Appeals would find no violation of the Fourth Amendment, thereby demonstrating that the supposed need for the good faith exception in this context is more apparent than real. Therefore, although the Court's decisions are clearly limited to the situation in which police officers reasonably rely upon an apparently valid warrant in conducting a search, I am not at all confident that the exception unleashed today will remain so confined. Indeed, the full impact of the Court's regrettable decision will not be felt until the Court attempts to extend this rule to situations in which the police have conducted a warrantless search solely on the basis of their own judgment about the existence of probable cause and exigent circumstances. When that question is finally posed, I for one will not be surprised if my colleagues decide once again that we simply cannot afford to protect Fourth Amendment rights.

* * *

JUSTICE STEVENS, concurring in the judgment in [Sheppard], and dissenting in [Leon].[i]

* * *

The Court assumes that the searches in these cases violated the Fourth Amendment, yet refuses to apply the exclusionary rule because the Court concludes that it was "reasonable" for the police to conduct them. In my opinion an official search and seizure cannot be both "unreasonable" and "reasonable" at the same time. The doctrinal vice in the Court's holding is its failure to consider the separate purposes of the two prohibitory clauses in the Fourth Amendment.

The first clause prohibits unreasonable searches and seizures and the second prohibits the issuance of warrants that are not supported by probable cause or that do not particularly describe the place to be searched and the persons or things to be seized. We have, of course, repeatedly held that warrantless searches are presumptively unreasonable, and that there are only a few carefully delineated exceptions to that basic presumption. But when such an exception has been recognized, analytically we have necessarily concluded that the warrantless activity was not "unreasonable" within the meaning of the first clause. Thus, any Fourth Amendment case may present two separate questions: whether the search was conducted pursuant to a warrant issued in accordance with the second clause, and, if not, whether it was nevertheless "reasonable" within the meaning of the first. On these questions, the constitutional text requires that we speak with one voice. We cannot intelligibly assume *arguendo* that a search was constitutionally unreasonable but that the seized evidence is admissible because the same search was reasonable.

* * *

In [Leon], there is * * * a substantial question whether the warrant complied with the Fourth Amendment. There was a strong dissent on the probable cause issue when *Leon* was before the Court of Appeals, and that dissent has been given added force by this Court's intervening decision in Illinois v. Gates, which constituted a significant development in the law. It is probable, though admittedly not certain, that the Court of Appeals would now conclude that the warrant in *Leon* satisfied the Fourth Amendment if it were given the opportunity to reconsider the issue in the light of *Gates.* Adherence to our normal practice following the announcement of a new rule would therefore postpone, and probably obviate, the need for the promulgation of the broad new rule the Court announces today.

* * *

i. Justice Stevens expressed the view that there was no constitutional violation in *Sheppard.*

The notion that a police officer's reliance on a magistrate's warrant is automatically appropriate is one the Framers of the Fourth Amendment would have vehemently rejected. The precise problem that the Amendment was intended to address was *the unreasonable issuance of warrants.* As we have often observed, the Amendment was actually motivated by the practice of issuing general warrants—warrants which did not satisfy the particularity and probable cause requirements. The resentments which led to the Amendment were directed at the issuance of *warrants* unjustified by particularized evidence of wrongdoing. Those who sought to amend the Constitution to include a Bill of Rights repeatedly voiced the view that the evil which had to be addressed was the issuance of warrants on insufficient evidence. * * *

In short, the Framers of the Fourth Amendment were deeply suspicious of warrants; in their minds the paradigm of an abusive search was the execution of a warrant not based on probable cause. The fact that colonial officers had magisterial authorization for their conduct when they engaged in general searches surely did not make their conduct "reasonable." The Court's view that it is consistent with our Constitution to adopt a rule that it is presumptively reasonable to rely on a defective warrant is the product of constitutional amnesia. * * *

The exclusionary rule is designed to prevent violations of the Fourth Amendment.[j] "Its purpose is to deter—to compel respect for the constitutional guaranty in the only effectively available way, by removing the incentive to disregard it." If the police cannot use evidence obtained through warrants issued on less than probable cause, they have less incentive to seek those warrants, and magistrates have less incentive to issue them.

Today's decisions do grave damage to that deterrent function. Under the majority's new rule, even when the police know their warrant application is probably insufficient, they retain an incentive to submit it to a magistrate, on the chance that he may take the bait. No longer must they hesitate and seek additional evidence in doubtful cases. * * *

The Court is of course correct that the exclusionary rule cannot deter when the authorities have no reason to know that their conduct is unconstitutional. But when probable cause is lacking, then by definition a reasonable person under the circumstances would not believe there is a fair likelihood that a search will produce evidence of a crime. Under such circumstances well-trained professionals must know that they are violating the Constitution. The Court's approach—which, in effect, encourages the police to seek a warrant even if they know the existence of probable cause is doubtful—can only lead to an increased number of constitutional violations.

Thus, the Court's creation of a double standard of reasonableness inevitably must erode the deterrence rationale that still supports the exclusionary rule. But we should not ignore the way it tarnishes the rule of the judiciary in enforcing the Constitution. * * * While, as the Court correctly notes, we have refused to apply the exclusionary rule to collateral contexts in which its marginal efficacy is questionable, until today every time the police have violat-

j. For at least two reasons, the exclusionary rule is a better remedy than a civil action against an offending officer. Unlike the fear of personal liability, it should not create excessive deterrence; moreover, it avoids the obvious unfairness of subjecting the dedicated officer to the risk of monetary liability for a misstep while endeavoring to enforce the law. Society, rather than the individual officer, should accept the responsibility for inadequate training or supervision of officers engaged in hazardous police work. * * *

ed the applicable commands of the Fourth Amendment a court has been prepared to vindicate that Amendment by preventing the use of evidence so obtained in the prosecution's case-in-chief against those whose rights have been violated. Today, for the first time, this Court holds that although the Constitution has been violated, no court should do anything about it at any time and in any proceeding. In my judgment, the Constitution requires more. * * * Nor should we so easily concede the existence of a constitutional violation for which there is no remedy. To do so is to convert a Bill of *Rights* into an unenforced honor code that the police may follow in their discretion. The Constitution requires more; it requires a *remedy.* If the Court's new rule is to be followed, the Bill of Rights should be renamed.

Note

The facts of the companion case, Massachusetts v. Sheppard, 468 U.S. 981 (1984), were as follows:

"The badly burned body of Sandra Boulware was discovered in a vacant lot in the Roxbury section of Boston at approximately 5 a.m., Saturday, May 5, 1979. An autopsy revealed that Boulware had died of multiple compound skull fractures caused by blows to the head. After a brief investigation, the police decided to question one of the victim's boyfriends, Osborne Sheppard. Sheppard told the police that he had last seen the victim on Tuesday night and that he had been at a local gaming house (where cards games were played) from 9 p.m. Friday until 5 a.m. Saturday. He identified several people who would be willing to substantiate the latter claim.

"By interviewing the people Sheppard had said were at the gaming house on Friday night, the police learned that although Sheppard was at the gaming house that night, he had borrowed an automobile at about 3 a.m. Saturday morning in order to give two men a ride home. Even though the trip normally took only fifteen minutes, Sheppard did not return with the car until nearly 5 a.m.

"On Sunday morning, police officers visited the owner of the car Sheppard had borrowed. He consented to an inspection of the vehicle. Bloodstains and pieces of hair were found on the rear bumper and within the trunk compartment. In addition, the officers noticed strands of wire in the trunk similar to wire strands found on and near the body of the victim. The owner of the car told the officers that when he last used the car on Friday night, shortly before Sheppard borrowed it, he had placed articles in the trunk and had not noticed any stains on the bumper or in the trunk.

"On the basis of the evidence gathered thus far in the investigation, Detective Peter O'Malley drafted an affidavit designed to support an application for an arrest warrant and a search warrant authorizing a search of Sheppard's residence. The affidavit set forth the results of the investigation and stated that the police wished to search for

'[a] fifth bottle of amaretto liquor, 2 nickel bags of marijuana, a woman's jacket that has been described as black-grey (charcoal), any possessions of Sandra D. Boulware, similar type wire and rope that match those on the body of Sandra D. Boulware, or in the above Thunderbird. A blunt instrument that might have been used on the victim, men's or women's

> clothing that may have blood, gasoline burns on them. Items that may have fingerprints of the victim.' [a]

Detective O'Malley showed the affidavit to the district attorney, the district attorney's first assistant, and a sergeant, who all concluded that it set forth probable cause for the search and the arrest.

> "Because it was Sunday, the local court was closed, and the police had a difficult time finding a warrant application form. Detective O'Malley finally found a warrant form previously in use in the Dorchester District. The form was entitled 'Search Warrant—Controlled Substance G.L. c. 276 §§ 1 through 3A.' Realizing that some changes had to be made before the form could be used to authorize the search requested in the affidavit, Detective O'Malley deleted the subtitle 'controlled substance' with a typewriter. He also substituted 'Roxbury' for the printed 'Dorchester' and typed Sheppard's name and address into blank spaces provided for that information. However, the reference to 'controlled substance' was not deleted in the portion of the form that constituted the warrant application and that, when signed, would constitute the warrant itself.
>
> "Detective O'Malley then took the affidavit and the warrant form to the residence of a judge who had consented to consider the warrant application. The judge examined the affidavit and stated that he would authorize the search as requested. Detective O'Malley offered the warrant form and stated that he knew the form as presented dealt with controlled substances. He showed the judge where he had crossed out the subtitles. After unsuccessfully searching for a more suitable form, the judge informed O'Malley that he would make the necessary changes so as to provide a proper search warrant. The judge then took the form, made some changes on it, and dated and signed the warrant. However, he did not change the substantive portion of the warrant, which continued to authorize a search for controlled substances; nor did he alter the form so as to incorporate the affidavit. The judge returned the affidavit and the warrant to O'Malley, informing him that the warrant was sufficient authority in form and content to carry out the search as requested. O'Malley took the two documents and, accompanied by other officers, proceeded to Sheppard's residence. The scope of the ensuing search was limited to the items listed in the affidavit, and several incriminating pieces of evidence were discovered. Sheppard was then charged with first degree murder."

The Court stated that "[t]here is no dispute that the officers believed that the warrant authorized the search that they conducted." It found that there was an objectively reasonable basis for the officers' mistaken belief. If an error of constitutional dimension was made, the Court found that the judge made it and declined to suppress the evidence. The Court concluded that the officers "took every step that could reasonably be expected of them," and that O'Malley was not required "to disbelieve a judge who has just advised him, by word and by action, that the warrant he possesses authorizes him to conduct the search he has requested." The Court refused to decide whether the warrant was in fact invalid for lack of particularity. It stated that this was "a fact-bound issue of little importance since similar situations are unlikely to arise with any regularity." Justice Stevens argued in his dissent that there was no error of constitutional dimension and therefore no need to suppress evidence.

a. The liquor and marihuana were included in the request because Sheppard had told the officers that when he was last with the victim, the two had purchased two bags of marihuana and a fifth of amaretto before going to his residence.

Assume that most people would agree that it is undesirable to suppress evidence obtained by the government when its officers have acted reasonably, in good faith, and with an eye on relevant constitutional provisions. On this assumption, is a good faith exception a necessary addition to the law that the Court already had established to limit the exclusionary rule?

Consider *Leon.* Do you agree with the dissenting Justices that after the Court's decision in *Gates,* establishing a totality of the circumstances approach to evaluating warrants, that the lower court would have upheld the warrant? If so, then is Justice Stevens correct in arguing that no good faith rule is needed on these facts? Since *Leon* was decided, only a few cases have reached the result found "virtually inconceivable" by Justice Brennan—that the warrant was not based upon probable cause but that the officer was nonetheless objectively reasonable in relying upon it. And in these cases it is clear that the reviewing court thought that *Gates* was satisfied in the first place. See United States v. Martin, 833 F.2d 752 (8th Cir.1987) (upholding district court's finding of lack of probable cause as not clearly erroneous, but applying the good faith exception because, if exercising *de novo* review, the court would have found probable cause to exist); People v. Camarella, 54 Cal.3d 592, 286 Cal.Rptr. 780, 818 P.2d 63 (1991) (accepting trial court's determination that affidavit did not provide probable cause, but applying the good faith exception since the officer obtained substantial information corroborating the tip of an anonymous informant; the affidavit was "sufficient to make the probable cause determination a close question for any objectively reasonable and well-trained officer and, indeed, for reasonable judicial officers as well."). A more common result is that a Court which finds that probable cause is lacking under *Gates* will also find that the officer was not objectively reasonable in relying on the warrant. See United States v. Baxter, 889 F.2d 731 (6th Cir.1989) (affidavit describing tip from anonymous informant, with corroboration only of defendant's address and prior conviction on drug charges, is a barebones affidavit, and officer was not objectively reasonable in relying on the warrant); United States v. Jackson, 818 F.2d 345 (5th Cir.1987) (barebones affidavit).

Next, consider *Sheppard.* Do you believe that the Constitution was violated on these facts? Did the magistrate screen the affidavit carefully, as we want magistrates to do? Did the magistrate endeavor to carefully circumscribe the search? Did the officers execute the warrant reasonably and without seeking to look for extra evidence? If the answers are all "yes" to these questions, what authority is there for holding the search warrant invalid as a matter of constitutional law? Would a misspelled street name invalidate a warrant? A misspelled suspect's name? One would have thought not. If not, is Justice Stevens correct again that no good faith exception is needed? In thinking about this question, you might want to know that on remand, the state supreme court found no reason to suppress the evidence in Commonwealth v. Sheppard under the state constitution. Commonwealth v. Sheppard, 394 Mass. 381, 476 N.E.2d 541 (1985).

A good faith exception is something of an oxymoron, as the majority's reasoning suggests. The majority in *Leon* indicates that there are two steps in analyzing search and seizure problems: deciding whether there has been a constitutional violation and what remedy to utilize. To have a violation when an officer acts without warrants, the Supreme Court has said that the officer must have acted unreasonably considering all of the circumstances confronting the officer. In other words, the officer must have acted as a reasonable person would not have acted. To have a violation when a magistrate issues a warrant, the Court has said that the magistrate must have reached a conclusion that there was probable cause or that items could be sought and seized that no reasonable person could have reached.

Now the good faith rule seems to establish a concept of good faith "unreasonableness." Does this make sense? It can be argued that it does. Reasonable minds can differ as to what is reasonable, as can be seen in probable cause cases like United States v. Valez, page 97. What the good faith exception appears to mean is that in cases where some or most people would think that an officer's conduct was unreasonable, the good faith exception will apply so long as reasonable minds can differ on the point. Where no reasonable argument can be made that the officer's conduct was lawful, then the good faith exception will not apply. Thus, the good faith exception is similar to the standard used for reviewing jury verdicts in civil cases—the standard is not whether the jury was correct or whether the reviewing court would have decided the case another way, but whether no reasonable person could have decided the way the jury did. So long as there is room for argument, then, the good faith exception will apply. Another useful analogy comes from the qualified immunity cases decided under the civil rights statute, 42 U.S.C. § 1983. Even if the plaintiff's constitutional rights are violated, there is no liability unless the officer violated clearly established law; if the law was not clearly established, then there is room for argument as to whether the officer's conduct was lawful. The Supreme Court has equated the standards of qualified immunity with the objective reasonableness standard of the good faith exception to the exclusionary rule. See Anderson v. Creighton, 483 U.S. 635 (1987) (rejecting the argument that an officer may not reasonably act unreasonably). See also People v. Camarella, 54 Cal.3d 592, 286 Cal.Rptr. 780, 818 P.2d 63 (1991) (noting that under Supreme Court holdings, "the same standard of objective reasonableness * * * applied in the context of a suppression hearing in *Leon*, defines the qualified immunity accorded an officer" under section 1983).

Because an officer can reasonably act unreasonably, there are three types of errors after *Leon:* (1) reasonable mistakes which are not a violation of the Fourth Amendment at all, such as a mistake of fact; (2) unreasonable mistakes which violate the Fourth Amendment, but at the time of the conduct reasonable minds could have differed about whether the officer was acting lawfully; and (3) unreasonable mistakes where the officer violated clearly established law, so that no reasonable argument could be made that the action was lawful. Illinois v. Rodriguez, (page 337), where the officers made a reasonable mistake concerning the authority of a third party to consent to a search, falls into the first category; *Leon* falls into the second, as do other cases discussed later in this Note; and reliance on a warrant issued on the basis of a barebones affidavit falls into the third.

In Maryland v. Garrison, 480 U.S. 79 (1987), officers applied for a search warrant for a "third floor apartment" at a certain address. Utility records showed one bill being sent to the third floor at that address. There were seven apartments in the three story building. When the officers executed the warrant, they found one door on the third floor corridor. Inside the door was a foyer, and two open doorways led off from that. Officers went in each direction from the foyer, and it was not until they discovered a kitchen in each direction that they realized that they were searching two separate apartments. The Court held that the search warrant authorizing the search of the entire third floor, rather than a particular apartment, was valid when issued, because it was reasonable, though erroneous, to assume that there was only one apartment on that floor. The Court also found that the execution of the warrant up until the time the error was discovered was valid because "the officers' failure to realize the overbreadth of the warrant was objectively understandable and reasonable." The majority opinion was written by Justice Stevens, who dissented in *Leon.* Some have argued that the Court in *Garrison* applied the good faith exception to the exclusionary rule. See Note,

Maryland v. Garrison, Extending the Good Faith Exception to Warrantless Searches, 40 Baylor L.Rev. 151 (1988). Do you agree?

Leon was held to be controlling in Illinois v. Krull, 480 U.S. 340 (1987). Illinois had enacted a statute authorizing warrantless searches by state officials to inspect the records of dealers in motor vehicles, automobile parts, or automobile scrap metal. Although the statute in existence when officials searched a particular wrecking yard was subsequently held to be unconstitutional, the Supreme Court held that suppression of evidence obtained in the search was not necessary. Justice Blackmun's majority opinion reasoned that exclusion was not necessary to deter legislators from violating the Constitution, especially since legislators enact statutes for "broad programmatic purposes, not for the purpose of procuring evidence in particular criminal investigations." Justice Blackmun reasoned that, as in *Leon,* the presence of an intermediary upon whom the officer could reasonably rely meant that the officer could not be deterred by the exclusionary rule. The error was that of the Legislature, which could not be deterred from passing unconstitutional laws by application of the exclusionary rule; and the officer, who is subject to the deterrent effect of the rule, had done nothing wrong. He was not persuaded that *Leon* should be distinguished "because a statute authorizing warrantless searches affects an entire industry and a large number of citizens, while the issuance of a defective warrant affects only one person." Justice Blackmun predicted that individuals would seek declaratory judgments and injunctions against invalid statutes and would continue to challenge such statutes. The Court decided, as in *Leon,* that a good faith claim must have an objective basis, so that "[a] statute cannot support objectively reasonable reliance if, in passing the statute, the legislature wholly abandoned its responsibility to enact constitutional laws," and "a law enforcement officer [cannot] be said to have acted in good-faith reliance upon a statute if its provisions are such that a reasonable officer should have known that the statute was unconstitutional."

Justice O'Connor, joined by Justices Brennan, Marshall and Stevens, dissented. She found "a powerful historical basis for the exclusion of evidence gathered pursuant to a search authorized by an unconstitutional statute" in the reaction of the Framers of the Constitution to Acts of Parliament authorizing general searches. She distinguished legislators from magistrates, finding that "[t]he judicial role is particularized, fact-specific and nonpolitical," and argued that "[p]roviding legislatures a grace period during which the police may freely perform unreasonable searches in order to convict those who might have otherwise escaped creates a positive incentive to promulgate unconstitutional laws."

Before long, the Court will undoubtedly confront the question whether the good faith exception applies to warrantless actions by police. If the exception is held not to apply to warrantless activity, then the warrant clause of the Fourth Amendment might benefit from the Court's recognition of the good faith exception. Its recognition might encourage police to seek more warrants and judicial supervision than they otherwise would. Justice White, the author of the opinions in the good faith cases, suggested in a case decided the same day, Immigration and Naturalization Service v. Lopez-Mendoza, 468 U.S. 1032 (1984) (White, J., dissenting), that good faith actions by INS agents would not result in suppression of evidence. This might suggest that he will vote to apply the good faith rule to warrantless police actions. Does the rationale he offers in *Leon* for the good faith exception support such an extension? Hasn't the Court in *Leon* and *Krull* painted itself into a corner by holding that while intermediary officials such as magistrates and legislators cannot be deterred by the exclusionary rule, an officer in the competitive enterprise of ferreting out crime can be deterred? Arguments against applying the good faith exception to warrantless conduct can be found in Greenhalgh, The Warrantless Good Faith Exception: Unprecedented, Indefensible, and Devoid of Necessity, 26 S.Tex.L.J. 129 (1985). Marsh, On Rollercoasters, Submarines, and Judicial Shipwrecks: Acoustic Separation and the Good Faith Exception to the Fourth Amendment Exclusionary Rule, 1989 U.Ill.L.Rev. 941, argues that the extension of the good faith exception to warrantless searches is probably unwise, but that the majority's analysis in *Leon* is broad enough to allow for such an extension.

The consequences of extending the good faith exception to warrantless searches can be seen in the Fifth Circuit, where the exception has been applied to all searches and seizures after United States v. Williams, supra. In United States v. De Leon—Reyna, 930 F.2d 396 (5th Cir.1991), an officer who suspected defendant of drug trafficking took down the license plate number of the truck defendant was driving and radioed it to the dispatcher. The officer relayed the number "WM-1438" to the dispatcher, but did not follow unit policy requiring the use of code words for communicating license plate letters. The dispatcher misunderstood the officer to say "WN-1438" and radioed back that the license check had (not surprisingly) revealed that the plates were issued to a different truck than the truck that defendant was driving. On the basis of the dispatcher's information, the officer stopped the truck and discovered cocaine. The district court and a panel of the Fifth Circuit found that the officer had acted negligently in failing to use a well-accepted and simple method by which mistaken stops could be avoided, and held that the good faith exception could not apply to acts of negligence. On review en banc, the court reversed, concluding that even if negligent, the officer's "good faith reliance on the license report information * * * was objectively reasonable." The court reasoned that the failure to use code words does not mean that "*all* communications * * * are *wholly* unreliable." In dissent, Judge Thornberry objected to the application of the good faith exception to warrantless searches.

> If a mistake is made by someone other than the law enforcement officer [as in *Leon* and *Krull*], it is possible for the officer to be reasonable in believing that he is justified in stopping a defendant even though the basis for his suspicions is not objectively reasonable, but when the officer is also the one who made the mistake, the reasonableness required by the good faith exception is analytically identical to the reasonableness required by the Fourth Amendment. Adding a good faith analysis to a Fourth Amendment analysis contributes nothing but confusion.

Does the result in *De Leon—Reyna* create any possibilities for abuse?

So far, the Supreme Court has applied the good faith exception only where the officer is reasonably relying on an intermediary. But there is another intermediary that an officer relies upon, and that is the Court itself. If the officer relies on the established law at the time of the conduct, and the conduct is later found to be unconstitutional by the Supreme Court (as in *Chimel,* which overruled *Rabinowitz,* or as in *Katz,* which overruled *Olmstead*), should the good faith exception apply to admit the evidence? In these circumstances, the officer has not made an error; and the Court, which has made the error that it has now corrected, can hardly be considered deterrable by the exclusionary rule.

However, if the good faith exception applies to conduct that was lawful under Court precedent at the time, what does that do to the retroactivity doctrine? In Griffith v. Kentucky, 479 U.S. 314 (1987), discussed in Chapter One, the Court held that decisions which overrule prior law must apply retroactively to all cases on direct review. Wouldn't application of the good faith exception to a change of law mean that the law would be applied only prospectively? Is the argument that the *law* applies retroactively, but the *remedy* applies prospectively, very comforting? If the good faith exception applies to changes of law, what incentive does a defendant have for arguing that the Court should reconsider one of its prior decisions? See United States v. Richardson, 848 F.2d 509 (5th Cir.1988) (good faith exception applied where searches were conducted in accordance with the law "as then reflected by our decisions" even though these decisions have since been overruled).

While *Leon* does not currently apply to warrantless searches (outside the Fifth Circuit), many warrantless searches are conducted in order to discover information upon which to obtain a warrant. Before *Leon,* if a search warrant was based upon illegally discovered evidence, then the warrant itself was tainted and evidence obtained upon executing the warrant was ordinarily excluded as fruit of the poisonous tree. See Murray v. United States, supra. Does *Leon* allow the officers to reasonably rely on the warrant that is issued on the basis of evidence obtained in an illegal warrantless search? In United States v. Thomas, 757 F.2d 1359 (2d Cir.1985), a DEA agent brought a trained dog to the outside of defendant's apartment to sniff for drugs. The dog gave a positive alert, and this information was used to obtain a warrant. The court held that the canine sniff was impermissible, distinguishing United States v. Place, supra. However, the court found that the evidence obtained pursuant to the warrant was admissible under the good faith exception. It reasoned as follows:

> There is nothing more the officer could have or should have done under these circumstances to be sure his search would be legal. The magistrate, whose duty it is to interpret the law, determined that the canine sniff could form the basis for probable cause; it was reasonable for the officer to rely on this determination.

Hasn't the court in *Thomas* applied *Leon* to a warrantless search? For a contrary approach, see United States v. Vasey, 834 F.2d 782 (9th Cir.1987), where the court held that the good faith exception could not apply when a warrant was issued on the basis of information obtained in a search that was not close enough in time to be justified as incident to arrest. The court reasoned that the issuance of the warrant did not necessarily mean that the magistrate had found that the original search was in fact incident to arrest; this was especially true where the affidavit did not give a complete indication of the circumstances of the original search. Professor Green, in The Good Faith Exception to the Fruit of the Poisonous Tree Doctrine, 26 Crim. Law Bull. 509 (1990) argues that the good faith exception should not apply to warrants based on illegally obtained information unless the magistrate "made an explicit determination [that the original search was legal] after being fully apprised of all the relevant facts and law," including facts and law adverse to the government's position. Do you agree?

A good faith exception for searches conducted pursuant to warrants assumes that magistrates are truly independent and carefully screen police conduct. Should the good faith rule apply to warrants issued by nonlawyers? Do you believe that the magistrates in the lower courts of the nation who traditionally issue most warrants are indifferent to the reactions of the police and prosecutors who seek warrants? In close cases, are they likely to refuse warrant requests after *Leon* and *Sheppard*?

The Mississippi Supreme Court declined to adopt a good faith exception in Stringer v. State, 477 So.2d 1335 (Miss.1985). Relying on the state constitution, the court reasoned that "[t]he fundamental flaw in *Leon* is that its new 'insight'—that in the type of cases we are concerned with it is the issuing magistrate who violates the accused's Fourth Amendment rights, not the officer—suggests a *greater* need for the exclusionary rule, not a lesser one." It concluded that the exclusionary rule is "our only practicable means of getting the attention of issuing magistrates who disregard the rights of persons to be free of searches except under warrants issued upon probable cause."

People v. Bigelow, 66 N.Y.2d 417, 497 N.Y.S.2d 630, 488 N.E.2d 451 (1985), also rejects the good faith exception to the warrant requirement. Other state courts have followed *Leon*. See, e.g., Potts v. State, 300 Md. 567, 479 A.2d 1335 (1984).

Whether the good faith rule permits police and magistrates too much free reign may well depend on how appellate courts deal with Fourth Amendment questions in subsequent cases. If appellate courts carefully review challenges to warrant applications (and warrantless actions as well) and provide guidance as to what is acceptable and unacceptable, officers will be on notice as to what they may and may not do. Once a court declares something unacceptable, presumably an officer cannot objectively act reasonably in engaging in that conduct. See United States v. Buck, 813 F.2d 588 (2d Cir.1987), where the court held that a warrant with a catch-all clause was insufficiently particular, but nonetheless applied the good faith exception because "what the officers failed to do was to anticipate our holding today that the particularity clause of the Fourth Amendment prohibits the use of a catch-all description in a search warrant, unaccompanied by any list of particular items or any other limiting language." However, the court stated in a footnote that "with respect to searches conducted hereafter, police officers may no longer invoke the reasonable-reliance exception to the exclusionary rule when they attempt to introduce as evidence the fruits of searches undertaken on the basis of warrants containing only a catch-all description of the property to be seized."

On the other hand, if appellate courts tend to examine searches and seizures cursorily simply to assure that the magistrate or officer at a minimum approached constitutional requirements so that they appear to have acted in good faith, they may water down the protections of the Fourth Amendment. Justice Blackmun warns that he would be prepared to take another look at the exception should this happen.

At this point you might want to look back at the Fourth Amendment law you have covered. You will see, perhaps to your dismay, that nothing is simpler than it was prior to the good faith decisions. The basic questions of what officers may do are still there. The exclusionary rule and its other limits are still there. Now there is also a new exception. If you reexamine the cases you have read thus far, consider how often would the good faith exception have produced different results? How often do you think it will change results in future cases?

There is some indication in the federal cases decided after *Leon* that the lower courts are doing what Justice White speculated they would not do—i.e., avoid deciding the substance of Fourth Amendment issues and instead find good faith. For example, in United States v. Henderson, 746 F.2d 619 (9th Cir.1984), defendants convicted of drug offenses challenged an order authorizing beeper surveillance. Rather than rule on whether the order was valid, the court sustained the search by citing *Leon* and relying upon the good faith of the agents. Thus, in future cases, the agents have no guidance as to the validity of the order challenged by the defendants. Presumably, they continue to act in good faith until a similar order actually is invalidated. Likewise, in United States v. Tedford, 875 F.2d 446 (5th Cir.1989), the court bypassed a probable cause question and proceeded directly to the issue of good faith. The court stated that the probable cause issue was fact-bound, and resolution would not provide important guidance on Fourth Amendment limitations. Compare United States v. Brewer, 841 F.2d 667 (6th Cir.1988) (no need to decide *Leon* issue where court finds that probable cause supported the warrant). In *Leon,* Justice White posited that magistrates would be deterred from errors by way of instruction from reviewing courts. Has the practice since *Leon* borne this out?

United States v. Accardo, 749 F.2d 1477 (11th Cir.1985), offers an interesting factual perspective from which to assess the possible impact of *Leon*. Federal agents in Chicago suspected several health care service companies of labor racketeering activities. At the conclusion of their investigation, the agents sought a warrant to search two offices. They filed an affidavit in support of the warrant describing a kickback scheme, and a federal magistrate issued a warrant to seize "all corporate records." A federal district court suppressed the evidence that was seized on the ground that the warrant was impermissibly general. The court of appeals vacated and remanded for further consideration in light of *Leon*, noting that the agents acted in good faith, they filed a complete affidavit, several assistant United States attorneys reviewed the application, and a magistrate issued the warrant. Is it conceivable that such a warrant could be deemed valid for any business that is not totally illegal? Does the participation of prosecutors—who cannot be considered neutral under the Supreme Court's cases—bolster the good faith claim of police officers? Most courts have held that if the officer has the affidavit reviewed by a prosecutor, this goes far toward showing reasonable reliance. See e.g., People v. Camarella, 54 Cal.3d 592, 286 Cal.Rptr. 780, 818 P.2d 63 (1991). The *Camarella* court also held, however, contrary to *Accardo*, that the magistrate's issuance of a warrant is irrelevant to whether the warrant was so lacking in probable cause that it could not reasonably be relied upon. The court reasoned that "because issuance of a warrant is a constant factor" in all cases where the warrant is unsupported by probable cause and yet the good faith exception is asserted, "it cannot logically serve to distinguish among them."

For an example of reliance on the good faith exception, see United States v. Savoca, 761 F.2d 292 (6th Cir.1985). The court summarized the affidavit supporting a warrant as follows:

> The affidavit, when read in a common sense and realistic fashion, indicated that (1) FBI agents in Phoenix had just arrested Thomas Savoca and James Carey pursuant to federal arrest warrants for a bank robbery which took place in Austinburg, Ohio at an unspecified prior date, (2) the two suspects had been seen in Room 135 on two prior occasions, and (3) the two suspects were allegedly responsible for several other bank robberies in northeast Ohio and northwest Pennsylvania.

Although the court had originally held that the affidavit failed to establish probable cause for a search of a room in Phoenix, it concluded in light of *Leon* that a reasonably well-trained police officer who was reasonably aware of applicable judicial decisions might not have concluded that the warrant was invalid. A dissenting judge argued that "the warrant was based on an affidavit so lacking in indicia of probable cause as to render official belief in its existence entirely unreasonable." Who has the better of the argument?

Some cases have found a warrant to be so deficient that it could not be reasonably relied upon. In United States v. Fuccillo, 808 F.2d 173 (1st Cir.1987), officers searched a clothing warehouse and retail clothing store, with search warrants authorizing the seizure of "women's clothing" believed to be stolen. They seized virtually all the clothing found at each of the premises (including men's clothing). The court ruled that the warrants were insufficiently particular, since the officers "could have obtained specific information for presentment to the magistrate and placement in the warrant which would have enabled the agents [executing the warrants] to differentiate contraband cartons of women's clothing from legitimate ones." In fact the officers had a detailed list of the stolen clothing, but they failed to include it in the warrant application. The court further held that the good faith exception could not justify the searches and seizures. It reasoned that the officers were "reckless in not including in the affidavit information which was known or easily accessible to them," and that the warrant was so overbroad that the executing officers could not reasonably presume it to be valid. See also United States v. Stubbs, 873 F.2d 210 (9th Cir.1989) (good faith exception unavailable where warrant authorizes seizure of virtually all business documents, and probable cause existed as to only one transaction).

The Supreme Court denied review over the dissent of Justice Brennan, joined by Justice Marshall, in McCommon v. Mississippi, 474 U.S. 984 (1985), a case involving the candid suppression hearing testimony of a state court "judge" who had issued a search warrant. The judge testified that "if Sheriff Jones walked in there and said, 'Judge, I need a Search Warrant to search John Doe for Marijuana,' or drugs or whatever—liquor or whatever it might be, I'm going to go on his word because he's—I take him to be an honest law enforcement officer and he needs my help to get in to search these places and it's my duty to help him fulfill that." Justice Brennan wrote that he found "the Court's refusal to take this case particularly disturbing in light of the good faith exception to the Fourth Amendment exclusionary rule created by United States v. Leon." See also United States v. Breckenridge, 782 F.2d 1317 (5th Cir.1986), where the court held that the good faith exception applied even though the judge who issued the warrant never read the affidavit. The court reasoned that the officer could reasonably rely on the warrant since, though the judge did not read the affidavit, he "appeared to Agent Alexander to be doing so." Does *Shadwick* make sense in a jurisdiction that adopts a good faith exception?

Recall the discussion on standing, where the Court declared that Fourth Amendment rights are personal rights, so that standing to assert a Fourth Amendment violation requires that a personal right have been violated. Is this consistent with the Court's statements in *Leon* that the exclusionary rule serves only deterrence principles, and is not a personal right of the party aggrieved?

In *Leon,* the Court clearly holds that the exclusionary rule is not constitutionally required. Why then are the states required to exclude evidence? Has *Mapp* been overruled?

Professor Burkoff, in Bad Faith Searches, 57 N.Y.U.L.Rev. 70 (1982) argues for a "bad faith" extension to the exclusionary rule. He proposes exclusion of evidence if the officer intended to violate the Fourth Amendment, even though the officer's conduct turned out to be objectively reasonable. So for example, if an officer thought he was searching a home without probable cause, evidence discovered in the search would be excluded even though probable cause in fact existed. Recall the discussion on pretext, supra, as well as *Rodriguez,* the third party consent case. Do you think courts would be receptive to a bad faith extension? What problems of proof would it present?

13. Alternatives to Exclusion

The most common—and perhaps strongest—argument in support of the exclusionary rule is the absence of alternative means of enforcing Fourth

Amendment protections.[37] The efficacy of the alternatives are, however, as hotly debated as the rule itself. In this section, other possible remedies will be evaluated, both in terms of deterrent value and workability. Consider whether there is, in fact, an effective alternative to the exclusionary rule.

The most frequently cited replacements for the rule are damage remedies, criminal prosecution of the offending officers, and internal police discipline. It should be noted at the outset that any of these remedies could be used as supplements to suppression of evidence, and if effective as deterrents, might reduce the frequency with which that doctrine need be relied upon.

At present several forms of damage actions are available to the victim of an illegal search or seizure. Common law tort actions include false arrest, false imprisonment and trespass. In addition, a civil rights action under 42 U.S.C.A. § 1983 is available when state officers, acting under color of law, violate a constitutional right. In Bivens v. Six Unknown Named Agents of Federal Bureau of Narcotics, 403 U.S. 388 (1971), the Supreme Court created a § 1983 counterpart for violations by federal officials. Chief Justice Burger dissented and proposed a legislative remedy which would replace the exclusionary rule. Features of the proposal would include waiver of sovereign immunity as to illegal acts committed in the performance of assigned duties, and the creation of a statutory right on the part of aggrieved persons to proceed against the government before a quasi-judicial body.

Remedies for Fourth Amendment violations are generally appraised in terms of their effectiveness as deterrents to illegal police conduct, rather than their adequacy in compensating individual victims. This is consistent, of course, with the rationale that gives the warrant clause a predominant influence over the reasonableness clause of the Amendment. The traditional tort remedies are criticized as falling short on both counts. They neither deter nor compensate adequately. A comprehensive study of the problem can be found in Foote, Tort Remedies for Police Violations of Individual Rights, 39 Minn. L.Rev. 493 (1955).

Tort remedies have seldom been invoked in the past 150 years for Fourth Amendment violations. The two major problems involved in a tort action against police are first, winning, and second, collecting on the judgment. Obstacles such as governmental immunity exist in many states. Magistrates who issue invalid warrants are immune from suit. Pierson v. Ray, 386 U.S. 547, 553–55 (1967).[38] Police officers exercising discretion are entitled to qualified immunity, so that even if they violate the Fourth Amendment, the citizen does not recover unless the law was clearly established at the time of the

37. For a recent, vigorous defense of the exclusionary rule, see Kamisar, Does (Did) (Should) the Exclusionary Rule Rest on a "Principled Basis" Rather than an "Empirical Proposition"? 16 Creighton L.Rev., 565 (1983).

38. Both Supreme Court of Virginia v. Consumers Union, 446 U.S. 719 (1980), and Lopez v. Vanderwater, 620 F.2d 1229 (7th Cir. 1980), hold that absolute judicial immunity does not apply when a court or judge assumes enforcement or prosecutorial duties.

The Supreme Court created an exception to the absolute immunity of judges by a 5–4 vote in Pulliam v. Allen, 466 U.S. 522 (1984), holding that "judicial immunity is not a bar to prospective injunctive relief against a judicial officer acting in her judicial capacity" and that judicial immunity is no bar to the award of attorneys fees to a plaintiff who successfully sues a judge under the civil rights laws.

conduct.[39] How much Fourth Amendment law can be considered clearly established? Even in jurisdictions where suits are permitted, the "moral aspects of the case" make recovery in a jury trial difficult. Foote suggests that most victims of illegal police practices "lack the minimum elements of respectability which must be present to form a base upon which the fiction of reparation can operate." In a false arrest action, even where a plaintiff is not convicted of a crime, proof of a prior criminal reputation can be used to impeach his credibility as a witness, or to mitigate damages by showing either that there was no damage to reputation and no real mental anguish, or that probable cause existed for the arrest. "Respectable" persons have the greatest chance of recovering, since past record or reputation cannot be used in mitigation, but, as Foote points out, the "respectable" person is least likely to be subject to arbitrary arrest and harassment, and thus least likely to require a tort remedy.

If a plaintiff succeeds in proving liability, the next obstacle is proving—and collecting—damages which are adequate to cover the costs of the suit. In a trespass action, where damages are limited to actual property loss, the award is usually small except in the most extreme search cases. Likewise, false imprisonment suits in states which permit punitive damages only upon a showing of actual monetary loss provide little chance of recovery, since actual loss is often small or non-existent. Nominal damages provide no incentive for an aggrieved citizen to sue, and thus prevent private persons from effectively enforcing the public policy against police illegality. Lawyers are reluctant to pursue tort actions against the police, not only because of their limited remunerative possibilities, but because of the fear of police or prosecutorial retribution against their other clients. Foote suggests that the maximum deterrent effect can be achieved through a tort remedy by providing for minimum liquidated damages. In this way, lower income or "less respectable" victims may be able to sue successfully. A § 1983 action, which provides for exemplary damages, avoids some of the drawbacks of common law tort remedies. However, proof of the requisite intent and measuring the value of constitutional rights impose additional problems.

If the plaintiff receives a substantial damage award, the final problem is collecting on the judgment. Where sovereign immunity prevents actions

39. In Malley v. Briggs, 475 U.S. 335 (1986), the Court adopted the good faith standard it had established in *Leon* in the context of liability of officers who seek a warrant without having probable cause. The Court rejected an argument that police should have absolute immunity if a magistrate issues a warrant. Justice White's opinion for the Court states that the question to be asked is "whether a reasonably well-trained officer * * * would have known that his affidavit failed to establish probable cause and that he should not have applied for the warrant." The opinion observes that "[i]t is true that in an ideal system an unreasonable request for a warrant would be harmless, because no judge would approve it," but that "ours is not an ideal system, and it is possible that a magistrate, working under docket pressures, will fail to perform as a magistrate should."

The Court specifically held in Anderson v. Creighton, 483 U.S. 635 (1987), that the qualified immunity doctrine applied to police officers. The case arose when an FBI agent searched the Creightons' home without a warrant in the unsuccessful attempt to find a robbery suspect.

Justice Scalia wrote for the Supreme Court as it held that the officer is entitled to summary judgment on qualified immunity grounds if he can establish as a matter of law that a reasonable officer could have believed that the search comported with the Fourth Amendment, even though it did not. He rejected the Creightons' argument that qualified immunity should only protect reasonable official action and that an unreasonable search under the Fourth Amendment cannot be reasonable official action.

against the government, a plaintiff is left to attempt recovery from the offending officers, who are often unable to pay. One proposed solution is to require an official bond for policemen that covers constitutional violations. Comment, Search and Seizure in Illinois: Enforcement of Constitutional Right of Privacy, 47 Nw.U.L.Rev. 493 (1952).

Foote recommends three steps which would strengthen the deterrent effects of the tort remedy. First, the government should be made liable for illegal police behavior. Not only would this provide a financially responsible defendant, but it would apply the deterrent at the level where policy is made. In economic terms, it would place liability on the party in the best position to spread the losses due to inevitable police illegality, and to control and minimize the risk. Second, a provision for minimum liquidated damages should be created. Third, evidence as to past reputation should be inadmissible either to prove probable cause or to mitigate damages, unless special damages are sought.

Would a fortified tort remedy alone provide adequate protection of Fourth Amendment rights? The purported success of the tort remedy in Canada has often been cited as proof of its potential in the United States. See Spiotto, Search and Seizure Problem—Two Approaches: The Canadian Tort Remedy and the United States Exclusionary Rule, 1 J. of Police Science Admin. 36 (1976). However, the Canadian experience differs in several major respects, which may make the analogy futile. In his study of law enforcement in Ontario, Spiotto noted that the attitudes of the police, and of the public toward the police, differed drastically from those found in the United States. Within police departments, greater emphasis was placed on fairness and the importance of maintaining a favorable image. These attitudes were reinforced by strict internal discipline. Toronto citizens were seen as more law-abiding, and more supportive and respectful of the police. In addition, there is less serious crime than in the United States. The government is liable in tort for police misconduct, and Canadian juries show little reluctance to find the police liable. In summary, police-community relations in Canada, until recently, appeared to be a model well worth emulating. However, it is not at all clear that the effective tort remedy was responsible for this "utopian" situation, as much as it was a product thereof. Rather than proving the potential benefits of a solid tort action in this country, it highlights the fact that the best way to protect constitutional rights is to improve the attitudes of both the police and the public toward law enforcement.[40]

Would a strengthened tort remedy be effective as a supplement to the exclusionary rule, or to some other judicial or administrative scheme? Recall Chief Justice Burger's proposal, in his *Bivens* dissent, for a quasi-judicial body to adjudicate damage claims.

Criminal prosecution of offending officers is often suggested as the only real deterrent to police misconduct. A federal statute has been in existence since 1921 which makes federal officers who participate in illegal searches guilty of a misdemeanor and subject to substantial fines. 18 U.S.C.A. § 2236.

40. For a discussion of the exclusionary rule in Germany, see Bradley, The Exclusionary Rule in Germany, 96 Harv.L.Rev. 1032 (1983). Pakter, Exclusionary Rules in France, Germany and Italy, 9 Hastings Int'l & Compar.L.Rev. 1, 34 (1985), concludes that the three European countries exclude evidence obtained through illegal searches, although "each country has reached this result in its own way."

However, no officer has ever been convicted under the statute. Many states have similar statutes, which remain dormant. See, e.g., Va.Code Ann. § 19.2–59.

Why has there been such a dearth of prosecutions? The most likely answer is that prosecutors are reluctant to press charges against the police, except in the most extreme cases, because they rely heavily on cooperation with the department. In addition, juries are reluctant to convict policemen of crime. More fundamentally, it can be argued that the threat of a direct criminal sanction on the officer is an over-deterrent. It may lead to an officer "second-guessing" himself in developing situations, in such a way that effective law enforcement would be hindered and public safety endangered. The systemic deterrence provided by the exclusionary rule is probably more appropriate in these circumstances.

A third alternative—or supplementary—remedy for Fourth Amendment violations is police regulation and discipline. The primary emphasis is on the development of respect for constitutional rights, so as to discourage infringements, rather than on compensation of individual victims. These goals can be achieved through a number of processes: internal disciplinary measures, civilian review boards, or "rulemaking."

Internal discipline, while probably the preferred remedy among police administrators, has not proved effective as a supplement to the suppression doctrine. In a study of the Chicago Police Department, J.E. Spiotto found that disciplinary action was taken against officers primarily for corrupt practices. Spiotto, An Empirical Study of the Exclusionary Rule and its Alternatives, 2 J. Legal Studies 243 (1973). Insofar as searches are concerned, suspension or dismissal were used almost exclusively in cases where officers failed to inventory all they seized. A search which was neither brutal nor outrageous would not result in disciplinary action, even if a citizen's complaint was filed. In part, this was a reflection of the Department's view that the exclusionary rule was the mechanism for punishing overzealous searches. But it could also be indicative of what several commentators have found to be the fundamental flaw of using internal disciplinary processes to deter illegal searches: Much of the illegality occurs in the normal scope of police activity and is subtly condoned by administrators and prosecutors who ignore violations as a matter of practice.

These same aspects of bureaucratic organization and personality tend to limit the effectiveness of citizen review boards as watchdogs of Fourth Amendment rights. Like police disciplinary committees, the review boards deal primarily with police corruption and brutality, or other outrageous police conduct. They have neither the time nor the resources to investigate routine illegal searches. Furthermore, the hostility and distrust with which these boards are often viewed by police make it unlikely that any action they take would significantly influence police attitudes. See J. Hudson, Police Review Boards and Police Accountability, 36 L. & Contemp.Prob. 515 (1971).

Another proposal which warrants consideration is the adoption of a constitutional requirement of "rulemaking." Rulemaking involves the publication of regulations and standards to govern the scope of searches and seizures. The rules could be formulated by either legislative or police committees, but the essence of the proposal is that the articulated standards are open to community scrutiny and input. The rules, which would necessarily meet all Fourth

Amendment requirements and would be subject to judicial review, would work in conjunction with the exclusionary rule—i.e., evidence obtained in a search which did not adhere to regulations would be excluded. In addition, promotions would be contingent on an officer's record of conformance to regulations.

The doctrinal and practical advantages of requiring rulemaking are discussed in Amsterdam, Perspectives on the Fourth Amendment, 58 Minn.L.Rev. 349 (1974). Amsterdam argues that rulemaking provides a safeguard against arbitrary search and seizure without requiring the creation of new exceptions to the warrant requirement. It allows for flexibility and local autonomy, and permits the Court to extend Fourth Amendment coverage to police activities which demand control against abuse, but do not lend themselves to regulation by warrants or probable cause standards—e.g., border searches and driver's license checks.

Amsterdam maintains that rulemaking also improves police performance. It enhances the quality of police decisions by focusing attention on the importance of making policy, rather than on case-by-case, after-the-fact line-drawing. Police actions are made fairer and more consistent because the rulemaking process, being subject to community scrutiny, is less influenced by bias than discretionary decisions by individual officers at the scene of a crime.

Rulemaking also increases the visibility of police policy decisions. Amsterdam concludes that the process offers the best possibility for changing police attitudes toward constitutional liberties because police-made rules are most likely to be understood, enforced and obeyed by the police.

Does rulemaking provide the answer to the problem of deterring illegal searches and seizures? If underlying attitudes remain the same, will rulemaking be seen as something other than an attempt to limit the power of the police? If the proposal successfully changed the attitudes of the public and the police, would the exclusionary rule still be necessary, or would internal discipline do the job? Is there any other way to litigate the constitutionality of a department's regulations than by invoking the protections of the exclusionary rule?

Injunctions against unconstitutional police practices are possible in rare cases, see e.g., Allee v. Medrano, 416 U.S. 802 (1974); Lankford v. Gelston, 364 F.2d 197 (4th Cir. 1966); Commonwealth v. Porter, 480 F.Supp. 686 (W.D.Pa. 1979). But Rizzo v. Goode, 423 U.S. 362 (1976), suggests that, before equitable relief is granted, practices must be widespread and involve policy-making officials in a department. Goldman & Puro, Decertification of Police: An alternative to Traditional Remedies for Police Misconduct, 15 Hastings Const. L.Q. 45 (1987), examines the possible remedy of revoking an officer's state certification for constitutional violations.

What remedies would you require for Fourth Amendment violations?

Chapter Three

SELF-INCRIMINATION AND CONFESSIONS

I. THE PRIVILEGE AGAINST SELF-INCRIMINATION

A. HISTORY OF THE RIGHT AGAINST SELF-INCRIMINATION

1. The English History

The right against compulsory self-incrimination cannot be found in the Magna Carta, the English Bill of Rights, or any of the legal documents proclaiming the fundamental liberties of Englishmen. However, by the end of the seventeenth century, the privilege was unquestionably established as a tenet of the common law, and a century later, it was explicitly incorporated into the Constitutions of the United States and nine of the original states. While the existence of some form of the privilege is clear throughout various stages of history, the reasons for the development into its present form are much less so. A comprehensive history of the privilege can be found in The Origins of the Fifth Amendment (1968) by Professor Leonard W. Levy. A brief summary and excerpts from that history follow.

The privilege had its roots in opposition to the oath *ex officio,* which was administered in the ecclesiastical courts and the Courts of Star Chamber and High Commission. Unlike the common law courts, these institutions employed an inquisitional style of adjudication, which bore some resemblance to that used during the Inquisition on the Continent. Suspects were forced to swear under oath to answer truthfully all questions put to them by the court. Objections arose because the oath was required of a suspect before he was informed of the charges against him, the identity of his accusers, or the nature of the evidence against him. Thus a defendant who had in fact committed a crime was forced to accuse himself or risk the temporal and spiritual consequences of perjury.

When the oath was abolished, along with the Courts of Star Chamber and High Commission in 1641, attention turned to the common law courts. The oath administered there had not been the subject of controversy because it was required of defendants only after a formal charge had been announced. A defendant could refuse to answer questions, but might thereby subject himself to pressure from the court, and his silence would be taken as evidence of guilt. By the late 17th century, the notion had developed that a defendant should not be forced to answer questions that would put his "life or limb" in jeopardy. Professor Levy explains the development of this principle:

> The *nemo tenetur* maxim [no man is bound to accuse himself] had come a long way from its mysterious origins. Reputedly a canon-law maxim, it had never existed in any canon-law text. At best there was the general principle in Gratian, wiped out by Innocent III, Aquinas, and the Inquisition, that no man had to come forward voluntarily to confess a crime for which he was not even suspected. Gradually that came to mean that no one was bound to take an oath requiring him to answer truthfully to interrogatories concerning his guilt if he was merely suspected and had not been formally charged with crime. There was a natural repugnance to self-destruction, opposition to the oath as a form of spiritual torment, and conscientious objection to forswearing oneself. Conscience and an unwillingness to supply the evidence to convict oneself remained major forces against the oath; when it was abolished, they remained reasons for refusing to answer incriminating interrogatories.
>
> * * * The customary accusatorial system of criminal justice, consecrated by the symbolism of Magna Carta and then by the Petition of Right, fortified depiction of the oath as an instrumentality of the inquisitorial system, alien and contrary to the old liberties of the subject. Opposition to the oath came to focus on the fact that it compelled self-incrimination. * * * To furnish testimonial evidence against himself, with or without oath, was likened to drawing one's blood, running oneself upon the pikes, or cutting one's throat with one's tongue. Thus, the initially vague maxim that no man is bound to accuse himself had come to mean that he was not required to answer against himself in any criminal cause or to any interrogatories that might tend to expose him to prosecution.
>
> * * *

The Origins of the Fifth Amendment, supra, at 329–30.

About this same time, criminal defendants were disqualified from testifying under oath at trial because of the belief that, as an interested party, a defendant could not be trusted to testify truthfully. Thus the privilege against self-incrimination lost its importance in the trial context. However, the common law had long sanctioned inquisitorial preliminary examinations. While physical torture was illegal as a means of procuring confessions, the coercive practices used often approached those of the secret inquisitions on the Continent. Gradually, the rule developed that confessions forced in this manner could not be used against the defendant at trial because coerced confessions were not reliable. Thus, this rule against forced confessions became the principal bulwark of the privilege in the eighteenth century.

Professor Levy discusses the political and philosophical forces which contributed to the development of the privilege in the following excerpt:

> The claim to the right emerged in inquisitorial examinations, initially conducted by the Church, then by the State. It emerged also in the context of the great political struggle for constitutional limitations on arbitrary prerogative; during the late sixteenth century and early seventeenth, it was a focal point in that struggle to establish individual liberties and more representative government.
>
> * * *

> The claim to this right also emerged in the context of a whole cluster of criminal procedures whose object was to ensure fair play to the criminally accused. It harmonized with the principles that the accused was innocent until proved guilty and that the burden of proof was on the prosecution. It was related to the idea that a man's home should not be promiscuously broken into and rifled for evidence of his reading and writing. It was intimately connected to the belief that torture or any cruelty in forcing a man to expose his guilt was unfair and illegal. It was indirectly associated with the right to counsel and to have witnesses on behalf of the defendant, so that his lips could be sealed against the government's questions or accusations. It was at first a privilege of the guilty, given the nature of the substantive law of religious and political crimes. It was also a protection of the innocent. But the right became neither a privilege of the guilty nor a protection of the innocent. It became merely one of the ways of fairly determining guilt or innocence, like trial by jury itself; it became part of the due process of the law, a fundamental principle of the accusatorial system. The right implied a humane or ethical standard in judging a person accused of crime, regardless how heinous the crime or strong the evidence of his guilt. It reflected consideration for the human personality in that respect, but it also reflected the view that society benefited by seeking his conviction without the aid of his involuntary admissions. Forcing self-incrimination was thought not only to brutalize the system of criminal justice but to produce weak and untrustworthy evidence.
>
> Above all, the right was most closely linked to freedom of religion and speech. It was, in its origins, unquestionably the invention of those who were guilty of religious crimes, like heresy, schism, and nonconformity, and, later, of political crimes like treason, seditious libel, and breach of parliamentary privilege—more often than not, the offense was merely criticism of the government, its policies, or its officers. The right was associated then with guilt for crimes of conscience, of belief, and of association. In the broadest sense it was a protection not of the guilty, or of the innocent, but of freedom of expression, of political liberty, of the right to worship as one pleased. * * * The symbolic importance and practical function of the right was certainly a settled matter, taken for granted, in the eighteenth century. And before that it was part of the heritage of liberty which the common law bequeathed to the English settlers in America.

The Origins of the Fifth Amendment, supra, at 331–32.

2. *The History in the Colonies*

Settlement of the American colonies began at a time when opposition to the oath in the ecclesiastical courts was strongest and when the privilege was beginning to take hold in the common law courts. In fact, the Puritans, who played a major role in colonizing the new world, had been the most adamant supporters of the right in England. By 1652, provisions had been enacted in Massachusetts, Connecticut, and Virginia that protected defendants from the use of torture to coerce confessions, and in Massachusetts, the inquisitional oath was also prohibited. Even where it remained uncodified, the privilege was generally recognized as part of that body of common law which had been collectively adopted in most of the colonies.

The American insistence on constitutionalizing the common law privilege has been attributed to abuses in the prerogative courts established in the colonies. A major source of discontent—and cause of the Revolution—was the perceived failure of the Crown to protect the colonists' rights as Englishmen. Those rights which had remained as unwritten principles of the common law were now thought to require the explicit protections of a written document.

In June 1776, shortly before the Declaration of Independence was signed, Virginia adopted a Declaration of Rights drafted by George Mason. Section 8 provided that in all capital or criminal prosecutions, a man cannot "be compelled to give evidence against himself." Eight states followed Virginia's example, enacting bills of rights which protected the privilege in language similar to that used by Mason. However, that language was significantly more restrictive than the common law right as it existed at that time in England or the colonies. Taken literally, it suggested that the privilege could only be invoked by a criminal defendant at trial, whereas the common law had extended the right to witnesses and parties in civil cases, preliminary examinations, and even legislative hearings. Professor Levy suggests that Section 8 was the product of poor draftsmanship, rather than a deliberate attempt to restrict the privilege. Mason could not have intended what he said, because criminal defendants had no right to testify under oath at trial, thereby rendering the provision meaningless as written. Furthermore, there is no evidence that the provision effected any restrictive changes in Virginia criminal procedure.

The language with which the right is expressed in the Fifth Amendment differs from that found in these earlier documents. As first proposed by James Madison, the principle that "no man * * * shall be compelled to be a witness against himself" was included in a miscellaneous article that included due process and double jeopardy clauses. Not only was his placement of the clause unusual, being separate from the articles enumerating procedural rights of criminal defendants, but the phrasing was unique. Both suggested a very broad privilege, extending to witnesses and parties in almost any legal proceeding, and permitting invocation whenever civil penalties or even public disgrace were at stake.

Madison's proposal was amended in the House, apparently without debate, to confine the privilege to criminal cases. The Senate adopted the clause as amended. Levy argued that its inclusion in the Fifth Amendment, rather than in the Sixth, which establishes post-indictment procedural rights, proves that the privilege was intended to extend to witnesses and to all stages of criminal proceedings. For a conflicting interpretation of colonial history, see L. Mayers, Shall We Amend the Fifth Amendment, 178–92 (1959). Mayers maintains that the language of the earliest state and federal provisions indicated the framers' intent not to constitutionalize the witness' privilege.

It is difficult to prove—or to disprove—whether the framers intended the Fifth Amendment to be co-extensive with the common law. Few references to the privilege can be found in records of debates in Congress or the ratifying state conventions. Those that do exist mention it only as a privilege against torture. The earliest state and federal cases after adoption of the Amendment were consistent with the historical applications of the common law right in England and the colonies. Thus, the framers' intent is more profitably sought in the history of the privilege than in literal construction of the ambiguous terms of the Amendment. In the words of Justice Frankfurter: "The privilege against self-incrimination is a specific provision of which it is peculiarly true that 'a page of history is worth a volume of logic' ". Ullmann v. United States, 350 U.S. 422, 438 (1956) (quoting New York Trust Co. v. Eisner, 256 U.S. 345, 349 (1921)).

For a further look at that history, see Pittman, The Colonial and Constitutional History of the Privilege Against Self-Incrimination in America, 21 Va.L.Rev. 763 (1935).

B. THE POLICIES OF THE PRIVILEGE AGAINST SELF-INCRIMINATION

1. The Need to Examine Policies

Judge Friendly pointed out the need for careful examination of the privilege in his oft-cited article, The Fifth Amendment Tomorrow: The Case For Constitutional Change, 37 U.Cin.L.Rev. 679–81, 698 (1968):

Reexamination of the policies of the privilege is not a task undertaken with alacrity. * * * But it is indispensable to any reconsideration of the proper scope of the fifth amendment and peculiarly necessary because of the extent to which eloquent phrases have been accepted as a substitute for thorough thought. It is still true, as Bentham wrote 140 years ago, that the main obstacle to rational discussion of the privilege is

> the *assumption of the propriety of the rule,* as a proposition too plainly true to admit of dispute * * *. By assuming it as true, you * * * represent all men * * * whose opinions are worth regarding, as joining in the opinion; and by this means * * * you present * * * the fear of incurring the indignation or contempt of all reasonable men, by presuming to disbelieve or doubt what all such reasonable men are assured of.

A good way to start dissipating the lyricism now generally accompanying any reference to the privilege is to note how exceptional it is in the general setting of jurisprudence and morality. While it carries the burden of impeding ascertainment of the truth that is common to all testimonial privileges, it has uncommon burdens as well. Most other privileges, for example, communications between husband and wife, attorney and client, doctor and patient, priest and penitent, promote and preserve relationships possessing social value. Yet the law has rather steadfastly resisted their expansion, even to a profession having such strong claims as accountancy. In contrast, the fifth amendment privilege extends, by hypothesis, only to persons who have been breakers of the criminal law or believe they may be charged as such.

Again, while the other privileges accord with notions of decent conduct generally accepted in life outside the court room, the privilege against self-incrimination defies them. No parent would teach such a doctrine to his children; the lesson parents preach is that while a misdeed, even a serious one, will generally be forgiven, a failure to make a clean breast of it will not be. Every hour of the day people are being asked to explain their conduct to parents, employers and teachers. Those who are questioned consider themselves to be morally bound to respond, and the questioners believe it proper to take action if they do not.

Finally, the privilege, at least in its pre-trial application, seriously impedes the state in the most basic of all tasks, "to provide for the security of the individual and his property," not only as against the individual asserting the privilege but as against others who it has reason to think were associated with him. The privilege not only stands in the way of convictions but often prevents restitution to the victim—of goods, of money, even of a kidnapped child. In contrast to the rare case where it may protect an innocent person, it often may do the contrary. A man in suspicious circumstances but not in fact guilty is deprived of official interrogation of another whom he knows to be the true culprit; if the former is brought to trial, the best he can do is call the latter as a witness and hope the jury will draw the inference from the witness' assertion of the privilege which the jury cannot be told it may do with respect to his own.

One would suppose that such a collection of detriments would have led the Supreme Court to expound the basis for the privilege thoughtfully and carefully before asking the country to accept extensions in no way called for by the fifth amendment's words or history. It thus is strange how rarely one encounters in the Court's opinions on the privilege the careful weighing of *pros* and *cons,* the objective investigation of how rules of law actually work, and, above all, the consideration whether a less extreme position might not adequately meet the needs of the accused without jeopardizing other important interests, which ought to characterize constitutional adjudication before the Court goes beyond the ordinary meaning of the language. Instead, the privilege is treated with almost religious adulation, of which Mr. Justice Douglas' footnote reference to the *Halakhah* which "discards confessions in toto, and this because of its psychological insight and its concern for saving man from his own destructive inclination," is a striking recent example.

See also Tague, The Fifth Amendment: If an Aid to the Guilty Defendant, an Impediment to an Innocent One, 78 Geo.L.J. 1 (1989) (Fifth Amendment "can shackle the innocent defendant from attempting to prove that another person committed the crime").

---

2. *A Chart to Assist Analysis*

The chart below lists the most commonly offered justifications for the privilege against self-incrimination, critical responses to those justifications, and sources wherein these arguments are discussed.[1] As you study the chart, consider which of the asserted policies are valid rationales for the privilege. Which responses adequately dispose of the policy arguments? Are there convincing responses to any of the criticisms? To all of them?

1. Sources that are referred to several times are cited in shorthand form. The full citations follow:

Murphy v. Waterfront Comm., 378 U.S. 52 (1964).

Fortas, The Fifth Amendment: Nemo Tenetur Prodere Seipsum, 25 Clev.Bar Assn.J. 91 (1954).

Friendly, The Fifth Amendment Tomorrow: The Case for Constitutional Change, 37 U.Cin. L.Rev. 671 (1968).

McKay, Self-Incrimination and the New Privacy, 1967 Sup.Ct.Rev. 193.

L. Mayers, Shall We Amend the Fifth Amendment (1959).

8 J. Wigmore, Evidence in Trials at Common Law (McNaughten rev. 1961).

The usual rationales for the privilege against self-incrimination are found wanting in Dolinko, Is There a Rationale for the Privilege Against Self-Incrimination, 33 U.C.L.A.L.Rev. 1963 (1986). For a discussion of the debate on the privilege in England, see Gerstein, The Self-Incrimination Debate in Great Britain, 27 Am.J.Comp.L. 81 (1979).

Justification	Criticisms
1. *Protection of the Innocent:* The privilege protects the innocent defendant from convicting himself by a bad performance on the witness stand. *Murphy,* 378 U.S. at 55 (quoting Quinn v. United States, 349 U.S. 155, 162 (1955); Mayers, at 61.	1. The Supreme Court has explicitly disclaimed this rationale. Tehan v. United States ex rel. Shott, 382 U.S. 406, 415–16 (1966). There is no proof that it protects the innocent. In fact, juries are unlikely to give a defendant the benefit of such an innocent explanation of his silence in the face of evidence against him. Mayers, at 26, 61–67. Nor should the innocent defendant fear taking the stand since jurors often sympathize with the defendant who is subjected to brutal questioning. A. Train, From the District Attorney's Office 97 (1939). It is possible that an innocent defendant will invoke the privilege to avoid impeachment with prior convictions. However, the problem of impeachment does not require a constitutionally-based solution protecting all defendants. A better solution is to impose appropriate limitations on the use of prior convictions. See Montana Rule of Evidence 609 (prior convictions not admissible to attack credibility). Finally, the privilege historically—and by hypothesis—protects the guilty, i.e., those whose testimony would implicate them of a crime. Fortas, at 98–100.
2. *The Cruel Trilemma:* We are unwilling to subject those suspected of crime to the cruel trilemma of self-accusation, perjury or contempt. Brown v. Walker, 161 U.S. 591, 637 (1896) (Field, J., dissenting).	2. First, this problem is not peculiar to self-incrimination: it exists whenever a witness is reluctant to testify for whatever reason. Wigmore, § 2251, at 316. Second, is it necessarily cruel to create a situation where perjury is an option? "The prevalence of perjury today leads one to doubt that it is thought by the average witness as a soul-destroying experience." Wigmore, § 2251, at 316–17. Finally, this argument can only justify the privilege at trial. Where police questioning is involved, false answers are not perjury and contempt cannot be used against one who refuses to answer. Wigmore, § 2252, n. 27. See also W. Schaefer, The Suspect and Society 17–18 (1967). We do subject friends, lovers, parents, teachers, and most people to the discomfort of having to testify against individuals about whom they might care the most.
3. *Deter Perjury:* The absence of a privilege encourages perjury which burdens the courts. Wigmore, § 2251, at 311.	3. Perjury is prevalent despite the existence of the privilege. Silence is also a burden on the truth-finding function of the criminal process. Friendly, at 680. There is no reason to believe that a defendant who concludes that perjury will succeed will not attempt it. Nor is there reason to believe that a defendant who concludes that perjury will fail will attempt it or succeed if an attempt is made.

Justification	Criticisms
4. *Unreliability of Coerced Statements:* We do not trust self-deprecatory statements, particularly when they are the product of coercion. *Murphy,* 378 U.S. at 55; Michigan v. Tucker, 417 U.S. 433, 448–49 (1974).	4. If reliability is the primary concern, there is no need to exclude compelled evidence that can be independently corroborated, nor physical evidence extracted from a defendant. Moreover, testimony at trial is likely to be cast by the defense in its most favorable light. It will not always be self-deprecatory. Also, it is more likely to be reliable than statements obtained by police interrogation, which are admitted as evidence.
5. *Preference for Accusatorial System:* We prefer an accusatorial rather than inquisitorial system of criminal justice. *Murphy,* 378 U.S. at 55.	5. "Language like this, no matter how often repeated, no matter how eloquently intoned, is merely restatement of the privilege itself." McKay, at 209.
6. *Deter Improper Police Practices:* Self-incriminating statements are likely to be elicited by inhumane treatment and abuses. The privilege has historically protected against such forms of torture. *Murphy,* 378 U.S. at 55.	6. Torture is unacceptable on its own merits, regardless of the existence of a privilege. Wigmore, § 2251, at 315. The privilege is unnecessary to guard against objectionable police practices—adequate protection is afforded by the Due Process clauses of the Fifth and Fourteenth Amendments. Cf. Rogers v. Richmond, 365 U.S. 534 (1961); Rochin v. California, 342 U.S. 165 (1952); Watts v. Indiana, 338 U.S. 49 (1949). Testimony in court is subject to the safeguards of the judicial process.
7. *Fair State-Individual Balance:* "The privilege contributes towards a fair state-individual balance by requiring the government to leave the individual alone until good cause is shown for disturbing him and by requiring the government in its contest with the individual to shoulder the entire load." Wigmore, § 2251, at 317.	7. First, the probable cause requirements for search and arrest provide adequate protection against unwarranted governmental disturbance. Second, the argument depends on unprovable assumptions about the terms of the Lockian social contract upon which our government is based, i.e., did the sovereign individual yield to the sovereign state the power to extract evidence of his own guilt? *Compare* Friendly, at 692–93, *with* Fortas, at 98–100. Third, the argument relies on a notion of the criminal trial as "a jousting contest where the rules bear equally on both participants and neither is expected to be of the slightest help to the other"—a concept which bears no relation to reality. For example, the state and the defendant operate under different rules for discovery, appeal and burdens of proof. Cf. Michigan v. Tucker, 417 U.S. 433, 449–50 (1974). Finally, even assuming that the ideal balance between state and defendant could be determined, manipulating the scope of the privilege is not necessarily the best way to achieve that balance. Friendly, at 693–94.
8. *Preservation of Official Morality:* "Any system * * * which permits the prosecution to trust habitually to com-	8. Wigmore's statement was based on two debatable assumptions: First, he believed the privilege applied only in the

Justification	Criticisms
pulsory self-disclosure as a source of proof must itself suffer morally thereby. 8 J. Wigmore, § 2251 (3d ed. 1940). *Cf.* Tehan v. Shott, 382 U.S. 406, 415 (1966).	courtroom. When extended to the stationhouse, this rationale would disallow most police questioning—an untenable proposition. Second, he assumed that the privilege developed historically because the balance struck by the English judicial system had become morally unacceptable. Friendly, at 691.
9. *Privacy Rationale:* "Our respect for the inviolability of the human personality and of the right of each individual 'to a private enclave where he may lead a private life'" justifies the privilege. *Murphy,* 378 U.S. at 55 (quoting United States v. Grunewald, 233 F.2d 556, 581–82 (2d Cir. 1956) (Frank, J., dissenting)). See also, Fried, Privacy, 77 Yale L.J. 475, 488–89 (1968); McKay, at 212.	9. If the basis for the privilege is a general freedom of silence to protect one's privacy, it is inconsistent first, with immunity statutes which require testimony; second, with rules requiring information of a far more private nature in civil suits (e.g., annulment suits); and third, with the Fourth Amendment, which clearly does protect privacy, but only to the extent that intrusions are unreasonable. This rationale enjoys historical support only when crimes of belief or association are involved. It is immoral to suggest that a murderer in a typical criminal case is justified in withholding his aid because he "prefers to remain in a 'private enclave.'" Friendly, at 689–90.
10. *First Amendment Rationale:* The privilege affords "a shelter against governmental snooping and oppression concerning political and religious beliefs." Friendly, at 696.	10. The First Amendment is the appropriate vehicle for dealing with this problem, as the Court implicitly recognized in cases such as NAACP v. Alabama, 357 U.S. 449 (1958). Furthermore, this justification, even if valid, would apply only in free speech, religion, or association situations, not in the typical criminal investigation and prosecution. Wigmore, § 2251, at 314.

Consider how one's choice of rationale necessarily affects one's view of the legitimate scope of the Amendment. For example, if the privilege is primarily intended to prevent "the cruel trilemma" and to deter perjury, then it should be applicable only when testimony under oath is involved. If one is concerned that the government bear its burden of proof without assistance, then voice or handwriting exemplars and other physical evidence extracted from a defendant would be protected. In the cases that follow, try to determine which policies underlie the Supreme Court's analysis of the privilege. Are those policies defensible? Do they emerge inexorably from the language or background of the privilege? Do the policies identified in particular cases support the result reached by the Court in these cases? Are the policies consistently applied?

C. SCOPE OF THE PRIVILEGE

1. Proceedings in Which the Privilege Applies

Read literally, the language of the Fifth Amendment privilege would seem to indicate that the privilege against self-incrimination applies only to testimony sought to be compelled in a criminal case. However, the Supreme Court has consistently given the privilege a very broad interpretation, holding that it

> not only protects the individual against being involuntarily called as a witness against himself in a criminal prosecution but also privileges him not to answer official questions put to him in any other proceeding, civil or criminal, formal or informal, where his answers might incriminate him in future criminal proceedings.

Lefkowitz v. Turley, 414 U.S. 70, 77 (1973).

This policy of liberal interpretation was first articulated in Boyd v. United States, 116 U.S. 616 (1886). *Boyd* involved a forfeiture proceeding, pursuant to a statute authorizing the government to appropriate any goods about which an owner had made false statements with intent to defraud the revenue. The trial court had ordered appellants to produce an invoice under the authority of a statute which provided that failure to comply with such an order was tantamount to a confession of guilt. The appellant complied under protest and subsequently suffered a forfeiture judgment. After first holding that the use of the subpoena was an unreasonable seizure in violation of the Fourth Amendment, the Court turned to the Fifth Amendment and the relationship between the two provisions.

> We have already noticed the intimate relation between the two amendments. They throw great light on each other. For the "unreasonable searches and seizures" condemned in the Fourth Amendment are almost always made for the purpose of compelling a man to give evidence against himself, which in criminal cases is condemned in the Fifth Amendment; and compelling a man "in a criminal case to be a witness against himself," which is condemned in the Fifth Amendment, throws light on the question as to what is an "unreasonable search and seizure" within the meaning of the Fourth Amendment. And we have been unable to perceive that the seizure of a man's private books and papers to be used in evidence against him is substantially different from compelling him to be a witness against himself. We think it is within the clear intent and meaning of those terms. We are also clearly of opinion that proceedings instituted for the purpose of declaring the forfeiture of a man's property by reason of offences committed by him, though they may be civil in form, are in their nature criminal. * * * If the government prosecutor elects to waive an indictment, and to file a civil information against the claimants—that is civil in form—can he by this device take from the proceeding its criminal aspect and deprive the claimants of their immunities as citizens, and extort from them a production of their private papers, or, as an alternative, a confession of guilt? This cannot be. The information, though technically a civil proceeding, is in substance and effect a criminal one. * * * As, therefore, suits for penalties and forfeitures incurred by the commission of offences against the law, are of this quasi-criminal nature, we think that they are within the reason of criminal proceedings for all the purposes of the Fourth Amendment of the Constitution, and of that portion of the Fifth Amendment which declares that no person shall be compelled in any criminal case to be a witness against himself; and we are further of opinion that a compulsory production of the private books and papers of the owner of goods sought to be forfeited in such a suit is compelling him to be a witness against himself, within the meaning of the Fifth Amendment to the Constitution, and is the equivalent of a search and seizure—and an unreasonable search and seizure—within the meaning of the Fourth Amendment.

In *Boyd,* the Court took an expansive view of the privilege, finding not only that a forfeiture proceeding was a "criminal case," but that the subpoenaing of business records was equivalent to compelling a person to be a witness against himself. The latter point will be considered in detail later in the chapter.

The broad construction of the "criminal case" requirement was reaffirmed a few years later in Counselman v. Hitchcock, 142 U.S. 547, 562 (1892). The issue in *Counselman* was whether a grand jury witness could claim the privilege. The Court held that a grand jury investigation of a criminal matter was a "criminal case," but the language and analysis of the opinion suggested that the privilege was available in *any* proceeding, when the testimony sought from a party or witness might later be used in a criminal prosecution against that person.

> It is impossible that the meaning of the constitutional provision can only be, that a person shall not be compelled to be a witness against himself in a criminal prosecution against himself. It would doubtless cover such cases; but it is not limited to them. The object was to insure that a person should not be compelled, when acting as a witness in any investigation, to give testimony which might tend to show that he himself had committed a crime. The privilege is limited to criminal matters, but it is as broad as the mischief against which it seeks to guard.

Thus, *Boyd* and *Counselman* established that a person called as a witness in any federal proceeding could invoke the privilege against self-incrimination to avoid testifying to matters that could possibly tend to be damaging in a subsequent criminal prosecution. These decisions now bind the states as well as the federal government.

2. *Criminal Cases*

Boyd and *Counselman* make clear that the privilege against self-incrimination is available whenever the proceeding in which testimony is sought can itself be characterized as a criminal case, or when the compelled testimony might be used against the witness in a later criminal proceeding. However, the *use* of compelled testimony other than in a criminal case does not implicate the Fifth Amendment. See Piemonte v. United States, 367 U.S. 556 (1961) (privilege does not prevent use of compelled testimony for purposes of private retribution). What makes a proceeding a "criminal case?" [2] *Boyd* held that the potential penalties made a forfeiture proceeding criminal. In *Counselman,* the grand jury investigation focused on violations of federal criminal law; the privilege claim was honored because the witness was concerned about a possible criminal trial, which is the undisputed criminal case. In re Gault, 387 U.S. 1 (1967), held that juvenile delinquency proceedings are criminal cases for Fifth Amendment purposes, even though they were labeled "civil" by most states.

When incarceration is not available as a penalty, a legislative determination that a proceeding is "civil" is more likely to be upheld today than when *Boyd* was decided. United States v. L. O. Ward, 448 U.S. 242 (1980), held for example, that a statute imposing a "civil penalty" upon persons discharging

2. This question was asked in Chapter One. It is repeated here to demonstrate how courts have struggled to answer it with respect to a particular constitutional provision.

hazardous material into navigable waters was not "quasi-criminal" so as to invalidate a reporting requirement imposed upon polluters. The Court distinguished *Boyd* and several other forfeiture cases, suggesting that they involved penalties that had no correlation with the damages sustained by society or the costs of enforcing the law. It also noted that in *Boyd* the forfeiture provision was listed along with fine and imprisonment as possible punishments for customs fraud. Finally, the Court noted that the applicable civil and criminal remedies are contained in separate statutes enacted 70 years apart and that the civil statute has a use immunity provision preventing reported information from being used in criminal prosecutions. Justice Stevens dissented.

In Allen v. Illinois, 478 U.S. 364 (1986), the Court held 5–4, that proceedings under Illinois' Sexually Dangerous Persons Act were not criminal for self-incrimination purposes. Thus, the state court properly relied upon statements made by an individual to psychiatrists who examined him to determine whether he should be committed for treatment under the Act. The argument for applying the privilege focused on the fact that the state could not file a petition under the Act unless it had already filed criminal charges, the Act provided some of the same safeguards found in criminal proceedings, and a person committed for treatment was kept in a maximum security institution that also housed prisoners in need of psychiatric care. Justice Rehnquist's majority opinion stated that the question of whether a proceeding is criminal for Fifth Amendment purposes was "first of all a question of statutory construction." The majority relied heavily on the fact that the Illinois Legislature had expressly provided that proceedings under the Act would "be civil in nature." Justice Rehnquist concluded that the fact that the state has chosen to limit proceedings under the Act to persons charged with criminal acts did not turn a civil proceeding into a criminal one. Nor did the presence of some safeguards also found in criminal cases do so. The majority found that the conditions of the institution were not incompatible with the state's interest in treatment. Finally, it held that due process did not require recognition of the privilege, since the privilege would decrease, not increase, the reliability of the fact finding.

Justice Stevens, joined by Justices Brennan, Marshall and Blackmun, dissented. He argued that the relationship between the Act and the state's criminal law—the requirement that a criminal charge precede a petition under the Act, the use of a beyond a reasonable doubt standard of proof, and the requirement that the state show that a person actually committed one act or attempted to do so—required that proceedings under the Act be deemed criminal for purposes of the privilege against self-incrimination. Justice Stevens reasoned that a treatment goal was insufficient to render the privilege inapplicable and that the Court was "permitting a State to create a shadow criminal law without the fundamental protection of the Fifth Amendment."

Does *Allen* look more like a civil or a criminal proceeding? Does it matter that only criminal defendants could be affected by the statute?

As noted earlier, the privilege can be invoked in almost any proceeding, whether judicial, administrative or legislative. Fifth Amendment claims have been upheld when asserted by a party in a bankruptcy case. McCarthy v. Arndstein, 266 U.S. 34 (1924). Fifth Amendment claims also can be asserted by the subject of an investigation into possible wrongdoing by public contractors, Lefkowitz v. Turley, 414 U.S. 70 (1973) (architect); by public employees, Garrity v. New Jersey, 385 U.S. 493 (1967) (policemen); by prisoners, Baxter v. Palmigiano, 425 U.S. 308 (1976); or by lawyers (in disbarment proceedings), Spevack v. Klein, 385 U.S. 511 (1967).[3] In none of these cases, however, did the Court hold that the proceeding itself was a "criminal case," although substantial penalties—loss of professional status or even more severe incarceration in the case of prisoners—were often at stake. The distinction between these cases and *Boyd, Counselman* and *In re Gault* is important, because the scope of the privilege is affected by the forum in which it is exercised.[4]

As will be discussed below, a grant of use immunity allows the state to compel a witness' testimony, since the immunity grant means that neither the statement nor its fruits can be used against the person in either a state or a Federal prosecution. But what if the witness is concerned not only with the risk of domestic prosecution, but also with the risk of foreign prosecution? It is clear that a grant of use immunity by an American prosecutor has no binding effect on a foreign government. Can the witness refuse to testify, regardless of a grant of immunity, if there is a risk of foreign prosecution? Is a foreign prosecution a "criminal" case within the meaning of the Fifth Amendment? In Zicarelli v. New Jersey State Commission of Investigation, 406 U.S. 472 (1972), the Court granted certiorari to decide this question, but ultimately held that the questions asked of Zicarelli dealt only with domestic conduct, and did not subject him to a risk of foreign prosecution.

Consider the consequences if the Fifth Amendment protects against the risk of foreign prosecution. The government would never be able to compel testimony in such situations by granting immunity; domestic law enforcement efforts against those other than the witness would depend upon the substantive criminal laws of foreign nations; and sophisticated lawbreakers could manufacture foreign contacts to bring domestic prosecutions to a halt. In the modern era of international transactions, it might be possible to credibly argue a risk of foreign prosecution for virtually everyone involved in organized crime. Given all these concerns, most courts have held that the Fifth Amendment does not protect against the risk of foreign prosecution. See United States v. (Under Seal), 794 F.2d 920 (4th Cir.1986); In re Parker, 411 F.2d 1067 (10th Cir.1969). But see In re Cardassi, 351 F.Supp. 1080 (D.Conn.1972).

D. WHAT IS COMPULSION?

1. *Use of the Contempt Power*

Use of the contempt power is the classic form of compulsion, since it imposes substantial punishment on the witness who is exercising the right to

3. Many of these cases are considered infra.

4. If a case is a criminal case the accused need not take the stand and no adverse inference can be drawn from the invocation of the privilege. In other cases, one accused or suspected of wrongdoing must invoke the privilege when specific questions are asked, and refusal to testify can be used against the person. See, e.g., Baxter v. Palmigiano, 425 U.S. 308 (1976).

In Minnesota v. Murphy, 465 U.S. 420 (1984), the Court held that a person has no right to refuse to answer questions on the ground that they might be used against him in subsequent probation revocation proceedings, since those proceedings are civil and not criminal.

For a discussion of what courts should do when the privilege against self-incrimination is raised in civil cases, see Heidt, The Conjurer's Circle, The Fifth Amendment Privilege in Civil Cases, 91 Yale L.J. 1062 (1982).

remain silent, and it presents the witness with a cruel trilemma: remain silent, and face imprisonment; tell the truth, and face imprisonment; or tell a lie, and face imprisonment for perjury.

2. *Other State–Imposed Sanctions*

The Supreme Court has extended the concept of compulsion well beyond its original limitations in the contempt power. For example, the Court in Miranda v. Arizona, discussed infra, found compulsion in the setting of custodial interrogation. The Court has also found other state-imposed sanctions, of less severity than contempt, to constitute compulsion.

LEFKOWITZ v. TURLEY

Supreme Court of the United States, 1973.
414 U.S. 70.

MR. JUSTICE WHITE delivered the opinion of the Court:

[New York statutes required public contracts to provide that if a contractor refuses to waive immunity or to testify concerning state contracts, existing contracts can be cancelled and future contracts can be denied for five years.]

II

* * *

It is true that the State has a strong, legitimate interest in maintaining the integrity of its civil service and of its transactions with independent contractors furnishing a wide range of goods and services; and New York would have it that this interest is sufficiently strong to override the privilege. The suggestion is that the State should be able to interrogate employees and contractors about their job performance without regard to the Fifth Amendment, to discharge those who refuse to answer or to waive the privilege by waiving the immunity to which they would otherwise be entitled, and to use any incriminating answers obtained in subsequent criminal prosecutions. But claims of overriding interests are not unusual in Fifth Amendment litigation and they have not fared well.

* * *

[I]n almost the very context here involved, this court has only recently held that employees of the State do not forfeit their constitutional privilege and that they may be compelled to respond to questions about the performance of their duties but only if their answers cannot be used against them in subsequent criminal prosecutions. Garrity v. New Jersey, 385 U.S. 493 (1967); Gardner v. Broderick, 392 U.S. 273 (1968); Sanitation Men v. Sanitation Comm'r, 392 U.S. 280 (1968).

III

In Garrity v. New Jersey, certain police officers were summoned to an inquiry being conducted by the Attorney General concerning the fixing of traffic tickets. They were asked questions following warnings that if they did not answer they would be removed from office and that anything they said might be used against them in any criminal proceeding. No immunity of any kind was offered or available under state law. The questions were answered and the answers later used over their objections, in their prosecutions for conspiracy. The Court held that "protection of the individual under the Fourteenth Amendment against coerced statements prohibits use in subsequent criminal proceedings of statements obtained under threat of removal from office, and that it extends to all, whether they are policemen or other members of our body politic." * * *

The issue in Gardner v. Broderick, supra, was whether the State might discharge a police officer who, after he was summoned before a grand jury to testify about the performance of his official duties and was advised of his right against compulsory self-incrimination, then refused to waive that right as requested by the State. Conceding that appellant could be discharged for refusing to answer questions about the performance of his official duties, if not required to waive immunity, the Court held that the officer could not be terminated, as he was, for refusing to waive his constitutional privilege. * * *

The companion case, Sanitation Men v. Sanitation Com'r, supra, was to the same effect. * * *

These cases, and their predecessors, ultimately rest on a reconciliation of the well-recognized policies behind the privilege of self-incrimination, and the need of the State, as well as the Federal Government, to obtain information "to assure the effective functioning of government." Immunity is required if there is to be "rational accommodation between the imperatives of the privilege and the legitimate demands of government to compel citizens to testify." It is in this sense that immunity statutes have "become part of our constitutional fabric."

We agree with the District Court that *Garrity, Gardner,* and *Sanitation Men* control the issue now before us. The State sought to interrogate appellees about their transactions with the State and to require them to furnish possibly incriminating testimony by demanding that they waive their immunity and by disqualifying them as public contractors when they refused. It seems to us that the State intended to accomplish what *Garrity* specifically prohibited—to compel testimony that had not been immunized. The waiver sought by the State, under threat of loss of contracts, would have been no less compelled than a direct request for the testimony without resort to the waiver device. A waiver secured under threat of substantial economic sanction cannot be termed voluntary. As already noted, *Garrity* specifically rejected the claim of an effective waiver when the policemen in that case, in the face of possible discharge, proceeded to answer the questions put to them. The same holding is implicit in both *Gardner* and *Sanitation Men.*

* * *

Note

Spevack v. Klein, 385 U.S. 511 (1967), forbids disbarment of a lawyer for invoking the privilege during a bar investigation. Can an applicant for the bar exam refuse to answer questions on an application and still insist on admission to the bar?

Note that if the contractor in *Lefkowitz* had been given immunity from criminal prosecution, he could then be denied public contracts for refusing to testify. More importantly, he could then be denied public contracts on the basis of incriminating statements made in his immunized testimony. This is because the Fifth Amendment only protects against use of a statement in a criminal case. See Allen v. Illinois, supra; Matt v. Larocca, 71 N.Y.2d 154, 524 N.Y.S.2d 180, 518 N.E.2d 1172 (1987) ("the state may compel any person enjoying a public trust to account for his activities and may terminate his services if he refuses to answer relevant questions, or furnishes information indicating that he is no longer entitled to public confidence").

In Minnesota v. Murphy, 465 U.S. 420 (1984), the Court concluded that a threat to revoke probation for refusing to answer questions about criminal activity would constitute Fifth Amendment compulsion. The Court found no such compulsion, however, in the probation condition at issue in the case. That condition required that truthful answers be given, but did not signify that probation would be revoked if the probationer properly invoked his privilege.

In Selective Service System v. Minnesota Public Interest Research Group, 468 U.S. 841 (1984), the Supreme Court addressed a Fifth Amendment challenge to a portion of a 1983 statute that denies federal financial assistance under Title IV of the Higher Education Act of 1965 to male students who fail to register for the draft. Six anonymous students obtained an injunction from a district court when they sued alleging that: they resided in Minnesota, they needed financial aid to pursue their educations, they intended to apply for Title IV assistance, and they were legally required to register for the draft but had failed to do so. The district court found it likely that the 1983 statute violated the Fifth Amendment's privilege against compelled self-incrimination.

Writing for the Court, Chief Justice Burger observed that the students were not compelled to seek financial aid and that they would have no reason to make any statement about registration unless they sought such aid. He concluded that "since a nonregistrant is bound to know that his application would be denied, he is in no sense under compulsion to seek that aid. He has no reason to make any statement to anyone as to whether or not he has registered." He also noted that a student could register late, as the law permits, without providing any information to his school that might incriminate him, since the statute required only a certification that a student is in compliance with the law, not a statement of when he came into compliance. But the Chief Justice recognized, and the government conceded, that "a late registrant must disclose that his action is untimely when he makes a late registration with the Selective Service; the draft registration card must be dated and contain the registrant's date of birth."

Chief Justice Burger analyzed the students' position in the light of Lefkowitz v. Turley and similar cases. He distinguished prior cases finding that a penalty had been threatened or imposed upon a person because he invoked his privilege against self incrimination on the ground that the students had not yet been confronted with a need to assert the privilege and "the Government has not refused any request for immunity for their answers or otherwise threatened them with penalties for invoking the privilege."

Justice Marshall dissented, and Justice Brennan indicated that he agreed with Justice Marshall's Fifth Amendment analysis. Justice Marshall reasoned that: "[t]he Fifth Amendment privilege against coerced self-incrimination extends to every means of government information gathering"; the 1983 statute does not require a student to admit nonregistration, but it coerces students to register and thereby concede prior nonregistration; a student who registers late indicates to the government his birth date and date of registration and thus identifies himself as one who has violated the law; and the possibility of incrimination is therefore real.

Justice Marshall urged that the threat of denial of student aid amounts to substantial economic pressure that coerces the self-incrimination that he identified. He disagreed with the majority's conclusion that the students could not raise their Fifth Amendment claim in this litigation because they had not yet claimed their privilege against self-incrimination. He concluded that "it would be just as incriminating for [the students] to exercise their privilege against self-incrimination when they registered as it would be to fill out the [draft registration] form without exercising the privilege." Only a statutory grant of immunity would insure that late registrants would not incriminate themselves in order to obtain financial aid. Without that grant of immunity, Justice Marshall concluded that federal aid could not be conditioned on compliance with the registration law.

Two aspects of this case warrant special attention. First, it should be noted that the majority did not hold that students who register late must admit that they previously violated the law. It suggested that students who violated the law by not registering might seek to register late and invoke their privilege against self-incrimination when asked their birthdates. The majority implies that students would not have to supply their birthdates absent a grant of immunity. Justice Marshall appeared to agree that students could invoke their privilege, but he believed that the very invocation of the privilege would be incriminating.

Second, this case illustrates a point that escapes discussion in most of the Court's decisions. Once a person invokes his privilege against self-incrimination, it is likely in many instances that government officials will view the assertion of the privilege as a strong clue that they should investigate the person. Thus, if a taxpayer feels the need on a tax return or during an IRS audit to invoke the privilege, it would not be surprising if the IRS responded with a more extensive investigation than it otherwise might conduct. Or, if prosecutors call a witness before a grand jury and the witness invokes the privilege, a greater effort might be made to investigate the witness than might be made to investigate people who make it appear that they have no desire to hide anything from the government.

So far the Court has not held that the government is prevented from focusing prosecutorial and investigative resources upon persons who invoke the privilege against self-incrimination. Thus, the situation in which the students found themselves was not so very different from the situation in which many persons who rely on the privilege find themselves. Are you disturbed by this situation? Do you find it a fair price to exact for such a broad privilege? Should the government have to grant use immunity every time it seeks to compel someone to answer questions or to provide information as a condition of obtaining a government benefit or avoiding a penalty?

A requirement of use immunity would mean that students worried about draft registration could provide any information necessary to comply with the laws governing distribution of benefits or avoidance of penalties without fear that the government could use the information or the fruits derived from it in criminal prosecutions. The government could use the information and fruits thereof for any purpose, except to prosecute the person who provided the information. Some burden would be imposed upon the government, however, to demonstrate that any criminal prosecution against a person who received immunity is not tainted by the use of information provided on forms or in response to questions. There would surely be litigation over the use the government made of the information provided to it. Thus, the rule that immunity must be provided would further the privilege, but it might also burden the government. What rule would you adopt? Under the Supreme Court's cases, does the right to claim the privilege rest, as a practical matter, on whether the government can make it appear that a citizen is seeking a benefit rather than defending against government conduct?

Federal Sentencing Guideline Section 3E.1 provides for a reduced sentence to a defendant who accepts responsibility for his "criminal conduct." The term "criminal conduct" refers not only to what the defendant has been convicted of or pleaded guilty to, but also to other crimes that were related to or in furtherance of that conduct. Defendants have argued that "criminal conduct" must be limited to the crimes for which a defendant has been adjudged guilty; otherwise, the defendant will be "compelled" to incriminate himself on uncharged crimes in order to receive a sentence reduction. Is the denial of a sentence reduction for invoking the privilege tantamount to compulsion? The court in United States v. Oliveras, 905 F.2d 623 (2d Cir.1990), held that such a denial was compulsion, and thus that the defendant need only express remorse for the adjudged crimes in order to be eligible for a sentence reduction. The *Oliveras* court found no distinction between denial of a benefit and active punishment; in either case, the defendant received a longer prison sentence for invoking his privilege. Most courts, however, have rejected this view. For example, the court in United States v. Mourning, 914 F.2d 699 (5th Cir.1990), distinguished *Lefkowitz* as a situation where, "if a defendant took no action that would incriminate himself, the government would exact or increase punishment." In contrast, with sentence reduction, "should the defendant choose not to accept responsibility for all of his relevant criminal conduct, nothing happens. No increase in punishment occurs. The previously calculated guideline range remains constant." See also United States v. Gonzalez, 897 F.2d 1018 (9th Cir.1990) ("the possibility of leniency in the statute does not make denial of lenient treatment impermissible"). Which view is more persuasive?

3. *Comment on the Invocation of the Privilege*

In Griffin v. California, 380 U.S. 609 (1965),[5] the Court held that adverse comment to the jury, by either the judge or the prosecutor, on the defendant's election not to testify constituted punishment for the invocation of silence and thus violates the Fifth Amendment.[6] Thus, the fact that the defendant did not take the stand is not evidence against him.

Less clear is whether a prior invocation of the privilege—at a preliminary hearing or in a grand jury proceeding, for example—can be the subject of adverse comment. In Raffel v. United States, 271 U.S. 494 (1926), the Court

5. For a criticism of *Griffin,* see Ayer, The Fifth Amendment and the Inference of Guilt from Silence: Griffin v. California After Fifteen Years, 78 Mich.L.Rev. 841 (1980) (arguing that *Griffin* is an ill-advised exception to the rule that attorneys may draw any reasonable inference from the facts legitimately within the jury's knowledge). For a defense of *Griffin,* see Saltzburg, Foreword: The Flow and Ebb of Constitutional Criminal Procedure in the Warren and Burger Courts, 69 Geo.L.J. 151, 204 (1980).

6. In Lakeside v. Oregon, 435 U.S. 333 (1978), the Court held that an instruction to the jury can be given directing it *not* to draw an adverse inference from the defendant's failure to testify, even if the defendant objects to the instruction. Carter v. Kentucky, 450 U.S. 288 (1981), held that "a state trial judge has the constitutional obligation, upon proper request, to minimize the danger that the jury will give evidentiary weight to a defendant's failure to testify" by giving a jury instruction on the right of the defendant to remain silent.

Justice White wrote for seven members of the Court in James v. Kentucky, 466 U.S. 341 (1984), that a state prisoner preserved his right to attack the trial judge's failure to instruct the jury that it should draw no adverse inference from his failure to testify by asking the judge to admonish the jury to give no emphasis to his failure to take the stand. Although the state supreme court held that a request for an admonition was not adequate to support a claim on appeal of a failure to give an instruction, the Supreme Court found that "[t]here can be no dispute that, for federal constitutional purposes, James adequately invoked his substantive right to jury guidance," and that "Kentucky's distinction between admonitions and instructions is not the sort of firmly established and regularly followed state practice that can prevent implementation of federal constitutional rights." Justice Rehnquist dissented, and Justice Marshall did not participate.

The Court distinguished *Griffin* in United States v. Robinson, 485 U.S. 25 (1988), and held that a prosecutor properly pointed out in closing argument that the defendant had an opportunity to testify in response to defense counsel's argument that the defendant had not been permitted to explain his side of the story.

held that a defendant's refusal to testify in his first trial could be used against him in a second trial. But, in Grunewald v. United States, 353 U.S. 391 (1957), the Court held that there was no inconsistency between a defendant's silence before a grand jury and testimony at trial, and that the silence therefore should not have been used against him. The ruling did not rest on constitutional grounds, and the question whether prior silence sometimes can be utilized remains open as the discussion of Doyle v. Ohio, Jenkins v. Anderson and Fletcher v. Weir, infra, will illustrate.

Since a defendant never knows whether a preliminary hearing, a grand jury investigation or a trial will be followed by other proceedings, would you accept the argument that fundamental fairness requires that the defendant be permitted to choose whether or not to testify in each separate proceeding without being concerned that there might be another one on the horizon in which silence could be used as impeachment evidence? Would you accept an argument that prior silence is too ambiguous to be used as part of the prosecution's case? See Schiller, On the Jurisprudence of the Fifth Amendment Right to Silence, 16 Am.Cr.L.Rev. 197 (1979).

Sometimes it is difficult to tell whether a prosecutor is commenting on the silence of the defendant or on the totality of the evidence in a case. The difficulty in distinguishing comments on the accused's failure to testify from permissible argument is apparent in United States v. Monaghan, 741 F.2d 1434 (D.C.Cir.1984). A majority of the court found that a prosecutor did not impermissibly comment on the defendant's silence by arguing that the government's evidence that the defendant had taken indecent liberties with a minor was uncontradicted. A dissenting judge reasoned that the only witness who could have contradicted the alleged victim was the defendant and that repeated emphasis on the absence of contradictory evidence was a clear signal to the jury to rely on the defendant's assertion of his right not to testify. See also United States v. Bartemio, 547 F.2d 341 (7th Cir.1974) (reference to uncontradicted and uncontested evidence held not error, but suggestion made that if defendant is "the only person who could have challenged or contradicted such evidence," then error would result from reference); United States v. McKenzie, 922 F.2d 1323 (7th Cir.1991) (statement that evidence was "uncontradicted" is permissible, where defendant was not the only person who could rebut the prosecution's case, and comment would therefore not "naturally and necessarily" remind the jury that the defendant refused to testify); Lent v. Wells, 861 F.2d 972 (6th Cir.1988) (statement that evidence was uncontradicted violates *Griffin* where defendant was the only person who could rebut the complainant's assertion that a sexual attack occurred). Compare Lindgren v. Lane, 925 F.2d 198 (7th Cir.1991) (no *Griffin* violation where the prosecutor argues that the testimony of a prosecution witness is undisputed because the defense witness offered in contradiction was not believable).

Can the prosecutor in a sentencing phase of a capital trial argue to the jury that the defendant has expressed no remorse for the crime? See Lesko v. Lehman, 925 F.2d 1527 (3d Cir.1991) (*Griffin* protection applies to penalty phase of capital trial, and the "natural and necessary interpretation" of the prosecutor's comments was to refer to the defendant's failure to testify during the sentencing phase). The government in *Lesko* argued that the prosecutor was merely referring to the defendant's demeanor during the trial. Why did that argument not persuade the court?

The Supreme Court found in United States v. Hasting, 461 U.S. 499 (1983), that a court of appeals misused its supervisory power when it reversed convictions for kidnapping and other crimes without considering whether a prosecutor's comments on the failure of the defense to offer evidence were harmless error. The Court examined the argument for itself and found that the error was harmless beyond a reasonable doubt. Justice Stevens concurred in the judgment, arguing that where the defense offered evidence it was permissible for the prosecutor to refer to weaknesses in the defense case so that no constitutional error was presented. Justice Brennan, joined by Justice Marshall, dissented in part.

E. TO WHOM DOES THE PRIVILEGE BELONG?

The privilege against self-incrimination is personal, belonging only to the person who is himself incriminated by his own testimony. For example, an attorney may not claim the privilege on the ground that his testimony might incriminate his client. Which of the rationales discussed above justify this limitation? Consider the Court's policy analysis in the following case.

FISHER v. UNITED STATES

Supreme Court of the United States, 1976.
425 U.S. 391.

MR. JUSTICE WHITE delivered the opinion of the Court.

[Taxpayers, who were under investigation for possible civil or criminal tax violations, obtained documents relating to the preparation of their tax returns from their accountants. Shortly thereafter, they transferred these documents to the lawyers handling their cases. The IRS served summonses on the attorneys directing them to produce the records, but the attorneys refused to comply on Fifth Amendment grounds.]

II

All of the parties in these cases and the Court of Appeals for the Fifth Circuit have concurred in the proposition that if the Fifth Amendment would have excused a *taxpayer* from turning over the accountant's papers had he possessed them, the *attorney* to whom they are delivered for the purpose of obtaining legal advice should also be immune from subpoena. Although we agree with this proposition for the reasons set forth in Part III, *infra,* we are convinced that, under our decision in Couch v. United States, 409 U.S. 322 (1973), it is not the taxpayer's Fifth Amendment privilege that would excuse the *attorney* from production.

The relevant part of that Amendment provides:

> "No person * * * shall be *compelled* in any criminal case to be a *witness against himself.*" (Emphasis added.)

The taxpayer's privilege under this Amendment is not violated by enforcement of the summonses involved in these cases because enforcement against a taxpayer's lawyer would not "compel" the taxpayer to do anything—and certainly would not compel him to be a "witness" against himself. The Court has held repeatedly that the Fifth Amendment is limited to prohibiting the use of "physical or moral compulsion" exerted on the person asserting the privilege. In Couch v. United States, supra, we recently ruled that the Fifth Amendment rights of a taxpayer were not violated by the enforcement of a documentary summons directed to her accountant and requiring production of the taxpayer's own records in the possession of the accountant. We did so on the ground that in such a case "the ingredient of personal compulsion against an accused is lacking."

Here, the taxpayers are compelled to do no more than was the taxpayer in *Couch.* The taxpayers' Fifth Amendment privilege is therefore not violated by enforcement of the summonses directed toward their attorneys. This is true whether or not the Amendment would have barred a subpoena directing the taxpayer to produce the documents while they were in his hands.

The fact that the attorneys are agents of the taxpayers does not change this result. *Couch* held as much, since the accountant there was also the taxpayer's agent, and in this respect reflected a longstanding view. In Hale v. Henkel, 201 U.S. 43, 69–70 (1906), the Court said that the privilege "was never intended to permit [a person] to plead the fact that some third person might be incriminated by his testimony, even though he were the agent of such person * * *. [T]he Amendment is limited to a person who shall be compelled in any criminal case to be a witness against *himself.*" (Emphasis in original.) "It is extortion of information from the accused himself that offends our sense of justice."

* * *

Nor is this one of those situations, which *Couch* suggested might exist, where constructive possession is so clear or relinquishment of possession so temporary and insignificant as to leave the personal compulsion upon the taxpayer substantially intact. * * *

* * *

The Court of Appeals for the Fifth Circuit suggested that because legally and ethically the attorney was required to respect the confidences of his client, the latter had a reasonable expectation of privacy for the records in the hands of the attorney and therefore did not forfeit his Fifth Amendment privilege with respect to the records by transferring them in order to obtain legal advice. It is true that the Court has often stated that one of the several purposes served by the constitutional privilege against compelled testimonial self-incrimination is that of protecting personal privacy. But the Court has never suggested that every invasion of privacy violates the privilege. Within the limits imposed by the language of the Fifth Amendment, which we necessarily observe, the privilege truly serves privacy interests; but the Court has never on any ground, personal privacy included, applied the Fifth Amendment to prevent the otherwise proper acquisition or use of evidence which, in the Court's view, did not involve compelled testimonial self-incrimination of some sort.

* * *

We cannot cut the Fifth Amendment completely loose from the moorings of its language, and make it serve as a general protector of privacy—a word not mentioned in its text and a concept directly addressed in the Fourth Amendment. We adhere to the view that the Fifth Amendment protects against "compelled self-incrimination, not [the disclosure of] private information."

Insofar as private information not obtained through compelled self-incriminating testimony is legally protected, its protection stems from other sources—the Fourth Amendment's protection against seizures without warrant or probable cause and against subpoenas which suffer from "too much indefiniteness or breadth in the things required to be 'particularly described,'" or evidentiary privileges such as the attorney-client privilege.

[In Part III, the Court held that the attorney-client privilege protects against disclosure of documents that would have been protected by the Fifth Amendment had they been in the taxpayer's possession. However, in Part IV it concluded that the documents in question would not be privileged even in the hands of the taxpayer. See section F, 2 of this chapter infra, for the Court's discussion of the latter issue.]

Note

Justice Marshall cited *Couch* and *Fisher* in his opinion for a unanimous Court in SEC v. Jerry T. O'Brien, Inc., 467 U.S. 735 (1984), holding that the self-incrimination clause of the Fifth Amendment imposed no burden on the SEC to give notice to a target of a "nonpublic investigation" as to subpoenas issued to third parties, since the target could not claim the privilege as to material sought from someone else.

Prior to *Fisher* the Court in Bellis v. United States, 417 U.S. 85 (1974) had extended the "personal compulsion" limitation to exclude partnerships from Fifth Amendment protection. The partnership in *Bellis* was a law firm with three partners, and a handful of employees. Justice Marshall, writing for the Court, stated broadly that "no artificial organization may utilize the personal privilege against compulsory self-incrimination." Justice Marshall concluded that the partnership in *Bellis* had "an established institutional identity independent of its individual partners." Thereafter in United States v. Doe, 465 U.S. 605 (1984), the Court held that a sole proprietorship was entitled to Fifth Amendment protection. Finally, in Braswell v. United States, 487 U.S. 99 (1988), the Court held that a corporation wholly owned and operated by a single individual was not itself entitled to Fifth Amendment protection. Chief Justice Rehnquist, writing for the Court, distinguished *Doe* as follows:

> Had petitioner conducted his business as a sole proprietorship, *Doe* would require that he be provided the opportunity to show that his act of production would entail testimonial self-incrimination. But petitioner has operated his business through the corporate form, and we have long recognized that for purposes of the Fifth Amendment, corporations and other collective entities are treated differently from individuals.

Corporations have Fourth Amendment rights (see Marshall v. Barlow's in Chapter Two); they have First Amendment rights (First National Bank v. Bellotti, 435 U.S. 765 (1978)); they have due process rights (International Shoe Co. v. Washington, 326 U.S. 310 (1945)); why don't they have Fifth Amendment rights? Why is it of constitutional importance that Braswell operated a business as a corporation rather than as a sole proprietorship?

What is the basis for the Court's rejection of the privilege in a partnership situation? Is it the need to protect the governmental interest in regulating economic activity? Can that rationale justify denying the privilege to such unincorporated organizations as the Communist Party of Denver (Rogers v. United States, 340 U.S. 367, 371–72 (1951)), or the Civil Rights Congress (McPhaul v. United States, 364 U.S. 372, 380 (1960))? Does it justify allowing it to a sole proprietor? Does a two-person law firm represent "the purely private interest of its constituents?" A 200-person firm surely embodies "their common or group interests only." What about the firm with 35 members, or 15 or 6?

F. WHAT IS PROTECTED

In the cases that follow, the Court attempts to define the scope of the privilege.

1. Non-testimonial Evidence

SCHMERBER v. CALIFORNIA

Supreme Court of the United States, 1966.
384 U.S. 757.

MR. JUSTICE BRENNAN delivered the opinion of the Court.

Petitioner was convicted in Los Angeles Municipal Court of the criminal offense of driving an automobile while under the influence of intoxicating liquor. He had been arrested at a hospital while receiving treatment for injuries suffered in an accident involving the automobile that he had apparently been driving. At the direction of a police officer, a blood sample was then withdrawn from petitioner's body by a physician at the hospital. The chemical analysis of this sample revealed a percent by weight of alcohol in his blood at the time of the offense which indicated intoxication, and the report of this analysis was admitted in evidence at the trial. Petitioner objected to receipt of this evidence of the analysis on the ground that the blood had been withdrawn despite his refusal, on the advice of his counsel, to consent to the test. He contended that in that circumstance the withdrawal of the blood and the admission of the analysis in evidence denied him due process of law under the Fourteenth Amendment, as well as specific guarantees of the Bill of Rights secured against the States by that Amendment: his privilege against self-incrimination under the Fifth Amendment; his right to counsel under the Sixth Amendment; and his right not to be subjected to unreasonable searches and seizures in violation of the Fourth Amendment.

[In the opinion, the Court rejects each claim. Only the Fifth Amendment issue is taken up here.]

* * *

II

* * *. We hold that the privilege protects an accused only from being compelled to testify against himself, or otherwise provide the State with evidence of a testimonial or communicative nature,[a] and that the withdrawal of blood and use of the analysis in question in this case did not involve compulsion to these ends.

It could not be denied that in requiring petitioner to submit to the withdrawal and chemical analysis of his blood the State compelled him to submit to an attempt to discover evidence that might be used to prosecute him for a criminal offense. He submitted only after the police officer rejected his ob-

a. A dissent suggests that the report of the blood test was "testimonial" or "communicative," because the test was performed in order to obtain the testimony of others, communicating to the jury facts about petitioner's condition. Of course, all evidence received in court is "testimonial" or "communicative" if these words are thus used. But the Fifth Amendment relates only to acts on the part of the person to whom the privilege applies, and we use these words subject to the same limitations. A nod or head-shake is as much a "testimonial" or "communicative" act in this sense as are spoken words. But the terms as we use them do not apply to evidence of acts noncommunicative in nature as to the person asserting the privilege, even though, as here, such acts are compelled to obtain the testimony of others.

jection and directed the physician to proceed. The officer's direction to the physician to administer the test over petitioner's objection constituted compulsion for the purposes of the privilege. The critical question, then, is whether petitioner was thus compelled "to be a witness against himself."

If the scope of the privilege coincided with the complex of values it helps to protect, we might be obliged to conclude that the privilege was violated. * * *

* * * [H]owever, the privilege has never been given the full scope which the values it helps to protect suggest. History and a long line of authorities in lower courts have consistently limited its protection to situations in which the State seeks to submerge those values by obtaining the evidence against an accused through "the cruel, simple expedient of compelling it from his own mouth. * * * In sum, the privilege is fulfilled only when the person is guaranteed the right 'to remain silent unless he chooses to speak in the unfettered exercise of his own will.' " * * *

It is clear that the protection of the privilege reaches an accused's communications, whatever form they might take, and the compulsion of responses which are also communications, for example, compliance with a subpoena to produce one's papers. Boyd v. United States, 116 U.S. 616. On the other hand, both federal and state courts have usually held that it offers no protection against compulsion to submit to fingerprinting, photographing, or measurements, to write or speak for identification, to appear in court, to stand, to assume a stance, to walk, or to make a particular gesture. The distinction which has emerged, often expressed in different ways, is that the privilege is a bar against compelling "communications" or "testimony," but that compulsion which makes a suspect or accused the source of "real or physical evidence" does not violate it.

Although we agree that this distinction is a helpful framework for analysis, we are not to be understood to agree with past applications in all instances. There will be many cases in which such a distinction is not readily drawn. Some tests seemingly directed to obtain "physical evidence," for example, lie detector tests measuring changes in body function during interrogation, may actually be directed to eliciting responses which are essentially testimonial. To compel a person to submit to testing in which an effort will be made to determine his guilt or innocence on the basis of physiological responses, whether willed or not, is to evoke the spirit and history of the Fifth Amendment. Such situations call to mind the principle that the protection of the privilege "is as broad as the mischief against which it seeks to guard," Counselman v. Hitchcock, 142 U.S. 547, 562.

In the present case, however, no such problem of application is presented. Not even a shadow of testimonial compulsion upon or enforced communication by the accused was involved either in the extraction or in the chemical analysis. Petitioner's testimonial capacities were in no way implicated; indeed, his participation, except as a donor, was irrelevant to the results of the test, which depend on chemical analysis and on that alone.[b] Since the blood test

b. This conclusion would not necessarily govern had the State tried to show that the accused had incriminated himself when told that he would have to be tested. Such incriminating evidence may be an unavoidable byproduct of the compulsion to take the test, especially for an individual who fears the extraction or opposes it on religious grounds. If it wishes to compel persons to submit to such attempts to discover evidence, the State may have to forgo the advantage of any *testimonial* products of administering the test—products which would fall within the privilege. Indeed, there may be circumstances in which the evidence, although an incriminating product of compulsion, was neither petitioner's testimony nor evidence relating to some communicative act or writing by the petitioner, it was not inadmissible on privilege grounds.

* * *

MR. JUSTICE BLACK with whom MR. JUSTICE DOUGLAS joins, dissenting.

* * * [T]o reach the conclusion that compelling a person to give his blood to help the State convict him is not equivalent to compelling him to be a witness against himself strikes me as quite an extraordinary feat. The Court, however, overcomes what had seemed to me to be an insuperable obstacle to its conclusion by holding that

> "* * * the privilege protects an accused only from being compelled to testify against himself, or otherwise provide the State with evidence of a testimonial or communicative nature, and that the withdrawal of blood and use of the analysis in question in this case did not involve compulsion to these ends."

I cannot agree that this distinction and reasoning of the Court justify denying petitioner his Bill of Rights' guarantee that he must not be compelled to be a witness against himself.

In the first place it seems to me that the compulsory extraction of petitioner's blood for analysis so that the person who analyzed it could give evidence to convict him had both a "testimonial" and a "communicative nature." The sole purpose of this project which proved to be successful was to obtain "testimony" from some person to prove that petitioner had alcohol in his blood at the time he was arrested. And the purpose of the project was certainly "communicative" in that the analysis of the blood was to supply information to enable a witness to communicate to the court and jury that petitioner was more or less drunk.

* * *

[The concurring opinion of Justices Harlan and Stewart and the dissenting opinions of Chief Justice Warren and Justice Fortas are omitted. Justice Douglas dissented on the grounds that "the Fifth Amendment marks 'a zone of privacy' which the Government may not force a person to surrender. * * * No clearer invasion of this right of privacy can be imagined than forcible bloodletting of the kind involved here."]

Note

Is Justice Brennan's distinction between "communicative" and physical evidence convincing in this case? How does the Court justify its limitation on the privilege—other than noting that it "has never been given the full scope which the values it helps to protect suggest?" Is the Court, as Justice Black suggests, really just balancing the necessities of law enforcement against the values underlying the privilege? Which policies are ill served by the Court's decision?

The holding in *Schmerber* has been reaffirmed and extended several times. One year after that decision, the Court held that requiring a suspect to participate in a police line-up did not violate the Fifth Amendment. In United States v. Wade, 388 U.S. 218 (1967), the defendant was arrested for robbing a bank. He was forced to stand in a line-up with several other prisoners, each of whom wore strips of tape

pain, danger, or severity of an operation would almost inevitably cause a person to prefer confession to undergoing the "search," and nothing we say today should be taken as establishing the permissibility of compulsion in that case. But no such situation is presented in this case.

on their faces, as had the actual robber. In addition, each man was required to utter the words allegedly spoken by the robber. The Court held:

> Neither the lineup itself nor anything shown by this record that Wade was required to do in the lineup violated his privilege against self-incrimination. We have only recently reaffirmed that the privilege "protects an accused only from being compelled to testify against himself, or otherwise provide the State with evidence of a testimonial or communicative nature * * *." Schmerber v. California, 384 U.S. 757, 761. * * *
>
> We have no doubt that compelling the accused merely to exhibit his person for observation by a prosecution witness prior to trial involves no compulsion of the accused to give evidence having testimonial significance. It is compulsion of the accused to exhibit his physical characteristics, not compulsion to disclose any knowledge he might have. It is no different from compelling Schmerber to provide a blood sample * * *. [C]ompelling Wade to speak within hearing distance of the witnesses, even to utter words purportedly uttered by the robber, was not compulsion to utter statements of a "testimonial" nature; he was required to use his voice as an identifying physical characteristic, not to speak his guilt. * * *

Justice Black again dissented on the Fifth Amendment issue, because requiring a suspect to stand in a line-up and speak certain words is "forcing [that] person to supply proof of his own crime."

Justice Fortas filed a separate opinion arguing that forced participation in a police line-up does not violate the Fifth Amendment because:

> [I]t is an incident of the State's power to arrest, and a reasonable and justifiable aspect of the State's custody resulting from arrest. It does not require that the accused take affirmative, volitional action, but only that, having been duly arrested he may be seen for identification purposes. * * *

However, he challenged the constitutionality of forcing a suspect to speak in the line-up.

> * * * It is more than passive, mute assistance to the eyes of the victim or of witnesses. It is the kind of volitional act—the kind of forced cooperation by the accused—which is within the historical perimeter of the privilege against compelled self-incrimination.
>
> * * * *Schmerber,* which authorized the forced extraction of blood from the veins of an unwilling human being, did not compel the person actively to cooperate—to accuse himself by a volitional act which differs only in degree from compelling him to act out the crime, which, I assume, would be rebuffed by the Court. It is the latter feature which places the compelled utterance by the accused squarely within the history and noble purpose of the Fifth Amendment's commandment.

What other physical characteristics are excepted from Fifth Amendment protection? In Gilbert v. California, 388 U.S. 263 (1967), a companion case to *Wade,* the Court held that handwriting exemplars may be compelled from an unwilling defendant. In United States v. Dionisio, 410 U.S. 1 (1973), the same rule was applied to voice-prints. While one's voice and handwriting are means of communication, the Court's view is that the sample itself, in contrast to the content of the communication, is merely an identifying physical characteristic, outside the protection of the Fifth Amendment. Of course, another view of voice and handwriting exemplars is that the suspect is saying "this is my real voice and handwriting." If, in fact, the suspect attempts to distort the exemplar, this may be considered as evidence of guilt. Viewed in this light, do the cases make sense? Note that your answer may depend upon the policy arguments that you accept as a valid basis for the privilege.

The Court in Pennsylvania v. Muniz, 110 S.Ct. 2638 (1990) held that the line between testimonial and non-testimonial evidence must be determined by whether the witness faces the cruel trilemma in disclosing the evidence. After failing sobriety tests, police officers transported Muniz to a booking center. There they asked Muniz, among other things, the date of his sixth birthday. The officers did not give Muniz *Miranda* warnings. Muniz responded with slurred speech, stumbled over his answers, and said that he did not know the date of his sixth birthday. Both the manner of speech and the content of Muniz's answers were used as evidence that he was under the influence of alcohol.

Writing for eight members of the Court, Justice Brennan concluded that evidence of the slurred nature of Muniz's speech was not testimonial under *Schmerber* and its progeny. The slurred speech in *Muniz* was held to be physical evidence, because its relevance was divorced from the content of the words themselves. The Court stated that "[r]equiring a suspect to reveal the physical manner in which he articulates words, like requiring him to reveal the physical properties of the sound produced by his voice, see *Dionisio* * * * does not, without more, compel him to provide a 'testimonial' response for purposes of the privilege." Only Justice Marshall dissented on this point.

The Court did not decide whether a person's performance on a sobriety test (e.g. standing on one leg for thirty seconds and counting) was testimonial, since Muniz did not challenge the lower court's decision that such evidence was non-testimonial under *Schmerber.* The Court noted however, that many lower courts have held that such tests measure physical capacity such as reflex, dexterity and balance, and consequently are not testimonial under *Schmerber.* See People v. Hager, 69 N.Y.2d 141, 512 N.Y.S.2d 794, 505 N.E.2d 237 (1987) ("physical performance tests do not reveal a person's subjective knowledge or thought processes but, rather, exhibit a person's degree of physical coordination.").

With respect to the answer to the sixth birthday question, Justice Brennan, writing on this point for five members of the court (including Justice Marshall), held that Muniz's response *was* testimonial. The State argued that an answer to the sixth birthday question did not trigger Fifth Amendment protection because the only evidence derived would concern the physiological functioning of Muniz's brain, which the State contended was physical and not testimonial. Justice Brennan rejected this argument, reasoning "that the 'fact' to be inferred might be said to concern the physical status of Muniz's brain merely describes the way in which the inference is incriminating. The correct question * * * is whether the incriminating inference of mental confusion is drawn from a testimonial act or from physical evidence." Thus, facts about a person's physical condition may be obtained either through physical or testimonial evidence. When they are obtained through testimonial evidence, the Fifth Amendment applies. If police had compelled Schmerber to answer questions about the alcohol in his blood, his responses would be testimonial even though the fact proven would concern Schmerber's physical condition.

Justice Brennan found that Muniz's answer to the sixth birthday question was protected by the "core meaning" of the self-incrimination clause. He explained as follows:

> Because the privilege was designed primarily to prevent a recurrence of the Inquisition and the Star Chamber * * * it is evident that a suspect is compelled to be a witness against himself at least whenever he must face the

> modern day analog of the historic trilemma. * * * Whenever a suspect is asked for a response requiring him to communicate an express or implied assertion of fact or belief, the suspect confronts the 'trilemma' of truth, falsity or silence and hence the response (whether based on truth or falsity) contains a testimonial component.

The State argued that Muniz did not face the cruel trilemma in answering the sixth birthday question, since the State was not interested in the actual date of Muniz's sixth birthday. Justice Brennan, concluded, however, that Muniz was "confronted with the trilemma." He reasoned as follows:

> By hypothesis, the inherently coercive environment created by the custodial interrogation precluded the option of remaining silent. * * * Muniz was left with the choice of incriminating himself by admitting that he did not then know the date of his sixth birthday, or answering untruthfully by reporting a date that he did not then believe to be accurate (an incorrect guess would be incriminating as well as untruthful). The content of his truthful answer supported an inference that his mental faculties were impaired, because his assertion (he did not know the date of his sixth birthday) was different from the assertion (he knew the date was [correct date]) that the trier of fact might reasonably have expected a lucid person to provide. Hence, the incriminating inference of impaired mental faculties stemmed, not just from the fact that Muniz slurred his response, but also from a testimonial aspect of that response.

Chief Justice Rehnquist, joined by Justices White, Blackmun and Stevens, dissented from the Court's holding that the content of Muniz's answer to the sixth birthday question was testimonial. The Chief Justice argued that the question was designed to elicit the physical fact of Muniz's mental coordination. The dissenters reasoned that since the police could extract Schmerber's blood "to determine how much that part of his system had been affected by alcohol," the police could likewise "examine the functioning of Muniz's mental processes for the same purpose."

The dissenters also took issue with the Court's analysis of the "trilemma" facing Muniz. According to the Chief Justice, "the potential for giving a bad guess does not subject the suspect to the truth-falsity-silence predicament that renders a response testimonial." The Chief Justice reasoned by analogy that if the condition of Muniz's eyes were relevant, a question concerning what Muniz saw on an eye chart would not require a testimonial response, even though Muniz might have to say "I don't know" or make a wrong guess. The dissenters could not see a distinction between oral responses to an eye chart and oral responses concerning defendant's mental faculties.

Which position—majority or dissent—is more consistent with the traditional policies behind the Fifth Amendment? Suppose police officers had said to Muniz, "We want you to speak as clearly as you can," and Muniz had responded. Would his response be testimonial, or is this virtually identical to *Dionisio?*

What about Chief Justice Rehnquist's hypothetical case of the eye test where the defendant's poor eyesight is relevant to a prosecution? When asked to read an eye chart during custodial interrogation, the suspect would appear to be subject to the modern analog of the cruel trilemma—the same one in which Muniz found himself. He cannot be silent due to the pressures of custodial interrogation. If he answers truthfully, that he cannot read the chart, such information can incriminate him where poor eyesight is relevant. If he answers untruthfully and ventures a guess about the chart, that information is incriminating as well. So despite Chief Justice Rehnquist's use of a hypothetical which he obviously feels does not present a testimonial problem, the fact is that a testimonial problem does exist after *Muniz.* Much to the dissenters' chagrin, the risk of making a wrong guess is now the modern day analog of the Star Chamber.

Muniz does not, however, stand for the proposition that all compelled oral statements are testimonial. If a compelled statement is not an express or implied assertion of fact which can be true or false, the Court has held that the statement is not testimonial, even though it is communicative: there is no risk of perjury since such a statement cannot be false. Thus, in Doe v. United States, 487 U.S. 201 (1988), the Court held that a person's compelled signature on a bank consent form, directing the release of bank records assuming such records existed, was not testimonial since there was no assertion of fact that the records did or did not exist. See In re Grand Jury Subpoena, 826 F.2d 1166 (2d Cir.1987) ("the directives here * * * do not contain any assertions by appellants regarding the existence of, or control over, foreign bank accounts. They authorize disclosure of records and information only if such accounts exist."). Compare United States v. Davis, 767 F.2d 1025 (2d Cir.1985) (consent form may be testimonial if there is an implied assertion that bank records actually exist).

When a suspect refuses to cooperate in supplying physical evidence or to participate in a line-up, what sanctions are available to the state? One possibility is an action for contempt. See Doss v. United States, 431 F.2d 601, 603 (9th Cir. 1970). A few courts have held that testimony about a suspect's non-cooperation is admissible at trial, and that a prosecutor may argue that such conduct is evidence of guilt. See United States v. Stembridge, 477 F.2d 874 (5th Cir. 1973) (evidence that handwriting samples were disguised is admissible at trial); United States v. Parhms, 424 F.2d 152 (9th Cir. 1970) (defendant's refusal to stand in line-up may be introduced during cross-examination and prosecutor may argue that refusal is evidence of guilt).

Justice O'Connor wrote for seven members of the court in South Dakota v. Neville, 459 U.S. 553 (1983), and explained how *Schmerber* affects a person who refuses to take a test. Neville was stopped for drunken driving and was asked to submit to a blood-alcohol test. He refused, saying he was too drunk to pass the test. The state courts suppressed evidence of the refusal on self-incrimination grounds and the Supreme Court reversed. It reasoned as follows: *Schmerber* authorized a state to force a person to take such a test; South Dakota, therefore, had the power to administer a test to Neville without his consent; the state could agree to respect Neville's refusal to take the test; and in doing so the state could condition its agreement to refrain from doing what it lawfully could do by providing that Neville's refusal would result in certain disadvantages being imposed upon him. The Court concluded that "a refusal to take a blood-alcohol test, after a police officer has lawfully requested it, is not an act coerced by the officer, and thus is not protected by the privilege against self-incrimination." Nor was the officer required to inform Neville that his refusal might be used as evidence against him. The Court found no "implicit promise to forego use of evidence that would unfairly 'trick' " a person.

Justice Stevens, joined by Justice Marshall, dissented and argued that the state courts had relied on the state, not the federal constitution. Whether or not Justice Stevens was correct in 1983, South Dakota had the last word in the *Neville* case. Relying on the state constitution, the state supreme court held that the failure to fully advise Neville of the consequences of refusing a blood alcohol test was a denial of due process and that the refusal to take the test could not be used as evidence against him. State v. Neville, 346 N.W.2d 425 (S.D.1984). Since the refusal could not be used as evidence, Neville's statement that he was too drunk to pass the test, which contained the substance of the refusal, also could not be used.

If the officer could have forcibly taken a blood sample from Neville, is there any reason why a state should be barred from permitting Neville to avoid having the sample taken?

Estelle v. Smith, 451 U.S. 454 (1981), holds that a defendant who is to be interviewed by a government psychiatrist who will testify at sentencing (in this case the death penalty was involved) has a right to be warned that what he says may be used against him in the sentencing proceeding. Writing for the Court, Chief Justice Burger rejected the state's argument that the statements made by the defendant to the doctor were not testimonial. The doctor based his testimony on the defendant's statements about the crime and omissions from his statements. Three Justices concurred in the judgment on right to counsel grounds.

In Jones v. Dugger, 839 F.2d 1441 (11th Cir.1988), Jones was arrested for sexually assaulting two women. He was questioned by Detective Holsberry, without *Miranda* warnings. In response to these questions, he answered that he had finished ninth grade and could read and write; he first denied involvement in the crime, then he confessed. Sanity was the central issue at trial. Holsberry testified as to his observations of Jones at the time, but he did not testify to the content of the statements. Holsberry stated that Jones appeared to be rational and well-oriented at the time of questioning, and appeared to know the difference between right and wrong. The court found that the Fifth Amendment was not violated because no testimonial communication of Jones had been used. The Court distinguished *Estelle* as a case where the doctor based his conclusion on the details of the story that defendant told him, whereas Holsberry's testimony merely related "demeanor evidence." How could Holsberry have testified that Jones knew the difference between right and wrong without considering the details of Jones' statement? For a view contrary to *Jones,* see United States v. Hinckley, 672 F.2d 115 (D.C.Cir.1982), affirming the suppression of opinion testimony of FBI agents that John Hinckley was sane, on the basis of statements taken in violation of *Miranda.*

Many cases hold what Chief Justice Burger implied in Estelle v. Smith: a defendant may be compelled to undergo an examination to determine competency to stand trial and an examination to determine mental state at the time of a crime when an insanity defense is raised. See, e.g. Rivera v. Collins, 934 F.2d 658 (5th Cir.1991). As long as any statements made during a competency examination are not used for any purpose other than to decide whether the defendant is capable of understanding the proceedings and assisting in his defense, are there self-incrimination problems with such an examination? Do the problems increase when a defendant raises an insanity defense and the government wishes to conduct an examination? Should it make any difference whether the government or the defendant bears the burden of persuasion on the insanity defense? Should it make any difference whether a jurisdiction treats a defendant who was insane at the time of an offense as not guilty by reason of insanity or as guilty but mentally ill?

In Buchanan v. Kentucky, 483 U.S. 402 (1987), the Court transformed the suggestion it made in Estelle v. Smith concerning the use of a defendant's statements to rebut an insanity defense into a formal holding, as it found no violation of the Fifth Amendment in the use of a psychiatric evaluation of the defendant to rebut a psychiatric defense. During his trial for murder and related crimes, Buchanan did not testify in support of the defense of "extreme emotional disturbance." He called a social worker, who formerly had been assigned to him, to read portions of evaluations of his mental state, which had been made when Buchanan had been arrested for an earlier offense. The prosecutor asked the social worker to read another report made during the period in which Buchanan was hospitalized as a result of the evaluation that had originally been made. The prosecutor also sought, over Buchanan's objection, to introduce a report of a psychological evaluation made when Buchanan's counsel and the prosecutor jointly requested a psychiatric examination for Buchanan pursuant to a state procedure for involuntary hospitalization. The report contained observations about Buchanan's mental state, but it did not describe any statements by Buchanan. Justice Blackmun wrote for the Court that "if a defendant requests such an evaluation or presents psychiatric evidence, then, at the very least, the prosecution may rebut this presentation with evidence from the reports of the examination that the defendant requested." Thus, the Court found a waiver of Fifth Amendment rights in these circumstances.

Justice Marshall, joined by Justice Brennan, dissented and argued that the state statute governing involuntary hospitalization and treatment was designed to assist the mentally ill person in need of treatment, not to generate evidence of criminal responsibility. Thus, Justice Marshall concluded that when Buchanan agreed to an examination, he implicitly limited his consent to an examination for purposes of hospitalization and treatment.

2. *Documents*

In *Boyd,* the Court held that a subpoena of one's private books and papers violates the Fifth Amendment. What are "private papers" and to what extent are they protected? In *Fisher,* the Court found that the privilege cannot be asserted to prevent the government from obtaining evidence from third parties. The rationale is that the incriminated person has not been *compelled* to do anything when the evidence is gathered from third parties. The same rationale served as a basis for the holding in Andresen v. Maryland, 427 U.S. 463 (1976) (discussed in the previous chapter), that the use at trial of the defendant's business records, seized pursuant to a valid warrant, did not violate the Fifth Amendment. The Court explained:

> [I]n this case, petitioner was not asked to say or to do anything. The records seized contained statements that petitioner had voluntarily committed to writing. The search for and seizure of these records were conducted by law enforcement personnel. Finally, when these records were introduced at trial, they were authenticated by a handwriting expert, not by petitioner. Any compulsion of petitioner to speak, other than the inherent psychological pressure to respond at trial to unfavorable evidence, was not present.
>
> This case thus falls within the principle stated by Mr. Justice Holmes: "A party is privileged from producing the evidence but not from its production." Johnson v. United States, 228 U.S. 457, 458 (1913). * * *

Fisher and *Andresen* probably mean that the portion of *Boyd* holding that a person may rely on the privilege to resist a formal governmental demand for private papers in existence when the demand is made no longer will be followed. *Fisher* does suggest, however, that in some circumstances a person may properly refuse to respond to a subpoena because of the tendency of the response to incriminate.

FISHER v. UNITED STATES

Supreme Court of the United States, 1976.
425 U.S. 391.

* * *

IV

* * *

Several of *Boyd's* express or implicit declarations have not stood the test of time. The application of the Fourth Amendment to subpoenas [has been limited] * * *. Purely evidentiary (but "nontestimonial") materials, as well as contraband and fruits and instrumentalities of crime, may now be searched for and seized under proper circumstances. [Warden v. Hayden, discussed in the previous chapter] * * * Also, any notion that "testimonial" evidence may never be seized and used in evidence is inconsistent with [*Katz, Osborn,* and *Berger,* all discussed in the previous chapter], approving the seizure under appropriate circumstances of conversations of a person suspected of crime.

It is also clear that the Fifth Amendment does not independently proscribe the compelled production of every sort of incriminating evidence but applies only when the accused is compelled to make a *testimonial* communication that is incriminating. * * *

The pronouncement in *Boyd* that a person may not be forced to produce his private papers has nonetheless often appeared as dictum in later opinions of this Court. To the extent, however, that the rule against compelling production of private papers rested on the proposition that seizures of or subpoenas for "mere evidence," including documents, violated the Fourth Amendment and therefore also transgressed the Fifth, the foundations for the rule have been washed away. In consequence, the prohibition against forcing the production of private papers has long been a rule searching for a rationale consistent with the proscriptions of the Fifth Amendment against compelling a person to give "testimony" that incriminates him. Accordingly, we turn to the question of what, if any, incriminating testimony within the Fifth Amendment's protection, is compelled by a documentary summons.

A subpoena served on a taxpayer requiring him to produce an accountant's workpapers in his possession without doubt involves substantial compulsion. But it does not compel oral testimony; nor would it ordinarily compel the taxpayer to restate, repeat, or affirm the truth of the contents of the documents sought. Therefore, the Fifth Amendment would not be violated by the fact alone that the papers on their face might incriminate the taxpayer, for the privilege protects a person only against being incriminated by his own compelled testimonial communications.

The accountant's workpapers are not the taxpayer's. They were not prepared by the taxpayer, and they contain no testimonial declarations by him. Furthermore, as far as this record demonstrates, the preparation of all of the papers sought in these cases was wholly voluntary, and they cannot be said to contain compelled testimonial evidence, either of the taxpayers or of anyone else.[a] The taxpayer cannot avoid com-

a. The fact that the documents may have been written by the person asserting the privilege is insufficient to trigger the privilege, and, unless the Government has compelled the subpoenaed person to write the document, the fact that it was written by him is not controlling with respect to the Fifth Amendment issue. Conversations may be seized and introduced in evidence under proper safeguards, if not compelled. In the case of a documentary subpoena the only thing compelled is the act of producing the document

pliance with the subpoena merely by asserting that the item of evidence which he is required to produce contains incriminating writing, whether his own or that of someone else.

The act of producing evidence in response to a subpoena nevertheless has communicative aspects of its own, wholly aside from the contents of the papers produced. Compliance with the subpoena tacitly concedes the existence of the papers demanded and their possession or control by the taxpayer. It also would indicate the taxpayer's belief that the papers are those described in the subpoena. The elements of compulsion are clearly present, but the more difficult issues are whether the tacit averments of the taxpayer are both "testimonial" and "incriminating" for purposes of applying the Fifth Amendment. These questions perhaps do not lend themselves to categorical answers; their resolution may instead depend on the facts and circumstances of particular cases or classes thereof. In light of the records now before us, we are confident that however incriminating the contents of the accountant's workpapers might be, the act of producing them—the only thing which the taxpayer is compelled to do—would not itself involve testimonial self-incrimination.

It is doubtful that implicitly admitting the existence and possession of the papers rises to the level of testimony within the protection of the Fifth Amendment. The papers belong to the accountant, were prepared by him, and are the kind usually prepared by an accountant working on the tax returns of his client. Surely the Government is in no way relying on the "truthtelling" of the taxpayer to prove the existence of or his access to the documents. The existence and location of the papers are a foregone conclusion and the taxpayer adds little or nothing to the sum total of the Government's information by conceding that he in fact has the papers. Under these circumstances by enforcement of the summons "no constitutional rights are touched. The question is not of testimony but of surrender."

When an accused is required to submit a handwriting exemplar he admits his ability to write and impliedly asserts that the exemplar is his writing. But in common experience, the first would be a near truism and the latter self-evident. In any event, although the exemplar may be incriminating to the accused and although he is compelled to furnish it, his Fifth Amendment privilege is not violated because nothing he has said or done is deemed to be sufficiently testimonial for purposes of the privilege. This Court has also time and again allowed subpoenas against the custodian of corporate documents or those belonging to other collective entities such as unions and partnerships and those of bankrupt businesses over claims that the documents will incriminate the custodian despite the fact that producing the documents tacitly admits their existence and their location in the hands of their possessor. * * *

Moreover, assuming that these aspects of producing the accountant's papers have some minimal testimonial significance, surely it is not illegal to seek accounting help in connection with one's tax returns or for the accountant to prepare workpapers and deliver them to the taxpayer. At this juncture, we are quite unprepared to hold that either the fact of existence of the papers or of their possession by the taxpayer poses any realistic threat of incrimination to the taxpayer.

As for the possibility that responding to the subpoena would authenticate the

and the compelled act is the same as the one performed when a chattel or document not authored by the producer is demanded.

workpapers, production would express nothing more than the taxpayer's belief that the papers are those described in the subpoena. The taxpayer would be no more competent to authenticate the accountant's workpapers or reports by producing them than he would be to authenticate them if testifying orally. The taxpayer did not prepare the papers and could not vouch for their accuracy. The documents would not be admissible in evidence against the taxpayer without authenticating testimony. Without more, responding to the subpoena in the circumstances before us would not appear to represent a substantial threat of self-incrimination.

Whether the Fifth Amendment would shield the taxpayer from producing his own tax records in his possession is a question not involved here; for the papers demanded here are not his "private papers." We do hold that compliance with a summons directing the taxpayer to produce the accountant's documents involved in these cases would involve no incriminating testimony within the protection of the Fifth Amendment.

* * *

Note

The Court applied *Fisher* in United States v. Doe, 465 U.S. 605 (1984), holding that the owner of several sole proprietorships properly invoked his privilege against self-incrimination in response to grand jury subpoenas for business documents and records. A district judge had found that the act of producing the documents would have required the owner to "admit that the records exist, that they are in his possession, and that they are authentic." Justice Powell's opinion for the Court stated that the privilege does not protect the contents of records prepared voluntarily by a taxpayer, since the government did not compel the owner to make incriminating records. Justice Powell recognized, however, that the privilege may be invoked when the act of producing documents involves "testimonial self-incrimination." All Justices agreed with him on this point. Justice O'Connor added a one paragraph concurring opinion stating "that the Fifth Amendment provides absolutely no protection for the contents of private papers of any kind." Justice Marshall, joined by Justice Brennan, offered a short opinion which argued that the Court had not decided whether some private papers might be protected by the privilege. Justice Stevens also wrote a separate opinion.

Most courts after *Doe* have agreed with Justice O'Connor that the contents of voluntarily prepared documents are never protected by the Fifth Amendment. See In re Grand Jury Proceedings on February 4, 1982, 759 F.2d 1418 (9th Cir.1985) (no distinction between business and personal records); In re Steinberg, 837 F.2d 527 (1st Cir.1988). Other courts still draw a business/personal distinction, and hold that the contents of personal records are protected. United States v. (Under Seal), 745 F.2d 834 (4th Cir.1984). Recall that the rationale of *Doe* and *Fisher* is that the contents of documents are not protected when the document is voluntarily prepared; all that is compelled is the act of production. Given that rationale, how can one validly distinguish between voluntarily prepared business records and voluntarily prepared personal records? Is the line between business and personal records an easy line to draw?

In *Fisher,* the Court found that the testimonial aspects of the act of production were not incriminating, since existence, control, and authenticity of the documents was a "foregone conclusion" given other evidence in the case. In *Doe,* the Court accepted the finding of the District Court that the act of production would have incriminated the taxpayer. When would the act of production, independent of the contents of the documents, be incriminating?

The mere existence of documents is rarely incriminating. For example, it is not incriminating for a corporation to have inventory records. However, in certain cases the fact that records exist can itself tend to incriminate. Thus, if a corporation has a second set of books and records, that is incriminating independent of the content of the records. See In re Doe, 711 F.2d 1187 (2d Cir.1983), where a doctor was suspected of dispensing quaaludes without a proper medical purpose. A subpoena for patient files for a certain time period was served. The court found that there were an inordinate number of files for this time period, and that "simply turning over these files could constitute incriminating testimony by Doe that he treated this unrealistic number of patients during the specified periods." See also United States v. Argomaniz, 925 F.2d 1349 (11th Cir.1991) (existence of documents would show that taxpayer had income for a year when he claimed not to have any).

The producer of documents in response to a subpoena admits not only existence but also that he controls the documents. Again, however, it is ordinarily not incriminating to control documents, independent of their content. Certainly, the fact that a records custodian has control of corporate records is not inherently incriminating. However, in some limited cases the admission of control creates an inference of affiliation with another person or business that itself tends to incriminate. Thus, in In re Sealed Case, 832 F.2d 1268 (D.C.Cir.1987), a person allegedly involved in the Iran–Contra scandal was served with a subpoena to produce the records of eight foreign companies involved in covert and illegal activity. The court found that producing the records would be an incriminating admission that he was intimately involved with these corporations.

Finally, the act of production is an admission that the documents are the ones demanded by the government, and this admission could be used in some cases to authenticate the documents at trial. See Federal Rule of Evidence 901. In *Fisher,* the Court found that the taxpayer's admission could not be used to authenticate the documents prepared by the accountant, but the contrary may be true if it is the taxpayer's own records which are demanded.

Even in the limited cases where the act of production would be incriminating, the Fifth Amendment will not apply if existence, control, and authentication are a "foregone conclusion." This will be the case when the government has substantial independent evidence that the records exist, that the witness controls them, and that the records produced are authentic. For example, existence and control can be shown through other witnesses, when the records have either been prepared by or shown to them. See United States v. Clark, 847 F.2d 1467 (10th Cir.1988) (existence and control of records that defendant had once given to his accountant to prepare tax return is proven by subpoenaing accountant to testify; existence and control of bank records can be proven through testimony of bank officials). Persons in similar situations can testify that in their jobs, records such as those subpoenaed exist and they have custody over them. See U.S. S.E.C. v. First Jersey Securities, Inc., 843 F.2d 74 (2d Cir.1988) (possession of parallel documents by other branch managers). Existence and control is often admitted, though perhaps unwittingly, by the witness at some time before the subpoena is served. See United States v. Rue, 819 F.2d 1488 (8th Cir.1987) (dentist demurs to voluntary inspection on grounds that his records are too voluminous to produce). Finally, authentication can be shown in a variety of ways, such as by handwriting exemplars, testimony by those who prepared the documents, and comparison to similar documents. See United States v. Clark, supra. Given all these considerations, how much protection is left for documents after *Fisher* and *Doe?*

Recall that in *Bellis,* the Court held that business entities were not entitled to Fifth Amendment protection. But a business entity itself cannot be compelled to produce incriminating evidence, except through individual agents of the entity. If the act of production of documents would be personally incriminating to an agent of the entity, can the agent invoke his personal Fifth Amendment privilege? This was the question in Braswell v. United States, 487 U.S. 99 (1988). Braswell formed two corporations in which he was the sole shareholder. When a grand jury issued a subpoena to him, in his capacity as agent, to produce the books and records of the two companies, Braswell invoked his personal privilege against self-incrimination on the ground that the act of production might be incriminating. Chief Justice Rehnquist, writing for the Court, relied on the "collective entity" rule to deny the Fifth Amendment claim. The Chief Justice described that rule as follows:

> The official records and documents of the organization that are held [by the agent] in a representative rather than in a personal capacity cannot be the subject of the personal privilege against self-incrimination, even though production of the papers might tend to incriminate [the agent] personally.

The Chief Justice expressed the following rationale for the collective entity rule:

> The custodian of corporate or entity records holds those documents in a representative rather than a personal capacity * * * and a custodian's assumption of his representative capacity leads to certain obligations, including the duty to produce corporate records on proper demand by the Government. Under those circumstances, the custodian's act of production is not deemed a personal act, but rather an act of the corporation.

Braswell sought support from Curcio v. United States, 354 U.S. 118 (1957), where Curcio was served with a subpoena to testify in his capacity as a secretary-treasurer of a local union. Curcio refused to answer any questions as to the whereabouts of the books and records of the union. The Court in *Curcio* held that the collective entity rule did not require "the giving of oral testimony by the custodian." The Chief Justice distinguished *Curcio* in *Braswell,* stating that a corporate agent assumes the risk of producing documents as part of the job, but not the risk of oral testimony.

The Chief Justice reasoned that recognizing a privilege on the part of records custodians would have a detrimental impact on the government's efforts to prosecute white collar crime; that the simple expedient of providing use immunity for the act of production so that it could not be used as evidence against the custodian posed a problem for the government because the act of production might taint other evidence; and that if the privilege were recognized any subpoena to the corporation rather than to a particular custodian might not be honored because the custodian might refuse to cooperate with any other representative of the corporation if cooperation might be incriminating.

Although a custodian like Braswell is not permitted to claim the privilege in response to a subpoena for corporate records, the Court recognized that "certain consequences flow from the fact that the custodian's act of production is one in his representative rather than personal capacity." The Court noted that the government had conceded that "it may make no use of the 'individual act' against the individual," which means, "[f]or example, in a criminal prosecution the Government may not introduce into evidence before the jury the fact that the subpoena was served upon and the corporation's documents were delivered by one particular individual, the custodian." This is not to say, however, that the government may not use the act of production as evidence, since the corporation's act of production may be used as evidence against the custodian. Moreover, "the jury may draw from the corporation's act of production the conclusion that the records in question are authentic corporate records, which the corporation possessed, and which it produced in response to the subpoena, [a]nd if the defendant held a prominent position within the corporation that produced the records, the jury may, just as it would had someone else produced the documents, reasonably infer that he had possession of the documents or knowledge of their contents."

As a result of the limits on the use of the act of production, the Court concluded that the custodian was not incriminated by the fact of personal production, only by the fact of corporate production. The Court left "open the question whether the agency rationale supports compelling a custodian to produce corporate records when the custodian is able to establish, by showing for example that he is the sole employee and officer of the corporation, that the jury would inevitably conclude that he produced the records."

Justice Kennedy, joined by Justices Brennan, Marshall and Scalia, dissented and argued that "[t]he Court today denies an individual his Fifth Amendment privilege against self-incrimination in order to vindicate the rule that a collective entity which employs him has no privilege itself." He found no prior decision of the Court which presented the claim that the act of production by a corporate custodian would be incriminating, and he concluded that the majority's approach to the privilege—i.e., holding that it did not apply to corporate custodians but that the custodians' act of production could not be used as evidence—"avoided and manipulated" basic Fifth Amendment principles. He added that in some instances like *Fisher* the existence of a privilege would not necessarily mean the claim of privilege would be sustained and that simple use immunity limited to the act of production would permit the government to obtain records without compelling a self-incriminating act.

It is easy to state the Court's holding with respect to the privilege but more difficult to understand what difference it would make if the dissenters had prevailed in *Braswell.* In order to understand the stakes in *Braswell,* it is important to know something about the law of immunity, discussed infra. At this point, it should suffice to state that a person loses the right to remain silent because of the privilege if the government, at a minimum, formally guarantees that no compelled testimony or evidence derived from it will be used against the person in a future criminal prosecution. This is called use immunity. The majority states that use immunity would pose problems for the government, and the dissent disagrees.

Suppose that Braswell had been given use immunity for the act of production. The fact that he provided documents to the grand jury could not be used as evidence against him. But, it cannot be used in any event, because of the nonconstitutional agency analysis that the majority holds flows naturally from the logic of its approach. The difference, if any, between the majority and the dissenters must focus, then, on derivative evidence. If Braswell were given use immunity, would the following facts be derived from the act of production: certain documents were prepared by or for the corporation, these documents still exist, and they are under the control of the corporation or its agent? The majority is concerned that the derivative use rule would cover these facts and that the government might have a difficult time proving that any other evidence of the same facts was not also derived from the production by the custodian. In the end, the majority permits the corporation's act of production to be used as evidence and implicitly recognizes that evidence derived from the corporation's act of production is also admissible.

The dissenters would not permit the act of production to be used against the custodian. They also assert that "[i]n appropriate cases the Government will be able to establish authenticity, possession, and control by means other than compelling assertions about them from a suspect."

The Court appears divided on both theoretical and empirical questions. The theoretical question is whether an individual gives up the right to complain of personal incrimination when he assumes an agency position with a collective entity. Is it offensive to refuse to expand the personal privilege to entity situations? The empirical question is whether the requirement of use immunity for acts of production by custodians would pose major problems under the derivative evidence rule.

Note

In Baltimore City Dept. of Social Services v. Bouknight, 493 U.S. 549 (1990), the Court relied in part upon the collective entity rule to find the Fifth Amendment inapplicable to an act of production of a child. Suspecting child abuse, the Department of Social Services obtained a court order removing Maurice Bouknight from his mother's control. The Department obtained a further order declaring Maurice to be a "child in need of assistance" under Maryland law. That court order gave the Department jurisdiction over Maurice. Maurice was returned to his mother, but only under extensive conditions imposed by a protective order. Ms. Bouknight did not comply with those conditions, and the Juvenile Court granted the Department's petition again to remove Maurice from his mother's control. Ms. Bouknight failed to produce Maurice, and Department officials feared that he might be dead. The case was referred to the police homicide division. The Juvenile Court directed that Ms. Bouknight be held in contempt for failing to produce Maurice. That court rejected her argument that the Fifth Amendment protected her from any incrimination that might result from the act of producing Maurice.

Justice O'Connor wrote the majority opinion for the Supreme Court. She assumed, without deciding, that Bouknight's act of producing Maurice could be potentially incriminating, as an "implicit communication of control over Maurice at the moment of production." However, Justice O'Connor concluded that Bouknight could not invoke the privilege "because she has assumed custodial duties related to production and because production is required as part of a noncriminal regulatory regime."

Justice O'Connor found an analogy to *Braswell*. She argued that by "accepting care of Maurice subject to the custodial order's conditions," Bouknight accepted the consequent obligations of production. However, because the act of production would be that of a custodian, Justice O'Connor also relied upon *Braswell's* nonconstitutional agency analysis:

> We are not called upon to define the precise limitations that may exist upon the State's ability to use the testimonial aspect of Bouknight's act of production in subsequent criminal proceedings. But we note that imposition of such limitations is not foreclosed. The same custodial role that limited the ability to resist the production order may give rise to corresponding limitations upon the direct and indirect use of that testimony.

Justice Marshall, joined by Justice Brennan, dissented. He rejected the analogy to the collective entity rule. He reasoned that Bouknight "is not the agent for an artificial entity that possesses no Fifth Amendment privilege. Her role as Maurice's parent is very different from the role of a corporate custodian who is merely the instrumentality through whom the corporation acts."

After *Bouknight,* assume that the Department of Social Services suspects that a child has been abused or murdered, but unlike Bouknight, the child's parent has never been the subject of a prior court order. Could the parent be held in contempt for refusing to produce the child at a juvenile proceeding?

In discussing the nonconstitutional agency analysis of *Braswell,* Justice O'Connor refers to the "direct and indirect" limitations upon the use of the act of production. Does she go farther than the Court did in *Braswell?* What protections after the fact are available to a custodian who is compelled to produce something? If Bouknight revealed the corpse of her son, would the body be admissible in evidence in a subsequent criminal case?

3. *Required Records*

Even if documents are not voluntarily prepared, their contents as well as the act of production will be unprotected if the government requires the documents to be kept for a legitimate administrative purpose that is not focussed solely on those inherently suspect of criminal activity. In Shapiro v. United States, 335 U.S. 1 (1948), a 5–4 decision, Chief Justice Vinson wrote for the Court as it held that the compelled production of defendant's customary business records, which were required to be kept under the Emergency Price Control Act, did not implicate the Fifth Amendment:

> It may be assumed at the outset that there are limits which the Government cannot constitutionally exceed in requiring the keeping of records which may be inspected by an administrative agency and may be used in prosecuting statutory violations committed by the record-keeper himself. But no serious misgiving that those bounds have been overstepped would appear to be evoked when there is a sufficient relation between the activity sought to be regulated and the public concern so that the Government can constitutionally regulate or forbid the basic activity concerned, and can constitutionally require the keeping of particular records, subject to inspection by the Administrator. It is not questioned here that Congress has constitutional authority to prescribe commodity prices as a war emergency measure, and that the licensing and record-keeping requirements of the Price Control Act represent a legitimate exercise of that power. * * *

In a dissenting opinion, Justice Frankfurter indicated what he considered to be the fallacy of the Court's conclusion.

The Court hardly finds a problem in disposing of an issue far-reaching in its implications, involving as they do a drastic change in the relations between the individual and the Government as hitherto conceived. The Court treats the problem as though it were almost self-evident that when records are required to be kept for some needs of Government, or to be kept in a particular form, they are legally considered governmental records and may be demanded as instruments of self-crimination.

* * *

* * * The underlying assumption of the Court's opinion is that all records which Congress in the exercise of its constitutional powers may require individuals to keep in the conduct of their affairs, because those affairs also have aspects of public interest, become "public" records in the sense that they fall outside the constitutional protection of the Fifth Amendment. The validity of such a doctrine lies in the scope of its implications. The claim touches records that may be required to be kept by federal regulatory laws, revenue measures, labor and census legislation in the conduct of business which the understanding and feeling of our people still treat as private enterprise, even though its relations to the public may call for governmental regulation, including the duty to keep designated records.

The majority opinion in *Shapiro* refers to "limits which the Government cannot constitutionally exceed" in requiring that records be kept or produced for inspection. What are those limits? In 1968, the Court decided several cases, in which the scope of the required records doctrine was an issue. Marchetti v. United States, 390 U.S. 39 (1968), involved a defendant who had been convicted for willfully failing to register and to pay an occupational tax for engaging in the business of accepting wagers, as required by 26 U.S.C.A. §§ 4411 and 4412. While acknowledging Congress' authority to tax unlawful activities, the Court reversed the convictions on the ground that "those who properly assert the constitutional privilege as to these provisions may not be criminally punished for failure to comply with their requirements." The Court overruled an earlier line of cases which had held the privilege inapplicable to registration statutes, because they "are entirely prospective in their application" while the privilege "offers protection only as to past and present acts." Justice Harlan, writing for the majority, saw "no reason to suppose that the force of the constitutional prohibition is diminished merely because confession of a guilty purpose precedes the act which it is subsequently employed to evidence." Furthermore, "timely assertion" did not require a claim of privilege at the time the registration and tax were due since that would be as much a confession of guilt as actual registration.[7] Rather, it could be asserted at

7. Anytime that a person is compelled to answer questions on a form that might tend to incriminate that person in a subsequent criminal case, the person can refuse to answer and rely on the Fifth Amendment privilege against self-incrimination. If the person does answer, the privilege will be lost with respect to the answer and it can be used as evidence. See Garner v. United States, 424 U.S. 648 (1976) (holding that a person who answered questions on tax return, rather than invoking the privilege, had not been compelled to testify against himself). *Marchetti* was a different case, because the filing of the return itself tended to incriminate.

In Minnesota v. Murphy, 465 U.S. 420 (1984), the Court reiterated its view that generally a person who is asked to answer questions must invoke his privilege against self-incrimination or lose its protection. It held that a probationer lost the protection of the privilege when he answered questions of his probation officer concerning crimes for which he had not yet been charged. The state supreme court had held that the probation officer should have warned Murphy of his right

trial, and, in fact, would constitute a complete defense to the indictments for failure both to register and to pay the occupational tax.

Justice Harlan compared this case with *Shapiro* and explained why the required records doctrine did not apply:

> Each of the three principal elements of the [required records] doctrine, as it is described in *Shapiro,* is absent from this situation. First, petitioner Marchetti was not, by the provisions now at issue, obliged to keep and preserve records "of the same kind as he has customarily kept"; he was required simply to provide information, unrelated to any records which he may have maintained, about his wagering activities. This requirement is not significantly different from a demand that he provide oral testimony. Second, whatever "public aspects" there were to the records at issue in *Shapiro,* there are none to the information demanded from Marchetti. The Government's anxiety to obtain information known to a private individual does not without more render that information public; if it did, no room would remain for the application of the constitutional privilege. Nor does it stamp information with a public character that the Government has formalized its demands in the attire of a statute; if this alone were sufficient, the constitutional privilege could be entirely abrogated by any Act of Congress. Third, the requirements at issue in *Shapiro* were imposed in "an essentially non-criminal and regulatory area of inquiry" while those here are directed to a "selective group inherently suspect of criminal activities." The United States' principal interest is evidently the collection of revenue, and not the punishment of gamblers, but the characteristics of the activities about which information is sought, and the composition of the groups to which inquiries are made, readily distinguish this situation from that in *Shapiro.*

In Haynes v. United States, 390 U.S. 85 (1968), decided the same day, the Court reversed a conviction for possession of a sawed-off shotgun which had not been registered as required by the National Firearms Act, 26 U.S.C.A. § 5841. The reversal was grounded on a finding that the registration statute created real and appreciable hazards of incrimination, because it was "directed principally at those persons who have obtained possession of a firearm without complying with the Act's other requirements, and who therefore are immediately threatened by criminal prosecution" under other sections of the Act.

Justice Harlan again found the required records doctrine to be inapplicable because the registration did not involve records of the kind "customarily kept," the statutory provisions were directed at "a highly selective group inherently suspect of criminal activities," they were not concerned essentially with noncriminal and regulatory inquiries, and the records involved were in no sense "public."

How does one distinguish between legislation that has a noncriminal or regulatory purpose, such as the production of tax revenue, and one that is essentially criminal? If both require self-reporting that may be incriminating, what is the basis for differential application of the Fifth Amendment? The Court's answers to these questions have been unsatisfactory.

In California v. Byers, 402 U.S. 424 (1971), the constitutionality of California's "hit and run" statute was in issue. Byers was convicted of a misdemean-

to refuse to answer her questions, but a majority of the Supreme Court held that no warnings were required. This case is considered in connection with the Miranda cases, infra.

or for failure to stop at the scene of an accident and to leave his name and address. The California Supreme Court had upheld the statute, but inserted a use restriction on the information provided (i.e., the information could not be used in a criminal prosecution), because disclosure created "substantial hazards of self-incrimination." The United States Supreme Court vacated the state court's judgment, finding that the statute did not infringe the privilege against self-incrimination and thus a use restriction was not constitutionally required. In a plurality opinion, Chief Justice Burger stressed that the public need for self-reporting must be balanced against the individual's claim to constitutional protection. Here, the statutory scheme was essentially regulatory and non-criminal; it was directed to the motoring public at large, rather than to "a highly selective group inherently suspect of criminal activities;" and self-reporting was indispensable to fulfillment of its purposes. On balance, the possibility of incrimination was not sufficiently great to justify invalidation of a statute which provided valuable protection to the public. Even if incrimination was a danger, Chief Justice Burger argued, the Fifth Amendment was not implicated. The act of stopping at the scene of an accident was no more "testimonial" than standing in a line-up, and disclosure of identity "is an essentially neutral act." It would be an extravagant extension of the Fifth Amendment, the Chief Justice concluded, to hold that there is a constitutional right "to flee the scene of an accident in order to avoid the possibility of legal involvement." Justice Harlan, in his opinion concurring in the result in *Byers,* disagreed with the Chief Justice's analysis. Justice Harlan was willing to call the information sought by the statute testimonial and he recognized that it was potentially incriminatory, but he argued that a use restriction would seriously undermine the state's legitimate interests in enforcing criminal sanctions to deter dangerous driving by making those sanctions unavailable in the most appropriate cases—those that involved accidents. A constitutionally mandated use restriction would thus deprive the government of its capacity to use all self-reporting schemes effectively.

Why was a use restriction necessary in the *Marchetti-Haynes* line of cases but not in *Byers?* Why can't the culpable driver who justifiably perceives a risk of self-incrimination claim the same privilege that gamblers and owners of unregistered guns are entitled to assert? Does the purpose of the statutory scheme make a difference? Note that in *Marchetti* and *Haynes,* the asserted legislative purpose was entirely non-criminal. Yet, there the privilege applied anyway. In *Byers,* regulation of driving habits by means of criminal sanctions was an explicit secondary purpose. But here the Court drew a line and refused to apply the privilege. If purpose is important, was the Court wrong in each case? How important is the strength of the governmental interests at stake? In *Marchetti,* a restriction on the use of reported information would in no way impair the interest in taxing gambling activity. However, as noted above, automatic immunity from prosecution for traffic offenses would be detrimental to the state's interest in regulating driving. Are the different results in these cases attributable to a distrust of self-executing assertions of the privilege? As Justice Harlan noted in his concurring opinion in *Byers,* a driver who stops and identifies himself is not automatically acknowledging guilt; the accident may be someone else's fault, and even if the driver is culpable, the state still has the burden of proving that he acted criminally. If we allow noncompliance based on a driver's own assessment of the incriminatory potential of compliance, then the primary purpose of the statute—ensuring financial responsibility for accidents—will be frustrated. However, in *Marchetti* and *Haynes* the mere act of paying an occupation tax or registering an illegal firearm amounted to confession of criminal conduct—the state had no further burden to carry, and there was no danger that the reporting person would over-estimate the incriminatory effect of his statements. See also United States v. Freed, 401 U.S. 601 (1971) (upholding the National Firearms Act disclosure requirements as amended). If the Court had come out the other way in *Marchetti* and *Haynes,* would the required records exception have swallowed the Fifth Amendment rule?

18 U.S.C. § 922(e) makes it a crime to knowingly fail to provide written notice to an airline before shipping firearms. Does a defendant who fails to comply have a Fifth Amendment defense? Courts have held that the statute is within the required records exception, as a legitimate exercise of regulatory activity. See United States v. Alkhafaji, 754 F.2d 641 (6th Cir.1985); United States v. Wilson, 721 F.2d 967 (4th Cir.1983). Isn't the statute targeted toward a group inherently suspect of illegal activity? What legitimate, non-criminal purpose can be found in the statute?

The City of Seattle recently experimented with an ordinance requiring "crack houses" (premises where crack cocaine is sold) to file "neighborhood impact" statements with the City, and imposing criminal sanctions for failure to file such a statement. Can this ordinance be justified under the required records exception?

Recall the discussion of searches based on "special needs" beyond criminal law enforcement in Chapter Two. Do you see any analogy between the law governing those searches and the required records exception?

In Baltimore City Dept. of Social Services v. Bouknight, discussed supra, the Court relied in part upon the required records exception to find the Fifth Amendment inapplicable to an act of production of a child who was feared dead. The mother, upon whom the order to produce the child was served, claimed that the Fifth Amendment protected her from the incriminating aspects of the act of production. The Court held that the collective entity rule and the required records exception each applied, so that the mother was not protected from incrimination.

With regard to the required records exception, Justice O'Connor, writing for the majority, relied heavily on *Shapiro* and *Byers.* As in those cases, the State's demand for information was imposed in an "essentially non-criminal and regulatory area of inquiry" and was not "directed to a selective group inherently suspect of criminal activities." Justice O'Connor reasoned that the State's efforts to gain access to "children in need of assistance" did not focus solely on criminal conduct, and were motivated by the proper regulatory purpose of concern for the child's safety and welfare.

Justice Marshall, joined by Justice Brennan, dissented. He rejected the analogy to the required records exception. He noted that as a matter of fact, the State's scheme was "narrowly targeted at parents who through abuse or neglect deny their children the minimal reasonable level of care and attention," and argued that the State's goal of protecting children from abuse "inevitably intersects" with criminal provisions that serve the same goal.

Note that in *Bouknight,* the matter had been referred to criminal authorities, though the order to produce was issued in a child protective proceeding. Does it matter whether the state is pursuing a civil, protective course or a criminal investigation?

In Bionic Auto Parts and Sales, Inc. v. Fahner, 721 F.2d 1072 (7th Cir.1983), the court held that the privilege against self-incrimination barred a state from enforcing against any person who had a right to claim the privilege a regulation requiring a record of any serial number or identifying mark that was removed from an auto or an auto part. It said that "[a]lthough there is a fine line between a regulatory purpose and the specific effort to root out criminal activity, we are hard pressed to articulate a regulatory rationale for the record-keeping requirement in question." Compare that same court's decision in United States v. Lehman, 887 F.2d 1328 (7th Cir.1989), which held that a statute requiring buyers and sellers of livestock to keep records was within the required records exception. The court stated that "there is nothing ordinarily criminally suspect in buying and selling livestock."

For a general approach to required records, see Saltzburg, The Required Records Doctrine: Its Lessons for the Privilege Against Self-Incrimination, 53 U.Chi.L.Rev. 6 (1986).

G. PROCEDURAL ASPECTS OF SELF-INCRIMINATION CLAIMS

1. *Determining the Risk of Incrimination*

If a criminal defendant decides not to take the stand, there is no need for the court to decide whether this exercise of the privilege is valid, for it clearly is. But when the privilege is invoked by someone who is on the stand in a proceeding, the trial judge must decide whether the privilege is properly invoked. To do this, the judge must determine whether the information requested of a witness might possibly tend to incriminate the witness in the future, and the judge must make the determination without compelling the witness to divulge the information that the witness claims is protected by the privilege. Thus, the task of the court is delicate and in most cases the court must sustain the privilege, because it cannot say that it is

> "*perfectly clear,* from a careful consideration of all the circumstances in the case, that the witness is mistaken, and that the answer[s] *cannot possibly* have such tendency" to incriminate.

Hoffman v. United States, 341 U.S. 479, 488 (1951).

> If a person cannot possibly be prosecuted in the future—e.g., a complete pardon has been issued, double jeopardy clearly bars future prosecution, or immunity (as discussed infra) has been granted—then the privilege cannot be relied upon. If the privilege is applicable, it "extends to answers that would in themselves support a conviction * * * but likewise embraces those which would furnish a link in the chain of evidence needed to prosecute * * *. [I]f the witness, upon interposing his claim, were required to prove the hazard * * * he would be compelled to surrender the very protection which the privilege is designed to guarantee. To sustain the privilege, it need only be evident from the implications of the question, in the setting in which it is asked, that a responsive answer to the question or an explanation of why it

> cannot be answered might be dangerous because injurious disclosure could result."
>
> Id.

See also Malloy v. Hogan, 378 U.S. 1 (1964) (even after Malloy was convicted and served a prison sentence for gambling activities, he could not be compelled to identify his associates in those activities, since disclosure of these names "might furnish a link in a chain of evidence sufficient to connect the petitioner with a more recent crime for which he might still be prosecuted").

2. *Immunity* [8]

If a witness is guaranteed that no criminal prosecution having anything to do with statements given to the government will take place, then there is no possibility of incrimination and no right to refuse to testify because of the privilege. A broad guarantee against future prosecution is often called transactional immunity, to signify that no transaction about which a witness testifies can be the subject of a future prosecution against the witness.

At one time, it appeared that the Supreme Court might require transactional immunity as the cost to the government of forcing a witness to testify. In Counselman v. Hitchcock, 142 U.S. 547 (1892), the Court held that a statute, providing that no "evidence obtained from a party or witness by means of a judicial proceeding * * * shall be given in evidence; or in any matter used against him * * * in any court of the United States," was insufficient to supplant the privilege against self-incrimination.

But, in the landmark case, Kastigar v. United States, 406 U.S. 441 (1972),[9] the Court explained that *Counselman* did not require transactional immunity; what it required was use and "derivative use" or "use-fruits" immunity. The defect in the statute rejected in *Counselman* was that it did not "prevent the use of his testimony to search out other testimony to be used in evidence against him [the immunized witness]." 142 U.S. at 464. In *Kastigar,* the Court upheld 18 U.S.C.A. § 6002, which provides an immunity that prevents the use of testimony or other information obtained from a person "or any information directly or indirectly derived from such testimony or other information." The Court stated that use immunity was "a rational accommodation between the imperatives of the privilege and the legitimate demands of government to compel citizens to testify" and that it "leaves the witness and the prosecutorial

8. It should be noted that immunity is granted in two ways. Usually, a witness refuses to testify and is granted immunity, forcing the witness to testify. If the witness does not initially refuse to talk, any statements made will be deemed to be voluntary. The other way in which immunity is granted is by statute—if a witness testifies, immunity is automatically granted.

In United States v. Doe, 465 U.S. 605 (1984), the Court held that a sole proprietor could rely on the privilege against self-incrimination and decline to produce records as long as the act of production might tend to incriminate. The government had stated that it would not use the act of production as evidence but did not seek a formal grant of immunity. The Court declined "to extend the jurisdiction of courts to include prospective grants of use immunity in the absence of the formal request that the statute requires."

9. Prior to *Kastigar,* the Court had held in Murphy v. Waterfront Comm., 378 U.S. 52 (1964), that a state grant of immunity prevented the federal government from using the compelled testimony or its fruits, and that this protection was sufficient to supplant the Fifth Amendment privilege against self-incrimination. Until *Kastigar,* no one was sure whether the *Murphy* rule applied when the same sovereign granted the immunity and subsequently sought to bring a criminal charge against an immunized witness.

authorities in substantially the same position as if the witness had claimed the Fifth Amendment privilege. The immunity therefore is coextensive with the privilege and suffices to supplant it."

The Court said that after immunity is granted and a witness is compelled to talk, the burden is on the government "to prove that the evidence it proposes to use is derived from a legitimate source wholly independent of the compelled testimony."

Justice Marshall dissented, arguing that the burden placed on the government was not adequate protection for the witness, "[f]or the paths of information through the investigative bureaucracy may well be long and winding, and even a prosecutor acting in the best of faith cannot be certain that somewhere in the depths of his investigative apparatus, often including hundreds of employees, there was not some prohibited use of the compelled testimony." [10]

When a witness gives immunized testimony and is later prosecuted, the question of whether the government has used the fruits of the immunized testimony inevitably arises. One way for the government to satisfy its burden of showing that its evidence is not the fruit of immunized testimony is to establish a "Chinese Wall" between the prosecutors exposed to the testimony and the prosecutors who bring the case against the witness. See United States v. Schwimmer, 882 F.2d 22 (2d Cir.1989) (recommending the "Chinese Wall" approach); U.S. Dep't of Justice, U.S. Attorneys' Manual, § 111.40 (1987) (to demonstrate that no use has been made of the compelled testimony, prosecution should be handled by an attorney unfamiliar with its substance). How likely is it that a "Chinese Wall" will be effective?

In United States v. North, 920 F.2d 940 (D.C.Cir.1990), North had been granted immunity by Congress to testify to his role in the Iran–Contra scandal. His testimony was nationally televised. The Independent Counsel (IC) who brought the case against North was not exposed to the testimony and did not use the immunized testimony at trial. The IC's documentary evidence was "canned" before the testimony began. However, many of the IC's witnesses had seen the testimony on their own. The court held that *Kastigar* is violated "whenever the prosecution puts on a witness whose testimony is shaped, directly or indirectly, by compelled testimony, regardless of *how or by whom* he was exposed to that compelled testimony." The court explained its rationale as follows:

> Were the rule otherwise, a private lawyer for a witness sympathetic to the government could listen to the compelled testimony and use it to prepare the witness for trial. The government would presumably thereby gain the advantage of use of the immunized testimony so long as it did not actually cooperate in that effort. This interpretation of *Kastigar,* ("Look ma, no hands") * * * if accepted, would enormously increase the risk of providing immunized testimony.

10. Justice Douglas also dissented. Justices Brennan and Rehnquist did not participate. Justice Brennan has indicated that he shares Justice Marshall's view. See, e.g., Lefkowitz v. Turley, 414 U.S. 70, 85 (concurring opinion); Piccirillo v. New York, 400 U.S. 548, 562 (1971) (Brennan, J., dissenting). States may still require transactional immunity as a matter of state constitutional or statutory law. See, e.g., Attorney General v. Colleton, 387 Mass. 790, 444 N.E.2d 915 (1982); N.Y.C.P.L. 190.40. Even though a State gives transactional immunity, the witness can still be prosecuted in a Federal court, so long as the testimony is not used. United States v. Gallo, 863 F.2d 185 (2d Cir.1988).

The *North* court was most concerned that the memory of the prosecution witnesses would be impermissibly refreshed by their exposure to the immunized testimony, and that therefore their testimony would carry more weight at trial than it otherwise would have. The court held that the prosecutor's burden of showing no use of the immunized testimony could be met by "canning the testimony beforehand, just as wise prosecutors meet their burden of showing independent investigation by canning the results of the investigation before the defendant gives immunized testimony." Chief Judge Wald argued in dissent that witnesses who wish to frustrate prosecutions will "line up to testify before Congress" in exchange for immunity, and that prospective witnesses at a trial "may seek to frustrate the conviction of a target by exposing themselves to immunized testimony." Under *North,* is there any practical difference between transactional and use immunity?

For cases which take a more permissive view of the prosecutor's burden of showing freedom from taint, see United States v. Serrano, 870 F.2d 1 (1st Cir.1989) (*Kastigar* does not protect against nonevidentiary uses of immunized testimony; a contrary rule "amounts to a per se rule that would in effect grant a defendant transactional immunity" once it is shown that prosecutors, investigators, or witnesses were exposed to it); United States v. Byrd, 765 F.2d 1524 (11th Cir.1985) (*Kastigar* does not prohibit non-evidentiary uses such as for the decision whether to indict, or whether to accept a plea bargain). See also Humble, Nonevidentiary Use of Compelled Testimony: Beyond the Fifth Amendment, 66 Tex.L.Rev. 351 (1987) (Fifth Amendment does not require the government to prove that it made no non-evidentiary use of compelled testimony). In United States v. Pantone, 634 F.2d 716 (3d Cir. 1980), the court said that it did "not believe mere access to immunized grand jury testimony [by the prosecutor] prevents the government from carrying its burden under *Kastigar.*" The court found that the heavy burden of proving an independent source of government evidence was satisfied.

In United States v. Gallo, 859 F.2d 1078 (2d Cir.1988), Gallo's immunized grand jury testimony was used along with other information to obtain a wiretap on another person's phone. Conversations were intercepted that incriminated Gallo, and these were used against him at trial. The court held that *Kastigar* was not violated, since the affidavit upon which the wiretap authorization was based contained sufficient information to support a wiretap even without the immunized testimony. Is this "independent source" analysis consistent with *Kastigar?*

The Supreme Court has made clear that once use immunity is granted, the testimony that is extracted from the immunized witness is coerced and cannot be used as evidence against the witness in a subsequent case involving the matter about which the witness testified, even for impeachment purposes. New Jersey v. Portash, 440 U.S. 450 (1979). Although the witness' testimony may not be used to prove the defendant guilty of acts to which the testimony relates the Supreme Court held in United States v. Apfelbaum, 445 U.S. 115 (1980), that grand jury testimony of a witness who was given use immunity before testifying could be used against him in a subsequent perjury prosecution. Justice Rehnquist's opinion for the Court reasoned that the allegedly false statements and any true statements that are relevant could be used as evidence. Justice Brennan and Justice Blackmun, joined by Justice Marshall, concurred in the result. For a discussion of *Apfelbaum* and *Portash,* see

Hoffman, The Privilege Against Self-Incrimination and Immunity Statutes: Permissible Uses of Immunized Testimony, 16 Crim.L.Bull. 421 (1980).

In Pillsbury Co. v. Conboy, 459 U.S. 248 (1983), the Court upheld the right of a witness at a deposition in a civil case to claim the privilege against self-incrimination even though he had previously been granted use immunity in related criminal proceedings. Conboy was a former executive of a company involved in an antitrust case. He testified before a grand jury after receiving use immunity. Subsequently, his grand jury testimony was provided to lawyers in related civil litigation. The lawyers decided to depose Conboy, and at the deposition, they read from the grand jury transcript in the course of asking questions. Conboy invoked his privilege against self-incrimination, but the district court found that the former immunity grant required him to answer and held him in contempt. A majority of the Court concluded that the prior grant of immunity was not sufficient protection to assure Conboy that nothing that he said at the deposition could be used against him in later criminal proceedings. It also reasoned that should the government ultimately decide to prosecute Conboy, it might have a difficult time proving that its evidence was not derived from the deposition in which the prior immunized testimony was used. To protect both the witness and the government, the Court held that a new immunity grant would be required before the witness could be forced to answer. Justice Marshall wrote a concurring opinion, and Justices Brennan and Blackmun concurred in the judgment. Justice Stevens, joined by Justice O'Connor, dissented.

In United States v. Rylander, 460 U.S. 752 (1983) the IRS served a subpoena on Rylander for corporate books and records. Following Rylander's failure to respond, a civil contempt hearing was held in district court. Rylander testified for the limited purpose of verifying an unsworn letter he sent to the court stating that he did not possess the records and had not disposed of them to other persons. He refused to submit to questions, claiming his privilege against self-incrimination. Rylander bore the burden of producing evidence indicating that he had no ability to comply with the subpoena, and the Court found that he had not met his burden. It refused to shift the burden of producing evidence to the government simply because Rylander invoked his privilege, saying that to do so would "convert the privilege from the shield against self-incrimination which it was intended to be into a sword whereby a claimant asserting the privilege would be freed from adducing proof in support of a burden which would otherwise have been his." Justice Marshall dissented. Should use immunity be required from someone caught in the situation in which Rylander found himself? To avoid contempt, Rylander had to speak. Yet, he could not speak without risking incrimination. Was he really seeking to abuse the privilege?

3. *Waiver of the Privilege*

If a defendant elects to testify, has the defendant waived the privilege completely? On direct examination, the defendant can control what she says, but not on cross-examination. The usual rule is that a defendant who takes the stand is treated like any other witness. American jurisdictions vary on the scope of cross-examination. Some restrict the scope to that of the direct examination and others permit the cross-examiner to raise new matters. If the evidence rule governs when the defendant testifies, then the scope of a constitutional right is dependent on a rule of evidence. See generally G. Lilly, An Introduction to the Law of Evidence § 4.10 (2d ed. 1987). The following suggestion has been made for a fair accommodation of the interests of the defendant and the government:

> "* * * We * * * recommend that the defendant be subject to cross-examination to the extent necessary to fairly test the statements made upon direct examination and inferences that might be drawn from such statements. This position respects the privilege, but insures that it does not give the defendant an extra tactical weapon not contemplated by the Constitution. As for claims that the Fifth Amendment privilege is already too costly and any intrusion should be welcome, we must reject such cavalier treatment of the Constitution. If the document is to be amended it should be amended directly. Moreover, the accused who elects to testify opens the door to impeachment under [other rules] that can be damaging. Thus, the decision to waive the privilege involves costs as well as benefits."

S. Saltzburg & M. Martin, 1 Federal Rules of Evidence Manual 686–87 (5th ed. 1990). Would you take the same or a different approach?

United States v. Panza, 612 F.2d 432 (9th Cir.1979), upholds a trial judge's decision striking a defendant's testimony for refusing to answer the prosecutor's questions. See also United States v. Hearst, 563 F.2d 1331 (9th Cir.1977), where the defendant testified that she was under duress from members of the Symbionese Liberation Army at the time of the bank robbery with which she was charged. The court held that she waived the privilege with respect to questions on cross-examination concerning a later period in which she allegedly lived with SLA members voluntarily. The court found that the Government's questions were "reasonably related" to the subjects covered by the direct testimony. Hearst unsuccessfully relied on Calloway v. Wainwright, 409 F.2d 59 (5th Cir.1968), a case in which the defendant testified at trial that his confession was involuntarily obtained. The *Calloway* court held that defendant had not waived the privilege concerning the substance of the charges against him, and therefore that the prosecutor's reference to Calloway's failure to testify on these matters violated *Griffin.* Why was *Calloway* not helpful to Hearst? See also Lesko v. Lehman, 925 F.2d 1527 (3d Cir.1991) (defendant who testifies at capital sentencing hearing concerning biographical information does not waive the privilege concerning the circumstances of the crime).

In Buchanan v. Kentucky, discussed in the material after *Schmerber,* the Court found a waiver of the Fifth Amendment right to exclude a psychiatric report when the defendant used an insanity defense based on psychiatric testimony.

II. CONFESSIONS AND DUE PROCESS

A. INTRODUCTION

The United States Supreme Court has relied on three constitutional provisions in determining the admissibility of confessions:

(1) From 1936–1964, the due process clauses of the Fifth and Fourteenth Amendments were used as the standard by which to judge the voluntariness of a confession.

(2) From 1964–1966, the Sixth Amendment right to counsel became important in determining whether a confession was properly obtained.

(3) Since 1966, the Fifth Amendment's privilege against self-incrimination has been the basis of coerced confession claims; a waiver analysis has prevailed, and the privilege must be shown to have been effectively waived before a confession is admissible. Sixth Amendment cases continue to supplement the Fifth Amendment protection. The due process test is still relevant, but it is invoked less frequently than the privilege against self-incrimination and the right to counsel.

These developments have not been as smooth as this brief description might suggest. The changing nature of coerced confession claims and of the Court's approach to them is an important part of the development of constitutionally-based criminal procedure. Thus, it warrants careful attention.

In 1884, the Court reviewed a federal criminal conviction in Hopt v. People of Territory of Utah, 110 U.S. 574.[11] It explicitly recognized that there was a common law rule prohibiting the use of confessions obtained by inducements, promises and threats. Because of their inherent unreliability, such confessions were not admitted into evidence. The same desire to prevent erroneous convictions led the Court to cite treatises on evidence and to follow the common law rule. (There is no indication that the Court was relying on any constitutional language.) See also Sparf v. United States, 156 U.S. 51 (1895); Pierce v. United States, 160 U.S. 355 (1896).

Thirteen years later, in Bram v. United States, 168 U.S. 532 (1897) (suspect in custody of police was stripped, searched and questioned), the Court abruptly departed from an emphasis on the reliability of confessions, and relied on the self-incrimination clause of the Fifth Amendment to find that statements of an accused, which were introduced to establish his guilt, were made involuntarily and therefore violated the constitutional prohibition against compelled incrimination. This decision was sharply criticized by a number of legal scholars as an erroneous union of the right against self-incrimination and the common law confessions rule.[12]

The proposition that the Fifth Amendment is the proper basis on which to assess the admissibility of confessions "was not itself developed in subsequent decisions," Miranda v. Arizona, 384 U.S. 436, 506 (1966) (Harlan, J., dissenting). This was so, even though the rule stated in Justice White's majority opinion in *Bram* was not challenged by Justice Brewer's dissent, in which Chief Justice Fuller and Justice Brown joined. Although it did not overrule *Bram,* for two-thirds of a century the Court never explicitly and exclusively relied on the privilege against self-incrimination to suppress the use of a confession in another federal case. It did assume in dicta, however, that *Bram* might have continued force. See, e.g., Burdeau v. McDowell, 256 U.S. 465 (1921). See generally, Developments in the Law: Confessions, 79 Harv.L.Rev. 935, 959–61 (1966). (The Court could not rely on *Bram* in reviewing state confession cases until 1964 when the Fifth Amendment's self-incrimination clause was incorporated into the Fourteenth Amendment and thereby made applicable to the

11. This section on the background of confessions law draws heavily from O. Stephens, The Supreme Court and Confessions of Guilt 19–26 (1973).

12. See, e.g., 3 J. Wigmore, Evidence § 823 (Chadbourn Rev. 1981).

states.) After *Bram* and until 1964, the Court turned to the due process clauses of the Constitution to decide coerced confession cases.

B. THE DUE PROCESS CASES

The Court made its first important decision on confessions under the due process clause of the Fourteenth Amendment in Brown v. Mississippi, 297 U.S. 278 (1936). Summarily reversing convictions obtained in the state court, the Supreme Court found that severe whippings, used to procure confessions from helpless defendants, made the confessions involuntary and violated basic due process rights. In reaching its decision, the Court emphasized the unreliability of confessions extracted by torture and, referred to the confessions in *Brown* as "spurious."

The Court decided thirty-five confession cases between *Brown* in 1936 and Massiah v. United States, 377 U.S. 201 in 1964.[13] It struggled in the ensuing cases, which involved more subtle and less physical methods of obtaining confessions, to define appropriate constitutional limitations on the interrogation methods used by police in light of the capacity of an individual possessed of free will to withstand coercion. Case-by-difficult case, the Court attempted to describe the reach of the due process clauses, and their role in controlling the methods by which government agents seek evidence.[14]

A summary, by no means exhaustive, might convey the breadth of circumstances that the Court considered when it tried to determine the validity of confessions. With respect to the personal characteristics of the accused, the Court was not only concerned with the youthfulness of the suspect, but also with the educational background of the accused in cases such as Payne v. Arkansas, 356 U.S. 560 (1958) (fifth grade education), and Fikes v. Alabama, 352 U.S. 191 (1957) (illiterate). In addition, the court was sensitive to any mental deficiency of the defendant as illustrated by Culombe v. Connecticut, 367 U.S. 568, 620 (1961) (illiterate mental defective of the moron class), and Blackburn v. Alabama, 361 U.S. 199, 207 (1960) (strong probability that the accused was insane and incompetent at the time he allegedly confessed). Conversely, the Court was less likely to find undue coercion if the defendant was well-educated as in Crooker v. California, 357 U.S. 433 (1958) (accused had completed one year of law school), or was a hardened veteran of criminal proceedings as in Stein v. New York, 346 U.S. 156, 185 (1953) (defendants were not "young, soft, ignorant or timid").

In considering circumstances of physical deprivation or mistreatment, the Court not only disapproved of severe brutality like that found in *Brown,* supra, but also of the denial of food, *Payne,* supra (accused was given no food for twenty-four hours), or sleep, Ashcraft v. Tennessee, 322 U.S. 143 (1944) (defendant was not permitted to sleep for thirty-six hours). If the accused was permitted certain amenities, the Court responded favorably. In *Crooker,* supra, for instance, the confession was found admissible and the Court pointed out that the defendant was provided with food and was permitted to smoke during interrogations.

13. See generally, G. James, Constitutional Limitations on Evidence in Criminal Cases, 260 (1973).

14. See generally, J. Cook, Constitutional Rights of the Accused: Trial Rights § 71, at 274 (1974).

A third factor, psychological influence, was also accorded great weight by the Court. Although the Court stated that a voluntary statement need not be volunteered, it refused to hold that only physical brutality was impermissible. In Watts v. Indiana, 338 U.S. 49, 53 (1949), the Court said that:

> if [the confession] is the product of sustained pressure by the police it does not issue from a free choice. When a suspect speaks because he is overborne, it is immaterial whether he has been subjected to a physical or mental ordeal. Eventual yielding to questioning under such circumstances is plainly the product of the suction process of interrogation and therefore the reverse of voluntary.

In *Watts,* as in Haley v. Ohio, 332 U.S. 596 (1948), and numerous other cases, the Court paid special attention to whether the accused was denied the aid of family, friends or counsel.[15] Incommunicado confinement consistently was viewed as coercive. Another form of psychological influence was trickery. See generally White, Police Trickery in Inducing Confessions, 127 U.Pa.L.Rev. 581 (1979).

The Court also recognized the pressure inherent in such psychological techniques as sustained interrogation, *Ashcraft,* supra, and the threat of mob violence, *Payne,* supra (defendant was told thirty to forty people would be waiting to get him unless he confessed). The Court also was concerned about rewards and inducements to confess, which had been condemned in *Hopt,* supra. New techniques as well as old were carefully scrutinized. For example, in Leyra v. Denno, 347 U.S. 556 (1954), the Court took exception to the use of a trained psychiatrist to extract a confession through skillful and suggestive questioning.

Finally, as will be considered in more detail later, in applying the voluntariness standard, the Court considered whether the accused was aware or had been apprised of his constitutional right to counsel, as well as his right to remain silent.

It should be apparent from this overview that the voluntariness standard required a case-by-case scrutiny of the circumstances surrounding a particular confession to determine if the methods by which it was obtained comported with due process. The Court considered both the police conduct in procuring the confession and the defendant's ability to withstand coercion; therefore, the "totality of the circumstances" test that was set forth in Fikes v. Alabama, 352 U.S. 191 (1957), was determinative of the voluntariness of the confession.

In reviewing confession cases, the Court made it clear that it would overturn a finding that a confession was voluntary if there was undisputed contrary evidence in the record. Chambers v. Florida, 309 U.S. 227, 228 (1940). Furthermore, as the emphasis shifted from the reliability of a coerced confession to concern about the manner in which the police extracted it, it soon became the rule that even if sufficient evidence existed from sources independent of the confession that the accused committed the crime charged, the conviction was still to be reversed if a coerced confession had been admitted at trial. The rationale behind this rule was that it was not known if the jury

15. Some other cases in which the accused was not permitted the support of friends or counsel include Chambers v. Florida, 309 U.S. 227 (1940); Ward v. Texas, 316 U.S. 547 (1942); Ashcraft v. Tennessee, 322 U.S. 143 (1944); Turner v. Pennsylvania, 338 U.S. 62 (1949); and Blackburn v. Alabama, 361 U.S. 199 (1960).

relied on the confession in reaching its verdict. Payne v. Arkansas, 356 U.S. 560, 568 (1958). Later, however, the Court held that admission of a coerced confession would not result in reversal if the error was harmless beyond a reasonable doubt. Arizona v. Fulminante, 111 S.Ct. 1246 (1991). However, the *Fulminante* Court recognized that, because of its evidentiary potency, the admission of a coerced confession would rarely be harmless error. The error in *Fulminante* was found not to be harmless. The Court's analysis of the harmless error rule is discussed in Chapter 13.

Although the Court refined its analysis of the voluntariness test in the course of handing down over 30 full-length opinions under the due process standard, some members of the Court recognized the shortcomings of the voluntariness approach. Justice Frankfurter, a supporter of the due process standard, noted in *Columbe* that "[n]o single litmus-paper test for constitutionally impermissible interrogations has been evolved. * * * " The word "voluntary" hardly offered clear guidance to law enforcement officers and to lower court judges. It had to be defined anew in every case. Because the Court could not possibly pass on all of the state confession cases in which review was sought, usually certiorari was limited to death penalty cases or others of special concern. Thus, the confusion in the lower courts was not something with which the High Court could concern itself. In fact, each totality of the circumstances decision, it might be argued, caused a greater division among lower trial and appellate courts. That the Justices themselves often disagreed on the proper application of the test compounded the problem.

C. RISING CONCERN WITH THE DUE PROCESS APPROACH

The growing dissatisfaction by certain members of the Court with the voluntariness standard became very apparent in 1959 when in Spano v. New York, 360 U.S. 315 (1959), four concurring justices expressed greater concern about the fact that the defendant Spano had been indicted and was refused permission to see his attorney than about the voluntariness of the confession under the totality of the circumstances.

SPANO v. NEW YORK

Supreme Court of the United States, 1959.
360 U.S. 315.

MR. CHIEF JUSTICE WARREN delivered the opinion of the Court.

This is another in the long line of cases presenting the question whether a confession was properly admitted into evidence under the Fourteenth Amendment. As in all such cases, we are forced to resolve a conflict between two fundamental interests of society; its interest in prompt and efficient law enforcement, and its interest in preventing the rights of its individual members from being abridged by unconstitutional methods of law enforcement. Because of the delicate nature of the constitutional determination which we must make, we cannot escape the responsibility of making our own examination of the record.

The State's evidence reveals the following: Petitioner Vincent Joseph Spano is a derivative citizen of this country, having been born in Messina, Italy. He was 25 years old at the time of the shooting in question and had graduated from junior high school. He had a record of regular employment. The shooting took place on January 22, 1957.

On that day, petitioner was drinking in a bar. The decedent, a former professional boxer weighing almost 200 pounds who had fought in Madison Square Garden, took some of petitioner's money from the bar. Petitioner followed him out of the bar to recover it. A fight ensued, with the decedent knocking petitioner down and then kicking him in the head three or four times. Shock from the force of these blows caused petitioner to vomit. After the bartender applied some ice to his head, petitioner left the bar, walked to his apartment, secured a gun, and walked eight or nine blocks to a candy store where the decedent was frequently to be found. He entered the store in which decedent, three friends of decedent, at least two of whom were ex-convicts, and a boy who was supervising the store were present. He fired five shots, two of which entered the decedent's body, causing his death. The boy was the only eyewitness; the three friends of decedent did not see the person who fired the shot. Petitioner then disappeared for the next week or so.

On February 1, 1957, the Bronx County Grand Jury returned an indictment for first-degree murder against petitioner. * * *

On February 3, 1957, petitioner called one Gaspar Bruno, a close friend of 8 or 10 years' standing who had attended school with him. Bruno was a fledgling police officer, having at that time not yet finished attending police academy. According to Bruno's testimony, petitioner told him "that he took a terrific beating, that the deceased hurt him real bad and he dropped him a couple of times and he was dazed; he didn't know what he was doing and that he went and shot at him." Petitioner told Bruno that he intended to get a lawyer and give himself up. Bruno relayed this information to his superiors.

The following day, February 4, at 7:10 p.m., petitioner, accompanied by counsel, surrendered himself to the authorities in front of the Bronx County Building, where both the office of the Assistant District Attorney who ultimately prosecuted his case and the courtroom in which he was ultimately tried were located. His attorney had cautioned him to answer no questions, and left him in the custody of the officers. He was promptly taken to the office of the Assistant District Attorney and at 7:15 p.m. the questioning began, being conducted by Assistant District Attorney Goldsmith, Lt. Gannon, Detectives Farrell, Lehrer and Motta, and Sgt. Clarke. The record reveals that the questioning was both persistent and continuous. Petitioner, in accordance with his attorney's instructions, steadfastly refused to answer. Detective Motta testified: "He refused to talk to me." "He just looked up to the ceiling and refused to talk to me." Detective Farrell testified:

"Q. And you started to interrogate him?

"A. That is right.

* * *

"Q. What did he say?

"A. He said 'you would have to see my attorney. I tell you nothing but my name.'

* * *

"Q. Did you continue to examine him?

"A. Verbally, yes, sir."

He asked one officer, Detective Ciccone, if he could speak to his attorney, but that request was denied. Detective Ciccone testified that he could not find the attorney's name in the telephone book. He was given two sandwiches, coffee and cake at 11 p.m.

At 12:15 a.m. on the morning of February 5, after five hours of questioning in which it became evident that petitioner was following his attorney's instructions, on the Assistant District Attorney's orders petitioner was transferred to the 46th Squad, Ryer Avenue Police Station. The Assistant District Attorney also went to the police station and to some extent continued to participate in the interrogation. Petitioner arrived at 12:30 and questioning was resumed at 12:40. The character of the questioning is revealed by the testimony of Detective Farrell:

> "Q. Who did you leave him in the room with?
>
> "A. With Detective Lehrer and Sergeant Clarke came in and Mr. Goldsmith came in or Inspector Halk came in. It was back and forth. People just came in, spoke a few words to the defendant or they listened a few minutes and they left."

But petitioner persisted in his refusal to answer, and again requested permission to see his attorney, this time from Detective Lehrer. His request was again denied.

It was then that those in charge of the investigation decided that petitioner's close friend, Bruno, could be of use. He had been called out on the case around 10 or 11 p.m., although he was not connected with the 46th Squad or Precinct in any way. Although, in fact, his job was in no way threatened, Bruno was told to tell petitioner that petitioner's telephone call had gotten him "in a lot of trouble," and that he should seek to extract sympathy from petitioner for Bruno's pregnant wife and three children. Bruno developed this theme with petitioner without success, and petitioner, also without success, again sought to see his attorney, a request which Bruno relayed unavailingly to his superiors. After this first session with petitioner, Bruno was again directed by Lt. Gannon to play on petitioner's sympathies, but again no confession was forthcoming. But the Lieutenant a third time ordered Bruno falsely to importune his friend to confess, but again petitioner clung to his attorney's advice. Inevitably, in the fourth such session directed by the Lieutenant, lasting a full hour, petitioner succumbed to his friend's prevarications and agreed to make a statement. Accordingly, at 3:25 a.m. the Assistant District Attorney, a stenographer, and several other law enforcement officials entered the room where petitioner was being questioned, and took his statement in question and answer form with the Assistant District Attorney asking the questions. The statement was completed at 4:05 a.m.

But this was not the end. At 4:30 a.m. three detectives took petitioner to Police Headquarters in Manhattan. On the way they attempted to find the bridge from which petitioner said he had thrown the murder weapon. They crossed the Triborough Bridge into Manhattan, arriving at Police Headquarters at 5 a.m., and left Manhattan for the Bronx at 5:40 a.m. via the Willis Avenue Bridge. When petitioner recognized neither bridge as the one from which he had thrown the weapon, they reentered Manhattan via the Third Avenue Bridge, which petitioner stated was the right one, and then returned to the Bronx well after 6 a.m. During that trip the officers also elicited a statement from petitioner that the deceased was always "on [his] back," "always pushing" him and that he was "not sorry" he had shot the deceased. All three detectives testified to that statement at the trial.

Court opened at 10 a.m. that morning and petitioner was arraigned at 10:15.

At the trial, the confession was introduced in evidence over appropriate objections. The jury was instructed that it could rely on it only if it was found to be voluntary. The jury returned a guilty verdict and petitioner was sentenced to death. * * *

Petitioner's first contention is that his absolute right to counsel in a capital case, Powell v. Alabama, 287 U.S. 45, became operative on the return of an indictment against him, for at that time he was in every sense a defendant in a criminal case, the grand jury having found sufficient cause to believe that he had committed the crime. He argues accordingly that following indictment no confession obtained in the absence of counsel can be used without violating the Fourteenth Amendment. He seeks to distinguish Crooker v. California, 357 U.S. 433, and Cicenia v. Lagay, 357 U.S. 504, on the ground that in those cases no indictment had been returned. We find it unnecessary to reach that contention, for we find use of the confession obtained here inconsistent with the Fourteenth Amendment under traditional principles.

The abhorrence of society to the use of involuntary confessions does not turn alone on their inherent untrustworthiness. It also turns on the deep-rooted feeling that the police must obey the law while enforcing the law; that in the end life and liberty can be as much endangered from illegal methods used to convict those thought to be criminals as from the actual criminals themselves. Accordingly, the actions of police in obtaining confessions have come under scrutiny in a long series of cases. Those cases suggest that in recent years law enforcement officials have become increasingly aware of the burden which they share, along with our courts, in protecting fundamental rights of our citizenry, including that portion of our citizenry suspected of crime. The facts of no case recently in this Court have quite approached the brutal beatings in Brown v. Mississippi, 297 U.S. 278 (1936), or the 36 consecutive hours of questioning present in Ashcraft v. Tennessee, 322 U.S. 143 (1944). But as law enforcement officers become more responsible, and the methods used to extract confessions more sophisticated, our duty to enforce federal constitutional protections does not cease. It only becomes more difficult because of the more delicate judgments to be made. Our judgment here is that, on all the facts, this conviction cannot stand.

Petitioner was a foreign-born young man of 25 with no past history of law violation or of subjection to official interrogation, at least insofar as the record shows. He had progressed only one-half year into high school and the record indicates that he had a history of emotional instability. He did not make a narrative statement, but was subject to the leading questions of a skillful prosecutor in a question and answer confession. He was subjected to questioning not by a few men, but by many. * * * All played some part, and the effect of such massive official interrogation must have been felt. Petitioner was questioned for virtually eight straight hours before he confessed, with his only respite being a transfer to an arena presumably considered more appropriate by the police for the task at hand. Nor was the questioning conducted during normal business hours, but began in early evening, continued into the night, and did not bear fruition until the not-too-early morning. The drama was not played out, with the final admissions obtained, until almost sunrise. In such circumstances slowly mounting fatigue does, and is calculated to, play its part. The questioners persisted in the face of his repeated refusals to answer on the advice of his attorney, and they ignored his reasonable requests to contact the local attorney whom he had already retained and who had personally delivered him into the custody of these officers * * *.

The use of Bruno, characterized in this Court by counsel for the State as a "childhood friend" of petitioner's, is another factor which deserves mention in the totality of the situation. Bruno's was the one face visible to petitioner in which he could put some trust. There was a bond of friendship between them going back a decade into adolescence. It was with this material that the officers felt that they could overcome petitioner's will. They instructed Bruno falsely to state that petitioner's telephone call had gotten him into trouble, that his job was in jeopardy, and that loss of his job would be disastrous to his three children, his wife and his unborn child. And Bruno played this part of a worried father, harried by his superiors, in not one, but four different acts, the final one lasting an hour.

* * *

We conclude that petitioner's will was overborne by official pressure, fatigue and sympathy falsely aroused, after considering all the facts in their post-indictment setting. Here a grand jury had already found sufficient cause to require petitioner to face trial on a charge of first-degree murder, and the police had an eyewitness to the shooting. The police were not therefore merely trying to solve a crime, or even to absolve a suspect. They were rather concerned primarily with securing a statement from defendant on which they could convict him. The undeviating intent of the officers to extract a confession from petitioner is therefore patent. * * *

* * *

MR. JUSTICE DOUGLAS, with whom MR. JUSTICE BLACK and MR. JUSTICE BRENNAN join, concurring.

While I join the opinion of the Court, I add what for me is an even more important ground of decision.

We have often divided on whether state authorities may question a suspect for hours on end when he has no lawyer present and when he has demanded that he have the benefit of legal advice. See Crooker v. California, and cases cited. But here we deal not with a suspect but with a man who has been formally charged with a crime. The question is whether after the indictment and before the trial the Government can interrogate the accused *in secret* when he asked for his lawyer and when his request was denied. This is a capital case; and under the rule of Powell v. Alabama, the defendant was entitled to be represented by counsel. This representation by counsel is not restricted to the trial. As stated in Powell v. Alabama:

> "during perhaps the most critical period of the proceedings against these defendants, that is to say, from the time of their arraignment until the beginning of their trial, when consultation, thoroughgoing investigation and preparation were vitally important, the defendants did not have the aid of counsel in any real sense, although they were as much entitled to such aid during that period as at the trial itself."

Depriving a person, formally charged with a crime, of counsel during the period prior to trial may be more damaging than denial of counsel during the trial itself.

* * *

This is a case of an accused, who is scheduled to be tried by a judge and jury, being tried in a preliminary way by the police. This is a kangaroo court procedure whereby the police produce the vital evidence in the form of a confession which is useful or necessary to obtain a conviction. They in effect deny him effective representation by counsel. * * * When he is deprived of that right after indictment and before trial, he may indeed be denied effective representation by counsel at the only stage when legal aid and advice would help him.

MR. JUSTICE STEWART, whom MR. JUSTICE DOUGLAS and MR. JUSTICE BRENNAN join, concurring.

While I concur in the opinion of the Court, it is my view that the absence of counsel when this confession was elicited was alone enough to render it inadmissible under the Fourteenth Amendment.

* * *

Our Constitution guarantees the assistance of counsel to a man on trial for his life in an orderly courtroom, presided over by a judge, open to the public, and protected by all the procedural safeguards of the law. Surely a Constitution which promises that much can vouchsafe no less to the same man under midnight inquisition in the squad room of a police station.

Note on Modern Due Process Cases

The concurring justices emphasized that once a person is formally charged by an indictment or information, his constitutional right to counsel begins, at least when counsel previously has been retained. Although the majority of the Court rejected the confession under the voluntariness standard, the majority did not reject the views expressed in the concurring opinions. It left the counsel question for another day, which was not long in coming, as we shall soon see.

Spano and later cases assumed that the problem of physical brutality and the related problem of unreliability of statements beaten from a suspect do not frequently arise today. Unfortunately, this may be an overly optimistic attitude. See generally Abramovitz, When Suspects are Abused, Nat'l L.J., June 11, 1979, at 1, col. 1.

Despite the Court's regulation of confessions through the Sixth Amendment in *Massiah* and through the Fifth Amendment in *Miranda,* the totality of the circumstances voluntariness test is in some cases a suspect's only protection from police coercion. The Sixth Amendment does not apply until the suspect has been formally charged (Moran v. Burbine, infra). *Miranda* applies only during police "custodial interrogation," and that term does not cover all potentially coercive police practices (Rhode Island v. Innis, infra). See United States v. Murphy, 763 F.2d 202 (6th Cir.1985) (sending an attack dog to apprehend the suspect is not custodial interrogation, but confession made while dog was attacking held involuntary). Moreover, *Miranda* rights can be waived. Finally, the Court has held that a violation of *Miranda* is not itself a violation of the Constitution, so that a *Miranda*–defective confession can be used for impeachment (Harris v. New York, infra), the fruits of such a confession are admissible (Oregon v. Elstad, infra), and the confession itself can be admitted if obtained under emergency circumstances (New York v. Quarles, infra). However, where *Miranda* and *Massiah* are inapplicable, the confession is still excluded under the Due Process Clause if obtained through police coercion.

It is the rare case in which a court will find that a suspect confessed involuntarily. See White, Interrogation Without Questions, 78 Mich.L.Rev. 1209 (1980). Examples of cases denying involuntariness claims are Sumpter v. Nix, 863 F.2d 563 (8th Cir.1988) (suspect with I.Q. of 89 and psychological problems, promised treatment, and interrogated for 7½ hours); McCall v. Dutton, 863 F.2d 454 (6th Cir.1988) (defendant was wounded, and officers interrogated with guns drawn); Moore v. Dugger, 856 F.2d 129 (11th Cir.1988) (suspect with an I.Q. of 62, who functioned at the level of an 11-year old, had been without food or sleep for 25 hours at the time he confessed).

Jurek v. Estelle, 623 F.2d 929 (5th Cir.1980) (en banc), well illustrates the difficulty of applying a "coercion" test to a mentally deficient suspect. One written confession, obtained after several oral statements were made, was deemed to be voluntary. A second statement was held to be involuntary because it was the subject of continuing purposeful and suggestive interrogation directed toward amending the first confession in an unreliable way that was designed to produce a death penalty. The majority found *Spano* to be helpful authority.

Grano, Voluntariness, Free Will, and the Law of Confessions, 65 Va.L.Rev. 859 (1979), argues that an involuntary confession is "any confession produced by interrogation pressures that a person of reasonable firmness, with some of the defendant's characteristics, would not resist." How would *Spano* be resolved under this standard?

What effect does the use of police deception and similar psychological ploys have on the voluntariness inquiry? The Court in *Bram* had stated that a confession induced by "any direct or implied promises, however slight" must be suppressed. But courts have not followed that language from *Bram.* For example, in Green v. Scully, 850 F.2d 894 (2d Cir.1988), Green was taken to the station by two New York detectives to be interrogated as a murder suspect. He waived his *Miranda* rights. Thereafter, Detective Byrnes threatened him with the electric chair, even though there is no capital punishment in New York. Then Byrnes left the room. During a lengthy interrogation, Detective Hazel consistently asserted that the police had all the evidence they needed to convict Green, stating that he had personally checked it out. This was false. When Green stated that he would never confess because he would not be able to face his and the victim's families, Hazel said he could help Green with that and suggested that Green must have been mentally ill when he committed the murder. Hazel referred to Green as "brother" and said that he would get psychiatric help for Green. Then Hazel took a different tack, appeared frustrated, and threatened to leave the interrogation over to the "bad cop," Byrnes. Byrnes then came in and stated that he had found Green's palm prints at the scene, with blood stains on them. This was not true. Byrnes told Green that he was lucky that Hazel was there, because Hazel cared about him while Byrnes did not. Green then began to consider cooperating, after again receiving assurance from Hazel that he would obtain psychiatric help. In the course of his confession, Green stated that he suffered from blackouts, that he was confessing out of fear that if he were not convicted on this crime he might kill someone else, and that confessing would be the only way to obtain psychiatric help.

The court held that the confession was voluntary. It concluded that despite *Bram,* "the presence of a direct or implied promise of help or leniency alone has not barred the admission of a confession" and that "promises do not require an analysis separate from or different than the totality of circumstances rule." The court found that Green was of above average intelligence, streetwise, that the interrogation session was only two hours long, and that Green was not handcuffed or in pain during that time. As to the psychological tactics, the court found the police conduct "troubling." The tactics were not dispositive however, because the court concluded that Green had his own motivation for confessing.

> [T]he scare tactics, false representation as to the evidence, good cop/bad cop routine, and whatever hopes were instilled from the promises or fears from the reference to the 'chair' considered together did not overbear Green's will and bring about his confession. He confessed—as he candidly admitted—

because he was afraid that what he had done to the victims in a blackout would be something he was going to do to his own family—maybe even his mother.

Did the court overlook the fact that Green confessed not precisely to take himself "off the street," but because in doing so he would obtain psychiatric help? Suppose Green had been taken before a judge for a bail hearing, and the judge had offered to obtain psychiatric help for Green if he would confess. Would the confession be coerced? If so, is it true that a judge has more coercive power over a suspect than the officers had in *Green?*

In Florida v. Cayward, 552 So.2d 971 (Fla.App.1989), police fabricated a scientific report for use as a ploy in interrogating the defendant. The report was prepared on stationery of Lifecodes, Inc., a testing service, and it indicated that DNA testing showed that bodily fluids on the victim came from the defendant. Defendant confessed when shown the false report. The court found the resulting confession involuntary, reasoning as follows:

> The reporters are filled with examples of police making false verbal assertions to a suspect, but * * * we perceive an intrinsic distinction between verbal assertions and manufactured documentation. * * * It may well be that a suspect is more impressed and thereby more easily induced to confess when presented with tangible, official-looking reports as opposed to merely being told that some tests have implicated him. In addition to our spontaneous distaste for the conduct we have reviewed in this matter, we have practical concerns regarding the use of the false reports beyond the inducement of a confession. Unlike oral misrepresentations, manufactured documents have the potential of indefinite life and the facial appearance of authenticity. * * * Such reports have the potential of finding their way into the courtroom.

Do you agree that there is a per se distinction between false verbal statements and false documentary evidence?

A divided court of appeals found in Miller v. Fenton, 796 F.2d 598 (3d Cir.1986), that a defendant was not denied due process when his confession was used in a state murder trial. The majority stated that "it is generally recognized that the police may use some psychological tactics in eliciting a statement from a suspect." It concluded that psychological ploys "may play a part in the suspect's decision to confess, but so long as that decision is a product of the suspect's own balancing of competing considerations, the confession is voluntary." For the majority, the issue was whether a police officer's statements "were so manipulative or coercive that they deprived Miller of his ability to make an unconstrained, autonomous decision to confess." The majority distinguished promises of leniency and promises of help with some collateral problem, reasoning that the latter are less coercive. It found that indirect promises to assist a suspect in getting psychological help did not taint the confession. Miller had passed out and hit the floor immediately after confessing, but the court dismissed this fact by stating that "the human psyche, upon being released from the terrible burden of concealing such a heinous crime, might well react just as Miller's did after a confession." The court concluded that it had "little doubt that Detective Boyce's encouraging words, perhaps in combination with the sad [false] announcement that the victim had just died, helped Miller to reach his decision to unburden himself," but that "the test for voluntariness is not a but-for test, but a question of whether the confession was a product of free choice."

The dissenting judge vigorously maintained that "[t]he circumstances of this case provide a classic illustration of the once common practice of obtaining guilty pleas in the back rooms of police stations rather than in open court." He also rejected the distinction between types of promises and suggested that "when promises, however slight, are made in the interrogation room rather than in the presence of counsel, those promises render the resulting confession inadmissible." Which analysis is more persuasive in *Miller*? Which is more consistent with *Spano*?

Justice White wrote for a majority in Arizona v. Fulminante, 111 S.Ct. 1246 (1991), as it found that a confession made by one prisoner to another was coerced and thus involuntary under the Fifth and Fourteenth Amendments. Fulminante was suspected of murdering his stepdaughter in Arizona, but had not been arrested or charged before he was incarcerated in New Jersey on a firearms conviction. He became friends with another inmate who was a paid informant for the FBI and who masqueraded as an organized crime figure. When the informant learned that Fulminante was suspected of killing a child, he suggested to Fulminante that he could protect him from other inmates, but only if Fulminante told him the truth about what had occurred. This resulted in the confession to which the informant testified.

Justice White observed that the *Bram* standard, which condemned any confession obtained by any direct or implied promises, however slight, or by the exertion of any improper influence, had been replaced by a totality of the circumstances test. In applying the test, he observed that state court findings ordinarily are given deference, and that, although the question was close, the state supreme court was correct in concluding that a credible threat of physical violence had existed, and the hope for protection from that violence had resulted in the confession. This overbore Fulminante's will. Justice White stressed that "a finding of coercion need not depend upon actual violence by a government agent; a credible threat is sufficient." The majority analogized Fulminante's plight to that of the defendant in Payne v. Arkansas, supra, where the interrogating officer promised that if Payne confessed, the officer would protect him from an angry mob just outside the jailhouse door.

Chief Justice Rehnquist, joined by Justices O'Connor, Kennedy and Souter, dissented. He emphasized that Fulminante offered no evidence that he believed his life was in danger or that he confessed to obtain protection; that the conversations between Fulminante and the informant were not lengthy; that Fulminante was free at all times to leave the informant's company; that the informant never threatened Fulminante and never demanded that he confess; and that Fulminante was "an experienced habitue of prisons." The Chief Justice asserted that the majority had embraced a "more expansive definition" of involuntariness than was warranted by previous case law.

After *Fulminante,* is a credible threat of physical violence a per se factor? If so, why is it different from a credible threat of the electric chair, as in *Green,* or a credible assertion that the suspect's fingerprints were found at the scene?

The Supreme Court emphasized in Colorado v. Connelly, 479 U.S. 157 (1986) that the due process focus is on whether police coerced statements. Connelly approached a uniformed officer in downtown Denver and stated that he had murdered someone and wanted to talk about it. The officer warned Connelly that he had the right to remain silent, that anything he said could be used against him in court, and that he had a right to an attorney before any questioning. Connelly stated that he understood his rights and wanted to talk about the murder. A homicide detective arrived and repeated the warnings. Connelly then confessed that he had come from Boston to confess to the murder of a young girl whom he had killed months earlier. The officers took him to the police station, examined their records, discovered that an unidentified female body had been found, talked with Connelly concerning the murder, and took Connelly in a police car to point out the location of the crime. The next morning Connelly began to appear disoriented, and he stated that "voices" had told him to come to Denver to confess. He was initially found incompetent to assist in his own defense, but later was declared fit to proceed to trial.

An expert witness testified in support of Connelly's motion to suppress his confessions that Connelly was experiencing "command hallucinations," which interfered with his ability to make free and rational choices. The state courts suppressed the confessions, and the Supreme Court reversed. Writing for the Court, Chief Justice Rehnquist reasoned that the police did nothing wrong in speaking with Connelly and that the state courts failed "to recognize the essential link between coercive activity of the State, on the one hand, and a resulting confession by a defendant, on the other." The Court held that "coercive police activity is a necessary predicate to the finding that a confession is not 'voluntary' within the meaning of the Due Process Clause." The Chief Justice reasoned that suppressing a statement in the absence of police coercion "would serve absolutely no purpose in enforcing constitutional guarantees" because it would not deter future police conduct. The Chief Justice concluded as follows:

> Only if we were to establish a brand new constitutional right—the right of a criminal defendant to confess to his crime only when totally rational and properly motivated—could respondent's present claim be sustained. * * * Respondent would now have us require sweeping inquiries into the state of mind of a criminal defendant who has confessed, inquiries quite divorced from any coercion brought to bear on the defendant by the State. We think the Constitution rightly leaves this sort of inquiry to be resolved by state laws governing the admission of evidence * * *. A statement rendered by one in the condition of respondent might be proved to be quite unreliable, but this is a matter to be governed by the evidentiary laws of the forum.

Justice Brennan, joined by Justice Marshall, dissented from this holding. He argued that the absence of police wrongdoing was not conclusive and "[t]he requirement that a confession be voluntary reflects a recognition of the importance of free will and of reliability in determining the admissibility of a confession, and thus demands an inquiry into the totality of the circumstances surrounding the confession." Justice Brennan conceded that "it is true that police overreaching has been an element of every confession case to date," but asserted that "it is also true that in every case the Court has made clear that ensuring that a confession is a product of free will is an independent concern." There is reason to fear, he argued, that confessions by mentally ill individuals who lack free will are insufficiently reliable to be used as evidence.

Had the dissenters prevailed, would there be any satisfactory way of distinguishing defendants moved to confess by uncontrollable feelings of guilt and those moved by other forces? Should these defendants be treated in the same way the dissenters would have treated Connelly?

The effect of *Connelly* can be seen in such cases as Snethen v. Nix, 885 F.2d 456 (8th Cir.1989), where the suspect's mother coerced him into confessing to the authorities. The court relied on *Connelly* to find no due process violation.

Is "free will" a workable standard for confession cases? Judge Posner in United States v. Rutledge, 900 F.2d 1127 (7th Cir.1990), had this to say about the "overbearing of free will" test:

> Taken seriously it would require the exclusion of virtually all fruits of custodial interrogation, since few choices to confess can be thought truly 'free' when made by a person who is incarcerated and is being questioned by * * * officers without the presence of counsel or anyone else to give him moral support. The formula is not taken seriously. *Connelly* may have driven the stake through its heart by holding that a confession which is not a product of the defendant's free choice * * * is admissible so long as whatever it was that destroyed the defendant's power of choice was not police conduct. In any event, very few incriminating statements, custodial or otherwise, are held to be involuntary, though few are the product of a choice that the interrogators left completely free.
>
> An alternative approach, which is implied by *Connelly* and may well describe the courts' actual as distinct from articulated standard, is to ask whether the government has made it impossible for the defendant to make a *rational* choice as to whether to confess—has made it in other words impossible for him to weigh the pros and cons of confessing and go with the balance as it appears at the time. This approach * * * implies, for example, that if the government feeds the defendant false information that seriously distorts his choice, by promising him that if he confesses he will be set free, or if the government drugs him so that he cannot make a conscious choice at all, then the confession must go out. * * * The police are allowed to play on a suspect's ignorance, his anxieties, his fears, and his uncertainties; they just are not allowed to magnify those fears, uncertainties and so forth to the point where rational decision becomes impossible.

Has Judge Posner fairly described the above cases? Is his analysis consistent with *Fulminante?*

III. THE SPECIAL FEDERAL STANDARD FOR CONFESSIONS

Before turning to the change in the Court's approach that followed *Spano,* it should be noted that during the period that the state confession cases were decided under the voluntariness approach, federal cases were governed by an identical standard. A coerced confession that violated the due process clause of the Fourteenth Amendment also violated the due process clause of the Fifth Amendment. But in federal court, a confession might be rejected even without a finding of coercion. In 1943, in McNabb v. United States, 318 U.S. 332, the Court, utilizing its supervisory power over the federal judiciary and the trial of criminal cases, decided to exclude confessions in federal cases if they were received during a period of illegal detention.[16] The record in *McNabb* revealed that the three McNabbs, who were charged with murdering a federal officer, had been subjected to protracted and repeated questioning and that they had had very little formal schooling. But the Court did not rely on due process grounds in overturning the convictions. Instead, the confessions were barred because they were obtained during a period of unnecessary delay in bringing the suspects before a United States (judicial) Commissioner for a preliminary

16. That is, in violation of congressional legislation. Justice Frankfurter wrote the majority opinion. Justice Reed alone dissented. Justice Rutledge did not participate. One year later, Justice Frankfurter authored a majority opinion in United States v. Mitchell, 322 U.S. 65 (1944), in which the Court upheld the use of confessions that were obtained before illegal detention began. Justice Black dissented without opinion.

hearing. In order to preclude federal law enforcement agents from questioning suspects under their exclusive control in violation of federal law, a new exclusionary rule was created.[17]

The *McNabb* decision was criticized for unduly handcuffing federal agents in their investigatory endeavors. Five years later, it looked as if the rule might be in trouble. In Upshaw v. United States, 335 U.S. 410 (1948), the Court rejected a confession under *McNabb* by a 5–4 vote. The four dissenters would have limited *McNabb* to cases involving great psychological pressure as well as delay in bringing a suspect before a magistrate. But the Court unanimously reaffirmed the *McNabb* decision in Mallory v. United States, 354 U.S. 449 (1957). See generally Hogan & Snee, The McNabb-Mallory Rule: Its Rise, Rationale and Rescue, 47 Geo.L.J. 1 (1958). In *Mallory,* the Court found a confession of a rape suspect to be inadmissible, because the method by which it was procured violated rule 5(a) of the Federal Rules of Criminal Procedure (which were not yet adopted when *McNabb* was decided), requiring that an arrested person be taken before a committing magistrate without "unnecessary delay." The accused in *Mallory* had been arrested in the early afternoon and was detained at headquarters within the vicinity of numerous committing magistrates. However, the police did not try to arraign him until that night, after they had secured a confession. The accused was not actually taken before a magistrate until the following morning. The Court opined that "[i]t is not the function of the police to arrest, as it were at large and to use an interrogating process at police headquarters in order to determine whom they should charge before a committing magistrate * * *."

The *McNabb-Mallory* approach to confessions raises the question whether Congress has the power to authorize police to detain and interrogate people. Does the Fourth Amendment have any importance here? If Congress does have the power, is it unlimited? If not, what are the limits? If Congress does not have the power, why is it relevant that a statute or congressionally approved court rule is violated?

In 1968, Congress enacted 18 U.S.C.A. § 3501(c). It provides that a delay of six hours in bringing a person before a magistrate does not by itself require exclusion of a confession obtained during the six hours. Delays of more than six hours probably are suspect, but there is no automatic ban on using confessions obtained as a result of interrogation and detention lasting more than six hours. See, e.g., United States v. Marrero, 450 F.2d 373 (2d Cir. 1971); United States v. Gaines, 555 F.2d 618 (7th Cir. 1977). What does this statute suggest about Congress' own view of its powers? Do you share this view? The need for a *McNabb-Mallory* exclusionary rule diminished as the Court turned from a totality of the circumstances test for confessions to reliance on particular provisions of the Bill of Rights. See generally United States v. Poole, 495 F.2d 115 (D.C.Cir. 1974). Discussion of the developments follows. At this point you might want to review a question asked in Chapter Two. What is the purpose of an arrest? A related question is whether Congress or the Supreme

17. That *McNabb* was not based on any constitutional provision must be emphasized. In a state case, Gallegos v. Nebraska, 342 U.S. 55, 63 (1951), in which the accused was not brought before a magistrate for twenty-five days after his arrest and fourteen days after his arrival in Nebraska, the Court specifically noted that the federal rule was not constitutionally mandated and was not applicable to trials in state courts.

Court may authorize arrests for the purpose of interrogation without "compelling" a person to be a witness and to risk incrimination.

IV. NEW EMPHASIS ON THE RIGHT TO COUNSEL

The previous discussion of the due process voluntariness standard observed that one important factor in determining the admissibility of a confession was whether the accused had been informed or had knowledge of his constitutional rights. Whether the accused had been apprised of his privilege against self-incrimination was considered as a factor, though not a dispositive one, in many confession cases, including Turner v. Pennsylvania, 338 U.S. 62 (1949), Harris v. South Carolina, 338 U.S. 68 (1949), Payne v. Arkansas, 356 U.S. 560 (1958), and Culombe v. Connecticut, 367 U.S. 568 (1961). Indeed, in sustaining the admissibility of the confession in Crooker v. California, 357 U.S. 433, 438 (1958), the Court observed that the accused, a former law student, knew of his constitutional right to keep silent.

The Court also took special notice when the accused had been denied access to counsel. See, e.g., Malinski v. New York, 324 U.S. 401 (1945); Haley v. Ohio, 332 U.S. 596 (1948); and Harris v. South Carolina, 338 U.S. 68 (1949). By the late 1950's, Justice Douglas, supported by Justice Black and frequently by Chief Justice Warren and Justice Brennan, was insisting that a suspect had a constitutional right to have counsel present during police interrogations.

In *Spano,* supra, we saw that the Court left open the question whether an accused has a right to see his retained attorney prior to his interrogation, but after his indictment. In Massiah v. United States, 377 U.S. 201 (1964), the Court addressed this question, and in so doing, took its first significant step away from the due process or totality of the circumstances approach to determining the admissibility of a confession.

MASSIAH v. UNITED STATES

Supreme Court of the United States, 1964.
377 U.S. 201.

MR. JUSTICE STEWART delivered the opinion of the Court.

* * *

The petitioner, a merchant seaman, was in 1958 a member of the crew of the S. S. *Santa Maria.* In April of that year federal customs officials in New York received information that he was going to transport a quantity of narcotics aboard that ship from South America to the United States. As a result of this and other information, the agents searched the *Santa Maria* upon its arrival in New York and found in the afterpeak of the vessel five packages containing about three and a half pounds of cocaine. They also learned of circumstances, not here relevant, tending to connect the petitioner with the cocaine. He was arrested, promptly arraigned, and subsequently indicted for possession of narcotics aboard a United States vessel. In July, a superseding indictment was returned, charging the petitioner and a man named Colson with the same substantive offense and in separate counts charging the petitioner, Colson, and others with having conspired to possess narcotics aboard a United States vessel, and to import, conceal, and facilitate the sale of narcotics. The petitioner, who had retained a lawyer, pleaded not guilty and was released on bail, along with Colson.

A few days later, and quite without the petitioner's knowledge, Colson decided to cooperate with the government agents in their continuing investigation of the narcotics activities in which the petitioner, Colson, and others had allegedly been engaged. Colson permitted an agent named Murphy to install a Schmidt radio transmitter under the front seat of Colson's automobile, by means of which Murphy, equipped with an appropriate receiving device, could overhear from some distance away conversations carried on in Colson's car.

On the evening of November 19, 1959, Colson and the petitioner held a lengthy conversation while sitting in Colson's automobile, parked on a New York street. By prearrangement with Colson, and totally unbeknown to the petitioner, the agent Murphy sat in a car parked out of sight down the street and listened over the radio to the entire conversation. The petitioner made several incriminating statements during the course of this conversation. At the petitioner's trial these incriminating statements were brought before the jury through Murphy's testimony, despite the insistent objection of defense counsel. The jury convicted the petitioner of several related narcotics offenses, and the convictions were affirmed by the Court of Appeals.

* * * [I]t is said that the petitioner's Fifth and Sixth Amendment rights were violated by the use in evidence against him of incriminating statements which government agents had deliberately elicited from him after he had been indicted and in the absence of his retained counsel.

[The Court discusses *Spano,* paying more attention to the concurring opinions than to the majority opinion. It also discusses right to counsel precedents, which are discussed in the chapter on counsel, infra, and ultimately finds the Sixth Amendment right to counsel to be determinative.]

* * * We hold that the petitioner was denied the basic protections of that guarantee when there was used against him at his trial evidence of his own incriminating words, which federal agents had deliberately elicited from him after he had been indicted and in the absence of his counsel. It is true that in the *Spano* case the defendant was interrogated in a police station, while here the damaging testimony was elicited from the defendant without his knowledge while he was free on bail. But, as Judge Hays pointed out in his dissent in the Court of Appeals, "if such a rule is to have any efficacy it must apply to indirect and surreptitious interrogations as well as those conducted in the jailhouse. In this case, Massiah was more seriously imposed upon * * * because he did not even know that he was under interrogation by a government agent."

The Solicitor General, in his brief and oral argument, has strenuously contended that the federal law enforcement agents had the right, if not indeed the duty, to continue their investigation of the petitioner and his alleged criminal associates even though the petitioner had been indicted. He points out that the Government was continuing its investigation in order to uncover not only the source of narcotics found on the S. S. *Santa Maria,* but also their intended buyer. He says that the quantity of narcotics involved was such as to suggest that the petitioner was part of a large and well-organized ring, and indeed that the continuing investigation confirmed this suspicion, since it resulted in criminal charges against many defendants. Under these circumstances the Solicitor General concludes that the government agents were completely "justified in making use of Colson's cooperation by having Colson continue his normal associations and by surveilling them."

* * * We do not question that in this case, as in many cases, it was entirely proper to continue an investigation of the suspected criminal activities of the defendant and his alleged confederates, even though the defendant had already been indicted. All that we hold is that the defendant's own incriminating statements, obtained by federal agents under the circumstances here disclosed, could not constitutionally be used by the prosecution as evidence against *him* at his trial.

MR. JUSTICE WHITE, with whom MR. JUSTICE CLARK and MR. JUSTICE HARLAN join, dissenting.

* * *

Whatever the content or scope of the rule may prove to be, I am unable to see how this case presents an unconstitutional interference with Massiah's right to counsel. Massiah was not prevented from consulting with counsel as often as he wished. No meetings with counsel were disturbed or spied upon. Preparation for trial was in no way obstructed. It is only a sterile syllogism—an unsound one, besides—to say that because Massiah had a right to counsel's aid before and during the trial, his out-of-court conversations and admissions must be excluded if obtained without counsel's consent or presence. The right to counsel has never meant as much before, and its extension in this case requires some further explanation, so far unarticulated by the Court.

* * *

[T]he Court's newly fashioned exclusionary principle goes far beyond the constitutional privilege against self-incrimination, which neither requires nor suggests the barring of voluntary pretrial admissions. * * *

At the time of the conversation in question, petitioner was not in custody but free on bail. He was not questioned in what anyone would call an atmosphere of official coercion.

* * *

Note

In Escobedo v. Illinois, 378 U.S. 478 (1964), the Court undertook a short-lived experiment of extending the Sixth Amendment right to counsel to a suspect who had not yet been formally charged. Escobedo was taken into custody on suspicion of murder. He asked for a lawyer several times, but his request was denied. His mother retained a lawyer for him, and the lawyer went to the police station, but the police would not let the lawyer speak to Escobedo. Escobedo was confronted with incriminating evidence, while handcuffed in a standing position, and was given false promises that if he confessed, he would be allowed to go home, since the police were more interested in his alleged accomplice. While these facts established a strong case for holding Escobedo's confession involuntary, the Court relied explicitly on the Sixth Amendment to invalidate the confession. Justice Goldberg, writing for the Court, recognized that unlike Spano and Massiah, Escobedo had not been indicted at the time he confessed; but he argued that "in the context of this case, that fact should make no difference." Justice Goldberg stated that when Escobedo was denied his request for counsel, "the investigation had ceased to be a general investigation of an unsolved crime" and that Escobedo had become the "accused." Justice Goldberg stated the holding as follows:

> [W]here, as here, the investigation is no longer a general inquiry into an unsolved crime, but has begun to focus on a particular suspect, the suspect has been taken into police custody, the police carry out a process of interrogations * * *, the suspect has requested and been denied [counsel], and the police have

> not effectively warned him of his absolute constitutional right to remain silent, the accused has been denied "the Assistance of Counsel" in violation of the Sixth Amendment * * *.

Justices Harlan, Stewart, White and Clark dissented. The dissenters were concerned that the majority's "focus" test would result in an extravagant extension of the Sixth Amendment right to counsel, which by its terms applies to criminal "prosecutions" not criminal "investigations." As Justice Stewart put it:

> [T]he institution of formal, meaningful judicial proceedings, by way of indictment, information, or arraignment, marks the point at which a criminal investigation has ended and adversary litigative proceedings have commenced. * * * [T]he Court today converts a routine police investigation of an unsolved murder into a distorted analogue of a judicial trial. It imports into this investigation constitutional concepts historically applicable only after the onset of formal prosecutorial proceedings.

As in *Massiah,* Justice White was concerned that the Court's grant of Sixth Amendment protection would "supersede the self-incrimination provision of the Fifth Amendment." Justice White stated that the Fifth Amendment "addresses itself to the very issue of incriminating admissions of an accused and resolves it by proscribing only compelled statements."

What is the concern in *Escobedo* and *Massiah?* Is it that confessions may not be reliable? Is it that the police are taking a shortcut to proving their case? Is it that police interrogation is basically unacceptable? Is it that suspects are not playing the game very well? Is it all of these things, perhaps? Or none? How do you think the *Escobedo* majority would answer this question: "Is it a good thing for the police to get people to confess, as long as brutal methods are not utilized?" How would the dissenters answer?

Does the *Escobedo* Court give any indication when an investigation can be said to have focused on the accused? In their dissenting opinions, Justices Stewart and White strongly criticize the indefiniteness of the Sixth Amendment right that is recognized in the majority ruling. But is the voluntariness standard they espouse any more definite? Which standard provides more guidance to the police? Assuming that both a voluntariness standard and a counsel standard are indefinite, are the costs of uncertainty the same under both? If not, which standard keeps the costs to society lower?

The *Escobedo* majority appears to argue that it cannot be viewed as undesirable for all persons to fully exercise their constitutional rights. But isn't this the heart of the disagreement between the majority and the dissenters? Arguably, the dissenters take the view that the government is free to try to discourage people from exercising their rights, as long as the government leaves the people free in the end to choose what to do. The majority seem to believe that the idea of a constitutional right is that it is to be nurtured by the government. Which approach appeals more to you?

As a Sixth Amendment case, *Escobedo* has little or no continuing relevance. In Moran v. Burbine, 475 U.S. 412 (1986), Burbine was being interrogated as a suspect in a murder. His family retained counsel for him, but police officers denied counsel's request to see Burbine. Burbine had not been formally charged at the time he confessed. Burbine relied on *Escobedo* to argue that his Sixth Amendment rights were violated, but Justice O'Connor, writing for the majority, rejected that argument. She stated that "subsequent decisions foreclose any reliance on *Escobedo* * * * for the proposition that the Sixth Amendment right, in any of its manifestations, applies prior to the initiation of adversary criminal proceedings." She stated that *Escobedo* is in retrospect best understood as a Fifth Amendment case, because the prime purpose of the Court in *Escobedo* was not to vindicate the right to counsel as such but rather to guarantee "the full effectuation of the privilege against self-incrimination."

While *Escobedo* is therefore mainly of historical note on the Court's road to *Miranda,* the Sixth Amendment right to counsel has significant contemporary relevance where information is sought from a person who has been formally charged. After the Court decided *Miranda,* it returned to *Massiah* and gave it a very broad reading. These cases are discussed infra.

The philosophical differences among the Justices continued after *Escobedo.* They became most evident in the next case, perhaps the most familiar one in all of criminal procedure.

V. THE FIFTH AMENDMENT APPROACH

A. MIRANDA v. ARIZONA

In 1964, the Court in Malloy v. Hogan, 378 U.S. 1, paved the way for its decision in *Miranda* by ruling that the Fifth Amendment privilege against self-incrimination is applicable to the states through the Fourteenth Amendment. Two years later, in *Miranda,* the Court declared that the Fifth Amendment is the touchstone for determining the admissibility of any statements obtained through custodial interrogation by government officials.

MIRANDA v. ARIZONA

Supreme Court of the United States, 1966.
384 U.S. 436.

MR. CHIEF JUSTICE WARREN delivered the opinion of the Court.

The cases before us raise questions which go to the roots of our concepts of American criminal jurisprudence: the restraints society must observe consistent with the Federal Constitution in prosecuting individuals for crime. More specifically, we deal with the admissibility of statements obtained from an individual who is subjected to custodial police interrogation and the necessity for procedures which assure that the individual is accorded his privilege under the Fifth Amendment to the Constitution not to be compelled to incriminate himself.

* * *

Our holding will be spelled out with some specificity in the pages which follow but briefly stated it is this: the prosecution may not use statements, whether exculpatory or inculpatory, stemming from custodial interrogation of the defendant unless it demonstrates the use of procedural safeguards effective to secure the privilege against self-incrimination. By custodial interrogation, we mean questioning initiated by law enforcement officers after a person has been taken into custody or otherwise deprived of his freedom of action in any significant way.[a] As for the procedural safeguards to be employed, unless other fully effective means are devised to inform accused persons of their

a. This is what we meant in *Escobedo* when we spoke of an investigation which had focused on an accused.

right of silence and to assure a continuous opportunity to exercise it, the following measures are required. Prior to any questioning, the person must be warned that he has a right to remain silent, that any statement he does make may be used as evidence against him, and that he has a right to the presence of an attorney, either retained or appointed. The defendant may waive effectuation of these rights, provided the waiver is made voluntarily, knowingly and intelligently. If, however, he indicates in any manner and at any stage of the process that he wishes to consult with an attorney before speaking there can be no questioning. Likewise, if the individual is alone and indicates in any manner that he does not wish to be interrogated, the police may not question him. The mere fact that he may have answered some questions or volunteered some statements on his own does not deprive him of the right to refrain from answering any further inquiries until he has consulted with an attorney and thereafter consents to be questioned.

I

The constitutional issue we decide in each of these cases is the admissibility of statements obtained from a defendant questioned while in custody or otherwise deprived of his freedom of action in any significant way. In each, the defendant was questioned by police officers, detectives, or a prosecuting attorney in a room in which he was cut off from the outside world. In none of these cases was the defendant given a full and effective warning of his rights at the outset of the interrogation process. In all the cases, the questioning elicited oral admissions, and in three of them, signed statements as well which were admitted at their trials. They all thus share salient features—incommunicado interrogation of individuals in a police-dominated atmosphere, resulting in self-incriminating statements without full warnings of constitutional rights.

An understanding of the nature and setting of this in-custody interrogation is essential to our decisions today. The difficulty in depicting what transpires at such interrogations stems from the fact that in this country they have largely taken place incommunicado. From extensive factual studies undertaken in the early 1930's, including the famous Wickersham Report to Congress by a Presidential Commission, it is clear that police violence and the "third degree" flourished at that time. * * *

* * *

Again we stress that the modern practice of in-custody interrogation is psychologically rather than physically oriented. * * * Interrogation still takes place in privacy. Privacy results in secrecy and this in turn results in a gap in our knowledge as to what in fact goes on in the interrogation rooms. A valuable source of information about present police practices, however, may be found in various police manuals and texts which document procedures employed with success in the past, and which recommend various other effective tactics. These texts are used by law enforcement agencies themselves as guides. It should be noted that these texts professedly present the most enlightened and effective means presently used to obtain statements through custodial interrogation. By considering these texts and other data, it is possible to describe procedures observed and noted around the country.

The officers are told by the manuals that the "principal psychological factor contributing to a successful interrogation is *privacy*—being alone with the person under interrogation." The efficacy of this tactic has been explained as follows:

"If at all practicable, the interrogation should take place in the investigator's office or at least in a room of his own choice. The subject should be deprived of every psychological advantage. In his own home he may be confident, indignant, or recalcitrant. He is more keenly aware of his rights and more reluctant to tell of his indiscretions or criminal behavior within the walls of his home. Moreover his family and other friends are nearby, their presence lending moral support. In his own office, the investigator possesses all the advantages. The atmosphere suggests the invincibility of the forces of the law."

To highlight the isolation and unfamiliar surroundings, the manuals instruct the police to display an air of confidence in the suspect's guilt and from outward appearance to maintain only an interest in confirming certain details. The guilt of the subject is to be posited as a fact. The interrogator should direct his comments toward the reasons why the subject committed the act, rather than court failure by asking the subject whether he did it. Like other men, perhaps the subject has had a bad family life, had an unhappy childhood, had too much to drink, had an unrequited desire for women. The officers are instructed to minimize the moral seriousness of the offense, to cast blame on the victim or on society. These tactics are designed to put the subject in a psychological state where his story is but an elaboration of what the police purport to know already—that he is guilty. Explanations to the contrary are dismissed and discouraged.

The texts thus stress that the major qualities an interrogator should possess are patience and perseverance. * * *

The manuals suggest that the suspect be offered legal excuses for his actions in order to obtain an initial admission of guilt. * * *

When the techniques described above prove unavailing, the texts recommend they be alternated with a show of some hostility. * * *

The interrogators sometimes are instructed to induce a confession out of trickery. The technique here is quite effective in crimes which require identification or which run in series. In the identification situation, the interrogator may take a break in his questioning to place the subject among a group of men in a line-up. "The witness or complainant (previously coached, if necessary) studies the line-up and confidently points out the subject as the guilty party." Then the questioning resumes "as though there were now no doubt about the guilt of the subject." A variation on this technique is called the "reverse line-up":

"The accused is placed in a line-up but this time he is identified by several fictitious witnesses or victims who associated him with different offenses. It is expected that the subject will become desperate and confess to the offense under investigation in order to escape from the false accusations."

* * *

Even without employing brutality, the "third degree" or the specific stratagems described above, the very fact of custodial interrogation exacts a heavy toll on individual liberty and trades on the weakness of individuals. * * *

In the cases before us today, given this background, we concern ourselves primarily with this interrogation atmosphere and the evils it can bring. In No. 759, Miranda v. Arizona, the police arrested the defendant and took him to a special interrogation room where they secured a confession. In No. 760, Vignera v. New York, the defendant made oral admissions to the police after interrogation in the afternoon, and then signed an inculpatory statement upon being questioned by an assistant district attorney later the same evening. In No. 761, Westover v. United States, the defendant was handed over to the Federal Bureau of Investigation by local authorities after they had detained and interrogated him for a lengthy period, both at night and the following morning. After some two hours of questioning, the federal officers had obtained signed statements from the defendant. Lastly, in No. 584, California v. Stewart, the local police held the defendant five days in the station and interrogated him on nine separate occasions before they secured his inculpatory statement.

In these cases, we might not find the defendants' statements to have been involuntary in traditional terms. Our concern for adequate safeguards to protect precious Fifth Amendment rights is, of course, not lessened in the slightest. In each of the cases, the defendant was thrust into an unfamiliar atmosphere and run through menacing police interrogation procedures. The potentiality for compulsion is forcefully apparent, for example, in *Miranda,* where the indigent Mexican defendant was a seriously disturbed individual with pronounced sexual fantasies, and in *Stewart,* in which the defendant was an indigent Los Angeles Negro who had dropped out of school in the sixth grade. To be sure, the records do not evince overt physical coercion or patent psychological ploys. The fact remains that in none of these cases did the officers undertake to afford appropriate safeguards at the outset of the interrogation to insure that the statements were truly the product of free choice.

It is obvious that such an interrogation environment is created for no purpose other than to subjugate the individual to the will of his examiner. This atmosphere carries its own badge of intimidation. To be sure, this is not physical intimidation, but it is equally destructive of human dignity. The current practice of incommunicado interrogation is at odds with one of our Nation's most cherished principles—that the individual may not be compelled to incriminate himself. Unless adequate protective devices are employed to dispel the compulsion inherent in custodial surroundings, no statement obtained from the defendant can truly be the product of his free choice.

From the foregoing, we can readily perceive an intimate connection between the privilege against self-incrimination and police custodial questioning. It is fitting to turn to history and precedent underlying the Self-Incrimination Clause to determine its applicability in this situation.

II

[The Court briefly traces the roots of the Fifth Amendment and how the privilege against self-incrimination obtained constitutional status in the United States.]

The question in these cases is whether the privilege is fully applicable during a period of custodial interrogation. * * * We are satisfied that all the principles embodied in the privilege apply to informal compulsion exerted by law-enforcement officers during in-custody questioning. An individual swept from familiar surroundings into police custody, surrounded by antagonistic forces, and subjected to the techniques of persuasion described above cannot be otherwise than under compulsion to speak. As a practical matter, the compulsion to speak in the isolated setting of the police station may well be greater than in courts or other official investigations, where there are often impartial observers to guard against intimidation or trickery.

This question, in fact could have been taken as settled in federal courts almost 70 years ago, when, in Bram v. United

States, 168 U.S. 532, 542 (1897), this Court held:

> "In criminal trials, in the courts of the United States, wherever a question arises whether a confession is incompetent because not voluntary, the issue is controlled by that portion of the Fifth Amendment * * * commanding that no person 'shall be compelled in any criminal case to be a witness against himself.' "

* * *

III

Today, then, there can be no doubt that the Fifth Amendment privilege is available outside of criminal court proceedings and serves to protect persons in all settings in which their freedom of action is curtailed in any significant way from being compelled to incriminate themselves. We have concluded that without proper safeguards the process of in-custody interrogation of persons suspected or accused of crime contains inherently compelling pressures which work to undermine the individual's will to resist and to compel him to speak where he would not otherwise do so freely. In order to combat these pressures and to permit a full opportunity to exercise the privilege against self-incrimination, the accused must be adequately and effectively apprised of his rights and the exercise of those rights must be fully honored.

It is impossible for us to foresee the potential alternatives for protecting the privilege which might be devised by Congress or the States in the exercise of their creative rule-making capacities. Therefore we cannot say that the Constitution necessarily requires adherence to any particular solution for the inherent compulsions of the interrogation process as it is presently conducted. Our decision in no way creates a constitutional straitjacket which will handicap sound efforts at reform, nor is it intended to have this effect. We encourage Congress and the States to continue their laudable search for increasingly effective ways of protecting the rights of the individual while promoting efficient enforcement of our criminal laws. However, unless we are shown other procedures which are at least as effective in apprising accused persons of their right of silence and in assuring a continuous opportunity to exercise it, the following safeguards must be observed.

At the outset, if a person in custody is to be subjected to interrogation, he must first be informed in clear and unequivocal terms that he has the right to remain silent. For those unaware of the privilege, the warning is needed simply to make them aware of it—the threshold requirement for an intelligent decision as to its exercise. More important, such a warning is an absolute prerequisite in overcoming the inherent pressures of the interrogation atmosphere. It is not just the subnormal or woefully ignorant who succumb to an interrogator's imprecations, whether implied or expressly stated, that the interrogation will continue until a confession is obtained or that silence in the face of accusation is itself damning and will bode ill when presented to a jury.[b] Further, the warning will show the individual that his interrogators are prepared to recognize his privilege should he choose to exercise it.

The Fifth Amendment privilege is so fundamental to our system of constitutional rule and the expedient of giving an adequate warning as to the availability of the privilege so simple, we will not

b. In accord with our decision today it is impermissible to penalize an individual for exercising his Fifth Amendment privilege when he is under police custodial interrogation. The prosecution may not, therefore, use at trial the fact that he stood mute or claimed his privilege in the face of accusation.

pause to inquire in individual cases whether the defendant was aware of his rights without a warning being given. Assessments of the knowledge the defendant possessed, based on information as to his age, education, intelligence, or prior contact with authorities, can never be more than speculation; a warning is a clearcut fact. More important, whatever the background of the person interrogated, a warning at the time of the interrogation is indispensable to overcome its pressures and to insure that the individual knows he is free to exercise the privilege at that point in time.

The warning of the right to remain silent must be accompanied by the explanation that anything said can and will be used against the individual in court. This warning is needed in order to make him aware not only of the privilege, but also of the consequences of forgoing it. It is only through an awareness of these consequences that there can be any assurance of real understanding and intelligent exercise of the privilege. Moreover, this warning may serve to make the individual more acutely aware that he is faced with a phase of the adversary system—that he is not in the presence of persons acting solely in his interest.

The circumstances surrounding in-custody interrogation can operate very quickly to overbear the will of one merely made aware of his privilege by his interrogators. Therefore, the right to have counsel present at the interrogation is indispensable to the protection of the Fifth Amendment privilege under the system we delineate today. Our aim is to assure that the individual's right to choose between silence and speech remains unfettered throughout the interrogation process. A once-stated warning, delivered by those who will conduct the interrogation, cannot itself suffice to that end among those who most require knowledge of their rights. A mere warning given by the interrogators is not alone sufficient to accomplish that end. Prosecutors themselves claim that the admonishment of the right to remain silent without more "will benefit only the recidivist and the professional." Even preliminary advice given to the accused by his own attorney can be swiftly overcome by the secret interrogation process. Thus, the need for counsel to protect the Fifth Amendment privilege comprehends not merely a right to consult with counsel prior to questioning, but also to have counsel present during any questioning if the defendant so desires.

That presence of counsel at the interrogation may serve several significant subsidiary functions as well. If the accused decides to talk to his interrogators, the assistance of counsel can mitigate the dangers of untrustworthiness. With a lawyer present the likelihood that the police will practice coercion is reduced, and if coercion is nevertheless exercised the lawyer can testify to it in court. The presence of a lawyer can also help to guarantee that the accused gives a fully accurate statement to the police and that the statement is rightly reported by the prosecution at trial.

An individual need not make a pre-interrogation request for a lawyer. While such request affirmatively secures his right to have one, his failure to ask for a lawyer does not constitute a waiver. No effective waiver of the right to counsel during interrogation can be recognized unless specifically made after the warnings we here delineate have been given. The accused who does not know his rights and therefore does not make a request may be the person who most needs counsel. * * *

* * *

Accordingly we hold that an individual held for interrogation must be clearly informed that he has the right to consult with a lawyer and to have the lawyer with him during interrogation under the system for protecting the privilege we delineate today. As with the warnings of the right to remain silent and that anything stated can be used in evidence against him, this warning is an absolute prerequisite to interrogation. No amount of circumstantial evidence that the person may have been aware of this right will suffice to stand in its stead. Only through such a warning is there ascertainable assurance that the accused was aware of this right.

If an individual indicates that he wishes the assistance of counsel before any interrogation occurs, the authorities cannot rationally ignore or deny his request on the basis that the individual does not have or cannot afford a retained attorney. The financial ability of the individual has no relationship to the scope of the rights involved here. The privilege against self-incrimination secured by the Constitution applies to all individuals. The need for counsel in order to protect the privilege exists for the indigent as well as the affluent. In fact, were we to limit these constitutional rights to those who can retain an attorney, our decisions today would be of little significance. The cases before us as well as the vast majority of confession cases with which we have dealt in the past involve those unable to retain counsel. While authorities are not required to relieve the accused of his poverty, they have the obligation not to take advantage of indigence in the administration of justice. Denial of counsel to the indigent at the time of interrogation while allowing an attorney to those who can afford one would be no more supportable by reason or logic than the similar situation at trial and on appeal. * * *

In order fully to apprise a person interrogated of the extent of his rights under this system then, it is necessary to warn him not only that he has the right to consult with an attorney, but also that if he is indigent a lawyer will be appointed to represent him. Without this additional warning, the admonition of the right to consult with counsel would often be understood as meaning only that he can consult with a lawyer if he has one or has the funds to obtain one. The warning of a right to counsel would be hollow if not couched in terms that would convey to the indigent—the person most often subjected to interrogation—the knowledge that he too has a right to have counsel present. As with the warnings of the right to remain silent and of the general right to counsel, only by effective and express explanation to the indigent of this right can there be assurance that he was truly in a position to exercise it.[c]

Once warnings have been given, the subsequent procedure is clear. If the individual indicates in any manner, at any time prior to or during questioning, that he wishes to remain silent, the interrogation must cease.[d] At this point he has shown that he intends to exercise his Fifth Amendment privilege; any statements taken after the person invokes his privilege cannot be other than the product of compulsion, subtle or otherwise. Without the right to cut off questioning, the setting of in-custody interrogation operates on the individual to overcome free choice in producing a

c. While a warning that the indigent may have counsel appointed need not be given to the person who is known to have an attorney or is known to have ample funds to secure one, the expedient of giving a warning is too simple and the rights involved too important to engage in *ex post facto* inquiries into financial ability when there is any doubt at all on that score.

d. If an individual indicates his desire to remain silent, but has an attorney present, there may be some circumstances in which further questioning would be permissible. In the absence of evidence of overbearing, statements then made in the presence of counsel might be free of the compelling influence of the interrogation process and might fairly be construed as a waiver of the privilege for purposes of these statements.

statement after the privilege has been once invoked. If the individual states that he wants an attorney, the interrogation must cease until an attorney is present. At that time, the individual must have an opportunity to confer with the attorney and to have him present during any subsequent questioning. If the individual cannot obtain an attorney and he indicates that he wants one before speaking to police, they must respect his decision to remain silent.

This does not mean, as some have suggested, that each police station must have a "station house lawyer" present at all times to advise prisoners. It does mean, however, that if police propose to interrogate a person they must make known to him that he is entitled to a lawyer and that if he cannot afford one, a lawyer will be provided for him prior to any interrogation. If authorities conclude that they will not provide counsel during a reasonable period of time in which investigation in the field is carried out, they may refrain from doing so without violating the person's Fifth Amendment privilege so long as they do not question him during that time.

If the interrogation continues without the presence of an attorney and a statement is taken, a heavy burden rests on the government to demonstrate that the defendant knowingly and intelligently waived his privilege against self-incrimination and his right to retained or appointed counsel. This Court has always set high standards of proof for the waiver of constitutional rights, and we reassert these standards as applied to in-custody interrogation. Since the State is responsible for establishing the isolated circumstances under which the interrogation takes place and has the only means of making available corroborated evidence of warnings given during incommunicado interrogation, the burden is rightly on its shoulders.

An express statement that the individual is willing to make a statement and does not want an attorney followed closely by a statement could constitute a waiver. But a valid waiver will not be presumed simply from the silence of the accused after warnings are given or simply from the fact that a confession was in fact eventually obtained. * * *

* * * Moreover, where in-custody interrogation is involved, there is no room for the contention that the privilege is waived if the individual answers some questions or gives some information on his own prior to invoking his right to remain silent when interrogated.

Whatever the testimony of the authorities as to waiver of rights by an accused, the fact of lengthy interrogation or incommunicado incarceration before a statement is made is strong evidence that the accused did not validly waive his rights. In these circumstances the fact that the individual eventually made a statement is consistent with the conclusion that the compelling influence of the interrogation finally forced him to do so. It is inconsistent with any notion of a voluntary relinquishment of the privilege. Moreover, any evidence that the accused was threatened, tricked, or cajoled into a waiver will, of course, show that the defendant did not voluntarily waive his privilege. The requirement of warnings and waiver of rights is a fundamental with respect to the Fifth Amendment privilege and not simply a preliminary ritual to existing methods of interrogation.

The warnings required and the waiver necessary in accordance with our opinion today are, in the absence of a fully effective equivalent, prerequisites to the admissibility of any statement made by a defendant. No distinction can be drawn between statements which are direct confessions and statements which amount to "admissions" of part or all of an offense. The privilege against self-incrimination protects the individual from being compelled to incriminate himself in any manner; it does not distinguish degrees of incrimination. Similarly, for precisely the same reason, no distinction may be drawn between inculpatory statements and statements alleged to be merely "exculpatory." If a statement made were in fact truly exculpatory it would, of course, never be used by the prosecution. In fact, statements merely intended to be exculpatory by the defendant are often used to impeach his testimony at trial or to demonstrate untruths in the statement given under interrogation and thus to prove guilt by implication. These statements are incriminating in any meaningful sense of the word and may not be used without the full warnings and effective waiver required for any other statement. * * *

The principles announced today deal with the protection which must be given to the privilege against self-incrimination when the individual is first subjected to police interrogation while in custody at the station or otherwise deprived of his freedom of action in any significant way. It is at this point that our adversary system of criminal proceedings commences, distinguishing itself at the outset from the inquisitorial system recognized in some countries. Under the system of warnings we delineate today or under any other system which may be devised and found effective, the safeguards to be erected about the privilege must come into play at this point.

Our decision is not intended to hamper the traditional function of police officers in investigating crime. When an individual is in custody on probable cause, the police may, of course, seek out evidence in the field to be used at trial against him. Such investigation may include inquiry of persons not under restraint. General on-the-scene questioning as to facts surrounding a crime or other general questioning of citizens in the fact-finding process is not affected by our holding. It is an act of responsible citizenship for individuals to give whatever information they may have to aid in law enforcement. In such situations the compelling atmosphere inherent in the process of in-custody interrogation is not necessarily present.

In dealing with statements obtained through interrogation, we do not purport to find all confessions inadmissible. Confessions remain a proper element in law enforcement. Any statement given freely and voluntarily without any compelling influences is, of course, admissible in evidence. * * *

* * *

IV

* * *

Over the years the Federal Bureau of Investigation has compiled an exemplary record of effective law enforcement while advising any suspect or arrested person, at the outset of an interview, that he is not required to make a statement, that any statement may be used against him in court, that the individual may obtain the services of an attorney of his own choice and, more recently, that he has a right to free counsel if he is unable to pay. A letter received from the Solicitor General in response to a question from the Bench makes it clear that the present pattern of warnings and respect for the rights of the individual followed as a practice by the FBI is consistent with the procedure which we delineate today.

The practice of the FBI can readily be emulated by state and local enforcement agencies. The argument that the FBI deals with different crimes than are dealt with by state authorities does not mitigate the significance of the FBI experience. * * *

[The Court also cites the experience of other countries.]

V

Because of the nature of the problem and because of its recurrent significance in numerous cases, we have to this point discussed the relationship of the Fifth Amendment privilege to police interrogation without specific concentration on the facts of the cases before us. We turn now to these facts to consider the application to these cases of the constitutional principles discussed above. In each instance, we have concluded that statements were obtained from the defendant under circumstances that did not meet constitutional standards for protection of the privilege.

* * *

MR. JUSTICE CLARK, dissenting in Nos. 759, 760, and 761, and concurring in the result in No. 584.

It is with regret that I find it necessary to write in these cases. However, I am unable to join the majority because its opinion goes too far on too little, while my dissenting brethren do not go quite far enough. Nor can I join in the Court's criticism of the present practices of police and investigatory agencies as to custodial interrogation. The materials it refers to as "police manuals" are, as I read them, merely writings in this field by professors and some police officers. * * *

I

* * * Such a strict constitutional specific inserted at the nerve center of crime detection may well kill the patient. Since there is at this time a paucity of information and an almost total lack of empirical knowledge on the practical operation of requirements truly comparable to those announced by the majority, I would be more restrained lest we go too far too fast.

[In parts II and III of his opinion, Justice Clark advocates a totality of the circumstances test.]

MR. JUSTICE HARLAN, whom MR. JUSTICE STEWART and MR. JUSTICE WHITE join, dissenting.

I believe the decision for the Court represents poor constitutional law and entails harmful consequences for the country at large. How serious these consequences may prove to be only time can tell. But the basic flaws in the Court's justification seem to me readily apparent now once all sides of the problem are considered.

I. INTRODUCTION

* * *

* * * The new rules are not designed to guard against police brutality or other unmistakably banned forms of coercion. Those who use third-degree tactics and deny them in court are equally able and destined to lie as skillfully about warnings and waivers. Rather, the thrust of the new rules is to negate all pressures, to reinforce the nervous or ignorant suspect, and ultimately to discourage any confession at all. The aim in short is toward "voluntariness" in a utopian sense, or to view it from a different angle, voluntariness with a vengeance.

* * *

II. CONSTITUTIONAL PREMISES

[Justice Harlan surveys the limits on confessions the Court evolved under the Due Process Clause of the Fourteenth Amendment.]

I turn now to the Court's asserted reliance on the Fifth Amendment, an approach which I frankly regard as a *trompe l'oeil.* The Court's opinion in my view reveals no adequate basis for extending the Fifth Amendment's privilege against self-incrimination to the police station. Far more important, it fails to show that the Court's new rules are well supported, let alone compelled, by Fifth Amendment precedents. Instead, the new rules actually derive from quotation and analogy drawn from precedents under the Sixth Amendment, which should properly have no bearing on police interrogation.

The Court's opening contention, that the Fifth Amendment governs police station confessions, is perhaps not an impermissible extension of the law but it has little to commend itself in the present circumstances. Historically, the privilege against self-incrimination did not bear at all on the use of extra-legal confessions, for which distinct standards evolved. * * * Even those who would readily enlarge the privilege must concede some linguistic difficulties since the Fifth Amendment in terms proscribes only compelling any person "in any criminal case to be a witness against himself."

Though weighty, I do not say these points and similar ones are conclusive, for, as the Court reiterates, the privilege embodies basic principles always capable of expansion. Certainly the privilege does represent a protective concern for the accused and an emphasis upon accusatorial rather than inquisitorial values in law enforcement, although this is similarly true of other limitations such as the grand jury requirement and the reasonable doubt standard. Accusatorial values, however, have openly been absorbed into the due process standard governing confessions. * * * Since extension of the general principle has already occurred, to insist that the privilege applies as such serves only to carry over inapposite historical details and engaging rhetoric and to obscure the policy choices to be made in regulating confessions.

Having decided that the Fifth Amendment privilege does apply in the police station, the Court reveals that the privilege imposes more exacting restrictions than does the Fourteenth Amendment's voluntariness test. * * *

The more important premise is that pressure on the suspect must be eliminated though it be only the subtle influence of the atmosphere and surroundings. The Fifth Amendment, however, has never been thought to forbid *all* pressure to incriminate one's self in the situations covered by it. * * * This is not to say that short of jail or torture any sanction is permissible in any case; policy and history alike may impose sharp limits. However, the Court's unspoken assumption that *any* pressure violates the privilege is not supported by the precedents and it has failed to show why the Fifth Amendment prohibits that relatively mild pressure the Due Process Clause permits.

The Court appears similarly wrong in thinking that precise knowledge of one's rights is a settled prerequisite under the Fifth Amendment to the loss of its protections. * * * No Fifth Amendment precedent is cited for the Court's contrary view. There might of course be reasons apart from Fifth Amendment precedent for requiring warning or any other safeguard on questioning but that is a different matter entirely.

A closing word must be said about the Assistance of Counsel Clause of the Sixth Amendment, which is never expressly relied on by the Court but whose judicial precedents turn out to be linchpins of the confession rules announced today. * * *

The only attempt in this Court to carry the right to counsel into the station house occurred in *Escobedo*, the Court repeating several times that that stage was no less "critical" than trial itself. This is hardly persuasive when we consider that a grand jury inquiry, the filing of a certiorari petition, and certainly the purchase of narcotics by an undercover agent from a prospective defendant may all be equally "critical" yet provision of counsel and advice on that score have never been thought compelled by the Constitution in such cases. The sound reason why this right is so freely extended for a criminal trial is the severe injustice risked by confronting an untrained defendant with a range of technical points of law, evidence, and tactics familiar to the prosecutor but not to himself. This danger shrinks markedly in the police station where indeed the lawyer in fulfilling his professional responsibilities of necessity may become an obstacle to truthfinding. * * *

* * *

[Justice Harlan points out that no state had imposed the newly announced interrogation rules on its own initiative, unlike cases such as Mapp v. Ohio, where more than half the states had already adopted the exclusionary rule before the Supreme Court approved it, and Gideon v. Wainwright, where 22 states filed an *amicus* brief in favor of the course taken by the court. By contrast, 27 states signed an *amicus* brief opposing the new restrictions on police interrogation not including the three other states which were parties. He also argued that other countries that strictly controlled confessions gave the prosecutor advantages not given in the United States. Finally, he applied his due process approach to the specific cases before the Court.]

MR. JUSTICE WHITE, with whom MR. JUSTICE HARLAN and MR. JUSTICE STEWART join, dissenting.

I

The proposition that the privilege against self-incrimination forbids in-custody interrogation without the warnings specified in the majority opinion and without a clear waiver of counsel has no significant support in the history of the privilege or in the language of the Fifth Amendment. As for the English authorities and the common-law history, the privilege, firmly established in the second half of the seventeenth century, was never applied except to prohibit compelled judicial interrogations. * * * Morgan, The Privilege Against Self-Incrimination, 34 Minn.L.Rev. 1, 18 (1949).

[Justice White surveyed the history of the Fifth Amendment and the Court's prior treatment of confession cases in support of this proposition.]

II

That the Court's holding today is neither compelled nor even strongly suggested by the language of the Fifth Amendment, is at odds with American and English legal history, and involves a departure from a long line of precedent does not prove either that the Court has exceeded its powers or that the Court is wrong or unwise in its present reinterpretation of the Fifth Amendment. It does, however, underscore the obvious—that the Court has not discovered or found the law in making today's decision, nor has it derived it from some irrefutable sources; what it has done is to make new law and new public policy in much the same way that it has in the course of interpreting other great clauses of the Constitution. This is what the Court historically has done. Indeed, it is what it must do and will continue to do until and unless there is some fundamental change in the constitutional distribution of governmental powers.

But if the Court is here and now to announce new and fundamental policy to govern certain aspects of our affairs, it is wholly legitimate to examine the mode of this or any other constitutional decision in this Court and to inquire into the advisability of its end product in terms of the long-range interest of the country. At the very least the Court's text and reasoning should withstand analysis and be a fair exposition of the constitutional provision which its opinion interprets. * * *

III

* * *

If the rule announced today were truly based on a conclusion that all confessions resulting from custodial interrogation are coerced, then it would simply have no rational foundation. * * * Even if one were to postulate that the Court's concern is not that all confessions induced by police interrogation are coerced but rather that some such confessions are coerced and present judicial procedures are believed to be inadequate to identify the confessions that are coerced and those that are not, it would still not be essential to impose the rule that the Court has now fashioned. Transcripts or observers could be required, specific time limits, tailored to fit the cause, could be imposed, or other devices could be utilized to reduce the chances that otherwise indiscernible coercion will produce an inadmissible confession.

On the other hand, even if one assumed that there was an adequate factual basis for the conclusion that all confessions obtained during in-custody interrogation are the product of compulsion, the rule propounded by the Court would still be irrational, for, apparently, it is only if the accused is also warned of his right to counsel and waives both that right and the right against self-incrimination that the inherent compulsiveness of interrogation disappears. But if the defendant may not answer without a warning a question such as "Where were you last night?" without having his answer be a compelled one, how can the Court ever accept his negative answer to the question of whether he wants to consult his retained counsel or counsel whom the court will appoint? And why if counsel is present and the accused nevertheless confesses, or counsel tells the accused to tell the truth, and that is what the accused does, is the situation any less coercive insofar as the accused is concerned? The Court apparently realizes its dilemma of foreclosing questioning without the necessary warnings but at the same time permitting the accused, sitting in the same chair in front of the same policemen, to waive his right to consult an attorney. It expects, however, that the accused will not often waive the right; and if it is claimed that he has, the State faces a severe, if not impossible burden of proof.

All of this makes very little sense in terms of the compulsion which the Fifth Amendment proscribes. That amendment deals with compelling the accused himself. It is his free will that is involved. Confessions and incriminating admissions, as such, are not forbidden evidence; only those which are compelled are banned. I doubt that the Court observes these distinctions today. * * *

* * *

IV

Criticism of the Court's opinion, however, cannot stop with a demonstration that the factual and textual bases for the rule it propounds are, at best, less than compelling. Equally relevant is an assessment of the rule's consequences measured against community values. * * *

The obvious underpinning of the Court's decision is a deep-seated distrust of all confessions. As the Court declares that the accused may not be interrogated without counsel present, absent a waiver of the right to counsel, and as the Court all but admonishes the lawyer to advise the accused to remain silent, the result adds up to a judicial judgment that evidence from the accused should not be used against him in any way, whether compelled or not. This is the not so subtle overtone of the opinion—that it is inherently wrong for the police to gather evidence from the accused himself. And this is precisely the nub of this dissent. I see nothing wrong or immoral, and certainly nothing unconstitutional, in the police's asking a suspect whom they have reasonable cause to arrest whether or not he killed his wife or in confronting him with the evidence on which the arrest was based, at least where he has been plainly advised that he may remain completely silent * * *. Particularly when corroborated, as where the police have confirmed the accused's disclosure of the hiding place of implements or fruits of the crime, such confessions have the highest reliability and significantly contribute to the certitude with which we may believe the accused is guilty. Moreover, it is by no means certain that the process of confessing is injurious to the accused. To the contrary it may provide psychological relief and enhance the prospects for rehabilitation.

[Justice White argues that the due process test worked well enough; that the Court's holding will impair the swift and sure apprehension of criminals; that release of the guilty is not necessarily in their best interests, and certainly not in society's best interest; and that the innocent may be reluctant to talk to the police after the decision.]

Note

As with any other important decision, it is important to ask what *Miranda* means and to examine the issues that arise in its wake. This task will be postponed briefly, however, in order to examine the broad significance of *Miranda* and the reaction to it.

Miranda merged self-incrimination and confession law and thus departed from the analytic framework of most of the Court's opinions in the Twentieth Century. Because of this, *Miranda* was viewed by many as a radical change in the law. The *Miranda* dissents nurtured this view. But, it is not difficult to find the seeds of Miranda in Bram v. United States, discussed at the beginning of the section on confessions. Moreover, the history of the privilege against self-incrimination is sufficiently unclear that reasonable people easily may reach different conclusions as to whether it should reach into the modern day stationhouse. For a defense of the majority's approach, see Kamisar, A Dissent From the Miranda Dissents: Some Comments on the "New" Fifth Amendment and the Old "Voluntariness" Test, 65 Mich.L.Rev. 59 (1966).

In thinking about *Miranda,* it might be useful to ask whether a suspect who is compelled to undergo interrogation in the police station might believe that the police have the power to keep him in custody and to ask questions until he confesses. If so, the warnings simply clarify that the suspect may be confined against his will but not compelled to speak. See Saltzburg, Miranda v. Arizona Revisited: Constitutional Law or Judicial Fiat, 26 Washburn L.Rev. 1 (1986).

There are two distinct aspects to *Miranda,* and it is useful to consider them separately. First, there is the problem of judicial review of police interrogation practices. The Supreme Court was concerned before *Miranda* that judges had enormous difficulty in making voluntariness determinations, because it was difficult after an interrogation to determine how coercive it really was, especially when the usual witnesses were police officers and the suspect—all of whom may have tended to have a skewed view of the process. One purpose of *Miranda* is to create a prophylactic rule to aid in judicial review: If the warnings are not given, then a confession is tainted. If they are given, then the confession still may not be voluntary, but at least courts have some greater confidence in any confession that is obtained. But, to the extent that *Miranda* was intended to ease the task of judicial review of confessions, it is subject to attack on the ground that taperecording of interrogations and the placement of a heavy burden on the government to demonstrate voluntariness would have been a sufficient, and perhaps a better, way to promote effective review. See Saltzburg, Standards of Proof and Preliminary Questions of Fact, 27 Stan.L.Rev. 271, 295–96 (1975). The wisdom of the Court's approach also is subject to challenge on the ground that the courts remain dependent on testimony to determine in what manner the warnings were given and what happened afterwards.

One of the ironies of *Miranda* is that it may detract from careful judicial review of police activities. Even if *Miranda* warnings are given, statements may be coerced. See, e.g., Mincey v. Arizona, 437 U.S. 385 (1978) (the murder scene search case discussed in the previous chapter), in which the Court made this clear. Investigating the murder of a police officer, a detective went to the hospital where the defendant was in the intensive care unit, and after giving the *Miranda* warnings, proceeded to interrogate the defendant. Justice Stewart wrote for eight Justices (with Justice Rehnquist alone dissenting) and described how the defendant was lying in bed barely conscious and "encumbered by tubes, needles, and breathing apparatus" during the interrogation while the detective persisted in his questioning, despite the fact that the defendant requested that the interrogation stop until he could get a lawyer.

The Court had no difficulty under these facts in concluding that "[d]ue process of law requires that statements obtained as these were cannot be used in any way against a defendant at his trial." But *Mincey* was that rare case in which the Court was outraged by the police officer's conduct. In most cases, police behavior is much more civilized, and the question is whether courts will screen confessions as carefully in light of the totality of the circumstances after *Miranda* warnings are given as they did before the warnings were required. If the warnings are really necessary, as the *Miranda* Court held, then lower courts may presume that they are meaningful and that, once given, they go a long way—all the way in most cases—toward establishing voluntariness. Green v. Scully and Miller v. Fenton, both discussed in the section on voluntariness, supra, are examples of this presumption. If the *Miranda* warnings really are not very meaningful, then the decision may do more harm than good. How you estimate the likely costs and benefits of the decision should affect your opinion of the decision.

Second, *Miranda* may signify the view of a majority of the Court in 1966 that no person should be deemed to confess voluntarily and intelligently unless he or she knows of the right to remain silent and that statements made can be used as evidence against the speaker. See generally Schrock, Welsh & Collins, Interrogational Rights: Reflections on Miranda v. Arizona, 52 So.Cal.L.Rev. 1 (1978). There is a powerful attraction in an argument that assumes, in a democracy like ours, that all persons should know what the Supreme Law of the Land is. If our educational process taught law, like reading, writing and arithmetic, *Miranda* probably would not have been necessary. But, prior to *Miranda* it was the rare, not the usual person, who could articulate her constitutional rights to refuse cooperation to the police. Although the Court could not compel that law be taught to all, it had a way of making the government the teacher in custody situations. Thus, part of *Miranda* involves educating suspects about the real choice they have to make in the interrogation process.

The educational aspect of *Miranda* has its own problems. The Court was depending on the very police officers about whom it was concerned to give the warnings. How effective could the Court have expected police officers to be as teachers of constitutional rights? We do not rely on an officer "in the competitive enterprise of ferreting out crime" to protect our Fourth Amendment rights, but rather impose a judicial officer as an intermediary. Why do we rely on a police officer to protect our Fifth Amendment rights? On the other hand, what is the alternative—that no custodial interrogation occur until the suspect is brought before a magistrate and given warnings? How would that rule affect the state's ability to obtain confessions? See Kamisar, Kauper's "Judicial Examination of the Accused" Forty Years Later—Some Comments on a Remarkable Article, 73 Mich. L.Rev. 15 (1974).

If knowledge of a choice is important before people say things that might incriminate them, why would the Court have required warnings only in custodial settings? In other words, custody would seem arguably relevant to a concern about judicial review, but not to a concern about knowing actions by people. Finally, there is the most important question of all: did the framers of the Fifth and Fourteenth Amendments have any intent or purpose to make the government educate people so that they would not say damaging things; or, were the framers concerned with forcible government action directed at people who refuse to say anything?

Even as a set of warnings, *Miranda* is not wholly adequate. Despite the fact that Chief Justice Warren repeats the Court's holding in several places, it is arguable that there are subtle differences in different parts of the opinion. Test yourself on this by stating what you think the Court's required warning is. Then ask someone else to do the same. Compare your warnings. You may find some significant differences. Even if you do not, ask yourself what you have not told the suspect. For example, have you communicated what happens if the suspect remains silent? Have you invited the person to ask questions to assure an understanding of the warnings? Have you informed the suspect that if he wants to talk, he can change his mind at any time?

What effect has *Miranda* had? In many jurisdictions, it has had very little measurable effect. See generally Stephens, The Supreme Court and Confessions of Guilt 179–200 (1973) and authorities cited therein. See also Medalie, Leitz and Alexander, Custodial Police Interrogation in Our Nation's Capital: The Attempt to Implement Miranda, 66 Mich.L.Rev. 1347 (1968). In some instances warnings are not given to all suspects, the warnings are incomplete, they are given in an unhelpful way, or the suspect has less than full understanding of the available options. See Interrogations in New Haven: The Impact of Miranda, 76 Yale L.J. 1519 (1967); Griffiths & Ayres, A Postscript to the Miranda Project: Interrogation of Draft Protesters, 77 Yale L.J. 300 (1967). Although in some places the absolute number of confessions may have fallen after *Miranda,* it does not appear that the conviction rates of law enforcement agencies has suffered. See Seeburger & Wettick, Miranda in Pittsburgh—A Statistical Study, 29 U.Pitt.L.Rev. 1 (1967). Debate continues over the effects of *Miranda*. Among the writings asserting that the decision has hurt law enforcement are Office of Legal Policy, Report on the Law of Pretrial Interrogation (Feb. 12, 1986), defended in Markman, The Fifth Amendment and Custodial Questioning: A Response to "Reconsidering Miranda," 54 U.Chi.L.Rev. 938 (1987), and Caplan, Questioning Miranda, 38 Vand.L.Rev. 1417 (1985). These claims are attacked in Schulhofer, The Fifth Amendment at Justice: A Reply, 54 U.Chi.L.Rev. 950 (1987); Schulhofer, Reconsidering Miranda, 54 U.Chi. L.Rev. 435 (1987); and White, Defending Miranda: A Reply to Professor Caplan, 39

Vand.L.Rev. 1 (1986). Professor White concludes that "the great weight of empirical evidence supports the conclusion that *Miranda's* impact on the police's ability to obtain confessions has not been significant." Recently, a special committee of the ABA Criminal Justice Section reported that a "very strong majority of those surveyed—prosecutors, judges and police officers—agree that compliance with *Miranda* does not present serious problems for law enforcement." Special Committee on Criminal Justice in a Free Society, Criminal Justice Section, ABA, Criminal Justice In Crisis 28–29 (1988).

Professors Inbau and Manak assess another cost of *Miranda* in Miranda v. Arizona: Is It Worth the Cost? (A Sample Survey, with Commentary, of the Expenditure of Court Time and Effort), 24 Cal.Western L.Rev. 185 (1988). They conclude that *Miranda* questions take up a disproportionate amount of time in trial and appellate courts. They do not factor in, however, the amount of court time that would be expended if *Miranda* were overruled and the courts returned to the old case-by-case voluntariness test to regulate confessions.

Part of the reason *Miranda* may not have much of an adverse effect on law enforcement is that the *Miranda* opinion is not as drastic as its opponents initially feared. *Miranda* does not put an end to confessions without counsel, or to stationhouse interrogation. *Miranda* does impose a warning requirement, but these warnings are given by a police officer, not a judicial officer. *Miranda* provides a right to silence and to counsel, but the decision whether to invoke these rights (and conversely whether to waive them) is made by the suspect in the very coercive atmosphere that the Court was so concerned about. The Court in *Miranda* specifically rejected the suggestion, which would seem to flow from the premise that stationhouse interrogation was coercive, that a suspect must have a nonwaivable right to an attorney before being interrogated. Thus, *Miranda* did not give significant advantages to suspects at the expense of law enforcement. Rather, it struck a compromise. See Benner, Requiem for *Miranda:* The Rehnquist Court's Voluntariness Doctrine in Historical Perspective, 67 Wash.U.L.Q. 59 (1989) ("confronted with the storm of controversy that *Escobedo* created, the Court retreated in *Miranda,* and struck a compromise" which "transformed the debate about self-incrimination into a debate about waiver"); Saltzburg, Miranda v. Arizona Revisited: Constitutional Law or Judicial Fiat, 26 Washburn L.J. 1 (1986) ("*Miranda* is more of a compromise than most critics would care to admit"). For an argument that the *Miranda* Court did not go far enough, and that "all suspects should have a nonwaivable right to consult with a lawyer before being interrogated by police," see Ogletree, Are Confessions Really Good for the Soul? A Proposal to Mirandize *Miranda,* 100 Harv.L.Rev. 1826 (1987). If *Miranda* had gone that far, would it have been overruled by now?

Whether or not *Miranda* significantly damages law enforcement, and whether or not it significantly protects suspect's rights, it is a decision of great symbolic importance. In fact, it became a lightning rod for criticism, sometimes undifferentiated, of the Warren Court's criminal procedure decisions. *Miranda* is a symbol, and much of the argument for and against *Miranda* is therefore broader than the opinion itself. Thus, the Office of Legal Policy of the Justice Department advocates that *Miranda* be overruled "because of its symbolic status as the epitome of Warren Court activism in the criminal law area." Report No. 1, Pretrial Interrogation, 22 U.Mich.J.L.Ref. 437 (1989). If *Miranda* is overruled, will the public forget about it? Will police officers? Will the courts?

In light of the controversy engendered by *Miranda,* one might assume that warnings are unique to the United States. The fact is, however, that other countries also require them. Pakter, Exclusionary Rules in France, Germany and Italy, 9 Hastings Int'l & Compar.L.Rev. 1, 27 (1985), found that "European Codes expressly require a right to silence warning. There is a dispute among scholars, however, as to the wisdom of excluding evidence in order to enforce the codes."

B. THE *MIRANDA* ISSUES

1. Impeaching the Defendant-Witness

One of the most significant cases limiting the Court's decision in *Miranda* is Harris v. New York, 401 U.S. 222 (1971).[18] In *Harris,* the defendant, charged with selling heroin to undercover police officers, took the stand in his own defense. On cross-examination, he was asked if he had made statements to the police immediately after his arrest that partially contradicted his direct testimony. Although the statements were not admissible as substantive evidence under *Miranda* since the accused was not warned of his right to counsel prior to his in-custody interrogation, Chief Justice Burger, writing for the Court, held that the statements could be admitted for purposes of impeaching the petitioner's credibility:

> Some comments in the *Miranda* opinion can indeed be read as indicating a bar to use of an uncounseled statement for any purpose, but discussion of that issue was not at all necessary to the Court's holding and cannot be regarded as controlling. *Miranda* barred the prosecution from making its case with statements of an accused made while in custody prior to having or effectively waiving counsel. It does not follow from *Miranda* that evidence inadmissible against an accused in the prosecution's case in chief is barred for all purposes, provided of course that the trustworthiness of the evidence satisfies legal standards. * * *
>
> * * * The impeachment process here undoubtedly provided valuable aid to the jury in assessing petitioner's credibility, and the benefits of this process should not be lost, in our view, because of the speculative possibility that impermissible police conduct will be encouraged thereby. Assuming that the exclusionary rule has a deterrent effect on proscribed police conduct, sufficient deterrence flows when the evidence in question is made unavailable to the prosecution in its case in chief.
>
> Every criminal defendant is privileged to testify in his own defense, or to refuse to do so. But that privilege cannot be construed to include the right to commit perjury. Having voluntarily taken the stand, petitioner was under an obligation to speak truthfully and accurately, and the prosecution here did no more than utilize the traditional truth-testing devices of the adversary process.[a] Had inconsistent statements been made by the accused to some third person, it

18. Justices Black, Brennan, Douglas and Marshall dissented. Arguably, the Court strained, to the point of distorting the record, to use this case to cabin *Miranda.* See Ely & Dershowitz, Harris v. New York: Some Anxious Observations on the Candor and Logic of the Emerging Nixon Majority, 80 Yale L.J. 1198 (1971).

a. If, for example, an accused confessed fully to a homicide and led the police to the body of the victim under circumstances making his confession inadmissible, the petitioner would have us allow that accused to take the stand and blandly deny every fact disclosed to the police or discovered as a "fruit" of his confession, free from confrontation with his prior statements and acts. The voluntariness of the confession would, on this thesis, be totally irrelevant. We reject such an extravagant extension of the Constitution.

could hardly be contended that the conflict could not be laid before the jury by way of cross-examination and impeachment.

The shield provided by *Miranda* cannot be perverted into a license to use perjury by way of a defense, free from the risk of confrontation with prior inconsistent utterances. We hold, therefore, that petitioner's credibility was appropriately impeached by use of his earlier conflicting statements.

Can the decision in *Harris* be reconciled with the language in *Miranda*?

The Court reaffirmed *Harris* in Oregon v. Hass, 420 U.S. 714 (1975).[19] In *Hass,* the defendant had received the full *Miranda* warnings and had said that he would like to call a lawyer. He was told that he could not telephone an attorney until he and the police officer reached the police station. Thereafter, the defendant made inculpatory statements before he was given an opportunity to call a lawyer. The Court stated that the only difference between the situations in *Harris* and *Hass* was that the *Miranda* warnings given in *Hass* were proper, whereas those given in *Harris* were defective. Finding that *Hass* was controlled by *Harris,* the Court held that the statements were admissible in evidence solely for impeachment purposes, after the defendant had taken the stand and offered direct testimony in conflict with the incriminating information with knowledge that the inculpatory statements had been ruled inadmissible as substantive evidence.

The Court's decisions in *Harris* and *Hass* leave a defendant with a practical problem. The defendant may not want to take the stand, because if he does the jury may learn about a confession obtained from him in violation of *Miranda.* Even though the jury will be told that the confession can be used for impeachment purposes only, the Court has recognized that juries are likely to be swayed by confessions and to use them improperly. See Bruton v. United States, 391 U.S. 123 (1968). If the defendant does not take the stand, he loses the opportunity to testify in his own behalf, and the chance of conviction increases appreciably. See H. Kalven & H. Zeisel, The American Jury 160 (1960). Given the value to the prosecution of a *Miranda*-defective confession after *Harris,* do you think the Chief Justice was correct in asserting that sufficient deterrence flows from exclusion of the confession in the case-in-chief?

In Mincey v. Arizona, 437 U.S. 385 (1978), the Court distinguished *Harris* and *Hass* and held that if a confession is involuntary, as opposed to merely *Miranda*-defective, it cannot be admitted even for impeachment purposes. The Court reasoned that the due process clause operated to prohibit the use of involuntary confessions for any purpose.

In James v. Illinois, discussed in Chapter Two, the Court held that the impeachment exception could not be used to allow impeachment of a defendant's witnesses with illegally obtained evidence. *James* dealt with a Fourth Amendment violation, but the Court has stated that the impeachment exception applies to both Fourth Amendment violations and *Miranda* violations in equal measure. See Capra, Prisoners of Their Own Jurisprudence: The Supreme Court's Fourth and Fifth Amendment Cases, 36 Vill.L.Rev. 1267 (1992). Thus, while Harris' confession could be used to impeach Harris, it could not be used to contradict Harris' witnesses.

19. Justices Brennan and Marshall dissented. Justice Douglas took no part in the decision.

Under standard evidentiary principles, a defendant can be impeached with prior silence if a reasonable person would have spoken at the time about the matter later testified to. In Doyle v. Ohio, 426 U.S. 610 (1976), the defendant had been given *Miranda* warnings at the time of his arrest and chose to remain silent. At his trial, he took the stand and related an exculpatory story that he had not previously told to the police. On cross-examination, he was asked why he had not given the exculpatory explanation before.

The Court held that the use for impeachment purposes of the defendant's silence at the time of arrest, after receiving the *Miranda* warnings, violated the due process clause of the Fourteenth Amendment.[20] In reaching this conclusion, the Court said that "while it is true that the *Miranda* warnings contain no express assurance that silence will carry no penalty, such assurance is implicit to any person who receives the warnings. In such circumstances, it would be fundamentally unfair and a deprivation of due process to allow the arrested person's silence to be used to impeach an explanation subsequently offered at trial." [21]

20. Justices Stevens, Blackmun, and Rehnquist dissented. Prior to *Doyle,* the Court had limited the use of silence upon arrest for impeachment, but as an evidentiary, not a constitutional, ruling. See United States v. Hale, 422 U.S. 171 (1975).

The Court later held that a person who waived his rights after receiving *Miranda* warnings and who spoke to the police could be asked at trial why his pretrial statement differed from his trial testimony, even if the question focused on a relevant omission in the pretrial statement. Anderson v. Charles, 447 U.S. 404 (1980).

In United States v. Cummiskey, 728 F.2d 200 (3d Cir.1984), the court of appeals read the Supreme Court's decision in Doyle v. Ohio as holding "that when the action of remaining silent occurs after the witness has received Miranda warnings, that action is not relevant as a prior inconsistent assertion." Since the relevance of the silence depends on the absence of warnings, the Court held "that when a testifying defendant makes an objection to the prosecutor's cross-examination with respect to post-arrest silence, it is the prosecutor's burden * * * to establish that Miranda warnings were not given prior to the silence relied upon for impeachment purposes."

21. Justice Stevens' majority opinion in Wainwright v. Greenfield, 474 U.S. 284 (1986), relied upon *Doyle* to hold that a defendant's silence after receiving Miranda warnings may not be used to rebut an insanity defense at trial. The Court indicated that the prosecution could have elicited testimony concerning the defendant's behavior at the time of his arrest as long as questions were carefully framed to avoid any reference to the defendant's assertion of his right to remain silent or his right to remain silent until appointment of counsel. Justice Rehnquist, joined by Chief Justice Burger, concurred in the judgment, but argued that a request for a lawyer after Miranda warnings should be treated differently from a decision to remain silent. He reasoned that the warnings do not imply that a defendant's request for counsel will not be used against him and that a request for counsel "may be highly relevant where the plea is based on insanity."

The Supreme Court found no violation of *Doyle* in Greer v. Miller, 483 U.S. 756 (1987). When Miller took the stand in his trial for kidnapping, robbery, and murder, he testified that he had taken no part in the criminal activity, and that two other defendants had come to his trailer and confessed to the crimes shortly after they occurred. The prosecutor asked Miller why he didn't tell his story to anyone after he was arrested. Miller's lawyer objected and moved for a mistrial. The trial judge denied the motion and instructed the jury to "ignore the question, for the time being."

The Supreme Court indicated that there was no doubt that Miller had received Miranda warnings when he was arrested. Justice Powell's opinion for the Court concluded, however, that the trial judge in Miller's case, unlike the judge in *Doyle,* did not permit the inquiry into silence after receipt of warnings. Once objection was made, no further question or argument concerning silence was heard. Thus, the fact of Miller's post-arrest silence was not submitted to the jury as evidence, and no *Doyle* violation occurred.

Justice Stevens filed an opinion concurring in the judgment. Justice Brennan filed a dissenting opinion, in which Justices Marshall and Blackmun joined.

It is important to note that *Doyle* did not say that the Fifth Amendment was violated by the use of the silence. Thus, the decision implied that if *Miranda* were overruled and no warnings were given to a suspect, silence might be used as impeachment evidence. Hence, *Doyle* furthered *Miranda* rights, but in a way that invited a narrower view of the Fifth Amendment in the future. It also is significant that the three dissenters were willing to permit the use of the evidence despite *Miranda.*

In Jenkins v. Anderson, 447 U.S. 231 (1980), the Court considered whether the use of pre-arrest silence for impeachment purposes was inconsistent with *Doyle.* Jenkins stabbed and killed Redding, and at his trial for murder he contended that the killing was in self-defense. Jenkins was not apprehended until he turned himself in two weeks after the killing. On cross-examination and in closing argument, the prosecutor emphasized that Jenkins' two-week waiting period was inconsistent with his later claim of self-defense. Justice Powell, writing for the Court, found *Doyle* inapplicable.

> In this case, no governmental action induced petitioner to remain silent before arrest. The failure to speak occurred before the petitioner was taken into custody and given *Miranda* warnings. Consequently, the fundamental unfairness present in *Doyle* is not present in this case. We hold that impeachment by use of prearrest silence does not violate the Fourteenth Amendment.

Justice Stevens, joined by Justice Stewart, concurred in the judgment, stating that "the admissibility of petitioner's failure to come forward with the excuse of self-defense shortly after the stabbing raised a routine evidentiary question that turns on the probative significance of that evidence and presented no issue under the Federal Constitution." Justices Marshall and Brennan dissented.

Surely the *Jenkins* Court is correct in wanting to uphold fair cross-examination of a defendant who takes the witness stand. Justice Stevens also must be correct in observing that what a person does without police influence generally does not violate the Fifth Amendment, even if the actions are incriminating. But does either opinion explain why the holding should not be read as an announcement that persons who may be involved in criminal activities must report their involvement to the police or risk having their failure to report used against them at trial, at least for impeachment purposes? Would such an announcement be the kind of government coercion that Justice Stevens finds missing in the case? Assume you are a criminal lawyer and a client comes to you and tells you facts that might indicate possible criminal activity, what do you advise? If you tell your client to tell the police everything she knows, you are a more effective agent for the government than the police can be under *Miranda.* If you tell your client to do nothing, *Jenkins* suggests that the client may suffer as a result. Could you tell your client to send an anonymous letter to the police stating that she is not guilty of criminal activity and that her failure to come forward represents a decision not to risk misinterpretation of the facts and concomitant incrimination? Would this bar use of silence as evidence under either the majority's view or that of Justice Stevens? What other advice could you give?

For a criticism of Jenkins, see Saltzburg, Foreword: The Flow and Ebb of Constitutional Criminal Procedure in the Warren and Burger Courts, 69 Geo.L.J. 151, 203–05 (1980).

In Fletcher v. Weir, 455 U.S. 603 (1982), the Court considered whether *Doyle* prohibited the use of a suspect's *post*-arrest silence for impeachment purposes, when that silence preceded *Miranda* warnings. Weir testified at trial that he acted in self-defense, and the prosecutor asked why he did not offer this explanation when he was arrested. The Court, per curiam, held that "in the absence of the sort of affirmative assurances embodied in the *Miranda* warnings," impeachment with post-arrest silence was constitutionally permissible. The Court stated that the arrest by itself does not implicitly induce a suspect to remain silent. Some state courts have rejected *Fletcher* as a matter of state law. See Nelson v. State, 691 P.2d 1056 (Alaska App.1984); State v. Davis, 38 Wn.App. 600, 686 P.2d 1143 (1984).

2. *The Fruit of the Poisonous Tree*

By its terms (and even after *Harris*), *Miranda* requires that if the police engage in custodial interrogation and give no warnings or incomplete warnings, the resulting confession must be excluded from the case-in-chief. But what about the fruits of that confession? Such fruits can consist of investigative leads pursued as a result of the confession, physical evidence, or a second confession by the suspect. In Michigan v. Tucker, 417 U.S. 433 (1974), and Oregon v. Elstad, 470 U.S. 298 (1985), the Court severely limited the exclusionary impact of *Miranda* on the fruits of confessions, and more importantly held that a violation of *Miranda* is not by itself a violation of the Fifth Amendment.

In *Tucker,* defendant was arrested for rape. Before he was interrogated, he was advised of his right to remain silent and his right to counsel, but was not told that he had the right to appointed counsel if he was indigent. The defendant thereafter told the police that he was with a friend at the time the crime was committed. However, when the police talked to the defendant's friend, Henderson, he gave information tending to incriminate the defendant. Before trial, the defendant moved to exclude Henderson's expected testimony because the defendant had told the police about Henderson without getting the full *Miranda* warnings. The motion was denied and the defendant was convicted.

The Court found that the failure to give the full *Miranda* warnings required exclusion of Tucker's confession but not Henderson's testimony. The Court stated:

> * * * There is plainly no reason to believe that Henderson's testimony is untrustworthy simply because *respondent* was not advised of *his* right to appointed counsel. Henderson was both available at trial and subject to cross-examination by respondent's counsel, and counsel fully used this opportunity, suggesting in the course of his cross-examination that Henderson's character was less than exemplary and that he had been offered incentives by the police to testify against respondent. Thus the reliability of his testimony was subject to the normal testing process of an adversary trial.

The *Tucker* Court held that the *Miranda* warnings were "procedural safeguards" that "were not themselves rights protected by the Constitution but were instead measures to insure that the right against compulsory self-incrimination was protected." As support for this assertion, the *Tucker* Court relied on language in *Miranda* inviting the states and the federal government to devise alternative solutions to protect the Fifth Amendment right. Justice

Rehnquist concluded that the failure to give warnings "did not abridge respondent's constitutional privilege against self-incrimination, but departed only from the prophylactic standards later laid down by the Court in *Miranda* to safeguard that privilege." Since violation of the *Miranda* procedural safeguards was not a violation of the Constitution, exclusion of the fruits of a *Miranda*-defective confession was not automatically required. Justice Rehnquist framed the question as whether the benefits of exclusion (deterring future *Miranda* violations) outweighed the costs of exclusion (the loss of reliable evidence). Justice Rehnquist found that the deterrent effect of excluding Henderson's testimony would be minimal, since sufficient deterrence already existed from exclusion of Tucker's confession from the case-in-chief. The Court weighed the minimal incremental deterrence against the cost of excluding Henderson's reliable testimony, and found that the exclusionary rule should not apply. The Court left open the question whether the fruit of the poisonous tree doctrine could ever be applied to a *Miranda* violation. Justice Rehnquist noted, however, that if Tucker's confession had been involuntary, the Due Process Clause would require exclusion of the confession as well as its fruits. Justices Brennan and Marshall concurred in the judgment.

Justice O'Connor, writing for the Court in *Elstad,* extended the *Tucker* analysis to a case where a second confession resulted from a *Miranda*-defective confession. The facts were as follows: Police investigating a burglary of a home suspected Elstad, an 18–year–old neighbor. They obtained a warrant for his arrest and served it at his house. One officer asked Elstad if he knew someone by the name of Gross (the burglarized family), and Elstad said that he did and that he had heard the Gross house was burglarized. The officer indicated that he thought Elstad was involved in the burglary, and Elstad replied "Yes, I was there." Elstad had not received *Miranda* warnings at that point. The officers took Elstad from his home to the Sheriff's headquarters and approximately an hour later gave him *Miranda* warnings. Elstad gave a full statement, which was typed, read back to him, initialed and signed by Elstad and the officers. The statement was used at the trial in which Elstad was convicted of burglary. The state supreme court overturned the conviction, reasoning that "the cat was sufficiently out of the bag to exert a coercive impact" on Elstad as a result of his oral statement obtained in violation of *Miranda.*

Justice O'Connor rejected the argument that the second confession had to be excluded as tainted by the first:

> The Court in *Miranda* required suppression of many statements that would have been admissible under traditional due process analysis by presuming that statements made while in custody and without adequate warnings were protected by the Fifth Amendment.
>
> Respondent's contention that his confession was tainted by the earlier failure of the police to provide *Miranda* warnings and must be excluded as "fruit of the poisonous tree" assumes the existence of a constitutional violation. It is settled law that "a confession obtained through custodial interrogation after an illegal arrest should be excluded unless intervening events break the causal connection between the illegal arrest and the confession so that the confession is 'sufficiently an act of free will to purge the primary taint.'" Taylor v. Alabama [Chapter Two, supra].

But as we explained in * * * *Tucker,* a procedural *Miranda* violation differs in significant respects from violations of the Fourth Amendment, which have traditionally mandated a broad application of the "fruits" doctrine. * * *

The *Miranda* exclusionary rule * * * sweeps more broadly than the Fifth Amendment itself. It may be triggered even in the absence of a Fifth Amendment violation. The Fifth Amendment prohibits use by the prosecution in its case in chief only of *compelled* testimony. Failure to administer *Miranda* warnings creates a presumption of compulsion. Consequently, unwarned statements that are otherwise voluntary within the meaning of the Fifth Amendment must nevertheless be excluded from evidence under *Miranda.* Thus, in the individual case, *Miranda's* preventive medicine provides a remedy even to the defendant who has suffered no identifiable constitutional harm.

But the *Miranda* presumption, though irrebutable for purposes of the prosecution's case in chief, does not require that the statements and their fruits be discarded as inherently tainted. Despite the fact that patently *voluntary* statements taken in violation of *Miranda* must be excluded from the prosecution's case, the presumption of coercion does not bar their use for impeachment purposes on cross-examination. Harris v. New York. * * * Where an unwarned statement is preserved for use in situations that fall outside the sweep of the *Miranda* presumption, "the primary criterion of admissibility [remains] the 'old' due process voluntariness test." Schulhofer, Confessions and the Court, 79 Mich.L.Rev. 865, 877 (1981).

Since exclusion of the second confession was not constitutionally required merely because it was the fruit of a *Miranda*-defective confession, the Court, as it had in *Tucker,* applied a cost-benefit analysis to determine whether exclusion would be appropriate. Justice O'Connor reasoned as follows:

In deciding "how sweeping the judicially imposed consequences" of a failure to administer *Miranda* warnings should be, the *Tucker* Court noted that neither the general goal of deterring improper police conduct nor the Fifth Amendment goal of assuring trustworthy evidence would be served by suppression of the witness' testimony. The unwarned confession must, of course, be suppressed, but the Court ruled that introduction of the third-party witness' testimony did not violate Tucker's Fifth Amendment rights.

We believe that this reasoning applies with equal force when the alleged "fruit" of a noncoercive *Miranda* violation is neither a witness nor an article of evidence but the accused's own voluntary testimony. As in *Tucker,* the absence of any coercion or improper tactics undercuts the twin rationales—trustworthiness and deterrence—for a broader rule. Once warned, the suspect is free to exercise his own volition in deciding whether or not to make a statement to the authorities.

* * * If errors are made by law enforcement officers in administering the prophylactic *Miranda* procedures, they should not breed the same irremediable consequences as police infringement of the Fifth Amendment itself. It is an unwarranted extension of *Miranda* to hold that a simple failure to administer the warnings, unaccompanied by any actual coercion or other circumstances calculated to undermine the suspect's ability to exercise his free will so taints the investigatory process that a subsequent voluntary and informed waiver is ineffective for some indeterminate period. Though *Miranda* requires that the unwarned admission must be suppressed, the admissibility of any subsequent statement should turn in these circumstances solely on whether it is knowingly and voluntarily made.

The lower court had held that Elstad's second confession was involuntary, despite the recital of *Miranda* warnings, because Elstad thought he had "let the cat out of the bag" after the first confession, and insufficient time had passed before the second confession to dissipate the coercive impact stemming from Elstad's faulty assumption. Justice O'Connor rejected this reasoning, and found that the second confession was voluntary and admissible.

> This Court has never held that the psychological impact of voluntary disclosure of a guilty secret qualifies as state compulsion or compromises the voluntariness of a subsequent informed waiver. The Oregon court, by adopting this expansive view of Fifth Amendment compulsion, effectively immunizes a suspect who responds to pre-*Miranda* warning questions from the consequences of his subsequent informed waiver of the privilege of remaining silent. This immunity comes at a high cost to legitimate law enforcement activity, while adding little desirable protection to the individual's interest in not being *compelled* to testify against himself. When neither the initial nor the subsequent admission is coerced, little justification exists for permitting the highly probative evidence of a voluntary confession to be irretrievably lost to the factfinder.
>
> There is a vast difference between the direct consequences flowing from coercion of a confession by physical violence or other deliberate means calculated to break the suspect's will and the uncertain consequences of disclosure of a "guilty secret" freely given in response to an unwarned but non-coercive question, as in this case. * * * We must conclude that, absent deliberately coercive or improper tactics in obtaining the initial statement, the mere fact that a suspect has made an unwarned admission does not warrant a presumption of compulsion. A subsequent administration of *Miranda* warnings to a suspect who has given a voluntary but unwarned statement ordinarily should suffice to remove the conditions that precluded admission of the earlier statement. In such circumstances, the finder of fact may reasonably conclude that the suspect made a rational and intelligent choice whether to waive or invoke his rights.

Justice O'Connor noted that if the officers had "exploit[ed] the unwarned admission to pressure respondent into waiving his right to remain silent," the second confession may well have been coerced. But that was not the case in *Elstad.*

Justice Brennan, joined by Justice Marshall, dissented. Justice Brennan argued that the majority had dealt a "crippling blow to *Miranda,*" by allowing police officers to obtain an unwarned confession virtually secure in the knowledge that by giving warnings they could then obtain a second confession which would be admissible. He reasoned as follows:

> For all practical purposes, the pre-warning and post-warning questioning are often but stages of one overall interrogation. Whether or not the authorities explicitly confront the suspect with his earlier illegal admissions makes no significant difference, of course, because the suspect knows that the authorities know of his earlier statements and most frequently will believe that those statements have already sealed his fate.

Justice Brennan concluded that "the correct approach, administered for almost 20 years by most courts with no untoward results, is to presume that an admission or confession obtained in violation of *Miranda* taints a subsequent confession unless the prosecution can show the taint is so attenuated as to justify [its] admission."

Justice Stevens wrote a separate dissent, arguing that the majority's distinction between "police misconduct that warrants a finding of actual coercion" and "police misconduct that establishes an irrebuttable presumption of coercion" was untenable as well as unfaithful to *Miranda.*

Do you agree with Justice Brennan that *Elstad* has dealt *Miranda* a "crippling blow"? Consider Bryant v. Vose, 785 F.2d 364 (1st Cir.1986), where officers obtained an unwarned confession, then gave warnings and obtained a second confession soon thereafter. Both confessions were admitted at trial. On review, the court found both confessions voluntary, and held that while the first confession should have been excluded under *Miranda,* its admission was harmless because the jury "learned no more from the improperly admitted confession than it did from the properly admitted one." Is this result consistent with *Elstad?*

In People v. Bethea, 67 N.Y.2d 364, 502 N.Y.S.2d 713, 493 N.E.2d 937 (1986), the court rejected *Elstad* as a matter of state constitutional law. It concluded that the state privilege against compelled self-incrimination "would have little deterrent effect if the police know that they can as part of a continuous chain of events question a suspect in custody without warning, provided only they thereafter question him or her again after warnings have been given."

In United States v. Carter, 884 F.2d 368 (8th Cir.1989), agents obtained an unwarned confession, and immediately thereafter gave *Miranda* warnings and obtained a signed waiver and confession. The court held that the second confession was properly excluded, and distinguished *Elstad* as follows:

> In this case, there was no passage of time to speak of between the unwarned confession and the subsequent warnings and confession, all of which occurred as part and parcel of a continuous process. * * * We think *Elstad* did not go so far as to fashion a rule permitting this sort of end run around *Miranda.*

The dissenting judge argued that the case was controlled by *Elstad.* With whom do you agree?

In New York v. Quarles, infra, Justice O'Connor in a concurring opinion argued that physical evidence obtained as a fruit of a *Miranda*-defective confession should not be excluded. This concurrence, together with the reasoning in *Tucker* and *Elstad,* has persuaded most courts that all evidentiary fruits of a *Miranda*-defective confession are admissible. See United States v. Gonzalez–Sandoval, 894 F.2d 1043 (9th Cir.1990) (reasoning of *Tucker* and *Elstad* "applies as well to non-testimonial physical evidence obtained as a result of a *Miranda* violation").

3. *Waiver and the Role of Counsel*

The *Miranda* Court stated that the accused may waive the rights to silence and counsel, but only if, under all the circumstances, the rights are waived "voluntarily, knowingly, and intelligently." Thus, the validity of a waiver is a question of fact in any particular case. According to *Miranda,* a valid waiver will not be assumed from the silence of the accused after the warnings are given, nor from the fact that a confession is eventually obtained. However, the Court later held in North Carolina v. Butler, 441 U.S. 369 (1979), that neither an express statement of waiver nor a written waiver is required, so long as there is sufficient evidence to show that the suspect understood his rights and voluntarily waived them. Even the suspect's refusal to sign a waiver form does not preclude a finding of waiver under the totality of the circumstances. See United States v. Frazier, 476 F.2d 891 (D.C.Cir.1973). Of course, while a written waiver is not required, it certainly supports the government's claim that a knowing and voluntary waiver was obtained. See Hyde v. Massey, 592 F.2d 249 (5th Cir.1979).

The Supreme Court in Moran v. Burbine, 475 U.S. 412 (1986) held that two requirements must be met before a suspect can be found to have waived his *Miranda* rights:

> First, the relinquishment of the right must have been voluntary in the sense that it was the product of a free and deliberate choice rather than intimidation, coercion, or deception. Second, the waiver must have been made with a full awareness both of the nature of the right being abandoned and the consequences of the decision to abandon it.

In Tague v. Louisiana, 444 U.S. 469 (1980) (per curiam), the Court held that a waiver of *Miranda* rights was not proven by testimony of an officer that he read a suspect his rights from a card. He could not remember what the rights were, whether he asked the suspect if he understood them, or whether he made an effort to determine if the suspect "was literate or otherwise capable of understanding his rights." Often *Miranda* issues turn on a "swearing contest" between police officers and defendants. Should there be a requirement that interrogations be videotaped with a sound recording? Even with videotaping, questions can arise as to the capacity of a defendant to understand and waive *Miranda* rights. See, e.g., Hampton v. State, 569 P.2d 138 (Alaska 1977). But would a good tape help resolve most cases?

It is important to keep in mind that even after *Miranda* warnings are given, a confession can still be coerced under traditional standards. See e.g., Mincey v. Arizona, supra; United States v. Brown, 557 F.2d 541 (6th Cir.1977) (even though *Miranda* warnings were given, the confession was involuntary because the defendant was in the inherently coercive atmosphere of the back seat of a police car when he made the statement and was afraid that he would be beaten by the police if he did not confess); Commonwealth v. Perry, 475 Pa. 1, 379 A.2d 545 (1977) (a confession was involuntary where a statement was taken while the defendant was in the hospital and in a great deal of pain).[22]

22. The Supreme Court extended the privilege against self-incrimination to minors in In re Gault, 387 U.S. 1 (1967). The alleged waiver by a juvenile of his rights is generally subjected to stricter scrutiny than waiver by adults. A fundamental question in the area of waiver by juveniles has been whether a minor should be able to waive his rights without first consulting with his parents or with an attorney. In State v. Jackson, 118 Ariz. 270, 576 P.2d 129 (1978), the Supreme Court of Arizona, rejecting a proposed per se rule that statements made by juveniles in response to police questioning should be suppressed unless parents are present, reasserted that the voluntariness of a statement by a juvenile shall be judged according to the totality of the circumstances. The court went on to say that the presence of parents was only one factor that enters into the voluntariness calculus. To the same effect, see Bluitt v. State, 269 Ind. 438, 381 N.E.2d 458 (1978). In Fare v. Michael C., 442 U.S. 707 (1979), the Court held 5–4, that a minor's request to see a probation officer was not the equivalent of a request for a lawyer.

The Supreme Court held in Colorado v. Connelly, 479 U.S. 157 (1986) (described supra), the decision holding that coercive police activity is a prerequisite to a finding that a confession is involuntary, that "[t]here is obviously no reason to require more in the way of a 'voluntariness' inquiry in the *Miranda* waiver context than in the Fourteenth Amendment confession context." Thus, "[t]he voluntariness of a waiver of this privilege [against self-incrimination] has always depended on the absence of police overreaching, not on 'free choice' in any broader sense of the word." The Court found that a defendant voluntarily waived his rights because he decided to confess after receiving warnings without the police engaging in any coercive behavior: "Respondent's perception of coercion flowing from the 'voice of God,' however important or significant such a perception may be in other disciplines, is a matter to which the United States Constitution does not speak." Chief Justice Rehnquist's majority opinion did not address the question whether Connelly's waiver was intelligent as well as voluntary, leaving the question for the state courts on remand.

Although Justice Stevens joined the majority in concluding that the first statements made to the uniformed officer were admissible, he dissented from the part of the decision upholding the use of the statements made after Connelly was in custody. Justice Stevens reasoned that a defendant who is incompetent to stand trial is not competent to waive his privilege against self-incrimination. Justice Brennan, joined by Justice Marshall, used similar reasoning in his dissent and added that Connelly was "clearly" unable to make an intelligent waiver.

If an individual like Connelly actually is compelled by some internal force or belief to speak, what difference does it make whether or not he is formally arrested when police officers speak with him? Is there a rationale for distinguishing the standard for competency to stand trial from the standard for agreeing to talk with the police?

Subsequent to *Connelly* and its remand on the issue of whether Connelly understood his rights, several courts have held that persons who are deranged or mentally defective cannot knowingly and intelligently waive their *Miranda* rights. In Smith v. Zant, 887 F.2d 1407 (11th Cir.1989) (en banc) the court concluded that "the *Connelly* Court addressed only voluntariness," and noted the "continued vitality of the knowing and intelligent requirement." The court found that the state did not satisfy its burden of showing that the defendant was capable of understanding his *Miranda* rights; the defendant had an I.Q. of 65, he was under extreme stress, and the warnings were read to him only once, very quickly.

It is possible for the suspect to give a limited or conditional waiver, and the resulting confession will be admissible so long as police comply with the imposed limitations. In Connecticut v. Barrett, 479 U.S. 523 (1987), Barrett received *Miranda* warnings and then signed a form indicating that he would talk to the police about a sexual assault investigation. He stated he had "no problem" in talking about the assault, but that he would not give a written statement. He was given *Miranda* warnings several times, and eventually gave an oral confession which was admitted at trial. In an opinion by Chief Justice Rehnquist, the Court held that Barrett had knowingly and voluntarily waived his *Miranda* rights. The Chief Justice reasoned that the police had complied with Barrett's conditions, because they never sought to obtain a written statement. He emphasized that Barrett gave affirmative indications that he was willing to make an oral statement. The fact that Barrett's decision may have been "illogical" was held irrelevant, "for we have never embraced the theory that a defendant's ignorance of the full consequences of his decisions vitiates their voluntariness."

Justice Brennan concurred in the judgment. He argued that if Barrett was laboring under the misimpression that oral statements could not be admitted against him at trial, his waiver would have been invalid. However, Barrett's testimony at trial that he understood the warnings (to the effect that *any* statement could be used against him) demonstrated a valid waiver. Justice Stevens, joined by Justice Marshall, dissented.

The court in Bruni v. Lewis, 847 F.2d 561 (9th Cir.1988) relied on *Barrett* to uphold a waiver when the defendant told the police to "ask your questions and I will answer those I see fit." Is this a limited waiver?

How much information must a suspect have to make a "knowing and intelligent" waiver of *Miranda* rights? This question arose in three Supreme Court cases, in each of which defendants argued that the *Miranda* warnings did not give them enough information. The Court rejected this argument in each case.

In Colorado v. Spring, 479 U.S. 564 (1987), Spring was arrested in Missouri when he tried to sell stolen firearms to an undercover agent. Agents also had information that Spring had been involved in a killing in Colorado. Spring was given warnings and signed a waiver form. He was first questioned about the firearms. Then the agents asked him whether he had ever shot anyone. He said that he had "shot another guy once." Eventually Spring gave a complete confession to the killing. Spring argued that he had not knowingly and intelligently waived his *Miranda* rights concerning the Colorado shooting, because the agents had not warned him that he would be questioned about that matter. Justice Powell, writing for seven members of the Court, rejected Spring's argument. Justice Powell reasoned as follows:

> Spring understood that he had the right to remain silent and that anything he said could be used as evidence against him. The Constitution does not require that a criminal suspect know and understand every possible consequence of a waiver of the Fifth Amendment privilege. * * * The *Miranda* warnings protect this privilege by ensuring that a suspect knows that he may choose not to talk to law enforcement officers, to talk only with counsel present, or to discontinue talking at any time. * * * [A] suspect's awareness of all the possible subjects of questioning in advance of interrogation is not relevant to determining whether the suspect voluntarily, knowingly, and intelligently waived his Fifth Amendment privilege.

Spring also argued that his waiver was invalid because the agents "tricked" him into believing that they were only concerned with the firearms charge. Justice Powell rejected this argument as well, stating that while trickery could vitiate the voluntariness of a waiver, trickery could not be found through "mere silence," and that the agents had not affirmatively misrepresented the intended scope of their questioning.

Justice Marshall, joined by Justice Brennan, dissented. He argued that a suspect's decision to waive the privilege will "necessarily be influenced by his awareness of the scope and seriousness of the matters under investigation."

He claimed that the majority's rule would allow officers to take "unfair advantage of the suspect's psychological state."

In Oregon v. Elstad, discussed supra, Elstad argued that the waiver he made before giving his second confession was not knowing and intelligent. Justice O'Connor described the argument, and rejected it, as follows:

> Respondent * * * has argued that he was unable to give a fully *informed* waiver of his rights because he was unaware that his prior statement could not be used against him. Respondent suggests that Deputy McAllister, to cure this deficiency, should have added an additional warning to those given him at the Sheriff's office. Such a requirement is neither practicable nor constitutionally necessary. In many cases, a breach of *Miranda* procedures may not be identified as such until long after full *Miranda* warnings are administered and a valid confession obtained. The standard *Miranda* warnings explicitly inform the suspect of his right to consult a lawyer before speaking. Police officers are ill equipped to pinch-hit for counsel, construing the murky and difficult questions of when "custody" begins or whether a given unwarned statement will ultimately be held admissible.
>
> This Court has never embraced the theory that a defendant's ignorance of the full consequences of his decisions vitiates their voluntariness. * * *

At the time *Miranda* was decided, it arguably signified the minimum showing required before the government could successfully claim that an individual had waived his privilege and voluntarily made a statement. If you go back to the language in the Warren opinion, is it consistent with the waiver approach evident in these cases? Is it possible that in the decisions since the original *Miranda* case, the Court has treated *Miranda* as setting the maximum requirements that will be imposed upon the government?

In thinking about the last question, consider the result in Moran v. Burbine, 475 U.S. 412 (1986). Justice O'Connor's majority opinion begins with a useful summary of the case:

> After being informed of his rights pursuant to Miranda v. Arizona, and after executing a series of written waivers, respondent confessed to the murder of a young woman. At no point during the course of the interrogation, which occurred prior to arraignment, did he request an attorney. While he was in police custody, his sister attempted to retain a lawyer to represent him. The attorney telephoned the police station and received assurances that respondent would not be questioned until the next day. In fact, the interrogation session that yielded the inculpatory statements began later that evening. The question presented is whether either the conduct of the police or respondent's ignorance of the attorney's efforts to reach him taints the validity of the waivers and therefore requires exclusion of the confessions.

Justice O'Connor, writing for five members of the Court, concluded first that Burbine's waiver was valid despite the fact that he was not informed that an attorney sought to contact him. She reasoned as follows:

> The voluntariness of the waiver is not at issue. As the Court of Appeals correctly acknowledged, the record is devoid of any suggestion that police resorted to physical or psychological pressure to elicit the statements. * * * Nor is there any question about respondent's comprehension of the full panoply of rights set out in the *Miranda* warnings and of the potential consequences of a decision to relinquish them. * * *

> Events occurring outside of the presence of the suspect and entirely unknown to him surely can have no bearing on the capacity to comprehend and knowingly relinquish a constitutional right. [Accepting Burbine's argument would mean that] the same defendant, armed with the same information and confronted with precisely the same police conduct, would have knowingly waived his *Miranda* rights had a lawyer not telephoned the police station to inquire about his status. Nothing in any of our waiver decisions or in our understanding of the essential components of a valid waiver requires so incongruous a result. No doubt the additional information would have been useful to respondent; perhaps even it might have affected his decision to confess. But we have never read the Constitution to require that the police supply a suspect with a flow of information to help him calibrate his self interest in deciding whether to speak or stand by his rights. Once it is determined that a suspect's decision not to rely on his rights was uncoerced, that he at all times knew he could stand mute and request a lawyer, and that he was aware of the state's intention to use his statements to secure a conviction, the analysis is complete and the waiver is valid as a matter of law.

In the majority's view, the fact that the police acted deliberately to deprive Burbine of information concerning counsel's attempt to reach him did not affect the validity of the waiver.

> [W]hether intentional or inadvertent, the state of mind of the police is irrelevant to the question of the intelligence and voluntariness of respondent's election to abandon his rights. Although highly inappropriate, even deliberate deception of an attorney could not possibly affect a suspect's decision to waive his *Miranda* rights unless he were at least aware of the incident. Nor was the failure to inform respondent of the telephone call the kind of "trick[ery]" that can vitiate the validity of a waiver. Granting that the "deliberate or reckless" withholding of information is objectionable as a matter or ethics, such conduct is only relevant to the constitutional validity of a waiver if it deprives a defendant of knowledge essential to his ability to understand the nature of his rights and the consequences of abandoning them. Because respondent's voluntary decision to speak was made with full awareness and comprehension of all the information *Miranda* requires the police to convey, the waivers were valid.

Burbine argued that apart from the waiver issue, *Miranda* should be read to prohibit the police from deliberately deceiving counsel, or from denying counsel's request to see the suspect. The majority declined "to further extend *Miranda's* reach." Justice O'Connor explained the Court's position as follows:

> [W]hile we share respondent's distaste for the deliberate misleading of an officer of the court, reading *Miranda* to forbid police deception of an *attorney* "would cut [the decision] completely loose from its own explicitly stated rationale." As is now well established, "[t]he ... *Miranda* warnings are 'not themselves rights protected by the Constitution but [are] instead measures to insure that the [suspect's] right against compulsory self-incrimination [is] protected.'" Michigan v. Tucker. Their objective is not to mold police conduct for its own sake. Nothing in the Constitution vests in us the authority to mandate a code of behavior for state officials wholly unconnected to any federal right or privilege. The purpose of the *Miranda* warnings instead is to dissipate the compulsion inherent in custodial interrogation and, in so doing, guard against abridgement of the suspect's Fifth Amendment rights. Clearly, a rule that focuses on how the police treat an attorney—conduct that has no relevance at all to the degree of compulsion experienced by the defendant

during interrogation—would ignore both *Miranda* 's mission and its only source of legitimacy.

Finally, the Court declined to "extend" *Miranda* to require the police to inform the suspect of an attorney's efforts to reach him. Justice O'Connor argued as follows:

> As we have stressed on numerous occasions, "[o]ne of the principal advantages" of *Miranda* is the ease and clarity of its application. We have little doubt that the approach urged by respondent * * * would have the inevitable consequence of muddying *Miranda* 's otherwise relatively clear waters. The legal questions it would spawn are legion: To what extent should the police be held accountable for knowing that the accused has counsel? Is it enough that someone in the station house knows, or must the interrogating officer himself know of counsel's efforts to contact the suspect? Do counsel's efforts to talk to the suspect concerning one criminal investigation trigger the obligation to inform the defendant before interrogation may proceed on a wholly separate matter? * * *
>
> Moreover, problems of clarity to one side, reading *Miranda* to require the police in each instance to inform a suspect of an attorney's efforts to reach him would work a substantial and, we think, inappropriate shift in the subtle balance struck in that decision. Custodial interrogations implicate two competing concerns. On the one hand, "the need for police questioning as a tool for effective enforcement of criminal laws" cannot be doubted. Admissions of guilt are more than merely "desirable," they are essential to society's compelling interest in finding, convicting and punishing those who violate the law. On the other hand, the Court has recognized that the interrogation process is "inherently coercive" and that, as a consequence, there exists a substantial risk that the police will inadvertently traverse the fine line between legitimate efforts to elicit admissions and constitutionally impermissible compulsion.
>
> *Miranda* attempted to reconcile these opposing concerns by giving the *defendant* the power to exert some control over the course of the interrogation. Declining to adopt the more extreme position that the actual presence of a lawyer was necessary to dispel the coercion inherent in custodial interrogation, see Brief for American Civil Liberties Union as *Amicus Curiae* in Miranda v. Arizona, the Court found that the suspect's Fifth Amendment rights could be adequately protected by less intrusive means. Police questioning, often an essential part of the investigatory process, could continue in its traditional form, the Court held, but only if the suspect clearly understood that, at any time, he could bring the proceeding to a halt or, short of that, call in an attorney to give advice and monitor the conduct of his interrogators.
>
> The position urged by respondent would upset this carefully drawn approach in a manner that is both unnecessary for the protection of the Fifth Amendment privilege and injurious to legitimate law enforcement. Because, as *Miranda* holds, full comprehension of the rights to remain silent and request an attorney are sufficient to dispel whatever coercion is inherent in the interrogation process, a rule requiring the police to inform the suspect of an attorney's efforts to contact him would contribute to the protection of the Fifth Amendment privilege only incidentally, if at all. This minimal benefit, however, would come at a substantial cost to society's legitimate and substantial interest in securing admissions of guilt. Indeed, the very premise of the Court of Appeals was not that awareness of Ms. Munson's phone call would have dissipated the coercion of the interrogation room, but that it might have

convinced respondent not to speak at all. Because neither the letter nor purposes of *Miranda* require this additional handicap on otherwise permissible investigatory efforts, we are unwilling to expand the *Miranda* rules to require the police to keep the suspect abreast of the status of his legal representation.

Justice Stevens, joined by Justices Brennan and Marshall, dissented. He argued that the Court's holding "flies in the face of this Court's repeated expressions of deep concern about incommunicado questioning," and that the holding "exalts incommunicado interrogation, sanctions police deception, and demeans the right to consult with an attorney." In his view, "[p]olice interference with communications between an attorney and his client is a recurrent problem." Referring to the heavy burden that *Miranda* placed on the government to prove waiver, Justice Stevens reasoned that "proof that the required warnings have been given is a necessary, but by no means sufficient, condition for establishing a valid waiver." He opined that "there can be no constitutional distinction * * * between a deceptive misstatement and the concealment by the police of the critical fact that an attorney retained by the accused or his family has offered assistance, either by telephone or in person." Justice Stevens responded to the majority's reliance on *Miranda's* careful balance with the observation that a rule requiring the police to inform a suspect of an attorney's call would serve *Miranda's* goal of dispelling the compulsion inherent in custodial interrogation, and to the majority's concern for clarity with the suggestion that no state that required the police to tell a suspect of an attorney's call had experienced problems. Justice Stevens argued that the police deliberately deceived the suspect's agent, his attorney, and that "as a matter of law, the police deception of Munson [the attorney] was tantamount to deception of Burbine himself."

Is Moran v. Burbine consistent with *Miranda?* For a view that it is, see Kamisar, Remembering the "Old World" of Criminal Procedure: A Reply to Professor Grano, 23 U.Mich.J.L.Ref. 537 (1990).

Imagine the following facts: in a commercial setting, two parties, A and B, are meeting in A's office and considering signing a contract when B's lawyer telephones A to say that she would come over immediately if there was any chance B was going to sign the contract because she did not want B to sign before B had a legal opinion on the contract; A tells B's lawyer that she need not bother to come to A's office, because no contract was going to be signed until the next day; A fails to relate the conversation to B and instead suggests that B sign the contract immediately; and B does so. If B later wishes to void the contract, would a court hold that B may do so? Should the answer to this question be the same as the answer to the question whether the police deception in Moran v. Burbine should require suppression of the defendant's statement?

The *Burbine* approach has been rejected as a matter of state constitutional law by some courts. See Haliburton v. Florida, 514 So.2d 1088 (Fla.1987). In Connecticut v. Stoddard, 206 Conn. 157, 537 A.2d 446 (1988), the Court rejected *Burbine* and held that a waiver could not be knowing unless the suspect was informed of counsel's attempt to contact him. The Court reasoned as follows:

> *Miranda* warnings refer only to an abstract right to counsel. That a suspect validly waives the presence of counsel only means that for the moment the suspect is forgoing the exercise of that conceptual privilege. Faced with a

> concrete offer of assistance, however, a suspect may well decide to reclaim his or her continuing right to legal assistance. We cannot therefore conclude that a decision to forgo the abstract offer contained in *Miranda* embodies an implied rejection of a specific opportunity to confer with a known lawyer.

Has the *Stoddard* court effectively addressed the concerns of the majority in *Burbine?*

4. *Waiver and Resumption of Questioning*

In all the above cases, the suspect had never invoked his *Miranda* rights, and the government argued that the suspect waived his rights and confessed. Can the government argue that waiver occurred if the suspect first invokes his *Miranda* rights and later confesses? Obviously it is a more difficult argument to make, since in the prior cases, the suspects may have at all times wanted to speak with the police. Where the suspect has initially invoked his rights, however, something must have changed his mind. The government must show that this change of mind came from the suspect, and not from the police. Where the suspect has invoked his rights, the Supreme Court has shown far greater sensitivity to the waiver issue than in cases where there was no invocation.

A suspect can invoke two rights in response to the *Miranda* warnings—the right to silence, and the right to counsel. The Court has held that the rules on waiver differ depending on which right is invoked.

In Michigan v. Mosley, 423 U.S. 96 (1975), the defendant was arrested in connection with certain robberies, given *Miranda* warnings, and told that he could remain silent. The defendant said that he did not want to discuss the robberies, and the detective refrained from questioning him further. Approximately two hours later *Miranda* warnings were given again, and a different detective questioned the defendant about a murder that was not related to the robberies. The defendant made an incriminating statement, which was admitted at his murder trial, in which he was convicted.

Justice Stewart, writing for the Court, found that the admission of the incriminating statements did not violate *Miranda.* In reaching this decision, the Court found it necessary to interpret language from *Miranda:*

> If the individual indicates in any manner, at any time prior to or during questioning, that he wishes to remain silent, the interrogation must cease. At this point he has shown that he intends to exercise his Fifth Amendment privilege; any statement taken after the person invokes his privilege cannot be other than the product of compulsion, subtle or otherwise. Without the right to cut off questioning, the setting of in-custody interrogation operates on the individual to overcome free choice in producing a statement after the privilege has been once invoked.

The Court concluded that the only sensible reading of the above language was not that the suspect could never be interrogated, but rather that the accused's right to cut off questioning must be scrupulously honored. Reviewing the circumstances around Mosley's second interrogation, the Court found:

> This is not a case, therefore, where the police failed to honor a decision of a person in custody to cut off questioning, either by refusing to discontinue the interrogation upon request or by persisting in repeated efforts to wear down his

resistance and make him change his mind. In contrast to such practices, the police here immediately ceased the interrogation, resumed questioning only after the passage of a significant period of time and the provision of a fresh set of warnings, and restricted the second interrogation to a crime that had not been a subject of the earlier interrogation.

Justice Stewart also indicated that the Court would not tolerate repetitive attempts, without respite, to interrogate a defendant who wanted to remain silent. But he concluded *Miranda* should not be a per se bar to resumption of questioning.

It may be wondered how an officer can "scrupulously honor" a suspect's right to remain silent and yet resume questioning. Generally speaking, courts have found the most important factor to be whether the officers gave the suspect a "cooling off" period after he invoked the right to silence. See Charles v. Smith, 894 F.2d 718 (5th Cir.1990) (no waiver where suspect was asked whether he owned a certain hat and coat, two minutes after invoking the right to silence); Grooms v. Keeney, 826 F.2d 883 (9th Cir.1987) (waiver found after four hour break in questioning). Multiple attempts to get the suspect to speak are considered problematic. See Vujosevic v. Rafferty, 844 F.2d 1023 (3d Cir.1988) (no waiver where suspect was approached four times to determine whether he had changed his mind about not talking, and where officers had no reason to believe that he changed his mind). On the other hand, if the officers give fresh *Miranda* warnings when they approach the suspect, this is evidence that they are scrupulously honoring the suspect's right to silence, as well as evidence that defendant knowingly and voluntarily waived his rights if a confession is obtained. See Otey v. Grammer, 859 F.2d 575 (8th Cir.1988) (waiver found where warnings were given frequently and defendant was allowed to control the subject matter of the questioning).

The *Mosley* standards presume that the suspect has invoked the right to silence after receiving *Miranda* warnings. But whether such an invocation has been made is often a close question. For example, in United States v. Pena, 897 F.2d 1075 (11th Cir.1990), the defendant Chitty was arrested for his involvement in a major drug conspiracy. After receiving the warnings, he was asked if he wished to cooperate with the government, and he said "I really want to but I can't; they will kill my parents." He was then confronted with incriminating evidence, and confessed to involvement after a series of questions. The court held that "where an individual in custody makes an equivocal invocation of his right to remain silent, further questioning must be restricted to clarifying that request until it in fact is clarified, and no statement taken after the request but before the clarification can clear the *Miranda* hurdle." The court found that Chitty's statement was ambiguous, because Chitty "expressed conflicting desires to cooperate and to remain silent," and that the failure of the officer to clarify the ambiguity precluded a finding of waiver of *Miranda* rights. Is this a fair resolution of the problem presented by ambiguous invocations?

In Edwards v. Arizona, 451 U.S. 477 (1981), the Court determined whether and under what circumstances a waiver can be found after the suspect invokes his right to counsel. The Court adopted a per se approach when it confronted the following facts:

> On January 19, 1976, a sworn complaint was filed against Edwards in Arizona state court charging him with robbery, burglary, and first-degree murder. An arrest warrant was issued pursuant to the complaint, and Edwards was arrested at his home later that same day. At the police station, he was informed of his rights as required by Miranda v. Arizona. Petitioner stated that he understood his rights, and was willing to submit to questioning. After being told that another suspect already in custody had implicated him in the crime, Edwards denied involvement and gave a taped statement presenting an alibi defense. He then sought to "make a deal." The interrogating officer told him that he wanted a statement, but that he did not have the authority to negotiate a deal. The officer provided Edwards with the number of a county attorney. Petitioner made the call, but hung up after a few moments. Edwards then said, "I want an attorney before making a deal." At that point, questioning ceased and Edwards was taken to county jail.
>
> At 9:15 the next morning, two detectives, colleagues of the officer who had interrogated Edwards the previous night, came to the jail and asked to see Edwards. When the detention officer informed Edwards that the detectives wished to speak with him, he replied that he did not want to talk to anyone. The guard told him that "he had" to talk and then took him to meet with the detectives. The officers identified themselves, stated they wanted to talk to him, and informed him of his *Miranda* rights. Edwards was willing to talk, but he first wanted to hear the taped statement of the alleged accomplice who had implicated him. After listening to the tape for several minutes, petitioner said that he would make a statement so long as it was not tape recorded. The detectives informed him that the recording was irrelevant since they could testify in court concerning whatever he said. Edwards replied "I'll tell you anything you want to know, but I don't want it on tape." He thereupon implicated himself in the crime.

The Court found that the defendant had not waived his *Miranda* rights, reasoning as follows:

> [A]dditional safeguards are necessary when the accused asks for counsel; and we now hold that when an accused has invoked his right to have counsel present during custodial interrogation, a valid waiver of that right cannot be established by showing only that he responded to further police-initiated custodial interrogation even if he has been advised of his rights. We further hold that an accused, such as Edwards, having expressed his desire to deal with the police only through counsel, is not subject to further interrogation by the authorities until counsel has been made available to him, unless the accused himself initiates further communication, exchanges or conversations with the police.

Chief Justice Burger and Justices Powell and Rehnquist agreed with the result, but expressed concern about the seemingly per se aspects of the majority rule which they found to be an unnecessary embellishment on the standard knowing and intelligent waiver rule. *Edwards* is one of the few Supreme Court cases reading *Miranda* as broadly as possible.

The Court has revisited the *Edwards* rule on several occasions. The Court found that *Edwards* did not require the suppression of statements in Wyrick v. Fields, 459 U.S. 42 (1982). Fields, a soldier, was convicted of rape. He had received the advice of a retained attorney and of defense counsel provided by the military and decided to request a polygraph examination. Prior to the examination, he signed a consent form that related Miranda rights and additional rights guaranteed by the Uniform Code of Military Justice. The examiner also informed Fields that he did not have to answer questions, that he could consult a lawyer before answering any questions, and that he could stop answering at any time. At the conclusion of the examination, the examiner told Fields that there had been some deceit and asked whether Fields could explain why some of his answers were bothering him. At this time Fields admitted intercourse with the 81 year old victim, but denied rape. Asked whether he would like to talk with another military agent and with the local chief of police, Fields said he would. After receiving additional warnings, he told the police chief that there had been consensual intercourse. The Supreme Court reversed a court of appeals' finding that the procedures violated *Edwards* and held that Fields had initiated the polygraph examination and thereby validly waived his right to post-test questioning "unless the circumstances changed so seriously that his answers no longer were voluntary," or unless he no longer was making a voluntary waiver. The Court found that Fields had initiated the inquiry and that nothing that occurred invalidated his waiver.[23]

Edwards requires that a suspect "initiate" further communication before a waiver can be found. Whether a suspect has initiated reinterrogation is often a difficult question. In Oregon v. Bradshaw, 462 U.S. 1039 (1983), Oregon police were investigating the death of Lowell Reynolds, who apparently died in the wreck of his pickup truck. Bradshaw was asked and consented to come to the police station for questioning. Once there, he was advised of his rights and admitted providing liquor to Reynolds. He was arrested for furnishing liquor to a minor. When an officer suggested that Bradshaw might have been driving Reynolds' truck, Bradshaw expressed a desire for an attorney. Questioning stopped. Thereafter, during or just before a 10 or 15 mile trip from the station to the jail, Bradshaw asked, "Well, what is going to happen to me now?" An officer answered that Bradshaw had requested an attorney and that Bradshaw should not be talking with the officer unless he desired to do so. The two had a conversation concerning where Bradshaw was being taken and with what he would be charged. The officer suggested that Bradshaw might help himself by taking a lie detector test, and Bradshaw agreed to take one. The next day, following new warnings, he took the test. The examiner expressed doubts that Bradshaw had told the truth and Bradshaw then admitted he was driving the vehicle in which Reynolds was killed. The trial court admitted Bradshaw's confession, and he was convicted of first degree manslaughter, driving while under the influence of intoxicants, and driving with a revoked license.

The Oregon Court of Appeals reversed, finding that the officer had violated *Edwards*. A majority of the Supreme Court disagreed. Justice Rehnquist's

23. *Wyrick* is distinguished in United States v. Gillyard, 726 F.2d 1426 (9th Cir. 1984). The court of appeals upheld a district judge's finding that a suspect who agreed to take a polygraph test did not waive his Miranda rights under the following circumstances: the polygraph examiner told him after the test that he was being deceptive; he denied any criminal involvement; and, after 30 minutes with the examiner following the test, the suspect was confronted with two agents who questioned him for an hour without giving Miranda warnings. The court pointed out several differences between this case and *Wyrick*: the defendant and his attorney suggested the examination in *Wyrick* whereas government agents suggested it in this case; Wyrick had counsel and Gillyard did not; Wyrick received a much more substantial warning than the standard Miranda warning and Gillyard did not; and Wyrick was asked questions only by the examiner, while Gillyard was questioned by additional officers.

plurality opinion, joined by Chief Justice Burger and Justices White and O'Connor, reasoned that Bradshaw initiated a conversation:

> There can be no doubt in this case that in asking, "Well, what is going to happen to me now?", respondent "initiated" further conversation in the ordinary dictionary sense of that word. While we doubt that it would be desirable to build a superstructure of legal refinements around the word "initiate" in this context, there are undoubtedly situations where a bare inquiry by either a defendant or by a police officer should not be held to "initiate" any conversation or dialogue. There are some inquiries, such as a request for a drink of water or a request to use a telephone that are so routine that they cannot be fairly said to represent a desire on the part of an accused to open up a more generalized discussion relating directly or indirectly to the investigation. Such inquiries or statements, by either an accused or a police officer, relating to routine incidents of the custodial relationship, will not generally "initiate" a conversation in the sense in which that word was used in *Edwards*.
>
> Although ambiguous, the respondent's question in this case as to what was going to happen to him evinced a willingness and a desire for a generalized discussion about the investigation; it was not merely a necessary inquiry arising out of the incidents of the custodial relationship. It could reasonably have been interpreted by the officer as relating generally to the investigation. That the police officer so understood it is apparent from the fact that he immediately reminded the accused that "you do not have to talk to me," and only after the accused told him that he "understood" did they have a generalized conversation. On these facts we believe that there was not a violation of the *Edwards* rule.

The plurality clarified that a finding of initiation by the suspect was not enough to constitute a waiver under *Edwards*. Justice Rehnquist stated that even if the suspect initiates communication, "where reinterrogation follows, the burden remains upon the prosecution to show that subsequent events indicated a waiver of the Fifth Amendment right to have counsel present during the interrogation." Thus, the plurality used a two-step analysis to determine whether a suspect waives his rights after invoking the right to counsel. The first step is the bright-line prophylactic safeguard of the initiation requirement, and the second step is the familiar totality of circumstances test of a knowing and voluntary waiver. The plurality found that after initiating communication, Bradshaw knowingly and voluntarily waived his *Miranda* rights, since he was given fresh warnings and it was clear he understood them.

Justice Marshall, joined by Justices Brennan, Blackmun and Stevens, dissented. The dissenters applied the same two-step approach as had the majority, but they differed as to the meaning of the initiation requirement. Justice Marshall argued that the plurality's definition of "initiation" was overbroad, and "drastically undermined" the protection erected in *Edwards*. In Justice Marshall's view, initiation could not be found unless the suspect expressed a willingness to discuss the specific subject matter of the investigation. He argued that Bradshaw's question was merely a response to his custodial surroundings, rather than an expression of willingness to discuss his crime.

The deciding vote was cast by Justice Powell, who concurred in the judgment reversing the Oregon court. He expressed concern about the two step approach: asking first whether the accused initiated communications, and if so, then asking whether there was a valid waiver. He observed that this analysis, if followed literally, "often would frustrate justice as well as common sense" and preferred to rely on the totality of the circumstances and "the judgment of the trial court that has had the benefit of hearing the evidence and assessing the weight and credibility of testimony."

Suppose the Supreme Court announced that once a suspect requested a lawyer, the police must be sure that any subsequent statements by the suspect are intended to initiate a discussion with the police concerning the offenses for which a suspect has been placed in custody. Would this unduly burden the police? What would police have to do to ascertain the intent of the suspect? Had they made an effort in *Bradshaw*, what would they have discovered?

While the Court split 4–4 in *Bradshaw* as to the proper test for initiation, the lower courts have consistently followed Justice Rehnquist's view. The court in United States v. Velasquez, 885 F.2d 1076 (3d Cir.1989), relied on the *Bradshaw* plurality to hold that the suspect's statement "what is going to happen?" was an initiation under *Edwards.* The court stated that the plurality's test was a reasonable compromise between individual and state interests, and that Justice Marshall's test "might convert the prophylactic value of the initiation requirement * * * into an overly stringent substantive hurdle." Do you agree?

In Henderson v. Dugger, 925 F.2d 1309 (11th Cir.1991), Henderson was suspected of a string of murders, and he was being transported by Officers Hord and Bakker from one county to another. He invoked his right to counsel before getting into the police car. Upon arrival in the county of destination, Officer Bakker stopped the car and got out to make a phone call. Henderson asked officer Hord, "what's going to happen next?" Hord responded that Henderson was going to be placed in a county detention facility. At the suppression hearing, Hord testified that in response to this statement, Henderson "had a look on his face like 'you've got to be kidding. I know all these things, and all you're going to do is take me to jail.' " Hord took it that Henderson wanted to show the officers where bodies were buried. Henderson was given fresh warnings, and signed a waiver form, and then led the officers to the bodies of three previously undiscovered murder victims. The court, relying on the plurality opinion in *Bradshaw,* held that Henderson had initiated conversation when he asked what was going to happen next. However, the court added this cautionary note:

> We are careful to add that this holding is a result of our conclusion that Henderson himself asked a question initially that could have been taken as relating to his crimes, * * *. A holding that Henderson initiated his confession through nonverbal communication would allow police to interrogate suspects who have invoked their right to counsel on the basis of police interpretations of suspects' demeanors, facial expressions, and so on. A twitch of the cheek could be taken as a desire to confess. Such a rule would effectively wipe out the protections that cases such as *Edwards* provide.

As with invocation of the right to silence, questions arise as to whether the suspect has invoked a right to counsel. If the invocation is ambiguous, most courts have held (as with invocations of silence) that the officer can only ask questions which clarify whether or not the suspect is invoking the right to counsel. See United States v. Fouche, 833 F.2d 1284 (9th Cir.1987); United States v. Gotay, 844 F.2d 971 (2d Cir.1988) ("Suspects should not be forced, on pain of losing a constitutional right, to select their words with lawyer-like precision").

In some cases the suspect's statement may not even rise to the level of an ambiguous invocation. Is Quadrini v. Clusen, 864 F.2d 577 (7th Cir.1989) such a case? Quadrini was given warnings, then made an incriminating statement; thereafter he showed the officers the business card of the public defender who was his lawyer, questioning continued, and the suspect made another, far more incriminating statement. The admissibility of the second statement was at issue. Quadrini claimed that by showing the officers the business card of his lawyer, he invoked the right to counsel, or at least that the invocation was ambiguous and so only clarifying questions could be asked. The court found *Edwards* inapplicable because Quadrini's action did not even rise to the level of an ambiguous invocation.

On the other side of the spectrum, arguments arise as to whether the suspect's invocation is clear enough so that no questions can be asked, or ambiguous enough that clarifying questions can be asked. In Smith v. Illinois, 469 U.S. 91 (1984), a suspect who was asked whether he understood his right to have a lawyer present stated, "Uh, yeah, I'd like that." The Court did not determine what questions if any are permissible when the suspect makes an ambiguous invocation of counsel, because the court found that "with the possible exception of the word 'uh' the defendant's statement in this case was neither indecisive nor ambiguous." The Court concluded that "where nothing about the request for counsel or the circumstances leading up to the request would render it ambiguous, all questioning must cease."

When the officer questioned Smith after his response to the warnings, ostensibly to clarify the request, Smith did make ambiguous statements concerning his desire for counsel. But the Court dismissed this later ambiguity as irrelevant. It declared that "using an accused's subsequent responses to cast doubt on the adequacy of the initial request *itself* is * * * intolerable" and that a contrary rule would lead to abusive use of "clarifying" questions. Justice Rehnquist, joined by Chief Justice Burger and Justice Powell, dissented. He argued that Smith's statement was ambiguous under the circumstances, and that the majority's rule preventing consideration of post-request statements was overbroad.

Does *Edwards* permit officers to initiate interrogation on crimes other than the one for which the suspect invoked his right to counsel? In Arizona v. Roberson, 486 U.S. 675 (1988), the Court answered this question in the negative and held that an invocation of counsel under *Edwards* was not offense-specific.

Roberson was arrested at the scene of a just-completed burglary. After he was given *Miranda* warnings, he stated that he wanted a lawyer before answering any questions. Three days later while the defendant remained in custody, another officer, who was unaware of the previous request for a lawyer, gave new *Miranda* warnings and obtained a statement concerning another burglary. Justice Stevens wrote for the Court as it declared that "*Edwards* serves the purpose of providing 'clear and unequivocal' guidelines to the law enforcement profession," and that "there is nothing ambiguous about the requirement that after a person in custody has expressed his desire to deal with the police only through counsel, he is not subject to further interrogation by the authorities until counsel has been made available to him, unless the accused himself initiates further communication, exchanges, or conversations with the police."

The Court concluded that "to a suspect who has indicated his inability to cope with the pressures of custodial interrogation by requesting counsel, any further interrogation without counsel having been provided will surely exacerbate whatever compulsion to speak the suspect may be feeling." In response to the suggestion of the United States as *amicus curiae* that a suspect might have good reason to want to speak to police about a new investigation, Justice Stevens wrote that "[t]he simple answer is that the suspect, having requested counsel, can determine how to deal with the separate investigations with counsel's advice." He added that "even if the police have decided temporarily not to provide counsel, they are free to inform the suspect of the facts of the second investigation as long as such communication does not constitute interrogation."

Justice Kennedy, joined by Chief Justice Rehnquist, dissented, complaining that the Court's ruling was unnecessary to protect a suspect's rights and unduly restricted legitimate investigations. He described the breadth of the Court's rule as follows: "The rule announced today will bar law enforcement officials, even those from some other city or other jurisdiction, from questioning a suspect about an unrelated matter if he is in custody and has requested counsel to assist in answering questions put to him about the crime for which he was arrested." Justice Kennedy attacked the Court's presumption "that a suspect has made the decision that he does not wish to talk about that [separate investigation] without counsel present, although that decision was made when the suspect was unaware of even the existence of a second investigation," and argued that "[a]llowing authorities who conduct a separate investigation to read the suspect his *Miranda* rights and ask him whether he wishes to invoke them strikes an appropriate balance."

Justice O'Connor did not participate in the case.

The Court distinguished *Roberson* in McNeil v. Wisconsin, 111 S.Ct. 2204 (1991) when it held that an invocation of Sixth Amendment rights was "offense-specific" and that police could therefore initiate questioning on crimes other than the crime with which the defendant was charged. The case arose when the State charged McNeil with armed robbery, and at his initial appearance before a judicial officer, McNeil invoked his right to counsel. Police thereafter initiated questioning of McNeil concerning armed robbery and murder committed in another part of the state. McNeil waived his *Miranda* rights and confessed to those crimes; he argued that this waiver was invalid under *Edwards* and *Roberson,* because police initiated interrogation after he had invoked his right to counsel. Justice Scalia, writing for a six-person majority, stated that McNeil's invocation of his offense-specific Sixth Amendment right at his initial appearance did not constitute an invocation of the non-offense specific *Miranda–Edwards* right. Justice Scalia explained as follows:

> To invoke the Sixth Amendment interest is, as a matter of fact, not to invoke the *Miranda–Edwards* interest. One might be quite willing to speak to the police without counsel present concerning many matters, but not the matter under prosecution. It can be said, perhaps, that it is likely that one

> who has asked for counsel's assistance in defending against a prosecution would want counsel present for all custodial interrogation, even interrogation unrelated to the charge. * * * But even if that were true, the likelihood that a suspect would wish counsel to be present is not the test for applicability of *Edwards*. The rule of that case * * * requires, at a minimum, some statement that can reasonably be construed to be expression of a desire for the assistance of an attorney in dealing with custodial interrogation by the police. Requesting the assistance of an attorney at a bail hearing does not bear that construction.

Justice Scalia rejected the defendant's argument that a total prohibition on police-initiated questioning after any invocation of counsel would provide a clear guideline for the police. He responded that "the police do not need our assistance to establish such a guideline; they are free, if they wish, to adopt it on their own." Justice Scalia recognized that clear guidelines are nonetheless important for judicial review. He responded, however, that bright-line rules should be used "only when they guide sensibly, and in a direction we are authorized to go." Justice Scalia concluded that the defendant's proposed bright-line rule "would do much more harm than good, and is not contained within, or even in furtherance of, the Sixth Amendment's right to counsel or the Fifth Amendment's right against compelled self-incrimination."

Justice Kennedy wrote a concurring opinion, reiterating the views of his *Roberson* dissent that an invocation of the *Miranda* right to counsel should be offense-specific as well.

Justice Stevens, joined by Justices Marshall and Blackmun, dissented. The dissenters argued that the Court's offense-specific test for a Sixth Amendment invocation would lead to ambiguity and consequent abuse. Justice Stevens argued that police might "file charges selectively in order to preserve opportunities for custodial interrogation."

The dissenters also contended that the majority's limited construction of a Sixth Amendment invocation would have little practical effect. Because *Roberson* held that an invocation of *Miranda* rights is *not* offense-specific, Justice Stevens asserted that "the entire offense-specific house of cards that the Court has erected" for the Sixth Amendment would collapse whenever defendant or counsel makes an explicit statement invoking *Miranda* rights at the initial appearance.

Is Justice Stevens correct that the holding in *McNeil* will affect very few cases, because a defendant can and will explicitly invoke his *Miranda* rights at the initial appearance? The practical effect of *McNeil* may lie in a footnote in Justice Scalia's opinion, responding to this argument in the dissent. Justice Scalia asserted that "we have never held that a person can invoke his *Miranda* rights anticipatorily, in a context other than custodial interrogation—which a preliminary hearing will not always, or even usually, involve." He stated that such reasoning would lead to the unacceptable conclusion that *Miranda* rights could be invoked "in a letter prior to arrest, or indeed even prior to identification as a suspect." He concluded as follows:

> Most rights must be asserted when the government seeks to take the action they protect against. The fact that we have allowed the *Miranda* right to counsel, once asserted, to be effective with respect to future custodial interrogation does not necessarily mean that we will allow it to be asserted

initially outside the context of custodial interrogation, with similar future effect.

The Court further clarified and arguably extended the *Edwards* rule when it held in Minnick v. Mississippi, 111 S.Ct. 486 (1990), that the protection of *Edwards* continues even after the suspect has consulted with an attorney. Justice Kennedy, who dissented in *Roberson,* wrote the majority opinion for six justices. Minnick committed murders in Mississippi, and was apprehended in California. After making inculpatory statements at an FBI interview (which were excluded from Minnick's trial as violative of *Edwards*), an appointed attorney met with Minnick on two or three occasions. The attorney told Minnick not to say anything, and not to sign any waiver forms. After these consultations, a Mississippi Deputy Sheriff initiated an interrogation of Minnick. Minnick was given *Miranda* warnings, refused to sign a waiver of rights form, and confessed. The trial court held that the confession to the Deputy Sheriff was not excluded by *Edwards,* reasoning that *Edwards* was inapplicable once counsel had been made available to Minnick.

The *Minnick* majority held that *Edwards* is not satisfied by mere consultations with counsel, and that police-initiated interrogation may only occur if counsel is actually present during the interrogation. The Court relied upon language in *Miranda, Edwards,* and the *Edwards* line of cases which stated that "the interrogation must cease until an attorney is present" and that the suspect has the right "to have counsel present during custodial interrogation." From this language, Justice Kennedy concluded that "a fair reading of *Edwards* and subsequent cases demonstrates that we have interpreted the rule to bar police-initiated interrogation unless the accused has counsel with him at the time of questioning * * *. We now hold that interrogation must cease, and officials may not reinitiate interrogation without counsel present, whether or not the accused has consulted with his attorney."

Justice Kennedy reasoned that two policies underlying *Edwards* rendered its application in this case "appropriate and necessary": (1) the bright line *Edwards* rule provides clarity and certainty, and (2) the rule guarantees that suspects will not be badgered by police officers and provides prophylactic protection against police coercion.

On the issue of clarity, the Court found that a rule allowing police-initiated interrogation after consultation with counsel "would undermine the advantages flowing from *Edwards'* clear and unequivocal character." Justice Kennedy observed that a rule denying *Edwards* protection after consultation would be vague because "consultation is not a precise concept, for it may encompass variations from a telephone call to say that the attorney is in route, to a hurried exchange, * * * to a lengthy in-person conference."

On the policy in *Edwards* of preventing badgering and coercion, the Court found that mere consultation with an attorney would be insufficient to protect against the risk of harassment and exploitation of the suspect by the police. Justice Kennedy stated that "a single consultation with an attorney does not remove the suspect from persistent attempts by officials to persuade him to waive his rights, or from the coercive pressures that accompany custody and that may increase as custody is prolonged."

In a vigorous dissent, Justice Scalia, joined by Chief Justice Rehnquist, attacked the Court's "irrebuttable presumption" that a suspect who has invoked his right to counsel "can never validly waive that right during any police-initiated encounter, even after the suspect has been provided multiple *Miranda* warnings and has actually consulted with his attorney." More fundamentally, Justice Scalia contended that *Edwards* itself was an unnecessary prophylactic rule. Even more fundamentally, Justice Scalia attacked what he thought was the underlying premise of *Miranda* and its progeny: that an honest confession is a "foolish mistake" which ought to be rejected as evidence.

Justice Scalia argued that *Edwards* was inconsistent with the Court's general case-by-case approach to waiver, which in other cases (such as *Mosley*) had rejected an irrebuttable presumption that a suspect could not voluntarily waive *Miranda* rights. Justice Scalia admitted that *Edwards* succeeded in providing assurance against coercion and in providing clear guidelines to the courts and to law enforcement. He responded, however, that

> so would a rule that simply excludes all confessions by all persons in police custody. The value of any prophylactic rule must be assessed not only on the basis of what is gained, but also on the basis of what is lost. * * * Undoubtedly some bright-line rules can be adopted to implement [the Fifth Amendment right], marking out the situations in which knowledge or voluntariness cannot possibly be established—for example, a rule excluding confessions obtained after five hours of continuous interrogation. But a rule excluding all confessions that follow upon even the slightest police inquiry cannot conceivably be justified on this basis. It does not rest upon a reasonable prediction that all such confessions, or even most such confessions will be unaccompanied by a knowing and voluntary waiver.

Justice Scalia noted that the *Edwards* rule, when combined with *Mosley,* resulted in the anomaly that "the suspect in custody who says 'I do not wish to discuss this matter' can be asked to change his mind; but if he should say, more tentatively 'I do not think I should discuss this matter without my attorney present' he can no longer be approached."

Justice Scalia stated that, even if *Edwards* struck an appropriate balance between the need to protect the suspect and proper law enforcement objectives, the extension of *Edwards* promulgated by the majority did not. He pointed out that a suspect who has consulted with counsel is in a different situation from a suspect who has not. After consultation, the suspect knows "that he has an advocate on his side, and that the police will permit him to consult with that advocate. He almost certainly also has a heightened awareness (above what the *Miranda* warning itself will provide) of his right to remain silent."

Justice Scalia concluded with a broad attack on the prophylactic rules of *Edwards* and *Miranda* itself:

> Today's extension of the *Edwards* prohibition is the latest stage of prophylaxis built upon prophylaxis, producing a veritable fairyland castle of imagined constitutional restriction upon law enforcement. The newest tower, according to the Court, is needed to avoid inconsistency with the purpose of *Edwards'* prophylactic rule, which was needed to protect *Miranda's* prophylactic right to have counsel present, which was needed to protect the right against compelled self-incrimination found (at last!) in the Constitution.
>
> It seems obvious to me that, even in *Edwards* itself but surely in today's decision, we have gone far beyond any genuine concern about suspects who do

not know their right to remain silent, or who have been coerced to abandon it. Both holdings are explicable * * * only as an effort to protect suspects against what is regarded as their own folly. The sharp-witted criminal would know better than to confess; why should the dull-witted suffer for his lack of mental endowment? Providing him an attorney at every stage where he might be induced or persuaded (though not coerced) to incriminate himself will even the odds. Apart from the fact that this protective enterprise is beyond our authority under the Fifth Amendment * * * it is unwise. The procedural protections of the Constitution protect the guilty as well as the innocent, but it is not their objective to set the guilty free. That some clever criminals may employ those protections to their advantage is poor reason to allow criminals who have not done so to escape justice.

Thus, even if I were to concede that an honest confession is a foolish mistake, I would welcome rather than reject it * * *. More fundamentally, however, it is wrong, and subtly corrosive of our criminal justice system, to regard an honest confession as a "mistake." While every person is entitled to stand silent, it is more virtuous for the wrongdoer to admit his offense and accept the punishment he deserves. * * * We should, then, rejoice at an honest confession, rather than pity the "poor fool" who has made it. * * * To design our laws on premises contrary to these is to abandon belief in either personal responsibility or the moral claim of just government to obedience.

Justice Souter did not participate in the decision.

Suppose a suspect said "I don't want you to ask questions without my lawyer here." Then he consults with his lawyer. At that point, why should there be a presumption that the suspect is not willing to talk to police? Is Justice Scalia correct that there should be no presumption either way?

In Riddle v. State, 580 So.2d 1195 (Miss.1991), Riddle said he wanted to talk to his lawyer, and the officer got the lawyer on the telephone. The lawyer advised Riddle to confess. Riddle hung up the phone and pursuant to questioning he confessed. The court found a valid waiver, though stating that if *Minnick* were taken "literally" a waiver could not be found. The court stated that the "spirit" of *Minnick* had been satisfied, and saw "no reason on principle why telephonic access to counsel is legally less significant that eyeball-to-eyeball access." Do you agree?

5. *Incomplete Warnings*

The Court summarily reversed the California Supreme Court in California v. Prysock, 451 U.S. 1301 (1981), and held that where a suspect was informed that he had "the right to talk to a lawyer before you are questioned, have him present while you are being questioned, and all during the questioning" and also that he had "the right to have a lawyer appointed to represent you at no cost to yourself," *Miranda* was satisfied even though the suspect was not informed of right to have an attorney appointed before further questioning. The Court declared that it had "never indicated that the rigidity of *Miranda* extends to the precise formulation of the warnings," and that "*Miranda* itself indicates that no talismanic incantation" is required.

Chief Justice Rehnquist wrote for the Court in Duckworth v. Eagan, 492 U.S. 195 (1989), as it found no *Miranda* violation in a police officer's reading a waiver form to a suspect, which provided:

"Before we ask you any questions, you must understand your rights. You have the right to remain silent. Anything you say can be used against you in court. *You have the right to talk to a lawyer for advice before we ask you any questions, and to have him with you during questioning.* You have this right to the advice and presence of a lawyer even if you cannot afford to hire one. We *have no way of giving you a lawyer, but one will be appointed for you, if you wish, if and when you go to court.* If you wish to answer questions now without a lawyer present, you have the right to stop answering questions at any time. You also have right to stop answering at any time until you've talked to a lawyer." (emphasis added)

The Chief Justice noted that the Court has never insisted that *Miranda* warnings be given in the exact form described in Chief Justice Warren's opinion, and concluded that the inclusion of the "if and when you go to court" language accurately described state procedure and did not fail to apprise the defendant of his rights.

Justice Marshall, joined by Justices Brennan, Blackmun, and Stevens, dissented. He argued that the "if and when" language led the defendant to believe that a lawyer will not be appointed until some future time after questioning takes place.

In United States v. Connell, 869 F.2d 1349 (9th Cir.1989), Connell received an oral warning that "you must make your own arrangements to obtain a lawyer, and this will be at no expense to the Government," and that "if you cannot afford to pay for a lawyer, one *may* be appointed to represent you." (emphasis added). He also received written warnings which stated that if he could not afford a lawyer, "arrangements will be made for you to obtain one in accordance with the law." The court held that these warnings together were insufficient, and that Connell's confession should have been excluded. The court reasoned that the oral warning was "misleading" because it appeared that the right to appointed counsel was subject to government discretion. It found the written warning to be "ambiguous" because "Connell is not expected to know what the requirements of the law are. In fact, conveying to the person in custody the requirements of the law is the whole purpose of the warning." Is *Connell* inconsistent with *Prysock* and *Eagan*?

6. Custody

The Supreme Court held in *Miranda* that the police must give an accused the *Miranda* warnings before commencing a custodial interrogation. If the defendant is not in custody, the *Miranda* warnings do not apply, and the test is one of the voluntariness of the confession under the totality of the circumstances. An important question, therefore, is "what constitutes 'custody'?" According to *Miranda,* the test is whether a person is deprived of his freedom of action in any significant way. In several cases subsequent to *Miranda,* the Court specifically addressed the custody question. In Orozco v. Texas, 394 U.S. 324 (1969), it held that the defendant was in custody in his bedroom when four policemen entered at 4:00 a. m. and tried to elicit incriminating information from him. In so deciding, the Court noted that one of the four officers had testified that the defendant was under arrest and not free to leave his bedroom. Clearly, if a person is arrested, he is in custody. Interestingly, however, it is not clear that Orozco knew or believed he was under arrest.

In Mathis v. United States, 391 U.S. 1 (1968), the defendant was interrogated in jail by I.R.S. agents about defendant's alleged tax evasion. The Court found that although the defendant was in jail for reasons unrelated to the tax investigation, he was still in custody, and the failure to give him his *Miranda* warnings violated his constitutional rights.

Conversely, in Beckwith v. United States, 425 U.S. 341 (1976), the Court found that the defendant was not in custody for purposes of receiving *Miranda* warnings where two I.R.S. agents arrived at his house at 8:00 p. m., were invited in and sat with the defendant at his dining room table to discuss their investigation of his federal income tax returns. The agents were looking at the possibility of criminal tax fraud. The Court maintained that although Beckwith was the focus of a tax investigation, he was not in a custodial situation when he talked with the agents in his home. Without custody, the Court stated that there is not the inherently coercive atmosphere which triggers the need for *Miranda* warnings.

In Oregon v. Mathiason, 429 U.S. 492 (1977), a per curiam opinion, the Court ruled that an individual at a police station is not necessarily in custody. An officer told Mathiason over the phone that he wanted to discuss something with him and asked if they could meet somewhere. Mathiason had no preference, so the policeman asked if he could come down to the station house. Mathiason agreed, and arriving a short time later, was told that he was not under arrest. Mathiason was ushered into an office, the door was closed and the two sat across a desk. The officer told the defendant about the burglary he was investigating, that he believed the defendant was involved, and that his fingerprints were found at the scene (which was not true).

The Court concluded that Mathiason's freedom was not restrained so as to render him in custody under *Miranda.* The Court stressed that Mathiason went down to the station voluntarily, was informed that he was not under arrest, and left the station without hindrance after he confessed. The dissenters, Justices Brennan, Marshall and Stevens, stressed that Mathiason was a parolee and so it could not be truly said that he went down to the station of his own accord. Does *Mathiason* encourage suspects to be cooperative with the police? If it is important that a suspect is allowed to leave, can't that factor be manipulated by officers after *Mathiason*?

In California v. Beheler, 463 U.S. 1121 (1983), the Court extended *Mathiason* to find that the suspect was not in custody when he agreed to accompany police officers down to the station for questioning. He was told he was not under arrest and was released after confessing. Should there be a difference between going to the station unaccompanied and going to the station with police officers?

Justice White wrote for six Justices in Minnesota v. Murphy, 465 U.S. 420 (1984), as the Court held that the privilege against self-incrimination was not violated when a probation officer called Murphy, a probationer, to her office and questioned him about the rape and murder of a teenage girl in 1974. Murphy had admitted the offenses to a counselor as part of the treatment prescribed as a condition of probation. The Court held that *Miranda* did not require the officer to warn Murphy of his rights prior to asking questions about crimes he might have committed, since Murphy was not arrested or otherwise in custody although he was required to meet with the officer. Although the

Court recognized that the officer sought incriminating information, it reiterated its statement in *Beckwith* that warnings are not required simply because an investigation has focused upon a suspect.

Justice Marshall, joined by Justice Stevens and in part by Justice Brennan, dissented. He argued that a reasonable man in Murphy's position would have believed that his duty to answer questions honestly as a condition of probation required him to respond to the questions put by the officer.

To test your view of the meaning of "custody" consider the following facts:

> On February 25, 1989, the Twin Cities Federal Savings and Loan Association (TCF) was robbed by two men armed with a shotgun and possibly a handgun. [Eyewitness descriptions and other information led the officers to focus on Griffin as a suspect. The officers telephoned Griffin's house].
>
> * * * Griffin's stepfather answered the phone and informed the agents that Griffin would be home early that evening. Agents Waldie and Tremper proceeded to Griffin's home, arriving at 7 p.m., and were invited into the living room by Griffin's stepfather. The purpose of the interview was to determine what Griffin knew of the bank robbery. The officers did not intend to arrest him at that time. The agents waited in the living room until 8:15 p.m. when Griffin was heard approaching the house outside. The agents moved to the hall near the front door to meet Griffin as he entered the house. Waldie and Tremper identified themselves as F.B.I. agents investigating a bank robbery and informed Griffin that they needed to speak with him. At that point, before any other words were spoken, Griffin stated, "The gun wasn't loaded."
>
> The agents explained to Griffin's parents that it was necessary for them to speak to Griffin in private and, accordingly, the three went into the dining room and sat down. The agents did not draw their guns, handcuff Griffin, or place him under formal arrest. Griffin's parents retired to the upstairs of the house where they remained throughout the course of the questioning.
>
> Neither of the agents informed Griffin that he was not under arrest, that he was free to request the agents to leave without speaking to them, nor did they inform him of his *Miranda* rights. Twice during the two-hour interview Griffin asked to obtain cigarettes from other places in the house and each time Agent Waldie required that Agent Tremper escort him. Griffin was told he was to stay in their view at all times. The agents used this procedure to ensure their personal safety because a weapon had been used in the course of the robbery, although this was not explained to Griffin at the time.
>
> During the interview, Griffin appeared nervous, "sort of choked up for words" and "fearful" of the agents. In the course of the questioning Griffin implicated himself and Chapman in the robbery. The agents questioned Griffin for approximately two hours. At the conclusion of the interview the agents placed Griffin under arrest. Griffin was then transported to the F.B.I. office where, three hours after his initial confrontation with the agents, he was advised of his *Miranda* rights for the first time.

In United States v. Griffin, 922 F.2d 1343 (8th Cir.1990), the court surveyed precedent and set forth extensive guidelines for determining whether a suspect is in custody under *Miranda:*

> Custody occurs either upon formal arrest or under *any other circumstances* where the suspect is deprived of his freedom of action in *any* significant way. In determining whether a suspect is "in custody" at a particular time we

examine the extent of the physical or psychological restraints placed on the suspect during interrogation in light of whether a "reasonable person in the suspect's position would have understood his situation" to be one of custody. * * * The determination of custody arises from an examination of the totality of the circumstances.

Relevant Factors

Previous decisions of this court have stated that the relevant factors to be considered in making a determination of custody include an accused's freedom to leave the scene, and the purpose, place and length of the interrogation. While the accused's freedom of action during the interrogation remains a critical factor, the purpose, place and length factors have been interpreted to have inconclusive, independent relevance to the determination of custody.

Purpose

It is insufficient to render an interrogation custodial that the purpose of the interrogation is to obtain potentially inculpatory information from a suspect that has become the focus of the investigation. Beckwith v. United States. Although custody is not inferred from the mere circumstance that the police are questioning the one whom they believe to be guilty, the fact that the individual has become the focus of the investigation is relevant "to the extent that the suspect is aware of the evidence against him" and this awareness contributes to the suspect's sense of custody. * * *

Place

The place of the interrogation, while relevant, has not developed as a determinative factor in custody analysis. *Miranda* tended to focus on the coercive aspects of the stationhouse interrogation, but subsequent authority indicates that deprivations of freedom may occur in places other than the police station. Orozco v. Texas; United States v. Mahar, 801 F.2d 1477, 1500 (6th Cir.1986) (suspect in custody when questioned at place of employment); United States v. Beraun–Panez, 830 F.2d 127, 127–28 (9th Cir.1987) (suspect in custody when questioned on isolated range near where he was herding cattle). Conversely, interrogation which occurs at the police station or jailhouse may be non-custodial.

Length

The length of the interrogation has been a similarly undeterminative factor in the analysis of custody. While *Miranda* was most obviously concerned with the "marathon" routine of questioning a suspect, custody has been found in relatively brief interrogations where the questioning is of a sort where "the detainee is aware that questioning will continue until he provides his interrogators the answers they seek." *Beraun–Panez,* 812 F.2d at 579 (questioning of suspect for approximately one hour together with other circumstances indicated custody); *Mahar,* 801 F.2d at 1500 (questioning of suspect for only twenty minutes at place of employment custodial in light of other indicia of custody); Davis v. Allsbrooks, 778 F.2d 168 (4th Cir.1985) (no custody though questioning occurred over the course of several hours where other circumstances demonstrated lack of restraint on suspect).

Indicia of Custody

A consistent line of inquiry has developed from this case-by-case approach which has identified several common indicia of custody. These indicia of custody relate to the specific police practices employed during questioning which tend to either mitigate or aggravate an atmosphere of custodial interrogation. This inquiry into the indicia of custody has generally focused on an examination of (1) whether the suspect was informed at the time of questioning that the questioning was voluntary, that the suspect was free to leave or request the officers to do so, or that the suspect was not considered under arrest; (2) whether the suspect possessed unrestrained freedom of movement during questioning; (3) whether the suspect initiated contact with authorities or voluntarily acquiesced to official requests to respond to questions; (4) whether strong arm tactics or deceptive stratagems were employed during questioning; (5) whether the atmosphere of the questioning was police dominated; or, (6) whether the suspect was placed under arrest at the termination of the questioning.

* * * The first three of these factors may be fairly characterized as mitigating factors, that is to say the affirmative presence of one or more of these factors during questioning would tend to mitigate the existence of custody at the time of the questioning. Conversely, the remaining three factors may be characterized as coercive factors, which is to say that the affirmative presence of one or more of these factors during questioning would tend to aggravate the existence of custody. It is not necessary to a finding of custody that all of the foregoing indicia be presented by the factual circumstances of a case, and a particularly strong showing with respect to one factor may compensate for a deficiency with respect to other factors. Realizing that the available means of coercion are as vast as the circumstances in which it may arise, we emphasize that the foregoing list is merely intended to be representative of those indicia of custody most frequently cited by this and other courts when undergoing the prescribed totality of the circumstances analysis.

I. Application of Indicia Factors

* * *

(1) Advice Given by Officers

The most obvious and effective means of demonstrating that a suspect has not been "taken into custody or otherwise deprived of . . . freedom of action," is for the police to inform the suspect that an arrest is not being made and that the suspect may terminate the interview at will. Where a suspect has been so advised, custody has frequently been found to not exist. * * * By the same token, the absence of police advisement that the suspect is not under formal arrest, or that the suspect is at liberty to decline to answer questions, has been identified as an important indicium of the existence of a custodial setting. See Minnick v. Mississippi (*Miranda* implicated by "formal interview which petitioner was compelled to attend").

(2) Restraint

We have often looked upon the lack of restraint on a suspect's freedom of movement during questioning, the second indicium of custody, as a factor indicating absence of custody. Circumstances of custody are frequently obviated where the suspect's freedom of action is not curtailed during questioning. * * * *Beckwith,* (no custody where suspect permitted to move about his home unaccompanied). This second factor is related to the first factor in that both concern the suspect's liberty during questioning and the suspect's subjective assessment of the circumstances. Though it is often the case that suspects are escorted or chaperoned during questioning for reasons unrelated to custody, as in this case where Agent Waldie testified that he was concerned for the safety of himself and his partner, "the relevant inquiry is the *effect on the suspect.*" * * * We realize that the likely effect on a suspect of being placed under guard during questioning, or told to remain in the sight of interrogating officials, is to associate these restraints with a formal arrest.

(3) Who Initiated Contact

The third indicium of custody concerns whether the interview was instigated by authorities or whether the suspect initiated contact or voluntarily acquiesced to official questions. As noted in *Miranda,* "custodial interrogation [means] questioning *initiated* by law enforcement officers." Applying this fundamental precept of *Miranda* to cases in this circuit, this Court has frequently found custody lacking where suspects take the initiative to offer statements or voluntarily arrange for questioning. Conversely, when the confrontation between the suspect and the criminal justice system is instigated at the direction of law enforcement authorities, rather than the suspect, custody is more likely to exist.

(4) Tactics Used

Police deployment of strong arm tactics or deceptive stratagems during interrogation, number four in the list of indicia of custody enumerated above, is a practice widely condemned in American law. * * * Because such strong arm tactics are more generally associated with formal arrest than with an informal encounter with police, the use of such tactics is identified as an indicium of custody. *Beraun–Panez,* 812 F.2d at 580 (custodial interrogation where officers confronted suspect with false or misleading witness statements, employed "Mutt and Jeff" routine, and took advantage of suspect's insecurities about his alien status). It goes without saying that a strong presumption of impropriety attaches to any circumstances where this Court detects the use of coercive interrogation techniques to obtain confessions. An interrogation can still be custodial even though no strong-arm tactics are used, but the absence of such tactics is a factor which can assist us in reaching an objective conclusion that the suspect could not have associated the questioning with formal arrest.

(5) Domination of Interview

An interrogation which occurs in an atmosphere dominated by the police, the fifth indicium of custody, is more likely to be viewed as custodial than one which does not. * * * The question is whether the entire context of the questioning, including such considerations as place and length of the interrogation, demonstrates that the course of the investigation was police dominated.

Other circumstances which indicate police domination of the custodial surroundings concern whether the police assume control of the interrogation site and "dictate the course of conduct followed by the [suspect]" or other persons present at the scene. Where the conduct of the police leads a suspect to believe that the police have taken full control of the scene, then we are more likely to recognize the existence of custody. * * * Officers diminish the public character of, and assert their dominion over, an interrogation site by removing a suspect from the presence of third persons who could lend moral support. *Beraun–Panez,* 812 F.2d at 582 (agents interrogating rancher in pasture demonstrated domination of interrogation by stopping co-worker from approaching suspect); [United States v.] *Jorgensen,* 871 F.2d at 729 (atmosphere not police dominated when suspect permitted to speak with brother in private during questioning). When police resort to domineering practices, we find there exists a greater probability that an objective, reasonable person would feel in custody during the interrogation.

Applying the foregoing standards to the facts of the case, the court found that Griffin's first statement about the gun not being loaded was "volunteered" and thus not subject to *Miranda.* However, the subsequent confession was excluded, because Griffin was in custody at that time, and he did not receive *Miranda* warnings.

> In this case, we find none of the mitigating factors cited in the list of indicia of custody, but most of the coercive factors. Griffin did not initiate or arrange for the questioning. Griffin himself did not invite the law enforcement officers into the house. He was not told he had the option to reject their request for an interview. Instead, the agents were admitted by Griffin's stepfather and Griffin was confronted in the hallway of his own home where questioning was initiated by the F.B.I. agents. Griffin was not informed that he was not under arrest, that he was at liberty to request the agents to leave, or that he could refuse to answer questions.
>
> Griffin's freedom of action was restrained to a degree commonly associated with formal arrest during questioning when he was accompanied by an officer when he retrieved cigarettes from other rooms in the house and was told to remain in view of the agents at all times. Though Agent Waldie testified that the purpose of escorting Griffin was for safety concerns, this fact was not disclosed to Griffin at the time. We must consider the "effect on the suspect" of the agents' actions and we find that appellant could not reasonably have understood that he was free to do as he pleased when he was not permitted to go to another room of his own home without being accompanied by an officer.
>
> The record does not reflect that strong arm tactics were employed in the questioning of Griffin; however, we note that we do not expect to find these tactics employed in every case, particularly when authority dictates that they should not be employed in any case. Strong arm tactics and deceptive strategems are one indicium of custody, and are not a pre-requisite to a finding of custody. Questioning which occurs in the suspect's own home may provide a margin of comfort, but, as previously noted, the setting of the interrogation is not so important to the inquiry as the question of police domination of that setting. Here we find ample evidence of a police dominated, custodial environment in the fact that as soon as Griffin arrived at home the agents took control of the scene. * * * By sending Griffin's parents away, the agents asserted their dominion over the interrogation site, isolated Griffin from family who may have provided moral support, and eliminated any last vestige of a public interrogation. Any objective reasonable person would conclude from these actions that the authorities were now in complete control of the defendant. * * *
>
> Finally, we believe Griffin's arrest at the conclusion of the interview is objective evidence which tends to support the reasonableness of Griffin's subjective belief that he was in custody from the inception of the encounter and that his arrest was imminent. Griffin had already implicated himself prior to questioning with his volunteered (and hence admissible) statement that "[t]he gun wasn't loaded." The level of police domination of his home, the restrictions on his actions during questioning, together with the fact that the agents never informed Griffin that he would not be arrested, reflects a pattern of conduct on the part of the officers that any reasonable person would associate with formal arrest.

We have undertaken an extended analysis for the reason that this case presents to us for the third time in as many years a situation where we must overrule a district court's ruling on the question of custody. * * * The motivation and purpose of the *Miranda* opinion, as well as the ease of its application, are undermined if its effect is to simply substitute the endless chain of voluntariness questions that crowded court dockets prior to its announcement with a new class of case-by-case determinations on the issue of what is custody. While not intending to establish a bright line rule of custody, the analysis we use is intended to provide law enforcement and prosecutors with some insight into the appropriate indicia of custody which should be taken into consideration when analyzing the totality of the circumstances.

The *Griffin* court concluded that doubtful cases should be called in favor of a finding of custody, so that officers would be encouraged to give *Miranda* warnings:

The application of the rule of *Miranda* is not a process to be avoided by law enforcement officers. Custody should not be a mystical concept to any law enforcement agency. We see no reason why doubts as to the presence or absence of custody should not be resolved in favor of providing criminal suspects with the simple expedient of *Miranda* warnings. As noted in the *Miranda* opinion, and as demonstrated by case law and legal authority appearing in the intervening years since the announcement of the *Miranda* decision, the effectiveness of law enforcement is not undermined by informing suspects of their rights.

Do you agree with the court that if custody is a close question, it should be decided against the government? Do you think the Supreme Court would agree? Do you think the Supreme Court would have found custody in *Griffin?*

If a police officer asks questions of a suspect during a *Terry* stop, must the officer give *Miranda* warnings? In Berkemer v. McCarty, 468 U.S. 420 (1984), the Court in an opinion by Justice Marshall held that *Terry* stops are not custodial for *Miranda* purposes. Justice Marshall noted that *Terry* stops are typically of brief duration; questioning is limited, because the officer can ask only a "moderate number of questions to determine identity and to try to obtain information confirming or dispelling the officer's suspicions;" the detainee is not obliged to respond; and unless probable cause arises in a short time, the detainee must be released. Justice Marshall concluded that *Terry* stops were "comparatively nonthreatening" and hence unlike the custodial situations required to trigger *Miranda.* If the stop escalates to an arrest, however, *Miranda* will apply. Thus, the law distinguishing *Terry* stops from arrests discussed in Chapter Two (see, e.g., Dunaway v. New York, supra) also determines whether custody exists under *Miranda.* See Saltzburg, Foreword: The Flow and Ebb of Constitutional Criminal Procedure in the Warren and Burger Courts, 69 Geo.L.J. 151, 200–03 (1980).

A plurality of the Court has indicated that *Miranda* warnings are not required before someone who is a "putative" defendant is called to testify before a grand jury. See United States v. Mandujano, 425 U.S. 564 (1976) (opinion by Chief Justice Burger, joined by Justices White, Powell and Rehnquist). Since a subpoened witness must appear before the grand jury, is the appearance really voluntary?

7. *Interrogation*

In addition to the custody requirement, the police must also be interrogating the individual before the need for *Miranda* warnings arises. Thus, volunteered statements or "threshold" confessions (where the defendant walks into the police station and immediately confesses) are not barred by the fact that they were not preceded by *Miranda* warnings.

The Government has the burden of proving the spontaneity of the challenged statement or confession. To preserve the evidence for trial, after the accused volunteers an incriminating statement, a cautious policeman will give the *Miranda* warnings before pursuing follow-up questioning.

Is a statement volunteered if the accused interrupts the officer who is giving him his *Miranda* rights? Any such statement would appear to be volunteered in view of the fact that in *Miranda* the Court observed that the police did not have to stop a person who is trying to confess to a crime in order to give that person his warnings. The case is clearly stronger for the police if they are attempting to notify the individual of his rights when he interrupts them.

The Supreme Court's most important decision on the concept of interrogation is Rhode Island v. Innis.

RHODE ISLAND v. INNIS

Supreme Court of the United States, 1980.
446 U.S. 291.

MR. JUSTICE STEWART delivered the opinion of the Court.

In Miranda v. Arizona, the Court held that, once a defendant in custody asks to speak with a lawyer, all interrogation must cease until a lawyer is present. The issue in this case is whether the respondent was "interrogated" in violation of the standards promulgated in the *Miranda* opinion.

I

On the night of January 12, 1975, John Mulvaney, a Providence, R.I., taxicab driver, disappeared after being dispatched to pick up a customer. His body was discovered four days later buried in a shallow grave in Coventry, R.I. He had died from a shotgun blast aimed at the back of his head.

On January 17, 1975, shortly after midnight, the Providence police received a telephone call from Gerald Aubin, also a taxicab driver, who reported that he had just been robbed by a man wielding a sawed-off shotgun. Aubin further reported that he had dropped off his assailant near Rhode Island College in a section of Providence known as Mount Pleasant. While at the Providence police station waiting to give a statement, Aubin noticed a picture of his assailant on a bulletin board. Aubin so informed one of the police officers present. The officer prepared a photo array, and again Aubin identified a picture of the same person. That person was the respondent. Shortly thereafter, the Providence police began a search of the Mount Pleasant area.

At approximately 4:30 a. m. on the same date, Patrolman Lovell, while cruising the streets of Mount Pleasant in a patrol car, spotted the respondent standing in the street facing him. When Patrolman Lovell stopped his car, the respondent walked towards it. Patrolman Lovell then arrested the respondent, who was unarmed, and advised him of his so-called *Miranda* rights. While the two men waited in the patrol car for other police officers to arrive, Patrolman Lovell did not converse with the respondent other than to respond to the latter's request for a cigarette.

Within minutes, Sergeant Sears arrived at the scene of the arrest, and he also gave the respondent the *Miranda* warnings. Immediately thereafter, Captain Leyden and other police officers arrived. Captain Leyden advised the respondent of his *Miranda* rights. The respondent stated that he understood those rights and wanted to speak with a lawyer. Captain Leyden then directed that the respondent be placed in a "caged wagon," a four-door police car with a wire screen mesh between the front and rear seats, and be driven to the central police station. Three officers, Patrolmen Gleckman, Williams, and McKenna, were assigned to accompany the respondent to the central station. They placed the respondent in the vehicle and shut the doors. Captain Leyden then instructed the officers not to question the respondent or intimidate or coerce him in any way. The three officers then entered the vehicle, and it departed.

While enroute to the central station, Patrolman Gleckman initiated a conversation with Patrolman McKenna concerning the missing shotgun. As Patrolman Gleckman later testified:

> "A. At this point, I was talking back and forth with Patrolman McKenna stating that I frequent this area while on patrol and [that because a school for handicapped children is located nearby,] there's a lot of handicapped children running around in this area, and God forbid one of them might find a weapon with shells and they might hurt themselves."

Patrolman McKenna apparently shared his fellow officer's concern:

> "A. I more or less concurred with him [Gleckman] that it was a safety factor and that we should, you know, continue to search for the weapon and try to find it."

While Patrolman Williams said nothing, he overheard the conversation between the two officers:

> "A. He [Gleckman] said it would be too bad if the little—I believe he said girl—would pick up the gun, maybe kill herself."

The respondent then interrupted the conversation, stating that the officers should turn the car around so he could show them where the gun was located. * * * At the time the respondent indicated that the officers should turn back, they had traveled no more than a mile, a trip encompassing only a few minutes.

The police vehicle then returned to the scene of the arrest where a search for the shotgun was in progress. There, Captain Leyden again advised the respondent of his *Miranda* rights. The respondent replied that he understood those rights but that he "wanted to get the gun out of the way because of the kids in the area in the school." The respondent then led the police to a nearby field, where he pointed out the shotgun under some rocks by the side of the road. [A motion to suppress was denied and Innis was convicted.]

* * * It was the view of the state appellate court that, even though the police officers may have been genuinely concerned about the public safety and even though the respondent had not been addressed personally by the police officers, the respondent nonetheless had been subjected to "subtle coercion" that was the equivalent of "interrogation" within the meaning of the *Miranda* opinion. * * *

* * *

II

* * *

In the present case, the parties are in agreement that the respondent was fully informed of his *Miranda* rights and that he invoked his *Miranda* right to counsel when he told Captain Leyden that he wished to consult with a lawyer. It is also uncontested that the respondent was "in custody" while being transported to the police station.

The issue, therefore, is whether the respondent was "interrogated" by the police officers in violation of the respondent's undisputed right under *Miranda* to remain silent until he had consulted with a lawyer.[a] In resolving this issue, we first define the term "interrogation" under *Miranda* before turning to a consideration of the facts of this case.

A

The starting point for defining "interrogation" in this context is, of course, the Court's *Miranda* opinion. There the Court observed that "[b]y custodial interrogation, we mean *questioning* initiated by law enforcement officers after a person has been taken into custody or otherwise deprived of his freedom of action in any significant way." This passage and other references throughout the opinion to "questioning" might suggest that the *Miranda* rules were to apply only to those police interrogation practices that involve express questioning of a defendant while in custody.

We do not, however, construe the *Miranda* opinion so narrowly. The concern of the Court in *Miranda* was that the "interrogation environment" created by the interplay of interrogation and custody would "subjugate the individual to the will of his examiner" and thereby undermine the privilege against compulsory self-incrimination. The police practices that evoked this concern included several that did not involve express questioning. * * *

This is not to say, however, that all statements obtained by the police after a person has been taken into custody are to be considered the product of interrogation. * * * It is clear therefore that the special procedural safeguards outlined in *Miranda* are required not where a suspect is simply taken into custody, but rather where a suspect in custody is subjected to interrogation. "Interrogation," as conceptualized in the *Miranda* opinion, must reflect a measure of compulsion above and beyond that inherent in custody itself.[b] * * *

We conclude that the *Miranda* safeguards come into play whenever a person in custody is subjected to either express questioning or its functional equivalent. That is to say, the term "interrogation" under *Miranda* refers not only to express questioning, but

a. Since we conclude that the respondent was not "interrogated" for *Miranda* purposes, we do not reach the question whether the respondent waived his right under *Miranda* to be free from interrogation until counsel was present.

b. There is language in the opinion of the Rhode Island Supreme Court in this case suggesting that the definition of "interrogation" under Miranda is informed by this Court's decision in Brewer v. Williams [discussed infra]. This suggestion is erroneous. Our decision in *Brewer* rested solely on the Sixth and Fourteenth Amendment right to counsel. That right, as we held in *Massiah*, prohibits law enforcement officers from "deliberately elicit[ing]" incriminating information from a defendant in the absence of counsel after a formal charge against the defendant has been filed. Custody in such a case is not controlling; * * *. By contrast, the right to counsel at issue in the present case is based not on the Sixth and Fourteenth Amendments, but rather on the Fifth and Fourteenth Amendments as interpreted in the *Miranda* opinion. The definitions of "interrogation" under the Fifth and Sixth Amendments, if indeed the term "interrogation" is even apt in the Sixth Amendment context, are not necessarily interchangeable, since the policies underlying the two constitutional protections are quite distinct.

also to any words or actions on the part of the police (other than those normally attendant to arrest and custody) that the police should know are reasonably likely to elicit an incriminating response [c] from the suspect.[d] The latter portion of this definition focuses primarily upon the perceptions of the suspect, rather than the intent of the police. This focus reflects the fact that the *Miranda* safeguards were designed to vest a suspect in custody with an added measure of protection against coercive police practices, without regard to objective proof of the underlying intent of the police. A practice that the police should know is reasonably likely to evoke an incriminating response from a suspect thus amounts to interrogation.[e] But, since the police surely cannot be held accountable for the unforeseeable results of their words or actions, the definition of interrogation can extend only to words or actions on the part of police officers that they *should have known* were reasonably likely to elicit an incriminating response.[f]

B

Turning to the facts of the present case, we conclude that the respondent was not "interrogated" within the meaning of *Miranda.* It is undisputed that the first prong of the definition of "interrogation" was not satisfied, for the conversation between Patrolmen Gleckman and McKenna included no express questioning of the respondent. Rather, that conversation was, at least in form nothing more than a dialogue between the two officers to which no response from the respondent was invited.

* * *

Moreover, it cannot be fairly concluded that the respondent was subjected to the "functional equivalent" of questioning. * * * There is nothing in the record to suggest that the officers were aware that the respondent was peculiarly susceptible to an appeal to his conscience concerning the safety of handicapped children, or that the police knew that the respondent was unusually disoriented or upset at the time of his arrest.

The case thus boils down to whether, in the context of a brief conversation, the officers should have known that the respondent would suddenly be moved to make a self-incriminating response. Given the fact that the entire conversation appears to have consisted of no more than a few off-hand remarks, we cannot say that the officers should have known that it was reasonably likely that Innis would so respond. This is not a case where the police carried on a lengthy harangue in the presence of the suspect. Nor does the record support the respondent's contention that, under the circumstances, the officers' comments were particularly "evocative."

* * *

c. By "incriminating response" we refer to any response—whether inculpatory or exculpatory—that the *prosecution* may seek to introduce at trial. * * *

d. One of the dissenting opinions seems totally to misapprehend this definition in suggesting that it "will almost certainly exclude every statement [of the police] that is not punctuated with a question mark."

e. This is not to say that the intent of the police is irrelevant, for it may well have a bearing on whether the police should have known that their words or actions were reasonably likely to evoke an incriminating response. In particular, where a police practice is designed to elicit an incriminating response from the accused, it is unlikely that the practice will not also be one which the police should have known was reasonably likely to have that effect.

f. Any knowledge the police may have had concerning the unusual susceptibility of a defendant to a particular form of persuasion might be an important factor in determining whether the police should have known that their words or actions were reasonably likely to elicit an incriminating response from the suspect.

[Justice White's concurring opinion is omitted].

CHIEF JUSTICE BURGER, concurring in the judgment.

Since the result is not inconsistent with Miranda v. Arizona, I concur in the judgment.

The meaning of *Miranda* has become reasonably clear and law enforcement practices have adjusted to its strictures; I would neither overrule *Miranda,* disparage it, nor extend it at this late date. I fear, however, that the rationale in Part II, A and B, of the Court's opinion * * * may introduce new elements of uncertainty; under the Court's test, a police officer in the brief time available, apparently must evaluate the suggestibility and susceptibility of an accused. Few, if any, police officers are competent to make the kind of evaluation seemingly contemplated; even a psychiatrist asked to express an expert opinion on these aspects of a suspect in custody would very likely employ extensive questioning and observation to make the judgment now charged to police officers.

Trial judges have enough difficulty discerning the boundaries and nuances flowing from post-*Miranda* opinions, and we do not clarify that situation today.

MR. JUSTICE MARSHALL, with whom MR. JUSTICE BRENNAN joins, dissenting.

I am substantially in agreement with the Court's definition of "interrogation" within the meaning of Miranda v. Arizona. In my view, the *Miranda* safeguards apply whenever police conduct is intended or likely to produce a response from a suspect in custody. * * *

I am utterly at a loss, however, to understand how this objective standard as applied to the facts before us can rationally lead to the conclusion that there was no interrogation. * * *

One can scarcely imagine a stronger appeal to the conscience of a suspect—*any* suspect—than the assertion that if the weapon is not found an innocent person will be hurt or killed. And not just any innocent person, but an innocent child—a little girl—a helpless, handicapped little girl on her way to school. The notion that such an appeal could not be expected to have any effect unless the suspect were known to have some special interest in handicapped children verges on the ludicrous.

* * *

I firmly believe that this case is simply an aberration, and that in future cases the Court will apply the standard adopted today in accordance with its plain meaning.

JUSTICE STEVENS, dissenting.

* * *

I

As the Court recognizes, Miranda v. Arizona, makes it clear that, once respondent requested an attorney, he had an absolute right to have any type of interrogation cease until an attorney was present. As it also recognizes, *Miranda* requires that the term "interrogation" be broadly construed to include "either express questioning or its functional equivalent." In my view any statement that would normally be understood by the average listener as calling for a response is the functional equivalent of a direct question, whether or not it is punctuated by a question mark. The Court, however, takes a much narrower view. It holds that police conduct is not the "functional equivalent" of direct questioning unless the police should have known that what they were saying or doing was likely to elicit an incriminating response from the suspect. This holding represents a plain departure from the principles set forth in *Miranda.*

* * *

From the suspect's point of view, the effectiveness of the warnings depends on whether it appears that the police are scrupulously honoring his rights. Apparent attempts to elicit information from a suspect after he has invoked his right to cut off questioning necessarily demean that right and tend to reinstate the imbalance between police and suspect that the *Miranda* warnings are designed to correct. Thus, if the rationale for requiring those warnings in the first place is to be respected, any police conduct or statements that would appear to a reasonable person in the suspect's position to call for a response must be considered "interrogation."

* * *

[T]he Court's test creates an incentive for police to ignore a suspect's invocation of his rights in order to make continued attempts to extract information from him. If a suspect does not appear susceptible to a particular type of psychological pressure, the police are apparently free to exert that pressure on him despite his request for counsel, so long as they are careful not to punctuate their statements with question marks. And if, contrary to all reasonable expectations, the suspect makes an incriminating statement, that statement can be used against him at trial. * * *

Note

Applying the *Innis* test to statements made by a suspect to his wife in the presence of a police officer who recorded the statements, the Supreme Court held, 5–4, in Arizona v. Mauro, 481 U.S. 520 (1987), that the police did not engage in interrogation. Police received a telephone call from a store stating that a man had entered the store claiming to have killed his son. When officers reached the store, Mauro freely admitted that he had killed his son and directed officers to the body. The police arrested Mauro and gave him two sets of *Miranda* warnings. After the second set, given at the police station, Mauro indicated that he wished to say nothing more without a lawyer. Mrs. Mauro, who was being questioned separately, asked to speak with her husband. The police were reluctant to permit her to do so, but ultimately agreed to her request. An officer told the Mauros, however, that they could speak together only if an officer were present to observe and hear what was said. The officer placed a tape recorder in plain view. Mrs. Mauro expressed despair, and Mr. Mauro consoled her by saying that "You tried to stop me as best you can." Mauro's defense at trial was insanity, and the prosecutor played the tape at trial in rebuttal, arguing that it demonstrated that Mauro was sane.

Justice Powell wrote for the majority, as it concluded that there was no evidence that the officers sent Mrs. Mauro in to see her husband for the purpose of eliciting statements. Even though the officers conceded that they recognized a possibility that Mauro would incriminate himself while talking with his wife, Justice Powell concluded that "officers do not interrogate a suspect simply by hoping that he will incriminate himself." Justice Powell determined that "Mauro was not subjected to compelling influences, psychological ploys, or direct questioning," and "his volunteered statements cannot properly be considered the result of police interrogation." He added that "[p]olice departments need not adopt inflexible rules barring suspects from speaking with their spouses, nor must they ignore legitimate security concerns by allowing spouses to meet in private."

Justice Stevens, joined by Justices Brennan, Marshall and Blackmun, dissented. He emphasized that the Arizona Supreme Court "unanimously and unequivocally concluded that the police intended to interrogate" Mauro and saw no reason to disturb that court's findings. He concluded that "it was not only likely, but highly probable, that one of the suspects would make a statement that the prosecutor might seek to introduce at trial," and that "[i]t follows that the police conduct in this case was the 'functional equivalent' of deliberate, direct interrogation."

Suppose the police officers refused to permit Mrs. Mauro to speak with her husband, and he had made a statement to the police. What argument, if any, would Mr. Mauro have made regarding the relationship between the refusal and his statement? Should the police be required to tell Mr. Mauro that his wife had asked to speak with him? If they were required to do so and Mr. Mauro demanded to see his wife, should the police be compelled to honor the demand? If they honor it but insist upon having an officer present, do they violate *Miranda*? Is this scenario different in any meaningful way from the actual facts of *Mauro* where the police told both suspects that they could speak together only if an officer was present to see and hear what was said? If the dissenters are correct in *Mauro,* what advice would they give to police confronted with the *Mauro* facts?

Deciding when an interrogation begins is not easy under any test. Consider United States v. Calisto, 838 F.2d 711 (3d Cir.1988), where officers searched Calisto's home and found large quantities of drugs in a bedroom. Calisto was placed under arrest by Officer McKeefry and invoked his right to silence. The officers knew that Calisto lived with his adult daughter. One of the searching officers came up to McKeefry and said that he had found both men's and women's clothing in the bedroom where the drugs had been located. Officer McKeefry responded, "Well, then we'll have to get an arrest warrant for the daughter." Calisto, who was a few feet away from McKeefry, said "Don't lock my daughter up. She has nothing to do with that stuff. That's mine. I'm the one you want." The court found that McKeefry's statement concerning the daughter was not interrogation, reasoning that his remark "was not directed at Calisto, was the kind of remark that an officer would normally make in carrying out his duties under the circumstances that confronted him, and was not made in a provocative manner." The court concluded that "even if it could be said that reasonable officers might have expected a protest of some kind from Calisto upon his hearing of his daughter's possible arrest, we do not think it was reasonable to expect an *inculpatory* response from Calisto." (emphasis added). Do you agree with the court? In contrast, see United States v. Green, 776 F.Supp. 565 (D.D.C.1991) (threat that drugs found in a car would be attributed to Green's mother constituted interrogation of Green). See also Plazinich v. Lynaugh, 843 F.2d 836 (5th Cir.1988) (informing the defendant of the attempted suicide of his lover and partner-in-crime was not interrogation but rather "food for thought").

In Edwards v. Arizona, supra, the Court found that Edwards had been interrogated when he was confronted with incriminating evidence, in that case a tape containing admissions by an associate. See also People v. Ferro, 63 N.Y.2d 316, 482 N.Y.S.2d 237, 472 N.E.2d 13 (1984) (interrogation found where officers placed the fruits of Ferro's crime in front of his jail cell). Why does confronting the suspect with incriminating evidence constitute interrogation, while confronting the same suspect with a risk of harm to innocent children does not? It should be noted that despite the holding in *Edwards,* courts have not uniformly found interrogation whenever the suspect is confronted with incriminating evidence. See Shedelbower v. Estelle, 885 F.2d 570 (9th Cir.1989) (lying to the defendant that he had just been identified by an eyewitness was not reasonably likely to elicit an incriminating response).

Customs officers investigated a house and discovered marijuana in United States v. Castro, 723 F.2d 1527 (11th Cir.1984). One officer called to a suspect upstairs in the house, identified himself and requested that he come down. As the suspect did so, the officer, with gun drawn, said "What in the world is going on here?" The suspect replied, "You want money. We got money." The court held, 2–1, that the statement was totally voluntary and clearly outside the protective umbrella of *Miranda*. A dissenting judge argued that it should not matter whether the answer was responsive to the question where the officer plainly directed his question to a suspect who was in custody.

As you think about *Innis,* consider whether the majority or Justice Stevens would provide a defendant with greater protection. Which test considers personal characteristics of a defendant that may be known to the police? [24]

Since *Innis* holds there was no interrogation, the decision would be the same even after Edwards v. Arizona, supra. *Edwards* holds that a suspect cannot waive the right to counsel after invoking it, unless he initiates the conversation. But if the police renew contact which does not rise to the level of custodial interrogation, *Miranda* itself is inapplicable to a resulting confession, and therefore so is *Edwards.*

In *Innis,* the Court's definition of interrogation excludes questions "attendant to custody." Thus, officers can ask questions attendant to custody without *Miranda* warnings, and if the suspect's answer is incriminating, it is admissible at trial. In Pennsylvania v. Muniz, 496 U.S. 582 (1990), a suspect who failed sobriety tests was brought to a booking center, where he was asked, among other things, his name, address, height, weight, eye color, date of birth, and current age. Muniz stumbled over the answers and gave incorrect information on some points. His responses were admitted at his trial as evidence of drunkenness. Justice Brennan, writing for a plurality of four members of the Court, held that Muniz's answers to the questions were admissible, even though in response to custodial interrogation, because they fell within a "routine booking question exception which exempts from *Miranda's* coverage questions to secure the biographical data necessary to complete booking or pretrial services." The plurality noted that the booking exception would not apply if such questions were "designed to elicit incriminatory admissions."

Chief Justice Rehnquist, joined by Justices White, Blackmun and Stevens, concurred in the result. The Chief Justice did not find it necessary to consider whether the questions to Muniz fell within a booking exception to *Miranda.* He found Muniz's answers to these questions to be non-testimonial, and hence not protected by the Fifth Amendment, since they were used at trial only to show that Muniz's mental processes were not operating properly. (This aspect of the case is discussed in Section I.F of this Chapter). However, Chief Justice Rehnquist assumed that a booking exception to *Miranda* does exist.

Justice Marshall dissented. He argued that a booking exception would lead to difficult, time-consuming litigation concerning its scope and application, contrary to the *Miranda* bright line approach.

Muniz may be important with respect to provision of pretrial services. In federal proceedings, an officer may inquire about a suspect's financial status before a magistrate rules on pretrial release. In some cases, this financial information

24. On the *Innis* case, see Grano, Rhode Island v. Innis, A Need to Reconsider the Constitutional Premises Underlying the Law of Confessions, 17 Am.Crim.L.Rev. 1 (1979); White, Rhode Island v. Innis, The Significance of a Suspect's Assertion of His Right to Counsel, 17 Am.Crim.L.Rev. 53 (1979).

might be relevant to prove guilt. It might show unexplained income for a tax violation, or that the defendant had money shortly after a crime occurred, or that the defendant had no money and thus a motive to commit a crime. Does *Muniz* mean that questions asked for routine administrative purposes never require *Miranda* warnings?

How is a court able to tell whether an officer's question about biographical information is, as *Muniz* puts it, "designed to elicit incriminatory admissions?" Is it a subjective test? Lower courts have looked to objective factors such as whether there could be a proper administrative purpose for the question, whether the question is asked by an officer who routinely books suspects, and whether the officer would need to know the information for booking purposes. See, e.g., Gladden v. Roach, 864 F.2d 1196 (5th Cir.1989) ("straightforward questions to secure the biographical data necessary to complete the booking process" are not covered by *Miranda*); United States v. Webb, 755 F.2d 382 (5th Cir.1985) (questions by classification officer concerning nature of defendant's crime were not booking questions where classification officer already knew what defendant was charged with, and testimony indicated that such questions were not ordinarily asked by classification officers); United States v. Hinkley, 672 F.2d 115 (D.C.Cir.1982) (questions are not within booking exception where they have clear investigative purpose, and interrogation was conducted by officers who did not ordinarily book suspects).

In United States v. Carmona, 873 F.2d 569 (2d Cir.1989), officers arresting Carmona asked his name, even though they knew who he was. He answered with a false name, and this answer was used as evidence of consciousness of guilt at his trial. The court held that the question "what's your name?" is always within the booking exception, even if the officer knows that information. The court noted that it was prudent practice for officers to make sure that the person arrested is the correct person. Was the question in *Carmona* "designed to elicit incriminating information?" Didn't the officers arrest Carmona even though he said he was someone else?

After the booking questions, the defendant in *Muniz* was asked to perform certain sobriety tests and to submit to a breathalyzer test. These tests, as well as the consequences of refusal to take the tests, were explained to Muniz by officers in the absence of *Miranda* warnings. While attempting to comprehend the explanations, Muniz gave responses admitting that he was impaired by alcohol. Writing for eight members of the Court, Justice Brennan concluded that Muniz's responses were admissible since the instructions from the officers "were not likely to be perceived as calling for any verbal response" and thus were not interrogation. The Court reasoned that the officers' instructions were "limited and focussed inquiries" which were "necessarily attendant to the legitimate police procedure."

Justice Marshall dissented from the Court's holding that questions and instructions attendant to sobriety tests and breathalyzer tests were not interrogation. Justice Marshall concluded that under the circumstances of Muniz's impaired state, such questions were reasonably likely to elicit an incriminating response.

After *Muniz,* explanations concerning custodial procedures, such as fingerprinting, transportation, inventorying, etc. will not be considered interrogation even though the defendant may make incriminating statements during the explanation. This is because such explanations cannot be considered to call for an incriminating response any more than did the explanations made in *Muniz.* Moreover, even direct questions about the suspect's understanding of such explanations will not be interrogation, since they are considered "necessarily attendant to" such explanations. Statements going beyond the subject matter of the explanation could still be considered interrogation after *Muniz,* since the Court emphasized that the officers therein strictly circumscribed the dialogue to the specific issues of a breathalyzer test and a sobriety test. Still, extended discussions with much incriminating information can occur in these explanatory situations. See State v. Whitehead, 458 N.W.2d 145 (Minn.App.1990) (advisory interview, where the defendant and the officer each made over 100 statements, does not constitute interrogation under *Muniz* because the discussion was within the scope of questioning attendant to the interview).

8. Undercover Activity

Does *Miranda* apply to undercover attempts to elicit information from a suspect in custody? In Illinois v. Perkins, 496 U.S. 292 (1990), an undercover agent was placed in Perkins' cell. Perkins was in prison on charges unrelated to those being investigated by the undercover officer. In the course of conversation concerning a planned escape, the agent asked Perkins whether he had killed anybody. Perkins said yes and described the murder that was being investigated. The Court held that "*Miranda* was not meant to protect suspects from boasting about their criminal activities in front of persons who they believe to be their cellmates." Justice Kennedy wrote the opinion for seven members of the Court. He reasoned that *Miranda* was concerned with the pressures upon a suspect in a police-dominated atmosphere. If the suspect does not even know that he is talking to a police officer, the problems with which the Court was concerned in *Miranda* do not exist. Justice Kennedy explained as follows:

> It is the premise of *Miranda* that the danger of coercion results from the interaction of custody and official interrogation. * * * Questioning by captors, who appear to control the suspect's fate, may create mutually reinforcing pressures that the Court has assumed will weaken the suspect's will, but where a suspect does not know that he is conversing with a government agent, these pressures do not exist.

One of the virtues of *Miranda,* recognized by the Court, is its bright-line character. Perkins argued that the creation of an "undercover investigations exception" to *Miranda* would destroy the clarity of the rule. The majority rejected this argument, on the ground that the *Perkins* rule itself is a bright-line rule: if there is an undercover investigation (and it is easy to determine whether there is) then *Miranda* is completely inapplicable. Justice Kennedy stated that "law enforcement officers will have little difficulty putting into practice our holding that undercover agents need not give *Miranda* warnings to incarcerated suspects."

Justice Brennan concurred in the judgment. He agreed that when a suspect does not know he is talking to a police agent, *Miranda* warnings are not required. Justice Brennan argued, however, that undercover activity constituted trickery which could raise a "substantial claim that the confession was obtained in violation of the Due Process Clause."

Justice Marshall dissented. He argued that undercover questioning of an incarcerated suspect constituted both "custody" and "interrogation," and that the majority's opinion was thus an unjustified "exception" to *Miranda.* Justice Marshall also expressed concern that police would use the majority's decision to circumvent *Miranda* requirements by the use of undercover agents.

9. *Nature of Offense*

The Court in Berkemer v. McCarty, 468 U.S. 420 (1984), established that there is no distinction between felonies and misdemeanors insofar as *Miranda* is concerned.

Writing for the Court, Justice Marshall rejected the felony-misdemeanor distinction on the ground that an exception would remove one of *Miranda's* principal advantages—i.e., the clarity of the rule.

> The exception to *Miranda* proposed by petitioner would substantially undermine this crucial advantage of the doctrine. The police often are unaware when they arrest a person whether he may have committed a misdemeanor or a felony. * * * Indeed, the nature of his offense may depend upon circumstances unknowable to the police, such as whether the suspect has previously committed a similar offense or has a criminal record of some other kind. It may even turn upon events yet to happen, such as whether a victim of the accident dies. It would be unreasonable to expect the police to make guesses as to the nature of the criminal conduct at issue before deciding how they may interrogate the suspect.
>
> Equally importantly, the doctrinal complexities that would confront the courts if we accepted petitioner's proposal would be byzantine. Difficult questions quickly spring to mind: For instance, investigations into seemingly minor offenses sometimes escalate gradually into investigations into more serious matters; at what point in the evolution of an affair of this sort would the police be obliged to give *Miranda* warnings to a suspect in custody? What evidence would be necessary to establish that an arrest for a misdemeanor offense was merely a pretext to enable the police to interrogate the suspect (in hopes of obtaining information about a felony) without providing him the safeguards prescribed by *Miranda?* The litigation necessary to resolve such matters would be time-consuming and disruptive of law enforcement. And the end result would be an elaborate set of rules, interlaced with exceptions and subtle distinctions, discriminating between different kinds of custodial interrogations. Neither the police nor criminal defendants would benefit from such a development.

10. *An Emergency Exception*

A defendant who is in custody and who is asked questions that plainly amount to interrogation is not always entitled to *Miranda* warnings—not since the Supreme Court's decision in New York v. Quarles, 467 U.S. 649 (1984). The Court, in an opinion by Justice Rehnquist, concluded that state courts had erred in suppressing a gun and statements obtained from a defendant charged with criminal possession of a weapon. The Court held "that under the circumstances involved in this case, overriding considerations of public safety justify the officer's failure to provide *Miranda* warnings before he asked questions devoted to locating the abandoned weapon." The opinion states the facts as follows:

> On September 11, 1980, at approximately 12:30 a.m., Officer Frank Kraft and Officer Sal Scarring were on road patrol in Queens, New York, when a young woman approached their car. She told them that she had just been raped by a black male, approximately six feet tall, who was wearing a black

jacket with the name "Big Ben" printed in yellow letters on the back. She told the officers that the man had just entered an A & P supermarket located nearby and that the man was carrying a gun.

The officers drove the woman to the supermarket, and Officer Kraft entered the store while Officer Scarring radioed for assistance. Officer Kraft quickly spotted respondent, who matched the description given by the woman, approaching a check-out counter. Apparently upon seeing the officer, respondent turned and ran toward the rear of the store, and Officer Kraft pursued him with a drawn gun. When respondent turned the corner at the end of an aisle, Officer Kraft lost sight of him for several seconds, and upon regaining sight of respondent, ordered him to stop and put his hands over his head.

Although more than three other officers had arrived on the scene by that time, Officer Kraft was the first to reach respondent. He frisked him and discovered that he was wearing a shoulder holster which was then empty. After handcuffing him, Officer Kraft asked him where the gun was. Respondent nodded in the direction of some empty cartons and responded, "the gun is over there." Officer Kraft thereafter retrieved a loaded .38 caliber revolver from one of the cartons.

The Court agreed with the state courts that the facts demonstrated custodial interrogation and thus would appear to fall within the coverage of *Miranda.* But it explained the need for an exception, which it treated as somewhat analogous to the Fourth Amendment exigent circumstances doctrine, as follows:

The police in this case, in the very act of apprehending a suspect, were confronted with the immediate necessity of ascertaining the whereabouts of a gun which they had every reason to believe the suspect had just removed from his empty holster and discarded in the supermarket. So long as the gun was concealed somewhere in the supermarket, with its actual whereabouts unknown, it obviously posed more than one danger to the public safety: an accomplice might make use of it, a customer or employee might later come upon it.

In such a situation, if the police are required to recite the familiar *Miranda* warnings before asking the whereabouts of the gun, suspects in Quarles' position might well be deterred from responding. Procedural safeguards which deter a suspect from responding were deemed acceptable in *Miranda* in order to protect the Fifth Amendment privilege; when the primary social cost of those added protections is the possibility of fewer convictions, the *Miranda* majority was willing to bear that cost. Here, had *Miranda* warnings deterred Quarles from responding to Officer Kraft's question about the whereabouts of the gun, the cost would have been something more than merely the failure to obtain evidence useful in convicting Quarles. Officer Kraft needed an answer to his question not simply to make his case against Quarles but to insure that further danger to the public did not result from the concealment of the gun in a public area.

We conclude that the need for answers to questions in a situation posing a threat to the public safety outweighs the need for the prophylactic rule protecting the Fifth Amendment's privilege against self-incrimination. We decline to place officers such as Officer Kraft in the untenable position of having to consider, often in a matter of seconds, whether it best serves society for them to ask the necessary questions without the *Miranda* warnings and render whatever probative evidence they uncover inadmissible, or for them to give the warnings in order to preserve the admissibility of evidence they might uncover but possibly damage or destroy their ability to obtain that evidence and neutralize the volatile situation confronting them.

Although the Court recognized that it had "to some degree * * * lessen[ed] the desirable clarity of" the *Miranda* rule, it stated that "we recognize here the importance of a workable rule 'to guide police officers, who have only limited time and expertise to reflect on and balance the social and individual interests involved in the specific circumstances they confront.' " It expressed the belief that "the exception we recognize today lessens the necessity of that on-the-scene balancing process." The Court held that the gun and the statement revealing its location need not be suppressed.

Justice O'Connor concurred in part and dissented in part. She dissented from the exception created by the Court on the ground that it would be confusing and contrary to *Miranda's* bright line approach. She offered the following criticism of the majority's exception:

> In my view, a "public safety" exception unnecessarily blurs the edges of the clear line heretofore established and makes *Miranda's* requirements more difficult to understand. In some cases, police will benefit because a reviewing court will find that an exigency excused their failure to administer the required warnings. But in other cases, police will suffer because, though they thought an exigency excused their noncompliance, a reviewing court will view the "objective" circumstances differently and require exclusion of admissions thereby obtained. The end result will be a finespun new doctrine on public safety exigencies incident to custodial interrogation, complete with the hair-splitting distinctions that currently plague our Fourth Amendment jurisprudence. * * *
>
> The justification the Court provides for upsetting the equilibrium that has finally been achieved—that police cannot and should not balance considerations of public safety against the individual's interest in avoiding compulsory testimonial self-incrimination—really misses the critical question to be decided. *Miranda* has never been read to prohibit the police from asking questions to secure the public safety. Rather, the critical question *Miranda* addresses is who shall bear the cost of securing the public safety when such questions are asked and answered: the defendant or the State. *Miranda,* for better or worse, found the resolution of that question implicit in the prohibition against compulsory self-incrimination and placed the burden on the State. When police ask custodial questions without administering the required warnings, *Miranda* quite clearly requires that the answers received be presumed compelled and that they be excluded from evidence at trial.

Justice Marshall dissented and was joined by Justices Brennan and Stevens. He disagreed as to the existence of an emergency, describing the facts in the following way:

> [C]ontrary to the majority's intimations, no customers or employees were wandering about the store in danger of coming across Quarles' discarded weapon. Although the supermarket was open to the public, Quarles' arrest took place during the middle of the night when the store was apparently deserted except for the clerks at the checkout counter. The police could easily have cordoned off the store and searched for the missing gun. Had they done so, they would have found the gun forthwith. The police were well aware that Quarles had discarded his weapon somewhere near the scene of the arrest.

Justice Marshall concluded that the public safety exception will result in police officers' coercing suspects into making statements to be used by the government. And he offered an alternative to police concerned with public safety:

> If a bomb is about to explode or the public is otherwise imminently imperiled, the police are free to interrogate suspects without advising them of their constitutional rights. Such unconsented questioning may take place not only when police officers act on instinct but also when higher faculties lead them to believe that advising a suspect of his constitutional rights might decrease the likelihood that the suspect would reveal life-saving information. If trickery is necessary to protect the public, then the police may trick a suspect into confessing. While the Fourteenth Amendment sets limits on such behavior, nothing in the Fifth Amendment or our decision in Miranda v. Arizona proscribes this sort of emergency questioning. All the Fifth Amendment forbids is the introduction of coerced statements at trial.

The extent to which Justices feel comfortable in creating exceptions to or limitations upon *Miranda* appears to turn on the extent to which they believe that *Miranda* extends a prophylactic protection beyond the demands of the Constitution. If *Miranda* is viewed as requiring much more than the Constitution demands, then exceptions and limitations can be defended as trimming only some of the extra-constitutional protection that the decision provided. But if Miranda is viewed as a necessary protection in most custodial situations of the right to remain silent, exceptions and limitations are more difficult to justify.

The majority states that "[w]e conclude that the need for answers to questions in a situation posing a threat to the public safety outweighs the need for the prophylactic rule protecting the Fifth Amendment privilege against self-incrimination." It had no occasion to indicate the scope of the emergency exception. Are the police permitted to keep a suspect in custody for an extended period without *Miranda* warnings if they claim to be seeking information to protect the public? For example, if a murder suspect is arrested and a firearm was used to commit the murder, may the police delay *Miranda* warnings for several hours so that they can interrogate the suspect about the whereabouts of the firearm? Or, it is critical that in *Quarles* the officer acted in the heat of the moment as he came upon a crime scene?

VI. THE RIGHT TO COUNSEL AFTER *MIRANDA*

A. BREWER v. WILLIAMS

Although the Supreme Court has narrowed the reach of *Miranda,* recently it has breathed new life into Massiah v. United States. *Massiah,* you will recall, held that the use of incriminating statements made in the absence of his lawyer by an individual who had been indicted violated the accused's Sixth Amendment right to legal representation. After *Miranda,* it was unclear whether the filing of an indictment or other formal charge, the test in *Massiah,* retained independent constitutional significance, especially since *Massiah* is ignored in the *Miranda* opinions. Brewer v. Williams and United States v. Henry establish that *Massiah* is still good law.

BREWER v. WILLIAMS

Supreme Court of the United States, 1977.
430 U.S. 387.[25]

MR. JUSTICE STEWART delivered the opinion of the Court.

I

On the afternoon of December 24, 1968, a 10-year-old girl named Pamela Powers went with her family to the YMCA in Des Moines, Iowa, to watch a wrestling tournament in which her brother was participating. When she failed to return from a trip to the washroom, a search for her began. The search was unsuccessful.

Robert Williams, who had recently escaped from a mental hospital, was a resident of the YMCA. Soon after the girl's disappearance Williams was seen in the YMCA lobby carrying some clothing and a large bundle wrapped in a blanket. He obtained help from a 14-year-old boy in opening the street door of the YMCA and the door to his automobile parked outside. When Williams placed the bundle in the front seat of his car the boy "saw two legs in it and they were skinny and white." Before anyone could see what was in the bundle Williams drove away. His abandoned car was found the following day in Davenport, Iowa, roughly 160 miles east of Des Moines. A warrant was then issued in Des Moines for his arrest on a charge of abduction.

On the morning of December 26, a Des Moines lawyer named Henry McKnight went to the Des Moines police station and informed the officers present that he had just received a long distance call from Williams, and that he had advised Williams to turn himself in to the Davenport police. Williams did surrender that morning to the police in Davenport, and they booked him on the charge specified in the arrest warrant and gave him the warnings required by Miranda v. Arizona. The Davenport police then telephoned their counterparts in Des Moines to inform them that Williams had surrendered. McKnight, the lawyer, was still at the Des Moines police headquarters, and Williams conversed with McKnight on the telephone. In the presence of the Des Moines chief of police and a police detective named Leaming, McKnight advised Williams that Des Moines police officers would be driving to Davenport to pick him up, that the officers would not interrogate him or mistreat him, and that Williams was not to talk to the officers about Pamela Powers until after consulting with McKnight upon his return to Des Moines. As a result of these conversations, it was agreed between McKnight and the Des Moines police officials that Detective Leaming and a fellow officer would drive to Davenport to pick up Williams, that they would bring him directly back to Des Moines, and that they would not question him during the trip.

In the meantime Williams was arraigned before a judge in Davenport on the outstanding arrest warrant. The judge advised him of his *Miranda* rights and committed him to jail. Before leaving the courtroom, Williams conferred with a lawyer named Kelly, who advised him not to make any statements until consulting with McKnight back in Des Moines.

Detective Leaming and his fellow officer arrived in Davenport about noon to pick up Williams and return him to Des Moines. Soon after their arrival they met with Williams and Kelly, who, they understood, was acting as

25. For an exhaustive analysis of this case, see Kamisar, Brewer v. Williams, Massiah and Miranda: What is "Interrogation"? When Does it Matter? 67 Geo.L.J. 1 (1978).

Williams' lawyer. Detective Leaming repeated the *Miranda* warnings, and told Williams:

> "[W]e both know that you're being represented here by Mr. Kelly and you're being represented by Mr. McKnight in Des Moines, and * * * I want you to remember this because we'll be visiting between here and Des Moines."

Williams then conferred again with Kelly alone, and after this conference Kelly reiterated to Detective Leaming that Williams was not to be questioned about the disappearance of Pamela Powers until after he had consulted with McKnight back in Des Moines. When Leaming expressed some reservations, Kelly firmly stated that the agreement with McKnight was to be carried out—that there was to be no interrogation of Williams during the automobile journey to Des Moines. Kelly was denied permission to ride in the police car back to Des Moines with Williams and the two officers.

The two detectives, with Williams in their charge, then set out on the 160-mile drive. At no time during the trip did Williams express a willingness to be interrogated in the absence of an attorney. Instead, he stated several times that "[w]hen I get to Des Moines and see Mr. McKnight, I am going to tell you the whole story." Detective Leaming knew that Williams was a former mental patient, and knew also that he was deeply religious.

The detective and his prisoner soon embarked on a wide-ranging conversation covering a variety of topics, including the subject of religion. Then, not long after leaving Davenport and reaching the interstate highway, Detective Leaming delivered what has been referred to in the briefs and oral arguments as the "Christian burial speech." Addressing Williams as "Reverend," the detective said:

> "I want to give you something to think about while we're traveling down the road. * * * Number one, I want you to observe the weather conditions, it's raining, it's sleeting, it's freezing, driving is very treacherous, visibility is poor, it's going to be dark early this evening. They are predicting several inches of snow for tonight, and I feel that you yourself are the only person that knows where this little girl's body is, that you yourself have only been there once, and if you get a snow on top of it you yourself may be unable to find it. And, since we will be going right past the area on the way into Des Moines, I feel that we could stop and locate the body, that the parents of this little girl should be entitled to a Christian burial for the little girl who was snatched away from them on Christmas [E]ve and murdered. And I feel we should stop and locate it on the way in rather than waiting until morning and trying to come back out after a snow storm and possibly not being able to find it at all."

Williams asked Detective Leaming why he thought their route to Des Moines would be taking them past the girl's body, and Leaming responded that he knew the body was in the area of Mitchellville—a town they would be passing on the way to Des Moines.[a] Leaming then stated: "I do not want you to answer me. I don't want to discuss it any further. Just think about it as we're riding down the road."

As the car approached Grinnell, a town approximately 100 miles west of Davenport, Williams asked whether the

a. The fact of the matter, of course, was that Detective Leaming possessed no such knowledge.

police had found the victim's shoes. When Detective Leaming replied that he was unsure, Williams directed the officers to a service station where he said he had left the shoes; a search for them proved unsuccessful. As they continued towards Des Moines, Williams asked whether the police had found the blanket, and directed the officers to a rest area where he said he had disposed of the blanket. Nothing was found. The car continued towards Des Moines, and as it approached Mitchellville, Williams said that he would show the officers where the body was. He then directed the police to the body of Pamela Powers.

Williams was indicted for first-degree murder. Before trial, his counsel moved to suppress all evidence relating to or resulting from any statements Williams had made during the automobile ride from Davenport to Des Moines. After an evidentiary hearing the trial judge denied the motion. He found that "an agreement was made between defense counsel and the police officials to the effect that the Defendant was not to be questioned on the return trip to Des Moines," and that the evidence in question had been elicited from Williams during "a critical stage in the proceedings requiring the presence of counsel on his request." The judge ruled, however, that Williams had "waived his right to have an attorney present during the giving of such information."

* * * The jury found Williams guilty of murder. [The Iowa Supreme Court affirmed 4–3. But Williams was successful below in his federal habeas corpus action.]

II

A

[The Court held that the District Judge acted properly in the federal habeas corpus action brought by Williams in not holding an evidentiary hearing.]

B

[T]he District Court based its judgment in this case on three independent grounds. The Court of Appeals appears to have affirmed the judgment on two of those grounds. We have concluded that only one of them need be considered here.

Specifically, there is no need to review in this case the doctrine of Miranda v. Arizona, a doctrine designed to secure the constitutional privilege against compulsory self-incrimination. It is equally unnecessary to evaluate the ruling of the District Court that Williams' self-incriminating statements were, indeed, involuntarily made. For it is clear that the judgment before us must in any event be affirmed upon the ground that Williams was deprived of a different constitutional right—the right to the assistance of counsel.

* * *

There can be no doubt in the present case that judicial proceedings had been initiated against Williams before the start of the automobile ride from Davenport to Des Moines. A warrant had been issued for his arrest, he had been arraigned on that warrant before a judge in a Davenport courtroom, and he had been committed by the court to confinement in jail. The State does not contend otherwise.

There can be no serious doubt, either, that Detective Leaming deliberately and designedly set out to elicit information from Williams just as surely as—and perhaps more effectively than—if he had formally interrogated him. Detective Leaming was fully aware before departing for Des Moines that Williams was being represented in Davenport by Kelly and in Des Moines by McKnight. Yet he purposely sought during Williams' isolation from his lawyers to obtain as much incriminating information as possible. Indeed, Detective Leaming conceded as much when he testified at Williams' trial:

"Q. In fact, Captain, whether he was a mental patient or not, you were trying to get all the information you could before he got to his lawyer, weren't you?

"A. I was sure hoping to find out where that little girl was, yes, sir.

* * *

"2. Well, I'll put it this way: You was [*sic*] hoping to get all the information you could before Williams got back to McKnight, weren't you?

"A. Yes, sir."

* * *

The circumstances of this case are thus constitutionally indistinguishable from those presented in Massiah v. United States. * * *

That the incriminating statements were elicited surreptitiously in the *Massiah* case, and otherwise here, is constitutionally irrelevant. Rather, the clear rule of *Massiah* is that once adversary proceedings have commenced against an individual, he has a right to legal representation when the government interrogates him.[b] It thus requires no wooden or technical application of the *Massiah* doctrine to conclude that Williams was entitled to the assistance of counsel guaranteed to him by the Sixth and Fourteenth Amendments.

III

The Iowa courts recognized that Williams had been denied the constitutional right to the assistance of counsel. They held, however, that he had waived that right during the course of the automobile trip from Davenport to Des Moines. * * *

* * *

[I]t was incumbent upon the State to prove "an intentional relinquishment or abandonment of a known right or privilege." That standard has been reiterated in many cases. We have said that the right to counsel does not depend upon a request by the defendant, and that courts indulge in every reasonable presumption against waiver. This strict standard applies equally to an alleged waiver of the right to counsel whether at trial or at a critical stage of pretrial proceedings.

* * * [J]udged by these standards, the record in this case falls far short of sustaining petitioner's burden. It is true that Williams had been informed of and appeared to understand his right to counsel. But waiver requires not merely comprehension but relinquishment, and Williams' consistent reliance upon the advice of counsel in dealing with the authorities refutes any suggestion that he waived that right. He consulted McKnight by long distance telephone before turning himself in. He spoke with McKnight by telephone again shortly after being booked. After he was arraigned, Williams sought out and obtained legal advice from Kelly. Williams again consulted with Kelly after Detective Leaming and his fellow officer arrived in Davenport. Throughout, Williams was advised not to make

b. The only other significant factual difference between the present case and *Massiah* is that here the police had *agreed* that they would not interrogate Williams in the absence of his counsel. This circumstance plainly provides petitioner with no argument for distinguishing away the protection afforded by *Massiah.*

It is argued that this agreement may not have been an enforceable one. But we do not deal here with notions of offer, acceptance, consideration, or other concepts of the law of contracts. We deal with constitutional law. And every court that has looked at this case has found an "agreement" in the sense of a commitment made by the Des Moines police officers that Williams would not be questioned about Pamela Powers in the absence of his counsel.

any statements before seeing McKnight in Des Moines, and was assured that the police had agreed not to question him. His statements while in the car that he would tell the whole story *after* seeing McKnight in Des Moines were the clearest expressions by Williams himself that he desired the presence of an attorney before any interrogation took place. But even before making these statements, Williams had effectively asserted his right to counsel by having secured attorneys at both ends of the automobile trip, both of whom, acting as his agents, had made clear to the police that no interrogation was to occur during the journey. Williams knew of that agreement and, particularly in view of his consistent reliance on counsel, there is no basis for concluding that he disavowed it.

Despite Williams' express and implicit assertions of his right to counsel, Detective Leaming proceeded to elicit incriminating statements from Williams. Leaming did not preface this effort by telling Williams that he had a right to the presence of a lawyer, and made no effort at all to ascertain whether Williams wished to relinquish that right. The circumstances of record in this case thus provide no reasonable basis for finding that Williams waived his right to the assistance of counsel.

The Court of Appeals did not hold, nor do we, that under the circumstances of this case Williams *could not,* without notice to counsel, have waived his rights under the Sixth and Fourteenth Amendments. It only held, as do we, that he did not.

IV

* * *

The judgment of the Court of Appeals is affirmed.[c]

MR. JUSTICE MARSHALL, concurring.

I concur wholeheartedly in my Brother Stewart's opinion for the Court, but add these words in light of the dissenting opinions filed today. The dissenters have, I believe, lost sight of the fundamental constitutional backbone of our criminal law. They seem to think that Detective Leaming's actions were perfectly proper, indeed laudable, examples of "good police work." In my view, good police work is something far different from catching the criminal at any price. It is equally important that the police, as guardians of the law, fulfill their responsibility to obey its commands scrupulously. * * *

In this case, there can be no doubt that Detective Leaming consciously and knowingly set out to violate Williams' Sixth Amendment right to counsel and his Fifth Amendment privilege against self-incrimination, as Leaming himself understood those rights. * * *

* * *

Leaming knowingly isolated Williams from the protection of his lawyers and during that period he intentionally "persuaded" him to give incriminating evidence. It is this intentional police misconduct—not good police practice—

c. The District Court stated that its decision "does not touch upon the issue of what evidence, if any, beyond the incriminating statements themselves must be excluded as 'fruit of the poisonous tree.'" 375 F.Supp. 170, 185. We, too, have no occasion to address this issue, and in the present posture of the case there is no basis for the view of our dissenting Brethren (White, J., dissenting) (Blackmun, J., dissenting), that any attempt to retry the respondent would probably be futile. While neither Williams' incriminating statements themselves nor any testimony describing his having led the police to the victim's body can constitutionally be admitted into evidence, evidence of where the body was found and of its condition might well be admissible on the theory that the body would have been discovered in any event, even had incriminating statements not been elicited from Williams. [The evidence concerning the body was admitted at the retrial, and Williams' conviction was upheld. See Nix v. Williams in Chapter Two].

that the Court rightly condemns. * * *

* * *

MR. JUSTICE POWELL, concurring.

* * *

I

* * *

I join the opinion of the Court which also finds that the efforts of Detective Leaming "to elicit information from Williams," as conceded by counsel for petitioner at oral argument, were a skillful and effective form of interrogation. Moreover, the entire setting was conducive to the psychological coercion that was successfully exploited. Williams was known by the police to be a young man with quixotic religious convictions and a history of mental disorders. The date was the day after Christmas, the weather was ominous, and the setting appropriate for Detective Leaming's talk of snow concealing the body and preventing a "Christian burial." * * *

The dissenting opinion of The Chief Justice states that the Court's holding today "conclusively presumes a suspect is legally incompetent to change his mind and tell the truth until an attorney is present." I find no justification for this view. * * *

* * *

MR. JUSTICE STEVENS, concurring.

* * *

Nothing that we write, no matter how well reasoned or forcefully expressed, can bring back the victim of this tragedy or undo the consequences of the official neglect which led to the respondent's escape from a state mental institution. The emotional aspects of the case make it difficult to decide dispassionately, but do not qualify our obligation to apply the law with an eye to the future as well as with concern for the result in the particular case before us.

Underlying the surface issues in this case is the question, whether a fugitive from justice can rely on his lawyer's advice given in connection with a decision to surrender voluntarily. The defendant placed his trust in an experienced Iowa trial lawyer who in turn trusted the Iowa law enforcement authorities to honor a commitment made during negotiations which led to the apprehension of a potentially dangerous person. Under any analysis, this was a critical stage of the proceeding in which the participation of an independent professional was of vital importance to the accused and to society. At this stage—as in countless others in which the law profoundly affects the life of the individual—the lawyer is the essential medium through which the demands and commitments of the sovereign are communicated to the citizen. If, in the long run, we are seriously concerned about the individual's effective representation by counsel, the State cannot be permitted to dishonor its promise to this lawyer.

MR. CHIEF JUSTICE BURGER, dissenting.

The result in this case ought to be intolerable in any society which purports to call itself an organized society. It continues the Court—by the narrowest margin—on the much-criticized course of punishing the public for the mistakes and misdeeds of law enforcement officers, instead of punishing the officer directly, if in fact he is guilty of wrongdoing. It mechanically and blindly keeps reliable evidence from juries whether the claimed constitutional violation involves gross police misconduct or honest human error.

Williams is guilty of the savage murder of a small child; no member of the Court contends he is not. While in custody, and after no fewer than *five* warnings of his rights to silence and to counsel, he led police to the concealed body of his victim. The Court concedes Williams was not threatened or coerced and that he spoke and acted voluntarily and with full awareness of his constitutional rights. In the face of all this, the Court now holds that because Williams was prompted by the detective's statement—not interrogation but a statement—the jury must not be told how the police found the body.

* * *

The evidence is uncontradicted that Williams had abundant knowledge of his right to have counsel present and of his right to silence. Since the Court does not question his mental competence, it boggles the mind to suggest that Williams could not understand that leading police to the child's body would have other than the most serious consequences. All of the elements necessary to make out a valid waiver are shown by the record and acknowledged by the Court; we thus are left to guess how the Court reached its holding.

One plausible but unarticulated basis for the result reached is that once a suspect has asserted his right not to talk without the presence of an attorney, it becomes legally impossible for him to waive that right until he has seen an attorney. But constitutional rights are *personal,* and an otherwise valid waiver should not be brushed aside by judges simply because an attorney was not present. * * *

* * *

MR. JUSTICE WHITE, with whom MR. JUSTICE BLACKMUN and MR. JUSTICE REHNQUIST join, dissenting.

* * *

II

* * * The majority creates no new rule preventing an accused who has retained a lawyer from waiving his right to the lawyer's presence during questioning. The majority simply finds that no waiver was *proved* in this case. I disagree. That respondent knew of his right not to say anything to the officers without advice and presence of counsel is established on this record to a moral certainty. He was advised of the right by three officials of the State—telling at least one that he understood the right—and by two lawyers. Finally, he further demonstrated his knowledge of the right by informing the police that he would tell them the story in the presence of McKnight when they arrived in Des Moines. The issue in this case, then, is whether respondent relinquished that right intentionally.

Respondent relinquished his right not to talk to the police about his crime when the car approached the place where he had hidden the victim's clothes. Men usually intend to do what they do and there is nothing in the record to support the proposition that respondent's decision to talk was anything but an exercise of his own free will. Apparently, without any prodding from the officers, respondent—who had earlier said that he would tell the whole story when he arrived in Des Moines—spontaneously changed his mind about the timing of his disclosures when the car approached the places where he had hidden the evidence. However, even if his statements were influenced by Detective Leaming's above-quoted statement, respondent's decision to talk in the absence of counsel can hardly be viewed as the product of an overborne will. The statement by Leaming was not coercive; it was accompanied by a request that respondent not respond to it; and it was delivered hours before respondent decided to make any statement. Respondent's waiver was thus knowing and intentional.

* * *

The majority recognizes that even after this "assertion" of his right to counsel, it would have found that respondent waived his right not to talk in counsel's absence if his waiver had been express—i.e., if the officers had asked him in the car whether he would be willing to answer questions in counsel's absence and if he had answered "yes." But waiver is not a formalistic concept. Waiver is shown whenever the facts establish that an accused knew of a right and intended to relinquish it. Such waiver, even if not express, was plainly shown here. * * *

* * *

MR. JUSTICE BLACKMUN, with whom MR. JUSTICE WHITE and MR. JUSTICE REHNQUIST join, dissenting.

* * *

First, the police did not deliberately seek to isolate Williams from his lawyers so as to deprive him of the assistance of counsel. The isolation in this case was a necessary incident of transporting Williams to the county where the crime was committed.

Second, Leaming's purpose was not solely to obtain incriminating evidence. The victim had been missing for only two days, and the police could not be certain that she was dead. Leaming, of course, and in accord with his duty, was "hoping to find out where that little girl was," but such motivation does not equate with an intention to evade the Sixth Amendment. Moreover, the Court seems to me to place an undue emphasis, and aspersion on what it and the lower courts have chosen to call the "Christian burial speech," and on Williams' "deeply religious" convictions.

Third, not every attempt to elicit information should be regarded as "tantamount to interrogation." I am not persuaded that Leaming's observations and comments, made as the police car traversed the snowy and slippery miles between Davenport and Des Moines that winter afternoon, were an interrogation, direct or subtle, of Williams.

In summary, it seems to me that the Court is holding that *Massiah* is violated whenever police engage in any conduct, in the absence of counsel, with the subjective desire to obtain information from a suspect after arraignment. Such a rule is far too broad.

* * *

Note

Reaffirming that the Sixth Amendment right to counsel attaches only after adversarial proceedings have begun, the Supreme Court held in United States v. Gouveia, 467 U.S. 180 (1984), that prison officials did not violate the right to counsel of inmates suspected of two murders when the officials placed them in administrative detention for periods of 19 and 8 months prior to their being indicted. Justice Rehnquist's opinion for the Court stated that "both inside and outside the prison, it may well be true that in some cases pre-indictment investigation could help a defendant prepare a better defense. But, * * * our cases have never suggested that the purpose of the right to counsel is to provide a defendant with a pre-indictment private investigator, and we see no reason to adopt that novel interpretation of the right to counsel in this case." His opinion recognizes the possible prejudice that can result from delay in the filing of charges and cites statutes of limitations and general concepts of due process as protections against unfairness. Justice Stevens, joined by Justice Brennan, concurred in the judgment and argued that while the right to counsel generally attaches after formal proceedings have commenced, "[i]f the authorities take a person into custody in order to interrogate him or to otherwise facilitate the process of making a case against him, then under the rationale of *Escobedo, Miranda,* and our other cases, the person is sufficiently 'accused' to be entitled to the protections of the Sixth Amendment." On the facts of this case, Justice Stevens found that administrative detention did not serve an accusatorial function. Justice Marshall agreed with Justice Stevens' analysis, but dissented as to its application to the facts and argued that administrative detention was part of an accusatorial process.[26]

The Supreme Court held in Moran v. Burbine, supra, that there was no violation of a suspect's right to counsel when police failed to disclose to him that a lawyer had called and had been falsely told that the suspect would not be interrogated until the next day. Justice O'Connor's majority opinion observed that the suspect had not been formally charged, cited *Gouveia* as well as *Massiah, Brewer,* and other cases drawing a line between pre- and post-charge situations, and declined to adopt a rule that would make the right to counsel depend "on the fortuity of whether the suspect or his family happens to have retained counsel prior to interrogation."

It is necessary to consider once more what there is about an indictment or an appearance in court that suggests that each triggers a special standard by which to judge interrogations? Do you think the Court confused Fifth and Sixth Amendment rights in *Massiah* and *Brewer*?

Massiah, the precedent for *Brewer,* itself involved a suspect who was not in custody. Is there any justification for establishing a counsel right in such a

26. The *Massiah–Brewer* line of cases was relied on in Estelle v. Smith, 451 U.S. 454 (1981), where all nine Justices agreed that a defendant's right to counsel was violated when he was interviewed by a government psychiatrist who was trying to get information that could be used at a capital sentencing hearing and the defendant had not waived his right to legal advice before answering questions. In a footnote the Court observed that it was not holding that the defendant had a right to have counsel present during a psychiatric interview, only that he had a right to consult counsel before deciding whether to speak.

In Buchanan v. Kentucky, 483 U.S. 402 (1987), the Court held that there was no Sixth Amendment violation in the admission of a report of a psychological evaluation to rebut a defense of extreme emotional disturbance, where the defendant's counsel had joined in the request for the evaluation. The Court assumed, without allegations to the contrary, that defense counsel consulted with Buchanan about the nature of the psychological evaluation. Thus, the defendant's right to counsel was not infringed.

The Court found in Satterwhite v. Texas, 486 U.S. 249 (1988), that *Estelle* was violated. Justice O'Connor wrote for the Court as it held that an *Estelle* error may be harmless, but that it was impossible to say beyond a reasonable doubt in this case that the psychiatrist's testimony did not influence the sentencing jury.

In Powell v. Texas, 492 U.S. 680 (1989), the Court, in a per curiam opinion, found a Sixth Amendment violation where Powell was subjected to a psychiatric examination and defense counsel was not informed that his client would be examined on the issue of future dangerousness. The Court held that Powell had not waived his Sixth Amendment right by introducing psychiatric testimony in support of a defense of insanity. The Court distinguished *Buchanan* as a case where it had found a waiver of Fifth Amendment rights. [The Fifth Amendment aspects of *Buchanan* are discussed earlier in this Chapter in the material on the privilege against self-incrimination]. The Court had also found no Sixth Amendment violation in *Buchanan,* but not because of waiver; rather counsel in *Buchanan* had been informed of the scope of the examination before it took place. The Court in *Powell* explained the difference between the Fifth and Sixth Amendment standards in this context as follows:

> While it may be unfair to the state to permit a defendant to use psychiatric testimony without allowing the state a means to rebut that testimony [Buchanan] it certainly is not unfair to require the state to provide counsel with notice before examining the defendant concerning future dangerousness. Thus, if a defendant were to surprise the prosecution on the eve of trial by raising an insanity defense to be supported by psychiatric testimony, the court might be justified in ordering a continuance and directing that the defendant submit to examination by a state-appointed psychiatrist. There would be no justification, however, for also directing that defense counsel receive no notice of this examination.

situation? *Brewer* may be a stronger case for a counsel right. But should a case like *Brewer* turn on whether or not there was an arraignment or indictment?

In *Massiah,* the "interrogation" really never took place; rather statements were obtained by trick—i.e., by using an undercover informant. In *Brewer,* the "interrogation" was indirect, but the state conceded that what the officer did was the equivalent of interrogation. If the officers had said nothing and Brewer had confessed, presumably his confession would have been admissible.

B. WAIVER

Under what circumstances can an accused be held to have waived his Sixth Amendment rights? Is the test for waiver similar or identical to that applied for waiver of *Miranda* violations? In Michigan v. Jackson, 475 U.S. 625 (1986), the accused formally requested counsel at an arraignment. Later, he was interrogated by police officers without having initiated contact, he signed a waiver form, and confessed. Justice Stevens wrote for the Court as it held that Jackson had not voluntarily waived his Sixth Amendment rights. He stated that when an accused invokes his Sixth Amendment right to counsel, the standards of Edwards v. Arizona, supra, govern the waiver of Sixth Amendment rights. Accordingly, Jackson could only have waived his Sixth Amendment rights if he had initiated a later conversation and knowingly and voluntarily waived his rights; this he had not done. Justice Stevens contended that "the reasons for prohibiting the interrogation of an uncounseled prisoner are even stronger after he has been formally charged with an offense than before." Justice Rehnquist, joined by Justice Powell and Justice O'Connor, dissented and argued that the majority had placed itself in "an analytical strait-jacket" because the Court's waiver rule did not apply unless the accused actually invoked his Sixth Amendment right to counsel. He explained as follows:

> The problem with the limitation the Court places on the Sixth Amendment version of the *Edwards* rule is that, unlike a defendant's 'right to counsel' under *Miranda,* which does not arise until affirmatively invoked by the defendant during custodial interrogation, a defendant's Sixth Amendment right to counsel does not depend at all on whether the defendant has requested counsel.
>
> The Court provides no satisfactory explanation for its decision to extend the *Edwards* rule to the Sixth Amendment, yet limit that rule to those defendants foresighted enough, or just plain lucky enough, to have made an explicit request for counsel which we have always understood to be completely unnecessary for Sixth Amendment purposes.

While the waiver standards are the same for Fifth and Sixth Amendment rights once those rights have been invoked, the consequences of an invocation of the Sixth Amendment right are more limited. In McNeil v. Wisconsin, 111 S.Ct. 2204 (1991), the Court held that an invocation of the Sixth Amendment right to counsel is "offense-specific." The state had charged McNeil with armed robbery, and at his initial appearance before a judicial officer, McNeil invoked his right to counsel. Police thereafter initiated questioning of McNeil concerning an armed robbery and murder committed in another part of the state. McNeil waived his rights and confessed to those crimes. He thereafter argued on the basis of Michigan v. Jackson that his waiver was not voluntary because when he invoked his right to counsel at the initial appearance, it applied as well to unrelated charges. Justice Scalia, writing for a 6–3 majority, held that an invocation of Sixth Amendment rights gave protection only as to the crime with which the accused had been charged. He concluded that "just as the right is offense-specific, so also its Michigan v. Jackson effect of invalidating subsequent waivers in police-initiated interviews is offense-specific." Accordingly, the rule of Arizona v. Roberson, prohibiting police-initiated interrogation as to unrelated crimes when a suspect invokes his *Miranda* right to counsel, does not apply when an accused invokes his Sixth Amendment right to counsel. Put another way, Michigan v. Jackson applied *Edwards* to Sixth Amendment invocations, but the Court in *McNeil* refused to apply the *Roberson* extension of *Edwards* to such invocations.

Justice Scalia argued that an invocation of counsel at an initial appearance could, as held in *Jackson,* be construed to imply a desire not to be questioned without counsel concerning the crime charged; but it could not reasonably be construed to imply a desire never to undergo custodial interrogation, about anything, without counsel present.

The Court further found that a broad construction of the invocation of counsel at an initial appearance would be unsound as a matter of policy. Justice Scalia asserted that such a broad rule would mean that "most persons in pretrial custody for serious offenses would be unapproachable by police officers suspecting them of involvement in other crimes, even though they have never expressed any unwillingness to be questioned." He concluded that "since the ready ability to obtain uncoerced confessions is not an evil but an unmitigated good, society would be the loser" from such a rule. Justice Scalia also stated that when a suspect invokes his Sixth Amendment right to counsel at an initial appearance, he does not thereby invoke a *Miranda/Roberson* right to counsel as to unrelated crimes. This aspect of *McNeil* is discussed in the section on *Miranda* waivers, supra.

Justice Kennedy wrote a concurring opinion, reiterating his dissenting arguments *Roberson,* that an invocation of the *Miranda* right to counsel should be considered offense-specific as well. He contended that "the Court should devote some attention to bringing its Fifth and Sixth Amendment jurisprudence into a logical alignment."

Justice Stevens, joined by Justices Marshall and Blackmun, dissented. He contended that the majority's offense-specific construction of a Sixth Amendment invocation "ignores the substance of the attorney-client relationship that the legal profession has developed over the years" since the scope of the relationship between attorney and client "is as broad as the subject matter that might reasonably be encompassed by negotiations for a plea bargain or the contents of a presentence investigation report."

If an accused has not invoked his Sixth Amendment right to counsel, what must he be told about that right before he can give a knowing and intelligent waiver? Recall that in Moran v. Burbine, the Court held that the *Miranda* warnings encompassed the sum and substance of all information required for a knowing and intelligent waiver of *Miranda* rights. In Patterson v. Illinois, 487 U.S. 285 (1988), Patterson was indicted, received *Miranda* warnings, and signed the waiver form and confessed. He had never invoked his right to counsel, so *Jackson* did not apply. He argued, however, that the *Miranda* warnings did not adequately inform him of his Sixth Amendment right to counsel, so his waiver was not knowing and intelligent. Justice White, writing for the Court, rejected this argument.

> By telling petitioner that he had a right to consult with an attorney, to have a lawyer present while he was questioned, and even to have a lawyer appointed for him if he could not afford to retain one on his own, [the officers] conveyed to petitioner the sum and substance of the rights that the Sixth Amendment provided him. * * * [The *Miranda*] warning also sufficed * * * to let petitioner know what a lawyer could 'do for him' during the postindictment questioning; namely, advise petitioner to refrain from making any [incriminating] statements * * *
>
> Our conclusion is supported by petitioner's inability, in the proceedings before this Court, to articulate with precision what additional information should have been provided to him before he would have been competent to waive his right to counsel. * * * The State's decision to take an additional step and commence formal adversarial proceedings against the accused does not substantially increase the value of counsel to the accused at questioning, or expand the limited purpose that an attorney serves when the accused is questioned by authorities. With respect to this inquiry, we do not discern a substantial difference between the usefulness of a lawyer to a suspect during custodial interrogation, and his value to an accused at postindictment questioning. * * * Because the role of counsel at questioning is relatively simple and limited, we see no problem in having a waiver procedure at that stage which is likewise simple and limited.

Justice White distinguished Faretta v. California, 422 U.S. 806 (1975), where the Court required copious warnings to be conveyed to an accused before a waiver of the right to counsel at trial would be found (the nature of these warnings is discussed in Chapter Ten). Justice White explained that the "full dangers and disadvantages of self-representation during questioning are less substantial and more obvious to an accused than they are at trial."

In a footnote, Justice White stressed that it was still possible that an accused would not have waived his Sixth Amendment rights, "even though the challenged practices would pass constitutional muster under *Miranda.*" He gave two examples where a Sixth Amendment waiver would not be found even though a Fifth Amendment waiver would. First, "we have permitted a waiver to stand where a suspect was not told that his lawyer was trying to reach him during questioning [Moran v. Burbine]; in the Sixth Amendment context, this waiver would not be valid." Second, "a surreptitious conversation between an undercover police officer and an unindicted suspect would not give rise to any *Miranda* violation [Illinois v. Perkins]; however, once the accused is indicted, such questioning would be prohibited" [*Massiah,* supra and *Henry,* infra], and a waiver could not be found. Justices Stevens, Brennan, Marshall and Blackmun dissented in *Patterson.* Justice Stevens argued that the majority had underplayed the significance of the initiation of formal proceedings, and the role of counsel after an indictment. He noted that the lawyer might examine the indictment for legal sufficiency, or might be able to negotiate a plea bargain, and that the *Miranda* warnings did not apprise the accused of these possibilities.

The Court in *Patterson* left open whether an indicted suspect is entitled to a warning that he has been indicted before a waiver of the Sixth Amendment right to counsel could be found; Patterson had been so informed. But the sweeping language in *Patterson* has led courts to hold that such an "indictment warning" is not required. See Riddick v. Edmiston, 894 F.2d 586 (3d Cir.1990).

C. DELIBERATE ELICITATION AND THE PASSIVE EAR

Chief Justice Burger, who so vigorously dissented in *Brewer,* may have extended *Massiah* in his opinion for the Court in United States v. Henry, 447 U.S. 264 (1980).

Henry was convicted of armed bank robbery and sought collateral relief after he learned that a cellmate (Nichols) who testified at trial had been a paid government informant. No hearing was held in the district court, and the facts of the case were not crystal clear in the Supreme Court. It appeared to be undisputed that Nichols was a government informant, paid in the past for expenses and services in connection with information he supplied. An affidavit supplied to the district court by an FBI agent stated that the agent had told Nichols, who was kept in the same jail as Henry, of the government's interest in several individuals who were housed in the jail, including Henry. The affidavit also reported that the agent told Nichols not to initiate conversations with Henry, but to pay attention to anything Henry said about the robbery.

Citing both *Massiah* and *Brewer,* the Chief Justice wrote that "[t]he question here is whether * * * a government agent 'deliberately elicited' incriminating statements from Henry within the meaning of *Massiah.*" The Chief Justice analyzed this question as follows:

> Three factors are important. First, Nichols was acting under instructions as a paid informant for the Government; second, Nichols was ostensibly no more than a fellow inmate of Henry; and third, Henry was in custody and under indictment at the time he was engaged in conversation by Nichols.
>
> * * * Even if the agent's statement that he did not intend that Nichols would take affirmative steps to secure incriminating information is accepted, he must have known that such propinquity would lead to that result.
>
> The Government argues that the federal agents instructed Nichols not to question Henry about the robbery. Yet according to his own testimony, Nichols was not a passive listener; rather, he had 'some conversations with Mr. Henry' while he was in jail and Henry's incriminatory statements were 'the product of this conversation.' While affirmative interrogation, absent waiver, would certainly satisfy *Massiah,* we are not persuaded, as the Government contends, that Brewer v. Williams modified *Massiah's* 'deliberately elicited' test. * * *
>
> The Government argues that this Court should apply a less rigorous standard under the Sixth Amendment [to undercover activity] than where the accused is speaking in the hearing of persons he knows to be Government officers. That line of argument, however, seeks to infuse Fifth Amendment concerns * * * into the Sixth Amendment protection * * *.
>
> Moreover, the concept of a knowing and voluntary waiver of Sixth Amendment rights does not apply in the context of communications with an undisclosed undercover informant acting for the Government. In that setting, Henry, being unaware that Nichols was a Government agent expressly commis-

sioned to secure evidence, cannot be held to have waived his right to the assistance of counsel.

Finally, Henry's incarceration at the time he was engaged in conversation by Nichols is also a relevant factor. * * * [T]he mere fact of custody imposes pressures on the accused; confinement may bring into play subtle influences that will make him particularly susceptible to the ploys of undercover Government agents.

The Court concluded that "[b]y intentionally creating a situation likely to induce Henry to make incriminating statements without the assistance of counsel, the government violated Henry's Sixth Amendment's right to counsel."

Justice Powell's concurring opinion emphasized that the case did not involve the introduction of spontaneous statements which were not barred by *Massiah*. He concluded that Henry had demonstrated "the functional equivalent of interrogation."

Justice Blackmun, joined by Justice White, dissented. He argued that the Court purported to retain the "deliberately elicited" test, but that in reality it was extending *Massiah* to "cover even a 'negligent' triggering of events resulting in reception of disclosures." He found troubling the language "likely to induce" in the majority opinion. As a matter of policy, he argued that undercover work that produces reliable evidence, obtained without coercion from a person willing to talk, ought not to be rejected as culpable or unfair police conduct. His view of *Massiah* is as follows:

While not out of line with the Court's prior right to counsel cases, *Massiah* certainly is the decision in which Sixth Amendment protections have been extended to their outermost point. I simply do not perceive any good reason to give *Massiah* the expansion it receives in this case.

Recognizing that the focus on "deliberateness" was not "an objective test," such as that established in Rhode Island v. Innis, Justice Blackmun noted that the proper focus of a Sixth Amendment claim was on an interference with the right to counsel, not on coercion, and concluded that a deliberateness standard "imposes the exclusionary sanction on that conduct that is most culpable, most likely to frustrate the purpose of having counsel, and most susceptible to being checked by a deterrent." He went on to criticize the Court's application of its own test to the facts, which in his view did not reveal that anything the government agent did was " 'likely to induce' Nichols' successful prompting of Henry."

Justice Rehnquist filed a separate dissent. He urged another look at the doctrinal underpinnings of the *Massiah* doctrine. After observing that in *Massiah* cases like this one the government has done nothing to impair the defendant's ability to consult with an attorney, Justice Rehnquist observed:

The role of counsel in an adversary system is to offer advice and assistance in the preparation of a defense and to serve as a spokesman for the accused in technical legal proceedings. And the Sixth Amendment, of course, protects the confidentiality of communications between the accused and his attorney. But there is no constitutional or historical support for concluding that an accused has a right to have his attorney serve as a sort of guru who must be present whenever an accused has an inclination to reveal incriminating information to anyone who acts to elicit such information at the behest of the prosecution. To the extent the accused is protected from revealing evidence that may be incriminatory, the focus must be on the Fifth Amendment privilege against compulsory self-incrimination.

Note

The Court distinguished *Henry* in Kuhlmann v. Wilson, 477 U.S. 436 (1986), as it held that the Sixth Amendment was not violated when police put a jailhouse informant in close proximity to a defendant, the defendant made statements to the informant which were used against the defendant, and the informant made no effort to stimulate conversations about the crimes charged. The Court stated that, to prove a Sixth Amendment violation, a defendant must show that the police took some action, beyond merely listening, that was designed deliberately to elicit incriminating remarks.

The basic facts were the following: Prior to a defendant's arrival at a jail following an arraignment for robbery and murder, an officer entered into an agreement with inmate Lee under which Lee would listen to the defendant's conversations and report them, but Lee would ask no questions and would "keep his ears open." The defendant told Lee that he had been present during the robbery but denied knowing the robbers. Lee responded that the explanation "didn't sound too good." The defendant changed details over the next few days. Finally, after a visit from his brother, the defendant admitted to Lee that he and two other men had committed the robbery and murder.

Justice Powell found that the informant in *Henry* had "stimulated" the conversations with Henry and that Lee had not done so in the instant case. The Court stated that a defendant does not show a Sixth Amendment violation "simply by showing that an informant, either through prior arrangement or voluntarily, reported his incriminating statements to the police." Justice Powell found it insignificant that Lee had said that the defendant's version of the crimes didn't sound too good; that one remark did not bring the case out of the realm of the "passive recording device." Justice Brennan, joined by Justice Marshall, dissented and found the case to be virtually indistinguishable on its facts from *Henry.* Justice Stevens also dissented briefly and agreed with Justice Brennan. Chief Justice Burger filed a short concurring opinion stating that "[t]here is a vast difference between placing an 'ear' in the suspect's cell and placing a voice in the cell to encourage conversation for the 'ear' to record." See also United States v. York, 933 F.2d 1343 (7th Cir.1991) (no deliberate elicitation where the informant responded with neutral comments when incriminating topics were brought up by the defendant; informants are not required to reveal their status by refusing to participate in the natural flow of conversation).

Sixth Amendment protection under *Henry* requires that the informant must have been working for the government at the time the information was obtained. Whether that is so is often a difficult question. In United States v. Watson, 894 F.2d 1345 (D.C.Cir.1990) Watson argued that the jailhouse informant was working as a government agent at the time Watson made incriminating statements. He noted that the informant had worked for the DEA for two years and was in regular contact with the DEA while he was in jail. But the court found "no evidence that the DEA in any way encouraged" the informant to talk to Watson; that the informant was in contact with the DEA on unrelated cases, and did not mention Watson until after Watson made incriminating statements; and that the informant "was acting as an entrepreneur." The court stated that the informant "may have hoped to make a sale to the government when he spoke with Watson, but that does not make the government responsible for his actions, any more than a person who has bought an article from a salesman in the past is responsible if the salesman then steals something similar in the hope of making a second sale." Do you agree? See also United States v. Sampol, 636 F.2d 621 (D.C.Cir.1980) (Sixth Amendment violated where informant "had been accepted by the government as an informant at large whose reports about any criminal activity would be gratefully received"); United States v. York, 933 F.2d 1343 (7th Cir.1991) (jailhouse plant was a state agent as a matter of law, where he had been promised a reward for suitable information obtained from any source about any inmate, and the informant was motivated by a concern to obtain that reward).

For an eloquent defense of the *Massiah* doctrine, in response to an attack on that doctrine by the Justice Department, see Tomkovicz, The Truth About *Massiah*, 23 U.Mich.J.L.Ref. 641 (1990).

D. CONTINUING INVESTIGATIONS

The Supreme Court elaborated on the concept of "deliberate elicitation" in Maine v. Moulton, 474 U.S. 159 (1985). Moulton and a codefendant, Colson, were charged with theft of automobiles and parts. Colson, along with his lawyer, informed the Chief of Police of threatening telephone calls to his house and of the fact that Moulton had spoken of killing a key witness. Colson cooperated with the police and agreed to have a recording device placed upon his telephone. Three calls from Moulton were received, but they were essentially nonincriminating. The police wired Colson with a transmitter when he agreed to meet with Moulton. They spoke of eliminating witnesses, Moulton rejected the idea, and Colson led Moulton into talking about their theft activities. Both the recorded telephone statements and the recorded meeting were used as evidence at trial. Moulton was convicted.

Justice Brennan wrote for the Court as it reversed. He rejected the argument that the Sixth Amendment is not violated if the police record conversations or meetings initiated by the suspect, not by a government agent: "knowing exploitation by the State of an opportunity to confront the accused without counsel being present is as much a breach of the State's obligation not to circumvent the right to the assistance of counsel as is the intentional creation of such an opportunity." Justice Brennan also rejected the argument that Moulton's statements should be admissible because the police were investigating new crimes, including threats to the safety of witnesses. Although he recognized that police may investigate crimes not yet charged and may use statements made by a suspect pertaining to those crimes, Justice Brennan concluded that "incriminating statements pertaining to pending charges are inadmissible at the trial of those charges, notwithstanding the fact that the police were also investigating other crimes, if, in obtaining the evidence, the State violated the Sixth Amendment by knowingly circumventing the accused's right to the assistance of counsel." He stated that the Sixth Amendment guarantees the accused "the right to rely on counsel as a 'medium' between him and the State." Justice Brennan rejected the argument that the officers' instructions to the informant to limit the scope of discussion was sufficient to protect Moulton. He stated that the agents should have known that despite their instructions, the conversation between the informant and Moulton would be likely to turn to the crime for which both were charged. Justice Brennan noted that "direct proof of the State's knowledge will seldom be available," but that "proof that the State must have known that its agent was likely to obtain incriminating statements" suffices to establish a Sixth Amendment violation.

Chief Justice Burger dissented, joined by Justices White and Rehnquist and in part by Justice O'Connor. He argued that the "deliberately eliciting" language focuses upon a purpose of using statements in connection with pending charges and that suppression should not be required unless police institute the investigation of separate charges in bad faith to avoid the dictates of *Massiah.*

Consider the impact of *Moulton* on police behavior. *Massiah* and subsequent cases taught that it was impermissible for the police to deliberately seek statements from a suspect who had been formally charged. *Moulton* holds that it is permissible to seek statements relating to crimes not charged, but that it is impermissible to seek statements regarding the crimes already charged. Suppose that the police use an undercover informant to seek the permissible statements, but the suspect changes the conversation to talk about the charged offenses. Are the statements admissible? Is there any deliberate elicitation? Suppose that the statements made with respect to the uncharged offenses are relevant—e.g., to show intent, plan, etc.—in the prosecution of the charged offenses. May they be used in that prosecution if the realization of their relevance came only after they were obtained? See Mealer v. Jones, 741 F.2d 1451 (2d Cir. 1984) (*Massiah* requires exclusion of uncharged offenses offered as "other crimes" evidence, where the government "must have known" that any statements covering the uncharged offense would incriminate the accused on the charged crime as well). Suppose that it is impossible to seek evidence about additional crimes without eliciting statements about charges already brought. Why should the statements be suppressed, as in *Moulton,* in the prosecution of the pending charges? Under Fourth Amendment cases, police who come upon evidence in a legal search may use it in any prosecution. If the "search" for statements is legal in cases like *Moulton,* does the suppression remedy make sense?

E. THE SIXTH AMENDMENT EXCLUSIONARY RULE

In *Moulton,* Chief Justice Burger argued in dissent that even if there were a Sixth Amendment violation, the exclusionary rule should not apply. Citing United States v. Leon (discussed in Chapter Two), he argued that "the Sixth Amendment claims at issue here closely parallel claims under the Fourth Amendment where we have found the exclusionary rule to be inapplicable by weighing the costs and benefits of its applications."

The Court has held that the Fourth Amendment exclusionary rule is not constitutionally required. It has also declared that the *Miranda* exclusionary rule is not constitutionally required. On the other hand, a violation of the Due Process Clause carries with it an automatic rule of exclusion, as the Court has consistently stated in cases such as Michigan v. Tucker, Oregon v. Elstad, and Mincey v. Arizona. Does the Constitution require exclusion of a confession obtained in violation of the Sixth Amendment, or is Chief Justice Burger correct in *Moulton*?

Despite the Chief Justice's assertions, several commentators have argued that the Constitution requires exclusion of evidence obtained as a result of a Sixth Amendment violation. They reason that a violation of the right to counsel is not complete until the confession is admitted at trial. It is only at that point that the effectiveness of counsel envisioned by *Massiah* is impaired. As such, a *Massiah* violation is unlike a Fourth Amendment violation, which occurs at the time of the intrusion; and it is unlike a *Miranda* violation, which is not a violation of a Constitutional right. See Schulhofer, Confessions and the Court, 79 Mich.L.Rev. 865 (1981); Loewy, Police Obtained Evidence and the Constitution: Distinguishing Unconstitutionally Obtained Evidence from Unconstitutionally Used Evidence, 87 Mich.L.Rev. 907 (1989).

If the commentators are right, the consequences are significant, especially if considered in relation to the rules on *Miranda*-defective confessions. As with involuntary confessions, it would mean that *Massiah*-defective confessions could not be used for impeachment purposes; that fruits of these confessions—such as physical evidence or a second confession—would be excluded (subjection to exceptions for attenuation, independent source, and inevitable discovery); that such confessions would be excluded even if the officer had a "public safety" excuse for deliberately eliciting information from the accused; and that such confessions would be excluded even if the officer was acting in good faith.

The question of whether the Constitution requires exclusion of a confession obtained in violation of the Sixth Amendment was discussed but not decided in Michigan v. Harvey, 494 U.S. 344 (1990). The Court in *Harvey* held that a statement obtained in violation of Michigan v. Jackson could be used for impeachment purposes. Harvey confessed after invoking his right to counsel at arraignment. The confession resulted from police-initiation, but Harvey received warnings, understood them, and was not coerced into waiving his rights. Chief Justice Rehnquist's opinion for the Court stressed that the *Jackson* rule was merely a transposition of the prophylactic standards of Edwards v. Arizona to the Sixth Amendment context. Accordingly, a violation of the prophylactic safeguards of *Jackson* was not a violation of the Constitution itself. Rather, *Jackson* "established a presumption which renders invalid some waivers that would be considered voluntary, knowing and intelligent under the traditional case-by-case inquiry." As a result, the holding in Harris v. New York, allowing *Miranda*-defective confessions to be used for impeachment purposes, was fully applicable. The Chief Justice specifically left open the "admissibility for impeachment purposes of a voluntary statement obtained in the absence of a knowing and voluntary waiver of the right to counsel." However, the majority intimated that a "true" violation of the Sixth Amendment (as opposed to prophylactic safeguards) would result in exclusion for all purposes.

Justice Stevens, joined by Justices Brennan, Marshall and Blackmun, dissented. He argued that the rule in *Jackson* was constitutionally based, and not a mere prophylactic safeguard of an underlying constitutional right. Justice Stevens also stated a proposition with which the majority did not necessarily disagree: that the Sixth Amendment (unlike the Fourth Amendment) contains its own constitutionally-based exclusionary rule. Justice Stevens reasoned that exclusion of a statement obtained in violation of the Sixth

Amendment "follows not as a remedy for a violation that has preceded trial, but as a necessary incident of the constitutional right itself."

Though the issue has not been decided by the Supreme Court, other courts have held that a *Massiah*-defective confession cannot be used for impeachment purposes (see United States v. Brown, 699 F.2d 585 (2d Cir.1983)), and that the fruits of *Massiah* confessions must be excluded from trial (see United States v. Kimball, 884 F.2d 1274 (9th Cir.1989)). Do you agree that a violation of *Massiah* should be treated differently from a violation of *Miranda* or a violation of the Fourth Amendment?

VII. PROCEDURES AT TRIAL REGARDING CONFESSIONS

Three approaches to determining the admissibility of confessions have been used by American courts: (1) In some states, the trial judge alone determines admissibility. (2) Under what has been referred to as the Massachusetts rule, the trial judge makes a separate determination of the voluntariness of the confession; if he decides the confession is voluntary and permits it to be admitted at trial, the jury may also pass on the voluntariness issue. (3) Before the Supreme Court rendered its decision in Jackson v. Denno, 378 U.S. 368 (1964), New York and several other states permitted the jury to decide the voluntariness of a confession, once there was a prima facie showing—enough evidence, if believed, to support a finding—of voluntariness.

The Supreme Court struck down the New York system in Jackson v. Denno because it did not have confidence that juries could separate the voluntariness question from the merits of the case. The Court first noted that "the evidence given the jury inevitably injects irrelevant and impermissible consideration of truthfulness of the confession into the assessment of voluntariness." The Court also expressed concern that the jury would be unable to totally disregard a confession that it decided was involuntary in its determination of guilt:

> It is difficult, if not impossible, to prove that a confession which a jury has found to be involuntary has nevertheless influenced the verdict or that its finding of voluntariness, if this is the course it took, was affected by the other evidence showing the confession was true. But the New York procedure poses substantial threats to a defendant's constitutional rights to have an involuntary confession entirely disregarded and to have the coercion issue fairly and reliably determined. These hazards we cannot ignore.

In light of these concerns, the Court held that the defendant is entitled to a clear-cut ruling by the court that a confession is voluntary before it is admitted.[27] If the judge finds that the confession is admissible, the defendant

27. At the *Jackson* hearing, the judge is not permitted to consider the reliability of the confession, since an involuntary confession is excluded even if it is reliable. See Doby v. South Carolina Department of Corrections, 741 F.2d 76 (4th Cir. 1984). A defendant's testimony at a *Jackson* hearing cannot be used against him at trial to prove guilt. See United States v. Dollard, 780 F.2d 1118 (4th Cir. 1985). Unless a request for a Jackson v. Denno hearing is made, none will be held in most cases. But in United States v. Powe, 591 F.2d 833 (D.C. Cir. 1978), the Court indicated that certain "alerting circumstances" may impose a duty on the trial judge to protect a criminal defendant and to conduct a hearing on the voluntariness of a confession, even if defense counsel fails to request one. A few

may still introduce evidence at trial to impugn the credibility of the confession. It seems that the judge can invite the jury to make its own determination of voluntariness, as long as the judge does not tell the jury that she has found the confession to be voluntary. Thus, the Massachusetts rule can still be used.

At the preliminary hearing on the voluntariness of the confession, the government has the burden of showing the validity of a waiver of *Miranda* rights or the voluntariness of statements. In making these decisions, several courts have insisted that the government have proof "beyond a reasonable doubt." But, in 1972, the Supreme Court held in Lego v. Twomey, 404 U.S. 477 (1972), that the government need only demonstrate by a preponderance of the evidence that the confession was voluntary in order to satisfy the constitutional requirement. Justice White wrote for the Court in the 4–3 decision, stating:

> Since the purpose that a voluntariness hearing is designed to serve has nothing whatever to do with improving the reliability of jury verdicts, we cannot accept the charge that judging the admissibility of a confession by a preponderance of the evidence undermines the mandate of In re Winship, 397 U.S. 358 (1970). Our decision in *Winship* was not concerned with standards for determining the admissibility of evidence or with the prosecution's burden of proof at a suppression hearing when evidence is challenged on constitutional grounds. *Winship* went no further than to confirm the fundamental right that protects "the accused against conviction except upon proof beyond a reasonable doubt of every fact necessary to constitute the crime with which he is charged." A high standard of proof is necessary, we said, to ensure against unjust convictions by giving substance to the presumption of innocence. A guilty verdict is not rendered less reliable or less consonant with *Winship* simply because the admissibility of a confession is determined by a less stringent standard. Petitioner does not maintain that either his confession or its voluntariness is an element of the crime with which he was charged. He does not challenge the constitutionality of the standard by which the jury was instructed to decide his guilt or innocence; nor does he question the sufficiency of the evidence that reached the jury to satisfy the proper standard of proof. Petitioner's rights under *Winship* have not been violated.

Justice Brennan, joined by Justices Douglas and Marshall, dissented. He argued that the preponderance standard "does not provide sufficient protection against the danger that involuntary confessions will be employed at trial." According to Justice Brennan, the majority's application of the preponderance standard meant that it was no more concerned with the erroneous admission of an involuntary confession than it was with the erroneous exclusion of reliable evidence. Justice Brennan found this view inconsistent with the substantive rule excluding involuntary confessions even if they are reliable; that rule presumes that protecting against involuntary confessions is more important than admitting reliable evidence.

For the view that voluntariness hearings may have a bearing on the reliability of guilty verdicts, and that in determining the appropriate standard of proof the ultimate effect of the preliminary fact issue on the case should be considered, see Saltzburg, Standards of Proof and Preliminary Questions of Fact, 27 Stan.L.Rev. 271 (1975).

courts seem to require a hearing in all cases. See, e.g., State v. Staley, 253 S.E.2d 66 (W.Va. 1979).

The Court did specifically note in *Lego* that the states were free to impose a higher burden of proof in state proceedings, and some have. See, e.g., People v. Jiminez, 21 Cal.3d 595, 147 Cal.Rptr. 172, 580 P.2d 672 (1978); State v. Verhasselt, 83 Wis.2d 647, 266 N.W.2d 342 (1978); State v. Gullick, 118 N.H. 912, 396 A.2d 554 (1978).

In Colorado v. Connelly, 479 U.S. 157 (1986), the decision (discussed above) holding that coercive police activity is a prerequisite to finding a coerced confession, the Court concluded that the government must prove that a suspect waived his *Miranda* rights by a preponderance of the evidence, the same standard it had adopted for a voluntariness determination in *Lego*. The Court stated that if a preponderance of the evidence was sufficient to establish the voluntariness of a confession, then "a waiver of the auxiliary protections established in *Miranda* should require no higher burden of proof." Justice Brennan, joined by Justice Marshall, dissented, adhering to the arguments made in his *Lego* dissent. He added that when a defendant is in custody the coercive atmosphere poses an increased danger of overreaching and the police are in a position to demonstrate by stronger proof that a waiver is voluntary. Is the case for a higher standard of proof stronger when the police have control over a suspect and are in a position to document their actions?

The Supreme Court relied upon language in *Lego* to hold in Crane v. Kentucky, 476 U.S. 683 (1986), that a court must permit a defendant to offer evidence at trial that attacks the credibility of a confession. To exclude such evidence is to bar the defendant from being heard on the probative value of the government's evidence and violates elementary notions of due process.

Chapter Four

IDENTIFYING SUSPECTS

I. INTRODUCTION

As one would expect, often it is easier for law enforcement officers to discover and prove that a crime has been committed and how it took place than it is to identify the perpetrator. At times the failure or absence of witnesses leads prosecutors to seek other ways of establishing identity. The development of handwriting analysis, the frequent use of fingerprint evidence, and current efforts to improve spectographic analysis of voices are, in part, responses to the felt need for better identification techniques. One of the most important scientific breakthroughs has been the use of DNA profiling, in which body fluid samples are "lifted," like fingerprints, from the crime scene, the DNA is extracted from the body fluid, and then compared with the DNA extracted from body fluid taken from the defendant. Most courts have found DNA profiling to be admissible, so long as the prosecution establishes that the laboratory performing the tests used techniques that are generally accepted as reliable in the scientific community. See United States v. Two Bulls, 918 F.2d 56 (8th Cir. 1990) (citing cases where DNA evidence has been admitted, but stressing that a showing must be made in each case that DNA profiling was reliably conducted). For an exhaustive discussion of the process used in DNA profiling, and the problems which can arise in that process, see People v. Castro, 144 Misc.2d 956, 545 N.Y.S.2d 985 (Bronx Cty. 1989) (excluding profile evidence because techniques used by particular laboratory were unreliable). A sample of the extensive legal literature on DNA identification evidence includes Giannelli, Criminal Discovery, Scientific Evidence, and DNA, 44 Vand. L.Rev. 791 (1991), and Burk, DNA Identification: Possibilities and Pitfalls Revisited, 31 Jurimetrics 53 (1990).

Unfortunately, science cannot replace identification by witnesses in all cases. In fact, most cases in which identity is disputed will turn on whether witnesses are believed. Yet, it is well known that eyewitness evidence is not very reliable and that police procedures may render identifications even less reliable than they otherwise would be. As the drafters of the ALI Model Code of Pre-Arraignment Procedure accurately observe, "a wide variety of experienced persons consider and have considered the pre-trial identification as a crucial factor in the fair and accurate determination of guilt or innocence, and a factor as to which certain kinds of error, once committed, are particularly hard to remedy and peculiarly likely to lead to unjust results." Commentary to § 160, at 422. Circuit Judge McGowan has explained that many experts believe that erroneous identifications are "conceivably the greatest single threat to the achievement of our ideal that no innocent man shall be punished." Constitutional Interpretation and Criminal Identification, 12 Wm. & Mary L.Rev. 235, 238 (1970).[1]

This chapter examines the very real dangers associated with identification evidence and the safeguards that the criminal justice system has fashioned to assure that, if we can help it, witness error will not irreparably taint criminal litigation.

II. THE JUDICIAL RESPONSE

A. LINEUPS

1. *The Warren Court and the Right to Counsel*

With so much evidence available casting doubt for so long on the identification techniques commonly used by the police, sooner or later the judiciary was going to have to examine them. Once the United States Supreme Court began to focus generally on police procedures in the 1960's, the time for an examination had come. One morning in June of 1967, the Court handed down three major opinions designed to protect those suspected and accused of crime from unfair tactics.

The first case was the following one:

UNITED STATES V. WADE

Supreme Court of the United States, 1967.
388 U.S. 218.

MR. JUSTICE BRENNAN delivered the opinion of the Court.

The question here is whether courtroom identifications of an accused at trial are to be excluded from evidence because the accused was exhibited to the witnesses before trial at a post-indictment lineup conducted for identification purposes without notice to and in the absence of the accused's appointed counsel.

The federally insured bank in Eustace, Texas, was robbed on September 21, 1964. A man with a small strip of tape on each side on his face entered the bank, pointed a pistol at the female cashier and the vice president, the only persons in the bank at the time, and forced them to fill a pillowcase with the

1. A shocking case in which two men were erroneously identified as the same "stocking mask" rapist before a third suspect was arrested is reported by Bauer, Two Wrongly Arrested Men Free; Third is Held in Staunton, Wash. Post., Jan. 23, 1980, at A1, col. 5. One man was kept nine months in the criminal ward of a state mental hospital before being released; the other was more fortunate, having been confined 71 days in a local jail before being released.

For a description of a well publicized case of mistaken identification of a priest as a gentleman robber, see Winer, Pagano Case Points Finger at Lineups, Nat'l L.J., Sept. 10, 1979, at 1, col. 4.

For an excellent summary of the literature on eyewitness identification, see Special Issue on Eyewitness Behavior, 4 L. & Hum.Behav. 237 (1980).

Two popular additions to the literature on eyewitness identification are E. Loftus, Eyewitness Testimony (1979) and A. Yarmey, The Psychology of Eyewitness Testimony (1979). Both are reviewed by Circuit Court Judge David Bazelon in Psychology Today, March 1980, at 102.

bank's money. The man then drove away with an accomplice who had been waiting in a stolen car outside the bank. On March 23, 1965, an indictment was returned against respondent, Wade, and two others for conspiring to rob the bank, and against Wade and the accomplice for the robbery itself. Wade was arrested on April 2, and counsel was appointed to represent him on April 26. Fifteen days later an FBI agent, without notice to Wade's lawyer, arranged to have the two bank employees observe a lineup made up of Wade and five or six other prisoners and conducted in a courtroom of the local county courthouse. Each person in the line wore strips of tape such as allegedly worn by the robber and upon direction each said something like "put the money in the bag," the words allegedly uttered by the robber. Both bank employees identified Wade in the lineup as the bank robber.

At trial, the two employees, when asked on direct examination if the robber was in the courtroom, pointed to Wade. The prior lineup identification was then elicited from both employees on cross-examination. * * *

* * *

III

The Government characterizes the lineup as a mere preparatory step in the gathering of the prosecution's evidence, not different—for Sixth Amendment purposes—from various other preparatory steps, such as systematized or scientific analyzing of the accused's fingerprints, blood sample, clothing, hair, and the like. We think there are differences which preclude such stages being characterized as critical stages at which the accused has the right to the presence of his counsel. Knowledge of the techniques of science and technology is sufficiently available, and the variables in techniques few enough, that the accused has the opportunity for a meaningful confrontation of the Government's case at trial through the ordinary processes of cross-examination of the Government's expert witnesses and the presentation of the evidence of his own experts. The denial of a right to have his counsel present at such analyses does not therefore violate the Sixth Amendment; they are not critical stages since there is minimal risk that his counsel's absence at such stages might derogate from his right to a fair trial.

IV

But the confrontation compelled by the State between the accused and the victim or witnesses to a crime to elicit identification evidence is peculiarly riddled with innumerable dangers and variable factors which might seriously, even crucially, derogate from a fair trial. The vagaries of eyewitness identification are well-known; the annals of criminal law are rife with instances of mistaken identification. * * * A major factor contributing to the high incidence of miscarriage of justice from mistaken identification has been the degree of suggestion inherent in the manner in which the prosecution presents the suspect to witnesses for pretrial identification. * * * Suggestion can be created intentionally or unintentionally in many subtle ways. And the dangers for the suspect are particularly grave when the witness' opportunity for observation was insubstantial, and thus his susceptibility to suggestion the greatest.

Moreover, "[i]t is a matter of common experience that, once a witness has picked out the accused at the line-up, he is not likely to go back on his word later on, so that in practice the issue of identity may (in the absence of other relevant evidence) for all practical purposes be determined there and then, before the trial."

The pretrial confrontation for purpose of identification may take the form of a lineup, also known as an "identification parade" or "showup," as in the present case, or presentation of the suspect alone to the witness. * * * It is obvious that risks of suggestion attend either form of confrontation and increase the dangers inhering in eyewitness identification. But as in the case with secret interrogations, there is serious difficulty in depicting what transpires at lineups and other forms of identification confrontations. * * * [T]he defense can seldom reconstruct the manner and mode of lineup identification for judge or jury at trial. Those participating in a lineup with the accused may often be police officers; in any event, the participants' names are rarely recorded or divulged at trial. The impediments to an objective observation are increased when the victim is the witness. Lineups are prevalent in rape and robbery prosecutions and present a particular hazard that a victim's understandable outrage may excite vengeful or spiteful motives. In any event, neither witnesses nor lineup participants are apt to be alert for conditions prejudicial to the suspect. And if they were, it would likely be of scant benefit to the suspect since neither witnesses nor lineup participants are likely to be schooled in the detection of suggestive influences.[a] Improper influences may go undetected by a suspect, guilty or not, who experiences the emotional tension which we might expect in one being confronted with potential accusers. Even when he does observe abuse, if he has a criminal record he may be reluctant to take the stand and open up the admission of prior convictions. Moreover, any protestations by the suspect of the fairness of the lineup made at trial are likely to be in vain; the jury's choice is between the accused's unsupported version and that of the police officers present. In short, the accused's inability effectively to reconstruct at trial any unfairness that occurred at the lineup may deprive him of his only opportunity meaningfully to attack the credibility of the witness' courtroom identification.

* * *

The few cases that have surfaced therefore reveal the existence of a process attended with hazards of serious unfairness to the criminal accused and strongly suggest the plight of the more numerous defendants who are unable to ferret out suggestive influences in the secrecy of the confrontation. We do not assume that these risks are the result of police procedures intentionally designed to prejudice an accused. Rather we assume they derive from the dangers inherent in eyewitness identification and the suggestibility inherent in the context of the pretrial identification. Williams & Hammelmann, in one of the most comprehensive studies of such forms of identification, said, "[T]he fact that the police themselves have, in a given case, little or no doubt that the man put up for identification has committed the offense, and that their chief pre-occupation is with the problem of getting sufficient proof, because he has not 'come clean,' involves a danger that this persuasion may communicate itself even in a doubtful case to the witness in some way * * *." Identification Parades, Part I, [1963] Crim.L.Rev. 479, 483.

Insofar as the accused's conviction may rest on a courtroom identification in fact the fruit of a suspect pretrial identification which the accused is helpless to subject to effective scrutiny at trial, the accused is deprived of that right of cross-examination which is an

a. An additional impediment to the detection of such influences by participants, including the suspect, is the physical conditions often surrounding the conduct of the lineup. In many, lights shine on the stage in such a way that the suspect cannot see the witness. In some a one-way mirror is used and what is said on the witness' side cannot be heard.

essential safeguard to his right to confront the witnesses against him. And even though cross-examination is a precious safeguard to a fair trial, it cannot be viewed as an absolute assurance of accuracy and reliability. Thus in the present context, where so many variables and pitfalls exist, the first line of defense must be the prevention of unfairness and the lessening of the hazards of eyewitness identification at the lineup itself. The trial which might determine the accused's fate may well not be that in the courtroom but that at the pretrial confrontation, with the State aligned against the accused, the witness the sole jury, and the accused unprotected against the overreaching, intentional or unintentional, and with little or no effective appeal from the judgment there rendered by the witness—"that's the man."

Since it appears that there is grave potential for prejudice, intentional or not, in the pretrial lineup, which may not be capable of reconstruction at trial, and since presence of counsel itself can often avert prejudice and assure a meaningful confrontation at trial, there can be little doubt that for Wade the post-indictment lineup was a critical stage of the prosecution at which he was "as much entitled to such aid [of counsel] * * * as at the trial itself." Thus both Wade and his counsel should have been notified of the impending lineup, and counsel's presence should have been a requisite to conduct of the lineup, absent an "intelligent waiver." No substantial countervailing policy considerations have been advanced against the requirement of the presence of counsel. Concern is expressed that the requirement will forestall prompt identifications and result in obstruction of the confrontations. As for the first, we note that in the two cases in which the right to counsel is today held to apply, counsel had already been appointed and no argument is made in either case that notice to counsel would have prejudicially delayed the confrontations. Moreover, we leave open the question whether the presence of substitute counsel might not suffice where notification and presence of the suspect's own counsel would result in prejudicial delay.[b] And to refuse to recognize the right to counsel for fear that counsel will obstruct the course of justice is contrary to the basic assumptions upon which this Court has operated in Sixth Amendment cases. * * * In our view counsel can hardly impede legitimate law enforcement; on the contrary, for the reasons expressed, law enforcement may be assisted by preventing the infiltration of taint in the prosecution's identification evidence.[c] That result cannot help the guilty avoid conviction but can only help assure that the right man has been brought to justice.[d]

Legislative or other regulations, such as those of local police departments, which eliminate the risks of abuse and

b. Although the right to counsel usually means a right to the suspect's own counsel, provision for substitute counsel may be justified on the ground that the substitute counsel's presence may eliminate the hazards which render the lineup a critical stage for the presence of the suspect's *own* counsel.

c. Concern is also expressed that the presence of counsel will force divulgence of the identity of government witnesses whose identity the Government may want to conceal. To the extent that this is a valid or significant state interest there are police practices commonly used to effect concealment, for example, masking the face.

d. Many other nations surround the lineup with safeguards against prejudice to the suspect. In England the suspect must be allowed the presence of his solicitor or a friend; Germany requires the presence of retained counsel; France forbids the confrontation of the suspect in the absence of his counsel; Spain, Mexico, and Italy provide detailed procedures prescribing the conditions under which confrontation must occur under the supervision of a judicial officer who sees to it that the proceedings are officially recorded to assure adequate scrutiny at trial. Murray, The Criminal Lineup at Home and Abroad, 1966 Utah L.Rev. 610, 621–627.

unintentional suggestion at lineup proceedings and the impediments to meaningful confrontation at trial may also remove the basis for regarding the stage as "critical." But neither Congress nor the federal authorities have seen fit to provide a solution. What we hold today "in no way creates a constitutional straitjacket which will handicap sound efforts at reform, nor is it intended to have this effect."

V

We come now to the question whether the denial of Wade's motion to strike the courtroom identification by the bank witnesses at trial because of the absence of his counsel at the lineup required, as the Court of Appeals held, the grant of a new trial at which such evidence is to be excluded. We do not think this disposition can be justified without first giving the Government the opportunity to establish by clear and convincing evidence that the in-court identifications were based upon observations of the suspect other than the lineup identification. Where, as here, the admissibility of evidence of the lineup identification itself is not involved, a *per se* rule of exclusion of courtroom identification would be unjustified. A rule limited solely to the exclusion of testimony concerning identification at the lineup itself, without regard to admissibility of the courtroom identification, would render the right to counsel an empty one. The lineup is most often used, as in the present case, to crystallize the witnesses' identification of the defendant for future reference. We have already noted that the lineup identification will have that effect. The State may then rest upon the witnesses' unequivocal courtroom identification, and not mention the pretrial identification as part of the State's case at trial. Counsel is then in the predicament in which Wade's counsel found himself—realizing that possible unfairness at the lineup may be the sole means of attack upon the unequivocal courtroom identification, and having to probe in the dark in an attempt to discover and reveal unfairness, while bolstering the government witness' courtroom identification by bringing out and dwelling upon his prior identification. Since counsel's presence at the lineup would equip him to attack not only the lineup identification but the courtroom identification as well, limiting the impact of violation of the right to counsel to exclusion of evidence only of identification at the lineup itself disregards a critical element of that right.

We think it follows that the proper test to be applied in these situations is that quoted in Wong Sun v. United States, 371 U.S. 471, 488, " '[W]hether, granting establishment of the primary illegality, the evidence to which instant objection is made has been come at by exploitation of that illegality or instead by means sufficiently distinguishable to be purged of the primary taint.' " Application of this test in the present context requires consideration of various factors; for example, the prior opportunity to observe the alleged criminal act, the existence of any discrepancy between any pre-lineup description and the defendant's actual description, any identification prior to lineup of another person, the identification by picture of the defendant prior to the lineup, failure to identify the defendant on a prior occasion, and the lapse of time between the alleged act and the lineup identification. It is also relevant to consider those facts which, despite the absence of counsel, are disclosed concerning the conduct of the lineup.

* * *

On the record now before us we cannot make the determination whether the in-court identifications had an independent origin. This was not an issue at trial, although there is some evidence relevant to a determination. That inquiry is most properly made in the District Court. We therefore think the appropriate procedure to be followed is to vacate the conviction pending a hearing to determine whether the in-court identifications had an independent source, or whether, in any event, the introduction of the evidence was harmless error, and for the District Court to reinstate the conviction or order a new trial, as may be proper.

* * *

[Separate opinions by Justice Fortas, joined by Chief Justice Warren, and by Justice Douglas are omitted.]

MR. JUSTICE CLARK, concurring.

With reference to the lineup point involved in this case I cannot, for the life of me, see why a lineup is not a critical stage of the prosecution. Identification of the suspect—a prerequisite to establishment of guilt—occurs at this stage, and with Miranda v. Arizona, 384 U.S. 436 (1966), on the books, the requirement of the presence of counsel arises, unless waived by the suspect. I dissented in *Miranda* but I am bound by it now, as we all are. * * *

MR. JUSTICE BLACK, dissenting in part and concurring in part.

* * *

The Court in Part I of its opinion rejects Wade's Fifth Amendment contention. From that I dissent. [See the discussion of this point in Chapter Three.] In Parts II–IV of its opinion, the Court sustains Wade's claim of denial of right to counsel in the out-of-court lineup, and in that I concur. * * * I would reverse the Court of Appeals' reversal of Wade's conviction, but I would not remand for further proceedings. Since the prosecution did not use the out-of-court lineup identification against Wade at his trial, I believe the conviction should be affirmed.

* * *

MR. JUSTICE WHITE, whom MR. JUSTICE HARLAN and MR. JUSTICE STEWART join, dissenting in part and concurring in part.

The Court has again propounded a broad constitutional rule barring use of a wide spectrum of relevant and probative evidence, solely because a step in its ascertainment or discovery occurs outside the presence of defense counsel. This was the approach of the Court in Miranda v. Arizona. I objected then to what I thought was an uncritical and doctrinaire approach without satisfactory factual foundation. * * *

The Court's opinion is far-reaching. It proceeds first by creating a new *per se* rule of constitutional law: a criminal suspect cannot be subjected to a pretrial identification process in the absence of his counsel without violating the Sixth Amendment. * * *

The rule applies to any lineup, to any other techniques employed to produce an identification and *a fortiori* to a face-to-face encounter between the witness and the suspect alone, regardless of when the identification occurs, in time or place, and whether before or after indictment or information. It matters not how well the witness knows the suspect, whether the witness is the suspect's mother, brother, or long-time associate, and no matter how long or well the witness observed the perpetrator at the scene of the crime. The kidnap victim who has lived for days with his abductor is in the same category as the witness who has had only a fleeting glimpse of the criminal. Neither may identify the suspect without defendant's counsel being present. The same strictures apply regardless of the number of other witnesses who positively identify the defendant and regardless of the corroborative evidence showing that it was the defendant who had committed the crime.

* * * The Court apparently believes that improper police procedures are so widespread that a broad prophylactic rule must be laid down, requiring the presence of counsel at all pretrial identifications, in order to detect recurring instances of police misconduct. I do not share this pervasive distrust of all official investigations. None of the materials the Court relies upon supports it. Certainly, I would bow to solid fact, but the Court quite obviously does not have before it any reliable, comprehensive survey of current police practices on which to base its new rule. Until it does, the Court should avoid excluding relevant evidence from state criminal trials.

* * *

Note

It is important to understand exactly what the result in *Wade* was. Clearly, the lineup was improper because of the absence of counsel, substitute counsel, or waiver of counsel. But, when Wade was tried, the lineup was not mentioned by the prosecution; its results were not a part of the evidence until brought up by the defense in cross-examination. Thus, the controlling question was whether the in-court identification was tainted by the unconstitutional lineup—i.e., whether the in-court identification, which the prosecutor used, would have been made had there been no lineup. The Court placed any "blame" for mentioning the lineup on the defense.

Evidence of an out-of-court identification, offered for its truth, was hearsay not subject to any exception at the time of the federal trial in *Wade.* Thus, the prosecution made no use of the prior identification until the defense "opened the door." A federal prosecutor would no longer be so constrained, since Rule 801(d)(1)(C) of the Federal Rules of Evidence provides for admissibility of prior identifications as "not hearsay" when the person who made the identification is "subject to cross-examination." In Gilbert v. California, 388 U.S. 263 (1967), one of the companion cases to *Wade,* the out-of-court identification made in the absence of counsel was admitted in the prosecution's case-in-chief under a state hearsay exception. Gilbert was convicted of armed bank robbery and the murder of a police officer who entered the bank during the course of the robbery. At the time of the challenged identification procedure, Gilbert had been indicted. Justice Brennan, writing for the Court, described the circumstances of the identification as follows:

> Three eyewitnesses to the Alhambra crimes who identified Gilbert at the guilt stage of the trial had observed him at a lineup conducted without notice to his counsel in a Los Angeles auditorium 16 days after his indictment and after appointment of counsel. The manager of the apartment house in which incriminating evidence was found, and in which Gilbert allegedly resided, identified Gilbert in the courtroom and also testified, in substance, to her prior lineup identification on examination by the State. Eight witnesses who identified him in the courtroom at the penalty stage were not eyewitnesses to the Alhambra crimes but to other robberies allegedly committed by him. In addition to their in-court identifications, these witnesses also testified that they identified Gilbert at the same lineup.
>
> The lineup was on a stage behind bright lights which prevented those in the line from seeing the audience. Upwards of 100 persons were in the audience, each an eyewitness to one of the several robberies charged to Gilbert.

In a footnote, Justice Brennan stated that doubtful witnesses were allowed to call Gilbert out of the line-up to make him repeat a phrase in a particular way or to walk in a particular way. He also stated that the witnesses talked to each other at some point, and that they made their identifications in each other's presence.

As in *Wade,* the Court held that the in-court identifications would be excluded unless they proceeded from a source independent of the tainted identification, such as a substantial opportunity to view the perpetrator at the time of the crime. As in *Wade,* the Court remanded for an independent source determination. However, as to the use of the out-of-court identification as evidence, the Court adopted a per se rule of exclusion. Justice Brennan explained as follows:

> Quite different considerations are involved as to the admission of the testimony of the manager of the apartment house at the guilt phase and of the eight witnesses at the penalty stage that they identified Gilbert at the lineup. That testimony is the direct result of the illegal lineup "come at by exploitation of [the primary] illegality." The State is therefore not entitled to an opportunity to show that that testimony had an independent source. Only a *per se* exclusionary rule as to such testimony can be an effective sanction to assure that law enforcement authorities will respect the accused's constitutional right to the presence of his counsel at the critical lineup. In the absence of legislative regulations adequate to avoid the hazards to a fair trial which inhere in lineups as presently conducted, the desirability of deterring the constitutionally objectionable practice must prevail over the undesirability of excluding relevant evidence. That conclusion is buttressed by the consideration that the witness' testimony of his lineup identification will enhance the impact of his in-court identification on the jury and seriously aggravate whatever derogation exists of the accused's right to a fair trial.

Without doubt, the Court in *Wade* and *Gilbert* was concerned about inadequate identification procedures and the lasting effect they may have in some cases. But did the Court fashion a suitable remedy for the problems it identified? The Court's remedy is criticized in Read, Lawyers at Lineups: Constitutional Necessity or Avoidable Extravagance, 17 U.C.L.A.L.Rev. 339, 362–367 (1969). Read makes the following arguments: *Wade* viewed counsel as essentially an observer, i.e., a passive participant. A passive observer is unlikely to be able to improve the quality of lineups. If the defendant is not a very good witness in a hearing on a lineup because of obvious bias, his lawyer is likely to be almost as biased and thus no better a witness. Moreover, various recording devices would recreate the lineup more effectively than testimony by participants. And counsel is no more schooled than other participants in psychology and may be insensitive to lineup conditions that might be prejudicial to a defendant.

The presence of a lawyer at a lineup might do some good, however. Even a passive observer is not barred from making suggestions to police and prosecutors. A lawyer who is used to bargaining with law enforcement officials may be able to persuade them as to the unfairness of some lineups. Moreover, knowledge that a lawyer is present may tend to make officials more careful. Lawyers may not be trained psychologists, but they should know the kinds of suggestive factors that make lineups vulnerable and can urge case law on police and prosecutors. Even without formal interdisciplinary training, lawyers may be careful listeners and should be able to identify certain forms of suggestiveness—e.g., leading questions to witnesses. Finally, jurors may be suspicious of a defendant's lawyer describing a lineup, but the jury might believe the lawyer if he has taken notes, or pictures, and if other persons do not dispute some of the things that the lawyer describes.

If the lawyer is inclined to be active, what can she do that will not work against her client's interests by calling attention to the client? If the lawyer is too passive, does she risk waiving her client's rights? Compare Gilligan, Eyewitness Identification, 58 Mil.L.Rev. 183, 201 (1972) with Panel Discussion, The Role of the Defense Lawyer at a Line-up in Light of the *Wade, Gilbert* and *Stovall* Decisions, 4 Crim.L.Bull. 273, 290 (1968).[2] Does the passive role demean the defense lawyer?

2. *The Burger Court and the Right to Counsel*

KIRBY v. ILLINOIS

Supreme Court of the United States, 1972.
406 U.S. 682.

MR. JUSTICE STEWART announced the judgment of the Court and an opinion in which THE CHIEF JUSTICE, MR. JUSTICE BLACKMUN, and MR. JUSTICE REHNQUIST join.

* * * In the present case we are asked to extend the *Wade-Gilbert per se* exclusionary rule to identification testimony based upon a police station show-up that took place *before* the defendant had been indicted or otherwise formally charged with any criminal offense.

On February 21, 1968, a man named Willie Shard reported to the Chicago police that the previous day two men had robbed him on a Chicago street of a wallet containing, among other things, traveler's checks and a Social Security card. On February 22, two police officers stopped the petitioner and a companion, Ralph Bean, on West Madison Street in Chicago. When asked for identification, the petitioner produced a wallet that contained three traveler's checks and a Social Security card, all bearing the name of Willie Shard. Papers with Shard's name on them were also found in Bean's possession. When asked to explain his possession of Shard's property, the petitioner first said that the traveler's checks were "play money," and then told the officers that he had won them in a crap game. The officers then arrested the petitioner and Bean and took them to a police station.

Only after arriving at the police station, and checking the records there, did the arresting officers learn of the Shard robbery. A police car was then dispatched to Shard's place of employment, where it picked up Shard and brought him to the police station. Immediately upon entering the room in the police station where the petitioner and Bean were seated at a table, Shard positively identified them as the men who had robbed him two days earlier. No lawyer was present in the room, and neither the petitioner nor Bean had asked for legal assistance, or been advised of any right to the presence of counsel.

More than six weeks later, the petitioner and Bean were indicted for the robbery of Willie Shard. Upon arraignment, counsel was appointed to represent them, and they pleaded not guilty. A pretrial motion to suppress Shard's identification testimony was denied, and at the trial Shard testified as a witness for the prosecution. In his testimony he described his identification of the two men at the police station on February 22, and identified them again in the courtroom as the men who had robbed him on February 20. He was cross-examined at length regarding the circumstances of his identification of the two defendants. The jury found both defendants guilty, and the petitioner's conviction was affirmed on appeal. * * *

I

* * *

2. See also ALI Model Code of Pre-Arraignment Procedure, Commentary to § 160.

In a line of constitutional cases in this Court stemming back to the Court's landmark opinion in Powell v. Alabama, 287 U.S. 45, it has been firmly established that a person's Sixth and Fourteenth Amendment right to counsel attaches only at or after the time that adversary judicial proceedings have been initiated against him.

This is not to say that a defendant in a criminal case has a constitutional right to counsel only at the trial itself. The *Powell* case makes clear that the right attaches at the time of arraignment, and the Court has recently held that it exists also at the time of a preliminary hearing. But the point is that, while members of the Court have differed as to existence of the right to counsel in the contexts of some of the above cases, *all* of those cases have involved points of time at or after the initiation of adversary judicial criminal proceedings—whether by way of formal charge, preliminary hearing, indictment, information, or arraignment.

* * *

The initiation of judicial criminal proceedings is far from a mere formalism. It is the starting point of our whole system of adversary criminal justice. For it is only then that the government has committed itself to prosecute, and only then that the adverse positions of government and defendant have solidified. It is then that a defendant finds himself faced with the prosecutorial forces of organized society, and immersed in the intricacies of substantive and procedural criminal law. It is this point, therefore, that marks the commencement of the "criminal prosecutions" to which alone the explicit guarantees of the Sixth Amendment are applicable.

In this case we are asked to import into a routine police investigation an absolute constitutional guarantee historically and rationally applicable only after the onset of formal prosecutorial proceedings. We decline to do so. Less than a year after *Wade* and *Gilbert* were decided, the Court explained the rule of those decisions as follows: "The rationale of those cases was that an accused is entitled to counsel at any 'critical stage of the *prosecution,*' and that a post-indictment lineup is such a 'critical stage.'" (Emphasis supplied.) Simmons v. United States, 390 U.S. 377, 382–383. * * *

II

What has been said is not to suggest that there may not be occasions during the course of a criminal investigation when the police do abuse identification procedures. Such abuses are not beyond the reach of the Constitution. As the Court pointed out in *Wade* itself, it is always necessary to "scrutinize *any* pretrial confrontation * * *." The Due Process Clause of the Fifth and Fourteenth Amendments forbids a lineup that is unnecessarily suggestive and conducive to irreparable mistaken identification. * * *

MR. CHIEF JUSTICE BURGER, concurring.

I agree that the right to counsel attaches as soon as criminal charges are formally made against an accused and he becomes the subject of a "criminal prosecution." Therefore, I join in the plurality opinion and in the judgment.

MR. JUSTICE POWELL, concurring in the result.

As I would not extend the *Wade-Gilbert per se* exclusionary rule, I concur in the result reached by the Court.

MR. JUSTICE BRENNAN with whom MR. JUSTICE DOUGLAS and MR. JUSTICE MARSHALL join, dissenting.

* * *

While it should go without saying, it appears necessary, in view of the plurality opinion today, to re-emphasize that

Wade did not require the presence of counsel at pretrial confrontations for identification purposes simply on the basis of an abstract consideration of the words "criminal prosecutions" in the Sixth Amendment. Counsel is required at those confrontations because "the dangers inherent in eyewitness identification and the suggestibility inherent in the context of the pretrial identification," mean that protection must be afforded to the "most basic right [of] a criminal defendant—his right to a fair trial at which the witnesses against him might be meaningfully cross-examined." * * * Hence, "the initiation of adversary judicial criminal proceedings," is completely irrelevant to whether counsel is necessary at a pretrial confrontation for identification in order to safeguard the accused's constitutional rights to confrontation and the effective assistance of counsel at his trial.

* * *

Wade and *Gilbert,* of course, happened to involve post-indictment confrontations. Yet even a cursory perusal of the opinions in those cases reveals that nothing at all turned upon that particular circumstance. In short, it is fair to conclude that rather than "declin[ing] to depart from [the] rationale" of *Wade* and *Gilbert,* the plurality today, albeit purporting to be engaged in "principled constitutional adjudication," refuses even to recognize that "rationale." For my part, I do not agree that we "extend" *Wade* and *Gilbert,* by holding that the principles of those cases apply to confrontations for identification conducted after arrest. Because Shard testified at trial about his identification of petitioner at the police station showup, the exclusionary rule of *Gilbert* requires reversal.

MR. JUSTICE WHITE, dissenting.

United States v. Wade and Gilbert v. California govern this case and compel reversal of the judgment below.

Note

It helps to remember that *Kirby* states that "[t]he Due Process Clause of the Fifth and Fourteenth Amendments forbids a lineup that is unnecessarily suggestive and conducive to irreparable mistaken identification." To discover whether *Kirby* was meant to gut *Wade* or to restate *Wade's* invitation to law enforcement officials to develop alternatives to counsel, it is necessary to examine the Court's approach to controlling suggestiveness in showups at which counsel for the accused is not provided. The cases examining claims of "unnecessary suggestiveness" are examined in the next section.

As a practical matter, the Court in *Kirby* must have been concerned with the implications of extending the *Wade* right to counsel rule to all or virtually all identifications. Many identifications are made on the street only minutes after the event. Application of the *Wade* rule in these circumstances obviously presents problems; the delay resulting from waiting for counsel to arrive may perversely decrease the reliability of the identification due to the fading memory of witnesses. In light of these problems, the result in *Kirby* is understandable, so long as the Due Process Clause provides meaningful protection against mistaken identifications in cases where the *Wade* rule does not apply. As we will see, though, this has not been the case.

The vast majority of identification procedures are conducted before a formal charge has been filed. Indeed they are conducted to obtain evidence with which to bring a formal charge. Thus, *Kirby* strips *Wade* of significant practical effect. Does *Kirby* create an incentive for the government to delay an indictment in order to conduct an identification in the absence of counsel? Does a suspect have a constitutional right to be indicted at a certain point? Courts have stated that if adversary proceedings are "deliberately delayed" in order to evade the *Wade* rule, the resulting identification will be invalidated. See U.S. ex rel. Burbank v. Warden, 535 F.2d 361 (7th Cir.1976). However, proving that an indictment was deliberately delayed is difficult, to say the least. See United States ex rel. Hall v. Lane, 804 F.2d 79 (7th Cir.1986) (no evidence that delay was caused by bad faith).

In United States v. Ash, 413 U.S. 300 (1973), the Court again restricted the *Wade* rule, and held that a defendant has no right to counsel at a photographic identification, whether conducted before or after indictment or formal charge. Justice Blackmun's majority opinion described the right to counsel as a defendant's right to have a spokesperson or advisor. Since an accused is not present at a photographic display, the Court concluded that no advisor or spokesperson is necessary. Little attention was paid by the majority to the dangers of eyewitness identification considered in *Wade.* Rather, the Court focused on the presence of the defendant. Justice Stewart concurred only in the result, because he concluded that "[a] photographic identification is quite different from a lineup, for there are substantially fewer possibilities of impermissible suggestion when photographs are used, and those unfair influences can be readily reconstructed at trial." 413 U.S. at 324. Professor Grano, in *Kirby, Biggers,* and *Ash*: Do Any Constitutional Safeguards Remain Against the Danger of Protecting the Innocent?, 72 Mich.L.Rev. 717 (1974), argues that each of Justice Stewart's assertions is subject to challenge and suggests that there are myriad possibilities of suggestiveness in photographic identifications.

Ash may be one signal that the Court now is concerned with eliminating only the worst kind of suggestiveness, not in assuring that eyewitness identification is as reliable as it might be. This majority simply refused to squarely address the question whether counsel is necessary to prevent the kind of suggestion that worried the *Wade* and *Gilbert* Courts.

B. UNNECESSARY SUGGESTIVENESS

1. *The Foundations of a Due Process Test*

On the same day that it decided *Wade* and *Gilbert,* the Court made it clear that those decisions applied prospectively only. Stovall v. Denno, 388 U.S. 293 (1967). The Court in *Stovall* held that a due process-fundamental fairness approach would be used in assessing identification procedures that were not governed by *Wade* and *Gilbert.* This approach has continuing relevance, even though *Stovall* dealt specifically with identifications occurring before the date that *Wade* and *Gilbert* were decided. As stated above, after *Kirby* and *Ash,* the application of *Wade* and *Gilbert* is limited to post-indictment corporeal identifications. The due process test set forth in *Stovall,* and developed in later cases discussed below, will govern the admissibility of most identification evidence. Justice Brennan, again writing for the Court, described the relevant facts in *Stovall*:

> Dr. Paul Behrendt was stabbed to death in the kitchen of his home in Garden City, Long Island, about midnight August 23, 1961. Dr. Behrendt's wife, also a physician, had followed her husband to the kitchen and jumped at the assailant. He knocked her to the floor and stabbed her 11 times. The police found a shirt on the kitchen floor and keys in a pocket which they traced to petitioner. They arrested him on the afternoon of August 24. An arraign-

ment was promptly held but was postponed until petitioner could retain counsel.

Mrs. Behrendt was hospitalized for major surgery to save her life. The police, without affording petitioner time to retain counsel, arranged with her surgeon to permit them to bring petitioner to her hospital room about noon of August 25, the day after the surgery. Petitioner was handcuffed to one of five police officers who, with two members of the staff of the District Attorney, brought him to the hospital room. Petitioner was the only Negro in the room. Mrs. Behrendt identified him from her hospital bed after being asked by an officer whether he "was the man" and after petitioner repeated at the direction of an officer a "few words for voice identification." None of the witnesses could recall the words that were used. Mrs. Behrendt and the officers testified at the trial to her identification of the petitioner in the hospital room, and she also made an in-court identification of petitioner in the courtroom.

Petitioner was convicted and sentenced to death. * * *

After holding that *Wade* and *Gilbert* would not be retroactively applied, the Court considered Stovall's contention that "in any event the confrontation conducted in this case was so unnecessarily suggestive and conducive to irreparable mistaken identification that he was denied due process of law." Justice Brennan analyzed this question by focussing on whether it was necessary for the police to act as they did.

The practice of showing suspects singly to persons for the purpose of identification, and not as part of a lineup, has been widely condemned. However, a claimed violation of due process of law in the conduct of a confrontation depends on the totality of the circumstances surrounding it, and the record in the present case reveals that the showing of Stovall to Mrs. Behrendt in an immediate hospital confrontation was imperative. The Court of Appeals, *en banc,* stated, 355 F.2d, at 735,

> "Here was the only person in the world who could possibly exonerate Stovall. Her words, and only her words, 'He is not the man' could have resulted in freedom for Stovall. The hospital was not far distant from the courthouse and jail. No one knew how long Mrs. Behrendt might live. Faced with the responsibility of identifying the attacker, with the need for immediate action and with the knowledge that Mrs. Behrendt could not visit the jail, the police followed the only feasible procedure and took Stovall to the hospital room. Under these circumstances, the usual police station line-up, which Stovall now argues he should have had, was out of the question."

Note that the Court in *Stovall* did not mention the possible unreliability of the identification, even though Stovall was handcuffed and was the only African-American man in the room. Does the Court mean that even unreliable identifications are constitutionally admissible so long as the police have a legitimate excuse for conducting a suggestive identification? Conversely, if the police had no good reason for acting as they did, would the Court then be concerned about whether the identification was reliable? One reading of *Stovall* is that the actual reliability of the identification is irrelevant; the only question is whether the police engaged in impermissible suggestion (which would result in automatic exclusion of the identification), or whether they had an excuse (which would result in automatic admissibility of the identification). Another reading is that the Court simply did not focus on how police suggestiveness could or could not affect the reliability of an identification, and that this question was left for another day. These issues resurface in Manson v. Brathwaite, infra.

Note that Mrs. Behrendt, the witness who made the identification in *Stovall,* survived her attack and testified at trial. Of course, her survival is a happy event; but could this lead you to question whether there was really such an emergency as to excuse the suggestive activity in *Stovall?* Also note that part of the reason the police activity was held permissible is that this was the only procedure that could have resulted in freedom for Stovall. But if that is the case, why not let Stovall decide whether he wants to be subject to a show-up identification in handcuffs? If Stovall had been given the option to exonerate himself in this way, what do you think he would have done?

Cases arise from time to time in which the government argues that there was a legitimate excuse for conducting a suggestive identification procedure. Usually these claims are rebuffed. For example, in Neil v. Biggers, 409 U.S. 188 (1972), defendant was identified in a one-on-one showup. The government offered as an excuse that the officers checked the city jail and the juvenile home and found no one at either place fitting the defendant's "unusual physical description." The Court stated that it was "inclined to agree with the courts below that the police did not exhaust all possibilities in seeking persons physically comparable to respondent." Similarly, in United States v. Drougas, 748 F.2d 8 (1st Cir.1984), a government witness was shown pictures of the defendant "and asked if he could identify the locations of the resorts depicted therein." The ostensible purpose of this identification was to ascertain whether the defendant was likely to flee (and where he was likely to flee to) if he were set free on bail. The pictures showed the defendant at a motel swimming pool with a cement deck and several palm trees. There was no evidence that the government witness had ever been to a tropical location. The witness identified the person in the pictures as the defendant, but could not identify the locations. The court held that the government's purported excuse for conducting a suggestive photo identification "stretches credulity." Yet in both *Biggers* and *Drougas,* the identifications were held admissible even though the police had engaged in impermissible suggestiveness. The following materials discuss how this could be so.

2. *Reaffirming the Due Process Approach*

In Simmons v. United States, 390 U.S. 377 (1968), a Chicago Savings and Loan Association was robbed by two men. Police learned from a bank employee that one of the men was seen in a car with a conspicuous dent. Police located a car matching the employee's description and as a result of investigation they began to suspect one Andrews, and an FBI search of his mother's home revealed evidence suggesting a connection with the robbery. From Andrews' sister the FBI obtained pictures of Andrews and of Simmons, because the sister said Andrews and Simmons were together when the bank was robbed. Bank employees identified Simmons as one of the robbers. At trial, the same employees identified Simmons, but the government did not elicit testimony about the photo identifications. Simmons argued that the identification procedure was unfair.

The FBI had shown the bank employees at least six pictures, mostly group photos of Andrews, Simmons and others, and some individual snapshots of

Simmons and Andrews. The Court recognized the danger of suggestive procedures and noted that a procedure is suggestive if it involves only one person or if one person's picture is repeated and others are not. It also observed that a suggestive identification might have a lasting effect. But, the Court declined to prohibit the use of photographic techniques, and preferred a totality of the circumstances test. "[W]e hold that each case must be considered on its own facts, and that convictions based on eyewitness identification at trial following a pretrial identification by photograph will be set aside on that ground only if the photographic identification procedure was so impermissibly suggestive as to give rise to a very substantial likelihood of irreparable misidentification."

Emphasizing the government's need for fast action, the fact that the witnesses had difficulty picking out Andrews (none identified him outside of court, although he appeared as prominently as Simmons in the photos) but no such problem with Simmons, the excellent opportunity the witnesses had to observe the robbery, and the short period of time that passed between robbery and identification, the Court found no due process violation "even though the identification procedure employed may have in some respects fallen short of the ideal."

In Foster v. California, 394 U.S. 440 (1969), the Court found for the first and so far only time that a police procedure was so impermissibly suggestive as to create a substantial risk of mistaken identification. The eyewitness was called to the station to view a three-person lineup. Foster, who was six feet tall, was placed between two men who were both six inches shorter. Only Foster wore a jacket similar to that of the perpetrator. The witness could not positively identify Foster. Foster was then brought into an office for a one-on-one showup. The witness could still not make a positive identification. A week later, the witness viewed a second line-up. Only Foster remained from the first line-up. At this point, the witness positively identified Foster. This identification was admitted at trial pursuant to the California hearsay exception discussed in *Gilbert.* The Supreme Court stated that the "suggestive elements in this identification procedure made it all but inevitable that [the witness] would identify petitioner whether or not he was in fact the man," and that the procedure "so undermined the reliability of the eyewitness identification as to violate due process."

3. *Weakening the Foundations*

In Neil v. Biggers, 409 U.S. 188 (1972), the defendant was convicted of rape, after the victim identified him at trial and described her earlier out-of-court identification. The latter was of concern to the Supreme Court. For seven months after the rape, the victim viewed lineups, one person showups, and photographs, but was unable to identify her assailant. One day the police arrested the defendant on an unrelated charge. They brought the victim to the police station, walked the defendant past her, and directed the defendant to utter certain words. The victim identified the defendant. Justice Powell's opinion for the Court stated "that the primary evil to be avoided is 'a very substantial likelihood of irreparable misidentification.'" He concluded that "[w]hile the phrase [in the inner quotes] was coined as a standard for determining whether an in-court identification would be admissible in the wake of a suggestive out-of-court identification, with the deletion of 'irreparable' it serves equally well as a standard for the admissibility of testimony concerning the out-of-court identification itself."

Justice Powell posed the question whether "unnecessary suggestiveness alone requires the exclusion of evidence" but he avoided answering it by saying that the only purpose of an affirmative answer "would be to deter the police from using a less reliable procedure where a more reliable one may be available." He concluded that such deterrence could not work where, as here, the lineup preceded *Stovall.* Thus, the question was whether the identification was reliable "even though the confrontation procedure was suggestive." On the facts, the Court found that the police suggestiveness did not cause the identification to be made, and therefore "the identification was reliable even though the confrontation procedure was suggestive." Essentially the Court found that the witness had an independent source for the identification:

> The victim spent a considerable period of time with her assailant, up to half an hour. She was with him under adequate artificial light in her house and under a full moon outdoors, and at least twice, once in the house and later in the woods, faced him directly and intimately. She was no casual observer, but rather the victim of one of the most personally humiliating of all crimes. Her description to the police, which included the assailant's approximate age, height, weight, complexion, skin texture, build, and voice, might not have satisfied Proust but was more than ordinarily thorough. She had 'no doubt' that respondent was the person who raped her. * * * The victim here, a practical nurse by profession, had an unusual opportunity to observe and identify her assailant. She testified * * * that there was something about his face 'I don't think I could ever forget.'
>
> There was, to be sure, a lapse of seven months between the rape and the confrontation. This would be a serious negative factor in most cases. Here, however, the testimony is undisputed that the victim made no previous identification at any of the showups, lineups, or photographic showings.

Thus, the question for admissibility under the Due Process Clause is whether the witness had a picture of the defendant in his mind *before* the police suggestiveness occurred, and whether that suggestiveness altered that picture in any way. To determine this question, a court must investigate how clear the witness' pre-identification picture was; this is determined by such factors as how good a look the witness got at the time of or before the crime, how attentive the witness was, and whether memory loss has faded the picture in the witness' mind by the time of the identification. Inferences are drawn about the clarity of the picture in the witness' mind by descriptions given by the witness, by whether the witness has mistakenly identified another person as the criminal, and by the certainty of the witness at the time the defendant is identified. Against all these factors, a court must look at the suggestive tactics used by the police and determine how likely they were to have had an effect on this witness. After *Biggers,* police suggestiveness is not the predominant inquiry that it may have appeared to be in *Stovall.* Rather, it is only one factor among the totality of circumstances to be considered. The following case makes this clear.

4. *Shifting the Emphasis of the Due Process Test*

MANSON v. BRATHWAITE

Supreme Court of the United States, 1977.
432 U.S. 98.

MR. JUSTICE BLACKMUN delivered the opinion of the Court.

This case presents the issue as to whether the Due Process Clause of the Fourteenth Amendment compels the exclusion, in a state criminal trial, apart from any consideration of reliability, of pretrial identification evidence obtained by a police procedure that was both suggestive and unnecessary. This Court's decisions in Stovall v. Denno and Neil v. Biggers are particularly implicated.

I

Jimmy D. Glover, a full-time trooper of the Connecticut State Police, in 1970 was assigned to the Narcotics Division in an undercover capacity. On May 5 of that year, about 7:45 p.m., e.d.t., and while there was still daylight, Glover and Henry Alton Brown, an informant, went to an apartment building at 201 Westland, in Hartford, for the purpose of purchasing narcotics from "Dickie Boy" Cicero, a known narcotics dealer. Cicero, it was thought, lived on the third floor of that apartment building. Glover and Brown entered the building, observed by backup Officers D'Onofrio and Gaffey, and proceeded by stairs to the third floor. Glover knocked at the door of one of the two apartments served by the stairway. The area was illuminated by natural light from a window in the third floor hallway. The door was opened 12 to 18 inches in response to the knock. Glover observed a man standing at the door and, behind him, a woman. Brown identified himself. Glover then asked for "two things" of narcotics. The man at the door held out his hand, and Glover gave him two $10 bills. The door closed. Soon the man returned and handed Glover two glassine bags. While the door was open, Glover stood within two feet of the person from whom he made the purchase and observed his face. Five to seven minutes elapsed from the time the door first opened until it closed the second time.

Glover and Brown then left the building. This was about eight minutes after their arrival. Glover drove to headquarters where he described the seller to D'Onofrio and Gaffey. Glover at that time did not know the identity of the seller. He described him as being "a colored man, approximately five feet eleven inches tall, dark complexion, black hair, short Afro style, and having high cheekbones, and of heavy build. He was wearing at the time blue pants and a plaid shirt." D'Onofrio, suspecting from this description that respondent might be the seller, obtained a photograph of respondent from the Records Division of the Hartford Police Department. He left it at Glover's office. D'Onofrio was not acquainted with respondent personally, but did know him by sight and had seen him "[s]everal times" prior to May 5. Glover, when alone, viewed the photograph for the first time upon his return to headquarters on May 7; he identified the person shown as the one from whom he had purchased the narcotics.

* * *

Respondent was charged, in a two-count information, with possession and sale of heroin * * *. At his trial in January 1971, the photograph from which Glover had identified respondent was received in evidence without objection on the part of the defense. Glover also testified that, although he had not seen respondent in the eight months that had elapsed since the sale, "there [was] no doubt whatsoever" in his mind that the person shown on the photograph was respondent. Glover also made a positive in-court identification without objection.

No explanation was offered by the prosecution for the failure to utilize a photographic array or to conduct a line-up.

* * *

The jury found respondent guilty on both counts of the information. * * *

[The Court discusses its precedents, all of which have been discussed, supra.]

II

* * *

Biggers well might be seen to provide an unambiguous answer to the question before us: the admission of testimony concerning a suggestive and unnecessary identification procedure does not violate due process so long as the identification possesses sufficient aspects of reliability.[a] In one passage, however, the Court observed that the challenged procedure occurred pre-*Stovall* and that a strict rule would make little sense with regard to a confrontation that preceded the Court's first indication that a suggestive procedure might lead to the exclusion of evidence. One perhaps might argue that by implication, the Court suggested that a different rule could apply post-*Stovall.* The question before us, then, is simply whether the *Biggers* analysis applies to post-*Stovall* confrontations as well as to those pre-*Stovall.*

[The Court discussed the District Court's and the Court of Appeals' opinions in the habeas corpus proceeding that ultimately reached the High Court.]

IV

Petitioner at the outset acknowledges that "the procedure in the instant case was suggestive [because only one photograph was used] and unnecessary" [because there was no emergency or exigent circumstance]. The respondent, in agreement with the Court of Appeals, proposes a *per se* rule of exclusion that he claims is dictated by the demands of the Fourteenth Amendment's guarantee of due process. He rightly observes that this is the first case in which this Court has had occasion to rule upon strictly post-*Stovall* out-of-court identification evidence of the challenged kind.

Since the decision in *Biggers,* the Courts of Appeals appear to have developed at least two approaches to such evidence. The first, or *per se* approach, employed by the Second Circuit in the

a. Mr. Justice Marshall argues in dissent that our cases have "established two different due process tests for two very different situations." Pretrial identifications are to be covered by *Stovall,* which is said to require exclusion of evidence concerning unnecessarily suggestive pretrial identifications without regard to reliability. In-court identifications, on the other hand, are to be governed by *Simmons* and admissibility turns on reliability. The Court's cases are sorted into one category or the other. *Biggers,* which clearly adopts the reliability of the identification as the guiding factor in the admissibility of both pretrial and in-court identifications, is condemned for mixing the two lines and for adopting a uniform rule.

Although it must be acknowledged that our cases are not uniform in their emphasis, they hardly suggest the formal structure the dissent would impose on them. If our cases truly established two different rules, one might expect at some point at least passing reference to the fact. There is none. And if *Biggers* departed so grievously from the past cases, it is surprising that there was not at least some mention of the point in Mr. Justice Brennan's dissent. In fact, the cases are not so readily sorted as the dissent suggests. Although *Foster* involved both in-court and out-of-court identifications, the Court seemed to apply only a single standard for both. * * * Thus, *Biggers* is not properly seen as a departure from the past cases, but as a synthesis of them.

present case, focuses on the procedures employed and requires exclusion of the out-of-court identification evidence, without regard to reliability, whenever it has been obtained through unnecessarily suggestive confrontation procedures.[b] The justifications advanced are the elimination of evidence of uncertain reliability, deterrence of the police and prosecutors, and the stated "fair assurance against the awful risks of misidentification."

The second, or more lenient, approach is one that continues to rely on the totality of the circumstances. It permits the admission of the confrontation evidence if, despite the suggestive aspect, the out-of-court identification possesses certain features of reliability. Its adherents feel that the *per se* approach is not mandated by the Due Process Clause of the Fourteenth Amendment. This second approach, in contrast to the other, is *ad hoc* and serves to limit the societal costs imposed by a sanction that excludes relevant evidence from consideration and evaluation by the trier of fact. See United States ex rel. Kirby v. Sturges, 510 F.2d 397, 407–408 (CA7) (opinion by Judge, now Mr. Justice, Stevens).

Mr. Justice Stevens, in writing for the Seventh Circuit in *Kirby,* supra, observed: "There is surprising unanimity among scholars in regarding such a rule [the *per se* approach] as essential to avoid serious risk of miscarriage of justice." He pointed out that well-known federal judges have taken the position that "evidence of, or derived from, a showup identification should be inadmissible unless the prosecutor can justify his failure to use a more reliable identification procedure." Indeed, the ALI Model Code of Pre-Arraignment Procedure §§ 160.1 and 160.2 (1975) (hereafter Model Code) frowns upon the use of a showup or the display of only a single photograph.

The respondent here stresses the same theme and the need for deterrence of improper identification practice, a factor he regards as pre-eminent. Photographic identification, it is said, continues to be needlessly employed. He notes that the legislative regulation "the Court had hoped *Wade* would engender," has not been forthcoming. He argues that a totality rule cannot be expected to have a significant deterrent impact; only a strict rule of exclusion will have direct and immediate impact on law enforcement agents. Identification evidence is so convincing to the jury that sweeping exclusionary rules are required. Fairness of the trial is threatened by suggestive confrontation evidence, and thus, it is said, an exclusionary rule has an established constitutional predicate.

There are, of course, several interests to be considered and taken into account. The driving force behind United States v. Wade and Gilbert v. California (right to counsel at a post-indictment lineup), and *Stovall,* all decided on the same day, was the Court's concern with the problems of eyewitness identification. Usually the witness must testify about an encounter with a total stranger under circumstances of emergency or emotional stress. The witness' recollection of the stranger can be distorted easily by the circumstances or by later actions of the police. Thus, *Wade* and its companion cases reflect the concern that the jury not hear eyewitness testimony unless that evidence has aspects of reliability. It must be observed

b. Although the *per se* approach demands the exclusion of testimony concerning unnecessarily suggestive identifications, it does permit the admission of testimony concerning a subsequent identification, including an in-court identification, if the subsequent identification is determined to be reliable. 527 F.2d, at 367. The totality approach, in contrast, is simpler: if the challenged identification is reliable, then testimony as to it and any identification in its wake is admissible.

that both approaches before us are responsive to this concern. The *per se* rule, however, goes too far since its application automatically and peremptorily, and without consideration of alleviating factors, keeps evidence from the jury that is reliable and relevant.

The second factor is deterrence. Although the *per se* approach has the more significant deterrent effect, the totality approach also has an influence on police behavior. The police will guard against unnecessarily suggestive procedures under the totality rule, as well as the *per se* one, for fear that their actions will lead to the exclusion of identifications as unreliable.

The third factor is the effect on the administration of justice. Here the *per se* approach suffers serious drawbacks. Since it denies the trier reliable evidence, it may result, on occasion, in the guilty going free. Also, because of its rigidity, the *per se* approach may make error by the trial judge more likely than the totality approach. And in those cases in which the admission of identification evidence is error under the *per se* approach but not under the totality approach—cases in which the identification is reliable despite an unnecessarily suggestive identification procedure—reversal is a Draconian sanction. Certainly, inflexible rules of exclusion, that may frustrate rather than promote justice, have not been viewed recently by this Court with unlimited enthusiasm.

* * *

We therefore conclude that reliability is the linchpin in determining the admissibility of identification testimony for both pre- and post-*Stovall* confrontations. The factors to be considered are set out in *Biggers.* These include the opportunity of the witness to view the criminal at the time of the crime, the witness' degree of attention, the accuracy of his prior description of the criminal, the level of certainty demonstrated at the confrontation, and the time between the crime and the confrontation. Against these factors is to be weighed the corrupting effect of the suggestive identification itself.

V

We turn, then, to the facts of this case and apply the analysis:

1. The opportunity to view. Glover testified that for two to three minutes he stood at the apartment door, within two feet of the respondent. The door opened twice, and each time the man stood at the door. The moments passed, the conversation took place, and payment was made. Glover looked directly at his vendor. It was near sunset, to be sure, but the sun had not yet set, so it was not dark or even dusk or twilight. Natural light from outside entered the hallway through a window. There was natural light, as well, from inside the apartment.

2. The degree of attention. Glover was not a casual or passing observer, as is so often the case with eyewitness identification. Trooper Glover was a trained police officer on duty—and specialized and dangerous duty—when he called at the third floor of 201 Westland in Hartford on May 5, 1970. Glover himself was a Negro and unlikely to perceive only general features of "hundreds of Hartford black males," as the Court of Appeals stated. It is true that Glover's duty was that of ferreting out narcotics offenders and that he would be expected in his work to produce results. But it is also true that, as a specially trained, assigned, and experienced officer, he could be expected to pay scrupulous attention to detail, for he knew that subsequently he would have to find and arrest his vendor. In addition, he knew that his claimed observations would be subject later to close scrutiny and examination at any trial.

3. The accuracy of the description. Glover's description was given to D'Onofrio within minutes after the transaction. It included the vendor's race, his height, his build, the color and style of his hair, and the high cheekbone facial feature. It also included clothing the vendor wore. No claim has been made that respondent did not possess the physical characteristics so described. D'Onofrio reacted positively at once. Two days later, when Glover was alone, he viewed the photograph D'Onofrio produced and identified its subject as the narcotics seller.

4. The witness' level of certainty. There is no dispute that the photograph in question was that of respondent. Glover, in response to a question whether the photograph was that of the person from whom he made the purchase, testified: "There is no question whatsoever." This positive assurance was repeated.

5. The time between the crime and the confrontation. Glover's description of his vendor was given to D'Onofrio within minutes of the crime. The photographic identification took place only two days later. We do not have here the passage of weeks or months between the crime and the viewing of the photograph.

These indicators of Glover's ability to make an accurate identification are hardly outweighed by the corrupting effect of the challenged identification itself. Although identifications arising from single-photograph displays may be viewed in general with suspicion, we find in the instant case little pressure on the witness to acquiesce in the suggestion that such a display entails. D'Onofrio had left the photograph at Glover's office and was not present when Glover first viewed it two days after the event. There thus was little urgency and Glover could view the photograph at his leisure. And since Glover examined the photograph alone, there was no coercive pressure to make an identification arising from the presence of another. The identification was made in circumstances allowing care and reflection.

Although it plays no part in our analysis, all this assurance as to the reliability of the identification is hardly undermined by the facts that respondent was arrested in the very apartment where the sale had taken place, and that he acknowledged his frequent visits to that apartment.

Surely, we cannot say that under all the circumstances of this case there is "a very substantial likelihood of irreparable misidentification." Short of that point, such evidence is for the jury to weigh. We are content to rely upon the good sense and judgment of American juries, for evidence with some element of untrustworthiness is customary grist for the jury mill. Juries are not so susceptible that they cannot measure intelligently the weight of identification testimony that has some questionable feature.

Of course, it would have been better had D'Onofrio presented Glover with a photographic array including "so far as practicable * * * a reasonable number of persons similar to any person then suspected whose likeness is included in the array." Model Code § 160.-2(2). The use of that procedure would have enhanced the force of the identification at trial and would have avoided the risk that the evidence would be excluded as unreliable. But we are not disposed to view D'Onofrio's failure as one of constitutional dimension to be enforced by a rigorous and unbending exclusionary rule. The defect, if there be one, goes to weight and not to substance.

We conclude that the criteria laid down in *Biggers* are to be applied in determining the admissibility of evidence offered by the prosecution concerning a post-*Stovall* identification, and that those criteria are satisfactorily met and complied with here.

* * *

MR. JUSTICE STEVENS, concurring.

While I join the Court's opinion, I would emphasize two points.

First, as I indicated in my opinion in United States ex rel. Kirby v. Sturges, 510 F.2d 397, 405–406 (CA7 1975), the arguments in favor of fashioning new rules to minimize the danger of convicting the innocent on the basis of unreliable eyewitness testimony carry substantial force. Nevertheless, for the reasons stated in that opinion, as well as those stated by the Court today, I am persuaded that this rulemaking function can be performed "more effectively by the legislative process than by a somewhat clumsy judicial fiat," and that the Federal Constitution does not foreclose experimentation by the States in the development of such rules.

Second, in evaluating the admissibility of particular identification testimony it is sometimes difficult to put other evidence of guilt entirely to one side. Mr. Justice Blackmun's opinion for the Court carefully avoids this pitfall and correctly relies only on appropriate indicia of the reliability of the identification itself. Although I consider the factual question in this case extremely close, I am persuaded that the Court has resolved it properly.

MR. JUSTICE MARSHALL, with whom MR. JUSTICE BRENNAN joins, dissenting.

Today's decision can come as no surprise to those who have been watching the Court dismantle the protections against mistaken eyewitness testimony erected a decade ago * * *. But it is still distressing to see the Court virtually ignore the teaching of experience embodied in those decisions and blindly uphold the conviction of a defendant who may well be innocent.

I

The magnitude of the Court's error can be seen by analyzing the cases in the *Wade* trilogy and the decisions following it. [The dissent analyzes the precedents previously discussed.]

* * * *Stovall* and *Simmons* established two different due process tests for two very different situations. Where the prosecution sought to use evidence of a questionable pretrial identification, *Stovall* required its exclusion, because due process had been violated by the confrontation, unless the necessity for the unduly suggestive procedure outweighed its potential for generating an irreparably mistaken identification. The *Simmons* test, on the other hand, was directed to ascertaining due process violations in the introduction of in-court identification testimony that the defendant claimed was tainted by pretrial procedures. In the latter situation, a court could consider the reliability of the identification under all the circumstances.

* * *

The Court inexplicably seemed to erase the distinction between *Stovall* and *Simmons* situations in Neil v. Biggers. In *Biggers* there was a pretrial confrontation that was clearly both suggestive and unnecessary. Evidence of this, together with an in-court identification, was admitted at trial. *Biggers* was, in short, a case plainly cast in the *Stovall* mold. Yet the Court, without explanation or apparent recognition of the distinction, applied the *Simmons* test. The Court stated "that the primary evil to be avoided is 'a very substantial likelihood of irreparable misidentification.' * * * It is the likelihood of misidentification which violates a defendant's right to due process * * *." While this statement accurately describes the lesson of *Simmons,* it plainly ignores the teaching of *Stovall* and *Foster* that an unnecessarily suggestive pretrial confrontation itself violates due process.

But the Court did not simply disregard the due process analysis of *Stovall.* It went on to take the *Simmons* standard for assessing the constitutionality of an in-court identification—" 'a very substantial likelihood of irreparable misidentification' "—and transform it into the "standard for the admissibility of testimony concerning [an] out-of-court identification." It did so by deleting the word "irreparable" from the *Simmons* formulation. This metamorphosis could be accomplished, however, only by ignoring the fact that *Stovall,* fortified only months earlier by Kirby v. Illinois, had established a test for precisely the same situation that focused on the need for the suggestive procedure. It is not surprising that commentators almost unanimously mourned the demise of *Stovall* in the *Biggers* decision.

II

* * * [I]n determining the admissibility of the post-*Stovall* identification in this case, the Court considers two alternatives, a *per se* exclusionary rule and a totality-of-the-circumstances approach. The Court weighs three factors in deciding that the totality approach, which is essentially the test used in *Biggers,* should be applied. In my view, the Court wrongly evaluates the impact of these factors.

First, the Court acknowledges that one of the factors, deterrence of police use of unnecessarily suggestive identification procedures, favors the *per se* rule. Indeed, it does so heavily, for such a rule would make it unquestionably clear to the police they must never use a suggestive procedure when a fairer alternative is available. I have no doubt that conduct would quickly conform to the rule.

Second, the Court gives passing consideration to the dangers of eyewitness identification recognized in the *Wade* trilogy. It concludes, however, that the grave risk of error does not justify adoption of the *per se* approach because that would too often result in exclusion of relevant evidence. In my view, this conclusion totally ignores the lessons of *Wade.* * * *

Finally, the Court errs in its assessment of the relative impact of the two approaches on the administration of justice. * * *

First, the *per se* rule here is not "inflexible." Where evidence is suppressed, for example, as the fruit of an unlawful search, it may well be forever lost to the prosecution. Identification evidence, however, can by its very nature be readily and effectively reproduced. The in-court identification, permitted under *Wade* and *Simmons* if it has a source independent of an uncounseled or suggestive procedure, is one example. Similarly, when a prosecuting attorney learns that there has been a suggestive confrontation, he can easily arrange another lineup conducted under scrupulously fair conditions. * * *

Second, other exclusionary rules have been criticized for preventing jury consideration of relevant and usually reliable evidence in order to serve interests unrelated to guilt or innocence, such as discouraging illegal searches or denial of counsel. Suggestively obtained eyewitness testimony is excluded, in contrast, precisely because of its unreliability and concomitant irrelevance. Its exclusion both protects the integrity of the truth-seeking function of the trial and discourages police use of needlessly inaccurate and ineffective investigatory methods.

* * *

III

Despite my strong disagreement with the Court over the proper standards to be applied in this case, I am pleased that its application of the totality test does recognize the continuing vitality of *Stovall.* In assessing the reliability of the identification, the Court mandates weighing "the corrupting effect of the suggestive identification itself" against the "indicators of [a witness'] ability to make an accurate identification." The Court holds, as Neil v. Biggers failed to, that a due process identification inquiry must take account of the suggestiveness of a confrontation and the likelihood that it led to misidentification, as recognized in *Stovall* and *Wade.* Thus, even if a witness did have an otherwise adequate opportunity to view a criminal, the later use of a highly suggestive identification procedure can render his testimony inadmissible. Indeed, it is my view that, assuming applicability of the totality test enunciated by the Court, the facts of the present case require that result.

I consider first the opportunity that Officer Glover had to view the suspect. Careful review of the record shows that he could see the heroin seller only for the time it took to speak three sentences of four or five short words, to hand over some money, and later after the door reopened, to receive the drugs in return. The entire face-to-face transaction could have taken as little as 15 or 20 seconds. But during this time, Glover's attention was not focused exclusively on the seller's face. He observed that the door was opened 12 to 18 inches, that there was a window in the room behind the door, and, most importantly, that there was a woman standing behind the man. Glover was, of course, also concentrating on the details of the transaction—he must have looked away from the seller's face to hand him the money and receive the drugs. The observation during the conversation thus may have been as brief as 5 or 10 seconds.

As the Court notes, Glover was a police officer trained in and attentive to the need for making accurate identifications. Nevertheless, both common sense and scholarly study indicate that while a trained observer such as a police officer "is somewhat less likely to make an erroneous identification than the average untrained observer, the mere fact that he has been so trained is no guarantee that he is correct in a specific case. This identification testimony should be scrutinized just as carefully as that of the normal witness." * * *

Another factor on which the Court relies—the witness' degree of certainty in making the identification—is worthless as an indicator that he is correct. Even if Glover had been unsure initially about his identification of respondent's picture, by the time he was called at trial to present a key piece of evidence for the State that paid his salary, it is impossible to imagine his responding negatively to such questions as "is there any doubt in your mind whatsoever" that the identification was correct. * * *

Next, the Court finds that because the identification procedure took place two days after the crime, its reliability is enhanced. While such temporal proximity makes the identification more reliable than one occurring months later, the fact is that the greatest memory loss occurs within hours after an event. After that, the dropoff continues much more slowly. Thus, the reliability of an identification is increased only if it was made within several hours of the crime. If the time gap is any greater, reliability necessarily decreases.

Finally, the Court makes much of the fact that Glover gave a description of the seller to D'Onofrio shortly after the incident. Despite the Court's assertion that because "Glover himself was a Negro and unlikely to perceive only general features of 'hundreds of Hartford black males,' as the Court of Appeals stated," the description given by Glover was actually no more than a general summary of the seller's appearance. We may discount entirely the seller's clothing, for that was of no significance later in the proceeding. Indeed, to the extent that Glover noticed clothes, his attention was diverted from the seller's face. Otherwise, Glover merely described vaguely the seller's height, skin color, hairstyle, and build. He did say that the seller had "high cheekbones," but there is no other mention of facial features, nor even an estimate of age. Conspicuously absent is any indication that the seller was a native of the West Indies, certainly something which a member of the black community could immediately recognize from both appearance and accent.

From all of this, I must conclude that the evidence of Glover's ability to make an accurate identification is far weaker than the Court finds it. In contrast, the procedure used to identify respondent was both extraordinarily suggestive and strongly conducive to error. * * *

* * *

Note

In Part II of the dissent, the *per se* rule rejected by the majority is defended. But does the dissent ever make clear what the *per se* rule really requires? No test that purports to focus on the reliability of an identification can entirely avoid looking at the identification procedure(s) used—e.g., blindfolding the witness and suggesting that the witness identify lineup participant number 3 (the suspect) is not likely to be acceptable, even after *Manson*. Is there any reason to believe, however, that very much attention will be paid to the identification procedures outside of the cases that shock the conscience? Uelman, Testing the Assumptions of Neil v. Biggers: An Experiment in Eyewitness Identification, 16 Crim.L.Bull. 358 (1980), questions the validity of the assumptions that the Court made in *Neil* and *Manson* in finding suggestive procedures reliable.

If the out-of-court identification is excluded after *Manson,* can the witness identify the defendant in court? Recall that under *Wade,* the witness could make an in-court identification if it was free from the taint of the line-up conducted in the absence of counsel. But if the prior identification was caused by police suggestiveness, as required for exclusion after *Manson* (and as distinguished from a counsel-free line-up which may not have changed the picture of the perpetrator in the witness' mind) there can by definition be no independent source for the in-court identification. If there were an independent source, then the out-of-court identification itself would be admissible. See Marsden v. Moore, 847 F.2d 1536 (11th Cir.1988) (single photograph procedure creates substantial risk of mistaken identification where witness had only a fleeting glimpse of the perpetrator two years before the identification; in-court identification must be excluded as well); Dispensa v. Lynaugh, 847 F.2d 211 (5th Cir.1988) (identification caused by police suggestiveness requires exclusion of both in-court and out-of-court identification).

In evaluating who has the better of the argument in *Manson,* consider the following hypothetical. A victim of a kidnapping, who lived in close quarters with the perpetrator for six months, finally escapes. He contacts the police and describes the kidnapper in perfect detail, including a distinctive scar on the kidnapper's forehead. The defendant is apprehended, and the victim sees him in a one-on-one showup. He has the distinctive scar described by the victim. The victim immediately identifies the defendant with absolute certainty. The police had no reason for failing to conduct a line-up. Under the *per se* rule rejected in *Manson,* this identification would be inadmissible; but the in-court identification would be admissible because it proceeded from an independent source. Does this make sense? One could argue that it does since otherwise police will not be deterred from conducting suggestive identifications. Moreover, the cost of exclusion to the state is not significant because the in-court identification will still be admissible, and the police could always conduct a line-up *after* this suggestive procedure. The identification from that subsequent line-up, like the in-court identification, would proceed from an independent source and would therefore be admissible. But if the rule of exclusion can be so easily evaded, is it worth having? If the line-up would be *pro forma* in these circumstances, does it make sense to require one?

Ultimately, the question is whether the *per se* rule would be a more effective deterrent than the totality of circumstances test chosen by the Court. There is certainly strong evidence that the *Manson* test, at least as applied by the courts, does little to deter the police from using suggestive identification procedures. For example, the Court has denounced the use of showups in most of the cases you have read. Yet, in 1990, the court in Rodriguez v. Young, 906 F.2d 1153 (7th Cir.), noted with distress "that we continue to review cases both of showups and other suggestive procedures," and that "in few of these cases do we ever find an explanation, by the prosecution, for the failure to conduct a lineup." Of course, the court in *Rodriguez* held that the identification was admissible despite the police suggestiveness, so it will undoubtedly be hearing more such cases in the future.

Recall that *Stovall* implied that if police suggestiveness was *permissible,* an identification could be admitted even if it were unreliable. But after *Manson,* reliability is the "linchpin." Does that mean that defendants can actually benefit from application of the *Manson* test in cases where the police have a good excuse for a suggestive procedure? Some courts have said yes. In United States v. Bouthot, 878 F.2d 1506 (1st Cir.1989), the witness was called by a district attorney at a parallel trial, and saw defendant in the courtroom. He based his identification in defendant's trial on that meeting. The government argued that the identification should be admitted because "there was no impermissibly suggestive identification procedure conducted by the government." The court relied on *Manson* and rejected this argument.

> Because the due process focus in the identification context is on the fairness of the trial and not exclusively on police deterrence, it follows that federal courts should scrutinize all suggestive identification procedures, not just those orchestrated by the police, to determine if they would sufficiently taint the trial so as to deprive the defendant of due process.

See also Thigpen v. Cory, 804 F.2d 893 (6th Cir.1986) citing *Biggers,* and stating that "the deterrence of police misconduct is not the basic purpose for excluding identification evidence" and that "only the effects of, and not the causes for, pre-identification encounters should be determinative of whether the confrontations were suggestive." Do these cases mean that an in-court identification cannot be made if the witness bases it on having seen the defendant alone on the street a week after the crime, or if he had seen the defendant driving by in the back of a police car? If so, the Court may want to re-think the implications of the totality of circumstances test.

Watkins v. Sowders, 449 U.S. 341 (1981), holds, 7–2, that a trial judge need not hold a hearing outside the presence of jurors whenever a defendant claims that a witness' identification was arrived at improperly. The Court said that cross-examination of the witness within the hearing of the jury is a valid way of eliciting the facts surrounding the identification and may supply a basis for the decision on admissibility. The Court did say that "[i]n some circumstances, not presented here, such a determination [outside the jury's hearing] may be constitutionally necessary," but did not elaborate. In the two companion cases before the Court, the out-of-court identification procedures were held to be constitutionally valid by lower courts. Thus, the cases did not present the question whether, once a jury had heard about an eyewitness identification that was subsequently held to be invalid, a simple instruction to disregard the particular eyewitness identification (or the in-court testimony if that were required) would be sufficient protection for a defendant. The question not reached by the majority most concerned the dissenters.

C. THE CURRENT STATE OF THE LAW

1. *Judicial Attitudes*

It should be clear that, for better or worse, after *Kirby, Ash, Neil,* and *Manson,* many courts are not very careful in their handling of eyewitness evidence.

Consider for example violations of *Wade* and *Gilbert.* Remember that those cases are still good law, at least in post-formal charge lineups. Moore v. Illinois, 434 U.S. 220 (1977), makes this clear[3] in applying *Gilbert* to an identification at a preliminary hearing when the defendant had no lawyer. Even when *Wade* and *Gilbert* govern, courts have liberally applied the independent source approach "to overcome almost any deficiency that exists at an identification confrontation." Trapp, Pretrial Identification Confrontation, 45 Miss.L.J. 489, 507 (1974). For some representative cases, see Commentary to § 160.7 of the ALI Model Code of Pre-Arraignment Procedure, at 455. Invocation of the harmless error rule is another way for courts to avoid reversing convictions because of *Wade* and *Gilbert* problems. Id. at 457–58. See also United States ex rel. Moore v. Illinois, 577 F.2d 411 (7th Cir. 1978). But see Kampshoff v. Smith, 698 F.2d 581 (2d Cir. 1983). When *Wade* and *Gilbert* do not apply, many lower courts view *Manson* as an invitation to ignore suggestiveness.

In United States v. Marchand, 564 F.2d 983 (2d Cir. 1977), the Court affirmed a conviction for possession of a large quantity of marijuana. A witness was shown 15 photos, two of which were of the same suspect. No other person's picture was repeated. There was a delay of 8 months between the witness' grand jury testimony and his identification. And there was little information before the Court to explain why an indictment was not handed down against Marchand earlier, in which case a lineup, rather than a photo

3. *Moore* establishes that *Wade* extends to all post-charge identifications of the suspect's person. Some lower court cases indicate that *Wade* extends to "the entire post-indictment lineup, including the witness' response stage." State v. McGhee, 350 So.2d 370 (La.1977) (but court recognized some federal decisions rejecting per se rule). Accord, People v. Williams, 3 Cal.3d 853, 92 Cal.Rptr. 6, 478 P.2d 942 (1971). But see United States v. Rich, 580 F.2d 929 (9th Cir. 1978); United States v. Banks, 485 F.2d 545 (5th Cir. 1973); United States v. Cunningham, 423 F.2d 1269 (4th Cir. 1970). In general *Wade* does not apply to an identification for a crime not yet formally charged to a defendant, even though the defendant is in custody. See, e.g., United States ex rel. Hall v. Lane, 804 F.2d 79 (7th Cir. 1986). When *Wade* does apply, it will not be satisfied by the presence of counsel for someone else, when counsel is not seeking to protect the interests of the formally charged suspect. See United States ex rel. Burton v. Cuyler, 439 F.Supp. 1173 (E.D.Pa.1977).

State v. Mitchell, 593 S.W.2d 280 (Tenn. 1980), held that a bail hearing was the beginning of the formal adjudicatory process and the right to counsel attached during any identification attempt.

identification procedure, could have been used.[4] In the same case there was evidence that an agent may have been highly suggestive in dealing with a second witness. Yet, the message of the Court was that "even impermissible suggestiveness is not a per se bar to the receipt of a photographic identification." The same court upheld a conviction in Haberstroh v. Montanye, 493 F.2d 483 (2d Cir. 1974), even though the identification procedure involved just three photos, only one of which resembled the description of the robber. The Court found no sufficient likelihood of misidentification.

Archuleta v. Kirby, 864 F.2d 709 (10th Cir.1989) is another example of current judicial attitudes toward identification evidence. Two men were eating in a restaurant when they saw a man break the window of their van with a tire iron. The van was parked across the street. The witnesses ran out of the restaurant, and one of them chased the perpetrator; when that witness and the perpetrator were about ten feet apart, the witness got an unobstructed look at the man's face. The witness lost the man after a two minute chase. The police arrived and the witnesses gave descriptions; the witness who chased the perpetrator described him as 5′9″, hispanic, with a mustache; the other witness said the man was 5′7″. Based on these descriptions, the police detained Archuleta and brought him back to the scene of the crime thirty minutes after the incident. The police displayed Archuleta to both witnesses while he was in the back of the police car, handcuffed. Both witnesses made a positive identification. The state conceded that the identification procedure was unnecessarily suggestive. Balancing the five *Manson* factors against the "corruptive effect" of the identification procedure, the court found: (1) both witnesses had "ample opportunity to view the criminal;" (2) the attention of both witnesses was focussed on the criminal, as evidenced by their ability to describe him; (3) while the witnesses overestimated Archuleta's height and did not tell the police that he had distinctive tattoos, "these appear to be minor errors;" (4) the witnesses were very certain about their identification; and (5) the identification occurred within a very short interval of time. The court cited cases in which identifications made over a year after the crime had been upheld.

How important is it that the witness is certain about an identification? The court in Rodriguez v. Young, 906 F.2d 1153 (7th Cir.1990) had this to say about the certainty factor:

> We are skeptical about equating certainty with reliability. Determinations of the reliability suggested by a witness's certainty after the use of suggestive procedures are complicated by the possibility that the certainty may reflect the corrupting effect of the suggestive procedures themselves. Also, the most certain witnesses are not invariably the most reliable ones. We consider certainty a relevant factor but consider it warily.

How important is the witness' character in determining whether police suggestiveness caused the witness to make an unreliable identification? Consider United States ex rel. Hudson v. Brierton, 699 F.2d 917 (7th Cir.1983), where a witness pursued armed bank robbers, and engaged in a high speed chase through city streets, while one of the robbers was shooting at him. For a part of the chase, the witness' car was within seven inches of the robbers' car. Eventually, the witness lost the robbers. The witness was later called down to

4. For a discussion of the advantages of a lineup, see Egan, Pittner & Goldstein, Eyewitness Identification Photographs v. Live Models, 1 L. & Human Behav. 199 (1977).

the police station, and identified the defendant while he was handcuffed in a jail cell. The court found that this impermissible suggestiveness did not cause a mistaken identification. It noted that the witness had an opportunity to view the defendant at close quarters; he had a desire to seek out and retain an image of the defendant, because he knew that he would be a witness at a later criminal trial; he had not given a prior description, but this was just one factor; the witness was certain; and the identification was made within a few hours after the event. Most important for the court, however, was the character of the witness. The court found it extremely unlikely that the witness "would be affected by the suggestive identification procedure in light of his serious attitude and diligence with respect to the episode."

Occasionally, a court will find the police procedure so suggestive, and the witness' pre-identification picture so vague, that the identification must be excluded under the due process clause. An example is United States v. Watkins, 741 F.2d 692 (5th Cir.1984). After a post office was robbed, Watkins was rounded up, and brought to the post office in a patrol car, handcuffed. He was viewed by those who had been in the post office at the time of the robbery. One witness identified the defendant at trial on the basis of the showup. The court found that the witness had no independent source for making the identification.

> Barbara Pollett had very little opportunity to view the robber; she was lying face down on the floor for all but a few seconds of the robbery and the assailant wore a stocking mask. There is no evidence that she was specially trained to observe people for later identification. Her description of the assailant immediately after the robbery related only to general size, body build, race, and clothing. * * * The only factor supporting reliability is the short span of time between the robbery and the showup. But taken as a whole, the overall factors suggest a substantial likelihood of misidentification.

The court found the error to be harmless.

If it is difficult in most cases and impossible in some cases to know the extent to which suggestive procedures corrupt the identification process, does Kirby v. Illinois make sense? Does Manson v. Brathwaite?[5]

2. *The Effect of Identification Procedures on Trials*

Some of the defects in pre-trial lineups may even have an impact on trials aside from possibly tainting identification evidence. If the government uses "mug shots" in a photo identification, the suggestion to the witness will be that the mug shot reflects a prior criminal record of the person photographed. This

5. The difficulty in deciding when an identification is insufficiently reliable after suggestiveness has occurred is evident in Graham v. Solem, 728 F.2d 1533 (8th Cir.1984) (en banc). A rape victim identified Graham as one of her attackers after three pretrial identification events. Nine days after the rape, police drove her to a construction site where Graham worked, and she stated that Graham bore a resemblance to the attacker but she could not be sure he was the man. Later the same day, police took the victim to an auto garage shop where a group of men were standing around, and she picked Graham out of the group, saying she was 90 per cent sure he was the attacker. Finally, the police took her to view Graham in a detention center in a one-on-one showup conducted through a glass door. The South Dakota Supreme Court found that the subsequent in-court identification by the victim was reliable. State v. Reiman, 284 N.W.2d 860 (S.D.1979), but a federal district judge granted Graham habeas corpus relief. Ultimately, the court of appeals reversed by a 5–4 vote.

may not be so bad before trial, if all the photos are mug shots. But if the photo identification is mentioned by the prosecution's witnesses and its reliability is challenged during trial by the defense, the government will offer the photographs as evidence. At this point the jury will learn that the defendant has a prior record, even though evidence rules often exclude this evidence as highly prejudicial. See Fed.R.Evid. 404(b); 609. Although the courts will balance the need for the evidence against its possible prejudicial effect, see United States v. Fosher, 568 F.2d 207 (1st Cir. 1978), in many cases the photos will be admitted. See, e.g., United States v. Stevens, 935 F.2d 1380 (3d Cir. 1991) (submitting "wanted board," with which defendant was identified, to the jury, was permissible under Federal Rule 403 even though others on the board were violent felons and defendant had no record of violent activity: "Allowing the jury to inspect the board in its unaltered condition would permit the jurors to determine what, if anything, drew the victims' attention to Stevens"). But see United States v. Torres-Flores, 827 F.2d 1031 (5th Cir. 1987) (introduction of book of mug shots held reversible error where government did not take easy steps to redact inflammatory material from the book). Compare United States v. McCoy, 848 F.2d 743 (6th Cir. 1988) (introducing mug shots prohibited by Rule 403 where the defendant never challenged the suggestiveness of the identification, and therefore did not "open the door"). Thus, the defendant identified by mug shot may have to choose between challenging the identification and protecting against disclosure of a prior record.

3. *Voice Identification*

Aside from the minimal scrutiny of lineups, show-ups and photographic identifications that courts provide, little attention is paid to related problems. Most courts do not yet require, for example, that more than one voice be used in voice identification procedures. One court, in rejecting the claim that voice identifications must be made in a nonsuggestive atmosphere, resembling lineup conditions, said that "[t]he due process procedure urged by appellant would, if generally applied, make a mockery of the new Federal Rules of Evidence." United States v. Albergo, 539 F.2d 860 (2d Cir. 1976). Why this should be the case is inexplicable. Fed.R.Evid. 901(b)(5) suggests that voice identifications can be made by a person who has heard the voice on any occasion; it says nothing about identification procedures. Most courts do use the eyewitness standards for voice identification. See, e.g., United States v. Pheaster, 544 F.2d 353 (9th Cir. 1976).[6] But even this may not be adequate, since it is not necessarily true that voice identifications present exactly the same problems as visual identifications. More fundamentally, the *Manson* test gives only minimal protection against police suggestiveness for any identification procedure whether by sight or voice. For example, in United States v. Patton, 721 F.2d 159 (6th Cir. 1983), the defendant was charged with making threatening phone calls. The witness identified the defendant's voice at a pretrial "show-up." The court held that the *Manson* test "applies with full force to aural identification." But then the court found that the show-up had not caused a mistaken identification. Applying the *Manson* factors, the court concluded that the

6. For an interesting case on voice identification in which Manson v. Brathwaite was deemed applicable and an out-of-court identification was suppressed, see State v. Pendergrass, 586 P.2d 691 (Mont.1978).

witness had an opportunity to hear the defendant's voice during four phone calls; that the witness was attentive to these calls, as evidenced by her description of their content; that the time between the crime and the voice "show-up" was only three weeks; and that, upon hearing the defendant's voice at the "show-up" the witness "immediately recoiled, instantly recognizing the voice." Is the likelihood of mistaken identification any greater with voice identifications than with visual identifications?

Chapter Five

THE RIGHT TO COUNSEL

I. THE BACKGROUND

The Sixth Amendment provides that "[i]n all criminal prosecutions, the accused shall enjoy the right * * * to have the Assistance of Counsel for his defence." The right to counsel embodied in the Amendment deviated from the English common law practice at the time of the American Revolution. Under English law, an accused had a right to have counsel in misdemeanor, but not felony, cases. Although Parliament granted special treatment to those accused under the Treason Act of 1695, and required the court to appoint counsel upon the request of the accused, in ordinary felony cases the defendant was not permitted to have counsel until 1836.[1] Despite the absence of a right to counsel, in practice English courts frequently allowed counsel to argue points of law and to assume other defense functions.[2]

When the Constitution was adopted, twelve of the thirteen original states had rejected the English common law rule and had fully recognized the right to counsel in criminal prosecutions. Powell v. Alabama, 287 U.S. 45, 64–65 (1932). Adoption of the Sixth Amendment formalized and perpetuated the elimination of the prohibition of counsel at criminal trials. It built upon the Judiciary Act of 1789, which was signed the day before the Sixth Amendment was proposed by both houses of Congress. Section 35 provided that "in all courts of the United States the parties may plead and manage their own causes personally or by the assistance of such counsel or attorneys at law as by the rules of the said courts respectively shall be permitted to manage and conduct cases therein." [3] Hence, it conveyed the idea that the right to counsel was a grant of privilege and not a requirement that counsel be appointed. This can be contrasted with the Federal Crimes Act of 1790, which imposed a statutory *duty* on federal courts in capital cases to assign counsel. 1 Stat. 118 (1790). Although no statute required appointment of counsel in noncapital cases and no one originally read the Sixth Amendment as so requiring, the practice developed of appointing counsel for indigents in serious federal cases.[4]

1. See Faretta v. California, 422 U.S. 806, 821–826 (1975); W. Beaney, The Right to Counsel in American Courts 8–15 (1955); F. Heller, The Sixth Amendment (1951); Holtzoff, The Right of Counsel Under the Sixth Amendment, 20 N.Y.U.L.Rev. 1–22 (1944).

2. W. Beaney, supra note 1, at 9–11.

3. Judiciary Act of 1789, § 35, 1 Stat. 73 (1789).

4. Before 1938, some courts would appoint counsel for indigents, but the practice was not uniform. See W. Beaney, supra note 1, at 29–33; Holtzoff, supra note 1, at 8.

In Johnson v. Zerbst, 304 U.S. 458 (1938), the Court gave new meaning to the Sixth Amendment by holding that the Amendment requires counsel in federal court in all criminal proceedings, unless the defendant waives the assistance of counsel. The Court viewed counsel as a jurisdictional prerequisite to a federal court's authority to deprive an accused of life or liberty.

The right to counsel in state prosecutions for many years was determined exclusively by state law. In 1932, even before Johnson v. Zerbst, supra, the famous "Scottsboro Case" raised the question of whether a failure to make an effective appointment of counsel to indigent defendants in a capital case could deprive the defendants of their rights without due process.

The right to counsel is important in many stages of the criminal process. This is already apparent from the previous chapters. The *Massiah* rule, for example, governed attempts to elicit statements from an accused following an indictment or other formal charge. And the *Wade* and *Gilbert* rules governing lineups following a formal charge also involved a right to counsel. The chapters that follow this one involve the decision to bring formal charges against a suspect, the treatment of the suspect while charges are pending, trials and guilty pleas, and post-trial procedures. Counsel is important in most of the stages of the criminal process that will be examined. At some point it is useful to look at the development of the right to counsel. That look is provided in this chapter. The discussion of counsel here is limited to establishing how the right to counsel developed and to examining the stages of the process to which the right extends. In Chapter Ten, which covers trial rights, the right to counsel at trial is more extensively examined. The doctrine of effective assistance will be discussed there, along with the right of self-representation.

II. THE EARLY DEVELOPMENT OF THE RIGHT

POWELL v. ALABAMA

Supreme Court of the United States, 1932.
287 U.S. 45.

MR. JUSTICE SUTHERLAND delivered the opinion of the Court.

These cases were argued together and submitted for decision as one case.

The petitioners, hereinafter referred to as defendants, are negroes charged with the crime of rape, committed upon the persons of two white girls. The crime is said to have been committed on March 25, 1931. The indictment was returned in a state court of first instance on March 31, and the record recites that on the same day the defendants were arraigned and entered pleas of not guilty. There is a further recital to the effect that upon the arraignment they were represented by counsel. But no counsel had been employed, and aside from a statement made by the trial judge several days later during a colloquy immediately preceding the trial, the record does not disclose when, or under what circumstances, an appointment of counsel was made, or who was appointed. During the colloquy referred to, the trial judge, in response to a question, said that he had appointed all the members of the bar for the purpose of arraigning the defendants and then of course anticipated that the members of the bar would continue to help the defendants if no counsel appeared. Upon the argument here both sides accepted that as a correct statement of the facts concerning the matter.

There was a severance upon the request of the state, and the defendants were tried in three several groups, as indicated above. * * * Each of the three trials was completed within a single day. Under the Alabama statute the punishment for rape is to be fixed by the jury, and in its discretion may be from ten years imprisonment to death. The juries found defendants guilty and imposed the death penalty upon all. * * *

* * *

The record shows that on the day when the offense is said to have been committed, these defendants, together with a number of other negroes, were upon a freight train on its way through Alabama. On the same train were seven white boys and the two white girls. A fight took place between the negroes and the white boys, in the course of which the white boys, with the exception of one named Gilley, were thrown off the train. A message was sent ahead, reporting the fight and asking that every negro be gotten off the train. The participants in the fight, and the two girls, were in an open gondola car. The two girls testified that each of them was assaulted by six different negroes in turn, and they identified the seven defendants as having been among the number. None of the white boys was called to testify, with the exception of Gilley, who was called in rebuttal.

Before the train reached Scottsboro, Alabama, a sheriff's posse seized the defendants and two other negroes. Both girls and the negroes then were taken to Scottsboro, the county seat. Word of their coming and of the alleged assault had preceded them, and they were met at Scottsboro by a large crowd. It does not sufficiently appear that the defendants were seriously threatened with, or that they were actually in danger of, mob violence; but it does appear that the attitude of the community was one of great hostility. The sheriff thought it necessary to call for the militia to assist in safeguarding the prisoners. * * * Soldiers took the defendants to Gadsden for safekeeping, brought them back to Scottsboro for arraignment, returned them to Gadsden for safekeeping while awaiting trial, escorted them to Scottsboro for trial a few days later, and guarded the court house and grounds at every stage of the proceedings. It is perfectly apparent that the proceedings, from beginning to end, took place in an atmosphere of tense, hostile and excited public sentiment. During the entire time, the defendants were closely confined or were under military guard. The record does not disclose their ages, except that one of them was nineteen; but the record clearly indicates that most, if not all, of them were youthful, and they are constantly referred to as "the boys." They were ignorant and illiterate. All of them were residents of other states, where alone [sic] members of their families or friends resided.

* * *

[First.] * * *

It is hardly necessary to say that, the right to counsel being conceded, a defendant should be afforded a fair opportunity to secure counsel of his own choice. Not only was that not done here, but such designation of counsel as was attempted was either so indefinite or so close upon the trial as to amount to a denial of effective and substantial aid in that regard. [The Court reviewed the record, which revealed that an out-of-state lawyer agreed to assist "all the members of the bar" who were appointed to represent the defendants. The out-of-stater did not know Alabama law and was unwilling to take over the case.]

It thus will be seen that until the very morning of the trial no lawyer had been named or definitely designated to represent the defendants. Prior to that time, the trial judge had "appointed all the members of the bar" for the limited "purpose of arraigning the defendants." Whether they would represent the defendants thereafter if no counsel appeared in their behalf, was a matter of speculation only, or, as the judge indicated, of mere anticipation on the part of the court. Such a designation, even if made for all purposes, would, in our opinion, have fallen far short of meeting, in any proper sense, a requirement for the appointment of counsel. How many lawyers were members of the bar does not appear; but, in the very nature of things, whether many or few, they would not, thus collectively named, have been given that clear appreciation of responsibility or impressed with that individual sense of duty which should and naturally would accompany the appointment of a selected member of the bar, specifically named and assigned.

[T]his action of the trial judge in respect of appointment of counsel was little more than an expansive gesture, imposing no substantial or definite obligation upon any one * * *. [The Court noted that, prior to the calling of the case for trial, a leading member of the local bar agreed to be employed to help the prosecution. Also during pretrial preparations defendants "did not have the aid of counsel in any real sense."]

The defendants, young, ignorant, illiterate, surrounded by hostile sentiment, haled back and forth under guard of soldiers, charged with an atrocious crime regarded with especial horror in the community where they were to be tried, were thus put in peril of their lives within a few moments after counsel for the first time charged with any degree of responsibility began to represent them.

It is not enough to assume that counsel thus precipitated into the case thought there was no defense, and exercised their best judgment in proceeding to trial without preparation. Neither they nor the court could say what a prompt and thoroughgoing investigation might disclose as to the facts. No attempt was made to investigate. No opportunity to do so was given. Defendants were immediately hurried to trial. * * * Under the circumstances disclosed, we hold that defendants were not accorded the right of counsel in any substantial sense.

* * *

[The Court cited numerous state decisions which supported its conclusion, and noted that legitimate concerns with prompt disposition of criminal cases do not justify eliminating any opportunity for counsel to prepare for trial.]

Second. The Constitution of Alabama provides that in all criminal prosecutions the accused shall enjoy the right to have the assistance of counsel; and a state statute requires the court in a capital case, where the defendant is unable to employ counsel, to appoint counsel for him. The state supreme court held that these provisions had not been infringed, and with that holding we are powerless to interfere. The question, however, which it is our duty and within our power, to decide, is whether the denial of the assistance of counsel contravenes the due process clause of the Fourteenth Amendment to the federal Constitution.

[The Court discussed the historical development of the right to counsel in England and the colonies. One test for determining whether due process has been accorded is to examine whether the settled "usages and modes of proceeding" were followed. The Court concluded that the procedures here deviated from traditionally accepted practices. In spite of sweeping language to the contrary in Hurtado v. California, 110 U.S. 516 (1884), the Fifth and

Fourteenth Amendments' due process clauses embrace certain fundamental principles of liberty and justice, even though they are specifically dealt with in other parts of the Constitution. Because the right to the assistance of counsel is of such a fundamental character, lack of counsel, said the Court, can impair a defendant's due process right to a hearing.]

* * *

What, then, does a hearing include? Historically and in practice, in our own country at least, it has always included the right to the aid of counsel when desired and provided by the party asserting the right. The right to be heard would be, in many cases, of little avail if it did not comprehend the right to be heard by counsel. Even the intelligent and educated layman has small and sometimes no skill in the science of law. If charged with crime, he is incapable, generally, of determining for himself whether the indictment is good or bad. He is unfamiliar with the rules of evidence. Left without the aid of counsel he may be put on trial without a proper charge, and convicted upon incompetent evidence, or evidence irrelevant to the issue or otherwise inadmissible. He lacks both the skill and knowledge adequately to prepare his defense, even though he have a perfect one. He requires the guiding hand of counsel at every step in the proceedings against him. Without it, though he be not guilty, he faces the danger of conviction because he does not know how to establish his innocence. If that be true of men of intelligence, how much more true is it of the ignorant and illiterate, or those of feeble intellect. If in any case, civil or criminal, a state or federal court were arbitrarily to refuse to hear a party by counsel, employed by and appearing for him, it reasonably may not be doubted that such a refusal would be a denial of a hearing, and, therefore, of due process in the constitutional sense.

* * *

In the light of the facts outlined in the forepart of this opinion—the ignorance and illiteracy of the defendants, their youth, the circumstances of public hostility, the imprisonment and the close surveillance of the defendants by the military forces, the fact that their friends and families were all in other states and communication with them necessarily difficult, and above all that they stood in deadly peril of their lives—we think the failure of the trial court to give them reasonable time and opportunity to secure counsel was a clear denial of due process.

* * * [W]e are of opinion that, under the circumstances just stated, the necessity of counsel was so vital and imperative that the failure of the trial court to make an effective appointment of counsel was likewise a denial of due process within the meaning of the Fourteenth Amendment. Whether this would be so in other criminal prosecutions, or under other circumstances, we need not determine. All that it is necessary now to decide, as we do decide, is that in a capital case, where the defendant is unable to employ counsel, and is incapable adequately of making his own defense because of ignorance, feeble mindedness, illiteracy, or the like, it is the duty of the court, whether requested or not, to assign counsel for him as a necessary requisite of due process of law; and that duty is not discharged by an assignment at such a time or under such circumstances as to preclude the giving of effective aid in the preparation and trial of the case. * * *

* * *

[Justice Butler dissented.]

Note

Powell v. Alabama articulated the basic underlying rationale for providing counsel and emphasized the fundamental importance of counsel. Although the defendants' due process rights were violated in *Powell,* the Court did not require counsel in all state prosecutions. Ten years later, in fact, the Court held explicitly that the due process clause of the Fourteenth Amendment does not incorporate the specific guarantees of the Sixth Amendment. Betts v. Brady, 316 U.S. 455 (1942). Counsel for indigent defendants was not considered a fundamental right essential to a fair trial. The Court endorsed a case-by-case inquiry into the fundamental fairness of the proceeding, in light of the totality of the facts in a given case. The defendant's conviction for robbery was affirmed even though the judge refused to appoint counsel upon request.

> [T]he accused was not helpless, but was a man forty-three years old, of ordinary intelligence, and ability to take care of his own interests on the trial of this narrow issue [alibi defense]. He had once before been in a criminal court, pleaded guilty to larceny and served a sentence and was not wholly unfamiliar with criminal procedure. It is quite clear that in Maryland, if the situation had been otherwise and it had appeared that the petitioner was, for any reason, at a serious disadvantage by reason of the lack of counsel, a refusal to appoint would have resulted in the reversal of judgment of conviction. * * *

The approach to appointment of counsel in *Betts* was undermined by a number of cases decided before *Betts* was overruled in Gideon v. Wainwright, 372 U.S. 335 (1963), set forth infra. The Court faced difficult problems in deciding in what special circumstances due process required appointment of counsel. Two cases in particular, in which counsel was not appointed, effectively undercut *Betts.* In Hudson v. North Carolina, 363 U.S. 697 (1960), the Court held that the defendant needed a lawyer to protect against the prejudicial effect of his co-defendant's plea of guilty to a lesser charge in the presence of the jury. In Chewning v. Cunningham, 368 U.S. 443 (1962), the Court reversed the defendant's conviction under a recidivist statute. The defendant was denied due process because the difficult legal questions in the case presented too great a potential for prejudice to the defendant. As one commentator noted, "(a)s this history of the 'special circumstances' case shows, the Court had consistently whittled away at the *Betts* rule until with *Chewning* and *Hudson* it was almost completely eroded." Israel, Gideon v. Wainwright: The "Art" of Overruling, 1963 Sup.Ct.Rev. 211, 260.

Chandler v. Fretag, 348 U.S. 3 (1954), overturned a defendant's conviction as a habitual criminal because he was denied an opportunity to retain counsel. The Court found it difficult to distinguish between an indigent's need for counsel and the need of one who can afford counsel. Furthermore, the court held in Hamilton v. Alabama, 368 U.S. 52 (1961), that there was an unqualified right to counsel in capital cases. The distinction between a case involving capital punishment, where counsel was provided, and one involving a maximum punishment of life imprisonment, where counsel was not provided, proved to be tenuous, at best. For a more extended discussion of the decisions following *Betts,* see generally Israel, supra, at 260; Kamisar, Betts v. Brady Twenty Years Later, 61 Mich.L.Rev. 219 (1962).

Application of the *Betts* rule was not easy for the Court. Nor was that rule entirely consistent with the language of *Powell.* Thus, it was only a matter of time before the Court would call for a more sweeping approach to appointment of counsel. That call came as Gideon's trumpet sounded (see A. Lewis, Gideon's Trumpet (1964)) in 1963.

III. A NEW AND SWEEPING RIGHT AND ITS LIMITS

GIDEON v. WAINWRIGHT

Supreme Court of the United States, 1963.
372 U.S. 335.

MR. JUSTICE BLACK delivered the opinion of the Court.

Petitioner was charged in a Florida state court with having broken and entered a poolroom with intent to commit a misdemeanor. This offense is a felony under Florida law. Appearing in court without funds and without a lawyer, petitioner asked the court to appoint counsel for him, whereupon the following colloquy took place:

> "The Court: Mr. Gideon, I am sorry, but I cannot appoint Counsel to represent you in this case. Under the laws of the State of Florida, the only time the Court can appoint Counsel to represent a Defendant is when that person is charged with a capital offense. I am sorry, but I will have to deny your request to appoint Counsel to defend you in this case.
>
> "The Defendant: The United States Supreme Court says I am entitled to be represented by Counsel."

Put to trial before a jury, Gideon conducted his defense about as well as could be expected from a layman. He made an opening statement to the jury, cross-examined the State's witnesses, presented witnesses in his own defense, declined to testify himself, and made a short argument "emphasizing his innocence to the charge contained in the Information filed in this case." The jury returned a verdict of guilty, and petitioner was sentenced to serve five years in the state prison. * * * Since 1942, when Betts v. Brady was decided by a divided Court, the problem of a defendant's federal constitutional right to counsel in a state court has been a continuing source of controversy and litigation in both state and federal courts. To give this problem another review here, we granted certiorari. Since Gideon was proceeding *in forma pauperis,* we appointed counsel to represent him and requested both sides to discuss in their briefs and oral arguments the following: "Should this Court's holding in Betts v. Brady be reconsidered?"

I

* * *

[The Court discussed the facts of Betts v. Brady, which were virtually indistinguishable from those in *Gideon.* The Court noted that *Betts* addressed the circumstance of an indigent charged with a felony.]

* * * Upon full reconsideration we conclude that Betts v. Brady should be overruled.

II

* * *

We accept Betts v. Brady's assumption, based as it was on our prior cases, that a provision of the Bill of Rights which is "fundamental and essential to a fair trial" is made obligatory upon the States by the Fourteenth Amendment. We think the Court in *Betts* was wrong, however, in concluding that the Sixth Amendment's guarantee of counsel is not one of these fundamental rights. Ten years before Betts v. Brady, this Court, after full consideration of all the historical data examined in *Betts,* had unequivocally declared that "the right to the aid of counsel is of this fundamental character." Powell v. Alabama. While the Court at the close of its *Powell* opinion did by its language, as this

Court frequently does, limit its holding to the particular facts and circumstances of that case, its conclusions about the fundamental nature of the right to counsel are unmistakable.

* * *

* * * The fact is that in deciding as it did—that "appointment of counsel is not a fundamental right, essential to a fair trial"—the Court in Betts v. Brady made an abrupt break with its own well-considered precedents. In returning to these old precedents, sounder we believe than the new, we but restore constitutional principles established to achieve a fair system of justice. Not only these precedents but also reason and reflection require us to recognize that in our adversary system of criminal justice, any person haled into court, who is too poor to hire a lawyer, cannot be assured a fair trial unless counsel is provided for him. This seems to us to be an obvious truth. Governments, both state and federal, quite properly spend vast sums of money to establish machinery to try defendants accused of crime. Lawyers to prosecute are everywhere deemed essential to protect the public's interest in an orderly society. Similarly, there are few defendants charged with crime, few indeed, who fail to hire the best lawyers they can get to prepare and present their defenses. That government hires lawyers to prosecute and defendants who have the money hire lawyers to defend are the strongest indications of the widespread belief that lawyers in criminal courts are necessities, not luxuries. The right of one charged with crime to counsel may not be deemed fundamental and essential to fair trials in some countries, but it is in ours. From the very beginning, our state and national constitutions and laws have laid great emphasis on procedural and substantive safeguards designed to assure fair trials before impartial tribunals in which every defendant stands equal before the law. This noble ideal cannot be realized if the poor man charged with crime has to face his accusers without a lawyer to assist him. * * *

The Court in Betts v. Brady departed from the sound wisdom upon which the Court's holding in Powell v. Alabama rested. Florida, supported by two other States, has asked that Betts v. Brady be left intact. Twenty-two States, as friends of the Court, argue that *Betts* was "an anachronism when handed down" and that it should now be overruled. We agree.

The judgment is reversed and the cause is remanded to the Supreme Court of Florida for further action not inconsistent with this opinion.

[Justices Douglas, Clark, and Harlan wrote separate concurring opinions. Justice Harlan questioned whether *Betts* was an abrupt break with history. He viewed the *Betts* rule as one that did not work, but argued that it was "entitled to a more respectful burial than has been accorded."]

Note

After *Betts,* the Court struggled to explain how a defendant charged with a crime carrying a possible life sentence as a penalty could defend himself without counsel when another defendant charged with the same crime was deemed incapable of effectively being heard as long as capital punishment were possible. Ultimately, the Court concluded that it had no satisfactory explanation. Thus came Gideon v. Wainwright. It should be noted, however, that the Supreme Court has often established more protective rules in death penalty sentencing proceedings, on the ground that "death is different." See Chapter Eleven, infra; so in retrospect the distinctions found insubstantial in *Gideon* are still applied by the Court, at least at the time of sentencing.

Gideon requires appointed counsel for indigents, but what does it mean to be "indigent?" Consider Barry v. Brower, 864 F.2d 294 (3d Cir. 1988), where the defendant was denied a request for the appointment of counsel on the ground that he and his wife had an $80,000 equity in their home and $7,500 in a money market fund. Barry claimed that his debts exceeded his assets, his wife opposed selling their property to pay for his legal expenses, and that he had consulted six attorneys recommended by the public defender, all of whom had refused to represent him without a substantial "up-front" payment. The court held that Barry was entitled to appointed counsel. It stated that "indigence is not equivalent to destitution," and that "if by their nature an accused's assets cannot be timely reduced to cash and cash is required, the present financial inability to obtain counsel which defines indigence for Sixth Amendment purposes appears." The court noted that the state may require reasonable reimbursement if the defendant's indigency is temporary.

In Fuller v. Oregon, 417 U.S. 40 (1974), the Court upheld a statute which conditioned probation on repayment to the state of the costs of a free legal defense, where the defendant had gained a subsequent ability to pay. While states may obtain reimbursement as a constitutional matter, section 5–6.2 of the A.B.A. Standards for Criminal Justice recommends that payment be sought only where defendants have made fraudulent representations concerning indigency in order to obtain free counsel. The commentary to the Standard states that reimbursement requirements "may serve to discourage defendants from exercising their right to counsel."

Many of the states have detailed statutes determining eligibility for appointed counsel. See, e.g., N.J.Stat.Ann. 2A:158A–14 (West 1988) (considering factors such as liquid assets, the ability to make bail, and the projected costs of defense). The federal standard for appointment of counsel "for any person financially unable to obtain adequate representation" is codified in 18 U.S.C. § 3006A (West 1988).

After *Gideon,* the Court was asked whether a defendant charged with a misdemeanor was inherently more capable of self-representation than a felony defendant. The right to counsel grew with the answer.

ARGERSINGER v. HAMLIN

Supreme Court of the United States, 1972.
407 U.S. 25.

MR. JUSTICE DOUGLAS delivered the opinion of the Court.

Petitioner, an indigent, was charged in Florida with carrying a concealed weapon, an offense punishable by imprisonment up to six months, a $1,000 fine, or both. The trial was to a judge, and petitioner was unrepresented by counsel. He was sentenced to serve 90 days in jail, and brought this habeas corpus action in the Florida Supreme Court, alleging that, being deprived of his right to counsel, he was unable as an indigent layman properly to raise and present to the trial court good and sufficient defenses to the charge for which he stands convicted. The Florida Supreme Court by a four-to-three decision, in ruling on the right to counsel, followed the line we marked out in Duncan v. Louisiana, 391 U.S. 145, 159, as respects the right to trial by jury and held that the right to court-appointed counsel extends only to trials "for non-petty offenses punishable by more than six months imprisonment."

[The Court noted that the Sixth Amendment was binding on the states through the Fourteenth Amendment and proceeded to examine the Amendment's requirements of a public trial, the right to be informed of the nature and cause of the accusation, the right of confrontation, and the right of compulsory process. These rights have never been limited to felonies or to serious offenses. Although Duncan v. Louisiana limited the right to trial by jury to trials where the potential punishment was imprisonment for six months or more, the Court concluded that "there is no support for a similar limitation on the right to assistance of counsel." The Court relied heavily on the rationale in *Powell* and *Gideon* and utilized lengthy quotations from both opinions.]

* * *

The requirement of counsel may well be necessary for a fair trial even in a petty-offense prosecution. We are by no means convinced that legal and constitutional questions involved in a case that actually leads to imprisonment even for a brief period are any less complex than when a person can be sent off for six months or more.

* * *

Beyond the problem of trials and appeals is that of the guilty plea, a problem which looms large in misdemeanor as well as in felony cases. Counsel is needed so that the accused may know precisely what he is doing, so that he is fully aware of the prospect of going to jail or prison, and so that he is treated fairly by the prosecution.

In addition, the volume of misdemeanor cases far greater in number than felony prosecutions, may create an obsession for speedy dispositions, regardless of the fairness of the result. * * *

There is evidence of the prejudice which results to misdemeanor defendants from this "assembly-line justice." * * *

We must conclude, therefore, that the problems associated with misdemeanor and petty offenses often require the presence of counsel to insure the accused a fair trial. Mr. Justice Powell suggests that these problems are raised even in situations where there is no prospect of imprisonment. We need not consider the requirements of the Sixth Amendment as regards the right to counsel where loss of liberty is not involved, however, for here petitioner was in fact sentenced to jail. And, as we said in Baldwin v. New York, 399 U.S., at 73, "the prospect of imprisonment for however short a time will seldom be viewed by the accused as a trivial or 'petty' matter and may well result in quite serious repercussions affecting his career and his reputation." * * *

We hold, therefore, that absent a knowing and intelligent waiver, no person may be imprisoned for any offense, whether classified as petty, misdemeanor, or felony, unless he was represented by counsel at his trial.[a]

* * *

[Justice Brennan filed a concurring opinion. Chief Justice Burger concurred in the result, and Justice Powell filed an opinion concurring in the result, in which Justice Rehnquist joined. Justice Brennan emphasized the availability of law students to assist indigents. The Chief Justice expressed con-

a. We do not share Mr. Justice Powell's doubt that the Nation's legal resources are sufficient to implement the rule we announce today. It has been estimated that between 1,575 and 2,300 full-time counsel would be required to represent *all* indigent misdemeanants, excluding traffic offenders. Note, Dollars and Sense of an Expanded Right to Counsel, 55 Iowa L.Rev. 1249, 1260–1261 (1970). These figures are relatively insignificant when compared to the estimated 355,200 attorneys in the United States (Statistical Abstract of the United States 153 (1971)), a number which is projected to double by the year 1985. See Ruud, That Burgeoning Law School Enrollment, 58 A.B.A.J. 146, 147. Indeed, there are 18,000 new admissions to the bar each year—3,500 more lawyers than are required to fill the "estimated 14,500 average annual openings." Id., at 148.

cern that trial judges would have difficulty deciding whether to appoint counsel before hearing evidence in a case. He pointed out that the judge probably will rely on representations of the prosecutor. Justice Powell preferred an approach that, like Betts v. Brady, would have afforded counsel when necessary to a fair trial whether a defendant is faced with a fine or imprisonment. He was bothered by the fact that indigents would receive counsel in cases in which relatively poor non-indigents would forego counsel. Also of concern to him was the lack of attorney resources available to courts in some areas and the increased burden that appointing counsel represented for overworked judges.]

Although *Argersinger* extended the right to appointed counsel to anyone actually imprisoned [5] the Court did not consider whether the right to counsel extends to one who is punished only with a fine. In Scott v. Illinois, 440 U.S. 367 (1979), the Court considered whether the Sixth Amendment requires appointed counsel when a defendant actually is fined, but the offense is punishable by fine or imprisonment.

In *Scott,* the Court stated that there was a line drawn in *Argersinger* between imprisonment and other forms of punishment. Even though the statute under which Scott was convicted authorized a year of incarceration, he was not entitled to counsel. Two paragraphs from the majority opinion follow:

> In *Argersinger* the Court rejected arguments that social cost or a lack of available lawyers militated against its holding, in some part because it thought these arguments were factually incorrect. But they were rejected in much larger part because of the Court's conclusion that incarceration was so severe a sanction that it should not be imposed as a result of a criminal trial unless an indigent defendant had been offered appointed counsel to assist in his defense, regardless of the cost to the States implicit in such a rule. The Court in its opinion repeatedly referred to trials "where an accused is deprived of his liberty," and to "a case that actually leads to imprisonment even for a brief period." The Chief Justice in his opinion concurring in the result also observed that "any deprivation of liberty is a serious matter."
>
> Although the intentions of the *Argersinger* Court are not unmistakably clear from its opinion, we conclude today that *Argersinger* did indeed delimit the constitutional right to appointed counsel in state criminal proceedings.[a] Even were the matter *res nova,* we believe that the central premise of *Argersinger*—that actual imprisonment is a penalty different in kind from fines or the mere threat of imprisonment—is eminently sound and warrants adoption of actual imprisonment as the line defining the constitutional right to appointment of counsel. *Argersinger* has proved reasonably workable, whereas any extension would create confusion and impose unpredictable, but necessarily substantial, costs on 50 quite diverse States. We therefore hold that the Sixth and Fourteenth Amendments to the United States Constitution require only that no indigent criminal defendant be sentenced to a term of imprison-

5. For a critique of the manner in which the requirements of *Argersinger* have been implemented, see Froyd, Is Argersinger a Shot in the Arm or a Coup de Grace? 62 A.B.A.J. 1154 (1976).

a. We note that the line drawn in *Argersinger* was with full awareness of the various options. Both the petitioner in that case and the Legal Aid Society of New York, as *amicus curiae,* argued that the right to appointed counsel should pertain in any case in which imprisonment was an authorized penalty for the underlying offense. * * * The Solicitor General argued for the standard that was finally adopted—that of actual imprisonment.

ment unless the State has afforded him the right to assistance of appointed counsel in his defense.

Justice Powell concurred, although he expressed reservations about the rule enunciated in *Argersinger* and reaffirmed in *Scott.* He argued that the constitution does not mandate the rule in *Argersinger,* and preferred a more flexible due process approach to the appointment of counsel. Nevertheless, in *Scott* he recognized a need to provide clear guidance to lower courts.

Justice Brennan, joined by Justices Marshall and Stevens, dissented. The dissenters asserted that *Argersinger* represented a cautious approach to the extension of the right to counsel principles underlying *Gideon.* In their view, the question of the right to counsel in cases in which incarceration is authorized but not imposed was expressly reserved in *Argersinger.* They focused on the need for counsel to defend against a charge, and concluded that counsel should be furnished whenever imprisonment is authorized for an offense. They noted that public defender systems are economically feasible, and that many states actually require counsel where any imprisonment is authorized. Justice Brennan argued that the actual imprisonment approach was unworkable because it forces the judge to consider sentencing factors before the case has even begun. He explained as follows:

> [T]he judge will be forced to decide in advance of trial—and without hearing the evidence—whether he will forego entirely his judicial discretion to impose some sentence of imprisonment and abandon his responsibility to consider the full range of punishments established by the legislature. His alternatives, assuming the availability of counsel, will be to appoint counsel and retain the discretion vested in him by law, or to abandon this discretion in advance and proceed without counsel.

In contrast, Justice Brennan argued that the authorized imprisonment approach to appointing counsel "respects the allocation of functions between legislatures and courts in the administration of the criminal justice system." He noted that another salutary effect of the authorized imprisonment approach would be to encourage state legislatures to update criminal statutes. As Justice Brennan put it, "a state legislature or local government might determine that it no longer desired to authorize incarceration for certain minor offenses in light of the expense of meeting the requirements of the Constitution. In my view, this re-examination is long overdue."

Justice Blackmun also dissented. He agreed that *Argersinger* did not decide this question, but would have held that an indigent defendant must be given counsel in any prosecution for an offense punishable by more than six months imprisonment (or, under *Argersinger,* when the defendant is actually subjected to a term of imprisonment). This approach would make the right to counsel co-extensive with the right to a jury trial, also guaranteed by the Sixth Amendment and discussed in Chapter Ten, infra.

With which approach do you agree? For a critical analysis of *Scott,* see Herman & Thompson, Scott v. Illinois and the Right to Counsel: A Decision in Search of a Doctrine? 17 Am.Crim.L.Rev. 71 (1979).

One lower court had this to say about *Scott:*

> In essence, the *Scott* holding set up a trade-off whereby states could choose between providing indigent defendants with appointed counsel and foregoing

> jail time for convictions obtained without appointed counsel. *Scott* holds that, if the state wants to incarcerate an indigent defendant, the state must provide appointed counsel.

Moore v. Jarvis, 885 F.2d 1565 (11th Cir.1989). Does the "trade-off" approach described have anything to do with the Sixth Amendment right to counsel in "all criminal prosecutions?" Does it have anything to do with the right to due process, which extends to deprivations of both liberty and property?

Recall that in Berkemer v. McCarty (Chapter Three) the Court held that the protections of Miranda v. Arizona applied to misdemeanors. Thus, an indigent person subject to custodial questioning for a misdemeanor has a right to appointed counsel during that questioning. But then at trial, he has no right to appointed counsel unless he receives a prison sentence. Is the *Miranda* right more important than the right to counsel at trial in misdemeanor cases?

As Justice Brennan noted in his dissent in *Scott,* many states require the appointment of counsel for indigents whenever imprisonment is authorized. See, e.g., N.Y.—McKinney's CPL 170.10.

Note

If a defendant is not provided counsel, can the court impose a suspended sentence under *Scott*? The court in United States v. Reilley, 948 F.2d 648 (10th Cir.1991) answered in the negative. The court explained that since a defendant who is not provided counsel "cannot be ordered to serve a sentence of imprisonment, it seems obvious that a conditional sentence of imprisonment is equally invalid. Since the court's conditional threat to imprison Reilley could never be carried out, the threat itself is hollow and should be considered a nullity."

In Baldasar v. Illinois, 446 U.S. 222 (1980), a divided Supreme Court held that a defendant was denied his right to counsel under *Argersinger* and *Scott* when his misdemeanor theft conviction was transformed into a felony because of a previous conviction for the same offense, where the defendant had not had counsel when previously convicted and fined. Justice Stewart's opinion, joined by Justices Brennan and Stevens, said simply that *Scott* was violated because Baldasar "was sentenced to an increased term of imprisonment *only* because he had been convicted in a previous prosecution in which he had *not* had the assistance of appointed counsel." Justice Marshall's concurring opinion, joined by Justices Brennan and Stevens, argued that Baldasar had been deprived of liberty because of his first trial in violation of *Argersinger,* and emphasized that convictions obtained without counsel are not reliable. Justice Blackmun's deciding vote was premised on his view in *Scott* that the right to counsel cases should be expanded to include any crime punishable by more than six months imprisonment; the first conviction in the instant case was such a crime. Justice Powell's dissent was joined by the Chief Justice and Justices White and Rehnquist. The dissent argued that since the first conviction was valid, as only a fine was imposed, it could be used in the second case.

Although *Baldasar* prevailed, when Justice Blackmun's vote is added to the four dissents, it seems that a defendant may receive an enhanced sentence because of a prior conviction for a misdemeanor that was punishable by 6 months or less imprisonment. See Santillanes v. United States Parole Commission, 754 F.2d 887 (10th Cir. 1985) (Justice Blackmun's concurring opinion, rather than the plurality opinion, represents the holding in *Baldasar).*

Whether uncounseled misdemeanor convictions are reliable enough to be used in sentencing is debatable. On the one hand, a probation report often will have information about arrests and other activities of a defendant that did not even result in a trial, let alone a conviction. This may suggest that *Baldasar* permits the use of evidence that is no worse than what ordinarily comes before sentencing decisionmakers. On the other hand, no other piece of information alone usually results in a conviction for a higher offense carrying a greater sentence.

Many courts have read *Baldasar* to hold that a prior uncounseled conviction cannot be used only if all of the following circumstances are present: (1) the later misdemeanor is *automatically* converted, (2) into a *felony,* and (3) the defendant receives a jail term which she could not otherwise have received, *because of* the prior offense. Under this view, the uncounseled conviction could be used for enhancement so long as the subsequent offense remains a misdemeanor; it could be used if the defendant receives a term of incarceration that is permissible for the subsequent offense alone; and it could be used if the sentencing judge considered the uncounseled conviction on a discretionary basis as it related to defendant's character. See United States v. Peagler, 847 F.2d 756 (11th Cir.1988) ("defendant's sentence was not automatically increased by statute from a non-jail offense to a jail offense because he had a criminal record"); Moore v. Jarvis, 885 F.2d 1565 (11th Cir.1989) (statute allowing consideration of prior uncounseled convictions is valid because "it allows judges to sentence first-time offenders to the same term of incarceration Moore received"); United States v. Castro-Vega, 945 F.2d 496 (2d Cir.1991) (uncounseled misdemeanor conviction can be used to determine the appropriate criminal history category under the Sentencing Guidelines, for a crime that was already a felony). Is this view of *Baldasar* acceptable? The court in Moore v. Jarvis, supra, also held that *Baldasar* was not applicable where the defendant had the assets to obtain counsel at the time of the prior conviction. Does that make sense?

Although *Gideon*, *Argersinger*, and *Scott* might appear to suggest that the line separating felonies and misdemeanors is clear, that is not the case in many jurisdictions. Thirty-nine states use and define the term "felony." Often, the definition turns on the place of imprisonment rather than the duration of punishment. Almost as often the definition turns on the duration but not the place. Some states use both place and duration to define a felony. Two states and the District of Columbia do not use the term felony, and nine others use it but do not define it. See Table 5 in U.S. Department of Justice, Bureau of Justice Statistics Bulletin, State Felony Courts and Felony Laws (August 1987).

IV. THE SCOPE OF THE RIGHT

A. CRITICAL STAGES

Gideon, Argersinger and *Scott* analyze the right of an indigent to appointed trial counsel. But as we have already seen in connection with confessions, and even identification procedures, counsel may be needed before a trial starts. And counsel may be needed also after it ends. Other "critical stages"—stages where the presence of counsel is critical—are so labeled when it is said that counsel is constitutionally required to protect against potential prejudice to a defendant's rights. The justification for and development of the "critical stage" analysis is expressed in United States v. Wade, 388 U.S. 218 (1967), a case examined in the preceding chapter on identification. The *Wade* Court wrote as follows:

> * * * When the Bill of Rights was adopted, there were no organized police forces as we know them today. The accused confronted the prosecutor and the witnesses against him, and the evidence was marshalled, largely at the trial itself. In contrast, today's law enforcement machinery involves critical confrontations of the accused by the prosecution at pretrial proceedings where the results might well settle the accused's fate and reduce the trial itself to a mere formality. In recognition of these realities of modern criminal prosecution, our cases have construed the Sixth Amendment guarantee to apply to "critical" stages of the proceedings. * * *
>
> [The Court discusses *Powell, Escobedo, Massiah, Miranda,* and other cases.]
>
> In sum, the principle of Powell v. Alabama and succeeding cases requires that we scrutinize *any* pretrial confrontation of the accused to determine whether the presence of his counsel is necessary to preserve the defendant's basic right to a fair trial as affected by his right meaningfully to cross-examine the witnesses against him and to have effective assistance of counsel at the trial itself. It calls upon us to analyze whether potential substantial prejudice to defendant's rights inheres in the particular confrontation and the ability of counsel to help avoid that prejudice.

The Court concluded, as Chapter Four revealed, that there was great potential for suggestiveness in a lineup, and "the accused's inability effectively to reconstruct at trial any unfairness that occurred at the lineup may deprive him of his only opportunity meaningfully to attack the credibility of the witness' courtroom identification." The Court reasoned that counsel would often avert prejudice and assure a meaningful confrontation at trial.

Using this method of analysis, the Court found in Coleman v. Alabama, 399 U.S. 1 (1970), that Alabama's preliminary hearing was a critical stage requiring the appointment of counsel. Although preliminary hearings have not yet been examined, it is sufficient for present purposes to note that the purposes of the preliminary hearing were to determine whether there was sufficient evidence against the accused to present the case to the grand jury, and to fix bail.

> Plainly the guiding hand of counsel at the preliminary hearing is essential to protect the indigent accused against an erroneous or improper prosecution. First, the lawyer's skilled examination and cross-examination of witnesses may expose fatal weaknesses in the State's case that may lead the magistrate to refuse to bind the accused over. Second, in any event, the skilled interrogation of witnesses by an experienced lawyer can fashion a vital impeachment tool for use in cross-examination of the State's witnesses at the trial, or preserve testimony favorable to the accused of a witness who does not appear at the trial. Third, trained counsel can more effectively discover the case the State has against his client and make possible the preparation of a proper defense to meet that case at the trial. Fourth, counsel can also be influential at the preliminary hearing in making effective arguments for the accused on such matters as the necessity for an early psychiatric examination or bail.

Id. at 9.[6]

6. The Court vacated defendants' convictions of assault with intent to murder, and remanded the case for determination of whether the failure to provide counsel was harmless error.

People v. Hodge, 53 N.Y.2d 313, 441 N.Y.S.2d 231, 423 N.E.2d 1060 (1981), held that the accused was denied effective assistance of counsel when a preliminary hearing proceeded in the unexplained absence of his retained counsel. Even though the grand jury

Since most of the cases cited in *Wade* have already been discussed, as have several other right to counsel cases in the identification chapter, already it should be clear that the Court has had more difficulty applying than defining the "critical stage" test. The right to counsel has not been extended to all pretrial phases of a criminal investigation. Kirby v. Illinois, 406 U.S. 682 (1972), for instance, limited the scope of the critical stage doctrine, in holding that a show-up identification before the defendant is charged with a criminal offense is not a critical stage. Unless counsel is provided to safeguard an independent constitutional right, as in *Miranda,* generally one can say that adversary proceedings must be formally initiated before a particular phase of a prosecution can be considered a critical stage. (Recall Massiah v. United States, and Brewer v. Williams.) Adversary criminal proceedings plainly can be initiated by formal charge, preliminary hearing, indictment, information, or arraignment. It is not yet clear what the Supreme Court means by "formal charge," but presumably the Court is focusing on the filing of some statement with the court that expresses the government's belief that the criminal process leading to conviction should begin against a suspect. Before this happens, an investigation generally does not trigger counsel rights. Thus, counsel is not constitutionally required to assist witnesses at a grand jury proceeding. See, e.g., In re Grand Jury Subpoenas, 906 F.2d 1485 (10th Cir. 1990) (subpoenaing attorney to testify before the grand jury to give information against his client does not violate defendant's right to counsel, even though it may result in defense attorney's disqualification from representation; no Sixth Amendment rights attach prior to indictment). Some states, however, statutorily permit counsel in the grand jury room under some circumstances.[7] The grand jury is considered at length in a subsequent chapter.

Even where the criminal process has begun, there are limitations on the extension of the right to counsel to pre-trial proceedings. United States v. Ash, 413 U.S. 300 (1973), holding that a photographic identification at which the accused was not present was not a critical stage illustrates this point. After reviewing the history and expansion of the Sixth Amendment counsel guarantee, the *Ash* Court redefined the approach used in extending the right to counsel: "[T]he test utilized by the Court has called for examination of the event in order to determine whether the accused required aid in coping with legal problems or assistance in meeting his adversary." The Court distinguished the lineup in *Wade* because in *Ash* there was no confrontation between the accused and the prosecution. After stating that there is no right to counsel because the accused has no right to be present,[8] the Court went on to make the following argument:

subsequently indicted and the defendant was found guilty beyond a reasonable doubt, the court, split 4–3, remanded the case for a new trial, reasoning that the accused lost valuable insights into the government's case at the preliminary hearing, that the first trial probably provided those insights, and that granting a new trial was therefore an appropriate disposition. The dissenters argued that since the grand jury is not bound by a preliminary hearing anyway, the defendant suffered no prejudice.

7. E.g., Ariz.Rules of Crim.Proc., Rule 12.6 (protecting "targets" of investigations only); Colo.Rev.Stat. § 16.5–204(4)(d) (all witnesses); 38 Ill.Ann.Stat. § 112–4(b) (protecting all witnesses); 40 Mich.Comp.Laws Ann. § 767.19e (same); Minn.Rules of Crim.Proc. Rule 18.04 (protecting if immunity is waived); 10 Rev. Code of Wash.Ann. § 10.27.120 (protecting unless immunity is granted).

8. Remember that one view of counsel under *Wade* is that counsel is more passive than active. If this view is correct, consider wheth-

A substantial departure from the historical test would be necessary if the Sixth Amendment were interpreted to give Ash a right to counsel at the photographic identification in this case. Since the accused himself is not present at the time of the photographic display, and asserts no right to be present, no possibility arises that the accused might be misled by his lack of familiarity with the law or overpowered by his professional adversary. Similarly, the counsel guarantee would not be used to produce equality in a trial-like adversary confrontation. * * *

Even if we were willing to view the counsel guarantee in broad terms as a generalized protection of the adversary process, we would be unwilling to go so far as to extend the right to a portion of the prosecutor's trial-preparation interviews with witnesses. * * * The traditional counterbalance in the American adversary system for these interviews arises from the equal ability of defense counsel to seek and interview witnesses himself.

That adversary mechanism remains as effective for a photographic display as for other parts of pretrial interviews.[a] No greater limitations are placed on defense counsel in constructing displays, seeking witnesses, and conducting photographic identifications than those applicable to the prosecution. Selection of the picture of a person other than the accused, or the inability of a witness to make any selection, will be useful to the defense in precisely the same manner that the selection of a picture of the defendant would be useful to the prosecution. * * * Although we do not suggest that equality of access to photographs removes all potential for abuse, it does remove any inequality in the adversary process itself and thereby fully satisfies the historical spirit of the Sixth Amendment's counsel guarantee.

At trial, can defense counsel "correct" any mistakes made during a photo identification procedure? The Court often talks about the test of whether a stage of the process is critical as if it involved only one question: is counsel's presence at the pre-trial stage necessary to assure a subsequent, fair trial? Might there be another aspect to the test, one that focuses on the skills a lawyer brings to trials and whether those kinds of skills are almost as important to a suspect at other stages? If attention is paid to this possible aspect of the critical stage test, it might be easier to understand cases like Commonwealth v. Holzer, 480 Pa. 93, 389 A.2d 101 (1978) (right to counsel at search and seizure suppression hearing). Also, it might help to explain how the right to counsel has been extended to certain stages of a criminal prosecution following trial.

er counsel could not perform the same role at a photographic identification.

a. Duplication by defense counsel is a safeguard that normally is not available when a formal confrontation occurs. Defense counsel has no statutory authority to conduct a preliminary hearing, for example, and defense counsel will generally be prevented by practical considerations from conducting his own lineup. Even in some confrontations, however, the possibility of duplication may be important. The Court [in *Gilbert*] noted this in holding that the taking of handwriting exemplars did not constitute a "critical stage":

"If, for some reason, an unrepresentative exemplar is taken, this can be brought out and corrected through the adversary process at trial since the accused can make an unlimited number of additional exemplars for analysis and comparison by government and defense handwriting experts." Gilbert v. California, 388 U.S. 263, 267 (1967).

B. POST-TRIAL STAGES

MEMPA v. RHAY

Supreme Court of the United States, 1967.
389 U.S. 128.

MR. JUSTICE MARSHALL delivered the opinion of the Court.

These consolidated cases raise the question of the extent of the right to counsel at the time of sentencing where the sentencing has been deferred subject to probation.

Petitioner Jerry Douglas Mempa was convicted in the Spokane County Superior Court on June 17, 1959, of the offense of "joyriding." This conviction was based on his plea of guilty entered with the advice of court-appointed counsel. He was then placed on probation for two years on the condition, *inter alia,* that he first spend 30 days in the county jail, and the imposition of sentence was deferred * * *.

About four months later the Spokane County prosecuting attorney moved to have petitioner's probation revoked on the ground that he had been involved in a burglary on September 15, 1959. A hearing was held in the Spokane County Superior Court on October 23, 1959. Petitioner Mempa, who was 17 years old at the time, was accompanied to the hearing by his stepfather. He was not represented by counsel and was not asked whether he wished to have counsel appointed for him. Nor was any inquiry made concerning the appointed counsel who had previously represented him.

At the hearing Mempa was asked if it was true that he had been involved in the alleged burglary and he answered in the affirmative. A probation officer testified without cross-examination that according to his information petitioner had been involved in the burglary and had previously denied participation in it. * * * [T]he court immediately entered an order revoking petitioner's probation and then sentenced him to 10 years in the penitentiary, * * *.

* * *

[Petitioner Walkling was sentenced without counsel under similar circumstances.]

* * *

In 1948 this Court held in Townsend v. Burke, 334 U.S. 736, that the absence of counsel during sentencing after a plea of guilty coupled with "assumptions concerning his criminal record which were materially untrue" deprived the defendant in that case of due process. Mr. Justice Jackson there stated in conclusion, "in this case, counsel might not have changed the sentence, but he could have taken steps to see that the conviction and sentence were not predicated on misinformation or misreading of court records, a requirement of fair play which absence of counsel withheld from this prisoner." [The Court discusses other pre-*Gideon* cases.]

There was no occasion in *Gideon* to enumerate the various stages in a criminal proceeding at which counsel was required, but [these earlier cases], when the *Betts* requirement of special circumstances is stripped away by *Gideon,* clearly stand for the proposition that appointment of counsel for an indigent is required at every stage of a criminal proceeding where substantial rights of a criminal accused may be affected. In particular, Townsend v. Burke, supra, illustrates the critical nature of sentencing in a criminal case and might well be considered to support by itself a holding that the right to counsel applies at sentencing. Many lower courts have concluded that the Sixth Amendment right to counsel extends to sentencing in federal cases.

The State, however, argues that the petitioners were sentenced at the time they were originally placed on probation and that the imposition of sentence following probation revocation is, in effect, a mere formality constituting part of the probation revocation proceeding. It is true that sentencing in Washington offers fewer opportunities for the exercise of judicial discretion than in many other jurisdictions. The applicable statute requires the trial judge in all cases to sentence the convicted person to the maximum term provided by law for the offense of which he was convicted. The actual determination of the length of time to be served is to be made by the Board of Prison Terms and Paroles within six months after the convicted person is admitted to prison.

On the other hand, the sentencing judge is required by statute, together with the prosecutor, to furnish the Board with a recommendation as to the length of time that the person should serve, in addition to supplying it with various information about the circumstances of the crime and the character of the individual. We were informed during oral argument that the Board places considerable weight on these recommendations, although it is in no way bound by them. Obviously to the extent such recommendations are influential in determining the resulting sentence, the necessity for the aid of counsel in marshaling the facts, introducing evidence of mitigating circumstances and in general aiding and assisting the defendant to present his case as to sentence is apparent.

Even more important in a case such as this is the fact that certain legal rights may be lost if not exercised at this stage. For one, Washington law provides that an appeal in a case involving a plea of guilty followed by probation can only be taken after sentence is imposed following revocation of probation. Therefore in a case where an accused agreed to plead guilty, although he had a valid defense, because he was offered probation, absence of counsel at the imposition of the deferred sentence might well result in loss of the right to appeal. While ordinarily appeals from a plea of guilty are less frequent than those following a trial on the merits, the incidence of improperly obtained guilty pleas is not so slight as to be capable of being characterized as *de minimis.*

Likewise the Washington statutes provide that a plea of guilty can be withdrawn at any time prior to the imposition of sentence, if the trial judge in his discretion finds that the ends of justice will be served. Without undertaking to catalog the various situations in which a lawyer could be of substantial assistance to a defendant in such a case, it can be reiterated that a plea of guilty might well be improperly obtained by the promise to have a defendant placed on the very probation the revocation of which furnishes the occasion for desiring to withdraw the plea. An uncounseled defendant might very likely be unaware of this opportunity.

The two foregoing factors assume increased significance when it is considered that, as happened in these two cases, the eventual imposition of sentence on the prior plea of guilty is based on the alleged commission of offenses for which the accused is never tried.

In sum, we do not question the authority of the State of Washington to provide for a deferred sentencing procedure coupled with its probation provisions. Indeed, it appears to be an enlightened step forward. All we decide here is that a lawyer must be afforded at this proceeding whether it be labeled a revocation of probation or a deferred sentencing. We assume that counsel appointed for the purpose of the trial or guilty plea would not be unduly burdened by being requested to follow through at the deferred sentencing stage of the proceeding.

* * *

Today, it is likely to come as no surprise that sentencing is treated as part of the trial process and as requiring the assistance of counsel. However, courts have held that *Mempa* does not mean that every step in the sentencing process is "critical" within the meaning of the Sixth Amendment. In United States v. Johnson, 935 F.2d 47 (4th Cir. 1991), defendant was sentenced in part on the basis of *ex parte* communications between his probation officer and the sentencing judge. The court rejected the argument that the right to counsel attached to those meetings. It found the communications to be "nonadversarial," reasoning that under the Federal Sentencing Guidelines, the probation officer is an agent of the court and assists the court in arriving at a just sentence. Do you agree that a conference between the probation officer and the judge is not a critical stage?

Before *Mempa,* the Court had ruled in Douglas v. California, 372 U.S. 353 (1963), a case in which the merits of the indigent defendant's one and only appeal as of right were decided without the benefit of counsel, that the defendant was treated unconstitutionally. Utilizing an equal protection rationale, the Court extended the right to counsel to this situation. Denial of counsel to the defendant constituted discrimination on the basis of indigency, which violated the Fourteenth Amendment. However, in Ross v. Moffitt, 417 U.S. 600 (1974), the Court did not extend the *Douglas* reasoning to require counsel for discretionary appeals. The Court said that absolute equality is not required and also noted that there are significant differences between a defendant's interest in having counsel during trial and on appeal. Justice Rehnquist essentially used a due process analysis, and stated that the right to appointed counsel would be mandated only if reasonably necessary for adequate access to the court. He found that counsel was not reasonably necessary for discretionary appeals:

> [P]rior to his seeking discretionary review in the State Supreme Court, [respondent's] claims had once been presented by a lawyer and passed upon by an appellate court. Douglas v. California. We do not believe it can be said, therefore, that a defendant in respondent's circumstances is denied meaningful access to the North Carolina Supreme Court simply because the State does not appoint counsel to aid him in seeking review in that court. At that stage he will have, at the every least, a brief on his behalf in the Court of Appeals setting forth his claims of error, and in many cases an opinion by the Court of Appeals disposing of his case. These materials, supplemented by whatever submission respondent may make *pro se,* would appear to provide the Supreme Court of North Carolina with an adequate basis on which to base its decision to grant or deny review. * * *
>
> This is not to say, of course, that a skilled lawyer * * * would not prove helpful to any litigant able to employ him. * * * [But] the fact that a particular service might be of benefit to an indigent defendant does not mean that the service is constitutionally required. The duty of the State under our cases is not to duplicate the legal arsenal that may be privately retained by a criminal defendant in a continuing effort to reverse his conviction, but only to assure the indigent defendant an adequate opportunity to present his claims fairly in the context of the State's appellate process.

Reasoning from Ross v. Moffitt, the Court held, in Wainwright v. Torna, 455 U.S. 586 (1982) (per curiam), that a defendant could not challenge his retained lawyer's failure to file a timely petition for discretionary review in the state supreme court. Since he had no right to counsel, there could be no claim of ineffective counsel. Justice Marshall, dissenting, argued that the defendant was denied due process. Can you identify reasons why counsel should be required in one appeal—as of right—and not another—discretionary appeal?

Chief Justice Rehnquist wrote for the Court in Pennsylvania v. Finley, 481 U.S. 551 (1987), as it relied on Ross v. Moffitt to hold that a defendant has no right to counsel in postconviction proceedings. Because such right is lacking, the Court held that a lawyer, who is appointed to represent a defendant in such a proceeding and who finds the defendant's claims to be frivolous, need not file a brief referring to anything in the record that would support the defendant's claims. Such a brief is required on direct appeal as of right under the Supreme Court's decision in Anders v. California, 386 U.S. 738 (1967), but the requirement is derived from the right to counsel itself. When the right is nonexistent, there is no requirement. The Chief Justice also rejected due process and equal protection arguments made in support of a briefing requirement.

In Murray v. Giarratano, 492 U.S. 1 (1989), the Court relied on *Ross* and *Finley* to hold that the state was not required to provide counsel for death-row inmates pursuing post-conviction habeas corpus remedies. The plurality opinion, written by Chief Justice Rehnquist, "declined to read either the Eighth Amendment or the Due Process Clause to require yet another distinction between the rights of capital case defendants and those in noncapital cases." The Chief Justice noted, however, that many states "automatically provide counsel to death-row inmates in state habeas corpus proceedings, as a matter of state law." Justice Kennedy concurred in the judgment "on the facts and record of this case" noting that "no prisoner on death row in Virginia has been unable to obtain counsel to represent him in postconviction proceedings." Justice Stevens, joined by Justices Blackmun, Marshall and Brennan, dissented. He noted that under Virginia law, some claims that would ordinarily be brought on direct review are deferred until habeas corpus proceedings, such as claims concerning ineffective assistance of counsel. So review of those claims in a habeas proceeding is tantamount to a first appeal covered by *Douglas.* He also argued that capital litigation is more complex, and subject to a greater time pressure, than the postconviction proceedings contemplated in *Finley.*

The indigent appellant has the constitutional right to a relevant transcript or adequate substitute when challenging trial errors on an appeal as of right. Griffin v. Illinois, 351 U.S. 12 (1956). This is so even though the conviction is for an ordinance violation punishable by fine only. Mayer v. Chicago, 404 U.S. 189 (1971). And a state cannot require an indigent to pay a filing fee as a condition precedent to an appeal. Burns v. Ohio, 360 U.S. 252 (1959). Although the Court often uses equal protection language in these cases, Ross v. Moffitt and noncriminal cases like San Antonio Independent School Dist. v. Rodriguez, 411 U.S. 1 (1973), suggest that the Court is more concerned with establishing a system that permits all criminal defendants to take advantage of procedures that the structure of the system itself implies are fundamental checks against erroneous results. This helps to explain why a preliminary hearing transcript will have to be afforded free of charge to an indigent standing trial. Roberts v. LaVallee, 389 U.S. 40 (1967).

Once the defendant has been properly convicted and sentenced, some constitutional protections diminish or disappear. A defendant has no absolute right to counsel at parole or probation revocation proceedings, for example. In Gagnon v. Scarpelli, 411 U.S. 778 (1973), the Court adopted a case-by-case approach to the appointment of counsel at these revocation hearings. Relying on Morrissey v. Brewer, 408 U.S. 471 (1972), which held that due process protections apply to parole revocation proceedings (in other words, that they have to be fundamentally fair because liberty interests are threatened), the *Gagnon* Court first determined that due process also applied to probation revocation hearings. However, the Court rejected the contention that states are under a constitutional duty to provide counsel for indigents in all probation and parole revocation cases. Acknowledging that its case-by-case approach to counsel is similar to the fundamental fairness approach of *Betts,* which was rejected in *Gideon,* the Court distinguished criminal trials from probation or parole revocation hearings, reasoning as follows:

> In a criminal trial, the State is represented by a prosecutor; formal rules of evidence are in force; a defendant enjoys a number of procedural rights which may be lost if not timely raised; and, in a jury trial, a defendant must make a presentation understandable to untrained jurors. In short, a criminal trial under our system is an adversary proceeding with its own unique characteristics. In a revocation hearing, on the other hand, the State is represented, not by a prosecutor, but by a parole officer with a different orientation; formal procedures and rules of evidence are not employed; and the members of the hearing body are familiar with the problems and practice of probation or parole. The need for counsel at revocation hearings derives, not from the invariable attributes of those hearings, but rather from the peculiarities of particular cases.

The Court in *Gagnon* articulated the relevant considerations:

> * * * Presumptively, it may be said that counsel should be provided in cases where, after being informed of his right to request counsel, the probationer or parolee makes such a request, based on a timely and colorable claim (i) that he has not committed the alleged violation of the conditions upon which he is at liberty; or (ii) that, even if the violation is a matter of public record or is uncontested, there are substantial reasons which justified or mitigated the violation and make revocation inappropriate, and that the reasons are complex or otherwise difficult to develop or present. In passing on a request for the appointment of counsel, the responsible agency also should consider, especially in doubtful cases, whether the probationer appears to be capable of speaking effectively for himself.

The line that the Court has drawn is between adjudication of guilt and innocence and imposition of punishment in a criminal trial, and regular procedures for reviewing the adjudication and sentence, on the one hand, and proceedings that are related, but collateral to, the merits of a criminal case, on the other hand. When guilt is adjudicated, the Court has shown a special sensitivity to the need for counsel. This helps to explain In re Gault, 387 U.S. 1 (1967), which involved a fifteen-year-old, who was confined to a State Industrial School until he reached majority for allegedly making lewd telephone calls. Before being committed as a juvenile delinquent, he was given a hearing without counsel. In holding that due process required that he be appointed counsel, the Court focused on the juvenile's need for assistance of counsel to cope with the problems of law. Underlying the majority's opinion is the concern that the proceeding, though civil in nature, involved the potential for incarceration that was as real as a similar threat in a criminal case.

But, in Middendorf v. Henry, 425 U.S. 25 (1976), the Court refused to hold, on the basis of *Argersinger,* that a summary court-martial is a criminal prosecution because it results in a loss of liberty. The peculiarities of the military setting and its procedures led the Court to distinguish the summary court-martial from the traditional criminal trial. Furthermore, the Court said that due process does not necessitate counsel in this situation. Counsel, thought the Court, would alter the nature of the proceeding, which is informal and flexible.

C. THE RIGHT EXTENDED TO EXPERTS

In Ake v. Oklahoma, 470 U.S. 68 (1985), the Court held that an indigent defendant may be entitled to expert assistance in addition to appointed counsel. Ake was arrested and charged with murdering a couple and wounding their two children. He was hospitalized after initially being found incompetent to stand trial. Subsequently, he responded sufficiently well to medication that he was declared fit to stand trial. At the guilt stage of the capital proceeding, he raised an insanity defense. Defense counsel called and questioned each psychiatrist who had examined Ake while he was hospitalized. But each doctor indicated on cross-examination that he had not diagnosed Ake's mental state at the time of the offense. The jury convicted. During the sentencing stage no new evidence was presented.

Justice Marshall's opinion for the Court reasoned that Ake should have had a psychiatrist to assist his defense at both stages. The Court borrowed a procedural due process test it uses in civil cases to balance the defendant's need for help against the burden on the state of providing help. It found a strong "private interest" in life and liberty and the importance of avoiding an unjust conviction; no governmental interest in prevailing at trial if the result "is to cast a pall on the accuracy of the verdict obtained"; and a great value in providing expert assistance to a defendant when his sanity at the time of the offense is to be a significant factor at trial and when the government presents psychiatric evidence concerning future dangerousness in a capital sentencing proceeding. Thus, it held that Ake had been denied due process when he was not afforded access to a competent psychiatrist who might have conducted an appropriate examination and assisted in the evaluation, preparation and presentation of the defense. Chief Justice Burger concurred in the result. Justice Rehnquist filed a dissenting opinion.

An indigent defendant's right to an appointed expert under *Ake* is not automatic. It is only triggered when the defendant will be deprived of a fair opportunity to present his defense without the expert assistance. For example, in Caldwell v. Mississippi, 472 U.S. 320 (1985), the defendant sought the provision of several experts, including a ballistics expert. As support for his request, he stated only that the expert "would be of great necessarius [sic] witness." The trial court denied the request. The Supreme Court stated that Caldwell's "undeveloped assertions" were not sufficient to require appointment of the expert. See also Bowden v. Kemp, 767 F.2d 761 (11th Cir.1985) (appointment of psychiatrist not required where no showing was made that sanity would be a real issue at trial).

Generally speaking the courts have read *Ake* narrowly, and have refused to require appointment of an expert unless it is absolutely essential to the defense. See Harris, *Ake* Revisited: Expert Psychiatric Witnesses Remain Beyond Reach for the Indigent, 68 No.Car.L.Rev. 763 (1990).

Chapter Six

THE SCREENING AND CHARGING PROCESS

I. INTRODUCTION

Once the police have made an arrest, or they have made the decision to arrest a person, the suspect's fate lies mainly in the hands of the prosecutor. The prosecutor has very broad discretion to decide whether to file a formal charge against the suspect, and if so, what crime to charge. As a practical matter, this is so even if the charge actually is made by a grand jury or is screened by a magistrate. The prosecutor's discretion continues even after the charging decision has been made, since a prosecutor usually can obtain a dismissal of a criminal case prior to trial or the entry of a guilty plea. The fact that a prosecutor chooses to bring a charge does not guarantee that a defendant will be convicted, but it does guarantee that the defendant will be significantly burdened as a result of the initiation of the criminal process. The costs of a defense and the stigma of the charge must be borne by a defendant, and they might never be erased, even though the defendant may be acquitted.

A decision to charge a defendant with criminal activity puts into motion several formal and informal procedures. These will be considered in this chapter. Two of the most important are the preliminary hearing and the grand jury investigation. These procedures and their relationship to the prosecutor's role in the screening of cases and the charging process receive most of the attention in the material that follows.

II. CHOICES AND THE CHARGING PROCESS

A. CONTROLLED AND UNCONTROLLED CHOICES

Choices must be made at all levels of our criminal justice system. The police must decide whether to arrest or to investigate. Prosecutors must decide whether to initiate cases or whether to plea bargain. Magistrates issuing search and arrest warrants, or sitting in preliminary hearings, must decide whether probable cause exists or whether a suspect should be released on bail or pursuant to other conditions of pre-trial release. Grand juries must decide whether to indict, and prosecutors must decide whether to seek dismissal of indictments. Trial judges must decide whether there is enough evidence for cases to go to petit juries, and petit juries must decide whether to convict or acquit. Judges or juries must determine the sentences to be imposed on convicted offenders. Correctional authorities must decide how to treat incarcerated offenders, and parole or pardon authorities must determine whether to release offenders before their formal sentences have been served.

Some of these choices are controlled by standards—e.g., whether probable cause exists, whether there is enough evidence to go to a jury, and how convinced the jury must be before it convicts—and the task of government officials or jurors is to apply the standards to particular facts. Other choices—sentencing in some states is an example—might be controlled at the margin by minimum and maximum provisions but provide the decisionmaker wide latitude in choosing where to settle within the permissible range. The standards channel decisionmaking to some extent, but not completely. Still other choices are virtually standardless; that is, the persons who make them are not bound to follow any constitutional, statutory or other guidelines and have articulated none of their own to explain their actions.

The screening and charging process involves many uncontrolled choices, and these are a cause of concern. As you proceed in this chapter, keep in mind what choices are possible and what controls, if any, are placed upon them by the agency making the choice, or by some external agency.

B. LESS THAN FULL ENFORCEMENT OF THE LAW

One of the realities of law enforcement is that not all crimes are investigated, not all criminals are prosecuted, and not all laws are enforced. Nowhere in the United States is there a full enforcement policy—i.e, one that seeks to impose a sanction on every criminal act that occurs.

One compelling reason is that full enforcement is just too costly. We are not willing to pay for the police, the prosecutors, the public defenders, the judges, the courtrooms, and the penal institutions that would be required to punish all criminal acts that occur. Since we are not willing to pay for full enforcement, it is apparent that we expect that the people who administer the criminal justice system will be able to focus on important cases and to disregard less important ones. We also expect that usually they will make decisions on the importance of various cases as early in the process as possible, since it is important not to expend resources in processing cases that will not be carried forward. Thus, one reason for choice in the screening and charging process is simple economics; with limited resources allocated to law enforcement, not all cases can be pursued, and it is therefore necessary to determine which cases are important and how important they are.

Apart from economics, there are reasons why choices are made in the processing of cases. The notion of individualized justice runs deep in this country. Actions which technically fall under the same statutory proscription may not be equally reprehensible. As Roscoe Pound wrote,

> [l]aw is something more than an aggregate of rules. Hence enforcement of law is much more than applying to definite detailed states of fact the preappointed definite detailed consequences. Law must govern life, and the very essence of life is change. No legislative omniscience can predict and appoint consequences for the infinite variety of detailed facts

which human conduct continually presents. * * * [1]

Unlike the concern about economics, however, individualized justice need not depend on the exercise of discretion by a prosecutor or by a charging authority. Judges or juries could decide culpability after trial. Yet, the leveling of a charge can have such a devastating impact on a person that we probably have come to expect prosecutors to refuse to charge in some cases, even though it is possible that a conviction might be obtained.

Finally, legislative "overcriminalization" has resulted in criminal codes which, if they were fully enforced, might be intolerable. Laws are sometimes passed as "state-declared ideals," such as adultery statutes, which are "unenforced because we want to continue our conduct, and unrepealed because we want to preserve our morals." [2] Other laws, e.g., gambling laws, are drafted broadly for administrative convenience but are never fully enforced, since there is a general feeling that the legislature never really wanted to prohibit private poker games among friends. Outdated laws, which would cause public outrage were they enforced, remain unrepealed. Sometimes this is because non-enforcement results in ignorance of the existence of the laws; sometimes it is because there is no group likely to lobby for reform.

It seems, then, that legislatures pass and refuse to repeal statutes that invite choices by those who screen cases and make charging decisions.

It should be noted that the concept of individualized justice runs counter to another fundamental concept of American law: that all citizens should be treated equally under the law. When a legislature passes a broad statute and depends upon government officials who enforce the statute to exercise their discretion as to who should be prosecuted, the distinctions between classes of people and individuals are less visible. If the legislature were to write the distinctions into the statute, they would be more accessible to citizens, more easily subject to review, and undoubtedly more controversial. For a long time now, legislatures have been permitted to delegate to others the task of refining a statutory scheme through enforcement. Whether this is desirable is one question. Whether it is a permissible delegation of authority is another. Assuming that it is both desirable and permissible, there is yet a third question: Are there mechanisms available to provide some guarantee of equal treatment?

Some other countries purport to operate on the principle that the police and prosecutor have no discretion to exercise at all. If the case is one in which there is sufficient evidence to prosecute, it must be prosecuted. Whether these systems operate in practice as they are designed to in theory is questionable. Two observers make the following comment:

> The principle of compulsory prosecution which formally permeates the German and Italian systems, and informally the French, demands the impossible: full enforcement of the law in a time of rising crime and fierce competition for resources. Inevitably, adjustments must be made in the way in which the principle is to be applied; where formal law or ideology does not permit these

1. R. Pound, Criminal Justice in America 36 (1945).

2. LaFave, The Prosecutor's Discretion in the United States, 18 J.Am.Comp.L. 532, 533 (1970).

adjustments, informal processes are created that do.[3]

This observation has been challenged.[4] Whether or not it is entirely accurate, it serves as a reminder that it may be more difficult to make a mandatory system of prosecutions work in practice than it is to posit such a system in theory.

Judge Miner, in The Consequences of Federalizing Criminal Law, 4 Crim. Just. 16 (1989) argues that a prosecutor's decision not to prosecute someone who is guilty of a crime invades the province of the jury and creates a public perception of unfairness. Professor Green, in "Hare and Hounds": The Fugitive Defendant's Constitutional Right to be Pursued, 56 Brooklyn L.Rev. 439 (1990) disagrees with Judge Miner and argues that it makes sense that the prosecutor enjoys "virtually unfettered discretion in deciding how to allocate investigative and prosecutorial resources." Professor Green contends that the prosecution is in the "best position" to decide how to use the finite resources allocated to prosecuting crime. With whom do you agree?

III. SCREENING BY THE POLICE

A. THE NATURE OF POLICE CHOICES

Before reaching the question of what choices should be available to those responsible for charging suspects with criminal offenses, it is necessary to focus on the police. Generally, officials who have the ultimate responsibility for charging decisions do not themselves investigate criminal conduct.[5] The job of investigation is left to the police. Obviously, then, if the police do not turn information over to the charging officials, it is unlikely that those officials will have any real choice to make.

In Chapter Two, the restrictions on police investigations, arrests and searches were examined. The assumption there was that the police wanted to proceed against citizens, and the question was what limits, if any, should be placed on police activity. Sometimes, the police decide they do not want to take action against individuals, even though such action might be permissible under the rules previously discussed. When the police decide not to act, often they effectively screen cases from the criminal justice process.

3. Goldstein & Marcus, The Myth of Judicial Supervision in Three Inquisitorial Systems: France, Italy, and Germany, 87 Yale L.J. 240, 280 (1977).

4. Langbein & Weinreb, Continental Criminal Procedure: Myth and Reality, 87 Yale L.J. 1549 (1978). See also, Langbein, Land Without Plea Bargaining: How the Germans Do It, 78 Mich.L.Rev. 204 (1979).

5. Prosecutors may be well advised not to become too active in investigating cases they will have to prosecute. See, e.g., Roby v. State, 587 P.2d 641 (Wyo.1978).

In United States v. Johnston, 690 F.2d 638 (7th Cir.1982), the court reversed a decision barring the prosecutor assigned to a case from testifying at a suppression hearing concerning a telephone conversation he had with the defendant about which the defendant had testified. The court noted that prosecutors should avoid interviewing prospective witnesses except in the presence of third parties and indicated that prosecutors generally ought to withdraw where they must testify during a part of a case. But where the defendant placed the telephone call to the prosecutor and voluntarily chose to testify to its contents, the court concluded that the prosecutor should be permitted to testify and, if there was no reasonable likelihood that he would again be called as a witness, he could continue in the case. In other situations, it warned, the government would be required to show that its case would be prejudiced by substitution of counsel before a prosecutor would be permitted to continue after having testified.

The first level of screening may be done when the police decide whom to arrest. Although a decision to make an arrest must be reviewed by an impartial magistrate, either before or after the arrest is made, a decision not to arrest is essentially unreviewable.

The suggestion has been made that police cannot properly be given the choice whether or not to arrest, and that they must arrest when they have probable cause to do so.[6] But some statutes arguably are now drafted so as to explicitly recognize police choices.[7] Even where statutes appear to eliminate the possibility of choice, choices are made anyway by the police. In fact, it appears that the police in all American jurisdictions make decisions not to arrest people whom they could arrest. Several explanations can be offered for this phenomenon.

Were the police to arrest every suspect who they reasonably believed committed a crime, an already overburdened judicial system would be further burdened. Thus, we tolerate choices by the police because we are not prepared to handle more cases. Actually, the police themselves are not prepared to handle more cases either. If they spent more time in processing cases, they would have less time to spend on the street to deal with crimes that they view as more serious than the ones they now choose to ignore. Also, police officers learn that courts and prosecutors will not proceed very far in processing certain kinds of cases. Rather than initiating a process that they know will be shortlived, the police may decide not to make an arrest and to devote their energies to other activities. Similarly, if police strongly believe that a case will be dropped by the prosecutor, they may choose not to arrest a person in order to avoid unnecessarily stigmatizing that person. Dismissal of a complaint may not entirely eliminate the stigma associated with the arrest.

Some of these reasons should cause concern. A prosecutor may drop charges against an individual, who might be convicted were the charge pursued, because the arrest itself is a sufficient stigma and the prosecutor believes that conviction would be overkill. If no arrest is made, the deterrent impact on the law may be reduced. Thus, the fact that a prosecutor may choose to drop a case does not necessarily mean that no arrest should be made. As a practical matter, however, the police do not like to see their work end in a dismissal of a case. Whether or not they should refuse to arrest, they may do so when they know that a case will not go very far in the prosecutor's office.

Another reason that police will refrain from arresting is that the function they perform is more than initiating the criminal process; they also attempt to maintain order, and to do so they may need to maintain good relations with community elements who would resent the filing of criminal charges in some instances. The police officer may approach a disruptive incident "not in terms of enforcing the law but in terms of 'handling the situation.' "[8] Arrest is only one of several tools that the officer may use to maintain order. Often he may rely on his personal qualities—his size, his ability to "talk tough," his ability to

6. Hall, Police and Law in a Democratic Society, 28 Ind.L.J. 133, 155 (1953).

7. See, e.g., Md.Ann.Code art. 27, § B (1957); N.Y.Crim.Pro. § 140.10 (McKinney 1970). They state an officer's power in permissive terms. An argument has been made, however, that these statutes do not confer discretion, but indicate when an arrest warrant is not needed. See Allen, The Police and Substantive Rulemaking: Reconciling Principle and Expediency, 125 U.Pa.L.Rev. 62, 72–73 n. 56 (1976).

8. J. Wilson, Varieties of Police Behavior 33 (1968).

reason, etc.—to command respect so that order may be restored. Once order is restored, the officer may decide that it would be unnecessary or inappropriate to make an arrest.

B. SOME TYPICAL CASES

Consider the following situations, which a police officer might expect to confront, and in which a choice to arrest or not will be made.

1. An officer responds to a call from a woman who says her husband is going to beat her. When the officer arrives, the woman has a broken nose and several facial bruises, but she refuses to sign a complaint. Should the officer arrest the husband anyway? Should he suggest that the couple see a marriage counselor? Should his decision be affected by whether the couple has children who witnessed the beating?

2. An officer watches an adult sell an ounce of marijuana to a juvenile. When he apprehends the seller, the seller offers to work as an informant in exchange for favorable treatment, but only if no arrest is made. What should the officer do?

3. Suppose two officers are operating a speed trap and a car whizzes by at 20 miles per hour over the speed limit. They usually issue tickets to anyone speeding more than 8 miles over the limit. Should they issue a ticket if the driver is a parent rushing to the hospital to see an ill child? If the driver is an employee who is late to work and may be facing the loss of a job if tardy one more time? If the driver is a 17-year-old youth who has only a probationary license and will lose it automatically if a ticket is issued? If the driver is from out of town and did not realize that he was speeding?

The recognition of police discretion and the various choices that officers must make as a routine matter has been of recent vintage. See generally, ABA Standards, The Urban Police Function (2d ed. 1980). Ironically, if police departments contemplate adopting rules that would indicate circumstances in which an arrest could be, but probably ought not be, made, they may be criticized. Yet, without rules, decisions are left to individual officers at the lowest enforcement level.

Police rules to govern reactions to criminal activity have been criticized. See Allen, supra note 7. If police were making decisions totally on their own, surely there would be reason for concern. But as Professor Davis points out—see Davis, Police Discretion (1975); Davis, Police Rulemaking on Selective Enforcement: A Reply, 125 U.Pa.L.Rev. 1167 (1977)—the police rules would be made in conjunction with prosecutors and community representatives in the light of what courts do with cases, and would be subject to modification, of course, by the legislature.

IV. THE PROSECUTORIAL DECISION WHETHER TO CHARGE

A. THE NATURE OF THE DECISION

The prosecutor's decision whether to charge a suspect with a crime is of a different character than the patrolman's decision whether to arrest. While the patrolman usually must make an on-the-spot decision, the prosecutor has time, a fuller knowledge of the facts, and the opportunity to consult with colleagues. The consequences of a decision to charge are far greater than those of the decision to arrest. A decision to charge is a decision that the suspect should bear the monetary and social costs of trial and, in some cases, that the suspect's freedom should be conditioned on payment of bail. That the defendant may reduce some of these costs by pleading guilty to a lesser charge only makes the prosecutor's decision more consequential.[9]

B. THE FACTS THAT ARE CONSIDERED

The prosecutor must decide whether to charge and what crime to charge. The decision whether to charge depends on the prosecutor's belief that (1) the suspect is guilty, (2) the evidence is sufficient to secure conviction, and (3) it is in the community's best interest to prosecute the suspect. General criteria to be employed by the prosecutor are set forth in the standards of the National Advisory Commission on Criminal Justice Standards and Goals: Courts 20–21 (1973).

Standard 1.1 Criteria for Screening

An accused should be screened out of the criminal justice system when the benefits to be derived from prosecution or diversion would be outweighed by the costs of such action. Among the factors to be considered in making this determination are the following:

1. Any doubt as to the accused's guilt;

2. The impact of further proceedings upon the accused and those close to him, especially the likelihood and seriousness of financial hardship or family life disruption;

3. The value of further proceedings in preventing future offenses by other persons, considering the extent to which subjecting the accused to further proceedings could be expected to have an impact upon others who might commit such offenses, as well as the seriousness of those offenses;

4. The value of further proceedings in preventing future offenses by the offender, in light of the offender's commitment to criminal activity as a way of life; * * *

5. The value of further proceedings in fostering the community's sense of security and confidence in the criminal justice system;

6. The direct cost of prosecution, in terms of prosecutorial time, court time, and similar factors;

7. Any improper motives of the complainant;

8. Prolonged nonenforcement of the statute on which the charge is based;

9. The likelihood of prosecution and conviction of the offender by another jurisdiction; and

9. F. Miller, Prosecution: The Decision to Charge a Suspect with a Crime 3 (1969).

A police department study of Manhattan felony arrests for two summer months showed that 51% of 3,000 felony arrests resulted in cases being processed as misdemeanors. 33.8% of the total were reduced for reasons that had nothing to do with police work or problems with the arrests. Basler, 51% of Manhattan Felony Charges Found Reduced, N.Y. Times, Feb. 12, 1982, at 1, col. 4.

10. Any assistance rendered by the accused in apprehension or conviction of other offenders, in the prevention of offenses by others, in the reduction of the impact of offenses committed by himself or others upon the victims, and any other socially beneficial activity engaged in by the accused that might be encouraged in others by not prosecuting the offender.

In practice, perhaps the most important factor in a prosecutor's decision to prosecute is whether the prosecutor thinks a case can be won. A prosecutor with a high conviction rate is not only more likely to be successful in a reelection bid, but also will have enhanced credibility when she does file charges.[10] Therefore, she is likely to want to carry all the way to trial only those cases which are supported by a great deal of evidence and to which she thinks the judge and jury will be sympathetic.

This orientation on the part of the prosecutors could produce some salutary effects on the criminal justice system. For example, if the prosecutor is likely to prosecute only those suspects who, she is sure, are guilty, conviction of innocent persons will be minimized. And, prosecuting only "winners" preserves judicial and law enforcement resources.

But there are problems with setting a goal of high conviction rates. They are not always sought by prosecutors who are concerned about the danger of convicting innocent persons. They can be reached by offering very favorable plea bargains to people against whom the evidence is quite weak and who might well be acquitted at trial. Also, the prosecutor who offers a bargain that is rejected may vindictively pursue a defendant to demonstrate to others the wisdom of pleading guilty.

In short, it is not clear that a prosecutor's office should be judged on the basis of its rate of conviction. But the reality is that it probably will be.

Justice Brennan wrote for the majority in Young v. United States ex rel. Vuitton et Fils S.A., 481 U.S. 787 (1987), as the Court held that district courts have the authority to appoint a private attorney to prosecute a criminal contempt case, but that ordinarily they should do so only as a last resort after requesting the appropriate prosecuting authority to initiate prosecution. The case arose as a result of the issuance of an injunction by a federal district court forbidding trademark infringement. Counsel for the company that obtained the injunction requested the district court to appoint them as special counsel to prosecute a criminal contempt action for violation of the injunction. The Supreme Court held that, under Fed.R.Crim.P. 42(b), a district court has the power to instigate contempt proceedings and to appoint counsel, but concluded that, by affording the appropriate prosecuting authority an opportunity to initiate the proceeding, a district court enhances "the prospect that investigative activity will be conducted by trained prosecutors pursuant to Justice Department guidelines." The Court used its supervisory power to declare "that counsel for a party that is the beneficiary of a court order may not be appointed as prosecutor in a contempt action alleging a violation of that order." The Court observed that the prosecutor is expected to represent the interests of the government, not private litigants, and reasoned that "[i]n a case where a prosecutor represents an interested party, * * * the ethics of the legal profes-

10. Skolnick, Social Control in the Adversary System, 11 J. of Conflict Resolution 52, 57–8 (1967).

sion *require* that an interest other than the government's be taken into account."

Justice Brennan commanded only a plurality (Justices Marshall, Blackmun and Stevens joining him), however, for the proposition that appointment of an interested prosecutor is an error that cannot be harmless. He wrote that "[a] concern for actual prejudice in such circumstances misses the point, for what is at stake is the public perception of the integrity of our criminal justice system."

Justice Blackmun added a concurring paragraph in which he stated that "appointing an interested party's counsel to prosecute for criminal contempt is a violation of due process." The majority opinion, relying on the Court's supervisory powers, had not reached the constitutional issue.

Justice Scalia concurred in the judgment reversing the conviction. He reasoned that the appointments of the independent prosecutors were void, because prosecution of individuals who violate court orders is not part of the judicial power entrusted to the courts. He concluded that the United States Attorney might have exercised discretion and chosen not to prosecute the contempt, and that the convictions must be reversed because "[i]t would be impossible to conclude with any certainty that these prosecutions would have been brought had the court simply referred the matter to the Executive Branch."

Justice Powell, joined by Chief Justice Rehnquist and Justice O'Connor, concurred with most of the reasoning of the Court, but rejected the notion that an error in appointing an interested lawyer to prosecute always requires reversal. He argued for a remand to determine whether the error in this case was prejudicial.

Justice White dissented alone. Although he agreed with much of the Court's reasoning as to the desirability of referring contempt cases to the prosecuting authority and of not appointing interested lawyers to prosecute, he found that Rule 42 had been written to embrace a prior practice of appointing interested parties. He indicated that he would leave amendment of the rule to the rule-making process.

C. THE DECISION NOT TO PROSECUTE

A prosecutor's decision not to prosecute a suspect is generally not subject to judicial review. This means that the effect of a prosecutor's decision not to charge a suspect is a final resolution of the case in favor of the suspect. Of course, the prosecutor may change her mind and decide to charge the suspect within the time prescribed by the applicable statute of limitations, but courts rarely attempt to compel the prosecutor to file charges.

Even when statutory language appears to make prosecution of all violations of a statute mandatory, courts have been extremely reluctant to require prosecution where the prosecutor has decided against it. See, e.g., Inmates of Attica v. Rockefeller, 477 F.2d 375 (2d Cir.1973) (statutory language that prosecutor is "required" to institute prosecutions "has never been thought to exclude the exercise of prosecutorial discretion"). The court in *Attica* relied on separation of powers principles and refused to order the prosecutor to instigate prosecutions against state officials.

United States v. Cox, 342 F.2d 167 (5th Cir.1965), reviewed a district court's decision holding a United States Attorney in contempt for failing to prepare or sign indictments for a federal grand jury in Mississippi. The United States Attorney was acting upon instructions from the Acting Attorney General, to whom the district court issued an order to show cause why he too should not be adjudged in contempt. Three members of the divided court of appeals would have held that the United States Attorney had no obligation to prepare and sign indictments, three would have held that he had the obligation to do both tasks, and one judge cast his vote to require the prosecutor to prepare but not to sign indictments. The absence of litigation since this case strongly suggests that federal judges will not interfere with the decision of prosecutors not to approve of charges, even where a grand jury might wish to indict. Is this deference sound? No federal prosecutor can lawfully sign an indictment not approved by the grand jury, but it appears that he or she may decline to sign off on charges which the grand jury wishes to prefer. In thinking about the prosecutor's role, can you see a difference between the failure to approve an indictment that the grand jury wishes to return and the filing of an indictment that the grand jury opposes?

Morrison v. Olson, 487 U.S. 654 (1988), upheld a federal statute which requires the Attorney General to conduct a preliminary investigation of allegations of criminal activity on the part of high-ranking federal officials and, unless the allegations are found to be insubstantial, to ask a three-judge federal panel to appoint an "independent counsel" to complete the investigation, to decide whether or not to prefer charges, and to conduct any trials. Seven justices voted to uphold the statute and rejected the dissenting argument of Justice Scalia that the statute violates separation of powers principles.

There are several theoretical checks on the prosecutor's decision not to prosecute. All have extremely limited practical effect. In many states a grand jury can return a valid indictment without the prosecutor's approval. When a grand jury is dissatisfied with the performance of the local prosecutor, it may also request the attorney general to appoint a special prosecutor.[11] In some states, the attorney general may supercede the local prosecutor and initiate prosecution. Finally, a few jurisdictions permit private prosecution by allowing a citizen to present a claim to the grand jury where the prosecutor has failed to do so.[12] But if the grand jury indicts, the prosecutor may take over and quickly dispose of the case as she wishes.

In highly publicized cases, elected prosecutors may have to worry about public opinion. But in most cases, the public is not well informed, and the electoral process is no check on the prosecutor. Finally, in most states local prosecutors are subject to removal by the legislature or by recall. These are obviously cumbersome and ineffective procedures, used only in cases of corruption or some other special circumstance.

11. See generally, Annot., 84 ALR 3d 29 (1978) (appointment of special prosecutor).

12. See e.g. Brack v. Wells, 184 Md. 86, 40 A.2d 319 (1944). There is no private right of prosecution in federal courts. See United States v. Panza, 381 F.Supp. 1133 (W.D.Pa. 1974). In State v. Boykin, 298 N.C. 687, 259 S.E.2d 883 (1979), the court upheld the use of a privately retained prosecutor in a capital case, rejecting the defendant's argument that it violates due process for the family of a deceased to pay counsel to prosecute and to make counsel more a representative of private than public interests.

In State ex rel. Unnamed Petitioners v. Connors, 136 Wis.2d 118, 401 N.W.2d 782 (1987), the state supreme court invalidated a statute which permitted a circuit judge to allow the filing of a criminal complaint when a district attorney refuses or is unavailable to issue one. The court reasoned that the statute violated state constitutional separation of powers principles.

Although a prosecutor has great discretion not to bring charges, once they are brought in federal court, some courts may attempt to exercise some control over the dismissal of the charges. See, e.g., United States v. Butler, 486 F.Supp. 1285 (E.D.Tex.1980) (discussing Fed.R.Crim.P. 48(a) and refusing to permit the government to dismiss indictments after defendants pleaded guilty but before they were sentenced), reversed 659 F.2d 624 (5th Cir.1981) (en banc).[13]

D. ALTERNATIVES TO PROSECUTION

1. *Diversion*

In some instances the goals of the criminal justice system are better served when an offender is neither prosecuted nor simply released, but is diverted to a non-criminal alternative. Diversion occurs when formal criminal proceedings are suspended on the condition that the defendant will do something in return.[14] Typically the prosecutor suspends prosecution in exchange for the defendant's agreement to make restitution for an offense or to submit to rehabilitative counseling. Although diversion may occur at any point during the criminal process, it is most significant when it occurs before a case is too far along and prosecutorial resources have been spent in preparation for a criminal prosecution.

In recent years, prosecutors and legislators have increasingly turned to the diversion alternative for several reasons. The familiar concerns about limited government resources and increasing criminal caseloads encourages the removal of cases from the criminal justice system. Moreover, in many situations diversion alternatives are thought to provide a better means of handling a person with a problem that has led to criminal activity than conviction and sentencing. Finally, there is a realization that unless incarceration is a necessary punishment, it should be avoided. Prisons and jails are facilities of last resort. The offender who receives counseling, but is allowed to continue as a member of society, will be better prepared to cope with society than if he is isolated from society by imprisonment.

Some jurisdictions have enacted statutes that specifically provide for counseling alternatives to prosecution. These statutes generally cover crimes involving youthful offenders, mentally disturbed offenders, alcohol abuse or

13. Professor Goldstein has written of the tremendous discretion vested in prosecutors and has urged judges to "use their authority more aggressively at hearings on dismissal, charge reductions, and guilty pleas in order to build a common law of prosecutorial discretion." The Passive Judiciary 8 (1981). Central to his thesis is the idea that prosecutors ought to have to explain departures from rules and that explanations should be subject to verification. His approach is criticized in Stern, Book Review, 82 Colum.L.Rev. 1275 (1982).

14. National Advisory Commission on Criminal Justice Standards and Goals: Courts 27 (1973).

drug abuse. If certain criteria are met, these statutes give authority to the prosecutor to divert the case to a counseling agency.[15]

Some statutes appear to limit the discretion of the prosecutor. At the very least they present standards against which the prosecutor's decision can be judged and criticized. Some such diversion procedures involve the courts, and when they and the prosecutors are involved together, the extent of prosecutorial discretion may be diminished.[16]

2. *Informal Procedures*

Three types of cases in which prosecutors usually employ informal procedures are nonsupport, family assault and bad check cases.[17] Each type may be handled differently.

In nonsupport cases, one spouse (in most cases the wife) usually is not interested in having the other (the husband) prosecuted. But the threat of prosecution is a means of securing support payments. It would harm the wife's interest to have the husband in jail, because he would then have no income from which to make the payments. When the wife first comes to the prosecutor, the prosecutor may simply write a letter to the husband threatening him with prosecution if he does not resume making payments. Usually, though, if the husband is within the jurisdiction, the prosecutor will arrange an informal conference between the husband and wife or refer the case to an adjustment agency. The adjustment agency may go through a formal interview process with both spouses before making an arrangement for the husband to resume regular payments. If an arrangement cannot be made, the husband may be prosecuted, but only if the wife is willing. Although jurisdictions vary, the sentence imposed on the husband is usually probation, conditioned upon his making regular payments.

In family assault cases, the prosecutor generally delays the charging decision for a couple of days in the hope that the complainant will cool down and withdraw the complaint. Prosecutors are reluctant to charge for a number of reasons, including the relatively minor nature of most disputes, the strain on judicial resources, and the strain that formal proceedings would place on a continuing relationship.

If mediation appears to be necessary, the prosecutor may refer the case to a social agency or arrange an informal hearing before a member of the

15. See, e.g., Cal.Penal Code § 1000.5.

16. See People v. Superior Court, 11 Cal.3d 59, 113 Cal.Rptr. 21, 520 P.2d 405 (1974), where the court declared a statutory provision, granting prosecutors the right to veto a judge's decision to apply the diversionary remedy, unconstitutional under the California Constitution. See also State v. Maddocks, 80 N.J. 98, 402 A.2d 224 (1979).

State v. Greenlee, 228 Kan. 712, 620 P.2d 1132 (1980), found that a diversion statute did not grant any individual defendant a right to diversion, but said that "[t]he prosecutor, although possessing wide discretion is not immune from judicial review of the exercise of that discretion for arbitrariness."

Congress provided in the Victim and Witness Protection Act of 1982 that federal prosecutors shall consult crime victims or in some cases the families of victims to confer about decisions to dismiss cases or refer offenders to diversion programs. For a discussion of the statute, see Goldstein, The Victim and Prosecutorial Discretion: The Federal Victim and Witness Protection Act of 1982, 47 L. & Contemp.Prob. 225 (1984).

17. These descriptions are summaries taken from material in F. Miller, Prosecution: The Decision to Charge a Suspect with a Crime 260–73 (1969).

prosecutor's office or police department. If neither party appears at the hearing, the prosecutor assumes the dispute has been resolved and drops the case. If only one party appears, the prosecutor will usually arrange a second meeting rather than charge the suspect. Where both parties appear, the dispute is usually talked out, and no prosecution ensues.

In most bad check cases, the recipient of the bad check is interested only in getting his money. In such cases the prosecutor's office serves as a type of collection agency. Typically the prosecutor will first advise the recipient to seek restitution from the offender. If this is unsuccessful, the prosecutor usually writes a letter to the check writer advising him that he will be charged if he does not make restitution within a specified period of time. The offender is required to pay the money to the prosecutor, who then pays the complainant. When the offender does not have enough money to make the payments, he often is allowed to make installment payments.

Although informal procedures can be a useful alternative to the overburdened judicial system, they may be costly, and as long as prosecutors are involved, they do not reduce caseloads. But if they are no more costly than prosecutions, they may provide a more effective remedy than a criminal sanction.

E. PROSECUTORIAL RULEMAKING

Just as there have been numerous calls for rulemaking by the police, there have been a number of suggestions that chief prosecutorial officers should formulate regulations to govern the conduct of their offices. See, e.g., ALI Model Code of Pre-Arraignment Procedure § 10.3 (calling for regulations); ABA Standards, The Prosecution Function § 3–3.4 (1992) (calling for policy guidelines to determine "whether criminal proceedings should be instituted").

Some guidelines have been drafted, but they leave much room for individualized judgment on the part of particular prosecutors. See, e.g., U. S. Dept. of Justice, Materials Relating to Prosecutorial Discretion (1978). The arguments for rulemaking are similar to those made in favor of police rulemaking, but they are even stronger, since policy-making executive officials are likely to be trusted with greater power to make enforcement decisions than are lower level police officers.

Arguments against rulemaking have been made, however. They are the following: the application of rules in particular cases would be challenged, thus raising the costs of the criminal process; rules would reduce the deterrent efficacy of the criminal law by announcing which laws would not be vigorously enforced; individual treatment would be sacrificed in order to have uniformity; problems in law enforcement change rapidly and rulemaking would inhibit a rapid prosecutorial response to new problems; and adequate rules cannot be devised.[18] Are these arguments persuasive?

18. See generally, Beck, The Administrative Law of Criminal Prosecution: The Development of Prosecutorial Policy, 27 Am. U.L.Rev. 310, 337–80 (1978). See also, Vorenberg, Decent Restraint of Prosecutorial Discretion, 94 Harv.L.Rev. 1521 (1981), which suggests appropriate ways of controlling discretion. Frase, The Decision to File Federal Criminal Charges: A Quantitative Study of Prosecutorial Discretion, 47 U.Chi.L.Rev. 246 (1980), focuses on one United States Attorney's office and documents the tremendous discretion afforded federal prosecutors and the

F. SELECTIVE ENFORCEMENT

Whether by rules or by ad hoc decisions, prosecutors operating in a world of partial enforcement must somehow choose whom to prosecute. One way or another, prosecutors will try to focus attention on the more important cases. However, the selection of a certain type of case for emphasis may raise equal protection problems.

1. Emphasis on Career or Dangerous Criminals

Special Task Force lawyers are being used by the federal government and some state prosecutors' offices to deal with important offenders. One such approach is discussed here.

The Bronx County District Attorney's Office has implemented a program aimed at speeding up the prosecution, and increasing the conviction rate, of "career criminals." The program utilizes objective screening criteria to evaluate the seriousness of the crime, the criminal history of the offender, and the strength of the case. If the case passes these criteria, it is prosecuted by the Major Offense Bureau (MOB), a separate department within the district attorney's office. MOB cases have special access to the courts and follow a clearly defined plea bargaining policy. As a result of this program, MOB cases reached final disposition in a median time of 97 days compared to 400 days in other parts of the office, resulted in a significantly higher conviction rate, and resulted in an average maximum sentence of 10 years (in comparison with an average sentence of 3.5 years for a control group).[19]

Does the establishment of special procedures deny MOB defendants equal protection of the law? Is it significant that MOB cases always would be prosecuted under normal procedures anyway? What criteria are specific enough and fair enough to justify the special MOB treatment? If all persons arrested for certain crimes are prosecuted as MOB defendants, is there much reason for concern? How certain should a prosecutor have to be that a suspect committed a serious offense before he can employ the special MOB procedures? Should a prosecutor be able to tell law enforcement officials to "go after X who I believe is an organized crime official. Check his tax records, his business dealings, everything"? [20]

2. Constitutional Limitations and Prosecutorial Immunity

Equal protection attacks are extensions of the doctrine of Yick Wo v. Hopkins, 118 U.S. 356 (1886). In that case, criminal enforcement of a San Francisco ordinance, which made it unlawful for any person to run a laundry without consent of the city's board of supervisors except in a brick or stone building, was held to violate the equal protection clause of the Fourteenth Amendment. Although the ordinance was fair on its face, it was principally

factors they most often consider in exercising it.

19. Bronx County District Attorney's Office, the Major Offense Bureau (1977).

20. For a study showing how incomplete and inaccurate some computerized criminal justice records are and how inadequacies may result in harsh treatment of suspects and convicted defendants, see Doernberg & Zeigler, Due Process Versus Data Processing: An Analysis of Computerized Criminal History Information Systems, 55 N.Y.U.L.Rev. 1110 (1980).

applied against Chinese merchants and was therefore unconstitutional. In Two Guys v. McGinley, 366 U.S. 582 (1961), the Court may have expanded this doctrine from the administrative context of *Yick Wo* to the prosecutorial context. There, a store owner sought an injunction against the discriminatory enforcement of a Pennsylvania Sunday closing or "blue law." The Court hinted that discriminatory enforcement might be a valid defense to the charges:

> Since appellant's employees may defend against any such proceeding that is actually prosecuted on the ground of unconstitutional discrimination, we do not believe that the court below was incorrect in refusing to exercise its injunctive powers at that time.

A year later, the court was more explicit. In Oyler v. Boles, 368 U.S. 448 (1962), a convict sought a writ of habeas corpus, alleging that the West Virginia habitual offender statute had been discriminatorily applied against him. The defendant alleged that a high percentage of persons in similar circumstances had not been prosecuted under the habitual offender statute, but the Court rejected his claim because the defendant failed to allege that the prosecutor had "a deliberate policy of proceeding only in a certain class of cases or against specific persons."

Oyler may have established a two-pronged test for discriminatory enforcement claims. Under this test, a defendant must show: (1) that the prosecutor deliberately prosecuted some people, but not others who were similarly situated; and (2) that the selection of people for prosecution was deliberately based on an "unjustified standard * * * or other arbitrary classification." See United States v. Berrios, 501 F.2d 1207 (2d Cir.1974).

The Supreme Court did not elaborate on the discriminatory prosecution test for a number of years after *Oyler*.[21] During these years, lower federal courts heard numerous cases claiming discriminatory treatment. Although they did not always agree on the correct statement of the *Oyler* test,[22] the courts almost always were reluctant to interfere with prosecutorial discretion. The exceptional case was United States v. Falk, 479 F.2d 616 (7th Cir.1973) (en banc). The court held (4–3) that a prosecutor should be required to explain the reasons for moving against the defendant. Falk, a leader in the anti-war movement during the Vietnam War era, had been found guilty of refusing to submit to induction into the Armed Forces, and of two charges of failing to possess selective service cards. During earlier proceedings Falk had twice been denied the right to be heard on his claim that the purpose behind his prosecution was to unconstitutionally abridge his First Amendment rights. The court held that he presented sufficient evidence to raise a reasonable doubt about the prosecutor's purpose in charging him and that he was entitled to be heard.

The decision sparked a lengthy dissent by Judge Cummings. After attacking the evidence which the majority found sufficient to rebut the presumption of proper prosecutorial purpose, he wrote:

21. Cox v. Louisiana, 379 U.S. 536 (1965), discusses unconstitutional vesting of discretionary power in the prosecutor under an overbroad statute.

22. Cardinale and Feldman, The Federal Courts and the Right to Nondiscriminatory Administration of the Criminal Law: A Critical View, 29 Syracuse L.Rev. 659 (1978); United States v. Steele, 461 F.2d 1148 (9th Cir.1972); United States v. Robinson, 311 F.Supp. 1063 (W.D.Mo.1969).

> [I]f indeed Falk's draft counseling activity is one of the reasons why the prosecution was brought, that is hardly an impermissible reason for prosecution. Quite the contrary. As stated in the panel decision, "select enforcement of a law against someone in a position to influence others is unquestionably a legitimate prosecutorial scheme to secure general compliance with the law." * * * It is well within the realm of prosecutorial discretion to take into account the personal characteristics of the defendant, and among those his visibility and influence over others may quite properly weigh heavily in the decision whether to prosecute. * * *

The holding in *Falk* can be attributed to the court's concern for the defendant's First Amendment rights. Other circuits have taken a similar approach where First Amendment rights have been involved. United States v. Berrios, 501 F.2d 1207 (2nd Cir.1974); United States v. Crowthers, 456 F.2d 1074 (4th Cir.1972). But where First Amendment rights have not been involved, those claiming discriminatory enforcement have found courts to be unsympathetic.[23]

One of the most important cases on selective prosecution is United States v. Wayte, 470 U.S. 598 (1985), which saw the Supreme Court elaborate on the *Oyler* test. The government charged Wayte with failure to register for the draft, and Wayte claimed that he had been singled out for prosecution because of his outspoken views. Wayte presented evidence at a hearing that a conservative figure of the number of nonregistrants was 500,000. The government had only prosecuted eleven men, including Wayte, at the time of the hearing, despite the fact that the Justice Department had sent a memo to United States Attorneys indicating that the Selective Service System had access to Social Security records, which could be used to implement an active enforcement policy. Wayte also produced evidence that all men prosecuted were "vocal opponents of draft registration." With a prima facie case having been made, the district court concluded that the government was conscious that its "passive enforcement" policy would have an effect on vocal nonregistrants. It concluded that it violates the first amendment to prosecute only those who are vocal in their disagreement with government policy. The court of appeals reversed, 2–1, and was affirmed by the Supreme Court.

Justice Powell's opinion for seven Justices described the government's policy as "passive enforcement" which involved several steps. The Selective Service System would investigate only cases of nonregistration that came to its attention as a result of letters from young men like Wayte who wrote to government officials telling them that they had not registered or as a result of

23. See, e.g., Butler v. Cooper, 554 F.2d 645 (4th Cir.1977) (fact that 98 percent of arrests for liquor law violations were of black persons was insufficient to show racially discriminatory enforcement of the laws); United States v. Kelly, 556 F.2d 257 (5th Cir.1977) (defendant failed to establish that the Justice Department had decided to prosecute criminal offenses committed by customs service personnel such as defendant while ignoring offenses committed by Jury Enforcement Administration personnel); United States v. Johnson, 577 F.2d 1304 (5th Cir.1978) (defendant charged with willfully failing to file an income tax return failed to establish, prima facie, that he was prosecuted for conduct for which other persons were not prosecuted).

Not all First Amendment claims succeed. A court rejected the Reverend Sun Myung Moon's claim that his tax prosecution was an effort to attack his religious group in United States v. Sun Myung Moon, 718 F.2d 1210 (2d Cir.1983). Prosecution of strike leaders and vocal opponents of the law for participating in a strike while employed by the federal government was held not to amount to impermissible selective prosecution in United States v. Hoover, 727 F.2d 387 (5th Cir.1984).

reports made by third parties. Selective Service sent a letter to each reported violator that explained the duty to register and requested compliance with the law. It transmitted to the Department of Justice the names of those who did not register in response to the letter. Names of those who were required to, but had not, registered were forwarded to the FBI for additional inquiry. The appropriate United States Attorney contacted nonregistrants by registered mail to inform them that prosecution would be considered if they did not register. Usually, an FBI agent sought to interview a nonregistrant in an effort to persuade him to register. This was known as the "beg" policy. Before prosecutions began, the President established a grace period. Thereafter, some prosecutions were brought.

Justice Powell reasoned that "[i]t is appropriate to judge selective prosecution claims according to equal protection standards" and to require Wayte "to show both that the passive enforcement system had a discriminatory effect and that it was motivated by a discriminatory purpose." He concluded that the government treated all reported nonregistrants similarly, not in a discriminatory manner. Moreover, he found that there was no showing of an impermissible intent. Finally, he rejected an argument that passive enforcement violated the First Amendment, since the government's interest in registration was substantial and its passive enforcement policy was related to its legitimate interest in defense and "placed no more limitation on speech than was necessary to assure registration for the national defense." Justice Powell also noted that it would be undesirable to permit individuals who report their violations of the law to claim an immunity from prosecution on the theory that the reporting is a form of protest that cannot be punished.

Justice Marshall, joined by Justice Brennan, dissented without reaching the merits of the selective prosecution question. He concluded that Wayte had demonstrated a right to discovery of government documents and that no decision on the merits should have been made before the discovery was made available.

It is not always obvious who qualifies as similarly situated when claims of selective prosecution are made. Suppose, for example, a group of people decide to set up a system to assist refugees from various countries to enter the United States illegally, members of the group are prosecuted for violating the immigration laws, and they complain that various ranchers or farmers have not been prosecuted for hiring illegal aliens. Is this a prima facie case of discrimination? Does it matter whether large scale importers of illegal aliens are prosecuted? One court said that it did matter in United States v. Aguilar, 871 F.2d 1436 (9th Cir.1989). Can you identify the government policy in prosecuting "movement member" and large scale violators and in not prosecuting isolated employers?

A claim of discriminatory prosecution cannot be turned into a suit for civil damages under 42 U.S.C. § 1983. In Imbler v. Pachtman, 424 U.S. 409 (1976), the Court held that a prosecutor has absolute immunity from liability for all claims concerning the initiation of charges and the trying of the case. However, the court did note that a prosecutor might be held criminally liable under 18 U.S.C.A. § 242, the criminal analog of § 1983.

Imbler was limited in part in Burns v. Reed, 111 S.Ct. 1934 (1991). A state prosecutor advised the police that they could question a suspect, whom the police thought had multiple personalities, under hypnosis and that they "probably had probable cause" to arrest the suspect. During a subsequent probable cause hearing on a search warrant, the prosecutor elicited testimony from an officer that the suspect had confessed, but neither the prosecutor nor the officer informed the judge that the confession was obtained under hypnosis or that the suspect had otherwise denied guilt. The warrant was issued and the suspect was charged with attempted murder, but a motion to suppress the statements made under hypnosis was later granted and the charges were dropped. The Court held that the *Imbler* absolute immunity applied to the prosecutor's appearance in court to support the search warrant and his presentation of evidence in the hearing. The Court reasoned that the prosecutor's role at a pre-trial hearing satisfies the *Imbler* requirement of being "intimately associated with the judicial phase of the criminal process."

The Court also held, however, that only qualified immunity applied with respect to the prosecutor's advice to the police concerning probable cause. Justice White's opinion reasoned that "it is incongruous to allow prosecutors to be absolutely immune from liability for giving advice to the police, but to allow police officers only qualified immunity for following the advice."

Justice White concluded that the only issue before the Court with respect to the search warrant hearing involved the prosecutor's conduct in the hearing. Justice Scalia concurred in part in the judgment and dissented in part. He was joined by Justice Blackmun, and in part by Justice Marshall. He argued that the suspect had also challenged the prosecutor's motive in seeking the warrant. Justice Scalia reasoned that there is no absolute immunity for procuring a search warrant. He argued that the prosecutor's act of procuring a search warrant is analogous to a policeman's act in seeking a search warrant, for which there is no absolute immunity.

In United States v. Batchelder, 442 U.S. 114 (1979), Justice Marshall wrote for the Court as it held that a defendant who was convicted of receiving a firearm that had traveled in interstate commerce could be sentenced to five years' imprisonment, the maximum term under the statute, and that he was not entitled to be sentenced under another statute which punished felons for transporting firearms with a maximum penalty of two years. Justice Marshall reasoned that a wrongdoer has notice that more than one statute covers his conduct. Thus, the fact that conduct violates two statutes does not require a prosecution under the more lenient of them. A defendant's sole complaint is against invidious discrimination. Justice Marshall observed that a trial judge has discretion to make sentencing choices after a prosecution is brought and a conviction is obtained. But, under sentencing guidelines, those choices might be rather narrowly constrained today (see Chapter Eleven). Thus, the charging decision may be determinative of sentence except for a modest choice by the sentencing judge within a guidelines range. Should prosecutorial discretion be more circumscribed when judicial discretion in sentencing is reduced? If the same conduct is punishable under two or more statutes and there are no regulations governing the prosecutor's choice, how can it be "just" for a court to impose a sentence for whatever offense the prosecutor has chosen? Justice Marshall reasons in *Batchelder* that it does not deny equal protection or due process for a prosecutor to deliberately choose to charge one offense because it will produce a higher sentence than another. Why is this choice permissible?

Prosecutors may be limited in their ability to charge a defendant in a certain way as punishment for a defendant's exercise of constitutional rights. The subject of vindictive prosecutions is considered in Chapter Twelve.

V. THE GRAND JURY

The American criminal justice system, like the American political system, has checks and balances to prevent against too much centralized authority being placed in the hands of the executive. In some instances, depending on the jurisdiction and the seriousness of the crime, the grand jury operates as a check on the prosecutor's decision to charge. In other instances, the preliminary hearing serves this function. In some rare instances, both checks are available. Where a minor offense is charged, no pretrial screening procedure may be utilized. The remainder of this chapter will focus on the checks that exist and how they operate.

A. BACKGROUND ON THE GRAND JURY

R. Younger, The People's Panel 1–2 (1963)

The Grand Jury originated in England as the accusing body in the administration of criminal justice. At the Assize of Clarendon, in 1166, Henry II provided that twelve knights or twelve "good and lawful men" of every hundred and four lawful men of every vill disclose under oath the names of those in the community believed guilty of criminal offenses. Members of this inquisitorial body were obliged to present to the judge sworn accusations against all suspected offenders. Unlike petit juries, grand juries were not to pass upon guilt or innocence but were to decide only whether an individual should be brought to trial. At first all accusations originated with the members of the inquest themselves, but gradually the juries came to consider accusations made by outsiders as well. The jurors then heard only witnesses against the accused and, if they were convinced that there were grounds for trial, indicted him. They also passed upon indictments laid before them by crown prosecutors, returning a "true bill" if they found the accusation true or a "no bill" if they found it false. However, the juries never lost their power to accuse on their own knowledge. This they did by making a presentment to the court. The presentment represented an accusation on the jury's own initiative while an indictment represented a charge that originated outside the membership. Under their power of presentment English grand juries could and did investigate any matter that appeared to them to involve a violation of the law.

Slowly the character of the institution changed. Originally an important instrument of the Crown, it gradually became instead a strong independent power guarding the rights of the English people. The juries did not have to divulge to the court the evidence upon which they acted, and when royal officials abused their authority, they intervened to protect citizens from unfounded accusations. With the growth of royal absolutism in England the inquests became highly prized as defenders of the liberties of the people and shields against royal persecution. The refusal, in 1681, of a grand jury to indict Lord Shaftesbury on charges of treason, in spite of the insistence of Charles II, led Englishmen to look upon the grand jury system with increased respect. John Somers, Lord Chancellor of England, in his tract The Security of Englishmen's Lives, noted that "Grand juries are our only security, in as much as our lives cannot be drawn into jeopardy by all the malicious crafts of the devil, unless such a number of our honest countrymen shall be satisfied in the truth of the accusations." By the end of the seventeenth century the grand jury had become an important bulwark of the rights and privileges of English citizens.

Thus, the grand jury served two major functions. On one hand, it was a "buffer" protecting citizens from unjust prosecution by the state. On the other hand, it served an enforcement function by investigating incidents or offenses which the jurors thought suspicious. The buffer function of the grand jury was considered so fundamental that it was included in the Bill of Rights. The Fifth Amendment states in relevant part:

> No person shall be held to answer for a capital, or otherwise infamous crime, unless on a presentment or indictment of a Grand Jury, except in cases arising in the land or naval forces, or in the Militia, when in actual service in time of War or public danger; * * *.

Unlike most other provisions of the Bill of Rights examined thus far, the right to a grand jury indictment does not extend to defendants accused of state crimes. In Hurtado v. California, 110 U.S. 516 (1884), the Supreme Court held that the right to a grand jury indictment is not incorporated in the due process clause of the Fourteenth Amendment. Today, approximately half the states require prosecution by indictment for serious crimes as a matter of state constitutional or statutory law.

An indictment was not constitutionally required to charge a corporation with an antitrust felony, said the court in United States v. Armored Transport, Inc., 629 F.2d 1313 (9th Cir.1980). The court said that "[a] crime may be classified infamous either because of the nature of the crime, or because the potential punishment is infamous." It emphasized the punishment as the key factor. Since a corporation is potentially subject only to a fine (up to a million dollars) and a fine is not an infamous punishment for a corporation, no indictment was required, even though an individual who faces a potential prison sentence would have to be charged by indictment.

B. THE CHARGE OF THE GRAND JURY

The following model instructions to the grand jury for New Jersey provide a useful introduction to the work of the grand jury and the expectations that the community has for this body. The charge is given by the judge who empanels and supervises the grand jury.

MODEL GRAND JURY CHARGE

* * *

Citizens in general have only a vague idea of what a grand jury is and what its functions are. Since you are now members of the grand jury * * * you should be clear as to the functions you fulfill and the responsibilities placed upon you under our law. The term "grand" jury is sometimes misunderstood. It must be differentiated from the term "petit" jury. Both expressions are French in origin. "Grand" means large; "petit" means small. The terms refer to the size of membership of each jury—not the importance of the respective functions. Both juries—grand and petit—are essential to our system of justice, although their size and function differ. The grand jury is composed of 23 members; the petit or trial jury is composed of 12 members.[24]

The function of the grand jury is not to determine whether someone is guilty or not guilty of a crime—that is the responsibility of a petit jury. Rather, the primary function of the grand jury is to make a determination whether there is probable cause to believe that a crime was committed and that the accused committed it. While I will shortly define your obligations in greater detail, suffice it to say at this point that the grand jury serves as a screening mechanism to protect citizens from having to respond to unfounded charges. * * *

As I have noted, your principal function will be to consider alleged violations of the criminal law. You will determine whether or not an indictment should be returned against a person accused of violating the law. Under our system of justice, it is not enough that someone simply accuses another of committing a crime. After the accusation and before the person is made to stand trial on the charge, there must be an inquiry made by a grand jury to determine whether there is a basis for the charge. If the grand jury determines that there is an adequate basis for the charge, it votes to return an indictment against the accused. An indictment is a formal document brought in the name of the State of New Jersey, naming the accused as defendant and setting forth in writing the specific date and place of the alleged offense; the name of the alleged victim; the facts and circumstances making the alleged conduct criminal and the specific section of the criminal statutes of this state violated by that alleged conduct. If the grand jury

24. New Jersey empanels the same number of grand jurors as in the federal system. Other jurisdictions establish different numerical requirements for their grand juries. See, e.g., § 19.2–195 of the Code of Virginia.

When you examine the right to jury trial in Chapter Ten, you will see that more federal grand jurors are required than petit jurors; yet, the federal grand jury need not be unanimous, although the trial jury must be. Why would there be more grand jurors than petit jurors? Virginia provides for fewer grand jurors than petit jurors and still does not require unanimity among grand jurors. What does size tell you, if anything, about the role the grand jury is to play? What does the absence of a unanimity requirement tell you about the grand jury?

Under the Fourteenth Amendment, it is clear that racial or ethnic discrimination in the selection of grand jurors will violate the equal protection clause, and perhaps notions of fundamental fairness under the due process clause as well. See Rose v. Mitchell, 443 U.S. 545 (1979); Carter v. Jury Commission, 396 U.S. 320 (1970); Turner v. Fouche, 396 U.S. 346 (1970). In Castaneda v. Partida, 430 U.S. 482 (1977), the Court established that statistics could be used to make out a prima facie case of discrimination against Mexican–Americans, even where a majority of a county's population were Mexican–Americans. Challenges under the Fourteenth Amendment are like all of the challenges to government action on the basis of suspect classifications. It would seem permissible for a state to have a "blue ribbon" grand jury as long as the selection process did not exclude groups whose negative treatment would trigger a strict scrutiny analysis under the Fourteenth Amendment.

Chief Justice Burger wrote for the Court in Hobby v. United States, 468 U.S. 339 (1984), as it held that discrimination in the selection of grand jury forepersons and deputy forepersons in a federal district did not require reversal of a conviction. Hobby, a white male, had complained of racial and sexual discrimination in the selection of the grand jury. A court of appeals assumed, without deciding, that there had been discrimination against African-Americans and women, but held that reversal of Hobby's conviction was not required. The Supreme Court agreed. Chief Justice Burger condemned all discrimination in the selection of grand jurors, but found that the ministerial functions of the foreperson and the deputy added little to the role that any particular grand juror plays. Thus, as long as the grand jury was validly selected, discrimination in the selection of the two ministerial leaders did not deny the defendant due process.

In most places, the grand jury is drawn from the same pool as the petit jury, as under the Jury Selection and Service Act of 1968, 28 U.S.C.A. § 1861 et seq. But in states like Virginia, random selection of trial jurors is required (with voting and other lists to be used)—see Va.Code § 8.01–345—whereas grand jurors are selected differently.

decides that there is not an adequate basis for the charge it votes not to return an indictment or, in legal parlance, "no bills" the charge.

Whether or not there is an adequate basis shown for an indictment is known in legal language as "probable cause." "Probable cause" is not a technical concept. It has a practical meaning. Probable cause exists where the evidence presented is sufficient to lead a reasonable person to believe that a crime has been committed and that the accused committed it. Again, be clear that your function is not to decide beyond a reasonable doubt whether the evidence presented indicates that the accused committed a crime. A full-blown trial is not conducted before you; the technical rules of evidence do not apply; lawyers for the accused are not present to present a defense; the accused and any witnesses he may produce at a trial are generally not heard. In short, an indictment is merely the mechanism by which the criminal trial process is commenced. What you have to decide, based on what is presented to you, is whether there is reasonable ground to believe that a crime has been committed and that the accused committed it. If you do not believe that to be so you should vote against returning an indictment.[25]

We have thus far limited our consideration of your function to criminal charges—to deciding whether or not to indict a person. But since the grand jury is that independent investigative body which represents the public concern of the community, you may also inquire into matters which, while not strictly of a criminal nature, still have overtones of wrongdoing. You may become aware of official acts or omissions which fall short of criminal conduct and yet those acts or omissions are not in the public interest. It is certainly in the public interest that such conduct be revealed in an effective, well-considered manner. To investigate such matters you have those broad, comprehensive and independent powers I have previously alluded to. If you feel, after a well considered investigation, that some problem of public concern or some aspect of public business or some evil ought to be brought to the attention of the general populace you may do so by way of a presentment. A presentment, then, is a formal document, presented by you to the public in which you set forth your findings as to some problem in public affairs or public concern or derelictions in duty of public officers.

A presentment requires the exercise of sensitive judgment on your part. It involves serious matters and may not be returned lightly. It cannot be used to single out persons in private or unofficial positions to impugn their motives or hold them up to scorn. A presentment has to do with matters of public concern, not idle curiosity. If there is a problem of which the public should be aware and if the problem is caused in whole or in part by the noncriminal misconduct of a public official that individual may be named and indeed criticized. But before such a presentment is voted you must be satisfied that the proof of such wrongdoing is conclusive for once the presentment is made public there is no reversing its effect. And so as a matter of fundamental fairness a presentment naming and censuring a specific individual in a position affected with a public interest will not be made public, after being handed up, until the assignment judge obtains and reviews the full record of the testimony and exhibits and determines that sufficient evidence has been presented to support such charges.[26]

25. Since a grand jury indictment often will result in the arrest of the defendant, probable cause is a constitutional minimum. The grand jury is treated as though it were an independent magistrate, and no further finding of probable cause is necessary after the arrest is made to justify custody. In some jurisdictions the grand jury is told to decide whether the evidence would warrant conviction by a jury. It is unclear whether the difference has an impact on grand jury deliberations.

26. The word presentment is used in different ways. In New Jersey, apparently it

With respect to both indictments and presentments, the proofs respecting the alleged offense or public condition will be presented to you in the grand jury room in the form of witnesses or documentation. For the orderliness of the proceeding the matters will be presented and the witnesses called, in the usual case, by the prosecuting attorney. If, after hearing those witnesses called you feel that you wish to hear from additional witnesses before deciding whether or not there is an adequate basis for an indictment or a presentment you have the right to ask the prosecutor to subpoena them and if he refuses you may request the assistance of the assignment judge.

As I have said, the prosecuting attorney will present the various matters to you for your consideration. But understand clearly that the grand jury is an independent legal institution. It is not the agent of the prosecutor. It functions under our Constitution as the representative of the community with its own separate and distinct powers. It may investigate matters of a criminal nature of which its members may be aware even though not presented by the prosecutor. The same is true with respect to a presentment. The prosecutor, as a lawyer, is available to advise you on legal questions and you should freely call upon him for such legal advice—as you may the Court if you deem it necessary. You may, if you wish, ask the prosecutor for his opinion as to the sufficiency or insufficiency of the evidence. However, the prosecutor is not the one who decides whether to indict or not, or whether to return a presentment or not.

The prosecutor is not entitled to be present during your discussions. If during your discussion you do not want the prosecutor present you may ask him to leave the room and he must comply. Such requests are requests of the grand jury not individual jurors, and are to be determined by a majority of the jurors present.

It should be obvious that because of the sensitive nature of the matters which may come before you, these proceedings must be conducted in complete confidence. It would be dereliction of your duty and a violation of your oath were you ever to discuss with anyone outside the grand jury room what you may have heard while there. Untold and irreversible harm could be done to individual reputations were it otherwise. Remember, one of the prime functions of a grand jury is to protect the good name of individuals from unfounded charges.

Therefore, all your deliberations and discussions must take place in the grand jury room while you are in session. It is wrong for jurors to confer or deliberate together privately or by telephone concerning grand jury matters outside the grand jury room. A grand jury must confer together and act as a body. Your deliberations must likewise be kept secret. Each juror has the right to expect that his or her communications with fellow jurors during deliberations will remain confidential. There must be the utmost freedom of expression and debate in the grand jury

means a report, not an indictment. In Virginia, "[a] presentment is a written accusation of crime prepared and returned by a grand jury from their knowledge or observation; without any bill of indictment laid before them." Va.Code § 19.2–216.

The idea of reports, not formal charges, by grand juries has been troublesome in recent years. When the reports criticize particular individuals, who have difficulty responding in an effective way, courts are most troubled. See, e.g., United States v. Briggs, 514 F.2d 794 (5th Cir.1975); Application of Jordan, 439 F.Supp. 199 (S.D.W.Va.1977). A federal statute grants individuals criticized in a report the opportunity to publish an official response. 18 U.S.C.A. § 3333(c). But that may not be nearly as powerful as the charge by the grand jury. Case-by-case analysis of reports is still the order of the day. See In re Report and Recommendation of June 5, 1972, [Grand Jury], 370 F.Supp. 1219 (D.D.C.1974); Annot., 28 ALR Fed. 851 (1976). See also, Biglieri v. Washoe County Grand Jury Report, 95 Nev. 696, 601 P.2d 703 (1979) (grand jury may not accuse individual of indictable offense in a report without actually indicting).

room uninhibited by fear on the part of any juror that his views or expressions will be revealed or "leaked" outside of the grand jury room.

If, during your service, anyone should attempt to influence you in the performance of your duties, it would be an unquestionable violation of the law on the part of that person. Bring any such conduct to my attention immediately. Such breach will be dealt with by me expeditiously.

An official certified court reporter will be present in the grand jury room at all times when you are in session. It is that person's obligation to faithfully and accurately record all that transpires during the session. That reporter takes an oath of secrecy also. The testimony of witnesses including that in response to your questions is later transcribed if an indictment or presentment is handed up in the matter and is available for the trial of the case. However, the comments of the grand jurors in their discussions and deliberations and their vote on indictments or presentments are never recorded or transcribed. Further, the court reporter is not to be present in the grand jury room during your deliberations.

Any indictments you vote to return shall be handed up to me as assignment judge in open court. If you vote not to indict; that is "no bill" a matter, that document should immediately be signed by your foreman and returned to the Court the same day it is voted upon so that the individual, if in custody on that pending charge, may be immediately released. If you decide to return a presentment your foreman shall notify me ahead of time so that I may arrange to be present to receive it.

Now that you understand what is required of you we will ask the clerk to call the roll and administer to you your oath as grand jurors.[27]

C. THE PROCEDURES OF THE GRAND JURY

The Federal Rule illustrates typical procedures of the grand jury.

FEDERAL RULES OF CRIMINAL PROCEDURE

Rule 6

The Grand Jury

(a) **Summoning Grand Juries.** The court shall order one or more grand juries to be summoned at such times as the public interest requires. The grand jury shall consist of not less than 16 nor more than 23 members. The court shall direct that a sufficient number of legally qualified persons be summoned to meet this requirement.

(b) **Objections to Grand Jury and to Grand Jurors.**

(1) **Challenges.** The attorney for the government or a defendant who has been held to answer in the district court may challenge the array of jurors on the ground that the grand jury was not selected, drawn or summoned in accordance with law, and may challenge an individual juror on the ground that the juror is not legally qualified. Challenges shall be made before the administration of the oath to the jurors and shall be tried by the court.[28]

27. The charge is reprinted in Hearings on Grand Jury Reform Before the Subcomm. on Immigration, Citizenship & Int'l Law of the House Comm. on the Judiciary, Pt. I, 95th Cong. 1st Sess. at 477–80 (1977).

28. Obviously, it is extremely difficult for a defendant to challenge the grand jury before the jurors are sworn.

(2) **Motion to Dismiss.** A motion to dismiss the indictment may be based on objections to the array or on the lack of legal qualification of an individual juror, if not previously determined upon challenge. It shall be made in the manner prescribed in 28 U.S.C.A. § 1867(e) and shall be granted under the conditions prescribed in that statute. An indictment shall not be dismissed on the ground that one or more members of the grand jury were not legally qualified if it appears from the record kept pursuant to subdivision (c) of this rule that 12 or more jurors, after deducting the number not legally qualified, concurred in finding the indictment.[29]

(c) **Foreman and Deputy Foreman.** The court shall appoint one of the jurors to be foreman and another to be deputy foreman. The foreman shall have power to administer oaths and affirmations and shall sign all indictments. He or another juror designated by him shall keep a record of the number of jurors concurring in the finding of every indictment and shall file the record with the clerk of the court, but the record shall not be made public except on order of the court. During the absence of the foreman, the deputy foreman shall act as foreman.

(d) **Who May Be Present.** Attorneys for the government,[30] the witness under examination, interpreters when needed and, for the purpose of taking the evidence, a stenographer or operator of a recording device may be present while the grand jury is in session, but no person other than the jurors may be present while the grand jury is deliberating or voting.[31]

29. Because 11 grand jurors could be disqualified without invalidating an indictment, such challenges rarely succeed. Most jurisdictions do not allow challenge to the bias of a grand jury, although some statutes and rules do allow particular forms of challenge. See, e.g., Me.R.Crim.P. 6(b). The Supreme Court has not ruled on whether an indictment by a biased grand jury is fundamentally unfair. It did not reach the question in Beck v. Washington, 369 U.S. 541 (1962). The fact that a state charges someone through a grand jury, which supposedly is an independent, impartial group of citizens, may enhance the significance of the charge. If so, should the grand jury at least have to have the votes of the designated number of unbiased jurors to charge an offense? Most courts probably would not entertain a claim that a grand jury was influenced improperly by pre-trial publicity. See People ex rel. Sears v. Romiti, 50 Ill.2d 51, 277 N.E.2d 705 (1972).

30. Usually the prosecutor may be present when evidence is presented. But see Va. R.Crim.P. 3A:6(b). Virginia gives the prosecutor a greater opportunity to be present before special grand juries. Va.Code § 19.2–210.

In United States v. Mechanik, 475 U.S. 66 (1986), the Supreme Court held that a violation of Rule 6(d) that occurred when two agents testified in tandem before a grand jury in support of a superseding indictment expanding a conspiracy charge was harmless error that had no effect on the outcome of the trial. Justice O'Connor, joined by Justices Brennan and Blackmun, concurred in the judgment, reasoning that a Rule 6 violation affects the grand jury proceeding rather than the trial, and that dismissal of the indictment is an appropriate remedy "if it is established that the violation substantially influenced the grand jury's decision to indict, or if there is grave doubt as to whether it had such effect." Justice Marshall dissented.

Justice Kennedy cited *Mechanik* in Bank of Nova Scotia v. United States, 487 U.S. 250 (1988), which held that a federal court may not invoke its supervisory power to circumvent the harmless error inquiry prescribed by Fed.R.Crim.P. 52(a). The Court concluded that a district court exceeds its powers in dismissing an indictment for prosecutorial misconduct not prejudicial to the defendant. For nonconstitutional errors, the Court adopted the standard of prejudice suggested by Justice O'Connor in her *Mechanik* concurrence.

31. If there is testimony by the prosecutor, some decisions say that the prosecutor can no longer remain as the legal advisor to the grand jury. See, e.g., United States v. Treadway, 445 F.Supp. 959 (N.D.Tex.1978). Does this make sense when a grand juror can testify and remain part of the grand jury? See also United States v. Samango, 450 F.Supp. 1097 (D.Hawaii 1978). If the prosecutor finds himself in a conflict of interest situation, any indictment may be dismissed. See United States v. Gold, 470 F.Supp. 1336 (N.D.Ill.1979).

(e) **Secrecy of Proceedings and Disclosure.—**[32]

(1) Recording of Proceedings. All proceedings, except when the grand jury is deliberating or voting, shall be recorded stenographically or by an electronic recording device. An unintentional failure of any recording to reproduce all or any portion of a proceeding shall not affect the validity of the prosecution. The recording or reporter's notes or any transcript prepared therefrom shall remain in the custody or control of the attorney for the government unless otherwise ordered by the court in a particular case.

(2) General Rule of Secrecy. A grand juror, an interpreter, a stenographer, an operator of a recording device,[33] a typist who transcribes recorded testimony, an attorney for the Government, or any person to whom disclosure is made under paragraph (3)(A)(ii) of this subdivision shall not disclose matters occurring before the grand jury, except as otherwise provided for in these rules. No obligation of secrecy may be imposed on any person except in accordance with this rule. A knowing violation of rule 6 may be punished as a contempt of court.

(3) Exceptions.—

(A) Disclosure otherwise prohibited by this rule of matters occurring before the grand jury, other than its deliberations and the vote of any grand juror, may be made to—

(i) an attorney for the government for use in the performance of such attorney's duty; [34] and

32. The Supreme Court and most states seek to assure secrecy in grand jury deliberations in order to promote cooperation of witnesses, to avoid signalling that a charge may be made to persons who might flee, to gather reliable evidence before witnesses attempt to manufacture, conceal or eliminate it, and to protect those who are not charged from public exposure of allegations. See United States v. Procter & Gamble Co., 356 U.S. 677, 681 n. 6 (1958); Douglas Oil Co. v. Petrol Stops Northwest, 441 U.S. 211 (1979).

Fed.R.Evid. 606(b) makes inadmissible grand jury evidence about the deliberations of the jury. Whether grand jurors may testify about extraneous influences brought to bear on the jury depends on the kind of challenges that can be raised to grand jury indictments. For example, if a challenge is made to the number of jurors who voted to indict, there is a split of authority as to whether a grand juror can testify about the vote. See State ex rel. Matko v. Ziegler, 154 W.Va. 872, 179 S.E.2d 735 (1971). And if grand jurors cannot be challenged for bias, then testimony about bias plainly would be irrelevant and excluded. But, if a ground for attack is recognized, secrecy may give way. See, e.g., subdivision (e)(2)(C)(ii) of Fed.R.Crim.P. 6.

Note that the federal rule, like most rules, imposes no obligation of secrecy on grand jury witnesses. See In re Russo, 53 F.R.D. 564 (C.D.Cal.1971). The argument has been made that a secrecy requirement would be impractical. See Dession, The New Federal Rules of Criminal Procedure: II, 56 Yale L.J. 197, 204 N. 100 (1947). Do you agree with this? If witnesses are free to talk, how effective do you think the secrecy rule is likely to be?

In Butterworth v. Smith, 494 U.S. 624 (1990) the Court unanimously held that a Florida statute violated the First Amendment insofar as it prohibited a grand jury witness from disclosing his own testimony after the grand jury's term has ended. Chief Justice Rehnquist's opinion noted in contrast that Federal Rule of Criminal Procedure 6 exempts witnesses from the obligation of secrecy as to their own statements.

33. Not all states mandate recording of grand jury testimony. See Knodsen, Pretrial Disclosure of Federal Grand Jury Testimony, 48 Wash.L.Rev. 422 (1973).

34. In United States v. Sells Engineering, Inc., 463 U.S. 418 (1983), the Court held, 5–4, that lawyers in the civil division of the Justice Department may not get automatic disclosure of evidence presented to a grand jury. The majority reasoned that automatic disclosure would increase the risk of inadvertent or illegal disclosure of grand jury proceedings and discourage witnesses from cooperating with grand juries. Thus, to obtain disclosure, civil division lawyers, like private litigants, must make a strong showing of particularized need for disclosure for use in another proceeding, demonstrate that this need is greater than the need for secrecy in the grand jury proceeding, and structure requests for disclosure so as to obtain only what is really needed.

The Supreme Court distinguished *Sells Engineering* in United States v. John Doe, Inc. I,

(ii) such government personnel as are deemed necessary by an attorney for the government to assist an attorney for the government in the performance of such attorney's duty to enforce Federal criminal law.

(B) Any person to whom matters are disclosed under subparagraph (A)(ii) of this paragraph shall not utilize that grand jury material for any purpose other than assisting the attorney for the government in the performance of such attorney's duty to enforce Federal criminal law. An attorney for the government shall promptly provide the district court, before which was impaneled the grand jury whose material has been so disclosed, with the names of the persons to whom such disclosure has been made.

(C) Disclosure otherwise prohibited by this rule of matters occurring before the grand jury may also be made—

(i) When so directed by a court [35] preliminarily to or in connection with a judicial proceeding; [36] or

(ii) when permitted by a court at the request of the defendant, upon a showing that grounds may exist for a motion to dismiss the indictment because of matters occurring before the grand jury; or

(iii) when the disclosure is made by an attorney for the government to another federal grand jury.

If the court orders disclosure of matters occurring before the grand jury, the disclosure shall be made in such manner, at such time, and under such conditions as the court may direct.

* * *

(4) Sealed Indictments. The federal magistrate to whom an indictment is returned may direct that the indictment be kept secret until the defendant is in custody or has been released pending trial. Thereupon the clerk shall seal the indictment and no person shall disclose the return of the indictment except when necessary for the issuance and execution of a warrant or summons.

481 U.S. 102 (1987), as it held that attorneys in the antitrust division of the Justice Department who conducted a grand jury investigation may make continued use of grand jury materials in the civil phase of a dispute without obtaining a court order to do so. The Court also affirmed a district judge who found particularized need for disclosure of grand jury material to Justice Department lawyers in the civil division and the United States Attorney. Justice Stevens' majority opinion reasoned that an attorney who conducted a grand jury investigation does not necessarily disclose any grand jury materials when continuing into a civil phase of a proceeding, and that the danger of abuse of the grand jury in the context of this case was small. Justice Brennan, joined by Justices Marshall and Blackmun, dissented and argued that the Court's approach to the word "disclosure" ignored the substantive concerns of Rule 6. Justice White did not participate in the case.

35. Douglas Oil Co. v. Petrol Stops Northwest, 441 U.S. 211 (1979), indicates that the supervising judge ideally should review a request for disclosure, but that after this judge makes a written evaluation of the need for continued grand jury secrecy, the better practice would be to send the requested materials to the court in which the case for which disclosure is sought is pending for an evaluation of the need of the requesting party for the evidence. See also Illinois v. Abbott & Assoc., Inc., 460 U.S. 557 (1983) (section 4F(b) of the Clayton Act does not implicitly exempt state attorneys general from showing particularized need for grand jury materials).

Some courts have suggested that documents obtained by grand juries may more readily be disclosed than testimony. See, e.g., In re Grand Jury Investigation, 441 F.Supp. 1299 (M.D.Fla.1977).

36. In United States v. Baggot, 463 U.S. 476 (1983), the Court held, 8–1, that an IRS tax audit is not conducted preliminarily to or in connection with a judicial proceeding. Thus, grand jury evidence could not be disclosed for use in such an audit. The Court found that disclosure is only permitted when there is pending or anticipated litigation, not where litigation is merely possible.

(5) Closed Hearing. Subject to any right to an open hearing in contempt proceedings, the court shall order a hearing on matters affecting a grand jury proceeding to be closed to the extent necessary to prevent disclosure of matters occurring before a grand jury.

(6) Sealed Records. Records, orders and subpoenas relating to grand jury proceedings shall be kept under seal to the extent and for such time as is necessary to prevent disclosure of matters occurring before a grand jury.

(f) **Finding and Return of Indictment.** An indictment may be found only upon the concurrence of 12 or more jurors. The indictment shall be returned by the grand jury to a federal magistrate in open court. If a complaint or information is pending against the defendant and 12 jurors do not concur in finding an indictment, the foreman shall so report to a federal magistrate in writing forthwith.

(g) **Discharge and Excuse.** A grand jury shall serve until discharged by the court but no grand jury may serve more than 18 months unless the court extends the service of the grand jury for a period of six months or less upon a determination that such extension is in the public interest. At any time for cause shown the court may excuse a juror either temporarily or permanently, and in the latter event the court may impanel another person in place of the juror excused.[37]

D. THE RELATIONSHIP OF THE GRAND JURY TO THE DEPARTMENTS OF GOVERNMNET

The roles played by the prosecutor, the court and the grand jury are not exactly the same in all jurisdictions. However, it is common for courts to view the prosecutor's relationship to the grand jury as subject to little, if any, judicial scrutiny. United States v. Chanen, 549 F.2d 1306 (9th Cir.1977), illustrates this. The government presented its case three times to a federal grand jury. The first time the government did not ask for an indictment, and no vote was taken before the grand jury was discharged. A second grand jury indictment was dismissed because no transcript was made, and the government failed to present the jury with the evidence presented to the first grand jury. On the third attempt, the government secured an indictment against defendants for statutory fraud. The government presented its evidence to the third grand jury by reading testimony from its first grand jury presentation. The district court quashed the indictment because the judge felt that where the first grand jury failed to indict on the basis of live testimony, a subsequent grand jury should hear live testimony as well. The court of appeals reversed. It held that the prosecutor's action was not "fundamentally unfair" and therefore did not constitute a basis for dismissal.

> Respecting the work of the grand jury, both court and prosecutor play supportive and complementary roles. As a practical matter, the grand jury generally relies on the prosecutor to determine what witnesses to call. Also, in practice the prosecutor conducts the examination of the witnesses and otherwise determines what evidence to present before the grand jury. In addition, it is the prosecutor who normally prepares the indictment, although of course the grand jury must review the indictment and adopt it as its own. Some of these

37. Some jurisdictions provide that a grand jury can only be discharged before its term expires for "legal" or good cause. E.g., N.J.Ct.R. 3, 6–10. Still others allow discharge when the grand jury's work is done. E.g., Cal.Penal Code § 915.

functions—such as initiating a criminal case by presenting evidence before the grand jury—qualifies as "an executive function within the exclusive prerogative of the Attorney General." In re Persico, 522 F.2d 41, 54–55 (2d Cir.1975).

The court, on the other hand, exercises its power to summon witnesses to attend and to give testimony before the grand jury. Also, "it is the court which must compel a witness to testify if, after appearing, he refuses to do so." Brown v. United States, supra, 359 U.S. at 49. In addition, the court exercises a form of authority over the grand jury when, for example, it dismisses an indictment for failure to charge all elements of the offense or to warn the defendant fairly of the charge against which he must defend. Likewise, the court exercises authority over the prosecutor when it dismisses an indictment because of prosecutorial misconduct. * * *

Nevertheless, given the constitutionally-based independence of each of the three actors—court, prosecutor and grand jury—we believe a court may not exercise its "supervisory power" in a way which encroaches on the prerogatives of the other two unless there is a clear basis in fact and law for doing so. If the district courts were not required to meet such a standard, their "supervisory power" could readily prove subversive of the doctrine of separation of powers.

Application of this standard to the present case requires reversal. The asserted legal basis for the district court's interference with a standard prosecutorial decision—what evidence to present to the grand jury and how to present it—is the need to preserve the integrity of the judicial process and to avoid any fundamental unfairness. But it is far from clear that the prosecutor's decision in this case regarding the presentation of evidence to the third grand jury implicates any of those interests.[38]

38. In United States v. Samango, 607 F.2d 877 (9th Cir.1979), the court affirmed the dismissal of an indictment by a district judge on the ground that the prosecutor's behavior produced a biased grand jury. Another of the unusual cases in which an indictment was dismissed because of improper prosecutorial conduct is Unites States v. Lawson, 502 F.Supp. 158 (D.Md.1980). The court found that the prosecutor intentionally asked misleading questions of a witness and failed to disclose known, exculpatory evidence. But the court's dismissal was without prejudice, because "[a]lthough defendants do have a constitutional right to an informed and unbiased grand jury, they have no concomitant right to bar forever investigation into their alleged criminal conduct."

United States v. McKenzie, 678 F.2d 629 (5th Cir.1982), indicates that an indictment will be quashed because of prosecutorial conduct before a grand jury "only when prosecutorial misconduct amounts to overbearing the will of the grand jury so that the indictment is, in effect, that of the prosecutor rather than the grand jury." The court indicated that a prosecutor could tell the jury that the evidence shows the defendant is guilty.

In United States v. Anderson, 577 F.Supp. 223 (D.Wyo.1983), a district judge dismissed an indictment charging several defendants with conspiracy to defraud the government and related offenses. The judge found: the government used undercover investigators to invade the "defense camp," one such investigator used questions prepared by the United States Attorney in his conversations with the defendants, the United States Attorney questioned the investigator before the grand jury about the defendants' legal strategy and defenses, the prosecution violated grand jury secrecy and showed grand jury material to an expert who testified before the grand jury, and law enforcement officers described themselves as "grand jury officers" during the course of interviews with prospective witnesses and purported to grant informal or "pocket" immunity to witnesses without court approval in order to compel them to testify. The Judge concluded that "[t]he manner in which the government conducted itself during the course of the grand jury proceedings which resulted in the indictments in this case obfuscated the important constitutional distinctions between prosecutor, law enforcement investigator and grand jury."

United States v. Udziela, 671 F.2d 995 (7th Cir.1982), holds that when a prosecutor discovers that perjured testimony has been presented to a grand jury, the government has the option of voluntarily withdrawing the tainted indictment and seeking a new one or appearing with defense counsel before the district court for an in camera inspection of the

---

Note

The role of the prosecutor does vary from place to place, but generally she serves the following functions: (a) She is the legal advisor to the grand jury. Many critics maintain that the grand jury should have separate counsel at its disposal to reduce the prosecutor's control over the grand jury. But traditionally the prosecutor is also the grand jury's counsel. (b) She presents evidence to the grand jury. The grand jury can always hear any additional evidence that it requests, but as a practical matter grand juries usually rely on the prosecutor to explain criminal offenses and to present the evidence that the grand jury considers. The prosecutor can subpoena witnesses to attend grand jury hearings, and once the witnesses are present the grand jury will hear them. (c) The prosecutor usually may negate a grand jury's decision to return an indictment by refusing to sign the indictment—see United States v. Cox, 342 F.2d 167 (5th Cir.1967)—or by nolle prosequi, which dismisses the charges. And a grand jury decision not to indict can be circumvented if the prosecutor resubmits the case to another grand jury. In some jurisdictions such action requires court approval.

E. THE GRAND JURY AS A PROTECTION AGAINST UNJUST PROSECUTION

The traditional view of the grand jury as a protection against unwarranted prosecution has been described as follows:

> Historically, this body has been regarded as a primary security to the innocent against hasty, malicious and oppressive persecution; it serves the invaluable function in our society of standing between the accuser and the accused, whether the latter be an individual, minority group, or other, to determine whether a charge is founded upon reason or was dictated by an intimidating power or by malice and personal ill will.

Wood v. Georgia, 370 U.S. 375, 390 (1962).

In recent years this view has been challenged. Commentators and courts have increasingly come to see a grand jury indictment as little more than a rubber stamp for the prosecutor's decision to go forward. In Hawkins v. Superior Court, 22 Cal.3d 584, 150 Cal.Rptr. 435, 586 P.2d 916 (1978), the California Supreme Court expressed its somewhat cynical view of the modern grand jury.

> The prosecuting attorney is typically in complete control of the total process in the grand jury room: he calls the witnesses, interprets the evidence, states and applies the law, and advises the grand jury on whether a crime has been committed. The grand jury is independent only in the sense that it is not formally attached to the prosecutor's office; though legally free to vote as they please, grand jurors virtually always assent to the recommendations of the prosecuting attorney, a fact borne out by available statistical and survey data. Indeed, the fiction of grand jury independence is perhaps best demonstrated by the following fact to which the parties herein have stipulated: between

grand jury transcript to determine whether sufficient untainted evidence supports the indictment.

January 1, 1974, and June 30, 1977, 235 cases were presented to the San Francisco grand jury and indictments were returned in all 235.

The pervasive prosecutorial influence reflected in such statistics has led an impressive array of commentators to endorse the sentiment expressed by United States District Judge William J. Campbell, a former prosecutor: "Today, the grand jury is the total captive of the prosecutor who, if he is candid, will concede that he can indict anybody, at any time, for almost anything, before any grand jury." (Campbell, Eliminate the Grand Jury (1973) 64 J.Crim.L. & C. 174.) Another distinguished federal jurist, Judge Marvin E. Frankel, put it this way: "The contemporary grand jury investigates only those whom the prosecutor asks to be investigated, and by and large indicts those whom the prosecutor wants to be indicted." (Frankel & Naftalis, The Grand Jury: An Institution on Trial (1977) p. 100.) * * *

The domination of grand jury proceedings by the prosecuting attorney no doubt derives at least in part from the grand jury's institutional schizophrenia: it is expected to serve two distinct and largely inconsistent functions—accuser and impartial factfinder. * * *

The high proportion of true bills (i.e. decisions to charge, rather than not to charge) compared to no bills is not surprising. The grand jury is neither a rubber stamp nor a body with no mind of its own. What it is, however, is a body that hears only one side of a case. And it reacts to that side. It is only natural that it agrees with the prosecutor in almost every case, since no counter to the prosecutor appears before the jury. Thus, in 1976 slightly more than 23,000 indictments were returned by federal grand juries as compared to 123 no bills.[39] The principal function of the grand jury today probably is not to refuse indictment, but to force the prosecution to gather and to offer evidence in some systematic way before a charge is brought. What often is overlooked in discussions of grand juries is the fact that when the evidence, once put together, turns out to be weak, prosecutors sometimes decide not to ask for indictments or to seek indictments on lesser offenses than they might have charged on their own. One reason that this function of the jury does not work better than it otherwise could is that prosecutors often are permitted to offer evidence to grand juries that could not be offered at trials. The next case is an illustration.

COSTELLO v. UNITED STATES

Supreme Court of the United States, 1956.
350 U.S. 359.

MR. JUSTICE BLACK delivered the opinion of the Court.

We granted certiorari in this case to consider a single question: "May a defendant be required to stand trial and a conviction be sustained where only hearsay evidence was presented to the grand jury which indicted him?"

Petitioner, Frank Costello, was indicted for wilfully attempting to evade payment of income taxes due the United States for the years 1947, 1948 and 1949. The charge was that petitioner falsely and fraudulently reported less income than he and his wife actually received during the taxable years in

39. See generally Morse, A Survey of the Grand Jury Systems, 10 Ore.L.Rev. 101 (1931). For a grand juror's personal account of an unsatisfactory experience, see McGaughey, Trials of a Grand Juror, 65 A.B.A.J. 725 (1979).

question. Petitioner promptly filed a motion for inspection of the minutes of the grand jury and for a dismissal of the indictment. His motion was based on an affidavit stating that he was firmly convinced there could have been no legal or competent evidence before the grand jury which indicted him since he had reported all his income and paid all taxes due. The motion was denied. At the trial which followed the Government offered evidence designed to show increases in Costello's net worth in an attempt to prove that he had received more income during the years in question than he had reported. To establish its case the Government called and examined 144 witnesses and introduced 368 exhibits. All of the testimony and documents related to business transactions and expenditures by petitioner and his wife. The prosecution concluded its case by calling three government agents. Their investigations had produced the evidence used against petitioner at the trial. They were allowed to summarize the vast amount of evidence already heard and to introduce computations showing, if correct, that petitioner and his wife had received far greater income than they had reported.

* * *

Counsel for petitioner asked each government witness at the trial whether he had appeared before the grand jury which returned the indictment. This cross-examination developed the fact that the three investigating officers had been the only witnesses before the grand jury. After the Government concluded its case, petitioner again moved to dismiss the indictment on the ground that the only evidence before the grand jury was "hearsay," since the three officers had no firsthand knowledge of the transactions upon which their computations were based. Nevertheless the trial court again refused to dismiss the indictment, and petitioner was convicted. * * *

The Fifth Amendment provides that federal prosecutions for capital or otherwise infamous crimes must be instituted by presentments or indictments of grand juries. But neither the Fifth Amendment nor any other constitutional provision prescribes the kind of evidence upon which grand juries must act. The grand jury is an English institution, brought to this country by the early colonists and incorporated in the Constitution by the Founders. There is every reason to believe that our constitutional grand jury was intended to operate substantially like its English progenitor. The basic purpose of the English grand jury was to provide a fair method for instituting criminal proceedings against persons believed to have committed crimes. Grand jurors were selected from the body of the people and their work was not hampered by rigid procedural or evidential rules. In fact, grand jurors could act on their own knowledge and were free to make their presentments or indictments on such information as they deemed satisfactory. * * *

In Holt v. United States, 218 U.S. 245, this Court had to decide whether an indictment should be quashed because supported in part by incompetent evidence. Aside from the incompetent evidence "there was very little evidence against the accused." The Court refused to hold that such an indictment should be quashed, pointing out that "The abuses of criminal practice would be enhanced if indictments could be upset on such a ground." The same thing is true where as here all the evidence before the grand jury was in the nature of "hearsay." If indictments were to be held open to challenge on the ground that there was inadequate or incompetent evidence before the grand jury, the resulting delay would be great indeed. The result of such a rule would be that before trial on the merits a defendant could always insist on a kind of preliminary trial to determine the competency and adequacy of the evidence before the grand jury. This is not required by the Fifth Amendment. An indictment returned by a legally constituted and unbiased grand jury, like an information drawn by the prosecutor, if valid on its face, is enough to call for trial of the charge on the merits. The Fifth Amendment requires nothing more.

Petitioner urges that this Court should exercise its power to supervise the administration of justice in federal courts and establish a rule permitting defendants to challenge indictments on the ground that they are not supported by adequate or competent evidence. No persuasive reasons are advanced for establishing such a rule. It would run counter to the whole history of the grand jury institution, in which laymen conduct their inquiries unfettered by technical rules. Neither justice nor the concept of a fair trial requires such a change. In a trial on the merits, defendants are entitled to a strict observance of all the rules designed to bring about a fair verdict. Defendants are not entitled, however, to a rule which would result in interminable delay but add nothing to the assurance of a fair trial.

MR. JUSTICE CLARK and MR. JUSTICE HARLAN took no part in the consideration or decision of this case.

MR. JUSTICE BURTON, concurring.

I agree with the denial of the motion to quash the indictment. In my view, however, this case does not justify the breadth of the declarations made by the Court. I assume that this Court would not preclude an examination of grand-jury action to ascertain the existence of bias or prejudice in an indictment. Likewise, it seems to me that if it is shown that the grand jury had before it no substantial or rationally persuasive evidence upon which to base its indictment, that indictment should be quashed.

* * *

Note

In Chapter Two, we saw that illegally seized evidence can be used as the basis of grand jury questioning and probably as the basis for a grand jury indictment—United States v. Calandra, 414 U.S. 338 (1974)—unless a Congressional statute specifically allows a witness to raise a claim that evidence is being improperly used—e.g., Gelbard v. United States, 408 U.S. 41 (1972).

Aside from historical justifications, several arguments can be offered in support of *Costello.* First, inadmissible evidence usually has probative value, and the grand jury's function is investigative, not adjudicative. Second, many evidentiary rules are designed to ensure fairness in an adversary proceeding, and the grand jury is not adversarial. (Related to this is the argument that a prosecutor cannot be expected to object to her own evidence, and that the general rule is that, even at trial, evidence that is technically inadmissible will be admitted if no objection is made). Third, any misleading effect of inadmissible evidence will be remedied at trial. Fourth, grand jury proceedings would be greatly burdened if the rules of evidence were applicable to them. The court would have to review decisions as to the admissibility of evidence. In order to make relevance and other rulings, supervising courts would have to ask grand juries why they wanted certain evidence, and this might infringe upon the independence of the grand jury.

In United States v. Al Mudarris, 695 F.2d 1182 (9th Cir.1983), two defendants convicted of mail fraud against a medical insurance carrier complained that the grand jury that indicted them heard a single witness who summarized the case against them. Other witnesses had testified before grand juries, but the terms of these grand juries had expired before indictments were returned. The court of appeals found no error in the use of a summary witness, but it expressed a concern that the grand jurors may not have had sufficient time to review the transcripts of prior grand jury testimony. The court warned that a prosecutor must not abuse the summary witness device "by pressuring grand jurors into a precipitous decision or otherwise discouraging them from evaluating the evidence" and suggested that "it would be better practice to remind the grand jury that it retains the option of calling percipient witnesses." In addition, the court criticized prejudicial remarks made by the prosecutor to the grand jury. It said that a prosecutor may not make prejudicial remarks in an effort to sway a grand jury toward indictment, but it found the remarks to be harmless in this case. In United States v. DiBernardo, 552 F.Supp. 1315 (S.D.Fla.1982), the court dismissed the indictment in an obscenity case where a special agent of the FBI had been an undercover agent and grand jury witness and it appeared that the agent was a pathological liar. The court found that the grand jury proceedings were tainted and also noted that the prosecutor may have created a false impression of facts before the grand jury by presenting irrelevant, prejudicial information.

Several courts have expressed concern about *Costello* and have attempted to narrow it somewhat. Some states—e.g., Alaska now provide that "[h]earsay evidence shall not be presented to the grand jury absent compelling justification for its introduction. If hearsay evidence is presented to the grand jury, the reasons for its use shall be stated on the record." Alaska R.Crim.P. 6(m).[40] The Model Code of Pre-Arraignment Procedure would allow hearsay to be used to avoid an unreasonable burden on the government or on a witness, if the grand jury is informed about the declarant's reliability, § 340.5. The Code would allow a defendant to challenge the use of illegally seized evidence to support an indictment on the theory that such evidence will not be available to the government at trial and therefore should not be used, over the complaint of the defendant, in deciding whether to impose the burden of trial upon him. The American Bar Association expressed concern about the presentation of hearsay evidence to grand juries as it adopted a standard stating that "absent some compelling necessity, a prosecutor should not present the grand jury with a hearsay version of critical eyewitness testimony as a substitute for such testimony when it is available." The vote in the ABA House of delegates was close. See 70 A.B.A.J. 42 (1984).

Even if grand juries hear witnesses with firsthand knowledge, the prosecutor will usually decide how many witnesses to call. There is no requirement that defense witnesses be heard. Alaska R.Crim.P. 6(p). Thus, the grand jury will still get a one-sided presentation. But rules that reduce the amount of hearsay evidence [41] and that require the prosecutor to present exculpatory evidence in her possession—see, e.g., Johnson v. Superior Court, 15 Cal.3d 248, 124 Cal.Rptr. 32, 539 P.2d 792 (1975) [42]—may serve the purpose discussed earlier: they force the prosecutor to examine the evidence that she actually has available, and enable her to see it in context. Sometimes prosecutorial decisions may be affected as a result. And in

40. See Adams v. State, 598 P.2d 503 (Alaska 1979). Violation of the rule can be harmless error, when there is sufficient other evidence to support the indictment. State v. Taylor, 566 P.2d 1016 (Alaska 1977).

41. Some decisions prohibit the prosecutor from leading the grand jury into thinking it is getting eyewitness evidence, when testimony really is hearsay. See, e.g., United States v. Estepa, 471 F.2d 1132 (2d Cir.1972).

42. Accord, Frink v. State, 597 P.2d 154 (Alaska 1979). See generally Comment, The Prosecutor's Duty to Present Exculpatory Evidence to an Indicting Grand Jury, 75 Mich. L.Rev. 1514 (1977).

rare cases, the grand jury itself may be moved to resist the prosecutor. If you were setting up a grand jury system, which rule would you choose?

F. CRITICISM OF THE GRAND JURY AS A SCREENING DEVICE

The grand jury is an institution that has come under heavy fire in recent years. Part of the attack has been directed at its failure to screen out many cases brought to it by prosecutors. As the previous sections have indicated, there is little doubt that the grand jury cannot effectively remove many cases from the system, since the grand jury hears one side of a case and is likely to indict only on the basis of what it hears. Moreover, the prosecutor, whom the grand jury theoretically is supposed to check, is the grand jury's legal advisor; she also is the person who calls the witnesses or suggests whom the grand jurors should call. When this prosecutor implicitly says to the jury "this person should be indicted for these offenses," the grand jury is likely to cooperate with this official in whom it has placed so much confidence. Thus, the idea of a grand jury being so independent that it is unaffected by a prosecutor's position with respect to the filing of charges probably is unrealistic. If such an independent body is desired, either the grand jury will have to be modified or some other institution will have to be created.

Yet, the symbiotic relationship of grand jury and prosecutor does not necessarily mean that people are indicted who should not be. As noted earlier, if the evidence that the grand jury hears does not support an indictment, the prosecutor may be the first to suggest that no charges be brought. If the prosecutor attempts to influence a grand jury into indicting in cases in which the grand jurors are troubled by the absence of evidence, the grand jury may begin to lose confidence in the prosecutor, and a close working relationship may be interrupted. Knowledge of this may lead prosecutors to ask for true bills only when they are relatively sure that the grand jury will feel comfortable with the evidence presented. If this is the case, then indictments only will issue in cases in which an independent body also would choose to indict. But the fact remains that any decision by the grand jury will rest on a presentation that is controlled in large measure by the prosecutor.

Much of the attack on the grand jury goes beyond criticism of the jury as a "rubber stamp" for the prosecutor. Much of it focuses on the grand jury's investigative function and potential abuses of that function, the subject of the next section.

G. THE GRAND JURY AS THE GRAND INQUEST

The Supreme Court has emphasized that the role of the grand jury is to investigate into the existence of any and all criminal conduct, and that the scope of the inquiry is broad. See, e.g., Branzburg v. Hayes, 408 U.S. 665 (1972); United States v. Nixon, 418 U.S. 683 (1974). To understand how broadly the grand jury can sweep, it is helpful to think back to the search and seizure material in Chapter Two. You will recall that the government cannot obtain a search warrant to gather evidence unless it has probable cause. The same is true of an arrest warrant. And no warrantless arrest can validly take place without probable cause. This is in sharp contrast with the standards used by a grand jury. The jury can call anyone to testify before it upon the hint of suspicion or on the basis of a prosecutor's speculation about possible criminal activity. People called before the grand jury can be asked to bring documents and other tangible objects with them. Although the usual privileges can be raised before the grand jury, the burden is on the person called to raise them and sometimes to be willing to litigate in order to preserve them.[43] Any aspect of a person's life that might shed light on some criminal activity by somebody is within the proper scope of a grand jury inquest. If a grand jury can issue reports as well as indictments, it may have power to investigate into non-criminal as well as criminal matters, and the scope of an already broad inquiry is broadened even further.

The scope of federal subpoena power is nationwide, which means that the burden of traveling to testify can be considerable. The state grand jury has no such nationwide reach, but it too can impose travel burdens on witnesses. When it is recognized that often the prosecutor subpoenas witnesses without prior consultation with the grand jurors, it is apparent that a prosecutor can call witnesses before grand juries who are considerably burdened by the duty of responding to a subpoena but who have little to tell the grand jury. Prosecutors can call witnesses who will add nothing to the grand jury's knowledge, but who suffer simply because they are called. For example, one of the cases consolidated for hearing in Branzburg v. Hayes, supra, involved Earl Caldwell, a New York Times reporter who covered the Black Panther Party. Caldwell claimed that his appearance before the grand jury would compromise his relationship with the Party. The Supreme Court held that this gave him neither the right to refuse to appear before the jury nor the right to refuse to answer questions based on information related to him in confidence. Under the Court's opinion, even if the grand jury did not have any significant need for answers to questions, and even if, by answering, Caldwell's ability to function as a reporter covering the Party would be destroyed, the grand jury had a right to the information. Justice Powell's concurring opinion suggested that some First Amendment protections might be afforded news reporters, but in light of the facts of the three consolidated cases, it appears that the power of the grand jury to subpoena the press is substantial.

Any person who can demonstrate that a grand jury is harassing him may move to quash a subpoena. But such motions are not likely to succeed. Early in this century the Supreme Court established the appropriate degree of deference to be accorded grand jury subpoenas by judicial officers.

> [I]t is clearly recognized that the giving of testimony and the attendance upon court or grand jury in order to testify are public duties which every person within the jurisdiction of the Government is bound to perform upon being properly summoned, and for performance of which he is entitled to no further compensation than that which the statutes provide. The personal sacrifice involved is a part of the necessary contribution of the individual to the welfare of the public. The duty, so onerous at times, yet so necessary to the administration of justice according to the forms and modes established in our system of

43. In SEC v. Jerry T. O'Brien, Inc., 467 U.S. 735 (1984), the Court declined to find that any provision in the Constitution or in federal statutes governing the SEC require that the agency give notice to a target of a "nonpublic investigation" as to subpoenas issued to third parties. In explaining its reading of federal law, the Court expressed concern over the administrative burden a notice provision would impose and over the possibility that "the imposition of a notice requirement * * * would substantially increase the ability of persons who have something to hide to impede legitimate investigations by the Commission."

government is subject to mitigation in exceptional circumstances; there is a constitutional exemption from being compelled in any criminal case to be a witness against oneself, entitling the witness to be excused from answering anything that will tend to incriminate him (see Brown v. Walker, 161 U.S. 591); some confidential matters are shielded from considerations of policy, and perhaps in other cases for special reasons a witness may be excused from telling all that he knows.

But, aside from exceptions and qualifications—and none such is asserted in the present case—the witness is bound not only to attend but to tell what he knows in answer to questions framed for the purpose of bringing out the truth of the matter under inquiry.

He is not entitled to urge objections of incompetency or irrelevancy, such as a party might raise, for this is no concern of his. Nelson v. United States, 201 U.S. 92, 115.

On familiar principles, he is not entitled to challenge the authority of the court or of the grand jury, provided they have a *de facto* existence and organization.

He is not entitled to set limits to the investigation that the grand jury may conduct. * * * [I]n our system examination of witnesses by a grand jury need not be preceded by a formal charge against a particular individual. Hale v. Henkel, 201 U.S. 43, 65. It is a grand inquest, a body with powers of investigation and inquisition, the scope of whose inquiries is not to be limited narrowly by questions of propriety or forecasts of the probable result of the investigation, or by doubts whether any particular individual will be found properly subject to an accusation of crime. As has been said before, the identity of the offender, and the precise nature of the offense, if there be one, normally are developed at the conclusion of the grand jury's labors, not at the beginning.

And, for the same reasons, witnesses are not entitled to take exception to the jurisdiction of the grand jury or the court over the particular subject-matter that is under investigation. In truth it is in the ordinary case no concern of one summoned as a witness whether the offense is within the jurisdiction of the court or not. At least, the court and grand jury have authority and jurisdiction to investigate the facts in order to determine the question whether the facts show a case within their jurisdiction.

Blair v. United States, 250 U.S. 273, 281–83 (1919).

The Court reiterated this point in United States v. Dionisio, 410 U.S. 1 (1973). The next excerpt contains the Court's description of the facts and its approach to grand jury subpoenas.

A special grand jury was convened in the Northern District of Illinois in February 1971, to investigate possible violations of federal criminal statutes relating to gambling. In the course of its investigation, the grand jury received in evidence certain voice recordings that had been obtained pursuant to court orders.

The grand jury subpoenaed approximately 20 persons, including the respondent Dionisio, seeking to obtain from them voice exemplars for comparison with the recorded conversations that had been received in evidence. Each witness was advised that he was a potential defendant in a criminal prosecution. Each was asked to examine a transcript of an intercepted conversation, and to go to a nearby office of the United States Attorney to read the transcript into a recording device. The witnesses were advised that they would be allowed to have their attorneys present when they read the transcripts. Dionisio and other witnesses refused to furnish the voice exemplars, asserting that these disclosures would violate their rights under the Fourth and Fifth Amendments.

* * *

Following a hearing, the District Judge rejected the witnesses' constitutional arguments and ordered them to comply with the grand jury's request. [The Fifth Amendment self-incrimination claim was rejected for reasons discussed in Chapter Three, supra.]

* * *

The Court of Appeals held that the Fourth Amendment required a preliminary showing of reasonableness before a grand jury witness could be compelled to furnish a voice exemplar, and that in this case the proposed "seizures" of the voice exemplars would be unreasonable because of the large number of witnesses summoned by the grand jury and directed to produce such exemplars. We disagree.

* * *

It is clear that a subpoena to appear before a grand jury is not a "seizure" in the Fourth Amendment sense, even though that summons may be inconvenient or burdensome. * * *

* * *

The Court of Appeals found critical significance in the fact that the grand jury had summoned approximately 20 witnesses to furnish voice exemplars. We think that fact is basically irrelevant to the constitutional issues here. The grand jury may have been attempting to identify a number of voices on the tapes in evidence, or it might have summoned the 20 witnesses in an effort to identify one voice. But whatever the case, "[a] grand jury's investigation is not fully carried out until every available clue has been run down and all witnesses examined in every proper way to find if a crime has been committed * * *." * * * The grand jury may well find it desirable to call numerous witnesses in the course of an investigation. It does not follow that each witness may resist a subpoena on the ground that too many witnesses have been called. Neither the order to Dionisio to appear nor the order to make a voice recording was rendered unreasonable by the fact that many others were subjected to the same compulsion.[44]

* * *

In dissent, Justice Marshall argued that a stigma often attaches to witnesses called to testify before grand juries, and that some protection against prosecutorial control of the grand jury is necessary. He was willing to concede that witnesses could be called to testify before the grand jury, but urged that before real evidence is gathered by the grand jury over the objection of a witness, the government should have to make a showing of reasonableness: to show (a) the investigation is authorized; (b) the authorized inquiry is permissible under the

44. Using its supervisory power, the District of Columbia Court of Appeals held that a prosecutor seeking judicial enforcement of a grand jury directive that a nondefendant-nonarrestee appear in a lineup must "make a minimum factual showing sufficient to permit the judge to conclude that there is a reason for the lineup which is consistent with the legitimate function of the grand jury." A majority of the court found lineups to be more of an intrusion than fingerprint or voiceprint procedures. In re Kelley, 433 A.2d 704 (D.C.App.1981) (en banc).

Constitution; (c) the evidence sought is relevant; and (d) the request is adequate, but not excessive, for the purposes of the inquiry.

Actually, the difference between the majority and the dissent is not as great as it may appear. If a grand jury witness refuses to answer a question or provide information requested by the grand jury, the government will request that the witness be held in contempt. A court could order the witness incarcerated until the witness cooperates or the grand jury dissolves, which would be civil contempt; the court could order the witness punished for failure to comply, which would be criminal contempt; or, the court could do both. Before holding the witness in contempt, the court will consider any claim by the witness that the grand jury acted improperly in putting questions or seeking information. At least one court has held that before holding a reluctant grand jury witness in contempt, the court must be satisfied that the information sought was relevant to an investigation, that the investigation was properly within the grand jury's jurisdiction, and that the grand jury was not being used primarily for another purpose (such as to gather evidence for a subsequent civil suit). In re Grand Jury Proceedings, 486 F.2d 85 (3d Cir. 1973).[45]

The Court in United States v. Nixon, 418 U.S. 683 (1974) held that a trial subpoena must satisfy a three pronged test of relevancy, admissibility and specificity. However, in United States v. R. Enterprises, Inc., 111 S.Ct. 722 (1991), the Court rejected the application of the *Nixon* standards to grand jury subpoenas. Justice O'Connor, writing for a unanimous Court on this point, stressed the distinction between a grand jury investigation and a trial proceeding. She stated that "the Government cannot be required to justify the issuance of a grand jury subpoena by presenting evidence sufficient to establish probable cause because the very purpose of requesting the information is to ascertain whether probable cause exists." The Court also noted that the multifactor *Nixon* test would produce unacceptable procedural delays which would frustrate the grand jury's investigation.

Justice O'Connor noted, however, that the grand jury's investigatory powers are "not unlimited." Under Federal Rule of Criminal Procedure 17(c), subpoenas may be quashed if compliance would be "unreasonable or oppressive." The Court held that a subpoena would be unreasonable under Rule 17(c) only if "there is no reasonable possibility that the category of materials the

45. In re Grand Jury Proceedings Harrisburg Grand Jury 79–1, 658 F.2d 211 (3d Cir. 1981), limits the earlier decision concerning grand jury subpoenas by holding that the showing the government must make relates to the matters about which a witness is asked to testify and not to the appearance of the witness before the grand jury.

In In re Grand Jury Proceedings, 686 F.2d 135 (3d Cir.1982), the Court held that a grand jury demand that a witness produce facial and scalp hair was not a search or seizure under the Fourth Amendment. A concurring opinion argued that the demand was a seizure, but a reasonable one because it was pursuant to a valid grand jury subpoena. The concurring opinion would find government action that involves "the uninvited laying on of hands to perform a search" or "an actual invasion of the body" to be within the reach of the Fourth Amendment. It distinguished *Dionisio* and *Mara* on the ground that there was no physical imposition involved in those cases.

In In re Grand Jury Proceeding (Schofield), 721 F.2d 1221 (9th Cir.1983), the court reversed an order requiring the government to make a preliminary showing of relevance before obtaining information concerning fees and expenses paid to a lawyer: "No preliminary affidavit, disclaiming ill intent, will be required of the government where a grand jury has subpoenaed testimony or material evidence in good faith." Accord, In re Grand Jury Subpoena Served Upon Doe, 781 F.2d 238 (2d Cir.1986) (en banc).

Government seeks will produce information relevant to the general subject of the grand jury's investigation." Justice O'Connor recognized that this standard would be extraordinarily difficult to meet in practice, especially given the difficult position of subpoena recipients, who may have no knowledge of the Government's purpose in seeking production of the requested information. The Court suggested that an *in camera* proceeding be employed in cases where the recipient of the subpoena is unaware of the nature of the investigation.

Justice Stevens, joined by Justices Marshall and Blackmun, wrote an opinion concurring in the majority's rejection of the *Nixon* standards, and concurring in the judgment on the Court's definition of unreasonableness under Federal Rule 17(c). He stressed that the Court's opinion "should not be read to suggest that the deferential relevance standard the Court has formulated will govern decision in every case, no matter how intrusive or burdensome the request." He suggested that reasonableness of the subpoena ought to be determined in light of the burden of producing the requested information.

When it becomes apparent that a grand jury is attempting to harass or abuse citizens, courts will take action. See, e.g., Ealy v. Littlejohn, 569 F.2d 219 (5th Cir.1978) (holding that a state grand jury investigation into a citizens' association having no arguable or colorable relationship to a shooting death violated First Amendment rights). Similarly, when it appears that a grand jury is being used as a discovery device for civil litigation—see e.g., United States v. Procter & Gamble Co., 187 F.Supp. 55 (D.N.J.1960); In re Grand Jury Proceedings, supra—a court will intervene. See also United States v. Gibbons, 607 F.2d 1320 (10th Cir.1979) (reiterating that it is improper to use a grand jury as a discovery device when an indictment already has been returned, although discovery may be an incidental benefit of investigation of additional crimes).

It is clearly improper for the prosecutor to call a person who already has been indicted by a grand jury to testify before that grand jury in order to gather evidence for the pending prosecution. One reason why courts condemn the tactic is that the grand jury completes its function under local law when it returns an indictment. Thus, the post-indictment evidence gathering function is not part of the grand jury's work. Another reason is that once the indictment is returned, arguably cases like Brewer v. Williams, 430 U.S. 387 (1977), discussed in Chapter Three, supra, and Kirby v. Illinois, 406 U.S. 682 (1972), discussed in Chapter Four, supra, require that the defendant be given complete access to counsel, since formal charges have been brought. If counsel were permitted to be with the defendant in the grand jury room, there still might be a problem, since counsel and the defendant might want questioning about the case to stop immediately. Could a grand jury be given power to question an indicted defendant against her will?

One court has held that "[w]here a substantial purpose of calling an indicted defendant before a grand jury is to question him secretly and without counsel present without his being informed of the nature and cause of the accusation about a crime for which he stands already indicted, the proceeding is an abuse of process which violates both the right to counsel provision of the Sixth Amendment and the due process clause of the Fifth Amendment." United States v. Doss, 563 F.2d 265 (6th Cir.1977) (en banc). The *Doss* court held that a witness improperly called before a grand jury under such circumstances could not be prosecuted for perjury on the basis of false statements made. Note, however, that the grand jury may call an indicted person to investigate new additional charges.[46]

The *Doss* case leads into what is perhaps the most significant charge made against the grand jury: i.e., it is an inherently unfair proceeding, because witnesses are called to testify without being told why they are being called, what the purpose of the inquiry is, and whether they are suspected of criminal wrongdoing. Ignorance of the nature of the proceeding is compounded by the absence of counsel in the grand jury room in most jurisdictions, and by the legal inability of the individual witness to simply say "I do not wish to talk with you." The complaint that no one should be asked to give information without being told why has a ring to it like that which gave birth to the privilege against self-incrimination in England. Because grand jurors and prosecutors can ask leading questions, a witness who might be a target of the grand jury has good reason to fear that a slip of the tongue may come back to haunt her. Yet, the witness will have difficulty in answering carefully without knowledge of what the investigation is all about. Without a lawyer present to assist, vague or confusing questions may be asked, and a witness may later discover that what she said to the grand jury can be cast in a more negative light than she would have supposed while testifying.

In response to these complaints, the Department of Justice has added to the guidelines for United States Attorneys, found in the United States Attorney's Manual (which guidelines are enforced through internal discipline within the Department), sections that require that a witness be advised of several things: of the general subject matter of the grand jury's inquiry (to the extent that an investigation would not be compromised); that the witness may refuse to answer questions that would tend to incriminate; that any answers may be used against the witness; and that the witness may step outside the grand jury room to consult with counsel. The guidelines provide that a target of an investigation may be subpoenaed, but known targets should be advised that they are targets and should be invited to testify voluntarily; if they refuse, a subpoena should be issued only after the grand jury and the responsible prosecutor have approved the subpoena. The prosecutor is encouraged to offer a target an opportunity to testify before the grand jury indicts.

There is a small trend toward recognizing the right of grand jury witnesses to be accompanied by counsel, and the trend is controversial. Compare, e.g., Silbert, Defense Counsel in the Grand Jury—The Answer to the White Collar Criminal's Prayers, 15 Am.Cr.L.Rev. 293 (1978) with Hixson, Bringing Down the Curtain on the Absurd Drama of Entrances and Exits—Witness Representation in the Grand Jury Room, 15 Am.Cr.L.Rev. 307 (1978). It is unclear whether a witness has a constitutional right to consult with counsel in some way during grand jury testimony. In re Groban, 352 U.S. 330 (1957), which held that there was no right to the assistance of counsel in a fire marshall's investigation, contains dictum that suggests there is no right to representation by counsel before a grand jury. But *Groban* came before many of the Court's right to counsel cases, and before *Miranda.* Whether it remains good law is questionable. Assuming that it does, the fact remains that nothing can be

46. Sometimes it may be difficult for a court to know whether the government is pursuing a new investigation. But the court may indicate to the government that it will carefully scrutinize the government's conduct when its use of the grand jury has been completed. See, e.g., United States v. Doe, 455 F.2d 1270 (1st Cir.1972).

done to prevent a witness from consulting a lawyer prior to testifying. More importantly, most jurisdictions recognize the right of a witness to consult with a lawyer outside the grand jury room, even though this may interrupt the flow of information to the grand jury. This limited opportunity to consult counsel probably reflects a practical consideration: if the witness refuses to answer, the grand jury would have to seek a contempt citation to make the witness answer; before going through that process, the grand jury may be better advised to let the witness discuss with counsel the question, since the witness may decide to answer voluntarily.

The argument against having counsel in the grand jury room is that whether or not counsel is theoretically limited to advising the witness rather than speaking to the jury, the presence of counsel will turn the grand jury inquiry into an adversary proceeding. "Even if the attorney himself is quieted, he could as a practical matter 'argue' through the witness." Silbert, supra, at 301. The response has been to cite the experience of states that permit counsel to accompany witnesses into the grand jury room as evidence that counsel would not disrupt the functioning of the grand jury. See, e.g., Hixson, supra, at 318–20.

There probably is merit in the argument that the grand jury will get somewhat less cooperation from some witnesses if those witnesses are given greater access to counsel. Indeed, if it makes no difference whether or not counsel is present, those who now attack the grand jury for not allowing counsel to accompany witnesses would have little to worry about. The real question is whether we are willing to accept a procedure in which a trained lawyer, the prosecutor, and a group of citizens advised by this trained lawyer can question a person in secret without giving that person the right to have somebody there to advise her when she wants advice. It may be constitutional to retain such a system, but is it consistent with the values that we claim to hold as we process criminal cases?

Although it may be true that at an actual trial a mere witness does not have full opportunity to consult with counsel, it also is probably the case that the witness knows what the case is about by that time and what questions will be asked (at least generally). Thus, consultation with counsel before trial should be adequate to protect the witness's rights. If an unexpected question is asked, most, perhaps all, courts would provide a witness an opportunity to consult a lawyer before saying something that might be incriminating or that might result in the loss of a privilege. The grand jury inquiry is different; the opportunity to prepare is not the same. And the question is whether we are willing to support an institution that conducts secret interrogations of citizens who wish to have someone trained in the law present to assist them in a manner that is intended to make it difficult, or impossible, for the citizen to benefit from the advice of counsel.

The American Bar Association has made recommendations for grand jury reform. These include allowing counsel into the grand jury room, warning every witness of the privilege against self-incrimination and the right to counsel, and requiring prosecutors to present exculpatory evidence to the grand jury. Those who fear the power entrusted to grand juries and the ways in which prosecutors may manipulate grand juries will find United States v. Kilpatrick, 594 F.Supp. 1324 (D.Colo.1984), a useful case to cite as an example of abuse of the grand jury system. The district court dismissed an indictment charging conspiracy, mail fraud and tax fraud after finding that the government engaged in a variety of improper acts. These included the following: misleading the grand jury as to the role that IRS agents played in an investigation, permitting IRS agents to appear before the grand jury without the presence of government counsel and to read transcripts to the jurors, failing to control the disclosure of information by the IRS, manipulating the grand jury to develop evidence for civil cases, publicizing the individuals and entities under investigation, improperly imposing secrecy obligations on witnesses who testified before the grand jury, using "pocket" (informal) immunity rather than the statutory immunity to obtain testimony, improperly questioning witnesses who invoked the privilege against self-incrimination to suggest that targets of the investigation were financing the witnesses' refusal to testify, misrepresenting the evidence in a summary to the jurors, and abusing an expert witness on taxation.

VI. THE PRELIMINARY HEARING AND ITS RELATIONSHIP TO INDICTMENTS AND INFORMATIONS

Federal Rule of Criminal Procedure 5 provides that when an arrest is made, the arrested person shall be taken without unnecessary delay before the nearest available federal magistrate. You will recall that Gerstein v. Pugh, 420 U.S. 103 (1975), discussed in Chapter Two, requires that, if there has been no previous probable cause determination, that one be made within a reasonable time period. Fed.R.Crim.P. 5 provides for such a determination when the person arrested is brought before the magistrate. The rule provides that a defendant is entitled to a preliminary examination for any crime except a petty offense. Fed.R.Crim.P. 5.1 governs preliminary examinations.

Note that an indictment cuts off the right to a preliminary hearing, since probable cause is held to be validly established by the indictment itself. It is common in some federal districts for prosecutors to avoid preliminary hearings by indicting as many defendants as possible. Rule 5 requires a preliminary hearing within a reasonable time, and it provides outer time limits. Whether a defendant's request for an examination as soon as the government can be ready must be granted is unclear. See Weinberg & Weinberg, The Congressional Invitation to Avoid a Preliminary Hearing, 67 Mich.L.Rev. 1361 (1969). But it would seem that the government can avoid a preliminary hearing if it presents its evidence to the grand jury as soon as it can.

Prior to the adoption of the Federal Rules of Criminal Procedure, a federal prosecutor needed leave of court to file an information, and leave of court depended on a finding of probable cause. See Albrecht v. United States, 273 U.S. 1. But Fed.R.Crim.P. 7(a), eliminated the leave of court requirement, without explanation.[47] Note that the filing of an information, like the filing of an indictment, cuts off the right to a preliminary examination.

47. Except in certain cases, such as capital cases, most jurisdictions permit a defendant to waive the requirement of indictment by grand jury. The standard by which waiver is judged is not well developed. This is somewhat surprising given the large number of defendants who waive indictment.

Virtually every state that requires felony prosecutions to commence by indictment establishes some right to a preliminary examination. In most, the filing of the indictment cuts off the right to a preliminary hearing, just as does Federal Rule 5. Almost half the states today do not require indictments in felony cases. In these states prosecutors can begin felony cases by filing informations. In special cases prosecutors may utilize grand jury indictments, but usually they will use the information, since it is a less burdensome way of beginning a case. Most states that permit the filing of an information in a felony case make a magistrate's decision to bind the defendant over for trial a prerequisite to the filing of the information. A few states do allow the prosecutor to file the information directly, however. The Supreme Court has upheld the direct filing of an information in Lem Woon v. Oregon, 229 U.S 586 (1913), and Ocampo v. United States, 234 U.S. 91 (1914). Of course, after Gerstein v. Pugh, supra, a magistrate will have to make a probable cause determination, if the accused is deprived of freedom. But the *Gerstein* opinion indicates that the limited hearing it requires is to protect against erroneous detention; it is not a screening device to check the prosecutor's decision to bring charges against a defendant. The language of the opinion makes it highly unlikely that the Court will hold that some check on the prosecutor's decision to charge is constitutionally mandated.

Most states have time limits in which the preliminary hearing must be held. But other aspects of the hearing are often not covered by rule. Even the standard to be used by the magistrate who conducts the preliminary hearing often is unclear. It is apparent that different judges sitting in the same jurisdiction have different ideas about what screening function the hearing is to serve. Some judges believe that their function is to determine probable cause, with the evidence viewed in the light most favorable to the government, ignoring credibility questions. Others take the view that there must be enough evidence for a trier of fact to find guilt beyond a reasonable doubt. Some magistrates probably consider whether a defendant should be burdened by going to trial in some cases, even if there is enough evidence to warrant a bindover.

The standard that is chosen indicates how much screening a jurisdiction wants its magistrates to do. It probably is true that if a prosecutor presents all her evidence to the magistrate and the magistrate concludes that no reasonable jury could convict, it is silly to bind the defendant over for trial, even if there technically is probable cause. But the question that may arise is whether the prosecutor should be required to present all of her evidence to the magistrate as a prerequisite to bringing charges. The more thorough the screening at the preliminary hearing, the more it resembles a trial, and the more costly it is.

Although some jurisdictions require magistrates to follow the usual rules of evidence at preliminary hearings, most others provide that the usual rules need not be followed, which means in most cases that hearsay evidence can be used, as it can be used before most grand juries. Again, the approach to the question whether evidence rules should be followed at the hearing depends on the kind of hearing that is to be held. Obviously, the more closely the evidence rules resemble the rules that will be used at trial, the more screening the magistrate is able to do. But the more screening that is done, the more time-consuming and expensive the procedure is likely to be. Fed.R.Crim.P. 5.1

represents the majority view; it admits hearsay evidence and allows a probable cause determination to be made in reliance on hearsay evidence.

Jurisdictions vary considerably on the scope of the hearing. One obvious difference is that some magistrates are only concerned with probable cause and take the evidence in the light most favorable to the government, and are not very concerned with affirmative defenses or with cross-examination of government witnesses for impeachment purposes. Other magistrates look for sufficient evidence for the trier of fact to find guilt beyond a reasonable doubt, and they are likely to want to hear more evidence.[48]

Another obvious difference among jurisdictions is in their approach to the hearing as a discovery device. If the hearing is not to serve a discovery purpose, as under Fed.R.Crim.P. 5.1, then questions asked for discovery reasons are unlikely to be permitted over objection.[49] If, however, a jurisdiction recognizes a discovery purpose, the scope of questioning may be quite broad.

Perhaps the most important difference among jurisdictions is the effect given the magistrate's decision. If the case is a felony case that will begin by a grand jury indictment, a decision by the magistrate that there is no cause for bindover generally is not binding on a grand jury. The grand jury still can indict. And a decision by the magistrate that bindover should be limited to designated offenses also is not binding on the grand jury in most jurisdictions. It can charge any offense for which it finds probable cause.

If the prosecution can begin by information, generally the prosecutor is limited by the bindover in the charges that can be brought. In some states only those charges designated by the magistrate can be brought. In other states the offense for which the defendant is bound over or others supported by the evidence at the preliminary hearing may be charged. Still others use a transactional test, which allows all crimes related to the same transactions and facts adduced at the examination to be charged. See, e.g., Kirby v. State, 86 Wisc.2d 292, 272 N.W.2d 113 (1978). Under all these approaches, the defendant can challenge the information in the trial court, although it is likely that the trial court will defer to the preliminary hearing judge (and the absence of a formal record may make a challenge especially difficult). If the prosecutor is not satisfied with the bindover decision, she may drop the prosecution, file a new complaint, and hope for a better bindover ruling from another magistrate. If the magistrate refuses to bind over the defendant, the prosecutor usually can try again before another magistrate. See, e.g., Commonwealth v. Prado, 481 Pa. 485, 393 A.2d 8 (1978). Generally, the refusal to bind the defendant over is not appealable,[50] although sometimes mandamus may be possible. If the

48. The role of the magistrate in preliminary hearings is examined in People v. Slaughter, 35 Cal.3d 629, 200 Cal.Rptr. 448, 677 P.2d 854 (1984), a decision reversing a magistrate's refusal to certify a murder charge against the defendant. The Court wrote as follows:

> [T]he magistrate is not a trier of fact. He does not decide whether defendant committed the crime, but only whether there is "some rational ground for assuming the possibility that an offense has been committed and the accused is guilty of it." If the record shows strong and credible evidence of defendant's guilt, the magistrate may reasonably assume the possibility of his guilt. Thus, in many cases he will not find it necessary to resolve all conflicts in the evidence, in order to find probable cause to hold the defendant for trial.

49. The preliminary hearing may be used not only as a discovery device, but also as a device to preserve testimony, and to precipitate bargaining that will lead to a guilty plea.

50. But see Wittke v. State ex rel. Smith, 80 Wisc.2d 332, 259 N.W.2d 515 (1977) (per-

prosecutor cannot get a favorable bindover decision, she might decide to present the case, even if it is a misdemeanor, to the grand jury, or decide to file charges directly against the defendant, if that is possible.

Note

In many instances an error at a preliminary hearing is likely to be considered harmless error once the defendant is tried and convicted. See, e.g., State v. McCloud, 357 So.2d 1132 (La.1978). For a defendant to preserve her rights, a prompt objection to the preliminary hearing should be made in the trial court. In some jurisdictions an adequate preliminary hearing is a jurisdictional prerequisite to prosecution, so that error cannot be harmless, if it renders the hearing inadequate.

A few states now provide for post-indictment preliminary hearings. Connecticut amended its state constitution to provide that defendants charged with an offense punishable by death or life imprisonment must be given a probable cause hearing. No longer is an indictment required. The constitutional provision is discussed in State v. Sanabria, 192 Conn. 671, 474 A.2d 760 (1984).

Many authorities favor abolishing the requirement of a grand jury indictment and urge that the use of grand juries be left to the option of prosecutors.[51] See, e.g., Nat'l Advisory Comm'n on Criminal Justice Standards and Goals: Courts, Standard 4.4 (1973) (recognizing that in some circumstances it may be wise to utilize the grand jury). See also McIntyre, Variation in the Operation of Grand Juries, A.B.F.Res.Rep. No. 11 (Winter 1977).

If the grand jury is abolished, there must be some mechanism to take its place if the government is to be able to carry out its necessary investigative functions. One option is to give the prosecutor subpoena power. See generally Hall, The Prosecutor's Subpoena Power, 33 Ark.L.Rev. 122 (1979). Another is to set up special investigative commissions. Still another is to utilize one-person grand juries, conducted by a judicial officer. See, e.g., State v. Washington, 83 Wisc.2d 808, 266 N.W.2d 597 (1978). Some of these investigative bodies may be restricted in ways that grand juries are not, but this is not always the case. In deciding whether you would do away with the requirement of a grand jury indictment, you must decide whether you think that it is likely that these other investigative alternatives will be more or less abusive than the grand jury. If you were to conclude that a prosecutor tempers an investigation in order to demonstrate good faith to a grand

mitting appeal, but barring refiling of charges); cf., Commonwealth v. Prado, 481 Pa. 485, 393 A.2d 8 (1978).

51. "The reasons usually given by prosecutors for choosing to initiate prosecutions by indictment include the following: indictment procedures (1) save time; (2) protect witnesses against embarrassing cross-examination; (3) protect an innocent accused when no indictment is returned; (4) protect the cover of an informant; (5) protect witnesses against harm or intimidation; (6) allow the prosecuting attorney to test his case and obtain a community viewpoint on its strength; (7) permit the evidentiary hearing to be held over an extended period of time; (8) facilitate investigations, e.g., by providing subpoena availability without the initiation of formal proceedings; (9) allow the prosecutor to toll the statute of limitations when the defendant is absent; (10) protect the defendant from prejudicial pretrial publicity; (11) protect society from the flight of the accused; and (12) permit the prosecuting attorney to share responsibility for the prosecution with the grand jury when there is great public interest in a case. (See Judicial Council of Cal., Annual Rep. (1974) pp. 47–51; Graham & Letwin, The Preliminary Hearings in Los Angeles: Some Field Findings and Legal-Policy Observations (1971) 18 UCLA L.Rev. 636, 679; Note, Some Aspects of the California Grand Jury System (1956) 8 Stan. L.Rev. 631, 644; Margolin & Arguimbau, Post-Indictment Preliminary Hearings in California, in Fourteenth Annual Defending Criminal Cases (PLI 1976) p. 286.)"

jury, then you might be concerned about abolition of a requirement of grand jury indictment. But if you believe that prosecutors sufficiently control grand juries so that their investigation would be the same even if conducted independently of a grand jury, then the abolition of an indictment requirement probably would be welcome.

VII. THE PROBLEM OF VARIANCE AND COMPLETENESS

In Stirone v. United States, 361 U.S. 212 (1960), the Supreme Court reversed a conviction for violation of the Hobbs Act (interfering with interstate commerce) because the government's proof of the defendants' effect on interstate commerce involved shipments of steel from inside Pennsylvania to points outside the state, whereas the indictment charged that the effect was on shipments from outside the state into Pennsylvania. The Court said that it could not permit a defendant to be tried on charges not made in the indictment, because to do so would threaten the protection afforded by grand jury scrutiny.[52]

Justice Marshall wrote for a unanimous Court (Justice Powell not participating) in United States v. Miller, 471 U.S. 130 (1985), holding that the Fifth Amendment's protection of indictment by grand jury is not violated "when a defendant is tried under an indictment that alleges a certain fraudulent scheme but is convicted based on trial proof that supports only a significantly narrower and more limited, though included, fraudulent scheme." The government had charged Miller with fraudulent acts in consenting to a burglary of his business and lying to the insurer about the value of his loss. The proof focused only on the value of the loss. Justice Marshall wrote that "[a]s long as the crime and the elements of the offense that sustain the conviction are fully and clearly set out in the indictment, the right to a grand jury is not normally violated by the fact that the indictment alleges more crimes or other means of submitting the same crime." He distinguished *Stirone* on the ground that the offense proved at trial was *not* fully charged in the indictment.

One aspect of a variance claim involves inadequate notice to the defendant of the charges made against him. If a defendant in a state court is denied adequate notice, he too has a constitutional claim, one that arises under the due process clause. See, e.g., Watson v. Jago, 558 F.2d 330 (6th Cir. 1977); State v. Armijo, 90 N.M. 614, 566 P.2d 1152 (1977). The other aspect of the claim is the denial of grand jury scrutiny of the charge made by the prosecutor. If a prosecutor files an information, should he be free to amend it? Does it matter what kind of preliminary hearing system a jurisdiction has? Notice may be a problem here also. See Green v. State, 94 Nev. 176, 576 P.2d 1123 (1978).

52. Sometimes indictments are attacked on the ground that they are confusing and would be difficult for jurors to understand. Rarely do such attacks succeed. An exception is United States v. Gonsalves, 691 F.2d 1310 (9th Cir. 1982), where a district court used its supervisory power to dismiss an indictment as unmanageable. The indictment charged drug trafficking and contained two conspiracy counts. It named thirteen defendants and identified seventeen alleged co-conspirators who were not named as defendants. The district court described the case as "a complex monstrosity" that was unmanageable. On appeal, the court affirmed and reasoned that "the degree of encroachment upon the prerogatives of the prosecutor that a dismissal entails in this case is minimal." The government remained free to break the case down into smaller, more manageable indictments.

One of the most common claims of variance concerns conspiracy prosecutions. Often a defendant claims that the government proved a conspiracy or several conspiracies different from the one alleged in the indictment. Although most such claims are unsuccessful, some do succeed. One example is United States v. Jackson, 696 F.2d 578 (8th Cir. 1982). Five defendants were charged with conspiracy to commit mail fraud, with substantive mail fraud violations, and with wrongful use of the mails. One of the defendants, charged with and convicted only of conspiracy, and another, charged with and convicted of conspiracy and substantive counts, claimed that the government had proved not one conspiracy but two. All charges related to four fires in buildings that the government claimed were deliberately set in order to enable the defendants to fraudulently collect insurance proceeds under homeowners' policies. Using an analysis that has become fairly standard in the courts of appeal, the reviewing court asked whether the government proved the overall agreement charged. Its answer was that no jury could have found that the two defendants were parties to a single overall scheme to commit mail fraud. It accepted the claim that one fire was separate from the other three. As a result it reversed the conspiracy convictions.

One example of the variance issues that can arise in conspiracy cases is United States v. Wright, 932 F.2d 868 (10th Cir.1991). An informant told the FBI that several people, including defendants Wright and Kirby, were involved in drug dealing. The informant claimed that he had obtained methamphetamine and cocaine from Wright for two years and that he had been operating a methamphetamine lab financed by Wright. Subsequently, the informant was wired with a tape recorder as he met with Wright. On one occasion, Kirby joined them in a restaurant and asked whether he had been implicated by a defendant in a methamphetamine bust. Ultimately, an undercover FBI agent arranged to purchase cocaine from an associate of Wright. The informant predicted the circumstances of the transaction, which involved Wright and his associate. The informant indicated that if Wright brought anyone with him, it would be Kirby for protection. A superseding indictment charged Kirby *inter alia* with conspiring to manufacture and distribute methamphetamine as well as with the distribution of cocaine.

The trial judge noted at the charging conference that it was "very difficult" to find evidence linking Kirby to the manufacture and distribution of methamphetamine, but instructed the jury that it could find Kirby guilty of conspiracy if it found he was a conspirator solely in the distribution of cocaine. Kirby contended on appeal that the jury should have been instructed to acquit if it did not find that he was a participant in the single, overall conspiracy relating to both methamphetamine and cocaine. Citing both *Stirone* and *Miller,* the court of appeals rejected Kirby's contention. It distinguished constructive amendments of indictments in jury instructions that broaden charges from constructive amendments that narrow charges and reasoned that *Miller* clearly established that the Fifth Amendment is not violated if the defendant is convicted upon evidence which tends to show a narrower scheme than that alleged in the indictment, so long as the narrower scheme is fully included within the charges actually made. It upheld the following charge to the jury:

> Although the indictment charges a single conspiracy, it would be possible to find separate conspiracies, one relating to the manufacture and distribution of methamphetamine and the other relating to the distribution of cocaine. Whether there was one conspiracy, or two conspiracies, or no conspiracy at all is a fact for you to determine in accordance with these instructions. If you find beyond a reasonable doubt that a defendant was involved in the single conspiracy charged in the indictment or in separate conspiracies to manufacture and distribute methamphetamine or to distribute cocaine, then you must find that defendant guilty.

The court focused on the possibility of a "spill over effect," *i.e.,* "a likelihood of transference of guilt to [Kirby] from evidence presented relating to the methamphetamine conspiracy," and identified three factors which earlier cases had regarded as relevant: (1) whether the proliferation of separate crimes impaired the jury's ability to segregate each individual defendant's actions, (2) whether confusion resulted among jurors concerning the legal limitations on the use of certain evidence, and (3) whether the evidence supporting the conviction was strong or weak. As to Kirby, the court found that evidence underlying his conviction for either conspiracy was strong enough to preclude the possibility of prejudice.

The case is interesting not only because it demonstrates appellate willingness to find strong evidence where the trial judge found weak evidence, but also because of the instruction actually given by the trial judge. Suppose that the jury believed that there were two conspiracies, not one, and that Kirby was only involved with cocaine. What does the trial judge's instruction suggest that the jury is required to do? The judge instructed the jury to decide whether there were two conspiracies, one conspiracy, or none. If, on the one hand, the jury first decided that there were two conspiracies, but that Kirby was only involved in one, is it clear whether they should acquit or convict Kirby? If, on the other hand, the jury concluded that there was one overall conspiracy but that Kirby was not involved with methamphetamine in that conspiracy, is it clear whether they should acquit or convict him?

Suppose that unlike the court of appeals, the jury found that there was too little evidence to tie Kirby to methamphetamine. Does this mean that spill-over prejudice is unlikely because the jury was obviously able to pay close attention to the respective guilt of the two defendants? What if the jury found the case against Kirby's involvement with methamphetamine to be close, and his involvement in the cocaine conspiracy also to be close? Would the argument about spill-over prejudice be stronger?

Chapter Seven

BAIL AND PRETRIAL RELEASE

I. INTRODUCTION TO THE PROBLEMS OF RESTRAINT PENDING TRIAL

A. THE SUSPECT'S CONCERNS

One half or more of the defendants who are arrested are released or convicted and sentenced within 24 hours of their arrest.[1] The remaining defendants await disposition of their cases for days, weeks, or months, depending on prosecutors' workloads, the gravity and complexity of the cases, the condition of court calendars, and the actions of defense attorneys. The magistrate must determine which defendants may and should be released pending trial.

At the time that the magistrate rules, the police have progressed sufficiently far in the investigatory process to have focused on an individual suspect. But there is some possibility that the suspect is innocent of all charges, or of most charges that are being considered or have been brought. In contrast to the final determination of guilt beyond a reasonable doubt at trial, the pre-trial determination of probable cause, which forms the basis for arrest and detention pending trial, has the limited function of establishing only a reasonable probability that a suspect committed a crime. The suspect and the accused claim that until a finding of guilt is made, it is improper to deprive them of liberty pending trial. The claim has considerable appeal. Given the probability of guilt that has been demonstrated by the state, however, the state has a substantial interest in detaining one who has been or will be accused to ensure her presence at trial, and her eventual punishment, if proven guilty. In short, once probable cause is demonstrated, the accused is legally presumed to be innocent, but is not treated as if no charge had been made and no probable cause found.

Aside from the suspect's claim of entitlement to a presumption of innocence, the suspect can point to significant personal costs associated with pretrial detention.[2] The consequences of incarceration include deprivation of

1. The Challenge of Crime in a Free Society, Report of the President's Commission on Law Enforcement and the Administration of Justice (1968).

2. As Professor Caleb Foote noted in his seminal article, The Coming Constitutional Crisis in Bail, 113 U.Pa.L.Rev. 959, 964 (1965) (hereinafter, Crisis in Bail):

contacts with friends and family, absence from employment and possibly loss of job, diminished ability to support family and to hire counsel, restrictions in the preparation of a defense, and stigmatizing effects on the prisoner's reputation and future employment prospects.[3] These factors, as well as the poor conditions that characterize most pretrial detention facilities,[4] effectively constitute punishment of a suspect who has yet to be proven guilty beyond a reasonable doubt, and who has not been afforded other rights associated with trial. Moreover, studies indicate that pretrial imprisonment prejudices the actual adjudication of guilt or innocence when it finally occurs. The self-fulfilling quality of pretrial detention is in part attributed to the factors described above. By limiting the defendant's participation in investigation and trial preparation, incarceration may affect the verdict.[5] In addition, prior detention erodes the rehabilitative prospects of the accused, placing him at a disadvantage both in conviction and sentencing. The defendant's demeanor, recognized as an essential element of the fact-finding determination, will reflect recent imprisonment: He is apt to be unshaven, unwashed, unkempt, and unhappy as he enters the courtroom under guard.[6] The hopelessness, the lowered self-esteem, and a decline in respect for the criminal justice system may produce a tendency to plead guilty in detained suspects, who lose their incentives to prolong the adjudication process.

There are social costs to pretrial detention, as well. In addition to the significant costs of maintenance and support of the prisoners, society must bear the secondary welfare costs incident to the imprisonment of a head of a household. There is a further, intangible social cost—"punishing" by detention individuals who are presumed innocent until proven guilty.

> Any resolution of the detention problem involves an allocation of inescapable costs. Someone has to pay a price for the fact we have to have a pretrial period between accusation and final adjudication. If defendants are kept locked up, the cost is borne by those among them who are innocent or prejudiced by the detention. If they are all released, society pays in those cases where the defendant flees or commits new crimes.

The costs described by Foote are exacerbated by the protracted length of the pretrial period between accusation and final adjudication in many jurisdictions. Implicit in our discussion of pretrial detention is the recognition that speedy trials and more expeditious adjudication of criminal matters would alleviate most problems in this area. The movement toward statutory and court-adopted speedy trial rules, discussed in Chapter Ten, has helped to reduce the delays.

Application of Haynes, 290 Or. 75, 619 P.2d 632 (1980), analyzes the relationship of denial of bail and the right to a speedy trial in a habeas corpus action brought by a defendant who had been awaiting trial for murder for 2½ years.

3. See Thaler, Punishing the Innocent: The Need for Due Process and the Presumption of Innocence Prior to Trial, 1978 Wis. L.Rev. 441.

4. See President's Commission on Law Enforcement and the Administration of Justice, Task Force Report: Corrections (1967).

5. See Kinney v. Lenon, 425 F.2d 209 (9th Cir. 1970), where the Court held that the defendant's release was necessary so that he might track down witnesses essential to his defense. See also, Note, Bail: An Ancient Practice Re-examined, 70 Yale L.J. 966, 969–970 n. 27 (1960), where student directors of the Yale Law School Public Defender Association reported difficulty in convincing blacks to discuss criminal matters with any white people: "They have found it impossible to locate Negro witnesses that the accused could probably find within a short period of time if permitted to search for them."

6. See P. Wald, Pretrial Detention and Ultimate Freedom: A Statistical Study, 39 N.Y.U.L.Rev. 631, 632 (1964).

In Zeisel, Bail Revisited, 4 A.B.F.Res.J. 769, the argument is made that defendants who do not make bail on less serious offenses often serve more time than they would serve if they were released pending disposition of their cases; jailed defendants are likely to cop pleas for time served in order to obtain release, whereas freed defendants are less likely to accept just any deal that is offered.

B. COUNTERVAILING CONCERNS

On the other hand, there are compelling societal interests that militate in favor of pretrial detention of a criminal suspect. The basic justification for imprisonment pending trial is to guarantee the presence of the suspect in order to ensure proper judicial disposition of the case. As a corollary, pretrial incarceration may protect the judicial processes by precluding any interference with evidence or witnesses on the part of the defendant. Detention may even serve to protect the accused from others who have a stake in the disposition of his case, or from himself, if the accused is violent or unstable or otherwise judged likely to harm himself.

The most controversial argument in support of pretrial detention focuses on its preventive (or preventative) aspects. Arguably, the state has an interest in the protection of the community that warrants imprisonment of those accused of criminal activity. Having established that there is probable cause to believe that the suspect committed a crime that is dangerous to society and for which he is likely to be punished, releasing him would seem repugnant to the legitimate needs of effective law enforcement. There are obvious problems with the argument. The lower the "cause" standard for arrest and detention, the less certain society must be that it is dealing with an actual offender in any case. You already know about the probable cause standard for arrest. Is it high enough to justify much of an assumption concerning guilt? Even if people are guilty of past crimes, preventive action suggests they are likely to commit future crimes as well. Thus, a preventive approach necessitates at the outset a prediction of the danger that an accused criminal poses to the community.

Although detention to assure presence at trial is less controversial, it too requires a prediction, a prediction of the likelihood of flight. We know all too little about how to ascertain the odds on flight, and aside from the difficulty of ascertaining probabilities, there exists the further problem of applying the information we can gather.

What mechanism will operate to release those who pose no threat to the judicial process or the community at large, while detaining criminal suspects who are dangerous or likely to flee? How can the system protect the presumption of innocence and the right to be free pending adjudication, without hampering the law enforcement process? These are the questions posed in this chapter as well as in the real world of processing criminal cases.

II. BAIL: ITS HISTORY AND THE CONSTITUTION

A. THE COMMON LAW ORIGINS OF BAIL [7]

The traditional mechanism for pretrial release, bail, originated in medieval England, where prisoners could be confined in disease-ridden and insecure prisons for years awaiting trial by travelling justices, whose visits were infrequent.

Sheriffs welcomed the opportunity to place custodial responsibility in third parties. A prisoner would seek a friend or master, usually a property owner,

7. See D. Freed & P. Wald, Bail in the United States: 1964, Working Paper for the National Conference on Bail and Criminal Justice, Washington, D.C.

who accepted custody or "bailment" of the accused, and promised to surrender himself if the defendant failed to appear. Of course, the law developed to permit the surety to forfeit property or money instead of his person, but the relationship remained a personal one, with a minimal risk of flight. Eventually Parliament specified which offenses were bailable, and the Habeas Corpus Act of 1679 provided procedures to free prisoners who were bailable by law. Some judges still circumvented these requirements by setting prohibitive levels of bail; so in 1689, Parliament responded with a Bill of Rights' provision forbidding excessive bail.

B. THE CONSTITUTIONAL BASIS FOR PRETRIAL RELEASE: THE EIGHTH AMENDMENT

The American Constitution incorporated the right of a person in custody to seek a writ of habeas corpus in Article I § 9, and the ban on excessive bail in the Eighth Amendment. The third aspect of British law regarding bail, that is, the actual right to bail for specific offenses, was not included in the Constitution.

> The bail clause was lifted with slight changes from the Bill of Rights Act. In England that clause has never been thought to accord a right to bail in all cases, but merely to provide that bail shall not be excessive in those cases where it is proper to grant bail. When this clause was carried over in our Bill of Rights, nothing was said that indicated any different concept. The Eighth Amendment has not prohibited Congress from defining the classes of cases in which bail shall be allowed in this country. * * *

Carlson v. Landon, 342 U.S. 524, 545–46 (1952).

In *Carlson,* a civil case, the Court denied bail to alien communists awaiting deportation hearings. The Court's interpretation of the Eighth Amendment has not gone unchallenged. Professor Caleb Foote, for example, points out that the bail clause standing alone "represents some of the most ambiguous language in the Bill of Rights," susceptible to several possible interpretations. Crisis in Bail, supra note 2, at 969.

The *Carlson* majority held that the Eighth Amendment prohibits excessive bail in cases where statute and court decisions provide for bail, but that the clause itself does not require bail. Critics of the holding point out that this interpretation would subsume the Constitution to some other law. "It requires one to believe that a basic human right would be deliberately inserted in the Constitution in a form which permitted Congress to restrict it at will, or even to render the eighth amendment entirely moot by enacting legislation denying the right to bail in all cases." Crisis in Bail, supra note 2, at 969. Some states have resolved this dilemma by adding a bail requirement, usually for all but capital crimes, to their state constitutions. In the federal system, however, this anomaly presents special problems, if the Eighth Amendment is to be incorporated into the Fourteenth Amendment and applied to the states.[8] To require

8. Sistrunk v. Lyons, 646 F.2d 64 (3d Cir. 1981), holds that the bail clause of the Eighth Amendment is binding on the states. A majority of the same court concluded in Cobb v. Aytch, 643 F.2d 946 (3d Cir. 1981) (en banc), that the bail clause, together with the rights to counsel and to a speedy trial, restricted a state's right to move pretrial detainees to places distant from the place of an offense.

One court of appeals held unconstitutional a state law precluding bail for a defendant accused of forcible rape where the "proof is

excessive bail would be violative of due process, but if no right to bail exists, the courts would retain discretion to disallow bail altogether.

This incongruity suggests to some that the Eighth Amendment must imply a right to bail, as the dissenters argued in Carlson v. Landon, supra. But others find it inexplicable that the framers did not expressly include that right in the Amendment. The concept of requiring bail was not unfamiliar to the framers, who incorporated it into the Judiciary Act of 1789. Professor Foote suggests that the omission of the bail guarantee may be ascribed to inadvertent draftsmanship, and that the only historically consistent reading of the Eighth Amendment

> reveals a right to bail secure against both legislative and judicial abridgment * * *. The alternative is to reduce the amendment to surplusage, and to disregard (1) the important role of bail as a fundamental right in the development of English liberty following Magna Charta; (2) the nondiscretionary character of contemporary English and colonial bail law; (3) the significant trends in colonial legislation which went far beyond English law in their liberality and excluded judicial discretion in determining the right to bail; and (4) the objective of the Bill of Rights to protect against congressional abuse.

Crisis in Bail, supra note 2, at 1125. See the discussion in United States v. Salerno, infra.

III. THE OPERATION OF A BAIL RELEASE SYSTEM

Before examining the scope of the right to bail that is recognized in most jurisdictions, an overview of bail procedures—the mechanics of the system—is in order.

A. THE ADMINISTRATION OF BAIL: THE PROCEDURES

P. WICE, BAIL AND ITS REFORM: A NATIONAL SURVEY

10–15 (1973)

* * *

The most frequently used procedure for obtaining one's pretrial release is through *cash bail.* Having learned of the bail figure, a defendant may raise the full amount of the bond through personal savings or those of his friends and family. If he shows up for all required court appearances, the entire amount is usually refunded to him.

However, the defendant may require the assistance of a bail bondsman, who has complete discretion in selecting clients. The bondsman's usual fee is 10

evident and the presumption great." Hunt v. Murphy, 648 F.2d 1148 (8th Cir. 1981). Although it appeared that the case might lead the Supreme Court to explain the Eighth Amendment's applicability to the states, the Court vacated the judgment of the lower court as moot. 454 U.S. 812 (1982).

In Meechaicum v. Fountain, 696 F.2d 790 (10th Cir. 1983), the Court found a constitutional problem with the way Kansas handled a suspect also wanted by another state. The suspect had been convicted of burglary and placed on probation in Texas before returning home to Kansas. While in Kansas, he was charged with additional criminal acts, and Texas began extradition proceedings. Kansas held the suspect without bail after the Governor of Texas executed an extradition warrant. The federal court of appeals found that the bail provision of the Eighth Amendment was binding on the states, that the crimes for which the suspect was charged by Kansas were bailable under state law, and that it was impermissible for Kansas to refuse to consider the suspect for bail simply because an outstanding warrant from Texas existed.

percent of bond amount, a payment not recoverable by the defendant. The bondsman will place the full amount of the bond with the court and the defendant gains pretrial freedom.

Results of the questionnaire mailed to 72 cities indicate that 65 percent of all defendants arrested for misdemeanors and felonies were able to obtain their release on cash bonds, also referred to as surety bonds.[9] Of this total, 44 percent utilized a bondsman and 21 percent raised the required amounts themselves. There is great variation among cities regarding the amount of bond associated with any given crime.

A second method by which pretrial release may be obtained is the *10 percent plan,* [10] whereby the defendant pays 10 percent of the bond directly to the court and recovers 90 percent of this deposit if he appears in court as scheduled. During 1969, 36 percent of those gaining pretrial release in Chicago used the 10 percent plan, whereas only 4.5 percent did so in Washington, D.C.

In 75 percent of the cities studied, the court permitted defendants [to be] released on *property bonds,* whereby the defendant or others offer property as bail in lieu of cash. Only two of the cities studied (Atlanta and St. Louis) use this method with any regularity. Interviews in both cities, however, revealed two basic problems.

First, in St. Louis, the author was told that forfeiture on property bonds created a moral dilemma for the criminal court clerk's office. The difficulty is caused by naive but good-hearted citizens who are willing to sign a property bond so that the defendant can secure his pretrial release. Usually being respectable citizens unfamiliar with the operation of the criminal courts, they have not investigated the implications if the defendant forfeits the bond, which would permit the city to claim their property at any time. The net result is that these claims are not pressed by the clerk's office.

Most prevalent in Atlanta, the second problem associated with property bonds was that businessmen who owned real estate throughout the city would use the same piece of property for several bonds. Charging defendants half of what they would have to pay bondsmen, the businessmen were shrewd enough to realize that because of the enforcement dilemma indicated above, they ran little risk of losing their property even if the defendant did forfeit and skip town.

In most cities where the judge is allowed a good deal of discretion in setting bonds, he may replace or supplement the surety bond by imposing such *conditions of release* as requiring the defendant to return to work or school, to avoid certain individuals or areas of the city, or to subject himself to treatments for drug addiction.

Personal bond is another method of release, which may be referred to as personal surety, nominal bond, or release on own recognizance. It is used when a judge determines that the defendant is sufficiently motivated to show up for his scheduled court appearance and can be released on his own signature without bail.

* * *

Defendants released on personal or surety bond by a nonjudicial officer, such as a police desk sergeant, have obtained freedom only until their first court appear-

9. Atlanta, Baltimore, Chicago, Detroit, Indianapolis, Los Angeles, Oakland, Philadelphia, San Francisco, St. Louis and Washington, D.C. were among the cities studied.

10. A constitutional challenge to the 10% plan was rebuffed in Schilb v. Kuebel, 404 U.S. 357 (1971).

ance, which usually occurs the following day. At that time, unless the case is disposed of then and there, the judge reviews the bail amount and may revise it upward or downward. Similarly, bail set by a lower court for those accused of felonies may be reviewed and revised by the higher court which conducts the actual trial.

* * *

B. THE BONDSMAN

Free of most political and governmental restraints, the private bail bondsman lurks in the background of any discussion of bail, and is one of the most important players in the pretrial drama. A uniquely American development,[11] the private surety replaces the personal guarantor of the British Common Law. When bail is set, the accused can pay a non-refundable premium—usually 10%, although rates differ markedly throughout the states—to a private bondsman, who then puts up the total amount of bail. Since the bondsman assumes the risk of forfeiture, he has traditionally been given much discretion in establishing collateral for bail, and in tracking down and retrieving a fleeing accused. The legal right of a bondsman to cancel the bond and keep the fee at any time that he surrenders the defendant to court gives the bondsman considerable leverage, especially when bail may be set anew at different stages of a trial. The threat of being "turned in" ties the defendant to his bondsman, who may demand new premiums as the trial progresses.

Proponents of the bond system point out that without the private bondsman, numerous defendants would remain in jail for lack of available assets. Also, bondsmen are often on call 24 hours a day. The profit motive provides them with the incentive to enforce a defendant's appearance in court. Thus, the system encourages private enterprise to assume part of the cost of administering the criminal justice process. In theory, the bondsmen reinforce the law enforcement system by preventing flight and helping to return fugitives. See ABA Standards, Pre-Trial Release § 10–5.4 (2d ed.1980).

Critics, however, argue that the private bond system undercuts the purposes of bail and contravenes the ideals of the criminal justice system. Release from jail on commercial bond can minimize the possibility of pecuniary loss to a defendant, so that his bail is no longer a direct deterrent to flight. The defendant loses the same amount to the bondsman whether or not he appears at trial. Theoretically, the court aims to set bail at a level that will ensure the appearance of the accused, but the intervening role of the bondsman supercedes the judicial determination. Thus, magistrates may fix bail with knowledge that the defendant has found a bondsman to advance funds or has been unable to secure help. Should a magistrate, aware of the existence of the bondsman, increase the bail so that the premium (assuming it is a percentage of the bail set) will approximate the bail intended by the court? Should the magistrate lower the bail for a prisoner who is not accepted for bail by a private bondsman?

11. Only the United States and the Philippines give the private bondsman a major role in the judicial process. See Bail in the U.S., supra note 7. See also Note, Bail: An Ancient Practice Re-examined, supra note 5.

Discretion in choosing clients provides one explanation for the low level of risk in the bonding business.[12] Bondsmen consider principally the type of crime for which the defendant was arrested, not necessarily the seriousness of the offense. Thus, those accused of organized crime or professional gambling are good risks, while a first time offender is considered a bad risk, unsophisticated as to the intricacies of the court system and prone to panic and jump bail. Narcotic addicts are considered good risks, prostitutes are not.[13] Bondsmen are free to incorporate their own political or personal prejudices in the bonding decision. The result can be disturbing. For example, civil rights activists who were arrested in the South often were unable to obtain the services of a bondsman.[14]

On the other hand, the private bonding mechanism may act as an effective shield for judges who are susceptible to competing public pressures regarding pretrial release. If may be impolitic for a judge to release a notorious suspect on bail, even if the risk of flight is minimal; but if he sets a high bail, the accused will be freed for the cost of the bondsman's fee. Also, there are numerous minor offenders for whom even temporary detention is not justified by the crime charged, who simply would have to stay in jail were it not for the private bondsman. When the bondsmen in New York went on strike in 1961 and 1964, refusing to write bonds except on 100% collateral in bankbooks or real estate, the population of the city jails swelled. The strikes were in retaliation for tighter collection policies enforced on forfeitures.[15]

Liberal forfeiture policies provide another explanation for the low level of financial risk in the bonding business. Studies have shown the forfeiture rate on private bondsmen to be very low,[16] and collection of the forfeitures has been lax. Some courts allow a "grace period" in which the bondsmen may produce the accused without loss of bail. This protects the bondsman's investment in most cases. The majority of forfeitures are not wilful, but result from mere oversight, since few jurisdictions have effective systems for notifying the accused of their appearance dates.[17] Some courts allow discretionary remittal of the forfeited bond within a few years if the defendant should appear.[18] In

12. See Bail in the United States, supra, note 7, at 33 (1963); J. Campbell, J. Sahid, and D. Staing, Law and Order Reconsidered, Report of the Task Force on Law & Law Enforcement to the National Commission on the Causes and Prevention of Violence, 462–466 (1970).

13. See A. Marticz, The Ups and Downs of a Bail Bondsman, L.A. Times, 8/2/76, reprinted in J. Snortum and I. Hader, Criminal Justice Allies and Adversaries (1978); The Bail System of the District of Columbia, Report of the ABA Junior Section, Washington, D.C. (1963).

14. R. Goldfarb, Ransom 2–3 (1965).

15. Bail or Jail, 19 Record of the Ass'n of the N.Y. City Bar 13 (1964).

16. See, e.g., The Manhattan Bail Project: An Interim Report, 38 N.Y.U.L.Rev. 67 (1963). For an example of a bail bond forfeiture, see United States v. Carr, 608 F.2d 886 (1st Cir. 1979). See also State v. Ascencio, 92 Wis.2d 822, 285 N.W.2d 910 (App.1979) (forfeiture of half of bond).

17. The grace privilege may be abused. Surveys in some states indicated that some defaults were intentionally planned in order to avoid or secure particular judges. Bail in the United States, supra note 7, at 28.

18. In United States v. Jeffers, 573 F.2d 1074 (9th Cir. 1978) the convicted defendant absconded, resulting in forfeiture of his bond, but was killed in a plane crash seven weeks later. The Court pointed out that although Federal R.Crim.P. 46(e)(1) makes forfeiture mandatory upon breach of a condition of bail, Rule 46(e)(2) permits the Court to set aside the forfeiture "if it appears that justice does not require" its enforcement. The two principle considerations regarding remission are (1) a forfeiture should bear some reasonable relation to the cost and inconvenience to the government and the courts, and (2) if a violation of a condition of release is not just technical, substantial forfeiture may be applied as a deterrent. Nonetheless, the court allowed partial remission, since the fugitive left a wife

some places, the bond system has been subject to abuses through corruption and collusion in the area of collection of forfeitures.[19]

Since the threat of forfeiture is minimal, and keeping track of clients in modern society is not easy, most bondsmen are lax about maintaining contact with the accused party. If the party flees and bail may be forfeited, some bondsmen use a system of informants and "skip tracers"—modern day bounty hunters, who often carry arms and have criminal records—to locate the fugitive. Recapture has been held to be a private remedy, arising from a private action, and usually is not limited like state action. Freed from the constraints of due process [20] and constitutional criminal procedure, a bondsman can seize a fugitive in another jurisdiction and present him to authorities, while the state must await extradition proceedings.[21]

Noting that "the methods often employed by bondsmen are hardly likely to promote respect for the administration of justice," the ABA Standards on Pretrial Release set forth a standard prohibiting, or at least severely limiting, private bonding:

and two children. See also People v. Manufacturers Cas. Ins. Co., 208 Misc. 504, 144 N.Y.S.2d 282 (1955) holding the standards for remission of forfeiture where the defendant is produced to be (1) whether the people have lost any rights, (2) whether the failure to appear was willful, (3) whether the bondsman expended money in an effort to produce the defendant, and (4) whether the defendant was produced as a result of those efforts. When the defendant is not produced, the test for remission of forfeiture is (1) whether the failure to produce was due to death, insanity, or imprisonment on another charge and (2) whether the personal surety will suffer hardship, such as will cause destitution to a family. (The courts are not concerned with losses to the corporate surety or bondsman.)

19. See W. Thomas, Bail Reform in America 16–17 (1976); R. Goldfarb, Ransom 92–127 (1965).

20. Bondsmen are not public officers and therefore are not bound by the constitutional restraints that were examined in Chapters Two and Three. Although they are not restrained by the Constitution, bondsmen rely upon it to protest forfeitures. In Wilshire Ins. Co. v. State, 546 Nev. 94, 582 P.2d 372 (1978), the Court held that due process requires that the bondsmen be given notice of bail forfeiture proceedings. In People v. Surety Ins. Co., 55 Cal.App.3d 197, 127 Cal.Rptr. 451 (1976), the Court upheld the general bond scheme against a due process challenge. Under the California rules, the clerk of the Court is required to give notice of forfeiture to the surety. Failure to do so frees the surety from responsibility. Upon receiving notice, the surety is required to locate the defendant and turn him in within 6 months to avoid default.

21. Some bondsmen have gone to great lengths to protect their investments. In United States v. Trunko, 189 F.Supp. 559 (E.D.Ark. 1960), the federal government prosecuted two bondsmen for willful deprivation of liberty without due process under color of state law. The Ohio bondsmen entered an Arkansas home before dawn, displayed guns, seized and handcuffed the fugitive, and drove away at high speed, despite the pleas of his wife that they call the sheriff. The fugitive had been placed on $500 bond for a misdemeanor, driving under the influence of alcohol. The court held that sufficient state action and a violation of constitutional rights were proven, but acquitted the bondsmen, stating that they lacked the requisite, specific criminal intent. In a civil suit against bondsmen under similar facts, the district court of Tennessee held there was no civil liability because of the contractual relationship between the parties. Thomas v. Miller, 282 F.Supp. 571 (E.D.Tenn. 1968). In Shine v. State, 44 Ala.App. 171, 204 So.2d 817 (1967) the defendant secured an appearance bond from a bondsman, appeared at trial, was convicted of a misdemeanor and was fined $100 which the bondsman paid, also arranging for release on an appeal bond. To collect $40 still owed to him, the bondsman, accompanied by several armed agents, surrounded the defendant's home at 5:00 a.m. and threatened to break in. When one agent broke down the front door and pointed an 18 inch shotgun through the opening, the defendant shot and killed him. Convicted of second degree murder, the defendant won reversal on appeal.

For an interesting case, see Kear v. Hilton, 699 F.2d 181 (4th Cir. 1983) (recognizing that "[p]rofessional bondsmen in the United States enjoy extraordinary powers to capture and use force to compel peremptory return of a bail jumper," but permitting extradition of bondsman to Canada for kidnapping a bail jumper).

§ 5.4 Prohibition of Compensated Sureties

> Compensated sureties should be abolished. Pending abolition, they should be licensed and carefully registered. The amount which a compensated surety can charge for writing a bond should be set by law. No licensed surety should be permitted to reject an applicant willing to pay the statutory fee or insist upon additional collateral other than specified by law.

Similar acts have been passed in a few states, although most states have hesitated to eliminate the private bondsman for fear that fewer persons would be released, and higher bonds would result for those who were released. Instead, critics of the bondsmen system have encouraged use of the Illinois 10% plan,[22] and other procedures for bail that are controlled by law enforcement authorities in the state.[23]

C. THE BAIL SETTING DECISION

Consistent with their distrust of governmental discretion, the American colonists favored an absolute right to bail established by law.[24] Thus, the Federal Judiciary Act of 1789 mandated that all persons be bailable by sureties except "in capital cases, where the proof of guilt is evident or the presumption is great." [25] A similar rule was adopted by most of the states.[26]

In most places, the judiciary is entrusted with vast discretion in implementing the controlling statutes or court rules. Bail criteria are not self-executing; it is the application of general criteria to particular cases that effectively determines which defendants are released. Often courts can choose among criteria in making bail decisions, and the choice often reflects a court's view of the purposes of bail. Broad discretion in applying and choosing criteria finds support in the leading Supreme Court precedent regarding bail: Stack v. Boyle, 342 U.S. 1 (1951). The Court has never held that bail or any form of pretrial release is constitutionally required.[27] However, Stack v. Boyle recognized that a federal court must set bail at an amount that appropriately furthers the purposes of bail. Although the Court indicated that judicial discretion in non-capital cases is limited to the setting of amount, it recognized that the decision to release an individual accused is necessarily fact-specific, leaving ample room for judicial discretion. The Court held that bail fixed in uniform amounts of $50,000 for each of twelve defendants charged with

22. See, e.g., Goals for Virginia's Criminal Justice System, Report of the Task Force on Criminal Justice Goals and Objectives, Va. Council on Criminal Justice and Va. Crime Commission, March 1977, suggesting a pilot program be instituted, modeled after the Illinois 10% plan, by which 10% of the bail amount is deposited with a clerk of the court, rather than a private bondsman. Upon appearance, all but a fixed fee to cover costs is returned to the defendant. See, C. Bowman, The Illinois 10% Bail Deposit Provision, 1975 U.Ill.Law Forum 35.

23. The Uniform Bail Bond Act, promulgated by the National Association of Insurance Commissioners, regulates the practices of bondsmen; however, it has only been adopted by a few jurisdictions.

24. See, P. Secret, The Constitutionality of Prevention Detention 54–76 (1977). The British System, however, moved to its current position of complete judicial discretion regarding bail. See Crisis in Bail, supra note 2, at 978.

25. 1 Stat. 91 § 33 (1789).

26. A few states adopted the British system, according complete discretion to the judiciary.

27. Despite provisions for appellate review of bail decisions, it is unusual for appellate courts to overrule lower courts in cases involving suspects in major crimes. An example of the unusual is Ex parte Hellenguard, 622 S.W.2d 875 (Tex.Cr.App.1981) (lowering bond in murder case from $100,000 to $25,000).

violations of the Smith Act could not be justified in the absence of evidence relating to the particular untrustworthiness of each defendant. Three paragraphs from the Court's opinion follow:

> The right to release before trial is conditioned upon the accused's giving adequate assurance that he will stand trial and submit to sentence if found guilty. Like the ancient practice of securing the oaths of responsible persons to stand as sureties for the accused, the modern practice of requiring a bail bond or the deposit of a sum of money subject to forfeiture serves as additional assurance of the presence of an accused. Bail set at a figure higher than an amount reasonably calculated to fulfill this purpose is 'excessive' under the Eighth Amendment.
>
> Since the function of bail is limited, the fixing of bail for any individual defendant must be based upon standards relevant to the purpose of assuring the presence of that defendant. The traditional standards as expressed in the Federal Rules of Criminal Procedure are to be applied in each case to each defendant. In this case petitioners are charged with offenses under the Smith Act and, if found guilty, their convictions are subject to review with the scrupulous care demanded by our Constitution. Upon final judgment of conviction, petitioners face imprisonment of not more than five years and a fine of not more than $10,000. It is not denied that bail for each petitioner has been fixed in a sum much higher than that usually imposed for offenses with like penalties and yet there has been no factual showing to justify such action in this case. The Government asks the courts to depart from the norm by assuming, without the introduction of evidence, that each petitioner is a pawn in a conspiracy and will, in obedience to a superior, flee the jurisdiction. To infer from the fact of indictment alone a need for bail in an unusually high amount is an arbitrary act. Such conduct would inject into our own system of government the very principles of totalitarianism which Congress was seeking to guard against in passing the statute under which petitioners have been indicted.
>
> If bail in an amount greater than that usually fixed for serious charges of crimes is required in the case of any of the petitioners, that is a matter to which evidence should be directed in a hearing so that the constitutional rights of each petitioner may be preserved. In the absence of such a showing, we are of the opinion that the fixing of bail before trial in these cases cannot be squared with the statutory and constitutional standards for admission to bail.

Trial courts have difficulty determining what bail is appropriate for different individuals. The next excerpt discusses how the bail determination is made and highlights some inequities.

P. Wice, Bail and Its Reform: A National Survey 15–17 (1973).

* * *

The criterion to which nearly all felony court judges assign the greatest significance when reaching decisions on bail amounts is the seriousness of offense, despite evidence indicating that this intention is unrelated to [the] primary purpose of bail—to guarantee that the defendant will appear for trial.[28]

28. In a study of pretrial release in New Haven, a Yale Law Student found that the offense charged was the primary consideration at bail hearings. His conclusion, based on interviews with 81 accused felons, was that nearly half of those who were held in jail because of inability to post bond had sufficient ties in the community to meet conditions of

The author believes that this criterion is used most frequently because it is so clear-cut and easy to apply. Thus the process of setting bail becomes a very rapid and smoothly operating procedure, a desirable objective in view of the tremendous workloads facing many courts.

However, this criterion does not result in a uniform bail-setting policy because each judge has his own conception of the seriousness of various offenses.[29]

Used in close conjunction with the judge's conception of the seriousness of the offense, a second yardstick employed in the bail-setting decision is the strength of the case against the defendant. This information is often relayed to the bench by prosecutors and police officers.

A third factor considered very relevant by the judiciary is the defendant's prior criminal record.

The three criteria above are felt to be the most crucial factors in setting bail by nearly all judges interviewed. They are the only factors that judges examine with any degree of regularity.

Other criteria relate to the defendant's background, such as his community ties, financial status, and character references. One of the most ironic aspects of the bail-setting procedure is that the factor explored least frequently by the judge has the greatest impact on the defendant's ability to secure pretrial release—his financial status and the amount of bail he can afford to pay.

There are three explanations for this lack of judicial interest in the defendant's background. First, many judges are too harried and overworked to have an opportunity to question the defendant about his background. Second, some judges consider such inquiries as so much wasted time since defendants cannot be trusted to supply truthful answers. Finally, judges believe the first three criteria to be the most valid predictors of defendant behavior.

Judges do not reach bail-setting decisions in a vacuum. The five most significant outside influences are the police, court officials, prosecutor's office, defense attorney, and newspapers.

The most important outside influence is that of the police, who can influence a judge's bail decision through (1) selection of the charge with which to accuse the defendant, (2) specific recommendations made at the bail hearing, (3) the provision of "rap sheets" to the judge, and (4) an indication of the strength of the case against the accused.

Prosecutors may alter the charge, notify the judge about the strength of the case, and make recommendations at the bail hearing.[30]

release. W. Brochett, Pre-Trial Detention: The Most Critical Period (Unpublished manuscript 1970), cited in W. Thomas, Bail Reform in America 143 (1976).

29. A 1978 Report to Congress by the General Accounting Office confirmed that judicial officers "use bail for differing purposes." The result of this "substantial judicial discretion" is that release conditions vary widely throughout federal districts. For example, 75% of the defendants charged with drug offenses in Northern Texas had to pay money to secure release, as compared with 21% faced with similar charges in Eastern Michigan. Report to Congress by the Comptroller General, The Federal Bail Process Fosters Inequities 5–8 (1978).

30. Prosecutors may not be unbiased in their recommendations to judges. One study in Kings County, Washington, indicates that the bail system is used to protect prosecutors from public criticism. By suggesting a high bail amount with the expectation that the judge will lower it, prosecutors seek to shield themselves from responsibility if the accused fails to appear in court. The court, in turn, is under pressure to keep the prison population down. Cole, The Decision to Prosecute, 4 Law & Soc'y Rev. 331 (1970).

Also influential are the various court officials who play such an essential role in running the daily operation of criminal courts. Judges tend to rely on these people and will use them as a source of information on several matters related to bail administration.

If the defendant's counsel is present at the bail hearing, he tries to supply facts in attempting to secure his client's release on the best conditions possible.[31]

Finally, pressures exerted on the judiciary by the press and general public influence the bail-setting decision. Fearful of adverse publicity resulting from releasing a defendant who might commit a crime while awaiting trial, one judge indicated that he and his associates were constantly looking over their shoulders at the press and general public when deliberating the amount of the defendant's bond.

* * *

Pressures from law enforcement officials and the public, in combination with the judge's own view that bail serves other purposes beyond simply securing presence at trial, lead judges to consider factors such as the dangerousness of the accused in setting bail, even if such factors are not relied upon explicitly because they are not recognized in a governing statute or court rule.[32] The practice of denying bail or setting it at an unattainably high amount is used either implicitly or explicitly to detain defendants who seem dangerous to the community, who are unpopular, or whom the judges would like to give a "taste of jail."

D. TWO SAMPLE CASES

In the following fact situations, consider what arguments you see for and against recommending bail for the accused. As judge, would you set bail? As a private bondsman, whose general practice is either to accept 10% of the bond as a non-refundable premium or to refuse the client, would you take the risk?

1. The 39–year–old defendant was arrested 2 days ago for attempted murder and aggravated battery. He has a prior record of 10 armed robberies and one attempted jailbreak while awaiting an earlier trial. Yesterday, he threatened the life of a cellmate, and boasted that he always carried a loaded gun. He has an excellent record for his prior experience on parole, and a perfect attendance record while free on bond for a prior conviction. He has been working part-time, and for the past 6 months has lived with his mother. The maximum sentence is 10 years. Would your answer differ if he had no job, and no permanent address? If he were charged with burglary? With armed robbery? With vagrancy? Would your decision be different if a statute or court rule provided that the sole purpose of bail is to compel the appearance of the accused?

2. A 36–year–old defendant is charged with breaking and entering. She is a heroin addict, and has a record of seven prior convictions for breaking and entering, as well as two convictions for possession of narcotics. She lives with

31. Is the bail hearing a "critical stage" warranting appointed counsel under the Sixth Amendment? Note that bail was mentioned in Coleman v. Alabama, discussed in Chapter Five, and that it also is mentioned in Gerstein v. Pugh, discussed in Chapter Two. In reality, it may be to the defendant's advantage to be eligible for bail before counsel is appointed. If bail is denied or set too high, counsel can always ask for reconsideration.

32. See, e.g., United States v. Wind, 527 F.2d 672 (6th Cir.1975).

her three children, and works part-time in the department store where she was arrested. Should she be released on bail? How much bail should be required?

IV. BEYOND BAIL: ALTERNATIVE SYSTEMS OF PRETRIAL RELEASE

A. THE BAIL REFORM MOVEMENT

Recognition that bail often was set arbitrarily, without regard to individual trustworthiness or ability to pay, led to bail reform projects in the early 1960's. Louis Schweitzer established the Vera Foundation in New York for the purpose of eliminating discriminatory aspects of the bail system. He designed the Manhattan Bail Project to expand the use of personal recognizance for defendants who, based on certain guidelines, could be released with a low probability of flight.

POINT SCORING SYSTEM MANHATTAN BAIL PROJECT

To be recommended, defendant needs:

1. A New York area address where he can be reached and
2. A total of five points from the following categories—

Prior Record

1 No convictions.

0 One misdemeanor conviction.

—1 Two misdemeanor or one felony conviction.

—2 Three or more misdemeanor or two or more felony convictions.

Family Ties (In New York area)

3 Lives in established family home AND visits other family members (immediate family only).

2 Lives in established family home (immediate family).

1 Visits others of immediate family.

Employment or School

3 Present job one year or more, steadily.

2 Present job 4 months OR present and prior 6 months.

1 Has present job which is still available.

OR Unemployed 3 months or less and 9 months or more steady prior job.

OR Unemployment Compensation.

OR Welfare.

3 Presently in school, attending regularly.

2 Out of school less than 6 months but employed, or in training.

1 Out of school 3 months or less, unemployed and not in training.

Residence (in New York area steadily)

3 One year at present residence.

2 One year at present or last prior residence OR 6 months at present residence.

1 Six months at present and last prior residence OR in New York City 5 years or more.

Discretion

+1 Positive, over 65, attending hospital, appeared on some previous case.

0 Negative—intoxicated—intention to leave jurisdiction.

The success of the Manhattan Bail Project [33] led many other cities to duplicate the project.[34] These projects, in combination with numerous studies pointing out the inadequacies of the bail system [35] and the work of the National Conference on Bail and Criminal Justice in 1964,[36] culminated in the Federal Bail Reform Act of 1966, considered infra, which established release on personal recognizance as the preferred device for pretrial release, with a presumption against monetary bail.

In general, the pretrial release programs were effective in releasing large numbers of defendants without adversely affecting either no-show rates or rates of rearrest for new crimes while on release.[37] The most effective programs have included mechanisms for supervised release, and for notifying defendants of their appearance dates.[38] The reform movement has had effects beyond the cases in which bail projects actually are utilized. It has demonstrated the feasibility of release upon one's own recognizance and it has educated judges in its use. Today, non-financial forms of release are used even where bail projects do not exist.[39]

There are numerous cases that remain unresolved by the emphasis on personal recognizance release. Consider, for example:

> Many addicts come into our court on petit larceny charges. They will tell you they have a $40–50 per day habit supported solely by stealing. To release them is to guarantee theft in the amount of $250 or more a week. But, they usually return to court on the appointed date. An addict with a bad habit cannot leave his source, so flight is almost non-existent. On the date of trial, the pusher will bring them in or they are quickly found in their neighborhood.

33. During the first three years, over ⅓ of the 10,000 detainees interviewed were released on their own recognizance following recommendations of VERA staff members. Only 1.6% of the total number released on their own recognizance failed to appear at trial. In the same time period 3% of these released on bail failed to appear. Ten Year Report of the Vera Institute of Justice, 1961–71.

34. At least 68 cities reported bail projects operational by the 1964 Conference on Bail and Criminal Justice or the 1965 Institute on the Operation of Pre-Trial Release Programs. W. Thomas, Bail Reform in America 24–25 (1976).

35. See, e.g., Attorney General's Committee on Poverty and the Administration of Federal Criminal Justice, Report (1963). For a description of influences on the development of the Bail Reform Act, see Ervin, The Legislative Role in Bail Reform, 35 Geo.Wash.L.Rev. 429 (1967).

36. Bail and Summons, National Conference on Bail & Criminal Justice: Proceedings (1965).

37. National Center for State Courts, An Evaluation of Policy Related Research on the Effectiveness of Pretrial Release Programs (1975).

38. P. Wice, Bail and Its Reform, A National Survey 65 (1973).

39. W. Thomas, Bail Reform in America 154 (1976).

> Since they are a good risk on personal bond, the Bail Act dictates that they be released. Yet they pose a double economic danger to the community in terms of future burglary, robbery or tampering offenses.

Prepared Statement of Chief Judge Harold H. Greene, D.C. Ct. of Gen'l Sess. Hearings on the Bail Reform Act of 1966, Before the Subcomm. on Constit. Rts. of Senate Comm. on the Judiciary, 91st Cong., 1st Sess. (1969). How should the community handle the problem of the addict?

B. THE FEDERAL STATUTE: REFORM AND PREVENTIVE DETENTION

Congress, concerned about the arbitrariness and unfairness of a system of pretrial release that depended heavily on bail bondsmen, enacted the Bail Reform Act of 1966, a statute emulated by many states. The most important provision of the Act was § 3146, which provided in relevant part as follows:

> (a) Any person charged with an offense, other than an offense punishable by death, shall, at his appearance before a judicial officer, be ordered released pending trial on his personal recognizance or upon the execution of an unsecured appearance bond in an amount specified by the judicial officer, unless the officer determines, in the exercise of his discretion, that such a release will not reasonably assure the appearance of the person as required. When such a determination is made, the judicial officer shall, either in lieu of or in addition to the above methods of release, impose the first of the following conditions of release which will reasonably assure the appearance of the person for trial or, if no single condition gives that assurance, any combination of the following conditions:
>
> (1) place the person in the custody of a designated person or organization agreeing to supervise him;
>
> (2) place restrictions on the travel, association, or place of abode of the person during the period of release;
>
> (3) require the execution of an appearance bond in a specified amount and the deposit in the registry of the court, in cash or other security as directed, of a sum not to exceed 10 per centum of the amount of the bond, such deposit to be returned upon the performance of the conditions of release;
>
> (4) require the execution of a bail bond with sufficient solvent sureties, or the deposit of cash in lieu thereof; or
>
> (5) impose any other condition deemed reasonably necessary to assure appearance as required, including a condition requiring that the person return to custody after specified hours.
>
> (b) In determining which conditions of release will reasonably assure appearance, the judicial officer shall, on the basis of available information, take into account the nature and circumstances of the offense charged, the weight of the evidence against the accused, the accused's family ties, employment, financial resources, character and mental condition, the length of his residence in the community, his record of convictions, and his record of appearance at court proceedings or of flight to avoid prosecution or failure to appear at court proceedings.
>
> * * *

The purpose of the 1966 Act was to encourage federal courts to release accused persons without requiring them to deal with bail bondsmen. Apparently, courts were to consider only whether pretrial release "will reasonably assure the appearance of the person for trial." No provision was made for confinement of an accused who might pose a "danger" to the community.

There is little doubt that most courts have historically applied criteria for pretrial release in such a manner as to satisfy their views of the proper purposes of pretrial release. As noted earlier, some jurisdictions recognize only one criterion for pretrial release: whether the accused will show up at trial. Other jurisdictions permit consideration of another factor: danger to the community.

It is not always clear what dangers can be considered, but any likelihood of additional criminal activity while released would be enough for some judges to deny release. Even where likelihood of appearance is the only permissible bail criterion, it is almost certain that danger to the community is considered sub rosa. It may be that the analytical distinctions between jurisdictions are exaggerated. Consider the following analysis of bail:

> Bail today may be defined as serving two functions. Its lawful purpose is said to be to assure the presence of the defendant at trial, and for this purpose we tend to acknowledge that bail can be set high to prevent flight. This purpose is contrasted with the supposedly unlawful practice of preventive detention, under which high bail is set to protect the community against a risk of danger from the defendant's future crime. * * *
>
> When a court sets high bail to detain on grounds of flight risk, let us speak not of assuring appearance but rather of the court's prediction that, if released, the defendant may jump bail and run away. And when a court sets high bail to detain on grounds of risk of danger, let us speak not of protecting the community but rather of the court's prediction that, if released, the defendant may injure persons or property rights. So rephrased, we find that both forms of high bail involve—
>
> (1) a prediction of the defendant's future conduct on the basis of past events;
>
> (2) a prediction that, if released, the defendant will do something illegal, i.e., jump bail or perform some other unlawful act; and
>
> (3) detention of a man who is presumed to be innocent of the present charge against him.
>
> * * *
>
> Once we analyze the two forms of detention in these terms, we find, *first,* that neither kind of detention alters the presumption of innocence with respect to the crime charged. For both released and detained defendants, the traditional presumption of innocence operates with respect to the current charge as an element in allocating the burden of proof at trial. Detention prior to trial is not based on a determination of guilt. It is designed not to punish the defendant for past acts but to prevent him from engaging in future acts. *Second,* we see that both forms of detention equally violate the due process clause, or are equally irrelevant to due process, because each equally deprives a man of his liberty by imposing a prior restraint to guard against anticipated misconduct. *Third,* we discover that both forms of detention equally merit the

description "preventive detention" because each equally restrains the accused's freedom in order to prevent misbehavior.

Statement of Daniel Freed, in Panel Discussion on Preventive Detention, in Bail and Summons, supra note 49, at 43–44 (1965).

Congress repealed the 1966 Bail Reform Act as part of its Comprehensive Crime Control Act of 1984, 18 U.S.C.A. §§ 3141–3150. The Bail Reform Act of 1984 was an important part of the comprehensive overhaul of federal criminal law. The most important changes are the explicit recognition that potential dangerousness to the community may be considered in pretrial release decisions and a prohibition against setting bail so high that a defendant cannot afford to post it.

Like the 1966 statute, the 1984 reform measure establishes a preference for pretrial release upon an accused's own recognizance or upon execution of an unsecured appearance bond. The 1984 statute requires a court to utilize one of these forms of release "unless the judicial officer determines that such release will not reasonably assure the appearance of the person as required or will endanger the safety of any other person or the community." [§ 3142(b)]. If the judicial officer makes such a determination, he must order release subject to certain conditions, which are set forth in the statute. [§ 3142(c)(1) & (2)]. The officer must select the least restrictive conditions that will assure the accused's appearance and protect public safety.

The 1984 statute explicitly provides for a hearing under certain circumstances [§ 3142(f)] at which the judicial officer will determine whether any condition or combination of conditions will reasonably assure the accused's appearance and protect public safety. If the officer finds that no condition or combination of conditions is adequate, "he shall order the detention of the person before trial." [§ 3142(e)].

A rebuttable presumption arises that no condition or conditions is adequate if an accused has been convicted of a crime of violence [defined in § 3156], a crime punishable by death or life imprisonment, or a drug offense punishable by ten years or more incarceration; the prior conviction was committed while the person was on release pending trial; and not more than five years has elapsed since the conviction or date of release from incarceration for the conviction. An additional rebuttable presumption arises if the judicial officer finds that there is probable cause to believe that an accused committed a federal drug offense punishable by ten years or more incarceration. [§ 3142(e)].

In United States v. Jessup, 757 F.2d 378 (1st Cir.1985), the Court sustained the presumption in the Bail Reform Act of 1984 that a defendant charged with a serious drug offense poses a serious risk of flight. It concluded that Congress shifted only the burden of production with respect to the flight issue to the defendant and that the government continued to bear the burden of persuasion with respect to likelihood of flight. The Court also concluded, however, the presumption did not disappear when the defendant offered rebuttal evidence. Instead, it adopted a "middle ground" which requires Judges and Magistrates to consider Congress' finding that suspects charged with serious drug offenses pose special risks of flight and to weigh that finding when deciding whether the government has satisfied its persuasion burden.

The Bail Reform Act of 1984 has caused a number of interpretive problems for the courts. There is a division of authority as to the scope of appellate review with respect to a finding that pretrial detention is appropriate. Some courts hold that a finding will be affirmed unless it is clearly erroneous; more hold that appellate review is plenary and independent as to facts and mixed questions of fact and law. The various approaches are discussed in United States v. Hurtado, 779 F.2d 1467 (11th Cir.1985). *Hurtado* also holds that probable cause to believe that the defendant has committed an offense is conclusively demonstrated by the return of an indictment. The opinion reasons that an indictment plus the government's request for detention is sufficient to require an inquiry into whether detention is necessary.[40]

In United States v. Montalvo–Murillo, 495 U.S. 711 (1990), the Government failed to comply with the provision in the Bail Reform Act of 1984 that a hearing to determine the propriety of pretrial release be held "immediately upon the person's first appearance before the judicial officer." The District Court ultimately found that Montalvo–Murillo posed a risk of flight and a danger to the community, and that no condition of release could give reasonable assurances against these risks. The court nonetheless released Montalvo–Murillo due to the lack of a timely hearing; he thereupon became a fugitive.

Justice Kennedy, writing for six Justices, acknowledged the importance of a prompt hearing, but asserted that "neither the timing requirements nor any other part of the Act can be read to require, or even suggest, that a timing error must result in release of a person who should otherwise be detained." The majority reasoned as follows:

> The safety of society does not become forfeit to the accident of noncompliance with statutory time limits where the Government is ready and able to come forward with the requisite showing to meet the burden of proof required by the statute. * * * An order of release in the face of the Government's ability to prove at once that detention is required by the law has neither causal nor proportional relation to any harm caused by the delay in holding the hearing.

Justice Kennedy concluded that release of Montalvo–Murillo was an unwarranted remedy since he had not been prejudiced by the delay:

> In this case, it is clear that the noncompliance with the timing requirement had no substantial influence on the outcome of the proceeding. Because respondent was dangerous and likely to flee, he would have been detained if his hearing had been held upon his first appearance rather than a few days later. On these facts, the detention was harmless.

The majority did not decide what remedies would be appropriate for a failure to comply with the timely hearing requirement, nor what remedies would be available to a person detained beyond the statutory limit and later found to have been eligible for release.

40. A good discussion of the problems arising under the 1984 bail statute can be found in Serr, The Federal Bail Reform Act of 1984: The First Wave of Case Law, 39 Ark.L.Rev. 169 (1985).

Justice Stevens wrote a dissenting opinion joined by Justices Brennan and Marshall. The dissenters argued that the majority had undervalued the importance of a prompt hearing concerning pretrial detention. Justice Stevens concluded that "Congress has written detailed legislation in a sensitive area that requires the Government to turn square corners. The Court today, however, permits federal prosecutors to violate the law with impunity."

After *Montalvo–Murillo,* what incentive does the prosecutor have to comply with the timely hearing requirement? What remedies other than release can be imposed by the court? Does it follow that because a person is found dangerous and likely to flee at a *later* hearing, the failure to provide an earlier hearing was harmless?

Unlike the 1966 statute, the 1984 reform legislation provides that a person who has been convicted shall be detained pending imposition or execution of sentence "unless the judicial officer finds by clear and convincing evidence that the person is not likely to flee or pose a danger to the safety of any other person of the community if released." [§ 3143(a)].

There is little doubt that the 1984 legislation will make it more difficult for some defendants to obtain release pending trial and for most defendants who are convicted to obtain release pending sentencing. It would be wrong to conclude, however, that the statute represents a generally negative attitude toward pretrial release.

As noted above, no accused may be detained pending trial without findings by the judicial officer. A defendant may seek review of these findings. [§ 3145]. For the first time, the statute explicitly provides that "[t]he judicial officer may not impose a financial condition that results in the pretrial detention of the person." [§ 3142(c)]. This means that, unless the judicial officer finds that no condition or conditions of release will provide that an accused will appear and will protect the community, the officer must provide for release of the accused.

Senate Report No. 98–225 explains the 1984 legislation as viewed by the Senate Judiciary Committee:

"The constraints of the Bail Reform Act [of 1966] fail to grant the courts the authority to impose conditions of release geared toward assuring community safety, or the authority to deny release to those defendants who pose an especially grave risk to the safety of the community. If a court believes that a defendant poses such a danger, it faces a dilemma—either it can release the defendant prior to trial despite these fears, or it can find a reason, such as risk of flight, to detain the defendant (usually by imposing high money bond). In the Committee's view, it is intolerable that the law denies judges the tools to make honest and appropriate decisions regarding the release of such defendants.

* * *

"In facing the problem of how to change current bail laws to provide appropriate authority to deal with dangerous defendants seeking release, the Committee concluded that while such measures as permitting consideration of community safety in setting release conditions and providing for revocation of release upon the commission of a crime during the pretrial period may serve to reduce the rate of pretrial recidivism, and that these measures therefore should be incorporated in this chapter, there is a small but identifiable group of particularly dangerous defendants as to whom neither the imposition of stringent release conditions nor the prospect of revocation of release can reasonably assure the safety of the community or other persons. It is with respect to this limited group of offenders that the courts must be given the power to deny release pending trial.

* * *

"The Committee has given thorough consideration to the issues which have arisen during the lengthy debate over pretrial detention. In particular, this consideration has focused on three questions: first, whether pretrial detention is constitutionally permissible; second, whether a preventive detention statute that is appropriately narrow in scope, and that provides necessarily stringent safeguards to protect the rights of defendants, will be sufficiently workable, as a practical matter, that it will be utilized to any significant degree; and third, whether the premise of a pretrial detention statute—that judges can predict with an acceptable degree of accuracy which defendants are likely to commit further crimes if released—is a reasonable one.

"With respect to the first two questions, experience with the preventive detention provision of the District of Columbia Code has been a useful reference. Although this statute was enacted in 1970, its constitutionality has been squarely addressed only recently. In *United States v. Edwards* [430 A.2d 1321 (D.C.App. 1981) (en banc), cert. denied 455 U.S. 1022 (1982)], the District of Columbia Court of Appeals *en banc* upheld the constitutionality of the statute. While the opinion of the court addressed a variety of constitutional issues, the decision focused on, and ultimately rejected, the two most commonly raised arguments that pretrial detention is unconstitutional: that the Eighth Amendment's prohibition on excessive bail impliedly guarantees an absolute right to release pending trial, and that pretrial detention is violative of the Due Process Clause of the Fifth Amendment in that it permits punishment of a defendant prior to an adjudication of guilt. In its review of the Eighth Amendment issue, the court exhaustively examined both the origins of the excessive bail clause and case law interpreting it, and concluded that the purpose of the amendment was to limit the discretion of the judiciary in setting money bail in individual cases, and not to limit the power of the Congress to deny release for certain crimes or certain offenders. With respect to the Due Process issue, the court concluded, correctly in the view of the Committee, that pretrial detention is not intended to promote the traditional aims of punishment such as retribution or deterrence, but rather that it is designed 'to curtail reasonably predictable conduct, not to punish for prior acts,' and thus, under the Supreme Court's decision in *Bell v. Wolfish,* is a constitutionally permissible regulatory, rather than a penal, sanction.

"Based on its own constitutional analysis and its review of the *Edwards* decision, the Committee is satisfied that pretrial detention is not *per se* unconstitutional. However, the Committee recognizes a pretrial detention statute may nonetheless be constitutionally defective if it fails to provide adequate procedural safeguards or if it does not limit pretrial detention to cases in which it is necessary to serve the societal interests it is designed to protect. The pretrial detention provisions of this section have been carefully drafted with these concerns in mind.

* * *

"The question whether future criminality can be predicted, an assumption implicit in permitting pretrial detention based on perceived defendant dangerousness, is one which neither the experience under the District of Columbia detention statute nor empirical analysis can conclusively answer. If a defendant is detained, he is logically precluded from engaging in criminal activity, and thus the correctness of the detention decision cannot be factually determined. However, the presence of certain combinations of offense and offender characteristics, such as the nature and seriousness of the offense charged, the extent of prior arrests and convictions, and a history of drug addiction, have been shown in studies to have a strong positive relationship to predicting the probability that a defendant will commit a new offense while on release. While predictions which attempt to identify those defendants who will pose a significant danger to the safety of others if released are not infallible, the Committee believes that judges can, by considering factors such as those noted above, make such predictions with an acceptable level of accuracy.

* * *

"While providing statutory authority for pretrial detention is a substantial change in Federal law, it is well known that a substantial minority of Federal defendants in the past have in fact been detained pending trial, primarily because of an inability to meet conditions of release. Under the Bail Reform Act, it is permissible for a defendant to be detained if he is unable to meet conditions of release that have been determined by a judge to be reasonably necessary to assure his appearance. However, it has been suggested that the phenomenon of pretrial detention under the Bail Reform Act is often the result of intentional imposition of excessively stringent release conditions, and in particular extraordinarily high money bonds, in order to achieve detention. Furthermore, it has been suggested that in many cases, while the imposition of such conditions has apparently been for the purpose of assuring the defendant's appearance at trial, the underlying concern has been the need to detain a particularly dangerous defendant, a concern which the Bail Reform Act fails to address.

* * *

"Providing statutory authority to conduct a hearing focusing on the issue of a defendant's dangerousness, and to permit an order of detention where a defendant poses such a risk to others that no form of conditional release is sufficient, would allow the courts to address the issue of pretrial criminality honestly and effectively. It would also be fairer to the defendant than the indirect method of achieving detention through the imposition of financial conditions beyond his reach. The defendant would be fully informed of the issue before the court, the government would be required to come forward with information to support a finding of dangerousness, and the defendant would be given an opportunity to respond directly. The new bail procedures promote candor, fairness, and effectiveness for society, the victims of crime—and the defendant as well.

"It is the intent of the Committee that the pretrial detention provisions of section 3142 are to replace any existing practice of detaining dangerous defendants through the imposition of excessively high money bond. Because of concern that the opportunity to use financial conditions of release to achieve pretrial detention would provide a means of circumventing the procedural safeguards and standard of proof requirements of a pretrial detention provision, the Committee was urged to do away with money bond entirely. * * * Instead, the bill assures the goal of precluding detention through use of high money bond by stating explicitly that '[t]he judge may not impose a financial condition that results in the detention of the person.' Retention of money bond was recommended by the Department of Justice, which noted that money bond has historically been one of the primary methods of securing the appearance of defendants and that this form of release has proved to be an effective deterrent to flight for certain defendants."

Which system of pretrial release is preferable, the one established by the 1966 Act or the one established in 1984? Will magistrates consider dangerousness in making release decisions no matter what the governing statute or rule provides? If some magistrates might, is it desirable to have some criteria set forth to govern decisionmaking? If Congress concluded that federal courts took dangerousness into account without saying so prior to 1984, what guarantee is there that the courts will not actually use criteria other than those set forth in the 1984 statute when making decisions?

V. THE CONSTITUTIONALITY OF PREVENTIVE DETENTION

There are practical problems in identifying "dangerous" suspects,[41] but, the most controversial aspect of preventive detention is its constitutionality. Professor Foote argued that the pretrial detainee "is being denied the fundamental fairness guaranteed by the due process of law because, although he alleges he is innocent, he is being punished by imprisonment before he has been tried." Crisis in Bail, supra note 2, at 1135. But see the statement of Daniel Freed, supra. If one relies on the presumption of innocence to criticize pretrial detention to protect the community, is any bail or pretrial release system constitutional in which not all suspects are released on their own recognizance immediately and without conditions?

Technically, the presumption of innocence is no more than a rule of evidence that allocates the burden of proof to the government and serves as the foundation for the procedural requirement of proof beyond a reasonable doubt. Those who argue that pretrial detention contravenes the "presumption of innocence" of the accused assign a broader meaning to the presumption. In view of the Eighth Amendment, can that meaning have a constitutional foundation? Apart from the dictum in Stack v. Boyle ("unless this right to bail is preserved, the presumption of innocence secured only after centuries of struggle would lose its meaning") and similar language in other decisions, there is little reason to think that the presumption of innocence and bail systems cannot co-exist.

It is important to recognize that nothing in the Constitution prohibits a legislature from extending the presumption of innocence into pretrial decisions. Nothing prevents the release of all persons pending trial. No jurisdiction currently operates this way. Rather, a balance is struck between the suspect's desire to be free and the community's insistence that, the criminal process proceed quickly, without endangering innocent persons.

UNITED STATES v. SALERNO

Supreme Court of the United States, 1987.
481 U.S. 739

CHIEF JUSTICE REHNQUIST delivered the opinion of the Court.

The Bail Reform Act of 1984 allows a federal court to detain an arrestee

41. See the analysis of the several studies that have been done in W. Thomas, Bail Reform in America 234 (1976). Compare also the views of Professor Dershowitz, Assistant Attorney General Santorelli, and Senators Ervin and Hruska, before the Subcomm. on Const. Rights of the Senate Comm. on the Judiciary, 91st Cong., 1st Sess. (1969), reprinted in Preventive Detention 305–17 (S. Cullen ed. 1971).

pending trial if the government demonstrates by clear and convincing evidence after an adversary hearing that no release conditions "will reasonably assure ... the safety of any person and the community." The United States Court of Appeals for the Second Circuit struck down this provision of the Act as facially unconstitutional, because, in that court's words, this type of pretrial detention violates "substantive due process." We granted certiorari because of a conflict among the Courts of Appeals regarding the validity of the Act. We hold that, as against the facial attack mounted by these respondents, the Act fully comports with constitutional requirements. We therefore reverse.

I

Responding to "the alarming problem of crimes committed by persons on release," Congress formulated the Bail Reform Act of 1984, 18 U.S.C. § 3141 et seq. (1982 ed., Supp. III), as the solution to a bail crisis in the federal courts. * * *

Respondents Anthony Salerno and Vincent Cafaro were arrested on March 21, 1986, after being charged in a 29-count indictment alleging various Racketeer Influenced and Corrupt Organizations Act (RICO) violations, mail and wire fraud offenses, extortion, and various criminal gambling violations. The RICO counts alleged 35 acts of racketeering activity, including fraud, extortion, gambling, and conspiracy to commit murder. At respondents' arraignment, the Government moved to have Salerno and Cafaro detained pursuant to § 3142(e), on the ground that no condition of release would assure the safety of the community or any person. The District Court held a hearing at which the Government made a detailed proffer of evidence. The Government's case showed that Salerno was the "boss" of the Genovese Crime Family of La Cosa Nostra and that Cafaro was a "captain" in the Genovese Family. According to the Government's proffer, based in large part on conversations intercepted by a court-ordered wiretap, the two respondents had participated in wide-ranging conspiracies to aid their illegitimate enterprises through violent means. The Government also offered the testimony of two of its trial witnesses, who would assert that Salerno personally participated in two murder conspiracies. Salerno opposed the motion for detention, challenging the credibility of the Government's witnesses. He offered the testimony of several character witnesses as well as a letter from his doctor stating that he was suffering from a serious medical condition. Cafaro presented no evidence at the hearing, but instead characterized the wiretap conversations as merely "tough talk."

The District Court granted the Government's detention motion, concluding that the Government had established by clear and convincing evidence that no condition or combination of conditions of release would ensure the safety of the community or any person * * *.

Respondents appealed, contending that to the extent that the Bail Reform Act permits pretrial detention on the ground that the arrestee is likely to commit future crimes, it is unconstitutional on its face. Over a dissent, the United States Court of Appeals for the Second Circuit agreed. Although the court agreed that pretrial detention could be imposed if the defendants were likely to intimidate witnesses or otherwise jeopardize the trial process, it found "§ 3142(e)'s authorization of pretrial detention [on the ground of future dangerousness] repugnant to the concept of substantive due process, which we believe prohibits the total deprivation of liberty simply as a means of preventing future crimes." * * *

It reasoned that our criminal law system holds persons accountable for past actions, not anticipated future actions. Although a court could detain an arrestee who threatened to flee before trial, such detention would be permissible because it would serve the basic objective of a criminal system—bringing the accused to trial. * * * The Court of Appeals also found our decision in Schall v. Martin, 467 U.S. 253 (1984), upholding postarrest pretrial detention of juveniles, inapposite because juveniles have a lesser interest in liberty than do adults. * * *

II

A facial challenge to a legislative Act is, of course, the most difficult challenge to mount successfully, since the challenger must establish that no set of circumstances exists under which the Act would be valid. The fact that the Bail Reform Act might operate unconstitutionally under some conceivable set of circumstances is insufficient to render it wholly invalid, since we have not recognized an "overbreadth" doctrine outside the limited context of the First Amendment. We think respondents have failed to shoulder their heavy burden to demonstrate that the Act is "facially" unconstitutional.[a]

* * *

A

* * *

Respondents first argue that the Act violates substantive due process because the pretrial detention it authorizes constitutes impermissible punishment before trial. The Government, however, has never argued that pretrial detention could be upheld if it were "punishment." The Court of Appeals assumed that pretrial detention under the Bail Reform Act is regulatory, not penal, and we agree that it is.

As an initial matter, the mere fact that a person is detained does not inexorably lead to the conclusion that the government has imposed punishment. To determine whether a restriction on liberty constitutes impermissible punishment or permissible regulation, we first look to legislative intent. Unless Congress expressly intended to impose punitive restrictions, the punitive/regulatory distinction turns on " 'whether an alternative purpose to which [the restriction] may rationally be connected is assignable for it, and whether it appears excessive in relation to the alternative purpose assigned [to it].' "

We conclude that the detention imposed by the Act falls on the regulatory side of the dichotomy. The legislative history of the Bail Reform Act clearly indicates that Congress did not formulate the pretrial detention provisions as punishment for dangerous individuals. Congress instead perceived pretrial detention as a potential solution to a pressing societal problem. There is no doubt that preventing danger to the community is a legitimate regulatory goal.

Nor are the incidents of pretrial detention excessive in relation to the regulatory goal Congress sought to achieve. The Bail Reform Act carefully limits the circumstances under which detention may be sought to the most serious of crimes. See 18 U.S.C. § 3142(f) (detention hearings available if case involves crimes of violence, offenses for which the sentence is life imprisonment or death, serious drug offenses, or certain repeat offenders). The arrestee is entitled to a prompt detention hearing, and the maximum length of pretrial detention is limited by the stringent time

a. We intimate no view on the validity of any aspects of the Act that are not relevant to respondents' case. Nor have respondents claimed that the Act is unconstitutional because of the way it was applied to the particular facts of their case.

limitations of the Speedy Trial Act.[b] See 18 U.S.C. § 3161 et seq. (1982 ed. and Supp. III). Moreover, as in Schall v. Martin, the conditions of confinement envisioned by the Act "appear to reflect the regulatory purposes relied upon by the government." As in *Schall* the statute at issue here requires that detainees be housed in a "facility separate, to the extent practicable, from persons awaiting or serving sentences or being held in custody pending appeal." 18 U.S.C. § 3142(i)(2). We conclude, therefore, that the pretrial detention contemplated by the Bail Reform Act is regulatory in nature, and does not constitute punishment before trial in violation of the Due Process Clause.

The Court of Appeals nevertheless concluded that "the Due Process Clause prohibits pretrial detention on the ground of danger to the community as a regulatory measure, without regard to the duration of the detention." Respondents characterize the Due Process Clause as erecting an impenetrable "wall" in this area that "no governmental interest—rational, important, compelling or otherwise—may surmount."

We do not think the Clause lays down any such categorical imperative. We have repeatedly held that the government's regulatory interest in community safety can, in appropriate circumstances, outweigh an individual's liberty interest. For example, in times of war or insurrection, when society's interest is at its peak, the government may detain individuals whom the government believes to be dangerous. Even outside the exigencies of war, we have found that sufficiently compelling governmental interests can justify detention of dangerous persons. Thus, we have found no absolute constitutional barrier to detention of potentially dangerous resident aliens pending deportation proceedings. We have also held that the government may detain mentally unstable individuals who present a danger to the public, and dangerous defendants who become incompetent to stand trial. We have approved of post-arrest regulatory detention of juveniles when they present a continuing danger to the community. Even competent adults may face substantial liberty restrictions as a result of the operation of our criminal justice system. If the police suspect an individual of a crime, they may arrest and hold him until a neutral magistrate determines whether probable cause exists. Finally, respondents concede and the Court of Appeals noted that an arrestee may be incarcerated until trial if he presents a risk of flight, or a danger to witnesses.

Respondents characterize all of these cases as exceptions to the "general rule" of substantive due process that the government may not detain a person prior to a judgment of guilt in a criminal trial. Such a "general rule" may freely be conceded, but we think that these cases show a sufficient number of exceptions to the rule that the congressional action challenged here can hardly be characterized as totally novel. Given the well-established authority of the government, in special circumstances, to restrain individuals' liberty prior to or even without criminal trial and conviction, we think that the present statute providing for pretrial detention on the basis of dangerousness must be evaluated in precisely the same manner that we evaluated the laws in the cases discussed above.

The government's interest in preventing crime by arrestees is both legitimate and compelling. In *Schall,* supra, we recognized the strength of the State's interest in preventing juvenile crime.

b. We intimate no view as to the point at which detention in a particular case might become excessively prolonged, and therefore punitive, in relation to Congress' regulatory goal.

This general concern with crime prevention is no less compelling when the suspects are adults. Indeed, "[t]he harm suffered by the victim of a crime is not dependent upon the age of the perpetrator." The Bail Reform Act of 1984 responds to an even more particularized governmental interest than the interest we sustained in *Schall.* The statute we upheld in *Schall* permitted pretrial detention of any juvenile arrested on any charge after a showing that the individual might commit some undefined further crimes. The Bail Reform Act, in contrast, narrowly focuses on a particularly acute problem in which the government interests are overwhelming. The Act operates only on individuals who have been arrested for a specific category of extremely serious offenses. 18 U.S.C. § 3142(f). Congress specifically found that these individuals are far more likely to be responsible for dangerous acts in the community after arrest. Nor is the Act by any means a scattershot attempt to incapacitate those who are merely suspected of these serious crimes. The government must first of all demonstrate probable cause to believe that the charged crime has been committed by the arrestee, but that is not enough. In a full-blown adversary hearing, the government must convince a neutral decisionmaker by clear and convincing evidence that no conditions of release can reasonably assure the safety of the community or any person. 18 U.S.C.A. § 3142(f). While the government's general interest in preventing crime is compelling, even this interest is heightened when the government musters convincing proof that the arrestee, already indicted or held to answer for a serious crime, presents a demonstrable danger to the community. Under these narrow circumstances, society's interest in crime prevention is at its greatest.

On the other side of the scale, of course, is the individual's strong interest in liberty. We do not minimize the importance and fundamental nature of this right. But, as our cases hold, this right may, in circumstances where the government's interest is sufficiently weighty, be subordinated to the greater needs of society. * * *. When the government proves by clear and convincing evidence that an arrestee presents an identified and articulable threat to an individual or the community, we believe that, consistent with the Due Process Clause, a court may disable the arrestee from executing that threat. Under these circumstances, we cannot categorically state that pretrial detention "offends some principle of justice so rooted in the traditions and conscience of our people as to be ranked as fundamental."

Finally, we may dispose briefly of respondents' facial challenge to the procedures of the Bail Reform Act. To sustain them against such a challenge, we need only find them "adequate to authorize the pretrial detention of at least some [persons] charged with crimes," whether or not they might be insufficient in some particular circumstances. We think they pass that test. As we stated in *Schall,* "there is nothing inherently unattainable about a prediction of future criminal conduct."

Under the Bail Reform Act, the procedures by which a judicial officer evaluates the likelihood of future dangerousness are specifically designed to further the accuracy of that determination. Detainees have a right to counsel at the detention hearing. 18 U.S.C. § 3142(f). They may testify in their own behalf, present information by proffer or otherwise, and cross-examine witnesses who appear at the hearing. Ibid. The judicial officer charged with the responsibility of determining the appropriateness of detention is guided by statutorily enumerated factors, which include the nature and the circumstances of the charges, the weight of the evidence, the history and characteristics of the putative offender, and the danger to the community. § 3142(g). The government must prove its case by clear and convincing evidence. § 3142(f). Finally, the judicial officer must include written findings of fact and a written statement of reasons for a decision to detain. § 3142(i). The Act's review provisions, § 3145(c), provide for immediate appellate review of the detention decision.

We think these extensive safeguards suffice to repel a facial challenge. * * *

B

Respondents also contend that the Bail Reform Act violates the Excessive Bail Clause of the Eighth Amendment. The Court of Appeals did not address this issue because it found that the Act violates the Due Process Clause. We think that the Act survives a challenge founded upon the Eighth Amendment.

The Eighth Amendment addresses pretrial release by providing merely that "Excessive bail shall not be required." This Clause, of course, says nothing about whether bail shall be available at all. Respondents nevertheless contend that this Clause grants them a right to bail calculated solely upon considerations of flight. They rely on Stack v. Boyle, 342 U.S. 1, 5 (1951), in which the Court stated that "Bail set at a figure higher than an amount reasonably calculated [to ensure the defendant's presence at trial] is 'excessive' under the Eighth Amendment." In respondents' view, since the Bail Reform Act allows a court essentially to set bail at an infinite amount for reasons not related to the risk of flight, it violates the Excessive Bail Clause. Respondents concede that the right to bail they have discovered in the Eighth Amendment is not absolute. A court may, for example, refuse bail in capital cases. And, as the Court of Appeals noted and respondents admit, a court may refuse bail when the defendant presents a threat to the judicial process by intimidating witnesses. Respondents characterize these exceptions as consistent with what they claim to be the sole purpose of bail—to ensure integrity of the judicial process.

While we agree that a primary function of bail is to safeguard the courts' role in adjudicating the guilt or innocence of defendants, we reject the proposition that the Eighth Amendment categorically prohibits the government from pursuing other admittedly compelling interests through regulation of pretrial release. The above-quoted *dicta* in Stack v. Boyle is far too slender a reed on which to rest this argument. The Court in *Stack* had no occasion to consider whether the Excessive Bail Clause requires courts to admit all defendants to bail, because the statute before the Court in that case in fact allowed the defendants to be bailed. Thus, the Court had to determine only whether bail, admittedly available in that case, was excessive if set at a sum greater than that necessary to ensure the arrestees' presence at trial.

The holding of *Stack* is illuminated by the Court's holding just four months later in Carlson v. Landon, 342 U.S. 524 (1952). In that case, remarkably similar to the present action, the detainees had been arrested and held without bail pending a determination of deportability. The Attorney General refused to release the individuals, "on the ground that there was reasonable cause to believe that [their] release would be prejudicial to the public interest and *would endanger the welfare and safety of the United States*." The detainees brought the same challenge that respondents bring to us today: The Eighth Amendment required them to be admitted to bail. The Court squarely rejected this proposition * * *.

Carlson v. Landon was a civil case, and we need not decide today whether the Excessive Bail Clause speaks at all to Congress' power to define the classes of criminal arrestees who shall be admitted to bail. For even if we were to conclude that the Eighth Amendment imposes some substantive limitations on the National Legislature's powers in this area, we would still hold that the Bail Reform Act is valid. Nothing in the text of the Bail Clause limits permissible government considerations solely to questions of flight. The only arguable substantive limitation of the Bail Clause is that the government's proposed conditions of release or detention not be "excessive" in light of the perceived evil. Of course, to determine whether the government's response is excessive, we must compare that response against the interest the government seeks to protect by means of that response. Thus, when the government has admitted that its only interest is in preventing flight, bail must be set by a court at a sum designed to ensure that goal, and no more. We believe that when Congress has mandated detention on the basis of a compelling interest other than prevention of flight, as it has here, the Eighth Amendment does not require release on bail.

III

* * *

Reversed.

JUSTICE MARSHALL with whom JUSTICE BRENNAN joins, dissenting.

* * *

II

The majority approaches respondents' challenge to the Act by dividing the discussion into two sections, one concerned with the substantive guarantees implicit in the Due Process Clause, and the other concerned with the protection afforded by the Excessive Bail Clause of the Eighth Amendment. This is a sterile formalism, which divides a unitary argument into two independent parts and then professes to demonstrate that the parts are individually inadequate.

On the due process side of this false dichotomy appears an argument concerning the distinction between regulatory and punitive legislation. The majority concludes that the Act is a regulatory rather than a punitive measure. The ease with which the conclusion is reached suggests the worthlessness of the achievement. * * *

* * * Let us apply the majority's reasoning to a similar, hypothetical case. After investigation, Congress determines (not unrealistically) that a large proportion of violent crime is perpetrated by persons who are unemployed. It also determines, equally reasonably, that much violent crime is committed at night. From amongst the panoply of "potential solutions," Congress chooses a statute which permits, after judicial proceedings, the imposition of a dusk-to-dawn curfew on anyone who is unemployed. Since this is not a measure enacted for the purpose of punishing the unemployed, and since the majority finds that preventing danger to the community is a legitimate regulatory goal, the curfew statute would, according to the majority's analysis, be a mere "regulatory" detention statute, entirely compatible with the substantive components of the Due Process Clause.

The absurdity of this conclusion arises, of course, from the majority's cramped concept of substantive due process. The majority proceeds as though the only substantive right protected by the Due Process Clause is a right to be free from punishment before conviction. The majority's technique for infringing this right is simple: merely redefine any measure which is claimed to be punishment as "regulation," and, magically, the Constitution no longer prohibits its imposition. Because * * * the Due Process Clause protects other substantive rights which are infringed by this legislation, the majority's argument is merely an exercise in obfuscation.

The logic of the majority's Eighth Amendment analysis is equally unsatisfactory. The Eighth Amendment, as the majority notes, states that "[e]xcessive bail shall not be required." The majority then declares, as if it were undeniable, that: "[t]his Clause, of course, says nothing about whether bail shall be available at all." If excessive bail is imposed the defendant stays in jail. The same result is achieved if bail is denied altogether. Whether the magistrate sets bail at $1 billion or refuses to set bail at all, the consequences are indistinguishable. It would be mere sophistry to suggest that the Eighth Amendment protects against the former decision, and not the latter. Indeed, such a result would lead to the conclusion that there was no need for Congress to pass a preventive detention measure of any kind; every federal magistrate and district judge could simply refuse, despite the absence of any evidence of risk of flight or danger to the community, to set bail. This would be entirely constitutional, since, according to the majority, the Eighth Amendment "says nothing about whether bail shall be available at all."

But perhaps, the majority says, this manifest absurdity can be avoided. Perhaps the Bail Clause is addressed only to the judiciary. "[W]e need not decide today," the majority says, "whether the Excessive Bail Clause speaks at all to Congress' power to define the classes of criminal arrestees who shall be admitted to bail." The majority is correct that this question need not be decided today; it was decided long ago. Federal and state statutes which purport to accomplish what the Eighth Amendment forbids, such as imposing cruel and unusual punishments, may not stand. See, e.g., Trop v. Dulles, 356 U.S. 86 (1958); Furman v. Georgia, 408 U.S. 238 (1972). The text of the Amendment, which provides simply that "[e]xcessive bail shall not be required, nor excessive fines imposed, nor cruel and unusual punishments inflicted," provides absolutely no support for the majority's speculation that both courts and Congress are forbidden to inflict cruel and unusual punishments, while only the courts are forbidden to require excessive bail.[c]

The majority's attempts to deny the relevance of the Bail Clause to this case are unavailing, but the majority is nonetheless correct that the prohibition of excessive bail means that in order "to determine whether the government's response is excessive, we must compare that response against the interest the government seeks to protect by means of that response." The majority concedes, as it must, that "when the government has admitted that its only interest is in preventing flight, bail must be set by a court at a sum designed to ensure that goal, and no more." But, the majority says, "when Congress had mandated detention on the basis of a

c. The majority refers to the statement in Carlson v. Landon, 342 U.S. 524, 545 (1952) that the Bail Clause was adopted by Congress from the English Bill of Rights Act of 1689, 1 Wm. & Mary, Sess. 2, ch. II, § I(10), and that "[i]n England that clause has never been thought to accord a right to bail in all cases, but merely to provide that bail shall not be excessive in those cases where it is proper to grant bail." A sufficient answer to this meagre argument was made at the time by Justice Black: "The Eighth Amendment is in the American Bill of Rights of 1789, not the English Bill of Rights of 1689." Carlson v. Landon, supra, at 557 (dissenting opinion). Our Bill or Rights is contained in a written Constitution one of whose purposes is to protect the rights of the people against infringement by the the Legislature, and its provisions, whatever their origins, are interpreted in relation to those purposes.

compelling interest other than prevention of flight, as it has here, the Eighth Amendment does not require release on bail." This conclusion follows only if the "compelling" interest upon which Congress acted is an interest which the Constitution permits Congress to further through the denial of bail. The majority does not ask, as a result of its disingenuous division of the analysis, if there are any substantive limits contained in both the Eighth Amendment and the Due Process Clause which render this system of preventive detention unconstitutional. The majority does not ask because the answer is apparent and, to the majority, inconvenient.

III

* * *

The statute now before us declares that persons who have been indicted may be detained if a judicial officer finds clear and convincing evidence that they pose a danger to individuals or to the community. The statute does not authorize the government to imprison anyone it has evidence is dangerous; indictment is necessary. But let us suppose that a defendant is indicted and the government shows by clear and convincing evidence that he is dangerous and should be detained pending a trial, at which trial the defendant is acquitted. May the government continue to hold the defendant in detention based upon its showing that he is dangerous? The answer cannot be yes, for that would allow the government to imprison someone for uncommitted crimes based upon "proof" not beyond a reasonable doubt. The result must therefore be that once the indictment has failed, detention cannot continue. But our fundamental principles of justice declare that the defendant is as innocent on the day before his trial as he is on the morning after his acquittal. Under this statute an untried indictment somehow acts to permit a detention, based on other charges, which after an acquittal would be unconstitutional.

* * *

* * * The detention purportedly authorized by this statute bears no relation to the government's power to try charges supported by a finding of probable cause, and thus the interests it serves are outside the scope of interests which may be considered in weighing the excessiveness of bail under the Eighth Amendment.

* * *

IV

There is a connection between the peculiar facts of this case and the evident constitutional defects in the statute which the Court upholds today. Respondent Cafaro was originally incarcerated for an indeterminate period at the request of the Government, which believed (or professed to believe) that his release imminently threatened the safety of the community. That threat apparently vanished, from the Government's point of view, when Cafaro agreed to act as a covert agent of the Government. There could be no more eloquent demonstration of the coercive power of authority to imprison upon prediction, or of the dangers which the almost inevitable abuses pose to the cherished liberties of a free society.

* * *

Throughout the world today there are men, women and children interned indefinitely, awaiting trials which may never come or which may be a mockery of the word, because their governments believe them to be "dangerous." Our Constitution, whose construction began two centuries ago, can shelter us forever from the evils of such unchecked power. Over two hundred years it has slowly, through our efforts, grown more durable, more expansive, and more just. But it cannot protect us if we lack the courage, and the self-restraint, to protect ourselves. Today a majority of the Court applies itself to an ominous exercise in demolition. Theirs is truly a decision which will go forth without authority, and come back without respect.

I dissent.

JUSTICE STEVENS, dissenting.

There may be times when the government's interest in protecting the safety of the community will justify the brief detention of a person who has not committed any crime. To use Judge Feinberg's example, it is indeed difficult to accept the proposition that the government is without power to detain a person when it is a virtual certainty that he or she would otherwise kill a group of innocent people in the immediate future. United States v. Salerno, 794 F.2d 64, 77 (CA2 1986) (dissenting opinion). Similarly, I am unwilling to decide today that the police may never impose a limited curfew during a time of crisis. These questions are obviously not presented in this case, but they lurk in the background and preclude me from answering the question that is presented in as broad a manner as Justice Marshall has. Nonetheless, I firmly agree with Justice Marshall that the provision of the Bail Reform Act allowing pretrial detention on the basis of future dangerousness is unconstitutional. Whatever the answers are to the questions I have mentioned, it is clear to me that a pending indictment may not be given any weight in evaluating an individual's risk to the community or the need for immediate detention.

If the evidence of imminent danger is strong enough to warrant emergency detention, it should support that preventive measure regardless of whether the person has been charged, convicted, or acquitted of some other offense. * * *

* * *

Note

Justice Marshall concludes that the majority opinion divides a "unitary argument" into two parts, one focusing on due process and the other on the Eighth Amendment, and that the division weakens both parts of the argument. Imagine that the arguments were combined. Would Chief Justice Rehnquist's opinion change? Does the Chief Justice fail to make clear the majority's conclusion that consideration of an accused's potential danger to the community is not necessarily impermissible in pretrial release decisionmaking?

Does Justice Marshall adequately explain why an accused may be detained on the ground that a court concludes there is a risk of flight? When a grand jury determines that there is probable cause to charge an individual with a crime, the grand jury has made a determination that there is sufficient likelihood that the individual is guilty to warrant a trial. This likelihood is sufficient to warrant arrest, booking and detention pending a pretrial release decision—all of this notwithstanding the fact that the individual is presumed to be innocent. The grand jury generally makes no determination concerning likelihood of flight. Yet, the dissenters appear to accept the proposition that it is consistent with the presumption of innocence to detain a person when the court determines that flight is likely. Is this determination a prediction of future behavior? What standards govern the prediction?

Justice Stevens leaves open the possibility that the government may have a valid interest in brief detention of a person who has not committed a crime or in a curfew to protect the community, but he agrees with Justice Marshall that "allowing pretrial detention on the basis of future dangerousness is unconstitutional." Does this mean that the dissenters would never permit an accused individual to be detained pending trial as long as he does not present a risk of flight? Consider the case of an accused as to whom the government has overwhelming evidence of several completed murders. Must a serial killer be released pending trial as long as flight is not expected?

The Chief Justice focuses on the findings that Congress made concerning the need for pretrial detention of dangerous individuals, the congressional specification of categories of accused persons who may be detained pending trial, and the procedural rights guaranteed to any person whom the government seeks to detain. Would the decision of the Court have been different if Congress had simply provided that a federal court could consider dangerousness along with likelihood of flight when making pretrial release decisions, and had not required clear and convincing evidence of dangerousness? The answer to this question might well be important in future cases. Approximately half of the states permitted dangerousness to be considered prior to *Salerno,* but many of these states did not limit consideration of dangerousness to specific categories of accused persons and did not provide procedural protections like those found in the federal statute. Thus, *Salerno* might not signify that all forms of preventive detention are necessarily valid.

The Court left open in *Salerno* the possibility that the federal statute might be unconstitutionally applied. Before the court of appeals struck down the federal statute in *Salerno,* a divided panel of the court had found in United States v. Melendez-Carrion, 790 F.2d 984 (2d Cir.1986), that the bail law was unconstitutionally applied. After *Salerno,* another panel of the court found that continued detention of a defendant for 12 months was unconstitutional. United States v. Frisone, 795 F.2d 1 (2d Cir.1986). However, in United States v. Infelise, 934 F.2d 103 (7th Cir.1991), the court held that continued detention for two years did not violate due process. The court noted that the Government cannot delay a trial in order to use preventive detention as a surrogate for punishment. But the court found the delay to be due to the complexity of the case, the presence of multiple defendants, and pre-trial motions by the defendants.

Is the statute unconstitutionally applied when a court distinguishes between "international drug traffickers" and "local drug dealers" in assessing whether to release a defendant? In United States v. Giampa, 755 F.Supp. 665 (W.D.Pa.1990), the court held that an indictment charging a defendant with violating sections of the Controlled Substance Act raises a presumption under the Bail Reform Act that no conditions of release would assure both defendant's presence at trial and the safety of the community. It noted that a defendant could rebut that presumption by presenting some credible evidence that he would appear at trial and not pose a threat. Upon presentation of such evidence, the burden of persuasion would then fall upon the government to prove by clear and convincing evidence that the defendant should be detained pending trial. In *Giampa,* the court held that the defendant rebutted the statutory presumption by showing his long residence in the area, his close ties to his family, steady employment history, lack of resources or contacts which would enable him to flee the country with ease, and the fact that he had no record and did not appear to live the life of a serious drug dealer. In releasing Giampa, the court focused on the fact that Giampa was differently situated from the "international narcotics trafficker" with whom Congress was most concerned when it enacted the Bail Reform Act.

In assessing dangerousness and the assurance of safety of the community, can membership in an Organized Crime Family be considered? If so, can any release conditions suffice to protect against the risk of flight and the risk to public safety? Consider the facts of United States v. Tortora, 922 F.2d 880 (1st Cir.1990):

> An alleged soldier in the Patriarca Family of the Mafia was indicted for violation of the RICO statute. His three predicate crimes in furtherance of the RICO enterprise were: extortion; violation of the Travel Act; and conspiracy to violate the Travel Act. Upon the grant of the government's motion for pretrial detention, the defendant proposed certain release conditions to assure the safety of the community. These conditions mandated, for example, that the defendant not violate the law, appear at scheduled proceedings, eschew possession of weapons and substance abuse, restrict his travel, etc. In granting the release order, the [district] court required the defendant to (1) remain at home twenty-four hours a day, except for a reasonable number of visits to doctors and lawyers, wearing an electronic bracelet; (2) refrain from communicating with any person not approved by the prosecutor and defense counsel; (3) meet with codefendants only in the presence of counsel for the purpose of preparing a defense; (4) allow only one telephone line into his residence, hooking it up to a pen register; and (5) post the residence—a house owned by his brother—as security.

The court of appeals vacated the order releasing Tortora. It agreed with the district court that Tortora was properly classified as dangerous. The court reasoned that membership in an Organized Crime Organization was clearly relevant to dangerousness, rejecting Tortora's argument that such "associational ties" could not be considered. It concluded that so long as the defendant was judged as an individual, his devotion to the Mafia was important evidence of his dangerous character, especially where Tortora, at a ritualistic Mafia ceremony, "threatened to kill his brother if the latter posed a danger to any member of the organization." The court also rejected Tortora's argument that devotion to his family precluded a finding of dangerousness. It responded that in light of Tortora's oath of fealty to the Mafia, "there is every reason to believe that he will prefer Family over family."

The court of appeals held that the release conditions were not adequate to assure the community's safety in view of the fact that virtually all of them hinged upon the defendant's good faith compliance. As such they could be too easily manipulated or circumvented. For instance, electronic monitoring "cannot be expected to prevent a defendant from committing crimes or deter him from participating in felonious activity within the monitoring radius"; and pen registers could be evaded by "the surreptitious introduction into his home of a cellular telephone." The court concluded that the "honor-dependent" nature of the restrictions took on great significance where "little about the defendant or his history suggests that good faith will be forthcoming." The court rejected the argument that the conditions of release could be amended to eliminate the risk of danger to the community:

> Given the breadth of human imagination, it will always be possible to envision some set of release conditions which might reasonably assure the safety of the community. For instance, agents could be posted by the government to watch Tortora at all times to ensure that he remains compliant; the guards could search all visitors, dog Tortora's footsteps en route to all appointments, and otherwise act as private jailers. But the Bail Reform Act, as we read it, does not require release of a dangerous defendant if the only combination of conditions that would reasonably assure societal safety consists of heroic

measures beyond those which can fairly be said to have been within Congress' contemplation.

Tortora further argued that the release conditions were sufficient because they were at least as restrictive as those imposed on another member of the Patriarca Family, who outranked Tortora. According to the court, this disparate treatment did not rise to the level of an unconstitutional application of the statute. The court reasoned that after *Salerno,* due process challenges to pretrial detention "must be resolved on a case-by-case basis," and that incarceration of Tortora was not unfair under the circumstances in light of his proven dangerousness.

Finally, Tortora argued that the release conditions were sufficient because, if kept in prison, he would have at least as much ability to commit crimes as he would have if released. The court viewed this argument as "perverse" and stated:

> The Bail Reform Act does not ordain that dangerousness upon release is to be measured relative to dangerousness if incarcerated, and for good reason: the ability of an incarcerated person to commit crimes while in jail is a problem for the Executive Branch to solve. The idea that someone who otherwise ought not to be released should be let loose by the courts because his jailers may not prevent him from committing crimes in prison comprises a classic non sequitur * * *.

Does *Salerno* stand for the proposition that there are certain defendants who cannot be freed no matter what the release conditions? Should the government in *Tortora* have been constitutionally required to implement more stringent release conditions? See United States v. Infelise, 934 F.2d 103 (7th Cir.1991) (statutory requirement of investigating and applying alternatives less intrusive than incarceration is applicable regardless of constitutional requirements). Do you agree with the court that the conditions imposed could have been easily evaded?

In Hilton v. Braunskill, 481 U.S. 770 (1987), a case decided the same day as *Salerno,* the Court held that when a federal court grants habeas corpus relief and orders the release of a state prisoner, the court may consider dangerousness in deciding whether a prisoner should be freed pursuant to Fed.R.Crim.P. 23 pending review of its order. Although the rule does not provide any standard by which dangerousness is to be assessed and does not guarantee any particular procedural rights, the Court decided that the factors governing the issuance of stays of district court orders in civil cases should govern the determination whether a prisoner should be free while the state appeals the granting of habeas corpus relief. It observed "that a successful habeas petitioner is in a considerably less favorable position than a pre-trial arrestee, such as the respondent in *Salerno,*" because "a state habeas petitioner has been adjudged guilty beyond a reasonable doubt by a judge or jury, and this adjudication of guilt has been upheld by the appellate courts of the state." *Hilton* is discussed infra in connection with bail following conviction.

VI. SPECIAL PROBLEMS IN THE OPERATION OF BAIL

A. CAPITAL OFFENSES

Historically, statutes categorically recognizing a right to bail have excluded capital crimes "where the proof is evident, or the presumption great" from those offenses for which bail is required. The granting or denial of bail is traditionally a matter of judicial discretion where a capital offense is charged. Is there any justification for distinguishing between capital and non-capital offenses? Wice's study, which has been quoted previously, indicates that there is little correlation between the seriousness of the crime and the actual forfeiture rate. If the only legitimate purpose of bail is to assure appearance, a distinction based on gravity of the offense, rather than the integrity of the defendant, might seem irrelevant. But the urge to flee is likely to be greatest when the accused faces the prospect of capital punishment.

If a distinction in bail treatment is preserved for capital offenses, what considerations are relevant to judicial discretion? Most statutes withhold pre-trial release in capital cases only when the "proof is evident" or the "presumption is great." The states differ over the allocation of the burden of proof on these issues. State v. Konigsberg, 33 N.J. 367, 164 A.2d 740 (1960), discusses the various approaches that are used.[42]

Although historically the courts have explicitly upheld the use of judicial discretion in capital cases, and legislatures have differentiated capital from non-capital cases in the pre-trial release context, the trend is to treat all cases similarly.[43]

B. JUVENILE OFFENDERS

In the legislative effort to afford complete treatment for juvenile offenders, many states do not provide a bail requirement for juveniles charged with offenses which would be crimes if committed by an adult.[44] These courts seem to suggest that if the juvenile offender wants to be treated like an adult he has to take the bad with the good—he can only have bail if his offense is adjudicated as a crime. Other courts have noted the possibility of release into parental custody, and have held that the existence of such an option precludes bail, even in a case when the possibility is foreclosed by a judicial determination that release into parental custody would be inappropriate. Is the total denial of bail consistent with the Supreme Court's analysis in *Schall*? In line with the general predilection against awarding bail after conviction (discussed infra), most courts disallow bail for juveniles after adjudication of their delin-

42. Although the majority of courts hold that the state bears the burden of proving that bail should be denied in capital cases, some courts have held otherwise. In State v. Green, 275 So.2d 184 (La.1973), for example, the Court rebuffed a constitutional challenge to a Louisiana statute placing the burden of proof on the defendant, pointing out that the presumption of innocence does not protect against arrest. "If it were absolute and operative at every stage of a prosecution, the defendant could never be jailed with conviction * * *. There is little relationship between the right to bail and the presumption of innocence."

43. Under the Bail Reform Act of 1984, 18 U.S.C. §§ 3141–3150, a judicial officer may consider dangerousness to the community with respect to crimes other than capital offenses. Although the Act no longer treats capital offenses differently from all other crimes, it recognizes the importance of a prior conviction for a crime punishable by death or life imprisonment that occurred while the accused was released pending trial. Unless more than five years has elapsed between the prior conviction or release from confinement for the conviction, the Act creates a rebuttable presumption against pretrial release pending trial on the current charge.

Denial of bail was upheld in United States v. Kostadinov, 721 F.2d 411 (2d Cir.1983), as the court of appeals held that a prosecution for espionage and conspiracy to commit espionage is a capital case irrespective of whether the government is seeking the death penalty that is facially available under the statute.

44. The same rationale has prevented bail for a person quarantined because of communicable disease, insanity, or narcotics addiction. Since this person is being held for purposes of treatment, bail has been held not to be required. At least one court has held, however, that if a person is charged with a criminal offense, his bail application cannot be rejected solely on the suspicion that he has a social disease. See generally Annots., 8 Am.Jur.2d § 24; 11 ALR 2d 1385.

quency, pending appeal. See, e.g., City of Warwick v. Robalewski, 120 R.I. 119, 385 A.2d 669 (1978). The courts adopt the view that the juvenile is a "ward" of the state, subject to "treatment," regardless of the existence or adequacy of such treatment.

C. BAIL AFTER THE TRIAL BEGINS AND ENDS

As early as 1894, the Supreme Court held that there is no constitutional right to bail pending appeal from a conviction. McKane v. Durston, 153 U.S. 684 (1894). Even some courts that recognize a constitutional right to pretrial release hold that it is lost after conviction; "since there is no constitutional right to appeal, there is no constitutional right to be free pending appeal." United States v. Sine, 461 F.Supp. 565 (D.S.C.1978). The fundamental rights of the convicted defendant differ in other respects, as well. "[T]he presumption of innocence and the right to participate in the preparation of a defense to ensure a fair trial—are obviously not present where the defendant has already been convicted." Gallie v. Wainwright, 362 So.2d 936, 941 (Fla.1978). At the same time, the risk of flight is arguably greater for a defendant who has already been convicted and who may have little hope of a reversal. For these reasons, the standards for postconviction release are stricter, and different criteria may be applied from those used prior to trial. After conviction, the court may consider factors such as the likelihood of reversal, the substantiality of issues on appeal, the length of the sentence imposed, future dangerousness, and the seriousness of the conviction.

The Bail Reform Act of 1966, and state statutes following the federal lead, required the release of convicted defendants pending appeal, unless the appeal was frivolous or a procrastinating maneuver, or the court had reason to believe no condition of release would reasonably assure that the defendant would neither flee nor pose danger to another or to the community. The 1966 Act "reflects a policy strongly favoring post-trial as well as pretrial release, but both its structure and its interpretation underscore the delicacy of the determinations which must precede any rulings on that score." United States v. Stanley, 469 F.2d 576, 580 (D.C.Cir.1972).

The Bail Reform Act of 1984 changed the 1966 statute and provided that a defendant may be released pending appeal only if the court finds "by clear and convincing evidence that the person is not likely to flee or pass a danger to the safety of any other person or the community" and "the appeal is not for purpose of delay and raises a substantial question of law or fact likely to result in reversal or an order for a new trial."

In United States v. Miller, 753 F.2d 19 (3d Cir.1985), the court held that the Act reverses the presumption in favor of release pending appeal to a presumption against release. A district judge must assess whether an appeal raises a substantial question and, if so, whether resolution of the question in the defendant's favor is likely to result in reversal or an order for a new trial on all counts on which imprisonment has been imposed. The court rejected the district court's approach that bail must be denied unless the defendant persuades the district court it is likely to be reversed. See also United States v. Giancola, 754 F.2d 898 (11th Cir.1985); United States v. Powell, 761 F.2d 1227 (8th Cir. 1985) (en banc); United States v. Handy, 761 F.2d 1279 (9th Cir. 1985).

United States v. Affleck, 765 F.2d 944 (10th Cir.1985) (en banc), adopts the *Miller* analysis, but applies a stricter standard of substantiality. A substantial question is more than a nonfrivolous one; it is a question that is close and might well be decided differently. Judge McKay dissented and argued that "the Bail Reform Act violates the eighth amendment by allowing the denial of bail on grounds unrelated to the defendant's likelihood of flight." Other courts have agreed with the majority's refinement of *Miller*.

Hilton v. Braunskill, 481 U.S. 770 (1987), posed an interesting question of federal-state relations. A defendant convicted in New Jersey state courts of sexual assault and unlawful possession of a weapon successfully challenged his convictions in a habeas corpus proceeding in federal district court. The district judge ordered that a writ of habeas corpus would issue unless the state provided a new trial within 30 days. The state asked the district court to stay its order pending an appeal, and the court determined that it could only grant the request if there was a risk that the defendant would not appear for subsequent proceedings. The court of appeals affirmed.

Chief Justice Rehnquist wrote for the Court as it held that the lower courts had erred and that Fed.R.Crim.P. 23 (c) and (d) created only a presumption that a defendant should be released from custody pending an appeal of a decision granting habeas corpus relief. In deciding whether the presumption may be overcome, the Court held that the general approach governing stays in civil cases should be applied. A court should evaluate the likelihood the state will succeed on the merits, whether there is a chance of irreparable injury absent a stay, whether issuance of a stay will substantially injure the other party in the proceeding, and where the public interest lies. The Chief Justice wrote that "if the state establishes that there is a risk that the prisoner will pose a danger to the public if released, the court may take that factor into consideration in determining whether or not to enlarge him." He added that "[t]he state's interest in continuing custody and rehabilitation pending a final determination of the case on appeal is also a factor to be considered; it will be strongest where the remaining portion of the sentence to be served is long, and weakest where there is little of the sentence remaining to be served."

Justice Marshall, joined by Justices Brennan and Blackmun, dissented. He noted that New Jersey law did not permit consideration of dangerousness in pretrial release decisionmaking and argued that the majority could not support its approach by reference to state law. Justice Marshall concluded that state bail law ought to apply to release decisions concerning state prisoners.

Should federal or state law govern release decisions in federal habeas corpus proceedings involving state prisoners? Would Justice Marshall have found state law to be so clearly applicable if the state law absolutely denied release pending appeal in collateral proceedings? Is there any constitutional infirmity in denying release until the completion of collateral proceedings?

Suppose that New Jersey state courts hold that dangerousness may not be considered in making the determination whether to release a prisoner pending an appeal by the state of an order of a state trial court granting habeas relief. Could New Jersey make a bona fide argument that a federal district court should consider dangerousness in deciding whether to release its prisoner pending the state's appeal of an order granting habeas relief on the basis of some "public interest" or the possibility of "irreparable injury?" If New Jersey determines as a matter of state policy that dangerousness should not be considered when a prisoner has established to the satisfaction of a trial court that his conviction was constitutionally invalid, is there any federal interest that would warrant overriding the policy?

Now make a different assumption. Suppose that New Jersey law is unclear as to whether dangerousness may be considered when a state appeals from a trial court's decision to overturn a conviction in a collateral proceeding, and that the only clear New Jersey law is that dangerousness is not to be considered in making release decisions prior to trial and while a defendant appeals a conviction. Does this mean that the state policy necessarily bars consideration of dangerousness in collateral proceedings? Or, might a state conclude, as did Chief Justice Rehnquist, that a prisoner who has been convicted and whose conviction has been affirmed on direct review should be treated differently from a person who has not yet been convicted or whose conviction has not yet been tested on appeal?

VII. THE CONTINUING PROBLEMS AND REFORM EFFORTS

As with many parts of the criminal justice system, the subject of pretrial release is largely ignored while vast resources are invested in litigating questions about searches and seizures and confessions. Yet, justice for many persons accused of crime may depend more on fair treatment before and after trial than on the success of suppression motions. In pretrial release decisions one wonders what standards trial judges employ, and whether there is discrimination against minorities, the poor, the powerless, and social misfits.

Statutes like the Federal Bail Reform Acts endeavor to make judges accountable for their pretrial decisions and to provide an opportunity for review of those decisions. By using statutory criteria to govern decision-making, Congress has attempted to foster evenhanded application of the law.

The attitude among many judges, especially federal judges who have become familiar with the Bail Reform Acts, is to assume (1) that, under the Eighth Amendment, a state might be able to deny bail to all those who are accused of crimes (although no state does); (2) that, if bail can be denied, other forms of pre-trial release could be denied also; but (3) that if a state establishes some form of pre-trial release system, it must be run in a way that assures all suspects of equal treatment under the law.[45]

Pugh v. Rainwater, 572 F.2d 1053 (5th Cir. 1978) (en banc) is a good example. A panel of the court had viewed money bail as inherently discriminatory. But a majority of the en banc court took a different view.

> At the outset we accept the principle that imprisonment solely because of indigent status is invidious discrimination and not constitutionally permissible. The punitive and heavily burdensome nature of pretrial confinement has been

45. In Griffith v. State, 641 P.2d 228 (Alaska 1982), the court held unconstitutional on equal protection grounds a state statute denying post-conviction bail to some, but not all, felony defendants. The court noted that a person convicted of second degree murder could be released on bail, but a person convicted of first degree robbery could not be. The court found that "[t]o the extent that it limits its burdens to a part of the class of violent or dangerous offenders, there is little in Alaska's classification scheme that is reasonably or rationally related to the state's purpose in denying the opportunity for post-conviction bail."

the subject of convincing commentary. We view such deprivation of liberty of one who is accused but not convicted of crime as presenting a question having broader effects and constitutional implications than would appear from a rule stated solely for the protection of indigents.

* * *

By definition an indigent is incapable of meeting any money bail requirement. Similarly disfavored is the non-indigent whose money bail is set in an amount higher than he can provide. Money bail, however, may not be the most burdensome requirement in all cases. A moneyed visitor in a city far removed from his home might find certain of the alternative forms of release infinitely more onerous.

* * *

The ultimate inquiry in each instance is what is necessary to reasonably assure defendant's presence at trial. Systems which incorporate a presumption favoring personal recognizance avoid much of the difficulty inherent in the entire subject area. * * * We have no doubt that in the case of an indigent, whose appearance at trial could reasonably be assured by one of the alternate forms of release, pretrial confinement for inability to post money bail would constitute imposition of an excessive restraint. We do not read the State of Florida's new rule to require such a result.

Now that the Bail Reform Act of 1984 bars federal judicial officers from detaining an accused prior to trial by setting high bail, state and federal courts almost certainly will be asked to review state bail systems that continue to rely upon money bail and to deny release to those unable to satisfy the bail that a court sets. Since the 1984 legislation represents a congressional judgment that high bail is unnecessary to assure an accused's appearance and to protect public safety, courts might well be more sympathetic to an attack on money bail premised on equal protection law.

Due process protections also have been established in the context of another pretrial detention issue: the conditions of confinement. Duran v. Elrod, 542 F.2d 998 (7th Cir. 1976), for example, held that as a matter of due process, pretrial detainees may suffer no more restrictions than are reasonably necessary to ensure their presence at trial. Prohibitions on telephone calls and visitation rights were held to be unreasonable.[46] In Bell v. Wolfish, 439 U.S. 816 (1978), the Supreme Court upheld the conditions of restraint in a modern federal facility in New York. By a 6–3 vote, the court suggested that conditions that were reasonably related to the security of the institution and were not intended as punishment would be sustained. Arbitrary and purposeless rules were deemed to be evidence of punitive intent. Intimate body searches following contact visits were permitted, even without reasonable suspicion, although the vote on this issue was 5–4. The Court did not require the prison officials to justify their actions by a compelling interest showing. But the

46. Most courts have concluded that denial of contact visitation to pretrial detainees is unconstitutional as a matter of law unless such is justified in a particular case by the need to preserve jail security or discipline. See, e.g. Miller v. Carson, 563 F.2d 741 (5th Cir. 1977); Rhem v. Malcolm, 507 F.2d 333 (2d Cir. 1974). But compare Feeley v. Sampson, 570 F.2d 364 (1st Cir. 1978), which, like the other cases, held that restrictions on pretrial detainees must bear a reasonable relationship to the purpose of producing the accused at trial, but specifically stated that pretrial detainees have no constitutional right to contact visitation.

Court did say that its decision was addressed to a modern prison, and the opinion does not necessarily apply to the more common, old, delapidated prisons found in many places. Justices Brennan, Marshall and Stevens dissented and were joined by Justice Powell on the body search issue.

Bell v. Wolfish proved to be determinative in Block v. Rutherford, 468 U.S. 576 (1984). A district judge had found that contact visits for detainees who had been confined for a month or more and were not determined to be drug oriented or escape risks must be permitted and that detainees should be able to observe from a distance while their cells are searched. The court of appeals affirmed. Chief Justice Burger wrote for the Court as it reversed. Since there was no finding or suggestion that the denial of contact visits was intended to be punishment, the Chief Justice cited *Bell* for the proposition that a blanket prohibition on contact visits must be sustained if it is reasonably related to the security of a facility. He found a reasonable relationship in the need to protect against the smuggling of contraband, to protect visitors, and to assure that dangerous detainees do not seek help from low security risk detainees in obtaining contraband or weapons. The Chief Justice observed that the Court did not denigrate the importance of family visits or suggest that they might not help a detainee reintegrate himself into society. Rather, the Court held that contact visits were not constitutionally required.

The Chief Justice found that *Bell* actually decided that searching the cells or rooms of detainees did not violate their constitutional rights. One of the practices challenged in that case involved the search of rooms in the absence of the detainees. Since it had been sustained, the Chief Justice reasoned that *Bell* governed the instant case and that the detainees had no right to witness the searches of their cells.

Justice Blackmun concurred in the judgment, but wrote separately to express disagreement with the extent to which the Court purported to defer to the judgment of prison administrators. He indicated that nonpunitive measures related to legitimate goals should be sustained, but that courts should not neglect their responsibility to assure that the measures are actually nonpunitive and reasonable. Justice Blackmun also indicated his view that *Bell* had not decided the cell search issue. He made an independent analysis of the detainees' contention that procedural due process concepts required that they be given an opportunity to witness the searches. In rejecting this contention, Justice Blackmun focused on the friction between officers and detainees that observation might engender and on the possibility that detainees might learn where to hide contraband as a result of watching searches.

Justice Marshall, joined by Justices Brennan and Stevens, dissented. After reiterating his view that *Bell* was "fundamentally misconceived," he added that, even if he believed that *Bell* was defensible, he could not accept the way it was applied in the instant case.

Attempts to improve upon pre-trial release procedures continue, with emphasis placed on releasing as many suspects as possible. At long last, many advocates of reform are pushing for release of offenders prior to bail hearings; in fact, they are pushing for greater use of summonses as an alternative to detention altogether. It should be readily apparent that only if arrest and booking begin a case is the bail decision so critical. If a person is informed of a criminal charge by summons, detention should only be required if something happens after the summons is served to indicate that the accused should not be permitted to remain free.

At this point you might want to reconsider whether arrest should be the preferred way of beginning a criminal case.

Chapter Eight

DISCOVERY

I. CRIMINAL DISCOVERY: UNLIKE CIVIL DISCOVERY

It is common knowledge that the promulgation of the Federal Rules of Civil Procedure in 1938 marked an important change in the theory and practice of civil litigation:

> [Before the new rules] a diligent lawyer could come into court well prepared on his own case, but he was frequently in the dark as to the exact nature of his opponent's case, and consequently unprepared to meet it. Surprise was a legitimate trial tactic. A lawsuit was viewed as a game or joust in which counsel for each side strove mightily for his client, and the theory was that justice would emerge triumphant when the dust of combat settled in the judicial arena.

M. Green, The Business of the Trial Courts, in The Courts, the Public and the Law Explosion 7, 21–22 (1965).

This "sporting theory of justice" gave way to the belief that a trial should be a "quest for truth." The federal civil rules which now have been adopted in most states provide opposing counsel and litigants with tools, such as depositions and interrogatories, for discovery of information prior to trial; they permit each party upon request to discover much of the evidence that is in the exclusive control of the other. This is not to say that discovery has not become a sport all its own. But, in theory at least, civil discovery means that one side rarely has monopoly power over the facts. Despite the almost universal condemnation of the "sporting theory" of litigation, that theory still prevails in criminal cases, in the sense that pretrial discovery has remained limited. This raises obvious questions: Are the arguments in favor of broad discovery for civil litigants any less persuasive in the criminal context; in other words, is the "quest for truth" inherently different in civil and criminal cases? If not, are there countervailing considerations in criminal cases that justify a different approach to discovery?

As you read further, remember that criminal and civil causes of action sometimes overlap, especially in antitrust, environmental, and other cases of governmental regulation. Should adjudicative procedures such as discovery be tied to the sanction that might be used by a court? To the charges made against a person? Within the criminal law, the wide range of possible cases makes it difficult to predict the need for discovery or its possible abuses in particular cases. Opponents of discovery tend to focus on violent criminals, citing the danger of revealing prosecutorial information to them.[1] Adherents of more liberal discovery often point to white collar crimes in order to align the accused with the civil defendant.[2] In truth, one may wonder whether a "white collar" defendant is more of a threat to criminal than to civil proceedings.[3] One may also wonder whether those charged with violent crimes are more likely to abuse discovery than other defendants. Although there is little evidence to suggest that defendants convicted of crimes of violence actually would abuse discovery, there is a widespread, and reasonable, belief that certain defendants—those with organized crime connections, for example—pose the greatest threat to witnesses and evidence. When a system of discovery is established, the most important issue is whether or not to presume that most defendants and most defense lawyers will abuse discovery or to presume that most will use discovery as it should be used—i.e., to prepare for trial or plea negotiations.

Most of the discovery questions considered in this chapter involve nonconstitutional issues. The Supreme Court has repeatedly stated that "there is no general constitutional right to discovery in a criminal case." Weatherford v. Bursey, 429 U.S. 545, 559 (1977). On the other hand, it is clear that constitutional considerations are implicated when a state establishes a discovery system. Some sharing of information by the government may be necessary if a fair trial is to result. And even though an accused may have to give the government notice of certain claims, if it is to have a fair chance to meet them, the accused must be permitted to preserve her privilege against self-incrimination, which can be a complicating factor.

This chapter examines the competing considerations in criminal discovery, and the rules that are generally applied in federal and state cases. Although the trend is to broaden criminal discovery, recommendations for reform still

1. * * * A criminal trial is as different from a civil trial as night is from day. In a civil trial the parties are ordinarily law-abiding citizens who are peacefully seeking to have the court resolve a dispute involving money or property. In a criminal trial, on the other hand, the stakes are much higher than mere money or property. The defendant's liberty, and sometimes his very life, depends on the outcome. Many defendants are desperate, vicious criminals who are guilty of most serious crimes against society and who would stop at nothing to win an acquittal.

Flannery, Prosecutor's Case Against Liberal Discovery, 33 F.R.D. 74, 78 (1963).

2. [T]he range of civil and criminal substantive law is too broad to permit the generalization that one involved in civil litigation is far less likely to suborn perjury or intimidate witnesses. It is difficult to believe that the defendant to charges of income tax evasion, false advertising, mail fraud, et cetera, will regularly tamper with justice on the criminal side of the court but that he will not do so when defending against the same or comparable charges on the civil side. * * * Far more likely, "bad" people will do bad things on both sides of the court; the kind of people involved in litigation, and the stakes at issue, are central to the intimidation-bribery-perjury nexus, not their involvement on any one side of the court.

A. Goldstein; The State & The Accused: Balance of Advantage 69 Yale L.J. 1149 (1960).

3. See generally Statement of Harris Steinberg, in Discovery in Criminal Cases, 44 F.R.D. 481, 508–510 (1968):

> Discovery, of course, is only one part of the criminal trial process, and it cannot do, nor should it be blamed for not doing, nor should it be judged in the light of whether it does, anything about crooked lawyers, perjurers or suborners. Crooked lawyers should be summarily dealt with, but that should be done by disbarment proceedings, and not by withholding from a presumptively innocent man, on trial for his liberty, information bearing on the issues of his case, which will enable him to defend himself. Perjurers and suborners should be sent to jail, but defendants on trial should not be deprived of discovery about their own cases, because we fear that tailor-made perjured evidence will be concocted to bolster the defense, if the facts are revealed.

are at this date "in a sense, revolutionary." American Bar Association Standards: Discovery and Procedure Before Trial (2d ed.1980). To understand the reform movement, it first is important to see the limited discovery procedures provided in most jurisdictions and to understand why they remain limited.

The federal discovery framework is discussed at some length herein. A number of states have used it as a model. Some states still regulate discovery by common law decisionmaking, in which appellate decisions and past practice tend to control basic approaches. In such jurisdictions, it is not uncommon to find variances among cities or counties and differences in attitudes among trial judges. Most states have court rules or statutes that regulate discovery. Those that do not follow the federal framework often borrow heavily from the ABA Standards, which also receive attention herein. States that follow the ABA Standards in some respects may depart in other respects. The initial ABA Standards were adopted in 1970 and are cited herein. A second edition was adopted in 1980 and is also cited, even though some of its principal modifications—e.g., open file defense discovery—have not been adopted.

II. THE BASIC ISSUES

A. ARGUMENTS AGAINST CRIMINAL DISCOVERY

Arguments against criminal discovery focus primarily on the implications of the defendant's access to prosecutorial information. Judge Learned Hand set the framework for such arguments in his oft-quoted opinion in United States v. Garsson, 291 F. 646, 679 (S.D.N.Y.1925):

> * * * Under our criminal procedure the accused has every advantage. While the prosecution is held rigidly to the charge, he need not disclose the barest outline of his defense. He is immune from question or comment on his silence; he cannot be convicted when there is the least fair doubt in the minds of any one of the twelve. Why in addition he should in advance have the whole evidence against him to pick over at his leisure, and make his defense, fairly or foully, I have never been able to see. No doubt grand juries err and indictments are calamities to honest men, but we must work with human beings and we can correct such errors only at too large a price. Our dangers do not lie in too little tenderness to the accused. Our procedure has been always haunted by the ghost of the innocent man convicted. It is an unreal dream. What we need to fear is the archaic formalism and the watery sentiment that obstructs, delays, and defeats the prosecution of crime.

Opponents of discovery argue that expansion would tip the balance too much on the side of the accused. Prosecutors already face a heavy burden of proof and the defendant has the benefit of a privilege against self-incrimination which allows her not to testify at all. Neither of these elements is found in a civil trial. As one prosecutor explained:

> A civil trial is a search for the truth by both sides. But is a criminal trial a search for the truth? As far as the Government is concerned, it certainly is, for the Government prosecutor has just as great a duty to protect the innocent as he has to prosecute the guilty. The defense lawyer, however, has no duty to reveal the truth. His responsibility is to insure that the defendant receives a fair trial and to require the Government to prove his client's guilt beyond a

> reasonable doubt. He may be convinced that his client is guilty; but if the defendant insists on a trial, the defense lawyer must require the Government to prove him guilty beyond a reasonable doubt. * * * There is, therefore, a vast difference between a civil and criminal case in that a civil case is a search for the truth and there can be a mutual exchange of information so that the truth may be ascertained, whereas in a criminal case involving a guilty defendant, there is a one-sided search for the truth and there can be no equal exchange of information due to the very nature of the proceedings.

Statement of Thomas A. Flannery, The Prosecutor's Case Against Liberal Discovery, 33 F.R.D. 74, 78–79 (1963).

Consider for a moment what such comments suggest. Apparently, the notion is that the accused can be treated poorly in some respects if she is treated well in other respects. But what does this say about our attitude toward constitutional rights? It is true that the privilege against self-incrimination as interpreted by the Supreme Court makes it more difficult for the prosecutor to gather evidence from a defendant than if no such broad privilege were recognized. It is true that the restrictions on evidence gathering attributable to the Fourth Amendment and the right to counsel under the Sixth Amendment sometimes impair the government's ability to gather evidence. But does this mean that trials are not conducted to get at the truth? Or does it mean that trials are designed to reconstruct relevant facts within a special procedural framework that recognizes the importance of extrajudicial activities as well as trial rights? Are you prepared to accept the argument that trial rights should be allocated so as to disadvantage a defendant on the ground that she has the benefit of constitutional rights outside the trial setting? What would be wrong with permitting equal discovery by prosecutors and defendants, except when constitutional rights require that the defendant be given more favorable treatment?

A related argument is that discovery will enable the defendant to prepare a perjured defense.[4] But is the danger of perjury appreciably greater in criminal than in civil cases? Assuming that it is, doesn't the government have opportunities to "freeze" evidence in criminal cases that are virtually unknown in civil cases and that make the danger of perjury attributable to discovery slight? For example, the government can obtain a search warrant to seize tangible evidence and to hold it for trial. The government can use sophisticated electronic eavesdropping pursuant to court order. The government can call witnesses to testify before a secret grand jury and obtain statements that are made under oath. The government can call witnesses to testify in a preliminary hearing to pin down their testimony before the defendant's very eyes. With such evidence-gathering devices available, does the government have to worry much about manufactured evidence? It is true that the government does not know what the defendant herself will say in many instances. But the government will disclose all its evidence at trial before the defendant testifies in any event, so is discovery much of an incremental inducement to perjury?

4. The search for truth may also be impaired if prosecutors, who know they will have to reveal information, are discouraged from making records and rely on memory instead. See Louisell, Criminal Discovery: Dilemma Real or Apparent? 49 Calif.L.Rev. 56 (1961). Do you think this really would happen?

In a classic opinion, Judge Vanderbilt described the specific dangers that he perceived:

> In criminal proceedings long experience has taught the courts that often discovery will lead not to honest factfinding, but on the contrary to perjury and the suppression of evidence. Thus the criminal who is aware of the whole case against him will often procure perjured testimony in order to set up a false defense, * * * Another result of full discovery would be that the criminal defendant who is informed of the names of all of the State's witnesses may take steps to bribe or frighten them into giving perjured testimony or into absenting themselves so that they are unavailable to testify. Moreover, many witnesses, if they know that the defendant will have knowledge of their names prior to trial, will be reluctant to come forward with information during the investigation of the crime, * * * All these dangers are more inherent in criminal proceedings where the defendant has much more at stake, often his own life, than in civil proceedings.

State v. Tune, 13 N.J. 203, 210–211, 98 A.2d 881, 884 (1953).

This may be the strongest argument against extensive discovery on behalf of criminal defendants. Whether the threat to witnesses and to the administration of justice is as great as the quote suggests is subject to fair debate, but it certainly is the case that many experienced prosecutors believe the threat to be real, as some of the material that follows will demonstrate.

One thing that you might want to ponder as you proceed in the chapter is whether it is necessary to take an all or nothing approach to various discovery issues. Opponents of liberal discovery claim that it poses dangers, but surely they would concede that the dangers do not exist in all cases. Advocates of discovery reform argue that the dangers are overstated in the run of the mine case, but surely they would concede that danger is real in some cases. Why should a rule be written to deny or grant discovery for all criminal cases? Another approach would be to permit discovery in some but not all cases. It is possible, for example, either to presume that discovery is to be permitted, but to allow the government to oppose it in a particular case, or to presume that it is not to be permitted absent a showing by the defendant of specialized need. Indeed, this is something like the approach of Fed.R.Crim.P. 16(d). One of the problems with this approach is that it may result in hearings when one side or the other tries to overcome the presumption. Early in a criminal case it may be hard for the side against whom the presumption operates to offer proof. Also, the hearing itself may tend to produce the discovery that the government opposes. But another tack might be taken. Discovery of relevant material could be presumed proper, but the prosecutor could be empowered to deny discovery if an affidavit were submitted under seal to the trial court explaining why discovery in a particular case might threaten the fair administration of justice. The natural response of a defendant would be to protest against any ex parte procedure. But if the choice is to deny all defendants discovery to protect against some defendants, or to grant discovery to all except those against whom an affidavit is submitted, isn't there a good argument that the latter procedure is the better one? [5]

5. For a similar proposal, see Uniform Rule 421(f) (permitting motions to restrict discovery to be made in camera).

Another argument against defense discovery is that it results in fishing expeditions into government records. This argument generally can be answered by providing in discovery rules that only relevant information can be requested and by indicating the classes of information that generally should be discoverable. This is what the ABA Standards do. They also adopt a relevance limitation on discovery, recognizing, however, that determining relevance is not always easy. The fact that the same prosecutors' offices appear in all criminal cases means that prosecutors should be able to learn quickly what material courts will require them to turn over to defendants.

B. ARGUMENTS FAVORING CRIMINAL DISCOVERY

Proponents of more liberal discovery hold that the gravity of the liberty and reputation interests at stake in criminal cases argues for liberalized discovery. In a dissent in *Tune,* supra, State Court Justice (later Supreme Court Justice) Brennan said:

> It shocks my sense of justice that in these circumstances counsel for an accused facing a possible death sentence should be denied inspection of his confession which, were this a civil case, could not be denied.

In a later article, The Criminal Prosecution: Sporting Event or Quest for Truth? 1963 Wash.U.L.Q. 279, Justice Brennan addressed the arguments against discovery. He pointed out that the privilege against self-incrimination has not prevented prosecutors from securing confessions or incriminating non-testimonial evidence from the criminally accused; that the best protections against manipulation are early exposure of the facts and emphasis on the ethical responsibilities of defense counsel; and that the trial judge can act to protect witnesses shown to be in danger. Justice Brennan and others have pointed out that, without discovery, indigent defendants are seriously handicapped in the preparation of a defense. In addition, as Dean Pye has noted:

> Most criminal cases result in a plea of guilty. The principal role of the capable advocate in many circumstances is to advise that his client plead guilty. For this advice to be meaningful, it must be based upon knowledge of the facts and the consequences. One of these consequences is the probability of conviction if the client goes to trial. It may be impossible for counsel to make any intelligent evaluation of the alternatives if he knows only what his client has told him and what he has discovered on his own.

The Defendant's Case for More Liberal Discovery, 33 F.R.D. 82, 83 (1963).

Finally, proponents seek to dispel the arguments against discovery by pointing to jurisdictions where it works. In many states, where discovery is a matter of prosecutorial discretion, there has been a general "open-file" policy, at least in particular cases, and the prosecutors take into account the same considerations discussed above. In still other states, legislatures have expanded criminal discovery, without apparent detriment to the criminal justice process. See, e.g., Langrock, Vermont's Experiment in Criminal Discovery, 53 A.B.A.J. 732 (1967); Fletcher, Pretrial Discovery in State Criminal Cases, 12 Stan.L.Rev. 293 (1960).

C. OBJECTIVES OF CRIMINAL DISCOVERY

In 1980, the ABA adopted discovery standards that emphasized the advantages to the courts of broad discovery:

Standard 11–1.1. Procedural needs prior to trial

(a) Procedures prior to trial should:

(i) promote an expeditious as well as a fair disposition of the charges, whether by diversion, plea, or trial;

(ii) provide the accused with sufficient information to make an informed plea;

(iii) permit thorough preparation for trial and minimize surprise at trial;

(iv) reduce interruptions and complications during trial and avoid unnecessary and repetitious trials by identifying and resolving prior to trial any procedural, collateral, or constitutional issues;

(v) eliminate as much as possible the procedural and substantive inequities among similarly situated defendants; and

(vi) effect economies in time, money, judicial resources, and professional skills by minimizing paperwork, avoiding repetitious assertions of issues, and reducing the number of separate hearings.

(b) These needs can be served by:

(i) full and free discovery;

(ii) simpler and more efficient procedures; and

(iii) procedural pressures for expediting the processing of cases.

The ABA standards urge trial courts to promote discovery, to encourage automatic disclosure of information, and to develop procedural devices to assist the litigants in discovery. Counsel are urged to engage in discovery without judicial supervision to the greatest possible extent. The Standards address three concerns that the ABA Advisory Committee recognized as "major impediments to criminal justice."

The first impediment is the proliferation of pre-trial motions necessitated by recent Supreme Court decisions in the area of criminal procedure. Each motion entails separate preparation, paperwork, and court and attorney time, all collateral to the issue of guilt or innocence. The Commentary to the ABA Standards makes the point as follows:

> Constitutional developments have focused attention on motions as a means for vindicating almost every criminal procedure right enumerated in the fourth, fifth, sixth, eighth and fourteenth amendments. In addition, state developments have added to the arsenal of available motions. A factor that has also contributed to the development of extensive motion practice is the increased incidence of postconviction challenges to the effectiveness of counsel's assistance. As the quality of counsel becomes a routine issue in the appellate review process, counsel are likely to make extensive pretrial motions as a form of self-defense.[6]

6. To reduce the amount of time spent hearing various motions, the ABA Standards divide discovery into three stages: an exploratory stage in which counsel are to cooperate

The second impediment is the short supply of experienced defense counsel available to meet the increased demand created by the right to counsel cases, discussed in Chapter Five, supra. Discovery would facilitate the task of criminal defense for sometimes inexperienced court-appointed attorneys.

The third impediment is the difficulty of achieving finality in convictions in the face of an increasing number of collateral attacks on convictions. See Chapter Thirteen, infra. Identification and resolution of important constitutional issues through discovery before trial would sometimes obviate the very need for a trial, and could go a long way toward safeguarding the integrity of any adjudication of guilt that is made.

D. A SYSTEMIC NEED FOR DEFENSE DISCOVERY

The previous arguments in favor of defense discovery emphasize that it will aid plea bargaining, that it will reduce the sporting aspects of litigation, that its evils can be controlled, and that it will improve the efficiency of the criminal justice system. These arguments are important. But there may be one that should be added to the usual list; it is based on an appreciation of the realities of the criminal justice system of which you are now aware.

Unlike civil cases, in which parties share control, criminal cases give monopoly power over important parts of the process to the prosecutor. It is the prosecutor, together with the police, who decides when to bring a suspect into custody. It is the prosecutor who decides what charges to bring. It is the prosecutor who has the right to seek a grand jury indictment. It is the prosecutor who may have the option of either filing an information and triggering a preliminary hearing, or utilizing the grand jury as a charging body. In some jurisdictions it is the prosecutor who has subpoena power. It is the prosecutor who makes decisions on granting immunity to witnesses. It is the prosecutor who can hold out the carrot of a sweet plea bargain to cooperative witnesses. It is the prosecutor who can call on uniformed police officers to seek out information from citizens who may feel bound to cooperate with officers of the law. And the prosecutor often exercises these functions without input from the defendant.

Putting aside any advantages that accrue to defendants from the adoption of a Bill of Rights and incorporation of most of it against the states, consider who has the advantage in preparing a case for trial, the prosecutor or the defendant? How great an advantage is it? If it is quite large, then the argument for defense discovery increases in strength. But some would resist the argument and point out the prosecutor has a heavy burden of persuasion, one that is not placed on the defendant, except in unusual circumstances. On the other hand, it could be argued that denying the defendant the factual data necessary to litigate a case effectively and thereby to raise the requisite doubt is inconsistent with the burden of persuasion that is placed on the prosecutor.

with each other in providing the discovery required under the standards; an omnibus hearing at which the court will resolve disputed questions, consider constitutional issues and rule on various motions (with a check-list form utilized to assure that "all requests, errors and issues are then considered"); and a pretrial conference to plan the actual trial. Standard 11–5.1 (2d ed.1980).

III. DISCOVERY ON BEHALF OF THE DEFENDANT

A. THE STATE OF THE LAW

In most jurisdictions, criminal discovery remains strictly circumscribed either by statute or court action.

> Most of the states have * * * limited a defendant's discovery by a variety of doctrines that had their origins in the halting and cautious growth of discovery. The most common of these doctrines holds that the question of whether to grant discovery is in the discretion of the trial court. A second limiting doctrine confines discovery to evidence that would be admissible in court. Another such doctrine requires the defendant to establish a foundation for discovery by demonstrating a particularized need for the information he requests. Some states surprisingly refuse discovery of evidence about which the defendant already knows on the ground that he has no need of it. * * * In addition, many states deny discovery of particular categories of information—for example, the defendant's confession, the confessions of co-defendants, the statements of prospective witnesses, and the transcript or minutes of grand jury testimony.[7]

On the other hand,

> in many jurisdictions, there is considerable discovery by grace—i.e., discovery provided by the prosecutor although not compelled by statute, rule, or decision. This fact is often ignored in judicial decisions and law review commentaries. While it is dangerous to generalize too much about the form and scope of this informal discovery in view of the differing attitudes of individual prosecutors, the differing relationships a prosecutor has with individual defense counsel, and the attitudes a prosecutor may have toward a particular case, it seems that the sine qua non of defense discovery is defense cooperation. If the defense attorney is willing to provide information, he may usually obtain access to information in return.
>
> Some might think such discovery by grace adequately protects the legitimate interests of criminal defendants. But clearly any system which relies wholly on discretion entrusted to one side is open to abuse and unfairness. The ability to withhold or grant information is one form of control which prosecutors hold over the defense bar. Information may be given selectively to encourage a guilty plea; a defense counsel who has "unreasonably" refused to plead certain clients guilty may find that his access to information has been shut off, and in the "big case" normal channels of communication may close. It is, of course, the client who suffers when an attorney falls from grace, or when the prosecutor, for other reasons, disregards usual procedures for trading information.

R. Lempert & S. Saltzburg, A Modern Approach to Evidence 127–8 (2d ed.1982).

B. SOME SPECIFICS OF DEFENSE DISCOVERY

The federal system, like the states, historically has afforded very limited discovery to criminal defendants. Rule 16 as originally adopted in 1946

7. Nakell, Criminal Discovery for the Defense and the Prosecution—The Developing Constitutional Considerations, 50 N.C.L.Rev. 437, 474–75 (1972). More than half the states and the federal system have statutes and rules controlling discovery. Even in the absence of affirmative discovery provisions, most courts today hold that they have power to order discovery.

essentially only gave the defendant access to material that would have been otherwise available to him had it not been impounded by the government. 1966 revisions of the Rule divided discovery by the defendant into two classes of materials: that which the court might order simply upon motion of the defendant, and that which the court might order upon a defendant's "showing of materiality to the preparation of his defense and that the request was reasonable." Although both classes implicated judicial discretion, the extra showing required for books, papers, tangible objects, or places, which fell in the latter class, gave rise to an inference that the defendant had a *right* to discovery of materials under the first class (defendant's statements, reports of examination and tests, and defendant's grand jury testimony.)

In 1975 the Supreme Court attempted to revise its rule. Although Congress did not adopt the recommendations in their entirety, Rule 16 was amended significantly that year. Subdivision (a) of the amended rule divides discovery by the defendant into four classes of information sought. The only completely new category added in 1975 covers the defendant's prior criminal record. The rule also establishes a duty of disclosure binding on the government, stating that "upon request of a defendant the government *shall* permit" instead of "upon motion of a defendant * * * the court may order the attorney for the government to permit * * *" (emphasis added).

The importance of the new rule is its shift in emphasis. "The issue now is not whether to allow discovery; it is rather how should the discovery process operate and what should comprise minimum mandatory discovery." Miller, Proposed Amendments to the Federal Rules of Criminal Procedure, 14 Washburn L.J. 76 (1975). By making discovery a matter of right, the rules place primary responsibility on defense attorneys and prosecutors, instead of on the court.

By examining the rule's approach to various aspects of discovery and by comparing it to other approaches that have been recommended or adopted, we can outline the current state of discovery in most American criminal cases.

1. *The Defendant's Statements*

The federal rule gives the defendant the right to discover her written or recorded statements within the custody or control of the government. The government must exercise due diligence in obtaining such statements upon request. Such discovery may not seem very controversial, but the fact that it has been indicates the kind of opposition to defense discovery that has existed for some time. Most courts have discretion to grant or deny this discovery.

The argument has been made that if the defendant's prior statements are disclosed, she can tailor her testimony at trial to eliminate any discrepancies and the prosecution will not be able to impeach her. This advantage, however, is already available for prosecution witnesses, who are "prepped" for cross-examination by the defense. Moreover, revelation of prior incriminating statements may persuade the defendant to plead guilty and avoid trial. Usually, the government will offer the defendant's statements during its case-in-chief. There, the defendant often will hear it before testifying anyway. Perhaps the most significant argument for disclosure is that the defendant should know what the government claims she told its agents, since the government can always use statements properly obtained in some fashion, and the importance of the defendant's words makes it imperative that she should know exactly what it is she may have to explain or deny.

There has been some controversy over the meaning of the word "statement" in the rule. The Jencks Act, discussed infra, defines statements of government witnesses discoverable for cross-examination purposes as:

(1) a written statement made by said witness and signed or otherwise adopted or approved by him;

(2) a stenographic, mechanical, electrical, or other recording, or a transcription thereof, which is a substantially verbatim recital of an oral statement made by said witness and recorded contemporaneously with the making of such oral statement; or

(3) a statement, however taken or recorded, or a transcription thereof, if any, made by said witness to a grand jury.

The Courts have read the Jencks Act to strictly limit discovery to statements that reproduce exact words or are substantially verbatim. The drafters of Rule 16 provided no definition. Can you think of an argument that would support a broader reading of statement under Rule 16(a)(1)(A) than under the Jencks Act? Oral statements are only discoverable if the government intends to use them at trial. Notice that oral statements made to undercover agents are not covered, nor are oral statements made to non-governmental people. Can you figure out why the rule is drafted as it is? Several courts have held that unsolicited admissions made by defendants to government agents are not discoverable.[8]

Have you any problem with turning over to the defendant her own statements?

2. *Co-Defendants' Statements*

The federal rule does not require that a defendant be given a copy of a co-defendant's statements, but ABA Standard § 11–2.1(a)(ii) does. The rationale for the ABA version rests in part on Bruton v. United States, 391 U.S. 123 (1968), discussed in Chapter Ten. *Bruton* held that it is constitutional error to try one defendant where the jury has before it a non-testifying codefendant's statement implicating her, even if the jury instructions specify that the statement only is admissible against the non-testifying co-defendant who confessed. Thus, knowledge of the statement in advance is necessary to allow defense counsel to move for appropriate remedies such as severance or redaction of the confession. But the ABA Standards go further, and note that even if it is clear that the confessing defendant will testify, so that there is no *Bruton* concern, there is still no good argument for denying one defendant a look at the other's statement. Defense counsel cannot work well without knowing what each defendant has previously said. Under the Federal Rule, each defendant could obtain her own statement and share it. Would any harm

8. See e.g. United States v. Johnson, 562 F.2d 515 (8th Cir. 1977); United States v. Green, 548 F.2d 1261 (6th Cir. 1977). Does it make sense to differentiate unsolicited statements from those which are made in response to a question? How does such a distinction relate to the purposes of discovery of the defendant's statements?

be done by providing for discovery directly by each defendant of all statements by all co-defendants?

3. *Discovery of Prior Criminal Records*

As the Advisory Committee on the Federal Rules noted in its comment to Fed.R.Crim.P. 16(a)(1)(B):

> A defendant may be uncertain of the precise nature of his prior record and it seems therefore in the interest of efficient and fair administration to make it possible to resolve prior to trial any disputes as to the correctness of the relevant criminal record of the defendant.

Disclosure of prior convictions should enable the defendant to seek pretrial rulings on the admissibility of such convictions to impeach her if she should choose to testify. Rules like Fed.R.Evid. 609(a), which permit the trial judge some discretion in admitting and rejecting some convictions as impeachment evidence, often invite such motions, and these motions often save time once trial commences.

4. *Documents and Tangible Objects*

Under Fed.R.Crim.P. 16(a)(1)(C) there is still room for judicial discretion. Few disputes arise concerning evidence obtained from or belonging to the defendant. And the government knows that it must disclose upon request material that it plans to use at trial. More difficult to apply is the language "material to the preparation of his defense." For example, in United States v. Phillip, 948 F.2d 241 (6th Cir. 1991), Phillip was on trial for murder and child abuse of one of his sons, Jamal. Jamal died after falling down a flight of stairs. The Government contended that Phillip hit Jamal so hard that he fell down the steps. Phillip admitted that he had beaten Jamal for a period of weeks, but contended that Jamal had fallen down the steps accidentally while Phillip had his back turned. The Government videotaped an interview with the defendant's six-year-old son, Roderick. Roderick stated that Phillip had not hit Jamal at the time of the dispute, but also stated that his mother had coached him; he also made several statements inculpating Phillip and describing acts of abuse. The court of appeals rejected Phillip's argument that the videotape was material to his defense:

> Phillip asserts in conclusory fashion that access to the videotape * * * would have aided him in the preparation of his defense, but he does not state convincingly how the videotape would have assisted him. He does suggest that viewing the videotape would have allowed him to reach a more informed decision concerning whether or not to depose Roderick or to subpoena him as a defense witness. However, since Roderick was his son, Phillip was aware of Roderick's potential availability to testify concerning Phillip's battering of Jamal. Moreover, early access to the videotape certainly could not have enlightened Phillip with respect to the *wisdom* of deposing Roderick or calling him as a witness. * * * On the whole, the videotape is inculpatory in nature and reveals a highly impressionable young child making highly inconsistent statements within a short period of time. * * *
>
> [E]arly access to the videotape would have informed Phillip that if deposed or placed on the witness stand, Roderick might 1) make exculpatory state-

ments, 2) make inculpatory statements, 3) make both exculpatory and inculpatory statements, and/or 4) have little memory of relevant events. After viewing the videotape, Phillip would have been in no better position to evaluate the wisdom of deposing Roderick or calling him as a witness. Accordingly, we conclude that the videotape was not material to the preparation of Phillip's defense, and that consequently the government and the district court did not violate Rule 16(a)(1)(C) by denying early access to the videotape.

Judicial discretion is also exercised in rejecting discovery requests that are insufficiently specific. The courts are properly concerned with preventing "fishing expeditions"; thus it has been held that a request for "anything exculpatory" is equivalent to no request at all, and the "trial judge need not accord the slightest heed to such shotgun approach." United States v. Wiener, 578 F.2d 757 (9th Cir. 1978). See also United States v. Haldeman, 559 F.2d 31 (D.C.Cir.1976).[9]

Because documents cannot be intimidated and cannot easily be tampered with, if the government retains control of the original, the fear of misuse by the defendant is not great. The limits of discovery here are to protect the government from having to respond to overbroad requests. If the documents would reveal the names of witnesses or other information not discoverable, then they will not be disclosed.

5. *Experts, Examinations and Tests*

Many jurisdictions, even those with restrictive discovery rules, allow discovery of results of examinations and tests such as autopsy reports, reports of medical or psychiatric examinations, blood tests, handwriting or fingerprinting comparisons, ballistic tests, and so forth. Because of its factual nature, such evidence is unlikely to be misused or distorted by disclosure. And it is practically impossible for the defense to test or rebut scientific or expert evidence without opportunities to examine that evidence before the trial. Reports should be disclosed whether the results are positive or negative from the standpoint of the prosecution.[10] Note that Federal Rule 16(a)(1)(D) allows disclosure of reports without regard to relevance, admissibility at trial, or probative value. Should those factors be considered?

Oral reports are not discoverable under Rule 16. Professor Gianelli, in Criminal Discovery, Scientific Evidence, and DNA, 44 Vand.L.Rev. 791 (1991), notes that when Rule 16(a)(1)(D) was drafted in 1966, "most scientific evidence consisted of autopsy reports and crime laboratory reports." However, "today experts have developed many new categories of scientific evidence. Examples include expert testimony on rape trauma syndrome, child sexual abuse accommodation syndrome, battered woman syndrome, and bite mark comparisons. Neither custom nor regulation requires these experts to write reports. Indeed

9. See also United States v. Williams, 580 F.2d 578 (D.C.Cir.1978) (holding that "tenuous claims are not sufficient to justify the trial court's indulgence of inquiry into the legitimacy of evidence in the government's possession"). In *Williams,* the government denied that the transcripts of wiretaps in its possession affected the defendant's claim of standing. In the absence of a showing by the accused that the electronic eavesdropping records would facilitate his proof of standing, the "government's denial must generally be accepted as conclusive."

10. It is possible that "negative" results, that is reports that would tend to be exculpatory, would have to be disclosed. See discussion in Section IV, infra.

* * * the prosecution loses the element of surprise by preparing the report." Professor Gianelli argues that, in light of these scientific advances, Rule 16 should be amended to provide for discovery of the substance and basis of expert testimony, and for the right to test and retest evidence.

6. *Names, Addresses and Statements of Witnesses*

This controversial area has been summarized in R. Lempert & S. Saltzburg, A Modern Approach to Evidence 128–29 (2d ed. 1982) as follows:

> Some states mandate disclosure of the names and/or the relevant written or recorded statements of certain potential trial witnesses, but few go as far as Florida does in providing that the prosecutor shall provide within 15 days of a demand by one charged with an offense "[t]he names and addresses of all persons known to the prosecutor to have information which may be relevant to the offense charged, and to any defense with respect thereto." Approximately a dozen states hold that disclosure of such statements rests within the discretion of the trial judge, and most require a significant showing of special need to justify discovery. Some states by statute ban disclosure of witnesses' statements, and most states do not affirmatively permit it.
>
> Federal courts have traditionally refused such discovery, relying on the Jencks Act, 18 U.S.C.A. § 3500. This statute followed the Supreme Court's decision in Jencks v. United States, 353 U.S. 657 (1957), in which the Court exercised its supervisory power to hold that a trial court erred in denying a defense request to examine during the trial statements of two undercover FBI agents. The Court rejected the notion that pretrial statements should only be made available where the defense could show a probable inconsistency between the witness' pretrial statements and his in-court testimony. Without the earlier statements the task of proving probable inconsistency would be difficult indeed. The Jencks Act affirmed the Court's basic requirement that the government disclose pretrial statements made by its witnesses. Subsections (b) and (e) of the Act provide that *after* a witness called by the United States has testified on direct examination, the defendant may move for and receive statements of the witness in the government's possession. Statements within the meaning of the act include only written statements approved by the witness, stenographic or mechanical transcripts that purport to be almost verbatim accounts of oral statements, and any statements, however recorded, made to a grand jury. The Court's ruling is modified in that *in camera* review is required for the purpose of separating portions of statements relating to the witness' trial testimony from unrelated portions.[11] Most states have followed the federal lead and patterned statutes upon the Jencks Act, but some states still require a showing of probable conflict between testimony and statement before requiring production. The Supreme Court has affirmed the limitations in the Act, making clear that its decision in *Jencks* was not constitutionally based.[a] In the case of Goldberg v. United States, 425 U.S. 94 (1976), the Court interpreted the Act to mean that statements made to government lawyers

11. United States v. Hinton, 719 F.2d 711 (4th Cir.1983), canvasses the cases that analyze whether the government has an obligation to preserve the rough notes used to prepare formal reports. Although it recognized that some courts have required that rough notes be preserved and made available, the court concluded that these notes were not statements within the meaning of the Jencks Act and that the government was not obliged to produce them.

a. United States v. Augenblick, 393 U.S. 348 (1969).

otherwise producible under the Act are not barred from production by the work product doctrine.

Some jurisdictions provide the defendant with a list of prospective witnesses who have made statements, and some require the prosecution to endorse on the indictment the names of grand jury witnesses. This latter requirement provides less disclosure than one might think since an indictment can be secured on the testimony of only a few witnesses. A few jurisdictions require the prosecution to list the names of the witnesses it intends to call at trial.

The ABA Standards would require the prosecutor to disclose "the names and addresses of witnesses, together with their relevant written or recorded statements" (Standards 11–2.1(a)(1)). But amended Federal Rule of Criminal Procedure 16, as enacted by the Congress, requires no disclosure of the names of prospective witnesses. The Supreme Court had approved an amendment that would have provided such discovery, but it fell before the complaints of federal prosecutors.[12]

The Department of Justice opposed the amendment and mustered the support of numerous United States Attorneys. The following excerpts are from the congressional hearings:

As the United States Attorney for the Western District of Pennsylvania has observed:

"Proposed Rule 16 eliminates any discretion of the court in denying discovery which the court presently possesses under Rule 16, and it requires the government to supply defendant with a list of the names and addresses of all of its witnesses. It is as if the proponents of that Rule had never heard of the murder of key witnesses in organized crime cases with which many of us are regrettably familiar."

"It seems clear that we have a hard enough time securing the cooperation of civilian witnesses who 'don't want to get involved' without putting them in a situation in which, months before trial, they become subject to such degradation and harassment as may occur to an ingenious defendant, who will have far more to gain under the new rules than the present post-conviction satisfaction of revenge. Indeed, we are of the view that the law should not, in the name of 'enlightened' discovery procedures, expose innocent members of the public, who have had the misfortune to be victims of or witnesses to criminal conduct, to the mercy of defendants any more than the confrontation clause presently requires."[13]

On the other hand, the ABA standards argue that disclosure is necessary to defense counsel in order to prepare adequately to cross-examine witnesses and test their credibility.[14]

12. Since the Congress rejected the idea that witnesses' names and addresses should be turned over to the defense, most courts will be reluctant to exercise any inherent power they have to authorize such discovery. See, e.g., United States v. Taylor, 542 F.2d 1023 (8th Cir. 1976). But if the defense need for such evidence is strong enough, disclosure may be ordered. See, e.g., United States v. Holmes, 346 A.2d 517 (D.C.App.1975).

13. Statement of W. Vincent Rakestraw, Ass't Att'y Gen'l, in House Hearings on Federal Rules of Criminal Procedure, 93rd Cong., 2nd Sess. (1974).

14. "In most cases the client admittedly knows something about the transaction, but rarely does he know everything about it. The average defendant is not gifted with the total recall which would permit him to remember every detail. He does not possess the legal acumen necessary to segregate those facts which are relevant to the question of guilt, innocence or mitigation. He does not know the names of all of the witnesses who know

Are there more direct ways to eliminate the problems perceived by the U.S. Attorneys? Earl Silbert suggested the following alternative:

> Alternatively, we would recommend that in the event witness disclosure is to be permitted, some burden be placed on the party seeking disclosure to show a reasonable need for the information sought, and that whatever disclosure in this regard is permitted, no party be required to disclose earlier than three days in advance of trial. Finally, it is particularly critical that in this area the trial Court retain discretion as to whether or not to grant the discovery sought.[15]

Would this have been a preferable approach?

The limitations that characterize discovery in many jurisdictions are illustrated by State v. Hines, 422 So.2d 1297 (La.1982), granting extraordinary writs to prevent a trial judge from requiring the prosecution to provide the defense in a first degree murder case with names of prospective government witnesses. The protection of witnesses is so important that it may take precedence over rules that appear to make discovery mandatory.

It is on this question, whether witnesses' names, addresses and statements should be disclosed, that the debate about discovery becomes most heated. Would this be an appropriate place to invoke the presumption of discovery, but to permit the prosecutor in any case to state in writing reasons for nondisclosure that would not be revealed to the defense, but that would be reviewed by the court?

7. *Grand Jury Minutes and Transcripts*

Chapter Six, supra, examined grand jury secrecy. Once an indictment is returned, do arguments for secrecy still hold? Will secrecy protect the reputations of those accused? Will secrecy inhibit flight once a defendant is formally charged? Will secrecy deter collusion among witnesses after an investigation is completed and charges have been brought? Will secrecy protect the identity of witnesses who will appear at trial? Will secrecy prevent tampering with a grand jury following a charge? Note that Fed.R.Crim.P. 16(a)(1)(A) allows a defendant to see his own grand jury testimony. The 1980 ABA Standard 11–2.1 provides that all relevant testimony of grand jury witnesses must be provided to the defendant.

something about the case. He does not have in his possession all of the demonstrative or documentary evidence which may be relevant at his trial. He may be unaware of the results of a scientific test, such as a blood test which was conducted after his arrest. He does not know what the Government witnesses have said in prior statements. Even the most gifted defendant may have forgotten much in the period of four to eight weeks which usually pass before the appearance of counsel in the case.

* * *

"The hallmark of our legal system is cross-examination. It is the major technique for the ascertainment of the truth in a trial.

* * *

Effective cross-examination without broad discovery is frequently impossible except in the unusual case where the defendant is sufficiently wealthy to hire private investigators. It is extremely difficult to develop inconsistencies or to effectively impeach any witness whose identity is unknown until he is sworn or until his name is divulged during voir dire."

Statement of Dean Pye, House Hearings, supra note 13, at 91. See also Palermo v. United States, 360 U.S. 343, 362–66 (1959).

15. Statement, Id., at 121.

8. *Work Product*

Fed.R.Crim.P. 16(a)(2) provides extensive work product protection for the fruits of government investigations. The 1980 ABA Standards provide more limited protection: [16]

11–2.6 Matters Not Subject to Disclosure.

(a) Disclosure shall not be required of legal research or of records, correspondence, reports or memoranda to the extent that they contain the opinions, theories or conclusions of the prosecuting attorney or members of his legal staff.

(b) Disclosure of an informant's identity shall not be required where his identity is a prosecution secret and a failure to disclose will not infringe the constitutional rights of the accused. Disclosure shall not be denied hereunder of the identity of witnesses to be produced at a hearing or trial.

(c) Disclosure shall not be required where it involves a substantial risk of grave prejudice to national security and a failure to disclose will not infringe the constitutional rights of the accused. Disclosure shall not thus be denied hereunder regarding witnesses or material to be produced at a hearing or trial.

Uniform Rule 421(b) is in accord. What theory justifies protecting police or FBI reports under the federal rule? If it is true that the government has easier access to information than the defendant in many situations, why should that information not be shared with the defense?

Work product is one of those areas in which prosecutors complain that discovery would be one-sided, since the privilege against self-incrimination or the attorney-client privilege will bar the government from finding out what the defendant or her attorney has done to prepare a case most of the time. Assume that the government could not force disclosure of much of the work product of the defense. Does that mean that one-sided disclosure of the government's work product is undesirable? Since the government has the power of the grand jury and the prosecutor may even have subpoena power, is there any information that the government will want to reach—other than that protected by the privilege against self-incrimination—that it cannot reach as easily as the defense? There will be many times when the converse is untrue—i.e., the defense will not have the same ease of access to information as the prosecutor. Is this important?

What rule on work product would you adopt?

9. *A Different Kind of Discovery System*

Uniform Rule 421 would provide for broad disclosure of information to the defendant upon request.

Rule 421. [Prosecuting Attorney to Allow Access.]

(a) **Duty of Prosecuting Attorney.** Upon the defendant's written request, the prosecuting attorney, except as provided in subdivision (b), shall allow access at any reasonable time to all matters within the prosecuting

16. An extensive review of the work product rule can be found in Feldman, The Work Product Rule in Criminal Practice and Procedure, 50 U.Cin.L.Rev. 495 (1981).

attorney's possession or control which relate in any way to the case, including statements, [portions of grand jury minutes or transcripts] [law enforcement officer] reports, expert reports, reports on prospective jurors, papers, photographs, objects, and places, and the identity of persons having information relating to the case. * * * In affording this access, the prosecuting attorney shall allow the defendant at any reasonable time and in any reasonable manner to inspect, photograph, copy, or have reasonable tests made. If a scientific test or experiment of any matter may preclude or impair any further tests or experiments, the prosecuting attorney shall give the defendant and any person known or believed to have an interest in the matter reasonable notice and opportunity to be present and to have an expert observe or participate in the test or experiment.

The exceptions are for limited work product, the opinions of the prosecutor or members of the legal staff; situations when a protective order is entered to protect witnesses or evidence; and for protecting the integrity of a continuing investigation. As noted earlier, a prosecutor who does not want to disclose information can make an ex parte showing before a court and explain why.

This type of system presumes that there is no valid purpose served by denying the defendant information that might be used as part of a defense. Would you be willing to go this far? In 1980, the ABA Standards opted for such an "open file" approach to criminal discovery. Standard 11–2.1.

C. MECHANISMS FOR DISCOVERY

The predominant means for discovery in civil cases are depositions and interrogatories. No jurisdiction expressly permits the defense to discover prosecutorial information through interrogatories, and if a Bill of Particulars is requested as a pretext for discovery, it is likely to be denied. Depositions are authorized in criminal cases, although usually they are not permitted as a matter of right at the instance of any party as they are in civil cases. In fact, they usually are limited to preserving testimony. Federal Rule 15 illustrates how restricted the use of depositions may be.

(a) **When Taken.** Whenever due to exceptional circumstances of the case it is in the interest of justice that the testimony of a prospective witness of a party be taken and preserved for use at trial, the court may upon motion of such party and notice to the parties order that testimony of such witness be taken by deposition and that any designated book, paper, document, record, recording, or other material not privileged, be produced at the same time and place.

* * *

Assume that somehow a defendant learns the names of witnesses. There is little that she can do in most jurisdictions to get the witnesses to talk with her or with counsel. It now seems clear that the prosecutor cannot advise the witnesses not to talk with the defendant or with defense counsel. See, e.g., Gregory v. United States, 369 F.2d 185 (D.C.Cir.1966); Annot., 90 ALR 3d 1231 (1979). But many witnesses may want to have nothing to do with the defense. Should there be some mechanism for the defense to find out what the witnesses know? Two possibilities exist. The first is that a preliminary hearing can be made a discovery hearing in part, so that witnesses can be called by the defense. The trouble with this approach is that at the time the hearing is held, the defense may not know what to ask. More importantly, if the defense is not careful, it will preserve the testimony of an unfavorable witness who may become unavailable and the witness' preliminary hearing testimony will be admitted, although the defense really did not effectively examine the witness. Also, early in the case, the defense may not have discovered the identities of all the witnesses. The advantage of this approach is that discovery takes place in one place, at one time, and under the supervision of the court.

The alternative is the one used in civil cases: to allow depositions to be taken for discovery. This is the approach taken by Uniform Rule 431. Do you believe that this rule would threaten legitimate government interests? Would it add substantially to the cost of criminal cases?[17] Does this depend on how many fewer motions and how much less abuse of preliminary hearings and other procedures would result by permitting direct discovery?

In complex cases, computer technology is critical to the success of an investigation and prosecution. The use of computer technology creates significant discovery problems, however. Is the defendant entitled to a relevant report generated by the government? To the data underlying the report? To the computer program? For an interesting discussion of these problems, see Garcia, "Garbage In, Gospel Out": Criminal Discovery, Computer Reliability, and the Constitution, 38 UCLA L.Rev. 1043 (1991). Professor Garcia proposes a broad materiality standard under Rule 16 and concludes that defense counsel should have access to computerized information as well as the "underlying information, programs, computers, manuals, procedures, tests and personnel, in order to protect a client against the use of unreliable information during plea discussions, at pretrial hearings, at trial, and at sentencing."

IV. THE PROSECUTOR'S DUTY TO DISCLOSE

In a series of cases dating back at least to 1935, the Supreme Court has established that even though pre-trial discovery rules generally are matters of local law, rather than constitutionally required rules, the government must disclose certain information to both the defendant and the trial court.

The 1935 decision was Mooney v. Holohan, 294 U.S. 103. The defendant sought habeas corpus relief, claiming "that the sole basis of his conviction was perjured testimony, which was knowingly used by the prosecuting authorities in order to obtain that conviction and also that the prosecution knowingly suppressed evidence that the defense could have used to impeach the perjured testimony. The Court said that the due process clause would be violated if the government engaged in "a deliberate deception of court and jury by the presentation of testimony known to be perjured." Seven years later, in Pyle v. Kansas, 317 U.S. 213 (1942), a habeas petitioner charged the prosecution with knowing use of perjured testimony and the deliberate suppression of evidence favorable to the defense by threats made to witnesses. The Court cited *Mooney* and held that the "allegations * * *, if proven, would entitle petitioner to release from his present custody."

Some time passed before the Court's next major decision on the subject in Napue v. Illinois, 360 U.S. 264 (1959). There the principal government witness

17. Some jurisdictions have adopted the approach and are staying with it. See, e.g., Alaska R.Crim.P. 15(a).

testified that he had received no promises of special consideration in exchange for his testimony. The prosecutor elicited the information from the witness and made no effort to correct it, although he knew the testimony was false. The Court found that the resulting conviction was invalid. A prior case, different on the facts, but similar in its rationale was Alcorta v. Texas, 355 U.S. 28 (1957), cited in *Napue.* The defendant was convicted of first degree murder; a defense claim of "sudden passion" was rejected after a witness named Castelleja answered the prosecutor's questions by saying that he had not kissed the defendant's wife (the victim) on the night of the murder and that he had only a casual relationship with her. Although the witness had previously told the prosecution that he had sexual intercourse with the victim on several occasions, the prosecution did not disclose this. The Supreme Court reversed because the prosecutor knowingly allowed the witness to create a false impression at trial.

In 1963, the Court decided one of its most important disclosure cases, Brady v. Maryland, 373 U.S. 83. Brady and a companion, Boblit, were charged with first degree murder, a capital offense. Brady was tried first; he admitted participation in the crime, but claimed that Boblit did the actual killing. Prior to trial Brady's lawyer asked the prosecutor to allow him to see Boblit's statements. Several statements were shown to counsel, but one in which Boblit admitted the homicide was not revealed. The defense did not learn about it until after Brady's conviction and death sentence were affirmed. Brady's state court post-conviction claim produced a victory in the Maryland Court of Appeals. Since Brady admitted participation, the victory resulted only in a resentencing. The Supreme Court affirmed. It said that "[a] prosecution that withholds evidence on demand of an accused which, if made available, would tend to exculpate him or reduce the penalty helps shape a trial that bears heavily on the defendant. That casts the prosecutor in the role of an architect of a proceeding that does not comport with standards of justice * * *." Justice White concurred, but expressed concern about some of the Court's language. Justice Harlan, joined by Justice Black, dissented and urged a remand to the state courts for a determination of whether Boblit's statement was admissible under state law on the issue of guilt. If so, they would have held that Brady was denied equal protection when his conviction was not reversed.

Next came Giles v. Maryland, 386 U.S. 66 (1967). Two brothers were convicted of rape. The complaining witness testified that the defendants came upon her and a date, demanded money from them and damaged their car; that she fled; and that she was captured and was frightened into submitting to intercourse. The defendants claimed that she offered to have sex with them. Justice Brennan's plurality opinion, joined by Chief Justice Warren and Justice Douglas, supported a remand for reconsideration in light of *Napue,* because there were basic inconsistencies between the testimony of the complaining witness and statements made in a public report that was not part of the record in the state court proceeding. Justice White favored a broader remand to inquire into the possible suppression of evidence concerning the mental condition of the complaining witness. Justice Fortas wanted to reverse, since the prosecution knew of evidence concerning a previous encounter involving the complaining witness and two youths at a party which resulted in a rape charge that was dropped and her attempted suicide.[18] Justice Harlan's dissenting opinion was joined by Justices Black, Clark and Stewart.[19]

In Giglio v. United States, 405 U.S. 150 (1972), the Court found a violation of due process when a key witness testified that he had never been told that he would not be prosecuted as a result of testifying for the government. Promises had been made by a predecessor in the prosecutor's office and the trial attorney for the government did not know it. Still, the Court reversed the conviction; it said that a promise by one attorney would be attributed to the government and suggested that procedures and regulations could be developed to avoid future problems of the *Giglio* type.

Later in the same term the Court divided 5–4 in upholding a defendant's conviction in Moore v. Illinois, 408 U.S. 786 (1972). Justice Blackmun, for the majority, and Justice Marshall, for the dissenters, each wrote lengthy opinions. Much of the dispute turned on different interpretations of the record. The majority opinion is significant because it demonstrates a willingness to read "materiality" under *Brady* as a concept that means something like "very important evidence." It was also significant because the prosecutor utilized a police officer at counsel table during the trial. The officer had his own files, and the dissenters concluded that evidence not turned over to the defense was probably in the officer's files. Although the majority disagreed with the dissenters' conclusion that the statement was not turned over, its opinion also states that "[w]e know of no constitutional requirement that the prosecution make a complete and detailed accounting to the defense of all police investigatory work on a case." The dissenters did not disagree with this assertion, but maintained that "[i]t makes no difference whatever whether the evidence that was suppressed was found in the file of a police officer who directly aided the prosecution or in the file of the prosecutor himself." The majority never indicated its position on this point.

UNITED STATES v. AGURS

Supreme Court of the United States, 1976.
427 U.S. 97.

MR. JUSTICE STEVENS delivered the opinion of the Court.

After a brief interlude in an inexpensive motel room, respondent repeatedly stabbed James Sewell, causing his death. She was convicted of second-degree murder. The question before us is whether the prosecutor's failure to provide defense counsel with certain background information about Sewell, which would have tended to support the argument that respondent

18. The Maryland Court of Appeals assumed that the evidence might have been admissible if known to and offered by the defense at trial, but found it insufficiently exculpatory to warrant a new trial. Justice Fortas disagreed, saying that even if the evidence could not have been admitted, the information might have been helpful to the defense, and that no state interest is served by concealment of information "which is material, generously conceived."

19. Justice Harlan responded to Justice Fortas and argued that the Fortas' view would impose overly broad discovery rules on the state and "alter the character and balance of our present systems of criminal justice."

Justice Fortas replied with an addendum to his opinion in which he cited Brady v. Maryland: "I believe that deliberate concealment and nondisclosure by the state are not to be distinguished in principle from misrepresentation."

acted in self-defense, deprived her of a fair trial under the rule of Brady v. Maryland.

* * *

I

At about 4:30 p.m. on September 24, 1971, respondent, who had been there before, and Sewell, registered in a motel as man and wife. They were assigned a room without a bath. Sewell was wearing a bowie knife in a sheath, and carried another knife in his pocket. Less than two hours earlier, according to the testimony of his estranged wife, he had had $360 in cash on his person.

About 15 minutes later three motel employees heard respondent screaming for help. A forced entry into their room disclosed Sewell on top of respondent struggling for possession of the bowie knife. She was holding the knife; his bleeding hand grasped the blade; according to one witness he was trying to jam the blade into her chest. The employees separated the two and summoned the authorities. Respondent departed without comment before they arrived. Sewell was dead on arrival at the hospital.

Circumstantial evidence indicated that the parties had completed an act of intercourse, that Sewell had then gone to the bathroom down the hall, and that the struggle occurred upon his return. The contents of his pockets were in disarray on the dresser and no money was found; the jury may have inferred that respondent took Sewell's money and that the fight started when Sewell re-entered the room and saw what she was doing.

On the following morning respondent surrendered to the police. She was given a physical examination which revealed no cuts or bruises of any kind, except needle marks on her upper arm. An autopsy of Sewell disclosed that he had several deep stab wounds in his chest and abdomen, and a number of slashes on his arms and hands, characterized by the pathologist as "defensive wounds."

Respondent offered no evidence. Her sole defense was the argument made by her attorney that Sewell had initially attacked her with the knife, and that her actions had all been directed toward saving her own life. The support for this self-defense theory was based on the fact that she had screamed for help. Sewell was on top of her when help arrived, and his possession of two knives indicated that he was a violence-prone person. It took the jury about 25 minutes to elect a foreman and return a verdict.

Three months later defense counsel filed a motion for a new trial asserting that he had discovered (1) that Sewell had a prior criminal record that would have further evidenced his violent character; (2) that the prosecutor had failed to disclose this information to the defense; and (3) that a recent opinion of the United States Court of Appeals for the District of Columbia Circuit made it clear that such evidence was admissible even if not known to the defendant. Sewell's prior record included a plea of guilty to a charge of assault and carrying a deadly weapon in 1963, and another guilty plea to a charge of carrying a deadly weapon in 1971. Apparently both weapons were knives.

The Government opposed the motion, arguing that there was no duty to tender Sewell's prior record to the defense in the absence of an appropriate request; that the evidence was readily discoverable in advance of trial and hence was not the kind of "newly discovered" evidence justifying a new trial; and that, in all events, it was not material.

The District Court denied the motion. * * *

The Court of Appeals reversed. The court found no lack of diligence on the part of the defense and no misconduct by the prosecutor in this case. It held, however, that the evidence was material, and that its nondisclosure required a new trial because the jury might have returned a different verdict if the evidence had been received.

The decision of the Court of Appeals represents a significant departure from this Court's prior holding; because we believe that that court has incorrectly interpreted the constitutional requirement of due process, we reverse.

II

The rule of Brady v. Maryland, arguably applies in three quite different situations. Each involves the discovery, after trial, of information which had been known to the prosecution but unknown to the defense.

In the first situation, typified by Mooney v. Holohan, the undisclosed evidence demonstrates that the prosecution's case includes perjured testimony and that the prosecution knew, or should have known, of the perjury.[20] In a series of subsequent cases, the Court has consistently held that a conviction obtained by the knowing use of perjured testimony is fundamentally unfair, and must be set aside if there is any reasonable likelihood that the false testimony could have affected the judgment of the jury.[21] It is this line of cases on which the Court of Appeals placed primary reliance. In those cases the Court has applied a strict standard of materiality, not just because they involve prosecutorial misconduct, but more importantly because they involve a corruption of the truth-seeking function of the trial process. Since this case involves no misconduct, and since there is no reason to question the veracity of any of the prosecution witnesses, the test of materiality followed in the *Mooney* line of cases is not necessarily applicable to this case.

The second situation, illustrated by the *Brady* case itself, is characterized by a pretrial request for specific evidence. In that case defense counsel had requested the extrajudicial statements made by Brady's accomplice, one Boblit. This Court held that the suppression of one of Boblit's statements deprived Brady of due process, noting specifically that the statement had been requested and that it was "material." A fair analysis of the holding in *Brady* indicates that implicit in the requirement of materiality is a concern that the suppressed evidence might have affected the outcome of the trial.

* * *

The test of materiality in a case like *Brady* in which specific information has been requested by the defense is not necessarily the same as in a case in which no such request has been made. Indeed, this Court has not yet decided whether the prosecutor has any obligation to provide defense counsel with exculpatory information when no request has been made. Before addressing that question, a brief comment on the function of the request is appropriate.

In *Brady* the request was specific. It gave the prosecutor notice of exactly

20. In the case of knowing use of perjured testimony, reversal of the conviction will be the only remedy available, since the Supreme Court has held that prosecutors have absolute immunity, Imbler v. Pachtman, 424 U.S. 409 (1976), and that police officers also have absolute immunity against claims that they perjured themselves when called to testify. Briscoe v. LaHue, 460 U.S. 325 (1983).

21. The Court held in Weatherford v. Bursey, 429 U.S. 545 (1977), that the due process clause was not violated when a government agent concealed from the defendant his true identity and denied up to the day of trial that he would testify against the defendant. At trial, there was no misrepresentation of fact.

what the defense desired. Although there is, of course, no duty to provide defense counsel with unlimited discovery of everything known by the prosecutor, if the subject matter of such a request is material, or indeed if a substantial basis for claiming materiality exists, it is reasonable to require the prosecutor to respond either by furnishing the information or by submitting the problem to the trial judge. When the prosecutor receives a specific and relevant request, the failure to make any response is seldom, if ever, excusable.

In many cases, however, exculpatory information in the possession of the prosecutor may be unknown to defense counsel. In such a situation he may make no request at all, or possibly ask for "all *Brady* material" or for "anything exculpatory." Such a request really gives the prosecutor no better notice than if no request is made. If there is a duty to respond to a general request of that kind, it must derive from the obviously exculpatory character of certain evidence in the hands of the prosecutor. But if the evidence is so clearly supportive of a claim of innocence that it gives the prosecution notice of a duty to produce, that duty should equally arise even if no request is made. Whether we focus on the desirability of a precise definition of the prosecutor's duty or on the potential harm to the defendant, we conclude that there is no significant difference between cases in which there has been merely a general request for exculpatory matter and cases, like the one we must now decide, in which there has been no request at all. The third situation in which the *Brady* rule arguably applies, typified by this case, therefore embraces the case in which only a general request for "*Brady* material" has been made.

We now consider whether the prosecutor has any constitutional duty to volunteer exculpatory matter to the defense, and if so, what standard of materiality gives rise to that duty.

III

We are not considering the scope of discovery authorized by the Federal Rules of Criminal Procedure, or the wisdom of amending those Rules to enlarge the defendant's discovery rights. We are dealing with the defendant's right to a fair trial mandated by the Due Process Clause of the Fifth Amendment to the Constitution. Our construction of that Clause will apply equally to the comparable clause in the Fourteenth Amendment applicable to trials in state courts.

* * *

The Court of Appeals appears to have assumed that the prosecutor has a constitutional obligation to disclose any information that might affect the jury's verdict. That statement of a constitutional standard of materiality approaches the "sporting theory of justice" which the Court expressly rejected in *Brady.* For a jury's appraisal of a case "might" be affected by an improper or trivial consideration as well as by evidence giving rise to a legitimate doubt on the issue of guilt. If everything that might influence a jury must be disclosed, the only way a prosecutor could discharge his constitutional duty would be to allow complete discovery of his files as a matter of routine practice.

Whether or not procedural rules authorizing such broad discovery might be desirable, the Constitution surely does not demand that much. * * * The mere possibility that an item of undisclosed information might have helped the defense, or might have affected the outcome of the trial, does not establish "materiality" in the constitutional sense.

Nor do we believe the constitutional obligation is measured by the moral culpability, or the willfulness, of the prosecutor. If evidence highly probative of innocence is in his file, he should be presumed to recognize its significance even if he has actually overlooked it. Cf. Giglio v. United States. Conversely, if evidence actually has no probative significance at all, no purpose would be served by requiring a new trial simply because an inept prosecutor incorrectly believed he was suppressing a fact that would be vital to the defense. If the suppression of evidence results in constitutional error, it is because of the character of the evidence, not the character of the prosecutor.

As the District Court recognized in this case, there are situations in which evidence is obviously of such substantial value to the defense that elementary fairness requires it to be disclosed even without a specific request. For though the attorney for the sovereign must prosecute the accused with earnestness and vigor, he must always be faithful to his client's overriding interest that "justice shall be done." He is the "servant of the law, the twofold aim of which is that guilt shall not escape or innocence suffer." Berger v. United States, 295 U.S. 78, 88. This description of the prosecutor's duty illuminates the standard of materiality that governs his obligation to disclose exculpatory evidence.

* * *

The proper standard of materiality must reflect our overriding concern with the justice of the finding of guilt.[a] Such a finding is permissible only if supported by evidence establishing guilt beyond a reasonable doubt. It necessarily follows that if the omitted evidence creates a reasonable doubt that did not otherwise exist, constitutional error has been committed. This means that the omission must be evaluated in the context of the entire record. If there is no reasonable doubt about guilt whether or not the additional evidence is considered, there is no justification for a new trial. On the other hand, if the verdict is already of questionable validity, additional evidence of relatively minor importance might be sufficient to create a reasonable doubt.

This statement of the standard of materiality describes the test which courts appear to have applied in actual cases although the standard has been phrased in different language. It is also the standard which the trial judge applied in this case. He evaluated the significance of Sewell's prior criminal record in the context of the full trial which he recalled in detail. Stressing in particular the incongruity of a claim that Sewell was the aggressor with the evidence of his multiple wounds and respondent's unscathed condition, the trial judge indicated his unqualified opinion that respondent was guilty. He noted that Sewell's prior record did not contradict any evidence offered by the prosecutor, and was largely cumulative of the evidence that Sewell was wearing a bowie knife in a sheath and carrying a second knife in his pocket when he registered at the motel.

Since the arrest record was not requested and did not even arguably give rise to any inference of perjury, since

a. It has been argued that the standard should focus on the impact of the undisclosed evidence on the defendant's ability to prepare for trial, rather than the materiality of the evidence to the issue of guilt or innocence. See Note, The Prosecutor's Constitutional Duty to Reveal Evidence to the Defense, 74 Yale L.J. 136 (1964). Such a standard would be unacceptable for determining the materiality of what has been generally recognized as "*Brady* material" for two reasons. First, that standard would necessarily encompass incriminating evidence as well as exculpatory evidence, since knowledge of the prosecutor's entire case would always be useful in planning the defense. Second, such an approach would primarily involve an analysis of the adequacy of the notice given to the defendant by the State, and it has always been the Court's view that the notice component of due process refers to the charge rather than the evidentiary support for the charge.

after considering it in the context of the entire record the trial judge remained convinced of respondent's guilt beyond a reasonable doubt, and since we are satisfied that his firsthand appraisal of the record was thorough and entirely reasonable, we hold that the prosecutor's failure to tender Sewell's record to the defense did not deprive respondent of a fair trial as guaranteed by the Due Process Clause of the Fifth Amendment. * * *

MR. JUSTICE MARSHALL with whom MR. JUSTICE BRENNAN joins, dissenting.

The Court today holds that the prosecutor's constitutional duty to provide exculpatory evidence to the defense is not limited to cases in which the defense makes a request for such evidence. But once having recognized the existence of a duty to volunteer exculpatory evidence, the Court so narrowly defines the category of "material" evidence embraced by the duty as to deprive it of all meaningful content.

* * *

Under today's ruling, if the prosecution has not made knowing use of perjury, and if the defense has not made a specific request for an item of information, the defendant is entitled to a new trial only if the withheld evidence actually creates a reasonable doubt as to guilt in the judge's mind. With all respect, this rule is completely at odds with the overriding interest in assuring that evidence tending to show innocence is brought to the jury's attention. The rule creates little, if any, incentive for the prosecutor conscientiously to determine whether his files contain evidence helpful to the defense. Indeed, the rule reinforces the natural tendency of the prosecutor to overlook evidence favorable to the defense, and creates an incentive for the prosecutor to resolve close questions of disclosure in favor of concealment.

More fundamentally, the Court's rule usurps the function of the jury as the trier of fact in a criminal case. The Court's rule explicitly establishes the judge as the trier of fact with respect to evidence withheld by the prosecution. The defendant's fate is sealed so long as the evidence does not create a reasonable doubt as to guilt in the judge's mind, regardless of whether the evidence is such that reasonable men could disagree as to its import—regardless, in other words, of how "close" the case may be.

* * * I would hold that the defendant in this case had the burden of demonstrating that there is a significant chance that the withheld evidence, developed by skilled counsel, would have induced a reasonable doubt in the minds of enough jurors to avoid a conviction. * * *

Note

Justice Blackmun wrote for the Court in United States v. Bagley, 473 U.S. 667 (1985), as the Court declined to overturn a conviction because of nondisclosure of exculpatory evidence. Bagley was charged with narcotics and firearms offenses and convicted in a bench trial only on the narcotics charges. Thereafter he learned that, despite his motion to discover any deals or promises between the government and its witnesses, the government had not disclosed that its two principal witnesses had signed contracts with the Bureau of Alcohol, Tobacco and Firearms to be paid for their undercover work. Although the trial judge ruled that the contracts would not have affected the outcome because the principal witnesses testified primarily concerning the firearms charges on which Bagley was acquitted, the court of appeals disagreed. The Supreme Court agreed with the trial judge and found that nondisclosure of impeachment evidence, like nondisclosure of other exculpatory evidence, requires reversal only if the evidence was material in the sense that it might have affected the outcome of the trial.

Justice Blackmun's opinion set forth a single "standard of materiality" applicable to nondisclosed exculpatory evidence. Justice Blackmun borrowed from the Court's ineffective assistance of counsel cases and derived the following standard: "[E]vidence is material only if there is a reasonable probability that, had the evidence been disclosed to the defense, the result of the proceeding would have been different. A 'reasonable probability' is a probability sufficient to undermine confidence in the outcome." Justice Blackmun noted that this test was "sufficiently flexible" to cover no request, general request, and specific request cases. In a part of the opinion joined only by Justice O'Connor, Justice Blackmun reasoned that "the more specifically the defense requests certain evidence . . . the more reasonable it is for the defense to assume from the nondisclosure that the evidence does not exist and to make pretrial and trial decisions on the basis of this assumption." Thus, specific request cases present special considerations in applying the single "reasonable probability" standard of materiality. Justice White, joined by the Chief Justice and Justice Rehnquist, concurred in the judgment. Although he expressed agreement with the single materiality standard developed by Justice Blackmun, he saw "no reason to attempt to elaborate on the relevance to the inquiry of the specificity of the defense's request for disclosure."

Justice Marshall, joined by Justice Brennan, dissented and argued that "[W]hen the Government withholds from a defendant evidence that might impeach the prosecution's *only witnesses,* that failure to disclose cannot be deemed harmless error." Justice Stevens, who authored *Agurs,* also dissented. He argued that, unlike *Agurs,* the instant case involved a specific request and that *Brady* requires reversal for failure to disclose evidence favorable to an accused upon a specific request if the evidence is material either to guilt or punishment. Thus, he would have remanded for a determination of whether there is "any reasonable likelihood" that the nondisclosure could have affected the judgment of the trier of fact.

Professor Stacy, in The Search for the Truth in Constitutional Criminal Procedure, 91 Colum.L.Rev. 1369, 1392 (1991), has this to say about the *Bagley* standard of materiality:

> The *Bagley* standard, which focuses on the likely impact of evidence on the ultimate result in the case, suffers from two interrelated deficiencies. The first problem is that the standard will frequently be misapplied. A prosecutor's lack of information about the planned defense and partisan inclinations impede her from making an accurate and objective assessment of the evidence's effect on the outcome. The second problem is that many misapplications of the *Bagley* standard will never be detected and remedied. Because the prosecution has exclusive possession of the evidence subject to the duty to disclose and a clear incentive to withhold it, the defense or a court will sometimes never learn of evidence wrongly withheld.
>
> In short, the Court has interpreted the prosecution's duty to disclose exculpatory evidence more narrowly than a true concern for accurate factfinding implies. For a Court genuinely interested in the search for the truth, neither the adversarial system, prosecutorial burdens, nor the constitutional text can justify the *Bagley* standard, which will result in important exculpatory evidence not being disclosed in a significant number of cases.

While the combination of the Blackmun and White opinions in *Bagley* produce a single standard of materiality for all nondisclosure cases, *Bagley* leaves ambiguity about the relevance of a specific defense request for the evidence. In *Agurs,* Justice

Stevens emphasized that the specific request increased the level of prosecutorial responsibility. In *Bagley,* Justice Blackmun emphasized the greater prejudicial impact of a denied specific request due to the possibility that defense counsel will be misled. Justice White thought it appropriate to leave the precise impact of a specific request for another day. Where a case involves a specific request, lower courts after *Bagley* have continued to take account of that factor, although not always stating why it is significant. See e.g. Jean v. Rice, 945 F.2d 82 (4th Cir.1991) (recordings and reports indicating that the prosecution's star witness had been hypnotized were *Brady* material: "We are persuaded that the audio recordings and accompanying reports—twice requested—should have been disclosed to defense counsel"). As the Fifth Circuit stated in Lindsey v. King, 769 F.2d 1034 (5th Cir.1985): "Viewing the [*Bagley*] opinions as a whole, it is fair to say that all the participating Justices agreed on one thing at least: that reversal for suppression of evidence by the government is most likely where the request for it was specific."

Dispute has arisen about whether exculpatory evidence is *Brady* material if it would be inadmissible at trial. Given the *Agurs* focus on the substantive exculpatory nature of the nondisclosed material itself, some courts have held that the prosecution's duty to disclose is limited to information which would be admissible as evidence. Other courts have held that the crucial question is whether the material would be likely to lead to admissible evidence as an end-product; if so, the prosecutor has a duty to disclose it. See the discussion in the majority and dissenting opinions in United States v. Phillip, 948 F.2d 241 (6th Cir.1991). The issue was whether a videotaped statement was *Brady* material. The majority stated that "the issue of materiality for *Brady* purposes pertains only to the question of a defendant's guilt or innocence, not to the issue of a defendant's inability to prepare for trial." The majority held that the tape was not *Brady* material because the exculpatory statements on the tape were "inadmissible hearsay" and that the statements were not admissible for impeachment purposes because the witness did not testify at the trial. In dissent, Chief Judge Merritt argued that limiting *Brady* protection to admissible evidence would mean that "a deposition given by the perpetrator or an eyewitness exonerating the defendant could be concealed because it is hearsay."

As a prosecutor, would you now be entitled to knowingly fail to turn over evidence that appears to be exculpatory but not sufficiently so to require a new trial under *Bagley* and *Agurs?* Should prosecutors be trusted with this responsibility? Would an opinion that held the prosecutor to a standard of turning over all evidence that reasonable persons would conclude might tend to exculpate the defendant be unacceptable?[22]

22. *Brady* claims usually are raised by defendants who went to trial. But Ex parte Lewis, 587 S.W.2d 697 (Tex.Cr.App.1979), holds that a prosecutor must meet a *Brady* obligation to one who pleads guilty. How far would you go in requiring a prosecutor to reveal exculpatory evidence to a defendant who is willing to admit that he committed the crime? For a strong argument that *Brady* disclosure is required for the factual accuracy in the guilty plea process, see McMunigal, Disclosure and Accuracy in the Guilty Plea Process, 40 Hastings L.J. 957 (1989).

Note that the *Brady* obligation falls upon prosecutors. For an interesting clash of views on the trial judge's duty to provide the defense with *Brady* type material, compare the district judge's opinion in United States v. Cuthbertson, 511 F.Supp. 375 (D.N.J.), with that of the court of appeals which reversed him, 651 F.2d 189 (3d Cir.1981).

Note also that it is not clear exactly when *Brady* material must be disclosed. United States v. Thevis, 84 F.R.D. 47 (N.D.Ga.1979), ordered early disclosure of *Brady* material, although the court noted that pretrial disclosure is not constitutionally compelled in every case. But see United States v. Algie, 503 F.Supp. 783 (E.D.Ky.1980), rev'd 667 F.2d 569 (6th Cir. 1982), where the prosecutor refused to comply with an early disclosure order, took

Justice Marshall wrote for a unanimous Supreme Court in California v. Trombetta, 467 U.S. 479 (1984). The Court held that law enforcement officers are not required by the due process clause to preserve breath samples of suspected drunk drivers in order for the results of the tests to be admissible. A device called an Intoxilyzer was used to test these samples. Suspects, including those challenging the police procedures in the instant case, breathed into the device and infrared light sensed their blood alcohol level. California officers purge the device after each test, thus destroying the breath samples. Although the state health department had approved a kit which officers could use to preserve breath samples, it was not standard practice for officers to use the kit. In his opinion, Justice Marshall noted that the Court had never squarely addressed whether the government has a duty to take affirmative steps to preserve evidence. One precedent, Killian v. United States, 368 U.S. 231 (1961) (finding no due process violation where FBI agents destroyed preliminary notes they used to make a report), supported the conclusion that "[w]hatever duty the Constitution imposes on the States to preserve evidence, that duty must be limited to evidence that might be expected to play a significant role in the suspect's defense." The Court found that the chances were extremely low that preserved samples would have assisted defendants, that the state had developed procedures to protect against machine malfunctions, and that some alternative attacks were possible when defendant raised one of the limited number of claims available to challenge the functioning of a testing machine. In a footnote, Justice Marshall indicated that in finding the state's procedures to be fair, the Court was not relying on the fact that the state provided an option for persons stopped for suspected drunk driving to elect a urine or blood test rather than to be tested by an Intoxilyzer and to have a second blood alcohol test conducted by independent experts. Since no notice of these options was provided to persons who were stopped, the Court found that they were irrelevant to a determination of whether the state acted unfairly in not requiring preservation of breath samples.

Chief Justice Rehnquist wrote for the Court in Arizona v. Youngblood, 488 U.S. 51 (1988), as it expanded *Trombetta* and held that "unless a criminal defendant can show bad faith on the part of the police, failure to preserve potentially useful evidence does not constitute a denial of due process of law." Youngblood was convicted of sexually assaulting a young boy. Although investigative authorities attempted to analyze semen obtained from the victim's person, they did not refrigerate the victim's clothing and were unable at a later date to test the semen found on the clothing. The Supreme Court found that the failure to preserve the evidence for testing was, at worst, negligent. The Chief Justice noted that there was no evidence that the police had any reason to believe that the semen samples might have exonerated the accused when they handled the clothing or of any bad faith on the part of the police.

Chief Justice Rehnquist recognized that the *Brady* cases made the good or bad faith of the police irrelevant when material exculpatory evidence is suppressed, but he concluded that "the Due Process Clause requires a different result when we deal with the failure of the State to preserve evidentiary material of which no more can be said than that it could have been subjected to tests, the results of which might have exonerated the defendant." He reasoned "that requiring a defendant to show bad faith on the part of the police both limits the extent of the police's obligation to preserve evidence to reasonable bounds and confines it to that class of cases where the interests of justice most clearly require it, i.e., those cases in which the police

an interlocutory appeal, and succeeded in reversing the trial judge.

themselves by their conduct indicate that the evidence could form a basis for exonerating the defendant."

The Chief Justice commented on language in the state appellate court's opinion, which indicated that newer tests could not be performed on the clothing as follows: "If the court meant * * * that the Due Process Clause is violated when the police fail to use a particular investigatory tool, we strongly disagree. The situation here is no different than [sic] a prosecution for drunk driving that rests on police observation alone; the defendant is free to argue to the finder of fact that a breathalizer test might have been exculpatory, but the police do not have a constitutional duty to perform any particular tests."

Justice Stevens, concurring in the judgment, agreed that the state has a strong incentive to preserve evidence that might enable it to prove guilt and noted that the defendant may argue to the jury the significance of the failure to preserve evidence. He declined to join the majority opinion, however, because he believed "there may well be cases in which the defendant is unable to prove that the State acted in bad faith but in which the loss or destruction of evidence is nonetheless so critical to the defense as to make a criminal trial fundamentally unfair."

Justice Blackmun, joined by Justices Brennan and Marshall, dissented. He argued that Youngblood may have been denied the opportunity to put on a full defense merely by "police ineptitude," but that such ineptitude denied him due process. Justice Blackmun argued against imposing a showing of bad faith upon a defendant and in favor of focusing on whether the state permitted evidence material to the defense to deteriorate. He suggested that the bad faith test was less than clear and might create more questions than it answers.

Reviewing *Trombetta,* Justice Blackmun concluded that the discarded evidence would have been of little value to the accused and at best could have been used to impeach the test results relied upon by the government. The potential value of the semen evidence to Youngblood was much greater, since it possibly would have provided complete exoneration. Thus, Justice Blackmun stated his due process test as follows: "[W]here no comparable evidence is likely to be available to the defendant, police must preserve physical evidence of a type that they reasonably should know has the potential, if tested, to reveal immutable characteristics of the criminal, and hence to exculpate a defendant charged with the crime." He briefly commented that "[t]here is no need in this case to discuss whether the police have a duty to test evidence, or whether due process requires that police testing be on the 'cutting edge' of technology."

The Supreme Court struggled in Pennsylvania v. Ritchie, 480 U.S. 39 (1987), to balance a defendant's need for discovery of information that might assist in confrontation of critical witnesses and protection of children who might be victims of child abuse. Ritchie was charged with rape and other sexual offenses; the alleged victim was his daughter. Prior to trial, Ritchie sought disclosure of the file maintained by the state protective service agency relating to his prosecution and the agency's records regarding a separate report that Ritchie's children were being abused. A state statute provided that all reports and information obtained in the agency's investigations must be kept confidential. The statute recognized exceptions, however. One exception permitted the agency to disclose information to a court of competent jurisdiction pursuant to a court order. The trial judge denied Ritchie's motions to compel discovery of the agency's records. His daughter was the principal witness against him. The jury believed her testimony and convicted Ritchie on all charges. The state supreme court found that Ritchie's Sixth

Amendment rights had been violated and ordered a remand so that Ritchie's lawyer could examine all of the agency's records.

Justice Powell wrote for the Supreme Court as it held that the Confrontation Clause is not a "constitutionally-compelled rule of pretrial discovery." The Court found no violation of Ritchie's confrontation right, since he was permitted to cross-examine his daughter at trial. It declined to decide whether the Compulsory Process Clause guarantees some pretrial discovery, relying instead on the Due Process Clause and stating that "[a]lthough we conclude that compulsory process provides no *greater* protections in this area than those afforded by Due Process, we need not decide today whether and how the guarantees of the Compulsory Process Clause differ from those of the Fourteenth Amendment."

Applying due process principles, the Court affirmed the decision to remand the case to the trial court and stated that Ritchie is entitled to have the agency's records reviewed by the trial court "to determine whether it contains information that probably would have changed the outcome of his trial." It disagreed, however, with the state supreme court's decision to require disclosure of the records to defense counsel. Justice Powell wrote "that Ritchie's interest (as well as that of the Commonwealth) in ensuring a fair trial can be protected fully by requiring that the [agency's] files be submitted only to the trial court for *in camera* review," and that "[t]o allow full disclosure to defense counsel in this type of case would sacrifice unnecessarily the Commonwealth's compelling interest in protecting its child abuse information."

Justice Blackmun concurred in part and in the judgment, writing separately to state his view that "there might well be a confrontation violation, if, as here, a defendant is denied pretrial access to information that would make possible effective cross-examination of a crucial prosecution witness." He indicated that he was in substantial agreement with Justice Brennan that the Confrontation Clause was not limited to assuring cross-examination at trial, and that the Clause required an examination of the effectiveness of cross-examination.

Justice Brennan, joined by Justice Marshall, dissented, and argued that "the right of cross-examination also may be significantly infringed by events occurring outside the trial itself, such as the wholesale denial of access to material that would serve as the basis for a significant line of inquiry at trial." Although he approved the trial court's conclusion that Ritchie's vague speculations that the records might be helpful were insufficient to warrant general access to the records, Justice Brennan concluded that "in denying access to the prior statements of the victim the court deprived Ritchie of material crucial to any effort to impeach the victim at trial."

Justice Stevens, joined by Justices Brennan, Marshall and Scalia, filed a separate dissent arguing that the decision below was not a final judgment and was not reviewable.

Capra, Access to Exculpatory Evidence: Avoiding the Agurs Problems of Prosecutorial Discretion and Retrospective Review, 53 Ford.L.Rev. 391 (1984), argues that a per se right to an in camera hearing at which the court would examine a prosecutor's files for *Brady* material would be more effective than retrospective review of claims that exculpatory evidence was suppressed.

V. DISCOVERY BY THE PROSECUTION

A. DISCLOSURE OF DEFENSE BEFORE TRIAL

Any attempt to force defendants to comply with government discovery requests runs into Fifth Amendment concerns. The next case disposes of some of these.

1. *Alibi Defense*

WILLIAMS v. FLORIDA

Supreme Court of the United States, 1970.
399 U.S. 78.

MR. JUSTICE WHITE delivered the opinion of the Court.

Prior to his trial for robbery in the State of Florida, petitioner filed a "Motion for a Protective Order," seeking to be excused from the requirements of Rule 1.200 of the Florida Rules of Criminal Procedure. That rule required a defendant, on written demand of the prosecuting attorney, to give notice in advance of trial if the defendant intends to claim an alibi, and to furnish the prosecuting attorney with information as to the place where he claims to have been and with the names and addresses of the alibi witnesses he intends to use. In his motion petitioner openly declared his intent to claim an alibi, but objected to the further disclosure requirements on the ground that the rule "compels the Defendant in a criminal case to be a witness against himself" in violation of his Fifth and Fourteenth Amendment rights. The motion was denied. * * * [The other aspect of the case involved a challenge to the six man jury provided by Florida. It also was unsuccessful. The jury issue is discussed in Chapter Ten]. Petitioner was convicted as charged and was sentenced to life imprisonment. * * *

I

Florida's notice-of-alibi rule is in essence a requirement that a defendant submit to a limited form of pretrial discovery by the State whenever he intends to rely at trial on the defense of alibi. In exchange for the defendant's disclosure of the witnesses he proposes to use to establish that defense, the State in turn is required to notify the defendant of any witnesses it proposes to offer in rebuttal to that defense. Both sides are under a continuing duty promptly to disclose the names and addresses of additional witnesses bearing on the alibi as they become available. The threatened sanction for failure to comply is the exclusion at trial of the defendant's alibi evidence—except for his own testimony—or, in the case of the State, the exclusion of the State's evidence offered in rebuttal of the alibi.

In this case, following the denial of his Motion for a Protective Order, petitioner complied with the alibi rule and gave the State the name and address of one Mary Scotty. Mrs. Scotty was summoned to the office of the State Attorney on the morning of the trial, where she gave pretrial testimony. At the trial itself, Mrs. Scotty, petitioner, and petitioner's wife all testified that the three of them had been in Mrs. Scotty's apartment during the time of the robbery. On two occasions during cross-examination of Mrs. Scotty, the prosecuting attorney confronted her with her earlier deposition in which she had given dates and times that in some respects did not correspond with the dates and times given at trial. Mrs. Scotty adhered to her trial story, insisting that she had been mistaken in her earlier testimony. The State also offered in rebuttal the testimony of one of the officers investigating the robbery who claimed that Mrs. Scotty had asked him for directions on the afternoon in question during the time when she claimed to have been in her apartment with petitioner and his wife.

We need not linger over the suggestion that the discovery permitted the State against petitioner in this case deprived him of "due process" or a "fair trial." Florida law provides for liberal discovery by the defendant against the State, and the notice-of-alibi rule is itself carefully hedged with reciprocal duties requiring state disclosure to the defendant. Given the ease with which an alibi can be fabricated, the State's interest in protecting itself against an eleventh-hour defense is both obvious and legitimate. Reflecting this interest, notice-of-alibi provisions, dating at least from 1927, are now in existence in a substantial number of States.[a] The adversary system of trial is hardly an end in itself; it is not yet a poker game in which players enjoy an absolute right always to conceal their cards until played. We find ample room in that system, at least as far as "due process" is concerned, for the instant Florida rule, which is designed to enhance the search for truth in the criminal trial by insuring both the defendant and the State ample opportunity to investigate certain facts crucial to the determination of guilt or innocence.

Petitioner's major contention is that he was "compelled * * * to be a witness against himself" contrary to the commands of the Fifth and Fourteenth Amendments because the notice-of-alibi rule required him to give the State the name and address of Mrs. Scotty in advance of trial and thus to furnish the State with information useful in convicting him. No pretrial statement of petitioner was introduced at trial; but armed with Mrs. Scotty's name and address and the knowledge that she was to be petitioner's alibi witness, the State was able to take her deposition in advance of trial and to find rebuttal testimony. Also, requiring him to reveal the elements of his defense is claimed to have interfered with his right to wait until after the State had presented its case to decide how to defend against it. We conclude, however, as has apparently every other court that has considered the issue, that the privilege against self-incrimination is not violated by a requirement that the defendant give notice of an alibi defense and disclose his alibi witnesses.[b]

The defendant in a criminal trial is frequently forced to testify himself and to call other witnesses in an effort to reduce the risk of conviction. When he presents his witnesses, he must reveal their identity and submit them to cross-examination which in itself may prove incriminating or which may furnish the State with leads to incriminating rebuttal evidence. That the defendant faces such a dilemma demanding a choice between complete silence and presenting a defense has never been thought

a. In addition to Florida, at least 15 States appear to have alibi-notice requirements of one sort or another. * * * [See also Fed. R.Crim.P. 12.1.]

We do not, of course, decide that each of these alibi-notice provisions is necessarily valid in all respects; that conclusion must await a specific context and an inquiry, for example, into whether the defendant enjoys reciprocal discovery against the State.

b. We emphasize that this case does not involve the question of the validity of the threatened sanction, had petitioner chosen not to comply with the notice-of-alibi rule. Whether and to what extent a State can enforce discovery rules against a defendant who fails to comply, by excluding relevant, probative evidence is a question raising Sixth Amendment issues which we have no occasion to explore. It is enough that no such penalty was exacted here.

an invasion of the privilege against compelled self-incrimination. The pressures generated by the State's evidence may be severe but they do not vitiate the defendant's choice to present an alibi defense and witnesses to prove it, even though the attempted defense ends in catastrophe for the defendant. However, "testimonial" or "incriminating" the alibi defense proves to be, it cannot be considered "compelled" within the meaning of the Fifth and Fourteenth Amendments.

Very similar constraints operate on the defendant when the State requires pretrial notice of alibi and the naming of alibi witnesses. Nothing in such a rule requires the defendant to rely on an alibi or prevents him from abandoning the defense; these matters are left to his unfettered choice.[c] That choice must be made, but the pressures that bear on his pretrial decision are of the same nature as those that would induce him to call alibi witnesses at the trial: the force of historical fact beyond both his and the State's control and the strength of the State's case built on these facts. Response to that kind of pressure by offering evidence or testimony is not compelled self-incrimination transgressing the Fifth and Fourteenth Amendments.

* * *

Petitioner concedes that absent the notice-of-alibi rule the Constitution would raise no bar to the court's granting the State a continuance at trial on the ground of surprise as soon as the alibi witness is called. Nor would there be self-incrimination problems if, during that continuance, the State was permitted to do precisely what it did here prior to trial: take the deposition of the witness and find rebuttal evidence. But if so utilizing a continuance is permissible under the Fifth and Fourteenth Amendments, then surely the same result may be accomplished through pretrial discovery, as it was here, avoiding the necessity of a disrupted trial.[d] We decline to hold that the privilege against compulsory self-incrimination guarantees the defendant the right to surprise the State with an alibi defense.

* * *

[Justice Blackmun did not participate in the case. The Chief Justice filed a short concurring opinion on the alibi point. Justice Marshall dissented on the jury issue, but concurred in the alibi ruling.]

MR. JUSTICE BLACK, with whom MR. JUSTICE DOUGLAS joins, concurring in part and dissenting in part.

* * *

c. Petitioner's apparent suggestion to the contrary is simply not borne out by the facts of this case. The mere requirement that petitioner disclose in advance his intent to rely on an alibi in no way "fixed" his defense as of that point in time. The suggestion that the State, by referring to petitioner's proposed alibi in opening or closing statements might have "compelled" him to follow through with the defense in order to avoid an unfavorable inference is a hypothetical totally without support in this record. The first reference to the alibi came from petitioner's own attorney in his opening remarks; the State's response did not come until after the defense had finished direct examination of Mrs. Scotty. Petitioner appears to raise this issue as a possible defect in alibi-notice requirements in general, without seriously suggesting that his choice of defense at trial in this case would have been different but for his prior compliance with the rule. Indeed, in his Motion for a Protective Order, petitioner freely disclosed his intent to rely on an alibi; his only objection was to the further requirement that he disclose the nature of the alibi and the name of the witness. On these facts, then, we simply are not confronted with the question of whether a defendant can be compelled in advance of trial to select a defense from which he can no longer deviate. We do not mean to suggest, though, that such a procedure must necessarily raise serious constitutional problems. * * *

d. It might also be argued that the "testimonial" disclosures protected by the Fifth Amendment include only statements relating to the historical facts of the crime, not statements relating solely to what a defendant proposes to do at trial.

I

The core of the majority's decision is an assumption that compelling a defendant to give notice of an alibi defense before a trial is no different from requiring a defendant, after the State has produced the evidence against him at trial, to plead alibi before the jury retires to consider the case. This assumption is clearly revealed by the statement that "the pressures that bear on [a defendant's] pretrial decision are of the same nature as those that would induce him to call alibi witnesses at the trial: the force of historical fact beyond both his and the State's control and the strength of the State's case built on these facts." That statement is plainly and simply wrong as a matter of fact and law, and the Court's holding based on that statement is a complete misunderstanding of the protections provided for criminal defendants by the Fifth Amendment and other provisions of the Bill of Rights.

A

When a defendant is required to indicate whether he might plead alibi in advance of trial, he faces a vastly different decision from that faced by one who can wait until the State has presented the case against him before making up his mind. Before trial the defendant knows only what the State's case *might* be. Before trial there is no such thing as the "strength of the State's case"; there is only a range of possible cases. At that time there is no certainty as to what kind of case the State will ultimately be able to prove at trial. Therefore any appraisal of the desirability of pleading alibi will be beset with guesswork and gambling far greater than that accompanying the decision at the trial itself. Any lawyer who has actually tried a case knows that, regardless of the amount of pretrial preparation, a case looks far different when it is actually being tried than when it is only being thought about.

* * *

The Court apparently also assumes that a defendant who has given the required notice can abandon his alibi without hurting himself. Such an assumption is implicit in and necessary for the majority's argument that the pretrial decision is no different from that at the trial itself. I, however, cannot so lightly assume that pretrial notice will have no adverse effects on a defendant who later decides to forgo such a defense. Necessarily the defendant will have given the prosecutor the names of persons who may have some knowledge about the defendant himself or his activities. Necessarily the prosecutor will have every incentive to question these persons fully, and in doing so he may discover new leads or evidence. Undoubtedly there will be situations in which the State will seek to use such information—information it would probably never have obtained but for the defendant's coerced cooperation.

B

It is unnecessary for me, however, to engage in any such intellectual gymnastics concerning the practical effects of the notice-of-alibi procedure, because the Fifth Amendment itself clearly provides that "[n]o person * * * shall be compelled in any criminal case to be a witness against himself." If words are to be given their plain and obvious meaning, that provision, in my opinion, states that a criminal defendant cannot be required to give evidence, testimony, or any other assistance to the State to aid it in convicting him of crime. The Florida notice-of-alibi rule in my opinion is a patent violation of that constitutional provision because it requires a defendant to disclose information to the State so that the State can use that information to destroy him. * * *

* * *

II

On the surface this case involves only a notice-of-alibi provision, but in effect the decision opens the way for a profound change in one of the most important traditional safeguards of a criminal defendant. The rationale of today's decision is in no way limited to alibi defenses, or any other type or classification of evidence. The theory advanced goes at least so far as to permit the State to obtain under threat of sanction complete disclosure by the defendant in advance of trial of all evidence, testimony, and tactics he plans to use at that trial. In each case the justification will be that the rule affects only the "timing" of the disclosure, and not the substantive decision itself. * * *

* * *

Note

In Wardius v. Oregon, 412 U.S. 470 (1973), the Court struck down a notice of alibi provision that was not reciprocal—i.e., that did not require the prosecution to disclose in advance its rebuttal evidence. The Court suggested "that if there is to be any unbalance in discovery rights, it should work in the defendant's favor."

2. *General Discovery*

The general federal discovery rule covering the defense is Rule 16(b) which provides for discovery of documents and tangible objects and reports of examinations and tests. The 1980 ABA Standards also provide for limited discovery by the government.

The federal rule conditions government discovery on a prior request by a defendant for discovery from the government. The 1975 changes approved by the Supreme Court, but rejected by the Congress, would have given the government a right to discovery even without a defense request. The idea of the change was to make clear that each side in a criminal case has a right to prepare for trial and that discovery is a necessary part of that preparation. By conditioning the government's right to discovery on a defense request, the federal rule is probably intended to avoid constitutional problems. But if it would violate a defendant's self-incrimination right to seek discovery directly, can the government avoid the constitutional problem so easily by providing for reciprocal discovery?

If you were establishing a discovery system, would you give each side a right to discovery irrespective of what the other side did or would you condition the government's right to discovery on a prior defense request?

As part of the proposed 1975 amendments to Rule 16, the Supreme Court approved a rule that would have required the defense, as well as the prosecutor, to disclose the names of witnesses to be called as part of the defense's case-in-chief. When the discovery opportunity for the defense was eliminated, the government lost its discovery right also. Should the 1975 expansion of discovery be implemented in your view?

Justice Black in *Williams* was plainly correct in foreseeing that states would not limit notice requirements to alibi defenses. See, e.g., Fed.R.Crim.P. 12.2 (insanity and mental state defenses). Mosteller, Discovery Against the Defense: Tilting the Adversarial Balance, 74 Cal.L.Rev. 1567 (1986), describes a discovery "revolution" in the states. Mosteller found that in addition to prosecutorial discovery with respect to alibi and insanity, which is available in the great majority of states, 25 states grant the prosecution an independent (non-reciprocal) right to discover at least one of the following: "defenses, witness names, statements of witnesses, reports of experts, or documents and tangible evidence." Seven states provide for broad defense disclosure upon a request for discovery from the prosecution. Twelve states give the prosecution an independent right to obtain the statements of all defense witnesses, and three more permit this discovery when the defendant seeks discovery from the government. Some states require a defendant to summarize the expected testimony of defense witnesses and to create a statement summarizing oral statements of witnesses. Other states require the defense to furnish the government with statements taken from government witnesses. Two questions naturally arise. Does this discovery, going as it does beyond *Williams*, violate the privilege against self-incrimination? If it does not, are defendants and prosecutors equally treated as required by *Wardius*? How would you answer these questions?

3. *Sanctions for Nondisclosure*

In Taylor v. Illinois, 484 U.S. 400 (1988) and Michigan v. Lucas, 111 S.Ct. 1743 (1991), the Court considered whether the Sixth Amendment prohibits trial courts from precluding evidence proffered by criminal defendants who violate legitimate statutory notice requirements. In *Taylor*, defendant wilfully violated a state procedural rule by failing to identify a particular defense witness in response to a pretrial discovery request. The trial court sanctioned this violation by refusing to allow the undisclosed witness to testify. The Court rejected the argument that, under the Sixth Amendment, preclusion is never a permissible sanction for a discovery violation. Justice Stevens wrote the majority opinion for five members of the Court. Justice Brennan, joined by Justices Marshall and Blackmun, dissented.

In *Lucas*, the defendant in a rape case proffered a defense of consent based in part upon the defendant's prior sexual relationship with the victim. The Michigan rape shield statute required that the defense give notice to the prosecution, within 10 days of the arraignment, of the intent to present evidence of past sexual conduct with the victim. The defendant did not comply with that notice requirement. Justice O'Connor, writing for a majority of six justices, treated the case as presenting a limited question: whether the lower court had erred in adopting a *per se* rule that preclusion of evidence of a rape victim's prior sexual relationship with a criminal defendant violates the Sixth Amendment. The majority held that such a *per se* rule was inappropriate, because the notice requirement could serve a legitimate state purpose in some cases, and a defendant's violation of the notice requirement could be so egregious as to warrant the sanction of preclusion. The Court did not decide whether the Michigan notice period (the shortest in the nation, requiring notice to be given well before trial) was in fact "arbitrary or disproportionate" to the State's legitimate interests. The Court remanded to determine whether preclusion was appropriate under the circumstances of the case. Justice Blackmun concurred in the judgment. Justice Stevens, joined by Justice Marshall, dissented, contending that the lower court had not in fact gone so far "as to adopt the *per se* straw man that the Court has decided to knock down today."

Taylor and *Lucas* do not hold that preclusion is permissible whenever a discovery rule is violated. They do hold that the Sixth Amendment does not absolutely prohibit the sanction of preclusion in all cases. What factors should a court take into account in determining whether a sanction of preclusion is warranted?

B. DISCOVERY AT TRIAL

UNITED STATES v. NOBLES

Supreme Court of the United States, 1975.
422 U.S. 225.

MR. JUSTICE POWELL delivered the opinion of the Court.

In a criminal trial, defense counsel sought to impeach the credibility of key prosecution witnesses by testimony of a defense investigator regarding statements previously obtained from the witnesses by the investigator. The question presented here is whether in these circumstances a federal trial court may compel the defense to reveal the relevant portions of the investigator's report for the prosecution's use in cross-examining him. The United States Court of Appeals for the Ninth Circuit concluded that it cannot. 501 F.2d 146. We granted certiorari, and now reverse.

I

Respondent was tried and convicted on charges arising from an armed robbery of a federally insured bank. The only significant evidence linking him to the crime was the identification testimony of two witnesses, a bank teller and a salesman who was in the bank during the robbery. Respondent offered an alibi but, as the Court of Appeals recognized, his strongest defense centered around attempts to discredit these eyewitnesses. Defense efforts to impeach them gave rise to the events that led to this decision.

In the course of preparing respondent's defense, an investigator for the defense interviewed both witnesses and preserved the essence of those conversations in a written report. When the witnesses testified for the prosecution, respondent's counsel relied on the report in conducting their cross-examination. Counsel asked the bank teller whether he recalled having told the investigator that he had seen only the back of the man he identified as respondent. The witness replied that he did not remember making such a statement. He was allowed, despite defense counsel's initial objection, to refresh his recollection by referring to a portion of the investigator's report. The prosecutor also was allowed to see briefly the relevant portion of the report. The witness thereafter testified that although the report indicated that he told the investigator he had seen only respondent's back, he in fact had seen more than that and continued to insist that respondent was the bank robber.

The other witness acknowledged on cross-examination that he too had spoken to the defense investigator. Respondent's counsel twice inquired whether he told the investigator that "all blacks looked alike" to him, and in each instance the witness denied having made such a statement. The prosecution again sought inspection of the relevant portion of the investigator's report, and respondent's counsel again objected. The court declined to order disclosure at that time, but ruled that it would be required if the investigator testified as to the witnesses' alleged statements from the witness stand. The court further advised that it would examine the investigator's report *in camera* and would excise all reference to matters not relevant to the precise statements at issue.

After the prosecution completed its case, respondent called the investigator as a defense witness. The court reiterated that a copy of the report, inspected and edited *in camera,* would have to be submitted to Government counsel at the completion of the investigator's impeachment testimony. When respondent's counsel stated that he did not intend to produce the report, the court ruled that the investigator would not be allowed to testify about his interviews with the witnesses.[a]

The Court of Appeals for the Ninth Circuit, while acknowledging that the trial court's ruling constituted a "very limited and seemingly judicious restriction," nevertheless considered it reversible error. * * *

II

* * *

While the adversary system depends primarily on the parties for the presentation and exploration of relevant facts, the judiciary is not limited to the role of a referee or supervisor. Its compulsory processes stand available to require the presentation of evidence in court or before a grand jury. * * * Decisions of this Court repeatedly have recognized the federal judiciary's inherent power to require the prosecution to produce the previously recorded statements of its witnesses so that the defense may get the full benefit of cross-examination and the truth-finding process may be enhanced. At issue here is whether, in a proper case, the prosecution can call upon that same power for production of witness statements that facilitate "full disclosure of all the [relevant] facts."

In this case, the defense proposed to call its investigator to impeach the identification testimony of the prosecution's eyewitnesses. It was evident from cross-examination that the investigator would testify that each witness' recollection of the appearance of the individual identified as respondent was considerably less clear at an earlier time than it was at trial. It also appeared that the investigator and one witness differed even as to what the witness told him during the interview. The investigator's contemporaneous report might provide critical insight into the issues of credibility that the investigator's testimony would raise. It could assist the jury in determining the extent to which the investigator's testimony actually discredited the prosecution's witnesses. If, for example, the report failed to mention the purported statement of one witness that "all blacks looked alike," the jury might disregard the investigator's version altogether. On the other hand, if this statement appeared in the contemporaneously recorded report, it would tend strongly to corroborate the investigator's version of the interview and to diminish substantially the reliability of that witness' identification.[b]

a. Although the portion of the report containing the bank teller's alleged statement previously was revealed and marked for identification, it was not introduced into evidence. When the discussion of the investigator's testimony subsequently arose, counsel for the Government noted that he had only a limited opportunity to glance at the statement, and he then requested disclosure of that portion of the report as well as the statement purportedly made by the salesman.

b. Rule 612 of the new Federal Rules of Evidence entitles an adverse party to inspect a writing relied on to refresh the recollection of a witness while testifying. The Rule also authorizes disclosure of writings relied on to refresh recollection before testifying if the court deems it necessary in the interests of justice. The party obtaining the writing thereafter can use it in cross-examining the witness and can introduce into evidence those portions that relate to the witness' testimony. As the Federal Rules of Evidence were not in effect at the time of respondent's trial, we have no occasion to consider them or their applicability to the situation here presented.

It was therefore apparent to the trial judge that the investigator's report was highly relevant to the critical issue of credibility. In this context, production of the report might substantially enhance "the search for truth," Williams v. Florida, 399 U.S., at 82. We must determine whether compelling its production was precluded by some privilege available to the defense in the circumstances of this case.

III

A

The Court of Appeals concluded that the Fifth Amendment renders criminal discovery "basically a one-way street." Like many generalizations in constitutional law, this one is too broad. The relationship between the accused's Fifth Amendment rights and the prosecution's ability to discover materials at trial must be identified in a more discriminating manner.

* * *

In this instance disclosure of the relevant portions of the defense investigator's report would not impinge on the fundamental values protected by the Fifth Amendment. The court's order was limited to statements allegedly made by third parties who were available as witnesses to both the prosecution and the defense. Respondent did not prepare the report, and there is no suggestion that the portions subject to the disclosure order reflected any information that he conveyed to the investigator. The fact that these statements of third parties were elicited by a defense investigator on respondent's behalf does not convert them into respondent's personal communications. Requiring their production from the investigator therefore would not in any sense compel respondent to be a witness against himself or extort communications from him.

* * *

B

The Court of Appeals also held that Fed.Rule Crim.Proc. 16 deprived the trial court of the power to order disclosure of the relevant portions of the investigator's report. Acknowledging that the Rule appears to control pretrial discovery only, the court nonetheless determined that its reference to the Jencks Act, 18 U.S.C.A § 3500, signaled an intention that Rule 16 should control trial practice as well. We do not agree.

Both the language and history of Rule 16 indicate that it addresses only pretrial discovery. * * *

* * * We conclude, therefore, that Rule 16 imposes no constraint on the District Court's power to condition the impeachment testimony of respondent's witness on the production of the relevant portions of his investigative report. In extending the Rule into the trial context, the Court of Appeals erred.

IV

Respondent contends further that the work-product doctrine exempts the investigator's report from disclosure at trial. While we agree that this doctrine applies to criminal litigation as well as civil, we find its protection unavailable in this case.

The work-product doctrine, recognized by this court in Hickman v. Taylor, 329 U.S. 495 (1947), reflects the strong "public policy underlying the orderly prosecution and defense of legal claims." * * * The Court therefore recognized a qualified privilege for certain materials prepared by an attorney "acting for his client in anticipation of litigation." Id., at 508.

Although the work-product doctrine most frequently is asserted as a bar to discovery in civil litigation, its role in assuring the proper functioning of the criminal justice system is even more vital. The interests of society and the accused in obtaining a fair and accurate resolution of the question of guilt or innocence demand that adequate safeguards assure the thorough preparation and presentation of each side of the case.[c]

At its core, the work-product doctrine shelters the mental processes of the attorney, providing a privileged area within which he can analyze and prepare his client's case. But the doctrine is an intensely practical one, grounded in the realities of litigation in our adversary system. One of those realities is that attorneys often must rely on the assistance of investigators and other agents in the compilation of materials in preparation for trial. It is therefore necessary that the doctrine protect material prepared by agents for the attorney as well as those prepared by the attorney himself.[d] Moreover, the concerns reflected in the work-product doctrine do not disappear once trial has begun. Disclosure of an attorney's efforts at trial, as surely as disclosure during pretrial discovery, could disrupt the orderly development and presentation of his case. We need not, however, undertake here to delineate the scope of the doctrine at trial, for in this instance it is clear that the defense waived such right as may have existed to invoke its protections.

The privilege derived from the work-product doctrine is not absolute. Like other qualified privileges, it may be waived. Here respondent sought to adduce the testimony of the investigator and contrast his recollection of the contested statements with that of the prosecution's witnesses. Respondent, by electing to present the investigator as a witness, waived the privilege with respect to matters covered in his testimony.[e] Respondent can no more advance the work-product doctrine to sustain a unilateral testimonial use of work-product materials than he could elect to testify in his own behalf and thereafter assert his Fifth Amendment privilege to resist cross-examination on matters reasonably related to those brought out in direct examination.

V

Finally, our examination of the record persuades us that the District Court properly exercised its discretion in this instance. The court authorized no general "fishing expedition" into the defense files or indeed even into the defense investigator's report. Rather, its considered ruling was quite limited in scope, opening to prosecution scrutiny only the portion of the report that related to the testimony the investigator would offer to discredit the witnesses'

c. A number of state and federal decisions have recognized the role of the work-product doctrine in the criminal law, and have applied its protections to the files of the prosecution and the accused alike. See, e.g., State v. Bowen, 104 Ariz. 138, 449 P.2d 603; Peel v. State, 154 So.2d 910 (Fla.App.1963); In re Grand Jury Proceedings (Duffy v. United States), 473 F.2d 840 (CA8 1973); In re Terkeltoub, 256 F.Supp. 683 (S.D.N.Y.1966).

d. The sole issue in *Hickman* related to materials prepared by an attorney, and courts thereafter disagreed over whether the doctrine applied as well to materials prepared on his behalf. See Proposed Amendments to the Federal Rules of Civil Procedure Relating to Discovery, 48 F.R.D. 487, 501 (1970); 4 J. Moore, Federal Practice ¶ 26.63[8] (2d ed. 1974). Necessarily, it must. This view is reflected in the Federal Rules of Civil Procedure, see Rule 26(b)(3), and in Rule 16 of the Criminal Rules as well, see Rules 16(b) and (c); cf. E. Cleary, McCormick on Evidence 208 (2d ed. 1972).

e. What constitutes a waiver with respect to work-product materials depends, of course, upon the circumstances. Counsel necessarily makes use throughout trial of the notes, documents, and other internal materials prepared to present adequately his client's case, and often relies on them in examining witnesses. When so used, there normally is no waiver. But where, as here, counsel attempts to make a testimonial use of these materials the normal rules of evidence come into play with respect to cross-examination and production of documents.

identification testimony. The court further afforded respondent the maximum opportunity to assist in avoiding unwarranted disclosure or to exercise an informed choice to call for the investigator's testimony and thereby open his report to examination.

The court's preclusion sanction was an entirely proper method of assuring compliance with its order. Respondent's argument that this ruling deprived him of the Sixth Amendment rights to compulsory process and cross-examination misconceives the issue. The District Court did not bar the investigator's testimony. It merely prevented respondent from presenting to the jury a partial view of the credibility issue by adducing the investigator's testimony and thereafter refusing to disclose the contemporaneous report that might offer further critical insights. * * *

MR. JUSTICE DOUGLAS took no part in the consideration or decision of this case.

MR. JUSTICE WHITE, with whom MR. JUSTICE REHNQUIST joins, concurring.

I concur in the judgment and in Parts II, III, and V of the opinion of the Court. I write only because of misgivings about the meaning of Part IV of the opinion. The Court appears to have held in Part IV of its opinion only that whatever protection the defense investigator's notes of his interviews with witnesses might otherwise have had, that protection would have been lost when the investigator testified about those interviews. With this I agree also. It seems to me more sensible, however, to decide what protection these notes had in the first place before reaching the "waiver" issue. Accordingly, and because I do not believe that the work-product doctrine of Hickman v. Taylor, 329 U.S. 495 (1947), can be extended wholesale from its historic role as a limitation on the nonevidentiary material which may be the subject of pretrial discovery to an unprecedented role as a limitation on the trial judge's power to compel production of evidentiary matter at trial, I add the following.

I

Up until now the work-product doctrine of Hickman v. Taylor has been viewed almost exclusively as a limitation on the ability of a party to obtain pretrial discovery. * * *

[Justice White points out that the *Hickman* Court analyzed the discovery question as a pretrial issue only, and that it did not hold that discovery was denied because of a privilege. Rather, the Court said the request was outside the reach of proper discovery.]

Since Hickman v. Taylor, Congress, the cases, and the commentators have uniformly continued to view the "work product" doctrine solely as a limitation on pretrial discovery and not as a qualified evidentiary privilege. * * * In the criminal area, Congress has enacted 18 U.S.C.A. § 3500 and accepted Fed. Rule Crim.Proc. 16(c). The former prevents pretrial discovery of witness statements from the Government; the latter prevents pretrial discovery of witness statements from the defense. Neither limits the power of the trial court to order production as evidence of prior statements of witnesses who have testified at trial.

* * *

The reasons for largely confining the work-product rule to its role as a limitation on pretrial discovery are compelling. First of all, the injury to the factfinding process is far greater where a rule keeps *evidence* from the factfinder than when it simply keeps advance disclosure of evidence from a party or keeps from him *leads* to evidence developed by his adversary and which he is just as well able to find by himself. In the main, where a party seeks to discover a statement made to an opposing party in order to *prepare* for trial, he can obtain the "substantial equivalent * * * by other means," Fed.Rule Civ. Proc. 26(b)(3), i.e., by interviewing the witness himself. A prior inconsistent statement in the possession of his adversary, however, when sought for evidentiary purposes—i.e., to impeach the witness after he testifies—is for that purpose unique. By the same token, the danger perceived in *Hickman* that each party to a case will decline to prepare in the hopes of eventually using his adversary's preparation is absent when disclosure will take place only at trial. Indeed, it is very difficult to articulate a reason why statements on the same subject matter as a witness' testimony should not be turned over to an adversary after the witness has testified. The statement will either be consistent with the witness' testimony, in which case it will be useless and disclosure will be harmless; or it will be inconsistent and of unquestioned value to the jury. Any claim that disclosure of such a statement would lead the trial into collateral and confusing issues was rejected by this Court in Jencks v. United States, 353 U.S. 657 (1957), and by Congress in the legislation which followed.

Accordingly, it would appear that with one exception to be discussed below, the work-product notions of Hickman v. Taylor impose no restrictions on the trial judge's ordering production of evidentiary matter at trial; that these notions apply in only a very limited way, if at all, to a party's efforts to obtain *evidence* pretrial pursuant to available discovery devices; and that these notions supply only a qualified discovery immunity with respect to witness statements in any event.

II

In one of its aspects, the rule of Hickman v. Taylor, supra, has application to evidentiary requests at trial. Both the majority and the concurring opinions in Hickman v. Taylor were at pains to distinguish between production of statements written by the witness and in the possession of the lawyer, and those statements which were made orally by the witness and written down by the lawyer. Production and use of oral statements written down by the lawyer would create a substantial risk that the lawyer would have to testify.[f] * * *

The remarks of the Court in Hickman v. Taylor, while made in the context of a request for pretrial discovery have application to the evidentiary use of lawyers' memoranda of witness interviews at trial. It is unnecessary, however, to decide in this case whether the policies against putting in issue the credibility of the lawyer who will sum up to the jury outweigh the jury's interest in obtaining all relevant information. * * * In this case, the creator of the memorandum was not the trial lawyer but an investigator and he was, in any event, to be called as a witness by the defense.[23]

f. If the witness does not acknowledge making an inconsistent statement to the lawyer—even though the lawyer recorded it—the cross-examiner may not offer the document in evidence without at least calling the lawyer as a witness to authenticate the document and otherwise testify to the prior statement.

23. Other courts have ordered disclosure of defense material as a result of the way defense counsel examined witnesses. See, e.g., United States v. Salsedo, 607 F.2d 318 (9th Cir. 1979). The court of appeals held that the trial judge acted properly in requiring defendant's counsel to turn over a transcript of a telephone conversation between the defendant and a government informant, after counsel made reference to the transcript in his cross-examination of the informant and another government witness.

Note

Following *Nobles,* the Supreme Court adopted Fed.R.Crim.P. 26.2. There is some question about how the Jencks Act, Fed.R.Crim.P. 26.2 and Fed.R.Evid. 612 relate to one another. The Jencks Act was the first to be adopted and covers only the prosecution. Fed.R.Crim.P. 26.2 covers both sides in a criminal case and largely supercedes the act. Fed.R.Evid. 612 applies in civil and criminal cases and establishes that, except where the Jencks Act dictates otherwise, a judge must give one party access to material used to refresh recollection prior to trial. Since the criminal procedure rule was adopted after the evidence rule, it is not mentioned along with the Jencks Act in the evidence rule. However, it would seem that under Fed.R.Evid. 612 statements covered by either the Jencks Act or the criminal procedure rule ought to receive similar treatment and that, since the procedure rule supercedes the Jencks Act, the evidence rule should defer to the procedure rule in the same way it defers to the statute.

It is important to note that none of these provisions authorizes disclosure of "work product" or other material in the files of counsel unless a witness testifies. Once a witness finishes direct examination, the Jencks Act and Fed.R.Crim.P. 26.2 compel disclosure, upon request, of the witness' prior statements, but of nothing else.

The evidence rule covers all material, not just witness statements, that a witness uses to refresh recollection. When the evidence rule defers to the Jencks Act and the criminal procedure rule, a trial judge should not order disclosure of a witness' prior statements until the conclusion of direct examination. This means there will never be pretrial disclosure of these statements. Other material used to refresh recollection may be disclosed prior to the end of direct examination, and in the case of material reviewed by a witness before trial, even before the witness testifies.

For a slightly different view, see Foster, The Jencks Act: Rule 26.2—Rule 612 Interface—"Confusion Worse Confounded," 34 Okla.L.Rev. 679 (1981).

C. TWO NOBLES PROBLEMS

To test the implications of *Nobles* and the new rule, consider the following two hypotheticals. Ask how the *Nobles* Court would have resolved the issues prior to the adoption of the rule and then compare your answer to the resolution under the rule.

> 1. * * * A fight occurs on a street corner between the defendant and the "victim," during which the latter is stabbed. In a trial charging the defendant with assault with a deadly weapon, the defendant's claim is self-defense. The victim testifies for the prosecution on direct that the assault was unprovoked. On cross-examination, he is asked whether it is not true that he told a passerby, just seconds before the fight began, that he intended to kill the defendant. The victim denies ever speaking with the passerby. In its case-in-chief, the defense calls the passerby who testifies to two things: first, that the conversation with the victim did occur, and second, that he, the passerby, actually saw the victim strike the initial blow. Previously, this defense witness had given the defense counsel a statement to the effect that (1) before the fight the victim had stated to the passerby that he intended to kill the defendant; (2) there was another witness to the fight; (3) the defendant admitted to the passerby after the fight that he overreacted; (4) it was actually too dark for the passerby to see what happened; and (5) the passerby had been a good friend of

the defendant for years. [Must the statement be turned over to the government? If so, the whole statement, or only parts of it?]

Scheininger, United States v. Nobles: A Prosecutor's Perspective, 14 Am.Cr. L.Rev. 1, 7 (1976). Compare Scheininger with Rosenbleet, United States v. Nobles: A Defense View, 14 Am.Cr.L.Rev. 17 (1976).

2. Powell is appointed by a state trial court to represent Jarv in a criminal case. Jarv is charged with robbing a convenience store and with unlawful possession of a firearm. Powell talks with Sharp, the store clerk and only eyewitness. Powell makes an accurate written record of everything Sharp has to say. Trial is delayed a year and a half due to the illness of Jarv. At trial Sharp has difficulty recalling details of the crime. The prosecution is worried because of Sharp's problems on the stand and defense evidence that Sharp is reputed to be a liar. At a recess Sharp tells the prosecutor that defense counsel has a written record of a statement made by Sharp shortly after Jarv's arrest. Sharp and the prosecutor believe the statement will bolster Sharp's testimony. The prosecutor demands its production. Should the Court accede to the demand? In answering this question, is it important that Powell is appointed, not retained by Jarv? Is it important that Powell made the record, or would your answer be the same if Sharp gave a written statement in his own hand? Is there any force to a contention by Powell that the posture of the case required that he seek a statement and that it is unfair to use the statement against the defense? Do you agree with Justice White that discovery of evidence is more important than discovery of leads?

R. Lempert & S. Saltzburg, A Modern Approach to Evidence 146, Problem II–20 (2d ed.1982).

Chapter Nine

PLEAS OF GUILTY

I. THE GENERAL ISSUES

Once the determination to press charges is made officially and a case not only begins to develop, but also survives pre-trial motions or preliminary screening, the government becomes committed to the idea that the accused should be punished. The accused, even if innocent, must be concerned with how the case will ultimately be resolved. Questions like "Will I be convicted?" and "What kind of sentence will be imposed on me if I am convicted?" become increasingly important. Uncertainty about how these and other questions would be answered by going to trial often leads an accused to respond favorably to, or to initiate, "settlement" discussions with the government. By agreeing to plead guilty (or nolo contendere perhaps) the accused accepts punishment for some criminal activity. In exchange for this acceptance, the system—i.e., the prosecutor and the court—permits the accused to avoid some of the uncertainty endemic in any litigation system in which human beings must decide crucial questions of fact and law and often can exercise broad discretion in implementing social policy.

The extent to which settlement negotiations actually take place, the nature of most settlements reached, the legitimacy of any settlements in criminal cases and the role of the various participants—i.e., the prosecutor, the trial judge, the defense counsel, the defendant, the victim, etc.—are all subjects that have been debated in the literature.

Although it is not possible in one chapter to capture all of the nuances of the debate, at least the surface of some of the principal issues can be scratched. A good place to start is with excerpts from the introduction to an interesting and comprehensive study of plea bargaining in a number of American jurisdictions. This excerpt comprises the remainder of this section of the chapter.

H. MILLER, W. McDONALD, J. CRAMER, PLEA BARGAINING IN THE UNITED STATES (1978) [1]

A primary rationale for plea bargaining is administrative efficiency and control of the calendar. Many judges and prosecutors have indicated that a substantial decrease in pleas would create chaos in the system of justice. They

1. The study utilized on-site interviews in jurisdictions with different populations.

believe that plea bargaining is the essential underpinning for the continued existence of an orderly system of justice.

Advocates of plea bargaining make several claims and assumptions. By pleading guilty the defendant: (1) Aids in ensuring prompt and certain application of correctional measures; (2) avoids delay and increases the probability of prompt and certain application of correctional measures to other offenders; (3) acknowledges guilt and manifests the willingness to accept responsibility for conduct; (4) avoids public trial when the consequences outweigh any legitimate need for such; (5) prevents undue harm to the defendant from the form of conviction; and (6) makes possible the granting of concessions to him when he has given or offered cooperation in the prosecution of other offenders.

* * *

Those opposed to plea bargaining believe it to be inherently undesirable, illegal and unreformable; that its existence and accompanying pressures will cause laxness in observing constitutional requirements. In short the evils of plea bargaining practices cannot be legitimized; purity is essential; and any negotiation renders the system impure. They explicitly assume the system will not collapse if bargaining is phased out properly.

A system of beliefs for those opposed to plea bargaining includes the following: (1) There is a real danger of innocent persons being convicted; (2) Prosecutors bargain primarily to move cases; (3) Bargaining distributes unevenly and inappropriately among the offenders the ability to get a deal providing a lenient disposition; (4) Bargaining is inefficient and wasteful; (5) It may reduce the deterrent impact of the law since it usually results in lower sentences; (6) It makes correctional rehabilitation more difficult by limiting judicial sentencing discretion; and (7) Those who opt for a jury trial generally receive longer sentences.

Finally, some believe the costs of abolishing plea bargaining are not acceptable. In 1970, Chief Justice Burger called the consequence of a 10% reduction (90% to 80%) in the rate of guilty pleas tremendous, requiring the assignment of twice the judicial manpower and facilities. He alleged that a further reduction to 70% would treble the demand.[a] Some question this estimate and others say the quality of justice should not be measured in fiscal terms.

* * *

What is Plea Bargaining?

There is no common definition of plea bargaining in general use throughout the United States, thus clouding discussions of plea bargaining issues. Moreover, the word "bargaining" has unpleasant connotations, causing some actors to deny that it exists. Allegations that plea bargaining has been abolished should therefore be approached skeptically. "Explicit" and "implicit" bargaining occurs. Explicit bargaining is specific. Where it is implicit defendants can "reasonably expect" certain dispositions, even though no overt bargaining has occurred. The kinds of agreements and dispositions can vary,

a. Chief Justice Warren Burger, State of the Judiciary 1970, 56 A.B.A.J. 929, 931 (1970).

depending on the circumstances of the case. Finally, not all criminal justice actors agree as to what elements constitute a plea bargain (whether it be some charge dismissals, a charge reduction, or an agreed upon sentence recommendation).

This study defines plea bargaining as "the defendant's agreement to plead guilty to a criminal charge with the reasonable expectation of receiving some consideration from the state."

The Extent of Plea Bargaining

Data available from 20 states indicate that the rates of pleas differ between jurisdictions. There appears to be little correlation between such rates and population size. One study indicates that rural prosecutors accept plea bargains more readily than prosecutors in larger jurisdictions; another that relationships within a court system are the dominant factor in plea bargaining, with no correlation between plea rates and size of jurisdiction. These studies and data raise questions concerning assumptions about costs and caseload pressure in relation to plea bargaining.

* * *

Types of Plea Bargaining

The project classified plea bargaining in two ways, explicit and implicit. Both kinds can occur in one jurisdiction; but in 27 or 30 jurisdictions explicit plea bargaining was dominant, particularly in felony cases. Explicit plea bargaining involves overt negotiations between two or three actors (prosecutor, defense attorney and judge) followed by an agreement on the terms of the bargain. Implicit bargaining involves an understanding by the defendant that a more severe sentence may be imposed for going to trial rather than pleading guilty. Defense attorneys can, however, be clear in advising the defendant of this probable outcome.

Where explicit plea bargaining occurs concessions may include charge modification, sentence agreement or both. The variety of sentence concessions or actors involved in the bargaining process may be virtually unlimited. Five major types of explicit plea bargaining were identified:

1. Judges participating and indicating the sentence.
2. Modification of charges by the prosecutor.
3. Prosecutorial agreement to make a sentencing recommendation.
4. Combination of 2 and 3.
5. Combination of 1 and 2.

Many jurisdictions had more than one type even though one or two types were dominant in each jurisdiction. The most common pattern involved charge modifications and sentence recommendations by the prosecutor (4). The second most common involved charge modifications alone (2). In one jurisdiction prosecutorial sentence recommendations are the dominant pattern; another combined charge bargaining and judicial indication of the sentence. In some jurisdictions judicial participation is substantial, although a minority of the judges may be so involved because of the way cases are assigned.

* * *

Judicial Participation in Plea Bargaining

Judicial participation in plea discussions is opposed by the American Bar Association and the National Advisory Commission on Criminal Justice Standards and Goals. It is also prohibited by the Federal Rules of Criminal Procedure. Some states disallow any form of judicial participation,[2] while others, such as Illinois, prohibit the judge from initiating plea bargaining but allow participation in the discussion.

In our observations we found at least some judges in more than half of the jurisdictions visited taking an active role in the negotiation process. This participation took place in scheduled and unscheduled pretrial conferences in chambers or at the bench. The prosecutor and defense counsel were usually present. In 12 of 25 states visited by project staff there is case or statutory law which speaks to the issue of judicial participation by the judge. Ten states prohibit it; two states permit it.

A major objection to judicial participation in negotiations is based on the powerful position of the judge. Plea negotiations involving direct judicial participation might be inherently coercive. A second major objection is that a judge cannot properly oversee a process in which he is a direct participant.

Those advocating a direct judicial role suggest that only through active judicial participation can a sufficient amount of predictability in the sentence be insured. Some believe that such participation may expedite the process. Contrary to those objecting to judicial participation, there is a belief that only through involvement can a judge effectively oversee the plea bargaining process.

* * *

Sentencing Differential Between Guilty Plea and Trial

It has been alleged that judges induce guilty pleas by imposing more severe sentences when a defendant chooses a trial rather than pleading guilty. Some studies suggest that differential sentencing exists at the misdemeanor and felony levels.

There is a split as to the propriety of differential sentencing. Proponents believe leniency is proper for those who accept responsibility for their conduct by pleading guilty and contribute to the efficient and economical administration of the law. They assert that those submitting themselves to prompt correctional measures should be granted sentence concessions, and that differential sentences for those demanding trial is not undue punishment if it is not excessive. Those opposed believe that guilty pleas have no direct relevance to the appropriate disposition of an offender and that the constitutional right to trial should not be the cause of enhanced punishment.

II. THE LEGITIMACY OF SENTENCING CONCESSIONS

A. RECOGNIZING THE IMPORTANCE OF UNCERTAINTY

One of the reasons that some defendants plead guilty is to obtain the advantages of sentencing concessions that are awarded those who spare the

2. See, e.g., State v. Buckalew, 561 P.2d 289 (Alaska, 1977).

state the expense and inconvenience of putting on a trial. Although there evidently is judicial reluctance to impose a penalty—i.e., a higher sentence than otherwise would be warranted—on an offender who chooses to go to trial,[3] many judges indicate that they are willing to give a preference to those who plead. See, e.g., Note, The Influence of the Defendant's Plea on Judicial Determination of Sentence, 66 Yale L.J. 204 (1956). Judge Bazelon explained one rationale for distinguishing in sentencing between those who plead guilty and those who do not in the next case.

SCOTT v. UNITED STATES

Court of Appeals of the United States, D.C.Cir., 1969.
419 F.2d 264.

BAZELON, CHIEF JUDGE:

[Vincent Scott was convicted of robbery and sentenced to prison for five to fifteen years.]

The trial judge * * * stated at the sentencing hearing, "If you had pleaded guilty to this offense, I might have been more lenient with you." The stark import of this comment is that the defendant paid a price for demanding a trial. In view of the prohibitions the Supreme Court has laid down against making the exercise of Fourth, and Fifth, and Sixth Amendment rights costly, the pricetag thus placed on the right to a fair trial which these amendments guarantee would, on first impression, seem clearly impermissible.

And yet, despite the startling incongruity, empirical evidence supports the proposition that judges do sentence defendants who have demanded a trial more severely. At least one Court of Appeals has taken approving "judicial notice of the fact that trial courts quite generally impose a lighter sentence on pleas of guilty than in cases where the accused pleaded not guilty but has been found guilty by a jury." An advisory committee of the American Bar Association has concluded that "it is proper for the court to grant charge and sentence concessions to defendants who enter a plea of guilty * * * when the interest of the public in the effective administration of criminal justice would thereby be served."

* * *

Two arguments inevitably appear whenever differential sentencing is discussed. The first is that the defendant's choice of plea shows whether he recognizes and repents his crime. One difficulty with this argument is that no court or commentator has explained why a defendant's insistence upon his self-incrimination privilege is not also evidence of a lack of repentance. Or his insistence that evidence unconstitutionally seized should not be admitted.

Repentance has a role in penology. But the premise of our criminal jurisprudence has always been that the time for repentance comes after trial. The adversary process is a fact-finding engine, not a drama of contrition in which a prejudged defendant is expected to knit up his lacerated bonds to society.

* * *

The second argument for differential sentencing is necessity. Most convictions, perhaps as many as 90 per cent in some jurisdictions, are the product of guilty pleas. Unless a large proportion of defendants plead guilty, the argument runs, the already crowded dockets

3. See, e.g., United States v. Wiley, 278 F.2d 500 (7th Cir. 1960); Commonwealth v. Bethea, 474 Pa. 571, 379 A.2d 102 (1977); In re Lewallen, 23 Cal.3d 274, 152 Cal.Rptr. 528, 590 P.2d 383 (1979).

in many jurisdictions would collapse into chaos. Since most defendants are indigent, the only price they can be forced to pay for pleading innocent is time in jail. Ergo, differential sentences are justified for those who plead guilty and those who plead innocent.

When approached from this perspective, the problem inevitably becomes entwined with that of plea bargaining. And the difficulties that practice presents are exceeded only by its pervasiveness. In many areas such bargaining dominates the criminal process. Its format may vary. The prosecutor may agree to reduce the charge in exchange for a guilty plea, or he may agree to recommend a lighter sentence. The judge may be aware of the agreement or he may not. If aware that a bargain has been struck, the court may or may not ratify the agreement before a plea is offered and accepted.

* * *

The fact that the trial judge must be aware of any bargain made before accepting a plea of guilty, and perhaps may ratify the agreement in appropriate circumstances, imposes an obligation upon the judge to supervise the fairness of the bargain. Since the trial judge determines the sentence a convicted defendant will receive, he cannot escape this responsibility if plea bargaining takes the form of a promised sentence recommendation. But the functional problem is the same if plea bargaining takes the form of a prosecutorial offer to reduce the charge, as seems to be the practice in the District of Columbia. By deciding what charge or charges to proceed with, the prosecutor can often effectively control the sentence the defendant is likely to receive. To the extent this decision is made independently by the prosecutor before the defendant is called upon to plead, there is no danger that the defendant will be deterred from exercising his right to trial. When, however, the prosecutor makes his decision by offering to reduce the charge in exchange for a plea of guilty, the situation is quite different. If the trial judge is to so supervise the bargain, the law must resolve the troubling issue * * *: what inducements to plead guilty are permissible? Since this case does not present that issue, it would be inappropriate to essay a comprehensive answer to the question. Because the problem is so closely entwined with the policy of differential sentencing, however, several brief comments are in order.

First, the prosecutor clearly cannot have carte blanche to apply whatever tactics he wishes to induce a guilty plea. A policy of deliberately overcharging defendants with no intention of prosecuting on all counts simply in order to have chips at the bargaining table would, for example, constitute improper harassment of the defendant.

Second, there may be circumstances under which the prosecutor may bargain with the defendant without raising the constitutional question of whether the exercise of the right to trial can be made costly. When there is substantial uncertainty concerning the likely outcome of a trial, "each side is interested in limiting these inherent litigation risks." * * *

Superficially it may seem that even in such a case the defendant who insists upon a trial and is found guilty pays a price for the exercise of his right when he receives a longer sentence than his less venturesome counterpart who pleads guilty. In a sense he has. But the critical distinction is that the price he has paid is not one imposed by the state to discourage others from a similar exercise of their rights, but rather one encountered by those who gamble and lose. After the fact, the defendant who pleads innocent and is convicted receives a heavier sentence. But, by the same token, the defendant who pleads innocent and is acquitted receives no sentence. To the extent that the bargain struck reflects only the uncertainty of conviction before trial, the "expected sentence before trial"—length of sentence discounted by probability of conviction—is the same for those who decide to plead guilty and those who hope for acquittal but risk conviction by going to trial.

* * * The danger presented by plea bargaining is that defendants deciding upon a plea will be deterred from exercising their right to a trial. The relevant vantage point is thus before trial, and the relevant comparison is between the expectations of those who decide to insist upon a trial and those who decide to eliminate the risk of trial by pleading guilty. If the sentence expectations of those two classes at that time are the same then there will be no chilling effect upon exercise of the right to trial, and it is accurate to say that no "price" has been placed upon exercise of the right.

To determine the expectations of those defendants who insist upon a trial, we must consider the probability of conviction as well as the sentences received by those who plead innocent and are later convicted. The argument that the defendant who receives a heavier sentence after trial has "paid a price" because he receives a heavier sentence than the defendant who is acquitted (and goes free) or pleads guilty (and receives a shorter sentence on the same or a reduced charge) errs on two counts: (1) the comparison is made at the wrong time—after trial, when the uncertainty of litigation has passed, rather than before trial—and (2) the comparison is made between the wrong categories of defendants—the class of defendants convicted after trial versus the class of defendants who plead guilty or are acquitted rather than the class of defendants who exercise their right to trial versus the class of defendants who do not.

The situation is quite different when the prosecutor engages in bargaining not because he is willing to take a sure half loaf rather than to await the outcome of a trial, but because his limited resources convince him he must deter defendants from demanding a trial. The divide between the two situations may be difficult to locate for even the best-intentioned prosecutor, and even more difficult for a trial judge to review. But the standards which guide prosecutors in the exercise of their discretion are as much a part of the law as the rules applied in court. * * * In the area of plea bargaining, the lodestar must be the realization that our law solemnly promises each man accused his day in court. If a prosecutor enters plea and charge negotiations not with the purpose of adjusting the charge to reflect the uncertainties of litigation but with the goal of deterring the defendant from the exercise of his right to a trial, the chasm between promise and reality is no narrower because the trial court affects a righteous air of non-involvement. Perhaps the promise must be tempered if society is unwilling to pay its price. But that decision should be made in sunlight, and not in the shrouded mist of unguided prosecutorial discretion.

* * *

B. RECOGNIZING THE IMPORTANCE OF AN EFFICIENT SYSTEM

The ABA Standards on Pleas of Guilty (1970) adopted a broader view of permissible bargaining:

1.8 Consideration of Plea in Final Disposition.

(a) It is proper for the court to grant charge and sentence concessions to defendants who enter a plea of guilty or nolo contendere when the interest of the public in the effective administration of criminal justice would thereby be served. Among the considerations which are appropriate in determining this question are:

(i) that the defendant by his plea has aided in ensuring the prompt and certain application of correctional measures to him;

(ii) that the defendant has acknowledged his guilt and shown a willingness to assume responsibility for his conduct;

(iii) that the concessions will make possible alternative correctional measures which are better adapted to achieving rehabilitative, protective, deterrent or other purposes of correctional treatment, or will prevent undue harm to the defendant from the form of conviction;

(iv) that the defendant has made public trial unnecessary when there are good reasons for not having the case dealt with in a public trial;

(v) that the defendant has given or offered cooperation when such cooperation has resulted or may result in the successful prosecution of other offenders engaged in equally serious or more serious criminal conduct;

(vi) that the defendant by his plea has aided in avoiding delay (including delay due to crowded dockets) in the disposition of other cases and thereby has increased the probability of prompt and certain application of correctional measures to other offenders.

(b) The court should not impose upon a defendant any sentence in excess of that which would be justified by any of the rehabilitative, protective, deterrent or other purposes of the criminal law because the defendant has chosen to require the prosecution to prove his guilt at trial rather than to enter a plea of guilty or nolo contendere.[4]

Do you approve of all of these factors? Which trouble you the most?

The trial judge in United States v. Medina-Cervantes, 690 F.2d 715 (9th Cir. 1982), indicated concern that the defendant, convicted of entering the United States illegally and of reentering the United States after having been deported, was "thumbing his nose at our judicial system" by insisting on a trial and the exercise of the full panoply of trial rights. He imposed a fine that was intended to reimburse the government for the costs of the trial. The court of appeals stated that it did not doubt the good faith of the trial judge, but remanded for resentencing, observing that "[i]t is well settled that an accused may not be subjected to more severe punishment simply because he exercised his right to stand trial." It directed the trial judge to state the reasons for the sentence imposed upon remand.

4. When it adopted a second set of Standards on Pleas of Guilty in 1980, the ABA modified its position. Standard 14–1.8 provides that a court should not treat the fact that a defendant entered a guilty plea as a mitigating factor. However, the court may consider whether the defendant who pleads guilty is genuinely contrite and willing to assume responsibility for his actions, whether sentencing concessions might provide more appropriate correctional measures, whether the defendant showed genuine concern for victims by avoiding trial, and whether the defendant has cooperated with the government. And the court may grant sentencing concessions. Do you think that it is possible for a court to assess the genuineness of professed motives for a plea as long as sentencing concessions are permissible?

Had the trial judge said nothing, the court of appeals presumably would have sustained the sentence. Do you think that a system that "encourages" pleas is likely to penalize those who insist on going to trial? Could a judge identify a lack of remorse as a basis for increasing the penalty? Should the judge do so?

Analyses like that provided by Judge Bazelon suggest that plea bargaining recognizes the absence of certainty in the trial process and the risk that both prosecutors and defendants must face in putting their cases before judges or juries. The ABA Standards purport to prohibit imposition of a higher sentence upon a defendant because he chooses trial as opposed to a guilty plea, but they also permit a reduction in sentence because a defendant acknowledges guilt and shows a willingness to accept responsibility for criminal acts. Is it satisfying to say that the defendant who goes to trial gets a fair sentence, even though it is higher than that imposed upon an identical defendant who pleads guilty, because the latter has accepted responsibility and therefore deserves a lower sentence? Or, do the ABA Standards provide camouflage for the reality that our system wants to encourage pleas in order to relieve courts of trial burdens, to protect witnesses from the burdens of testifying, and to keep conviction rates high? Cases like *Medina–Cervantes* indicate that excessive candor on the part of trial judges may be ill received by courts of appeals. But, there are many cases in which judges impose differential sentences on defendants who plead guilty and those who go to trial and offer little justification.

Suppose that a jurisdiction announced that it would reduce by 40% or some other percentage the sentence that would otherwise be imposed upon a defendant who is convicted after trial. Would such a system be invalid because it is explicitly a reward for giving up the right to trial? Is such a system objectionable because the same percentage reduction would be available to all defendants regardless of the seriousness of their crimes and the probability that they would be convicted at trial?

These questions are no longer of merely theoretical interest. The United States Sentencing Commission's guidelines, discussed at greater length in Chapter Eleven, infra, actually incorporate a two level reduction in the guideline range that will be applied to an offender who accepts responsibility for criminal conduct. Section 3E1.1. Such a reduction amounts to a 25–35% reduction in the sentence.

Acceptance of responsibility does not require a guilty plea, but the Commission apparently envisioned that a defendant who goes to trial rarely will be able to qualify for the reduction. The Commission's review of acceptance cases found that as many as 20% of the defendants who go to trial are able to obtain the reduction, a higher percentage than the Commission foresaw. The Department of Justice at one point recommended clarification of the acceptance criteria, but the Commission has not yet chosen to provide clarification.

Some of the Commission discussions indicate that Commission members are concerned that any explicit statement that a guilty plea automatically entitles a defendant to a reduction or that the decision to go to trial automatically disqualifies a defendant would raise constitutional problems, because of the appearance of a reward or penalty in the guidelines. This may explain why the acceptance criteria are not as clear as some prosecutors would prefer.

Would the guidelines be unconstitutional if they conditioned acceptance of responsibility on a plea of guilty? See e.g. United States v. White, 869 F.2d 822 (5th Cir. 1989) (Section 3E1.1 does not impinge on defendant's Sixth Amendment right to trial: "It is not unconstitutional for the Government to bargain for a guilty plea in exchange for a reduced sentence. The fact that a more lenient sentence is imposed on a contrite defendant does not establish a corollary that those who elect to stand trial are penalized.").

The Commission's approach does not focus in the slightest on the probability of conviction or the strength of the government's evidence. Nor does it focus on the seriousness of the offense charged. All defendants are treated equally. This is consistent with the mandate of the Commission to reduce unjustified disparities in sentencing, but arguably it may result in disparity. A defendant against whom the evidence is weak might well have negotiated a more favorable plea arrangement prior to the adoption of guidelines than a defendant against whom the evidence is strong. Does it make sense to treat these two defendants as though they were similarly situated? Does it make sense to provide the same sentencing reduction in percentage terms for all offenders regardless of the punishment they would otherwise receive?

The Commission's guidelines restrict "plea bargaining" to the extent that the amount of the reduction in sentence is fixed. The guidelines cannot control the charges brought against a defendant, however. Some members of the Commission have asserted that prosecutors at times evade the guidelines by their charging decisions. See, e.g., Schulhofer & Nagel, Negotiated Pleas Under the Federal Sentencing Guidelines: The First Fifteen Months, 27 Am.Crim.L.Rev. 231 (1989). The Department of Justice has attempted to control plea bargaining. It issued a Prosecutor's Handbook on Sentencing Guidelines and Other Provisions of the Sentencing Reform Act of 1984 (Nov. 1, 1987), a memorandum of the Assistant Attorney General of the Criminal Division to All Litigating Division Heads and All United States Attorneys (Nov. 3, 1987), and Attorney General Dick Thornburgh's Memorandum to Federal Prosecutors (Nov. 13, 1989). All of these pronouncements endeavored to assure appropriate punishment for offenders. Charges were to reflect the most serious conduct of an offender, and plea arrangements were not to subvert the guidelines. Schulhofer & Nagel, supra, at 285, conclude that "the mechanisms for preventing and exposing Guideline circumvention are incomplete and often ineffective." In part, this is because of dissatisfaction among some prosecutors with the guidelines and the incentives for defendants to plead.

The guidelines represent an effort to control the sentencing effects of plea bargaining. They raise new questions of policy. Should the same percentage reduction be used for all crimes and all offenders? If prosecutors inevitably must consider the strength or weaknesses of their cases, something which the Department of Justice permits, is it not inevitable that their charging decisions will reflect a desire to make the guidelines work so as to arrive at a result not very different from the result that would obtain without guidelines? If this is true, is it better to have a system that may encourage prosecutors to charge in ways that permit an agreed upon sentence to be obtained, but without judicial input, than a system that permits prosecutors and defendants to bargain subject to judicial review?

Which system is more just, one that permits bargaining in light of the facts of a particular case, or one that regulates the extent to which a bargain can effect sentences in all cases? Is fairness better defined in terms of percentage reduction equality or in terms of individualized justice? For an argument that some specified reward is necessary in a presumptive sentencing system, see Alschuler, Sentencing Reform and Prosecutorial Power: A Critique of Recent Proposals for "Fixed" and "Presumptive" Sentencing, 126 U.Pa.L.Rev. 550, 557–76 (1978).

The Senate Judiciary Committee, in Senate Report No. 98–225, at 63, wrote as follows:

> Some critics expressed the concern that a sentencing guidelines system will simply shift discretion from sentencing judges to prosecutors. The concern is that the prosecutor will use the plea bargaining process to circumvent the guidelines recommendation if he doesn't agree with the guidelines recommendation.
>
> The bill contains a provision designed to avoid this possibility. * * * [T]he Sentencing Commission is directed to issue policy statements for consideration by Federal judges in deciding whether to accept a plea agreement. This guidance will assure that judges can examine plea agreements to make certain that prosecutors have not used plea bargaining to undermine the sentencing guidelines. Professor Stephen J. Schulhofer, who initially raised the question of whether sentencing guidelines would shift too much discretion to prosecutors, has stated that judicial review of plea bargaining under such policy statements should alleviate any potential problem in this area.

Are you convinced? Schulhofer, Due Process of Sentencing, 128 U.Pa.L.Rev. 733 (1980), suggests a framework for judicial control of prosecutorial charge reduction decisions that would work to promote greater sentencing equality.

Professor Alschuler ultimately concludes that "neither a transfer of discretion to the prosecutor's office nor an increase in prosecutorial bargaining power is inevitable" under the new guideline sentencing, but suggests that the guidelines "permit the judicial control of prosecutorial power—again if judges will do the job." Alschuler, Departures and Plea Agreements Under the Sentencing Guidelines, 117 F.R.D. 459 (1988).

The suggestion is made in Pope, How Unreliable Factfinding Can Undermine Sentencing Guidelines, 95 Yale L.J. 1258 (1986), that too little attention has been paid to the procedural trappings that will promote fair sentencing under a guideline approach.

C. EFFICIENCY AT WHAT PRICE

Some commentators have argued that plea bargaining does not promote an efficient criminal justice system and that it produces unfairness.[5] Other commentators have pointed out some jurisdictions which might rely less on bargaining than do most American jurisdictions.[6] Yet, the study that began

5. Alschuler, The Changing Plea-Bargaining Debate, 69 Cal.L.Rev. 652 (1981), attacks plea bargaining as an efficiency, sentencing and dispute resolution device.

6. Schulhofer, Is Plea Bargaining Inevitable?, 97 Harv.L.Rev. 1037 (1984), suggests that it might be possible to have fewer plea bargains and more adversarial contests, even in major cities, than many analysts of plea

this chapter suggests that plea bargaining is a well-established institution.[7] Since most prosecutors and defense attorneys appear to accept bargaining, and influential figures such as the former Chief Justice of the United States insist that cases would grind to a halt, it is doubtful that plea bargaining will disappear in the near future.

Does plea bargaining produce acceptable results? The *Scott* case argues that in some cases it might, but bargaining is almost certain to produce disturbing results in other cases. Consider, for example, the following problem:

Problem

A defendant is charged with first degree murder, and he pleads self-defense. The two witnesses for the state are the daughter and wife of the deceased. Both claim that the defendant fired a gun without provocation. At a preliminary hearing the magistrate believes that the question of sufficiency of the evidence to hold the defendant is a close one because the eyewitnesses are less believable than the defendant, but ultimately binds the defendant over because a jury could believe them and return a guilty verdict. The grand jury charges first degree murder.

Assume that the prosecutor says to the defense lawyer in the course of plea bargaining, "I agree with the magistrate. The greater probability is self-defense here, but I figure that there is about a 40% chance that the defendant will be convicted of first degree murder. This surely is a case of premeditated murder or self-defense. It was one or the other, pure and simple." The prosecutor goes on to say: "If I am right, the expected minimum penalty from your client's perspective is 40% multiplied by the minimum sentence he can receive which is twenty years, or 8 years as the bottom line. In other words, your client will be found innocent and serve no time in 6 out of 10 cases, and in 4 out of 10 cases your client will serve a minimum of twenty years. The way I see it the jury either believes my witnesses or yours and that kind of case is always unpredictable. Like the magistrate implied, reasonable juries have leeway in determining whom to believe. Since your client has a 40% chance of serving a minimum of 20 years, a conservative, but impartial, observer would say that your client should be looking to reduce his exposure to jail. Here is what I am prepared to do: I will let your client plead to negligent homicide and recommend a two year sentence. Because your client has no prior record, the court will probably accept that recommendation." The defense lawyer takes

bargaining have assumed. The article describes bench trials in Philadelphia and concludes that the bench trials are more than "slow pleas" of guilty. The trials are described as adversarial and as producing results often favorable to defendants. See also Schulhofer, No Job Too Small: Justice Without Bargaining in the Lower Criminal Courts, 1986 ABA Res.J. 519.

Hughes, English Criminal Justice: Is it Better Than Ours?, 26 Ariz.L.Rev. 507, 559–87 (1984), points out that the English system, which is sometimes cited as an example of justice without bargaining, operates with far more pressure upon defendants to plead than many commentators like to admit. He does conclude, however, that the English system is less coercive than the American system. The English defendant has a fairly reasonable expectation of the sentencing concession awarded for a guilty plea. The confrontational case-by-case approach to bargaining that is familiar to Americans is not evident in the English system, perhaps because of the absence of a corps of professional prosecutors.

7. If you are interested in some history on plea bargaining, see Alschuler, Plea Bargaining and Its History, 79 Colum.L.Rev. 1 (1979). For a general exchange of views on the subject, see the numerous articles in 13 Law & Soc.Rev. 189–687 (1979).

this offer back to the client who is afraid of the possibility of a minimum twenty year sentence.

If the defense lawyer agrees on the odds and so informs the defendant, should the defendant be permitted to plead to the negligent homicide charge? Does it matter whether it is impossible that negligent homicide was committed?[8] If a factual basis requirement is in effect, must there be a factual basis for negligent homicide, or is it sufficient that there is a basis for the greater offense? If a basis for the lesser offense must be shown, can the prosecutor ethically permit the defendant to state to the court a distorted version of the facts? Could the prosecutor put on only part of the state's evidence in an effort to create for the court an appearance of negligent homicide? If the answer to either or both of the last two questions is "no," what incentive does the system provide for anyone to challenge an improper plea? If the defense lawyer agrees with the prosecutor about the odds but, in fact, better lawyers would calculate the chance of conviction as 20%, is ineffective assistance of counsel demonstrated? Is it ethical for the prosecutor to prosecute a case where the odds of getting a guilty verdict are less than even? Does it matter whether the prosecutor has a subjective belief in the guilt of the defendant?

Is it unrealistic to assume that the odds against conviction in some cases would be quite high? H. Kalven & H. Zeisel, The American Jury (1965) suggests that there may be reason to believe that an attractive defendant, a stiff penalty and the circumstances of a case may make the prosecutor's burden more onerous than it usually is. If the illustration uses numbers that you believe are unrealistic, change them so that there is a 60% chance of conviction. Should the defendant accept an offer to plead to second degree murder with an 8-year sentence recommendation? Could a rational lawyer advise against such a plea? If you like plea bargaining, consider whether there is any prosecutorial offer that would be so coercive as to be unreasonable. If you don't like plea bargaining, consider whether there is any offer that you would deem proper.

The problem of the deal that it is too good to turn down represents for some people one evil of plea bargaining. Some critics view such plea agreements as compromising society's interests; some view them as a threat to the innocent; some see problems of uncontrolled and unreviewable discretion; and some see all of these problems. See generally Parnas and Atkins, Abolishing Plea Bargaining: A Proposal, 14 Crim.L.Bull. 101 (1978); Langbein, Torture and Plea Bargaining, 46 Chi.L.Rev. 3 (1978).

As the previous section indicated, plea bargaining appears to be somewhat regulated by the federal sentencing guidelines. Ironically, however, there are circumstances in which the pressure on a federal defendant to plead can be tremendous notwithstanding the two level reduction for acceptance of responsibility that has been discussed. This pressure results from two factors: (1) the existence of mandatory minimum sentencing statutes; and (2) the possibility of

8. Some courts are more concerned with legal than with factual impossibility. But courts have approved pleas to non-existent crimes. See, e.g., People v. Foster, 19 N.Y.2d 150, 225 N.E.2d 200 (1967). Other courts have refused to do so, but have tried to suggest how an impermissible bargain could be restructured so that both sides can retain the benefits. See, e.g., People v. Collins, 21 Cal.3d 208, 145 Cal.Rptr. 686, 577 P.2d 1026 (1978). What are the most powerful arguments against pleas to nonexistent crimes? Are there arguments to support such pleas? If plea bargaining comes down to sentence bargaining, does it really matter to what crime a defendant pleads? Why? See the discussion in United States v. Briggs in the next section.

a reduction in sentence below a mandatory minimum for substantial assistance to the prosecution in the investigation and prosecution of other defendants.

Congress has provided with respect to various offenses, particularly drugs and firearms, a substantial minimum sentence. The Sentencing Commission provided Congress in August, 1991 with a "Special Report" entitled Mandatory Minimum Penalties in the Federal Criminal Justice System. This lengthy document observes that there are more than 60 criminal statutes in the federal criminal code that contain mandatory minimum penalties, and that only four of the 60 frequently result in convictions. All four relate to drug and weapon offenses. The Commission found that, despite the expectation that the mandatory minimum would be applied in all cases in which the defendant seemed eligible for the penalty, a considerable number of cases resulted in a lesser sentence. Indeed, the Commission found that in 35% of these cases, defendants pled guilty to offenses carrying either nonmandatory or reduced mandatory minimum penalties. The Commission was unable to determine whether the pleas were justified by evidentiary concerns or other legitimate governmental interests.

The presence of a mandatory minimum penalty can produce great pressure on a defendant to plead guilty to escape the minimum. In a number of instances, the guidelines adopted by the Commission would not impose a sentence as strict as required by a mandatory minimum statute. If a prosecutor is willing to charge under a nonmandatory or reduced mandatory statute, the defendant may leap at a plea offer, particularly if the mandatory penalty that is avoided by the plea is 10 years or more. See DeBenedectis, Mandatory Minimum Sentences Hit, A.B.A.J. Dec. 1991, p. 36 (noting that "mandatory minimums give federal prosecutors wide discretion over sentencing through the crimes they charge and bargains they accept").

Additionally, section 5K1.1 of the Guidelines contains a policy statement on substantial assistance, which recognizes that where a defendant provides substantial assistance, a trial court may depart from the guidelines. Because Congress has provided in 18 U.S.C. § 3553(e) that a substantial assistance departure may go below a mandatory minimum, the defendant who can provide substantial assistance may be able to avoid a very high penalty even if he or she cannot persuade a prosecutor to reduce or amend charges. The defendant may be encouraged to plead to obtain the benefits of the substantial assistance rule.

The higher the mandatory minimum and the greater the reduction associated with cooperation, the more pressure there is for the defendant to abandon a defense and to cooperate. Thus, in the end, it may be that in drug and firearm cases the federal system is as coercive as any found in the states. Is this a problem? Should mandatory minimum penalties be permitted to go hand in hand with plea bargaining? If not, which should be abolished?

D. PROSECUTORIAL VINDICTIVENESS

Not all plea bargaining involves settlements that look like a wonderful deal for the defendant. Consider, for example, Bordenkircher v. Hayes, 434 U.S. 357 (1978). Hayes was indicted by a Kentucky grand jury on a charge of uttering a forged instrument in the amount of $88.30, an offense punishable by

2–10 years imprisonment. During pre-trial negotiations, the prosecutor told Hayes that if he did not plead guilty and "save the court the inconvenience and necessity of a trial," the prosecutor would seek a new indictment under the then existing Kentucky Habitual Criminal Act, which carried a mandatory life sentence. Hayes chose not to plead guilty, was indicted under the Act and received a life sentence. The Supreme Court affirmed, holding that the decision whether to charge an offense rests with prosecutors and grand juries and that "a rigid constitutional rule that would prohibit a prosecutor from acting forthrightly in his dealings with the defense could only invite unhealthy subterfuge that would drive the practice of plea bargaining back into the shadows from which it has so recently emerged." In sum, the Court concluded that "this case would be no different if the grand jury had indicted Hayes as a recidivist from the outset, and the prosecutor had offered to drop that charge as part of the plea bargain." [9] Justice Blackmun, joined by Justices Brennan and Marshall, dissented. He disagreed with the Court's analysis that the timing of the indictment made no difference and suggested that prior to *Hayes* the Court "ha[d] never openly sanctioned such deliberate overcharging or taken such a cynical view of the bargaining process." He added that "[e]ven if overcharging is to be sanctioned, there are strong reasons of fairness why the charge should be presented at the beginning of the bargaining process, rather than as a filliped thread at the end." Justice Powell also dissented on the ground that the prosecutor effectively conceded that his strategy did not reflect the public interest in an appropriate sentence, but simply a desire to avoid trial even if the means of doing so was the imposition of an unreasonable sentence. Which view, if any, would you support?[10]

Bordenkircher v. Hayes, illustrates how much discretion the prosecution has in charging offenses with an eye to plea bargaining. Would you control this discretion? Could you? See generally Gifford, Meaningful Reform of Plea Bargaining: The Control of Prosecutorial Discretion, 1983 U.Ill.L.Rev. 37.

III. THE REQUIREMENTS FOR A VALID GUILTY PLEA

A. DISTINGUISHING BARGAINING FROM THE PLEA PROCEDURE

Sections I and II of the chapter demonstrate that American courts do not treat plea bargaining as though it were inherently evil. On the contrary, prosecutors regularly offer to drop charges or to recommend lower sentences in

9. Although the government can use a bargain to induce a defendant to go to trial, it cannot use one to induce a witness' silence. See Jones v. United States, 386 A.2d 308 (D.C.App.1978). Can you see a distinction that you can defend?

10. In Corbitt v. New Jersey, 439 U.S. 212 (1978), the Court upheld a New Jersey statute that mandated life sentences for defendants convicted by a jury, but permitted lesser terms for those who pleaded guilty. The Court relied on Bordenkircher v. Hayes.

In United States v. Richburg, 478 F.Supp. 535 (M.D.Tenn.1979), the court distinguished *Bordenkircher* and held that where a defendant was not told during plea negotiations that his failure to plead would lead to the filing of additional charges, it was unconstitutional for the government to bring new charges after bargaining was unsuccessful. A majority of the court in Twiggs v. Superior Court, 34 Cal.3d 360, 194 Cal.Rptr. 152, 667 P.2d 1165 (1983), also found that the prosecutor's amendment of an information to charge five additional felonies after a defendant refused an offered plea gave rise to a presumption of vindictiveness. The majority distinguished *Bordenkircher* on the ground that the additional charges were not made as part of a bargaining process, since bargaining had ended before the charges were brought.

exchange for guilty pleas. The hypothetical problem posed in Section II highlights how attractive prosecutors' offers might appear, especially when defendants face charges carrying huge maximum sentences.

Courts tend to distinguish the bargaining that takes place, which is largely unregulated as Bordenkircher v. Hayes illustrates, from the procedures surrounding the judicial acceptance of a guilty plea. These procedures have grown more formal over time. The unanswered question is whether the formality provides realistic protection for defendants or only trappings to persuade a watchful public that justice is being done.

B. THE REQUIREMENT OF SOME KIND OF A RECORD

In two cases decided in 1969, McCarthy v. United States, 394 U.S. 459, and Boykin v. Alabama, 395 U.S. 238, the Supreme Court made it clear that, because a defendant who pleads guilty gives up several constitutional rights, a valid guilty plea requires "an intentional relinquishment or abandonment of a known right or privilege." (Citing Johnson v. Zerbst, 304 U.S. 458, 464 (1938).)[11] The Court said that "[c]onsequently, if a defendant's guilty plea is not equally voluntary and knowing, it has been obtained in violation of due process and is therefore void."

In *McCarthy*, the Court set aside the guilty plea of a defendant who had pleaded to one count of a three count indictment charging willful and knowing attempts to evade federal income tax payments. After discussing in dictum the constitutional requirements for a valid plea, the Court based its decision on Fed.R.Crim.P. 11. The trial judge did not comply with the rule, since he failed both to ask the defendant whether he understood the nature of the charges against him and to inquire adequately into the voluntariness of the plea, the Court said that the defendant had to be afforded the opportunity to plead anew. Rule 11 was viewed as an attempt to avoid post-plea hearings on waiver, and the Court refused to remand the case for such a hearing into the intelligent and voluntary nature of McCarthy's plea.

Boykin v. Alabama overturned death sentences imposed by an Alabama jury on a 27 year old black man who pleaded guilty to five indictments charging common law robbery. (In Alabama at the time, the jury determined punishment following a plea except where state law required otherwise.) The Supreme Court said that "[i]t was error, plain on the face of the record, for the trial judge to accept petitioner's guilty plea without an affirmative showing that it was intelligent and voluntary." Citing another right to counsel case, Carnley v. Cochran, 369 U.S. 506 (1962), the Court said that it was impermissible to presume, on the basis of a silent record, waiver of constitutional rights as important as the privilege against self-incrimination, trial by jury and confrontation. Justice Harlan, joined by Justice Black, would have remanded for a hearing, apparently because the absence of a good record showing waiver did not establish that no constitutionally valid waiver took place. The dissent emphasized that *McCarthy* was decided under the Federal Rules of Criminal Procedure, not the Constitution.

11. The *Johnson* standard has been examined in several places thus far—e.g., in connection with Brewer v. Williams in Chapter Three.

Justice Harlan's dissent voices reasonable concern that *Boykin* "in effect fastens upon the States, as a matter of federal constitutional law, the rigid prophylactic requirements of Rule 11 of the Federal Rules of Criminal Procedure." Prior to 1975, Rule 11 was unclear as to exactly what a trial judge had to say to a defendant in order to comply. *Boykin* itself did not tell the states exactly what to do, other than to develop a record relating to a guilty plea. Arguably, the *Boykin* majority at least wanted a specific warning about the three constitutional rights identified as especially important. This interpretation often has been rejected by lower courts, however. See, e.g., United States v. Henry, 933 F.2d 553 (7th Cir. 1991) (guilty plea held valid even though the defendant was not precisely informed of rights listed in *Boykin*; literal compliance with *Boykin* is not required, so long as the defendant understands that by pleading guilty, he waives his right to trial); United States v. Colston, 936 F.2d 312 (7th Cir. 1991) (when the judge described what would occur at trial, defendant who pleaded guilty must have known that he was waiving his right to confrontation).

Boykin's requirement of an explicit record has also been flexibly applied. See e.g., United States v. Ferguson, 935 F.2d 862 (7th Cir. 1991) (absence of transcript of guilty plea hearing is not fatal; the court relies on the custom, practice and law applicable to guilty pleas in Illinois state courts, all of which leads to a presumption that the defendant was informed of the necessary rights under *Boykin*).

If a state court develops no record at the time a plea is entered but subsequently holds a habeas corpus hearing in response to a defendant's challenge to a guilty plea, is the habeas record an adequate substitute for a hearing at time of the plea? North Carolina v. Alford, 400 U.S. 25, 29 n. 3 (1970), suggests an affirmative answer. See also Smith v. State, 264 Ark. 329, 571 S.W.2d 591 (1978).[12] Also unclear is whether *Boykin* applies to misdemeanor pleas. Whelan v. State, 472 S.W.2d 140 (Tex.Crim.App.1971), suggests a negative answer, but can this be squared with the right to counsel cases (*Argersinger,* for example)[13] previously examined, especially in view of the fact that both *McCarthy* and *Boykin* cite right to counsel cases? State v. Vensel, 88 Wn.2d 552, 564 P.2d 326 (1977), treats courts not of record the same as higher courts; compliance with *Boykin* is mandated. Thus, the true significance of *Boykin* is not clear.

12. In People v. Sumstine, 36 Cal.3d 909, 206 Cal.Rptr. 707, 687 P.2d 904 (1984), the court analyzed a *Boykin* problem when a defendant challenged a prior conviction that was used to enhance his sentence. Records regarding the conviction had been destroyed. The court concluded that a defendant cannot simply rely upon the silence or absence of records and must allege that he was not warned of rights. The government is permitted to prove that, in fact, warnings were given.

13. Note that *Whelan* came before *Argersinger.*

Although *Boykin* does not appear to be limited to felony cases, it is well known that in many courts that handle misdemeanors, particularly courts not of record, guilty pleas are taken en masse without personal warnings of constitutional rights to individual defendants. In State v. Toney, 412 So.2d 1034 (La.1982), and State v. Jones, 404 So.2d 1192 (La.1981), the court indicated that "whenever a misdemeanor guilty plea will be used as a basis for actual imprisonment, enhancement of actual imprisonment or conversion of a subsequent misdemeanor into a felony," the three rights specified in *Boykin* must be explained to a defendant.

C. VOLUNTARY AND INTELLIGENT PLEAS AND THE ADVANTAGES OF A COMPLETE RECORD

1. *A Voluntary Plea*

To be valid, a guilty plea must be voluntary; that is, it must not be the product of improper coercion by government officials. The standard of voluntariness is similar to that employed in connection with confessions, a standard that was examined in Chapter Three, supra. As the Supreme Court said in Brady v. United States, discussed infra, "the agents of the State may not produce a plea by actual or threatened physical harm or by mental coercion overbearing the will of the defendant." Thus, it is clear that if a defendant were threatened with physical torture or actually harmed as part of an effort to get him to plead guilty, any resulting plea would be involuntary. Most challenges to guilty pleas do not raise these kinds of claims, however. Unlike the interrogation process, the procedure for accepting pleas affords opportunities for trial judges to see whether a defendant is apparently exercising free will in choosing to plead. Whether it is the degree of control exercised by the courts or the fact that prosecutors, as lawyers, tend to be less coercive than police officers, or both, is unclear, but for some reason there seem to be fewer complaints about threats of physical harm or improper mental coercion when guilty pleas are challenged than when confessions are attacked.

Perhaps the most interesting thing about guilty pleas is that they are deemed to be voluntary in circumstances in which it is doubtful that a confession would be called voluntary—i.e., when the state explicitly offers something of value to the defendant who agrees to plead guilty and give up trial rights. As noted earlier this aspect of voluntariness has not troubled most courts.

2. *A Knowing and Intelligent Plea*

In Henderson v. Morgan, 426 U.S. 637 (1976), a 19 year old defendant, with substantially less than average intelligence, pleaded guilty to second degree murder, after he was advised by counsel that a 25 year sentence would be imposed. The defendant had been indicted for first degree murder as a result of stabbing to death a woman who employed him while he was on release from a state school for mental defectives. The stabbing took place when she discovered him in her room at night trying to get his wages so that he could leave the premises unnoticed. Because the defendant was not advised that an intent to cause the victim's death was an element of second degree murder, the Court held that even if his lawyers would have given the defendant the same advice—i.e., to plead guilty—had the defendant been specifically informed of every element of the offense, and even though the Court was willing to "assume that he probably would have pleaded anyway," the plea could not be voluntary [14] unless the defendant knew the nature of the offense to which he pleaded. In its footnote 18, the Court assumed that notice of a charge did not always require a description of every element of an offense, but said that

14. The Court used the word "voluntary" to mean the same thing as "intelligent." Why this choice was made is unexplained.

For a discussion of the standard of competency to plead guilty, see Note, Competence to Plead Guilty and to Stand Trial: A New Standard When a Criminal Defendant Waives Trial, 68 Va.L.Rev. 1139 (1982).

"intent is such a critical element of the offense of second-degree murder that notice of that element is required." Justice White, joined by Justices Stewart, Blackmun and Powell, concurred and emphasized that the decision whether or not to plead to a specific offense is the defendant's alone, not his lawyer's. Justice Rehnquist, joined by Chief Justice Burger, dissented.

Under *Henderson,* it is normally presumed that the defendant is informed by his attorney of the charges against him and the elements of those charges. See Oppel v. Meachum, 851 F.2d 34 (2d Cir.1988). Furthermore, testimony of an accused's counsel that it is his standard practice to advise his clients of the elements of the charged offense and potential defenses has been held sufficient to defeat a due process challenge. United States v. Butcher, 926 F.2d 811 (9th Cir.1991). However, as illustrated in Tamayo–Reyes v. Keeney, 926 F.2d 1492 (9th Cir.1991), when an accused does not speak English, an additional inquiry is necessary. Even if the court will assume that the attorney described to the translator certain essential elements of the crime, the critical issue remains whether the translator accurately translated that communication.

Henderson establishes that a defendant must know about some "crucial" elements of the offense to which the guilty plea is addressed.[15] What else must a defendant know? Generally, a defendant must know the penalty that can be imposed. See, e.g., Chavez v. Wilson, 417 F.2d 584 (9th Cir. 1969); Stephen v. United States, 426 F.2d 257 (5th Cir. 1970). Is a general idea of the maximum penalty enough? See Pilkington v. United States, 315 F.2d 204 (4th Cir. 1963) (implying that defendant should have been told not only about statutory maximums, but also about possibility he would serve more time if sentenced under Youth Corrections Act). If the defendant is to understand the potential consequences of pleading, the general rule should be that a defendant must know whether several counts or indictments will produce concurrent or consecutive sentences. See ABA Standards, Pleas of Guilty, § 11–1.4 (requiring such an understanding). Some courts would not hold a plea invalid because the defendant did not know of a statutory minimum penalty. See, e.g., People v. Kontopoulos, 26 Ill.2d 388, 186 N.E.2d 312 (1962). Would you call a plea without knowledge of the minimum penalty a knowing one? Is it sufficient to know the maximum?

Is a plea knowing and voluntary when the judge explains the elements of a more severe offense but the defendant pleads to a lesser offense? In United States v. Wildes, 910 F.2d 1484 (7th Cir.1990), the court held that the defendant's guilty plea to aiding and abetting delivery of marijuana was not involuntary because the trial court recited more complex elements of the party to crime offense rather than the elements of the aiding and abetting offense prior to accepting the defendant's guilty plea. The court emphasized that the defendant never stated that he did not know the elements of an aiding and abetting offense. Did the defendant really know the crucial elements of the offense?

Most decisions distinguish knowledge of sentence possibilities from knowledge of "collateral consequences." For example, most courts do not require that a defendant be told of the possibility (or even of a mandatory requirement)

15. See also Harned v. Henderson, 588 F.2d 12 (2d Cir. 1978); Commonwealth v. Tabb, 477 Pa. 115, 383 A.2d 849 (1978).

of deportation following conviction. See Vizcarra-Delgadillo v. United States, 395 F.2d 70 (9th Cir. 1968) (Browning, J., dissenting). Most do not require that a defendant be told about the possibility of future prosecution under a multiple offender (or habitual or repeat offender) law, of the loss of driver's license, of the loss of business opportunities, of parole revocation, or of parole generally. See generally Note, Guilty Plea Bargains and Compromises By Prosecutor to Secure Guilty Pleas, 112 U.Pa.L.Rev. 865 (1964). But see Annot., 8 ALR Fed. 760 (knowledge of ineligibility for parole), Annot., 42 ALR Fed. 707 (1979) (failure to advise accused of mandatory minimum parole term).[16]

Can a guilty plea be valid if the defendant did not commit the crime? Consider the following facts:

> Susan Briggs stole over $5 million dollars from her employers by initiating wire transfers from their accounts to hers and others. She pleaded guilty in 1986 to charges of bank fraud and transportation of stolen money and was sentenced to a total of thirty years imprisonment. Subsequently, she challenged the validity of her guilty plea on the ground that it was not knowing and intelligent. In essence, she maintained that she did not obtain funds by means of false or fraudulent pretenses, representations, or promises, as required by the bank fraud statute, and therefore, her plea of guilty to that charge was not an informed one.

Was her plea knowing and intelligent? When presented with these facts, the court in United States v. Briggs, 939 F.2d 222 (5th Cir.1991), held that an evidentiary hearing was necessary because defendant's plea might not have been knowing and intelligent. The court reasoned as follows:

> The record of Briggs' guilty plea does not reflect any representations, pretenses, or promises at all—false or otherwise—from which we might conclude that Briggs' conduct constituted a violation of [the statute].
>
> * * * A plea is not voluntary if the accused "has such incomplete understanding of the charge that his plea cannot stand as an intelligent admission of guilt." * * *
>
> Simply put, to convict someone of a crime on the basis of conduct that does not constitute the crime offends the basic notions of justice and fair play embodied in the Constitution.
>
> Briggs contends that she pleaded guilty in the mistaken belief that the act of ordering funds transferred, in itself, amounted to a sufficient misrepresentation under the bank fraud statute. She also maintains that she did not make a misrepresentation in connection with the wire transfer order. In sum, she alleges that she pleaded guilty to a crime which she now understands not to encompass her conduct, and therefore, her plea of guilty was not knowing and intelligent. Since we hold that the ordering of transfer of funds, without more,

16. See also Strader v. Garrison, 611 F.2d 61 (4th Cir. 1979) (although defendant pleading guilty generally need not be informed of parole eligibility date, a defendant who asks and is grossly misinformed by counsel has been denied constitutional rights; state could avoid retrial by reducing the sentence so the bad advice would be rendered harmless); Meyer v. State, 95 Nev. 855, 603 P.2d 1066 (1979) (withdrawal of guilty plea must be allowed when defendant was not told that statute did not allow probation). Hunter v. Fogg, 616 F.2d 55 (2d Cir. 1980), distinguished the shortest statutory mandatory sentence (about which a defendant must be told) from a possibility of parole ineligibility (about which he need not be told).

Federal Rule of Criminal Procedure 11(c)(1), set forth infra, was amended in 1982 to require that the defendant be told about special parole terms.

> does not amount to a violation of the bank fraud statute, we agree with Briggs that her motion sufficiently alleges a due process challenge to the validity of her guilty plea.

Is this consistent with *Henderson?* Is the court saying that a person can only knowingly and intelligently plead guilty when they actually are guilty of the underlying offense? Don't people routinely plead to lesser offenses to obtain shorter sentences when they really did not commit the elements of that particular crime?

3. *The Amended Federal Rule*

To provide better guidance to federal trial judges as to what information a defendant should have when pleading and what the court should know in deciding whether or not to accept a plea, Fed.R.Crim.P. 11 was amended in 1975 and again in 1982.[17] It now specifically requires that the trial judge inform the defendant of the rights listed in the rule and that the judge require disclosure on the record of any plea agreement.

Some appellate courts have taken the requirements of Rule 11 to heart and indicated to trial judges that noncompliance will render pleas nullities. See, e.g., United States v. Kahn, 588 F.2d 964 (5th Cir. 1979); United States v. Adams, 566 F.2d 962 (5th Cir. 1978); United States v. Journet, 544 F.2d 633 (2d Cir. 1976). But there has been a tendency today to treat the rule more flexibly in collateral attack cases and to require a showing of prejudice before a complaint of noncompliance will be entertained. See, e.g., Lepera v. United States, 587 F.2d 433 (9th Cir. 1978); Del Vecchio v. United States, 556 F.2d 106 (2d Cir. 1977). In United States v. Timmreck, 441 U.S. 780 (1979), Justice Stevens' opinion for a unanimous court established that a conviction based on a guilty plea cannot be collaterally attacked for a Rule 11 violation, unless the violation is constitutional or jurisdictional.

The idea of subdivision (d) of Rule 11 is not only to assure that a plea is tendered for the right reasons, but also to make a record that will be sufficient to assure that a guilty plea is really final and can withstand a subsequent attack. No matter how careful a court is, however, some post-conviction claims probably will require hearings. See generally Note, Rule 11 and Collateral Attack on Guilty Pleas, 86 Yale L.J. 1393 (1977). The Supreme Court has recognized with respect to the rule that "like any procedural mechanism, its exercise is neither always perfect nor uniformly invulnerable to subsequent challenge calling for an opportunity to prove the allegations." Fontaine v. United States, 411 U.S. 213, 215 (1973). Although the rule is not a sure guarantor of finality, it results in fewer post-plea hearings than otherwise would be required, and it can impart much information to the criminal defendant who has an important decision to make. See Spritzer, Criminal Waiver, Procedural Default and the Burger Court, 126 U.Pa.L.Rev. 473, 494 (1978).

United States v. Bachynsky, 934 F.2d 1349 (5th Cir.1991) (en banc), analyzes the various approaches taken by federal circuits to plea colloquies that

17. Several state courts have followed the federal lead and have stated explicitly what trial judges must do in accepting pleas. See, e.g., State v. Mackey, 553 S.W.2d 337 (Tenn. 1977). See generally Annot., 41 ALR Fed. 874 (1979).

fail to satisfy Rule 11. It defined the issue before it and summarized its conclusion as follows:

> Today we consider whether there may be circumstances under which the harmless error provision of Rule 11(h), * * * obviates the need to vacate a plea of guilty or nolo contendere even though, during the plea colloquy specified in Rule 11(c)(1) for determining the defendant's understanding of the maximum possible penalty provided by law, the district court fails totally to mention or explain the effect of any supervised release term to which the defendant is exposed. For the reasons set forth below, we respond affirmatively, concluding that a district court's total failure during the plea colloquy to mention or explain the effect of supervised release does not constitute a total failure to address a Rule 11 core concern, and thus does not automatically mandate reversal. Consequently, when a total failure to address supervised release is determined to constitute only a partial failure to address a core concern of Rule 11, the door is open to a determination of whether the district court's failure to explain the effects of supervised release affected the substantial rights of the defendant. * * *

The defendant was a Ph.D.–M.D. who pleaded guilty to racketeering and a tax conspiracy. The scheme giving rise to the convictions involved weight loss and smoking cessation clinics in which innumerable unnecessary medical tests were conducted for which insurance companies were billed. The defendant's plea agreement stated that he was aware of the maximum sentences for both charges to which he pleaded and that he could be sentenced to the maximum sentence allowable under the law. At the plea hearing, the district court explained the nature of the charges and the maximum penalties, but did not explain supervised release or advise the defendant that his sentence could or would include a term of supervised release. The defendant was sentenced to 121 months imprisonment and three years of supervised release.

The court of appeals reasoned that, even if supervised release were considered to be the equivalent of prison, and even if it assumed that the three years or 36 months of such release could be extended to five years and would be revoked so that the defendant would spend every day of the sentence (including the supervised release portion) incarcerated, the total sentence was less than the maximum sentence that could have been imposed. It concluded that "the core concern * * * is that the defendant understand the consequences of his plea," and that, once the district court explains the statutory maxima for offenses, a failure to inform a defendant of supervised release is a partial failure to address a core concern.

On the facts of the case, the en banc court found harmless error. It warned that "[o]ur decision today should be viewed by this circuit's criminal defense bar as a caution not to 'lie behind the log' in hopes of getting a second bite at the plea bargain apple when and if counsel should notice an inadvertent omission in the district court's plea colloquy," and that "our decision should not be interpreted by prosecutors or district courts as a signal to relax their dedication to total compliance with all provisions of Fed.R.Crim.P. 11, particularly those of section c(1)." It added that "this court has no intention of abdicating its obligation to scrutinize plea colloquies for adherence to Rule 11."

Later, in United States v. Bounds, 943 F.2d 541 (5th Cir.1991), the court was presented with the problem that did not exist in *Bachynsky:* the aggregate amount of supervised release and actual prison sentence imposed exceeded the statutory maximum explained to the defendant. The lower court informed the defendant of a twenty-five year maximum, whereas he actually received a twenty-five year prison sentence and three years of supervised release. Accordingly, the Court of Appeals found a violation of a "core concern" of Rule 11. The question was what remedy to apply. The court noted that one possible remedy would be to remove the supervised release period and uphold the plea. But the court found that not possible where, as here, the statute under which the defendant pleaded required the imposition of supervised release. Therefore, the court reversed the conviction and vacated the sentence, giving the defendant leave to plead anew.

Should defense counsel be required in all cases to submit to the court a statement declaring that the defendant has been informed of all possible consequences of a guilty plea and to state what those consequences are? This would permit both the prosecution and the trial court to focus on any misunderstandings or omissions which might later serve as the basis for challenging a plea. Would such a requirement violate the attorney-client privilege? Is there any argument that it would be unfair to impose such a burden on counsel? If such a burden were imposed, should the prosecutor be required to submit in writing a written statement of the possible consequences so that it could be compared with that submitted by the defense? Were counsel required to make such submissions, would the trial court's role be improperly invaded in any way?

4. The Problem Case; Secret Promises

Blackledge v. Allison, 431 U.S. 63 (1977), illustrates the kind of case that Rule 11 is designed to filter out. Allison pleaded guilty to attempted safe robbery in a North Carolina state court. The trial court judge read questions to Allison from a printed form.

Three days after answering the questions, Allison was sentenced to 17–21 years in prison. He sought habeas corpus relief to attack his conviction, alleging that he was told by counsel that the trial judge told counsel that Allison would only get 10 years if he pleaded guilty. The Court noted that "[t]he litany of form questions * * * nowhere indicated to Allison (or indeed to the lawyers involved) that plea bargaining was a legitimate practice that could be freely disclosed in open court. * * * The process thus did nothing to dispel a defendant's belief that any bargain struck must remain concealed. * * *" Thus, the court held that Allison had a right to have his claim heard. Justice Powell concurred and stated that the case was "an example * * * of how finality can be frustrated by failure to adhere to proper procedures at the trial court level." [18]

One of the claims that is difficult to cut off at a plea hearing is that the defendant was not mentally competent when he pleaded. If there is any doubt about competency prior to plea, qualified experts should examine the defendant. Trial judges are well advised to pay scrupulous attention to the mental

18. Chief Justice Burger concurred in the judgment. Justice Rehnquist did not participate in the decision of the case.

condition of the defendant.[19] See Suggs v. LaVallee, 570 F.2d 1092 (2d Cir. 1978).

Special promises of leniency, threats of harm, and other improper influences should be more easily ferreted out at a plea hearing if the court addresses the prosecutor and defense counsel as well as the defendant. Once rules like Fed.R.Crim.P. 11 make an effort to force plea bargains out in the open, should courts be more reluctant to allow a defendant to allege that promises or threats were made to induce a plea, when the defendant and counsel represented otherwise to a trial judge who asked about bargains, threats, etc.? See Walters v. Harris, 460 F.2d 988 (4th Cir. 1972) (suggesting that treating a plea as final in such circumstances is desirable). But see Comment, United States v. Barker; Presentence Withdrawal of Guilty Pleas, 71 Nw.U.L.Rev. 86 (1976).

In re Ibarra, 34 Cal.3d 277, 193 Cal.Rptr. 538, 666 P.2d 980 (1983), recognizes a special duty of judicial scrutiny into possible coercion when prosecutors offer "package deal" bargains to several defendants. Professor Green, in "Package" Plea Bargaining and the Prosecutor's Duty of Good Faith, 25 Crim.L.Bull. 507 (1989), argues that courts do not take sufficient account of the coercive aspects of package plea bargaining, but that prosecutors who offer multi-defendant deals have an ethical responsibility to avoid overreaching.

5. *Prosecutorial Recommendations*

Fed.R.Crim.P. 11 permits the government (1) to move to dismiss some charges, (2) to recommend a sentence or not to oppose a sentence, (3) or to agree that a specific sentence is the appropriate disposition of the case. What difference is there between 2 and 3? Note that no recommendation is binding on the court. There is a way the prosecutor can bind the court, however—by negotiating before filing charges and thus limiting the court's sentencing alternatives. Similarly, the prosecutor can work out informal arrangements to suspend a contemplated prosecution while the defendant seeks rehabilitative help, an agreement beyond the normal control of a court[20] (although a breakdown in the agreement may bring the court into the picture and the court may have to decide what, if any, impact the past agreement should have on future proceedings). See Model Code of Pre-Arraignment Procedure § 320.5.

One of the most important parts of Rule 11 is subdivision (11)(e)(4), which permits a defendant to withdraw a plea if the court rejects a specific agreement. The idea is to permit judges some role in screening plea bargains, but to allow the parties to start anew when the judge rejects a bargain.[21]

19. See generally Annots., 31 ALR Fed. 375 (1976); 38 ALR Fed. 238 (1978).

20. See Dearborne v. State, 575 S.W.2d 259 (Tenn.1978).

21. Note how this effectively makes the judge a participant in bargaining. At some point the judge may accept a bargain and both the prosecutor and the defendant must realize this.

A trial judge's blanket policy of rejecting plea agreements that permit a defendant charged with multiple counts to plead to only one was condemned in United States v. Miller, 722 F.2d 562 (9th Cir.1983). The court of appeals reasoned that trial judges must exercise their discretion in particular cases rather than establish blanket rules regarding acceptable pleas.

In United States v. Cruz, 539 F.Supp. 231 (D.Puerto Rico 1982), one of four defendants charged with cocaine distribution agreed to a plea bargain in which the government moved to dismiss an indictment and file a superceding information charging a misdemeanor and to recommend probation at the time of sentencing. The judge indicated that he would

Potential unfairness arises when the prosecutor recommends a sentence—e.g., 10 years—that is not binding on the court and the judge accepts the plea but then sentences the defendant to more than the recommended sentence. Consider, for example, Lilly v. Commonwealth, 218 Va. 960, 243 S.E.2d 208 (1978).

In *Lilly,* the prosecutor made the agreed upon recommendation when the plea was entered and reiterated it at sentencing.[22] The judge rejected the 10 year suspended sentence recommended by the prosecutor, refused to let Lilly withdraw his plea and gave him 10 years with no part suspended. Although Lilly was told that the judge would impose sentence, do you believe that any defendant situated like Lilly would believe that 10 years suspended was not going to be the sentence?[23] Do you find this procedure acceptable? If any part of it bothers you, what changes would you suggest?[24]

D. CLAIMS OF INNOCENCE

The Model Code of Pre-Arraignment Procedure § 350.4(4) addresses a subject not explicitly covered by Rule 11. It provides that "[t]he court may accept the defendant's guilty plea even though the defendant does not admit that he is in fact guilty if the court finds that it is reasonable for someone in the defendant's position to plead guilty. The court shall advise the defendant that if he pleads guilty he will be treated as guilty whether he is guilty or not." This approach is consistent with North Carolina v. Alford, 400 U.S. 25 (1970).

Alford was indicted by North Carolina for the capital crime of first-degree murder. He pleaded guilty to second-degree murder, but at the plea hearing he took the stand and testified in part as follows:

> I pleaded guilty on second degree murder because they said there is too much evidence, but I ain't shot no man, but I take the fault for the other man. We never had an argument in our life and I just pleaded guilty because they said if I didn't they would gas me for it, and that is all.

Subsequently, Alford sought post-conviction relief on the ground that his plea was produced by fear and coercion. After noting that "[s]tate and lower federal

accept the plea, but reserved a ruling on the sentencing recommendation until he saw a presentence report. Once having seen the report, the judge decided to vacate the plea because it appeared that the defendant was involved in an operation too extensive to be disposed of by a misdemeanor plea. The opinion emphasizes the importance of the "public interest" in plea bargains.

22. In United States v. Benchimol, 471 U.S. 453 (1985), the Court held that the government did not breach its plea agreement when it recommended, as promised, probation without restitution for a defendant convicted of mail fraud, but it made no effort to explain its reason for agreeing to recommend a lenient sentence. The Court found that it was error for the court of appeals to imply a condition—i.e., explanation of the recommendation—that the parties had not made part of their agreement. Justice Stevens concurred in the judgment. Justice Brennan, joined by Justice Marshall, dissented.

23. The point that what a defendant believes is critical is made in United States v. Marzgliano, 588 F.2d 395 (3d Cir. 1978) (requiring hearing on what defendant was told about the effect of his plea, not on what actually transpired between trial judge and defense counsel).

24. One possible approach is found in Model Code of Pre-Arraignment Procedure § 350.6.

> The court after pronouncing the sentence * * * shall inquire of the defendant personally whether the sentence pronounced violates any agreement or understanding the defendant had with respect to the sentence. If the court determines that the sentence is inconsistent with an agreement or that it differs from the defendant's understanding in such a way that it would be unjust to permit the defendant's plea to stand it shall vacate the plea.

courts are divided upon whether a guilty plea can be accepted when it is accompanied by protestations of innocence and hence contains only a waiver of trial but no admission of guilt," the Court concluded that "[i]n view of the strong factual basis for the plea demonstrated by the State and Alford's clearly expressed desire to enter it despite his professed belief in his innocence, we hold that the trial judge did not commit constitutional error in accepting it." [25]

One of the reasons for sustaining the plea in *Alford* was the factual basis for it. Note that Fed.R.Crim.P. 11(f) also requires an inquiry into the factual basis for a plea. See also State v. Goulette, 258 N.W.2d 758 (Minn.1977) (emphasizing the importance of factual inquiry in *Alford*-type cases). In United States v. Briggs, 939 F.2d 222 (5th Cir. 1991), discussed supra, Briggs pleaded guilty to bank fraud resulting from a wire transfer. The court found, however, that a wire transfer is not a fraudulent communication as defined in the bank fraud statute. It held that if Briggs pleaded to conduct which did not constitute the crime for which she was convicted, the guilty plea would have to be vacated as a violation of due process. The court distinguished *Alford* as a case in which there was a factual basis for the guilty plea, irrespective of the defendant's protestations of innocence.

E. FACTUAL BASIS FOR PLEAS

It is unclear whether the Supreme Court intended in *Alford* to make a judicial determination that a plea has a factual basis as a constitutional prerequisite to acceptance of some or all guilty pleas. Such a determination can help to assure that defendants who are innocent do not plead guilty. The advantages of a judicial determination are analyzed in Barkai, Accuracy Inquiries for All Felony and Misdemeanor Pleas: Voluntary Pleas But Innocent Defendants, 126 U.Pa.L.Rev. 88 (1977).

Barkai observes that courts that make inquiries into the factual bases for pleas use two different approaches. Some use a "trial-factual-basis procedure," by which they insist that sufficient facts be shown to warrant a conviction if the defendant were to stand trial. Facts may be shown in various ways, some of which are more reliable than others. A court might insist, for example, on personal interrogation of the defendant or testimony of witnesses, or it might accept representations of counsel as to the facts. Other courts use a "notice-factual-basis procedure," by which they inform defendants of any factual defects but permit defendants to plead guilty notwithstanding factual defects. Many jurisdictions simply do not require any judicial determination into the facts supporting a plea.

Would you require a determination that the facts support a guilty plea? Thinking back to the problem of the defendant charged with murder who is offered a chance to plead to involuntary manslaughter, would you reject pleas that appear to represent compromises that cannot fairly be said to fit the facts? Would you permit a defendant to plead guilty notwithstanding a defect in the facts presented?

25. Justice Brennan, joined by Justices Douglas and Marshall, dissented. Justice Black concurred in "substantially all of the opinion in this case."

The Indiana Supreme Court held that an Indiana judge may not accept an *Alford* plea in Ross v. Indiana, 456 N.E.2d 420 (Ind.1983).

F. THE FINALITY OF GUILTY PLEAS

1. *Withdrawal of a Plea*

Once it is recognized that American jurisdictions are very willing to promote plea bargains, some aspects of guilty pleas are more easily understood. Many jurisdictions, for example, limit the period in which a plea can be withdrawn. Some bar any attempt at withdrawal after sentence is imposed; others make the day the judgment is entered the final day for any withdrawal attempt; and still others, like Fed.R.Crim.P. 32(d), allow a motion to withdraw after sentence "to correct manifest injustice."[26] Courts are most reluctant to find manifest injustice. Even before sentence is imposed, most jurisdictions give the trial judge discretion to hold a defendant to his plea. Uniform Rule 444(e) provides that the defendant shall be allowed to withdraw a plea before sentencing "for any fair and just reason unless the prosecution shows it has been substantially prejudiced by reliance on the plea."

How one feels about the freedom a defendant should have to withdraw a plea may depend on one's confidence that defendants understand what they are doing when they are considering plea bargaining and that their counsel do not pressure them in any way to plead. Also relevant is how final a defendant believes the entry of the plea will be. Which system—one that is reluctant to set aside pleas, or one that is willing to allow a defendant to second guess the plea decision—is most consistent with the theoretical ideals of the American criminal justice system? Which is most consistent with the realities of the system? [27]

26. If a defendant starts a trial, has a change of heart and pleads guilty, and then seeks to withdraw the plea, courts are not inclined to allow withdrawal. See, e.g., Commonwealth v. Whelan, 481 Pa. 418, 392 A.2d 1362 (1978). Do you see why?

27. Generally, either side can withdraw an offer to accept a certain plea prior to court approval, but reliance by the defendant might require enforcement of a government offer in some circumstances. See Cooper v. United States, 594 F.2d 12 (4th Cir. 1979); People v. Heiler, 79 Mich.App. 714, 262 N.W.2d 890 (1977).

Kisamore v. State, 286 Md. 654, 409 A.2d 719 (1980), holds that when a plea bargain had been reached by the state and the defendant but was not consummated because of a postponement of the trial date, "[i]t was not fair and equitable" for the state later to renege on the bargain. See also Cooper v. United States, 594 F.2d 12 (4th Cir. 1979) (withdrawal by government of plea offer interfered with counsel's relationship with defendant). But see Government of the Virgin Islands v. Scotland, 614 F.2d 360 (3d Cir. 1980) (absent detrimental reliance by defendant, prosecutor can withdraw plea bargain).

The Supreme Court unanimously reversed the court of appeals in Mabry v. Johnson, 467 U.S. 504 (1984). It found that Johnson, who was serving time for burglary and assault, entered a valid guilty plea to a related murder charge, after his conviction on that charge had been overturned on appeal.

Prior to Johnson's second trial, the prosecutor offered to recommend a concurrent 21 year term in exchange for a guilty plea. Johnson decided to accept the offer, but when his lawyer phoned the prosecutor to indicate Johnson's decision, the prosecutor stated that the offer was an error, withdrew it, and offered to recommend a consecutive 21 year term if Johnson pleaded guilty. Johnson pled not guilty and went to trial, only to see a mistrial declared on the second day. Thereafter, he accepted the prosecutor's second offer and pleaded guilty.

Writing for the Court, Justice Stevens reasoned that "[a] plea bargain standing alone is without constitutional significance; in itself it is a mere executory agreement which, until embodied in the judgment of a court, does not deprive an accused of liberty or any other constitutionally protected interest." Since Johnson made a knowing and voluntary plea with the advice of counsel, Justice Stevens reasoned that he could not attack the resulting judgment by way of habeas corpus; the judgment of conviction was valid and was unaffected by the prosecutor's first offer. He

2. *Remedies for Breach of a Bargain*

Courts that are reluctant to allow withdrawal because of a defendant's change of mind also are reluctant to allow automatic withdrawal when a bargain has been breached by the government. Consider, for example, Santobello v. New York, 404 U.S. 257 (1971). Charged with two gambling felonies, Santobello agreed to plead guilty to a lesser included offense and the prosecutor agreed to make no recommendation as to sentence. Before sentencing Santobello retained a new lawyer and unsuccessfully moved prior to sentencing to withdraw the plea. Meanwhile, a second prosecutor took over the case and, ignorant of the terms of the bargain, made a sentence recommendation. In an opinion by the Chief Justice, the Court held that even an inadvertent breach of a plea agreement was unacceptable. But the Court remanded to afford the state courts the option of allowing Santobello to withdraw the plea or to have a new sentencing proceeding before a different judge. Justice Marshall, joined by Justices Brennan and Stewart, argued that Santobello "must be permitted to withdraw his guilty plea." Justice Douglas said that "[i]n choosing a remedy, * * * a court ought to accord a defendant's preference considerable, if not controlling, weight inasmuch as the fundamental rights flouted by a prosecutor's breach of a plea bargain are those of the defendant, not of the state." [28]

wrote that "[t]he Due Process Clause is not a code of ethics for prosecutors; its concern is with the manner in which persons are deprived of their liberty," and he found no constitutional infirmity in the taking of the guilty plea.

Once the court approves a plea arrangement, it, as well as the government may be bound by the plea agreement. In United States v. Blackwell, 694 F.2d 1325 (D.C.Cir. 1982), for example, the Court found that the trial judge erred in telling a defendant's common law wife—who was going to testify that she, not he, brought certain guns to a room that the two rented—that if she so testified a plea bargain that she had arranged with the government might be undone and she might be prosecuted for perjury. The appellate court said that its reading of Rule 11 led it to conclude that the plea agreement accepted by the court bound the government and that the trial judge therefore erred in his warning to the wife. It concluded, however, that the error did not warrant reversal where no objection was made during the trial.

Analyzing the structure of Rule 11(e) in United States v. Holman, 728 F.2d 809 (6th Cir.1984), the court of appeals held that when a trial judge was informed that the government's attorney had agreed under (e)(1)(C) that a particular sentence was the appropriate one for the defendant and the judge accepted the plea without indicating whether or not he was accepting or rejecting the plea agreement and without stating that he was deferring a judgment pending consideration of a presentence report, the judge implicitly accepted the plea agreement and could not later reject it in light of the presentence report. The prosecutor had agreed that a sentence of no greater than a year and a day was appropriate. After reading the presentence report, the trial judge rejected the plea agreement. Holman withdrew his plea and later entered another plea pursuant to an agreement under which he could receive 30 months imprisonment. Although the appeals court found that the trial judge erred, Holman did not benefit from the finding. The court of appeals said that if Holman had been forced to trial, any sentence of more than a year and a day would have been set aside. But, since Holman did not go to trial and instead entered into a new agreement, the acceptance of the new agreement cured any prejudice visited upon him by the trial judge's mishandling of the first plea.

28. There were only seven Justices who participated in this case.

In Patrick v. Camden County Prosecutor, 630 F.2d 206 (3d Cir. 1980), the district court found that the prosecutor breached a plea bargain agreement when he made a recommendation to the court as to the defendant's sentence. The district court ordered that the defendant be resentenced before a different judge without any prosecutorial recommendation as to sentence. But the court of appeals said that the district court should have permitted the state judge to consider whether the plea bargain should be specifically enforced or whether the defendant should be permitted to withdraw his plea.

If the prosecutor reneges on a bargain,[29] should the defendant have a choice of starting all over again by withdrawing the plea or of specific enforcement of the promise? If you are inclined to answer "no" because you think that specific performance leaves the defendant in as good a position as she otherwise would have been in, ask yourself whether this is really the case. Is the defendant no worse off when she had to bear the burden of obtaining performance of a promise? *Santobello* is the situation in which the defendant wants to withdraw his plea. Sometimes the defendant will want specific performance. If courts are reluctant to allow defendants to withdraw pleas, should they be any more willing to let prosecutors out of their bargains?

If a defendant manages to set aside a guilty plea and decides to go to trial, is the prosecutor entitled to charge a higher offense than the one to which the defendant pleaded? Most courts treat the withdrawal of the plea as an erasure that allows both sides to proceed anew. See, e.g., United States ex rel. Williams v. McMann, 436 F.2d 103 (2d Cir.1970). However, the *Williams* court acknowledged that although general principles of fundamental fairness do not bar every prosecution, certain allegations such as prosecutorial vindictiveness could pose a reasonable challenge on the basis of due process. Nonetheless, "no presumption of vindictiveness arises when the prosecutor simply reinstates the indictment that was in effect before the plea agreement was entered." Taylor v. Kincheloe, 920 F.2d 599 (9th Cir.1990), citing Blackledge v. Perry, 417 U.S. 21 (1974). See also Annotation, Retrial on Greater Offense Following Reversal of Plea-Based Conviction of Lesser Offense, 14 A.L.R.4th 970 (1990). Would you require that the defendant be permitted to plead again pursuant to the original bargain whenever the prosecutor changes or raises the charges? See Borman, The Chilled Right to Appeal from a Plea Bargain Conviction: A Due Process Cure, 69 Nw.U.L.Rev. 663 (1974).

In Ricketts v. Adamson, 483 U.S. 1 (1987), the Court held that the double jeopardy clause did not bar a state from filing a new information seeking a capital conviction against a defendant who had entered a guilty plea in return for a specific prison term and subsequently violated the terms of the plea agreement. Adamson was one of three individuals charged with first-degree murder in the dynamiting of a reporter's car. He agreed to plead guilty to second-degree murder and to testify against the other defendants in exchange

When a defendant who admitted a probation violation pursuant to an agreement that he would not be imprisoned was sentenced to prison, he was entitled to withdraw from his agreement but not to specific performance in People v. Calloway, 29 Cal.3d 666, 175 Cal. Rptr. 596, 631 P.2d 30 (1981). Specific performance would have bound the Court, as well as the prosecutor.

Some of the problems of fashioning appropriate remedies for breaches, as well as the sordid state of some plea bargaining, are illustrated in Palermo v. Warden, 545 F.2d 286 (2d Cir. 1976).

29. Sometimes it is difficult to determine when a bargain has been breached. For example, if a prosecutor agrees to drop two counts of a three count indictment in exchange for a plea to the remaining count, and the sentencing judge relies on the fact that three offenses were committed, has the bargain been breached? In deciding how to answer, would you view an objective or subjective test of the bargain as more appropriate?

In United States v. Arnett, 628 F.2d 1162 (9th Cir. 1979), the Court said that "[p]lea bargaining * * * though a matter of criminal jurisprudence, is subject to contract law standards. Therefore, the terms of the agreement, if disputed, are to be determined by objective standards." See also United States v. Hayes, 946 F.2d 230 (3d Cir. 1991) (where government promised to "make no recommendation as to the specific sentence to be imposed" and then emphasized the seriousness of the offense at the sentencing hearing, the government breached the terms of the plea agreement; principles of contract control whether plea agreement has been breached).

for a designated prison sentence. Although Adamson testified as promised and the other defendants were convicted, the State Supreme Court reversed the convictions and remanded their cases for new trials. Adamson's lawyer informed the prosecutor that Adamson would only testify at second trials if certain conditions were met, including his release from prison following his testimony. The state informed the lawyer that it viewed Adamson in breach of the agreement. Adamson nevertheless invoked his privilege against self-incrimination when called to testify at a pretrial proceeding. Thereafter, the state filed a new information and convicted Adamson of first-degree murder. He was sentenced to death. An en banc court of appeals found that Adamson was placed in jeopardy twice, but the Supreme Court disagreed.

Justice White wrote for the Court. He indicated that the Court assumed that jeopardy attached when Adamson was sentenced pursuant to his guilty plea and that, because second-degree murder is a lesser included offense of first-degree murder, absent special circumstances Adamson could not have been retried for first-degree murder. Justice White agreed with the state that special circumstances arose from the plea agreement which specifically provided that the entire agreement would be null and void if Adamson refused to testify. He was unimpressed with the court of appeals' reasoning that Adamson acted in good faith, since it was unclear whether Adamson was obliged to testify at retrials. Justice White concluded that Adamson knew that if he breached the agreement he could be retried, "it is incredible to believe that he did not anticipate that the extent of his obligation would be decided by a court," and the end "result was that respondent was returned to the position that he occupied prior to execution of the plea bargain; he stood charged with first-degree murder."

Justice White reasoned that it was "of no moment" that Adamson offered to comply with the agreement after the state supreme court decision interpreting it, since "[t]he parties did not agree that respondent would be relieved of the consequences of his refusal to testify if he were able to advance a colorable argument that a testimonial obligation was not owing." Justice White ended his opinion with the observation that "[t]he parties could have struck a different bargain, but permitting the State to enforce the agreement the parties actually made does not violate the Double Jeopardy Clause."

Justice Brennan, joined by Justices Marshall, Blackmun and Stevens, dissented. He disagreed that Adamson ever breached the plea agreement and argued that, assuming such a breach occurred, Adamson never made a conscious decision to violate the agreement. Justice Brennan focused on the provision of the agreement which stated that Adamson was to be sentenced at the conclusion of his promised testimony, and noted that Adamson was sentenced after he had provided extensive testimony. Thus, Justice Brennan found that Adamson reasonably could have concluded that he had met his contractual obligations. After observing that "[t]he Court has yet to address in any comprehensive way the rules of construction appropriate for disputes involving plea agreements," Justice Brennan suggested that "the law of commercial contract may in some cases prove useful as an analogy or point of departure in construing a plea agreement, or in framing the terms of the debate." Relying on commercial law, he reasoned that the state failed to explain why a letter from Adamson's lawyer to the state, which indicated that the lawyer concluded that Adamson did not have to testify at re-trials of the other defendants, was a breach of contract. Even assuming that somehow Adamson breached his contract, Justice Brennan reasoned that the state had failed completely to mitigate any damage it suffered. It dropped the prosecution of the other two defendants despite Adamson's willingness to comply with the agreement once it was construed by the state supreme court. He found that the state was delayed a month in its other prosecutions and that its reinstatement of capital charges as punishment for this delay violated principles of fundamental fairness. Justice Brennan also concluded that Adamson never deliberately decided to breach his agreement, and that he could not be deemed to have waived his double jeopardy protection.

Is a prosecutor who breaches a plea agreement treated more favorably than a defendant who breaches? How useful is the contract analogy in these cases?

3. *Collateral Attack*

Jurisdictions that do not like to see guilty pleas withdrawn or vacated often do not like to see them challenged on appeal or collaterally attacked.[30] Thus, they generally establish a regime in which a voluntary and intelligent guilty plea is a waiver of all claims that the pleader has. The Supreme Court has promoted this approach in four cases: the *Brady* trilogy—Brady v. United States, 397 U.S. 742 (1970); McMann v. Richardson, 397 U.S. 759 (1970); Parker v. North Carolina, 397 U.S. 790 (1970)—and Tollett v. Henderson, 411 U.S. 258 (1973).

The defendant in *Brady* was charged with kidnapping under a federal statute that authorized the death penalty if a jury recommended it but not in a bench trial. Brady pleaded guilty when it appeared that the trial judge would not try the case without a jury, but Brady sought to challenge his guilty plea via habeas corpus on the ground that the statute unconstitutionally infringed his right to jury trial. The Supreme Court held that even if Brady would not have pleaded guilty but for the death penalty provision, he pleaded knowingly and intelligently with the advice of counsel. Thus, he was not entitled to withdraw his plea, even if a Supreme Court decision rendered after his plea was entered suggested that the kidnapping statute was invalid in burdening the right to jury trial.

In *Parker,* the Court reached a similar result with respect to a state court defendant who was charged with first-degree burglary and who pleaded guilty to avoid a possible jury-imposed death sentence. The Court also said in *Parker* and in *McMann* that a defendant who pleaded guilty could not attack the plea in a subsequent collateral proceeding on the ground that it was motivated by a prior coerced confession. Following this trilogy, the Court held in *Tollett* that a defendant who pleaded guilty to first-degree murder could not challenge in subsequent habeas corpus proceedings the racial composition of the grand jury that indicted him.

30. For a discussion of the defendant's right to appeal a guilty plea conviction, see Borman, The Hidden Right to Direct Appeal from a Federal Plea Conviction, 64 Cornell L.Rev. 319 (1979) (discussing Fed.R.Crim.P. 32(a)(2): "There shall be no duty on the court to advise the defendant of any right of appeal after sentence is imposed following a plea of guilty or nolo contendere.")

The four cases appeared to hold that a guilty plea represents acceptance by a defendant of his conviction and that the conviction was valid unless the defendant was not adequately represented by counsel. But, the Court soon muddied the waters in Blackledge v. Perry, 417 U.S. 21 (1974), as it held that a prison inmate who pleaded guilty to a felony charge in a North Carolina court after seeking a trial de novo following a conviction on a misdemeanor charge could attack his plea on the ground that the prosecutor acted improperly in retaliating against the defendant by raising the charge to a felony from a misdemeanor (a ground discussed in Chapter Twelve, infra). Thereafter, the Court held in Menna v. New York, 423 U.S. 61 (1975), that a defendant who pleaded guilty did not lose the right to challenge the plea as a violation of double jeopardy rights.

The Court held in United States v. Broce, 488 U.S. 563 (1989), that defendants, who pleaded guilty to two separate counts charging bidrigging conspiracies, could not successfully move to vacate their sentences on the ground that they actually were involved in a single, large conspiracy. Justice Kennedy reasoned for the Court that the indictments charged two conspiracies and that the defendants conceded by their pleas that they committed two separate crimes. He observed that *Blackledge* and *Menna* were resolved on the basis of the existing record and did not require an inquiry into evidence outside the record, but the instant case involved indictments which on their face charged separate offenses. Thus, Justice Kennedy concluded that the defendants could not make a double jeopardy claim without contradicting their pleas and, therefore, it was not necessary to "consider the degree to which the decision by an accused to enter into a plea bargain which incorporates concessions by the Government, such as the one agreed to here, heightens the already substantial interest the Government has in the finality of the plea." Justice Stevens filed a concurring opinion.

Justice Blackmun, joined by Justices Brennan and Marshall, dissented. He argued that the government did not challenge the district court's finding that there was a single conspiracy and that two convictions cannot stand for a single conspiracy. Although no evidentiary hearing was needed in *Blackledge* and *Menna,* he argued that the reasoning of those decisions was not dependent on the absence of a hearing.

It is clear that the Supreme Court has attempted to promote plea bargaining. Yet, the Court has identified a narrow range of cases in which guilty pleas cannot bar a subsequent collateral attack. Can you think of any rule that would rationalize the cases?[31]

In Haring v. Prosise, 462 U.S. 306 (1983), the Court held that a defendant who pleaded guilty in state court was not barred from pursuing a civil rights action in which he claimed that a search and seizure was illegal. State law did

31. For two attempts at stating such a rule, see Saltzburg, Pleas of Guilty and the Loss of Constitutional Rights: The Current Price of Pleading Guilty, 76 Mich.L.Rev. 1265 (1978); Westen, Away from Waiver: A Rationale for the Forfeiture of Constitutional Rights in Criminal Procedure, 75 Mich.L.Rev. 1214 (1977). See also Alschuler, The Supreme Court, the Defense Attorney, and the Guilty Plea, 47 U.Colo.L.Rev. 1 (1975); Dix, Waiver in Criminal Procedure: A Brief for More Careful Analysis, 55 Tex.L.Rev. 193 (1977); Israel, Criminal Procedure, The Burger Court, and the Legacy of the Warren Court, 75 Mich. L.Rev. 1320, 1357–65 (1977).

not collaterally estop such an action and the Court declined to adopt a special federal rule of preclusion.

4. *Conditional Pleas*

Although many jurisdictions do everything possible to make a guilty plea as final as possible, others have found that plea bargaining can be promoted if defendants who plead guilty are permitted to raise some post-plea claims. In these jurisdictions a defendant need not go to trial just to preserve a search and seizure or confession challenge. Rather, the defendant can plead guilty and after conviction still make the claim. What claims can be preserved—beyond those required in Blackledge v. Perry and Menna v. New York—depends upon state law. But if a state permits federal constitutional claims to be raised following a guilty plea, a federal court also will entertain those claims in a habeas corpus action if they would have been entertained following a trial. See Lefkowitz v. Newsome, 420 U.S. 283 (1975). State courts may even entertain non-constitutional claims following a guilty plea, if they wish.[32] The Supreme Court approved conditional pleas of guilty for federal courts when it amended Rule 11 in 1983.

The Supreme Court indicated it could not find that the introduction of a statement made by an arrestee who had not been given Miranda warnings was harmless error in Berkemer v. McCarty, 468 U.S. 420 (1984). The defendant had pleaded "no contest" pursuant to a state rule that allowed him to appeal a pretrial denial of a motion to suppress evidence. The Court observed that it is difficult even on the basis of a complete trial record to decide whether the erroneous admission of evidence might have affected the outcome and that the difficulty is enhanced when there is no trial record whatever.

United States v. Burns, 684 F.2d 1066 (2d Cir. 1982), approves conditional guilty pleas, but also urges trial courts to consent to the reservation of issues only where they can be adequately reviewed without a full trial and are likely to be dispositive of the case. In United States v. Guerro, 694 F.2d 898 (2d Cir. 1982), the court of appeals affirmed a district court's decision not to dismiss an indictment on the ground that it was barred by the statute of limitations. The appeal was brought by a defendant who had pleaded guilty pursuant to a court-approved agreement preserving his right to appeal. At the conclusion of its opinion the court rejected the defendant's contention that the government had waived the right to rely on certain acts in responding to the statute of limitations claim. The court added that "[a] conditional plea that reserves for appeal issues that cannot be decided without full development at trial is inappropriate. And as to a conditional plea that properly reserves only issues that will be dispositive and are ripe for appellate review, the precise terms and conditions of the plea should be embodied in a written stipulation or set forth accurately in the transcript of record."

United States v. Hall, 724 F.2d 1055 (2d Cir.1983), is a case in which the district judge accepted a guilty plea to bank robbery charges with the statement that the defendant would be permitted to withdraw the plea "if there is any disturbance by the United States Court of Appeals of my decision filed

32. Note, Conditional Guilty Pleas, 93 Harv.L.Rev. (1980), argues that a defendant has a constitutional right to enter a conditional guilty plea.

today." The district court had denied a motion to suppress. A majority of the court of appeals affirmed the conviction, but commented that district courts should not accept conditional pleas with a promise that suggests that even a finding of harmless error by the court of appeals would permit a defendant to withdraw his plea. A dissenting judge agreed that an oral confession by the defendant was harmless beyond a reasonable doubt, but would have held that the district court abused its discretion in accepting a plea accompanied by its guarantee to the defendant.

In Heuga v. State, 609 P.2d 547 (Alaska 1980), a defendant pleaded guilty to robbery, but at the time of pleading reserved his right to appeal the trial court's rejection of his motion to suppress a confession. The Alaska Supreme Court refused to hear the appeal because "appeals from such conditional pleas will not be accepted unless the issue reserved for appeal is dispositive of the case, and a stipulation of the parties to that effect, approved by the court, appears in the record." In the instant case, there was a known eyewitness to the crime at the time the defendant pleaded, and the court declined to determine "hypothetical and abstract questions which are not dispositive of the case as to which appeal is sought."

Chapter Ten

TRIAL AND TRIAL–RELATED RIGHTS

I. THE RIGHT TO A SPEEDY TRIAL

A. THE BACKGROUND OF AND POLICIES SUPPORTING THE RIGHT

The Sixth Amendment provides that "[i]n all criminal prosecutions, the accused shall enjoy the right to a speedy and public trial * * *" It is a guarantee of deliberate speed in the prosecution of a case and a protection against several evils associated with delayed litigation. The Supreme Court has long recognized that "[t]he right of a speedy trial is necessarily relative. It is consistent with delays and depends upon circumstances." Beavers v. Haubert, 198 U.S. 77, 87 (1905). Careful analysis of the facts of each case, rather than bright line tests, has been, and is still, the preferred approach of the Court to constitutionally based speedy trial claims.

This should not suggest, however, that the Court does not value speedy trials. In Klopfer v. North Carolina, 386 U.S. 213 (1967), the Court established that the right is fundamental and part of the bundle of rights binding upon the states through the due process clause of the Fourteenth Amendment.[1]

> We hold here that the right to a speedy trial is as fundamental as any of the rights secured by the Sixth Amendment. That right has its roots at the very foundation of our English law heritage. Its first articulation in modern jurisprudence appears to have been made in Magna Carta (1215), wherein it was written, "We will sell to no man, we will not deny or defer to any man either justice or right"; but evidence of recognition of the right to speedy justice in even earlier times is found in the Assize of Clarendon (1166). By the late thirteenth century, justices, armed with commissions of gaol delivery and/or oyer and terminer were visiting the countryside three times a year. These justices, Sir Edward Coke wrote in Part II of his Institutes, "have not suffered the prisoner to be long detained, but at their next coming have given the prisoner full and speedy justice, * * * without detaining him long in prison." To Coke, prolonged detention without trial would have been contrary to the law and custom of England; but he also believed that the delay in trial, by itself, would be an improper denial of justice. In his explication of Chapter 29 of the Magna Carta, he wrote that the words "We will sell to no man, we will not deny or defer to any man either justice or right" had the following effect:

1. Justices Harlan and Stewart concurred in the result.

"And therefore, every subject of this realme, for injury done to him in bonis, terris, vel persona, by any other subject, be he ecclesiasticall, or temporall, free, or bond, man, or woman, old, or young, or be he outlawed, excommunicated, or any other without exception, may take his remedy by the course of the law, and have justice, and right for the injury done to him, freely without sale, fully without any deniall, and speedily without delay."

Coke's Institutes were read in the American Colonies by virtually every student of the law. Indeed, Thomas Jefferson wrote that at the time he studied law (1762–1767), "Coke Lyttleton was the universal elementary book of law students." And to John Rutledge of South Carolina, the Institutes seemed "to be almost the foundation of our law." To Coke, in turn, Magna Carta was one of the fundamental bases of English liberty. Thus, it is not surprising that when George Mason drafted the first of the colonial bills of rights, he set forth a principle of Magna Carta, using phraseology similar to that of Coke's explication: "[I]n all capital or criminal prosecutions," the Virginia Declaration of Rights of 1776 provided, "a man hath a right * * * to a speedy trial * * *." That this right was considered fundamental at this early period in our history is evidenced by its guarantee in the constitutions of several of the States of the new nation, as well as by its prominent position in the Sixth Amendment. Today, each of the 50 States guarantees the right to a speedy trial to its citizens.

The history of the right to a speedy trial and its reception in this country clearly establish that it is one of the most basic rights preserved by our Constitution.

There are three interests protected by the right. First is the interest of an accused person in avoiding prolonged detention prior to trial. Innocent persons are never compensated for the losses that result from such detention. Those who are convicted following trial may have been confined for long periods in inadequate jails. Some who receive probation would never have spent time incarcerated except for pretrial delay. Second is the interest of the accused in avoiding prolonged anxiety concerning the charges made and public suspicion while charges are pending. Third is the accused's interest in litigating a case before evidence disappears and memories fade. Not all of these concerns are present in all cases, but they can be. See generally Godbold, Speedy Trial—Major Surgery for a National Ill, 24 Ala.L.Rev. 265 (1972).

Supreme Court cases establish that any one concern is sufficient to trigger application of speedy trial principles. In Klopfer v. North Carolina, supra, for example, the Court found a speedy trial violation when a Duke University professor, who was indicted for criminal trespass for participation in a sit-in at a restaurant, saw the prosecutor obtain a "nolle prosequi with leave" following a trial that ended in a hung jury. The nolle prosequi permitted the prosecutor to reinstate the case without further order. Because the procedure indefinitely prolonged the anxiety and concern accompanying public accusation, the Court found that it violated the defendant's right to a speedy trial.

In Smith v. Hooey, 393 U.S. 374 (1969), the Court held that speedy trial rights extend to people imprisoned on other offenses.

At first blush it might appear that a man already in prison under a lawful sentence is hardly in a position to suffer from "undue and oppressive incarceration prior to trial." But the fact is that delay in bringing such a person to trial on a pending charge may ultimately result in as much oppression as is suffered by one who is jailed without bail upon an untried charge. First, the possibility that the defendant already in prison might receive a sentence at least partially concurrent with the one he is serving may be forever lost if trial of the pending charge is postponed. Secondly, under procedures now widely practiced, the duration of his present imprisonment may be increased, and the conditions under which he must serve his sentence greatly worsened, by the pendency of another criminal charge outstanding against him.

And while it might be argued that a person already in prison would be less likely than others to be affected by "anxiety and concern accompanying public accusation," there is reason to believe that an outstanding untried charge (of which even a convict may, of course, be innocent) can have fully as depressive an effect upon a prisoner as upon a person who is at large.

* * *

Finally, it is self-evident that "the possibilities that long delay will impair the ability of an accused to defend himself" are markedly increased when the accused is incarcerated in another jurisdiction. Confined in a prison, perhaps far from the place where the offense covered by the outstanding charge allegedly took place, his ability to confer with potential defense witnesses, or even to keep track of their whereabouts, is obviously impaired. And, while "evidence and witnesses disappear, memories fade, and events lose their perspective," a man isolated in prison is powerless to exert his own investigative efforts to mitigate these erosive effects of the passage of time.

One year later, in Dickey v. Florida, 398 U.S. 30 (1970), the Court ordered a prosecution dismissed, when a federal prisoner made persistent requests for a speedy trial on an armed robbery charge, and for seven years Florida took no action to bring him to trial. In the interim, potential defense witnesses had died or disappeared. Chief Justice Burger wrote the opinion for a unanimous court, stating that "[s]tale claims have never been favored by the law, and far less so in criminal cases. Although a great many accused persons seek to put off the confrontation as long as possible, the right to a prompt inquiry into criminal charges is fundamental and the duty of the charging authority is to provide a prompt trial." [2]

B. WHEN DOES THE RIGHT TO SPEEDY TRIAL ATTACH?

Klopfer, Smith and Dickey all wanted the charges against them disposed of promptly. Because each was charged in some fashion or other with an offense, speedy trial rights attached. If no formal charge is made against a person but it is clear that one might be forthcoming at some future time, what protection, if any, can be claimed? That is the issue in the next two cases.

2. Justice Harlan wrote a short concurring opinion. Justice Brennan wrote a longer opinion, in which Justice Marshall joined, discussing the standards under which a speedy trial claim should be judged.

Almost every state has adopted the Interstate Agreement on Detainers, which means that states can provide speedy trials to persons incarcerated in other states. On the relationship of the federal courts to the states, see Note, The Interrelationship Between Habeas Corpus Ad Prosequendum, the Interstate Agreement on Detainers, and the Speedy Trial Act of 1974: United States v. Mauro [436 U.S. 340 (1978)], 40 U.Pitt.L.Rev. 285 (1979).

1. *Speedy Trial Clause Analysis*

UNITED STATES v. MARION

Supreme Court of the United States, 1971.
404 U.S. 307.

MR. JUSTICE WHITE delivered the opinion of the Court.

This appeal requires us to decide whether dismissal of a federal indictment was constitutionally required by reason of a period of three years between the occurrence of the alleged criminal acts and the filing of the indictment.

On April 21, 1970, the two appellees were indicted and charged in 19 counts with operating a business known as Allied Enterprises, Inc., which was engaged in the business of selling and installing home improvements such as intercom sets, fire control devices, and burglary detection systems. Allegedly, the business was fraudulently conducted and involved misrepresentations, alterations of documents, and deliberate nonperformance of contracts. The period covered by the indictment was March 15, 1965, to February 6, 1967; the earliest specific act alleged occurred on September 3, 1965, the latest on January 19, 1966.

On May 5, 1970, appellees filed a motion to dismiss the indictment "for failure to commence prosecution of the alleged offenses charged therein within such time as to afford [them their] rights to due process of law and to a speedy trial under the Fifth and Sixth Amendments to the Constitution of the United States." No evidence was submitted, but from the motion itself and the arguments of counsel at the hearing on the motion, it appears that Allied Enterprises had been subject to a Federal Trade Commission cease-and-desist order on February 6, 1967, and that a series of articles appeared in the Washington Post in October 1967, reporting the results of that newspaper's investigation of practices employed by home improvement firms such as Allied. The articles also contained purported statements of the then United States Attorney for the District of Columbia describing his office's investigation of these firms and predicting that indictments would soon be forthcoming. Although the statements attributed to the United States Attorney did not mention Allied specifically, that company was mentioned in the course of the newspaper stories. In the summer of 1968, at the request of the United States Attorney's office, Allied delivered certain of its records to that office, and in an interview there appellee Marion discussed his conduct as an officer of Allied Enterprises. The grand jury that indicted appellees was not impaneled until September 1969, appellees were not informed of the grand jury's concern with them until March 1970, and the indictment was finally handed down in April.

Appellees moved to dismiss because the indictment was returned "an unreasonably oppressive and unjustifiable time after the alleged offenses." They argued that the indictment required memory of many specific acts and conversations occurring several years before, and they contended that the delay was due to the negligence or indifference of the United States Attorney in investigating the case and presenting it to a grand jury. No specific prejudice was claimed or demonstrated. * * *

* * *

II

Appellees * * * claim that their rights to a speedy trial were violated by the period of approximately three years between the end of the criminal scheme charged and the return of the indictment; it is argued that this delay is so substantial and inherently prejudicial that the Sixth Amendment required the dismissal of the indictment. In our view, however, the Sixth Amendment speedy trial provision has no application until the putative defendant in some way becomes an "accused," an event that occurred in this case only when the appellees were indicted on April 21, 1970.

The Sixth Amendment provides that "[i]n all criminal prosecutions, the accused shall enjoy the right to a speedy and public trial * * *." On its face, the protection of the Amendment is activated only when a criminal prosecution has begun and extends only to those persons who have been "accused" in the course of that prosecution. These provisions would seem to afford no protection to those not yet accused, nor would they seem to require the Government to discover, investigate, and accuse any person within any particular period of time. The Amendment would appear to guarantee to a criminal defendant that the Government will move with the dispatch that is appropriate to assure him an early and proper disposition of the charges against him. * * *

Our attention is called to nothing in the circumstances surrounding the adoption of the Amendment indicating that it does not mean what it appears to say, nor is there more than marginal support for the proposition that, at the time of the adoption of the Amendment, the prevailing rule was that prosecutions would not be permitted if there had been long delay in presenting a charge. The framers could hardly have selected less appropriate language if they had intended the speedy trial provision to protect against pre-accusation delay. * * *

III

It is apparent also that very little support for appellees' position emerges from a consideration of the purposes of the Sixth Amendment's speedy trial provision, a guarantee that this Court has termed "an important safeguard to prevent undue and oppressive incarceration prior to trial, to minimize anxiety and concern accompanying public accusation and to limit the possibilities that long delay will impair the ability of an accused to defend himself." United States v. Ewell, 383 U.S. 116, 120 (1966). Inordinate delay between arrest, indictment, and trial may impair a defendant's ability to present an effective defense. But the major evils protected against by the speedy trial guarantee exist quite apart from actual or possible prejudice to an accused's defense. To legally arrest and detain, the Government must assert probable cause to believe the arrestee has committed a crime. Arrest is a public act that may seriously interfere with the defendant's liberty, whether he is free on bail or not, and that may disrupt his employment, drain his financial resources, curtail his associations, subject him to public obloquy, and create anxiety in him, his family and his friends. * * * So viewed, it is readily understandable that it is either a formal indictment or information or else the actual restraints imposed by arrest and holding to answer a criminal charge that engage the particular protections of the speedy trial provision of the Sixth Amendment.

Invocation of the speedy trial provision thus need not await indictment, information, or other formal charge. But we decline to extend the reach of the amendment to the period prior to arrest.[3] Until this event occurs, a citizen suffers no restraints on his liberty

3. Arrest does trigger speedy trial rights. Dillingham v. United States, 423 U.S. 64 (1975).

and is not the subject of public accusation; his situation does not compare with that of a defendant who has been arrested and held to answer. Passage of time, whether before or after arrest, may impair memories, cause evidence to be lost, deprive the defendant of witnesses, and otherwise interfere with his ability to defend himself. But this possibility of prejudice at trial is not itself sufficient reason to wrench the Sixth Amendment from its proper context. Possible prejudice is inherent in any delay, however short; it may also weaken the Government's case.

The law has provided other mechanisms to guard against possible as distinguished from actual prejudice resulting from the passage of time between crime and arrest or charge. As we said in United States v. Ewell, supra, "the applicable statute of limitations * * * is * * * the primary guarantee against bringing overly stale criminal charges." Such statutes represent legislative assessments of relative interests of the State and the defendant in administering and receiving justice; they "are made for the repose of society and the protection of those who may [during the limitation] * * * have lost their means of defence." Public Schools v. Walker, 9 Wall. 282, 288 (1870). These statutes provide predictability by specifying a limit beyond which there is an irrebuttable presumption that a defendant's right to a fair trial would be prejudiced.[4] * * * There is thus no need to press the Sixth Amendment into service to guard against the mere possibility that pre-accusation delays will prejudice the defense in a criminal case since statutes of limitation already perform that function.

Since appellees rely only on potential prejudice and the passage of time between the alleged crime and the indictment, * * * we perhaps need go no further to dispose of this case, for the indictment was the first official act designating appellees as accused individuals and that event occurred within the statute of limitations. Nevertheless, since a criminal trial is the likely consequence of our judgment and since appellees may claim actual prejudice to their defense, it is appropriate to note here that the statute of limitations does not fully define the appellees' rights with respect to the events occurring prior to indictment. Thus, the Government concedes that the Due Process Clause of the Fifth Amendment would require dismissal of the indictment if it were shown at trial that the pre-indictment delay in this case caused substantial prejudice to appellees' rights to a fair trial and that the delay was an intentional device to gain tactical advantage over the accused. * * * However, we need not, and could not now, determine when and in what circumstances actual prejudice resulting from preaccusation delays requires the dismissal of the prosecution. Actual prejudice to the defense of a criminal case may result from the shortest and most necessary delay; and no

4. Sometimes a question arises as to whether an accused can waive statute of limitations' protections. See generally, Comment, The Statute of Limitations in a Criminal Case: Can It be Waived, 18 Wm. & Mary L.Rev. 823 (1977); Case Comment, 90 Harv.L.Rev. 1550 (1977), discussing United States v. Wild, 551 F.2d 418 (D.C.Cir. 1977).

United States v. Williams, 684 F.2d 296 (4th Cir. 1982), concluded that a defendant charged with first degree murder waived the statute of limitations for second degree murder when he asked for a jury charge on the lesser offense. The court reasoned that without an instruction on the lesser offense, the jury would have been asked to return an all or nothing verdict—i.e., not guilty or guilty of first degree murder, a capital offense—and that the defendant probably benefited from the charge.

The Supreme Court's decision in Spaziano v. Florida, 468 U.S. 447 (1984), holding that a state court could refuse to instruct a jury on lesser included offenses in a capital murder case where the statute of limitations had run on the lesser offenses and the defendant refused to waive the statute, should provide some guidance to lower courts faced with similar problems in noncapital cases.

one suggests that every delay-caused detriment to a defendant's case should abort a criminal prosecution. To accommodate the sound administration of justice to the rights of the defendant to a fair trial will necessarily involve a delicate judgment based on the circumstances of each case. * * *

IV

[The Court found no denial of a speedy trial or of due process.]

MR. JUSTICE DOUGLAS, with whom MR. JUSTICE BRENNAN and MR. JUSTICE MARSHALL join, concurring in the result.

I assume that if the three-year delay in this case had occurred *after* the indictment had been returned, the right to a speedy trial would have been impaired and the indictment would have to be dismissed. I disagree with the Court that the guarantee does not apply if the delay was at the pre-indictment stage of a case.

* * *

The Sixth Amendment, to be sure, states that "the accused shall enjoy the right to a speedy and public trial." But the words "the accused," as I understand them in their Sixth Amendment setting, mean only the person who has standing to complain of prosecutorial delay in seeking an indictment or filing an information. The right to a speedy trial is the right to be brought to trial speedily which would seem to be as relevant to pre-indictment delays as it is to post-indictment delays.

* * *

The right * * * protects several demands of criminal justice: the prevention of undue delay and oppressive incarceration prior to trial; the reduction of anxiety and concern accompanying public accusation; and limiting the possibilities that long delay will impair the ability of an accused to defend himself.

At least some of these values served by the right to a speedy trial are not unique to any particular stage of the criminal proceeding. Undue delay may be as offensive to the right to a speedy trial before as after an indictment or information. The anxiety and concern attendant on public accusation may weigh more heavily upon an individual who has not yet been formally indicted or arrested for, to him, exoneration by a jury of his peers may be only a vague possibility lurking in the distant future. Indeed, the protection underlying the right to a speedy trial may be denied when a citizen is damned by clandestine innuendo and never given the chance promptly to defend himself in a court of law. Those who are accused of crime but never tried may lose their jobs or their positions of responsibility, or become outcasts in their communities.

The impairment of the ability to defend oneself may become acute because of delays in the pre-indictment stage. Those delays may result in the loss of alibi witnesses, the destruction of material evidence, and the blurring of memories. At least when a person has been accused of a specific crime, he can devote his powers of recall to the events surrounding the alleged occurrences. When there is no formal accusation, however, the State may proceed methodically to build its case while the prospective defendant proceeds to lose his.

* * *

[Justice Douglas concurred in the result on the ground that the case against the defendants was complex and required extensive investigation, so that the government's three-year delay in bringing the prosecution was permissible under the circumstances.]

2. *Due Process Clause Analysis*

UNITED STATES v. LOVASCO

Supreme Court of the United States, 1977.
431 U.S. 783.

MR. JUSTICE MARSHALL delivered the opinion of the Court.

* * *

I

On March 6, 1975, respondent was indicted for possessing eight firearms stolen from the United States mails, and for dealing in firearms without a license. The offenses were alleged to have occurred between July 25 and August 31, 1973, more than 18 months before the indictment was filed. Respondent moved to dismiss the indictment due to the delay.

The District Court conducted a hearing on respondent's motion at which the respondent sought to prove that the delay was unnecessary and that it had prejudiced his defense. In an effort to establish the former proposition, respondent presented a Postal Inspector's report on his investigation that was prepared one month after the crimes were committed, and a stipulation concerning the post-report progress of the probe. The report stated, in brief, that within the first month of the investigation respondent had admitted to Government agents that he had possessed and then sold five of the stolen guns, and that the agents had developed strong evidence linking respondent to the remaining three weapons. The report also stated, however, that the agents had been unable to confirm or refute respondent's claim that he had found the guns in his car when he returned to it after visiting his son, a mail handler, at work. The stipulation into which the Assistant United States Attorney entered indicated that little additional information concerning the crimes was uncovered in the 17 months following the preparation of the Inspector's report.

To establish prejudice to the defense, respondent testified that he had lost the testimony of two material witnesses due to the delay. The first witness, Tom Stewart, died more than a year after the alleged crimes occurred. At the hearing respondent claimed that Stewart had been his source for two or three of the guns. The second witness, respondent's brother, died in April 1974, eight months after the crimes were completed. Respondent testified that his brother was present when respondent called Stewart to secure the guns, and witnessed all of respondent's sales. Respondent did not state how the witnesses would have aided the defense had they been willing to testify.

* * *

II

* * *

* * * *Marion* makes clear that proof of prejudice is generally a necessary but not sufficient element of a due process claim, and that the due process inquiry must consider the reasons for the delay as well as the prejudice to the accused.

The Court of Appeals found that the sole reason for the delay here was "a hope on the part of the Government that others might be discovered who may have participated in the theft * * *." It concluded that this hope did not justify the delay, and therefore affirmed the dismissal of the indictment. But the Due Process Clause does not permit courts to abort criminal prosecutions simply because they disagree with a prosecutor's judgment as to when to seek an indictment. * * *

It requires no extended argument to establish that prosecutors do not deviate from "fundamental conceptions of justice" when they defer seeking indictments until they have probable cause to believe an accused is guilty; indeed it is unprofessional conduct for a prosecutor to recommend an indictment on less than probable cause. It should be equally obvious that prosecutors are under no duty to file charges as soon as probable cause exists but before they are satisfied they will be able to establish the suspect's guilt beyond a reasonable doubt. To impose such a duty "would have a deleterious effect both upon the rights of the accused and upon the ability of society to protect itself." From the perspective of potential defendants, requiring prosecutions to commence when probable cause is established is undesirable because it would increase the likelihood of unwarranted charges being filed, and would add to the time during which defendants stand accused but untried. These costs are by no means insubstantial since, as we recognized in *Marion*, a formal accusation may "interfere with the defendant's liberty, * * * disrupt his employment, drain his financial resources, curtail his associations, subject him to public obloquy, and create anxiety in him, his family and his friends." From the perspective of law enforcement officials, a requirement of immediate prosecution upon probable cause is equally unacceptable because it could make obtaining proof of guilt beyond a reasonable doubt impossible by causing potentially fruitful sources of information to evaporate before they are fully exploited. And from the standpoint of the courts, such a requirement is unwise because it would cause scarce resources to be consumed on cases that prove to be insubstantial, or that involve only some of the responsible parties or some of the criminal acts. Thus, no one's interests would be well served by compelling prosecutors to initiate prosecutions as soon as they are legally entitled to do so.

It might be argued that once the Government has assembled sufficient evidence to prove guilt beyond a reasonable doubt, it should be constitutionally required to file charges promptly, even if its investigation of the entire criminal transaction is not complete. Adopting such a rule, however, would have many of the same consequences as adopting a rule requiring immediate prosecution upon probable cause.

First, compelling a prosecutor to file public charges as soon as the requisite proof has been developed against one participant on one charge would cause numerous problems in those cases in which a criminal transaction involves more than one person or more than one illegal act. In some instances, an immediate arrest or indictment would impair the prosecutor's ability to continue his investigation, thereby preventing society from bringing lawbreakers to justice. In other cases, the prosecutor would be able to obtain additional indictments despite an early prosecution, but the necessary result would be multiple trials involving a single set of facts. Such trials place needless burdens on defendants, law enforcement officials, and courts.

Second, insisting on immediate prosecution once sufficient evidence is developed to obtain a conviction would pressure prosecutors into resolving doubtful cases in favor of early—and possibly unwarranted—prosecutions. The determination of when the evidence available to the prosecution is sufficient to obtain a conviction is seldom clear-cut, and reasonable persons often will reach conflicting conclusions. In the instant case, for example, since respondent admitted possessing at least five of the firearms, the primary factual issue in dispute was whether respondent knew the guns were stolen as required by 18 U.S.C.A.

§ 1708. Not surprisingly, the Postal Inspector's report contained no direct evidence bearing on this issue. The decision whether to prosecute, therefore, required a necessarily subjective evaluation of the strength of the circumstantial evidence available and the credibility of respondent's denial. Even if a prosecutor concluded that the case was weak and further investigation appropriate, he would have no assurance that a reviewing court would agree. To avoid the risk that a subsequent indictment would be dismissed for preindictment delay, the prosecutor might feel constrained to file premature charges, with all the disadvantages that would entail.[a]

Finally, requiring the Government to make charging decisions immediately upon assembling evidence sufficient to establish guilt would preclude the Government from giving full consideration to the desirability of not prosecuting in particular cases. The decision to file criminal charges, with the awesome consequences it entails, requires consideration of a wide range of factors in addition to the strength of the Government's case, in order to determine whether prosecution would be in the public interest. Prosecutors often need more information than proof of a suspect's guilt, therefore, before deciding whether to seek an indictment. Again the instant case provides a useful illustration. Although proof of the identity of the mail thieves was not necessary to convict respondent of the possessory crimes with which he was charged, it might have been crucial in assessing respondent's culpability, as distinguished from his legal guilt. If, for example, further investigation were to show that respondent had no role in or advance knowledge of the theft and simply agreed, out of paternal loyalty, to help his son dispose of the guns once respondent discovered his son had stolen them, the United States Attorney might have decided not to prosecute, especially since at the time of the crime respondent was over 60 years old and had no prior criminal record. Requiring prosecution once the evidence of guilt is clear, however, could prevent a prosecutor from awaiting the information necessary for such a decision.

We would be most reluctant to adopt a rule which would have these consequences absent a clear constitutional command to do so. We can find no such command in the Due Process Clause of the Fifth Amendment. In our view, investigative delay is fundamentally unlike delay undertaken by the Government solely "to gain tactical advantage over the accused," precisely because investigative delay is not so one-sided. Rather than deviating from elementary standards of "fair play and decency," a prosecutor abides by them if he refuses to seek indictments until he is completely satisfied that he should prosecute and will be able promptly to establish guilt beyond a reasonable doubt. Penalizing prosecutors who defer action for these reasons would subordinate the goal of "orderly expedition" to that of "mere speed." This the Due Process Clause does not require. We therefore hold that to prosecute a defendant following investigative delay does not deprive him of due process, even if his defense might have been somewhat prejudiced by the lapse of time.

In the present case, the Court of Appeals stated that the only reason the Government postponed action was to await the results of additional investigation. Although there is, unfortunately, no evidence concerning the reasons for

a. In addition, if courts were required to decide in every case when the prosecution should have commenced, it would be necessary for them to trace the day-by-day progress of each investigation. Maintaining daily records would impose an administrative burden on prosecutors, and reviewing them would place an even greater burden on the courts.

the delay in the record, the court's "finding" is supported by the prosecutor's implicit representation to the District Court, and explicit representation to the Court of Appeals, that the investigation continued during the time that the Government deferred taking action against respondent. The finding is, moreover, buttressed by the Government's repeated assertions in its petition for certiorari, its brief, and its oral argument in this Court, "that the delay was caused by the government's efforts to identify persons in addition to respondent who may have participated in the offenses." We must assume that these statements by counsel have been made in good faith. In light of this explanation, it follows that compelling respondent to stand trial would not be fundamentally unfair. The Court of Appeals therefore erred in affirming the District Court's decision dismissing the indictment.

* * *

MR. JUSTICE STEVENS, dissenting.

If the record presented the question which the Court decides today, I would join its well-reasoned opinion. I am unable to do so because I believe our review should be limited to the facts disclosed by the record developed in the District Court and the traditional scope of review we have exercised with regard to issues of fact.

* * *

Note

In United States v. MacDonald, 456 U.S. 1 (1982), military charges had been brought against the defendant for murdering his wife and children. Those charges were dismissed and MacDonald was honorably discharged. Four years later the Justice Department presented the case against MacDonald to a grand jury, and the grand jury returned an indictment on murder charges. MacDonald brought an interlocutory appeal alleging a speedy trial violation. The Supreme Court held that a defendant could not bring an appeal from the denial of a motion to dismiss on speedy trial grounds until after completion of the trial. 435 U.S. 850 (1978). MacDonald was tried and convicted. On appeal, the court of appeals found a speedy trial violation because the long delay allowed the prosecution to refresh the memory of its witnesses, and the defense could not adequately probe the recollection of the witnesses whose memories were refreshed. The Supreme Court rejected these concerns as irrelevant and held that the time between the dropping of charges and a later indictment does not count toward the speedy trial determination. The Court noted that the speedy trial guarantee is designed to "minimize the possibility of lengthy incarceration prior to trial" and that after charges are dismissed, the citizen, as in *Marion,* suffers no restraints on his liberty. Chief Justice Burger, writing for the majority, concluded that once charges are dismissed, "the formerly accused is, at most, in the same position as any other subject of a criminal investigation." Justice Marshall, joined by Justices Brennan and Blackmun dissented, arguing that the Speedy Trial Clause continues to protect one who has been accused of a crime until the government has completed its attempts to try him for that crime. Whereas Chief Justice Burger distinguished *Klopfer* in a footnote as a case in which the prosecution was only suspended and never really dismissed, the dissenters relied on *Klopfer* to argue that MacDonald suffered continuous anxiety, disruption of employment, financial strain and public obloquy while the same government that arrested him continued to investigate him from the time that formal charges were dropped in 1970 until he was indicted in 1975. After concluding that the Speedy Trial Clause applied, the dissenters conceded that the question whether the delay violated the clause was close, but ultimately they agreed with the court of appeals. Justice Stevens also agreed that the clause applied and that the case was close, but he found no violation because the government had a need "to proceed cautiously and deliberately before making a final decision to prosecute for such a serious offense." Recall the concerns of the court of appeals in United States v. North (Chapter Three, page 485), that witnesses' memories may be refreshed through immunized testimony. Why should similar concerns be irrelevant in *MacDonald*?

A majority of the Court relied upon *MacDonald* in United States v. Loud Hawk, 474 U.S. 302 (1986), which held that the time after a district court dismissed an indictment, and before the dismissal was reversed on appeal, should be excluded from the length of delay considered under the Speedy Trial Clause where defendants were not subject to any restraints during this time period. Justice Powell's opinion for the Court reasoned that even if the defendants remained under public suspicion, their liberty was not impaired, and impairment of liberty is the "core concern" of the Clause. Justice Marshall, joined by Justices Brennan, Blackmun and Stevens, dissented. He argued that the district court could have conditioned the release of the defendants by restricting travel, association and other rights, and that the defendants' position during the time that the government appealed "is most closely analogous to that of a defendant who has been arrested but not yet indicted."

In its opinion in United States v. Gouveia, 467 U.S. 180 (1984), holding that the Sixth Amendment right to counsel does not attach to inmates placed in administrative detention pending investigation of suspected criminal acts, the Court noted that its cases distinguish speedy trial claims from right to counsel claims in assessing when Sixth Amendment rights arise. It stated that "an analogy between an arrest and an inmate's administrative detention pending investigation may have some relevance in analyzing when the speedy trial right attaches in this context, but it is not relevant to a proper determination of when the right to counsel attaches."

The Sixth Amendment begins "In all criminal prosecutions" and then lists the rights protected, including the right to speedy trial and the right to counsel. *Gouveia* and Kirby v. Illinois (Chapter Four, supra) construe the term "criminal prosecutions" and conclude that the right to counsel does not begin until a formal charge. *Dillingham* (footnote 3, supra) and *Marion* construe the term "criminal prosecutions" and hold that the right to speedy trial attaches at arrest. How can the same term mean something different depending on the right invoked?

A comprehensive analysis of delay between criminal activity and the filing of a charge is found in Townsend, Pre-Accusation Delay, 24 S.Tex.L.Rev. 69 (1983). See also Dickerson v. Guste, 932 F.2d 1142 (5th Cir. 1991) (Speedy Trial right did not attach as to state prosecution while the defendant was in federal custody; nor was the Due Process Clause violated by pre-indictment delay; defendant made no showing that the state intentionally delayed prosecution to obtain a tactical advantage—the state had attempted to exercise custody over the defendant but Federal authorities refused to release him).

Are you persuaded that there is a good reason to distinguish pre-charge and post-charge rights to speedy process? The Court has demonstrated a propensity in recent cases to read the speedy trial clause narrowly. See, e.g., Moody v. Daggett, 429 U.S. 78 (1976) (holding that a federal parolee imprisoned for a crime committed while on parole is not constitutionally entitled to a prompt parole revocation hearing when a parole violator warrant is issued and lodged with the institution of his confinement but not served on him, despite a dissent by Stevens, J., joined by Brennan J., relying on *Klopfer* and *Smith*).

Not all state courts have read their state constitutions to limit the reach of the Speedy Trial Clause. Alaska recognizes speedy trial rights even before formal charges are brought. Dixon v. State, 605 P.2d 882 (Alaska 1980). State ex rel. Leonard v. Hey, 269 S.E.2d 394 (W.Va.1980), holds that an eleven year delay between identification, location and connection of a defendant with a criminal act is prima facie prejudicial and thus a denial of due process requiring dismissal unless the government could justify the delay by proving its reasonableness.

In deciding whether you would be inclined to give the speedy trial clause a broader reach, consider the next section. See whether you believe the difference between a speedy trial analysis and a due process analysis matters very much.

C. ASSESSING SPEEDY TRIAL CLAIMS

BARKER v. WINGO

Supreme Court of the United States, 1972.
407 U.S. 514.

MR. JUSTICE POWELL delivered the opinion of the Court.

* * *

I

On July 20, 1958, in Christian County, Kentucky, an elderly couple was beaten to death by intruders wielding an iron tire tool. Two suspects, Silas Manning and Willie Barker, the petitioner, were arrested shortly thereafter. The grand jury indicted them on September 15. Counsel was appointed on September 17, and Barker's trial was set for October 21. The Commonwealth had a stronger case against Manning, and it believed that Barker could not be convicted unless Manning testified against him. Manning was naturally unwilling to incriminate himself. Accordingly, on October 23, the day Silas Manning was brought to trial, the Commonwealth sought and obtained the first of what was to be a series of 16 continuances of Barker's trial. Barker made no objection. By first convicting Manning, the Commonwealth would remove possible problems of self-incrimination and would be able to assure his testimony against Barker.

The Commonwealth encountered more than a few difficulties in its prosecution of Manning. The first trial ended in a hung jury. A second trial resulted in a conviction, but the Kentucky Court of Appeals reversed because of the admission of evidence obtained by an illegal search. At his third trial, Manning was again convicted, and the Court of Appeals again reversed because the trial court had not granted a change of venue. A fourth trial resulted in a hung jury. Finally, after five trials, Manning was convicted, in March 1962, of murdering one victim, and after a sixth trial, in December 1962, he was convicted of murdering the other.

The Christian County Circuit Court holds three terms each year—in February, June, and September. Barker's initial trial was to take place in the September term of 1958. The first continuance postponed it until the February 1959 term. The second continuance was granted for one month only. Every term thereafter for as long as the Manning prosecutions were in process, the Commonwealth routinely moved to continue Barker's case to the next term. When the case was continued from the June 1959 term until the following September, Barker, having spent 10 months in jail, obtained his release by posting a $5,000 bond. He thereafter remained free in the community until his trial. Barker made no objection, through his counsel, to the first 11 continuances.

When on February 12, 1962, the Commonwealth moved for the twelfth time to continue the case until the following term, Barker's counsel filed a motion to dismiss the indictment. The motion to dismiss was denied two weeks later, and the Commonwealth's motion for a continuance was granted. The Commonwealth was granted further continuances in June 1962 and September 1962, to which Barker did not object.

In February 1963, the first term of court following Manning's final conviction, the Commonwealth moved to set Barker's trial for March 19. But on the day scheduled for trial, it again moved for a continuance until the June term. It gave as its reason the illness of the ex-sheriff who was the chief investigating officer in the case. To this continuance, Barker objected unsuccessfully.

The witness was still unable to testify in June, and the trial, which had been set for June 19, was continued again until the September term over Barker's objection. This time the court announced that the case would be dismissed for lack of prosecution if it were not tried during the next term. The final trial date was set for October 9, 1963. On that date, Barker again moved to dismiss the indictment, and this time specified that his right to a speedy trial had been violated. The motion was denied; the trial commenced with Manning as the chief prosecution witness; Barker was convicted and given a life sentence.

* * *

II

The right to a speedy trial is generically different from any of the other rights enshrined in the Constitution for the protection of the accused. In addition to the general concern that all accused persons be treated according to decent and fair procedures, there is a societal interest in providing a speedy trial which exists separate from, and at times in opposition to, the interests of the accused. The inability of courts to provide a prompt trial has contributed to a large backlog of cases in urban courts which, among other things, enables defendants to negotiate more effectively for pleas of guilty to lesser offenses and otherwise manipulate the system. In addition, persons released on bond for lengthy periods awaiting trial have an opportunity to commit other crimes. It must be of little comfort to the residents of Christian County, Kentucky, to know that Barker was at large on bail for over four years while accused of a vicious and brutal murder of which he was ultimately convicted. Moreover, the longer an accused is free awaiting trial, the more tempting becomes his opportunity to jump bail and escape. Finally, delay between arrest and punishment may have a detrimental effect on rehabilitation.

If an accused cannot make bail, he is generally confined, as was Barker for 10 months, in a local jail. This contributes to the overcrowding and generally deplorable state of those institutions. Lengthy exposure to these conditions "has a destructive effect on human character and makes the rehabilitation of the individual offender much more difficult." At times the result may even be violent rioting. Finally, lengthy pretrial detention is costly. * * * In addition, society loses wages which might have been earned, and it must often support families of incarcerated breadwinners.

A second difference between the right to speedy trial and the accused's other constitutional rights is that deprivation of the right may work to the accused's advantage. Delay is not an uncommon defense tactic. As the time between the commission of the crime and trial lengthens, witnesses may become unavailable or their memories may fade. If the witnesses support the prosecution, its case will be weakened, sometimes seriously so. And it is the prosecution which carries the burden of proof. Thus, unlike the right to counsel or the right to be free from compelled self-incrimination, deprivation of the right to speedy trial does not *per se* prejudice the accused's ability to defend himself.

Finally, and perhaps most importantly, the right to speedy trial is a more vague concept than other procedural rights. It is, for example, impossible to determine with precision when the right has been denied. We cannot definitely say how long is too long in a system where justice is supposed to be swift but deliberate. As a consequence, there is no fixed point in the criminal process when the State can put the defendant to the choice of either exercising or waiving the right to a speedy trial. If, for example, the State moves for a 60-day continuance, granting that continuance is not a violation of the right to speedy trial unless the circumstances of the case are such that further delay would endanger the values the right protects. It is impossible to do more than generalize about when those circumstances exist. There is nothing comparable to the point in the process when a defendant exercises or waives his right to counsel or his right to a jury trial. * * *

The amorphous quality of the right also leads to the unsatisfactorily severe remedy of dismissal of the indictment when the right has been deprived. This is indeed a serious consequence because it means that a defendant who may be guilty of a serious crime will go free, without having been tried. Such a remedy is more serious than an exclusionary rule or a reversal for a new trial, but it is the only possible remedy.

III

Perhaps because the speedy trial right is so slippery, two rigid approaches are urged upon us as ways of eliminating some of the uncertainty which courts experience in protecting the right. The first suggestion is that we hold that the Constitution requires a criminal defendant to be offered a trial within a specified time period. The result of such a ruling would have the virtue of clarifying when the right is infringed and of simplifying courts' application of it. Recognizing this, some legislatures have enacted laws, and some courts have adopted procedural rules which more narrowly define the right. The United States Court of Appeals for the Second Circuit has promulgated rules for the district courts in that Circuit establishing that the government must be ready for trial within six months of the date of arrest, except in unusual circumstances, or the charge will be dismissed. This type of rule is also recommended by the American Bar Association.

But such a result would require this Court to engage in legislative or rulemaking activity, rather than in the adjudicative process to which we should confine our efforts. We do not establish procedural rules for the States, except when mandated by the Constitution. We find no constitutional basis for holding that the speedy trial right can be quantified into a specified number of days or months. The States, of course, are free to prescribe a reasonable period consistent with constitutional standards, but our approach must be less precise.

The second suggested alternative would restrict consideration of the right to those cases in which the accused has demanded a speedy trial. Most States have recognized what is loosely referred to as the "demand rule," although eight States reject it. It is not clear, however, precisely what is meant by that term. Although every federal court of appeals that has considered the question has endorsed some kind of demand rule, some have regarded the rule within the concept of waiver, whereas others have viewed it as a factor to be weighed in assessing whether there has been a deprivation of the speedy trial right. We shall refer to the former approach as the demand-waiver doctrine. The demand-waiver doctrine provides that a defendant waives any consideration of his right to speedy trial for any period prior to which he has not demanded a trial. Under this rigid approach, a prior demand is a necessary condition to the consideration of the speedy trial right. This essentially was the approach the Sixth Circuit took below.

Such an approach, by presuming waiver of a fundamental right from inaction, is inconsistent with this Court's pronouncements on waiver of constitutional rights. * * *

In excepting the right to speedy trial from the rule of waiver we have applied to other fundamental rights, courts that have applied the demand-waiver rule have relied on the assumption that delay usually works for the benefit of the accused and on the absence of any readily ascertainable time in the criminal process for a defendant to be given the choice of exercising or waiving his right. But it is not necessarily true that delay benefits the defendant. There are cases in which delay appreciably harms the defendant's ability to defend himself. Moreover, a defendant confined to jail prior to trial is obviously disadvantaged by delay as is a defendant released on bail but unable to lead a normal life because of community suspicion and his own anxiety.

The nature of the speedy trial right does make it impossible to pinpoint a precise time in the process when the right must be asserted or waived, but that fact does not argue for placing the burden of protecting the right solely on defendants. A defendant has no duty to bring himself to trial; the State has that duty as well as the duty of insuring that the trial is consistent with due process. Moreover, for the reasons earlier expressed, society has a particular interest in bringing swift prosecutions, and society's representatives are the ones who should protect that interest.

It is also noteworthy that such a rigid view of the demand-waiver rule places defense counsel in an awkward position. Unless he demands a trial early and often, he is in danger of frustrating his client's right. If counsel is willing to tolerate some delay because he finds it reasonable and helpful in preparing his own case, he may be unable to obtain a speedy trial for his client at the end of that time. Since under the demand-waiver rule no time runs until the demand is made, the government will have whatever time is otherwise reasonable to bring the defendant to trial after a demand has been made. Thus, if the first demand is made three months after arrest in a jurisdiction which prescribes a six-month rule, the prosecution will have a total of nine months—which may be wholly unreasonable under the circumstances. The result in practice is likely to be either an automatic, *pro forma* demand made immediately after appointment of counsel or delays which but for the demand-waiver rule, would not be tolerated. Such a result is not consistent with the interests of defendants, society, or the Constitution.

We reject, therefore, the rule that a defendant who fails to demand a speedy trial forever waives his right. This does not mean, however, that the defendant has no responsibility to assert his right. We think the better rule is that the defendant's assertion of or failure to assert his right to a speedy trial is one of the factors to be considered in an inquiry into the deprivation of the right. Such a formulation avoids the rigidities of the demand-waiver rule and the resulting possible unfairness in its application. It allows the trial court to exercise a judicial discretion based on the circumstances, including due consideration of any applicable formal procedural rule. It would permit, for example, a court to attach a different weight to a situation in which the defendant knowingly fails to object from a situation in which his attorney acquiesces in long delay without adequately informing his client, or from a situation in which no counsel is appointed. It would also allow a court to weigh the frequency and force of the objections as opposed to attaching significant weight to a purely *pro forma* objection.

In ruling that a defendant has some responsibility to assert a speedy trial claim, we do not depart from our holdings in other cases concerning the waiver of fundamental rights, in which we have placed the entire responsibility on the prosecution to show that the claimed waiver was knowingly and voluntarily made. Such cases have involved rights which must be exercised or waived at a specific time or under clearly identifiable circumstances, such as the rights to plead not guilty, to demand a jury trial, to exercise the privilege against self-incrimination, and to have the assistance of counsel. We have shown above that the right to a speedy trial is unique in its uncertainty as to when and under what circumstances it must be asserted or may be deemed waived. But the rule we announce today, which comports with constitutional principles, places the primary burden on the courts and the prosecutors to assure that cases are brought to trial. We hardly need add that if delay is attributable to the defendant, then his waiver may be given effect under standard waiver doctrine, the demand rule aside.

* * *

IV

A balancing test necessarily compels courts to approach speedy trial cases on an *ad hoc* basis. We can do little more than identify some of the factors which courts should assess in determining whether a particular defendant has been deprived of his right. Though some might express them in different ways, we identify four such factors: Length of delay, the reason for the delay, the defendant's assertion of his right, and prejudice to the defendant.

The length of the delay is to some extent a triggering mechanism. Until there is some delay which is presumptively prejudicial, there is no necessity for inquiry into the other factors that go into the balance. Nevertheless, because of the imprecision of the right to speedy trial, the length of delay that will provoke such an inquiry is necessarily dependent upon the peculiar circumstances of the case.[a] To take but one example, the delay that can be tolerated for an ordinary street crime is considerably less than for a serious, complex conspiracy charge.

Closely related to length of delay is the reason the government assigns to justify the delay. Here, too, different weights should be assigned to different reasons. A deliberate attempt to delay the trial in order to hamper the defense should be weighted heavily against the government. A more neutral reason such as negligence or overcrowded courts should be weighted less heavily but nevertheless should be considered since the ultimate responsibility for such circumstances must rest with the government rather than with the defen-

a. Nothing we have said should be interpreted as disapproving a presumptive rule adopted by a court in the exercise of its supervisory powers which establishes a fixed time period within which cases must normally be brought.

dant. Finally, a valid reason, such as a missing witness, should serve to justify appropriate delay.

We have already discussed the third factor, the defendant's responsibility to assert his right. Whether and how a defendant asserts his right is closely related to the other factors we have mentioned. The strength of his efforts will be affected by the length of the delay, to some extent by the reason for the delay, and most particularly by the personal prejudice, which is not always readily identifiable, that he experiences. The more serious the deprivation, the more likely a defendant is to complain. The defendant's assertion of his speedy trial right, then, is entitled to strong evidentiary weight in determining whether the defendant is being deprived of the right. We emphasize that failure to assert the right will make it difficult for a defendant to prove that he was denied a speedy trial.

A fourth factor is prejudice to the defendant.[5] Prejudice, of course, should be assessed in the light of the interests of defendants which the speedy trial right was designed to protect. This Court has identified three such interests: (i) to prevent oppressive pretrial incarceration; (ii) to minimize anxiety and concern of the accused; and (iii) to limit the possibility that the defense will be impaired. Of these, the most serious is the last, because the inability of a defendant adequately to prepare his case skews the fairness of the entire system. If witnesses die or disappear during a delay, the prejudice is obvious. There is also prejudice if defense witnesses are unable to recall accurately events of the distant past. Loss of memory, however, is not always reflected in the record because what has been forgotten can rarely be shown.

We have discussed previously the societal disadvantages of lengthy pretrial incarceration, but obviously the disadvantages for the accused who cannot obtain his release are even more serious. The time spent in jail awaiting trial has a detrimental impact on the individual. It often means loss of a job; it disrupts family life; and it enforces idleness. Most jails offer little or no recreational or rehabilitative programs. The time spent in jail is simply dead time. Moreover, if a defendant is locked up, he is hindered in his ability to gather evidence, contact witnesses, or otherwise prepare his defense. Imposing those consequences on anyone who has not yet been convicted is serious. It is especially unfortunate to impose them on those persons who are ultimately found to be innocent. Finally, even if an accused is not incarcerated prior to trial, he is still disadvantaged by restraints on his liberty and by living under a cloud of anxiety, suspicion, and often hostility.

We regard none of the four factors identified above as either a necessary or sufficient condition to the finding of a deprivation of the right of speedy trial. Rather, they are related factors and must be considered together with such other circumstances as may be relevant. In sum, these factors have no talismanic qualities; courts must still engage in a difficult and sensitive balancing process. But, because we are dealing with a fundamental right of the accused, this process must be carried out with full recognition that the accused's interest in a speedy trial is specifically affirmed in the Constitution.

V

The difficulty of the task of balancing these factors is illustrated by this case, which we consider to be close. It is

5. See also Moore v. Arizona, 414 U.S. 25 (1973) (noting that a showing of prejudice is not required by *Barker*).

clear that the length of delay between arrest and trial—well over five years—was extraordinary. Only seven months of that period can be attributed to a strong excuse, the illness of the ex-sheriff who was in charge of the investigation. Perhaps some delay would have been permissible under ordinary circumstances, so that Manning could be utilized as a witness in Barker's trial, but more than four years was too long a period, particularly since a good part of that period was attributable to the Commonwealth's failure or inability to try Manning under circumstances that comported with due process.

Two counterbalancing factors, however, outweigh these deficiencies. The first is that prejudice was minimal. Of course, Barker was prejudiced to some extent by living for over four years under a cloud of suspicion and anxiety. Moreover, although he was released on bond for most of the period, he did spend 10 months in jail before trial. But there is no claim that any of Barker's witnesses died or otherwise became unavailable owing to the delay. The trial transcript indicates only two very minor lapses of memory—one on the part of a prosecution witness—which were in no way significant to the outcome.

More important than the absence of serious prejudice, is the fact that Barker did not want a speedy trial. Counsel was appointed for Barker immediately after his indictment and represented him throughout the period. No question is raised as to the competency of such counsel. Despite the fact that counsel had notice of the motions for continuances, the record shows no action whatever taken between October 21, 1958, and February 12, 1962, that could be construed as the assertion of the speedy trial right. On the latter date, in response to another motion for continuance, Barker moved to dismiss the indictment. The record does not show on what ground this motion was based, although it is clear that no alternative motion was made for an immediate trial. Instead the record strongly suggests that while he hoped to take advantage of the delay in which he had acquiesced, and thereby obtain a dismissal of the charges, he definitely did not want to be tried.

* * *

The probable reason for Barker's attitude was that he was gambling on Manning's acquittal. The evidence was not very strong against Manning, as the reversals and hung juries suggest, and Barker undoubtedly thought that if Manning were acquitted, he would never be tried.

* * *

That Barker was gambling on Manning's acquittal is also suggested by his failure, following the *pro forma* motion to dismiss filed in February 1962, to object to the Commonwealth's next two motions for continuances. Indeed, it was not until March 1963, after Manning's convictions were final, that Barker, having lost his gamble began to object to further continuances. At that time, the Commonwealth's excuse was the illness of the ex-sheriff, which Barker has conceded justified the further delay.

We do not hold that there may never be a situation in which an indictment may be dismissed on speedy trial grounds where the defendant has failed to object to continuances. There may be a situation in which the defendant was represented by incompetent counsel, was severely prejudiced, or even cases in which the continuances were granted *ex parte.* But barring extraordinary circumstances, we would be reluctant indeed to rule that a defendant was denied this constitutional right on a record that strongly indicates as does this one, that the defendant did not want a speedy trial. We hold, therefore, that Barker was not deprived of his due process right to a speedy trial.

The judgment of the Court of Appeals is affirmed.

MR. JUSTICE WHITE, with whom MR. JUSTICE BRENNAN joins, concurring.

Although the Court rejects petitioner's speedy trial claim * * *, it is apparent that had Barker not so clearly acquiesced in the major delays * * * the result would have been otherwise. * * *

[M]any defendants will believe that time is on their side and will prefer to suffer whatever disadvantages delay may entail. But, for those who desire an early trial, these personal factors should prevail if the only countervailing considerations offered by the State are those connected with crowded dockets and prosecutorial case loads. A defendant desiring a speedy trial, therefore, should have it within some reasonable time; and only special circumstances presenting a more pressing public need with respect to the case itself should suffice to justify delay. Only if such special considerations are in the case and if they outweigh the inevitable personal prejudice resulting from delay would it be necessary to consider whether there has been or would be prejudice to the defense at trial. * * *

Note

One critic has suggested that the Court slighted the importance of the length of a delay, bent the waiver doctrine, unduly disparaged the inchoate aspects of prejudice, and too readily accepted all but the most unfair reasons for state delay. Uviller, Barker v. Wingo, Speedy Trial Gets a Fast Shuffle, 72 Colum.L.Rev. 1376 (1972). Another critic has suggested that except for cases "in which the defendant is disabled or substantially impeded from making a demand for trial" and in cases in which "unwarranted delay gives rise to possibilities of impairment of a defendant's defense," there is good reason to require that a defendant who wants to claim a speedy trial violation must have gone "on record with a request for a speedy trial while it was still possible for the trial court to give him one." Amsterdam, Speedy Criminal Trial: Rights and Remedies, 27 Stan.L.Rev. 525 (1975). Do you find Barker v. Wingo satisfying? If not, can you state a better rule?

The Supreme Court used the *Barker* standard to determine whether the government's delay in instituting forfeiture proceedings under the Bank Secrecy Act of 1970 after seizing property without a hearing violated due process. United States v. Eight Thousand Eight Hundred and Fifty Dollars, 461 U.S. 555 (1983). The Court reasoned that a person who has been deprived of the use of property is in a situation comparable to a defendant who no longer retains his complete liberty. Applying the four-part *Barker* test, the Court concluded that there was no due process violation on the facts.

In United States v. Loud Hawk, 474 U.S. 302 (1986), a majority of the Supreme Court concluded that "an interlocutory appeal by the Government ordinarily is a valid reason that justifies delay." Justice Powell's opinion observed that in assessing such an appeal the factors that might be examined "include the strength of the Government's position on the appealed issue, the importance of the issue in the posture of the case, and—in some cases—the seriousness of the crime." The opinion also stated that defendants ordinarily cannot use the delay caused by their own interlocutory appeals to support a speedy trial claim, although they might be able to do so if they "bear the heavy burden of showing an unreasonable delay caused by the prosecution in that appeal, or a wholly unjustifiable delay by the appellate court." Justice Marshall's dissenting opinion, joined by Justices Brennan, Blackmun and Stevens, argued that the court of appeals, which took over five years to decide two appeals, one of which was expedited, delayed a "patently unreasonable" amount of time and that the prosecutor's good faith could not discharge the responsibility of a court to decide an appeal within a reasonable period of time.

Some courts have balanced the factors so as to give more weight to the defendant's interests. Wilson v. State, 44 Md.App. 1, 408 A.2d 102 (1979), is a rare case in which application of the Barker v. Wingo test through a "scoresheet" resulted in a finding of a speedy trial violation following an unexcused delay of 7½ months and an excused delay of 6 months. See also Ex parte Slaughter, 377 So.2d 632 (Ala.1979) (denial of speedy trial following 2½ year delay from indictment to trial); United States v. Ellis, 408 A.2d 971 (D.C.App.1979) (22 month delay between arrest and trial date denied speedy trial). In Bean v. United States, 409 A.2d 1064 (D.C.App.1979), the court said that "a showing of a delay greater than one year makes out a prima facie case of prejudicial delay."

Others have held inaction by a defendant to be especially significant. See, e.g., Commonwealth v. Look, 379 Mass. 893, 402 N.E.2d 470 (1980), which states that inaction by a defendant in pressing a claim is to be weighed heavily against him. See also United States v. Juarez-Fierro, 935 F.2d 672 (5th Cir. 1991) (four month delay due to negligent failure to procure attendance of a witness did not violate the right to a speedy trial, where the defendant's speedy trial claim was made for the first time on appeal).

People v. Johnson, 26 Cal.3d 557, 162 Cal.Rptr. 431, 606 P.2d 738 (1980), makes it clear that the asserted inability of a public defender to resolve a calendar conflict because of a need to accommodate other clients is not good cause for violating a speedy trial rule.

Consider the prejudice factor of *Barker*. Won't it almost always be the prosecution, rather than the defense, that suffers prejudice from delay? See Green, "Hare and Hounds": The Fugitive Defendant's Constitutional Right to be Pursued, 56 Brooklyn L.Rev. 439, 507 (1990) ("the passage of time is more likely to hurt the prosecution than the defense which, after all, has no obligation to call witnesses or present evidence, but need only, and in many cases does only, put the government to its proof").

Does the Sixth Amendment right to speedy trial include a right to speedy appeal? The court in Rheuark v. Shaw, 477 F.Supp. 897 (N.D.Tex.1979) said yes. Is the right determined by resort to the *Barker* factors? If so, it would seem that all speedy appeal claims would founder on the prejudice prong of *Barker,* unless the appeal itself was meritorious. Delay of an appeal does not result in the loss of evidence that would be relevant for the appeal; nor is incarceration problematic if the defendant has been justly convicted. Is the result of this reasoning that a defendant with an unmeritorious appeal has no right to a speedy appeal? What is the remedy for a defendant with a meritorious appeal—an order that the appeal be heard? Professor Arkin, in Speedy Criminal Appeal: A Right Without a Remedy, 74 Minn.L.Rev. 437 (1990) argues that the *Barker* prejudice factor is inapposite in the appellate context, and that remedies for a denial of the right to speedy appeal should include reduction of sentence or discharge from custody in egregious cases.

In Simmons v. Reynolds, 898 F.2d 865 (2d Cir.1990), the court held that the defendant, a state prisoner, was not entitled to be released from custody, even though a six-year delay in hearing his appeal violated his due process rights, since the disposition of his state appeal while his habeas corpus petition was pending transformed the prisoner's custody from illegal to legal. The Court concluded that any prejudice the prisoner suffered from the delay did not harm his ability to have a fair review of his conviction. It noted that the prisoner could seek redress through a federal civil rights action for damages.

In United States v. Blanco, 861 F.2d 773 (2d Cir.1988), Blanco was indicted on narcotics charges in April, 1975. At that time she was living in Colombia. From then until her arrest in February, 1985, Blanco was aware of the charges against her, but made no attempt to answer them. Federal agents kept track of her through an informant. In May, 1984, she was spotted in California by a DEA agent, but the agent did not arrest her because the arrest would have jeopardized a continuing investigation. She was arrested nine months later. Blanco argued that she was prejudiced by the ten year delay, as well as by the nine month delay after she was spotted in California. She claimed that these delays were attributable to the government's lack of diligence in pursuing her. She cited Smith v. Hooey, 393 U.S. 374 (1969), where the Court held that a Texas prosecutor was to blame for pretrial delay occasioned by his failure to secure the presence of an indicted defendant who was serving a federal prison sentence. The Court in *Smith* concluded that the federal authorities would upon request have produced the defendant, even though they were not legally required to do so.

The court in *Blanco* rejected the speedy trial claim. It found that *Smith* did not apply, and that the government had acted with "due diligence" in all respects. Do you agree? Does it make a difference that at the time of *Blanco,* there was no extradition treaty between Colombia and the United States? Why should the government even be required to exercise "due diligence" to secure the attendance of a fugitive defendant? See Green, "Hare and Hounds": The Fugitive Defendant's Constitutional Right to be Pursued, 56 Brooklyn L.Rev. 439 (1990) (approving of the result in *Blanco,* and arguing further that the government has no constitutional or ethical obligation to pursue a fugitive defendant who is aware of the charges against her).[6]

D. ENFORCING SPEEDY TRIAL CLAIMS

In Strunk v. United States, 412 U.S. 434 (1973), Chief Justice Burger's opinion for a unanimous Court held that, after finding a speedy trial violation when it reviewed Strunk's conviction for interstate transportation of a stolen vehicle, the court of appeals erred in holding that the "extreme" remedy of dismissal of the charges was unwarranted and in remanding the case to the district court for a reduction in sentence to compensate for the period of unnecessary delay. The Chief Justice wrote that "[i]n light of the policies which underlie the right to a speedy trial, dismissal must remain, as *Barker* noted, 'the only possible remedy.' "

This approach has been criticized. "If it is once admitted that the sixth amendment protects against at least three separate sorts of harm to the criminal defendant when it guarantees him a speedy trial, then it seems apparent that a given delay, in the context of a particular prosecution, may infringe upon one of the defendant's interests but not the others, and may violate the sixth amendment for one purpose but not for all purposes." Amsterdam, supra, at 537–38. Can you imagine situations in which you might find a speedy trial violation but not require dismissal?

6. For an interesting case in which a court found a speedy trial violation, see United States v. New Buffalo Amusement Corp., 600 F.2d 368 (2d Cir. 1979) (obscenity case; prejudice as result of change in public attitude toward obscenity during delay).

If *Strunk* really means that there is only one remedy for all speedy trial violations and that remedy is dismissal, how likely is it that many courts will find such violations? Is an all or nothing approach the best method of indicating the interests that are to be protected by the speedy trial guarantee? Professor Arkin, in Speedy Criminal Appeal: A Right Without a Remedy, 74 Minn.L.Rev. 437, 482 (1990), states that because of the extreme, exclusive remedy provided by *Strunk,* courts have "refused to find speedy trial violations except in the most outlandish cases" and that the *Strunk* remedy "effectively gutted the right."

E. BEYOND THE CONSTITUTION: STATUTORY AND JUDICIAL TIME LIMITS

Although not required by the Sixth Amendment, a large number of jurisdictions have followed the recommendation of the ABA that time limits be set by statute or rule for bringing cases to trial. ABA Standards, Speedy Trial § 12–2.1 (2d ed. 1980). The statutes and rules that have been adopted differ greatly, since each jurisdiction is free to set up any protective system that it wishes. Because of these statutes and rules, there has been "a shift from the amorphousness of constitutional litigation to the relative certainty of legislative enforcement. The final outcome is a more effective protection of the right to a speedy trial." Arkin, supra at 440. It should be noted, however, that these enactments do not in all cases ensure prompt adjudication of criminal cases. See R. Misner, Speedy Trial: Federal and State Practice § 17.13 (1983).

One important statute is the Speedy Trial Act of 1974. 18 U.S.C.A. §§ 3161–74. The Act provides definite time periods for bringing an accused to trial. For example, any indictment or information shall be filed within 30 days of arrest (or, if no grand jury is in session, 60 days); arraignment of a defendant pursuant to Fed.R.Crim.P. 10 shall be within ten days of either the public filing date of the indictment or information or the date a defendant has been ordered held to answer and has appeared before a judicial officer of the court in which the charge is pending, whichever date is later; and trial shall commence within 60 days of arraignment.[7] The Act also provides for a number of periods of delay that do not count in computing the time periods between various events—e.g., time needed to determine the competency of the defendant; delay resulting from other trials of the defendant; delay resulting from interlocutory appeals and pretrial motions. If the applicable time limits are not adhered to, charges against the defendant are to be dismissed *either with or without prejudice.*[8] See 18 U.S.C.A. § 3162(a)(1)(2). Several factors that are to be considered, among others, when a court decides what the effect of a dismissal should be are: the seriousness of the offense; the facts and circum-

7. The Act did not make these limits effective at the outset. Time periods were gradually reduced between 1975 and 1979. In Public Law 96–43, enacted August 2, 1979, the Act was amended to allow seventy days for trial. The Amendment followed complaints by prosecutors and judges that the Act placed too onerous a burden of moving cases on them.

In United States v. Pringle, 751 F.2d 419 (1st Cir.1984), the court held that the Speedy Trial Act requires a district judge to reject a defendant's offer to waive statutory speedy trial rights. It also held, however, that if the attempted waiver causes delay, the defendant is responsible for that delay.

8. Some states require dismissals to be with prejudice. See, e.g., Alaska Crim.R. 45(g); Wash.Sup.Ct.Rule 33(i).

stances which led to the dismissal; and the impact of a reprosecution on the administration of the Act and the administration of justice. Some commentators have discussed these and other factors and have analyzed how the Act has been implemented by federal judges.[9]

In United States v. Taylor, 487 U.S. 326 (1988), the Supreme Court reversed the dismissal of an indictment with prejudice where the defendant failed to appear for his trial on federal narcotics charges, which was scheduled one day prior to expiration of the statutory period, and subsequently the government exceeded by 15 days the period permitted between the defendant's arrest and the filing of a superseding indictment. Justice Blackmun wrote for the court and reasoned that the statute favors neither dismissals with or without prejudice; it permits district courts to exercise sound discretion. The Court noted that the statute sets forth specific factors—seriousness of the offense, facts and circumstances leading to dismissal, and the impact of a reprosecution on the speedy trial process and the administration of justice—as being "among others" that the Court may consider in ruling on a motion to dismiss. The Court determined that prejudice to the defendant was also a factor. It observed that the district court did not explain why these factors justified a dismissal with prejudice and that it had ignored the "brevity of the delay" as well as Taylor's own "illicit contribution to the delay." Justice White added a one sentence concurrence. Justice Scalia concurred in part. Justice Stevens, joined by Justices Brennan and Marshall, dissented.

Many cases have construed the statutory requirements of the Speedy Trial Act. One of the most difficult questions is whether a given delay constitutes "excludible delay" within the meaning of the Act. See 18 U.S.C. § 3161(h). For example, the court in United States v. Andress, 943 F.2d 622 (6th Cir.1991) held that the period of time between the issuance of a magistrate's report and recommendations on a pretrial motion and the government's filing of objections to that report should be treated as excludible delay. Accordingly, the court rejected the defendant's claim that the eight-day delay should be counted as part of the Speedy Trial Act's 70–day indictment-to-trial limit. The court in United States v. Thomas, 788 F.2d 1250 (7th Cir.1986) took the contrary view. In Henderson v. United States, 476 U.S. 321 (1986), the Court held that periods of time in which a court awaits post-hearing submissions are excludible under the Act. See also United States v. Tanner, 941 F.2d 574 (7th Cir.1991) (excludible delay of one co-defendant is ascribed to all).

In United States v. Brainer, 691 F.2d 691 (4th Cir. 1982), a district judge refused to dismiss a drug prosecution when the government failed to comply with the terms of the Speedy Trial Act. The judge found the act to be an unconstitutional encroachment upon the judiciary. The government joined the defendant in arguing on appeal that the Act was valid, and counsel was appointed to argue in favor of the district judge's conclusion as amicus curiae. The court of appeals reversed, finding that the Act regulated procedure in the federal courts and did not impermissibly interfere with inherent judicial power to control dockets.

9. See, e.g., Steinberg, Dismissal With or Without Prejudice Under the Speedy Trial Act: A Proposed Interpretation, 68 J.Crim.L. & Cr. 1 (1977).

Misner, Speedy Trial: Federal and State Practice (1983), analyzes speedy trial statutes and rules throughout the United States.

II. JOINDER AND SEVERANCE

A. SOME GENERAL RULES AND PROBLEMS

The outcome of a criminal case can be affected by the number and nature of charges and defendants joined together. There was a time at which the government could only charge one offense in an indictment and was greatly restricted in trying defendants jointly over objection. But that time is long past in many jurisdictions. In Richardson v. Marsh, 481 U.S. 200 (1987), Justice Scalia, writing for the Court, had this to say about the advantages of a joint trial:

> Joint trials play a vital role in the criminal justice system, accounting for almost one third of federal criminal trials in the past five years. Many joint trials—for example, those involving large conspiracies to import and distribute illegal drugs—involve a dozen or more codefendants. * * * It would impair both the efficiency and the fairness of the criminal justice system to require * * * that prosecutors bring separate proceedings, presenting the same evidence again and again, requiring victims and witnesses to repeat the inconvenience (and sometimes trauma) of testifying, and randomly favoring the last-tried defendants who have the advantage of knowing the prosecution's case beforehand. Joint trials generally serve the interests of justice by avoiding inconsistent verdicts and enabling more accurate assessment of relative culpability—advantages which sometimes operate to the defendant's benefit. Even apart from these tactical considerations, joint trials generally serve the interests of justice by avoiding the scandal and inequity of inconsistent verdicts.

There are economies associated with trying multiple offenses and defendants together.[10] Sometimes the economies benefit the government, sometimes they benefit the defendants and sometimes they benefit both sides. But there also are dangers when joinder is effected.

The Federal Rules of Criminal Procedure attempt to strike a balance through three separate but related rules: Rules 8, 13 and 14. The text of those rules is set forth in the Supplement.[11]

The ABA Standards on Joinder and Severance (App. Drafts 1968, 1978) take the view that the government can charge similar offenses that are not

10. But see Dawson, Joint Trials of Defendants in Criminal Cases: An Analysis of Efficiencies and Prejudices, 77 Mich.L.Rev. 1379 (1979) (challenges the wisdom of trying jointly charged defendants together).

One recent study of joinder of offenses, Tanford, Decision-Making Processes in Joined Criminal Trials, 12 Crim. Justice & Behavior 367 (1985), found, as a result of empirical research with jurors and students, that joinder of offenses "fosters a negative impression of the defendant that affects memory, evaluation of evidence, and social interference processes." Interestingly, the study concludes that "joining charges within a realistic trial setting increases the likelihood that a defendant will be convicted on a particular charge, regardless of the similarity of the charges or the evidence." United States v. Lewis, 787 F.2d 1318 (9th Cir.1986), cites the Tanford article in an opinion that reverses a defendant's conviction for killing in order to secure a getaway vehicle for a bank robbery. The indictment charged the defendant with being a felon in receipt of a firearm as well as with the killing and bank larceny. The trial judge did not give instructions telling the jury to be careful to consider the prior conviction only with respect to the firearms charge until the third day of trial, and the court of appeals found that the failure to sever the gun charge from the killing charge was prejudicial.

11. See generally Decker, Joinder and Severance in Federal Criminal Cases: An Examination of Judicial Interpretation of the Federal Rules, 53 Notre Dame Law. 147 (1977).

related to one another, but that the defendant has a right to have the cases tried separately. Also, they give a defendant the right to have related charges tried together. (The 1978 standards give the prosecutor a right also to sever unrelated offenses.) In some respects the ABA Standards attempt to permit defendants to ask for compulsory joinder of issues in much the same manner that a civil litigant could under Fed.R.Civ.P. 13(a). Fed.R.Crim.P. 13 affords similar opportunities, but only if the court orders cases tried together.

All of the principal criticisms of joinder center around two assertions: (1) One side, usually the government, is seeking an unfair advantage by having charges combined in order to brand the defendant as a bad person, to show that "birds of a feather flock together," to reduce a jury's regret at convicting the defendant in a world of imperfect proof, or to establish a "where there's smoke, there's fire" attitude in the trier of fact.[12] (2) One side, usually the government, is trying to separate out issues to wear down the other side, to compartmentalize a case in order to weaken it, to increase the odds that witnesses and evidence will become unavailable or to increase the odds of winning at least one case.[13]

The competing policy considerations—efficiency in the presentation of evidence versus a fair trial on each charge made against a defendant—are best understood in the context of actual cases.

B. JOINDER OF CLAIMS

United States v. Mullen, 550 F.2d 373 (6th Cir. 1977), illustrates a simple problem of joinder of claims. Mullen was charged with two bank robberies which took place 19 days apart. He requested a severance, but it was denied. The Court of Appeals affirmed per curiam, disposing of the joinder claim in one short paragraph: "We find no abuse of discretion in the district court's denial of the motion for a severance." Judge Engel dissented. He recognized that under Federal Rule 8(a) the claims were properly joined originally.

> However, under Rule 14, Federal Rules of Criminal Procedure, the court may order separate trials of counts "if it appears that a defendant or the government is prejudiced by a joinder of offenses * * * " The general test to determine whether severance is warranted involves weighing the possible prejudice to the defendant from the joinder against the public interest in avoiding duplicitous, time consuming trials in which the same factual and legal issues must be litigated. * * *
>
> Of the three grounds for joinder under Rule 8(a), that based on the "similar character" of offenses combines the greatest danger of real prejudice to a defendant with the least promise of judicial economy. Very little time is saved since the charges usually involve different transactions. * * *
>
> Three potential sources of prejudice to the defendant by joinder of two or more offenses solely on this similar character theory are described in Drew v. United States, 118 U.S.App.D.C. 11, 331 F.2d 85, 88 (1964):
>
> > (1) he may become embarrassed or confounded in presenting separate defenses; (2) the jury may use the evidence of one of the crimes charged to

12. The defendant sometimes may want weak charges combined with strong ones in the hope that reasonable doubts as to the weak ones will carry over to the others.

13. Usually the government wants to win at least one case. But defendants may believe that their best strategy is "divide and conquer."

infer a criminal disposition on the part of the defendant from which is found his guilt of the other crime or crimes charged; or (3) the jury may cumulate the evidence of the various crimes charged and find guilt when, if considered separately, it would not so find.

* * *

The problems inherent in joinder of similar offenses are especially clear where the defendant has a good defense on one charge (and perhaps is innocent), but no defense on the other. * * *

Potentially the defendant might also be prejudiced in a trial of two entirely unrelated charges by the jury's use of the evidence of one of the offenses to infer a criminal disposition on the part of the defendant to commit the other. The injection into a trial of proof that the defendant has also been guilty of the commission of other crimes has been consistently condemned in the absence of any legitimate reasons for its injection.

Frequently when two similar charges are joined for trial, their relationship enables the prosecutor to introduce evidence of one of the crimes in the trial of the other to prove motive, opportunity, intent, preparation, plan, knowledge, identity or absence of mistake or accident. Rule 404(b), Federal Rules of Evidence. Thus if the evidence of the two crimes is admissible under Rule 404(b) the danger from trying both offenses together is largely dissipated.[14] It appears from the record in this case that the trial judge was persuaded to deny severance because he believed that the evidence could be brought in to "show intent, to show state of mind". Upon the facts here, I cannot agree.

The issue at trial was primarily one of identity and at no time was the intent of the robber disputed. The government argues that the evidence was relevant to the identity and *modus operandi* of the robber, but an examination of the record here does not persuade me that it would have been admissible in separate trials.

Here the evidence showed robberies occurring 19 days apart at different banks, although in the same general vicinity. Witnesses described the culprit in each as a young slim black male with prominent cheekbones and of a height between five-feet-six and five-feet-ten, with weight from between 145 and 160 pounds. In both cases, money was demanded from the teller, and a withdrawal slip was left behind each time, although under different circumstances. Each time a light colored coat was worn as was a knit hat. On the other hand, a sawed-off shotgun was used in the first robbery while the second robber was armed possibly with a knife or was unarmed. In one case the robber wore red slacks, while in the other the slacks went unnoticed but he wore gloves. The crimes occurred at different times of the day. One robbery was initiated by a note (on the back of a withdrawal slip) demanding the money, while the other was by a vocal demand. In one robbery the teller was asked to put money in a brown paper bag and in the other, no bag was used. The robber of the first bank exited and walked around the corner. In the second, he walked out and drove away in a taxi.

* * * The evidence here falls short of earmarking the robberies as the handiwork of the defendant. * * *

14. The evidentiary standard that permits proof of modus operandi—see, e.g., Fed.R.Evid. 404(b)—was borrowed and used as the permissible test for joinder of offenses of similar character in Commonwealth v. Morris, 493 Pa. 164, 425 A.2d 715 (1981). In that court's view, the offenses must show an unusual or distinctive modus operandi, or they may not be joined.

* * *

Does Judge Engel overlook any proper interest of the government?[15] See also Leach v. Kolb, 911 F.2d 1249 (7th Cir.1990) (improper joinder of attempted murder, armed robbery, and attempted armed robbery charges arising from separate incidents did not deprive defendant of a fair trial, where evidence of the defendant's guilt on each charge was overwhelming, and the trial court gave explicit limiting instructions requiring the jury to determine guilt or innocence on each count without reference to guilt or innocence on other charged counts).[16]

Mullen illustrates the problem of joinder against the wishes of a defendant. The converse problem is nonjoinder. A prosecutor who fails to join similar offenses may run afoul of the Double Jeopardy Clause when the subsequent prosecution is brought. Consider, for example, the facts of Ashe v. Swenson, 397 U.S. 436 (1970). Three or four masked men robbed six other men who were playing poker. Four men were charged with the crime, including Ashe. The government charged six separate robberies and the theft of a car of one of the robbery victims. Ashe was first tried for one robbery and was acquitted. Then he was tried again for a second of the robberies and was convicted. The Court held that the rule of collateral estoppel was part of the protection provided by the Double Jeopardy Clause, and that the state was collaterally estopped from showing that Ashe was a robber at the poker game. Even if Ashe had been convicted of the single robbery in the first case, the Double Jeopardy Clause may have prevented a subsequent prosecution. While the Court has not adopted the "transactional test" suggested by Justice Brennan (i.e. that the government must join all charges against a defendant which arise from a single transaction or occurrence), it has held that subsequent prosecution is precluded if the government "must prove conduct that constitutes an offense for which the defendant has already been convicted." Grady v. Corbin, 495 U.S. 508 (1990). In *Corbin,* a subsequent prosecution for homicide resulting from a traffic accident was barred by a prior prosecution for driving while intoxicated. The subject of double jeopardy will be taken up in detail in Chapter Twelve; for present purposes it is important to note that the Double Jeopardy Clause serves as a mandatory joinder rule in many cases.[17]

C. JOINDER OF DEFENDANTS

Some jurisdictions that allow the prosecutor to join claims over a defendant's objection do not allow additional defendants to be joined without the

15. Complete coverage of Rules like 404(b) is left for a course in evidence.

16. People v. Shapiro, 50 N.Y.2d 747, 431 N.Y.S.2d 422, 409 N.E.2d 897 (1980), is one of the rare cases in which convictions were set aside for failure to grant a severance. Shapiro was accused on 64 counts of "homosexual sodomitic acts" in one indictment and in two other indictments with promoting prostitution and various sexual offenses arising out of activities that took place on one particular night. The court of appeals found that joining the first indictment with the other two raised a possibility of his being convicted improperly on those two as a result of "propensity" evidence.

Social scientists appear to confirm the intuition of defense lawyers that a defendant is more likely to be convicted on a particular charge when that charge is tried together with other charges. See Tanford & Penrod, Social Inference Processes In Juror Judgments of Multiple-Offense Trials, 47 J. Personality & Soc. Psych. 749 (1984). The study indicates that joinder produced confusion of evidence and negative inferences about the defendant.

17. See generally Thomas, An Elegant Theory on Double Jeopardy, 1988 U.Ill.L.Rev. 827.

consent of all defendants. See, e.g., Va.Code § 19.2–263; Uniform R.Crim.P. 472(a). See also Langrock, Joint Trials: A Short Lesson from Little Vermont, 9 Crim.L.Bull. 612 (1973).[18] The ABA Standards give no absolute right of severance to a defendant, but attempt to limit joinder to situations in which it is most efficient and, even then, to grant authority for severance. Rules 8 and 14 of the Federal Rules of Criminal Procedure do not distinguish between joinder of claims and parties.

It is common to find joinder in several classes of cases, especially conspiracy cases. Generally, courts express sympathy for the plight if defendants joined in conspiracy cases, but find the Government interest in efficiency to be paramount. See, e.g. United States v. Gonzales, 933 F.2d 417 (7th Cir.1991).

See also United States v. Jackson, 549 F.2d 517 (8th Cir. 1977). In this complex conspiracy case—a drug prosecution—the court approved the joinder of defendants. It noted that the general rule is that persons charged with conspiracy should be tried together. There is an exception that is discussed in this case for situations in which some defendants might be able to exculpate one particular defendant but refuse to do so if they are joined together. In order to avail oneself of this exception, a defendant must make a showing that co-defendants are willing and able to render help to him if a severance is granted. Bald and conclusory allegations will not be sufficient. See also United States v. Tolliver, 937 F.2d 1183 (7th Cir.1991) (joint trial permissible where co-defendant with exculpatory information stated that he would not testify for the defendant even if the cases were severed; the fact that the co-defendant often changed his mind was irrelevant, since the mere possibility of exculpatory testimony is not sufficient to warrant a severance). The defendant must also show that the prospective testimony is substantially exculpatory. See United States v. Gonzalez, 933 F.2d 417 (7th Cir.1991) (severance not required where co-defendant would testify that the defendant took a certain trip for a legitimate business purpose; the testimony would not exclude the possibility that the defendant took trips for drug-related purposes on other occasions).

Another, limited exception to the general rule of joinder in conspiracy and other cases is where there is a gross disparity in the evidence against various joined defendants. In these cases, "the danger is that the bit players may not be able to differentiate themselves in the jurors' minds from the stars." United States v. Zafiro, 945 F.2d 881 (7th Cir.1991) cert. granted 60 U.S.L.W. 3652 (1992). In order to obtain a severance on this ground, the defendant will have to show a disparity in the evidence so great that the jury will not be able to follow limiting instructions. See e.g., United States v. Farmer, 924 F.2d 647 (7th Cir.1991) (defendants arguing gross disparity were not prejudiced from a joint trial, where the record showed that the jury meticulously considered the evidence against each defendant; the jury returned 62 findings of guilty and 38 findings of not guilty, and all defendants but one were acquitted on at least one count); United States v. Gonzalez, 933 F.2d 417 (7th Cir.1991) (some disparity between defendants is permissible if it is within the jury's capacity to follow the court's limiting instructions). Given the institutional interest in trying all

18. See State ex rel. Whitman v. Fox, 160 W.Va. 633, 236 S.E.2d 565 (1977) (joinder impermissible).

members of the conspiracy together, the gross disparity argument is rarely successful. See *Zafiro,* supra.

Although many jurisdictions give prosecutors power to determine when defendants will be charged together and courts are reluctant to grant severances that result in multiple trials, some cases hold that where defendants have antagonistic defenses a severance must be granted. For example in United States v. Walters, 913 F.2d 388 (7th Cir.1990), Walters and Bloom sought to represent professional athletes. They enticed football players who were still in college to sign contracts by providing cash bonuses and other incentives. These contracts were post-dated so that the athlete would retain his college eligibility; the agreements were in violation of National Collegiate Athletic Association ("NCAA") rules. The athletes would then have to lie to their colleges on eligibility forms in order to continue to receive scholarships. Prior to their enterprise, Walters and Bloom consulted a noted sports attorney to obtain advice concerning the legal ramifications of these agreements. The attorney opined that Walters and Bloom were violating NCAA rules, but that they were not violating any laws. It was unclear whether the attorney factored in that the athletes would be lying on the college eligibility forms. Walters and Bloom were charged with mail fraud, RICO violations, and conspiracy. Walters defended on the ground that his actions were taken in good faith on the advice of counsel. Bloom's motion to sever was denied, and both Bloom and Walters were convicted. On appeal, Bloom argued that Walters' pursuit of an advice of counsel defense required Bloom to assert the same defense, and also to waive his attorney-client privilege. The court of appeals analyzed this claim as follows:

> [S]everances are called for where the defenses of codefendants are mutually antagonistic or irreconcilable, such that the acceptance of one party's defense will preclude the acquittal of the other. Even where defenses are not mutually antagonistic, a severance may be granted if the actual conduct of one defendant's defense unduly prejudices his or her codefendant. * * *
>
> When Walters pursued his advice-of-counsel defense, Bloom was forced to observe his own attorneys testify about the intimate discussions to which he had been a party. Bloom could not pursue his own defense, but was forced to skittle along behind that of Walters. Details which Bloom chose to share with his attorney were not available to the prosecution and broadcast to the jury. Bloom's counsel did not wish to pursue the advice of counsel gambit with Walters. In fact, Bloom's counsel stated to the court that Walters' theory had "gone over like a lead balloon" with the jury. * * *
>
> We recognize that joint trials are an essential element of the quick administration of justice. If every defendant who wanted a severance was given one, the slow pace of our court system would go from a crawl to paralysis; any motion for severance must be balanced against the need for judicial economy. Here, no such balance can be reasonably struck. * * * Once Walters pursued his advice of counsel defense, as was his right, Bloom must have been provided the option of a separate trial. Any other course of action forced Bloom to waive his attorney-client privilege. We cannot tolerate such devil's bargains.

Is it important that the court in *Walters* never describes what Bloom's defense would have been, and whether it would have been more viable than the advice of counsel defense? Is it important that in another part of the opinion, the court reversed Walters' conviction on the ground that he had presented sufficient evidence to the jury on the advice of counsel defense to be entitled to a jury instruction on that issue? Aren't antagonistic defenses something that the jury can sort out?

In *Walters* severance was held required because Walters' defense impaired the defense of Bloom. Is severance required if defendants are "pointing fingers" at each other, such that if one defense is believed the other cannot be? Consider the analysis of Judge Posner in United States v. Zafiro, 945 F.2d 881 (7th Cir.1991) cert. granted 60 U.S.L.W. 3652 (1992), a case in which four defendants were tried for a narcotics conspiracy. Officers discovered a large amount of cocaine at a residence to which all four defendants were connected. Soto and Garcia argued lack of knowledge and that Martinez and Zafiro were the drug dealers. Martinez and Zafiro argued lack of knowledge and that Soto and Garcia were the drug dealers. Judge Posner concluded that joinder of all defendants was proper.

> The fact that it is certain that a crime was committed by one of two defendants is a reason for trying them together, rather than a reason against, to avoid the scandal and inequity of inconsistent verdicts. * * *
>
> Each member of each pair of defendants * * * was accusing the other of being the drug dealer. In this symmetrical situation, each defendant had to defend himself against the prosecutor and one other defendant but at the same time had a live body to offer the jury in lieu of himself (or herself). * * * This was apt to be a more persuasive line than telling the jury to let everyone go, when the one thing no one could question is that the government had found 75 pounds of cocaine on premises connected with these defendants. * * *
>
> We remind the defense bar that they are not obliged to make futile arguments on behalf of their clients. The argument that a conviction should be reversed because the district judge failed to sever properly joined defendants for trial is nearly always futile even when the defendants can be said to be presenting mutually antagonistic defenses.

In Schaffer v. United States, 362 U.S. 511 (1960), defendants were joined on the basis of a conspiracy charge, though the substantive counts charged each defendant with different acts of theft. At the close of the government's case, the trial court dismissed the conspiracy count for lack of proof. But the substantive counts were submitted to the jury and the defendants were convicted. The Supreme Court found that defendants had not suffered any prejudice warranting severance, since the proof at trial was "carefully compartmentalized" as to each defendant. It noted that as of the beginning of the trial, the joinder was authorized by Rule 8(b), and it refused to adopt "a hard-and-fast formula that, when a conspiracy count fails, joinder is error as a matter of law." Justice Douglas, joined by Chief Justice Warren and Justices Black and Brennan, in dissent, found "implicit prejudice" in trying separate offenses in a joint trial, because "a subtle bond is likely to be created between the several defendants even though they have never met nor acted in unison."

In United States v. Andrews, 754 F.Supp. 1161 (N.D.Ill.1990), the court encountered the recent phenomenon of a "megatrial." Thirty-eight defendants were charged in a 175 count indictment under the RICO statute. 18 U.S.C. § 1962. The government alleged that the defendants were involved in a street gang, and the indictment related over 250 factually separate criminal acts committed over a 23 year period. The court held that joinder of these claims and parties was permissible under Fed.R.Crim.P. 8, since the defendants were each alleged members of a single and unified RICO conspiracy. The court commented as follows:

> This case provides a vivid example of the broad charging authority that RICO has conferred to the government. Prior to RICO, the scope of a proper indictment under Rule 8(b) was largely restricted to the number of individuals who could conspire to commit a single substantive crime. RICO removes this natural ceiling by making it a crime to agree to the commission of a pattern of racketeering, which can include a limitless number of substantive crimes and, consequently, a limitless number of conspirators. Thus, RICO evades the practical limitations of group conduct that Rule 8(b) places on the scope of an indictment.

The court found, however, that though joinder was technically proper under Rule 8, severance was required under Rule 14 because the defendants would be prejudiced by the megatrial. The court divided various actors and charges into five trial units. It expressed general concern about mega-trials, and doubted their efficiency. Following the lead of several other courts, the judge adopted a "presumption *against* a joint trial and *for* severance when faced with the prospect of a mega-trial." It defined a "mega-trial" as one in which the prosecution estimates the length of trial to be greater than four months, and ten or more defendants are joined. The court explained as follows:

> [A]t some point, the oft-cited advantages of a joint trial are outweighed by the manifest disadvantages of a large and protracted trial. * * * One disadvantage * * * is the significant exacerbation of the public cost of providing defense counsel to each defendant. All but one of the defense attorneys currently representing a defendant in this case are being federally funded. Testimony directly implicating most of their clients is projected to last not more than a few weeks, and, for many, not more than a few days. Thus, in a single trial, [the attorneys] would be compelled to sit idly by for the duration of a lengthy trial where the vast majority of evidence deals solely with the criminal activities of other attorneys' clients. * * * The cost of twenty-one court-appointed attorneys for a one-year trial is at least $1.6 million. Here, a significant majority of this total would be wasted as compensation to defense counsel for idle time.

The court also noted other disadvantages of a mega-trial: the management aspect of the case would wreak havoc upon an already overburdened docket; the trial would place "enormous personal burdens on the jurors, the defendants, defense counsel and the Court"; and the the search for truth would be impaired due to the "massive and complex evidence making it almost impossible for the jury to separate evidence as it relates to each defendant." The court concluded that these costs were "too high a price to pay for the government's ill-conceived desire to prosecute all these defendants in one spectacular trial extravaganza."

D. MISJOINDER

The Supreme Court held in United States v. Lane, 474 U.S. 438 (1986), that misjoinder of counts in violation of Fed.R.Crim.P. 8(b) does not automatically compel reversal of convictions. A father and son were charged with various offenses arising out of an arson conspiracy. They persuaded a court of appeals that one count, brought solely against the father, was improperly joined with four counts naming them both and another count charging the son with perjury. The court of appeals concluded that misjoinder is prejudicial per se. Chief Justice Burger's opinion for the Court disagreed, reasoning that misjoinder, which does not rise to the level of a constitutional violation, surely can be harmless in light of decisions holding that even constitutional errors do not inevitably require reversal of convictions. Justice Brennan, joined by Justice Blackmun, dissented in part, and would have left the determination of whether the error was harmless to the court of appeals. Justice Stevens, joined by Justice Marshall, dissented and argued that misjoinder affects substantial rights within the meaning of the harmless error rule, Fed.R.Crim.P. 52(a), and the harmless error statute, 28 U.S.C. § 2111. He also concluded that if a harmless error inquiry is proper, it should be conducted by the court of appeals.

While the misjoinder in *Lane* was not of constitutional dimension, constitutional error can occur in a joint trial that could not arise if the defendants were tried separately. For example, in Bruton v. United States, 391 U.S. 123 (1968), the Court found constitutional error when Bruton's co-defendant made a post-custodial confession which was offered at the joint trial. The confession was admissible against the co-defendant as a party admission, but it was inadmissible hearsay as to Bruton. The trial judge gave a limiting instruction that the statement could only be used against the co-defendant, but the Court held that in light of the "powerfully incriminating" nature of the confession, the instruction was insufficient to protect Bruton's constitutional right to confront his accuser.

The Court suggested separate trials to avoid a "*Bruton*" problem, but courts after *Bruton* have often used means short of separate trials to protect against the use of the confession of one co-defendant against another. The Supreme Court has approved redaction of a confession, to exclude all reference to the defendant's existence. See Richardson v. Marsh, 481 U.S. 200 (1987). In *Marsh,* the confession was redacted to refer only to the confessing co-defendant and another perpetrator who had absconded. The court did not imply that a redaction such as "X and I did it" would be sufficient when the jury could easily find that "X" was the defendant. See People v. Wheeler, 62 N.Y.2d 867, 478 N.Y.S.2d 254, 466 N.E.2d 846 (1984) (redaction to "we did it" held insufficient); United States v. Van Hemelryck, 945 F.2d 1493 (11th Cir.1991) (reference to "another individual" held insufficient redaction).

Some courts have experimented with empaneling two juries in a single trial to resolve the *Bruton* problem. The jury hearing the case against the non-confessing co-defendant is excused when the statement is introduced or referred to. A judge who tried such a case stated that before the confession was introduced, she excused both juries, and then called the confessing defendant's jury back to hear the confession. In that way, the jurors for the non-confessing defendant would not think that they were missing anything. See Santagata, One Trial, Two Juries—It Works in Extraordinary Cases, N.Y.L.J., May 11, 1988, p. 1. In People v. Ricardo B., 73 N.Y.2d 228, 538 N.Y.S.2d 796, 535 N.E.2d 1336 (1989), the court held that the use of multiple juries "does not deny defendants their constitutional right to a jury trial or, in the absence of identified prejudice, to due process of law." The court noted, however, that multiple juries should be used sparingly, because their use "can only magnify the problems inherent in joint trials because of the need to insulate the juries from inadmissible evidence or argument."

Bruton has been held inapplicable to a bench trial of joined defendants, since the problem that the Court was concerned about in *Bruton* was the jury's inability to follow the judge's instruction not to use one co-defendant's confession against another. Rogers v. McMackin, 884 F.2d 252 (6th Cir.1989).

Does the prosecutor in a joint trial assume the risk of one co-defendant prejudicing another? Consider Toolate v. Borg, 828 F.2d 571 (9th Cir.1987), where Toolate's codefendant, Frazier, took the stand and on direct examination shifted the blame to Toolate. He refused to be cross-examined, and the judge gave an instruction to the jury to disregard his testimony. Toolate's motion for a mistrial was denied. The court of appeals held that *Bruton* required a mistrial under these circumstances, since Frazier's testimony was powerfully incriminating against Toolate, and the instruction was insufficient to protect Toolate's right to confrontation. The government argued that mistrial was not required because, unlike in *Bruton* where the prosecutor proffered the co-defendant's confession, the prosecutor in *Toolate* had done nothing wrong. The court rejected this argument and reasoned that the prosecutor who tries defendants jointly assumes certain risks.

> Codefendants * * * have the opportunity to sabotage each other's trial through unethical tactics. For example, if one codefendant comments prejudicially on another's refusal to testify, the latter's conviction must ordinarily be reversed. See United States v. Patterson, 819 F.2d 1495 (9th Cir.1987). The result is the same if one codefendant calls the other as a witness, requiring him to invoke his Fifth Amendment privilege in the jury's presence. United States v. Kaplan, 576 F.2d 598 (5th Cir.1978). One codefendant could also produce a mistrial for another by testifying to irrelevant, highly prejudicial matter, such as the latter's prior criminal record. [See United States v. Bovain, 708 F.2d 606 (11th Cir.1983)]. These dangers are inherent in the joint trial process.
>
> * * *
>
> True, the government did not perpetrate the prejudice in this case, as it did in *Bruton,* and could not have prevented it. This is significant because the *Bruton* rule emerged in part to stop the government from using joint trials to circumvent the evidentiary rules that would apply in separate ones. That concern does not exist here. But *Bruton* rests, for good or ill, on the presumed inability of juries to disregard an incriminatory codefendant's confession. In that crucial respect, this case is identical to *Bruton.*

In light of *Toolate* and the cases discussed in the above quote, when would it ever be prudent to try multiple defendants in a single trial?

III. CONSTITUTIONALLY BASED PROOF REQUIREMENTS

A. PROOF BEYOND A REASONABLE DOUBT GENERALLY

In re Winship, 397 U.S. 358 (1970), decided that proof beyond a reasonable doubt was a constitutional requirement in criminal cases. Samuel Winship, a 12–year–old boy, was brought before a juvenile court and charged with delinquency for taking $112 from a woman's pocketbook in a locker. The judge acknowledged that the conduct might not have been proved beyond a reasonable doubt, but determined that Winship could be adjudged a delinquent by a preponderance of the evidence. *Winship* held that the requirement of proof beyond a reasonable doubt is one of the "essentials of due process and fair treatment" required during the adjudicatory stage when a juvenile is charged with an act which would constitute a crime if committed by an adult. Justice Brennan's majority opinion traced the history of proof in American criminal trials and found "virtually unanimous" authority supporting the reasonable doubt standard. He concluded that the criminal defendant has a transcending liberty interest in criminal trials that requires the narrowest margin for error.

> Moreover, use of the reasonable-doubt standard is indispensable to command the respect and confidence of the community in applications of the criminal law. It is critical that the moral force of the criminal law not be diluted by a standard of proof that leaves people in doubt whether innocent men are being condemned. It is also important in our free society that every individual going about his ordinary affairs have confidence that his government cannot adjudge him guilty of a criminal offense without convincing a proper factfinder of his guilt with utmost certainty.
>
> Lest there remain any doubt about the constitutional stature of the reasonable-doubt standard, we explicitly hold that the Due Process Clause protects the accused against conviction except upon proof beyond a reasonable doubt of every fact necessary to constitute the crime with which he is charged.

Justice Harlan concurred and added some thoughts about the reasonable doubt standard.

> Professor Wigmore, in discussing the various attempts by courts to define how convinced one must be to be convinced beyond a reasonable doubt, wryly observed: "The truth is that no one has yet invented or discovered a mode of measurement for the intensity of human belief. Hence there can be yet no successful method of communicating intelligibly * * * a sound method of self-analysis for one's belief," 9 J. Wigmore, Evidence 325 (3d ed. 1940).
>
> Notwithstanding Professor Wigmore's skepticism, we have before us a case where the choice of the standard of proof has made a difference: the juvenile court judge below forthrightly acknowledged that he believed by a preponderance of the evidence, but was not convinced beyond a reasonable doubt, that appellant stole $112 from the complainant's pocketbook. Moreover, even though the labels used for alternative standards of proof are vague and not a very sure guide to decisionmaking, the choice of the standard for a particular variety of adjudication does, I think, reflect a very fundamental assessment of the comparative social costs of erroneous factual determinations.
>
> To explain why I think this so, I begin by stating two propositions, neither of which I believe can be fairly disputed. First, in a judicial proceeding in which there is a dispute about the facts of some earlier event, the factfinder cannot acquire unassailably accurate knowledge of what happened. Instead, all the factfinder can acquire is a belief of what *probably* happened. The intensity of this belief—the degree to which a factfinder is convinced that a given act actually occurred—can, of course, vary. In this regard, a standard of proof represents an attempt to instruct the factfinder concerning the degree of confidence our society thinks he should have in the correctness of factual conclusions for a particular type of adjudication. Although the phrases "preponderance of the evidence" and "proof beyond a reasonable doubt" are

quantitatively imprecise, they do communicate to the finder of fact different notions concerning the degree of confidence he is expected to have in the correctness of his factual conclusions.

A second proposition, which is really nothing more than a corollary of the first, is that the trier of fact will sometimes, despite his best efforts, be wrong in his factual conclusions. In a lawsuit between two parties, a factual error can make a difference in one of two ways. First, it can result in a judgment in favor of the plaintiff when the true facts warrant a judgment for the defendant. The analogue in a criminal case would be the conviction of an innocent man. On the other hand, an erroneous factual determination can result in a judgment for the defendant when the true facts justify a judgment in plaintiff's favor. The criminal analogue would be the acquittal of a guilty man.

The standard of proof influences the relative frequency of these two types of erroneous outcomes. If, for example, the standard of proof for a criminal trial were a preponderance of the evidence rather than proof beyond a reasonable doubt, there would be a smaller risk of factual errors that result in freeing guilty persons, but a far greater risk of factual errors that result in convicting the innocent. Because the standard of proof affects the comparative frequency of these two types of erroneous outcomes, the choice of the standard to be applied in a particular kind of litigation should, in a rational world, reflect an assessment of the comparative social disutility of each.

When one makes such an assessment, the reason for different standards of proof in civil as opposed to criminal litigation becomes apparent. In a civil suit between two private parties for money damages, for example, we view it as no more serious in general for there to be an erroneous verdict in the defendant's favor than for there to be an erroneous verdict in the plaintiff's favor. * * *

In a criminal case, on the other hand, we do not view the social disutility of convicting an innocent man as equivalent to the disutility of acquitting someone who is guilty. * * *

In this context, I view the requirement of proof beyond a reasonable doubt in a criminal case as bottomed on a fundamental value determination of our society that it is far worse to convict an innocent man than to let a guilty man go free. It is only because of the nearly complete and long-standing acceptance of the reasonable-doubt standard by the States in criminal trials that the Court has not before today had to hold explicitly that due process, as an expression of fundamental procedural fairness, requires a more stringent standard for criminal trials than for ordinary civil litigation.

Chief Justice Burger, joined by Justice Stewart, implicitly accepted the proof requirement in criminal proceedings, but would have treated juvenile cases differently. Justice Black dissented on the ground that proof beyond a reasonable doubt was not found in the language of the Constitution and could not properly be read into the "due process of law" language of the Fourteenth Amendment.

In Taylor v. Kentucky, 436 U.S. 478 (1978), the Court reversed a conviction where the judge refused to give a requested instruction that the defendant was presumed innocent. Later, however, in Kentucky v. Whorton, 441 U.S. 786 (1979), the Court held that a presumption of innocence instruction was not constitutionally required in every case. It stressed the facts of *Taylor,* where the trial judge's instructions were "spartan," the prosecutor made improper remarks, and the evidence against the defendant was weak. The Court concluded that the failure to give a requested instruction on the presumption of innocence "must be evaluated in light of the totality of the circumstances—including all the instructions to the jury, the arguments of counsel, whether the weight of the evidence was overwhelming, and other relevant factors—to determine whether the defendant received a constitutionally fair trial.". See also United States v. Payne, 944 F.2d 1458 (9th Cir.1991) (underlying purposes of a presumption of innocence instruction were "served adequately by other instructions which squarely placed the burden on the government of proving its case beyond a reasonable doubt, defined beyond a reasonable doubt, and clearly confined the scope of the evidence properly before the jury").

What should the judge say to the jury about the meaning of reasonable doubt? The instruction in Cage v. Louisiana, 111 S.Ct. 328 (1990) defined reasonable doubt as one creating "a grave uncertainty" and "an actual substantial doubt." The trial court elaborated that a "moral certainty" was required to convict. The Supreme Court in a per curiam opinion held that the words "grave" and "substantial" "suggest a higher degree of doubt than is required for acquittal under the reasonable doubt standard." The Court concluded that the instruction was constitutionally defective; the references to grave and substantial doubt, combined with the reference to moral certainty, as opposed to evidentiary certainty, could have led a reasonable juror to find guilt on a lesser standard than that required by *Winship.*

A first degree murder conviction was reversed in Commonwealth v. Rembiszewski, 391 Mass. 123, 461 N.E.2d 201 (1984), because the trial judge told the jury that "proof beyond a reasonable doubt is the same kind of proof and degree of satisfaction or conviction which you wanted for yourself when you were considering one of those very important decisions" such as whether to get married, whether to buy a house, whether to change jobs after having held one for a long time, and whether to undergo surgery. According to the state supreme court, "[t]he judge's use of examples of decisions in the personal lives of the jurors detracted from the seriousness of the issue before them."

Winship itself hardly had a remarkable impact on the typical criminal case, since proof beyond a reasonable doubt was the standard proof requirement in all criminal cases. But the reach of *Winship* to concepts like affirmative defenses was and is uncertain.

B. PUTTING PERSUASION BURDENS ON DEFENDANTS

The Court's first attempt to identify *Winship's* scope came in Mullaney v. Wilbur, 421 U.S. 684 (1975). Maine required a defendant charged with murder to prove that he acted "in the heat of passion on sudden provocation" in order to reduce the homicide to manslaughter. Under the Maine system, the prosecutor had to show beyond a reasonable doubt that a homicide was both intentional and unlawful. Unless the defendant proved heat of passion or sudden provocation by a preponderance of the evidence, the defendant was convicted of murder. The Maine statute defined murder as the killing of a person "with malice aforethought." After briefly tracing the history of homicide statutes in the United States, Justice Powell's majority opinion stated the Court's holding "that the Due Process Clause requires the prosecution to prove beyond a reasonable doubt the absence of the heat of passion or sudden provocation when the issue is properly presented in a homicide case." [19] The Court reasoned as follows:

> Petitioners, the warden of the Maine Prison and the State of Maine, argue that * * * *Winship* should not be extended to the present case. They note that as a formal matter the absence of the heat of passion on sudden provocation is not a "fact necessary to constitute the *crime*" of felonious homicide in Maine.
>
> This distinction is relevant, according to petitioners, because in *Winship* the facts at issue were essential to establish criminality in the first instance, whereas the fact in question here does not come into play until the jury already has determined that the defendant is guilty and may be punished at least for manslaughter. In this situation, petitioners maintain, the defendant's critical interests in liberty and reputation are no longer of paramount concern since, irrespective of the presence or absence of the heat of passion on sudden provocation, he is likely to lose his liberty and certain to be stigmatized. In short, petitioners would limit *Winship* to those facts which, if not proved, would wholly exonerate the defendant.
>
> This analysis fails to recognize that the criminal law of Maine, like that of other jurisdictions, is concerned not only with guilt or innocence in the abstract but also with the degree of criminal culpability. Maine has chosen to distinguish those who kill in the heat of passion from those who kill in the absence of this factor. Because the former are less "blameworth[y]," State v. Lafferty, 309 A.2d, at 671, 673 (concurring opinion), they are subject to substantially less severe penalties. By drawing this distinction, while refusing to require the prosecution to establish beyond a reasonable doubt the fact upon which it turns, Maine denigrates the interests found critical in *Winship*.
>
> The safeguards of due process are not rendered unavailing simply because a determination may already have been reached that would stigmatize the defendant and that might lead to a significant impairment of personal liberty. The fact remains that the consequences resulting from a verdict of murder, as compared with a verdict of manslaughter, differ significantly. Indeed, when viewed in terms of the potential difference in restrictions of personal liberty attendant to each conviction, the distinction established by Maine between murder and manslaughter may be of greater importance than the difference between guilt or innocence for many lesser crimes.
>
> Moreover, if *Winship* were limited to those facts that constitute a crime as defined by state law, a State could undermine many of the interests that decision sought to protect without effecting any substantive change in its law. It would only be necessary to redefine the elements that constitute different crimes, characterizing them as factors that bear solely on the extent of punishment. An extreme example of this approach can be fashioned from the law challenged in this case. Maine divides the single generic offense of felonious homicide into three distinct punishment categories—murder, voluntary manslaughter, and involuntary manslaughter. Only the first two of these

19. In contrast to the burden of persuasion is the burden of production. Many jurisdictions put the burden on a defendant to raise sufficient evidence to bring a defense into a case, at which time the prosecutor must disprove the defense beyond a reasonable doubt. Even if the Constitution permits a jurisdiction to impose the persuasion burden on a defendant, a jurisdiction may be satisfied with imposing the production burden instead. Whenever it is constitutional to put a burden of persuasion on a defendant, it will be constitutional to impose the lesser burden. *Mullaney* establishes that in some cases only a production burden may be imposed. Courts differ as to when the production burden is satisfied by a defendant. See Christie v. State, 580 P.2d 310 (Alaska, 1978).

> categories require that the homicidal act either be intentional or the result of criminally reckless conduct.
>
> But under Maine law these facts of intent are not general elements of the crime of felonious homicide.
>
> Instead, they bear only on the appropriate punishment category. Thus, if petitioners' argument were accepted, Maine could impose a life sentence for any felonious homicide—even those that traditionally might be considered involuntary manslaughter—unless the *defendant* was able to prove that his act was neither intentional nor criminally reckless.
>
> *Winship* is concerned with substance rather than this kind of formalism. * * *

Justice Rehnquist, joined by Chief Justice Burger, concurred and noted that he saw no inconsistency between *Mullaney* and Leland v. Oregon, 343 U.S. 790 (1952) (upholding placement upon defendant of burden of persuasion beyond a reasonable doubt on issue of insanity).

Although Justice Rehnquist saw no inconsistency,[20] few others could find an adequate handle to reconcile the cases. Lower courts were most puzzled by what the Court had in mind. The puzzle became more intricate with the subsequent decision in Patterson v. New York, 432 U.S. 197 (1977). This time Justice White wrote the majority opinion and Justice Powell dissented. The majority upheld a New York scheme which placed the burden on the defendant to prove extreme emotional disturbance by a preponderance of the evidence, after the prosecutor proved an intentional homicide beyond a reasonable doubt, in order to reduce second degree murder to manslaughter. After citing Leland v. Oregon, and Rivera v. Delaware (see note 20 supra) the majority reasoned as follows:

> We cannot conclude that Patterson's conviction under the New York law deprived him of due process of law. The crime of murder is defined by the statute, which represents a recent revision of the state criminal code, as causing the death of another person with intent to do so. The death, the intent to kill, and causation are the facts that the State is required to prove beyond a reasonable doubt if a person is to be convicted of murder. No further facts are either presumed or inferred in order to constitute the crime. The statute does provide an affirmative defense—that the defendant acted under the influence of extreme emotional disturbance for which there was a reasonable explanation—which, if proved by a preponderance of the evidence, would reduce the crime to manslaughter, an offense defined in a separate section of the statute. It is plain enough that if the intentional killing is shown, the State intends to deal with the defendant as a murderer unless he demonstrates the mitigating circumstances.
>
> Here, the jury was instructed in accordance with the statute, and the guilty verdict confirms that the State successfully carried its burden of proving the facts of the crime beyond a reasonable doubt. Nothing in the evidence, including any evidence that might have been offered with respect to Patterson's mental state at the time of the crime, raised a reasonable doubt about his guilt as a murderer; and clearly the evidence failed to convince the jury that

20. Nor did the majority of the Court. In Rivera v. Delaware, 429 U.S. 877 (1976), over the dissent of Justice Brennan joined by Justice Marshall, the Court dismissed, for want of a substantial federal question, an appeal from the Delaware Supreme Court's holding that it was constitutional to put the burden of persuasion on insanity on the defendant.

Patterson's affirmative defense had been made out. It seems to us that the State satisfied the mandate of Winship that it prove beyond a reasonable doubt "every fact necessary to constitute the crime with which [Patterson was] charged."

In convicting Patterson under its murder statute, New York did no more than *Leland and Rivera* permitted it to do without violating the Due Process Clause. Under those cases, once the facts constituting a crime are established beyond a reasonable doubt, based on all the evidence including the evidence of the defendant's mental state, the State may refuse to sustain the affirmative defense of insanity unless demonstrated by a preponderance of the evidence.

The New York law on extreme emotional disturbance follows this pattern. This affirmative defense, which the Court of Appeals described as permitting "the defendant to show that his actions were caused by a mental infirmity not arising to the level of insanity, and that he is less culpable for having committed them," does not serve to negative any facts of the crime which the State is to prove in order to convict of murder. It constitutes a separate issue on which the defendant is required to carry the burden of persuasion; and unless we are to overturn *Leland and Rivera*, New York has not violated the Due Process Clause, and Patterson's conviction must be sustained.

We are unwilling to reconsider *Leland* and *Rivera*. But even if we were to hold that a State must prove sanity to convict once that fact is put in issue, it would not necessarily follow that a State must prove beyond a reasonable doubt every fact, the existence or nonexistence of which it is willing to recognize as an exculpatory or mitigating circumstance affecting the degree of culpability or the severity of the punishment. Here, in revising its criminal code, New York provided the affirmative defense of extreme emotional disturbance, a substantially expanded version of the older heat-of-passion concept; but it was willing to do so only if the facts making out the defense were established by the defendant with sufficient certainty. The State was itself unwilling to undertake to establish the absence of those facts beyond a reasonable doubt, perhaps fearing that proof would be too difficult and that too many persons deserving treatment as murderers would escape that punishment if the evidence need merely raise a reasonable doubt about the defendant's emotional state. It has been said that the new criminal code of New York contains some 25 affirmative defenses which exculpate or mitigate but which must be established by the defendant to be operative. The Due Process Clause, as we see it, does not put New York to the choice of abandoning those defenses or undertaking to disprove their existence in order to convict of a crime which otherwise is within its constitutional powers to sanction by substantial punishment.

The requirement of proof beyond a reasonable doubt in a criminal case is "bottomed on a fundamental value determination of our society that it is far worse to convict an innocent man than to let a guilty man go free." The social cost of placing the burden on the prosecution to prove guilt beyond a reasonable doubt is thus an increased risk that the guilty will go free. While it is clear that our society has willingly chosen to bear a substantial burden in order to protect the innocent, it is equally clear that the risk it must bear is not without limits; and Mr. Justice Harlan's aphorism provides little guidance for determining what those limits are. Due process does not require that every conceivable step be taken, at whatever cost, to eliminate the possibility of convicting an innocent person. Punishment of those found guilty by a jury, for example, is not forbidden merely because there is a remote possibility in some instances that an innocent person might go to jail.

* * *

We thus decline to adopt as a constitutional imperative, operative countrywide, that a State must disprove beyond a reasonable doubt every fact constituting any and all affirmative defenses related to the culpability of an accused. Traditionally due process has required that only the most basic procedural safeguards be observed; more subtle balancing of society's interests against those of the accused have been left to the legislative branch. We therefore will not disturb the balance struck in previous cases holding that the Due Process Clause requires the prosecution to prove beyond a reasonable doubt all of the elements included in the definition of the offense of which the defendant is charged. Proof of the nonexistence of all affirmative defenses has never been constitutionally required; and we perceive no reason to fashion such a rule in this case and apply it to the statutory defense at issue here.

This view may seem to permit state legislatures to reallocate burdens of proof by labeling as affirmative defenses at least some elements of the crimes now defined in their statutes. But there are obviously constitutional limits beyond which the States may not go in this regard. "It is not within the province of a legislature to declare an individual guilty or presumptively guilty of a crime." The legislature cannot "validly command that the finding of an indictment, or mere proof of the identity of the accused, should create a presumption of the existence of all the facts essential to guilt."

Long before *Winship*, the universal rule in this country was that the prosecution must prove guilt beyond a reasonable doubt. At the same time, the long-accepted rule was that it was constitutionally permissible to provide that various affirmative defenses were to be proved by the defendant. This did not lead to such abuses or to such widespread redefinition of crime and reduction of the prosecution's burden that a new constitutional rule was required. This was not the problem to which *Winship* was addressed. Nor does the fact that a majority of the States have now assumed the burden of disproving affirmative defenses—for whatever reasons—mean that those States that strike a different balance are in violation of the Constitution.

In a footnote, Justice White quoted extensively from Chief Judge Breitel's concurring opinion in the New York Court of Appeals:

It would be an abuse of affirmative defenses, as it would be of presumptions in the criminal law, if the purpose or effect were to unhinge the procedural presumption of innocence which historically and constitutionally shields one charged with crime. Indeed, a by-product of such abuse might well be also to undermine the privilege against self-incrimination by in effect forcing a defendant in a criminal action to testify in his own behalf.

Nevertheless, although one should guard against such abuses, it may be misguided, out of excess caution, to forestall or discourage the use of affirmative defenses, where defendant may have the burden of proof but no greater than by a preponderance of the evidence. In the absence of affirmative defenses the impulse to legislators, especially in periods of concern about the rise of crime, would be to define particular crimes in unqualifiedly general terms, and leave only to sentence the adjustment between offenses of lesser and greater degree. In times when there is also a retrogressive impulse in legislation to restrain courts by mandatory sentences, the evil would be compounded.

The affirmative defense, intelligently used, permits the gradation of offenses at the earlier stages of prosecution and certainly at the trial, and thus offers the opportunity to a defendant to allege or prove, if he can, the distinction between the offense charged and the mitigating circumstances which should ameliorate the degree or kind of offense. The instant homicide case is a good example. Absent the affirmative defense, the crime of murder or manslaughter could legislatively be defined simply to require an intent to kill, unaffected by the spontaneity with which that intent is formed or the provocative or mitigating circumstances which should legally or morally lower the grade of crime. The placing of the burden of proof on the defense, with a lower threshold, however, is fair because of defendant's knowledge or access to the evidence other than his own on the issue. To require the prosecution to negative the 'element' of mitigating circumstances is generally unfair, especially since the conclusion that the negative of the circumstances is necessarily a product of definitional and therefore circular reasoning, and is easily avoided by the likely legislative practice mentioned earlier.

In sum, the appropriate use of affirmative defenses enlarges the ameliorative aspects of a statutory scheme for the punishment of crime, rather than the other way around—a shift from primitive mechanical classifications based on the bare antisocial act and its consequences, rather than on the nature of the offender and the conditions which produce some degree of excuse for his conduct, the mark of an advanced criminology.

Justice Powell's dissent was joined by Justices Brennan and Marshall. He was plainly correct in arguing that the distinction between Maine and New York law was "formalistic rather than substantive." But that aside, the real question for the Court was whether *Mullaney* was correctly decided. Justice Powell thought that it was, and he wrote as follows:

The Court beats its retreat from *Winship* apparently because of a concern that otherwise the federal judiciary will intrude too far into substantive choices concerning the content of a State's criminal law. The concern is legitimate, but misplaced. *Winship* and *Mullaney* are no more than what they purport to be: decisions addressing the procedural requirements that States must meet to comply with due process. They are not outposts for policing the substantive boundaries of the criminal law.

The *Winship/Mullaney* test identifies those factors of such importance, historically, in determining punishment and stigma that the Constitution forbids shifting to the defendant the burden of persuasion when such a factor is at issue. *Winship* and *Mullaney* specify only the procedure that is required when a State elects to use such a factor as part of its substantive criminal law. They do not say that the State must elect to use it. For example, where a State has chosen to retain the traditional distinction between murder and manslaughter, as have New York and Maine, the burden of persuasion must remain on the prosecution with respect to the distinguishing factor, in view of its decisive historical importance. But nothing in *Mullaney* or *Winship* precludes a State from abolishing the distinction between murder and manslaughter and treating all unjustifiable homicide as murder. In this significant respect, neither *Winship* nor *Mullaney* eliminates the substantive flexibility that should remain in legislative hands.

* * *

Furthermore, as we indicated in *Mullaney*, even as to those factors upon which the prosecution must bear the burden of persuasion, the State retains an important procedural device to avoid jury confusion and prevent the prosecution from being unduly hampered. The State normally may shift to the defendant the burden of production, that is, the burden of going forward with sufficient evidence "to justify [a reasonable] doubt upon the issue." ALI, Model Penal Code § 1.13, Comment, p. 110 (Tent.Draft No. 4, 1955). If the defendant's evidence does not cross this threshold, the issue—be it malice, extreme emotional disturbance, self-defense, or whatever—will not be submitted to the jury. Ever since this Court's decision in Davis v. United States, 160 U.S. 469 (1895), federal prosecutors have borne the burden of persuasion with respect to factors like insanity, self-defense, and malice or provocation, once the defendant has carried this burden of production. I know of no indication that this practice has proven a noticeable handicap to effective law enforcement.

To be sure, there will be many instances when the *Winship/Mullaney* test as I perceive it will be more difficult to apply than the Court's formula. Where I see the need for a careful and discriminating review of history, the Court finds a brightline standard that can be applied with a quick glance at the face of the statute. But this facile test invites tinkering with the procedural safeguards of the presumption of innocence, an invitation to disregard the principles of *Winship* that I would not extend.

The Court found that *Patterson* rather than *Mullaney* applied in McMillan v. Pennsylvania, 477 U.S. 79 (1986), as it upheld a state statute providing that anyone convicted of certain enumerated felonies is subject to a mandatory minimum sentence of five years' imprisonment if the sentencing judge finds by a preponderance of the evidence (evidence introduced at trial and additional evidence offered at a sentencing proceeding) that the defendant "visibly possessed a firearm" during the commission of the offense. Justice Rehnquist wrote for the Court and reasoned that the finding did not involve an element of the offense, but was a part of sentencing. The state statute did not create a new offense, nor did it change the maximum punishment that could be imposed for an offense. Instead, it limited judicial discretion in sentencing. The Court found no due process violation, no deprivation of the right to jury trial, and no need for a standard of proof higher than the preponderance standard. Justice Rehnquist stated that "*Patterson* stressed that in determining what facts must be proved beyond a reasonable doubt the state legislature's definition of the elements of the offense is usually dispositive," and that the Pennsylvania statute did not go beyond the minimal limitations set by *Patterson*: it did not create a presumption of guilt, and did not relieve the prosecution of its burden of proving guilt. The statute's applicability depended on the conviction of the defendant. Justice Rehnquist concluded as follows:

> Finally, we note that the spectre raised by petitioners of States restructuring existing crimes in order to evade the commands of *Winship* just does not appear in this case. * * * The Pennsylvania Legislature did not change the definition of any existing offense. It simply took one factor that has always been considered by sentencing courts to bear on punishment—the instrumentality used in committing a violent felony—and dictated the precise weight to be given that factor if the instrumentality is a firearm. Pennsylvania's decision to do so has not transformed a sentencing factor into an element of some hypothetical offense.

Justice Stevens dissented arguing that "a state legislature may not dispense with the requirement of proof beyond a reasonable doubt for conduct that it targets for severe criminal penalties." He concluded that under *Patterson* "the Due Process Clause requires proof beyond a reasonable doubt of conduct which exposes a criminal defendant to greater stigma or punishment, but does not likewise constrain state reductions of criminal penalties, even if such reductions are conditioned on a prosecutor's failure to prove a fact by a preponderance of the evidence or on proof supplied by the criminal defendant." Although Justice Stevens recognized that "[t]he distinction between aggravating and mitigating facts has been criticized as formalistic," he reasoned as follows: it was unlikely that a legislature would enact a statute imposing excessively harsh punishment for conduct unless the defendant proved it was not criminal, but it was conceivable that a legislature might seek to subject defendants to increased punishment for aggravating conduct not proved beyond a reasonable doubt.

Justice Marshall, joined by Justices Brennan and Blackmun, also dissented. He indicated agreement with much of Justice Stevens' dissent, but declined to "rely in this case on the formalistic distinction between aggravating and mitigating facts." To decide the instant case, he agreed with Justice Stevens that the fact that the Pennsylvania statute operated to create a special stigma and a special punishment upon a finding of specific conduct was sufficient to mandate that the prosecution prove the conduct beyond a reasonable doubt.

The *McMillan* approach has been utilized to reject due process challenges to the Federal Sentencing Guidelines. These guidelines consider the quantity of narcotics possessed by the defendant as part of the sentencing determination rather than as an element of the offense itself. Courts have stated broadly that "in determining which facts must be proven beyond a reasonable doubt, the legislature's definition of the elements of the offense controls." United States v. Cross, 916 F.2d 622, 623 (11th Cir.1990), and that the "due process clause, according to the Supreme Court, acts only to insure that legislative decisions to criminalize conduct do not offend deeply held values; it does not protect against legislative decisions to punish conduct, even when they offend the same values." United States v. Ebbole, 917 F.2d 1495 (7th Cir.1990). Under these broad standards, courts have concluded that quantity can permissibly be considered an element of sentencing and not the offense, and therefore may be proven by a preponderance of the evidence.

The *Patterson* approach prevailed again in Martin v. Ohio, 480 U.S. 228 (1987). Justice White again wrote for the Court as it sustained an Ohio rule placing the burden of persuasion on self-defense on the defendant. Martin was charged with aggravated murder, and the trial judge instructed the jury that the prosecution was required by state law to prove beyond a reasonable doubt that the defendant purposefully, and with prior calculation and design, caused the death of her husband. Although the majority recognized that evidence offered to prove self-defense may also negate a purposeful killing by prior calculation and design, it appeared to reject the claim that the overlap was complete. Justice White explained that a jury would be required to acquit a defendant if it had a reasonable doubt about the defendant's calculation and design, but a jury might believe beyond a reasonable doubt that the defendant purposefully killed someone with prior calculation and design and still excuse the killing as having been done in self-defense. Thus, even though Ohio and South Carolina were the only two states that imposed the burden of proving self-defense on a defendant, their allocation of the burden was constitutionally sound. Justice White stated that it would be "quite different if the jury had been instructed that self-defense evidence could not be considered in determining whether there was a reasonable doubt about the State's case, i.e., that self-defense evidence must be put aside for all purposes unless it satisfied the preponderance standard. Such an instruction would plainly relieve the State of its burden and plainly run afoul of *Winship's* mandate." But in this case, the judge instructed the jury that all of the evidence, including the evidence going to self-defense, had to be considered in deciding whether there was reasonable doubt about the sufficiency of the State's proof of the elements of the crime.

Justice Powell, joined by Justices Brennan and Marshall and in large part by Justice Blackmun, dissented. He reasoned that "[t]he reason for treating a defense that negates an element of the crime differently from other affirmative defenses is plain. If the jury is told that the prosecution has the burden of proving all of the elements of a crime, but then also is instructed that defendant has the burden of *dis*proving one of those same elements, there is a danger that the jurors will resolve the inconsistency in a way that lessens the presumption of innocence." He concluded that the danger of juror confusion was present in Ohio's allocation of burdens and that "the Court's reliance on *Patterson* is puzzling," since the *Patterson* majority emphasized that the affirmative defense did "not serve to negative any facts of the crime which the State is to prove in order to convict of murder." Justice Powell expressed concern that "[t]oday's decision could be read to say that virtually all state attempts to shift the burden of proof for affirmative defenses will be upheld, regardless of the relationship between the elements of the defense and the elements of the crime" and specifically noted that "[t]he Court today fails to discuss or even cite *Mullaney,* despite our unanimous agreement in that case that this danger [of unchecked discretion to shift burdens] would justify judicial intervention in some cases." In the portion of the opinion not joined by Justice Blackmun, Justice Powell reasserted the approach he presented in his *Patterson* dissent.

In Flores v. Minnesota, 906 F.2d 1300 (8th Cir.1990), the court applied *Martin* and held that a state could permissibly place the burden of proof on the defendant to prove intoxication by a preponderance of the evidence in order to negate the element of premeditation incorporated in the State's murder offense. The court reasoned as follows:

> Here, as in *Martin,* proof of the affirmative defense seemingly negates one of the elements of the crime. While the state must prove premeditation beyond a reasonable doubt, the defendant may prove by a preponderance of the evidence that he was too intoxicated to form premeditation. Thus, the jury may acquit if the defendant's evidence either (1) raises a reasonable doubt about premeditation, or (2) establishes by a preponderance that he was too intoxicated to form the intent required for premeditated murder. *Martin* teaches that so long as the jury is instructed to consider all of the evidence of premeditation and intoxication, this situation creates no constitutional violation. The instructions in this case explicitly charged the jury to consider the evidence of intoxication in relation to the defendant's intent. According to *Martin* we must therefore find no due process violation.

In a footnote the court commented that "there is little to be gained here from re-examining the difficulties found by courts and commentators in reconciling *Mullaney* and *Patterson*." Instead, the court based its holding on *Martin*.

In State v. Belcher, 161 W.Va. 660, 245 S.E.2d 161 (1978), the state supreme court said that a state could not presume malice from the fact of a killing and place the burden of disproving malice on a defendant. If the state were forced to prove an intentional homicide and the defendant were permitted to prove that it was without malice to lower the degree of the offense, would *Patterson* require that this system be set aside?

Professor Stacy, in The Search for the Truth in Constitutional Criminal Procedure, 91 Colum.L.Rev. 1369 (1991), has this to say about the Court's treatment of *Winship* in *Mullaney* and subsequent cases:

> At first, in Mullaney v. Wilbur, the Court made the reasonable doubt standard applicable to any factor having an important bearing on the stigma attaching to the crime. The Court now rejects this approach, instead distinguishing between those factors state law treats as elements of the offense and those treated as affirmative defenses. * * * Because the Court has articulated no meaningful limits on a state's ability to treat a given factor as an affirmative defense rather than as an element of the offense, it has effectively given states discretion to opt out of the reasonable doubt standard.

Without much doubt, identifying the path between *Mullaney* and *Patterson* is not easy. Some commentators have suggested that the task is not worth the candle, because *Mullaney* essentially is an unsupportable decision. The following excerpt states the arguments that have been raised against *Mullaney*:

> In *Mullaney*, the Court noted that the interests protected by the reasonable doubt standard are implicated when a state chooses to distinguish murder from manslaughter. That is true enough, but what the Court failed to note was that these interests are implicated *every time* a state draws a distinction between offenses by the use of an affirmative defense. Thus *Mullaney*, carried to its logical extreme, would seem to forbid the use of all affirmative defenses. Yet, consider once again the genesis of this analysis in *Winship*. There the Court relied heavily on the existing state of the law in order to demonstrate the constitutional interest in the reasonable doubt standard. The existing state of the law, however, included affirmative defenses. Thus, on the basis of *Winship*, states should indeed be forbidden generally from employing the preponderance standard in criminal cases, but, in light of the Court's analysis, *should they be allowed to employ affirmative defenses in that setting*? The answer is obviously yes; or if that is not so obvious, the analytical structure of *Winship*, as distinguished from Justice Brennan's dicta, unmistakably provides no basis for the contrary conclusion.
>
> One can now see more clearly the shift of analysis in *Mullaney* that permitted it to accomplish a result that *Winship* could not sustain. *Mullaney* invoked *Winship* not to invalidate a burden-of-proof practice demonstrably inconsistent with the "traditions and conscience of our people," but instead used that case in a fashion that would provide the means to invalidate a practice long accepted throughout the country. * * *
>
> * * *
>
> An example may help to clarify [my] argument. Consider a state with an intentional homicide statute that punishes every intentional homicide with

thirty-years' imprisonment; if the state proves that the defendant intentionally killed the victim, then a flat sentence of thirty years is imposed regardless of the presence of any mitigating factor. Assume that such a statute is constitutional. Now, consider the effect on the constitutionality of that statute of simply adding to it a provision that no more than twenty years of imprisonment may be imposed if the defendant proves by a preponderance of the evidence that he acted under the influence of extreme emotional disturbance. If the constitutional interest in the reasonable doubt standard centers on liberty deprivation, how can the addition of a chance to mitigate a constitutional punishment invalidate the statute? Or, to put it another way, if a state may constitutionally imprison all intentional murderers for thirty years by proving beyond reasonable doubt only intent and causation, then whatever liberty interest the defendant constitutionally possesses in the context of homicide prosecutions surely is fully accommodated by such a statute. How, then, can the addition of a mitigating circumstance in the form of an affirmative defense—a factor that reduces punishment—possibly violate the already fully accommodated interest?

Patterson appears on close inspection to have adopted this line of reasoning, [where the Court states that]:

> The Due Process Clause, as we see it, does not put New York to the choice of abandoning [affirmative] defenses or undertaking to disprove their existence in order to convict of a crime which otherwise is within its constitutional powers to sanction by substantial punishment.

The key to this passage is the word "otherwise." What the Court is saying, I think, is that if a state may "otherwise" impose a particular sentence on the basis of what the state has proven beyond a reasonable doubt, then permitting a defendant to reduce the sentence he receives below the permissible level through proof of an affirmative defense is constitutional.

If the Court now subscribes to this theory * * * the analysis of the constitutionality of an affirmative defense must proceed to another level. One must ask whether the greater punishment—the punishment authorized in the event the defendant fails to establish the affirmative defense—is constitutional.[21]

This analysis has been criticized, however.

The error in this analysis is that it arises from only one of the two liberty-based reasons the Supreme Court has recognized as requiring proof beyond a reasonable doubt. While one reason is the above recognized desire to protect the defendant's freedom, a second reason is to protect a defendant from stigmatization, a separate liberty interest. In fact, protection against stigmatization by the state gives rise to due process protections even in civil contexts. The greater the chance of stigma, the greater the protections are likely to be; and where the chance of severe stigmatization is great, the burden of persuasion may be elevated. Stigma is a special concern of the criminal law. When a criminal charge is pressed in a case in which jail is not even a possible sanction, proof beyond a reasonable doubt is still required. Once the state chooses to avail itself of the criminal sanction and to label a defendant a

21. Allen, The Restoration of In re Winship: A Comment on Burdens of Persuasion in Criminal Cases After Patterson v. New York, 76 Mich.L.Rev. 30, 39–46 (1977). A similar argument is made in Jeffries & Stephan, Defenses, Presumptions and Burden of Proof in the Criminal Law, 88 Yale L.J. 1325 (1979).

"criminal," the defendant is guaranteed the highest degree of protection against harmful error available in a legal dispute. * * *

Once stigma is interjected into the analysis of the greater-includes-the-lesser approach, the fundamental flaw in that approach becomes evident. The following example illustrates the flaw. Assume that a state adopts a statute that declares that any killing—whether negligent, reckless, malicious, or malicious and premeditated—is murder punishable by five years' to life imprisonment. The statute probably could withstand a facial constitutional attack, even if a sentence in a particular case might be cruel and unusual. As long as there are no lesser offenses, all killers would be classified the same way. Such a statute would homogenize all killings, something that is not done in American law. It would prevent the state from signifying by label that one offense was more blameworthy than another and from identifying one offender as having committed a crime different in kind or degree from that of another offender. If, during sentencing, the state attempted to increase the penalty automatically upon finding certain aggravating circumstances, such as premeditation, the proof beyond a reasonable doubt requirement might possibly be imposed with respect to those circumstances. Although some differences in punishment might give clues to individual culpability, sentences might be based on other, different factors as well.

Now suppose the state rejects the homogenized approach, deciding instead to classify offenses and to provide different punishment ranges for each classification. Murder is presumed once the prosecution proves a killing and any mens rea previously mentioned, but defendants may reduce a murder conviction to "lesser" murder, voluntary manslaughter, or involuntary manslaughter by bearing certain burdens of persuasion. The greater-includes-the-lesser theorists argue that defendants are better off under this system. They are, in the sense that they have a chance to reduce the level of the offense and to limit punishment. But they are worse off in another way. Any defendant who fails to assume and satisfy the persuasion burden on a lesser offense is now clearly classified as a more serious murderer than a defendant who does satisfy the burden. In addition, he may be punished more severely than he would have been under the homogenized approach. The scheme obviously tends to stigmatize those who lose in a very different way than those who win. What looks like an opportunity has thus become a burden. If the burden is not met, there is undoubtedly greater stigmatization, and also the possibility of greater punishment.

The greater-includes-the-lesser approach therefore must be rejected because it permits the imposition of stigma without requiring the government to prove that there is a difference between greater and lesser offenders. The analytical approach undertaken by the Supreme Court is more sensitive to the stigma problem and thus more consistent with the rationale for imposing a proof beyond a reasonable doubt requirement on the government.

* * *

The argument has been made that it is not possible to measure degrees of stigma, but the Supreme Court has implicitly, but correctly, rejected this position. The basic components of a criminal prosecution, the act and mens rea elements, which serve to provide little protection as constitutional minima under the greater-includes-the-lesser approach, are very useful in identifying the traditional distinctions that have delineated more and less serious categories of offenses. It is worse to be a first-degree murderer than a second-degree murderer; the statutory scheme almost everywhere makes some clear differentiation between degrees of homicide. It might be true that a lay person could not state with much confidence the difference between the degrees, but a chief executive with pardon power might be more successful. A parole board could. A future employer might be interested in the difference. Even a lay person probably could make a fair guess as to the difference between first degree murder and an unintentional but reckless killing.

Mullaney and *Patterson* appear to embrace the idea that where a jurisdiction draws traditional distinctions between or among degrees of offenses, and the distinctions represent judgments about culpability which would be likely to increase or decrease the stigma associated with a conviction, the prosecution must prove the greater offense. It is this rationale that explains why the prosecution need not necessarily prove beyond a reasonable doubt a jurisdictional element, competence of the defendant, or fair notice. The Constitution and its due process clauses afford several different kinds of protections, of which the proof beyond a reasonable doubt requirement is only one. Whenever the government seeks to impose a criminal sanction that suggests a certain level of culpability within a scheme that sets forth a range of offenses, the government must demonstrate that particular level of culpability according to a standard that assures a justification for any punishment and stigmatization. * * * [22]

Which approach do you find more persuasive?

In Hicks on Behalf of Feiock v. Feiock, 485 U.S. 624 (1988), a father was held in civil contempt for failing to make support payments as ordered by a state court. Under state law, the ability to comply with a court order was an element of the offense of contempt, and the alleged contemnor bore the burden of persuasion on that element. The Supreme Court held that a statute could permissibly shift the burden of persuasion on an element of the offense in a civil case, but that if this had been a criminal contempt proceeding *Mullaney* would have required the prosecutor to prove beyond a reasonable doubt that the defendant had the ability to comply with the court order.

C. PROOF OF ALTERNATIVE MEANS OF COMMITTING A SINGLE CRIME

Closely related to the burden-shifting question is the question whether a state can constitutionally determine that a single crime can be committed by alternative means: whether it is constitutionally acceptable to permit jurors to reach one verdict based on any combination of alternative findings. In Schad v. Arizona, 111 S.Ct. 2491 (1991), defendant was charged with first-degree murder. At trial, the prosecutor advanced both premeditated and felony murder theories. Under Arizona law, first-degree murder includes both felony murder and premeditated murder. The jury returned a general verdict of guilty. Justice Souter, writing for a plurality of four justices, stated that it was constitutionally permissible to define first-degree murder in such a way that it

22. Saltzburg, Burdens of Persuasion in Criminal Cases: Harmonizing the Views of the Justices, 20 Am.Cr.L.Rev. 393, 405–409 (1983). This article explains *Patterson* as a case in which the Court declined to reconsider its approach to the insanity defense in *Leland* and treated New York's affirmative defense as an expanded insanity defense. See also Underwood, The Thumb on the Scales of Justice: Burdens of Persuasion in Criminal Cases, 86 Yale L.J. 1299 (1977).

could be committed by alternative means, so long as such means "reasonably reflect notions of equivalent blameworthiness or culpability." Justice Souter recognized that the Due Process Clause would not permit a state "to convict anyone under a charge of 'Crime' so generic that any combination of jury findings of embezzlement, reckless driving, murder, burglary, tax evasion, or littering, for example, would suffice for conviction." However, the Arizona statute did not create such a disparate collection of alternative means to commit first degree murder. Justice Souter concluded that felony murder and premeditated murder were of sufficient "moral equivalence" to be grouped together as two ways of committing the same crime, and that therefore the general verdict of guilt was constitutionally permissible. Justice Souter found it highly relevant that many states have traditionally considered felony murder and premeditated murder as alternative means of committing first degree murder. He stated that the "historical and contemporary acceptance of Arizona's definition of the offense and verdict practice is a strong indication" that it did not violate due process, because "legal definitions, and the practices comporting with them, are unlikely to endure for long, or to retain wide acceptance, if they are at odds with notions of fairness and rationality sufficiently fundamental to be comprehended in due process."

Justice Scalia concurred in the judgment. In his view, the fact that the Arizona statutory definition of first-degree murder is traditionally and currently accepted in most states was dispositive of the due process issue. He concluded as follows:

> Submitting killing in the course of a robbery and premeditated killing to the jury under a single charge is not some novel composite that can be subjected to the indignity of fundamental fairness review. It was the norm when this country was founded, * * * and remains the norm today. Unless we are here to invent a Constitution rather than enforce one, it is impossible that a practice as old as the common law and still in existence in the vast majority of States does not provide that process which is due.

Justice White, joined by Justices Marshall, Blackmun and Stevens, dissented. He noted that felony murder and premeditated murder contain separate elements of conduct and state of mind and argued that these elements could not "be mixed and matched at will." He asserted that "it is particularly fanciful to equate an intent to do no more than rob with a premeditated intent to murder."

The prosecution in *Schad* was required to prove all elements beyond a reasonable doubt, and the defendant was not required to prove anything. So how does the *Schad* issue relate to the burden-shifting cases previously decided by the Court? The answer lies in the possibility that by combining alternative theories of guilt, a prosecutor may manage to convict a defendant without proving beyond a reasonable doubt all of the elements of any one theory to a constitutionally adequate number of jurors. At the logical limit of the analysis, for example, a prosecutor could argue twelve alternatives to a twelve-person jury and persuade only one juror beyond a reasonable doubt of each theory. Were the theories set forth in separate counts, a defendant would never be convicted. In fact, the vote would be 11–1 for acquittal on each count. But, by combining the theories, all twelve jurors would agree that the defendant is "guilty" of a "crime." All members of the Court in *Schad* agreed that at some point this tactic would be impermissible under the Due Process Clause.

They disagreed, however, on where that point lies. Four Justices gave traditional and current acceptance significant weight, and one found traditional and current acceptance dispositive. However, in the burden-shifting cases, the Court has (at least in *Mullaney*) repudiated presumptions used for many years; and in *Martin* it upheld a burden-shifting statute which had been rejected in 48 states. How important is it that states traditionally gave, and currently give, alternative theories of first-degree murder to a jury in a single count with a general verdict form?

D. PRESUMPTIONS

An alternative to placing a burden of persuasion on a defendant in order to reduce the burden on the government of presenting evidence is to utilize a presumption or a judicially recognized inference.[23] Few aspects of procedural law can be more confusing than presumptions, since the word "presumption" is used to mean several different things in different contexts.

In criminal cases the word "presumption" has taken on a special meaning because of several constitutional decisions by the Supreme Court. In these cases, presumption is used as follows: the government proves one fact (A) and the court tells the jury that it can use A as proof of another fact (B), unless in light of all the evidence the jury has a reasonable doubt that B is untrue. In other words, the burden remains on the government to prove guilt beyond a reasonable doubt, but a presumption is a special type of judicial comment that tells the jury that proof of A is also, or may be, tantamount to proof of B.

The following case illustrates how the Supreme Court has approached many criminal presumptions.

BARNES v. UNITED STATES

Supreme Court of the United States, 1973.
412 U.S. 837.

MR. JUSTICE POWELL delivered the opinion of the Court.

Petitioner Barnes was convicted in United States District Court on two counts of possessing United States Treasury checks stolen from the mails, knowing them to be stolen, two counts of forging the checks, and two counts of uttering the checks, knowing the endorsements to be forged. The trial court instructed the jury that ordinarily it would be justified in inferring from unexplained possession of recently stolen mail that the defendant possessed the mail with knowledge that it was stolen. * * *

The evidence at petitioner's trial established that on June 2, 1971, he opened a checking account using the pseudonym "Clarence Smith." On July 1, and July 3, 1971, the United States Disbursing Office at San Francisco mailed four Government checks in the amounts of $269.02, $154.70, $184 and $268.80 to Nettie Lewis, Albert Young, Arthur Salazar, and Mary Hernandez, respectively. On July 8, 1971, petitioner deposited these four checks into the "Smith" account. Each check

23. In this section, the word presumption will be used to cover situations in which the court instructs a jury that proof of one fact entitles the jury to infer, assume, or presume the existence of another fact.

bore the apparent endorsement of the payee and a second endorsement by "Clarence Smith."

At petitioner's trial the four payees testified that they had never received, endorsed, or authorized endorsement of the checks. A Government handwriting expert testified that petitioner had made the "Clarence Smith" endorsement on all four checks and that he had signed the payees' names on the Lewis and Hernandez checks. Although petitioner did not take the stand, a postal inspector testified to certain statements made by petitioner at a post-arrest interview. Petitioner explained to the inspector that he received the checks in question from people who sold furniture for him door to door and that the checks had been signed in the payees' names when he received them. Petitioner further stated that he could not name or identify any of the salespeople. Nor could he substantiate the existence of any furniture orders because the salespeople allegedly wrote their orders on scratch paper that had not been retained. Petitioner admitted that he executed the Clarence Smith endorsements and deposited the checks but denied making the payees' endorsements.

The District Court instructed the jury that "[p]ossession of recently stolen property, if not satisfactorily explained, is ordinarily a circumstance from which you may reasonably draw the inference and find, in the light of the surrounding circumstances shown by the evidence in the case, that the person in possession knew the property had been stolen."

The jury brought in guilty verdicts on all six counts, and the District Court sentenced petitioner to concurrent three-year prison terms. The Court of Appeals for the Ninth Circuit affirmed, finding no lack of "rational connection" between unexplained possession of recently stolen property and knowledge that the property was stolen. * * * We affirm.

I

We begin our consideration of the challenged jury instruction with a review of four recent decisions which have considered the validity under the Due Process Clause of criminal law presumptions and inferences. Turner v. United States, 396 U.S. 398, 610 (1970); Leary v. United States, 395 U.S. 6 (1969); United States v. Romano, 382 U.S. 136 (1965); United States v. Gainey, 380 U.S. 63 (1965).

In United States v. Gainey, the Court sustained the constitutionality of an instruction tracking a statute which authorized the jury to infer from defendant's unexplained presence at an illegal still that he was carrying on "the business of a distiller or rectifier without having given bond as required by law." Relying on the holding of Tot v. United States, 319 U.S. 463, 467 (1943), that there must be a "rational connection between the fact proved and the ultimate fact presumed," the Court upheld the inference on the basis of the comprehensive nature of the "carrying on" offense and the common knowledge that illegal stills are secluded, secret operations. The following Term the Court determined, however, that presence at an illegal still could not support the inference that the defendant was in possession, custody, or control of the still, a narrower offense. "Presence is relevant and admissible evidence in a trial on a possession charge; but absent some showing of the defendant's function at the still, its connection with possession is too tenuous to permit a reasonable inference of guilt—'the inference of the one from proof of the other is arbitrary * * *.' "

Three and one-half years after *Romano*, the Court in Leary v. United States, considered a challenge to a statutory inference that possession of marihuana, unless satisfactorily explained, was sufficient to prove that the defendant knew that the marihuana had been illegally imported into the United States. The Court concluded that in view of the significant possibility that any given marihuana was domestically grown and the improbability that a marihuana user would know whether his marihuana was of domestic or imported origin, the inference did not meet the standards set by *Tot, Gainey,* and *Romano*. Referring to these three cases, the Leary Court stated that an inference is " 'irrational' or 'arbitrary,' and hence unconstitutional, unless it can at least be said with substantial assurance that the presumed fact is more likely than not to flow from the proved fact on which it is made to depend." In a footnote the Court stated that since the challenged inference failed to satisfy the more-likely-than-not standard, it did not have to "reach the question whether a criminal presumption which passes muster when so judged must also satisfy the criminal 'reasonable doubt' standard if proof of the crime charged or an essential element thereof depends upon its use."

Finally, in Turner v. United States, decided the year following *Leary*, the Court considered the constitutionality of instructing the jury that it may infer from possession of heroin and cocaine that the defendant knew these drugs had been illegally imported. The Court noted that *Leary* reserved the question of whether the more-likely-than-not or the reasonable-doubt standard controlled in criminal cases, but it likewise found no need to resolve that question. It held that the inference with regard to heroin was valid judged by either standard. With regard to cocaine, the inference failed to satisfy even the more-likely-than-not standard.

The teaching of the foregoing cases is not altogether clear. To the extent that the "rational connection," "more likely than not," and "reasonable doubt" standards bear ambiguous relationships to one another, the ambiguity is traceable in large part to variations in language and focus rather than to differences of substance. What has been established by the cases, however, is at least this: that if a statutory inference submitted to the jury as sufficient to support conviction satisfies the reasonable-doubt standard (that is, the evidence necessary to invoke the inference is sufficient for a rational juror to find the inferred fact beyond a reasonable doubt) as well as the more-likely-than-not standard, then it clearly accords with due process.

In the present case we deal with a traditional common-law inference deeply rooted in our law. For centuries courts have instructed juries that an inference of guilty knowledge may be drawn from the fact of unexplained possession of stolen goods. * * * This longstanding and consistent judicial approval of the instruction, reflecting accumulated common experience, provides strong indication that the instruction comports with due process.

This impressive historical basis, however, is not in itself sufficient to establish the instruction's constitutionality. Common-law inferences, like their statutory counterparts, must satisfy due process standards in light of present-day experience. In the present case the challenged instruction only permitted the inference of guilt from unexplained possession of recently stolen property. The evidence established that petitioner possessed recently stolen Treasury checks payable to persons he did not know, and it provided no plausible explanation for such possession consistent with innocence. On the basis of this evidence alone common sense and experience tell us that petitioner must have known or been aware of the high probability that the checks were stolen.

Such evidence was clearly sufficient to enable the jury to find beyond a reasonable doubt that petitioner knew the checks were stolen. Since the inference thus satisfies the reasonable-doubt standard, the most stringent standard the Court has applied in judging permissive criminal law inferences, we conclude that it satisfies the requirements of due process.[a]

* * *

MR. JUSTICE BRENNAN, with whom MR. JUSTICE MARSHALL joins, dissenting.

* * *

We held in In re Winship, that the Due Process Clause requires "proof beyond a reasonable doubt of every fact necessary to constitute the crime * * *." Thus, in Turner v. United States, we approved the inference of "knowledge" from the fact of possessing smuggled heroin because " '[c]ommon sense' * * *, tells us that those who traffic in heroin will *inevitably* become aware that the product they deal in is smuggled * * *." (Emphasis added.) The basis of that "common sense" judgment was, of course, the indisputable fact that all or virtually all heroin in this country is necessarily smuggled. Here, however, it cannot be said that all or virtually all endorsed United States Treasury checks have been stolen. Indeed, it is neither unlawful nor unusual for people to use such checks as direct payment for goods and services. Thus, unlike *Turner*, "common sense" simply will not permit the inference that the possessor of stolen Treasury checks "*inevitably*" knew that the checks were stolen.

In short, the practical effect of the challenged instruction was to permit the jury to convict petitioner even if it found insufficient or disbelieved all of the Government's evidence bearing directly on the issue of "knowledge." By authorizing the jury to rely exclusively on the inference in determining the element of "knowledge," the instruction relieved the Government of the burden of proving that element beyond a reasonable doubt. The instruction thereby violated the principle of *Winship* that every essential element of the crime must be proved beyond a reasonable doubt.

[The separate dissenting opinion of Justice Douglas is omitted.]

In the following case the Court emphasized the importance of the language used by the trial judge in jury instructions.

a. It is true that the practical effect of instructing the jury on the inference arising from unexplained possession of recently stolen property is to shift the burden of going forward with evidence to the defendant. If the Government proves possession and nothing more, this evidence remains unexplained unless the defendant introduces evidence, since ordinarily the Government's evidence will not provide an explanation of his possession consistent with innocence. In Tot v. United States, the Court stated that the burden of going forward may not be freely shifted to the defendant. *Tot* held, however, that where there is a "rational connection" between the facts proved and the fact presumed or inferred, it is permissible to shift the burden of going forward to the defendant. Where an inference satisfies the reasonable-doubt standard, as in the present case, there will certainly be a rational connection between the fact presumed or inferred (in this case, knowledge) and the facts the Government must prove in order to shift the burden of going forward (possession of recently stolen property).

We do not decide today whether a judge-formulated inference of less antiquity or authority may properly be emphasized by a jury instruction.

COUNTY COURT v. ALLEN

Supreme Court of the United States, 1979.
442 U.S. 140.

MR. JUSTICE STEVENS delivered the opinion of the Court.

A New York statute provides that, with certain exceptions, the presence of a firearm in an automobile is presumptive evidence of its illegal possession by all persons then occupying the vehicle. The United States Court of Appeals for the Second Circuit held that respondents may challenge the constitutionality of this statute in a federal habeas corpus proceeding and that the statute is "unconstitutional on its face." * * *

Four persons, three adult males (respondents) and a 16-year-old girl (Jane Doe, who is not a respondent here), were jointly tried on charges that they possessed two loaded handguns, a loaded machinegun, and over a pound of heroin found in a Chevrolet in which they were riding when it was stopped for speeding on the New York Thruway shortly after noon on March 28, 1973. The two large-caliber handguns, which together with their ammunition weighed approximately six pounds, were seen through the window of the car by the investigating police officer. They were positioned crosswise in an open handbag on either the front floor or the front seat of the car on the passenger side where Jane Doe was sitting. Jane Doe admitted that the handbag was hers. The machinegun and the heroin were discovered in the trunk after the police pried it open. The car had been borrowed from the driver's brother earlier that day; the key to the trunk could not be found in the car or on the person of any of its occupants, although there was testimony that two of the occupants had placed something in the trunk before embarking in the borrowed car. The jury convicted all four of possession of the handguns and acquitted them of possession of the contents of the trunk.

Counsel for all four defendants objected to the introduction into evidence of the two handguns, the machinegun, and the drugs, arguing that the State had not adequately demonstrated a connection between their clients and the contraband. The trial court overruled the objection, relying on the presumption of possession created by the New York statute. Because that presumption does not apply if a weapon is found "upon the person" of one of the occupants of the car, the three male defendants also moved to dismiss the charges relating to the handguns on the ground that the guns were found on the person of Jane Doe. * * *

At the close of the trial, the judge instructed the jurors that they were entitled to infer possession from the defendants' presence in the car. He did not make any reference to the "on the person" exception in his explanation of the statutory presumption, nor did any of the defendants object to this omission or request alternative or additional instructions on the subject.

* * *

Inferences and presumptions are a staple of our adversary system of factfinding. It is often necessary for the trier of fact to determine the existence of an element of the crime—that is, an "ultimate" or "elemental" fact—from the existence of one or more "evidentiary" or "basic" facts. The value of these evidentiary devices, and their validity under the Due Process Clause, vary from case to case, however, depending on the strength of the connection between the particular basic and elemental facts involved and on the degree to which the device curtails the factfinder's freedom to assess the evidence independently. Nonetheless, in criminal cases, the ultimate test of any device's constitutional validity in a given case remains constant; the device must not undermine the factfinder's responsibility at trial, based on evidence adduced by the State, to find the ultimate facts beyond a reasonable doubt.

The most common evidentiary device is the entirely permissive inference or presumption, which allows—but does not require—the trier of fact to infer the elemental fact from proof by the prosecutor of the basic one and that places no burden of any kind on the defendant. In that situation the basic fact may constitute prima facie evidence of the elemental fact. When reviewing this type of device, the Court has required the party challenging it to demonstrate its invalidity as applied to him. Because this permissive presumption leaves the trier of fact free to credit or reject the inference and does not shift the burden of proof, it affects the application of the "beyond a reasonable doubt" standard only if, under the facts of the case, there is no rational way the trier could make the connection permitted by the inference. For only in that situation is there any risk that an explanation of the permissible inference to a jury, or its use by a jury, has caused the presumptively rational factfinder to make an erroneous factual determination.

A mandatory presumption is a far more troublesome evidentiary device. For it may affect not only the strength of the "no reasonable doubt" burden but also the placement of that burden; it tells the trier that he or they must find the elemental fact upon proof of the basic fact, at least unless the defendant has come forward with some evidence to rebut the presumed connection between the two facts.[a] In this

a. This class of more or less mandatory presumptions can be subdivided into two parts; presumptions that merely shift the burden of production to the defendant, following the satisfaction of which the ultimate burden of persuasion returns to the prosecution; and presumptions that entirely shift the burden of proof to the defendant. The mandatory presumptions examined by our cases have almost uniformly fit into the former subclass, in that they never totally removed the ultimate burden of proof beyond a reasonable doubt from the prosecution. E.g., Tot v. United States.

To the extent that a presumption imposes an extremely low burden of production—e.g., being satisfied by "any" evidence—it may well be that its impact is no greater than that of a permissive inference, and it may be proper to analyze it as such.

In deciding what type of inference or presumption is involved in a case, the jury instructions will generally be controlling, although their interpretation may require recourse to the statute involved and the cases decided under it. * * *

The importance of focusing attention on the precise presentation of the presumption to the jury and the scope of that presumption is illustrated by a comparison of United States v. Gainey with United States v. Romano. Both cases involved statutory presumptions based on proof that the defendant was present at the site of an illegal still. In Gainey the Court sustained a conviction "for carrying on" the business of the distillery in violation of 26 U.S.C. § 5601(a)(4), whereas in Romano, the Court set aside a conviction for being in "possession, or custody, or * * * control" of such a distillery in violation of § 5601(a)(1). The difference in outcome was attributable to two important differences between the cases. Because the statute involved in Gainey was a sweeping prohibition of almost any activity associated with the still, whereas the Romano statute involved only one narrow aspect of the total undertaking, there was a much higher probability that mere presence could support an inference of guilt in the former case than in the latter.

Of perhaps greater importance, however, was the difference between the trial judge's instructions to the jury in the two cases. In Gainey, the judge had explained that the presumption was permissive; it did not require the jury to convict the defendant even if it was convinced that he was present at the site. On the contrary, the instructions made it clear that presence was only " 'a circumstance to be considered along with all the other circumstances in the case.' " As we emphasized, the "jury was thus specifically told that the statutory inference was not conclusive." In Romano, the trial judge told the jury that the defendant's presence at the still " 'shall be deemed sufficient evidence to authorize conviction.' " Although there was other evidence of guilt, that instruction authorized conviction

situation, the Court has generally examined the presumption on its face to determine the extent to which the basic and elemental facts coincide. To the extent that the trier of fact is forced to abide by the presumption, and may not reject it based on an independent evaluation of the particular facts presented by the State, the analysis of the presumption's constitutional validity is logically divorced from those facts and based on the presumption's accuracy in the run of cases.[b] It is for this reason that the Court has held it irrelevant in analyzing a mandatory presumption, but not in analyzing a purely permissive one, that there is ample evidence in the record other than the presumption to support a conviction.

Without determining whether the presumption in this case was mandatory, the Court of Appeals analyzed it on its face as if it were. In fact, it was not, as the New York Court of Appeals had earlier pointed out.

The trial judge's instructions make it clear that the presumption was merely a part of the prosecution's case, that it gave rise to a permissive inference available only in certain circumstances, rather than a mandatory conclusion of possession, and that it could be ignored by the jury even if there was no affirmative proof offered by defendants in rebuttal. The judge explained that possession could be actual or constructive, but that constructive possession could not exist without the intent and ability to exercise control or dominion over the weapons. He also carefully instructed the jury that there is a mandatory presumption of innocence in favor of the defendants that controls unless it, as the exclusive trier of fact, is satisfied beyond a reasonable doubt that the defendants possessed the handguns in the manner described by the judge. In short, the instructions plainly directed the jury to consider all the circumstances tending to support or contradict the inference that all four occupants of the car had possession of the two loaded handguns and to decide the matter for itself without regard to how much evidence the defendants introduced.

Our cases considering the validity of permissive statutory presumptions such as the one involved here have rested on an evaluation of the presumption as ap-

even if the jury disbelieved all of the testimony except the proof of presence at the site. This Court's holding that the statutory presumption could not support the Romano conviction was thus dependent, in part, on the specific instructions given by the trial judge. Under those instructions it was necessary to decide whether, regardless of the specific circumstances of the particular case, the statutory presumption adequately supported the guilty verdict.

b. In addition to the discussion of Romano in n. a, supra, this point is illustrated by Leary v. United States. In that case, Dr. Timothy Leary, a professor at Harvard University, was stopped by customs inspectors in Laredo, Tex., as he was returning from the Mexican side of the international border. Marihuana seeds and a silver snuffbox filled with semirefined marihuana and three partially smoked marihuana cigarettes were discovered in his car. He was convicted of having knowingly transported marihuana which he knew had been illegally imported into this country in violation of 21 U.S.C. § 176a (1964 ed.) That statute included a mandatory presumption: "possession shall be deemed sufficient evidence to authorize conviction [for importation] unless the defendant explains his possession to the satisfaction of the jury." Leary admitted possession of the marihuana and claimed that he had carried it from New York to Mexico and then back.

* * *

Despite the fact that the defendant was well educated and had recently traveled to a country that is a major exporter of marihuana to this country, the Court found the presumption of knowledge of importation from possession irrational. It did so, not because Dr. Leary was unlikely to know the source of the marihuana, but instead because "a majority of possessors" were unlikely to have such knowledge. Because the jury had been instructed to rely on the presumption even if it did not believe the Government's direct evidence of knowledge of importation (unless, of course, the defendant met his burden of "satisfying" the jury to the contrary), the Court reversed the conviction.

plied to the record before the Court. None suggests that a court should pass on the constitutionality of this kind of statute "on its face." It was error for the Court of Appeals to make such a determination in this case.

III

As applied to the facts of this case, the presumption of possession is entirely rational. * * * [R]espondents were not "hitch-hikers or other casual passengers," and the guns were neither "a few inches in length" nor "out of [respondents'] sight." The argument against possession by any of the respondents was predicated solely on the fact that the guns were in Jane Doe's pocketbook. But several circumstances—which, not surprisingly, her counsel repeatedly emphasized in his questions and his argument—made it highly improbable that she was the sole custodian of those weapons.

Even if it was reasonable to conclude that she had placed the guns in her purse before the car was stopped by police, the facts strongly suggest that Jane Doe was not the only person able to exercise dominion over them. The two guns were too large to be concealed in her handbag. The bag was consequently open, and part of one of the guns was in plain view, within easy access of the driver of the car and even, perhaps, of the other two respondents who were riding in the rear seat.

Moreover, it is highly improbable that the loaded guns belonged to Jane Doe or that she was solely responsible for their being in her purse. As a 16-year-old girl in the company of three adult men she was the least likely of the four to be carrying one, let alone two, heavy handguns. It is far more probable that she relied on the pocketknife found in her brassiere for any necessary self-protection. Under these circumstances, it was not unreasonable for her counsel to argue and for the jury to infer that when the car was halted for speeding, the other passengers in the car anticipated the risk of a search and attempted to conceal their weapons in a pocketbook in the front seat. The inference is surely more likely than the notion that these weapons were the sole property of the 16-year-old girl.

Under these circumstances, the jury would have been entirely reasonable in rejecting the suggestion—which, incidentally, defense counsel did not even advance in their closing arguments to the jury—that the handguns were in the sole possession of Jane Doe. Assuming that the jury did reject it, the case is tantamount to one in which the guns were lying on the floor or the seat of the car in plain view of the three other occupants of the automobile. In such a case, it is surely rational to infer that each of the respondents was fully aware of the presence of the guns and had both the ability and the intent to exercise dominion and control over the weapons.

MR. JUSTICE POWELL, with whom MR. JUSTICE BRENNAN, MR. JUSTICE STEWART, and MR. JUSTICE MARSHALL join, dissenting.

* * *

Legitimate guidance of a jury's deliberations is an indispensable part of our criminal justice system. Nonetheless, the use of presumptions in criminal cases poses at least two distinct perils for defendants' constitutional rights. The Court accurately identifies the first of these as being the danger of interference with "the factfinder's responsibility at trial, based on evidence adduced by the State, to find the ultimate facts beyond a reasonable doubt." If the jury is instructed that it must infer some ultimate fact (that is, some element of the offense) from proof of other facts unless the defendant disproves the ultimate fact by the preponderance of the evidence, then the presumption shifts the burden of proof to the defendant concerning the element thus inferred.

But I do not agree with the Court's conclusion that the only constitutional difficulty with presumptions lies in the danger of lessening the burden of proof the prosecution must bear. As the Court notes, the presumptions thus far reviewed by the Court have not shifted the burden of persuasion; instead, they either have required only that the defendant produce some evidence to rebut the inference suggested by the prosecution's evidence, or merely have been suggestions to the jury that it would be sensible to draw certain conclusions on the basis of the evidence presented. Evolving from our decisions, therefore, is a second standard for judging the constitutionality of criminal presumptions which is based—not on the constitutional requirement that the State be put to its proof—but rather on the due process rule that when the jury is encouraged to make factual inferences, those inferences must reflect some valid general observation about the natural connection between events as they occur in our society.

* * *

In sum, our decisions uniformly have recognized that due process requires more than merely that the prosecution be put to its proof. In addition, the Constitution restricts the court in its charge to the jury by requiring that, when particular factual inferences are recommended to the jury, those factual inferences be accurate reflections of what history, common sense, and experience tell us about the relations between events in our society. Generally, this due process rule has been articulated as requiring that the truth of the inferred fact be more likely than not whenever the premise for the inference is true. Thus, to be constitutional a presumption must be at least more likely than not true.

II

* * *

Undeniably, the presumption charged in this case encouraged the jury to draw a particular factual inference regardless of any other evidence presented: to infer that respondents possessed the weapons found in the automobile "upon proof of the presence of the machine gun and the hand weapon" and proof that respondents "occupied the automobile at the time such instruments were found." I believe that the presumption thus charged was unconstitutional because it did not fairly reflect what common sense and experience tell us about passengers in automobiles and the possession of handguns. People present in automobiles where there are weapons simply are not "more likely than not" the possessors of those weapons.

* * *

It seems to me that the Court mischaracterizes the function of the presumption charged in this case. As it acknowledges was the case in *Romano*, supra, the "instruction authorized conviction even if the jury disbelieved all of the testimony except the proof of presence" in the automobile. The Court nevertheless relies on all of the evidence introduced by the prosecution and argues that the "permissive" presumption could not have prejudiced defendants. The possibility that the jury disbelieved all of this evidence, and relied on the presumption, is simply ignored.

* * *

Note

After deciding *Allen*, the Court held in Sandstrom v. Montana, 442 U.S. 510 (1979), that an instruction to the jury in a homicide case that "the law presumes that a person intends the ordinary consequences of his voluntary acts" violated the Constitution, because it may have removed from the prosecution some of its burden to prove beyond a reasonable doubt all elements of the crime charged. The Court observed that unlike in *Allen*, a reasonable jury could have interpreted the instruction as a legal command that was not rebuttable. Second, the jury may have interpreted the instruction as a direction to find intent once voluntary action was proven unless the defendant proved the lack of intent. Finally, the jury could have read the instruction as authorizing it to draw a permissive inference. Since the first two interpretations would have shifted a constitutionally required burden from the prosecutor, and since the Court could not be sure how the jury may have treated the instruction, the Court found that reversal of the conviction was required.

One way of reading the presumption cases is as establishing two rules: "[T]he first rule is that where the prosecution bears the burden of persuasion, a trial judge may not encourage the jury to make logical jumps not supported by the evidence. Otherwise the persuasion burden would be compromised." The second rule, which would apply where a persuasion burden could be shifted to a defendant, is that any "instruction must be a fair statement about evidence actually produced in the case." Saltzburg, supra note 22, at 415–16.[24]

Justice Brennan, who authored *Sandstrom* wrote for five members of the Court in Francis v. Franklin, 471 U.S. 307 (1985), as it held invalid the following jury instructions:

> A crime is a violation of a statute of this State in which there shall be a union of joint operation of act or omission to act, and intention or criminal negligence. A person shall not be found guilty of any crime committed by misfortune or accident where it satisfactorily appears there was no criminal scheme or undertaking or intention or criminal negligence. *The acts of a person of sound mind and discretion are presumed to be the product of the person's will, but the presumption may be rebutted. A person of sound mind and discretion is presumed to intend the natural and probable consequences of his acts but the presumption may be rebutted.* A person will not be presumed to act with criminal intention but the trier of facts, that is, the jury, may find criminal intention upon a consideration of the words, conduct, demeanor, motive and all other circumstances connected with the act for which the accused is prosecuted. [Emphasis added]

The defendant escaped from custody and attempted to obtain a car to speed his flight. He pounded on the door of a house until a 72-year-old resident opened the door. When the defendant pointed a gun and demanded the keys to the resident's car, the resident slammed the door and the gun fired and killed him. The defendant claimed that he did not intend to kill and that the firing was accidental.

Justice Brennan began his analysis by restating the principles the Court had laid down for determining the constitutionality of presumptions:

24. An excellent discussion of problems with County Court v. Allen is found in Lushing, Faces Without Features: The Surface Validity of Criminal Inferences, 72 J.Crim.L. & Crim. 82 (1981).

For a discussion of the Supreme Court's presumption cases as applied to the federal bank robbery statute, see Ponsoldt, A Due Process Analysis of Judicially-Authorized Presumptions in Federal Aggravated Bank Robbery Cases, 74 J.Crim.L. & Crim. 363 (1983). For an argument against treating instructions on permissible inferences differently from mandatory presumptions, see Note, The Improper Use of Presumptions in Recent Criminal Law Adjudication, 38 Stan.L.Rev. 423 (1986).

> The threshold inquiry in ascertaining the constitutional analysis applicable to this kind of jury instruction is to determine the nature of the presumption it describes. The court must determine whether the challenged portion of the instruction creates a mandatory presumption or merely a permissive inference. A mandatory presumption instructs the jury that it must infer the presumed fact if the State proves certain predicate facts. A permissive inference suggests to the jury a possible conclusion to be drawn if the State proves predicate facts, but does not require the jury to draw the conclusion.
>
> Mandatory presumptions must be measured against the standards of *Winship* as elucidated in *Sandstrom.* Such presumptions violate the Due Process Clause if they relieve the State of the burden of persuasion on an element of an offense. A permissive inference does not relieve the State of its burden of persuasion because it still requires the State to convince the jury that the suggested conclusion should be inferred based on the predicate facts involved. Such inferences do not necessarily implicate the concerns of *Sandstrom.* A permissive inference violates the Due Process Clause only if the suggested conclusion is not one that reason and common sense justify in light of the proven facts before the jury. County Court v. Allen.

Justice Brennan concluded that the challenged instruction created a mandatory presumption, because it was "cast in the language of command." The fact that the judge said the presumption "may be rebutted" did not affect the mandatory nature of the presumption itself. According to Justice Brennan, a mandatory rebuttable presumption can be just as constitutionally infirm as a mandatory irrebuttable presumption.

> A mandatory rebuttable presumption does not remove the presumed element from the case if the State proves the predicate facts, but it nonetheless relieves the State of the affirmative burden of persuasion on the presumed element by instructing the jury that it must find the presumed element unless the defendant persuades the jury not to make such a finding. A mandatory rebuttable presumption is perhaps less onerous from the defendant's perspective, but it is no less unconstitutional. * * * In Mullaney v. Wilbur we explicitly held unconstitutional a mandatory rebuttable presumption that shifted to the defendant a burden of persuasion on the question of intent.

Justice Brennan reasoned that a reasonable juror could have concluded that it was to find an intent to kill unless the defendant persuaded it that it should not infer intent. Although the presumption in this case was plainly rebuttable, whereas the *Sandstrom* presumption was subject to several interpretations, Justice Brennan found that it might have led the jury to impermissibly place a burden of persuasion on the defendant.

Justice Powell dissented and argued that the combination of instructions on reasonable doubt, the presumption of innocence, and interpretation of circumstantial evidence, and the portion of the challenged instructions stating that "criminal intention" cannot be presumed sufficiently removed any danger that a reasonable jury would have imposed a persuasion burden on the defendant. Justice Rehnquist dissented, joined by the Chief Justice and Justice O'Connor. He made an argument similar to that made by Justice Powell and suggested that instead of focusing on what a reasonable jury *might* have interpreted the instructions to mean, the Court should find it *likely* that a juror so understood the charge before finding constitutional error.

The Court decided that a *Sandstrom* error may be harmless in Rose v. Clark, 478 U.S. 570 (1986). In a murder case, the trial judge instructed the jury that malice was "an intent to do any injury to another, a design formed in the mind of doing mischief to another" and that "[a]ll homicides are presumed to be malicious in the absence of evidence which would rebut the implied presumption." Lower federal courts held that the instructions violated *Sandstrom* and that the error could not be harmless. Justice Powell wrote for a majority of the Court as it found that "the erroneous malice instruction does not compare with the kinds of errors that automatically require reversal of an otherwise valid conviction." The Court remanded the case for a determination of the effect of the error on the judgment.

Justice Blackmun, joined by Justices Brennan and Marshall, dissented. Reasoning that "[a] jury that receives a constitutionally flawed, burden-shifting instruction on intent, is, in effect, directed to return a verdict against the defendant," he concluded that it was impossible for a reviewing court to know whether the jury relied upon the instruction or whether it actually found malice beyond a reasonable doubt. In the face of this uncertainty, Justice Blackmun would not have applied a harmless error analysis. Chief Justice Burger filed a brief concurring opinion indicating his view that the error was harmless. Justice Stevens concurred in the judgment, but did not join the majority's "dictum" on harmless error analysis generally.

The Court remanded in Carella v. California, 491 U.S. 263 (1989), for a determination whether two erroneous jury instructions—one stating that a person is presumed to embezzle a vehicle if it is not returned within five days of the expiration of the rental agreement, and a second stating that intent to commit theft by fraud is presumed from failure to return rented property within 20 days of remand—were harmless under *Rose.*

Justice Scalia, joined by Justices Brennan, Marshall and Blackmun, concurred in the judgment. He argued that a mandatory irrebuttable presumption invades the jury's function and denies the jury its proper role. According to Justice Scalia, an instruction which essentially directs a verdict cannot be cured by an appellate court's determination that the record unmistakably established guilt, since that would be a finding of fact by judges rather than jurors. (As will be discussed later in this Chapter, a trial judge cannot direct a guilty verdict, even if the evidence of guilt is overwhelming). Justice Scalia argued that an impermissible conclusive presumption could only be deemed harmless where it played no role in the jury's verdict, such as where it addressed an element of the crime which the defendant admitted—for example, a *Sandstrom* error where defendant stipulated intent and contested only identity.

In Yates v. Evatt, 111 S.Ct. 1884 (1991), the trial court instructed the jury that malice is implied or presumed from the wilful doing of a wrongful act, or from the use of a deadly weapon. The judge further instructed that these presumptions were rebuttable by the rest of the evidence. The state court found that the instructions violated *Sandstrom* and *Francis,* but that the error was harmless. The Supreme Court disagreed, and set forth a particularized methodology for determining harmless error with respect to unlawful presumptions.

Justice Souter, writing for the Court, described the procedure for determining harmless error as follows:

> To say that an instruction to apply an unconstitutional presumption did not contribute to the verdict is to make a judgment about the significance of the presumption to reasonable jurors, when measured against the other evidence considered by those jurors independently of the presumption. * * *

> It will not be enough that the jury considered evidence from which it could have come to the verdict without reliance on the presumption. Rather, the issue * * * is whether the jury actually rested its verdict on evidence establishing the presumed fact beyond a reasonable doubt, independently of the presumption. Since that enquiry cannot be a subjective one into the jurors' minds, a court must approach it by asking whether the force of the evidence presumably considered by the jury in accordance with the instructions is so overwhelming as to leave it beyond a reasonable doubt that the verdict resting on that evidence would have been the same in the absence of the presumption.

Justice Souter cautioned that the entire record review used for most harmless error analysis (see e.g. Chapman v. California, Chapter Thirteen, page 1283) may not always be permissible when determining whether erroneous presumptions were harmless error. He explained as follows:

> [T]he terms of some presumptions so narrow the jury's focus as to leave it questionable that a reasonable juror would look to anything but the evidence establishing the predicate fact in order to infer the fact presumed. When applying a harmless-error analysis in presumption cases, therefore, it is crucial to ascertain from the trial court's instructions that the jurors, as reasonable persons, would have considered the entire trial record, before looking to that record to assess the significance of the erroneous presumption.

Justice Souter concluded that the lower court had applied an improper test for harmless error when it sought merely to determine whether it was beyond a reasonable doubt that the jury "would have found it unnecessary to rely on the unconstitutional presumptions." This "less rigorous standard" was inadequate, because it failed to take two important considerations into account:

> Enquiry about the necessity for reliance * * * can tell us that the verdict could have been the same without the presumptions, when there was evidence sufficient to support the verdict independently of the presumptions' effect. But the enquiry will not tell us whether the jury's verdict did rest on that evidence as well as on the presumptions, or whether that evidence was of such compelling force as to show beyond a reasonable doubt that the presumptions must have made no difference in reaching the verdict obtained.

Justice Souter then proceeded to determine whether the erroneous presumptions were harmless under the facts of the case. He first found that since the jury was instructed to consider all the evidence together with the presumption, the whole record could be reviewed in assessing the significance of the errors. However, Justice Souter concluded that the evidence independent of the presumption was insufficient to prove beyond a reasonable doubt that the jury rested its verdict on that evidence.

Justice Scalia, joined by Justice Blackmun, concurred in part and concurred in the judgment. He reiterated his position in Carella v. California, concluding that while the Court's "hypothetical inquiry ensures that the State has, in fact, proved malice beyond a reasonable doubt, it does not ensure that it has proved that element beyond a reasonable doubt *to the satisfaction of a jury.*"

After *Sandstrom, Francis,* and *Allen,* why would a trial court choose to instruct the jury with a presumption, unless the defendant stipulated to it? If the presumption is mandatory, it runs the risk of violating *Winship* and *Mullaney.* If the instruction is permissive, it must be in accord with reason and common sense and as such it would seem to be superfluous to a jury of reasonable people. Since the prosecutor could argue to the jury that it should draw reasonable inferences from the evidence, do you see any value to the use of presumptions? Does it matter that the permissible inference is explained by the judge?

IV. TRIAL BY JURY

A. THE FUNDAMENTAL RIGHT

Article III, Section 2, clause 3 of the Constitution provides that "[t]he trial of all Crimes, except in Cases of Impeachment, shall be by Jury; and such Trial shall be held in the State where the said Crimes shall have been committed; but when not committed within any State, the Trial shall be at such Place or Places as the Congress may by Law have directed." The Sixth Amendment is, in part, redundant; it provides that "[i]n all criminal prosecutions, the accused shall enjoy the right to a speedy and public trial, by an impartial jury of the State and district wherein the crime shall have been committed, which district shall have been previously ascertained by law * * *." Certainly, a right found in two places in the Constitution is likely to be regarded as fundamental. And that is just how the Supreme Court viewed it when it incorporated the Sixth Amendment through the Fourteenth and made it binding on the states.

DUNCAN v. LOUISIANA

Supreme Court of the United States, 1968.
391 U.S. 145.

MR. JUSTICE WHITE delivered the opinion of the Court.

Appellant, Gary Duncan, was convicted of simple battery in the Twenty-fifth Judicial District Court of Louisiana. Under Louisiana law simple battery is a misdemeanor, punishable by a maximum of two years' imprisonment and a $300 fine. Appellant sought trial by jury, but because the Louisiana Constitution grants jury trials only in cases in which capital punishment or imprisonment at hard labor may be imposed, the trial judge denied the request. Appellant was convicted and sentenced to serve 60 days in the parish prison and pay a fine of $150. * * *

* * *

I

[The Court discusses its prior incorporation tests.]

* * * The claim before us is that the right to trial by jury guaranteed by the Sixth Amendment meets these tests. The position of Louisiana, on the other hand, is that the Constitution imposes upon the State no duty to give a jury trial in any criminal case, regardless of the seriousness of the crime or the size of the punishment which may be imposed. Because we believe that trial by jury in criminal cases is fundamental to the American scheme of justice, we hold that the Fourteenth Amendment guarantees a right of jury trial in all criminal cases which—were they to be tried in a federal court—would come within the Sixth Amendment's guarantee. Since we consider the appeal before us to be such a case, we hold that the Constitution was violated when appellant's demand for jury trial was refused.

The history of trial by jury in criminal cases has been frequently told. It is sufficient for present purposes to say that by the time our Constitution was written, jury trial in criminal cases had been in existence in England for several centuries and carried impressive credentials traced by many to Magna Carta.

Its preservation and proper operation as a protection against arbitrary rule were among the major objectives of the revolutionary settlement which was expressed in the Declaration and Bill of Rights of 1689. * * *

* * *

The guarantees of jury trial in the Federal and State Constitutions reflect a profound judgment about the way in which law should be enforced and justice administered. A right to a jury trial is granted to criminal defendants in order to prevent oppression by the Government. Those who wrote our constitutions knew from history and experience that it was necessary to protect against unfounded criminal charges brought to eliminate enemies and against judges too responsive to the voice of higher authority. The framers of the constitutions strove to create an independent judiciary but insisted upon further protection against arbitrary action. Providing an accused with the right to be tried by a jury of his peers gave him an inestimable safeguard against the corrupt or overzealous prosecutor and against the compliant, biased, or eccentric judge. If the defendant preferred the common-sense judgment of a jury to the more tutored but perhaps less sympathetic reaction of the single judge, he was to have it. Beyond this, the jury trial provisions in the Federal and State Constitutions reflect a fundamental decision about the exercise of official power—a reluctance to entrust plenary powers over the life and liberty of the citizen to one judge or to a group of judges. Fear of unchecked power, so typical of our State and Federal Governments in other respects, found expression in the criminal law in this insistence upon community participation in the determination of guilt or innocence. The deep commitment of the Nation to the right of jury trial in serious criminal cases as a defense against arbitrary law enforcement qualifies for protection under the Due Process Clause of the Fourteenth Amendment, and must therefore be respected by the States.

Of course jury trial has "its weaknesses and the potential for misuse," Singer v. United States, 380 U.S. 24, 35 (1965). We are aware of the long debate, especially in this century, among those who write about the administration of justice, as to the wisdom of permitting untrained laymen to determine the facts in civil and criminal proceedings. * * *

The State of Louisiana urges that holding that the Fourteenth Amendment assures a right to jury trial will cast doubt on the integrity of every trial conducted without a jury. Plainly, this is not the import of our holding. Our conclusion is that in the American States, as in the federal judicial system, a general grant of jury trial for serious offenses is a fundamental right, essential for preventing miscarriages of justice and for assuring that fair trials are provided for all defendants. We would not assert, however, that every criminal trial—or any particular trial—held before a judge alone is unfair or that a defendant may never be as fairly treated by a judge as he would be by a jury. Thus we hold no constitutional doubts about the practices common in both federal and state courts, of accepting waivers of jury trial and prosecuting petty crimes without extending a right to jury trial. However, the fact is that in most places more trials for serious crimes are to juries than to a court alone; a great many defendants prefer the judgment of a jury to that of a court. Even where defendants are satisfied with bench trials, the right to a jury trial very likely serves its intended purpose of making judicial or prosecutorial unfairness less likely.

II

Louisiana's final contention is that even if it must grant jury trials in serious criminal cases, the conviction before us is valid and constitutional because here the petitioner was tried for simple battery and was sentenced to only 60 days in the parish prison. We are not persuaded. It is doubtless true that there is a category of petty crimes or offenses which is not subject to the Sixth Amendment jury trial provision and should not be subject to the Fourteenth Amendment jury trial requirement here applied to the States. Crimes carrying possible penalties up to six months do not require a jury trial if they otherwise qualify as petty offenses, Cheff v. Schnackenberg, 384 U.S. 373 (1966). But the penalty authorized for a particular crime is of major relevance in determining whether it is serious or not and may in itself, if severe enough, subject the trial to the mandates of the Sixth Amendment. * * * In the case before us the Legislature of Louisiana has made simple battery a criminal offense punishable by imprisonment for up to two years and a fine. The question, then, is whether a crime carrying such a penalty is an offense which Louisiana may insist on trying without a jury.

We think not. So-called petty offenses were tried without juries both in England and in the Colonies and have always been held to be exempt from the otherwise comprehensive language of the Sixth Amendment's jury trial provisions. There is no substantial evidence that the Framers intended to depart from this established common-law practice, and the possible consequences to defendants from convictions for petty offenses have been thought insufficient to outweigh the benefits to efficient law enforcement and simplified judicial administration resulting from the availability of speedy and inexpensive nonjury adjudications. These same considerations compel the same results under the Fourteenth Amendment. Of course the boundaries of the petty offense category have always been ill-defined, if not ambulatory. In the absence of an explicit constitutional provision, the definitional task necessarily falls on the courts, which must either pass upon the validity of legislative attempts to identify those petty offenses which are exempt from jury trial or, where the legislature has not addressed itself to the problem, themselves face the question in the first instance. In either case it is necessary to draw a line in the spectrum of crime, separating petty from serious infractions. This process, although essential, cannot be wholly satisfactory, for it requires attaching different consequences to events which, when they lie near the line, actually differ very little.

In determining whether the length of the authorized prison term or the seriousness of other punishment is enough in itself to require a jury trial, we * * * refer to objective criteria, chiefly the existing laws and practices in the Nation. In the federal system, petty offenses are defined as those punishable by no more than six months in prison and a $500 fine. In 49 of the 50 States crimes subject to trial without a jury, which occasionally include simple battery, are punishable by no more than one year in jail. Moreover, in the late 18th century in America crimes triable without a jury were for the most part punishable by no more than a six-month prison term, although there appear to have been exceptions to this rule. We need not, however, settle in this case the exact location of the line between petty offenses and serious crimes. It is sufficient for our purposes to hold that a crime punishable by two years in prison is, based on past and contemporary standards in this country, a serious crime and not a petty offense. Consequently, appellant was entitled to a jury trial and it was error to deny it.

* * *

MR. JUSTICE BLACK, with whom MR. JUSTICE DOUGLAS joins, concurring.

[Justice Black sets forth his total incorporation view.]

MR. JUSTICE HARLAN, whom MR. JUSTICE STEWART joins, dissenting.

Every American jurisdiction provides for trial by jury in criminal cases. The question before us is not whether jury trial is an ancient institution, which it is; nor whether it plays a significant role in the administration of criminal justice, which it does; nor whether it will endure, which it shall. The question in this case is whether the State of Louisiana, which provides trial by jury for all felonies, is prohibited by the Constitution from trying charges of simple battery to the court alone. In my view, the answer to that question, mandated alike by our constitutional history and by the longer history of trial by jury, is clearly "no."

* * *

MR. JUSTICE FORTAS, concurring.

* * * I agree that the Due Process Clause of the Fourteenth Amendment requires that the States accord the right to jury trial in prosecutions for offenses that are not petty. A powerful reason for reaching this conclusion is that the Sixth Amendment to the Constitution guarantees the right to jury trial in federal prosecutions for such offenses. * * *

* * *

But although I agree with the decision of the Court, I cannot agree with the implication, that the tail must go with the hide: that when we hold, influenced by the Sixth Amendment, that "due process" requires that the States accord the right of jury trial for all but petty offenses, we automatically import all of the ancillary rules which have been or may hereafter be developed incidental to the right to jury trial in the federal courts. I see no reason whatever, for example, to assume that our decision today should require us to impose federal requirements such as unanimous verdicts or a jury of 12 upon the States. We may well conclude that these and other features of federal jury practice are by no means fundamental—that they are not essential to due process of law—and that they are not obligatory on the States.

* * *

Note

Duncan's declaration that "petty offenses" may be tried without a jury, notwithstanding the *Duncan* holding, was subsequently affirmed in Baldwin v. New York, 399 U.S. 66 (1969). In *Baldwin* the Court defined "petty" by considering the severity of the maximum penalty and concluded that "no offense can be deemed petty for purposes of the right to trial by jury where imprisonment for more than six months is authorized."[25]

The "petty" offense definition also appears in cases involving criminal contempt and the right to jury trial. In Bloom v. Illinois, 391 U.S. 194 (1968), the Court ruled that criminal contempt is a crime to which the jury trial provisions of the Constitution apply, but also noted that criminal contempt cases follow the rule

25. In several other respects, the U.S. Supreme Court has sanctioned discretion in the operation of the state court jury system. See for example, McKeiver v. Pennsylvania, 403 U.S. 528 (1971) (a juvenile has no constitutional right to trial by jury, in part because the nonadversary nature of the juvenile hearing promotes what is "an intimate, informal protective proceeding"); and Ludwig v. Massachusetts, 427 U.S. 618 (1975) (upholding a two tier court system which denies a jury trial in the first tier, but grants a jury de novo in the second tier because it "absolutely guarantees trial by jury to persons accused of serious crimes" in a fair and not unduly burdensome manner).

that "petty" crimes need not be tried to a jury. The Court again defined petty by considering the penalty imposed, here noting that where the legislature has not authorized a specific penalty for contempt, the state may not impose a jail sentence greater than six months without providing a jury trial.[26]

Several years later, the Court considered the effect of aggregate and concurrent contempt sentences on the jury trial right in Taylor v. Hayes, 418 U.S. 488 (1974), and Codispoti v. Pennsylvania, 418 U.S. 506 (1974). The trial court in *Taylor* imposed sentences for several contempt violations; the appellate court affirmed the sentences but ran them concurrently so that the total penalty imposed was six months in jail. The Court affirmed the decision, noting that there is no difference between permitting a state to reduce the sentence after conviction, and permitting the state to proceed without a jury where the sentence imposed is six months or less.

However, in *Codispoti,* a decision announced the same day as *Taylor,* the Court held that in a post-verdict adjudication, the Sixth Amendment requires a jury trial when the contempt sentences aggregate more than six months, even though no individual sentence is greater than six months. *Codispoti* implies that summary contempt adjudications during trial might amount to more than six months in the aggregate without triggering a right to jury trial. But it remains to be seen how much freedom the Supreme Court will give lower court judges to utilize summary contempt as opposed to post-verdict adjudications of contempt.

Justice Marshall wrote for a unanimous Court in Blanton v. City of North Las Vegas, 489 U.S. 538 (1989), holding that a defendant has no Sixth Amendment right to a trial by jury when charged under Nevada law with driving under the influence (DUI). A convicted defendant is subject to a minimum term of two days' imprisonment and a maximum term of six months' imprisonment. Alternatively, a trial court may order the defendant to perform 48 hours of community work while wearing distinctive garb which identifies him as a DUI offender. A convicted defendant may also be fined from $200 to $1,000, he automatically loses his license for 90 days, and he must attend an alcohol abuse education class at his own expense.

Justice Marshall relied upon prior cases for the proposition that the primary emphasis in assessing the right to jury trial is on the maximum authorized period of incarceration. Although he recognized that a legislature's view of the seriousness of an offense might also be reflected in other penalties, he reasoned that incarceration is intrinsically different from other penalties and is the most powerful indication of whether an offense is "serious." Justice Marshall wrote that it is appropriate to presume for Sixth Amendment purposes that an offense is petty if it carries a maximum prison term of six months or less, and that "[a] defendant is entitled to a jury trial in such circumstances only if he can demonstrate that any additional statutory penalties, viewed in conjunction with the maximum authorized period of incarceration, are so severe that they clearly reflect a legislative determination that the offense in question is a 'serious' one." The Nevada penalties, he concluded, reflected no such legislative determination.

26. In Frank v. United States, 395 U.S. 147 (1969), the Court refused to require a jury trial for contempt punished by three years probation, holding that Congress, by statute, had classified as petty any offense that provides a term of probation for less than five years and that the contempt statute did not specify penalties of more than six months. Of course, no more than six months imprisonment could have been imposed without a jury trial. Three justices dissented.

Recall Scott v. Illinois, Chapter Five, supra, where the Court held that Scott was not entitled to appointed counsel because he was not imprisoned after his conviction. The offense for which Scott was convicted authorized imprisonment for up to a year. Did Scott have the right to a jury trial? Does it make sense to have a right to jury trial but no right to appointed counsel?

B. WHAT THE JURY DECIDES

One of the decisions that has to be made is what questions of fact should not be given to the jury, but should be reserved to the court. This issue underlies much of the law concerning the use of presumptions, supra.

We have seen that elements of a crime are tried to juries and must be proved beyond a reasonable doubt. The same is true of the elements of some defenses. Other issues, such as those that arise in sentencing (discussed in Chapter Eleven, infra), are tried neither to juries nor under a proof beyond a reasonable doubt requirement. In some jurisdictions, venue is one of these issues. Just as Art. III, Section 3, cl. 3 requires the trial of all crimes to be "in the State where the said Crimes shall have been committed," and the Sixth Amendment gives an accused the right to "an impartial jury of the State and district wherein the crime shall have been committed," state constitutions and laws specify venue provisions. There is enormous confusion in most jurisdictions as to how venue should be handled. One finds many federal cases holding that there need not be direct proof of venue, as long as circumstantial evidence in the record proves proper venue. See, e.g., United States v. Turner, 586 F.2d 395 (5th Cir. 1978). But it is unclear whether proof beyond a reasonable doubt is required and whether the jury is instructed on venue.[27] Other jurisdictions are clear. In some, proof beyond a reasonable doubt to a jury is required. See, e.g., State v. Hamilton, 185 Mont. 522, 605 P.2d 1121 (1980); State v. Hastings, 31 Or.App. 981, 571 P.2d 1284 (1977).[28] In others, venue is not a jury question, see, e.g., State v. Wise, 90 N.M. 659, 567 P.2d 970 (1977), and a venue hearing is held by the court under a preponderance of the evidence standard. See, e.g., State v. Allen, 293 N.W.2d 16 (Iowa 1980); State v. Batdorf, 293 N.C. 486, 238 S.E.2d 497 (1977). Still other jurisdictions require proof beyond a reasonable doubt to a jury, but refuse appellate review on the sufficiency of the evidence once some evidence of venue is presented, no matter how little. See, e.g., State v. Rheams, 352 So.2d 615 (La.1977). One court of appeals discussed a defendant's rights when venue is challenged, United States v. Winship, 724 F.2d 1116 (5th Cir.1984), and found that a defendant can waive his right to challenge venue by silence and that venue requires proof by a preponderance of the evidence. It held, however, that "failure to instruct on venue is reversible error when trial testimony puts venue in question and the defendant requests the instruction," although it found that the testimony had not sufficiently put venue in question to require an instruction in the instant case. What reason is there to send venue questions to a jury? Questions of the

27. Hance v. Zant, 696 F.2d 940 (11th Cir. 1983), found no constitutional problem with a state court's failing to instruct a jury on venue, which Georgia required the government to prove beyond a reasonable doubt. The court said that venue was a jurisdictional element, not an element of the offense, and the state could establish a system which did not require a specific instruction to the jury, especially where the defendant did not contest venue.

28. But the *Hastings* court left open the question whether binding judicial notice of venue would be permissible.

jurisdiction of the court to hear a case are usually questions of law reserved to the judge, unless the legislature includes them as elements of an offense. Should venue be treated differently? In the portion of this chapter devoted to fair-trial, free press issues, you will see that judges rule on change of venue motions. Is there some good reason why the same judges should not rule on challenges to venue? And, unless venue is challenged, shouldn't it be deemed to be proper? See United States v. McDonough, 603 F.2d 19 (7th Cir. 1979) (venue objection waived when not raised in motion for judgment of acquittal); cf. State v. Lemay, 390 A.2d 7 (Me.1978) ("[i]n this case tried by both parties on the assumption that the crime occurred in Maine, the trial court was justified in assuming that it had jurisdiction").

C. REQUISITE FEATURES OF THE JURY

1. Size

WILLIAMS v. FLORIDA

Supreme Court of the United States, 1970.
399 U.S. 78.

MR. JUSTICE WHITE delivered the opinion of the court.

[Petitioner filed a pretrial motion to impanel a 12–person jury instead of the six person jury provided by Florida law in all but capital cases. The motion was denied and petitioner was convicted of robbery and sentenced to life imprisonment. In Part I of the opinion, the Court rejected the petitioner's attack on a state rule requiring notice of an alibi defense.]

II

In Duncan v. Louisiana, we held that the Fourteenth Amendment guarantees a right to trial by jury in all criminal cases that—were they to be tried in a federal court—would come within the Sixth Amendment's guarantee. Petitioner's trial for robbery on July 3, 1968, clearly falls within the scope of that holding. The question in this case then is whether the constitutional guarantee of a trial by "jury" necessarily requires trial by exactly 12 persons, rather than some lesser number—in this case six. We hold that the 12–man panel is not a necessary ingredient of "trial by jury," and that respondent's refusal to impanel more than the six members provided for by Florida law did not violate petitioner's Sixth Amendment rights as applied to the States through the Fourteenth.

We had occasion in Duncan v. Louisiana to review briefly the oft-told history of the development of trial by jury in criminal cases. That history revealed a long tradition attaching great importance to the concept of relying on a body of one's peers to determine guilt or innocence as a safeguard against arbitrary law enforcement. That same history, however, affords little insight into the considerations that gradually led the size of that body to be generally fixed at 12. Some have suggested that the number 12 was fixed upon simply because that was the number of the presentment jury from the hundred, from which the petit jury developed. Other, less circular but more fanciful reasons for the number 12 have been given, "but they were all brought forward after the number was fixed," and rest on little more than mystical or superstitious insights into the significance of "12." Lord Coke's explanation that the "*number of twelve* is much respected *in holy writ,* as 12 *apostles,* 12 *stones,* 12 *tribes, etc.,*" is typical. In short, while sometime in the 14th century the size of the jury at common law came to be fixed generally at 12, that particular feature of the jury system appears to have been a historical accident, unrelated to the great purposes which gave rise to the jury in the first place. The question before us is whether this accidental feature of the jury has been immutably codified into our Constitution.

* * *

While "the intent of the Framers" is often an elusive quarry, the relevant constitutional history casts considerable doubt on the easy assumption in our past decisions that if a given feature existed in a jury at common law in 1789, then it was necessarily preserved in the Constitution. Provisions for jury trial were first placed in the Constitution in Article III's provision that "[t]he Trial of all Crimes * * * shall be by Jury; and such Trial shall be held in the State where the said Crimes shall have been committed." The "very scanty history [of this provision] in the records of the Constitutional Convention" sheds little light either way on the intended correlation between Article III's "jury" and the features of the jury at common law. Indeed, pending and after the adoption of the Constitution, fears were expressed that Article III's provision failed to preserve the common-law right to be tried by a "jury of the vicinage." That concern, as well as the concern to preserve the right to jury in civil as well as criminal cases, furnished part of the impetus for introducing amendments to the Constitution that ultimately resulted in the jury trial provisions of the Sixth and Seventh Amendments. As introduced by James Madison in the House, the Amendment relating to jury trial in criminal cases would have provided that:

> "The trial of all crimes * * * shall be by an impartial jury of freeholders of the vicinage, with the requisite of unanimity for conviction, of the right of challenge, and other accustomed requisites * * *."

The Amendment passed the House in substantially this form, but after more than a week of debate in the Senate it returned to the House considerably altered. * * * [The Court discusses more history, including appointment of a Conference committee.] The version that finally emerged from the Committee was the version that ultimately became the Sixth Amendment, ensuring an accused:

> "the right to a speedy and public trial, by an impartial jury of the State and district wherein the crime shall have been committed, which district shall have been previously ascertained by law * * *."

Gone were the provisions spelling out such common-law features of the jury as "unanimity," or "the accustomed requisites." And the "vicinage" requirement itself had been replaced by wording that reflected a compromise between broad and narrow definitions of that term, and that left Congress the power to determine the actual size of the "vicinage" by its creation of judicial districts.

Three significant features may be observed in this sketch of the background of the Constitution's jury trial provisions. First, even though the vicinage requirement was as much a feature of the common-law jury as was the 12-man requirement, the mere reference to "trial by jury" in Article III was not interpreted to include that feature. * * * Second, provisions that would have explicitly tied the "jury" concept to the "accustomed requisites" of the time were eliminated. * * * Finally, contemporary legislative and constitutional provisions indicate that where Congress wanted to leave no doubt that it was incorporating existing common-law features of the jury system, it knew how to use express language to that effect. Thus, the Judiciary bill, signed by the President on the same day that the House and Senate finally agreed on the form of the Amendments to be submitted to the States, provided in certain cases for the narrower "vicinage" requirements that the House had wanted to include in the Amendments. And the Seventh Amendment, providing for jury trial in civil cases, explicitly added that "no fact tried by a jury, shall be otherwise re-examined in any Court of the United States, than according to the rules of the common law."

We do not pretend to be able to divine precisely what the word "jury" imported to the Framers, the First Congress, or the States in 1789. It may well be that the usual expectation was that the jury would consist of 12, and that hence, the most likely conclusion to be drawn is simply that little thought was actually given to the specific question we face today. But there is absolutely no indication in "the intent of the Framers" of an explicit decision to equate the constitutional and common-law characteristics of the jury. Nothing in this history suggests, then, that we do violence to the letter of the Constitution by turning to other than purely historical considerations to determine which features of the jury system, as it existed at common law, were preserved in the Constitution. The relevant inquiry, as we see it, must be the function that the particular feature performs and its relation to the purposes of the jury trial. Measured by this standard, the 12–man requirement cannot be regarded as an indispensable component of the Sixth Amendment.

The purpose of the jury trial, as we noted in *Duncan,* is to prevent oppression by the Government. * * * Given this purpose, the essential feature of a jury obviously lies in the interposition between the accused and his accuser of the commonsense judgment of a group of laymen, and in the community participation and shared responsibility that results from that group's determination of guilt or innocence. The performance of this role is not a function of the particular number of the body that makes up the jury. To be sure, the number should probably be large enough to promote group deliberation, free from outside attempts at intimidation, and to provide a fair possibility for obtaining a representative cross-section of the community. But we find little reason to think that these goals are in any meaningful sense less likely to be achieved when the jury numbers six, then when it numbers 12—particularly if the requirement of unanimity is retained. And, certainly the reliability of the jury as a factfinder hardly seems likely to be a function of its size.

It might be suggested that the 12–man jury gives a defendant a greater advantage since he has more "chances" of finding a juror who will insist on acquittal and thus prevent conviction. But the advantage might just as easily belong to the State which also needs only one juror out of twelve insisting on guilt to prevent acquittal. What few experiments have occurred—usually in the civil area—indicate that there is no discernible difference between the results reached by the two different-sized juries. In short, neither currently available evidence nor theory suggests that the 12-man jury is necessarily more advantageous to the defendant than a jury composed of fewer members.

Similarly, while in theory the number of viewpoints represented on a randomly selected jury ought to increase as the size of the jury increases, in practice the difference between the 12–man and the six-man jury in terms of the cross-section of the community represented seems likely to be negligible. Even the

12-man jury cannot insure representation of every distinct voice in the community, particularly given the use of the peremptory challenge. * * *

* * *

MR. JUSTICE HARLAN, concurring in the result.

[Justice Harlan reiterated his concern that incorporation of the Sixth Amendment dilutes federal guarantees in order to reconcile the logic of "incorporation," the "jot-for-jot and case-for-case" application of the federal right to the states, with the reality of federalism.]

[The Chief Justice concurred. Mr. Justice Black and Mr. Justice Douglas concurred in part and dissented in part. Mr. Justice Marshall dissented in part. Mr. Justice Stewart concurred in the result. Mr. Justice Blackmun took no part in the decision of the case.]

In Ballew v. Georgia, the Court reaffirmed *Williams,* yet held that a six person jury is the absolute minimum jury size.

BALLEW v. GEORGIA

Supreme Court of the United States, 1978.
435 U.S. 223.

MR. JUSTICE BLACKMUN announced the judgment of the court and delivered an opinion in which MR. JUSTICE STEVENS joined.

[Petitioner was convicted on two-misdemeanor counts of distributing obscene material by a five person jury impaneled according to Georgia law. The opinion recites the facts and describes *Williams*].

* * *

III

When the Court in *Williams* permitted the reduction in jury size—or, to put it another way, when it held that a jury of six was not unconstitutional—it expressly reserved ruling on the issue whether a number smaller than six passed constitutional scrutiny. The Court refused to speculate when this so-called "slippery slope" would become too steep. We face now, however, the two-fold question whether a further reduction in the size of the state criminal trial jury does make the grade too dangerous, that is, whether it inhibits the functioning of the jury as an institution to a significant degree, and, if so, whether any state interest counterbalances and justifies the disruption so as to preserve its constitutionality.

Williams v. Florida * * * generated a quantity of scholarly work on jury size.[a] These writings do not draw or

a. E.g., M. Saks, Jury Verdicts (1977) (hereinafter cited as Saks); Bogue & Fritz, The Six-Man Jury, 17 S.D.L.Rev. 285 (1972); Davis Kerr, Atkin, Holt & Mech, The Decision Processes of 6- and 12-Person Mock Juries Assigned Unanimous and Two-Thirds Majority Rules, 32 J. of Personality & Soc. Psych. 1 (1975); Diamond, A Jury Experiment Reanalyzed, 7 U.Mich.J.L. Reform 520 (1974); Friedman, Trial by Jury: Criteria for Convictions, Jury Size and Type I and Type II Errors, 26-2 Am.Stat. 21 (April 1972); Institute of Judicial Administration, A Comparison of Six- and Twelve-Member Civil Juries in New Jersey Superior and County Courts (1972); Lempert, Uncovering "Nondiscernible" Differences: Empirical Research and the Jury-Size Cases, 73 Mich.L.Rev. 643 (1975); Nagel & Neef, Deductive Modeling to Determine an Optimum Jury Size and Fraction Required to Convict, 1975 Wash.U.L.Q. 933 (hereinafter cited as Nagel & Neef); Pabst, Statistical Studies of the Cost of Six-Man versus Twelve-Man Juries, 14 Wm. & Mary L.Rev. 326 (1972); Zeisel, * * * And Then There Were None: The Diminution of the Federal Jury, 38 U.Chi.L.Rev. 710 (1971); Zeisel, The Waning of the American Jury, 58 A.B.A.J. 367 (1972); Zeisel & Diamond, "Convincing Empirical Evidence" on the Six Member Jury, 41 U.Chi.Rev. 281 (1974); Note, Six-Member and Twelve-Mem-

identify a bright line below which the number of jurors would not be able to function as required by the standards enunciated in *Williams.* On the other hand, they raise significant questions about the wisdom and constitutionality of a reduction below six. We examine these concerns:

First, recent empirical data suggest that progressively smaller juries are less likely to foster effective group deliberation. At some point, this decline leads to inaccurate fact-finding and incorrect application of the common sense of the community to the facts. Generally, a positive correlation exists between group size and the quality of both group performance and group productivity. A variety of explanations have been offered for this conclusion. Several are particularly applicable in the jury setting. The smaller the group, the less likely are members to make critical contributions necessary for the solution of a given problem. Because most juries are not permitted to take notes, memory is important for accurate jury deliberations. As juries decrease in size, then, they are less likely to have members who remember each of the important pieces of evidence or argument. Furthermore, the smaller the group, the less likely it is to overcome the biases of its members to obtain an accurate result. When individual and group decisionmaking were compared, it was seen that groups performed better because prejudices of individuals were frequently counterbalanced, and objectivity resulted. Groups also exhibited increased motivation and self-criticism. All of these advantages, except, perhaps, self-motivation, tend to diminish as the size of the group diminishes. Because juries frequently face complex problems laden with value choices, the benefits are important and should be retained. In particular, the counterbalancing of various biases is critical to the accurate application of the common sense of the community to the facts of any given case.

Second, the data now raise doubts about the accuracy of the results achieved by smaller and smaller panels. Statistical studies suggest that the risk of convicting an innocent person rises as the size of the jury diminishes * * *. [The studies posit that by considering the risk of not convicting a guilty party, an optimal jury size between six and eight is identified.] As the size diminished to five and below, the weighted sum of errors increased because of the enlarging risk of the conviction of innocent defendants.

Another doubt about progressively smaller juries arises from the increasing inconsistency that results from the decreases. [Several studies suggest that 12-person panels considering the same case will reach the same result, or compromise to the same result, with greater consistency than a six person panel.]

Third, the data suggest that the verdicts of jury deliberation in criminal cases will vary as juries become smaller, and that the variance amounts to an imbalance to the detriment of one side, the defense. [The Court noted that hung juries will diminish because a person in the minority is less likely to have an ally on the six-person panel, and thus is less likely to speak up.]

ber Juries: An Empirical Study of Trial Results, 6 U.Mich.J.L.Ref. 671 (1973); Note, An Empirical Study of Six- and Twelve-Member Jury Decision-Making Processes, 6 U.Mich. J.L.Ref. 712 (1973).

We have considered them carefully because they provide the only basis, besides judicial hunch, for a decision about whether smaller and smaller juries will be able to fulfill the purpose and functions of the Sixth Amendment. Without an examination about how juries and small groups actually work, we would not understand the basis for the conclusion of Mr. Justice Powell that "a line has to be drawn somewhere."

Fourth, what has just been said about the presence of minority viewpoint as juries decrease in size foretells problems not only for jury decisionmaking, but also for the representation of minority groups in the community. * * * [The Court commented that meaningful and appropriate representation decreases with a decrease in jury size.] Further reduction in size will erect additional barriers to representation.

Fifth, several authors have identified in jury research methodological problems tending to mask differences in the operation of smaller and larger juries. [Several commentators have explained that although differences in jury verdicts as a function of size may be hard to identify, the fact that differences do exist in even a small percentage of cases is important in evaluating the operation of the jury system.] Nationwide, however, these small percentages will represent a large number of cases. And it is with respect to those cases that the jury trial right has its greatest value. When the case is close, and the guilt or innocence of the defendant is not readily apparent, a properly functioning jury system will insure evaluation by the sense of the community and will also tend to insure accurate factfinding. * * *

IV

While we adhere to, and reaffirm our holding in Williams v. Florida, these studies, most of which have been made since *Williams* was decided in 1970, lead us to conclude that the purpose and functioning of the jury in a criminal trial is seriously impaired, and to a constitutional degree, by a reduction in size to below six members. We readily admit that we do not pretend to discern a clear line between six members and five. But the assembled data raise substantial doubt about the reliability and appropriate representation of panels smaller than six. Because of the fundamental importance of the jury trial to the American system of criminal justice, any further reduction that promotes inaccurate and possibly biased decisionmaking, that causes untoward differences in verdicts, and that prevents juries from truly representing their communities, attains constitutional significance.

* * *

V

* * * We find no significant state advantage in reducing the number of jurors from six to five. * * *

[The concurring opinion of Justice Stevens is omitted.]

MR. JUSTICE WHITE concurring in the judgment.

Agreeing that a jury of fewer than six persons would fail to represent the sense of the community and hence not satisfy the fair cross-section requirement of the Sixth and Fourteenth Amendments, I concur in the judgment of reversal.

MR. JUSTICE POWELL, with whom THE CHIEF JUSTICE and MR. JUSTICE REHNQUIST join, concurring in the judgment.

I concur in the judgment, as I agree that use of a jury as small as five members, with authority to convict for serious offenses, involves grave questions of fairness. As the opinion of Mr. Justice Blackmun indicates, the line between five- and six-member juries is difficult to justify, but a line has to be drawn somewhere if the substance of jury trial is to be preserved.

I do not agree, however,that every feature of jury trial practice must be the same in both federal and state courts. * * * Also, I have reservations as to the wisdom—as well as the necessity—of Mr. Justice Blackmun's heavy reliance on numerology derived from statistical studies. Moreover, neither the validity nor the methodology employed by the studies cited was subjected to the traditional testing mechanisms of the adversary process. The studies relied on merely represent unexamined findings of persons interested in the jury system.

For these reasons I concur only in the judgment.

MR. JUSTICE BRENNAN, with whom MR. JUSTICE STEWART and MR. JUSTICE MARSHALL join.

I join Mr. Justice Blackmun's opinion insofar as it holds that the Sixth and Fourteenth Amendments require juries in criminal trials to contain more than five persons. * * *

2. *Unanimity*

In the companion cases of Johnson v. Louisiana and Apodaca v. Oregon, the Court considered the unanimity feature of the jury. In *Johnson,* the non-retroactivity of *Duncan's* incorporation of the Sixth Amendment to a pre-*Duncan* trial caused the petitioner to challenge the validity of a less than unanimous jury verdict (9 to 3) under the due process and equal protection clauses of the Fourteenth Amendment. Mr. Justice White delivered the opinion of the Court and rejected petitioner's challenge, holding that unanimity is not essential to the required finding of guilt beyond a reasonable doubt, and that a state provision requiring unanimous verdicts in some cases and non-unanimous verdicts in others is not an invidious classification prohibited by the equal protection clause. The court's reasoning is set forth in the *Apodaca* case, which analyzed the right to jury trial in a post-*Duncan* proceeding.

APODACA v. OREGON

Supreme Court of the United States, 1972.
406 U.S. 404.

MR. JUSTICE WHITE announced the judgment of the Court and an opinion in which THE CHIEF JUSTICE, MR. JUSTICE BLACKMUN and MR. JUSTICE REHNQUIST joined.

[The three petitioners were convicted of various criminal charges by three separate, less than unanimous Oregon juries. Two juries returned 11–1 votes, the third returned the minimum 10–2 verdict.]

In Williams v. Florida, 399 U.S. 78 (1970), we had occasion to consider a related issue: whether the Sixth Amendment's right to trial by jury requires that all juries consist of 12 men. After considering the history of the 12-man requirement and the functions it performs in contemporary society, we concluded that it was not of constitutional stature. We reach the same conclusion today with regard to the requirement of unanimity.

I

* * *

As we observed in *Williams,*, one can draw conflicting inferences from this legislative history. One possible inference is that Congress eliminated references to unanimity and to the other "accustomed requisites" of the jury because those requisites were thought already to be implicit in the very concept of jury. A contrary explanation, which we found in *Williams* to be the more plausible, is that the deletion was intended to have some substantive effect. Surely one fact that is absolutely clear from this history is that, after a proposal had been made to specify precisely which of the common-law requisites of the jury were to be preserved by the Constitution, the Framers explicitly rejected the proposal and instead left such specification to the future. As in *Williams,* we must accordingly consider what is meant by the concept "jury" and determine whether a feature commonly associated with it is constitutionally required. And, as in *Williams,* our inability to divine "the intent of the Framers" when they eliminated references to the "accustomed requisites" requires that in determining what is meant by a jury we must turn to other than purely historical considerations.

II

Our inquiry must focus upon the function served by the jury in contemporary society. As we said in *Duncan,* the purpose of trial by jury is to prevent oppression by the Government by providing a "safeguard against the corrupt or overzealous prosecutor and against the compliant, biased, or eccentric judge." "Given this purpose, the essential feature of a jury obviously lies in the interposition between the accused and his accuser of the commonsense judgment of a group of laymen * * *." A requirement of unanimity, however, does not materially contribute to the exercise of this commonsense judgment. As we said in *Williams,* a jury will come to such a judgment as long as it consists of a group of laymen representative of a cross section of the community who have the duty and the opportunity to deliberate, free from outside attempts at intimidation, on the question of a defendant's guilt. In terms of this function we perceive no difference between juries required to act unanimously and those permitted to convict or acquit by votes of 10 to two or 11 to one. Requiring unanimity would obviously produce hung juries in some situations where nonunanimous juries will convict or acquit. But in either case, the interest of the defendant in having the judgment of his peers interposed between himself and the officers of the State who prosecute and judge him is equally well served.

III

Petitioners nevertheless argue that unanimity serves other purposes constitutionally essential to the continued operation of the jury system. Their principal contention is that a Sixth Amendment "jury trial" made mandatory on the States by virtue of the Due Process Clause of the Fourteenth Amendment, should be held to require a unanimous jury verdict in order to give substance to the reasonable-doubt standard otherwise mandated by the Due Process Clause.

We are quite sure, however, that the Sixth Amendment itself has never been held to require proof beyond a reasonable doubt in criminal cases. The reasonable-doubt standard developed separately from both the jury trial and the unanimous verdict. As the Court noted in the *Winship* case, the rule requiring proof of crime beyond a reasonable doubt did not crystallize in this country until after the Constitution was adopted. And in that case, which held such a burden of proof to be constitutionally required, the Court purported to draw no support from the Sixth Amendment.

Petitioners' argument that the Sixth Amendment requires jury unanimity in order to give effect to the reasonable-doubt standard thus founders on the fact that the Sixth Amendment does not require proof beyond a reasonable doubt at all. * * *

IV

Petitioners also cite quite accurately a long line of decisions of this Court upholding the principle that the Fourteenth Amendment requires jury panels to reflect a cross section of the community. They then contend that unanimity is a necessary precondition for effective application of the cross-section requirement, because a rule permitting less than unanimous verdicts will make it possible for convictions to occur without the acquiescence of minority elements within the community.

There are two flaws in this argument. One is petitioners' assumption that every distinct voice in the community has a right to be represented on every jury and a right to prevent conviction of a defendant in any case. All that the Constitution forbids, however, is systematic exclusion of identifiable segments of the community from jury panels * * *.

We also cannot accept petitioners' second assumption—that minority groups, even when they are represented on a jury, will not adequately represent the viewpoint of those groups simply because they may be outvoted in the final result. They will be present during all deliberations, and their views will be heard. We cannot assume that the majority of the jury will refuse to weigh the evidence and reach a decision upon rational grounds, just as it must now do in order to obtain unanimous verdicts, or that a majority will deprive a man of his liberty on the basis of prejudice when a minority is presenting a reasonable argument in favor of acquittal. We simply find no proof for the notion that a majority will disregard its instructions and cast its votes for guilt or innocence based on prejudice rather than the evidence.

* * *

MR. JUSTICE POWELL, concurring in the judgment.

[Mr. Justice Powell, subscribing to the views of Mr. Justice Harlan, rejected the theory that all elements of the jury trial within the meaning of the Sixth Amendment are incorporated into the due process clause of the Fourteenth Amendment and applied against the states. He thus joined the plurality in holding that unanimity is not required in state trials, thus permitting state deviation from the federal blueprint in order to advance valuable jury trial innovations.] [29]

MR. JUSTICE DOUGLAS, with whom MR. JUSTICE BRENNAN and MR. JUSTICE MARSHALL concur, dissenting.

[Dissent applies to both *Johnson* and *Apodaca*]

* * * With due respect to the majority, I dissent from this radical departure from American traditions.

I

The Constitution does not mention unanimous juries. Neither does it mention the presumption of innocence, nor does it say that guilt must be proved beyond a reasonable doubt in all criminal cases. Yet it is almost inconceivable that anyone would have questioned whether proof beyond a reasonable doubt was in fact the constitutional standard. * * *

* * *

I had similarly assumed that there was no dispute that the Federal Constitution required a unanimous jury in all criminal cases. * * * Like proof beyond a reasonable doubt, the issue of unanimous juries in criminal cases simply never arose. Yet in cases dealing with juries it had always been assumed that a unanimous jury was required. Today

29. Note the split of the Court in *Apodaca.* Eight Justices agreed that the Fourteenth Amendment incorporated all aspects of the Sixth Amendment jury trial right. Justice Powell alone advanced the theory of a different conception of jury trials for federal and state courts. Five Justices (the dissenters and Justice Powell) agreed that the Sixth Amendment requires unanimity. So why didn't Apodaca win? Most state courts still require unanimity. *Johnson* and *Apodaca* have caused few states to change pre-existing practice.

the bases of those cases are discarded and two centuries of American history are shunted aside.

* * *

II

The plurality approves a procedure which diminishes the reliability of a jury. * * *

The diminution of verdict reliability flows from the fact that nonunanimous juries need not debate and deliberate as fully as must unanimous juries. As soon as the requisite majority is attained, further consideration is not required either by Oregon or by Louisiana even though the dissident jurors might, if given the chance, be able to convince the majority. Such persuasion does in fact occasionally occur in States where the unanimous requirement applies: "In roughly one case in ten, the minority eventually succeeds in reversing an initial majority, and these may be cases of special importance."[a] * * * The Court now extracts from the jury room this automatic check against hasty factfinding by relieving jurors of the duty to hear out fully the dissenters.

It is said that there is no evidence that majority jurors will refuse to listen to dissenters whose votes are unneeded for conviction. Yet human experience teaches that polite and academic conversation is no substitute for the earnest and robust argument necessary to reach unanimity. * * * [I]n Apodaca's case, whatever courtesy dialogue transpired could not have lasted more than 41 minutes. I fail to understand why the Court should lift from the States the burden of justifying so radical a departure from an accepted and applauded tradition and instead demand that these defendants document with empirical evidence what has always been thought to be too obvious for further study.

To be sure, in Williams v. Florida, we held that a State could provide a jury less than 12 in number in a criminal trial. We said: "What few experiments have occurred—usually in the civil area—indicate that there is no discernible difference between the results reached by the two different-sized juries. In short, neither currently available evidence nor theory suggests that the 12-man jury is necessarily more advantageous to the defendant than a jury composed of fewer members."

That rationale of *Williams* can have no application here. *Williams* requires that the change be neither more nor less advantageous to either the State or the defendant. It is said that such a showing is satisfied here since a 3:9 (Louisiana) or 2:10 (Oregon) verdict will result in acquittal. Yet experience shows that the less-than-unanimous jury overwhelmingly favors the States.

Moreover, even where an initial majority wins the dissent over to its side, the ultimate result in unanimous-jury States may nonetheless reflect the reservations of uncertain jurors. I refer to many compromise verdicts on lesser-included offenses and lesser sentences. Thus, even though a minority may not be forceful enough to carry the day, their doubts may nonetheless cause a majority to exercise caution. Obviously, however, in Oregon and Louisiana, dissident jurors will not have the opportunity through full deliberation to temper the opposing faction's degree of certainty of guilt.

It is my belief that a unanimous jury is necessary if the great barricade known as proof beyond a reasonable doubt is to be maintained. This is not to equate proof beyond a reasonable doubt with the requirement of a unanimous jury. That would be analytically

a. H. Kalven & H. Zeisel, The American Jury 490 (1966). See also The American Jury: Notes For an English Controversy, 48 Chi. B.Rec. 195 (1967).

fallacious since a deadlocked jury does not bar, as double jeopardy, retrial for the same offense. Nevertheless, one is necessary for a proper effectuation of the other. * * *

Suppose a jury begins with a substantial minority but then in the process of deliberation a sufficient number changes to reach the required 9:3 or 10:2 for a verdict. Is not there still a lingering doubt about that verdict? Is it not clear that the safeguard of unanimity operates in this context to make it far more likely that guilt is established beyond a reasonable doubt?

* * *

[Justice Blackmun filed a concurring opinion. Justices Brennan, Stewart and Marshall filed dissenting opinions.]

Note

Go back to *Duncan* and examine the reasons that the Court gave for holding that the right to jury trial is fundamental and binding on the states. Do these reasons suggest that the Court should be more concerned with the punishment that triggers the right or with the manner in which the jury is selected? If protection against eccentric or biased judges and vindictive prosecutions underlies the right, what would common sense tell you about the likelihood that a six person, as opposed to a twelve person jury, would provide such protection? If a 9-3 verdict is acceptable, can you think of any good reason why a 7-5 verdict would not be acceptable? Do you think that conviction or acquittal by a divided jury is consistent with the values that make the jury trial right fundamental? If a state provided a five person jury but required unanimity, are you as sure as the *Ballew* Court that this would have been worse than a 9-3 verdict? If the intent of the framers in 1791 is still valid today and binds not only the federal government but the states as well, shouldn't twelve person juries and unanimity be viewed as parts of what the framers thought the concept of jury trial was all about? In *Ballew* the Court relied on a series of jury studies and statistics gathered therein. Do you think that the arguments recited by the Court justify a requirement of a jury of six rather than five? What about a reduction in size from twelve to six? It is one thing to use statistics to justify a departure from tradition. But in *Williams* and *Johnson-Apodaca* the Court had little statistical evidence available to bolster its decisions; rather, it chose to discount the social science evidence that might have cast doubt on the decisions. When no clear case for a break with tradition is made, should the usual elements associated with a fundamental right be subject to modification on the basis of unsupported conjecture? Indeed, absent contrary evidence, should tradition be regarded as the best guide to the intent of the framers? See Justice Scalia's concurring opinion in Schad v. Arizona, supra this Chapter.

One of the strongest arguments against unanimous verdicts is that it forces compromises. For example, if ten jurors decide a defendant is guilty of first degree murder and two believe that the defendant is innocent, the jury might compromise on second degree murder as an alternative to continued deliberation. Critics of unanimity argue that such compromise is acceptable in ordinary political life, but not in litigation.[30] Do you find this criticism persuasive? If so, re-examine what happens when a 9-3 or 10-2 jury verdict is accepted. Does the absence of a unanimity requirement promote deliberation? It does remove the need for some compromises. But is a compromise by a jury that follows the instructions of a court (requiring each juror to support the verdict) an evil? Is it arguable that any

30. For an argument against unanimity premised on political theory, see Jacobson, The Unanimous Verdict: Politics and the Jury Trial, 1977 Wash.U.L.Q. 39.

compromise by a unanimous jury is a final agreement by all jurors on a just verdict?

In federal courts and in most state courts, jurors have to be unanimous, but it is sometimes difficult to determine what they have to be unanimous about. For example, if two findings could each lead to the same guilty verdict, must the jury be unanimous about at least one of the findings, or only about the ultimate conclusion that the defendant is guilty? In Schad v. Arizona, 111 S.Ct. 2491 (1991), defendant was tried for murder under separate theories of felony murder and premeditated murder. The jury returned a general verdict of guilty. Schad argued that there was no showing that the jury had unanimously agreed that he had committed felony murder, nor could it be determined that they were unanimous about premeditated murder. The Court reasoned that Schad's argument was really addressed to whether the state could permissibly characterize several alternative actions and mental states as a single crime. The Court stated that the issue "is one of the permissible limits in defining criminal conduct, * * * not one of jury unanimity." The Court held that Arizona did not violate defendant's due process rights by grouping felony murder and premeditated murder as two alternative means of committing the single crime of first-degree murder.

Suppose that a court gave a twelve-person jury a special verdict form and six jurors agreed that a defendant was guilty of premeditation but not of felony murder, while the other six agreed that the defendant was guilty of felony murder but not of premeditation. Could the court add six votes on one theory with six votes on the other to find that the jury had found the defendant guilty? A general verdict form permits a jury to aggregate votes in just this way. At what point must a jury agree on basic elements before finding a defendant guilty? Which elements are basic? See Viveros v. State, 606 P.2d 790 (Alaska 1980) (court reverses where it is uncertain whether jury agreed on one finding).

In United States v. Holley, 942 F.2d 916 (5th Cir.1991), the defendant was tried on a perjury count which set forth several statements, each alleged to be perjurious. The jury was not instructed that it had to unanimously agree that at least one particular statement in the count was perjurious. A general verdict of guilty was returned. The court of appeals reversed the conviction on the ground that the defendant had been deprived of his right to a unanimous verdict: each juror found that the defendant had committed perjury, but there was no indication that they had all agreed that any particular statement was an act of perjury. The court distinguished *Schad* as a case in which the jury was allowed to choose among alternative means of committing a crime, whereas the prosecution in *Holley* sought to group several different acts in a single count; in *Schad* it could at least be said that the jury was unanimous that defendant, when he acted on a certain occasion, was committing a crime. Is the court in *Holley* relying on the distinction between *actus reus* and *mens rea*? Why should that distinction make a difference in terms of unanimity?

3. *The Interplay Between Size and Unanimity*

The interplay between the constitutionally sufficient six person jury, and the issue of unanimity was delineated in Burch v. Louisiana, 441 U.S. 130 (1979). In an opinion by Justice Rehnquist, the Court held that "conviction by a nonunanimous six-person jury in a state criminal trial for a nonpetty offense deprives an accused of his constitutional right to trial by jury." The Court conceded that drawing lines was difficult, but found it essential. It concluded that use of nonunanimous six-person juries threatened the substance of the right to jury trial. There were no dissents.

In *Burch,* Justice Rehnquist stated that the "near-uniform judgment of the Nation," as reflected by the fact that only two states permitted non-unanimous verdicts by a six-person jury, "provides a useful guide in delimiting the line between those jury practices that are constitutionally permissible and those that are not." But when *Apodaca* was decided, the vast majority of states used unanimous verdicts. How, then, did *Apodaca* get decided the way it did?

D. JURY SELECTION AND COMPOSITION

1. *The Jury Pool*

The Sixth Amendment assures the defendant "an impartial jury of the State and district wherein the crime shall have been committed." This language, with its emphasis on both the impartial and community character of the jury, has served as a touchstone in the regulation of the pool from which the petit jury is drawn.

In Glasser v. United States, 315 U.S. 60, 85–86 (1942), the Court observed as follows:

> [The jury selection process] must always accord with the fact that the proper functioning of the jury system, and, indeed, our democracy itself, requires that the jury be a "body truly representative of the community," and not the organ of any special group or class. If that requirement is observed, the officials charged with choosing federal jurors may exercise some discretion to the end that competent jurors may be called. But they must not allow the desire for competent jurors to lead them into selections which do not comport with the concept of the jury as a cross-section of the community.

Thus, the selection of the jury panel must be unbiased and indiscriminate; it must generate a panel representing a cross-section of the community. Additionally, each individual juror must be impartial, unbiased and free from outside influences.

2. *The Cross-Section Requirement*

The concept of an unbiased selection of a cross-section of the community initially developed under the rubric of the Fourteenth Amendment in response to race-related challenges. In Strauder v. West Virginia, 100 U.S. 303 (1879), the Court struck down a West Virginia state statute that excluded blacks from grand and petit jury service as violative of the Fourteenth Amendment's equal protection clause. Importantly, the *Strauder* Court noted that more than race was at issue:

> [T]he constitution of juries is a very essential part of the protection such a mode of trial is intended to secure. The very idea of a jury is a body of men composed of the peers or equals of the person whose rights it is selected or summoned to determine; that is, of his neighbors, fellows, associates, persons having the same legal status in society as that which he holds.

In subsequent challenges to state systems that were administered so as to preclude blacks from jury service, the Court ruled that a system which provides the opportunity to discriminate, and that generates a low number of participating blacks (evidencing discrimination) is invalid. See, e.g., Smith v. Texas, 311 U.S. 128 (1940) (grand jury lists of sixteen people were drawn by 3–5 jury commissioners; few blacks served as jurors.)

Other race-related challenges led to the development of a set of rules summarized by the Court in Akins v. Texas, 325 U.S. 398, 403 (1945):

> Defendants under our criminal statutes are not entitled to demand representatives of their racial inheritance upon juries before whom they are tried. But such defendants are entitled to require that those who are trusted with jury selection shall not pursue a course of conduct which results in discrimination "in the selection of jurors on racial grounds." Our directions that indictments be quashed when Negroes, although numerous in the community, were excluded from grand jury lists have been based on the theory that their continual exclusion indicated discrimination and not on the theory that racial groups must be recognized.

The Court first recognized the impact of the exclusion of a non-race-related class in a civil case, Thiel v. Southern Pacific Co., 328 U.S. 217 (1946). The Court held that the deliberate and intentional exclusion of daily wage earners from a federal court jury panel impermissibly violated the jury cross-section requirement. In *Thiel,* the jury commissioner and clerk used a city directory to identify and exclude daily wage earners from a federal court jury panel. The Court ruled that although a judge may exclude a person from jury service when participation entails a financial hardship, complete exclusion in the absence of such a finding is forbidden by its power of supervision over lower federal courts.

In the same year, the Court ruled in Ballard v. United States, 329 U.S. 187 (1946), that women constitute a cognizable class which could not be intentionally and systematically excluded from federal jury service in a state in which women were eligible for jury service.[31] The Court again relied upon its supervisory authority to prohibit the exclusion.

It was not until the 1954 case of Hernandez v. Texas, 347 U.S. 475 (1954), where the Court prohibited a state's selection of jurors on ethnic grounds, that the Court cited constitutional authority to strike down a selection process that discriminated on a non-racial basis.

In recognizing the existence of cognizable classes other than race, the Court has been careful to delineate the scope of the defendant's challenge. Both *Thiel* and *Ballard* noted that a defendant has no standing to challenge a particular jury as failing to represent all social, economic and political groups, but is restricted to challenging the selection procedure as systematically excluding a cognizable group. That is, the fair cross-section requirement is applicable to the jury pool, but not to the ultimate petit jury that hears the defendant's case. This was confirmed in Holland v. Illinois, 493 U.S. 474 (1990), where a five-person majority explicitly held that the fair cross-section requirement does not apply to the petit jury. Consequently, the Sixth Amendment did not protect the defendant, who was white, from the prosecutor's discriminatory use of peremptory challenges to exclude African-Americans

31. Congress provided that jurors in a federal court shall have the same qualifications as those of the highest court of law in the State. California, the state at issue in *Ballard,* included women on its juries.

from the petit jury. Justice Scalia wrote the majority opinion. He contended that the fair cross-section requirement guarantees only that

> in the process of selecting the petit jury the prosecution and defense will compete on an equal basis. But to say that the Sixth Amendment deprives the State of the ability to 'stack the deck' in its favor is not to say that each side may not, once a fair hand is dealt, use peremptory challenges to eliminate prospective jurors belonging to groups it believes would unduly favor the other side.

Justice Scalia also stressed two practical problems in applying the fair cross-section requirement to the petit jury. First, it would lead to the curtailment if not elimination of the "venerable" practice of peremptory challenges. Second, it would be all but impossible to form a petit jury that mirrored the community. The impact of *Holland* has been severely curtailed, however, by the Court's use of the equal protection clause to limit the exercise of peremptory challenges. See Batson v. Kentucky, page 928, infra.

The Court's initial interpretation of the meaning of "exclusion" was quite narrow. In Hoyt v. Florida, 368 U.S. 57 (1961), the Court held that a state statute providing that no woman shall be taken for jury service unless she volunteers did not violate the Fourteenth Amendment. The Court reasoned that the statute created an exemption, not an exclusion, and thereby complied with the equal protection clause.

But, over the years the Court became more vigorous in demanding that classes of people not be excluded from the selection process. The Court made it clear that exclusion was a sufficient evil that any defendant victimized by unconstitutional exclusion of classes of jurors could challenge the jury. In Peters v. Kiff, 407 U.S. 493 (1972), for example, the Court held that a defendant, irrespective of his own race, may challenge the systematic exclusion of a racial group from the jury process. The Court ruled that such an exclusion is a denial of due process.

After *Peters,* the Court indicated that it is insufficient for the government to be satisfied with a selection process that does not exclude classes of citizens from participation, but that treats some classes more favorably than others; the government may have to promote inclusion of all citizens to foster the idea of a cross-section of the community.

TAYLOR v. LOUISIANA

Supreme Court of the United States, 1975.
419 U.S. 522.

MR. JUSTICE WHITE delivered the opinion of the Court.

[The Louisiana Code provided that a woman should not be selected for jury service unless she had previously filed a written declaration of her desire to be subject to jury service. Appellant, a male, alleged that the statute violated his Sixth and Fourteenth Amendment right to an impartial jury trial. The Court related the facts of the case—i.e., Taylor was convicted of aggravated kidnapping and sentenced to death, although the death sentence was subsequently annulled on the ground that the state's death penalty statute was unconstitutional.]

II

The Louisiana jury-selection system does not disqualify women from jury service, but in operation its conceded systematic impact is that only a very few women, grossly disproportionate to the number of eligible women in the community, are called for jury service. In this case, no women were on the venire from which the petit jury was drawn. The issue we have, therefore, is whether a jury-selection system which operates to exclude from jury service an identifiable class of citizens constituting 53% of eligible jurors in the community comports with the Sixth and Fourteenth Amendments.

The State first insists that Taylor, a male, has no standing to object to the exclusion of women from his jury. But Taylor's claim is that he was constitutionally entitled to a jury drawn from a venire constituting a fair cross section of the community and that the jury that tried him was not such a jury by reason of the exclusion of women. Taylor was not a member of the excluded class; but there is no rule that claims such as Taylor presents may be made only by those defendants who are members of the group excluded from jury service. [The court cited Peters v. Kiff.] Taylor, in the case before us, was similarly entitled to tender and have adjudicated the claim that the exclusion of women from jury service deprived him of the kind of factfinder to which he was constitutionally entitled.

III

The background against which this case must be decided includes our holding in Duncan v. Louisiana that the Sixth Amendment's provision for jury trial is made binding on the States by virtue of the Fourteenth Amendment. Our inquiry is whether the presence of a fair cross section of the community on venires, panels, or lists from which petit juries are drawn is essential to the fulfillment of the Sixth Amendment's guarantee of an impartial jury trial in criminal prosecutions.

* * *

We accept the fair-cross-section requirement as fundamental to the jury trial guaranteed by the Sixth Amendment and are convinced that the requirement has solid foundation. The purpose of a jury is to guard against the exercise of arbitrary power—to make available the commonsense judgment of the community as a hedge against the overzealous or mistaken prosecutor and in preference to the professional or perhaps over-conditioned or biased response of a judge. This prophylactic vehicle is not provided if the jury pool is made up of only special segments of the populace or if large, distinctive groups are excluded from the pool. Community participation in the administration of the criminal law, moreover, is not only consistent with our democratic heritage but is also critical to public confidence in the fairness of the criminal justice system. Restricting jury service to only special groups or excluding identifiable segments playing major roles in the community cannot be squared with the constitutional concept of jury trial. * * *

IV

We are also persuaded that the fair-cross-section requirement is violated by the systematic exclusion of women, who in the judicial district involved here amounted to 53% of the citizens eligible for jury service. This conclusion necessarily entails the judgment that women are sufficiently numerous and distinct from men and that if they are systematically eliminated from jury panels, the Sixth Amendment's fair-cross-section requirement cannot be satisfied. This very matter was debated in Ballard v. United States. Positing the fair-cross-section rule—there said to be a statutory one—the Court concluded that the systematic exclusion of women was unacceptable. The dissenting view that an all-male panel drawn from various groups in the community would be as truly representative as if women were included, was firmly rejected:

> "The thought is that the factors which tend to influence the action of women are the same as those which influence the action of men—personality, background, economic status—and not sex. Yet it is not enough to say that women when sitting as jurors neither act nor tend to act as a class. Men likewise do not act as a class. But, if the shoe were on the other foot, who would claim that a jury was truly representative of the community if all men were intentionally and systematically excluded from the panel? The truth is that the two sexes are not fungible; a community made up exclusively of one is different from a community composed of both; the subtle interplay of influence one on the other is among the imponderables. To insulate the courtroom from either may not in a given case make an iota of difference. Yet a flavor, a distinct quality is lost if either sex is excluded. The exclusion of one may indeed make the jury less representative of the community than would be true if an economic or racial group were excluded." 329 U.S., at 193–194.

In this respect, we agree with the Court in *Ballard:* If the fair-cross-section rule is to govern the selection of juries, as we have concluded it must, women cannot be systemically excluded from jury panels from which petit juries are drawn. This conclusion is consistent with the current judgment of the country, now evidenced by legislative or constitutional provisions in every State and at the federal level qualifying women for jury service.

V

There remains the argument that women as a class serve a distinctive role in society and that jury service would so substantially interfere with that function that the state has ample justification for excluding women from service unless they volunteer, even though the result is that almost all jurors are men. * * *

The States are free to grant exemptions from jury service to individuals in case of special hardship or incapacity and to those engaged in particular occupations the uninterrupted performance of which is critical to the community's welfare. It would not appear that such exemptions would pose substantial threats that the remaining pool of jurors would not be representative of the community. A system excluding all women, however, is a wholly different matter. It is untenable to suggest these days that it would be a special hardship for each and every woman to perform jury service or that society cannot spare *any* women from their present duties. This may be the case with many, and it may be burdensome to sort out those who should be exempted from those who should serve. But that task is performed in the case of men, and the administrative convenience in dealing with women as a class is insufficient justification for diluting the quality of community judgment represented by the jury in criminal trials.

* * *

Note

In Duren v. Missouri, 439 U.S. 357 (1979), the Court held that in order to establish a prima facie violation of the fair cross-section requirement, a defendant must show three things: (1) the group excluded from the jury array is a distinctive group within the community; (2) the representation of the group in the venire from which jurors are selected is not fair and reasonable in relation to the number of such persons in the community; and (3) this underrepresentation was the result of a systematic exclusion of the group in the jury selection process. At that point, the burden shifts to the state to show that the inclusion of the underrepresented group would be "incompatible with a significant state interest." On the facts, the Court found that Duren had made out a prima facie case by showing that 54% of the adult inhabitants of the county were women, while only 15% of the persons placed on venires were women, and a woman could decline jury service by simply not reporting for jury duty. Justice White, writing for the Court, stated that an exemption tailored to women who could not leave their children might effectuate a state interest sufficient to satisfy the fair cross-section requirement, but that no such limited exemption was operative in this case.

Two years before *Taylor,* the Court considered a jury selection challenge that alleged that the systematic exclusion of a cognizable group, young adults (ages 18 to 24), constituted an improper jury selection system. The Court rejected the challenge, holding that systematic exclusion is not established where the jury list is refilled only once every four years. The Court assumed, without deciding, that the young did form a cognizable class. Hamling v. United States, 418 U.S. 87 (1974). Does the holding in *Taylor* suggest that the young are such a group? Commonwealth v. Bastarache, 382 Mass. 86, 414 N.E.2d 984 (1980), found that the class of people of 18–34 years of age was not an identifiable group whose underrepresentation on juries made the jury selection system suspect. See also People v. Bartolomeo, 126 A.D.2d 375, 513 N.Y.S.2d 981 (1987) (18–20 year-olds are not a distinctive group).

Consider again the Court's holding in *Thiel,* forbidding the systematic exclusion of daily wage earners from a federal jury. After *Taylor,* is a constitutional challenge alleging that blue collar workers are excluded from state juries likely to succeed? Do blue collar workers comprise a cognizable class for purposes of constitutional analysis? How would you articulate the factors that identify a group as one that must not be excluded from juries? Would you distinguish blue collar workers from women? From young adults? See generally Zeigler, Young Adults as a Cognizable Group in Jury Selection, 76 Mich.L.Rev. 1045 (1978). One jury study has suggested that in three out of every ten federal districts such workers are underrepresented, relative to their proportion in the community, by more than 20%. J. Van Dyke, Jury Selection Procedures 25 (1977). Should a challenge based in part on such data prevail? The court held that ex-felons and resident aliens could be excluded in Rubio v. Superior Court, 24 Cal.3d 93, 154 Cal.Rptr. 734, 593 P.2d 595 (1979). Do you agree? In deciding future jury cases, the Court may have to decide whether a statistical demonstration of underrepresentation of religious sects, political parties, and welfare recipients is constitutionally significant.

In the course of reviewing a murder conviction and death sentence in Willis v. Zant, 720 F.2d 1212 (11th Cir.1983), the court reasoned that "[t]he distinctiveness and homogeneity of a group under the sixth amendment depends upon the time and location of the trial. For example, Latinos have been held to be a cognizable group in Miami, Florida. In another community they might not be." It suggested that a group is cognizable under the Sixth Amendment if: it is defined by some definite factor; there is a common thread or similarity of ideas, attitudes or experiences among its members; and there is a community of interest among its members that cannot be adequately represented if the group is excluded from jury selection. The court remanded for factfinding on the question whether young adults were improperly excluded in the community in which the defendant was charged and convicted.

Barber v. Ponte, 772 F.2d 982 (1st Cir.1985) (en banc), held, 3-2, that "young adults" are not a distinctive group for jury selection purposes. In Anaya v. Hansen, 781 F.2d 1 (1st Cir.1986), the same court held that neither young adults nor blue collar workers constituted a cognizable group for cross-section analysis.

If a state can show a truly random selection process, and if the state uses a source (or sources) of jury names—e.g., driver's license lists as well as voting lists—that is likely to include most members of a community, most jury selection challenges can be avoided.[32] See, e.g., United States v. Di Pasquale, 864 F.2d 271 (3d Cir.1988) (even if there is statistical underrepresentation of distinctive groups, the use of voter and drivers lists to obtain a jury pool is permissible and does not constitute systematic exclusion). In fact, underrepresentation should be rare. But if a state refuses to follow clear, visible selection procedures, suspicion of disparities is likely to continue.[33] Assuming that random selection procedures are used to call jurors, the questions that almost surely will arise will involve who can be excused from jury service on hardship grounds. Can all lawyers be excused? Can all wage earners? Can all single parents? Remember that exclusion of these people would be at their request only. Thus, their rights to serve would be unimpaired. But would the criminal defendant be permitted to complain about the diminishment of chances to have a real cross-section of the community? How would you approach the problem of excusing jurors upon request?

32. The Federal Jury Selection and Service Act of 1968, 28 U.S.C.A. §§ 1861–69, provides for random selection. The Act calls for the use of voter registration lists or lists of actual voters and "some other source or sources of names in addition to voter lists where necessary to foster the policy and protect the rights [set forth in the Act]." The federal statute was followed by the Uniform Jury Selection and Service Act (1970). See McKusick & Bixer, Uniform Jury Selection and Service Act, 8 Harv.J.Legis. 280 (1971).

Some citizens may decline to register to vote to avoid jury service. Contentions have been made that certain groups are especially likely not to register to vote and that such lists do not produce a cross-section of the community. As long as voter lists do not have racial identifications—see e.g., King v. Cook, 298 F.Supp. 584 (N.D.Miss.1969); Caston v. State, 240 So.2d 443 (Miss.1970)—and are used as part of some non-discriminatory selection scheme, their use is likely to be sustained. See People v. Hicks, 59 A.D.2d 251, 399 N.Y.S.2d 316 (1977) (persons who do not register to vote are not a cognizable class of qualified jurors, and no proof was shown that the jury selection system based on voter lists was the product of intentional and systematic exclusion of African-Americans); People v. Wai Ming Lee, 92 Misc.2d 204, 399 N.Y.S.2d 962 (1977) (use of voter registration list and income tax mailing list was proper for making up the pool of prospective jurors, despite the fact that Asian-Americans were underrepresented).

For an argument that the Constitution requires multiple source lists, see Kairys, Kadane & Lehoczky, Jury Representativeness: A Mandate for Multiple Source Lists, 65 Calif.L.Rev. 776 (1977).

An en banc court held in United States v. Gometz, 730 F.2d 475 (7th Cir.1984), that the federal statute did not require a district court clerk to take steps to assure that the jury pool is a representative cross-section of the community when a large percentage of the prospective jurors who are sent qualification forms fail to return the forms. The court reasoned that nothing in the statute indicates a congressional intent to compel inclusion of "anti-authoritarian" personalities in a jury pool and that as long as the number of responses is high enough to generate enough names for the jury wheel the clerk need not take measures to correct a low response rate.

33. Jurisdictions vary on whether a defendant has a right to inspect and copy jury lists. In Test v. United States, 420 U.S. 28 (1975), the Court held that a federal criminal defendant has the right to inspect in order to prepare challenges to petit and grand jury selection procedures. In some cases—e.g., treason or capital cases—statutes may require that the defendant be served with a list. See 18 U.S.C.A. § 3432.

Generally a defendant has not been given access to "jury books" or information on juries prepared by the government. See, e.g., Hamer v. United States, 259 F.2d 274 (9th Cir. 1958). Should the *Brady* doctrine—which requires the prosecutor to disclose exculpatory information, as discussed in the discovery chapter—be read as requiring the government to share its information on jurors with the defense?

State v. Williams, 659 S.W.2d 778 (Mo.1983), sustains the exclusion of lawyers from jury venires on the ground that there are substantial public policy rationales for exclusion: e.g., lawyers might exert undue influence and might be inclined to assess cases in light of their knowledge of the trial lawyers' reputations and skills. In Prejean v. Blackburn, 570 F.Supp. 985 (W.D.La.1983), the court denied habeas corpus relief to a defendant who had received the death penalty in state court. The court found that the exclusion of doctors and lawyers from the jury venire did not violate the cross-section of the community requirement.

Would a blue ribbon jury pool—i.e., one composed of specially trained people—be constitutional today?

E. THE IMPARTIAL AND UNBIASED JUROR

1. *Voir Dire and Court Control*

The establishment of a panel representing a fair cross-section of the community is only the first stage in the jury selection procedure. The second stage required by the Sixth Amendment is to assure that the actual trial jury is impartial and fairly chosen. Because preconceived notions about the case at issue threaten impartiality, each juror must be free of bias. Accordingly, in a process called voir dire, meaning "to speak the truth," prospective jurors are subject to two kinds of challenges: an unlimited number of challenges for cause based on a "narrowly specified, provable and legally cognizable basis of partiality," and a specified (by statute or rule) number of peremptory challenges which, at least until recently, could be exercised for any reason or no reason—though as we will see the use of peremptory challenges has been limited by Batson v. Kentucky and its progeny, infra.

Voir dire may be conducted in any of several methods: by addressing all questions to the panel at one time, or by addressing each juror individually;[34] by having the judge put questions to the jurors or by allowing counsel to ask the questions; and by allowing a broad inquiry into juror attitudes or by limiting the number and scope of questions that may be asked to the narrow issues presented in a specific case. Voir dire vests broad authority in the trial judge.[35] In many jurisdictions the manner in which voir dire is conducted is

34. Voir dire must be conducted with care. See, e.g., State v. Jackson, 358 So.2d 1263 (La.1978) (voir dire is improperly conducted where the trial court fails to instruct all prospective jurors to listen to all questions propounded to the first panel of prospective jurors and subsequently limits questioning of other panels by asking if they heard earlier questions, and if their answers would be the same). The record suggested that many jurors failed to hear or understand the initial set of questions.

In questioning one prospective juror about bias, the Court must be careful to avoid eliciting prejudicial information in the presence of other prospective jurors. See State v. McCorgary, 224 Kan. 677, 585 P.2d 1024 (1978).

35. See, e.g., Fed.R.Crim.P. 24(a) (court *may* allow attorneys to question). Annot., 28 ALR Fed. 26 (1976). Some jurisdictions give parties or their counsel a right to conduct voir dire. See State v. Burns, 173 Conn. 317, 377 A.2d 1082 (1977).

United States v. Ible, 630 F.2d 389 (5th Cir. 1980), expresses concern that "voir dire may have little meaning if it is not conducted at least in part by counsel. The 'federal' practice of almost exclusive voir dire examination by the court does not take into account the fact that it is parties, rather than the court, who have a full grasp of the nuances and the strength and weaknesses of the case". The court added in a footnote the following thought:

> "During the past fifteen to twenty years there has been a trend by federal district judges to conduct the voir dire questioning themselves. Such a course was a result of many abuses by counsel including the consumption of excessive time periods and delv-

left up to the judge.[36] In all jurisdictions, the judge has discretion to consider the relevance of the questions in a particular case, and has the right to refuse to allow and to strike questions deemed irrelevant or inappropriate. The judge's relevance determinations are fact-specific; they frequently turn on the particular aspects of the case to be tried. In most instances the appellate court will defer considerably to the trial court, believing that the trial judge has a better feel than an appellate court for the need to put questions to prospective jurors. But the Constitution requires that some inquiries be made at the request of a defendant if there is to be voir dire.

In Ham v. South Carolina, 409 U.S. 524 (1973), a young, bearded African-American, active in the civil rights movement, was charged with possession of marijuana. He alleged, in defense, that police officials had framed him, because of his civil rights activities. During voir dire, he requested that the trial judge ask four questions relating to potential juror prejudice: two related to prejudice against African-Americans, the third related to prejudice against individuals with beards, and the fourth related to pretrial publicity. The request was refused. The Supreme Court granted review to consider whether the refusal violated federal constitutional rights.

Justice Rehnquist, writing for the Court, declared as follows:

> Since one of the purposes of the Due Process Clause of the Fourteenth Amendment is to insure these "essential demands of fairness," and since a principal purpose of the adoption of the Fourteenth Amendment was to prohibit the States from invidiously discriminating on the basis of race, we think that the Fourteenth Amendment required the judge in this case to interrogate the jurors upon the subject of racial prejudice. South Carolina law permits challenges for cause, and authorizes the trial judge to conduct *voir dire* examination of potential jurors. The State having created this statutory framework for the selection of juries, the essential fairness required by the Due Process Clause of the Fourteenth Amendment requires that under the facts shown by this record the petitioner be permitted to have the jurors interrogated on the issue of racial bias.
>
> We agree with the dissenting justices of the Supreme Court of South Carolina that the trial judge was not required to put the question in any particular form, or to ask any particular number of questions on the subject, simply because requested to do so by petitioner. * * * In this context, either of the brief, general questions urged by the petitioner would appear sufficient to

ing into improper areas during voir dire examination. More recently, records reviewed in this court reflect a new pattern by trial courts. The trial judge will explain the nature of the case in general terms, point out the parties and counsel, cover the most basic points of law (burden of proof, presumption of innocence, right to remain silent, etc.), explain the procedures and schedule to be followed and then turn the questioning over to trial counsel. We encourage this approach. Trial judges have a duty to control this and every other aspect of the trial, but all proper areas of inquiry must be covered fairly."

See McMillion, Advocating Voir Dire Reform, 77 A.B.A.J., Nov. 1991, p. 114 (discussing legislation proposed in the Senate to give attorneys a limited right to conduct questioning of jurors in the Federal courts).

36. Although the trial judge exercises control over voir dire, certain subjects, such as the physical or mental capacity of persons to serve as jurors, must be the subject of inquiry where it appears from the information supplied by the prospective jurors themselves that there may be a problem. See United States v. Rucker, 557 F.2d 1046 (4th Cir. 1977).

Voir dire is important enough that the defendant has a right to have his lawyer present. See Eason v. State, 563 S.W.2d 945 (Tex.Cr.App.1978).

focus the attention of prospective jurors on any racial prejudice they might entertain.

The third of petitioner's proposed questions was addressed to the fact that he wore a beard. While we cannot say that prejudice against people with beards might not have been harbored by one or more of the potential jurors in this case, this is the beginning and not the end of the inquiry as to whether the Fourteenth Amendment required the trial judge to interrogate the prospective jurors about such possible prejudice. Given the traditionally broad discretion accorded to the trial judge in conducting *voir dire,* and our inability to constitutionally distinguish possible prejudice against beards from a host of other possible similar prejudices, we do not believe the petitioner's constitutional rights were violated when the trial judge refused to put this question. The inquiry as to racial prejudice derives its constitutional stature from * * * a principal purpose as well as from the language of those who adopted the Fourteenth Amendment. The trial judge's refusal to inquire as to particular bias against beards, after his inquiries as to bias in general, does not reach the level of a constitutional violation.

* * *

Ham was distinguished in the following case.

RISTAINO v. ROSS

Supreme Court of the United States, 1976.
424 U.S. 589.

[An African-American, charged in a state court with violent crimes against a white security guard, requested the trial court to ask during voir dire a question specifically directed to racial prejudice. The trial court refused and was affirmed on appeal. The Supreme Court was reviewing a federal court of appeals' decision granting relief on the basis of *Ham.*]

MR. JUSTICE POWELL delivered the opinion of the Court.

* * *

II

The Constitution does not always entitle a defendant to have questions posed during *voir dire* specifically directed to matters that conceivably might prejudice veniremen against him. *Voir dire* "is conducted under the supervision of the court, and a great deal must, of necessity, be left to its sound discretion." Connors v. United States, 158 U.S. 408, 413 (1895). This is so because the "determination of impartiality, in which demeanor plays such an important part, is particularly within the province of the trial judge." Rideau v. Louisiana, 373 U.S. 723, 733 (1963) (Clark, J., dissenting). Thus, the State's obligation to the defendant to impanel an impartial jury generally can be satisfied by less than an inquiry into a specific prejudice feared by the defendant.

In *Ham,* however, we recognized that some cases may present circumstances in which an impermissible threat to the fair trial guaranteed by due process is posed by a trial court's refusal to question prospective jurors specifically about racial prejudice during *voir dire. Ham* involved a Negro tried in South Carolina courts for possession of marihuana. He was well known in the locale of his trial as a civil rights activist, and his defense was that law enforcement officials had framed him on the narcotics charge to "get him" for those activities. Despite the circumstances, the trial judge denied Ham's request that the court-conducted *voir dire* include questions specifically directed to racial prejudice. We reversed * * *.

By its terms *Ham* did not announce a requirement of universal applicability. Rather, it reflected an assessment of whether under all of the circumstances presented there was a constitutionally significant likelihood that, absent questioning about racial prejudice, the jurors would not be as "indifferent as [they stand] unsworne." Coke on Littleton 155b (19th ed. 1832). In this approach *Ham* was consistent with other determinations by this Court that a State had denied a defendant due process by failing to impanel an impartial jury.

The circumstances in *Ham* strongly suggested the need for *voir dire* to include specific questioning about racial prejudice. Ham's defense was that he had been framed because of his civil rights activities. His prominence in the community as a civil rights activist, if not already known to veniremen, inevitably would have been revealed to the members of the jury in the course of his presentation of that defense. Racial issues therefore were inextricably bound up with the conduct of the trial. Further, Ham's reputation as a civil rights activist and the defense he interposed were likely to intensify any prejudice that individual members of the jury might harbor. In such circumstances we deemed a *voir dire* that included questioning specifically directed to racial prejudice, when sought by Ham, necessary to meet the constitutional requirement that an impartial jury be impaneled.

We do not agree with the Court of Appeals that the need to question veniremen specifically about racial prejudice also rose to constitutional dimensions in this case.[a] The mere fact that the victim of the crimes alleged was a white man and the defendants were Negroes was less likely to distort the trial than were the special factors involved in *Ham.* The victim's status as a security officer, also relied upon by the Court of Appeals, was cited by respective defense counsel primarily as a separate source of prejudice, not as an aggravating racial factor, and the trial judge dealt with it by his question about law-enforcement affiliations. The circumstances thus did not suggest a significant likelihood that racial prejudice might infect Ross' trial. This was made clear to the trial judge when Ross was unable to support his motion concerning *voir dire* by pointing to racial factors such as existed in *Ham* or others of comparable significance. In these circumstances, the trial judge acted within the Constitution in determining that the demands of due process could be satisfied by his more generalized but thorough inquiry into the impartiality of the veniremen.

* * *

MR. JUSTICE STEVENS took no part in the consideration or decision of this case.

[The opinion of JUSTICE WHITE, concurring in the result, is omitted.]

MR. JUSTICE MARSHALL, with whom MR. JUSTICE BRENNAN joins, dissenting.

* * * Today, in reversing the Court of Appeals' affirmance of the District Court's grant of a writ of habeas corpus, the Court emphatically confirms that the promises inherent in *Ham* * * * will not be fulfilled. * * * I cannot join in this confirmation. Accordingly, I respectfully dissent.

a. Although we hold that *voir dire* questioning directed to racial prejudice was not constitutionally required, the wiser course generally is to propound appropriate questions designed to identify racial prejudice if requested by the defendant. Under our supervisory power we would have required as much of a federal court faced with the circumstances here. * * *

Note

A divided Supreme Court held that there was no reversible error in a district court's refusal to voir dire prospective jurors on their racial prejudices in Rosales-Lopez v. United States, 451 U.S. 182 (1981). The defendant was a Mexican charged with smuggling aliens into the United States. The trial judge asked jurors about attitudes toward "the alien problem" and aliens, but not about racial or ethnic prejudices. Justice White, writing for a plurality (Justices Stewart, Blackmun and Powell) concluded that "it is usually best to allow the defendant * * * to have the inquiry into racial or ethnic prejudice pursued," but refused to require deference to defendants in all cases since an inquiry into racial matters may create an impression that justice turns on race. The plurality said that prior cases "fairly imply that federal trial courts must make such an inquiry when requested by a defendant accused of a violent crime and where the defendant and the victim are members of different racial or ethnic groups." The plurality said this was a supervisory rule for federal courts and might be extended to other circumstances that suggest a reasonable possibility that racial or ethnic prejudice will affect the jury. Justice Rehnquist, joined by Chief Justice Burger, rejected the supervisory rule and preferred to rely on the discretion of trial judges. Justice Stevens, joined by Justices Brennan and Marshall, dissented and argued that "[m]uch as we wish it were otherwise, we should acknowledge the fact that there are many potential jurors who harbor strong prejudices against all members of certain racial, religious or ethnic groups for no reason other than hostility to the group as a whole." It appears that upon request by the defendant an inquiry into racial prejudice must be made under the dissenters' view.

One of the most telling arguments for the defendant was the fact that the trial judge apparently assumed that "the alien problem" was a familiar one. Exactly what is this problem? Any recognition of a special problem concerning aliens, especially in a part of the country where many aliens come from Mexico, might have been used to support a claim that under *Ham* the defendant's questions should have been asked.

The Supreme Court departed from *Ristaino* in capital cases as it held in Turner v. Murray, 476 U.S. 28 (1986), that a death sentence was invalid where a trial judge refused a black defendant's request to voir dire prospective jurors on racial prejudice in a prosecution charging him with murdering a white man. Justice White wrote for the Court as it held that "a capital defendant accused of an interracial crime is entitled to have prospective jurors informed of the race of the victim and questioned on the issue of racial bias." He noted that the trial judge retains discretion as to the form and number of questions, including whether to question jurors individually or collectively, and that a defendant cannot complain unless he has specifically asked for voir dire questions concerning race.

Only three other justices joined the portions of Justice White's opinion that distinguished capital sentencing from the guilt phase of a trial. Justice White reasoned that the jury has broad discretion during the sentencing phase and that there is a special risk of improper sentencing. Justices Brennan and Marshall agreed with Justice White as to sentencing, but would have held that "a criminal defendant is entitled to inquire on voir dire about the potential racial bias of jurors whenever the case involves a violent interracial crime." Justice Powell, joined by Justice Rehnquist, dissented and defended the *Ristaino* approach. The Chief Justice concurred in the judgment without opinion.

Chief Justice Rehnquist relied on *Ristaino* in his opinion for the Court in Mu'Min v. Virginia, 111 S.Ct. 1899 (1991), holding that a state trial judge is not obliged to question prospective jurors individually about the contents of pretrial publicity to which they may have been exposed. Mu'Min was a state prisoner serving time for first-degree murder when he was charged with capital murder while on a work detail. The case was widely publicized, as it arose during the 1988 presidential campaign in which another case of a murder by a prisoner on furlough became an issue of national debate. Articles in the newspapers revealed details of the prior murder for which Mu'Min was incarcerated, the fact that the death penalty was unavailable at that time, the denial of parole six times to Mu'Min, his confession to the crime charged, and criticism of the supervision of work gangs in Virginia. Prior to trial, the defendant submitted proposed voir dire questions and asked for individual voir dire concerning the content of the publicity to which the juror had been exposed. The trial judge instead asked jurors whether they heard or read anything about the case and whether they could be fair. Jurors who indicated that they had received information about the case were examined in panels of four; they were asked to respond if they had an opinion about the case, and if they could not enter the Jury box with an open mind. Prospective jurors who remained silent were considered to have asserted that they could remain fair.

As the Court had done in *Ristaino,* Chief Justice Rehnquist distinguished the requirements of the Due Process Clause concerning voir dire in state trials from the more extensive supervisory power of federal courts over federal trials. He reasoned that there was no stronger argument for a requirement of individual voir dire about the content of pretrial publicity than there is for voir dire about racial or ethnic prejudice. He observed that if the contents of pretrial publicity must be the subject of inquiry, burdensome individual voir dire would be required, to prevent jurors from infecting each other with the publicity giving rise to the inquiry. He rejected the less burdensome alternative of written questions concerning content of publicity to which each juror had been exposed, reasoning that written answers would not give counsel or the court access to the demeanor of jurors. Thus, because efforts to fully protect the defendant from jurors affected by pre-trial publicity were too onerous, the constitution did not require the court to take less effective efforts.

Justice O'Connor wrote a concurring opinion. She concluded that a trial judge could realistically assess whether jurors could be fair without knowing what each juror had heard about a case. Justice O'Connor agreed with Justice Marshall's dissenting view that the trial judge could have done more, but ultimately concluded that "content" questions are not so indispensable to a fair trial that it violates the Constitution for a trial court to evaluate jurors without asking them.

Justice Marshall's dissenting opinion was joined by Justice Blackmun and Justice Stevens. His basic principle was that "[w]hen a prospective juror has been exposed to prejudicial pretrial publicity, a trial court cannot realistically assess the juror's impartiality without first establishing what the juror already has learned about the case." He offered three reasons: (1) "content questioning is necessary to determine whether the type and extent of the publicity to which a prospective juror has been exposed would disqualify that juror as a matter of law"; (2) "even when pretrial publicity is not so extreme as to make a juror's exposure to it *per se* disqualifying, content questioning still is essential to give legal depth to the trial court's finding of impartiality"; and (3) "content questioning facilitates accurate trial court factfinding."

Justice Kennedy also dissented. He agreed with Justice Marshall that the voir dire in the instant case was insufficient to insure an informed ruling that the jurors were qualified to sit. Justice Kennedy wrote that "[i]n my view, a juror's acknowledgement of exposure to pretrial publicity initiates a duty to assess that individual juror's ability to be impartial." He contended that "the trial judge should have substantial discretion in conducting the voir dire, but, in my judgment, findings of impartiality must be based on something more than the mere silence of the individual in response to questions asked *en masse*."

As indicated in *Mu'Min,* the regulation of voir dire under the Federal supervisory power is more rigorous than that required by the Constitution. Generally speaking, individual voir dire has been required in three situations in the Federal courts, although trial judges have significant discretion as to how to frame the questions. These three situations are: 1) where a case has racial overtones; 2) where the case involves matters concerning which the local community is known to harbor strong feelings, that may stop short of a need for a change of venue but may nonetheless affect the trial—such as child abuse or narcotics distribution; and 3) where testimony from law enforcement agents is likely to be overvalued. See generally United States v. Payne, 944 F.2d 1458 (9th Cir.1991) for a discussion and application of these considerations. In *Payne* the court held that the trial court's refusal to ask venire members if they would be unduly influenced by the testimony of law enforcement officers was not reversible error. The court noted that officers' testimony had only a minor role in the government's case, and distinguished United States v. Contreras–Castro, 825 F.2d 185 (9th Cir.1987) where a similar error was held reversible because the government's entire case rested on the testimony of government agents.

Chief Justice Burger's majority opinion in Press-Enterprise Co. v. Superior Court, 464 U.S. 501 (1984) (a case holding invalid the closing to the public of voir dire and the sealing of the voir dire transcript in a rape-murder prosecution), contains a footnote stating that a six-week voir dire "in and of itself undermines public confidence in the courts and the legal profession. Properly conducted it is inconceivable that the process could extend over such a period." The Court took notice of the fact that jury selection of such length was "not unknown" in California. Justice Stevens' concurring opinion added that the First Amendment's right of access to proceedings rests on the idea that public access will improve public understanding and that lengthy voir dire proceedings undermine public understanding. Justice Marshall concurred only in the judgment of the Court, noting that the case involved "an interracial sexual attack and murder," and commenting that "[g]iven the history and continuing legacy of racism in our country, that fact alone should suggest that a greater than usual amount of inquiry may have been needed in order to obtain a fair and impartial jury in this case." He found "it not at all 'inconceivable' that the voir dire process could have legitimately extended over six weeks."

2. *Illustrative Voir Dire Problems*

After *Ristaino* and *Mu'Min* it is unlikely that federal courts will attempt to dictate to the states how voir dire should be conducted in the usual case. But the policy question of how much voir dire to permit will remain. Consider the scope of voir dire permitted in three specific situations. Is the scope sufficient? Too restrictive?

a. The facts in this case are brutal, but unfortunately such cases arise.

> The record discloses that early on the morning of July 9, 1974, a seventy-nine year old resident was forcibly removed from her home and taken to a nearby isolated swamp where she was raped and sodomized. Her body was discovered later the same day, face down in the swampy area. The medical evidence established that the cause of death was drowning. Christian was arrested and charged with the murder and rape on September 27, 1974.

The appellant, an African–American man, was convicted on the basis of circumstantial evidence that included testimony from a white woman neighbor, alleging that he had made sexual advances to her, which she refused, the morning of the crime. During voir dire, the trial court denied appellant's request to ask questions relating to each venireman's beliefs about the difference, if any, in the sexual drives of African–American and white men, and their attitudes toward inter-racial sexual relations. The appellate court reversed, holding that the circumstances established a need for inquiry into possible racial prejudices and that the defense questions were "suited to elicit the prospective jurors' racial prejudices in a manner germane to issues which would crystalize at trial." Commonwealth v. Christian, 480 Pa. 131, 389 A.2d 545, 549 (1978). Would you have permitted the inquiry? Was it required under *Ham?*

b. If a defendant is contemplating an insanity defense, does she have a right to ask the prospective jurors whether they would be hostile to such a defense? See United States v. Allsup, 566 F.2d 68 (9th Cir.1977); cf. State v. Johnson, 383 A.2d 1012 (R.I.1978).

These questions raise two issues. The first is whether counsel should be able to "argue" about a case during voir dire, which can happen if counsel is asking numerous questions of jurors. The second is whether voir dire is a device to screen out biased jurors who should be excused for cause—see, e.g., Schlinsky v. United States, 379 F.2d 735 (1st Cir.1967)—or to help the parties exercise peremptory challenges. See, e.g., State v. Stuit, 176 Mont. 84, 576 P.2d 264 (1978). As you read on, think about the purpose(s) that voir dire should serve.

c. In United States v. Barnes, 604 F.2d 121 (2d Cir.1979), a divided court approved the trial judge's decision to keep the names and addresses of jurors secret from counsel and to bar defense counsel from inquiring into the jurors' ethnic and religious backgrounds. The trial judge permitted an inquiry of prospective jurors as to their county and length of residence and certain family history. The limitations on voir dire were intended to protect the jurors from harassment and threats to themselves and their families. Do you believe that it is necessary for a party to know where a juror lives in order to make an intelligent decision whether to challenge the juror peremptorily? *Barnes* is commented upon in 93 Harv.L.Rev. 782 (1980). United States v. Thomas, 757 F.2d 1359 (2d Cir.1985), also sustained a jury selection procedure in which the jurors' names and addresses were not revealed, but the defendants were told the part of the Bronx or Manhattan that the jurors were from. The court noted that it did not intend to say that that the practice of impanelling an anonymous jury would be valid in all cases. In United States v. Tutino, 883 F.2d 1125 (2d Cir.1989), the judge permitted the impanelling of an anonymous jury in a trial alleging a heroin distribution conspiracy when presented with the following submission from the government:

> The government requested an anonymous jury for five reasons: (1) the defendants faced serious penalties, including substantial prison terms and a possible parole revocation, and, according to the government, were therefore likely to bribe or threaten the jury; (2) [defendant] Tutino had attempted to tamper with a jury in a prior trial; (3) [defendants] Tutino and Guarino were known associates of organized crime figures; (4) Tutino had a prior extortion conviction and Guarino and [defendant] Larca had prior narcotics convictions; and (5) the jury had to be protected from the media.

In affirming the decision to use an anonymous jury, the court of appeals noted that the trial court issued instructions regarding the presumption of innocence more than once. The court believed that "these instructions were carefully framed to avoid any risk that the anonymous procedures would appear extraordinary or reflect adversely on the defendants." Do you believe that any instructions would suffice to protect the presumption of innocence when a jury is anonymous? See also United States v. Vario, 943 F.2d 236 (2d Cir.1991) (pretrial publicity, and co-conspirator's tampering with grand jury, warrant anonymous jury). In *Vario,* the court took pains to note that "the invocation of the words 'organized crime,' 'mob' or 'Mafia,' unless there is something more, does not warrant an anonymous jury."

3. Challenges for Cause

The cognizable, specific biases that permit a challenge for cause are defined by statute. The typical statute permits such a challenge where the juror is of unsound mind or lacks the qualifications required by law, is related to a party, has served in a related case or on the indicting grand jury, or has a "state of mind" that will prevent him or her from acting with entire impartiality. See e.g., ABA Standards, Trial by Jury 58–59 (2d ed. 1980).

a. Jurors Who Cannot Be Excused for Cause

Usually the question is whether a person *must* be excused for cause. However, one line of cases focuses on when persons may not be so excused. In Witherspoon v. Illinois, 391 U.S. 510 (1968), a statute provided that the prosecutor could challenge a juror for cause if the prospective juror stated "that he has conscientious scruples against capital punishment, or that he is opposed to the same." At Witherspoon's trial 47 veniremen, referred to by the trial court as "conscientious objectors," were successfully challenged on the basis of their negative attitude toward the death penalty. These jurors were not asked whether their scruples would invariably compel them to vote against capital punishment. Justice Stewart, writing for the Court, first rejected Witherspoon's argument that a jury which had a favorable attitude toward the death penalty would also be partial to the prosecution in the guilt phase. He found Witherspoon's data on this point "too tentative and fragmentary" and concluded that "we are not prepared to announce a *per se* constitutional rule requiring the reversal of every conviction returned by a jury selected as this one was." [37]

37. For an argument that a jury that is biased on the punishment question also is biased on the guilt issue, see White, The Constitutional Invalidity of Convictions Imposed by Death-qualified Juries, 58 Cornell L.Rev. 1176 (1973).

However, Justice Stewart found that Witherspoon's death sentence was invalid because "in its role as arbiter of the punishment to be imposed, this jury fell woefully short of that impartiality to which the petitioner was entitled under the Sixth and Fourteenth Amendments." Justice Stewart reasoned as follows:

> A man who opposes the death penalty, no less than one who favors it, can make the discretionary judgment entrusted to him by the State and can thus obey the oath he takes as a juror. But a jury from which all such men have been excluded cannot perform the task demanded of it. * * *
>
> If the State had excluded only those prospective jurors who stated in advance of trial that they would not even consider returning a verdict of death, it could argue the resulting jury was simply neutral with respect to the penalty. But when it swept from the jury all who expressed conscientious or religious scruples against capital punishment and all who opposed it in principle, the State crossed the line of neutrality. In its quest for a jury capable of imposing the death penalty, the State produced a jury uncommonly willing to condemn a man to die. * * *
>
> [W]e hold that a sentence of death cannot be carried out if the jury that imposed or recommended it was chosen by excluding veniremen for cause simply because they voiced general objections to the death penalty or expressed conscientious or religious scruples against its infliction.

The Court in *Witherspoon* emphasized the narrowness of its holding. It did not prohibit the State from impanelling a "death-qualified" jury. It simply prohibited the exclusion for cause of a juror who expresses reservations about the death penalty, where the juror states that these reservations would not preclude a vote for the death penalty in the proper case.

Adams v. Texas, 448 U.S. 38 (1980), held unconstitutional a Texas procedure that excluded jurors in a capital case who were unable to take an oath that the mandatory penalty of death or imprisonment for life would not "affect [their] deliberations on any issue of fact." The Court said that *Witherspoon* and subsequent cases establish "the general proposition that a juror may not be challenged for cause based on his views about capital punishment unless those views would prevent or substantially impair the performance of his duties as a juror in accordance with his instructions and his oath. The State may insist, however, that jurors will consider and decide the facts impartially and conscientiously apply the law as charged by the court." Differences between the Texas procedures and the Illinois procedures in *Witherspoon* were not deemed significant. The Court emphasized that "*Witherspoon* is not a ground for challenging any prospective juror. It is a limitation on the State's power to exclude * * *." In order to exclude a juror for cause, the state must show that the juror's beliefs about capital punishment would lead him to violate his oath or ignore the law, not simply that a juror might be affected by the possibility of the death penalty.

The Court limited the impact of *Witherspoon* and *Adams* in Wainwright v. Witt, 469 U.S. 412 (1985). One of the prospective jurors in Witt's capital murder trial indicated that personal beliefs concerning the death penalty would "interfere" with her judging the guilt or innocence of the defendant. That juror was excluded for cause and Witt argued that *Witherspoon* was violated because the juror did not state that she would automatically vote against the death penalty, or that she would be prevented from making an impartial decision as to guilt. Justice Rehnquist, writing for the Court, stated that *Witherspoon* did not require a "ritualistic adherence" to a requirement that a prospective juror make it "unmistakably clear that he would automatically vote against the death penalty." Justice Rehnquist set forth the following standard for determining whether a juror could be excluded for cause due to a negative attitude about the death penalty:

> [The] standard is whether the juror's views would prevent or substantially impair the performance of his duties as a juror in accordance with his instructions and his oath. We note that, in addition to dispensing with *Witherspoon's* reference to automatic decisionmaking, this standard likewise does not require that a juror's bias be proved with unmistakable clarity. This is because determinations of juror bias cannot be reduced to question-and-answer sessions which obtain results in the manner of a catechism. What common sense should have realized experience has proved: many veniremen simply cannot be asked enough questions to reach the point where their bias has been made 'unmistakably clear'; these veniremen may not know how they will react when faced with imposing the death sentence, or may be unable to articulate, or may wish to hide their true feelings. Despite this lack of clarity in the printed record, however, there will be situations where the trial judge is left with the definite impression that a prospective juror would be unable to faithfully and impartially apply the law. * * * [T]his is why deference must be paid to the trial judge who sees and hears the juror.

Justice Rehnquist concluded that, giving proper deference to the trial judge, the juror in Witt's case was properly excused for cause. Despite the fact that the juror had stated only that her beliefs might "interfere" with her impartiality, Justice Rehnquist stated that "whatever ambiguity respondent may find in this record, we think that the trial court, aided as it undoubtedly was by its assessment of [the juror's] demeanor, was entitled to resolve it in favor of the State."

Justice Stevens concurred in the judgment. Justice Brennan, joined by Justice Marshall, dissented and argued that "the inevitable result of the quest for such purity in the jury room in a capital case is not a neutral jury drawn from a fair cross-section of the community but a jury biased against the defendant, at least with respect to penalty, and a jury from which an identifiable segment of the community has been excluded."

A majority of the Court found *Witt* dispositive in Darden v. Wainwright, 477 U.S. 168 (1986), a case in which the Court affirmed a murder conviction and death sentence. The trial judge had excused one juror for cause after the juror indicated that he had strong personal views against the death penalty. Justice Powell wrote for the majority and concluded that the question put to the juror and his answers were not sufficient by themselves to compel the conclusion that the juror could not recommend the death penalty under any circumstances. He reasoned, however, that the trial court was entitled to take account of the entire series of questions put to other jurors in the presence of the excused juror and found that these questions stated the correct standard for excusing a juror for cause. Justice Blackmun, joined by Justices Brennan, Marshall and Stevens, dissented.

The Court found a *Witherspoon* violation in Gray v. Mississippi, 481 U.S. 648 (1987), and reaffirmed Davis v. Georgia, 429 U.S. 122 (1976) (per curiam), which effectively established a per se rule requiring the vacation of a death sentence imposed by a jury from which a potential juror was improperly excluded as a result of such a violation. In *Gray,* the prosecutor had used all twelve peremptory challenges prior to the time that a prospective juror, Mrs. Bounds, was called to the jury box. Eight of the twelve challenges were directed at potential jurors who had expressed doubts about the death penalty. The trial judge had refused to excuse any of these jurors for cause. The prosecutor asked the trial judge to reconsider his rulings in order to give the prosecution an additional challenge that could be used against Mrs. Bounds. Although the judge expressed some concern about denying challenges for cause to five previous jurors, he excused Mrs. Bounds for cause and denied reconsideration of the earlier challenges. The state supreme court held that the trial judge had failed to follow proper voir dire procedures in questioning the earlier jurors and concluded that they should have been excused for cause after stating they unequivocally opposed the death penalty. The court held that the trial judge did not err in taking affirmative action to correct the error by excusing Mrs. Bounds.

Justice Blackmun's opinion for the Court rejected the state supreme court's analysis to the extent it relied on the reasoning that any error was harmless because, but for the trial judge's error in denying earlier challenges for cause, the prosecutor, would have had an additional challenge available and would have removed Mrs. Bounds. Justice Blackmun found that "[t]he inadequate questioning regarding the venire members' views in effect precludes an appellate court from determining whether the trial judge erred in refusing to remove them for cause." Justice Blackmun stated that "the relevant inquiry is 'whether the composition of the *jury panel as a whole* could have been affected by the trial court's error,'" and reasoned that the prosecutor might not always use a peremptory challenge against a juror who had reservations about capital punishment since that juror had to be compared with other venire members. He concluded that "[t]he nature of the jury selection process defies any attempt to establish that an erroneous *Witherspoon-Witt* exclusion of a juror is harmless." Justice Blackmun was concerned with the practical implications of the prosecutor's argument that a *Witherspoon* violation should be deemed harmless whenever the prosecutor has an unexercised peremptory challenge that she said she would have exercised on the juror improperly excused for cause:

> The practical result of this unexercised peremptory argument would be to insulate jury-selection error from meaningful appellate review. By simply stating during voir dire that the State is prepared to exercise a peremptory challenge if the court denies its motion for cause, a prosecutor would ensure that a reviewing court would consider any erroneous exclusion harmless.

Finally, Justice Blackmun rejected the state's argument that the trial judge, in excluding Mrs. Bounds, was merely trying to correct his erroneous denial of challenges for cause as to prior jurors who could have been excluded under *Witherspoon.* The Court refused to "condone the correction of one error by the commitment of another."

Joined in part of his opinion only by Justices Brennan, Marshall, and Stevens, Justice Blackmun added that a court "cannot say with confidence that an erroneous exclusion of a scrupled, yet eligible, venire member is an isolated incident" in a case in which "the State exercised its peremptory challenges to remove all venire members who expressed any degree of hesitation against the death penalty," and the error could not be harmless in light of the state's manipulation of its challenges.

Justice Powell concurred in all but the last part of Justice Blackmun's opinion. He concluded that prosecutors may remove peremptorily jurors who may not be willing to impose lawful punishment and that, irrespective of the fact that the prosecutor challenged other jurors who had doubts about the death penalty, "the improper exclusion of even a single juror is sufficient to require resentencing in a capital case."

Justice Scalia, joined by Chief Justice Rehnquist and Justices White and O'Connor, dissented, arguing that the trial judge realized that he had erred in failing to sustain challenges for cause made to five jurors and that he effectively gave back a peremptory challenge to be used for the removal of Mrs. Bounds. He also expressed disagreement with dictum in the plurality portion of Justice Blackmun's opinion that suggested it was unconstitutional for prosecutors to exclude jurors who had reservations about capital punishment.

Ross v. Oklahoma, 487 U.S. 81 (1988) presented the opposite situation from *Gray:* the challenged juror stated that he would automatically vote for capital punishment, and so should have been excluded for cause, but defendant exercised a peremptory challenge at any rate. The state conceded that the juror should have been disqualified under *Witt,* but argued that defendant's use of one of his nine peremptory challenges rectified the trial court's error. The defendant responded that he ultimately exhausted all of his peremptories, and would have used the one that he expended due to the trial court's error to excuse another juror who ultimately sat on his panel.

Chief Justice Rehnquist, writing for the Court, concluded that Ross had not been denied an impartial jury because the juror who would have automatically imposed the death penalty was "removed from the jury as effectively as if the trial court excused him for cause." The Chief Justice rejected the argument that the loss of a peremptory challenge constitutes a violation of the right to be tried by an impartial jury, since "peremptory challenges are not of constitutional dimension." He reasoned that the state may define the purpose and manner of exercise of peremptory challenges, and that Oklahoma had properly qualified its grant of such challenges "by the requirement that the defendant must use those challenges to cure erroneous refusal by the trial court to excuse jurors for cause." He concluded that Ross made no claim that any of the jurors who convicted him and sentenced him to death was biased or partial, and that an error with respect to a juror who did not sit did not mandate reversal. The Chief Justice added that *Gray* could not stand for the proposition that any error that affects the composition of the jury must result in a reversal, since the *Gray* majority conceded that the trial judge in *Gray,* had he recognized a mistake, could have dismissed the entire venire and started anew.

Justice Marshall, joined by Justices Brennan, Blackmun, and Stevens, wrote that "[a] man's life is at stake," and "[w]e should not be playing games." He argued as follows:

> [T]he loss of a peremptory challenge in this case affected the composition of the jury panel in precisely the same way as the trial court's error in *Gray* itself. In *Gray,* the defendant was deprived of a juror who, although inexcusable for cause, seemed to be sympathetic to the defense in that she had expressed reservations about the death penalty. The defense in the instant case was

deprived of an opportunity to remove an otherwise qualified juror whom it perceived to be sympathetic to the prosecution."

Justice Marshall complained that the majority erred in comparing the dismissal of the entire venire with the instant case: "The *Gray* Court did not hold that a defendant has the right to any particular venire or panel; rather, the Court held that a defendant has a right to a jury selection procedure untainted by constitutional error."

From the perspective of the defendants in *Gray* and *Ross,* was the trial judge's error obviously more detrimental in one case than the other? What difference, if any, is there between the harm suffered by the defendant in the two cases?

In *Witherspoon,* the Court rejected the defendant's argument that a "death-qualified" jury could not render an impartial verdict as to guilt. The basis for this rejection was that Witherspoon's empirical evidence was tentative and sketchy. The defendant in Lockhart v. McCree, 476 U.S. 162 (1986), made a similar argument with updated empirical evidence, and met a similar fate. The Court held that the Constitution does not prohibit the removal for cause, prior to the guilt phase of a bifurcated trial, of prospective jurors whose opposition to the death penalty is so strong that it would prevent or substantially impair the performance of their duties as jurors at the sentencing phase of the trial.

Writing for the Court, Justice Rehnquist found fault with various empirical studies relied upon by the lower courts. But, even assuming that the studies supported the argument that "death qualified" juries were more prone to convict than juries on which persons were not excluded because of their opposition to capital punishment, he reasoned that the Constitution does not bar exclusion of jurors who are unwilling or unable to perform one of their duties as jurors.

The Court refused to find that a jury is biased when it is "death qualified," since an impartial jury is one that will conscientiously apply the law and find the facts and there was no showing that any of the twelve jurors in the case under review was partial. Finally, the Court distinguished *Witherspoon* and *Adams,* finding that they involved a deliberate attempt to slant a jury to make the death penalty more likely, whereas the removal of "*Witherspoon*-excludables" serves the proper interest of attaining a jury that could impartially decide all of the issues in a case.

Justice Marshall, joined by Justices Brennan and Stevens, dissented. He argued that "the Court upholds a practice that allows a State a special advantage in those prosecutions where the charges are the most serious and the possible punishments, the most severe." The advantage is that "[t]he State's mere announcement that it intends to seek the death penalty if the defendant is found guilty of a capital offense will give the prosecution a license to empanel a jury especially likely to return that very verdict." Justice Marshall joined the lower courts in crediting the studies done by researchers. He argued that *Witherspoon* struck down a system that was stacked against a defendant and that a "death-qualified" jury is stacked because it excludes jurors less prone than others to convict. The dissent relied upon *Ballew* (striking down 5 person jury) as well as the research on death-qualification to argue that juries from which jurors opposed to capital punishment have been excluded are less able to judge blameworthiness and to function as the representatives of the community. Justice Marshall concluded that the State's interest in submitting the penalty issue to a jury capable of imposing capital punishment could be accommodated by excluding jurors at the sentencing stage, not when guilt is determined. Justice Blackmun concurred in the judgment without opinion.

Relying on *McCree,* the Supreme Court held, in Buchanan v. Kentucky, 483 U.S. 402 (1987), that a defendant as to whom the capital portion of an indictment was dismissed was not denied an impartial jury when he was tried together with another defendant facing a capital charge by a jury from which prospective jurors opposed to the death penalty were excluded. Justice Blackmun's opinion for the Court reasoned that "*McCree* requires rejection of petitioner's claim that 'death qualification' violated his right to a jury selected from a representative cross-section of the community." He added that the state had not excluded the jurors opposed to the death penalty for arbitrary reasons unrelated to their ability to serve as jurors. Finally, he concluded that the state's interest in a joint trial is as compelling an interest as that recognized in *McCree* as sufficient to justify exclusion of jurors.

Justice Marshall, joined by Justices Brennan and Stevens, argued in dissent that the additional costs to a state of implementing a system of separate juries, or of providing alternate jurors who would replace those who opposed the death penalty after the guilt determination had been made, are minimal in comparison to a defendant's interest in an impartial jury at the guilt determination stage.

See also Winick, Prosecutorial Peremptory Challenge Practices in Capital Cases: An Empirical Study and A Constitutional Analysis, 81 Mich.L.Rev. 1 (1982) (suggesting that prosecutors may deprive defendants of fair sentencing juries in capital cases by systematically excluding jurors whose tendency is to vote for life imprisonment, not a death sentence); Note, Peremptory Challenges and the Meaning of Jury Representation, 89 Yale L.J. 1177 (1980).

b. *Jurors Who Must Be Excused for Cause*

Justus v. Commonwealth, 220 Va. 971, 266 S.E.2d 87 (1980), illustrates the question that courts face more frequently: when must a juror be excused? The Court reversed a capital conviction because one juror was improperly seated. The court said that the fact that the juror said she could give the defendant a fair trial was not enough to overcome her positive and unequivocal testimony that she thought Justus was guilty from what she heard and read. The court added that any reasonable doubt that a venireman does not stand indifferent in a case must be resolved in favor of the accused. A different approach is taken by many courts. For example, Jordan v. State, 247 Ga. 328, 276 S.E.2d 224 (1981), a capital case growing out of a prison riot in which a guard was killed, upholds the trial judge's ruling that a prospective juror who had worked previously as a deputy sheriff for 17 years, knew the district attorney when the attorney had been a detective, was working at the time of trial as a parole supervisor at the prison, knew the deceased prison guard, had worked with him two days before the riot, and expressed the view that it would be hard for him to base his decision strictly on what he heard in court, was not subject to challenge for cause when he said "he would do his best to keep an open mind during the trial but could not say positively whether he could do so or not."

Generally, the broad scope of the statutory language, particularly as embodied in "the state of mind" ground, vests considerable discretion in the trial judge. The following cases illustrate the kinds of challenges for cause that are attempted.

a. Appellant was convicted on two counts of aggravated bank robbery and attempted bank robbery. Evidence adduced at trial showed that appellant participated in three bank robberies and engaged in a shoot out with police at a residence. During the voir dire, one venireman stated he was "not interested in convicting anybody," and when asked if he would be prejudiced against conviction, he said there was a "reasonable doubt in my mind, [and] it would take an awful lot." He was removed for cause, by the state over appellant's objection. The trial court thereafter denied appellant's two motions to strike for cause. One was directed at a juror who was a senior vice-president of another bank and had previously served on a grand jury. The other was directed at a juror whose daughter had been robbed and raped. Both jurors said they believed they could give appellant a fair trial.[38] The appellate court sustained the trial court's rulings in both instances. United States v. Young, 553 F.2d 1132 (8th Cir.1977). How would you have ruled as a trial judge? As an appellate court?

b. Appellant was convicted for robbery and sentenced to twelve years' imprisonment. During the trial court voir dire, the following exchange took place.

"Mr. Pickard (Defense Counsel): Has anybody been robbed? Due to the fact that you have recently been robbed do you think you might be a little bit more inclined to convict regardless of the evidence?

"Juror Spencer: Yes sir, I probably would.

"Mr. Pickard: You think you may be a little biased?

"Juror Spencer: Yes sir.

"Mr. Pickard: You're saying in all probability you wouldn't be able to give him a fair trial and view the evidence objectively?

"Juror Spencer: Yes sir.

"Mr. Pickard: We challenge for cause.

"The Court: In spite of your experience a couple of weeks ago, could you still listen to the evidence that comes from this witness stand, and this evidence alone, and render a fair and impartial decision concerning the defendant, Beauford Harold Johnson?[39]

38. One commentator has suggested that "[c]ourts, feeling helpless before questions of human psychology, are unable to decide whether a person can be fair in spite of having an opinion on the matter at issue—thus the technique of 'just asking her.' Once having asked, however, the court cannot easily impugn the credibility of a citizen who has professed her impartiality." B. Babcock, Voir Dire: Preserving "Its Wonderful Power", 27 Stan.L.Rev. 545, 550 (1975).

Allowing jurors with preconceived ideas about guilt to sit simply because they state they will be fair is a practice that is vigorously attacked in Yount v. Patton, 710 F.2d 956 (3d Cir. 1983) (Stern, J., concurring).

39. Worthington v. State, 76 Ind. 506, 405 N.E.2d 913 (1980), held that a challenge for cause was properly rejected even though a witness said she had an opinion about the defendant's guilt, since she also said she

"Juror Spencer: Yes sir, I believe I could.

"The Court: You wouldn't let that experience that you had affect you?

"Juror Spencer: No sir.

"The Court: Challenge denied.

Juror Spencer became the foreman of the jury. (Emphasis added.)

The appellate court sustained the trial court's denial of challenge. Johnson v. State, 356 So.2d 769 (Ala.Cr.App.1978). Would you have sustained the lower court?

c. Is a juror who is a county commissioner and also a part-time deputy sheriff subject to a challenge for cause? See State v. Radi, 176 Mont. 451, 578 P.2d 1169 (1978) (statute does not permit challenge). How does a decision like this affect the impartial appearance of the jury? In Dennis v. United States, 339 U.S. 162 (1950), the Court held that where the government was a party in a litigation, jurors could not be excused for cause merely because they were government employees. The Court stated that actual bias must be shown. Should the result in *Dennis* have been affected by the fact that the defendant was charged with failure to comply with a subpoena issued by the House Un-American Activities Committee? Would jurors who are government employees be less impartial in cases where the substantive offense is a wrong done to the government itself?

d. Must a court strike an entire panel because of the conduct of one juror? In United States v. Khoury, 901 F.2d 948 (11th Cir.1990), the court sustained the trial court's refusal to strike the entire panel based on the conduct of one juror. During the voir dire in a trial for a drug related conspiracy, one juror said that her son had been charged with a crime and murdered in a drug related incident and proceeded to cry in the presence of the rest of the jury. The trial court struck this juror for cause and instructed the rest of the jurors that her statements were not evidence and had nothing to do with the case. The appellate court affirmed. Would this type of conduct prejudice the remaining jurors?

4. *The Use of Peremptory or Discretionary Challenges* [40]

The Supreme Court has described the peremptory challenge as follows:

> The essential nature of the peremptory challenge is that it is one exercised without a reason stated, without inquiry, and without being subject to the court's control. While challenges for cause permit rejection of jurors on a narrowly specified, provable and legally cognizable basis of partiality, the peremptory permits rejection for a real or imagined partiality that is less easily designated or demonstrable.

Swain v. Alabama, 380 U.S. 202 (1965). The Court in *Swain* stated that the peremptory challenge serves salutary purposes in the adversary system:

> The function of the challenge is not only to eliminate extremes of partiality on both sides, but to assure the parties that the jurors before whom they try

would decide the case on the evidence presented.

40. One study suggests that the effective use of peremptory challenges can significantly affect the outcome of some cases. See Zeisel & Diamond, The Effect of Peremptory Challenges on Jury and Verdict: An Experiment in a Federal District Court, 30 Stan.L.Rev. 491 (1978).

the case will decide on the basis of the evidence placed before them, and not otherwise. * * * Indeed the very availability of peremptories allows counsel to ascertain the possibility of bias through probing questions on the *voir dire* and facilitates the exercise of challenges for cause by removing the fear of incurring a juror's hostility through examination and challenge for cause.

Another purpose for the peremptory is to encourage a litigant to accept the jury and its decision because it belongs to him in a vivid sense: he picked it and was able to exclude those he feared. See Babcock, Voir Dire: Preserving "Its Wonderful Power," 27 Stan.L.Rev. 545, 552 (1975). Finally, as Ross v. Oklahoma points out, the peremptory challenge serves as a "backstop" when the trial judge erroneously refuses to excuse a juror for cause.

The relationship between peremptory challenges and voir dire should be apparent. In cases like *Mu'Min,* supra, the defendant argues that extensive voir dire is essential not only to determine whether a juror should be excluded for cause, but also to give defense counsel the information necessary to decide whether to expend a peremptory. As you go through the materials on peremptory challenges, see if the Court has been consistent in protecting peremptories at the same time as it has, in cases like *Mu'Min,* approved of limitations on voir dire. Note also that the Court in *Mu'Min* and Ross v. Oklahoma, supra, stressed that there is no constitutional right to peremptory challenges. Does this explain how the Court can approve of limitations on voir dire?

In felony cases, Fed.R.Crim.P. 24(b) gives the defense ten peremptory challenges and the prosecution six. Most states allocate equal numbers of challenges to prosecutors and defendants. In multiple defendant cases, the court will allocate challenges to defendants if they cannot agree on how to use them. Fed.R.Crim.P. 24(b)(2) states that in multiple defendant cases "the court may allow the parties additional challenges and permit them to be exercised separately or jointly."

There are several different procedural approaches to the exercise of peremptory challenges. Some jurisdictions use the strike system, in which the parties get to see the entire panel and to strike the least desirable (from their viewpoints) jurors first. Some use the challenge system, where a party will not be sure who will take the seat of a challenged juror. In many courts, the defendant must strike all jurors to whom she objects and then give the prosecutor a chance to do the same. Once a juror is "passed" (that is, not struck) the juror remains. See, e.g., United States v. Anderson, 562 F.2d 394 (6th Cir.1977). Other courts permit challenges to any member of the panel until challenges are exhausted. Can you see a problem with the system prohibiting a challenge after a pass?

While the peremptory challenge ostensibly allows the litigant to exclude a prospective juror on any grounds, the equal protection clause imposes some limits on this choice. In Swain v. Alabama, supra, defendant argued that the prosecutor exercised peremptories to exclude African–Americans from serving on petit juries. The Court held that if this allegation could be proven, the prosecutor's action would violate the equal protection clause. However, such a violation could not be proven by the use of peremptory challenges in a single case. Rather, the defendant would have to show that the prosecutor "in case after case, whatever the circumstances" was responsible for the removal of prospective jurors who survived challenges for cause "with the result that no Negroes ever serve on petit juries." It should be apparent that such a burden is all but impossible to meet. See People v. Wheeler, 22 Cal.3d 258, 148 Cal.Rptr. 890, 583 P.2d 748 (1978) (noting that data on such practices is inaccessible, and that at the time a peremptory is exercised, trial judges would be reluctant to allow a continuance for an investigation into a pattern of discrimination in other cases). Moreover, *Swain* did nothing to protect the first several victims of discrimination in the use of peremptories. As the court in *Wheeler* stated, "each and every defendant, not merely the last in this artificial sequence," ought to be entitled to the same constitutional protection.

The following case reconsiders *Swain* and finds that its proof requirements are too stringent. But in allowing defendants to show discrimination in their particular cases, whom is the Court trying to protect? And what kind of costs are involved in this protection?

BATSON v. KENTUCKY

Supreme Court of the United States, 1986.
476 U.S. 79.

JUSTICE POWELL delivered the opinion of the Court.

This case requires us to reexamine that portion of Swain v. Alabama, 380 U.S. 202 (1965), concerning the evidentiary burden placed on a criminal defendant who claims that he has been denied equal protection through the State's use of peremptory challenges to exclude members of his race from the petit jury.

I

Petitioner, a black man, was indicted in Kentucky on charges of second-degree burglary and receipt of stolen goods. * * * The prosecutor used his peremptory challenges to strike all four black persons on the venire, and a jury composed only of white persons was selected. Defense counsel moved to discharge the jury before it was sworn on the ground that the prosecutor's removal of the black veniremen violated petitioner's rights under the * * * Fourteenth Amendment to equal protection of the laws. * * * The judge then denied petitioner's motion * * *.

The jury convicted petitioner on both counts. On appeal to the Supreme Court of Kentucky, petitioner pressed, among other claims, the argument concerning the prosecutor's use of peremptory challenges. * * *

The Supreme Court of Kentucky affirmed. * * * We granted certiorari, and now reverse.

II

In Swain v. Alabama, this Court recognized that a "State's purposeful or deliberate denial to Negroes on account of race of participation as jurors in the administration of justice violates the Equal Protection Clause." This principle has been "consistently and repeatedly" reaffirmed, in numerous decisions of this Court both preceding and following *Swain.* We reaffirm the principle today.

A

More than a century ago, the Court decided that the State denies a black defendant equal protection of the laws when it puts him on trial before a jury from which members of his race have been purposefully excluded. Strauder v. West Virginia, 100 U.S. 303 (1880). That decision laid the foundation for the Court's unceasing efforts to eradicate racial discrimination in the procedures used to select the venire from which individual jurors are drawn. * * *

In holding that racial discrimination in jury selection offends the Equal Protection Clause, the Court in *Strauder* recognized, however, that a defendant has no right to a "petit jury composed in whole or in part of persons of his own race." * * * But the defendant does have the right to be tried by a jury whose members are selected pursuant to nondiscriminatory criteria. * * *

Purposeful racial discrimination in selection of the venire violates a defendant's right to equal protection because it denies him the protection that a trial by jury is intended to secure. * * * The petit jury has occupied a central position in our system of justice by safeguarding a person accused of crime against the arbitrary exercise of power by prosecutor or judge. Duncan v. Louisiana. Those on the venire must be "indifferently chosen," to secure the defendant's right under the Fourteenth Amendment to "protection of life and liberty against race or color prejudice."

Racial discrimination in selection of jurors harms not only the accused whose life or liberty they are summoned to try. Competence to serve as a juror ultimately depends on an assessment of individual qualifications and ability impartially to consider evidence presented at a trial. A person's race simply "is unrelated to his fitness as a juror." As long ago as *Strauder,* therefore, the Court recognized that by denying a person participation in jury service on account of his race, the State unconstitutionally discriminated against the excluded juror.

The harm from discriminatory jury selection extends beyond that inflicted on the defendant and the excluded juror to touch the entire community. Selection procedures that purposefully exclude black persons from juries undermine public confidence in the fairness of our system of justice. * * *

B

In *Strauder,* the Court invalidated a state statute that provided that only white men could serve as jurors. We can be confident that no State now has such a law. The Constitution requires, however, that we look beyond the face of the statute defining juror qualifications and also consider challenged selection practices to afford "protection against action of the State through its administrative officers in effecting the prohibited discrimination." * * * While decisions of this Court have been concerned largely with discrimination during selection of the venire, the principles announced there also forbid discrimination on account of race in selection of the petit jury. Since the Fourteenth Amendment protects an accused throughout the proceedings bringing him to justice, the State may not draw up its jury lists pursuant to neutral procedures but then resort to discrimination at "other stages in the selection process."

Accordingly, the component of the jury selection process at issue here, the State's privilege to strike individual jurors through peremptory challenges, is subject to the commands of the Equal Protection Clause. Although a prosecutor ordinarily is entitled to exercise permitted peremptory challenges "for any reason at all, as long as that reason is related to his view concerning the outcome" of the case to be tried, the Equal Protection Clause forbids the prosecutor to challenge potential jurors solely on account of their race or on the assumption that black jurors as a group will be unable impartially to consider the State's case against a black defendant.

III

The principles announced in *Strauder* never have been questioned in any subsequent decision of this Court. Rather, the Court has been called upon repeatedly to review the application of those principles to particular facts. A recurring question in these cases, as in any case alleging a violation of the Equal Protection Clause, was whether the defendant had met his burden of proving purposeful discrimination on the part of the State. That question also was at the heart of the portion of Swain v. Alabama we reexamine today.

A

* * * To preserve the peremptory nature of the prosecutor's challenge, the Court in *Swain* declined to scrutinize his actions in a particular case by relying on a presumption that he properly exercised the State's challenges.

* * *

A number of lower courts following the teaching of *Swain* reasoned that proof of repeated striking of blacks over a number of cases was necessary to establish a violation of the Equal Protection Clause. Since this interpretation of *Swain* has placed on defendants a crippling burden of proof, prosecutors' peremptory challenges are now largely immune from constitutional scrutiny. For reasons that follow, we reject this evidentiary formulation as inconsistent with standards that have been developed since *Swain* for assessing a prima facie case under the Equal Protection Clause.

B

[Justice Powell discusses and relies on general equal protection cases outside the peremptory challenge context].

[S]ince *Swain,* we have recognized that a black defendant alleging that members of his race have been impermissibly excluded from the venire may make out a prima facie case of purposeful discrimination by showing that the totality of the relevant facts gives rise to an inference of discriminatory purpose. Once the defendant makes the requisite showing, the burden shifts to the State to explain adequately the racial exclusion. The State cannot meet this burden on mere general assertions that its officials did not discriminate or that they properly performed their official duties. Rather, the State must demonstrate that "permissible racially neutral selection criteria and procedures have produced the monochromatic result." [a]

* * *

Since the ultimate issue is whether the State has discriminated in selecting the defendant's venire * * * the defendant may establish a prima facie case "in other ways than by evidence of long-continued unexplained absence" of members of his race "from many panels." * * *

[T]his Court has recognized that a defendant may make a prima facie showing of purposeful racial discrimination in selection of the venire by relying solely on the facts concerning its selection *in his case.* * * * "A single invidiously discriminatory governmental act" is not "immunized by the absence of such discrimination in the making of other comparable decisions." For evidentiary requirements to dictate that "several must suffer discrimination" before one could object, would be inconsistent with the promise of equal protec-

a. Our decisions concerning "disparate treatment" under Title VII of the Civil Rights Act of 1964 have explained the operation of prima facie burden of proof rules. See McDonnell Douglas Corp. v. Green, 411 U.S. 792 (1973); Texas Dept. of Community Affairs v. Burdine, 450 U.S. 248 (1981); United States Postal Service Board of Governors v. Aikens, 460 U.S. 711 (1983). The party alleging that he has been the victim of intentional discrimination carries the ultimate burden of persuasion. Texas Dept. of Community Affairs v. Burdine, supra, at 252–256.

tion to all.[b]

C

The standards for assessing a prima facie case in the context of discriminatory selection of the venire have been fully articulated since *Swain.* These principles support our conclusion that a defendant may establish a prima facie case of purposeful discrimination in selection of the petit jury solely on evidence concerning the prosecutor's exercise of peremptory challenges at the defendant's trial. To establish such a case, the defendant first must show that he is a member of a cognizable racial group, and that the prosecutor has exercised peremptory challenges to remove from the venire members of the defendant's race. Second, the defendant is entitled to rely on the fact, as to which there can be no dispute, that peremptory challenges constitute a jury selection practice that permits "those to discriminate who are of a mind to discriminate." Finally, the defendant must show that these facts and any other relevant circumstances raise an inference that the prosecutor used that practice to exclude the veniremen from the petit jury on account of their race. This combination of factors in the empaneling of the petit jury, as in the selection of the venire, raises the necessary inference of purposeful discrimination.

In deciding whether the defendant has made the requisite showing, the trial court should consider all relevant circumstances. For example, a "pattern" of strikes against black jurors included in the particular venire might give rise to an inference of discrimination. Similarly, the prosecutor's questions and statements during *voir dire* examination and in exercising his challenges may support or refute an inference of discriminatory purpose. These examples are merely illustrative. We have confidence that trial judges, experienced in supervising *voir dire,* will be able to decide if the circumstances concerning the prosecutor's use of peremptory challenges creates a prima facie case of discrimination against black jurors.

Once the defendant makes a prima facie showing, the burden shifts to the State to come forward with a neutral explanation for challenging black jurors. Though this requirement imposes a limitation in some cases on the full peremptory character of the historic challenge, we emphasize that the prosecutor's explanation need not rise to the level justifying exercise of a challenge for cause. But the prosecutor may not rebut the defendant's prima facie case of discrimination by stating merely that he challenged jurors of the defendant's race on the assumption—or his intuitive judgment—that they would be partial to the defendant because of their shared race. * * * The core guarantee of equal protection, ensuring citizens that their State will not discriminate on account of race, would be meaningless were we to approve the exclusion of jurors on the basis of such assumptions, which arise solely from the jurors' race. Nor may the prosecutor rebut the defendant's case merely by denying that he had a discriminatory motive or "affirm[ing] [his] good faith in making individual selections." If these general assertions were accepted as rebutting a defendant's prima facie case, the Equal Protection Clause "would be but a vain and illusory requirement." The prosecutor therefore must articulate a neutral explanation related to the particular case to be tried. The trial court then will have the duty to determine if the

b. Decisions under Title VII also recognize that a person claiming that he has been the victim of intentional discrimination may make out a prima facie case by relying solely on the facts concerning the alleged discrimination against him.

defendant has established purposeful discrimination.

IV

The State contends that our holding will eviscerate the fair trial values served by the peremptory challenge. Conceding that the Constitution does not guarantee a right to peremptory challenges and that *Swain* did state that their use ultimately is subject to the strictures of equal protection, the State argues that the privilege of unfettered exercise of the challenge is of vital importance to the criminal justice system.

While we recognize, of course, that the peremptory challenge occupies an important position in our trial procedures, we do not agree that our decision today will undermine the contribution the challenge generally makes to the administration of justice. The reality of practice, amply reflected in many state- and federal-court opinions, shows that the challenge may be, and unfortunately at times has been, used to discriminate against black jurors. By requiring trial courts to be sensitive to the racially discriminatory use of peremptory challenges, our decision enforces the mandate of equal protection and furthers the ends of justice. In view of the heterogeneous population of our Nation, public respect for our criminal justice system and the rule of law will be strengthened if we ensure that no citizen is disqualified from jury service because of his race.

Nor are we persuaded by the State's suggestion that our holding will create serious administrative difficulties. * * * We decline, however, to formulate particular procedures to be followed upon a defendant's timely objection to a prosecutor's challenges.

V

In this case, petitioner made a timely objection to the prosecutor's removal of all black persons on the venire. Because the trial court flatly rejected the objection without requiring the prosecutor to give an explanation for his action, we remand this case for further proceedings. If the trial court decides that the facts establish, prima facie, purposeful discrimination and the prosecutor does not come forward with a neutral explanation for his action, our precedents require that petitioner's conviction be reversed.

JUSTICE WHITE, concurring.

The Court overturns the principal holding in Swain v. Alabama, 380 U.S. 202 (1965), that the Constitution does not require in any given case an inquiry into the prosecutor's reasons for using his peremptory challenges to strike blacks from the petit jury panel in the criminal trial of a black defendant and that in such a case it will be presumed that the prosecutor is acting for legitimate trial-related reasons. The Court now rules that such use of peremptory challenges in a given case may, but does not necessarily, raise an inference, which the prosecutor carries the burden of refuting, that his strikes were based on the belief that no black citizen could be a satisfactory juror or fairly try a black defendant.

I agree that, to this extent, *Swain* should be overruled. I do so because *Swain* itself indicated that the presumption of legitimacy with respect to the striking of black venire persons could be overcome by evidence that over a period of time the prosecution had consistently excluded blacks from petit juries. This should have warned prosecutors that using peremptories to exclude blacks on the assumption that no black juror could fairly judge a black defendant would violate the Equal Protection Clause.

It appears, however, that the practice of peremptorily eliminating blacks from petit juries in cases with black defendants remains widespread, so much so that I agree that an opportunity to inquire should be afforded when this occurs. If the defendant objects, the judge, in whom the Court puts considerable trust, may determine that the prosecution must respond. * * *

Much litigation will be required to spell out the contours of the Court's equal protection holding today, and the significant effect it will have on the conduct of criminal trials cannot be gainsaid. But I agree with the Court that the time has come to rule as it has, and I join its opinion and judgment.

* * *

JUSTICE MARSHALL, concurring.

I join JUSTICE POWELL's eloquent opinion for the Court, which takes a historic step toward eliminating the shameful practice of racial discrimination in the selection of juries. The Court's opinion cogently explains the pernicious nature of the racially discriminatory use of peremptory challenges, and the repugnancy of such discrimination to the Equal Protection Clause. The Court's opinion also ably demonstrates the inadequacy of any burden of proof for racially discriminatory use of peremptories that requires that "justice . . . sit supinely by" and be flouted in case after case before a remedy is available. I nonetheless write separately to express my views. The decision today will not end the racial discrimination that peremptories inject into the jury-selection process. That goal can be accomplished only by eliminating peremptory challenges entirely.

* * *

* * * Merely allowing defendants the opportunity to challenge the racially discriminatory use of peremptory challenges in individual cases will not end the illegitimate use of the peremptory challenge.

* * * First, defendants cannot attack the discriminatory use of peremptory challenges at all unless the challenges are so flagrant as to establish a prima facie case. * * * [W]here only one or two black jurors survive the challenges for cause, the prosecutor need have no compunction about striking them from the jury because of their race. Prosecutors are left free to discriminate against blacks in jury selection provided that they hold that discrimination to an "acceptable" level.

Second, when a defendant can establish a prima facie case, trial courts face the difficult burden of assessing prosecutors' motives. Any prosecutor can easily assert facially neutral reasons for striking a juror, and trial courts are ill equipped to second-guess those reasons. How is the court to treat a prosecutor's statement that he struck a juror because the juror had a son about the same age as defendant, or seemed "uncommunicative," or "never cracked a smile" and, therefore "did not possess the sensitivities necessary to realistically look at the issues and decide the facts in this case"? If such easily generated explanations are sufficient to discharge the prosecutor's obligation to justify his strikes on nonracial grounds, then the protection erected by the Court today may be illusory.

Nor is outright prevarication by prosecutors the only danger here. * * * A prosecutor's own conscious or unconscious racism may lead him easily to the conclusion that a prospective black juror is "sullen," or "distant," a characterization that would not have come to his mind if a white juror had acted identically. A judge's own conscious or unconscious racism may lead him to accept such an explanation as well supported. * * * Even if all parties approach the Court's mandate with the best of conscious intentions, that mandate requires them to confront and overcome their own racism on all levels—a challenge I doubt all of them can meet. * * *

The inherent potential of peremptory challenges to distort the jury process by permitting the exclusion of jurors on racial grounds should ideally lead the Court to ban them entirely from the criminal justice system. * * *

Some authors have suggested that the courts should ban prosecutors' peremptories entirely, but should zealously guard the defendant's peremptory as "essential to the fairness of trial by jury," and "one of the most important of the rights secured to the accused". I would not find that an acceptable solution. Our criminal justice system "requires not only freedom from any bias against the accused, but also from any prejudice against his prosecution. Between him and the state the scales are to be evenly held." We can maintain that balance, not by permitting both prosecutor and defendant to engage in racial discrimination in jury selection, but by banning the use of peremptory challenges by prosecutors and by allowing the States to eliminate the defendant's peremptories as well.

* * *

[The concurring opinion of JUSTICE STEVENS, joined by JUSTICE BRENNAN, and the concurring opinion of JUSTICE O'CONNOR, are omitted.]

CHIEF JUSTICE BURGER, joined by JUSTICE REHNQUIST, dissenting.

* * *

Today the Court sets aside the peremptory challenge, a procedure which has been part of the common law for many centuries and part of our jury system for nearly 200 years. It does so on the basis of a constitutional argument that was rejected, without a single dissent, in Swain v. Alabama. * * *

* * *

Instead of even considering the history or function of the peremptory challenge, the bulk of the Court's opinion is spent recounting the well-established principle that intentional exclusion of racial groups from jury venires is a violation of the Equal Protection Clause. I too reaffirm that principle, which has been a part of our constitutional tradition since at least Strauder v. West Virginia. But if today's decision is nothing more than mere "application" of the "principles announced in *Strauder,*" as the Court maintains, some will consider it curious that the application went unrecognized for over a century. The Court in *Swain* had no difficulty in unanimously concluding that cases such as *Strauder* did not require inquiry into the basis for a peremptory challenge. * * *

A moment's reflection quickly reveals the vast differences between the racial exclusions involved in *Strauder* and the allegations before us today:

"Exclusion from the venire summons process implies that the government (usually the legislative or judicial branch) ... has made the general determination that those excluded are unfit to try *any* case. Exercise of the peremptory challenge, by contrast, represents the discrete decision, made by one of two or more opposed *litigants* in the trial phase of our adversary system of justice, that the challenged venireperson will likely be more unfavorable to that litigant in that *particular case* than others on the same venire.

"Thus, excluding a particular cognizable group from all venire pools is stigmatizing and discriminatory in several interrelated ways that the peremptory challenge is not. The former singles out the excluded group, while individuals of all groups are equally subject to peremptory challenge on any basis, including their group affiliation. Further, venire-pool exclusion bespeaks *a priori* across-the-board total unfitness, while peremptory-strike exclusion merely suggests potential partiality in a particular isolated case. Exclusion from venires focuses on the inherent attributes of the excluded group and infers its *inferiority,* but the peremptory does not. To suggest that a particular race is unfit to judge in any case necessarily is racially insulting. To suggest that each race may have its own special concerns, or even may tend to favor its own, is not." United States v. Leslie, 783 F.2d 541, 554 (CA5 1986) (en banc).

Unwilling to rest solely on jury venire cases such as *Strauder,* the Court also invokes general equal protection principles in support of its holding. But peremptory challenges are often lodged, of necessity, for reasons "normally thought irrelevant to legal proceedings or official action, namely, the race, religion, nationality, occupation or affiliations of people summoned for jury duty." * * * [U]nadulterated equal protection analysis is simply inapplicable to peremptory challenges exercised in any particular case. A clause that requires a minimum "rationality" in government actions has no application to " 'an arbitrary and capricious right' " * * *.

* * *

Our system permits two types of challenges: challenges for cause and peremptory challenges. Challenges for cause obviously have to be explained; by definition, peremptory challenges do not. * * * Analytically, there is no middle ground: A challenge either has to be explained or it does not. It is readily apparent, then, that to permit inquiry into the basis for a peremptory challenge would force "the peremptory challenge [to] collapse into the challenge for cause." * * *

Confronted with the dilemma it created, the Court today attempts to decree a middle ground. To rebut a prima facie case, the Court requires a "neutral explanation" for the challenge, but is at pains to "emphasize" that the "explanation need not rise to the level justifying exercise of a challenge for cause." I am at a loss to discern the governing principles here. A "clear and reasonably specific" explanation of "legitimate reasons" for exercising the challenge will be difficult to distinguish from a challenge for cause. * * * Apparently the Court envisions permissible challenges short of a challenge for cause that are just a little bit arbitrary—but not too much. While our trial judges are "experienced in supervising *voir dire,*" they have no experience in administering rules like this.

* * *

Today we mark the return of racial differentiation as the Court accepts a positive evil for a perceived one. Prosecutors and defense attorneys alike will build records in support of their claims that peremptory challenges have been exercised in a racially discriminatory fashion by asking jurors to state their racial background and national origin for the record, despite the fact that "such questions may be offensive to some jurors and thus are not ordinarily asked on voir dire." This process is sure to tax even the most capable counsel and judges since determining whether a prima facie case has been established will "require a continued monitoring and recording of the 'group' composition of the panel present and prospective."

* * *

JUSTICE REHNQUIST, with whom THE CHIEF JUSTICE joins, dissenting.

* * *

I cannot subscribe to the Court's unprecedented use of the Equal Protection Clause to restrict the historic scope of the peremptory challenge, which has been described as "a necessary part of trial by jury." In my view, there is simply nothing "unequal" about the State's using its peremptory challenges to strike blacks from the jury in cases involving black defendants, so long as such challenges are also used to exclude whites in cases involving white defendants, Hispanics in cases involving Hispanic defendants, Asians in cases involving Asian defendants, and so on. This case-specific use of peremptory challenges by the State does not single out blacks, or members of any other race for that matter, for discriminatory treatment. Such use of peremptories is at best based upon seat-of-the-pants instincts, which are undoubtedly crudely stereotypical and may in many cases be hopelessly mistaken. But as long as they are applied across-the-board to jurors of all races and nationalities, I do not see—and the Court most certainly has not explained—how their use violates the Equal Protection Clause.

* * *

Note

Batson left a number of open questions, including: Is *Batson* only applicable to exclusion of African-Americans? Does it apply to discriminatory use of peremptories by defense counsel? Must the defendant be a member of the excluded group? What kind of neutral explanation, short of a challenge for cause, will suffice? The Court has decided several cases in an attempt to answer some of these questions.

In Powers v. Ohio, 111 S.Ct. 1364 (1991), the defendant, a white man, alleged that the prosecutor exercised peremptory challenges to exclude African-American jurors on the basis of race. In a 7–2 decision, the Court held that Powers had standing to bring an equal protection claim on behalf of the excluded African-American jurors. The case was remanded to determine whether the prosecutor had in fact excluded African-Americans on the basis of race.

The majority opinion, written by Justice Kennedy, downplayed the numerous references in *Batson* to the racial identity between the defendant and the excused prospective juror. Justice Kennedy asserted that "*Batson* was designed to serve multiple ends, only one of which was to protect individual defendants from discrimination in the selection of jurors. * * * *Batson* recognized that a prosecutor's discriminatory use of peremptory challenges harms the excluded jurors and the community at large."

Does the above passage mean that the community at large has a cause of action when prospective jurors are excluded on account of race? What if a defendant intentionally decides not to object to race-based strikes? Does the defendant waive the community's right to challenge exclusion?

The majority saw the question in *Powers* as one of third party standing. Could the defendant, whose rights were not infringed, assert the equal protection rights of the excluded prospective jurors? Justice Kennedy noted three requirements for third party standing, based on the Court's previous cases: (1) the litigant must have suffered an "injury in fact;" (2) the litigant must have a "close relation to the third party;" and (3) there must exist some hindrance to the third party's ability to protect his or her own interests.

As to the first requirement of injury in fact, Justice Kennedy argued that a criminal defendant suffers injury in fact from exclusion of jurors of a different race because "racial discrimination in the selection of jurors casts doubt on the integrity of the judicial process * * * and places the fairness of a criminal proceeding in doubt." On this point, the Court concluded as follows:

> The purpose of the jury system is to impress upon the criminal defendant and the community as a whole that a verdict * * * is given in accordance with law by persons who are fair. The verdict will not be accepted or understood in these terms if the jury is chosen by unlawful means at the outset. Upon these considerations, we find that a criminal defendant suffers a real injury when the prosecutor excludes jurors at his or her own trial on account of race.

As to the second requirement of a close relationship between the litigant and the third party, the Court stated that "the excluded juror and the criminal defendant have a common interest in eliminating racial discrimination from the courtroom. * * * The rejected juror may lose confidence in the court and its verdicts, as may the defendant if his or her objections cannot be heard." Justice Kennedy also asserted that "*voir dire* permits a party to establish a relation, if not a bond of trust, with the jurors."

Concerning the third requirement for third party standing, the majority found that it was very unlikely that the excluded prospective juror would assert his or her own equal protection rights. Justice Kennedy noted that the barriers to bringing an individual action are "daunting," and concluded that "the reality is that a juror dismissed because of his race probably will leave the courtroom possessing little incentive to set in motion the arduous process needed to vindicate his own rights."

Justice Scalia, joined by Chief Justice Rehnquist, filed a stinging dissent. Justice Scalia noted that a grant of third party standing assumes that the first party has rights at stake to begin with. He contended that African-American jurors excluded by peremptory challenge because of their race in fact suffer no equal protection violation, since all other groups are equally subject to peremptory challenge. Justice Scalia argued that when one group, "like all others, has been made subject to peremptory challenge on the basis of its group characteristic, its members have been treated not differently but the same." Justice Scalia also complained that "to affirm that the Equal Protection Clause applies to strikes of individual jurors is effectively to abolish the peremptory challenge."

Even assuming that excluded jurors had an equal protection right, Justice Scalia argued that the jurors' claims could not be asserted by the defendant. The dissenters objected most strongly to the Court's assertion that a white defendant suffered an "injury in fact" by the exclusion of African-American jurors. Justice Scalia noted that the majority relied on the "perceptions of unfairness" that would occur upon exclusion of jurors on account of race. He responded that "injury in perception would seem to be the very antithesis of injury in fact." Justice Scalia recognized that Powers had "a concrete interest in challenging the practice at issue here; he would have a concrete interest in challenging a mispronunciation of one of the jurors' names, if that would overturn his conviction. But none of this has anything to do with injury in fact."

Justice Scalia contended that the majority had improperly applied the holding and reasoning of *Batson:*

> This case * * * involves not a clarification of *Batson,* but the creation of an additional, *ultra-Batson* departure from established law. Petitioner seeks not some further elaboration of the right to have his racial identity disregarded in the selection of the jury, but rather the announcement of a new right to have his jury immune from the exclusion of people of *any* race. * * * Not only does this exceed the rationale of *Batson,* but it exceeds *Batson's* emotional and symbolic justification as well. Notwithstanding history, precedent, and the significant benefits of the peremptory challenge system, it is intolerably offensive for the State to imprison a person on the basis of a conviction rendered by

a jury from which members of that person's minority race were carefully excluded. I am unmoved, however, and I think most Americans would be, by this white defendant's complaint that he was sought to be tried by an all-white jury * * *.

How can the grant of third party standing in *Powers* be squared with the Court's denial of third party standing in Fourth Amendment cases such as United States v. Payner and Rakas v. Illinois (Chapter Two, supra)? Is there some difference between a Fourth and Sixth Amendment violation that can account for such disparate treatment?

In light of *Powers,* can a *Batson* violation ever be harmless error?

Recall that in Holland v. Illinois, supra, the Court held that a white defendant could not challenge the exclusion of African–Americans from the petit jury under the fair cross-section requirement of the Sixth Amendment. The Court reasoned that the fair cross-section requirement was not applicable to the petit jury. After *Powers,* does *Holland* have any practical effect?

In the per curiam opinion of Alvarado v. United States, 110 S.Ct. 2995 (1990), the Court stated that a *Batson* violation could be found even if the resulting jury represented a fair cross-section of the community. The Court noted that a *Batson* claim is not premised on the fair cross-section requirement (which does not apply to the petit jury at any rate, after *Holland*), or on the resulting makeup of the jury, but rather on the striking of jurors on purely racial grounds.

Can the prosecutor object to race-based peremptory challenges by the defendant? After *Powers,* the fact that the objecting party is not of the same race as the excluded juror is irrelevant. However, in *Powers,* the party exercising the peremptory challenge was a government actor. If the party exercising the peremptory is a private actor, the issue is whether their activity, even though racially discriminatory, constitutes state action. In Edmonson v. Leesville Concrete Co., 111 S.Ct. 2077 (1991), the Court held that a private litigant in a civil case may not use peremptory challenges to exclude jurors on account of race. Justice Kennedy, writing for six members of the Court, found the necessary state action in the trial judge's excusing of the juror once a peremptory challenge is exercised: "By enforcing a discriminatory peremptory challenge, the court has not only made itself a party to the biased act, but has elected to place its power, property and prestige behind the alleged discrimination."

Justice O'Connor, joined by Chief Justice Rehnquist and Justice Scalia, dissented. She asserted that "not everything that happens in a courtroom is state action" and that "the peremptory is, by design, an enclave of private action in a government-managed proceeding." She concluded that "it is antithetical to the nature of our adversarial process * * * to say that a private attorney acting on behalf of a private client represents the government for constitutional purposes."

Justice Scalia filed a separate dissenting opinion, arguing that the majority's decision would have a negative effect on criminal defendants:

> The effect of today's decision (which logically must apply to criminal prosecutions) will be to prevent the defendant from [striking jurors on account of race]—so that the minority defendant can no longer seek to prevent an all-white jury, or to seat as many jurors of his own race as possible. * * * So in criminal cases, today's decision represents a net loss to the minority litigant.

Justice Scalia also lamented the costs imposed by the majority's application of *Batson* to peremptory strikes by private parties:

When combined with our decision this Term in *Powers* * * * today's decision means that *both* sides, in *all* * * * jury cases, no matter what their race * * * may lodge racial-challenge objections and, after those objections have been considered and denied, appeal the denials—with the consequence, if they are successful, of having the judgments against them overturned. Thus, yet another complexity is added to an increasingly Byzantine system of justice that devotes more and more of its energies to side shows and less and less to the merits of the case.

See also United States v. Greer, 939 F.2d 1076 (5th Cir.1991) (after *Edmonson, Batson* applies to peremptory strikes by defense counsel). The Court has recently granted certiorari to determine whether defense counsel's peremptory strikes constitute state action sufficient to trigger *Batson* protections. See Georgia v. McCollum, 112 S.Ct. 370 (1991). cf. Polk County v. Dodson, 454 U.S. 312 (1981) (public defender's representation of an indigent defendant did not constitute action "under color of state law" for purposes of 42 U.S.C. § 1983).

If a party makes out a prima facie case of racial discrimination by the adversary's use of peremptory challenges, *Batson* requires that the striking party give a race-neutral explanation sufficient to rebut the prima facie case. In Hernandez v. New York, 111 S.Ct. 1859 (1991), the defendant claimed that the prosecutor struck Latino jurors on account of race. The prosecutor did not wait for the trial court's ruling on whether a prima facie case of discrimination had been established. Rather, the prosecutor defended his strikes on the ground that since the prospective jurors were bilingual and many witnesses would be Spanish-speaking, he "was very uncertain that they would be able to listen and follow the interpreter." The prosecutor based his assertion on the answers given by the prospective jurors to whether they could accept the interpreter as the final arbiter of what was said by the Spanish-speaking witnesses. According to the prosecutor, the excluded prospective jurors "looked away from me and said with some hesitancy that they would try * * * to follow the interpreter." The trial court and the State appellate courts found that this explanation was race-neutral and sufficient to rebut the defendant's prima facie case. The Supreme Court agreed, but there was no majority opinion.

Justice Kennedy wrote an opinion joined by Chief Justice Rehnquist, Justice White, and Justice Souter. Justice Kennedy defined a race-neutral explanation as one "based on something other than the race of the juror. * * * Unless a discriminatory intent is inherent in the prosecutor's explanation, the reason offered will be deemed race neutral." Justice Kennedy found that the prosecutor's explanation "rested neither on the intention to exclude Latino or bilingual jurors, nor on stereotypical assumptions about Latinos or bilinguals." According to Justice Kennedy, the prosecutor properly divided jurors into two potential classes: "those whose conduct during *voir dire* would persuade him they might have difficulty in accepting the translator's rendition of Spanish-language testimony and those potential jurors who gave no reason for such doubt. Each category would include both Latinos and non-Latinos."

Justice Kennedy recognized that the prosecutor's criterion for exclusion would have a disparate impact on prospective Latino jurors, since they were more likely to be fluent in Spanish than non-Latino jurors. He responded, however, that while disparate impact was relevant in determining whether the prosecutor acted with discriminatory intent, "it will not be conclusive in the preliminary race-neutrality step of the *Batson* inquiry. * * * Unless the government actor adopted a criterion with the intent of causing the impact asserted, that impact itself does not violate the principle of race-neutrality. Nothing in the prosecutor's explanation shows that he chose to exclude jurors * * * *because* he wanted to prevent bilingual Latinos from serving on the jury."

Justice Kennedy then proceeded to determine whether the trial court erred in holding that in light of the prosecutor's explanation, the defendant had failed to carry his burden of proving purposeful discrimination. Justice Kennedy found that the issue of intent to discriminate was a pure issue of fact that was based on the credibility of the prosecutor's explanation. Accordingly, Justice Kennedy asserted that the trial court's finding on the issue of discriminatory intent should not be overturned unless it was clearly erroneous. The plurality found no clear error in the trial court's decision that the prosecutor's explanation was credible.

Justice Kennedy cautioned that his opinion did not imply that the prosecutor had untrammeled discretion to exclude bilingual jurors. He noted that the case would be different if the prosecutor had merely stated that he did not want Spanish-speaking jurors. Justice Kennedy concluded:

> It may well be, for certain ethnic groups and in some communities, that proficiency in a particular language, like skin color, should be treated as a surrogate for race under an equal protection analysis. * * * And, as we make clear, a policy of striking all who speak a given language without regard to the particular circumstances of the trial or the individual responses of the jurors, may be found by the trial judge to be a pretext for racial discrimination. But that case is not before us.

Justice O'Connor, joined by Justice Scalia, concurred in the judgment. She agreed with much of Justice Kennedy's opinion, but felt that the plurality went "farther than it needs to in assessing the constitutionality of the prosecutor's asserted justification for his peremptory strikes." According to Justice O'Connor, "if the trial court believes the prosecutor's nonracial justification, and that finding is not clearly erroneous, that is the end of the matter." Justice O'Connor stressed that disparate impact was no substitute for a finding of intentional discrimination.

Justice Stevens, joined by Justices Marshall and Blackmun, dissented. He argued that the prosecutor's explanation was insufficient to overcome the prima facie case of discrimination because, among other things, "the justification would inevitably result in a disproportionate disqualification of Spanish-speaking venirepersons." According to Justice Stevens "an explanation that is race-neutral on its face is nonetheless unacceptable if it is merely a proxy for a discriminatory practice." Justice Stevens also noted that the prosecutor's concerns could have been alleviated by methods short of striking the prospective jurors, such as by a charge to the jury that the official translation alone is evidence.

What limitations are placed on a prosecutor's explanation for exercising peremptory challenges after *Hernandez?* Will a prosecutor who is intentionally discriminating on the basis of race always be able to assert some credible race-neutral explanation? See also United States v. Nichols, 937 F.2d 1257 (7th Cir.1991) (neutral explanation found where the prospective juror was young and living with a man to whom she was not married); United States v. Cartlidge, 808 F.2d 1064 (5th Cir.1987) (neutral explanation found where prospective juror was young, single and unemployed); People v. Simpson, 121 A.D.2d 881, 504 N.Y.S.2d 115 (1986) (neutral explanation found where prospective African-American jurors showed some sympathy toward criminals on voir dire); United States v. Biaggi, 853 F.2d 89 (2d Cir.1988) (*Batson* limits exclusion of Italian-Americans, but prosecutor gave neutral explanation for exclusion; prospective jurors had displayed angry, arrogant or flippant demeanors).

In Ford v. Georgia, 111 S.Ct. 850 (1991), a defendant, prior to the Court's decision in *Batson,* raised a claim of discrimination under *Swain.* Justice Souter, writing for a unanimous Court, held that the defendant had properly preserved a *Batson* claim for direct appeal. The Court reasoned that *Batson* did not change the nature of the violation in *Swain,* but merely provided a more lenient burden of proof to substantiate the claim. Justice Souter therefore concluded that "a defendant alleging a violation of equal protection of the law under *Swain* necessarily states an equal protection violation subject to proof under the *Batson* standard of circumstantial evidence as well." See also Jimeno v. Texas, 112 S.Ct. ___ (1992) (Applying *Ford* and holding that reliance on *Swain* preserved the defendant's equal protection argument). *Ford* also approved a state procedure requiring a *Batson* claim to be raised in the period between the selection of the jurors and the administration of their oaths. But the Court held that the rule could not be applied retroactively to preclude federal review of a *Batson* claim.

Hernandez clearly indicates that Latinos are protected by the equal protection clause under *Batson.* What about other groups? United States v. De Gross, 1992 WL 63082 (9th Cir.1992) found a *Batson* violation where defense counsel exercised peremptory challenges on the basis of gender. Other courts have disagreed. See United States v. Nichols, 937 F.2d 1257 (7th Cir.1991) (*Batson* is only concerned with the racially discriminatory use of peremptory challenges; therefore, the prosecutor's exclusion of all prospective African–American women jurors did not establish a prima facie case of discrimination; African–American men were seated on the jury, and the prosecutor had unexpended peremptories with which he could have excluded these men). See also United States v. Greer, 939 F.2d 1076 (5th Cir.1991) (*Batson* applies to exclusion of prospective Jewish jurors; therefore, the trial court did not err in refusing to require Jewish venire-members to identify themselves, even though defendants were being prosecuted for hate crimes against Jews). Some groups, while probably protected by *Batson,* will often be so difficult to discern that a prima facie case of discrimination will not be made. For example, in United States v. Di Pasquale, 864 F.2d 271 (3d Cir.1988), defendant challenged the exclusion of prospective Italian–American jurors. The court held that a prima facie case had not been made, since the defendant's only proof was that the excluded jurors had Italian surnames. What should Di Pasquale have done to prove a prima facie case of discrimination?

What exactly constitutes a prima facie case of discrimination under *Batson?* What if the prosecutor strikes three of six prospective African–American jurors? What if five of six are struck, but the prosecutor still has a peremptory to use and does not use it against the sixth African–American? Is it relevant that the prosecutor exercised peremptory challenges against non-minorities? Are questions asked on voir dire relevant? See generally United States v. Esparsen, 930 F.2d 1461 (10th Cir.1991) (courts have looked to questions asked on voir dire, the answers of those included as compared to those who were struck, the number of challenges used on a certain group, whether members of the group actually sat on the jury, whether the litigant had unexpended peremptories, the rate at which members of the group were struck compared to the rate at which non-members were struck, and other factors particular to the case). While no single factor is usually dispositive, a prima facie case will ordinarily be found if the litigant strikes all prospective jurors from a racial group. As the court in *Esparsen* put it, "the striking of a single juror will not always constitute a prima facie case, but when no members of a racial group remain because of that strike, it does." See also People v. James, 132 A.D.2d 932, 518 N.Y.S.2d 266 (1987) (prima facie case of race discrimination where the prosecutor challenged five out of six African–Americans, which constituted half of his peremptory challenges); People v. Howard, 128 A.D.2d

804, 513 N.Y.S.2d 506 (1987) (where prosecutor's only peremptory challenges were to the only two African–Americans on the venire, a prima facie case of discrimination was established); United States v. Hughes, 864 F.2d 78 (8th Cir.1988) (questioning on voir dire did not reveal sufficient independent reasons, other than race, for the striking of two African–Americans). The court in *Hughes* also found it relevant that there had been frequent charges of systematic exclusion of African–Americans from juries in the judicial district.

For a thorough discussion of *Batson* and its implications, see Alschuler, The Supreme Court and the Jury: Voir Dire, Peremptory Challenges, and the Review of Jury Verdicts, 56 Chi.L.Rev. 153 (1989).

Consider Judge Gee's comments about *Batson,* which were made in dissent in the court of appeals decision in *Edmonson,* 860 F.2d 1308 (5th Cir.1988), the case in which the Court ultimately extended *Batson* to civil cases:

> What remains after [*Batson*] is not the peremptory challenge which our procedure has known for decades—or not one which can be freely exercised against all jurors in all cases, at any rate. Justice Marshall would dispense with strikes entirely, and perhaps this will be the final outcome. In this much at least he is surely correct, that we must go on or backward; to stay here is to rest content with a strange procedural creature indeed: a challenge for semi-cause, * * * a skewed and curious device, exercisable without giving reasons in some cases but not in others, all depending on race.

After *Batson* and its progeny, does retaining the system of peremptory challenges make any sense?

5. *Jury Misconduct*

The conduct of the individual jurors during the trial proceedings and the subsequent deliberations must comport with the requirement of impartiality. The trial judge must deal with any particular action that could undermine a juror's impartiality. Where jurors learn of highly inflammatory information that will not be brought out in evidence, they may be disqualified. See, e.g., United States v. Williams, 568 F.2d 464 (5th Cir. 1978) (jurors saw newscast); People v. Honeycutt, 20 Cal.3d 150, 141 Cal.Rptr. 698, 570 P.2d 1050 (1977) (information and advice from an attorney friend of the foreman was prejudicial.) Even if the juror is adversely affected by events outside her control, she may have to be excused. See, e.g., United States v. Taylor, 554 F.2d 200 (5th Cir. 1977).

Additionally, a juror must remain able and qualified to perform his duty. See United States v. Smith, 550 F.2d 277 (5th Cir. 1977) (sleeping juror and juror whose conduct suggests that tampering has occurred are disqualified). Of course, the trial judge must be careful not to excuse a juror too quickly, and to excuse jurors in a way that does not prejudice either of the parties.

Habeas corpus relief was granted in Phillips v. Smith, 485 F.Supp. 1365 (S.D.N.Y.1980), affirmed, 632 F.2d 1019 (2d Cir.), on the ground that the defendant was denied a fair trial when the prosecutor learned during the trial that one juror's employment application was pending in his office, and the prosecutor did not disclose this fact to the court or the defense until after the jury returned its guilty verdict. The Supreme Court reversed, 455 U.S. 209 (1982), holding that due process does not require a new trial every time a juror is placed in a potentially compromising situation, and reasoning that where a post-trial hearing resulted in a finding that the juror was not actually biased, a federal court should not set aside a state conviction.

During the course of trial, the judge has discretion to sequester the jury. See United States v. Johnson, 584 F.2d 148 (6th Cir. 1978). See generally Annot., 72 ALR3d 131 (1976). Some jurisdictions require sequestration, unless it is waived. See N.Y.C.P.L. § 310.10; Davidson v. Commonwealth, 555 S.W.2d 269 (Ky.1977). Once deliberations begin, sequestration will be required. If a claim is made that some external influence has affected jury deliberations, an inquiry may be made. But the internal deliberations of the jury ordinarily will not be questioned by the court. See Federal Rule of Evidence 606(b).

In Rushen v. Spain, 464 U.S. 114 (1983), the Court reversed lower federal courts that had granted habeas corpus relief to a petitioner who complained about ex parte communications between a trial judge and a juror. The juror had indicated to the judge that she was an acquaintance of a woman who had been murdered by one of the defense witnesses, although she expressed the view that she could be fair to the defendants. The lower courts had reasoned that the contact between judge and juror could not be deemed harmless, since no contemporaneous record had been made. But the Supreme Court ruled that the lower federal courts should have deferred to the "presumptively correct" state court finding that the jury's deliberations had not been affected by the ex parte contact. See also United States v. Strickland, 935 F.2d 822 (7th Cir.1991) (a juror acted improperly when he asked a question of a government witness outside of court; but this was not prejudicial because the witness did not answer, curative instructions were given, and the trial judge determined after questioning that the juror could remain impartial).

The Supreme Court held, 5–4, in Tanner v. United States, 483 U.S. 107 (1987), that two defendants, who were convicted of conspiring to defraud the United States and mail fraud, were properly denied a hearing concerning juror misconduct. The defendants called to the trial judge's attention one juror's statement that several jurors had consumed alcohol at lunch throughout the trial, causing them to sleep during the afternoons. The only other evidence offered in the trial court in support of a hearing was defense counsel's testimony that he had observed one of the jurors "in a sort of giggly mood" during the trial, something not called to the judge's attention. While the case was pending on appeal, the defendants presented a second juror's affidavit indicating that numerous members of the jury, including the affiant, consumed alcohol during the trial and some jurors used illegal drugs. Writing for the majority, Justice O'Connor relied upon Fed.R.Evid. 606(b) and rejected the defendants' claim that substance abuse was an "outside" or "extraneous" influence that could impeach a jury verdict. She also rejected the argument that the failure to inquire into juror intoxication denies a defendant a fair trial before an impartial and competent jury, reasoning that other aspects of the trial process—voir dire of jurors, observations by the trial judge and courtroom participants, and observations and reports by fellow jurors—are adequate to assure defendants fair trials. Justice O'Connor expressed concern that routine impeachment of jury verdicts would have a negative effect on finality and on jury deliberations.

> There is little doubt that post-verdict investigation into juror misconduct would in some instances lead to the invalidation of verdicts reached after

irresponsible or improper behavior. It is not at all clear, however, that the jury system could survive such efforts to perfect it. Allegations of juror misconduct, incompetency, or inattentiveness, raised for the first time days, weeks, or months after the verdict seriously disrupt the finality of the process. Moreover, full and frank discussion in the jury room, jurors' willingness to return an unpopular verdict, and the community's trust in a system that relies on the decisions of laypeople would all be undermined by a barrage of post-verdict scrutiny of juror conduct.

Justice Marshall, joined by Justices Brennan, Blackmun and Stevens, dissented. He concluded that "[e]very criminal defendant has a constitutional right to be tried by competent jurors," and that "[i]f, as charged, members of petitioners' jury were intoxicated as a result of their use of drugs and alcohol to the point of sleeping through material portions of the trial, the verdict in this case must be set aside." Justice Marshall concluded that the evidence of alcohol and drug use was an outside influence about which jurors may testify under Rule 606(b), since it was unrelated to juror deliberations. He concluded that voir dire of jurors prior to trial cannot disclose whether they will use drugs during the trial, and the type of misconduct alleged would not have been easily verified by courtroom personnel.

Tanner states that the voir dire process is preferable to post-conviction review for determining whether jurors are competent and impartial. But what if the witness lies at the voir dire? In United States v. Colombo, 869 F.2d 149 (2d Cir.1989), defendant submitted a post-conviction affidavit from an alternate juror, averring that a juror deliberately failed to reveal on voir dire that her brother-in-law was an attorney for the government. Her motivation for concealment was that she thought it would hurt her chances to sit on the case. The court held that if it could be shown that the juror's brother-in-law was a government attorney, "the conviction cannot stand, because such conduct obstructed the voir dire and indicated an impermissible partiality on the juror's part." The court rejected as irrelevant the argument that merely having a government attorney as a brother-in-law would not have been enough to challenge the juror for cause.

> The point is not that her relationship with her brother-in-law tainted the proceedings but that her willingness to lie about it exhibited an interest strongly suggesting partiality. * * *
>
> [C]ourts cannot administer justice in circumstances in which a juror can commit a federal crime in order to serve as a juror in a criminal case and do so with no fear of sanction so long as a conviction results.

Presuming the truth of the allegations in *Tanner* and *Colombo,* which case presents the more serious threat to the defendant's right to an impartial jury?

F. THE TRIAL JUDGE AND THE RIGHT TO JURY TRIAL

1. *The Role of the Judge Generally*

If the right to jury trial is to work as intended—i.e., to provide protection against eccentric, biased or bureaucratic judges and public officials—it is necessary that the judge not take action that unduly invades the independence of the jury.

In any trial system with evidence and procedural rules like those found in the United States, it is almost certain that the trial judge will be called upon to decide what evidence will get to a jury and what will be excluded. To some extent, the development of modern evidence codes may control the judge's decisionmaking power, but even under codes judges are left with broad discretion. See Saltzburg, The Federal Rules of Evidence and the Quality of Practice in Federal Courts, 27 Cleve.St.L.Rev. 173 (1978). Appellate review of decisions in individual cases and careful selection of judges provide some assurance that evidentiary and procedural decisions will be fair, but the fact is that appellate courts reviewing a cold record are likely to defer on "judgment calls" to trial judges, and the selection of judges is neither careful, nor apolitical in many instances. Thus, there is little doubt that trial judges have an impact on jury decisions through their decisions on questions of evidence and procedure.

There is no doubt that judges have enormous powers reserved to them, powers that are exercised more or less independently of juries. For example, trial judges decide whether or not to accept guilty pleas and plea bargains; there is no right to jury trial on the advisability of any contract between the prosecutor and the defendant. Earlier in this chapter, we saw that judges rule on questions of joinder and severance, that judges rule on speedy trial questions and that judges even control the selection process of the jury. It is not difficult, then, to demonstrate that the meaningfulness of the jury trial right will depend in part on the role played by the trial judge.

2. *Selection of Judges*

Who are these trial judges and how are they selected? Federal trial judges are, of course, nominated by the President and confirmed, with life tenure as long as there is good behavior, by the Senate. Nominees are screened by an ABA Committee on the Federal Judiciary, although the ABA can do no more than make a judgment that may or may not be accepted by the President and the Senate. See Miller, The ABA's Role in Judicial Selection, 65 A.B.A.J. 516 (1979).

State judges are selected by a variety of different methods; often they must win elections to continue in office. See generally, Winters, Selection of Judges—An Historical Introduction, 44 Tex.L.Rev. 1081 (1966). The quality of judges may differ at different stages of the criminal process and in different geographical areas. For example, one commentator concluded that "[m]unicipal court judges in most urban centers are chosen neither because they have demonstrated great legal talent nor for their compassion. On the contrary, they are chosen by partisan political machines for their faithfulness to the party and their past work on behalf of the party." Katz, Municipal Courts—Another Urban Ill, 20 Case W.Res.L.Rev. 87, 119–39 (1968). Although the conclusion is somewhat dated, many observers would agree that it remains accurate today. The differences among judges sitting on the same court often are well known. See Smith & Blumberg, The Problem of Objectivity in Judicial Decisionmaking, 46 Social Forces 96 (1967).

Proposals are often made to make judicial selection and retention decisions less political. See, e.g., Nat'l Advisory Comm'n on Criminal Justice Standards and Goals: Courts, Standards 7.1 and 7.2 (1973), and authorities cited therein. But, in many states, political officials resist any attempt to limit the use of judicial positions as patronage or to remove the political constraints on the day-to-day actions of trial judges.

3. *Peremptory and Other Challenges*

Some jurisdictions recognize the potential impact that a judge can have on the ultimate disposition of any case, even one tried to a jury; some provide for a right to challenge one judge peremptorily—i.e., as a matter of right. See, e.g., Alaska Stat. 22.20.022. And all allow judges to be challenged for cause, although the standards by which such challenges are measured differ.[41]

4. *Specific Judicial Powers*

Although it is clear that the trial judge can influence the outcome of a jury trial, there are things that trial judges cannot do without violating a defendant's rights. Most of these limitations are not constitutionally based.[42] Rather, they are created by local law.

For example, most states will not allow a trial judge to comment on the weight of the evidence or on the credibility of witnesses, although some of these states will allow the judge to sum up the evidence presented by both sides.

The federal courts and a minority of the states give much more power to the trial judge and allow comment and summation. Because they do not allow unlimited comment and find it difficult to demarcate when the limits of

41. There would be a constitutional problem if the judge were biased or had an interest in the case. See Ward v. Village of Monroeville, 409 U.S. 57 (1972) (traffic offense; judge not impartial where he is also the Mayor, responsible for village finances); Tumey v. Ohio, 273 U.S. 510 (1926).

Brown v. Vance, 637 F.2d 272 (5th Cir. 1981), struck down a Mississippi scheme that provided no salary for "justice court" judges, but that permitted them to charge a fee for each criminal case docketed, regardless of disposition. The court said that a judge under this system may be biased against defendants, since such a bias may increase police officers' willingness to file cases and thereby raise the judge's income.

In Coleman v. State, 378 So.2d 640 (Miss. 1979), the court in a capital case held that a judge who was the third or fourth cousin of the murder victim was not required to recuse himself. In Corbett v. Bordenkircher, 615 F.2d 722 (6th Cir. 1980), the court concluded that a trial judge need not recuse himself simply because he has represented a defendant in the past.

42. One constitutionally based rule is that the trial judge may not direct a verdict of guilty in a criminal case, even if the defendant admits every material element of an offense. See Rucker v. State, 580 P.2d 1005 (Okl.Cr.App.1978). Thus, a jury can nullify the application of the law to the facts of a case by refusing to convict. In United States v. Dougherty, 473 F.2d 1113 (D.C.Cir. 1972), Judge Leventhal argued that the jury should not be told that it may refuse to apply the law given it by the court.

> What makes for health as an occasional medicine would be disastrous as a daily diet. The fact that there is widespread existence of the jury's prerogative, and approval of its existence as a "necessary counter to case-hardened judges and arbitrary prosecutors," does not establish as an imperative that the jury must be informed by the judge of that power. On the contrary, it is pragmatically useful to structure instructions in such wise that the jury must feel strongly about the values involved in the case, so strongly that it must itself identify the case as establishing a call of high conscience, and must independently initiate and undertake an act in contravention of the established instructions. This requirement of independent jury conception confines the happening of the lawless jury to the occasional instance that does not violate, and viewed as an exception may even enhance, the over-all normative effect of the rule of law.

Judge Bazelon disagreed.

> If, as the Court appears to concede, awareness is preferable to ignorance, then I simply do not understand the justification for relying on a haphazard process of informal communication whose effectiveness is likely to depend, to a large extent, on whether or not any of the jurors are so well-educated and astute that they are able to receive the message. If the jury should know of its power to disregard the law, then the power should be explicitly described by instruction of the court or argument of counsel.
>
> * * *

permissible comment are exceeded, it is difficult to know how much leeway the trial judge actually has. It appears that the practice is less expansive than the theory.

Virtually all jurisdictions allow the trial judge to call and to question witnesses, but none provides unlimited authority to the judge. Again, drawing lines is difficult.

It is sufficient here to note that the more active the judge is, the greater the threat to the independence of the jury. See, e.g., People v. Cook, 33 Cal.3d 400, 189 Cal.Rptr. 159, 658 P.2d 86 (1983) (trial court's comments on evidence after jury failed to reach a verdict interfered with defendant's right to jury trial). See generally Saltzburg, The Unnecessarily Expanding Role of the American Trial Judge, 64 Va.L.Rev. 1 (1978).

The judge is expected to be neutral and not to assume the role of prosecutor. See Petway v. United States, 391 A.2d 798 (D.C.App.1978). Gratuitous comments and interruptions by the judge are disfavored.[43] See Keane v. State, 357 So.2d 457 (Fla.Ct.App.1978). If the judge distorts important testimony in commenting to the jury on the evidence, reversal may be required. See Owens v. State, 561 S.W.2d 167 (Tenn.Cr.App.1977). But appellate courts will try to avoid reversals where the trial judge has a slip of the tongue. See generally Varela v. State, 561 S.W.2d 186 (Tex.Cr.App.1978) (comment must be reasonably calculated to prejudice defendant's rights to be prejudicial).

The most important aspect of judicial control may be the judge's instructions to the jury and responses to their inquiries after instructions are given. Since in most states the judge instructs the jury on the law and binds them to follow the instructions, what the judge says is critical to the disposition of the case by the jurors. It is common to find provisions like Fed.R.Crim.P. 30, which requires the court to accept or reject proposed instructions by counsel before closing argument, and before the instructions as a whole are given.[44]

5. *Judicial Control Over Jury Deliberations*

Once the jury retires to deliberate, there is good reason to be concerned about any further contact with the judge.

In United States v. Walker, 575 F.2d 209, 214 (9th Cir.1978), the Court described the trial judge's role in responding to jury questions.

> We are aware that the trial court faces a difficult task in attempting to respond to a jury's communication. A trial judge is often reluctant to respond to questions in language similar to that used by the jury, particularly where inquiries are phrased as hypothetical cases or as questions requiring a categorical yes or no answer. Questions or illustrations from the jury may be phrased so that a simple affirmative or negative response might favor one party's

43. It may be difficult to control nonverbal messages from the judge to the jury. See Note, Judges' Nonverbal Behavior in Jury Trials: A Threat to Judicial Impartiality, 61 Va. L.Rev. 1266 (1975).

44. Aside from instructing the jurors on the law, the trial judge controls the jury in many ways. For example, some judges do not allow note-taking by jurors, while others do. See United States v. Maclean, 578 F.2d 64 (3d Cir.1978); ABA Standards, Trial By Jury § 15–4.2 (2d ed. 1980). Trial judges differ in their attitude toward questions by the jurors to witnesses during the trial. For a suggested procedure, see Saltzburg, The Unnecessarily Expanding Role of the American Trial Judge, 64 Va.L.Rev. 1, 63–65 (1978).

> position, place undue weight on certain evidence, or indicate that the trial judge believes certain facts to be true when such matters should properly be determined by the jury. Because the jury may not enlist the court as its partner in the factfinding process, the trial judge must proceed circumspectly in responding to inquiries from the jury. The court may properly attempt to avoid intrusion on the jury's deliberations by framing responses in terms of supplemental instructions rather than following precisely the form of question asked by the jury.

Dixon v. State, 605 P.2d 882 (Alaska 1980), recognizes the critical importance of a court's responding to a jury's request to review evidence, but only after consulting with the defendant and his counsel, who should be able "to offer comments, suggestions, and objections to guide both the substance and phrasing of the court's response to the jury's request."

One of the most controversial questions is whether the trial judge can put some pressure on the jury to return a verdict when it indicates that it is unable to agree. One common, but controversial, charge is drawn from Allen v. United States, 164 U.S. 492 (1896), and is commonly referred to as the "Allen charge" or the "dynamite" charge:

> In a large proportion of cases absolute certainty cannot be expected. Although your verdict must be the verdict of each of you individually and not a mere acquiescence in the conclusion of your fellows, yet you should examine the question submitted with candor and with a proper regard for and deference to the opinions of each other. It is your duty to decide the case if you can conscientiously do so. You should listen, with a disposition to be convinced, to each other's arguments. If much the larger number are for conviction, a dissenting juror should consider whether his doubts are reasonable ones when they make no impression upon the minds of so many others, equally honest and equally intelligent. If, upon the other hand, the majority is for acquittal, the minority ought to ask themselves whether they might not reasonably doubt the correctness of a judgment which was not concurred in by the majority.

Some judges have been highly critical of it. See, e.g., Huffman v. United States, 297 F.2d 754, 759 (5th Cir.1962) (Brown, J., dissenting). Some courts have rejected it. In the case that follows, you will find references to the case law that has developed and an example of a modified *Allen* charge that asks all jurors, not just those in the minority, to reconsider their positions. See whether you think the modifications remove any problems you may have with the original *Allen* charge.

UNITED STATES v. SEAWELL

United States Court of Appeals, Ninth Circuit, 1977.
550 F.2d 1159.

MERRILL, CIRCUIT JUDGE:

The question presented is whether the giving of a second modified *Allen* charge, in response to a jury's report of deadlock, has such coercive implications that it should, as a sound rule of practice, be prohibited. We conclude that it has.

Seawell was convicted for armed bank robbery and the use of a firearm in its commission. He was found to be one of three masked robbers and, specifically, the one who guarded the front door of the bank during the robbery. His trial lasted four and one-half days, from Monday to Friday, in the course of which the jury heard the testimony of twenty-two witnesses. There followed closing arguments and the court's instructions. The jury then deliberated for two hours on Friday afternoon before recessing for the weekend.

On Monday, two notes were sent to the judge after the jury had deliberated approximately one and one-half hours. The first note said, "[t]he jury is at a ten-to-two impasse. The two state that nothing we can say will convince them otherwise. What course of action should we now take?" The second note, received minutes later, asked that a certain witness's testimony be read. Assuming that the second note had superseded the first, the judge had the testimony reread and then indicated to counsel his intention to give a modified *Allen* charge if the jury remained unable to agree.

Ten minutes after resuming deliberations, the jury sent another note indicating a ten-to-two deadlock, and a modified *Allen* charge was given.[a] Approxi-

a. The form of the *Allen* charge given was:

"The Court wishes to suggest a few thoughts which you may desire to consider in your deliberations, along with the evidence in the case, and all the instructions previously given.

This is an important case. The trial has been expensive in time, and effort, and money, to both the defense and the prosecution. If you should fail to agree on a verdict, the case is left open and undecided. Like all cases it must be disposed of sometime. There appears no reason to believe that another trial would not be costly to both sides. Nor does there appear any reason to believe that the case can be tried again, by either side, better or more exhaustively than it has been tried before you. Any future jurors must be selected in the same manner and from the same source from which you have been chosen. So there appears no reason to believe that the case would ever be submitted to twelve men and women more conscientious, more impartial, or more competent to decide it, or that more or clearer evidence could be produced on behalf of either side.

Of course, these things suggest themselves, upon brief reflection, to all of us who sat through this trial. The only reason they are mentioned now is because some of them may have escaped your attention, which must have been fully occupied up to this time in reviewing the evidence in the case. They are matters which, along with other and perhaps more obvious ones, remind us how desirable it is that you unanimously agree upon a verdict.

As stated in the instructions given at the time the case was submitted for your decision, you should not surrender your honest convictions as to the weight or the effect of evidence, solely because of the opinion of other jurors, or for the mere purpose of returning a verdict.

However, it is your duty as jurors to consult with one another and deliberate with a view to reaching an agreement, if you can do so without violence to individual judgment. Each of you must decide the case for yourself, but you should do so only after a consideration of the evidence in the case with your fellow jurors. And in the course of your deliberations, you should not hesitate to reexamine your own views, and change your opinion, if convinced it is erroneous.

In order to bring twelve minds to a unanimous result, you must examine the questions submitted to you with candor and frankness, and with proper deference to and regard for the opinions of each other. That is to say, in conferring together, each of you should pay due attention and respect to the view of others and listen to each other's arguments with a disposition to reexamine your own views.

If much the greater number of you are for a conviction, each dissenting juror ought to consider whether a doubt in his or her own mind is a reasonable one, since it makes no effective impression upon the minds of so many equally honest, equally conscientious fellow jurors, who bear the same responsibility, serve under the same oath, and have heard the same evidence with, we may assume, the same attention and equal desire to arrive at the truth. On the other hand, if a majority or even a lesser number of you are for acquittal, other jurors ought seriously to ask themselves again, and most thoughtfully whether they do not have reason to doubt the correctness of a judgment which is not concurred in by many of their fellow jurors, and whether they should not distrust the weight and sufficiency of the evidence, which fails to convince the minds of several of their fellows beyond a reasonable doubt.

You are not partisans, you are judges—judges of the facts. Your sole interest here is to seek the truth from the evidence in the case. You are the exclusive judges of the credibility of all the witnesses and the weight and effect of all the evidence. In the performance of this high duty, you are at liberty to disregard all comments of both Court and

mately three and one-half hours later, after some intervening discussion between judge and jury, the judge received another note from the jury which read in part:

> "No amount of argument has persuaded their convictions, these are the others who do not agree with the majority of the jurors. We therefore submit to you that we are at an impasse and are not likely to change our minds until fatigue becomes a deciding factor which we believe is neither fair to the defendant or the people."

The court, after stating that the jury would not in any event have to deliberate later than 6:30 P.M. that night or beyond the point of fatigue, then reread the *Allen* charge. The jury retired at 4:10 P.M. and the guilty verdict was returned at 5:00 P.M. Timely objections were made by defense counsel.

Problems arising from the inherently coercive effect of the *Allen* charge have caused other courts of appeals [b] and state courts [c] to prohibit or to restrict severely its use. Nevertheless, the content,[d] timing [e] and circumstances sur-

counsel, including of course the remarks I am now making.

Remember, at all times, that no juror is expected to yield a conscientious conviction he or she may have as to the weight and effect of the evidence. But remember also that, after full deliberation and consideration of all the evidence in the case, it is your duty to agree upon a verdict, if you can do so without violating your individual judgment and conscience. Remember too, if the evidence in the case fails to establish guilt beyond a reasonable doubt, the accused should have your unanimous verdict of not guilty.

In order to make a decision more practicable, the law imposes the burden of proof upon one party or the other, in all cases. In the present case, the burden of proof is on the Government.

Above all, keep constantly in mind that, unless your final conscientious appraisal of the evidence in the case clearly requires it, the accused should never be exposed to the risk of having to run twice the gauntlet of criminal prosecution; and to endure a second time the mental, emotional, and financial strain of a criminal trial.

You may conduct your deliberations as you choose, but I suggest that you now carefully reexamine and reconsider all the evidence in the case bearing upon the questions before you.

You may be as leisurely in your deliberations as the occasion may require; and you shall take all the time which you may feel is necessary.

You may now retire and continue your deliberations in such manner as shall be determined by your good and conscientious judgment as reasonable men and women.

The jury will be sent to deliberate."

b. United States v. Thomas, 146 U.S.App. D.C. 101, 449 F.2d 1177, 1184–88 (1971); United States v. Fioravanti, 412 F.2d 407, 417 (3d Cir.), cert. denied, 396 U.S. 837 (1969); United States v. Brown, 411 F.2d 930, 934 (7th Cir. 1969), cert. denied, 396 U.S. 1017 (1970). See also Green v. United States, 309 F.2d 852, 854 n.3 (5th Cir.1962), but compare with United States v. Bailey, 468 F.2d 652 (5th Cir.1972).

c. Many state courts have banned or restricted the use of the *Allen* charge on the basis of their supervisory powers. See e.g., Fields v. State, 487 P.2d 831, 836 (Alaska 1971); State v. Thomas, 86 Ariz. 161, 342 P.2d 197, 200 (1959); State v. Nicholson, 315 So.2d 639, 641 (La.1975); State v. Martin, 297 Minn. 359, 211 N.W.2d 765, 772 (1973); State v. Randall, 137 Mont. 534, 353 P.2d 1054, 1058 (1960); State v. Marsh, 260 Or. 416, 490 P.2d 491, 503 (1971); Kersey v. State, 525 S.W.2d 139, 144 (Tenn.1975).

At least one state court has found the *Allen* charge violative of constitutional rights. Commonwealth v. Spencer, 442 Pa. 328, 275 A.2d 299, 304 (1971).

See also People v. Prim, 53 Ill.2d 62, 289 N.E.2d 601, 609–10 (1972); State v. White, 285 A.2d 832, 838 (Me.1972); State v. Garza, 185 Neb. 445, 176 N.W.2d 664, 666 (1970); Azbill v. State, 88 Nev. 240, 495 P.2d 1064, 1069 (1972); State v. Champagne, 198 N.W.2d 218, 238 (N.D.1972); State v. Ferguson, 84 S.D. 605, 175 N.W.2d 57, 61 (1970).

d. Sullivan v. United States, 414 F.2d 714, 717–18 (9th Cir.1969); Dearinger v. United States, 378 F.2d 346, 347 n.2 (9th Cir.1967); Kawakita v. United States, 190 F.2d 506, 521–28 (9th Cir.), aff'd, 343 U.S. 717 (1952).

e. The timing of the *Allen* charge here was similar to that in Dearinger v. United States, 378 F.2d 346, 347 (9th Cir.1967), where the jury received the case at 3:15 P.M. and the charge was given at 12:45 P.M. the following day, as well as that in Walsh v. United States, 371 F.2d 135, 136 (9th Cir.1967), where the jury received the case at 11:55 A.M. and the charge was given at 5:45 P.M. the same day.

rounding[f] the *Allen* charges given here have been upheld by this circuit and we do not now undertake to re-examine those decisions. * * *

If the charge is to pass muster as instruction on the law there is little need to repeat it save at the jury's request. (Here, for example, it was repeated three and one-half hours after it was first given. Nothing had intervened to cause the jury to overlook what last had been said to them.) Repetition of the charge, together with rejection of the jury's second report of deadlock, is almost certain to convey the thought that by failing to come to an agreement—by once again reporting themselves at impasse—the jurors have acted contrary to the earlier instruction as that instruction was properly to be understood. * * *

Ordinarily, the general test of whether a supplemental jury instruction is in error is to consider all the circumstances to determine if the instruction was coercive. Jenkins v. United States, 380 U.S. 445, 446, (1965). Pragmatic considerations weigh against the application of this test when an *Allen* charge is given more than once. A case-by-case determination would provide little, if any, guidance for a trial judge. Defendants would also face insurmountable difficulties in attempting to show prejudice. A single *Allen* charge, without more, stands at the brink of impermissible coercion. We believe that the protection of a defendant's right to an impartial jury compels a per se rule.[g] Such a rule is not at odds with prior decisions of this court or other courts of appeals.[h] We conclude that as a sound rule of practice it is reversible error to repeat an *Allen* charge in a federal prosecution in this circuit after a jury has reported itself deadlocked and has not itself requested a repetition of the instruction.[i]

* * *

See also Sullivan v. United States, 414 F.2d 714, 717 (9th Cir.1969), where the *Allen* charge was given after approximately five and one-half hours of deliberations over two days. The *Sullivan* court, however, indicated that it was not deciding whether the timing was appropriate because the issue was not raised by defense counsel. Id. at 717 n.5. Cf. United States v. Contreras, 463 F.2d 773, 774 (9th Cir.1972), where the *Allen* charge was premature when given on the second day of deliberations, but before there was an indication of deadlock.

f. The fact that the jury disclosed its exact numerical division has not, by itself, precluded the use of the *Allen* charge. United States v. Williams, 444 F.2d 108, 109 (9th Cir.1971). Contra, Mullin v. United States, 123 U.S.App. D.C. 29, 356 F.2d 368, 370 (1966). It would, however, be reversible error for a trial judge to inquire into the numerical split of a jury before giving an *Allen* charge. Brasfield v. United States, 272 U.S. 448 (1926).

g. A per se rule, such as the one we have adopted here, always poses the risk that it may sweep within its embrace cases which do not warrant its protection. We believe, however, that this "cost" of adopting a per se rule is outweighed by the importance of a defendant's right to an impartial jury trial and the insurmountable problems of proof and appellate review that a less definite rule would occasion. [For a totality of the circumstances approach, see United States v. Fossler, 597 F.2d 478 (5th Cir. 1979).]

h. On those rare occasions when the use of two *Allen* charges has been upheld by other courts the second charge was at the request of the jury, United States v. Kahaner, 317 F.2d 459, 484 (2d Cir.), cert. denied, 375 U.S. 836 (1963); White v. United States, 279 F.2d 740, 750 (4th Cir.), cert. denied, 364 U.S. 850 (1960); or the first charge was a part of the general jury instructions delivered before the jury had begun its deliberations and thus was not in response to a report of deadlock. United States v. Washington, 144 U.S.App.D.C. 338, 447 F.2d 308, 310 (1970).

i. We do not intimate that after one *Allen* charge has been given any indication of deadlock must be accepted without question. If an indication of deadlock is ambiguous and the trial judge has reasonable grounds to believe the jury is not in fact deadlocked, then the trial judge may take reasonable steps to assure that the jury is in fact deadlocked. This may include asking the jury to determine carefully whether they are deadlocked, and, if so, to communicate that fact to the trial judge unambiguously. The trial judge may not, however, repeat the *Allen* charge or ask minority jurors to reexamine their stand.

WRIGHT, CIRCUIT JUDGE, concurring and dissenting:

* * *

With due respect to the views of the majority, I dissent from that portion of the opinion which holds that it was reversible error to repeat the so-called *Allen* charge under the circumstances of this case. I strongly disagree with the per se rule that is now adopted because I feel that it is an unwarranted intrusion into the area of trial court discretion.

* * *

Note

Would you join the majority in favoring a per se rule? Another case finding the giving of two "deadlock" instructions to be prejudicial error is Epperson v. United States, 471 A.2d 1016 (D.C.App.1984). Should the judge be able to tell a jury that a case will have to be retried if the jury fails to reach a verdict? The California Supreme Court said "no" in People v. Barraza, 23 Cal.3d 675, 153 Cal.Rptr. 459, 591 P.2d 947 (1979).

The circuit which decided *Seawell* has in some cases refused to apply the per se rule. For example, in United States v. Nickell, 883 F.2d 824 (9th Cir.1989), the judge gave one *Allen* charge on Friday immediately before the jurors recessed for the weekend, and another when they resumed deliberations on Monday. The court found no error as it distinguished the case from *Seawell.* The court reasoned as follows:

> In this case the danger of reproof and coercive disapproval of further deliberations inherent in a second instruction after a second report of deadlock does not exist. There was no intervening deliberation by the jury after the *Allen* charge was first given before the weekend recess. There was no second deadlock. In these circumstances there could have been no suggestion of criticism of intervening behavior by the jury in the second supplemental instruction, since the judge addressed the jury the second time only as a reminder of the instructions given before the break. In this case, the remarks of the judge before the jury resumed its deliberations after the break can be viewed not as a second modified *Allen* charge, but as a continuation of the first. The threat of coercion that the *Seawell* rule is designed to prevent was not presented in this case.

See also United States v. Ruggiero, 928 F.2d 1289 (2d Cir.1991) ("we do not regard a repeated *Allen* charge as inevitably coercive").

The time period between the giving of the *Allen* charge and the jury's return of a verdict has not been considered dispositive evidence of coercion. See United States v. Hiland, 909 F.2d 1114 (8th Cir.1990) (*Allen* charge not coercive even though jury returned verdict ten minutes thereafter).

The Supreme Court held, 5–3, in Lowenfield v. Phelps, 484 U.S. 231 (1988), that the trial judge did not act improperly in a capital case in giving a modified *Allen* charge during the sentencing phase of the case. When the jury indicated to the trial judge that it was unable to reach a decision on sentence, the judge gave each juror a piece of paper and asked each to indicate whether further deliberations would be helpful in obtaining a verdict. Eight jurors initially answered affirmatively, and three others subsequently indicated that they had misunderstood the question. The judge then asked each to indicate whether further deliberations would enable the jury to reach a verdict, and eleven jurors responded affirmatively. At this point, the judge told the jurors that they should consider each other's views with the objective of reaching a verdict without surrendering their honest beliefs in doing so, and that the court would impose a sentence of life imprisonment without possibility of probation, parole or suspension of sentence if the jury failed to agree on a sanction. Chief Justice Rehnquist's majority opinion reasoned that the trial judge had not coerced the jury into reaching a decision and distinguished Brasfield v. United States, 272 U.S. 448 (1926), which had used the Court's supervisory powers to condemn judicial inquiry into the numerical division of jurors. The Court also distinguished Jenkins v. United States, 380 U.S. 445 (1965), where the trial judge told the jury that "you have got to reach a decision in this case." Justice Marshall, joined by Justices Brennan and Stevens, dissented and argued that the two polls of the jury whittled the minority jurors from four to one. He condemned the fact that in the instant case, as in *Brasfield,* the jurors were asked to identify themselves by name in the polls. He also expressed doubts as to the wisdom of the *Allen* charge, especially in a case in which a hung jury would produce a life sentence rather than a new proceeding.

For a Supreme Court suggestion that the trial judge put improper pressure on the jury in a long case, see United States v. United States Gypsum Co., 438 U.S. 422 (1978).

G. THE JURY VERDICT

Generally the verdict that the jury returns must be in writing. See, e.g., Uniform Rule 535(a). It must be returned by the jury in open court. See Fed.R.Crim.P. 31(a); Uniform Rule 535(b). "If there are two or more defendants, the jury at any time during its deliberations may return a verdict or verdicts with respect to a defendant or defendants as to whom it has agreed * * *" Fed.R.Crim.P. 31(b). "If there are two or more offenses for which the jury could return a verdict, it may return a verdict with respect to any offense, including a lesser included offense for which verdict forms are submitted, as to which it agrees." Uniform Rule 535(d). Some jurisdictions provide that unless the parties waive the right to a poll, the clerk will ask each juror individually whether the verdict announced is his verdict. See, e.g., Uniform Rule 535(e). But others require a request before the jury is polled. See, e.g., Fed.R.Crim.P. 31(d). Verdicts are usually general verdicts of guilty or not guilty (or not guilty by reason of insanity) on each count. In rare instances a special interrogatory is used. See, e.g., Fed.R.Crim.P. 31(e) (special verdict shall indicate property subject to forfeiture).

The fact that jury verdicts are inconsistent does not invalidate convictions. See Dunn v. United States, 284 U.S. 390 (1932). The idea is that the inconsistent jury may be attempting to mitigate the force of its verdicts. See United States v. Carbone, 378 F.2d 420 (2d Cir. 1967). Of course, jury inconsistency may be a reason for a trial judge to grant a new trial.

Justice Rehnquist wrote for a unanimous Court in United States v. Powell, 469 U.S. 57 (1984), holding that the general rule that a defendant convicted on one count of an indictment cannot attack the verdict as being inconsistent with acquittal on another count applies to a case in which the defendant was convicted of using the telephone in connection with a cocaine conspiracy and possession charges but was acquitted of the conspiracy and possession counts. The Court recognized that the verdict could not be rationally reconciled, but reasoned that it is always uncertain as to why the jury returns such a verdict and "whose ox has been gored." Since the government may not appeal an acquittal, the Court declined to give the defendant a new trial on the conviction as a matter of course. Moreover, the Court expressed the view that inconsistent verdicts are often a matter of lenity and rejected as unworkable a rule that would permit criminal defendants to challenge verdicts by arguing that in particular cases they are not the product of lenity.

The question whether special interrogatories can and should be used in a criminal case is touched upon in United States v. Ruggiero, 726 F.2d 913 (2d Cir.1984). In a complicated prosecution for racketeering and other offenses, the government alleged various predicate acts to support its racketeering charges. (At least two predicate acts must be proved to support a conviction.) The court of appeals found that one of the predicate acts alleged was improper. Since it was impossible to determine whether the jury relied upon this particular act in returning its guilty verdict on the racketeering charges, the court found that reversal was required. The majority opinion stated that "in a complex RICO [racketeering] trial such as this one, it can be extremely useful for a trial judge to request the jury to record their specific dispositions of the separate predicate acts charged, in addition to their verdict of guilt or innocence on the RICO charge." Judge Newman wrote a separate opinion analyzing the subject of special interrogatories at greater length. He explained the reasons for judicial reluctance to use interrogatories in criminal cases: "There is apprehension that eliciting 'yes' or 'no' answers to questions concerning the elements of an offense may propel a jury toward a logical conclusion of guilt, whereas a more generalized assessment might have yielded an acquittal"; and "[t]he possibility also exists that fragmenting a single count into the various ways an offense may be committed affords a divided jury an opportunity to resolve its differences to the defendant's disadvantage by saying 'yes' to some means and 'no' to others, although unified consideration of the count might have produced an acquittal or at least a hung jury." He noted that "[i]nterrogatories are especially objectionable when they make resolution of a single fact issue determinative of guilt or innocence, without regard to the elements of an offense, * * * or when their wording shifts the burden of proof to the defendant." On balance, he concluded that a trial judge "should have the discretion to use a jury interrogatory in cases where risk of prejudice to the defendant is slight and the advantage of securing particularized factfinding is substantial."[45]

The jury may find the defendant guilty of the crime charged or of any lesser included offense. The doctrine of lesser included offense was described well in United States v. King, 567 F.2d 785, 790 (8th Cir. 1977):

> This Court has held that a defendant is entitled to a lesser-included offense instruction when the following five elements are present: (1) a proper request is made; (2) the elements of the lesser offense are identical to part of the elements of the greater offense; (3) there is some evidence that would justify conviction of the lesser offense; (4) the proof on the element or elements differentiating the two crimes is sufficiently in dispute so that the jury may

45. In Harris v. Rivera, 454 U.S. 339 (1981), the Court concluded that the federal Constitution places no burden on a state trial judge in a bench trial to explain why he acquits one defendant and convicts another even when the verdicts appear to be inconsistent. Should a presumption that the trial judge may have been drawing fine lines between defendants be employed? Should it be employed if the judge is not legally trained?

Rarely, if ever, do we ask criminal juries to make specific findings of fact. Under rules like Fed.R.Crim.P. 23, trial judges must make special findings in bench trials upon request. See United States v. Silberman, 464 F.Supp. 866 (M.D.Fla.1979).

consistently find the defendant innocent of the greater and guilty of the lesser-included offense; and (5) there is mutuality, i.e., a charge may be demanded by either the United States or the defense.

It does not follow that a lesser included offense instruction is mandatory every time a lesser offense is included within the offense charged in the indictment. The instruction need not be given when "from the evidence adduced at the trial there is no rational basis upon which the jury could find the defendant guilty of the lesser offense."[46]

In People v. Geiger, 35 Cal.3d 510, 199 Cal.Rptr. 45, 674 P.2d 1303 (1984), the court reversed a defendant's conviction for second-degree burglary because the trial judge refused to give an instruction on a related, but not lesser-included, offense of vandalism. It emphasized the importance of giving the jury a choice when a defendant's actions might arguably fall within the definitions of several different offenses, stating that the benefit of an instruction on lesser related offenses flows to the government as well as to the defendant.

The Model Penal Code, § 1.07(4) provides that one offense is included in another when

(a) it is established by proof of the same or less than all the facts required to establish the commission of the offense charged; or

(b) it consists of an attempt or solicitation to commit the offense charged or to commit an offense otherwise included therein; or

(c) it differs from the offense charged only in the respect that a less serious injury or risk of injury to the same person, property or public interest or a lesser kind of culpability suffices to establish its commission.

In Schmuck v. United States, 489 U.S. 705 (1989), the Court adopted the "elements" test for determining whether a trial court must give a lesser included offense instruction under Fed.R.Crim.P. 31(c). Under this test, a lesser included offense is one in which all of its elements are also required to prove a more serious offense. For example, the elements required to prove involuntary manslaughter in most states are also required to prove the more serious offense of murder. The Court in *Schmuck* rejected the broader "inherent relationship" test, under which an offense is included within another when the facts proven at trial support the inference that the defendant committed the less serious offense, and an inherent relationship exists between the two offenses. Under this test, the lower court held that Schmuck was entitled to an instruction concerning odometer tampering, when he was charged with mail fraud arising from a scheme to sell cars with turned-back odometers. However, under the elements test, an instruction on odometer tampering was not required, since Schmuck could have been convicted of mail fraud without a showing that he actually turned back any odometers; thus, the elements of odometer tampering were not a "subset" of the elements of mail fraud. In adopting the elements approach to Rule 31(c), the Court noted that it was

46. For a discussion of the concept, see Koenig, The Many-Headed Hydra of Lesser Included Offenses: A Herculean Task for the Michigan Courts, 1975 Det.L.Rev. 41; George, Lesser Included Offenses in Michigan, 1975 Det.L.Rev. 35 (1975); Barnett, The Lesser-Included Offense Doctrine: A Present Day Analysis for Practitioners, 5 Conn.L.Rev. 255 (1972); Note, The Doctrine of Lesser Included Offenses in Kansas, 15 Washburn L.J. 40 (1976); Note, Lesser Included Offenses: Application of Equal Standards to the Prosecution and Defense in Lesser Included Offense Situations, 4 Toledo L.Rev. 273 (1973).

"grounded in the language and history of the Rule and provides greater certainty in its application." The Court also reasoned that the inherent relationship test may create notice problems where the prosecutor asks for a jury charge on an offense whose elements were not charged in the indictment. In contrast, the elements approach, which "involves a textual comparison of criminal statutes and does not depend on inferences that may be drawn from evidence introduced at trial * * * permits both sides to know in advance what jury instructions will be available and to plan their trial strategy accordingly." The Court found the inherent relationship approach to be "rife with the potential for confusion."

In capital cases, the constitution may require the court to instruct on lesser included offenses. See Beck v. Alabama and Schad v. Arizona in Chapter Eleven. The concept of lesser included offense is also discussed in Chapter Twelve, in connection with double jeopardy rules. Are there any circumstances in which the defendant may not want to have the jury instructed on a lesser included offense?

While verdicts can be inconsistent, does it follow that defendants ought to be allowed to assert inconsistent defenses, such as "I wasn't there and if I was, it was self-defense"? In Mathews v. United States, 485 U.S. 58 (1988), Chief Justice Rehnquist wrote for the Court as it held that "even if the defendant denies one or more elements of the crime, he is entitled to an entrapment instruction whenever there is sufficient evidence from which a reasonable jury could find entrapment." The Court rejected the government's argument "that allowing a defendant to rely on inconsistent defenses will encourage perjury" and confuse a jury. Justice White, joined by Justice Blackmun, dissented.

H. WAIVER OF JURY TRIAL; TRIAL BY THE COURT

Even though a defendant may have a right to a jury trial, she may desire to be tried by a judge. Certain crimes—e.g., narcotics offenses in some jurisdictions—may be difficult for lay jurors to view dispassionately. See generally H. Kalven and H. Zeisel, The American Jury (1966). Defendants with prior records may believe that in reaching a decision on the merits of a case, a judge can discount prior convictions offered for impeachment purposes somewhat better than a jury can. Jurisdictions differ on whether the defendant can waive a jury trial at all, on whether the prosecutor can force a jury trial when the defendant prefers a judge trial, and on whether the court can refuse to try a case without a jury when neither side wants one. In Singer v. United States, 380 U.S. 24 (1965), the Supreme Court upheld Fed.R.Crim.P. 23(a), which allows a defendant to waive a jury trial only "with the approval of the court and the consent of the government," against a constitutional attack. The Court rejected the argument that the Sixth Amendment's right to jury trial implies a correlative right to waive a jury if the defendant wants to. The Court did say that it would not "assume that federal prosecutors would demand a jury trial for an ignoble purpose." And it left open the possibility that in some circumstances the defendant's reasons for wanting to avoid a jury would be so compelling that the government would deny "an impartial trial" if it insisted on a jury.[47] See also United States v. Clark, 943 F.2d 775 (7th Cir.1991)

47. For a discussion of the proper procedure for a court to use in accepting a waiver of jury trial, see Countess v. State, 286 Md. 444, 408 A.2d 1302 (1979).

(no violation of the Constitution where "the result is simply that the defendant is subject to an impartial trial by jury—the very thing that the Constitution guarantees him"; in dictum, the court states that a defendant may have a right to a bench trial in a case involving "very complex facts").

The defendant who faces a trial by judge has the right to an impartial judge. Does the defendant have a right to a judge who knows much of the law? In North v. Russell, 427 U.S. 328 (1976), the Supreme Court held that an accused is not denied due process "when tried before a nonlawyer police court judge with a later trial de novo available under a State's two-tier court system." The Court, per Chief Justice Burger, recognized that the accused had the right to counsel at the first trial, but concluded that since lay magistrates can issue warrants, they could try cases in the first instance. Justice Stewart, joined by Justice Marshall, dissented, taking the view that "the essential presupposition of this basic constitutional right [of counsel] is that the judge conducting the trial will be able to understand what the defendant's lawyer is talking about." Can you reconcile *North* with the right-to-counsel cases?

When trial judges sit without juries, they need not fear that their comments, questions and expressions will bias some other fact-finder. But there are reasons to be concerned with a judge who interferes with the presentation of evidence by the parties who have prepared a case for trial. It may make some sense in the case of a traffic infraction, when no prosecutor is present, for the judge to ask the few relevant questions that need to be asked. See People v. Carlucci, 23 Cal.3d 249, 152 Cal.Rptr. 439, 590 P.2d 15 (1979). But in cases in which counsel is present and prepared, the active judge may unfairly impair one side of a case and may cast doubt on the overall fairness of the proceedings. Usually, trial judges can get away with trial comments and active participation in bench trials and can hear evidence that is not actually admissible, because appellate courts will assume that the trial judge put aside any improper considerations at the time of decision in the case. See Rogers v. McMackin, 884 F.2d 252 (6th Cir. 1989) (*Bruton* rule, requiring severance if co-defendant's confession is admitted at trial, did not apply in a bench trial, because trial judge can exclude it from consideration as to non-confessing defendant). However, if it is clear that the trial judge has relied upon inadmissible evidence, closer scrutiny will follow. See Lee v. Illinois, 476 U.S. 530 (1986) (reversible error where trial judge explicitly considers co-defendant's confession against the other defendant). For an argument that trial judges should be more careful asking questions and calling witnesses in bench trials, see Saltzburg, The Unnecessarily Expanding Role of the American Trial Judge, 64 Va.L.Rev. 1 (1978).

V. THE IMPARTIALITY OF THE TRIBUNAL AND THE INFLUENCE OF THE PRESS

Our philosophically ideal judges and juries are totally impartial, very thorough, eminently fair and incredibly accurate. Although there is little that

Dolchok v. State, 639 P.2d 277 (Alaska 1982), presents the interesting situation of a first degree murder defendant who waived a jury after his lawyer and the prosecutor both agreed that he was not guilty by reason of insanity and the prosecutor also agreed not to argue for a guilty verdict. The judge convicted the defendant and subsequent proceedings resulted in a finding that the waiver of a jury was valid.

we can or will do to assure thoroughness and accuracy once a jury begins to deliberate, often it is possible to keep from a jury information that might lead to a decision that is not in accord with the rules that are established to govern litigation. We have already seen one way of protecting against a biased jury—i.e., voir dire of prospective jurors in order to eliminate those whose partiality would threaten the integrity of the jury as factfinder.

Another way of preventing or inhibiting jury bias is to control the flow of information to the potential pool of jurors in a community and, even more importantly, to control the flow of information to those selected as jurors in any case.

Whenever any government agency wants to control the flow of information to the public, it is likely to be resisted by the press and many willing recipients of information. Efforts to afford all parties a fair trial can threaten some of the interests served by a free press. How to accommodate the competing interests has become known as the "fair trial—free press" issue and is the subject of this section of the chapter.

A. CRITICISM OF TRIALS AND COURTS

One of the early cases to reach the Supreme Court was Bridges v. California, 314 U.S. 252 (1941). *Bridges* arose out of state court litigation involving a dispute between an A.F.L. Union and a C.I.O. Union of which Harry Bridges was an officer. Bridges wrote a letter to the Secretary of Labor in which he stated that the C.I.O. did not intend to let state courts override the union's selection of its officers and representatives. For this he was held in contempt. The Supreme Court was willing to assume that Bridges' letter threatened a strike if the state court decided against his union, but it reversed the contempt ruling. The Court said that such a strike would not have run afoul of state law, and that it would not assume that the trial judge was unaware of strike possibilities. In another case decided with Bridges', union men were awaiting pronouncement of sentences for assaults when a newspaper published editorials urging the trial judge to make an example of the defendants. The newspaper and its managing editor were held in contempt. Again the Court reversed. Two editorials were viewed as presenting no threat to the administration of justice in the state court, and the third "did no more than threaten future adverse criticism which was reasonably to be expected anyway in the event of a lenient disposition of the pending case."

Justice Black's majority opinion recognized that "free speech and fair trials are two of the most cherished policies of our civilization, and it would be a trying task to choose between them." Ultimately, he concluded that "the substantive evil must be extremely serious and the degree of imminence extremely high before utterances can be punished." (This built upon the clear and present danger test advocated in earlier cases.) Justice Frankfurter, joined by Chief Justice Stone and Justices Roberts and Byrnes, dissented:

> A trial is not a "free trade in ideas," nor is the best test of truth in a courtroom "the power of the thought to get itself accepted in the competition of the market." * * *
>
> The dependence of society upon an unswerved judiciary is such a commonplace in the history of freedom that the means by which it is maintained are

too frequently taken for granted without heed to the conditions which alone make it possible.

The dissent would have distinguished general comment and criticism from attempts to influence judicial behavior in particular cases. For the dissent "[t]he question concerning the narrow power we recognize always is—was there a real and substantial threat to the impartial decision by a court of a case actively pending before it." The dissent would have affirmed the contempt convictions arising out of the publication of the one editorial and Bridges' letter.

Five years later, in Pennekamp v. Florida, 328 U.S. 331 (1946), the Court was much less divided. An associate newspaper editor and his paper were held in contempt for publishing two editorials, one of which was accompanied by a cartoon. The editorials discussed particular cases that had been before the circuit court of Dade County, Florida (some of which were still pending) and complained of legal technicalities that blocked conviction and punishment of criminals. Justice Reed's opinion for the Court emphasized that the newspaper attacks were on judges, not juries, and concluded that there was no clear and present danger to a fair administration of justice. Justice Frankfurter's concurring opinion distinguished *Pennekamp* from *Bridges*, largely because in *Pennekamp* there was no effort to influence particular cases.

Craig v. Harney, 331 U.S. 367 (1947), divided the Justices once again. Justice Douglas' opinion for the Court overturned contempt convictions of a newspaper's publisher, editorial writer and reporter, who were punished because of an editorial and several news stories criticizing a trial judge's[48] handling of a suit between private litigants (a forcible detainer case). The majority concluded that news articles about the trial "were partial reports of what transpired at the trial" and said that "[t]hose who see and hear what transpired can report it with impunity" since "[a] trial is a public event." The Court said this despite its recognition that "the news articles were by any standard an unfair report of what transpired." Similarly, the Court found that news reports of what citizens planned to do about the judge's ruling were reports of "community events of legitimate interest." As for the editorial attacking the judge, the Court found no threat that would "immediately imperil" the administration of justice. Justice Murphy concurred briefly to urge the importance of giving the press breathing room to criticize judges and courts. As in *Bridges*, Justice Frankfurter dissented. Chief Justice Vinson joined him. Justice Jackson also dissented. Justice Frankfurter concluded that "[t]he thrust of the articles was directed to what the judge should do on a matter immediately before him, namely to grant a motion for a new trial." Justice Jackson agreed. He focused on the monopoly position of the newspaper, the unusual interest it took in the proceeding, the elected position the judge held, and the fact that a non-lawyer had no professional association to stand behind him.

The clear and present danger test in the context of criminal contempt was reaffirmed in Wood v. Georgia, 370 U.S. 375 (1962). Chief Justice Warren's majority opinion overturned the contempt conviction of an elected sheriff for

48. The judge was a layperson (non-lawyer) holding elective office, a fact that the paper deplored.

expressing in a written statement to the press his feeling that a local elected judge, in issuing a charge to a regularly-impaneled grand jury which advised them to investigate "an inane and inexplicable pattern of Negro bloc voting," was using "race agitation" and intimidation. The judge's charge was given in the midst of a local political campaign, and in order to publicize the investigation, the judge had requested reporters for all local news media to be present in the courtroom when the charge was delivered. The majority emphasized that no individual was on trial when the sheriff spoke, that the judge's charge was directed against one group in the community, that a discussion of both sides of the issue might have assisted the grand jury, and that "it is difficult to imagine how the voting problem may be alleviated by an abridgment of talk and comment regarding its solution." Justice Harlan, joined by Justice Clark, dissented. The dissent argued that the Sheriff's remarks were not general criticisms with respect to rulings already made, but specific attacks directed toward the disposition of the pending investigation.

These four cases involved criticisms, express or implied, of judges and not of juries, although *Wood* presented a situation in which a grand jury's actions could have been influenced by the statements made by the defendant sheriff. Although the right to speak was sustained in all four cases, all recognized that some speech—that which presented a clear and present imminent danger to the administration of justice—could be punished. None of the four cases examined a violation of a previously established legislative or judicial ban on speech; all the speech was objected to after it was made. It is clear that under some circumstances direct attempts to influence the behavior of a tribunal can be regulated. There can be no doubt, for example, that a newspaper has no greater authority to threaten or bribe a judge or jury than does anyone else. If a jury is sequestered throughout a case, a newspaper has no special right to violate the sequestration order and to smuggle information to jurors. These cases are not hard. What is hard, however, is to define the scope of judicial authority to control the general circulation of information because of fear that chances for a fair trial for the government and/or the defendant will be reduced.

B. THE IMPACT OF PRESS COVERAGE ON LITIGATION

1. *Breaking Ground*

In Irvin v. Dowd, 366 U.S. 717 (1961), a unanimous Supreme Court struck down for the first time a state conviction because of the effect of pretrial publicity.[49] Irvin had been convicted of murder and sentenced to death. The charge arose after six murders were committed in the vicinity of Evansville, Indiana. Police issued releases saying that Irvin had confessed to the murder. Although one change of venue was granted, it was from Evansville to an adjoining rural county which had received some of the publicity concerning the crimes and Irvin's arrest. A second change of venue was denied. Justice Clark's opinion for the Court said that "[i]t is not required * * * that jurors be totally ignorant of the facts and issues involved. In these days of swift,

49. Prior to *Irvin*, the Court set aside a conviction in Marshall v. United States, 360 U.S. 310 (1959), under its supervisory powers because of news articles the jurors had read. See also Janko v. United States, 366 U.S. 716 (1961), rev'g, 281 F.2d 156 (8th Cir. 1960).

widespread and diverse methods of communication, an important case can be expected to arouse the interest of the public in the vicinity, and scarcely any of those best qualified to serve as jurors will not have formed some impression or opinion as to the merits of the case. * * * To hold that the mere existence of any preconceived notion as to the guilt or innocence of the accused, without more, is sufficient to rebut the presumption of a prospective juror's impartiality would be to establish an impossible standard. It is sufficient if the juror can lay aside his impression or opinion and render a verdict based on the evidence presented in court." The Court described the publicity that accompanied the case, and evaluated its effect on Irvin's trial, as follows:

> Here the build-up of prejudice is clear and convincing. An examination of the then current community pattern of thought as indicated by the popular news media is singularly revealing. For example, petitioner's first motion for a change of venue from Gibson County alleged that the awaited trial of petitioner had become the cause célèbre of this small community—so much so that curbstone opinions, not only as to petitioner's guilt but even as to what punishment he should receive, were solicited and recorded on the public streets by a roving reporter, and later were broadcast over the local stations. A reading of the 46 exhibits which petitioner attached to his motion indicates that a barrage of newspaper headlines, articles, cartoons and pictures was unleashed against him during the six or seven months preceding his trial. The motion further alleged that the newspapers in which the stories appeared were delivered regularly to approximately 95% of the dwellings in Gibson County and that, in addition, the Evansville radio and TV stations, which likewise blanketed that county, also carried extensive newscasts covering the same incidents. These stories revealed the details of his background, including a reference to crimes committed when a juvenile, his convictions for arson almost 20 years previously, for burglary and by a court-martial on AWOL charges during the war. He was accused of being a parole violator. The headlines announced his police line-up identification, that he faced a lie detector test, had been placed at the scene of the crime and that the six murders were solved but petitioner refused to confess. Finally, they announced his confession to the six murders and the fact of his indictment for four of them in Indiana. They reported petitioner's offer to plead guilty if promised a 99-year sentence, but also the determination, on the other hand, of the prosecutor to secure the death penalty, and that petitioner had confessed to 24 burglaries (the modus operandi of these robberies was compared to that of the murders and the similarity noted). One story dramatically relayed the promise of a sheriff to devote his life to securing petitioner's execution by the State of Kentucky, where petitioner is alleged to have committed one of the six murders, if Indiana failed to do so. Another characterized petitioner as remorseless and without conscience but also as having been found sane by a court-appointed panel of doctors. In many of the stories petitioner was described as the "confessed slayer of six," a parole violator and fraudulent-check artist. Petitioner's court-appointed counsel was quoted as having received "much criticism over being Irvin's counsel" and it was pointed out, by way of excusing the attorney, that he would be subject to disbarment should he refuse to represent Irvin. On the day before the trial the newspapers carried the story that Irvin had orally admitted the murder of Kerr (the victim in this case) as well as "the robbery-murder of Mrs. Mary Holland; the murder of Mrs. Wilhelmina Sailer in Posey County, and the slaughter of three members of the Duncan family in Henderson County, Ky."
>
> * * *

Finally, and with remarkable understatement, the headlines reported that "impartial jurors are hard to find." The panel consisted of 430 persons. The court itself excused 268 of those on challenges for cause as having fixed opinions as to the guilt of petitioner; 103 were excused because of conscientious objection to the imposition of the death penalty;[50] 20, the maximum allowed, were peremptorily challenged by petitioner and 10 by the State; 12 persons and two alternates were selected as jurors and the rest were excused on personal grounds, e.g., deafness, doctor's orders, etc. An examination of the 2,783-page voir dire record shows that 370 prospective jurors or almost 90% of those examined on the point (10 members of the panel were never asked whether or not they had any opinion) entertained some opinion as to guilt—ranging in intensity from mere suspicion to absolute certainty. A number admitted that, if they were in the accused's place in the dock and he in theirs on the jury with their opinions, they would not want him on a jury.

Here the "pattern of deep and bitter prejudice" shown to be present throughout the community, was clearly reflected in the sum total of the voir dire examination of a majority of the jurors finally placed in the jury box. Eight out of the 12 thought petitioner was guilty. With such an opinion permeating their minds, it would be difficult to say that each could exclude this preconception of guilt from his deliberations. The influence that lurks in an opinion once formed is so persistent that it unconsciously fights detachment from the mental processes of the average man. Where one's life is at stake—and accounting for the frailties of human nature—we can only say that in the light of the circumstances here the finding of impartiality does not meet constitutional standards. Two-thirds of the jurors had an opinion that petitioner was guilty and were familiar with the material facts and circumstances involved, including the fact that other murders were attributed to him, some going so far as to say that it would take evidence to overcome their belief. One said that he "could not * * * give the defendant the benefit of the doubt that he is innocent." Another stated that he had a "somewhat" certain fixed opinion as to petitioner's guilt. No doubt each juror was sincere when he said that he would be fair and impartial to petitioner, but the psychological impact requiring such a declaration before one's fellows is often its father. Where so many, so many times, admitted prejudice, such a statement of impartiality can be given little weight. As one of the jurors put it, "you can't forget what you hear and see." With his life at stake, it is not requiring too much that petitioner be tried in an atmosphere undisturbed by so huge a waive of public passion and by a jury other than one in which two-thirds of the members admit, before hearing any testimony, to possessing a belief in his guilt.

Thus, the Court set aside the conviction. Justice Frankfurter's concurring opinion suggested both that the problem of undue publicity was not isolated in Evansville, and that its impact on the *Irvin* case was not atypical.

The Court overturned another state conviction, in Rideau v. Louisiana, 373 U.S. 723 (1963). The Court began its opinion with a description of the facts of the case.

On the evening of February 16, 1961, a man robbed a bank in Lake Charles, Louisiana, kidnapped three of the bank's employees, and killed one of them. A few hours later the petitioner, Wilbert Rideau, was apprehended by

50. Could these jurors have been excused under the later case of Witherspoon v. Illinois, supra?

the police and lodged in the Calcasieu Parish jail in Lake Charles. The next morning a moving picture film with a sound track was made of an "interview" in the jail between Rideau and the Sheriff of Calcasieu Parish. This "interview" lasted approximately 20 minutes. It consisted of interrogation by the sheriff and admissions by Rideau that he had perpetrated the bank robbery, kidnapping, and murder. Later the same day the filmed "interview" was broadcast over a television station in Lake Charles, and some 24,000 people in the community saw and heard it on television. The sound film was again shown on television the next day to an estimated audience of 53,000 people. The following day the film was again broadcast by the same television station, and this time approximately 29,000 people saw and heard the "interview" on their television sets. Calcasieu Parish has a population of approximately 150,000 people.

Some two weeks later, Rideau was arraigned on charges of armed robbery, kidnapping, and murder, and two lawyers were appointed to represent him. His lawyers promptly filed a motion for a change of venue, on the ground that it would deprive Rideau of rights guaranteed to him by the United States Constitution to force him to trial in Calcasieu Parish after the three television broadcasts there of his "interview" with the sheriff. After a hearing, the motion for change of venue was denied, and Rideau was accordingly convicted and sentenced to death on the murder charge in the Calcasieu Parish trial court.

Three members of the jury which convicted him had stated on voir dire that they had seen and heard Rideau's televised "interview" with the sheriff on at least one occasion. Two members of the jury were deputy sheriffs of Calcasieu Parish. Rideau's counsel had requested that these jurors be excused for cause, having exhausted all of their peremptory challenges, but these challenges for cause had been denied by the trial judge.

The record in this case contains as an exhibit the sound film which was broadcast. What the people of Calcasieu Parish saw on their television sets was Rideau, in jail, flanked by the sheriff and two state troopers, admitting in detail the commission of the robbery, kidnapping, and murder, in response to leading questions by the sheriff. The record fails to show whose idea it was to make the sound film, and broadcast it over the local television station, but we know from the conceded circumstances that the plan was carried out with the active cooperation and participation of the local law enforcement officers. And certainly no one has suggested that it was Rideau's idea, or even that he was aware of what was going on when the sound film was being made.

It held that "it was a denial of due process of law to refuse the request for a change of venue, after the people of Calcasieu Parish had been exposed repeatedly and in depth to the spectacle of Rideau personally confessing in detail to the crimes with which he was later to be charged." The Court stated that the televised confession "in a very real sense *was* Rideau's trial—at which he pleaded guilty to murder," and that a later trial in a community so pervasively exposed to the confession "could be but a hollow formality." Justice Clark, joined by Justice Harlan, dissented, complaining that the defendant had not established any "substantial nexus" between the televised confession and any prejudice suffered at the trial.

In *Rideau,* there was no indication that the confession was coerced, and therefore it was undoubtedly admissible against Rideau at trial. Since the jurors would hear the confession at trial, what prejudice could Rideau have suffered from the pre-trial publicity?

In Patton v. Yount, 467 U.S. 1025 (1984), the Supreme Court reinstated a state defendant's murder conviction. Justice Powell's opinion for the Court emphasized that the court of appeals' reliance on *Irvin* was misplaced since the trial in *Irvin* took place six or seven months after extensive publicity began, whereas Yount was convicted in a second trial four years after most of the publicity occurred in connection with his first trial. That most jurors remembered the case was not decisive. The Court stated that "[t]he relevant question is not whether the community remembered the case, but whether the jurors at Yount's trial had such fixed opinions that they could not judge impartially the guilt of the defendant." Justice Powell reasoned as follows:

> It is not unusual that one's recollection of the fact that a notorious crime was committed lingers long after the feelings of revulsion that create prejudice have passed. It would be fruitless to attempt to identify any particular lapse of time that in itself would distinguish the situation that existed in *Irvin*. But it is clear that the passage of time between a first and a second trial can be a highly relevant fact. In the circumstances of this case, we hold that it clearly rebuts any presumption of partiality or prejudice that existed at the time of the initial trial.

The Court also held that whether a particular juror had such a predisposition as to be "partial" is a question of historical fact, not a mixed question of fact and law. Thus, a federal habeas corpus court must presume that state court findings that a juror was fair are valid. Justice Stevens, joined by Justice Brennan, dissented. Justice Marshall did not participate.

In Mu'Min v. Virginia, 111 S.Ct. 1899 (1991), the defendant was a state prisoner serving time for first-degree murder when he was charged with capital murder while on a work detail. The case was widely publicized. Articles in the newspapers revealed details of the prior murder for which Mu'Min was incarcerated, the fact that the death penalty was unavailable at that time, the denial of parole six times to Mu'Min, his confession to the crime charged, and criticism of the supervision of work gangs in Virginia. Mu'Min claimed that the jurors could not be impartial in such a setting, despite the judge's finding on voir dire that the jurors had not been substantially affected by the publicity.

The Chief Justice quoted prior decisions stating that a trial court's finding of juror impartiality may be overturned only where there is manifest error. He stated that "particularly with respect to pretrial publicity, we think this primary reliance on the judgment of the trial court makes good sense. The judge of that court sits in the locale where the publicity is said to have had its effect, and brings to his evaluation of any such claim his own perception of the depth and extent of news stories that might influence a juror." This was so even though the judge had not questioned individual jurors to determine whether they had been affected by pre-trial publicity.

The majority rejected Mu'Min's reliance on Irvin v. Dowd on the ground that the pretrial publicity in the instant case was not of the same kind or extent as in *Irvin*. The majority also rejected the defendant's reliance upon the ABA Standards for Criminal Justice, which require individual interrogation of jurors concerning pretrial publicity. Chief Justice Rehnquist refused to hold the A.B.A. standards controlling. He reasoned as follows:

> [The A.B.A. Standards] are based on a substantive rule that renders a potential juror subject to challenge for cause, without regard to his state of mind, if he has been exposed to and remembers highly significant information or other incriminating matters that may be inadmissible in evidence. That is a stricter standard of juror eligibility than that which we have held the Constitution to require. * * * Under the constitutional standard * * * the relevant question is not whether the community remembered the case, but whether the jurors had such fixed opinions that they could not judge impartially the guilt of the defendant. * * * It is not required that the jurors be totally ignorant of the facts and issues involved.

The Chief Justice concluded that it was therefore not necessary for the trial judge to ask each juror individually whether they had been affected by pre-trial publicity.

Justice O'Connor wrote a concurring opinion. She cited Patton v. Yount for the proposition that even jurors who had read about inadmissible confessions are not disqualified as a matter of law, and concluded that a trial judge could realistically assess whether jurors could be fair without knowing what each juror had heard about a case. Justices Marshall, Blackmun, Stevens, and Kennedy dissented.

Are prospective jurors impartial because they honestly believe they are? Or are they impartial only if they are free of subconscious bias? Is there any way for a defendant to be guaranteed subconscious neutrality? Do peremptory challenges provide adequate protection? Should the standard for challenges for cause recognize the possibility of subconscious bias?

2. *Television in the Courtroom*

In Estes v. Texas, 381 U.S. 532 (1965), the Court held that the defendant was denied a fair trial due to the pervasive media coverage of his trial. Justice Clark, writing for the Court, described the effect that the media had on the courtroom during both pre-trial hearings and at the trial:

> The initial hearings were carried live by both radio and television, and news photography was permitted throughout. The videotapes of these hearings clearly illustrate that the picture presented was not one of that judicial serenity and calm to which petitioner was entitled. Indeed, at least 12 cameramen were engaged in the courtroom throughout the hearing taking motion and still pictures and televising the proceedings. Cables and wires were snaked across the courtroom floor, three microphones were on the judge's bench and others were beamed at the jury box and the counsel table. It is conceded that the activities of the television crews and news photographers led to considerable disruption of the hearings. Moreover, veniremen had been summoned and were present in the courtroom during the entire hearing but were later released after petitioner's motion for continuance had been granted. * * * The trial witnesses present at the hearing, as well as the original jury panel, were undoubtedly made aware of the peculiar public importance of the case by the press and television coverage being provided, and by the fact that they themselves were televised live and their pictures rebroadcast on the evening show. * * *
>
> Because of continual objection, the rules governing live telecasting, as well as radio and still photos, were changed as the exigencies of the situation

seemed to require. As a result, live telecasting was prohibited during a great portion of the actual trial. Only the opening and closing arguments of the State, the return of the jury's verdict and its receipt by the trial judge were carried live with sound. Although the order allowed videotapes of the entire proceeding without sound, the cameras operated only intermittently, recording various portions of the trial for broadcast on regularly scheduled newscasts later in the day and evening. At the request of the petitioner, the trial judge prohibited coverage of any kind, still or television, of the defense counsel during their summations to the jury.

Because of the varying restrictions placed on sound and live telecasting the telecasts of the trial were confined largely to film clips shown on the stations' regularly scheduled news programs. The news commentators would use the film of a particular part of the day's trial activities as a backdrop for their reports. Their commentary included excerpts from testimony and the usual reportorial remarks. On one occasion the videotapes of the September hearings were rebroadcast in place of the "late movie."

The Court held that the First Amendment did not extend a right to the news media to televise from the courtroom, and that the disruption of the proceedings created by television coverage required a new trial, even though Estes had not made a showing of actual prejudice. Justice Clark concluded with these critical comments about televised coverage of courtroom proceedings:

[T]he chief function of our judicial machinery is to ascertain the truth. The use of television, however, cannot be said to contribute materially to this objective. Rather its use amounts to the injection of an irrelevant factor into court proceedings. In addition experience teaches that there are numerous situations in which it might cause actual unfairness—some so subtle as to defy detection by the accused or control by the judge. We enumerate some in summary:

1. The potential impact of television on the jurors is perhaps of the greatest significance. * * *

2. The quality of the testimony in criminal trials will often be impaired. The impact upon a witness of the knowledge that he is being viewed by a vast audience is simply incalculable. Some may be demoralized and frightened, some cocky and given to overstatement; memories may falter, as with anyone speaking publicly, and accuracy of statement may be severely undermined. Embarrassment may impede the search for the truth, as may a natural tendency toward overdramatization. * * *

In addition the invocation of the rule against [sequestration of] witnesses is frustrated. In most instances witnesses would be able to go to their homes and view broadcasts of the day's trial proceedings, notwithstanding the fact that they had been admonished not to do so. * * *

* * *

3. A major aspect of the problem is the additional responsibilities the presence of television places on the trial judge. His job is to make certain that the accused receives a fair trial. This most difficult task requires his undivided attention. Still when television comes into the courtroom he must also supervise it. * * *

* * *

4. Finally, we cannot ignore the impact of courtroom television on the defendant. Its presence is a form of mental—if not physical—harassment, resembling a police lineup or the third degree. The inevitable close-ups of his gestures and expressions during the ordeal of his trial might well transgress his personal sensibilities, his dignity, and his ability to concentrate on the proceedings before him—sometimes the difference between life and death—dispassionately, freely and without the distraction of wide public surveillance. A defendant on trial for a specific crime is entitled to his day in court, not in a stadium, or a city or nationwide arena. The heightened public clamor resulting from radio and television coverage will inevitably result in prejudice. Trial by television is, therefore, foreign to our system. Furthermore, telecasting may also deprive an accused of effective counsel. The distractions, intrusions into confidential attorney-client relationships and the temptation offered by television to play to the public audience might often have a direct effect not only upon the lawyers, but the judge, the jury and the witnesses.

* * *

Chief Justice Warren, joined by Justices Douglas and Goldberg, wrote a concurring opinion concluding that "televising of criminal proceedings is inherently a denial of due process." Justice Harlan wrote a separate opinion, agreeing with the Court that the First Amendment does not require that television be allowed in the courtroom, but disagreeing with the Court that televised proceedings were *per se* prohibited by the constitution. He suggested a case-by-case approach. Justice Stewart's dissent, joined by Justices Black, Brennan and White concluded that "in the present state of the art" televised judicial proceedings were unwise, but found no denial of Estes' constitutional rights. Justice White's short dissent noted that advances in technology might make televised judicial proceedings more acceptable. Justice Brennan's separate statement noted that because of Justice Harlan's vote, *Estes* could not be read as an absolute bar to televised trials. In the next case, the Court clearly agreed with Justice Brennan's view.

CHANDLER v. FLORIDA

Supreme Court of the United States, 1981.
449 U.S. 560.

CHIEF JUSTICE BURGER delivered the opinion of the Court.

The question presented on this appeal is whether, consistent with constitutional guarantees, a state may provide for radio, television, and still photographic coverage of a criminal trial for public broadcast, notwithstanding the objection of the accused.

I

A

* * *

[In May, 1975, the Florida Supreme Court] announced an experimental program for televising one civil and one criminal trial under specific guidelines. These initial guidelines required the consent of all parties. It developed, however, that in practice such consent could not be obtained. The Florida Supreme Court then supplemented its order and established a new one-year pilot program during which the electronic media were permitted to cover all judicial proceedings in Florida without reference to the consent of participants, subject to detailed standards with respect to technology and the conduct of operators. The experiment began in

July 1977 and continued through June 1978.

When the pilot program ended, the Florida Supreme Court received and reviewed briefs, reports, letters of comment, and studies. It conducted its own survey of attorneys, witnesses, jurors, and court personnel through the Office of the State Court Coordinator. A separate survey was taken of judges by the Florida Conference of Circuit Judges. The court also studied the experience of six states that had, by 1979, adopted rules relating to electronic coverage of trials, as well as that of the 10 other states that, like Florida, were experimenting with such coverage.

Following its review of this material, the Florida Supreme Court concluded "that on balance there [was] more to be gained than lost by permitting electronic media coverage of judicial proceedings subject to standards for such coverage." The Florida court was of the view that because of the significant effect of the courts on the day-to-day lives of the citizenry, it was essential that the people have confidence in the process. It felt that broadcast coverage of trials would contribute to wider public acceptance and understanding of decisions. Consequently, after revising the 1977 guidelines to reflect its evaluation of the pilot program, the Florida Supreme Court promulgated a revised Canon 3A(7). The canon provides:

> "Subject at all times to the authority of the presiding judge to (i) control the conduct of proceedings before the court, (ii) ensure decorum and prevent distractions, and (iii) ensure fair administration of justice in the pending cause, electronic media and still photography coverage of public judicial proceedings in the appellate and trial courts of this state shall be allowed in accordance with standards of conduct and technology promulgated by the Supreme Court of Florida."

The implementing guidelines specify in detail the kind of electronic equipment to be used and the manner of its use. For example, no more than one television camera and only one camera technician are allowed. Existing recording systems used by court reporters are used by broadcasters for audio pickup. Where more than one broadcast news organization seeks to cover a trial, the media must pool coverage. No artificial lighting is allowed. The equipment is positioned in a fixed location, and it may not be moved during trial. Videotaping equipment must be remote from the courtroom. Film, videotape, and lenses may not be changed while the court is in session. No audio recording of conferences between lawyers, between parties and counsel, or at the bench is permitted. The judge has sole and plenary discretion to exclude coverage of certain witnesses, and the jury may not be filmed. The judge has discretionary power to forbid coverage whenever satisfied that coverage may have a deleterious effect on the paramount right of the defendant to a fair trial. The Florida Supreme Court has the right to revise these rules as experience dictates, or indeed to bar all broadcast coverage of photography in courtrooms.

B

In July 1977, appellants were charged with conspiracy to commit burglary, grand larceny, and possession of burglary tools. The counts covered breaking and entering a well-known Miami Beach restaurant.

The details of the alleged criminal conduct are not relevant to the issue before us, but several aspects of the case distinguish it from a routine burglary. At the time of their arrest, appellants were Miami Beach policemen. The State's principal witness was John Sion, an amateur radio operator who, by sheer chance, had overheard and recorded conversations between the appellants over their police walkie-talkie radios during the burglary. Not surprisingly, these novel factors attracted the attention of the media.

By pretrial motion, counsel for the appellants sought to have Experimental Canon 3A(7) declared unconstitutional on its face and as applied. The trial court denied relief but certified the issue to the Florida Supreme Court. However, the Supreme Court declined to rule on the question. * * *

After several additional fruitless attempts by the appellants to prevent electronic coverage of the trial, the jury was selected. At *voir dire*, the appellants' counsel asked each prospective juror whether he or she would be able to be "fair and impartial" despite the presence of a television camera during some, or all, of the trial. Each juror selected responded that such coverage would not affect his or her consideration in any way. A television camera recorded the *voir dire*.

A defense motion to sequester the jury because of the television coverage was denied by the trial judge. However, the court instructed the jury not to watch or read anything about the case in the media and suggested that jurors "avoid the local news and watch only the national news on television." Subsequently, defense counsel requested that the witnesses be instructed not to watch any television accounts of testimony presented at trial. The trial court declined to give such an instruction, for "no witness' testimony was [being] reported or televised [on the evening news] in any way."

A television camera was in place for one entire afternoon, during which the state presented the testimony of Sion, its chief witness. No camera was present for the presentation of any part of the case for the defense. The camera returned to cover closing arguments. Only two minutes and fifty-five seconds of the trial below were broadcast—and those depicted only the prosecution's side of the case.

The jury returned a guilty verdict on all counts. [The conviction was upheld on appeal.]

II

At the outset, it is important to note that in promulgating the revised Canon 3A(7), the Florida Supreme Court pointedly rejected any state or federal constitutional right of access on the part of photographers or the broadcast media to televise or electronically record and thereafter disseminate court proceedings. * * * [51]

* * *

III

Appellants rely chiefly on Estes v. Texas, and Chief Justice Warren's separate concurring opinion in that case. They argue that the televising of criminal trials is inherently a denial of due process, and they read *Estes* as announcing a *per se* constitutional rule to that effect.

* * *

Parsing the six opinions in *Estes*, one is left with a sense of doubt as to precisely how much of Justice Clark's opinion was joined in, and supported by, Justice Harlan. In an area charged with constitutional nuances, perhaps more

51. Zimmerman, Overcoming Future Shock: Estes Revisited, Or a Modest Proposal for the Constitutional Protection of the News-Gathering Process, 1980 Duke L.J. 641, argues for First Amendment protection for technological access to judicial proceedings, and urges that the government may "impose no more restrictions on the means by which its performance is reported than are strictly necessary to accommodate the countervailing constitutional requirements of orderly process."

should not be expected. Nonetheless, it is fair to say that Justice Harlan viewed the holding as limited to the proposition that "*what was done in this case* infringed the fundamental right to a fair trial assured by the Due Process Clause of the Fourteenth Amendment * * *."

* * *

IV

Since we are satisfied that *Estes* did not announce a constitutional rule that all photographic or broadcast coverage of criminal trials is inherently a denial of due process, we turn to consideration, as a matter of first impression, of the petitioner's suggestion that we now promulgate such a *per se* rule.

A

Any criminal case that generates a great deal of publicity presents some risks that the publicity may compromise the right of the defendant to a fair trial. Trial courts must be especially vigilant to guard against any impairment of the defendant's right to a verdict based solely upon the evidence and the relevant law. Over the years, courts have developed a range of curative devices to prevent publicity about a trial from infecting jury deliberations.

An absolute constitutional ban on broadcast coverage of trials cannot be justified simply because there is a danger that, in some cases, prejudicial broadcast accounts of pretrial and trial events may impair the ability of jurors to decide the issue of guilt or innocence uninfluenced by extraneous matter. The risk of juror prejudice in some cases does not justify an absolute ban on news coverage of trials by the printed media; so also the risk of such prejudice does not warrant an absolute constitutional ban on all broadcast coverage. * * *

B

As we noted earlier, the concurring opinions in *Estes* expressed concern that the very presence of media cameras and recording devices at a trial inescapably gives rise to an adverse psychological impact on the participants in the trial. This kind of general psychological prejudice, allegedly present whenever there is broadcast coverage of a trial, is different from the more particularized problem of prejudicial impact discussed earlier. If it could be demonstrated that the mere presence of photographic and recording equipment and the knowledge that the event would be broadcast invariably and uniformly affected the conduct of participants so as to impair fundamental fairness, our task would be simple; prohibition of broadcast coverage of trials would be required.

* * *

Not unimportant to the position asserted by Florida and other states is the change in television technology since 1962, when Estes was tried. It is urged, and some empirical data are presented, that many of the negative factors found in *Estes*—cumbersome equipment, cables, distracting lighting, numerous camera technicians—are less substantial factors today than they were at that time.

It is also significant that safeguards have been built into the experimental programs in state courts, and into the Florida program, to avoid some of the most egregious problems envisioned by the six opinions in the *Estes* case. Florida admonishes its courts to take special pains to protect certain witnesses—for example, children, victims of sex crimes, some informants, and even the very timid witness or party—from the glare of publicity and the tensions of being "on camera."

The Florida guidelines place on trial judges positive obligations to be on guard to protect the fundamental right of the accused to a fair trial. The Florida statute, being one of the few permitting broadcast coverage of criminal trials over the objection of the accused, raises problems not present in the statutes of other states. Inherent in electronic coverage of a trial is the risk that the very awareness by the accused of the coverage and the contemplated broadcast may adversely affect the conduct of the participants and the fairness of the trial, yet leave no evidence of how the conduct or the trial's fairness was affected. Given this danger, it is significant that Florida requires that objections of the accused to coverage be heard and considered on the record by the trial court. In addition to providing a record for appellate review, a pretrial hearing enables a defendant to advance the basis of his objection to broadcast coverage and allows the trial court to define the steps necessary to minimize or eliminate the risks of prejudice to the accused. Experiments such as the one presented here may well increase the number of appeals by adding a new basis for claims to reverse, but this is a risk Florida has chosen to take after preliminary experimentation. Here, the record does not indicate that appellants requested an evidentiary hearing to show adverse impact or injury. Nor does the record reveal anything more than generalized allegations of prejudice.

* * *

Whatever may be the "mischievous potentialities [of broadcast coverage] for intruding upon the detached atmosphere which should always surround the judicial process," at present no one has been able to present empirical data sufficient to establish that the mere presence of the broadcast media inherently has an adverse effect on that process. The appellants have offered nothing to demonstrate that their trial was subtly tainted by broadcast coverage—let alone that all broadcast trials would be so tainted.

Amici members of the defense bar vigorously contend that displaying the accused on television is in itself a denial of due process. This was a source of concern to Chief Justice Warren and Justice Harlan in *Estes*: that coverage of select cases "singles out certain defendants and subjects them to trials under prejudicial conditions not experienced by others." Selection of which trials, or parts of trials, to broadcast will inevitably be made not by judges but by the media, and will be governed by such factors as the nature of the crime and the status and position of the accused—or of the victim; the effect may be to titillate rather than to educate and inform. The unanswered question is whether electronic coverage will bring public humiliation upon the accused with such randomness that it will evoke due process concerns * * *.

The concurring opinion of Chief Justice Warren joined by Justices Douglas and Goldberg in *Estes* can fairly be read as viewing the very broadcast of some trials as potentially a form of punishment in itself—a punishment before guilt. This concern is far from trivial. But, whether coverage of a few trials will, in practice, be the equivalent of a "Yankee Stadium" setting—which Justice Harlan likened to the public pillory long abandoned as a barbaric perversion of decent justice—must also await the continuing experimentation.

D

To say that the appellants have not demonstrated that broadcast coverage is inherently a denial of due process is not to say that the appellants were in fact accorded all of the protections of due process in their trial. As noted earlier, a defendant has the right on review to show that the media's coverage of his case—printed or broadcast—compromised the ability of the jury to judge him fairly. Alternatively, a defendant might show that broadcast coverage of his particular case had an adverse impact on the trial participants sufficient to constitute a denial of due process. Neither showing was made in this case.

To demonstrate prejudice in a specific case a defendant must show something more than juror awareness that the trial is such as to attract the attention of broadcasters.

* * *

V

* * * We are not empowered by the Constitution to oversee or harness state procedural experimentation; only when the state action infringes fundamental guarantees are we authorized to intervene. We must assume state courts will be alert to any factors that impair the fundamental rights of the accused.

The Florida program is inherently evolutional in nature; the initial project has provided guidance for the new canons which can be changed at will, and application of which is subject to control by the trial judge. The risk of prejudice to particular defendants is ever present and must be examined carefully as cases arise. * * *

[The Court affirmed the convictions.]

JUSTICE STEWART, concurring in the result.

Although concurring in the judgment, I cannot join the opinion of the Court because I do not think the convictions in this case can be affirmed without overruling Estes v. Texas. * * *

* * *

JUSTICE WHITE, concurring in the judgment.

* * *

Whether the decision in *Estes* is read broadly or narrowly, I agree with Justice Stewart that it should be overruled. * * *

* * *

Note

Whether or not the changes in television technology are sufficient to distinguish 1965 from 1981, it seems clear that the assumptions made by Justice Clark in his *Estes* opinion are different from those made by Chief Justice Burger in his *Chandler* opinion. Which assumptions find more support in your own experience? In thinking about a defendant's challenge to televised trials, consider the following questions: Is a witness who might be inclined to admit weaknesses in his testimony as likely to do so if the testimony may be broadcast throughout the community? Is a witness' testimony accusing a defendant likely to have a lingering effect if televised even though the defendant may be acquitted? Is it possible that prosecutors will use "grandstand" tactics in the cases that are important enough to be considered for television coverage? Will there ever be clear answers to any of these questions? If not, is the better constitutional rule one that permits states to experiment or one that entitles a defendant to protection from the risks of prejudice?

State v. Green, 395 So.2d 532 (Fla.1981), indicates that where a trial court finds that an otherwise competent defendant would be rendered incompetent by the presence of cameras, they should be excluded as the case is "qualitatively different" from the ordinary case. What if the cameras simply make a defendant nervous? Does this require exclusion?

3. *Protecting the Integrity of Judicial Proceedings*

In Sheppard v. Maxwell, 384 U.S. 333 (1966), Sheppard was tried and convicted for murdering his wife. He claimed that she was killed by an intruder. The case obtained substantial notoriety in the community. In his opinion for the Court, Justice Clark describes the pre-trial publicity and the media coverage during the trial:

> On July 7, the day of Marilyn Sheppard's funeral, a newspaper story appeared in which Assistant County Attorney Mahon—later the chief prosecutor of Sheppard—sharply criticized the refusal of the Sheppard family to permit his immediate questioning. From there on headline stories repeatedly stressed Sheppard's lack of cooperation with the police and other officials. Under the headline "Testify Now In Death, Bay Doctor Is Ordered," one story described a visit by Coroner Gerber and four police officers to the hospital on July 8. When Sheppard insisted that his lawyer be present, the Coroner wrote out a subpoena and served it on him. Sheppard then agreed to submit to questioning without counsel and the subpoena was torn up. The officers questioned him for several hours. On July 9, Sheppard, at the request of the Coroner, re-enacted the tragedy at his home before the Coroner, police officers, and a group of newsmen, who apparently were invited by the Coroner. The home was locked so that Sheppard was obliged to wait outside until the Coroner arrived. Sheppard's performance was reported in detail by the news media along with photographs. The newspapers also played up Sheppard's refusal to take a lie detector test and "the protective ring" thrown up by his family. Front-page newspaper headlines announced on the same day that "Doctor Balks At Lie Test; Retells Story." A column opposite that story contained an "exclusive" interview with Sheppard headlined: " 'Loved My Wife, She Loved Me,' Sheppard Tells News Reporter." The next day, another headline story disclosed that Sheppard had "again late yesterday refused to take a lie detector test" and quoted an Assistant County Attorney as saying that "at the end of a nine-hour questioning of Dr. Sheppard, I felt he was now ruling [a test] out completely." But subsequent newspaper articles reported that the Coroner was still pushing Sheppard for a lie detector test. More stories appeared when Sheppard would not allow authorities to inject him with "truth serum." [a]
>
> On the 20th, the "editorial artillery" opened fire with a front-page charge that somebody is "getting away with murder." The editorial attributed the ineptness of the investigation to "friendships, relationships, hired lawyers, a husband who ought to have been subjected instantly to the same third-degree to which any other person under similar circumstances is subjected. * * *" The following day, July 21, another page-one editorial was headed: "Why No Inquest? Do It Now, Dr. Gerber." The Coroner called an inquest the same day and subpoenaed Sheppard. It was staged the next day in a school gymnasium; the Coroner presided with the County Prosecutor as his advisor and two detectives as bailiffs. In the front of the room was a long table occupied by reporters, television and radio personnel, and broadcasting equipment. The hearing was broadcast with live microphones placed at the Coroner's seat and the witness stand. A swarm of reporters and photographers attended. Shep-

a. At the same time, the newspapers reported that other possible suspects had been "cleared" by the lie detector tests. One of these persons was quoted as saying that he could not understand why an innocent man would refuse to take such a test.

pard was brought into the room by police who searched him in full view of several hundred spectators. Sheppard's counsel were present during the three-day inquest but were not permitted to participate. When Sheppard's chief counsel attempted to place some documents in the record, he was forcibly ejected from the room by the Coroner, who received cheers, hugs, and kisses from ladies in the audience. Sheppard was questioned for five and one-half hours about his actions on the night of the murder, his married life, and a love affair with Susan Hayes.[b] At the end of the hearing the Coroner announced that he "could" order Sheppard held for the grand jury, but did not do so.

Throughout this period the newspapers emphasized evidence that tended to incriminate Sheppard and pointed out discrepancies in his statements to authorities. * * * During the inquest on July 26, a headline in large type stated: "Kerr [Captain of the Cleveland Police] Urges Sheppard's Arrest." In the story, Detective McArthur "disclosed that scientific tests at the Sheppard home have definitely established that the killer washed off a trail of blood from the murder bedroom to the downstairs section," a circumstance casting doubt on Sheppard's accounts of the murder. No such evidence was produced at trial. The newspapers also delved into Sheppard's personal life. Articles stressed his extramarital love affairs as a motive for the crime. The newspapers portrayed Sheppard as a Lothario, fully explored his relationship with Susan Hayes, and named a number of other women who were allegedly involved with him. The testimony at trial never showed that Sheppard had any illicit relationships besides the one with Susan Hayes.

On July 28, an editorial entitled "Why Don't Police Quiz Top Suspect" demanded that Sheppard be taken to police headquarters. * * *

That night at 10 o'clock Sheppard was arrested at his father's home on a charge of murder. He was taken to the Bay Village City Hall where hundreds of people, newscasters, photographers and reporters were awaiting his arrival. He was immediately arraigned—having been denied a temporary delay to secure the presence of counsel—and bound over to the grand jury.

The publicity then grew in intensity until his indictment on August 17. * * *

With this background the case came on for trial two weeks before the November general election at which the chief prosecutor was a candidate for common pleas judge and the trial judge, Judge Blythin, was a candidate to succeed himself. Twenty-five days before the case was set, 75 veniremen were called as prospective jurors. All three Cleveland newspapers published the names and addresses of the veniremen. * * *

The courtroom in which the trial was held measured 26 by 48 feet. A long temporary table was set up inside the bar, in back of the single counsel table. It ran the width of the courtroom, parallel to the bar railing, with one end less than three feet from the jury box. Approximately 20 representatives of newspapers and wire services were assigned seats at this table by the court. Behind the bar railing there were four rows of benches. These seats were likewise assigned by the court for the entire trial. The first row was occupied by representatives of television and radio stations, and the second and third rows by reporters from out-of-town newspapers and magazines. * * * Representatives of the news media also used all the rooms on the courtroom floor,

b. The newspapers had heavily emphasized Sheppard's illicit affair with Susan Hayes, and the fact that he had initially lied about it.

including the room where cases were ordinarily called and assigned for trial. Private telephone lines and telegraphic equipment were installed in these rooms so that reports from the trial could be speeded to the papers. Station WSRS was permitted to set up broadcasting facilities on the third floor of the courthouse next door to the jury room, where the jury rested during recesses in the trial and deliberated. Newscasts were made from this room throughout the trial, and while the jury reached its verdict.

On the sidewalk and steps in front of the courthouse, television and newsreel cameras were occasionally used to take motion pictures of the participants in the trial, including the jury and the judge. Indeed, one television broadcast carried a staged interview of the judge as he entered the courthouse. In the corridors outside the courtroom there was a host of photographers and television personnel with flash cameras, portable lights and motion picture cameras. This group photographed the prospective jurors during selection of the jury. After the trial opened, the witnesses, counsel, and jurors were photographed and televised whenever they entered or left the courtroom. Sheppard was brought to the courtroom about 10 minutes before each session began; he was surrounded by reporters and extensively photographed for the newspapers and television. A rule of court prohibited picture-taking in the courtroom during the actual sessions of the court, but no restraints were put on photographers during recesses, which were taken once each morning and afternoon, with a longer period for lunch.

All of these arrangements with the news media and their massive coverage of the trial continued during the entire nine weeks of the trial. The courtroom remained crowded to capacity with representatives of news media. Their movement in and out of the courtroom often caused so much confusion that, despite the loud-speaker system installed in the courtroom, it was difficult for the witnesses and counsel to be heard. Furthermore, the reporters clustered within the bar of the small courtroom made confidential talk among Sheppard and his counsel almost impossible during the proceedings. They frequently had to leave the courtroom to obtain privacy. And many times when counsel wished to raise a point with the judge out of the hearing of the jury it was necessary to move to the judge's chambers. Even then, news media representatives so packed the judge's anteroom that counsel could hardly return from the chambers to the courtroom. The reporters vied with each other to find out what counsel and the judge had discussed, and often these matters later appeared in newspapers accessible to the jury.

* * *

The jurors themselves were constantly exposed to the news media. Every juror, except one, testified at voir dire to reading about the case in the Cleveland papers or to having heard broadcasts about it. * * * During the trial, pictures of the jury appeared over 40 times in the Cleveland papers alone. The court permitted photographers to take pictures of the jury in the box, and individual pictures of the members in the jury room. One newspaper ran pictures of the jurors at the Sheppard home when they went there to view the scene of the murder. Another paper featured the home life of an alternate juror. The day before the verdict was rendered—while the jurors were at lunch and sequestered by two bailiffs—the jury was separated into two groups to pose for photographs which appeared in the newspapers.

The Court held that the trial judge's failure to control the media coverage of the judicial proceedings deprived Sheppard of his right to a fair trial. Justice Clark reasoned as follows:

> While we cannot say that Sheppard was denied due process by the judge's refusal to take precautions against the influence of pretrial publicity alone, the court's later rulings must be considered against the setting in which the trial was held. In light of this background, we believe that the arrangements made by the judge with the news media caused Sheppard to be deprived of that "judicial serenity and calm to which [he] was entitled." The fact is that bedlam reigned at the courthouse during the trial and newsmen took over practically the entire courtroom, hounding most of the participants in the trial, especially Sheppard. At a temporary table within a few feet of the jury box and counsel table sat some 20 reporters staring at Sheppard and taking notes. The erection of a press table for reporters inside the bar is unprecedented. The bar of the court is reserved for counsel, providing them a safe place in which to keep papers and exhibits, and to confer privately with client and co-counsel. It is designed to protect the witness and the jury from any distractions, intrusions or influences, and to permit bench discussions of the judge's rulings away from the hearing of the public and the jury. Having assigned almost all of the available seats in the courtroom to the news media, the judge lost his ability to supervise that environment. * * *

Justice Clark emphasized that the trial court had substantial authority to control media coverage in order to protect the defendant's right to a fair trial, and that the trial court in *Sheppard* should have exercised this authority. The Court gave the following suggestions as to what could and should have been done:

> The carnival atmosphere at trial could easily have been avoided since the courtroom and courthouse premises are subject to the control of the court. As we stressed in *Estes*, the presence of the press at judicial proceedings must be limited when it is apparent that the accused might otherwise be prejudiced or disadvantaged. Bearing in mind the massive pretrial publicity, the judge should have adopted stricter rules governing the use of the courtroom by newsmen, as Sheppard's counsel requested. The number of reporters in the courtroom itself could have been limited at the first sign that their presence would disrupt the trial. They certainly should not have been placed inside the bar. Furthermore, the judge should have more closely regulated the conduct of newsmen in the courtroom. For instance, the judge belatedly asked them not to handle and photograph trial exhibits lying on the counsel table during recesses.
>
> Secondly, the court should have insulated the witnesses. All of the newspapers and radio stations apparently interviewed prospective witnesses at will, and in many instances disclosed their testimony. * * * Although the witnesses were barred from the courtroom during the trial the full verbatim testimony was available to them in the press. This completely nullified the judge's imposition of the rule [sequestering witnesses].
>
> Thirdly, the court should have made some effort to control the release of leads, information, and gossip to the press by police officers, witnesses, and the counsel for both sides. * * *

* * *

More specifically, the trial court might well have proscribed extrajudicial statements by any lawyer, party, witness, or court official which divulged prejudicial matters, such as the refusal of Sheppard to submit to interrogation or take any lie detector tests; any statement made by Sheppard to officials; the identity of prospective witnesses or their probable testimony; any belief in guilt or innocence; or like statements concerning the merits of the case. * * * Being advised of the great public interest in the case, the mass coverage of the press, and the potential prejudicial impact of publicity, the court could also have requested the appropriate city and county officials to promulgate a regulation with respect to dissemination of information about the case by their employees. In addition, reporters who wrote or broadcast prejudicial stories, could have been warned as to the impropriety of publishing material not introduced in the proceedings.

Justice Clark concluded that "where there is a reasonable likelihood that prejudicial news prior to trial will prevent a fair trial, the judge should continue the case until the threat abates, or transfer it to another county not so permeated with publicity." With respect to publicity during the proceedings, he concluded that "courts must take such steps by rule and regulation that will protect their processes from prejudicial outside interferences."

Note

Taking a cue from *Estes* and *Sheppard,* most courts exercise considerable control over the courtroom today. Rarely, if ever, do reporters or other non-participants dominate the atmosphere at trial. In some highly publicized cases the courts adopt special safeguards. Consider, for example, the order entered in the case of James Earl Ray, accused, and convicted upon his plea of guilty, of killing Dr. Martin Luther King, Jr.

In the Criminal Court of Shelby County, Tennessee

Order on Courthouse and Courtroom Procedures and Publicity

The Constitutions of the United States and the State of Tennessee guarantee defendants in criminal cases due process of law and the right to a fair trial by an impartial jury. It is the duty of the trial Court to see that every defendant receives all his constitutional rights.

From the worldwide attention attracted to this case at bar resulting in massive and pervasive publicity in the news media, the Court is of the opinion that the following rules are necessary to a constitutionally guaranteed, orderly and fair trial by an impartial jury, and therefore orders:

I

The term "Criminal Courts Buildings" as used herein shall mean the Criminal Courts Building, 150 Washington, and the adjoining Shelby County Building, 157 Poplar Avenue, Memphis, Tennessee.

All entrance ways, corridors, and approaches to courtrooms, offices, and other rooms in the Criminal Courts Buildings will be kept clear at all times for free access thereto by those using them in the course of their employment or those having business to transact therein.

II

No cameras, photographic, television, radio or sound equipment, including tape recorders, will be permitted in the Criminal Courts Buildings or upon the alley-ways, parking lots, yards or grounds immediately surrounding said buildings. No photographs will be taken of the Jury, nor will they be televised. No sketches will be made in the Criminal Courts Buildings.

III

All persons seeking admission to the courtroom will submit voluntarily to a search of his person before being admitted.

IV

No one will enter the courtroom after a session has begun without permission of the Court, but must wait until the next recess. No one will leave the courtroom except at recess or adjournment except in an emergency. At noon recess and adjournment, and at any other time the Jury is retiring from the second floor, or the prisoner is being removed to the jail, the spectators shall remain seated in the courtroom until the Jury and prisoner have had ample time to withdraw, and said spectators have been given permission to disperse.

V

The bar of the Court within the rail is reserved for the defendant, counsel, members of the Bar, court personnel and such witnesses as counsel may desire to be within the bar for consultation purposes. No one else will enter without permission of the Court.

VI

No one except attorneys of record, their agents, court personnel, witnesses and jurors may handle exhibits except by order of the Court.

VII

All lawyers participating in this case, their assistants, office associates, staff members, investigators and employees under their supervision and control are forbidden to take part in interviews for publicity and from making extrajudicial statements about this case from this date until such time as a verdict is returned in this case in open Court.

VIII

The County Medical Examiner, Jury Commissioners, Criminal Court Clerk, County Sheriff, Police Officials and other law enforcement officers, employees of this Court, all other persons employed in the "Criminal Courts Buildings," their associates, deputies, assistants, staff members and personnel under their supervision and control are forbidden to participate in interviews for publicity and from making extrajudicial statements about this case from this date and until such time as a verdict in this case is returned in open Court.

IX

All witnesses, persons subpoenaed to Grand Jury or Court, jurors, and those persons summoned but excused from serving as jurors, are forbidden to participate in interviews for publicity and from making extrajudicial statements about this case from this date and until such time as a verdict in this case is returned in open Court.

X

Nothing in this order shall prohibit any witness from discussing any matter in connection with the case with any of the attorneys representing the defendant or the State, or any representative of such attorneys.

Following the suggestion of the *Sheppard* Court, the trial judge in the *Ray* case barred lawyers, their employees, law enforcement and court personnel, and witnesses from making extrajudicial statements prior to the entry of a verdict. Similar "gag" orders are common today. DR7–107 of the ABA Code of Professional Responsibility and Rule 3.6 of the Model Rules of Professional Conduct make disclosure of information by lawyers an ethical violation under some circumstances. See e.g. United States v. Bingham, 769 F.Supp. 1039 (N.D.Ill.1991) (defense attorneys' conduct was referred to disciplinary committee, where attorneys criticized the empanelment of an anonymous jury in televised interviews the night before jury selection, despite a court order to refrain from such publicity).

Gag orders and disciplinary rules raise questions of First Amendment rights of trial participants. Is it fair to restrict the defense as well as the prosecution from making pre-trial statements? What likely harm is associated with defense statements? Is a plea of not guilty likely to dissipate the taint of an indictment? If not, shouldn't the defense be able to attempt to restore a semblance of a presumption of innocence? Can a defendant in a big case raise funds to support a defense without publicly discussing the case? Should the defendant who claims he is the victim of politics or harassment be barred from protesting prior to the conclusion of litigation?

Are restrictions on all attorneys, including defense attorneys, less worrisome than restrictions on criminal defendants? Is it a sufficient answer to any challenge to restrictions to say that attorneys are officers of the court?

In Gentile v. State Bar of Nevada, 111 S.Ct. 2720 (1991), the Supreme Court upheld the validity of a state disciplinary rule proscribing "an extrajudicial statement that a reasonable person would expect to be disseminated by means of media communication if the lawyer knows or reasonably should know that it will have a substantial likelihood of materially prejudicing an adjudicative proceeding." Chief Justice Rehnquist's opinion upholding this standard was joined by Justices White, O'Connor, Scalia, and Souter. However, Justice Kennedy wrote for the Court, joined by Justices Marshall, Blackmun, Stevens and O'Connor, as it held that the particular Nevada rule was void for vagueness. Consequently, the Court held that the rule could not support a private reprimand of counsel for remarks made at a press conference following the indictment of his client.

The case arose after cocaine and traveler's checks used in an undercover police operation were missing from a vault, and an investigation led to the indictment of Gentile's client. Gentile held a press conference in which he suggested that the thief was a police officer, not his client, and that his client was not guilty. Gentile's main purpose in holding the press conference was to counter the adverse publicity which had already occurred. Gentile's client was ultimately acquitted.

Justice Kennedy found it unnecessary to address the constitutionality of the "substantial likelihood of material prejudice" standard, or to determine whether the First Amendment provides less protection for lawyers than for the press. He reasoned that the Nevada rule was vague because of its safe harbor provision, which set forth examples of some statements that would not violate the rule. He stated that a lawyer seeking to avail himself of the Nevada safe harbor provision "must guess at its contours." The safe harbor provision gave defense counsel the right to "explain the general nature of the defense" but "without elaboration." Justice Kennedy concluded that this provision gave insufficient guidance because "general and elaboration are both classic terms of degree" with "no settled usage or tradition of interpretation in law." According to Justice Kennedy, Gentile was given "no principle for determining when his remarks pass from the safe harbor of the general to the forbidden sea of the elaborated." Justice Kennedy noted that Gentile had spent several hours researching the requirements of the Nevada rule, and that at his press conference his remarks were guarded and general. He asserted that "the fact Gentile was found in violation of the Rules after studying them and making a conscious effort at compliance demonstrates that [the Nevada Rule] creates a trap for the wary as well as the unwary."

Justice O'Connor, who wrote a brief concurring opinion, agreed with Justice Kennedy's void for vagueness analysis. She also agreed, however, with Chief Justice Rehnquist's opinion that the "substantial likelihood of prejudice" standard set forth in the Nevada rule was constitutional, even though it provided less protection to lawyers than the "clear and present danger" standard applicable to the press. Justice Kennedy suggested, without purporting to decide, that the ABA's model rule, which is similar to Nevada's, was intended to approximate the clear and present danger standard. Chief Justice Rehnquist's opinion for the Court rejected that suggestion and held that the First Amendment does not require that lawyers representing clients in pending cases must be given the same latitude as the press. The Chief Justice reasoned that "lawyers representing clients in pending cases are key participants in the criminal justice system, and the State may demand some adherence to the precepts of that system in regulating their speech as well as their conduct." He noted that a lawyer's extrajudicial statements can have significant impact on the trial "since lawyers' statements are likely to be received as especially authoritative." He concluded that the "substantial likelihood" test was an appropriate balance of the interests of the lawyer and the state, since it imposes "only narrow and necessary limitations on lawyers' speech," and "it merely postpones the attorney's comments until after the trial."

In the end, the Court invalidated the sanction imposed upon Gentile, indicated that state rules which provide ambiguous examples may be invalidated as a result of vagueness, and upheld the standard that lawyers in pending cases may not make public comments when they know or should know that such comments will have a substantial likelihood of materially prejudicing an adjudicative proceeding. The Court emphasized that lawyers pose a greater risk of tainting the trial because their extrajudicial comments are likely to be taken as authoritative; and conversely, the Court noted that comments likely to prejudice the trial are sanctionable even if an untainted jury is ultimately found.

Justice Kennedy questioned whether, as an empirical matter, statements by defense counsel in all but a few cases could realistically threaten to prejudice a trial, especially when the statements are made shortly after charges are brought and well before the trial is to be held. What types of prejudice might a state reasonably fear when public comments are made by a trial counsel? Is a defense lawyer as capable as a prosecutor of creating a prejudicial environment? Suppose that police officers or witnesses who are not lawyers have made public statements. Should a defendant have a right to respond through counsel? When it is common practice for prosecutors to draft "speaking indictments," i.e. charging instruments that set forth in detail the crime charged, should a defendant be permitted to make a public response through counsel and to set forth the defense position in as much detail as is found in the indictment?

Chief Justice Rehnquist's opinion in *Gentile* stresses the state's legitimate concern that jurors will be affected by pre-trial publicity, and that Gentile was properly disciplined for making general comments well before trial. Yet in Mu'Min v. Virginia, supra, a case he wrote in the same term, the community had been barraged with newspaper and television reports prejudicial to the defendant, and the Chief Justice stated that the publicity did not rise even to a level requiring questioning of individual jurors about the content of the publicity. How can the two cases be reconciled?

Gentile is concerned with prejudicial pre-trial publicity. What if the lawyer criticizes what has occurred in a completed case? Obviously, there is no risk of prejudicing the jury, and, as the Chief Justice noted in *Gentile,* the Nevada Rule therein merely postponed rather than prohibited Gentile's comments. However, other disciplinary rules may apply to post-trial comments. Does the state have any interest in controlling lawyers' speech at this point? In Matter of Holtzman, 78 N.Y.2d 184, 573 N.Y.S.2d 39, 577 N.E.2d 30 (1991), the court upheld a disciplinary sanction imposed on a District Attorney who, after a defendant was acquitted in a rape trial, publicly criticized the judge's conduct. Holtzman issued a press release stating that the judge had forced the rape complainant to reenact the rape in open court. This allegation was based on a report to Holtzman from the assistant district attorney who tried the case. After the press release was issued, defense counsel called the allegations false, and the rape complainant vacillated as to what had occurred. Holtzman was disciplined under DR 1–102(A)(5) and (6) of the Code of Professional Responsibility. These rules prohibit conduct "prejudicial to the administration of justice" and conduct "adversely reflecting on the lawyer's fitness to practice law." The Court of Appeals upheld lower court findings that Holtzman's report was false, and held that she knew or should have known that attacks such as hers are "unwarranted and unprofessional" and "serve to bring the bench and bar into disrepute, and tend to undermine public confidence in the judicial system." Holtzman argued that her press release, even if false, was protected under the "constitutional malice" standard of New York Times Co. v. Sullivan, 376 U.S. 254 (1964), but the Court of Appeals held that this standard was not applicable to lawyer discipline:

> Accepting petitioner's argument would immunize all accusations, however reckless or irresponsible, from censure as long as the attorney uttering them did not actually entertain serious doubts as to their truth. * * * In order to adequately protect the public interest and maintain the integrity of the judicial system, there must be an objective standard, of what a reasonable attorney would do in similar circumstances. It is the reasonableness of the belief, not the state of mind of the attorney, that is determinative.

What more should Holtzman have done before sending out the press release? If an extensive investigation was required, isn't it possible that other rape complainants would have been mistreated in the interim? Didn't the press release have the salutary effect of notifying the public of the District Attorney's interest in protecting rape complainants? Aren't lawyers uniquely qualified to criticize judges?

Witnesses complain of their treatment by criminal courts. Can a gag order prohibiting discussion of a case by any potential witness be justified without a showing of clear and present danger to the administration of justice?

C. PROTECTING AGAINST PREJUDICIAL PUBLICITY

Whether the legal profession paid sufficient attention to press coverage of trials before the 1960's is debatable. Whatever the answer, it seems clear that during the 60's the level of concern increased.[52]

Most observers since have agreed that it is wise to attempt to solve some problems of undue or unfair press coverage by limiting the information disseminated to the public. This can be accomplished in two ways: by controlling press access to information and by restricting what the press prints.

1. *Controlling Access to Courts; Public Trials*

Pell v. Procunier, 417 U.S. 817 (1974), Saxbe v. Washington Post Co., 417 U.S. 843 (1974), and Houchins v. KQED, Inc., 438 U.S. 1 (1978), establish that news media have no special right of access to all sources of information within government control. However, language supported by most of the *Estes* justices suggested that the right to public judicial proceedings may not be exclusively the defendant's and a number of lower court decisions recognized a strong presumption in favor of open proceedings for the benefit of the public.

52. After *Sheppard* was decided the ABA issued its well known report in 1966 on fair-trial, free-press questions. ABA Standards, Fair Trial and Free Press (Tent. Draft, 1966); (App. Draft 1968). And the Judicial Conference of the United States did its own report. 45 F.R.D. 391 (1968). See also ABA Standards, Fair Trial and Free Press, Ch. 8 (2d ed. 1980).

See, e.g., United States v. Cianfrani, 573 F.2d 835 (3d Cir. 1978) (recognizing strong presumption in favor of public pre-trial suppression hearing even when defendant wants to waive public trial, but allowing temporary restrictions on public access).

But, in Gannett Co., Inc. v. DePasquale, 443 U.S. 368 (1979), the Supreme Court held 5–4 that the right to a public trial is conferred upon the defendant, not the general public. A state trial judge had granted two defendants' motions to exclude the press and public from a pretrial hearing on a motion to suppress confessions and physical evidence. A newspaper owner challenged the judge's decision, only to lose in the highest state court and in the Supreme Court. The Court stated that the Framers of the Sixth Amendment did not intend "to create a constitutional right in strangers to attend a pretrial proceeding, when all that they actually did was to confer upon the accused an explicit right to demand a public trial." The Court also noted that, assuming the First Amendment granted a right of access to pretrial proceedings, the trial court had appropriately balanced the First Amendment interests with the defendant's right to be free from prejudicial pretrial publicity. Justice Powell's concurring opinion suggested that he would recognize some such right, but Justice Rehnquist's concurring opinion indicated that he thought the Court's prior decisions had rejected the idea that the First Amendment guaranteed access to government facilities. Chief Justice Burger also concurred, noting that a pretrial hearing was not a "trial" within the meaning of the Sixth Amendment. Justice Blackmun's dissenting opinion was joined by Justices Brennan, White and Marshall.

Gannett left its readers confused as to its precise scope. See, e.g., Goodale, Gannett Means What It Says; But Who Knows What It Says? Nat'l L.J., Oct. 15, 1979, at 20, col. 1. Despite the fact that the Court had before it a pretrial proceeding, the reasoning of the majority opinion was not confined to such proceedings. Did *Gannett* mean to allow any and all exclusions of the public from any and all parts of trials? If not, what limitations does the Constitution place on the closing of proceedings?

In Richmond Newspapers, Inc. v. Virginia, 448 U.S. 555 (1980), the Supreme Court held that the First Amendment does give the public and the press a limited right of access to criminal trials. Chief Justice Burger's plurality opinion commanded the most votes in the case. Only Justices White and Stevens joined the opinion, however. Justice Stevens also added a separate concurrence, and Justice White added a concurring statement. The Chief Justice distinguished *Gannett* as dealing with pretrial proceedings, looked to the history of American criminal trials, and found that they had long been conducted in public places in which the public and the media were welcome. He observed that the presence of the public added something of importance to the proceedings. Finally, he concluded that the right of the public and the press to be present was not absolute and would give way to overriding governmental interests articulated in findings of a court, but suggested that alternatives must be explored before closure is ordered. Justice Brennan, joined by Justice Marshall, concurred in the judgment and would have held the underlying Virginia statute unconstitutional for giving trial judges too much discretion. Justice Brennan was reluctant to specify the countervailing government interests that might justify overriding the presumption of open trials. Justices Stewart and Blackmun wrote separate opinions concurring in the result. Justice Stewart distinguished the trial setting from places like jails not generally open to the public. Justice Blackmun had some extremely harsh words for the *Gannett* opinion. Justice Rehnquist dissented. Justice Powell did not participate in the decision. The case provides some answers to questions left open in *Gannett*, but it raised some new and difficult problems: What showing of governmental interest will satisfy a court that proceedings should be closed? [53] Does the First Amendment right extend to pretrial proceedings? If so, must the government make the same showing of overriding interest to close those proceedings? What procedures must be employed before any proceeding is closed? [54]

The Court relied on *Richmond Newspapers* in Globe Newspaper Co. v. Superior Court, 457 U.S. 596 (1982), to invalidate a state statute that was construed by the Massachusetts Supreme Judicial Court to require exclusion of the press and general public from the courtroom during the testimony of a sex offense victim under the age of 18. Justice Brennan's opinion for the Court observed that where "the State attempts to deny the right of access in order to inhibit the disclosure of sensitive information, it must be shown that the denial is necessitated by a compelling governmental interest, and is narrowly tailored to serve that interest." Although the Court agreed that safeguarding the physical and psychological well-being of a minor is a compelling state interest, it found that this could be accomplished on a case-by-case basis with the trial judge weighing "the minor victim's age, psychological maturity and understanding, the nature of the crime, the desires of the victim, and the interests of parents and relatives." It rejected the assertion that the statute was necessary to encourage minor victims to come forward and to provide accurate testimony, saying that "[n]ot only is the claim speculative in empirical terms, but it is also open to serious question as a matter of logic and common sense." Chief Justice Burger, joined by Justice Rehnquist, dissented. He argued that there was historical support for exclusion of the public from trials involving sexual assaults, particularly those against minors; that it was paradoxical to permit states to close trials of juveniles to protect defendants but not to permit them to protect victims; that the law was a rational response to the undisputed problem of the underreporting of rapes and other sexual offenses; and that the states should have room to experiment before a court demands empirical data to justify a law like Massachusetts'. Justice O'Connor concurred in the judgment, emphasizing that *Richmond Newspapers* applies only to criminal

53. United States v. Hernandez, 608 F.2d 741 (9th Cir. 1979), upheld the exclusion of the public from trial during the testimony of one witness whose safety or whose family's safety might have been threatened by public viewing of testimony. In contrast, see People v. Kan, 78 N.Y.2d 54, 571 N.Y.S.2d 436, 574 N.E.2d 1042 (1991), where error was found when the trial court excluded the public, including the defendant's family, during the testimony of the key cooperating witness-accomplice to the defendant's crime. The witness stated that he feared retaliation from testifying in open court, but not from the defendant's family, who knew him already anyway. The court found that "the expulsion of everyone during this accomplice's testimony was broader than constitutionally tolerable and constituted a violation of Kan's overriding right to a public trial."

54. In United States v. Criden, 648 F.2d 814 (3d Cir. 1981) a case arising out of one of the Abscam prosecutions, the court relied on *Richmond Newspapers* to hold that the trial judge erred in denying an application by television networks for permission to copy for broadcasting purposes those video and audio tapes admitted into evidence and played to the jury in open court.

Stephens v. Van Arsdale, 227 Kan. 676, 608 P.2d 972 (1980), upholds against a First Amendment attack by the press a statute denying access to criminal records following expungement.

trials. Justice Stevens dissented on procedural grounds. *Globe Newspaper Co.* answered some of the questions raised by *Richmond Newspapers*, but did not decide whether the First Amendment right of access applied in pretrial proceedings.[55]

Richmond Newspapers was the authority that Chief Justice Burger cited in his opinion for the Court in Press-Enterprise Co. v. Superior Court, 464 U.S. 501 (1984). The important facts were as follows: Jury selection in a capital prosecution for rape and murder took six weeks. Only three days of the voir dire of the jury was open to the public, since the trial judge was concerned about the privacy of the jurors. After the jury was selected, the trial judge denied a request by Press-Enterprise to release a transcript of the voir dire. A state appellate court sustained the trial judge and the state supreme court denied review.

Citing neither the First nor the Sixth Amendment, the Court stated that "how we allocate the 'right' to openness as between the accused and the public, or whether we view it as a component inherent in the system benefitting both, is not crucial. No right ranks higher than the right of the accused to a fair trial. But the primacy of the accused's right is difficult to separate from the right of everyone in the community to attend the voir dire which promotes fairness." It reasoned that openness has "a community therapeutic value" and that secret proceedings would deny an outlet for community reaction to serious crime.

Openness, while prized, was not absolutely required. "The presumption of openness may be overcome only by an overriding interest based on findings that closure is essential to preserve higher values and is narrowly tailored to serve that interest. The interest is to be articulated along with findings specific enough that a reviewing court can determine whether the closure order was properly entered." As an example of proper closure, the Court suggested that in a rape trial a prospective juror might privately inform the judge that she or a member of her family had been raped, but had declined to seek prosecution because of the associated emotional trauma. It also suggested that "[b]y requiring the prospective juror to make an affirmative request, the trial judge can ensure that there is in fact a valid basis for a belief that disclosure infringes a significant interest in privacy," and that "[w]hen limited closure is ordered, the constitutional values sought to be protected by holding open proceedings may be satisfied later by making a transcript of the closed proceedings available within a reasonable time, if the judge determines that disclosure can be accomplished while safeguarding the juror's valid privacy interests." On the facts presented, the Court found that the closure order and the sealing of the transcript were unwarranted. It observed that parts of the transcript might have been sealed and other parts disclosed and that the judge could have considered revealing the substance of answers without disclosing the identity of jurors. It remanded for further proceedings.

55. Westchester Rockland Newspapers, Inc. v. Leggett, 48 N.Y.2d 430, 423 N.Y.S.2d 630, 399 N.E.2d 518 (1979), involved a pretrial mental competency hearing of a defendant charged with rape. The court distinguished *Gannett* and emphasized the important public purposes served by open hearings. It concluded that "[t]he right of the public to attend court proceedings generally includes pretrial proceedings in criminal cases." The burden is on the defendant to show a "strong likelihood that evidence relevant and admissible at this particular hearing * * * would prejudice the defendant's trial if it were disclosed to potential jurors." Reasons for any closure must be given in open court by the judge.

Justice Blackmun concurred, stating that he saw no need to decide whether privacy interests of jurors might outweigh a defendant's need for information about jurors. Justice Marshall, who concurred in the judgment, also expressed concern about denying the public and the press private information about jurors. He argued that before closing proceedings the trial judge "should be obliged to show that the order in question constitutes *the least restrictive means available* for protecting compelling state interests" and that some transcript of proceedings should be available in all but the most extraordinary cases. Justice Stevens also concurred. He explicitly relied upon a First Amendment right of access.

Justice Powell wrote for a unanimous Court in Waller v. Georgia, 467 U.S. 39 (1984). An indictment charged a number of people with racketeering and other offenses. Prior to the trial of one group of defendants, a motion was made to suppress evidence obtained through wiretaps and searches of homes. The prosecution moved to have the suppression hearing closed to all persons other than those involved in the prosecution on the ground that the taps would "involve" some persons who were indicted but not on trial in this case and other persons not indicted at all. Over the objection of some defendants, the trial judge granted the motion. The suppression hearing lasted seven days, although only two and a half hours were devoted to playing tapes of intercepted conversations. The trial judge suppressed some, but not all, evidence. At trial the defendants were acquitted of racketeering and convicted on gambling charges. Thereafter, but before other persons named in the indictment were tried, a transcript of the suppression hearing was released. The Georgia Supreme Court found that the trial judge had properly balanced the defendants' right to a public hearing against the privacy rights of other persons. The United States Supreme Court disagreed.

Justice Powell cited the Court's First Amendment decisions and included *Press-Enterprise* in his discussion of these cases. He reasoned that "there can be little doubt that the explicit Sixth Amendment right of the accused is no less protective than the implicit First Amendment right of the press and public." He also observed that "suppression hearings often are as important as the trial itself. In *Gannett*, as in many cases, the suppression hearing was the *only* trial, because the defendants thereafter pleaded guilty pursuant to a plea bargain." And he concluded that a suppression hearing often resembles a bench trial in which witnesses are sworn and testify, making the need for an open proceeding especially strong. Thus, the court held "that under the Sixth Amendment any closure of a suppression hearing over the objections of the accused must meet the tests set out in *Press-Enterprise* and its predecessors."

The Court found that the trial judge erred in not considering alternatives to closing the entire hearing and in not requiring the government to provide more details about its need for closure. One option the Court cited was to close only the part of the hearing—e.g., the playing of the tapes—that jeopardized the interests articulated by the government. Rather than reverse the convictions, the Court remanded the case for a new suppression hearing to be conducted in accordance with the constitutional standards articulated in this and prior cases.

Lower courts have read *Waller* as articulating a four-prong test by which to assess the propriety of closure:

> (1) The party seeking to close the hearing must advance an overriding interest that is likely to be prejudiced; (2) the closure must be no broader than necessary to protect that interest; (3) the trial court must consider reasonable alternatives to closing the proceeding; and (4) the trial court must make findings adequate to support the closure.

People v. Kan, 78 N.Y.2d 54, 571 N.Y.S.2d 436, 574 N.E.2d 1042 (1991).

Despite the Supreme Court's recent decisions and a 1982 statute requiring that a preliminary hearing shall be open to the public unless the magistrate finds that exclusion is necessary to protect the defendant's right to a fair trial, the state supreme court held in Press-Enterprise Co. v. Superior Court, 37 Cal.3d 772, 209 Cal.Rptr. 360, 691 P.2d 1026 (1984), that a preliminary hearing may be closed to the public if there is "a reasonable likelihood of substantial prejudice which would impinge upon the right to a fair trial."

The Supreme Court reversed in Press-Enterprise Co. v. Superior Court, 478 U.S. 1 (1986). Chief Justice Burger wrote for the majority as it concluded "that the qualified First Amendment right of access to criminal proceedings applies to preliminary hearings as they are conducted in California." He reasoned that preliminary hearings have usually been open, and that preliminary hearings are sufficiently like trials in California to justify the conclusion that public access is essential. Thus, preliminary hearings may only be closed "if specific findings are made demonstrating that, first, there is a substantial probability that the defendant's right to a fair trial will be prejudiced by publicity that closure would prevent and, second, reasonable alternatives to closure cannot adequately protect the defendant's free trial rights."

Justice Stevens, joined in part by Justice Rehnquist, dissented. He challenged the majority's observation that pretrial proceedings are generally open, by citing *Gannett*, which had noted that the public had no general right to attend pretrial proceedings, and by pointing out that states differed in the ways they approached these proceedings. He also challenged the reliance on the value of openness as proving too much, since the same argument could be made with respect to grand jury proceedings, resulting in charges being brought against individuals, even though these proceedings have historically been secret. In the end, Justice Stevens found the test adopted by the majority to be inconsistent with *Gannett*.

For an illustration of a limited closing order that was sustained, see People v. Glover, 60 N.Y.2d 783, 469 N.Y.S.2d 677, 457 N.E.2d 783 (1983). In the second trial of a rape case, the trial judge, having presided over the previous trial and seeing that the complainant's testimony was sensitive and that court employees tended to "traffic" in the courtroom during the sensitive portions, made a limited closure order. No spectator was present at the time the order was made nor was anyone seeking admission. The judge informed the defendant that anyone he wished to have in the courtroom would be admitted. The court of appeals upheld the order. In contrast, in People v. Clemons, 78 N.Y.2d 48, 571 N.Y.S.2d 433, 574 N.E.2d 1039 (1991), the same court held that the defendant's right to a public trial was violated when the trial court ordered that the public be excluded from the courtroom during the rape complainant's testimony. The court noted that closure was ordered "solely on the basis of a brief colloquy between the presiding judge and counsel during which the prosecutor merely informed the court that the complainant desired that the courtroom be closed." The court distinguished *Glover* as a case where the trial judge had presided over the defendant's previous trial on the same charges and thus knew of the highly embarrassing nature of the complainant's testimony. The court recognized that "the Sixth Amendment does not require a judicial insensitivity to the very real problems that rape victims may face in having to testify in open court," but concluded that the Amendment "does demand a more careful balancing of interests than that conducted by the trial court here."

In United States v. Chagra, 701 F.2d 354 (5th Cir. 1983), the court of appeals upheld a trial judge who closed a pretrial bond reduction hearing involving a defendant charged with arranging the murder of a federal judge. The Court said that a defendant seeking closure of a hearing overcomes the First Amendment right of access if he shows that his right to a fair trial will be prejudiced if the hearing is open to the public, alternatives to closure cannot guarantee a fair trial, and closure will probably protect against the perceived danger of prejudice. See also In re South Carolina Press Association, 946 F.2d 1037 (4th Cir.1991), which held that a judge presiding over corruption trials of African–American state legislators involved in a "sting" operation was justified in closing jury selection proceedings, in order to avoid chilling the honest responses of veniremembers to very personal questions concerning their racial biases, prior convictions, and other relevant matters. Defendants claimed that they were being persecuted, as well as prosecuted, because of their race and that a disproportionately large number of African–American legislators have been targeted for prosecution. The case had received substantial notoriety. The court of appeals found that the trial judge made necessary findings concerning the need for closure and the importance of truthful answers on voir dire, and that given the "very unusual circumstances," no reasonable alternatives to closure would adequately protect the fair trial rights of the defendants.

2. *Controlling What Is Printed*

Once information about judicial proceedings is discovered by observers, including the press, the rule is that only in the most exceptional cases, if at all, can courts control dissemination of the information to the public.

NEBRASKA PRESS ASS'N v. STUART

Supreme Court of the United States, 1976.
427 U.S. 539.

MR. CHIEF JUSTICE BURGER delivered the opinion of the court.

* * *

I

On the evening of October 18, 1975, local police found the six members of the Henry Kellie family murdered in their home in Sutherland, Neb., a town of about 850 people. Police released the description of a suspect, Erwin Charles Simants, to the reporters who had hastened to the scene of the crime. Simants was arrested and arraigned in Lincoln County Court the following morning, ending a tense night for this small rural community.

The crime immediately attracted widespread news coverage, by local, regional, and national newspapers, radio and television stations. Three days after the crime, the County Attorney and Simants' attorney joined in asking the County Court to enter a restrictive order relating to "matters that may or may not be publicly reported or disclosed to the public," because of the "mass coverage by news media" and the "reasonable likelihood of prejudicial news which would make difficult, if not impossible, the impaneling of an impartial jury and tend to prevent a fair trial." The County Court heard oral argument but took no evidence; no attorney for members of the press appeared at this stage. The County Court granted the prosecutor's motion for a restrictive order and entered it the next day, October 22. The order prohibited everyone in attendance from "releas[ing] or authoriz[ing] the release for public dissemination in any form or manner whatsoever any testimony given or evidence adduced"; the order also required members of the press to observe the Nebraska Bar-Press Guidelines.[a]

Simants' preliminary hearing was held the same day, open to the public but subject to the order. The County Court bound over the defendant for trial to the State District Court. The charges, as amended to reflect the autopsy findings, were that Simants had committed the murders in the course of a sexual assault.

Petitioners—several press and broadcast associations, publishers, and individual reporters—moved on October 23 for leave to intervene in the District Court, asking that the restrictive order imposed by the County Court be vacated. The District Court conducted a hearing, at which the County Judge testified and newspaper articles about the Simants case were admitted in evidence. The District Judge granted petitioners' motion to intervene and, on October 27, entered his own restrictive order. The judge found "because of the nature of the crimes charged in the complaint that there is a clear and present danger that pre-trial publicity could impinge upon the defendant's right to a fair trial." The order applied only until the jury was impaneled, and specifically prohibited petitioners from reporting five subjects: (1) the existence or contents of a confession Simants had made to law enforcement officers, which had been introduced in open court at arraignment; (2) the fact or nature of statements Simants had made to other persons; (3) the contents of a note he had written the night of the crime; (4) certain aspects of the medical testimony at the preliminary hearing; and (5) the identity of the victims of the alleged sexual assault and the nature of the assault. It also prohibited reporting the exact nature of the restrictive order itself. Like the County Court's order, this order incorporated the Nebraska Bar-Press Guidelines. Finally, the order set out a plan for attendance, seating and courthouse traffic control during the trial.[56]

* * *

a. These Guidelines are voluntary standards adopted by members of the state bar and news media to deal with the reporting of crimes and criminal trials. They outline the matters of fact that may appropriately be reported, and also list what items are not generally appropriate for reporting, including confessions, opinions on guilt or innocence, statements that would influence the outcome of a trial, the results of tests or examinations, comments on the credibility of witnesses, and evidence presented in the jury's absence. The publication of an accused's criminal record should, under the Guidelines, be "considered very carefully." The Guidelines also set out standards for taking and publishing photographs, and set up a joint bar-press committee to foster cooperation in resolving particular problems that emerge.

56. That portion of the opinion discussing the attempts by the press to have the restrictions lifted is omitted. Often, the press is unable to seek review by mandamus or similar extraordinary remedy. See, e.g., English v. McCrary, 348 So.2d 293 (Fla.1977). But see Gannett Pacific Corp. v. Richardson, 59 Hawaii 224, 580 P.2d 49 (1978).

The Nebraska Supreme Court * * * modified the District Court's order to accommodate the defendant's right to a fair trial and the petitioners' interest in reporting pretrial events. The order as modified prohibited reporting of only three matters: (a) the existence and nature of any confessions or admissions made by the defendant to law enforcement officers, (b) any confessions or admissions made to any third parties, except members of the press, and (c) other facts "strongly implicative" of the accused. The Nebraska Supreme Court did not rely on the Nebraska Bar-Press Guidelines. * * *

[Much of the procedural history is deleted, as is the Court's discussion of mootness.]

The state trial judge in the case before us acted responsibly, out of a legitimate concern, in an effort to protect the defendant's right to a fair trial. What we must decide is not simply whether the Nebraska courts erred in seeing the possibility of real danger to the defendant's rights, but whether in the circumstances of this case the means employed were foreclosed by another provision of the Constitution.

V

[The Court discusses its prior restraint cases: E.g., Near v. Minnesota ex rel. Olson, 283 U.S. 697, 707 (1931); Organization for a Better Austin v. Keefe, 402 U.S. 415 (1971); New York Times Co. v. United States, 403 U.S. 713 (1971).]

The thread running through all these cases is that prior restraints on speech and publication are the most serious and the least tolerable infringement on First Amendment rights. A criminal penalty or a judgment in a defamation case is subject to the whole panoply of protections afforded by deferring the impact of the judgment until all avenues of appellate review have been exhausted. Only after judgment has become final, correct or otherwise, does the law's sanction become fully operative.

A prior restraint, by contrast and by definition, has an immediate and irreversible sanction. If it can be said that a threat of criminal or civil sanctions after publication "chills" speech, prior restraint "freezes" it at least for the time.

The damage can be particularly great when the prior restraint falls upon the communication of news and commentary on current events. Truthful reports of public judicial proceedings have been afforded special protection against subsequent punishment. * * *

* * *

The authors of the Bill of Rights did not undertake to assign priorities as between First Amendment and Sixth Amendment rights, ranking one as superior to the other. In this case, the petitioners would have us declare the right of an accused subordinate to their right to publish in all circumstances. But if the authors of these guarantees, fully aware of the potential conflicts between them, were unwilling or unable to resolve the issue by assigning to one priority over the other, it is not for us to rewrite the Constitution by undertaking what they declined to do. It is unnecessary, after nearly two centuries, to establish a priority applicable in all circumstances. Yet it is nonetheless clear that the barriers to prior restraint remain high unless we are to abandon what the Court has said for nearly a quarter of our national existence and implied throughout all of it. * * *

* * *

VI

We turn now to the record in this case to determine whether, as Learned Hand put it, "the gravity of the 'evil,' discounted by its improbability, justifies such invasion of free speech as is necessary to avoid the danger." To do so, we must examine the evidence before the trial judge when the order was entered to determine (a) the nature and extent of pretrial news coverage; (b) whether other measures would be likely to mitigate the effects of unrestrained pretrial publicity; and (c) how effectively a restraining order would operate to prevent the threatened danger. The precise terms of the restraining order are also important. We must then consider whether the record supports the entry of a prior restraint on publication, one of the most extraordinary remedies known to our jurisprudence.

A

In assessing the probable extent of publicity, the trial judge had before him newspapers demonstrating that the crime had already drawn intensive news coverage, and the testimony of the County Judge, who had entered the initial restraining order based on the local and national attention the case had attracted. The District Judge was required to assess the probable publicity that would be given these shocking crimes prior to the time a jury was selected and sequestered. He then had to examine the probable nature of the publicity and determine how it would affect prospective jurors.

Our review of the pretrial record persuades us that the trial judge was justified in concluding that there would be intense and pervasive pretrial publicity concerning this case. He could also reasonably conclude, based on common human experience, that publicity might impair the defendant's right to a fair trial. He did not purport to say more, for he found only "a clear and present danger that pre-trial publicity *could* impinge upon the defendant's right to a fair trial." (Emphasis added.) His conclusion as to the impact of such publicity on prospective jurors was of necessity speculative, dealing as he was with factors unknown and unknowable.

B

We find little in the record that goes to another aspect of our task, determining whether measures short of an order restraining all publication would have insured the defendant a fair trial. Although the entry of the order might be read as a judicial determination that other measures would not suffice, the trial court made no express findings to that effect; the Nebraska Supreme Court referred to the issue only by implication.

Most of the alternatives to prior restraint of publication in these circumstances were discussed with obvious approval in Sheppard v. Maxwell: (a) change of trial venue to a place less exposed to the intense publicity that seemed imminent in Lincoln County; (b) postponement of the trial to allow public attention to subside; (c) searching questioning of prospective jurors, as Mr. Chief Justice Marshall used in the [Aaron] Burr case, to screen out those with fixed opinions as to guilt or innocence; (d) the use of emphatic and clear instructions on the sworn duty of each juror to decide the issues only on evidence presented in open court. Sequestration of jurors is, of course, always available. Although that measure insulates jurors only after they are sworn, it also enhances the likelihood of dissipating the impact of pretrial publicity and emphasizes the elements of the jurors' oaths.

This Court has outlined other measures short of prior restraints on publication tending to blunt the impact of pretrial publicity. Professional studies have filled out these suggestions, recommending that trial courts in appropriate cases limit what the contending lawyers, the police, and witnesses may say to anyone. See American Bar Association Project on Standards for Criminal Justice, Fair Trial and Free Press 2–15 (App.Draft 1968).

We have noted earlier that pretrial publicity, even if pervasive and concentrated, cannot be regarded as leading automatically and in every kind of criminal case to an unfair trial. The decided cases "cannot be made to stand for the proposition that juror exposure to information about a state defendant's prior convictions or to news accounts of the crime with which he is charged alone presumptively deprives the defendant of due process." Murphy v. Florida, 421 U.S. at 799. Appellate evaluations as to the impact of publicity take into account what other measures were used to mitigate the adverse effects of publicity. The more difficult prospective or predictive assessment that a trial judge must make also calls for a judgment as to whether other precautionary steps will suffice.

We have therefore examined this record to determine the probable efficacy of the measures short of prior restraint on the press and speech. There is no finding that alternative measures would not have protected Simants' rights, and the Nebraska Supreme Court did no more than imply that such measures might not be adequate. Moreover, the record is lacking in evidence to support such a finding.

C

We must also assess the probable efficacy of prior restraint on publication as a workable method of protecting Simants' right to a fair trial, and we cannot ignore the reality of the problems of managing and enforcing pretrial restraining orders. The territorial jurisdiction of the issuing court is limited by concepts of sovereignty. The need for in personam jurisdiction also presents an obstacle to a restraining order that applies to publication at large as distinguished from restraining publication within a given jurisdiction. * * * [b]

The Nebraska Supreme Court * * * opinion reflects awareness of the tensions between the need to protect the accused as fully as possible and the need to restrict publication as little as possible. The dilemma posed underscores how difficult it is for trial judges to predict what information will in fact undermine the impartiality of jurors, and the difficulty of drafting an order that will effectively keep prejudicial information from prospective jurors. When a restrictive order is sought, a court can anticipate only part of what will develop that may injure the accused. But information not so obviously prejudicial may emerge, and what may properly be published in these "gray zone" circumstances may not violate the restrictive order and yet be prejudicial.

Finally, we note that the events disclosed by the record took place in a community of 850 people. It is reasonable to assume that, without any news accounts being printed or broadcast, rumors would travel swiftly by word of mouth. One can only speculate on the accuracy of such reports, given the generative propensities of rumors; they could well be more damaging than rea-

b. Assuming, arguendo, that these problems are within reach of legislative enactment, or that some application of evolving concepts of long-arm jurisdiction would solve the problems of personal jurisdiction, even a cursory examination suggests how awkwardly broad prior restraints on publication, directed not at named parties but at large, would fit into our jurisprudence. The British experience is in sharp contrast for a variety of reasons; Great Britain has a smaller and unitary court system permitting the development of a manageable system of prior restraints by the application of the constructive contempt doctrine. Moreover, any comparison between the two systems must take into account that although England gives a very high place to freedom of the press and speech, its courts are not subject to the explicit strictures of a written constitution.

sonably accurate news accounts. But plainly a whole community cannot be restrained from discussing a subject intimately affecting life within it.

Given these practical problems, it is far from clear that prior restraint on publication would have protected Simants' rights.

D

Finally, another feature of this case leads us to conclude that the restrictive order entered here is not supportable. At the outset the County Court entered a very broad restrictive order, the terms of which are not before us; it then held a preliminary hearing open to the public and the press. There was testimony concerning at least two incriminating statements made by Simants to private persons; the statement—evidently a confession—that he gave to law enforcement officials was also introduced. The State District Court's later order was entered after this public hearing and, as modified by the Nebraska Supreme Court, enjoined reporting of (1) "[c]onfessions or admissions against interest made by the accused to law enforcement officials"; (2) "[c]onfessions or admissions against interest, oral or written, if any, made by the accused to third parties, excepting any statements, if any, made by the accused to representatives of the news media"; and (3) all "[o]ther information strongly implicative of the accused as the perpetrator of the slayings."

To the extent that this order prohibited the reporting of evidence adduced at the open preliminary hearing, it plainly violated settled principles * * *.

The third prohibition of the order was defective in another respect as well. As part of a final order, entered after plenary review, this prohibition regarding "implicative" information is too vague and too broad to survive the scrutiny we have given to restraints on First Amendment rights. The third phase of the order entered falls outside permissible limits.

E

* * *

Our analysis ends as it began, with a confrontation between prior restraint imposed to protect one vital constitutional guarantee and the explicit command of another that the freedom to speak and publish shall not be abridged. We reaffirm that the guarantees of freedom of expression are not an absolute prohibition under all circumstances, but the barriers to prior restraint remain high and the presumption against its use continues intact. We hold that, with respect to the order entered in this case prohibiting reporting or commentary on judicial proceedings held in public, the barriers have not been overcome; to the extent that this order restrained publication of such material, it is clearly invalid. To the extent that it prohibited publication based on information gained from other sources, we conclude that the heavy burden imposed as a condition to securing a prior restraint was not met and the judgment of the Nebraska Supreme Court is therefore reversed.

MR. JUSTICE WHITE, concurring.

Technically there is no need to go farther than the Court does to dispose of this case, and I join the Court's opinion. I should add, however, that for the reasons which the Court itself canvasses there is grave doubt in my mind whether orders with respect to the press such as were entered in this case would ever be justifiable. * * *

MR. JUSTICE POWELL, concurring.

* * *

In my judgment a prior restraint properly may issue only when it is shown to be necessary to prevent the dissemination of prejudicial publicity that otherwise poses a high likelihood of preventing, directly and irreparably, the impaneling of a jury meeting the Sixth Amendment requirement of impartiality. This requires a showing that (i) there is a clear threat to the fairness of trial, (ii) such a threat is posed by the actual publicity to be restrained, and (iii) no less restrictive alternatives are available. Notwithstanding such a showing, a restraint may not issue unless it also is shown that previous publicity or publicity from unrestrained sources will not render the restraint inefficacious. * * *

I believe these factors are sufficiently addressed in the Court's opinion to demonstrate beyond question that the prior restraint here was impermissible.

MR. JUSTICE BRENNAN, with whom MR. JUSTICE STEWART and MR. JUSTICE MARSHALL join, concurring in the judgment.

* * * The right to a fair trial by a jury of one's peers is unquestionably one of the most precious and sacred safeguards enshrined in the Bill of Rights. I would hold, however, that resort to prior restraints on the freedom of the press is a constitutionally impermissible method for enforcing that right; judges have at their disposal a broad spectrum of devices for ensuring that fundamental fairness is accorded the accused without necessitating so drastic an incursion on the equally fundamental and salutary constitutional mandate that discussion of public affairs in a free society cannot depend on the preliminary grace of judicial censors.

* * *

Justice Stevens' opinion concurring in the judgment is omitted.

Note

After *Stuart,* it is doubtful that a prior restraint would be upheld in any but the most exceptional case. The separate opinions support the assertion that it is difficult to imagine a case in which none of the alternatives to prior restraint would work, and in which the press will not have covered the case so fully before any restraint is ordered that it would be likely to work effectively.

The *Nebraska Press* case is a good context in which to ask what the benefits of press coverage are, and whether you agree with the Court's approach that prevents trial courts from inhibiting press coverage, even temporarily.

On the subject of the right of the press to print the information that it obtains, see Landmark Communications, Inc. v. Virginia, 435 U.S. 829 (1978); Cox Broadcasting Corp. v. Cohn, 420 U.S. 469 (1975); Oklahoma Publishing Co. v. District Court, 430 U.S. 308 (1977). The first two cases involved attempts to impose sanctions on newspapers for violating state laws prohibiting publication of certain facts bearing upon investigations or cases. *Landmark Communications, Inc.* upholds the right of the press to publish truthful information concerning "confidential proceedings" of a commission investigating the conduct of a judge. *Cohn* upheld the right of a publisher to reveal the name of a deceased rape victim once it was revealed in the courtroom. Citing *Cohn* and *Nebraska Press,* the Court held in *Oklahoma Publishing* that publication of the name of a minor child obtained in the course of a juvenile hearing open to the public and a picture obtained outside the courthouse could not be prohibited. See also State ex rel. Daily Mail Publishing Co. v. Smith, 161 W.Va. 684, 248 S.E.2d 269 (1978), affirmed, 443 U.S. 97 (1979), (holding unconstitutional a state statute making it a crime to publish the name of a child in any proceeding under child welfare statutes without prior approval of the trial court).

In United States v. Noriega, 752 F.Supp. 1045 (S.D.Fla.1990), the defendant, a deposed Panamanian dictator being tried on drug charges, made telephone calls to his attorney from the correctional center where he was awaiting trial. These calls were recorded by correctional facility officials, and obtained by the Cable News Network (CNN) from an undisclosed source. Noriega moved to enjoin CNN from broadcasting the recordings insofar as they disclosed privileged communications. The court, citing *Stuart,* refused to grant the injunction, reasoning that less intrusive alternatives could be used to protect the defendant. Specifically the court required "sequestration" of the prosecuting attorneys and prosecution witnesses, so that Noriega's communications would not be revealed to them and could not be used against him. The court noted that the danger of prejudicial pretrial publicity could be controlled through change of venue, continuance, careful voir dire, and emphatic jury instructions.

3. *Change of Venue and Continuance*

Sometimes press coverage is greater in one part of a jurisdiction than another, and coverage often is greater immediately after a crime is committed or an arrest takes place than later. By transferring a case from one part of a jurisdiction to another or by continuing a trial until passions cool, some of the ill effects of pretrial publicity might be avoided. In Patton v. Yount, supra, the Court emphasized that the passage of time would go far to dissipate the taint of prejudicial pretrial publicity.

Fed.R.Crim.P. 21(a) provides for transfer of proceedings to another district if the judge is "satisfied that there exists in the district where the prosecution is pending so great a prejudice against the defendant that he cannot obtain a fair and impartial trial." In *Sheppard* the Court said that "where there is a *reasonable likelihood* that the prejudicial news prior to trial will prevent a fair trial, the judge should continue the case until the threat abates, or transfer it to another county not so permeated with publicity." (Emphasis added.) See also Rideau v. Louisiana, and Irvin v. Dowd, supra. Accord, ABA Standards, Fair Trial and Free Press § 8–3.3(c). There is reason to believe that most courts do not grant changes of venue upon showings of reasonable likelihood of prejudice from pre-trial publicity. A showing of actual prejudice usually is required unless the state effectively concedes prejudice. See Durrough v. State, 562 S.W.2d 488 (Tex.Cr.App.1978). In United States v. Faul, 748 F.2d 1204 (8th Cir.1984), a widely publicized case in which two defendants—tax protesters and members of an organization known as the Posse Comitatus—were charged with murdering United States Marshals and assaulting other officials, the court of appeals divided, 2–1, on whether the trial judge erred in failing to grant a change of venue. The judges agreed that publicity had been widespread, but they disagreed on its nature. The majority found the publicity to be largely factual while the dissenting judge argued that "[t]he emotionalism running through this rural district caused even 'factual' reporting to fan the flames of the community's shock and anger."

Martinez v. Superior Court, 29 Cal.3d 574, 174 Cal.Rptr. 701, 629 P.2d 502 (1981), is one of the few cases that takes the reasonable likelihood of prejudice standard seriously. The court granted a mandamus petition and ordered a change of venue in a murder prosecution. It emphasized extensive publicity over the course of a year, the small size of the county, and the gravity of the charge. It also observed that the status of the victim and the accused in the community are significant, but not controlling, factors in ruling on a venue change request.

The more typical approach, demanding a showing of actual prejudice, is evident in cases such as United States v. Angiulo, 897 F.2d 1169 (1st Cir.1990), a widely publicized Mafia/RICO case, in which the court denied defendant's motion for change of venue due to pretrial publicity. The court, relying on Patton v. Yount, held that the mere fact that a majority of the impanelled jurors had been exposed to the Patriarca-Angiulo names, or that some linked the Angiulo name with the Mafia, was not sufficient to support a finding of actual prejudice. The court deferred to the trial court's conclusion that the jurors could lay aside their impressions and render a verdict based on the evidence in court. See also Swindler v. State, 267 Ark. 418, 592 S.W.2d 91 (1979) (upholding death penalty and rejecting challenges to jury bias and denial of change of venue motion where three jurors were seated who had read and heard about the case, and over 80% of jurors called were excused for cause).

Although the Supreme Court held in Groppi v. Wisconsin, 400 U.S. 505 (1971), that a state cannot ban a change of venue in misdemeanor cases, the Court has never closely scrutinized denials of venue changes except in the extraordinary cases discussed earlier. Because courts focus more on actual prejudice than on the likelihood of prejudice, it is common for the ruling on a change of venue motion to be reserved until jury selection.[57] What happens then is predictable. Courts invest resources in voir dire of potential jurors, and the more they invest the more they want to get a return—to go ahead and try the case. It is the rare case in which a change of venue is granted once the jury is empaneled. Williams v. Superior Court, 34 Cal.3d 584, 194 Cal.Rptr. 492, 668 P.2d 799 (1983), is a case in which an appellate court granted a special writ prior to trial ordering a change of venue. The Court emphasized the racial overtones of the case: two African–American brothers were charged with the murder, rape and kidnapping of a white woman in a small county; the case had received extensive publicity, especially since one brother was tried, convicted and sentenced to death before the second brother sought the change of venue; and there was the additional publicity given to the second brother's two arrests while the first brother was being tried.

The hostility of some courts to change of venue motions can be attributed to feelings that trial at a distant location will burden witnesses, that the community in which the crime was committed has a substantial interest in seeing the law enforced against wrongdoers by means of the criminal justice system, and that a change of prosecutors may be required, which may be disruptive to the legitimate interests of the government.[58] Courts may also be

57. Mallott v. State, 608 P.2d 737 (Alaska 1980), illustrates the way in which voir dire, once begun, makes a change of venue unlikely.

58. Sometimes the government wants a change of venue despite the burden it may place on prosecutors. Because the defendant generally has a right to be tried in the jurisdiction where the crime was committed, courts are most reluctant to recognize change of venue requests by the government. See State v. Mendoza, 80 Wis.2d 122, 258 N.W.2d 260 (1977). But see Uniform R.Crim.P. 462(a). Some states have upheld the prosecutor's right to seek a venue change. Others have limited the right to defendants. See Comment to Uniform R.Crim.P. 462(a), at 203–04. An alternative to a change of venue is a change of prospective jurors. If publicity in parts of a jurisdiction is much less than in the place where the crime was committed, jurors could be brought from the other parts to the original venue. There are obvious advantages to witnesses and to the prosecution from such a procedure. Are there disadvantages to the

concerned that the selection of the transferee jurisdiction may be viewed as unfair to one side or the other. These interests in not changing venue often are weighed against the benefits to the defendant of a venue change.

If a change of venue is requested, some opportunity for a hearing should be provided. See Henley v. State, 576 S.W.2d 66 (Tex.Cr.App.1978); Pamplin v. Mason, 364 F.2d 1 (5th Cir. 1966). Uniform Rule 462(a) provides that the request may be accompanied by qualified public opinion polls or by opinion testimony. But such supporting evidence is not required. Can you see why?

A continuance may be less disruptive, since it does not change the place where trial is held. 18 U.S.C.A. § 3161(8)(A) indicates that a continuance can be granted if the judge determines that "the ends of justice served by taking such action outweigh the best interest of the public and the defendant in a speedy trial." One factor to be considered is whether the failure to continue the case would be "likely" to "result in a miscarriage of justice."

4. *Selecting and Controlling the Jury*

If publicity threatens the fairness of a trial, great care must be taken in the selection of a jury. Voir dire of prospective jurors should be done more carefully though this is not necessarily Constitutionally required, see Mu'Min v. Virginia, supra. Challenges for cause might be more liberally allowed, and the number of peremptory challenges might be increased. After the jury is picked it can be sequestered to isolate it from extrajudicial influences, and a careful caution by the trial judge to the jurors should be sufficient to keep them from listening to news reports of the trial. Of course, the jury should not be told that either side has requested sequestration, lest it be biased against that side.

It is doubtful that courts routinely take care to protect defendants from the adverse effects of publicity. Only in the unusual case of massive pretrial publicity that is familiar to many members of the petit jury pool is individual questioning of jurors outside the hearing of others likely to be deemed constitutionally necessary. See, e.g., United States v. Hawkins, 658 F.2d 279 (5th Cir. 1981); United States v. Davis, 583 F.2d 190 (5th Cir. 1978).

In Murphy v. Florida, 421 U.S. 794 (1975), the Supreme Court affirmed the convictions of the well-known "Murph-the-Surf" for breaking and entering and assault despite extensive press coverage. After citing prior cases the Court concluded that the defendant must show "the actual existence of such an opinion in the mind of the juror[s] as will raise the presumption of partiality." (Citing Irvin v. Dowd). Chief Justice Burger concurred in the judgment, although he found that the trial judge was remiss in protecting the defendant against the possible unfairness attributable to extensive media coverage of the case. Justice Brennan dissented.

defendant? Are the attitudes of jurors brought into a courtroom outside their localities likely to differ from those that would exist in their home courthouse? If so, how? Once the point is reached at which a local jury cannot be trusted, can the local judge be trusted? The local prosecutor?

VI. CONFRONTATION AND COMPULSORY PROCESS

A. THE CONSTITUTIONAL STRUCTURE

The Sixth Amendment to the United States Constitution provides in relevant part that "[i]n all criminal prosecutions, the accused shall enjoy the right * * * to be confronted with the Witnesses against him [and] to have compulsory process for obtaining witnesses in his favor * * *." The two clauses can be referred to as the confrontation and compulsory process clauses of the Constitution. Their importance in the trial of criminal cases is obvious, for they, at a minimum, establish as threshold rules for criminal litigation two propositions: that the defendant can examine the government's witnesses and that she can produce her own witnesses by the use of process issuing from the courts.

Despite the obvious significance of these rights, there was little major litigation, particularly in the Supreme Court, involving them for the first 150 years of American history. This is due partly to the fact that confrontation was not incorporated into the Fourteenth Amendment and recognized as binding upon the states until Pointer v. Texas, 380 U.S. 400 (1965), and compulsory process was not incorporated and recognized as binding on the states until two years later, in Washington v. Texas, 388 U.S. 14 (1967).

Beginning with *Pointer,* the confrontation and cross-examination cases have raised serious questions about the relationship between nonconstitutional rules of evidence and the Sixth Amendment. In the debate that has ensued in the wake of the Supreme Court's opinions, some facts often have been overlooked. First, basic evidence law has been modernized and bears little relation to that which existed in colonial or early American days. Second, most nonconstitutional evidence doctrines attempt to assure that trials are fairer than they would be without the existence of evidence rules or that the trial process does not violate interests which, although they have nothing to do with enhancing the litigation process, are valued sometimes so much so that they are constitutionally protected. Thus, there is reason to believe that today's evidence rules are designed to promote fair trials and other important values and that historical anomalies in the law of evidence have become less significant. In the process of promoting fair trials, evidence rules are drafted so as to encourage admissibility, especially when the need for the evidence is strong. Thus, in many cases there is no need for defendants to raise confrontation and compulsory process claims, because the rules are set up to allow defendants to produce and examine evidence, except when a good reason exists—i.e., some other important social policy is served—for excluding the evidence. As we shall see, the hardest cases involve nice judgments about what it is that promotes fair trials or what social policies are important enough to be promoted at the expense of trial rights.

Some question has arisen concerning the relationship between the confrontation and compulsory process clauses.[59] Although there may be some elusive cases, the language of the Amendment strongly suggests that a defendant has a

59. For an example of the difficulty in distinguishing confrontation and compulsory process claims, see McLemore v. State, 87 Wis.2d 739, 275 N.W.2d 692 (1979). The Court overturned an armed robbery conviction because the court refused to allow the defendant to call his own expert to testify in a hearing on an evidence ruling about the polygraph procedures used by the state, when the defendant stipulated prior to trial that the test should be taken and the results introduced in evidence. The defendant wanted to impeach the examiner and challenge the test. Whether this is done as part of confrontation or as part of compulsory process probably does not matter, as long as it is done.

confrontation right to confront the witnesses against him—i.e., those who testify adversely to him—and a compulsory process right to compel the appearance of witnesses in his behalf. If the word "witnesses" is read broadly—to include physical evidence, experiments and tests, and out-of-court statements—the basic distinction between challenging adverse witnesses and compelling testimony of favorable ones is sound.[60]

In Nelson v. Farrey, 874 F.2d 1222 (7th Cir.1989), the defendant claimed that his right to confrontation was denied when witnesses testified to statements made by the victim, and those statements were offered as proof of guilt. Judge Posner had this to say about the confrontation clause and its relationship to the compulsory process clause:

> If the literal sense of the confrontation clause were its only sense, Nelson would have no case. He would be entitled to confront only those persons who actually testified at trial, and T. [the victim] was not one of them. But interpreted literally the clause could be easily evaded: instead of calling eyewitnesses to a crime to testify, the state could put on witnesses who would merely recite what those eyewitnesses had told them. This might not be the end of the world. The defendant might be able to use his Sixth Amendment right of compulsory process to get the eyewitnesses into court, where he could confront them. Of course, this would require a nonliteral reading of the compulsory process clause, which as written merely entitles the defendant 'to have compulsory process for obtaining witnesses *in his favor,*' and we are speaking here of *prosecution* witnesses. * * * Additional interpretation would be required to expand the compulsory process clause from a help in mounting a defense to a help in confronting the prosecution's nontestifying witnesses. * * * There is no escaping the uncertainties of interpretation by switching the focus from the confrontation clause to the compulsory process clause.

Both the compulsory process clause and the confrontation clause (and for that matter the Due Process Clause and the Sixth Amendment right to effective counsel) have the same goal: to guarantee that the defendant is able to mount a reasonably effective defense. See California v. Trombetta, 467 U.S. 479 (1984) (noting that several clauses of the Constitution work together "to require that criminal defendants be afforded a meaningful opportunity to present a complete defense").

B. THE RIGHT OF THE DEFENDANT TO BE PRESENT

One aspect of the Sixth Amendment involves the defendant's right to be present during the trial. The right is discussed in the next case.

60. One commentator suggests that witnesses "against" the accused are those on whose statements the prosecution relies at trial. This commentator would distinguish between these witnesses and those on whom the defendant relies. See Westen, Confrontation and Compulsory Process: A Unified Theory of Evidence for Criminal Cases, 91 Harv. L.Rev. 567 (1978).

Another commentator would read the Amendment so that a witness against a defendant is one who makes the statement that "was accusatory in nature when made." See Graham, The Confrontation Clause, the Hearsay Rule, and the Forgetful Witness, 56 Tex. L.Rev. 151, 192 (1973). Do you think that it matters whether the person was making an accusation? Or does it matter whether the evidence is an important part of the government's case, or an important part of the totality of the evidence that might be used by the jury to convict?

ILLINOIS v. ALLEN

Supreme Court of the United States, 1970.
397 U.S. 337.

MR. JUSTICE BLACK delivered the opinion of the Court.

The Confrontation Clause of the Sixth Amendment to the United States Constitution provides that: "In all criminal prosecutions, the accused shall enjoy the right * * * to be confronted with the witnesses against him * * *." * * * One of the most basic of the rights guaranteed by the Confrontation Clause is the accused's right to be present in the courtroom at every stage of his trial. Lewis v. United States, 146 U.S. 370 (1892). The question presented in this case is whether an accused can claim the benefit of this constitutional right to remain in the courtroom while at the same time he engages in speech and conduct which is so noisy, disorderly, and disruptive that it is exceedingly difficult or wholly impossible to carry on the trial.

[Allen lost an appeal but won relief on federal habeas corpus in the Court of Appeals on his claim that his rights were violated when he was removed from the courtroom following disruptive behavior.]

* * *

It is essential to the proper administration of criminal justice that dignity, order, and decorum be the hallmarks of all court proceedings in our country. The flagrant disregard in the courtroom of elementary standards of proper conduct should not and cannot be tolerated. We believe trial judges confronted with disruptive, contumacious, stubbornly defiant defendants must be given sufficient discretion to meet the circumstances of each case. No one formula for maintaining the appropriate courtroom atmosphere will be best in all situations. We think there are at least three constitutionally permissible ways for a trial judge to handle an obstreperous defendant like Allen: (1) bind and gag him, thereby keeping him present; (2) cite him for contempt; (3) take him out of the courtroom until he promises to conduct himself properly.

I

Trying a defendant for a crime while he sits bound and gagged before the judge and jury would to an extent comply with that part of the Sixth Amendment's purposes that accords the defendant an opportunity to confront the witnesses at the trial. But even to contemplate such a technique, much less see it, arouses a feeling that no person should be tried while shackled and gagged except as a last resort. Not only is it possible that the sight of shackles and gags might have a significant effect on the jury's feelings about the defendant, but the use of this technique is itself something of an affront to the very dignity and decorum of judicial proceedings that the judge is seeking to uphold. Moreover, one of the defendant's primary advantages of being present at the trial, his ability to communicate with his counsel, is greatly reduced when the defendant is in a condition of total physical restraint. It is in part because of these inherent disadvantages and limitations in this method of dealing with disorderly defendants that we decline to hold with the Court of Appeals that a defendant cannot under any possible circumstances be deprived of his right to be present at trial. However, in some situations which we need not attempt to foresee, binding and gagging might possibly be the fairest and most reasonable way to handle a defendant * * *.

* * *

Allen's behavior was clearly of such an extreme and aggravated nature as to justify either his removal from the courtroom or his total physical restraint. Prior to his removal he was repeatedly warned by the trial judge that he would be removed from the courtroom if he persisted in his unruly conduct, and * * * the record demonstrates that Allen would not have been at all dissuaded by the trial judge's use of his criminal contempt powers. Allen was constantly informed that he could return to the trial when he would agree to conduct himself in an orderly manner. Under these circumstances we hold that Allen lost his right guaranteed by the Sixth and Fourteenth Amendments to be present throughout his trial.

* * *

Note

Are you satisfied with the Court's directions to trial judges as to the proper response to cases of disruption? Some courts require that the shackling of a defendant be reserved for cases in which a clear showing of necessity—to prevent escape in exceptional circumstances, for example—is made. See, e.g., Kennedy v. Cardwell, 487 F.2d 101 (6th Cir. 1973); State v. Stewart, 276 N.W.2d 51 (Minn. 1979); State v. Brewster, 164 W.Va. 173, 261 S.E.2d 77 (1979). Would you take this approach? Is there a hierarchy of appropriate responses to disruption that you would urge on trial judges? Harrell v. Israel, 672 F.2d 632 (7th Cir. 1982), recommends a hearing to determine the need for shackling before a defendant is restrained. See generally, Annot., 90 ALR 3d 17 (1979).

The Supreme Court held in Holbrook v. Flynn, 475 U.S. 560 (1986), that deployment of uniformed law enforcement officers in a courtroom during a trial for security reasons is not inherently prejudicial to a defendant. It found no denial of due process or equal protection when four uniformed state troopers sat in the spectator section of the courtroom behind the defense table. Justice Marshall's unanimous opinion for the Court stated that it would never be possible "to eliminate from trial procedures every reminder that the State has chosen to marshal its resources against a defendant to punish him for allegedly criminal conduct." According to Justice Marshall, the Due Process Clause prohibits only such procedures which are so inherently prejudicial that they "brand the defendant with an unmistakable mark of guilt." The use of security officers was not considered inherently prejudicial because "the presence of guards at a defendant's trial need not be interpreted as a sign that he is particularly dangerous or culpable." Justice Marshall concluded that four troopers, sitting in the first row of the spectator's section, "are unlikely to have been taken as a sign of anything other than a normal official concern for the safety and order of the proceedings." The Court distinguished Estelle v. Williams, 425 U.S. 501 (1976), where it had found a due process violation when the defendant was forced to wear prison garb at the trial. Justice Marshall concluded that even if the presence of the guards was somewhat prejudicial, "sufficient cause for this level of security could be found in the State's need to maintain custody over defendants who had been denied bail after an individualized determination that their presence at trial could not otherwise be ensured." In contrast, there was no need in *Williams* to dress the defendant in prison garb.

Rules like Fed.R.Crim.P. 43 describe when the defendant has a right to be present. Rogers v. United States, 422 U.S. 35 (1975), indicates the importance of the words "at every stage of the trial" in the federal rule. Rogers' conviction for threatening the President was overturned because the jury sent a note to the trial judge inquiring whether the court would "accept the Verdict—'Guilty as charged with extreme mercy of the Court,'" and the judge answered in the affirmative without notifying Rogers or his counsel. Despite the fact that Rogers did not know of the judge's action until after certiorari was granted and therefore never questioned it, the Court, in a unanimous opinion by Chief Justice Burger, concluded that Rule 43 was violated and that the error was not harmless,[61] because the response that the judge gave the jury could have been improved considerably and might have induced unanimity among jury members.

In United States v. Alikpo, 944 F.2d 206 (5th Cir.1991), a defendant charged with heroin distribution was over an hour late for scheduled jury selection. The judge began the jury selection process without him, and the defendant arrived just before the parties began to exercise peremptory challenges. The court of appeals found that conducting jury selection in the defendant's absence violated Rule 43 as well as the defendant's constitutional right to be present at trial. The court refused to find waiver on the facts, and rejected the argument that the error was harmless because the defendant was present for the exercise of peremptory challenges. It stated that the defendant can be of little use at the challenge stage if he did not hear a prospective juror's response on voir dire. The court also relied upon the prejudice that could arise because the veniremembers would be adversely affected by "an accused heroin smuggler cavalierly walking in late for his trial." Would it have been less prejudicial to delay the jury selection process until the defendant saw fit to come to court? Compare United States v. Moore, 936 F.2d 1508 (7th Cir.1991) (defendant had no absolute right to be present at a conference in which his counsel advised the court that he would call a co-defendant to testify, the co-defendant's counsel advised the court that his client would declare the privilege, and the judge found a reasonable basis for the exercise of the privilege; the defendant's presence was not required to assure "a reasonable opportunity to defend against the charge").

Federal Rule 43 provides that a defendant loses his right to be present by disruptive conduct or by voluntarily absenting himself after the trial starts. See also State v. Lister, 119 N.H. 713, 406 A.2d 967 (1979) (defendant could be tried for murder in absentia when he absented himself from proceedings following suppression hearing and selection of five jurors).

People v. Parker, 57 N.Y.2d 136, 454 N.Y.S.2d 967, 440 N.E.2d 1313 (1982), reversed a conviction obtained without the defendant being present. Insisting that only a knowing and intelligent waiver could justify a trial in absentia, the

61. The harmless error question can be close. Compare, e.g., Cox v. State, 575 P.2d 297 (Alaska 1978) (court's ex parte denial of jury's request to hear playback of two alibi witnesses' testimony is reversible error) with State v. Hannagan, 559 P.2d 1059 (Alaska 1977) (defendant's absence during playback of testimony was harmless error).

The Supreme Court reversed a court of appeals summarily in United States v. Gagnon, 470 U.S. 522 (1985), and found that four defendants waived a right to be present when a trial judge questioned a juror in chambers concerning his statement of concern to a bailiff about one defendant's drawing pictures of the jury. The Court held that the presence of counsel and the defendants was not necessary to ensure fundamental fairness and that the defendants waived any right to be present under Fed.R.Crim.P. 43 by not objecting to the procedure used by the trial judge.

court reasoned that there could be no finding of waiver without evidence that the defendant understood not only that there was a trial date fixed, but also that trial would proceed without her if she failed to appear.

The Supreme Court held, in Kentucky v. Stincer, 482 U.S. 730 (1987), that a defendant was not denied his right of confrontation when he was barred from an in-chambers hearing to determine the competency to testify of two minors who allegedly were sodomized by the defendant. Justice Blackmun reasoned in his majority opinion that the primary purpose of the Confrontation Clause is to promote reliability in criminal trials by ensuring a defendant an opportunity to cross-examine witnesses, and that there was no indication that the defendant's presence at the competency hearing, which was limited to competency issues and involved no questions about the substantive testimony the victims would give, would have promoted a more reliable competency determination. The defendant was represented at the hearing by counsel who was permitted to question the victims on competency issues. After the judge found the victims to be competent, they testifed in open court in the presence of the defendant and were asked by defense counsel questions about their memory and understanding of the difference between the truth and a lie.

Justice Blackmun declined to decide whether a competency hearing is a trial or pretrial proceeding and stated that "it is more useful to consider whether excluding the defendant from the hearing interferes with his opportunity for effective cross-examination." He emphasized that state law permitted the defendant to cross-examine the victims completely at trial and to address their competency, even to the point of repeating questions asked at the competency hearing. He also emphasized that "the determination of competency is an ongoing one for the judge to make based on the witness' actual testimony at trial." Because the defendant had the opportunity for full and effective cross-examination of the two witnesses during trial, and because of the nature of the competency hearing, Justice Blackmun reasoned that the defendant was not denied his right to confront his accusers.

Justice Blackmun also rejected the defendant's argument that he was denied due process. He placed great weight on the fact that at the competency hearing "[n]o question regarding the substantive testimony that the two girls would have given during trial was asked," and stated that "although a competency hearing in which a witness is asked to discuss upcoming substantive testimony might bear a substantial relationship to a defendant's opportunity better to defend himself at trial, that kind of inquiry is not before us in this case."

Justice Marshall, joined by Justices Brennan and Stevens, dissented. He argued that the defendant has the right to have witnesses testify in his presence and that the right of cross-examination, while a primary concern of the Confrontation Clause, is not its exclusive focus. Justice Marshall reasoned that "[p]hysical presence of the defendant enhances the reliability of the fact-finding process"; the findings that the trial judge must make concerning a witness' competency "often concern matters about which the defendant, and not his counsel, possesses the knowledge needed to expose the inaccuracies in the witness' answers"; and "[i]t is both functionally inefficient and fundamentally unfair to attribute to the defendant's attorney complete knowledge of the facts which the trial judge, in the defendant's involuntary absence, deems relevant to the competency determination."

The Supreme Court held in Coy v. Iowa, 487 U.S. 1012 (1988), that a defendant's Confrontation Clause rights were violated when he was convicted on two counts of lascivious acts with a child after a jury trial in which a screen was placed between him and the two 13–year-old victims while they testified. The defendant could dimly perceive the witnesses through the screen but they could not see him.

Justice Scalia wrote for the Court and reasoned that "[w]e have never doubted * * * that the Confrontation Clause guarantees the defendant a face-to-face meeting with witnesses appearing before the trier of fact." This guarantee, he reasoned, "serves ends related both to appearances and to reality," since it is more difficult for a witness to lie about a defendant to his face. Although he recognized that "face-to-face presence may, unfortunately, upset the truthful rape victim or abused child," Justice Scalia stated that "by the same token it may confound and undo the false accuser, or reveal the child coached by a malevolent adult."

In response to the state's argument that the Confrontation Clause may have to give way to other values, Justice Scalia questioned whether there could be an exception from the core right of confrontation addressed in the case, but left "for another day, however, the question whether any exceptions exist." He stated that whatever exceptions might exist would require a showing of necessity to further an important public policy, and that a legislatively imposed presumption of trauma from testimony "could not be sustained by any conceivable exception."

Justice O'Connor, joined by Justice White, filed a concurring opinion. Although she agreed with the conclusion that Iowa's procedure in this case violated the Confrontation Clause, Justice O'Connor noted that numerous states have permitted child witnesses to testify on closed circuit television and she emphasized that "nothing in today's decision necessarily dooms such efforts by state legislatures to protect child witnesses." She argued that the case would have been different had the trial court found that these witnesses would have been traumatized by testifying in the defendant's presence.

Justice Blackmun, joined by Chief Justice Rehnquist, dissented. He would have recognized a preference for face-to-face confrontation, but would have held that there was a significant state interest in this case in departing from the presumptive approach to confrontation. Justice Blackmun relied upon a cautionary instruction given to the jury by the trial judge to reject the defendant's argument that the screen placed in front of him was inherently prejudicial. Justice Kennedy took no part in the case.

Justice O'Connor transformed her concurring views in *Coy* into an opinion for the Court in Maryland v. Craig, 110 S.Ct. 3157 (1990). The *Craig* majority upheld the use of one-way closed circuit television testimony of a child in a sex abuse prosecution. The trial judge in *Craig* found, after an evidentiary hearing, that the child would suffer serious emotional distress from testifying in the defendant's presence. Justice O'Connor noted that *Coy* left open the question of whether exceptions could exist to the "irreducible literal meaning of the clause: a right to meet face to face all those who appear and give evidence at trial." Relying on cases where the Court upheld the admission of reliable hearsay testimony, the majority stated that "we have never insisted on an actual face-to-face encounter at trial in every instance in which testimony is admitted against a defendant" and that face-to-face confrontation is not "an indispensable element" of the Sixth Amendment right.

The majority noted, however, that the right to face-to-face confrontation "may not be easily dispensed with." Denial of face-to-face confrontation was held permissible only where "necessary to further an important public policy and only where the reliability of the testimony is otherwise assured."

The majority found that testimony pursuant to one-way closed circuit television was sufficiently reliable because such a procedure

> preserves all of the other elements of the confrontation right: the child witness must be competent to testify and must testify under oath; the defendant retains full opportunity for contemporaneous cross-examination; and the judge, jury and defendant are able to view (albeit by video monitor) the demeanor (and body) of the witness as he or she testifies. * * * The presence of these other elements of confrontation * * * adequately assures that the testimony is both reliable and subject to rigorous adversarial testing in a manner functionally equivalent to that accorded live, in-person testimony.

The Court also found that there was a significant state interest in preserving the emotional well-being of child abuse victims, which was sufficient to dispense with face-to-face confrontation, "at least in some cases." Justice O'Connor held that the state must make "an adequate showing of necessity" that was "case-specific." The Court noted that the mere fact that the witness would be traumatized by testifying in a courtroom setting would not be enough; rather, the child must be traumatized by testifying in the presence of the defendant. Justice O'Connor found it unnecessary to determine the minimum showing of emotional trauma necessary for use of a substitute for in-person testimony since the Maryland statute, which requires a showing of serious emotional distress such that the child cannot communicate, "clearly met" constitutional standards.

Finally, the Court held that it was not necessary for a trial court to observe the child-witness' behavior in the defendant's presence or to explore less restrictive alternatives before ordering the use of one-way closed circuit television. Since the state appellate court had held that such procedural limitations were constitutionally required and had not been conducted, the Court remanded the case for a redetermination of whether the trial court properly found that the child-witness would suffer severe emotional trauma from testifying in the defendant's presence.

Justice Scalia, joined by Justices Brennan, Marshall and Stevens, dissented. Justice Scalia reiterated his suggestion in *Coy* that the right to face-to-face confrontation was absolute, and contended that the majority's balancing approach was "antitextual." He elaborated as follows:

> The Court today has applied "interest-balancing" analysis where the text of the Constitution simply does not permit it. We are not free to conduct a cost-benefit analysis of clear and explicit constitutional guarantees, and then to adjust their meaning to comport with our findings. The Court has convincingly proved that the Maryland procedure * * * gives the defendant virtually everything the Confrontation Clause guarantees (everything, that is, except confrontation). I am persuaded, therefore, that the Maryland procedure is

virtually constitutional. * * * [I]t is not, however, actually constitutional * * *.

The dissenters further contended that even if the guarantee of face-to-face confrontation could be balanced away, the articulated state interest was not sufficient to do so: the child could be protected from severe emotional trauma by not calling him or her as a witness. Justice Scalia explained:

> The State's interest here is in fact no more and no less than what the State's interest always is when it seeks to get a class of evidence admitted in criminal proceedings: more convictions of guilty defendants. That is not an unworthy interest, but it should not be dressed up as a humanitarian one.
>
> And the interest on the other side is also what it usually is when the State seeks to get a new class of evidence admitted: fewer convictions of innocent defendants—specifically, in the present context, innocent defendants accused of particularly heinous crimes. The "special" reasons that exist for suspending one of the usual guarantees of reliability in the case of children's testimony are perhaps matched by "special" reasons for being particularly insistent upon it in the case of children's testimony.

If, as Justice O'Connor contends, the use of closed-circuit television is the "functional equivalent" of in-court testimony, why must a state interest be found to support it? Why could it not be used whenever the prosecutor wished? Does *Craig* allow the state to use videotaped testimony of child-witnesses? See Vigil v. Tansy, 917 F.2d 1277 (10th Cir.1990) (videotape of cross-examined testimony admissible where psychiatrist testifies that child would be traumatized by testifying in court). Is an instruction to the jury not to draw a negative inference against the defendant from the use of closed-circuit television testimony sufficient to protect the defendant from prejudice?

C. THE RIGHT OF THE DEFENDANT TO EXAMINE ACCUSERS

In addition to guaranteeing the defendant a right to be present at all stages of the prosecution, the confrontation clause assures a defendant that she will be able to examine and "test" the accuracy of proof offered by the government. This aspect of the confrontation clause is very much related to the hearsay rule that exists in one form or another in all American jurisdictions.

Whenever a statement (or a declaration or a writing) is made outside of the context of actual, ongoing litigation in a courtroom, and someone offers the statement with the hope that it will be relied upon as if the speaker asserted the truth of her statement under oath in the courtroom while the speaker was on the stand, a hearsay problem is presented. American courts have been concerned that such untested statements—i.e., untested by examination at the time they were made—are not generally reliable enough to use as evidence. The speaker may have been lying, exaggerating, kidding, etc.; the speaker may have misspoken or spoken ambiguously; the speaker may have suffered memory lapses; and the speaker may not have been able to perceive things as clearly as she might think she did.

Now, testimony at trial can be unreliable for all of the same reasons, but we believe, or profess to anyway, that cross-examination can demonstrate the defects of trial testimony. Since extra-judicial statements that are not examined when made cannot be relied upon as readily, American courts tend to exclude these statements when they are offered as if the speaker had asserted the truth of her statement from the witness stand, unless the statement falls within what are called "hearsay exceptions." These exceptions purport to admit an out-of-court statement as an assertion of truth, if some special features of the statement and the circumstances in which it was made provide some guarantee that the usual worries about untested statements are alleviated. See Joseph & Saltzburg, Evidence in America, Ch. 58 (1989).

Because the hearsay rule itself historically has excluded many of the most worrisome statements offered against defendants, there are not as many confrontation cases in which damaging, untested extra-judicial statements have been admitted as one might think. But there is a trend today to remove barriers to the admissibility of evidence previously considered likely to distort factfinding, and to increase the admissibility of hearsay evidence. The adoption of the "residual" exception to the hearsay rule in the Federal Rules of Evidence and in most states has been the principal source of this increased admissibility. Under the residual exception, hearsay can be admitted if the judge finds it to have sufficient circumstantial guarantees of reliability, and also finds that it is necessary for the proponent's case. This case-by-case approach has led to the admission of many hearsay statements that would not have been admitted previously under the categorical exceptions to the hearsay rule. See Joseph & Saltzburg, supra, Chapter 58.

It is likely that an understanding of the Court's confrontation cases is promoted by examining them in conjunction with a study of the hearsay rule. This approach is a typical aspect of a basic Evidence course in American law schools. In light of the fact that confrontation and compulsory process concepts are like to be treated in detail in Evidence, this part of the chapter only highlights the Sixth Amendment issues raised by the two witness clauses.

Until the Court made the clauses binding on the States, it had infrequent occasion to analyze their impact on the presentation of evidence at trial. The Court as a whole did not speak about the compulsory process clause, and the confrontation clause received only a little attention.

In Mattox v. United States, 156 U.S. 237 (1895), the Court faced a situation in which Mattox had been convicted of murder, had won a reversal, was retried, and was convicted again when a transcript of the reporter's notes summarizing the testimony of two witnesses from the first trial was admitted in evidence. The witnesses had died between the two trials. The Supreme Court found that admission of the transcript did not violate the confrontation clause. It explained the purpose of the clause as follows:

> The primary object of the constitutional provision in question was to prevent depositions or ex parte affidavits, such as were sometimes admitted in civil cases, being used against the prisoner in lieu of a personal examination and cross-examination of the witness, in which the accused has an opportunity, not only of testing the recollection and sifting the conscience of the witness, but of compelling him to stand face to face with the jury in order that they may look at him, and judge by his demeanor upon the stand and the manner in which he gives his testimony whether he is worthy of belief.

Four years later, in Kirby v. United States, 174 U.S. 47 (1899), the Court found a confrontation violation when a defendant was convicted of receiving stolen goods, and the proof that the goods had been stolen from the government was a record of the conviction of the thief. The fact of theft, an element of the offense, could not be proved in a way that denied the defendant the right to confront witnesses.

In recent cases, several themes emerge as significant. First, the Court has shown a preference for the live testimony of witnesses rather than a transcript of their prior testimony. It has required the government to make a good faith effort to produce witnesses before upholding the admission of prior recorded testimony.

The first important case was Barber v. Page, 390 U.S. 719 (1968). Oklahoma sought to introduce the preliminary hearing testimony of a witness who was in federal prison in Texas at the time of trial. Justice Marshall's opinion for the Court reasoned that the state did not make a good faith effort to produce the witness at trial.[62]

The Court backed away from its emphasis on a good faith effort in Mancusi v. Stubbs, 408 U.S. 204 (1972). At Stubbs' retrial on a murder charge, the testimony of the state's key witness at the first trial was used as evidence, since the witness had moved to Sweden between trials. The Court distinguished *Barber* on the ground that the state could not have compelled the witness to return from Sweden to testify, and that his former testimony was fully cross-examined. The state had never even tried to get the witness to return, but the Court found that the Constitution did not require the doing of a futile act.

The good faith requirement was reaffirmed in Ohio v. Roberts, 448 U.S. 56 (1980). Roberts was charged in Ohio with forgery of a check and possession of stolen credit cards. The check was in the name of Bernard Issacs and the credit cards belonged to Issacs and his wife. The Issacs' daughter was called to testify for the defense at a preliminary hearing. She said that the defendant had been permitted to use her apartment, but denied that she had given him checks and credit cards belonging to her parents. The state used her testimony at trial when it became clear that she had left the state and her parents did not know how to contact her.[63]

In United States v. Inadi, 475 U.S. 387 (1986), the Court held that a statement offered against a defendant under the co-conspirator exception to the hearsay rule could be admitted despite the fact that the declarant was avail-

62. On the ability of states to secure the attendance of witnesses, see Uniform Act to Secure Attendance of Witnesses from Without State in Criminal Proceedings, 11 U.L.A. 1 (1974) (adopted in virtually every state). For cases discussing the showing that must be made under the uniform act, see Annots., 12 ALR 4th 742, 771 (1982); Martinez v. Sullivan, 881 F.2d 921 (10th Cir.1989) (citing and applying cases).

See also United States v. Kelly, 892 F.2d 255 (3d Cir.1989) (admission into evidence of videotaped depositions taken in Belgium without the defendant's presence did not violate his right to confrontation; the witnesses could not be compelled to attend the trial, the depositions were taken in accordance with American procedure, and the defendant had telephone contact with his attorney, who cross-examined the witnesses at the depositions).

63. Compare United States v. Quinn, 901 F.2d 522 (6th Cir.1990), where the court found that the prosecution had not met its duty of good faith effort to produce the declarant. An officer pounded on the window of the declarant's apartment, and found nobody at home. He left a Marshal's sticker. He checked the declarant's mother's house, and was told that the declarant would be there that evening. He drove by the house and did not see the declarant's car, and did not bother to stop or call. No one checked her place of employment. The court concluded that "while we decline to attribute bad faith to the Government's effort, we are compelled to observe that it was singularly unenthusiastic."

able but was not produced by the prosecution. The Court distinguished the *Roberts* rule of production as applicable only when the hearsay statement is a weak substitute for in-court testimony (such as the testimony at a preliminary hearing which was considered in *Roberts*). In contrast, hearsay statements of co-conspirators are made under informal circumstances and thus have evidentiary significance different from that provided by in-court testimony. The Court found that this different evidentiary significance justified dispensing with the production of the declarant for cross-examination.

The Court in *Inadi* stated that *Roberts* was not intended to provide a general approach to evaluating hearsay under the Confrontation Clause, but rather dealt with the discrete problem of prior testimony. This statement left an important issue up in the air: whether the Confrontation Clause generally requires production of available declarants even though a hearsay exception does not. For instance, Rule 803 of the Federal Rules of Evidence sets forth 24 hearsay exceptions allowing admission of hearsay even though the declarant is available to testify. These exceptions (such as for excited utterances and business records) are based on the *Inadi*-like premise that a statement meeting the admissibility requirements has evidentiary significance equal to or greater than in-court testimony. If the *Roberts* rule of preference applies to these exceptions, the Confrontation Clause may require that a declarant be produced even though the hearsay exception does not require it. However, if *Inadi's* "evidentiary significance" test establishes the general approach to producing hearsay declarants, then a statement which qualifies under a Rule 803 exception would be admissible even though the declarant is available but not produced. In White v. Illinois, 112 S.Ct. 736 (1992), the Court rejected the *Roberts* rule of production outside its limited context of prior testimony, and applied the *Inadi* analysis to statements which qualified under the excited utterance and medical diagnosis exceptions to the hearsay rule. White was charged with sexual assault of a child; the hearsay statements offered against him were made by the victimized child. The child was available for trial, but neither the prosecution nor the defense sought to call her. Chief Justice Rehnquist, writing for the Court, emphasized that the child's statements—some made while she was in an upset state and some made for purposes of treatment—"had substantial probative value, value that could not be duplicated simply by the declarant later testifying in court." He stated that "to exclude such probative statements under the strictures of the Confrontation Clause would be the height of wrongheadedness, given that the Confrontation Clause has as a basic purpose the promotion of the integrity of the fact-finding process." He concluded that there was "no basis in *Roberts* or *Inadi,* for excluding from trial, under the aegis of the Confrontation Clause, evidence embraced within such exceptions to the hearsay rule as those for spontaneous declarations and statements made for purposes of medical treatment." He found such statements "materially different from the statements at issue in *Roberts,* where the out-of-court statements sought to be introduced were themselves made in the course of a judicial proceeding, and where there was consequently no threat of lost evidentiary value if the out-of-court statements were replaced with live testimony." Finally, the Chief Justice rejected the defendant's argument that production of the hearsay declarant was required under *Coy* and *Craig,* supra. He noted that "*Coy* and *Craig* involved only the question of what *in-court* procedures are constitutionally required to guarantee a defendant's confrontation right once a witness is testifying." The Court found "no basis for importing the necessity requirement announced in those cases into the much different context of out-of-court declarations admitted under established exceptions to the hearsay rule." Justice Thomas, joined by Justice Scalia, concurred in part and in the judgment.

Two principles underly *Inadi* and *White.* The first is that if the hearsay statement has evidentiary value which cannot be duplicated by in-court testimony, it makes no sense to exclude the hearsay. This argument is flawed, however, since White was not arguing that the hearsay statements should be excluded; he was arguing that *if* the declarant is available, admissibility of the statements should be conditioned on the prosecution producing the declarant. If White's argument were accepted, the jury could evaluate *both* the hearsay statement and the in-court testimony. The jury would be getting more, not less, information. Thus, contrary to the Court's assertion, a production requirement is completely consistent with the truth-seeking function of the Confrontation Clause.

The other principle underlying *Inadi* and *White* is that if neither party bothers to call an available declarant, the in-court testimony is probably not very important anyway. But there are many reasons for a defendant to demand production by the prosecution, even though the defendant would not wish to call the witness himself. One reason is that the declarant would be called by the defendant as an adverse witness. While that is permitted under Federal Rule 607, it is obviously preferable to attack a witness on cross-examination rather than direct. Can you think of any other reasons why the defendant would demand that the prosecution produce witnesses who the defendant would not wish to call himself?

Second, the Court has indicated that where a witness is present at trial, the witness' prior statements generally may be used as evidence against a defendant, if the defendant has an opportunity to examine the witness on those statements. Thus, if a jurisdiction admits prior statements as an exception or exemption from the hearsay rule, the confrontation clause will not bar their use. In United States v. Owens, 484 U.S. 554 (1988), the Court held that admission of a prior statement of a witness who testifies at trial satisfies the right to confrontation even if the witness has no memory of the truthfulness of the statement or of the underlying event. In *Owens*, a prison guard was attacked and suffered serious head injuries. Shortly after the attack, he identified Owens as the perpetrator. At trial, he remembered making the statement, but due to his head injuries he could not remember anything about the attack, or about what he was thinking when he made the identification. The jury was allowed to consider the guard's identification as proof of guilt. Owens argued that since the guard had no memory, cross-examination could not effectively test the truthfulness of his identification. But Justice Scalia, writing for the Court, stated that "the Confrontation Clause guarantees only an *opportunity* for effective cross-examination, not cross-examination that is effective in whatever way, and to whatever extent, the defense might wish," and that "successful cross-examination is not the constitutional guarantee." Justice Scalia emphasized that demonstrating a witness' lack of memory is "often a prime objective of cross-examination." See also Frank v. Brookhart, 877 F.2d 671 (8th Cir.1989) (cross-examination of schizophrenic witness satisfies the confrontation clause, relying on *Owens*).

Third, physical presence of the person whose out-of-court statements are offered is not enough to satisfy confrontation requirements, if the person is unwilling to testify. Douglas v. Alabama, 380 U.S. 415 (1965), illustrates why. The prosecutor called Douglas' co-defendant to testify. He invoked his privilege against self-incrimination and refused to answer as the prosecutor, reading from a document purporting to be a confession that implicated Douglas, stopped every few lines to ask whether the witness made the statements. The Court found that this violated the right to confrontation.

In Bruton v. United States, 391 U.S. 123 (1968), discussed in the section on joinder, supra, the Court held that introduction of one non-testifying defendant's confession, which implicated another defendant, was impermissible in a trial of the other defendant. The Court found that a limiting instruction to a jury would not be sufficient to cure the problem that would arise from the fact that one defendant would have damaged another without being subject to cross-examination.[64] The fact that both co-defendants have confessed does not cure the *Bruton* problem, because each defendant's confession tends to confirm the other, and in such cases each defendant is seeking to attack his own confession by claiming that it was inaccurately reported or untrue when made. Accordingly, the co-defendant's confession has a "devastating" impact that cannot be instructed away. See Cruz v. New York, 481 U.S. 186 (1987) (rejecting an "interlocking confessions" exception to *Bruton*). However, if the co-defendant's confession is redacted to eliminate all reference to the existence of the defendant, the *Bruton* problem is solved and the defendants can be tried jointly. See Richardson v. Marsh, 481 U.S. 200 (1987).

Fourth, statements that are not offered for their truth are not likely to raise serious confrontation concerns. Chief Justice Burger wrote for a unanimous Court in Tennessee v. Street, 471 U.S. 409 (1985), which distinguished *Bruton*. The state relied on Street's detailed confession in prosecuting him for murder. Street claimed that his confession was coerced and that the Sheriff read him the confession of Peele (who was tried separately for the murder) and directed him to say the same thing. The Sheriff denied this, and Peele's statement was admitted so that the jury could compare it to Street's confession and assess the relative credibility of Street and the Sheriff. The trial judge instructed the jury to consider Peele's statement only as rebuttal and not for the truth of its contents. This nonhearsay use by the state raised no confrontation concern in the eyes of the Supreme Court. The Court noted that cross-examination of Peele "would have been ineffective to undermine the prosecutor's limited purpose in introducing Peele's confession," and that the constitution did not require the State "to call a witness who could offer no relevant testimony on the immediate issue of coercion." The Court concluded that there was no alternative that would have allowed the jury to decide who was telling the truth and simultaneously that would have assured that the jury would not misuse Peele's statement. Justice Brennan, joined by Justice Marshall, added a brief concurring opinion which emphasized that the state

64. Haddad, Post-Bruton Developments: A Reconsideration of the Confrontation Rationale, and a Proposal for a Due Process Evaluation of Limiting Instructions, 18 Am.Crim. L.Rev. 1 (1980), argues that the confrontation rationale of *Bruton* is unsatisfactory and that the case is better understood as focusing on the likelihood that jury instructions under some circumstances are inadequate to assure fair trials.

had a need for admission of the statement to rebut a claim made by Street. Justice Powell did not participate in the case.

Fifth, the defendant has a right to fairly cross-examine and impeach a government witness. In Davis v. Alaska, 415 U.S. 308 (1974), the Court held that a defendant had the right to elicit evidence that a witness was on probation as a result of a juvenile adjudication, notwithstanding a state law that protected the juvenile from disclosure of the delinquency adjudication. See also Smith v. Illinois, 390 U.S. 129 (1968) (reversing conviction because the defendant was denied an opportunity to question a witness about his real name and address).

In Delaware v. Van Arsdall, 475 U.S. 673 (1986), Justice Rehnquist wrote for the Court as it reasoned that a state trial judge denied a defendant his confrontation right when he prohibited a defendant charged with murder from questioning a government witness concerning the dismissal of his pending public drunkenness charge. The Court stated that "[b]y thus cutting off all questioning about an event that the State conceded had taken place and that a jury might reasonably have found furnished the witness a motive for favoring the prosecution in his testimony, the court's ruling violated respondent's rights secured by the Confrontation Clause." The Court rejected the State's argument that in order to state a violation of the Confrontation Clause a defendant must show that "the particular limitation on cross-examination created a reasonable possibility that the jury returned an inaccurate guilty verdict." Instead, the Court concluded that "the focus of the prejudice inquiry in determining whether the confrontation right has been violated must be on the particular witness, not on the outcome of the entire trial" and that "a criminal defendant states a violation of the Confrontation Clause by showing that he was prohibited from engaging in otherwise appropriate cross-examination designed to show a prototypical form of bias on the part of the witness." It remanded the case to the state courts for a determination of whether the confrontation violation was harmless, as it rejected the defendant's argument that a confrontation violation requires automatic reversal of a conviction.

In Olden v. Kentucky, 488 U.S. 227 (1988) Olden was tried for rape, and asserted a defense of consent. The evidence showed that the defendant dropped the complainant off at her home after they had intercourse. Defendant's theory was that the complainant had concocted a rape story to protect her relationship with the man she was living with. That man was African-American, while the complainant was white. The trial judge prohibited inquiry into the complainant's living arrangements on the ground that the information would prejudice the jury against her. The Supreme Court rejected this reasoning and held that the limitation on cross-examination violated Olden's right of confrontation. The Court stated that "speculation as to the effect of jurors' racial biases cannot justify exclusion of cross-examination with such strong potential to demonstrate the falsity of [the complainant's] testimony." The Court noted that a trial court may constitutionally limit cross-examination as to a witness' bias if the defendant's purpose is to harass or prejudice, or if the evidence of bias is repetitive or only marginally relevant. But it concluded that "the limitation here was beyond reason."

Sixth, if "evidence" is transmitted to the trier of fact outside the courtroom, confrontation rights may be violated. See Parker v. Gladden, 385 U.S.

363 (1966) (bailiff made prejudicial remarks to jury); cf. Turner v. Louisiana, 379 U.S. 466 (1965) (police officer witnesses too close to jurors). And prosecutors are not permitted to smuggle claims that cannot be cross-examined into their arguments. See Frazier v. Cupp, 394 U.S. 731 (1969); cf. Donnelly v. DeChristoforo, 416 U.S. 637, 643 n. 15 (1974).

Seventh, as the Court said in Ohio v. Roberts, supra, generally there must be "indicia of reliability" to warrant admitting hearsay statements of an unavailable witness against a defendant. Ohio v. Roberts stated that hearsay falling within a firmly rooted hearsay exception need not be analyzed for indicia of reliability to satisfy the Confrontation Clause. The Supreme Court held, 6–3, in Bourjaily v. United States, 483 U.S. 171 (1987), that statements falling within the federal rule governing coconspirator statements made during and in furtherance of a conspiracy satisfy confrontation concerns. Chief Justice Rehnquist wrote for the majority as it held that coconspirator statements satisfy the Confrontation Clause as long as there is some evidence corroborating the statements. The Court left open whether coconspirator statements could be admitted pursuant to a finding that the declarant and a defendant were coconspirators based solely upon the challenged statements.[65] Justice Blackmun, joined by Justices Brennan and Marshall, suggested that a reliability inquiry might be appropriate even for statements satisfying the traditional approach to coconspirator statements—i.e., admitted pursuant to a finding by the trial judge based upon evidence independent of the coconspirator statements that the declarant and the defendant were members of a conspiracy. He urged that some indicia of reliability must be required when the foundation for coconspirator statements is lowered.[66]

In White v. Illinois, supra, the Court held that the hearsay exceptions for excited utterances and for statements for purposes of medical diagnosis and treatment were both "firmly rooted," so that statements which qualify under these exceptions automatically satisfy the reliability requirement of the Confrontation Clause. The Court noted that the excited utterance exception was at least two centuries old, and recognized in the Federal Rules and more than 40 states. The Court also noted the wide acceptance of the hearsay exception for statements for purposes of medical treatment, though it neither relied upon nor even mentioned its historical pedigree.

The Court has imposed stringent reliability requirements for hearsay statements that do not fall within firmly rooted exceptions. In Lee v. Illinois, 476 U.S. 530 (1986), Lee and Thomas were tried jointly for murder. Lee admitted some involvement in the killing, but argued that she did not plan the killing and that she acted in self-defense and in "sudden and intense passion." Thomas had confessed to police officers, and this confession implicated Lee not

65. Should traditional hearsay exceptions automatically be deemed to satisfy the hearsay rule? For a discussion of this question and an analysis of which hearsay exceptions are and should be considered firmly rooted, see Mosteller, Child Sexual Abuse and Statements for the Purpose of Medical Diagnosis or Treatment, 67 N.C.L.Rev. 257 (1989); Joseph & Saltzburg, Evidence in America, Ch. 58 (1991 Supp.). See generally Haddad, The Future of Confrontation Clause Developments: What Will Emerge When the Supreme Court Synthesizes the Diverse Lines of Confrontation Decisions?, 81 J.Crim.L. & Crim. 77 (1990).

66. One commentator suggests that the emphasis should be on sufficiency of the evidence, rather than on admissibility. See Graham, The Right of Confrontation and the Hearsay Rule: Sir Walter Raleigh Loses Another One, 8 Crim.L.Bull. 99 (1972). Do you think that this will avoid hard confrontation cases?

only in the killing itself but in the plan to kill the victim. This confession was admitted as evidence of Lee's state of mind. Justice Brennan, writing for the Court, concluded that Thomas' post-custodial confession was insufficiently reliable to satisfy the confrontation clause. He noted that "the post-arrest statements of a codefendant have traditionally been viewed with special suspicion" due to the risk that the codefendant might be shifting blame or attempting to make a deal. The Court stated that hearsay statements which do not fit firmly rooted hearsay exceptions carry a heavy presumption of unreliability, and that there was nothing about the circumstances of Thomas' confession which would overcome that presumption.

The Court in Idaho v. Wright, 110 S.Ct. 3139 (1990), considered whether the hearsay statements of a three year-old child in a sex abuse prosecution contained sufficient "indicia of reliability" to be admissible under the Confrontation Clause. The challenged statements were made to a doctor in response to questions he asked regarding the alleged abuse. The doctor used leading questions, and the question and answer session was not recorded on videotape. However, the child's statements were corroborated by testimony from her older sister and by physical evidence of sex abuse occurring at the time the child was in the custody of defendant. The Idaho courts admitted the statement under the State's "residual" hearsay exception, which covers statements not admissible under other exceptions, but which have "equivalent guarantees of trustworthiness."

Justice O'Connor, writing for a five-person majority, held that the child's statements did not have sufficient "indicia of reliability" under *Roberts,* and thus that their admission violated the defendant's right to confrontation.

Justice O'Connor quickly passed over the State's contention that the residual exception was firmly rooted. This could not be so, since unlike traditional exceptions, the residual exception "accommodates ad hoc instances in which statements not falling within a recognized hearsay exception might nevertheless be sufficiently reliable to be admissible at trial." She noted that the residual exception therefore does not have the "tradition of reliability" required of firmly rooted exceptions. Since the statement did not fit within a firmly rooted exception, Justice O'Connor concluded that it was presumptively unreliable, and that the State was required to show "particularized guarantees of trustworthiness" in order to admit it.

The State argued, consistently with almost all lower courts, that the corroborative evidence (i.e. the testimony of the sister and the evidence of the physical abuse) could be considered in determining whether the statement was reliable. The majority rejected this contention. Justice O'Connor wrote that "the relevant circumstances include only those that surround the making of the statement and that render the declarant particularly worthy of belief," and that hearsay "must possess indicia of reliability by virtue of its inherent trustworthiness, not by reference to other evidence at trial."

The majority reasoned that allowing corroborative evidence to be considered "would permit admission of a presumptively unreliable statement by bootstrapping on the trustworthiness of other evidence at trial," and that the presence of evidence corroborating the truth of a hearsay statement "would be no substitute for cross-examination of the declarant at trial." The Court further noted that corroboration could be misused by the jury, especially if only some parts of a statement were corroborated:

> Corroboration of a child's allegation of sexual abuse, for example, sheds no light on the reliability of the child's allegations regarding the identity of the abuser. There is a very real danger that a jury will rely on partial corroboration to mistakenly infer the trustworthiness of the entire statement.

Thus, the sister's statements and the physical evidence of sexual abuse could not be used to determine reliability because such evidence was not relevant to the circumstances under which the child's statements were made. Justice O'Connor found that the circumstances in which the child made her statements were not sufficient to guarantee reliability. She emphasized the presumption of unreliability and noted that the doctor had used leading questions. Justice O'Connor concluded that there was "no special reason for supposing that the incriminating statements were particularly trustworthy."

Justice Kennedy, joined by Chief Justice Rehnquist and Justices White and Blackmun, dissented. The dissenters attacked the majority's premise, that corroboration was irrelevant to reliability, as illogical and unprecedented:

> It is a matter of common sense for most people that one of the best ways to determine whether what someone says is trustworthy is to see if it is corroborated by other evidence. In the context of child abuse, for example, if part of the child's hearsay statement is that the assailant tied her wrists or had a scar on his lower abdomen, and there is physical evidence or testimony to corroborate the child's statement, evidence which the child could not have fabricated, we are more likely to believe that what the child says is true. * * * Whatever doubt the Court has with the weight to be given the corroborating evidence found in this case is no justification for rejecting the considered wisdom of virtually the entire legal community that corroborating evidence is relevant to reliability and trustworthiness.

Under the Federal Rules of Evidence, a declaration against penal interest can be offered against a criminal defendant if there are corroborating circumstances indicating trustworthiness. See e.g. United States v. Garcia, 897 F.2d 1413 (7th Cir.1990). Will a statement admitted under that exception survive Confrontation Clause scrutiny after *Wright?* See United States v. York, 933 F.2d 1343 (7th Cir.1991) (the fact that a declaration against interest is corroborated is irrelevant after *Wright;* however, the statement in this case was admitted as sufficiently reliable since the declarant, though implicating the defendant, made his statement to friends under informal circumstances, and not to police officers while in custody—thus, the circumstances indicated no motive to falsify). Also, many Federal courts have admitted grand jury testimony against a criminal defendant under the residual exception of the Federal Rules. Most of these courts have relied on corroboration. See e.g. United States v. Curro, 847 F.2d 325 (6th Cir.1988). Can these decisions be defended after *Wright?* See United States v. Gomez–Lemos, 939 F.2d 326 (6th Cir.1991) (after *Wright,* corroboration can no longer be considered in determining whether grand jury statements are sufficiently reliable under the Confrontation Clause).

The Court in *Wright* rejects the proposition that hearsay can be found reliable because it is supported by corroborative evidence. Is this position consistent with the Court's view of the importance of corroboration in evaluating the reliability of an informant's hearsay statement to determine probable cause or reasonable suspicion? Recall Illinois v. Gates and Alabama v. White (Chapter Two) where the Court reasoned that if the informant is right about some things, an inference can be drawn that he is right about his conclusion that a suspect is involved in criminal activity.

D. THE RIGHT OF COMPULSORY PROCESS

The Supreme Court has had fewer compulsory process cases than confrontation cases. Its first major compulsory process case was Washington v. Texas, 388 U.S. 14 (1967), which held that the compulsory process clause applied to the states as well as to the federal government. A defendant convicted of murder challenged Texas statutes that provided that persons charged or convicted as coparticipants in the same crime could not testify for one another, although there was no bar to their testifying for the state. On the basis of these statutes, a trial judge excluded a defense witness who, the defendant claimed, was the person who did the shooting for which the defendant was charged and whom the defendant claimed he tried to stop.

Chief Justice Warren wrote as follows:

[I]t could hardly be argued that a State would not violate the clause if it made all defense testimony inadmissible as a matter of procedural law. It is difficult to see how the Constitution is any less violated by arbitrary rules that prevent whole categories of defense witnesses from testifying on the basis of *a priori* categories that presume them unworthy of belief.

The rule disqualifying an alleged accomplice from testifying on behalf of the defendant cannot even be defended on the ground that it rationally sets apart a group of persons who are particularly likely to commit perjury. The absurdity of the rule is amply demonstrated by the exceptions that have been made to it. For example, the accused accomplice may be called by the prosecution to testify against the defendant. Common sense would suggest that he often has a greater interest in lying in favor of the prosecution rather than against it, especially if he is still awaiting his own trial or sentencing. To think that criminals will lie to save their fellows but not to obtain favors from the prosecution for themselves is indeed to clothe the criminal class with more nobility than one might expect to find in the public at large. Moreover, under the Texas statutes the accused accomplice is no longer disqualified if he is acquitted at his own trial. Presumably, he would then be free to testify on behalf of his comrade, secure in the knowledge that he could incriminate himself as freely as he liked in his testimony, since he could not again be prosecuted for the same offense. The Texas law leaves him free to testify when he has a great incentive to perjury, and bars his testimony in situations where he has a lesser motive to lie.

We hold that the petitioner in this case was denied his right to have compulsory process for obtaining witnesses in his favor because the State arbitrarily denied him the right to put on the stand a witness who was physically and mentally capable of testifying to events that he had personally observed, and whose testimony would have been relevant and material to the defense. The Framers of the Constitution did not intend to commit the futile act of giving to a defendant the right to secure the attendance of witnesses whose testimony he had no right to use. The judgment of conviction must be reversed.

The most typical compulsory process claim is closely related to the Washington v. Texas situation; it arises when a court treats defense witnesses less favorably than government witnesses. Plainly, the compulsory process clause affords an accused the opportunity to subpoena witnesses who are "relevant, material and useful to an adequate defense." United States v. Barker, 553 F.2d 1013 (6th Cir. 1977). See Fed.R.Crim.P. 17(b).[67] That a witness might prefer not to testify is irrelevant. See Keshishian v. State, 386 A.2d 666 (Del.1978). The clause assures that the defense is no less able than the government to *compel* witnesses to appear and testify. In view of the importance that the Supreme Court attaches to the right, arbitrary restrictions on defense subpoenas are not likely to be viewed with favor. Thus, a refusal to grant a short adjournment to secure the presence of an important defense witness will not be tolerated. See Singleton v. Lefkowitz, 583 F.2d 618 (2d Cir. 1978). Also, it is likely that appellate courts will carefully scrutinize the exclusion of defense evidence in circumstances in which the prosecutor is allowed to offer similar evidence. See e.g., Rivera v. Director, 915 F.2d 280 (7th Cir. 1990) (defendant's right to an effective defense was violated when the trial court refused to admit an exculpatory confession made by a co-defendant, even though the confession was held reliable enough for the state to use to implicate a defendant in a related trial; at a minimum, the compulsory process clause requires reciprocity). And trial courts will not be allowed to bar defense evidence that is relevant and competent under evidence rules and is directed at a crucial element of the offense. See Hughes v. Mathews, 576 F.2d 1250 (7th Cir. 1978), and State ex rel. Boyd v. Green, 355 So.2d 789 (Fla.1978), both suggesting that a defendant cannot be denied an opportunity to negate the intent charged by the government. The Supreme Court cited both the Confrontation and Compulsory Process Clauses in Crane v. Kentucky, 476 U.S. 683 (1986), as it held that a court must permit a defendant to offer evidence that attacks the reliability of a confession. It reasoned that a defendant would be denied a chance to be heard if defense evidence that challenged the probative value of the government's evidence were excluded.

If the trial judge makes comments to a defense witness that are not made to other witnesses and that discourage the witness from testifying, compulsory process rights may be infringed. See Webb v. Texas, 409 U.S. 95 (1972).

Finding that a trial judge "blatantly interfered" with a state defendant's right to present alibi witnesses, a court of appeals granted habeas corpus relief in Anderson v. Warden, 696 F.2d 296 (4th Cir. 1982) (en banc). Anderson had been found guilty by a jury of rape, felony murder and burglary. Two alibi witnesses testified that Anderson was with them at the time the criminal activity took place. During cross-examination the prosecutor asked both witnesses whether they were familiar with the penalty for perjury. After the witnesses testified, the trial judge asked the prosecutor whether he wanted one witness held. The prosecutor said that he did and the sheriff was directed to put the witness in custody. Both witnesses were taken from the courtroom (possibly in the jury's presence). In chambers the judge lectured both and

67. United States v. Goodwin, 625 F.2d 693 (5th Cir. 1980), found a denial of a defendant's compulsory process right and reasoned that unless the government can show a request for a subpoena to be frivolous, a request for relevant evidence must be granted.

In People v. Carey, 77 Ill.2d 259, 32 Ill.Dec. 904, 396 N.E.2d 17 (1979), the court said that the defendant's right to compulsory process included the right to subpoenas duces tecum, to be issued prior to a preliminary hearing or trial to gather evidence for use therein.

indicated that he was upset at the falsity of their testimony. Subsequently, the judge told the jury that the witnesses had indicated to him that they had not told the truth and that they would be recalled so that they would have another chance to tell the truth. Their subsequent testimony weakened the alibi defense. Four judges dissented and reasoned that the trial judge had done nothing wrong.[68]

In United States v. Valenzuela-Bernal, 458 U.S. 858 (1982), the Supreme Court found no violation of compulsory process or due process rights where the government deported as illegal aliens persons whom the defendant wanted to call at trial. Justice Rehnquist's majority opinion reasoned that, to show a violation of compulsory process, the defendant must make a plausible showing of how the testimony of the missing witnesses would be material and favorable to the defense in a way that is not merely cumulative. At least the same showing would be required to show a violation of due process. Justice Blackmun's opinion concurring in the judgment indicated that he would have required at least a plausible theory as to how the testimony of the missing witnesses would have been helpful. Justice O'Connor expressed some concern about quick deportations, on the one hand, and unnecessary dismissal of charges, on the other. She suggested that under the Court's supervisory power it could require the government to delay deportation for a very brief interval during which time both the government and defense counsel would have an opportunity to interview a witness. Then a judgment could be made about the legitimacy of deportation before, rather than after, the event. Justice Brennan's dissent was joined by Justice Marshall.[69]

The Supreme Court rejected Texas' arbitrary rule in Washington v. Texas, but it did not provide much guidance to lower courts in determining when a state statute or evidence rule would fall before a compulsory process attack. In the next case, the Court again found a problem with state evidence rules.

CHAMBERS v. MISSISSIPPI

Supreme Court of the United States, 1973.
410 U.S. 284.

MR. JUSTICE POWELL delivered the opinion of the Court.

Petitioner, Leon Chambers, was tried by a jury in a Mississippi trial court and convicted of murdering a policeman. * * * [Chambers claimed that McDonald had murdered the policeman. McDonald had confessed to the crime

68. But see Everhart v. State, 358 So.2d 1058 (Ala.Cr.App.1978) (no error in judge's "blistering admonition" to government witness who may have surprised the prosecutor), and State v. Whiting, 117 N.H. 701, 378 A.2d 736 (1977) (trial judge warns two defense witnesses that they might be prosecuted for perjury if they contradicted their prior statements to government).

69. See United States v. Theresius Filippi, 918 F.2d 244 (1st Cir.1990) (right to compulsory process violated where a material witness for the defense, who was living in Ecuador, offered to testify at trial if American immigration hurdles could be cleared; the prosecutor failed to request clearance from the Immigration and Naturalization Service, even though clearances were routinely granted upon request from a prosecutor); Buie v. Sullivan, 923 F.2d 10 (2d Cir.1990) (right to compulsory process not violated where the prosecutor ordered the arrest of a defense witness on eve of trial, and the witness thereafter invoked his privilege against self-incrimination; there was no showing that the arrest was made in bad faith, since probable cause clearly existed to arrest the witness as a co-conspirator in the crime for which the defendant was charged).

on several occasions--once to Chambers' attorney, and to at least three other members of the community. At trial, Chambers tried to get McDonald's confessions before the jury, either by way of McDonald himself, or by calling three witnesses who would testify to McDonald's out-of-court statements.]

Chambers filed a pretrial motion requesting the court to order McDonald to appear. Chambers also sought a ruling at that time that, if the State itself chose not to call McDonald, he be allowed to call him as an adverse witness. * * * The trial court granted the motion requiring McDonald to appear but reserved ruling on the adverse-witness motion. At trial, after the State failed to put McDonald on the stand, Chambers called McDonald, laid a predicate for the introduction of his sworn out-of-court confession, had it admitted into evidence, and read it to the jury. The State, upon cross-examination, elicited from McDonald the fact that he had repudiated his prior confession. [McDonald further testified that he did not shoot the policeman].

At the conclusion of the State's cross-examination, Chambers renewed his motion to examine McDonald as an adverse witness. The trial court denied the motion, stating: "He may be hostile, but he is not adverse in the sense of the word, so your request will be overruled." On appeal, the State Supreme Court upheld the trial court's ruling, finding that "McDonald's testimony was not adverse to appellant" because "[n]owhere did he point the finger at Chambers."

Defeated in his attempt to challenge directly McDonald's renunciation of his prior confession, Chambers sought to introduce the testimony of the three witnesses to whom McDonald had admitted that he shot the officer. * * * The State objected to the admission of this testimony on the ground that it was hearsay. The trial court sustained the objection.

* * *

In sum, then, this was Chambers' predicament. As a consequence of the combination of Mississippi's "party witness" or "voucher" rule and its hearsay rule, he was unable either to cross-examine McDonald or to present witnesses in his own behalf who would have discredited McDonald's repudiation and demonstrated his complicity. * * * Chambers' defense was far less persuasive than it might have been had he been given an opportunity to subject McDonald's statements to cross-examination or had the other confessions been admitted.

III

The right of an accused in a criminal trial to due process is, in essence, the right to a fair opportunity to defend against the State's accusations. The rights to confront and cross-examine witnesses and to call witnesses in one's own behalf have long been recognized as essential to due process. * * * Both of these elements of a fair trial are implicated in the present case.

A

Chambers was denied an opportunity to subject McDonald's damning repudiation and alibi to cross-examination. He was not allowed to test the witness' recollection, to probe into the details of his alibi, or to "sift" his conscience so that the jury might judge for itself whether McDonald's testimony was worthy of belief. * * *

* * *

Whatever validity the "voucher" rule may have once enjoyed, and apart from whatever usefulness it retains today in the civil trial process, it bears little present relationship to the realities of the criminal process. It might have been logical for the early common law to require a party to vouch for the credibility of witnesses he brought before the jury to affirm his veracity. Having selected them especially for that purpose, the party might reasonably be expected to stand firmly behind their testimony. But in modern criminal trials, defendants are rarely able to select their witnesses: they must take them where they find them. Moreover, as applied in this case, the "voucher" rule's impact was doubly harmful to Chambers' efforts to develop his defense. Not only was he precluded from cross-examining McDonald, but, as the State conceded at oral argument, he was also restricted in the scope of his direct examination by the rule's corollary requirement that the party calling the witness is bound by anything he might say. He was, therefore, effectively prevented from exploring the circumstances of McDonald's three prior oral confessions and from challenging the renunciation of the written confession.

* * *

* * * The "voucher" rule, as applied in this case, plainly interfered with Chambers' right to defend against the State's charges.

B

We need not decide, however, whether this error alone would occasion reversal since Chambers' claimed denial of due process rests on the ultimate impact of that error when viewed in conjunction with the trial court's refusal to permit him to call other witnesses. * * * Each would have testified to the statements purportedly made by McDonald, on three separate occasions shortly after the crime, naming himself as the murderer. The State Supreme Court approved the exclusion of this evidence on the ground that it was hearsay.

* * *

Few rights are more fundamental than that of an accused to present witnesses in his own defense. In the exercise of this right, the accused, as is required of the State, must comply with established rules of procedure and evidence designed to assure both fairness and reliability in the ascertainment of guilt and innocence. Although perhaps no rule of evidence has been more respected or more frequently applied in jury trials than that applicable to the exclusion of hearsay, exceptions tailored to allow the introduction of evidence which in fact is likely to be trustworthy have long existed. The testimony rejected by the trial court here bore persuasive assurances of trustworthiness and thus was well within the basic rationale of the exception for declarations against interest. That testimony also was critical to Chambers' defense. In these circumstances, where constitutional rights directly affecting the ascertainment of guilt are implicated, the hearsay rule may not be applied mechanistically to defeat the ends of justice.

We conclude that the exclusion of this critical evidence, coupled with the State's refusal to permit Chambers to cross-examine McDonald, denied him a trial in accord with traditional and fundamental standards of due process. In reaching this judgment, we establish no new principles of constitutional law. Nor does our holding signal any diminution in the respect traditionally accorded to the States in the establishment and implementation of their own criminal trial rules and procedures. Rather, we hold quite simply that under the facts and circumstances of this case the rulings of the trial court deprived Chambers of a fair trial.

* * *

[The concurring opinion of Justice White, and the dissenting opinion of Justice Rehnquist are omitted.]

Note

In Green v. Georgia, 442 U.S. 95 (1979), the Court relied on *Chambers* to hold that due process required admission of a co-defendant's confession on behalf of a defendant in a capital sentencing proceeding. Some authorities view *Chambers* as solely a compulsory process case. Do you agree with this interpretation? Exactly what right did the Court recognize that Chambers possessed?

The Supreme Court held that a defendant's constitutional right to testify in her own behalf was violated in Rock v. Arkansas, 483 U.S. 44 (1987). Rock was charged with manslaughter for shooting her husband. She underwent hypnosis with a trained neuropsychologist to refresh her memory of the shooting. After the hypnosis she remembered details indicating that her gun had misfired that were supported by expert testimony. The trial judge excluded her refreshed testimony and ruled that she could only testify as to matters remembered and stated to the psychologist before being hypnotized. The state supreme court affirmed her conviction, but was reversed by the U.S. Supreme Court.[70]

Justice Blackmun's opinion for the Court observed that a defendant's right to testify in her own behalf is not only guaranteed by the Due Process Clause and the Compulsory Process Clause, but also is a necessary corollary to the Fifth Amendment's guarantee against compelled testimony. Citing Washington v. Texas and Chambers v. Mississippi, he reasoned that "[j]ust as a State may not apply an arbitrary rule of competence to exclude a material defense witness from taking the stand, it also may not apply a rule of evidence that permits a witness to take the stand, but arbitrarily excludes material testimony."

Justice Blackmun recognized that "the right to present relevant testimony is not without limitation," but cautioned that "restrictions of a defendant's right to testify may not be arbitrary or disproportionate to the purposes they are designed to serve." He found that in establishing a *per se* bar against post-hypnosis testimony, Arkansas had established a rule that "operates to the detriment of any defendant who undergoes hypnosis, without regard to the reasons for it, the circumstances under which it took place, or any independent verification of the information it produced." Justice Blackmun noted the possibility that procedural safeguards might reduce the possibility of suggestiveness during hypnosis and that some information recalled in hypnosis might be verified by corroborative evidence. Although the Court was "not now prepared to endorse without qualifications the use of hypnosis as an investigative tool," Justice Blackmun concluded that Arkansas "has not justified the exclusion of *all* of a defendant's testimony that the defendant is unable to prove to be the product of prehypnosis memory." Because the state courts had not considered the arguments for admitting Rock's testimony in light of the corroboration of recalled details, the Supreme Court remanded the case to the Arkansas Supreme Court for further proceedings.[71]

Chief Justice Rehnquist, joined by Justices White, O'Connor and Scalia dissented. He argued that "no known set of procedures * * * can insure against the inherently unreliable nature of such testimony," and that the state supreme court's approach to hypnotized witnesses "was an entirely permissible response to a novel

70. See Williams v. Armontrout, 877 F.2d 1376 (8th Cir.1989) for a discussion of the problems associated with hypnotically refreshed testimony.

71. Why is corroboration relevant to the reliability of the statement in *Rock*, but not in Idaho v. Wright, supra?

and difficult question." See also United States v. Contreras, 937 F.2d 1191 (7th Cir.1991) (Sentencing Guideline § 3C1.1, which authorizes a two-level increase for obstruction of justice, is applicable if the defendant takes the stand and commits perjury; the Guideline does not violate the defendant's constitutional right to testify, since there is no constitutional right to testify falsely).

After *Chambers,* and *Rock* it is easier to ask when the compulsory process clause overrides evidence rules than it is to answer the question. Consider the following situations.

1. In In re Farber (State v. Jascalevich), 78 N.J. 259, 394 A.2d 330 (1978), the State Supreme Court held that a doctor on trial for murder had a right to subpoena a news-reporter's notes, gathered in the course of investigative journalism that resulted in published stories that apparently led the prosecutor to charge the defendant. The court held that the Sixth Amendment took precedence over a state news-reporter shield law.[72] In Salazar v. State, 559 P.2d 66 (Alaska 1976), the State Supreme Court held that a defendant had a constitutional right to the testimony of a government witness' spouse, who may have been told by the witness in confidence that he, not the defendant, committed the murder charged.[73] In contrast, most courts have held where a third party confesses to his attorney that he has committed the crime for which the defendant is charged, the third party's attorney-client privilege predominates over the defendant's Sixth Amendment right. See Valdez v. Winans, 738 F.2d 1087 (10th Cir.1984). Similar conflicts between evidentiary privileges and compulsory process arise in rape prosecutions, where rape shield statutes prevent introduction of the character and prior sexual activity of the complainant. Can the statute apply even where it would prevent the defendant from introducing evidence that may be probative as to his state of mind? See Federal Rule of Evidence 412, excluding character evidence and prior acts of the complainant in a rape case, but noting that the constitution may require evidence otherwise excluded by the rule to be admitted in some cases. See also State v. Moats, 156 Wis.2d 74, 457 N.W.2d 299 (1990) (rape shield statute unconstitutional where it precludes introduction of other alleged acts of sexual abuse suffered by the victim, offered by the defendant to show where she obtained her precocious knowledge); Galvin, Shielding Rape Victims in the State and Federal Courts: A Proposal for the Second Decade, 70 Minn.L.Rev. 763 (1986).

Professor White has suggested that evidentiary privileges should be overridden by the defendant's compulsory process rights when the privileges protect governmental interests, as opposed to societal relationships. See White, Evidentiary Privileges and the Defendant's Constitutional Right to an Effective Defense, 80 J.Crim.L. & Crim. 377 (1989). Under this view, the attorney-client privilege and the interspousal privilege would remain inviolate, while the informer's privilege, the state secret privilege, and rape shield statutes would be overridden if they denied the defendant access to important probative evidence. Other commentators have gone further and argued that evidentiary privileges can never be weighted more heavily than a constitutional right. See Note, Defendant v. Witness: Measuring Confrontation and Compulsory Process Rights Against Statutory Communications Privileges, 30 Stan.L.Rev. 935 (1978). There is a problem with most of the judicial and scholarly writing in this area. It is this: When the compulsory process clause was adopted, privileges were recognized, and there apparently was no thought that privileges could not be viewed as consistent with compulsory process.

72. The reporter, Farber, refused to comply with an order that he turn over his notes. He was held in comtempt and imprisoned until the trial ended. The doctor was acquitted.

73. The Alaska court called this a confrontation case. Some commentators would call it a compulsory process case. Perhaps you can see from this case that the label chosen is not nearly as significant as the result reached.

Assuming that the Fourteenth Amendment was intended to or should incorporate compulsory process, why should long-standing privileges suddenly be ignored in the face of a constitutional claim that hardly is new? More troublesome is the question why the Congress of the United States and state legislatures should be barred from deciding that the First Amendment activities of reporters or the sanctity of marital privacy (which itself has been constitutionally protected) should give way to an interpretation of the compulsory process clause that is suddenly elastic, perhaps infinitely so. How would you strike the balance between a defendant's desire to seek out and present evidence and a society's attempts to promote other fundamental values? See Campbell v. Klevenhagen, 760 F.Supp. 1206 (S.D.Tex.1991) (contempt order imposed against newspersons was unconstitutional where the defendant made no showing that newspersons could identify their sources, or that if they could, the disclosure would lead to materially exculpatory information); Stephens v. Morris, 756 F.Supp. 1137 (N.D.Ind.1991) (rape shield statute properly applied where the exclusion of the complainant's prior sexual behavior did not deprive the defendant of materially exculpatory evidence).

2. In a number of cases, defendants have requested the government to seek grants of use immunity so that witnesses, who otherwise would invoke the Fifth Amendment, would be required to testify for the defense. Most courts have rejected the defense requests. See Blissett v. Lefevre, 924 F.2d 434 (2d Cir.1991), and the cases cited therein.[74] Since the government can grant immunity to its own witnesses and does so in cases like *Blissett,* is the case for holding that the defendant should have the benefits of immunity laws a stronger one than it would be if the government also could not immunize witnesses? The court in *Blissett* did say that immunity for a defense witness may be ordered under "exceptional circumstances" and listed three requirements for this exception:

> where (a) prosecutorial overreaching, through threats, harassment, or other forms of intimidation, has effectively forced the witness to invoke the Fifth Amendment, or the prosecutor has engaged in discriminatory use of immunity grants to gain a tactical advantage; (b) the witness's testimony is also material, exculpatory, and not cumulative; and (c) the defendant has no other way to obtain the evidence.

In the absence of these circumstances, courts are clearly concerned about interfering with a prosecutor's decision concerning whom to prosecute and whom to immunize. The courts also note that as a general rule, "a person suspected of crime should not be empowered to give his confederates an immunity bath." Id. But if use immunity and not transactional immunity is all that is required, are these legitimate concerns?

74. United States v. Klauber, 611 F.2d 512 (4th Cir. 1979), rejects a claim that the government must make its immunity powers available to any defendant who wishes to call a witness. Accord, United States v. Lenz, 616 F.2d 960 (6th Cir.1980); United States v. Turkish, 603 F.2d 769 (2d Cir. 1980). But see Government of Virgin Islands v. Smith, 615 F.2d 964 (3d Cir. 1980) (requiring immunity for defense witness); United States v. Westerdahl, 945 F.2d 1083 (9th Cir.1991) (defendant denied due process because of broad immunity granted to government witnesses while defendant's witnesses denied immunity).

The discretion afforded the prosecutor in seeking or refusing to seek use immunity for witnesses is illustrated by United States v. Taylor, 728 F.2d 930 (7th Cir.1984). The court of appeals affirmed Taylor's bank robbery conviction and said that the prosecutor's decision about immunity will not be reviewed except in the case of clear abuse of discretion amounting to a violation of due process. It held that the record supported the prosecutor's decision to revoke the immunity given to a witness on the second day of trial when he had evidence that the witness had lied to a grand jury while under a grant of immunity.

3. In People v. Scarola, 71 N.Y.2d 769, 530 N.Y.S.2d 83, 525 N.E.2d 728 (1988), the defendant was charged with robbery. The prosecution witness identified him as having spoken fluently, with a mellifluous voice. Scarola wished to take the stand not to testify, but only to show that he had a speech impediment and spoke nasally. The Court of Appeals held that it was constitutionally permissible to exclude the voice exemplar evidence, because of the "inherent lack of trustworthiness" and "the difficulty of testing the authenticity" of the speech that would be displayed on the witness stand. The court distinguished cases holding that the constitution requires the trial court to allow the defendant to take the stand to display physical evidence, such as scars and tattoos, unmentioned by prosecution witnesses. Is that a meaningful distinction? Is *Scarola* consistent with *Rock* and *Chambers?*

4. In State v. Gremillion, 542 So.2d 1074 (La.1989), the defendant was charged with killing his longtime friend in a fight. Nineteen hours after he was injured, the victim told a police officer who was investigating the crime that he could not identify his attackers. Gremillion attempted to call the police officer to testify to this statement, but it was hearsay, and there was no exception for it under the state hearsay rules. The court, citing *Chambers,* held that even though the statement was excluded under the hearsay rule "it should nevertheless be admitted into evidence due to its reliability and trustworthy nature." Does *Chambers* stand for this proposition? See also Rivera v. Director, State Department of Corrections, 915 F.2d 280 (7th Cir.1990) (exculpatory statement of codefendant must be admitted despite the fact that no state hearsay exception applies). Compare Gomez v. Greer, 896 F.2d 252 (7th Cir.1990) (exculpatory statement of a codefendant properly excluded; *Chambers* was based on the "conjunctive effect" of the hearsay rule and the voucher rule: "restrictions on the use of hearsay by themselves have no similar effect").

VII. THE KIND OF COUNSEL THAT IS GUARANTEED

In Chapter Five we saw that the accused is guaranteed the right to counsel. Here we examine the kind of counsel that the accused has a right to expect.

A. SOME MINIMAL LEVEL OF COMPETENCE

Although counsel is constitutionally required at trial and at many pre- and post-trial stages of a criminal prosecution, the quality of representation afforded defendants is uneven. A defendant who is acquitted has little reason to complain, even if her lawyer made serious errors at trial. But a defendant who is convicted may believe that her lawyer did not provide sufficiently competent representation. If so, she may challenge her conviction on the theory that she was denied "effective" assistance of counsel.

The notion that counsel must provide at least some minimal level of representation first appeared in Powell v. Alabama, 287 U.S. 45 (1932). Justice Sutherland's opinion concluded that the trial judge's failure to make an effective appointment of counsel resulted in the "denial of effective and substantial aid. * * * [D]efendants were not accorded the right of counsel in any substantial sense." When *Powell* was decided, the Sixth Amendment right to counsel did not apply to the states, and the Court's decision rested on due process considerations of fundamental fairness.

After *Powell,* the Court reiterated in several cases the importance of meaningful representation by counsel. In Avery v. Alabama, 308 U.S. 444 (1940), defense counsel's motion for a continuance in order to have more time to prepare for trial was denied. The defendant alleged that the denial of the motion deprived him of effective assistance of counsel. Although the court found no constitutional violation, it emphasized that "[t]he Constitution's guarantee of assistance of counsel cannot be satisfied by mere formal appointment." Unless counsel has the opportunity to consult with the accused and to prepare his defense, the appointment of counsel could be converted "into a sham and nothing more than a formal compliance with the Constitution's requirement that an accused be given the assistance of counsel." In the actual case, counsel had performed well, and there was no indication that more could have been done if additional time had been granted.

In Glasser v. United States, 315 U.S. 60 (1942), the Court reinforced the idea developed in *Avery* that counsel's inadequacy could require reversal of a defendant's conviction. The Court overturned Glasser's conviction because the trial court, over Glasser's objection, appointed the same counsel to represent both Glasser and a codefendant. The judge created a situation in which counsel inherently could not, and did not, protect Glasser's interests. Finding that Glasser's Sixth Amendment right to effective assistance of counsel was denied, the Court stated:

> The right to have the assistance of counsel is too fundamental and absolute to allow courts to indulge in nice calculations as to the amount of prejudice arising from its denial. * * * Of equal importance with the duty of the court to see that an accused has the assistance of counsel is its duty to refrain from embarrassing counsel in the defense of an accused by insisting, or indeed, even suggesting that counsel undertake to concurrently represent interests which might diverge from those of his first client * * *.

The decision in *Glasser* rested on the Sixth Amendment, because a federal defendant was involved.

Several other cases following *Glasser* considered the right to effective assistance of counsel as a due process right because, as in *Avery,* supra, state defendants were involved. A particularly notable decision is Michel v. Louisiana, 350 U.S. 91 (1955), which articulated the generally accepted rule that trial tactics are not a proper basis for an ineffective assistance of counsel claim. Defense counsel's failure to make a timely motion to quash an indictment on the ground that there was a systematic exclusion of blacks from the grand jury did not deny the defendant effective assistance of counsel. "The mere fact that a timely motion to quash was not filed does not overcome the presumption of effectiveness. * * * The delay might be considered sound trial strategy, particularly since the co-defendant could not be found. We cannot infer lack of effective counsel from this circumstance alone."

McMann v. Richardson, 397 U.S. 759, 771 n. 14 (1970), offered the only guidance the Court would provide for almost fifteen years as the definition of effective assistance. The Court explicitly recognized that "the right to counsel is the right to the effective assistance of counsel." But it rejected defendants' argument that their guilty pleas, which were motivated largely by allegedly coerced confessions, were invalid because counsel misjudged the admissibility of the confessions. An attorney's advice, in this context, must be "within the range of competence demanded of attorneys in criminal cases. * * * [I]f the right to counsel guaranteed by the Constitution is to serve its purpose, defendants cannot be left to the mercies of incompetent counsel, and * * * judges should strive to maintain proper standards of performance by attorneys who are representing defendants in criminal cases in their courts."

B. INCREASING CONCERN FOR THE DEFENDANT

The task of developing a standard for evaluating ineffective assistance of counsel claims had been left largely to lower courts before *McMann.* Initially, they granted relief only when counsel's incompetence reduced the trial to a "farce or mockery of justice." This approach was enunciated in Diggs v. Welch, 148 F.2d 667 (D.C.Cir.1945). Although the court recognized that counsel must be "effective," it chose a restrictive definition of that term because "[t]o allow a prisoner to try the issue of the effectiveness of his counsel under a liberal definition of that phrase is to give every convict the privilege of opening a Pandora's box of accusations which trial courts near large penal institutions would be compelled to hear." The farce or mockery standard prevailed at some point in most jurisdictions.[75] Gradually, the majority of federal circuits and many state courts adopted a higher standard for effective representation.[76]

After denying certiorari for a decade and a half in cases raising the question of the proper standard for assessing the adequacy of counsel, the Supreme Court finally addressed the standard in 1984 in the next two cases.

STRICKLAND v. WASHINGTON

Supreme Court of the United States, 1984.
466 U.S. 668.

JUSTICE O'CONNOR delivered the opinion of the Court.

This case requires us to consider the proper standards for judging a criminal defendant's contention that the Constitution requires a conviction or death sentence to be set aside because counsel's assistance at the trial or sentencing was ineffective.

I

A

During a ten-day period in September 1976, respondent planned and committed three groups of crimes, which included three brutal stabbing murders, torture, kidnapping, severe assaults, attempted murders, attempted extortion, and theft. After his two accomplices were arrested, respondent surrendered to police and voluntarily gave a lengthy statement confessing to the third of the

75. See Comment, Ineffective Assistance of Counsel: Who Bears the Burden of Proof? 29 Baylor Law Rev. 29, 32 n. 25 (1977).

76. E.g., Rummel v. Estelle, 590 F.2d 103 (5th Cir. 1979) (reasonably effective assistance of counsel); Marzullo v. Maryland, 561 F.2d 540 (4th Cir. 1977) (defense counsel's representation must be within the range of competence demanded of attorneys in criminal cases); United States v. Easter, 539 F.2d 663 (8th Cir. 1976) (trial counsel must exercise the customary skills and diligence that a reasonably competent attorney would perform under similar circumstances); United States v. DeCoster, 487 F.2d 1197 (D.C.Cir. 1973), modified 598 F.2d 311 (1979) (en banc), 624 F.2d 196 (D.C.Cir. 1979) (en banc) (defendant entitled to the reasonably competent assistance of an attorney acting as his diligent conscientious advocate).

criminal episodes. The State of Florida indicted respondent for kidnapping and murder and appointed an experienced criminal lawyer to represent him.

Counsel actively pursued pretrial motions and discovery. He cut his efforts short, however, and he experienced a sense of hopelessness about the case, when he learned that, against his specific advice, respondent had also confessed to the first two murders. By the date set for trial, respondent was subject to indictment for three counts of first degree murder and multiple counts of robbery, kidnapping for ransom, breaking and entering and assault, attempted murder, and conspiracy to commit robbery. Respondent waived his right to a jury trial, again acting against counsel's advice, and pleaded guilty to all charges, including the three capital murder charges.

In the plea colloquy, respondent told the trial judge that, although he had committed a string of burglaries, he had no significant prior criminal record and that at the time of his criminal spree he was under extreme stress caused by his inability to support his family. He also stated, however, that he accepted responsibility for the crimes. The trial judge told respondent that he had "a great deal of respect for people who are willing to step forward and admit their responsibility" but that he was making no statement at all about his likely sentencing decision.

Counsel advised respondent to invoke his right under Florida law to an advisory jury at his capital sentencing hearing. Respondent rejected the advice and waived the right. He chose instead to be sentenced by the trial judge without a jury recommendation.

In preparing for the sentencing hearing, counsel spoke with respondent about his background. He also spoke on the telephone with respondent's wife and mother, though he did not follow up on the one unsuccessful effort to meet with them. He did not otherwise seek out character witnesses for respondent. Nor did he request a psychiatric examination, since his conversations with his client gave no indication that respondent had psychological problems.

Counsel decided not to present and hence not to look further for evidence concerning respondent's character and emotional state. That decision reflected trial counsel's sense of hopelessness about overcoming the evidentiary effect of respondent's confessions to the gruesome crimes. It also reflected the judgment that it was advisable to rely on the plea colloquy for evidence about respondent's background and about his claim of emotional stress: the plea colloquy communicated sufficient information about these subjects, and by foregoing the opportunity to present new evidence on these subjects, counsel prevented the State from cross-examining respondent on his claim and from putting on psychiatric evidence of its own.

Counsel also excluded from the sentencing hearing other evidence he thought was potentially damaging. He successfully moved to exclude respondent's "rap sheet." Because he judged that a presentence report might prove more detrimental than helpful, as it would have included respondent's criminal history and thereby undermined the claim of no significant history of criminal activity, he did not request that one be prepared.

At the sentencing hearing, counsel's strategy was based primarily on the trial judge's remarks at the plea colloquy as well as on his reputation as a sentencing judge who thought it important for a convicted defendant to own up to his crime. Counsel argued that respondent's remorse and acceptance of responsibility justified sparing him from the death penalty. Counsel also argued that respondent had no history of criminal activity and that respondent committed the crimes under extreme mental or emotional disturbance, thus coming within the statutory list of mitigating circumstances. He further argued that respondent should be spared death because he had surrendered, confessed, and offered to testify against a co-defendant and because respondent was fundamentally a good person who had briefly gone badly wrong in extremely stressful circumstances. The State put on evidence and witnesses largely for the purpose of describing the details of the crimes. Counsel did not cross-examine the medical experts who testified about the manner of death of respondent's victims.

The trial judge found several aggravating circumstances with respect to each of the three murders. He found that all three murders were especially heinous, atrocious, and cruel, all involving repeated stabbings. All three murders were committed in the course of at least one other dangerous and violent felony, and since all involved robbery, the murders were for pecuniary gain. All three murders were committed to avoid arrest for the accompanying crimes and to hinder law enforcement. In the course of one of the murders, respondent knowingly subjected numerous persons to a grave risk of death by deliberately stabbing and shooting the murder victim's sisters-in-law, who sustained severe—in one case, ultimately fatal—injuries.

With respect to mitigating circumstances, the trial judge made the same findings for all three capital murders. First, although there was no admitted evidence of prior convictions, respondent had stated that he had engaged in a course of stealing. In any case, even if respondent had no significant history of criminal activity, the aggravating circumstances "would still clearly far outweigh" that mitigating factor. Second, the judge found that, during all three crimes, respondent was not suffering from extreme mental or emotional disturbance and could appreciate the criminality of his acts. Third, none of the victims was a participant in, or consented to, respondent's conduct. Fourth, respondent's participation in the crimes was neither minor nor the result of duress or domination by an accomplice. Finally, respondent's age (26) could not be considered a factor in mitigation, especially when viewed in light of respondent's planning of the crimes and disposition of the proceeds of the various accompanying thefts.

In short, the trial judge found numerous aggravating circumstances and no (or a single comparatively insignificant) mitigating circumstance. * * * He therefore sentenced respondent to death on each of the three counts of murder and to prison terms for the other crimes. The Florida Supreme Court upheld the convictions and sentences on direct appeal.

B

Respondent subsequently sought collateral relief in state court on numerous grounds, among them that counsel had rendered ineffective assistance at the sentencing proceeding. Respondent challenged counsel's assistance in six respects. He asserted that counsel was ineffective because he failed to move for a continuance to prepare for sentencing, to request a psychiatric report, to investigate and present character witnesses, to seek a presentence investigation report, to present meaningful arguments to the sentencing judge, and to investigate the medical examiner's reports or cross-examine the medical experts. In support of the claim, respondent submitted fourteen affidavits from friends, neighbors, and relatives stating that they would have testified if asked to do so. He also submitted one psychiatric report and one psychological report stating that respondent, though not under the influence of extreme mental or emotional disturbance, was "chronically frustrated and depressed because of his economic dilemma" at the time of his crimes.

The trial court denied relief without an evidentiary hearing, finding that the record evidence conclusively showed that the ineffectiveness claim was meritless. Four of the assertedly prejudicial errors required little discussion. First, there were no grounds to request a continuance, so there was no error in not requesting one when respondent pleaded guilty. Second, failure to request a presentence investigation was not a serious error because the trial judge had discretion not to grant such a request and because any presentence investigation would have resulted in admission of respondent's rap sheet and thus undermined his assertion of no significant history of criminal activity. Third, the argument and memorandum given to the sentencing judge were "admirable" in light of the overwhelming aggravating circumstances and absence of mitigating circumstances. Fourth, there was no error in failure to examine the medical examiner's reports or to cross-examine the medical witnesses testifying on the manner of death of respondent's victims, since respondent admitted that the victims died in the ways shown by the unchallenged medical evidence.

The trial court dealt at greater length with the two other bases for the ineffectiveness claim. The court pointed out that a psychiatric examination of respondent was conducted by state order soon after respondent's initial arraignment. That report states that there was no indication of major mental illness at the time of the crimes. Moreover, both the reports submitted in the collateral proceeding state that, although respondent was "chronically frustrated and depressed because of his economic dilemma," he was not under the influence of extreme mental or emotional disturbance. All three reports thus directly undermine the contention made at the sentencing hearing that respondent was suffering from extreme mental or emotional disturbance during his crime spree. Accordingly, counsel could reasonably decide not to seek psychiatric reports; indeed, by relying solely on the plea colloquy to support the emotional disturbance contention, counsel denied the State an opportunity to rebut his claim with psychiatric testimony. In any event, the aggravating circumstances were so overwhelming that no substantial prejudice resulted from the absence at sentencing of the psychiatric evidence offered in the collateral attack.

The court rejected the challenge to counsel's failure to develop and to present character evidence for much the same reasons. The affidavits submitted in the collateral proceeding showed nothing more than that certain persons would have testified that respondent was basically a good person who was worried about his family's financial problems. Respondent himself had already testified along those lines at the plea colloquy. Moreover, respondent's admission of a course of stealing rebutted many of the factual allegations in the affidavits. For those reasons, and because the sentencing judge had stated that the death sentence would be appropriate even if respondent had no significant prior criminal history, no substantial prejudice resulted from the absence at sentencing of the character evidence offered in the collateral attack.

* * *

The Florida Supreme Court affirmed the denial of relief.

C

Respondent next filed a petition for a writ of habeas corpus in the United

States District Court for the Southern District of Florida. * * *

The District Court disputed none of the state court factual findings concerning trial counsel's assistance and made findings of its own that are consistent with the state court findings. The account of trial counsel's actions and decisions given above reflects the combined findings. On the legal issue of ineffectiveness, the District Court concluded that, although trial counsel made errors in judgment in failing to investigate nonstatutory mitigating evidence further than he did, no prejudice to respondent's sentence resulted from any such error in judgment. * * *

[The Court of Appeals, en banc, reversed the judgment of the District Court and remanded].

* * *

II

* * *

Because of the vital importance of counsel's assistance, this Court has held that, with certain exceptions, a person accused of a federal or state crime has the right to have counsel appointed if retained counsel cannot be obtained. That a person who happens to be a lawyer is present at trial alongside the accused, however, is not enough to satisfy the constitutional command. The Sixth Amendment recognizes the right to the assistance of counsel because it envisions counsel's playing a role that is critical to the ability of the adversarial system to produce just results. An accused is entitled to be assisted by an attorney, whether retained or appointed, who plays the role necessary to ensure that the trial is fair.

For that reason, the Court has recognized that "the right to counsel is the right to the effective assistance of counsel." McMann v. Richardson, 397 U.S. 759, 771, n. 14 (1970). Government violates the right to effective assistance when it interferes in certain ways with the ability of counsel to make independent decisions about how to conduct the defense. See, e.g., Geders v. United States, 425 U.S. 80 (1976) (bar on attorney-client consultation during overnight recess); Herring v. New York, 422 U.S. 853 (1975) (bar on summation at bench trial); Brooks v. Tennessee, 406 U.S. 605, 612-613 (1972) (requirement that defendant be first defense witness); Ferguson v. Georgia, 365 U.S. 570, 593-596 (1961) (bar on direct examination of defendant). Counsel, however, can also deprive a defendant of the right to effective assistance, simply by failing to render "adequate legal assistance," Cuyler v. Sullivan, [446 U.S. 335] at 344. (Actual conflict of interest adversely affecting lawyer's performance renders assistance ineffective).

The Court has not elaborated on the meaning of the constitutional requirement of effective assistance in the latter class of cases—that is, those presenting claims of "actual ineffectiveness." In giving meaning to the requirement, however, we must take its purpose—to ensure a fair trial—as the guide. The benchmark for judging any claim of ineffectiveness must be whether counsel's conduct so undermined the proper functioning of the adversarial process that the trial cannot be relied on as having produced a just result.

The same principle applies to a capital sentencing proceeding such as that provided by Florida law. * * *

III

A convicted defendant's claim that counsel's assistance was so defective as to require reversal of a conviction or death sentence has two components. First, the defendant must show that counsel's performance was deficient. This requires showing that counsel made errors so serious that counsel was

not functioning as the "counsel" guaranteed the defendant by the Sixth Amendment. Second, the defendant must show that the deficient performance prejudiced the defense. This requires showing that counsel's errors were so serious as to deprive the defendant of a fair trial, a trial whose result is reliable. Unless a defendant makes both showings, it cannot be said that the conviction or death sentence resulted from a breakdown in the adversary process that renders the result unreliable.

A

As all the Federal Courts of Appeals have now held, the proper standard for attorney performance is that of reasonably effective assistance. The Court indirectly recognized as much when it stated in McMann v. Richardson, that a guilty plea cannot be attacked as based on inadequate legal advice unless counsel was not "a reasonably competent attorney" and the advice was not "within the range of competence demanded of attorneys in criminal cases." When a convicted defendant complains of the ineffectiveness of counsel's assistance, the defendant must show that counsel's representation fell below an objective standard of reasonableness.

More specific guidelines are not appropriate. * * *

Representation of a criminal defendant entails certain basic duties. Counsel's function is to assist the defendant, and hence counsel owes the client a duty of loyalty, a duty to avoid conflicts of interest. From counsel's function as assistant to the defendant derive the overarching duty to advocate the defendant's cause and the more particular duties to consult with the defendant on important decisions and to keep the defendant informed of important developments in the course of the prosecution. Counsel also has a duty to bring to bear such skill and knowledge as will render the trial a reliable adversarial testing process.

These basic duties neither exhaustively define the obligations of counsel nor form a checklist for judicial evaluation of attorney performance. In any case presenting an ineffectiveness claim, the performance inquiry must be whether counsel's assistance was reasonable considering all the circumstances. Prevailing norms of practice as reflected in American Bar Association standards and the like, e.g., ABA Standards for Criminal Justice 4–1.1 to 4–8.6 (2d ed. 1980) ("The Defense Function"), are guides to determining what is reasonable, but they are only guides. No particular set of detailed rules for counsel's conduct can satisfactorily take account of the variety of circumstances faced by defense counsel or the range of legitimate decisions regarding how best to represent a criminal defendant. Any such set of rules would interfere with the constitutionally protected independence of counsel and restrict the wide latitude counsel must have in making tactical decisions. Indeed, the existence of detailed guidelines for representation could distract counsel from the overriding mission of vigorous advocacy of the defendant's cause. Moreover, the purpose of the effective assistance guarantee of the Sixth Amendment is not to improve the quality of legal representation, although that is a goal of considerable importance to the legal system. The purpose is simply to ensure that criminal defendants receive a fair trial.

Judicial scrutiny of counsel's performance must be highly deferential. It is all too tempting for a defendant to second-guess counsel's assistance after conviction or adverse sentence, and it is all too easy for a court, examining counsel's defense after it has proved unsuccessful, to conclude that a particular act or omission of counsel was unreasonable. A fair assessment of attorney performance requires that every effort be made to eliminate the distorting effects of hindsight, to reconstruct the circumstances of counsel's challenged conduct, and to evaluate the conduct from counsel's perspective at the time. Because of the difficulties inherent in making the evaluation, a court must indulge a strong presumption that counsel's conduct falls within the wide range of reasonable professional assistance; that is, the defendant must overcome the presumption that, under the circumstances, the challenged action "might be considered sound trial strategy." There are countless ways to provide effective assistance in any given case. Even the best criminal defense attorneys would not defend a particular client in the same way.

The availability of intrusive post-trial inquiry into attorney performance or of detailed guidelines for its evaluation would encourage the proliferation of ineffectiveness challenges. * * *

Thus, a court deciding an actual ineffectiveness claim must judge the reasonableness of counsel's challenged conduct on the facts of the particular case, viewed as of the time of counsel's conduct. A convicted defendant making a claim of ineffective assistance must identify the acts or omissions of counsel that are alleged not to have been the result of reasonable professional judgment. The court must then determine whether, in light of all the circumstances, the identified acts or omissions were outside the wide range of professionally competent assistance. In making that determination, the court should keep in mind that counsel's function, as elaborated in prevailing professional norms, is to make the adversarial testing process work in the particular case. At the same time, the court should recognize that counsel is strongly presumed to have rendered adequate assistance and made all significant decisions in the exercise of reasonable professional judgment.

These standards require no special amplification in order to define counsel's duty to investigate, the duty at issue in this case. As the Court of Appeals concluded, strategic choices made after thorough investigation of law and facts relevant to plausible options are virtually unchallengeable; and strategic choices made after less than complete investigation are reasonable precisely to the extent that reasonable professional judgments support the limitations on investigation. * * *

The reasonableness of counsel's actions may be determined or substantially influenced by the defendant's own statements or actions. Counsel's actions are usually based, quite properly, on informed strategic choices made by the defendant and on information supplied by the defendant. In particular, what investigation decisions are reasonable depends critically on such information. For example, when the facts that support a certain potential line of defense are generally known to counsel because of what the defendant has said, the need for further investigation may be considerably diminished or eliminated altogether. And when a defendant has given counsel reason to believe that pursuing certain investigations would be fruitless or even harmful, counsel's failure to pursue those investigations may not later be challenged as unreasonable. * * *

B

An error by counsel, even if professionally unreasonable, does not warrant setting aside the judgment of a criminal proceeding if the error had no effect on the judgment. * * * Accordingly, any deficiencies in counsel's performance must be prejudicial to the defense in order to constitute ineffective assistance under the Constitution.

In certain Sixth Amendment contexts, prejudice is presumed. Actual or constructive denial of the assistance of counsel altogether is legally presumed to result in prejudice. So are various kinds of state interference with counsel's assistance. Prejudice in these circumstances is so likely that case by case inquiry into prejudice is not worth the cost. Moreover, such circumstances involve impairments of the Sixth Amendment right that are easy to identify and, for that reason and because the prosecution is directly responsible, easy for the government to prevent.

One type of actual ineffectiveness claim warrants a similar, though more limited, presumption of prejudice. In Cuyler v. Sullivan, the Court held that prejudice is presumed when counsel is burdened by an actual conflict of interest. In those circumstances, counsel breaches the duty of loyalty, perhaps the most basic of counsel's duties. Moreover, it is difficult to measure the precise effect on the defense of representation corrupted by conflicting interests. Given the obligation of counsel to avoid conflicts of interest and the ability of trial courts to make early inquiry in certain situations likely to give rise to conflicts, see, *e.g.*, Fed.Rule Crim.Proc. 44(c), it is reasonable for the criminal justice system to maintain a fairly rigid rule of presumed prejudice for conflicts of interest. Even so, the rule is not quite the *per se* rule of prejudice that exists for the Sixth Amendment claims mentioned above. Prejudice is presumed only if the defendant demonstrates that counsel "actively represented conflicting interests" and "that an actual conflict of interest adversely affected his lawyer's performance."

Conflict of interest claims aside, actual ineffectiveness claims alleging a deficiency in attorney performance are subject to a general requirement that the defendant affirmatively prove prejudice. The government is not responsible for, and hence not able to prevent, attorney errors that will result in reversal of a conviction or sentence. Attorney errors come in an infinite variety and are as likely to be utterly harmless in a particular case as they are to be prejudicial. * * * Representation is an art, and an act or omission that is unprofessional in one case may be sound or even brilliant in another. * * *

It is not enough for the defendant to show that the errors had some conceivable effect on the outcome of the proceeding. Virtually every act or omission of counsel would meet that test, and not every error that conceivably could have influenced the outcome undermines the reliability of the result of the proceeding. Respondent suggests requiring a showing that the errors "impaired the presentation of the defense." That standard, however, provides no workable principle. * * *

On the other hand, we believe that a defendant need not show that counsel's deficient conduct more likely than not altered the outcome in the case. This outcome-determinative standard has several strengths. It defines the relevant inquiry in a way familiar to courts, though the inquiry, as is inevitable, is anything but precise. The standard also reflects the profound importance of finality in criminal proceedings. Moreover, it comports with the widely used standard for assessing motions for new trial based on newly discovered evidence. Nevertheless, the standard is not quite appropriate.

Even when the specified attorney error results in the omission of certain evidence, the newly discovered evidence standard is not an apt source from which to draw a prejudice standard for ineffectiveness claims. The high standard for newly discovered evidence claims presupposes that all the essential elements of a presumptively accurate and fair proceeding were present in the proceeding whose result is challenged. An ineffective assistance claim asserts the absence of one of the crucial assurances that the result of the proceeding is reliable, so finality concerns are somewhat weaker and the appropriate standard of prejudice should be somewhat lower. The result of a proceeding can be rendered unreliable, and hence the proceeding itself unfair, even if the errors of counsel cannot be shown by a preponderance of the evidence to have determined the outcome.

Accordingly, the appropriate test for prejudice finds its roots in the test for materiality of exculpatory information not disclosed to the defense by the prosecution, United States v. Agurs, and in the test for materiality of testimony made unavailable to the defense by Government deportation of a witness, United States v. Valenzuela-Bernal. The defendant must show that there is a reasonable probability that, but for counsel's unprofessional errors, the result of the proceeding would have been different. A reasonable probability is a probability sufficient to undermine confidence in the outcome.

In making the determination whether the specified errors resulted in the required prejudice, a court should presume, absent challenge to the judgment on grounds of evidentiary insufficiency, that the judge or jury acted according to law. * * *

The governing legal standard plays a critical role in defining the question to be asked in assessing the prejudice from counsel's errors. When a defendant challenges a conviction, the question is whether there is a reasonable probability that, absent the errors, the factfinder would have had a reasonable doubt respecting guilt. When a defendant challenges a death sentence such as the one at issue in this case, the question is whether there is a reasonable probability that, absent the errors, the sentencer—including an appellate court, to the extent it independently reweighs the evidence—would have concluded that the balance of aggravating and mitigating circumstances did not warrant death.

In making this determination, a court hearing an ineffectiveness claim must consider the totality of the evidence before the judge or jury. * * *

IV

* * *

The principles governing ineffectiveness claims should apply in federal collateral proceedings as they do on direct appeal or in motions for a new trial. * * * [T]he presumption that a criminal judgment is final is at its strongest in collateral attacks on that judgment. An ineffectiveness claim, however, as our articulation of the standards that govern decision of such claims makes clear, is an attack on the fundamental fairness of the proceeding whose result is challenged. Since fundamental fairness is the central concern of the writ of habeas corpus, no special standards ought to apply to ineffectiveness claims made in habeas proceedings.

* * *

Although we have discussed the performance component of an ineffectiveness claim prior to the prejudice component, there is no reason for a court deciding an ineffective assistance claim to approach the inquiry in the same order or even to address both components of the inquiry if the defendant makes an insufficient showing on one. * * *

V

* * *

Application of the governing principles is not difficult in this case. The facts as described above make clear that the conduct of respondent's counsel at and before respondent's sentencing proceeding cannot be found unreasonable. They also make clear that, even assuming the challenged conduct of counsel was unreasonable, respondent suffered insufficient prejudice to warrant setting aside his death sentence.

With respect to the performance component, the record shows that respondent's counsel made a strategic choice to argue for the extreme emotional distress mitigating circumstance and to rely as fully as possible on respondent's acceptance of responsibility for his crimes. Although counsel understandably felt hopeless about respondent's prospects, nothing in the record indicates, as one possible reading of the District Court's opinion suggests, that counsel's sense of hopelessness distorted his professional judgment. Counsel's strategy choice was well within the range of professionally reasonable judgments, and the decision not to seek more character or psychological evidence than was already in hand was likewise reasonable.

* * *

With respect to the prejudice component, the lack of merit of respondent's claim is even more stark. The evidence that respondent says his trial counsel should have offered at the sentencing hearing would barely have altered the sentencing profile presented to the sentencing judge. * * *

* * *

Failure to make the required showing of either deficient performance or sufficient prejudice defeats the ineffectiveness claim. Here there is a double failure. More generally, respondent has made no showing that the justice of his sentence was rendered unreliable by a breakdown in the adversary process caused by deficiencies in counsel's assistance. Respondent's sentencing proceeding was not fundamentally unfair.

* * *

JUSTICE BRENNAN, concurring in part and dissenting in part.

* * *

I

* * *

I join the Court's opinion because I believe that the standards it sets out today will both provide helpful guidance to courts considering claims of actual ineffectiveness of counsel and also permit those courts to continue their efforts to achieve progressive development of this area of the law. * * *

With respect to the performance standard, I agree with the Court's conclusion that a "particular set of detailed rules for counsel's conduct" would be inappropriate. * * *

II

Because of their flexibility and the requirement that they be considered in light of the particular circumstances of the case, the standards announced today can and should be applied with concern for the special considerations that must attend review of counsel's performance in a capital sentencing proceeding. In contrast to a case in which a finding of ineffective assistance requires a new trial, a conclusion that counsel was ineffective with respect to only the penalty phase of a capital trial imposes on the state the far lesser burden of reconsideration of the sentence alone. On the other hand, the consequences to the defendant of incompetent assistance at a capital sentencing could not, of course, be greater. * * *

* * *

JUSTICE MARSHALL, dissenting.

* * *

I

The opinion of the Court revolves around two holdings. First, the majority ties the constitutional minima of attorney performance to a simple "standard of reasonableness." Second, the majority holds that only an error of counsel that has sufficient impact on a trial to "undermine confidence in the outcome" is grounds for overturning a conviction. I disagree with both of these rulings.

A

My objection to the performance standard adopted by the Court is that it is so malleable that, in practice, it will either have no grip at all or will yield excessive variation in the manner in which the Sixth Amendment is interpreted and applied by different courts. * * *

The debilitating ambiguity of an "objective standard of reasonableness" in this context is illustrated by the majority's failure to address important issues concerning the quality of representation mandated by the Constitution. It is an unfortunate but undeniable fact that a person of means, by selecting a lawyer and paying him enough to ensure he prepares thoroughly, usually can obtain better representation than that available to an indigent defendant, who must rely on appointed counsel, who, in turn, has limited time and resources to devote to a given case. Is a "reasonably competent attorney" a reasonably competent adequately paid retained lawyer or a reasonably competent appointed attorney? It is also a fact that the quality of representation available to ordinary defendants in different parts of the country varies significantly. Should the standard of performance mandated by the Sixth Amendment vary by locale? The majority offers no clues as to the proper responses to these questions.

The majority defends its refusal to adopt more specific standards primarily on the ground that "[n]o particular set of detailed rules for counsel's conduct can satisfactorily take account of the variety of circumstances faced by defense counsel or the range of legitimate decisions regarding how best to represent a criminal defendant." I agree that counsel must be afforded "wide latitude" when making "tactical decisions" regarding trial strategy, but many aspects of the job of a criminal defense attorney are more amenable to judicial oversight. For example, much of the work involved in preparing for a trial, applying for bail, conferring with one's client, making timely objections to significant, arguably erroneous rulings of the trial judge, and filing a notice of appeal if there are colorable grounds therefor could profitably be made the subject of uniform standards.

* * *

B

I object to the prejudice standard adopted by the Court for two independent reasons. First, it is often very difficult to tell whether a defendant convicted after a trial in which he was ineffectively represented would have fared better if his lawyer had been competent. Seemingly impregnable cases can sometimes be dismantled by good defense counsel. On the basis of a cold record, it may be impossible for a reviewing court confidently to ascertain how the government's evidence and arguments would have stood up against rebuttal and cross-examination by a shrewd, well prepared lawyer. The difficulties of estimating prejudice after the fact are exacerbated by the possibility that evidence of injury to the defendant may be missing from the record precisely because of the incompetence of defense counsel. * * *

Second and more fundamentally, the assumption on which the Court's holding rests is that the only purpose of the constitutional guarantee of effective assistance of counsel is to reduce the chance that innocent persons will be convicted. In my view, the guarantee also functions to ensure that convictions are obtained only through fundamentally fair procedures. * * *

* * *

II

* * *

A

In defining the standard of attorney performance required by the Constitution, the majority appropriately notes that many problems confronting criminal defense attorneys admit of "a range of legitimate" responses. And the majority properly cautions courts, when reviewing a lawyer's selection amongst a set of options, to avoid the hubris of hindsight. The majority goes on, however, to suggest that reviewing courts should "indulge a strong presumption that counsel's conduct" was constitutionally acceptable, and should "apply[ ] a heavy measure of deference to counsel's judgments."

I am not sure what these phrases mean, and I doubt that they will be self-explanatory to lower courts. If they denote nothing more than that a defendant claiming he was denied effective assistance of counsel has the burden of proof, I would agree. But the adjectives "strong" and "heavy" might be read as imposing upon defendants an unusually weighty burden of persuasion. If that is the majority's intent, I must respectfully dissent. The range of acceptable behavior defined by "prevailing professional norms" seems to me sufficiently broad to allow defense counsel the flexibility they need in responding to novel problems of trial strategy. To afford attorneys more latitude, by "strongly presuming" that their behavior will fall within the zone of reasonableness, is covertly to legitimate convictions and sentences obtained on the basis of incompetent conduct by defense counsel.

* * *

UNITED STATES v. CRONIC

Supreme Court of the United States, 1984.
466 U.S. 648.

JUSTICE STEVENS delivered the opinion of the Court.

Respondent and two associates were indicted on mail fraud charges involving the transfer of over $9,400,000 in checks between banks in Tampa, Florida, and Norman, Oklahoma, during a four-month period in 1975. Shortly before the scheduled trial date, respondent's retained counsel withdrew. The court appointed a young lawyer with a real estate practice to represent respondent, but allowed him only 25 days for pretrial preparation, even though it had taken the Government over four and one-half years to investigate the case and it had reviewed thousands of documents during that investigation. The two codefendants agreed to testify for the Government; respondent was convicted on 11 of the 13 counts in the indictment and received a 25-year sentence.

The Court of Appeals reversed the conviction because it concluded that respondent did not "have the Assistance of Counsel for his defence" that is guaranteed by the Sixth Amendment to the Constitution. This conclusion was not supported by a determination that respondent's trial counsel had made any specified errors, that his actual performance had prejudiced the defense, or that he failed to exercise "the skill, judgment, and diligence of a reasonably competent defense attorney"; instead the conclusion rested on the premise that no such showing is necessary "when circumstances hamper a given lawyer's preparation of a defendant's case." The question presented by the Government's petition for certiorari is whether the Court of Appeals has correctly interpreted the Sixth Amendment.

I

The indictment alleged a "check kiting" scheme. At the direction of respondent, his codefendant Cummings opened a bank account in the name of Skyproof Manufacturing, Inc. (Skyproof), at a bank in Tampa, Florida, and codefendant Merritt opened two accounts, one in his own name and one in the name of Skyproof, at banks in Norman, Oklahoma. Knowing that there were insufficient funds in either account, the defendants allegedly drew a series of checks and wire transfers on the Tampa account aggregating $4,841,073.95, all of which were deposited in Skyproof's Norman bank account during the period between June 23, 1975, and October 16, 1975; during approximately the same period they drew checks on Skyproof's Norman account for deposits in Tampa aggregating $4,600,881.39. The process of clearing the checks involved the use of the mails. By "kiting" insufficient funds checks between the banks in those two cities, defendants allegedly created false or inflated balances in the accounts. After outlining the overall scheme, Count I of the indictment alleged the mailing of two checks each for less than $1,000 early in May. Each of the additional 12 counts realleged the allegations in Count I except its reference to the two specific checks, and then added an allegation identifying other checks issued and mailed at later dates.

At trial the Government proved that Skyproof's checks were issued and deposited at the times and places, and in the amounts, described in the indictment. Having made plea bargains with defendants Cummings and Merritt, who had actually handled the issuance and delivery of the relevant written instruments, the Government proved through their testimony that respondent had conceived and directed the entire scheme, and that he had deliberately concealed his connection with Skyproof because of prior financial and tax problems.

After the District Court ruled that a prior conviction could be used to impeach his testimony, respondent decided not to testify. Counsel put on no defense. By cross-examination of Government witnesses, however, he established that Skyproof was not merely a sham, but actually was an operating company with a significant cash flow, though its revenues were not sufficient to justify as large a "float" as the record disclosed. Cross-examination also established the absence of written evidence that respondent had any control over Skyproof, or personally participated in the withdrawals or deposits.

The four-day jury trial ended on July 17, 1980, and respondent was sentenced on August 28, 1980. * * *

The Court of Appeals reversed the conviction because it inferred that respondent's constitutional right to the effective assistance of counsel had been violated. That inference was based on its use of five criteria: "(1) [T]he time afforded for investigation and preparation; (2) the experience of counsel; (3) the gravity of the charge; (4) the complexity of possible defenses; and (5) the accessibility of witnesses to counsel." Under the test employed by the Court of Appeals, reversal is required even if the lawyer's actual performance was flawless. By utilizing this inferential approach, the Court of Appeals erred.

II

* * *

* * * The right to the effective assistance of counsel is * * * the right of the accused to require the prosecution's case to survive the crucible of meaningful adversarial testing. When a true adversarial criminal trial has been conducted—even if defense counsel may have made demonstrable errors—the kind of testing envisioned by the Sixth Amendment has occurred.[a] But if the process loses its character as a confrontation between adversaries, the constitutional guarantee is violated.[b] * * *

III

While the Court of Appeals purported to apply a standard of reasonable competence, it did not indicate that there had been an actual breakdown of the adversarial process during the trial of this case. Instead it concluded that the circumstances surrounding the representation of respondent mandated an inference that counsel was unable to discharge his duties.

[B]ecause we presume that the lawyer is competent to provide the guiding hand that the defendant needs, the burden rests on the accused to demonstrate a constitutional violation. There are, however, circumstances that are so likely to prejudice the accused that the cost of litigating their effect in a particular case is unjustified.

Most obvious, of course, is the complete denial of counsel. The presumption that counsel's assistance is essential requires us to conclude that a trial is unfair if the accused is denied counsel at a critical stage of his trial. Similarly, if counsel entirely fails to subject the prosecution's case to meaningful adversarial testing, then there has been a denial of Sixth Amendment rights that makes the adversary process itself presumptively unreliable. * * *

Circumstances of that magnitude may be present on some occasions when although counsel is available to assist the accused during trial, the likelihood that any lawyer, even a fully competent one, could provide effective assistance is so small that a presumption of prejudice is appropriate without inquiry into the actual conduct of the trial. Powell v. Alabama, 287 U.S. 45 (1932), [set forth in Chapter Five] was such a case.

* * *

But every refusal to postpone a criminal trial will not give rise to such a presumption. * * *

The Court of Appeals did not find that respondent was denied the presence of counsel at a critical stage of the prosecution. Nor did it find, based on the actual conduct of the trial, that there was a breakdown in the adversarial process that would justify a presumption that respondent's conviction was insufficiently reliable to satisfy the Constitution. The dispositive question in this

a. Of course, the Sixth Amendment does not require that counsel do what is impossible or unethical. If there is no *bona fide* defense to the charge, counsel cannot create one and may disserve the interests of his client by attempting a useless charade. See Nickols v. Gagnon, 454 F.2d 467, 472 (CA7 1971), cert. denied, 408 U.S. 925 (1972). At the same time, even when no theory of defense is available, if the decision to stand trial has been made, counsel must hold the prosecution to its heavy burden of proof beyond reasonable doubt. And, of course, even when there is a *bona fide* defense, counsel may still advise his client to plead guilty if that advice falls within the range of reasonable competence under the circumstances.

b. The Court of Appeals focused on counsel's overall representation of respondent, as opposed to any specific error or omission counsel may have made. Of course, the type of breakdown in the adversarial process that implicates the Sixth Amendment is not limited to counsel's performance as a whole—specific errors and omissions may be the focus of a claim of ineffective assistance as well. See Strickland v. Washington. Since this type of claim was not passed upon by the Court of Appeals, we do not consider it here.

case therefore is whether the circumstances surrounding respondent's representation—and in particular the five criteria identified by the Court of Appeals—justified such a presumption.

IV

The five factors listed in the Court of Appeals' opinion are relevant to an evaluation of a lawyer's effectiveness in a particular case, but neither separately nor in combination do they provide a basis for concluding that competent counsel was not able to provide this respondent with the guiding hand that the Constitution guarantees.

Respondent places special stress on the disparity between the duration of the Government's investigation and the period the District Court allowed to newly appointed counsel for trial preparation. The lawyer was appointed to represent respondent on June 12, 1980, and on June 19, filed a written motion for a continuance of the trial that was then scheduled to begin on June 30. Although counsel contended that he needed at least 30 days for preparation, the District Court reset the trial for July 14—thus allowing 25 additional days for preparation.

Neither the period of time that the Government spent investigating the case, nor the number of documents that its agents reviewed during that investigation, is necessarily relevant to the question whether a competent lawyer could prepare to defend the case in 25 days. The Government's task of finding and assembling admissible evidence that will carry its burden of proving guilt beyond a reasonable doubt is entirely different from the defendant's task in preparing to deny or rebut a criminal charge. Of course, in some cases the rebuttal may be equally burdensome and time consuming, but there is no necessary correlation between the two. In this case, the time devoted by the Government to the assembly, organization, and summarization of the thousands of written records evidencing the two streams of checks flowing between the banks in Florida and Oklahoma unquestionably simplified the work of defense counsel in identifying and understanding the basic character of the defendants' scheme. When a series of repetitious transactions fit into a single mold, the number of written exhibits that are needed to define the pattern may be unrelated to the time that is needed to understand it.

The significance of counsel's preparation time is further reduced by the nature of the charges against respondent. Most of the Government's case consisted merely of establishing the transactions between the two banks. A competent attorney would have no reason to question the authenticity, accuracy or relevance of this evidence—there could be no dispute that these transactions actually occurred. As respondent appears to recognize, the only *bona fide* jury issue open to competent defense counsel on these facts was whether respondent acted with intent to defraud. When there is no reason to dispute the underlying historical facts, the period of 25 days to consider the question whether those facts justify an inference of criminal intent is not so short that it even arguably justifies a presumption that no lawyer could provide the respondent with the effective assistance of counsel required by the Constitution.

That conclusion is not undermined by the fact that respondent's lawyer was young, that his principal practice was in real estate, or that this was his first jury trial. Every experienced criminal defense attorney once tried his first criminal case. Moreover, a lawyer's experience with real estate transactions might be more useful in preparing to try a criminal case involving financial transactions than would prior experience in handling, for example, armed robbery prosecutions. The character of a particular lawyer's experience may shed light in an evaluation of his actual performance, but it does not justify a presumption of ineffectiveness in the absence of such an evaluation.[c]

The three other criteria—the gravity of the charge, the complexity of the case, and the accessibility of witnesses—are all matters that may affect what a reasonably competent attorney could be expected to have done under the circumstances, but none identifies circumstances that in themselves make it unlikely that respondent received the effective assistance of counsel.

* * *

JUSTICE MARSHALL concurs in the judgment.

Note

At last the Supreme Court has set forth a test for assessing adequacy of counsel. It appears that the Court adopted a middle ground between presuming that lawyer errors require reversal of convictions (absent some overwhelming showing of harmlessness), which would have called into question many convictions and placed a heavy burden on the government to support convictions tainted in any way by lawyer mistakes, and requiring defendants to show with some degree of certainty that they would have received a more favorable judgment but for mistakes by counsel, which would have resulted in defendants' bearing an exceptionally difficult burden. Do you find that the Court has struck a fair balance? Is Justice Marshall correct in asserting that the Court should have provided more specific guidance concerning what is expected of counsel?

In thinking about the *Cronic* case, recall that counsel asked for 30 days to prepare because 25 days was not sufficient time. If counsel in a future case were to ask for a continuance to seek a specific witness or to examine specific documents and the trial judge were to deny the request, would the claim of ineffectiveness be stronger than in *Cronic*? If counsel in a future case were able to specifically identify matters that could not be explored prior to a scheduled trial date despite the exercise of reasonable diligence, and if the trial judge were to refuse a motion for a delay in the trial, would the claim of ineffectiveness be stronger than in *Cronic*? Once counsel makes a claim that additional time or effort is needed to prepare adequately for trial and supports the claim with a specific statement (to the extent that the statement would not reveal privileged material), should the trial judge be compelled to at least make an inquiry into the bona fides of the claim? Note that the Court in *Cronic* did not hold that Cronic had received effective assistance of counsel. Rather, it rejected the per se rule of reversal applied by the lower court. On remand in *Cronic,* the court of appeals reviewed counsel's actual performance and held that it was ineffective and that Cronic was prejudiced. See United States v. Cronic, 839 F.2d 1401 (10th Cir.1988). The court found that defense counsel ignored the issues of the defendant's intent and good faith, which were really the only issues of dispute in the case. Cronic's attorney testified at the hearing on ineffectiveness that the defense he used was one seeking to "cloud the issues." The court of appeals held that "this cannot be a satisfactory explanation under *Strickland* or any other authority for a selection of a defense." The court also noted that defense counsel failed to object to evidence due to a misunderstanding of the statute under which Cronic was tried.

c. We consider in this case only the commands of the Constitution. We do not pass on the wisdom or propriety of appointing inexperienced counsel in a case such as this. It is entirely possible that many courts should exercise their supervisory powers to take greater precautions to ensure that counsel in serious criminal cases are qualified.

In Cuyler v. Sullivan, 446 U.S. 335 (1980), the Court said that "[a] proper respect for the Sixth Amendment disarms petitioner's [the State's] contention that defendants who retain their own lawyers are entitled to less protection than defendants for whom the State appoints counsel. * * * Since the State's conduct of a criminal trial itself implicates the State in the defendant's conviction, we see no basis for drawing a distinction between retained and appointed counsel that would deny equal justice to defendants who must choose their own lawyers."

Justice Brennan wrote for the majority in Evitts v. Lucey, 469 U.S. 387 (1985), which holds that the Fourteenth Amendment's due process clause guarantees criminal defendants in state courts the effective assistance of counsel on their first appeal as of right. Lucey had been convicted of trafficking in drugs. He appealed, but his counsel failed to file a "statement of appeal," as required by state law, along with the appellate brief. For this reason, the state appellate courts refused to review the conviction. Justice Brennan reasoned that cases holding that a defendant has a right to counsel on a first appeal as of right and that the right to counsel includes such things as a right to a necessary transcript for an indigent dispositively established that a defendant has a right to effective counsel on a first appeal as of right. He noted that an ineffective attorney may be sanctioned by the state or a state may establish a postconviction substitute for an appeal that a defendant lost as a result of ineffective assistance of counsel. But, he concluded that "[a] State may not extinguish this right [of appeal] because another right of the appellant—the right to effective assistance of counsel—has been violated." Although Kentucky argued that it should be permitted to deny appeals for noncompliance with procedural rules, since appeals need not be granted to defendants, the Court reasoned that "when a State opts to act in a field where its action has significant discretionary elements, it must nonetheless act in accord with the dictates of the Constitution—and, in particular, in accord with the Due Process Clause." The Court affirmed lower court rulings that a conditional writ of habeas corpus should issue, requiring the state to release the defendant unless it either reinstated his appeal or granted him a new trial. Justice Rehnquist, joined by Chief Justice Burger, dissented. The Chief Justice added two short dissenting paragraphs of his own.

The Court in Anders v. California, 386 U.S. 738 (1967), determined how appointed counsel should proceed if she believes that an appeal lacks merit. The Court held that if, after a "conscientious examination" of the case, counsel finds an appeal to be "wholly frivolous," counsel should advise the court and request permission to withdraw. However, that request must be accompanied by a brief (now called an "*Anders* brief") "referring to anything in the record that might arguably support the appeal." If the court thereafter finds that there are non-frivolous arguments to be made, counsel must be appointed to bring the appeal. In McCoy v. Court of Appeals of Wisconsin, 486 U.S. 429 (1988), the Court upheld a state rule which required an *Anders* brief to include a discussion of why the appeal lacks merit. The Court noted that the point of an *Anders* brief is to inform the court that the defendant's right to counsel has been satisfied, and a requirement of stated reasons would further that goal. The Court rejected the argument that it would be unethical for counsel to explain why she thought the appeal was frivolous. It stated that "if an attorney can advise the court of his or her conclusion that an appeal is frivolous without impairment of the client's fundamental rights, it must follow that no constitutional deprivation occurs when the attorney explains the basis for that conclusion."

In Penson v. Ohio, 488 U.S. 75 (1988), the Court held that no showing of prejudice is required by a defendant whose counsel fails to file an *Anders* brief.

The Court concluded that judicial scrutiny of the record is not an adequate substitute for counsel. It noted that "the denial of counsel in this case left petitioner completely without representation during the appellate court's actual decisional process."

It is important to note that the right to effective assistance of counsel on appeal, of which *Anders* is a part, extends only to the first appeal of right. It is not applicable to any attacks on the judgment thereafter. See Pennsylvania v. Finley, 481 U.S. 551 (1987) (no right to *Anders* brief in postconviction proceedings, therefore no claim of ineffective assistance of counsel is cognizable); Wainwright v. Torna, 455 U.S. 586 (1982) (no right to counsel at certiorari stage, therefore no claim of ineffective assistance can be asserted, even though defendant had retained counsel); Murray v. Giarratano, 492 U.S. 1 (1989) (no right to effective assistance of counsel in collateral attack of conviction of capital offense).

In Coleman v. Thompson, 111 S.Ct. 2546 (1991), counsel for a state prisoner failed to file a timely notice of appeal from the lower court's denial of a state habeas petition. The habeas petition claimed that counsel at Coleman's trial was constitutionally ineffective. State law required that claims of ineffectiveness of trial counsel be brought on collateral attack rather than on appeal. Coleman brought a collateral attack on this issue, and his ineffectiveness claim was rejected by the state habeas trial court. His appeal from that decision was dismissed because no notice of appeal had been timely filed. Coleman claimed that his counsel's failure to file a timely appeal from the denial of state habeas constituted another act of ineffective assistance of counsel. Justice O'Connor, writing for the Court, held that Coleman had no right to counsel on appeal from a denial of a state habeas petition, citing Pennsylvania v. Finley, and that in the absence of a right to counsel, Coleman had no right to claim constitutionally ineffective assistance of counsel.

Coleman argued that the appeal from the state habeas proceeding was tantamount to a first appeal of right, and thus was controlled by Evitts v. Lucey, because of the state law mandate that claims of ineffective assistance of trial counsel could only be asserted on habeas. Justice O'Connor responded that, presuming a state collateral proceeding could be treated as a first appeal of right in those cases where collateral review is the first place that a challenge can be presented, Coleman had that "appeal" of right when he petitioned the state trial court and that court denied habeas relief. His appeal from the state court's denial of habeas was therefore not a first appeal of right under *Evitts.*

Justice Blackmun, joined by Justices Marshall and Stevens, dissented. The dissenters argued that "fundamental fairness dictates that the State, having removed certain claims from the process of direct review, bear the burden of ineffective assistance of counsel in the proceeding to which the claim has been removed."

Dispute has arisen concerning application of the prejudice prong of *Strickland* to claims of ineffective assistance of counsel on appeal. For example, in Lozada v. Deeds, 111 S.Ct. 860 (1991), the defendant alleged that his counsel failed to inform him of his right to appeal or of the procedures and time limitations for an appeal, and that counsel had misled him into thinking that his case had been forwarded to the public defender's office. The district court dismissed Lozada's habeas corpus petition on the ground that Lozada had not indicated what issues he would have raised on appeal and had not demonstrated that the appeal might have succeeded. Both the district court and the court of appeals denied a certificate of probable cause to appeal the denial of habeas relief under 28 U.S.C. § 2253. The Supreme

Court in a per curiam opinion held that the certificate of probable cause should have been granted. The standard for granting such a certificate is that a court "could resolve the issues" in petitioner's favor. The Court held that Lozada had met that standard, since the issue of prejudice "could be resolved in a different manner than the one followed by the District Court." The Court noted that "at least two Courts of Appeals have presumed prejudice in this situation." See Abels v. Kaiser, 913 F.2d 821 (10th Cir.1990); Estes v. United States, 883 F.2d 645 (8th Cir.1989). Why should prejudice be presumed if the petitioner's claims on appeal would have had no merit? If the habeas court actually reviews the merits of petitioner's claims to determine prejudice under *Strickland,* is that tantamount to the appeal that never occurred due to counsel's ineffectiveness? See McCrae v. Blackburn, 793 F.2d 684 (5th Cir.1986) (no prejudice under *Evitts* where habeas court rejects on the merits the arguments that petitioner would have presented on appeal). See also Matire v. Wainwright, 811 F.2d 1430 (11th Cir.1987) (court notes an open question of whether prejudice should be determined by the likelihood of success on appeal, or by the likelihood of acquittal in an eventual retrial).

In Darden v. Wainwright, 477 U.S. 168 (1986), the Court held that a defendant convicted of murder and sentenced to death failed to satisfy the first prong of *Strickland* and did not demonstrate that his trial lawyers' performance fell below an objective standard of reasonableness. At the sentencing hearing, defense counsel failed to introduce any evidence in mitigation and relied solely on a simple plea for mercy from Darden himself. The Court, emphasizing the deference to defense counsel required by *Strickland,* noted several reasons why counsel may have made this strategic decision. If Darden's non-violence were introduced in mitigation, it would have opened the door to Darden's prior convictions. Any evidence of psychological impairment could have been rebutted by a state psychiatric report which opined that Darden was a sociopath. Evidence that he was a family man could have been rebutted by his extramarital affairs. The Court concluded that Darden had failed to "overcome the presumption that, under the circumstances, the challenged action might be considered sound trial strategy." See also Stewart v. Dugger, 847 F.2d 1486 (11th Cir.1988) (counsel's decision to reargue innocence at capital sentencing hearing, rather than to present mitigating evidence, held reasonable strategy under *Strickland:* "Trial counsel cannot be faulted for attempting to make the best of a bad situation.").

The Court finally found that a lawyer had acted ineffectively in Kimmelman v. Morrison, 477 U.S. 365 (1986). Justice Brennan's opinion for the Court noted that a defendant's trial counsel "failed to file a timely suppression motion, not due to strategic considerations, but because, until the day of trial, he was unaware of the search and of the State's intention to introduce the ... evidence," "because he had conducted no pretrial discovery." Counsel mistakenly believed that the State was required to turn over all inculpatory evidence to the defense. Although the Court indicated that generally a reviewing court should assess counsel's overall performance in order to determine whether identified acts or omissions overcome the presumption that reasonable professional assistance was provided, it found that the total failure to conduct pretrial discovery was sufficient to justify the determination in this case. Justice Brennan noted that "the justifications Morrison's attorney offered for his omission betray a startling ignorance of the law—or a weak attempt to shift blame for inadequate preparation," and that "such a complete lack of pretrial preparation puts at risk both the defendant's right to meet the case of the prosecution and the reliability of the adversarial testing process." The Court remanded for an examination of possible prejudice. It noted that if the error alleged is counsel's failure to move to suppress evidence, the defendant must show both a reasonable probability of a successful suppression motion and a reasonable probability that without the suppressed evidence, the fact finder would have had a reasonable doubt as to guilt. Justice Powell, joined by Chief Justice Burger and Justice Rehnquist, concurred in the judgment. He noted that a strong argument, neither made by the parties nor discussed by the lower courts, could be made that the admission of illegally seized but reliable evidence could not constitute prejudice.

In Hill v. Lockhart, 474 U.S. 52 (1985), the Court held that the *Strickland* standards apply to the plea process. Hill's counsel told him that if he accepted a plea bargain, he would be eligible for parole after serving one-third of his sentence. A two-year old Arkansas statute provided, however, that individuals with prior convictions such as Hill were not eligible for parole until they served one-half of their sentence. This meant Hill would have to serve nine years, rather than six, before parole eligibility. The Supreme Court refused to decide whether counsel failed the performance prong of *Strickland,* since it found that Hill had not shown that he had been prejudiced. The Court stated that to prove prejudice in the guilty plea context, the defendant must show that "but for counsel's errors, he would not have pleaded guilty and would have insisted on going to trial." In a subsequent habeas petition, Hill prevailed. See Hill v. Lockhart, 877 F.2d 698 (8th Cir.1989). The court of appeals found that Hill's counsel was clearly ineffective, due to his failure "to ascertain, through minimal research, the applicable statute governing parole eligibility for second offenders," and that parole eligibility "is normally one of the most important factors to a criminal client." The court concluded that but for the misadvice, Hill would have proceeded to trial. Hill had previously rejected a deal in which he would have been eligible for parole in nine years; and the court credited his testimony that if he had been correctly informed by counsel, he would have "rolled the dice" and gone to trial because he believed that he would have "just as good a chance on a life sentence imposed at trial of getting out after nine years." The court stated that "to succeed under *Strickland,* Hill need not show prejudice in the sense that he probably would have been acquitted or given a shorter sentence at trial." Compare Czere v. Butler, 833 F.2d 59 (5th Cir.1987), where the court found that the defendant had not shown prejudice from counsel's advice that he would be eligible for parole in forty years, when in fact he would not be eligible for eighty years as provided by statute. The court found that in accepting the plea, Czere was concerned more about avoiding the electric chair than he was about parole, and that the difference between parole eligibility in eighty rather than forty years could not have affected Czere's decision.

Hill is a case of ineffectiveness where counsel advised the defendant to accept a plea on erroneous information. The opposite situation can also implicate *Strickland.* See Toro v. Fairman, 940 F.2d 1065 (7th Cir.1991), where counsel was found ineffective for advising the defendant to reject a plea. The court noted that the defendant had no defense to the charges, and that he received a much longer sentence after being tried and found guilty. According to the court, counsel's judgment was clouded by his emotional involvement in the case. Interestingly, though, the court found no prejudice from this misadvice, since the defendant did not prove that but for counsel's error, he would have accepted the plea and *not* gone to trial. The defendant's conclusory statements on this point were held insufficient. But if the defendant had no case, as the court admits, why would he have gone to trial only to obtain a more severe sentence?

In *Strickland,* the Court held that lower courts could proceed directly to the prejudice prong, without having to evaluate defense counsel's performance. Many lower courts have done so. See, e.g., United States ex. rel. Cross v. DeRobertis, 811 F.2d 1008 (7th Cir.1987) (performance issue requires "a particularly subtle assessment," so court proceeds directly to prejudice prong). Is it important for courts to provide guidance on effectiveness standards? If so, is it acceptable for a court to proceed directly to the prejudice prong of *Strickland?*

Strickland indicated that the performance prong will be satisfied if, using appropriate deference, counsel's actions fall within the realm of sound trial strategy. Consider the following cases. Has counsel been ineffective, or has counsel merely used an unsuccessful strategy?

1. Martin was charged with sexual abuse of his two stepdaughters. He denied the charges, and claimed that he had a witness who would testify that the children had been encouraged to falsify their charges. Martin's counsel, shortly before trial, filed a motion for a continuance, alleging that he was unprepared to try the case. This motion was denied. Counsel decided to "rely on his motion" and therefore he did not put on any proof, and did not cross-examine or participate in the trial, other than to make an opening statement to the jury. This opening statement indicated that the defense was relying on its motion for continuance, and that the jury should not think "that my lack of participation is, uh, that I'm a dummy over here, and I don't know what's going on." The court of appeals stated that "even deliberate trial tactics may constitute ineffective assistance of counsel if they fall outside the wide range of professionally competent assistance." The court asserted that by calling the defendant and his witness to testify, the attorney could have presented a strong defense "without compromising" the motion for continuance. The court concluded that "the decision of Martin's attorney not to participate cannot be considered sound trial strategy," and that the total failure of counsel to put on a defense was per se prejudicial under *Cronic.* Is the court second-guessing defense counsel? Is that permissible after *Strickland?* See also United States v. Wolf, 787 F.2d 1094 (7th Cir.1986), where the court criticized defense counsel's "tactic of no objections" and held it ineffective:

> It is true that lawyers will frequently not object to objectionable questions, believing either that the witness will give an answer helpful to the defense (or at least not harmful to it) or that too-frequent objecting will irritate the jury or make it think the defendant is trying to hide the truth. But to have a *policy* of never objecting to improper questions is forensic suicide. It shifts the main responsibility for the defense from defense counsel to the judge. It would make no sense in a case like this where the prosecutor was intent on bringing in extraneous and at times unfounded charges in order to blacken the defendant's character.

Compare Warner v. Ford, 752 F.2d 622 (11th Cir.1985) (strategy of silence not ineffective in multi-defendant trial, where other defendants were defending aggressively and evidence was overwhelming; under these circumstances, it was reasonable to keep a "low profile"). Moore v. Deputy Commissioners, 946 F.2d 236 (3d Cir.1991) (proper strategy to fail to object to the introduction of inadmissible inculpatory evidence; defense counsel decided that "the less said about it the better").

2. Chambers was tried for the murder of Oestricker. Chambers was a small man and his victim was large. The prosecution called Ieppert, who testified that Chambers and Oestricker had a fight in a bar, that they decided to take the argument outside, and that Ieppert thereupon moved from his chair to the door of the bar to watch the fight, taking a few seconds to do so. At that point he saw Chambers point a gun at Oestricker and shoot him in the chest. After that, Chambers pistol-whipped his victim and said "take that, tough guy" and ran away. Another witness, Jones, had been outside the bar trying to start his car. He

testified that Chambers came out of the bar first and waited for Oestricker. Then Oestricker hit Chambers in the face and knocked him to the ground. Chambers then got up, pulled a gun, shot Oestricker, pistol-whipped him, said "take that, tough guy," yelled into the bar "Do any of you want any of this?" and ran to a parked car that had its engine running; the car sped quickly away. Chambers' attorney requested that a self-defense instruction be submitted to the jury. The trial court refused, and Chambers was found guilty of capital murder and sentenced to death. On appeal, the state supreme court reversed the conviction, holding that there was sufficient evidence to justify a self-defense instruction; the court pointed specifically to Jones' testimony that the victim hit Chambers first, and that the victim was a foot taller and 100 pounds heavier than the defendant. On re-trial, Chambers had newly appointed counsel. He did not call Jones to testify, and neither did the state. Other than that, the second trial proceeded much as the first. Chambers' defense counsel proceeded on a self-defense theory, and his questions on cross-examination were focused solely on the issue of self-defense. He pointed out that the victim was a foot taller and 100 pounds heavier than Chambers. As in the first trial, the trial court refused to give a self-defense instruction, and Chambers was found guilty of capital murder. Chambers' attorney later stated at the ineffectiveness hearing that, after reading the transcript of the first trial, he decided not to call Jones because much of Jones' testimony was "damaging" and because Jones "lacked credibility," although he admitted that he had never spoken to Jones. The court in Chambers v. Armontrout, 907 F.2d 825 (8th Cir.1990) (en banc) held that the failure to call Jones at the second trial deprived Chambers of effective assistance of counsel. The dissenters argued that "*Strickland* is not violated when a counsel, in the exercise of professional judgment, decides not to produce mitigating evidence that could reasonably be considered more damaging than helpful." With whom do you agree? The majority's decision in *Chambers* may give you the impression that courts are receptive to claims that counsel acted ineffectively. This is not at all the case. Most courts appear to bend over backwards to justify defense counsel's actions as proper strategy. See, e.g., Stringer v. Jackson, 862 F.2d 1108 (5th Cir.1988) (failure to present mitigating evidence is not ineffective); People v. Russell, 71 N.Y.2d 1016, 530 N.Y.S.2d 101, 525 N.E.2d 747 (1988) (failure to move to suppress evidence is a strategic decision); Brown v. Dixon, 891 F.2d 490 (4th Cir.1989) (not ineffective to argue inconsistent defenses); Rogers–Bey v. Lane, 896 F.2d 279 (7th Cir.1990) (proper strategy to inculpate the defendant in order to impeach a prosecution witness); United States v. Guerrero, 938 F.2d 725 (7th Cir.1991) (in light of overwhelming evidence of the defendant's involvement with narcotics, it was not ineffective to argue that the defendant was involved in a drug conspiracy different from that which was charged).

3. Willis was charged with murdering his son. At trial, the victim's wife testified that Willis came to his son's home to get a deer rifle. She then saw Willis shoot his son with a handgun. Willis denied this claim. No handgun was ever found or linked with the killing. No autopsy was ever performed. No bullet or bullet fragments were ever found. The medical examiner was unable to identify the caliber or type of gun used. Upon his arrest, Willis had stated with respect to his son "it was either him or me," and that statement was introduced at trial. The prosecution also introduced a trace metal test which showed that Willis had fired a gun on the day of his son's death. Willis' first trial ended in a deadlocked jury. He was convicted at the second trial. He claimed ineffective assistance because counsel failed to have an autopsy performed on the victim and to obtain ballistics

evidence therefrom. The court held that the failure to obtain an autopsy was a "reasonable tactical decision." It explained as follows:

> Appellant's defense was built entirely on the theory that the state had failed to prove appellant guilty beyond a reasonable doubt. Appellant's counsel decided that it was better for there to be uncertainty concerning the weapon used than to chance that an autopsy would reveal that a handgun was the murder weapon, thereby confirming the daughter-in-law's testimony. In their arguments to the jury, his defense attorneys played on this uncertainty regarding the murder weapon to establish reasonable doubt in the minds of the jurors. Appellant's counsel also thought that an attempt to exhume the body and perform an autopsy would have been opposed by appellant's ex-wife and daughters, who were also the victim's mother and sisters. Counsel feared that pursuit of an exhumation would have prompted them to reveal to the prosecution very damaging evidence regarding the appellant.

Are you convinced? Consider that defense counsel's explanation for making a certain decision is given at a hearing long after the trial, and that counsel has been charged at that point with ineffectiveness. Is there a risk that counsel will "color" his or her testimony under these circumstances?

Cases have arisen where counsel cannot even come up with a reason for acting (or not acting) as they did at trial. In these cases, courts have not been hesitant to find ineffectiveness. See, e.g., Jones v. Thigpen, 788 F.2d 1101 (5th Cir.1986) (no explanation for failure to argue mental retardation in mitigation at a capital sentencing hearing; defendant had an I.Q. of 41); Harding v. Davis, 878 F.2d 1341 (11th Cir.1989) (failure to object to judge's entry of directed verdict is ineffective and per se prejudicial); Burley v. Cabana, 818 F.2d 414 (5th Cir.1987) (failure to inform trial court of sentencing alternatives for a defendant who was a minor); Nixon v. Newsome, 888 F.2d 112 (11th Cir.1989) (failure to introduce prior inconsistent statement of star prosecution witness, made at another trial, that someone else did the shooting for which defendant was charged, held ineffective and prejudicial, given the lack of overwhelming evidence).

According to *Strickland,* pre-trial investigation is one component of effective assistance. Courts have found that a complete failure to investigate cannot be considered strategic, since a counsel who has done no investigation does not have enough information with which to make a strategic decision. See United States v. Gray, 878 F.2d 702 (3d Cir.1989) (counsel fails to contact 25 neutral eyewitnesses identified by the defendant, in a case in which the jury must make a credibility determination between the defendant and the complainant).

However, as *Strickland* also indicates, the duty to investigate depends critically on information supplied by the defendant. Consider Johnson v. Cabana, 805 F.2d 579 (5th Cir.1986). Johnson told his attorney that he had been convicted of several crimes, including aggravated assault and armed robbery. At the trial Johnson testified in his own defense and admitted these convictions on direct examination. After trial, Johnson's attorney obtained Johnson's "rap sheet" and discovered that it did not reveal an armed robbery conviction. The attorney learned that Johnson was under the misimpression that he had pled guilty to armed robbery, when in fact he had acquiesced in the revocation of his parole on his assault conviction following his arrest for armed robbery. Johnson petitioned for a writ of habeas corpus alleging that his counsel was ineffective because of his failure to examine Johnson's "rap sheet" before trial. He argued that a "rap sheet" was easy for counsel to obtain, and that he should not have relied on Johnson's description of his criminal record. The court rejected this argument, reasoning as follows:

> Johnson urges us to adopt a rule that would require counsel to always investigate all information that is readily available to him, including a defendant's criminal record. We decline to impose such an inflexible requirement * * *. [I]f counsel receives information from his client, the accuracy of which counsel has no reason to doubt, it will ordinarily be unnecessary for counsel to verify the information from an alternate source even if the information from that source is readily available. * * * [C]ounsel could reasonably infer that Johnson was familiar enough with criminal proceedings to know what charges he had been convicted of.

Judge Wisdom dissented, arguing that the attorney had a duty to investigate the defendant's prior convictions:

> I would take judicial knowledge of the fact that laymen as a rule and particularly black defendants in the Deep South have a very limited understanding of criminal legal processes. A reasonably effective defense of a black accused in this part of the country imposes on the defense attorney the duty of obtaining and examining the records—the "rap sheet."

With whom do you agree? Would the court have reached the same result if there were a conviction on the "rap sheet" that Johnson had not told his counsel about, and Johnson was impeached with that conviction at trial?

Concerning the prejudice prong of *Strickland,* it is obvious that the defendant is more likely to prove prejudice if the prosecution's evidence is weak. For example, in Atkins v. Attorney General of Alabama, 932 F.2d 1430 (11th Cir.1991), counsel failed to object to the introduction of a fingerprint card offered to make a comparison between Atkins' fingerprints and those found at the scene of the crime. The card included a printed notation of a prior arrest that would not have been admissible. The court found that the failure to object constituted ineffectiveness, and that without the error there was a reasonable probability that the outcome of the trial would have been different. Atkins' fingerprints had been found at the scene, but the victim testified that Atkins had worked for him at the house two days prior to the crime; no other physical evidence tied Atkins to the crime. The court asserted that "the introduction of a previous arrest can have an almost irreversible impact on the minds of the jurors" and that the evidence against Atkins was "not overwhelming." See also United States v. Gray, 878 F.2d 702 (3d Cir.1989) (where trial was basically a credibility determination between defendant and complainant, the failure to call disinterested witnesses who would support the defendant's testimony was prejudicial).

Cronic holds that in some limited cases, ineffectiveness and prejudice will be presumed without having to investigate counsel's performance. But it is clear that this rule of per se reversal is rarely applicable. If it did not apply under the facts of *Cronic,* where could it apply? Consider Solina v. United States, 709 F.2d 160 (2d Cir.1983), where the court concluded that per se reversal was required because defendant's trial counsel had held himself out as an attorney but had never passed a bar exam. The evidence against Solina was overwhelming, and Solina could point to no error of judgment on the part of his counsel at trial. Yet the court reasoned as follows:

> The problem of representation by [one not admitted to the bar] is not simply one of competence * * * but that he was engaging in a crime. Such a person cannot be wholly free from fear of what might happen if a vigorous defense should lead the prosecutor or the trial judge to inquire into his background and discover his lack of credentials.

The court found that Solina had been denied "counsel," as that term is used in the Sixth Amendment, and that this total denial of counsel was per se prejudicial. *Solina* preceded *Cronic,* but it has been followed by lower courts even after *Cronic.* See e.g. United States v. Novak, 903 F.2d 883 (2d Cir.1990) (per se reversal where defense counsel had obtained admission to the bar by fraud). Do you think that the Supreme Court would require per se reversal in a case like *Solina?* Compare Reese v. Peters, 926 F.2d 668 (7th Cir.1991) (*Solina* distinguished; no per se reversal where attorney's license had been suspended for failure to pay dues: "mountebanks, as in *Solina,* and persons who obtain credentials by fraud, are classes apart from persons who satisfied the court of their legal skills but later ran afoul of some technical legal rule."). See also Pilchak v. Camper, 935 F.2d 145 (8th Cir.1991) (per se reversal where defense counsel was suffering from Alzheimer's disease at the time of trial).

Ordinarily, ineffectiveness claims are not considered on direct appeal, because the trial record and the appellate briefs rarely provide sufficient information with which to evaluate counsel's performance and its impact on the trial. Thus, *Strickland* claims are almost always deferred to a collateral attack in which an evidentiary hearing is conducted. See United States v. Bounds, 943 F.2d 541 (5th Cir.1991) (declining to address ineffectiveness claim on appeal, where the only information in the record is the defendant's own assertions in his brief). Compare United States v. Guerrero, 938 F.2d 725 (7th Cir.1991) (ordinarily, *Strickland* claims are not considered on direct appeal, but an exception exists if the record is sufficiently developed with regard to the issue).

C. A SPECIAL PROBLEM: JOINT REPRESENTATION

The right to effective assistance of counsel may be denied because defense counsel has a conflict of interest, and cannot or does not properly protect her client's interests. This problem arises particularly when counsel represents multiple defendants. Codefendants may have divergent interests at all stages of a prosecution. A plea-bargain advantageous to one defendant may produce testimony adverse to another defendant.[77] Defendants may have inconsistent defenses, or wish to testify in ways that incriminate codefendants. Evidence inculpating one defendant might exculpate another, forcing counsel to make unsatisfactory choices in response to offered testimony. Separate counsel also might choose differing approaches to closing argument. See Green, "Through a Glass, Darkly": How the Court Sees Motions to Disqualify Criminal Defense Lawyers, 89 Colum.L.Rev. 1202 (1989), for an extensive discussion of conflicts of interest that can arise in the course of representation of criminal defendants.

In Holloway v. Arkansas, 435 U.S. 475 (1978), the Court made it clear that requiring or permitting a single attorney to represent codefendants is not a *per se* violation of the right to effective assistance of counsel. The Court noted that

77. For example, in State v. Ray, 273 N.W.2d 652 (Minn.1978), defense counsel represented codefendants in a burglary and aggravated assault case. One defendant, Ray, was offered the opportunity to plead guilty to a charge of aggravated assault, provided that he would testify against his codefendant. He did not accept the offer and was convicted of burglary and aggravated assault and was given a 20-year sentence for burglary, and a 10-year consecutive sentence for aggravated assault. If Ray had accepted the offer, he would have received only one sentence of 10 years. The court concluded that defense counsel had a conflict of interest which prevented him from advising Ray to accept the plea offer. Although the conviction was affirmed, the court noted that Ray could commence post-conviction proceedings. If he could show that he would have accepted the offer if counsel had advised him to do so, he would be entitled to reversal of the 20-year burglary sentence.

a common defense often gives strength against a common attack. Under some circumstances, however, joint representation can deny a defendant effective assistance of counsel. In *Holloway,* the defense counsel made pretrial motions for appointment of separate counsel for each defendant because of possible conflicts of interest. The trial court denied the motion, and refused defense counsel's renewed request, during the trial, for separate counsel when the three codefendants each wished to testify. Counsel felt that he would be unable to examine or cross-examine any defendant to protect the interests of the others. The Court reversed the defendants' convictions because the judge, after timely motions, failed either to appoint separate counsel or to take adequate steps to determine whether the risk was too remote to warrant separate counsel. The Court presumed prejudice to the defendants.

> Joint representation of conflicting interests is suspect because of what it tends to prevent the attorney from doing. For example, in this case it may well have precluded defense counsel for Campbell from exploring possible plea negotiations and the possibility of an agreement to testify for the prosecution, provided a lesser charge or a favorable sentencing recommendation would be acceptable. Generally speaking a conflict may also prevent an attorney from challenging the admission of evidence prejudicial to one client but perhaps favorable to another, or from arguing at the sentencing hearing the relative involvement and culpability of his clients in order to minimize the culpability of one by emphasizing that of another. Examples can be readily multiplied. The mere physical presence of an attorney does not fulfill the Sixth Amendment guarantee when the advocate's conflicting obligations have effectively sealed his lips on crucial matters.
>
> Finally, a rule requiring a defendant to show that a conflict of interests—which he and his counsel tried to avoid by timely objections to the joint representation—prejudiced him in some specific fashion would not be susceptible to intelligent, evenhanded application. In the normal case where a harmless error rule is applied, the error occurs at trial and its scope is readily identifiable. Accordingly, the reviewing court can undertake with some confidence its relatively narrow task of assessing the likelihood that the error materially affected the deliberations of the jury. But in a case of joint representation of conflicting interests the evil—it bears repeating—is in what the advocate finds himself compelled to *refrain* from doing, not only at trial but also as to possible pretrial plea negotiations and in the sentencing process. It may be possible in some cases to identify from the record the prejudice resulting from an attorney's failure to undertake certain trial tasks, but even with a record of the sentencing hearing available it would be difficult to judge intelligently the impact of a conflict on the attorney's representation of a client. And to assess the impact of a conflict of interests on the attorney's options, tactics and decisions in plea negotiations would be virtually impossible. Thus, an inquiry into a claim of harmless error here would require, unlike most cases, unguided speculation.

* * *

The Supreme Court has amended Fed.R.Crim.P. 44 to cover joint representation.[78]

78. For an argument in favor of a per se rule against joint representation, see Lowenthal, Joint Representation in Criminal Cases: A Critical Appraisal, 64 Va.L.Rev. 939 (1978). For an argument against such a rule see Margolin & Coliver, Pretrial Disqualification of

Rule 44. Right to and assignment of counsel

* * *

(c) Joint representation.—Whenever two or more defendants have been jointly charged pursuant to Rule 8(b) or have been joined for trial pursuant to Rule 13, and are represented by the same retained or assigned counsel or by retained or assigned counsel who are associated in the practice of law, the court shall promptly inquire with respect to such joint representation and shall personally advise each defendant of his right to the effective assistance of counsel, including separate representation. Unless it appears that there is good cause to believe no conflict of interest is likely to arise, the court shall take such measures as may be appropriate to protect each defendant's right to counsel.[79]

In Cuyler v. Sullivan, 446 U.S. 335 (1980), the Supreme Court held that a state prisoner may seek federal habeas corpus relief by claiming that his retained attorney represented conflicting interests and therefore was ineffective. Justice Powell's opinion for the Court rejected the petitioner's claim that *Holloway* requires a trial judge to inquire in every case into the propriety of joint representation. He wrote that

> [d]efense counsel have an ethical obligation to avoid conflicting representations and to advise the court promptly when a conflict of interest arises during the course of a trial. Absent special circumstances, therefore, trial courts may assume that multiple representation entails no conflict or that the lawyer and his clients knowingly accept such risk of conflict as may exist.

The opinion reiterated the suggestion in *Holloway* that multiple representation does give rise to a possibility of an improper conflict of interest and that a defendant who objects to multiple representation "must have the opportunity to show that potential conflicts impermissibly imperil his right to a fair trial." But, said the Court, "a defendant who raised no objection at trial must demonstrate that an actual conflict of interest adversely affected his lawyer's performance." Thus, the Court created a limited presumption of prejudice: prejudice is presumed, but only if the defendant demonstrates that counsel "actively represented conflicting interests" and that "an actual conflict of interest adversely affected his lawyer's performance." Justice Brennan's concurring opinion would have required trial judges to conduct an inquiry into possible conflicts in all cases of multiple representation. Justice Marshall's opinion, concurring in part and dissenting in part, argued that the Court's test was "not only unduly harsh, but incurably speculative as well," and that "[t]he appropriate question under the Sixth Amendment is whether an actual, relevant conflict of interests existed during the proceedings," whether or not a petitioner could show that it adversely affected his lawyer's performance.[80]

Criminal Defense Counsel, 20 Am.Crim.L.Rev. 227 (1982).

79. In United States v. Martorano, 620 F.2d 912 (1st Cir. 1980), the court held that written and oral advice by defense counsel concerning the risks of joint representation and a letter to the court signed by the defendant and stating that he accepted the risks did not satisfy the circuit's requirement of on the record warnings by the court. But the court found that the government proved that no prejudice occurred as a result of the absence of a formal judicial ruling.

80. When the Supreme Court remanded *Cuyler*, the court of appeals found that there was an actual conflict of interest that required reversal of Sullivan's conviction. Sullivan v. Cuyler, 723 F.2d 1077 (3d Cir.1983). Counsel, representing both a prospective witness and Sullivan, admitted at an evidentiary hearing that he did not call the witness on Sullivan's behalf because he had to take the witness'

The Court expressed concern in Wood v. Georgia, 450 U.S. 261 (1981), about "the inherent dangers that arise when a criminal defendant is represented by a lawyer hired and paid by a third party, particularly when the third party is the operator of the alleged criminal enterprise." The Court remanded for a hearing on whether a conflict tainted revocation of probation in this case.

The Supreme Court found no ineffective assistance of counsel in Burger v. Kemp, 483 U.S. 776 (1987), a capital case in which Burger and a codefendant were represented by law partners. The defendants were soldiers charged with the murder of a fellow soldier who worked part-time driving a taxi. Each defendant confessed, and Burger took military police to the place where the victim had been drowned. Leaphart, an experienced lawyer, was appointed to represent Burger, and he insisted that his law partner represent the codefendant. The two defendants were tried separately, and at their trials each defendant sought to avoid the death penalty by emphasizing the other's culpability. Burger was sentenced to death, and attacked his representation in a habeas corpus proceeding on the ground that Leaphart's partnership relationship created a conflict of interest for him. A federal district court denied relief, and the court of appeals affirmed. One judge dissented, however, and argued that a conflict of interest between the lawyers was present, and that Leaphart failed to investigate the case fully and to offer mitigating evidence.

Justice Stevens wrote for the Court as it affirmed the denial of relief. He conceded that "[t]here is certainly much substance to petitioner's argument that the appointment of two partners to represent coindictees in their respective trials creates a possible conflict of interest that could prejudice either or both clients," and that "the risk of prejudice is increased when the two lawyers cooperate with one another in planning and conduct of trial strategy." He observed, however, that the Court's decisions do not presume prejudice in all cases, and he concluded that "the overlap of counsel, if any, did not so infect Leaphart's representation as to constitute an active representation of competing interests." Justice Stevens added that "[p]articularly in smaller communities where the supply of qualified lawyers willing to accept the demanding and unrewarding work of representing capital prisoners is extremely limited, the two defendants may actually benefit from the joint efforts of two partners who supplement one another in their preparation." He noted that "we generally presume that the lawyer is fully conscious of the overarching duty of complete loyalty to his or her client," and that trial courts "appropriately and necessarily rely in large measure upon the good faith and good judgment of defense counsel." Justice Stevens also emphasized that each defendant was tried separately, and that separate trials significantly reduce the risk of a conflict of interest. The Court declined to disturb the lower courts' findings that there was no actual conflict of interest.

Justice Stevens added that, even if an actual conflict had been established, counsel's advocacy was unaffected by it. He concluded that there was no evidence that the prosecutor would have been receptive to a plea bargain and no doubt that Leaphart sought to negotiate for a life sentence, there was no reason to believe that Leaphart attempted to protect the other defendant who was not on trial with Burger, and the decision not to offer mitigating evidence and open the door to cross-examination about Burger's background was not

interests into account as well as those of Sullivan.

unreasonable even if it was erroneous. Although Justice Stevens stated that the evidence at the habeas corpus hearing "does suggest that Leaphart could well have made a more thorough investigation than he did," he added that "counsel's decision not to mount an all-out investigation into petitioner's background in search of mitigating circumstances was supported by reasonable professional judgment." Counsel had interviewed all potential witnesses who were called to his attention, and "there was a reasonable basis for his strategic decision that an explanation of petitioner's history would not have minimized the risk of the death penalty."

Justice Blackmun filed a dissenting opinion, in which Justices Brennan and Marshall joined, and in which Justice Powell joined in part. Justice Powell filed a separate dissenting opinion, in which Justice Brennan joined.[81]

In People v. Robinson, 79 Ill.2d 147, 37 Ill.Dec. 267, 402 N.E.2d 157 (1979), the court addressed the problem that arises when one public defender is disqualified from representing a defendant because of a conflict of interest, but another defender from the same office is appointed.

> Upon review of the authorities and consideration of the diversity of organization of the offices of the public defenders, we conclude that the avoidance of conflicts of interest which result in failure to provide effective assistance of counsel does not require us to hold that the individual attorneys who comprise the staff of a public defender are members of an entity which should be subject to the rule that if one attorney is disqualified by reason of a conflict of interest then no other member of the entity may continue with the representation. In many instances the application of such a *per se* rule would require the appointment of counsel with virtually no experience in the trial of criminal matters, thus raising, with justification, the question of competency of counsel. Balanced against this is the possibility, in most instances quite remote, that an experienced member of the public defender's staff might labor under a conflict of interest because another member of the staff was so burdened. * * *

The facts of United States v. Laura, 667 F.2d 365 (3d Cir. 1981), illustrate why many judges are uncomfortable with joint representation. A husband and wife indicted for cocaine importation jointly hired counsel. The district judge ordered them to retain separate lawyers, but their lawyer prepared affidavits stating they desired that he continue to represent them both. Both spouses indicated that they did not wish to consider plea bargaining and saw no other conflict of interest. The district judge permitted the defendants to waive their right to separate counsel and ultimately they pleaded guilty. Subsequently, the wife moved to withdraw her guilty plea and alleged a conflict of interest on counsel's part. She stated that she had only met with the lawyer for 10 minutes outside the presence of her husband before signing her affidavit; that before she pleaded guilty the lawyer had indicated to her that the government would only accept a plea bargain that covered both spouses; and that he told her she probably could be acquitted at trial, but her husband would be worse off without the plea agreement. A majority of the court of appeals found a valid waiver. A dissenting judge argued for a one-lawyer, one-client rule and persuasively demonstrated that the lawyer never clearly explained that there

81. A comprehensive discussion of the problems that can result when one lawyer, firm or public agency represents successive defendants is found in Lowenthal, Successive Representation By Criminal Lawyers, 93 Yale L.J. 1 (1983).

was a real conflict of interest between the spouses and that there was no waiver of her right to be advised by a lawyer loyal to her.

The difficult question raised by cases like *Laura* is whether a trial judge can ever be confident that codefendants have a full and complete understanding of the risks of joint representation. Because of the attorney-client privilege, there is a definite limit to how far the court can go in examining the advice the attorney has given to joint clients. This and the privilege against self-incrimination force judges to rely on the lawyer, who may have a personal stake in joint representation, or who may have been retained by one defendant (the husband in *Laura*) and thus may have a special loyalty to him. A judge can warn a defendant in the abstract about the ills associated with sharing a lawyer, but do defendants faced with a criminal prosecution understand? Can the judge trust the lawyer to help the defendants understand?

In cases involving "organized criminal activity," a lawyer may be selected by one defendant for all, or even by someone not charged. Such counsel may be more a screen to protect the organization than an advocate for particular defendants. Even if a judge orders defendants to obtain separate counsel, it is uncertain whether those counsel will be independent and not tied in some way to the organization. In some cases there may be nothing the judge can do to assure that the lawyers hired for defendants truly have their clients' best interest at heart. By ordering separate counsel, however, the judge does all that he can to protect the defendant, even if the protection ultimately is not successful.

Evaluating whether an actual conflict of interest adversely affected counsel's performance is obviously fact-dependent. Consider United States v. Gambino, 864 F.2d 1064 (3d Cir.1988). Gambino was charged with masterminding a heroin transaction at a cafe in Brooklyn. Surveillance showed that Gambino's car was at the cafe at the time the buyer took delivery of the heroin. Gambino was never identified at the scene, he had an alibi, and the buyer testified at trial that "Ignacio in Italy" had supplied the heroin. There was no proof that such a person existed. However, Gambino's counsel, Evseroff, received information that Mazzara was at the cafe that night. Mazzara was a known heroin supplier, whom Evseroff was simultaneously representing in the famous "Pizza Connection" Mafia trial. Evseroff chose not to bring what the court of appeals called "the Mazzara defense" at Gambino's trial. At the ineffectiveness hearing, the government argued that the Mazzara defense would have undermined the exculpatory testimony of the buyer. The court of appeals held that counsel had not labored under an actual conflict of interest. It reasoned as follows:

> Here, the alleged Sixth Amendment violation is that Evseroff did not advance the Mazzara defense because to do so would have been adverse to Mazzara. * * * It is clear that the multiple representation did not give rise to an actual conflict of interest in the sense that anything which Evseroff could have done at the trial on behalf of appellant but omitted to do could have prejudiced Mazzara. Mazzara, of course, was not a defendant at the trial nor was he even named in the indictment against appellant * * *. Thus, he could not have been directly affected by the outcome of the case. Further, while Mazzara presumably would have preferred not to see his name advanced as a possible source of the heroin, appellant has not demonstrated how Mazzara would have been injured or prejudiced if this had happened * * * and thus it follows that appellant and Mazzara did not have conflicting interests in

> Evseroff's performance at appellant's trial. * * * While appellant * * * is free with his criticism of Evseroff, a conflict of interest cannot be invented on his behalf simply so he can be given a new trial. Appellant should attribute his current predicament to his unlawful conduct, not to failings of his trial attorney.

The court discounted the fact that at the ineffectiveness hearing, Evseroff filed an affidavit stating that the reason he did not assert the Mazzara defense was that he didn't want to bring Mazzara's name into the trial. The court stated that "while there was no direct evidence that Evseroff had been coerced when he signed the affidavit * * * Evseroff had defended a person involved in serious organized criminal matters and had not succeeded in obtaining his acquittal." Therefore, "Evseroff might think it prudent to take steps to assist his client in obtaining a new trial, even if Evseroff thereby raised an ethical problem for himself."

In dissent, Judge Mansmann argued that Mazzara could have been prejudiced by the introduction of his name into the Gambino trial, and therefore defense counsel had labored under an actual conflict of interest.

> If Evseroff had presented a full-fledged Mazzara defense, he might have called witnesses who would provide testimony which might incriminate Mazzara. This testimony, if inconsistent, might later be used to impeach those witnesses when testifying [in the Pizza Connection] case. If Evseroff uncovered new evidence or witnesses to support an argument that Mazzara was the source of the heroin, and presented the witnesses and evidence at Gambino's trial, he could have provided further ammunition for the government to use against Mazzara in [the Pizza Connection] case. The effort to present Mazzara as the source of heroin would obviously undermine Evseroff's relationship with Mazzara. It goes without saying that most clients would not appreciate their attorney naming them as heroin sources.

Judge Mansmann further argued that the Mazzara defense would have probably been used by a conflict-free counsel despite the fact that the informant had named another supplier. There was no proof that the person named by the informant ever existed. Mazzara was a known heroin dealer who was at the scene. In any case, Evseroff could have raised the Mazzara defense as an alternative.

Who has the better of the argument? Interestingly, the government reported Evseroff to a lawyer's disciplinary committee for his conduct in *Gambino*. The majority found that fact irrelevant. Does that change your analysis? See also Nealy v. Cabana, 782 F.2d 1362 (5th Cir.1986) (actual conflict of interest where counsel fails to call defendant's brother, whom counsel was simultaneously representing in a separate trial). Foxworth v. Wainwright, 516 F.2d 1072 (5th Cir.1975) (actual conflict where counsel represented four defendants in a joint trial, and argued misidentification as to all, rather than seeking to shift blame from some defendants to others who were more culpable); Thomas v. Foltz, 818 F.2d 476 (6th Cir.1987) (actual conflict where counsel negotiates plea bargains as a package deal).

Conflicts of interest can arise even where counsel is representing a single client. In some cases, counsel's personal interests may be in conflict with the duty of loyalty owed the client. Courts have applied the *Cuyler* standards in such situations. For example, in United States v. Cancilla, 725 F.2d 867 (2d

Cir.1984), the defendant's counsel was engaged in criminal conduct with the defendant's co-conspirators. The court reasoned that "with the similarility of counsel's criminal activities to Cancilla's schemes and the link between them, it must have occurred to counsel that a vigorous defense might uncover evidence or prompt testimony revealing his own crimes." The court found an actual conflict of interest which adversely affected the representation. See also United States ex rel. Duncan v. O'Leary, 806 F.2d 1307 (7th Cir.1986) (reversal under *Cuyler* where defense counsel is the prosecutor's campaign manager and the prosecutor is running on a "law and order" ticket).

In People v. Winkler, 71 N.Y.2d 592, 528 N.Y.S.2d 360, 523 N.E.2d 485 (1988), the court held that if defense counsel negotiates a contingent fee in a criminal case, reversal is required if the fee arrangement adversely affected the representation. It refused to mandate per se reversal, however, since the contingent fee is entered into confidentially and "no advance State protection can be imposed or is even available." As such, per se reversal was a "disproportionate" remedy. How does the existence of a contingent fee even give rise to a conflict of interest warranting application of the *Cuyler* limited presumption of prejudice?

D. INEFFECTIVE ASSISTANCE WITHOUT FAULT ON THE PART OF DEFENSE COUNSEL

Governmental or prosecutorial action also can deprive a defendant of effective assistance of counsel. In Brooks v. Tennessee, 406 U.S. 605 (1972), a Tennessee rule required the defendant to testify first or not at all. The Court held that the rule violated the defendant's right to remain silent, and deprived him of the aid of counsel in planning his defense, particularly in the decision to testify or remain silent.

> By requiring the accused and his lawyer to make that choice without an opportunity to evaluate the actual worth of their evidence, the state restricts the defense—particularly counsel—in the planning of its case. Furthermore, the penalty for not testifying first is to keep the defendant off the stand entirely, even though as a matter of professional judgment his lawyer might want to call him later in the trial. The accused is thereby deprived of the "guiding hand of counsel" in the timing of this critical element of his defense.

The Court reversed his conviction and ordered a new trial. Similarly, in Herring v. New York, 422 U.S. 853 (1975), a New York statute giving a judge in a nonjury criminal trial the power to deny absolutely the opportunity for defense counsel to make a closing argument was held to be unconstitutional. New York denied Herring the assistance of counsel by permitting the judge to dispense with his counsel's summation.[82] In Geders v. United States, 425 U.S. 80 (1976), the defendant was prohibited from consulting with counsel during a 17-hour overnight recess between the direct and cross-examination of the defendant. Although recognizing the problem of "coached" witnesses, the Court decided that this method of preventing coaching violated the defendant's right to the assistance of counsel.

82. See also United States v. Bohn, 890 F.2d 1079 (9th Cir.1989) (exclusion of counsel from hearing to assess validity of defendant's Fifth Amendment claim required per se reversal; such a hearing is a critical stage of the proceedings).

Justice Stevens wrote for a majority in Perry v. Leeke, 488 U.S. 272 (1989), as it distinguished *Geders* and held that a state trial judge did not commit constitutional error in declaring a 15 minute recess after the defendant's direct testimony in his murder trial and in ordering that the defendant talk to no one, including his lawyer, during the recess. Although Justice Stevens recognized that "[t]here is merit in petitioner's argument that a showing of prejudice is not an essential component of a violation of the rule announced in *Geders,*" he reasoned that "when a defendant becomes a witness, he has no constitutional right to consult with his lawyer while he is testifying." Justice Stevens recognized that nondiscussion orders can prevent coaching of witnesses that interfere with the search for truth. He described *Geders* as a case involving an overnight recess in which matters that go beyond a defendant's own testimony would be discussed with counsel and stated that "in a short recess in which it is appropriate to presume that nothing but the testimony will be discussed, the testifying defendant does not have a constitutional right to advice."

Justice Marshall, joined by Justices Brennan and Blackmun, dissented. He argued that a defendant cannot be prevented from consulting with counsel during a recess and that the petitioner was not arguing for a right to interrupt cross-examination in order to consult with his lawyer.

Outside of the formal trial process, the government may undermine a defendant's right to effective assistance of counsel—e.g., when an informant interferes with the attorney-client relationship. The Supreme Court addressed this problem in Weatherford v. Bursey, 429 U.S. 545 (1977). Even though an undercover agent and informant attended two meetings between the defendant and counsel, the Court concluded that the defendant received effective assistance of counsel. Those meetings resulted in no tainted evidence, and no communication of defense strategy to the government. Despite an intrusion into the attorney-client relationship, there was not sufficient prejudice to require reversal. Justices Marshall and Brennan dissented, because they believed that when the prosecution acquires information about the defense, the fairness and integrity of the adversary system are impaired. Concerned with the potential chilling effect on freedom of communication between lawyer and client, they maintained that the essence of the Sixth Amendment right to counsel is the privacy of communications with counsel.

In United States v. Morrison, 449 U.S. 361 (1981), the Supreme Court unanimously concluded that "absent demonstrable prejudice, or substantial threat thereof, dismissal of the indictment is plainly inappropriate, even though the [Sixth Amendment] violation may have been deliberate," and even though the conduct of drug investigators in meeting with a defendant, after she was indicted and had counsel, outside of counsel's presence and suggesting that her lawyer might not be adequate and that she should cooperate with the government was "egregious."

United States v. Melvin, 650 F.2d 641 (5th Cir. 1981), discusses *Morrison* and concludes that to have a violation of Sixth Amendment rights, there must be an invasion of a confidential relationship between client and attorney. See also United States v. Noriega, 752 F.Supp. 1045 (S.D.Fla.1990), which held that despite outrageous, unconscionable conduct of law enforcement officers in eavesdropping on two conversations between the defendant and his counsel, dismissal of the prosecution was not warranted where there was no showing that trial strategy was revealed or that the defendant's ability to work in confidence with his attorney was impaired.

Although the defendant in *Weatherford* received effective assistance of counsel, interference with the attorney-client relationship may result in the denial of that right in other circumstances. In United States v. Levy, 577 F.2d 200 (3d Cir. 1978), a government informer, who was also a codefendant, relayed information about defense strategy to the government. The court distinguished *Weatherford* because in this case the government actually sought the information, and defense strategy actually was disclosed.

Can you think of an argument, other than that made by the *Weatherford* dissenters, that would justify overturning a conviction any time that the government invades the privacy of lawyer-client communications? What implicit message might an undercover agent be sending to the prosecutor when the agent is silent about what the defendant and defense counsel have been planning?

E. THE PERJURY PROBLEM

When a defense attorney believes that her client is about to commit perjury, she faces a particularly difficult dilemma.

In a highly publicized case, Nix v. Whiteside, 475 U.S. 157 (1986), a defense lawyer told a client, who pleaded self-defense in response to a murder charge, that if he took the stand and falsely claimed to have seen the victim with a gun, contrary to what he had told counsel, the lawyer would advise the court of the perjury, probably would be permitted to impeach the testimony, and would seek to withdraw. As a result, the client testified honestly that he believed the victim was reaching for a gun, but he had not seen one. The client challenged his second degree murder conviction on an ineffective assistance of counsel ground. Although the state courts commended the lawyer's integrity, a federal court of appeals granted habeas corpus relief.

The Supreme Court unanimously reversed in an opinion by Chief Justice Burger. He reasoned that no defendant has a right to commit perjury, so that no defendant has a right to rely upon counsel to assist in the development of false testimony. The Court noted that under *Strickland,* the defendant must prove prejudice, and Whiteside "has no valid claim that confidence in the result of his trial has been diminished by his desisting from the contemplated perjury." Even if the jury would have been persuaded by the perjury, the Court concluded that under *Strickland,* "a defendant has no entitlement to the luck of a lawless decisionmaker." The Chief Justice also rejected Whiteside's argument that the *Cuyler* limited presumption of prejudice should apply. Whatever conflict existed between Whiteside and his counsel "was imposed on the attorney by the client's proposal to commit the crime of fabricating testimony." The Chief Justice reasoned that "if a 'conflict' between a client's proposal and counsel's ethical obligation gives rise to a presumption that counsel's assistance was prejudicially ineffective, every guilty criminal's conviction would be suspect if the defendant had sought to obtain an acquittal by illegal means."

Although this was enough to decide the case, the Chief Justice went further and held that Whiteside's counsel had not been ineffective in discouraging his client from committing perjury. He concluded that for the purposes of this case, effectiveness could be determined by reference to the prevailing rules of professional responsibility governing the conduct of lawyers. He noted that Disciplinary Rule 7–102(A)(4) of the ABA Code of Professional Responsibility (in effect in Iowa and in a minority of states) provides that a lawyer shall not "knowingly use perjured testimony or false evidence"; and that Rule 3.3 of the more recent Model Rules of Professional Conduct (in effect in a majority of states) requires disclosure of client perjury to the tribunal as a last resort. The Chief Justice found that the prevailing ethical standards "confirm that the legal profession has accepted that an attorney's ethical duty to advance the interests of his client is limited by an equally solemn duty to comply with the law and standards of professional conduct." He concluded as follows:

> [U]nder no circumstances may a lawyer either advocate or passively tolerate a client's giving false testimony. * * * The rule adopted by the Court of Appeals, which seemingly would require an attorney to remain silent while his client committed perjury, is wholly incompatible with the established standards of ethical conduct and the laws of Iowa and contrary to professional standards promulgated by that State. The position advanced by the [Government], on the contrary, is wholly consistent with the Iowa standards of professional conduct and law, with the overwhelming majority of courts, and with codes of professional ethics. Since there has been no breach of any recognized professional duty, it follows that there can be no deprivation of the right to assistance of counsel under the *Strickland* standard.

Justice Brennan wrote an opinion concurring in the judgment. He agreed with the majority's analysis on the prejudice prong of *Strickland.* As to the performance prong, however, he argued that the Court "has no constitutional authority to establish rules of ethical conduct for lawyers practicing in the state courts," and that "the Court's essay regarding what constitutes the correct response to a criminal client's suggestion that he will perjure himself is pure discourse without force of law." Justice Blackmun wrote an opinion concurring in the judgment, joined by Justices Brennan, Marshall, and Stevens. He agreed that Whiteside had not shown prejudice from his lawyer's conduct, and saw no need to "grade counsel's performance." He rejected the Court's establishment of a per se rule of effective representation based on ethical codes.

> Whether an attorney's response to what he sees as a client's command to commit perjury violates a defendant's Sixth Amendment rights may depend on many factors: how certain the attorney is that the proposed testimony is false, the stage of the proceedings at which the attorney discovers the plan, or the ways in which the attorney may be able to dissuade his client, to name just three. The complex interaction of factors, which is likely to vary from case to case, makes inappropriate a blanket rule that defense attorneys must reveal, or threaten to reveal, a client's anticipated perjury to the court. Except in the rarest of cases, attorneys who adopt the role of the judge or jury to determine the facts, pose a danger of depriving their clients of the zealous and loyal advocacy required by the Sixth Amendment.
>
> I am therefore troubled by the Court's implicit adoption of a set of standards of professional responsibility for attorneys in state criminal proceedings. * * * It is for the States to decide how attorneys should conduct themselves in state criminal proceedings, * * *. Thus, I would follow the suggestion made in the joint brief amici curiae filed by 37 states * * * that we

allow the States to maintain their differing approaches to a complex ethical question.

Justice Stevens also wrote an opinion concurring in the judgment, emphasizing that it is often difficult to determine whether the client's proposed testimony is perjurious.

> From the perspective of an appellate judge, after a case has been tried and the evidence has been sifted by another judge, a particular fact may be as clear and certain as a piece of crystal or a small diamond. A trial lawyer, however, must often deal with mixtures of sand and clay. Even a pebble that seems clear enough at first glance may take on a different hue in a handful of gravel. * * *
>
> A lawyer's certainty that a change in his client's recollection is a harbinger of intended perjury—as well as judicial review of such apparent certainty—should be tempered by the realization that, after reflection, the most honest witness may recall (or sincerely believe he recalls) details that he previously overlooked.

Even if the propriety of counsel's performance is considered, *Whiteside* is an easy case. Most lawyers would think it entirely appropriate to try to discourage the client from a planned course of perjury. Indeed, discouragement of perjury is effective advocacy, because the jury may disbelieve the lie, the prosecutor may easily tear it apart on cross-examination, and obviously the client may subject himself to a perjury charge. Moreover, if the trial judge believes that a defendant lied on the stand, this may be taken into account at sentencing. See United States v. Grayson, 438 U.S. 41 (1978).

The difficult questions, not presented by *Whiteside,* are three. First, what if the client refuses to be dissuaded from a course of perjury and demands to testify? Second, what if the client appears to have been dissuaded from testifying falsely, but then commits perjury after taking the stand? Third, what if the lawyer learns after the testimony that the client has perjured himself? See Freedman, Client Confidences and Client Perjury: Some Unanswered Questions, 136 U.Pa.L.Rev. 1939 (1988) (arguing that all of these problems should be left to the adversary system and to cross-examination by the prosecutor). After *Whiteside,* the A.B.A. Standing Committee on Ethics issued Formal Opinion 87–353 (1987) to suggest an appropriate response to these problems under the Code of Professional Responsibility and the Model Rules of Professional Conduct. Portions of that opinion follow.[83]

Formal Opinion 87–353, April 20, 1987

Lawyer's Responsibility with Relation to Client Perjury

> * * * Model Rule 3.3(a) and (b) require a lawyer to disclose the client's perjury to the court if other remedial measures are ineffective, even if the information is otherwise protected under Rule 1.6, which prohibits a lawyer from revealing information relating to representation of a client. However, under Rule 3.3(b), the duty to disclose continues only "to the conclusion of the

83. In the opinion, the reference to "DR" means one of the Disciplinary Rules of the Code of Professional Responsibility, adopted by the A.B.A. in 1969 and in effect in a minority of states. The reference to "Rule" means one of the Model Rules of Professional Conduct, adopted by the A.B.A. in 1983 and in effect in most of the states. See generally C. Wolfram, Modern Legal Ethics § 2.6 (1986).

proceeding ...." From the Comment to Rule 3.3, it would appear that the Rule's disclosure requirement was meant to apply only in those situations where the lawyer's knowledge of the client's fraud or perjury occurs prior to final judgment and disclosure is necessary to prevent the judgment from being corrupted by the client's unlawful conduct.

* * *

Model Rule 3.3(a) and (b) represent a major policy change with regard to the lawyer's duty * * * when the client testifies falsely. It is now mandatory, under these Model Rule provisions, for a lawyer, who knows the client has committed perjury, to disclose this knowledge to the tribunal if the lawyer cannot persuade the client to rectify the perjury.

The relevant provisions of Rule 3.3(a) are: "(a) A lawyer shall not knowingly: ... (2) fail to disclose a material fact to a tribunal when disclosure is necessary to avoid assisting a criminal or fraudulent act by the client; ... (4) offer evidence that the lawyer knows to be false. If a lawyer has offered material evidence and comes to know of its falsity, the lawyer shall take reasonable remedial measures." Rule 3.3(a)(2) and (4) complement each other. While (a)(4), itself, does not expressly require disclosure by the lawyer to the tribunal of the client's false testimony after the lawyer has offered it and learns of its falsity, such disclosure will be the only "reasonable remedial [measure]" the lawyer will be able to take if the client is unwilling to rectify the perjury.

* * *

[Contrary to] the exception provided in DR 7–102(B)(1) of the Model Code [preventing disclosure if the information is a confidence or a secret] the disclosure requirement of Model Rule 3.3(a)(2) and (4) is not excused because of client confidences. Rule 3.3(b) provides in pertinent part: "The duties stated in paragraph (a) ... apply even if compliance requires disclosure of information otherwise protected by Rule 1.6." Thus, the lawyer's responsibility to disclose client perjury to the tribunal under Rule 3.3(a)(2) and (4) supersedes the lawyer's responsibility to the client under [the confidentiality requirements of] Rule 1.6.

* * *

Without doubt, the vitality of the adversary system, certainly in criminal cases, depends upon the ability of the lawyer to give loyal and zealous service to the client. And this, in turn, requires that the lawyer have the complete confidence of the client and be able to assure the client that the confidence will be protected and honored. However, the ethical rules of the bar which have supported these basic requirements of the adversary system have emphasized from the time they were first reduced to written form that the lawyer's duties to the client in this regard must be performed within the bounds of law.

For example, these ethical rules clearly recognize that a lawyer representing a client who admits guilt in fact, but wants to plead not guilty and put the state to its proof, may assist the client in entering such a plea and vigorously challenge the state's case at trial through cross-examination, legal motions and argument to the jury. However, neither the adversary system nor the ethical rules permit the lawyer to participate in the corruption of the judicial process by assisting the client in the introduction of evidence the lawyer knows is false. A defendant does not have the right, as part of the right to a fair trial and zealous representation by counsel, to commit perjury. And the lawyer owes no duty to the client, in providing the representation to which the client is entitled, to assist the client's perjury.

On the contrary, the lawyer, as an officer of the court, has a duty to prevent the perjury, and if the perjury has already been committed, to prevent its playing any part in the judgment of the court. This duty the lawyer owes the court is not inconsistent with any duty owed to the client. More particularly, it is not inconsistent with the lawyer's duty to preserve the client's confidences. For that duty is based on the lawyer's need for information from the client to obtain for the client all that the law and lawful process provide. Implicit in the promise of confidentiality is its nonapplicability where the client seeks the unlawful end of corrupting the judicial process by false evidence.

It must be emphasized that this opinion does not change the professional relationship the lawyer has with the client and require the lawyer now to judge, rather than represent, the client. The lawyer's obligation to disclose client perjury to the tribunal, discussed in this opinion, is strictly limited by Rule 3.3 to the situation where the lawyer *knows* that the client has committed perjury, ordinarily based on admissions the client has made to the lawyer. (The Committee notes that some trial lawyers report that they have avoided the ethical dilemma posed by Rule 3.3 because they follow a practice of not questioning the client about the facts in the case and, therefore, never "know" that a client has given false testimony. Lawyers who engage in such practice may be violating their duties under Rule 3.3 and their obligation to provide competent representation under Rule 1.1.) * * *.

So far, this opinion has discussed the duty of the lawyer when the lawyer learns that the client has committed perjury. The lawyer is presented with a different dilemma when, prior to trial, the client states an intention to commit perjury at trial. This was the situation addressed in ABA Informal Opinion 1314 (1975) [interpreting the Code of Professional Responsibility]. The Committee, in that opinion, stated that the lawyer in that situation must advise the client that the lawyer must take one of two courses of action: withdraw prior to the submission of the false testimony, or, if the client insists on testifying falsely, report to the tribunal the falsity of the testimony.

The Committee distinguished, in Informal Opinion 1314, the situation where the lawyer does not know in advance that the client intends to commit perjury. In that case, the Committee stated that when the client does commit perjury, and the lawyer later learns of it, the lawyer may not disclose the perjury to the tribunal because of the lawyer's primary duty to protect the client's confidential communications. The Committee believes that Model Rule 3.3 calls for a different course of action by the lawyer.

The duty imposed on the lawyer by Informal Opinion 1314—when the lawyer knows in advance that the client intends to commit perjury, to advise the client that if the client insists on testifying falsely, the lawyer must disclose the client's intended perjury to the tribunal—was based on the Committee's reading of DR 7–102(A)(4), (6) and (7). These provisions prohibit a lawyer from: (1) knowingly using perjured testimony or false evidence; (2) participating in the creation or preservation of evidence the lawyer knows to be false, and (3) counseling or assisting the client in conduct the lawyer knows to be illegal or fraudulent. However, none of these prohibitions *requires* disclosure to the tribunal of any information otherwise protected by DR 4–101. Although DR 4–101(C)(3) permits a lawyer to reveal a client's stated intention to commit perjury, this exception to the lawyer's duty to preserve the client's confidences and secrets is only discretionary on the part of the lawyer.

* * * Ordinarily, after warning the client of the consequences of the client's perjury, including the lawyer's duty to disclose it to the court, the lawyer can reasonably believe that the client will be persuaded not to testify falsely at trial. That is exactly what happened in Nix v. Whiteside. Under these circumstances, the lawyer may permit the client to testify and may examine the client in the normal manner. If the client does in fact testify falsely, the lawyer's obligation to make disclosure to the court is covered by Rule 3.3(a)(2) and (4).

In the unusual case, where the lawyer does know, on the basis of the client's clearly stated intention, that the client will testify falsely at trial, and the lawyer is unable to effectively withdraw from the representation, the lawyer cannot examine the client in the usual manner. Under these circumstances, when the client has not yet committed perjury, the Committee believes that the lawyer's conduct should be guided in a way that is consistent, as much as possible, with the confidentiality protections provided in Rule 1.6, and yet not violative of Rule 3.3. This may be accomplished by the lawyer's refraining from calling the client as a witness when the lawyer knows that the only testimony the client would offer is false; or, where there is some testimony, other than the false testimony, the client can offer in the client's defense, by the lawyer's examining the client on only those matters and not on the subject matter which would produce the false testimony. Such conduct on the part of the lawyer would serve as a way for the lawyer to avoid assisting the fraudulent or criminal act of the client without having to disclose the client's confidences to the court. However, if the lawyer does not offer the client's testimony, and, on inquiry by the court into whether the client has been fully advised as to the client's right to testify, the client states a desire to testify, but is being prevented by the lawyer from testifying, the lawyer may have no other choice than to disclose to the court the client's intention to testify falsely.

This approach must be distinguished from the solution offered in the initially ABA-approved Defense Function Standard 7.7 (1971). This proposal, no longer applicable, permitted a lawyer, who could not dissuade the client from committing perjury and who could not withdraw, to call the client solely to give the client's own statement, without being questioned by the lawyer and without the lawyer's arguing to the jury any false testimony presented by the client.

The Committee believes that under Model Rule 3.3(a)(2) and the recent Supreme Court decision of Nix v. Whiteside, the lawyer can no longer rely on the narrative approach to insulate the lawyer from a charge of assisting the client's perjury. Despite differences on other issues in Nix v. Whiteside, the Justices were unanimous in concluding that a criminal defendant does not have the constitutional right to testify falsely. More recently, this ruling was made the basis of the holding by the Seventh Circuit in U.S. v. Henkel, 799 F.2d 369 (7th Cir.1986), that the defendant "had no right to lie" and, therefore, was not deprived of the right to counsel when the defense lawyer refused to present the defendant's testimony which he knew was false.

Can you think of anything more destructive to the attorney-client relationship than the knowledge that the attorney must inform on her client in certain circumstances? Can the perjury problem be handled through cross-examination? When a District Attorney was asked what the defense lawyer should do when a client proposes to commit perjury, he responded "Do me a favor. Let him try it." (Quoted in Freedman, Client Confidences and Client Perjury: Some Unanswered Questions, 136 U.Pa.L.Rev.1939 (1988)). Would most prosecutors respond the same way? Is the existence of a lawyer-client relationship a sufficient reason to permit defense lawyers but not prosecutors to offer perjured testimony? See Saltzburg, Lawyers, Clients, and the Adversary System, 37 Mercer L.Rev. 674 (1986). Compare the solutions proposed by the A.B.A. Ethics Committee with those proposed by Professor Monroe Freedman, who addressed the perjury problem in Lawyer's Ethics in an Adversary System (31–37) (1985).

In my opinion, the attorney's obligation in such a situation would be to advise the client that the proposed testimony is unlawful, but to proceed in the normal fashion in presenting the testimony and arguing the case to the jury if the client makes the decision to go forward. Any other course would be a betrayal of the assurances of confidentiality given by the attorney in order to induce the client to reveal everything, however damaging it might appear.

The most obvious way to avoid the ethical difficulty is for the lawyer to withdraw from the case, at least if there is sufficient time before trial for the client to retain another attorney. The client will then go to the nearest law office, realizing that the obligation of confidentiality is not what it has been represented to be, and withhold incriminating information or the fact of guilt from the new attorney. In terms of professional ethics, the practice of withdrawing from a case under such circumstances is difficult to defend, since the identical perjured testimony will ultimately be presented. Moreover, the new attorney will be ignorant of the perjury and therefore will be in no position to attempt to discourage the client from presenting it. Only the original attorney, who knows the truth, has that opportunity, but loses it in the very act of evading the ethical problem.

The difficulty is all the more severe when the client is indigent. In that event, the client cannot retain other counsel, and in many jurisdictions it is impossible for appointed counsel or a public defender to withdraw from a case except for extraordinary reasons. Thus, the attorney can successfully withdraw only by revealing to the judge that the attorney has received knowledge of the client's guilt, or by giving the judge a false or misleading reason for moving for leave to withdraw. However, for the attorney to reveal knowledge of the client's guilt would be a gross violation of the obligation of confidentiality, particularly since it is entirely possible in many jurisdictions that the same judge who permits the attorney to withdraw will subsequently hear the case and sentence the defendant. Not only will the judge then have personal knowledge of the defendant's guilt before the trial begins, but it will be knowledge of which the newly appointed counsel for the defendant will very likely be ignorant.

* * *

The question remains: what should the lawyer do when faced with the client's insistence upon taking the stand and committing perjury? [Freedman describes the "Free Narrative" proposal, in which defense counsel lets the defendant tell his story on the stand, without asking questions and without referring to the statement in closing argument.]

There are at least two critical flaws in that proposal. The first is purely practical: The prosecutor might well object to testimony from the defendant in narrative form rather than in the conventional manner, because it would give the prosecutor no opportunity to object to inadmissible evidence prior to the jury's hearing it. * * *

More importantly, experienced trial attorneys have often noted that jurors assume that the defendant's lawyer knows the truth about the case, and that the jury will frequently judge the defendant by drawing inferences from the attorney's conduct in the case. There is, of course, only one inference that can be drawn if the defendant's own attorney turns his or her back on the defendant at the most critical point in the trial, and then, in closing argument, sums up the case with no reference to the fact that the defendant has given exculpatory testimony.

Despite the rejection of the "free narrative" solution by the A.B.A., the Court in *Whiteside,* and Professor Freedman, the narrative "continues to be a commonly accepted method of dealing with client perjury." Shockley v. State, 565 A.2d 1373 (Del.1989) (holding that use of free narrative was ethically permissible and did not constitute ineffective assistance of counsel). See also Florida Bar v. Rubin, 549 So.2d 1000 (Fla.1989) (lawyer jailed for thirty days for refusing to defend client who intended to commit perjury; proper solution would have been to use a free narrative). Can the free narrative be prohibited in practice? Suppose a defendant volunteers perjured testimony that goes beyond the scope of defense counsel's questions. Would it constitute ineffective assistance for defense counsel to move to strike the volunteered testimony as unresponsive? Should defense counsel be required to inform the judge that the volunteered testimony is perjurious? Does anyone tell the jury?

F. THE HIDDEN PROBLEM

The overall quality and effectiveness of court-appointed attorneys may be limited by low compensation for services. For example, in New Hampshire the legislature in 1966 set statutory limits of $10 per hour for preparation time and $15 per hour for in-court time. The legislature set $500 per case as the maximum permissible compensation. In Smith v. New Hampshire, 118 N.H. 764, 394 A.2d 834 (1978), the New Hampshire Supreme Court invalidated these limits. The New Hampshire constitution requires the state to furnish defendants with counsel at the state's expense. The court concluded that, due to inflation, the statutory compensation scheme effectively shifted the burden of providing counsel to the New Hampshire bar. Because the obligations of the bar are matters of judicial concern only, the court assumed responsibility for determining reasonable compensation in each case. "The rate awarded by the court should neither unjustly enrich nor, as the present fee schedule does, unduly impoverish the court-appointed attorney." Underlying the court's decision is the concern that, without adequate compensation, counsel will not, or cannot, provide adequate representation.[84]

84. Interestingly, one study indicates that defendants are less satisfied with public defenders (including court-appointed attorneys) than with retained lawyers. Only 56% of public defender clients believed that their lawyers fought hard for them, compared to 75% of private lawyer clients. Evaluations of retained and appointed counsel reflected a comparable disparity on most criteria used. See J. Casper, Criminal Courts: The Defendant's Perspective 30–31 (1978). The differing perceptions of retained and appointed counsel may or may not reflect actual differences in effectiveness. To what extent do you think an indigent's inability to choose particular counsel accounts for the different confidence in

Smith brings to the surface a problem that few judges and fewer lawyers like to talk about: namely, whether there are systemic flaws in the process of appointing counsel for indigents. Public defenders often have enormous caseloads and, like prosecutors, may have to choose to dispose of cases in ways that maximize the overall output of the agency, rather than the welfare of any one client. Is an overworked public defender ineffective per se? Is it acceptable to give defenders excessive caseloads, if prosecutors operate under similar burdens? As pressured as the public defender may be, the public service instincts that drew her into defense work may encourage her to resist the natural tendency to focus on an overall success rate at the expense of particular clients. It is the absence of such instincts that poses problems for some lawyers appointed by courts to represent indigents. Some lawyers, especially young ones, may take appointed cases for the extra income they provide. Others are coerced by the courts into taking appointed cases. In either event, the lawyer has an incentive to end the case as quickly as possible, and usually no incentive to drag it out, even to prove her client's innocence.[85] We have already examined the conflict of interest that may arise when a lawyer represents two clients. There also can be a conflict of interest when a low flat fee (or no fee) for representation is set and a lawyer is asked to take a loss to represent a criminal defendant. Lawyers may have ethical provisions that praise public service, but like other people they prefer not to take an involuntary loss. Thus, what is in the best interests of the lawyer may not be in the best interests of the client. Is it possible that assignment schemes may be violative of the spirit of the counsel cases?

Even at the Supreme Court level, there may be a problem with adequate compensation for appointed attorneys. In In re Berger, 111 S.Ct. 628 (1991), counsel appointed to represent a capital defendant before the Supreme Court requested compensation well in excess of the statutory maximum of $2500 permitted by the Criminal Justice Act. She argued, and the Court agreed, that the Anti–Drug Abuse Amendments Act of 1988 (21 U.S.C. § 801 et seq.) permits the federal courts in capital cases to award compensation in an amount "reasonably necessary" to assure competent representation, without regard to CJA compensation maximums. In determining the amount to be awarded, the Court, in a *per curiam* opinion, stated:

> It could be reasonably argued, on the basis of our practice to date, that there is no need to award attorney's fees in an amount greater than the $2500 cap in order to induce capable counsel to represent capital defendants in this Court. But we think this argument is outweighed by the possibility that the cap of $2500 may, at the margins, deter otherwise willing and qualified attorneys from offering their services to represent indigent capital defendants. Given the rising costs of practicing law today, we believe that appointed

and satisfaction with appointed counsel? The limitations on a defendant's choice of counsel are discussed, infra.

85. Once in a while, a notorious case may result in good publicity. But most criminal cases do not establish "reputations" for defense counsel.

A number of jurisdictions have struggled with the problem of insufficient funds to pay defense counsel. For a description of the problem, see Ranii, The Criminal Defense Crisis, Nat'l L.J., April 26, 1982, at 1, col. 1.

Inadequate funding and support for public defender systems are discussed in Mounts, Public Defender Programs, Professional Responsibility, and Competent Representation, 1982 Wis.L.Rev. 473.

counsel in capital cases should be able to receive compensation in an amount not to exceed $5,000.

The Court rejected, as unduly time-consuming, a case-by-case determination of compensation which might have resulted in awards greater than $5000 in many cases. Will lower courts guarantee the same effective representation found by the Supreme Court if they apply the Court's $5,000 maximum in capital cases? Note that the compensation scheme at issue in *Berger* is only applicable in federal courts.

The Arizona Supreme Court held in State v. Smith, 140 Ariz. 355, 681 P.2d 1374 (1984), that a "bid system" of obtaining defense representation for indigents created a presumption of constitutionally inadequate representation, although the state rebutted the presumption in the instant case. The bid system invited all attorneys in a county to submit sealed bids for contracts to represent indigents. The four lowest bids were accepted without regard to the experience or ability of the attorneys or recommendations from judges, bar associations or other lawyers. Although the bid invitation stated that additional compensation might be paid for unusually complex cases, it also indicated that there had been no such case in fourteen years. The state supreme court found that the system "results in an attorney being so overburdened that he cannot adequately represent all his clients properly and be reasonably effective." Because the decision invalidated a long-standing practice, the court made its decision prospective rather than retroactive.

Once you recognize these problems with appointing lawyers, what sort of a system would you set up to provide incentives for good lawyering?

G. LIMITATIONS ON THE RIGHT TO COUNSEL OF CHOICE

Gideon guarantees an absolute right to counsel for all serious crimes. But there is no absolute right to choose a particular counsel. Whether there is any right at all to choose a particular counsel depends on whether the defendant can afford it. The Supreme Court has held that so long as an indigent receives effective representation, he has no right to choose a particular counsel. In Morris v. Slappy, 461 U.S. 1 (1983), Slappy was appointed counsel whom he trusted, but that counsel became ill before trial, and another was substituted. Slappy argued that a continuance should have been granted until trusted counsel could return. He did not contend that substitute counsel was ineffective. Chief Justice Burger, writing for the Court, interpreted Slappy's request, and the lower court's holding, as assuming that the indigent had the right to a "meaningful attorney-client relationship." He rejected this argument in no uncertain terms.

> No authority was cited for this novel ingredient of the Sixth Amendment guarantee, and of course none could be. No court could possibly guarantee that a defendant will develop the kind of rapport with his attorney * * * that the Court of Appeals thought part of the Sixth Amendment guarantee of counsel.

See also United States v. Pina, 844 F.2d 1 (1st Cir.1988) (court has no obligation to appoint a lawyer outside the public defender's office, simply because the defendant believes that all lawyers from that office are incompetent).

If the defendant can afford it, there is a *qualified* right to retain counsel of choice. The nature of these qualifications are discussed in the next two cases.

WHEAT v. UNITED STATES

Supreme Court of the United States, 1988.
486 U.S. 153.

CHIEF JUSTICE REHNQUIST delivered the opinion of the Court.

The issue in this case is whether the District Court erred in declining petitioner's waiver of his right to conflict-free counsel and by refusing to permit petitioner's proposed substitution of attorneys.

I

Petitioner Mark Wheat, along with numerous codefendants, was charged with participating in a farflung drug distribution conspiracy. * * *

Also charged in the conspiracy were Juvenal Gomez–Barajas and Javier Bravo, who were represented in their criminal proceedings by attorney Eugene Iredale. Gomez–Barajas was tried first and was acquitted on drug charges overlapping with those against petitioner. To avoid a second trial on other charges, however, Gomez–Barajas offered to plead guilty to tax evasion and illegal importation of merchandise. At the commencement of petitioner's trial, the District Court had not accepted the plea; Gomez–Barajas was thus free to withdraw his guilty plea and proceed to trial.

Bravo, evidently a lesser player in the conspiracy, decided to forgo trial and plead guilty to one count of transporting approximately 2,400 pounds of marijuana from Los Angeles to a residence controlled by Victor Vidal. At the conclusion of Bravo's guilty plea proceedings on August 22, 1985, Iredale notified the District Court that he had been contacted by petitioner and had been asked to try petitioner's case as well. In response, the Government registered substantial concern about the possibility of conflict in the representation. * * *

* * * The Government's position was premised on two possible conflicts. First, the District Court had not yet accepted the plea and sentencing arrangement negotiated between Gomez–Barajas and the Government; in the event that arrangement were rejected by the court, Gomez–Barajas would be free to withdraw the plea and stand trial. He would then be faced with the prospect of representation by Iredale, who in the meantime would have acted as petitioner's attorney. Petitioner, through his participation in the drug distribution scheme, was familiar with the sources and size of Gomez–Barajas' income, and was thus likely to be called as a witness for the Government at any subsequent trial of Gomez–Barajas. This scenario would pose a conflict of interest for Iredale, who would be prevented from cross-examining petitioner and thereby from effectively representing Gomez–Barajas.

Second, and of more immediate concern, Iredale's representation of Bravo would directly affect his ability to act as counsel for petitioner. The Government believed that a portion of the marijuana delivered by Bravo to Vidal's residence eventually was transferred to petitioner. In this regard, the Government contacted Iredale and asked that Bravo be made available as a witness to testify against petitioner, and agreed in exchange to modify its position at the time of Bravo's sentencing. In the likely event that Bravo were called to testify, Iredale's position in representing both men would become untenable, for ethical proscriptions would forbid him to cross-examine Bravo in any meaningful way. By failing to do so, he would also fail to provide petitioner with effective assistance of counsel. Thus because of Iredale's prior representation of Gomez–Barajas and Bravo and the potential for serious conflict of interest, the Government urged the District Court to reject the substitution of attorneys.

In response, petitioner emphasized his right to have counsel of his own choosing and the willingness of Gomez–Barajas, Bravo, and petitioner to waive the right to conflict-free counsel. Petitioner argued that the circumstances posited by the Government that would create a conflict for Iredale were highly speculative and bore no connection to the true relationship between the coconspirators. If called to testify, Bravo would simply say that he did not know petitioner and had no dealings with him; no attempt by Iredale to impeach Bravo would be necessary. Further, in the unlikely event that Gomez–Barajas went to trial on the charges of tax evasion and illegal importation, petitioner's lack of involvement in those alleged crimes made his appearance as a witness highly improbable. Finally, and most importantly, all three defendants agreed to allow Iredale to represent petitioner and to waive any future claims of conflict of interest. In petitioner's view, the Government was manufacturing implausible conflicts in an attempt to disqualify Iredale, who had already proved extremely effective in representing Gomez–Barajas and Bravo.

[The District Court found for the Government and rejected the substitution of Iredale. Wheat was convicted and the court of appeals confirmed the conviction.]

II

The Sixth Amendment to the Constitution guarantees that "[i]n all criminal prosecutions, the accused shall enjoy the right ... to have the Assistance of Counsel for his defence." * * * Realizing that an unaided layman may have little skill in arguing the law or in coping with an intricate procedural system, we have held that the Sixth Amendment secures the right to the assistance of counsel, by appointment if necessary, in a trial for any serious crime. Gideon v. Wainwright. We have further recognized that the purpose of providing assistance of counsel "is simply to ensure that criminal defendants receive a fair trial," and that in evaluating Sixth Amendment claims, "the appropriate inquiry focuses on the adversarial process, not on the accused's relationship with his lawyer as such." Thus, while the right to select and be represented by one's preferred attorney is comprehended by the Sixth Amendment, the essential aim of the Amendment is to guarantee an effective advocate for each criminal defendant rather than to ensure that a defendant will inexorably be represented by the lawyer whom he prefers. See Morris v. Slappy.

The Sixth Amendment right to choose one's own counsel is circumscribed in several important respects. Regardless of his persuasive powers, an advocate who is not a member of the bar may not represent clients (other than himself) in court.[a] Similarly, a defendant may not insist on representation by an attorney he cannot afford or who for other reasons declines to represent the defendant. Nor may a defendant insist on the counsel of an attorney who has a previous or ongoing relationship with an opposing party, even when the opposing party is the Government.

a. Our holding in Faretta v. California, [discussed infra], that a criminal defendant has a Sixth Amendment right to represent *himself* if he voluntarily elects to do so, does not encompass the right to choose any advocate if the defendant wishes to be represented by counsel.

The question raised in this case is the extent to which a criminal defendant's right under the Sixth Amendment to his chosen attorney is qualified by the fact that the attorney has represented other defendants charged in the same criminal conspiracy.

In previous cases, we have recognized that multiple representation of criminal defendants engenders special dangers of which a court must be aware. While "permitting a single attorney to represent codefendants ... is not per se violative of constitutional guarantees of effective assistance of counsel," Holloway v. Arkansas, a court confronted with and alerted to possible conflicts of interest must take adequate steps to ascertain whether the conflicts warrant separate counsel. See also Cuyler v. Sullivan.

* * *

Petitioner insists that the provision of waivers by all affected defendants cures any problems created by the multiple representation. But no such flat rule can be deduced from the Sixth Amendment presumption in favor of counsel of choice. Federal courts have an independent interest in ensuring that criminal trials are conducted within the ethical standards of the profession and that legal proceedings appear fair to all who observe them. Both the American Bar Association's Model Code of Professional Responsibility and its Model Rules of Professional Conduct, as well as the rules of the California Bar Association (which governed the attorneys in this case), impose limitations on multiple representation of clients. See ABA Model Code of Professional Responsibility DR5–105(C) (1980); ABA Model Rules of Professional Conduct, Rule 1.7 (1984); Rules of Professional Conduct of the State Bar of California, Rules 5 and 7, Cal.Bus. & Prof.Code Ann. § 6076 (West 1974). Not only the interest of a criminal defendant but the institutional interest in the rendition of just verdicts in criminal cases may be jeopardized by unregulated multiple representation.

For this reason, the Federal Rules of Criminal Procedure direct trial judges to investigate specially cases involving joint representation. * * *

To be sure, this need to investigate potential conflicts arises in part from the legitimate wish of district courts that their judgments remain intact on appeal. As the Court of Appeals accurately pointed out, trial courts confronted with multiple representations face the prospect of being "whipsawed" by assertions of error no matter which way they rule. If a district court agrees to the multiple representation, and the advocacy of counsel is thereafter impaired as a result, the defendant may well claim that he did not receive effective assistance. See, e.g., Burger v. Kemp. On the other hand, a district court's refusal to accede to the multiple representation may result in a challenge such as petitioner's in this case. Nor does a waiver by the defendant necessarily solve the problem, for we note, without passing judgment on, the apparent willingness of Courts of Appeals to entertain ineffective-assistance claims from defendants who have specifically waived the right to conflict-free counsel. See, e.g., United States ex rel. Tonaldi v. Elrod, 716 F.2d 431 (CA7 1983).

Thus, where a court justifiably finds an actual conflict of interest, there can be no doubt that it may decline a proffer of waiver, and insist that defendants be separately represented.

* * *

Unfortunately for all concerned, a district court must pass on the issue of whether or not to allow a waiver of a conflict of interest by a criminal defendant not with the wisdom of hindsight after the trial has taken place,[86] but in the murkier pre-trial context when relationships between parties are seen through a glass, darkly. The likelihood and dimensions of nascent conflicts of interest are notoriously hard to predict, even for those thoroughly familiar with criminal trials. It is a rare attorney who will be fortunate enough to learn the entire truth from his own client, much less be fully apprised before trial of what each of the Government's witnesses will say on the stand. A few bits of unforeseen testimony or a single previously unknown or unnoticed document may significantly shift the relationship between multiple defendants. These imponderables are difficult enough for a lawyer to assess, and even more difficult to convey by way of explanation to a criminal defendant untutored in the niceties of legal ethics. Nor is it amiss to observe that the willingness of an attorney to obtain such waivers from his clients may bear an inverse relation to the care with which he conveys all the necessary information to them.

For these reasons we think the district court must be allowed substantial latitude in refusing waivers of conflicts of interest not only in those rare cases where an actual conflict may be demonstrated before trial, but in the more common cases where a potential for conflict exists which may or may not burgeon into an actual conflict as the trial progresses. In the circumstances of this case, with the motion for substitution of counsel made so close to the time of trial the District Court relied on instinct and judgment based on experience in making its decision. We do not think it can be said that the court exceeded the broad latitude which must be accorded it in making this decision. Petitioner of course rightly points out that the Government may seek to "manufacture" a conflict in order to prevent a defendant from having a particularly able defense counsel at his side; but trial courts are undoubtedly aware of this possibility, and must take it into consideration along with all of the other factors which inform this sort of a decision.

Here the District Court was confronted not simply with an attorney who wished to represent two coequal defendants in a straightforward criminal prosecution; rather, Iredale proposed to defend three conspirators of varying stature in a complex drug distribution scheme. The Government intended to call Bravo as a witness for the prosecution at petitioner's trial.[b] The Government might readily have tied certain deliveries of marijuana by Bravo to petitioner, necessitating vigorous cross-examination of Bravo by petitioner's counsel. Iredale, because of his prior representation of Bravo, would have been unable ethically to provide that cross-examination.

Iredale had also represented Gomez–Barajas, one of the alleged kingpins of the distribution ring, and had succeeded in obtaining a verdict of acquittal for him. Gomez–Barajas had agreed with the Government to plead guilty to other charges, but the District Court had not yet accepted the plea arrangement. If the agreement were rejected, petitioner's probable testimony at the resulting trial of Gomez–Barajas would create an ethical dilemma for Iredale from which one or the other of his clients would likely suffer.

Viewing the situation as it did before trial, we hold that the District Court's refusal to permit the substitution of

86. Pretrial disqualification of defense counsel is not immediately appealable. Flanagan v. United States, 465 U.S. 259 (1984).

b. Bravo was in fact called as a witness at petitioner's trial. His testimony was elicited to demonstrate the transportation of drugs that the prosecution hoped to link to petitioner.

counsel in this case was within its discretion and did not violate petitioner's Sixth Amendment rights. Other district courts might have reached differing or opposite conclusions with equal justification, but that does not mean that one conclusion was "right" and the other "wrong." The District Court must recognize a presumption in favor of petitioner's counsel of choice, but that presumption may be overcome not only by a demonstration of actual conflict but by a showing of a serious potential for conflict. The evaluation of the facts and circumstances of each case under this standard must be left primarily to the informed judgment of the trial court.

The judgment of the Court of Appeals is accordingly affirmed.

JUSTICE MARSHALL, with whom JUSTICE BRENNAN joins, dissenting.

* * * In the course of discussing the District Court's ruling, the court sets forth several principles with which I agree. The Court acknowledges, as it must, that the Sixth Amendment's guarantee of assistance of counsel comprehends the right to select one's own attorney. The Court also states that, although this constitutional right is not absolute, it mandates a presumption in favor of accepting a criminal defendant's choice of counsel. Having articulated these principles, however, the Court unaccountably grants broad discretion to the trial court to decide whether this presumption has been overcome. As a consequence of this unwarranted deference to a trial court's decision respecting a constitutional right, the Court countenances a ruling that is patently incorrect. * * *

* * *

The mere fact of multiple representation, as the Court concedes, will not support an order preventing a criminal defendant from retaining counsel of his choice. As this Court has stated on prior occasions, such representation will not invariably pose a substantial risk of a serious conflict of interest and thus will not invariably imperil the prospect of a fair trial. The propriety of the District Court's order thus depends on whether the Government showed that the particular facts and circumstances of the multiple representation proposed in this case were such as to overcome the presumption in favor of petitioner's choice of counsel. * * *

At the time of petitioner's trial, Iredale's representation of Gomez-Barajas was effectively completed. * * * Gomez-Barajas was not scheduled to appear as a witness at petitioner's trial; thus, Iredale's conduct of that trial would not require him to question his former client. The only possible conflict this Court can divine from Iredale's representation of both petitioner and Gomez-Barajas rests on the premise that the trial court would reject the negotiated plea agreement and that Gomez-Barajas then would decide to go to trial. In this event, the Court tells us, "petitioner's probable testimony at the resulting trial of Gomez-Barajas would create an ethical dilemma for Iredale."

This argument rests on speculation of the most dubious kind. The Court offers no reason to think that the trial court would have rejected Gomez-Barajas' plea agreement; neither did the Government posit any such reason in its argument or brief before this Court. The most likely occurrence at the time petitioner moved to retain Iredale as his defense counsel was that the trial court would accept Gomez-Barajas' plea agreement, as the court in fact later did. Moreover, even if Gomez-Barajas had gone to trial, petitioner probably would not have testified. The record contains no indication that petitioner had any involvement in or information about crimes for which Gomez-Barajas might yet have stood trial. The only alleged connection between petitioner and Gomez–Barajas sprang from the conspiracy to distribute marijuana, and a jury already had acquitted Gomez–Barajas of that charge. It is therefore disingenuous to say that representation of both petitioner and Gomez–Barajas posed a serious potential for a conflict of interest.

Similarly, Iredale's prior representation of Bravo was not a cause for concern. The Court notes that the prosecution intended to call Bravo to the stand at petitioner's trial and asserts that Bravo's testimony could well have "necessitat[ed] vigorous cross-examination . . . by petitioner's counsel." The facts, however, belie the claim that Bravo's anticipated testimony created a serious potential for conflict. Contrary to the Court's inference, Bravo could not have testified about petitioner's involvement in the alleged marijuana distribution scheme. As all parties were aware at the time, Bravo did not know and could not identify petitioner; indeed, prior to the commencement of legal proceedings, the two men never had heard of each other. Bravo's eventual testimony at petitioner's trial related to a shipment of marijuana in which petitioner was not involved; the testimony contained not a single reference to petitioner. Petitioner's counsel did not cross-examine Bravo, and neither petitioner's counsel nor the prosecutor mentioned Bravo's testimony in closing argument. All of these developments were predictable when the District Court ruled on petitioner's request that Iredale serve as trial counsel; the contours of Bravo's testimony were clear at that time. Given the insignificance of this testimony to any matter that petitioner's counsel would dispute, the proposed joint representation of petitioner and Bravo did not threaten a conflict of interest.[c]

Moreover, even assuming that Bravo's testimony might have "necessitat[ed] vigorous cross-examination," the District Court could have insured against the possibility of any conflict of interest without wholly depriving petitioner of his constitutional right to the counsel of his choice. Petitioner's motion requested that Iredale either be substituted for petitioner's current counsel or be added to petitioner's defense team. Had the District Court allowed the addition of Iredale and then ordered that he take no part in the cross-examination of Bravo, any possibility of a conflict would have been removed. Especially in light of the availability of this precautionary measure, the notion that Iredale's prior representation of Bravo might well have caused a conflict of interest at petitioner's trial is nothing short of ludicrous.

* * *

JUSTICE STEVENS, with whom JUSTICE BLACKMUN joins, dissenting.

* * * [T]he Court gives inadequate weight to the informed and voluntary character of the clients' waiver of their right to conflict-free representation.

c. The very insignificance of Bravo's testimony, combined with the timing of the prosecutor's decision to call Bravo as a witness, raises a serious concern that the prosecutor attempted to manufacture a conflict in this case. The prosecutor's decision to use Bravo as a witness was an 11th-hour development. * * * Only after the prosecutor learned of the substitution motion and decided to oppose it did he arrange for Bravo's testimony by agreeing to recommend to the trial court a reduction in Bravo's sentence. Especially in light of the scarce value of Bravo's testimony, this prosecutorial behavior very plausibly may be viewed as a maneuver to prevent Iredale from representing petitioner at trial. Iredale had proved to be a formidable adversary; he previously had gained an acquittal for the alleged kingpin of the marijuana distribution scheme. * * * As the Court notes, governmental maneuvering of this kind is relevant to a trial court's decision as to whether to accept a criminal defendant's chosen counsel. The significant possibility that the prosecutor was engaging in such bad-faith conduct provides yet another reason to dispute the Court's resolution of this case.

Particularly, the Court virtually ignores the fact that additional counsel representing petitioner had provided him with sound advice concerning the wisdom of a waiver and would have remained available during the trial to assist in the defense. Thus, this is not a case in which the District Judge faced the question whether one counsel should be substituted for another; rather the question before him was whether petitioner should be permitted to have *additional* counsel of his choice. I agree with Justice Marshall that the answer to that question is perfectly clear.

Accordingly, although I agree with the Court's premise that district judges must be afforded wide latitude in passing on motions of this kind,[d] in this case it is abundantly clear to me that the District Judge abused his discretion and deprived this petitioner of a constitutional right of such fundamental character that reversal is required.

Note

Wheat is criticized in Green, "Through a Glass, Darkly": How the Court Sees Motions to Disqualify Criminal Defense Lawyers, 89 Colum.L.Rev. 1201 (1989). Among other criticisms, Professor Green notes that "the Court relied on an unwarranted assumption that if the defendant is willing to waive potential conflict of interest claims his attorney probably has not complied with the ethical standards governing the investigation and disclosure of potential conflicts." If that is so, isn't the Court's position in *Wheat* contrary to its statement in Burger v. Kemp, supra, where the Court said that "we generally presume that the lawyer is fully conscious of the overarching duty of complete loyalty to his or her client"? How can the two positions be reconciled? Professor Green also contends that the Court in *Wheat* "inexplicably retreated from the concern expressed in previous cases for the attorney-client relationship and for the defendant's autonomy," and that it "exaggerated the significance of judicial interests" which justify disqualification of counsel despite a client's waiver. Do you agree?

Wheat is defended in Stuntz, Waiving Rights in Criminal Procedure, 75 Va.L.Rev. 761 (1989). Professor Stuntz argues that clients jointly represented by a single counsel may have improper motives, especially in large conspiracy cases. It may be that joint counsel is there to deter conspirators from cutting an individual deal and cooperating with the government. On the other hand, it may be that the clients have proper motives—they all want the same lawyer because that lawyer is excellent. Stuntz argues that the capability of the lawyer is likely to be known by the trial judge; if the lawyer is known to be merely average, bad motives can be inferred. Therefore a broad grant of discretion to the trial judge is necessary to allow the judge to separate good from bad motives in joint representation. Professor Stuntz's arguments are not borne out under the facts in *Wheat,* however, where the trial judge specifically noted that Iredale was an excellent and highly successful defense attorney, and disqualified him nonetheless.

Why must a lawyer be disqualified if he has represented one client who is now testifying against another? Of course, the lawyer cannot cross-examine the witness-client with confidential information. But if the lawyer cross-examines the witness-client with only non-confidential information, as she must, who does the cross-examination hurt? How is that cross-examination different from that which

d. In my view, deference to the trial judge is appropriate in light of his or her greater familiarity with such factors as the ability of the defendant knowingly and voluntarily to waive a potential conflict (including the possibility that a codefendant may be exerting undue influence over the defendant), the character of the lawyers, the particular facts of the case, and the availability of alternative counsel of a like caliber.

would be conducted by substitute counsel? And if there is some limited impairment in the cross-examination, why can't the client consent to it? Is Professor Green correct that "the Court in *Wheat* upheld the denial of Wheat's choice of counsel in a case where the ethical rules plainly would have permitted that choice"? See United States v. Cunningham, 672 F.2d 1064 (2d Cir.1982) (no disqualification required where defense attorney would be able to avoid using non-public information in cross-examining the witness).

CAPLIN & DRYSDALE v. UNITED STATES

Supreme Court of the United States, 1989.
491 U.S. 617.

JUSTICE WHITE delivered the opinion of the Court.

We are called on to determine whether the federal drug forfeiture statute includes an exemption for assets that a defendant wishes to use to pay an attorney who conducted his defense in the criminal case where forfeiture was sought. Because we determine that no such exemption exists, we must decide whether that statute, so interpreted, is consistent with the Fifth and Sixth Amendments. We hold that it is.

I

In January 1985, Christopher Reckmeyer was charged in a multi-count indictment with running a massive drug importation and distribution scheme. The scheme was alleged to be a continuing criminal enterprise (CCE), in violation of 21 U.S.C. § 848. Relying on a portion of the CCE statute that authorized forfeiture to the Government of "property constituting, or derived from ... proceeds ... obtained" from drug-law violations, § 853(a),[a] the indictment sought forfeiture of specified assets in Reckmeyer's possession. At this time, the District Court, acting pursuant to § 853(e)(1)(A),[b] entered a restraining order forbidding Reckmeyer to transfer any of the listed assets that were potentially forfeitable.

Sometime earlier, Reckmeyer had retained petitioner, a law firm, to represent him in the ongoing grand jury investigation which resulted in the January 1985 indictments.

* * * Reckmeyer moved to modify the District Court's earlier restraining order to permit him to use some of the restrained assets to pay petitioner's fees; Reckmeyer also sought to exempt from any postconviction forfeiture order the assets that he intended to use to pay petitioner. However, one week later, before the District Court could conduct a hearing on this motion, Reckmeyer

a. The forfeiture statute provides, in relevant part, that any person convicted of a particular class of criminal offenses

"shall forfeit to the United States, irrespective of any provision of State law—

"(1) any property constituting, or derived from, any proceeds the person obtained, directly or indirectly, as the result of such violation;

.....

"The court, in imposing sentence on such person, shall order, in addition to any other sentence imposed ..., that the person forfeit to the United States all property described in this subsection." 21 U.S.C. § 853(a). * * *

b. The pretrial restraining order provision states that

"[u]pon application of the United States, the court may enter a restraining order or injunction ... or take any other action to preserve the availability of property described in subsection (a) of [§ 853] for forfeiture under this section—

"(A) upon the filing of an indictment or information charging a violation ... for which criminal forfeiture may be ordered under [§ 853] and alleging that the property with respect to which the order is sought would, in the event of conviction, be subject to forfeiture under this section." § 853(e)(1).

entered a plea agreement with the Government. Under the agreement, Reckmeyer pleaded guilty to the drug-related CCE charge, and agreed to forfeit all of the specified assets listed in the indictment. * * * Subsequently, an order forfeiting virtually all of the assets in Reckmeyer's possession was entered by the District Court in conjunction with his sentencing.

After this order was entered, petitioner filed a petition under § 853(n), which permits third parties with an interest in forfeited property to ask the sentencing court for an adjudication of their rights to that property; specifically, § 853(n)(6)(B) gives a third party who entered into a bona fide transaction with a defendant a right to make claims against forfeited property, if that third party was "at the time of [the transaction] reasonably without cause to believe that the [defendant's assets were] subject to forfeiture." * * * Petitioner argued alternatively that assets used to pay an attorney were exempt from forfeiture under § 853, and if not, the failure of the statute to provide such an exemption rendered it unconstitutional. The District Court granted petitioner's claim for a share of the forfeited assets.

[The Court of Appeals reversed in an en banc decision.]

II

[The Court, relying on the companion case of United States v. Monsanto, 491 U.S. 600, held that the statute did not exempt attorney's fees from forfeiture.]

III

We therefore address petitioner's constitutional challenges to the forfeiture law. Petitioner contends that the statute infringes on criminal defendants' Sixth Amendment right to counsel of choice, and upsets the "balance of power" between the Government and the accused in a manner contrary to the Due Process Clause of the Fifth Amendment. We consider these contentions in turn.

A

Petitioner's first claim is that the forfeiture law makes impossible, or at least impermissibly burdens, a defendant's right "to select and be represented by one's preferred attorney." Wheat v. United States. Petitioner does not, nor could it defensibly do so, assert that impecunious defendants have a Sixth Amendment right to choose their counsel. The Amendment guarantees defendants in criminal cases the right to adequate representation, but those who do not have the means to hire their own lawyers have no cognizable complaint so long as they are adequately represented by attorneys appointed by the courts. * * * Petitioner does not dispute these propositions. Nor does the Government deny that the Sixth Amendment guarantees a defendant the right to be represented by an otherwise qualified attorney whom that defendant can afford to hire, or who is willing to represent the defendant even though he is without funds. Applying these principles to the statute in question here, we observe that nothing in § 853 prevents a defendant from hiring the attorney of his choice, or disqualifies any attorney from serving as a defendant's counsel. Thus, unlike *Wheat,* this case does not involve a situation where the Government has asked a court to prevent a defendant's chosen counsel from representing the accused. Instead, petitioner urges that a violation of the Sixth Amendment arises here because of the forfeiture, at the instance of the Government, of assets that defendants intend to use to pay their attorneys.

Even in this sense, of course, the burden the forfeiture law imposes on a criminal defendant is limited. The forfeiture statute does not prevent a defendant who has nonforfeitable assets from retaining any attorney of his choosing. Nor is it necessarily the case that a defendant who possesses nothing but assets the Government seeks to have forfeited will be prevented from retaining counsel of choice. Defendants like Reckmeyer may be able to find lawyers willing to represent them, hoping that their fees will be paid in the event of acquittal, or via some other means that a defendant might come by in the future. The burden placed on defendants by the forfeiture law is therefore a limited one.

Nonetheless, there will be cases where a defendant will be unable to retain the attorney of his choice, when that defendant would have been able to hire that lawyer if he had access to forfeitable assets, and if there was no risk that fees paid by the defendant to his counsel would later be recouped under § 853(c).[c] It is in these cases, petitioner argues, that the Sixth Amendment puts limits on the forfeiture statute.

This submission is untenable. Whatever the full extent of the Sixth Amendment's protection of one's right to retain counsel of his choosing, that protection does not go beyond "the individual's right to spend his own money to obtain the advice and assistance of ... counsel." A defendant has no Sixth Amendment right to spend another person's money for services rendered by an attorney, even if those funds are the only way that that defendant will be able to retain the attorney of his choice. A robbery suspect, for example, has no Sixth Amendment right to use funds he has stolen from a bank to retain an attorney to defend him if he is apprehended. The money, though in his possession, is not rightfully his; the Government does not violate the Sixth Amendment if it seizes the robbery proceeds and refuses to permit the defendant to use them to pay for his defense. * * *

* * *

There is no constitutional principle that gives one person the right to give another's property to a third party, even where the person seeking to complete the exchange wishes to do so in order to exercise a constitutionally protected right. * * *

Petitioner's "balancing analysis" to the contrary rests substantially on the view that the Government has only a modest interest in forfeitable assets that may be used to retain an attorney. Petitioner takes the position that, in large part, once assets have been paid over from client to attorney, the principal ends of forfeiture have been achieved: dispossessing a drug dealer or racketeer of the proceeds of his wrongdoing. We think that this view misses the mark for three reasons.

First, the Government has a pecuniary interest in forfeiture that goes beyond merely separating a criminal from his ill-gotten gains; that legitimate interest extends to recovering all forfeitable assets, for such assets are deposited in a Fund that supports law-enforcement efforts in a variety of important and useful ways. The sums of money that can be raised for law-enforcement activities this way are substantial,[d] and the

c. That section of the statute, which includes the so-called "relation back" provision, states:

"All right, title, and interest in property described in [§ 853] vests in the United States upon the commission of the act giving rise to forfeiture under this section. Any such property that is subsequently transferred to a person other than the defendant may be the subject of a special verdict of forfeiture and thereafter shall be forfeited to the United States, unless the transferee establishes" his entitlement to such property pursuant to § 853(n), discussed supra. 21 U.S.C. § 853(c).

d. For example, just one of the assets which Reckmeyer agreed to forfeit, a parcel of land known as "Shelburne Glebe," was recently sold by federal authorities for $5.3 million.

Government's interest in using the profits of crime to fund these activities should not be discounted.

Second, the statute permits "rightful owners" of forfeited assets to make claims for forfeited assets before they are retained by the Government. The Government's interest in winning undiminished forfeiture thus includes the objective of returning property, in full, to those wrongfully deprived or defrauded of it. * * *

Finally, as we have recognized previously, a major purpose motivating congressional adoption and continued refinement of the racketeer influenced and corrupt organizations (RICO) and CCE forfeiture provisions has been the desire to lessen the economic power of organized crime and drug enterprises. This includes the use of such economic power to retain private counsel. As the Court of Appeals put it: "Congress has already underscored the compelling public interest in stripping criminals such as Reckmeyer of their undeserved economic power, and part of that undeserved power may be the ability to command high-priced legal talent." The notion that the Government has a legitimate interest in depriving criminals of economic power, even insofar as that power is used to retain counsel of choice, may be somewhat unsettling. But when a defendant claims that he has suffered some substantial impairment of his Sixth Amendment rights by virtue of the seizure or forfeiture of assets in his possession, such a complaint is no more than the reflection of "the harsh reality that the quality of a criminal defendant's representation frequently may turn on his ability to retain the best counsel money can buy." Again, the Court of Appeals put it aptly: "The modern day Jean Valjean must be satisfied with appointed counsel. Yet the drug merchant claims that his possession of huge sums of money ... entitles him to something more. We reject this contention, and any notion of a constitutional right to use the proceeds of crime to finance an expensive defense." [e]

It is our view that there is a strong governmental interest in obtaining full recovery of all forfeitable assets, an interest that overrides any Sixth Amendment interest in permitting criminals to use assets adjudged forfeitable to pay for their defense. * * *

We therefore reject petitioner's claim of a Sixth Amendment right of criminal defendants to use assets that are the Government's—assets adjudged forfeitable, as Reckmeyer's were—to pay attorney's fees, merely because those assets are in their possession.[f] See also

The proceeds of the sale will fund federal, state, and local law-enforcement activities.

e. We also reject the contention, advanced by amici, see, e.g., Brief for American Bar Association as Amicus Curiae 20–22, * * * that a type of "per se" ineffective assistance of counsel results—due to the particular complexity of RICO or drug-enterprise cases—when a defendant is not permitted to use assets in his possession to retain counsel of choice, and instead must rely on appointed counsel. If such an argument were accepted, it would bar the trial of indigents charged with such offenses, because those persons would have to rely on appointed counsel—which this view considers per se ineffective.

If appointed counsel is ineffective in a particular case, a defendant has resort to the remedies discussed in Strickland v. Washington. But we cannot say that the Sixth Amendment's guarantee of effective assistance of counsel is a guarantee of a privately retained counsel in every complex case, irrespective of a defendant's ability to pay.

f. Petitioner advances three additional reasons for invalidating the forfeiture statute, all of which concern possible ethical conflicts created for lawyers defending persons facing forfeiture of assets in their possession.

Petitioner first notes the statute's exemption from forfeiture of property transferred to a bona fide purchaser who was "reasonably without cause to believe that the property was subject to forfeiture." 21 U.S.C. § 853(n)(6)(B). This provision, it is said, might give an attorney an incentive not to investigate a defendant's case as fully as possible, so that the lawyer can invoke it to protect from forfeiture any fees he has received. Yet given the requirement that any assets which the

Monsanto, which rejects a similar claim with respect to pretrial orders and assets not yet judged forfeitable.

B

Petitioner's second constitutional claim is that the forfeiture statute is invalid under the Due Process Clause of the Fifth Amendment because it permits the Government to upset the "balance of forces between the accused and his accuser." We are not sure that this contention adds anything to petitioner's Sixth Amendment claim, because, while "[t]he Constitution guarantees a fair trial through the Due Process Clauses ... it defines the basic elements of a fair trial largely through the several provisions of the Sixth Amendment." * * * Even if, however, the Fifth Amendment provides some added protection not encompassed in the Sixth Amendment's more specific provisions, we find petitioner's claim based on the Fifth Amendment unavailing.

Forfeiture provisions are powerful weapons in the war on crime; like any such weapons, their impact can be devastating when used unjustly. But due process claims alleging such abuses are cognizable only in specific cases of prosecutorial misconduct (and petitioner has made no such allegation here) or when directed to a rule that is inherently unconstitutional. * * * Petitioner's claim—that the power available to prosecutors under the statute *could* be abused—proves too much, for many tools available to prosecutors can be misused in a way that violates the rights of innocent persons.

[The Court notes that it rejected a similar argument—that the risk of abuse warranted a per se rule—in *Wheat*].

* * * Cases involving particular abuses can be dealt with individually by the lower courts, when (and if) any such cases arise.

JUSTICE BLACKMUN, with whom JUSTICES BRENNAN, MARSHALL and STEVENS join, dissenting. [Dissent also applicable to *Monsanto*].

Those jurists who have held forth against the result the majority reaches in these cases have been guided by one core insight: that it is unseemly and unjust for the Government to beggar those it prosecutes in order to disable their defense at trial. The majority trivializes "the burden the forfeiture law

Government wishes to have forfeited must be specified in the indictment, see Fed.Rule Crim.Proc. 7(c)(2), the only way a lawyer could be a beneficiary of § 853(n)(6)(B) would be to fail to read the indictment of his client. In this light, the prospect that a lawyer might find himself in conflict with his client, by seeking to take advantage of § 853(n)(6)(B), amounts to very little. * * *

The second possible conflict arises in plea bargaining: petitioner posits that a lawyer may advise a client to accept an agreement entailing a more harsh prison sentence but no forfeiture—even where contrary to the client's interests—in an effort to preserve the lawyer's fee. Following such a strategy, however, would surely constitute ineffective assistance of counsel. We see no reason why our cases such as Strickland v. Washington are inadequate to deal with any such ineffectiveness where it arises. * * *

Finally, petitioner argues that the forfeiture statute, in operation, will create a system akin to "contingency fees" for defense lawyers: only a defense lawyer who wins acquittal for his client will be able to collect his fees, and contingent fees in criminal cases are generally considered unethical. See ABA Model Rule of Professional Conduct 1.5(d)(2) (1983); ABA Model Code of Professional Responsibility DR 2–106(C) (1979). But there is no indication here that petitioner, or any other firm, has actually sought to charge a defendant on a contingency basis; rather the claim is that a law firm's prospect of collecting its fee may turn on the outcome at trial. This, however, may often be the case in criminal defense work. Nor is it clear why permitting contingent fees in criminal cases—if that is what the forfeiture statute does—violates a criminal defendant's Sixth Amendment rights. The fact that a federal statutory scheme authorizing contingency fees—again, if that is what Congress has created in § 853 (a premise we doubt)—is at odds with model disciplinary rules or state disciplinary codes hardly renders the federal statute invalid.

imposes on a criminal defendant." Instead, it should heed the warnings of our district court judges, whose day-to-day exposure to the criminal-trial process enables them to understand, perhaps far better than we, the devastating consequences of attorney's fee forfeiture for the integrity of our adversarial system of justice.

* * *

I

[JUSTICE BLACKMUN argues that the statute exempts attorney's fees from forfeiture.]

II

* * * [T]he majority pauses hardly long enough to acknowledge "the Sixth Amendment's protection of one's right to retain counsel of his choosing," let alone to explore its "full extent." Instead, it moves rapidly from the observation that " '[a] defendant may not insist on representation by an attorney he cannot afford,' " quoting Wheat v. United States, to the conclusion that the Government is free to deem the defendant indigent by declaring his assets "tainted" by criminal activity the Government has yet to prove. That the majority implicitly finds the Sixth Amendment right to counsel of choice so insubstantial that it can be outweighed by a legal fiction demonstrates, still once again, its " 'apparent unawareness of the function of the independent lawyer as a guardian of our freedom.' "

A

Over 50 years ago, this Court observed: "It is hardly necessary to say that the right to counsel being conceded, a defendant should be afforded a fair opportunity to secure counsel of his own choice." Powell v. Alabama. For years, that proposition was settled; the controversial question was whether the defendant's right to use his own funds to retain his chosen counsel was the outer limit of the right protected by the Sixth Amendment. * * * [W]hile court appointment of effective counsel plays a crucial role in safeguarding the fairness of criminal trials, it has never defined the outer limits of the Sixth Amendment's demands. The majority's decision in *Caplin & Drysdale* reveals that it has lost track of the distinct role of the right to counsel of choice in protecting the integrity of the judicial process, a role that makes "the right to be represented by privately retained counsel . . . the primary, preferred component of the basic right" protected by the Sixth Amendment.

The right to retain private counsel serves to foster the trust between attorney and client that is necessary for the attorney to be a truly effective advocate. See ABA Standards for Criminal Justice 4–3.1, p. 4–29 (commentary) (2d ed 1980). Not only are decisions crucial to the defendant's liberty placed in counsel's hands, but the defendant's perception of the fairness of the process, and his willingness to acquiesce in its results, depend upon his confidence in his counsel's dedication, loyalty, and ability. When the Government insists upon the right to choose the defendant's counsel for him, that relationship of trust is undermined: counsel is too readily perceived as the Government's agent rather than his own. * * *

The right to retain private counsel also serves to assure some modicum of equality between the Government and those it chooses to prosecute. The Government can be expected to "spend vast sums of money . . . to try defendants accused of crime," and of course will devote greater resources to complex cases in which the punitive stakes are high. Precisely for this reason, "there are few defendants charged with crime, few indeed, who fail to hire the best lawyers they can get to prepare and present their defenses." But when the Government provides for appointed counsel, there is no guarantee that levels of compensation and staffing will be even average. * * * Over the long haul, the result of lowered compensation levels will be that talented attorneys will "decline to enter criminal practice. ... This exodus of talented attorneys could devastate the criminal defense bar." Winick, Forfeiture of Attorneys' Fees under RICO and CCE and the Right to Counsel of Choice: The Constitutional Dilemma and How to Avoid It, 43 U.Miami L.Rev. 765, 781 (1989). Without the defendant's right to retain private counsel, the Government too readily could defeat its adversaries simply by outspending them.

The right to privately chosen and compensated counsel also serves broader institutional interests. The "virtual socialization of criminal defense work in this country" that would be the result of a widespread abandonment of the right to retain chosen counsel, Brief for Committees on Criminal Advocacy and Criminal Law of the Association of the Bar of the City of New York et al. as Amici Curiae, too readily would standardize the provision of criminal-defense services and diminish defense counsel's independence. There is a place in our system of criminal justice for the maverick and the risk taker and for approaches that might not fit into the structured environment of a public defender's office, or that might displease a judge whose preference for nonconfrontational styles of advocacy might influence the judge's appointment decisions. There is also a place for the employment of "specialized defense counsel" for technical and complex cases. * * * Only a healthy, independent defense bar can be expected to meet the demands of the varied circumstances faced by criminal defendants, and assure that the interests of the individual defendant are not unduly "subordinat[ed] ... to the needs of the system."

* * *

B

Had it been Congress' express aim to undermine the adversary system as we know it, it could hardly have found a better engine of destruction than attorney's-fee forfeiture. The main effect of forfeitures under the Act, of course, will be to deny the defendant the right to retain counsel, and therefore the right to have his defense designed and presented by an attorney he has chosen and trusts.[g] If the Government restrains the defendant's assets before trial, private counsel will be unwilling to continue, or to take on, the defense. Even if no restraining order is entered, the possiblity of forfeiture after conviction will itself substantially diminish the likelihood that private counsel will agree to take the case. * * *

The resulting relationship between the defendant and his court-appointed counsel will likely begin in distrust, and be exacerbated to the extent that the defendant perceives his new-found "indigency" as a form of punishment imposed by the Government in order to weaken his defense. * * * Appointed counsel may be inexperienced and undercompensated and, for that reason, may not have adequate opportunity or resources to deal with the special problems presented by what is likely to be a complex trial. The already scarce resources of a public defender's office will

g. There is reason to fear that, in addition to depriving a defendant of counsel of choice, there will be circumstances in which the threat of forfeiture will deprive the defendant of *any* counsel. If the Government chooses not to restrain transfers by employing § 853(e)(1), it is likely that the defendant will not qualify as "indigent" under the Criminal Justice Act. Potential private counsel will be aware of the threat of forfeiture, and, as a result, will likely refuse to take the case. * * *

be stretched to the limit. Facing a lengthy trial against a better armed adversary, the temptation to recommend a guilty plea will be great. The result, if the defendant is convicted, will be a sense, often well grounded, that justice was not done.

Even if the defendant finds a private attorney who is "so foolish, ignorant, beholden or idealistic as to take the business," the attorney-client relationship will be undermined by the forfeiture statute. Perhaps the attorney will be willing to violate ethical norms by working on a contingent-fee basis in a criminal case. But if he is not—and we should question the integrity of any criminal-defense attorney who would violate the ethical norms of the profession by doing so—the attorney's own interests will dictate that he remain ignorant of the source of the assets from which he is paid. Under § 853(c), a third-party transferee may keep assets if "the transferee establishes ... that he is a bona fide purchaser for value of such property who at the time of purchase was reasonably without cause to believe that the property was subject to forfeiture under this section." The less an attorney knows, the greater the likelihood that he can claim to have been an "innocent" third party. The attorney's interest in knowing nothing is directly adverse to his client's interest in full disclosure. The result of the conflict may be a less vigorous investigation of the defendant's circumstances, leading in turn to a failure to recognize or pursue avenues of inquiry necessary to the defense. Other conflicts of interest are also likely to develop. The attorney who fears for his fee will be tempted to make the Government's waiver of fee forfeiture the sine qua non for any plea agreement, a position which conflicts with his client's best interests.

Perhaps most troubling is the fact that forfeiture statutes place the Government in the position to exercise an intolerable degree of power over any private attorney who takes on the task of representing a defendant in a forfeiture case. * * * The Government will be ever tempted to use the forfeiture weapon against a defense attorney who is particularly talented or aggressive on the client's behalf—the attorney who is better than what, in the Government's view, the defendant deserves. The specter of the Government's selectively excluding only the most talented defense counsel is a serious threat to the equality of forces necessary for the adversarial system to perform at its best. * * *

The long-term effects of the fee-forfeiture practice will be to decimate the private criminal-defense bar. As the use of the forfeiture mechanism expands to new categories of federal crimes and spreads to the States, only one class of defendants will be free routinely to retain private counsel: the affluent defendant accused of a crime that generates no economic gain. As the number of private clients diminishes, only the most idealistic and the least skilled of young lawyers will be attracted to the field, while the remainder seek greener pastures elsewhere.

* * *

Note

Isn't the forfeitability of the assets the very point to be decided at trial? Hasn't the majority, by presuming the assets are ill-gotten and thus not the defendant's, begged the question? Maybe not, because according to the dissenters, it is the risk that assets will later be adjudicated forfeitable at trial which prevents the defendant from being able to retain an attorney. Still, where assets are restrained prior to trial, as in *Monsanto* (the companion case to *Caplin & Drysdale*), an argument can be made that the defendant is entitled at a minimum to notice and an opportunity to defend against the restraining order. See Mitchell v. W.T. Grant Co., 416 U.S. 600 (1974), requiring a hearing promptly after a seizure made pursuant to a pre-judgment remedy. The forfeiture statute does not provide for a hearing if assets are restrained after the defendant has been indicted on a forfeiture count (though there is a hearing requirement for pre-indictment restraint on assets). The statute provides that the fact of indictment is enough to show that the government is entitled to an order restraining the defendant's assets. How significant is this protection?

On remand in *Monsanto,* the court of appeals held that defendants subject to pre-trial restraint of assets are entitled to a hearing at which the government must show evidence independent of the indictment itself. This evidence must indicate that the restrained assets are likely to be found forfeitable by the jury. A hearing is not required before a temporary restraining order is issued, however, since the very point is to surprise the defendant and prevent his disposition of forfeitable assets. See 924 F.2d 1186 (2d Cir.1991). How can a defendant whose assets have been restrained afford to pay counsel for the hearing provided by *Monsanto?*

There are other situations in which the right to chosen counsel has been overridden by a state interest. Thus defense attorneys have been subpoenaed before grand juries, as well as after indictment, to give non-privileged evidence against their client, such as information concerning fee arrangements. This may result in disqualification of the attorney under relevant ethical codes. See Disciplinary Rule 5–102 of the Code of Professional Responsibility and Rule 3.7 of the Model Rules of Professional Conduct (both disqualifying the lawyer when he may be called as a witness against the client). In these cases, the qualified right to chosen counsel has usually been held outweighed by the state's interest in investigating and prosecuting crime. See In re Grand Jury Subpoena Served Upon John Doe, 781 F.2d 238 (2d Cir.1985) (en banc). Prosecutors are not allowed to subpoena defense counsel solely to create a disqualification, but it is the rare case where such bad intent will be found. See In re Antitrust Grand Jury Investigation, 714 F.2d 347 (4th Cir.1983) (where subpoena might aid in the investigation or prosecution, "the subpoena should issue even though there is also the possibility that the prosecutor will use it for some purpose other than obtaining evidence"). Compare In re Grand Jury Matters, 751 F.2d 13 (1st Cir.1984) (subpoena on defense attorney quashed where it was issued right before trial in circumstances indicating that the prosecutor was retaliating for successful motions by defense counsel). Problems created when defense attorneys are subpoenaed are discussed in Capra, Deterring the Formation of the Attorney–Client Relationship: Disclosure of Client Identity, Payment of Fees, and Communications by Fiduciaries, 4 Geo.J.Leg.Eth. 235 (1990).

If defendant's chosen counsel is from out-of-state, counsel must apply for *pro hac vice* admission. In Leis v. Flynt, 439 U.S. 438 (1979), the Court held that the attorney had no due process right to be admitted *pro hac vice.* But the Court in *Leis* did not consider whether a criminal defendant's right to chosen counsel would be violated if out-of-state counsel is denied *pro hac vice* admission. Generally, courts have found that the state has a legitimate interest in regulating the practice of out-of-state lawyers trying cases in local courts, and that *pro hac vice* admission can be denied so long as the exclusion is not arbitrary. See Panzardi–Alvarez v. United States, 879 F.2d 975 (1st Cir.1989) (denial of *pro hac vice* admission does not violate right to chosen counsel where counsel had previously represented joint clients with conflicting interests). Compare Fuller v. Diesslin, 868 F.2d 604 (3d Cir.1989), where the trial court denied *pro hac vice* admission on the ground that local lawyers were always better prepared on local practice rules, that out-of-state attorneys created delays due to traveling and that there were many local attorneys who could effectively represent the defendant. The court of appeals found that the right to chosen counsel had been violated:

> [T]he trial court's wooden approach and its failure to make record-supported findings balancing the right to [chosen] counsel with the demands of the administration of justice resulted in an arbitrary denial [which] constituted per se constitutional error * * *. We conclude that [the argument that if there is adequate local counsel, then *pro hac vice* admission can be denied] is without merit, because it collapses the right to counsel of choice into the right to effective assistance of counsel. * * * [A]lthough the core value in the sixth amendment is effective assistance of counsel, the amendment also comprehends other related rights, such as the right to select and be represented by one's preferred attorney.

VIII. SELF-REPRESENTATION

A. THE CONSTITUTIONAL RIGHT

Although a defendant has a right to the assistance of counsel in all criminal prosecutions, sometimes she may prefer to defend herself. Beginning with the Judiciary Act of 1789, the right of self-representation in federal courts has been protected by statute.[87] Before Faretta v. California, 422 U.S. 806 (1975), established that a defendant in a state criminal trial has a constitutional right to proceed pro se, most states also granted that right. But California, where Anthony Faretta was convicted of grand theft, did not. It allowed a judge to appoint counsel over Faretta's objection and despite his knowing and intelligent waiver of his right to counsel.

FARETTA v. CALIFORNIA

Supreme Court of the United States, 1975.
422 U.S. 806.

MR. JUSTICE STEWART delivered the opinion of the Court.

* * *

I

Anthony Faretta was charged with grand theft in an information filed in the Superior Court of Los Angeles County, Cal. At the arraignment, the Superior Court Judge assigned to preside at the trial appointed the public defender to represent Faretta. Well before the date of trial, however, Faretta requested that he be permitted to represent himself. Questioning by the judge revealed that Faretta had once represented himself in a criminal prosecution, that he had a high school education, and that he did not want to be represented by the public defender because he believed that that office was "very loaded down with * * * a heavy case load." The judge responded that he believed Faretta was "making a mistake" and emphasized that in further proceedings Faretta would receive no special favors. Nevertheless, after establishing that Faretta wanted to represent himself and did not want a lawyer,

87. Section 35 of the Judiciary Act of 1789, 1 Stat. 73, 92 (1789) (current version at 28 U.S.C.A. § 1654 (1970)) provided that "in all courts of the United States, the parties may plead and manage their own causes personally or by the assistance of * * * counsel. * * *"

the judge, in a "preliminary ruling," accepted Faretta's waiver of the assistance of counsel. The judge indicated, however, that he might reverse this ruling if it later appeared that Faretta was unable adequately to represent himself.

Several weeks thereafter, but still prior to trial, the judge *sua sponte* held a hearing to inquire into Faretta's ability to conduct his own defense, and questioned him specifically about both the hearsay rule and the state law governing the challenge of potential jurors. After consideration of Faretta's answers, and observation of his demeanor, the judge ruled that Faretta had not made an intelligent and knowing waiver of his right to the assistance of counsel, and also ruled that Faretta had no constitutional right to conduct his own defense. The judge, accordingly, reversed his earlier ruling permitting self-representation and again appointed the public defender to represent Faretta. Faretta's subsequent request for leave to act as cocounsel was rejected, as were his efforts to make certain motions on his own behalf. Throughout the subsequent trial, the judge required that Faretta's defense be conducted only through the appointed lawyer from the public defender's office. At the conclusion of the trial, the jury found Faretta guilty as charged, and the judge sentenced him to prison.

[The appellate court affirmed Faretta's conviction.]

II

[The Court reviewed federal and state statutes according the right of self-representation, and decisions supporting such a right.]

This Court's past recognition of the right of self-representation, the federal-court authority holding the right to be of constitutional dimension, and the state constitutions pointing to the right's fundamental nature form a consensus not easily ignored. "[T]he mere fact that a path is a beaten one," Mr. Justice Jackson once observed, "is a persuasive reason for following it." We confront here a nearly universal conviction, on the part of our people as well as our courts, that forcing a lawyer upon an unwilling defendant is contrary to his basic right to defend himself if he truly wants to do so.

III

This consensus is soundly premised. The right of self-representation finds support in the structure of the Sixth Amendment, as well as in the English and colonial jurisprudence from which the Amendment emerged.

A

The Sixth Amendment includes a compact statement of the rights necessary to a full defense * * *. Because these rights are basic to our adversary system of criminal justice, they are part of the "due process of law" that is guaranteed by the Fourteenth Amendment to defendants in the criminal courts of the States. The rights to notice, confrontation, and compulsory process, when taken together, guarantee that a criminal charge may be answered in a manner now considered fundamental to the fair administration of American justice—through the calling and interrogation of favorable witnesses, the cross-examination of adverse witnesses, and the orderly introduction of evidence. In short, the Amendment constitutionalizes the right in an adversary criminal trial to make a defense as we know it.

The Sixth Amendment does not provide merely that a defense shall be made for the accused; it grants to the accused personally the right to make his defense. It is the accused, not counsel, who must be "informed of the nature and cause of the accusation," who must be "confronted with the witnesses against him," and who must be accorded "compulsory process for obtaining witnesses in his favor." Although not stated in the Amendment in so many words, the right to self-representation—to make one's own defense personally—is thus necessarily implied by the structure of the Amendment. The right to defend is given directly to the accused; for it is he who suffers the consequences if the defense fails.

The counsel provision supplements this design. It speaks of the "assistance" of counsel, and an assistant, however expert, is still an assistant. The language and spirit of the Sixth Amendment contemplate that counsel, like the other defense tools guaranteed by the Amendment, shall be an aid to a willing defendant—not an organ of the State interposed between an unwilling defendant and his right to defend himself personally. To thrust counsel upon the accused, against his considered wish, thus violates the logic of the Amendment. In such a case, counsel is not an assistant, but a master; and the right to make a defense is stripped of the personal character upon which the Amendment insists. It is true that when a defendant chooses to have a lawyer manage and present his case, law and tradition may allocate to the counsel the power to make binding decisions of trial strategy in many areas. This allocation can only be justified, however, by the defendant's consent, at the outset, to accept counsel as his representative. An unwanted counsel "represents" the defendant only through a tenuous and unacceptable legal fiction. Unless the accused has acquiesced in such representation, the defense presented is not the defense guaranteed him by the Constitution, for, in a very real sense, it is not *his* defense.

* * *

[The Court explored in detail the historical development of the right to counsel in England and in the United States. It found that both English and colonial legal history support interpreting the Sixth Amendment to imply a right of self-representation].

* * *

IV

There can be no blinking the fact that the right of an accused to conduct his own defense seems to cut against the grain of this Court's decisions holding that the Constitution requires that no accused can be convicted and imprisoned unless he has been accorded the right to the assistance of counsel. For it is surely true that the basic thesis of those decisions is that the help of a lawyer is essential to assure the defendant a fair trial. And a strong argument can surely be made that the whole thrust of those decisions must inevitably lead to the conclusion that a State may constitutionally impose a lawyer upon even an unwilling defendant.

But it is one thing to hold that every defendant, rich or poor, has the right to the assistance of counsel, and quite another to say that a State may compel a defendant to accept a lawyer he does not want. The value of state-appointed counsel was not unappreciated by the Founders, yet the notion of compulsory counsel was utterly foreign to them. And whatever else may be said of those who wrote the Bill of Rights, surely there can be no doubt that they understood the inestimable worth of free choice.

It is undeniable that in most criminal prosecutions defendants could better defend with counsel's guidance than by their own unskilled efforts. But where the defendant will not voluntarily accept representation by counsel, the potential advantage of a lawyer's training and experience can be realized, if at all, only imperfectly. To force a lawyer on a defendant can only lead him to believe that the law contrives against him. Moreover, it is not inconceivable that in some rare instances, the defendant might in fact present his case more effectively by conducting his own defense. Personal liberties are not rooted in the law of averages. The right to defend is personal. The defendant, and not his lawyer or the State, will bear the personal consequences of a conviction. It is the defendant, therefore, who must be free personally to decide whether in his particular case counsel is to his advantage. And although he may conduct his own defense ultimately to his own detriment, his choice must be honored out of "that respect for the individual which is the lifeblood of the law." [a]

V

When an accused manages his own defense, he relinquishes, as a purely factual matter, many of the traditional benefits associated with the right to counsel. For this reason, in order to represent himself, the accused must "knowingly and intelligently" forego those relinquished benefits. Although a defendant need not himself have the skill and experience of a lawyer in order competently and intelligently to choose self-representation, he should be made aware of the dangers and disadvantages of self-representation, so that the record will establish that "he knows what he is doing and his choice is made with eyes open."

Here, weeks before trial, Faretta clearly and unequivocally declared to the trial judge that he wanted to represent himself and did not want counsel. The record affirmatively shows that Faretta was literate, competent, and understanding, and that he was voluntarily exercising his informed free will. The trial judge had warned Faretta that he thought it was a mistake not to accept the assistance of counsel, and that Faretta would be required to follow all the "ground rules" of trial procedure. We need make no assessment of how well or poorly Faretta had mastered the intricacies of the hearsay rule and the California code provisions that govern challenges of potential jurors on *voir dire.* For his technical legal knowledge, as such, was not relevant to an assessment of his knowing exercise of the right to defend himself.

In forcing Faretta, under these circumstances, to accept against his will a state-appointed public defender, the California courts deprived him of his constitutional right to conduct his own defense. Accordingly, the judgment before us is vacated, and the case is remanded for further proceedings not inconsistent with this opinion.

MR. CHIEF JUSTICE BURGER, with whom MR. JUSTICE BLACKMUN and MR. JUSTICE REHNQUIST join, dissenting.

* * *

This case * * * is an example of the judicial tendency to constitutionalize what is thought "good." That effort fails on its own terms here, because there is nothing desirable or useful in permitting every accused person, even the most uneducated and inexperienced, to insist upon conducting his own defense to criminal charges. Moreover, there is no constitutional ba-

a. Of course, a State may—even over objection by the accused—appoint a "standby counsel" to aid the accused if and when the accused requests help, and to be available to represent the accused in the event that termination of the defendant's self-representation is necessary.

The right of self-representation is not a license to abuse the dignity of the courtroom. Neither is it a license not to comply with relevant rules of procedural and substantive law. Thus, whatever else may or may not be open to him on appeal, a defendant who elects to represent himself cannot thereafter complain that the quality of his own defense amounted to a denial of "effective assistance of counsel."

sis for the Court's holding, and it can only add to the problems of an already malfunctioning criminal justice system. I therefore dissent.

I

The most striking feature of the Court's opinion is that it devotes so little discussion to the matter which it concedes is the core of the decision, that is, discerning an independent basis in the Constitution for the supposed right to represent oneself in a criminal trial. Its ultimate assertion that such a right is tucked between the lines of the Sixth Amendment is contradicted by the Amendment's language and its consistent judicial interpretation.

As the Court seems to recognize, the conclusion that the rights guaranteed by the Sixth Amendment are "personal" to an accused reflects nothing more than the obvious fact that it is he who is on trial and therefore has need of a defense. But neither that nearly trivial proposition nor the language of the Amendment, which speaks in uniformly mandatory terms, leads to the further conclusion that the right to counsel is merely supplementary and may be dispensed with at the whim of the accused. Rather, this Court's decisions have consistently included the right to counsel as an integral part of the bundle making up the larger "right to a defense as we know it."

* * *

II

[The dissent also differed with the majority's use of precedent and history, and concluded that the majority improperly found a new right in the Constitution.]

* * *

IV

Society has the right to expect that, when courts find new rights implied in the Constitution, their potential effect upon the resources of our criminal justice system will be considered. However, such considerations are conspicuously absent from the Court's opinion in this case.

It hardly needs repeating that courts at all levels are already handicapped by the unsupplied demand for competent advocates, with the result that it often takes far longer to complete a given case than experienced counsel would require. If we were to assume that there will be widespread exercise of the newly discovered constitutional right to self-representation, it would almost certainly follow that there will be added congestion in the courts and that the quality of justice will suffer. * * *

* * *

[Justice Blackmun also wrote a dissenting opinion in which the Chief Justice and Justice Rehnquist joined. He argued that the procedural problems spawned by the case "will far outweigh whatever tactical advantage the defendant may feel he has gained by electing to represent himself." Referring to the old proverb that "one who is his own lawyer has a fool for a client," Justice Blackmun opined that "the Court * * * now bestows a *constitutional* right on one to make a fool of himself."]

Note

In order to exercise the independent right of self-representation, a defendant must knowingly and intelligently relinquish the right to assistance of counsel. A criminal defendant usually is untrained and unskilled in law and trial procedures. Studies indicate that representation by an attorney substantially improves an accused's chances of receiving a preliminary hearing and release on bail. A

defendant represented by an attorney more frequently receives a jury trial, dismissal or acquittal and, if convicted, more frequently receives a suspended sentence, a relatively short sentence, or probation. See Nagel, Effects of Alternative Types of Counsel on Criminal Procedure Treatment, 48 Ind.L.J. 404 (1972–73) (based on data in 1 L. Silverstein, Defense of the Poor in Criminal Cases in American State Courts: A Field Study and Report (1965)). Should a defendant be advised of these and other dangers of self-representation before he waives the assistance of counsel? See Brown v. Smith, 470 F.Supp. 131 (S.D.N.Y.1979) (inadequate waiver of counsel). See also United States v. Robinson, 913 F.2d 712 (9th Cir.1990) (for a knowing and intelligent waiver, "a criminal defendant must be aware of the nature of the charges against him, the possible penalties, and the dangers and disadvantages of self-representation").

A model inquiry for Federal District Judges to use with defendants who wish to proceed *pro se* is contained in 1 Bench Book for United States District Judges 1.02–2 to –5 (3d ed. 1986):

> When a defendant states that he wishes to represent himself, you should . . . ask questions similar to the following:
>
> (a) Have you ever studied law?
>
> (b) Have you ever represented yourself or any other defendant in a criminal action?
>
> (c) You realize, do you not, that you are charged with these crimes: (Here state the crimes with which the defendant is charged.)
>
> (d) You realize, do you not, that if you are found guilty of the crime charged in Count I the court must impose an assessment of at least $50 ($25 if a misdemeanor) and could sentence you to as much as ______ years in prison and fine you as much as $______?
>
> (Then ask him a similar question with respect to each other crime with which he may be charged in the indictment or information.)
>
> (e) You realize, do you not, that if you are found guilty of more than one of those crimes this court can order that the sentences be served consecutively, that is, one after another?
>
> (f) You realize, do you not, that if you represent yourself, you are on your own? I cannot tell you how you should try your case or even advise you as to how to try your case.
>
> (g) Are you familiar with the Federal Rules of Evidence?
>
> (h) You realize, do you not, that the Federal Rules of Evidence govern what evidence may or may not be introduced at trial and, in representing yourself, you must abide by those rules?
>
> (i) Are you familiar with the Federal Rules of Criminal Procedure?
>
> (j) You realize, do you not, that those rules govern the way in which a criminal action is tried in federal court?
>
> (k) You realize, do you not, that if you decide to take the witness stand, you must present your testimony by asking questions of yourself? You cannot just take the stand and tell your story. You must proceed question by question through your testimony.
>
> (*l*) (Then say to the defendant something to this effect):

I must advise you that in my opinion you would be far better defended by a trained lawyer than you can be by yourself. I think it is unwise of you to try to represent yourself. You are not familiar with the law. You are not familiar with court procedure. You are not familiar with the rules of evidence. I would strongly urge you not to try to represent yourself.

(m) Now, in light of the penalty that you might suffer if you are found guilty and in light of all of the difficulties of representing yourself, is it still your desire to represent yourself and to give up your right to be represented by a lawyer?

(n) Is your decision entirely voluntary on your part?

(*o*) If the answers to the two preceding questions are in the affirmative, [and in your opinion the waiver of counsel *is* knowing and voluntary,] you should then say something to the following effect:

"I find that the defendant has knowingly and voluntarily waived his right to counsel. I will therefore permit him to represent himself."

(p) You should consider the appointment of standby counsel to assist the defendant and to replace him if the court should determine during trial that the defendant can no longer be permitted to represent himself.

Failure to conduct a waiver inquiry at least similar to that suggested in the Bench Book has been held reversible error. See United States v. McDowell, 814 F.2d 245 (6th Cir.1987); United States v. Balough, 820 F.2d 1485 (9th Cir.1987) (noting "limited exception" to per se reversal where the record on the whole reveals a knowing and intelligent waiver).

Numerous courts have held that a defendant's waiver of the right to assistance of counsel must be "unequivocal." For example, in Meeks v. Craven, 482 F.2d 465 (9th Cir. 1973), the defendant argued in a petition for habeas corpus that he was denied his right to proceed pro se. The court refused habeas corpus relief because the defendant's demand to proceed without counsel was not unequivocal.

Meeks' demand in this case was certainly not "unequivocal." He made no demand to proceed without counsel at the beginning of his trial. It is during the afternoon session that there appear in the record three statements which could be construed as demands by Meeks to proceed *pro se:*

"The Defendant: Your Honor, I have a motion before me. I got a hernia. Motion is whether or not I can proceed on pro per status, and my motion is based on points and authorities if you'd like to hear them.

"The Court: Why do you want to proceed in pro per?

"The Defendant: Well, there is another motion I would like to make after this one and counsel is against it."

* * *

"The Defendant: * * * I do believe in this case, as the Federal right points out, that I be allowed to conduct my own defense due to the fact that counsel feels very, very strongly about a motion that I would like to present before the Court this afternoon. If it was not for this motion, I would be more than willing to let counsel proceed. But I believe that this motion should be entered into the record because I believe it has, in effect, law that has been overlooked."

* * *

"The Court: * * * Motion denied. You still want to represent yourself?"

"The Defendant: Yes, Your Honor, I think I will."

The first two demands were conditional: Meeks stated that he wished to waive counsel only in order to present his motion and that he had no objection to counsel otherwise. The judge permitted Meeks to represent himself for purposes of making his motion. Meeks' "I think I will" is a prototype of equivocation. His so-called "demands" are not made more effective by the intervening discussion about Meeks' inability to present a defense. All this discussion was prior to the second "demand"; none of it was calculated to make the judge believe that Meeks wished anything more than to present his motion. Meeks made no further requests to proceed *pro se.*

An "unequivocal" demand to proceed *pro se* should be, at the very least, sufficiently clear that if it is granted the defendant should not be able to turn about and urge that he was improperly denied counsel. "I think I will" hardly meets the constitutional criteria for waiver of counsel.

In Adams v. Carroll, 875 F.2d 1441 (9th Cir.1989), Public Defender Carroll was appointed to represent Adams. Their relationship deteriorated quickly. Citing "lack of trust and communication with Mr. Carroll", Adams requested the appointment of a different attorney. He said that "if I can't have another lawyer, I will have to go pro per." Eventually, the court granted Adams' motion and reappointed the Public Defender's office. To Adams' "evident astonishment" the Public Defender's office promptly reassigned Carroll to the case. Adams objected, saying that while he didn't think himself competent to defend himself, he would have to do so if representation by Carroll was his only other choice. The trial court refused to appoint substitute counsel, and refused to allow Adams to represent himself, on the ground that Adams had declared himself not competent to do so. The case proceeded to trial with Carroll as defense counsel, and Adams was convicted. The court found that Adams had made an unequivocal request to proceed *pro se* and that Adams' conviction therefore had to be reversed. The court first noted that the "unequivocal request" requirement served two purposes:

> First, it acts as a backstop for the defendant's right to counsel, by ensuring that the defendant does not inadvertently waive that right through occasional musings on the benefits of self-representation. Because a defendant normally gives up more than he gains when he elects self-representation, we must be reasonably certain that he in fact wishes to represent himself.
>
> The requirement that a request for self-representation be unequivocal also serves an institutional purpose: It prevents a defendant from taking advantage of the mutual exclusivity of the rights to counsel and self-representation. A defendant who vacillates at trial between wishing to be represented by counsel and wishing to represent himself could place the trial court in a difficult position: If the court appoints counsel, the defendant could, on appeal, rely on his intermittent requests for self-representation in arguing that he had been denied the right to represent himself; if the court permits self-representation, the defendant could claim he had been denied the right to counsel. The requirement of unequivocality resolves this dilemma by forcing the defendant to make an explicit choice. If he equivocates, he is presumed to have requested the assistance of counsel.

According to the court, Adams had consistently expressed his desire to represent himself if Carroll was the only alternative. The court reasoned that "while his requests were *conditional,* they were not equivocal" and that "none of the purposes served by the [unequivocality] requirement would be furthered by treating a conditional request for self-representation as equivocal." Compare Burton v. Collins, 937 F.2d 131 (5th Cir.1991) (a defendant who expressed dissatisfaction with defense counsel, and asked whether he could represent himself, had not made a clear and unequivocal invocation of his right to self-representation; the colloquy with the judge was reasonably construed as an inquiry into alternatives rather than a waiver of counsel).

The reverse situation from *Adams,* anticipated by the court therein, is where the defendant is allowed to proceed pro se because he doesn't like the counsel he was appointed, and the court refuses to appoint a substitute counsel. Can the defendant argue that under these circumstances, his waiver of the right to counsel was not voluntary? Since there is no constitutional right to choose a particular counsel to be appointed, courts have rejected the notion that an election of *pro se* status is involuntary merely because of dissatisfaction with appointed counsel. See United States v. Robinson, 913 F.2d 712 (9th Cir.1990). On the other hand, when the defendant's only choice is between self-representation and *incompetent* counsel, choice of *pro se* status does not indicate a voluntary waiver of the right to counsel, and reversal is required. Therefore, if the defendant states that he wishes to defend himself because he believes appointed counsel to be incompetent, the trial court must conduct a thorough inquiry into the allegations, and must appoint substitute counsel if the allegations are meritorious. See United States v. Silkwood, 893 F.2d 245 (10th Cir.1989) (trial court failed to conduct inquiry to ensure that the defendant was not forced to make the "Hobson's choice * * * between incompetent or unprepared counsel and appearing *pro se*").

Courts are frequently unsympathetic to a defendant's desire for self-representation. In Russell v. State, 270 Ind. 55, 383 N.E.2d 309 (1978), the defendant attempted to assert his *Faretta* right on the day of trial. The defendant complained that he and his lawyer had very little pretrial contact. The trial court denied his request to proceed pro se. Consider the following excerpt from the Indiana Supreme Court's opinion:

> It is clear that the right to counsel can be relinquished only by a knowing, voluntary, and intelligent waiver of this right, under the rule of Johnson v. Zerbst (1938), 304 U.S. 458. However, it does not follow that the relinquishment of the right of self-representation can only come about through a process measured by such waiver standard. It is not enough to say that both the right to counsel and the right of self-representation are constitutional rights, and that both arise from the Sixth Amendment. Rather, the standards for establishing the relinquishment of constitutional rights vary with the nature of the right under consideration, and the interests protected by the rights. The right to counsel ensures that all defendants have access to the professional skill and knowledge needed to make the necessary procedural and substantive decisions in their trials; this right is also important to the implementation of the other constitutional rights of the accused, and helps ensure the accuracy of trial outcome in our adversary system. The right of self-representation, on the other hand, is not recognized because it furthers these types of fair trial interests; it may actually hinder such interests. The sole value furthered by the right of self-representation is that of personal autonomy.
>
> We thus do not think that a knowing, voluntary, and intelligent waiver of the right of self-representation is constitutionally mandated. Further, there is no reason why we should create such a new procedural requirement, and hold that advisement of the right of self-representation is necessary. * * * [S]uch

advices [sic] might suggest to the average defendant that he could in fact adequately represent himself and does not need an attorney, and it would be "fundamentally unwise" to impose a requirement to advise of the self-representation procedure which, if opted for by the defendant, "is likely to be to no one's benefit."

The Court then concluded that any request for self-representation must be unequivocal, and must be made within a reasonable time prior to the first day of trial. "Then, and only then, must a hearing be held on the self-representation question, under the guidelines of *Faretta.* Any self-representation request made the day of trial or later may be summarily denied, for self-representation after this point is completely a matter of the trial court's discretion." Is this hostility to the right of self-representation justifiable? Should the right to counsel be preferred to the right of self-representation? See also Horton v. Dugger, 895 F.2d 714 (11th Cir.1990) (request to proceed *pro se,* made on first day of trial, held untimely); Stano v. Dugger, 921 F.2d 1125 (11th Cir.1991) (en banc) ("trial courts are not required to divine when a criminal defendant is proceeding pro se * * *. The right of self-representation must be manifested to the trial court by an oral or written request in order to be recognized and to trigger the requisite examination by the court.").

The majority in *Faretta* recognized that "the right to self-representation is not a license to abuse the dignity of the courtroom." What type of acts can be considered so "obstructionist" that the right to self-representation is lost? In United States v. Flewitt, 874 F.2d 669 (9th Cir.1989), the trial court appointed counsel, against the Flewitts' wishes, because the Flewitts were unprepared at the time of trial, they had made excessive and "poorly formulated" discovery motions, and they had refused to cooperate with the government in utilizing discovery opportunities. On appeal, they argued that their right to self-representation had been violated, and the government argued that the Flewitts had lost their right due to their "obstructionist" tactics. The court found that the reference in *Faretta* to obstructionist tactics spoke of "disruption in the courtroom." The court noted that the Flewitts' pretrial activity may have been ill-advised and detrimental to them, but "that was their choice to make." See also Savage v. Estelle, 924 F.2d 1459 (9th Cir.1990) (defendant with a severe speech impediment is found unable to "abide by rules of procedure and courtroom protocol"; therefore, the right to self-representation was properly denied).

What is the remedy for the denial of the right to self-representation? Is per se reversal required even where counsel did a better job at trial than defendant would have done? In McKaskle v. Wiggins, 465 U.S. 168 (1984), the Court held that the denial of the right to proceed *pro se* was a violation of the defendant's right to personal autonomy. It had nothing to do with the likelihood of a successful outcome at trial. The Court concluded that "the right is either respected or denied; its deprivation cannot be harmless."

Thus, per se reversal is required for a violation of *Gideon,* and for the opposite violation of *Faretta.* But what if the defendant's *Faretta* rights are violated, and on re-trial, the trial judge refuses to appoint counsel and requires the defendant to represent himself? Is there a per se reversal for denial of the right to counsel, or can the state argue that they just gave the defendant what he wanted so badly in the first trial? Why must the state give him what he so strongly objected to in the first trial? In Johnstone v. Kelly, 812 F.2d 821 (2d Cir.1987), the court stated that counsel must be provided on retrial unless the defendant makes an unequivocal invocation of the right of self-representation. The court explained as follows:

If Johnstone elects to be represented by counsel at a retrial, it is not quite true, as the State contends, that he will again receive what the State once provided him. Though the State previously provided him with counsel, it denied him the choice whether to have counsel or proceed *pro se.* It is that choice that must be accorded at a retrial * * *.

The concept of personal autonomy was crucial in *Faretta.* Faretta was allowed his right to choose, even though various state interests would be negatively affected. Yet in *Wheat,* the defendant was denied his right to choose when state interests would be impaired. Can *Faretta* and *Wheat* be reconciled?

Faretta indicates that a state may appoint standby counsel, even over the defendant's objection, to aid the defendant and to be available to represent him if self-representation is for some reason terminated. The limits of standby counsel's role were explored in McKaskle v. Wiggins, 465 U.S. 168 (1984), where the Court found that advisory counsel's conduct did not unconstitutionally interfere with Wiggins' right to self-representation. Wiggins, convicted of robbery and sentenced to life imprisonment as a recidivist, waived counsel, then requested counsel, and finally decided to represent himself. The trial court appointed, at his request, two counsel to advise him. Disagreements between counsel and Wiggins occurred and at times counsel quarreled openly with Wiggins.

Justice O'Connor wrote for the majority and stated that *Faretta* requires that a defendant be given more than just the chance to be heard along with others: he must be given control over the defense. *Faretta* held that the right to self-representation was based on two factors: first, the defendant has the right to choose to control his own defense; second, self-representation may in some cases be an effective strategy, because it would allow the jury to sympathize with the defendant, matched up against overwhelming prosecutorial forces. Accordingly, standby counsel cannot seize actual control over the defendant's case, or else the first, "core" aspect of the right to self-representation would be violated. And standby counsel cannot without the defendant's consent "destroy the jury's perception that the defendant is representing himself" or else the strategy aspect of the right to self-representation would be undermined. The Court noted that "participation by standby counsel outside the presence of the jury engages only the first of these two limitations." It further noted that "*Faretta* rights are adequately vindicated in proceedings outside the presence of the jury if the *pro se* defendant is allowed to address the court freely" and if "all disagreements between counsel and the *pro se* defendant are resolved in the defendant's favor whenever the matter is one that would normally be left to the discretion of counsel." It found that most of the incidents of which Wiggins complained occurred outside the jury's presence. And it emphasized that all conflicts between Wiggins and his counsel were resolved in Wiggins' favor, although it opined that several incidents in which counsel engaged in acrimonious exchanges with their client were "regrettable."

The majority also found that Wiggins' problems largely occurred because he frequently changed his mind about the role he wanted counsel to play. It concluded that once Wiggins asked counsel to participate, the trial judge could assume that subsequent appearances were with his acquiescence unless he indicated otherwise.

The majority reasoned that standby counsel may assist the defendant in overcoming routine procedural and evidentiary problems and to ensure that the defendant complies with the basic rules of the courtroom. Thus, the trial judge may rely on counsel to provide the necessary procedural guidance to a defendant. On the facts of the case, the majority found that Wiggins had been permitted to make the key strategic choices and that he appeared to the jury as a man who was defending himself. The Court concluded as follows:

> *Faretta* affirmed the defendant's constitutional right to appear on stage at his trial. We recognize that a *pro se* defendant may wish to dance a solo, not a *pas de deux.* Standby counsel must generally respect that preference. But counsel need not be excluded altogether, especially when the participation is outside the presence of the jury or is with the defendant's express consent. The defendant in this case was allowed to make his own appearances as he saw fit. In our judgment counsel's unsolicited involvement was held within reasonable limits.

In dissent, Justice White, joined by Justices Brennan and Marshall, argued that the court of appeals correctly found that standby counsel continuously participated in the trial, disrupted the proceedings, and turned the trial into an ordeal for the jury. He agreed that a trial judge may insist that a defendant learn what he needs to know about procedural rules from standby counsel, but he found that the majority's test of when counsel becomes excessively involved was unworkable. He expressed concern about the subtle influences that squabbles between counsel and client can have on the outcome of a case and about the defendant's (not the jury's) perception of fairness, observing that *Faretta* is premised on the importance of the appearance of justice to the accused.

The dissenters concluded that the Court should encourage standby counsel to accept a limited role, and not encourage their participation and the inevitable post-hoc review of conflicts that participation will require. Justice Blackmun concurred in the result without opinion.

It is worth noting that in later proceedings, Wiggins maintained that he was impermissibly denied his right to counsel at his trial, because he had not unequivocally invoked his right to self-representation. The court in Wiggins v. Procunier, 753 F.2d 1318 (5th Cir.1985), rejected his claim. Does this give you some perspective on why courts require the right of self-representation to be unequivocally invoked?

In United States v. Flewitt, 874 F.2d 669 (9th Cir.1989), the court held that the defendants' failure to cooperate with standby counsel was not sufficient reason to deny them the right of self-representation. The court stated that "it indeed would be a paradox to justify revoking a defendant's *pro se* status on the basis that the defendant failed to consult counsel." But isn't that the very "paradox" that the Court imposed in *Wiggins* when it held that standby counsel could have significant input into the defense even over the defendant's objection?

Frequently a defendant wants to appear as "co-counsel" or to defend partially *pro se* and partially by counsel. The Court in *Wiggins* held that there was no constitutional right to "hybrid representation," but stated that a court could allow it in the exercise of its discretion. Only a few courts have exercised their discretion and permitted hybrid representation. See e.g. State v. McCleary, 149 N.J.Super. 77, 373 A.2d 400 (1977). See also United States v. Turnbull, 888 F.2d 636 (9th Cir.1989) ("if the defendant assumes any of the 'core functions' of the lawyer, the hybrid scheme is acceptable only if the defendant has voluntarily waived counsel"). What arguments support and oppose hybrid representation? When should a judge permit it? If the costs of the representation do not increase, what purpose, other than to discourage the exercise of *Faretta* rights, is served by denying hybrid representation? See generally Note, The Accused as Co–Counsel: The Case for the Hybrid Defense, 12 Valparaiso L.Rev. 329 (1978). Does *Wiggins* suggest an answer?

If the defendant exercises the right to defend himself at the trial and loses, does he have the right to appointed counsel for later proceedings such as post-trial motions and sentencing? In Menefield v. Borg, 881 F.2d 696 (9th Cir.1989), the court held that the defendant had the right to appointed counsel to prepare a motion for a new trial. The court reasoned as follows:

> We are certainly unwilling to deny counsel because of some conception that the defendant's initial decision to exercise his *Faretta* right and represent himself at trial is cast in stone. It is not surprising that a criminal defendant, having decided to represent himself and then having suffered a defeat at trial, would realize that he would be better served during the remainder of the case by the assistance of counsel. * * * Forcing the defendant to stumble through post-trial proceedings serves neither the individual nor our system of adversarial justice well.

See also United States v. Robinson, 913 F.2d 712 (9th Cir.1990) (right to appointed counsel at sentencing even though defendant represented himself at trial).

Does the defendant have the right to self-representation on appeal? The Court in Price v. Johnston, 334 U.S. 266 (1948), upheld the denial of a request of the defendant to participate in oral argument. *Price* was decided well before *Faretta,* but courts have continued to follow its holding that there is no right to make a *pro se* oral argument. See Horton v. Dugger, 895 F.2d 714 (11th Cir.1990). At least one court, however, has distinguished *Price* and held that there is a constitutional right to address the appellate court with a *pro se* brief. See Chamberlain v. Ericksen, 744 F.2d 628 (8th Cir.1984). Since the right to counsel extends to the first appeal of right, is there any reason why the right to self-representation should not extend that far?

Does the fact that *Faretta* raises hard questions signify that it is wrongly decided? If *Faretta* had gone the other way, what explanation would you give to a defendant who wanted to defend herself, who felt that appointed lawyers were ineffectual and that trial judges often appoint lawyers who are not likely to raise a fuss by asserting too many rights for a client? Could you explain to a defendant why she is given the power to consent to a search, to confess, to plead guilty, to waive lawyers during an investigation, to choose whether or not to remain silent before a grand jury, and to determine whether or not to testify at trial, but not to choose to represent herself at trial? Could the answer possibly be protection for the defendant, if the defendant is told of the possible costs and benefits and is mentally competent to understand them and to choose how to proceed? Could the answer be to protect the government, in view of the fact that those opposed to self-representation believe the pro se litigant has a fool for a client? If not, the answer must be to protect the courts, and possibly society, by forcing all defendants to have lawyers. How are courts and society protected if defendants are compelled to watch lawyers, whom they reject as spokespersons, purport to make representations on behalf of the defense? Can there be effective assistance of counsel if the client refuses to cooperate?

Unless hybrid representation is granted, a defendant who chooses the right to counsel over the right to self-representation gives up substantial control over the defense. Strategic choices are left to the lawyer; the lawyer can veto the client's wishes as to what defenses can be raised, what arguments will be made, how to cross-examine a witness, etc. See, e.g., United States v. Padilla, 819 F.2d 952 (10th Cir.1987), where the court found no constitutional violation where counsel refused to structure a defense as defendant directed. The court stated that "the Sixth

Amendment provides no right to counsel blindly following a defendant's instructions."

There are three notable exceptions to counsel's control over the defense. It is ultimately the defendant's decision (1) whether to waive a jury trial, (2) whether to testify, and (3) whether to plead guilty. See e.g., Stano v. Dugger, 921 F.2d 1125 (11th Cir.1991) (counsel cannot be deemed ineffective where defendant pleads guilty against counsel's advice). See also Rule 1.2 of the Model Rules of Professional Conduct (lawyer shall abide by client's decision "after consultation with the lawyer" as to these three matters).

In Jones v. Barnes, 463 U.S. 745 (1983), the Court held that the Sixth Amendment does not require appointed appellate counsel to raise all nonfrivolous claims on appeal. The Court reasoned that a contrary rule would seriously undermine "the ability of counsel to present the client's case in accord with counsel's professional evaluation." The Court stated that the right of personal autonomy recognized in *Faretta* did not extend to strategic choices once the right to counsel has been invoked. Justice Brennan, joined by Justice Marshall, dissented and argued that the defendant's right to "the assistance of counsel" requires that counsel raise all issues of arguable merit that his client insists upon raising. Justice Blackmun concurred in the result, reasoning that an attorney should, as an ethical, not a constitutional, requirement, raise all nonfrivolous claims upon which his client insists.

B. THE LIMITS OF THE RIGHT

It is generally recognized that there is no constitutional right to non-lawyer representation.[88] See, e.g., United States v. Turnbull, 888 F.2d 636 (9th Cir. 1989) ("'Counsel' means 'attorney'"); Comment, Denial of Defendant's Request for Representation by a Nonattorney Does Not Abuse Sixth Amendment, 26 Emory L.J. 457, 459 n. 26 (1977). The reasoning of the court in

88. Whether or not a person has a right to appointed counsel, she has a right to seek to develop her legal claims and to present them in court. See Bounds v. Smith, 430 U.S. 817 (1977) ("the fundamental constitutional right of access to the courts requires prison authorities to assist inmates in the preparation and filing of meaningful legal papers by providing prisoners with adequate law libraries or adequate assistance from persons trained in the law"). Some law libraries can be more helpful than others when they attempt to assist persons untrained in the law in their research. All law libraries must be somewhat concerned about the unauthorized practice of law. See generally Abrams & Dunn, The Law Library's Institutional Response to the Pro Se Patron: A Post-*Faretta* Review, 1 W.N.E.L.Rev. 47 (1978). By appointing lawyers for inmates, states can avoid some of the administrative problems of assuring adequate access to law libraries. See, e.g., Graham v. Hutto, 437 F.Supp. 118 (E.D.Va.1977). But the Court in Murray v. Giarratano, 492 U.S. 1 (1989) (discussed in Chapter Five) held that *Bounds* did not require that the state appoint counsel for prisoners who bring habeas corpus petitions. For recent cases illustrating the problems of providing meaningful access to the courts, see, e.g., Smith v. Bounds, 813 F.2d 1299 (4th Cir.1987) (legal assistance plan ordered, pre-*Giarratano*); Straub v. Monge, 815 F.2d 1467 (11th Cir.1987) (law library access); Valentine v. Beyer, 850 F.2d 951 (3d Cir.1988) (untrained legal research staff is insufficient to provide meaningful access to court); Procup v. Strickland, 792 F.2d 1069 (11th Cir.1986) (proper to enjoin prisoners from bringing frivolous litigation).

When the government decides not to appoint counsel for someone who believes that she wants or needs assistance, the government may be barred from inhibiting the unrepresented person from seeking help from non-traditional sources. See, e.g., Johnson v. Avery, 393 U.S. 483 (1969) (holding that state prison regulations may not unduly interfere with prisoners' access to courts and that "unless and until the State provides some reasonable alternative to assist inmates in the preparation of petitions for post-conviction relief, it may not validly enforce a regulation * * * barring inmates from furnishing such assistance to other prisoners").

United States v. Kelley, 539 F.2d 1199 (9th Cir. 1976) is typical. Kelley wanted his friend Hurd, a roofer, to serve as trial counsel, but the district court denied that request and appointed "standby counsel." The court of appeals held that a defendant has no Sixth Amendment right to delegate his power of self-representation to a non-lawyer.

> An independent right to the assistance of a non-lawyer cannot be mechanically inferred from the right to waive the assistance of a lawyer and to represent oneself, even though self-representation will usually result in advocacy by a non-lawyer. * * * The Court in *Faretta* did not mechanically infer the right to self-representation from the power to waive the assistance of counsel. It held that the right has an independent source in the structure and history of the Constitution. No such independent source can be found for the alleged right to the assistance of a non-lawyer.
>
> The personal autonomy protected by the right of self-representation does not require that a delegation of this right to a non-lawyer be respected. It is true that autonomy is to some extent vindicated by allowing a right to be exercised by a designated proxy. However, such an interpretation of autonomy is at odds with the whole tenor of the *Faretta* opinion and runs counter to the competing institutional interest in seeing that justice is administered fairly and efficiently with the assistance of competent lawyers.

A judge may, in her discretion, permit hybrid representation, but may she allow representation by a layperson? [89] Some courts would say "no," since they would be concerned about unauthorized practice of law problems. Can monopolistic bar practices stand in the way of a defendant's choice of counsel?

Can a law student ever provide effective assistance of counsel? A California appellate court in People v. Perez, 82 Cal.App.3d 89, 147 Cal.Rptr. 34 (1978), held that a bar-certified law student's representation of an indigent burglary defendant was the unauthorized practice of law and denied the defendant effective assistance of counsel. The court concluded that Perez had not voluntarily and intelligently waived his right to counsel. The court focused on the inexperience of law students.

> The dangers inherent in the practice of law by a student has been articulated thus:
>
> > "[A]ny law student * * * is apt to overlook relevant facts, to base his opinion of the law on a century-old case in a minority jurisdiction, to be unaware of statutory or administrative regulation which has supplanted the common law, and to fail to recognize the available defenses. Because the law is, in fact, a 'seamless web,' it is impossible to give competent advice in one area without a partial understanding of all the law."

Does it matter that Perez was convicted of a felony? Does it make sense to allow a new law school graduate to try her first case with no supervision, but to forbid a third year law student, who may be supervised by an experienced lawyer, from defending an accused? If a defendant acquiesces in a law student's representation, should it be permitted? See Solina v. United States, 709 F.2d 160 (2d Cir.1983) (law school graduate who never passed the bar examination is not "Counsel" for Sixth Amendment purposes; per se reversal required).

89. For an argument in favor of a defendant's right to elect lay representation, see Comment, The Criminal Defendant's Sixth Amendment Right to Lay Representation, 52 U.Chi.L.Rev. 460 (1985).

Chapter Eleven

SENTENCING

I. INTRODUCTION

A. THE IMPORTANCE OF SENTENCING

Before and during trial, the constitutional and other protections afforded one accused of crime are various and important. These protections are the focus of most of this book, and many have previously been examined. The most striking thing about the criminal process following a conviction is the absence of constitutional and nonconstitutional safeguards to assure evenhanded, fair, and accurate decisionmaking. One veteran attorney has noted that American lawyers have been pre-occupied with the pre-verdict stages of the criminal process: "[O]ur almost total emphasis on the pre-trial and trial phases of the criminal process, important as they are, reflects the romantic image of the criminal trial contest and the freeing of innocent defendants." Dash, The Defense Lawyer's Role at the Sentencing Stage of a Criminal Case, 54 F.R.D. 315 (1972). Yet, "[t]he consequences of a sentence are of the highest order. If too short or of the wrong type, it can deprive the law of its effectiveness and result in the premature release of a dangerous criminal. If too severe or improperly conceived, it can reinforce the criminal tendencies of the defendant and lead to a new offense by one who otherwise might not have offended so seriously again." ABA Standards, Sentencing Alternatives and Procedures § 18–1 (2d ed. 1980). Despite the importance of sentencing to the operation of the criminal justice system, the sentencing process is as much—and probably more—of a mystery to most Americans as any other part of our criminal procedure.

Understanding why this is so requires knowing the answers to four questions. These questions and their answers will be examined in the remainder of this section.

B. THE RESPONSIBILITY FOR SENTENCING

First, who does sentencing in American courts? The usual answer is that in the federal courts and in most states judges sentence convicted defendants, while in a minority of jurisdictions (and in many cases in which a capital sanction is possible) the jury sentences those who are convicted. But this is a most misleading answer, since the sentencing function hardly is confined to judges and juries. The prosecutor plainly has the power to affect the sentence that will be imposed on an offender through sentence and charge bargaining. Although the prosecutor never will pronounce the sentence in the sense of making it official, the power of the prosecutor to choose the charge upon which to proceed before a judge or jury and to press for either harsh or lenient treatment is substantial.

But even the prosecutor and the courts (judges and juries, that is) together do not set "final" sentences in many jurisdictions. If they collectively impose a prison sentence on a defendant, then a parole board often will determine the time which a prisoner actually will serve in prison and when the prisoner should be released on parole—i.e., released upon conditions. If parole is granted, parole boards decide whether conditions are satisfied and, if not, whether to revoke parole. If probation is imposed in lieu of a prison term, probation officers will work with the courts to decide whether the terms of probation have been satisfied by offenders. If not, probation may be revoked. Thus, administrative officials play a role in the sentencing scheme. The Governor—who either alone, or with the advice of some agency, possesses the power to commute sentences or to grant pardons—also may have a voice in the penalty finally imposed on a convicted defendant.

Despite the real power exercised by these participants in the sentencing process, there undoubtedly is one more force, potentially the most powerful of all, to consider—namely, the legislature. Since the legislature prescribes punishments, it can narrow the range of choices available to judges and juries. In theory, it can abolish plea bargaining, although it is unclear that the legislature ever could totally eliminate prosecutorial discretion. The legislature can expand or contract parole schemes, and it can raise or lower overall punishment levels.

C. THE DETERMINATION OF SENTENCES

Second, how are sentences determined? The answer to this question reveals why the legislative potential to control sentencing in order to promote fairness and equality is rarely realized in American jurisdictions. For much of this century, American jurisdictions selected the penalty for any particular crime that the legislature, acting at the time a statute was enacted, thought appropriate. Little effort was made to make the punishments for different crimes consistent with one another or to explain how minimum and maximum punishments were chosen, and the range between the minimum and maximum often was considerable. There was an absence of "disciplined restriction on the size and number of discriminations * * * taken at the legislative level * * *." Wechsler, Sentencing, Correction and the Model Penal Code, 109 U.Pa.L.Rev. 465 (1961). In 1962, the Model Penal Code endeavored to fashion a more orderly system. It divided felonies into three degrees and specified two kinds of sentencing ranges for each degree—one for ordinary felony offenders, and one for persistent, professional, multiple or specially dangerous offenders.[1] See Sections 6.06, 6.07 and 7.03. Misdemeanors were not classified since the maximum punishment was usually one year, and the problem of varying punishment schemes apparently was not thought to be a great problem.

1. Many jurisdictions have habitual offender statutes, that raise maximum punishments, often dramatically, for repeat offenders.

Numerous states have followed the lead of the Code and classified their crimes, although they may have used a different classification scheme than that proposed in the Code. See, e.g., Code of Virginia § 18.2–9 (6 classes of felonies and 4 classes of misdemeanors). But many jurisdictions have a variety of statutes that define crimes and prescribe punishment levels. Often, the result is a system in which particular, albeit haphazard, punishments are prescribed in particular sections of the criminal code. See, e.g., Title 39, Tenn.Code Ann. Although there has been a tendency to prescribe particular penalties for common law offenses that previously permitted unlimited punishment, the penalties prescribed for various offenses may not reflect a consistent approach to punishment.

Whether a classification or a more ad hoc system is used to prescribe punishments, the typical American state legislature has left the sentencing authority, judge or jury, with enormous flexibility in setting a sentence—subject of course to the influence of the prosecutor, parole board, etc. For example, a Class 2 felony in Virginia (e.g., nighttime arson § 18.2–77; first degree murder § 18.2–32) can be punished by 20 years to life and a Class 3 felony (e.g., nighttime arson with no person in dwelling § 18.2–77; burglary, § 18.2–89) by 5 to 20 years. If no plea bargain has been made or accepted, a judge or jury doing the sentencing in Virginia has uncontrolled discretion to choose a sentence within the prescribed range. Actually, the choice of sentence is somewhat broader, since a trial judge can grant probation, almost without limitation. In addition, judges can suspend portions of sentences, a procedure that is tantamount to partial probation after some time is served. They also can impose additional sanctions, such as fines or restitution, in many instances.

The Sentencing Reform Act of 1984 established the U.S. Sentencing Commission. The Act and the Commission's Guidelines are discussed later in the Chapter. With the advent of guidelines, the federal system contains statutes prescribing broad ranges of punishment for many offenses and guidelines that restrict the discretion of sentencing courts. In theory, the guidelines limit disparity in sentencing. In practice, there is concern that they actually shift greater control over sentencing to prosecutors, since the charges that are brought can limit the sentencing court's power to sentence. This is because the Guidelines severely circumscribe judicial discretion in setting the length of a sentence, yet leave the prosecutor considerable room to pick a precise sentence by way of charging decisions and suggestions for upward and downward departures. See United States v. Kikumura, 918 F.2d 1084 (3d Cir.1990) (the Guidelines have "replaced judicial discretion over sentencing with prosecutorial discretion"). With greater prosecutorial discretion comes the risk of disparity in sentencing that the Guidelines ostensibly sought to avoid. See Heaney, The Reality of Guidelines Sentencing: No End to Disparity, 28 Am.Crim.L.Rev. 161 (1991). See the discussion in Chapter Nine in connection with guilty pleas.

Also discussed in Chapter Nine were mandatory minimum penalties. These penalties "trump" the guidelines and require that courts impose what are often stiff penalties for various offenses, the most important of which are for firearm and narcotics offenses. Some states have guidelines fashioned by courts. But, no state has a commission that is exactly like the U.S. Sentencing Commission, and no state's guidelines closely parallel those of the Commission.

The federal approach is a reminder of the power the legislature has to influence sentencing by increasing or decreasing prescribed penalties, providing mandatory minimums, requiring the Sentencing Commission to fix guidelines above or below legislatively prescribed levels, and abolishing parole. The federal approach is a reminder also of the influence that prosecutors may have over sentencing. Although judges are thought of as having the most direct role in sentencing, in the federal system, their power is considerably less at the current time than it was before enactment of the 1984 statute. Where should power to determine sentences reside? The answer may depend on how important a value individualization is, and how vital it is to do away with allegedly unjustified disparities. The choices are explored as the Chapter continues.

D. SAMPLE JURISDICTIONS

Jurisdictions vary in the way they authorize judges and juries to sentence. Some impose sentences with uniform minimum and maximum specifications on all convicted of a certain crime.[2] For example, if the punishment for burglary is two to ten years, that sentence would be imposed on all who are convicted of burglary. Some states allow the judge to adjust either the minimum or the maximum or both to differentiate among offenders who commit the same crime. Still other states ask the judge or jury to set a specified number of years between the statutory minimum and maximum. Yet another approach is to allow the judge some authority to choose between a specific term of years and a maximum-minimum approach. Until recently, almost all states provided parole eligibility for those offenders sentenced to prison, the date of eligibility depending on the particular parole scheme utilized.[3] Virtually all states awarded good time credit to those who served their terms on good behavior, the credits reducing the actual amount of time served.

This outline obviously is general, as it is difficult to capture in a short space the numerous procedures used to sentence in the fifty states and the federal system. Some examples of sentencing procedures in individual states might assist an understanding of the approaches currently in vogue. In Connecticut, for instance, there are 4 classes of felonies. A judge can fix maximum and minimum sentences, but the minimum cannot exceed one-half the maximum imposed. Thus, class B felonies, which have a maximum of twenty years allow the trial judge to fix a maximum sentence of up to 20 years, and to specify a minimum of up to ten years (but, except in unusual circumstances not more than half the maximum). Conn.Gen.Stat.Ann. § 53a–35.

Kentucky has four classes of felonies also. It allows the trial judge to set the maximum anywhere within a range specified by statute. Ky.Rev.Stat. § 532.060.

Michigan lists its crimes and sentences individually, not by class. Statutes fix the maximum sentence, and the minimum is flexible, so that the trial judge

2. The ABA Standards on Sentencing Alternatives and Procedures, § 18–3.2 (2d ed. 1980) state that minimum sentences are rarely appropriate and should be short. Mandatory minimum terms are criticized.

Limits on the flexibility that legislatures can give sentencing courts are imposed in State v. Goode, 380 So.2d 1361 (La.1980) and State v. LeCompte, 406 So.2d 1300 (La.1981), which hold unconstitutional statutes providing for a minimum term of imprisonment but no maximum and for a minimum fine but no maximum. The court found that the statutes authorized excessive punishment.

3. More recent schemes are considered, infra.

can fix it anywhere up to two-thirds of the maximum sentence. Mich.Comp. L.A. § 769.8.

All three of these states, then, make some flexibility available to the trial judge who does the sentencing.[4] All have parole systems and all award good time credit.

Texas and Virginia are similar to these states except that juries may be involved in sentencing, at least when a trial on the merits is to the jury. Texas has three classes of felonies and Virginia has six. Statutes specify a sentencing range and the jury fixes the maximum sentence that a defendant will serve within the range. See Vernon's Tex.Code Ann.—Penal Code § 37.07; Va.Code § 19.2–295. Both have parole systems and good time. One difference between Texas and Virginia is that parole eligibility in Texas is fixed at one-third of the minimum sentence fixed by statute, whereas parole eligibility in Virginia is based on one-quarter of the sentence actually fixed. Another difference is that in Texas the defendant can have a jury trial on guilt and have a judge sentence.[5]

In Florida (West's Fla.Stat.Ann. § 775.082), and in most cases in North Carolina (N.C.Gen.Stat. § 15A–1351), there are specified maximum sentences and the judge chooses a fixed number of years. Georgia, which does not divide offenses into classes, has both minimum and maximum limits and the judge sets a definite number of years as the sentence. Arkansas, which does divide offenses into classes (four of them), also sets minimum and maximum sentences, but a jury sets a definite sentence. Ark.Stat.Ann. § 5–4–103. All of these states have parole and good time systems.[6]

4. Sometimes a jury makes a recommendation of leniency even when it is not asked to do so by a judge with sentencing power. If this happens, defense lawyers may argue that the jury has compromised its guilt determining function. See, generally Annot., Petit Jury Recommendations for Leniency in Federal Prosecutions, 33 ALR Fed. 774 (1977).

5. In a state like Virginia the defendant who fears an excessively high jury sentence cannot escape jury sentencing unless he pleads guilty, because the prosecutor has a right to insist on a jury trial. The judge can reduce a jury sentence, however. See Vines v. Muncy, 553 F.2d 342 (4th Cir. 1977). In Virginia, a jury trial produces a jury sentence. When a jury sentences, generally the judge can grant probation and suspend sentence.

6. Sentencing ranges increase when multiple convictions are obtained. Most proposals for sentencing reform recommend a limitation on the maximum sentence that can be achieved by adding sentences together. The 1968 ABA Standards, § 3.4, for example, recommend use of concurrent sentences in most instances. These ABA Standards § 3.5 also recommend coordination between federal and state courts and among various state courts in order to obtain a consistent and coherent penal program. The 1980 ABA Standards, § 18–4.5, also recommend a limit on the use of consecutive sentences. The Uniform Commissioner's Model Sentencing and Corrections Act, § 3–106 provides that sentences shall run consecutively, but places limits on maximums.

If there is a choice between concurrent and consecutive sentences, it may be important that the decisionmaker understand the option it is given. Cf. Hicks v. Oklahoma, 447 U.S. 343 (1980), where the Court found that a defendant was denied due process in sentencing. His jury had been instructed that if it found the defendant to be a habitual offender, it must sentence him to 40 years. After he was convicted, a state appellate court held that the mandatory sentencing provision was unconstitutional. But in Hicks' case, the appellate court reasoned that he was not prejudiced, because his sentence was within the range that validly could be imposed. Since the state provided for jury sentencing, and since the jury could have imposed a lesser sentence had it been properly instructed, the Supreme Court found the assumption of no prejudice to be unacceptable.

E. CONSTITUTIONAL LIMITATIONS ON PUNISHMENT

Third, are there constitutional limitations on punishment? It should be noted that federal and state constitutions place few limitations on the choice of penalty ranges. As we shall see in the next section of the chapter on sentencing procedures, due process challenges to sentencing are unlikely to succeed. The only other challenges likely to be made are grounded in equal protection [7] or cruel and unusual punishment analyses.

Most cruel and unusual punishment claims stand little chance of succeeding after Rummel v. Estelle, 445 U.S. 263 (1980). Justice Rehnquist's majority opinion concluded that it was unnecessary to decide whether a life sentence for obtaining $120.75 by false pretenses would be cruel and unusual punishment, since Rummel was sentenced for a third felony (the other two were fraudulent use of a credit card to obtain $80, and passing a forged check in the amount of $28.36). The fact of the third offense and the possibility of parole after 12 years made the punishment justifiable and not necessarily as severe as it might first appear, said the Court. Justice Powell dissented and was joined by Justices Brennan, Marshall and Stevens. He argued that the possibility of parole should not be considered in deciding the cruel and unusual punishment question since it was not guaranteed, and that the penalty for the offense was unconstitutionally disproportionate in view of the nonviolent nature of the offenses, the number of offenses, the habitual offender statutes used by the vast majority of states, and the punishment that Texas provides for other crimes.[8]

Before the Supreme Court decided *Rummel,* a district court found that a sentence of 40 years imposed upon a defendant convicted of possession of marijuana with intent to distribute and of distribution was cruel and unusual punishment where the total marijuana involved in the offenses was less than nine ounces. Davis v. Zahradnick, 432 F.Supp. 444 (W.D.Va.1977). The Court of Appeals affirmed. A per curiam Court, in Hutto v. Davis, 454 U.S. 370 (1982), reinstated the conviction:

> In short, *Rummel* stands for the proposition that federal courts should be "reluctan[t] to review legislatively mandated terms of imprisonment," and that "successful challenges to the proportionality of particular sentences" should be "exceedingly rare." By affirming the District Court decision after our decision in *Rummel,* the Court of Appeals sanctioned an intrusion into the basic line-

7. If a defendant cannot obtain pre-trial release, does the Constitution require that credit be given for time served in jail prior to trial or pending appeal? Some courts have suggested an affirmative answer. See, e.g., Johnson v. Prast, 548 F.2d 699 (7th Cir.1977). See also United States v. Wilson, 112 S.Ct. 1351 (1992) (it is the Attorney General who computes the amount of credit for time served after the defendant has begun to serve his sentence).

8. See also Carmona v. Ward, 439 U.S. 1091 (1979) (Marshall, J., joined by Powell, J., dissenting from denial of certiorari; defendants received mandatory life sentences for possession of a substance containing an ounce of cocaine); United States v. Lewis, 759 F.2d 1316 (8th Cir.1985) (upholding life sentence on defendant convicted of involvement in continuing criminal enterprise); United States v. Darby, 744 F.2d 1508 (11th Cir.1984) (upholding 60 year sentence and $100,000 fine in continuing drug enterprise case); Terrebonne v. Blackburn, 646 F.2d 997 (5th Cir.1981) (en banc) (upholding mandatory life sentence for distributing heroin where commutation is possible); United States v. Valenzuela, 646 F.2d 352 (9th Cir.1980) (upholding life imprisonment without possibility of parole for a continuing criminal enterprise); United States v. Baer, 575 F.2d 1295 (10th Cir.1978) (suspended sentence and probation for parking violation not excessive sentence despite usual penalty of $5 fine); State v. Curtis, 363 So.2d 1375 (La. 1978) (sentence of 198 years for armed robber convicted as multiple offender not cruel and unusual punishment). See generally Annot., Validity of State Statute Imposing Mandatory Sentence or Prohibiting Granting of Probation or Suspension of Sentence for Narcotics Offenses, 81 A.L.R.3d 1192 (1977).

drawing process that is "properly within the province of legislatures, not courts." More importantly, however, the Court of Appeals could be viewed as having ignored, consciously or unconsciously, the hierarchy of the federal court system created by the Constitution and Congress. Admittedly, the members of this Court decide cases "by virtue of their commissions, not their competence." And arguments may be made one way or the other whether the present case is distinguishable, except as to its facts, from *Rummel.* But unless we wish anarchy to prevail within the federal judicial system, a precedent of this Court must be followed by the lower federal courts no matter how misguided the judges of those courts may think it to be.

Justice Powell concurred in the judgment. Justice Brennan, joined by Justices Marshall and Stevens, dissented.[9] The next case finds a sentence to be constitutionally disproportionate. Does the Court depart from *Rummell* and *Davis?* If so, the departure was short-lived. See the discussion in the note following the case.

SOLEM v. HELM

Supreme Court of the United States, 1983.
463 U.S. 277.

JUSTICE POWELL delivered the opinion of the Court.

The issue presented is whether the Eighth Amendment proscribes a life sentence without possibility of parole for a seventh nonviolent felony.

I

By 1975 the State of South Dakota had convicted respondent Jerry Helm of six nonviolent felonies. In 1964, 1966, and 1969 Helm was convicted of third-degree burglary. In 1972 he was convicted of obtaining money under false pretenses. In 1973 he was convicted of grand larceny. And in 1975 he was convicted of third-offense driving while intoxicated. The record contains no details about the circumstances of any of these offenses, except that they were all nonviolent, none was a crime against a person, and alcohol was a contributing factor in each case.

In 1979 Helm was charged with uttering a "no account" check for $100. The only details we have of the crime are those given by Helm to the state trial court:

> " 'I was working in Sioux Falls, and got my check that day, was drinking and I ended up here in Rapid City with more money than I had when I started. I knew I'd done something I didn't know exactly what. If I would have known this, I would have picked the check up. I was drinking and didn't remember, stopped several places.' "

After offering this explanation, Helm pleaded guilty.

Ordinarily the maximum punishment for uttering a "no account" check would have been five years imprisonment in the state penitentiary and a $5,000 fine. As a result of his criminal record, however, Helm was subject to South Dakota's recidivist statute:

9. For a description of Davis' continuing efforts to obtain relief from his sentence, see Sager, Cruel and Unusual Punishment, Wash. Post, Jan. 22, 1981, B1, col. 2. The article also provides information about Davis' background, including the following: "Davis was convicted of the marijuana offenses in Wythe County Circuit Court, the same court where 21 years earlier a judge sentenced a white man who killed Davis' father in a traffic accident to a $150 fine and a 90-day suspended jail sentence." Roger Davis' sentence was commuted to twenty years by the Governor of Virginia, and he finally was paroled in 1984.

"When a defendant has been convicted of at least three prior convictions [*sic*] in addition to the principal felony, the sentence for the principal felony shall be enhanced to the sentence for a Class 1 felony." S.D.Codified Laws § 22-7-8 (1979) (amended 1981).

The maximum penalty for a "Class 1 felony" was life imprisonment in the state penitentiary and a $25,000 fine. Moreover, South Dakota law explicitly provides that parole is unavailable * * *. The Governor[a] is authorized to pardon prisoners, or to commute their sentences, but no other relief from sentence is available even to a rehabilitated prisoner.

Immediately after accepting Helm's guilty plea, the South Dakota Circuit Court sentenced Helm to life imprisonment under § 22-7-8. * * * The South Dakota Supreme Court, in a 3-2 decision, affirmed the sentence despite Helm's argument that it violated the Eighth Amendment.

[A federal district court denied habeas corpus relief and was reversed by the court of appeals, which distinguished Rummel v. Estelle.]

II

The Eighth Amendment declares: "Excessive bail shall not be required, nor excessive fines imposed, nor cruel and unusual punishments inflicted." The final clause prohibits not only barbaric punishments, but also sentences that are disproportionate to the crime committed.

A

The principle that a punishment should be proportionate to the crime is deeply rooted and frequently repeated in common-law jurisprudence. * * *

[The Court found that protection against disproportionate punishments was an important part of English law prior to the adoption of the Bill of Rights.]

When the Framers of the Eighth Amendment adopted the language of the English Bill of Rights, they also adopted the English principle of proportionality. Indeed, one of the consistent themes of the era was that Americans had all the rights of English subjects. * * *

B

The constitutional principle of proportionality has been recognized explicitly in this Court for almost a century. In the leading case of Weems v. United States, 217 U.S. 349 (1910), the defendant had been convicted of falsifying a public document and sentenced to 15 years of "cadena temporal," a form of imprisonment that included hard labor in chains and permanent civil disabilities. The Court noted "that it is a precept of justice that punishment for crime should be graduated and proportioned to offense," and held that the sentence violated the Eighth Amendment. The Court endorsed the principle of proportionality as a constitutional standard and determined that the sentence before it was "cruel in its excess of imprisonment," as well as in its shackles and restrictions.

The Court next applied the principle to invalidate a criminal sentence in Robinson v. California, 370 U.S. 660 (1962). A 90-day sentence was found to be excessive for the crime of being "addicted to the use of narcotics." The Court explained that "imprisonment for ninety days is not, in the abstract, a punishment which is either cruel or unusual." Thus there was no question of an inherently barbaric punishment.

a. The board of pardons and paroles is authorized to make recommendations to the Governor, but the Governor is not bound by the recommendation.

"But the question cannot be considered in the abstract. Even one day in prison would be a cruel and unusual punishment for the 'crime' of having a common cold."

Most recently, the Court has applied the principle of proportionality to hold capital punishment excessive in certain circumstances. Enmund v. Florida, 458 U.S. 782 (1982) (death penalty excessive for felony murder when defendant did not take life, attempt to take life, or intend that a life be taken or that lethal force be used); Coker v. Georgia, 433 U.S. 584, 592 (1977) (plurality opinion) ("sentence of death is grossly disproportionate and excessive punishment for the crime of rape"); id., at 601 (Powell, J., concurring in the judgment in part and dissenting in part) ("ordinarily death is disproportionate punishment for the crime of raping an adult woman"). * * *

C

There is no basis for the State's assertion that the general principle of proportionality does not apply to felony prison sentences. The constitutional language itself suggests no exception for imprisonment. We have recognized that the Eighth Amendment imposes "parallel limitations" on bail, fines, and other punishments, and the text is explicit that bail and fines may not be excessive. It would be anomalous indeed if the lesser punishment of a fine and the greater punishment of death were both subject to proportionality analysis, but the intermediate punishment of imprisonment were not. There is also no historical support for such an exception. The common-law principle incorporated into the Eighth Amendment clearly applied to prison terms. * * *

[The Court notes that it has said that capital punishment is different from other penalties and that capital cases are of limited assistance in deciding the validity of punishments in noncapital cases. But it had never said that a proportionality analysis is inapplicable to all noncapital cases.]

In sum, we hold as a matter of principle that a criminal sentence must be proportionate to the crime for which the defendant has been convicted. Reviewing courts, of course, should grant substantial deference to the broad authority that legislatures necessarily possess in determining the types and limits of punishments for crimes, as well as to the discretion that trial courts possess in sentencing convicted criminals. But no penalty is *per se* constitutional.

III

A

When sentences are reviewed under the Eighth Amendment, courts should be guided by objective factors that our cases have recognized. First, we look to the gravity of the offense and the harshness of the penalty. In *Enmund,* for example, the Court examined the circumstances of the defendant's crime in great detail. In *Coker* the Court considered the seriousness of the crime of rape, and compared it to other crimes, such as murder. In *Robinson* the emphasis was placed on the nature of the "crime." And in *Weems,* the Court's opinion commented in two separate places on the pettiness of the offense. Of course, a court must consider the severity of the penalty in deciding whether it is disproportionate.

Second, it may be helpful to compare the sentences imposed on other criminals in the same jurisdiction. If more serious crimes are subject to the same penalty, or to less serious penalties, that is some indication that the punishment at issue may be excessive. Thus in *Enmund* the Court noted that all of the other felony murderers on death row in Florida were more culpable than the petitioner there. The *Weems* Court identified an impressive list of more serious crimes that were subject to less serious penalties.

Third, courts may find it useful to compare the sentences imposed for commission of the same crime in other jurisdictions. In *Enmund* the Court conducted an extensive review of capital punishment statutes and determined that "only about a third of American jurisdictions would ever permit a defendant [such as Enmund] to be sentenced to die." Even in those jurisdictions, however, the death penalty was almost never imposed under similar circumstances. The Court's review of foreign law also supported its conclusion. The analysis in *Coker* was essentially the same. And in *Weems* the Court relied on the fact that, under federal law, a similar crime was punishable by only two year's imprisonment and a fine.

In sum, a court's proportionality analysis under the Eighth Amendment should be guided by objective criteria, including (i) the gravity of the offense and the harshness of the penalty; (ii) the sentences imposed on other criminals in the same jurisdiction; and (iii) the sentences imposed for commission of the same crime in other jurisdictions.

B

Application of these factors assumes that courts are competent to judge the gravity of an offense, at least on a relative scale. In a broad sense this assumption is justified, and courts traditionally have made these judgments—just as legislatures must make them in the first instance. Comparisons can be made in light of the harm caused or threatened to the victim or society, and the culpability of the offender. Thus in *Enmund* the Court determined that the petitioner's conduct was not as serious as his accomplices' conduct. Indeed, there are widely shared views as to the relative seriousness of crimes. For example, as the criminal laws make clear, nonviolent crimes are less serious than crimes marked by violence or the threat of violence.

There are other accepted principles that courts may apply in measuring the harm caused or threatened to the victim or society. The absolute magnitude of the crime may be relevant. Stealing a million dollars is viewed as more serious than stealing a hundred dollars—a point recognized in statutes distinguishing petty theft from grand theft. Few would dispute that a lesser included offense should not be punished more severely than the greater offense. Thus a court is justified in viewing assault with intent to murder as more serious than simple assault. It also is generally recognized that attempts are less serious than completed crimes. Similarly, an accessory after the fact should not be subject to a higher penalty than the principal.

Turning to the culpability of the offender, there are again clear distinctions that courts may recognize and apply. In *Enmund* the Court looked at the petitioner's lack of intent to kill in determining that he was less culpable than his accomplices. Most would agree that negligent conduct is less serious than intentional conduct. South Dakota, for example, ranks criminal acts in ascending order of seriousness as follows: negligent acts, reckless acts, knowing acts, intentional acts, and malicious acts. A court, of course, is entitled to look at a defendant's motive in committing a crime. Thus a murder may be viewed as more serious when committed pursuant to a contract.

This list is by no means exhaustive. It simply illustrates that there are generally accepted criteria for comparing the severity of different crimes on a broad scale, despite the difficulties courts face in attempting to draw distinctions between similar crimes.

C

Application of the factors that we identify also assumes that courts are able to compare different sentences. This assumption, too, is justified. The easiest comparison, of course, is between capital punishment and noncapital punishments, for the death penalty is different from other punishments in kind rather than degree. For sentences of imprisonment, the problem is not so much one of ordering, but one of line-drawing. It is clear that a 25–year sentence generally is more severe than a 15–year sentence,[b] but in most cases it would be difficult to decide that the former violates the Eighth Amendment while the latter does not. Decisions of this kind, although troubling, are not unique to this area. The courts are constantly called upon to draw similar lines in a variety of contexts.

[The Court draws analogies to speedy trial and right to jury trial cases.]

IV

It remains to apply the analytical framework established by our prior decisions to the case before us. We first consider the relevant criteria, viewing Helm's sentence as life imprisonment without possibility of parole. We then consider the State's argument that the possibility of commutation is sufficient to save an otherwise unconstitutional sentence.

A

Helm's crime was "one of the most passive felonies a person could commit." State v. Helm, 287 N.W.2d, at 501 (Henderson, J., dissenting). It involved neither violence nor threat of violence to any person. The $100 face value of Helm's "no account" check was not trivial, but neither was it a large amount. One hundred dollars was less than half the amount South Dakota required for a felonious theft. It is easy to see why such a crime is viewed by society as among the less serious offenses.

Helm, of course, was not charged simply with uttering a "no account" check, but also with being an habitual offender.[c] And a State is justified in punishing a recidivist more severely than it punishes a first offender. Helm's status, however, cannot be considered in the abstract. His prior offenses, although classified as felonies, were all relatively minor. All were nonviolent and none was a crime against a person. * * *

Helm's present sentence is life imprisonment without possibility of parole. Barring executive clemency, Helm will spend the rest of his life in the state penitentiary. This sentence is far more severe than the life sentence we considered in Rummel v. Estelle. Rummel was likely to have been eligible for parole within 12 years of his initial confinement,[d] a fact on which the Court relied heavily. Helm's sentence is the most severe punishment that the State could have imposed on any criminal for any crime. Only capital punishment, a penalty not authorized in South Dakota when Helm was sentenced, exceeds it.

We next consider the sentences that could be imposed on other criminals in the same jurisdiction. When Helm was sentenced, * * * there were a handful of crimes that were necessarily punished by life imprisonment: murder, and, on

b. The possibility of parole may complicate the comparison, depending upon the time and conditions of its availability.

c. We must focus on the principal felony—the felony that triggers the life sentence—since Helm already has paid the penalty for each of his prior offenses. But we recognize, of course, that Helm's prior convictions are relevant to the sentencing decision.

d. We note that Rummel was, in fact, released within eight months of the Court's decision in his case. See L.A. Times, Nov. 16, 1980, p. 1, col. 3.

a second or third offense, treason, first degree manslaughter, first degree arson, and kidnapping. There was a larger group for which life imprisonment was authorized in the discretion of the sentencing judge, including: treason, first degree manslaughter, first degree arson, and kidnapping; attempted murder, placing an explosive device on an aircraft, and first degree rape on a second or third offense; and any felony after three prior offenses. Finally, there was a large group of very serious offenses for which life imprisonment was not authorized, including a third offense of heroin dealing or aggravated assault.

Criminals committing any of these offenses ordinarily would be thought more deserving of punishment than one uttering a "no account" check—even when the bad-check writer had already committed six minor felonies. Moreover, there is no indication in the record that any habitual offender other than Helm has ever been given the maximum sentence on the basis of comparable crimes. It is more likely that the possibility of life imprisonment under § 22–7–8 generally is reserved for criminals such as fourth-time heroin dealers, while habitual bad-check writers receive more lenient treatment. In any event, Helm has been treated in the same manner as, or more severely than, criminals who have committed far more serious crimes.

Finally, we compare the sentences imposed for commission of the same crime in other jurisdictions. The Court of Appeals found that "Helm could have received a life sentence without parole for his offense in only one other state, Nevada," and we have no reason to doubt this finding. At the very least, therefore, it is clear that Helm could not have received such a severe sentence in 48 of the 50 States. * * *

B

The State argues that the present case is essentially the same as Rummel v. Estelle, for the possibility of parole in that case is matched by the possibility of executive clemency here. * * * We conclude, however, that the South Dakota commutation system is fundamentally different from the parole system that was before us in *Rummel.*

As a matter of law, parole and commutation are different concepts, despite some surface similarities. Parole is a regular part of the rehabilitative process. Assuming good behavior, it is the normal expectation in the vast majority of cases. The law generally specifies when a prisoner will be eligible to be considered for parole, and details the standards and procedures applicable at that time. Thus it is possible to predict, at least to some extent, when parole might be granted. * * *

* * *

The possibility of commutation is nothing more than a hope for "an *ad hoc* exercise of clemency." It is little different from the possibility of executive clemency that exists in every case in which a defendant challenges his sentence under the Eighth Amendment. Recognition of such a bare possibility would make judicial review under the Eighth Amendment meaningless.

* * *

CHIEF JUSTICE BURGER, with whom JUSTICE WHITE, JUSTICE REHNQUIST, and JUSTICE O'CONNOR join, dissenting.

The controlling law governing this case is crystal clear, but today the Court blithely discards any concept of *stare decisis,* trespasses gravely on the authority of the States, and distorts the concept of proportionality of punishment by tearing it from its moorings in capital cases. Only two Terms ago, we held in Rummel v. Estelle that a life sentence imposed after only a *third* nonviolent felony conviction did not constitute cruel and unusual punishment under the

Eighth Amendment. Today, the Court ignores its recent precedent and holds that a life sentence imposed after a *seventh* felony conviction constitutes cruel and unusual punishment under the Eighth Amendment. * * *

I

A

The Court's starting premise is that the Eighth Amendment's Cruel and Unusual Punishments Clause "prohibits not only barbaric punishments, but also sentences that are disproportionate to the crime committed." What the Court means is that a sentence is unconstitutional if it is more severe than five justices think appropriate. In short, all sentences of imprisonment are subject to appellate scrutiny to ensure that they are "proportional" to the crime committed.

* * *

B

* * *

The lesson the *Rummel* Court drew from *Weems* and from the capital punishment cases was that the Eighth Amendment did not authorize courts to review sentences of *imprisonment* to determine whether they were "proportional" to the crime. * * *

The *Rummel* Court categorically rejected the very analysis adopted by the Court today. Rummel had argued that various objective criteria existed by which the Court could determine whether his life sentence was proportional to his crimes. In rejecting Rummel's contentions, the Court explained why each was insufficient to allow it to determine in an *objective* manner whether a given sentence of imprisonment is proportionate to the crime for which it is imposed.

* * *

In short, *Rummel* held that the length of a sentence of imprisonment is a matter of legislative discretion; this is so particularly for recidivist statutes. I simply cannot understand how the Court can square *Rummel* with its holding that "a criminal sentence must be proportionate to the crime for which the defendant has been convicted."

If there were any doubts as to the meaning of *Rummel,* they were laid to rest last Term in Hutto v. Davis. * * *

* * * *Hutto* makes crystal clear that under *Rummel* it is error for appellate courts to second-guess legislatures as to whether a given sentence of imprisonment is excessive in relation to the crime,[e] as the Court does today.

* * *

II

* * *

The Court's traditional abstention from reviewing sentences of imprisonment to ensure that punishment is "proportionate" to the crime is well founded in history, in prudential considerations, and in traditions of comity. Today's conclusion by five Justices that they are able to say that one offense has less "gravity" than another is nothing other than a bald substitution of individual subjective moral values for those of the legislature. Nor, as this case well

e. Both *Rummel* and Hutto v. Davis leave open the possibility that in extraordinary cases—such as a life sentence for overtime parking—it might be permissible for a court to decide whether the sentence is grossly disproportionate to the crime. I agree that the Cruel and Unusual Punishments Clause might apply to those rare cases where reasonable men cannot differ as to the inappropriateness of a punishment. In all other cases, we should defer to the legislature's linedrawing. However, the Court does not contend that this is such an extraordinary case that reasonable men could not differ about the appropriateness of the punishment.

illustrates, are we endowed with Solomonic wisdom that permits us to draw principled distinctions between sentences of different length for a chronic "repeater" who has demonstrated that he will not abide by the law.

* * *

By asserting the power to review sentences of imprisonment for excessiveness the Court launches into uncharted and unchartable waters. Today it holds that a sentence of life imprisonment, without the possibility of parole, is excessive punishment for a seventh allegedly "nonviolent" felony. How about the eighth "nonviolent" felony? The ninth? The twelfth? Suppose one offense was a simple assault? Or selling liquor to a minor? Or statutory rape? Or price-fixing? The permutations are endless and the Court's opinion is bankrupt of realistic guiding principles. Instead, it casually lists several allegedly "objective" factors and arbitrarily asserts that they show respondent's sentence to be "significantly disproportionate" to his crimes. Must all these factors be present in order to hold a sentence excessive under the Eighth Amendment? How are they to be weighed against each other? Suppose several States punish severely a crime that the Court views as trivial or petty? I can see no limiting principle in the Court's holding.

* * *

Note

Was *Rummel* good law after *Solem*? The *Solem* majority does not express doubts about the validity of Rummel's sentence and distinguishes it from the sentence Helm received. Does this mean that if parole were possible for Helm his sentence would have been upheld?

Do you find Helm's prior convictions to be more serious or less serious than Rummel's? Do you find Helm's convictions to be more serious or less serious than Davis'? Can you work with the factors the majority provides in *Solem*?

On remand, Helm received a 20 year sentence. Is it constitutionally valid? Would 25 years have been too much? Will *Solem* offer much guidance to lower courts in future cases that raise similar questions?

The Court substantially limited the application of the *Solem* three-factor test of disproportionality in Harmelin v. Michigan, 111 S.Ct. 2680 (1991), although there was no majority opinion for the Court. Harmelin received a life sentence without parole for possession of 672 grams of cocaine. The Michigan statute was unique in the United States in the severity of punishment for possession of large amounts of cocaine. Moreover, the statute prescribed the same penalty, life without parole, for possession and for distribution of a large amount of cocaine. Harmelin argued that under the *Solem* three-factor test, his sentence was constitutionally disproportionate.

Justice Scalia, joined by Chief Justice Rehnquist, engaged in an extensive historical analysis of the Eighth Amendment, and concluded that "there is no proportionality requirement in the Eighth Amendment." He therefore concluded that *Solem* should be overruled. He argued that the *Solem* factors were indeterminate, and led to judicial subjectivity. He explained as follows:

> We think it enough that those who framed and approved the Federal Constitution chose, for whatever reason, not to include within it the guarantee against disproportionate sentences that some State Constitutions contained. It is worth noting, however, that there was good reason for that choice—a reason that reinforces the necessity of overruling *Solem.* While there are relatively

clear historical guidelines and accepted practices that enable judges to determine which modes of punishment are cruel and unusual, proportionality does not lend itself to such analysis. Neither Congress nor any state legislature has ever set out with the objective of crafting a penalty that is "disproportionate" yet * * * many enacted dispositions seem to be so—because they were made for other times or other places, with different social attitudes, different criminal epidemics, different public fears, and different theories of penology.

Justice Scalia did not completely rule out the possibility that a certain sentence could be constitutionally disproportionate, at least in theory. As he explained:

> This is not to say that there are no absolutes; one can imagine extreme examples that no rational person, in no time or place, could accept. But for the same reason these examples are easy to decide, they are certain never to occur. The real function of a proportionality principle, if it exists, is to enable judges to evaluate a penalty that some assemblage of men and women has considered proportionate—and to say that it is not. For that real-world enterprise, the standards seem so inadequate that the proportionality principle becomes an invitation to imposition of subjective values.

Justice Scalia dismissed the third factor of *Solem*—the character of the sentences imposed by other States for the same crime—as having no relevance to the Eighth Amendment. Thus, the fact that the Michigan statute was unique in its severity of punishment was of no moment. Justice Scalia concluded that "the Eighth Amendment is not a ratchet, whereby a temporary consensus on leniency for a particular crime fixes a permanent constitutional maximum, disabling the States from giving effect to altered beliefs and responding to changed social conditions."

Justice Scalia recognized that the Court had previously invalidated death sentences because of disproportionality. He stated, however, that proportionality review "is one of several respects in which we have held that death is different, and have imposed protections that the Constitution nowhere else provides."

Justice Kennedy, joined by Justices O'Connor and Souter, stated that "stare decisis counsels our adherence to the narrow proportionality principle that has existed in our Eighth Amendment jurisprudence for 80 years." He saw the Eighth Amendment's limitations on severity of sentencing to be governed by four principles: (1) the fixing of prison terms, as a general matter, is properly within the province of the legislature; (2) the Eighth Amendment "does not mandate adoption of any one penological theory;" (3) divergences in the length of prison terms "are the inevitable, often beneficial, result of the federal structure;" and (4) proportionality review should be informed by objective factors, such as consideration of the type of punishment imposed (especially the objective line between capital punishment and noncapital punishment).

From the above factors, Justice Kennedy concluded that the Eighth Amendment "forbids only extreme sentences that are grossly disproportionate to the crime." He stated that the second and third factors of *Solem*—which mandate an intra and inter-jurisdictional comparative analysis—are appropriate "only in the rare case in which a threshold comparison of the crime committed and the sentence imposed leads to an inference of gross disproportionality."

In Justice Kennedy's view, a comparative analysis was not required for Harmelin's sentence, because life imprisonment without parole was not grossly disproportionate to the crime. Justice Kennedy emphasized the pernicious effects of the drug epidemic, and stated that "the Michigan Legislature could with reason conclude that the threat imposed to the individual and society by possession of this large an amount of cocaine—in terms of violence, crime, and social displacement—is momentous enough to warrant the deterrence and retribution of a life sentence without parole."

Justice White, joined by Justices Marshall, Blackmun and Stevens, dissented. Justice White attacked Justice Scalia's historical analysis, and reasoned that the Framers would not have included an excessive fines clause in the Eighth Amendment (which specifically refers to proportionality) without also intending to prevent excessive sentences that could be imposed in lieu of fines. He argued that Justice Scalia's view failed to explain why the words "cruel and unusual punishment" would impose a proportionality requirement in capital cases but not in noncapital cases. He contended that the *Solem* analysis "has worked well in practice" and stated that "Justice Kennedy's abandonment of the second and third factors set forth in *Solem* makes any attempt at an objective proportionality analysis futile."

Applying the *Solem* analysis to Harmelin's sentence, Justice White found it to be disproportionate. On the first factor—the gravity of the offense and the severity of the punishment—he found that mere possession of drugs, even in a large quantity, "is not so serious an offense that it will always warrant, much less mandate, life imprisonment without possibility of parole." He noted that the statute was undifferentiated in that it applied to first-time offenders as well as to recidivists. Justice White was also concerned that Michigan imposed the same sentence for possession and distribution of large amounts of cocaine. He stated that "the State succeeded in punishing Harmelin as if he had been convicted of the more serious crime without being put to the test of proving his guilt on those charges."

On the second *Solem* factor of intra-jurisdictional comparison, Justice White noted that Michigan imposed a life sentence without parole for three crimes: first-degree murder, possession or manufacture with intent to distribute 650 grams or more of narcotics, and the possession offense for which Harmelin was convicted. Justice White concluded that Harmelin had been treated the same as "criminals who have committed far more serious crimes."

On the third factor of inter-jurisdictional comparison, Justice White emphasized that "no other jurisdiction imposes a punishment nearly as severe as Michigan's for possession of the amount of drugs at issue here." Justice White pointed out that under the Federal Sentencing Guidelines, Harmelin would have received a ten-year sentence.

Suppose a state mandates a life sentence without parole for possession of *any* amount of cocaine. Would Justice Scalia find such a sentence to be constitutionally disproportionate? Would Justice Kennedy?

Harmelin also attacked the constitutionality of his sentence on the ground that, even if it was not disproportionate, it was cruel and unusual to impose a mandatory life sentence without any consideration of mitigating factors. Justice Scalia, writing for five members of the Court, held that a sentence which is not otherwise cruel and unusual cannot become so simply because it is mandatory. Justice Scalia recognized that in capital cases, the Eighth Amendment requires individualized sentencing and consideration of all relevant mitigating evidence. He stated, however, that "we have drawn the line of required individualized sentencing at capital cases, and see no basis for extending it further." Justice Kennedy, joined by Justices O'Connor and Souter, wrote a concurring opinion. He argued that "the Michigan scheme may be as fair, if not more so, than other sentencing systems in which the sentencer's discretion or the complexity of the scheme obscures the possible sanction for a crime, resulting in a shock to the offender who learns the severity of his sentence only after he commits the crime." Justices White, Marshall, Blackmun and Stevens did not find it necessary to consider Harmelin's "required mitigation" argument in light of their view that the sentence was constitutionally disproportionate at any rate.

Does *Harmelin* restore the approach that the Court took in *Rummel?* Or does *Harmelin* suggest a different approach? Is *Harmelin* somewhere between *Rummel* and *Solem?* Or is *Harmelin* closer to one or the other of the prior opinions? Now that Justice Marshall has retired, his dissenting vote will not be present in future cases. It is possible that Justice Scalia and the Chief Justice will adhere to their *Harmelin* analysis, but they may choose to join other Justices in order to form a majority and provide clearer guidance to lower courts. How much difference is there between Justice Kennedy's approach and the dissenters'? Is there more help for lower courts in one approach or the other?

The *Solem* majority opinion cites Robinson v. California, which indicates that punishing a person for being addicted to narcotics is impermissible. *Robinson* has not prevented courts from punishing addicts for criminal acts. And, the Supreme Court has never decided whether it is permissible to punish someone who was insane at the time he committed a crime. In Jones v. United States, 463 U.S. 354 (1983), the Court upheld commitment to a mental institution of an insanity acquittee for purposes of treatment and protection until he could demonstrate that he was no longer mentally ill and dangerous, even if the commitment exceeded the maximum sentence provided for the crime charged. In a dissenting opinion, Justice Brennan, joined by Justices Marshall and Blackmun, wrote that "[p]unishing someone acquitted by reason of insanity would undoubtedly implicate important constitutional concerns. It is questionable that confinement to a mental hospital would pass constitutional muster as appropriate punishment for any crime." Would it pass muster under any of the *Harmelin* opinions?

F. OPTIONS OTHER THAN INCARCERATION

Fourth, what sentencing options other than traditional imprisonment are available? The answer is that a number of options exist; some are substitutes for imprisonment, and others amount to punishment in addition to imprisonment.

1. *The Fine*

One of the most familiar alternatives is the fine. The ABA has noted that "[i]t is no less the case with fines than it is with other types of penal sanctions that there is little logic to the statutory framework as it applies to different offenses within a given jurisdiction." ABA Standards, Sentencing Alternatives and Procedures, § 12–2.7 (2d ed. 1980).

There are several problems with the fine as a sanction. One problem is that it works better for middle-class or wealthier defendants who might be better able to pay the fine than poorer defendants.[10] Should ability to pay dictate the choice between jail and an alternative such as a fine? Another

10. For contrasting views on the relative benefits of imprisonment and fines for white collar criminals, compare Posner, Optimal Sentences for White-Collar Criminals, 17 Am. Crim.L.Rev. 409 (1980) with Coffee, Corporate Crime and Punishment: A Non-Chicago View of the Economics of Criminal Sanctions, 17 Am.Crim.L.Rev. 419 (1980).

problem is that judges often are not well enough informed about a defendant's ability to pay or to earn money to arrive at a realistic fine. Many defendants find that they are unable to pay the fine that the judge sets. A related problem is what to do with the defendant who attempts to pay the fine, but is unable to do so. A fourth problem is designating the kinds of offenses that are appropriately punished by fines. Is it ever appropriate to respond to violent crime with a fine? Are fines more appropriate for nonviolent theft crimes? Fifth, a question arises as to whether one who is imprisoned also should be fined. Finally, there is the question whether corporations should be penalized by fine in a different and harsher manner than natural persons. In many jurisdictions, the fine is provided as an option, but there is little in the way of statutes or rules to guide judges in choosing or rejecting the option.

Williams v. Illinois, 399 U.S. 235 (1970), and Tate v. Short, 401 U.S. 395 (1970), protect indigents against oppressive fine systems. In *Williams,* the Court held that it denied an indigent defendant equal protection of the laws to imprison him beyond the maximum term authorized by a state statute because of an inability to pay a fine and court costs. Tate v. Short held that an indigent defendant could not be imprisoned for failure to pay a fine when the state statute made traffic offenses punishable by fine only. How would you achieve deterrence for indigent offenders when jail is not an appropriate sanction?

The Supreme Court again considered the permissible treatment of indigents unable to pay fines in Bearden v. Georgia, 461 U.S. 660 (1983). Bearden was convicted of burglary and theft by receiving stolen property. Under the state's first offender statute, the trial judge did not enter a judgment of guilt, but deferred further proceedings and sentenced Bearden to three years on probation on the burglary charge and a concurrent one year on probation for the theft charge. As a condition of probation he ordered Bearden to pay a $500 fine and $250 restitution. Bearden borrowed $200 to make the initial payments required by the order, but was unable to make further payments. Subsequently, the court revoked Bearden's probation for failure to pay the balance of the fine and restitution, entered a judgment of conviction, and sentenced him to serve the remaining portion of the probationary period (more than two years) in prison.

Justice O'Connor's opinion for the Court observed that the Court's past cases dealing with indigents contained elements of both equal protection and due process analyses. Under either analysis, she reasoned that "[a] defendant's poverty in no way immunizes him from punishment." Thus, a state court may consider a defendant's entire background including employment and financial resources in arriving at a sentence. She reasoned further that "[t]he decision to place the defendant on probation * * * reflects a determination by the sentencing court that the State's penological interests do not require imprisonment"; that a state could imprison a probationer who willfully refused to pay a fine or restitution or to make bona fide efforts to seek employment or borrow money to pay a fine; and that "if the probationer has made all reasonable efforts to pay the fine or restitution, and yet cannot do so through no fault of his own, it is fundamentally unfair to revoke probation automatically without considering whether adequate alternative methods of punishing the defendant are available." Alternatives might include an extension of time to make payments, a reduction of the fine, or a requirement of some form of public service. "Only if the sentencing court determines that alternatives to imprisonment are not adequate in a particular situation to meet the State's interest in punishment and deterrence may the State imprison a probationer who has made sufficient bona fide efforts to pay."

Justice White, joined by Chief Justice Burger and Justices Powell and Rehnquist, concurred in the judgment. He argued that nothing in the Constitution prohibited a state from making "a good-faith effort to impose a jail sentence that in terms of the state's sentencing objectives will be roughly equivalent to the fine and restitution that the defendant failed to pay." He found no such effort by the trial court in this case.

A variation on the fine is forfeiture of property used in or the proceeds of criminal activity. It is increasingly common for both federal and state laws to provide for forfeiture upon conviction and also for civil forfeiture, which does not require a conviction. Congress has provided that a court shall order forfeiture where appropriate in addition to imposing other sanctions upon a defendant. 18 U.S.C. § 3554. As part of its Comprehensive Crime Control Act of 1984, Congress enacted the Comprehensive Forfeiture Act of 1984, which expands the forfeiture provisions in racketeering and drug cases. For a discussion of these forfeiture provisions, see Caplin & Drysdale v. United States in Chapter Ten.

An interesting study of the use of fines is the National Institute of Justice's Executive Summary "Fines in Sentencing" (Nov. 1984), by Hillsman, Sichel and Mahoney. The study is unsurprising in its finding that fines are widely used in limited jurisdiction courts, but more surprising in its finding that a number of courts frequently impose fines upon offenders of limited means and manage to collect them. The study also finds that some courts use fines extensively in felony cases. Judges impose these fines according to the gravity of the offense and the resources of the defendant. They find that use of such fines results in a dramatic drop in the number of short-term custodial sentences that courts impose. Should wealthy defendants be fined more than poor defendants? Does the answer depend on whether both wealthy and poor defendants are incarcerated as well as fined? See, e.g., United States v. Salerno, 937 F.2d 797 (2d Cir.1991) (in a racketeering case, the trial judge sentenced the defendant to 70 years in prison and ordered him to pay a fine of $376,000 plus twice the gross profits of his racketeering activities).

2. *Probation*

Another option is probation. The judicial determination of whether or not to incarcerate a defendant is one of the most important decisions a criminal trial judge is called upon to make. Both the Model Penal Code § 301.1 (1962) and the Nat'l Adv. Comm'n on Crim. Justice Standards and Goals: Corrections § 16.11 (1973) recommend the enactment of legislation that would specify the conditions that can be imposed as part of probation. Familiar conditions are that the probationer meet his family obligations, pay a fine if possible, keep a job, undergo medical (including psychiatric treatment), follow a prescribed course of study or training, report regularly to a probation officer and remain within a specified geographical area. See generally Annots., 35 A.L.R. Fed. 631 (condition that defendant give up profession or employment); 79 A.L.R.3d 976 (condition that defendant make reparations to victim); 79 A.L.R.3d 1025 (condition that defendant reimburse defense costs); 79 A.L.R.3d 1068 (condition that defendant post bond). Community service requirements may also be imposed today by some judges. More controversial conditions are those that call upon probationers to forego personal liberties that the unconvicted citizen may claim under the Bill of Rights. Although a majority of states place some statutory restriction on the judges' power to grant probation, there is no consistent pattern among the jurisdictions and there is some move toward elimination of those restrictions.[11] See, e.g., The President's Comm'n on Law Enforcement and Administration of Justice, Task Force Report: Corrections 34 (1967). When no statutory restrictions exist, judges themselves develop de facto limitations on the use of probation to sentence persons convicted of some of the most serious crimes. But there are few statutory, administrative or other guidelines to govern the judicial choice between probation and incarceration in the run of the mill case. For a discussion of some factors that courts may consider, see R. Dawson, Sentencing 79–99 (1969).

Although some jurisdictions place a statutory maximum on probation periods for felonies, often there is no such limitation for misdemeanors. Thus, a defendant who could be jailed for only one year might be placed on probation for five or ten years. The trial judge usually has broad discretion to select a probation period. In United States v. Thomas, 934 F.2d 840 (7th Cir.1991), the defendant found the conditions and length of the imposed probation to be onerous, and argued that he had an absolute right to reject probation and opt for a prison sentence. The court of appeals held that the defendant had no such option. It reasoned that it is the court, not the defendant, who is given the task of determining the sentence for a crime. The court was concerned that giving defendants the option to choose one form of sentence over another would have a negative effect on the sentencing process.

As part of the Sentencing Reform Act of 1984, Congress elaborated upon and modified the law governing probation. The relevant statutory sections are 18 U.S.C. §§ 3561–3566, and 3601–3607. The statute now explicitly empowers, and sometimes requires judges to make payment of a fine or restitution as a condition of probation.

3. *Restitution*

A third option is restitution. There is increasing concern in the United States with the plight of victims of crime. Hence, it is not surprising that courts are ordering more defendants to make financial restitution to victims. See Drapkin & Viano, Victimology: A New Focus (1973); Hudson & Galaway, Restitution in Criminal Justice (1977). Several states have statutes that make restitution a "policy" of criminal sentencing. See, e.g., Iowa Code Ann. § 910.2; Pa.Const.Stat.Ann., tit. 42, § 9721(C). One of the difficulties with restitution is that some "damages" awards may require jury trials and greater procedural rights than are presently provided in sentencing. Thus, restitution may be limited to pecuniary losses, not general damages for pain and suffering.

11. Some courts jealously protect their authority to grant probation. See, e.g., People v. Tanner, 24 Cal.3d 514, 156 Cal.Rptr. 450, 596 P.2d 328 (1979) (especially the separate opinion of the Chief Justice which concludes that the state constitution requires that courts have probation power—a rather startling doctrine).

See, e.g., Me.Rev.Stat.Ann. tit. 17–A §§ 1321–1325; Iowa Code Ann. § 910.3. An interesting 1979 sentencing statute in Colorado provides that restitution must be made a condition of probation (taking into account the defendant's ability to pay).[12] The growing interest in providing restitution for crime victims is explored in Harland, Monetary Remedies for the Victims of Crime: Assessing the Role of the Criminal Courts, 30 U.C.L.A.L.Rev. 52 (1982).

The Victim and Witness Protection Act of 1982 amended Title 18 of the United States Code in significant respects. Two new sections on restitution, 18 U.S.C.A. §§ 3663 and 3664, provide for restitution for victims of certain offenses and require a court to justify a sentence that does not include restitution. 18 U.S.C.A. § 3664(c) requires that the defendant and the government be informed of provisions of the presentence report relating to restitution. The prosecution must bear the burden of persuasion as to the victim's loss, while the defendant has the burden of persuasion as to his financial resources.

An en banc court summarized some significant aspects of the federal statute on restitution in United States v. Missouri Valley Constr. Co., 741 F.2d 1542 (8th Cir.1984). It observed in dictum that "where a defendant has been charged with crimes against several persons, but convicted on only some of the counts, the court may not order the defendant, as a condition of probation, to make payments to any persons who were not aggrieved by the precise acts charged in those counts on which conviction was had"; and "a defendant [may not] be ordered, as a condition of probation, to reimburse the government for fees paid to his court-appointed attorney, for in such circumstances neither the government nor the attorney is an 'aggrieved party' who suffered losses 'caused by the offense for which conviction was had.'" The court held that federal district judges lack power to impose upon a willing corporation, as a condition of probation, a requirement of contributions of money to charitable entities that did not suffer losses from the corporation's criminal conduct.

Congress again demonstrated its concern for crime victims and its interest in promoting restitution in the Sentencing Reform Act of 1984. The Act recognizes that restitution may be a condition of probation, 18 U.S.C. § 3563, provides that a defendant may have to give notice to victims of fraud or deception in connection with sentencing, 18 U.S.C. § 3555, provides that a court may order portions of a fine remitted if a defendant makes restitution, 18 U.S.C. § 3572, and states that restitution may be imposed in addition to other sanctions, 18 U.S.C. § 3556. As part of the Comprehensive Crime Control Act of 1984, Congress also enacted the Victims of Crime Act of 1984, which creates a crime victims fund and provides for crime victim compensation. A summary of legislation that has been passed to aid victims and witnesses is provided in the U.S. Department of Justice's Bureau of Justice Statistics' "Victim/Witness Legislation: An Overview (July 1984)." [13]

12. The statute provides that restitution shall be ordered only as a condition of probation. Colo.Rev.Stat. § 16–11–204.5. Why should an incarcerated offender be exempt from restitution?

13. The Crime Victim's Fund is supported in part by monies derived from 18 U.S.C. § 3013, which requires courts to impose a monetary special assessment on any person convicted of a federal misdemeanor. The Court in United States v. Munoz–Flores, 495 U.S. 385 (1990), upheld this statute against a challenge that it was passed in violation of the Origination Clause of the Constitution. Justice Marshall, writing for the majority, concluded that the statute was not a "Bill for raising Revenue." Justice Stevens (joined by Justice O'Connor) and Justice Scalia wrote opinions concurring in the judgment.

The Supreme Court held in Kelly v. Robinson, 479 U.S. 36 (1986), that a restitution obligation imposed as a condition of probation in a state criminal proceeding is not dischargeable in bankruptcy proceedings. *Kelly* dealt with bankruptcy proceedings brought under Chapter 7 of the Bankruptcy Code. In Pennsylvania Department of Public Welfare v. Davenport, 495 U.S. 552 (1990), the Court held that the exception to discharge relied on in *Kelly* did not extend to personal bankruptcy proceedings brought under Chapter 13 of the Bankruptcy Code, and therefore that state restitution obligations are dischargeable in Chapter 13 proceedings. Justice Marshall wrote the majority opinion for seven members of the Court. Justice Blackmun wrote a dissenting opinion joined by Justice O'Connor.

United States v. Florence, 741 F.2d 1066 (8th Cir.1984), rejected a defendant's argument that a restitution order, entered as part of the sentence imposed following conviction, amounted to an entry of a civil judgment in violation of the defendant's Seventh Amendment right to trial by jury. It found that the sentencing proceedings satisfied the due process clause. United States v. Brown, 744 F.2d 905 (2d Cir.1984), looked to the background of the Seventh Amendment and found that judicially ordered restitution in criminal cases was in accord with common law practice when the Bill of Rights was adopted. Thus, the court sustained a restitution order entered as part of the sentence imposed upon a defendant convicted of fraudulently holding himself out to be a lawyer.

In United States v. Lemire, 720 F.2d 1327 (D.C.Cir.1983), the court upheld convictions of three individuals and a corporation for wire fraud and other offenses. It sustained a sentence that required two defendants to make restitution to a company that was injured by their actions in the amounts of $1 million and $750 thousand. It rejected the defendants' argument that the statute, 18 U.S.C.A. § 3651 ("While on probation and among other conditions thereof, the defendant ... [m]ay be required to make restitution or reparation to aggrieved parties for actual damages or loss caused by the offense for which conviction was had"), precluded imposition of restitution unless the jury verdict included a determination of amount of loss to the victim. The court held that the sentencing judge may order restitution for the amount of loss she finds the criminal violation caused. It cautioned, however, that where the trial record does not clearly support the district court's assessment of loss due to illegal activity, the court must support its restitution order with additional findings of fact.

A trial judge's order that defendants, who pleaded guilty to conduct that resulted in the destruction of two vacation cottages, make restitution to the owners, adjacent property owners and their insurers was upheld in Pratt v. State, 486 A.2d 1154 (Del.1983). The amounts of restitution were determined according to statements of loss given by the injured parties to a presentence officer. The trial judge held a hearing on restitution before making the award. In its opinion, the state supreme court established guidelines for determining the value of losses in future cases.

Despite the growing trend toward imposing restitution requirements upon defendants, there may be limits upon a judge's power to insist upon restitution. In United States v. Elkin, 731 F.2d 1005 (2d Cir.1984), for example, the court of appeals found that a trial judge erred in imposing a restitution requirement upon a corporate defendant which was not placed on probation. The court concluded that the trial judge had no authority under the governing statute to suspend a sentence and to order restitution without placing the defendant on probation.

Another limitation on the power to award restitution is that the amount may not exceed the actual losses flowing from the precise offense for which the defendant has been convicted. The defendant in Hughey v. United States, 495 U.S. 411 (1990), was indicted on several counts of theft and unauthorized use of credit cards, and pleaded guilty to a single count. Justice Marshall, writing for a unanimous court, held that the trial court erred in ordering restitution for acts other than that to which the defendant pled guilty. The Court rejected the Government's policy argument that plea bargaining should not be allowed to hamper a victim's interest in compensation. Justice Marshall noted that "the essence of a plea agreement is that both the prosecution and the defense make concessions to avoid potential losses. Nothing in the statute suggests that Congress intended to exempt victims of crime from the effect of such a bargaining process."

In response to several celebrated cases in which convicted defendants published books about their criminal activity, many states enacted statutes requiring payment of the proceeds from the sale of such books to the state's Crime Victims Board. (The Federal counterpart is 18 U.S.C. § 3671). The law in New York was known as the "Son of Sam" Law. In Simon & Schuster, Inc. v. Members of New York State Crime Victims Board, 112 S.Ct. 501 (1991), the Court invalidated the Son of Sam Law as inconsistent with the First Amendment. Justice O'Connor, writing for the Court, explained that the Son of Sam law was a "content-based statute" which "singles out income derived from expressive activity for a burden the State places on no other income, and it is directed only at works with a specified content." Because the law was content-based, the State was required to show that the law served a compelling state interest and was narrowly drawn to achieve that interest.

Justice O'Connor noted that while the State had a compelling interest in compensating victims from the fruits of crime, "the Son of Sam law is significantly overinclusive." She stressed that the statute "applies to works on *any* subject, provided that they express the author's thoughts or recollections about his crime, however tangentially or incidentally." She noted that the statute would have covered works such as "The Autobiography of Malcolm X" and the "Confessions of St. Augustine." The Court emphasized that a more narrowly tailored statute—such as a statute covering works predominantly rather than tangentially about the author's criminal activity—could possibly pass constitutional muster.

4. *Pretrial Diversion And Partial Confinement*

Other sentencing alternatives are still in the early stages of development. Pretrial diversion programs may encourage some offenders, especially drug addicts (including alcoholics), to seek treatment instead of contesting charges. Successful completion of a treatment program usually results in the dismissal of charges. The federal program is discussed in Marshall v. United States, 414 U.S. 417 (1974), which holds that Congress can permissibly distinguish from other addicts those with two or more felony convictions and deny those with prior convictions the benefit of diversion programs. The judgment of the prosecutor as to the appropriateness of treatment may be central to some diversion schemes. Compare, e.g., People v. Superior Court, 11 Cal.3d 59, 113 Cal.Rptr. 21, 520 P.2d 405 (1974) with Sledge v. Superior Court, 11 Cal.3d 70, 113 Cal.Rptr. 28, 520 P.2d 412 (1974).

Even if incarceration is used as a sanction, there are alternatives to the typical prison sentence. For example, a sentence of partial confinement—for selected periods—may be imposed. Or, an offender might serve a sentence on nights and weekends. For an analysis of jail and prison populations, see U.S. Department of Justice, Bureau of Justice Statistics, Jail Inmates, 1985; U.S. Department of Justice, Bureau of Justice Statistics, 1984 Census of State Adult Correctional Facilities. The growth in the prison and jail populations of many jurisdictions has greatly increased the costs of running the criminal justice system and has led to a search for less expensive forms of incarceration. Some jurisdictions have experimented with "house arrest," a sentence imposed by the court in which offenders are legally ordered to remain confined in their own residences. Petersilia, A Man's Home is His Prison, 2 Criminal Justice, No. 4, 16, 17 (1988).

5. *Special Offender Status*

Finally, where incarceration is anticipated, the particularly dangerous offender and the professional criminal might be singled out for harsher treatment than the typical offender, and facilities might be developed to provide special treatment for certain types of offenders, particularly the young.

One statutory scheme "designed to provide a better method for treating young offenders convicted in federal courts in that vulnerable age bracket [16–22], to rehabilitate them and restore normal behavior patterns," Dorszynski v. United States, 418 U.S. 424, 432 (1974), was the Federal Youth Corrections Act, which provided the trial judge with special sentencing options for offenders under 22 years of age. Although the result of sentencing under the Act could have been a longer sentence than would be served by an adult, there was greater emphasis on treatment under the Act. More treatment facilities were made available to youth offenders; more individualized treatment for youth offenders was expected; and special release provisions (in lieu of parole) applied to youth offenders. In the Comprehensive Crime Control Act of 1984, Congress decided to replace the Youth Corrections Act with its general guideline approach to sentencing. In United States v. R.L.C., 112 S.Ct. 1329 (1992), the Court held that the maximum permissible sentence in Federal juvenile-delinquency proceedings must be limited to that which could have been imposed upon an adult under the Sentencing Guidelines.

Whether special statutes are intended to toughen or soften sentences for classes of offenders, they typically vest broad discretion in the sentencing authority.[14]

14. What is often a crucial question to a juvenile is whether he will be treated as a "child" or as an adult. See, e.g., Kent v. United States, 383 U.S. 541 (1966). Perhaps no advantage is more significant than the limit on incarceration to a designated age. If a person is transferred to the typical criminal court, the potential range of prison sentences may increase, so the transfer decision is of critical importance; yet it is a decision that is guided by few standards. Like most sentencing decisions "discretion" is almost uncontrolled. It is not surprising, therefore, that movements to reform sentencing by guiding

II. THE EXTENT OF THE DISPARITY PROBLEM AND ATTEMPTS TO REDUCE IT

A. STATE PROVISIONS

Several states have chosen alternatives to a system that gives judges or juries virtually uncontrolled discretion to choose any sentence within a broad range established by statute. California, for example, has adopted one of the least discretionary systems. See generally Oppenheim, Computing a Determinate Sentence * * * New Math Hits the Courts, 51 Cal.St.B.J. 604 (1976). Felonies, other than those punishable by death or life imprisonment, each are assigned three basic punishments; the following groupings are used: 16 months, 2 and 3 years; 2, 3, and 4 years; 3, 4, and 5 years; and 5, 6, and 7 years. The judge must choose the middle term in the range as the base term unless there are aggravating circumstances justifying the higher term or mitigating circumstances justifying the lower term. These factors are to be prescribed by the California Judicial Council. The base term may be increased upon certain findings, such as use of a firearm, the intentional causing of great bodily injury, or the exercise of previous offenses. Parole is abolished (although a period of supervised release is specified), and the inmate's release is determined by the court's sentence minus good time credits.[15]

judges and juries in their decisionmaking have also eyed juvenile courts as potential beneficiaries of reform. See, e.g., Feld, Reference of Juvenile Offenders for Adult Prosecution: The Legislative Alternative to Asking Unanswerable Questions, 62 Minn.L.Rev. 514 (1978). For a suggestion that juvenile courts should be abolished and that all juveniles should be tried as adults (where they would, on balance, obtain greater protection), see Ainsworth, Reimagining Childhood and Reconstructing the Legal Order: The Case for Abolishing the Juvenile Court, 69 N.C.L.Rev. 1083 (1991).

In Jones v. United States, 463 U.S. 354 (1983), Justice Powell's opinion for the Court upheld District of Columbia laws that required a defendant found not guilty by reason of insanity to prove by a preponderance of the evidence that he is no longer mentally ill or dangerous in order to obtain release from a mental hospital. Although other persons may be civilly committed only if the government proves by clear and convincing evidence that they are mentally ill and likely to injure themselves or others, the Court found that insanity acquittees constituted a special class who could be treated differently and who could be kept in a mental hospital beyond the maximum periods prescribed as penalties in criminal statutes. Jones had been charged with a misdemeanor, attempted petit larceny, punishable by a maximum prison sentence of one year. He raised insanity as a defense and proved it by a preponderance of the evidence as required by local law. The Court reasoned that because there had been proof beyond a reasonable doubt that Jones committed a crime, and he himself proved insanity, it was permissible to presume that he continued to be mentally ill and dangerous. Justice Brennan, joined by Justices Marshall and Blackmun, dissented and argued that an acquittal by reason of insanity of a single, nonviolent misdemeanor is not a constitutionally adequate substitute for the due process protections of clear and convincing evidence of dangerousness. Justice Stevens dissented on the ground that a plea of not guilty by reason of insanity could not justify confinement for a longer period than the maximum punishment for a crime.

15. Experience with the California sentencing law in three counties of the state is described in Casper, Brereton & Neal, The Implementation of the California Determinate Sentencing Law (May 1982). The authors found that following enactment of the statute there was a slight increase in the proportion of defendants sentenced to prison, but they cautioned that the increase might be attributable to factors other than the new statute. They found little evidence that the statute affected plea bargaining rates. In their conclusion, the authors state that interviews with court personnel, lobbyists and legislative aides suggested "that the coalition that came together to support the DSL is well on the way to dissolution, if it has not been pronounced dead already." Liberals see legislators raising prison terms while law enforcement officials believe that the terms are not long enough. The authors speculate that if sentences be-

Maine also has seen fit to abolish parole. See Maine Rev.Stat.Ann., tit. 17–A, § 1151 et seq. But it has left its 5 felony classes with broad sentencing ranges from which the trial judge chooses a "flat sentence"—i.e., the sentence that will be served less good time.[16] Although there is no parole, all sentences in excess of one year are deemed "tentative" and a positive assessment of the offender's "progress toward a non-criminal way of life" may result in resentencing.

B. THE CHANGE IN FEDERAL SENTENCING

Congress enacted the Sentencing Reform Act of 1984 as part of the Comprehensive Crime Control Act of 1984. The Sentencing Act takes the approach recommended by the Model Sentencing and Corrections Act.[17] It classifies federal criminal offenses and designates the sentencing range for the new classes, states the purposes to be served by any sentence, establishes a Commission to promulgate guidelines, requires judges to give reasons for sentencing and for departing from the guidelines, provides for appellate review when judges depart from the guidelines or from the sentence provided in a plea agreement, and abolishes parole. The Senate Judiciary Committee, in Senate Report No. 98–225, at 52–62, explained the new legislation as follows:

> "A primary goal of sentencing reform is the elimination of unwarranted sentencing disparity. The bill requires the judge, before imposing sentence, to consider the history and characteristics of the offender, the nature and circum-

come longer, their determinate nature may cause problems of prison overcrowding, which eventually might lead people to question the idea of determinacy. It is not surprising that there should be uncertainty about the appropriate balance between determinacy and indeterminacy. Historically, there has been uncertainty. See generally, Radzinowicz & Hood, Judicial Discretion and Sentencing Standards: Victorian Attempts to Solve a Perennial Problem, 127 U.Pa.L.Rev. 1288 (1979).

16. See also Ill.Annot.Stat. § 1005–5–1 et seq. (judge given broad range to choose sentence, but directed to consider certain aggravating and mitigating factors and to assign weight to them as seems appropriate).

17. That Act provides in part as follows:

(1) The sentence imposed should be no greater than that which is deserved for the offense committed.

(2) Inequalities in sentences that are unrelated to a purpose of this Article should be avoided.

(3) The sentence imposed should be the least severe measure necessary to achieve the purpose for which the sentence is imposed.

(4) Sentences not involving confinement should be preferred unless:

(i) confinement is necessary to protect society by restraining the defendant who has a long history of criminal conduct;

(ii) confinement is necessary to avoid deprecating the seriousness of the offense or justly to punish the defendant;

(iii) confinement is particularly suited to provide an effective deterrent to others likely to commit similar offenses;

(iv) measures less restrictive than confinement have been frequently or recently applied unsuccessfully to the defendant; or

(v) the purposes of this Article would be fulfilled only by a sentence involving confinement.

(5) The potential or lack of potential for the rehabilitation or treatment of the defendant should not be considered in determining the sentence alternative or length of term to be imposed, but the length of a term of community supervision may reflect the length of a treatment or rehabilitation program in which participation is a condition of the sentence.

(6) The prediction of the potential for future criminality by a particular defendant, unless based on prior criminal conduct or acts designated as a crime under the law, should not be considered in determining his sentence alternative or the length of term to be imposed.

stances of the offense, and the purposes of sentencing. He is then to determine which sentencing guidelines and policy statements apply to the case. Either he may decide that the guideline recommendation appropriately reflects the offense and offender characteristics and impose sentence according to the guideline recommendation or he may conclude that the guidelines fail to reflect adequately a pertinent aggravating or mitigating circumstance and impose sentence outside the guidelines. A sentence outside the guidelines is appealable, with the appellate court directed to determine whether the sentence is reasonable. Thus, the bill seeks to assure that most cases will result in sentences within the guideline range and that sentences outside the guidelines will be imposed only in appropriate cases.

"The Committee does not intend that the guidelines be imposed in a mechanistic fashion. It believes that the sentencing judge has an obligation to consider all the relevant factors in a case and to impose a sentence outside the guidelines in an appropriate case. The purpose of the sentencing guidelines is to provide a structure for evaluating the fairness and appropriateness of the sentence for an individual offender, not to eliminate the thoughtful imposition of individualized sentences. Indeed, the use of sentencing guidelines will actually enhance the individualization of sentences as compared to current law. Under a sentencing guidelines system, the judge is directed to impose sentence after a comprehensive examination of the characteristics of the particular offense and the particular offender. This examination is made on the basis of a presentence report that notes the presence or absence of each relevant offense and offender characteristics. This will assure that the probation officer and the sentencing judge will be able to make informed comparisons between the case at hand and others of a similar nature.

"The Parole Commission has argued that, even if a sentencing guidelines system is adopted, the Commission should be retained to set the actual release date for a person sentenced by a judge to a term of imprisonment. Under its proposal, the judge, after considering the sentencing guidelines, would determine whether to send a defendant to prison and, if so, would set the maximum prison term that could be served by the defendant. Shortly after the defendant begins his term, the Parole Commission, using its own guidelines, would set a presumptive release date subject to good behavior and could later adjust that date for noncompliance with prison rules. It bases this belief on the argument that a small collegial body will be better able than the Federal judges to achieve the goal of elimination of unwarranted sentencing disparity. The Committee strongly disagrees with the Parole Commission. The proposal is based on the same discredited assumptions as the present system and is entirely at odds with the rationale of the proposed guidelines system. Moreover, it has several practical deficiencies that would result in continuing some of the unfairness and uncertainty in the current system.

"First, it would perpetuate the current problem that judges do not control the determination of the length of a prison term even though this function is particularly judicial in nature. The better view is that sentencing should be within the province of the judiciary. Indeed, it is arguable that the Parole Commission by basing its decision on factors already known at the time of sentencing, has already usurped a function of the judiciary.

"Second, the argument that the Parole Commission, because it is a 'small collegial body,' is able to render more consistent decisions than the Federal judges would be, is debatable. Initial decisions of the Parole Commission are made by at least 35 hearing examiners, not by the nine Commissioners. It seems unlikely that more than 40 people making administrative decisions would result in substantially less inconsistency than a few hundred people making judicial decisions after hearing arguments presented by counsel for both sides, which are subject to appellate review by eleven courts of appeals sitting in panels and, ultimately, by a single Supreme Court. The recent GAO study of the operations of the United States Parole Commission concluded that the hearing examiners made errors in applying the guidelines in 53 percent of the cases studied, and most of these errors were not corrected in the internal appeals process. GAO specifically found that one reason the appellate process did not result in correction of errors in application of the guidelines was a Parole Commission policy that barred a decision more adverse to the prisoner than the decision appealed, even if the early release date was the result of an erroneous application of the guidelines.

"Third, it would draw an artificial line between imprisonment and probation, forcing the sentencing guidelines system and the judges to formulate sentencing policy that assumes that a term of imprisonment, no matter how brief, is necessarily a more stringent sentence than a term of probation with restrictive conditions and a heavy fine. Such an assumption would be a roadblock to the development of sensible comprehensive sentencing policy.

"Fourth, it would continue the current law problem that actual terms of imprisonment are determined in private rather than public proceedings.

"Fifth, the Parole Commission might be basing decisions on a different sentencing philosophy than is reflected in the sentencing guidelines. The Parole Commission has suggested that, at least for the first few years of sentencing guidelines, the Parole Commission should issue its own guidelines for lengths of prison terms rather than rely on guidelines promulgated by the Sentencing Commission.

"Finally, under the Parole Commission's proposal the procedures for review of a sentence outside the guidelines—for example, when both a term of imprisonment and a fine outside the guidelines are imposed—would be virtually unworkable. Apparently, the fine level would be reviewed publicly in the courts of appeals while the term of imprisonment would be reviewed privately by the Parole Commission. It is even possible that the Parole Commission under its proposal would review and amend a sentence after a United States court of appeals had already found it to be reasonable—a situation that the Committee finds totally unacceptable.

"The Committee believes that there may be unusual cases in which an eventual reduction in the length of a term of imprisonment is justified by changed circumstances. These would include cases of severe illness, cases in which other extraordinary and compelling circumstances justify a reduction of an unusually long sentence, and some cases in which the sentencing guidelines for the offense of which the defender was convicted have been later amended to provide a shorter term of imprisonment. The Committee believes, however, that it is unnecessary to continue the expensive and cumbersome Parole Commission to deal with the relatively small number of cases in which there may be justification for reducing a term of imprisonment. The bill, as reported, provides instead * * * for court determination, subject to consideration of Sentencing Commission standards, of the question whether there is justification for reducing a term of imprisonment in situations such as those described.

"Under the bill, the sentence imposed by the judge will be the sentence actually served. A sentence that exceeds one year may be adjusted at the end of each year by 36 days for a prisoner's compliance with institutional regulations. Should a prisoner demonstrate less than satisfactory compliance with prison rules, however, he may receive a small adjustment, or no adjustment at all. Once this credit has been given by the Bureau of Prisons, it cannot be withdrawn. Nor may credit that has been denied later be granted. The prisoner, the public, and the corrections officials will be certain at all times how long the prison term will be, and of the consequences of causing institutional discipline problems.

* * *

"[B]ecause of the increased certainty of release dates, the bill should enhance prison rehabilitation efforts because prison officials will be able to work with prisoners to develop realistic work programs and goals within a set term of imprisonment. As Professor Norval Morris of the University of Chicago Law School has illustrated, parole boards are not able to predict with any degree of certainty which prisoners are likely to be "good" release risks and which are not. Indeed, such determinations seem especially suspect when made on the basis of how a prisoner responds to prison rehabilitative programs.

* * *

"For the first time, Federal law will assure that the Federal criminal justice system will adhere to a consistent sentencing philosophy. Further, each participant in the system will know what purpose is to be achieved by the sentence in each particular case.

* * *

"The bill requires the sentencing judge to announce how the guidelines apply to each defendant and to give his reasons for the sentence imposed. The judge is also required to give the reason for imposing sentence at a particular point within the guidelines or, if the sentence is outside the guidelines, specific reasons for imposing a sentence of a different kind or length than recommended in the guidelines.

"The statement of reasons can be used by each participant in the Federal criminal justice system charged with reviewing or implementing a sentence. It will assist the appellate courts in reviewing the reasonableness of a sentence outside the guidelines, and in determining whether a sentence within the guidelines is the result of correct or incorrect application of the guidelines. The statement of reasons can be used by probation or prison officials, working in conjunction with the defendant, in achieving the goals sought by the sentencing judge.

"Finally, the abolition of the Parole Commission will eliminate its second-guessing of the judge's sentencing, and will obviate the need for the judge to anticipate how the Parole Commission may alter the sentence he imposed."

* * *

The U.S. Sentencing Commission found that adoption of guidelines satisfactory to legislators, prosecutors, defense lawyers, and judges was no simple task. It circulated two preliminary drafts before it delivered its final report to Congress in April, 1987.

In its first draft, circulated in September, 1986, the Commission indicated that it had considered three basic approaches to sentencing guidelines: real offense sentencing, modified real offense sentencing, and charge of conviction offense sentencing. The Commission described real offense sentencing as an approach that considered all of the offender's relevant behavior. It described charge of conviction sentencing as an approach that considered only the elements of behavior that formed part of the charge of which the offender was convicted. Modified real offense sentencing, falling somewhere in between the other two approaches, focuses on three items: the conduct necessarily involved in the offense of conviction, the conduct done in furtherance of the offense of conviction, and any injuries resulting from such conduct.

The Commission indicated that it had rejected real offense sentencing for several reasons: 1) A jury does not necessarily find the facts that would be considered in real offense sentencing. 2) A defendant who pleads to one offense may view as unfair a judge's considering other conduct for which the defendant might never have been convicted at trial. 3) Plea bargaining would be diminished and significant additional judicial resources would be required. 4) Deciding what conduct is relevant to sentencing is a difficult task.

The Commission also set forth reasons for rejecting charge of conviction sentencing: 1) Because of the way federal criminal statutes often are drafted, an offense might include widely different behavior, and the differences may be relevant in sentencing. 2) Any fair sentencing system ought to consider some uncharged elements—e.g., how much money a bank robber stole, or whether an assault resulted in physical injury. 3) Pure charge of conviction sentencing increases the power of prosecutors to determine sentences.

The Commission concluded that the traditional system of sentencing is largely a system of real offense sentencing, notwithstanding the fact that it usually is described differently. The Commission reasoned that the sentencing judge traditionally exercises broad discretion in choosing from an array of facts in a presentence report and adopts an appropriate sentence based on the facts that he or she deems relevant. In adopting modified real offense sentencing, the Commission purported to focus on only the real elements, whether charged as elements or not, that are importantly bound up with the conduct that constitutes the crime charged. When a fact has not necessarily been proved, or when a guilty plea is entered and the parties disagree as to the facts, the Commission proposed that the government would have to prove relevant facts, other than those offered in mitigation, by a preponderance of the evidence.

In its second draft, circulated in January, 1987, the Commission largely abandoned the approach it had taken in its first draft. It observed that its modified real offense approach had treated unadjudicated misconduct as a suitable object of punishment rather than as an aggravating factor in fixing the punishment for the offense of conviction. It also noted that the original approach created a potential for extensive litigation over disputed harms and a danger that fact or charge bargaining would increase the influence of prosecutors in sentencing.

The January draft adopted traditional offense categories and used as the base for sentencing guidelines the offense of conviction. Related conduct not included in the offense of conviction could be used to aggravate or mitigate a sentence, but it could not carry the weight of a separately charged and convicted offense. There was considerable criticism of the second draft, and the Committee scrambled to produce a final set of guidelines for submission to the Congress.

The April 1987 guidelines, like the January draft, include a sentencing table with 43 offense levels. The vertical column of the table begins with level 1 and ends with level 43. Six criminal history categories comprise the horizontal column of the table. A separate table for fines specifies minimum and maximum fines for all offense levels, unless a specific statutory provision governs.

One of the members of the Sentencing Commission, Ilene Nagel, has described the major decisions that the Commission made in the difficult process of creating guidelines in Foreword, Structuring Sentencing Discretion: The New Federal Sentencing Guidelines, 80 J.Crim.L. & Crimin. 883 (1990). The first decision the Commission made was whether to adopt an explicit rationale to govern its work—e.g., a just desert or utilitarian based theory of punishment. The Commission ultimately concluded that Congress had several goals in mind in the 1984 legislation and that no one rationale could further the legislative ends. As a result of the circulation of various drafts and extensive debate within the Commission, the Commission finally agreed to the following principles:

(1) Similar offense categories—e.g., for various kinds of fraud—would be grouped together under a single generic heading.

(2) The base sentence for each offense would be determined by a discussion process, "*anchored, but not bound by,*" estimates of the average time served in past years by offenders convicted of that offense and the percentage of offenders given a nonincarceration sentence.

(3) For articulated policy reasons—e.g., to increase deterrence—sentences could be raised or lowered with respect to past practice.

(4) Base offense sentences would be modified by a set of specific offense characteristics that would be determined by looking to past sentencing practices, to statutory aggravating or mitigating factors, to factors that are taken into consideration in similar offenses, to the vulnerability of victims, the offender's role in an offense, acceptance of responsibility, and the criminal history of the offender.

Thus, the Commission began with past practice, focussed on the importance of rationalizing sentences, and adopted an approach that focuses on the charges actually brought and the real offense behavior of the offender. It decided that conspiracies and attempts would generally be treated the same as the object offense, with a modest downward adjustment.

To understand how the guidelines work, it is useful to consider a hypothetical case. Suppose that a defendant is convicted of securities fraud. The guidelines describe offenses generically and contain an index indicating which guidelines cover various code sections. Securities fraud is governed by guideline § 2F1.1. The base offense level is 6, but the level increases as the estimated probable or intended loss increases. Thus, if the estimated loss were $150,000, the offense level would be 13 (base of 6 plus 7 added). If the securities fraud involved insider trading, the base would be 8 and the same increases would apply depending on the amount of the loss. § 2F1.2.

Certain adjustments of sentence must be considered. There are victim-related adjustments—e.g., adjustments that increase punishment when the victim is a child or especially vulnerable, § 3A1.1, or when the victim is a law enforcement officer. § 3A1.2. Adjustments are provided when the defendant had an aggravating or mitigating role in an offense. §§ 3B1.1, 3B1.2. A third adjustment increases punishment for obstruction of justice. § 3C1.1. See United States v. Thompson, 944 F.2d 1331 (7th Cir.1991) (enhancement for obstruction of justice not permitted where the defendant merely denies wrongdoing).

Section 1B1.3 of the Guidelines provides that "conduct which is not formally charged or is not an element of the offense of conviction may enter into the determination of the applicable sentencing range." Under this section, the sentencing range can be based not only on evidence for which the defendant was convicted, but also on evidence that is related to the conduct forming the basis of the conviction. See, e.g., United States v. Santiago, 906 F.2d 867 (2d Cir.1990) (in a drug distribution case, quantities and types of drugs not specified in the count of conviction are to be included in determining the base offense level if they were part of the same course of conduct or part of a common scheme or plan as the count of conviction; court properly considered previous, uncharged sales to the same buyer). "Relevant conduct" must be proven by a preponderance of the evidence. United States v. Mourning, 914 F.2d 699 (5th Cir.1990) (trial court properly considered uncharged acts of money laundering). Thus, in our hypothetical, if the Government could show that the defendant engaged in related acts of securities fraud, these acts would be considered in setting the base offense level.

The punishment level for the securities fraud defendant would rise by 4 if the defendant was the organizer of an illegal scheme that involved either five or more participants or was otherwise extensive. § 3B1.1(a). Thus, the defendant convicted of extensive illegal conduct involving $150,000 would be at level 17 (base of 6 plus 7 for amount plus 4 for extensiveness).

If the defendant is convicted on several counts, the calculation is usually made separately for each count, and a set of rules is applied to the totality. But there are special rules that aggregate some conduct. §§ 3D1.1–3D1.5. See generally Alschuler, The Failure of Sentencing Guidelines: A Plea for Less Aggregation, 58 U.Chi.L.Rev. 901 (1991). Assume, for example, that the securities fraud defendant was convicted of defrauding three victims whose estimated losses were $250,000, $100,000, and $500,000. For crimes in which offense level is determined primarily on the basis of the amount of the loss, the three estimated losses are added together for a total of $850,000. The addition would result in a punishment increase of 11 levels above the base offense level .

The final determinant of the offense level is the defendant's acceptance of responsibility. § 3E1.1. A defendant who "clearly demonstrates a recognition and affirmative acceptance of personal responsibility for the offense of conviction" will receive a reduction of 2 levels, whether or not he pleaded guilty. For example, if the securities fraud defendant who created an expected loss of $850,000 made voluntary restitution, his level might drop from 17 to 15. See, e.g., United States v. Phillip, 948 F.2d 241 (6th Cir.1991) (defendant not entitled to reduction for acceptance of responsibility where he gave a false alibi to the investigating officers); United States v. Burns, 925 F.2d 18 (1st Cir.1991) (defendant who enters *Alford* plea—pleading guilty while protesting his innocence—is not entitled to reduction for acceptance of responsibility).

Once the offense level is fixed, the sentencing judge must determine the defendant's criminal history. §§ 4A1.1–4A1.3. Criminal history points are determined by a defendant's prior convictions. Three points are allocated, for example, for each prior sentence of imprisonment exceeding one year and one month, and two points are added for each sentence of imprisonment of at least 60 days but less than one year and one month. Some offenses are excluded, and time periods are designated to exclude stale convictions. The sentencing judge is permitted to depart from the computational approach if reliable information indicates that the criminal history category understates the seriousness of the defendant's past criminal conduct. Special provision is made for "career offenders"—i.e., defendants at least 18 at the time they commit the crime of conviction, which is a crime of violence or trafficking in a controlled substance, and the defendant has at least two prior felony convictions for violent crimes or trafficking in controlled substances. § 4B1.1. Using this formula, the securities fraud defendant with no prior criminal record would have a criminal history of 0.

Using the sentencing table, and assuming no prior criminal history, a securities fraud defendant convicted of one count involving $150,000 would fall within a guideline for offense level 13 calling for a sentence of 12–18 months. Had the expected loss been less than $2,000, the defendant would fall within a guideline for offense level 6 calling for a sentence of 0–6 months. The sentence would be 24–30 months for level 17.

If instead of no criminal record, a defendant had a category III criminal record, the sentence for a level 13 offense increases to 18–24 months and for a level 17 offense to 30–37 months. Defendants in the worst criminal category (VI) would face a guideline of 33–41 months at level 13 and 51–63 months at level 17.

Each row of the sentencing table contains levels that overlap with the levels in the preceding and succeeding rows. By overlapping the levels, the Commission intended to discourage unnecessary litigation. Both the prosecutor and the defendant are expected to realize that the difference between one level and another will not necessarily make a difference in sentencing.

The securities fraud defendant would also be fined. The maximum fine would be twice the estimated loss caused by the offense or three times the estimated gain to the defendant.

The guidelines contain a section on "departures." They authorize departures from the guidelines when a defendant has provided substantial assistance to authorities, death or serious injury has resulted from conduct, the defendant's conduct was unusually extreme or cruel, and in other circumstances. §§ 5K1, 5K2. See, e.g., United States v. Phillip, 948 F.2d 241 (6th Cir.1991) (three-level upward departure under § 5K2.8 for extreme cruelty inflicted by the defendant on his four-year-old son); United States v. Williams, 937 F.2d 979 (5th Cir.1991) (upward departure because of the defendant's advantageous social background is not permitted). See generally Selya & Kipp, An Examination of Emerging Departure Jurisprudence Under the Federal Sentencing Guidelines, 67 Notre Dame L.Rev. 1 (1991).

In Williams v. United States, 112 S.Ct. ___ (1992), the Court considered the scope of appellate review of a district court's departure from a guideline range, where the departure was based on both valid and invalid considerations. The district court imposed an upward departure on the basis of two outdated convictions which it found were "reliable information" indicating more extensive criminal conduct than that reflected by Williams' criminal history category, and also on the basis of several arrests. The court of appeals held that the outdated convictions could be used for departure under Guideline § 4A1.3, but that the arrests could not be used for departure under that same Guideline. The court of appeals affirmed the sentence on the ground that a departure can be affirmed if it is reasonable in light of the proper factors standing alone. That court did not find it necessary to consider whether the district court would actually have imposed the departure if it had relied on the old convictions alone.

Justice O'Connor, writing for the majority, declared that "it is an incorrect application of the Guidelines for a district court to depart from the applicable sentencing range based on a factor that the Commission has already fully considered in establishing the guideline range or, as in this case, on a factor that the Commission has expressly rejected as an appropriate ground for departure." On the issue of appellate review, she concluded that "once the court of appeals has decided that the district court misapplied the Guidelines, a remand is appropriate unless the reviewing court concludes, on the record as a whole, that the error was harmless, i.e. that the error did not affect the district court's selection of the sentence imposed." The Court found this result mandated by 18 U.S.C. § 3742(f), which governs appellate review of sentences under the Guidelines. Since the affirmance by the court of appeals was based not on the ground of harmless error, but rather on the ground that the resulting sentence was reasonable, the Court vacated and remanded for a harmless error analysis. Justice White, joined by Justice Kennedy, dissented and argued that a remand to the district court is not required if the departure is reasonable, even though the district court may not itself have imposed the departure if not for its error.

The guidelines also indicate when probation is authorized and the method for fixing the term of probation. § 5B1.1–4. Recommended conditions of probation and supervised release, and recommended "special conditions" are set forth. The guidelines classify as serious offenses, which require a prison term, some offenses for which probation has been common—e.g., tax evasion and antitrust offenses. However, the guidelines permit the sentencing judge to impose a short prison term.

Because the guidelines are a radical departure from traditional sentencing practices in federal courts, it is not surprising that they are unattractive to many judges and lawyers. It is more surprising that the most biting attack on the Commission's work product has come from inside rather than outside the Commission. The attack appeared in the dissenting statement of Commissioner Paul Robinson. Robinson identified the failures that he saw in the guidelines: no adequate studies justified the sentencing levels, which he described as an incoherent and irrational approach to guidelines based upon past sentencing averages; offenses were not ranked systematically according to seriousness; many harms associated with criminal conduct were omitted from consideration; and fragmented and overlapping offenses resulted in similar guidelines.

Robinson's most disturbing charge is that the guidelines might produce as much disparity as the system they replace. He complained of the skeletal and vague nature of the guidelines and of the invitation to sentencing judges to depart from them. Commissioner Robinson sets forth his views on optimal sentencing reform in A Sentencing System for the 21st Century?, 66 Tex.L.Rev. 1 (1977).

The majority of the Commission responded with "Preliminary Observations on Commissioner Robinson's dissent." The majority described Robinson's approach, which was circulated in a July, 1986 draft, as calling for a highly detailed, mechanical guideline system that would aggravate punishments for each and every harm and reduce punishment for each and every mitigating factor. It concluded that the reaction to such an approach had been negative and might not have survived a congressional veto.

It is clear, however, that sentencing judges retain some flexibility to depart from the guidelines if they choose to do so. 18 U.S.C. § 3553(b) permits the sentencing court to depart from the guidelines if an aggravating or mitigating factor exists that was not adequately taken into consideration by the Sentencing Commission in formulating the guidelines. The Commission provides in a policy statement that where it has taken into account a factor, departures from the guidelines are warranted only if the factor is present to a degree substantially in excess of that ordinarily involved in the offense of conviction. The Commission's list of factors that might justify a departure is broad enough to include most factors that sentencing judges have traditionally considered as aggravating—e.g., harm to the victim, abduction or hostage taking, property damage, use of a weapon or dangerous instrumentality, disruption of a governmental function or threat to the public health or welfare, extreme or brutal conduct, and criminal purpose—and most factors that sentencing judges have considered as mitigating—victim's conduct, coercion and duress, diminished capacity, and avoidance of greater harms. Still, recent experience with the Guidelines shows that departures—either upward or downward—have been limited to truly unusual or egregious circumstances. See Selya & Kipp, An Examination of Emerging Departure Jurisprudence Under the Federal Sentencing Guidelines, 67 Notre Dame L.Rev. 1 (1991), discussing, among other cases, United States v. Roberson, 872 F.2d 597 (5th Cir.1989). In *Roberson,* the court departed upward in sentencing a defendant convicted of credit card fraud for using someone else's access card. The proprietor of the card lived with the defendant, had died of a coughing fit in the defendant's presence, and the defendant panicked in fear of being blamed for the death. He took the body to a dumpster and burned it. The court of appeals upheld the departure and opined that "the Commission did not contemplate that a credit card fraud case would also involve concealing, disposing of, and burning a corpse." See also United States v. Pena, 930 F.2d 1486 (10th Cir.1991) (downward departure for defendant convicted of possession with intent to distribute marijuana; defendant was a single parent of a two-month-old child, was the sole provider for that child as well as for her sixteen-year-old daughter and infant grandchild, and had an excellent employment record).

Justice Blackmun wrote for an 8–1 majority in Mistretta v. United States, 488 U.S. 361 (1989), which upheld the constitutionality of the guidelines promulgated by the United States Sentencing Commission. The Court rejected claims that Congress delegated excessive legislative power to the Commission, and that the statute violated separation of powers principles by requiring federal judges to serve on the Commission or by having them serve with non-judges on a Commission whose members were removable by the President for cause. Justice Scalia dissented.

The Supreme Court has recently decided several cases which deal with various details and ambiguities of the Sentencing Guidelines. In Braxton v. United States, 111 S.Ct. 1854 (1991), the Court considered the proviso in section 1B1.2(a) that in the case of a guilty plea containing a stipulation that "specifically establishes" a more serious offense, the district court should apply the Guideline most applicable to the stipulated offense, rather than the offense of conviction. Justice Scalia, writing for a unanimous Court, held that determination of the meaning and effect of a stipulation is not a factual finding, and therefore is subject to *de novo* review. He also concluded that under the particular circumstances of the case, the defendant in pleading guilty to assault had not stipulated to facts "specifically establishing" the more serious offense of attempt to kill. The Court found that the defendant had not admitted that he was shooting at somebody, nor that he had intent to kill.

The Court in *Braxton* also served notice that it may not need to resolve intercircuit conflicts on the meaning of the Guidelines. Justice Scalia stated that Congress contemplated that the Sentencing Commission would periodically review the work of the courts, and would make "whatever clarifying revisions to the Guidelines conflicting judicial decisions might suggest." Justice Scalia therefore concluded that the Court would be "more restrained and circumspect in using our certiorari power as the primary means of resolving such conflicts." The Court declined to resolve whether, under Guideline section 1B1.2(a), a stipulation must be part of a formal plea agreement in order to permit application of the sentence appropriate to the more serious offense stipulated. Justice Scalia noted that the Sentencing Commission had issued a call for public comment on whether the Guideline should be amended to resolve the ambiguity which had created a conflict among the circuits.

Gozlon–Peretz v. United States, 111 S.Ct. 840 (1991), emphasized that Congress in the Sentencing Reform Act replaced most forms of parole with a new system of supervised release, in which the sentencing court rather than the Parole Commission would oversee the defendant's post-confinement monitoring. Justice Kennedy, writing for a unanimous Court, held that supervised release was mandated for drug offenses under the Anti–Drug Abuse Act of 1986, even though the Act went into effect before the Sentencing Guidelines.

In Chapman v. United States, 111 S.Ct. 1919 (1991), the Court considered whether the Sentencing Guidelines pertaining to LSD allowed consideration of the carrier medium in determining the base offense level. Defendants argued that the carrier medium should not be included, since LSD is sold by dosage, not by weight, and the same dosage could be put on carrier mediums of various weights. If the carrier medium is considered in determining the base offense level, a person who sells five doses of LSD on sugar cubes could be subject to a greater sentence than a person caught with 20,000 doses in pure form. Chief Justice Rehnquist, writing for six members of the Court, noted that Congress had determined that sentences for trafficking in LSD should be based on the weight of the "mixture or substance"; and that the LSD together with the carrier medium could properly be termed a "mixture." The majority therefore held that the weight of the carrier medium should be included in determining the base offense level. The Court rejected the argument that inclusion of the carrier medium would result in arbitrary punishment. The Chief Justice stated that it was rational to increase the penalty for persons who possess large quantities of drugs, regardless of their purity. Justice Stevens, joined by Justice Marshall, dissented.

In thinking about the Commission's approach to sentencing individuals and the tradeoff between preventing unjustified disparities and recognizing justifiable distinctions among offenders, consider the policy statements which the Commission has adopted with respect to individual offenders. Do you agree with the Commission as to the factors that should and should not be taken into consideration?

§ 5H1.1. *Age* (Policy Statement)

Age is not ordinarily relevant in determining whether a sentence should be outside the guidelines. Neither is it ordinarily relevant in determining the type of sentence to be imposed when the guidelines provide sentencing options. Age may be a reason to go below the guidelines when the offender is elderly *and* infirm and where a form of punishment (*e.g.,* home confinement) might be equally efficient as and less costly than incarceration. If, independent of the consideration of age, a defendant is sentenced to probation or supervised release, age may be relevant in the determination of the length and conditions of supervision.

§ 5H1.2. *Education and Vocational Skills* (Policy Statement)

Education and vocational skills are not ordinarily relevant in determining whether a sentence should be outside the guidelines, but the extent to which a defendant may have misused special training or education to facilitate criminal activity is an express guideline factor. * * * Neither are education and vocational skills relevant in determining the type of sentence to be imposed when the guidelines provide sentencing options. If, independent of consideration of education and vocational skills, a defendant is sentenced to probation or supervised release, these considerations may be relevant in the determination of the length and conditions of supervision for rehabilitative purposes, for public protection by restricting activities that allow for the utilization of a certain skill, or in determining the type or length of community service.

§ 5H1.3. *Mental and Emotional Conditions* (Policy Statement)

Mental and emotional conditions are not ordinarily relevant in determining whether a sentence should be outside the guidelines, except as provided in the general provisions in Chapter Five. Mental and emotional conditions, whether mitigating or aggravating, may be relevant in determining the length and conditions of probation or supervised release.

§ 5H1.4. *Physical Condition, Including Drug Dependence and Alcohol Abuse* (Policy Statement)

Physical condition is not ordinarily relevant in determining whether a sentence should be outside the guidelines or where within the guidelines a sentence should fall. However, an extraordinary physical impairment may be a reason to impose a sentence other than imprisonment.

Drug dependence or alcohol abuse is not a reason for imposing a sentence below the guidelines. Substance abuse is highly correlated to an increased propensity to commit crime. Due to this increased risk, it is highly recommended that a defendant who is incarcerated also be sentenced to supervised release with a requirement that the defendant participate in an appropriate substance abuse program. If participation in a substance abuse program is required, the length of supervised release should take into account the length of time necessary for the supervisory body to judge the success of the program.

This provision would also apply in cases where the defendant received a sentence of probation. The substance abuse condition is strongly recommended and the length of probation should be adjusted accordingly. Failure to comply would normally result in revocation of probation.

§ 5H1.5. *Previous Employment Record* (Policy Statement)

Employment record is not ordinarily relevant in determining whether a sentence should be outside the guidelines or where within the guidelines a sentence should fall. Employment record may be relevant in determining the type of sentence to be imposed when the guidelines provide for sentencing options. If, independent of the consideration of employment record, a defendant is sentenced to probation or supervised release, considerations of employment record may be relevant in the determination of the length and conditions of supervision.

§ 5H1.6. *Family Ties and Responsibilities, and Community Ties* (Policy Statement)

Family ties and responsibilities and community ties are not ordinarily relevant in determining whether a sentence should be outside the guidelines. Family responsibilities that are complied with are relevant in determining whether to impose restitution and fines. Where the guidelines provide probation as an option, these factors may be relevant in this determination. If a defendant is sentenced to probation or supervised release, family ties and responsibilities that are met may be relevant in the determination of the length and conditions of supervision.

§ 5H1.7. *Role in the Offense* (Policy Statement)

A defendant's role in the offense is relevant in determining the appropriate sentence. * * *

§ 5H1.8. *Criminal History* (Policy Statement)

A defendant's criminal history is relevant in determining the appropriate sentence. * * *

§ 5H1.9. *Dependence upon Criminal Activity for a Livelihood* (Policy Statement)

The degree to which a defendant depends upon criminal activity for a livelihood is relevant in determining the appropriate sentence. * * *

§ 5H1.10. *Race, Sex, National Origin, Creed, Religion, and Socio–Economic Status* (Policy Statement)

These factors are not relevant in the determination of a sentence.

The Sentencing Commission sent guidelines for the sentencing of organizations to Congress on May 1, 1991, to take effect on November 1, 1991. On August 30, 1991, the Commission filed a Supplementary Report on Sentencing Guidelines for Organizations to provide additional information concerning the background, rationale and estimated effects of the organizational guidelines. The Supplemental Report, page 6, summarizes the governing principles of these guidelines:

> Because an organization is vicariously liable for actions taken by its agents, the Commission determined that the base fine, which measures the seriousness of the offense, should not be the sole basis for determining an appropriate sentence. Rather, the applicable culpability score, which is determined primarily by "the steps taken by the organization prior to the offense to prevent and detect criminal conduct, the level and extent of involvement in or tolerance of the offense by certain personnel, and the organization's actions after an offense has been committed" also influences the determination of a fine range. [Quoting from the Introductory Commentary to the Organizational Guidelines.]
>
> Specifically, the organization's culpability is determined by the level or extent of involvement in or tolerance of the offense by certain personnel, the organization's prior history, whether an order was violated when the organization committed the offense, whether the organization obstructed or attempted to obstruct justice, whether the organization had an effective program to prevent and detect violations of law, and whether the organization reported the offense, cooperated fully in the investigation, and accepted responsibility for its criminal conduct. The guidelines increase the fine range when organizations are more culpable and reduce the fine range when organizations are less culpable.

The Supplemental Report explains that the Commission found it difficult to decide whether to punish large and small corporations in the same way. Its general approach treats all organizations similarly, but the guidelines provide certain offsets for fines imposed on owners of closely held corporations. The report also explains that the Commission concluded that as a general rule the greater of pecuniary loss or gain should be used in setting a fine, provided that pecuniary loss should only be used if the loss was caused intentionally, knowingly or recklessly.

Some lawyers and economists have criticized the Commission's approach. The approach plainly relies less on past practice than the approach taken in the individual guidelines. This is largely the result of large increases in fine maxima and little experience on the part of courts in imposing fines under the higher statutory figures. To the extent that the criticism focuses on the Commission's writing on a blank slate, the Commission has responded by relying on the language Congress chose in its sentencing statute and the recognition that vicarious liability offenses require that some principles be recognized which may not have been fully recognized in the past when fine levels were much lower. The criticism is not limited to the absence of empirical support for the guidelines; it rests also on a notion that the sanctions are too severe and that they may deter lawful and desirable economic activity.

What are the arguments for punishing corporations and other organizations? Should they be punished if individuals who committed offenses are identifiable and can also be prosecuted? Should deterrence play a more significant role in organizational sentencing than in individual sentencing? The Guidelines clearly encourage corporate cooperation, but isn't it likely that this will come at the expense of corporate employees involved in the alleged wrongdoing? Does corporate counsel have a conflict of interest in advising the corporation to cooperate and accept responsibility, when that could mean that directors and other corporate agents will be incriminated? See generally Saltzburg, The Control of Criminal Conduct in Organizations, (Symposium on Sentencing of the Corporation), 71 B.U.L.Rev. 189, 421 (1991).

The Sentencing Commission indicated that it would continue to study sentencing and monitor the sentencing ranges it recommended. Any changes that work to the detriment of a defendant may have to be limited to prospective application in light of the Supreme Court's decision in Miller v. Florida, 482 U.S. 423 (1987). In *Miller,* the Court held that Florida courts violated the prohibition in Article I, § 10 of the Constitution against ex post facto laws when they approved application of a presumptive sentencing range of 5½ to 7 years to a defendant convicted of a crime for which the presumptive range was only 3½ to 4½ years at the time he committed the crime. The Court reached the following conclusions: a state may not avoid the ex post facto limitation by providing notice that a penalty might be changed in the future; the revised guidelines substantially disadvantaged the defendant without having any ameliorative effects, since the defendant could not have been sentenced to more than 4½ years under the guideline in effect at the time of the crime unless the trial judge made specific findings supported by proof beyond a reasonable doubt, and the defendant had an opportunity for appellate review of the departure from the guidelines; and the presumptive sentencing provisions were enacted by the legislature and had the force of law. Compare United States v. Chambers, 944 F.2d 1253 (6th Cir.1991) (Ex Post Facto clause is not violated by applying the Federal Sentencing Guidelines to a conspiracy which began before and continues after the effective date of the Guidelines).

In Collins v. Youngblood, 110 S.Ct. 2715 (1990), the defendant was sentenced to life imprisonment and a $10,000 fine, in violation of state law which did not authorize both a fine and a prison term for his crime. The State thereafter passed a statute allowing an appellate court to reform a sentence that was not authorized by law. Chief Justice Rehnquist, writing for the Court, held that the use of the subsequent statute to reform defendant's sentence by deleting the fine was consistent with the Ex Post Facto clause, since the defendant's sentence was not retroactively increased. Justice Stevens, joined by Justices Brennan and Marshall, concurred in the judgment.

III. SENTENCING PROCEDURES

A. GENERAL PROCEDURES

One might suppose that if a part of the criminal justice system as important as sentencing allows the sentencing authority such great latitude in fixing a sentence, at least extensive procedural protections would be implemented to protect against abuse of authority. But one's supposition would be largely unfounded. Due process rights in sentencing have been hard to establish since 1949.

WILLIAMS v. NEW YORK

Supreme Court of the United States, 1949.
337 U.S. 241.

MR. JUSTICE BLACK delivered the opinion of the court.

A jury in a New York state court found appellant guilty of murder in the first degree. The jury recommended life imprisonment, but the trial judge imposed sentence of death. In giving his reason for imposing the death sentence the judge discussed in open court the evidence upon which the jury had convicted stating that this evidence had been considered in the light of additional information obtained through the court's "Probation Department, and through other sources." Consideration of this additional information was pursuant to § 482 of New York Criminal Code which provides:

> * * * Before rendering judgment or pronouncing sentence the court shall cause the defendant's previous criminal record to be submitted to it, including any reports that may have been made as a result of a mental, phychiatric [*sic*] or physical examination of such person, and may seek any information that will aid the court in determining the proper treatment of such defendant.

The Court of Appeals of New York affirmed the conviction and sentence over the contention that as construed and applied the controlling penal statutes are in violation of the due process clause of the Fourteenth Amendment of the Constitution of the United States "in that the sentence of death was based upon information supplied by witnesses with whom the accused had not been confronted and as to whom he had no opportunity for cross-examination or rebuttal. * * *".

The narrow contention here makes it unnecessary to set out the facts at length. The record shows a carefully conducted trial lasting more than two weeks in which appellant was represented by three appointed lawyers who conducted his defense with fidelity and zeal. The evidence proved a wholly indefensible murder committed by a person engaged in a burglary. * * *

About five weeks after the verdict of guilty with recommendation of life imprisonment, and after a statutory pre-sentence investigation report to the judge, the defendant was brought to court to be sentenced. Asked what he had to say, appellant protested his innocence. After each of his three lawyers had appealed to the court to accept the jury's recommendation of a life sentence, the judge gave reasons why he felt that the death sentence should be imposed. He narrated the shocking details of the crime as shown by the trial evidence, expressing his own complete belief in appellant's guilt. He stated that the pre-sentence investigation revealed many material facts concerning appellant's background which though relevant to the question of punishment could not properly have been brought to the attention of the jury in its consideration of the question of guilt. He referred to the experience appellant "had had on thirty other burglaries in and about the same vicinity" where the murder had been committed. The appellant had not been convicted of these burglaries although the judge had information that he had confessed to some and had been identified as the perpetrator of some of the others. The judge also referred to certain activities of appellant as shown by the probation report that indicated appellant possessed "a morbid sexuality" and classified him as a "menace to society." The accuracy of the statements made by the judge as to appellant's background and past practices was not challenged by appellant or his counsel, nor was the judge asked to disregard any of them or to afford appellant a chance to refute or discredit any of them by cross-examination or otherwise.[18]

The case presents a serious and difficult question. The question relates to the rules of evidence applicable to the manner in which a judge may obtain information to guide him in the imposition of sentence upon an already convicted defendant. * * * To aid a judge in exercising * * * discretion intelligently the New York procedural policy encourages him to consider information about the convicted person's past life, health, habits, conduct, and mental and moral propensities. The sentencing judge may consider such information even though obtained outside the courtroom from persons whom a defendant has not been permitted to confront or cross-examine. It is the consideration of information obtained by a sentencing judge in this manner that is the basis for appellant's broad constitutional challenge to the New York statutory policy.

* * *

Tribunals passing on the guilt of a defendant always have been hedged in by strict evidentiary procedural limitations. But both before and since the American colonies became a nation, courts in this country and in England practiced a policy under which a sentencing judge could exercise a wide discretion in the sources and types of evidence used to assist him in determining the kind and extent of punishment to be imposed within limits fixed by law. Out-of-court affidavits have been used frequently, and of course in the smaller communities sentencing judges naturally have in mind their knowledge of the personalities and backgrounds of convicted offenders. A recent manifestation of the historical latitude allowed sentencing judges appears in Rule 32 of the Federal Rules of Criminal Procedure. That rule provides for consideration by federal judges of reports made by probation officers containing information about a convicted defendant, including such information "as may be helpful in imposing sentence or in granting probation or in the correctional treatment of the defendant. * * *"

In addition to the historical basis for different evidentiary rules governing trial and sentencing procedures there are sound practical reasons for the distinction. In a trial before verdict the issue is whether a defendant is guilty of having engaged in certain criminal conduct of which he has been specifically accused. Rules of evidence have been fashioned for criminal trials which narrowly confine the trial contest to evidence that is strictly relevant to the particular offense charged. These rules rest in part on a necessity to prevent a time-consuming and confusing trial of collateral issues. They were also designed to prevent tribunals concerned solely with the issue of guilt of a particular offense from being influenced to convict for that offense by evidence that the defendant had habitually engaged in other misconduct. A sentencing judge, however, is not confined to the narrow issue of guilt. His task within fixed statutory or constitutional limits is to determine the type and extent of punishment after the issue of guilt has been determined. Highly relevant—if not essential—to his selection of an appropriate sentence is the possession of the fullest information possible concerning the defendant's life and characteristics.

18. This sentence in the opinion often is ignored. It may be very important, since it limits the holding of the Court. United States v. Stephens, 699 F.2d 534 (11th Cir. 1983), recognizes that the defendant has a right to be sentenced on the basis of accurate information, although the court held that this did not require a sentencing proceeding to be a full-scale evidentiary-type hearing.

And modern concepts individualizing punishment have made it all the more necessary that a sentencing judge not be denied an opportunity to obtain pertinent information by a requirement of rigid adherence to restrictive rules of evidence properly applicable to the trial.

* * *

Modern changes in the treatment of offenders makes it more necessary now than a century ago for observance of the distinctions in the evidential procedure in the trial and sentencing processes. For indeterminate sentences and probation have resulted in an increase in the discretionary powers exercised in fixing punishments. * * *

Under the practice of individualizing punishments, investigational techniques have been given an important role. Probation workers making reports of their investigations have not been trained to prosecute but to aid offenders. Their reports have been given a high value by conscientious judges who want to sentence persons on the best available information rather than on guesswork and inadequate information. * * * We must recognize that most of the information now relied upon by judges to guide them in the intelligent imposition of sentences would be unavailable if information were restricted to that given in open court by witnesses subject to cross-examination. And the modern probation report draws on information concerning every aspect of a defendant's life. The type and extent of this information make totally impractical if not impossible open court testimony with cross-examination. Such a procedure could endlessly delay criminal administration in a retrial of collateral issues.

The considerations we have set out admonish us against treating the due process clause as a uniform command that courts throughout the Nation abandon their age-old practice of seeking information from out-of-court sources to guide their judgment toward a more enlightened and just sentence. New York criminal statutes set wide limits for maximum and minimum sentences. Under New York statutes a state judge cannot escape his grave responsibility of fixing sentence. In determining whether a defendant shall receive a one-year minimum or a twenty-year maximum sentence, we do not think the Federal Constitution restricts the view of the sentencing judge to the information received in open court.

* * *

MURPHY, J., dissenting:

* * *

* * * The record before us indicates that the judge exercised his discretion to deprive a man of his life, in reliance on material made available to him in a probation report, consisting almost entirely of evidence that would have been inadmissible at the trial. Some, such as allegations of prior crimes, was irrelevant. Much was incompetent as hearsay. All was damaging, and none was subject to scrutiny by the defendant.

Due process of law includes at least the idea that a person accused of crime shall be accorded a fair hearing through all the stages of the proceedings against him. I agree with the Court as to the value and humaneness of liberal use of probation reports as developed by modern penologists, but, in a capital case, against the unanimous recommendation of a jury where the report would concededly not have been admissible at the trial, and was not subject to examination by the defendant, I am forced to conclude that the high commands of due process were not obeyed.

In the Sentencing Reform Act of 1984, Congress provided that when guidelines are used to sentence offenders, Rule 32(c)(2) will require that a presentence report inform the defendant of the guidelines which govern his case and of pertinent policy statements by the Sentencing Commission.[19]

The district court can disregard the mechanical dictates of the federal sentencing guidelines when it finds "that there exists an aggravating or mitigating circumstance of a kind, or to a degree, not adequately taken into consideration by the Sentencing Commission." 18 U.S.C. § 991(b)(1)(B). In Burns v. United States, 111 S.Ct. 2182 (1991), the district court departed upward from the prescribed sentencing range without first notifying the parties of its intent to depart. Justice Marshall, writing for a five-person majority, held that Federal Rule of Criminal Procedure 32 requires that the district court give the parties reasonable notice that it is contemplating an upward or downward departure. Justice Souter, joined by Chief Justice Rehnquist and Justices White and O'Connor, dissented.

Notice that Rule 32 requires that a presentence report be prepared, unless the defendant waives a report or the record is otherwise complete without one, and that the defendant be told at a minimum the substance of the report.[20] Section 7.07 of the Model Penal Code would require a presentence investigation in all felony cases, and some jurisdictions have adopted this approach. Others have a much more flexible approach and leave the court with discretion to order a report. What arguments can be made against requiring pre-sentence reports in all cases, except those in which the trial or plea proceeding and the sentencing hearing together are so complete that the report would be superfluous?[21] Is there any reason why the prosecutor should not be able to request such a report?

In United States v. Grayson, 438 U.S. 41 (1978), the Court per Chief Justice Burger cited *Williams* and held that a trial judge, who must "consider the defendant's whole person and personality," may take into account in sentencing a defendant whether the defendant testified truthfully at trial. Justice Stewart, joined by Justices Brennan and Marshall, dissented on the ground "that all defendants who choose to testify, and only those who do so, face the very real prospect of a greater sentence based upon the trial judge's unreviewable perception that the testimony was untruthful," that "[o]ther witnesses risk punishment for perjury only upon indictment and conviction in accord with the full protections of the Constitution," and that "[o]nly the defendant himself,

19. Fennell & Hall, Due Process at Sentencing: An Empirical and Legal Analysis of the Disclosure of Presentence Reports in Federal Courts, 93 Harv.L.Rev. 1615 (1980), reports that disclosure of information in presentence reports to defendants has not had an adverse impact on the willingness of people in most places to supply information to the government and argues that disclosure of information to the defendant and counsel, at least its general thrust if not its particulars, is necessary for fair sentencing.

The Supreme Court held in United States Department of Justice v. Julian, 486 U.S. 1 (1988), that prison inmates may obtain access to the nonconfidential aspects of their presentence reports pursuant to the Freedom of Information Act. Although the Court noted that the parties agreed that in both civil and criminal cases federal courts had been reluctant to give third parties access to the reports, it found "[t]here is no indication, however, that similar restrictions on discovery of presentence investigation reports have been recognized by the courts when the individual requesting discovery is the subject of the report."

20. If the jury sentences, the opportunity to obtain a presentence report is diminished, although the judge still may find a report useful in deciding whether to grant probation, suspend all or part of a sentence, or to reduce a jury sentence.

21. It has been held that the defendant has no right to challenge the expertise of the persons who prepared the report. See People v. Arbuckle, 22 Cal.3d 749, 150 Cal.Rptr. 778, 587 P.2d 220 (1978).

whose testimony is likely to be of critical importance to his defense, faces the additional risk that the disbelief of a single listener will itself result in time in prison."

There are some limits to the things that a Court may consider. Race, for example, clearly would be an impermissible factor; the same is true of sex. See United States v. Maples, 501 F.2d 985 (4th Cir. 1974). In Townsend v. Burke, 334 U.S. 736 (1948) the Court indicated that a sentence based on inaccurate information may be set aside. In that case, the defendant was sentenced on the basis of prior convictions which did not in fact exist. Although the defendant has a right of allocution—to make a statement on his own behalf—the defendant may not know what the judge is concerned about.[22] In the exceptional case the appellate court may vacate a sentence because it is possible that the trial judge relied on information that the defendant might have contested had he known it was before the trial judge. See, e.g., United States v. Harris, 558 F.2d 366 (7th Cir. 1977). In United States v. Tucker, 404 U.S. 443 (1972), the Court held that a sentencing court could not rely on prior convictions that were obtained when the defendant was unconstitutionally deprived of representation by counsel.[23] A trial judge must not explicitly add a penalty because the defendant chose to go to trial and/or requested a jury. See, e.g., United States v. Wiley, 267 F.2d 453 (7th Cir. 1959).

Justice Powell wrote for eight members of the Court in Roberts v. United States, 445 U.S. 552 (1980), finding no impropriety in the district court's using as one factor in sentencing the refusal of a convicted defendant to cooperate with officials investigating a criminal conspiracy in which he was a confessed participant. The Court noted that the defendant had raised no privilege against self-incrimination claim in the trial court. Justice Marshall dissented. See generally Nemerson, Coercive Sentencing, 64 Minn.L.Rev. 669 (1980).

United States v. Messer, 785 F.2d 832 (9th Cir.1986), remanded a case to the trial court for a determination of whether the trial judge relied on contested information in a presentence report in sentencing a defendant who pleaded guilty to tax evasion. The Court stated that "when a trial judge relies upon materially false or unreliable information in sentencing, the defendant's due process rights are violated." The provision in Fed.R.Crim.P. 32(c)(3)(D) works to implement the due process standard by requiring the trial judge to make findings concerning challenged information or to state that no such findings are necessary because the information will be disregarded in the sentencing.

B. SPECIAL PROCEDURES FOR SENTENCING

The sentencing system reviewed in *Williams* was a non-adversarial, indeterminate, individualized system granting unfettered discretion to trial judges.

22. Some states require judges to explain their sentences. See, e.g., State v. Voelkel, 377 So.2d 1204 (La.1979), vacating a sentence for failure of trial judge to state facts relied upon and reasons as required by law.

23. But see Baldasar v. Illinois, 446 U.S. 222 (1980), discussed in Chapter Five, supra. It is unclear whether convictions tainted by illegal searches and seizures that do not relate to the integrity of the factfinding process can be used in sentencing. Compare Verdugo v. United States, 402 F.2d 599 (9th Cir. 1968) with United States v. Schipani, 435 F.2d 26 (2d Cir. 1970), and United States v. Lee, 540 F.2d 1205 (4th Cir. 1976). See also United States v. Washington, 586 F.2d 1147 (7th Cir. 1978) (convictions under unconstitutional statute considered).

If the sentencing system changes—as it has in some states and in the Federal system under the Guidelines—then the constitution may require greater procedural protections than were established in *Williams.* The next case and the note following it demonstrate this point.

SPECHT v. PATTERSON

Supreme Court of the United States, 1967.
386 U.S. 605.

MR. JUSTICE DOUGLAS delivered the opinion of the Court.

We held in Williams v. New York that the Due Process Clause of the Fourteenth Amendment did not require a judge to have hearings and to give a convicted person an opportunity to participate in those hearings when he came to determine the sentence to be imposed. [The Court quotes from *Williams.*]

That was a case where at the end of the trial and in the same proceeding the fixing of the penalty for first degree murder was involved—whether life imprisonment or death.

The question is whether the rule of the *Williams* case applies to this Colorado case where petitioner, having been convicted for indecent liberties under one Colorado statute that carries a maximum sentence of 10 years (Colo.Rev. Stat.Ann. § 40–2–32 (1963)) but not sentenced under it, may be sentenced under the Sex Offenders Act, Colo.Rev. Stat.Ann. §§ 39–19–1 to 10 (1963), for an indeterminate term of from one day to life without notice and full hearing. [The Colorado courts approved the procedure and habeas corpus relief was sought in federal court.]

The Sex Offenders Act may be brought into play if the trial court "is of the opinion that any * * * person [convicted of specified sex offenses], if at large, constitutes a threat of bodily harm to members of the public, or is an habitual offender and mentally ill." § 1. He then becomes punishable for an indeterminate term of from one day to life on the following conditions as specified in § 2:

"(2) A complete psychiatric examination shall have been made of him by the psychiatrists of the Colorado psychopathic hospital or by psychiatrists designated by the district court; and

"(3) A complete written report thereof submitted to the district court. Such report shall contain all facts and findings, together with recommendations as to whether or not the person is treatable under the provisions of this article; whether or not the person should be committed to the Colorado state hospital or to the state home and training schools as mentally ill or mentally deficient. Such report shall also contain the psychiatrist's opinion as to whether or not the person could be adequately supervised on probation."

This procedure was followed in petitioner's case; he was examined as required and a psychiatric report prepared and given to the trial judge prior to the sentencing. But there was no hearing in the normal sense, no right of confrontation and so on.

Petitioner insists that this procedure does not satisfy due process because it allows the critical finding to be made under § 1 of the Sex Offenders Act (1) without a hearing at which the person so convicted may confront and cross-examine adverse witnesses and present evidence of his own by use of compulsory process, if necessary; and (2) on the basis of hearsay evidence to which the person involved is not allowed access.

We adhere to Williams v. New York, supra; but we decline the invitation to extend it to this radically different situation. * * * We hold that the requirements of due process were not satisfied here.

The Sex Offenders Act does not make the commission of a specified crime the basis for sentencing. It makes one conviction the basis for commencing another proceeding under another Act to determine whether a person constitutes a threat of bodily harm to the public, or is an habitual offender and mentally ill. That is a new finding of fact that was not an ingredient of the offense charged. The punishment under the second Act is criminal punishment even though it is designed not so much as retribution as it is to keep individuals from inflicting future harm.

The Court of Appeals for the Third Circuit in speaking of a comparable Pennsylvania statute said:

> "It is a separate criminal proceeding which may be invoked after conviction of one of the specified crimes. Petitioner therefore was entitled to a full judicial hearing before the magnified sentence was imposed. At such a hearing the requirements of due process cannot be satisfied by partial or niggardly procedural protections. A defendant in such a proceeding is entitled to the full panoply of the relevant protections which due process guarantees in state criminal proceedings. He must be afforded all those safeguards which are fundamental rights and essential to a fair trial, including the right to confront and cross-examine the witnesses against him." Gerchman v. Maroney, 3d Cir., 355 F.2d 302, 312.

We agree with that view. Under Colorado's criminal procedure, here challenged, the invocation of the Sex Offenders Act means the making of a new charge leading to criminal punishment. The case is not unlike those under recidivist statutes where an habitual criminal issue is "a distinct issue" (Graham v. West Virginia, 224 U.S. 616, 625) on which a defendant "must receive reasonable notice and an opportunity to be heard." Due process, in other words, requires that he be present with counsel, have an opportunity to be heard, be confronted with witnesses against him, have the right to cross-examine, and to offer evidence of his own. And there must be findings adequate to make meaningful any appeal that is allowed. * * * None of these procedural safeguards we have mentioned is present under Colorado's Sex Offenders Act. We therefore hold that it is deficient in due process as measured by the requirements of the Fourteenth Amendment.

[Justice Harlan concurred, but for reasons set forth in Pointer v. Texas, 380 U.S. 400, 408 (1965) (setting forth his views on due process rights that are "implicit in the concept of ordered liberty").]

Note

In McMillan v. Pennsylvania, 477 U.S. 79 (1986), the Court held that it was permissible for a state to impose a mandatory minimum sentence upon a defendant found by the trial judge to have "visibly possessed a firearm" during the commission of a specified offense. It rejected the defendant's argument that the finding should be supported by at least clear and convincing evidence and concluded that there was no constitutional infirmity in the state's use of a preponderance of the evidence standard. Is *McMillan* consistent with *Specht*? With your views of due process?

The federal sentencing guidelines provide for modified real offense sentencing. This means that a defendant convicted of fraud or drug distribution may have a sentence increased pursuant to a finding by the sentencing court that the fraud involved a certain sum of money or a certain amount of drugs. The Commission has provided for certain upward and downward adjustments in the guidelines. The structure is not unlike the grading of offenses which in the past was a legislative task. If the legislature created a statute with various grades and provided increasing penalties to correspond to increasing grades, the government might well have to prove a defendant's increasing culpability beyond a reasonable doubt. Whether or not this would be required depends on the reading that is given to the line of cases on burdens of persuasion that is discussed in Chapter Ten. Guidelines can serve to grade offenses in much the same way as legislation. In light of *McMillan,* it is likely that the preponderance of the evidence standard will be deemed appropriate for most decisions that sentencing courts make under guidelines. See United States v. Ebbole, 917 F.2d 1495 (7th Cir.1990) (quantity of drugs possessed proven by preponderance of the evidence). But even if the Constitution does not require proof beyond a reasonable doubt, there is reason to ask whether some additional protection—e.g., stricter enforcement of hearsay rules—is required when sentencing decisions depend on findings that are much more structured than they were before the adoption of guidelines. If it is the case that, although guidelines control judicial discretion in order to reduce disparity, they also require judges to consider factors that result in different treatment of offenders convicted of the same offense, are special procedures needed to assure that the judges' findings are sufficiently accurate to justify treating defendants in disparate ways?

In United States v. Silverman, 945 F.2d 1337 (6th Cir.1991) (later vacated for rehearing en banc), the court held that the Confrontation Clause applies to the determination of disputed facts in adversary sentencing hearings conducted under the Federal Sentencing Guidelines. The court distinguished *Williams* as applying to a system (such as the Federal system before the Guidelines) which "did not require the judge to find facts or to base his sentence on the existence or nonexistence of a particular fact * * * because district judges had an absolute and unreviewable discretion so long as the sentence imposed did not exceed the statutory maximum for the offense." The court noted:

> [T]he new system completely changes the discretionary, nonadversary, nonfactual nature of the sentencing process by introducing the adversary sentencing hearing and the need for precise and accurate findings of disputed facts. * * * The existence or nonexistence of a particular fact—for example, the amount of money involved or drugs possessed * * *—may automatically double or even in some cases multiply tenfold the particular sentence that judges are required to impose under the code.

The court relied on *Specht* for the proposition that "when the sentencing system changes, the nature of the applicable constitutional limitations may also change." It noted that "the *Specht* case expressly distinguishes the sentencing system reviewed in *Williams* on the ground that the Colorado scheme requires fact finding in an adversary setting rather than the exercise of pure unreviewable discretion without the necessity of finding facts." For a case in accord with *Silverman,* see United States v. Fortier, 911 F.2d 100 (8th Cir.1990). For a contrary result, adhering to *Williams,* see United States v. Kikumura, 918 F.2d 1084 (3d Cir.1990). For a comprehensive treatment of sentencing procedures, see A. Campbell, The Law of Sentencing §§ 41–68 (1978 & 1991 supp.).

C. PAROLE AND PROBATION PROCEDURES

1. *Probation and Parole Denials; Classification Decisions*

A person is placed on probation as part of the usual sentencing process, and the *Williams* attitude toward procedural rights prevails. In People v. Edwards, 18 Cal.3d 796, 135 Cal.Rptr. 411, 557 P.2d 995 (1976), for example, the court held that a trial judge need not state reasons for denying probation. But parole is a different concept altogether. The parole board makes a determination whether someone who has been sentenced should be released before the sentence is fully served (though as we have seen, this is no longer the case under the Federal Sentencing Guidelines). The American Bar Association has recommended that prisoners should have access to the prison file considered by the parole board, that a prisoner should have the right to have counsel or some other representative of his choice present at the examination of his file and at the hearing, that statements of reasons should be given for denial of parole and that the parole board's decisions should be open to public inspection. But in the past, procedures have varied from state to state. For some time courts differed over the question of what, if any, procedural protections are constitutionally required in parole-release decisionmaking. Finally, the Supreme Court provided an answer.

In Greenholtz v. Inmates, 439 U.S. 817 (1979), the Court, per Chief Justice Burger, held that the possibility of parole does not create an entitlement to due process protections. The Court did conclude that some parole systems, including Nebraska's, create legitimate expectations of release that require some procedural protections. But these are confined to some opportunity to be heard and some indication of the reasons why parole is not granted. Justice Marshall's dissenting opinion was joined by Justices Brennan and Stevens. Justice Powell agreed with these dissenters that parole decisionmaking triggered due process safeguards, but was unwilling to provide as many safeguards as the others would have. However, he concluded that Nebraska provided an inadequate opportunity for prisoners to present information to parole authorities.[24] The Court relied upon *Greenholtz* in Board of Pardons v. Allen, 482 U.S. 369 (1987), which held, 6–3, that Montana parole law created a liberty interest.

No constitutionally protected expectancy interest was found in an explicitly discretionary pardon system despite the frequency with which pardons were granted. Connecticut Bd. of Pardons v. Dumschat, 452 U.S. 458 (1981). See also Jago v. Van Curen, 454 U.S. 14 (1981) (inmate told that he was being paroled had no protected interest that was violated when parole was rescinded before release from custody).

The Court distinguished *Greenholtz* in Vitek v. Jones, 445 U.S. 480 (1980), and held that the involuntary transfer of a prisoner to a mental hospital implicates a liberty interest if a state creates an expectation that such a transfer would not take place without a finding of mental illness, or the transfer stigmatizes the prisoner in a way that imposes a "grievous loss" upon him. Finding both the necessary expectation and the grievous loss in this case,

24. More elaborate procedural safeguards for parole release decisionmaking, including a prisoner's access to the information in his record on which the decisionmaker will rely, were required under state law in Tasker v. Mohn, 267 S.E.2d 183 (W.Va.1980).

the Court upheld the district court's order, which required the following procedures prior to a transfer: written notice, a hearing, opportunity to be heard and to cross-examine witnesses unless there is a finding of good cause for not allowing production and cross-examination, an independent decisionmaker, a written statement of the evidence relied on and the reasons for a transfer decision, and timely notice of all rights. A plurality of the Court (Justices White, Brennan, Marshall and Stevens) would have found a right to counsel. Justice Powell believed that assistance to the prisoner need not be in the form of legal counsel, and that it might be provided by a licensed psychiatrist or other mental health professional. The four dissenters went off on procedural grounds and did not reach the merits.

The Court reasoned in Hewitt v. Helms, 459 U.S. 460 (1983), that a prisoner has no right to procedural protections with respect to terms of confinement "ordinarily contemplated by a prison sentence" and that ordinarily "administrative segregation" is one of these terms. The Court rejected the claim that when a state provides procedural safeguards in connection with the use of administrative segregation it thereby recognizes a protected liberty interest. However, in this case the Court concluded that the state had gone beyond simple procedural guidelines and used "language of an unmistakably mandatory character," thus creating a liberty interest. Such an interest required, in the Court's view, only an informal, nonadversary review of evidence. Justice Stevens' dissenting opinion was joined by Justices Brennan and Marshall. Justice Stevens argued that all citizens, including prisoners, enjoy a residuum of liberty and that the due process clause is "implicated when the State singles out one person for adverse treatment significantly different from that imposed on the community at large." Justice Blackmun joined the second part of Justice Stevens' opinion, which argued that once a liberty interest attaches with respect to administrative segregation, an inmate should have the right to present his views in person, to periodic review of his administrative confinement and to a brief written statement explaining the reasons for continued administrative segregation. See also Olim v. Wakinekona, 461 U.S. 238 (1983) (no liberty interest in confinement in one state rather than another); Meachum v. Fano, 427 U.S. 215 (1976) (no liberty interest in confinement in particular prison within a state); Montanye v. Haymes, 427 U.S. 236 (1976) (same as *Meachum*). For a thorough discussion of this line of cases, see Herman, The New Liberty: The Procedural Due Process Rights of Prisoners and Others under the Burger Court, 59 N.Y.U.L.Rev. 482 (1984).

2. *Probation and Parole Revocations*

MORRISEY v. BREWER

Supreme Court of the United States, 1972.
408 U.S. 471.

MR. CHIEF JUSTICE BURGER delivered the opinion of the Court.

[Morrisey and Booher both were paroled from Iowa state prisons. Each subsequently had his parole revoked because of violations of parole conditions, and each sued, challenging the revocation procedures. One principal line of attack was that the absence of a revocation hearing violated due process.]

I

* * * The essence of parole is release from prison, before the comple-

tion of sentence, on the condition that the prisoner abide by certain rules during the balance of the sentence. Under some systems parole is granted automatically after the service of a certain portion of a prison term. Under others, parole is granted by the discretionary action of a board which evaluates an array of information about a prisoner and makes a prediction whether he is ready to reintegrate into society.

To accomplish the purpose of parole, those who are allowed to leave prison early are subjected to specified conditions for the duration of their terms. These conditions restrict their activities substantially beyond the ordinary restrictions imposed by law on an individual citizen. * * * Additionally, parolees must regularly report to the parole officer to whom they are assigned and sometimes they must make periodic written reports of their activities.

* * *

The enforcement leverage which supports the parole conditions derives from the authority to return the parolee to prison to serve out the balance of his sentence if he fails to abide by the rules. In practice not every violation of parole conditions automatically leads to revocation. Typically a parolee will be counseled to abide by the conditions of parole, and the parole officer ordinarily does not take steps to have parole revoked unless he thinks that the violations are serious and continuing so as to indicate that the parolee is not adjusting properly and cannot be counted on to avoid antisocial activity. The broad discretion accorded the parole officer is also inherent in some of the quite vague conditions, such as the typical requirement that the parolee avoid "undesirable" associations or correspondence. Yet revocation of parole is not an unusual phenomenon, affecting only a few parolees. It has been estimated that 35–45% of all parolees are subjected to revocation and return to prison. Sometimes revocation occurs when the parolee is accused of another crime; it is often preferred to a new prosecution because of the procedural ease of recommitting the individual on the basis of a lesser showing by the State.

Implicit in the system's concern with parole violations is the notion that the parolee is entitled to retain his liberty as long as he substantially abides by the conditions of his parole. The first step in a revocation decision thus involves a wholly retrospective factual question: whether the parolee has in fact acted in violation of one or more conditions of his parole. Only if it is determined that the parolee did violate the conditions does the second question arise: should the parolee be recommitted to prison or should other steps be taken to protect society and improve chances of rehabilitation? The first step is relatively simple; the second is more complex. The second question involves the application of expertise by the parole authority in making a prediction as to the ability of the individual to live in society without committing antisocial acts. This part of the decision, too, depends on facts, and therefore it is important for the Board to know not only that some violation was committed but also to know accurately how many and how serious the violations were. Yet this second step, deciding what to do about the violation once it is identified, is not purely factual but also predictive and discretionary.

If a parolee is returned to prison, he often receives no credit for the time "served" on parole. Thus the returnee may face a potential of substantial imprisonment.

II

We begin with the proposition that the revocation of parole is not part of a criminal prosecution and thus the full panoply of rights due a defendant in such a proceeding does not apply to parole revocations. Parole arises after the end of the criminal prosecution, including imposition of sentence. Supervision is not directly by the court but by an administrative agency, which is sometimes an arm of the court and sometimes of the executive. Revocation deprives an individual not of the absolute liberty to which every citizen is entitled, but only of the conditional liberty properly dependent on observance of special parole restrictions.

We turn therefore to the question whether the requirements of due process in general apply to parole revocations. * * *

We turn to an examination of the nature of the interest of the parolee in his continued liberty. The liberty of a parolee enables him to do a wide range of things open to persons who have never been convicted of any crime. * * * Subject to the conditions of his parole, he can be gainfully employed and is free to be with family and friends and to form the other enduring attachments of normal life. Though the State properly subjects him to many restrictions not applicable to other citizens, his condition is very different from that of confinement in a prison. He may have been on parole for a number of years and may be living a relatively normal life at the time he is faced with revocation. The parolee has relied on at least an implicit promise that parole will be revoked only if he fails to live up to the parole conditions. * * *.

We see, therefore, that the liberty of a parolee, although indeterminate, includes many of the core values of unqualified liberty and its termination inflicts a "grievous loss" on the parolee and often on others. * * * Its termination calls for some orderly process, however informal.

Turning to the question what process is due, we find that the State's interests are several. The State has found the parolee guilty of a crime against the people. That finding justifies imposing extensive restrictions on the individual's liberty. Release of the parolee before the end of his prison sentence is made with the recognition that with many prisoners there is a risk that they will not be able to live in society without committing additional antisocial acts. Given the previous conviction and the proper imposition of conditions, the State has an overwhelming interest in being able to return the individual to imprisonment without the burden of a new adversary criminal trial if in fact he has failed to abide by the conditions of his parole.

Yet the State has no interest in revoking parole without some informal procedural guarantees. Although the parolee is often formally described as being "in custody," the argument cannot even be made here that summary treatment is necessary as it may be with respect to controlling a large group of potentially disruptive prisoners in actual custody. Nor are we persuaded by the argument that revocation is so totally a discretionary matter that some form of hearing would be administratively intolerable. A simple factual hearing will not interfere with the exercise of discretion. Serious studies have suggested that fair treatment on parole revocation will not result in fewer grants of parole.

This discretionary aspect of the revocation decision need not be reached unless there is first an appropriate determination that the individual has in fact breached the conditions of parole.

* * * What is needed is an informal hearing structured to assure that the finding of a parole violation will be based on verified facts and that the exercise of discretion will be informed by an accurate knowledge of the parolee's behavior.

III

We now turn to the nature of the process that is due, bearing in mind that the interest of both State and parolee will be furthered by an effective but informal hearing. In analyzing what is due, we see two important stages in the typical process of parole revocation.

(a) Arrest of Parolee and Preliminary Hearing. The first stage occurs when the parolee is arrested and detained, usually at the direction of his parole officer. The second occurs when parole is formally revoked. There is typically a substantial time lag between the arrest and the eventual determination by the parole board whether parole should be revoked. Additionally, it may be that the parolee is arrested at a place distant from the state institution, to which he may be returned before the final decision is made concerning revocation. Given these factors, due process would seem to require that some minimal inquiry be conducted at or reasonably near the place of the alleged parole violation or arrest and as promptly as convenient after arrest while information is fresh and sources are available. Such an inquiry should be seen as in the nature of a "preliminary hearing" to determine whether there is probable cause or reasonable grounds to believe that the arrested parolee has committed acts which would constitute a violation of parole conditions.

In our view due process requires that after the arrest, the determination that reasonable grounds exist for revocation of parole should be made by someone not directly involved in the case. It would be unfair to assume that the supervising parole officer does not conduct an interview with the parolee to confront him with the reasons for revocation before he recommends an arrest. It would also be unfair to assume that the parole officer bears hostility against the parolee which destroys his neutrality; realistically the failure of the parolee is in a sense a failure for his supervising officer. However, we need make no assumptions one way or the other to conclude that there should be an uninvolved person to make this preliminary evaluation of the basis for believing the conditions of parole have been violated. The officer directly involved in making recommendations cannot always have complete objectivity in evaluating them. * * *

This independent officer need not be a judicial officer. The granting and revocation of parole are matters traditionally handled by administrative officers. * * * It will be sufficient, therefore, in the parole revocation context, if an evaluation of whether reasonable cause exists to believe that conditions of parole have been violated is made by someone such as a parole officer other than the one who has made the report of parole violations or has recommended revocation. A State could certainly choose some other independent decisionmaker to perform this preliminary function.

With respect to the preliminary hearing before this officer, the parolee should be given notice that the hearing will take place and that its purpose is to determine whether there is probable cause to believe he has committed a parole violation. The notice should state what parole violations have been alleged. At the hearing the parolee may appear and speak in his own behalf; he may bring letters, documents, or individuals who can give relevant information to the hearing officer. On request of the parolee, persons who have given adverse information on which parole revocation is to be based are to be made available for questioning in his presence. However, if the hearing officer determines that the informant would be subjected to risk of harm if his identity were disclosed, he need not be subjected to confrontation and cross-examination.

The hearing officer shall have the duty of making a summary, or digest, of what transpires at the hearing in terms of the responses of the parolee and the substance of the documents or evidence given in support of parole revocation and of the parolee's position. Based on the information before him, the officer should determine whether there is probable cause to hold the parolee for the final decision of the parole board on revocation. Such a determination would be sufficient to warrant the parolee's continued detention and return to the state correctional institution pending the final decision. * * *

(b) The Revocation Hearing. There must also be an opportunity for a hearing, if it is desired by the parolee, prior to the final decision on revocation by the parole authority. This hearing must be the basis for more than determining probable cause; it must lead to a final evaluation of any contested relevant facts and consideration of whether the facts as determined warrant revocation. The parolee must have an opportunity to be heard and to show, if he can, that he did not violate the conditions, or, if he did, that circumstances in mitigation suggest the violation does not warrant revocation. The revocation hearing must be tendered within a reasonable time after the parolee is taken into custody. A lapse of two months, as the State suggests occurs in some cases, would not appear to be unreasonable.

We cannot write a code of procedure; that is the responsibility of each State. Most States have done so by legislation, others by judicial decision usually on due process grounds. Our task is limited to deciding the minimum requirements of due process. They include (a) written notice of the claimed violations of parole; (b) disclosure to the parolee of evidence against him; (c) opportunity to be heard in person and to present witnesses and documentary evidence; (d) the right to confront and cross-examine adverse witnesses (unless the hearing officer specifically finds good cause for not allowing confrontation); (e) a "neutral and detached" hearing body such as a traditional parole board, members of which need not be judicial officers or lawyers; and (f) a written statement by the factfinders as to the evidence relied on and reasons for revoking parole. We emphasize that there is no thought to equate this second stage of parole revocation to a criminal prosecution in any sense; it is a narrow inquiry; the process should be flexible enough to consider evidence including letters, affidavits, and other material that would not be admissible in an adversary criminal trial.

We do not reach or decide the question whether the parolee is entitled to the assistance of retained counsel or to appointed counsel if he is indigent.

We have no thought to create an inflexible structure for parole revocation procedures. The few basic requirements set out above, which are applicable to future revocations of parole, should not impose a great burden on any State's parole system. Control over the required proceedings by the hearing officers can assure that delaying tactics and other abuses sometimes present in the traditional adversary trial situation do not occur. Obviously a parolee cannot relitigate issues determined against him in other forums, as in the situation presented when the revocation is based on conviction of another crime.

* * *

[Justice Brennan, joined by Justice Marshall, concurred in the result. He expressed his view that prisoners who can afford to retain and wish to retain counsel must be permitted to do so. They left open the question of whether counsel must be appointed for indigents. Justice Douglas dissented in part; although his view was not very different from the majority's, he would not as readily allow revocation upon a preliminary showing.]

Note

A unanimous Supreme Court held in Black v. Romano, 471 U.S. 606 (1985), that the due process clause does not require a sentencing court to indicate that it has considered alternatives to incarceration before revoking probation. Romano pleaded guilty to two counts of transferring and selling a controlled substance. The trial judge imposed two concurrent twenty year sentences, suspended execution of the sentences, and placed Romano on probation for five years. Two months later Romano was arrested for leaving the scene of an accident after he had run over a pedestrian. The trial judge held a probation revocation hearing during which no suggestion was made by Romano or his two lawyers that an alternative to incarceration be considered. Instead, Romano's argument was that he had not violated his probation conditions. Justice O'Connor's opinion for the Court analyzes *Morrissey* and Gagnon v. Scarpelli, 411 U.S. 778 (1973) (providing right to counsel in certain parole and probation revocation proceedings) and concludes that although the Court did "not question the desirability of considering possible alternatives to imprisonment before probation is revoked," the "decision to revoke probation is generally predictive and subjective in nature" and "incarceration for violation of a probation condition is not constitutionally limited to circumstances where that sanction represents the only means of promoting the State's interest in punishment and deterrence." A statement of reasons for revocation is not required because "[t]he written statement required by *Gagnon* and *Morrissey* helps to insure accurate factfinding with respect to any alleged violation and provides an adequate basis for review to determine if the decision rests on permissible grounds supported by the evidence." The opinion distinguishes *Bearden* on the ground that it involved a situation in which a defendant violated a probation condition through no fault of his own [inability to pay a fine] and leaves open the question "whether concerns for fundamental fairness would preclude the automatic revocation of probation in [other] circumstances." It rejects an argument that the revocation was improper because it was unrelated to the prior convictions. Justice Marshall added a concurring opinion in which Justice Brennan joined. Justice Powell did not participate in the case.

D. APPELLATE REVIEW OF SENTENCING GENERALLY

Not only is enormous discretion vested in the sentencing authority in most states, but there is little review in most jurisdictions of how that discretion is exercised. The absence of much effective appellate supervision cannot be very surprising. To the extent that a rehabilitative or personalized sentence is imposed upon an offender, and to the extent we believe that trial judges can pierce the offender's soul to judge moral worth, an appellate court which sits away from the real life trial or plea proceedings and has little, if any, opportunity to see the participants will defer to the sentencing authority at trial. For a summary of existing appellate review provisions, see Labbe, Appellate Review of Sentences, 68 J.Crim.L. & Crim. 122 (1977). One must be careful in assessing these provisions, however, since "the existence of explicit statutory authority is not prima facie proof of the vitality of sentence review in any jurisdiction." Labbe, supra, at 127.

One of the most controversial aspects of appellate review is whether the state should be permitted to appeal a sentence. American jurisdictions generally forbid the raising of a sentence on appeal. A few permit some government appeal, however, see, e.g., Alaska Stat. § 12.55.120(b) (allowing a government appeal of sentence to provide guidance to lower courts, but not to raise sentence). In the Williams v. New York type of sentencing system, unfettered as it is by guidelines, you can see why one would fear that, if the opportunity presented itself, prosecutors would threaten to appeal sentences in order to discourage defendants from taking appeals or challenging sentences. In a system of unchecked discretion, risk-averse defendants might well choose not to subject themselves to an unguided appellate tribunal's sentence. If a guideline or presumptive system of sentences is adopted, the opportunities for arbitrariness are reduced, and arguably, the case for permitting the prosecutor to have some appellate review (at least where the guidelines are not followed by the trial court) may be more attractive.

Under the Federal Sentencing Guidelines, either party may appeal if (1) the sentence was imposed in violation of law; (2) the sentence was based on an incorrect application of the Guidelines; or (3) the sentence, imposed for an offense which lacked a guideline, was plainly unreasonable. In addition, the defendant may appeal a sentence which contains an upward departure, and the government may appeal a sentence which contains a downward departure. See 18 U.S.C. § 3742. In the absence of the above circumstances, neither party may obtain review. See generally Selya & Kipp, An Examination of Emerging Departure Jurisprudence Under the Federal Sentencing Guidelines, 67 Notre Dame L.Rev. 1 (1991). United States v. DiFrancesco, 449 U.S. 117 (1980), upholds the constitutionality of appellate review of sentences at the request of the government.

One of the most interesting disputes about appellate review of sentencing in a state supreme court is found in Wright v. State, 670 P.2d 1090 (Wyo.1983), in which the court held, 3–2, that the trial judge did not abuse his discretion in denying probation to a defendant convicted of unlawful delivery of marijuana and in sentencing him to 2–4 years in prison. The presentence report recommended probation and the trial judge gave no reasons for denying it. A majority of the court recognized that it had power to review sentence determinations but emphasized the importance of deference to trial judges. One judge concurred and noted that the power to review sentences had been exercised in such a way as to make review perfunctory if the sentence is within the limits set by the legislature. One dissenting judge opined that appellate "standards are useless" if the court is willing to affirm sentences like the one given to *Wright*. A second dissenting judge expressed concern that the court was too concerned with semantics—whether delivery was different from dealing, etc.—and not concerned enough with determining the right sentence for a 20 year old youth with no prior criminal record.

IV. THE DEATH PENALTY AND ITS PROCEDURES

A. THE RISK OF ARBITRARINESS

In June of 1972, the Supreme Court in a 5–4 decision vacated the death sentences of approximately 600 inmates throughout the nation on the ground that the then existing capital punishment schemes resulted in the infliction of cruel and unusual punishment in violation of the Eighth and Fourteenth Amendments. Furman v. Georgia, 408 U.S. 238 (1972). The majority agreed only on a one paragraph per curiam opinion. Accompanying it were separate concurring opinions by Justices Douglas, Brennan, Stewart, White, and Marshall. Justices Blackmun, Powell and Rehnquist and Chief Justice Burger dissented. In the Douglas, Stewart and White opinions the emphasis was on the infrequent, "bolt of lightning" character of capital punishment, with suggestions of arbitrariness or discrimination in its utilization. Justices Brennan and Marshall focused on the argument that death was an excessive, unnecessary punishment that violated modern views of human dignity.

Four years later, the Court responded to legislative efforts to restore capital sanctions in a series of cases. In Gregg v. Georgia, 428 U.S. 153 (1976), the Georgia death penalty statute was upheld. Justices Stewart, Powell and Stevens announced the judgment of the Court. They reasoned that the Eighth Amendment's meaning must be drawn from evolving standards of decency; that, although punishments must not be excessive in form or severity and must respect human dignity, a legislature need not select the least severe sanction available; that capital punishment could be justified on retributive and deterrent theories; and that a sentencing authority could impose a death sentence if properly guided by statutory standards. The Georgia system withstood scrutiny, since the sentencing authority—a jury in a jury trial (after it returns a guilty verdict)[25] or a judge in a bench trial—was told to consider certain aggravating circumstances set forth in the statute and any mitigating evidence and was directed that it could not impose a death sentence without stating in writing that it found an aggravating circumstance beyond a reasonable doubt. In addition, the state supreme court would automatically review any death sentence to see if it were excessive or disproportionate to the penalty imposed in similar cases.[26]

Justice White, with whom the Chief Justice and Justice Rehnquist joined, concurred in the judgment. Justice Blackmun did likewise. Justices Brennan and Marshall reiterated their *Furman* views that capital punishment was virtually a per se violation of the Eighth Amendment.

In companion cases, Proffitt v. Florida, 428 U.S. 242 (1976), and Jurek v. Texas, 428 U.S. 262 (1976), the Court upheld the Florida and Texas death

25. In McGautha v. California, 402 U.S. 183 (1971) the Court sustained a single verdict capital trial. It was frowned upon by the *Gregg* plurality, however. A bifurcated trial was preferred.

26. The Supreme Court took a look at the Georgia death penalty statute as applied in Godfrey v. Georgia, 446 U.S. 420 (1980). Justice Stewart's plurality opinion concluded that the Georgia Supreme Court had adopted too broad and vague a construction of the following language: "[an offense that] was outrageously or wantonly vile, horrible or inhuman in that it involved torture, depravity of mind, or an aggravated battery to the victim." The plurality concluded that "[t]here is no principled way to distinguish this case, in which the death penalty was imposed, from the many cases in which it was not," and voted to vacate the death sentence. Justice Marshall, joined by Justice Brennan, concurred in the judgment and urged that the Court's approach in *Gregg* "increasingly appears to be doomed to failure," since "appellate courts are incapable of guaranteeing the kind of objectivity and evenhandedness that the Court contemplated and hoped for in *Gregg*." Chief Justice Burger dissented, and Justice White also dissented and was joined by Justice Rehnquist.

penalty statutes. The breakdown of the votes was the same as in *Gregg*. In Florida, aggravating and mitigating factors are set forth in the statute. In a jury trial, after the jury declares that the defendant is guilty it is instructed to consider whether mitigating circumstances outweigh aggravating circumstances and, based on this calculus, whether a death sentence should be imposed. The jury decides punishment by majority vote, and its decision serves as a recommendation to the trial judge, who is empowered to impose a different sentence. If the sentence is death, written findings by the judge are required. Automatic review in the state supreme court is provided.

The Texas system asks a jury that returns a guilty verdict in a capital case to decide whether (1) the conduct of the defendant was a deliberate act that the defendant reasonably expected would cause death; (2) there is a probability that the defendant's future violent acts would be a continuing threat to society; and (3) if raised by the defendant, whether the conduct of the defendant was an unreasonable response to actions by the deceased. If the answer to any question is no, the sentence must be life imprisonment. If the answer to all questions is yes, then the death penalty is imposed. The Stewart, Powell and Stevens plurality found that the Texas system allowed the jury to consider mitigating circumstances, although the statute is not explicit on the point.

In Woodson v. North Carolina, 428 U.S. 280 (1976), and Roberts v. Louisiana, 428 U.S. 325 (1976), this plurality joined Justices Brennan and Marshall in striking down "mandatory" death penalty statutes. Tracing the history of the death penalty in America, the plurality concluded that a mandatory death penalty "papered over the problem of unguided and unchecked jury discretion," because many juries will refuse to convict a person accused of a capital sanction. The plurality found that contemporary values require rejection of a mandatory death sentence and that a valid capital punishment system requires that the sentencing authority engage in "particularized consideration of relevant aspects of the character and record of each convicted defendant before the imposition upon him of a sentence of death." At this point, Justice White, joined by the Chief Justice and Justices Blackmun and Rehnquist, dissented. They believed that a mandatory penalty removed most of the danger of arbitrariness, that it was not possible to conclude with sufficient certainty that the public had rejected mandatory capital punishment in designated circumstances as unacceptable, and that most juries would do their duty and do it fairly.

B. MITIGATING EVIDENCE AND THE REQUIREMENT OF INDIVIDUALIZED SENTENCING

Two more years passed and votes shifted slightly. In Lockett v. Ohio, 438 U.S. 586 (1978), the Chief Justice joined the plurality view of Justices Stewart, Powell and Stevens and delivered another plurality opinion—this time for four—striking down the Ohio death penalty statute as being too restrictive on a defendant's ability to introduce evidence of mitigating factors. The standards adopted by the plurality were ultimately accepted by a majority of the Court, as the Note following the case indicates.

LOCKETT v. OHIO

Supreme Court of the United States, 1978.
438 U.S. 586.

MR. CHIEF JUSTICE BURGER delivered the opinion of the Court with respect to the constitutionality of petitioner's conviction (Parts I and II) together with an opinion (Part III) in which MR. JUSTICE STEWART, MR. JUSTICE POWELL, and MR. JUSTICE STEVENS joined, on the constitutionality of the statute under which petitioner was sentenced to death, and announced the judgment of the Court.

* * *

III

Lockett challenges the constitutionality of Ohio's death penalty statute on a number of grounds. We find it necessary to consider only her contention that her death sentence is invalid because the statute under which it was imposed did not permit the sentencing judge to consider, as mitigating factors, her character, prior record, age, lack of specific intent to cause death, and her relatively minor part in the crime. To address her contention from the proper perspective, it is helpful to review the developments in our recent cases where we have applied the Eighth and Fourteenth Amendments to death penalty statutes. We do not write on a "clean slate."

A

Prior to Furman v. Georgia, every State that authorized capital punishment had abandoned mandatory death penalties, and instead permitted the jury unguided and unrestrained discretion regarding the imposition of the death penalty in a particular capital case. Mandatory death penalties had proven unsatisfactory, as the plurality noted in Woodson v. North Carolina, in part because juries "with some regularity disregarded their oaths and refused to convict defendants where a death sentence was the automatic consequence of a guilty verdict."

This Court had never intimated prior to *Furman* that discretion in sentencing offended the Constitution. As recently as McGautha v. California, 402 U.S. 183 (1971), the Court had specifically rejected the contention that discretion in imposing the death penalty violated the fundamental standards of fairness embodied in Fourteenth Amendment due process, and had asserted that States were entitled to assume that "jurors confronted with the truly awesome responsibility of decreeing death for a fellow human [would] act with due regard for the consequences of their decision."

The constitutional status of discretionary sentencing in capital cases changed abruptly, however, as a result of the separate opinions supporting the judgment in *Furman*. * * *

Predictably, the variety of opinions supporting the judgment in *Furman* engendered confusion as to what was required in order to impose the death penalty in accord with the Eighth Amendment. Some States responded to what was thought to be the command of *Furman* by adopting mandatory death penalties for a limited category of specific crimes, thus eliminating all discretion from the sentencing process in capital cases. Other States attempted to continue the practice of individually assessing the culpability of each individual defendant convicted of a capital offense and, at the same time, to comply with *Furman*, by providing standards to guide the sentencing decision.

* * *

The signals from this Court have not * * * always been easy to decipher. The States now deserve the clearest guidance that the Court can provide; we have an obligation to reconcile previously differing views in order to provide that guidance.

B

With that obligation in mind we turn to Lockett's attack on the Ohio statute. Essentially she contends that the Eighth and Fourteenth Amendments require that the sentencer be given a full opportunity to consider mitigating circumstances in capital cases and that the Ohio statute does not comply with that requirement. She relies, in large part, on the plurality opinions in *Woodson*, *Roberts*, and *Jurek*, but she goes beyond them.

We begin by recognizing that the concept of individualized sentencing in criminal cases generally, although not constitutionally required, has long been accepted in this country. Consistent with that concept, sentencing judges traditionally have taken a wide range of factors into account. That States have authority to make aiders and abettors equally responsible, as a matter of law, with principals, or to enact felony murder statutes is beyond constitutional challenge. But the definition of crimes generally has not been thought automatically to dictate what should be the proper penalty. And where sentencing discretion is granted, it generally has been agreed that the sentencing judge's "possession of the fullest information possible concerning the defendant's life and characteristics" is "[h]ighly relevant—*if not essential*—[to the] selection of an appropriate sentence * * *." Williams v. New York, 337 U.S., at 247 (emphasis added).

The opinions of this Court going back many years in dealing with sentencing in capital cases have noted the strength of the basis for individualized sentencing. * * *

Although legislatures remain free to decide how much discretion in sentencing should be reposed in the judge or jury in noncapital cases, the plurality opinion in *Woodson*, after reviewing the historical repudiation of mandatory sentencing in capital cases, concluded that:

> "in capital cases the fundamental respect for humanity underlying the Eighth Amendment * * * requires consideration of the character and record of the individual offender and the circumstances of the particular offense as a constitutionally indispensable part of the process of inflicting the penalty of death."

That declaration rested "on the predicate that the penalty of death is qualitatively different" from any other sentence. We are satisfied that this qualitative difference between death and other penalties calls for a greater degree of reliability when the death sentence is imposed. The mandatory death penalty statute in *Woodson* was held invalid because it permitted *no* consideration of "relevant facets of the character and record of the individual offender or the circumstances of the particular offense." The plurality did not attempt to indicate, however, which facets of an offender or his offense it deemed "relevant" in capital sentencing or what degree of consideration of "relevant facets" it would require.

We are now faced with those questions and we conclude that the Eighth and Fourteenth Amendments require that the sentencer, in all but the rarest kind of capital case,[a] not be precluded from considering *as a mitigating factor*, any aspect of a defendant's character or record and any of the circumstances of

a. We express no opinion as to whether the need to deter certain kinds of homicide would justify a mandatory death sentence, as, for example, when a prisoner—or escapee—under a life sentence is found guilty of murder. See Roberts (Harry) v. Louisiana, 431 U.S. 633, 637 n. 5 (1977).

the offense that the defendant proffers as a basis for a sentence less than death. We recognize that, in noncapital cases, the established practice of individualized sentences rests not on constitutional commands but public policy enacted into statutes. The considerations that account for the wide acceptance of individualization of sentences in noncapital cases surely cannot be thought less important in capital cases. Given that the imposition of death by public authority is so profoundly different from all other penalties, we cannot avoid the conclusion that an individualized decision is essential in capital cases. The need for treating each defendant in a capital case with that degree of respect due the uniqueness of the individual is far more important than in noncapital cases. A variety of flexible techniques—probation, parole, work furloughs, to name a few—and various post conviction remedies, may be available to modify an initial sentence of confinement in noncapital cases. The nonavailability of corrective or modifying mechanisms with respect to an executed capital sentence underscores the need for individualized consideration as a constitutional requirement in imposing the death sentence.

There is no perfect procedure for deciding in which cases governmental authority should be used to impose death. But a statute that prevents the sentencer in all capital cases from giving independent mitigating weight to aspects of the defendant's character and record and to circumstances of the offense proffered in mitigation creates the risk that the death penalty will be imposed in spite of factors which may call for a less severe penalty. When the choice is between life and death, that risk is unacceptable and incompatible with the commands of the Eighth and Fourteenth Amendments.

C

The Ohio death penalty statute does not permit the type of individualized consideration of mitigating factors we now hold to be required by the Eighth and Fourteenth Amendments in capital cases. Its constitutional infirmities can best be understood by comparing it with the statutes upheld in *Gregg, Proffitt,* and *Jurek*.

In upholding the Georgia statute in *Gregg*, Justices Stewart, Powell, and Stevens noted that the statute permitted the jury "to consider any aggravating or mitigating circumstances," * * * and that the Georgia Supreme Court had approved "open and far ranging argument" in presentence hearings. Although the Florida statute approved in *Proffitt* contained a list of mitigating factors, six members of this Court assumed, in approving the statute, that the range of mitigating factors listed in the statute was not exclusive. *Jurek* involved a Texas statute which made no explicit reference to mitigating factors. Rather the jury was required to answer three questions in the sentencing process, the second of which was "whether there is a probability that the defendant would commit criminal acts of violence that would constitute a continuing threat to society." The statute survived the petitioner's Eighth and Fourteenth Amendment attack because three Justices concluded that the Texas Court of Criminal Appeals had broadly interpreted the second question—despite its facial narrowness—so as to permit the sentencer to consider "whatever mitigating circumstances" the defendant might be able to show. None of the statutes we sustained in *Gregg* and the companion cases clearly operated at that time to prevent the sentencer from considering any aspect of the defendant's character and record or any circumstances of his offense as an independently mitigating factor.

In this regard the statute now before us is significantly different. Once a defendant is found guilty of aggravated murder with at least one of seven specified aggravating circumstances, the death penalty must be imposed unless, considering "the nature and circumstances of the offense and the history, character, and conditions of the offender," the sentencing judge determines that at least one of the following mitigating circumstances is established by a preponderance of the evidence:

"(1) The victim of the offense induced or facilitated it.

"(2) It is unlikely that the offense would have been committed, but for the fact that the offender was under duress, coercion, or strong provocation.

"(3) The offense was primarily the product of the offender's psychosis or mental deficiency, though such condition is insufficient to establish the defense of insanity." Ohio Rev.Code Ann. § 2929.04(B) (1975 Repl. Vol.).

The Ohio Supreme Court has concluded that there is no constitutional distinction between the statute approved in *Proffitt*, supra, and Ohio's statute, because the mitigating circumstances in Ohio's statute are "liberally construed in favor of the accused," and because the sentencing judge or judges may consider factors such as the age and criminal record of the defendant in determining whether any of the mitigating circumstances is established. But even under the Ohio court's construction of the statute, only the three factors specified in the statute can be considered in mitigation of the defendant's sentence. We see, therefore, that once it is determined that the victim did not induce or facilitate the offense, that the defendant did not act under duress or coercion, and that the offense was not primarily the product of the defendant's mental deficiency, the Ohio statute mandates the sentence of death. The absence of direct proof that the defendant intended to cause the death of the victim is relevant for mitigating purposes only if it is determined that it sheds some light on one of the three statutory mitigating factors. Similarly, consideration of a defendant's comparatively minor role in the offense, or age, would generally not be permitted, as such, to affect the sentencing decision.

The limited range of mitigating circumstances which may be considered by the sentencer under the Ohio statute is incompatible with the Eighth and Fourteenth Amendments. To meet constitutional requirements, a death penalty statute must not preclude consideration of relevant mitigating factors.

Accordingly, the judgment under review is reversed to the extent that it sustains the imposition of the death penalty; the case is remanded for further proceedings.

Note

Justice Marshall reiterated his *Furman* views. Justice Blackmun concurred in the judgment on a narrower ground. Justice Brennan did not participate. Justices White and Rehnquist wrote separate dissenting opinions. The breakdown in a companion case, Bell v. Ohio, 438 U.S. 637 (1978), was similar, except that Justice White would have vacated the death sentence.

A majority of the Court relied on *Lockett* in holding that the state courts impermissibly restricted the mitigating circumstances that could support a life sentence in the case of a 16 year old defendant. Eddings v. Oklahoma, 455 U.S. 104 (1982).

Beck v. Alabama, 447 U.S. 625 (1980), held unconstitutional an Alabama statute under which a jury was not permitted to consider lesser included offenses in a capital case. The majority noted that, except under the challenged statute, a defendant in Alabama and in most jurisdictions has the universal benefit of having a jury instructed on lesser included offenses. Referring to the standard practice as one that avoids unwarranted convictions where the evidence establishes that the defendant is guilty of a violent offense but leaves some doubt as to an element, the Court concluded that the risk of an unwarranted conviction "cannot be tolerated in a case in which the defendant's life is at stake." Justice Rehnquist, joined by Justice White, dissented on procedural grounds. Subsequently, in Hopper v. Evans, 456 U.S. 605 (1982), the Court held that *Beck* only required a lesser included offense instruction where the evidence supports such an instruction. In *Hopper* the Court found that where the evidence affirmatively negated any claim that the defendant did not intend to kill his victim, an instruction on the offense of unintentional killing was not warranted.

Beck was distinguished in Spaziano v. Florida, 468 U.S. 447 (1984). The defendant had been indicted for murder after the statute of limitations for lesser included offenses had run. The trial judge informed the defendant that he would instruct the jury on the lesser included offenses if the defendant waived the statute of limitations as to them, and the defendant refused. The trial judge instructed the jury only on capital murder and the jury convicted the defendant.

Justice Blackmun's opinion for the Court stated that "[t]he goal of the *Beck* rule * * * is to eliminate the distortion of the fact-finding process that is created when the jury is forced into an all-or-nothing choice between capital murder and innocence. Requiring that the jury be instructed on lesser included offenses for which the defendant may not be convicted, however, would simply introduce another type of distortion into the fact-finding process." Justice Blackmun added that *Beck* does not require that a jury be misled into thinking that it has a choice when it has none. "Such a rule not only would undermine the public's confidence in the criminal justice system, but it would do a serious disservice to the goal of rationality on which the *Beck* rule is based." He indicated that when the statute of limitations has run on lesser offenses, the defendant should not be forced to waive the statute; he should have a choice. Justice White added a one sentence opinion stating that he did not agree that *Beck* required a state court to permit the defendant to waive the statute and to give a lesser included offense instruction. Justice Rehnquist joined his opinion.

A five-person majority of the Court distinguished *Beck* in Schad v. Arizona, 111 S.Ct. 2491 (1991). Schad was indicted for first-degree murder, and the prosecutor advanced both premeditated and felony murder theories; Schad argued that the evidence established that he was at most a thief, not a murderer. The trial court refused to instruct the jury on theft as a lesser included offense, but did instruct the jury on second-degree murder; in Arizona, second-degree murder is a lesser included offense only of premeditated murder, not of felony murder. Schad argued that the failure to charge on theft violated *Beck,* because if the jury believed he was guilty of theft but not murder, they would be presented with the "all-or-nothing" choice of capital murder or innocence prohibited by *Beck.*

Justice Souter's majority opinion held that *Beck* was inapplicable, because the jury in Schad's case was instructed on a lesser included offense: that of second-degree murder. Thus, the "central concern of *Beck* simply is not implicated * * * for petitioner's jury was not faced with an all-or-nothing choice between the offense of conviction (capital murder) and innocence." Justice Souter rejected Schad's argument that second-degree murder was not a legitimate "third option" for the jurors if they found that Schad was guilty of theft but not murder. He explained as follows:

> To accept the contention advanced by petitioner and the dissent, we would have to assume that a jury unconvinced that petitioner was guilty either of capital or second-degree murder, but loath to acquit him completely (because it was convinced he was guilty of robbery), might choose capital murder rather than second-degree murder as its means of keeping him off the streets. Because we see no basis to assume such irrationality, we are satisfied that the second-degree murder instruction in this case sufficed to ensure the verdict's reliability.

Justice Souter cautioned that the *Beck* requirement of providing a third option when warranted by the evidence would not be satisfied "by instructing the jury on just any lesser included offense, even one without any support in the evidence." But in this case the evidence would have supported a second-degree murder conviction.

Justice White, joined by Justices Marshall, Blackmun, and Stevens, dissented. Justice White argued that the second-degree murder instruction provided no legitimate "third option" if the jury believed that defendant was guilty of theft but not murder. He concluded that "when the state chooses to proceed on various theories, each of which has lesser included offenses, the relevant lesser included instructions and verdict forms on each theory must be given in order to satisfy *Beck.*"

A majority of the Court found *Lockett* and *Eddings* controlling in Skipper v. South Carolina, 476 U.S. 1 (1986). A defendant charged with capital murder was denied the right to present the testimony of two jailors and a "regular visitor" to the jail that he had made a good adjustment between the time of his arrest and trial. Justice White's majority opinion reasoned that "[c]onsideration of a defendant's past conduct as indicative of his probable future behavior is an inevitable and not undesirable element of criminal sentencing," and that evidence such as the testimony proffered in this case is potentially mitigating and may not be excluded from a capital sentencer's consideration. Justice Powell, joined by the Chief Justice and Justice Rehnquist, concurred in the judgment on the ground that the defendant was barred from rebutting evidence and argument presented by the prosecution. He argued, however, that a state ought to be able to exclude such evidence, when unnecessary as rebuttal, since the evidence has no bearing on the offense or the defendant's culpability. Justice Powell noted that the defendant has an obvious, self-interested motive to behave while incarcerated pending trial, which has little to do with the notions of retribution and deterrence that support capital punishment.

In Hitchcock v. Dugger, 481 U.S. 393 (1987), a unanimous Court found that "it could not be clearer that the advisory jury was instructed not to consider, and the sentencing judge refused to consider, evidence of nonstatutory mitigating circumstances, and that the proceedings therefore did not comport with the requirements of *Eddings* and *Skipper.*"

The Court reiterated in Sumner v. Shuman, 483 U.S. 66 (1987), the importance of permitting sentencing juries or judges to consider all circumstances before imposing a death sentence. Justice Blackmun wrote for the Court as it held unconstitutional a statute, later repealed, that mandated the death penalty for prisoners serving life sentences without parole who are convicted of first degree murder. Shuman, who was incarcerated for first degree murder, was convicted of murdering a fellow inmate. Justice Blackmun reasoned that "[t]he simple fact that a particular inmate is serving a sentence of life imprisonment without possibility of parole does not contribute significantly to the profile of that person for purposes of determining whether he should be sentenced to death." He observed that Nevada law permitted a life sentence without parole for crimes other than first degree murder. He added that, even as applied to convicted murderers, the mandatory scheme failed to consider the circumstances surrounding the murder giving rise to incarceration. Justice White, joined by Chief Justice Rehnquist and Justice Scalia, dissented.

The Supreme Court held, 6–2, in Lowenfield v. Phelps, 484 U.S. 231 (1988), that a defendant was properly sentenced to death for murder committed with the intent "to kill or inflict great bodily harm upon more than one person." It found no defect in Louisiana's treating as an aggravating circumstance the knowing creation of a risk of death or great bodily harm to more than one person. Chief Justice Rehnquist reasoned for the Court that the function of aggravating circumstances is to narrow the class of persons eligible for the death penalty and that there is "no reason why this narrowing function may not be performed by jury findings at either the sentencing phase of the trial or the guilt phase. Justice Marshall, joined by Justice Brennan, dissented. He argued that "[t]he only conceivable reason for making narrowing a constitutional requirement is its function in structuring sentencing deliberations," and added that "[b]y permitting the removal of the narrowing function from the sentencing process altogether, the Court reduces it to a mechanical formality entirely unrelated to the choice between life and death" that "will inevitably tilt the sentencing scales toward the imposition of the death penalty."

The Supreme Court struggled in Franklin v. Lynaugh, 487 U.S. 164 (1988), to reconcile the principle that sentencing discretion must be guided with the cases holding that a defendant must be permitted to offer mitigating evidence for the sentencing authority's consideration. After a jury found Franklin guilty of capital murder, the trial court submitted two issues for its consideration: 1) whether murder was committed deliberately and with the reasonable expectation that death would result, and 2) whether there was a probability that the defendant would constitute a continuing threat to society. The trial judge told the jury that if it gave affirmative responses on both issues, the defendant would be sentenced to death. The judge refused the defendant's request for five jury instructions which would have told the jury that it could consider any mitigating evidence in deciding the two issues and that any mitigating evidence could justify a negative answer to either or both questions, even if the jury otherwise believed that "yes" answers were warranted. The defendant complained in particular that the jury was not instructed that it could take into account doubts about guilt or the defendant's disciplinary record during his period of incarceration in deciding on the sentence.

Justice White, joined by Chief Justice Rehnquist and Justices Scalia and Kennedy, reasoned that the Court had never held that a capital defendant has a right to an instruction telling the jury to consider whether it had a "residual doubt" about guilt in deciding on sentence, and that, even if a defendant had such a right, it was unimpaired in this case where no limits were placed on the defendant's opportunity to argue residual doubt to the jury. The plurality also rejected the defendant's argument that the jury should have been told that if his record in prison established sufficiently good character, this alone might warrant a sentence of imprisonment rather than death. The plurality concluded that a state could provide a sentencing jury with a framework for considering mitigating evidence and that nothing in *Skipper* required that a jury be told that it could consider character evidence on an issue other than future dangerousness if a state chose to focus the jury's attention on dangerousness as a sentencing criterion. The plurality added that the defendant had not suggested how his prison record was probative of any fact other than future dangerousness.

Justice White wrote that in deciding cases like *Eddings* and *Lockett* "this Court has never held that jury discretion must be undirected or unfocused; we have never concluded that States cannot channel jury discretion in capital sentencing in an effort to achieve a more rational and equitable administration of the death penalty."

Justice O'Connor, joined by Justice Blackmun, expressed "doubts" about a sentencing scheme that would "limit the ability of the sentencing authority to give effect to mitigating evidence relevant to a defendant's character or background or to the circumstances of the offense that mitigate against the death penalty." She observed that if a defendant offers mitigating evidence that is not relevant to the issues that are submitted to the jury, a question arises whether the jury must be instructed as to the effect it may give that evidence. But, in the instant case, Justice O'Connor concluded that the only mitigating evidence offered by the defendant related to his prison record, and the jury was free to give mitigating effect to this evidence in deciding the second issue submitted to it. She also concluded that "[o]ur cases to not support the proposition that a defendant who has been found guilty beyond a reasonable doubt has a constitutional right to reconsideration by the sentencing body of lingering doubts about his guilt."

Justice Stevens, joined by Justices Brennan and Marshall, dissented and argued that evidence of past good behavior in prison is relevant in sentencing in the same way as evidence of honorable military service or past kindness—i.e., it tells the sentencer something about the defendant's personality and the appropriateness of a sentence of imprisonment as well as about future dangerousness. He reasoned that the defendant was entitled to an instruction that the jury could answer one of the issues "no" if it found that the defendant's character was such that he should not receive the death penalty, and that the notion that a state could provide a framework for the jury's consideration of mitigating evidence could not be reconciled with the Court's holdings that required all mitigating evidence to be admitted on behalf of a defendant.

Does *Franklin* mean that a state judge may tell a jury that it cannot use mitigating evidence in certain ways while making a sentencing determination? If not, is there a meaningful difference between an instruction that limits a jury to two issues and one that tells the jury not to consider evidence on other issues?

The Supreme Court held in Johnson v. Mississippi, 486 U.S. 578 (1988), that Mississippi violated a defendant's Eighth Amendment rights by declining to vacate a capital sentence after a New York state court had set aside the defendant's earlier conviction for assault with intent to commit rape. The New York conviction was an aggravating circumstance which the prosecutor relied upon in asking the jury to return a death sentence, and the sole evidence of the New York conduct was an authenticated copy of the judgment of conviction which demonstrated that the defendant had been convicted and incarcerated. Justice Stevens wrote for the Court "[t]hat petitioner was imprisoned is not proof that he was guilty of the offense; indeed, it would be perverse to treat the imposition of punishment pursuant to an invalid conviction as an aggravating circumstance." The Court remanded the case to the state courts for further proceedings.

Justice Brennan, joined by Justice Marshall, and Justice White, joined by Chief Justice Rehnquist, filed brief concurring opinions. Justice O'Connor concurred in the judgment.

Although the Supreme Court held, 5–4, in Penry v. Lynaugh, 492 U.S. 302 (1989), that there is no categorical Eighth Amendment bar to execution of mentally retarded defendants, it also held by a different, 5–4, vote that a sentencing body must be allowed to consider retardation in considering whether the death penalty is appropriate in a particular case. Justice O'Connor delivered the opinion of the Court with respect to all issues. Justice Scalia, joined by Chief Justice Rehnquist and Justices White and Kennedy, concurred with respect to the permissibility of executing a mentally retarded defendant, but argued that a state had an interest in channeling the way in which a decisionmaker considered evidence such as mental retardation. Justice Brennan, joined by Justice Marshall, and Justice Stevens, joined by Justice Blackmun, wrote separately and dissented from the holding that mentally retarded persons may be executed for their crimes, but agreed that a decisionmaker must be permitted to consider evidence of mental retardation in assessing blameworthiness of the defendant. Justice O'Connor distinguished *Franklin* on the ground that the majority in that case concluded that the jury was able to give full effect to the mitigating evidence, whereas the jury in the instant case was never instructed on the relevance of mental retardation to the "deliberate" nature of the killing or to general notions of mitigation. For a discussion of *Penry* and the issues it leaves, see Hayman, Beyond *Penry*: The Remedial Use of the Mentally Retarded Label in Death Penalty Sentencing, 59 U.M.K.C.L. Rev. 17 (1990).

In Saffle v. Parks, 494 U.S. 484 (1990), a five-person majority refused to decide whether the Eighth Amendment prohibited a judge from giving an anti-sympathy instruction. Justice Kennedy, writing for the Court, stated that the principle urged was a "new rule" which could not be announced on collateral review after Teague v. Lane (Chapter One). Justice Kennedy noted that the Court had previously decided in *Lockett* and *Eddings* that the State could not bar relevant mitigating evidence from being presented and considered during the penalty phase of a capital trial. But Justice Kennedy argued that these cases spoke only "to *what* mitigating evidence the jury must be permitted to consider," not "to *how* it must consider the mitigating evidence." Justice Kennedy concluded, therefore, that existing precedent did not mandate the invalidation of anti-sympathy instructions.

Justice Brennan, joined by Justices Marshall, Blackmun and Stevens, dissented. The dissenters found no meaningful distinction between an instruction from the judge to avoid sympathy, and the exclusion of evidence pertaining to sympathy. Justice Brennan argued that in either case, the jury was effectively deprived from considering relevant mitigating evidence. Justice Brennan also contended that the second *Teague* exception, for new rules bearing upon fundamental fairness, should be applied with special solicitude in capital cases.

In contrast, the Court in McKoy v. North Carolina, 494 U.S. 433 (1990), held that the Eighth Amendment prohibits a state from requiring mitigating circumstances to be found unanimously. Justice Marshall, writing for the Court, found that a unanimity requirement violated the principles of *Lockett,* since it would allow one holdout juror to prevent the other jurors from giving effect to all mitigating evidence. The State argued that the unanimity requirement was permissible because the statute also required that aggravating circumstances be found unanimously. Justice Marshall rejected this argument, concluding that a State "may not limit a sentencer's consideration of mitigating evidence merely because it places the same limitation on consideration of aggravating circumstances." Justice White concurred with the understanding that the Eighth Amendment does not prevent a state from placing the burden of persuasion on the defendant with respect to mitigating circumstances. Justice Blackmun wrote a concurring opinion.

Justice Kennedy concurred in the result. He argued that the "one juror veto" system was "the height of arbitrariness," and concluded: "I would recognize the arbitrary operation of the North Carolina system as the exclusive basis of our decision, for the unanimity requirement, standing alone, is not invalid under our *Lockett* line of cases. * * * *Lockett* and its progeny stand only for the proposition that a state may not cut off in an absolute manner the presentation of mitigating evidence. * * * "

Justice Scalia, joined by Chief Justice Rehnquist and Justice O'Connor, dissented in *McKoy.* Justice Scalia argued that under *Saffle,* there is a constitutional distinction between what the sentencer is allowed to consider and the manner in which it is allowed to do so. The dissenters contended that a unanimity requirement determined how the jury would consider mitigating evidence, but did not preclude the jury from considering all mitigating evidence presented to it. Justice Scalia also noted that the unanimity requirement served the salutary purpose of furthering group deliberation. Without such a requirement, "[e]ach juror must presumably decide in splendid isolation, on the basis of his uniquely determined mitigating circumstance, whether death should be imposed. What was supposed to be jury trial has degenerated into a poll."

Are the decisions in *Saffle* and *McKoy* consistent? Which decision, *Saffle* or *McKoy,* better applies the principles of *Lockett?* What effect does an antisympathy instruction have on a jury's freedom to weigh mitigating evidence? What effect does a unanimity instruction with respect to mitigating evidence have on a jury's freedom to weigh such evidence?

The Pennsylvania death penalty statute considered in Blystone v. Pennsylvania, 494 U.S. 299 (1990), requires the jury to impose a death sentence if it finds at least one listed aggravating circumstance and no mitigating circumstances. Blystone argued that the statute was unconstitutional because it was mandatory, and also because it did not allow the jury to consider whether the severity of a listed aggravating circumstance warranted a death sentence. Chief Justice Rehnquist, writing for the majority, found the statute consistent with the Eighth Amendment, since it allowed the jury "to consider and give full effect to all relevant mitigating evidence." Nor was the statute impermissibly mandatory, as were the statutes struck down in *Woodson* and *Roberts* (striking down mandatory death penalty statutes). In Pennsylvania, death is not automatically imposed for certain types of murder, but only after it is found that aggravating circumstances outweigh mitigating circumstances in the particular case. Justice Rehnquist concluded that the Eighth Amendment did not require that the jury independently weigh aggravating circumstances: "The requirement of individualized sentencing in capital cases is satisfied by allowing the jury to consider all relevant mitigating evidence."

Justice Brennan, joined by Justices Marshall, Blackmun and Stevens in dissent, argued that under *Penry,* "a jury must be able to consider the weight of *both* the aggravating *and* mitigating circumstances when choosing whether to impose a death sentence."

The Court applied *Blystone* in Boyde v. California, 494 U.S. 370 (1990). The judge in *Boyde* instructed the jury that if the aggravating circumstances outweighed the mitigating circumstances "you shall impose a sentence of death." Writing for the same majority as in *Blystone,* Chief Justice Rehnquist found this instruction permissible since it did not prevent the jury from considering all relevant mitigating evidence.

Boyde also challenged the judge's instructions as impermissibly limiting the jury's consideration of mitigating evidence. The state contended that the judge's catch-all instruction, to consider "any other circumstance which extenuates the gravity of the crime," was sufficiently broad to allow consideration of all mitigating evidence. Boyde argued that that instruction could have been interpreted by the jury to refer only to evidence concerning the crime itself, and not to evidence of defendant's background and character. The Chief Justice agreed with the state's contention. According to the majority, the appropriate standard for reviewing jury instructions is "whether there is a reasonable likelihood that the jury has applied the challenged instruction in a way that prevents the consideration of constitutionally relevant evidence." The Court found no reasonable likelihood of misconception in this case. Chief Justice Rehnquist argued that the "reasonable likelihood" standard was an appropriate balance between the conflicting policies of accuracy and finality.

Justice Marshall, joined by Justices Brennan, Stevens and Blackmun, dissented. Justice Marshall contended that the majority's "reasonable likelihood" standard was inconsistent with prior case law such as Francis v. Franklin (Chapter Ten) (using the test of whether a reasonable juror could have concluded on an impermissible basis), and that it "places too much of the risk of error in capital sentencing on the defendant."

The Arizona capital sentencing scheme at issue in Walton v. Arizona, 110 S.Ct. 3047 (1990) allows the judge to determine whether the sentence shall be death or life imprisonment. The statute defines ten aggravating circumstances, one of which is that the defendant committed the offense in an "especially heinous, cruel or depraved manner." The statute allows consideration of all relevant mitigating circumstances, but the burden is on the defendant to prove the existence of a mitigating circumstance by a preponderance of the evidence. If the trial court finds both aggravating and mitigating circumstances, the burden is on the defendant to show that the mitigating factors outweigh the aggravating factors.

Walton challenged the Arizona sentencing scheme on several grounds, all of which were rejected by the Court in an opinion by Justice White.

First, Walton argued that every finding of fact underlying the sentencing decision must be made by the jury and not the judge. The Court found this claim precluded by Hildwin v. Florida, discussed infra (upholding system where jury returns advisory verdict and judge imposes capital sentence).

Second, Walton argued that the Arizona statute impermissibly placed the burden on the defendant of proving mitigating circumstances, and of proving that such circumstances outweighed the aggravating factors. Relying on cases allowing the state to shift the burden of proof of affirmative defenses, (see Patterson v. New York, Chapter Ten) the Court held as follows:

> So long as a State's method of allocating the burdens of proof does not lessen the State's burden to prove every element of the offense charged, or in this case to prove the existence of aggravating circumstances, a defendant's constitutional rights are not violated by placing on him the burden of proving mitigating circumstances sufficiently substantial to call for leniency.

Finally, Walton contended that the "especially heinous, cruel or depraved" aggravating circumstance was impermissibly broad and failed to channel the sentencer's discretion. Walton relied on Godfrey v. Georgia, 446 U.S. 420 (1980) and Maynard v. Cartwright, 486 U.S. 356 (1988), cases in which the Court had struck down similarly worded statutes as impermissibly broad and subject to arbitrary application. Justice White gave two reasons for finding that the risk of arbitrary application did not exist, given the way the statute was applied in Arizona. First, the judge, not the jury, was the final sentencer. Second, on review, the Arizona appellate court applied a limited definition of the aggravating circumstance to the facts presented.

As to the first point, the majority found that the judge would not be subject to unguided discretion in the same way as would a jury. Justice White explained as follows:

> When the jury is the final sentencer, it is essential that the jurors be properly instructed regarding all facets of the sentencing process. It is not enough to instruct the jury in the bare terms of an aggravating circumstance that is unconstitutionally vague on its face. * * * Trial judges are presumed to know the law and apply it in making their decisions. If the Arizona Supreme Court has narrowed the definition of the "especially heinous, cruel or depraved" aggravating circumstance, we presume that Arizona trial judges are applying the narrower definition.

On the second point, Justice White found that the Arizona Supreme Court "has sought to give substance to the operative terms" of the broad aggravating circumstance, and that the Arizona Supreme Court's construction of the statute sufficiently channeled the discretion of the factfinder. The following is the entirety of the majority's analysis of the Arizona Supreme Court's effort to limit the broad terms of the statute:

> Recognizing that the proper degree of definition of an aggravating factor of this nature is not susceptible of mathematical precision, we conclude that the definition given to the "especially cruel" provision by the Arizona Supreme Court is constitutionally sufficient because it gives meaningful guidance to the sentencer. Nor can we fault the state court's statement that a crime is committed in an especially "depraved" manner when the perpetrator "relishes the murder, evidencing debasement or perversion," or "shows indifference to the suffering of the victim and evidences a sense of pleasure in the killing."

Finally, Justice White rejected Walton's challenge to the proportionality review of the Arizona Supreme Court. The majority held that so long as the sentencer's discretion is reasonably channeled, a proportionality review is not constitutionally required, since it can be presumed that a death sentence proceeding from controlled discretion is not disproportionate or freakishly imposed. See also United States v. Pretlow, 770 F.Supp. 239 (D.N.J.1991) (the absence of proportionality review in the Federal Drug Kingpin law's death penalty provision does not violate the Eighth Amendment, where appellate review provisions sufficiently address the risk of an arbitrary death sentence).

In an extensive concurring opinion in *Walton*, Justice Scalia stated that he "will not, in this case or in the future, vote to uphold an Eighth Amendment claim that the sentencer's discretion has been unlawfully restricted." Justice Scalia contended that the *Lockett* line of cases, which prevents the state from controlling the discretion of the sentencer as to mitigating circumstances, is fatally inconsistent with the *Furman* line of cases, which requires the state to channel the discretion of the sentencer in determining whether death should be imposed. Addressing the command of stare decisis, Justice Scalia stated that "stare decisis cannot command the impossible. Since I cannot possibly be guided by what seems to me to be incompatible principles, I must reject the one that is plainly in error." Justice Scalia described the inconsistency between *Lockett* and *Furman* as follows:

> Today a petitioner before this Court says that a State sentencing court (1) had unconstitutionally broad discretion to sentence him to death instead of imprisonment, and (2) had unconstitutionally narrow discretion to sentence him to imprisonment instead of death. An observer unacquainted with our death penalty jurisprudence (and in the habit of thinking logically) would probably say these positions cannot both be right. * * * But that just shows that our jurisprudence and our logic have long since parted ways.

Justice Scalia contended that to argue, as the Court had previously done, that the *Furman* and *Lockett* lines of cases pursue "twin objectives," is "rather like referring to the twin objectives of good and evil. They cannot be reconciled."

Justice Brennan wrote a dissenting opinion joined by Justice Marshall. Justice Brennan criticized the majority's "cavalier application today of longstanding Eighth Amendment doctrines developed over the course of two decades of careful and sustained inquiry." Addressing Justice Scalia's rejection of *Lockett* and its progeny, Justice Brennan responded as follows:

> The *Lockett* and *Furman* principles speak to different concerns underlying our notion of civilized punishment. The *Lockett* rule flows primarily from the Amendment's core concern for human dignity * * * whereas the *Furman* principle reflects the understanding that the Amendment commands that punishment not be meted out in a wholly arbitrary and irrational manner.

Justice Blackmun wrote a dissenting opinion, joined by Justices Brennan, Marshall and Stevens. Justice Blackmun first took issue with the majority's holding that the state could impose the burden of proof as to mitigation on the defendant. Justice Blackmun found the cases allowing the state to impose upon defendant the burden of proving affirmative defenses to be inapposite. He noted that those cases proceeded from the proposition that the state had no obligation to allow an affirmative defense, and could therefore require the defendant to prove it if allowed. According to Justice Blackmun, "that reasoning is simply inapposite when a capital defendant introduces mitigating evidence, since the state lacks the power to exclude the evidence entirely."

Justice Blackmun further contended that requiring the defendant to prove mitigating factors by a preponderance was impermissible under *Lockett,* in that it imposes a limitation on the sentencing body's consideration of mitigating evidence. Justice Blackmun explained as follows:

> Mitigating evidence that fails to meet [the preponderance] standard is not so unreliable that it has no proper place in the sentencing decision; decisions as to punishment, like decisions as to guilt or innocence, will often be based on the cumulative effect of several pieces of evidence, no one of which by itself is fully persuasive. The problems with the preponderance standard are compounded when the defendant presents several possible mitigating factors. A trial judge might be 49% convinced as to each of ten mitigating circumstances;

yet he would be forced to conclude, as a matter of law, that there was no mitigation to weigh against the aggravating factors. * * *

The Arizona rule at issue here falls well within the prohibition announced in *Lockett* and its progeny. The statute defines a wide range of relevant mitigating evidence—evidence with some degree of persuasiveness which has not been proved by a preponderance—that cannot be given effect by the capital sentencer.

Justice Blackmun also attacked the majority's ruling that the state could permissibly place the burden on the defendant to show that mitigating factors outweighed aggravating factors. According to Justice Blackmun, the principle that the death penalty is qualitatively different from other penalties is inconsistent with a capital sentencing scheme "which provides that doubtful cases should be resolved in favor of a sentence of death."

Finally, Justice Blackmun voiced strong disagreement with the majority's conclusion that the "heinous, cruel, or depraved" aggravating circumstance, as applied by the Arizona courts, sufficiently channeled the sentencer's discretion. Justice Blackmun criticized the majority for failing to carefully analyze whether the Arizona Supreme Court had actually placed limitations on the application of the impermissibly broad aggravating circumstance. Conducting his own detailed analysis of Arizona Supreme Court cases construing the statute, Justice Blackmun stated that "there would appear to be few first-degree murders which the Arizona Supreme Court would not define as especially heinous or depraved—and those murders which do fall outside this aggravating circumstance are likely to be covered by some other aggravating factor." Under these circumstances, Justice Blackmun contended that the majority's reliance on the trial court's ability to apply a narrow definition of the aggravating circumstance was misplaced. He explained as follows:

The defective nature of the trial court's sentence did not stem from the judge's failure to abide by limitations announced by the Arizona Supreme Court. Rather, the trial-level sentencing procedure was defective because, even assuming that the trial judge correctly applied the relevant precedents, those decisions had failed to articulate a constitutionally sufficient narrowing construction of the statutory language.

Justice Blackmun closed with a parting comment about the majority's brusque treatment of Walton's claims:

Earlier this Term the very same majority of this Court severely restricted the regime of federal habeas corpus that had previously helped to safeguard the constitutional rights of criminal defendants, including those accused of capital crimes. See Butler v. McKellar (discussed in Chapter One); Saffle v. Parks. Today this majority serves notice that capital defendants no longer should expect from this Court on direct review a considered examination of their constitutional claims. In adjudicating claims that will mean life or death * * * the majority makes only the most perfunctory effort to reconcile its holding with this Court's prior Eighth Amendment jurisprudence. Nor does the majority display any recognition that a decision concerning the constitutionality of a State's capital punishment scheme may require an understanding of the manner in which that scheme actually operates.

Perhaps the current majority has grown weary of explicating what some Members no doubt choose to regard as hypertechnical rules. * * * Today's decision is either an abdication of the Court's constitutional role, or it is a silent repudiation of previously settled legal principles.

Justice Stevens wrote a separate dissenting opinion, contending that the Sixth Amendment requires a jury determination of facts that must be established before the death penalty is imposed.

After *Walton,* can a state require the defendant to prove the existence of a mitigating circumstance beyond a reasonable doubt? Does *Walton* mean that there will no longer be a qualitative distinction between capital sentences and other sentences? Twenty-four states have statutory aggravating circumstances for a murder which is "heinous, atrocious or cruel." These statutes are impermissibly vague, unless the state appellate courts impose some limitations on discretion in applying the statute. After *Walton,* how does a state court go about imposing limitations? What standards should it apply? For a thorough discussion of the problems presented by *Lockett* and *Walton,* see Sundby, The *Lockett* Paradox: Reconciling Guided Discretion and Unguided Mitigation in Capital Sentencing, 38 UCLA L.Rev. 1147 (1991).

C. MINIMUM MENS REA

The Court held, 5–4, that imposition of a capital sanction for aiding and abetting a murder without regard to the intent of the defendant was cruel and unusual punishment. Enmund v. Florida, 458 U.S. 782 (1982). Enmund was a participant in a robbery in which two people were killed, but he was not present at the murders and there was no showing that he intended to take a life. The majority held that the focus must be on the defendant's culpability, not on that of others. Justice White wrote for the majority. Justice O'Connor dissented and was joined by Chief Justice Burger and Justices Powell and Rehnquist.

Note

The Supreme Court explained the requirements of *Enmund* in Cabana v. Bullock, 474 U.S. 376 (1986). Bullock was convicted of murder and sentenced to death in a state court proceeding that permitted the jury to return a death penalty solely on the basis of his participation in a robbery, without considering whether Bullock killed, attempted to kill, or intended to kill anyone. Justice White's opinion for the Court reasoned that "[t]he Eighth Amendment is satisfied so long as the death penalty is not imposed upon a person ineligible under *Enmund* for such punishment" and that "[a]t what point in its criminal process a State chooses to make the *Enmund* determination is of little concern from the standpoint of the Constitution." Thus, the Court concluded that a death sentence may stand "provided only that the requisite findings are made in an adequate proceeding before some appropriate tribunal—be it an appellate court, a trial judge, or a jury." It also held that a federal habeas corpus court should give the state courts the initial opportunity to make factual findings that were not made in the course of direct review in the state system.

Justice Blackmun dissented and was joined by Justices Brennan and Marshall. He argued that *Enmund* required individualized consideration of a defendant by a factfinder and that it is important to require the sentencer to determine that the defendant had sufficient *mens rea* in order to assure that the sentencer truly focuses on his personal responsibility. Justice Stevens dissented and was joined by

Justice Brennan. He argued that the question of the defendant's intent was part of the determination of "moral culpability" that must be determined by a single decisionmaker, judge or jury. Justice Brennan also filed a short dissent of his own.

In Tison v. Arizona, 481 U.S. 137 (1987), Justice O'Connor wrote for the Court as it explained that *Enmund* did not require proof that a particular defendant intended to kill as a necessary foundation for imposition of a capital sentence. Although the Court did "not attempt to precisely delineate the particular types of conduct and states of mind warranting imposition of the death penalty," it held "that major participation in the felony committed, combined with reckless indifference to human life, is sufficient to satisfy the *Enmund* culpability requirement." The Court remanded the case to the state courts for consideration in light of its opinion.

Justice Brennan, joined by Justice Marshall and in large part by Justices Blackmun and Stevens, dissented. He argued that where the defendant did not actually kill, finding that the defendant intended to kill "seems indispensable to establishing capital culpability," and criticized the majority's reliance on doctrines like felony murder in cases involving the death penalty.

D. JURY CONSIDERATION OF INVALID AGGRAVATING FACTORS, AND JUDGE VERSUS JURY FUNCTIONS

In Zant v. Stephens, 462 U.S. 862 (1983), the Court held that a death sentence could stand even though one aggravating circumstance found by the jury was invalid. A jury found that Stephens committed murder. It found two aggravating circumstances: 1) that Stephens had a prior conviction for a capital felony *and* alternatively that he had a substantial history of serious assaultive crimes, and 2) that he committed murder as an escapee from custody. While Stephens' appeal was pending, the Georgia Supreme Court held that a substantial history of assaultive crimes was too vague an aggravating circumstance to withstand scrutiny. Nevertheless, it affirmed Stephens' death sentence. A federal court of appeals granted habeas corpus relief and was reversed.

The Supreme Court had certified to the Georgia Supreme Court the following question: "What are the premises of state law that support the conclusion that the death sentence is not impaired by the invalidity of one of the statutory aggravating circumstances found by the jury?" That court responded by stating *inter alia* that the purpose of the aggravating circumstance requirement is to limit discretion so that only persons who have at least one aggravating circumstance may possibly receive the death penalty and that Stephens was such a person. It also noted that the evidence of Stephens' prior crimes was properly admitted.

Justice Stevens wrote for the majority that the Court's cases "indicate * * * that statutory aggravating circumstances * * * play a constitutionally necessary function at the stage of legislative definition: they circumscribe the class of persons eligible for the death penalty. But the Constitution does not require the jury to ignore other possible aggravating factors in the process of selecting, from among that class, those defendants who will actually be sentenced to death. What is important at the selection stage is an *individualized* determination on the basis of the character of the individual and the circumstances of the crime." The majority found Georgia's capital punishment scheme to be valid and concluded that even though the statutory label "aggravating circumstance" might have caused the jury to give Stephens' prior record more weight than it otherwise would have, the Georgia Supreme Court did not err in concluding that the label's impact was inconsequential. It expressed no opinion as to what would happen if an aggravating circumstance relied upon by a jury that had been asked to weigh aggravating and mitigating factors were subsequently invalidated. Justice White concurred in part and in the judgment. Justice Rehnquist concurred in the judgment. Justice Marshall, joined by Justice Brennan, dissented.

The court also upheld a death sentence in Barclay v. Florida, 463 U.S. 939 (1983). The jury had recommended a life sentence for a defendant, but the trial judge imposed the death penalty after reviewing a presentence report. The Florida Supreme Court remanded so that the defendant could offer evidence as to any aspect of the presentence report, and the trial judge reaffirmed his sentence. Although the trial judge relied on one aggravating factor that was not recognized by state law, the prior bad record of the defendant, he also found aggravating factors listed in the Florida statute. The Florida Supreme Court affirmed the sentence despite its finding that the judge erred in considering a nonstatutory aggravating factor. Justice Rehnquist—writing for himself, Chief Justice Burger, and Justices White and O'Connor—found that the sentence was neither unprincipled nor arbitrary. The trial judge had properly considered the past record of the defendant to decide that there were no mitigating factors to be weighed on his behalf. His reliance on a nonstatutory aggravating factor, in addition to statutory aggravating factors, could properly be regarded by the state supreme court as harmless error. Justice Stevens, joined by Justice Powell, concurred in the judgment and emphasized that Florida offered more procedural protections than the Constitution required. Justice Marshall, joined by Justice Brennan, and Justice Blackmun filed dissenting opinions.

Zant was distinguished and *Barclay* clarified in Stringer v. Black, 112 S.Ct. ___ (1992). Unlike the Georgia procedure at issue in *Zant,* the Mississippi procedure requires the jury to weigh the aggravating circumstances against the mitigating circumstances. The death penalty is imposed only if the aggravating factors outweigh the mitigating factors. The jury in Stringer's case found three aggravating circumstances, but one aggravating factor was that the murder was "heinous, atrocious and cruel." As established in Walton v. Arizona, and Maynard v. Cartwright, supra, this aggravating factor, absent case law elaboration or a clarifying instruction, is impermissibly vague and subject to arbitrariness. Thus it could not constitutionally support Stringer's death sentence. Still, the jury had found two valid aggravating factors, and that the three aggravating factors outweighed the mitigating factors. The State relied on *Zant,* which held that the vagueness of one among several aggravating circumstances was irrelevant so long as there was mandatory appellate review for any arbitrariness or disproportionality stemming from some other source. The State recognized that the Court left open in *Zant* whether its analysis would be different if applied to a weighing state; but it argued that reasonable jurists could find that *Zant* was applicable to Stringer's case, and therefore Stringer, in arguing that *Zant* was not applicable, was asking for a new rule to be applied to his case. This would violate the principles of Teague v. Lane, discussed in Chapter Two, where the Court held that new rules could not generally be applied on habeas, and that any rule as to which reasonable minds could differ before its promulgation was a new rule.

Justice Kennedy, writing the opinion for a majority of six justices, concluded that *Zant* was clearly inapplicable in a weighing state, and that Stringer was not asking for a new rule. Rather, he was asking for application of a "well-settled principle: use of a vague or imprecise aggravating factor in the weighing process invalidates the sentence and at the very least requires constitutional harmless-error analysis or reweighing in the state judicial system." Justice Kennedy elaborated as follows:

> The principal difference between the sentencing schemes in Georgia and Mississippi is that Mississippi is what we have termed a "weighing" state while Georgia is not. * * * That Mississippi is a weighing State only gives emphasis to the requirement that aggravating factors be defined with some degree of precision. * * *
>
> In a nonweighing State, so long as the sentencing body finds at least one valid aggravating factor, the fact that it also finds an invalid aggravating factor does not infect the formal process of deciding whether death is an appropriate penalty. Assuming a determination by the state appellate court that the invalid factor would not have made a difference to the jury's determination, there is no constitutional violation resulting from the introduction of the invalid factor in an earlier stage of the proceedings. But when the sentencing body is told to weigh an invalid factor in its decision, a reviewing court may not assume it would have made no difference if the thumb had been removed from death's side of the scale. When the weighing process itself has been skewed, only constitutional harmless-error analysis or reweighing at the trial or appellate level suffices to guarantee that the defendant received an individualized sentence.

In *Barclay*, the Court had considered the use of an invalid aggravating factor in Florida, which like Mississippi is a "weighing" state. Justice Kennedy explained *Barclay* as a case in which the Court had "focused on the weight the sentencer gave to an invalid aggravating factor." Therefore, *Barclay* "demonstrates that a reviewing court in a weighing State may not make the automatic assumption that [an invalid aggravating factor] has not infected the weighing process." Since the Mississippi Supreme Court had made an automatic assumption of harmless error in Stringer's case, the Court remanded the case for a constitutional harmless-error analysis or a reweighing in the state judicial system.

Justice Souter, joined by Justices Scalia and Thomas, dissented. He argued that the Court's result was not dictated by precedent, but was rather a "leap of reason" from *Zant* and *Barclay,* and hence a new rule which could not be retroactively applied to Stringer.

By a 6–3 vote, the Supreme Court held in Spaziano v. Florida, 468 U.S. 447 (1984), that there is no constitutional requirement that a jury's recommendation of life imprisonment in a capital case be final so as to preclude the trial judge from overriding the jury's recommendation and imposing the death sentence. Justice Blackmun wrote for the majority. He responded to the defendant's argument that the primary purpose of capital punishment is retribution (i.e., "an expression of community outrage"), which is something a jury is especially well-suited to consider, with the observation that deterrence and incapacitation also are justifications for capital punishment while retribution is an element of all punishment. Furthermore, he reasoned that it is not required that a retributive scheme be administered by a jury. Although 30 of 37 states with capital punishment give the life-or-death decision to a jury, and only 3 of the remaining 7 allow a judge to override a jury's recommendation of life, Justice Blackmun indicated that the Court was "unwilling to say that there is any one right way for a State to set up its capital-sentencing scheme." In affirming the defendant's sentence, Justice Blackmun noted that the trial judge was required to make an independent examination of the evidence, to make his own findings as to aggravating and mitigating circumstances, and to set forth in writing his reasons for imposing a death sentence. The Florida Supreme Court then reviewed this sentence. He found nothing arbitrary or irrational in the punishment imposed.

Justice Stevens, joined by Justices Brennan and Marshall, dissented. He argued that capital punishment "is the one punishment that cannot be prescribed by a rule of law as judges normally understand such rules, but rather is ultimately understood only as an expression of the community's outrage—its sense that an individual has lost his moral entitlement to live" and that "the danger of an excessive response can only be avoided if the decision to impose the death penalty is made by a jury rather than by a single government official."

In Baldwin v. Alabama, 472 U.S. 372 (1985), the Court sustained the validity of a death sentence under a 1975 Alabama statute, later repealed, which required a jury that convicted a defendant of one of a number of specified aggravated circumstances to "fix the punishment at death." Justice Blackmun's majority opinion relied on the fact that the trial judge conducted a hearing after the jury fixed the sentence at which mitigating and aggravating factors were considered, and the judge had the power to impose a life sentence. The Court found that the trial judge was bound to impose a sentence without regard to what the jury had done, and the Court rejected an argument that the judge might have been influenced by the mandatory jury sentence. Justice Stevens, joined by Justices Brennan and Marshall, dissented. He relied upon the arguments he had made in *Spaziano*. Justice Brennan also filed a short dissent.

In a per curiam opinion in Hildwin v. Florida, 490 U.S. 638 (1989), the Court relied upon *Spaziano* to hold that a death penalty was valid where the jury unanimously returned an advisory verdict calling for that penalty, and the trial judge entered an order imposing the penalty and finding four aggravating circumstances. See also Walton v. Arizona, supra (judge can make findings of fact underlying the sentencing determination).

E. IMPROPER JUDICIAL COMMENT

Justice O'Connor wrote for the Court in California v. Ramos, 463 U.S. 992 (1983), as it held, 5–4, that the Constitution does not prohibit a state trial court from telling a jury of a governor's power to commute a life sentence without parole. The majority found that a jury instruction on the governor's power did not invite undue speculation and did not divert the jury's attention from its own responsibilities. And it found no infirmity in the absence of an instruction on the governor's power to commute a death sentence, since such an instruction would be more likely to encourage than to inhibit such a sentence. Justice Marshall, joined by Justice Brennan and in part by Justice Blackmun, and Justices Blackmun and Stevens filed dissenting opinions.

The California Supreme Court had the last word in *Ramos.* In People v. Ramos, 37 Cal.3d 136, 207 Cal.Rptr. 800, 689 P.2d 430 (1984), the court held, 6–1, that the instruction upheld by the United States Supreme Court violated the state constitution because it "invites the jury to second-guess a future Governor's exercise of his constitutional authority and to impose a harsher sentence than it might otherwise impose simply out of fear that the Governor and the parole authorities will make a mistake and will release the defendant while he is still dangerous."

F. IMPROPER PROSECUTORIAL ARGUMENT

Justice Marshall wrote for the Court in Caldwell v. Mississippi, 472 U.S. 320 (1985) as it distinguished *Ramos.* The Court invalidated a conviction because a prosecutor argued to the jury that its decision was not "final" and was automatically reviewable. It concluded that "it is constitutionally impermissible to rest a death sentence on a determination made by a sentencer who has been led to believe that the responsibility for determining the appropriateness of the defendant's death rests elsewhere." The Court found several problems with the prosecutor's argument: the jury might not have understood that appellate review involves "a presumption of correctness"; the jury might have been prone to return a death sentence to "send a message" while believing that an appellate court would set the sentence aside; the jury might have assumed that a life sentence could not be changed to a death sentence on appeal and determined that only by returning a death sentence could it delegate the final decision to an appellate court; and the jury might have underestimated the importance of its role.

Justice Marshall commanded only a plurality for his distinction of *Ramos* as involving an instruction to the jury that "was both accurate and relevant to a legitimate state penological interest—that interest being a concern for the future dangerousness of the defendant should he ever return to society." He found that "the argument at issue here cannot be said to be either accurate or relevant to a valid state penological interest." Justice O'Connor concurred in the judgment on this point. She distinguished *Ramos* on the ground that the prosecutor's remarks in the instant case were inaccurate and also tended to diminish the jury's sense of responsibility. But she added that it would not be impermissible for a state to instruct jurors "on the sentencing procedure, including the existence and limited nature of appellate review."

Justice Rehnquist, joined by Chief Justice Burger and Justice White, dissented. He argued that the Court overstated the seriousness of the prosecutor's comments.

The Court in Sawyer v. Smith, 110 S.Ct. 2822 (1990), found that the rule in *Caldwell* could not be applied to a person whose conviction had become final before the date of that decision. Under Teague v. Lane (Chapter One) if a decision establishes a new rule of law, that rule can not be used to attack a conviction on habeas corpus, subject to two limited exceptions, one of which is that the new rule is a "watershed" rule of criminal procedure necessary to fundamental fairness. The Court in *Sawyer* held that *Caldwell* established a new rule since it was not dictated by then-existing precedent, and that *Caldwell* did not establish a "watershed" rule of criminal procedure necessary to the fundamental fairness of a criminal proceeding.

Justice Kennedy, writing for the majority, agreed with Sawyer that *Caldwell* was designed to ensure accuracy in capital sentencing. But he reasoned that a new rule must also be essential to fundamental fairness in order to be retroactive in habeas cases; and the rule in *Caldwell* did not rise to this level. According to the majority, if promoting accuracy was enough to trigger the *Teague* exception, then all decisions establishing new rules concerning capital sentencing would be retroactive, since "[a]ll of our Eighth Amendment jurisprudence concerning capital sentencing is directed toward the enhancement of reliability and accuracy in some sense."

Justice Marshall dissented in an opinion joined by Justice Brennan, and in large part by Justices Blackmun and Stevens. Justice Marshall argued that the rule in *Caldwell* triggered the *Teague* exception, since it was designed to guarantee the fundamental fairness of a sentencing determination by assuring that the jury will take its obligations seriously.

In Darden v. Wainwright, 477 U.S. 168 (1986), the Court affirmed a murder conviction and death sentence. The prosecutor made a closing argument that suggested that only the death penalty would guarantee that the defendant would not commit another such act, incorporated the use of the word "animal," and included offensive comments regarding an emotional reaction to the case. Although the majority found that the argument "deserves the condemnation it has received from every court to review it," it found that the argument did not deny the defendant a fair trial or sentencing. The majority noted that much of the argument was invited by the defense, the trial judge carefully instructed the jury to decide the case on the basis of the evidence and that arguments were not evidence, and the defendants had the opportunity to argue first and last and to rebut the prosecutor's argument. Justice Blackmun, joined by Justices Brennan, Marshall and Stevens, responded that the majority opinion "reveals a Court willing to tolerate not only imperfection but a level of fairness and reliability so low it should make conscientious prosecutors cringe."

G. VICTIM IMPACT STATEMENTS

Justice Powell wrote for the Court in Booth v. Maryland, 482 U.S. 496 (1987), as it held that the introduction of a victim impact statement, which set forth personal characteristics of two murder victims and the emotional impact of the crime on the family, in the sentencing phase of a capital case violates the Eighth Amendment. The Court reasoned that such a statement creates a constitutionally unacceptable risk that the jury may impose the death penalty in an arbitrary and capricious manner, the material in the statement "may be wholly unrelated to the blameworthiness of a particular defendant," and "it would be difficult—if not impossible—to provide a fair opportunity to rebut such evidence without shifting the focus of the sentencing hearing away from the defendant." It observed in one footnote that information similar to that found in a victim impact statement may be admissible for various reasons at trial.

Justice White, joined by Chief Justice Rehnquist and Justices O'Connor and Scalia, dissented. He argued that "[t]here is nothing aberrant in a juror's inclination to hold a murderer accountable not only for his internal disposition in committing the crime but also for the full extent of the harm he caused," and he stated that "I fail to see why the State cannot, if it chooses, include as a sentencing consideration the particularized harm that an individual's murder causes to the rest of society and in particular to his [the victim's] family."

Justice Brennan wrote for the Court in South Carolina v. Gathers, 490 U.S. 805 (1989), as it relied upon *Booth* to set aside a death penalty on the ground that the prosecutor read to the jury from a religious tract carried by the victim and inferred personal qualities about the victim from both the tract and the voter registration card he carried. Since there was no evidence that the tract or the card were related to the crime, the Court concluded that they shed no light on the defendant's culpability.

Justice White concurred, stating that the result is correct unless *Booth* is overruled. Chief Justice Rehnquist and Justices O'Connor, Kennedy and Scalia dissented reiterating the arguments of the dissent in *Booth*.

Booth and *Gathers* held three categories of evidence categorically inadmissible in the sentencing phase: evidence revealing the individuality of the victim, evidence concerning the impact of the crime on the victims' survivors, and evidence from the victim's family members concerning their opinions about the crime, the defendant, and the appropriate sentence. In Payne v. Tennessee, 111 S.Ct. 2597 (1991), the Court overruled *Booth* and *Gathers* as to the first two categories of evidence; no evidence from the third category was offered in *Payne*.

Chief Justice Rehnquist, writing for six members of the Court, reasoned that "the assessment of harm caused by the defendant as a result of the crime charged has understandably been an important concern of the criminal law." He argued that *Booth* had "unfairly weighted the scales in a capital trial" because "no limits are placed on the relevant mitigating evidence a capital defendant may offer." He concluded that "by turning the victim into a faceless stranger * * * *Booth* deprives the State of the full moral force of its evidence and may prevent the jury from having before it all the information necessary to determine the proper punishment."

The Chief Justice noted that victim impact evidence could occasionally be inflammatory, but that this did not warrant a per se rule of exclusion. He stated that if evidence were so prejudicial as to create a fundamentally unfair proceeding, the Due Process Clause would provide a mechanism for relief.

Chief Justice Rehnquist recognized that adherence to *stare decisis* was the "preferred course," but that *stare decisis* was not as compelling in cases involving procedural and evidentiary rules as in cases involving property and contract rights. He concluded that "*Booth* and *Gathers* were decided by the narrowest of margins, over spirited dissents challenging the basic underpinnings of those decisions," and that "they have been questioned by members of the Court in later decisions, and have defied consistent application by the lower courts."

Justice O'Connor wrote a concurring opinion joined by Justices White and Kennedy. She stated that "murder is the ultimate act of depersonalization

* * * taking away all that is special and unique about the person" and concluded that "the Constitution does not preclude a State from deciding to give some of that back."

Justice Scalia wrote a concurring opinion joined by Justices O'Connor and Kennedy. He concluded that *Booth,* by announcing "a novel rule, contrary to long and unchallenged practice * * * compromised the fundamental values underlying the doctrine of *stare decisis.*"

Justice Souter, joined by Justice Kennedy, wrote a concurring opinion. He noted that much of the evidence excluded by *Booth* at the sentencing proceeding, such as information concerning the victim's occupation and family, will have been admitted at trial for contextual purposes. He criticized *Booth* as promising "more than it can deliver, given the unresolved tension between common evidentiary standards at the guilt phase, and *Booth's* promise of a sentencing determination free from the consideration of facts unknown to the defendant and irrelevant to his decision to kill." He concluded that the only way to enforce the premise of *Booth* would be to empanel a separate jury for sentencing purposes, which would be a major and unwarranted imposition on the States.

Justice Marshall, in his last opinion on the Court, was joined by Justice Blackmun in dissent. He stated that "[p]ower, not reason, is the new currency of this Court's decisionmaking." He contended that "neither the law nor the facts supporting *Booth* and *Gathers* underwent any change in the last four years. Only the personnel of this Court did."

Justice Stevens wrote a separate dissent, restating the arguments in the majority opinions of *Booth* and *Gathers* to the effect that victim impact evidence is irrelevant to the defendant's moral responsibility.

H. INSANE CONVICTS

In Ford v. Wainwright, 477 U.S. 399 (1986), the Court held that a state may not validly execute a prisoner who is insane. Justice Marshall announced the judgment of the Court and delivered an opinion commanding five votes for the first two sections and the votes of Justices Brennan, Blackmun, and Stevens as to the last three sections. In section II, Justice Marshall concluded "that the Eighth Amendment prohibits a State from carrying out a sentence of death upon a prisoner who is insane." He explained that "[w]hether its aim be to protect the condemned from fear and pain without comfort of understanding, or to protect the dignity of society itself from the barbarity of exacting mindless vengeance, the restriction finds enforcement in the Eighth Amendment." In the plurality sections of his opinion, Justice Marshall reasoned that Florida's procedures, under which the Governor appointed three psychiatrists to evaluate the prisoner's sanity and the Governor evaluated their conclusions, were inadequate to assure an accurate determination as to sanity and that the prisoner was entitled to a de novo hearing on sanity in the district court. The state procedures failed to include the prisoner in the process for determining sanity and gave no opportunity for the prisoner to impeach the psychiatrist who examined him.

Justice Powell concurred in the first two sections of the Court's opinion and in the judgment. He found fault with the Florida statute because it did not require the Governor to consider materials submitted by the prisoner, but he disagreed with Justice Marshall's more elaborate procedural requirements. Justice O'Connor, joined by Justice White, dissented from the conclusion that the Eighth Amendment bars execution of an insane prisoner, but found that Florida had created a liberty interest in avoiding execution while incompetent. She agreed with Justice Powell that the failure of Florida to require the Governor to consider material submitted by the prisoner violated basic notions of a fair hearing. Justice Rehnquist, joined by Chief Justice Burger, dissented. He argued that Florida's procedures were "more faithful to both traditional and modern practice" than was the judgment reached by the Court.

I. CLAIMS OF RACIAL DISCRIMINATION

McCleskey v. Kemp, 481 U.S. 279 (1987), raised one of the most controversial capital punishment issues that the Supreme Court faced since it upheld capital sentencing statutes: Does evidence of racial disparity in the implementation of the death penalty invalidate it? By a 5–4 vote, the Court held that there was neither an Eighth Amendment violation nor a denial of equal protection in Georgia's enforcement of the death penalty, even assuming a comprehensive study of capital sentencing in Georgia to be valid.

McCleskey, a black man, was convicted of two counts of armed robbery and of the murder of a white police officer during the course of a robbery. His habeas corpus attack on his conviction relied upon studies of more than 2,000 murder cases in Georgia that purported to show various ways in which the Georgia system of imposing capital punishment produced results that disfavored blacks. Justice Powell's opinion for the Court observed that the study found that "defendants charged with killing white persons received the death penalty in 11% of the cases, but defendants charged with killing blacks received the death penalty in only 1% of the cases." Justice Powell also cited the study's finding that "the death penalty was assessed in 22% of the cases involving black defendants and white victims; 8% of the cases involving white defendants and white victims; 1% of the cases involving black defendants and black victims; and 3% of the cases involving white defendants and black victims." Justice Powell added that the study indicated that "prosecutors sought the death penalty in 70% of the cases involving black defendants and white victims; 32% of the cases involving white defendants and white victims; 15% of the cases involving black defendants and black victims; and 19% of the cases involving white defendants and black victims."

Although the district court found various methodological problems with the study, the court of appeals assumed that it was valid and nonetheless affirmed the denial of habeas relief. The Supreme Court took the same approach and reached the same result.

Justice Powell reasoned that the statistics did not prove any discrimination in McCleskey's case. He observed that "[b]ecause discretion is essential to the criminal justice process, we would demand exceptionally clear proof before we would infer that the discretion has been abused." Finding no such clear proof, Justice Powell concluded that McCleskey had failed to establish an equal protection violation.

Justice Powell also reasoned that McCleskey "cannot base a constitutional claim on an argument that his case differs from other cases in which defendants *did* receive the death penalty," since the state courts found that his sentence was "not disproportionate to other death sentences," and that "absent a showing that the Georgia capital punishment system operates in an arbitrary and capricious manner, McCleskey cannot prove a constitutional violation by demonstrating that other defendants who may be similarly situated did *not* receive the death penalty." Justice Powell described the study of discrimination as showing at most "a discrepancy that appears to correlate with race," and stated that "[a]pparent disparities in sentencing are an inevitable part of our criminal justice system." He voiced concern that a decision for McCleskey might generate attacks on various aspects of sentencing and might result in judges interfering with proper legislative judgments.

Justice Brennan, joined by Justice Marshall and for the most part by Justices Blackmun and Stevens, dissented and argued that McCleskey's death sentence violated the Eighth and Fourteenth Amendments. He relied on the study of Georgia capital punishment to conclude that the jury *more likely than not* would have spared McCleskey's life if his victim had been black. Justice Brennan not only relied on the statistics, but also traced "Georgia's legacy of a race-conscious criminal justice system." He concluded that "we have demanded a uniquely high degree of rationality in imposing the death penalty" and that "[a] capital sentencing scheme in which race more likely than not plays a role does not meet this standard." He identified four reasons in the Court's opinion for rejecting McCleskey's challenge to the Georgia capital punishment system—the desirability of discretion for actors in the system, the existence of safeguards against abuse of discretion, the potential consequences for broader challenges to criminal sentencing, and concern over judicial usurpation of legislative judgments—and found each of them insufficient to overcome the strong showing made by McCleskey.

Justice Blackmun, joined by Justices Marshall and Stevens and for the most part by Justice Brennan, filed another dissenting opinion. His stated intention was to "concentrate on the decisions within the prosecutor's office through which the State decided to seek the death penalty and, in particular, the point at which the State proceeded to the penalty phase after conviction." Using this approach, he found that McCleskey showed he was a member of a distinct class that had been singled out for different treatment, there was a substantial likelihood that his death sentence was due to racial factors, and the process by which the State decided to seek a death penalty in his case was susceptible to abuse. Justice Blackmun found that a prima facie case of discrimination was made and was unrebutted. Although he was sympathetic to the problem of attempting to have juries explain verdicts, he objected to the Court's refusal to require the prosecutor to explain his actions. Justice Blackmun added that if granting McCleskey relief "were to lead to a closer examination of the effects of racial considerations throughout the criminal-justice system, the system, and hence society, might benefit."

Justice Stevens also filed his own dissenting opinion, in which Justice Blackmun joined. He concluded that "[t]he Court's decision appears to be based on a fear that the acceptance of McCleskey's claim would sound the death knell for capital punishment in Georgia," but that such a fear was unfounded. He observed that the study of capital cases demonstrated that there exist categories of extremely serious cases in which capital punishment is consistently sought and imposed and that Georgia could narrow the class of death-eligible defendants to those cases.

J. APPELLATE REVIEW

Justice White wrote for the Court in Pulley v. Harris, 465 U.S. 37 (1984), as it held that its death penalty decisions do not require that a state appellate court compare every case in which capital punishment is imposed with other capital cases in the state to assure that punishment is not disproportionate in a particular case. The majority was willing to assume that there could be a capital sentencing system so lacking in checks on arbitrariness that it would not pass constitutional muster without comparative proportionality review, but it found that California had adequate protections against disproportionate imposition of the death penalty in its requirements that special circumstances be alleged, its specification of aggravating and mitigating circumstances, its provision for jury consideration followed by review by the trial judge who must state a reason for his findings, and its provision for appellate review. Justice Stevens concurred in part and in the judgment. Justice Brennan, joined by Justice Marshall, dissented. See also Walton v. Arizona, supra (proportionality review not required).

In Clemons v. Mississippi, 494 U.S. 738 (1990), the Court held that an appellate court could reweigh the balance of aggravating and mitigating factors when the jury relied on an invalid aggravating circumstance. The jury had found as an aggravating circumstance that Clemons' crime was "especially heinous, atrocious or cruel." An identical aggravating circumstance had been held impermissibly vague in Maynard v. Cartwright, 486 U.S. 356 (1988). Yet, the jury found another aggravating circumstance, i.e. that Clemons committed the crime for pecuniary gain. Justice White, writing for the Court, held that the Mississippi Supreme Court could affirm the capital sentence by reweighing the valid aggravating circumstance against the mitigating evidence presented at the sentencing phase. Justice White stated: "It is a routine task of appellate courts to decide whether the evidence supports a jury verdict and in capital cases in 'weighing' States, to consider whether the evidence is such that the sentencer could have arrived at the death sentence that was imposed."

Justice Blackmun, joined by Justices Brennan, Marshall and Stevens, dissented. He attacked the majority's "bloodless" approach, and argued that appellate courts are incapable of weighing mitigating and aggravating factors on a cold record. Justice Blackmun concluded:

> An appellate court is ill-suited to undertake the task of capital sentencing, not simply because of its general deficiencies as a factfinder, or because the costs of erroneous factfinding are so high, but also because the capital sentencing decision by its very nature is peculiarly likely to turn on considerations that cannot adequately be conveyed through the medium of a written record * * * More than any other decision known to our law, the decision whether to impose the death penalty involves an assessment of the defendant himself, not simply a determination as to the facts surrounding a particular event.

Can the situation in *Clemons* be distinguished from *Spaziano,* where the Court held that the trial court could override the jury's recommendation of a life sentence and impose the death penalty?

The Court in Lewis v. Jeffers, 110 S.Ct. 3092 (1990), held that federal habeas challenges to a state court's application of its own statutory aggravated circumstance are subject to a "rational factfinder" standard of review. Justice O'Connor wrote the opinion for five members of the Court. Justice Blackmun wrote a dissenting opinion joined by Justices Brennan, Marshall, and Stevens.

The Court elaborated on its holdings in *Clemons* and *Lewis* in Parker v. Dugger, 111 S.Ct. 731 (1991). Parker was convicted of two murders arising out of the sale of drugs. The Florida jury found that aggravating circumstances existed, but that mitigating factors outweighed them, and recommended that Parker be sentenced to life imprisonment for both murders. The trial judge, who has ultimate sentencing authority under Florida law (see *Spaziano*), accepted the jury's recommendation for one murder but overrode it for the other, and sentenced Parker to death. The trial judge found six aggravating circumstances, and concluded that there were "no mitigating circumstances that outweigh the aggravating circumstances." The Florida Supreme Court determined that there was insufficient evidence to support two of the aggravating circumstances found by the trial judge. That Court nonetheless affirmed the death sentence, stating that the trial court found "no mitigating circumstances," and that the existence of the four remaining aggravating circumstances adequately supported the jury override. Justice O'Connor, in an opinion for five justices, held that the Florida Supreme Court acted arbitrarily and capriciously by failing to consider Parker's mitigating evidence. The Court found an absence of "meaningful appellate review" in violation of the Eighth Amendment, and vacated the death sentence.

Justice O'Connor applied the rational factfinder standard of *Lewis,* and held that the Florida Supreme Court's ruling did not meet this standard. Justice O'Connor concluded that the State Supreme Court's interpretation of the trial court's decision as having found no mitigating circumstances was "not fairly supported by the record." She reasoned that the trial judge had to find mitigating circumstances in order to accept the jury's recommendation of a life sentence as to one of the murders; if he had found no mitigating circumstances, "he would have had nothing to balance against the aggravating circumstances for either murder;" and since the evidence in mitigation was pertinent to both murders, the judge must have found mitigation as to both.

Justice O'Connor recognized that, under *Clemons,* an appellate court in a weighing state can strike aggravating factors on which the sentencer relied, and yet affirm a death sentence by reweighing the evidence or conducting a harmless error analysis. However, the majority held that the Florida Supreme Court did not conduct a reweighing consistent with *Clemons,* since it did not consider and explicitly balance the mitigating circumstances; it erroneously proceeded on the assumption that the trial judge had found no mitigating circumstances. For the same reason, the Florida Supreme Court did not conduct a proper harmless error analysis; that could only have been done by considering the mitigating circumstances. Justice O'Connor stated:

> Following *Clemons,* a reviewing court * * * may reweigh the evidence or conduct a harmless error analysis based on what the sentencer actually found. What the Florida Supreme Court could not do, but what it did, was to ignore the evidence of mitigating circumstances in the record and misread the trial judge's findings regarding mitigating circumstances, and affirm the sentence based on a mischaracterization of the trial judge's findings.

Justice O'Connor concluded that the Florida Supreme Court's reliance on "nonexistent findings" deprived Parker of "meaningful appellate review" and of "the individualized treatment to which he is entitled under the Constitution." The Court stressed that it would have been a different case if the appellate court had conducted its own independent factual inquiry, or had relied on findings actually made by the trial judge.

Justice White, joined by Chief Justice Rehnquist and Justices Scalia and Kennedy, dissented. Justice White accused the majority of "second-guessing" state supreme courts in violation of the rational factfinder standard of *Lewis.* To Justice White, the trial court's finding or lack thereof as to mitigating circumstances was ambiguous, and the Florida Supreme Court could rationally conclude that the trial judge had found no mitigating circumstances. Justice White also criticized the majority for its "creation of a new and unexplained 'meaningful appellate review' standard to apply in habeas proceedings." According to Justice White, the majority's holding "suggests that the Eighth Amendment will have been violated any time a federal court decides that a state appellate court has committed an error of state law in a capital case or has not rigorously followed some state appellate procedure. The Court points to no cases supporting this radical revision of our Eighth Amendment jurisprudence."

Can the defendant waive his right to appeal a death sentence? In Whitmore v. Arkansas, 495 U.S. 149 (1990), Ronald Simmons waived his right to direct appeal of his conviction and death sentence. The trial court conducted a hearing and found that Simmons was competent to make such a waiver. Whitmore, a fellow death-row inmate, sought to intervene in Simmons' proceeding both individually and as "next friend" of Simmons. The Arkansas courts denied Whitmore's petition. In the Supreme Court, Whitmore contended that the State was required by the Eighth Amendment to conduct appellate review of Simmons' conviction.

Chief Justice Rehnquist, writing for the majority, held that Whitmore lacked standing to bring this claim. According to the Court, Whitmore had no standing to bring the claim on his own behalf, since any injury to him from Simmons' execution would be too attenuated. The Court rejected the argument that an exception to traditional standing doctrine should be made for capital cases: "The short answer to this suggestion is that the requirement of an Art. III 'case or controversy' is not merely a traditional 'rule or practice,' but rather is imposed directly by the Constitution."

The majority also rejected Whitmore's claim of standing as "next friend" of Simmons. The Chief Justice stated that the "next friend" doctrine, found in federal common law, was premised on the inability of the real party in interest to appear on his own behalf. Since Simmons had been found competent to waive his right to appeal, the "next friend" doctrine could not apply.

Justice Marshall, joined by Justice Brennan, dissented. Justice Marshall argued that the limitations on the "next friend" doctrine should be relaxed for death penalty cases; otherwise the Court would "permit an unconstitutional execution on the basis of a common law doctrine that the Court has the power to amend."

K. PREDICTIONS OF DANGEROUSNESS

In Barefoot v. Estelle, 463 U.S. 880 (1983), the Court held that predictions of future behavior by psychiatrists were not too speculative or unreliable to be used in capital cases and that psychiatrists could offer expert opinions in response to hypothetical questions without examining a defendant. Justice Blackmun, joined by Justices Brennan and Marshall, dissented.

L. STAYS OF EXECUTION

The Supreme Court also addressed in *Barefoot* the problem of when stays of execution should be granted in habeas corpus proceedings initiated by prisoners facing execution. The Court concluded that a court of appeals had examined the merits of Barefoot's constitutional claim and found it lacking in substance when it denied a stay and that the court of appeals had not erred. Justice White's opinion for the Court recommended procedural guidelines for lower courts asked to stay executions. It suggested that certificates of probable cause to appeal from denials of habeas corpus relief should not be granted simply because a nonfrivolous claim is raised, and that a substantial showing must be made that a federal right has been denied; that, when a certificate is granted, a habeas petitioner must be afforded a full opportunity to address the merits of his claim and the court of appeals must decide the merits; that courts of appeals may adopt expedited procedures, but should inform petitioners and their counsel that the merits may be disposed of when a stay is requested; that district courts may expedite consideration of successive petitions, even though those petitions may raise new or different claims; and that stays are not automatic when petitions for certiorari are sought from the Supreme Court. Justice Stevens concurred in the judgment. Justice Marshall, joined by Justice Brennan, dissented.

In a per curiam opinion, the Court in Delo v. Stokes, 495 U.S. 320 (1990), held that the district court abused its discretion in issuing a stay of execution pending consideration of a fourth federal habeas petition. The Court concluded that the successive petition failed to satisfy the *Barefoot* requirement of providing "substantial grounds upon which relief might be granted." The Court found an abuse of the writ because the claims asserted in the fourth habeas petition were "not novel and could have been developed long before this last minute application for stay of execution." Justice Kennedy wrote a concurring opinion joined by Chief Justice Rehnquist and Justice Scalia.

Justice Brennan wrote a dissenting opinion joined by Justices Marshall and Blackmun. The dissenters argued that the Court had not given sufficient deference to the discretion of the courts below.

In the Supreme Court, a stay of execution requires the vote of five Justices, while a grant of a petition for certiorari requires four. Because of this anomaly a person was executed after the Court had decided to hear his claim. See Hamilton v. Collins, 111 S.Ct. 244 (1990) (Brennan, J., dissenting from denial of stay of execution).

The Court expressed its frustration with delayed executions in In re Blodgett, 112 S.Ct. 674 (1992). Campbell was convicted of multiple murders in

1982 and sentenced to death. His first habeas petition was filed in 1985, and proceedings in that matter were completed when the Court denied certiorari in 1988. Campbell filed a second habeas petition in March, 1989, which the district court dismissed within days. The Ninth Circuit Court of Appeals granted Campbell an indefinite stay of execution, pending appeal. The case was argued and submitted in June, 1989. As of January, 1992, no decision had been announced and the stay was still in effect. The State of Washington petitioned the Supreme Court for a writ of mandamus, ordering the Ninth Circuit to issue its opinion. The Court refused to issue the writ on the ground that the State should have first petitioned the Ninth Circuit for an expedited decision. But the Court had harsh words for what it considered an inordinately delayed execution. It stated that "the State of Washington has sustained severe prejudice" which has prevented the State "from exercising its sovereign power to enforce the criminal law." The Court noted that expedited review of Campbell's second habeas petition was warranted under *Barefoot.* It denied the writ "without prejudice to the right of the State to again seek mandamus relief or to request any other extraordinary relief by motion or petition if unnecessary delays or unwarranted stays occur in the panel's disposition of the matter."

For an example of a death penalty review significantly more expedited than that in *Blodgett,* see Clark v. Collins, 112 S.Ct. 925 (1992) (Stevens, J., dissenting from denial of stay of execution in a first habeas petition, after the petition was denied by both the district court and the court of appeals within 33 hours of its filing).

M. NON-HOMICIDE CASES

All of the preceding cases were homicide cases. Between *Gregg* et al. and *Lockett*, the Court held (again without a majority opinion) in Coker v. Georgia, 433 U.S. 584 (1977), that rape not resulting in death could not be punished by death. Justices Stewart, White, Blackmun and Stevens took this view in a plurality opinion, arguing that the death penalty would be excessive for rape. Justice Powell agreed with the result of the case, but was not willing to say that no rape would warrant imposition of the death penalty. Justices Brennan and Marshall adhered to their *Furman* positions. The Chief Justice, joined by Justice Rehnquist, dissented. They emphasized the facts of the particular case, including the offender's prior record, and the seriousness of the crime of rape. ("Rape thus is not a crime 'light years' removed from murder in the degree of its heinousness; it certainly poses a serious potential danger to the life and safety of innocent victims—apart from the devastating psychic consequences.") Compare the result in the non-capital case of Harmelin v. Michigan, supra.

N. SPECIAL PROCEDURES

In addition to suggesting that capital punishment may be confined to homicide cases and to statutes giving the judge or jury not only guidance on implementation of the death penalty but also full access to evidence of mitigating circumstances, the Court has established another rule for death cases. In Gardner v. Florida, 430 U.S. 349 (1977), Justice Stevens authored a plurality opinion, joined by Justices Stewart and Powell, holding that it was a denial of due process for a trial judge in Florida to impose a death sentence in partial reliance on a presentence report, portions of which were not disclosed to counsel for the parties. Although the trial judge made the findings required by statute, did not comment on the confidential portion of the report, and did not indicate that there was anything important in this portion, the plurality distinguished Williams v. New York on several grounds: "It is first significant that in *Williams* the material facts concerning the defendant's background which were contained in the presentence report were described in detail by the trial judge in open court. * * * It is also significant that Mr. Justice Black's opinion recognized that the passage of time justifies a re-examination of capital sentencing procedures." The opinion went on to explain that death was now recognized as "a different kind of punishment from any other which may be imposed in this country," and that "it is now clear that the sentencing process * * * must satisfy the requirements of the Due Process Clause." The plurality concluded that "[w]ithout full disclosure of the basis for the death sentence, the Florida capital-sentencing procedure would be subject to the defects which resulted in the holding of unconstitutionality in Furman v. Georgia." The Chief Justice concurred in the judgment without opinion. Justice White also concurred in the judgment, preferring to rely on the Eighth Amendment, not the due process clause. Justice Blackmun concurred in the result with a short paragraph indicating that he felt bound to do so by *Woodson* and *Roberts*. Justices Brennan and Marshall agreed that disclosure of the report was required, but remained committed to the idea that no death penalty would pass muster. Justice Rehnquist dissented in one paragraph. See also Green v. Georgia, 442 U.S. 95 (1979) (holding that defendant had due process right to offer codefendant's confession in capital sentencing hearing).

The Court in Lankford v. Idaho, 111 S.Ct. 1723 (1991) relied on *Gardner* to strike down a death sentence on the ground that defendant had not received adequate notice that the judge might sentence him to death. Justice Stevens, writing for a five-person majority, held that the Due Process Clause imposes stringent notice requirements in capital cases, in order to guarantee that a defendant has a meaningful opportunity to argue against a sentence of death. The "unique circumstance" creating the due process violation in *Lankford* was the trial court's presentencing order requiring the State to advise the court and the defendant of its intent to seek a death sentence. The State responded that it would not recommend death. At the subsequent sentencing hearing, neither the State nor the defense mentioned the death penalty. The judge nonetheless imposed a sentence of death.

Justice Stevens found that the trial court's presentencing order "was comparable to a pretrial order limiting the issues to be tried." Justice Stevens recognized that, under Idaho law, the trial judge has sole responsibility for capital sentencing, and is not bound by the State's decision not to seek the death penalty. The majority stated nonetheless that the judge's "silence following the State's response to the presentencing order had the practical effect of concealing from the parties the principal issue to be decided at the hearing." Justice Stevens concluded that the defendant's "lack of adequate notice that the judge was contemplating the imposition of the death sentence created an impermissible risk that the adversary process may have malfunctioned in this case." The Court noted as in *Gardner* that its special procedural requirements were limited to capital cases.

Justice Scalia, joined by Chief Justice Rehnquist and Justices White and Souter, dissented. Justice Scalia argued that the Idaho statutory scheme, authorizing the judge to impose a death sentence *sua sponte*, gave Lankford sufficient notice of the possibility of a death sentence. He further contended that the presentencing order relied on by the majority was meant only to bind the State in its intentions, and not to bind the judge. Justice Scalia accused the majority of adopting "the topsy-turvy principle that the capital defendant cannot be presumed to know the law, but must be presumed to have detrimentally relied upon a misunderstanding of the law or a misinterpretation of the judge."

Thus, capital cases are treated as being an order of magnitude different from other serious cases. Are you persuaded that they are? No matter what your position on this question, ask yourself how much protection the defendant charged with a capital sanction really gets from the Supreme Court's opinions. How much protection is there when proof of aggravating factors beyond a reasonable doubt is not required in Florida, when "aggravating factors" can be cast in the form they take in Texas, when the defendant has the burden of establishing mitigating factors in Arizona, when a jury recommendation of life imprisonment is not binding in Florida on a trial judge, and when a jury is left free in Georgia and Florida once it finds an aggravating factor to return a death sentence regardless of how it comes out on mitigating factors? Are you satisfied with the procedures? If not, are there any procedures that would satisfy you? If you are satisfied, or if you can imagine a set of procedures that might satisfy you in capital cases, would you extend some of the same procedures to non-capital cases?

O. EXECUTION OF JUVENILE OFFENDERS

A plurality of the Supreme Court held in Thompson v. Oklahoma, 487 U.S. 815 (1988), that it would be cruel and unusual punishment to execute a defendant convicted of a brutal murder when the defendant was only 15 years old at the time of the murder. Justice Stevens, joined by Justices Brennan, Marshall and Blackmun, found a near universal trend among the states to treat a person under 16 as a minor for several important purposes. The plurality noted, for example, that all states have enacted legislation designating the maximum age for juvenile court jurisdiction at no less than 16. The four Justices focused on a number of factors supporting their conclusion that there was a national consensus against executing youths who commit murder before reaching the age of 16: the states that have set a minimum age for execution have chosen 16 at a minimum, the pattern of past jury sentences in the United States demonstrates that the community has rejected the death penalty for 15-year-olds, the Anglo-American tradition does not support the death penalty for youths under 16, and it is understood that a normal 15-year-old is not prepared to assume the full responsibilities of an adult.

Justice O'Connor provided the fifth vote to overturn Thompson's death sentence. She stated that "[a]lthough I believe that a national consensus forbidding the execution of any person for a crime committed before the age of 16 very likely does exist, I am reluctant to adopt this conclusion as a matter of constitutional law without better evidence than we now possess." Noting that "[t]he history of the death penalty instructs that there is danger in inferring a settled societal consensus from statistics like those relied on in this case," Justice O'Connor confined her concurrence to the particular facts of the case, and observed that Oklahoma enacted a statute authorizing capital punishment for murder without setting any minimum age. She concluded that the state's separate determination that 15–year-old defendants may be tried as adults did not demonstrate that the state had focused on the minimum age for execution, and stated that "there is a considerable risk that the Oklahoma legislature either did not realize that its actions would have the effect of rendering 15–year-old defendants death-eligible or did not give the question the serious consideration that would have been reflected in the explicit choice of some minimum age for death-eligibility." Thus, she stated "[i]n this unique situation, I am prepared to conclude that petitioner and others who were below the age of 16 at the time of their offense may not be executed under the authority of a capital punishment statute that specifies no minimum age at which the commission of a capital crime can lead to the offender's execution."

Justice Scalia, joined by Chief Justice Rehnquist and Justice White, dissented. Although he agreed that an automatic death penalty for individuals younger than 16 when they committed their crimes would be opposed by a national consensus, and he stated that he might agree that a person under 16 at the time of a crime is entitled to a rebuttable presumption of insufficient maturity and responsibility to justify execution, Justice Scalia could not agree that "there is a national consensus that no criminal so much as one day under 16, after individuated consideration of his circumstances, including the overcoming of a presumption that he should not be tried as an adult, can possibly be deemed mature and responsible enough to be punished with death for any crime." Justice Scalia cited Blackstone's Commentaries on the Law of England (1769) for the two propositions concerning the common law: (1) a person above the age of 7 could be executed, and (2) a 15–year-old was above the age (14) up to which there was a rebuttable presumption of incapacity to commit a capital or other felony. He observed that the trend among the states was to lower rather than to raise the age of juvenile criminal responsibility, and noted that most states with capital punishment have not set a minimum age for the death penalty. Justice Scalia recognized that the statistics on executions demonstrate that society has always agreed that executions of 15–year-olds should be rare, but reasoned that this agreement did not support a conclusion that no person under 16 ever could be sufficiently mature and responsible to be executed for murder.

Finally, Justice Scalia rejected on several grounds the approach taken by Justice O'Connor. He argued as follows: there is no consensus against the execution of a 15–year-old no matter what the circumstances of a murder; if there were a doubt about this, even if Oklahoma were to make it absolutely clear that it wished to execute 15–year-olds, one state's action would not disprove the national consensus; the death sentence imposed in this case was neither an accident nor unknown to the people of Oklahoma; and Justice O'Connor's opinion would require Oklahoma to legislate in a manner not required by the Constitution and open the door to invalidation of legislation because of uncertainty concerning the existence of a national consensus.

Justice Kennedy did not participate in the case.

A majority of the Supreme Court held in Stanford v. Kentucky, 492 U.S. 361 (1989), that the imposition of capital punishment on an individual for a crime committed at age 16 or 17 years of age does not constitute cruel and unusual punishment. Justice Brennan, joined by Justices Marshall, Blackmun, and Stevens dissented.

P. FIRST AMENDMENT CONSIDERATIONS

In Dawson v. Delaware, 112 S.Ct. 1093 (1992), the Court held that where associational activity is not relevant to capital sentencing, its admission violates the First Amendment. At Dawson's capital sentencing hearing, the prosecutor introduced evidence showing that the defendant was a member of the Aryan Brotherhood, a white supremacist prison gang. Chief Justice Rehnquist, writing for an eight-person majority, noted that Dawson's right to associate with the Aryan Brotherhood was constitutionally protected. He rejected Dawson's broad argument that the Constitution forbids the consideration in sentencing of any evidence of First Amendment activity, noting that in Barclay v. Florida, 463 U.S. 939 (1983), the Court permitted consideration of "the elements of racial hatred" in the defendant's crime. The Chief Justice concluded, however, that the mere evidence of Dawson's association with the Aryan Brotherhood was not relevant to any issue in his sentencing proceeding. Unlike the defendant in *Barclay* whose crime was racially motivated, Dawson was convicted of murdering a white woman.

The state in *Dawson* proffered several ways in which the membership in the Aryan Brotherhood was relevant to sentencing issues, but the Chief Justice rejected all of them. According to the Court, the membership was not relevant to any aggravating circumstance, since the prosecution did not prove that the Aryan Brotherhood had committed or endorsed any unlawful or violent acts. Mere evidence of association was therefore not relevant to future dangerousness. Nor was the evidence relevant to prove the defendant's "character." The Chief Justice reasoned that "Delaware might have avoided this problem if it had presented evidence showing more than mere abstract beliefs on Dawson's part, but on the present record one is left with the feeling that the Aryan Brotherhood evidence was employed simply because the jury would find these beliefs morally reprehensible."

Finally, the Court rejected the argument that Aryan Brotherhood membership was relevant to rebut Dawson's mitigating evidence, which consisted of testimony about his kindness to family members, good time credits while in prison, and enrollment in drug and alcohol programs. The Chief Justice recognized that the State was entitled to "broad" rebuttal, but concluded that the mere association with a white supremacist group was in no way responsive to the mitigating evidence. The Court left open the question of whether the wrongful admission of the Aryan Brotherhood evidence was harmless error.

Justice Blackmun concurred, and stressed that "because of the potential chilling effect that consideration of First Amendment activity at sentencing might have, there is a substantial argument that harmless-error analysis is not appropriate."

Justice Thomas dissented, claiming that even the mere association with a white supremacist prison group was relevant to Dawson's sentencing. He argued that membership in a prison gang was proof of an aggravating factor, even if the prosecution did not present proof of any unlawful gang activity. He reasoned that "a jury reasonably could conclude from Dawson's membership in a prison gang that he had engaged in some sort of forbidden activities while in prison." According to Justice Thomas, it was common knowledge that prison gangs do not "meet every month to discuss 'The Critique of Pure Reason' * * *. Gangs affiliate for mutual support, but not the kind contemplated by the National Labor Relations Act." Justice Thomas also contended that Dawson's membership in a prison gang was relevant to future dangerousness because it tended to establish that he "has not been a well-behaved and well-adjusted prisoner." He concluded that in light of the defendant's broad right to present all evidence in mitigation, the Court had imposed "a double standard for determining relevance: a standard easy for defendants to satisfy, but difficult for prosecutors." Is *Dawson* inconsistent with Payne v. Tennessee, where the Court upheld the admission of victim impact statements on the ground that it was unfair to allow the defendant to show that he was a real person, while not allowing the prosecutor to show that the victim was a real person as well?

Chapter Twelve

DOUBLE JEOPARDY

I. INTRODUCTION

The double jeopardy clause of the Fifth Amendment provides: "[N]or shall any person be subject for the same offense to be twice put in jeopardy of life or limb."[1] Made applicable to the states in Benton v. Maryland, 395 U.S. 784 (1969), the clause provides three basic related protections: "It protects against a second prosecution for the same offense after acquittal. It protects against a second prosecution for the same offense after conviction. And it protects against multiple punishments for the same offense." North Carolina v. Pearce, 395 U.S. 711, 717 (1969). As you will see, interpretation and application of the double jeopardy clause have resulted in a careful accommodation between the finality interests of the defendant and the government's interest in having one fair opportunity to prosecute and convict.

Like many of the constitutional provisions which have been examined previously, the double jeopardy clause is not easily understood. Although its history suggests some answers to a few questions, most hard questions were not debated, perhaps not even contemplated, during the drafting and discussion of the Bill of Rights and the Fourteenth Amendment. The historical material is no less satisfactory, however, than the language of the Amendment itself. When the words of the double jeopardy clause are parsed, it appears that the language offers few clues as to the intent of its drafters.

II. THE EFFECT OF AN ACQUITTAL

Traditionally, the government has been unable to initiate a second prosecution on the theory that an acquittal was mistaken, and it has been forbidden to appeal from an acquittal or legal rulings that produced the acquittal, even if the rulings underlying an acquittal were erroneous.[2] And if a jury acquits a defendant, the trial judge cannot grant the government a second trial, even if he believes the jury erred badly. The government cannot appeal from an

1. The Double Jeopardy Clause originated with the common-law pleas of autrefois acquit, autrefois convict and pardon. The clause adopts the traditional language of "jeopardy." For a history of the Double Jeopardy Clause, see J. Sigler, Double Jeopardy (1969); United States v. Wilson, 420 U.S. 332, 339–42 (1975).

2. When the prosecution is appealing a question of law that will not result in a retrial after a finding of innocence, an appeal may not be barred by the double jeopardy clause. Whether an appeal will be permitted depends on local law.

acquittal, even if it has a reasonable claim that the jury would have convicted but for errors committed by the trial judge, since the defendant's interest in finality is held to preclude a retrial. See Sanabria v. United States, 437 U.S. 54 (1978); Fong Foo v. United States, 369 U.S. 141 (1962). In *Sanabria*, for example, discussed infra, the trial court erroneously excluded evidence of the alleged crime and then granted an acquittal based on the insufficiency of the remaining evidence. The double jeopardy clause barred retrial.

In view of the preclusive effect of an acquittal on future adjudication, it is important to know what constitutes an acquittal and when the government can appeal an adverse ruling or dismissal of a case on the ground that the trial court did something other than acquit the defendant. The Supreme Court considered these questions in United States v. Scott. Note carefully the Court's discussion of the history of the Double Jeopardy Clause and the basic double jeopardy principles in Part II of the opinion. The mistrial cases noted in Part III are discussed infra.

UNITED STATES v. SCOTT

Supreme Court of the United States, 1978.
437 U.S. 82.

MR. JUSTICE REHNQUIST delivered the opinion of the Court.

On March 5, 1975, respondent, a member of the police force in Muskegon, Mich., was charged in a three-count indictment with distribution of various narcotics. Both before his trial in the United States District Court for the Western District of Michigan, and twice during the trial, respondent moved to dismiss the two counts of the indictment which concerned transactions that took place during the preceding September, on the ground that his defense had been prejudiced by preindictment delay. At the close of all the evidence, the court granted respondent's motion. Although the court did not explain its reasons for dismissing the second count, it explicitly concluded that respondent had "presented sufficient proof of prejudice with respect to Count I." The court submitted the third count to the jury, which returned a verdict of not guilty.

The Government sought to appeal the dismissals of the first two counts to the United States Court of Appeals for the Sixth Circuit. That court, relying on our opinion in United States v. Jenkins, 420 U.S. 358 (1975),[3] concluded that any further prosecution of respondent was barred by the Double Jeopardy Clause of the Fifth Amendment, and therefore dismissed the appeal. The Government has sought review in this Court only with regard to the dismissal of the first count. * * * We now reverse.

I

The problem presented by this case could not have arisen during the first

3. In *Jenkins*, the defendant was prosecuted for failure to report for induction into military service. The defendant waived a jury and was tried by a judge who filed written findings of fact and conclusions of law. The judge ordered the indictment dismissed on the ground that the draft board had not proceeded properly. The Supreme Court held that double jeopardy barred retrial (and therefore the government could not appeal because the trial judge had not indicated whether he would have convicted but for the legal point about the draft board's procedures); thus, further factfinding would be required and would violate the double jeopardy clause. In *Wilson*, cited in Section I of the opinion, the Court held that when the trial judge set aside a jury verdict of guilty by dismissing an indictment because of delay, the government could appeal, because the appellate court could simply reinstate the jury verdict without subjecting the defendant to additional factfinding.

century of this Court's existence. The Court has long taken the view that the United States has no right of appeal in a criminal case, absent explicit statutory authority. United States v. Sanges, 144 U.S. 310 (1892). Such authority was not provided until the enactment of the Criminal Appeals Act, Act of Mar. 2, 1907, ch. 2564, 34 Stat. 1246, which permitted the United States to seek a writ of error in this Court from any decision dismissing an indictment on the basis of "the invalidity, or construction of the statute upon which the indictment is founded." Our consideration of Government appeals over the ensuing years ordinarily focused upon the intricacies of the Act and its amendments.[a] In 1971, however, Congress adopted the current language of the Act, permitting Government appeals from any decision dismissing an indictment, "except that no appeal shall lie where the double jeopardy clause of the United States Constitution prohibits further prosecution." 18 U.S.C.A. § 3731. Soon thereafter, this Court remarked in a footnote with more optimism than prescience that "[t]he end of our problems with this Act is finally in sight." United States v. Weller, 401 U.S. 254, 255 n. 1 (1971). For in fact the 1971 amendment did not end the debate over appeals by the Government in criminal cases; it simply shifted the focus of the debate from issues of statutory construction to issues as to the scope and meaning of the Double Jeopardy Clause.

In our first encounter with the new statute, we concluded that "Congress intended to remove all statutory barriers to Government appeals and to allow appeals whenever the Constitution would permit." United States v. Wilson, 420 U.S. 332, 337 (1975). Since up to that point Government appeals had been subject to statutory restrictions independent of the Double Jeopardy Clause, our previous cases construing the statute proved to be of little assistance in determining when the Double Jeopardy Clause of the Fifth Amendment would prohibit further prosecution. A detailed canvass of the history of the double jeopardy principles in English and American law led us to conclude that the Double Jeopardy Clause was primarily "directed at the threat of multiple prosecutions," and posed no bar to Government appeals "where those appeals would not require a new trial." We accordingly held in *Jenkins*, that, whether or not a dismissal of an indictment after jeopardy had attached amounted to an acquittal on the merits, the Government had no right to appeal, because "further proceedings of some sort, devoted to the resolution of factual issues going to the elements of the offense charged, would have been required upon reversal and remand."[b]

a. A thorough account of the enactment and development of the Act is set out in Mr. Justice Harlan's opinion for the Court in United States v. Sisson, 399 U.S. 267, 291–296 (1970).

b. The rule established in *Wilson* and *Jenkins* was later described in the following terms:

"[D]ismissals (as opposed to mistrials) if they occurred at a stage of the proceeding after which jeopardy had attached, but prior to the factfinder's conclusion as to guilt or innocence, were final so far as the accused defendant was concerned and could not be appealed by the Government because retrial was barred by double jeopardy. This made the issue of double jeopardy turn very largely on temporal considerations—if the Court granted an order of dismissal during the factfinding stage of the proceedings, the defendant could not be reprosecuted, but if the dismissal came later, he could." Lee v. United States, 432 U.S. 23, 36 (1977) (Rehnquist, J., concurring).

[In *Lee*, a defendant, after the prosecutor's opening statement, moved to dismiss an information because it failed to allege specific intent. Following a two hour trial, the court noted that the defendant had been proved guilty beyond a reasonable doubt, but granted the motion to dismiss the information. Subsequently, the defendant was charged again with the same crime and convicted. The Court held that retrial was not barred by the

If *Jenkins* is a correct statement of the law, the judgment of the Court of Appeals relying on that decision, as it was bound to do, would in all likelihood have to be affirmed. Yet, though our assessment of the history and meaning of the Double Jeopardy Clause in *Wilson, Jenkins,* and Serfass v. United States, 420 U.S. 377 (1975),[4] occurred only three Terms ago, our vastly increased exposure to the various facets of the Double Jeopardy Clause has now convinced us that *Jenkins* was wrongly decided. It placed an unwarrantedly great emphasis on the defendant's right to have his guilt decided by the first jury empaneled to try him so as to include those cases where the defendant himself seeks to terminate the trial before verdict on grounds unrelated to factual guilt or innocence. We have therefore decided to overrule *Jenkins*, and thus to reverse the judgment of the Court of Appeals in this case.[5]

II

The origin and history of the Double Jeopardy Clause are hardly a matter of dispute. The constitutional provision had its origin in the three common-law pleas of *autrefois acquit, autrefois convict,* and pardon. These three pleas prevented the retrial of a person who had previously been acquitted, convicted, or pardoned for the same offense. As this Court has described the purpose underlying the prohibition against double jeopardy:

> "The underlying idea, one that is deeply ingrained in at least the Anglo-American system of jurisprudence, is that the State with all its resources and power should not be allowed to make repeated attempts to convict an individual for an alleged offense, thereby subjecting him to embarrassment, expense and ordeal and compelling him to live in a continuing state of anxiety and insecurity, as well as enhancing the possibility that even though innocent he may be found guilty." *Green* [v. United States, 355 U.S. 184] at 187–188.

These historical purposes are necessarily general in nature, and their application has come to abound in often subtle distinctions which cannot by any means all be traced to the original three commonlaw pleas referred to above.

Part of the difficulty arises from the development of other protections for criminal defendants in the years since the adoption of the Bill of Rights. At the time the Fifth Amendment was adopted, its principles were easily applied, since most criminal prosecutions proceeded to final judgment, and neither the United States nor the defen-

double jeopardy clause. The Court reasoned that the trial court granted the motion to dismiss in contemplation of a second prosecution, and that it was permissible under the circumstances to delay a ruling on the motion to dismiss until the trial was completed.]

4. In *Serfass*, the Court held that the government could appeal a pre-trial dismissal of an indictment, because the defendant, having never been subjected to factfinding on the guilt and innocence question, could be tried if the trial judge erred in dismissing the indictment.

5. The appellate scheme in the federal courts is described in this opinion. Note that there can be no appeal in circumstances where new trial court proceedings would be necessary for there to be a valid conviction and those proceedings are barred by the double jeopardy clause. For purposes of this chapter, it is not critical to master the federal statute governing appeals; it is sufficient to remember that when the Supreme Court holds that there can be no appeal because of the jeopardy clause, the Supreme Court is saying that there can be no further trial proceedings. The Court would say the same thing if the government tried to bring a second action instead of appealing, and the defendant complained.

Arizona v. Manypenny, 451 U.S. 232 (1981), holds that in a state criminal proceeding removed to a federal court (see 28 U.S.C. § 1442, removal by Federal officers), a state may appeal under 28 U.S.C. § 1291 a district court's entry of judgment of acquittal following a jury verdict of guilty when state law would have permitted such an appeal in state court.

dant had any right to appeal an adverse verdict. See Act of Sept. 24, 1789, ch. 20, § 22, 1 Stat. 84. The verdict in such a case was unquestionably final, and could be raised in bar against any further prosecution for the same offense.

* * * It was not until 1889 that Congress permitted criminal defendants to seek a writ of error in this Court, and then only in capital cases. Act of Feb. 6, 1889, ch. 113, § 6, 25 Stat. 656.[c] Only then did it become necessary for this Court to deal with the issues presented by the challenge of verdicts on appeal.

And, in the very first case presenting the issues, United States v. Ball, 163 U.S. 662 (1896), the Court established principles that have been adhered to ever since. Three persons had been tried together for murder; two were convicted, the other acquitted. This Court reversed the convictions, finding the indictment fatally defective, Ball v. United States, 140 U.S. 118 (1891), whereupon all three defendants were tried again. This time all three were convicted and they again sought review here. This Court held that the Double Jeopardy Clause precluded further prosecution of the defendant who had been *acquitted* at the original trial but that it posed no such bar to the prosecution of those defendants who had been *convicted* in the earlier proceeding. The Court disposed of their objection almost peremptorily:

> "Their plea of former conviction cannot be sustained, because upon a writ of error sued out by themselves the judgment and sentence against them were reversed, and the indictment ordered to be dismissed. * * * [I]t is quite clear that a defendant, who procures a judgment against him upon an indictment to be set aside, may be tried anew upon the same indictment, or upon another indictment, for the same offence of which he had been convicted." 163 U.S., at 671–672.

Although *Ball* firmly established that a successful appeal of a conviction precludes a subsequent plea of double jeopardy, the opinion shed no light on whether a judgment of acquittal could be reversed on appeal consistently with the Double Jeopardy Clause. Because of the statutory restrictions upon Government appeals in criminal cases, this Court in the years after *Ball* was faced with that question only in unusual circumstances, such as were present in Kepner v. United States, 195 U.S. 100 (1904). That case arose out of a criminal prosecution in the Philippine Islands, to which the principles of the Double Jeopardy Clause had been expressly made applicable by Act of Congress. Although the defendant had been acquitted in his original trial, traditional Philippine procedure provided for a trial *de novo* upon appeal. This Court, in reversing the resulting conviction, remarked:

> "The court of first instance, having jurisdiction to try the question of the guilt or innocence of the accused, found Kepner not guilty; to try him again upon the merits, even in an appellate court, is to put him a second time in jeopardy for the same offense * * *" Id., at 133.

More than 50 years later, in Fong Foo v. United States, 369 U.S. 141 (1962), this Court reviewed the issuance of a writ of mandamus by the Court of Appeals for the First Circuit instructing a District Court to vacate certain judgments of acquittal. Although indicating its agreement with the Court of Appeals

c. Two years later, review was provided for all "infamous" crimes. Act of Mar. 3, 1891, ch. 517, § 5, 26 Stat. 827.

that the judgments had been entered erroneously, this Court nonetheless held that a second trial was barred by the Double Jeopardy Clause. Only last Term, this Court relied upon these precedents in United States v. Martin Linen Supply Co., 430 U.S. 564 (1977), and held that the Government could not appeal the granting of a motion to acquit pursuant to Fed.Rule Crim.Proc. 29 where a second trial would be required upon remand.[6] The Court, quoting language in *Ball* stated: "Perhaps the most fundamental rule in the history of double jeopardy jurisprudence has been that '[a] verdict of acquittal * * * could not be reviewed, on error or otherwise, without putting [a defendant] twice in jeopardy, and thereby violating the Constitution."

These, then, at least, are two venerable principles of double jeopardy jurisprudence. The successful appeal of a judgment of conviction, on any ground other than the insufficiency of the evidence to support the verdict, Burks v. United States, 437 U.S. 1, poses no bar to further prosecution on the same charge. A judgment of acquittal, whether based on a jury verdict of not guilty or on a ruling by the court that the evidence is insufficient to convict, may not be appealed and terminates the prosecution when a second trial would be necessitated by a reversal.[d] What may seem superficially to be a disparity in the rules governing a defendant's liability to be tried again is explainable by reference to the underlying purposes of the Double Jeopardy Clause. As *Kepner* and *Fong Foo* illustrate, the law attaches particular significance to an acquittal. To permit a second trial after an acquittal, however mistaken the acquittal may have been, would present an unacceptably high risk that the Government, with its vastly superior resources, might wear down the defendant so that "even though innocent he may be found guilty." *Green*, 355 U.S., at 188. On the other hand, to require a criminal defendant to stand trial again after he has successfully invoked a statutory right of appeal to upset his first conviction is not an act of governmental oppression of the sort against which the Double Jeopardy Clause was intended to protect. * * *

III

Although the primary purpose of the Double Jeopardy Clause was to protect the integrity of a final judgment, this Court has also developed a body of law guarding the separate but related interest of a defendant in avoiding multiple prosecutions even where no final determination of guilt or innocence has been made. Such interests may be involved in two different situations: the first, in which the trial judge declares a mistrial; the second, in which the trial judge terminates the proceedings favorably to the defendant on a basis not related to factual guilt or innocence.

A

When a trial court declares a mistrial, it all but invariably contemplates that

6. In this case the jury was hopelessly deadlocked and was discharged. Subsequently, the trial judge entered a judgment of acquittal. The Court held that any retrial would violate the double jeopardy clause.

d. In *Jenkins* we had assumed that a judgment of acquittal could be appealed where no retrial would be needed on remand:

> "When this principle is applied to the situation where the jury returns a verdict of guilt but the trial court thereafter enters a judgment of acquittal, an appeal is permitted. In that situation a conclusion by an appellate court that the judgment of acquittal was improper does not require a criminal defendant to submit to a second trial; the error can be corrected on remand by the entry of a judgment on the verdict." 420 U.S., at 365.

Despite the Court's heavy emphasis on the finality of an acquittal in *Martin Linen* and Sanabria v. United States, 437 U.S. 54, neither decision explicitly repudiates this assumption.

the prosecutor will be permitted to proceed anew notwithstanding the defendant's plea of double jeopardy. See Lee v. United States, 432 U.S. 23, 30 (1977). Such a motion may be granted upon the initiative of either party or upon the court's own initiative. The fact that the trial judge contemplates that there will be a new trial is not conclusive on the issue of double jeopardy; in passing on the propriety of a declaration of mistrial granted at the behest of the prosecutor or on the court's own motion, this Court has balanced "the valued right of a defendant to have his trial completed by the particular tribunal summoned to sit in judgment on him," Downum v. United States, 372 U.S. 734, 736 (1963), against the public interest in insuring that justice is meted out to offenders.

Our very first encounter with this situation came in United States v. Perez, 9 Wheat. 579 (1824), in which the trial judge had on his own motion declared a mistrial because of the jury's inability to reach a verdict. The Court said that trial judges might declare mistrials "whenever, in their opinion, taking all the circumstances into consideration, there is a manifest necessity for the act, or the ends of public justice would otherwise be defeated." In our recent decision in Arizona v. Washington, 434 U.S. 497 (1978), we reviewed this Court's attempts to give content to the term "manifest necessity." That case, like *Downum*, supra, arose from a motion of the prosecution for a mistrial, and we noted that the trial court's discretion must be exercised with a careful regard for the interests first described in United States v. Perez.

Where, on the other hand, a *defendant* successfully seeks to avoid his trial prior to its conclusion by a motion for mistrial, the Double Jeopardy Clause is not offended by a second prosecution. * * * Such a motion by the defendant is deemed to be a deliberate election on his part to forego his valued right to have his guilt or innocence determined before the first trier of fact. * * * [7]

B

We turn now to the relationship between the Double Jeopardy Clause and reprosecution of a defendant who has successfully obtained not a mistrial but a termination of the trial in his favor before any determination of factual guilt or innocence. Unlike the typical mistrial, the granting of a motion such as this obviously contemplates that the proceedings will terminate then and there in favor of the defendant. The prosecution, if it wishes to reinstate the proceedings in the face of such a ruling, ordinarily must seek reversal of the decision of the trial court.

The Criminal Appeals Act, 18 U.S.C.A. § 3731, as previously noted, makes appealability of a ruling favorable to the defendant depend upon whether further proceedings upon reversal would be barred by the Double Jeopardy Clause. *Jenkins* held that, regardless of the character of the midtrial termination, appeal was barred if "further proceedings of some sort, devoted to the resolution of factual issues going to the elements of the offense charged, would have been required upon reversal and remand." However, only last Term, in *Lee*, supra, the Government was permitted to institute a second prosecution after a midtrial dismissal of an indictment. The Court found the circumstances presented by that case "functionally indistinguishable from a declaration of mistrial." Thus, *Lee* demonstrated that, at least in some cases, the dismissal of an indictment

7. But see the limited exception to this principle, established in the later case of Oregon v. Kennedy, discussed infra.

may be treated on the same basis as the declaration of a mistrial.

In the present case, the District Court's dismissal of the first count of the indictment was based upon a claim of preindictment delay and not on the court's conclusion that the Government had not produced sufficient evidence to establish the guilt of the defendant. Respondent Scott points out quite correctly that he had moved to dismiss the indictment on this ground prior to trial, and that had the District Court chosen to grant it at that time the Government could have appealed the ruling under our holding in Serfass v. United States, 420 U.S. 377 (1975). He also quite correctly points out that jeopardy had undeniably "attached" at the time the District Court terminated the trial in his favor; since a successful Government appeal would require further proceedings in the District Court leading to a factual resolution of the issue of guilt or innocence, *Jenkins* bars the Government's appeal. However, our growing experience with Government appeals convinces us that we must re-examine the rationale of *Jenkins* in light of *Lee, Martin Linen*, and other recent expositions of the Double Jeopardy Clause.

IV

Our decision in *Jenkins* was based upon our perceptions of the underlying purposes of the Double Jeopardy Clause * * *. Upon fuller consideration, we are now of the view that this language from *Green* [see Part II of the opinion, supra.], while entirely appropriate in the circumstances of that opinion,[8] is not a principle which can be expanded to include situations in which the defendant is responsible for the second prosecution. It is quite true that the Government with all its resources and power should not be allowed to make repeated attempts to convict an individual for an alleged offense. This truth is expressed in the three common-law pleas of *autrefois acquit, autrefois convict*, and pardon, which lie at the core of the area protected by the Double Jeopardy Clause. As we have recognized * * * a defendant once acquitted may not be again subjected to trial without violating the Double Jeopardy Clause.

But that situation is obviously a far cry from the present case, where the Government was quite willing to continue with its production of evidence to show the defendant guilty before the jury first empaneled to try him, but the defendant elected to seek termination of the trial on grounds unrelated to guilt or innocence. This is scarcely a picture of an all-powerful state relentlessly pursuing a defendant who had either been found not guilty or who had at least insisted on having the issue of guilt submitted to the first trier of fact. It is instead a picture of a defendant who chooses to avoid conviction and imprisonment, not because of his assertion that the Government has failed to make out a case against him, but because of a legal claim that the Government's case against him must fail even though it might satisfy the trier of fact that he was guilty beyond a reasonable doubt.

We have previously noted that "the trial judge's characterization of his own action cannot control the classification of the action." Despite respondent's contentions, an appeal is not barred simply because a ruling in favor of a defendant "is based upon facts outside the face of the indictment," or because it "is granted on the ground * * * that

8. The *Green* Court held that a conviction on a lesser included offense was the equivalent of an acquittal on the greater offense and barred retrial on the greater offense even if the defendant appealed and obtained a reversal of the conviction on the lesser offense. Of course, the defendant could be prosecuted again for the lesser crime of which he was convicted.

the defendant simply cannot be convicted of the offense charged." Rather, a defendant is acquitted only when "the ruling of the judge, whatever its label, actually represents a resolution [in the defendant's favor], correct or not, of some or all of the factual elements of the offense charged." Where the court, before the jury returns a verdict, enters a judgment of acquittal pursuant to Fed.Rule Crim.Proc. 29, appeal will be barred only when "it is plain that the District Court * * * evaluated the Government's evidence and determined that it was legally insufficient to sustain a conviction."

* * *

We think that in a case such as this the defendant, by deliberately choosing to seek termination of the proceedings against him on a basis unrelated to factual guilt or innocence of the offense of which he is accused, suffers no injury cognizable under the Double Jeopardy Clause if the Government is permitted to appeal from such a ruling of the trial court in favor of the defendant. We do not thereby adopt the doctrine of "waiver" of double jeopardy rejected in *Green*. Rather, we conclude that the Double Jeopardy Clause, which guards against Government oppression, does not relieve a defendant from the consequences of his voluntary choice. In *Green* the question of the defendant's factual guilt or innocence of murder in the first degree was actually submitted to the jury as a trier of fact; in the present case, respondent successfully avoided such a submission of the first count of the indictment by persuading the trial court to dismiss it on a basis which did not depend on guilt or innocence. He was thus neither acquitted nor convicted, because he himself successfully undertook to persuade the trial court not to submit the issue of guilt or innocence to the jury which had been empaneled to try him.

* * * [W]here the defendant, instead of obtaining a reversal of his conviction on appeal, obtains the termination of the proceedings against him in the trial court without any finding by a court or jury as to his guilt or innocence [h]e has not been "deprived" of his valued right to go to the first jury; only the public has been deprived of its valued right to "one complete opportunity to convict those who have violated its laws." Arizona v. Washington, 434 U.S., at 509. No interest protected by the Double Jeopardy Clause is invaded when the Government is allowed to appeal and seek reversal of such a midtrial termination of the proceedings in a manner favorable to the defendant.[e]

* * *

MR. JUSTICE BRENNAN, with whom MR. JUSTICE WHITE, MR. JUSTICE MARSHALL, and MR. JUSTICE STEVENS join, dissenting.

* * *

[T]he Court today overrules the principle recognized in *Jenkins* and *Lee.* While reaffirming that the Government

e. We should point out that it is entirely possible for a trial court to reconcile the public interest in the Government's right to appeal from an erroneous conclusion of law with the defendant's interest in avoiding a second prosecution. In *Wilson*, supra, the court permitted the case to go to the jury, which returned a verdict of guilty, but it subsequently dismissed the indictment for preindictment delay on the basis of evidence adduced at trial. More recently in United States v. Ceccolini, 435 U.S. 268 (1978), we described similar action with approval: "The District Court had sensibly first made its finding on the factual question of guilt or innocence, and then ruled on the motion to suppress; a reversal of these rulings would require no further proceedings in the District Court, but merely a reinstatement of the finding of guilt."

We, of course, do not suggest that a midtrial dismissal of a prosecution, in response to a defense motion on grounds unrelated to guilt or innocence, is necessarily improper. Such rulings may be necessary to terminate proceedings marred by fundamental error. But where a defendant prevails on such a motion, he takes the risk that an appellate court will reverse the trial court.

may not appeal from judgments of "acquittal" when reversals would require new trials, the Court holds that appeals by the United States will lie from all other final judgments favorable to the accused. The Court implements this new rule by fashioning a more restrictive definition of "acquittal" than heretofore followed—i.e., "a resolution, correct or not, of some or all of the factual elements of the offense"—and holds, without explanation, that, under the restrictive definition, respondent was not "acquitted" when the District Judge concluded that the facts adduced at trial established that unjustifiable and prejudical preindictment delay gave respondent a complete defense to the charges contained in count one.

I dissent. I would not overrule the rule announced in *Jenkins* and reaffirmed in *Lee*. This principle is vital to the implementation of the values protected by the Double Jeopardy Clause; indeed, it follows necessarily from the very rule the Court today reaffirms. The Court's attempt to draw a distinction between "true acquittals" and other final judgments favorable to the accused, quite simply, is unsupportable in either logic or policy. Equally fundamental, the decision today indefensibly adopts an overly restrictive definition of "acquittal." Its definition, moreover, in sharp contrast to the rule of *Jenkins*, is incapable of principled application. * * *

* * *

A

While the Double Jeopardy Clause often has the effect of protecting the accused's interest in the finality of particular favorable determinations, this is not its objective. For the Clause often permits Government appeals from final judgments favorable to the accused. See United States v. Wilson, 420 U.S. 332 (1975) (whether or not final judgment was an acquittal, Government may appeal if reversal would not necessitate a retrial). The purpose of the Clause, which the Court today fails sufficiently to appreciate, is to protect the accused against the agony and risks attendant upon undergoing more than one criminal trial for any single offense. * * *

* * *

B

The whole premise for today's retreat from *Jenkins* and *Lee*, of course, is the Court's new theory that a criminal defendant who seeks to avoid conviction on a "ground unrelated to factual innocence" somehow stands on a different constitutional footing from a defendant whose participation in his criminal trial creates a situation in which a judgment of acquittal has to be entered. This premise is simply untenable. The rule prohibiting retrials following acquittals does not and could not rest on a conclusion that the accused was factually innocent in any meaningful sense. If that were the basis for the rule, the decisions that have held that even egregiously erroneous acquittals preclude retrials, see, e.g., Fong Foo v. United States, supra (acquittal entered after three of many prosecution witnesses had testified); Sanabria v. United States, were erroneous.

It is manifest that the reasons that bar a retrial following an acquittal are equally applicable to a final judgment entered on a ground "unrelated to factual innocence." The heavy personal strain of the second trial is the same in either case. So too is the risk that, though innocent, the defendant may be found guilty at a second trial. If the appeal is allowed in either situation, the Government will, following any reversal, not only obtain the benefit of the favorable appellate ruling but also be permitted to shore up any other weak points of its case and obtain all the other advantages at the second trial that the Double Jeopardy Clause was designed to forbid.

Moreover, the Government's interest in retrying a defendant simply cannot vary depending on the ground of the final termination in the accused's favor. I reject as plainly erroneous the Court's suggestion that final judgments not based on innocence deprive the public of "its valued right to 'one complete opportunity to convict those who have violated its laws,'" and therefore differ from "true acquittals." The Government has the same "complete opportunity" in either situation by virtue of its participation as an adversary at the criminal trial.

[The dissenters also objected to the difficulties in applying the Court's approach. They questioned the difference between a dismissal based on the defenses of insanity and entrapment and a dismissal for pre-indictment delay. The decision, in their view, needlessly complicates an area of law which was "crystal clear."]

Problem

In Sanabria v. United States, 437 U.S. 54 (1978), the defendant was charged with the federal offense of conducting an illegal gambling business, in violation of the law of the place where the business was located—in this case, Massachusetts law. The single count indictment alleged that Sanabria and his co-defendants engaged in both numbers betting and betting on horse races. At the end of the defense presentation, the judge concluded that the Massachusetts statute cited in the indictment did not prohibit numbers betting and excluded all evidence of numbers betting. This was error, since the government only had to show that the gambling operation violated state law. Once this was demonstrated, any evidence that showed participation in the gambling operation was admissible. The error led the trial judge to erroneously grant a defense motion for an acquittal, because there was insufficient evidence to connect the defendant with the horse-betting activities, as opposed to the overall gambling business. Seeking a new trial only on the part of the indictment related to numbers betting, the government appealed, urging that the district court's action should be construed as a dismissal of the numbers betting part of the case, rather than as an acquittal. The Court of Appeals accepted this characterization and remanded for a new trial because Sanabria voluntarily had moved to terminate the trial.

The Supreme Court reversed and held that a new trial was barred. It held that the district court acquitted the defendant, and that the action could not be characterized as a dismissal, since the trial judge believed that he was construing the indictment and ruling on the merits. Moreover, the indictment alleged one offense, with two theories of liability: numbers betting and horse betting. Thus, the Court said that even if the action could be characterized as a "dismissal," a retrial would subject the defendant to two trials for the same offense, after the defendant had been acquitted of the offense.

Assume that after the government offered its evidence, the following colloquy took place: the trial judge asked: "Do you claim that the defendant was involved in horse betting?" The prosecutor answered: "No, only in numbers betting, but as part of the same gambling operation as the horse betting." The trial judge said: "Well, you have not charged an offense under the statute then, because there can be no offense without a violation of a specific state gambling statute by this defendant himself. Thus, I am dismissing the indictment because there is no offense charged."

Would a reversal and a retrial be permissible if an appellate court concluded that an offense was properly charged? See generally Cooper, Government Appeals in Criminal Cases: The 1978 Decisions, 81 F.R.D. 539 (1979). For a thoughtful and scholarly discussion of double jeopardy problems generally, see Westen & Drubel, Toward a General Theory of Double Jeopardy, 1978 Sup.Ct.Rev. 81.

Note

If a trial judge enters a judgment of acquittal, before the jury reaches a verdict, that determination is final. United States v. Martin Linen Supply, 430 U.S. 564 (1977), so indicates. In fact, it holds that a judgment of acquittal following a mistrial is as final as a directed verdict.[9]

In Smalis v. Pennsylvania, 476 U.S. 140 (1986), Justice White wrote for a unanimous Court as it found that a husband and wife, charged with various crimes in connection with a fire in a building they owned that killed two tenants, were acquitted for double jeopardy purposes when a state trial judge sustained a demurrer at the close of the prosecution's case in a bench trial. Since the state trial judge determined that the state's evidence was insufficient to establish factual guilt, the double jeopardy clause barred a post-judgment appeal by the government. Even if the state trial court was incorrect, jeopardy had attached and was terminated by the acquittal. The Court held that an acquittal would be found not only where the judge assessed the evidence as a matter of credibility and found it insufficient, but also where the judge determined that evidence was insufficient "as a matter of law."

One extremely interesting question concerning the effect of a ruling is disposed of in three paragraphs in Rodrigues v. Gudeman, 794 F.2d 1458 (9th Cir.1986). A defendant charged with rape and sodomy was acquitted by a trial judge on the basis of an insanity defense. The prosecution appealed, however, and the state supreme court held that the insanity question should have been given to a jury. The trial judge then granted a motion for reconsideration and vacated the acquittal. The federal court of appeals rejected the defendant's habeas corpus claim that he could not be tried for the crimes in light of his acquittal, finding that the defendant was not in jeopardy because the judge was not the appropriate finder of fact. Does this seem consistent with the Supreme Court's rulings that a judgment of acquittal entered by a trial judge prior to a jury's verdict bars retrial?

If a judge waits until after a jury convicts to enter a judgment of acquittal, may the government appeal that ruling? Footnote d in *Scott* suggests that an appeal in those circumstances is permissible. The lower courts have agreed. See cases cited in United States v. Blasco, 581 F.2d 681, 683 at n. 2 (7th Cir. 1978). See also United States v. Maddox, 944 F.2d 1223 (1991).

Consider footnote e of the Court's opinion in *Scott*. Does it suggest that it is best for a trial judge to allow a case to be decided by a jury before she rules on a

9. The Court noted that Rule 29 is similar to the directed verdict mechanism in Fong Foo v. United States, 369 U.S. 141 (1962). Compare *Martin Linen Supply* with United States v. Sanford, 429 U.S. 14 (1976) (no double jeopardy problem where trial court dismissed indictment after mistrial was declared, even though based on evidence presented at trial). For a criticism of *Martin Linen* as a constitutional decision, see Cooper, Government Appeals in Criminal Cases: The 1978 Decisions, 81 F.R.D. 539, 541–42 (1979). See also United States v. Maddox, 944 F.2d 1223 (6th Cir.1991) (no double jeopardy violation where the trial judge granted a post-trial motion for acquittal, then changed his mind and reinstated the conviction; *Martin Linen* distinguished as a case in which the jury never reached a verdict, and therefore further proceedings would have been necessary).

motion to dismiss on grounds unrelated to guilt or innocence? This approach would benefit both the defendant and the government, would it not?

United States v. Steed, 646 F.2d 136 (4th Cir. 1981), recognizes, albeit reluctantly, that the government may appeal a judgment of acquittal entered after the jury returns a verdict, but holds that the standard of review is "nonreview" when the trial judge has found the evidence to be insufficient. The court also refers to this standard as "absolute deference" which is designed to enhance the power of the trial judge to protect criminal defendants from the possibility of jury abuses or excesses.

Scott indicates that a defendant is not necessarily placed twice in jeopardy because he is subjected to two trials.[10] Sometimes a second trial is permissible, and sometimes it is not. Drawing lines between permissible and impermissible attempts by the government to litigate a case that has been litigated once previously is the Court's task under the double jeopardy clause. *Scott* indicates that the Court has not found it to be easy.

Which approach—that of *Jenkins* or that of *Scott*—makes more sense? *Jenkins* focused on whether further factfinding would be necessary in a case. *Scott* focuses on whether there has been some determination by judge or jury relating to factual guilt or innocence. *Jenkins* attempted to prevent repetitive litigation. *Scott* attempts to protect an unimpaired statement by the trial court (judge or jury) that the defendant is not guilty. Which is the more justifiable protection?

In thinking about this, it might be helpful to first consider what happens when the defendant is convicted in the trial court and appeals.

III. THE CONVICTED DEFENDANT APPEALS

When a defendant successfully appeals a conviction, may he be retried? United States v. Ball, 163 U.S. 662 (1896), mentioned in *Scott* and discussed in the following case, established that a retrial following a reversal of a conviction is permissible. In the next case, the Court considered whether a defendant may be retried when the reversal was based on insufficiency of the evidence rather than on trial error.

10. The Court has recognized the importance of not making a defendant with a good double jeopardy claim stand trial twice. In Abney v. United States, 431 U.S. 651 (1977), for example, the Court held that under 18 U.S.C.A. § 1291 a defendant could appeal a denial of a pre-trial motion to dismiss on double jeopardy grounds.

In Justices v. Lydon, 466 U.S. 294 (1984), the Court reaffirmed *Abney* and emphasized that a defendant who has a claim that a second trial would place him in jeopardy twice is entitled to seek federal habeas corpus relief to bar the second trial. In a case such as Lydon's, which arose in state court, the defendant must exhaust state remedies before seeking federal relief. The Court found that Lydon had done so and therefore that he was entitled to federal review of his double jeopardy claim. On the merits, the Court rejected the claim.

Abney led the Court to conclude in Richardson v. United States, 468 U.S. 317 (1984), that a defendant could appeal the denial of his motion for a judgment of acquittal where a jury indicated that it was unable to agree on a verdict and the trial judge granted a mistrial and scheduled a second trial. Justice Rehnquist's opinion for the Court reasoned that the first trial was over and the defendant was not seeking to interrupt or delay that trial by filing his appeal. The opinion reiterated that an immediate appeal requires a showing of a colorable, non-frivolous claim. Justice Stevens was the only dissenter on the appealability issue. On the merits, the Court held that a defendant is not placed in jeopardy twice when a mistrial is declared due to a genuinely deadlocked jury and he is retried, irrespective of the sufficiency of the evidence in the first proceeding.

A. INSUFFICIENT EVIDENCE TO CONVICT

BURKS v. UNITED STATES

Supreme Court of the United States, 1978.
437 U.S. 1.

MR. CHIEF JUSTICE BURGER delivered the opinion of the Court.

We granted certiorari to resolve the question of whether an accused may be subjected to a second trial when conviction in a prior trial was reversed by an appellate court solely for lack of sufficient evidence to sustain the jury's verdict.

I

Petitioner Burks was tried in the United States District Court for the crime of robbing a federally insured bank by use of a dangerous weapon * * *. Burks' principal defense was insanity. To prove this claim petitioner produced three expert witnesses who testified, albeit with differing diagnoses of his mental condition, that he suffered from a mental illness at the time of the robbery, which rendered him substantially incapable of conforming his conduct to the requirements of the law. In rebuttal the Government offered the testimony of two experts, one of whom testified that although petitioner possessed a character disorder, he was not mentally ill. The other prosecution witness acknowledged a character disorder in petitioner, but gave a rather ambiguous answer to the question of whether Burks had been capable of conforming his conduct to the law. Lay witnesses also testified for the Government, expressing their opinion that petitioner appeared to be capable of normal functioning and was sane at the time of the alleged offense.

Before the case was submitted to the jury, the court denied a motion for a judgment of acquittal. The jury found Burks guilty as charged. Thereafter, he filed a timely motion for a new trial, maintaining, among other things, that "[t]he evidence was insufficient to support the verdict." The motion was denied by the District Court, which concluded that petitioner's challenge to the sufficiency of the evidence was "utterly without merit."

On appeal petitioner narrowed the issues by admitting the affirmative factual elements of the charge against him, leaving only his claim concerning criminal responsibility to be resolved. With respect to this point, the Court of Appeals agreed with petitioner's claim that the evidence was insufficient to support the verdict and reversed his conviction. * * *

[The Court of Appeals, rather than terminating the case, remanded to the District Court for a determination of whether a directed verdict of acquittal should be entered or a new trial ordered.]

* * *

[In Part II of the opinion, the Court examined several prior decisions—Bryan v. United States, 338 U.S. 552 (1950); Sapir v. United States, 348 U.S. 373 (1955); Yates v. United States, 354 U.S. 298 (1957); Forman v. United States, 361 U.S. 416 (1960)—which indicated that a defendant who requests a new trial, as did Burks, may be required to stand trial even when his conviction is reversed for failure of proof.]

III

It is unquestionably true that the Court of Appeals' decision "represente[d] a resolution, correct or not, of some or all of the factual elements of the offense charged." United States v. Martin Linen Supply Co., 430 U.S. 564, 571 (1977). By deciding that the Government had failed to come forward with sufficient proof of petitioner's capacity to be responsible for criminal acts, that court was clearly saying that Burks' criminal culpability had not been established. If the District Court had so held in the first instance, as the reviewing court said it should have done, a judgment of acquittal would have been entered and, of course, petitioner could not be retried for the same offense. Consequently, as Mr. Justice Douglas correctly perceived in *Sapir*, it should make no difference that the *reviewing* court, rather than the trial court, determined the evidence to be insufficient. The appellate decision unmistakably meant that the District Court had erred in failing to grant a judgment of acquittal. To hold otherwise would create a purely arbitrary distinction between those in petitioner's position and others who would enjoy the benefit of a correct decision by the District Court.

The Double Jeopardy Clause forbids a second trial for the purpose of affording the prosecution another opportunity to supply evidence which it failed to muster in the first proceeding. This is central to the objective of the prohibition against successive trials. * * *

Nonetheless, as the discussion in Part II, supra, indicates, our past holdings do not appear consistent with what we believe the Double Jeopardy Clause commands. A close reexamination of those precedents, however, persuades us that they have not properly construed the Clause, and accordingly should no longer be followed.

* * *

[Reconsideration of the prior cases involves an examination of United States v. Ball, 163 U.S. 662 (1896), which permitted a new trial when the accused successfully sought review of a conviction.]

* * *

Ball came before the Court twice, the first occasion being on writ of error from federal convictions for murder. On this initial review, those defendants who had been found guilty obtained a reversal of their convictions due to a fatally defective indictment. On remand after appeal, the trial court dismissed the flawed indictment and proceeded to retry the defendants on a new indictment. They were again convicted and the defendants came once more to this Court, arguing that their second trial was barred because of former jeopardy. The Court rejected this plea in a brief statement * * *. The reversal in *Ball* was therefore based not on insufficiency of evidence but rather on trial error, i.e., failure to dismiss a faulty indictment. Moreover, the cases cited as authority by *Ball* were ones involving trial errors.

We have no doubt that *Ball* was correct in allowing a new trial to rectify *trial error* * * *.

Various rationales have been advanced to support the policy of allowing retrial to correct trial error,[a] but in our view the most reasonable justification is that advanced by *Tateo,*[11] supra, 377 U.S., at 466:

> "It would be a high price indeed for society to pay were every accused granted immunity from punishment

a. It has been suggested, for example, that an appeal from a conviction amounts to a "waiver" of double jeopardy protections, or that the appeal somehow continues the jeopardy which attached at the first trial.

11. United States v. Tateo, 377 U.S. 463 (1964) (holding that a defendant could be retried after pleading guilty in the middle of a trial following a statement by the trial judge as to the sentence he would impose if the defendant were convicted and then setting aside the guilty plea).

because of any defect sufficient to constitute reversible error in the proceedings leading to conviction."

* * * In short, reversal for trial error, as distinguished from evidentiary insufficiency, does not constitute a decision to the effect that the government has failed to prove its case. As such, it implies nothing with respect to the guilt or innocence of the defendant. Rather, it is a determination that a defendant has been convicted through a judicial process which is defective in some fundamental respect, e.g., incorrect receipt or rejection of evidence, incorrect instructions, or prosecutorial misconduct. When this occurs, the accused has a strong interest in obtaining a fair readjudication of his guilt free from error, just as society maintains a valid concern for insuring that the guilty are punished. * * *

The same cannot be said when a defendant's conviction has been overturned due to a failure of proof at trial, in which case the prosecution cannot complain of prejudice, for it has been given one fair opportunity to offer whatever proof it could assemble.[b] Moreover, such an appellate reversal means that the government's case was so lacking that it should not have even been *submitted* to the jury. Since we necessarily afford absolute finality to a jury's *verdict* of acquittal—no matter how erroneous its decision—it is difficult to conceive how society has any greater interest in retrying a defendant when, on review, it is decided as a matter of law that the jury could not properly have returned a verdict of guilty.

The importance of a reversal on grounds of evidentiary insufficiency for purposes of inquiry under the Double Jeopardy Clause is underscored by the fact that a federal court's role in deciding whether a case should be considered by the jury is quite limited. Even the trial court, which has heard the testimony of witnesses firsthand, is not to weigh the evidence or assess the credibility of witnesses when it judges the merits of a motion for acquittal. The prevailing rule has long been that a district judge is to submit a case to the jury if the evidence and inferences therefrom most favorable to the prosecution would warrant the jury's finding the defendant guilty beyond a reasonable doubt. Obviously a federal appellate court applies no higher a standard; rather, it must sustain the verdict if there is substantial evidence, viewed in the light most favorable to the Government, to uphold the jury's decision. While this is not the appropriate occasion to re-examine in detail the standards for appellate reversal on grounds of insufficient evidence, it is apparent that such a decision will be confined to cases where the prosecution's failure is clear. Given the requirements for entry of a judgment of acquittal, the purposes of the Clause would be negated were we to afford the government an opportunity for the proverbial "second bite at the apple."

In our view it makes no difference that a defendant has sought a new trial as one of his remedies, or even as the sole remedy. It cannot be meaningfully said that a person "waives" his right to a judgment of acquittal by moving for a new trial. * * * Since we hold today that the Double Jeopardy Clause precludes a second trial once the reviewing court has found the evidence legally insufficient, the only "just" remedy available for that court is the direction of a judgment of acquittal. To the extent that our prior decisions suggest that by moving for a new trial, a defendant waives his right to a judgment of

b. In holding the evidence insufficient to sustain guilt, an appellate court determines that the prosecution has failed to prove guilt beyond a reasonable doubt.

acquittal on the basis of evidentiary insufficiency, those cases are overruled.

* * *

MR. JUSTICE BLACKMUN took no part in the consideration or decision of this case.

B. INSUFFICIENT EVIDENCE AND TRIAL COURT ERROR

In Greene v. Massey, 437 U.S. 19 (1978), the per curiam opinion of the Florida Supreme Court and the concurrence of three judges did not make clear whether the reversal was for insufficiency of the evidence or trial error. The United States Supreme Court remanded the case to the Court of Appeals for reconsideration consistent with *Burks*, making clear that *Burks* applied to state cases. The Court noted that the concurring state court justices may have thought that once inadmissible hearsay evidence was discounted, there was insufficient evidence to permit the jury to convict.

Does *Burks* apply when the evidence actually introduced at trial is sufficient to sustain the convictions, but the legally competent evidence (i.e. excluding from consideration evidence erroneously admitted by the trial court) is insufficient? The Court in Lockhart v. Nelson, 488 U.S. 33 (1988) answered in the negative. The prosecutor used Nelson's prior convictions at a sentencing hearing, to prove that Nelson should receive an enhanced sentence as a habitual offender. This was error under state law as to one conviction, because Nelson had been pardoned. On habeas review, the district court found the sentence invalid. The State announced its intention to resentence Nelson as a habitual offender, by using a prior conviction not offered or admitted at the initial sentencing hearing. Nelson interposed a claim of double jeopardy. Chief Justice Rehnquist, writing for the Court, concluded that the *Burks* exception was inapplicable and that Nelson's resentencing would not implicate Double Jeopardy concerns.

> *Burks* was based on the view that an appellate court's reversal for insufficiency of the evidence is in effect a determination that the government's case against the defendant was so lacking that the trial court should have entered a judgment of acquittal, rather than submitting the case to the jury. * * *
>
> *Burks* was careful to point out that a reversal based solely on evidentiary insufficiency has fundamentally different implications * * * than a reversal based on such ordinary 'trial errors' as the 'incorrect receipt or rejection of evidence.' While the former is in effect a finding 'that the government has failed to prove its case' against the defendant, the latter 'implies nothing with respect to the guilt or innocence of the defendant,' but is simply 'a determination that [he] has been convicted through a judicial *process* which is defective in some fundamental respect.'
>
> It appears to us to be beyond dispute that this is a situation described in *Burks* as reversal for 'trial error' * * * It is quite clear from our opinion in *Burks* that a reviewing court must consider all of the evidence admitted by the trial court in deciding whether retrial is permissible under the Double Jeopardy Clause—indeed, that is the *ratio decidendi* of *Burks* * * *. The basis for the *Burks* exception to the general rule is that a reversal for insufficiency of the evidence should be treated no differently than a trial court's granting a judgment of acquittal at the close of all the evidence. A trial court in passing on such a motion considers all the evidence it has admitted, and to make the

analogy complete it must be this same quantum of evidence which is considered by the reviewing court. * * *

Had the defendant offered evidence at the sentencing hearing to prove that the conviction had become a nullity by reason of the pardon, the trial judge would presumably have allowed the prosecutor an opportunity to offer evidence of another prior conviction to support the habitual offender charge. Our holding today thus merely recreates the situation that would have been obtained if the trial court had excluded the evidence of the conviction because of the showing of a pardon.

Justice Marshall, joined by Justices Brennan and Blackmun, dissented. Justice Marshall argued that if the State had produced a "blank piece of paper" at the sentencing hearing "no one would doubt that Arkansas had produced insufficient evidence and that the Double Jeopardy Clause barred retrial." He concluded that "there is no constitutionally significant difference between that hypothetical and this case."

How did the Court know that the State would have introduced another prior conviction if the judge had properly excluded the inadmissible conviction at Nelson's sentencing hearing? If the State is prepared to introduce the admissible conviction on resentencing, why didn't the State introduce that conviction the first time around? Is it possible that the State only became aware of this further conviction *after* Nelson was sentenced? Consider the explanation in State v. Boone, 284 Md. 1, 393 A.2d 1361 (1978):

> The prosecution, we believe, in proving its case is entitled to rely upon the correctness of the rulings of the court and proceed accordingly. If the evidence offered by the State is received after challenge and is legally sufficient to establish the guilt of the accused, the State is not obligated to go further and adduce additional evidence that would be, for example, cumulative. Were it otherwise, the State, to be secure, would have to consider every ruling by the court on the evidence to be erroneous and marshall and offer every bit of relevant and competent evidence. The practical consequences of this would seriously affect the orderly administration of justice, if for no other reason, because of the time which would be required to prepare for trial and try the case. Furthermore, if retrial were precluded because discounting erroneously admitted evidence results in evidentiary insufficiency, there would be no opportunity to correct an error by the court as distinguished from the mistaken belief by the prosecution that it had proved its case.

Do you agree? Should the government have to show that it had additional evidence that it did not offer at the first trial? Is *Nelson* consistent with *Burks'* focus on whether a rational jury should have acquitted?

In Tate v. Armontrout, 914 F.2d 1022 (8th Cir.1990), the court permitted the resentencing of a defendant after a remand because the trial court had failed to make a sufficient record of his prior convictions which had enhanced his sentence. The court held that this was trial error, and reasoned as follows:

> The point is that it is the sufficiency of the evidence that determines whether or not double jeopardy bars retrial because an acquittal should have been granted in the first instance, it is not the sufficiency of the record that determines a bar. * * * While the state may not have a second opportunity to produce sufficient evidence, we do not believe double jeopardy can bar the state from an opportunity to show that it did in fact produce sufficient evidence,

particularly where the record was not properly made and prevents the reviewing court from making the proper constitutional inquiry.

For a case applying the Burks exception, see United States v. Londono–Villa, 930 F.2d 994 (2d Cir.1991) (evidence insufficient to find that defendant knew or intended that cocaine would be imported into the United States, thus indictment dismissed).

In Montana v. Hall, 481 U.S. 400 (1987), the Supreme Court summarily reversed a state supreme court decision that a defendant whose conviction was overturned could not be retried on another charge. Hall was originally charged with sexual assault of the daughter of his ex-wife. He successfully moved to dismiss the charge, persuading the trial court that he could only be prosecuted for incest. After his conviction for incest, he persuaded the state supreme court that the incest statute did not apply on the facts of the case since the statute had not been in effect on the date of the charged criminal act. That court concluded that Hall could not be retried on the original charge because sexual assault and incest were the same offense, so that a retrial after a conviction for committing a nonexistent crime (incest under these circumstances) would violate double jeopardy. The Supreme Court disagreed, finding no constitutional bar to Hall's reprosecution for sexual assault, since a reversal of a conviction on grounds other than insufficiency of the evidence such as, in this case, a "defect in the charging instrument," does not bar a retrial. Justice Marshall dissented from the summary handling of the case, and Justice Stevens filed a separate dissent suggesting that the state supreme court may have rested its decision on state law.

In Parker v. State, 300 Ark. 360, 779 S.W.2d 156 (1989), Parker was charged with felony capital murder, and on appeal his conviction was reversed on the ground that the state had not proved that the murder was committed in furtherance of the underlying felony, as required by state law. The defendant was retried and convicted of ordinary capital murder. The court relied on Montana v. Hall and held that the original conviction had been reversed not because the evidence was insufficient, but because the State had committed "the trial error of charging and trying Parker under the wrong capital murder provision." Dissenting from denial of certiorari (111 S.Ct. 218 (1990)), Justice Marshall argued as follows:

> In my view, the reasoning in *Hall* is wholly inapposite to this case. In *Hall,* the Court concluded that the State had prosecuted the defendant under the 'wrong' statute not because the state *could not prove* that the defendant had violated the state incest statute, but because that statute was *legally inapplicable* to the defendant's conduct [having been enacted after the conduct]. In this case, the inapplicability of the capital felony murder statute to petitioner's conduct was *factual,* not legal.

Why should there be a retrial if the statute under which the defendant is charged is legally inapplicable, but not if the statute is factually inapplicable?

When *Scott, Burks* and *Hall* are put together, they establish that the defendant has a right to one conclusive disposition of the merits of a case—i.e., a decision that is properly rendered. But the government also may get an opportunity to challenge rulings that prevent it from obtaining a decision on the guilt or innocence of the defendant.

Hudson v. Louisiana, 450 U.S. 40 (1981), held that *Burks* was violated when a second trial was held after the trial judge at the first trial granted a motion for a new trial on the ground that the evidence was insufficient to support the jury's verdict. But in Tibbs v. Florida, 457 U.S. 31 (1982), the Supreme Court held 5–4 that a defendant could be retried after an appellate court overturned an initial conviction on the ground that it was against the weight of the evidence. Writing for the majority, Justice O'Connor reasoned that "[a] reversal based on the weight of the evidence * * * can occur only after the State both has presented sufficient evidence to support conviction and has persuaded the jury to convict. The reversal simply affords the defendant a second opportunity to seek a favorable judgment." Her opinion distinguished cases in which reviewing courts find that a defendant is entitled to a not guilty verdict as a matter of law from those in which the defendant is convicted on the basis of sufficient evidence but is given a second chance nonetheless. Justice White's dissent, joined by Justices Brennan, Marshall and Blackmun, argued that whether a reversal is based on insufficiency or weight of the evidence, a retrial gives the prosecution a second chance to do what it was unable to do in the first trial—i.e., put on stronger evidence. The dissenters suggested that appellate judges might use weight-of-the-evidence reasoning to permit retrial where it ought to be prohibited under *Burks*. In response, the majority observed that the prosecutor might present no additional evidence where reversal was on weight of the evidence reasoning, since an appellate court might afford a defendant a second chance but still affirm a conviction rendered by a second jury on the same evidence presented to the first. The majority also commented that "trial and appellate judges commonly distinguish between the weight and the sufficiency of the evidence. We have no reason to believe that today's decision will erode the demonstrated ability of judges to distinguish legally insufficient evidence from evidence that rationally supports a verdict."

Despite the optimism expressed by the majority in *Tibbs,* it has not always been easy to determine whether a dismissal is based on insufficiency rather than weight. Thus, in Freer v. Dugger, 935 F.2d 213 (11th Cir.1991), the defendant was found guilty. After the verdict, he moved for a judgment of acquittal. The trial judge remarked that no evidence placed the defendant at the scene of the crime, and that witnesses had in fact testified that he was not there. Evidence that the defendant's palm print was found at the scene was discounted by the fact that he had been there earlier. The judge ruled that he was "going to set aside the verdict;" in response to the Government's request, the judge stated that he would grant its motion for a new trial, "because I'm not satisfied the evidence proves guilt beyond a reasonable doubt." The defendant was convicted on retrial, but the court of appeals relied on *Burks* and *Hudson* and held that the second trial violated the defendant's double jeopardy rights. The court stated that the question is whether "the substance of the court's judgment was an acquittal, even though, in form, the court granted a new trial." It noted that the trial judge's comments and rulings were made in response to a motion for acquittal, and that the judge apparently felt that the state had failed to prove identity beyond a reasonable doubt. Therefore, only the form, and not the substance of the trial court's ruling changed when the judge attempted to modify the effect of his ruling by granting a new trial rather than entering a judgment of acquittal. The court noted that it was irrelevant whether, in fact, the evidence was sufficient to sustain a conviction. The question is whether the trial court, correctly or not, found the evidence to be insufficient. If so, there was a functional acquittal, which is final for purposes of the Double Jeopardy Clause.

Note

A jury decision that the defendant is not guilty or innocent cannot be set aside by any judge, nor can a trial judge's decision in a bench trial that the defendant is not guilty be set aside by a higher court. However, once a judge or jury finds the defendant guilty and thereafter the trial judge attempts to eradicate the verdict on some legal ground, review is possible at the request of the government.

If a judgment of guilty is challenged by the defendant and the appellate court holds that no reasonable trier of fact could have convicted, then the appellate court will reverse the conviction and treat the case as if the error were remedied—i.e., by barring a new trial because the defendant is deemed as a matter of law to be proved not guilty. If the defendant's conviction is reversed because of a trial error not amounting to a misestimation of the sufficiency of the evidence, the government can try again because neither it nor the defendant has had a final judgment on the merits.

Justice Brennan's position in *Scott* may now be usefully re-examined. The *Ball* case, discussed in *Burks*, indicates that a defendant who is convicted and who successfully appeals may be tried again. One difference between *Ball* and *Scott* is that the trier of fact never reached the merits in the latter case. Hence, it is arguable that the trier of fact may have acquitted, whereas in *Ball* the trier's decision to convict in the first trial actually was made. Arguably, then, the *Scott* trial judge denied the defendant a decision on the merits in the first litigation. But as long as the defendant acquiesced in the judge's approach, the majority saw no bar to retrial. The majority may have been treating the case as if the trial judge had said this to the defendant: "You have moved to dismiss this case. I am inclined to grant your motion, but I don't want to deny the government a chance to litigate the merits in the event that my decision to dismiss on a technical, legal ground is wrong. Thus, I shall give you a choice: I'll dismiss now before the verdict is returned if you want, but if I do this, you must understand that there will be a second trial if I am reversed. Or, I'll let the motion to dismiss remain undecided until after the verdict is in. If you are acquitted, you will be free. If you are convicted, I'll dismiss the case and the government can appeal and seek to have the conviction reinstated without further ado." Is this a fair characterization of the majority's approach in *Scott*? Is this a defensible approach? How would Justice Brennan argue against it?

C. TRIAL DE NOVO AND CONTINUING JEOPARDY

The Court distinguished *Burks* in Justices v. Lydon, 466 U.S. 294 (1984). Lydon was arrested after breaking into an automobile in Boston. He was charged with the knowing possession of implements "adapted and designed for forcing and breaking open a * * * depository [an automobile] in order to steal therefrom * * *" with the intent "to use and employ them therefor." Lydon had a right to choose a jury trial or an initial trial to the bench. An acquittal before either a judge or a jury would have been final, but only a jury's verdict of guilty would have been final; a defendant who elected a bench trial had an absolute right to a trial de novo if convicted.

Lydon, like most Massachusetts defendants, opted for the bench trial. He was convicted. He then requested a trial de novo to a jury, but he attempted in state court, and then in federal court, to bar the second trial on the ground that there had been insufficient evidence to warrant a conviction in the bench trial. He claimed that *Burks* barred retrial. The Court disagreed.

Justice White wrote for the Court and reasoned that *Burks* prohibited a second trial after a reviewing court found that a conviction was based on insufficient evidence. Under the Massachusetts system, no such determination had been made. The policies underlying *Burks* did not apply, he said, because this was not a case in which the prosecution had an incentive to offer a weak case first, in order to discover the defendant's evidence and theories, since an acquittal would be a final victory for the defendant; and the prosecutor received no education as to how to present a better case from reviewing judges, since there had been no review. Justice White explained that the two-tiered option granted to a defendant offered benefits not generally available in a single-tiered system and that a defendant who opted for the two-tiered process had no complaint that he could not challenge a mistake at the first level. He noted that if the defendant were convicted on insufficient evidence at the trial de novo, *Burks* would apply at that point.

Justice Brennan, joined by Justice Marshall, concurred separately and objected to the majority's treatment of the Massachusetts system as a single system of continuing jeopardy with two interrelated parts. Since an acquittal at the first trial would have barred a retrial, Justice Brennan thought that the completion of the first trial had enormous significance, and he argued that the fact that Massachusetts did not provide for an opportunity to obtain review of the sufficiency of the evidence following a bench trial was not determinative. Rather, the question was whether a defendant who sought a determination on the sufficiency issued by way of habeas corpus, as he had a right to, could prevent a second trial by demonstrating that the evidence at the first was not adequate to support a conviction. Justice Brennan concluded that "the guilty verdict rendered by the first-tier judge undeniably ended a set of proceedings in that courtroom that would be most naturally understood as a single, completed trial." Thus, he would have relied upon *Burks* and held that Lydon could not be tried a second time if the evidence at the bench trial was constitutionally insufficient.

Justice Stevens wrote a separate opinion in which he agreed with Justice Brennan that the majority's notion of "continuing jeopardy" was unhelpful and also that Lydon was entitled to a judgment of acquittal if the evidence at the bench trial was insufficient. He disagreed, however, with the idea that the assessment of the sufficiency of the evidence should take place prior to the second-tier trial. He would not disrupt state proceedings by permitting federal habeas corpus review prior to the second-tier trial. Although this would mean that some defendants would stand trial a second time unnecessarily, Justice Stevens argued that the state system is not unnecessarily harsh and that the balance of state and individual interests was fair under his suggested approach.

Justice Rehnquist relied on the Court's reasoning in *Lydon* in his majority opinion in Richardson v. United States, 468 U.S. 317 (1984). The Court held that a defendant was not placed in jeopardy twice when a mistrial was declared due to a genuine jury deadlock, Richardson's motion for judgment of acquittal was denied and the trial judge scheduled a second trial. As it had in *Lydon,* the Court read *Burks* as holding only that "once a defendant obtained an unreversed appellate ruling that the Government had failed to introduce sufficient evidence to convict him at trial, a second trial was barred by the Double Jeopardy Clause." Examining Richardson's claim, the Court said that "[w]here, as here, there has been only a mistrial resulting from a hung jury, *Burks* simply does not require that an appellate court rule on the sufficiency of the evidence because retrial might be barred by the Double Jeopardy Clause." The Court found that the declaration of a mistrial was not the equivalent of an acquittal, it did not terminate jeopardy, and that "[r]egardless of the sufficiency of the evidence at petitioner's first trial, he has no valid double jeopardy claim to prevent his retrial." Justice Brennan, joined by Justice Marshall, relied on the analysis he used in *Lydon* and dissented. He agreed with the majority that a new trial is not barred simply because a jury could not reach a verdict, but urged that "[w]hen the prosecution has failed to present constitutionally sufficient evidence, it cannot complain of unfairness in being denied a second chance, and the interests in finality, shared by the defendant and society, strongly outweigh the reasons for a retrial."

IV. THE CONVICTED DEFENDANT IS TRIED AGAIN

A. THE SAME OFFENSE

Double jeopardy bars not only the retrial of a defendant who is acquitted;[12] it also bars the reprosecution of a defendant who is convicted. Here the policies are obvious. First, the defendant may be forced to defend, but not repetitively. Once the government gets the conviction it originally sought, further proceedings might well be vexatious. Moreover, further proceedings might produce multiple punishments for the same offense and result in unequal application of the law. Thus, there is no doubt that after a valid conviction, the same offense cannot be prosecuted again. But what constitutes the same offense?

In Brown v. Ohio, 432 U.S. 161 (1977), the defendant stole a car in East Cleveland, Ohio. Nine days later, he was arrested in another city and charged with joyriding. He pled guilty and served his sentence. After his release, he was returned to East Cleveland and charged with auto theft and joyriding. He pled guilty to auto theft, but reserved his double jeopardy claim for a motion to withdraw his plea. The court overruled his double jeopardy objection and sentenced him. The Supreme Court concluded that the conviction violated the Double Jeopardy Clause, because joyriding is a lesser included offense of auto

12. Two Supreme Court cases consider the application of the Double Jeopardy Clause to juvenile proceedings. In Breed v. Jones, 421 U.S. 519 (1975), the defendant committed an armed robbery and was adjudicated a delinquent in juvenile court. At a subsequent disposition hearing, the judge found him unfit for treatment as a juvenile and ordered him to be prosecuted as an adult. His trial and conviction as an adult violated the double jeopardy clause, because he was subjected to the burden of two trials. The judge could and should have transferred the defendant to adult court before holding the factfinding adjudicatory hearing.

In Swisher v. Brady, 438 U.S. 204 (1978), the Court found that allowing the state to file exceptions to proposed nondelinquency findings made by juvenile court masters does not violate the prohibition against double jeopardy. The nature of the proceeding was crucial. Pursuant to a Maryland rule of procedure, a master makes preliminary findings and proposals at a hearing. The judge, who makes the final adjudication, retains the power to accept, reject, or modify the master's proposals, to remand for further hearings, and to supplement the record in some circumstances.

theft under Ohio law. Adhering to the test of different offenses established in Blockburger v. United States, 284 U.S. 299 (1932), for the purpose of determining whether it is permissible to cumulate punishment, the Court asked whether each statutory provision contains an element which the other does not.[13] The Court noted that "[w]here the judge is forbidden to impose cumulative punishment for two crimes at the end of a single proceeding, the prosecutor is forbidden to strive for the same result in successive proceedings." Because the Ohio statute defined auto theft as joyriding with the intent to permanently deprive the owner of possession, the only difference in proof was the intent. (I.e., only one crime required something that the other did not). The Court held that Brown could not be convicted of both offenses because they were based on different parts of the same joyride. The nine-day joyride could not be divided into a series of temporal or spatial units, because Ohio law did not create separate offenses for each day someone was joyriding. Concurring, Justices Brennan and Marshall expressed the view that the Double Jeopardy Clause requires that all charges stemming from one criminal act, occurrence, episode, or transaction be prosecuted in one proceeding. Justices Blackmun, Burger and Rehnquist argued in dissent that Brown committed a separate offense when he operated the car nine days after stealing it.

It is important under *Blockburger* that *each* provision must require something that the other does not for there to be separate offenses. In Illinois v. Vitale, 447 U.S. 410 (1980), the Court cited the *Blockburger* test as the appropriate one to use in judging whether a driver of an automobile that struck and killed two children could be prosecuted for involuntary manslaughter following his conviction for failing to reduce speed to avoid the collision. The Court remanded the case for further development of state law, observing that "if manslaughter by automobile does not always entail proof of a failure to slow, then the two offenses are not the 'same' under the *Blockburger* test," but cautioning also that if the state would "find it necessary to prove a failure to slow or to rely on conduct necessarily involving such failure" Vitale's double jeopardy claim "would be substantial." Four dissenters argued that no further proceedings were appropriate.

The following case makes it clear that the *Blockburger* test is not the only hurdle that the prosecution must satisfy when it brings a second prosecution against the defendant.

GRADY v. CORBIN

Supreme Court of the United States, 1990.
495 U.S. 508.

JUSTICE BRENNAN delivered the opinion of the Court.

We have long held, see Blockburger v. United States, that the Double Jeopardy Clause of the Fifth Amendment

13. The Supreme Court cited Harris v. Oklahoma, 433 U.S. 682 (1977) (per curiam), in a two-paragraph per curiam opinion in Payne v. Virginia, 468 U.S. 1062 (1984), sustaining a defendant's double jeopardy challenge to his conviction for robbery following another conviction for capital murder committed during the perpetration of the robbery while armed with a deadly weapon. It said that where "conviction of a greater crime, murder, cannot be had without conviction of the lesser crime, robbery ... the Double Jeopardy Clause bars prosecution for a lesser crime after conviction of the greater one."

prohibits successive prosecutions for the same criminal act or transaction under two criminal statutes whenever each statute does not "requir[e] proof of a fact which the other does not." In Illinois v. Vitale, we suggested that even if two successive prosecutions were not barred by the *Blockburger* test, the second prosecution would be barred if the prosecution sought to establish an essential element of the second crime by proving the conduct for which the defendant was convicted in the first prosecution. Today we adopt the suggestion set forth in *Vitale.* We hold that the Double Jeopardy Clause bars a subsequent prosecution if, to establish an essential element of an offense charged in that prosecution, the government will prove conduct that constitutes an offense for which the defendant has already been prosecuted.

I

* * * At approximately 6:35 p.m. on October 3, 1987, respondent Thomas Corbin drove his automobile across the double yellow line of Route 55 in LaGrange, New York, striking two oncoming vehicles. Assistant District Attorney (ADA) Thomas Dolan was called to the scene, where he learned that both Brenda Dirago, who had been driving the second vehicle to be struck, and her husband Daniel had been seriously injured. Later that evening, ADA Dolan was informed that Brenda Dirago had died from injuries sustained in the accident. That same evening, while at the hospital being treated for his own injuries, respondent was served with two uniform traffic tickets directing him to appear at the LaGrange Town Justice Court on October 29, 1987. One ticket charged him with the misdemeanor of driving while intoxicated in violation of N.Y. Veh. & Traf. Law § 1192(3), the other charged him with failing to keep right of the median in violation of § 1120(a). A blood test taken at the hospital that evening indicated a blood alcohol level of 0.19%, nearly twice the level at which it is *per se* illegal to operate a motor vehicle in New York.

Three days later, Assistant District Attorney Frank Chase began gathering evidence for a homicide prosecution in connection with the accident. "Despite his active involvement in building a homicide case against [Corbin], however, Chase did not attempt to ascertain the date [Corbin] was scheduled to appear in Town Justice Court on the traffic tickets, nor did he inform either the Town Justice Court or the Assistant District Attorney covering that court about his pending investigation." Thus, Assistant District Attorney Mark Glick never mentioned Brenda Dirago's death in the statement of readiness for trial and other pretrial pleadings he submitted to respondent and the LaGrange Town Justice Court on October 14, 1987.

Accordingly, when respondent pleaded guilty to the two traffic tickets on October 27, 1987, a date on which no member of the District Attorney's office was present in court, the presiding judge was unaware of the fatality stemming from the accident. Corbin was never asked if any others had been injured on the night in question and did not voluntarily incriminate himself by providing such information.[a] The presiding judge accepted his guilty plea, but because the District Attorney's of-

a. The New York Court of Appeals held that, although an attorney may not misrepresent facts, "a practitioner representing a client at a traffic violation prosecution should not be expected to *volunteer* information that is likely to be highly damaging to his client's position." Because the Court of Appeals refused to characterize as misconduct the behavior of either Corbin or his attorney, we need not decide whether our double jeopardy analysis would be any different if affirmative misrepresentations of fact by a defendant or his counsel were to mislead a court into accepting a guilty plea it would not otherwise accept.

fice had not submitted a sentencing recommendation, the judge postponed sentencing until November 17, 1987, when an Assistant District Attorney was scheduled to be present in court. The Assistant District Attorney present at sentencing on that date, Heidi Sauter, was unaware that there had been a fatality, was unable to locate the case file, and had not spoken to ADA Glick about the case. Nevertheless, she did not seek an adjournment so that she could ascertain the facts necessary to make an informed sentencing recommendation. Instead, she recommended a "minimum sentence," and the presiding judge sentenced Corbin to a $350 fine, a $10 surcharge, and a 6-month license revocation.

Two months later, on January 19, 1988, a grand jury investigating the October 3, 1987, accident indicted Corbin, charging him with reckless manslaughter, second-degree vehicular manslaughter, and criminally negligent homicide for causing the death of Brenda Dirago; third-degree reckless assault for causing physical injury to Daniel Dirago; and driving while intoxicated. The prosecution filed a bill of particulars that identified the three reckless or negligent acts on which it would rely to prove the homicide and assault charges: (1) operating a motor vehicle on a public highway in an intoxicated condition, (2) failing to keep right of the median, and (3) driving approximately 45 to 50 miles per hour in heavy rain, "which was a speed too fast for the weather and road conditions then pending." Respondent moved to dismiss the indictment on statutory and constitutional double jeopardy grounds. * * *

[The trial court denied the motion], but the New York Court of Appeals reversed. The court prohibited prosecution of the driving while intoxicated counts pursuant to New York's statutory double jeopardy provision, N.Y.Crim.Proc.Law § 40.20. The court further ruled that prosecution of the two vehicular manslaughter counts would violate the Double Jeopardy Clause of the Fifth Amendment pursuant to the *Blockburger* test because, as a matter of state law, driving while intoxicated "is unquestionably a lesser included offense of second degree vehicular manslaughter." Finally, relying on the "pointed dictum" in this Court's opinion in *Vitale,* the court barred prosecution of the remaining counts because the bill of particulars expressed an intention to "rely on the prior traffic offenses as the acts necessary to prove the homicide and assault charges." * * * We granted certiorari, and now affirm.

II

* * *

We believe that [the *Vitale*] analysis is correct and governs this case.[b] To determine whether a subsequent prosecution is barred by the Double Jeopardy Clause, a court must first apply the traditional *Blockburger* test. If application of that test reveals that the offenses have identical statutory elements or that one is a lesser included offense of the other, then the inquiry must cease, and the subsequent prosecution is barred.

The State argues that this should be the last step in the inquiry and that the Double Jeopardy Clause permits successive prosecutions whenever the offenses charged satisfy the *Blockburger* test. We

b. We recognized in Brown v. Ohio, 432 U.S. 161, 169, and n. 7 (1977), that when application of our traditional double jeopardy analysis would bar a subsequent prosecution, "[a]n exception may exist where the State is unable to proceed on the more serious charge at the outset because the additional facts necessary to sustain that charge have not occurred or have not been discovered despite the exercise of due diligence. See Diaz v. United States, 223 U.S. 442, 448–449 (1912)." Because ADA Dolan was informed of Brenda Dirago's death on the night of the accident, such an exception is inapplicable here.

disagree. The Double Jeopardy Clause embodies three protections: "It protects against a second prosecution for the same offense after acquittal. It protects against a second prosecution for the same offense after conviction. And it protects against multiple punishments for the same offense." North Carolina v. Pearce. The *Blockburger* test was developed "in the context of multiple punishments imposed in a single prosecution." Garrett v. United States, 471 U.S. 773 (1985). In that context, "the Double Jeopardy Clause does no more than prevent the sentencing court from prescribing greater punishment than the legislature intended." Missouri v. Hunter, 459 U.S. 359 (1983). The *Blockburger* test is simply a "rule of statutory construction," a guide to determining whether the legislature intended multiple punishments.

Successive prosecutions, however, whether following acquittals or convictions, raise concerns that extend beyond merely the possibility of an enhanced sentence:

> "The underlying idea, one that is deeply ingrained in at least the Anglo–American system of jurisprudence, is that the State with all its resources and power should not be allowed to make repeated attempts to convict an individual for an alleged offense, thereby subjecting him to embarrassment, expense and ordeal and compelling him to live in a continuing state of anxiety and insecurity ...." Green v. United States [discussed supra].

Multiple prosecutions also give the State an opportunity to rehearse its presentation of proof, thus increasing the risk of an erroneous conviction for one or more of the offenses charged. See, e.g., Tibbs v. Florida [discussed supra] (noting that the Double Jeopardy Clause "prevents the State from honing its trial strategies and perfecting its evidence through successive attempts at conviction"); Ashe v. Swenson, 397 U.S. 436 (1970) (the State conceded that, after the defendant was acquitted in one trial, the prosecutor did, at a subsequent trial, "what every good attorney would do—he refined his presentation in light of the turn of events at the first trial"). Even when a State can bring multiple charges against an individual under *Blockburger,* a tremendous additional burden is placed on that defendant if he must face each of the charges in a separate proceeding.

Because of these independent concerns, we have not relied exclusively on the *Blockburger* test to vindicate the Double Jeopardy Clause's protection against multiple prosecutions.

* * *

If *Blockburger* constituted the entire double jeopardy inquiry in the context of successive prosecutions, the State could try Corbin in four consecutive trials: for failure to keep right of the median, for driving while intoxicated, for assault, and for homicide. The State could improve its presentation of proof with each trial, assessing which witnesses gave the most persuasive testimony, which documents had the greatest impact, which opening and closing arguments most persuaded the jurors. Corbin would be forced either to contest each of these trials or to plead guilty to avoid the harassment and expense.

Thus, a subsequent prosecution must do more than merely survive the *Blockburger* test. As we suggested in *Vitale,* the Double Jeopardy Clause bars any subsequent prosecution in which the government, to establish an essential element of an offense charged in that prosecution, will prove conduct that constitutes an offense for which the defendant has already been prosecuted.[c] This is not an "actual evidence" or "same evidence" test.[d] The critical inquiry is what conduct the State will prove, not the evidence the State will use to prove that conduct. As we have held, the presentation of specific evidence in one trial does not forever prevent the government from introducing that same evidence in a subsequent proceeding. See Dowling v. United States, 493 U.S. 342 (1990) [discussed infra]. On the other hand, a State cannot avoid the dictates of the Double Jeopardy Clause merely by altering in successive prosecutions the evidence offered to prove the same conduct. For example, if two bystanders had witnessed Corbin's accident, it would make no difference to our double jeopardy analysis if the State called one witness to testify in the first trial that Corbin's vehicle crossed the median (or if nobody testified in the first trial because Corbin, as he did, pleaded guilty) and called the other witness to testify to the same conduct in the second trial.

Applying this analysis to the facts of this case is straightforward. Respondent concedes that *Blockburger* does not bar prosecution of the reckless manslaughter, criminally negligent homicide, and third-degree reckless assault offenses. The rest of our inquiry in this case is simplified by the bill of particulars filed by the State on January 25, 1988.[e] That statement of the prosecution's theory of proof is binding on the State until amended, and the State has not amended it to date. * * * By its own pleadings, the State has admitted that it will prove the entirety of the conduct for which Corbin was convicted—driving while intoxicated and failing to keep right of the median—to establish essential elements of the homicide and assault offenses. Therefore, the Double Jeopardy Clause bars this successive prosecution, and the New York Court of Appeals properly granted respondent's petition for a writ of prohibition. This holding would not bar a subsequent prosecution on the homicide and assault charges if the bill

c. Similarly, if in the course of securing a conviction for one offense the State necessarily has proved the conduct comprising all of the elements of another offense not yet prosecuted (a "component offense"), the Double Jeopardy Clause would bar subsequent prosecution of the component offense. See Harris v. Oklahoma, 433 U.S. 682 (1977) ("When, as here, conviction of a greater crime, murder, cannot be had without conviction of the lesser crime, robbery with firearms, the Double Jeopardy Clause bars prosecution for the lesser crime after conviction of the greater one") (footnote omitted); cf. Brown v. Ohio, 432 U.S. 161 (1977) (noting that it is irrelevant for the purposes of the Double Jeopardy Clause whether the conviction of the greater offense precedes the conviction of the lesser offense or vice-versa).

d. Terminology in the double jeopardy area has been confused at best. Commentators and judges alike have referred to the *Blockburger* test as a "same evidence" test. This is a misnomer. The *Blockburger* test has nothing to do with the *evidence* presented at trial. It is concerned solely with the statutory elements of the offenses charged. A true "same evidence" or "actual evidence" test would prevent the government from introducing in a subsequent prosecution any evidence that was introduced in a preceding prosecution. It is in this sense that we discuss, and do not adopt, a "same evidence" or "actual evidence" test.

e. Application of the test we adopt today will not depend, as JUSTICE SCALIA's dissent argues, on whether the indictment "happens to show that the same evidence is at issue" or whether the jurisdiction "happen[s] to require the prosecution to submit a bill of particulars that cannot be exceeded." The Courts of Appeals, which long ago recognized that the Double Jeopardy Clause requires more than a technical comparison of statutory elements when a defendant is confronting successive prosecutions, have adopted an essential procedural mechanism for assessing double jeopardy claims prior to a second trial. All nine federal Circuits which have addressed the issue have held that "when a defendant puts double jeopardy in issue with a non-frivolous showing that an indictment charges him with an offense for which he was formerly placed in jeopardy, the burden shifts to the government to establish that there were in fact two separate offenses." United States v. Ragins, 840 F.2d 1184, 1192 (CA4 1988) (collecting cases). * * *

of particulars revealed that the State would not rely on proving the conduct for which Corbin had already been convicted (*i.e.,* if the State relied solely on Corbin's driving too fast in heavy rain to establish recklessness or negligence).[f]

III

* * * With adequate preparation and foresight, the State could have prosecuted Corbin for the offenses charged in the traffic tickets and the subsequent indictment in a single proceeding, thereby avoiding this double jeopardy question. We have concluded that the Double Jeopardy Clause of the Fifth Amendment demands application of the standard announced today, but we are confident that with proper planning and attention prosecutors will be able to meet this standard and bring to justice those who make our Nation's roads unsafe.

The judgment of the New York Court of Appeals is

Affirmed.

JUSTICE O'CONNOR, dissenting.

I agree with much of what Justice SCALIA says in his dissenting opinion. I write separately, however, to note that my dissent is premised primarily on my view that the inconsistency between the Court's opinion today and Dowling v. United States, decided earlier this Term, indicates that the Court has strayed from a proper interpretation of the scope of the Double Jeopardy Clause.

In *Dowling,* we considered whether an eyewitness' testimony regarding a robbery for which Dowling had been acquitted was admissible at a second trial of Dowling for an unrelated robbery. The eyewitness had testified at the first trial that a man had entered her house "wearing a knitted mask with cutout eyes and carrying a small handgun" and that his mask had come off during a struggle, revealing his identity. Based on this evidence, Dowling had been charged with burglary, attempted robbery, assault, and weapons offenses, but was acquitted of all charges. At a second trial for an unrelated bank robbery, the government attempted to use the witness' testimony to prove Dowling's identity as a robber. We held that the Double Jeopardy Clause did not bar the introduction of the evidence: Because the prior acquittal did not necessarily represent a jury determination that Dowling was not the masked man who had entered the witness' home, the testimony was admissible in the second trial to prove identity.

The Court's ruling today effectively renders our holding in *Dowling* a nullity in many circumstances. If a situation identical to that in *Dowling* arose after today's decision, a conscientious judge attempting to apply the test enunciated by the Court, would probably conclude that the witness' testimony was barred by the Double Jeopardy Clause. The record in *Dowling* indicated that the Government was offering the eyewitness testimony to establish the defendant's identity, "an essential element of an offense charged in [the subsequent] prosecution," and that the testimony would likely "prove conduct that constitutes an offense for which the defendant has already been prosecuted." * * * As a practical matter, this means that

f. Adoption of a "same transaction" test would bar the homicide and assault prosecutions even if the State were able to establish the essential elements of those crimes without proving the conduct for which Corbin previously was convicted. The Court, however, has "steadfastly refused to adopt the 'single transaction' view of the Double Jeopardy Clause." Garrett v. United States [discussed infra]. But see Jones v. Thomas [discussed infra]. (BRENNAN, J., joined by MARSHALL, J., dissenting) (maintaining that "the Double Jeopardy Clause requires, except in very limited circumstances, that all charges against a defendant growing out of a single criminal transaction be tried in one proceeding").

the same evidence ruled admissible in *Dowling* is barred by *Grady.*

* * *

JUSTICE SCALIA, with whom CHIEF JUSTICE REHNQUIST and JUSTICE KENNEDY join, dissenting.

The State of New York seeks to prosecute respondent a second time for the actions that he took at 6:35 p.m. on October 3, 1987. If the Double Jeopardy Clause guaranteed the right not to be twice put in jeopardy for the same conduct, it would bar this second prosecution. But that Clause guarantees only the right not to be twice put in jeopardy for the same *offense,* and has been interpreted since its inception, as was its common-law antecedent, to permit a prosecution based upon the same acts but for a different crime. The Court today holds otherwise, departing from clear text and clear precedent with no justification except the citation of dictum in a recent case (dictum that was similarly unsupported, and inconclusive to boot). The effects of this innovation upon our criminal-justice system are likely to be substantial. In practice, it will require prosecutors to observe a rule we have explicitly rejected in principle: that all charges arising out of a single occurrence must be joined in a single indictment. * * *

I

* * *

* * * I would adhere to the *Blockburger* rule that successive prosecutions under two different statutes do not constitute double jeopardy if each statutory crime contains an element that the other does not, regardless of the overlap between the proof required for each prosecution in the particular case. That rule best gives effect to the language of the Clause, which protects individuals from being twice put in jeopardy "for the same *offence,* " not for the same *conduct* or *actions.* "Offence" was commonly understood in 1791 to mean "transgression," that is, "the Violation or Breaking of a Law." Dictionarium Britannicum (Bailey ed. 1730); see N. Webster, An American Dictionary of the English Language (1828). If the same conduct violates two (or more) laws, then each offense may be separately prosecuted. Of course, this is not to say that two criminal provisions create "distinct" offenses simply by appearing under separate statutory headings; but if each contains an element the other does not, i.e., if it is possible to violate each one without violating the other, then they cannot constitute the "*same* offence."

Another textual element also supports the *Blockburger* test. Since the Double Jeopardy Clause protects the defendant from being "twice put in jeopardy," i.e., made to stand trial for the "same offence," it presupposes that sameness can be determined before the second trial. Otherwise, the Clause would have prohibited a second "conviction" or "sentence" for the same offense. A court can always determine, before trial, whether the second prosecution involves the "same offence" in the *Blockburger* sense, since the Constitution entitles the defendant "to be informed of the nature and cause of the accusation." But since the Constitution does not entitle the defendant to be informed of the *evidence* against him, the Court's "proof-of-same-conduct" test will be implementable before trial only if the indictment happens to show that the same evidence is at issue, or only if the jurisdiction's rules of criminal procedure happen to require the prosecution to submit a bill of particulars that cannot be exceeded. More often than not, in other words, the Court's test will not succeed in preventing the defendant from being tried twice.

Relying on text alone, therefore, one would conclude that the Double Jeopardy Clause meant what *Blockburger* said. But there is in addition a wealth of historical evidence to the same effect. [Justice Scalia engages in an extensive historical analysis of the Double Jeopardy Clause].

II

The Court today abandons text and long-standing precedent to adopt the theory that double jeopardy bars "any subsequent prosecution in which the government, to establish an essential element of an offense charged in that prosecution, *will prove* conduct that constitutes an offense for which the defendant has already been prosecuted." The Court purports to derive that standard from our decision in Illinois v. Vitale, in which a motorist who caused a fatal accident was first convicted of unlawful failure to reduce speed, and later charged with involuntary manslaughter. * * * We did not decide in *Vitale* that the second prosecution would constitute double jeopardy if it required proof of the conduct for which Vitale had already been convicted. We could not possibly have decided that, since the issue was not presented on the facts before us. But beyond that, we did not even *say* in *Vitale,* by way of *dictum,* that such a prosecution would violate the Double Jeopardy Clause. We said only that a claim to that effect would be "substantial," deferring to another day the question whether it would be *successful.* That day is today, and we should answer the question no.

* * *

The principle the Court adopts today is not only radically out of line with our double jeopardy jurisprudence; its practical effect, whenever it applies, will come down to a requirement that where the charges arise from a " 'single criminal act, occurrence, episode, or transaction,' " they "must be tried in a single proceeding," a requirement we have hitherto "steadfastly refused" to impose. Suppose, for example, that the State prosecutes a group of individuals for a substantive offense, and then prosecutes them for conspiracy. In the conspiracy trial it *will prove* (if it can) that the defendants actually committed the substantive offense—even though there is evidence of other overt acts sufficient to sustain the conspiracy charge. For proof of the substantive offense, though not an *element* of the conspiracy charge, will assuredly be *persuasive* in establishing that a conspiracy existed. Or suppose an initial prosecution for burglary and a subsequent prosecution for murder that occurred in the course of the same burglary. In the second trial the State *will prove* (if it can) that the defendant was engaged in a burglary—not because that is itself an element of the murder charge, but because by providing a motive for intentional killing it will be *persuasive* that murder occurred. Under the analysis embraced by the Court today, I take it that the second prosecution in each of these cases would be barred, because the State, "to establish an essential element of an offense charged in that prosecution, will prove conduct that constitutes an offense for which the defendant has already been prosecuted." * * *

The Court seeks to shrink the apparent application of its novel principle by saying that repetitive proof violates the Double Jeopardy Clause only if it is introduced "to establish an essential element of an offense charged in [the second] prosecution." That is a meaningless limitation, of course. *All* evidence pertaining to guilt seeks "to establish an essential element of [the] offense," and should be excluded if it does not have that tendency.

* * *

It is not at all apparent how a court is to go about deciding whether the evidence that has been introduced (or that will be introduced) at the second trial "proves conduct" that constitutes an offense for which the defendant has already been prosecuted. Is the judge in the second trial supposed to pretend that he is the judge in the first one, and to let the second trial proceed *only if* the evidence would not be enough to go to the jury on the earlier charge? Or (as the language of the Court's test more readily suggests) is the judge in the second trial supposed to decide on his own whether the evidence before him really "proves" the earlier charge (perhaps beyond a reasonable doubt)? Consider application of the Court's new rule in the unusually simple circumstances of the present case: Suppose that, in the trial upon remand, the prosecution's evidence shows, among other things, that when the vehicles came to rest after the collision they were located on what was, for the defendant's vehicle, the wrong side of the road. The prosecution also produces a witness who testifies that prior to the collision the defendant's vehicle was "weaving back and forth"—*without* saying, however, that it was weaving back and forth over the center line. Is this enough to meet today's requirement of "proving" the offense of operating a vehicle on the wrong side of the road? If not, suppose in addition that defense counsel asks the witness on cross-examination, "When you said the defendant's vehicle was 'weaving back and forth,' did you mean weaving back and forth across the center line?"—to which the witness replies yes. Will this self-inflicted wound count for purposes of determining what the prosecution has "proved?" If so, can the prosecution then seek to impeach its own witness by showing that his recollection of the vehicle's crossing the center line was inaccurate? Or can it at least introduce another witness to establish that fact? There are many questions here, and the answers to all of them are ridiculous. Whatever line is selected as the criterion of "proving" the prior offense—enough evidence to go to the jury, more likely than not, or beyond a reasonable doubt—the prosecutor in the second trial will presumably seek to introduce as much evidence as he can without crossing that line; and the defense attorney will presumably seek to provoke the prosecutor into (or assist him in) proving the defendant guilty of the earlier crime. This delicious role-reversal, discovered to have been mandated by the Double Jeopardy Clause lo these 200 years, makes for high comedy but inferior justice. Often, the performance will even have an encore. If the judge initially decides that the previously prosecuted offense "will not be proved" (whatever that means) he will have to decide at the conclusion of the trial whether it "has been proved" (whatever that means). Indeed, he may presumably be asked to make the latter determination periodically during the course of the trial, since the Double Jeopardy Clause assuredly entitles the defendant to have the proceedings terminated as soon as its violation is evident. Even if we had no constitutional text and no prior case-law to rely upon, rejection of today's opinion is adequately supported by the modest desire to protect our criminal legal system from ridicule.

A limitation that is so unsupported in reason and so absurd in application is unlikely to survive. Today's decision to extend the Double Jeopardy Clause to prosecutions that *prove* a previously prosecuted offense will lead predictably to extending it to prosecutions that *involve the same facts as* a previously prosecuted offense. We will thus have fully embraced JUSTICE BRENNAN'S "same transaction" theory, which has as little support in the text and history of the Double Jeopardy Clause, but at least has the merit of being rational and easy to apply. One can readily imagine the words of our first opinion effecting this extension: "When we said in *Grady* that the second prosecution is impermissible if it 'will prove conduct' that constitutes the prior offense, we did not mean that it will establish commission of that offense with the degree of completeness that would permit a jury to convict. It suffices if the evidence in the second prosecution 'proves' the previously prosecuted offense in the sense of tending to establish one or more of the elements of that offense." The Court that has done what it has today to 200 years of established double jeopardy jurisprudence should find this lesser transmogrification easy. It may, however, prove unnecessary, since prosecutors confronted with the inscrutability of today's opinion will be well advised to proceed on the assumption that the "same transaction" theory has already been adopted. It is hard to tell what else has.

* * *

Note

In Payne v. Tennessee, discussed in Chapter Eleven, the Court indicated its willingness to reconsider 5–4 decisions in which "vigorous" dissents had been filed. Is *Grady* such a case?

If the Court had adopted a "transactional" approach, Corbin could not have been retried even if the prosecution were to limit its proof to Corbin's driving too fast in heavy rain to establish recklessness or negligence. Even though the proof would be different, the transaction would be the same. In practical effect, however, Justice Scalia has a point. A prosecutor is all but forced to charge all crimes in a single transaction at one time, since it is rather unlikely that totally different conduct arising from the same transaction could make a subsequent prosecution successful. In *Grady,* for instance, it is unlikely that Corbin would be convicted on a serious charge for driving too fast in a heavy rain. The most damaging conduct is that of drunkenness, and that cannot be punished after *Grady.*

What are the arguments for and against a transactional test? In civil cases, the plaintiff is required by the doctrine of res judicata to join in one case all claims against a single defendant arising from the same transaction. See Restatement, Second of Judgments, § 24 (1980). Why should we demand any less of a prosecutor?

A problem left by *Grady* is that in the second prosecution, there will often have to be a trial before a trial to determine which conduct the government intends to prove to support the conviction, as well as which conduct was proven at the prior prosecution. At this "pre"-trial, the defendant may suffer at least to some degree from the same burdens of duplicate litigation, uncertainty and harassment that Justice Brennan found of such concern. Moreover, the burden on the courts and on the prosecution is obvious. Whatever the drawbacks of the *Blockburger* test, at least its required comparison of statutory elements (as opposed to conduct) can be done without an extensive pre-trial hearing. See Capra, Prisoners of Their Own Jurisprudence: Fourth and Fifth Amendment Cases in the Supreme Court, 36 Vill.L.Rev. 1267 (1991) for a discussion of some of the problems left in the wake of *Grady.*

Grady did not involve a conspiracy case, but the Court's conduct test leaves substantial questions as to how to deal with subsequent prosecutions where a conspiracy is charged in either the former or latter case. There are three separate questions which must be resolved.

1. Can a conspiracy and the underlying substantive crime be successively prosecuted? Although Justice Scalia in his dissent in *Grady* said that this would

not be possible given the similarity of conduct, his argument should be evaluated in context: he was using a "parade of horribles" approach. The lower courts after *Grady* have generally allowed successive prosecutions, reasoning that the conspiracy is based upon separate conduct, i.e. the agreement. See United States v. Clark, 928 F.2d 639 (4th Cir.1991) (defendant convicted for possession of heroin and cocaine can later be prosecuted for conspiracy to commit those offenses; evidence of his previous possession did not constitute an "essential element" of the conspiracy charge). There is no indication in *Grady* that it intended to overrule the long line of cases such as Pinkerton v. United States, 328 U.S. 640 (1946) to the effect that the collective criminal agreement is sufficiently distinct from the substantive offense for double jeopardy purposes. *Grady* prohibits a subsequent prosecution only where the government will prove, as an essential element of the crime, conduct that constitutes an offense for which the defendant has already been prosecuted. An overt act is not always an essential element of a conspiracy. See e.g., United States v. Savaiano, 843 F.2d 1280 (10th Cir.1988) ("an overt act is not a necessary element of conspiracy under the federal drug enforcement statutes"). See J. Potuto, S. Saltzburg, and H. Perlman, Federal Criminal Jury Instructions, § 11.01 (2d ed. 1991). In the United States v. Felix, 112 S.Ct. 1377 (1992), the defendant was prosecuted for conspiracy, manufacture and possession with intent to distribute narcotics. Of the nine overt acts supporting the conspiracy charge against Felix, two were based on conduct for which he had been previously prosecuted. Chief Justice Rehnquist, writing for the majority, declared that the Court in *Grady* had not disturbed the time-honored rule that "a substantive crime, and a conspiracy to commit that crime, are not the 'same offense' for double jeopardy purposes." The Chief Justice cited *Pinkerton* for the proposition that the essence of a conspiracy offense "is in the agreement or confederation to commit a crime" and that "the agreement to do the act is distinct from the act itself." He noted that several lower courts (such as *Clark*, supra) had engaged in subtle inquiries after *Grady* to determine whether the previously proven conduct establishes an "essential element" of the subsequently charged offense. He concluded, however, that it was "best not to enmesh in such subtleties the established doctrine that a conspiracy to commit a crime is a separate offense from the crime itself. Justice Stevens, joined by Justice Blackmun, concurred in the judgment. He argued that the overt acts proven against Felix did not establish an essential element of the conspiracy "because there is no overt act requirement in the federal drug conspiracy statute and the overt acts did not establish an agreement between Felix and his coconspirators".

2. Can an enterprise and the predicate acts be successively prosecuted? In Garrett v. United States, 471 U.S. 773 (1985) the Court held that a prosecution under the Continuing Criminal Enterprise statute could be brought after predicate acts had been prosecuted. *Grady* cites *Garrett* without an apparent intent to overrule it. Again, as with conspiracy, the enterprise is different conduct from that of the predicate acts. Lower courts have generally held that *Grady* does not bar successive prosecutions of predicate acts and the enterprise. On the other hand, unlike overt acts in conspiracy, predicate acts constitute an element of the crime in enterprise prosecutions. So an argument can be made that if the defendant was previously prosecuted for a predicate act, and the prosecution relies upon that act as a predicate for the enterprise prosecution, such conduct will establish an essential element of the enterprise. Courts have not to this point distinguished *Grady's* possibly different applications to conspiracies and enterprises. See e.g.,

United States v. Farmer, 924 F.2d 647 (7th Cir.1991) (error, if any, in proving two previously prosecuted predicate acts was harmless, because the defendant was found to have committed thirty-seven other predicate acts which had not been the subject of a former prosecution). In United States v. Felix, supra, the Court cited *Garrett* favorably and appeared to reject any application of *Grady* to "multilayered conduct, both as to time and to place" involved in enterprise prosecutions. The Court drew no distinction between subsequent conspiracy prosecutions, at issue in *Felix*, and subsequent enterprise prosecutions, at issue in *Garrett*.

3. When is a subsequent conspiracy prosecution barred by a previous one? Before *Grady,* lower courts looked at several factors, including overlapping time frame, congruence of co-conspirators, identity of overt acts, and location of relevant acts. See, e.g., United States v. Bryan, 896 F.2d 68 (5th Cir.1990) (double jeopardy bars second prosecution for conspiracy where the time frame of the "two conspiracies" substantially overlap, and the personnel, overt acts and location of the relevant acts are all substantially identical). These seem to be factors focussing on whether previously prosecuted conduct "establishes" the subsequently charged conspiracy, and that is precisely the test that *Grady* espouses. See United States v. Calderone, 917 F.2d 717 (2d Cir.1990), where the first prosecution was for a massive international drug conspiracy. The government then prosecuted the defendants on charges of a small conspiracy to distribute heroin in New York. The court dismissed the case under *Grady,* noting that the conduct proven in the first case and alleged in the second were overlapping to such a point that the previously proven conduct "constituted the entirety of" an element of the subsequently charged conspiracy.

Grady is discussed in Thomas, A Modest Proposal to Save the Double Jeopardy Clause, 69 Wash.Univ.L.Q. 195 (1991). Professor Thomas agrees with the result in *Grady,* but argues that the "same conduct" test should only apply where the initial prosecution is for a "grave" offense, which he defines as one for which imprisonment is authorized. He contends that such a limitation on *Grady* is required, or else the case will surely be overruled as inimical to state interests. Do you agree?

The Court found that an adequate remedy for a double jeopardy violation was provided by the state in Morris v. Mathews, 475 U.S. 237 (1986). The defendant pleaded guilty to aggravated robbery of a bank. Subsequently, he was charged with and convicted of aggravated murder, which was defined as causing the death of another while fleeing immediately after committing aggravated robbery. A state appellate court concluded that the double jeopardy clause barred the conviction for aggravated murder under the *Vitale* decision. But the court held that the jury had properly found the defendant guilty of murder, and it reduced his sentence accordingly.

Justice White's opinion for the Supreme Court reasoned that there is no per se rule requiring a new trial following a double jeopardy violation and that "when a jeopardy-barred conviction is reduced to a conviction for a lesser included offense which is not jeopardy barred, the burden shifts to the defendant to demonstrate a reasonable probability that he would not have been convicted of the non-jeopardy-barred offense absent the presence of the jeopardy-barred offense."[14] See also Daniels v. Bronson, 932 F.2d 102 (2d Cir.1991)

14. He cited *Strickland v. Washington,* an ineffective assistance of counsel case, discussed in connection with Chapter Ten. Justice White explained that a reasonable proba-

(reduction of the greater inclusive jeopardy-barred count to a non-duplicative lesser offense avoids double jeopardy without prejudice to the defendant).

B. DEFENSE RESPONSIBILITY FOR MULTIPLE TRIALS

The requirement of a single trial for the same conduct does not apply if the defendant is responsible for multiple prosecutions. In Jeffers v. United States, 432 U.S. 137 (1977), the defendant was charged with conspiracy to distribute drugs and with engaging in a continuing criminal enterprise to violate the drug laws. Jeffers opposed a government motion to consolidate the indictments. He successfully argued that his Sixth Amendment right to a fair trial would be endangered because much of the evidence which would be admitted against him and his co-defendants on the conspiracy charge would be inadmissible in his trial for conducting a continuing criminal enterprise. Jeffers requested and obtained a severance. Subsequently, he maintained that his prosecution for engaging in a continuing criminal enterprise violated the double jeopardy clause because the conspiracy charge was a lesser included offense. The Supreme Court rejected the claim.

> In this case, trial together of the conspiracy and continuing criminal enterprise charges could have taken place without undue prejudice to petitioner's Sixth Amendment right to a fair trial.[a] If the two charges had been tried in one proceeding, it appears that petitioner would have been entitled to a lesser-included-offense instruction. * * * Nevertheless, petitioner did not adopt that course. Instead, he was solely responsible for the successive prosecutions for the conspiracy offense and the continuing-criminal-enterprise offense. Under the circumstances, we hold that his action deprived him of any right that he might have had against consecutive trials.

If a trial judge accepts a guilty plea to a lesser offense over the objection of a prosecutor who seeks to convict on a greater offense, the fact that the trial judge dismisses the greater charges does not bar reprosecution on those charges. So the Supreme Court held in Ohio v. Johnson, 467 U.S. 493 (1984).

bility is one that is "sufficient to undermine confidence in the outcome." Later, he added that "[t]o prevail in a case like this, the defendant must show that, but for the improper inclusion of the jeopardy-barred charge, the result of the proceeding would have been different." The Court remanded the case for further proceedings.

Justice Blackmun, joined by Justice Powell, concurred in the judgment. He argued that the usual harmless error test should apply and that reversal should be required unless the error was harmless beyond a reasonable doubt. He objected to the test set forth by the majority, since the threshold question in ineffective assistance of counsel cases is whether the Constitution was violated. In the instant case, a violation was found, so the harmless error test should be used.

Justice Brennan dissented. He agreed with Justice Blackmun's argument that the harmless error test should apply, but found the error harmful. Justice Marshall also agreed that the harmless error test should apply, but argued that the court of appeals properly found the error to be prejudicial.

a. Petitioner argues that a finding of waiver is inconsistent with the decision in Simmons v. United States, 390 U.S. 377, 389–394 (1968), where the Court held that a defendant could not be required to surrender his Fifth Amendment privilege against compulsory self-incrimination in order to assert an arguably valid Fourth Amendment claim. In petitioner's case, however, the alleged Hobson's choice between asserting the Sixth Amendment fair trial right and asserting the Fifth Amendment double jeopardy claim is illusory. Had petitioner asked for a Rule 14 severance from the other defendants, the case might be different. In that event, he would have given the court an opportunity to ensure that prejudicial evidence relating only to other defendants would not have been introduced in his trial. * * * No such motion, however, was made. Under the circumstances of this case, therefore, no dilemma akin to that in *Simmons* arose.

Johnson was charged with four offenses, including murder. He offered to plead guilty to involuntary manslaughter and grand theft, but not to murder and aggravated robbery. The trial judge accepted his offer and dismissed the remaining charges on the ground that to prosecute him on these charges would place him in jeopardy twice. The prosecutor objected to this procedure and appealed from the dismissals. Two state appellate courts upheld the trial judge, but the Supreme Court, in an opinion by Justice Rehnquist, reversed.

The Court accepted, as it was required to, the Ohio courts' interpretation of state law as not intending cumulative punishment for murder and manslaughter. Thus, it stated that should Johnson be convicted on the more serious charges, the trial court would have to confront the question of cumulative punishments and assure that state law was followed. The Court rejected, however, the claim that the federal Constitution barred a trial on the more serious charges.

Justice Brennan concurred on the double jeopardy point, but expressed the view that the Ohio state courts had relied on state, not federal, law. Justice Stevens, joined by Justice Marshall, dissented. He agreed with Justice Brennan that the judgment rested on state law, but, since the Court reached the merits, he expressed his view that a conviction based on a plea of guilty produces the same result as a conviction upon a jury verdict. He concluded, therefore, that double jeopardy principles barred reprosecution of Johnson for a greater offense when he had already been convicted of a lesser offense. For an analysis of the problems created by Ohio v. Johnson, see Ohio v. Johnson: Prohibiting the Offensive Use of Guilty Pleas to Invoke Double Jeopardy Protection, 19 Ga.L.Rev. 159 (1984). See also Taylor v. Whitley, 933 F.2d 325 (5th Cir.1991) (defendant waives a double jeopardy attack by pleading guilty, unless the double jeopardy violation is apparent on the face of the indictment; relying on United States v. Broce, 488 U.S. 563 (1989) (discussed in Chapter Nine)).

C. SUBSEQUENT DEVELOPMENTS AND JEOPARDY

In Garrett v. United States, 471 U.S. 773 (1985), the Court held that a defendant who had pleaded guilty to importing marijuana in a federal court in Washington state could subsequently be prosecuted in Florida and punished for engaging in a "continuing criminal enterprise," even though the marijuana importation to which he had pleaded was used as evidence of the enterprise. Since the enterprise charged had not been completed when the defendant was indicted in Washington, the Court held that Diaz v. United States, 223 U.S. 442 (1912) (prosecution of homicide allowed following prosecution for assault and battery where victim died following the first trial), controlled and the defendant was not impermissibly placed in double jeopardy as a result of the second prosecution. Justice Stevens, joined by Justices Brennan and Marshall, agreed that a second prosecution could be brought, but argued that the Washington importation could not be used as a predicate offense. He reasoned that all of the facts necessary to sustain the Florida charge were known before the defendant was indicted in Washington. Thus, there was no necessity for two prosecutions. Justice Powell did not participate.

D. MULTIPLE PUNISHMENTS

The double jeopardy clause prohibits multiple punishment for the *same* crime. This principle was established in Ex parte Lange, 85 U.S. (18 Wall.) 163 (1873). In *Lange*, the defendant was sentenced to both a fine and imprisonment. After the defendant fully paid the fine, the judge realized that the statute allowed only a fine *or* imprisonment. He vacated the sentence and imposed a new sentence of imprisonment. Because the defendant had suffered complete punishment for the crime by paying the fine, no further punishment could be imposed. In a subsequent case, United States v. Benz, 282 U.S. 304 (1931), the Court held that a trial judge could lower a sentence without violating the double jeopardy clause. In dictum, the Court indicated that increasing a penalty being served would constitute multiple punishment in violation of the double jeopardy clause. Bozza v. United States, 330 U.S. 160 (1947), qualified this approach by allowing a district court to increase a sentence to conform to the statutory minimum sentence.[15]

The Court distinguished *Lange* and In re Bradley, 318 U.S. 50 (1943) in Jones v. Thomas, 491 U.S. 376 (1989). Thomas had been convicted of attempted robbery and of first-degree felony murder for a killing during the commission of a felony and was sentenced to 15 years and life respectively, with the 15 years to be served first. He sought state postconviction relief, arguing that it was improper for him to receive separate punishment for the enhanced murder and the underlying felony. After the state supreme court accepted this argument in another case, the Governor commuted Thomas' sentence, and he remained in custody pursuant to the murder conviction with credit for the time served on the underlying felony. The Supreme Court held that the Double Jeopardy Clause did not require that Thomas be released, simply because he had completed his sentence on the underlying felony offense.

Justice Kennedy wrote for the Court, and acknowledged that the Double Jeopardy Clause protects against "additions to a sentence in a subsequent proceeding that upset a defendant's legitimate expectation of finality." He nonetheless concluded that the state had properly cured the double jeopardy problem under Morris v. Matthews, supra. He distinguished *Lange* as involv-

15. The prohibition against multiple punishment also requires that time served on an original sentence be credited toward a sentence imposed after retrial. North Carolina v. Pearce, 395 U.S. 711 (1969). The credit must include accumulated good-time credits.

The Supreme court held in Weaver v. Graham, 450 U.S. 24 (1981), that Florida enacted an ex post facto law when it repealed a statute and thereby reduced the amount of "gain time" deducted from a prisoner's sentence for good conduct.

The double jeopardy clause itself may not speak to problems like the permissibility of denying credit for pre-trial incarceration toward any sentence that is imposed, since pre-trial incarceration is not viewed as punishment. Also, the double jeopardy clause may not be strictly applicable when a prisoner accepts a parole on the condition that any time spent on parole will not be credited toward time served if parole is revoked. See, e.g., Lashley v. Florida, 413 F.Supp. 850 (M.D.Fla.1976) and cases cited therein.

If a person is convicted of a crime and serves time before overturning the conviction and the person is not retried, should the person have a right to credit for the time served on any future sentence? There is a strong moral argument that she should, at least if the future sentence is for a crime that occurred prior to the overturning of the conviction on which time was served. If the crime occurred thereafter and an automatic credit applied, a person might have a constitutional right to commit an offense without fear of punishment. Whether the moral argument can be grounded in the double jeopardy clause is doubtful, especially in light of the Court's definition of the same offense.

ing more punishment than the legislature authorized. He conceded that *Bradley* was more analogous to Thomas' case, since Bradley was sentenced for contempt to a $500 fine and six months imprisonment under a statute that made fine and imprisonment alternative sanctions. Bradley was taken to prison and two days later paid the fine. The Supreme Court held that he was entitled to be released from prison, even if the state would have preferred to have returned the fine. Justice Kennedy reasoned that *Bradley* involved alternative punishments prescribed for the same crime, whereas the instant case involved separate sentences for what the sentencing court thought were separately punishable offenses. He concluded that the legislature in *Bradley* intended one punishment or the other, but the legislature in the instant case intended that Thomas should be convicted of felony murder or of both murder and the underlying felony. He added that extension of *Bradley* would result in the case turning on whether the 15–year sentence was imposed prior to or after the life sentence, and opined that there was no reason to believe that the order of the sentences was of the slightest importance to the sentencing judge.

Justice Scalia dissented and was joined by Justice Stevens, and in all but one footnote by Justices Brennan and Marshall. He argued that, even though the sentencing judge erroneously thought that the 15–year and life sentences were punishments for separate offenses, state law established that these were alternative punishments. Thus, he concluded that the instant case could not be distinguished from *Lange* and *Bradley.* Justice Scalia candidly stated that "[t]he Double Jeopardy Clause is and has always been, not a provision designed to assure reason and justice in the particular case, but the embodiment of technical, prophylactic rules that require the Government to turn square corners," and that "[w]henever it is applied to release a criminal deserving of punishment it frustrates justice in the particular case, but for the greater purpose of assuring repose in the totality of circumstances." He added that "[w]ith technical rules, above all others, it is imperative that we adhere to what we have stated the rules to be," since "[a] technical rule with equitable exceptions is no rule at all."

What constitutes "punishment" for purposes of the Double Jeopardy Clause? In United States v. Halper, 490 U.S. 435 (1989), the Court unanimously held that in rare instances where a defendant has previously sustained a criminal penalty and the government seeks an additional civil penalty which bears no rational relationship to compensating for loss, imposition of the second penalty might constitute double punishment which is prohibited by the Double Jeopardy Clause. Justice Blackmun wrote for the Court that the general approach to deciding whether a proceeding is civil or criminal is not well suited to analyzing Double Jeopardy issues, since "a civil as well as a criminal sanction constitutes punishment when the sanction as applied in the individual case serves the goal of punishment."

The facts involved a manager of a medical service company who was convicted of submitting 65 false claims for government reimbursement and fined $5,000. Thereafter, the government sought summary judgment under the False Claims Act, which provided for a civil penalty of $2,000 on each claim, as well as a penalty for twice the amount of the government's actual damages of $585 and the costs of the action. Thus, the government sought a sanction of $130,000 for a $585 fraud.

Justice Blackmun wrote as follows:

> What we announce now is a rule for the rare case, the case such as the one before us, where a fixed-penalty provision subjects a prolific but small-gauge offender to a sanction overwhelmingly disproportionate to the damages he has caused. The rule is one of reason: Where a defendant previously has sustained a criminal penalty and the civil penalty sought in the subsequent proceeding bears no rational relation to the goal of compensating the Government for its loss, but rather appears to qualify as "punishment" in the plain meaning of the word, then the defendant is entitled to an accounting of the Government's damages and costs to determine if the penalty sought in fact constitutes a second punishment. We must leave to the trial court the discretion to determine on the basis of such an accounting, the size of the civil sanction the Government may receive without crossing the line between remedy and punishment. * * * While the trial court's judgment in these matters often may amount to no more than an approximation, even an approximation will go far towards ensuring both that the Government is fully compensated for the costs of corruption and that, as required by the Double Jeopardy Clause, the defendant is protected from a sanction so disproportionate to the damages caused that it constitutes a second punishment."

Justice Blackmun concluded that "under the Double Jeopardy Clause a defendant who has already been punished in a criminal prosecution may not be subjected to an additional civil sanction to the extent that the second sanction may not fairly be characterized as remedial, but only as a deterrent or retribution." The Court stressed that it was not precluding the government "from seeking the full civil penalty against a defendant who previously has not been punished for the same conduct, even if the civil sanction imposed is punitive." The Court remanded for a determination of the government's actual damages; it noted that if the damage figure of $16,000, as originally projected by the district court, were correct, Halper's liability would be "sufficiently disproportionate that the sanction constitutes a second punishment." For a discussion of *Halper* and the growing trend toward using civil remedies for criminal law enforcement, see Cheh, Constitutional Limits on Using Civil Remedies To Achieve Criminal Law Objectives: Understanding and Transcending the Criminal-Civil Law Distinction, 42 Hast.L.J. 1325 (1991).

Although it is not immediately obvious, it seems that the protection against multiple punishments is directed more against prosecutors and trial courts than against legislators. If a legislature decides that it wants a robber or burglar to serve twice as much time for an offense, it can increase the maximum sentence (and raise the minimum also, if necessary). But a prosecutor who wants someone to serve more time than the legislature has prescribed may try to charge the same offense more than once. Generally, a legislature that establishes a hierarchy of lesser and greater offenses increases the punishment for each greater offense. The increased punishment represents punishment for the additional elements that distinguish the greater from the lesser offense. Thus, courts properly assume that prosecutors and trial courts cannot add together sentences for greater and lesser offenses. It is doubtful that a legislature would or could pass the same statute twice, give it two different numbers, and have a person prosecuted for the exact same thing twice. (It is never necessary to do this, since increasing the punishment for a single offense accomplishes almost the same thing. The only difference is that a prosecutor who brings two cases has two chances to win. But if he loses the first time, he cannot try again because of collateral estoppel.)

In several cases, the Court has emphasized that a legislature may provide separate, cumulative penalties for offenses that might appear to be greater and lesser included offenses—i.e., the legislature may separate criminal acts if it wishes to do so.

In Whalen v. United States, 445 U.S. 684 (1980), Justice Stewart's opinion for the Court held that the defendant was improperly sentenced when he was given one sentence for felony (first-degree) murder and another for the underlying offense of rape. Justice Stewart found that Congress had not authorized multiple sentences for these crimes. He stated that "[t]he Double Jeopardy Clause at the very least precludes federal courts from imposing consecutive sentences unless authorized by Congress to do so. * * * If a federal court exceeds its own authority by imposing multiple punishments not authorized by Congress, it violates not only the specific guarantee against double jeopardy, but also the constitutional principle of separation of powers in a manner that trenches particularly harshly on individual liberty." Separate opinions by Justice Blackmun and Justice White emphasized that their votes turned solely on the intent of Congress, not on double jeopardy principles. Justice Rehnquist dissented and was joined by the Chief Justice. See also Busic v. La Rocca, 446 U.S. 398 (1980) (Blackmun, J., concurring and Rehnquist, J., dissenting) (emphasizing that the double jeopardy clause does not bar multiple punishments for what the legislature decides are two crimes).

United States v. Rodriguez, 612 F.2d 906 (5th Cir. 1980) (en banc), held that consecutive offenses could be imposed on defendants convicted of conspiracy to import and conspiracy to distribute marijuana. Both convictions were under the Comprehensive Drug Abuse and Control Act of 1970. The court focused on Congressional intent and found no double jeopardy problem, since "the Double Jeopardy Clause imposes no limits on Congress' power to define the allowable unit of prosecution and punishment, at least so long as all charges are brought in a single proceeding." The Supreme Court affirmed in Albernaz v. United States, 450 U.S. 333 (1981), saying that "the question of what punishments are constitutionally permissible is not different from the question of what punishment the Legislative Branch intended to be imposed." Justice Stewart, joined by Justices Marshall and Stevens concurring in the judgment agreed that there were two offenses under the scheme but said that "[n]o matter how clearly it spoke, Congress could not constitutionally provide for cumulative punishments unless each statutory offense required proof of a fact that the other did not. * * *".

Justice Stewart's argument in *Albernaz* was based on Blockburger v. United States, discussed in detail in Grady v. Corbin. The Court has held that the *Blockburger* test, focussing on whether each statutory offense requires proof of an element that the other does not, provides an appropriate starting point for determining whether the legislature has authorized multiple punishments. See *Grady*. That is, if the elements of the two offenses are the same, the presumption is that multiple punishments are not intended. However, the Court in Missouri v. Hunter, 459 U.S. 359 (1983), held that *Blockburger* is merely a rule of statutory construction, which can be overcome by a clear showing that the legislature intended multiple punishments. The Court stated that where "a legislature specifically authorizes cumulative punishments under two statutes, regardless of whether those two statutes proscribe the same conduct under *Blockburger,* a court's task of statutory construction is at an end" and cumulative punishments can be imposed in a single trial.

Hunter was convicted of first degree robbery of a grocery store, which meant that he used a dangerous and deadly weapon in the robbery, and also of armed criminal action, which meant that he committed a felony with a dangerous or deadly weapon. The state supreme court held that the state legislature intended to provide two punishments for what it found to be the same offense. Writing for the majority, Chief Justice Burger observed that Hunter had not been subjected to two trials, only to two punishments. He reasoned that there is nothing in the double jeopardy clause to prohibit a state from punishing conduct by means of cumulative statutes. Justice Marshall, joined by Justice Stevens, dissented. The dissent argued that where multiple charges for the same conduct are brought, the prosecution obtains an unfair advantage because a jury is more likely to convict on one count, even as a compromise; that several convictions, rather than one, mean greater collateral consequences for the defendant; and that the stigma resulting from more than one conviction for the same conduct would be excessive.

For applications of *Blockburger* and *Hunter,* see, e.g., United States v. Holloway, 905 F.2d 893 (5th Cir.1990) (cumulative punishment for even the same offense is not prohibited by the Double Jeopardy Clause, so long as legislative intent is clear; under the Crime Control Act of 1984, the defendant can be punished both for armed bank robbery and for use of a firearm in a crime of violence, since Congress intended that offenses committed with firearms should be subject to cumulative punishment); United States v. Marrero, 904 F.2d 251 (5th Cir.1990) (*Blockburger* test applied to permit cumulative punishments for presenting false insurance claims to a government agency and for theft of government services; insurance claim statute required proof that a false claim was submitted while theft statute did not, and theft statute required proof of a conversion but insurance claim statute did not).

In United States v. York, 888 F.2d 1050 (5th Cir.1989) the defendant was cumulatively sentenced under 18 U.S.C. § 1001 and 18 U.S.C. § 1014. Both crimes concern the use of fraudulent documents to mislead the government. Section 1014 specifically applies to intent to influence a financial institution, while section 1001 generally prohibits lying on forms submitted to government officials. The court applied the *Blockburger* test and found that section 1014 has an element (influencing a financial institution) that section 1001 does not. The court had more trouble with finding an element in section 1001 that is not included in section 1014. But the court held that even if all of the section 1001 elements were included in section 1014, and thus the *Blockburger* test were failed (since *each* crime must have an element that the other does not), multiple punishment was still permissible. The court relied on *Hunter* and found a clear Congressional intent to punish these crimes separately. It reasoned that if multiple punishments were not intended, section 1014 would be superfluous: section 1001 crimes are easier to prove and carry a higher sentence. Also, the statutes were passed at different times and were in response to different problems. Does this mean that if the elements are different, multiple punishments are permissible under *Blockburger,* and if the elements are the same, multiple punishments are permissible under *Hunter* because otherwise one of the statutes would be superfluous?

Chief Justice Burger wrote for the Court in Ball v. United States, 470 U.S. 856 (1985), as it found that Congress did not intend that a felon could be convicted and concurrently sentenced for both receiving a firearm and possessing it in violation of federal law. The Court concluded, however, that a defendant could be charged with two offenses. Should the defendant be found guilty of both, the trial judge may enter a judgment as to only one offense. Justice Stevens concurred in the judgment. He suggested that, since Ball was not only tried but was also convicted of both offenses, it was unnecessary for the Court to decide whether a defendant could be charged with the two offenses as long as he was convicted of only one. He added that "I see no reason why this Court should go out of its way to encourage prosecutors to tilt the scales of justice against the defendant by employing such tactics," and quoted from Justice Marshall's dissent in Missouri v. Hunter. Justice Marshall concurred in the judgment without opinion, and Justice Powell did not participate in the case.

Note

You may have realized that in one sense many punishments for criminal activity may involve additional sanctions for previous convictions. This is because one of the familiar factors that courts take into account in imposing sentences is whether the defendant has a prior record. Some judges, in sentencing repeat offenders, will impose a sentence on new convictions that is higher than they would impose on first offenders, because they take into account previous convictions. Can you think of a rationale for this that would take it out of the double jeopardy prohibition? In thinking about your answer, consider what happens to a defendant who never is convicted a second time.

V. COLLATERAL ESTOPPEL

The same offense definition also applies when the defendant is acquitted and the government seeks to reprosecute. Separate offenses generally may be tried separately. But even where separate trials on distinct offenses are held, the double jeopardy clause still may be important.

Closely related to the double jeopardy prohibition against retrial after an acquittal is the collateral estoppel bar to relitigation of any ultimate fact determined in favor of the defendant in a prior prosecution. In the following case, which held that the rule of collateral estoppel is a constitutional requirement of the double jeopardy clause, note what the prosecutor was trying to do.

ASHE v. SWENSON

Supreme Court of the United States, 1970.
397 U.S. 436.

MR. JUSTICE STEWART delivered the opinion of the Court.

* * *

Sometime in the early hours of the morning of January 10, 1960, six men were engaged in a poker game in the basement of the home of John Gladson at Lee's Summit, Missouri. Suddenly three or four masked men, armed with a shotgun and pistols, broke into the basement and robbed each of the poker players of money and various articles of personal property. The robbers—and it has never been clear whether there were three or four of them—then fled in a car belonging to one of the victims of the robbery. Shortly thereafter the stolen car was discovered in a field, and later that morning three men were arrested by a state trooper while they were walking on a highway not far from where the abandoned car had been found. The petitioner was arrested by another officer some distance away.

The four were subsequently charged with seven separate offenses—the armed robbery of each of the six poker players and the theft of the car. In May 1960 the petitioner went to trial on the charge of robbing Donald Knight, one of the participants in the poker game. At the trial the State called Knight and three of his fellow poker players as prosecution witnesses. Each of them described the circumstances of the holdup and itemized his own individual losses. The proof that an armed robbery had occurred and that personal property had been taken from Knight as well as from each of the others was unassailable. The testimony of the four victims in this regard was consistent both internally and with that of the others. But the State's evidence that the petitioner had been one of the robbers was weak. Two of the witnesses thought that there had been only three robbers altogether, and could not identify the petitioner as one of them. Another of the victims, who was the petitioner's uncle by marriage, said that at the "patrol station" he had positively identified each of the other three men accused of the holdup, but could say only that the petitioner's voice "sounded very much like" that of one of the robbers. The fourth participant in the poker game did identify the petitioner, but only by his "size and height, and his actions."

The cross-examination of these witnesses was brief, and it was aimed primarily at exposing the weakness of their identification testimony. Defense counsel made no attempt to question their testimony regarding the holdup itself or their claims as to their losses. Knight testified without contradiction that the robbers had stolen from him his watch, $250 in cash, and about $500 in checks. His billfold, which had been found by the police in the possession of one of the three other men accused of the robbery, was admitted in evidence. The defense offered no testimony and waived final argument.

The trial judge instructed the jury that if it found that the petitioner was one of the participants in the armed robbery, the theft of "any money" from Knight would sustain a conviction. He also instructed the jury that if the petitioner was one of the robbers, he was guilty under the law even if he had not personally robbed Knight. The jury—though not instructed to elaborate upon its verdict—found the petitioner "not guilty due to insufficient evidence."

Six weeks later the petitioner was brought to trial again, this time for the robbery of another participant in the poker game, a man named Roberts. The petitioner filed a motion to dismiss, based on his previous acquittal. The motion was overruled, and the second trial began. The witnesses were for the most part the same, though this time their testimony was substantially stronger on the issue of the petitioner's identity. For example, two witnesses who at the first trial had been wholly unable to identify the petitioner as one of the robbers, now testified that his features, size, and mannerisms matched those of one of their assailants. Another witness who before had identified the petitioner only by his size and actions now also remembered him by the unusual sound of his voice. The State further refined its case at the second trial by declining to call one of the participants in the poker game whose identification testimony at the first trial had been conspicuously negative. The case went to the jury on instructions virtually identical to those given at the first trial. This time the jury found the petitioner guilty, and he was sentenced to a 35-year term in the state penitentiary.

[The State Supreme Court affirmed the conviction. Petitioner's request for a writ of habeas corpus was denied on the authority of Hoag v. New Jersey, 356 U.S. 464 (1958). In *Hoag*, the facts were virtually identical to those in *Ashe*. The Court accepted the state's determination that the previous acquittal did not give rise to an estoppel. Because *Hoag* was decided before Benton v. Maryland made the due process clause applicable to the states, the *Hoag* Court did not examine whether collateral estoppel is an ingredient of the Fifth Amendment guarantee against double jeopardy.]

The doctrine of Benton v. Maryland, 395 U.S. 784, puts the issues in the present case in a perspective quite different from that in which the issues were perceived in Hoag v. New Jersey, supra. The question is no longer whether collateral estoppel is a requirement of due process, but whether it is a part of the Fifth Amendment's guarantee against double jeopardy. And if collateral estoppel is embodied in that guarantee, then its applicability in a particular case is no longer a matter to be left for state court determination within the broad bounds of "fundamental fairness," but a matter of constitutional fact we must decide through an examination of the entire record.

"Collateral estoppel" is an awkward phrase, but it stands for an extremely important principle in our adversary system of justice. It means simply that when an issue of ultimate fact has once been determined by a valid and final judgment, that issue cannot again be litigated between the same parties in any future lawsuit. Although first developed in civil litigation, collateral estoppel has been an established rule of federal criminal law at least since this Court's decision more than 50 years ago in United States v. Oppenheimer, 242 U.S. 85. * * *

The federal decisions have made clear that the rule of collateral estoppel in criminal cases is not to be applied with the hypertechnical and archaic approach of a 19th century pleading book, but with realism and rationality. Where a previous judgment of acquittal was based upon a general verdict, as is usually the case, this approach requires a court to "examine the record of a prior proceeding, taking into account the pleadings, evidence, charge, and other relevant matter, and conclude whether a rational jury could have grounded its verdict upon an issue other than that which the defendant seeks to foreclose from consideration." * * * Any test more technically restrictive would, of course, simply amount to a rejection of the rule of collateral estoppel in criminal proceedings, at least in every case where the first judgment was based upon a general verdict of acquittal.

Straightforward application of the federal rule to the present case can lead to but one conclusion. For the record is utterly devoid of any indication that the first jury could rationally have found that an armed robbery had not occurred, or that Knight had not been a victim of that robbery. The single rationally conceivable issue in dispute before the jury was whether the petitioner had been one of the robbers. And the jury by its verdict found that he had not. The federal rule of law, therefore, would make a second prosecution for the robbery of Roberts wholly impermissible.

The ultimate question to be determined, then, in the light of Benton v. Maryland, supra, is whether this established rule of federal law is embodied in the Fifth Amendment guarantee against double jeopardy. We do not hesitate to hold that it is. For whatever else that constitutional guarantee may embrace, it surely protects a man who has been acquitted from having to "run the gantlet" a second time.

The question is not whether Missouri could validly charge the petitioner with six separate offenses for the robbery of the six poker players. It is not whether he could have received a total of six punishments if he had been convicted in a single trial of robbing the six victims. It is simply whether, after a jury determined by its verdict that the petitioner was not one of the robbers, the State could constitutionally hale him before a new jury to litigate that issue again.

After the first jury had acquitted the petitioner of robbing Knight, Missouri could certainly not have brought him to trial again upon that charge. Once a jury had determined upon conflicting testimony that there was at least a reasonable doubt that the petitioner was one of the robbers, the State could not present the same or different identification evidence in a second prosecution for the robbery of Knight in the hope that a different jury might find that evidence more convincing. The situation is constitutionally no different here, even though the second trial related to another victim of the same robbery. For the name of the victim, in the circumstances of this case, had no bearing whatever upon the issue of whether the petitioner was one of the robbers.

In this case the State in its brief has frankly conceded that following the petitioner's acquittal, it treated the first trial as no more than a dry run for the second prosecution: "No doubt the prosecutor felt the state had a provable case on the first charge and, when he lost, he did what every good attorney would do—he refined his presentation in light of the turn of events at the first trial." But this is precisely what the constitutional guarantee forbids.

[Justices Black and Harlan concurred separately. Justice Brennan, joined by Justices Douglas and Marshall, urged in concurrence that the double jeopardy clause bars prosecution in separate trials for crimes stemming from a single criminal act, occurrence, episode or transaction. Chief Justice Burger dissented.]

Note

Ashe provides some protection for a defendant who is unable to face all charges in one trial. As commentators and courts have often noted,[16] however, juries frequently return general verdicts. The defense of collateral estoppel may not be available because several issues might have been the basis for the acquittal. Again the question posed in Grady v. Corbin arises: would it be better to require that all offenses stemming from one transaction be joined together? Does the government have a good reason for not wanting to join multiple counts in some cases?

Only a party to the prior criminal proceeding may take advantage of the collateral estoppel rule. A unanimous Court in Standefer v. United States, 447

16. See, e.g., Schaefer, Unresolved Issues in the Law of Double Jeopardy: Waller and Ashe, 58 Calif.L.Rev. 387 (1970); Note, 69 Mich.L.Rev. 762 (1971).

See also United States v. Clark, 613 F.2d 391 (2d Cir. 1980) (placing a heavy burden on a defendant claiming collateral estoppel to show that the fact he seeks to foreclose was actually resolved in his favor in previous litigation).

U.S. 10 (1980), held that a defendant accused of aiding and abetting in the commission of a federal offense may be convicted after the named principal has been acquitted of that offense. Chief Justice Burger's opinion rejected the attempt to extend the concept of "nonmutual collateral estoppel," developed in civil cases, into constitutional criminal procedure. Among the special attributes of criminal cases relied upon were the following: the government's limited discovery rights; the impossibility of a directed verdict for the government; the limitations on the government's right to appeal; the existence of exclusionary rules that may exclude evidence as to one defendant but not another; and the governmental interest in enforcement of the criminal law.

Non-parties cannot be bound by a prior adjudication of facts. See Vestal, Issue Preclusion and Criminal Prosecutions, 65 Iowa L.Rev. 281 (1980). So, for example, the suppression of evidence in a state prosecution does not automatically prevent the United States from using that evidence in a federal proceeding. "Since the United States was not a party to the state action, and had no way of making its views on the issue known to the state judge, it cannot be fairly considered to have had its day in court." United States v. Davis, 906 F.2d 829 (2d Cir.1990). The same principles would apply to a subsequent prosecution in a different state.

There is an exception to this rule if "the relationship between federal and state prosecutors is so close that it placed the federal government in privity with the state prosecution." Id. To find a privity relationship, some courts have required the defendant to show that "the state proceeding was merely a sham and a cover for a federal prosecution." United States v. Ng, 699 F.2d 63 (2d Cir.1983) (state must be the tool of the federal government). Other courts have required the lesser showing that the federal government "actively participated" in the state prosecution. United States v. Nasworthy, 710 F.Supp. 1353 (S.D.Fla.1989) (federal government had a "laboring oar" in the state court litigation). How much participation would you require before finding that one sovereign was bound by an adjudication against another? It should be noted that even if privity is found, "collateral estoppel would be inappropriate unless the issue resolved in the first proceeding was the same as the issue sought to be relitigated." United States v. Davis, supra. So if, for instance, a state court's suppression order is based on state law rather than the Fourth Amendment, collateral estoppel will not apply in the federal proceeding, or in a proceeding in another state. Id. See the material on the exclusionary rule in Chapter Two.

A fact once determined against a defendant is not binding upon him in a subsequent criminal prosecution. He is entitled to relitigate the claim. Evidence of the prior judgment might be admissible to prove facts necessarily found beyond a reasonable doubt. See, e.g., Fed.R.Evid. 803(22). As the Court suggested in *Ashe*, and reaffirmed in Simpson v. Florida, 403 U.S. 384 (1971) (holding that *Ashe* applied after acquittal in second trial even though defendant was convicted in first trial, which was reversed on appeal), mutuality of estoppel is not required, and not permitted. In a civil proceeding following a conviction, in which the parties are the same, such as a civil enforcement proceeding, collateral estoppel may be invoked against a convicted defendant. See, e.g., United States v. Podell, 572 F.2d 31 (2d Cir. 1978) (guilty plea to substantive violation of a conflict of interest statute prevented the defendant from denying his breach of fiduciary duties when the government tried to impose a constructive trust on money he received in breach of his fiduciary duty).

May an acquittal of a substantive charge ever be used by a defendant in a subsequent civil forfeiture case? In One Lot Emerald Cut Stones v. United States,

409 U.S. 232, 233 (1972), the Court concluded that a prior acquittal for "willfully and knowingly, with intent to defraud the United States, smuggling * * * articles into the United States without submitting to the required customs procedures" did not bar a civil forfeiture action. The civil action only required proof that the property was brought into the United States without the required customs declaration. Collateral estoppel could not apply because the acquittal might have been based on the lack of the requisite intent. The Court also noted that the difference in burden of proof in the civil and criminal cases precluded the application of collateral estoppel.

Chief Justice Burger wrote for a unanimous Court in United States v. One Assortment of 89 Firearms, 465 U.S. 354 (1984), holding that a gun owner's acquittal on criminal charges involving firearms does not preclude a subsequent in rem forfeiture proceeding. The Court reasoned that since a lesser burden of proof applies in the forfeiture proceeding, collateral estoppel was no bar. Moreover, the Court found that the proceeding is civil in nature and not within the scope of the double jeopardy clause.

In Dowling v. United States, 493 U.S. 342 (1990), the Court refused to apply the collateral estoppel doctrine when facts underlying a prior acquittal were used as evidence of an unrelated offense. Dowling was charged with bank robbery. On the issue of identification, the prosecution offered evidence that the defendant had participated in another robbery under similar circumstances. See Federal Rule of Evidence 404(b). Dowling had been acquitted of that robbery, and argued that its introduction at the later trial was prohibited by *Ashe*. Justice White's majority opinion distinguished *Ashe* on the ground that Dowling's prior acquittal "did not determine the ultimate issue in the present case." The Court further noted that, to introduce evidence of an unrelated crime, the prosecution was not required to show that the defendant committed that crime beyond a reasonable doubt. Under the Federal Rules of Evidence, similar act evidence is admissible if the jury could reasonably conclude that the act occurred and the defendant was the actor. Justice Rehnquist therefore found support in the cases permitting civil forfeiture actions after an acquittal on a criminal conviction.

Justice Brennan, joined by Justices Marshall and Stevens, dissented. Justice Brennan argued that the majority took insufficient account of the burdens imposed upon a defendant if facts are relitigated in a subsequent criminal prosecution.

As pointed out in the dissents in Grady v. Corbin, supra, *Dowling* appears inconsistent with *Grady*. Despite their apparent inconsistency, the cases can be reconciled. *Grady* bars situations in which "to establish an essential element of an offense charged" in a subsequent prosecution, the government attempts to prove conduct for which the defendant has already been prosecuted. In *Dowling*, the evidence of the prior crime did not "establish" an element of the later offense. It was evidence of a later offense, but the Court in *Grady* specifically rejected a "same evidence" test as overbroad. The Court in United States v. Felix, 112 S.Ct. 1377 (1992) made this point by stating that "introduction of relevant evidence of particular misconduct in a case is not the same thing as prosecution for that conduct." The Court in *Felix* found no Double Jeopardy violation where uncharged drug activity was offered to show defendant's intent in one case, and then subsequently prosecuted in another.

Dowling has been interpreted to permit a sentencing court to consider acquitted conduct. See United States v. Averi, 922 F.2d 765 (11th Cir.1991) (the fact that the crime was not proved beyond a reasonable doubt does not preclude consideration where the governing standard of proof is lower).

VI. DUAL SOVEREIGNS

The double jeopardy clause only prohibits successive prosecutions by the same "sovereign." The dual sovereignty doctrine is well-explained in United States v. Davis, 906 F.2d 829 (2d Cir.1990):

> One of the by-products of our nation's federal system is the doctrine of 'dual sovereignty.' Under this well-established principle, a federal prosecution does not bar a subsequent state prosecution of the same person for the same acts, and a state prosecution does not bar a federal one. This doctrine rests upon the basic structure or our polity. The states and the national government are distinct political communities, drawing their separate sovereign power from different sources, each from the organic law that established it. Each has the power, inherent in any sovereign, independently to determine what shall be an offense against its authority and to punish such offenses. When a single act violates the laws of two sovereigns, the wrongdoer has committed two distinct offenses. See generally United States v. Wheeler, 435 U.S. 313 (1978).
>
> In practice, successive prosecutions for the same conduct remain rarities. In the normal exercise of prosecutorial discretion, one sovereign usually defers to the other. For example, as a matter of policy the federal government ordinarily will not pursue criminal charges against a defendant who has already been prosecuted in state court. See United States Department of Justice, United States Attorneys' Manual, Tit. 9, § 2.142. However, this is no limitation on the government's sovereign right to vindicate its interests and values, and nothing prevents a federal prosecution whenever the state proceeding has not adequately protected the federal interest.
>
> The only legally binding exception to the dual sovereignty doctrine is a narrow one carved out by the Supreme Court in Bartkus v. Illinois, 359 U.S. 121 (1959). Successive prosecutions will be barred where one prosecuting sovereign can be said to be acting as a 'tool' of the other, or where one prosecution is merely a 'sham and a cover' for another. Except for this extraordinary type of case, successive state and federal prosecutions may, in fact as well as form, be brought by different sovereigns and the outcome in a state proceeding is not binding upon the later prosecution.

As implied by the discussion in *Davis,* the dual sovereignty principle also allows two different states to prosecute the defendant for the same conduct. Heath v. Alabama, 474 U.S. 82 (1985) (discussed below). Also, it does not matter that the defendant is acquitted by one sovereign, since the point is that another sovereign is not bound by the prior adjudication. See Bartkus v. Illinois, 359 U.S. 121 (1959) (upholding state conviction for robbery where defendant had previously been acquitted of federal charges stemming from the same robbery); United States v. Farmer, 924 F.2d 647 (7th Cir.1991) (previous acquittal on predicate acts in state court does not prohibit subsequent RICO prosecution in federal court).

In Abbate v. United States, 359 U.S. 187 (1959), the Court upheld a federal prosecution following a state conviction based upon the same criminal act. The Court reaffirmed *Bartkus,* and expressed concern that one sovereign could hinder the law enforcement efforts of another. Shortly after the decision in *Abbate,* the Justice Department established the "Petite Policy" of not prosecuting an individual after a state prosecution for the same act, unless there are compelling reasons for the second proceedings. The policy is reprinted, in large part, in United States v. Mechanic, 454 F.2d 849, 856 n. 5 (8th Cir.1971), and is now set forth in the United States Attorneys' Manual, § 9–2.142. United States Attorneys must obtain approval from an Assistant Attorney General before instituting the second prosecution.[17]

In Waller v. Florida, 397 U.S. 387 (1970), the Court refused to consider a municipality a separate sovereign from the state of which it is a part. The defendant, who removed a mural from a wall in the St. Petersburg city hall, was convicted in municipal court of violating a city ordinance prohibiting destruction of city property and of disorderly breach of the peace. The state of Florida subsequently charged him with grand larceny. The Court refused to permit successive municipality-state prosecutions, and analogized the relationship to that of the federal government and a federal territory.

Although the dual sovereign rule of *Bartkus* and *Abbate* has been criticized greatly,[18] the Court reaffirmed the rationale in United States v. Wheeler, 435 U.S. 313 (1978), and Heath v. Alabama, 474 U.S. 82 (1985). In *Wheeler*, federal prosecution of an Indian for statutory rape was permitted even though he had been convicted of a lesser offense by a tribal court.

In Heath v. Alabama, 474 U.S. 82 (1985), the Supreme Court affirmed an Alabama capital murder conviction of a man who had previously pleaded guilty in Georgia to murder based on the same homicide. Heath was found guilty of hiring two men to kill his wife, who was nine months pregnant at the time of her death. The men kidnapped her in Alabama and apparently killed her in Georgia. Heath pleaded guilty in Georgia and received a life sentence. Thereafter, Alabama indicted him and convicted him of a murder during a kidnapping. Justice O'Connor wrote for the Court and stated that "in applying the dual sovereignty doctrine * * * the crucial determination is whether the two entities that seek successively to prosecute a defendant for the same course of conduct can be termed separate sovereigns. This determination turns on

17. The policy has resulted in the dismissal of convictions at the government's request when the policy has inadvertently been violated and a conviction has resulted. See, e.g., Petite v. United States, 361 U.S. 529 (1960).

In Rinaldi v. United States, 434 U.S. 22 (1977), the district court rejected the government's motion to dismiss an indictment after trial when the government represented before trial that it had authority to proceed with the case. Although the court of appeals affirmed, the Supreme Court reversed. It noted that the policy involved efficiency considerations for the government and fairness considerations for the defendant. Because the government's post-trial efforts to dismiss the indictment were not "tainted with impropriety," a majority of the Court concluded that the most important thing was to protect the individual defendant from unfairness associated with needless multiple prosecutions and that "[t]he defendant * * * should receive the benefit of the policy whenever its application is urged by the Government." Chief Justice Burger dissented without opinion. Justice Rehnquist's brief dissenting opinion, urging that no reason was given to justify overturning a conviction because of an administrative error, was joined by Justice White.

The court held in United States v. Renfro, 620 F.2d 569 (6th Cir. 1980), that the decision whether or not to prosecute was left to the government and a defendant could not challenge the government's failure to comply with its *Petite* policy.

18. See, e.g., Pontikes, Dual Sovereignty and Double Jeopardy: A Critique of Bartkus v. Illinois and Abbate v. United States, 14 W.Res.L.Rev. 700 (1963); Note, 66 Nw. U.L.Rev. 248 (1971) (suggesting that unless state and federal laws reflect different social interests, only one prosecution should be permitted); Note, 14 Wake Forest L.Rev. 823 (1978). Compare Harrison, Federalism & Double Jeopardy: A Study in the Frustration of Human Rights, 17 U.Miami L.Rev. 306 (1963).

whether the two entities draw their authority to punish the offender from distinct sources of power." She cited *Waller* as confirmation that "it is the presence of independent authority to prosecute, not the relation between the States and the Federal Government in our federalist system, that constitutes the basis for the dual sovereignty doctrine." Justice O'Connor asserted that "to deny a State its power to enforce its criminal laws because another state won the race to the courthouse would be a shocking and untoward deprivation of the historic right and obligation of the States to maintain peace and order within their confines." She rejected the argument that a state's interest could be vindicated by a prosecution in another state, asserting that "a State's interest in vindicating its sovereign authority through enforcement of its laws by definition can never be satisfied by another State's enforcement of its own laws." She concluded that "[t]he States are no less sovereign with respect to each other than they are with respect to the Federal Government." Thus, the Court assumed that the crimes charged in the two states were essentially the same, but found that each state may independently decide whether and how to prosecute a defendant for violations of its laws.

Justice Marshall, joined by Justice Brennan, dissented and argued that the fact that the federal government and the states have differing interests in criminal prosecutions does not necessarily mean that two states have differing interests in prosecuting the same crime. He argued that "[a]lthough the two States may have opted for different policies within their assigned territorial jurisdictions, the sovereign concerns with whose vindication each State has been charged are identical," so that "in contrast to the federal-state context, barring the second prosecution would still permit one government to act upon the broad range of sovereign concerns that have been reserved to the States by the Constitution." Justice Marshall also argued that since Georgia had assisted Alabama in its prosecution, double jeopardy concerns were implicated. Justice Brennan added a short dissent, joined by Justice Marshall.

Heath's Supreme Court lawyer has criticized the reasoning of the Supreme Court. See Allen & Ratnaswamy, Heath v. Alabama: A Case Study of Doctrine and Rationality in the Supreme Court, 76 J.Crim.L. & Crim. 801 (1985). The article predicts that ambitious prosecutors will abuse the authority conferred upon them in noteworthy cases in order to further their political advancement.

States are free to provide greater double jeopardy protection than the federal constitution provides. The additional guarantees may be statutory or constitutional. For example, section 793 of the California Penal Code provides: "When an act charged as a public offense is within the jurisdiction of another State or country, as well as of this State, a conviction or acquittal thereof in the former is a bar to the prosecution or indictment therefore in this State." Section 793 was held to bar a prosecution for grand theft auto and unlawful driving or taking of a vehicle following a conviction in Oregon for unauthorized use of a vehicle, which was based on the same acts. See People v. Comingore, 20 Cal.3d 142, 141 Cal.Rptr. 542, 570 P.2d 723 (1977).

Several states have rejected the dual sovereignty theory, at least in some circumstances. In State v. Hogg, 118 N.H. 262, 385 A.2d 844 (1978), the New Hampshire Supreme Court construed the state double jeopardy clause to prohibit a state prosecution for robbery after a federal court acquittal on charges arising from the same criminal transaction. In Commonwealth v.

Mills, 447 Pa. 163, 286 A.2d 683 (1971), the Supreme Court of Pennsylvania barred second prosecutions for the same offense unless the interests of the state and the other jurisdiction are substantially different. Accord, People v. Cooper, 398 Mich. 450, 247 N.W.2d 866 (1976).

VII. ABORTED PROCEEDINGS

A. PROSECUTORIAL OR JUDICIAL ERROR

As noted earlier, the Double Jeopardy Clause is derived from English law, which provided that a defendant was put in jeopardy only after a conviction or an acquittal. The protection was afforded to a defendant only after a complete trial. A related principle, that a defendant may be put in jeopardy in a prosecution that does not terminate in a conviction or acquittal, was incorporated gradually into the Double Jeopardy Clause. The defendant's finality interest could be undermined if the prosecution could terminate a trial before the verdict, and institute a new proceeding. This protection, like other double jeopardy guarantees, becomes operative when jeopardy "attaches." In Crist v. Bretz, 437 U.S. 28 (1978), the Court concluded that the federal rule that jeopardy attaches when the jury is impaneled and sworn is an integral part of the constitutional guarantee against double jeopardy, and applies in state proceedings. The rule reflects and protects the defendant's interest in retaining a chosen jury, which is at the core of double jeopardy concerns.[19] See United States v. Juarez-Fierro, 935 F.2d 672 (5th Cir.1991) (pre-voir dire oath to the venire does not constitute attachment of jeopardy; a jury is not empaneled until all parties have exercised their challenges, and jurors have been selected to serve on the petit jury). In a non-jury trial, jeopardy attaches when the court begins to hear evidence.

The following cases consider when a retrial is permissible following a mistrial. The next case discusses the major prior cases.

B. MISTRIAL DECLARED OVER DEFENDANT'S OBJECTION

ILLINOIS v. SOMERVILLE

Supreme Court of the United States, 1973.
410 U.S. 458.

MR. JUSTICE REHNQUIST delivered the opinion of the Court.

We must here decide whether declaration of a mistrial over the defendant's objection, because the trial court concluded that the indictment was insufficient to charge a crime, necessarily prevents a State from subsequently trying the defendant under a valid indictment. We hold that the mistrial met the "manifest necessity" requirement of our cases, since the trial court could reasonably have concluded that the "ends of public justice" would be defeated by

19. Justice Powell's dissent documents the origin of the double jeopardy protection of a "defendant's valued right to have his trial completed by a particular tribunal." This special double jeopardy rule evolved from the common law rule barring the needless discharge of a jury. Without the rule, discharges might become common, especially when acquittal seems likely. Justice Powell argued that the rule that jeopardy attaches at the swearing of the jury was adopted without careful evaluation. He argued that jeopardy should not attach until witnesses testify.

having allowed the trial to continue. Therefore, the Double Jeopardy Clause of the Fifth Amendment, made applicable to the States through the Due Process Clause of the Fourteenth Amendment, did not bar retrial under a valid indictment.

[The defendant was indicted for theft. After the jury was sworn, but before any evidence was presented, the trial court granted the State's motion for a mistrial, because the indictment was fatally defective for failure to allege the requisite intent. After a retrial and conviction, the defendant sought a writ of habeas corpus. He alleged that conviction constituted double jeopardy.]

II

The fountainhead decision construing the Double Jeopardy Clause in the context of a declaration of a mistrial over a defendant's objection is United States v. Perez, 9 Wheat. 579 (1824). Mr. Justice Story, writing for a unanimous Court, set forth the standards for determining whether a retrial, following a declaration of a mistrial over a defendant's objection, constitutes double jeopardy within the meaning of the Fifth Amendment. In holding that the failure of the jury to agree on a verdict of either acquittal or conviction did not bar retrial of the defendant, Mr. Justice Story wrote:

> "We think that in all cases of this nature, the law has invested Courts of justice with the authority to discharge a jury from giving any verdict, whenever, in their opinion, taking all the circumstances into consideration, there is a manifest necessity for the act, or the ends of public justice would otherwise be defeated. They are to exercise a sound discretion on the subject; and it is impossible to define all the circumstances, which would render it proper to interfere. To be sure, the power ought to be used with the greatest caution, under urgent circumstances, and for very plain and obvious causes; and, in capital cases especially, Courts should be extremely careful how they interfere with any of the chances of life, in favour of the prisoner. But, after all, they have the right to order the discharge * * *."

This formulation, consistently adhered to by this Court in subsequent decisions, abjures the application of any mechanical formula by which to judge the propriety of declaring a mistrial in the varying and often unique situations arising during the course of a criminal trial. The broad discretion reserved to the trial judge in such circumstances has been consistently reiterated in decisions of this Court. * * *

In reviewing the propriety of the trial judge's exercise of his discretion, this Court, following the counsel of Mr. Justice Story, has scrutinized the action to determine whether, in the context of that particular trial, the declaration of a mistrial was dictated by "manifest necessity" or the "ends of public justice." The interests of the public in seeing that a criminal prosecution proceed to verdict, either of acquittal or conviction, need not be forsaken by the formulation or application of rigid rules that necessarily preclude the vindication of that interest. This consideration, whether termed the "ends of public justice," or, more precisely, "the public's interest in fair trials designed to end in just judgments," has not been disregarded by this Court.

In United States v. Perez, supra, and Logan v. United States, 144 U.S. 263 (1892), this Court held that "manifest necessity" justified the discharge of juries unable to reach verdicts, and, therefore, the Double Jeopardy Clause did not bar retrial. In Simmons v. United States, 142 U.S. 148 (1891), a trial judge dismissed the jury, over defendant's objection, because one of the jurors had been acquainted with the defendant, and, therefore, was probably prejudiced against the Government; this Court held that the trial judge properly exercised his power "to prevent the defeat of the ends of public justice." In Thompson v. United States, 155 U.S. 271 (1894), a mistrial was declared after the trial judge learned that one of the jurors was disqualified, he having been a member of the grand jury that indicted the defendant. Similarly, in Lovato v. New Mexico, 242 U.S. 199 (1916), the defendant demurred to the indictment, his demurrer was overruled, and a jury sworn. The district attorney, realizing that the defendant had not pleaded to the indictment after the demurrer had been overruled, moved for the discharge of the jury and arraignment of the defendant for pleading; the jury was discharged, the defendant pleaded not guilty, the same jury was again impaneled, and a verdict of guilty rendered. In both of those cases this Court held that the Double Jeopardy Clause did not bar reprosecution.

While virtually all of the cases turn on the particular facts and thus escape meaningful categorization, it is possible to distill from them a general approach, premised on the "public justice" policy enunciated in United States v. Perez, to situations such as that presented by this case. A trial judge properly exercises his discretion to declare a mistrial if an impartial verdict cannot be reached, or if a verdict of conviction could be reached but would have to be reversed on appeal due to an obvious procedural error in the trial. If an error would make reversal on appeal a certainty, it would not serve "the ends of public justice" to require that the Government proceed with its proof when, if it succeeded before the jury, it would automatically be stripped of that success by an appellate court. This was substantially the situation in both Thompson v. United States, supra, and Lovato v. New Mexico, supra. While the declaration of a mistrial on the basis of a rule or a defective procedure that would lend itself to prosecutorial manipulation would involve an entirely different question, such was not the situation in the above cases or in the instant case.

In Downum v. United States [372 U.S. 734 (1963)], the defendant was charged with six counts of mail theft, and forging and uttering stolen checks. A jury was selected and sworn in the morning, and instructed to return that afternoon. When the jury returned, the Government moved for the discharge of the jury on the ground that a key prosecution witness, for two of the six counts against defendant, was not present. The prosecution knew, prior to the selection and swearing of the jury, that this witness could not be found and had not been served with a subpoena. The trial judge discharged the jury over the defendant's motions to dismiss two counts for failure to prosecute and to continue the other four. This Court, in reversing the convictions on the ground of double jeopardy, emphasized that "[e]ach case must turn on its facts," and held that the second prosecution constituted double jeopardy, because the absence of the witness and the reason therefore did not there justify, in terms of "manifest necessity," the declaration of a mistrial.

In United States v. Jorn [400 U.S. 470 (1971)], the Government called a taxpayer witness in a prosecution for willfully assisting in the preparation of fraudulent income tax returns. Prior to his testimony, defense counsel suggested he be warned of his constitutional right against compulsory self-incrimination. The trial judge warned him of his rights, and the witness stated that he was willing to testify and that the Internal Revenue Service agent who first contacted him warned him of his rights. The trial judge, however, did not believe the witness' declaration that the

IRS had so warned him, and refused to allow him to testify until after he had consulted with an attorney. After learning from the Government that the remaining four witnesses were "similarly situated," and after surmising that they, too, had not been properly informed of their rights, the trial judge declared a mistrial to give the witnesses the opportunity to consult with attorneys. In sustaining a plea in bar of double jeopardy to an attempted second trial of the defendant, the plurality opinion of the Court, emphasizing the importance to the defendant of proceeding before the first jury sworn, concluded:

> "It is apparent from the record that no consideration was given to the possibility of a trial continuance; indeed, the trial judge acted so abruptly in discharging the jury that, had the prosecutor been disposed to suggest a continuance, or the defendant to object to the discharge of the jury, there would have been no opportunity to do so. When one examines the circumstances surrounding the discharge of this jury, it seems abundantly apparent that the trial judge made no effort to exercise a sound discretion to assure that, taking all the circumstances into account, there was a manifest necessity for the *sua sponte* declaration of this mistrial. Therefore, we must conclude that in the circumstances of this case, appellee's reprosecution would violate the double jeopardy provision of the Fifth Amendment."

* * *

[The Court rejected Somerville's argument that any trial on a defective indictment precludes retrial, and then considered whether the circumstances of the case justified the mistrial.]

In the instant case, the trial judge terminated the proceeding because a defect was found to exist in the indictment that was, as a matter of Illinois law, not curable by amendment. The Illinois courts have held that even after a judgment of conviction has become final, the defendant may be released on habeas corpus, because the defect in the indictment deprives the trial court of "jurisdiction." The rule prohibiting the amendment of all but formal defects in indictments is designed to implement the State's policy of preserving the right of each defendant to insist that a criminal prosecution against him be commenced by the action of a grand jury. The trial judge was faced with a situation similar to those in *Simmons, Lovato,* and *Thompson*, in which a procedural defect might or would preclude the public from either obtaining an impartial verdict or keeping a verdict of conviction if its evidence persuaded the jury. If a mistrial were constitutionally unavailable in situations such as this, the State's policy could only be implemented by conducting a second trial after verdict and reversal on appeal, thus wasting time, energy, and money for all concerned. Here, the trial judge's action was a rational determination designed to implement a legitimate state policy, with no suggestion that the implementation of that policy in this manner could be manipulated so as to prejudice the defendant. This situation is thus unlike *Downum*, where the mistrial entailed not only a delay for the defendant, but also operated as a post-jeopardy continuance to allow the prosecution an opportunity to strengthen its case. Here, the delay was minimal, and the mistrial was, under Illinois law, the only way in which a defect in the indictment could be corrected. Given the established standard of discretion * * *, we cannot say that the declaration of a mistrial was not required by "manifest necessity" or the "ends of public justice."

Our decision in *Jorn*, relied upon by the court below and respondent, does not support the opposite conclusion.

While it is possible to excise various portions of the plurality opinion to support the result reached below, divorcing the language from the facts of the case serves only to distort its holdings. That opinion dealt with action by a trial judge that can fairly be described as erratic. The Court held that the lack of apparent harm to the defendant from the declaration of a mistrial did not itself justify the mistrial, and concluded that there was no "manifest necessity" for the mistrial, as opposed to less drastic alternatives. The Court emphasized that the absence of any manifest need for the mistrial had deprived the defendant of his right to proceed before the first jury, but it did not hold that that right may never be forced to yield, as in this case, to "the public's interest in fair trials designed to end in just judgments." The Court's opinion in *Jorn* is replete with approving references to Wade v. Hunter, supra * * *.

The determination by the trial court to abort a criminal proceeding where jeopardy has attached is not one to be lightly undertaken, since the interest of the defendant in having his fate determined by the jury first impaneled is itself a weighty one. Nor will the lack of demonstrable additional prejudice preclude the defendant's invocation of the double jeopardy bar in the absence of some important countervailing interest of proper judicial administration. But where the declaration of a mistrial implements a reasonable state policy and aborts a proceeding that at best would have produced a verdict that could have been upset at will by one of the parties, the defendant's interest in proceeding to verdict is outweighed by the competing and equally legitimate demand for public justice.

[Justice White, joined by Justices Douglas and Brennan, dissented. Relying on *Downum* and *Jorn*, they argued that even when prosecutorial misconduct consists of a mistake or oversight, the defendant's interest in having the trial completed by the first tribunal prevails. This should be true even when no specific prejudice to the defendant is shown. In this case, the reason for the mistrial was the state's error.

Justice Marshall dissented separately. Also relying on *Downum* and *Jorn*, he argued that the court's "balancing" approach underemphasized the defendant's interest in continuing with the trial. Continuation was a viable alternative to a mistrial in his view.]

Note

Somerville generally has been considered a retreat from the heightened scrutiny of mistrials granted without the defendant's consent in *Downum* and *Jorn*. What factors are relevant to the Court's "balancing" approach? Consider the Court's treatment of the following issues in both *Somerville* and in Arizona v. Washington, the next case: Whose conduct or what event is responsible for the mistrial? What is the purpose, nature and effect of that conduct? Is there prosecutorial overreaching or harassment? Does the potential for prosecutorial manipulation exist? Is there any actual prejudice to the defendant from the mistrial? Has the court considered all viable alternatives to a mistrial? For cases relying on *Downum* and *Jorn* and distinguishing *Somerville*, see Randall v. Rothwax, 78 N.Y.2d 494, 577 N.Y.S.2d 211, 583 N.E.2d 924 (1991) (where the defendant pleaded guilty during jury deliberations due to misadvice from the judge that the jury was leaning toward conviction, when in fact they were leaning toward acquittal, the guilty plea must be vacated and double jeopardy bars a retrial; the trial court, without manifest necessity, eliminated the defendant's right to have a resolution from the jury); United States v. Meza-Soria, 935 F.2d 166 (9th Cir.1991) (trial court declares a mistrial over the defendant's objection, on the ground that evidence admitted on defendant's behalf should not have been introduced; retrial barred by double jeopardy because the evidence was in fact admissible).

C. VARYING LEVELS OF APPELLATE SCRUTINY

ARIZONA v. WASHINGTON

Supreme Court of the United States, 1978.
434 U.S. 497.

MR. JUSTICE STEVENS delivered the opinion of the Court.

An Arizona trial judge granted the prosecutor's motion for a mistrial predicated on improper and prejudicial comment during defense counsel's opening statement. In a subsequent habeas corpus proceeding, a Federal District Court held that the Double Jeopardy Clause protected the defendant from another trial. The Court of Appeals for the Ninth Circuit affirmed. The questions presented are whether the record reflects the kind of "necessity" for the mistrial ruling that will avoid a valid plea of double jeopardy, and if so, whether the plea must nevertheless be allowed because the Arizona trial judge did not fully explain the reasons for his mistrial ruling.

I

In 1971 respondent was found guilty of murdering a hotel night clerk. In 1973, the Superior Court of Pima County, Ariz., ordered a new trial because the prosecutor had withheld exculpatory evidence from the defense. The Arizona Supreme Court affirmed the new trial order in an unpublished opinion.

Respondent's second trial began in January 1975. During the *voir dire* examination of prospective jurors, the prosecutor made reference to the fact that some of the witnesses whose testimony the jurors would hear had testified in proceedings four years earlier. Defense counsel told the prospective jurors "that there was evidence hidden from [respondent] at the last trial." In his opening statement, he made this point more forcefully:

> "You will hear testimony that notwithstanding the fact that we had a trial in May of 1971 in this matter, that the prosecutor hid those statements and didn't give those to the lawyer for George saying the man was Spanish speaking, didn't give those statements at all, hid them.
>
> "You will hear that that evidence was suppressed and hidden by the prosecutor in that case. You will hear that that evidence was purposely withheld. You will hear that because of the misconduct of the County Attorney at that time and because he withheld evidence, that the Supreme Court of Arizona granted a new trial in this case."

[The prosecutor moved for a mistrial, because there was no theory on which the basis for the new trial ruling could be admissible, and the prejudice to the jury could not be repaired by any cautionary instruction. The judge granted the motion, but did not expressly find that there was "manifest necessity" for a mistrial, and did not expressly state that he had considered and found alternative solutions to be inadequate.]

II

A State may not put a defendant in jeopardy twice for the same offense. The constitutional protection against double jeopardy unequivocally prohibits a second trial following an acquittal. The public interest in the finality of criminal judgments is so strong that an acquitted defendant may not be retried even though "the acquittal was based upon an egregiously erroneous foundation." If the innocence of the accused has been confirmed by a final judgment, the Constitution conclusively presumes that a second trial would be unfair.

Because jeopardy attaches before the judgment becomes final, the constitutional protection also embraces the defendant's "valued right to have his trial completed by a particular tribunal." The reasons why this "valued right" merits constitutional protection are worthy of repetition. Even if the first trial is not completed, a second prosecution may be grossly unfair. It increases the financial and emotional burden on the accused, prolongs the period in which he is stigmatized by an unresolved accusation of wrongdoing, and may even enhance the risk that an innocent defendant may be convicted. The danger of such unfairness to the defendant exists whenever a trial is aborted before it is completed. Consequently, as a general rule, the prosecutor is entitled to one, and only one, opportunity to require an accused to stand trial.

Unlike the situation in which the trial has ended in an acquittal or conviction, retrial is not automatically barred when a criminal proceeding is terminated without finally resolving the merits of the charges against the accused. Because of the variety of circumstances that may make it necessary to discharge a jury before a trial is concluded, and because those circumstances do not invariably create unfairness to the accused, his valued right to have the trial concluded by a particular tribunal is sometimes subordinate to the public interest in affording the prosecutor one full and fair opportunity to present his evidence to an impartial jury. Yet in view of the importance of the right, and the fact that it is frustrated by any mistrial, the prosecutor must shoulder the burden of justifying the mistrial if he is to avoid the double jeopardy bar. His burden is a heavy one. The prosecutor must demonstrate "manifest necessity" for any mistrial declared over the objection of the defendant.

The words "manifest necessity" appropriately characterize the magnitude of the prosecutor's burden. For that reason Mr. Justice Story's classic formulation of the test has been quoted over and over again to provide guidance in the decision of a wide variety of cases. Nevertheless, those words do not describe a standard that can be applied mechanically or without attention to the particular problem confronting the trial judge. Indeed, it is manifest that the key word "necessity" cannot be interpreted literally; instead, contrary to the teaching of Webster, we assume that there are degrees of necessity and we require a "high degree" before concluding that a mistrial is appropriate.

The question whether that "high degree" has been reached is answered more easily in some kinds of cases than in others. At one extreme are cases in which a prosecutor requests a mistrial in order to buttress weaknesses in his evidence. Although there was a time when English judges served the Stuart Monarchs by exercising a power to discharge a jury whenever it appeared that the Crown's evidence would be insufficient to convict, the prohibition against double jeopardy as it evolved in this country was plainly intended to condemn this "abhorrent" practice. As this Court noted in United States v. Dinitz, 424 U.S. 600, 611: [20]

> "The Double Jeopardy Clause does protect a defendant against governmental actions intended to provoke mistrial requests and thereby to subject defendants to the substantial burdens imposed by multiple prosecu-

20. *Dinitz* is described in a problem following Oregon v. Kennedy, infra.

> tions. It bars retrials where 'bad-faith conduct by judge or prosecutor,' * * * threatens the '[h]arassment of an accused by successive prosecutions or declaration of a mistrial so as to afford the prosecution a more favorable opportunity to convict' the defendant."

Thus, the strictest scrutiny is appropriate when the basis for the mistrial is the unavailability of critical prosecution evidence,[a] or when there is reason to believe that the prosecutor is using the superior resources of the State to harass or to achieve a tactical advantage over the accused.[b]

At the other extreme is the mistrial premised upon the trial judge's belief that the jury is unable to reach a verdict, long considered the classic basis for a proper mistrial. The argument that a jury's inability to agree establishes reasonable doubt as to the defendant's guilt, and therefore requires acquittal, has been uniformly rejected in this country. Instead, without exception, the courts have held that the trial judge may discharge a genuinely deadlocked jury and require the defendant to submit to a second trial. This rule accords recognition to society's interest in giving the prosecution one complete opportunity to convict those who have violated its laws.

Moreover, in this situation there are especially compelling reasons for allowing the trial judge to exercise broad discretion in deciding whether or not "manifest necessity" justifies a discharge of the jury. On the one hand, if he discharges the jury when further deliberations may produce a fair verdict, the defendant is deprived of his "valued right to have his trial completed by a particular tribunal." But if he fails to discharge a jury which is unable to reach a verdict after protracted and exhausting deliberations, there exists a significant risk that a verdict may result from pressures inherent in the situation rather than the considered judgment of all the jurors. If retrial of the defendant were barred whenever an appellate court views the "necessity" for a mistrial differently from the trial judge, there would be a danger that the latter, cognizant of the serious societal consequences of an erroneous ruling, would employ coercive means to break the apparent deadlock. Such a rule would frustrate the public interest in just judgments. The trial judge's decision to declare a mistrial when he considers the jury deadlocked is therefore accorded great deference by a reviewing court.[c]

We are persuaded that, along the spectrum of trial problems which may warrant a mistrial and which vary in their amenability to appellate scrutiny,

a. If, for example, a prosecutor proceeds to trial aware that key witnesses are not available to give testimony and a mistrial is later granted for that reason, a second prosecution is barred. Downum v. United States, 372 U.S. 734. The prohibition against double jeopardy unquestionably "forbids the prosecutor to use the first proceeding as a trial run of his case." Note, Twice in Jeopardy, 75 Yale L.J. 262, 287–288 (1965).

b. * * * The "particular tribunal" principle is implicated whenever a mistrial is declared over the defendant's objection and without regard to the presence or absence of governmental overreaching. If the "right to go to a particular tribunal is valued, it is because, independent of the threat of bad-faith conduct by judge or prosecutor, the defendant has a significant interest in the decision whether or not to take the case from the jury." United States v. Jorn, 400 U.S., at 485.

c. It should be noted, however, that the rationale for this deference in the "hung" jury situation is that the trial court is in the best position to assess all the factors which must be considered in making a necessarily discretionary determination whether the jury will be able to reach a just verdict if it continues to deliberate. If the record reveals that the trial judge has failed to exercise the "sound discretion" entrusted to him, the reason for such deference by an appellate court disappears. Thus, if the trial judge acts for reasons completely unrelated to the trial problem which purports to be the basis for the mistrial ruling, close appellate scrutiny is appropriate.

the difficulty which led to the mistrial in this case also falls in an area where the trial judge's determination is entitled to special respect.

In this case the trial judge ordered a mistrial because the defendant's lawyer made improper and prejudicial remarks during his opening statement to the jury. Although respondent insists that evidence of prosecutorial misconduct was admissible as a matter of Arizona law, and therefore that the opening statement was proper, we regard this issue as foreclosed by respondent's failure to proffer any Arizona precedent supportive of his contention and by the state court's interpretation of its own law, buttressed by the consistent opinion of the Federal District Court and the Court of Appeals. We therefore start from the premise that defense counsel's comment was improper and may have affected the impartiality of the jury.

We recognize that the extent of the possible bias cannot be measured, and that the District Court was quite correct in believing that some trial judges might have proceeded with the trial after giving the jury appropriate cautionary instructions. In a strict, literal sense, the mistrial was not "necessary." Nevertheless, the overriding interest in the evenhanded administration of justice requires that we accord the highest degree of respect to the trial judge's evaluation of the likelihood that the impartiality of one or more jurors may have been affected by the improper comment.

[The Court concluded that the mistrial was proper because the judge did not act irrationally or irresponsibly.]

* * * We are therefore persuaded by the record that the trial judge acted responsibly and deliberately, and accorded careful consideration to respondent's interest in having the trial concluded in a single proceeding. Since he exercised "sound discretion" in handling the sensitive problem of possible juror bias created by the improper comment of defense counsel, the mistrial order is supported by the "high degree" of necessity which is required in a case of this kind.[d] Neither party has a right to have his case decided by a jury which may be tainted by bias; in these circumstances, "the public's interest in fair trials designed to end in just judgments" must prevail over the defendant's "valued right" to have his trial concluded before the first jury impaneled.

IV

One final matter requires consideration. The absence of an explicit finding of "manifest necessity" appears to have been determinative for the District Court and may have been so for the Court of Appeals. If those courts regarded that omission as critical, they required too much. Since the record provides sufficient justification for the state-court ruling, the failure to explain that ruling more completely does not render it constitutionally defective.

Review of any trial court decision is, of course, facilitated by findings and by an explanation of the reasons supporting the decision. No matter how desirable such procedural assistance may be, it is not constitutionally mandated in a case such as this. The basis for the trial judge's mistrial order is adequately disclosed by the record, which includes the extensive argument of counsel prior to

d. Two considerations, while not determinative, add support to this conclusion. First, crowded calendars throughout the Nation impose a constant pressure on our judges to finish the business at hand. Generally, they have an interest in having the trial completed as promptly as possible, an interest which frequently parallels the constitutionally protected interest of the accused in having the trial concluded by a particular tribunal. Second, respondent does not attempt to demonstrate specific prejudice from the mistrial ruling, other than the harm which always accompanies retrial.

the judge's ruling. The state trial judge's mistrial declaration is not subject to collateral attack in a federal court simply because he failed to find "manifest necessity" in those words or to articulate on the record all the factors which informed the deliberate exercise of his discretion.

* * *

[Justice White argued in dissent that the case should have been remanded to the district court for a new determination of manifest necessity for the mistrial. Justice Marshall, joined by Justice Brennan, dissented on the ground that in this case a finding of manifest necessity must be explicit, rather than implied from the record. The record should make clear that there were no meaningful and practical alternatives to a mistrial or that the trial court carefully considered and rejected all others.]

Note

In Arizona v. Washington, the Court suggests that different levels of scrutiny are appropriate for mistrials granted for different reasons.[21] Does the "manifest necessity" requirement for a mistrial have any identifiable meaning? Lower court decisions are inconsistent. For an extensive survey of mistrials under different circumstances, see Schulhofer, Jeopardy and Mistrials, 125 U.Pa.L.Rev. 449 (1977). The inquiry into the permissibility of a retrial following a mistrial is largely fact specific. How should the following situations be analyzed?

a. The defendant's primary defense in a murder case was insanity. Prospective jurors were questioned carefully about their views of the defense and knowledge of the case. After the jurors were selected, but before they were sworn, one juror made a "passing comment" to his friend, the bailiff, that after seeing the defendant he thought "the poor man was crazy" and "didn't know what he was doing." The bailiff told the prosecutor about the incident, but did not notify the judge or defense counsel. The jurors were sworn, but before any evidence was introduced the prosecutor moved for a mistrial because the juror's opinion would preclude a fair trial. The judge examined the juror, who maintained that he had no prejudgment or fixed opinion on the defendant's sanity. The judge also heard argument on the motion before granting the mistrial. Should the retrial have been barred? Why or why not? See Smith v. Mississippi, 478 F.2d 88 (5th Cir.1973), which held that retrial was not barred. The court stated that "what is of controlling importance is that the state trial judge first painstakingly weighed all the factors present and thereupon exercised the discretion invested in him. His declaration of a mistrial was not unreasonable." But compare United States v. Pierce, 593 F.2d 415 (1st Cir.1979) (new trial barred where trial judge granted mistrial motion over defense objection, because a juror's husband told several jurors about some things that happened during hearing on motion to suppress; curative instruction should have been considered and a greater showing of prejudice to the case made before a mistrial was declared); Larios v. Superior Court, 24 Cal.3d 324, 155 Cal.Rptr. 374, 594 P.2d 491 (1979) (new trial barred after mistrial granted when a juror said that he would be inclined to rely on his independent investigation in deciding the case and no alternate was available).

b. In Arizona v. Washington, the Court indicated that great deference should be given to a judge's determination to declare a mistrial when the jury is hopelessly deadlocked. In United States v. Horn, 583 F.2d 1124 (10th Cir.1978), after a two-

21. Arizona v. Washington is one of the cases discussed in Note, Double Jeopardy Consequences of Mistrial, Dismissal and Reversal of Conviction on Appeal, 16 Am.Crim.L.Rev. 235 (1979).

day trial the jury deliberated for three or four hours. The jury then notified the judge that it was deadlocked. The judge recessed for the night. The following morning, the judge talked with the jury about their duty to agree, if possible, "without violence to individual judgment." He then gave a formal *Allen* charge (discussed in Chapter Ten). After the jury deliberated for a little more than an hour, they were brought back into court. Without further inquiry, the court declared a mistrial. The Court of Appeals held that a retrial was impermissible because there was no manifest necessity for the mistrial. Did the appellate court rule correctly? What factors should a court consider in determining whether a judge properly exercised his discretion to declare a deadlocked jury? One court has isolated seven criteria:

> (1) a timely objection by defendant, (2) the jury's collective opinion that it cannot agree, (3) the length of the deliberations of the jury, (4) the length of the trial, (5) the complexity of the issues presented to the jury, (6) any proper communications which the judge has had with the jury, and (7) the effects of possible exhaustion and the impact which coercion of further deliberations might have on the verdict.

See Arnold v. McCarthy, 566 F.2d 1377 (9th Cir.1978). Are these the factors that you would use? See also Escobar v. O'Leary, 943 F.2d 711 (7th Cir.1991) (manifest necessity existed for mistrial, where the jury was deadlocked after three days of deliberations in a short trial posing relatively simple issues; the fact that the jury was split eleven to one in favor of acquittal does not show that the judge believed this to be the case when he granted the mistrial).

c. In a joint trial, one of the co-defendants had retained counsel who had a series of "scheduling conflicts" requiring several delays in setting a trial date. Eventually, the trial judge offered the co-defendant the immediate services of an attorney who had previously worked with him on the case. The co-defendant refused. The trial judge, sensing bad faith, proceeded with the trial. The co-defendant disrupted the proceedings with continual requests for counsel during the testimony of government witnesses. Two days into trial, the judge received word that the attorney for another co-defendant had been arrested in an unrelated case for aggravated perjury. This was widely publicized. The judge consulted with counsel for each defendant, but they offered "no uniform curative measure" for any prejudice that they would suffer from these various problems. Some wanted a mistrial, some (defendants Talamas and Cary) a severance, some a continuance. The judge interviewed the jury, but did not make direct reference to the news stories concerning the arrest of the defense counsel. Three jurors admitted to hearing media reports about the case. Over the objections of defendants Talamas and Cary, the judge declared a mistrial. Should the retrial have been barred? In United States v. Bauman, 887 F.2d 546 (5th Cir.1989), the court answered in the negative. It stated that the doctrine of manifest necessity frees the trial court from the Hobson's Choice of continuing with an unfair trial or permanently ending the prosecution of the defendant. The court recognized that the Supreme Court has left the "manifest necessity" standard deliberately ambiguous, but that the term sounds more onerous than it is. The court concluded that a trial court has the discretion to order a mistrial even though severance may be a possible alternative. It rejected the argument "that the trial court must always agree to sever certain defendants if possible." The court noted that "reasonable judges may differ on the proper curative measure" in such circumstances and that under Arizona v. Washington "appellate courts are not meant to second-guess the sound discretion of the trial judge in declaring a mistrial for juror prejudice when that judge is closest to the compromising events." The court was satisfied that the trial court "evaluated, with due deliberation, whether a mistrial or some other curative measure was appropriate." Are you satisfied? What interests, if any, would not have been served by a severance of the defendants who objected to a mistrial?

d. The defendant was charged with murder and his defense was self-defense. When the jury was deliberating, a juror knocked on the jury room door and asked the sheriff who opened the door how far 92 feet was. The evidence at trial had indicated that the defendant shot the victim from that distance. The sheriff began pacing off the distance down the hallway while some jurors watched. After learning about this incident, the trial judge gave a curative instruction to the jury and they returned to their deliberations. The judge had a conference with the attorneys to decide what to do about this incident. The judge decided that a mistrial must be declared. As the lawyers and the judge were preparing to return to the court, the jury reported that it had reached a verdict. The judge stated that since he had declared the mistrial he would have the verdict reported only for the purpose of completing the record. The jury reported a verdict of not guilty. Would a retrial violated the Double Jeopardy Clause?

In the actual case, Corey v. District Court of Vermont, Unit No. 1, Rutland Circuit, 917 F.2d 88 (2d Cir.1990), the court held that there was no manifest necessity to declare a mistrial, once the trial judge learned that the jury had reached a verdict and that the verdict was not guilty. The court recognized that the sheriff acted improperly in demonstrating the distance to the jury and that the judicial response to it was appropriate. However, it reasoned that the trial judge should have refrained from immediately declaring a mistrial because: (1) an acquittal would reveal the absence of prejudice to the defendant; and (2) if the verdict were guilty, the court, concluding that the sheriff's conduct could have prejudiced the defendant, could have ordered a new trial. Did the reviewing court give the proper deference to the trial court under Arizona v. Washington?

D. MISTRIAL DECLARED UPON DEFENDANT'S MOTION

Under what circumstances, if any, can the defendant who moves for a mistrial invoke double jeopardy protections against a retrial? This question was considered in Oregon v. Kennedy, 456 U.S. 667 (1982). After defense counsel had brought out during cross-examination of the state's expert witness that the expert had previously filed a criminal complaint against the defendant, the prosecutor suggested on redirect examination that the reason for the filing was that the defendant was "a crook." The trial court granted Kennedy's motion for a mistrial, and when the state sought to retry him, he moved to dismiss the charges because of double jeopardy. Justice Rehnquist, writing for the Court, concluded that a retrial was not barred. He reasoned as follows:

> Where the trial is terminated over the objection of the defendant, the classical test for lifting the double jeopardy bar to a second trial is the 'manifest necessity' standard * * *. But in the case of a mistrial declared at the behest of the defendant, quite different principles come into play. Here the defendant himself has elected to terminate the proceedings against him, and the 'manifest necessity' standard has no place in the application of the Double Jeopardy Clause. * * *
>
> Our cases, however, have indicated that even where the defendant moves for a mistrial, there is a narrow exception to the rule that the Double Jeopardy Clause is no bar to retrial. See, e.g., United States v. Dinitz. * * *

> Since one of the principal threads making up the protection embodied in the Double Jeopardy Clause is the right of the defendant to have his trial completed before the first jury empaneled to try him, it may be wondered as a matter of original inquiry why the defendant's election to terminate the first trial by his own motion should not be deemed a renunciation of that right for all purposes. We have recognized, however, that there would be great difficulty in applying such a rule where the prosecutor's actions giving rise to the mistrial were done in order to goad the defendant into requesting a mistrial. In such a case, the defendant's valued right to complete his trial before the first jury would be a hollow shell if the inevitable motion for mistrial were held to prevent a later invocation of the bar of double jeopardy in all circumstances. But the precise phrasing of the circumstances which *will* allow a defendant to interpose the defense of double jeopardy * * * have been stated with less than crystal clarity * * *.

Justice Rehnquist rejected the argument that double jeopardy should apply whenever the prosecutor's conduct at the first trial indicated "overreaching." He argued that such a test offered "virtually no standards" for application. He opted for an approach which examined the intent of the prosecutor:

> [A] standard that examines the intent of the prosecutor, though certainly not entirely free from practical difficulties, is a manageable standard to apply. It merely calls for the court to make a finding of fact. Inferring the existence or nonexistence of intent from objective facts and circumstances is a familiar process in our criminal justice system. * * *
>
> Prosecutorial conduct that might be viewed as harassment or overreaching, even if sufficient to justify a mistrial on defendant's motion, therefore, does not bar retrial absent intent on the part of the prosecutor to subvert the protections afforded by the Double Jeopardy Clause. * * * Only where the governmental conduct in question is intended to 'goad' the defendant into moving for a mistrial may a defendant raise the bar of double jeopardy. * * *
>
> We do not by this opinion lay down a flat rule that where a defendant in a criminal trial successfully moves for a mistrial, he may not thereafter invoke the bar of double jeopardy against a second trial. But we do hold that the circumstances under which such a defendant may invoke the bar of double jeopardy to try him are limited to those cases in which the conduct giving rise to the successful motion for a mistrial was intended to provoke the defendant into moving for a mistrial. Since the Oregon trial court found, and the Oregon Court of Appeals accepted, that the prosecutorial conduct culminating in the termination of the first trial in this case was not so intended by the prosecutor, that is the end of the matter * * *.

Justice Powell's concurring opinion emphasized that a court determining the intent of the prosecutor "should rely primarily upon the objective facts and circumstances of the particular case." He noted that in the instant case, the prosecutor had made only a single comment, and that the prosecutor was surprised by and resisted the defendant's motion for a mistrial. Justice Stevens, joined by Justices Brennan, Marshall and Blackmun, concurred in the judgment. He argued that "[i]t is almost inconceivable that a defendant could prove that the prosecutor's deliberate misconduct was motivated by an intent to provoke a mistrial," and asserted that an "overreaching" standard was preferable even though it would be a "rare and compelling case" in which retrial would be barred.

Note

When Oregon v. Kennedy returned to state court, the state supreme court relied upon the state constitution to find that Kennedy's rights were violated. State v. Kennedy, 295 Or. 260, 666 P.2d 1316 (1983). It reasoned that retrial should be barred when the prosecution "either intends or is indifferent to the resulting mistrial or reversal."

Arizona found the Oregon approach attractive in Pool v. Superior Court, 139 Ariz. 98, 677 P.2d 261 (1984), as it held that a defendant could not be tried a second time where a mistrial occurred as a result of a prosecutor's persistent effort to cross-examine the defendant about irrelevant and prejudicial matters and attempted to amend an indictment in the middle of trial to add a charge to the one originally brought. The court said that a defendant is placed in jeopardy and cannot be retried after a mistrial is declared under the following conditions: the mistrial is granted because of the prosecutor's improper conduct or actions; such conduct is not simply negligent or mistaken, but, "taken as a whole, amounts to intentional conduct which the prosecutor knowns to be improper and prejudicial, and which he pursues for any improper purpose with indifference to a significant resulting danger of mistrial or reversal; and the conduct causes prejudice to the defendant which cannot be cured by means short of a mistrial."

Ponsoldt, When Guilt Should be Irrelevant: Government Overreaching as a Bar to Reprosecution Under the Double Jeopardy Clause After Oregon v. Kennedy, 69 Cornell L.Rev. 76 (1983), argues that the Supreme Court has given criminal defendants insufficient protection against prosecutorial conduct that is designed to force mistrial requests.

In Robinson v. Wade, 686 F.2d 298 (5th Cir. 1982), a state defendant who had been convicted and sentenced to death for a murder three times and who had been granted a new trial each time sought habeas corpus relief barring a fourth trial. Although the court criticized some of the prosecutor's actions, it found no prosecutorial overreaching sufficient to bar a retrial. Should there be a limit to the number of chances a prosecutor is given?

How should the following cases be decided in light of Oregon v. Kennedy?

a. The lead defense counsel was excluded from the trial because he repeatedly tried to make improper comments in opening argument. When the defendant desired the excluded counsel to continue to represent him, the judge gave him three alternatives: a stay or recess pending application to the court of appeals to review the propriety of expelling counsel; to continue the trial with assisting counsel; or a mistrial to enable the defendant to obtain other counsel. The defendant moved for a mistrial and was retried and convicted.

In the actual case, United States v. Dinitz, 424 U.S. 600 (1976), the Court concluded that the retrial did not violate the Double Jeopardy Clause and reversed the court of appeals, which had found no manifest necessity for aborting the first trial. Is this a sound decision if the record shows that the trial judge might have overreacted in excluding lead counsel?

b. The defendant was indicted for making a false oath and account in a bankruptcy proceeding, and for fraudulently transferring and concealing assets in contemplation of bankruptcy. He asked the court to prohibit the prosecutor from reading his grand jury testimony to the jury, because it contained many irrelevant and prejudicial statements. The government's attorney assured the court that irrelevant statements had been excluded, and the court denied the request. The prosecutor nevertheless read improper and prejudicial remarks by the grand jury to the trial jury. The defendant moved for a mistrial, which the court granted. He was retried and convicted. Under the Supreme Court's analysis, did the retrial violate the Double Jeopardy Clause?

In the actual case, United States v. Martin, 561 F.2d 135 (8th Cir. 1977), the court asked whether there was prosecutorial overreaching. Although "mere negligence" by the prosecutor is not prosecutorial overreaching designed to provoke a mistrial request, the court found that the prosecutor's gross negligence was undertaken to harass or prejudice the defendant. As a result, Martin had no choice but to move for a mistrial, and thus his retrial violated the Double Jeopardy Clause. Do you agree? Would this case be decided the same way under Oregon v. Kennedy?

Under Oregon v. Kennedy, the manifest necessity standard is inapplicable if the defendant moves for a mistrial. What if the defendant consents to a mistrial? In United States v. Dinitz, supra, the Court held that the manifest necessity standard was inapplicable in this situation as well. Why should this be so?

Is the failure to object tantamount to consent? In United States v. Buljubasic, 808 F.2d 1260 (7th Cir.1987) the court looked at several factors to determine whether the defendant's silence creates an inference of consent to a mistrial. These factors include (1) whether the defendant previously requested mistrial; (2) whether there was sufficient time to object; (3) whether the trial court indicated that it would declare a mistrial no matter what; and (4) whether the trial to that point had been "going the defendant's way." On the facts, the court found that the defendant had consented to a mistrial—he had moved for a mistrial several times, the court had held an hour-long hearing on the propriety of a mistrial, and the defense had not gone well to that point. Therefore, Oregon v. Kennedy was applicable, and since the defendant could not show that the prosecutor had "baited" him into seeking a mistrial, a retrial was not barred by the Double Jeopardy Clause. In Corey v. District Court of Vermont, Unit No. 1, Rutland Circuit, 917 F.2d 88 (2d Cir.1990), discussed in the Note after Arizona v. Washington, defense counsel did not object to the mistrial, but specifically stated that the defendant intended to assert his double jeopardy rights if there was a retrial. The court found that this action was sufficient to trigger the application of the manifest necessity standard. See also Escobar v. O'Leary, 943 F.2d 711 (7th Cir.1991) (the defendant sufficiently objected to a mistrial, which was granted by the court on the ground of jury deadlock; the defendant had raised a strong defense, had repeatedly requested more jury deliberations, and asked for an *Allen* charge, after the possibility of a mistrial arose).

In Beringer v. Sheahan, 934 F.2d 110 (7th Cir.1991), the prosecutor engaged in intentional misconduct, but the defendant never moved for a mistrial. The defendant was convicted, and his conviction was reversed on appeal due to the prosecutorial misconduct. The defendant claimed that a retrial would be impermissible under Oregon v. Kennedy, but the court found that case inapplicable to a situation where defendant fails to move for a mistrial; it held that the right to claim double jeopardy was waived, so that neither the "manifest necessity" standard nor the "intentional goading" standard were applicable. The court was concerned that a contrary result would allow defendants to refuse to move for a mistrial in the hope of obtaining a reversal and a double jeopardy bar on appeal.

VIII. CONTROLS ON JUDICIAL AND PROSECUTORIAL VINDICTIVENESS

A. JUDICIAL VINDICTIVENESS

NORTH CAROLINA v. PEARCE

Supreme Court of the United States, 1969.
395 U.S. 711.

MR. JUSTICE STEWART delivered the opinion of the Court.

When at the behest of the defendant a criminal conviction has been set aside and a new trial ordered, to what extent does the Constitution limit the imposition of a harsher sentence after conviction upon retrial? That is the question presented by these two cases.

In No. 413 the respondent Pearce was convicted in a North Carolina court upon a charge of assault with intent to commit rape. The trial judge sentenced him to prison for a term of 12 to 15 years. Several years later he initiated a state post-conviction proceeding which culminated in the reversal of his conviction by the Supreme Court of North Carolina, upon the ground that an involuntary confession had unconstitutionally been admitted in evidence against him. He was retried, convicted, and sentenced by the trial judge to an eight-year prison term, which, when added to the time Pearce had already spent in prison, the parties agree amounted to a longer total sentence than that originally imposed. * * *

In No. 418 the respondent Rice pleaded guilty in an Alabama trial court to four separate charges of second-degree burglary. He was sentenced to prison terms aggregating 10 years. Two and one-half years later the judgments were set aside in a state *coram nobis* proceeding, upon the ground that Rice had not been accorded his constitutional right to counsel. He was retried upon three of the charges, convicted, and sentenced to prison on terms aggregating 25 years. No credit was given for the time he had spent in prison on the original judgments.

* * *

The problem before us involves two related but analytically separate issues. One concerns the constitutional limitations upon the imposition of a more severe punishment after conviction for the same offense upon retrial. * * * [22]

* * *

II

* * * We turn, therefore, to consideration of the broader problem of what constitutional limitations there may be upon the general power of a judge to impose upon reconviction a longer prison sentence than the defendant originally received.

A

Long-established constitutional doctrine makes clear that, beyond the requirement already discussed, the guarantee against double jeopardy imposes no restrictions upon the length of a sentence imposed upon reconviction. At least since 1896, when United States v. Ball, 163 U.S. 662, was decided, it has been settled that this constitutional guarantee imposes no limitations whatever upon the power to *retry* a defendant who has succeeded in getting his

22. The other involved the question of whether credit must be given for time served, and the Court said that it must be given.

first conviction set aside. * * * And at least since 1919, when Stroud v. United States, 251 U.S. 15, was decided, it has been settled that a corollary of the power to retry a defendant is the power, upon the defendant's reconviction, to impose whatever sentence may be legally authorized, whether or not it is greater than the sentence imposed after the first conviction.[a] * * *

Although the rationale for this "well-established part of our constitutional jurisprudence" has been variously verbalized, it rests ultimately upon the premise that the original conviction has, at the defendant's behest, been wholly nullified and the slate wiped clean. As to whatever punishment has actually been suffered under the first conviction, that premise is, of course, an unmitigated fiction * * *. But, so far as the conviction itself goes, and that part of the sentence that has not yet been served, it is no more than a simple statement of fact to say that the slate *has* been wiped clean. The conviction *has* been set aside, and the unexpired portion of the original sentence will never be served. A new trial may result in an acquittal. But if it does result in a conviction, we cannot say that the constitutional guarantee against double jeopardy of its own weight restricts the imposition of an otherwise lawful single punishment for the offense in question. To hold to the contrary would be to cast doubt upon the whole validity of the basic principle enunciated in United States v. Ball, supra, and upon the unbroken line of decisions that have followed that principle for almost 75 years. We think those decisions are entirely sound, and we decline to depart from the concept they reflect.

B

[The Court rejected an argument that the equal protection clause forbids the imposition of a more severe sentence upon retrial.]

C

We hold, therefore, that neither the double jeopardy provision nor the Equal Protection Clause imposes an absolute bar to a more severe sentence upon reconviction. A trial judge is not constitutionally precluded, in other words, from imposing a new sentence, whether greater or less than the original sentence, in the light of events subsequent to the first trial that may have thrown new light upon the defendant's "life, health, habits, conduct, and mental and moral propensities." Such information may come to the judge's attention from evidence adduced at the second trial itself, from a new presentence investigation, from the defendant's prison record, or possibly from other sources. * * *

To say that there exists no absolute constitutional bar to the imposition of a more severe sentence upon retrial is not, however, to end the inquiry. There remains for consideration the impact of the Due Process Clause of the Fourteenth Amendment.

It can hardly be doubted that it would be a flagrant violation of the Fourteenth Amendment for a state trial court to follow an announced practice of imposing a heavier sentence upon every reconvicted defendant for the explicit purpose of punishing the defendant for his having succeeded in getting his original conviction set aside. Where, as in each of the cases before us, the original conviction has been set aside because of a constitutional error,

a. In *Stroud* the defendant was convicted of first-degree murder and sentenced to life imprisonment. After reversal of this conviction, the defendant was retried, reconvicted of the same offense, and sentenced to death. This Court upheld the conviction against the defendant's claim that his constitutional right not to be twice put in jeopardy had been violated.

the imposition of such a punishment, "penalizing those who choose to exercise" constitutional rights, "would be patently unconstitutional." United States v. Jackson, 390 U.S. 570, 581. And the very threat inherent in the existence of such a punitive policy would, with respect to those still in prison, serve to "chill the exercise of basic constitutional rights." But even if the first conviction has been set aside for nonconstitutional error, the imposition of a penalty upon the defendant for having successfully pursued a statutory right of appeal or collateral remedy would be no less a violation of due process of law. * * * A court is "without right to * * * put a price on an appeal. A defendant's exercise of a right of appeal must be free and unfettered. * * * [I]t is unfair to use the great power given to the court to determine sentence to place a defendant in the dilemma of making an unfree choice." "This Court has never held that the States are required to establish avenues of appellate review, but it is now fundamental that, once established, these avenues must be kept free of unreasoned distinctions that can only impede open and equal access to the courts." Rinaldi v. Yeager, 384 U.S. 305, 310–11 (1966).

Due process of law, then, requires that vindictiveness against a defendant for having successfully attacked his first conviction must play no part in the sentence he receives after a new trial. And since the fear of such vindictiveness may unconstitutionally deter a defendant's exercise of the right to appeal or collaterally attack his first conviction, due process also requires that a defendant be freed of apprehension of such a retaliatory motivation on the part of the sentencing judge.

In order to assure the absence of such a motivation, we have concluded that whenever a judge imposes a more severe sentence upon a defendant after a new trial, the reasons for his doing so must affirmatively appear. Those reasons must be based upon objective information concerning identifiable conduct on the part of the defendant occurring after the time of the original sentencing proceeding. And the factual data upon which the increased sentence is based must be made part of the record, so that the constitutional legitimacy of the increased sentence may be fully reviewed on appeal.

We dispose of the two cases before us in the light of these conclusions. In No. 418 Judge Johnson noted that "the State of Alabama offers no evidence attempting to justify the increase in Rice's original sentences * * *." He found it "shocking that the State of Alabama has not attempted to explain or justify the increase in Rice's punishment—in these three cases, over threefold." And he found that "the conclusion is inescapable that the State of Alabama is punishing petitioner Rice for his having exercised his post-conviction right of review * * *." In No. 413 the situation is not so dramatically clear. Nonetheless, the fact remains that neither at the time the increased sentence was imposed upon Pearce, nor at any stage in this habeas corpus proceeding, has the State offered any reason or justification for that sentence beyond the naked power to impose it.

[The Court upheld the relief granted to Pearce and Rice by the lower courts. Justices Douglas and Marshall concurred, but would have held that the Double Jeopardy Clause bars a higher penalty upon reconviction in every case. Analogizing to Green v. United States, 355 U.S. 184 (1957), they believed that a defendant should face the risk of a higher punishment only once. The fact that *Green* involved two different crimes with different punishments "is a matter of semantics." Justice Harlan's separate opinion largely agreed with the view of Justices Douglas and Marshall. Justice Harlan wrote as follows:

> "Every consideration enunciated by the Court in support of the decision in *Green* applies with equal force to the situation at bar. In each instance, the defendant was once subjected to the risk of receiving a maximum punishment, but it was determined by legal process that he should receive only a specified punishment less than the maximum. And the concept or fiction of an 'implicit acquittal' of the greater offense applies equally to the greater sentence: in each case it was determined at the former trial that the defendant or his offense was of a certain limited degree of 'badness' or gravity only, and therefore merited only a certain limited punishment. Most significantly, perhaps, in each case a contrary rule would place the defendant considering whether to appeal his conviction in the same 'incredible dilemma' and confront him with the same 'desperate' choice. His decision whether or not to appeal would be burdened by the consideration that success, followed by retrial and conviction, might place him in a far worse position than if he remained silent and suffered what seemed to be an unjust punishment. In terms of *Green*, that the imposition of a more severe sentence on retrial is a matter of pure *chance*, rather than the result of purposeful retaliation for having taken an appeal, renders the choice no less 'desperate.' "

Justice Black wrote a concurring and dissenting opinion. He concluded that due process prohibited a higher sentence imposed on appeal for the purpose of punishing a defendant for appealing, but that the detailed procedure mandated by the Court was not required. Justice White wrote an opinion concurring in part.]

That *Pearce* was decided as a due process and not a double jeopardy case is of great importance. The more flexible due process approach produced subsequent rulings that narrowed the potential reach of *Pearce*, rulings that would have been more difficult had *Pearce* rested on the double jeopardy language of the Fifth Amendment.

The Supreme Court explained in Wasman v. United States, 468 U.S. 559 (1984), that *Pearce* did not prevent the imposition of a higher sentence upon reconviction of a defendant who had been convicted of additional offenses between the first and second trials. The trial judge who sentenced Wasman carefully explained that he gave him a greater sentence after the second trial than he had after the first because he had additional convictions at the time of the second trial. The Court found this explanation sufficient to rebut the presumption of vindictiveness established by *Pearce.* Chief Justice Burger wrote for the Court. Justice Powell, joined by Justice Blackmun, added an opinion concurring in part of the Court's opinion and in the judgment. Justice Brennan, joined by Justice Marshall, added a sentence stating that he concurred in the judgment largely for the reasons stated by Justice Powell. Justice Stevens concurred in the judgment. The separate opinions reflected some dissatisfaction with the Chief Justice's treatment of the "vindictiveness" concept and a belief that, as Justice Powell wrote, "this case involves a straightforward application of the Court's holding in North Carolina v. Pearce."

Chief Justice Burger wrote for the Court in Texas v. McCullough, 475 U.S. 134 (1986), as it upheld a trial judge's imposition of a 50 year sentence in a second trial necessitated by the judge's granting a mistrial after a jury had imposed a 20 year sentence in the first trial. The Court held that the *Pearce* presumption of vindictiveness was inapplicable because the second trial occurred only "because the trial judge herself concluded that the prosecutor's misconduct required it" and "because different sentencers assessed the varying sentences that McCullough received." Moreover, the Court found that even if *Pearce* were to apply, the trial judge's findings—i.e., two new witnesses testified in the second case concerning the murder, and the judge learned for the first time that the defendant had been released from prison only four months before the murder—rebutted the presumption. It rejected the argument that *Pearce* permitted consideration only of events occurring subsequent to the original sentencing. The Chief Justice recognized that "a defendant may be more reluctant to appeal if there is a risk that new, probative evidence supporting a longer sentence may be revealed on retrial." But he stated that "this Court has never recognized this 'chilling effect' as sufficient reason to create a constitutional prohibition against considering relevant information in assessing sentences."

Justice Marshall, joined by Justices Blackmun and Stevens, dissented, arguing that "the mere grant of a new trial motion can in no way be considered a guarantee, or even an indication, that the judge will harbor no resentment toward defendant as a result of his decision to exercise his statutory right to make such a motion." Thus, he would have applied the *Pearce* presumption. He also argued that the *Pearce* Court plainly intended to limit rebuttal of the presumption to use of events or conduct taking place after the first sentencing, and that the Court's new approach would "chill" defendants from exercising their rights to seek correction of trial errors. Justice Brennan concurred in the judgment on the ground that "the possibility that an increased sentence upon retrial resulted from judicial vindictiveness is sufficiently remote that the presumption ... should not apply here." But he added that if he were to presume vindictiveness, he would agree with Justice Marshall that the reasons given by the trial judge were inadequate to rebut the presumption.

In Colten v. Kentucky, 407 U.S. 104 (1972), the Court held that *Pearce* did not apply when a second sentence was handed down by a higher court in a two-tiered trial court system. The Court emphasized that the de novo court "was not the court that is asked to do over what it thought it had already done correctly," and that therefore a presumption of vindictiveness would be unwarranted.

In Chaffin v. Stynchcombe, 412 U.S. 17 (1973), the Court held that due process does not require the extension of *Pearce* to jury sentencing. In *Chaffin* the defendant was tried for and convicted of robbery by force or violence. The jury sentenced him to fifteen years, but his appeal was successful. Thereafter, he was retried, convicted, and sentenced to life imprisonment. The jury knew that he had been tried previously on the same charge but did not know of his prior conviction or sentence. The following excerpt represents the Court's treatment of *Pearce*:

> Petitioner seeks the extension of the *Pearce* rationale to jury resentencing. That decision, as we have said, was premised on the apparent need to guard against *vindictiveness* in the resentencing process. *Pearce* was not written with a view to protecting against the mere possibility that, once the slate is wiped clean and the prosecution begins anew, a fresh sentence may be higher for some valid reason associated with the need for flexibility and discretion in the

sentencing process. The possibility of a higher sentence was recognized and accepted as a legitimate concomitant of the retrial process.

Subsequent cases have dispelled any doubt that *Pearce* was premised on the hazard of vindictiveness. * * * [A] focus on actual vindictiveness is reflected in the decision last Term in Colten v. Kentucky. The question in that case was whether the *Pearce* principle applied to bar the imposition of a higher sentence after a *de novo* trial in those jurisdictions that employ a two-tier system of trial courts. While noting that "[i]t may often be that the [*de novo* "appeal" court] will impose a punishment more severe than that received from the inferior court," we were shown nothing to persuade us that "the hazard of being *penalized* for seeking a new trial, which underlay the holding of *Pearce*, also inheres in the *de novo* trial arrangement." In short, the Due Process Clause was not violated because the "possibility of vindictiveness" was not found to inhere in the two-tier system.

This case, then, is controlled by the inquiry into possible vindictiveness counseled by *Pearce* * * *. The potential for such abuse of the sentencing process by the jury is, we think, *de minimis* in a properly controlled retrial. The first prerequisite for the imposition of a retaliatory penalty is knowledge of the prior sentence. It has been conceded in this case that the jury was not informed of the prior sentence. We have no reason to suspect that this is not customary in a properly tried jury case. It is more likely that the jury will be aware that there was a prior trial, but it does not follow from this that the jury will know whether that trial was on the same charge, or whether it resulted in a conviction or mistrial. Other distinguishing factors between jury and judicial sentencing further diminish the possibility of impropriety in jury sentencing. As was true in *Colten*, the second sentence is not meted out by the same judicial authority whose handling of the prior trial was sufficiently unacceptable to have required a reversal of the conviction. Thus, the jury, unlike the judge who has been reversed, will have no personal stake in the prior conviction and no motivation to engage in self-vindication. Similarly, the jury is unlikely to be sensitive to the institutional interests that might occasion higher sentences by a judge desirous of discouraging what he regards as meritless appeals.[a]

In light of these considerations, and where improper and prejudicial information regarding the prior sentence is withheld, there is no basis for holding that jury resentencing poses any real threat of vindictiveness.

Justice Douglas dissented. Justice Stewart also dissented and was joined by Justice Brennan; he argued that the judge and the prosecutor present threats of vindictiveness.

a. It has been suggested that higher sentences on retrial might result from vindictiveness on the part of the prosecutor. As punishment for a successful appeal, for instance, a prosecutor might recommend to the jury, and strenuously argue in favor of, a higher sentence than he previously sought. No such indication exists on this record since the prosecutor vigorously urged the imposition of the death penalty at the first trial. In any event, it would be erroneous to infer a vindictive motive merely from the severity of the sentence recommended by the prosecutor. Prosecutors often request more than they can reasonably expect to get, knowing that the jury will customarily arrive at some compromise sentence. The prosecutor's strategy also might well vary from case to case depending on such factors as his assessment of the jury's reaction to the proof and to the testimony of witnesses for and against the State. Given these practical considerations, and constrained by the bar against his informing the jury of the facts of prior conviction and sentence, the possibility that a harsher sentence will be obtained through prosecutorial malice seems remote.

> Either or both might have personal and institutional reasons for desiring to punish a defendant who has successfully challenged his conviction. Out of vindictiveness the prosecutor might well ask for a sentence more severe than that meted out after the first trial, and a judge by the manner in which he charges the jury might influence the jury to impose a higher sentence at the second trial.

They urged that a trial judge should be required to reduce any sentence imposed by the jury after retrial to that imposed after the first trial, unless she can state reasons for any increased sentence, as required by *Pearce.* Justice Marshall's dissent argued that vindictiveness by juries was a real concern, because they often know of the prior conviction and sentence. Moreover, he argued, different rules for judges and juries place an unnecessary burden on the defendant's right to choose a jury trial after a successful appeal. This argument was made by all the dissenters.

Chief Justice Rehnquist wrote for eight Justices in Alabama v. Smith, 490 U.S. 794 (1989), which held that the *Pearce* presumption of vindictiveness does not apply when a sentence imposed after a trial is greater than that previously imposed after a guilty plea. The Court asserted that post-*Pearce* cases had established that the *Pearce* presumption should apply only to circumstances where there is "a reasonable likelihood that the increase in sentence is the product of actual vindictiveness." The Chief Justice observed that "when a greater penalty is imposed after trial than was imposed after a prior guilty plea, the increase in sentence is not more likely than not attributable to the vindictiveness on the part of the sentencing judge." He reasoned that "[e]ven when the same judge imposes both sentences, the relevant sentencing information available to the judge after the plea will usually be considerably less than that available after a trial," and "after trial, the factors that may have indicated leniency as consideration for the guilty plea are no longer present." Justice Marshall dissented.

B. PROSECUTORIAL VINDICTIVENESS

Although the arguments about prosecutorial vindictiveness did not carry the day in *Chaffin*, they were more successful in Blackledge v. Perry, 417 U.S. 21 (1974). Perry, an inmate in a North Carolina prison, was involved in a fight with another inmate and was charged with misdemeanor assault with a deadly weapon. After he was convicted in the lower trial court, he appealed as of right to the higher trial court where he was entitled to a trial de novo. After the filing of the notice of appeal, the prosecutor obtained an indictment from a grand jury, charging Perry with felonious assault with intent to kill or inflict serious bodily injury. Perry pleaded guilty to the felony charge and received a sentence that was less favorable than that imposed by the lower trial court on the misdemeanor conviction. The Supreme Court held that a person who is convicted of an offense and who has an opportunity for a trial de novo has a right to avail himself of the opportunity without apprehension that the state will substitute a more serious charge for the one brought in the lower court. The Court reasoned as follows:

> The question is whether the opportunities for vindictiveness [on the part of the prosecutor] are such as to impel the conclusion that due process of law

> requires a rule analogous to that of the *Pearce* case. We conclude that the answer must be in the affirmative.
>
> A prosecutor clearly has a considerable stake in discouraging [appeals which] will clearly require increased expenditures of prosecutorial resources before the defendant's conviction becomes final, and may even result in a formerly convicted defendant going free. And, if the prosecutor has the means readily at hand to discourage such appeals—by 'upping the ante' through a felony indictment * * * the state can insure that only the most hardy defendants will brave the hazards of a de novo trial.
>
> There is, of course, no evidence that the prosecutor in this case acted in bad faith or maliciously in seeking a felony indictment against Perry. The rationale of [*Pearce*], however, was not grounded upon the proposition that actual retaliatory motivation must inevitably exist. Rather, we emphasized that since the fear of such vindictiveness may unconstitutionally deter a defendant's exercise of the right to appeal * * * due process also requires that a defendant be freed of apprehension of such a retaliatory motivation on the part of the sentencing judge. We think it clear that the same considerations apply here.

The Court noted that the presumption of vindictiveness would be overcome if the State shows "that it was impossible to proceed on the more serious charge at the outset" and cited Diaz v. United States, 223 U.S. 442 (1912), discussed supra. In *Diaz,* the Double Jeopardy Clause was held not to bar a later murder trial where the victim did not die until after the defendant's trial for assault and battery. See also United States v. York, 933 F.2d 1343 (7th Cir. 1991), where the defendant was subjected to an additional charge of obstruction of justice after a successful appeal of his murder conviction. The court concluded that the testimony required to support the obstruction charge came from the defendant's son, who had expressed an unwillingness to testify against his father at the first trial. When the son changed his mind and approached the authorities two years later, the prosecution could not be presumed vindictive when it added the obstruction charge.

The Court found that *Blackledge* clearly controlled in Thigpen v. Roberts, 468 U.S. 27 (1984). The defendant was convicted in a lower level court of several misdemeanors, he sought a de novo trial in a higher level court, and he was indicted for a felony offense arising out of the same conduct. Finding that the same prosecutor was involved in both prosecutions, the Court stated that it "need not determine the correct rule when two independent prosecutors are involved." It observed that the *Blackledge* presumption of vindictiveness is rebuttable and that no attempt at rebuttal had been made in the lower courts. Three Justices suggested that the case should be remanded to the court of appeals for consideration of the applicability of *Blackledge,* since that court had decided the case on a different ground.

It is not yet clear what restrictions *Blackledge* places on prosecutors. In *Blackledge* itself, it appears that the conviction in the lower trial court was for a lesser included offense of the felony prosecuted in the higher trial court. The Supreme Court said that the state was seeking a greater conviction in the higher court for "the same conduct" for which Perry had been convicted in the lower trial court. Hence, the holding of the Court was that the greater offense could not be charged, because to permit a lesser offense to be elevated to a greater offense afforded a prosecutor an improper opportunity for vindictiveness. But what if the prosecutor files new charges after an appeal is taken—i.e., charges that are based on different offenses than the offense for which a conviction has been obtained? The lower courts divide on the permissibility of this behavior. Compare, e.g., United States v. Preciado-Gomez, 529 F.2d 935 (9th Cir. 1976) (permitting additional counts to be added) with United States v. Johnson, 537 F.2d 1170 (4th Cir. 1976) (barring additional counts). Cf. Miracle v. Estelle, 592 F.2d 1269 (5th Cir. 1979) (two indictments were originally filed and trial was held on one; following a conviction the court granted the defendant a new trial; prosecutor sought to proceed on the other indictment; held to be improper). Is it wrong for a prosecutor to bring one part of her claims against a defendant first in order to see what, if any, sentence the defendant gets, and then to bring additional charges only if necessary to vindicate the public interest? Is it wrong for a prosecutor to respond to a defendant's appeal that might be meritorious by bringing a new charge that might prove to be less troublesome legally than the one originally brought, which is the subject of the appeal?

In United States v. Goodwin, 454 U.S. 1138 (1982), the Court again addressed the problem of when the possibility of vindictiveness is sufficient to require a prosecutor to explain and justify his actions. Goodwin was charged with several misdemeanors, including assault, following an incident in which a police officer stopped his car for speeding. After he indicated his desire for a jury trial and the case moved from a Magistrate to the District Court, an Assistant United States Attorney obtained a four count indictment against Goodwin that included a felony charge of forcibly assaulting a federal officer. Goodwin was convicted on the felony count and one misdemeanor count. The Supreme Court, in an opinion by Justice Stevens, reversed a court of appeals' holding that the Due Process Clause prohibits the government from bringing more serious charges against a defendant after he has exercised his right to jury trial. Distinguishing *Pearce* and *Blackledge* as decisions reflecting "a recognition by the Court of the institutional bias inherent in the judicial system against the retrial of issues that have already been decided," Justice Stevens' opinion reasoned that "[t]here is good reason to be cautious before adopting an inflexible presumption of prosecutorial vindictiveness in a pre-trial setting. In the course of preparing for trial, the prosecutor may uncover additional information that suggests a basis for further prosecution or he simply may come to realize that information possessed by the State has a broader significance." Although the opinion declined to adopt a presumption of vindictiveness, it stated that "we of course do not foreclose the possibility that a defendant in an appropriate case might prove objectively that the prosecutor's decision was motivated by a desire to punish him for doing something that the law plainly allowed him to do." Justice Blackmun would have presumed vindictiveness but found that the prosecutor's reasons for seeking a felony indictment adequately rebutted the presumption. Justice Brennan, joined by Justice Marshall, dissented.[23]

23. Recognizing that *Goodwin* makes a presumption of vindictiveness impossible, State v. Halling, 66 Or.App. 180, 672 P.2d 1386 (1983), nevertheless upholds a trial judge who found actual vindictiveness in the filing of two indictments against a defendant who refused to plead guilty to attempted murder. The prosecutor had not mentioned additional offenses during a pretrial conference and had phoned defense counsel to say that she had found a way "to cause further evil" to the defendant.

In United States v. Nichols, 937 F.2d 1257 (7th Cir.1991), the court relied on *Goodwin* to hold that no presumption of vindictiveness arises when a prosecutor obtains a superseding indictment charging more serious crimes after a mistrial has been declared because of a deadlocked jury. Such a situation does not involve "a retrial of issues that have already been decided." The court further held that the superseding indictment was not the result of actual vindictiveness. It noted that the prosecutor had no personal stake in the case.

The presumption of prosecutorial vindictiveness has not been readily found by lower courts. For example, in United States v. Sinigaglio, 925 F.2d 339 (9th Cir.1991), the court stated that "when increased charges are filed in the routine course of prosecutorial review or as a result of continuing investigation, there is no realistic likelihood of prosecutorial abuse, and therefore no appearance of vindictive prosecution arises merely because the prosecutor's action was taken after a defense right was exercised." It has also been held that the increase in charges due to the prosecutor's discovery of a new law does not warrant a presumption of vindictiveness. United States v. Austin, 902 F.2d 743 (9th Cir.1990). In United States v. Muldoon, 931 F.2d 282 (4th Cir.1991), the court held that a presumption of vindictiveness "does not arise from plea negotiations when the prosecutor threatens to bring additional charges if the accused refuses to plead guilty to pending charges. The Due Process Clause does not bar the prosecutor from carrying out his threat."

IX. DOUBLE JEOPARDY AND APPELLATE REVIEW OF SENTENCING

A. GOVERNMENT APPEALS GENERALLY

We have previously seen that an appellate court cannot set aside a jury or judge verdict of not guilty (except where the judge attempts to set aside a prior jury verdict of guilt) and a judge generally may not increase the sentence imposed upon a defendant who successfully appeals from a conviction. But can the prosecutor ask an appellate court to increase the sentence imposed by a trial court?

Justice Blackmun wrote for the majority in United States v. DiFrancesco, 449 U.S. 117 (1980), upholding the government's right to appeal the sentence imposed upon a "dangerous special offender." The majority said that the prohibition against multiple trials is the controlling constitutional principle in double jeopardy cases and that the problem with appellate review of acquittals is the necessity of a second trial. Appellate review of sentencing need not require a second trial. Moreover, the majority noted that "the pronouncement of sentence has never carried the finality that attaches to an acquittal." It also observed that the defendant is not subjected to multiple sentences when resentenced following an appeal, since the defendant understands that an initial sentence is not final. Justice Brennan, joined by Justices White, Marshall and Stevens, dissented and argued that "[i]n both acquittals and sentences, the trier of fact makes a factual adjudication that removes from the defendant's burden of risk the charges of which he was acquitted and the potential sentence which he did not receive." The dissent argued "that most defendants are more concerned with how much time they must spend in prison than with whether their record shows a conviction" and that the anxiety associated with multiple trials is equally present when the government can take an appeal from sentencing. Justice Stevens also filed a separate dissent.[24]

The case presented a strict double jeopardy claim, not a due process vindictiveness claim. The vindictiveness claim may not have been raised because the statute provided that "[a]ny review of the sentence by the United States shall be taken at least five days before expiration of the time for taking a review * * * by the defendant * * *" Does this provision eliminate vindictiveness concerns?

DiFrancesco is distinguished in United States v. Jones, 722 F.2d 632 (11th Cir.1983). A trial judge originally sentenced a defendant to four years imprisonment with all but six months suspended and five years probation. After discovering that he had misunderstood certain facts, through no fault of the defendant, the judge modified the sentence to a straight four year term. The court of appeals found that *DiFrancesco* would uphold a defendant's legitimate expectations as to the length of his sentence and concluded that the double jeopardy clause is violated by a trial court's resentencing a defendant to a greater sentence after he has begun to serve his original sentence. The court warned, however, that a defendant who is responsible for a trial court's misunderstanding would not have a legitimate expectation and could be subject to resentencing.

B. APPEALS IN CAPITAL CASES

The Supreme Court distinguished *DiFrancesco* in Bullington v. Missouri, 451 U.S. 430 (1981), and held that it would violate the Double Jeopardy Clause to impose a death penalty at a second trial when the jury in the first trial returned a verdict of life imprisonment in a bifurcated proceeding in which the prosecution had the burden of proving certain elements beyond a reasonable doubt. The majority noted that the capital sentencing procedure was more like a trial on guilt or innocence than are most sentencing proceedings and that the prior jury determination was tantamount to an acquittal on the death sentence. Four dissenters argued that the purpose of double jeopardy protection is to protect the innocent from wrongful conviction and that sentencing procedures present no danger of convicting the innocent.

Bullington proved to be controlling in Arizona v. Rumsey, 467 U.S. 203 (1984), as the Supreme Court held that a state judge's finding that there were no aggravating factors warranting imposition of capital punishment had the same effect as an "acquittal" and that the state supreme court violated the double jeopardy clause when it remanded a defendant's case back for resentencing and a death sentence was imposed. Like Missouri, Arizona placed the burden of proving aggravating circumstances on the prosecution beyond a reasonable doubt. The Court declined to distinguish Missouri's jury findings from Arizona's judge findings. Even though the state supreme court held that the trial judge had erred as a matter of law in construing one of the statutory

24. For a scholarly debate on the appeal question, see Stern, Government Appeals of Sentences: A Constitutional Response to Arbitrary and Unreasonable Sentences, 18 Am. Crim.L.Rev. 51 (1980); Freeman & Early, United States v. DiFrancesco: Government Appeal of Sentences, 18 Am.Cr.L.Rev. 91 (1980). See also Westen, The Three Faces of Double Jeopardy: Reflections on Government Appeals of Criminal Sentences, 78 Mich. L.Rev. 1001 (1980).

aggravating circumstances and thus prejudiced the government, the Supreme Court held that "[r]eliance on an error of law * * * does not change the double jeopardy effects of a judgment that amounts to an acquittal on the merits." Justice O'Connor wrote for the Court. Justice Rehnquist dissented and was joined by Justice White. He argued that the implied acquittal analysis of *Bullington* ought not to apply to a case in which the state proved an aggravating circumstance but the trial judge improperly applied state law to the state's proof.

The Supreme Court distinguished *Bullington* and *Rumsey* in Poland v. Arizona, 476 U.S. 147 (1986). The defendants were convicted of robbing a bank van and killing its guards. The trial court, making the same error made in *Rumsey* found that the offense was not committed for "pecuniary gain," because the statutory aggravating circumstance applied only to contract killings. But, the court found that the crime was committed in "an especially heinous" circumstance and imposed death sentences. On appeal, the state supreme court, reversing and remanding on another ground, held both that there was insufficient evidence of heinousness and that the trial judge erred in ruling that the crime was not for pecuniary gain under the statute.

Justice White's majority opinion found that both prior cases involved the equivalent of acquittals during sentencing, while there was no finding in the instant case that the prosecution failed to prove its case. The Court rejected the argument that a capital sentencer's failure to find a particular aggravating circumstance constitutes an acquittal of that circumstance for double jeopardy purposes and held instead that the proper inquiry is whether the sentencer or reviewing court has decided that the prosecution has failed to prove that death is an appropriate sentence. Thus, the Court ruled that the state supreme court acted properly in reviewing the "pecuniary gain" ruling by the trial judge and in permitting the judge to consider this aggravating circumstance once again upon retrial.

Justice Marshall, joined by Justices Brennan and Blackmun, dissented and argued that the only difference between this case and *Rumsey* is that the sentencing judge in this case made two errors of state law while the *Rumsey* judge made only one. The dissent reasoned that the state supreme court effectively held that the defendants were entitled to acquittals on the only aggravating circumstance that the trial court found to have been validly proved. Thus, any remand for further factfinding should be prohibited under *Burks* and *Rumsey*.

C. RESENTENCING FOLLOWING PARTIAL REVERSAL

The Supreme Court cited *DiFrancesco* in its per curiam opinion in Pennsylvania v. Goldhammer, 474 U.S. 28 (1985), which held that the double jeopardy clause did not prevent a state court from resentencing a defendant after some of his convictions had been overturned on appeal. Goldhammer had been convicted on 56 counts of forgery and 56 counts of theft, but he was sentenced to 2–5 years on a single theft count and five years of probation on a single forgery count with sentence on all other counts suspended. The state supreme court overturned 34 of the theft convictions, including the one count on which Goldhammer had been sentenced to prison, because the statute of limitations had run. The Supreme Court remanded the case for a determination of whether state law permitted resentencing.

Chapter Thirteen

POST-CONVICTION CHALLENGES

I. INTRODUCTION

Because of the double jeopardy clause and the constitutional right to a jury trial, the prosecutor generally will be unable to seek review of an acquittal unless it occurs in a case in which there has been a verdict of guilty which was set aside by the trial judge whose decision, if erroneous, can be reversed so that the original verdict can be reinstated without an additional trial.[1] The criminal defendant who is convicted has greater opportunities to challenge the trial court's judgment.[2] This chapter addresses the opportunities most likely to be made available in the typical criminal case.

Three types of proceedings will be examined in this chapter: some involve trial court motions, some involve direct appellate review of convictions, and some involve collateral attacks on convictions. The assumption is made that everyone has a basic familiarity with the following facts: criminal cases are tried in both federal and state courts; an appeal of one sort or another (e.g., in Virginia a defendant petitions for review, but the denial of the petition is similar to a summary affirmance of a conviction, as noted in D. Meador, Appellate Courts 169–171 (1974)), generally is provided a convicted defendant; the time period in which an appeal must be taken is set forth in applicable

1. This Chapter addresses only claims by persons who have litigated; it does not examine the status of those who have pleaded guilty. That has been taken up, supra, in Chapter Nine. Also not considered here are problems of when a decision becomes final for purposes of appeal. See, e.g., United States v. Nixon, 418 U.S. 683, 690–92 (1974). Nor are special techniques of avoiding review examined—*e.g.*, the concurrent sentence doctrine, see, e.g., Benton v. Maryland, 395 U.S. 784 (1969) (discretion to avoid review of one of concurrent judgments); the mootness doctrine, see, e.g., Sibron v. New York, 392 U.S. 40 (1968) (case not moot on direct appeal where adverse collateral consequences are possible); Dove v. United States, 423 U.S. 325 (1976), (certiorari petition dismissed when petitioner dies). In Ray v. United States, 481 U.S. 736 (1987), the Supreme Court announced in a two paragraph per curiam opinion that the "concurrent sentence doctrine" could not be invoked to bar appellate review of one of three counts on which a defendant was convicted, since the defendant was assessed $50 on each count and therefore had a right to review of all counts.

2. As noted in the previous chapter on double jeopardy, not all government appeals are constitutionally barred. Generally, if the prosecutor is not challenging an acquittal or seeking a second adjudication on the guilt-innocence question, the Constitution will not stand in the way of an appeal. However, in many jurisdictions the government cannot appeal unless a statute authorizes appeal. Kronenberg, Right of a State to Appeal in Criminal Cases, 49 J.Crim.L.C. & P.S. 473 (1959). Hence, although Congress had acted to open the doors to government appeals virtually to the limits of the Constitution in 18 U.S.C.A. § 3731, not all states permit the government such review.

statutes and rules of court (see, e.g., Fed.R.Crim.P. 4(b) (notice of appeal to be filed within 10 days of entry of judgment); Va.Sup.Ct.R. 56 (notice of appeal to be filed within 30 days of judgment)); the decision whether to appeal is the client's and, in order to render effective assistance of counsel, a lawyer must inform the client of the right to appeal (see, e.g., Nelson v. Peyton, 415 F.2d 1154 (4th Cir. 1969)). The defendant may raise claims concerning almost any trial errors, defects in trial procedure problems with the substantive law or the overall fairness of the results on appeal; but crowded appellate courts may screen some appeals and decide them on the basis of written briefs, reserving oral argument for special cases. See generally ABA Task Force on Appellate Procedure, Efficiency and Justice in Appeals; Methods and Selected Materials (1977). Questions concerning the right to counsel and to the effective assistance of counsel in post-conviction proceedings are addressed in Chapters Five and Ten. The special aspects of appellate review of sentences have been examined in Chapters Eleven and Twelve.

II. THE SUFFICIENCY OF THE EVIDENCE AND THE EFFECTS OF ERROR

A. INSUFFICIENCY AS A MATTER OF LAW

1. The General Standard

A defendant may move during trial or after a verdict is returned for an acquittal on the ground that the evidence is insufficient to sustain a conviction. Federal Rule of Criminal Procedure 29 indicates the opportunities available to a defendant to make and repeat such a motion.

As Professor Wright has noted, "[a] directed verdict for defendant * * * or judgment of acquittal as it is now called, is an important safeguard to the defendant. It tests the sufficiency of the evidence against him, and avoids the risk that a jury may capriciously find him guilty though there is no legally sufficient evidence of his guilt." 2 C. Wright, Federal Practice and Procedure, § 461, at 637–8 (1982). It should be obvious that it is going to be a rare case in which a post-verdict motion will not have been preceded by other motions. "It would be a rash defense counsel who waited to make such a motion until after the verdict, in view of the impact a guilty verdict is likely to have on the court's determination of the motion." Rezneck, The New Federal Rules of Criminal Procedure, 54 Geo.L.J. 1276, 1313 (1966).

The same standard is used in judging post-verdict as mid-trial motions. Courts have wisely adopted the general rule that a guilty verdict can only stand if there is sufficient evidence to support a finding beyond a reasonable doubt of all necessary elements of the government's case.[3] See American Tobacco Co. v. United States, 328 U.S. 781 (1946); United States v. Mariani, 725 F.2d 862 (2d Cir.1984). After In re Winship, discussed in Chapter Ten, supra, this rule probably is well grounded in the Constitution. When the burden of persuasion on a defense is placed upon the defendant, a guilty verdict will be

3. In conspiracy cases, an ill-defined and objectionable "slight evidence" standard has been utilized by some courts, but it never has been justified. See United States v. Malatesta, 583 F.2d 748 (5th Cir. 1978) (Coleman, J., concurring) and 590 F.2d 1379 (en banc) (rejecting the "slight evidence rule") (1979); Note, Connecting Defendants to Conspiracies, the Slight Evidence Rule and the Federal Courts, 64 Va.L.Rev. 881 (1978).

set aside if no reasonable jury could have rejected the defendant's evidence, when measured under the appropriate standard of proof. For example, if a defendant bears the burden of proving insanity by a preponderance of the evidence, a jury verdict of guilty will be set aside if the defendant's evidence is so strong that any *reasonable* jury would have found the proof of insanity to be preponderant.

Several federal circuits once held that acquittal is required in a circumstantial evidence case unless the evidence excludes every reasonable hypothesis except guilt. Wisely, the United States Supreme Court held that such an instruction is confusing and incorrect, Holland v. United States, 348 U.S. 121, 139–40 (1954). Today it is clear that "circumstantial evidence alone can sustain a guilty verdict and to do so, circumstantial evidence need not remove every reasonable hypothesis except that of guilt." United States v. White, 932 F.2d 588 (6th Cir.1991).

The standard for review by a trial judge upon a motion for acquittal is well-stated by the court in United States v. Mariani, 725 F.2d 862 (2d Cir.1984):

> When a defendant moves for a judgment of acquittal, the court must determine whether upon the evidence, giving full play to the right of the jury to determine credibility, weigh the evidence, and draw justifiable inferences of fact, a reasonable mind might fairly conclude guilt beyond a reasonable doubt. If it concludes that upon the evidence there must be such a doubt in a reasonable mind, it must grant the motion; or, to state it another way, if there is no evidence upon which a reasonable mind might fairly conclude guilt beyond a reasonable doubt, the motion must be granted. If it concludes that either of the two results, a reasonable doubt or no reasonable doubt, is fairly possible, it must let the jury decide the matter.

In *Mariani,* the court held that the trial court had used the correct standard but applied it improperly. Mariani was charged with conspiracy to steal money from the United States. An undercover agent had arranged a narcotics transaction with Mariani's friend, Miller. Mariani was parked at the scene where the deal was to be made. Miller went to the undercover agent, pointed toward Mariani and said "my man's over there, wait here and I'll get the package." Miller then went to Mariani's car, spoke to Mariani through the driver's side window, got into the car through the door on the passenger's side, and came out of the car carrying a package. Miller brought the package to the undercover agent, and received money. Miller and Mariani were then arrested. After their arrest, Miller stated that the agents should check the package because it did not contain drugs. Mariani then said, "you guys don't got what you think you got." Subsequent tests showed that the package did not contain drugs; hence the charge of stealing money from the United States. Mariani claimed that while he was present at the scene, he knew nothing about the transaction and was merely giving his friend a ride. The trial judge granted Mariani's motion for acquittal; he found that the evidence showed only that Mariani was present at the scene, and that mere presence was not sufficient to convict. He discounted Mariani's post-arrest statement as "merely echoing what he had heard Miller say earlier." The court of appeals agreed that mere presence is not sufficient for a conviction. But it held that the trial court had erred in discounting the post-arrest statement, and in refusing to draw reasonable inferences from the fact that Miller spoke with Mariani before taking the package from Mariani's car. The court concluded that "the district court substituted its own determination of the weight of the evidence and the reasonable inferences to be drawn for that of the jury." The court of appeals noted that "conspiracy can be proven circumstantially," that "seemingly innocent acts taken individually may indicate complicity when viewed collectively and with reference to the circumstances in general," and that "the evidence is to be viewed not in isolation but in conjunction." Compare Mikes v. Borg, 947 F.2d 353 (9th Cir. 1991) (in a case in which fingerprints are the only evidence against the defendant, the prosecution must establish that the defendant could only have left his fingerprints at the scene during the commission of the crime; habeas relief granted because the prosecution offered no evidence to exclude the possibility that the defendant may have been at the scene at a different time).

Mariani also makes clear that appellate courts will apply the same standard as trial courts in reviewing the sufficiency of the evidence, with one small difference. Generally, a trial judge will rule on the sufficiency of evidence only if a motion for judgment of acquittal is made, but she can enter a judgment of acquittal *sua sponte*. Appellate courts will not assess the sufficiency of the evidence absent a proper challenge. There is authority for the proposition that an appellate court will not review the sufficiency of the evidence if no motion for judgment of acquittal was made below, see, e.g., United States v. Luther, 521 F.2d 408 (9th Cir. 1975), but appellate courts generally will consider the sufficiency of the evidence in bench trials whether or not any motion was made in the trial court for judgment of acquittal. See, e.g., Hall v. United States, 286 F.2d 676 (5th Cir. 1960).

Why a motion for judgment in the lower court should be a prerequisite to appellate review of sufficiency of the evidence questions is difficult to see. Every defendant who stands trial challenges the government to prove its case. If the government has not done so, appellate review would seem to be appropriate. The only governmental interest in the anti-review rule that is readily recognizable is the avoidance of unnecessary appeals—that is, those that would not take place if a trial judge granted a judgment of acquittal. But it hardly appears likely that the typical defendant would intentionally forego a chance for an acquittal in the trial court in order to impose on the government the costs of appeal. As a practical matter, experienced and effective lawyers make routine motions for judgment of acquittal to preserve all appellate rights. It is difficult, in fact, to understand the failure of some lawyers to make the boilerplate motion, since it involves little preparation and almost no skill.

Fed.R.Crim.P. 29(a), provides, as does the law of most states, that a motion for judgment of acquittal (or a motion to strike the evidence) must be granted after the evidence of either side is concluded if it is insufficient to warrant conviction. It is well established that the defendant can rest, present no evidence, and if convicted, appeal on the ground that a motion for judgment of acquittal was improperly denied. But the authorities divide on whether a defendant can offer evidence without waiving the right to have the acquittal motion judged on appeal solely on the basis of the government's evidence, without reference to the evidence offered after the government rests. The waiver rule probably is used by most courts today, although it has been roundly criticized by commentators. See, e.g., 2 C. Wright, Federal Practice and Procedure § 463; Comment, The Motion for Acquittal: A Neglected Safeguard, 70 Yale L.J. 1151 (1961). But see United States v. Foster, 783 F.2d 1082

(D.C.Cir.1986) (en banc) (returning to the waiver rule after having rejected it). The problem for the defendant with the waiver rule is not that he loses the right to appeal by putting on evidence. At the close of the evidence, he can move again for an acquittal. But under the waiver rule, it is only the later motion that can be reviewed. The defendant, by putting on evidence, waives the prior motion. Thus, the conviction will be affirmed, even though the prosecution may have failed to put on a prima facie case, if the evidence brought forth in the defendant's case, or any rebuttal evidence, filled the gap, and the whole record is sufficient to sustain a conviction. If the waiver rule applies, the defendant has a tactical decision to make at the end of the government's case—i.e., whether to offer defense evidence to increase the chances of acquittal at trial or to refrain from doing so to preserve for appeal the acquittal motion directed solely at the government's evidence.

2. *The Standard of Appellate Review of Sufficiency of the Evidence*

Before Jackson v. Virginia, discussed infra, there had been some tendency among appellate courts to uphold verdicts supported by *any* evidence. Only "no evidence" cases produced reversals. See, e.g., Thompson v. Louisville, 362 U.S. 199 (1960) ("[t]he record is entirely lacking in evidence to support any of the charges"); Garner v. Louisiana, 368 U.S. 157 (1961) ("no evidence to support a finding that petitioners disturbed the peace"). The "no evidence" cases may have been decided by the Supreme Court as they were to avoid more difficult problems of federal-state relations. Justice Stewart, dissenting from denial of certiorari in Freeman v. Zahradnick, 429 U.S. 1111 (1977), argued that under *Winship*, a different test was required:

> The *Winship* case held that the Due Process Clause requires proof beyond a reasonable doubt of every element of a criminal offense. A jury must be instructed accordingly. Properly instructed juries, however, occasionally convict even when it can be said that no rational trier of fact could find guilt beyond a reasonable doubt—even when it is clear that the defendant was entitled to a directed verdict of acquittal as a matter of law. In a federal trial, such improper application of law (as defined by *Winship*) to fact requires reversal of the conviction on the ground of insufficient evidence.
>
> The power of a federal court to review the application of federal law to the facts as found also operates, however, in criminal cases originating in state courts. On direct review of a state court conviction, this Court reviews the application of the "voluntariness" standard to the historical facts to determine whether a confession was admissible, or the application of First Amendment standards to the facts as found to determine whether the conduct in issue was constitutionally protected, to take but two examples. The same rule is applied in federal habeas corpus actions. It is not immediately apparent why application of the beyond a reasonable doubt standard of *Winship* to the historical facts should be any more immune from constitutional scrutiny. If, after viewing the evidence in the light most favorable to the State, a federal court determines that no rational trier of fact could have found a defendant guilty beyond a reasonable doubt of the state offense with which he was charged, it is surely arguable that the court must hold, under *Winship*, that the convicted defendant was denied due process of law.
>
> * * *

The Supreme Court adopted Justice Stewart's analysis in Jackson v. Virginia, 443 U.S. 307 (1979). Writing for the Court, Justice Stewart opined that the "no evidence" rule was inadequate to protect against misapplication of the proof beyond a reasonable doubt requirement and that the critical question on review of a criminal conviction is whether the record evidence could reasonably support a finding of guilt beyond a reasonable doubt. He also wrote that the standard should be utilized by federal courts hearing habeas corpus attacks on state convictions. Justice Stewart concluded as follows:

> After *Winship* the critical inquiry on review of the sufficiency of the evidence to support a criminal conviction must be not simply to determine whether the jury was properly instructed, but to determine whether the record evidence could reasonably support a finding of guilt beyond a reasonable doubt. But this inquiry does not require a court to ask itself whether *it* believes that the evidence at the trial established guilt beyond a reasonable doubt. Instead, the relevant question is whether, after viewing the evidence in the light most favorable to the prosecution, *any* rational trier of fact could have found the essential elements of the crime beyond a reasonable doubt. This familiar standard gives full play to the responsibility of the trier of fact fairly to resolve conflicts in the testimony, to weigh the evidence, and to draw reasonable inferences from basic facts to ultimate facts. * * * The criterion thus impinges upon jury discretion only to the extent necessary to guarantee the fundamental protection of due process of law.

Thus, the standard for appellate review of sufficiency is the same as the standard used by the trial court in ruling on a motion for acquittal. See United States v. Mariani, supra.

Justice Stevens dissented and was joined by Chief Justice Burger and Justice Rehnquist. He argued that *Winship* did not address appellate or habeas corpus procedures and that the very premise of *Winship* was that judges and properly instructed juries act rationally and that a verdict of guilty beyond a reasonable doubt that survives post-verdict motions and appellate review is not likely to be erroneous. Furthermore, he expressed concern not only about federal review of state convictions and the concomitant intrusion of the federal judiciary into state affairs, but also about the increased workload for federal judges hearing habeas corpus challenges to state convictions. Justice Powell did not participate. Ironically, Jackson, who was convicted of first degree murder, did not benefit from his victory. The Court found that because Jackson, among other things, admitted firing several shots into the ground and reloading his gun before killing the deceased, a rational trier of fact could have found that the killing was premeditated.[4]

It is a rare case in which a federal habeas corpus court overturns a conviction under *Jackson,* and when it happens, it is done with reluctance. See West v. Wright, 931 F.2d 262 (4th Cir.1991), where the court, while finding that

4. Appellate courts will defer to trial judges and juries. But should they defer where all evidence is written? In United States v. Chesher, 678 F.2d 1353 (9th Cir. 1982), the defendant lost a motion to suppress evidence, waived a jury trial, and submitted the issue of guilt to the court on a written stipulation of facts. Upon conviction, he appealed and urged that the evidence was insufficient to support the conviction. Although the court of appeals remanded for a hearing on a suppression issue, it found that the trial judge's finding of guilt was not clearly erroneous. A dissenting judge would not have used this deferential approach, but would have determined on appeal de novo the issue of guilt on the basis of the stipulation.

the evidence was insufficient to sustain a conviction, stressed that it did not undertake its task lightly:

> A determination in federal collateral review that a state court conviction by jury verdict was not supported by constitutionally sufficient evidence is one to be made with special caution and anxiety. Where, as here, it is made in the process of reversing a federal district court, it involves disagreement on this fundamental matter with a properly instructed state jury of twelve, a state trial judge, the state's supreme court, and a federal district judge. And it involves disagreement from a vantage point far removed from the immediacy of the testimonial evidence whose sufficiency is at issue. Indeed, there may be no more delicate constitutional determination in federal collateral review, given its unique rejection not only of state judicial rulings but of state jury findings.

The court nonetheless found the evidence insufficient to convict. West was convicted of grand larceny on the basis of possession of stolen goods. The court of appeals noted that the theft occurred several weeks before the items were found in West's house; only a few of the stolen items were found there; West had made no attempt to conceal the items; West's testimony that he had bought the items at a flea market was plausible; and there was no conflicting evidence refuting his testimony. Thus, this was a "mere possession" case, and a rational trier of fact could not conclude that West had the intent to commit grand larceny. It is notable that the Court has granted certiorari in *West* to determine whether the court of appeals showed sufficient deference to the state court's application of law to fact. 112 S.Ct. 672 (1991).

Jackson was a habeas corpus case, but the standards set forth in *Jackson* apply for direct appeals as well. See, e.g., United States v. White, 932 F.2d 588 (6th Cir.1991).

Appellate review of sufficiency "is necessarily a fact-specific judgment call." West v. Wright, supra. Generally, the only challenges which are seriously entertained are (1) in theft cases, where the evidence shows little more than "mere possession," as in *West,* and (2) where the evidence shows that the defendant was present at the scene, but there is a dispute as to whether more has been shown than "mere presence," as in *Mariani.* In *Mariani,* the evidence was found to show more than "mere presence." In contrast, in United States v. White, 932 F.2d 588 (6th Cir.1991), the court held that a rational juror could not have found anything more than "mere presence," and reversed the conviction. White was charged with intentionally manufacturing a controlled substance. Officers observed a fifteen-by-thirty foot patch of marijuana growing three feet behind White's trailer home. The patch was cultivated and fertilized. The property on which the marijuana was grown was not owned by White. White's trailer was searched, and no marijuana was found; some fertilizer was found in the trailer, but it was never compared with the fertilizer used in the marijuana patch. White was partially disabled with a bad back and a bad arm. He lived with three family members, and there were two residences on each side of the trailer within 100 feet. The court concluded that "the only evidence linking White to the marijuana was the fact that he lived three feet from the patch," and that "mere presence in an area where drugs are found is not sufficient." The court rejected the government's argument that the jury's verdict was supported by the inferences which could be drawn from the circumstantial evidence. It stated that "a line must be drawn between valid circumstantial evidence, and evidence which requires a leap of faith in order to support a conviction." Compare United States v. Franklin, 728 F.2d 994 (8th Cir.1984) (intent to distribute controlled substance can be inferred solely from possession of a large quantity of the substance).

Is reversal required where a defendant is charged with multiple acts or means of committing a crime in a single count, and the evidence is insufficient as to one of the acts or means? In Griffin v. United States, 112 S.Ct. 466 (1991), the Court relied on the common law rule that a general verdict is valid so long as it is legally supportable on one of the submitted grounds—"even though that gave no assurance that a valid ground, rather than an invalid one, was actually the basis for the jury's action."

Griffin was charged, with others, in a conspiracy which was alleged to have two objects: (1) impairing the efforts of the Internal Revenue Service to ascertain income taxes (the "IRS object"); and (2) impairing the efforts of the Drug Enforcement Administration to ascertain forfeitable assets (the "DEA object"). The evidence introduced at trial implicated Griffin's co-defendants in both conspiratorial objects, but it did not sufficiently connect Griffin with the DEA object. The trial court over objection instructed the jury that it could return a guilty verdict if it found Griffin to have participated in either one of the two objects of the conspiracy. The jury returned a general verdict of guilty. The Court of Appeals found the evidence tying Griffin to the DEA object insufficient, but nonetheless affirmed Griffin's conviction on the ground that sufficient evidence existed tying her to the IRS object. Griffin argued that this result violated her right to due process, but the Supreme Court disagreed in an opinion by Justice Scalia.

Justice Scalia recognized that despite the general common law rule upholding an ambiguous general verdict, the Court had held in Stromberg v. California, 283 U.S. 359 (1931), that "where a provision of the Constitution forbids conviction on a particular ground, the constitutional guarantee is violated by a general verdict that may have rested on that ground." He also recognized that in Yates v. United States, 354 U.S. 298 (1957) the Court used a similar principle to void a conviction in which one means alleged in a single count was insufficient in law because barred by the statute of limitations. But Justice Scalia found these precedents to be exceptions to the general rule, and inapposite to a case where one of the objects in a single count was void not because of a legal error but rather due to factual insufficiency. He explained the *Stromberg–Yates* exception, and distinguished it from the general rule, as follows:

> Jurors are not generally equipped to determine whether a particular theory of conviction submitted to them is contrary to law—whether, for example, the action in question is protected by the Constitution, is time barred, or fails to come within the statutory definition of the crime. When, therefore, jurors have been left the option of relying upon a legally inadequate theory, there is no reason to think that their own intelligence and expertise will save them from that error. Quite the opposite is true, however, when they have been left the option of relying upon a factually inadequate theory, since jurors *are* well equipped to analyze the evidence. * * * It is one thing to negate a verdict that, while supported by evidence, may have been based on an erroneous view of the law; it is another to do so merely on the chance—remote, it seems to us—that the jury convicted on a ground that was not supported by

adequate evidence when there existed alternative grounds for which the evidence was sufficient.

Thus, the Court found it fair to presume from the general verdict that the jury convicted on the factually sufficient ground. Justice Blackmun concurred in the judgment. Justice Thomas did not participate.

B. MOTIONS FOR NEW TRIAL: INSUFFICIENCY AS A MATTER OF GRACE

Federal Rule of Criminal Procedure 33, providing for a new trial on motion if required "in the interest of justice", affords another avenue for attack on a conviction.[5] Note that, as was true of motions for acquittal, post-verdict new trial motions are defendants' remedies.

The standards governing a trial judge's ruling on a motion for a new trial are well-stated by the court in United States v. Martinez, 763 F.2d 1297 (11th Cir.1985):

> [A] motion for new trial on the ground that the verdict is contrary to the weight of the evidence raises issues very different from a motion for judgment of acquittal * * *. On a motion for judgment of acquittal, the court must view the evidence in the light most favorable to the verdict, and, under that light, determine whether the evidence is sufficient to support the verdict. Thus, on this motion, the court assumes the truth of the evidence offered by the prosecution. On a motion for a new trial based on the weight of the evidence, the court need not view the evidence in the light most favorable to the verdict. It may weigh the evidence and consider the credibility of the witnesses. If the court concludes that despite the abstract sufficiency of the evidence to sustain the verdict, the evidence preponderates sufficiently heavily against the verdict that a serious miscarriage of justice may have occurred, it may set aside the verdict, grant a new trial, and submit the issues for determination by another jury.
>
> * * * While the district court's discretion is quite broad, there are limits to it. The court may not reweigh the evidence and set aside the verdict simply because it feels some other result would be more reasonable. The evidence must preponderate heavily against the verdict, such that it would be a miscarriage of justice to let the verdict stand. Motions for new trials based on weight of the evidence are not favored. Courts are to grant them sparingly and with caution, doing so only in those really exceptional cases.
>
> Applying these principles, courts have granted new trial motions based on weight of the evidence only where the credibility of the government's witnesses had been impeached and the government's case had been marked by uncertainties and discrepancies.

The court in *Martinez* reversed the trial court's order granting a new trial. The disputed issue was whether the government could prove that the defendant knew there was cocaine on board a boat. To establish this knowledge, the government showed that the defendant was the captain of the boat, that 454 pounds of cocaine were found on board, that the boat had made a long journey from Colombia to Miami, and that there were only a few crew members. The

5. See the discussion of 28 U.S.C.A. § 2255, infra, since the statute and the Federal Rule overlap. Many states limit new trial motions by providing less time than the 2 years allowed by the Federal Rule.

court found that "the government's case against [the defendant] was not marked by uncertainties and discrepancies. It was not based on compound inferences. It was not presented through the testimony of impeached and suspect witnesses." The court concluded that this was not "one of those exceptional cases in which the court had the power to interfere with the jury's factual findings."

Some states give appellate courts authority to vacate a conviction as to which reversal is not warranted on the law or the facts, but there is a grave risk that an innocent person has been convicted. New York is such a state. Although its highest court recognizes this appellate power, it has held in People v. Carter, 63 N.Y.2d 530, 483 N.Y.S.2d 654, 473 N.E.2d 6 (1984), that trial judges cannot exercise similar power.

C. NEWLY DISCOVERED EVIDENCE CLAIMS

It is understandable that American judges, both trial and appellate, would be reluctant to overturn verdicts supported by sufficient evidence to amount to proof beyond a reasonable doubt. Reluctance to retry cases that are technically correct after the government has shouldered the load of a criminal prosecution also helps to explain the limitation on newly discovered evidence claims. If courts readily accepted newly discovered evidence claims, litigants who discovered that a tactical judgment made in one trial did not work would ask for another chance to litigate, and litigation would become interminable. The line between discovery of new evidence and discovery of new theories of how to use evidence is fuzzy—see, e.g., United States v. Pordum, 451 F.2d 1015 (2d Cir. 1971)—but rarely must it be sharpened in light of the reluctance of courts to take seriously either discovery claim.

Essentially, a defendant must meet a four prong test before a court will grant him a retrial based on any newly discovered evidence. As stated in United States v. Seago, 930 F.2d 482 (6th Cir.1991), the defendant must establish the following: (1) the new evidence was discovered after the trial; (2) the evidence could not have been discovered earlier with due diligence; (3) the evidence is material and not merely cumulative or impeaching; and (4) the evidence would likely produce an acquittal. In *Seago,* the court concluded that evidence of ineffective assistance of counsel is not newly discovered evidence for purposes of a motion for a new trial where the facts supporting the claim were within the defendant's knowledge at the time of the trial. See also United States v. Gonzalez, 933 F.2d 417 (7th Cir.1991) (defendants were not entitled to a new trial on the basis of newly discovered evidence where it would merely impeach a government witness' testimony that he had never had anything to do with cocaine, and evidence of the defendants' guilt was overwhelming).

Evidence is not "new" merely because it has been generated after the conviction. For example, in Harris v. Vasquez, 913 F.2d 606 (9th Cir.1990), the court concluded that defendant's new psychiatric reports did not justify another penalty hearing. Since defendant's counsel possessed evidence of defendant's brain damage at the original hearing, and no new psychiatric techniques or theories were alleged, the court concluded that the new reports were not new evidence but merely new opinions from new psychiatrists.

Advances in forensic testing techniques have occasionally given rise to new evidence claims. But they are not always, or even often, successful. When the forensic testing is done after a significant time period has elapsed, it rarely will be sufficiently conclusive to show that defendant would probably be acquitted on retrial. See Dumond v. Lockhart, 911 F.2d 104 (8th Cir.1990), where the court held that evidence of a genetic marker test done on a semen sample, showing that the sample was unlikely to be defendant's, was newly discovered evidence. Yet the defendant's motion for a new trial was denied because it was not probable that the evidence would produce an acquittal on retrial.

Once a verdict is rendered and judgment is imposed, experienced judges know that the participants in the trial process have second thoughts if they may be responsible for sending a person to prison, or even to death. See, e.g., Mastrian v. McManus, 554 F.2d 813 (8th Cir.1977) (recantation by star witness does not warrant new trial). Most second thoughts are treated as routine and ignored. For example, jurors cannot attack their verdicts by raising questions about the quality of the deliberations or the firmness of their votes. See e.g., Fed.R.Evid. 606(b). Similarly, witnesses who recant their trial testimony and change stories are viewed with utmost suspicion, United States ex rel. Sostre v. Festa, 513 F.2d 1313 (2d Cir. 1975), not only because of the commonness of feelings of remorse, but also because of a judicial fear that improper post-trial influence may be encouraged by ready judicial acceptance of recantations. Third party confessions, which are viewed with suspicion even if offered during a trial, see, e.g., Fed.R.Evid. 804(b)(3), are scrutinized with great care and a new trial will be denied if the trial judge does not believe the evidence.[6] See, e.g., United States v. Schoepflin, 442 F.2d 407 (9th Cir. 1971).

It is understandable that courts are unwilling to encourage post-conviction attacks, and there are good reasons to question the legitimacy of many such attempts. But, it is not clear that rules like Federal Rule of Criminal Procedure 33 are consistent with the values claimed for our criminal justice system.

The easy case to justify under Rule 33 is one in which the defendant holds evidence in reserve in order to guarantee the availability of a post-conviction motion should trial go badly. This type of behavior is to be discouraged, and strict enforcement of the rule against those who intentionally secrete evidence appears to be wise.

A case only slightly more difficult is one in which a defendant does not seek out evidence that she has reason to believe might be found. This defendant is playing a risky game; there is no reason to encourage the behavior, and the rule should apply in order to assure that defendants have incentives to gather all available evidence before trial, not after.

6. One of the rare cases in which a motion for a new trial on newly discovered evidence grounds was denied and an appellate court reversed is State v. Shannon, 388 So.2d 731 (La.1980). The new evidence consisted of the testimony of an eye-witness to a shooting, a friend of the victim, who contradicted the government's other witnesses and corroborated the defendant. On the question of the defendant's due diligence, the court observed that there was no way for the defendant to suspect prior to trial that an eyewitness was available, that during the seven hour trial the information that the defendant obtained could not have been verified in time to be of any use to the defense, and that a request for a recess would have been premature since the defendant's information was tenuous.

Although encouraging litigants to bring all claims and defenses in one proceeding is laudable on efficiency grounds, countervailing considerations emerge clearly when the defendant is not attempting to conceal evidence. If the defendant and her lawyer were negligent in gathering evidence and they discover new evidence some months after trial that establishes in the eyes of even the most skeptical observer that the defendant could not be guilty, must we depend solely on the pardon power and the parole process to do justice? What if the defendant's lawyer, but not the defendant, was negligent? Presumably, serious negligence might result in the overturning of a conviction on ineffective assistance of counsel grounds. Recognition of this possibility is a short step away from realization of the ultimate irony of Rule 33: a defendant who is diligent, who has a diligent lawyer, and who discovers evidence after being convicted will receive less sympathy from courts than the defendant whose lawyer was negligent. Yes, there is a rationale—to wit, all defendants are entitled to the benefit of the evidence that reasonably competent counsel would have adduced at trial, but not to the benefit of evidence that could not be discovered before trial. But why should this rationale be accepted?

Note that the time limit placed on newly discovered evidence motions generally does not exist with respect to ineffective assistance of counsel claims. The Advisory Committee on Criminal Rules had suggested that newly discovered evidence motions could be made "at any time before or after final judgment," but the Supreme Court adopted its own time limit.

Notice also that a federal trial judge cannot grant a new trial while an appeal is pending (although she can deny a new trial motion and her ruling is then appealable). In the federal system, if a new trial motion is made in the trial court before an appeal is disposed of, the appellate court can hold the appeal in abeyance while the district court indicates an intention to grant the motion or to deny it. If the former is indicated, the appellate court will ordinarily remand the case to the district court without reaching the merits of the appeal. See, e.g., Gordon v. United States, 383 F.2d 936 (D.C.Cir. 1967). The advantage of the Federal Rule is that it assures that two levels of the judicial system are not unknowingly considering the same case, when the decision by one level may render superfluous the work of the other.

D. ERROR IN THE PROCEEDINGS

In order to preserve a right to complain in a post-trial motion or on direct appeal, a defendant must raise all appropriate claims in a timely manner. For example, certain suppression claims must be raised before trial or they are deemed waived, unless good cause for delay in raising them is shown. See, e.g., Fed.R.Crim.P. 12. If the defense wishes to object at trial to other evidence offered by the government, a timely objection must be made. See Fed.R.Evid. 103(a). And, if the defendant wants to complain about the rejection of defense evidence, an appropriate offer of proof is required. See id. Failure to raise claims in an appropriate and timely manner generally bars review by post-conviction motion and direct appeal. However, if plain error is committed, a court may take cognizance of a claim not properly raised before or during trial. See, e.g., Fed.R.Crim.P. 52(b); Fed.R.Evid. 103(d). It is difficult to determine when plain error occurs, but it appears to be when a trial "flouts fundamental concepts of justice basic to our system." Virgil v. State, 84 Wis.2d 166, 267

N.W.2d 852 (1978). Courts are reluctant to allow parties to raise claims belatedly for many of the same reasons that they do not welcome newly discovered evidence claims. Here too, the door is not entirely closed to post-verdict challenges, but the threshold showing needed to trigger the court's concern is high. Often the same showing that satisfies a plain error standard also establishes ineffective assistance of counsel, since it is the rare case in which a clear error is made and the defense lawyer is not in a position to realize it.

Assuming that defense claims have been properly preserved, there is an opportunity under rules like Fed.R.Evid. 33 for a new trial motion raising any errors as grounds for a new trial. One might expect that the same trial judge who erred once is unlikely to be quick to change her mind, but it sometimes happens. Today, the trial judge knows that it is likely that a convicted defendant will appeal, and the post-trial motion enables the trial judge to correct any error that an appellate court would correct. There is no doubt that, to avoid an unnecessary appeal, the trial judge should grant a new trial to correct any mistake that would result in reversal on appeal. In close cases, the trial judge probably has authority to grant a new trial even if an appellate court, acting on the basis of a cold record, would not, since the trial judge should be particularly well situated to see or feel the prejudicial impact of an error that on paper does not appear to be significant.

If the trial judge should grant a new trial whenever an appellate court would reverse a conviction, the question arises as to when reversal would occur. The answer is that reversal occurs when the appellate court finds that there was error and that the error sufficiently taints the judgment to require another trial. Without error, no ground for reversal exists. Without harm attributable to error, the mistake is viewed as costless. But what sort of harm is costly enough to require another trial? The Supreme Court has partly answered the question with a constitutional mandate.

CHAPMAN v. CALIFORNIA

Supreme Court of the United States, 1967.
386 U.S. 18.

MR. JUSTICE BLACK delivered the opinion of the Court.

[Two petitioners were convicted in a California state court on charges that they robbed, kidnapped and murdered a bartender. One was sentenced to life imprisonment and the other to death. At trial the prosecutor commented on the petitioners' failure to testify and the trial court told the jury it could draw adverse inferences from their silence. The comment and the instruction violated petitioners' privilege against self-incrimination under Griffin v. California, 380 U.S. 609 (1965). Although it recognized this, the California Supreme Court held that the error was harmless. Justice Black indicated at the outset of his opinion that two questions were presented: (1) whether a *Griffin* error ever could be harmless, and (2) if so, was the error harmless in this case?]

I

Before deciding the two questions here—whether there can ever be harmless constitutional error and whether the error here was harmless—we must first decide whether state or federal law governs. The application of a state harmless-error rule is, of course, a state question where it involves only errors of state procedure or state law. But the error from which these petitioners suffered was a denial of rights guaranteed against invasion by the Fifth and Fourteenth Amendments, rights rooted in the Bill of Rights, offered and championed in the Congress by James Madison, who told the Congress that the "independent" federal courts would be the "guardians of those rights." Whether a conviction for crime should stand when a State has failed to accord federal constitutionally guaranteed rights is every bit as much of a federal question as what particular federal constitutional provisions themselves mean, what they guarantee, and whether they have been denied. With faithfulness to the constitutional union of the States, we cannot leave to the States the formulation of the authoritative laws, rules, and remedies designed to protect people from infractions by the States of federally guaranteed rights. We have no hesitation in saying that the right of these petitioners not to be punished for exercising their Fifth and Fourteenth Amendment right to be silent—expressly created by the Federal Constitution itself—is a federal right which, in the absence of appropriate congressional action, it is our responsibility to protect by fashioning the necessary rule.

II

We are urged by petitioners to hold that all federal constitutional errors, regardless of the facts and circumstances, must always be deemed harmful. Such a holding, as petitioners correctly point out, would require an automatic reversal of their convictions and make further discussion unnecessary. We decline to adopt any such rule. All 50 States have harmless-error statutes or rules, and the United States long ago through its Congress established for its courts the rule that judgments shall not be reversed for "errors or defects which do not affect the substantial rights of the parties." 28 U.S.C.A. § 2111.[a] * * * All of these rules, state or federal, serve a very useful purpose insofar as they block setting aside convictions for small errors or defects that have little, if any, likelihood of having changed the result of the trial. We conclude that there may be some constitutional errors which in the setting of a particular case are so unimportant and insignificant that they may, consistent with the Federal Constitution, be deemed harmless, not requiring the automatic reversal of the conviction.

III

In fashioning a harmless-constitutional-error rule, we must recognize that harmless-error rules can work very unfair and mischievous results when, for example, highly important and persuasive evidence, or argument, though legally forbidden, finds its way into a trial in which the question of guilt or innocence is a close one. What harmless-error rules all aim at is a rule that will save the good in harmless-error practices while avoiding the bad, so far as possible.

The federal rule emphasizes "substantial rights" as do most others. The California constitutional rule emphasizes "a miscarriage of justice," but the California courts have neutralized this to some extent by emphasis, and perhaps

a. 28 U.S.C.A. § 2111 provides:

"On the hearing of any appeal or writ of certiorari in any case, the court shall give judgment after an examination of the record without regard to errors or defects which do not affect the substantial rights of the parties."

Fed.Rule Crim.Proc. 52(a) provides:

"Any error, defect, irregularity or variance which does not affect substantial rights shall be disregarded."

overemphasis, upon the court's view of "overwhelming evidence." We prefer the approach of this Court in deciding what was harmless error in our recent case of Fahy v. Connecticut, 375 U.S. 85. There we said: "The question is whether there is a reasonable possibility that the evidence complained of might have contributed to the conviction." Although our prior cases have indicated that there are some constitutional rights so basic to a fair trial that their infraction can never be treated as harmless error,[b] this statement in *Fahy* itself belies any belief that all trial errors which violate the Constitution automatically call for reversal. At the same time, however, like the federal harmless-error statute, it emphasizes an intention not to treat as harmless those constitutional errors that "affect substantial rights" of a party. An error in admitting plainly relevant evidence which possibly influenced the jury adversely to a litigant cannot, under *Fahy,* be conceived of as harmless. Certainly error, constitutional error, in illegally admitting highly prejudicial evidence or comments, casts on someone other than the person prejudiced by it a burden to show that it was harmless. * * * There is little, if any, difference between our statement in Fahy v. Connecticut about "whether there is a reasonable possibility that the evidence complained of might have contributed to the conviction" and requiring the beneficiary of a constitutional error to prove beyond a reasonable doubt that the error complained of did not contribute to the verdict obtained. We, therefore, do no more than adhere to the meaning of our *Fahy* case when we hold, as we now do, that before a federal constitutional error can be held harmless, the court must be able to declare a belief that it was harmless beyond a reasonable doubt. While appellate courts do not ordinarily have the original task of applying such a test, it is a familiar standard to all courts, and we believe its adoption will provide a more workable standard, although achieving the same result as that aimed at in our *Fahy* case.

* * *

[The Court went on to hold that the error was not harmless. Justice Stewart concurred in the result and opted for automatic reversal for *Griffin* violations. Justice Harlan dissented on the ground that application of a state harmless error rule was an independent state ground barring Supreme Court review.]

Note

The Court has invoked *Chapman* in several cases to hold errors harmless. See Harrington v. California, 395 U.S. 250 (1969) (holding harmless the improper introduction of confessions of non-testifying co-defendants); Milton v. Wainwright, 407 U.S. 371 (1972) (declaring that any error in obtaining statements of accused in violation of right to counsel was harmless); Brown v. United States, 411 U.S. 223 (1973) (similar to *Harrington*, supra). One case in particular raises a question whether the *Chapman* standard as applied today is less rigorous than Justice Black intended. It is Schneble v. Florida, 405 U.S. 427 (1972). Like *Harrington*, supra, the case involved the improper introduction of a non-testifying co-defendant's statement against Schneble. Although it cited the *Chapman* test, the majority concluded that exclusion of the erroneously admitted evidence would not have caused reasonable jurors to have found the government's evidence significantly less persuasive and that the error was therefore harmless. The three dissenters suggested that this recasting of the *Chapman* test weakened it. Does saying an

b. See, e.g., Payne v. Arkansas, 356 U.S. 560 (coerced confession); Gideon v. Wainwright, 372 U.S. 335 (right to counsel); Tumey v. Ohio, 273 U.S. 510 (impartial judge).

error is harmless beyond a reasonable doubt mean the same thing as saying that an average jury would not have found the government's proper evidence significantly less persuasive?

In Kotteakos v. United States, 328 U.S. 750, 1557 (1946), the test of harmlessness—that still applies in federal courts to nonconstitutional errors—was whether an appellate court "is sure that the error did not influence the jury or had but very slight effect." Reversal is required for a non-constitutional error only if it "had substantial and injurious effect or influence in determining the jury's verdict." United States v. Lane, 474 U.S. 438 (1986) (applying the *Kotteakos* standard to a misjoinder under Fed.R.Crim.P. 8(b)). See also Fed.R.Crim.P. 52(a). The *Kotteakos-Lane* standard is clearly less protective of defendants than the harmless error rule applied by *Chapman.* See Brecht v. Abrahamson, 944 F.2d 1363 (7th Cir.1991) (because evidence of guilt was not overwhelming, it would be difficult to say that the error was harmless beyond a reasonable doubt; but it was clear that the error had no substantial and injurious effect on the verdict); United States v. Owens, 789 F.2d 750 (9th Cir.1986) (if admission of prior identification was merely a violation of the hearsay rule, it was harmless; but if admission also violated the defendant's right to confrontation, the error was harmful and reversal was required). In *Brecht,* supra, the court held that a violation of Doyle v. Ohio (commenting on the defendant's invocation of silence after receiving *Miranda* warnings) was subject to the *Kotteakos-Lane* standard of harmlessness. The court reasoned that *Doyle* was not a constitutional rule but was merely a prophylactic safeguard designed to protect the defendant's Fifth Amendment rights. Under the analysis in *Brecht,* violations of all of the *Miranda* safeguards would be analyzed under the harmless error standard applicable to nonconstitutional errors. This is because the Court has held that a violation of *Miranda* is not itself a violation of the constitution. See Chapter Three. Likewise, a court's misapplication of the Fourth Amendment exclusionary rule would be reviewed under *Kotteakos* rather than *Chapman,* because the exclusionary rule is not constitutionally-based. See Chapter Two.

Some state courts utilize the *Chapman* test for assessing the impact of state constitutional errors. See, e.g., Aldridge v. State, 584 P.2d 1105 (Alaska 1978). But others use a less demanding standard that is intended to save more convictions from reversal. Saltzburg, The Harm of Harmless Error, 59 Va.L.Rev. 988 (1973), argues that the *Chapman* test should be utilized generally in criminal cases. This approach has been followed in several jurisdictions. See, e.g., Commonwealth v. Story, 476 Pa. 391, 383 A.2d 155 (1978); Dorsey v. State, 276 Md. 638, 350 A.2d 665 (1976); State v. Okura, 56 Hawaii 455, 541 P.2d 9 (1975).

The Supreme Court has held that most constitutional violations are subject to the harmless error rule, but, as it recognized in the footnote in *Chapman,* certain errors can never be harmless. The question is how to determine which errors can be harmless and which cannot.

The Court has specifically held that certain errors require automatic reversal and a new trial. These errors include: (1) total deprivation of the right to counsel (*Gideon,* cited in footnote b in *Chapman;* see also Penson v. Ohio, discussed in Chapter Ten); (2) a biased judge (Tumey v. Ohio, cited in footnote b in *Chapman*); (3) unlawful exclusion of members of the defendant's race from the grand jury (Vasquez v. Hillery, 474 U.S. 254 (1986)); (4) violation of the right to a public trial (Waller v. Georgia, 467 U.S. 39 (1984)); (5) violation of the right of self-representation (McKaskle v. Wiggins, discussed in Chapter Ten); and (6) improper exclusion of a juror under *Witherspoon* (Gray v. Mississippi, discussed in Chapter Ten). In addition, harmless error analysis cannot apply if a retrial would in itself be the harm. Thus, violations of the right to speedy trial or of the Double Jeopardy Clause have never been considered harmless error. Finally, some errors require a showing of prejudice before a constitutional violation can even be found. This is so under the *Strickland* standard for ineffective assistance of counsel and under the *Brady* standard for disclosure of exculpatory evidence by the prosecution. In these two areas, a court which finds a constitutional violation has by definition determined that the error is harmful, and the *Chapman* standard becomes superfluous. See Capra, Access to Exculpatory Evidence: Resolving the *Agurs* Problems of Prosecutorial Discretion and Retrospective Review, 53 Ford.L.Rev. 391 (1984).

In Arizona v. Fulminante, 111 S.Ct. 1246 (1991) the Court retreated from the *Chapman* footnote insofar as it implied that admission of an involuntary confession could never be harmless error. Chief Justice Rehnquist explained the *Chapman* footnote as a "historical reference." He argued that Payne v. Arkansas, cited in *Chapman* for the proposition that admission of an involuntary confession could not be harmless, did not in fact reject the harmless error test of *Chapman* but rather rejected "a much more lenient rule which would allow affirmance of a conviction if the evidence other than the confession was sufficient to sustain the verdict."

The Chief Justice distinguished a trial error, "error which occurred during the presentation of the case to the jury, and which may therefore be quantitatively assessed in the context of other evidence presented in order to determine whether its admission was harmless beyond a reasonable doubt," from an error that is not subject to such an assessment, "a structural defect affecting the framework in which the trial proceeds * * *." According to the majority, admission of an involuntary confession falls into the category of trial error, while total deprivation of counsel as in *Gideon,* or a biased judge as in *Tumey,* falls into the category of structural defect. The Chief Justice saw no reason to distinguish coerced confessions from confessions obtained in violation of the defendant's Sixth Amendment rights or in violation of *Miranda.* Since these violations could be harmless, admission of a coerced confession could similarly be harmless. The Chief Justice noted, however, that due to the substantial impact that a confession has on the trial, it would be the rare case in which admission of a coerced confession would be harmless on the facts.

Justice White, joined by Justices Marshall, Blackmun and Stevens, dissented and argued that a defendant's confession is probably the most probative and damaging evidence against him and that it is impossible to know what weight and credit a jury might give a coerced confession.

The facts of the case are important to determine whether the introduction of the involuntary confession was harmless. Fulminante reported his 11 year-old stepdaughter, Jeneane, missing; he had been caring for her while his wife was in the hospital. Two days later, Jeneane's body was found; she had been shot twice, and a ligature was around her neck. The body had decomposed, so it could not be determined whether she had been sexually assaulted. There was evidence that Fulminante and Jeneane did not get along, and his statements about her disappearance were inconsistent. While Fulminante became a suspect, there was not enough evidence with which to file charges. Fulminante moved to New Jersey, where he was convicted on federal charges of possession of a firearm by a felon. While serving this term, Fulminante became friends with Anthony Sarivola, who masqueraded as an organized crime figure, but who in fact was a government informant. Rumors began to circulate that Fulminante was suspected of murdering a child. Sarivola offered to protect Fulminante from his fellow inmates, on the condition that Fulminante tell the truth about whether he killed Jeneane. Fulminante then admitted that he had driven Jeneane to the desert on his motorcycle, where he had choked her, sexually assaulted her, and made her beg for her life, before shooting her twice in the head. This confession was partially corroborated by physical evidence: motorcycle tire tracks were found at the scene, and the victim had been choked and shot twice in the head. A majority of the Court in *Fulminante* held that this confession was coerced, and thus it was constitutional error for the court to admit it at Fulminante's trial. This aspect of the case is discussed in Chapter Three.

Sarivola was released from prison one month later, and Fulminante six months thereafter. Fulminante was picked up from prison by Sarivola and his fiancee Donna. Donna and Fulminante had never met. Donna testified at trial that when she asked Fulminante why he was not returning to his family in Arizona, Fulminante confessed his sexual assault and murder of Jeneane. Donna did not report this confession to the authorities for over a year. Fulminante did not seriously contest the admissibility of this second confession.

The state in *Fulminante* argued that the coerced confession to Anthony Sarivola was harmless beyond a reasonable doubt, on the ground that it was cumulative, given Fulminante's later confession to Donna Sarivola. Justice White, writing for the majority on this point, rejected this argument. He concluded that without the first confession, the jury might not have believed that the second confession was ever made. According to the majority, Donna's story lacked plausibility. She contended that Fulminante, a total stranger, confessed to a heinous crime after Donna asked him an innocent and open-ended question. Moreover, she did not report this confession until more than a year later, and continued to associate with Fulminante. Most importantly, the confession to Donna was only partly corroborated by the physical evidence; the physical evidence did show that Jeneane was murdered, but not that she was sexually assaulted. Nor could the condition of the body show the state of mind of the killer. So the only piece of evidence which corroborated Donna's testimony as to crucial points of state of mind (such as that Fulminante made Jeneane beg for her life) was the coerced confession to Sarivola. Thus, the coerced confession was important to the State's case on two points: it made Donna's testimony that Fulminante had confessed more believable (since he had also confessed to someone else under different circumstances); and it made the important details concerning the crime more likely to be true by way of cross-corroboration. Justice White concluded that the coerced confession had a significant impact on the trial, and could not be deemed harmless beyond a reasonable doubt.

The Chief Justice, dissenting on this point, argued that this was a "classic case of harmless error: a second confession giving more details of the crime than the first was admitted in evidence and found free of any constitutional objection." Who has the better of the argument?

Does Chief Justice Rehnquist's reference to "structural" error fully explain why certain errors can never be harmless? Could it also be that in some cases, the harmless error analysis is simply not responsive to the error that occurred? Consider the defendant who is deprived of the right to proceed *pro se.* It is no answer to say that at his trial, his counsel performed very well and the evidence against him was overwhelming. The right to self-representation is not based upon an effective defense and a correct verdict, but rather upon personal autonomy. Is a violation of this right a structural defect, or is the harmless error doctrine simply irrelevant to the wrong suffered?

Is it possible that the application of the harmless error standard to coerced confessions will make a reviewing court more likely to find certain police tactics impermissible? Is anyone better off when a court holds that a confession was coerced but that it was harmless, where if automatic reversal were required, the court would hold the confession voluntary?

III. COLLATERAL ATTACK

A. REMEDIES GENERALLY

1. Collateral Attacks

After new trial motions have been made and all appeals are exhausted (or lost, perhaps for failure to comply with an appellate rule, such as a time limit on filing a notice of appeal), a defendant whose conviction emerges unscathed has a natural incentive to attempt additional attacks on the conviction. The stigma and the actual punishment that flow from a conviction are hardly more attractive once the normal appeals process has ended than they were before trial or judgment.

Post-conviction remedies, of which habeas corpus is the most common, have always been regarded as *collateral* remedies, "providing an avenue for upsetting judgments that have become otherwise final." Mackey v. United States, 401 U.S. 667, 683 (1971) (Harlan, J., separate opinion). They are not designed to substitute for direct review of convictions, nor can all the questions properly subject to appeal be raised collaterally.

In many states, the scope and nature of collateral attacks on criminal convictions are determined in large measure by the availability of common law writs, although statutes and court rules also may be important. In the past, observers of state remedies were moved to make comments like the following: "There is considerable duplication and overlapping, with resultant uncertainty as to the individual scope and purpose of each [remedy]." ABA Standards, Post Conviction Remedies, Commentary to § 22–1.1, at 7 (2d ed. 1980). In some jurisdictions it was observed that the addition of supplementary remedies to those provided at common law "adds to, rather than diminishes confusion." Id.

2. Coram Nobis

Of the common law writs, two are most significant: coram nobis (or vobis) and habeas corpus. Coram nobis is a remedy of last resort, available only to one otherwise remediless. It can be used to attack convictions on the basis of an error in fact, or a defense in fact, that does not appear on the face of the record that produced the judgment, as long as the defendant's failure to raise the factual claim was not negligent and the errors complained of are constitutional errors of sufficient magnitude to have significantly affected the verdict of the trier of fact.[7] The United States Supreme Court held that the writ is available in federal courts in United States v. Morgan, 346 U.S. 502 (1954). After Morgan was convicted in federal court and served his sentence, he was convicted in a state court and sentenced to a longer term as a second offender on the basis of the federal conviction. Collateral attack on the federal conviction under 28 U.S.C.A. § 2255, discussed infra, was not possible because Morgan was not in federal custody. But the Court held that an attack in the nature of coram nobis—in *Morgan* the challenge was that he had not been represented by counsel—was a step in a criminal case and available. The burden of proving a right to relief was placed upon the convicted person.

Subsequently the Court recognized "the obvious fact of life that most criminal convictions do in fact entail adverse collateral legal consequences." Sibron v. New York, 392 U.S. 40, 55 (1968). Coram nobis, in the absence of other remedies, will allow a convicted person to attempt to avoid these consequences, even though they may be minor. See, e.g., Holloway v. United States, 393 F.2d 731 (9th Cir. 1968). *Morgan* and its lower court progeny establish that coram nobis is to be used "only under circumstances compelling such action to achieve justice," 346 U.S. at 511, and that it is limited to cases in which the record does not reveal whether the facts alleged are true, and a non-negligent person has no other way to challenge a conviction. Because the Supreme Court held that coram nobis was a part of a criminal proceeding, one might assume that criminal rules of procedure govern. Whether this is what the Court intended is unclear. See, e.g., United States v. Keough, 391 F.2d 138 (2d Cir. 1968).

One of the most celebrated uses of the writ of coram nobis in recent years is Korematsu v. United States, 584 F.Supp. 1406 (N.D.Cal.1984), in which the court vacated the notorious conviction of an American citizen of Japanese ancestry for being in a place where all persons of Japanese ancestry had been excluded following the declaration of war by the United States against Japan in 1941. The conviction had been sustained by the Supreme Court in 1944. 323 U.S. 214 (1944). The district court relied upon a Report of the Commission on Wartime Relocation and Internment of Civilians (1982), which concluded that military necessity did not warrant the exclusion and detention of ethnic Japanese. It also relied upon internal government documents that demonstrated that the government knowingly withheld information from the courts when they were considering the critical question of military necessity in this case.

3. *Habeas Corpus*

In many instances coram nobis will not lie because habeas corpus or a remedy in the nature of habeas corpus exists. The habeas corpus writ referred to here is habeas corpus ad subjiciendum, which the Supreme Court referred to as "that great writ" as early as 1807 in Ex parte Bollman, 8 U.S. (4 Cranch) 75,

7. Coram nobis has been used in civil and criminal cases.

95 (1807). See also McNally v. Hill, 293 U.S. 131, 136–37 (1934). One commentary explains the writ as follows:

> Habeas corpus means literally "you have the body." Perhaps because of this, there has always been some confusion in the terminology of the writ. It has generally stemmed from a misunderstanding of what it means to grant the writ of habeas corpus. To grant the writ means only that the person to whom it is directed, the respondent, must "have the body," before the court. If the writ is granted, the respondent must produce the body of the person detained before the court in which the petition for the writ was filed. The court then inquires into the lawfulness of the detention. If the detention is found to be illegal, the relief requested in the petition will be granted. This may be, for example, discharge from the illegal detention. If the restraint on the prisoner's liberty is found to be lawful, then the request for relief is denied. In either case the writ itself has already been granted; the respondent has produced the body before the court.
>
> Often the relief requested in the petition for the writ can be granted without ever granting the writ itself. While this might seem odd, there is a simple explanation. It is not always necessary to produce the prisoner before the court in order to determine the lawfulness of his detention. Ordinarily, the prisoner need only be produced before the court if he must testify to some matter. Often the facts are agreed upon and not in dispute. What is being contested is the applicable law. In such cases there is no necessity for the prisoner to be present. * * *
>
> The confusion in the terminology of the writ arises from a failure to distinguish between granting the writ and granting the relief requested in the petition. As a sort of shorthand, lawyers and judges frequently use the expression "granting the writ" as if it were equivalent to granting the relief requested. There is certainly no harm in this as long as everyone knows what everyone else means. Like most forms of shorthand, it has a certain utility.

R. Sokol, Federal Habeas Corpus § 3, at 36–37 (2d ed. 1969).[8]

Although it is difficult to discover the precise depth of the writ's roots in English history—see generally Cohen, Some Considerations on the Origins of Habeas Corpus, 16 Canadian Bar Rev. 92, 115 (1938)—it seems that "[t]he early function of the writ, say from 1150, was simply to get an unwilling party into court regardless of the kind of case involved." R. Sokol, supra, § B, at 4. It did not begin a proceeding; rather, it assured that once a proceeding was otherwise begun, it would not be futile because of the absence of a party. In the fourteenth century, the writ, in addition to its earlier function, also became an independent action to test the cause of a detention. In this latter capacity it was known as habeas corpus cum causa. With the development of this aspect of the writ, it took its place in the struggle between the common law and the chancery courts. "Time and again * * * the common law judges through habeas corpus released from custody persons committed by other courts," and thus undercut the authority of the Chancellor. D. Meador, Habeas Corpus and Magna Carta: Dualism of Power and Liberty 12 (1966).

Darnel's Case, 3 St.Trials 1, arose in 1627 and probably accounts significantly for the development of the writ. Darnel and four other knights were

8. Other forms of habeas corpus are not discussed here. For a listing see Blackstone's Commentaries in R. Sokol, supra, at 320.

sent to prison for refusing to "loan" money to a demanding monarch. They sought habeas corpus to inquire into the power of the monarch to imprison them. Unsuccessful though they were, they invoked the concept of "due process of law," and they relied on Magna Carta in a way that led parliament to modify the decision by providing in its Petition of Right that no person should be imprisoned without being charged in some way that allowed an opportunity for an answer. Fifty years later the writ of habeas corpus was the established vehicle for challenging confinement as denying due process of law. In 1641 the first Habeas Corpus Act was passed to explicitly provide that the courts of King's Bench or Common Pleas could examine into the legality of detention. Amendments were made from time to time, including one in 1650 that permitted poor persons awaiting final decision on the validity of detention to be released on their own recognizance. Cohen, supra, at 176. In the famous decision in *Bushell's case*, 124 Eng.Rep. 1006, 6 St.Trials 999 (1670), Chief Justice Vaughan utilized habeas corpus to order the release of a juror committed for contempt for returning a not guilty verdict in the trial of William Penn and others. A century later Blackstone would call the writ "the most celebrated in the English law." R. Sokol, supra, at 15. But the writ was far from a perfect remedy for all illegal detentions. It developed that one court would not order the release of a person held by order of another court if the latter had proper jurisdiction. And, with respect to detentions ordered by the King, it was generally sufficient that the King asserted a right to detain a person despite the Petition of Right.

With the utilization of English common law in the American colonies, the writ of habeas corpus became a part of American law. See generally Oaks, Habeas Corpus in the States—1776–1865, 32 U.Chi.L.Rev. 243 (1965). At the time of the constitutional convention, 4 of the 12 states with written constitutions had provisions regarding habeas corpus. Id. In Article I of the Constitution, which sets forth the powers of Congress and restrictions upon those powers, clause 2 of section 9 provides that "[t]he Privilege of the Writ of Habeas Corpus shall not be suspended, unless when in Cases of Rebellion or Invasion the public Safety may require it." [9] It is unclear how far Congress could go in generally restricting the habeas corpus power of federal courts. If, for example, Congress did not authorize lower federal courts to hear any habeas corpus cases, would the anti-suspension clause be violated? That Congress need not create federal courts at all might suggest that no habeas power necessarily must be placed in lower courts. A related argument would be that, assuming some habeas corpus power may have to be lodged in lower federal courts, the power need not extend to review of most criminal convictions because, the traditional function of the writ was to test executive detentions and that convictions by a criminal court of competent jurisdiction could not be reexamined on habeas corpus at all. Bator et al., The Federal Courts and the Federal System 1467–9 (3d ed. 1988). See generally Developments in the Law—Federal Habeas Corpus, 83 Harv.L.Rev. 1038, 1049–50, 1263–66 (1970). Some suggestions have been made that even without statutory authority federal courts could grant writs of habeas corpus. See, e.g., Chafee, The Most Important Human Right in the Constitution, 32 B.U.L.Rev. 143 (1952). Our history suggests that Congress has always acted as though some

9. After the adoption of the Constitution, it became more common for states to include habeas corpus provisions in their own constitutions.

habeas powers should be vested in federal courts, and although federal courts have not invalidated congressional limitations, at times they have read statutes broadly to increase the scope of habeas corpus.

In section 14 of the First Judiciary Act of 1789, 1 Stat. 81–82, authority to grant various writs, including habeas corpus, was granted to federal judges. Judges of the district court and Justices of the Supreme Court could "grant writs of *habeas corpus* for the purpose of an inquiry into the cause of commitment,"[10] but only to prisoners in the custody of the United States, not the individual states.

Over time Congress broadened the reach of federal habeas corpus power, usually in response to a political problem.[11] In 1867, it permitted habeas corpus writs to be issued to state prisoners restrained of liberty in violation of the Constitution or any treaty or law of the United States and provided for an appeal to the Supreme Court from a denial of the writ.[12]

Only after 1867 did the writ assume an important place in the arsenal of weapons available to a convicted defendant who desired to attack the validity of the conviction. This, of course, is our concern here: to what extent can the writ be used to collaterally attack a state or federal criminal conviction.

Obviously, the answer depends in part on the court in which relief is sought. At one time the Supreme Court granted certiorari to decide whether state courts are obliged under the federal Constitution to provide persons convicted in state court with some post-conviction process to correct judgments of conviction obtained in violation of federal law. But the Court remanded the case to the Nebraska Supreme Court when the state legislature passed a post-conviction statute. Case v. Nebraska, 381 U.S. 336 (1965). Since then, all states appear to have recognized some form of post-conviction attack. See generally Whitmore v. State, 299 Ark. 55, 771 S.W.2d 266 (1989), for a discussion of the costs of allowing state post-conviction proceedings and the problems involved in integrating state and federal post-conviction proceedings.

The extent to which claims can be raised and the procedures that must be followed in raising the claims in state court depend upon state law, just as 28 U.S.C.A. § 2255 covers federal defendants in federal courts. If a convicted person wins relief in state court, further proceedings will be unnecessary. But failure to win in state court often will not bar a subsequent federal action to set aside a state conviction. The remainder of this chapter will focus on federal actions and two basic questions: (1) What issues should be cognizable in collateral actions? (2) Should it matter (and if so, why) whether the collateral action is brought by a person convicted in a state or federal court? Because this material involves, in part, nice questions of federal-state relations, only the surface is scratched here. An in-depth look at the problem is available in the standard advanced course in Federal Courts or Federal Procedure.

10. Circuit judges could grant the writ under the "all writs" statute, 28 U.S.C.A. § 1651, in aid of appellate jurisdiction.

11. The enactments are set forth in R. Sokol, supra, at 325–34.

12. Appellate jurisdiction was withdrawn the next year, see Ex parte McCardle, 74 U.S. (7 Wall.) 506 (1869), and was not restored until 1885, 23 Stat. 437.

B. THE FEDERAL HABEAS CORPUS SCHEME: THE PROCEDURAL FRAMEWORK

1. The Statutes

28 U.S.C.A. § 2241 et seq. sets forth the powers of federal judges to issue writs of habeas corpus and the procedures to be utilized in habeas corpus actions. Section 2241(a) does not clearly authorize federal district judges (rather than courts) to issue writs, but it has been read (and reasonably so) as if it did. The remainder of the section sets forth the reach of the writ and identifies the courts from which it should be sought.

§ 2241. Power to grant writ

(a) Writs of habeas corpus may be granted by the Supreme Court, any justice thereof, the district courts and any circuit judge within their respective jurisdictions. The order of a circuit judge shall be entered in the records of the district court of the district wherein the restraint complained of is had.

(b) The Supreme Court, any justice thereof, and any circuit judge may decline to entertain an application for a writ of habeas corpus and may transfer the application for hearing and determination to the district court having jurisdiction to entertain it.

(c) The writ of habeas corpus shall not extend to a prisoner unless—

(1) He is in custody under or by color of the authority of the United States or is committed for trial before some court thereof; or

(2) He is in custody for an act done or omitted in pursuance of an Act of Congress, or an order, process, judgment or decree of a court or judge of the United States; or

(3) He is in custody in violation of the Constitution or laws or treaties of the United States; * * *

* * *

Although the section extends to prisoners in both state and federal custody, 28 U.S.C.A. § 2255 takes precedence over § 2241 for federal prisoners challenging their convictions in federal courts.

§ 2255. Federal custody; remedies on motion attacking sentence

A prisoner in custody under sentence of a court established by Act of Congress claiming the right to be released upon the ground that the sentence was imposed in violation of the Constitution or laws of the United States, or that the court was without jurisdiction to impose such sentence, or that the sentence was in excess of the maximum authorized by law, or is otherwise subject to collateral attack, may move the court which imposed the sentence to vacate, set aside or correct the sentence.

A motion for such relief may be made at any time.

* * *

An application for a writ of habeas corpus in behalf of a prisoner who is authorized to apply for relief by motion pursuant to this section, shall not be entertained if it appears that the applicant has failed to apply for relief, by motion, to the court which sentenced him, or that such court has denied him relief, unless it also appears that the remedy by motion is inadequate or ineffective to test the legality of his detention.

This is the equivalent of the habeas corpus remedy provided to state prisoners by 28 U.S.C. § 2254. Hill v. United States, 368 U.S. 424 (1962). In United States v. Hayman, 342 U.S. 205 (1952), the Supreme Court explained that the purpose of the statute was to avoid having habeas corpus petitions filed and heard in the district in which a prisoner is confined, since the witnesses often would live in the district of conviction, and the courts sitting in localities with federal prisons could be overwhelmed with petitions. Like the habeas corpus remedy, the § 2255 remedy is a civil one; it is not part of a federal criminal proceeding. Because § 2255 exists, "it is the exclusive remedy and habeas corpus is barred for a federal prisoner." 2 Wright, Federal Practice and Procedure § 591.[13] Habeas corpus will lie, however, if someone is confined in federal prison before any judgment is rendered that can be attacked under § 2255. See, e.g., Brown v. Hunter, 187 F.2d 543 (10th Cir. 1951).

2. *Custody; The Erratic Development of a Concept*

Whether relief is sought under § 2241 or under § 2255, the applicant must be in custody. The meaning of "custody" has run an uncertain course in the Supreme Court. Early cases required something more than a "moral restraint," see Wales v. Whitney, 114 U.S. 564 (1885). That something was not satisfied by a showing that a person was free on bail, Stallings v. Splain, 253 U.S. 339 (1920), or parole, Weber v. Squier, 315 U.S. 810 (1942). In 1957, the Court entertained an attack under § 2255 by a prisoner who was in custody when he filed his petition but who had been released before his case was heard on the merits by the Supreme Court. Pollard v. United States, 352 U.S. 354, 358 (1957). Language in the majority opinion, with which the four dissenters on the merits of the underlying claim apparently agreed, suggested that "[t]he possibility of consequences collateral" to conviction justified going forward under § 2255. Two years later, however, the Court found that § 2255 was not available to challenge a future consecutive sentence. Heflin v. United States, 358 U.S. 415 (1959). Earlier the Court had reached the same result in a habeas case. McNally v. Hill, 293 U.S. 131 (1934). In 1960, the Court, over four dissents, dismissed as moot a claim brought by a state prisoner who was released under circumstances similar to those that produced the 1957 decision. Parker v. Ellis, 362 U.S. 574 (1960).

3. *Custody; An Expanding Concept*

In 1963, the Court found that parole was a custody status. Jones v. Cunningham, 371 U.S. 236 (1963). And a decade after *Pollard,* the subsequent course of decisions that had eroded its force was reversed.[14] In Peyton v. Rowe, 391 U.S. 54 (1968), the Court held that habeas corpus could be used by a

13. In Swain v. Pressley, 430 U.S. 372 (1977), the Court upheld the constitutionality of 23 D.C.Code § 110(g), which requires prisoners seeking to collaterally attack a District of Columbia conviction to use the District's post-conviction process, not federal habeas corpus.

14. Although "custody" has been an expanding concept, it has not always worked to the advantage of the habeas petitioner. In Preiser v. Rodriguez, 411 U.S. 475 (1973), prisoners challenging the method by which good time credit was taken from them brought a civil rights suit under 42 U.S.C.A. § 1983. But the Court held that the prisoners were really seeking a habeas corpus remedy and that, therefore, they had to exhaust state remedies. For an example of the difficulty of distinguishing § 1983 claims from habeas claims, see Wolff v. McDonnell, 418 U.S. 539 (1974).

prisoner serving one sentence who wished to attack a consecutive sentence. In so holding the Court expressly overruled McNally v. Hill, supra, and implicitly rejected Heflin v. United States, supra, as well. In Carafas v. LaVallee, 391 U.S. 234 (1968), the Court overruled Parker v. Ellis without a dissent. Thus, discharge of a prisoner once properly before the court will not result in a finding of "no custody." Subsequently, the Court found custody in Hensley v. Municipal Court, 411 U.S. 345 (1973), where a defendant sentenced to prison for one year had his sentence stayed pending appellate and post-conviction attacks. After *Hensley,* release on bail would seem to be custody for purposes of federal habeas corpus.[15] See. e.g., Campbell v. Shapp, 385 F.Supp. 305 (E.D.Pa.1974), affirmed, 521 F.2d 1398 (3d Cir.1975). If a person is in custody in one jurisdiction and wishes to attack a conviction mandating future custody in another jurisdiction, Braden v. 30th Judicial Circuit Ct., 410 U.S. 484 (1973), suggests that any "detainer" or formal demand for custody by the expectant jurisdiction is "custody." See also Nelson v. George, 399 U.S. 224 (1970). If no detainer or demand is made, the prospect of future custody remains real, but the Court has not yet determined whether this satisfies the federal statutes, although Rule 1(a) of the Rules Covering Section 2254 Cases in the United States District Courts (hereinafter "§ 2254 Rules") [16] and Rule 1(a) of the Rules Governing Section 2255 Proceedings for the United States District Court (hereafter "§ 2255 Rules") imply that it is.

The first case in many years to restrict the "collateral harm" concept and to find a habeas corpus action moot was Lane v. Williams, 455 U.S. 624 (1982). Two defendants pleaded guilty to burglary charges. Each was incarcerated, released on parole, found to be a parole violator, and reincarcerated. When parole was revoked each challenged his plea on the ground that he had not known of the mandatory parole requirement when he pleaded. But before the case reached the Supreme Court, each was released from custody. Since the parole terms had expired, Justice Stevens' opinion for the Court concluded that the case was moot. "No civil disabilities such as those present in *Carafas* result from a finding that an individual has violated parole. At most, certain non-statutory consequences may occur; employment prospects, or the sentence imposed in a future criminal proceeding, could be affected." Justice Marshall, joined by Justices Brennan and Blackmun, dissented, arguing that federal courts should presume the existence of collateral consequences to avoid the

15. Section 22–2.3 of the ABA Standards, Post Conviction Remedies (2d ed. 1980), recommends abolition of the custody requirement. Only a few states followed the recommendation.

16. Note that federal courts historically have been able to grant relief before judgment in exceptional cases. This authority continues to be recognized. See Braden v. 30th Judicial Circuit Ct., 410 U.S. 484 (1973). If habeas is sought before judgment, the § 2254 Rules "may be applied at the discretion of the United States district court." Rule 1(b).

In Justices v. Lydon, 466 U.S. 294 (1984), the Court held, 6–3, that the court of appeals was correct in holding that a state defendant who requested a trial de novo following a conviction in a bench trial, and who was released on his own recognizance during this time, was "in custody" for purposes of the federal habeas corpus statute and could raise a claim that the evidence at the bench trial was insufficient to sustain a conviction. Justice Powell, joined by Chief Justice Burger, argued that *Hensley* was wrongly decided, and that even if it were correct, it should not extend to a person who is free on his own recognizance pending a trial de novo. Justice O'Connor offered a similar view in a separate opinion, arguing that a state prisoner is not "in custody" simply because he faces minor restraints on his freedom as a result of an ongoing state trial. She would have read *Hensley* as "holding that the minimal constraints of a release on personal recognizance constitute 'custody' only when the state stands ready to incarcerate the habeas petitioner without further judicial hearing."

necessity of predicting how a state might use a conviction or parole revocation in future proceedings.

The Court held in Maleng v. Cook, 490 U.S. 488 (1989) (per curiam), that it was crucial in *La Vallee* that the petitioner had filed his petition prior to being released from incarceration, and that a former prisoner whose sentence had expired could not challenge the conviction for which the sentence was served, even though the former conviction might lead to an enhanced sentence in a subsequent proceeding. The Court reaffirmed *McNally,* however, and held that a federal prisoner as to whom a detainer had been lodged by a State could challenge the state conviction. The Court left open the question whether, in the course of attacking an enhanced conviction which follows an earlier conviction for which the sentence has been served, a prisoner may challenge the earlier conviction.

4. *Procedures for Seeking Relief*

28 U.S.C.A. §§ 2242–2243 and part of § 2255 set forth procedures for habeas and § 2255 cases. These are supplemented by the § 2254 and § 2255 rules. § 2255 cases begin by motion, whereas § 2254 cases begin with a petition for habeas corpus, naming the officer having custody of the petitioner and the state attorney-general as respondents. However, the model forms provided with both sets of rules are substantially identical. Both sets of rules provide for preliminary consideration by the judge, which could result in summary dismissal.[17] If not, the respondent in § 2254 cases and the United States Attorney in § 2255 cases are ordered to answer.[18] The respondent in § 2254 cases not only responds, but indicates what transcripts are available,[19] and the federal judge examines court files in § 2255 cases to determine the existence of transcripts and other records.[20] Discovery is permitted under the Federal Rules of Civil Procedure to the extent that the judge permits; the record may be expanded to include material designated by the judge, and the judge may appoint counsel to assist in discovery.[21] If a hearing is held, counsel must be appointed for indigents.[22] A magistrate may hold the hearing and propose findings and recommendations that are binding on the parties, unless objection is made within 10 days after service, in which case the judge decides de novo those matters objected to.[23]

5. *Procedural Rules*

Sections 2245–2250 provide certain evidence and evidence-related rules for habeas proceedings.[24] A certificate of the trial judge setting forth the facts

17. § 2254 Rules, Rule 4; § 2255 Rules, Rule 4(b).

18. § 2254 Rules, Rule 4; § 2255 Rules, Rule 4(b).

19. § 2254 Rules, Rule 5.

20. § 2255 Rules, Rule 5(b).

21. § 2254 Rules, Rules 6 & 7; § 2255 Rules, Rules 6 & 7.

22. § 2254 Rules, Rule 8(c); § 2255 Rules, Rule 8(c).

23. § 2254 Rules, Rule 8(b); § 2255 Rules, Rule 8(b). See also 28 U.S.C.A. § 636(b)(1).

24. Fed.R.Evid. 1101(e) provides that when a statute or rule does not apply, the Federal Rules of Evidence do. Also, Rule 11 of the § 2254 Rules provides that the Federal Rules of Civil Procedure may be used where they are appropriate and Rule 12 of the § 2255 Rules permits the use of either the Federal Rules of Civil Procedure or the Federal Rules of Criminal Procedure, whichever are more appropriate.

occurring at trial is admissible (§ 2245), as are depositions and affidavits, in the discretion of the trial judge (§ 2246). Documentary evidence and transcripts of prior proceedings are admissible (§ 2249), and indigent prisoners may be furnished with necessary documents pursuant to court order (§ 2250). Between the petitioner and the respondent, copies of the indictment, plea and judgment, if relevant, are to be submitted (§ 2249).

6. *Exhaustion of State Remedies*

An attack on a federal conviction can be made at any time under § 2255. But there is a condition precedent to an attack on a state conviction: exhaustion of state remedies. The exhaustion requirement originated in Ex parte Royall, 117 U.S. 241 (1886),[25] and it was codified in 28 U.S.C.A. § 2254.

As the Supreme Court pointed out in Darr v. Burford, 339 U.S. 200 (1950), the exhaustion requirement is rooted in federal-state comity. It allows the states the first opportunity to apply controlling legal principles to the facts bearing on the constitutional claim of a defendant in a state criminal action. It thereby preserves for state courts a role in the application and enforcement of federal law and prevents interruption of state adjudication by federal habeas proceedings. Consequently, it is not enough that the petitioner has been to the state courts; he must have presented there the same ground he seeks to advance in his federal habeas corpus petition. Darr v. Burford, supra.

In Sanders v. United States, 373 U.S. 1, 16 (1963), the Supreme Court explained what is meant by the same ground:

> By "ground" we mean simply a sufficient legal basis for granting the relief sought by the applicant. * * * [I]dentical grounds may often be proved by different factual allegations. So also, identical grounds may often be supported by different legal arguments, * * * or be couched in different language, * * * or vary in immaterial respects. * * * Should doubts arise in particular cases as to whether two grounds are different or the same, they should be resolved in favor of the applicant.

Subsequently, the Court refined the test by stating that "the substance of a federal habeas corpus claim must first be presented to the state courts." Picard v. Connor, 404 U.S. 270, 278 (1971). Connor challenged the legality of the indictment, which had originally named John Doe, and then was amended to name him. In the state courts, he contended that the amending procedure did not comply with the Massachusetts statute, with the result that he had not been lawfully indicted. In his habeas petition, he alleged a violation of equal protection. Justice Black, writing for the Court, concluded that this claim had not been exhausted in the state courts. He stated as follows:

> It would be unseemly in our dual system of government for a federal district court to upset a state court conviction without an opportunity to the state courts to correct a constitutional violation. It follows, of course, that once the federal claim has been fairly presented to the state courts, the exhaustion requirement is satisfied.
>
> We emphasize that the federal claim must be fairly presented to the state courts. If the exhaustion doctrine is to prevent unnecessary conflict between

25. Royall sought to challenge a Virginia statute before trial. The Court recognized discretion on the part of federal courts to defer to a state court in the first instance.

courts equally bound to guard and protect rights secured by the Constitution, it is not sufficient merely that the federal habeas applicant has been through the state courts. The rule would serve no purpose if it could be satisfied by raising one claim in the state courts and another in the federal courts. * * *

Until he reached this Court, respondent never contended that the method by which he was brought to trial denied him equal protection of the laws. * * * To be sure, respondent presented all the facts. Yet the constitutional claim * * * in those facts was never brought to the attention of the state courts. * * * [We] do not imply that respondent could have raised the equal protection claim only by citing book and verse on the federal constitution. We simply hold that the substance of a federal habeas corpus claim must first be presented to the state courts. The claim that an indictment is invalid is not the substantial equivalent of a claim that it results in an unconstitutional discrimination.

In Anderson v. Harless, 459 U.S. 4 (1982), six Justices concluded that a state prisoner had not exhausted state remedies where he challenged a jury instruction in state court by citing state law and in federal court raised a constitutional challenge for the first time. Three dissenters agreed with the court of appeals that the "substance" of the federal claim had been put before the state courts.

Mabry v. Klimas, 448 U.S. 444 (1980) (per curiam), suggests that exhaustion is especially appropriate when the proper construction of a state statute is in doubt. The importance of exhaustion in federal habeas corpus law is reiterated in the per curiam opinion in Duckworth v. Serrano, 454 U.S. 1 (1981) (reversing court of appeals for hearing ineffective assistance of counsel claim not previously presented to state courts).

In Rose v. Lundy, 455 U.S. 509 (1982), a majority of the Supreme Court held that the federal statute requires that a federal district court dismiss a petition that combines unexhausted and exhausted claims. Dismissal leaves the prisoner with the choice of returning to state court to finish exhaustion of all claims or resubmitting only the exhausted claims to the federal court. Thus, the Court in *Lundy* made clear that the exhaustion requirement does not preclude habeas review; it merely delays habeas review. The exhaustion requirement is therefore unlike other limitations on collateral review, such as the bar of procedural default in the state court, or the related bar of adequate state ground, both of which prevent claims from ever being heard on habeas. These doctrines are discussed below.

In *Lundy,* Justice O'Connor considered the consequences which should follow if a habeas petitioner chose to proceed only with his exhausted claims, deferring the unexhausted claims for a subsequent habeas petition. She wrote for a plurality of the court that such a petitioner "risks dismissal of subsequent federal petitions" under § 2254 Rule 9(b). Justices Brennan, White, Marshall, Blackmun and Stevens all refused to join Justice O'Connor's views. Some of these Justices would not have required that the district court dismiss mixed petitions in the first place, and some thought that § 2254 Rule 9(b) would not permit later dismissal of claims put aside. However, as a practical matter, Justice O'Connor's views may have largely prevailed on the subsequent dismissal issue. This is because, after *Lundy,* the Court has imposed substantial limitations on successive habeas petitions pursuant to the "abuse of the writ" doctrine. See McCleskey v. Zant, discussed below.

In Granberry v. Greer, 481 U.S. 129 (1987), Justice Stevens wrote for a unanimous Court as it held that a court of appeals is not required to dismiss a habeas corpus petition when a state raises for the first time on appeal a claim that a petitioner has failed to exhaust state remedies. The state's failure to raise an arguably meritorious exhaustion defense indicates that it has not met its duty to inform the district court as to any problem with exhaustion. Thus, a court of appeals "should determine whether the interests of comity and federalism will be better served by addressing the merits forthwith or by requiring a series of additional state and district court proceedings before reviewing the merits of the petitioner's claim."

A habeas petitioner is not required to bring his claims in the state court if that would be futile. For example, in Harris v. DeRobertis, 932 F.2d 619 (7th Cir.1991), the district court held that Harris had an unexhausted right to post-conviction relief under an Illinois statute. Harris had failed to assert his constitutional claim in his state appeal. An Illinois statute allowed claims such as Harris' to be brought on collateral attack; but if the proceedings were commenced more than ten years after final judgment, the petitioner had to prove that the delay was for some reason other than "culpable negligence." Harris' petition was filed twenty years after his conviction. The district court held that Harris could have tried to invoke the state remedy by demonstrating a lack of culpable negligence, and therefore his claim was unexhausted. The court of appeals disagreed. It noted that the Illinois statute had been in effect more than forty years, and in that time "the Illinois courts have failed to produce even a single published opinion in which the court found a lack of culpable negligence." Based on the Illinois case law, the court found that "the culpable negligence standard is an exceptional means of relief which will be unavailable to virtually all prisoners." The court concluded as follows:

> We believe the better approach is to forego resort to the Illinois post-conviction process if a petition would be untimely, absent judicial precedent indicating that the culpable negligence exception would be met. Such a holding avoids the 'merry-go-round procedure' * * * by which prisoners are shuttled back and forth between the state and federal courts before any decision on the merits is ever reached in order to exhaust meaningless remedies.

The court in *Harris* assumes that if the Illinois limitations period would be excused, or if it did not exist at all, then Harris would have been required to exhaust the state process of collateral review. Suppose Harris had asserted his constitutional claim in the state court appeal, and it was rejected. Would the court in *Harris* have proceeded under the same assumption that state collateral review must be exhausted? Suppose the state provides for collateral review without limitation as to number of petitions or the time in which they may be brought. Would it follow that a federal habeas petition could never be brought because the state post-conviction remedy is never exhausted? The Court in Castille v. Peoples, 489 U.S. 346 (1989), addressed this question. Justice Scalia wrote for a unanimous Court as follows:

> Title 28 U.S.C. § 2254(c) provides that a claim shall not be deemed exhausted so long as a petitioner 'has the right under the law of the State to raise, by any available procedure, the question presented.' Read narrowly, this language appears to preclude a finding of exhaustion if there exists any possibility of further state-court review. We have, however, expressly rejected

such a construction, Brown v. Allen, 344 U.S. 443 (1953), holding instead that once the state courts have ruled upon a claim, it is not necessary for the petitioner 'to ask the state for collateral relief, based upon the same evidence and issues already decided by direct review.' It would be inconsistent * * * to mandate recourse to state collateral review whose results have effectively been predetermined, or permanently to bar from federal habeas prisoners in States whose post-conviction procedures are technically inexhaustible.

Thus, the rule is that state collateral review is relevant for exhaustion purposes only if direct appeal has been bypassed and only if the collateral review process is meaningful and not itself inexhaustible.

On the facts in *Peoples,* the Court held that the petitioner had not exhausted state court remedies. Peoples presented his constitutional claim for the first time by filing a petition for allocatur with the Pennsylvania Supreme Court. Under Pennsylvania law, allocatur review is only allowed where there are "special and important reasons therefor." Justice Scalia found that in rejecting the petition for allocatur, the state court had not actually passed upon the claim so as to render further state proceedings useless. He noted the limitations on allocatur review in Pennsylvania and concluded that "raising the claim in such a fashion does not, for the relevant purpose, constitute fair presentation." He recognized, however, that "the requisite exhaustion may nonetheless exist, of course, if it is clear that respondent's claims are now procedurally barred under Pennsylvania law." Note, however, that if that is so, Peoples has jumped from the exhaustion frying pan into the procedural bar fire, and so federal habeas review is probably precluded at any rate. See Wainwright v. Sykes, infra.

To fully exhaust state remedies, the petitioner must utilize all state remedies available, including appellate remedies, but no longer must he petition the Supreme Court for certiorari.[26] See Fay v. Noia, 372 U.S. 391, 435–38 (1963).

7. *The Requirement of a Hearing*

§ 2254 originally did not indicate when a hearing should or must be held. The answer was found in Townsend v. Sain, 372 U.S. 293 (1963). There, the Court held that "[w]here the facts are in dispute, the federal court in habeas corpus must hold an evidentiary hearing if the habeas applicant did not receive a full and fair evidentiary hearing in a state court, either at the time of the trial or in a collateral proceeding." The Court explained "that a federal court must grant an evidentiary hearing to a habeas applicant under the following circumstances:

> * * * If (1) the merits of the factual dispute were not resolved in the state hearing; (2) the state factual determination is not fairly supported by the record as a whole; (3) the fact-finding procedure employed by the state court was not adequate to afford a full and fair hearing; (4) there is a substantial allegation of newly discovered evidence; (5) the material facts were not adequately developed at the state court hearing; or (6) for any reason it

26. The prisoner need not run through the state system more than once. But if he fails to appeal on a point and is permitted by the state to renew the point in a state collateral proceeding which provides appellate review, he must utilize the state procedure. Ex parte Hawk, 321 U.S. 114 (1944).

appears that the state trier of fact did not afford the habeas applicant a full and fair fact hearing.

(1) There cannot even be the semblance of a full and fair hearing unless the state court actually reached and decided the issues of fact tendered by the defendant. Thus, if no express findings of fact have been made by the state court, the District Court must initially determine whether the state court has impliedly found material facts. No relevant findings have been made unless the state court decided the constitutional claim tendered by the defendant on the merits. If relief has been denied in prior state collateral proceedings after a hearing but without opinion, it is often likely that the decision is based upon a procedural issue—that the claim is not collaterally cognizable—and not on the merits. On the other hand, if the prior state hearing occurred in the course of the original trial—for example, on a motion to suppress allegedly unlawful evidence, as in the instant case—it will usually be proper to assume that the claim was rejected on the merits.

If the state court has decided the merits of the claim but has made no express findings, it may still be possible for the District Court to reconstruct the findings of the state trier of fact, either because his view of the facts is plain from his opinion or because of other indicia. In some cases this will be impossible, and the Federal District Court will be compelled to hold a hearing.

Reconstruction is not possible if it is unclear whether the state finder applied correct constitutional standards in disposing of the claim. Under such circumstances the District Court cannot ascertain whether the state court found the law or the facts adversely to the petitioner's contentions. Since the decision of the state trier of fact may rest upon an error of law rather than an adverse determination of the facts, a hearing is compelled to ascertain the facts. Of course, the possibility of legal error may be eliminated in many situations if the fact finder has articulated the constitutional standards which he has applied. Furthermore, the coequal responsibilities of state and federal judges in the administration of federal constitutional law are such that we think the district judge may, in the ordinary case in which there has been no articulation, properly assume that the state trier of fact applied correct standards of federal law to the facts, * * *. Thus, if third-degree methods of obtaining a confession are alleged and the state court refused to exclude the confession from evidence, the district judge may assume that the state trier found the facts against the petitioner, the law being, of course, that third-degree methods necessarily produce a coerced confession.

In any event, even if it is clear that the state trier of fact utilized the proper standard, a hearing is sometimes required if his decision presents a situation in which the "so-called facts and their constitutional significance [are] * * * so blended that they cannot be severed in consideration." Unless the district judge can be reasonably certain that the state trier would have granted relief if he had believed petitioner's allegations, he cannot be sure that the state trier in denying relief disbelieved these allegations. If any combination of the facts alleged would prove a violation of constitutional rights and the issue of law on those facts presents a difficult or novel problem for decision, any hypothesis as to the relevant factual determinations of the state trier involves the purest speculation. The federal court cannot exclude the possibility that the trial judge believed facts which showed a deprivation of constitutional rights and yet (erroneously) concluded that relief should be denied.

Under these circumstances it is impossible for the federal court to reconstruct the facts, and a hearing must be held.

(2) This Court has consistently held that state factual determinations not fairly supported by the record cannot be conclusive of federal rights. * * *

* * *

(3) However, the obligation of the Federal District Court to scrutinize the state-court findings of fact goes farther than this. Even if all the relevant facts were presented in the state-court hearing, it may be that the fact-finding procedure there employed was not adequate for reaching reasonably correct results. If the state trial judge has made serious procedural errors (respecting the claim pressed in federal habeas) in such things as the burden of proof, a federal hearing is required. Even where the procedure employed does not violate the Constitution, if it appears to be seriously inadequate for the ascertainment of the truth, it is the federal judge's duty to disregard the state findings and take evidence anew. Of course, there are procedural errors so grave as to require an appropriate order directing the habeas applicant's release unless the State grants a new trial forthwith. * * *

(4) Where newly discovered evidence is alleged in a habeas application, evidence which could not reasonably have been presented to the state trier of facts, the federal court must grant an evidentiary hearing. Of course, such evidence must bear upon the constitutionality of the applicant's detention; the existence merely of newly discovered evidence relevant to the guilt of a state prisoner is not a ground for relief on federal habeas corpus. Also, the district judge is under no obligation to grant a hearing upon a frivolous or incredible allegation of newly discovered evidence.

(5) The conventional notion of the kind of newly discovered evidence which will permit the reopening of a judgment is, however, in some respects too limited to provide complete guidance to the federal district judge on habeas. If, for any reason not attributable to the inexcusable neglect of petitioner, evidence crucial to the adequate consideration of the constitutional claim was not developed at the state hearing, a federal hearing is compelled. * * *

(6) Our final category is intentionally open-ended because we cannot here anticipate all the situations wherein a hearing is demanded. It is the province of the district judges first to determine such necessities in accordance with the general rules. The duty to try the facts anew exists in every case in which the state court has not after a full hearing reliably found the relevant facts.

It was after *Townsend* that Congress enacted Public Law 89–711, 80 Stat. 1105 (1976), adding § 2254(d) to the habeas corpus statute.

If the six situations in which a hearing must be granted under *Townsend* are compared to § 2254(d), it is apparent that three statutory provisions are not found in *Townsend*, and one aspect of *Townsend* is not reflected in the statute. But the differences between the decision and the statute are probably not important as far as criteria for a hearing go, since the provisions of each can be matched as follows:

Townsend Reason For Hearing	Statutory Provision § 2254(d)
1. Merits not resolved in state court	1. Merits not resolved in state court
2. State determination not supported by record	8. State determination not supported by record
3. Inadequate state fact-finding procedure	2. Inadequate state fact-finding procedure
4. Substantial allegation of newly discovered evidence 5. Inadequate state development of material facts	3. Inadequate state development of material facts
6. Other reasons why state hearing was not full and fair	4. Lack of jurisdiction in state court 5. Lack of counsel in state proceeding 6. Absence of full and fair state hearing 7. Other denial of due process

Thus, a number of decisions hold that the statute codifies the *Townsend* criteria. See, e.g., Maxwell v. Turner, 411 F.2d 805 (10th Cir. 1969). But *Townsend* states that a hearing is mandatory under any of the enumerated circumstances. § 2255 requires a hearing "[u]nless the motion and the files and the records of the case conclusively show that the prisoner is entitled to no relief." The statute does not speak of mandatory hearings.

8. *Factual Findings and Mixed Questions of Law and Fact*

Section 2254(d) provides that "a determination made by a State court * * * shall be presumed to be correct" unless one of the eight criteria set forth in the chart is present, and the burden is on the petitioner to show that the factual determination by the state court was erroneous.

Thus, under the statute, factual findings are presumed correct. The Court has held, however, that deference is not required for legal findings or for decisions on mixed questions of fact and law. For example, in Cuyler v. Sullivan, 446 U.S. 335 (1980), the Court held that a finding as to the effectiveness of a lawyer involved in multiple representation of defendants was "a mixed determination of law and fact" fully open to review on collateral attack in a federal court.

In her opinion for the Court in Strickland v. Washington, 466 U.S. 668 (1984), setting forth the standards by which courts must assess effectiveness of counsel under the Constitution, Justice O'Connor wrote that "a state court conclusion that counsel rendered effective assistance is not a finding of fact binding on a federal court to the extent stated by 28 U.S.C.A. § 2254(d). * * * Rather, like the question whether multiple representation in a particular case gave rise to a conflict of interest, it is a mixed question of law and fact."

However, factual components necessary to establish counsel's ineffectiveness will be entitled to the presumption of correctness. Thus, in Burden v. Zant, 111 S.Ct. 862 (1991), the defendant alleged that his attorney labored under an actual conflict of interest by negotiating transactional immunity for the star witness in the defendant's trial. The State trial court had found that the witness was granted immunity from prosecution. On collateral review, the court of appeals disregarded this finding as "without factual support." In a per curiam opinion, the Supreme Court held that the court of appeals had failed to give a presumption of correctness to the trial court's finding.

Writing for the Court in Patton v. Yount, 467 U.S. 1025 (1984), Justice Powell reasoned that a state court's finding that a juror was not partial and could be fair was entitled to a presumption of correctness. It was a finding of historical fact rather than a mixed question of fact and law. Justice Stevens, joined by Justice Brennan, dissented. Justice Marshall did not participate. In Wainwright v. Witt, 469 U.S. 412 (1985), the Court relied upon *Patton* to hold that a trial judge's determination that a prospective juror was properly excluded for cause in a capital case is sufficiently factual that it is subject to § 2254(d).

The Supreme Court held in Miller v. Fenton, 474 U.S. 104 (1985), that a state court's decision that a confession was voluntary is a mixed question of fact and law which federal courts do not presume to be correct. Writing for the Court, Justice O'Connor observed that the decision to label a question as purely legal, purely factual or mixed "is sometimes as much a matter of allocation as it is of analysis." She analyzed *Patton* and *Witt* as involving credibility determination more properly made by state trial judges and observed that for a long time the Court had assumed that voluntariness was a question deserving of de novo review by a federal court. Although federal courts will presume that subsidiary factual questions—e.g., "the length and circumstances of the interrogation, the defendant's prior experience with the legal process, and familiarity with the *Miranda* warnings"—were correctly decided, Justice O'Connor wrote that "once such underlying factual issues have been resolved, * * * the state-court judge is not in an appreciably better position than the federal habeas court" to determine voluntariness under the totality of the circumstances test. Only Justice Rehnquist dissented.

In Sumner v. Mata, 449 U.S. 539 (1981), the Court considered a case in which the federal habeas court rejected the conclusion of the California Supreme Court. The California court had held that a photographic identification of Mata was not so impermissibly suggestive as to cause a substantial risk of mistaken identification. Justice Rehnquist, writing for the Court, asserted that the habeas court's findings (e.g. that substantial pressure had been brought to bear on the witnesses and that the witnesses had failed to give detailed descriptions of the perpetrator before the identification) were "considerably at odds" with the findings of the California Supreme Court. The Court held that the presumption of correctness under § 2254(d) applied to findings made by a state appellate court after a hearing. Justice Rehnquist reasoned that the statute "makes no distinction between the factual determinations of a state trial court and those of a state appellate court." He noted that the habeas court gave no indication that it had even considered § 2254(d) when it rejected the state court's findings. Justice Rehnquist concluded as follows:

> When Congress provided in § 2254(d) that a habeas court could not dispense with the presumption of correctness embodied therein unless it concluded that the factual determinations were not supported by the record, it

> contemplated at least some reasoned written references to § 2254(d) and the state-court findings. * * * [It] is clear that * * * Congress in § 2254(d) intended * * * to establish that the findings made by the state-court system shall be presumed to be correct unless one of seven conditions specifically set forth in § 2254(d) was found to exist by the habeas court. If none of those seven conditions were found to exist, or unless the habeas court concludes that the relevant state-court determination is not fairly supported by the record, 'the burden shall rest upon the applicant to establish by clear and convincing evidence that the factual determination by the State court was erroneous.' * * *
>
> * * * In order to ensure that this mandate of Congress is enforced, we now hold that a habeas court should include in its opinion granting the writ the reasoning which led it to conclude that any of the first seven factors were present, or the reasoning which led it to conclude that the state finding was not fairly supported by the record. * * * No court reviewing the grant of an application for habeas corpus should be left to guess as to the habeas court's reasons for granting relief notwithstanding the provisions of § 2254(d).

On remand, the court of appeals again refused to resort to the § 2254(d) presumption of correctness. It reasoned that its disagreement with the California court was "over the legal and constitutional significance of certain facts" and that whether a photographic identification procedure was impermissibly suggestive was a mixed question of law and fact to which the presumption of correctness did not apply. Again the Supreme Court reversed and remanded. 455 U.S. 591 (1981). The Court stated as follows:

> We agree with the Court of Appeals that the ultimate question as to the constitutionality of the pretrial identification procedures used in this case is a mixed question of law and fact that is not governed by § 2254(d). In deciding this question, the federal court may give different weight to the facts as found by the state court and may reach a different conclusion in light of the legal standard. But the questions of fact that underlie this ultimate conclusion *are* governed by the statutory presumption * * *. Thus, whether the witnesses in this case had an opportunity to observe the crime or were too distracted; whether the witnesses gave a detailed, accurate description; and whether the witnesses were under pressure from prison officials or others are all questions of fact as to which the statutory presumption applies.
>
> * * * Although the distinction between fact and law is not always easily drawn, we deal here with a statute that requires the federal courts to show a high measure of deference to the factfindings made by the state courts.

After *Mata,* is it possible for a state court to preclude habeas review by making broad findings of fact which are dispositive of a legal question?

Marshall v. Lonberger, 459 U.S. 422 (1983) afforded the Court another opportunity to emphasize that federal judges are not totally free to decide de novo factual questions previously decided against a habeas petitioner in state court. Lonberger was charged in Ohio with aggravated murder and a "specification" by a prosecutor who sought the death penalty. The "specification," which had to be proved beyond a reasonable doubt, was a prior conviction for an attempt to kill. Lonberger had pleaded guilty previously in an Illinois state court, and the Illinois judgment showed aggravated battery as the offense. The Ohio prosecutor claimed, however, that the plea had been to attempted murder. After an in limine hearing on the voluntariness of the Illinois plea, the Ohio trial judge admitted the indictment from the Illinois case as evidence. The jury returned a verdict finding aggravated murder and also the specification. The trial judge sentenced Lonberger to death. A state appellate court reversed the aggravated murder finding, but upheld the specification. A federal court of appeals overturned the conviction. It found that Lonberger never understood that in Illinois he was pleading guilty to a charge of attempted murder. A majority of the Supreme Court, in an opinion by Justice Rehnquist, agreed with the court of appeals that the question whether a plea of guilty was voluntary is a legal question on which federal courts may disagree with state courts, but the majority found that the question of what the Illinois records actually demonstrated was a factual question to which § 2254(d) applied. The Court reasoned that the state trial judge rejected Lonberger's claim after a hearing and that a federal court was not free to reject the state court's implicit or explicit findings unless it could find that the factual determination was not fairly supported by the record. After observing that federal appellate courts generally defer to trial judges' assessment of witness testimony, the majority reasoned that Congress would not have intended broader review of state court credibility determinations. Marshall v. Lonberger was cited in Maggio v. Fulford, 462 U.S. 111 (1983), a per curiam disposition in which the Court found that a federal court of appeals should have deferred to a state trial judge's findings as to why a hearing on a defendant's competency to stand trial was not necessary.

The Supreme Court relied on *Mata* and *Marshall* in Rushen v. Spain, 464 U.S. 114 (1983), a per curiam reversal of the grant of habeas corpus relief to a state prisoner who claimed that ex parte communications between the trial judge and a juror denied him his right to be present at all critical stages of the proceedings and that one juror was biased against him. The majority reasoned that the federal courts should have deferred to state court findings supporting the ultimate conclusion that the error was harmless. Here, the state court determined that the jury's deliberations, as a whole, were not biased, and the Court stated that this was a finding of "fact." Justice Marshall's dissenting opinion argued that the state court's finding that the juror was not biased lacked support in the record and that the state court made no findings as to the possible impact on the defense of the judge's ex parte communications.

In Wright v. West, 112 S.Ct. 672 (1991), the Supreme Court has directed the parties to brief and argue the following question: "In determining whether to grant a petition for a writ of habeas corpus by a person in custody pursuant to the judgment of a state court, should a federal court give deference to the state court's application of law to the specific facts of the petitioner's case or should it review the state court's determination *de novo?*" In *Wright,* the court of appeals found the evidence insufficient to convict, despite rulings to the contrary by the state trial and appellate courts. The question posed by the Court in *Wright* is whether a presumption of correctness should apply to mixed questions of law and fact decided by the state courts. Thus, the holdings previously discussed in *Cuyler, Strickland,* and Miller v. Fenton are apparently being reconsidered by the Court.

C. CLAIMS COGNIZABLE IN COLLATERAL PROCEEDINGS

Section 2254(a) makes clear that a district court can only entertain an application for habeas corpus relief on behalf of a state prisoner if the prisoner alleges that state custody "is in violation of the Constitution or laws or treaties of the United States." In almost every case the prisoner claims that the state conviction was obtained in violation of the Constitution. § 2255 allows an attack on a federal conviction alleged to be in violation of the Constitution or laws of the United States and adds other grounds for attack. But not every claim of a violation of federal law is cognizable when raised by a federal prisoner. If it were, the collateral remedy might serve as a substitute for appeal.

A violation of state law does not automatically rise to the level of a due process violation, which would be cognizable on collateral review. For example, in Estelle v. McGuire, 112 S.Ct. 475 (1991), McGuire was convicted in state court of the murder of his infant daughter. At the trial, the state offered medical evidence which showed that the infant had suffered severe injuries several weeks before her death. This prior injury evidence was offered to prove "battered child syndrome." The Ninth Circuit granted McGuire's habeas petition, reasoning that the prior injury evidence was "incorrectly admitted pursuant to California law," and that McGuire's due process rights were violated because no evidence linked McGuire to the prior injuries and no claim of accident had been made at trial.

The Supreme Court, in an opinion by Chief Justice Rehnquist, held that the alleged error did not "rise to the level of a due process violation" and reversed the granting of habeas relief. The Chief Justice concluded that "it is not the province of a federal habeas court to reexamine state court determinations on state law questions," and that "in conducting habeas review, a federal court is limited to deciding whether a conviction violated the Constitution, laws, or treaties of the United States." Thus it was irrelevant that the prior injuries evidence may have been inadmissible under state law. The only question was whether admission of the evidence violated McGuire's right to due process, and Court held that it did not. The Chief Justice reasoned that the prior injuries were admissible even if they were not linked to McGuire, since they tended to show that the infant's death "was the result of an intentional act by *someone,* and not an accident." The Court concluded that evidence which tended to prove lack of accident was relevant even though the defendant never claimed at trial that the infant's death was an accident. The Chief Justice noted that the prosecution was required to prove the element of intent beyond a reasonable doubt, and by eliminating the possibility of accident "the evidence regarding battered child syndrome was clearly probative of that element." He asserted that "the prosecution's burden to prove every element of the crime is not relieved by the defendant's tactical decision not to contest an essential element of the offense." Since the evidence was relevant, the Court concluded that its admission did not violate due process. The Chief Justice stated that "we need not explore further the apparent assumption of the Court of Appeals that it is a violation of the due process guaranteed by the Fourteenth Amendment for evidence that is not relevant to be received at a criminal trial." Justice O'Connor, joined by Justice Stevens, wrote a separate opinion. Justice Thomas did not participate.

1. Federal Defendants

In Sunal v. Large, 332 U.S. 174, 179 (1947), the Court wrote that "[i]t is plain * * * that the writ is not designed for collateral review of errors of [non-constitutional] law committed by the trial court—the existence of any evidence to support the conviction, irregularities in the grand jury procedure, departure from a statutory grant of time in which to prepare for trial, and other errors in trial procedure which do not cross the jurisdictional line." See also Hill v. United States, 368 U.S. 424 (1962) (defendant denied opportunity to make a statement before sentencing; no attack permitted); United States v. Timmreck, 441 U.S. 780 (1979) (technical violation of rule establishing procedures for accepting guilty pleas; no attack permitted); United States v. Addonizio, 442 U.S. 178 (1979) (no collateral attack on sentence allegedly frustrated by parole board's changed standards). Although the Court's opinions have left open for some time the possibility that a non-constitutional claim of sufficient seriousness could be raised in a collateral proceeding if no other remedy is available, the lower courts have been virtually unanimous in barring nonconstitutional claims on § 2255 motions. Bator et al., The Federal Courts and the Federal System 1586 (3d ed. 1988).

The Supreme Court held in Davis v. United States, 417 U.S. 333 (1974), that a conviction for refusal to submit to induction into the military could be challenged via § 2255 by a defendant who had appealed and lost in the Ninth Circuit before a second appellate opinion in the same Circuit interpreted the law in a manner favorable to him. The majority relied on the fact that the defendant was in custody in violation of the laws of the United States. Justice Rehnquist in dissent attempted to argue that the first and third paragraphs of § 2255 address illegal sentences, and that when the third paragraph refers to judgments it does not mention the "laws" of the United States. It seems that the majority properly gave § 2255 the same reach as § 2254, although it is unclear how far the majority would go. The most limited reading of the opinion would focus on the fact that the Solicitor General opposed Davis' original petition for certiorari following his direct appeal, on the ground that the intra-circuit conflict between Davis' case and the subsequent case would be worked out in the Circuit. This argument might have implied that Davis would get the benefit of the final resolution. A broader reading would allow a § 2255 claim to be brought where an administrative regulation exceeded the authority of an agency acting pursuant to a statutory scheme and, hence, there was no "jurisdiction" in the agency to promulgate the regulation. A third view is that federal non-constitutional claims can be brought under § 2255 whenever the Supreme Court is sufficiently bothered by the thought of barring such claims that it chooses to depart from *Sunal.*

2. *Constitutional Claims Generally*

From the foregoing it is apparent that federal habeas review is generally limited to constitutional claims. See also Smith v. Phillips, 455 U.S. 209 (1982) (only federal constitutional claims are cognizable in a § 2254 proceeding). The next question is whether all constitutional claims can be raised in § 2254 and § 2255 proceedings. On the face of the statutes, the answer might appear to be "yes," but that would not be a correct statement of the current state of the law. Nor would it reflect the status of the writ through most of our history.

In the early days, as our brief historical exegesis noted, the writ was used most frequently to attack the jurisdiction of the court imposing judgment. However, in cases like Ex parte Lange, 85 U.S. (18 Wall.) 163 (1873) (permitting a challenge to a court's authority to impose sentence) and Ex parte Siebold, 100 U.S. 371 (1879) (permitting a challenge to the constitutionality of a statute), the writ also was used.

As noted above, the first Judiciary Act gave the Supreme Court habeas corpus jurisdiction, but only as to federal prisoners. And the Court had no general appellate jurisdiction in criminal cases. The Court construed the habeas jurisdiction narrowly. Subsequently, the 1867 statute expanded habeas corpus jurisdiction to reach state prisoners and used language that was quite different from that used in the first Judiciary Act. The argument has been made that even after the adoption of the 1867 statute, the Supreme Court considered habeas corpus as extending only to jurisdictional defects in a proceeding. Bator, Finality in Criminal Law and Federal Habeas Corpus for State Prisoners, 76 Harv.L.Rev. 441 (1963). This argument has been challenged and it has been asserted that all constitutional claims have been cognizable in habeas corpus proceedings. Peller, In Defense of Federal Habeas Corpus Relitigation, 16 Harv.Civ.Rights & Civ.Lib.Rev. 579 (1982). In Saltzburg, Habeas Corpus: The Supreme Court and the Congress, 44 Ohio St.L.J. 367 (1983), the Court's opinions are described as confusing and the assessment is that the Court itself was not clear as to the scope of habeas corpus jurisdiction.

In Brown v. Allen, 344 U.S. 443 (1953) claims of racial injustice in the South were at the heart of three consolidated cases. Brown, convicted of rape and sentenced to death, alleged racial discrimination in the selection of the grand and petit juries and also the use of a coerced confession. Speller, also convicted of rape and sentenced to death, charged racial discrimination in the selection of the jury array in his case. Bernie and Lloyd Daniels were sentenced to death upon convictions for murder. They claimed that coerced confessions were used against them, that the procedure to determine the voluntariness of their confessions was invalid, and that there was racial bias in the selection of both grand and petit juries. Justice Reed delivered the opinion of the Court on most issues, and Justice Frankfurter delivered the opinion for the Court on the effect of a denial of certiorari on direct review.[27] The Reed opinion assumed that the lower federal courts had the power to issue writs of habeas corpus: "A way is left open to redress violations of the Constitution." The Court considered the merits of the Brown and Speller claims in affirming the denial of habeas corpus relief. But the Daniels' claims were barred because of the noncompliance with state procedures and the petitioners' failure to file a timely appeal: "A failure to use a state's available remedy in the absence of some interference or incapacity * * * bars federal habeas corpus."

Justice Frankfurter's opinion referred to the Act of 1867 as an enlargement of the scope of habeas corpus jurisdiction. He suggested that Congress could have left the enforcement of federal rights in state courts exclusively to the state courts, as it did until the 1867 Act, but that Congress chose to confer greater power on the federal courts. Although he observed that habeas proceedings are not a substitute for appeals, he remarked that the observation "does not touch one of those extraordinary cases in which a substantial claim

27. The majority held that no weight was to be given a denial of certiorari. The minority would have allowed district judges to give such weight to a denial of certiorari as they thought the record justified.

goes to the very foundation of a proceeding." He counseled appropriate deference to state findings, but relied on the congressional expansion of the writ as authority for federal courts to redetermine facts previously decided in state courts and to independently decide mixed fact-law questions. He said that "[i]t is not the boasting of empty rhetoric that has treated the writ of habeas corpus as the basic safeguard of freedom in the Anglo-American world," but recognized that "the writ has potentialities for evil as well as for good. Abuse of the writ may undermine the orderly administration of justice and therefore weaken the forces of authority that are essential for civilization." In a separate opinion, he together with Justices Black and Douglas, would not have barred the Daniels petitioners from seeking federal habeas corpus relief. Justice Jackson concurred in the result reached by Justice Reed and argued that "this Court has sanctioned progressive trivialization of the writ."

After Brown v. Allen, it appeared that all constitutional claims were cognizable in habeas corpus cases. No Justice actually argued otherwise in *Brown*. Kaufman v. United States, 394 U.S. 217 (1969), established that the same scope of review was available to § 2255 litigants.

Later, however, the Court held that certain constitutional claims could not be brought on collateral attack. The first step came in Schneckloth v. Bustamonte, 412 U.S. 218 (1973) (the consent search case considered in Chapter Two, supra). Justice Powell, joined by Chief Justice Burger and Justice Rehnquist in a concurring opinion, argued that "federal collateral review of a state prisoner's Fourth Amendment claims—claims which rarely bear on innocence—should be confined solely to the question of whether the petitioner was provided a full and fair opportunity to raise and have adjudicated the question in state courts." Justice Blackmun's concurring opinion indicated that he was in agreement, and Justice Stewart, the author of the majority opinion, indicated only that it was not necessary to reach the issue raised by Justice Powell.

Three years later Justice Powell had a majority for the result he had sought in *Schneckloth*. The landmark decision came in Stone v. Powell, 428 U.S. 465 (1976). After commenting that the primary purpose of the exclusionary rule is deterrence of illegal police conduct, the majority concluded that the benefits of extending the exclusionary rule to collateral review of Fourth Amendment claims were outweighed by the costs—not only the costs of losing reliable evidence, but also the dislocation costs associated with upsetting criminal convictions and thereby increasing (1) the prosecutorial burdens on the government, (2) the sense of frustration of state and federal judges whose decisions are set aside, and (3) the general uncertainty costs associated with non-final judgments. Justice Powell concluded as follows:

> [W]here the State has provided an opportunity for full and fair litigation of a Fourth Amendment claim, a state prisoner may not be granted federal habeas relief on the ground that evidence obtained in an unconstitutional search or seizure was introduced at his trial. In this context the contribution of the exclusionary rule, if any, to the effectuation of the Fourth Amendment is minimal and the societal costs of the application of the rule persist with special force.

Justice Brennan, joined by Justice Marshall, dissented. He urged that the Court was rewriting jurisdictional statutes, those governing § 2254 and § 2255 cases, and arrogating Congressional power into itself. Justice White also dissented and argued that "[u]nder the amendments to the habeas corpus statute, which * * * represented an effort by Congress to lend a modicum of finality to state criminal judgments, I cannot distinguish between Fourth Amendment and other constitutional issues."

In Kimmelman v. Morrison, 477 U.S. 365 (1986), Justice Brennan wrote for the Court as it held that Stone v. Powell did not bar a habeas corpus petitioner from claiming ineffective assistance of counsel based upon his trial counsel's failure to file a timely motion to suppress evidence. The Court declined "to hold either that the guarantee of effective assistance of counsel belongs solely to the innocent or that it attaches only to matters affecting the determination of actual guilt." Instead, it stated that "federal courts may grant habeas relief in appropriate cases, regardless of the nature of the underlying attorney error." Justice Brennan reasoned as follows:

> Were we to extend *Stone* and hold that criminal defendants may not raise ineffective assistance claims that are based primarily on incompetent handling of Fourth Amendment issues on federal habeas, we would deny most defendants whose trial attorneys performed incompetently in this regard the opportunity to vindicate their right to effective trial counsel. We would deny all defendants whose appellate counsel performed inadequately with respect to Fourth Amendment issues the opportunity to protect their right to effective appellate counsel. * * * Thus, we cannot say, as the Court was able to say in *Stone,* that restriction of federal habeas review would not severely interfere with the protection of the constitutional right asserted by the habeas petitioner.

Justice Brennan also noted that unlike Fourth Amendment claims, there is usually no full and fair opportunity to bring ineffective assistance claims at trial or on direct review. It should be noted, however, that *Kimmelman* creates a certain anomaly when juxtaposed with *Stone.* If two defendants have the same meritorious Fourth Amendment claim, and both are prejudiced by the admission of the tainted evidence at trial, the defendant with the incompetent lawyer can reap the benefit of exclusion on habeas while the defendant with the competent lawyer cannot. See Friedman, A Tale of Two Habeas, 73 Minn.L.Rev. 247 (1988).

It is a truly rare case in which the State fails to meet the *Stone* requirement that it provide a full and fair opportunity for litigation of Fourth Amendment claims. The requirement has been held to mean that on factual issues there must be an opportunity to offer evidence, and that some appellate review must be provided. See generally O'Berry v. Wainwright, 546 F.2d 1204 (5th Cir. 1977). For a collection of lower court cases on this subject, see C. Wright, Federal Practice and Procedure § 4263. It remains to be seen what claims other than Fourth Amendment claims might receive similar treatment. The Supreme Court applied *Stone* in summarily holding in Cardwell v. Taylor, 461 U.S. 571 (1983), that a court of appeals erred in considering whether statements admitted in a state criminal proceeding were the product of illegal detention since the state defendant was afforded an adequate opportunity to have that issue considered in state court. The Court stated, however, that a federal court could consider the voluntariness of the statements under the fifth and fourteenth amendments. See generally, Brewer v. Williams, 430 U.S. 387, 413–14 (1977) (Powell, J., concurring) (set forth in Chapter Three, supra); Wainwright v. Sykes, 433 U.S. 72, 87 n. 11 (1977) (infra). The Court refused to apply *Stone* in Rose v. Mitchell, 443 U.S. 545, 99 S.Ct. 2993, 61 L.Ed.2d 739 (1979) (permitting habeas challenge to racial discrimination in selection of grand jury). The Supreme Court reaffirmed in Vasquez v. Hillery, 474 U.S. 254 (1986), the position that commanded a majority in *Rose*: a defendant may challenge his state court conviction in a federal habeas corpus proceeding on the ground that a grand jury was selected in a racially discriminatory manner. Thus, the Court affirmed the grant of habeas corpus relief to a petitioner who had been convicted of murder in 1963. Justice Marshall's majority opinion observed that the rule invalidating a conviction because of racial discrimination in selection of the grand jury had stood since Strauder v. West Virginia, 100 U.S. 303 (1880), and reasoned that reversal of conviction is the only effective remedy against discrimination. Justice Powell, joined by Chief Justice Burger and Justice Rehnquist, dissented, and would have found the constitutional error harmless. Justice O'Connor indicated agreement on the merits with the dissenters, but concurred in the judgment in light of the Court's prior decisions.

In Duckworth v. Eagan, 492 U.S. 195 (1989), discussed infra in Chapter Three's section on incomplete *Miranda* warnings, Justice O'Connor, who was joined by Justice Scalia, relied upon Stone v. Powell and suggested in a concurring opinion that *Miranda* claims should not be cognizable in habeas corpus proceedings. Justice Marshall, joined by Justice Brennan, disagreed in his dissenting opinion. A majority of the Court did not address the question.

Halpern, Federal Habeas Corpus and the Mapp Exclusionary Rule After Stone v. Powell, 82 Colum.L.Rev. 1 (1982), suggests that "habeas corpus relief should be available under *Stone's* exception to correct judicial errors which, if otherwise uncorrected, could lead to diminished police adherence to fourth amendment values," errors that are "likely to become widespread among the courts of a particular state." But Stone v. Powell was held to bar a federal court from reconsidering a state court's decision that the exclusionary rule does not apply in probation revocation proceedings in Grimsley v. Dodson, 696 F.2d 303 (4th Cir. 1982).

3. *Procedural Bars to Claims by State Defendants*

a. State Procedural Bars and Deliberate Bypass

Brown v. Allen, while recognizing the broad scope of habeas proceedings, refused to hear a claim that had not been properly raised in state court. Like the exhaustion requirement, the procedural default doctrine is rooted in principles of federalism and comity. If the habeas remedy were always available despite a procedural default, state procedures (such as the requirement of a timely objection and the requirement of a timely notice of appeal) could be routinely disregarded. See Wainwright v. Sykes, infra. Unlike the exhaustion requirement, however, which merely delays a collateral attack, the procedural default doctrine precludes it. The question, then, is whether and under what circumstances a habeas petitioner can be excused from a procedural default in the state courts.

In Fay v. Noia, 372 U.S. 391 (1963), the Court created a very permissive test for lifting a state procedural bar. Noia sought habeas relief, arguing that the confession admitted against him at trial was coerced. However, Noia had not brought an appeal on this or any issue in the state courts; he had failed to a file a timely notice of appeal. Justice Brennan, writing for the Court, held that a procedural bar would be lifted unless it could be shown that the petitioner had deliberately bypassed a state remedy. Justice Brennan argued that lifting a procedural bar in all other cases—including where the default was caused by inadvertence or neglect—was necessary to effectuate federal interests. He asserted that petitioners would be unlikely to flaunt state procedural requirements and that state interests would not be unduly impaired. He reasoned as follows:

> We fully grant that the exigencies of federalism warrant a limitation whereby the federal judge has the discretion to deny relief to one who has deliberately sought to subvert or evade the orderly adjudication of his federal defenses in the state courts. Surely no stricter rule is a realistic necessity. A man under conviction for crime has an obvious inducement to do his very best to keep his state remedies open, and not stake his all on the outcome of a federal habeas proceeding which, in many respects, may be less advantageous to him than a state court proceeding. And if because of inadvertence or neglect he runs afoul of a state procedural requirement, and thereby forfeits his state remedies, appellate and collateral, as well as direct review thereof in this Court, those consequences should be sufficient to vindicate the State's valid interest in orderly procedure. Whatever residuum of state interest there may be under such circumstances is manifestly insufficient in the face of the federal policy, drawn from the ancient principles of the writ of habeas corpus, embodied both in the Federal Constitution and in the habeas corpus provisions of the Judicial Code, and consistently upheld by this Court, of affording an effective remedy for restraints contrary to the Constitution. * * *
>
> * * * We therefore hold that the federal habeas judge may in his discretion deny relief to an applicant who has deliberately by-passed the orderly procedure of the state courts and in so doing has forfeited his state court remedies.

Justice Clark dissented in *Fay,* contending that the decision was an affront to legitimate state interests. He argued as follows:

> Habeas corpus is in effect substituted for appeal, seriously disturbing the orderly disposition of state prosecutions and jeopardizing the finality of state convictions in disregard of the States' comprehensive procedural safeguards which, until today, have been respected by the federal courts. Essential to the administration of justice is the prompt enforcement of judicial decrees. After today state judgments will be relegated to a judicial limbo, subject to federal collateral attack—as here—a score of years later despite a defendant's willful failure to appeal.

Justice Harlan also dissented, in an opinion joined by Justices Clark and Stewart. He argued that since a state procedural bar would be respected by the Court if the defendant had petitioned for certiorari, there was no reason for the bar to receive any less respect on habeas review. He further contended that the deliberate bypass standard, "if it is meant to constitute a limitation on interference with state administration of criminal justice, falls far short of the mark" and in fact "amounts to no limitation at all."

b. A Required Showing of Cause and Prejudice

Soon the Court began to cut back on Fay v. Noia, and ultimately it was overruled. The first step was in Davis v. United States, 411 U.S. 233 (1973). Davis, who was convicted of entering a bank with intent to commit larceny, lost his right to challenge the racial composition of the grand jury that indicted him, because he failed to comply with Fed.R.Crim.P. 12(b)(2), which provides that such a challenge is waived unless made by motion before trial, although for cause shown the court may grant relief from waiver. The Court held that this express waiver provision was binding in collateral proceedings as well as on direct appeal, and that a claim once waived under the rule may not be resurrected in the absence of a showing of cause which the Court implied might require an inquiry into the prejudicial effect of the waiver on the applicant for relief. Justice Marshall, joined by Justices Douglas and Brennan, dissented. The Court relied upon *Davis* to hold in Francis v. Henderson, 425 U.S. 536 (1976), that the failure of a defendant to comply with the state equivalent of Federal Rule 12(b) barred subsequent habeas corpus relief out of deference to state procedure. *Francis* makes clear that a showing of "cause" is not enough; a showing of "actual prejudice" also is required. Justices Marshall and Stevens did not participate. Justice Brennan dissented.

Together with *Francis,* the Court decided Estelle v. Williams, 425 U.S. 501 (1976), holding (7–2) that, although the state denies due process if it forces a defendant to stand trial in prison garb, a defendant's failure to raise an objection at trial "is sufficient to negate the presence of compulsion necessary to establish a constitutional violation." This case was followed by Henderson v. Kibbe, 431 U.S. 145 (1977), in which the Court concluded that a trial judge's error in instructing the jury in an arguably incomplete way—which might have undermined the constitutional requirement of proof beyond a reasonable doubt—could not justify habeas corpus relief when no request for more complete instructions had been made, unless a stronger showing of prejudice were made than that necessary to support a finding of plain error. These decisions paved the way for the next case.

WAINWRIGHT v. SYKES

Supreme Court of the United States, 1977.
433 U.S. 72.

MR. JUSTICE REHNQUIST delivered the opinion of the Court.

* * *

Respondent Sykes was convicted of third-degree murder after a jury trial in the Circuit Court of DeSoto County. He testified at trial that on the evening of January 8, 1972, he told his wife to summon the police because he had just shot Willie Gilbert. Other evidence indicated that when the police arrived at respondent's trailer home, they found Gilbert dead of a shotgun wound, lying a few feet from the front porch. Shortly after their arrival, respondent came from across the road, and volunteered that he had shot Gilbert, and a few minutes later respondent's wife approached the police and told them the same thing. Sykes was immediately arrested and taken to the police station.

Once there, it is conceded that he was read his *Miranda* rights, and that he declined to seek the aid of counsel and indicated a desire to talk. He then made a statement, which was admitted into evidence at trial through the testimony of the two officers who heard it, to the effect that he had shot Gilbert from the front porch of his trailer home. There were several references during the trial to respondent's consumption of alcohol during the preceding day and to his apparent state of intoxication, facts which were acknowledged by the officers who arrived at the scene. At no time during the trial, however, was the admissibility of any of respondent's statements challenged by his counsel on the ground that respondent had not understood the *Miranda* warnings. Nor did the trial judge question their admissibility on his own motion or hold a factfinding hearing bearing on that issue.

Respondent appealed his conviction, but apparently did not challenge the admissibility of the inculpatory statements. [He unsuccessfully sought relief in state court habeas proceedings, but was successful in the lower federal courts.]

* * *

[The Court of Appeals held that noncompliance with Florida's contemporaneous objection rule did not bar review by way of habeas corpus.] The Court of Appeals distinguished our decision in *Davis,* supra (where failure to comply with a rule requiring pretrial objection to the indictment was found to bar habeas review of the underlying constitutional claim absent showing of cause for the failure and prejudice resulting), for the reason that "[a] major tenet of the *Davis* decision was that no prejudice was shown" to have resulted from the failure to object. It found that prejudice is "inherent" in any situation, like the present one, where the admissibility of an incriminating statement is concerned. Concluding that "[t]he failure to object in this case cannot be dismissed as a trial tactic, and thus a deliberate by-pass," the court affirmed the District Court order that the State hold a hearing on whether respondent knowingly waived his *Miranda* rights at the time he made the statements.

* * *

To the extent that the dicta of Fay v. Noia may be thought to have laid down an all-inclusive rule rendering state timely objection rules ineffective to bar review of underlying federal claims in federal habeas proceedings—absent a "knowing waiver" or a "deliberate bypass" of the right to so object—its effect was limited by *Francis*, which applied a different rule and barred a habeas challenge to the makeup of a grand jury. Petitioner Wainwright in this case urges that we further confine its effect by applying the principle enunciated in *Francis* to a claimed error in the admission of a defendant's confession.

* * *

[S]ince Brown v. Allen, it has been the rule that the federal habeas petitioner who claims he is detained pursuant to a final judgment of a state court in violation of the United State Constitution is entitled to have the federal habeas court make its own independent determination of his federal claim, without being bound by the determination on the merits of that claim reached in the state proceedings. This rule of Brown v. Allen is in no way changed by our holding today. Rather, we deal only with contentions of federal law which were *not* resolved on the merits in the state proceeding due to respondent's failure to raise them there as required by state procedure. We leave open for resolution in future decisions the precise definition of the "cause"-and-"prejudice" standard, and note here only that it is narrower than the standard set forth in dicta in Fay v. Noia, which would make federal habeas review generally available to state convicts absent a knowing and deliberate waiver of the federal constitutional contention. It is the sweeping language of Fay v. Noia, going far beyond the facts of the case eliciting it, which we today reject.[a]

The reasons for our rejection of it are several. The contemporaneous-objection rule itself is by no means peculiar to Florida, and deserves greater respect than *Fay* gives it, both for the fact that it is employed by a coordinate jurisdiction within the federal system and for the many interests which it serves in its own right. A contemporaneous objection enables the record to be made with respect to the constitutional claim when the recollections of witnesses are freshest, not years later in a federal habeas proceeding. It enables the judge who observed the demeanor of those witnesses to make the factual determinations necessary for properly deciding the federal constitutional question. * * *

A contemporaneous-objection rule may lead to the exclusion of the evidence objected to, thereby making a major contribution to finality in criminal litigation. Without the evidence claimed to be vulnerable on federal constitutional grounds, the jury may acquit the defendant, and that will be the end of the case; or it may nonetheless convict the defendant, and he will have one less federal constitutional claim to assert in his federal habeas petition. If the state trial judge admits the evidence in question after a full hearing, the federal habeas court pursuant to the 1966 amendment to § 2254 will gain significant guidance from the state ruling in this regard. Subtler considerations as well militate in favor of honoring a state contemporaneous-objection rule. An objection on the spot may force the prosecution to take a hard look at its hole card, and even if the prosecutor thinks that the state trial judge will admit the evidence he must contemplate the possibility of reversal by the state appellate courts or the ultimate issuance of a federal writ of habeas corpus based on the impropriety of the state court's rejection of the federal constitutional claim.

We think that the rule of Fay v. Noia, broadly stated, may encourage "sandbagging" on the part of defense lawyers, who may take their chances on a verdict of not guilty in a state trial court with the intent to raise their constitutional claims in a federal habeas court if their initial gamble does not pay off. The refusal of federal habeas courts to honor contemporaneous-objection rules may also make state courts themselves less stringent in their enforcement. Under the rule of Fay v. Noia, state appellate courts know that a federal constitutional issue raised for the first time in the proceeding before them may well be decided in any event by a federal *habeas* tribunal. Thus, their choice is between addressing the issue notwithstanding the petitioner's failure to timely object, or else face the prospect that the federal habeas court will decide the question without the benefit of their views.

The failure of the federal habeas courts generally to require compliance with a contemporaneous-objection rule tends to detract from the perception of the trial of a criminal case in state court as a decisive and portentous event. * * *

We believe that the adoption of the *Francis* rule in this situation will have the salutary effect of making the state

a. The Court in *Fay* stated its knowing-and-deliberate-waiver rule in language which applied not only to the waiver of the right to appeal, but to failures to raise individual substantive objections in the state trial. Then, with a single sentence in a footnote, the Court swept aside all decisions of this Court "to the extent that [they] may be read to suggest a standard of discretion in federal habeas corpus proceedings different from what we lay down today * * *." 372 U.S., at 439 n. 44. We do not choose to paint with a similarly broad brush here.

trial on the merits the "main event," so to speak, rather than a "tryout on the road" for what will later be the determinative federal habeas hearing. There is nothing in the Constitution or in the language of § 2254 which requires that the state trial on the issue of guilt or innocence be devoted largely to the testimony of fact witnesses directed to the elements of the state crime, while only later will there occur in a federal habeas hearing a full airing of the federal constitutional claims which were not raised in the state proceedings. If a criminal defendant thinks that an action of the state trial court is about to deprive him of a federal constitutional right there is every reason for his following state procedure in making known his objection.

The "cause"-and-"prejudice" exception of the *Francis* rule will afford an adequate guarantee, we think, that the rule will not prevent a federal habeas court from adjudicating for the first time the federal constitutional claim of a defendant who in the absence of such an adjudication will be the victim of a miscarriage of justice. Whatever precise content may be given those terms by later cases, we feel confident in holding without further elaboration that they do not exist here. Respondent has advanced no explanation whatever for his failure to object at trial, and, as the proceeding unfolded, the trial judge is certainly not to be faulted for failing to question the admission of the confession himself. The other evidence of guilt presented at trial, moreover, was substantial to a degree that would negate any possibility of actual prejudice resulting to the respondent from the admission of his inculpatory statement.

* * *

[The concurring opinion of CHIEF JUSTICE BURGER is omitted].

MR. JUSTICE STEVENS, concurring.

Although the Court's decision today may be read as a significant departure from the "deliberate bypass" standard, I am persuaded that the holding is consistent with the way other federal courts have actually been applying *Fay*. The notion that a client must always consent to a tactical decision not to assert a constitutional objection to a proffer of evidence has always seemed unrealistic to me. Conversely, if the constitutional issue is sufficiently grave, even an express waiver by the defendant himself may sometimes be excused.[b] Matters such as the competence of counsel, the procedural context in which the asserted waiver occurred, the character of the constitutional right at stake, and the overall fairness of the entire proceeding, may be more significant than the language of the test the Court purports to apply. I therefore believe the Court has wisely refrained from attempting to give precise content to its "cause" and "prejudice" exception to the rule of Francis v. Henderson, 425 U.S. 536.

* * *

[The opinion of JUSTICE WHITE, concurring in the judgment, is omitted].

MR. JUSTICE BRENNAN, with whom MR. JUSTICE MARSHALL joins, dissenting.

* * *

I believe that *Fay's* commitment to enforcing intentional but not inadvertent procedural defaults offers a realistic measure of protection for the habeas corpus petitioner seeking federal review of federal claims that were not litigated before the State. The threatened creation of a more "airtight system of for-

b. The test announced in *Fay* was not actually applied in that case. The Court held that habeas relief was available notwithstanding the client's participation in the waiver decision, and notwithstanding the fact that the decision was made on a tactical basis. The client apparently feared that the State might be able to convict him even without the use of his confession, and that he might be sentenced to death if reconvicted.

feitures" would effectively deprive habeas petitioners of the opportunity for litigating their constitutional claims before any forum and would disparage the paramount importance of constitutional rights in our system of government. Such a restriction of habeas corpus jurisdiction should be countenanced, I submit, only if it fairly can be concluded that *Fay's* focus on knowing and voluntary forfeitures unduly interferes with the legitimate interests of state courts or institutions. The majority offers no suggestion that actual experience has shown that *Fay's* bypass test can be criticized on this score. And, as I now hope to demonstrate, any such criticism would be unfounded.

III

A regime of federal habeas corpus jurisdiction that permits the reopening of state procedural defaults does not invalidate any state procedural rule as such;[c] Florida's courts remain entirely free to enforce their own rules as they choose, and to deny any and all state rights and remedies to a defendant who fails to comply with applicable state procedure. The relevant inquiry is whether more is required—specifically, whether the fulfillment of important interests of the State necessitates that federal courts be called upon to impose additional sanctions for inadvertent noncompliance with state procedural requirements such as the contemporaneous-objection rule involved here.

Florida, of course, can point to a variety of legitimate interests in seeking allegiance to its reasonable procedural requirements, the contemporaneous-objection rule included. As *Fay* recognized, a trial, like any organized activity, must conform to coherent process, and "there must be sanctions for the flouting of such procedure." The strict enforcement of procedural defaults, therefore, may be seen as a means of deterring any tendency on the part of the defense to slight the state forum, to deny state judges their due opportunity for playing a meaningful role in the evolving task of constitutional adjudication, or to mock the needed finality of criminal trials. All of these interests are referred to by the Court in various forms.

The question remains, however, whether any of these policies or interests are efficiently and fairly served by enforcing both intentional and inadvertent defaults pursuant to the identical stringent standard. I remain convinced that when one pierces the surface justifications for a harsher rule posited by the Court, no standard stricter than *Fay's* deliberate-bypass test is realistically defensible.

Punishing a lawyer's unintentional errors by closing the federal courthouse door to his client is both a senseless and misdirected method of deterring the slighting of state rules. It is senseless because unplanned and unintentional action of any kind generally is not subject to deterrence; and, to the extent that it is hoped that a threatened sanction addressed to the defense will induce greater care and caution on the part of trial lawyers, thereby forestalling negligent conduct or error, the potential loss of all valuable state remedies would be sufficient to this end. And it

c. This is not to suggest that the availability of collateral review has no bearing on the States' selection and enforcement of procedural requirements. On the contrary, to the extent that a State desires to have input into the process of developing federal law, and seeks to guarantee its primary factfinding role as authorized by § 2254 and Townsend v. Sain, 372 U.S. 293 (1963), the existence of broad federal habeas power will tend to encourage the liberalizing and streamlining of state rules that otherwise might serve to bar such state participation. From every perspective, I would suppose that any such effect of *Fay* would be considered a salutary one, see, e.g., Shapiro, Federal Habeas Corpus: A Study in Massachusetts, 87 Harv.L.Rev. 321, 348 (1973), although the Court implies the contrary.

is a misdirected sanction because even if the penalization of incompetence or carelessness will encourage more thorough legal training and trial preparation, the habeas applicant, as opposed to his lawyer, hardly is the proper recipient of such a penalty. Especially with fundamental constitutional rights at stake, no fictional relationship of principal-agent or the like can justify holding the criminal defendant accountable for the naked errors of his attorney. This is especially true when so many indigent defendants are without any realistic choice in selecting who ultimately represents them at trial. * * *

Hence, while I can well agree that the proper functioning of our system of criminal justice, both federal and state, necessarily places heavy reliance on the professionalism and judgment of trial attorneys, I cannot accept a system that ascribes the absolute forfeiture of an individual's constitutional claims to situations where his lawyer manifestly exercises *no* professional judgment at all—where carelessness, mistake, or ignorance is the explanation for a procedural default. Of course, it is regrettable that certain errors that might have been cured earlier had trial counsel acted expeditiously must be corrected collaterally and belatedly. I can understand the Court's wistfully wishing for the day when the trial was the sole, binding and final "event" of the adversarial process—although I hesitate to agree that in the eyes of the criminal defendant it has ever ceased being the "main" one. But it should be plain that in the real world, the interest in finality is repeatedly compromised in numerous ways that arise with far greater frequency than do procedural defaults. The federal criminal system, to take one example, expressly disapproves of interlocutory review in the generality of cases even though such a policy would foster finality by permitting the authoritative resolution of all legal and constitutional issues prior to the convening of the "main event." Instead, it relies on the belated correction of error, through appeal and collateral review, to ensure the fairness and legitimacy of the criminal sanction. Indeed, the very existence of the well-established right collaterally to reopen issues previously litigated before the state courts, represents a congressional policy choice that is inconsistent with notions of strict finality—and probably more so than authorizing the litigation of issues that, due to inadvertence, were never addressed to any court. Ultimately, all of these limitations on the finality of criminal convictions emerge from the tension between justice and efficiency in a judicial system that hopes to remain true to its principles and ideals. Reasonable people may disagree on how best to resolve these tensions. But the solution that today's decision risks embracing seems to be the most unfair of all: the denial of any judicial consideration of the constitutional claims of a criminal defendant because of errors made by his attorney which lie outside the power of the habeas petitioner to prevent or deter and for which, under no view of morality or ethics, can he be held responsible.

* * *

Note

The Court finally overruled Fay v. Noia and its deliberate bypass standard in Coleman v. Thompson, 111 S.Ct. 2546 (1991). Cases such as *Sykes* had limited *Fay* to its facts, so that the deliberate bypass standard essentially applied only when a state prisoner defaulted his entire appeal. That was the situation in *Coleman,* where the prisoner, by filing a late notice of appeal, defaulted his entire state post-conviction appeal. Justice O'Connor, writing for six members of the Court, recognized that the error in filing a late notice was "inadvertent" and the State admitted that Coleman had not deliberately bypassed his state post-conviction remedy. The Court nonetheless held that Coleman's habeas petition was barred in the absence of cause and prejudice. Justice O'Connor reasoned that the cause and prejudice standard was more compatible with interests of comity and finality than the deliberate bypass standard. She concluded as follows:

> In all cases in which a state prisoner has defaulted his federal claims in state court pursuant to an independent and adequate state procedural rule, federal habeas review of the claims is barred unless the prisoner can demonstrate cause for the default and actual prejudice as a result of the alleged violation of federal law, or demonstrate that failure to consider the claims will result in a fundamental miscarriage of justice. *Fay* was based on a conception of federal/state relations that undervalued the importance of state procedural rules. The several cases after *Fay* that applied the cause and prejudice standard to a variety of state procedural defaults represent a different view. We now recognize the important interest in finality served by state procedural rules, and the significant harm to the States that results from the failure of federal courts to respect them.

Justices Blackmun, Stevens and Marshall dissented.

United States v. Frady, 456 U.S. 152 (1982), holds that on collateral attack under § 2255 a petitioner convicted in federal court may not rely on the "plain error" doctrine of Fed.R.Crim.P. 52(b) to challenge an error as to which there was a procedural default. Frady, convicted of a vicious killing in 1963, moved to vacate his sentence on the ground that the jury instructions erroneously equated intent with malice and told the jury that the law presumes malice from the use of weapon. For the majority, Justice O'Connor wrote that the plain error standard, which "was intended to afford a means for the prompt redress of miscarriages of justice," "is out of place when a prisoner launches a collateral attack against a criminal conviction after society's legitimate interest in the finality of the judgment has been perfected by the expiration of the time allowed for direct review or by the affirmance of the conviction on appeal." To prevail, Frady would have had to show cause and prejudice under Wainwright v. Sykes. The majority found, without reaching the question of cause, that he could not show prejudice. The Court noted that Frady had admitted the killing for which he had been convicted. Justice O'Connor stated that prejudice does not follow simply from the fact that a jury instruction was erroneous. Rather, prejudice must be evaluated by the effect of the error in the context of the whole trial. She concluded that a petitioner must show that errors at the trial "worked to his *actual* and substantial disadvantage, infecting his entire trial with error of constitutional dimensions." Frady had failed to contradict strong evidence in the record that he had acted with malice, and therefore the instruction was not prejudicial. Justice Stevens concurred. Justice Blackmun concurred in the judgment, stating that "the cause and prejudice standard should not be a barrier to relief when the plain error exception to the federal contemporaneous objection requirement is applicable." He observed that some states permit exceptions from their contemporaneous objection rules so that the majority's approach to federal cases effectively denied federal prisoners the opportunity to raise claims that state prisoners might be able to raise. Justice Brennan dissented and argued that the Court obscured the distinction between § 2254, a civil proceeding, and § 2255, a part of a criminal case. Justices Blackmun and Brennan both appeared to agree that federalism concerns were not present in a § 2255 proceeding. Chief Justice Burger and Justice Marshall did not participate in the case. See also United States v. Shaid, 937 F.2d 228 (5th Cir.

1991) (en banc), where the court, citing *Frady,* held that the cause and prejudice standard is "designed to be significantly more difficult than the plain error test that we employ on direct appeal." The court concluded that "Shaid's argument that the jury may have misinterpreted the trial court's instruction on *mens rea* * * * suggests only the *possibility* that he was prejudiced by the erroneous instruction. Shaid has not challenged the sufficiency of the *mens rea* evidence at his trial, and he has not presented new evidence indicating his actual innocence." After *Frady,* is a procedural bar lifted only for those who can establish their actual innocence?

c. *The Meaning of "Cause"*

One of the Court's first attempts to explain the cause and prejudice standard of Wainwright v. Sykes is Engle v. Isaac, 456 U.S. 107 (1982), where the Court held that three habeas corpus petitioners, who had failed to comply with an Ohio rule mandating contemporaneous objections to jury instructions, could not collaterally challenge those instructions in federal court. The petitioners contended that Ohio had impermissibly shifted the burden of persuasion on self-defense issues to them, but none had objected to the trial court's instructions. Justice O'Connor observed for the majority that "[c]ollateral review of a conviction extends the ordeal of trial for both society and the accused," that "liberal allowance of the writ * * * degrades the prominence of the trial itself," and that "writs of habeas corpus frequently cost society the right to punish admitted offenders" as a result of "passage of time, erosion of memory and dispersion of witnesses." The majority declined to "limit *Sykes* to cases in which the constitutional error did not affect the truth-finding function of the trial"—e.g., a *Miranda* violation as in *Sykes.* The Court reasoned that the costs of habeas corpus do not depend upon the type of claim raised and that "[w]hile the nature of a constitutional claim may affect the calculation of cause and actual prejudice, it does not alter the need to make that threshold showing." Without reaching the question of prejudice, the Court found that the basis of petitioners' constitutional claim was apparent since In re Winship, decided before the petitioners were tried. Justice O'Connor rejected the argument that an objection to the instruction would have been futile, despite *Winship,* because Ohio courts had long required defendants to prove self-defense. She stated that "[e]ven a state court that has previously rejected a constitutional argument may decide, upon reflection, that the contention is valid." She noted that *Winship* had been relied on by some lawyers making similar claims at that time, even before Mullaney v. Wilbur (discussed in Chapter Ten) had specifically applied the *Winship* analysis to affirmative defenses. Thus, it could not be said that the petitioners had "lacked the tools to construct" an argument based on *Winship.* Justice O'Connor recognized that not "every astute counsel" would have made a constitutional objection in these circumstances. However, she concluded that the Constitution "does not insure that defense counsel will recognize and raise every constitutional claim." Justice Blackmun concurred in the result without opinion, and Justice Stevens concurred in part and dissented in part in a brief opinion. Justice Brennan, joined by Justice Marshall, dissented. He declined to "blame the 'offender' for the logistical and temporal difficulties arising from retrial: If the writ of habeas corpus has been granted, then it is at least as reasonable to blame the State for having prosecuted the first trial 'in violation of the Constitution or laws of the United States' * * *."

The Court examined "cause" again in Reed v. Ross, 468 U.S. 1 (1984). Ross was convicted of first-degree murder in 1969, prior to the Supreme Court's holding in *Winship* that the due process clause requires the state to prove beyond a reasonable doubt all of the elements necessary to constitute the crime with which a defendant is charged. Jury instructions had imposed upon Ross the burden of showing that he lacked malice and that he acted in self-defense. Ross did not contemporaneously object to the instructions, since state law did not require an objection. His appeal did not challenge the instructions either, and it was his failure to raise any objection on direct appeal that led the state courts to rule that he could not pursue a challenge to his convictions on collateral attack. Ross then sought federal habeas corpus relief.

The Supreme Court held, 5–4, in an opinion by Justice Brennan, that the court of appeals correctly found that Ross had shown sufficient cause for his failure to challenge the instructions on appeal to justify proceeding in federal court by way of habeas corpus. The Court observed the strong state interest in the integrity of its rules and procedures and in the finality of its judgments. It stated that "[i]n general, * * * defense counsel may not make a tactical decision to forgo a procedural opportunity—for instance, an opportunity to object at trial or to raise an issue on appeal—and then, when he discovers that the tactic has been unsuccessful, pursue an alternative strategy in federal court. The encouragement of such conduct by a federal court on habeas corpus review would not only offend generally accepted principles of comity, but would also undermine the accuracy and efficiency of the state judicial systems to the detriment of all concerned."

But the Court also noted that "[c]ounsel's failure to raise a claim for which there was no reasonable basis in existing law does not seriously implicate any of the concerns that might otherwise require deference to a State's procedural bar" and that "if we were to hold that the novelty of a constitutional question does not give rise to cause for counsel's failure to raise it, we might actually disrupt state-court proceedings by encouraging defense counsel to include any and all remotely plausible constitutional claims that could, some day, gain recognition." And it held, therefore, "that where a constitutional claim is so novel that its legal basis is not reasonably available to counsel, a defendant has cause for his failure to raise the claim in accordance with applicable state procedures." He concluded as follows:

> Whether an attorney had a reasonable basis for pressing a claim challenging a practice that this Court has arguably sanctioned depends on how direct this Court's sanction of the prevailing practice had been, how well entrenched the practice was in the relevant jurisdiction at the time of defense counsel's failure to challenge it, and how strong the available support is from sources opposing the prevailing practice.

The Court looked to the law as it existed prior to *Winship* and found only scant, indirect support for the challenge that Ross mounted in his habeas corpus petition. So while Ross' claim of error was similar to that of petitioners in *Engle,* those petitioners had the benefit of *Winship* in constructing their arguments at trial, while Ross did not. Therefore, Ross had cause for his procedural fault while the petitioners in *Engle* did not.[29]

Justice Rehnquist dissented, joined by the Chief Justice and Justices Blackmun and O'Connor. He reasoned as follows:

> [T]his equating of novelty with cause pushes the Court into a conundrum which it refuses to recognize. The more "novel" a claimed constitutional right, the more unlikely a violation of that claimed right undercut the fundamental fairness of the trial. To untie this knot in logic, the Court proposes a definition of novelty that makes a claim novel if the legal basis for asserting the claim is not reasonably available. This standard, of course, has no meaningful content independent of the factual setting in which it is applied. The Court's attempt to give content to this novelty standard, however, is simply too facile; under its application, virtually any new constitutional claim can be deemed "novel."

Ross holds that if a later rule could not have been reasonably anticipated by the petitioner, then there is cause for not invoking the rule in the state proceedings. But can the petitioner then rely on the rule in habeas proceedings to show a violation of the constitution? Recall the discussion of nonretroactivity of new rules on habeas, and particularly Teague v. Lane, in Chapter One. Under *Teague,* new rules are inapplicable to habeas cases, unless they are (1) landmark, "watershed" rules of criminal procedure such as the Court never expects to see again, or (2) rules which indicate that the defendant should not have been tried or sentenced in the first place. A new rule is defined as any rule as to which reasonable minds could have differed before it was adopted. How can the petitioner establish cause and yet have the rule apply retroactively to him? The "whipsaw" effect of *Ross* and *Teague* is described by Professor Arkin in The Prisoner's Dilemma: Life in the Lower Federal Courts After Teague v. Lane, 69 No.Car.L.Rev. 371, 408 (1991):

> [I]f a petitioner is able to show that his claim is based on a 'new' rule of law, the habeas court will excuse his state procedural default, assuming petitioner can show actual prejudice. But, having shown that the rule under which he seeks relief was not available to him at the time he should have raised it in the state courts, the petitioner may well have won the battle under *Wainwright* only to lose the war to *Teague.* Under most circumstances, the petitioner will have just shown that the very rule under which he seeks relief is not retroactive unless he can fit it into one of the two [extremely limited] *Teague* exceptions.

See also Hopkinson v. Shillinger, 888 F.2d 1286 (10th Cir.1989) ("a holding that a claim is so novel that there is no reasonably available basis for it, thus establishing cause, must also mean that the claim was too novel to be dictated by past precedent"). The reverse situation can also occur. If the rule could have been anticipated and therefore is not "new" under *Teague,* there will by definition be no cause for the failure to assert it in state proceedings. Fierro v. Lynaugh, 879 F.2d 1276 (5th Cir.1989).

29. Compare Dugger v. Adams, 489 U.S. 401 (1989), where a defendant who did not object to an instruction by the trial judge in a capital case, which explained to the jury that the court was responsible for sentencing, could not show cause for failing to challenge the instruction in a timely manner. Although the federal case on which Adams relied (Caldwell v. Mississippi, discussed in Chapter Eleven) was not decided at that time, the defendant had available a claim that the instruction misdescribed state law, and this claim was a necessary element of a *Caldwell* federal attack.

However, the *Ross* standard can still have utility where the failure to assert a claim is due to a lack of *facts* that were not reasonably available to the defendant at the time of the state proceedings. A unanimous Supreme Court held in Amadeo v. Zant, 486 U.S. 214 (1988), that a state defendant who was convicted of murder and sentenced to death showed cause for a late challenge to the racial composition of the grand jury by demonstrating that local officials had concealed a handwritten memorandum from the District Attorney to jury commissioners which indicated that underrepresentation of black members of the grand jury was intentional. The memorandum was discovered by a lawyer for the plaintiffs in a civil suit challenging voting procedures and was the basis for a federal district court's finding of intentional discrimination. The defendant's lawyer relied upon the finding on the defendant's direct appeal, but the state supreme court found that the challenge to the grand jury's composition came too late. The defendant obtained habeas corpus relief from a federal district judge, only to have a divided appellate panel reverse.

Justice Marshall wrote for the Court as it held that the federal district court's findings that there had been discrimination in the selection of the grand jury and that the defendant had raised the discrimination claim as soon as the memorandum surfaced were not clearly erroneous. Although the court of appeals had reasoned that the defendant was a white man with a history of assaulting black people and would not have been eager to have more black grand jury members, the court stated that there was significant evidence to support both the district judge and the court of appeals, and that the factfinder's choice between two permissible views of the evidence cannot be clearly erroneous.

In articulating the meaning of "cause," the Court cited *Ross* and reasoned as follows:

> If the District Attorney's memorandum was not reasonably discoverable because it was concealed by Putnam County officials, and if that concealment, rather than tactical considerations, was the reason for the failure of petitioner's lawyers to raise the jury challenge in the trial court, then petitioner established cause to excuse his procedural default under this Court's precedents.

In Murray v. Carrier, 477 U.S. 478 (1986), Justice O'Connor wrote for the Court as it held that a federal habeas petitioner cannot show cause for a procedural default by establishing that competent defense counsel's failure to raise a substantive claim of error was inadvertent rather than deliberate. In a rape and abduction case, the defendant's trial counsel had twice unsuccessfully requested an opportunity to review the victim's statements. On appeal, counsel failed to attack the trial judge's rulings in his petition for appeal, despite a state court rule limiting judicial consideration on appeal to errors raised in the petition. The Court held that this failure barred federal habeas corpus review even if it resulted from ignorance or inadvertence. It declined to distinguish failures to raise a claim on appeal from failures to raise them at trial. Justice O'Connor wrote that "we discern no inequity in requiring [the defendant] to bear the risk of attorney error that results in a procedural default" by "counsel whose performance is not constitutionally ineffective." To establish cause for a procedural default, a prisoner must ordinarily "show that some objective factor external to the defense impeded counsel's efforts to comply with the State's procedural rule." Justice O'Connor elaborated as follows:

> Without attempting an exhaustive catalog * * *, we note that a showing that the factual or legal claim was not reasonably available to counsel * * *, or that some interference by officials, Brown v. Allen, * * *, made compliance impracticable, would constitute cause under this standard.
>
> Similarly, if the procedural default is the result of ineffective assistance of counsel, the Sixth Amendment itself requires that responsibility for the default be imputed to the State [and it is therefore] cause for a procedural default. However, we think that the exhaustion doctrine * * * generally requires that a claim of ineffective assistance be presented to the state courts as an independent claim before it may be used to establish cause for a procedural default.

Justice Stevens, joined by Justice Blackmun, concurred in the judgment. He argued that the cause and prejudice formula "is not dispositive when the fundamental fairness of a prisoner's conviction is at issue" and advocated an "overall inquiry into justice." Justice O'Connor responded that the Stevens approach would actually replace the showing of cause requirement with a manifest injustice standard. She observed that the relationship of this standard to prejudice was uncertain. But in recognition of the fact that the cause and prejudice standard might produce a miscarriage of justice in some cases, Justice O'Connor provided that "in an extraordinary case, where a constitutional violation has probably resulted in the conviction of one who is actually innocent, a federal habeas corpus court may grant the writ even in the absence of a showing of cause for the procedural default." Thus, the Court remanded for an inquiry into whether the victim's statements contained material that would establish the defendant's innocence.

Justice Brennan, joined by Justice Marshall, dissented and argued that the cause and prejudice limitation, a judicial form of abstention not required by the language of the habeas corpus statute, should permit federal consideration of claims not raised because of inadvertence or ignorance. He found no deterrent efficacy in the use of the limitation in situations in which lawyers are not consciously deciding whether or not to raise a claim.

Decided with Murray v. Carrier was Smith v. Murray, 477 U.S. 527 (1986), a capital case. Once again Justice O'Connor found no cause for a procedural default. A psychiatrist who examined the defendant was called to testify by the state at the sentencing phase of the trial. He described, over the defendant's objection, an incident that the defendant had related to him. On appeal, the defendant's counsel did not challenge the testimony. In his habeas corpus petition, the defendant claimed that the use of the statements violated his constitutional rights under the Fifth and Sixth Amendments. Justice O'Connor found that a deliberate decision had been made not to put the claim before the state supreme court and that, even if the decision was made out of ignorance of the claim's strength, this was not sufficient to demonstrate cause. She also concluded that the application of the cause and prejudice standard would not result in a fundamental miscarriage of justice, since "the alleged constitutional error neither precluded the development of true facts nor resulted in the admission of false ones." The Court assumed that if the trial court had properly suppressed Smith's statements, the sentencing body probably would have imposed life imprisonment rather than the death penalty. The Court nonetheless held that Smith's claim was unrelated to *actual* innocence because the sentencing body in *Smith* would still have remained free, even if the trial court had excluded Smith's statements, to impose the death penalty.

Justice Stevens dissented, joined in full by Justices Marshall and Blackmun, and in part by Justice Brennan. He disagreed with the idea that only a claim implicating "actual innocence" could rise to the level of a miscarriage of justice, and argued that accuracy is not the only value protected by the Constitution.

The "actual innocence" exception set forth in *Carrier* and *Smith* was described and applied by the court in Johnson v. Singletary, 940 F.2d 1540 (11th Cir.1991) (en banc):

> [A]lthough factual inaccuracy in the guilt or sentencing context may well be *necessary* to a claim of actual innocence, factual inaccuracy is not *sufficient* unless the inaccuracy demonstrates, at least colorably, that the petitioner is * * * ineligible for either an adjudication of guilt or the sentence imposed. If prejudicial factual inaccuracy alone is enough to warrant review of a defaulted claim, then the actual innocence standard is meaningless.

In *Johnson,* the jury gave an advisory sentence of life imprisonment, but the trial judge (who has this power in Florida) sentenced Johnson to death. The judge found four aggravating factors, any of which were sufficient to qualify Johnson for the death penalty. The judge also relied on a psychological evaluation; but that evaluation was flawed by defense counsel's failure to inquire about Johnson's long history of drug abuse. The psychiatrist who conducted the evaluation later filed an affidavit stating that he would have testified in Johnson's favor if he had known about the drug abuse. The habeas court recognized that the trial judge, faced with a favorable report, and an advisory sentence for life imprisonment, would probably have imposed life imprisonment. But that did not trigger the actual innocence exception of *Carrier* and *Smith.* The court held that Johnson was required to show that absent the alleged constitutional error, he would have been "*ineligible* for the death penalty." This he could not do, since even with a favorable psychological report, at least one of the aggravating factors could still have been found. The Fifth Circuit took a similar approach to the actual innocence standard in Sawyer v. Whitley, 945 F.2d 812 (5th Cir.1991), holding that while the constitutional error would probably have resulted in a life sentence rather than a death penalty, this was not enough to lift the procedural bar: the actual innocence standard requires that if not for the constitutional error, the defendant would have been ineligible for the death penalty (or a guilty verdict, where the error occurs during the trial). Other circuits have stated that a procedural bar is lifted, despite absence of cause, when the constitutional error "probably" resulted in a guilty verdict or a death penalty that otherwise would not have been rendered. See Stokes v. Armontrout, 893 F.2d 152 (8th Cir.1989). The Supreme Court has granted certiorari in Sawyer v. Whitley, 112 S.Ct. 434 (1991), to resolve the conflict concerning the scope of the "actual innocence" exception.

Seidman, Factual Guilt and the Burger Court: An Examination of Continuity and Change in Criminal Procedure, 80 Colum.L.Rev. 436, 469 (1980), argues that

> the *Wainwright* Court's reluctance to look behind the presumption [of lawyer client identity] and its willingness to enforce procedural forfeitures undermine the reliability of our declarations of criminal responsibility in two ways: they mean that factually innocent defendants will nonetheless be punished because

of procedural defaults, and they mean that defendants not even responsible for the procedural defaults will be punished because of the misconduct of their attorney.

Murray v. Carrier held that constitutionally ineffective assistance of counsel would establish the "cause" necessary to excuse a procedural default. In Coleman v. Thompson, 111 S.Ct. 2546 (1991), the state prisoner's counsel failed to file a timely notice of appeal from the state trial court's denial of post-conviction relief. Coleman argued that his counsel's failure constituted ineffective assistance and lifted the procedural bar. Justice O'Connor, writing for the Court, rejected this argument. She relied on Pennsylvania v. Finley (discussed in Chapter Ten), which held that the defendant has no right to counsel in post-conviction proceedings, and reasoned that since Coleman had no constitutional right to counsel in the state habeas proceedings, there could be no claim of constitutionally ineffective counsel. She concluded that "Coleman must bear the risk of attorney error that results in a procedural default."

Justice O'Connor also rejected the argument that cause to excuse a procedural default should be found whenever counsel was so ineffective as to violate the standards of Strickland v. Washington (discussed in Chapter Ten), even though no Sixth Amendment claim is possible because the ineffectiveness did not occur in the trial or on a first appeal. She stated that this argument "is inconsistent not only with the language of *Carrier,* but the logic of that opinion as well." She reasoned that "cause" must be something "external to the petitioner, something that cannot be fairly attributed to him." She asserted that the only type of attorney error for which the State must take responsibility independent of the petitioner is where the Sixth Amendment has been violated. She explained as follows:

> Where a petitioner defaults a claim as a result of the denial of the right to effective assistance of counsel, the State, which is responsible for the denial as a constitutional matter, must bear the cost of any resulting default and the harm to state interests that federal habeas review entails. A different allocation of costs is appropriate in those circumstances where the State has no responsibility to ensure that the petitioner was represented by competent counsel. As between the State and the petitioner, it is the petitioner who must bear the burden of a failure to follow state procedural rules.

Justice Blackmun, joined by Justices Marshall and Stevens in dissent, attacked the majority's holding as "patently unfair." He argued that to permit a procedural default to preclude habeas review, when it was caused by attorney error egregious enough to constitute ineffective assistance of counsel, "in no way serves the State's interest in preserving the integrity of its rules and proceedings."

Note that the procedural bar in *Coleman* was the failure to file a notice of appeal from the state habeas trial court. Under the exhaustion doctrine, Coleman was not even required to bring his claims to the state habeas court (other than his claim of ineffective assistance of counsel at trial, which under state law could not be brought on direct appeal). See Castille v. Peoples, supra. Does it make sense that Coleman should be precluded from federal habeas review by a procedural bar imposed in a state proceeding that Coleman was not required to pursue as to most of his claims? What state interest is vindicated by the application of a procedural bar in a case such as *Coleman*?

4. *Adequate and Independent State Grounds*

If the state decision rests on an adequate and independent state ground, a federal court on habeas may not resolve federal issues asserted by the petitioner. The Supreme Court has stated that "in the habeas context, the application of the independent and adequate state ground doctrine is grounded in concerns of comity and federalism" and that without this doctrine "habeas petitioners would be able to avoid the exhaustion requirement by defaulting their federal claims in state court." Coleman v. Thompson, 111 S.Ct. 2546 (1991). A valid procedural bar is an adequate state ground, so long as the state courts rely on it and rest their decision on it. Id.

The Court has recognized, however, that whether a state court has in fact relied on an adequate and independent state ground is not an easy question. In another context—to determine whether a state court rested on state or federal grounds when it held that a defendant's constitutional rights had been violated—the Court established the following conclusive presumption:

> When a state court decision fairly appears to rest primarily on federal law, or to be interwoven with federal law, and when the adequacy and independence of any possible state law ground is not clear from the face of the opinion, we will accept as the most reasonable explanation that the state court decided the case the way it did because it believed that federal law required it to do so.

Michigan v. Long, 463 U.S. 1032, 1041–1042 (1983).

In Harris v. Reed, 489 U.S. 255 (1989), the Court applied the *Long* presumption to determine whether a state court's decision rested on adequate and independent state grounds so as to deny federal habeas review. The Court reasoned that since it was "faced with a common problem," it would "adopt a common solution."

The question in Coleman v. Thompson, 111 S.Ct. 2546 (1991) was whether an adequate and independent state ground could be found in a state appellate court's summary order of dismissal. Coleman brought a state habeas proceeding alleging various federal constitutional errors. The trial court denied relief. Coleman's notice of appeal to the Virginia Supreme Court from the trial court's decision was untimely under Virginia law. The Commonwealth moved to dismiss the appeal on the sole ground that it was untimely. The Virginia Supreme Court delayed ruling on the motion to dismiss, and consequently briefs on both the motion and the merits were filed. Six months later, stating that it had considered all the briefs, the Virginia Supreme Court summarily granted the motion to dismiss the appeal and dismissed the petition for appeal.

Justice O'Connor, writing for the Court, began her opinion with a preamble:

> This is a case about federalism. It concerns the respect that federal courts owe the States and the States' procedural rules when reviewing the claims of state prisoners in federal habeas corpus.

Justice O'Connor found that the summary order rested on the adequate and independent state ground, i.e. the state law allowing dismissal of an appeal which was untimely filed. She rejected, for two reasons, Coleman's argument that the state court should be required to explicitly state that it is relying on an independent state ground. First, she asserted that an absolute requirement of an explicit statement misreads *Long* which requires an explicit statement only upon a predicate finding that the state decision "must fairly appear to rest primarily on federal law or to be interwoven with federal law." Second, the proposal for a per se plain statement rule would "greatly and unacceptably expand the risk" that federal habeas courts would review state decisions that were in fact based on adequate and independent state grounds. Justice O'Connor explained that where it does not fairly appear that the state court decision is based primarily on federal grounds, "it is simply not true that the most reasonable explanation is that the state judgment rested on federal grounds," and that a conclusive presumption to that effect "is simply not worth the cost in the loss of respect for the State that such a rule would entail." She concluded that "we will not impose on state courts the responsibility for using particular language in every case in which a state prisoner presents a federal claim * * * in order that federal courts might not be bothered with reviewing state law and the record in the case." Rather, federal courts would have to consider the nature of the disposition and the surrounding circumstances of the order to determine whether the state court relied on an adequate state ground.

On the facts, the Court found that the Virginia Supreme Court's summary order did not "fairly appear" to rest on or to be interwoven with federal law. Justice O'Connor noted that the summary order granted the Commonwealth's motion to dismiss, which was based solely upon Coleman's failure to meet the time requirements for a notice of appeal. Federal law was not mentioned in the order. She recognized that the Virginia Supreme Court's explicit consideration of briefs discussing the merits "adds some ambiguity," but concluded that this did not override the "explicit grant of a dismissal motion based solely on procedural grounds." Compare Brown v. Collins, 937 F.2d 175 (5th Cir.1991) (state court fairly addressed federal constitutional claims where the government claimed a procedural bar, and the state court specifically noted that it "considered the petition" of the defendant alleging constitutional error).

If the State makes application of a procedural bar dependent on an antecedent ruling of federal law, the state rule is not an independent ground so as to preclude direct review. Ake v. Oklahoma, 470 U.S. 68 (1985). Coleman argued that the Virginia Supreme Court applied its procedural bar in his case only after determining that doing so would not abridge one of his federal rights. Justice O'Connor responded to this argument by stating that the Court would not decide whether the principle set forth in *Ake,* a direct review case, would apply to the determination of independent grounds in federal habeas. Assuming the principle did apply, the Court found nothing in Virginia Supreme Court jurisprudence to indicate that that court passed on the merits before determining whether to apply a procedural bar.

Justice White wrote a concurring opinion, emphasizing that he was not convinced that the Virginia Supreme Court followed a practice of waiving a procedural bar when constitutional issues are at stake.

Justice Blackmun, joined by Justices Marshall and Stevens, filed a lengthy dissent, criticizing the Court's "crusade to erect petty procedural barriers in the path of any state prisoner seeking review of his federal constitutional claims." He argued that the Court "is creating a Byzantine morass of arbitrary, unnecessary and unjustifiable impediments to the vindication of federal rights" and "subordinates fundamental constitutional rights to mere utilitarian interests." He asserted that the majority had "lost sight of the animating principles of federalism," and added:

> Federalism * * * has no normative value: it does not, as the majority appears to assume, blindly protect the interests of States from any incursion by the federal courts. Rather, federalism secures to citizens the liberties that derive from the diffusion of sovereign power. * * * In this context, it cannot lightly be assumed that the interests of federalism are fostered by a rule that impedes federal review of federal constitutional claims.

Justice Blackmun argued that states should be required to make a plain statement of reliance on state law in order to establish an independent state ground precluding habeas review. He asserted that "the plain-statement rule provides a simple mechanism by which a state court may invoke the discretionary deference of the federal court and virtually insulate its judgment from federal review." He contended that the majority's approach of looking to the nature of the disposition and the circumstances surrounding a summary order was "inherently indeterminate" and that the plain statement rule "effectively and equitably eliminates this unacceptable uncertainty."

After *Coleman,* is there anything left of the Harris v. Reed "plain statement" rule? Consider the views of Judge Williams, concurring in Young v. Herring, 938 F.2d 543 (5th Cir.1991) (en banc).

> [The plain statement] requirement is to be applied narrowly—only in those cases where the state court considers both the procedural bar and explicitly the federal constitutional issue on the merits. The fact that the [state] court is fully aware of the presence of the federal constitutional issue is not enough even though the court does not clearly and expressly rely upon the procedural bar.

In Ylst v. Nunnemaker, 111 S.Ct. 2590 (1991), the California Supreme Court denied without explanation Nunnemaker's state petition for habeas corpus. Twelve years earlier, the California Court of Appeal had affirmed Nunnemaker's conviction, rejecting his constitutional claims solely and explicitly on the ground of failure to object at trial. Nunnemaker's petition for state habeas to the California Supreme Court specifically addressed both procedural and constitutional issues. Justice Scalia, writing for a six-person majority, held that the California Supreme Court's unexplained denial of Nunnemaker's habeas petition was based on the independent and adequate state ground of procedural default. Justice Scalia noted that "procedural bars are not immortal" and that "if the last state court to be presented with a particular federal claim reaches the merits, it removes any bar to federal court review that might otherwise have been available." He recognized that it is often difficult to determine whether the later court lifted the procedural bar or instead rested on the independent state ground. Justice Scalia stated that the process used in *Coleman* of determining the nature of the disposition and the circumstances surrounding the unexplained order could not be used in every case, since "such clues will not always, or even ordinarily, be available." He noted that "many formulary orders are not meant to convey anything as to the reason for the decision" and that attributing a reason in these circumstances was "difficult and artificial." He stated the rule to guide such circumstances as follows:

> We think that the attribution necessary for federal habeas purposes can be facilitated, and sound results more often assured, by applying the following presumption: where there has been one reasoned state judgment rejecting a federal claim, later unexplained orders upholding that judgment or rejecting the same claim rest upon the same ground. * * * The maxim is that silence implies consent, not the opposite. * * * The essence of unexplained orders is that they say nothing. We think that a presumption which gives them no effect—which simply "looks through" them to the last reasoned decision—most nearly reflects the role that they are ordinarily intended to play.

Justice Scalia emphasized that the presumption of acceptance derived from "looking through" silent orders was rebuttable. He gave as an example a situation where the last reasoned state court decision relied on a procedural default, but a retroactive change in law eliminated that ground as a basis for decision, and the reviewing court directed briefing on the merits.

Applying the "looking through" analysis to the facts of *Nunnemaker,* the Court looked through the California Supreme Court's unexplained denial of habeas to the last reasoned state court decision, that of the California Court of Appeal twelve years earlier. Since that decision had expressly relied on the independent state ground of procedural default, the California Supreme Court's unexplained order was deemed to have done so as well.

Justice Blackmun, joined by Justices Stevens and Marshall, dissented. Justice Blackmun argued that the process of "looking through" silent orders would complicate the efforts of state courts to understand and accommodate the Court's federal habeas jurisprudence. He pointed out that "a state court that does not intend to rely on a procedural default but wishes to deny a meritless petition in a summary order must now remember that its unexplained order will be ignored by the federal habeas court. Thus, the state court must review the procedural history of the petitioner's claim and determine which state court judgment a federal habeas court is likely to recognize" as the last reasoned decision. Justice Blackmun concluded that he saw "no benefit in abandoning a clear rule to create chaos."

Coleman and *Nunnemaker* were decided on the same day. After these cases, how does a habeas court, in evaluating a summary order, determine whether to consider the nature of the disposition and the surrounding circumstances, as set forth in *Coleman,* or whether to use the "looking through" process of *Nunnemaker?*

A state ground will not be deemed "adequate" if it is not regularly followed and firmly established in practice. See James v. Kentucky, 466 U.S. 431 (1984), where the defendant asked the judge to admonish the jury not to draw an inference from his failure to testify. The judge refused the request, and James appealed the refusal. The state supreme court held that a request for an admonition was not adequate to support a claim on appeal for a failure to give an instruction. But the U.S. Supreme Court stated that "for federal constitutional purposes, James adequately invoked his substantive right to jury guidance." The Court held that "Kentucky's distinction between admonitions and instructions is not the sort of firmly established and regularly followed state practice that can prevent implementation of federal constitutional rights." In Ford v. Georgia, 111 S.Ct. 850 (1991), a unanimous Supreme Court held that a state procedural rule could not be retroactively applied to prevent federal review of a constitutional claim. Justice Souter's opinion for the Court concluded that a rule unannounced at the time of petitioner's trial could not have been firmly established at that time, and was thus "inadequate to serve as an independent state ground within the meaning of *James.*" See also Johnson v. Mississippi, 486 U.S. 578 (1988) (no adequate state ground where Mississippi law did not consistently require a claim such as defendant's to be asserted on direct appeal).

5. *Abuse of the Writ*

Successive habeas petitions can constitute abuse of the writ, which generally precludes review regardless of the merits of the subsequent petition. In McCleskey v. Zant, 111 S.Ct. 1454 (1991), the Court held that a petitioner could only bring successive habeas petitions if he could establish cause and prejudice under *Sykes* for the failure to bring all claims in a single petition. Otherwise, abuse of the writ would be found and the successive petitions dismissed. Justice Kennedy wrote the opinion for six members of the Court. The majority held that it was not necessary for the state to show that the petitioner had deliberately abandoned a claim in a prior habeas petition; a petitioner may also abuse the writ by failing to raise a claim through neglect. The Court determined that the cause and prejudice standards of procedural default properly defined whether a claim was not raised due to neglect.

Justice Kennedy recognized that the comity notions behind the procedural default doctrine were not applicable to successive federal habeas petitions. He responded as follows:

> Nonetheless, the doctrines of procedural default and abuse of the writ are both designed to lessen the injury to a State that results through reexamination of a state conviction on a ground that the State did not have the opportunity to address at a prior, appropriate time; and both doctrines seek to vindicate the State's interest in the finality of its criminal judgments.
>
> We conclude from the unity of structure and purpose in the jurisprudence of state procedural defaults and abuse of the writ that the standard for excusing a failure to raise a claim at the appropriate time should be the same in both contexts.

To satisfy the cause requirement, the petitioner must show under *Carrier* that some objective factor external to the defense impeded counsel's efforts, or else that defense counsel was constitutionally ineffective. Justice Kennedy noted, however, the limited exception to the cause requirement set forth in *Carrier:* "Federal courts retain the authority to issue the writ of habeas corpus in * * * extraordinary instances when a constitutional violation probably has caused the conviction of one innocent of the crime."

McCleskey asserted a *Massiah* claim in a second habeas petition, which had not been asserted in the first. Justice Kennedy proceeded to determine whether there was cause for McCleskey to have omitted the *Massiah* claim from his first petition. McCleskey argued that after the first petition was dismissed, he obtained access to a statement from a jailhouse informant to whom McCleskey had confessed. This statement had been withheld by the State up until that time. The statement indicated that the informant was working in concert with state officials to obtain information from McCleskey.

Justice Kennedy concluded that the State's suppression of the informant's statement did not constitute cause for failing to assert the *Massiah* claim in the first petition. He explained as follows:

> That McCleskey did not possess or could not reasonably have obtained certain evidence fails to establish cause if other known or discoverable evidence could have supported the claim in any event. * * * For cause to exist, the external impediment * * * must have prevented petitioner from raising the claim. * * * If what petitioner knows or could discover upon reasonable investigation supports a claim for relief in a federal habeas petition, what he does not know is irrelevant. Omission of the claim will not be excused merely because evidence discovered later might have also supported or strengthened the claim.

Justice Kennedy found that the suppression of the informant's statement did not establish cause, because McCleskey knew that he had confessed to the informant, knew that the informant told the police about the confessions, and knew that he had participated in the conversations related in the informant's statement.

Finally, the majority found that McCleskey had not satisfied the narrow "miscarriage of justice" exception to the cause requirements. According to Justice Kennedy, the *Massiah* violation, "if it be one, resulted in the admission at trial of truthful inculpatory evidence which did not affect the reliability of the guilt determination."

Justice Marshall, joined by Justices Blackmun and Stevens, dissented. He complained that the majority's application of the cause and prejudice requirement to successive habeas petitions "radically redefines the content of the abuse of the writ doctrine." According to Justice Marshall, abuse of the writ had previously been found only where a claim had been deliberately abandoned in a previous petition, or where successive petitions were used for harassment or some other bad-faith purpose. Justice Marshall accused the majority of substituting the "strict liability standard" of cause and prejudice for the more permissive good faith standard. He argued that application of the cause and prejudice standard to successive petitions would give rise to frivolous claims in the first petition:

> Rather than face the cause and prejudice bar, a petitioner will assert all conceivable claims, whether or not these claims reasonably appear to have merit. The possibility that these claims will be adversely adjudicated and thereafter be barred from relitigation under the successive-petition doctrine will not effectively discourage the petitioner from asserting them, for the petitioner will have virtually no expectation that any withheld claim could be revived should his assessment of its merit later prove mistaken. Far from promoting efficiency, the majority's rule thus invites the very type of baseless claims * * * that the majority seeks to avert.

Justice Marshall also took issue with the Court's application of the cause requirement to McCleskey's case. He argued that, while McCleskey may have been aware of his conversations with the informant, he was not aware of the informant's relationship with the State. That information was contained in the informant's statement, to which McCleskey had no access at the time of his first petition. Justice Marshall asserted that "the majority's analysis of this case is dangerous precisely because it treats as irrelevant the effect that the

State's disinformation strategy had on counsel's assessment of the reasonableness of pursuing the *Massiah* claim." He concluded that the majority's application of the cause requirement creates an incentive for state officials to engage in misconduct.

After *McCleskey,* are there any claims that counsel can properly save for a future habeas petition? Can counsel protect against a charge of having brought frivolous claims (and possible sanctions) by arguing that if the claims were not brought, they would be forever barred by the cause requirement? Recall the petitioner in Rose v. Lundy, who had both exhausted and unexhausted claims. Should such a petitioner proceed immediately in a federal habeas action with the exhausted claims?

*

Index

References are to Pages

References are to Pages

References are to Pages

†

0-314-00351-7
90000
9 780314 003515